5167745 0

5167745 0

RAND M\:NALLY

GOODE'S
W O R L D   A T L A S

19TH EDITION

Edward B. Espenshade, Jr.
EDITOR

John C. Hudson
ASSOCIATE EDITOR

Joel L. Morrison
SENIOR CONSULTANT

RAND M\:NALLY

CONTENTS

Goode's World Atlas
Copyright © 1995 by Rand McNally & Company; Fifth printing, Revised.
Copyright © 1922, 1923, 1932, 1933, 1937, 1939, 1943, 1946, 1949, 1954, 1957, 1960, 1964, 1970, 1974, 1978, 1982, 1986, 1990 by Rand McNally & Company
Formerly *Goode's School Atlas*
Made in U.S.A.

Library of Congress Catalog Card Number 94–68645

CONTENTS, *continued*

Major Cities Maps   *Scale 1:300,000* [226–244]

Geographical Tables and Indexes [245–372]

Map Projections

Every cartographer is faced with the problem of transforming the curved surface of the earth onto a flat plane with a minimum of distortion. The systematic transformation of locations on the earth (spherical surface) to locations on a map (flat surface) is called projection.

It is not possible to represent on a flat map the spatial relationships of angle, distance, direction, and area that only a globe can show faithfully. As a result, projection systems inevitably involve some distortion. On large-scale maps representing a few square miles, the distortion is generally negligible. But on maps depicting large countries, continents, or the entire world, the amount of distortion can be significant. Some maps of the Western Hemisphere, because of their projection, incorrectly portray Canada and Alaska as larger than the United States and Mexico, while South America looks considerably smaller than its northern neighbors.

One of the more practical ways map readers can become aware of projection distortions and learn how to make allowances for them is to compare the projection grid of a flat map with the grid of a globe. Some important characteristics of the globe grid are found listed on page xi.

There are an infinite number of possible map projections, all of which distort one or more of the characteristics of the globe in varying degrees. The projection system that a cartographer chooses depends on the size and location of the area being projected and the purpose of the map. In this atlas, most of the maps are drawn on projections that give a consistent area scale; good land and ocean shape; parallels that are parallel; and as consistent a linear scale as possible throughout the projection.

The transformation process is actually a mathematical one, but to aid in visualizing this process, it is helpful to consider the earth reduced to the scale of the intended map and then projected onto a simple geometric shape—a cylinder, cone, or plane. These geometric forms are then flattened to two dimensions to produce cylindrical, conic, and plane projections (see Figures 4, 5, and 6). Some of the projection systems used in this atlas are described on the following pages. By comparing these systems with the characteristics of a globe grid, readers can gain a clearer understanding of map distortion.

Mercator: This transformation—bearing the name of a famous sixteenth century cartographer—is conformal; that is, land masses are represented in their true shapes. Thus, for every point on the map, the angles shown are correct in every direction within a limited area. To achieve this, the projection increases latitudinal and longitudinal distances away from the equator. As a result, land *shapes* are correct, but their *areas* are distorted. The farther away from the equator, the greater the area distortion. For example, on a Mercator map, Alaska appears far larger than Mexico, whereas in fact Mexico's land area is greater. The Mercator projection is used in nautical navigation, because a line connecting any two points gives the compass direction between them. (See Figure 4.)

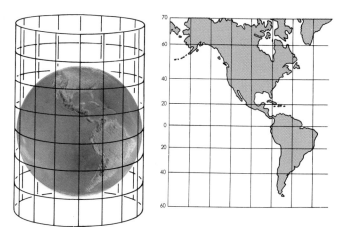

Figure 4. Mercator Projection (right), based upon the projection of the globe onto a cylinder.

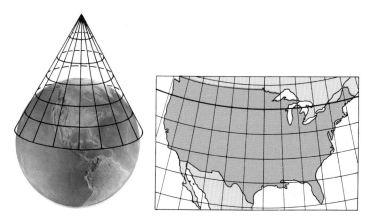

Figure 5. Projection of the globe onto a cone and a resultant Conic Projection.

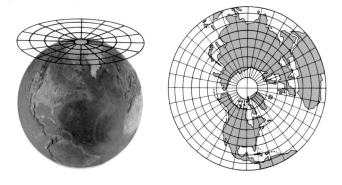

Figure 6. Lambert Equal-Area Projection (right), which assumes the projection of the globe onto a plane surface.

Conic: In this transformation—a globe projected onto a tangent cone—meridians of longitude appear as straight lines, and lines of latitude appear as parallel arcs. The parallel of tangency (that is, where the cone is presumed to touch the globe) is called a standard parallel. In this projection, distortion increases in bands away from the standard parallel. Conic projections are helpful in depicting middle-latitude areas of east-west extension. (See Figure 5.)

Lambert Equal Area *(polar case):* This projection assumes a plane touching the globe at a single point. It shows true distances close to the center (the tangent point) but increasingly distorted ones away from it. The equal-area quality (showing land areas in their correct proportion) is maintained throughout; but in regions away from the center, distortion of shape increases. (See Figure 6.)

Miller Cylindrical: O. M. Miller suggested a modification to the Mercator projection to lessen the severe area distortion in the higher latitudes. The Miller projection is neither conformal nor equal-area. Thus, while shapes are less accurate than on the Mercator, the exaggeration of *size* of areas has been somewhat decreased. The Miller cylindrical is useful for showing the entire world in a rectangular format. (See Figure 7.)

Mollweide Homolographic: The Mollweide is an equal-area projection; the least distorted areas are ovals centered just above and below the center of the projection. Distance distortions increase toward the edges of the map. The Mollweide is used for world-distribution maps where a pleasing oval look is desired along with the equal-area quality. It is one of the bases used in the Goode's Interrupted Homolosine projection. (See Figure 8.)

Sinusoidal, or Sanson-Flamsteed: In this equal-area projection the scale is the same along all parallels and the central meridian. Distortion of shapes is less along the two main axes of the projection but increases markedly toward the edges. Maps depicting areas such as South America or Africa can make good use of the Sinusoidal's favorable characteristics by situating the land masses along the central meridian, where the shapes will be virtually undistorted. The Sinusoidal is also one of the bases used in the Goode's Interrupted Homolosine. (See Figure 9.)

Goode's Interrupted Homolosine: An equal-area projection, Goode's is composed of the Sinusoidal grid from the equator to about 40° N and 40° S latitudes; beyond these latitudes, the Mollweide is used. This grid is interrupted so that land masses can be projected with a minimum of shape distortion by positioning each section on a separate central meridian. Thus, the shapes as well as the sizes of land masses are represented with a high degree of fidelity. Oceans can also be positioned in this manner. (See Figure 10.)

Robinson: This projection was designed for Rand McNally to present an uninterrupted and visually correct map of the earth. It maintains overall shape and area relationships without extreme distortion and is widely used in classrooms and textbooks. (See Figure 11.)

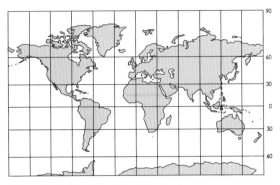

Figure 7. Miller Cylindrical Projection.

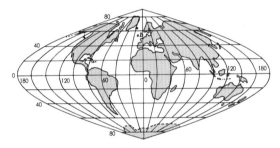

Figure 8. Mollweide Homolographic Projection.

Figure 9. Sinusoidal Projection.

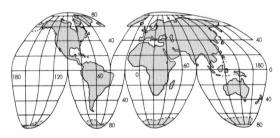

Figure 10. Goode's Interrupted Homolosine Projection.

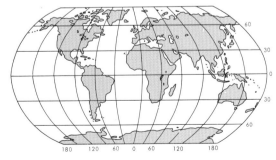

Figure 11. Robinson Projection.

Bonne: This equal-area transformation is mathematically related to the Sinusoidal. Distances are true along all parallels and the central meridian. Farther out from the central meridian, however, the increasing obliqueness of the grid's angles distorts shape and distance. This limits the area that can be usefully projected. Bonne projections, like conics, are best employed for relatively small areas in middle latitudes. (See Figure 12.)

Conic with Two Standard Parallels: The linear scale of this projection is consistent along two standard parallels instead of only one as in the simple conic. Since the spacing of the other parallels is reduced somewhat between the standard parallels and progressively enlarged beyond them, the projection does not exhibit the equal-area property. Careful selection of the standard parallels, however, provides good representation of limited areas. Like the Bonne projection, this system is widely used for areas in middle latitudes. (See Figure 13.)

Polyconic: In this system, the globe is projected onto a series of strips taken from tangent cones. Parallels are nonconcentric circles, and each is divided equally by the meridians, as on the globe. While distances along the straight central meridian are true, they are increasingly exaggerated along the curving meridians. Likewise, general representation of areas and shapes is good near the central meridian but progressively distorted away from it. Polyconic projections are used for middle-latitude areas to minimize all distortions and were employed for large-scale topographic maps. (See Figure 14.)

Lambert Conformal Conic: This conformal transformation system usually employs two standard parallels. Distortion increases away from the standard parallels, being greatest at the edges of the map. It is useful for projecting elongated east-west areas in the middle latitudes and is ideal for depicting the forty-eight contiguous states. It is also widely used for aeronautical and meteorological charts. (See Figure 15.)

Lambert Equal Area (oblique and polar cases): This equal-area projection can be centered at any point on the earth's surface, perpendicular to a line drawn through the globe. It maintains correct angles to all points on the map from its center (point of tangency), but distances become progressively distorted toward the edges. It is most useful for roughly circular areas or areas whose dimensions are nearly equal in two perpendicular directions.

The two most common forms of the Lambert projection are the oblique and the polar, shown in Figures 6 and 16. Although the meridians and parallels for the forms are different, the distortion characteristics are the same.

Important characteristics of the globe grid

1. All meridians of longitude are equal in length and meet at the Poles.
2. All lines of latitude are parallel and equally spaced on meridians.
3. The length, or circumference, of the parallels of latitude decreases as one moves from the equator to the Poles. For instance, the circumference of the parallel at 60° latitude is one-half the circumference of the equator.
4. Meridians of longitude are equally spaced on each parallel, but the distance between them decreases toward the Poles.
5. All parallels and meridians meet at right angles.

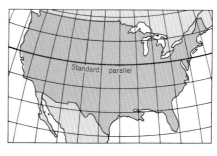

Figure 12.
Bonne Projection.

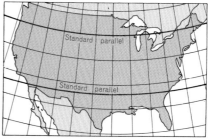

Figure 13.
Conic Projection with Two Standard Parallels.

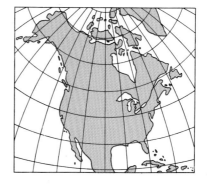

Figure 14.
Polyconic Projection.

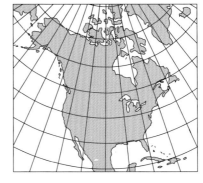

Figure 15.
Lambert Conformal Conic Projection.

Figure 16.
Lambert Equal-Area Projection (oblique case).

EDWARD B. ESPENSHADE, JR.
JOHN C. HUDSON

xi

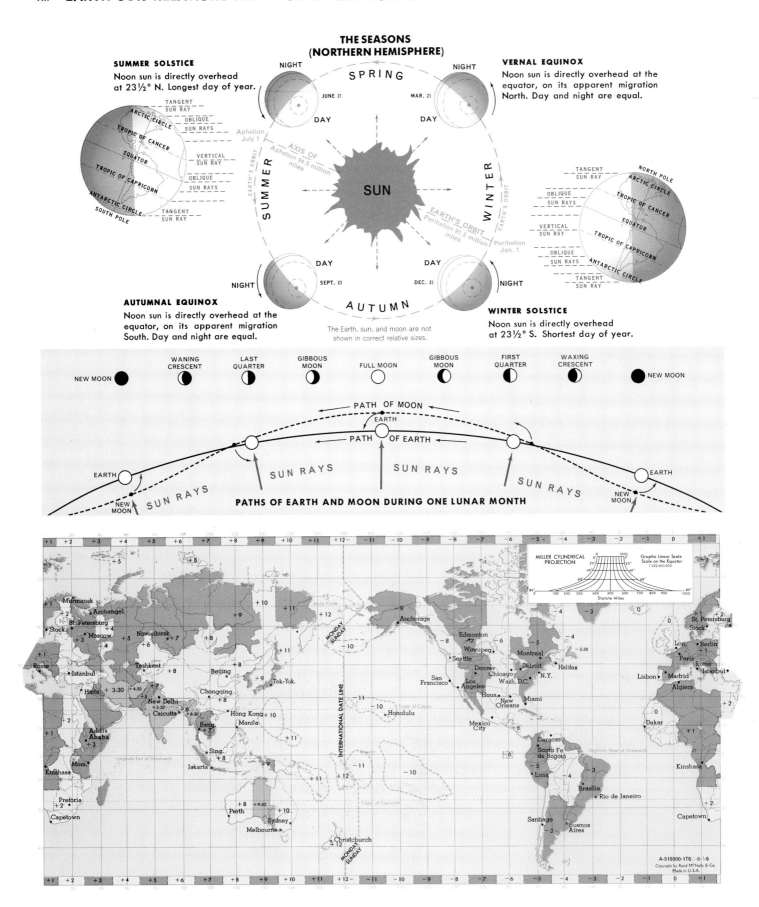

THE SEASONS
(NORTHERN HEMISPHERE)

SUMMER SOLSTICE
Noon sun is directly overhead at 23½° N. Longest day of year.

VERNAL EQUINOX
Noon sun is directly overhead at the equator, on its apparent migration North. Day and night are equal.

AUTUMNAL EQUINOX
Noon sun is directly overhead at the equator, on its apparent migration South. Day and night are equal.

The Earth, sun, and moon are not shown in correct relative sizes.

WINTER SOLSTICE
Noon sun is directly overhead at 23½° S. Shortest day of year.

SPRING   JUNE 21   MAR. 21
WINTER
SUMMER
AUTUMN   SEPT. 23   DEC. 22
NIGHT   DAY   NIGHT   DAY
SUN
AXIS OF
Aphelion July 1
Aphelion 94.5 million miles
EARTH'S ORBIT
Perihelion 91.5 million miles
Perihelion Jan. 1
EARTH'S ORBIT

TANGENT SUN RAY
ARCTIC CIRCLE
OBLIQUE SUN RAYS
TROPIC OF CANCER
EQUATOR
VERTICAL SUN RAY
TROPIC OF CAPRICORN
OBLIQUE SUN RAYS
ANTARCTIC CIRCLE
TANGENT SUN RAY
SOUTH POLE

TANGENT SUN RAY
NORTH POLE
OBLIQUE SUN RAYS
ARCTIC CIRCLE
TROPIC OF CANCER
VERTICAL SUN RAY
EQUATOR
OBLIQUE SUN RAYS
TROPIC OF CAPRICORN
ANTARCTIC CIRCLE
TANGENT SUN RAY

NEW MOON   WANING CRESCENT   LAST QUARTER   GIBBOUS MOON   FULL MOON   GIBBOUS MOON   FIRST QUARTER   WAXING CRESCENT   NEW MOON

PATH OF MOON
EARTH
PATH OF EARTH
SUN RAYS   SUN RAYS   SUN RAYS
EARTH   EARTH
NEW MOON   NEW MOON
PATHS OF EARTH AND MOON DURING ONE LUNAR MONTH

MILLER CYLINDRICAL PROJECTION
Graphic Linear Scale
Scale on the Equator
1:222,000,000
Statute Miles

Time Zones

The surface of the earth is divided into 24 time zones. Each zone represents 15° of longitude or one hour of time. The time of the initial, or zero, zone is based on the central meridian of Greenwich and is adopted eastward and westward for a distance of 7½° of longitude. Each of the zones in turn is designated by a number representing the hours (+ or −) by which its standard time differs from Greenwich mean time. These standard time zones are indicated by bands of orange and yellow. Areas which have a fractional deviation from standard time are shown in an intermediate color. The irregularities in the zones and the fractional deviations are due to political and economic factors.

(After U.S. Defense Mapping Agency)

This section of the atlas consists of more than sixty thematic maps presenting world patterns and distributions. Together with accompanying graphs, these maps communicate basic information on mineral resources, agricultural products, trade, transportation, and other selected aspects of the natural and cultural geographical environment.

A thematic map uses symbols to show certain characteristics of, generally, one class of geographical information. This "theme" of a thematic map is presented upon a background of basic locational information—coastline, country boundaries, major drainage, etc. The map's primary concern is to communicate visually basic impressions of the distribution of the theme. For instance, on page 43 the distribution of cattle shown by point symbols impresses the reader with relative densities—the distribution of cattle is much more uniform throughout the United States than it is in China, and cattle are more numerous in the United States than in China.

Although it is possible to use a thematic map to obtain exact values of a quantity or commodity, it is not the purpose intended, any more than a thematic map is intended to be used to give precise distances from New York to Moscow. If one seeks precise statistics for each country, he may consult the bar graph on the map or a statistical table.

The map on this page is an example of a special class of thematic maps called cartograms. The cartogram assigns to a named earth region an area based on some value other than land surface area. In the cartogram below the areas assigned are proportional to their countries' populations and tinted according to their rate of natural increase. The result of mapping on this base is a meaningful way of portraying this distribution since natural increase is causally related to existing size of population. On the other hand, natural increase is not causally related to earth area. In the other thematic maps in this atlas, relative earth sizes have been considered when presenting the distributions.

Real and hypothetical geographical distributions of interest to man are practically limitless but can be classed into point, line, area, or volume information relative to a specific location or area in the world. The thematic map, in communicating these fundamental classes of information, utilizes point, line, and area symbols. The symbols may be employed to show *qualitative* differences (differences in *kind*) of a certain category of information and may also show *quantitative* differences in the information (differences in *amount*). For example, the natural-vegetation map (page 18) was based upon information gathered by many observations over a period of time. It utilizes area symbols (color and pattern) to show the difference in the *kind* of vegetation as well as the extent. Quantitative factual information was shown on the annual-precipitation map, page 16, by means of isohyets (lines connecting points of equal rainfall). Also, area symbols were employed to show the intervals between the lines. In each of these thematic maps, there is one primary theme, or subject; the map communicates the information far better than volumes of words and tables could.

One of the most important aspects of the thematic-map section is use of the different maps to show comparisons and relationships among the distributions of various types of geographical information. For example, the relationship of dense population (page 24) to areas of intensive subsistence agriculture (page 34) and to manufacturing and commerce (page 32) is an important geographic concept.

The statistics communicated by the maps and graphs in this section are intended to give an idea of the relative importance of countries in the distributions mapped. The maps are not intended to take the place of statistical reference works. No single year affords a realistic base for production, trade, and certain economic and demographic statistics. Therefore, averages of data for three or four years have been used. Together with the maps, the averages and percentages provide the student with a realistic idea of the importance of specific areas.

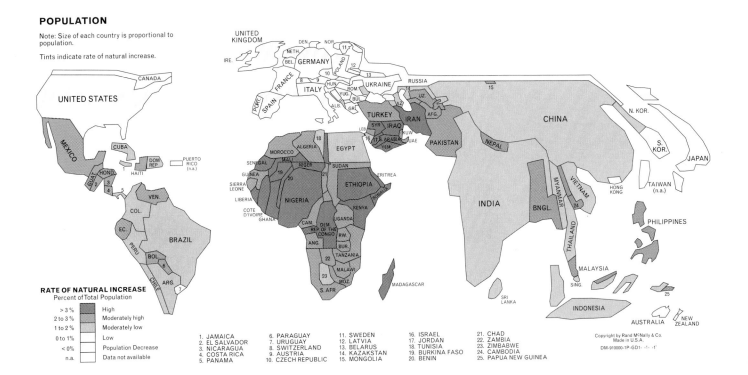

POPULATION

Note: Size of each country is proportional to population.

Tints indicate rate of natural increase.

RATE OF NATURAL INCREASE
Percent of Total Population

>3%	High
2 to 3%	Moderately high
1 to 2%	Moderately low
0 to 1%	Low
<0%	Population Decrease
n.a.	Data not available

1. JAMAICA	6. PARAGUAY	11. SWEDEN	16. ISRAEL	21. CHAD
2. EL SALVADOR	7. URUGUAY	12. LATVIA	17. JORDAN	22. ZAMBIA
3. NICARAGUA	8. SWITZERLAND	13. BELARUS	18. TUNISIA	23. ZIMBABWE
4. COSTA RICA	9. AUSTRIA	14. KAZAKSTAN	19. BURKINA FASO	24. CAMBODIA
5. PANAMA	10. CZECH REPUBLIC	15. MONGOLIA	20. BENIN	25. PAPUA NEW GUINEA

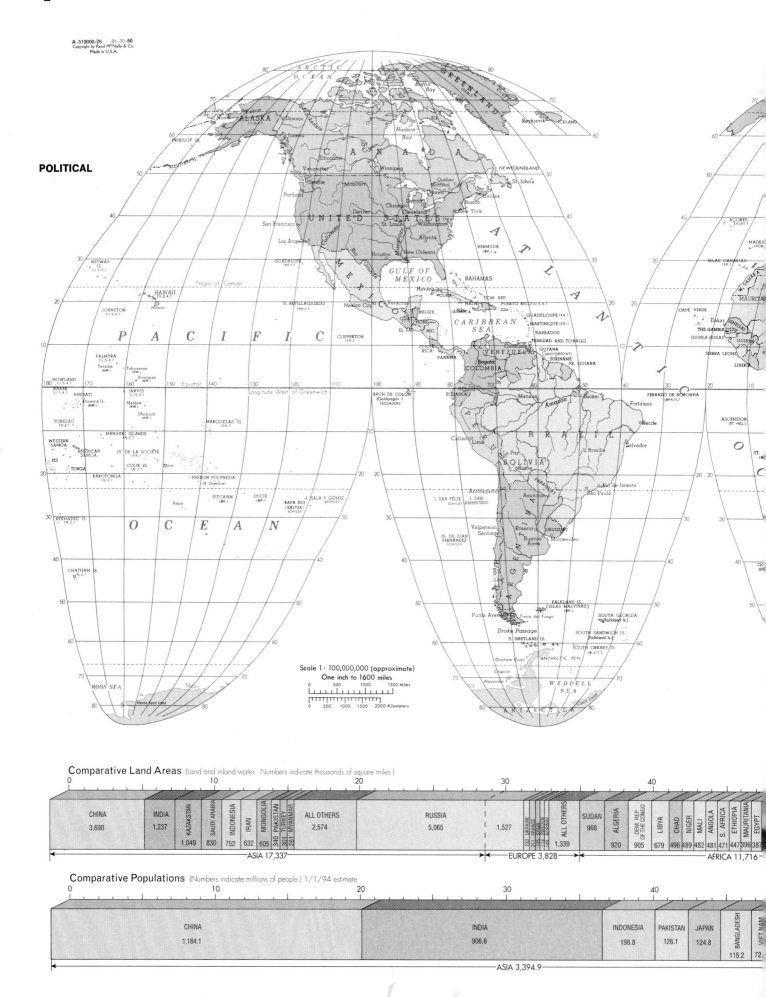

RUSSIA
KAZAKSTAN
MONGOLIA
CHINA
INDIA
IRAN
TURKEY
SAUDI ARABIA
LIBYA
EGYPT
SUDAN
CHAD
NIGER
ETHIOPIA
SOMALIA
KENYA
DEM. REP. OF THE CONGO
TANZANIA
ANGOLA
ZAMBIA
NAMIBIA
BOTSWANA
SOUTH AFRICA
MADAGASCAR
JAPAN
PHILIPPINES
INDONESIA
NEW GUINEA
AUSTRALIA
NEW ZEALAND
PACIFIC OCEAN
INDIAN OCEAN
ARABIAN SEA
BAY OF BENGAL
CORAL SEA
SEA OF OKHOTSK
BERING SEA
ALASKA
Tropic of Cancer
Tropic of Capricorn
Equator
Arctic Circle
Antarctic Circle
Longitude East of Greenwich
Moscow
Beijing
Tokyo
New Delhi
Jakarta
Sydney
Canberra
Cape Town
Conflicting Political Claims by U.K., Austl., Arg., Chile, Fr., etc., none of which is recognized by the U.S.A.

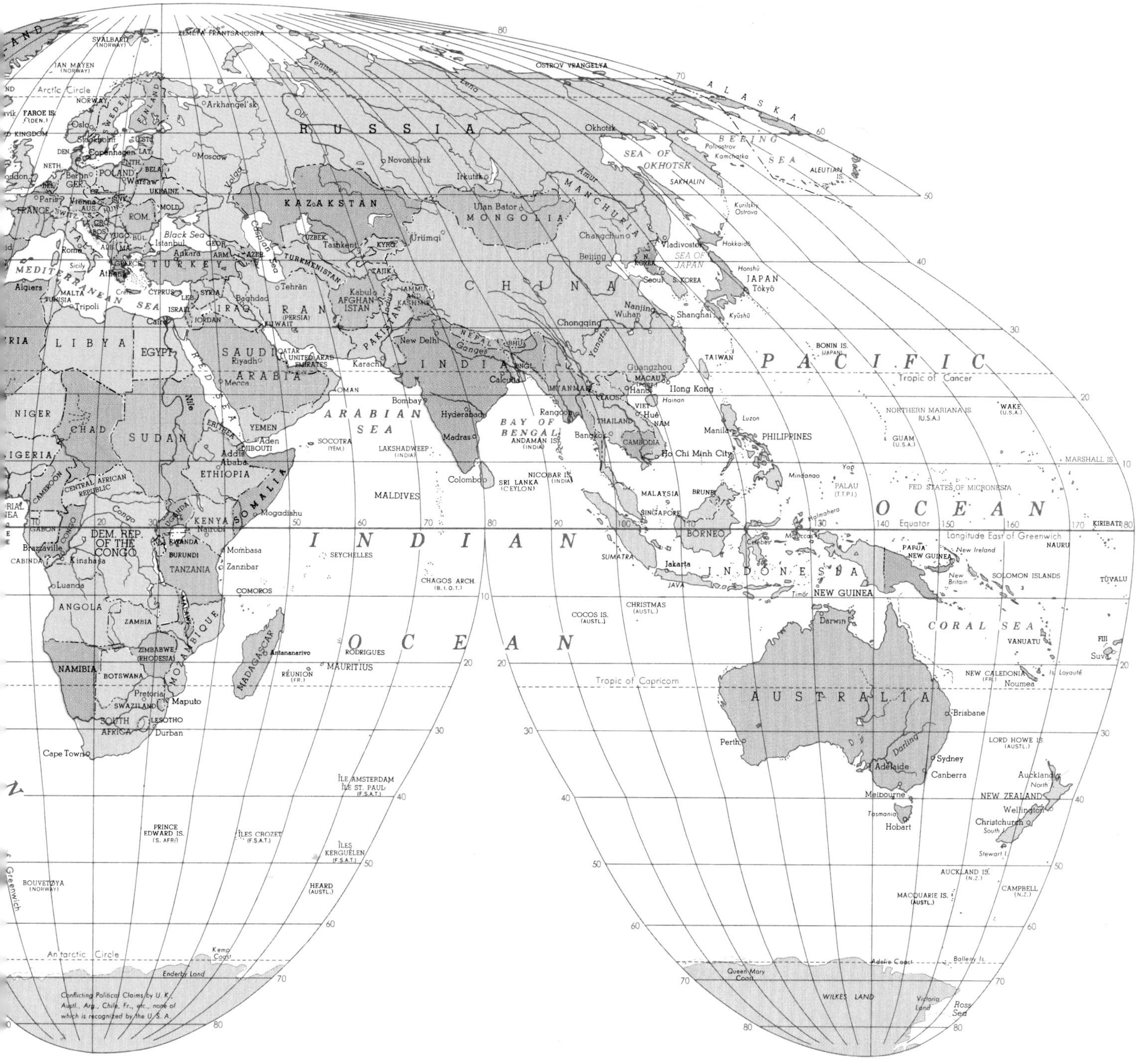

Goode's Homolosine Equal Area Projection

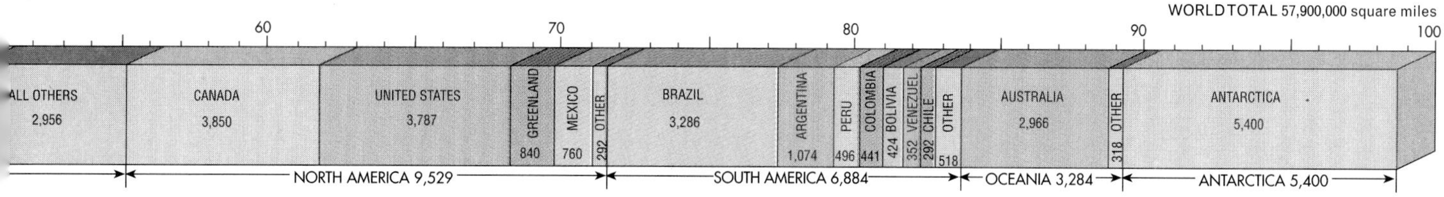

WORLD TOTAL 57,900,000 square miles
ALL OTHERS 2,956
CANADA 3,850
UNITED STATES 3,787
GREENLAND 840
MEXICO 760
OTHER 292
BRAZIL 3,286
ARGENTINA 1,074
PERU 496
COLOMBIA 441
BOLIVIA 424
VENEZUEL 352
CHILE 292
OTHER 518
AUSTRALIA 2,966
OTHER 318
ANTARCTICA 5,400
NORTH AMERICA 9,529
SOUTH AMERICA 6,884
OCEANIA 3,284
ANTARCTICA 5,400

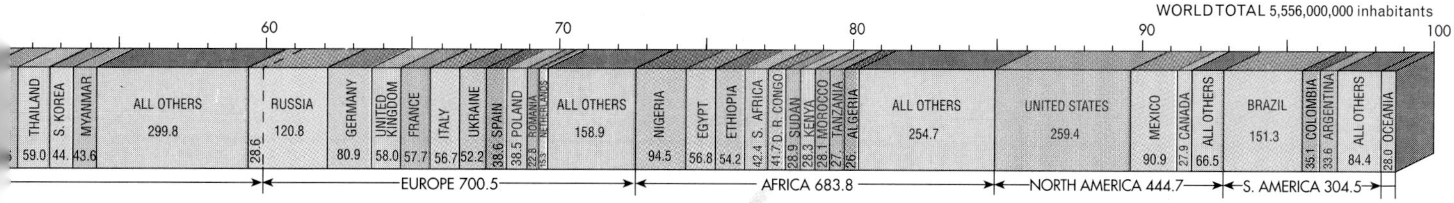

WORLD TOTAL 5,556,000,000 inhabitants
THAILAND 59.0
S. KOREA 44.
MYANMAR 43.6
ALL OTHERS 299.8
28.6
RUSSIA 120.8
GERMANY 80.9
UNITED KINGDOM 58.0
FRANCE 57.7
ITALY 56.7
UKRAINE 52.2
SPAIN 38.6
POLAND 38.5
ROMANIA 22.8
NETHERLANDS 15.3
ALL OTHERS 158.9
NIGERIA 94.5
EGYPT 56.8
ETHIOPIA 54.2
S. AFRICA 42.4
D. R. CONGO 41.7
SUDAN 28.9
KENYA 28.3
MOROCCO 28.1
TANZANIA 27.
ALGERIA 26.
ALL OTHERS 254.7
UNITED STATES 259.4
MEXICO 90.9
CANADA 27.9
ALL OTHERS 66.5
BRAZIL 151.3
COLOMBIA 35.1
ARGENTINA 33.6
ALL OTHERS 84.4
OCEANIA 28.0
EUROPE 700.5
AFRICA 683.8
NORTH AMERICA 444.7
S. AMERICA 304.5

4

PHYSICAL

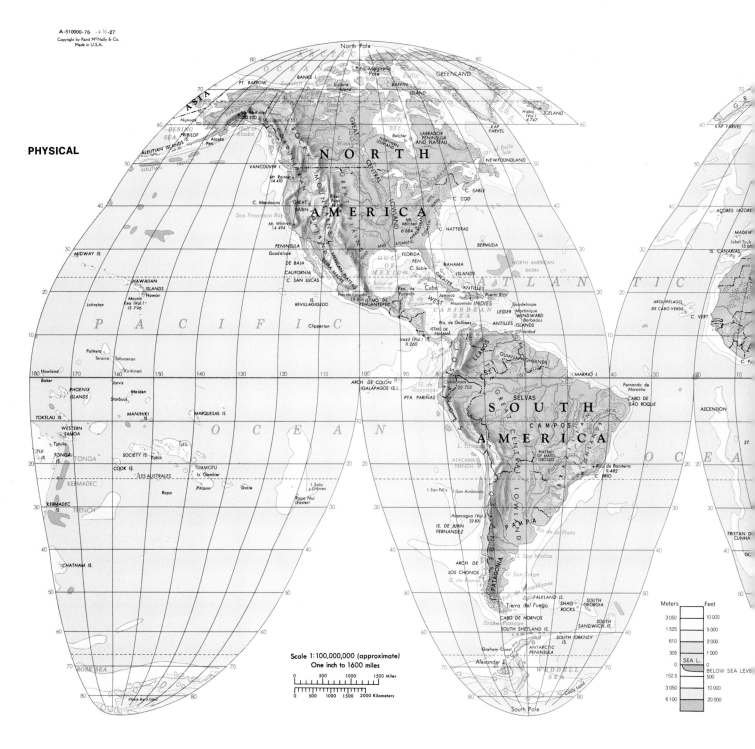

Scale 1:100,000,000 (approximate)
One inch to 1600 miles

Meters		Feet
3 050		10 000
1 525		5 000
610		2 000
305		1 000
0	SEA L.	
		BELOW SEA LEVEL
152.5		500
3 050		10 000
6 100		20 000

Land Elevations in Profile

Ocean Depths in Profile

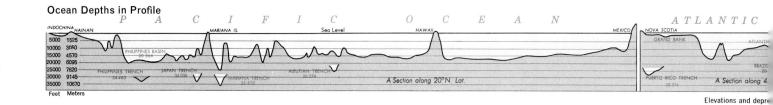

Elevations and depr

A Section along 20°N. Lat.

A Section along 4

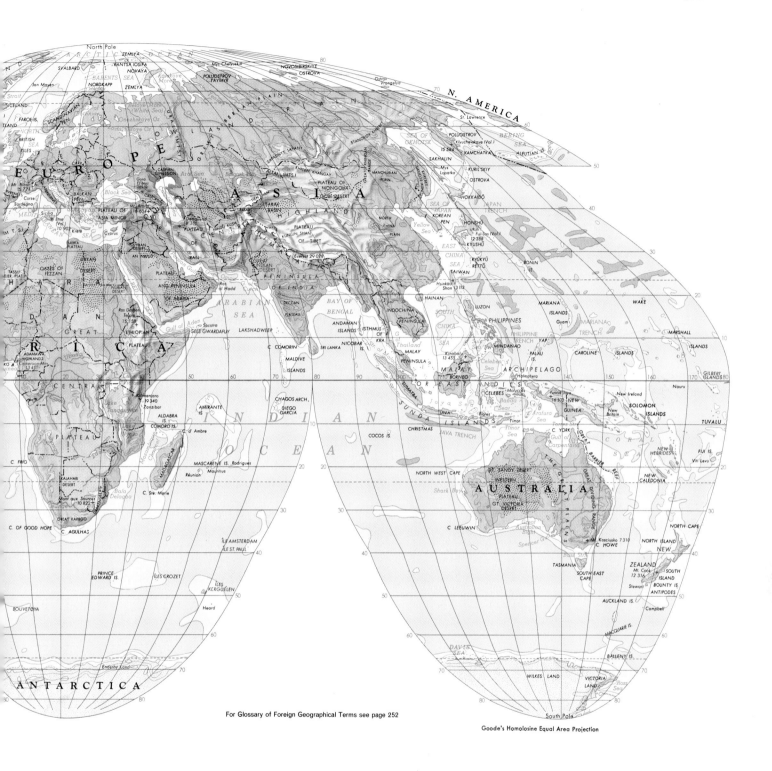

For Glossary of Foreign Geographical Terms see page 252

Goode's Homolosine Equal Area Projection

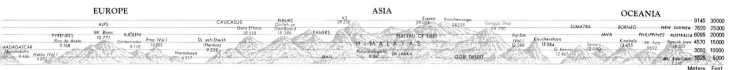

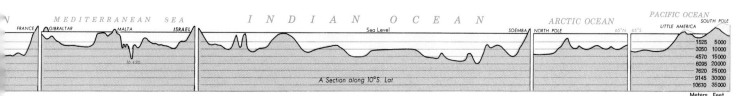

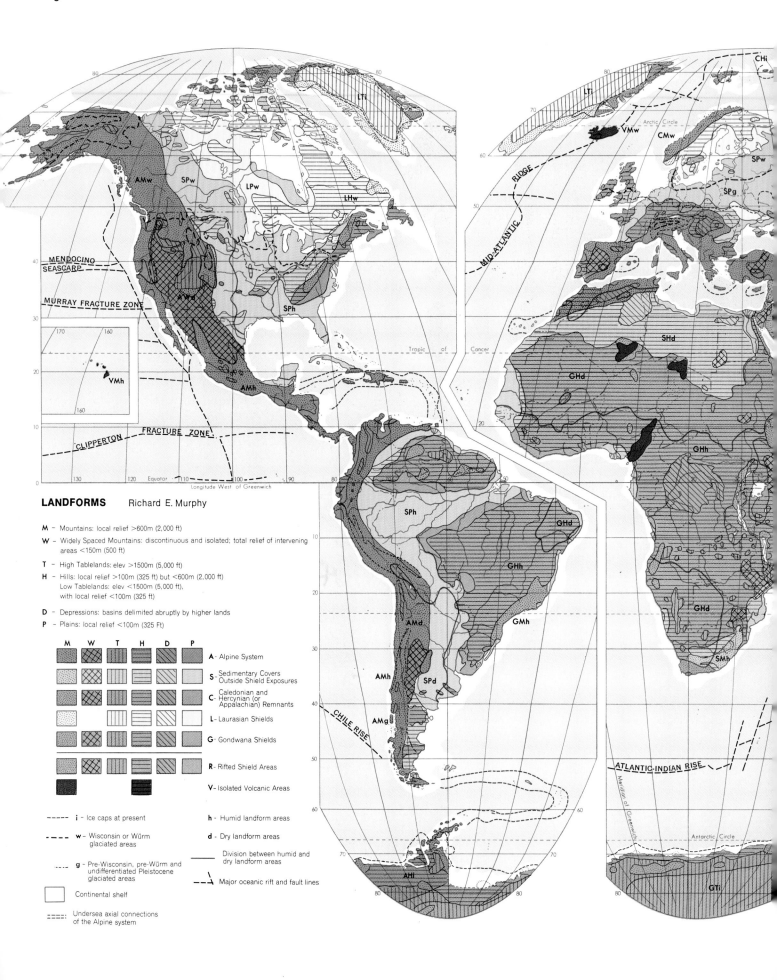

LANDFORMS   Richard E. Murphy

M – Mountains: local relief >600m (2,000 ft)

W – Widely Spaced Mountains: discontinuous and isolated; total relief of intervening
        areas <150m (500 ft)

T – High Tablelands: elev >1500m (5,000 ft)

H – Hills: local relief >100m (325 ft) but <600m (2,000 ft)
        Low Tablelands: elev <1500m (5,000 ft),
        with local relief <100m (325 ft)

D – Depressions: basins delimited abruptly by higher lands

P – Plains: local relief <100m (325 Ft)

M	W	T	H	D	P	
						A - Alpine System
						S - Sedimentary Covers Outside Shield Exposures
						C - Caledonian and Hercynian (or Appalachian) Remnants
						L - Laurasian Shields
						G - Gondwana Shields
						R - Rifted Shield Areas
						V - Isolated Volcanic Areas

– – – –   **i** - Ice caps at present

– – – –   **w** - Wisconsin or Würm glaciated areas

– – – –   **g** - Pre-Wisconsin, pre-Würm and undifferentiated Pleistocene glaciated areas

☐   Continental shelf

=====   Undersea axial connections of the Alpine system

h - Humid landform areas

d - Dry landform areas

———   Division between humid and dry landform areas

– – –   Major oceanic rift and fault lines

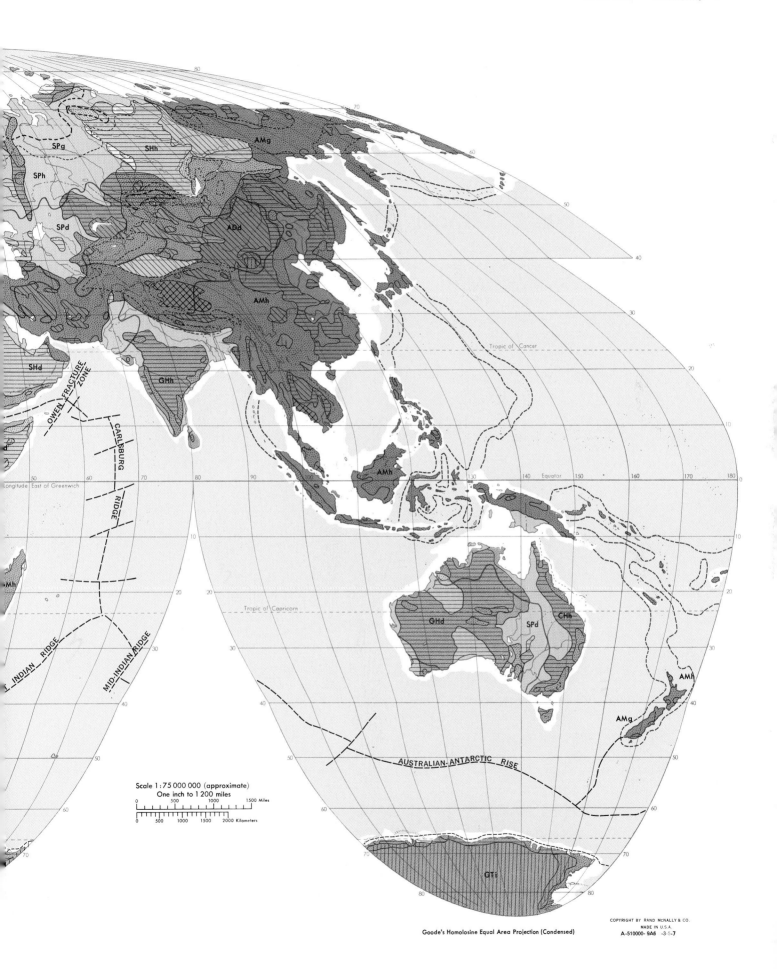

SPg

SHh

AMg

SPh

SPd

ADd

AMh

SHd

OWEN FRACTURE ZONE

CARLSBURG RIDGE

GHh

Tropic of Cancer

AMh

Longitude East of Greenwich

Equator

MID-INDIAN RIDGE

INDIAN RIDGE

AMh

Tropic of Capricorn

GHd

SPd

CHh

AMh

AMg

AUSTRALIAN-ANTARCTIC RISE

Scale 1:75 000 000 (approximate)
One inch to 1 200 miles

0   500   1000   1500 Miles

0   500   1000   1500   2000 Kilometers

GTi

Goode's Homolosine Equal Area Projection (Condensed)

A-510000- 9A6 -3-5-7

CONTINENTAL DRIFT

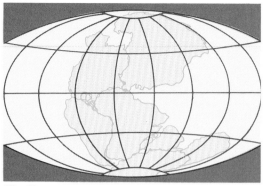

225 million years ago the supercontinent of Pangaea exists and Panthalassa forms the ancestral ocean. Tethys Sea separates Eurasia and Africa.

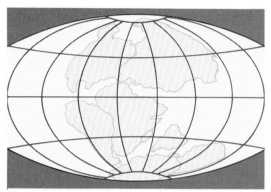

180 million years ago Pangaea splits, Laurasia drifts north. Gondwanaland breaks into South America/Africa, India, and Australia/Antarctica.

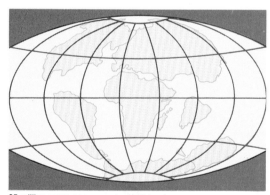

65 million years ago ocean basins take shape as South America and India move from Africa and the Tethys Sea closes to form the Mediterranean Sea.

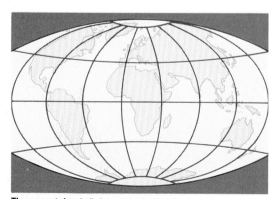

The present day: India has merged with Asia, Australia is free of Antarctica, and North America is free of Eurasia.

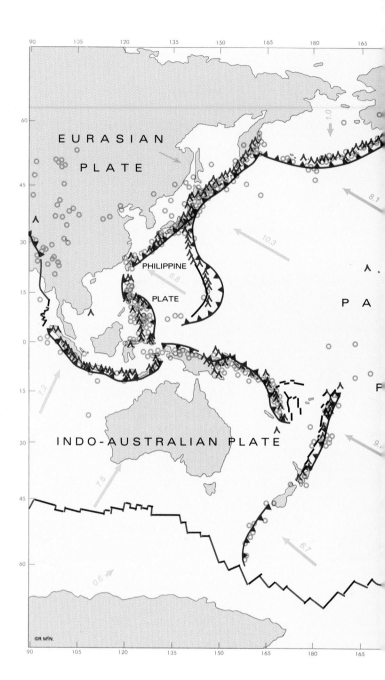

PLATE TECTONICS

Types of plate boundaries

Divergent: magma emerges from the earth's mantle at the mid-ocean ridges forming new crust and forcing the plates to spread apart at the ridges.

Convergent: plates collide at subduction zones where the denser plate is forced back into the earth's mantle forming deep ocean trenches.

Transform: plates slide past one another producing faults and fracture zones.

Other map symbols

Direction of plate movement

Length of arrow is proportional to the amount of plate movement (number indicates centimeters of movement per year)

Earthquake of magnitude 7.5 and above (from 10 A.D. to the present)

Volcano (eruption since 1900)

Selected hot spots

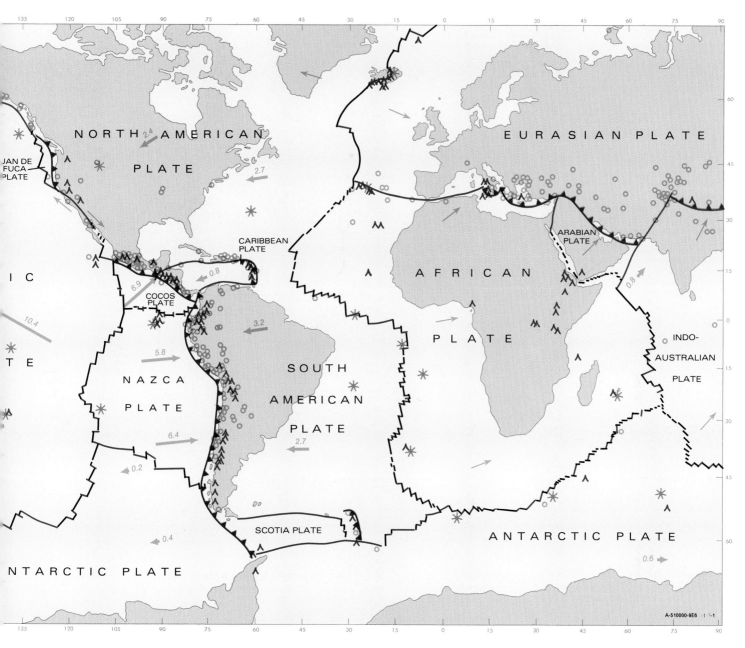

NORTH AMERICAN PLATE

JUAN DE FUCA PLATE

PACIFIC PLATE

CARIBBEAN PLATE

COCOS PLATE

NAZCA PLATE

SOUTH AMERICAN PLATE

SCOTIA PLATE

ANTARCTIC PLATE

EURASIAN PLATE

AFRICAN PLATE

ARABIAN PLATE

INDO-AUSTRALIAN PLATE

ANTARCTIC PLATE

A-510000-9E6

The plate tectonic theory describes the movement of the earth's surface and subsurface and explains why surface features are where they are.

Stated concisely, the theory presumes the lithosphere - the outside crust and uppermost mantle of the earth - is divided into about a dozen major rigid plates and several smaller platelets that move relative to one another. The position and names of the plates are shown on the map above.

The motor that drives the plates is found deep in the mantle. The theory states that because of temperature differences in the mantle, slow convection currents circulate there. Where two molten currents converge and move upward, they separate, causing the crustal plates to bulge and move apart in mid-ocean regions. Transverse fractures disrupt these broad regions. Lava wells up at these points to cause volcanic activity and to form ridges. The plates grow larger by accretion along these mid-ocean ridges, cause vast regions of the crust to move apart, and force the plates to collide with one another. As the plates do so, they are destroyed at subduction zones, where the plates are consumed downward, back into the earth's mantle, forming deep ocean trenches. The diagrams to the right illustrate the processes.

Most of the earth's volcanic and seismic activities

occur where plates slide past each other at transform boundaries or collide along subduction zones. The friction and heat caused by the grinding motion of the subducted plates causes rock to liquify and rise to the surface as volcanoes and eventually form vast mountain ranges. Strong and deep earthquakes are common here.

Volcanoes and earthquakes also occur at random locations around the earth known as "hot spots". Hot rock from deep in the mantle rises to the surface creating some of the earth's tallest mountains. As the lithospheric plates move slowly over these stationary plumes of magma, island chains (such as the Hawaiian Islands) are formed.

The overall result of tectonic movement is that the crustal plates move slowly and inexorably as relatively rigid entities, carrying the continents along with them. The history of this continental drifting is illustrated in the four maps to the left. It began with a single landmass called the supercontinent of Pangaea and the ancestral sea, the Panthalassa Ocean. Pangaea first split into a northern landmass called Laurasia and a southern block called Gondwanaland and subsequently into the continents we map today. The map of the future will be significantly different as the continents continue to drift.

Subduction Zone

Ocean Ridge Zone

10

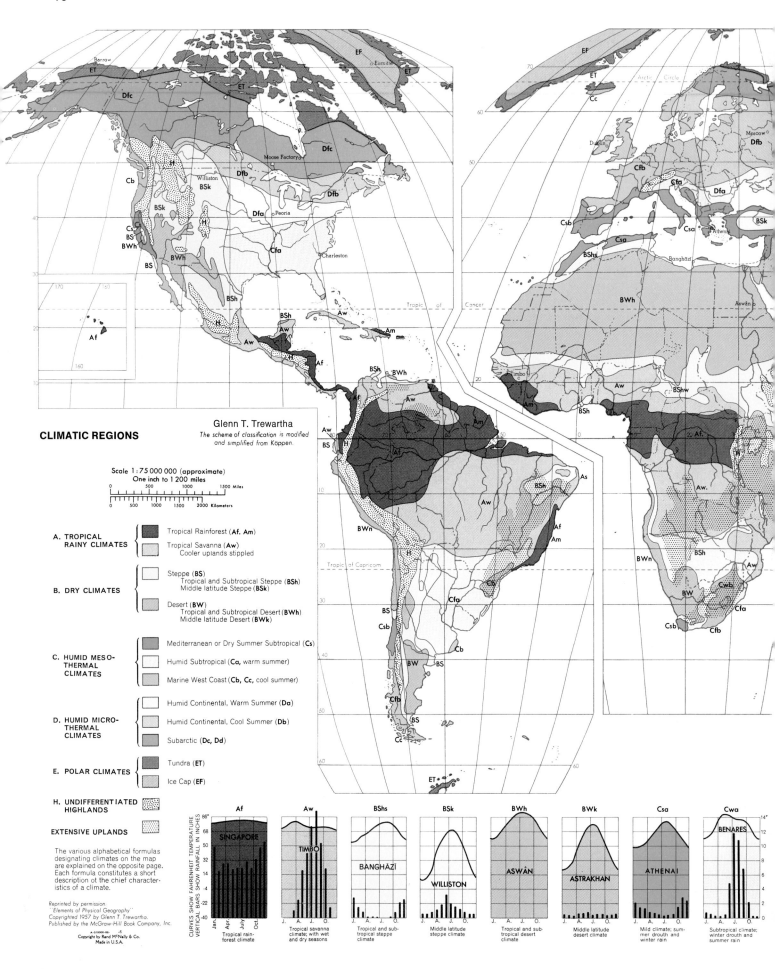

CLIMATIC REGIONS

Glenn T. Trewartha

The scheme of classification is modified and simplified from Köppen.

Scale 1:75 000 000 (approximate)
One inch to 1 200 miles

A. TROPICAL RAINY CLIMATES
- Tropical Rainforest (**Af, Am**)
- Tropical Savanna (**Aw**)
  Cooler uplands stippled

B. DRY CLIMATES
- Steppe (**BS**)
  Tropical and Subtropical Steppe (**BSh**)
  Middle latitude Steppe (**BSk**)
- Desert (**BW**)
  Tropical and Subtropical Desert (**BWh**)
  Middle latitude Desert (**BWk**)

C. HUMID MESOTHERMAL CLIMATES
- Mediterranean or Dry Summer Subtropical (**Cs**)
- Humid Subtropical (**Ca**, warm summer)
- Marine West Coast (**Cb, Cc**, cool summer)

D. HUMID MICROTHERMAL CLIMATES
- Humid Continental, Warm Summer (**Da**)
- Humid Continental, Cool Summer (**Db**)
- Subarctic (**Dc, Dd**)

E. POLAR CLIMATES
- Tundra (**ET**)
- Ice Cap (**EF**)

H. UNDIFFERENTIATED HIGHLANDS

EXTENSIVE UPLANDS

The various alphabetical formulas designating climates on the map are explained on the opposite page. Each formula constitutes a short description of the chief characteristics of a climate.

CURVES SHOW FAHRENHEIT TEMPERATURE
VERTICAL BARS SHOW RAINFALL IN INCHES

Af — SINGAPORE
Tropical rainforest climate

Aw — TIMBO
Tropical savanna climate; with wet and dry seasons

BShs — BANGHĀZĪ
Tropical and subtropical steppe climate

BSk — WILLISTON
Middle latitude steppe climate

BWh — ASWÂN
Tropical and subtropical desert climate

BWk — ASTRAKHAN
Middle latitude desert climate

Csa — ATHENAI
Mild climate; summer drouth and winter rain

Cwa — BENARES
Subtropical climate; winter drouth and summer rain

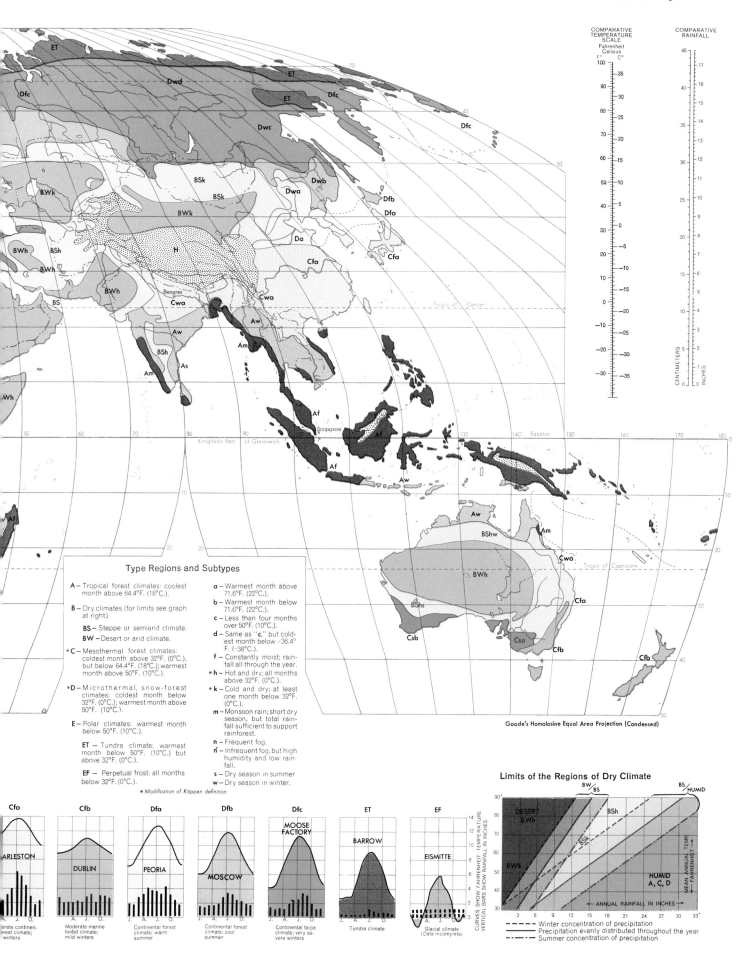

COMPARATIVE
TEMPERATURE
SCALE
Fahrenheit
Celsius

COMPARATIVE
RAINFALL

Goode's Homolosine Equal Area Projection (Condensed)

Type Regions and Subtypes

A – Tropical forest climates: coolest month above 64.4°F. (18°C.).

B – Dry climates (for limits see graph at right)

   BS – Steppe or semiarid climate.

   BW – Desert or arid climate.

***C** – Mesothermal forest climates: coldest month above 32°F. (0°C.). but below 64.4°F. (18°C.); warmest month above 50°F. (10°C.).

***D** – Microthermal, snow-forest climates: coldest month below 32°F. (0°C.); warmest month above 50°F. (10°C.).

E – Polar climates: warmest month below 50°F. (10°C.).

   ET – Tundra climate: warmest month below 50°F. (10°C.) but above 32°F. (0°C.).

   EF – Perpetual frost: all months below 32°F. (0°C.).

a – Warmest month above 71.6°F. (22°C.).

b – Warmest month below 71.6°F. (22°C.).

c – Less than four months over 50°F. (10°C.).

d – Same as "**c**," but coldest month below –36.4° F. (–38°C.).

f – Constantly moist; rainfall all through the year.

***h** – Hot and dry; all months above 32°F. (0°C.).

***k** – Cold and dry; at least one month below 32°F. (0°C.).

m – Monsoon rain; short dry season, but total rainfall sufficient to support rainforest.

n – Frequent fog.

n̄ – Infrequent fog, but high humidity and low rainfall.

s – Dry season in summer

w – Dry season in winter.

* Modification of Köppen definition

Limits of the Regions of Dry Climate

CURVES SHOW FAHRENHEIT TEMPERATURE
VERTICAL BARS SHOW RAINFALL IN INCHES

Cfa	**Cfb**	**Dfa**	**Dfb**	**Dfc**	**ET**	**EF**
CHARLESTON	DUBLIN	PEORIA	MOSCOW	MOOSE FACTORY	BARROW	EISMITTE
Moderate continental forest climate; mild winters	Moderate marine forest climate; mild winters	Continental forest climate; warm summer	Continental forest climate; cool summer	Continental taiga climate; very severe winters	Tundra climate	Glacial climate (Data Incomplete)

DESERT
BWh

BSh

BWk

BSk

BS/HUMID

HUMID
A, C, D

MEAN ANNUAL TEMP. FAHRENHEIT

ANNUAL RAINFALL IN INCHES

– – – – Winter concentration of precipitation
————— Precipitation evenly distributed throughout the year
– · – · – Summer concentration of precipitation

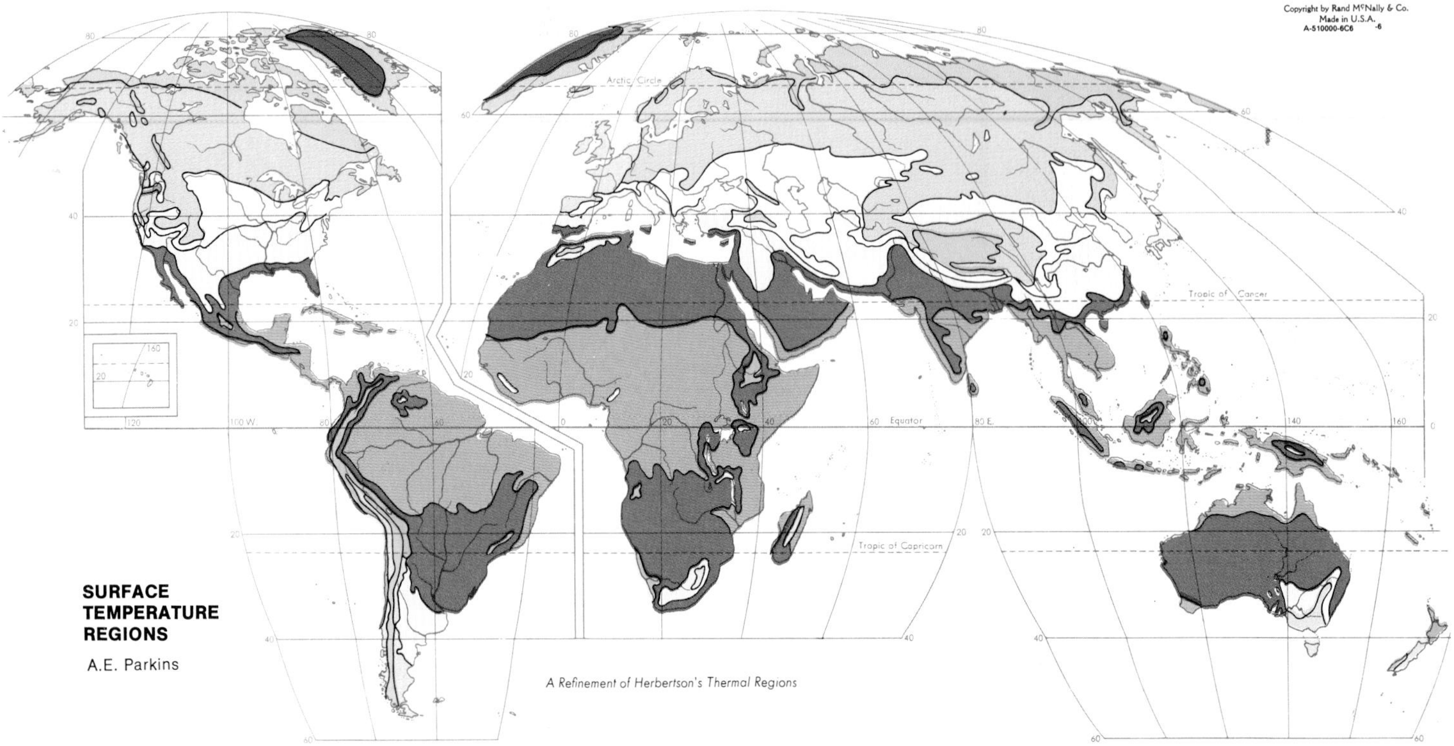

**SURFACE
TEMPERATURE
REGIONS**

A.E. Parkins

A Refinement of Herbertson's Thermal Regions

Hot = above 20°C
Mild = 10° to 20°
Cool = 0° to 10°
Cold = below 0°

Always cold;
Polar regions and high altitudes

Cold winter and cool summer;
always cool in the Andes

Cold winter and mild summer

Cool winter and mild summer

Hot summer and cold winter

Hot summer and cool winter

Hot summer and mild winter

Always hot

Always mild

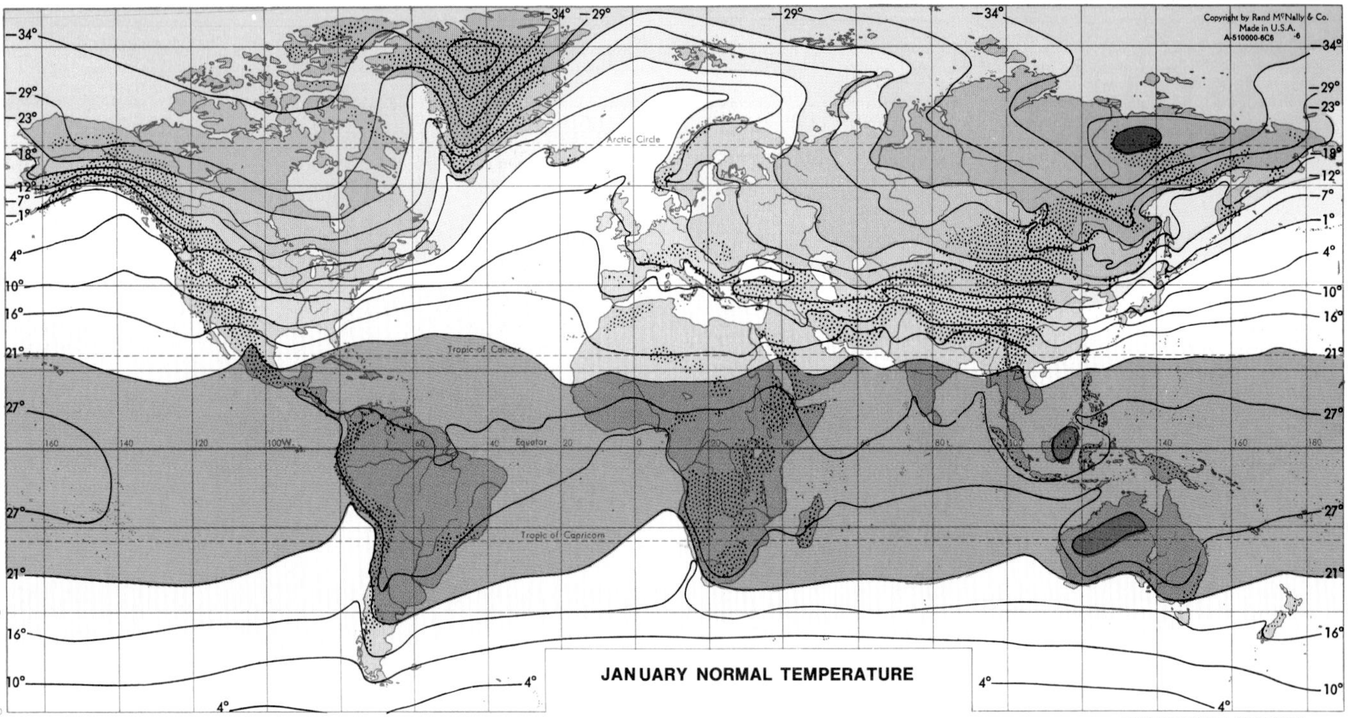

JANUARY NORMAL TEMPERATURE

MILLER CYLINDRICAL PROJECTION
Courtesy of the American Geographical Society.

Reduced to Sea Level

Below −46°C. (−50°F.)

−34° to −46° (−30° to −50°)

−23° to −34° (−10° to −30°)

−23° to −12° (−10° to +10°)

−12° to −1° (10° to 30°)

−1° to 10° (30° to 50°)

10° to 21° (50° to 70°)

21° to 32° (70° to 90°)

Over 32° (90°)

Highlands above 1000 meters

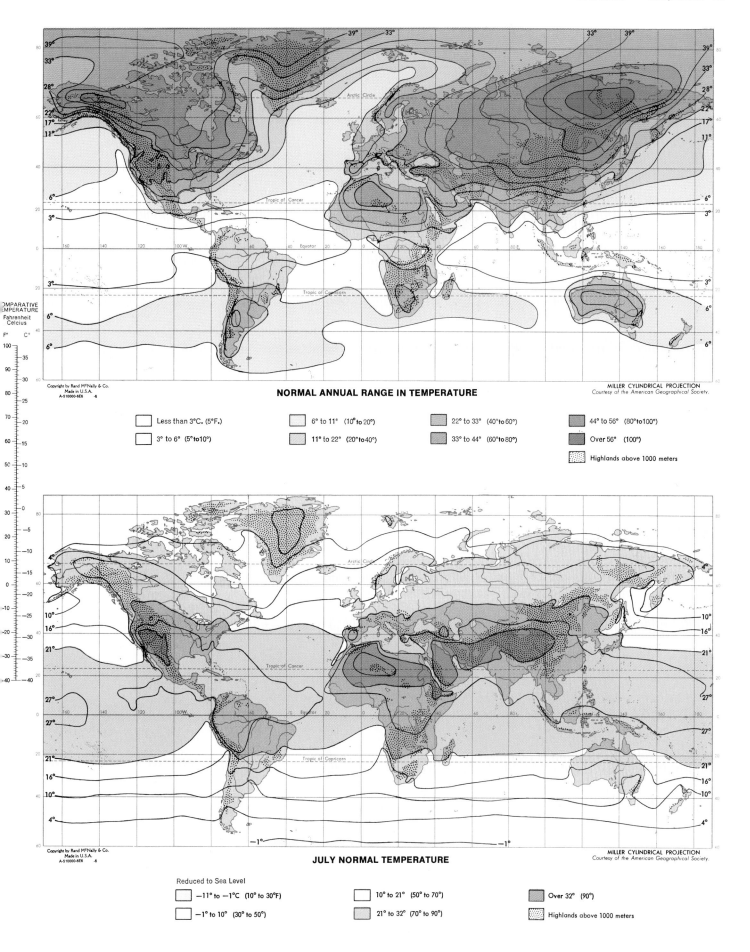

NORMAL ANNUAL RANGE IN TEMPERATURE

MILLER CYLINDRICAL PROJECTION
Courtesy of the American Geographical Society.

Less than 3°C. (5°F.)	6° to 11° (10° to 20°)	22° to 33° (40° to 60°)	44° to 56° (80° to 100°)
3° to 6° (5° to 10°)	11° to 22° (20° to 40°)	33° to 44° (60° to 80°)	Over 56° (100°)

Highlands above 1000 meters

JULY NORMAL TEMPERATURE

MILLER CYLINDRICAL PROJECTION
Courtesy of the American Geographical Society.

Reduced to Sea Level

−11° to −1°C (10° to 30°F)	10° to 21° (50° to 70°)	Over 32° (90°)
−1° to 10° (30° to 50°)	21° to 32° (70° to 90°)	Highlands above 1000 meters

Copyright by Rand McNally & Co.
Made in U.S.A.
A-510000-6E6 -6

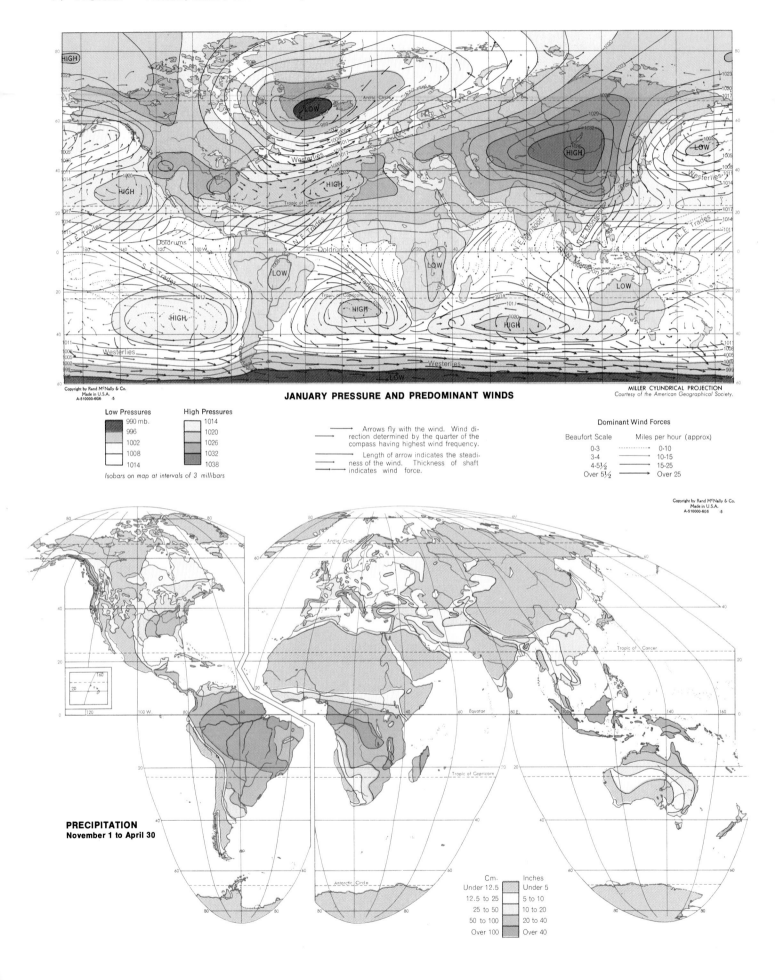

JANUARY PRESSURE AND PREDOMINANT WINDS

Copyright by Rand McNally & Co.
Made in U.S.A.
A-510000-6G6   -5

MILLER CYLINDRICAL PROJECTION
Courtesy of the American Geographical Society.

Low Pressures
- 990 mb.
- 996
- 1002
- 1008
- 1014

High Pressures
- 1014
- 1020
- 1026
- 1032
- 1038

Isobars on map at intervals of 3 millibars

→ Arrows fly with the wind. Wind direction determined by the quarter of the compass having highest wind frequency.

→ Length of arrow indicates the steadiness of the wind. Thickness of shaft indicates wind force.

Dominant Wind Forces

Beaufort Scale	Miles per hour (approx)
0-3	0-10
3-4	10-15
4-5½	15-25
Over 5½	Over 25

Copyright by Rand McNally & Co.
Made in U.S.A.
A-510000-6G6   -5

PRECIPITATION
November 1 to April 30

Cm.	Inches
Under 12.5	Under 5
12.5 to 25	5 to 10
25 to 50	10 to 20
50 to 100	20 to 40
Over 100	Over 40

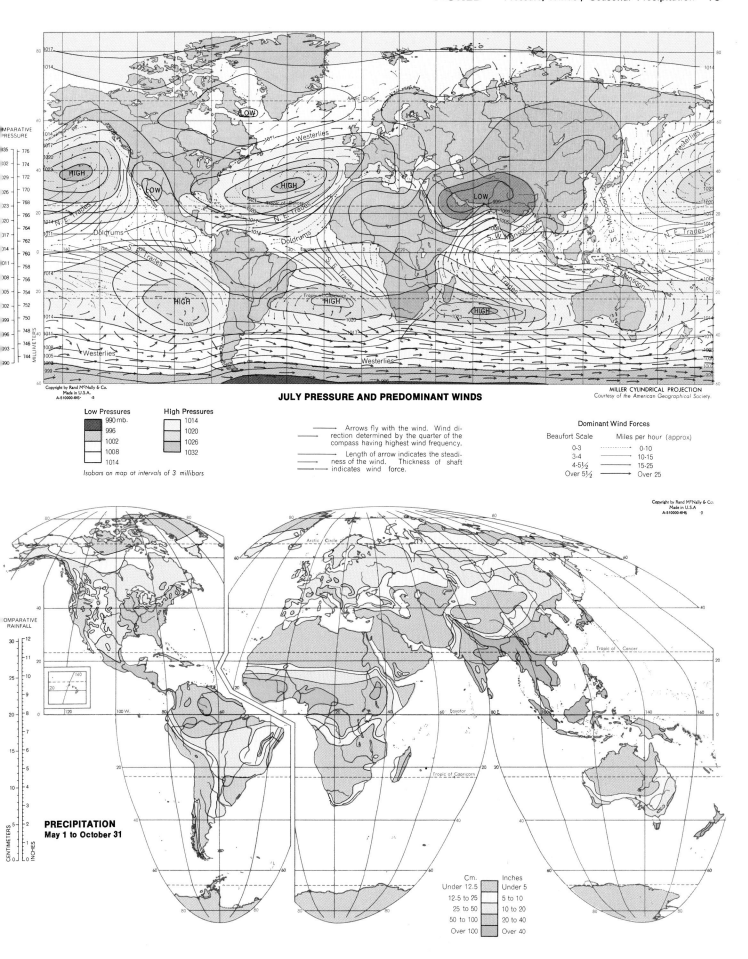

JULY PRESSURE AND PREDOMINANT WINDS

MILLER CYLINDRICAL PROJECTION
Courtesy of the American Geographical Society.

Copyright by Rand McNally & Co.
Made in U.S.A.
A-510000-6H5   -5

Low Pressures
990 mb.
996
1002
1008
1014

High Pressures
1014
1020
1026
1032

Isobars on map at intervals of 3 millibars

Arrows fly with the wind. Wind direction determined by the quarter of the compass having highest wind frequency.

Length of arrow indicates the steadiness of the wind. Thickness of shaft indicates wind force.

Dominant Wind Forces

Beaufort Scale	Miles per hour (approx)
0-3	0-10
3-4	10-15
4-5½	15-25
Over 5½	Over 25

Copyright by Rand McNally & Co.
Made in U.S.A
A-510000-6H6   -5

PRECIPITATION
May 1 to October 31

Cm.	Inches
Under 12.5	Under 5
12.5 to 25	5 to 10
25 to 50	10 to 20
50 to 100	20 to 40
Over 100	Over 40

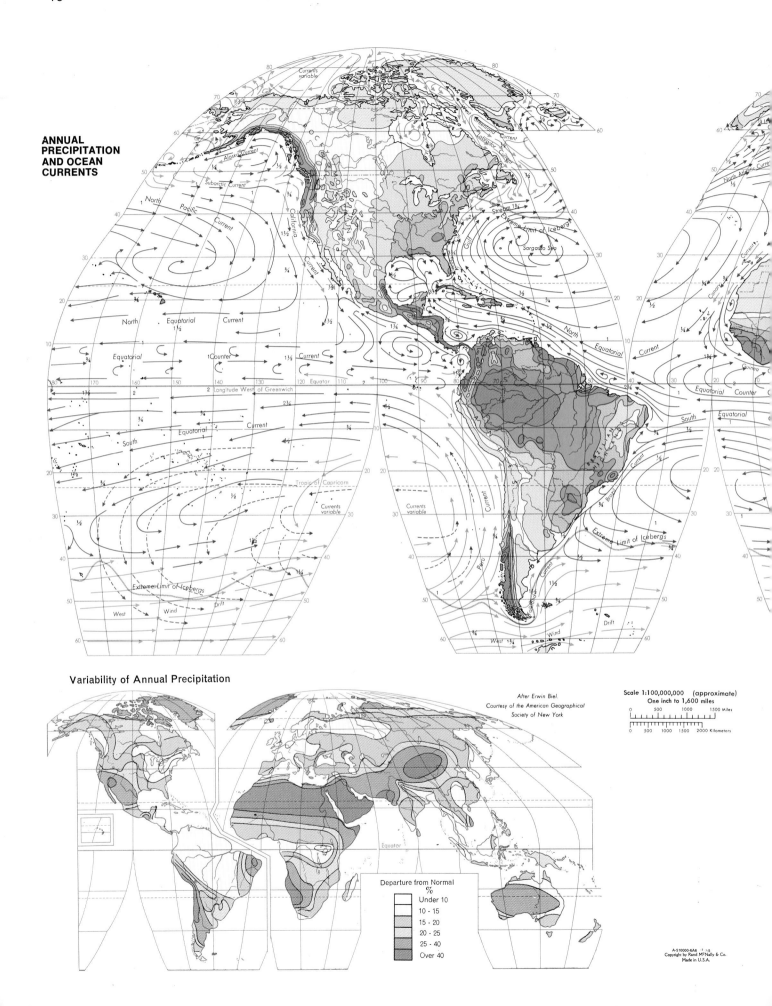

**ANNUAL
PRECIPITATION
AND OCEAN
CURRENTS**

Variability of Annual Precipitation

After Erwin Biel.
Courtesy of the American Geographical
Society of New York

Scale 1:100,000,000 (approximate)
One inch to 1,600 miles

Departure from Normal
%
Under 10
10 - 15
15 - 20
20 - 25
25 - 40
Over 40

A-510000-6A6
Copyright by Rand M°Nally & Co.
Made in U.S.A.

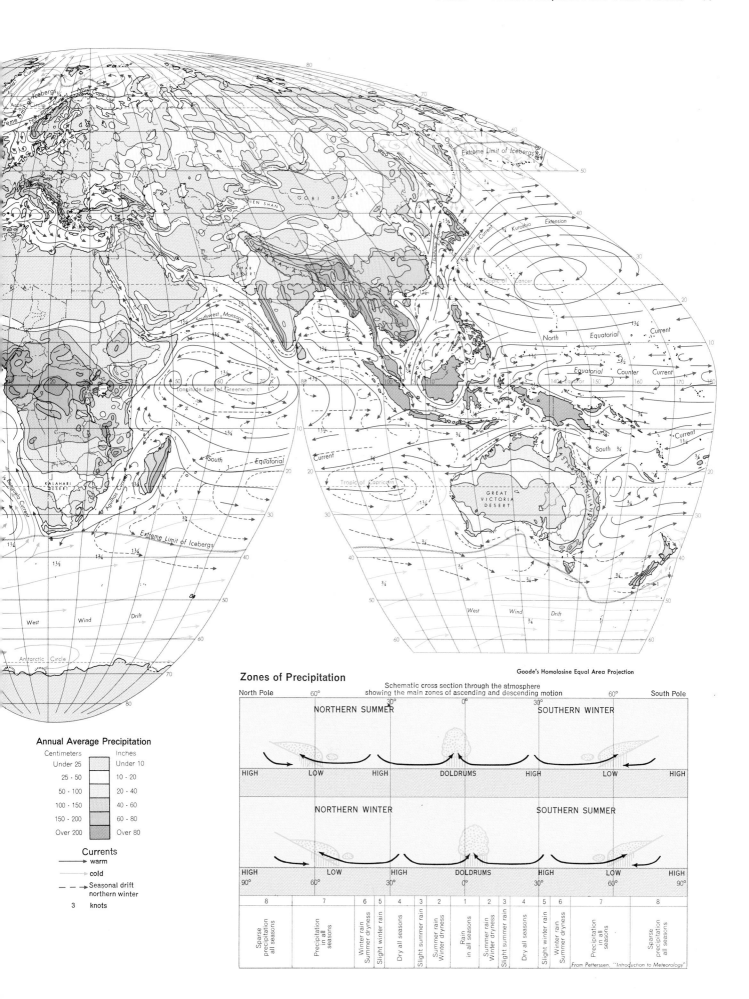

Goode's Homolosine Equal Area Projection

Zones of Precipitation

Schematic cross section through the atmosphere
showing the main zones of ascending and descending motion

Annual Average Precipitation

Centimeters		Inches
Under 25		Under 10
25 - 50		10 - 20
50 - 100		20 - 40
100 - 150		40 - 60
150 - 200		60 - 80
Over 200		Over 80

Currents

→ warm
→ cold
- - → Seasonal drift
northern winter

3 knots

From Petterssen, "Introduction to Meteorology"

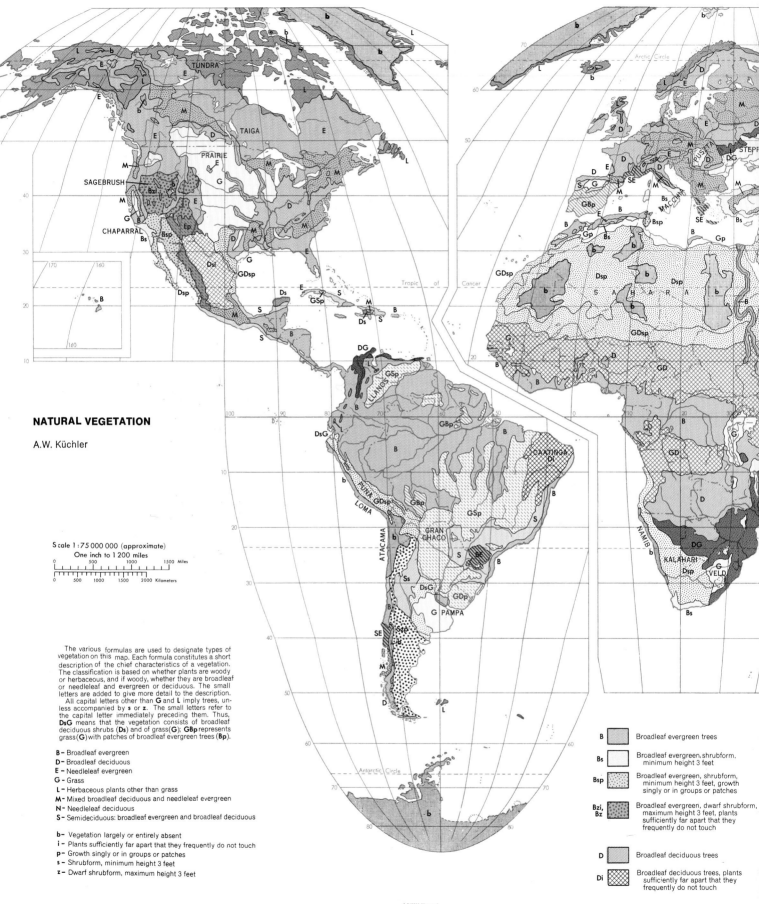

NATURAL VEGETATION

A.W. Küchler

Scale 1:75 000 000 (approximate)

One inch to 1 200 miles

0   500   1000   1500 Miles

0   500   1000   1500   2000 Kilometers

The various formulas are used to designate types of
vegetation on this map. Each formula constitutes a short
description of the chief characteristics of a vegetation.
The classification is based on whether plants are woody
or herbaceous, and if woody, whether they are broadleaf
or needleleaf and evergreen or deciduous. The
small letters are added to give more detail to the description.

All capital letters other than **G** and **L** imply trees, un-
less accompanied by **s** or **z**. The small letters refer to
the capital letter immediately preceding them. Thus,
DsG means that the vegetation consists of broadleaf
deciduous shrubs (**Ds**) and of grass (**G**); **GBp** represents
grass (**G**) with patches of broadleaf evergreen trees (**Bp**).

B – Broadleaf evergreen
D – Broadleaf deciduous
E – Needleleaf evergreen
G – Grass
L – Herbaceous plants other than grass
M – Mixed broadleaf deciduous and needleleaf evergreen
N – Needleleaf deciduous
S – Semideciduous: broadleaf evergreen and broadleaf deciduous

b – Vegetation largely or entirely absent
i – Plants sufficiently far apart that they frequently do not touch
p – Growth singly or in groups or patches
s – Shrubform, minimum height 3 feet
z – Dwarf shrubform, maximum height 3 feet

B	Broadleaf evergreen trees
Bs	Broadleaf evergreen, shrubform, minimum height 3 feet
Bsp	Broadleaf evergreen, shrubform, minimum height 3 feet, growth singly or in groups or patches
Bzi, Bz	Broadleaf evergreen, dwarf shrubform, maximum height 3 feet, plants sufficiently far apart that they frequently do not touch
D	Broadleaf deciduous trees
Di	Broadleaf deciduous trees, plants sufficiently far apart that they frequently do not touch

Goode's Homolosine
Equal Area Projection
(Condensed)

Broadleaf deciduous, shrubform, minimum height 3 feet	**E** Needleleaf evergreen trees	**GDsp** Grass and other herbaceous plants Broadleaf deciduous, shrubform, minimum height 3 feet, growth singly or in groups or patches	**S** Semideciduous: broadleaf evergreen and broadleaf deciduous trees
Broadleaf deciduous, shrubform, minimum height 3 feet, plants sufficiently far apart that they frequently do not touch	**Ep** Needleleaf evergreen trees, growth singly or in groups or patches	**GSp** Grass and other herbaceous plants Semideciduous: broadleaf evergreen and broadleaf deciduous trees, growth singly or in groups or patches	**Ss** Semideciduous: broadleaf evergreen and broadleaf deciduous, shrubform, minimum height 3 feet
Broadleaf deciduous, shrubform, minimum height 3 feet, growth singly or in groups or patches			**SsG** Semideciduous: broadleaf evergreen and broadleaf deciduous, shrubform, minimum height 3 feet Grass and other herbaceous plants
Broadleaf deciduous, dwarf shrubform, maximum height 3 feet, growth singly or in groups or patches	**G** Grass and other herbaceous plants	**L** Herbaceous plants other than grass	**Szp** Semideciduous: broadleaf evergreen and broadleaf deciduous, dwarf shrub-form, maximum height 3 feet, growth singly or in groups or patches
Broadleaf deciduous, shrubform, minimum height 3 feet Grass and other herbaceous plants	**Gp** Grass and other herbaceous plants, growth singly or in groups or patches		
Broadleaf deciduous trees Grass and other herbaceous plants	**GBp** Grass and other herbaceous plants Broadleaf evergreen trees, growth singly or in groups or patches	**M** Mixed: broadleaf deciduous and needleleaf evergreen trees	**SE** Semideciduous: broadleaf evergreen and broadleaf deciduous trees Needleleaf evergreen trees
Broadleaf deciduous trees Broadleaf evergreen, shrubform, minimum height 3 feet	**GD** Grass and other herbaceous plants Broadleaf deciduous trees	**N** Needleleaf deciduous trees	
	GDp Grass and other herbaceous plants Broadleaf deciduous trees, growth singly or in groups or patches	**ND** Needleleaf deciduous trees Broadleaf deciduous trees	**b** Vegetation largely or entirely absent

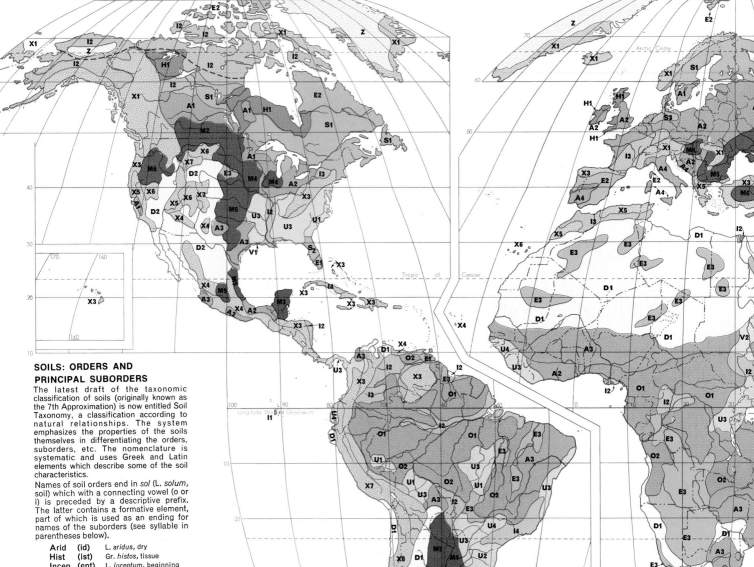

SOILS: ORDERS AND PRINCIPAL SUBORDERS

The latest draft of the taxonomic classification of soils (originally known as the 7th Approximation) is now entitled Soil Taxonomy, a classification according to natural relationships. The system emphasizes the properties of the soils themselves in differentiating the orders, suborders, etc. The nomenclature is systematic and uses Greek and Latin elements which describe some of the soil characteristics.

Names of soil orders end in *sol* (L. *solum*, soil) which with a connecting vowel (o or i) is preceded by a descriptive prefix. The latter contains a formative element, part of which is used as an ending for names of the suborders (see syllable in parentheses below).

Arid	(id)	L. *aridus*, dry
Hist	(ist)	Gr. *histos*, tissue
Incep	(ept)	L. *inceptum*, beginning
Moll	(oll)	L. *mollis*, soft
Ox	(ox)	F. *oxide*, oxide
Spod	(od)	Gr. *spodus*, wood ash
Ult	(ult)	L. *ultimus*, last
Vert	(ert)	L. *verto*, turn

Names of suborders have two parts. The first suggest diagnostic properties of the soil (see below), and second is the formative element from the order name, eg. Id (Arid).

Alb	L. *albus*, white bleached alluvial horizon soils
And	modified from ando soils from vitreous parent materials
Aqu	L. *aqua*, water soils which are wet for long periods
Arg	L. *argilla*, clay soils with a horizon of clay accumulation
Bor	Gr. *boreas*, northern cool
Cry	Gr. *kryes*, icy cold cold
Hum	L. *humus*, earth presence of organic matter
Ochr	Gr. *orchras*, pale soils with little organic matter
Psamm	Gr. *psammas*, sand sandy soils
Rend	from Rendzina high carbonate content
Torr	L. *torridus*, hot and dry soils of very dry climate
Ud	L. *udus*, humid soils of humid climate
Umbr	L. *umbra*, shade dark color reflecting relatively high organic matter
Ust	L. *ustus*, burnt soils of dry climates with summer rains
Xer	Gr. *xeros*, dry soils of dry climates with winter rains

Only dominant orders and suborders are shown and each area delineated may include other kinds of soil.

ALFISOLS — Podzolic soils of middle latitudes: soils with gray to brown surface horizons; subsurface horizons of clay accumulation; medium to high base supply.

Boralfs A1	Cool to cold, freely drained.
Udalfs A2	Temperate to hot; usually moist (Gray-brown Podzolic*)
Ustalfs A3	Warm subhumid to semi-arid; dry > 90 days (some Reddish Chestnut and Red & Yellow Podzolic soils*)
Xeralfs A4	Warm, dry in summer; moist in winter.

ARIDISOLS — Pedogenic horizons lower in organic matter and dry for > 6 mo. of the year. (Desert and Reddish Desert*) Salts may accumulate on or near surface.

Aridisols D1	Undifferentiated.
Argids D2	With horizon of clay accumulation.

ENTISOLS — Soils without pedogenic horizons on recent alluvium, dune sands, etc.; varied in appearance.

Aquents E1	Seasonally or perennially wet; bluish or gray and mottled.
Orthents E2	Shallow; or recent erosional surfaces (Lithosols*). A few on recent loams.
Psamments E3	Sandy soils on shifting and stabilized sands.

HISTOSOLS — Organic soils; bogs, peats and mucks; wholly or partly saturated with water.

INCEPTISOLS — Immature, weakly developed soils; pedogenic horizons show alteration but little illuviation; usually moist.

Andepts I1	Soil formed on amorphous clay or vitric volcanic ash.
Aquepts I2	Seasonally saturated with water (includes some Humic Gley, alluvial tundra soils*).
Ochrepts I3	Thin, light-colored surface horizons; little organic matter.
Tropepts I4	Continuously warm to hot; brownish to reddish.
Umbrepts I5	Dark colored surface horizons; rich in organic matter; medium to low base supply.

Scale 1 : 75 000 000 (approximate)
One inch to 1 200 miles

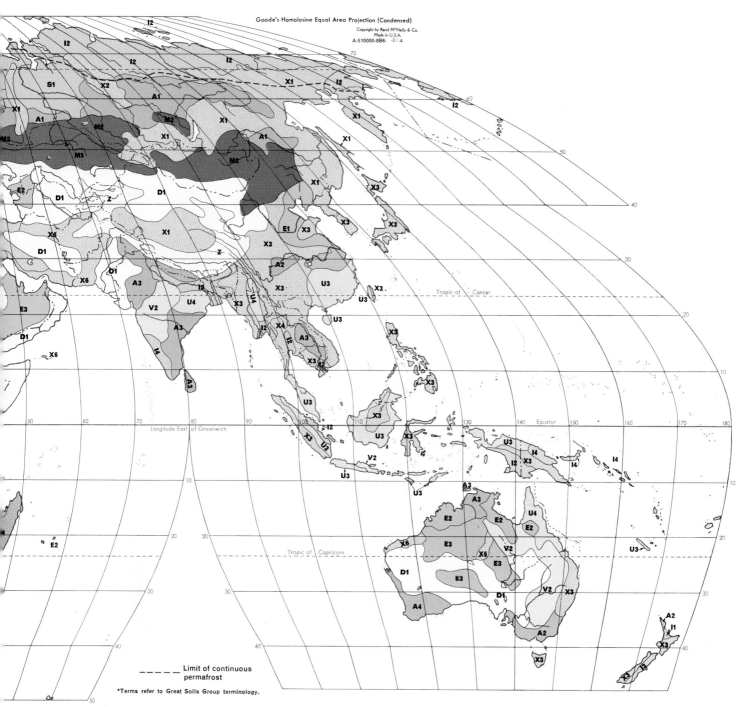

Goode's Homolosine Equal Area Projection (Condensed)
Copyright by Rand M⁰Nally & Co.
Made in U.S.A.
A-510000-8B6-

Longitude East of Greenwich

Tropic of Cancer

Equator

Tropic of Capricorn

- - - - Limit of continuous permafrost

*Terms refer to Great Soils Group terminology.

MOLLISOLS	Soils of the steppe (incl. Chernozem and Chestnut soils*). Thick, black organic rich surface horizons and high base supply.
Albolls M1	Seasonally saturated with water; light gray subsurface horizon.
Borolls M2	Cool or cold (incl. some Chernozem, Chestnut and Brown soils*).
Rendolls M3	Formed on highly calcareous parent materials (Rendzina*).
Udolls M4	Temperate to warm; usually moist (Prairie soils*).
Ustolls M5	Temperate to hot; dry for > 90 days (incl. some Chestnut and Brown soils*).
Xerolls M6	Cool to warm; dry in summer; moist in winter.

OXISOLS	Deeply weathered tropical and subtropical soils (Laterites*); rich in sesquioxides of iron and aluminum; low in nutrients; limited productivity without fertilizer.
Orthox O1	Hot and nearly always moist.
Ustox O2	Warm or hot; dry for long periods but moist > 90 consecutive days.

SPODOSOLS	Soils with a subsurface accumulation of amorphous materials overlaid by a light colored, leached sandy horizon.
Spodosols S1	Undifferentiated (mostly high latitudes).
Aquods S2	Seasonally saturated with water; sandy parent materials.
Humods S3	Considerable accumulations of organic matter in subsurface horizon.
Orthods S4	With subsurface accumulations of iron, aluminum and organic matter (Podzols*).

ULTISOLS	Soils with some subsurface clay accumulation; low base supply; usually moist and low inorganic matter; low in organic matter; can be productive with fertilization.
Aquults U1	Seasonally saturated with water; subsurface gray or mottled horizon.
Humults U2	High in organic matter; dark colored; moist, warm to temperate all year.
Udults U3	Low in organic matter; moist, temperate to hot (Red-Yellow Podzolic; some Reddish-Brown Lateritic soils*).
Ustults U4	Warm to hot; dry > 90 days.

VERTISOLS	Soils with high content of swelling clays; deep, wide cracks in dry periods dark colored.
Uderts V1	Usually moist; cracks open < 90 days.
Usterts V2	Cracks open > 90 days; difficult to till (Black tropical soils*).

MOUNTAIN SOILS Soils with various moisture and temperature regimes; steep slopes and variable relief and elevation; soils vary greatly within short distance.

X1 Cryic great groups of Entisols, Inceptisols and Spodosols.

X2 Boralfs and Cryic groups of Entisols and Inceptisols.

X3 Udic great groups of Alfisols, Entisols and Ultisols; Inceptisols.

X4 Ustic great groups of Alfisols, Entisols, Inceptisols, Mollisols and Ultisols.

X5 Xeric great groups of Alfisols, Entisols, Inceptisols, Mollisols and Ultisols.

X6 Torric great groups of Entisols; Aridisols.

X7 Ustic and cryic great groups of Alfisols, Entisols; Inceptisols and Mollisols; ustic great groups of Ultisols; cryic great groups of Spodosols.

X8 Aridisols; torric and cryic great groups of Entisols, and cryic great groups of Spodosols and Inceptisols.

Z Areas with little or no soil; icefields, and rugged mountain.

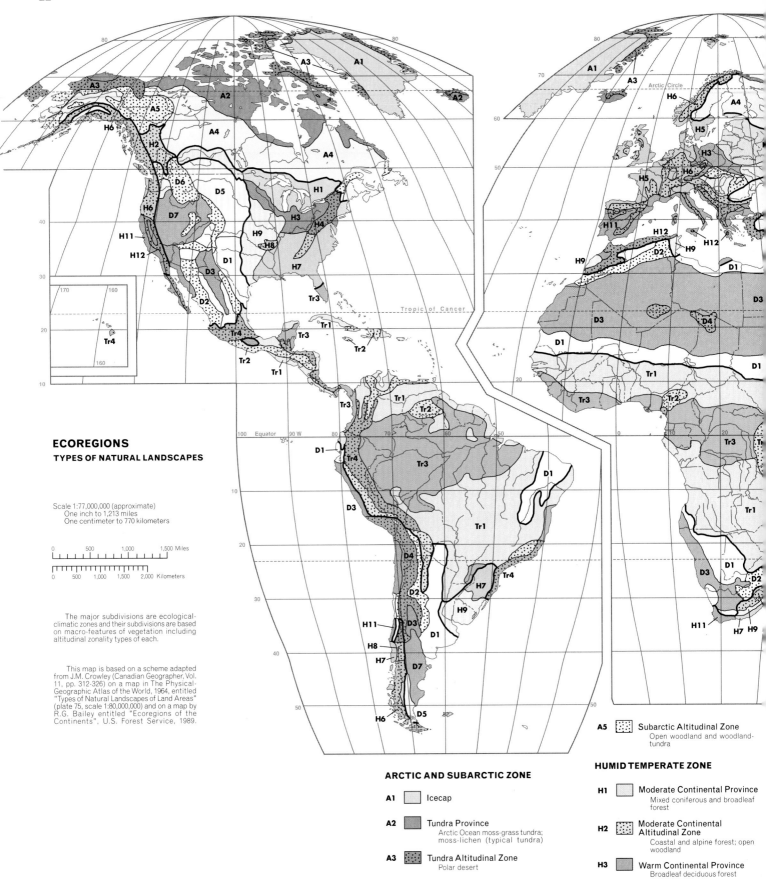

22

ECOREGIONS
TYPES OF NATURAL LANDSCAPES

Scale 1:77,000,000 (approximate)
One inch to 1,213 miles
One centimeter to 770 kilometers

| 0 | 500 | 1,000 | 1,500 Miles |

| 0 | 500 | 1,000 | 1,500 | 2,000 Kilometers |

The major subdivisions are ecological-climatic zones and their subdivisions are based on macro-features of vegetation including altitudinal zonality types of each.

This map is based on a scheme adapted from J.M. Crowley (Canadian Geographer, Vol. 11, pp. 312-326) on a map in The Physical-Geographic Atlas of the World, 1964, entitled "Types of Natural Landscapes of Land Areas" (plate 75, scale 1:80,000,000) and on a map by R.G. Bailey entitled "Ecoregions of the Continents", U.S. Forest Service, 1989.

A5 Subarctic Altitudinal Zone
Open woodland and woodland-tundra

ARCTIC AND SUBARCTIC ZONE

A1 Icecap

A2 Tundra Province
Arctic Ocean moss-grass tundra; moss-lichen (typical tundra)

A3 Tundra Altitudinal Zone
Polar desert

A4 Subarctic Province
Dark evergreen forest; needleleaf taiga; mixed coniferous and small-leafed forest

HUMID TEMPERATE ZONE

H1 Moderate Continental Province
Mixed coniferous and broadleaf forest

H2 Moderate Continental Altitudinal Zone
Coastal and alpine forest; open woodland

H3 Warm Continental Province
Broadleaf deciduous forest

H4 Warm Continental Altitudinal Zone
Upland broadleaf and alpine needleleaf forest

Copyright by Rand McNally & Co.
Made in U.S.A.
DM-510000-8D-GD1- -1- -1

A5 ☐ Marine Province
Lowland, west-coastal humid forest

A6 ▦ Marine Altitudinal Zone
Humid coastal and alpine coniferous forest

A7 ☐ Humid Subtropical Province
Broadleaf evergreen and broadleaf deciduous forest

A8 ▦ Humid Subtropical Altitudinal Zone
Upland, subtropical broadleaf forest

A9 ☐ Prairie Province

A0 ▦ Prairie Altitudinal Zone
Upland mixed prairie and woodland

H11 ▦ Mediterranean Province
Sclerophyll woodland, shrub, and steppe

H12 ▦ Mediterranean Altitudinal Zone
Upland shrub and steppe

DRY AND DESERT ZONE

D1 ☐ Tropical/Subtropical Steppe Province
Dry steppe, desert shrub, semi-desert savanna

D2 ▦ Tropical/Subtropical Steppe Altitudinal Zone
Upland steppe and desert shrub

D3 ▦ Tropical/Subtropical Desert Province
Hot, lowland desert at subtropical and coastal locations

D4 ▦ Tropical/Subtropical Desert Altitudinal Zone
Desert shrub

D5 ☐ Temperate Steppe Province
Medium to short steppe grassland

D6 ▦ Temperate Steppe Altitudinal Zone
Alpine meadow and coniferous woodland

D7 ▦ Temperate Desert Province
Midlatitude rainshadow desert

D8 ▦ Temperate Desert Altitudinal Zone
Extreme continental desert-steppe

HUMID TROPICAL ZONE

Tr1 ☐ Savanna Province
Seasonally dry forest, open woodland, tall grass

Tr2 ▦ Savanna Altitudinal Zone
Open woodland-steppe

Tr3 ▦ Rainforest Province
Constantly humid, broadleaf evergreen forest

Tr4 ▦ Rainforest Altitudinal Zone
Broadleaf evergreen and subtropical deciduous forest

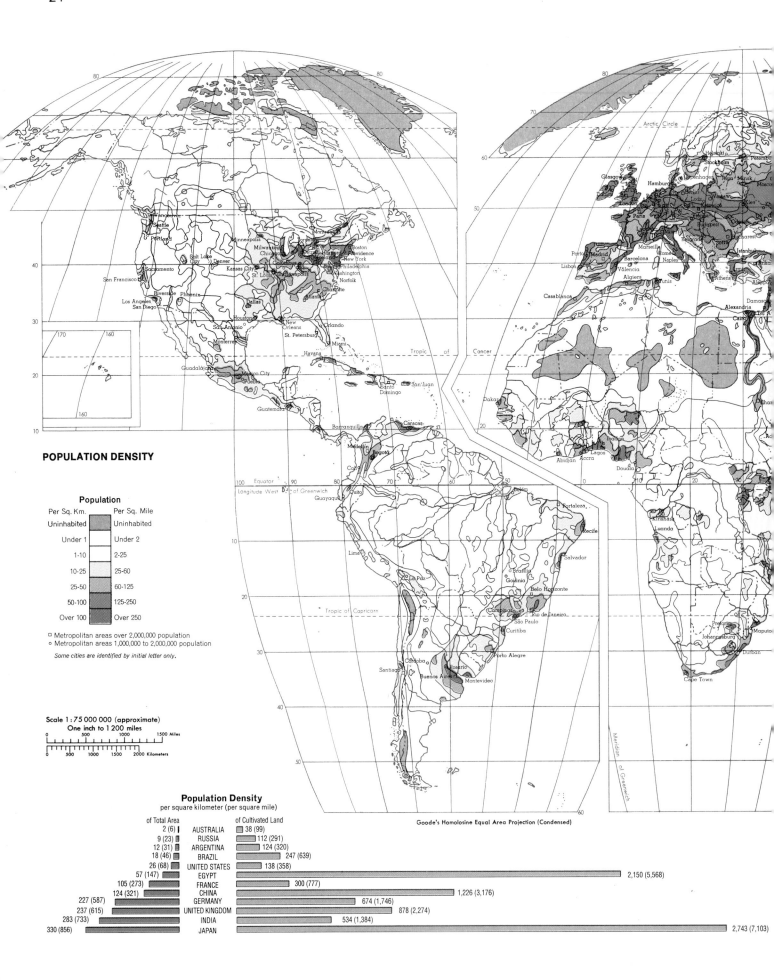

POPULATION DENSITY

Population

Per Sq. Km.	Per Sq. Mile
Uninhabited	Uninhabited
Under 1	Under 2
1-10	2-25
10-25	25-60
25-50	60-125
50-100	125-250
Over 100	Over 250

□ Metropolitan areas over 2,000,000 population
○ Metropolitan areas 1,000,000 to 2,000,000 population

Some cities are identified by initial letter only.

Scale 1 : 75 000 000 (approximate)
One inch to 1 200 miles

0   500   1000   1500 Miles

0   500   1000   1500   2000 Kilometers

Population Density
per square kilometer (per square mile)

of Total Area		of Cultivated Land
2 (6)	AUSTRALIA	38 (99)
9 (23)	RUSSIA	112 (291)
12 (31)	ARGENTINA	124 (320)
18 (46)	BRAZIL	247 (639)
26 (68)	UNITED STATES	138 (358)
57 (147)	EGYPT	2,150 (5,568)
105 (273)	FRANCE	300 (777)
124 (321)	CHINA	1,226 (3,176)
227 (587)	GERMANY	674 (1,746)
237 (615)	UNITED KINGDOM	878 (2,274)
283 (733)	INDIA	534 (1,384)
330 (856)	JAPAN	2,743 (7,103)

Goode's Homolosine Equal Area Projection (Condensed)

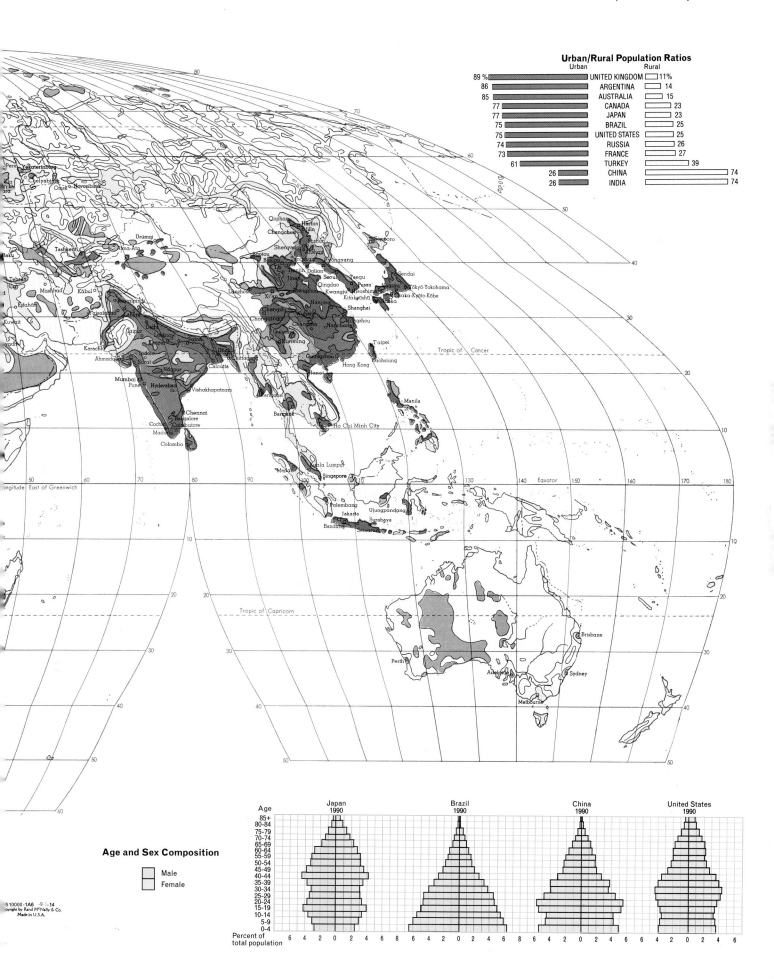

Urban/Rural Population Ratios

	Urban		Rural	
89 %		UNITED KINGDOM	11%	
86		ARGENTINA	14	
85		AUSTRALIA	15	
77		CANADA	23	
77		JAPAN	23	
75		BRAZIL	25	
75		UNITED STATES	25	
74		RUSSIA	26	
73		FRANCE	27	
61		TURKEY	39	
26		CHINA	74	
26		INDIA	74	

Age and Sex Composition

Male
Female

Age | Japan 1990 | Brazil 1990 | China 1990 | United States 1990

85+
80-84
75-79
70-74
65-69
60-64
55-59
50-54
45-49
40-44
35-39
30-34
25-29
20-24
15-19
10-14
5-9
0-4

Percent of
total population

6 4 2 0 2 4 6   6 4 2 0 2 4 6   6 4 2 0 2 4 6   6 4 2 0 2 4 6

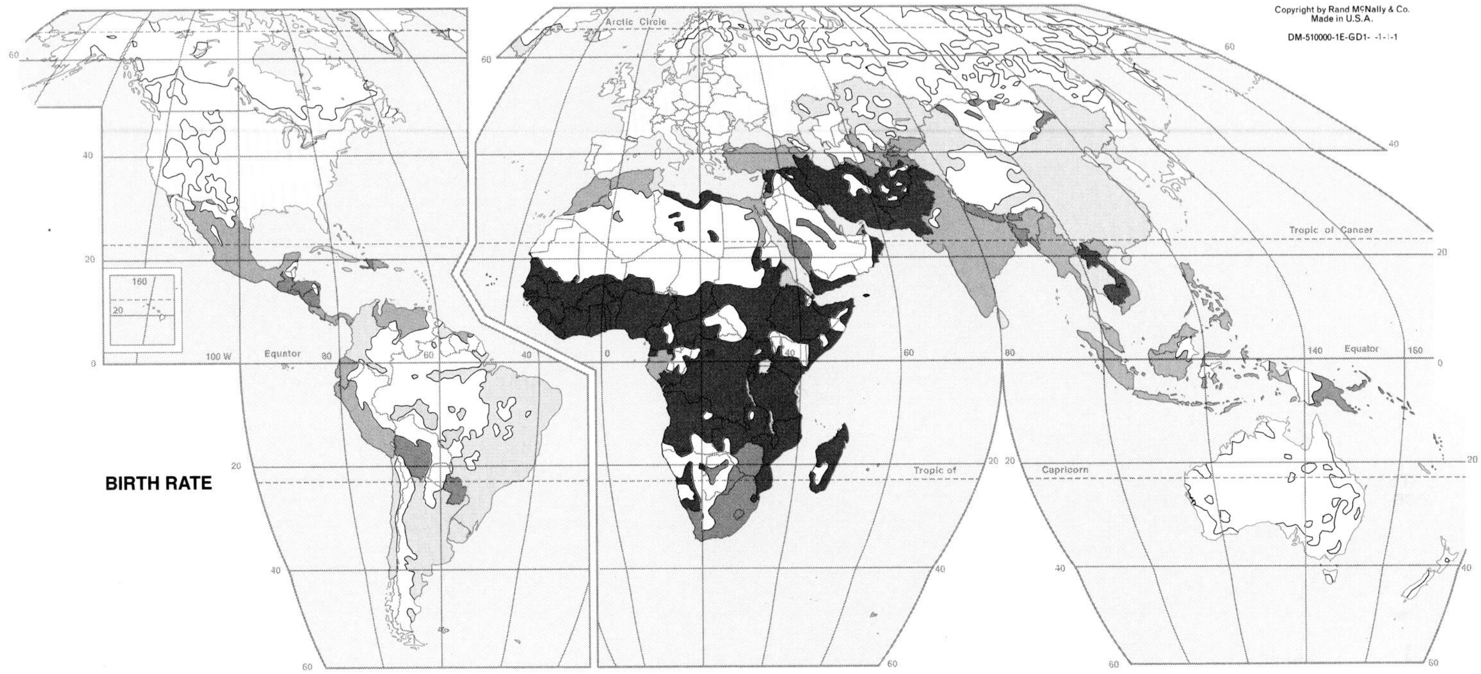

BIRTH RATE

Birth Rate (Crude)
per 1,000 population

	Over 40	High
	32 - 40	Moderately high
World Avg. →	24 - 32	Moderately low
25	16 - 24	Low
	Under 16	Very Low
		Uninhabited or sparsely populated
		Data not available

Life Expectancy at Birth

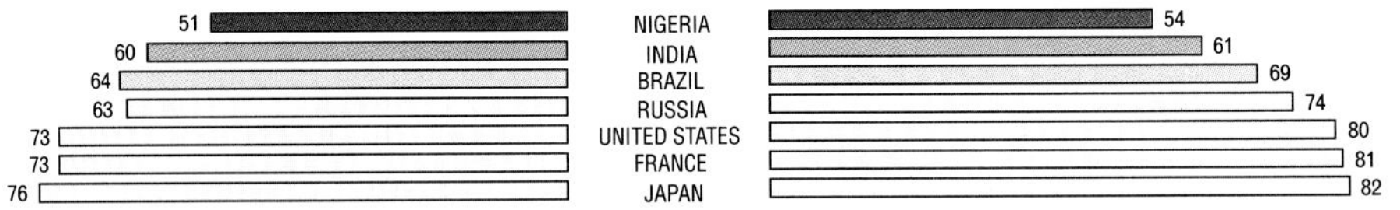

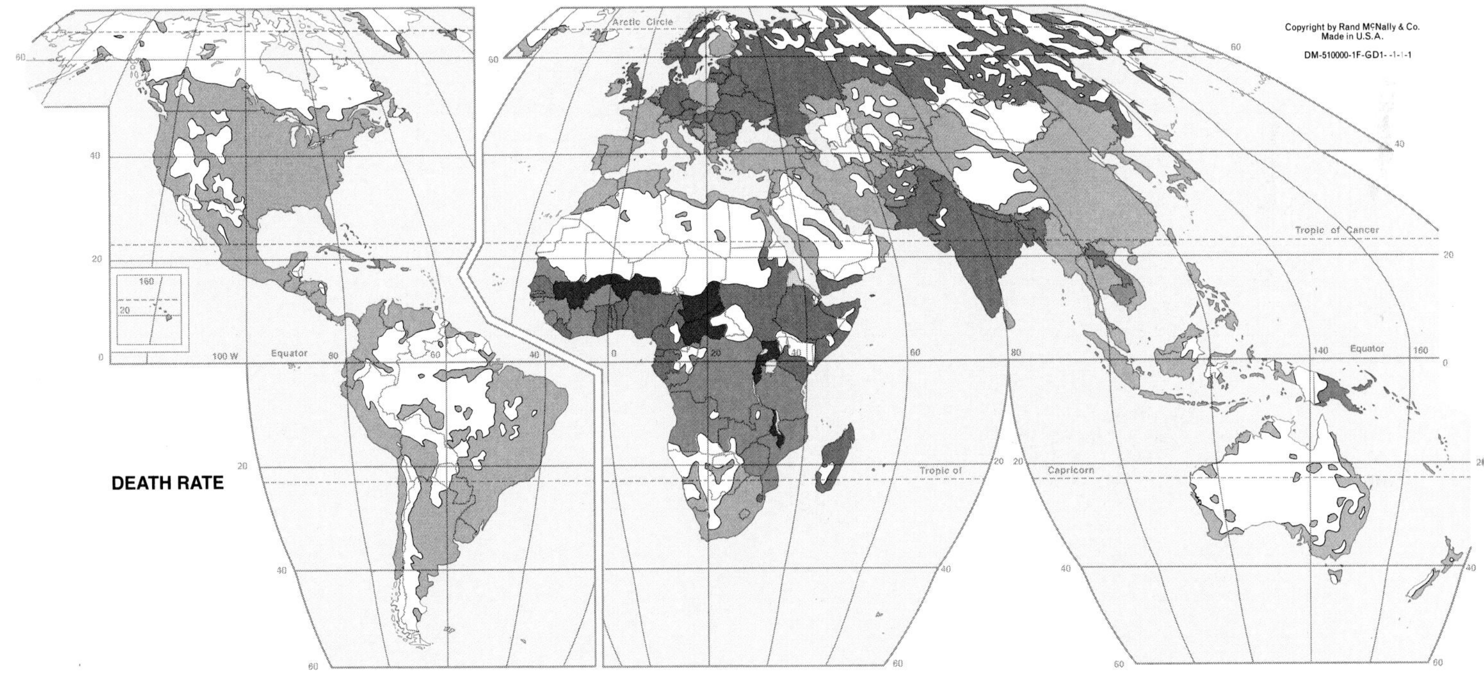

Years Male Female **Years**

	Male		Female	
NIGERIA	51		54	
INDIA	60		61	
BRAZIL	64		69	
RUSSIA	63		74	
UNITED STATES	73		80	
FRANCE	73		81	
JAPAN	76		82	

DEATH RATE

Death Rate (Crude) for all ages
per 1,000 population

	Over 20	High
	15 - 20	Moderately high
	10 - 15	Moderately low
World Avg. →	Under 10	Low
9		Uninhabited or sparsely populated
		Data not available

Infant Mortality Rate

Deaths under one year of age per 1,000 live births

JAPAN	4
FRANCE	7
UNITED STATES	9
RUSSIA	18
BRAZIL	63
INDIA	80
NIGERIA	105

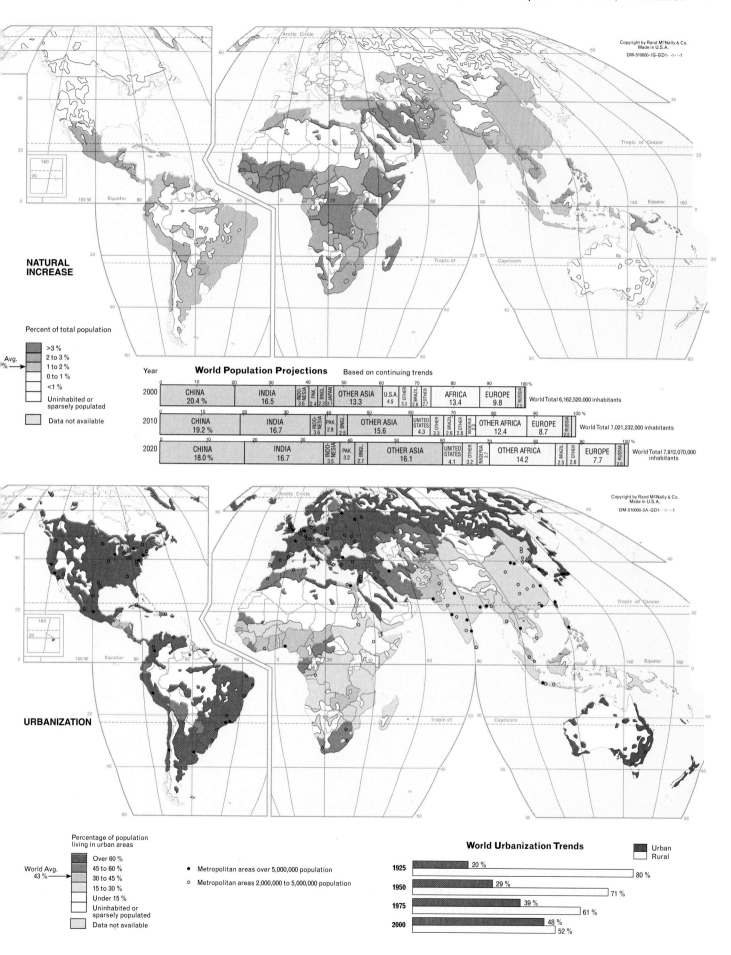

Copyright by Rand McNally & Co.
Made in U.S.A.
DM-510000-1G-GD1- -!-!-1

NATURAL INCREASE

Percent of total population

- >3 %
- 2 to 3 %
- 1 to 2 %
- 0 to 1 %
- <1 %
- Uninhabited or sparsely populated
- Data not available

Avg. % →

World Population Projections — Based on continuing trends

Year		World Total
2000	CHINA 20.4 % · INDIA 16.5 · INDO-NESIA 3.6 · PAK. 2.4 · BNGL 2.3 · JAPAN 2.1 · OTHER ASIA 13.3 · U.S.A. 4.5 · OTHER 3.3 · BRAZIL 2.8 · OTHER 2.7 · AFRICA 13.4 · EUROPE 9.8 · RUSSIA 2.5	World Total 6,162,520,000 inhabitants
2010	CHINA 19.2 % · INDIA 16.7 · INDO-NESIA 3.6 · PAK. 2.8 · BNGL 2.5 · OTHER ASIA 15.6 · UNITED STATES 4.3 · OTHER 3.3 · BRAZIL 2.6 · OTHER 2.8 · NIGERIA 2.7 · OTHER AFRICA 12.4 · EUROPE 8.7 · RUSSIA 2.2	World Total 7,021,232,000 inhabitants
2020	CHINA 18.0 % · INDIA 16.7 · INDO-NESIA 3.5 · PAK. 3.2 · BNGL 2.7 · OTHER ASIA 16.1 · UNITED STATES 4.1 · OTHER 3.2 · NIGERIA 2.7 · OTHER AFRICA 14.2 · BRAZIL 2.5 · OTHER 2.6 · EUROPE 7.7 · RUSSIA 2.0	World Total 7,912,070,000 inhabitants

Copyright by Rand McNally & Co.
Made in U.S.A.
DM-510000-3A-GD1- -!-!-1

URBANIZATION

Percentage of population living in urban areas

- Over 60 %
- 45 to 60 %
- 30 to 45 %
- 15 to 30 %
- Under 15 %
- Uninhabited or sparsely populated
- Data not available

World Avg. 43 % →

- ● Metropolitan areas over 5,000,000 population
- ○ Metropolitan areas 2,000,000 to 5,000,000 population

World Urbanization Trends

■ Urban   □ Rural

Year	Urban	Rural
1925	20 %	80 %
1950	29 %	71 %
1975	39 %	61 %
2000	48 %	52 %

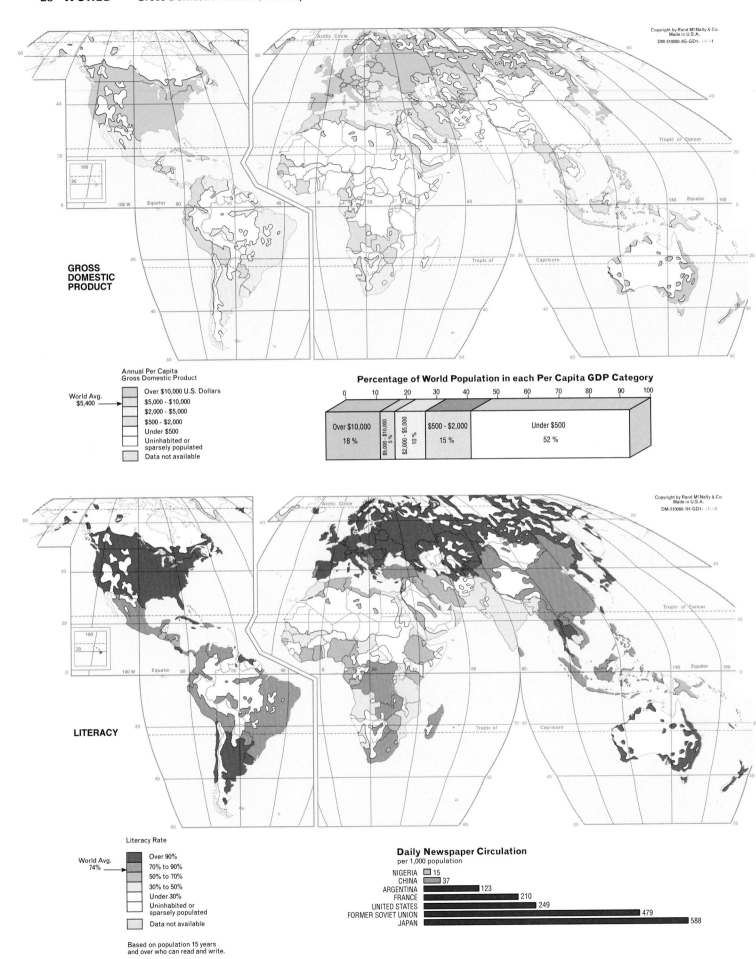

GROSS DOMESTIC PRODUCT

Annual Per Capita
Gross Domestic Product

World Avg. $5,400

	Over $10,000 U.S. Dollars
	$5,000 - $10,000
	$2,000 - $5,000
	$500 - $2,000
	Under $500
	Uninhabited or sparsely populated
	Data not available

Percentage of World Population in each Per Capita GDP Category

0 10 20 30 40 50 60 70 80 90 100

Over $10,000	$5,000 - $10,000	$2,000 - $5,000	$500 - $2,000	Under $500
18 %	5 %	10 %	15 %	52 %

LITERACY

Literacy Rate

World Avg. 74%

	Over 90%
	70% to 90%
	50% to 70%
	30% to 50%
	Under 30%
	Uninhabited or sparsely populated
	Data not available

Based on population 15 years
and over who can read and write.

Daily Newspaper Circulation
per 1,000 population

NIGERIA	15
CHINA	37
ARGENTINA	123
FRANCE	210
UNITED STATES	249
FORMER SOVIET UNION	479
JAPAN	588

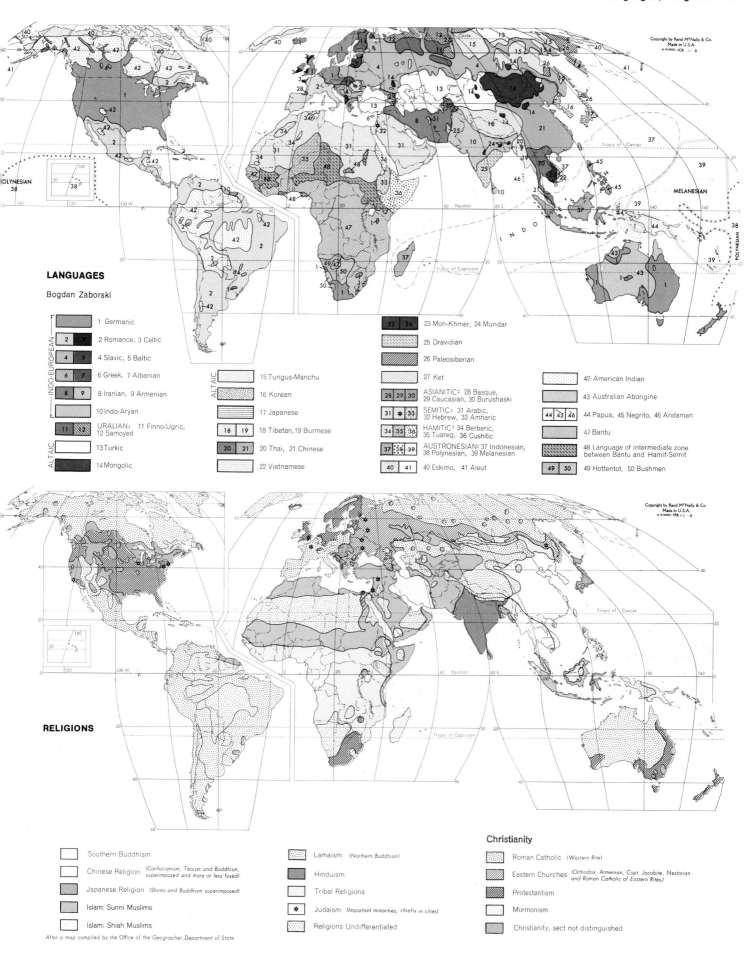

Copyright by Rand McNally & Co.
Made in U.S.A.
A-510000-1C6 -3-: -5

LANGUAGES

Bogdan Zaborski

INDO-EUROPEAN
- 1 Germanic
- 2 Romance, 3 Celtic
- 4 Slavic, 5 Baltic
- 6 Greek, 7 Albanian
- 8 Iranian, 9 Armenian
- 10 Indo-Aryan

URALIAN: 11 Finno-Ugric, 12 Samoyed

ALTAIC
- 13 Turkic
- 14 Mongolic
- 15 Tungus-Manchu
- 16 Korean
- 17 Japanese
- 18 Tibetan, 19 Burmese
- 20 Thai, 21 Chinese
- 22 Vietnamese

- 23 Mon-Khmer, 24 Mundar
- 25 Dravidian
- 26 Paleosiberian
- 27 Ket
- ASIANITIC: 28 Basque, 29 Caucasian, 30 Burushaski
- SEMITIC: 31 Arabic, 32 Hebrew, 33 Amharic
- HAMITIC: 34 Berberic, 35 Tuareg, 36 Cushitic
- AUSTRONESIAN: 37 Indonesian, 38 Polynesian, 39 Melanesian
- 40 Eskimo, 41 Aleut

- 42 American Indian
- 43 Australian Aborigine
- 44 Papua, 45 Negrito, 46 Andaman
- 47 Bantu
- 48 Language of intermediate zone between Bantu and Hamit-Semit
- 49 Hottentot, 50 Bushmen

Copyright by Rand McNally & Co.
Made in U.S.A.
A-510000-1R6 3-3 -5

RELIGIONS

Christianity

- Southern Buddhism
- Chinese Religion (Confucianism, Taoism and Buddhism, superimposed and more or less fused)
- Japanese Religion (Shinto and Buddhism superimposed)
- Islam: Sunni Muslims
- Islam: Shiah Muslims
- Lamaism (Northern Buddhism)
- Hinduism
- Tribal Religions
- Judaism (Important minorities, chiefly in cities)
- Religions Undifferentiated
- Roman Catholic (Western Rite)
- Eastern Churches (Orthodox, Armenian, Copt, Jacobite, Nestorian and Roman Catholic of Eastern Rites.)
- Protestantism
- Mormonism
- Christianity, sect not distinguished

After a map compiled by the Office of the Geographer, Department of State

CALORIE SUPPLY

Note: Size of each country is proportional to population.

Calorie supply per capita
(percentage of requirements*)

≥120%	Well above requirements
110 to 120%	Above requirements
100 to 110%	Adequate nutrition
90 to 100%	Some malnutrition
<90%	Serious malnutrition and/or hunger
n.a.	Data not available

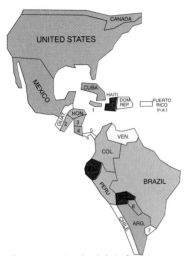

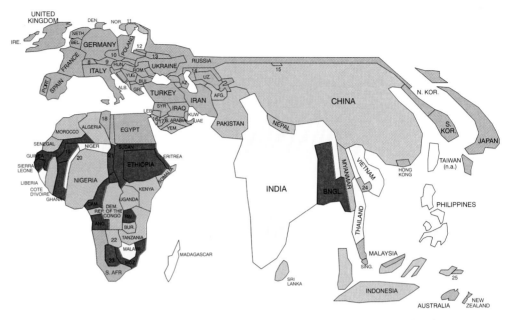

*Requirements estimated on the basis of
physiological needs for normal activity with
consideration of environmental temperature,
body weight, and age and sex distribution of
the population in various countries.
Estimates are for 1990.

Copyright by Rand McNally & Co.
Made in U.S.A.
DM-910000-1V-GD1- -1- -1'

1. JAMAICA	6. PARAGUAY	11. SWEDEN	16. ISRAEL	21. CHAD
2. EL SALVADOR	7. URUGUAY	12. LATVIA	17. JORDAN	22. ZAMBIA
3. NICARAGUA	8. SWITZERLAND	13. BELARUS	18. TUNISIA	23. ZIMBABWE
4. COSTA RICA	9. AUSTRIA	14. KAZAKSTAN	19. BURKINA FASO	24. CAMBODIA
5. PANAMA	10. CZECH REPUBLIC	15. MONGOLIA	20. BENIN	25. PAPUA NEW GUINEA

PROTEIN CONSUMPTION

Note: Size of each country is proportional to population.

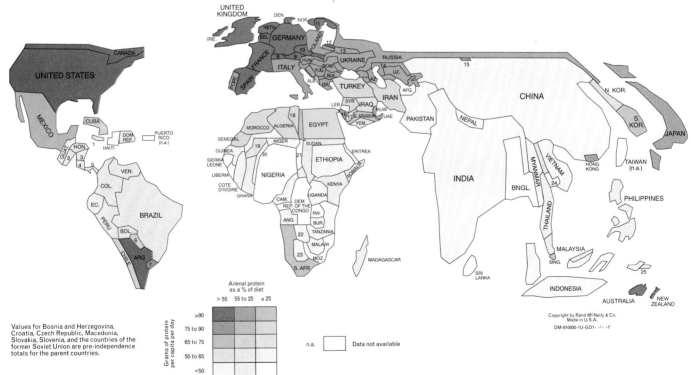

Values for Bosnia and Herzegovina,
Croatia, Czech Republic, Macedonia,
Slovakia, Slovenia, and the countries of the
former Soviet Union are pre-independence
totals for the parent countries.

Copyright by Rand McNally & Co.
Made in U.S.A.
DM-910000-1U-GD1- -1- -1'

Animal protein
as a % of diet

Grams of protein per capita per day	> 55	55 to 25	≤ 25
≥90			
75 to 90			
65 to 75			
50 to 65			
<50			
	< 45	45 to 75	≥ 75

Vegetable protein
as a % of diet

n.a.   Data not available

PHYSICIANS

Note: Size of each country is proportional to population.

Population per Physician

- Less than 1,000
- 1,000 to 6,000
- 6,000 to 18,000
- Greater than 18,000

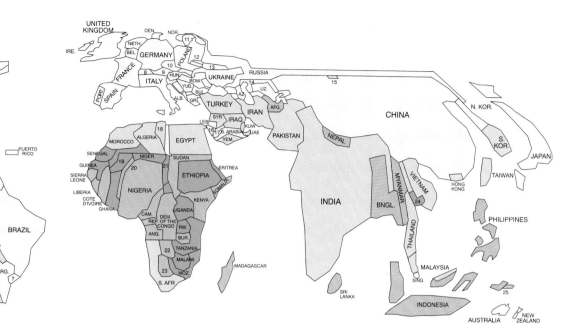

Copyright by Rand McNally & Co.
Made in U.S.A.
DM-910000-1L-GD1- - -!- -1'

1. JAMAICA	6. PARAGUAY	11. SWEDEN	16. ISRAEL	21. CHAD
2. EL SALVADOR	7. URUGUAY	12. LATVIA	17. JORDAN	22. ZAMBIA
3. NICARAGUA	8. SWITZERLAND	13. BELARUS	18. TUNISIA	23. ZIMBABWE
4. COSTA RICA	9. AUSTRIA	14. KAZAKSTAN	19. BURKINA FASO	24. CAMBODIA
5. PANAMA	10. CZECH REPUBLIC	15. MONGOLIA	20. BENIN	25. PAPUA NEW GUINEA

LIFE EXPECTANCY

Note: Size of each country is proportional to population.

Life Expectancy at Birth

- Greater than 70 years
- 60 to 70
- 50 to 60
- Less than 50
- Data not available

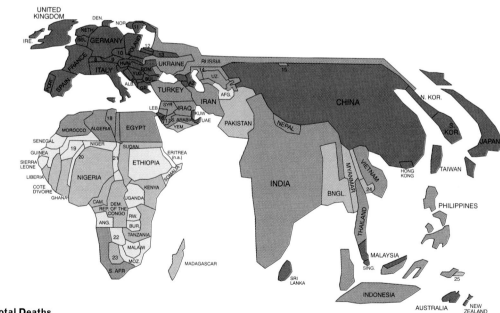

Copyright by Rand McNally & Co.
Made in U.S.A.
DM-910000-1M-GD1- -!- -!- -1'

Deaths by Age Group as a Percent of Total Deaths

DEVELOPING COUNTRIES: Low Income (excluding China and India)*

0 - 5 YEARS 50.4 %	5 - 15 7.5	15 - 50 18.1	50 - 65 8.8	OVER 65 15.2

INDUSTRIAL MARKET COUNTRIES*

15 - 50 YEARS 8.6 %	50 - 65 16.5	OVER 65 72.3

Life Expectancy at Birth

LOW INCOME* — 62 years
LOWER-MIDDLE INCOME* — 67
UPPER-MIDDLE INCOME* — 69
HIGH INCOME* — 77

*as defined by the World Bank

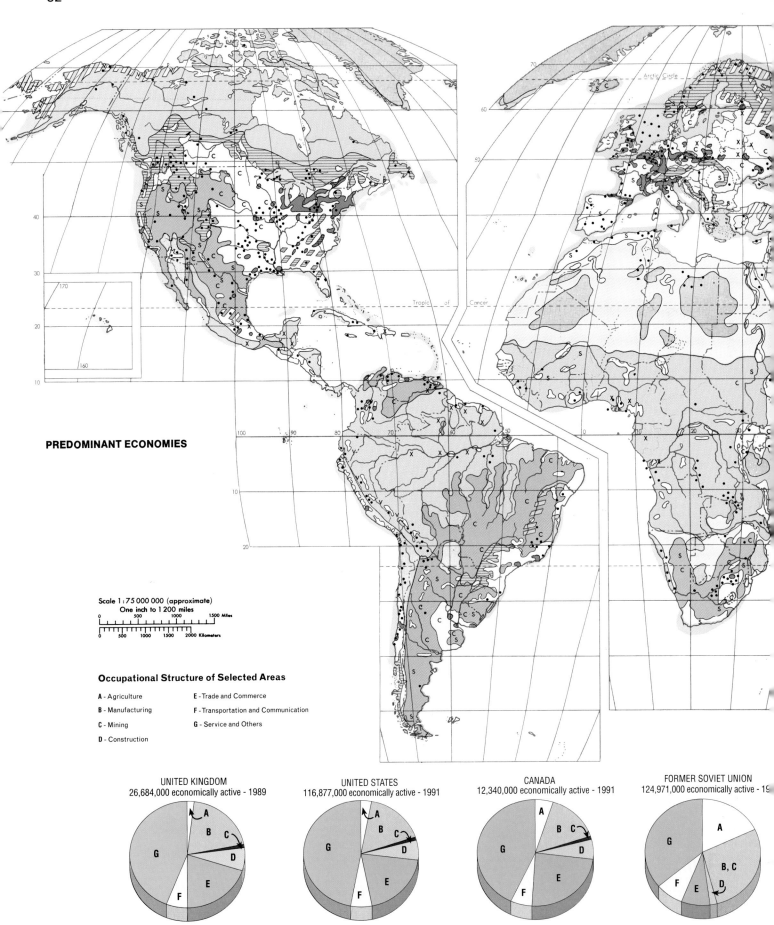

PREDOMINANT ECONOMIES

Scale 1:75 000 000 (approximate)
One inch to 1 200 miles

0   500   1000   1500 Miles

0   500   1000   1500   2000 Kilometers

Occupational Structure of Selected Areas

A - Agriculture   E - Trade and Commerce

B - Manufacturing   F - Transportation and Communication

C - Mining   G - Service and Others

D - Construction

UNITED KINGDOM
26,684,000 economically active - 1989

UNITED STATES
116,877,000 economically active - 1991

CANADA
12,340,000 economically active - 1991

FORMER SOVIET UNION
124,971,000 economically active - 19

A-510000-36-7-7-6-7
Copyright by Rand McNally & Co.
Made in U.S.A.

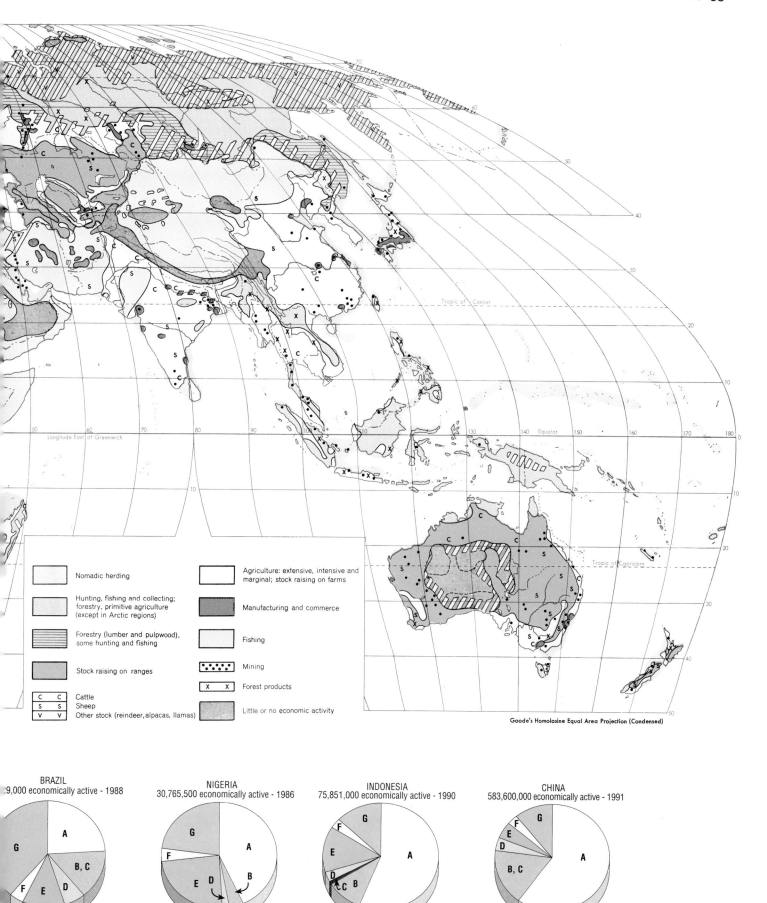

Nomadic herding

Hunting, fishing and collecting;
forestry, primitive agriculture
(except in Arctic regions)

Forestry (lumber and pulpwood),
some hunting and fishing

Stock raising on ranges

C	C	Cattle
S	S	Sheep
V	V	Other stock (reindeer, alpacas, llamas)

Agriculture: extensive, intensive and
marginal; stock raising on farms

Manufacturing and commerce

Fishing

Mining

| X | X | Forest products |

Little or no economic activity

Goode's Homolosine Equal Area Projection (Condensed)

BRAZIL
9,000 economically active - 1988

NIGERIA
30,765,500 economically active - 1986

INDONESIA
75,851,000 economically active - 1990

CHINA
583,600,000 economically active - 1991

MAJOR
AGRICULTURAL
REGIONS

Derwent Whittlesey

Scale 1 : 75 000 000 (approximate)
One inch to 1 200 miles

A	Nomadic Herding
B	Livestock Ranching
C	Shifting Cultivation
D	Rudimental Sedentary Cultivation
E	Intensive Subsistence Tillage, Rice Dominant
F	Intensive Subsistence Tillage, Rice Unimportant
G	Plantation Agriculture
H	Mediterranean Agriculture
	Crop Farming, Grain or Cotton Dominant
J	Commercial Livestock and Crop Farming
	Subsistence Crop and Livestock Farming
L	Dairy Farming
M	Specialized Horticulture
X	Non-Agricultural Areas

Goode's Homolosine Equal Area Projection (Condensed)

(Revision of Agricultural Regions by Whittlesey,
Annals Assoc. Am. Geographers, 1936)

A-510000-56- -2 -5
Copyright by Rand McNally & Co.
Made in U.S.A.

Probable Origins of Cultivated Plants

BEET
OLIVE
GRAPE
ONION GARLIC
LETTUCE

APPLE
ALMOND

SOYBEAN

BARLEY
DATE   BUCKWHEAT
FIG   PEACH
APRICOT   GINGER
FLAX   TEA   RICE
LENTIL   SUGAR RICE   BAMBOO
WHEAT   CANE   LIME
                       LEMON
                       ORANGE
                       GRAPEFRUIT
MILLET   SORGHUM   BANANA
COLA RICE
YAM OKRA   COFFEE
     OIL   COTTON
     PALM

AVOCADO
CACAO   WATERMELON   CLOVE
COMMON BEANS   POTATO   NUTMEG SUGAR
COTTON   PEANUT   FORAGE   CANE   COCONUT
MAIZE   TOMATO   GRASSES
PEPPER
SQUASH
SUNFLOWER   PEANUT
SWEET POTATO   SQUASH
TOBACCO   SWEET
TOMATO   POTATO

Hearth Areas

Based on Jack R. Harlan, Crops and Man
(Madison: American Society of Agronomy,
1975) and Erich Isaac, Geography of
Domestication (Prentice Hall, 1970)

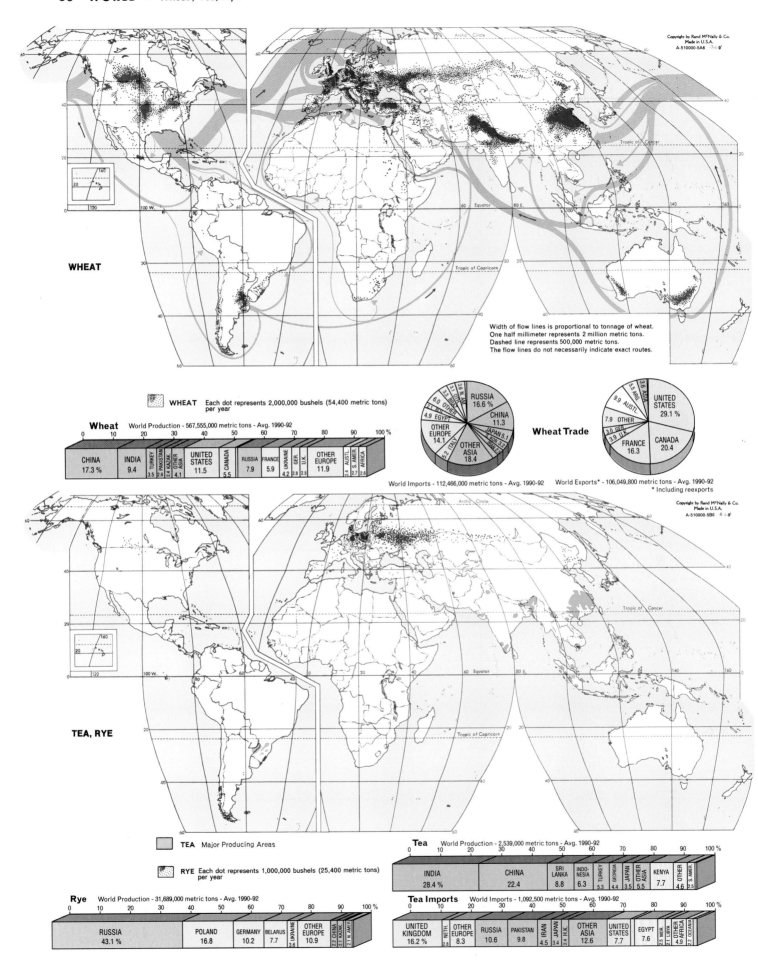

WHEAT

Width of flow lines is proportional to tonnage of wheat.
One half millimeter represents 2 million metric tons.
Dashed line represents 500,000 metric tons.
The flow lines do not necessarily indicate exact routes.

WHEAT   Each dot represents 2,000,000 bushels (54,400 metric tons) per year

Wheat World Production - 567,555,000 metric tons - Avg. 1990-92

0	10	20	30	40	50	60	70	80	90	100 %

| CHINA 17.3 % | INDIA 9.4 | TURKEY 3.5 | PAKISTAN 2.6 | KAZAK 2.4 | OTHER ASIA 4.1 | UNITED STATES 11.5 | CANADA 5.5 | RUSSIA 7.9 | FRANCE 5.9 | UKRAINE 4.2 | GER. 2.8 | U.K. 2.5 | OTHER EUROPE 11.9 | AUSTL. 2.4 | S. AMER. 2.7 | AFRICA 2.6 |

Wheat Trade

World Imports - 112,466,000 metric tons - Avg. 1990-92

RUSSIA 16.6 %
CHINA 11.3
JAPAN 5.1
S. KOR. 3.2
OTHER ASIA 18.4
ITALY 5.2
EGYPT 4.9
OTHER EUROPE 14.1
U.K. 2.1
BRAZIL 3.5
OTHER 6.0
N. AMER. 3.6

World Exports* - 106,049,800 metric tons - Avg. 1990-92
* Including reexports

UNITED STATES 29.1 %
CANADA 20.4
FRANCE 16.3
U.K. 3.9
GER. 3.0
OTHER 7.9
AUSTL. 9.9
ARG. 5.5
ASIA 3.6

TEA, RYE

TEA   Major Producing Areas

RYE   Each dot represents 1,000,000 bushels (25,400 metric tons) per year

Rye World Production - 31,689,000 metric tons - Avg. 1990-92

0	10	20	30	40	50	60	70	80	90	100 %

| RUSSIA 43.1 % | POLAND 16.8 | GERMANY 10.2 | BELARUS 7.7 | UKRAINE 3.6 | OTHER EUROPE 10.9 | CHINA 2.2 | KAZAK. | N. AMER. 2.1 |

Tea World Production - 2,539,000 metric tons - Avg. 1990-92

0	10	20	30	40	50	60	70	80	90	100 %

| INDIA 28.4 % | CHINA 22.4 | SRI LANKA 8.8 | INDO-NESIA 6.3 | TURKEY 5.3 | GEORGIA 4.4 | JAPAN 3.5 | OTHER ASIA 5.5 | KENYA 7.7 | OTHER 4.6 | S. AMER. 2.5 |

Tea Imports World Imports - 1,092,500 metric tons - Avg. 1990-92

0	10	20	30	40	50	60	70	80	90	100 %

| UNITED KINGDOM 16.2 % | NETH. 2.8 | OTHER EUROPE 8.3 | RUSSIA 10.6 | PAKISTAN 9.8 | IRAN 4.5 | JAPAN 3.4 | H.K. 2.4 | OTHER ASIA 12.6 | UNITED STATES 7.7 | EGYPT 7.6 | MOR. 2.5 | LIBYA 2.1 | OTHER AFRICA 3.4 | OCEANIA 2.2 |

Copyright by Rand McNally & Co.
Made in U.S.A.
A-510000-5A6

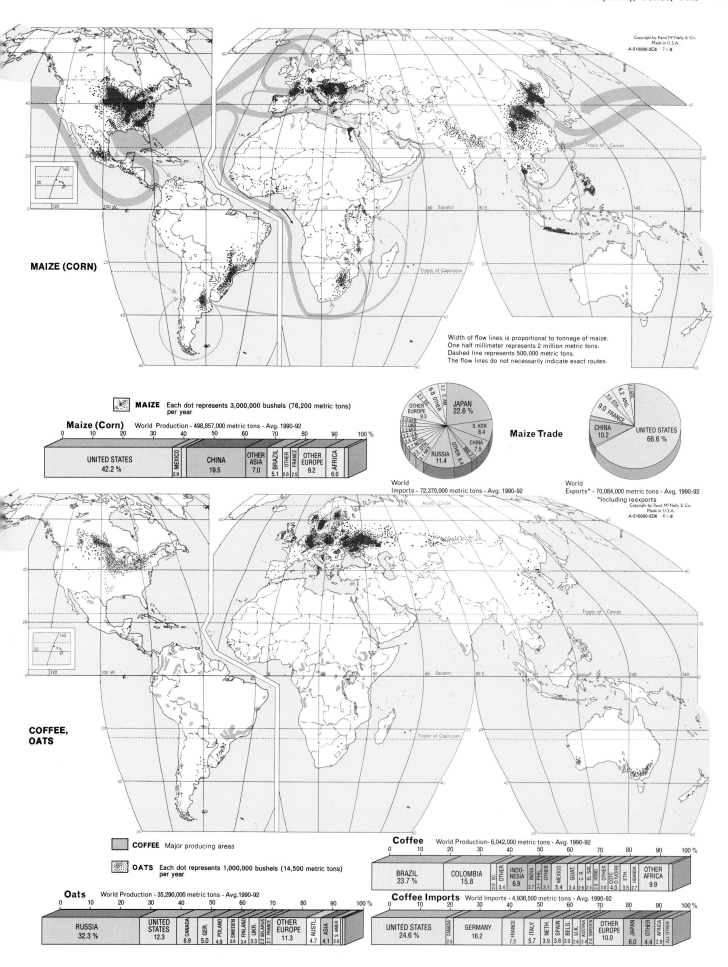

MAIZE (CORN)

Width of flow lines is proportional to tonnage of maize.
One half millimeter represents 2 million metric tons.
Dashed line represents 500,000 metric tons.
The flow lines do not necessarily indicate exact routes.

MAIZE Each dot represents 3,000,000 bushels (76,200 metric tons) per year

Maize (Corn) World Production - 498,857,000 metric tons - Avg. 1990-92

UNITED STATES 42.2 %	MEXICO 2.9	CHINA 19.5	OTHER ASIA 7.0	BRAZIL 5.1	OTHER 2.6	FRANCE 2.5	OTHER EUROPE 9.2	AFRICA 6.0

Maize Trade

World Imports - 72,370,000 metric tons - Avg. 1990-92
(JAPAN 22.6%, S. KOR 8.4, CHINA 7.5, OTHER 6.4, RUSSIA 11.4, MEX 3.1, SP 3.3, NETH 2.7, UK 2.4, MOV 2.2, UKR 2.0, GER 2.0, OTHER EUROPE 9.3, OTHER 6.8, S. AM 2.1, OTHER 3.2)

World Exports* - 70,084,000 metric tons - Avg. 1990-92
*Including reexports
(UNITED STATES 66.6%, CHINA 10.2, FRANCE 9.0, ARG. 3.3, OTHER 6.2, 2.2)

COFFEE, OATS

COFFEE Major producing areas

OATS Each dot represents 1,000,000 bushels (14,500 metric tons) per year

Coffee World Production- 6,042,000 metric tons - Avg. 1990-92

BRAZIL 23.7 %	COLOMBIA 15.8	EC 2.0	OTHER 3.4	INDO-NESIA 6.9	INDIA 2.7	PHIL 2.1	OTHER 3.1	MEXICO 5.4	GUAT 3.4	C.R. 2.6	EL SAL 2.5	HOND 2.0	OTHER 4.0	COTE D'IVOIRE 3.5	ETH. 2.7	UGANDA	OTHER AFRICA 9.9

Oats World Production - 35,290,000 metric tons - Avg.1990-92

RUSSIA 32.3 %	UNITED STATES 12.3	CANADA 6.9	GER. 5.0	POLAND 4.9	SWEDEN 3.6	FINLAND 3.4	UKR. 2.2	BELARUS 2.1	FRANCE	OTHER EUROPE 11.3	AUSTL. 4.7	ASIA 4.1	S. AMER 2.6

Coffee Imports World Imports - 4,936,500 metric tons - Avg. 1990-92

UNITED STATES 24.6 %	CANADA 2.5	GERMANY 16.2	FRANCE 7.3	ITALY 5.7	NETH. 3.9	SPAIN 3.6	BELG. 3.0	U.K. 2.6	AUSTRIA 2.4	SWEDEN 2.0	OTHER EUROPE 10.0	JAPAN 6.0	OTHER 4.4	AFRICA 2.9	ALL OTHER

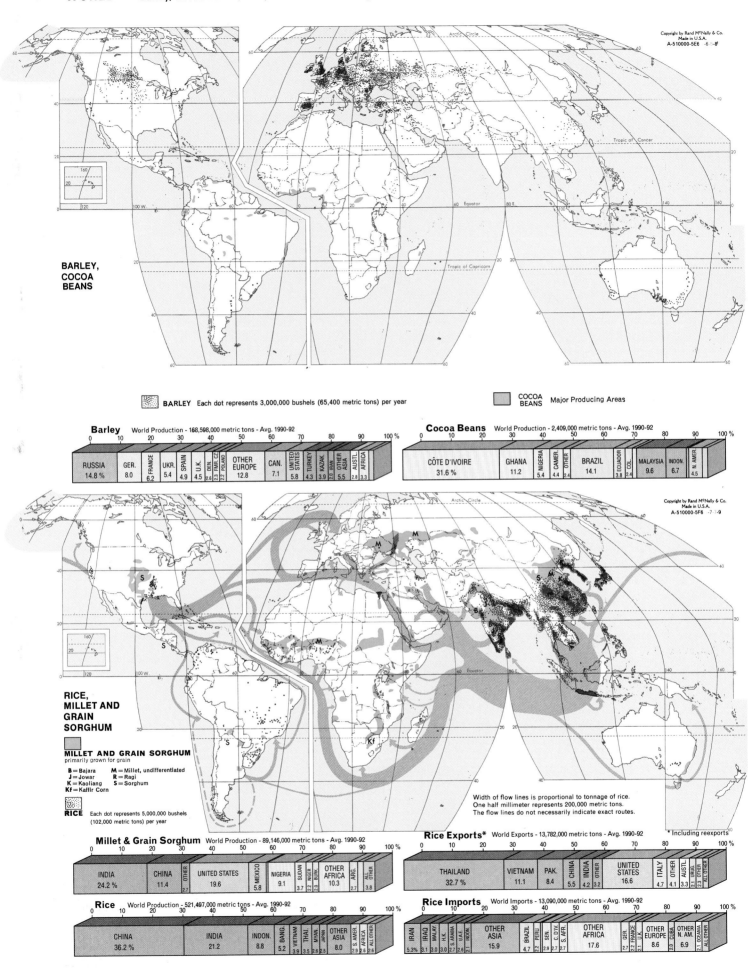

Copyright by Rand McNally & Co.
Made in U.S.A.
A-510000-5E6 -6 -8'

**BARLEY,
COCOA
BEANS**

⬚ **BARLEY** Each dot represents 3,000,000 bushels (65,400 metric tons) per year

▨ **COCOA BEANS** Major Producing Areas

Barley World Production - 168,598,000 metric tons - Avg. 1990-92

RUSSIA 14.8 %	GER. 8.0	FRANCE 6.2	UKR. 5.4	SPAIN 4.9	U.K. 4.5	DEN. 2.6	FMR. CZ. 2.3	POLAND 2.2	OTHER EUROPE 12.8	CAN. 7.1	UNITED STATES 5.8	TURKEY 4.3	KAZAK. 3.9	IRAN 2.0	OTHER ASIA 5.5	AUSTL. 2.8	AFRICA 3.3

Cocoa Beans World Production - 2,409,000 metric tons - Avg. 1990-92

CÔTE D'IVOIRE 31.6 %	GHANA 11.2	NIGERIA 5.4	CAMER. 4.4	OTHER 2.4	BRAZIL 14.1	ECUADOR 3.8	COL. 2.4	MALAYSIA 9.6	INDON. 6.7	N. AMER. 4.5

Copyright by Rand McNally & Co.
Made in U.S.A.
A-510000-5F6 -7 -9

**RICE,
MILLET AND
GRAIN
SORGHUM**

▨ **MILLET AND GRAIN SORGHUM**
primarily grown for grain

B = Bajara   **M** = Millet, undifferentiated
J = Jowar   **R** = Ragi
K = Kaoliang   **S** = Sorghum
Kf = Kaffir Corn

⬚ **RICE** Each dot represents 5,000,000 bushels
(102,000 metric tons) per year

Width of flow lines is proportional to tonnage of rice.
One half millimeter represents 200,000 metric tons.
The flow lines do not necessarily indicate exact routes.

Millet & Grain Sorghum World Production - 89,146,000 metric tons - Avg. 1990-92

INDIA 24.2 %	CHINA 11.4	OTHER 2.7	UNITED STATES 19.6	MEXICO 5.8	NIGERIA 9.1	SUDAN 3.7	NIGER 2.2	BURK. 2.0	OTHER AFRICA 10.3	ARG. 2.7	ALL OTHER 3.8

Rice Exports* World Exports - 13,782,000 metric tons - Avg. 1990-92   * Including reexports

THAILAND 32.7 %	VIETNAM 11.1	PAK. 8.4	CHINA 5.5	INDIA 4.2	UNITED STATES 16.6	ITALY 4.7	AUSTL. 4.1	URUG. 2.1	OTHER ALL OTHER

Rice World Production - 521,497,000 metric tons - Avg. 1990-92

CHINA 36.2 %	INDIA 21.2	INDON. 8.8	BANG. 5.2	VIETNAM 3.9	THAI. 3.5	MYAN. 2.6	JAPAN 2.5	OTHER ASIA 8.0	S. AMER. 2.9	AFRICA 2.6 ALL OTHER

Rice Imports World Imports - 13,090,000 metric tons - Avg. 1990-92

IRAN 5.3%	IRAQ 3.1	MALAY. 3.0	H.K. 2.7	S. ARABIA 2.7	U.A.E. 2.2	INDON. 2.1	OTHER ASIA 15.9	BRAZIL 4.7	PERU 2.9	SEN. 2.7	C. DIV.	S. AFR.	OTHER AFRICA 17.6	GER. 2.7	FRANCE 2.2	U.K.	OTHER EUROPE 8.6	CUBA 2.0	OTHER N. AM. 6.9	OCEANIA	ALL OTHER

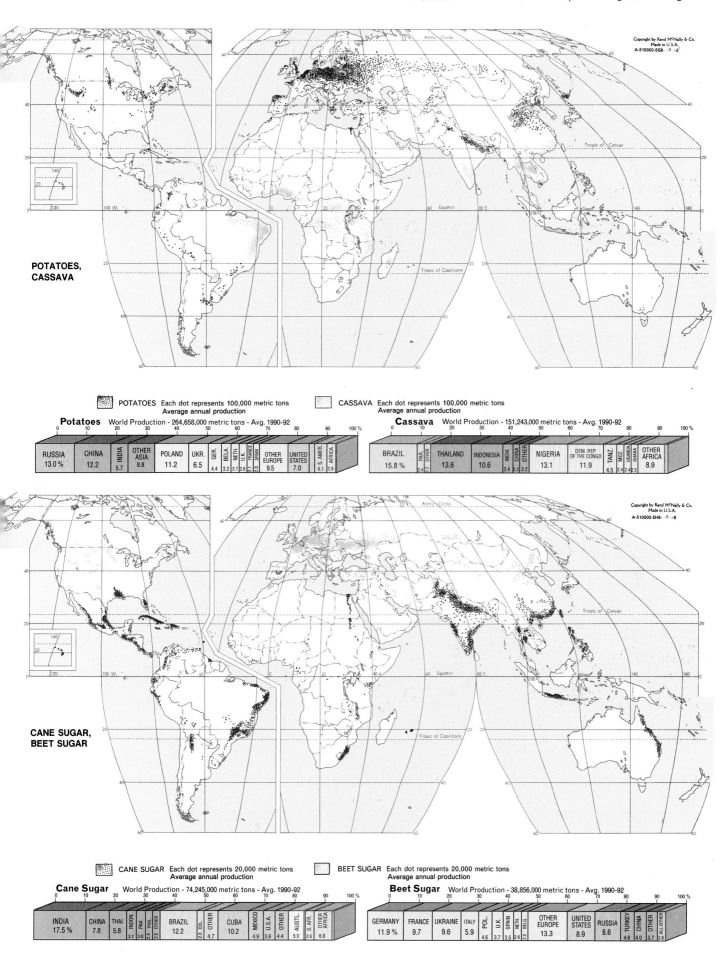

POTATOES, CASSAVA

Copyright by Rand McNally & Co.
Made in U.S.A.
A-510000-5G6- -2- -2'

▒ POTATOES Each dot represents 100,000 metric tons
Average annual production

▒ CASSAVA Each dot represents 100,000 metric tons
Average annual production

Potatoes World Production - 264,658,000 metric tons - Avg. 1990-92

0	10	20	30	40	50	60	70	80	90	100 %

| RUSSIA 13.0 % | CHINA 12.2 | INDIA 5.7 | OTHER ASIA 8.8 | POLAND 11.2 | UKR. 6.5 | GER. 4.4 | BELA. 3.2 | NETH. 2.7 | U.K. 2.6 | FRANCE 2.1 | SPAIN | OTHER EUROPE 9.5 | UNITED STATES 7.0 | S. AMER. 4.1 | AFRICA 2.9 |

Cassava World Production - 151,243,000 metric tons - Avg. 1990-92

0	10	20	30	40	50	60	70	80	90	100 %

| BRAZIL 15.8 % | PAR. 2.4 | OTHER 2.7 | THAILAND 13.6 | INDONESIA 10.6 | INDIA 3.4 | CHINA 2.2 | OTHER 3.2 | NIGERIA 13.1 | DEM. REP. OF THE CONGO 11.9 | TANZ. 4.5 | MOZ. 2.4 | UGANDA 2.4 | GHANA 2.3 | OTHER AFRICA 8.9 |

CANE SUGAR, BEET SUGAR

Copyright by Rand McNally & Co.
Made in U.S.A.
A-510000-5H6- -5- -9

▒ CANE SUGAR Each dot represents 20,000 metric tons
Average annual production

▒ BEET SUGAR Each dot represents 20,000 metric tons
Average annual production

Cane Sugar World Production - 74,245,000 metric tons - Avg. 1990-92

0	10	20	30	40	50	60	70	80	90	100 %

| INDIA 17.5 % | CHINA 7.8 | THAI. 5.8 | INDON. 3.2 | PAK. 3.0 | PHIL. 2.4 | OTHER 2.5 | BRAZIL 12.2 | COL. 2.3 | OTHER 4.7 | CUBA 10.2 | MEXICO 4.9 | U.S.A. 3.9 | AUSTL. 4.4 | S. AFR. 5.0 | OTHER AFRICA 6.0 |

Beet Sugar World Production - 38,856,000 metric tons - Avg. 1990-92

0	10	20	30	40	50	60	70	80	90	100 %

| GERMANY 11.9 % | FRANCE 9.7 | UKRAINE 9.6 | ITALY 5.9 | POL. 4.6 | U.K. 3.7 | SPAIN 3.5 | NETH. 2.6 | BELG. 2.2 | OTHER EUROPE 13.3 | UNITED STATES 8.9 | RUSSIA 8.6 | TURKEY 4.6 | CHINA 4.0 | OTHER 3.7 | ALL OTHER 2.8 |

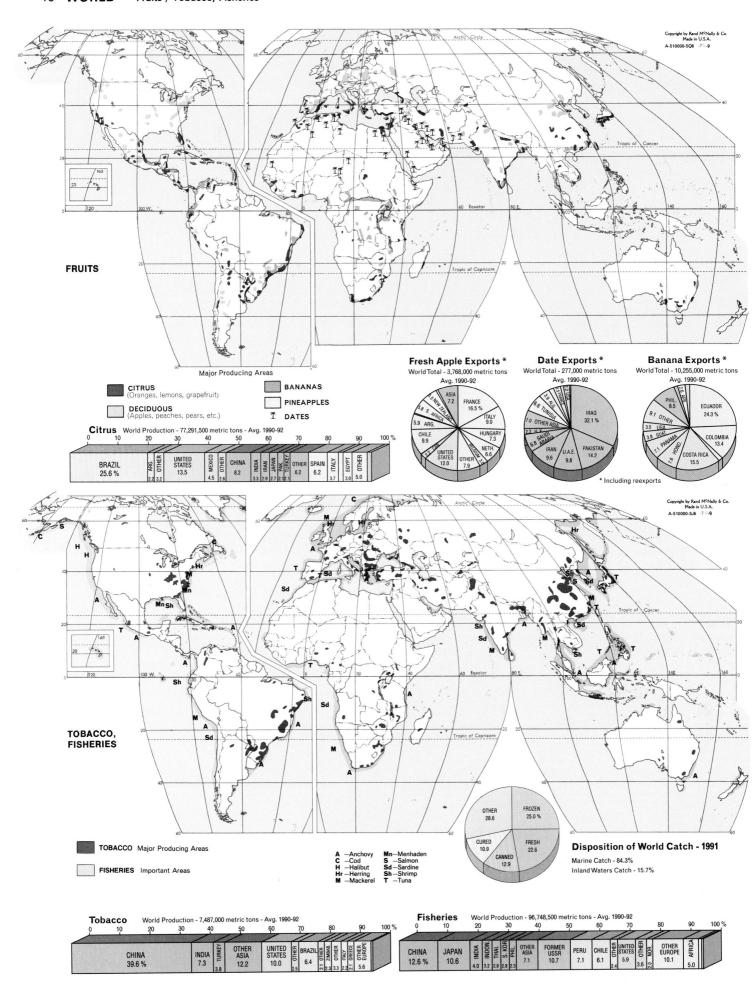

Copyright by Rand McNally & Co.
Made in U.S.A.
A-510000-5Q6 -7 -9

FRUITS

Major Producing Areas

CITRUS
(Oranges, lemons, grapefruit)

DECIDUOUS
(Apples, peaches, pears, etc.)

BANANAS

PINEAPPLES

DATES

Citrus World Production - 77,291,500 metric tons - Avg. 1990-92

	0	10	20	30	40	50	60	70	80	90	100 %

| BRAZIL 25.6 % | ARG. 2.2 | OTHER 3.2 | UNITED STATES 13.5 | MEXICO 4.5 | OTHER 2.6 | CHINA 8.2 | INDIA 3.3 | IRAN 2.9 | JAPAN 2.7 | PAK. 2.1 | TURKEY 2.1 | OTHER 6.2 | SPAIN 6.2 | ITALY 3.7 | EGYPT 3.0 | OTHER 5.0 |

Fresh Apple Exports*
World Total - 3,768,000 metric tons
Avg. 1990-92

- ASIA 7.2
- FRANCE 16.5 %
- ITALY 9.0
- HUNGARY 7.3
- NETH. 6.6
- BELGIUM 5.3
- OTHER 7.9
- UNITED STATES 12.0
- CANADA 2.2
- CHILE 9.9
- ARG. 5.9
- S. AFRICA 5.8
- S. NEW ZEALAND

Date Exports*
World Total - 277,000 metric tons
Avg. 1990-92

- IRAQ 32.1 %
- PAKISTAN 14.2
- U.A.E. 9.8
- IRAN 9.6
- SAUDI ARABIA 6.8
- H.K. 2.2
- OTHER ASIA 7.0
- TUNISIA 6.6
- ALG. 3.9
- FRANCE 3.9
- U.S. 2.4

Banana Exports*
World Total - 10,255,000 metric tons
Avg. 1990-92

- ECUADOR 24.3 %
- COLOMBIA 13.4
- COSTA RICA 15.5
- HOND. 7.5
- PANAMA 7.1
- GUAT. 3.9
- USA 3.5
- OTHER 9.1
- PHIL. 8.5
- 2.6

*** Including reexports**

Copyright by Rand McNally & Co.
Made in U.S.A.
A-510000-3J6 -7 -9

TOBACCO, FISHERIES

TOBACCO Major Producing Areas

FISHERIES Important Areas

A	—Anchovy	Mn	—Menhaden
C	—Cod	S	—Salmon
H	—Halibut	Sd	—Sardine
Hr	—Herring	Sh	—Shrimp
M	—Mackerel	T	—Tuna

Disposition of World Catch - 1991

- FROZEN 25.0 %
- FRESH 22.6
- CANNED 12.9
- CURED 10.9
- OTHER 28.6

Marine Catch - 84.3%
Inland Waters Catch - 15.7%

Tobacco World Production - 7,487,000 metric tons - Avg. 1990-92

	0	10	20	30	40	50	60	70	80	90	100 %

| CHINA 39.6 % | INDIA 7.3 | TURKEY 3.8 | OTHER ASIA 12.2 | UNITED STATES 10.0 | OTHER 2.5 | BRAZIL 6.4 | OTHER 2.1 | ZIMBAB. 2.3 | ITALY 3.3 | GREECE 2.2 | OTHER EUROPE 5.6 |

Fisheries World Production - 96,748,500 metric tons - Avg. 1990-92

	0	10	20	30	40	50	60	70	80	90	100 %

| CHINA 12.6 % | JAPAN 10.6 | INDIA 4.0 | INDON. 3.2 | THAI. 2.9 | S. KOR. 2.8 | PHIL. 2.3 | OTHER ASIA 7.1 | FORMER USSR 10.7 | PERU 7.1 | CHILE 6.1 | OTHER 2.4 | UNITED STATES 5.9 | OTHER 3.6 | NOR. 2.0 | OTHER EUROPE 10.1 | AFRICA 5.0 |

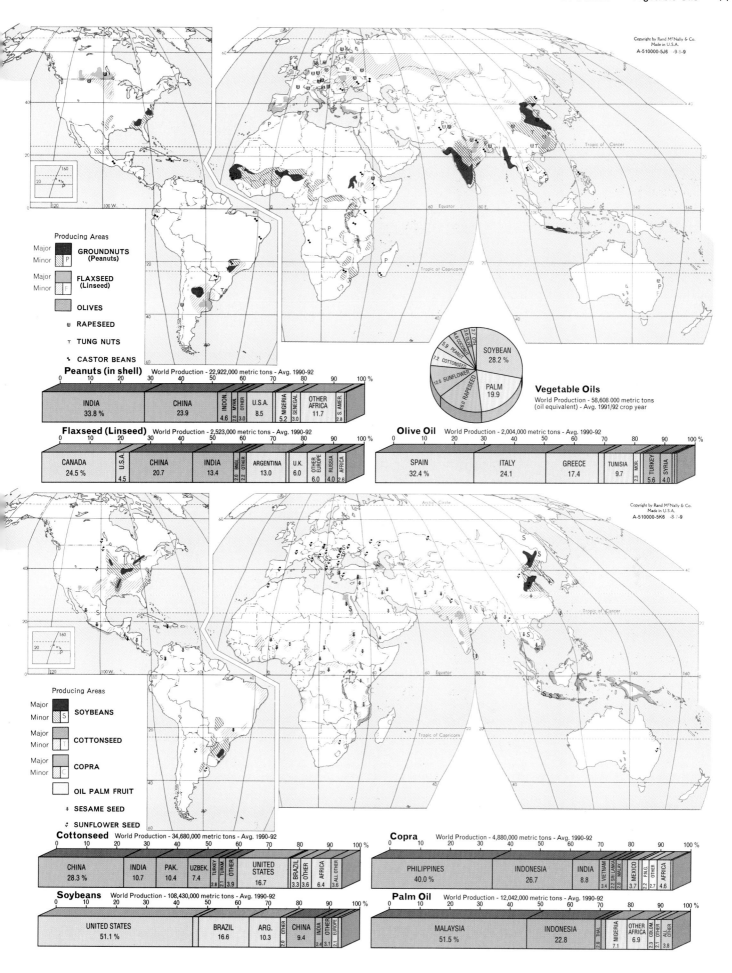

Producing Areas

Major / Minor	**P**	GROUNDNUTS (Peanuts)
Major / Minor	**F**	FLAXSEED (Linseed)
		OLIVES
	ш	RAPESEED
	T	TUNG NUTS
	⸙	CASTOR BEANS

Vegetable Oils

SOYBEAN 28.2 %
PALM 19.9
RAPESEED 16.0
SUNFLOWER 12.5
COTTONSEED 7.2
PEANUT 5.9
COCONUT 4.9
OTHER 2.7

World Production - 58,608,000 metric tons
(oil equivalent) - Avg. 1991/92 crop year

Peanuts (in shell)
World Production - 22,922,000 metric tons - Avg. 1990-92

INDIA 33.8 %	CHINA 23.9	INDON. 4.6	MYAN. 2.0	OTHER 3.0	U.S.A. 8.5	NIGERIA 5.2	SENEGAL 3.0	OTHER AFRICA 11.7	S. AMER. 2.8

Flaxseed (Linseed)
World Production - 2,523,000 metric tons - Avg. 1990-92

CANADA 24.5 %	U.S.A. 4.5	CHINA 20.7	INDIA 13.4	BNGL. 2.0	OTHER 2.2	ARGENTINA 13.0	U.K. 6.0	OTHER EUROPE 6.0	RUSSIA 4.0	AFRICA 2.6

Olive Oil
World Production - 2,004,000 metric tons - Avg. 1990-92

SPAIN 32.4 %	ITALY 24.1	GREECE 17.4	TUNISIA 9.7	MOR. 2.3	TURKEY 5.6	SYRIA 4.0

Producing Areas

Major / Minor	**S**	SOYBEANS
Major / Minor		COTTONSEED
Major / Minor		COPRA
		OIL PALM FRUIT
	⌘	SESAME SEED
	❀	SUNFLOWER SEED

Cottonseed
World Production - 34,680,000 metric tons - Avg. 1990-92

CHINA 28.3 %	INDIA 10.7	PAK. 10.4	UZBEK. 7.4	TURKEY 2.8	OTHER 3.9	UNITED STATES 16.7	BRAZIL 3.3	OTHER 3.6	AFRICA 6.4	ALL OTHER 3.6

Soybeans
World Production - 108,430,000 metric tons - Avg. 1990-92

UNITED STATES 51.1 %	BRAZIL 16.6	ARG. 10.3	OTHER 2.0	CHINA 9.4	INDIA 2.4	OTHER 3.1	EUROPE 2.1

Copra
World Production - 4,880,000 metric tons - Avg. 1990-92

PHILIPPINES 40.0 %	INDONESIA 26.7	INDIA 8.8	VIETNAM 3.4	SRI LANKA 2.2	MALAY. 2.0	MEXICO 3.7	P.N.G. 2.7	OTHER 2.7	AFRICA 4.6

Palm Oil
World Production - 12,042,000 metric tons - Avg. 1990-92

MALAYSIA 51.5 %	INDONESIA 22.8	THAI. 2.0	NIGERIA 7.1	OTHER AFRICA 6.9	COLOM. 2.3	OTHER 2.1	ALL OTHER 3.8

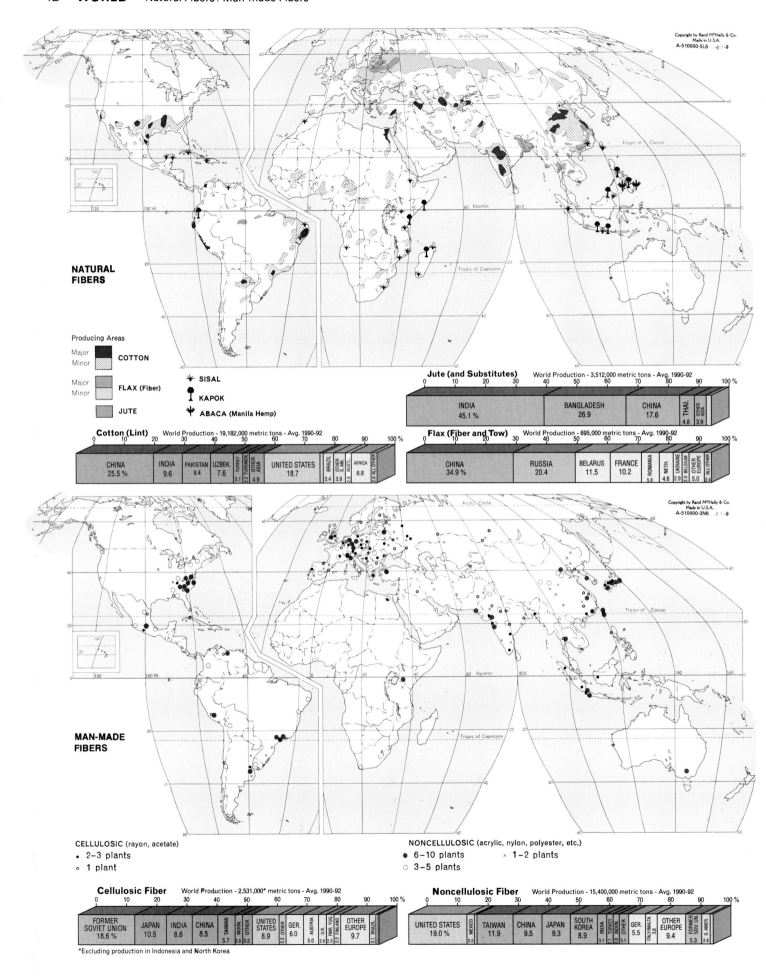

Copyright by Rand M℃Nally & Co.
Made in U.S.A.
A-510000-5L6

NATURAL FIBERS

Producing Areas

Major / Minor	COTTON
Major / Minor	FLAX (Fiber)
	JUTE

✹ SISAL
♟ KAPOK
✹ ABACA (Manila Hemp)

Cotton (Lint) — World Production - 19,182,000 metric tons - Avg. 1990-92

| 0 | 10 | 20 | 30 | 40 | 50 | 60 | 70 | 80 | 90 | 100 % |

| CHINA 25.5 % | INDIA 9.6 | PAKISTAN 9.4 | UZBEK. 7.6 | TURKEY 3.1 | OTHER ASIA 4.9 | UNITED STATES 18.7 | BRAZIL 3.4 | OTHER S. AM. 3.9 | AUSTL. 2.0 | AFRICA 6.8 | ALL OTHER 2.0 |

Jute (and Substitutes) — World Production - 3,512,000 metric tons - Avg. 1990-92

| 0 | 10 | 20 | 30 | 40 | 50 | 60 | 70 | 80 | 90 | 100 % |

| INDIA 45.1 % | BANGLADESH 26.9 | CHINA 17.6 | THAI. 4.8 | OTHER ASIA 3.9 |

Flax (Fiber and Tow) — World Production - 695,000 metric tons - Avg. 1990-92

| 0 | 10 | 20 | 30 | 40 | 50 | 60 | 70 | 80 | 90 | 100 % |

| CHINA 34.9 % | RUSSIA 20.4 | BELARUS 11.5 | FRANCE 10.2 | ROMANIA 5.8 | NETH. 4.6 | UKRAINE 2.9 | BELGIUM 2.3 | OTHER EUROPE 5.0 | ALL OTHER 2.4 |

Copyright by Rand M℃Nally & Co.
Made in U.S.A.
A-510000-3N6

MAN-MADE FIBERS

CELLULOSIC (rayon, acetate)
● 2-3 plants
○ 1 plant

NONCELLULOSIC (acrylic, nylon, polyester, etc.)
● 6-10 plants　　× 1-2 plants
○ 3-5 plants

Cellulosic Fiber — World Production - 2,531,000* metric tons - Avg. 1990-92

| 0 | 10 | 20 | 30 | 40 | 50 | 60 | 70 | 80 | 90 | 100 % |

| FORMER SOVIET UNION 18.6 % | JAPAN 10.5 | INDIA 8.6 | CHINA 8.5 | TAIWAN 5.7 | INDON. 2.5 | OTHER 3.2 | UNITED STATES 8.9 | GER. 2.3 | AUSTRIA 6.0 | U.K. 5.0 | FMR. YUG. 2.6 | FINLAND 2.2 | OTHER EUROPE 9.7 | BRAZIL 2.1 |

*Excluding production in Indonesia and North Korea

Noncellulosic Fiber — World Production - 15,400,000 metric tons - Avg. 1990-92

| 0 | 10 | 20 | 30 | 40 | 50 | 60 | 70 | 80 | 90 | 100 % |

| UNITED STATES 19.0 % | MEXICO 2.5 | TAIWAN 11.9 | CHINA 9.5 | JAPAN 9.3 | SOUTH KOREA 8.9 | INDIA 3.1 | TURKEY 2.0 | INDON. 3.1 | GER. 5.5 | ITALY/MALTA 3.8 | OTHER EUROPE 9.4 | FORMER SOV. UN. 5.3 | S. AMER. |

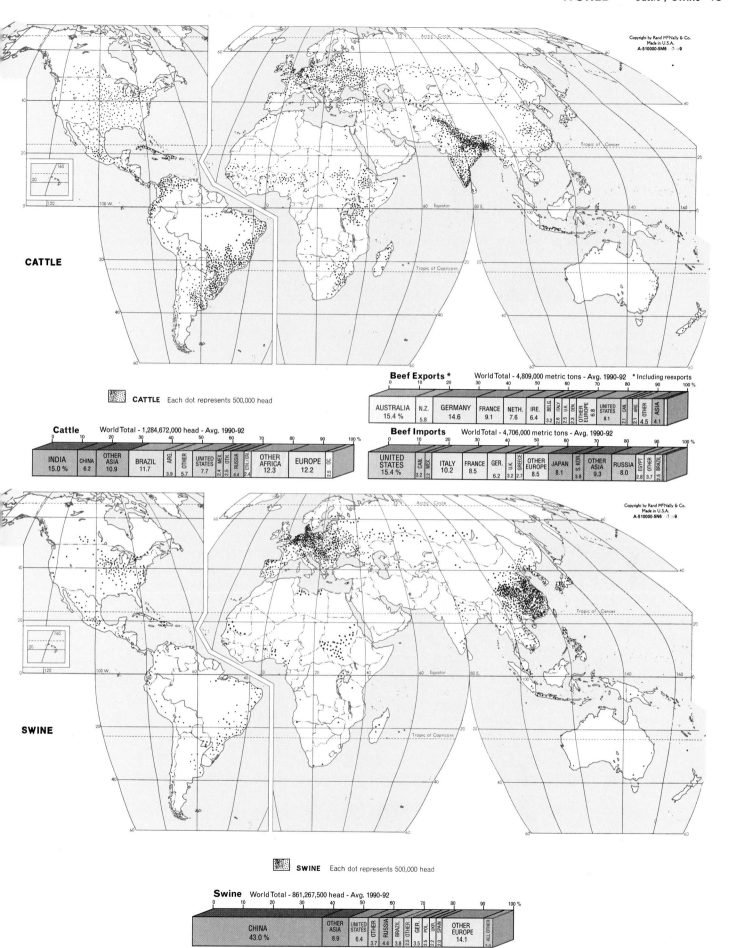

CATTLE

CATTLE Each dot represents 500,000 head

Cattle   World Total - 1,284,672,000 head - Avg. 1990-92

| INDIA 15.0 % | CHINA 6.2 | OTHER ASIA 10.9 | BRAZIL 11.7 | ARG. 3.9 | OTHER 5.7 | UNITED STATES 7.7 | MEX. 2.4 | OTH. 2.5 | RUSSIA 4.4 | ETH./ERI. 2.4 | OTHER AFRICA 12.3 | EUROPE 12.2 | OC. 2.5 |

Beef Exports *   World Total - 4,809,000 metric tons - Avg. 1990-92   * Including reexports

| AUSTRALIA 15.4 % | N.Z. 5.8 | GERMANY 14.6 | FRANCE 9.1 | NETH. 7.6 | IRE. 6.4 | BELG. 3.2 | ITALY 2.6 | U.K. 2.5 | DEN. 2.3 | OTHER EUROPE 6.8 | UNITED STATES 8.1 | CAN. 2.1 | ARG. 2.1 | OTHER 4.5 | ASIA 4.1 |

Beef Imports   World Total - 4,706,000 metric tons - Avg. 1990-92

| UNITED STATES 15.4 % | CAN. 3.2 | MEX. 2.2 | ITALY 10.2 | FRANCE 8.5 | GER. 6.2 | U.K. 3.2 | GREECE 2.7 | OTHER EUROPE 8.5 | JAPAN 8.1 | S. KOR. 3.8 | OTHER ASIA 9.3 | RUSSIA 8.0 | EGYPT 2.8 | OTHER 3.7 | BRAZIL 2.5 |

SWINE

SWINE Each dot represents 500,000 head

Swine   World Total - 861,267,500 head - Avg. 1990-92

| CHINA 43.0 % | OTHER ASIA 8.9 | UNITED STATES 6.4 | OTHER 3.7 | RUSSIA 4.4 | BRAZIL 3.8 | GER. 2.5 | POL. 3.5 | UKR. 2.2 | SPAIN 2.0 | OTHER EUROPE 14.1 | ALL OTHER |

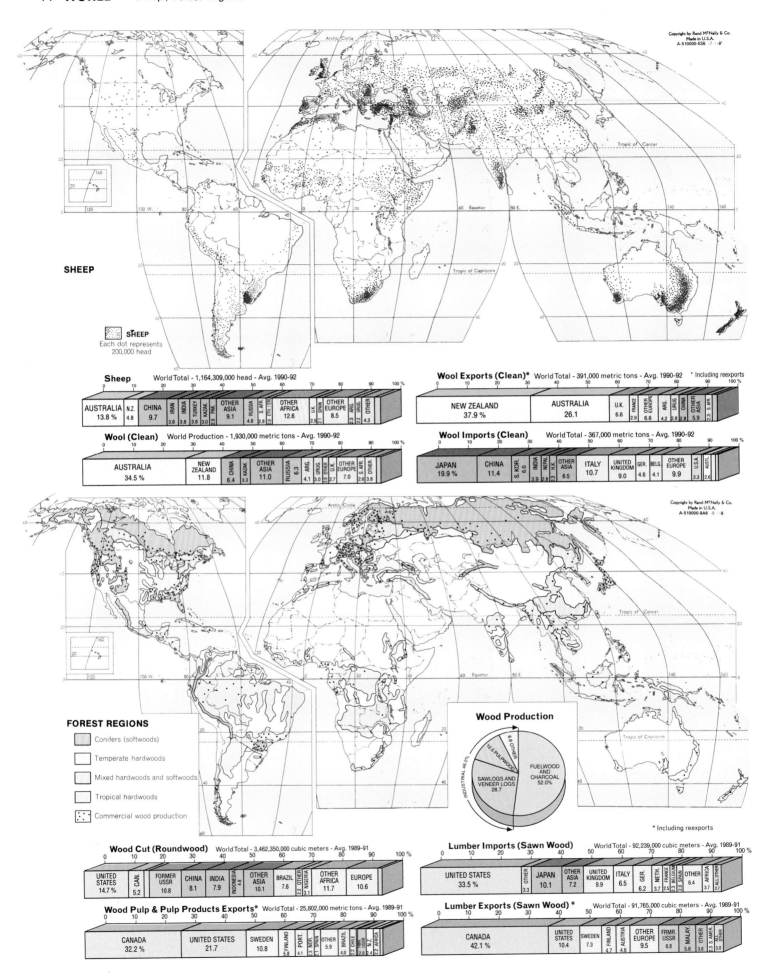

Copyright by Rand McNally & Co.
Made in U.S.A.
A-510000-5S6 -7 -9'

SHEEP

SHEEP
Each dot represents
200,000 head

Sheep World Total - 1,164,309,000 head - Avg. 1990-92

AUSTRALIA 13.8 %	N.Z. 4.8	CHINA 9.7	IRAN 3.8	INDIA 3.8	TURKEY	KAZAK. 2.3	PAK.	OTHER ASIA 9.1	RUSSIA 4.8	S. AFR. 2.8	ETH./ER. 2.0	OTHER AFRICA 12.6	U.K. 2.5	SPAIN 2.1	OTHER EUROPE 8.5	ARG. 2.3	URUG. 4.2	OTHER 4.3

Wool (Clean) World Production - 1,930,000 metric tons - Avg. 1990-92

AUSTRALIA 34.5 %	NEW ZEALAND 11.8	CHINA 6.4	KAZAK.	OTHER ASIA 11.0	RUSSIA 6.3	ARG. 4.1	URUG. 3.0	OTHER 2.7	U.K.	OTHER EUROPE 7.0	S. AFR. 2.6	OTHER 3.8

Wool Exports (Clean)* World Total - 391,000 metric tons - Avg. 1990-92   * Including reexports

NEW ZEALAND 37.9 %	AUSTRALIA 26.1	U.K. 6.6	FRANCE 2.9	OTHER EUROPE 6.6	ARG. 4.2	URUG. 2.8	CHINA 2.8	OTHER ASIA 5.9	S. AFR. 2.3

Wool Imports (Clean) World Total - 367,000 metric tons - Avg. 1990-92

JAPAN 19.9 %	CHINA 11.4	S. KOR. 6.0	INDIA 3.9	NEPAL	H.K. 2.3	OTHER ASIA 6.5	ITALY 10.7	UNITED KINGDOM 9.0	GER. 4.6	BELG. 4.1	OTHER EUROPE 9.9	U.S.A. 3.3	AUSTL. 2.6

Copyright by Rand McNally & Co.
Made in U.S.A.
A-510000-8A6 -8 -9

FOREST REGIONS

Conifers (softwoods)

Temperate hardwoods

Mixed hardwoods and softwoods

Tropical hardwoods

Commercial wood production

Wood Production

INDUSTRIAL 48.0%
6.8 OTHER
12.5 PULPWOOD
SAWLOGS AND VENEER LOGS 28.7
FUELWOOD AND CHARCOAL 52.0%

* Including reexports

Wood Cut (Roundwood) World Total - 3,462,350,000 cubic meters - Avg. 1989-91

UNITED STATES 14.7 %	CAN. 5.2	FORMER USSR 10.8	CHINA 8.1	INDIA 7.9	INDONESIA 4.8	OTHER ASIA 10.1	BRAZIL 7.6	OTHER	NIGERIA 3.1	OTHER AFRICA 11.7	EUROPE 10.6

Lumber Imports (Sawn Wood) World Total - 92,239,000 cubic meters - Avg. 1989-91

UNITED STATES 33.5 %	OTHER 3.3	JAPAN 10.1	OTHER ASIA 7.2	UNITED KINGDOM 9.9	ITALY 6.5	GER. 6.2	NETH. 3.7	FRANCE	BELGIUM 2.3	SPAIN 2.0	OTHER 6.4	AFRICA 3.7	ALL OTHER

Wood Pulp & Pulp Products Exports* World Total - 25,802,000 metric tons - Avg. 1989-91

CANADA 32.2 %	UNITED STATES 21.7	SWEDEN 10.8	FINLAND 5.8	PORT. 4.1	NOR. 2.1	SPAIN	OTHER 5.9	BRAZIL 4.0	CHILE 2.2	OTHER 2.9	N.Z. 2.2	AFRICA 2.4

Lumber Exports (Sawn Wood) * World Total - 91,765,000 cubic meters - Avg. 1989-91

CANADA 42.1 %	UNITED STATES 10.4	SWEDEN 7.3	FINLAND 4.7	AUSTRIA 4.6	OTHER EUROPE 9.5	FRMR. USSR 6.8	MALAY. 5.6	OTHER 3.8	S. AMER. 3.0	N.Z. OTHER

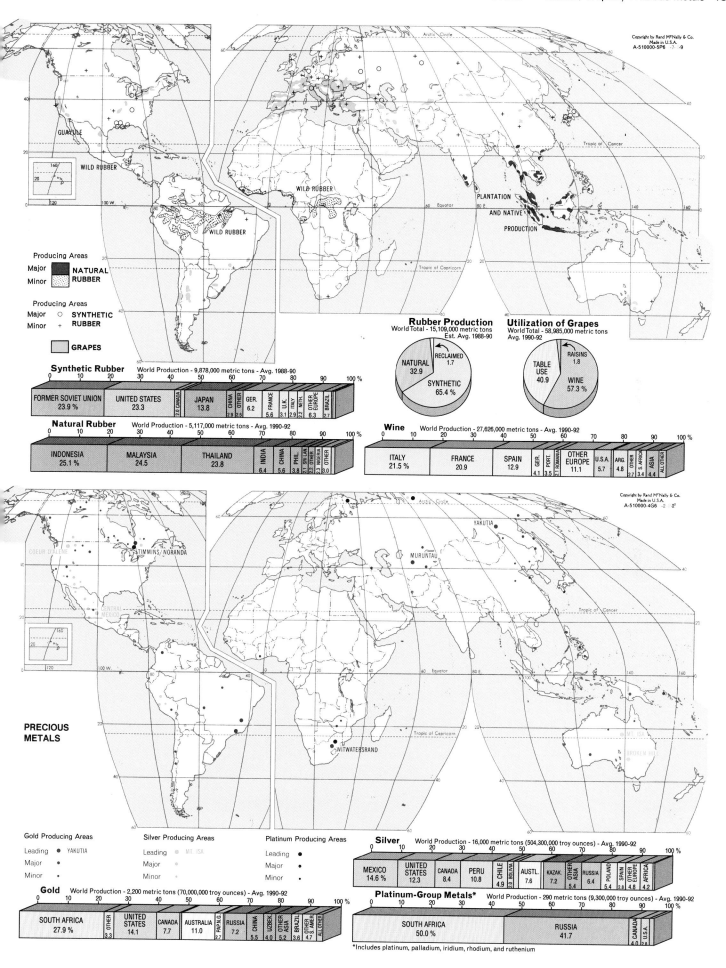

Copyright by Rand McNally & Co.
Made in U.S.A.
A-510000-5P6 -7- -9

GUAYULE
WILD RUBBER
WILD RUBBER
WILD RUBBER
PLANTATION
AND NATIVE
PRODUCTION

Producing Areas
Major ■ NATURAL
Minor ⋮ RUBBER

Producing Areas
Major ○ SYNTHETIC
Minor + RUBBER

▨ GRAPES

Synthetic Rubber
World Production - 9,878,000 metric tons - Avg. 1988-90

| FORMER SOVIET UNION 23.9 % | UNITED STATES 23.3 | CANADA 2.0 | JAPAN 13.8 | CHINA 2.9 | OTHER 2.5 | GER. 6.2 | FRANCE 5.6 | U.K. 3.1 | ITALY 2.9 | NETH. | OTHER EUROPE 6.3 | BRAZIL 2.7 |

Natural Rubber
World Production - 5,117,000 metric tons - Avg. 1990-92

| INDONESIA 25.1 % | MALAYSIA 24.5 | THAILAND 23.8 | INDIA 6.4 | CHINA 5.6 | PHIL. 3.8 | SRI LAN. 2.1 | NIGERIA 2.2 | OTHER 2.3 | OTHER 3.0 |

Rubber Production
World Total - 15,109,000 metric tons
Est. Avg. 1988-90

NATURAL 32.9
RECLAIMED 1.7
SYNTHETIC 65.4 %

Utilization of Grapes
World Total - 58,985,000 metric tons
Avg. 1990-92

TABLE USE 40.9
RAISINS 1.8
WINE 57.3 %

Wine
World Production - 27,626,000 metric tons - Avg. 1990-92

| ITALY 21.5 % | FRANCE 20.9 | SPAIN 12.9 | GER. 4.1 | ROMANIA 3.5 | OTHER EUROPE 11.1 | U.S.A. 5.7 | ARG. 4.8 | OTHER 2.7 | S. AFRICA 3.4 | ASIA 4.1 | ALL OTHER |

Copyright by Rand McNally & Co.
Made in U.S.A.
A-510000-4G6 -2- -2'

YAKUTIA
COEUR D'ALENE
TIMMINS / NORANDA
MURUNTAU
CENTRAL MEXICO
MT. ISA
BROKEN HILL
WITWATERSRAND

PRECIOUS METALS

Gold Producing Areas
Leading ● YAKUTIA
Major •
Minor ·

Silver Producing Areas
Leading ● MT. ISA
Major •
Minor ·

Platinum Producing Areas
Leading ●
Major •
Minor ·

Silver
World Production - 16,000 metric tons (504,300,000 troy ounces) - Avg. 1990-92

| MEXICO 14.6 % | UNITED STATES 12.3 | CANADA 8.4 | PERU 10.8 | CHILE 4.9 | BOLIVIA 2.0 | AUSTL. 7.6 | KAZAK. 7.2 | OTHER ASIA 5.4 | RUSSIA 6.4 | POLAND 5.4 | SPAIN 2.8 | OTHER EUROPE 4.8 | AFRICA 4.2 |

Gold
World Production - 2,200 metric tons (70,000,000 troy ounces) - Avg. 1990-92

| SOUTH AFRICA 27.9 % | OTHER 3.3 | UNITED STATES 14.1 | CANADA 7.7 | AUSTRALIA 11.0 | PAP.N.G. 2.7 | RUSSIA 7.2 | CHINA 5.5 | UZBEK. 4.0 | OTHER ASIA 5.2 | BRAZIL 3.6 | OTHER S. AMER. 4.7 | ALL OTHER |

Platinum-Group Metals*
World Production - 290 metric tons (9,300,000 troy ounces) - Avg. 1990-92

| SOUTH AFRICA 50.0 % | RUSSIA 41.7 | CANADA 4.0 | U.S.A. |

*Includes platinum, palladium, iridium, rhodium, and ruthenium

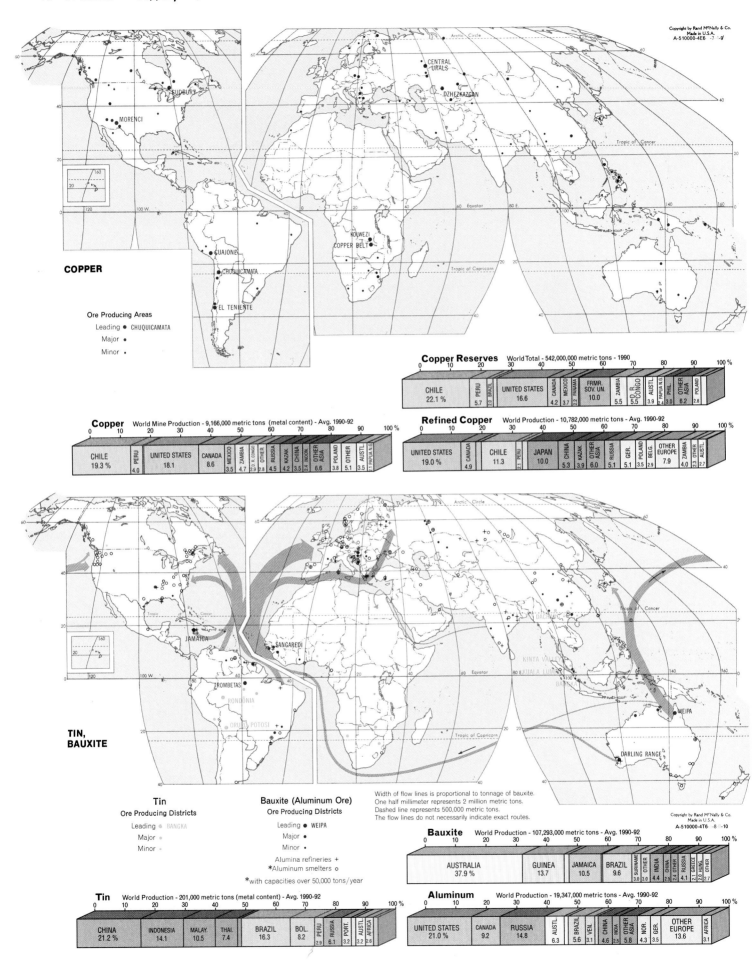

CENTRAL
URALS

DZHEZKAZGAN

SUDBURY

MORENCI

Tropic of Cancer

Equator   80 E.

KOLWEZI
COPPER BELT

CUAJONE

COPPER

CHUQUICAMATA

EL TENIENTE

Ore Producing Areas

Leading ● CHUQUICAMATA

Major ●

Minor ·

Copper Reserves World Total - 542,000,000 metric tons - 1990

0	10	20	30	40	50	60	70	80	90	100 %

CHILE 22.1 %	PERU 5.7	BRAZIL 2.0	UNITED STATES 16.6	CANADA 4.2	MEXICO 3.7	PANAMA 2.2	FRMR. SOV. UN. 10.0	ZAMBIA 5.5	D. R. CONGO 2.4	AUSTL. 3.9	PAPUA N.G. 3.0	PHIL. 3.0	OTHER ASIA 6.2	POLAND 2.8

Copper World Mine Production - 9,166,000 metric tons (metal content) - Avg. 1990-92

0	10	20	30	40	50	60	70	80	90	100 %

CHILE 19.3 %	PERU 4.0	UNITED STATES 18.1	CANADA 8.6	MEXICO 3.5	ZAMBIA 4.7	D. R. CONGO 2.9	OTHER 2.8	RUSSIA 4.5	KAZAK. 2.4	CHINA 3.5	INDON. 2.4	OTHER ASIA 6.6	POLAND 3.8	OTHER 5.1	AUSTL. 3.5	PAPUA N.G. 2.1

Refined Copper World Production - 10,782,000 metric tons - Avg. 1990-92

0	10	20	30	40	50	60	70	80	90	100 %

UNITED STATES 19.0 %	CANADA 4.9	CHILE 11.3	PERU 2.1	JAPAN 10.0	CHINA 5.3	KAZAK. 3.9	OTHER ASIA 6.0	RUSSIA 5.1	GER. 5.1	POLAND 3.5	BELG. 2.9	OTHER EUROPE 7.9	ZAMBIA 4.0	OTHER 2.3	AUSTL. 2.7

Arctic Circle

DACHANG

Tropic of Cancer

KINTA VALLEY

KUALA LUMPUR

BANGKA

JAMAICA

SANGAREDI

TROMBETAS

RONDONIA

ORURO POTOSI

Equator   80 E.

WEIPA

DARLING RANGE

Tropic of Capricorn

**TIN,
BAUXITE**

Tin
Ore Producing Districts

Leading ● BANGKA

Major ●

Minor ·

Bauxite (Aluminum Ore)
Ore Producing Districts

Leading ● WEIPA

Major ●

Minor ·

Alumina refineries +

*Aluminum smelters o

*with capacities over 50,000 tons/year

Width of flow lines is proportional to tonnage of bauxite.
One half millimeter represents 2 million metric tons.
Dashed line represents 500,000 metric tons.
The flow lines do not necessarily indicate exact routes.

Bauxite World Production - 107,293,000 metric tons - Avg. 1990-92

0	10	20	30	40	50	60	70	80	90	100 %

AUSTRALIA 37.9 %	GUINEA 13.7	JAMAICA 10.5	BRAZIL 9.6	SURINAME 3.0	OTHER 3.0	INDIA 4.4	CHINA 2.5	OTHER 2.4	RUSSIA 4.1	GREECE 2.1	HUNG. 2.0	OTHER 2.7

Tin World Production - 201,000 metric tons (metal content) - Avg. 1990-92

0	10	20	30	40	50	60	70	80	90	100 %

CHINA 21.2 %	INDONESIA 14.1	MALAY. 10.5	THAI. 7.4	BRAZIL 16.3	BOL. 8.2	PERU 2.9	RUSSIA 6.1	PORT. 3.2	AUSTL. 3.2	AFRICA 2.6

Aluminum World Production - 19,347,000 metric tons - Avg. 1990-92

0	10	20	30	40	50	60	70	80	90	100 %

UNITED STATES 21.0 %	CANADA 9.2	RUSSIA 14.8	AUSTL. 6.3	BRAZIL 5.6	VEN. 3.1	CHINA 4.6	INDIA 2.5	OTHER ASIA 5.8	NOR. 4.3	GER. 3.5	OTHER EUROPE 13.6	AFRICA 3.1

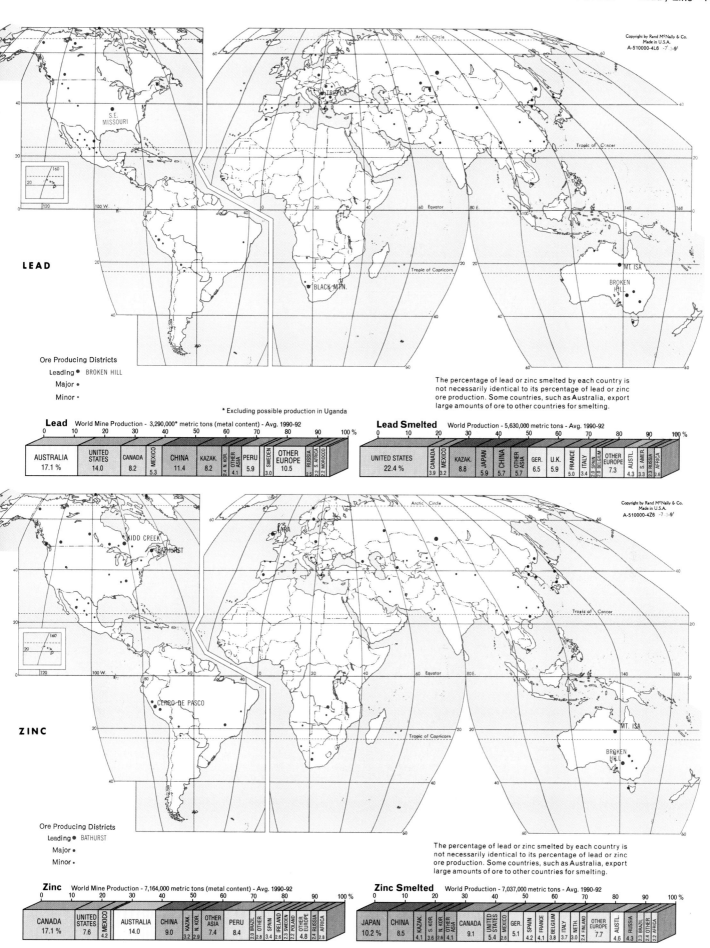

Copyright by Rand McNally & Co.
Made in U.S.A.
A-510000-4L6 -7 -9

LEAD

S.E. MISSOURI

TREPCA

BLACK MTN.

MT. ISA

BROKEN HILL

Ore Producing Districts

Leading ● BROKEN HILL

Major ●

Minor ·

The percentage of lead or zinc smelted by each country is not necessarily identical to its percentage of lead or zinc ore production. Some countries, such as Australia, export large amounts of ore to other countries for smelting.

* Excluding possible production in Uganda

Lead World Mine Production - 3,290,000* metric tons (metal content) - Avg. 1990-92

AUSTRALIA 17.1 %	UNITED STATES 14.0	CANADA 8.2	MEXICO 5.3	CHINA 11.4	KAZAK. 8.2	N. KOR 2.4	OTHER ASIA 4.1	PERU 5.9	SWEDEN 3.0	OTHER EUROPE 10.5	RUSSIA 2.3	S. AFRICA 2.2	MOROCCO 2.2

Lead Smelted World Production - 5,630,000 metric tons - Avg. 1990-92

UNITED STATES 22.4 %	CANADA 3.9	MEXICO 3.2	KAZAK. 8.8	JAPAN 5.9	CHINA 5.7	OTHER ASIA 5.7	GER. 6.5	U.K. 5.9	FRANCE 5.0	ITALY 3.4	SPAIN 2.8	BELGIUM 2.6	OTHER EUROPE 7.3	AUSTL. 4.3	S. AMER. 2.3	AFRICA 2.6

Copyright by Rand McNally & Co.
Made in U.S.A.
A-510000-4Z6 -7 -9

KIDD CREEK
BATHURST

JAVA

CERRO DE PASCO

MT. ISA

BROKEN HILL

ZINC

Ore Producing Districts

Leading ● BATHURST

Major ●

Minor ·

The percentage of lead or zinc smelted by each country is not necessarily identical to its percentage of lead or zinc ore production. Some countries, such as Australia, export large amounts of ore to other countries for smelting.

Zinc World Mine Production - 7,164,000 metric tons (metal content) - Avg. 1990-92

CANADA 17.1 %	UNITED STATES 7.6	MEXICO 4.2	AUSTRALIA 14.0	CHINA 9.0	KAZAK. 3.2	N. KOR 2.9	OTHER ASIA 7.4	PERU 8.4	BRAZIL 2.0	OTHER 2.8	SPAIN 3.4	IRELAND 2.8	SWEDEN 2.3	POLAND 2.3	OTHER EUROPE 4.8	RUSSIA 2.4	AFRICA 2.3

Zinc Smelted World Production - 7,037,000 metric tons - Avg. 1990-92

JAPAN 10.2 %	CHINA 8.5	KAZAK. 4.1	S. KOR. 3.6	N. KOR 2.6	OTHER ASIA 4.1	CANADA 9.1	UNITED STATES 5.4	MEXICO 2.6	GER. 5.1	SPAIN 4.2	FRANCE 4.1	ITALY 3.8	NETH. 3.7	FINLAND 3.0	OTHER EUROPE 7.7	AUSTL. 4.6	RUSSIA 4.3	BRAZIL 2.8	AFRICA 2.4

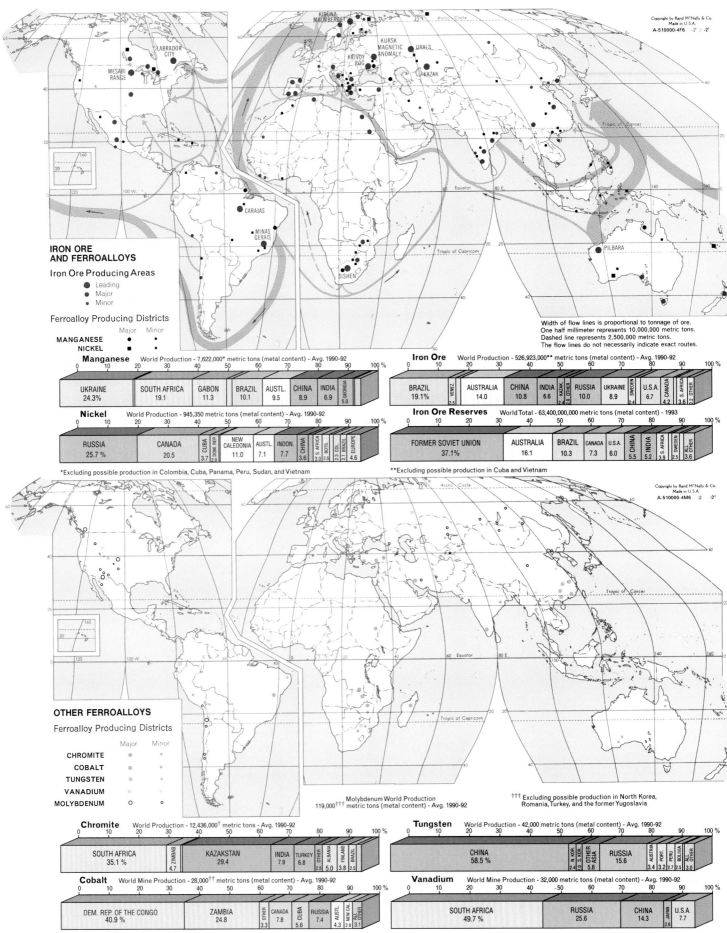

IRON ORE AND FERROALLOYS

Iron Ore Producing Areas

- Leading
- Major
- Minor

Ferroalloy Producing Districts

	Major	Minor
MANGANESE	●	•
NICKEL	■	▪

Width of flow lines is proportional to tonnage of ore.
One half millimeter represents 10,000,000 metric tons.
Dashed line represents 2,500,000 metric tons.
The flow lines do not necessarily indicate exact routes.

Manganese
World Production - 7,622,000* metric tons (metal content) - Avg. 1990-92

0	10	20	30	40	50	60	70	80	90	100 %

| UKRAINE 24.3% | SOUTH AFRICA 19.1 | GABON 11.3 | BRAZIL 10.1 | AUSTL. 9.5 | CHINA 8.9 | INDIA 6.9 | GEORGIA 5.0 |

Nickel
World Production - 945,350 metric tons (metal content) - Avg. 1990-92

0	10	20	30	40	50	60	70	80	90	100 %

| RUSSIA 25.7 % | CANADA 20.5 | CUBA 3.7 | DOM. REP. 2.8 | NEW CALEDONIA 11.0 | AUSTL. 7.1 | INDON. 7.7 | CHINA 3.0 | S.AFRICA 2.5 | BOTS. 2.5 | COL. 2.1 | BRAZIL 2.8 | EUROPE 4.6 |

*Excluding possible production in Colombia, Cuba, Panama, Peru, Sudan, and Vietnam

Iron Ore
World Production - 526,923,000** metric tons (metal content) - Avg. 1990-92

0	10	20	30	40	50	60	70	80	90	100 %

| BRAZIL 19.1% | VENEZ. 2.5 | AUSTRALIA 14.0 | CHINA 10.8 | INDIA 6.6 | KAZAK. 2.0 | OTHER | RUSSIA 10.0 | UKRAINE 8.9 | SWEDEN 6.7 | U.S.A. 4.2 | CANADA 3.6 | S.AFRICA 2.2 | OTHER |

Iron Ore Reserves
World Total - 63,400,000,000 metric tons (metal content) - 1993

0	10	20	30	40	50	60	70	80	90	100 %

| FORMER SOVIET UNION 37.1% | AUSTRALIA 16.1 | BRAZIL 10.3 | CANADA 7.3 | U.S.A. 6.0 | CHINA 5.5 | INDIA 5.2 | S.AFRICA 3.9 | SWEDEN 2.5 | ALL OTHER |

**Excluding possible production in Cuba and Vietnam

OTHER FERROALLOYS

Ferroalloy Producing Districts

	Major	Minor
CHROMITE	●	•
COBALT	■	▪
TUNGSTEN	●	•
VANADIUM	●	•
MOLYBDENUM	○	○

Molybdenum World Production
119,000[†††] metric tons (metal content) - Avg. 1990-92

††† Excluding possible production in North Korea, Romania, Turkey, and the former Yugoslavia

Chromite
World Production - 12,436,000[†] metric tons - Avg. 1990-92

0	10	20	30	40	50	60	70	80	90	100 %

| SOUTH AFRICA 35.1 % | ZIMBAB. 4.7 | KAZAKSTAN 29.4 | INDIA 7.9 | TURKEY 6.8 | OTHER | ALBANIA 3.8 | FINLAND 2.5 | BRAZIL 2.5 |

Cobalt
World Mine Production - 28,000[††] metric tons (metal content) - Avg. 1990-92

0	10	20	30	40	50	60	70	80	90	100 %

| DEM. REP. OF THE CONGO 40.9 % | ZAMBIA 24.8 | OTHER 3.3 | CANADA 7.8 | CUBA 5.6 | RUSSIA 7.4 | AUSTL. 4.3 | NEW CAL. 2.8 | ALL OTHER 3.1 |

Tungsten
World Production - 42,000 metric tons (metal content) - Avg. 1990-92

0	10	20	30	40	50	60	70	80	90	100 %

| CHINA 58.5 % | N. KOR. 2.4 | S. KOR. 2.0 | OTHER ASIA 5.8 | RUSSIA 15.6 | AUSTRIA 3.4 | PORT. 3.2 | PERU 2.7 | BOLIVIA 2.5 | ALL OTHER 3.0 |

Vanadium
World Mine Production - 32,000 metric tons (metal content) - Avg. 1990-92

0	10	20	30	40	50	60	70	80	90	100 %

| SOUTH AFRICA 49.7 % | RUSSIA 25.6 | CHINA 14.3 | JAPAN 2.6 | U.S.A. 7.7 |

† Excluding possible production in Bulgaria and North Korea   †† Excluding possible production in Bulgaria, China, Germany, Indonesia, and Poland

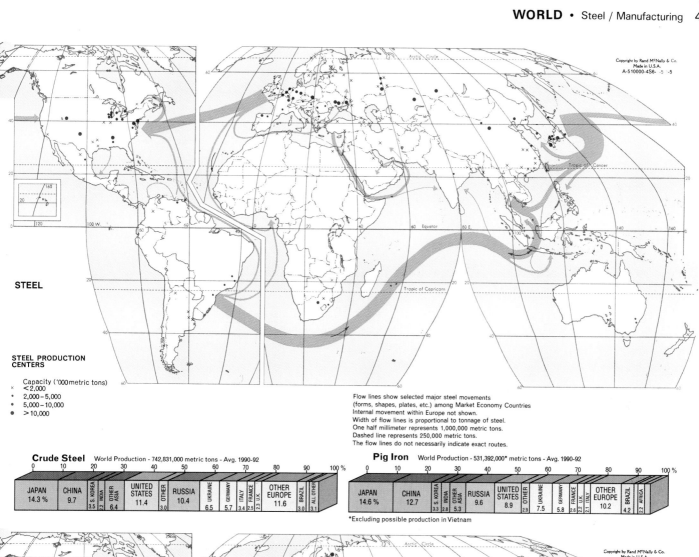

STEEL

STEEL PRODUCTION CENTERS

Capacity ('000 metric tons)
- × <2,000
- • 2,000–5,000
- • 5,000–10,000
- ● >10,000

Flow lines show selected major steel movements
(forms, shapes, plates, etc.) among Market Economy Countries
Internal movement within Europe not shown.
Width of flow lines is proportional to tonnage of steel.
One half millimeter represents 1,000,000 metric tons.
Dashed line represents 250,000 metric tons.
The flow lines do not necessarily indicate exact routes.

Crude Steel World Production - 742,831,000 metric tons - Avg. 1990-92

JAPAN 14.3 %	CHINA 9.7	S. KOREA 3.5	INDIA 2.2	OTHER ASIA 6.4	UNITED STATES 11.4	OTHER 3.0	RUSSIA 10.4	UKRAINE 6.5	GERMANY 5.7	ITALY 3.4	FRANCE 2.5	U.K. 2.3	OTHER EUROPE 11.6	BRAZIL 3.0	ALL OTHER 3.1

Pig Iron World Production - 531,392,000* metric tons - Avg. 1990-92

JAPAN 14.6 %	CHINA 12.7	S. KOREA 3.3	INDIA 2.8	OTHER ASIA 5.3	RUSSIA 9.6	UNITED STATES 8.9	OTHER 2.9	UKRAINE 7.5	GERMANY 5.8	FRANCE 2.6	U.K. 2.1	ITALY 2.1	OTHER EUROPE 10.2	BRAZIL 4.2	AFRICA 2.2

*Excluding possible production in Vietnam

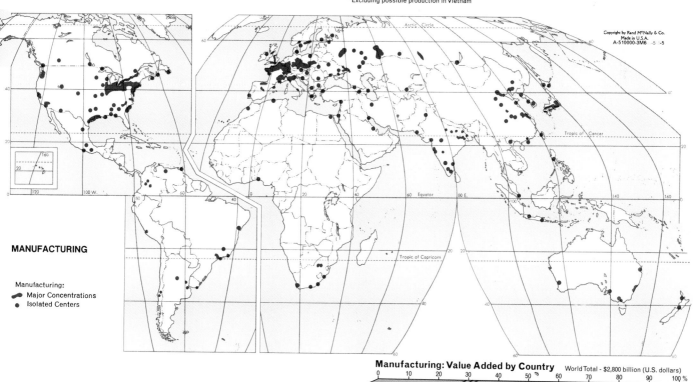

MANUFACTURING

Manufacturing:
- ⟳ Major Concentrations
- • Isolated Centers

Manufacturing: Value Added by Country World Total - $2,800 billion (U.S. dollars)

UNITED STATES 29.4 %	CANADA 2.1	WESTERN EUROPE 24.1	E. EUROPE 4.2	JAPAN 14.4	CHINA 3.5	OTHER ASIA 4.9	FORMER SOV. UN. 10.5	S. AMER. 3.7

Manufacturing: Employment by Product World Total - 218,600,000 people - 1985

FOOD 15.4 %	TEXTILES AND APPAREL 19.3	WOOD AND PAPER PRODUCTS 11.9	CHEM. 8.1	NON-METAL MINERAL PRODUCTS 5.8	BASIC METALS 3.9	METAL PRODUCTS 32.1	OTHER 3.5

Manufacturing: Employment by Country World Total - 280,501,000 people - 1991

CHINA 35.4 %	JAPAN 5.7	INDON. 2.8	OTHER ASIA 9.2	FORMER SOV. UN. 12.6	UNITED STATES 7.3	GERMANY 3.3	OTHER EUROPE 13.9	SOUTH AMERICA 4.9

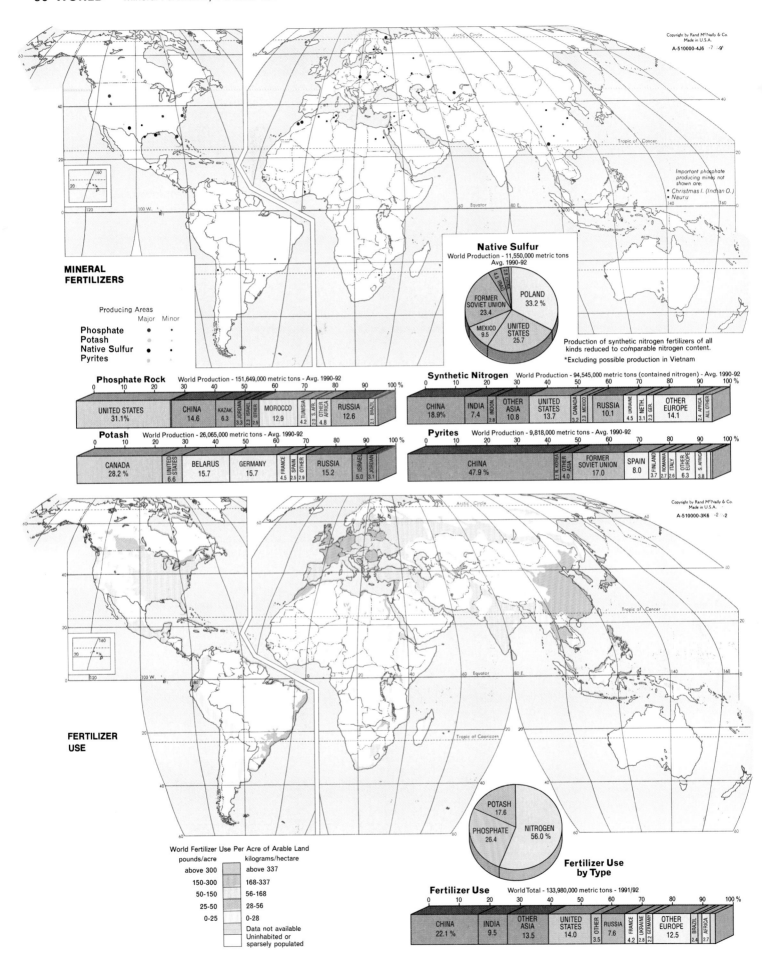

**MINERAL
FERTILIZERS**

Producing Areas

	Major	Minor
Phosphate	•	·
Potash	•	·
Native Sulfur	•	·
Pyrites	•	·

Copyright by Rand M°Nally & Co.
Made in U.S.A.
A-510000-4J6 -7 -9¹

*Important phosphate
producing mines not
shown are:*
• Christmas I. (Indian O.)
• Nauru

Native Sulfur
World Production - 11,550,000 metric tons
Avg. 1990-92

POLAND 33.2%
UNITED STATES 25.7
FORMER SOVIET UNION 23.4
MEXICO 9.5
4.5 IRAQ
3.8 CHINA

Production of synthetic nitrogen fertilizers of all
kinds reduced to comparable nitrogen content.

*Excluding possible production in Vietnam

Phosphate Rock World Production - 151,649,000 metric tons - Avg. 1990-92

| UNITED STATES 31.1% | CHINA 14.6 | KAZAK. 6.3 | JORDAN 3.3 | ISRAEL 2.3 | OTHER 2.6 | MOROCCO 12.9 | TUNISIA 4.2 | S. AFR. 2.0 | OTHER AFRICA 4.8 | RUSSIA 12.6 | BRAZIL 2.1 |

Synthetic Nitrogen World Production - 94,545,000 metric tons (contained nitrogen) - Avg. 1990-92

| CHINA 18.9% | INDIA 7.4 | INDON. 2.8 | OTHER ASIA 10.8 | UNITED STATES 13.7 | CANADA 3.2 | MEXICO 2.3 | RUSSIA 10.1 | UKRAINE 4.5 | NETH. 3.1 | GER. 2.3 | OTHER EUROPE 14.1 | AFRICA 2.4 | ALL OTHER |

Potash World Production - 26,065,000 metric tons - Avg. 1990-92

| CANADA 28.2% | UNITED STATES 6.6 | BELARUS 15.7 | GERMANY 15.7 | FRANCE 4.5 | SPAIN 2.5 | OTHER 2.9 | RUSSIA 15.2 | ISRAEL 5.0 | JORDAN 3.1 |

Pyrites World Production - 9,818,000 metric tons - Avg. 1990-92

| CHINA 47.9% | N. KOREA 2.1 | OTHER ASIA 4.0 | FORMER SOVIET UNION 17.0 | SPAIN 8.0 | FINLAND 3.7 | ROMANIA 2.7 | ITALY 2.6 | OTHER EUROPE 6.3 | S. AFRICA 3.8 |

**FERTILIZER
USE**

Copyright by Rand M°Nally & Co.
Made in U.S.A.
A-510000-3K6 -2 -2

World Fertilizer Use Per Acre of Arable Land

pounds/acre	kilograms/hectare
above 300	above 337
150-300	168-337
50-150	56-168
25-50	28-56
0-25	0-28
	Data not available
	Uninhabited or sparsely populated

**Fertilizer Use
by Type**

POTASH 17.6
NITROGEN 56.0%
PHOSPHATE 26.4

Fertilizer Use World Total - 133,980,000 metric tons - 1991/92

| CHINA 22.1% | INDIA 9.5 | OTHER ASIA 13.5 | UNITED STATES 14.0 | OTHER 3.5 | RUSSIA 7.6 | FRANCE 4.2 | UKRAINE 2.8 | GERMANY 2.2 | OTHER EUROPE 12.5 | BRAZIL 2.4 | AFRICA 2.7 |

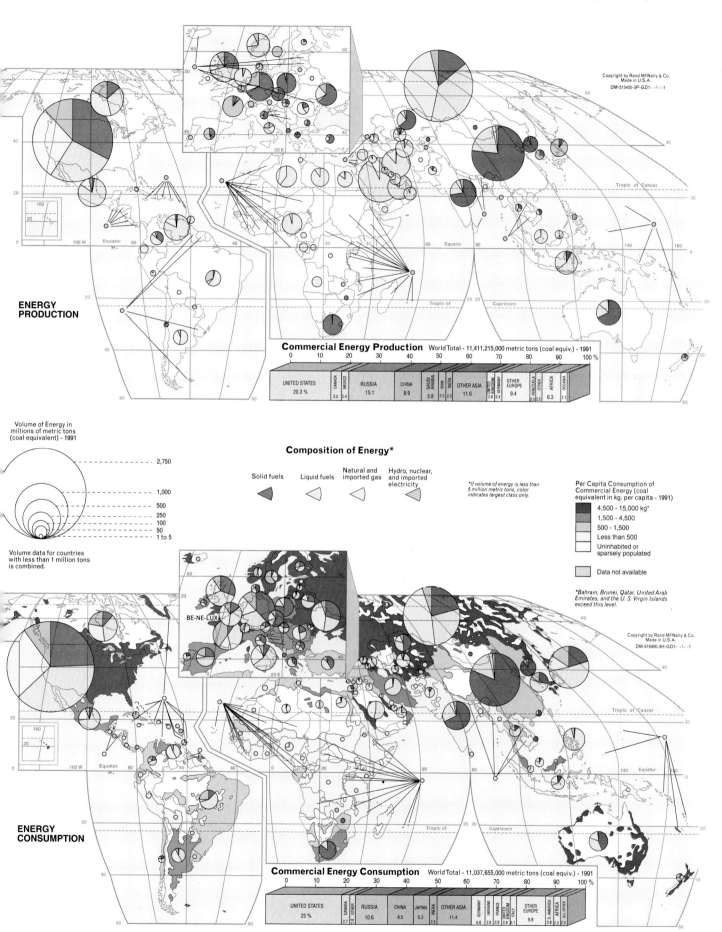

ENERGY PRODUCTION

Copyright by Rand McNally & Co.
Made in U.S.A.
DM-515400-3P-GD1- -1- -1

Commercial Energy Production World Total - 11,411,215,000 metric tons (coal equiv.) - 1991

0	10	20	30	40	50	60	70	80	90	100 %				

| UNITED STATES 20.3 % | CANADA 3.5 | MEXICO 2.4 | RUSSIA 15.1 | CHINA 8.9 | SAUDI ARABIA 5.8 | IRAN 2.5 | INDIA 2.2 | OTHER ASIA 11.6 | UNITED KINGDOM | GERMANY 2.4 | OTHER EUROPE 9.4 | VENEZUELA 2.0 | OTHER 2.2 | AFRICA 6.3 | OCEANIA 2.1 |

Volume of Energy in millions of metric tons (coal equivalent) - 1991

2,750
1,000
500
250
100
50
1 to 5

Volume data for countries with less than 1 million tons is combined.

Composition of Energy*

Solid fuels — Liquid fuels — Natural and imported gas — Hydro, nuclear, and imported electricity

*If volume of energy is less than 5 million metric tons, color indicates largest class only.

Per Capita Consumption of Commercial Energy (coal equivalent in kg. per capita - 1991)

4,500 - 15,000 kg*
1,500 - 4,500
500 - 1,500
Less than 500
Uninhabited or sparsely populated

Data not available

*Bahrain, Brunei, Qatar, United Arab Emirates, and the U. S. Virgin Islands exceed this level.

Copyright by Rand McNally & Co.
Made in U.S.A.
DM-515400-3H-GD1- -1- -1

BE-NE-LUX

ENERGY CONSUMPTION

Commercial Energy Consumption World Total - 11,037,655,000 metric tons (coal equiv.) - 1991

0	10	20	30	40	50	60	70	80	90	100 %	

| UNITED STATES 25 % | CANADA 2.7 | OTHER 1.8 | RUSSIA 10.6 | CHINA 8.5 | JAPAN 5.3 | INDIA 2.5 | OTHER ASIA 11.4 | GERMANY 4.6 | UKRAINE 2.8 | FRANCE 2.8 | UNITED KINGDOM 2.8 | ITALY 2.1 | OTHER EUROPE 9.8 | S. AMERICA 2.8 | AFRICA 2.2 | ALL OTHER |

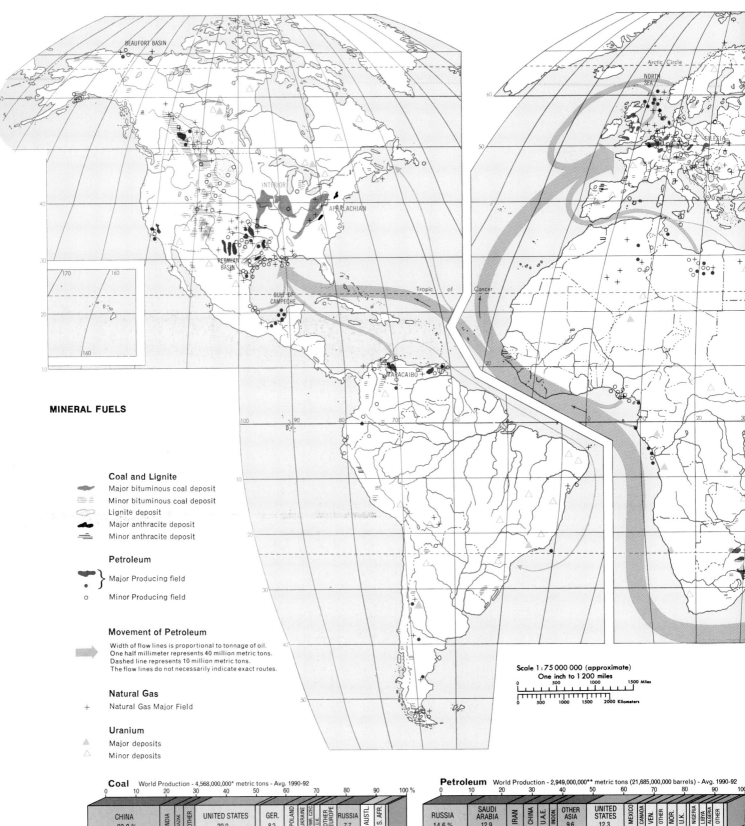

MINERAL FUELS

Coal and Lignite
Major bituminous coal deposit
Minor bituminous coal deposit
Lignite deposit
Major anthracite deposit
Minor anthracite deposit

Petroleum
⟩ Major Producing field

o Minor Producing field

Movement of Petroleum

Width of flow lines is proportional to tonnage of oil.
One half millimeter represents 40 million metric tons.
Dashed line represents 10 million metric tons.
The flow lines do not necessarily indicate exact routes.

Natural Gas
+ Natural Gas Major Field

Uranium
▲ Major deposits
△ Minor deposits

Scale 1 : 75 000 000 (approximate)
One inch to 1 200 miles

BEAUFORT BASIN
INTERIOR
APPALACHIAN
PERMIAN BASIN
GULF OF CAMPECHE
MARACAIBO
NORTH SEA
Arctic Circle
Tropic of Cancer

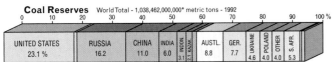

Coal World Production - 4,568,000,000* metric tons - Avg. 1990-92

| CHINA 23.8% | INDIA 5.0 | KAZAK. 2.9 | OTHER 3.8 | UNITED STATES 20.0 | GER. 8.2 | POLAND 4.6 | UKRAINE 3.1 | FMR. CZEC. 2.2 | U.K. 2.0 | OTHER EUROPE 5.7 | RUSSIA 7.7 | AUSTL. 4.7 | S. AFR. 3.8 |

Anthracite and Bituminous: World Total - 3,472,000,000 metric tons

Coal Reserves World Total - 1,038,462,000,000* metric tons - 1992

| UNITED STATES 23.1% | RUSSIA 16.2 | CHINA 11.0 | INDIA 6.0 | INDON. 3.1 | KAZAK. 2.1 | AUSTL. 8.8 | GER. 7.7 | UKRAINE 4.6 | POLAND 4.0 | OTHER 4.0 | S. AFR. 5.3 |

Anthracite and Bituminous: World Total - 519,231,000,000 metric tons
* Includes anthracite, subanthracite, bituminous, subbituminous, lignite, and brown coal

Petroleum World Production - 2,949,000,000** metric tons (21,685,000,000 barrels) - Avg. 1990-92

| RUSSIA 14.6% | SAUDI ARABIA 12.9 | IRAN 5.5 | CHINA 4.7 | U.A.E. 3.8 | INDON. 2.6 | OTHER ASIA 9.6 | UNITED STATES 12.3 | MEXICO 4.4 | CANADA 2.6 | VEN. 3.4 | NOR. 3.2 | U.K. 3.1 | NIGERIA 2.4 | ALGERIA 2.0 | OTHER 3.6 |

Petroleum Reserves World Total - 148,893,000,000** metric tons (1,094,800,000,000 barrels)

| SAUDI ARABIA 23.8% | IRAQ 9.1 | KUWAIT 8.7 | U.A.E. 7.5 | IRAN 7.0 | CHINA 2.4 | OTHER ASIA 5.0 | RUSSIA 14.3 | VEN. 5.8 | MEXICO 4.7 | U.S.A. 2.2 | LIBYA 2.8 | ALL OTHER 3.1 |

** Crude Petroleum

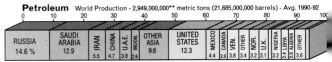
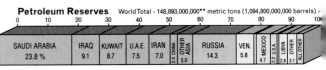

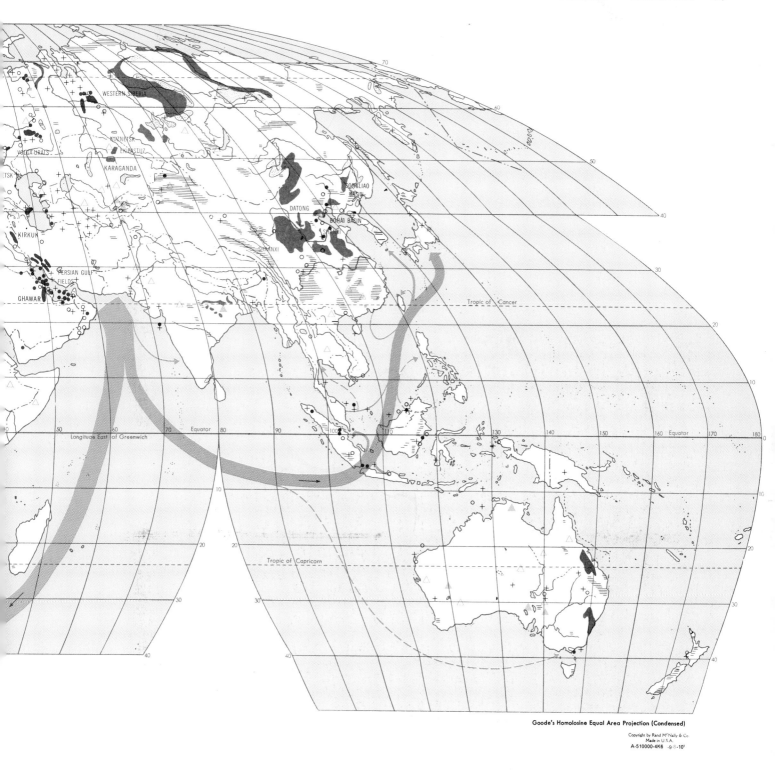

WESTERN SIBERIA

KUZNETSK
EKIBASTUZ

KARAGANDA

VOLGA-URALS

TSK

KIRKUK

PERSIAN GULF
FIELDS

GHAWAR

SONGLIAO
BASIN

DATONG

BOHAI BASIN

SHANXI

Tropic of Cancer

Longitude East of Greenwich   Equator

Tropic of Capricorn

Goode's Homolosine Equal Area Projection (Condensed)

Copyright by Rand M*Nally & Co.
Made in U.S.A.
A-510000-4K6 -9-II-10¹

Natural Gas   World Production - 2,076,000,000,000 cubic meters - Avg. 1990-92

0	10	20	30	40	50	60	70	80	90	100 %

| RUSSIA 30.9 % | UNITED STATES 24.2 | CANADA 5.7 | NETH. 4.0 | U.K. 2.6 | OTHER EUROPE 6.0 | TURKMEN. 3.7 | INDON. 2.0 | UZBEK. | OTHER ASIA 9.7 | ALGERIA 2.6 | S. AMER. 2.2 |

Natural Gas Reserves   World Total - 134,947,000,000,000 cubic meters - 1992

0	10	20	30	40	50	60	70	80	90	100 %

| RUSSIA 36.1 % | IRAN 13.7 | U.A.E. 4.2 | QATAR 4.1 | S. ARAB. 3.9 | IRAQ 2.3 | TURKMEN. 2.1 | OTHER ASIA 10.5 | U.S.A. 3.5 | CANADA 2.0 | ALGERIA 2.7 | NIGERIA 2.5 | VEN. 2.7 | EUROPE 5.0 |

Uranium   World Production - 43,500 metric tons - Avg. 1990-92

0	10	20	30	40	50	60	70	80	90	100 %

| CANADA 20.2 % | U.S.A. 6.7 | RUSSIA 8.7 | KAZAK. 8.4 | UZBEK. 8.1 | OTHER 2.8 | AUSTL. 7.4 | NIGER 6.7 | NAMIBIA 5.6 | S. AFR. 4.5 | FRANCE 5.7 | FRMR. CZECH. 4.2 | GER. 3.4 | UKRAINE 3.0 | OTHER 3.2 |

Uranium Reserves   World Total - 2,512,000 metric tons† - 1990/91

0	10	20	30	40	50	60	70	80	90	100 %

| AUSTRALIA 20.3 % | FORMER SOVIET UNION 18.5 | SOUTH AFRICA 12.4 | NIGER 6.8 | NAMIBIA 3.8 | OTHER 2.6 | UNITED STATES 10.8 | CANADA 7.6 | BRAZIL 5.6 | CHINA 2.0 | INDIA 2.0 | EUROPE 4.2 |

† Excluding possible reserves in Cuba, North Korea, Mongolia, and Vietnam

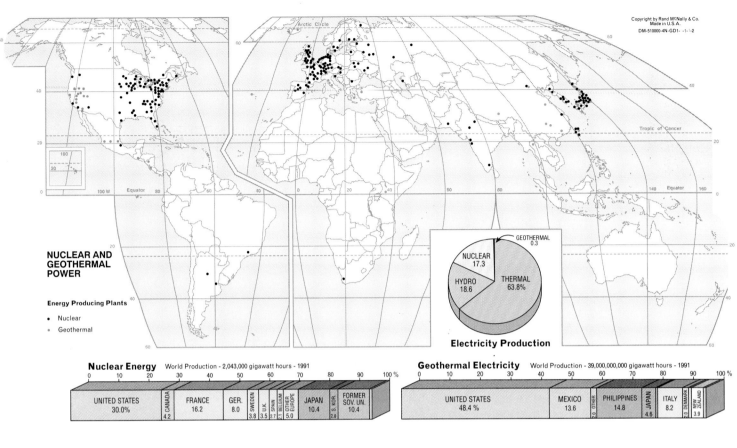

NUCLEAR AND GEOTHERMAL POWER

Energy Producing Plants

- Nuclear
- Geothermal

Electricity Production

GEOTHERMAL 0.3
NUCLEAR 17.3
HYDRO 18.6
THERMAL 63.8%

Nuclear Energy World Production - 2,043,000 gigawatt hours - 1991

0	10	20	30	40	50	60	70	80	90	100 %

| UNITED STATES 30.0% | CANADA 4.2 | FRANCE 16.2 | GER. 8.0 | SWEDEN 3.8 | U.K. 3.5 | SPAIN 2.7 | BELGIUM 2.1 | OTHER EUROPE 5.0 | JAPAN 10.4 | S. KOR. 2.8 | FORMER SOV. UN. 10.4 |

Geothermal Electricity World Production - 39,000,000,000 gigawatt hours - 1991

0	10	20	30	40	50	60	70	80	90	100 %

| UNITED STATES 48.4 % | MEXICO 13.6 | OTHER 2.0 | PHILIPPINES 14.8 | JAPAN 4.6 | ITALY 8.2 | DENMARK 2.0 | NEW ZEALAND 3.9 |

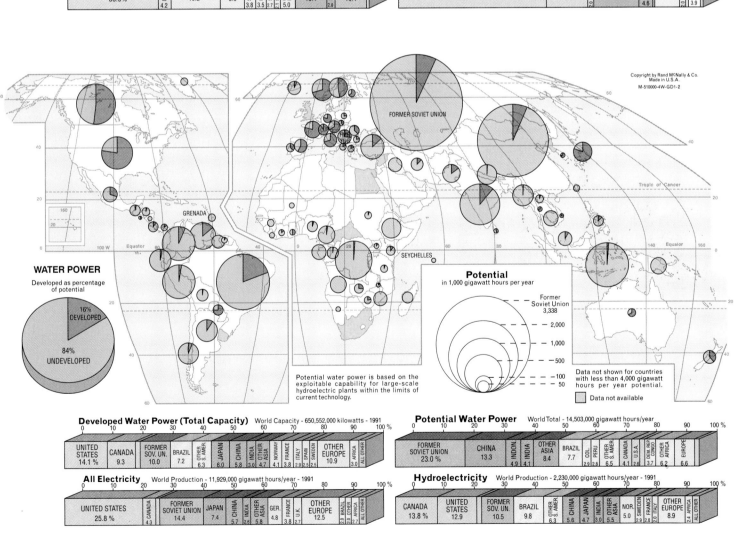

WATER POWER

Developed as percentage of potential

16% DEVELOPED
84% UNDEVELOPED

Potential
in 1,000 gigawatt hours per year

Former Soviet Union 3,338
— 2,000
— 1,000
— 500
— 100
— 50

Data not shown for countries with less than 4,000 gigawatt hours per year potential.

Data not available

Potential water power is based on the exploitable capability for large-scale hydroelectric plants within the limits of current technology.

Developed Water Power (Total Capacity) World Capacity - 650,552,000 kilowatts - 1991

0	10	20	30	40	50	60	70	80	90	100 %

| UNITED STATES 14.1 % | CANADA 9.3 | FORMER SOV. UN. 10.0 | BRAZIL 7.2 | OTHER S. AMER. 6.3 | JAPAN 6.0 | CHINA 5.8 | INDIA 3.0 | OTHER ASIA 4.7 | NORWAY 3.8 | FRANCE 2.5 | ITALY 2.5 | SPAIN 2.5 | OTHER EUROPE 10.9 | AFRICA 3.0 | ALL OTHER |

Potential Water Power World Total - 14,503,000 gigawatt hours/year

0	10	20	30	40	50	60	70	80	90	100 %

| FORMER SOVIET UNION 23.0 % | CHINA 13.3 | INDON. 4.9 | INDIA 4.1 | OTHER ASIA 8.4 | BRAZIL 7.7 | COL. 2.9 | PERU 2.6 | OTHER S. AMER. 6.5 | U.S.A. 4.1 | DEM. REP. CONGO 3.7 | OTHER AFRICA 6.2 | EUROPE 6.6 |

All Electricity World Production - 11,929,000 gigawatt hours/year - 1991

0	10	20	30	40	50	60	70	80	90	100 %

| UNITED STATES 25.8 % | CANADA 4.3 | FORMER SOVIET UNION 14.4 | JAPAN 7.4 | CHINA 5.7 | INDIA 2.8 | OTHER ASIA 5.8 | GER. 4.8 | FRANCE 3.8 | U.K. 2.7 | OTHER EUROPE 12.5 | BRAZIL 2.0 | AFRICA 2.0 | ALL OTHER 2.7 |

Hydroelectricity World Production - 2,230,000 gigawatt hours/year - 1991

0	10	20	30	40	50	60	70	80	90	100 %

| CANADA 13.8 % | UNITED STATES 12.9 | FORMER SOV. UN. 10.5 | BRAZIL 9.8 | OTHER S. AMER. 6.3 | CHINA 5.6 | JAPAN 4.7 | INDIA 3.0 | OTHER ASIA 5.0 | NOR. 5.0 | SWEDEN 2.9 | FRANCE 2.0 | ITALY 2.0 | OTHER EUROPE 8.9 | AFRICA 2.4 | ALL OTHER |

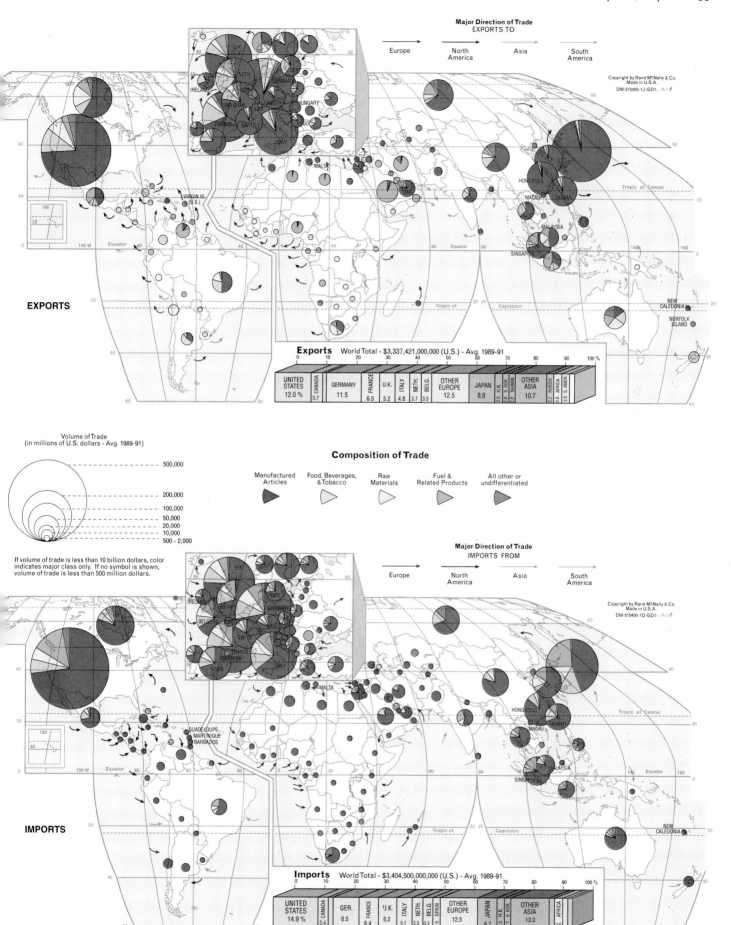

Major Direction of Trade
EXPORTS TO

Europe → North America → Asia → South America

EXPORTS

Exports World Total - $3,337,421,000,000 (U.S.) - Avg. 1989-91

| UNITED STATES 12.0 % | CANADA 3.7 | GERMANY 11.5 | FRANCE 6.0 | U.K. 5.2 | ITALY 4.8 | NETH. 3.7 | BELG. 3.5 | OTHER EUROPE 12.5 | JAPAN 8.8 | H.K. 2.5 | S. KOR. 2.0 | OTHER ASIA 10.7 | RUSSIA 2.6 | AFRICA 2.5 | S. AMER. 2.5 |

Volume of Trade
(in millions of U.S. dollars - Avg. 1989-91)

500,000
200,000
100,000
50,000
20,000
10,000
500 - 2,000

If volume of trade is less than 10 billion dollars, color indicates major class only. If no symbol is shown, volume of trade is less than 500 million dollars.

Composition of Trade

Manufactured Articles   Food, Beverages, & Tobacco   Raw Materials   Fuel & Related Products   All other or undifferentiated

Major Direction of Trade
IMPORTS FROM

Europe → North America → Asia → South America

IMPORTS

Imports World Total - $3,404,500,000,000 (U.S.) - Avg. 1989-91

| UNITED STATES 14.9 % | CANADA 3.4 | GER. 8.5 | FRANCE 6.4 | U.K. 6.2 | ITALY 5.1 | NETH. 3.5 | BELG. 3.3 | SPAIN 2.5 | OTHER EUROPE 12.5 | JAPAN 6.7 | H.K. 2.1 | S. KOR. | OTHER ASIA 13.0 | AFRICA 2.6 |

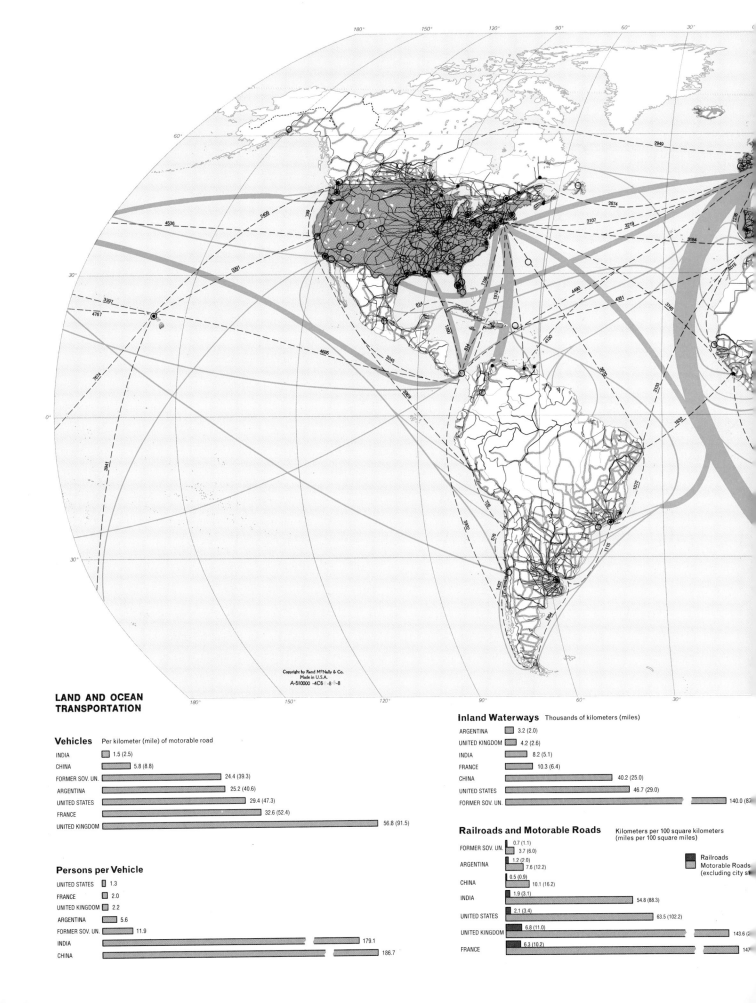

LAND AND OCEAN TRANSPORTATION

Vehicles   Per kilometer (mile) of motorable road

INDIA	1.5 (2.5)
CHINA	5.8 (8.8)
FORMER SOV. UN.	24.4 (39.3)
ARGENTINA	25.2 (40.6)
UNITED STATES	29.4 (47.3)
FRANCE	32.6 (52.4)
UNITED KINGDOM	56.8 (91.5)

Persons per Vehicle

UNITED STATES	1.3
FRANCE	2.0
UNITED KINGDOM	2.2
ARGENTINA	5.6
FORMER SOV. UN.	11.9
INDIA	179.1
CHINA	186.7

Inland Waterways   Thousands of kilometers (miles)

ARGENTINA	3.2 (2.0)
UNITED KINGDOM	4.2 (2.6)
INDIA	8.2 (5.1)
FRANCE	10.3 (6.4)
CHINA	40.2 (25.0)
UNITED STATES	46.7 (29.0)
FORMER SOV. UN.	140.0 (87

Railroads and Motorable Roads   Kilometers per 100 square kilometers (miles per 100 square miles)

Railroads
Motorable Roads (excluding city st

	Railroads	Motorable Roads
FORMER SOV. UN.	0.7 (1.1)	3.7 (6.0)
ARGENTINA	1.2 (2.0)	7.6 (12.2)
CHINA	0.5 (0.9)	10.1 (16.2)
INDIA	1.9 (3.1)	54.8 (88.3)
UNITED STATES	2.1 (3.4)	63.5 (102.2)
UNITED KINGDOM	6.8 (11.0)	143.6 (2
FRANCE	6.3 (10.2)	147

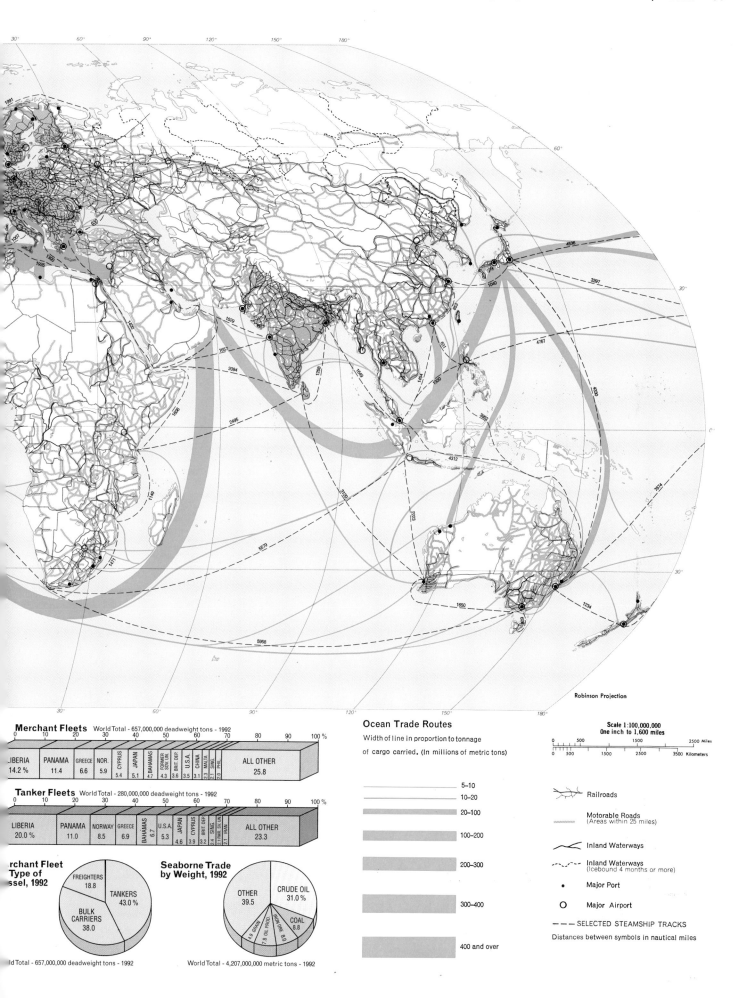

Merchant Fleets World Total - 657,000,000 deadweight tons - 1992

| | 0 | 10 | 20 | 30 | 40 | 50 | 60 | 70 | 80 | 90 | 100 % |

| LIBERIA 14.2 % | PANAMA 11.4 | GREECE 6.6 | NOR. 5.9 | CYPRUS 5.4 | JAPAN 5.1 | BAHAMAS 4.7 | FORMER SOV. UN. 4.3 | BRIT. DEP. 3.6 | U.S.A. 3.5 | CHINA 2.3 | MALTA 2.1 | SING. 2.0 | PHIL. | ALL OTHER 25.8 |

Tanker Fleets World Total - 280,000,000 deadweight tons - 1992

| | 0 | 10 | 20 | 30 | 40 | 50 | 60 | 70 | 80 | 90 | 100 % |

| LIBERIA 20.0 % | PANAMA 11.0 | NORWAY 8.5 | GREECE 6.9 | BAHAMAS 6.7 | U.S.A. 5.3 | JAPAN 4.6 | CYPRUS 3.9 | BRIT. DEP. 3.2 | FMR. SV. UN. 2.1 | SING. 2.1 | IRAN | ALL OTHER 23.3 |

Merchant Fleet by Type of Vessel, 1992

FREIGHTERS 18.8
TANKERS 43.0 %
BULK CARRIERS 38.0

World Total - 657,000,000 deadweight tons - 1992

Seaborne Trade by Weight, 1992

OTHER 39.5
CRUDE OIL 31.0 %
COAL 8.0
IRON ORE 8.0
OIL PROD. 7.8
GRAIN 4.9

World Total - 4,207,000,000 metric tons - 1992

Ocean Trade Routes

Width of line in proportion to tonnage of cargo carried. (In millions of metric tons)

	5–10
	10–20
	20–100
	100–200
	200–300
	300–400
	400 and over

Scale 1:100,000,000
One inch to 1,600 miles

0   500   1500   2500 Miles
0   500   1500   2500   3500 Kilometers

Railroads

Motorable Roads
(Areas within 25 miles)

Inland Waterways

Inland Waterways
(Icebound 4 months or more)

• Major Port

○ Major Airport

– – – SELECTED STEAMSHIP TRACKS

Distances between symbols in nautical miles

Robinson Projection

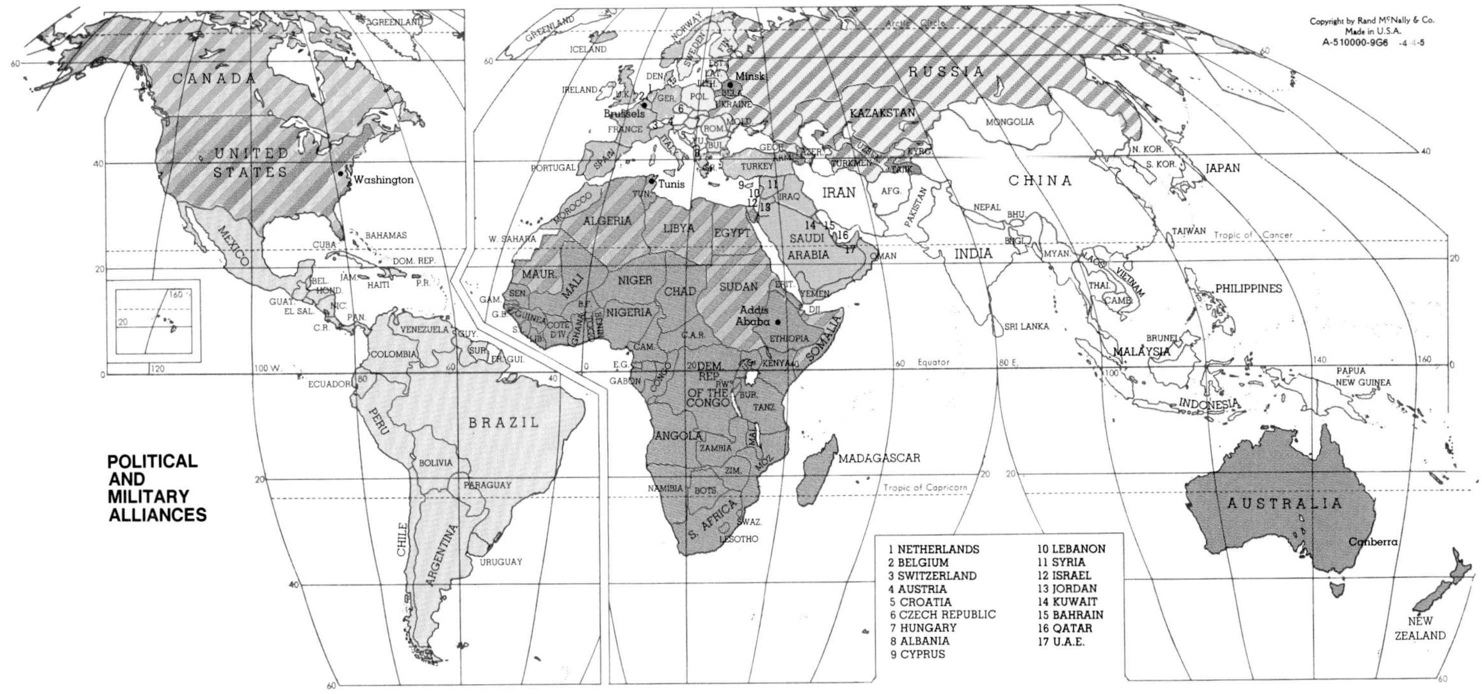

POLITICAL AND MILITARY ALLIANCES

Copyright by Rand M&cNally & Co.
Made in U.S.A.
A-510000-9G6 -4 4 5

1 NETHERLANDS	10 LEBANON
2 BELGIUM	11 SYRIA
3 SWITZERLAND	12 ISRAEL
4 AUSTRIA	13 JORDAN
5 CROATIA	14 KUWAIT
6 CZECH REPUBLIC	15 BAHRAIN
7 HUNGARY	16 QATAR
8 ALBANIA	17 U.A.E.
9 CYPRUS	

NATO-North Atlantic Treaty Organization, founded 1949. Headquarters in Brussels, Belgium.

NATO-Partnership for Peace Program

ANZUS-Australia-New Zealand-U.S. Security Treaty, founded 1952. Headquarters in Canberra, Australia.

OAS-Organization of American States, founded 1948. Headquarters in Washington, D.C., United States.

CIS-Commonwealth of Independent States, founded 1991. Headquarters in Minsk, Belarus.

AL-Arab League (League of Arab States), founded 1945. Headquarters in Tunis, Tunisia.

OAU-Organization of African Unity, founded 1963. Headquarters in Addis Ababa, Ethiopia.

Not affiliated with above organizatons.

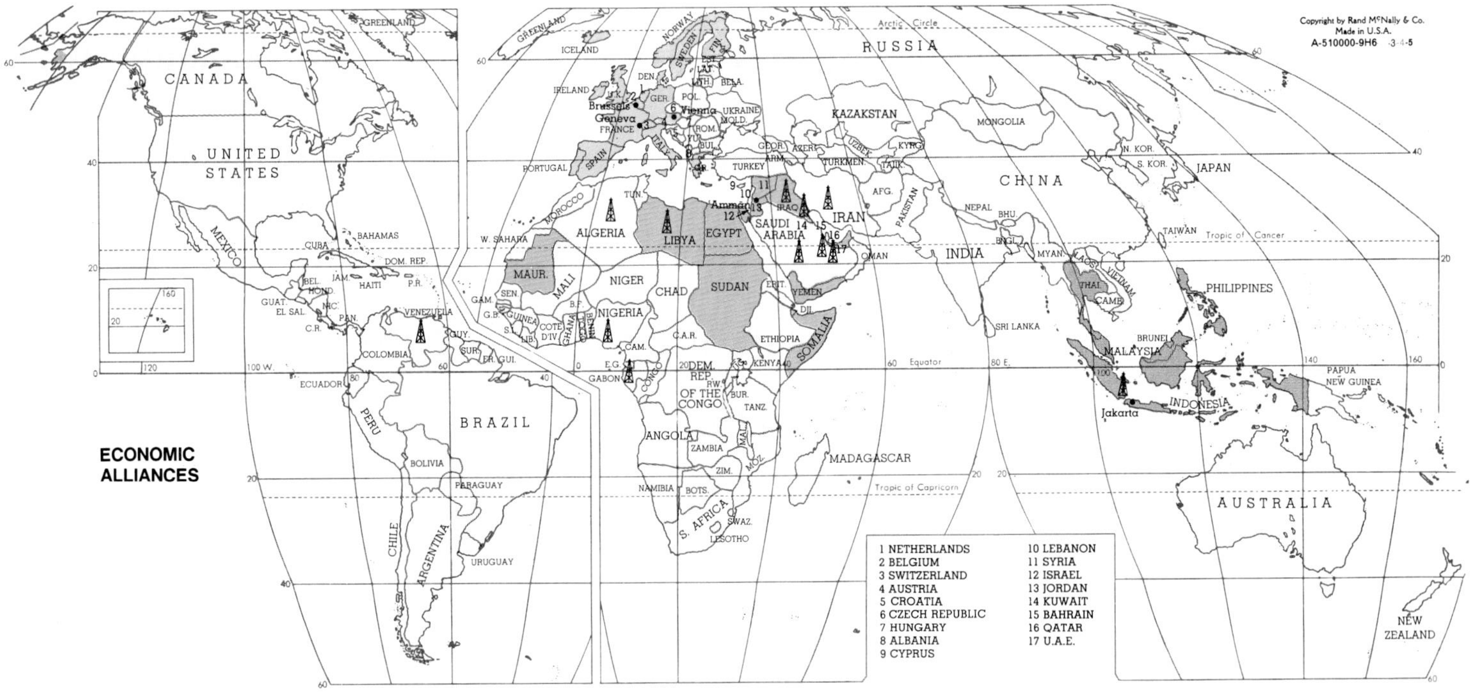

ECONOMIC ALLIANCES

Copyright by Rand M&cNally & Co.
Made in U.S.A.
A-510000-9H6 -3 4-5

1 NETHERLANDS	10 LEBANON
2 BELGIUM	11 SYRIA
3 SWITZERLAND	12 ISRAEL
4 AUSTRIA	13 JORDAN
5 CROATIA	14 KUWAIT
6 CZECH REPUBLIC	15 BAHRAIN
7 HUNGARY	16 QATAR
8 ALBANIA	17 U.A.E.
9 CYPRUS	

EU (Common Market)-European Union, founded 1957. Headquarters in Brussels, Belgium.

EFTA-European Free Trade Association, founded 1960. Headquarters in Geneva, Switzerland.

OPEC-Organization of Petroleum Exporting Countries, founded 1960. Headquarters in Vienna, Austria.

ASEAN-Association of Southeast Asian Nations, founded 1967. Headquarters in Jakarta, Indonesia.

CAEU-Council of Arab Economic Unity, founded 1964. Headquarters in 'Ammān, Jordan. Includes Arab Common Market countries.

Not affiliated with above organizations.

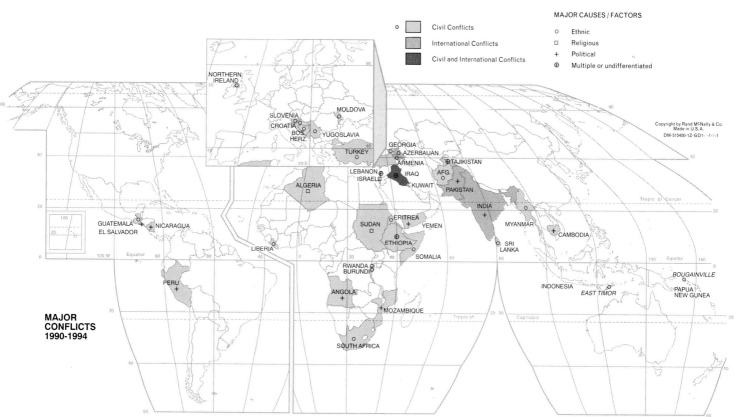

WORLD REFUGEES 1990-1993

Percent of population seeking asylum elsewhere

- Less than 0.1%
- 0.1 to 1.0%
- 1.0 to 5.0 %
- 5.0 to 10.0%
- Greater than 10.0%

Map data for Rwanda, Tanzania, and Dem. Rep. of the Congo revised 07/20/94

Number of Refugees Receiving Asylum
(by host country)

- 4,000,000
- 1,000,000
- 100,000
- 10,000

If number of resident refugees is less than 10,000 people, no symbol is shown.

Refugee Population (by Host Country)   World Total - 18,998,700 people - 1993

IRAN 21.9 %	PAKISTAN 8.6	OTHER ASIA 7.7	MALAWI 5.6	SUDAN 3.8	GUINEA 2.5	ETHIOPIA 2.3	KENYA 2.1	D. R. CONGO 2.0	OTHER AFRICA 10.0	GERMANY 4.4	BOS.-HERZ. 4.3	CROATIA 3.4	YUGO 2.7	OTHER EUROPE 8.3	CANADA 3.0	U.S.A. 2.4	S. AMER. 4.7

Labels on upper map: YUGO., CROATIA, BOS., PAK, IRAN, DEM. REP. CONGO, RWANDA, BURUNDI, MALAWI

MAJOR CAUSES / FACTORS

- ○ Ethnic
- ☐ Religious
- + Political
- ⊕ Multiple or undifferentiated

- Civil Conflicts
- International Conflicts
- Civil and International Conflicts

MAJOR CONFLICTS 1990-1994

Labels on lower map: NORTHERN IRELAND, SLOVENIA, CROATIA, BOS. HERZ., YUGOSLAVIA, MOLDOVA, GEORGIA, AZERBAIJAN, ARMENIA, TAJIKISTAN, TURKEY, LEBANON, ISRAEL, IRAQ, AFG., KUWAIT, PAKISTAN, ALGERIA, INDIA, ERITREA, YEMEN, MYANMAR, SUDAN, ETHIOPIA, SOMALIA, SRI LANKA, CAMBODIA, LIBERIA, GUATEMALA, EL SALVADOR, NICARAGUA, PERU, RWANDA, BURUNDI, ANGOLA, INDONESIA, EAST TIMOR, BOUGAINVILLE, PAPUA NEW GUINEA, MOZAMBIQUE, SOUTH AFRICA

REGIONAL MAPS

Basic continental and regional coverage of the world's land areas is provided by the following section of physical-political reference maps. The section falls into a continental arrangement: North America, South America, Europe, Asia, Australia, and Africa. (Introducing each regional reference-map section are basic thematic maps and the environment maps.)

To aid the student in acquiring concepts of the relative sizes of continents and of some of the countries and regions, uniform scales for comparable areas were used so far as possible. Continental maps are at a uniform scale of 1:40,000,000. In addition, most of the world is covered by a series of regional maps at scales of 1:16,000,000 and 1:12,000,000.

Maps at 1:10,000,000 provide even greater detail for parts of Europe, Africa, and Southeast Asia. The United States, parts of Canada, and much of Europe are mapped at 1:4,000,000. Seventy-six urbanized areas are shown at 1:1,000,000. The new, separate metropolitan-area section contains larger-scale maps of selected urban areas.

Many of the symbols used are self-explanatory. A complete legend below provides a key to the symbols on the reference maps in this atlas.

General elevation above sea level is shown by layer tints for altitudinal zones, each of which has a different hue and is defined by a generalized contour line. A legend is given on each map, reflecting this color gradation.

The surface configuration is represented by hill-shading, which gives the three-dimensional impression of landforms. This terrain representation is superimposed on the layer tints to convey a realistic and readily visualized impression of the surface. The combination of altitudinal tints and hill-shading best shows elevation, relief, steepness of slope, and ruggedness of terrain.

If the world used one alphabet and one language, no particular difficulty would arise in understanding place-names. However, some of the people of the world, the Chinese and the Japanese, for example, use nonalphabetic languages. Their symbols are transliterated into the Roman alphabet. In this atlas a "local-name" policy generally was used for naming cities and towns and all local topographic and water features. However, for a few major cities the Anglicized name was preferred and the local name given in parentheses, for instance, Moscow *(Moskva)*, Vienna *(Wien)*, Cologne *(Köln)*. In countries where more than one official language is used, a name is in the dominant local language. The generic parts of local names for topographic and water features are self-explanatory in many cases because of the associated map symbols or type styles. A complete list of foreign generic names is given in the Glossary.

Place-names on the reference maps are listed in the Pronouncing Index, which is a distinctive feature of *Goode's World Atlas*.

Physical-Political Reference Map Legend

Cultural Features

Political Boundaries

International (over water) (Demarcated, Undemarcated, and Administrative)

Disputed de facto

Claim Boundary

Indefinite or Undefined

Secondary, State, Provincial, etc. (over water)

Parks, Indian Reservations

City Limits — Urbanized Areas

Neighborhoods, Sections of City

Populated Places

⦿ 1,000,000 and over

◎ 250,000 to 1,000,000

☉ 100,000 to 250,000

• 25,000 to 100,000

○ 0 to 25,000

TŌKYŌ National Capitals

Boise Secondary Capitals

Note: On maps at 1:20,000,000 and smaller the town symbols do not follow the specific population classification shown above. On all maps, type size indicates the relative importance of the city.

Transportation

Railroads

Railroads On 1:1,000,000 scale maps

Railroad Ferries

Roads

Major Other On 1:1,000,000 scale maps

Major Other On 1:4,000,000 scale maps

On other scale maps

Caravan Routes

✈ Airports

Other Cultural Features

Dams

Pipelines

▲ Points of Interest

Ruins

Land Features

△ Peaks, Spot Heights

= Passes

Sand

Contours

Water Features

Lakes and Reservoirs

Fresh Water

Fresh Water: Intermittent

Salt Water

Salt Water: Intermittent

Other Water Features

Salt Basins, Flats

Swamps

Ice Caps and Glaciers

Rivers

Intermittent Rivers

Aqueducts and Canals

Ship Channels

Falls

Rapids

Springs

△ Water Depths

Fishing Banks

Sand Bars

Reefs

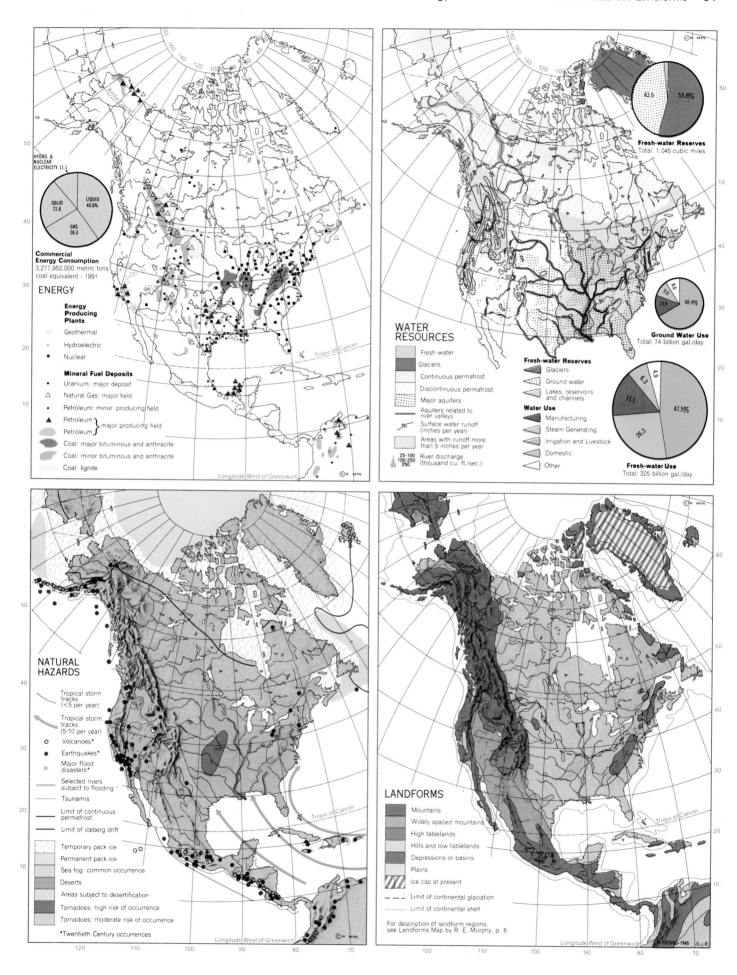

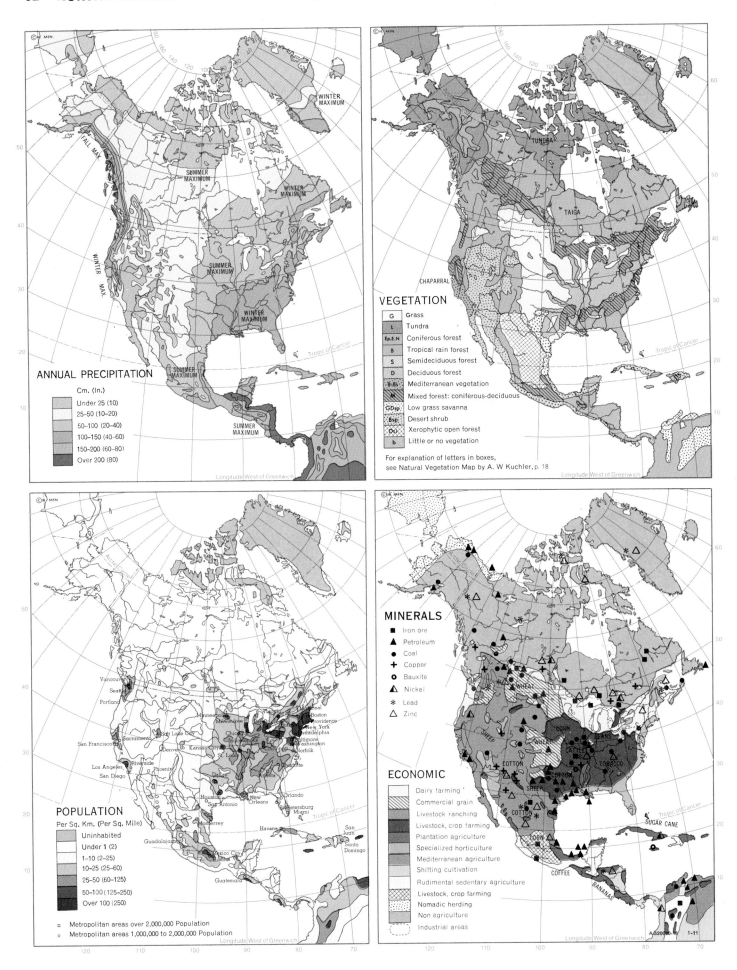

ANNUAL PRECIPITATION

Cm. (In.)

	Under 25 (10)
	25–50 (10–20)
	50–100 (20–40)
	100–150 (40–60)
	150–200 (60–80)
	Over 200 (80)

VEGETATION

G	Grass
L	Tundra
Ep.E.N	Coniferous forest
B	Tropical rain forest
S	Semideciduous forest
D	Deciduous forest
B-Bs	Mediterranean vegetation
M	Mixed forest: coniferous-deciduous
GDp	Low grass savanna
Bsp	Desert shrub
Dx	Xerophytic open forest
b	Little or no vegetation

For explanation of letters in boxes,
see Natural Vegetation Map by A. W Kuchler, p. 18

POPULATION

Per Sq. Km. (Per Sq. Mile)

	Uninhabited
	Under 1 (2)
	1–10 (2–25)
	10–25 (25–60)
	25–50 (60–125)
	50–100 (125–250)
	Over 100 (250)

□ Metropolitan areas over 2,000,000 Population

○ Metropolitan areas 1,000,000 to 2,000,000 Population

MINERALS

■	Iron ore
▲	Petroleum
●	Coal
+	Copper
○	Bauxite
△	Nickel
✳	Lead
△	Zinc

ECONOMIC

	Dairy farming
	Commercial grain
	Livestock ranching
	Livestock, crop farming
	Plantation agriculture
	Specialized horticulture
	Mediterranean agriculture
	Shifting cultivation
	Rudimental sedentary agriculture
	Livestock, crop farming
	Nomadic herding
	Non agriculture
	Industrial areas

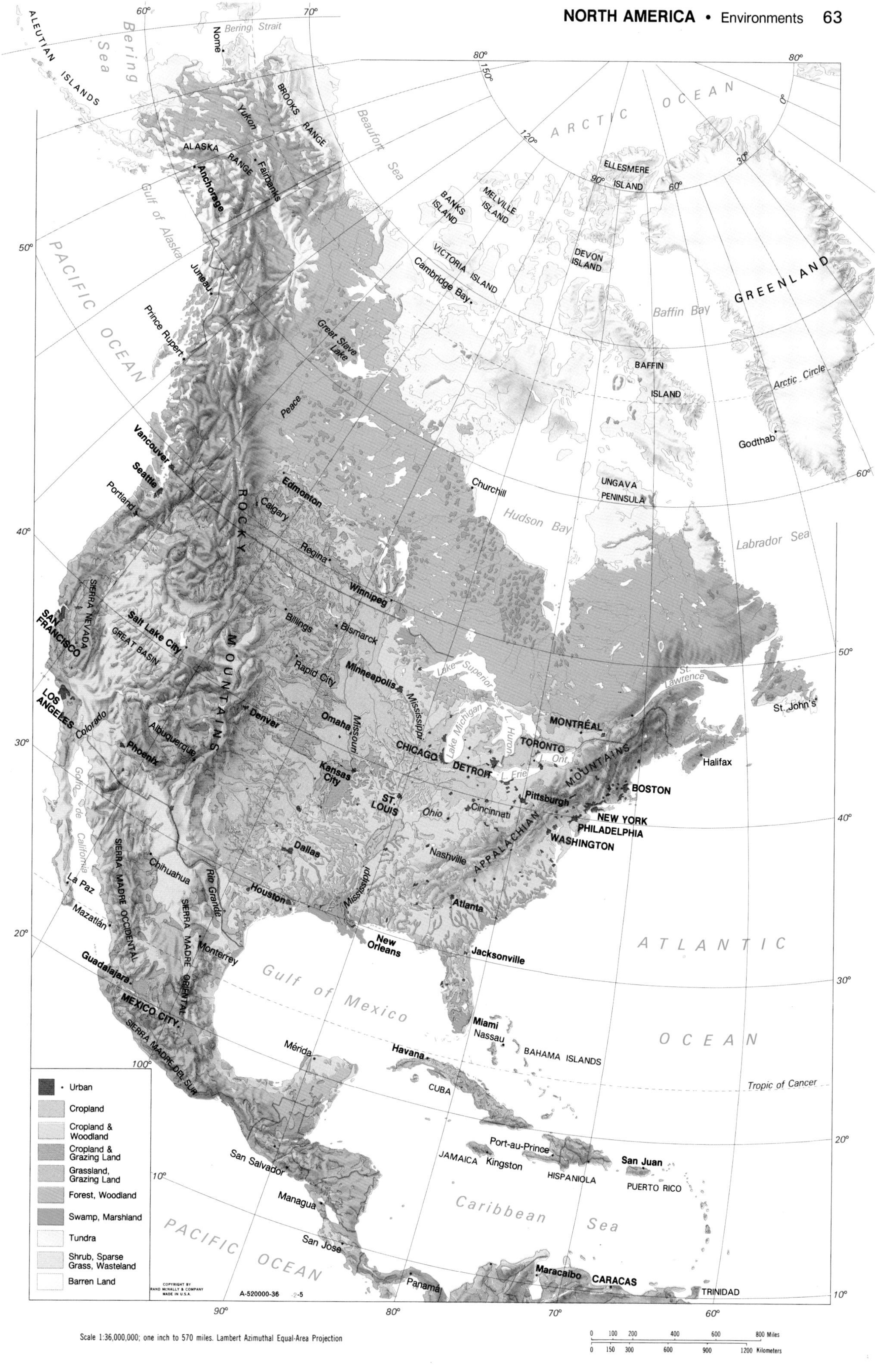

ARCTIC OCEAN

ALEUTIAN ISLANDS

Bering Sea
Bering Strait
Nome

BROOKS RANGE
ALASKA RANGE
Fairbanks
Anchorage
Yukon

Beaufort Sea

Gulf of Alaska

PACIFIC OCEAN

Juneau
Prince Rupert

BANKS ISLAND
MELVILLE ISLAND
VICTORIA ISLAND
Cambridge Bay

ELLESMERE ISLAND
DEVON ISLAND

GREENLAND

Baffin Bay

BAFFIN ISLAND

Arctic Circle

Godthab

Great Slave Lake

Peace

Vancouver
Seattle
Portland

Edmonton
Calgary

Regina

Winnipeg

Churchill

Hudson Bay

UNGAVA PENINSULA

Labrador Sea

ROCKY MOUNTAINS

SIERRA NEVADA

SAN FRANCISCO
Salt Lake City
GREAT BASIN

Billings
Bismarck

Rapid City

Minneapolis

Lake Superior
St. Lawrence

Lake Michigan
Lake Huron

St. John's

LOS ANGELES

Colorado

Denver

Omaha

Missouri

Mississippi

MONTRÉAL
TORONTO

L. Ont.

Halifax

Albuquerque
Phoenix

Kansas City

ST. LOUIS

CHICAGO
DETROIT
L. Erie

Pittsburgh
Cincinnati

APPALACHIAN MOUNTAINS

BOSTON
NEW YORK
PHILADELPHIA
WASHINGTON

Ohio

Nashville

Dallas

Chihuahua

SIERRA MADRE OCCIDENTAL

Golfo de California

Rio Grande

Houston

Mississippi

Atlanta

La Paz
Mazatlán

Monterrey

SIERRA MADRE ORIENTAL

New Orleans

Jacksonville

Gulf of Mexico

ATLANTIC OCEAN

Guadalajara

MEXICO CITY

SIERRA MADRE DEL SUR

Mérida

Havana

CUBA

Miami
Nassau
BAHAMA ISLANDS

Tropic of Cancer

San Salvador

Managua

San Jose

Panama

Port-au-Prince
JAMAICA Kingston
HISPANIOLA

San Juan
PUERTO RICO

Caribbean Sea

Maracaibo CARACAS
TRINIDAD

PACIFIC OCEAN

Legend

- Urban
- Cropland
- Cropland & Woodland
- Cropland & Grazing Land
- Grassland, Grazing Land
- Forest, Woodland
- Swamp, Marshland
- Tundra
- Shrub, Sparse Grass, Wasteland
- Barren Land

COPYRIGHT BY
RAND McNALLY & COMPANY
MADE IN U.S.A.

A-520000-36   2-5

Scale 1:36,000,000; one inch to 570 miles. Lambert Azimuthal Equal-Area Projection

0   100   200   400   600   800 Miles
0   150   300   600   900   1200 Kilometers

PACIFIC

OCEAN

Vancouver

Seattle

Spokane

Portland

Columbia

CASCADE RANGE

Medford

Boise

Great Salt Lake

Reno

GREAT BASIN

SIERRA NEVADA

SAN FRANCISCO

Fresno

Las Vegas

LOS ANGELES

Colorado

San Diego

Phoenix

PACIFIC

OCEAN

Hermosillo

Gulf of California

SIERRA MADRE OCCIDENTAL

Chihuahua

Torreón

Calgary

ROCKY MOUNTAINS

Billings

Rapid City

Casper

Salt Lake City

ROCKY MOUNTAINS

Denver

Albuquerque

El Paso

Rio Grande

SIERRA MADRE ORIENTAL

Regina

Lake Winnipeg

Bismarck

Missouri

Wichita

Amarillo

Red

Odessa

San Antonio

Rio Grande

Monterrey

50°

45°

40°

35°

30°

25°

125°

120°

115°

110°

105°

100°

Scale 1:12,000,000; one inch to 190 miles.
Albers Conical Equal Area Projection

0	50	100	200	300	400 Miles
0	75	150	300	450	600 Kilometers

Legend:
- Urban
- Cropland
- Cropland & Woodland
- Cropland & Grazing Land
- Grassland, Grazing Land
- Forest, Woodland
- Swamp, Marshland
- Shrub, Sparse Grass, Wasteland
- Barren Land

PHYSIOGRAPHIC DIVISIONS

1 Pacific Mountain System
2 Intermontane Plateaus
3 Rocky Mountain System
4 Interior Plains
5 Ozark-Ouachita Highlands
6 Gulf-Atlantic Plain
7 Appalachian Highlands
8 Laurentian Upland (Canadian Shield)
9 Hudson Bay Lowland

0 25 50 75 100   200   300   400   500 Miles
0   50   100   200   400   600   800 Kilometers

Scale 1: 12 000 000; One inch to 190 miles.   POLYCONIC PROJECTION

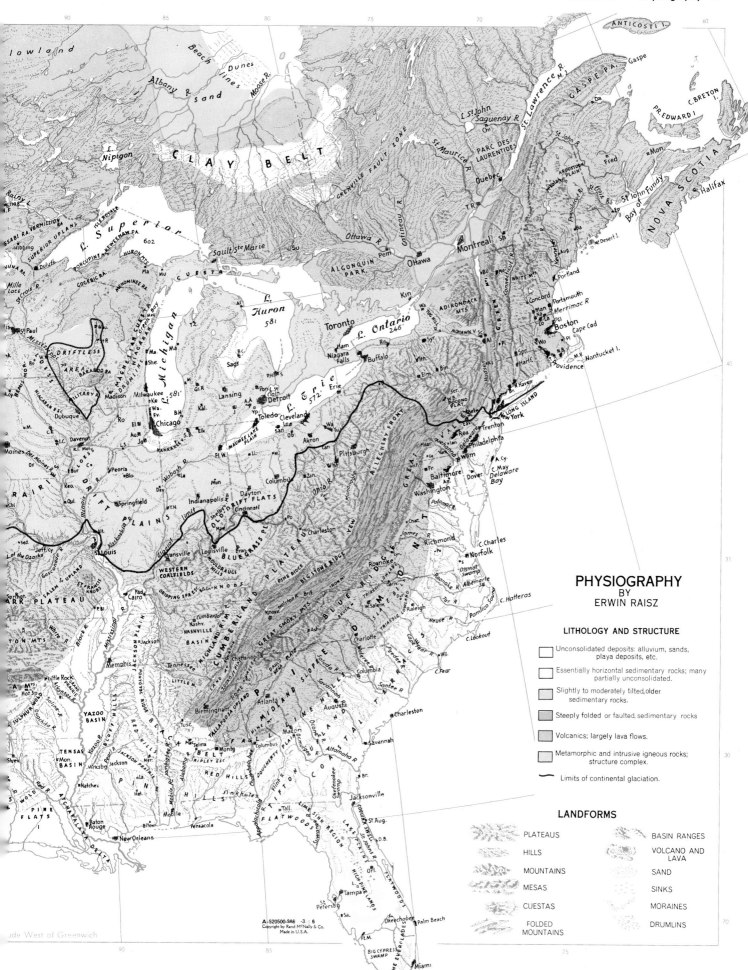

PHYSIOGRAPHY
BY
ERWIN RAISZ

LITHOLOGY AND STRUCTURE

Unconsolidated deposits: alluvium, sands,
playa deposits, etc.

Essentially horizontal sedimentary rocks; many
partially unconsolidated.

Slightly to moderately tilted, older
sedimentary rocks.

Steeply folded or faulted, sedimentary rocks

Volcanics; largely lava flows.

Metamorphic and intrusive igneous rocks;
structure complex.

Limits of continental glaciation.

LANDFORMS

PLATEAUS

HILLS

MOUNTAINS

MESAS

CUESTAS

FOLDED
MOUNTAINS

BASIN RANGES

VOLCANO AND
LAVA

SAND

SINKS

MORAINES

DRUMLINS

A-520500-9A6 -3 : 6
Copyright by Rand McNally & Co.
Made in U.S.A.

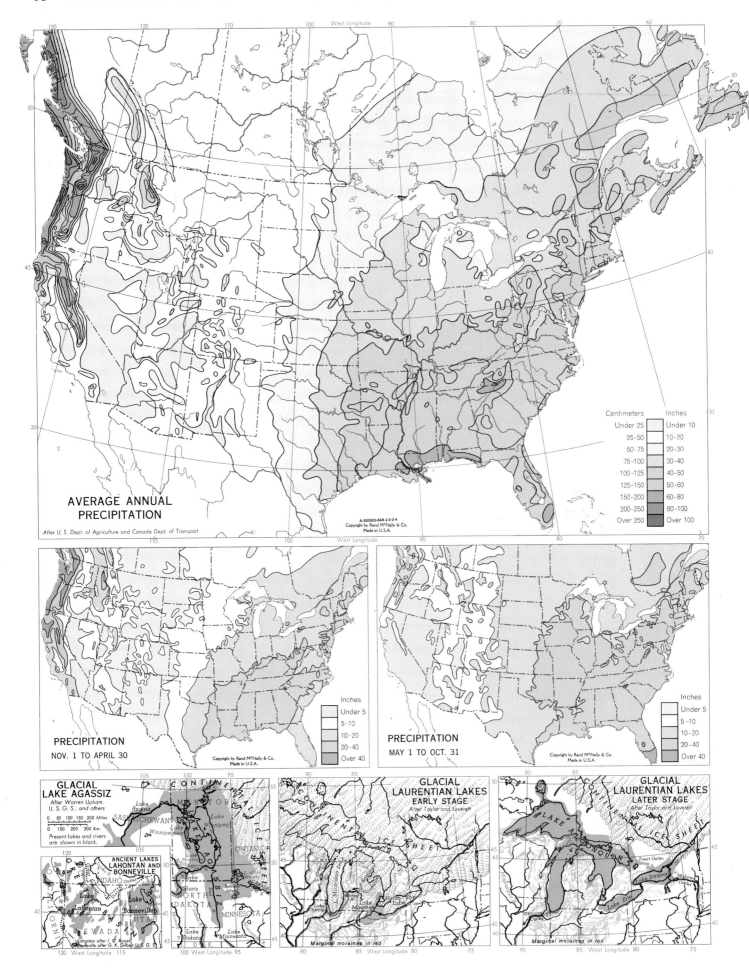

AVERAGE ANNUAL PRECIPITATION

After U. S. Dept. of Agriculture and Canada Dept. of Transport

A-520500-6A8-2-2-2-4
Copyright by Rand McNally & Co.
Made in U.S.A.

Centimeters	Inches
Under 25	Under 10
25–50	10–20
50–75	20–30
75–100	30–40
100–125	40–50
125–150	50–60
150–200	60–80
200–250	80–100
Over 250	Over 100

PRECIPITATION

NOV. 1 TO APRIL 30

Copyright by Rand McNally & Co.
Made in U.S.A.

Inches
Under 5
5–10
10–20
20–40
Over 40

PRECIPITATION

MAY 1 TO OCT. 31

Copyright by Rand McNally & Co.
Made in U.S.A.

Inches
Under 5
5–10
10–20
20–40
Over 40

GLACIAL LAKE AGASSIZ

After Warren Upham.
U. S. G. S. and others

0 50 100 150 200 Miles
0 100 200 300 Km.

Present lakes and rivers
are shown in black.

ANCIENT LAKES LAHONTAN AND BONNEVILLE

Lahontan after I. C. Russell
Bonneville after G. K. Gilbert, U. S. G. S.

GLACIAL LAURENTIAN LAKES EARLY STAGE

After Taylor and Leverett

Marginal moraines in red

GLACIAL LAURENTIAN LAKES LATER STAGE

After Taylor and Leverett

Marginal moraines in red

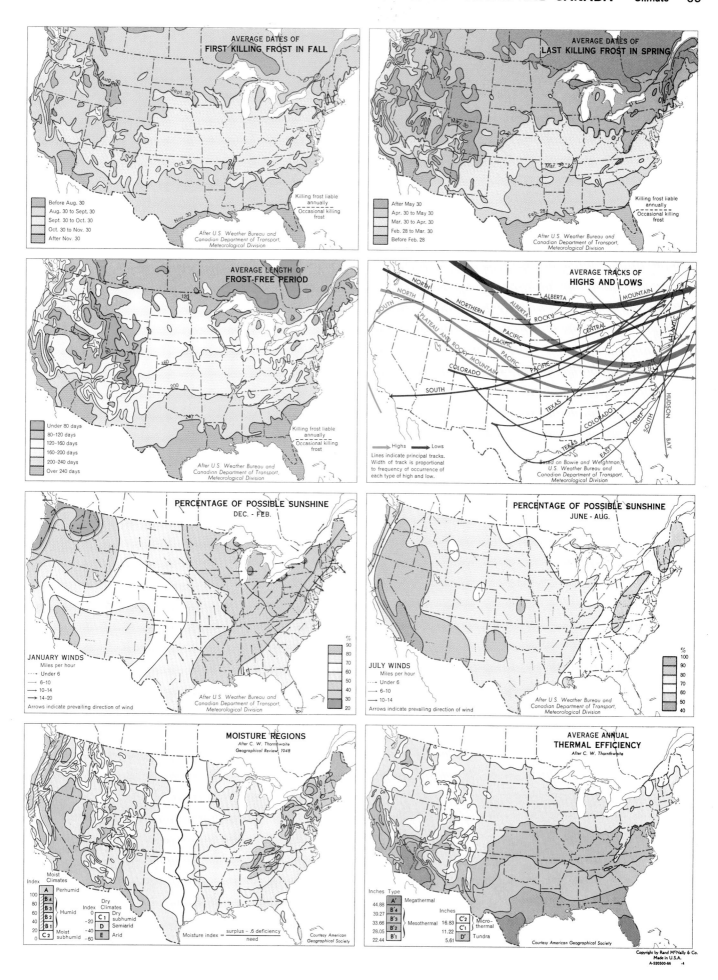

AVERAGE DATES OF
FIRST KILLING FROST IN FALL

Before Aug. 30
Aug. 30 to Sept. 30
Sept. 30 to Oct. 30
Oct. 30 to Nov. 30
After Nov. 30

Killing frost liable
annually
Occasional killing
frost

After U.S. Weather Bureau and
Canadian Department of Transport,
Meteorological Division

AVERAGE DATES OF
LAST KILLING FROST IN SPRING

After May 30
Apr. 30 to May 30
Mar. 30 to Apr. 30
Feb. 28 to Mar. 30
Before Feb. 28

Killing frost liable
annually
Occasional killing
frost

After U.S. Weather Bureau and
Canadian Department of Transport,
Meteorological Division

AVERAGE LENGTH OF
FROST-FREE PERIOD

Under 80 days
80–120 days
120–160 days
160–200 days
200–240 days
Over 240 days

Killing frost liable
annually
Occasional killing
frost

After U.S. Weather Bureau and
Canadian Department of Transport,
Meteorological Division

AVERAGE TRACKS OF
HIGHS AND LOWS

Highs   Lows
Lines indicate principal tracks.
Width of track is proportional
to frequency of occurrence of
each type of high and low.

Based on Bowie and Weightman,
U.S. Weather Bureau and
Canadian Department of Transport,
Meteorological Division

PERCENTAGE OF POSSIBLE SUNSHINE
DEC. - FEB.

JANUARY WINDS
Miles per hour
Under 6
6–10
10–14
14–20
Arrows indicate prevailing direction of wind

%
90
80
70
60
50
40
30
20

After U.S. Weather Bureau and
Canadian Department of Transport,
Meteorological Division

PERCENTAGE OF POSSIBLE SUNSHINE
JUNE - AUG.

JULY WINDS
Miles per hour
Under 6
6–10
10–14
Arrows indicate prevailing direction of wind

%
100
90
80
70
60
50
40

After U.S. Weather Bureau and
Canadian Department of Transport,
Meteorological Division

MOISTURE REGIONS
After C. W. Thornthwaite
Geographical Review, 1948

Index
Moist
Climates
100   A   Perhumid
80   B4
60   B3   Humid
40   B2
20   B1
0   C2   Moist
                 subhumid

Dry Climates
Index
       C1 Dry
           subhumid
-20   D   Semiarid
-40
-60   E   Arid

Moisture index = surplus − .6 deficiency / need

Courtesy American
Geographical Society

AVERAGE ANNUAL
THERMAL EFFICIENCY
After C. W. Thornthwaite

Inches Type
44.88   A'   Megathermal
39.27   B'4
33.66   B'3   Mesothermal   Inches
28.05   B'2   16.83 C'2 Micro-
22.44   B'1   11.22 C'1 thermal
                               5.61 D'   Tundra

Courtesy American Geographical Society

70

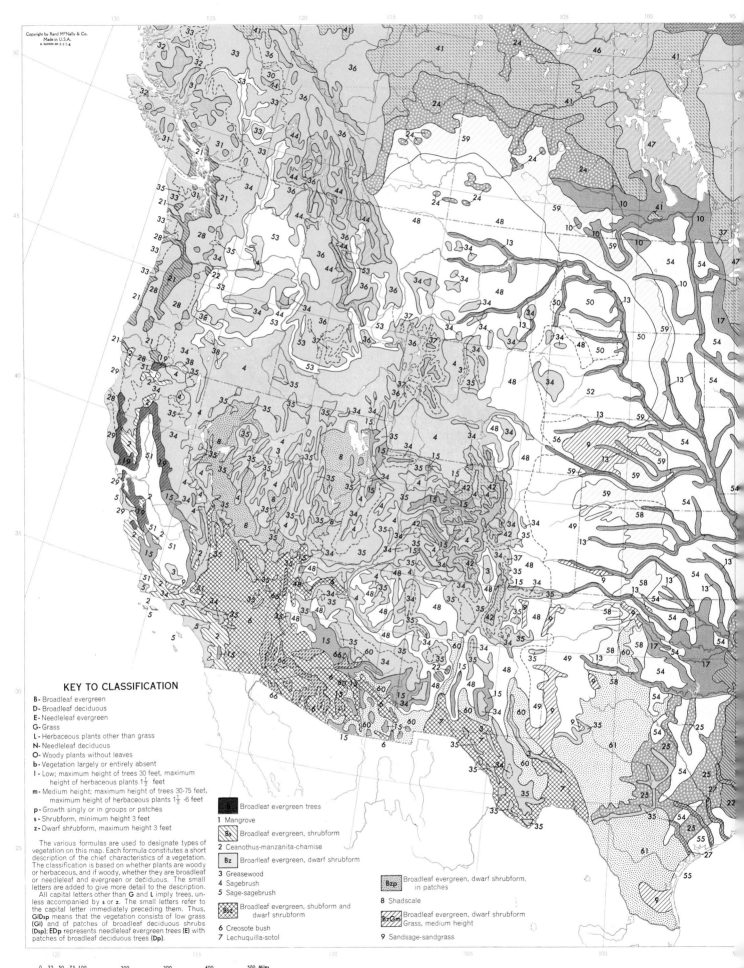

KEY TO CLASSIFICATION

B - Broadleaf evergreen
D - Broadleaf deciduous
E - Needleleaf evergreen
G - Grass
L - Herbaceous plants other than grass
N - Needleleaf deciduous
O - Woody plants without leaves
b - Vegetation largely or entirely absent
l - Low; maximum height of trees 30 feet, maximum
    height of herbaceous plants 1½ feet
m - Medium height; maximum height of trees 30-75 feet,
    maximum height of herbaceous plants 1½ -6 feet
p - Growth singly or in groups or patches
s - Shrubform, minimum height 3 feet
z - Dwarf shrubform, maximum height 3 feet

    The various formulas are used to designate types of
vegetation on this map. Each formula constitutes a short
description of the chief characteristics of a vegetation.
The classification is based on whether plants are woody
or herbaceous, and if woody, whether they are broadleaf
or needleleaf and evergreen or deciduous. The small
letters are added to give more detail to the description.
    All capital letters other than G and L imply trees, un-
less accompanied by s or z. The small letters refer to
the capital letter immediately preceding them. Thus,
GlDsp means that the vegetation consists of low grass
(Gl) and of patches of broadleaf deciduous shrubs
(Dsp); EDp represents needleleaf evergreen trees (E) with
patches of broadleaf deciduous trees (Dp).

■ Broadleaf evergreen trees
1 Mangrove
▨ **Bs** Broadleaf evergreen, shrubform
2 Ceanothus-manzanita-chamise
▧ **Bz** Broadleaf evergreen, dwarf shrubform
3 Greasewood
4 Sagebrush
5 Sage-sagebrush
▨ **Bsz** Broadleaf evergreen, shubform and
    dwarf shrubform
6 Creosote bush
7 Lechuquilla-sotol

▨ **Bzp** Broadleaf evergreen, dwarf shrubform,
    in patches
8 Shadscale
▨ **BzGm** Broadleaf evergreen, dwarf shrubform
    Grass, medium height
9 Sandsage-sandgrass

0 25 50 75 100   200   300   400   500 Miles
0 50 100   200   400   600   800 Kilometers

Scale 1: 14 000 000;   One inch to 2

NATURAL VEGETATION

BY A. W. KÜCHLER

Based on "A Physiognomic Classification of Vegetation"
Annals of the Assoc. of American Geographers, Vol 39, September, 1949

D Broadleaf deciduous trees

10 Aspen-oak
11 Beech-maple
12 Beech-tulip tree-maple-basswood
13 Cottonwood-willow
14 Maple-basswood
15 Oak
16 Oak-ash-maple
17 Oak-hickory
18 Oak-tulip tree

DB Broadleaf deciduous trees / Broadleaf evergreen trees

19 Oak-madrone

DE Broadleaf deciduous trees / Needleleaf evergreen trees

20 Maple-yellow birch-hemlock-pine
21 Oak-Douglas fir
22 Oak-pine
23 Maple-beech-hemlock

D / Gmp Broadleaf deciduous trees / Grass, medium height, in patches

24 Aspen-needle grass-wheat grass
25 Oak-hickory-bluestem

DN Broadleaf deciduous trees / Needleleaf deciduous trees

26 Bay trees-bald cypress
27 Tupelo-gum-bald cypress

E Needleleaf evergreen trees

28 Douglas fir
29 Douglas fir-redwood
30 Hemlock-arbor vitae
31 Hemlock-arbor vitae-Douglas fir
32 Hemlock-arbor vitae-fir
33 Hemlock-spruce
34 Pine
35 Pine-juniper
36 Pine-spruce
37 Spruce-fir

Esp Needleleaf evergreen, shrubform, in patches

38 Juniper

EDp Needleleaf evergreen trees / Broadleaf deciduous trees, in patches

39 Douglas fir-pine-aspen
40 Pine-spruce-birch
41 Spruce-aspen
42 Spruce-fir-aspen
43 Spruce-poplar-birch

EN Needleleaf evergreen trees / Needleleaf deciduous trees

44 Hemlock-arbor vitae-Douglas fir-larch
45 Pine-bald cypress
46 Pine-spruce-larch
47 Spruce-larch

Gl Grass, low

48 Grama grass
49 Grama grass-buffalo grass
50 Grama grass-needle grass
51 Needle grass-blue grass
52 Wheat grass
53 Wheat grass-blue grass

Gm Grass, medium height

54 Bluestem
55 Broom grass-water grass
56 Marsh grass
57 Saw grass

Gml Grass, medium and low height

58 Bluestem-bunch grass
59 Needle grass-wheat grass

Gl / Dsp Grass, low / Broadleaf deciduous, shrubform, in patches

60 Bunch grass-oak

Gm / Dsp Grass, medium height / Broadleaf deciduous, shrubform, in patches

61 Mesquite grass-mesquite

L Herbaceous plants other than grass

62 Lichens, etc.

LEp Herbaceous plants other than grass / Needleleaf evergreen trees, in patches

63 Lichens-spruce

LEp / Np Herbaceous plants other than grass / Needleleaf evergreen trees, in patches / Needleleaf deciduous trees, in patches

64 Lichens-spruce-larch

N Needleleaf deciduous trees

65 Bald cypress

Op Woody plants without leaves, in patches

66 Palo verde-cacti-ocotillo

b Vegetation largely or entirely absent

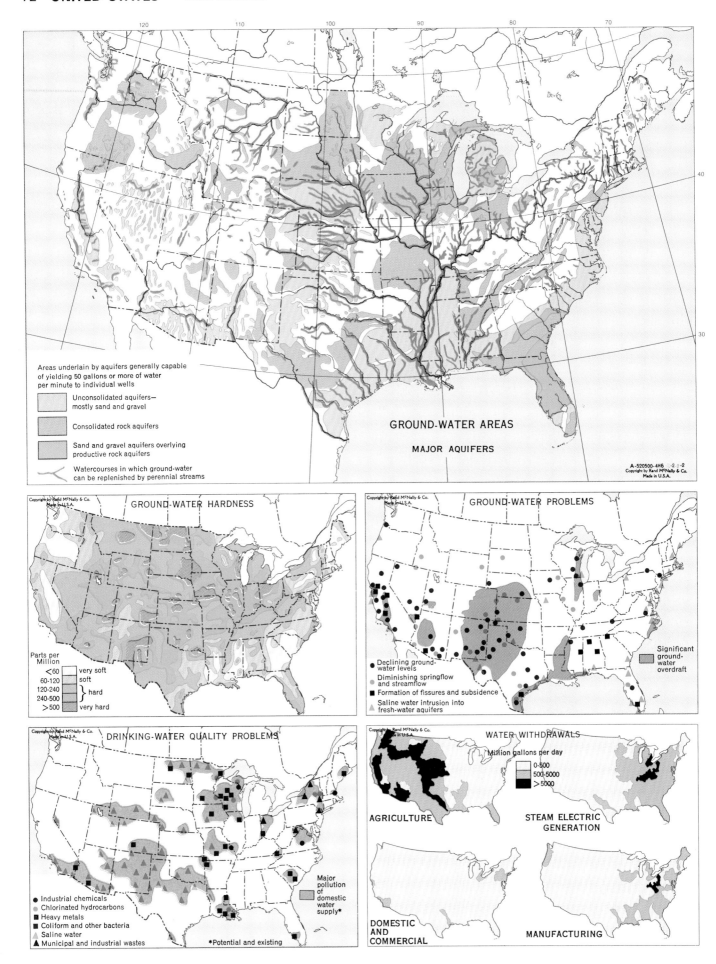

GROUND-WATER AREAS

MAJOR AQUIFERS

Areas underlain by aquifers generally capable
of yielding 50 gallons or more of water
per minute to individual wells

Unconsolidated aquifers—
mostly sand and gravel

Consolidated rock aquifers

Sand and gravel aquifers overlying
productive rock aquifers

Watercourses in which ground-water
can be replenished by perennial streams

A-520500-4H6 -2-2-2
Copyright by Rand McNally & Co.
Made in U.S.A.

GROUND-WATER HARDNESS

Parts per
Million
<60   very soft
60-120   soft
120-240 } hard
240-500
>500   very hard

GROUND-WATER PROBLEMS

● Declining ground-
water levels
● Diminishing springflow
and streamflow
■ Formation of fissures and subsidence
▲ Saline water intrusion into
fresh-water aquifers

Significant
ground-
water
overdraft

DRINKING-WATER QUALITY PROBLEMS

● Industrial chemicals
● Chlorinated hydrocarbons
■ Heavy metals
■ Coliform and other bacteria
▲ Saline water
▲ Municipal and industrial wastes

Major
pollution
of
domestic
water
supply*

*Potential and existing

WATER WITHDRAWALS

Million gallons per day
0-500
500-5000
>5000

AGRICULTURE

STEAM ELECTRIC
GENERATION

DOMESTIC
AND
COMMERCIAL

MANUFACTURING

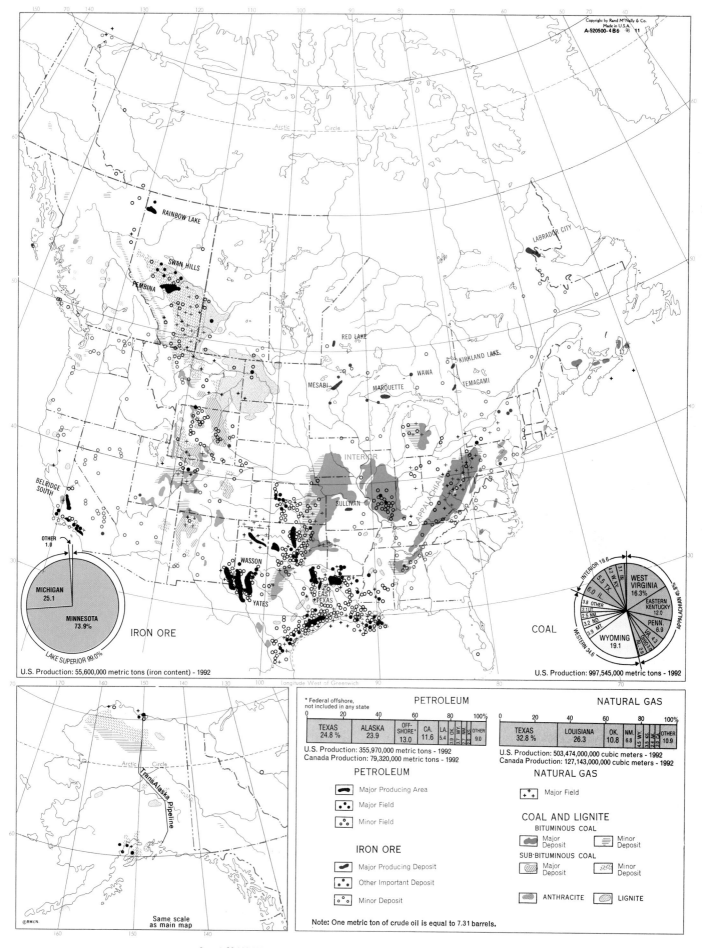

Copyright by Rand McNally & Co.
Made in U.S.A.
A-520500-4 B 6 98 11

RAINBOW LAKE

LABRADOR CITY

SWAN HILLS

PEMBINA

RED LAKE

KIRKLAND LAKE

WAWA

MESABI

MARQUETTE

TEMAGAMI

INTERIOR

APPALACHIAN

BELRIDGE
SOUTH

SULLIVAN

OTHER
1.0

WASSON

EAST
TEXAS

YATES

IRON ORE

MICHIGAN
25.1

MINNESOTA
73.9%

LAKE SUPERIOR 99.0%

U.S. Production: 55,600,000 metric tons (iron content) - 1992

COAL

INTERIOR 19.6

3.1 IN
4.2 W. KY
5.5 TX
6.0 IL

3.8 Other
2.0 UT
2.5 NM
3.2 ND
3.9 MT

WESTERN 34.6

WYOMING
19.1

WEST
VIRGINIA
16.3%

APPALACHIAN 45.8

EASTERN
KENTUCKY
12.0

PENN.
6.9

VA. 4.3
OHIO 3.5
ALA. 2.9

U.S. Production: 997,545,000 metric tons - 1992

TransAlaska Pipeline

Arctic Circle

Same scale
as main map

©RMCN.

* Federal offshore,
not included in any state

PETROLEUM

0		20		40		60		80		100%
TEXAS 24.8 %		ALASKA 23.9		OFF-SHORE* 13.0		CA. 11.6	LA. 5.4			OTHER 9.0

U.S. Production: 355,970,000 metric tons - 1992
Canada Production: 79,320,000 metric tons - 1992

NATURAL GAS

0		20		40		60		80		100%
TEXAS 32.8 %		LOUISIANA 26.3		OK. 10.8	NM. 6.8				OTHER 10.9

U.S. Production: 503,474,000,000 cubic meters - 1992
Canada Production: 127,143,000,000 cubic meters - 1992

PETROLEUM

⬛ Major Producing Area

⬛ Major Field

◌ Minor Field

IRON ORE

⬛ Major Producing Deposit

⬛ Other Important Deposit

◌ Minor Deposit

NATURAL GAS

+ Major Field

COAL AND LIGNITE

BITUMINOUS COAL

Major Deposit   Minor Deposit

SUB-BITUMINOUS COAL

Major Deposit   Minor Deposit

ANTHRACITE   LIGNITE

Note: One metric ton of crude oil is equal to 7.31 barrels.

Scale 1: 32 000 000; One inch to 500 miles.   LAMBERT CONFORMAL CONIC PROJECTION

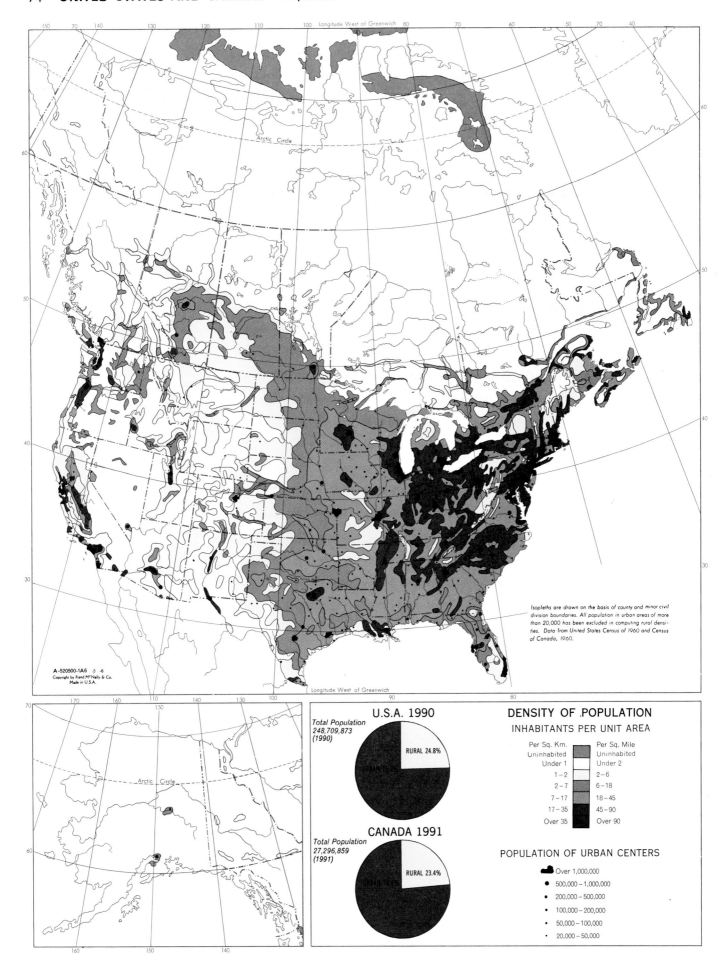

Isopleths are drawn on the basis of county and minor civil division boundaries. All population in urban areas of more than 20,000 has been excluded in computing rural densities. Data from United States Census of 1960 and Census of Canada, 1960.

A-520500-1A6 -5 -6
Copyright by Rand McNally & Co.
Made in U.S.A.

U.S.A. 1990

Total Population
248,709,873
(1990)

RURAL 24.8%

URBAN 75.2%

CANADA 1991

Total Population
27,296,859
(1991)

RURAL 23.4%

URBAN 76.6%

DENSITY OF POPULATION

INHABITANTS PER UNIT AREA

Per Sq. Km.		Per Sq. Mile
Uninhabited		Uninhabited
Under 1		Under 2
1–2		2–6
2–7		6–18
7–17		18–45
17–35		45–90
Over 35		Over 90

POPULATION OF URBAN CENTERS

Over 1,000,000
500,000 – 1,000,000
200,000 – 500,000
100,000 – 200,000
50,000 – 100,000
20,000 – 50,000

Scale 1:32 000 000; One inch to 500 miles.   LAMBERT CONFORMAL CONIC PROJECTION

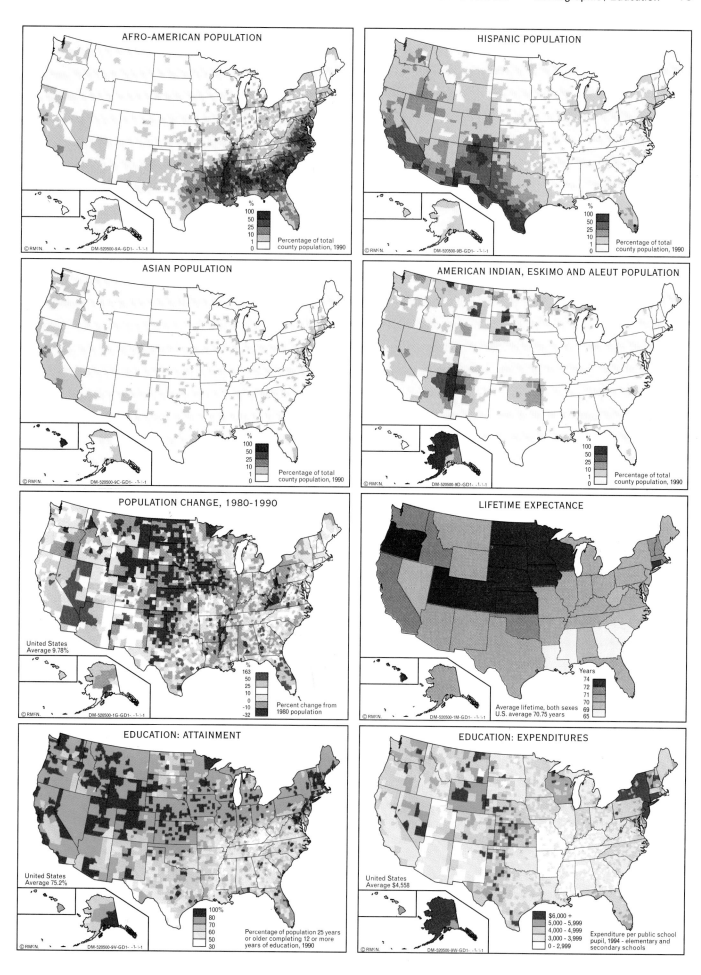

AFRO-AMERICAN POPULATION

%
100
50
25
10
1
0
Percentage of total
county population, 1990

© RMcN.   DM-520500-9A-GD1- -1-1-1

HISPANIC POPULATION

%
100
50
25
10
1
0
Percentage of total
county population, 1990

© RMcN.   DM-520500-9B-GD1- -1-1-1

ASIAN POPULATION

%
100
50
25
10
1
0
Percentage of total
county population, 1990

© RMcN.   DM-520500-9C-GD1- -1-1-1

AMERICAN INDIAN, ESKIMO AND ALEUT POPULATION

%
100
50
25
10
1
0
Percentage of total
county population, 1990

© RMcN.   DM-520500-9D-GD1- -1-1-1

POPULATION CHANGE, 1980-1990

United States
Average 9.78%

%
163
50
25
10
0
-10
-32
Percent change from
1980 population

© RMcN.   DM-520500-1G-GD1- -1-1-1

LIFETIME EXPECTANCE

Years
74
72
71
70
69
65

Average lifetime, both sexes
U.S. average 70.75 years

© RMcN.   DM-520500-1M-GD1- -1-1-1

EDUCATION: ATTAINMENT

United States
Average 75.2%

100%
80
70
60
50
30
Percentage of population 25 years
or older completing 12 or more
years of education, 1990

© RMcN.   DM-520500-9V-GD1- -1-1-1

EDUCATION: EXPENDITURES

United States
Average $4,558

$6,000 +
5,000 - 5,999
4,000 - 4,999
3,000 - 3,999
0 - 2,999
Expenditure per public school
pupil, 1994 - elementary and
secondary schools

© RMcN.   DM-520500-9W-GD1- -1-1-1

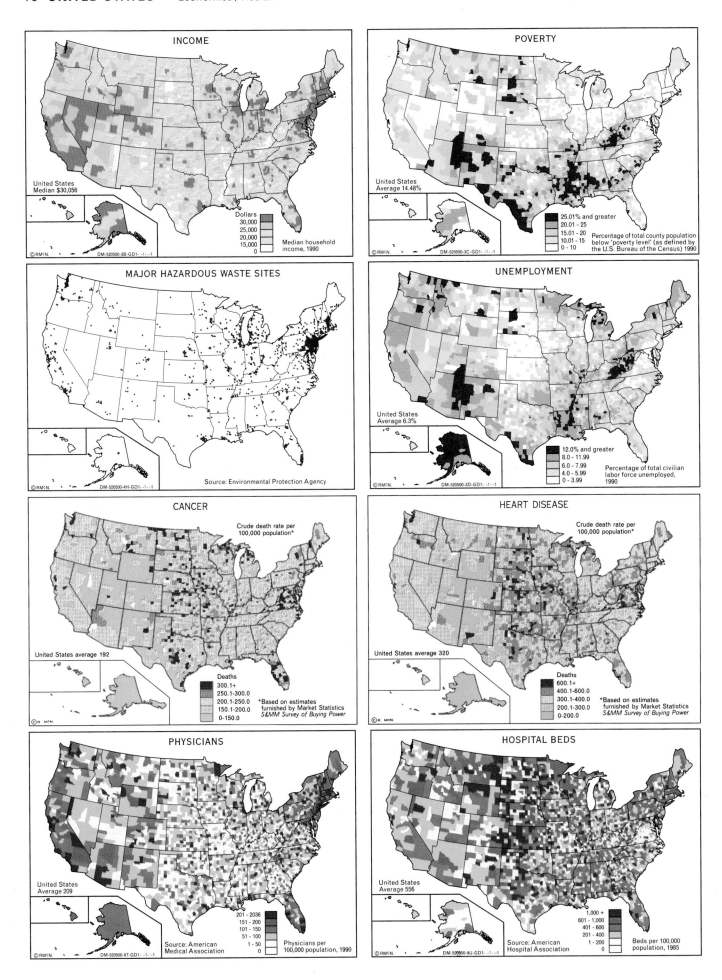

INCOME

United States
Median $30,056

Dollars
30,000
25,000
20,000
15,000
0

Median household
income, 1990

© RM©N.   DM-520500-3B-GD1- -1- -:-1

POVERTY

United States
Average 14.48%

25.01% and greater
20.01 - 25
15.01 - 20
10.01 - 15
0 - 10

Percentage of total county population
below 'poverty level' (as defined by
the U.S. Bureau of the Census) 1990

© RM©N.   DM-520500-3C-GD1- -1- -:-1

MAJOR HAZARDOUS WASTE SITES

Source: Environmental Protection Agency

© RM©N.   DM-520500-4H-GD1- -1- -:-1

UNEMPLOYMENT

United States
Average 6.3%

12.0% and greater
8.0 - 11.99
6.0 - 7.99
4.0 - 5.99
0 - 3.99

Percentage of total civilian
labor force unemployed,
1990

© RM©N.   DM-520500-3D-GD1- -1- -:-1

CANCER

Crude death rate per
100,000 population*

United States average 192

Deaths
300.1+
250.1-300.0
200.1-250.0
150.1-200.0
0-150.0

*Based on estimates
furnished by Market Statistics
S&MM Survey of Buying Power

©R. M©N.

HEART DISEASE

Crude death rate per
100,000 population*

United States average 320

Deaths
600.1+
400.1-600.0
300.1-400.0
200.1-300.0
0-200.0

*Based on estimates
furnished by Market Statistics
S&MM Survey of Buying Power

©R. M©N.

PHYSICIANS

United States
Average 209

201 - 2036
151 - 200
101 - 150
51 - 100
1 - 50
0

Physicians per
100,000 population, 1990

Source: American
Medical Association

© RM©N.   DM-520500-9T-GD1- -1- -:-1

HOSPITAL BEDS

United States
Average 556

1,000 +
601 - 1,000
401 - 600
201 - 400
1 - 200
0

Beds per 100,000
population, 1985

Source: American
Hospital Association

© RM©N.   DM-520500-9U-GD1- -1- -:-1

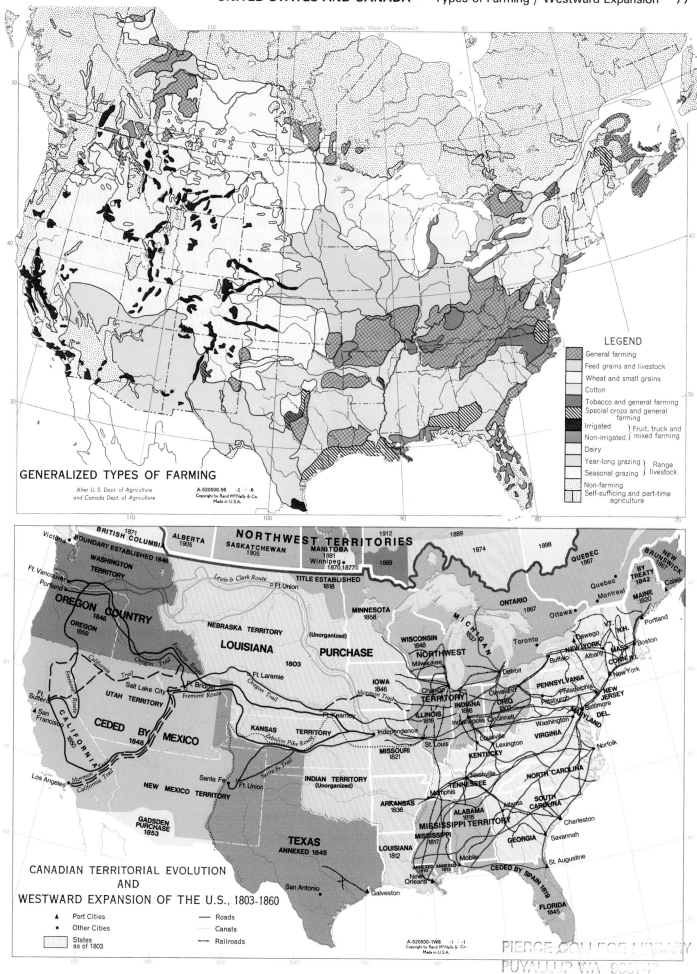

GENERALIZED TYPES OF FARMING

After U. S. Dept. of Agriculture
and Canada Dept. of Agriculture

A-520500-56   -3 -3 -6
Copyright by Rand McNally & Co.
Made in U.S.A.

LEGEND

General farming
Feed grains and livestock
Wheat and small grains
Cotton
Tobacco and general farming
Special crops and general farming
Irrigated } Fruit, truck and
Non-irrigated } mixed farming
Dairy
Year-long grazing } Range
Seasonal grazing } livestock
Non-farming
Self-sufficing and part-time agriculture

CANADIAN TERRITORIAL EVOLUTION
AND
WESTWARD EXPANSION OF THE U.S., 1803-1860

▲ Port Cities
● Other Cities
States as of 1803

— Roads
— Canals
—+— Railroads

A-520500-1W6   -1- -1
Copyright by Rand McNally & Co.
Made in U.S.A.

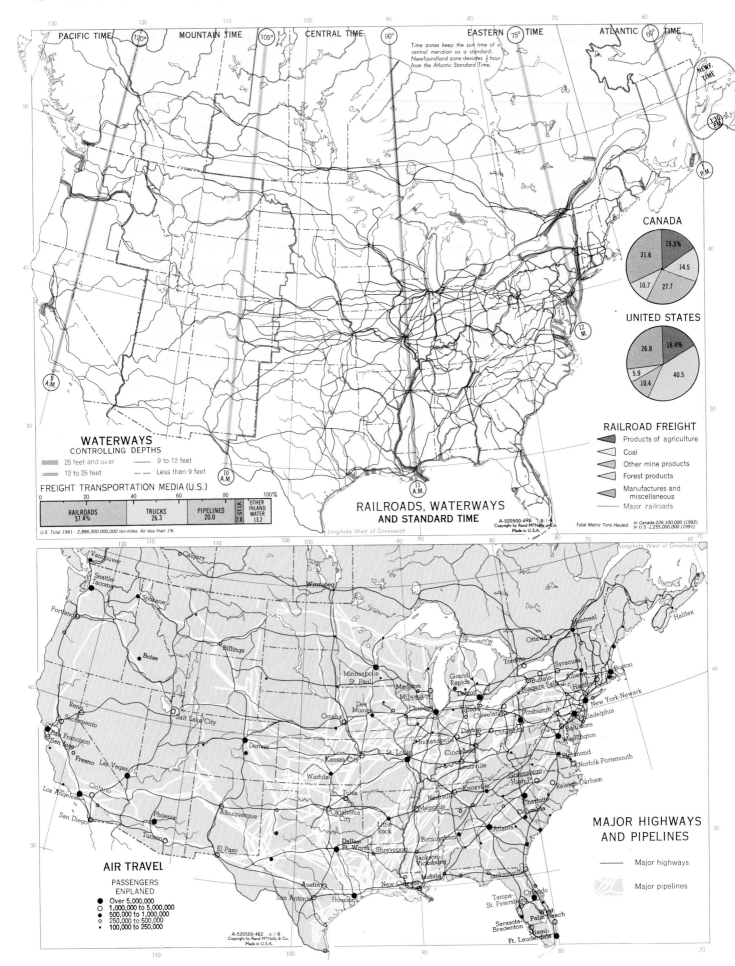

Time zones keep the sun time of a
central meridian as a standard.
Newfoundland zone deviates ½ hour
from the Atlantic Standard Time.

CANADA

15.5%
31.6
14.5
10.7   27.7

UNITED STATES

16.4%
26.8
40.5
5.9
10.4

RAILROAD FREIGHT

Products of agriculture
Coal
Other mine products
Forest products
Manufactures and
  miscellaneous
Major railroads

WATERWAYS
CONTROLLING DEPTHS

25 feet and over   9 to 12 feet
12 to 25 feet   Less than 9 feet

FREIGHT TRANSPORTATION MEDIA (U.S.)

0   20   40   60   80   100%

RAILROADS 37.4%	TRUCKS 26.3	PIPELINES 20.0	GT.LK. 2.8	OTHER INLAND WATER 13.2

U.S. Total 1991 - 2,886,000,000,000 ton-miles. Air less than 1%

RAILROADS, WATERWAYS
AND STANDARD TIME

A-520500-4R6
Copyright by Rand McNally & Co.
Made in U.S.A.

Total Metric Tons Hauled: In Canada-226,100,000 (1992)
In U.S.-1,255,000,000 (1991)

Longitude West of Greenwich

MAJOR HIGHWAYS
AND PIPELINES

——— Major highways

Major pipelines

AIR TRAVEL

PASSENGERS
ENPLANED

● Over 5,000,000
○ 1,000,000 to 5,000,000
◉ 500,000 to 1,000,000
○ 250,000 to 500,000
• 100,000 to 250,000

A-520500-462
Copyright by Rand McNally & Co.
Made in U.S.A.

Scale 1: 28 000 000; One inch to 440 miles.   LAMBERT CONFORMAL CONIC PROJECTION

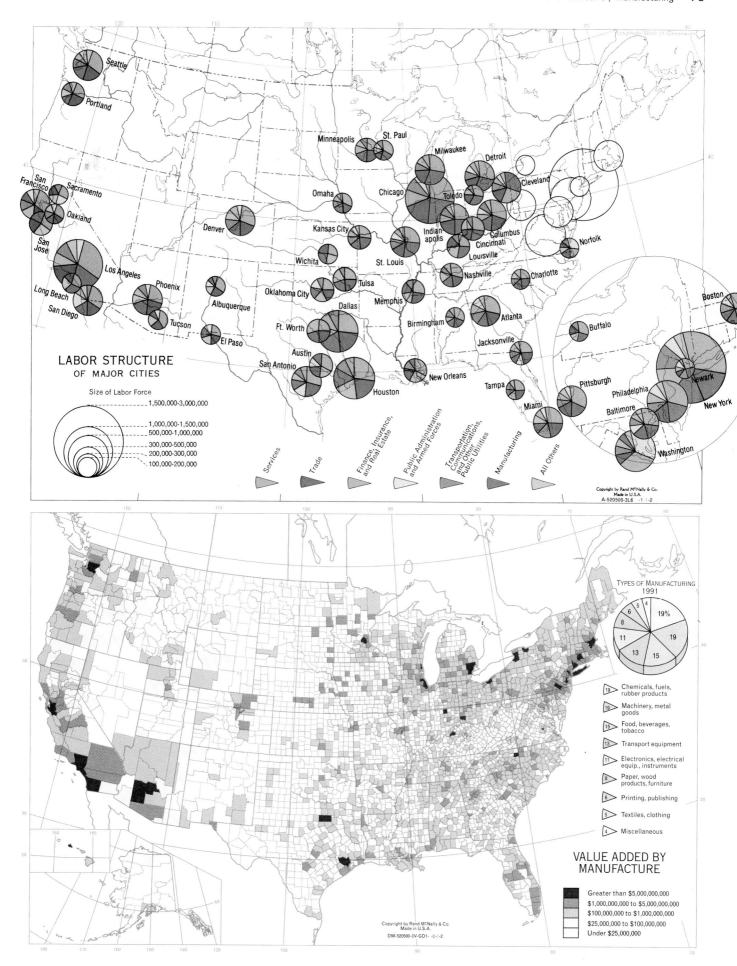

LABOR STRUCTURE
OF MAJOR CITIES

Size of Labor Force

1,500,000-3,000,000

1,000,000-1,500,000
500,000-1,000,000
300,000-500,000
200,000-300,000
100,000-200,000

Services

Trade

Finance, Insurance, and Real Estate

Public Administration and Armed Forces

Transportation, Communications, and Other Public Utilities

Manufacturing

All Others

Copyright by Rand McNally & Co.
Made in U.S.A.
A-520500-3L6   -1-1-2

TYPES OF MANUFACTURING
1991

19%
19
15
13
11
8
6
5
4

19 Chemicals, fuels, rubber products

19 Machinery, metal goods

15 Food, beverages, tobacco

13 Transport equipment

11 Electronics, electrical equip., instruments

8 Paper, wood products, furniture

6 Printing, publishing

5 Textiles, clothing

4 Miscellaneous

VALUE ADDED BY
MANUFACTURE

Greater than $5,000,000,000
$1,000,000,000 to $5,000,000,000
$100,000,000 to $1,000,000,000
$25,000,000 to $100,000,000
Under $25,000,000

Copyright by Rand McNally & Co.
Made in U.S.A.
DM-520500-3V-GD1- -2-2-2

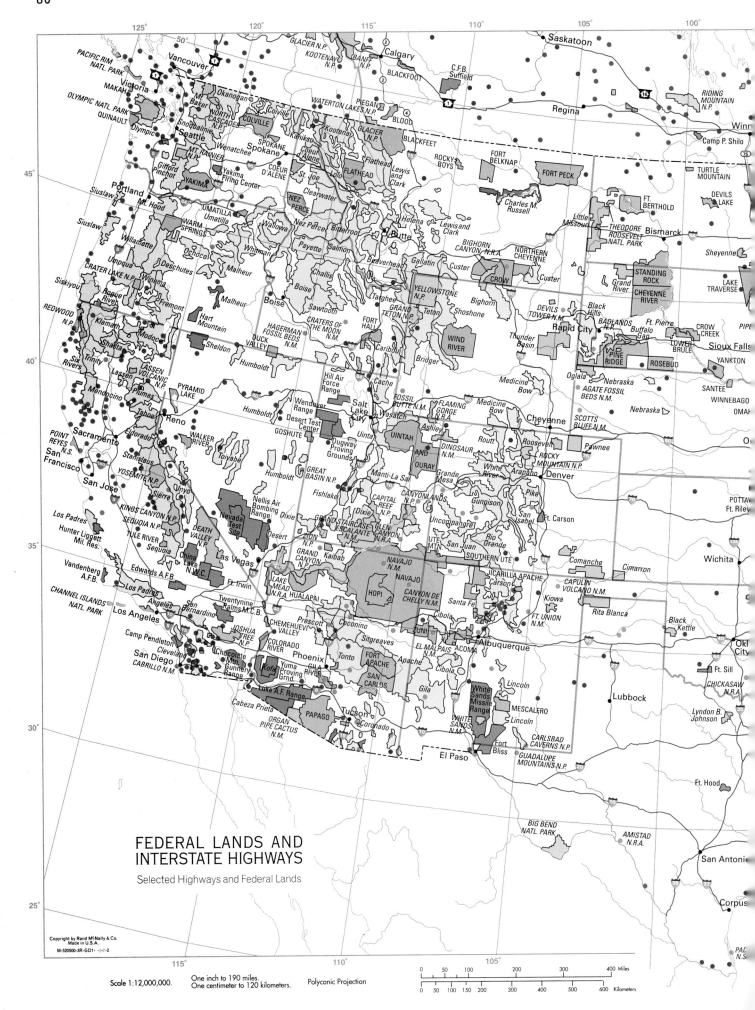

FEDERAL LANDS AND INTERSTATE HIGHWAYS

Selected Highways and Federal Lands

Copyright by Rand McNally & Co.
Made in U.S.A.
M-520500-3R-GD1- -2-2-2

Scale 1:12,000,000.

One inch to 190 miles.
One centimeter to 120 kilometers.

Polyconic Projection

0   50 100   200   300   400 Miles

0 50 100 150 200   300   400   500   600 Kilometers

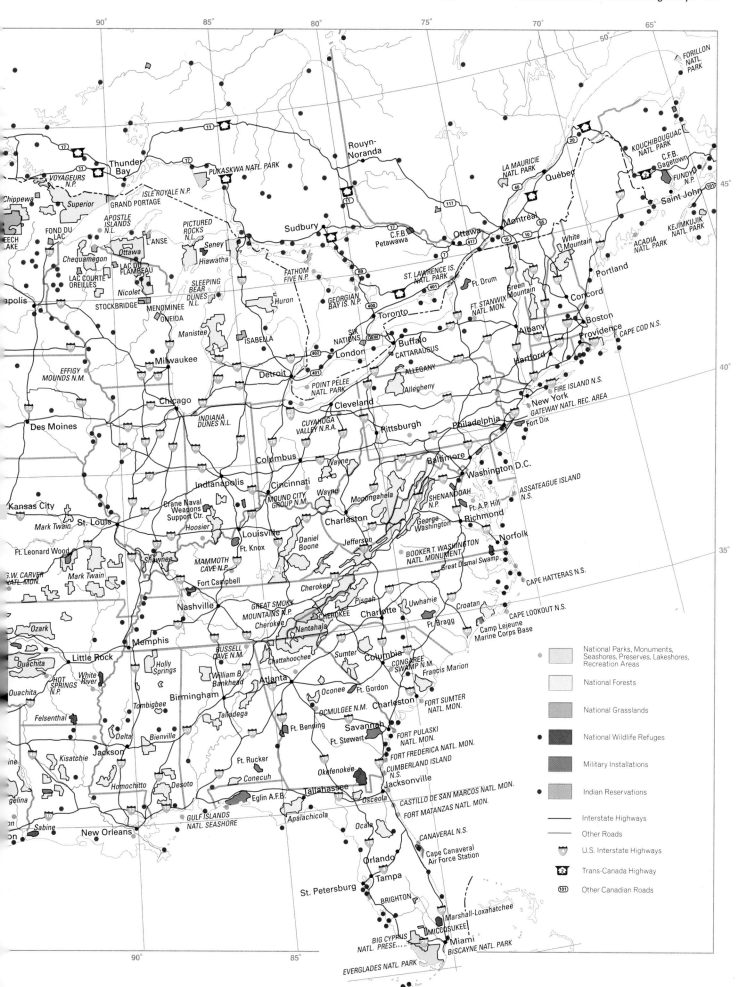

National Parks, Monuments, Seashores, Preserves, Lakeshores, Recreation Areas

National Forests

National Grasslands

National Wildlife Refuges

Military Installations

Indian Reservations

Interstate Highways

Other Roads

U.S. Interstate Highways

Trans-Canada Highway

Other Canadian Roads

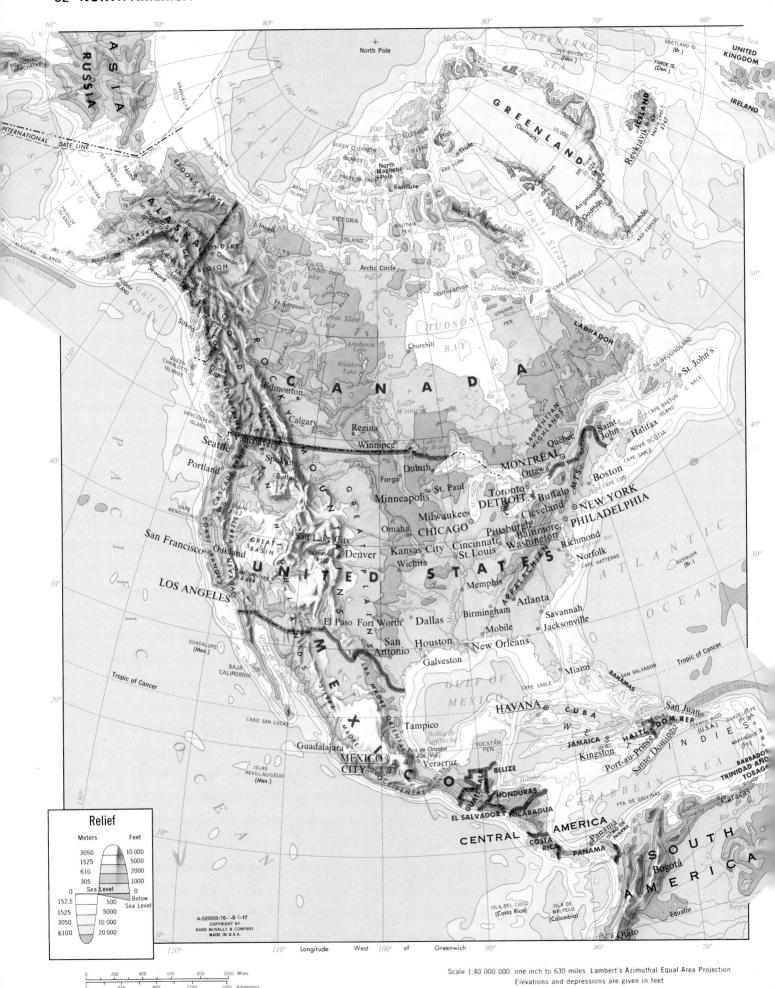

Relief

Meters	Feet
3050	10 000
1525	5000
610	2000
305	1000
0 Sea Level	0 Sea Level
	Below
152.5	500
1525	5000
3050	10 000
6100	20 000

A-520000-76- -5-17
COPYRIGHT BY
RAND McNALLY & COMPANY
MADE IN U.S.A.

0 200 400 600 800 1000 Miles
0 400 800 1200 1600 Kilometers

Scale 1:40 000 000; one inch to 630 miles. Lambert's Azimuthal Equal Area Projection
Elevations and depressions are given in feet

Longitude   West   of   Greenwich

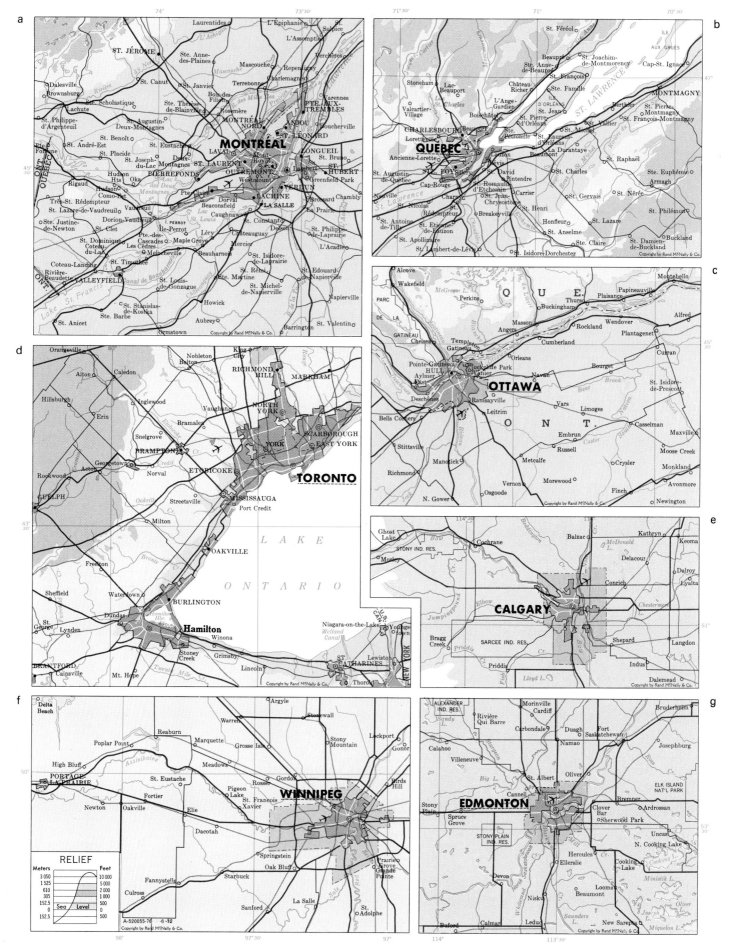

Scale 1:1 000 000; One inch to 16 miles.
Elevations and depressions are given in feet.

For larger scale coverage of
Montréal and Toronto see page 227.

84

Scale 1: 12 000 000; one inch to 190 miles. Conic Project

Elevations and depressions are given in feet

Longitude West of Greenwich

a

Longitude West of Greenwich

Same scale as
main map

QUEBEC

Gulf of
St. Lawrence

LONG RANGE MTS.

CAPE BAULD

C. ST. JOHN

GROS MORNE
NAT'L PARK

Deer Lake
Corner Brook
Stephenville
C. ST. GEORGE

Botwood
Grand Falls

Windsor
Gander

Twillingate

Bonavista

TERRA NOVA
NAT'L PARK

NEWFOUNDLAND

St.
George's

Trinity

CAPE RAY

Channel-Port-aux-Basques

CAPE NORTH

CAPE BRETON
ISLAND

Grand Bank

Burin

St. John's

ST. PIERRE AND MIQUELON (Fr.)

ATLANTIC OCEAN

BAFFIN
ISLAND
NAT'L PARK

Igloolik

Pangnirtung

BAFFIN

CUMBERLAND
SOUND

PRINCE
CHARLES
ISLAND

MELVILLE
PENINSULA

Foxe
Basin

Arctic Circle

ISLAND

Cumberland Sound

C. MERCY

Iqaluit

HALL PEN.

Frobisher Bay

EVERETT
MTS.

Lake Harbour

RESOLUTION

FOXE
PEN.

Foxe
Channel

SALISBURY

Hudson

Strait

C. DE
NOUVELLE
FRANCE

C. HOPES
ADVANCE

AKPATOK

KILLINIQ I.

SOUTHAMPTON
ISLAND

BELL
PEN.

NOTTINGHAM
ISLAND

COATS

MANSEL

C. LOW

Roes Welcome Sound

Fisher Strait

TORNGAT
MTS.

Hebron

Nain

Hopedale

Makkovik

Rigolet

Cartwright

Battle Harbour

LONG RANGE MTS.

St. Anthony

GROS MORNE
NAT'L PARK

Corner Brook
Stephenville
St. George's

IWUJIVIK

PENINSULE
D'UNGAVA

Payne

Ungava
Bay

Kuujjuaq

MEALY MTS.

Happy
Valley
Goose Bay

LABRADOR

Churchill Falls

Schefferville

NEWFOUNDLAND

Hamilton Inlet

HUDSON

BAY

All islands within bays and straits
lie within Northwest Territories.

OTTAWA
ISLANDS

Povungnituk

Minto

Lac
Bienville

Lac Mistassini

BELCHER
ISLANDS

Grande de la Baleine

Caniapiscau

Nichicun

MTS.
OTISH

MTS.
MANICOUAGAN

Réservoir Manicouagan

Natashquan

ILE D'ANTICOSTI

QUEBEC

Ft. Severn

C. HENRIETTA MARIA

PTE. LOUIS-XIV

Chisasibi

James
Bay

AKIMISKI

Ft. Albany

Moosonee

ONTARIO

St.
Joseph

Lac Seul

Lookout

Dryden

Lake of
the Woods

Rainy

Winisk

Severn

Attawapiskat

Albany

Missinaibi

Coral Rapids
Fraserdale

Armstrong Sta.
Nakina

Hearst

La Sarre

Rouyn

Amos

Senneterre

Parent

Reservoir Gouin

Gulf of
St. Lawrence

Sept-Iles

Clarke City

Mingan

Betsiamites

R. aux Outardes

St. Lawrence River

MTS.
CHIC-CHOCS

Cap-Chat
Matane

PEN. DE GASPE

Gaspé

New Carlisle

ILES DE LA
MADELEINE

P.E.I.

Chandler

Chaleur Bay

Caraquet

Bathurst

PRINCE EDWARD
ISLAND NAT'L PARK

Charlottetown

Summerside

Newcastle

Chatham

Richibucto

Moncton

NEW
BRUNSWICK

NOVA SCOTIA

New Glasgow

Sydney Mines
Sydney

CAPE BRETON
HIGHLANDS NAT'L PARK

Springhill

Amherst
Truro

Lunenburg
Bridgewater
Liverpool

Dartmouth
Halifax

Rimouski

Rivière-du-Loup

Edmundston

Woodstock

Fredericton

FUNDY
NAT'L PARK

Sussex

Saint John

Kentville

St. George

Digby

Shelburne

CAPE SABLE

Yarmouth

Armstrong Sta.
Nakina

Geraldton
Longlac

Kapuskasing

Cochrane
Iroquois Falls
Timmins

Kirkland Lake

Cobalt

Ville-Marie

Témiscaming

La Tuque

Shawinigan

Trois-
Rivières

Quebec

Lévis

Montmagny

Victoriaville

Drummondville

Sherbrooke

MAINE

St.-Jean

St. Andrews
St. Stephen

Augusta

Portland

ATLANTIC
OCEAN

Nipigon

Marathon

PUKASKWA
NAT'L PARK

MICHIPICOTEN

Chapleau

Blind River
Espanola

Sudbury

Sturgeon Falls
North
Bay

Mattawa

Pembroke
Renfrew
Huntsville
Bancroft
Smiths Falls

Parry Sound

Georgian
Bay

MANITOULIN

Orillia

Lindsay

Peterborough

Cobourg
Trenton

Ottawa
Hull

Brockville

Kingston

Alexandria
Bay

Ogdensburg

Cornwall

MONTREAL

Joliette

Sorel

St.-Hyacinthe

Valleyfield

Frontiere

VERMONT

NEW
HAMPSHIRE

Concord

BOSTON

CAPE COD

Thunder Bay

Lake Superior

Marquette

Escanaba

Sault Ste. Marie

Thessalon

Sault Ste. Marie

Lake Huron

Wiarton
Owen Sound

Kincardine

Midland
Barrie

Oshawa
Whitby

Port Hope

Lake Ontario

Rochester

Albany

Hartford

MASS.

CONN.

R.I.

Providence

NEW YORK

Duluth

Superior

St.
Paul

Green Bay

Saginaw
Flint

Lansing

Grand
Rapids

Detroit

Windsor

Chatham

Leamington

Sarnia

London
St. Thomas

Port
Huron

Kitchener

TORONTO

Hamilton

St. Catharines

Niagara
Falls

BUFFALO

Scranton

PENNSYLVANIA

NEW
YORK

N.J.

WISCONSIN

MILWAUKEE

CHICAGO

Toledo

OHIO

Lake Erie

Madison

MINNESOTA

MICHIGAN

A-520200-76   9-9-21

COPYRIGHT BY
RAND MCNALLY & COMPANY
MADE IN U.S.A.

Relief

Meters	Feet
3050	10 000
1525	5000
610	2000
305	1000
152.5	500
Sea Level	0
152.5	500
1525	5000
3050	10 000

0 25 50 75 100   200   300   400   500 Miles

0   100   200   400   600   800 Kilometers

134° 132° 130° 128° 126° 124°

54°

52°

50°

48°

Relief

Meters		Feet
3050		10 000
1525		5000
610		2000
305		1000
152.5		500
0	Sea Level	0
152.5		500
1525		5000

A-520220-76 6-8
COPYRIGHT BY
RAND McNALLY & COMPANY
MADE IN U.S.A.

132°

Continued on pages 104-105 130° 128° Longitude West of Greenwich 126° 124°

Scale 1:4 000 000; one inch to 64 miles. Conic Projec
Elevations and depressions are given in feet.

PRINCE
OF
WALES
ISLAND
DALL
ISLAND

LOLU
ISLAND
Klawock
Hydaburg
Copper Mtn.
3316
Metlakatla
ANNETTE
ISLAND
Ketchikan
Kelchican

Mt. Reid
4592
REVILLAGIGEDO
ISLAND

UNITED STATES
CANADA

DUNDAS
ISLAND

Dixon Entrance

CAPE KNOX

QUEEN

Masset

CHARLOTTE

Skidegate Inlet

QUEEN CHARLOTTE RANGES

GRAHAM ISLAND

MORESBY ISLAND
Mount Kermode
3550

ISLANDS

Hecate Strait

CAPE ST. JAMES

PORCHER
ISLAND

BANKS
ISLAND

PITT
ISLAND

Chatham Sound

Prince Rupert

Alice Arm

HAZELTON

Hazelton

Terrace

Smithers

SKEENA
MOUNTAINS
Shedin Pk.
8750

Mt. Thomlinson
8050

OMINECA
MOUNTAINS

Williston
Lake

Tchentlo
Lake

Babine
Lake

Takla
Lake

McLeo

Fort
St. James

KITIMAT

Kitimat

COAST

BULKLEY
MOUNTAINS RANGES
Hawson Pk.
9050

Morice Lake

Burns Lake

NECHAKO

Endako

Vanderhoof

BRITIS

MOUNTAINS

Ootsa
Lake

Michel Pk.
7396

Whitesail
Lake

Eutsuk Lake

Nechako
Reservoir

Tetachuck
Lake

KENNEY DAM

PLATEAU

NECHAKO
RANGE

HARTLEY BAY
Hartley Bay

ESTEVAN
GROUP

PRINCESS
ROYAL
ISLAND

ARISTAZABAL
ISLAND

Mt. Parry
3450

RODERICK
ISLAND

DOOLEY
ISLAND

SWINGLE
ISLAND

Ocean Falls

Bella Coola

COLU

Bella Bella

Namu

RANGES

PACIFIC

Charlotte
Lake

Redstone

Monarch Mtn.
11590

Rivers Inlet

FRA

Queen

Charlotte

Sound

CALVERT ISLAND

CAPE
CAUTION

Razorback Mtn.
10432

Silverthrone Mtn.
9700

Mt. Waddington
13163

Mt. Queen Bess
10791

Mt. Tatlow
10058

Good Hope Mtn.
10615

Monmouth
10480

PL

Queen Charlotte Strait

Bull Harbour

CAPE SCOTT

Port Hardy

Smood
Sound

Simood
Sound

Mt. Gilbert
3109

RANGES

Quatsino Sound

Port Alice

Kelsey Bay

REDONDA
ISLANDS

QUADRA
ISLAND

PACIFIC

OCEAN

CAPE COOK

VANCOUVER

Victoria Pk.
7095

Bloedel

Campbell
River

Powell River

Mr. G

NOOTKA
ISLAND

Golden Hinde
7291

Courtenay

Comox

Vananda

TEXADA
ISLAND

Squami

VANCOUVER

ISLAND

Nootka
Sound

ISLAND

RANGES

Tofino

Port Alberni

Nanaimo

Mt. Whymper
5056

North Vanco
Vancouv
Bur
New Wes
Lo
Ladysmith

PACIFIC RIM
NATIONAL PARK

Barkley
Sound

CAPE BEALE

Lake Cowichan

Duncan

Esquimalt

Strait of Juan de Fuca

CAPE FLATTERY

OLYMPIC
NATIONAL
PARK

OLYMPIC
NATIONAL
PARK

Port
Ange
V

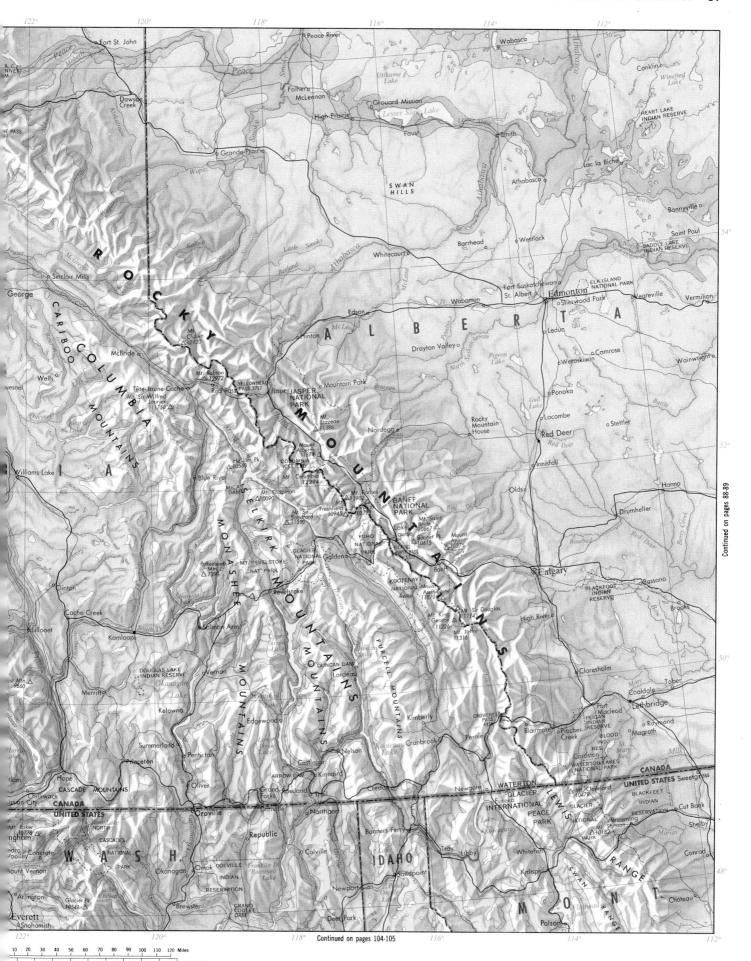

Continued on pages 88-89

Continued on pages 104-105

10 20 30 40 50 60 70 80 90 100 110 120 Miles
20 40 60 80 100 120 140 160 180 200 Kilometers

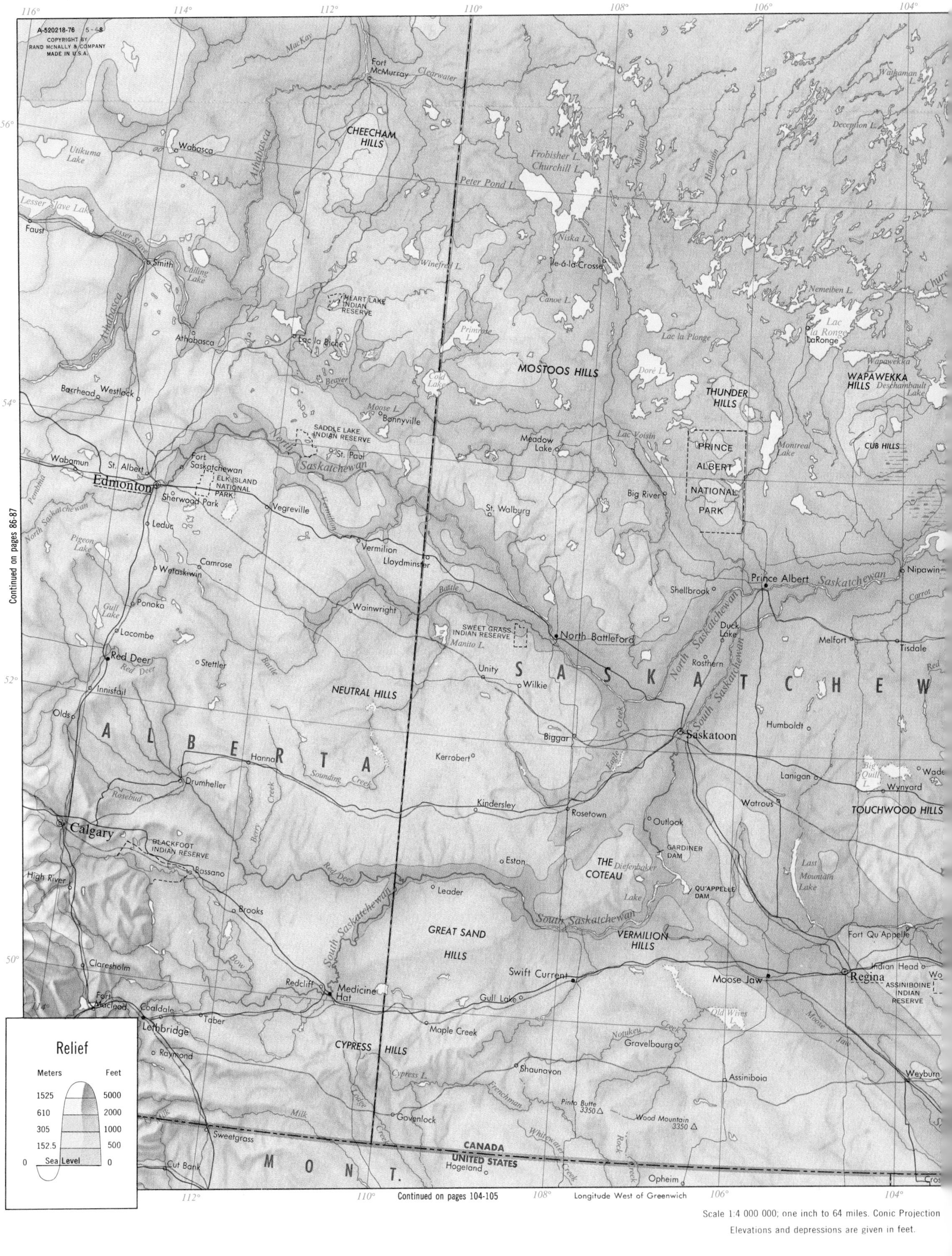

A-520218-76 5--8
COPYRIGHT BY
RAND McNALLY & COMPANY
MADE IN U.S.A.

Continued on pages 86-87

116° 114° 112° 110° 108° 106° 104°

56°

54°

52°

50°

Utikuma Lake
Wabasca
CHEECHAM HILLS
Fort McMurray
Clearwater
Deception L.
Frobisher L.
Churchill L.
Peter Pond L.
Nemeiben L.
Niska L.
Île-à-la-Crosse
Lac la Ronge
LaRonge
Wapawekka L.
WAPAWEKKA HILLS
Deschambault Lake
Lesser Slave Lake
Faust
Smith
Calling Lake
Athabasca
HEART LAKE INDIAN RESERVE
Lac la Biche
Beaver
Winefred L.
Primrose L.
Cold Lake
MOSTOOS HILLS
Lac la Plonge
Doré L.
Lac Voisin
THUNDER HILLS
Montreal Lake
CUB HILLS
Churc
Birchead
Westlock
Moose L.
Bonnyville
SADDLE LAKE INDIAN RESERVE
St. Paul
Meadow Lake
PRINCE ALBERT NATIONAL PARK
Wabamun
St. Albert
Edmonton
Fort Saskatchewan
North Saskatchewan
ELK ISLAND NATIONAL PARK
Sherwood Park
Vegreville
St. Walburg
Big River
Shellbrook
Prince Albert
Saskatchewan
Nipawin
Leduc
Pigeon Lake
Pembina
Wetaskiwin
Vermilion
Lloydminster
Battle
Duck Lake
Rosthern
Melfort
Tisdale
Camrose
Wainwright
SWEET GRASS INDIAN RESERVE
Manito L.
North Battleford
Gull Lake
Ponoka
Lacombe
Red Deer
Red Deer
Stettler
Battle
NEUTRAL HILLS
Unity
Wilkie
S A S K A T C H E W A
Rosthern
Humboldt
Innisfail
Olds
A L B E R T A
Hanna
Sounding Creek
Kerrobert
Biggar
Saskatoon
Lanigan
Big Quill L.
Wade
Wynyard
Drumheller
Rosebud
Berry Creek
Kindersley
Rosetown
Outlook
Watrous
TOUCHWOOD HILLS
Calgary
BLACKFOOT INDIAN RESERVE
Bassano
Red Deer
Eston
THE COTEAU
Diefenbaker
GARDINER DAM
Last Mountain Lake
High River
Brooks
Leader
QU'APPELLE DAM
QU'Appelle
Claresholm
Fort Macleod
Coaldale
Redcliff
Medicine Hat
South Saskatchewan
Bow
GREAT SAND HILLS
Swift Current
VERMILION HILLS
South Saskatchewan
Fort Qu'Appelle
Indian Head
Moose Jaw
Regina
Wo
Lethbridge
Taber
Gull Lake
Old Wives L.
ASSINIBOINE INDIAN RESERVE
Raymond
CYPRESS HILLS
Maple Creek
Notukeu Creek
Gravelbourg
Assiniboia
Weyburn
Cypress L.
Shaunavon
Milk
Govenlock
Pinto Butte 3350 △
Wood Mountain 3350 △
Cut Bank
Sweetgrass
Trenchman
Whitewater Creek
Rock Creek
CANADA
UNITED STATES
M O N T.
Hogeland
Opheim
Cros

Continued on pages 104-105

Longitude West of Greenwich

112° 110° 108° 106° 104°

Relief

Meters	Feet
1525	5000
610	2000
305	1000
152.5	500
0 Sea Level	0

Scale 1:4 000 000; one inch to 64 miles. Conic Projection
Elevations and depressions are given in feet.

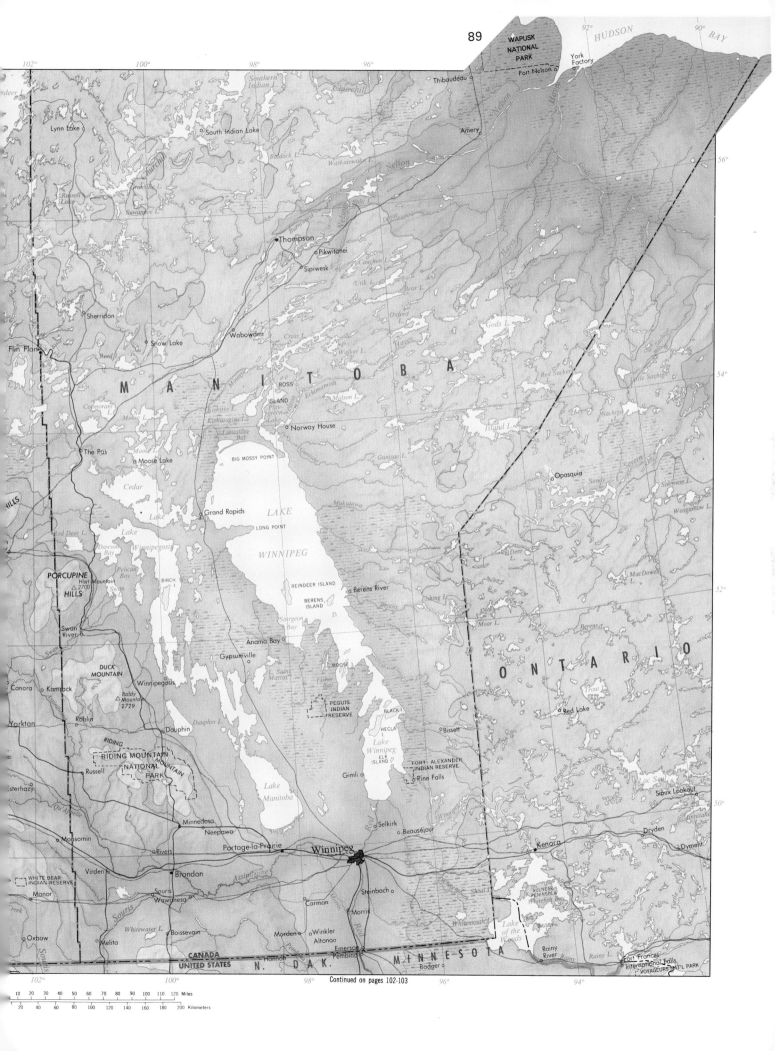

HUDSON BAY

WAPUSK
NATIONAL
PARK

York Factory

Port Nelson

Thibaudeau

Amery

Lynn Lake

South Indian Lake

Southern
Indian L.

Baldock L.

Churchill

Nelson

Russell
Lake

Granville L.

Suwannee L.

Waskaiowaka L.

Thompson

Pikwitonei

Sipiwesk

Utik L.

Burntwood

Bear L.

Oxford

Sherridon

Wabowden

Cross L.

Walker L.

Hayes

Gods L.

Flin Flon

Snow Lake

Reed

Cormorant L.

MANITOBA

Minago

ROSS
ISLAND

Echimamish

Molson L.

Island L.

Red Sucker L.

Little Sachigo

Sachigo

The Pas

Moose L.

Moose Lake

Kiskitto L.

Kiskittogisu L.

Limestone
Bay

Play
Green
L.

Norway House

Gunisao L.

Gunisao L.

Opasquia

Sandy

Sakwaso L.

Cedar

BIG MOSSY POINT

LAKE

Grand Rapids

LONG POINT

Mukutawa

Weagamow L.

Lake

Winnipegosis

Dawson
Bay

BIRCH

WINNIPEG

Deer L.

MacDowell
L.

PORCUPINE
HILLS

Hart Mountain
2700

Pelican
Bay

Swan

REINDEER ISLAND

BERENS
ISLAND

Berens River

Berens

Fishing L.

Swan
River

Sturgeon
Bay

Moar L.

Berens L.

Anama Bay

L. Saint
Martin

MOOSE I.

Fisher
Bay

Trout
L.

Gypsumville

Canora

Kamsack

DUCK
MOUNTAIN

Winnipegosis

Baldy Mountain
2729

PEGUIS
INDIAN
RESERVE

BLACK I.

ONTARIO

Red
Lake

Roblin

Dauphin L.

Dauphin

HECLA
I.

Bissett

Yorkton

RIDING

RIDING MOUNTAIN

NATIONAL
PARK

Russell

Lake
Winnipeg

ELK
ISLAND

FORT ALEXANDER
INDIAN RESERVE

Sioux Lookout

Esterhazy

Minnedosa

Neepawa

Gimli

Pine Falls

Lac Seul

Qu'Appelle

Lake
Manitoba

Selkirk

Kenora

Dryden

Moosomin

Rivers

Portage-la-Prairie

Winnipeg

Beauséjour

Dyment

White Bear
Indian Reserve

Virden

Brandon

Assiniboine

Red

AULNEAU
PENINSULA
Whitefish Bay

Manor

Souris

Wawanesa

Carman

Steinbach

Shoal L.

BIG
GRSBY

Oxbow

Melita

Whitewater L.

Boissevain

Morden

Winkler

Altona

Morris

Emerson

Pembina

Whitemouth

Lake
of the
Woods

Rainy
River

Fort Frances

International Falls
VOYAGEURS NAT'L PARK

CANADA
UNITED STATES

Hannah

Bodger

N. DAK.

MINNESOTA

Continued on pages 102-103

10 20 30 40 50 60 70 80 90 100 110 120 Miles

20 40 60 80 100 120 140 160 180 200 Kilometers

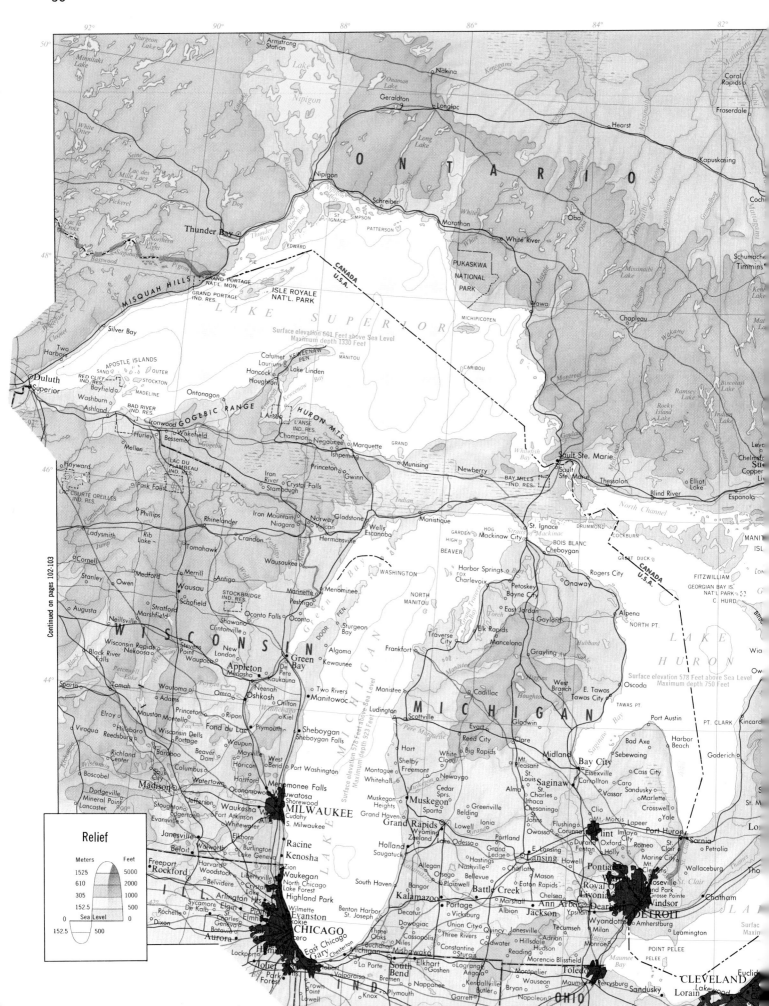

ONTARIO

LAKE SUPERIOR
Surface elevation 601 Feet above Sea Level
Maximum depth 1330 Feet

PUKASKWA NATIONAL PARK

ISLE ROYALE NAT'L. PARK

CANADA U.S.A.

MISQUAH HILLS

GRAND PORTAGE NAT'L. MON.
GRAND PORTAGE IND. RES.

Thunder Bay

Silver Bay

Two Harbors

APOSTLE ISLANDS
RED CLIFF IND. RES.
Bayfield
MADELINE
BAD RIVER IND. RES.

Duluth
Superior
Washburn
Ashland

GOGEBIC RANGE
Ironwood
Hurley
Mellen
Bessemer
Wakefield

HURON MTS.
L'ANSE IND. RES.
L'Anse
Champion
Negaunee
Ishpeming
Marquette

Munising

Newberry

BAY MILLS IND. RES.
Sault Ste. Marie
Sault Ste. Marie

Thessalon
Blind River
Espanola

Hayward

LAC DU FLAMBEAU IND. RES.
Park Falls

LAC COURTE OREILLES IND. RES.

Phillips

Ladysmith

Cornell

Stanley
Owen

Medford

Merrill
Antigo

Wausau
Schofield

STOCKBRIDGE IND. RES.

WISCONSIN

Iron River
Crystal Falls
Stambaugh

Iron Mountain
Norway
Vulcan
Niagara

Crandon

Rhinelander

Tomahawk

Wausaukee

Marinette
Menominee
Peshtigo

Oconto Falls
Oconto

Shawano

New London

Green Bay
De Pere
Kaukauna

Appleton
Menasha
Neenah

Oshkosh

Princeton
Gwinn

Gladstone
Escanaba
Wells

Hermansville

Manistique

GARDEN PEN.
Mackinac City
St. Ignace

HOG
HIGH
BEAVER

WASHINGTON

Frankfort

Traverse City

NORTH MANITOU

FOX
Harbor Springs
Charlevoix
Petoskey
Boyne City
East Jordan

BOIS BLANC
Cheboygan

Rogers City

Onaway

Gaylord

Alpena

NORTH PT.

CANADA U.S.A.

MICHIGAN

Elk Rapids
Mancelona

Grayling

West Branch

Oscoda

E. Tawas
Tawas City
TAWAS PT.

LAKE HURON
Surface elevation 578 Feet above Sea Level
Maximum depth 750 Feet

Stevens Point
Waupaca

Wisconsin Rapids
Nekoosa

Black River Falls

Sparta

Tomah

Wautoma
Omro
Adams

Ripon
Fond du Lac

Chilton
Manitowoc
Two Rivers

Kewaunee
Algoma

Sturgeon Bay

DOOR

Ludington

Scottville

Cadillac

Reed City
Evart
Clare

Gladwin

Bad Axe
Sebewaing
Caro
Cass City

Harbor Beach

PT. CLARK

Port Austin

Mt. Pleasant
St. Louis
Alma

Midland
Bay City
Essexville
Carrollton
Saginaw

Vassar
Marlette
Crosswell

Kingsley

Cudahy
MILWAUKEE

Racine
Kenosha

Muskegon
Muskegon Heights

Grand Rapids
Wyoming

Holland
Saugatuck

South Haven

Benton Harbor
St. Joseph

Battle Creek

Kalamazoo

Portage

Jackson

Ann Arbor

Lansing
E. Lansing

Flint

Pontiac

Livonia
Dearborn

DETROIT
Windsor

Port Huron
Sarnia

CLEVELAND

OHIO

Toledo

Continued on pages 102-103

Relief

Meters	Feet
1525	5000
610	2000
305	1000
152.5	500
0 Sea Level	0
152.5	500

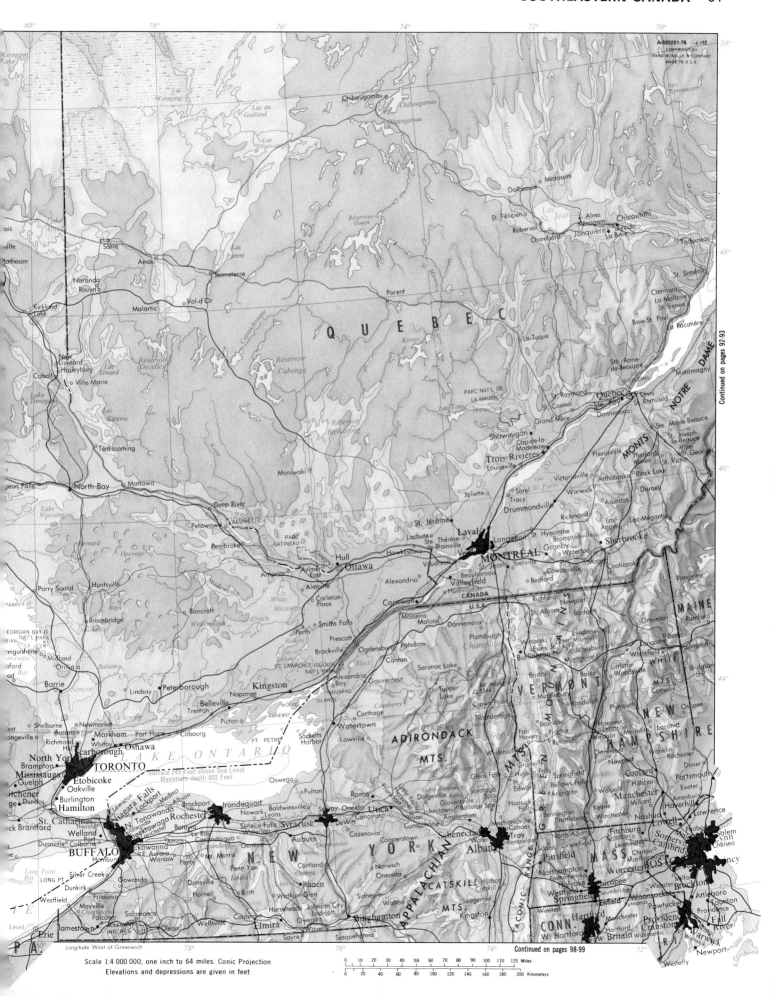

Continued on pages 92-93

Continued on pages 98-99

Scale 1:4 000 000; one inch to 64 miles. Conic Projection
Elevations and depressions are given in feet

Longitude West of Greenwich

0 10 20 30 40 50 60 70 80 90 100 110 120 Miles

0 20 40 60 80 100 120 140 160 180 200 Kilometers

QUEBEC

ONTARIO

LAKE ONTARIO

Surface 245 feet above Sea Level
Maximum depth 802 Feet

N E W   Y O R K

ADIRONDACK MTS.

VERMONT

MAINE

NEW HAMPSHIRE

MASS.

CONN.

APPALACHIAN MTS.

CATSKILL MTS.

TORONTO

BUFFALO

MONTREAL

BOSTON

Continued on pages 90-91

Continued on pages 98-99

Chibougamau
Mistassini

Mistassini
Manouane

Rivière

B
E
E

Clarke City
Sept-Iles
Port-Cartier
Mingan

Détroit de J

Chibougamau

Chibougamau

U
E

Dolbeau
Mistassini

St. Félicien
Roberval

Chambord
Alma
Kénogami
Jonquière
Arvida
La Baie
Chicoutimi

Q

Hauterive
Baie-Comeau
POINTE DES MONTS

Cap-Chat

Mt. Jacques-Cartier
4160

Détroit

Lac Jean
Forestville
Betsiamites
River

St. Lawrence

Matane
Ste. Félicité
Gaspé
PARC
FOR
CAP

La Tuque

Portneuf-Sur-Mer
Sault-au-Mouton

Mont-Joli
Amqui
CHIC-CHOCS

Saguenay
Tadoussac

Bic
Rimouski
Causapscal
MTS.

Nouvelle
Maria
New
Carlisle
GASPÉ
Chandler
Grand-Rivière
Percé

PARC NAT'L
DE LA
MAURICIE

St. Siméon

Clermont

La Malbaie
Ste. Irénée
Baie-St. Paul

Rivière-Trois-Pistoles

Matapédia
Campbellton
Dalhousie
Chaleur
Bay
MISCOU PT.
MISCOU
SHIPPEGAN

Grand'Mère
Shawinigan
St. Raymond
St. Casimir

ILE
AUX
COUDRES

Cacouna
Rivière-du-Loup
Temiscouata

Kedgwick
Jacquet River

Caraquet
Burnsville
Shippegan

Cap-de-la-Madeleine
Trois-Rivières
Louiseville

Ste. Anne
de Beaupré
ILE
D'ORLÉANS
Québec
Ste. Foy
Lévis
St. Romuald

St. Pascal
La Pocatière

DAME

Notre-Dame-
du-Lac
Cabano

Edmundston
Fort
Kent
Van Buren
St. Leonard

Bathurst

NEW

Newcastle
Chatham
Millerton
KOUCHIBOUGUAC
NAT'L PARK

Miramichi
Bay

Joliette
Tracy
Soret

Donnacona

Montmagny

St. Marie-Beauce
Ste.
Joseph-
Beauce
Ville-St. Georges

NOTRE

CANADA
U.S.A.

St. John

Lac-Frontière

Eagle
Lake
Caribou
Washburn

Grand Falls
Plaster Rock

BRUNSWICK

Blackville
Richibucto

Alberton
O'Leary

Plessisville
Victoriaville
Arthabaska
Black Lake
Thetford
Mines St. Victor

Warwick
Drummondville
Asbestos
Disraeli

DAME

Ashland
Mars Hill
Presque
Isle

Fort Fairfield

Monticello
Hartland
Stanley

Boiestown

Chipman

Buctouche
Harcourt

Shediac

MONTRÉAL
Laval
Longueuil
Verdun

St. Hyacinthe
Granby
Richmond
Bromptonville

MONTS

Lac-Mégantic

Mt. Katahdin
5267

Oakfield
Patten
Houlton
Woodstack
Benton

Marysville
Fredericton
Oromocto

Minto

Moncton
Dieppe

Salisbury
Havelock
Petitcodiac
Port Elgin
Sackville

Amherst

St. Jean
Beauharnois

Iberville
Cowansville
Magog
Sherbrooke

East
Angus

Rockwood

Moosehead

Millinocket

Danforth
McAdam

Oromocto
Grand

Sussex
Harvey
Hampton

FUNDY
NAT'L PARK
Alma
Joggins

Springh

COBEQUID
Landonderr

Platts-
burgh
Winooski
Burlington
Essex Jc.

St. Albans
Newport
CANADA
U.S.A.

Richford
Bedford

Coaticook

Greenville
Brownville
Junction

Monson

Lincoln

St. Stephen

Lepreau

Millirawook
St. George
St. Andrews

Eastport

Lubec

Bay
of Fundy

NOVA

Parrsboro

Canning
Wolfville
Kentville
Bridgetown
Middleton

Minas
Basin
Chignecto

Mt. Mansfield
4393
Barton

Lyndonville

St.
Johnsbury

MAINE

Rangeley
Dover-
Foxcroft

Dexter
Old Town

Lancaster
Berlin

Madison
Farmington
Pittsfield
Skowhegan

Bangor
Brewer

Cherryfield
Machias

GRAND
MANAN

Windsor

Digby

Annapolis
Royal

KEJIMKUJIK
NAT'L PARK

Middleton

Bridgewater

Mahone Bay

Dartmou
Halifax

Montpelier
Bristol
Middlebury
Brandon
Proctor
Rutland

Whitefield
WHITE
Mt.
Washington
6288
MTS.
Norway
S. Paris

Mexico
Rumford

Waterville

Winthrop

Augusta
Gardiner

Belfast
Camden
Rockland

Searsport

Bar Harbor
ACADIA NAT'L PARK
Mt
DESERT

Ellsworth

Brier I.

St. Mary's
Kejimkujik

Liverpool
Lunenburg

Randolph
Plymouth
Haven
Fair

NEW

Lebanon
Hanover
Windsor
Claremont

Meredith
Ossipee

Conway

Bridgton
Mechanic Falls
Auburn
Lewiston
Lisbon Falls
Brunswick
Bath

Westbrook

Boothbay Harbor

DEER I.

Vinalhaven
ISLE AU HAUT

Yarmouth
Wedgeport

Clark's Harbour
CAPE SABLE

Shelburne
Lockeport

ATLANTIC

Springfield
Bellows
Falls
Arlington

Newport
Franklin

HAMPSHIRE
Concord

Laconia
Rochester
N. Berwick
Somersworth
Dover

Sanford
Saco
Biddeford
Kennebunk

Portland
S. Portland

Bennington
Brattleboro

N. Adams
Adams
Greenfield
Northampton

MASS.

GREEN
MTS.

NEW YORK

Walpole
Hillsboro

Keene
Winchester
Nashua
Milford

Manchester

Fitchburg
Leominster
Gardner
Clinton
Marlborough
Hudson

Haverhill
Lawrence

Newburyport
CAPE ANN
Gloucester

Amesbury
Exeter
Kittery
Portsmouth

Holyoke
Chicopee
Springfield

Easthampton

Southbridge
Webster

Worcester

Putnam

Woonsocket
Pawtucket

CONN.
Hartford

R.I.
PROV.

Attleboro
Taunton

Lowell
Somerville
Cambridge
Chelsea

Peabody
Salem
Lynn

BOSTON
Quincy
Dedham
Norwood
Milford
Weymouth
Brockton
Plymouth

Massachusetts
Bay

Provincetown
CAPE COD

ATLANTIC

Longitude West of Greenwich

Scale 1:4 000 000; one inch to 64 miles. Conic Proje
Elevations and depressions are given in feet.

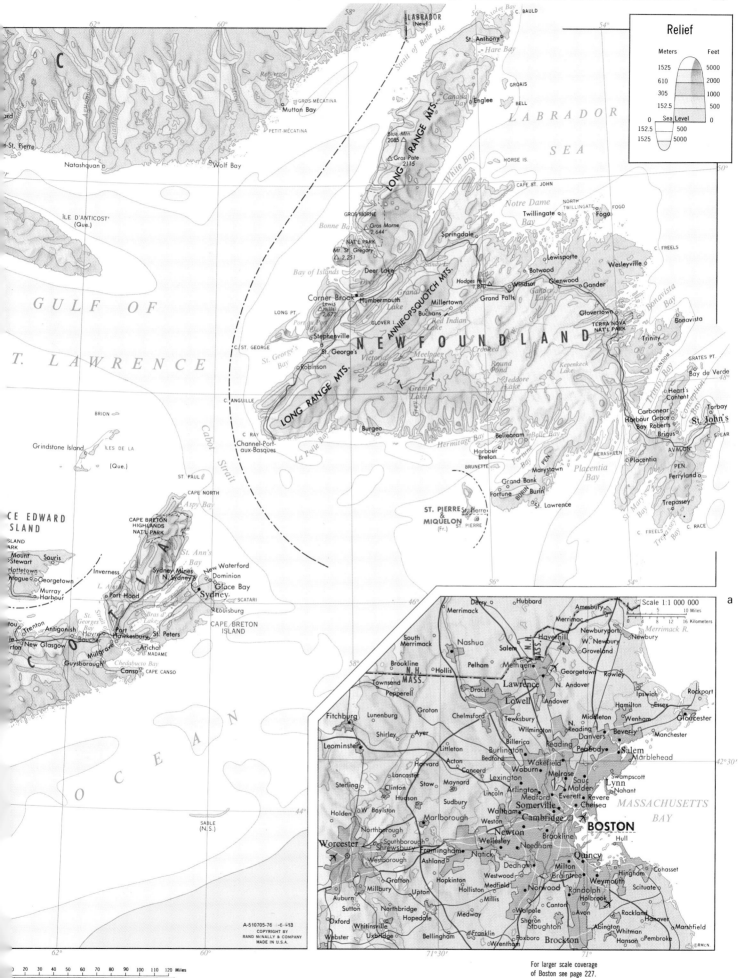

Relief

Meters	Feet
1525	5000
610	2000
305	1000
152.5	500
0	Sea Level	0
152.5	500
1525	5000

Scale 1:1 000 000

For larger scale coverage
of Boston see page 227.

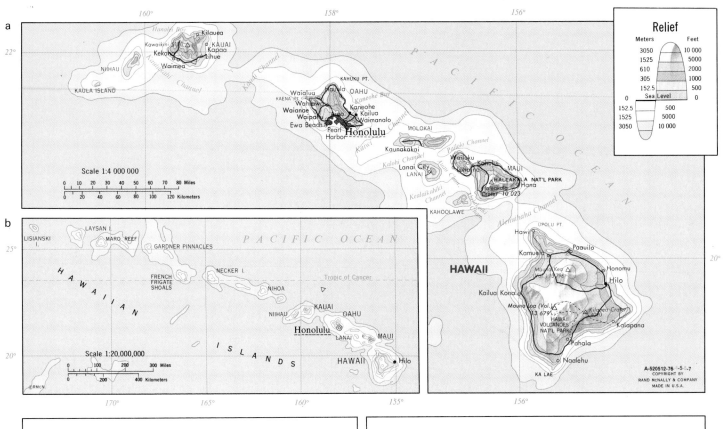

a

Scale 1:4 000 000

Relief		
Meters		Feet
3050		10 000
1525		5000
610		2000
305		1000
152.5		500
0	Sea Level	0
152.5		500
1525		5000
3050		10 000

b

Scale 1:20,000,000

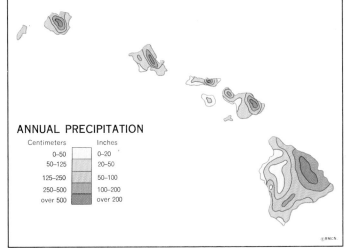

ANNUAL PRECIPITATION

Centimeters	Inches
0–50	0–20
50–125	20–50
125–250	50–100
250–500	100–200
over 500	over 200

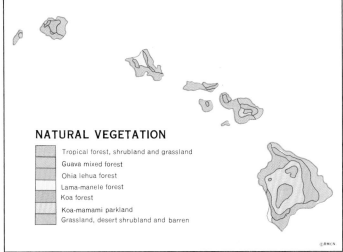

NATURAL VEGETATION

- Tropical forest, shrubland and grassland
- Guava mixed forest
- Ohia lehua forest
- Lama-manele forest
- Koa forest
- Koa-mamami parkland
- Grassland, desert shrubland and barren

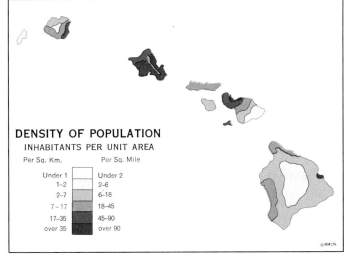

DENSITY OF POPULATION

INHABITANTS PER UNIT AREA

Per Sq. Km.	Per Sq. Mile
Under 1	Under 2
1–2	2–6
2–7	6–18
7–17	18–45
17–35	45–90
over 35	over 90

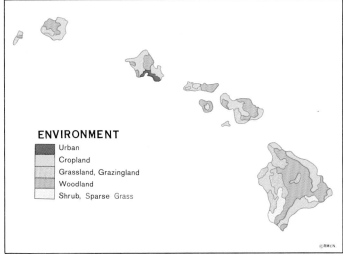

ENVIRONMENT

- Urban
- Cropland
- Grassland, Grazingland
- Woodland
- Shrub, Sparse Grass

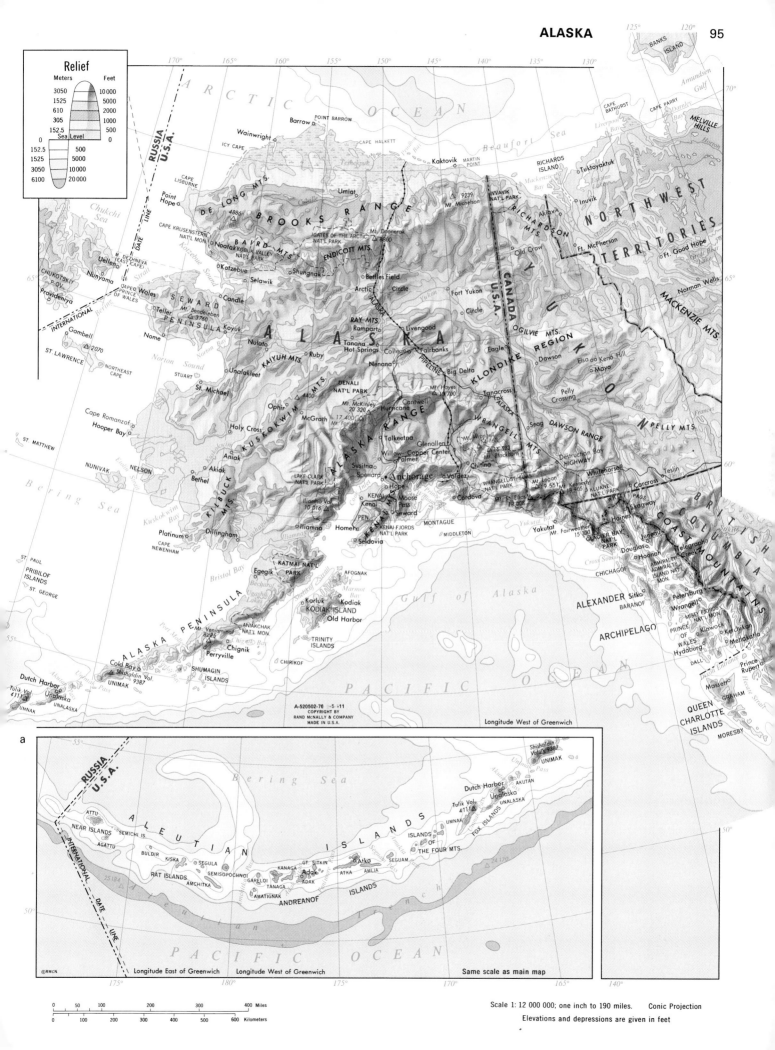

Relief

Meters	Feet
3050	10 000
1525	5000
610	2000
305	1000
152.5	500
0	Sea Level	0
152.5	500
1525	5000
3050	10 000
6100	20 000

A-520502-76 5 11
COPYRIGHT BY
RAND McNALLY & COMPANY
MADE IN U.S.A.

Longitude West of Greenwich

a

Longitude East of Greenwich   Longitude West of Greenwich   Same scale as main map

0 50 100 200 300 400 Miles
0 100 200 300 400 500 600 Kilometers

Scale 1: 12 000 000; one inch to 190 miles.   Conic Projection

Elevations and depressions are given in feet

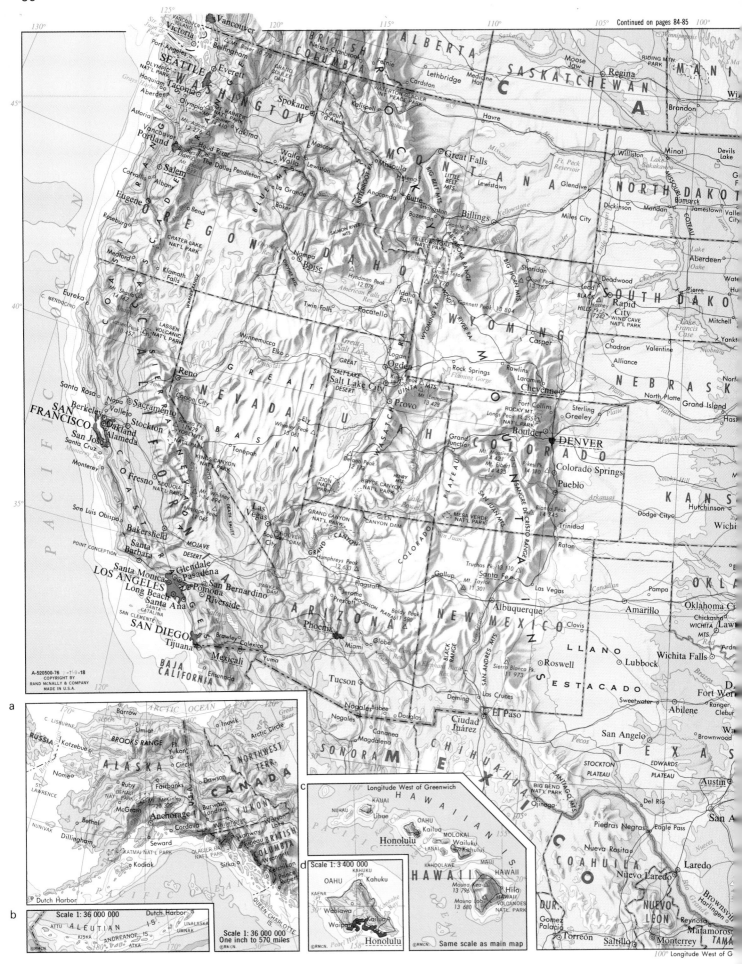

96

Continued on pages 84-85

Scale 1:12 000 000; one inch to 190 miles. Polyconic Pr
Elevations and depressions are given in feet

100° Longitude West of G

Scale 1:36 000 000
One inch to 570 miles

Scale 1:3 400 000

Same scale as main map

A-520500-76   -7-9-18
COPYRIGHT BY
RAND MCNALLY & COMPANY
MADE IN U.S.A.

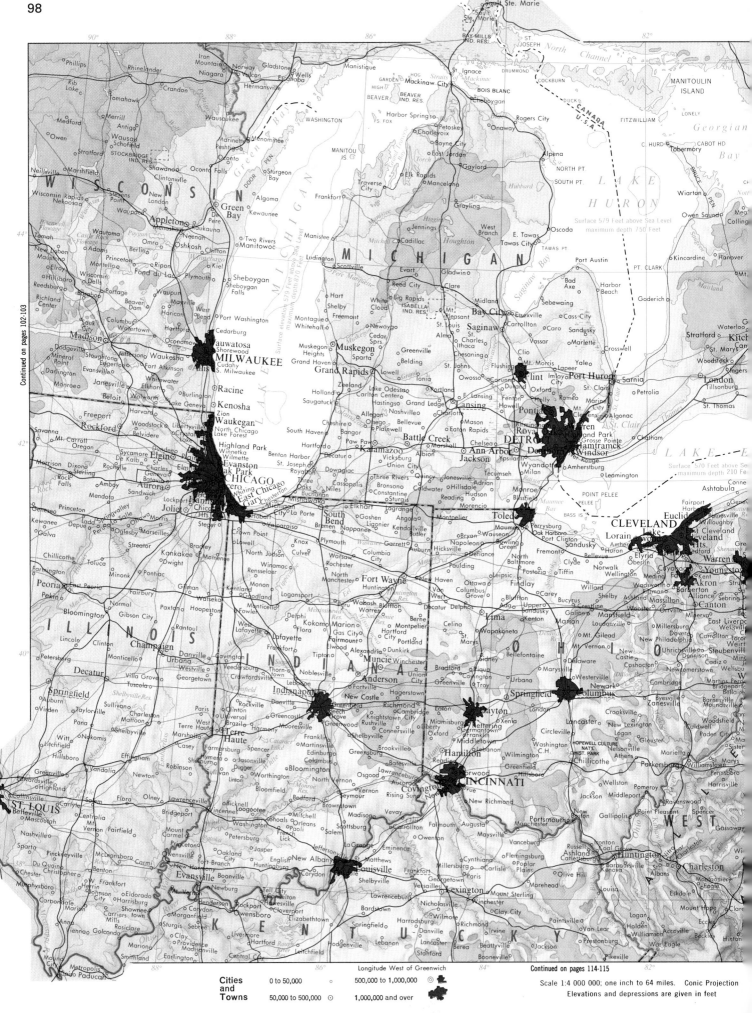

Continued on pages 102-103

Continued on pages 114-115

**Cities
and
Towns**

0 to 50,000   ○   500,000 to 1,000,000   ◎

50,000 to 500,000   ⊙   1,000,000 and over

Longitude West of Greenwich

Scale 1:4 000 000; one inch to 64 miles. Conic Projection

Elevations and depressions are given in feet

Continued on pages 90-91

Relief

Meters		Feet
1525		5000
610		2000
305		1000
152.5		500
0	Sea Level	0
152.5		500
1525		5000
3050		10 000

A-520596-76
COPYRIGHT BY
RAND McNALLY & COMPANY
MADE IN U.S.A.

0 20 40 60 80 100 120 Miles
0 20 40 60 80 100 120 160 180 200 Kilometers

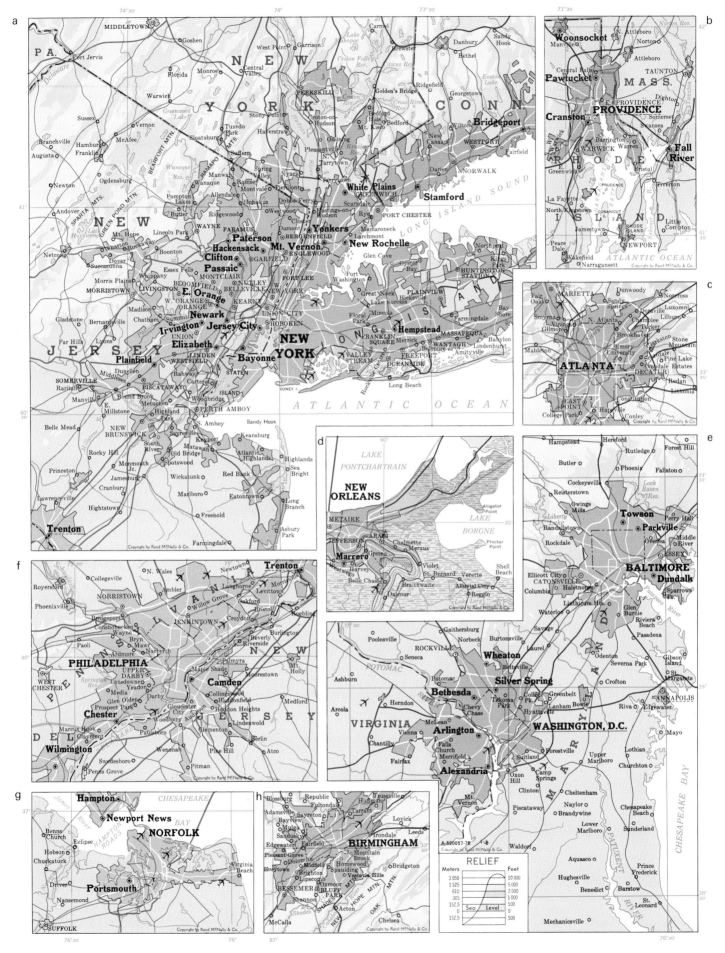

Scale 1:1 000 000; One inch to 16 miles.
Elevations and depressions are given in feet.

For larger scale coverage of New York, Baltimore,
Washington, D.C. and Philadelphia see pages 228 and 229.

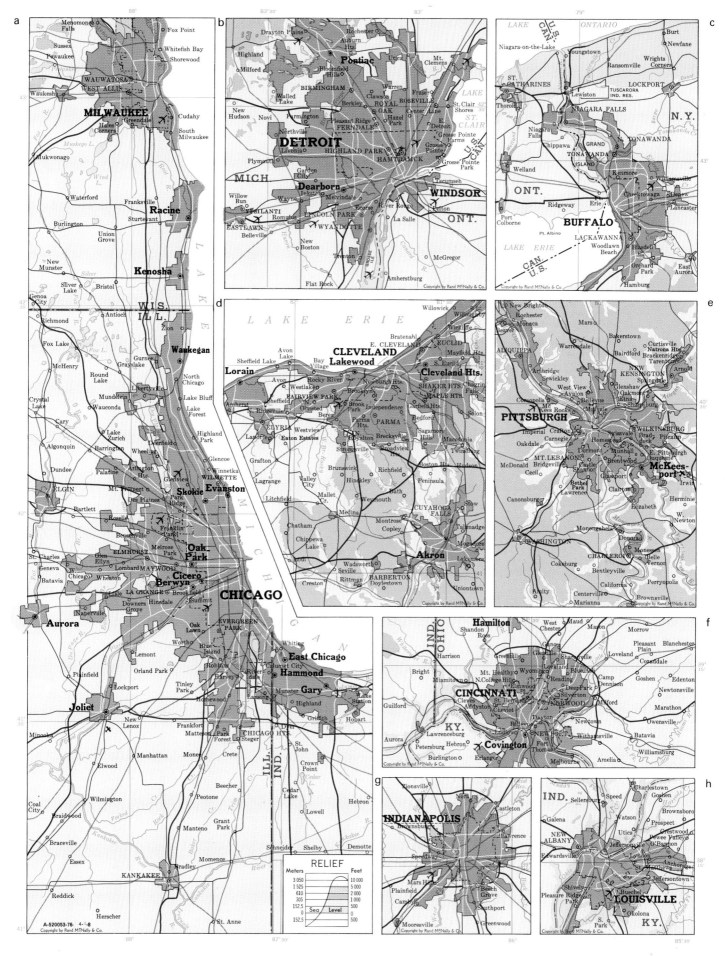

a — Milwaukee / Racine / Kenosha area

Menomonee Falls, Sussex, Pewaukee, Whitefish Bay, Shorewood, Fox Point, Waukesha, WAUWATOSA, WEST ALLIS, MILWAUKEE, Greendale, Hales Corners, Cudahy, South Milwaukee, Mukwonago, Waterford, Franksville, Racine, Sturtevant, Burlington, Union Grove, New Munster, Silver Lake, Bristol, Kenosha, Genoa City, WIS., ILL.

b — Detroit area

Drayton Plains, Highland, Milford, Pontiac, Auburn Hts., Rochester, Utica, Mt. Clemens, Bloomfield Hills, BIRMINGHAM, Warren, Fraser, ROSEVILLE, St. Clair Shores, New Hudson, Walled Lake, Berkley, Clawson, ROYAL OAK, Center Line, E. Detroit, LAKE ST. CLAIR, Novi, Farmington, Pleasant Ridge, Hazel Park, Grosse Pointe Farms, Northville, FERNDALE, HIGHLAND PARK, HAMTRAMCK, Grosse Pointe, Grosse Pointe Park, Plymouth, Garden City, Livonia, DETROIT, Willow Run, Wayne, Inkster, Melvindale, Ecorse, River Rouge, Trecumseh, WINDSOR, YPSILANTI, Romulus, LINCOLN PARK, La Salle, Fighton, ONT., EASTLAWN, Belleville, WYANDOTTE, New Boston, Trenton, GROSSE ILE, McGregor, Flat Rock, Amherstburg, MICH.

c — Buffalo / Niagara area

LAKE ONTARIO, U.S. CAN., Niagara-on-the-Lake, Youngstown, Burt, Newfane, ST. CATHARINES, Lewiston, Ransomville, Wrights Corners, LOCKPORT, Thorold, NIAGARA FALLS, TUSCARORA IND. RES., N.Y., Niagara Falls, Chippawa, GRAND ISLAND, TONAWANDA, Welland, ONT., Kenmore, Williamsville, Ridgeway, Erie, Cheektowaga, Depew, Lancaster, Port Colborne, Pt. Albino, BUFFALO, LACKAWANNA, Woodlawn Beach, Blasdell, Orchard Park, East Aurora, LAKE ERIE, CAN. U.S., Hamburg

d — Chicago area

Antioch, Richmond, Zion, Fox Lake, Waukegan, McHenry, Gurnee, Grayslake, North Chicago, Round Lake, Libertyville, Lake Bluff, Crystal Lake, Wauconda, Mundelein, Lake Forest, Cary, Lake Zurich, Deerfield, Highland Park, Algonquin, Barrington, Wheeling, Glencoe, Dundee, Palatine, Arlington Hts., Winnetka, WILMETTE, ELGIN, Mt. Prospect, Glenview, Evanston, Bartlett, Des Plaines, Park Ridge, Skokie, Roselle, Franklin Park, Bensenville, St. Charles, ELMHURST, Melrose Park, Oak Park, Geneva, W. Chicago, Wheaton, Lombard, MAYWOOD, Cicero, Berwyn, Batavia, Glen Ellyn, Lisle, LA GRANGE, Brookfield, Summit, CHICAGO, Naperville, Downers Grove, Hinsdale, Aurora, Oak Lawn, EVERGREEN PARK, Plainfield, Lemont, Worth, Blue Island, Whiting, Lockport, Orland Park, Robbins, Riverdale, Calumet City, East Chicago, Harvey, Munster, Hammond, Gary, Joliet, Homewood, Lansing, Highland, Lake Station, New Lenox, Frankfort, Dyer, Griffith, Hobart, Minooka, Matteson, Park Forest, Steger, CHICAGO HTS., St. John, Crown Point, Manhattan, Mokena, Crete, Cedar Lake, Hebron, Elwood, Peotone, Lowell, ILL. IND., Wilmington, Beecher, Grant Park, Schneider, Demotte, Coal City, Braidwood, Manteno, Momence, Braceville, Essex, Bradley, KANKAKEE, Reddick, Herscher, St. Anne, LAKE MICHIGAN

RELIEF

Meters	Feet
3 050	10 000
1 525	5 000
610	2 000
305	1 000
152.5	500
0	Sea Level 0
152.5	500

d (Cleveland inset) — Cleveland / Akron area

LAKE ERIE, Willowick, Willoughby, Avon Lake, Bratenahl, E. CLEVELAND, EUCLID, Wickliffe, Sheffield Lake, CLEVELAND, Lakewood, Maynard Hts., S. Euclid, Lorain, Bay Village, Rocky River, Newburgh Hts., Cleveland Hts., Chagrin Falls, Avon, Westlake, Brooklyn, SHAKER HTS., FAIRVIEW PARK, Berea, Independence, Garfield Hts., MAPLE HTS., Solon, Amherst, Sheffield, Olmsted, Brook Park, Bedford, N. Ridgeville, ELYRIA, Westview, Royalton, PARMA, Parma Hts., Sagamore Hills, Macedonia, LaPorte, Eaton Estates, Strongsville, Brecksville, Broadview, Twinsburg, Grafton, Brunswick, Richfield, Boston Hts., Hudson, Lagrange, Valley City, Hinckley, Peninsula, Litchfield, Mallet Cr., Weymouth, Bath, Stow, Medina, Montrose, Copley, CUYAHOGA FALLS, Talmadge, Chatham, Chippewa Lake, Seville, Akron, Moglbore, Kent, Lodi, Wadsworth, Creston, Rittman, BARBERTON, Doylestown, Lakemore

e — Pittsburgh area

New Brighton, Rochester, Monaca, Mars, Bakerstown, Curtisville, Natrona Hts., Beaver Falls, Warrendale, Bairdford, Brackenridge, Tarentum, ALIQUIPPA, NEW KENSINGTON, Springdale, Arnold, Ambridge, West View, Glenshaw, Oakmont, Sewickley, Avalon, Belleville, Etna, Shatpsburg, Coraopolis, Mt. Lebanon, Millvale, Imperial, Crafton, PITTSBURGH, WILKINSBURG, Oakdale, Carnegie, Dormont, Swissvale, Brad, Pitcairn, Duck, McDonald, Bridgeville, Homestead, Munhall, E. Pittsburgh, Cecil, Castle Shannon, Brentwood, Glassport, McKeesport, Irwin, Canonsburg, Bethel Park, Clairton, Herminie, Lawrence, Elizabeth, W. Newton, Washington, Monongahela, Donora, Monessen, Belle Vernon, CHARLEROI, Cokeburg, Bentleyville, Perryopolis, Amity, California, Centerville, Brownsville, Marianna, Uniontown

f — Cincinnati area

IND., OHIO, Hamilton, Shandon, Ross, West Chester, Maud, Mason, Morrow, Harrison, Greenhills, Glendale, Sharonville, Pleasant Plain, Blanchester, Bright, Miamitown, Mt. Healthy, Wyoming, Lockland, Blue Ash, Loveland, Cozaddale, Guilford, Cleves, N. College Hill, Reading, Camp Dennison, Goshen, Edenton, St. Bernard, Silverton, Deep Park, Newtonsville, Aurora, Addyston, CINCINNATI, NORWOOD, Milford, Marathon, Cheviot, Dayton, Newtown, Owensville, Lawrenceburg, Bellevue, NEWPORT, Withamsville, Batavia, KY., Petersburg, Hebron, Ludlow, Covington, Fort Thomas, Williamsburg, Burlington, Erlanger, Melbourne, Amelia

g — Indianapolis area

Zionsville, Nora, Castleton, Brownsburg, INDIANAPOLIS, Lawrence, Speedway, Mars Hill, Beech Grove, Plainfield, Camby, Southport, Mooresville, Greenwood

h — Louisville area

IND., Charlestown, Sellersburg, Speed, Goshen, Brownsboro, Galena, Watson, Prospect, NEW ALBANY, Utica, Crestwood, O'Bannon, Jeffersonville, Valley Sta., Edwardsville, Lyndon, St. Matthews, Anchorage, Jeffersontown, Shively, Buechel, Pleasure Ridge Park, LOUISVILLE, S. Park, Okolona, KY.

A-520053-76 4-4-8

Copyright by Rand McNally & Co.

| Miles | 0 2 4 6 8 10 12 14 16 18 20 22 24 |
| Kilometers | 0 4 8 12 16 20 24 28 32 36 40 |

Scale 1:1 000 000; One inch to 16 miles.
Elevations and depressions are given in feet.

For larger scale coverage of Cleveland, Buffalo, Pittsburgh, Detroit and Chicago see pages 229-231.

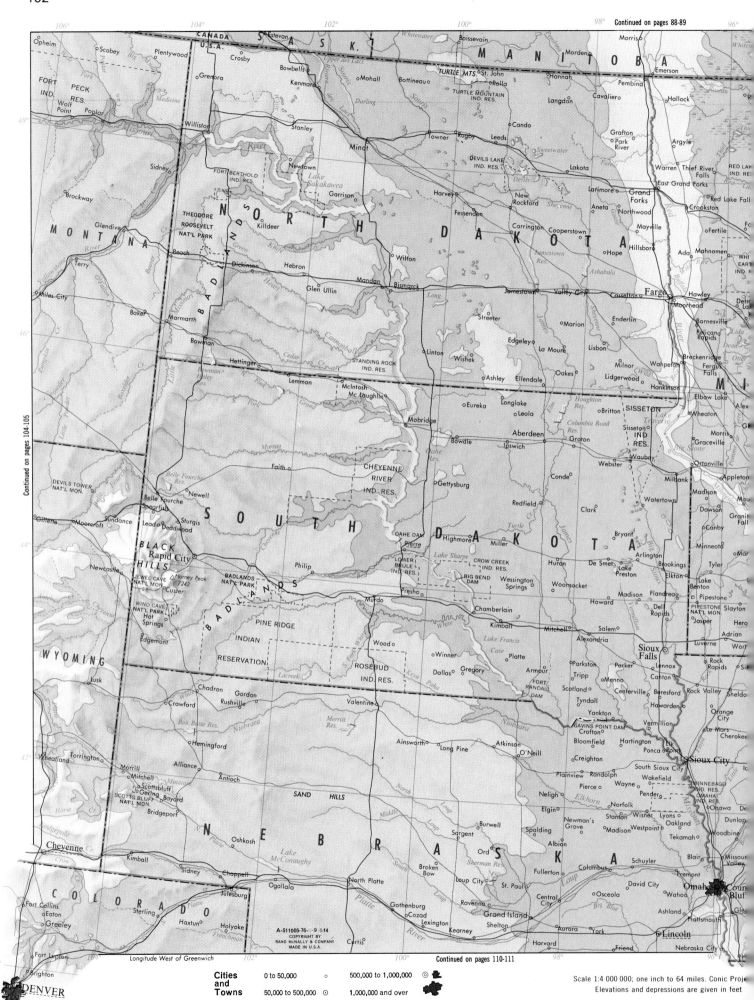

Continued on pages 88-89

Continued on pages 104-105

Continued on pages 110-111

A-511005-76- -9-8-14
COPYRIGHT BY
RAND McNALLY & COMPANY
MADE IN U.S.A.

Longitude West of Greenwich

Cities and Towns

| | 0 to 50,000 | ○ | 500,000 to 1,000,000 | ◎ |
| | 50,000 to 500,000 | ⊙ | 1,000,000 and over | |

Scale 1:4 000 000; one inch to 64 miles. Conic Proj
Elevations and depressions are given in feet

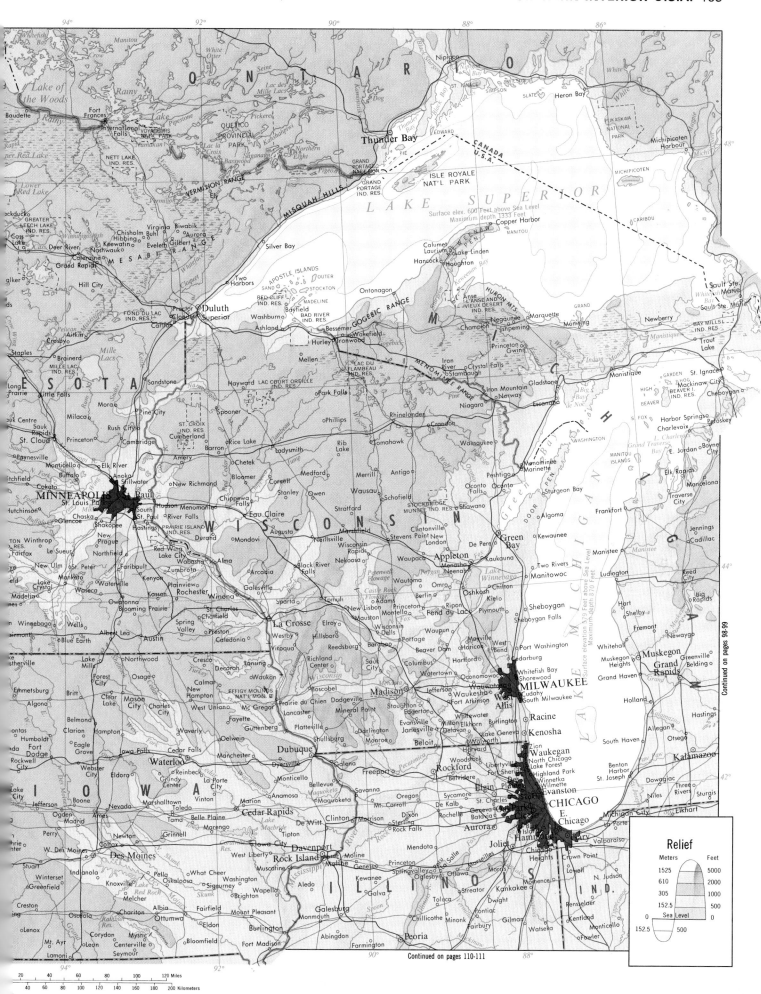

Continued on pages 98-99

Continued on pages 110-111

Relief

Meters	Feet
1525	5000
610	2000
305	1000
152.5	500
0	Sea Level
152.5	500

LAKE SUPERIOR
Surface elev. 600 Feet above Sea Level
Maximum depth 1333 Feet

LAKE MICHIGAN
Surface elevation 579 Feet above Sea Level
Maximum depth 870 Feet

0   20   40   60   80   100   120 Miles
0   20 40 60 80 100 120 140 160 180 200 Kilometers

124° · 120° Continued on pages 86-87 · 118° · 116°

BRITISH COLUMBIA
CANADA
U.S.A.

VANCOUVER ISLAND
Nanaimo · Ladysmith · Strait of Georgia · Steveston
N. Vancouver · Vancouver · New Westminster · Chilliwack
Blaine · Lynden
Duncan · Bellingham · Sedro Woolley · Concrete · Newhalem · Mt. Baker 10,778 · Ross Lake · Oroville · Grand Forks · Rossland · Trail · Northport · Porthill · Bonners Ferry · Lake Koocanusa · Troy
CAPE FLATTERY · MAKAH IND. RES. · Esquimalt · Victoria · San Juan Islands · Anacortes · Mount Vernon · Arlington · Glacier Peak 10,541 · Okanogan · COLVILLE IND. RES. · Colville · Chewelah · KALISPEL IND. RES. · Sandpoint · Libby · CABINET MTS. · Noxon Res.
Port Angeles · Port Townsend · Lake Chelan · Franklin D. Roosevelt Lake · Newport · Lake Pend Oreille
OLYMPIC MTS. · OLYMPIC NATIONAL PARK · TULALIP IND. RES. · Everett · Snohomish · Leavenworth · Chelan · WELLS DAM · GRAND COULEE DAM · Mansfield · SPOKANE DEER IND. RES. PARK · Spirit Lake · Coeur d'Alene
Mt. Olympus 7,965 · SEATTLE · Kirkland · Bellevue · Cashmere · Waterville · Davenport · Spokane · Opportunity · Kellogg · Thompson Falls
QUINAULT IND. RES. · Bremerton · Cascade Tunnel · Ephrata · Medical Lake · Cheney · COEUR D'ALENE IND. RES. · Wallace · Mullan
Moclips · Tacoma · Auburn · Enumclaw · Roslyn · Wenatchee · ROCK ISLAND DAM · Odessa · St. Maries
Shelton · Lakewood Center · Puyallup · Cle Elum · Ellensburg · Moses Lake · Ritzville · Tekoa
Hoquiam · Aberdeen · Montesano · Olympia · Carbonado · WENATCHEE MTS. · Colfax · Palouse
Grays Harbor · Cosmopolis · Elma · Mt. Rainier 14,410 · Yakima · PRIEST RAPIDS DAM · Pullman · Moscow · Elk River
Raymond · Centralia · Chehalis · MOUNT RAINIER NATIONAL PARK · PRIEST RAPIDS LAKE · LOWER MONUMENTAL DAM · Pomeroy · LOWER GRANITE DAM · Dworshak Res.
Willapa Bay · South Bend · Toppenish · Sunnyside · Richland · Pasco · LITTLE GOOSE DAM · Clarkston · Lewiston · NEZ PERCE IND. RES. · Winchester · Nez Perce
Ilwaco · Castle Rock · Mt. Saint Helens 8,307 · Mt. Adams 12,276 · YAKIMA INDIAN RESERVATION · Prosser · Kennewick · ICE HARBOR DAM · Waitsburg · Dayton · Asotin
Columbia · Warrenton · Astoria · Longview · Kelso · Kalama · Prosser · Wallula · Walla Walla · CLEARWATER
Seaside · Rainier · Goldendale · JOHN DAY DAM · MCNARY DAM · Milton-Freewater · MOUNTAINS
CAPE · Saint Helens · Vancouver · Camas · Hood River · The Dalles · Wasco · Pendleton · UMATILLA IND. RES. · Elgin · Grangeville
Tillamook Bay · Hillsboro · Portland · Gresham · BONNEVILLE DAM · THE DALLES DAM · Heppner · Wallowa · CLEARW MOUNTA
Tillamook · Forest Grove · Milwaukie · Lake Oswego · Oregon City · Mt. Hood 11,239 · Condon · La Grande · Enterprise · HELLS CANYON
McMinnville · Newberg · W. Linn · WARM SPRINGS IND. RES. · Union · WALLOWA MTS. · New Meadows
Sheridan · Woodburn · Silverton · Baker · Oxbow Res.
Dallas · Salem · Mt. Jefferson 10,497 · Lake Simtustus · Brownlee Res.
Newport · Independence · Albany · Lebanon · Lake Billy Chinook · John Day · Weiser
Toledo · Corvallis · Green Peter Lake · Prineville · Bend · Prineville Res. · Payette · Ontario
Eugene · Springfield · Diamond Peak 8,744 · Crooked R. · OREGON · Vale · Emmett
Reedsport · Cottage Grove · Hills Creek Lake · GREAT SANDY DESERT · Beulah Res. · Caldwell · Boise
North Bend · Coos Bay · CRATER LAKE NATIONAL PARK · Mt. Scott 8,926 · HARNEY BASIN · Burns · Nampa
Coos Bay · Coquille · Roseburg · Mt. McLoughlin 9,495 · Lake Abert · Harney Lake · Malheur Lake · Lake Owyhee · OWYHEE MTS. · Mountain Home
Bandon · Myrtle Point · Lake Sumner · Jordan Cr. · Glenns Ferry
CAPE BLANCO · Grants Pass · CASCADE · STEENS MTN. · C. J. Strike Res.
Medford · Ashland · OREGON CAVES NAT'L MON. · Klamath Falls · KLAMATH MTS. · Lakeview · WARNER MTS. · FORT MCDERMITT IND. RES. · DUCK VALLEY IND. RES.
Brookings · Upper Klamath Lake · LAVA BEDS NAT'L MON. · Lower Klamath Lake · Clear Lake · Goose Lake · Upper Lake · Paradise Valley · INDEPENDENCE MTS.
Crescent City · Happy Camp · Yreka · Weed · Mt. Shasta 14,162 · Altura · SUMMIT LAKE IND. RES. · PINE FOREST RA. · Midas · Tuscarora
HOOPA VALLEY IND. RES. · Dunsmuir · Eagle Peak 9,892 · Lower Lake · BLACK ROCK DESERT · SANTA ROSA RA.
Arcata · Fieldbrook · CALIFORNIA · NEVADA · Humboldt
Eureka · Fortuna · Scotia · Weaverville · Redding · LASSEN VOLCANIC NATIONAL PARK · Eagle Lake · Winnemucca · Elko
Ferndale · CAPE MENDOCINO · Anderson · Lassen Peak (Vol.) 10,457 · SMOKE CREEK DESERT · Battle Mountain · Rye Patch Res.

PACIFIC OCEAN

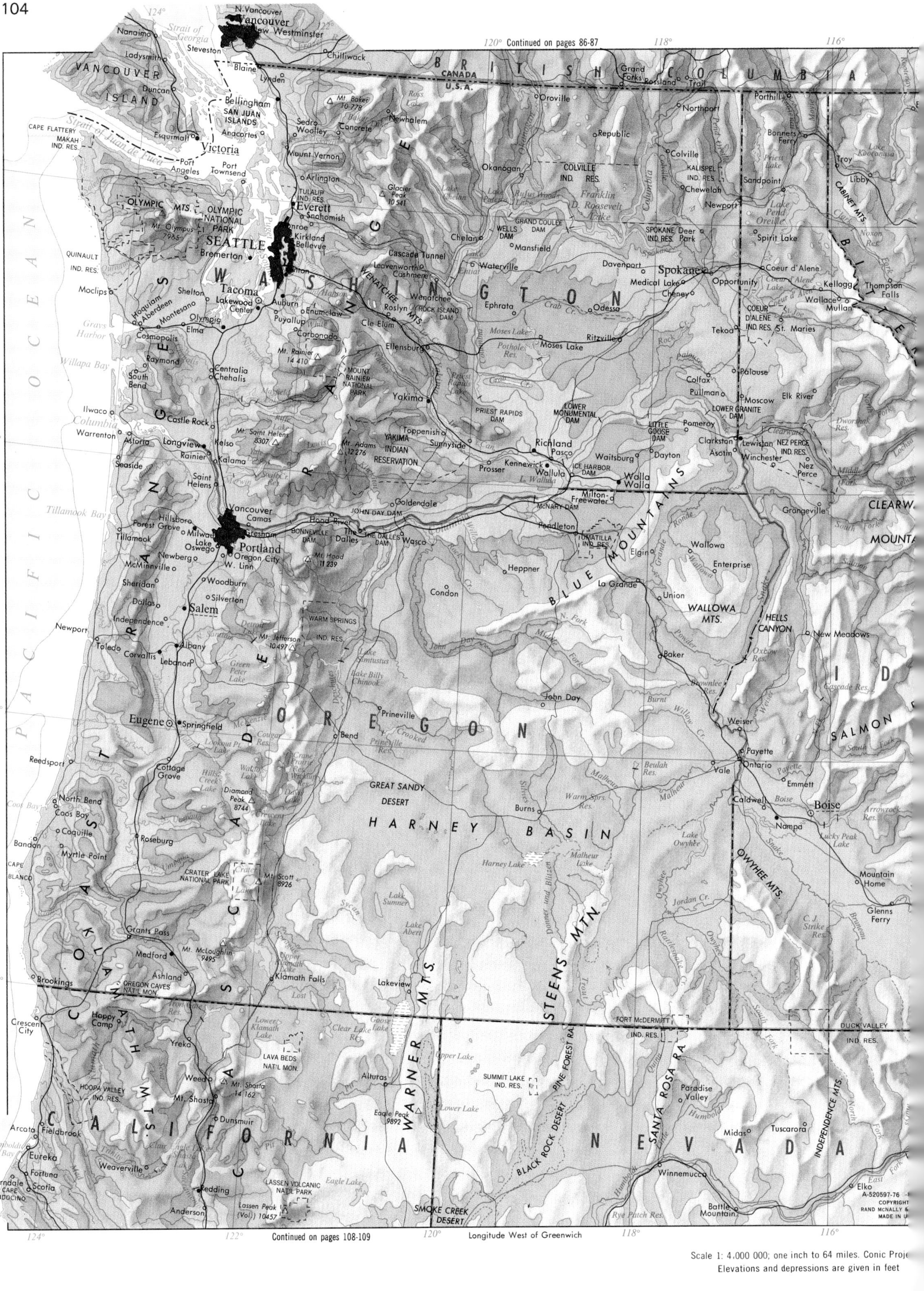

Continued on pages 108-109 · Longitude West of Greenwich

A-520597-76 COPYRIGHT RAND MCNALLY & MADE IN U

Scale 1: 4,000,000; one inch to 64 miles. Conic Proje
Elevations and depressions are given in feet

Continued on pages 88-89

114°   112°   110°   108°   106°

ALBERTA   CANADA   U.S.A.   **SASKATCHEWAN**

WATERTON-GLACIER INTERNATIONAL PEACE PARK

Plentywood

Morgan   Opheim   Scobey   Grenora

Hogeland

Sunburst   Milk   Willow   Cr.   Chinook   Harlem   FORT PECK IND. RES.

BLACKFEET IND. RES.   Cut Bank   Shelby   Havre   Malta   Glasgow   Wolf Point   Poplar   Williston

Browning   Fresna Res.   FT. BELKNAP IND. RES.   Ft. Peck   Missouri   N. DAK.

Valier   Conrad   ROCKY BOYS IND. RES.   Sidney

Choteau   Fort Benton   Fort Peck Lake   Brockway   Glendive   Beach

SWAN RANGE   Missouri   Winifred

NATIONAL BISON RANGE   Ronan   Belt   Lewistown   Winnett   Terry   Baker   Marmarth

Missoula   Lolo   Great Falls   LITTLE BELT MTS.   Neihart   **M O N T A N A**   Miles City

Stevensville   Helena   White Sulphur Spgs.   Harlowton   Roundup   Forsyth

Hamilton   East Helena   Townsend   Colstrip

Philipsburg   Deer Lodge   CRAZY MTS.   Huntley   Billings   Hardin   Lame Deer

Anaconda   Walkerville   Three Forks   Big Timber   LITTLE BIGHORN BATTLEFIELD NAT'L MON.   NORTHERN CHEYENNE IND. RES.

Butte   Bozeman   Livingston   Columbus   Laurel   Crow Agency   CROW IND. RES.

BIG HOLE NAT'L BATTLEFIELD   PIONEER MTS.   Red Lodge   Granite Peak 12,799   Bear Creek

Homer Youngs Peak 10,621   Twin Bridges   Electric Peak 10,992   Gardiner   Sheridan   DEVILS TOWER NAT'L MON.

Dillon   Mammoth Hot Springs   Mt. Washburn 10,243   Lovell   Buffalo   Sundance

Salmon   LEMHI RANGE   BEAVERHEAD MTS.   **YELLOWSTONE NATIONAL PARK**   Powell   BIGHORN MOUNTAINS   Gillette   Moorcroft

LOST RIVER RA.   7733 ft. above sea level   Cody   Greybull   Basin   Cloud Peak 13,167

Borah Pk. 12,662   St. Anthony   Ashton   Ten Sleep   Kaycee

Mackay   Rexburg   GRAND TETON NAT'L PARK   Worland   Geba

Hyndman Peak 12,009   Arco   Rigby   Grand Teton 13,770   Thermopolis   WIND RIVER IND. RES.   Midwest

CRATERS OF THE MOON NAT'L MON.   Idaho Falls   Gannett Peak 13,804   Shoshoni   Powder River   Glenrock

SNAKE RIVER PLAIN   Shelley   Fremont Peak 13,745   Riverton   Casper   Douglas   Orin

Blackfoot   FORT HALL   Lander

American Falls   Pocatello   **W Y O M I N G**

Rupert   Soda Springs   GREAT DIVIDE BASIN   Wheatland

Burley   Lava Hot Sprs.   Meade Peak 9957   Afton   Sweetwater   Seminoe Res.   Hanna

Oakley   Montpelier   GREAT DIVIDE BASIN   Rawlins

Malad City   Superior   Wheatland No. 2

Lewiston   Preston   Kemmerer   Granger   Green River   Rock Springs

Richmond   Smithfield   Logan   Providence   Wellsville   FLAMING GORGE RES.   PARK RANGE

Garland   Brigham

Lucin   Huntsville   Evanston   Craig

GREAT SALT LAKE DESERT   Ogden   Morgan   Farmington   Steamboat Spgs.

Wendover   Bountiful   UINTA MTS.   Kings Peak 13,528   DINOSAUR NAT'L MON.   COLO.

Salt Lake City   Mt. Emmons 13,440   Vernal   Oak Creek

Murray   Park City   UINTAH AND OURAY IND. RES.

Tooele   Midvale   Heber City   **U T A H**

110°

Continued on pages 108-109

Continued on pages 102-103

Relief

Meters		Feet
3050		10000
1525		5000
610		2000
305		1000
152.5		500
Sea Level		0
1525		500

Miles
20 40 60 80 100 120
20 40 60 80 100 120 140 160 180 200 Kilometers

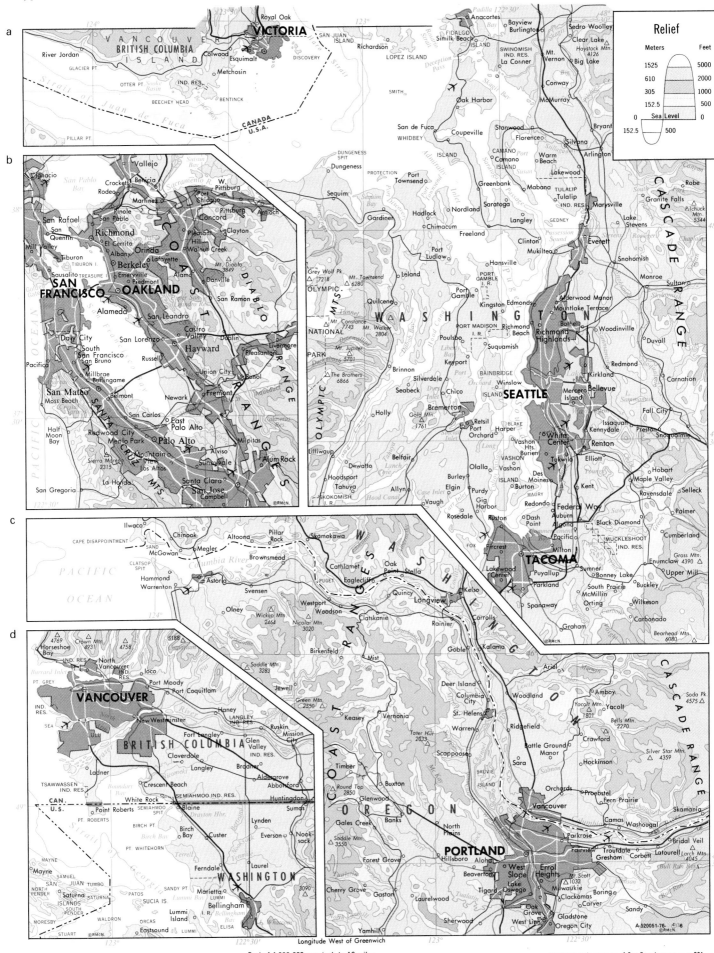

Scale 1:1 000 000; one inch to 16 miles.
Elevations and depressions are given in feet.

For larger scale coverage of San Francisco see page 231.

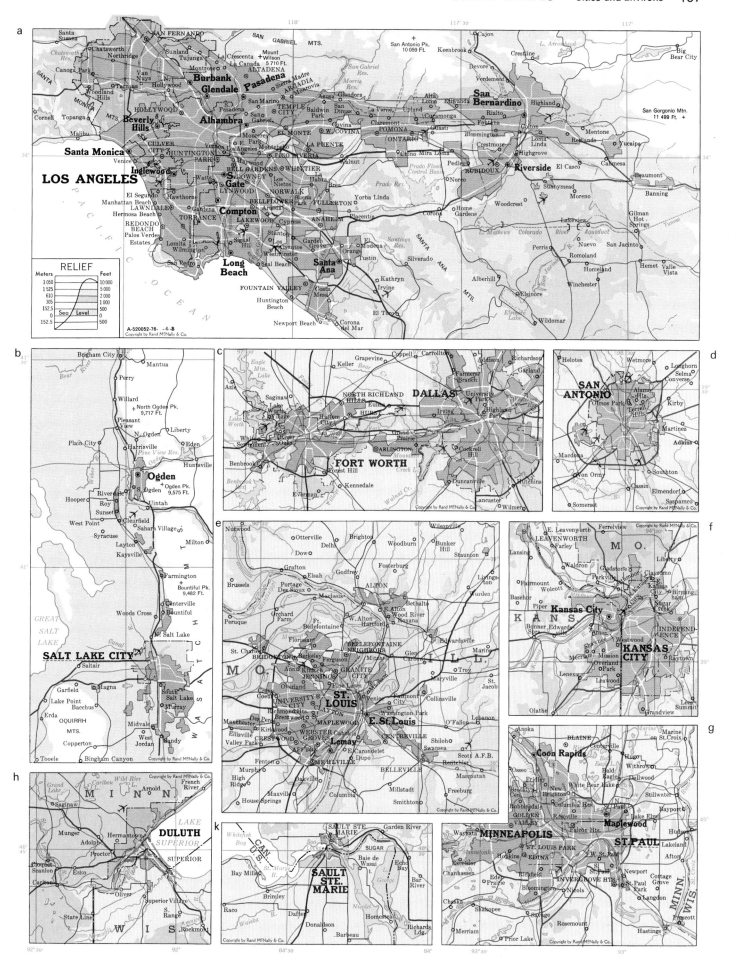

Scale 1:1 000 000; One inch to 16 miles.
Elevations and depressions are given in feet.

For larger scale coverage
of Los Angeles see page 232.

Continued on pages 104-105

Scale 1:4 000 000; one inch to 64 miles. Conic Projection
Elevations and depressions are given in feet

Longitude West of Greenwich

SAN DIEGO

Scale 1:1 000 000

A-520599-76 -8 6-18
COPYRIGHT BY
RAND McNALLY & COMPANY
MADE IN U.S.A.

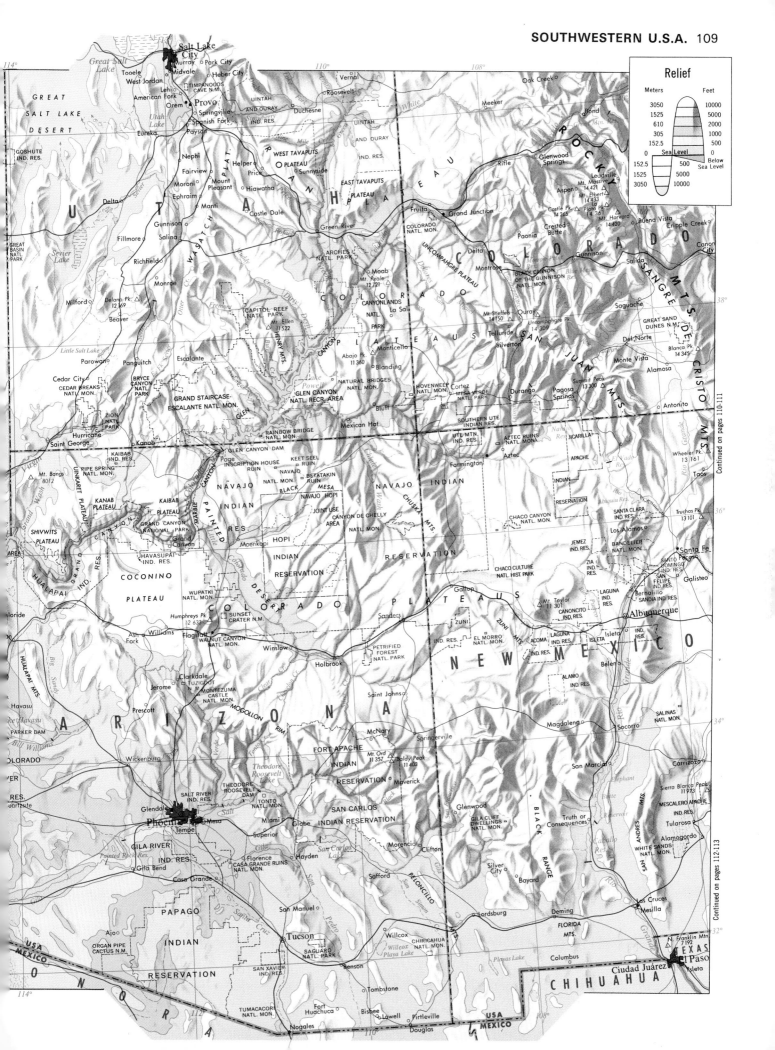

Relief

Meters		Feet
3050		10000
1525		5000
610		2000
305		1000
152.5		500
	Sea Level	0
152.5		500 Below
		Sea Level
1525		5000
3050		10000

Continued on pages 110-111

Continued on pages 112-113

110

Continued on pages 102-103

Continued on pages 108-109

Continued on pages 112-113

Longitude West of Greenwich

Scale 1:4 000 000; one inch to 64 miles. Conic Project
Elevations and depressions are given in feet.

Relief

Meters	Feet
3050	10 000
1525	5000
610	2000
305	1000
152.5	500
0 Sea Level	0

Cities and Towns

0 to 50,000 ○
50,000 to 500,000 ⊙
500,000 to 1,000,000 ◉
1,000,000 and over

A-511006-76- -7- -11
COPYRIGHT BY
RAND MCNALLY & COMPANY
MADE IN U.S.A.

Continued on pages 102-103

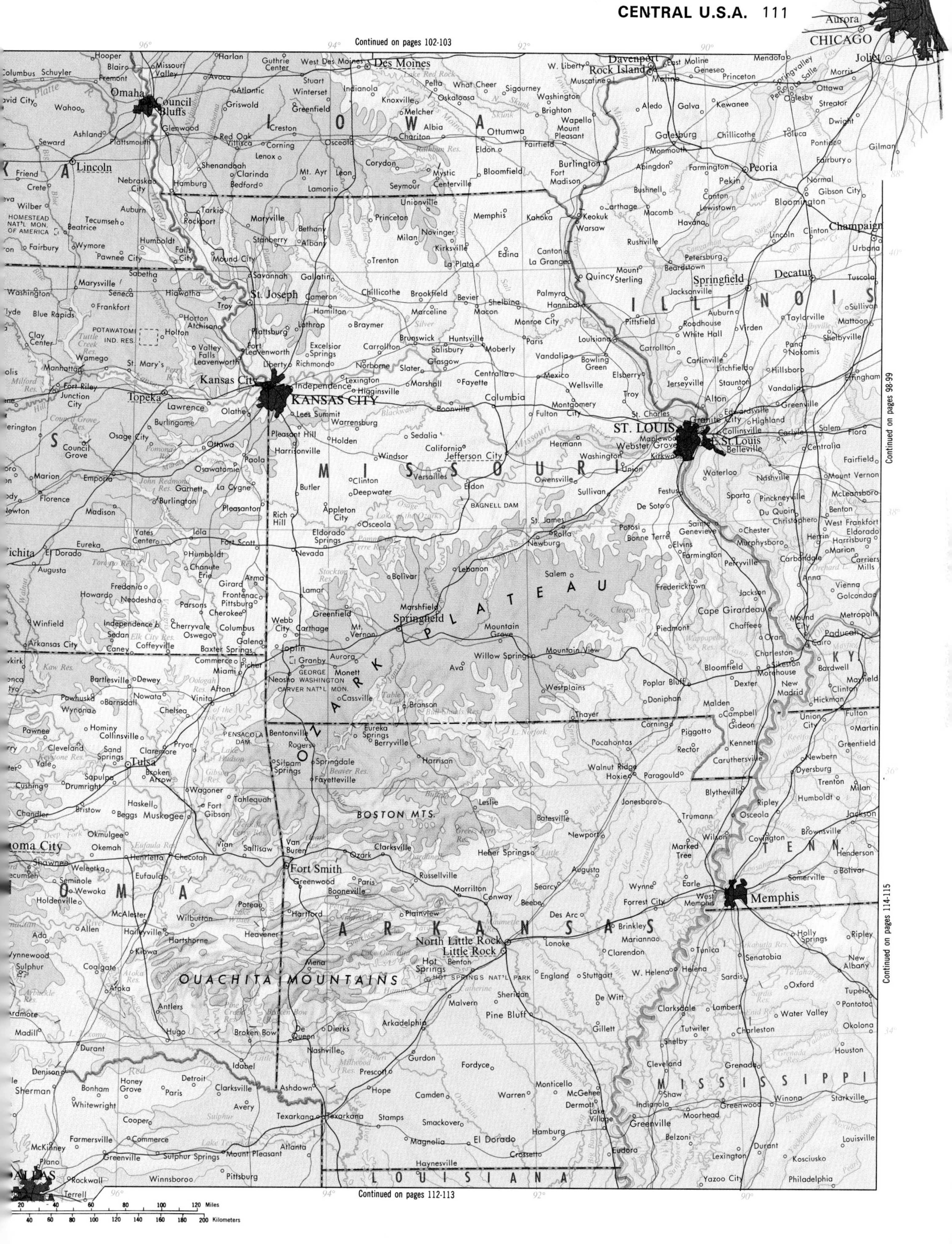

Aurora
CHICAGO
Joliet

I O W A
ILLINOIS
MISSOURI
O K L A H O M A
A R K A N S A S
TENN
MISSISSIPPI
LOUISIANA
KANSAS

Omaha
Council Bluffs
Lincoln
Des Moines
W. Des Moines
Davenport
Rock Island
East Moline
Moline

St. Joseph
Kansas City
KANSAS CITY
Topeka
Lawrence

ST. LOUIS
St. Louis

Springfield
Decatur
Champaign

Peoria
Bloomington

Tulsa
Fort Smith
Muskogee

OZARK PLATEAU
BOSTON MTS.
OUACHITA MOUNTAINS
OZARK

North Little Rock
Little Rock
Hot Springs
HOT SPRINGS NAT'L PARK

Memphis
West Memphis

Pine Bluff
Texarkana
El Dorado

Dallas

GEORGE WASHINGTON
CARVER NAT'L MON.

BAGNELL DAM
PENSACOLA DAM

Continued on pages 98-99

Continued on pages 114-115

Continued on pages 112-113

20   40   60   80   100   120 Miles
40   60   80   100   120   160   180   200 Kilometers

96°   94°   92°   90°

112

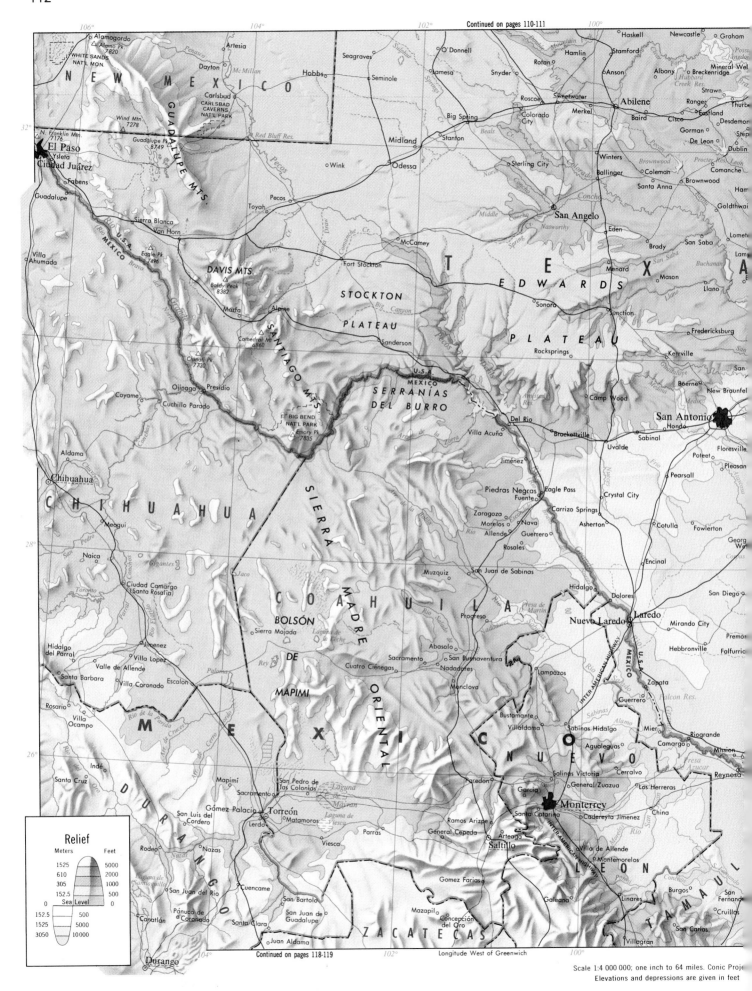

Continued on pages 110-111

NEW MEXICO

Alamogordo
△ Alamo Pk.
7820

WHITE SANDS
NAT'L MON.

Artesia
Dayton
McMillan

Seagraves
O'Donnell
Haskell
Newcastle
Graham

Carlsbad
Hobbs
Lamesa
Snyder
Rotan
Hamlin
Stamford
Mineral Wel

Wind Mtn.
7278
CARLSBAD
CAVERNS
NAT'L PARK
Seminole
Roscoe
Sweetwater
Anson
Albany
Breckenridge

N. Franklin Mtn.
7176
Red Bluff Res.
Big Spring
Colorado
City
Abilene
Baird
Ranger
Eastland
Thurbe
Cisco

El Paso
Guadalupe Pk.
8749
Midland
Stanton
Merkel
Gorman
Desdemon
Step

Ysleta
Ciudad Juárez
Odessa
Sterling City
De Leon
Dublin

Fabens
Wink
Ballinger
Coleman
Comanche

Guadalupe
Santa Anna
Brownwood
Ham

Villa
Ahumada
Pecos
Toyah
San Angelo
Eden
Goldthwai

Sierra Blanca
Van Horn
McCamey
Sonora
Brady
San Saba
Lomet
Lam

Eagle Pk.
7496
DAVIS MTS.
Baldy Peak
8382
Fort Stockton
STOCKTON
EDWARDS
Menard
Mason
Llano

Marfa
Alpine
PLATEAU
Sanderson
PLATEAU
Junction
Fredericksburg

Cathedral Mt.
6860
Rocksprings
Kerrville

Chinati Pk.
7730
Ojinaga
Presidio
SERRANÍAS
DEL BURRO
Camp Wood
Boerne
New Braunfel

Coyame
Cuchillo Parado
BIG BEND
NAT'L PARK
Emory Pk.
7835
Del Rio
Villa Acuña
Brackettville
San Antonio

CHIHUAHUA
Aldama
Jiménez
Uvalde
Hondo
Floresville
Poteet
Pleasan
Sabinal

Chihuahua
SIERRA
Piedras Negras
Fuente
Eagle Pass
Crystal City
Pearsall

Meoqui
Zaragoza
Morelos
Nava
Asherton
Cotulla
Fowlerton
Georg
We

Naica
Gigantes
Jaco
MADRE
Allende
Guerrero
Rosales
Encinal
Corpus

COAHUILA
Muzquiz
San Juan de Sabinas
Hidalgo
San Diego

Ciudad Camargo
(Santa Rosalia)
ORIENTAL
Presa de
Martin
Dolores
Nuevo Laredo
Laredo
Mirando City
Premor

BOLSÓN
Sierra Mojada
Laguna de
la Leche
Progreso
DURANGO
Hidalgo
del Parral
Jiménez
Villa Lopez
Valle de Allende
Abasolo
San Buenaventura
Nadadores
Lampazos
Hebbronville
Falfurri

Santa Barbara
Villa Coronado
Escalón
Sacramento
Cuatro Ciénegas
Monclova
Bustamante
Sabinas Hidalgo
Zapata
Falcon Res.

Rosario
Villa
Ocampo
DE
Rey
Villaldama
Aguaeguas
Mier
Camargo
Riograncie

MEXICO
MAPIMI
NUEVO
Paredon
Salinas Victoria
General Zuazua
Cerralvo
Los Herreras
Reynes
Mission

Indé
Mapimí
San Pedro de
las Colonias
Laguna de
Mayran
Garcia
China
Cadereyta Jimenez

Santa Cruz
Sacramento
Gómez Palacio
Torreón
Laguna de
Viesca
Ramos Arizpe
Monterrey
LEON

Rodeo
Nazas
Lerdo
Matamoros
Parras
Santa Catarina
Arteaga
Villa de Allende
Montemorelos

San Luis del
Cordero
Viesca
General Cepeda
Saltillo
Galeana

San Juan del Rio
Cuencame
San Bartolo
Gomez Farias
Linares
Burgos
San Fernando

Canatlán
Pánuco de
Coronado
San Juan de
Guadalupe
Mazapil
Concepción
del Oro
TAMAUL
San Carlos

Durango
Santa Clara
Juan Aldama
ZACATECAS
Villagrán
Cruillas

Continued on pages 118-119
Longitude West of Greenwich

Relief

Meters		Feet
1525		5000
610		2000
305		1000
152.5		500
0	Sea Level	0
152.5		500
1525		5000
3050		10 000

Scale 1:4 000 000; one inch to 64 miles. Conic Proje
Elevations and depressions are given in feet

Continued on pages 110-111

Continued on pages 114-115

Scale 1:1 000 000

Cities and Towns	0 to 50,000 ○	500,000 to 1,000,000 ◉
	50,000 to 500,000 ⊙	1,000,000 and over

A-511007-76- 5L-5-7
COPYRIGHT BY
RAND McNALLY & COMPANY
MADE IN U.S.A.

114

Continued on pages 98-99

Continued on pages 110-111

Continued on pages 112-113

A-520598-76   -7-7-13
COPYRIGHT BY
RAND McNALLY & COMPANY
MADE IN U.S.A.

Longitude West of Greenwich

Scale 1:4 000 000; one inch to 64 miles. Conic Pro
Elevations and depressions are given in fee

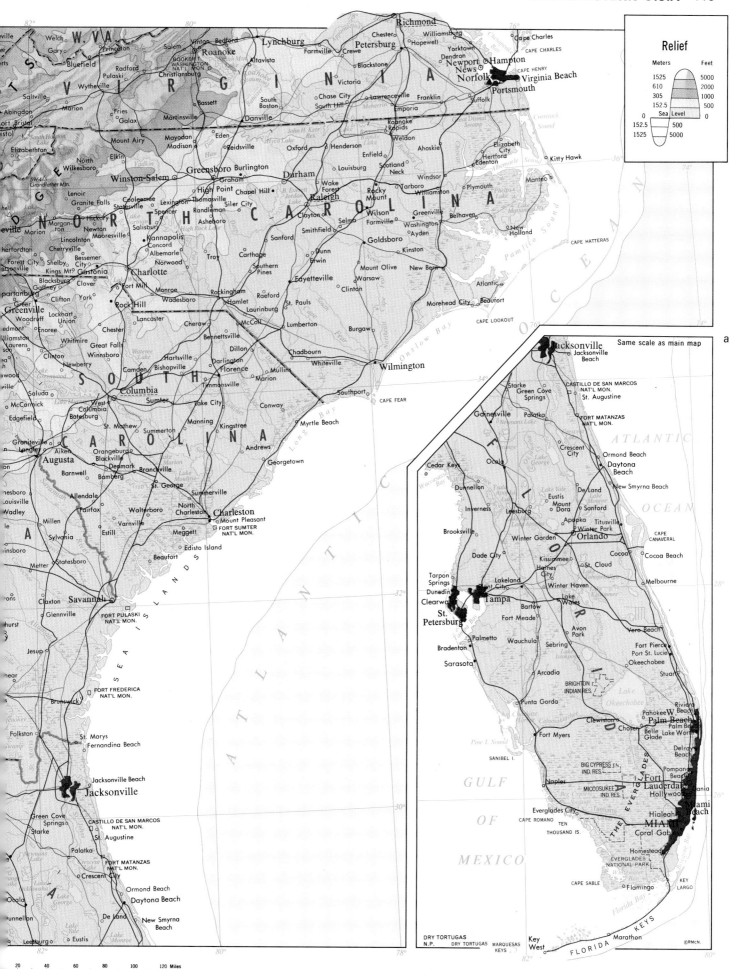

Scale 1:16 000 000; one inch to 250 miles. Polyconic Proj
Elevations and depressions are given in feet

a

Scale 1:1 000 000

PANAMA

A-530000-76-9 8-26
COPYRIGHT BY
RAND McNALLY & COMPANY
MADE IN U.S.A.

b

ATLANTIC OCEAN

Arecibo • • San Juan
• Aguadilla PTA. HIGUERO • Bayamón   CABEZAS DE   ST. THOMAS   TORTOLA (Br.)
Utuado   SAN JUAN   (U.S.A.)   Charlotte
PUERTO RICO   Fajardo   CULEBRA   Amalie   ST. JOHN
Mayagüez (U.S.A.) Caguas   Vieques   (U.S.A.)
Coamo   • Cayey Humacao   VIEQUES
CABO ROJO   Ponce   • Guayama
Salinas
CARIBBEAN   SEA   Christiansted

SAINT CROIX
(U.S.A.)

Scale 1:4 000 000
0   10   20   30   40 Miles
0 10 20 30 40 50 60 Kilometers
©RMcN.

c

OUTER BRASS   LITTLE
HANS LOLLICK
INNER BRASS   PICARA PT   HANS LOLLICK   GRASS
STORMY PT   THATCH CAY   CAY
ST △ THOMAS
Crown Mt.   (U.S.A.)
1558   • Charlotte Amalie
WATER   (St. Thomas)
FLAMINGO PT   St. Thomas   Nadir
©RMcN.   Harbor   Scale 1:500 000

Continued on pages 130-131

Relief
Meters   Feet
3050   10 000
1525   5000
610   2000
305   1000
152.5   500
0   Sea Level   0
152.5   500
1525   5000
3050   10 000
6100   20 000

Cities
and
Towns

0 to 50,000   ○   500,000 to 1,000,000   ◎
50,000 to 500,000   ⊙   1,000,000 and over

Continued on pages 112-113

24°

S I N A L O A

D U R A N G O

Sierra de Nayarit

N A Y A R I T

22°

Laguna
de Agua Brava

PUNTA
DE MITA

Bahía de
Banderas

CABO
CORRIENTES

SIERRA DE VALLEJO

SA. DEL CUALE

J A L I S C O

O C C I D E N T A L

20°

PTA. FARALLÓN

Bahía de
Manzanillo

C O L I M A

P A C I F I C

PUNTA TEJUPAN

18°

SIERRA DE COALCOMÁN

M I C H O A C Á N

O C E A N

16°

San Dimas
Durango
El Salto
Nombre de Dios
Mezquital
Miguel Auza
Juan Aldama
Nieves
Río Grande
Sombrerete
Chalchihuites
Sain Alto
Cañitas

Pánuco
Siqueros
Concordia
Rosario
Escuinapa
Villa Unión
Pueblo
Nuevo
El Salto
Santa María
de Ocotán
C. Pimal
11 700
Fresnillo
Calera
Víctor Rosales
Morelos
Troncoso
Gruñidora

Z A C A T E C A S

A L T I P L A N I C I E

S A N   L U I S

Vanegas
Cedral
Catorce
La Paz
Matehuala
Ascensión
Aramberri
Hidalgo
Zaragoza
Doctor Arroyo
Miquihuana
Peña Nevada
13 300

N U E V O
L E O N

Ciudad Victoria

T A M A U L I P

Jaumave
Llera
Ocampo
Magiscatzin
Ciudad Mante
Xicotencatl

Huajicori
Acaponeta
Tecuala
San Felipe
Rosamorada
Ruiz
Tuxpan
San Blas
Jalisco
Tepic
Pachotitán
Compostela
Sta. María del Oro
San Pedro
Lagunillas
Jala
Jomulco
Ahuacatlán
Amatlán de Cañas
Ixtlán
del Río
Etzatlán

Valparaíso
Huejuquilla el Alto
Ciudad
García
Zacatecas
Mezquitic
Huejúcar
Villanueva
Sta. María de
los Angeles
Rincón de Romoso
Colotlán
Monte
Escobedo

Ojocaliente
Luis Moya
Salinas
11 000
Asientos
Tepezalá
Villa García

Charcas
Venado
Ramos
Moctezuma

A G U A S C A L I E N T E S

M E X I C A N A

Calvillo
Aguascalientes

Tabasco
(Tlaltenango)
Sanchez Román
Bolaños
Chimaltitán
Jiménez del Téul
García de la Cadena
Moyahua
Nochistlán
Juchipila
Villa
Hidalgo
Encarnación
de Díaz
Teocaltiche
San Juan
de los Lagos
Lagos de
Moreno

San Luis
Potosí
Gogorrón
Pozos
Zaragoza
Ciudad Fernández
Ojo Caliente
Sta. María del Río
Villa de
Reyes
San Felipe
San Diego
de la Unión
San Luis
de la Paz

Soledad Díez Gutiérrez
Cerritos
Guadalcázar
Peotillos
Bocas

Ciudad del Maíz
Pastora
Alaquines
Cárdenas

P O T O S I

El Ebano
Tamuín
Ciudad de Valles

Rioverde
Rayón
General Pedro
Antonio Santos
Lagunillas
Arroyo Seco
Xilitla
San Martín Chalch
Tamazunchale
Huejutl
Huai
Jacala
Chapulhuacán

San Juan
Capistrano

Teocaltiche
Jalostotitlán
Yahualica
Cuquío
San Miguel
el Alto
Tepatitlán de Morelos
Unión de
San Antonio
Arandas
Atotonilco el Alto
San Miguel
el Alto
León
La Luz
Guanajuato
Silao
Romita
San José
Iturbide

Q U E R É T A R O

10 469
Tolimán
Cadereyta
Colón
Zimapán
Tasquillo
Zacualtipán
Metztitlán

Puerto Vallarta
Mascota
Talpa de Allende
San Martín
Hidalgo
Cocula
Ayutla
Zacoalco
de Torres
Juchitlán
Tecolotlán
Teocuitatlán
de Corona
Atoyac
Sayula
Tamazula
de Gordiano

Tequila
Ameca
Tala
Zapopan
Guadalajara
Tlaquepaque
Tonalá
Zapotlanejo
Ocotlán
Tlajomulco
de Zúñiga
Chapala
Jocotepec
Jamay
La Barca
Degollado
Yurécuaro

G U A N A J U A T O

Ciudad Manuel
Doblado
San Francisco
del Rincón
Cuerámaro
Pénjamo
La Piedad
Cabadas
Salamanca
Irapuato
Juventino
Rosas
Cortazar
Celaya
Valle de
Santiago
Jaral del Progreso
Salvatierra
Apaseo
Tarimoro

Querétaro
Cayetano Rubio
San Juan
del Río
Amealco
El Oro

H I D A L G O

Huichapan
Mixquiahuala
Actopan
Tula
Tulancingo
Pachuca
Tepeji
del Río

Union
de Tula
El Grullo
Autlán
Purificación
Venustiano
Carranza
Ciudad Guzmán
Zapotiltic
Tuxpan
Tecalitlán
Ixtlahuacán
Jiquilpan
de Juárez
Zamora
Chavinda
Tangancícuaro
Purépero
Chilchota
Zacapú
Cherán
Los Reyes
Paricutín
Uruapan
Villa Escalante
Pátzcuaro

Tingüindín
Cotija
de la Paz

Nevado de Colima
13 911
V. de Colima
12 620
Comala
Villa de Alvarez
Minatitlán
Colima
Tecomán
Cuyutlán
Manzanillo

Coalcomán de Matamoros
Aguililla
Apatzingán
de la Constitución
Tancítaro
Cerro de Tancítaro
9186
12 660

Coeneo
de la Libertad
Quiroga
Morelia
Angangueo
Ciudad
Hidalgo
Zinapécuaro
Maravatío
Contepec
Acámbaro
Tlalpujahua

Zitácuaro
Villa Victoria
Temascalcingo
Atlacomulco
Ixtlahuaca

México
City
Toluca

D I S T R I T O
F E D E R A L

M O R E L O S

Cuernavaca

G U E R R E R O

S I E R R A   M A D R E

Longitude West of Greenwich

Cities
and
Towns

0 to 50,000
50,000 to 500,000
500,000 to 1,000,000
1,000,000 and over

Scale 1:4 000 000; one inch to 64 miles. Conic Proje
Elevations and depressions are given in feet

Relief

Meters	Feet
3050	10 000
1525	5000
610	2000
305	1000
152.5	500
0	Sea Level	0
152.5	500
1525	5000
3050	10 000

A-531695-76
COPYRIGHT BY
RAND McNALLY & COMPANY
MADE IN U.S.A.

a

Morelos
Tecamac
Otumba
Apan
HIDALGO
Teotihuacán
Acolman
Cuautitlán
Chiconautla
Pyramids of Teotihuacán
Nicolás Romero
Tutitlán
Tepexpan
Cahuacán
Coacalco
Tepetlaoxtoc
Calpulalpan
TLAXCALA
San Bartolo
Atizapán
Tulpetlac
San Jerónimo
Nanacamilpa
Ixtlahuaca
Tlalnepantla
M É X I C O
Texcoco
Jiquipilco
Mazatla
Lago de
Coatlinchán
Cerro La Catedral 13 000
Atzcapotzalco
Gustavo A. Madero
Texcoco (Dry Lake)
Temoaya
Naucalpan de Juárez
Chicoloapan
Mimiapan
Chimalpa
MEXICO CITY
Los Reyes
Nezahualcóyotl
Cuajimalpa
Ixtacalco
Huixquilucan
Ixtapalapa
Ayotla INTER-AMERICAN
Ixtapaluca
Río Frío
Río Lerma
Lerma
Villa Obregón
Coyoacán
Tláhuac
HY.
Toluca
Contreras
Tláhuac
Texmelucan
Tlalpan
Xochimilco
San Andrés
Capultitlán
Chalco
PUEBLA
Metepec
Mexicalcingo
Ajusco
Topilejo
Tecómitl
Tlalmanalco
Almoloya
Cerro Muneca 12 655
Milpa Alta
Iztaccihuatl 17 343
Coatepec
Cerro Ajusco 12 850
Tenango
Oxtotepec
Nevado de Toluca 14 409
Amecameca
Tenango
DISTRITO FEDERAL
Tres Cumbres
Volcán Popocatépetl 17 887
Huitzilac
Ozumba
19°
Scale 1:1 000 000
Tepoztlán
Tlalnepantla
MORELOS
0 4 8 12 16 Kilometers
0   5   10 Miles
Tlayacapan
©RMcN
Cuernavaca

Sisal
YUCATÁN
Hunucmá
Maxcanú
Halachó
Calkini o Dzitbalché
Hecelchakán

GULF OF MEXICO

Lerma
Campeche
Seybaplaya
Champotón
Pustunich
Sabancuy
CAMPECHE
Chicbul
Mamantel

B A H Í A   D E   C A M P E C H E

ISLA DEL CARMEN
Laguna de Términos
San Pedro
Ciudad del Carmen
PUNTA FONTERA
Frontera
Paraíso
Allende
Palizada
Coatzacoalcos (Puerto México)
Comalcalco
Jálpa
Cunduacán
Cárdenas
TABASCO
Villahermosa
Huimanguillo
San Carlos
Balancán
Tacotalpa
Teapa
Emiliano Zapata
Palenque
Tenosique

For larger scale coverage
of Mexico City see page 233.

120

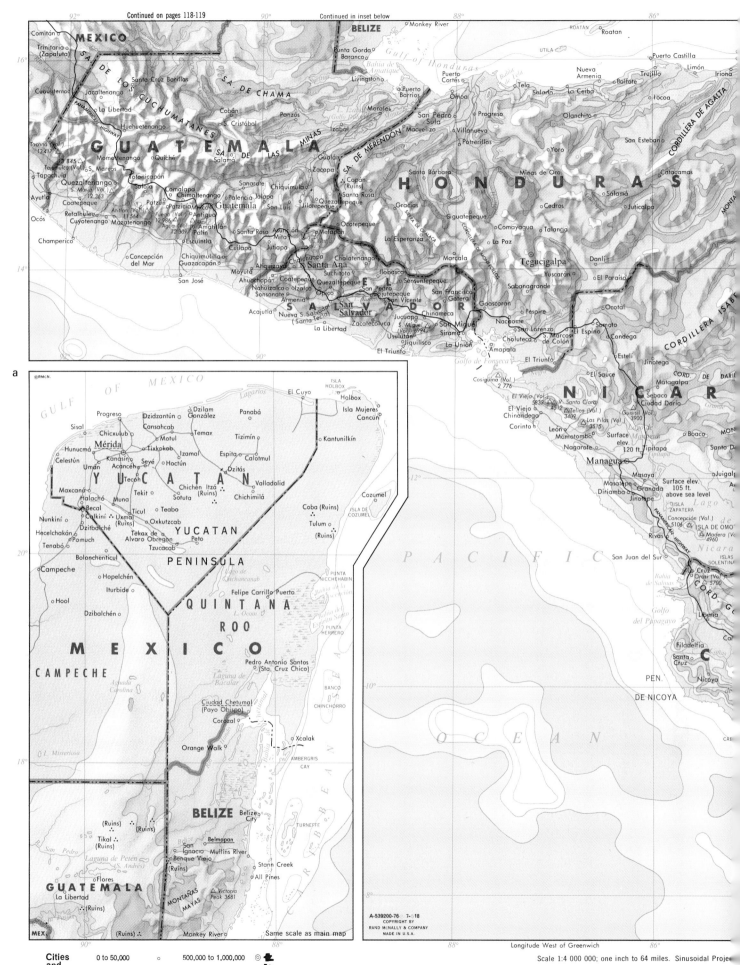

Continued on pages 118-119
Continued in inset below

MEXICO

BELIZE

Monkey River

ROATAN

Roatan

UTILA

Puerto Castilla

Limón

Iriona

Comitán
Trinitaria
(Zapaluta)

Cuauhtémoc

Jacaltenango

La Libertad

Santa Cruz Barillas

SA. DE LOS CUCHUMATANES

SA. DE CHAMA

Punta Gorda
Barranco

Bahía de
Amatique

Gulf of Honduras

Bahía de
Tela

Nueva
Armenia

Balfate

Trujillo

Tocoa

Huehuetenango

Cobán

S. Cristóbal

Panzós

Livingston

Puerto
Barrios

Puerto
Cortés

Omoa

Tela

Salado

La Ceiba

Tacaná (Vol.)
13,417

845

Tapachula

S. Marcos

Momostenango

Quiché

SA. DE LAS MINAS

Salamá

Izabal

Morales

San Pedro
Sula

Macuelizo

Villanueva

Santa Bárbara

Progreso

Olanchito

San Esteban

CORDILLERA DE AGALTA

Tajumulco (Vol.)
13,814

Quezaltenango

Totonicapán

Comalapa

Chimaltenango

Salama

Sanarate

Chiquimula

Zacapa

SA. DE MERENDÓN

Copán
(Ruins)

Potrerillos

Yoro

HONDURAS

Catacamas

Salamá

Ayutla

Coatepeque

S. María (Vol.)
12,363

Sololá

Patzún

Palencia

Jalapa

San Luis

Quezaltepeque

Santa Rosa

Gracias

Siguatepeque

Cedros

Juticalpa

Ocós

Retalhuleu

Cuyotenango

Mazatenango

Atitlán (Vol.)
11,564

Fuego (Vol.)
12,986

Antigua

Patzicía

Guatemala

San Luis

Jilotepeque

Ocotepeque

SIERRA DE OPALACA

La Esperanza

CORDILLERA DE MONTECILLOS

Comayagua

Talanga

Champerico

Concepción
del Mar

Agua (Vol.)
12,309

Palín

Escuintla

Santa Rosa

Mita

Asunción

Metapán

La Paz

Marcala

Tegucigalpa

Danlí

El Paraíso

Chiquimulilla
Guazacapán

Cuilapa

Jutiapa

Chalchuapa

Chalatenango

Yuscarán

Sabanagrande

El Paraíso

Atiquizaya

Santa Ana

Suchitoto

Ilobasco

Sensuntepeque

Goascorán

Pespire

Ocotal

CORDILLERA ISABE

Moyuta

Ahuachapán

Coatepeque

Quezaltepeque

San Pedro

San Francisco
Gotera

Nacaome

San Lorenzo

Somoto

Condega

Nahuizalco

Olzalco

EL

San Vicente

Usulután

San Miguel
(Vol.) 6994

Siramá

San Marcos
de Colón

El Espino

Estelí

Acajutla

Nueva S. Salvador
(Santa Tecla)

San
Salvador

SALVADOR

Jucuapa

Chinameca

Choluteca

El Triunfo

Jinotega

La Libertad

Zacatecoluca

La Unión

Amapala

Golfo de Fonseca

Jiquilisco

El Triunfo

Cosigüina (Vol.)
2 776

El Sauce

CORD. DE DARIE

Sébaco

Ciudad Darío

Matagalpa

NICAR

El Viejo (Vol.)
5839

Santa Clara
4512

Telica (Vol.)
3409

Las Pilas (Vol.)
3515

Güisisil (Vol.)
3900

Boaco

El Viejo

Chinandega

Corinto

León

Momotombo (Vol.)

Surface
elev.
120 ft.

Santo D

Nagarote

Managua

Masaya

Juigalp

Masatepe

Granada

Surface elev.
105 ft.
above sea level

ISLA
ZAPATERA

Concepción (Vol.)
5106

ISLA DE OMO

Diriamba

Jinotepe

Madera (Vol.)
4960

Rivas

Nicara

ISLAS
SOLENTIN

San Juan del Sur

Cruz

Orosí (Vol.)
5700

CORD. GU

Liberia

Car

Filadelfia

Santa
Cruz

C

PEN.

Nicoya

DE NICOYA

CAB

Inset map (a):

a

®RMcN.

GULF OF MEXICO

Lagartos

El Cuyo

ISLA
HOLBOX

Progreso

Dzidzantún

Dzilam
González

Panabá

Holbox

Sisal

Chicxulub

Cansahcab

Temax

Tizimín

Isla Mujeres
Cancún

Hunucmá

Mérida

Kanasín

Motul

Espita

Calotmul

Kantunilkín

Celestún

Uman

Acanceh

Seyé

Hoctún

Izamal

Tixkokob

Dzitás

YUCATÁN

Chichén Itzá
(Ruins)

Valladolid

Chichimilá

Coba (Ruins)

Cozumel

Maxcanú

Tecoh

Tekit

Sotuta

Teabo

ISLA DE
COZUMEL

Halachó

Muna

Ticul

Oxkutzcab

YUCATAN

Nunkiní

Becal

Uxmal
(Ruins)

Tekax de
Alvaro Obregón

Peto

Tulum
(Ruins)

Hecelchakán

Calkiní

Dzitbalché

Pomuch

Tzucacab

PENINSULA

Tenabó

Bolonchenticul

PUNTA
NICCHEHABIN

Campeche

Hopelchén

Iturbide

QUINTANA

Laguna de
Chichancanab

Bahía de la
Ascensión

Dzibalchén

Hool

ROO

L. Ocom

PUNTA
HERRERO

Bahía del
Espíritu Santo

MEXICO

CAMPECHE

Aguada
Carolina

Pedro Antonio Santos
(Sta. Cruz Chico)

BANCO
CHINCHORRO

L. Misterioso

Ciudad Chetumal
(Payo Obispo)

Corozal

Xcalak

Orange Walk

AMBERGRIS
CAY

CARIBBEAN

BELIZE

Belize
City

TURNEFF

(Ruins)

(Ruins)

Belmopan

San
Ignacio

Mullins River

Tikal
(Ruins)

Benque Viejo

Stann Creek

All Pines

GUATEMALA

La Libertad

Laguna de Petén
(S. Andrés)

Flores

MONTAÑAS
MAYAS

Victoria
Peak 3681

(Ruins)

MEX

(Ruins)

Monkey River

Same scale as main map

A-539200-76 7- 18
COPYRIGHT BY
RAND McNALLY & COMPANY
MADE IN U.S.A.

Longitude West of Greenwich

Scale 1:4 000 000; one inch to 64 miles. Sinusoidal Proje

Elevations and depressions are given in feet

Cities and Towns

Symbol	Population
○	0 to 50,000
◉	50,000 to 500,000
◎	500,000 to 1,000,000
●	1,000,000 and over

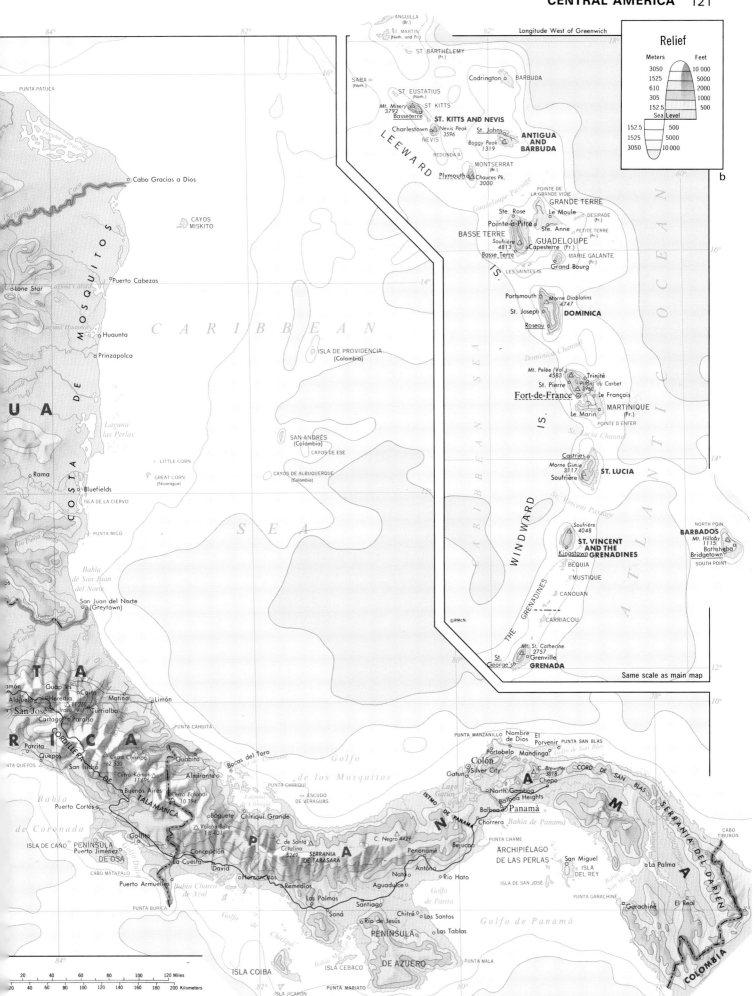

a

Scale 1:1 000 000

HAVANA
(La Habana)

GULF OF MEXICO

Playa de Guanabo
Cojimar
Guanabacoa
Campo Florido
Playa de Santa Fé
Regla
Baracoa
Marianao
San Francisco de Paula
Cotorro
Calabazar
Cuatro Caminos
Arroya Arena
Rancho Boyeros
Managua
Bauta
Santiago de las Vegas
San José de las Lajas
La Sabina
Caimito del Guayabal
Bejucal
Buenaventura
Ceiba del Agua
San Antonio de los Baños
San Antonio de las Vegas
△ 950
©RMcN

S PT.
Governor's Harbour
PALMETTO PT.
ELEUTHERA

Rock Sound

Arthur's Town
NORTHEAST PT.
CAT
LITTLE SAN SALVADOR

Old Bight

A T L A N T I C

HAWKS NEST PT.
COLUMBUS PT.
CAT CAY
SAN SALVADOR
(WATLING)
(Columbus, Oct. 12, 1492)
SOUTHWEST PT.

CONCEPTION

LEE STOCKING
Rolleville
CAPE STA. MARIA
RUM CAY

O C E A N

EAT EXUMA
George Town
LITTLE EXUMA
HOG CAY
LONG
Tropic of Cancer

JUMENTO CAYS
Clarence Town

WATER CAY

FLAMINGO CAY
CAP VERDE
SAMANA OR ATWOOD CAY

of War Channel
JAMAICA CAY
BIRD ROCK
CROOKED

SEAL CAYS
FORTUNE
NORTHEAST PT.
PLANA OR FLAT CAYS

NURSE CAY
DIANA BANK
The Bight of Acklins
FISH CAY
ACKLINS

RACCOON CAY
Abraham's Bay
MAYAGUANA

GREAT RAGGED
SALINA PT.
CASTLE
COLUMBUS BANK
CAY VERDE
MIRA POR VOS ISLETS

Caicos Passage
NORTH CAICOS

PROVIDENCIALES
GRAND CAICOS
CAY STA. DOMINGO
HOGSTY REEF
WEST CAICOS
CAICOS IS.
(Br.)
CAPE COMETE
EAST CAICOS

BROWN BANK
LITTLE INAGUA
CAICOS BANK
SOUTH CAICOS
GRAND TURK
Grand Turk
TURKS IS. (Br.)

NORTHEAST PT.
WEST SAND SPIT
AMBERGRIS CAYS
SALT CAY

PALMETTO PT.
Ocean Bight
SEAL CAYS
Turks I. Passage
Mouchoir Passage

CABO LUCRECIA
Man of War Bay
The Lake
GREAT INAGUA
MOUCHOIR BANK

Banes
Matthew Town
South Bay

Antilla
Bahía de Nipe

olguin
Mayari
Sagua de Tánamo
SILVER BANK

ÍN
Baracoa
CUCHILLAS DE TOA
Silver Bank Passage

SA. DE NIPE
GUANTANAMO
3100
SA. DE PURIAL
Alto Songo

SANTIAGO DE CUBA
San
Caney
Cent. Piedra
401
Guantánamo
PUNTA MAISÍ
NAVIDAD BANK

Santiago de Cuba
Guaimanera
Yateras
Bahía de Orando

Naval Station
(U.S.A.)
ILE DE LA TORTUE
CABO ISABELA
Monte Cristi
Puerto Plata

Bahía de Guantánamo
Canal de la Tortue
CORDILLERA SEPTENTRIONAL
Pico Diego

Port de Paix
Cap-Haitien
7434
Gaspar Hernández
CABO FRANCÉS VIEJO

CAP ST. NICOLAS
Le Borgne
Guayubin
Mao
San Francisco de Macoris
Bahía Escocesa

Le Môle
Limbé
Fort Liberté
Dajabón
Santiago Rodriguez
Nagua

PTE. PLATEFORME
Grande Rivière du Nord
Ouanaminthe
Moca
Salcedo
San
CABO SAMANÁ

Gonaïves
St. Michel de l'Atalaye
Valliere
Hinche
Santiago de los Caballeros
VEGA
Vega
Sánchez
Samaná

GOLFE DES GONAÏVES
Pico Bonhomme
DOMINICAN
Bahía de Samaná
CABO SAN RAFAEL

St. Marc
5883
CORDILLERA
Mte. Miro
7434
Pico Duarte
10417
Jarabacoa
Sabana de la Mar
CORDILLERA ORIENTAL

POINT OUEST
ÎLE DE LA GONÂVE
2546
Mirebalais
Lascahobas
CENTRAL
Cotui
Hato Mayor

HAITI
Port-au-Prince
Mte. Tina
9285
Bonao
Bayaguana
Los Llanos
Seibo

Jérémie
ÎLE GRANDE CAYEMITE
SIERRA DE NEIBA
REPUBLIC
La Romana

CAP DAME MARIE
Anse à Veau
Léogane
Pétionville
Neiba
San Cristóbal
S. Pedro de Macoris
CATALINA

Anse d'Hainault
Miragoâne
Petit Goave
SIERRA DE LA
8774
Azua
Santo Domingo
Higüey

FORMIGAS BANK
CAP DES IROIS
MASSIF DE LA HOTTE
7920
MASSIF DE LA SELLE
CUL DE SAC
SELLE
Baní
SAONA

NAVASSA
(U.S.A.)
Pico de Macaya
Duverge
Enriquillo

Tiburon
Coteaux
Aquin
Jacmel
Belle-Anse
SIERRA DE BAHORUCO
PTA. PALENQUE

nio
Roche à Bateau
Les Cayes
ÎLE A VACHE
HAITI
Enriquillo
H I S P A N I O L A

MORANT PT.
POINTE À GRAVOIS
CABO FALSO
Oviedo

BEATA
CABO BEATA
ALTO VELO

For larger scale coverage of Havana see page 233.

20 30 40 50 60 70 80 90 100 110 120 Miles
40 60 80 100 120 140 160 180 200 Kilometers

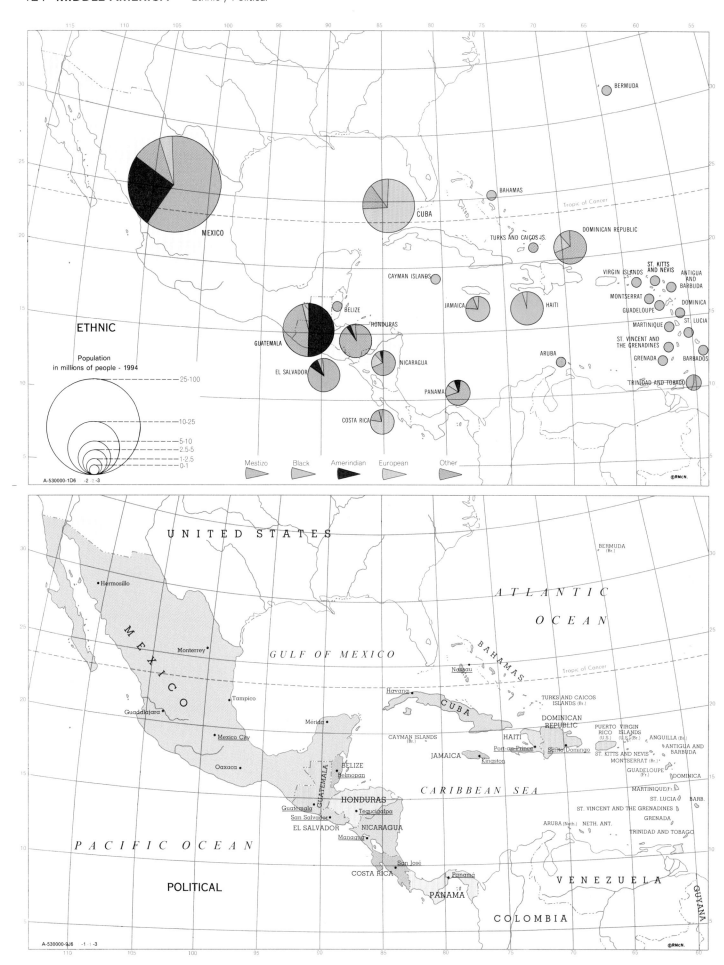

ETHNIC

Population
in millions of people - 1994

25-100

10-25

5-10
2.5-5
1-2.5
0-1

A-530000-1D6   -2 -2 -3

Mestizo   Black   Amerindian   European   Other

MEXICO

BAHAMAS

CUBA

TURKS AND CAICOS IS.

DOMINICAN REPUBLIC

BERMUDA

CAYMAN ISLANDS

JAMAICA

HAITI

VIRGIN ISLANDS

ST. KITTS AND NEVIS

ANTIGUA AND BARBUDA

MONTSERRAT

GUADELOUPE

DOMINICA

MARTINIQUE

ST. LUCIA

ST. VINCENT AND THE GRENADINES

GRENADA

BARBADOS

ARUBA

TRINIDAD AND TOBAGO

BELIZE

HONDURAS

GUATEMALA

EL SALVADOR

NICARAGUA

PANAMA

COSTA RICA

©RMCN

UNITED STATES

BERMUDA (Br.)

ATLANTIC OCEAN

• Hermosillo

M E X I C O

• Monterrey

GULF OF MEXICO

BAHAMAS

Nassau •

Tropic of Cancer

• Tampico

Guadalajara •

Havana •

CUBA

TURKS AND CAICOS ISLANDS (Br.)

DOMINICAN REPUBLIC

PUERTO RICO (U.S.)

VIRGIN ISLANDS (U.S.) (Br.)

ANGUILLA (Br.)

ANTIGUA AND BARBUDA

• Mérida

CAYMAN ISLANDS (Br.)

HAITI

Santo Domingo •

ST. KITTS AND NEVIS

MONTSERRAT (Br.)

• Mexico City

Port-au-Prince •

JAMAICA

Kingston •

GUADELOUPE (Fr.)

DOMINICA

• Oaxaca

CARIBBEAN SEA

MARTINIQUE (Fr.)

BELIZE

ST. LUCIA

GUATEMALA

Belmopan •

BARB.

HONDURAS

ST. VINCENT AND THE GRENADINES

Guatemala •

• Tegucigalpa

ARUBA (Neth.)

GRENADA

San Salvador •

NETH. ANT.

EL SALVADOR

NICARAGUA

TRINIDAD AND TOBAGO

Managua •

PACIFIC OCEAN

San José •

V E N E Z U E L A

COSTA RICA

• Panamá

GUYANA

POLITICAL

PANAMA

C O L O M B I A

A-530000-9J6   -1 -1 -3

©RMCN

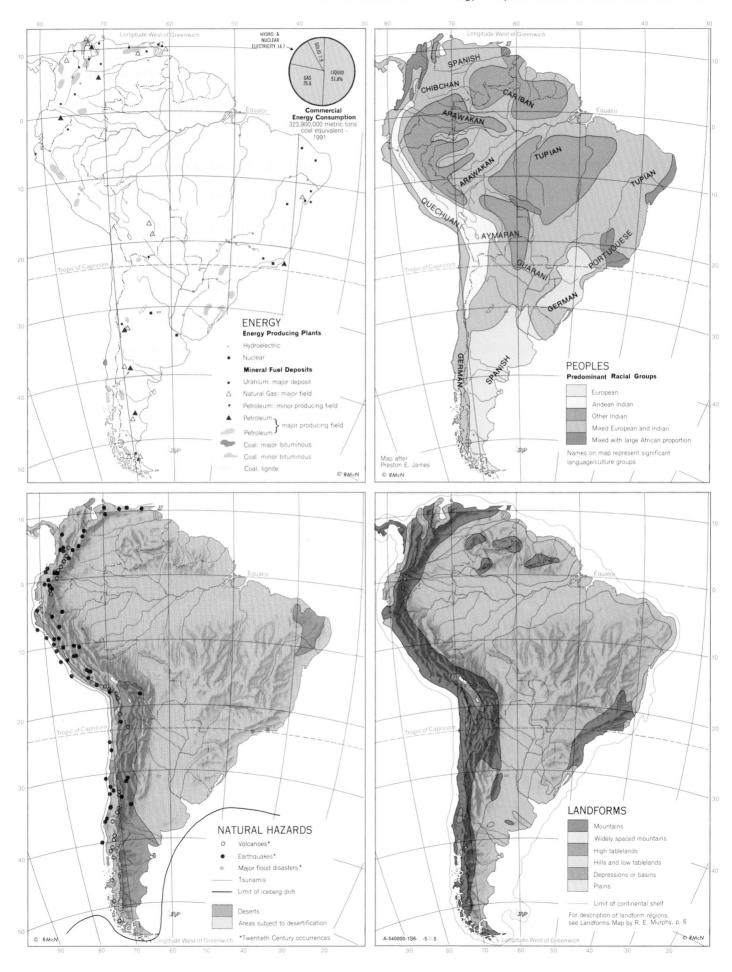

ENERGY

Energy Producing Plants
- · Hydroelectric
- ■ Nuclear

Mineral Fuel Deposits
- □ Uranium: major deposit
- △ Natural Gas: major field
- ▲ Petroleum: minor producing field
- ▲ Petroleum } major producing field
- Petroleum
- Coal: major bituminous
- Coal: minor bituminous
- Coal: lignite

HYDRO. & NUCLEAR ELECTRICITY 14.7
SOLID 7.9
LIQUID 51.8%
GAS 25.6

Commercial Energy Consumption
323,900,000 metric tons coal equivalent - 1991

© RMcN

PEOPLES
Predominant Racial Groups
- European
- Andean Indian
- Other Indian
- Mixed European and Indian
- Mixed with large African proportion

Names on map represent significant language/culture groups

Map after Preston E. James
© RMcN

SPANISH
CHIBCHAN
CARIBAN
ARAWAKAN
QUECHUAN
AYMARAN
ARAWAKAN
TUPIAN
TUPIAN
GUARANÍ
PORTUGUESE
GERMAN
GERMAN
SPANISH

NATURAL HAZARDS
- ○ Volcanoes*
- ● Earthquakes*
- ● Major flood disasters*
- Tsunamis
- Limit of iceberg drift
- Deserts
- Areas subject to desertification

*Twentieth Century occurrences

© RMcN

LANDFORMS
- Mountains
- Widely spaced mountains
- High tablelands
- Hills and low tablelands
- Depressions or basins
- Plains
- Limit of continental shelf

For description of landform regions, see Landforms Map by R. E. Murphy, p. 6

A-540000-1S6- -5-3-5
© RMcN

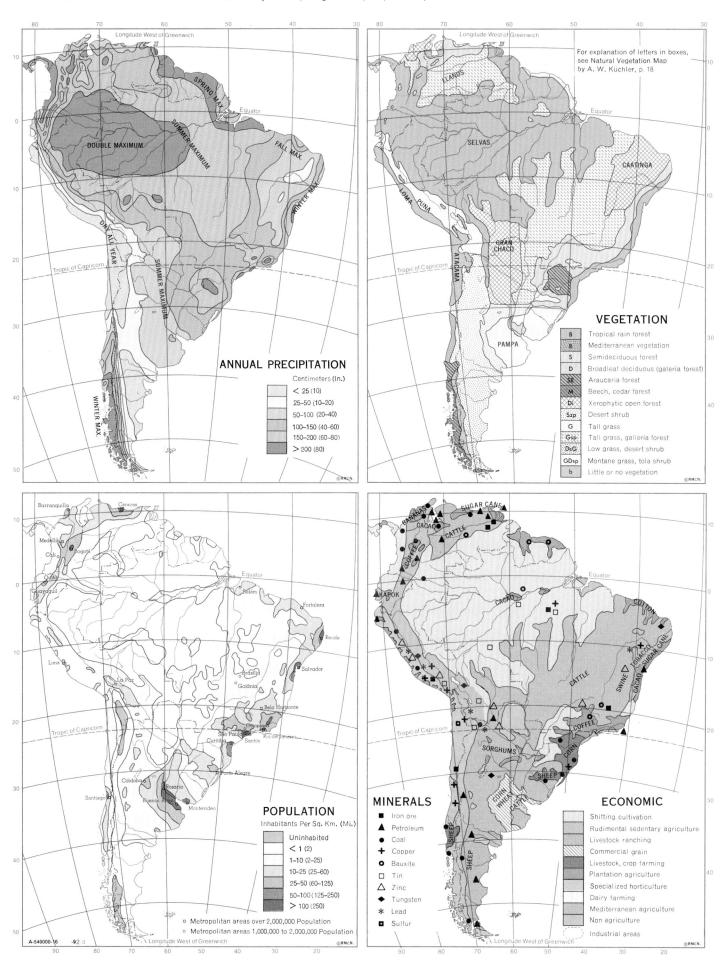

ANNUAL PRECIPITATION

Centimeters (In.)

- < 25 (10)
- 25–50 (10–20)
- 50–100 (20–40)
- 100–150 (40–60)
- 150–200 (60–80)
- > 200 (80)

VEGETATION

For explanation of letters in boxes, see Natural Vegetation Map by A. W. Küchler, p. 18

B	Tropical rain forest
B	Mediterranean vegetation
S	Semideciduous forest
D	Broadleaf deciduous (galeria forest)
SE	Araucaria forest
M	Beech, cedar forest
Di	Xerophytic open forest
Szp	Desert shrub
G	Tall grass
Gsp	Tall grass, galleria forest
DaG	Low grass, desert shrub
GDsp	Montane grass, tola shrub
b	Little or no vegetation

POPULATION

Inhabitants Per Sq. Km. (Mi.)

- Uninhabited
- < 1 (2)
- 1–10 (2–25)
- 10–25 (25–60)
- 25–50 (60–125)
- 50–100 (125–250)
- > 100 (250)

□ Metropolitan areas over 2,000,000 Population
○ Metropolitan areas 1,000,000 to 2,000,000 Population

MINERALS

- ■ Iron ore
- ▲ Petroleum
- ● Coal
- ✚ Copper
- ◎ Bauxite
- □ Tin
- △ Zinc
- ◆ Tungsten
- ✳ Lead
- ▣ Sulfur

ECONOMIC

- Shifting cultivation
- Rudimental sedentary agriculture
- Livestock ranching
- Commercial grain
- Livestock, crop farming
- Plantation agriculture
- Specialized horticulture
- Dairy farming
- Mediterranean agriculture
- Non agriculture
- Industrial areas

CUBA

JAMAICA

San Juan

Kingston   HISPANIOLA   PUERTO
RICO

Caribbean   Sea

ATLANTIC

Panamá

Barranquilla   Maracaibo   CARACAS   Port of Spain
TRINIDAD

OCEAN

Orinoco

LLANOS

Georgetown

BOGOTÁ

Quito

Negro

Belém

Equator

Iquitos

Manaus

Amazon

Fortaleza

SELVAS

Rio Branco

São Francisco

Recife

LIMA

ANDES

La Paz

Cuiabá

Brasília

Salvador

MATO
GROSSO

Iquique

Tropic of Capricorn

GRAN CHACO

Belo Horizonte

Paraná

Asunción

SÃO
PAULO

RIO DE JANEIRO

ANDES

San Miguel
de Tucumán

PACIFIC

Córdoba

Porto Alegre

SANTIAGO

BUENOS AIRES

Montevideo

ATLANTIC

PAMPA

OCEAN

Bahía Blanca

OCEAN

PATAGONIA

Puerto Montt

Punta Arenas

TIERRA
DEL FUEGO

FALKLAND
ISLANDS

SOUTH
GEORGIA

Drake   Passage

Legend:
- Urban
- Cropland
- Cropland & Woodland
- Cropland & Grazing Land
- Grassland, Grazing Land
- Forest, Woodland
- Swamp, Marshland
- Shrub, Sparse Grass, Wasteland
- Barren Land

Scale 1:36,000,000; one inch to 570 miles   Lambert Azimuthal Equal-Area Projection

0   100   200   400   600   800 Miles
0   150   300   600   900   1200 Kilometers

HAVANA

Tropic of Cancer

CUBA WEST

NORTH AMERICAN BASIN

HISPANIOLA San Juan

PEN. DE YUCATÁN

JAMAICA PUERTO RICO (U.S.A.)

GUADELOUPE (Fr.)

ATLANTIC

CARIBBEAN SEA MARTINIQUE (Fr.)

BARBADOS

INDIES

OCEAN

CENTRAL

Lago de Nicaragua

PUNTA DE GALLINAS

TRINIDAD AND TOBAGO
Port of Spain

Barranquilla
Cartagena Maracaibo La Guaira

AMERICA Panamá IST. DE PAN. Valencia CARACAS

Golfo de Panamá Mérida Ciudad Bolívar

LLANOS

Cerro Curú 7800 Georgetown

VENEZUELA GUYANA Paramaribo

ISLA DEL COCO (Costa Rica) Medellín BOGOTÁ Boa Vista do Rio Branco SURINAME FR. GUIANA Cayenne

ISLA DE MALPELO (Colombia) GUIANA HIGHLANDS

COLOMBIA

ILHA DE MARAJÓ Equator ROCEDOS SÃO PEDRO E SÃO PAULO (Brazil)

Quito Cotopaxi 19 347

ARCHIPIÉLAGO DE COLÓN (GALÁPAGOS ISLANDS) (Ec.) ECUADOR Rio Negro Belém (Pará) São Luís (Maranhão)

Guayaquil Chimborazo 20 702 Manaus (Manáos) Rio Amazonas

Golfo de Guayaquil Iquitos Leticia Japurá Putumayo Rio Solimões (Amazonas) ARQUIPÉLAGO FERNANDO DE NORONHA (Brazil)

Fortaleza (Ceará)

Chiclayo Juruá Purús Rio Madeira Teresina CABO DE SÃO ROQUE

Trujillo Rio Branco Pôrto Velho Natal

Nevo Huascarán 22 133 João Pessoa (Paraíba)

PERU Tapajós RECIFE (Pernambuco)

LIMA B R A Z I L Maceió

Cusco CHAPADA DE MATO GROSSO

Callao ANDES MTS. Xingu SERRA DO PIAUÍ

Volcán Misti 19 101 Brasília Salvador (Bahia)

Arequipa Nev. Illimani 20 741 Cuiabá

Mollendo La Paz BOLIVIA Diamantina

Sucre Belo Horizonte Pico da Bandeira 9482

Iquique Potosí CHACO Vitória

BRAZILIAN HIGHLANDS

Antofagasta GRAN CHACO PARAGUAY SÃO PAULO CABO FRIO

Salta Asunción Santos RIO DE JANEIRO

Cerro Azufre Copiapó 19 947 Tucumán

Copiapó Corrientes Florianópolis

ARGENTINA Pôrto Alegre

Coquimbo Córdoba Santa Fe Salto

ISLA DE SAN FÉLIX (Chile) ISLA DE SAN AMBROSIO (Chile) Cerro Aconcagua 22 89? Rosario URUGUAY Rio Grande

Valparaíso Mendoza BUENOS AIRES MONTEVIDEO

SANTIAGO La Plata

ISLAS DE JUAN FERNÁNDEZ (Chile) PAMPAS

Concepción

CHILE Bahía Blanca

Valdivia

Puerto Montt Viedma Golfo San Matías

ISLA DE CHILOÉ

ANDES MTS.

ARCHIPIÉLAGO DE LOS CHONOS Comodoro Rivadavia Golfo San Jorge

Monte San Valentín 13 314

FALKLAND IS. (ISLAS MALVINAS) (Br.)

WELLINGTON Río Gallegos Stanley

HANOVER Estrecho de Magallanes

Punta Arenas TIERRA DEL FUEGO

DESOLACIÓN ISLA DE LOS ESTADOS

Mt. Sarmiento 8100 CABO DE HORNOS (CAPE HORN)

SOUTH GEORGIA (Br.)

PACIFIC OCEAN ATLANTIC OCEAN

Tropic of Capricorn

Drake Passage SOUTH SANDWICH ISLANDS (Br.)

SOUTH SHETLAND ISLANDS (Br.) SOUTH ORKNEY IS. (Br.)

JOINVILLE

ANTARCTIC PENINSULA JAMES ROSS

Longitude West of Greenwich Antarctic Circle

Relief

Meters		Feet
3050		10 000
1525		5000
610		2000
305		1000
0	Sea Level	0
152.5		500
1525		5000
3050		10 000
6100		20 000

A-540000-76-3---15
COPYRIGHT BY
RAND McNALLY & COMPANY
MADE IN U.S.A.

| 0 | 200 | 400 | 600 | 800 | 1000 Miles |

| 0 | 400 | 800 | 1200 | 1600 Kilometers |

Scale 1:40 000 000; one inch to 630 miles. Lambert's Azimuthal, Equal Area Projection
Elevations and depressions are given in feet

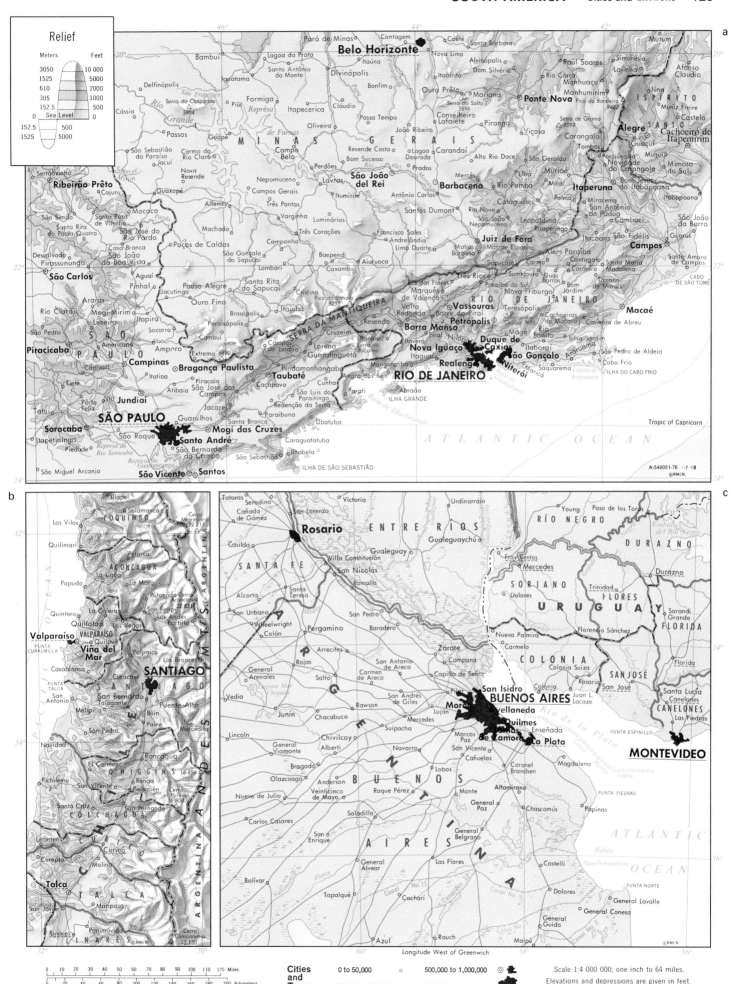

Relief

Meters		Feet
3050		10 000
1525		5000
610		2000
305		1000
152.5		500
0	Sea Level	0
152.5		500
1525		5000

a

b

c

Cities
and
Towns

| 0 to 50,000 | ○ | 500,000 to 1,000,000 | ◎ |
| 50,000 to 500,000 | ⊙ | 1,000,000 and over | ⬤ |

Scale 1:4 000 000; one inch to 64 miles.
Elevations and depressions are given in feet.

Longitude West of Greenwich

Continued on pages 130-131

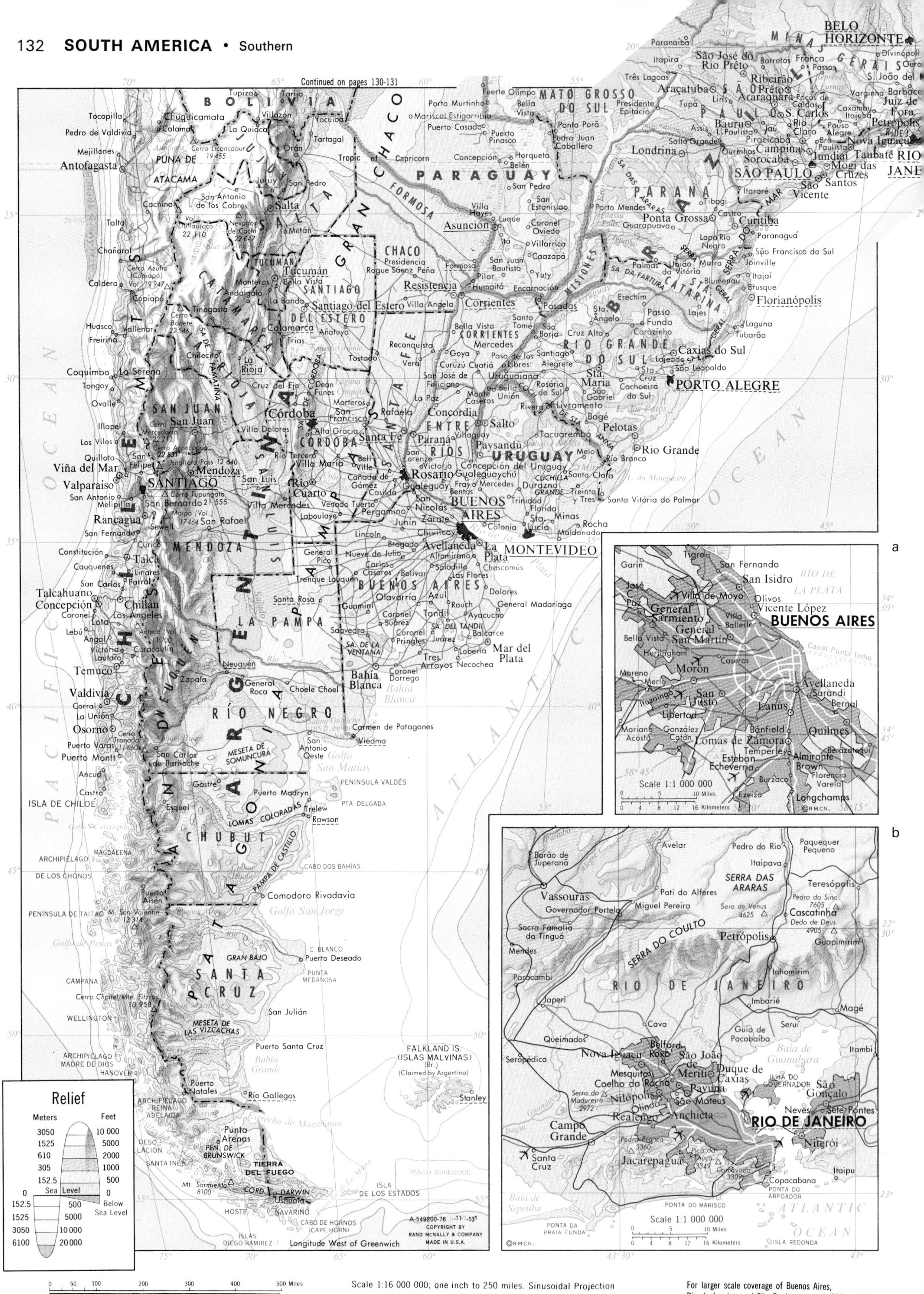

BOLIVIA

PARAGUAY

GRAN CHACO

CHACO

FORMOSA

URUGUAY

ARGENTINA

CHILE

PATAGONIA

LA PAMPA

BUENOS AIRES

RIO NEGRO

CHUBUT

SANTA CRUZ

TIERRA DEL FUEGO

BRASIL

MATO GROSSO DO SUL

SÃO PAULO

PARANÁ

SANTA CATARINA

RIO GRANDE DO SUL

MINAS GERAIS

BELO HORIZONTE

SÃO PAULO

PORTO ALEGRE

SANTIAGO

BUENOS AIRES

MONTEVIDEO

PACIFIC OCEAN

ATLANTIC OCEAN

FALKLAND IS. (ISLAS MALVINAS) (Br.) (Claimed by Argentina)

Stanley

Tropic of Capricorn

Longitude West of Greenwich

a

BUENOS AIRES

Scale 1:1 000 000

0 4 8 12 16 Kilometers

0 5 10 Miles

RIO DE LA PLATA

b

RIO DE JANEIRO

SERRA DAS ARARAS

RIO DE JANEIRO

Scale 1:1 000 000

0 5 10 Miles

0 4 8 12 16 Kilometers

Relief

Meters	Feet
3050	10 000
1525	5000
610	2000
305	1000
152.5	500
0 Sea Level	0 Sea Level
152.5	500
1525	5000
3050	10 000
6100	20 000

Below Sea Level

0 50 100 200 300 400 500 Miles

0 100 200 400 600 800 Kilometers

Scale 1:16 000 000; one inch to 250 miles. Sinusoidal Projection
Elevations and depressions are given in feet

COPYRIGHT BY
RAND MCNALLY & COMPANY
MADE IN U.S.A.
A-549200-76

For larger scale coverage of Buenos Aires, Rio de Janeiro, and São Paulo see pages 233 and 234.

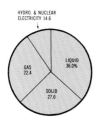

HYDRO. & NUCLEAR
ELECTRICITY 14.6

GAS
22.4

LIQUID
36.0%

SOLID
27.0

**Commercial
Energy Consumption**
2,768,953,000 metric tons
coal equivalent - 1991

ENERGY

Energy Producing Plants

▽ Geothermal

· Hydroelectric

■ Nuclear

Mineral Fuel Deposits

· Uranium: major deposit

△ Natural Gas: major field

· Petroleum: minor producing field

▲ Petroleum ⎫
            ⎬ major producing field
  Petroleum ⎭

  Coal: major bituminous and anthracite

  Coal: minor bituminous and anthracite

  Coal: lignite

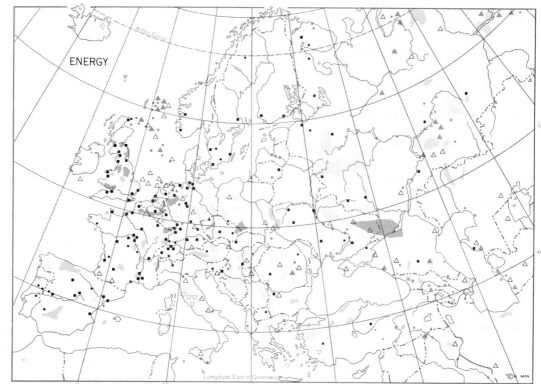

NATURAL HAZARDS

○ Volcanoes*

● Earthquakes*

● Major flood disasters*

—— Tsunamis

—— Limit of iceberg drift

  Temporary pack ice

  Areas subject to desertification

*Twentieth Century occurrences

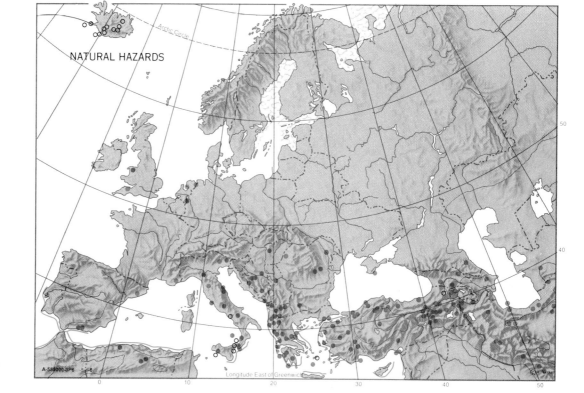

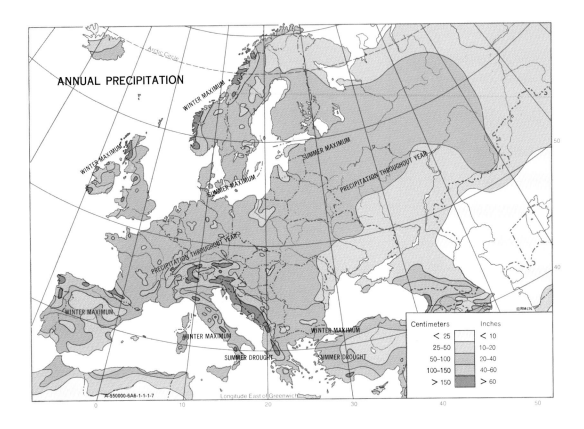

ANNUAL PRECIPITATION

WINTER MAXIMUM
WINTER MAXIMUM
SUMMER MAXIMUM
SUMMER MAXIMUM
PRECIPITATION THROUGHOUT YEAR
PRECIPITATION THROUGHOUT YEAR
WINTER MAXIMUM
WINTER MAXIMUM
WINTER MAXIMUM
SUMMER DROUGHT
SUMMER DROUGHT

Centimeters	Inches
< 25	< 10
25–50	10–20
50–100	20–40
100–150	40–60
> 150	> 60

Longitude East of Greenwich

A-550000-6A6-1-1-1-7

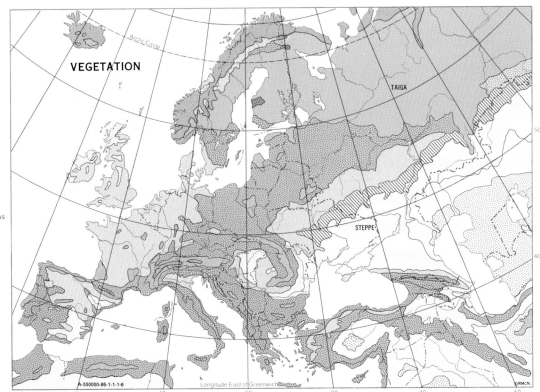

VEGETATION

TAIGA

STEPPE

Longitude East of Greenwich

A-550000-86-1-1-1-6

VEGETATION

E	Coniferous forest
B, B₂	Mediterranean vegetation
M	Mixed forest: coniferous-deciduous
S	Semi-deciduous forest
D	Deciduous forest
DG	Wooded steppe
G	Grass (steppe)
Gp	Short grass
Dsp	Desert shrub
L	Heath and moor
L	Alpine vegetation, tundra
b	Little or no vegetation

For explanation of letters in boxes,
see Natural Vegetation Map
by A. W. Kuchler, p. 18

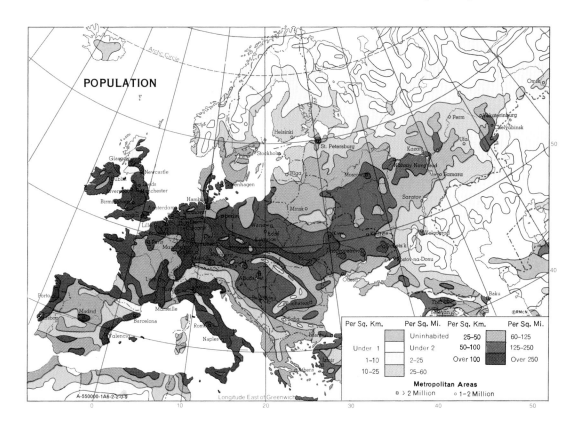

POPULATION

Per Sq. Km.	Per Sq. Mi.	Per Sq. Km.	Per Sq. Mi.
	Uninhabited	25–50	60–125
Under 1	Under 2	50–100	125–250
1–10	2–25	Over 100	Over 250
10–25	25–60		

Metropolitan Areas
□ > 2 Million   ○ 1–2 Million

A-550000-1A6-2-2-0-9   Longitude East of Greenwich

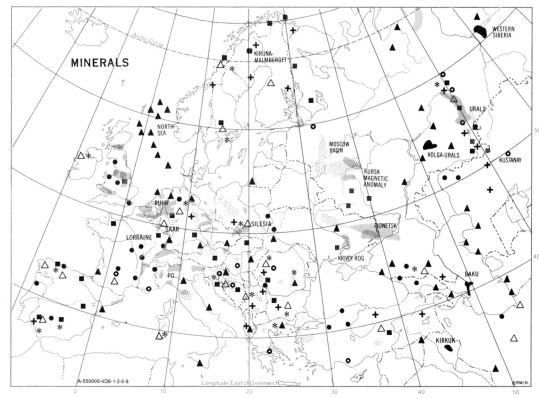

MINERALS

- Industrial areas
- Major coal deposits
- ● Major petroleum deposits
- Lignite deposits
- ▲ Minor petroleum deposits
- ● Minor coal deposits
- ■ Major iron ore
- ■ Minor iron ore
- ✳ Lead
- ⊙ Bauxite
- △ Zinc
- ✛ Copper

A-550000-4D6-1-3-0-8   Longitude East of Greenwich

Urban

Cropland

Cropland & Woodland

Cropland & Grazing Land

Grassland, Grazing Land

Forest, Woodland

Swamp, Marshland

Tundra

Shrub, Sparse Grass,
Wasteland (pattern)

Barren Land

Oasis

Scale 1: 16,000,000; one inch to 250 miles. Conic Projection

Longitude West of Greenwich   0°   Longitude East of Greenwich

| 0 | 50 | 100 | 200 | 300 | 400 | 500 Miles |

| 0 | 100 | 200 | 400 | 600 | 800 Kilometers |

Nar'yan-Mar

Ob'

Novosibirsk

Ob'

Pechora

Irtysh

ite Sea

Archangelsk

Omsk

URALS

Vologda

Kirov

Perm'

YEKATERINBURG

Qaraghandy

Volga

Kazan

Kama

Ufa

Nizhniy
Novgorod

Magnitogorsk

Balqash

MOSCOW

Samara

Orsk

Tula

Volga

Qyzylorda

Saratov

Ural

Syr Darya

Aral
Sea

DEPRESSION

KYZYL-KUM
(DESERT)

Kharkiv

Don

VOLGOGRAD

CASPIAN

Volga

Amu Dar'ya

Dnipropetrovs'k

Donets'k

MANYCH

DEPRESSION

Astrakhan'

KARA-KUM (DESERT)

Dnieper

Odesa

Krasnodar

Caspian

Ashgabat

C A U C A S U S

Black   Sea

TBILISI

BAKU

Sea

Yerevan

NBUL

ELBURZ MTS.

Ankara

DASHT-E KAVIR

TEHRAN

TOROS

AĞLARI

Kerman

Nicosia

Tigris

ZAGROS

CYPRUS

Euphrates

Baghdad

MOUNTAINS

Beirut

Abādān

COPYRIGHT BY
RAND McNALLY & COMPANY
MADE IN U.S.A.
A-550000-9IAE-1-1-2-3

Scale 1:16 000 000; one inch to 250 miles. Conic Proje
Elevations and depressions are given in feet.

PHYSIOGRAPHIC PROVINCES

0   400
Miles

Legend:
- Western Uplands (Mostly old rocks)
- Great European Plain
- Central Uplands
- Alpine System

EUROPE DURING THE ICE AGE

Legend:
- Tundra
- Forest
- Steppe

PHYSIOGRAPHY
BY
ERWIN RAISZ

LITHOLOGY AND STRUCTURE

- Unconsolidated deposits: alluvium, sands, bottom lands.
- Essentially horizontal sediments, also uplands and terraces in the plains.
- Moderately folded sedimentary rocks.
- Strongly folded and faulted rocks. The "Younger Series" in Norway.
- Metamorphic and intrusive igneous rocks.
- volcanics, lava flows, basalts, etc.

LANDFORMS

- PLATEAUS
- HILLS
- MOUNTAINS
- MESAS
- CUESTAS
- FOLDED MOUNTAINS
- BASIN RANGES
- VOLCANO AND LAVA
- SAND
- SINKS
- MORAINES
- DRUMLINS

50   100   200   300   400   500 Miles
100   200   400   600   800 Kilometers

EUROPE LANGUAGES
BY
BOGDAN ZABORSKI

Scale 1:16,500,000; one inch to 260 miles Conic Projection

B-550000-1C6-1-1-3
COPYRIGHT BY
RAND McNALLY & COMPANY
MADE IN U.S.A

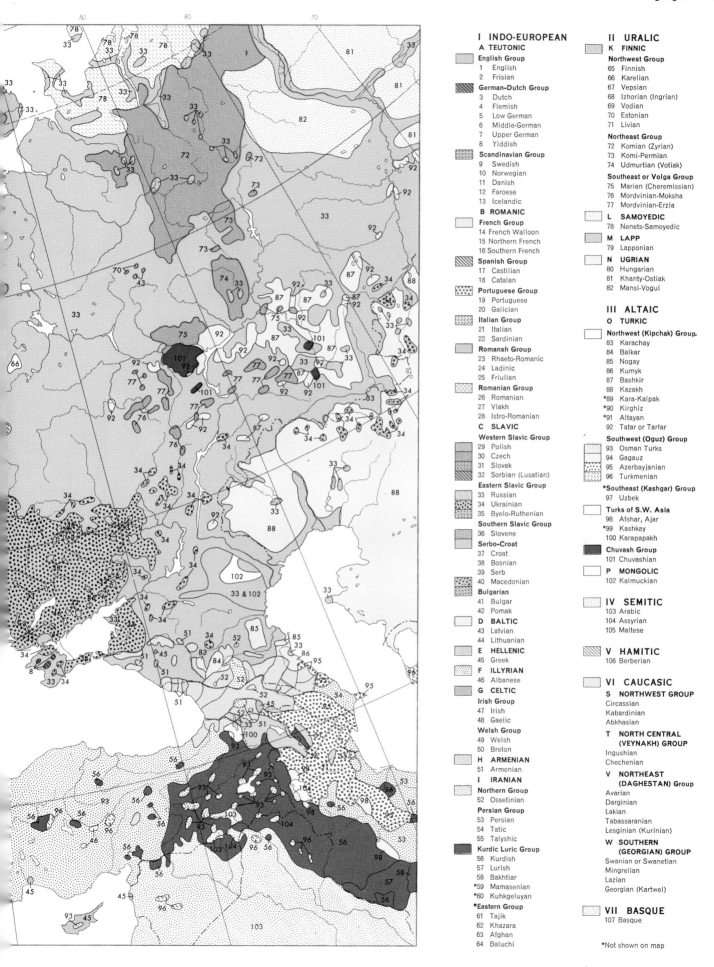

I INDO-EUROPEAN

A TEUTONIC

English Group
1 English
2 Frisian

German-Dutch Group
3 Dutch
4 Flemish
5 Low German
6 Middle-German
7 Upper German
8 Yiddish

Scandinavian Group
9 Swedish
10 Norwegian
11 Danish
12 Faroese
13 Icelandic

B ROMANIC

French Group
14 French Walloon
15 Northern French
16 Southern French

Spanish Group
17 Castilian
18 Catalan

Portuguese Group
19 Portuguese
20 Galician

Italian Group
21 Italian
22 Sardinian

Romansh Group
23 Rhaeto-Romanic
24 Ladinic
25 Friulian

Romanian Group
26 Romanian
27 Vlakh
28 Istro-Romanian

C SLAVIC

Western Slavic Group
29 Polish
30 Czech
31 Slovak
32 Sorbian (Lusatian)

Eastern Slavic Group
33 Russian
34 Ukrainian
35 Byelo-Ruthenian

Southern Slavic Group
36 Slovene

Serbo-Croat
37 Croat
38 Bosnian
39 Serb
40 Macedonian

Bulgarian
41 Bulgar
42 Pomak

D BALTIC
43 Latvian
44 Lithuanian

E HELLENIC
45 Greek

F ILLYRIAN
46 Albanese

G CELTIC

Irish Group
47 Irish
48 Gaelic

Welsh Group
49 Welsh
50 Breton

H ARMENIAN
51 Armenian

I IRANIAN

Northern Group
52 Ossetinian

Persian Group
53 Persian
54 Tatic
55 Talyshic

Kurdic Luric Group
56 Kurdish
57 Lurish
58 Bakhtiar
*59 Mamasenian
*60 Kuhgeluyan

*Eastern Group
61 Tajik
62 Khazara
63 Afghan
64 Baluchi

II URALIC

K FINNIC

Northwest Group
65 Finnish
66 Karelian
67 Vepsian
68 Izhorian (Ingrian)
69 Vodian
70 Estonian
71 Livian

Northeast Group
72 Komian (Zyrian)
73 Komi-Permian
74 Udmurtian (Votiak)

Southeast or Volga Group
75 Marian (Cheremissian)
76 Mordvinian-Moksha
77 Mordvinian-Erzia

L SAMOYEDIC
78 Nenets-Samoyedic

M LAPP
79 Lapponian

N UGRIAN
80 Hungarian
81 Khanty-Ostiak
82 Mansi-Vogul

III ALTAIC

O TURKIC

Northwest (Kipchak) Group
83 Karachay
84 Balkar
85 Nogay
86 Kumyk
87 Bashkir
88 Kazakh
*89 Kara-Kalpak
*90 Kirghiz
*91 Altayan
92 Tatar or Tartar

Southwest (Oguz) Group
93 Osman Turks
94 Gagauz
95 Azerbayjanian
96 Turkmenian

*Southeast (Kashgar) Group
97 Uzbek

Turks of S.W. Asia
98 Afshar, Ajar
*99 Kashkay
100 Karapapakh

Chuvash Group
101 Chuvashian

P MONGOLIC
102 Kalmuckian

IV SEMITIC
103 Arabic
104 Assyrian
105 Maltese

V HAMITIC
106 Berberian

VI CAUCASIC

S NORTHWEST GROUP
Circassian
Kabardinian
Abkhasian

T NORTH CENTRAL (VEYNAKH) GROUP
Ingushian
Chechenian

V NORTHEAST (DAGHESTAN) Group
Avarian
Darginian
Lakian
Tabassaranian
Lesginian (Kurinian)

W SOUTHERN (GEORGIAN) GROUP
Swanian or Swanetian
Mingrelian
Lazian
Georgian (Kartwel)

VII BASQUE
107 Basque

*Not shown on map

Relief

Meters	Feet
3050	10 000
1525	5000
610	2000
305	1000
152.5	500
0 Sea Level	0
152.5	Below Sea Level
1525	500
3050	5000
	10 000

Continued on pages 210-211

Longitude West of Greenwich   Longitude East of Greenwich

Scale 1: 16 000 000; one inch to 250 miles. Conic Projection

Elevations and depressions are given in feet

0	50	100	200	300	400	500 Miles
0	100	200	400	600	800 Kilometers

Continued on pages 170-171

Continued on pages 182-183

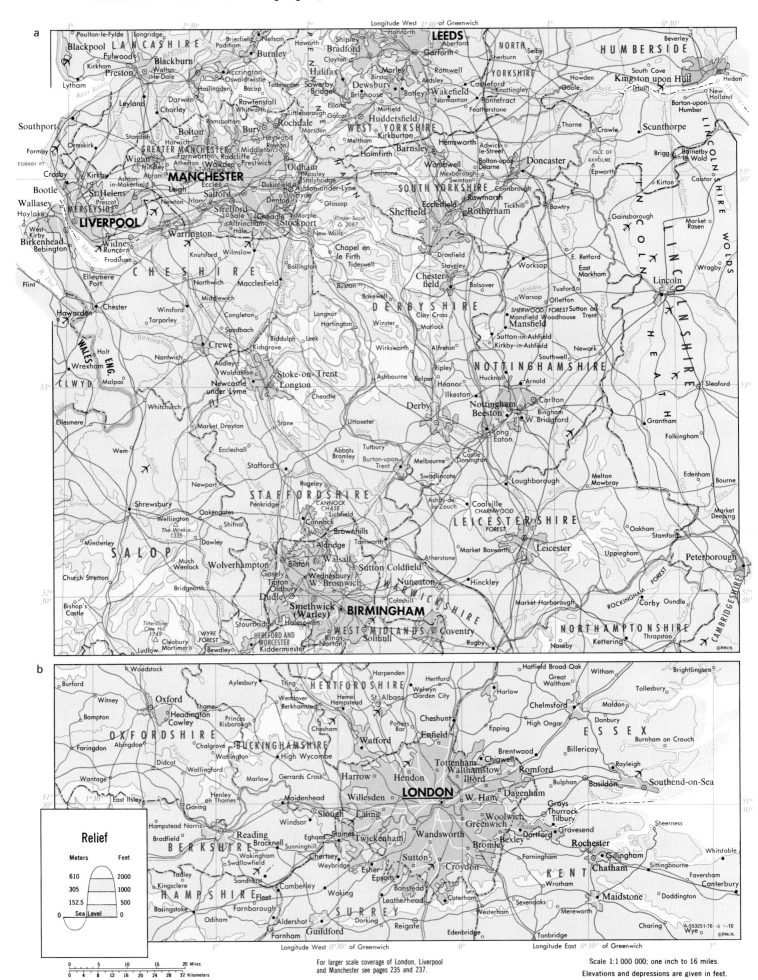

a

Longitude West 1°30′ of Greenwich

LANCASHIRE
Blackpool
Poulton-le-Fylde Longridge
Fulwood Kirkham Blackburn
Lytham Preston Walton-le-Dale
Southport Leyland Chorley Darwen
Formby Ormskirk Standish
Crosby Kirkby Wigan
Bootle St. Helens
Wallasey Prescot
Hoylake West Kirby Birkenhead Bebington
MERSEYSIDE
LIVERPOOL
Widnes Runcorn
Frodsham
Flint
Hawarden
Chester
WALES
ENG.
CLWYD
Wrexham
Holt
Malpas
Whitchurch
Ellesmere
Wem
Ellesmere Port
CHESHIRE
Northwich
Middlewich
Winsford
Tarporley
Nantwich
Crewe
Audley
Wolstanton
Newcastle under Lyme
Market Drayton
Eccleshall
Stafford
Newport
SALOP
Shrewsbury
Wellington
The Wrekin 1335
Oakengates
Shifnal
Dawley
Minsterley
Church Stretton
Much Wenlock
Bridgnorth
Bishop's Castle
Ludlow
Cleobury Mortimer
Titterstone Clee Hill 1749
Brierfield Nelson
Burnley
Haworth
Padiham
Accrington Oswaldtwistle
Haslingden
Rawtenstall
Whitworth
Ramsbottom
Bury
Heywood
Rochdale
Littleborough
Bolton Bradford Shipley
Horwich Clayton
GREATER MANCHESTER
Farnworth Radcliffe Prestwich
Atherton Walkden
Leigh Eccles Salford
MANCHESTER
Newton Irlam Stretford
Warrington Sale Altrincham Hale
Knutsford Wilmslow
Bollington
Macclesfield
Congleton
Sandbach
Biddulph
Kidsgrove
Stoke-on-Trent Longton
Cheadle
Stone
Uttoxeter
Abbots Bromley
Tutbury
Burton-upon-Trent
Rugeley
Penkridge
CANNOCK CHASE
Lichfield
Cannock
Brownhills
Aldridge
Tamworth
WARWICKSHIRE
Wolverhampton
Bilston
Walsall
Sutton Coldfield
Gosely
Wednesbury
Tipton Oldbury
W. Bromwich
Dudley
Smethwick (Warley)
BIRMINGHAM
Coleshill
Stourbridge Halesowen
WEST MIDLANDS
Solihull Coventry
HEREFORD AND WORCESTER
Kings Norton
Bewdley Kidderminster
WYRE FOREST
Halifax
Sowerby Bridge
Elland
LEEDS
Morley
Brighouse
Dewsbury
Batley
Mirfield
Huddersfield
Golcar
Kirkburton
Meltham
Holmfirth
WEST YORKSHIRE
Penistone
Barnsley
Wombwell
Hemsworth
Adwick le-Street
Bolton-upon-Dearne
Mexborough
Swinton
NORTH YORKSHIRE
Garforth
Rothwell
Ardsley
Wakefield
Normanton
Featherstone
Castleford
Pontefract
Knottingley
Goole
Doncaster
Conisbrough
Rawmarsh
Tickhill
Bawtry
SOUTH YORKSHIRE
Sheffield
Ecclesfield
Rotherham
Dronfield
Staveley
Chesterfield
Bolsover
Worksop
Warsop
Ollerton
SHERWOOD FOREST
Mansfield Woodhouse
Mansfield
Sutton-in-Ashfield
Kirkby-in-Ashfield
Hucknall
Arnold
Carlton
Nottingham
Beeston
W. Bridgford
Bingham
NOTTINGHAMSHIRE
DERBYSHIRE
Kinder Scout △ 2087
New Mills
Chapel en le Frith
Tideswell
Buxton
Bakewell
Longnor
Hartington
Winster
Matlock
Wirksworth
Clay Cross
Alfreton
Ashbourne
Belper
Ripley
Heanor
Ilkeston
Derby
Long Eaton
Melbourne
Castle Donington
Swadlincote
Ashby-de-la-Zouch
Coalville
CHARNWOOD FOREST
LEICESTERSHIRE
Loughborough
Market Bosworth
Atherstone
Hinckley
Nuneaton
Rugby
Naseby
Leicester
Melton Mowbray
Oakham
Uppingham
Market Harborough
ROCKINGHAM FOREST
Corby
Kettering
Thrapston
NORTHAMPTONSHIRE
HUMBERSIDE
Beverley
Kingston upon Hull (Hull)
South Cave
Hedon
New Holland
Barton-upon-Humber
Scunthorpe
Brigg
Barnetby le Wold
ISLE OF AXHOLME
Epworth
Crowle
Thorne
Howden
Selby
Sherburn
Gainsborough
Lincoln
LINCOLNSHIRE
Caistor
Market Rasen
Wragby
WOLDS
Kirton
E. Retford
East Markham
Tuxford
Newark
Southwell
Grantham
Sleaford
Folkingham
Edenham
Bourne
Market Deeping
Stamford
Oundle
Peterborough
CAMBRIDGESHIRE
River Ribble
River Mersey
River Dee
R. Trent
R. Severn
R. Witham
R. Ouse
R. Don
Manchester Ship Canal
3° 2°30′ 2° 1°30′ 1° 0°30′ Greenwich 0°30′
53°30′
53°
52°30′

b

Longitude West 0°30′ of Greenwich
Woodstock
Burford
Witney
Bampton
Faringdon
OXFORDSHIRE
Oxford
Headington Cowley
Abingdon
Didcot
Wallingford
Wantage
East Ilsley
Hampstead Norris
Bradfield
Reading
BERKSHIRE
Bracknell
Wokingham
Swallowfield
Tadley
Kingsclere
Sandhurst
Camberley
Aldershot
Fleet
Farnborough
Basingstoke
Odiham
HAMPSHIRE
Aylesbury
Tring
Wendover
Princes Risborough
Thame
Chalgrove
Watlington
BUCKINGHAMSHIRE
High Wycombe
Marlow
Gerrards Cross
Henley on Thames
Goring
Maidenhead
Windsor
Slough
Egham
Sunninghill
Chertsey
Weybridge
Esher
Woking
Leatherhead
Dorking
Guildford
Farnham
SURREY
Reigate
HERTFORDSHIRE
Harpenden
Welwyn Garden City
Hemel Hempstead
Berkhamsted
Chesham
St. Albans
Potters Bar
Watford
Harrow
Hendon
Willesden
Ealing
Staines
Twickenham
Wandsworth
Sutton
Epsom
Banstead
Caterham
Westerham
Sevenoaks
Hertford
Cheshunt
Enfield
Tottenham
Walthamstow
Ilford
LONDON
W. Ham
Woolwich
Greenwich
Bromley
Croydon
Hatfield Broad Oak
Great Waltham
Harlow
Epping
High Ongar
Brentwood
Chigwell
Romford
Dagenham
Grays
Thurrock
Tilbury
Bexley
Dartford
Farningham
Wrotham
Maidstone
Doddington
Witham
Chelmsford
Maldon
Danbury
Billericay
Burnham on Crouch
Basildon
Rayleigh
Southend-on-Sea
Gravesend
Rochester
Gillingham
Chatham
Sittingbourne
Faversham
Canterbury
Whitstable
Sheerness
Charing
Wye
Tonbridge
Edenbridge
Mereworth
KENT
ESSEX
Bulphan
Brightlingsea
Tollesbury
R. Thames
51°30′
1°30′ 1° 0°30′ Greenwich 0° Longitude East 0°30′ of Greenwich 1°

Relief
Meters	Feet
610	2000
305	1000
152.5	500
0 Sea Level	0

0 5 10 15 20 Miles
0 4 8 12 16 20 24 28 32 Kilometers

For larger scale coverage of London, Liverpool and Manchester see pages 235 and 237.

Scale 1:1 000 000; one inch to 16 miles.
Elevations and depressions are given in feet.

A-553251-76-6-4-10
©RMcN.

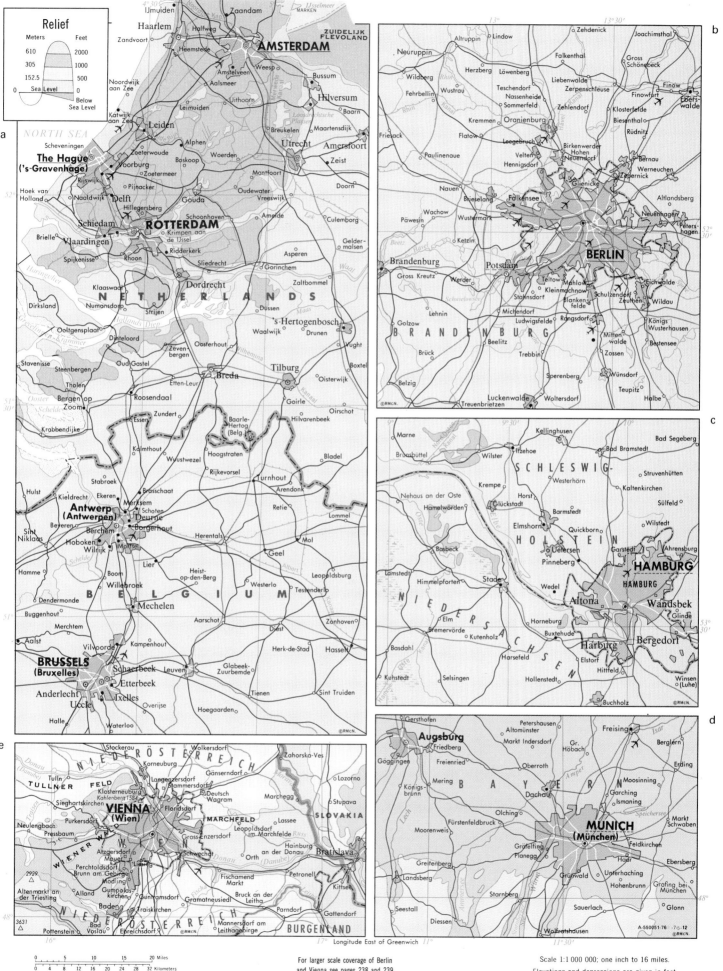

Relief
Meters	Feet
610	2000
305	1000
152.5	500
0 Sea Level	0
	Below Sea Level

a

NORTH SEA

IJmuiden
Haarlem
Zaandam
ZUIDELIJK FLEVOLAND
MARKEN
Halfweg
Zandvoort
Heemstede
AMSTERDAM
Amstelveen
Weesp
Noordwijk aan Zee
Aalsmeer
Bussum
Uithoorn
Hilversum
Katwijk aan Zee
Leiden
Breukelen
Maartensdijk
Baarn
Scheveningen
The Hague ('s-Gravenhage)
Voorburg
Zoeterwoude
Alphen
Woerden
Boskoop
Utrecht
Amersfoort
Zeist
Hoek van Holland
Rijswijk
Zoetermeer
Pijnacker
Gouda
Montfoort
Doorn
Naaldwijk
Delft
Hillegersberg
Schoonhoven
Vreeswijk
Oudewater
Schiedam
ROTTERDAM
Krimpen aan de IJssel
Amelde
Culemborg
Brielle
Vlaardingen
Rhoon
Ridderkerk
Sliedrecht
Gorinchem
Asperen
Gelder-malsen
Spijkenisse
Dordrecht
Zaltbommel
Klaaswaal
NETHERLANDS
Dussen
's-Hertogenbosch
Dirksland
Numansdorp
Strijen
Waalwijk
Drunen
Vught
Stavenisse
Oud Gastel
Oosterhout
Breda
Tilburg
Boxtel
Steenbergen
Zevenbergen
Etten-Leur
Oisterwijk
Bergen op Zoom
Roosendaal
Goirle
Oirschot
Krabbendijke
Zundert
Essen
Baarle-Hertog (Belg.)
Hilvarenbeek
Bladel
Kalmthout
Hoogstraten
Wuustwezel
Rijkevorsel
Turnhout
Arendonk
Hulst
Stabroek
Brasschaat
Retie
Lommel
Kieldrecht
Ekeren
Merksem
Schoten
Mol
Antwerp (Antwerpen)
Deurne
Borgerhout
Herentals
Geel
Sint Niklaas
Berchem
Hoboken
Wilrijk
Mortsel
Lier
Heist-op-den-Berg
Leopoldsburg
Hamme
Boom
Willebroek
Westerlo
Tessenderlo
Dendermonde
BELGIUM
Mechelen
Aarschot
Diest
Zonhoven
Buggenhout
Merchtem
Herk-de-Stad
Hasselt
Aalst
Vilvoorde
Kampenhout
BRUSSELS (Bruxelles)
Schaerbeek
Leuven
Glabbeek-Zuurbemde
Sint Truiden
Anderlecht
Etterbeek
Tienen
Uccle
Ixelles
Halle
Overijse
Hoegaarden
Waterloo

b

Neuruppin
Altruppin
Lindow
Zehdenick
Joachimsthal
Wildberg
Herzberg
Löwenberg
Falkenthal
Gross Schönebeck
Fehrbellin
Wustrau
Teschendorf
Liebenwalde
Finow
Finowfurt
Eberswalde
Friesack
Flatow
Nassenheide
Sommerfeld
Zehlendorf
Zerpenschleuse
Klosterfelde
Kremmen
Oranienburg
Biesenthal
Rüdnitz
Nauen
Birkenwerder
Hohen Neuendorf
Bernau
Werneuchen
Brieselang
Velten
Hennigsdorf
Zepernick
Altlandsberg
Päwesin
Wachow
Falkensee
Glienicke
Neuenhagen
Wustermark
Petershagen
Brandenburg
BERLIN
Gross Kreutz
Werder
Potsdam
Teltow
Mahlow
Eichwalde
Golzow
Kleinmachnow
Schulzendorf
Wildau
Lehnin
Michendorf
Blankenfelde
Zeuthen
BRANDENBURG
Ludwigsfelde
Rangsdorf
Königs Wusterhausen
Beelitz
Mittenwalde
Bestensee
Brück
Trebbin
Zossen
Belzig
Sperenberg
Wünsdorf
Teupitz
Halbe
Luckenwalde
Woltersdorf
Treuenbrietzen

c

Marne
Kellinghusen
Bad Segeberg
Brunsbüttel
Wilster
Itzehoe
Bad Bramstedt
SCHLESWIG-
Struvenhütten
Nehaus an der Oste
Krempe
Westerhörn
Kaltenkirchen
Hamelwörden
Glückstadt
Horst
Barmstedt
Sülfeld
Wilstedt
Lamstedt
Elmshorn
Quickborn
HOLSTEIN
Basbeck
Uetersen
Garstedt
Ahrensburg
Himmelpforten
Pinneberg
Stade
Wedel
HAMBURG
Altona
Wandsbek
Elm
Horneburg
Glinde
Bremervörde
Kutenholz
Buxtehude
HAMBURG
NIEDERSACHSEN
Basdahl
Harburg
Bergedorf
Harsefeld
Elstorf
Hittfeld
Kuhstedt
Selsingen
Hollenstedt
Winsen (Luhe)
Buchholz

d

Gersthofen
Petershausen
Freising
Augsburg
Friedberg
Altomünster
Markt Indersdorf
Gr. Höbach
Berglern
Göggingen
Freienried
Oberroth
Erding
Königs-brunn
Mering
BAYERN
Dachau
Moosinning
Garching
Ismaning
Olching
Fürstenfeldbruck
Moorenweis
MUNICH (München)
Markt Schwaben
Grafrath
Gräfelfing
Planegg
Haar
Feldkirchen
Greifenberg
Grünwald
Unterhaching
Ebersberg
Landsberg
Starnberg
Hohenbrunn
Grafing bei München
Seestall
Sauerlach
Glonn
Diessen
Wolfratshausen

e

Stockerau
Wolkersdorf
Zahorska-Ves
NIEDERÖSTERREICH
Tulln
Korneuburg
Gänserndorf
Langenzersdorf
Deutsch Wagram
Lozorno
FELD
Klosterneuburg
Kahlenberg 1584
Stupava
Sieghartskirchen
Floridsdorf
Marchegg
Neulengbach
VIENNA (Wien)
MARCHFELD
Lassee
Purkersdorf
Gross Enzersdorf
SLOVAKIA
Pressbaum
Leopoldsdorf im Marchfelde
2929
W I E N
Schwechat
Hainburg an der Donau
Bratislava
Atzgersdorf
Mauer
Liesing
Fischamend Markt
Orth
Perchtoldsdorf
Brunn am Gebirge
Petronell
Kittsee
Altenmarkt an der Triesting
Mödling
Guntramsdorf
Bruck an der Leitha
Alland
Gumpolds-kirchen
3631
NIEDERÖSTERREICH
Baden
Traiskirchen
Gramatneusiedl
Parndorf
Gattendorf
Pottenstein
Bad Vöslau
Mannersdorf am Leithagebirge
BURGENLAND
Pottenstein
Ebreichsdorf

Longitude East of Greenwich

For larger scale coverage of Berlin and Vienna see pages 238 and 239.

Scale 1:1 000 000; one inch to 16 miles.
Elevations and depressions are given in feet.

0 5 10 15 20 Miles
0 4 8 12 16 20 24 28 32 Kilometers

A-550051-76 · 7-6-12

Continued on pages 166-167

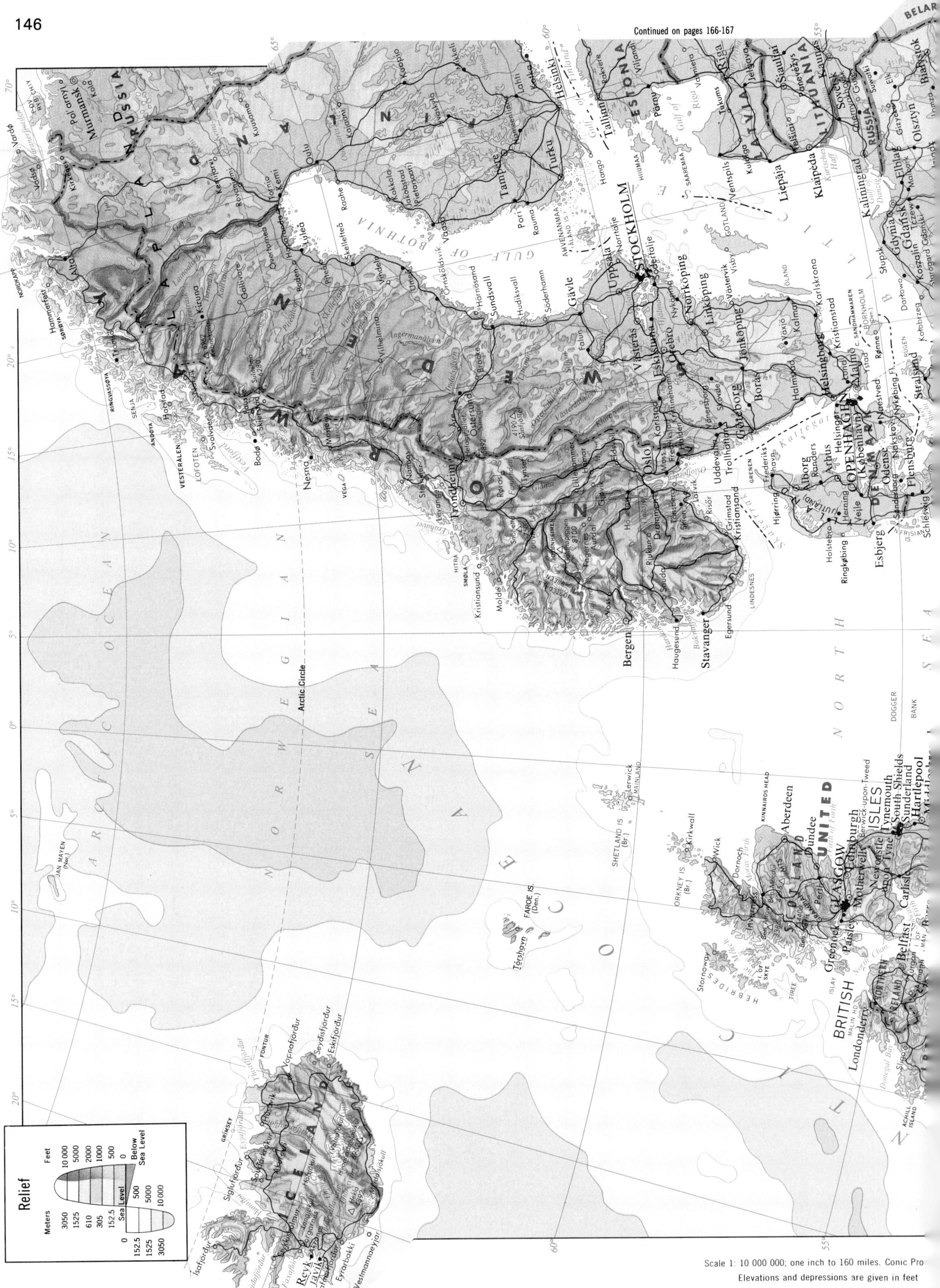

BELARUS

Relief

Meters	Feet	
3050	10 000	
1525	5000	
610	2000	
305	1000	
152.5	500	Below Sea Level
0	Sea Level	500
	0	5000
152.5		10 000
1525		
3050		

Scale 1: 10 000 000; one inch to 160 miles. Conic Pro
Elevations and depressions are given in feet

ARCTIC OCEAN

NORWEGIAN SEA

NORTH SEA

GULF OF BOTHNIA

RUSSIA

LAPLAND

FINLAND

SWEDEN

NORWAY

DENMARK

ESTONIA

LATVIA

LITHUANIA

ICELAND

FAROE IS. (Den.)

SHETLAND IS. (Br.)

ORKNEY IS. (Br.)

HEBRIDES

BRITISH ISLES

NORTHERN IRELAND

SCOTLAND

Murmansk

Helsinki

STOCKHOLM

COPENHAGEN

Oslo

Bergen

Stavanger

Trondheim

Reykjavik

Glasgow

Edinburgh

Aberdeen

Belfast

Londonderry

A-559400-76 13-10-23
COPYRIGHT BY
RAND MCNALLY & COMPANY
MADE IN U.S.A.

Continued on pages 146-147

ATLANTIC OCEAN

BAY OF BISCAY

FRANCE

PARIS

GERMANY

FRANKFURT

MANNHEIM

STUTTGART

MUNICH

SWITZERLAND

PORTUGAL

LISBON

SPAIN

MADRID

BARCELONA

ITALY

ROME
(Roma)

NAPLES
(Napoli)

CORSICA
(Fr.)

SARDINIA
(It.)

LIGURIAN SEA

TYRRHENIAN SEA

MEDITERRANEAN

SICILY

MALTA

MOROCCO

ATLAS MOUNTAINS

HAUT ATLAS

MOYEN ATLAS

SAHARAN ATLAS

ALGERIA

TUNISIA

GRAND ERG OCCIDENTAL

GRAND ERG ORIENTAL

TARABUL
(TRIPOLITANI)

Tripoli

Relief

Meters	Feet
3050	10000
1525	5000
610	2000
305	1000
152.5	500
0 Sea Level	0 Sea Level
	Below
152.5	500 Sea Level
1525	5000
3050	10000

A-558300-76
COPYRIGHT BY
RAND McNALLY & COMPANY
MADE IN U.S.A.

Longitude West of Greenwich 0° Longitude East of Greenwich

Scale 1:10 000 000; one inch to 160 miles. Bonne's Proj
Elevations and depressions are given in feet

Continued on pages 166-167

The Turkish Republic of Northern Cyprus
unilaterally declared its independence
on Nov. 15, 1983.

Areas occupied by Israel since 1967.

50   100   150   200   250   300 Miles
100   200   300   400   500 Kilometers

150

Relief

Meters		Feet
610		2000
305		1000
152.5		500
0	Sea Level	0
152.5	Below	500
1525	Sea Level	5000

Same scale as main map

SHETLAND
ISLANDS (Br.)

ORKNEY
ISLANDS (Br.)

SCOTLAND

Scale 1: 4 000 000; one inch to 64 miles. Conic Pro
Elevations and depressions are given in feet

Longitude West of Greenwich

Continued on pages 152-153

Continued on pages 154-155

Continued on pages 156-157

Longitude East of Greenwich

20 30 40 50 60 70 80 90 100 110 120 Miles
20 40 60 80 100 120 140 160 180 200 Kilometers

NORWAY

Egersund
Flekkefjord
Farsund
Kristiansand
Mandal
LINDESNES
Arendal
Grimstad
Lillesand

SWEDEN

Kungälv Alingsås Ulricehamn
Göteborg Borås
Mölndal
Varberg
Falkenberg
Oskarström
Helsingborg
Halmstad
Landskrona
Laholm Ängelholm
Lund
Malmö
Trelleborg

Skagen GRENEN
Hjørring
Frederikshavn LÆSØ
Brønderslev
Ålborg
Thisted
Løgstør
Nykøbing Hobro Mariager
Skive Viborg Randers Grenå
Struer
Holstebro Silkeborg Århus
Herning Skanderborg
Ringkøbing
Horsens
Vejle
Varde Fredericia
Esbjerg Kolding Odense
Ribe Middelfart
Haderslev Assens Nyborg Korsør
Åbenrå Fåborg
Tønder Sønderborg
ALS
AERØ
Flensburg
SCHLESWIG-
Schleswig
Husum
Eckernförde
Rendsburg Kiel Neustadt
Tönning Holstein
HOLSTEIN
Heide Neumünster
Itzehoe Bad Oldesloe
Elmshorn

DENMARK

Nykøbing S.
COPENHAGEN (København)
Holbæk Roskilde
SJAELLAND
Ringsted Køge
Slagelse
Næstved
Vordingborg
Svendborg
Rudkøbing
MØN
Nakskov Nykøbing
Maribo FALSTER
LOLLAND
LANGELAND
FEHMARN
Rostock
Wismar Güstrow
Teterow
Lübeck
Schwerin Parchim
MECKLENBURG
Ludwigslust
Pritzwalk Perleberg
Wittenberge
Salzwedel
Stendal Tangermünde
Gardelegen

Skagerrak

NORTH SEA

DOGGER
BANK
60—120 Ft.

Great Yarmouth
Lowestoft
Ipswich
Harwich
Southend-on-Sea
Margate
NORTH FORELAND
Canterbury
Dover
Strait of Dover
Calais
Boulogne-sur-Mer
Étaples
St. Valéry-sur-Somme
Le Tréport
Abbeville

FRISIAN ISLANDS
TERSCHELLING
VLIELAND
TEXEL
Den Helder
Alkmaar
Haarlem
Zaandam
AMSTERDAM
Leiden
The Hague ('s-Gravenhage)
Delft
Vlaardingen
ROTTERDAM
Dordrecht
Bergen op Zoom
Breda
Tilburg
Turnhout
Vlissingen
Oostende
Brugge Gent
ANTWERP
Mechelen
BRUSSELS
BELGIUM
Lille
Roubaix
Tourcoing
Armentières
Béthune
Douai
Arras
Cambrai
FLANDERS
Ieper
Kortrijk
Roeselare
Torhout
Dunkerque
St. Omer
Aalst
Leuven
Nivelles
Mons
La Louvière
Charleroi
Namur
Denain
Valenciennes
Maubeuge
Hautmont
Givet
Bastogne
LUX.
Fourmies

NETHERLANDS
Leeuwarden
Harlingen
Groningen
Delfzijl
Assen
Emmen
Meppel
Zwolle
Almelo
Hengelo
Enschede
Apeldoorn
Deventer
Utrecht
Arnhem
Nijmegen
Kleve
Wesel
Eindhoven
Helmond
Weert
's-Hertogenbosch
Heerlen
Maastricht
Aachen
Eupen
Verviers
Spa
Malmédy
Liège
Seraing
Herstal
Huy
Düren
Mönchengladbach
Solingen
Remscheid
Wuppertal
DÜSSELDORF
COLOGNE (Köln)
Siegburg
Bonn
Siegen
Gummersbach
Lüdenscheid
Hagen
Iserlohn
Arnsberg
Soest
Lippstadt
Paderborn
Gütersloh
Hamm
Ahlen
Münster
Osnabrück
Gronau
Rheine
Nordhorn
Lingen
Meppen
Papenburg
Leer
Emden
Norden
Wilhelmshaven
Cuxhaven
HELGOLAND
BORKUM
ISLANDS
NORDERNEY LANGEOOG
JUIST
AMELAND

FRISIAN ISLANDS

Oldenburg
Delmenhorst
Bremen
BREMERHAVEN
Stade
HAMBURG
Lüneburg
LÜNEBURGER
HEIDE
Verden
Soltau
Uelzen
Celle
Nienburg
Minden
Hannover
Hameln
Hildesheim
Braunschweig
Wolfenbüttel
Goslar
Helmstedt
Schöningen
Magdeburg
Schönebeck
Bernburg
HARZ
Blankenburg
Quedlinburg
Aschersleben
Staßfurt
Halberstadt
Oschersleben
NIEDERSACHSEN
GERMANY
Bielefeld
Herford
Detmold
Einbeck
Northeim
Göttingen
Nordhausen
Sangerhausen
Halle
Merseburg
Heiligenstadt
Mühlhausen
Sondershausen
Eschwege
Kassel
THÜRINGEN
Eisenach
Gotha
Erfurt
Weimar
Jena
Arnstadt
Rudolstadt
Saalfeld
Schmalkalden
Zella-Mehlis
Suhl
Meiningen
Sonneberg
Neustadt b.C.
Coburg
Kulmbach
Bayreuth
Bamberg
FRANKFURT AM MAIN
Offenbach
Hanau
Aschaffenburg
Wiesbaden
Mainz
Darmstadt
Würzburg
Erlangen
WESTERWALD
Limburg an der Lahn
Bad Homburg
Bad Nauheim
Marburg an der Lahn
Gießen
Fulda
Bad Hersfeld
Hünfeld
Hildburghausen
Schweinfurt
Neuwied
Koblenz
Andernach
Mayen
Ahrweiler
Bad Kreuznach
Bad Kissingen
RHEINLAND
EIFEL
PFALZ
RHÖN
Wittlich
Kirn
Bingen

FRANCE

Bayeux

ARDENNES
Dinant

North Foreland

Roskilde

Kiel Bay
BALTIC SEA
NORTH FRISIAN IS.
FÖHR
SYLT
FANØ
RØMØ
AMRUM

MORS
Nissum Fjord
Ringkøbing Fjord
Limfjord
ANHOLT

SAMSØ
FYN

Bogense
Nyborg

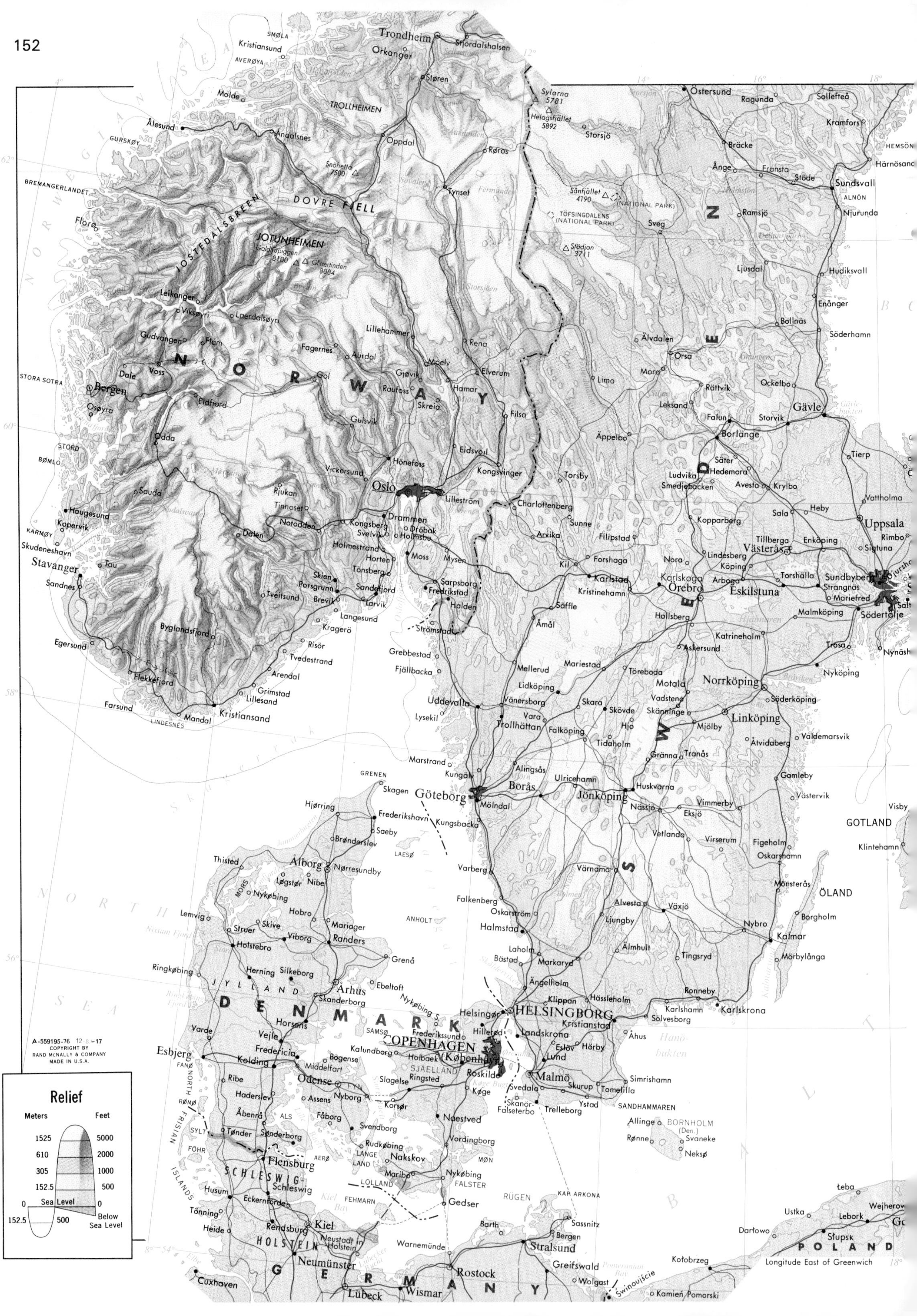

NORWEGIAN SEA

SMØLA
Trondheim
Kristiansund
Stjørdalshalsen
Orkanger
AVERØYA
Molde
Åndalsnes
Ålesund
TROLLHEIMEN
Støren
Oppdal
Røros
Sylarna 5781
Helagsfjället 5892
Østersund
Ragunda
Sollefteå
Kramfors
HEMSÖN
Härnösand
GURSKØY
Storsjö
Ånge
Fransta
Stöde
Sundsvall
ALNÖN
Njurunda
BREMANGERLANDET
Snøhetta 7500
Sånfjället 4190 (NATIONAL PARK)
TÖFSINGDALENS (NATIONAL PARK)
Sveg
Ramsjö
Flora
DOVRE FJELL
JOTUNHEIMEN
Galdhøpiggen 8100
Glittertinden 8984
Stödjan 3711
Ljusdal
Hudiksvall
Enånger
Leikanger
Vikøyri
Lærdalsøyri
Flåm
Lillehammer
Rena
Älvdalen
Orsa
Bollnäs
Söderhamn
Gudvangen
Fagernes
Aurdal
Gjøvik
Moelv
Elverum
Lima
Mora
Rättvik
Ockelbo
NORWAY
Dale
Voss
Gol
Raufoss
Hamar
Leksand
Falun
Storvik
Gävle
Bergen
Eldfjord
Gulsvik
Skreia
Filsa
Äppelbo
Borlänge
STORA SOTRA
Osøyra
Odda
Hønefoss
Eidsvoll
Kongsvinger
Torsby
Ludvika
Smedjebacken
Avesta
Krylbo
Säter
Hedemora
Tierp
Vattholma
STORD
BØMLO
Vickersund
Kongsberg
Drammen
Charlottenberg
Sunne
Kopparberg
Sala
Heby
Uppsala
Rimbo
Sauda
Rjukan
Svelvik
Holmsbu
Arvika
Filipstad
Nora
Köping
Arboga
Tillberga
Enköping
Sigtuna
Haugesund
Tinnoset
Notodden
Holmestrand
Horten
Moss
Mysen
Kil
Forshaga
Karlstad
Karlskoga
Lindesberg
Västerås
Eskilstuna
Sundbyberg
Strängnäs
Mariefred
Södertälje
Kopervik
KARMØY
Skien
Porsgrunn
Tønsberg
Sandefjord
Sarpsborg
Fredrikstad
Kristinehamn
Örebro
Hallsberg
Katrineholm
Malmköping
KVARKEN
Stavanger
Sandnes
Tveitsund
Brevik
Larvik
Halden
Säffle
Åmål
Askersund
Trosa
Nynäshamn
Egersund
Byglandsfjord
Langesund
Kragerø
Strömstad
Mellerud
Mariestad
Töreboda
Motala
Söderköping
Nyköping
Flekkefjord
Risør
Tvedestrand
Arendal
Grebbestad
Fjällbacka
Vänersborg
Lidköping
Skara
Skövde
Skänninge
Vadstena
NORRKÖPING
Farsund
Grimstad
Lillesand
Uddevalla
Vara
Hjo
Linköping
LINDESNES
Mandal
Kristiansand
Lysekil
Trollhättan
Falköping
Tidaholm
Mjölby
Valdemarsvik
Åtvidaberg
Marstrand
Alingsås
Ulricehamn
Huskvarna
Gränna
Tranås
Gamleby
GRENEN
Kungälv
Borås
Jönköping
Nässjö
Vimmerby
Västervik
Skagen
Göteborg
Mölndal
Eksjö
Visby
GOTLAND
Hjørring
Frederikshavn
Kungsbacka
Vetlanda
Virserum
Figeholm
Klintehamn
Brønderslev
Sæby
LÆSØ
Varberg
Värnamo
Oskarshamn
ÖLAND
Thisted
Ålborg
Nørresundby
Falkenberg
Oskarström
Alvesta
Växjö
Nybro
Borgholm
MORS
Løgstør
Nibe
ANHOLT
Ljungby
Kalmar
Lemvig
Nykøbing
Hobro
Mariager
Halmstad
Älmhult
Tingsryd
Mörbylånga
Struer
Skive
Viborg
Randers
Laholm
Markaryd
Ringkøbing
Holstebro
Grenå
Båstad
Ängelholm
Ronneby
Herning
Silkeborg
Ebeltoft
Nykøbing S.
Helsingør
Klippan
Hässleholm
Karlshamn
Karlskrona
JYLLAND
Århus
Skanderborg
HELSINGBORG
Landskrona
Kristianstad
Sölvesborg
DENMARK
Varde
Vejle
Horsens
SAMSØ
Frederikssund
Hillerød
Eslöv
Hörby
Åhus
HANÖ BUKTEN
Esbjerg
FANØ
Kolding
Fredericia
Middelfart
Bogense
Kalundborg
Holbæk
COPENHAGEN København
Roskilde
Svedala
Lund
Malmö
Skurup
Tomelilla
Simrishamn
Ribe
Åbenrå
FYN
Odense
Nyborg
Slagelse
Ringsted
Køge
Køge Bugt
Skanör Falsterbo
Trelleborg
Ystad
SANDHAMMAREN
Haderslev
ALS
Assens
Fåborg
Svendborg
Korsør
Næstved
Allinge
BORNHOLM (Den.)
Sønderborg
ÆRØ
Rudkøbing
LANGE LAND
Nakskov
Vordingborg
MØN
Rønne
Svaneke
Neksø
SYLT
Tønder
Flensburg
Maribo
Nykøbing FALSTER
KAP ARKONA
Husum
Eckernförde
LOLLAND
Gedser
RÜGEN
Leba
Ustka
FÖHR
SCHLESWIG
Schleswig
Kiel Bay
FEHMARN
Barth
Sassnitz
Bergen
Słupsk
FRISIAN ISLANDS
RØMØ
Tønning
Heide
Rendsburg
Kiel
Neustadt in Holstein
HOLSTEIN
Neumünster
Warnemünde
Stralsund
Greifswald
Świnoujście
Kamień Pomorski
Kołobrzeg
Darłowo
POLAND
Cuxhaven
Lübeck
Wismar
Rostock
GERMANY
Wolgast
Relief

Meters		Feet
1525		5000
610		2000
305		1000
152.5		500
0	Sea Level	0
152.5		Below Sea Level 500

A-559195-76 12 -17
COPYRIGHT BY
RAND McNALLY & COMPANY
MADE IN U.S.A.

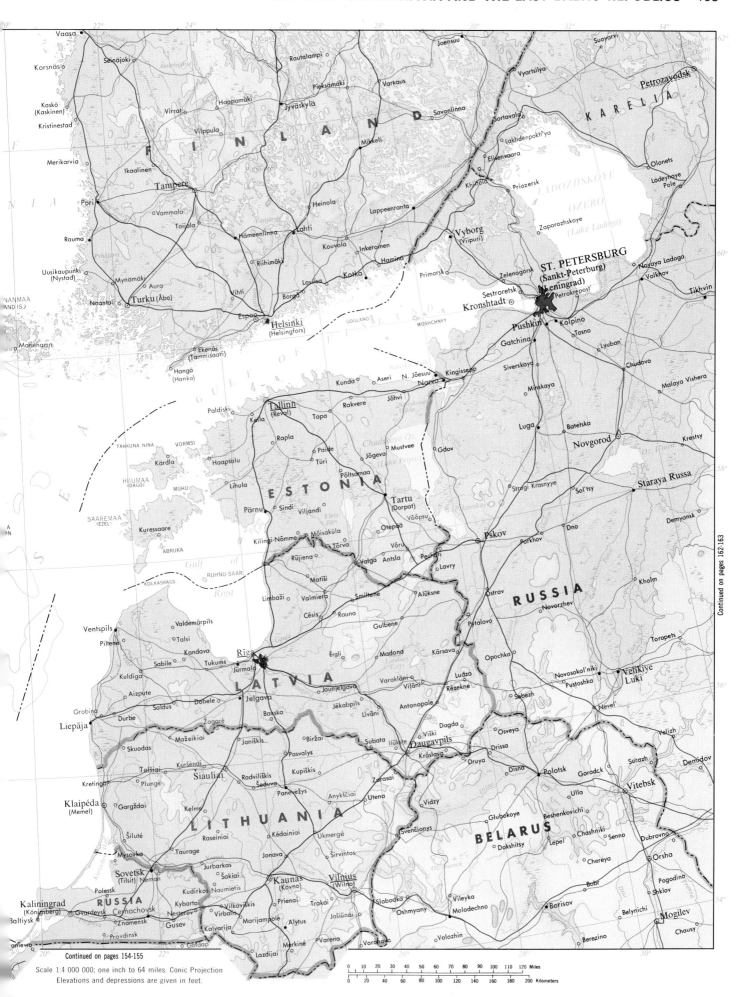

Continued on pages 162-163

Continued on pages 154-155

Scale 1:4 000 000; one inch to 64 miles. Conic Projection
Elevations and depressions are given in feet.

0 10 20 30 40 50 60 70 80 90 100 110 120 Miles

0 20 40 60 80 100 120 140 160 180 200 Kilometers

Continued on pages 152-153

DENMARK

NORTH SEA

FRISIAN ISLANDS

NETHERLANDS

AMSTERDAM

BELGIUM

LUXEMBOURG

FRANCE

SWITZERLAND

GERMANY

DÜSSELDORF
COLOGNE (Köln)
ESSEN
Dortmund
Wuppertal
Bonn
Duisburg
Bochum
Mönchengladbach
Aachen

HAMBURG
Bremen
Bremerhaven
Wilhelmshaven
Oldenburg
Delmenhorst
Groningen
Leeuwarden
Den Helder
Alkmaar

NIEDERSACHSEN
Hannover
Braunschweig
Hildesheim
Wolfsburg
Celle
Lüneburger HEIDE

SCHLESWIG-HOLSTEIN
Kiel
Flensburg
Schleswig
Neumünster
Rendsburg
Husum
Heide

Lübeck
Wismar
Schwerin
Rostock
Stralsund
Rügen
Greifswald

MECKLENBURG

POMERANIA
Szczecin (Stettin)
Stargard Szczeciński
Kołobrzeg
Koszalin

BERLIN
Potsdam
Brandenburg
Magdeburg
BRANDENBURG
Frankfurt an der Oder
Cottbus
Zielona Góra
Gorzów Wlkp.

POLAND

Leipzig
Halle
Dessau
Dresden
Görlitz
Chemnitz
Zwickau
Gera
Jena
Erfurt
Weimar
Gotha
Eisenach

THÜRINGEN
HARZ
Göttingen
Kassel
Paderborn
Münster
Bielefeld
Osnabrück

HESSEN
FRANKFURT AM MAIN
Wiesbaden
Mainz
Offenbach
Darmstadt
Hanau
Aschaffenburg
Würzburg
Schweinfurt
Fulda
Marburg
Giessen
Koblenz

RHEINLAND-PFALZ
SAARLAND
Saarbrücken
Kaiserslautern
Trier
Luxembourg

MANNHEIM
Heidelberg
Ludwigshafen
Speyer
Karlsruhe
Pforzheim
STUTTGART
Esslingen
Tübingen
Reutlingen
Heilbronn
Ulm
Ne Ulm
Augsburg

BADEN-WÜRTTEMBERG
Freiburg
Offenburg
SCHWARZWALD

Nürnberg
Fürth
Erlangen
Bamberg
Bayreuth
Hof
Regensburg
Ingolstadt
Landshut
Passau

BAYERN (BAVARIA)

MUNICH (München)
Dachau
Freising
Garmisch-Partenkirchen

CZECH REPUBLIC
PRAGUE (Praha)
Plzeň
Kladno
Hradec Králové
Pardubice
Liberec
Jelenia Góra
Wałbrzych
BOHEMIA (ČECHY)
ČESKOMORAVSKÁ
České Budějovice
Jihlava
Brno

BOHEMIAN FOREST
ERZGEBIRGE

AUSTRIA
VIENNA (Wien)
Linz
Salzburg
Innsbruck
Graz
Klagenfurt
OBERÖSTERREICH
SALZBURG
STEIERMARK
KÄRNTEN
HOHE TAUERN
NIEDERE TAUERN
Villach
Wiener Neustadt

SWITZERLAND
Zürich
Basel
Bern
Geneva (Genève)
Lausanne
Neuchâtel
St. Gallen
Luzern
Winterthur
Schaffhausen
LIECHTENSTEIN
VORARLBERG

SLOVENIA
Maribor
CROATIA
Udine

BALTIC

Continued on pages 156-157

Continued on pages 160-161

Longitude East of Greenwich

Scale 1:4 000 000; one inch to 64 miles. Conic Projection
Elevations and depressions are given in feet.

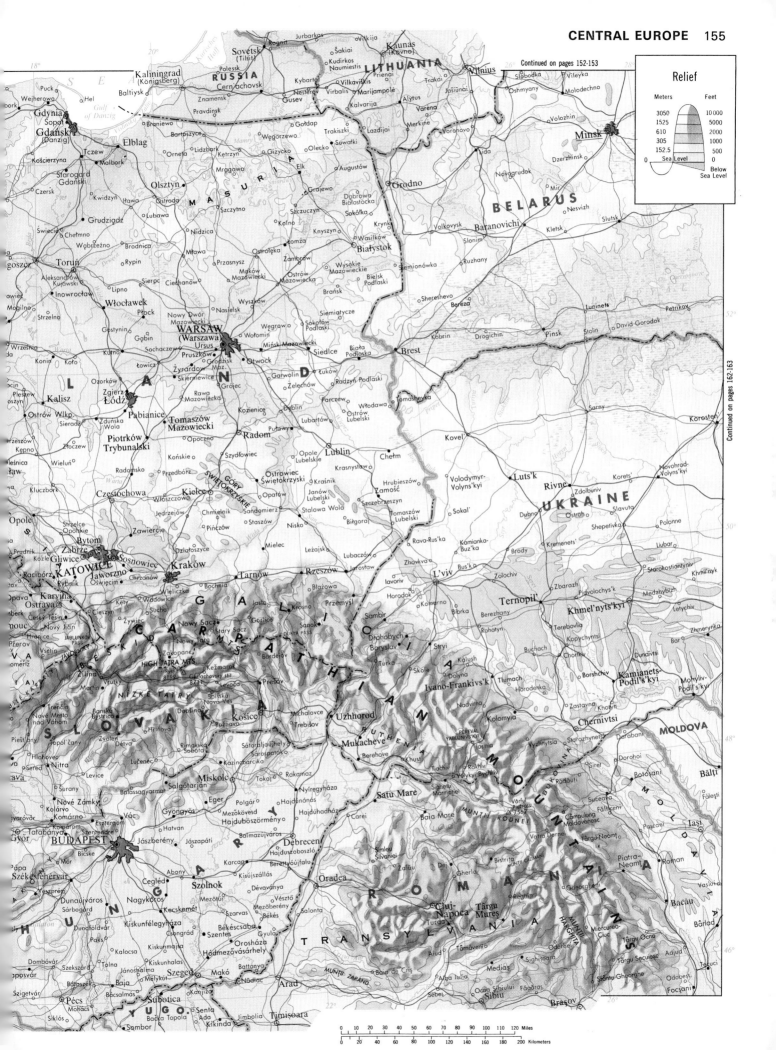

Continued on pages 152-153

Continued on pages 162-163

Relief

Meters	Feet
3050	10 000
1525	5000
610	2000
305	1000
152.5	500
Sea Level	0
	Below Sea Level

RUSSIA

LITHUANIA

Kaliningrad (Königsberg)

Gdynia
Sopot
Gdańsk
(Danzig)

Kaunas
(Kovno)

Vilnius

Minsk

BELARUS

MASURIA

WARSAW
(Warszawa)
Ursus

Łódź

P O L A N D

Brest

UKRAINE

Lublin

Kraków

Katowice

G A L I C I A

C A R P A T H I A N

L'viv

Ternopil'

Khmel'nyts'kyi

Uzhhorod

RUTHENIA

M O U N T A I N S

MOLDOVA

SLOVAKIA

Košice

Mukacheve

BUDAPEST

H U N G A R Y

Miskolc

Satu Mare

Debrecen

Oradea

R O M A N I A

T R A N S Y L V A N I A

Cluj-Napoca

Târgu Mureş

Sibiu

Braşov

YUGO.

Timişoara

Arad

MOLDAVIA

Iaşi

Bacău

0   10 20 30 40 50 60 70 80 90 100 110 120 Miles

0   20   40   60   80   100 120 140 160 180 200 Kilometers

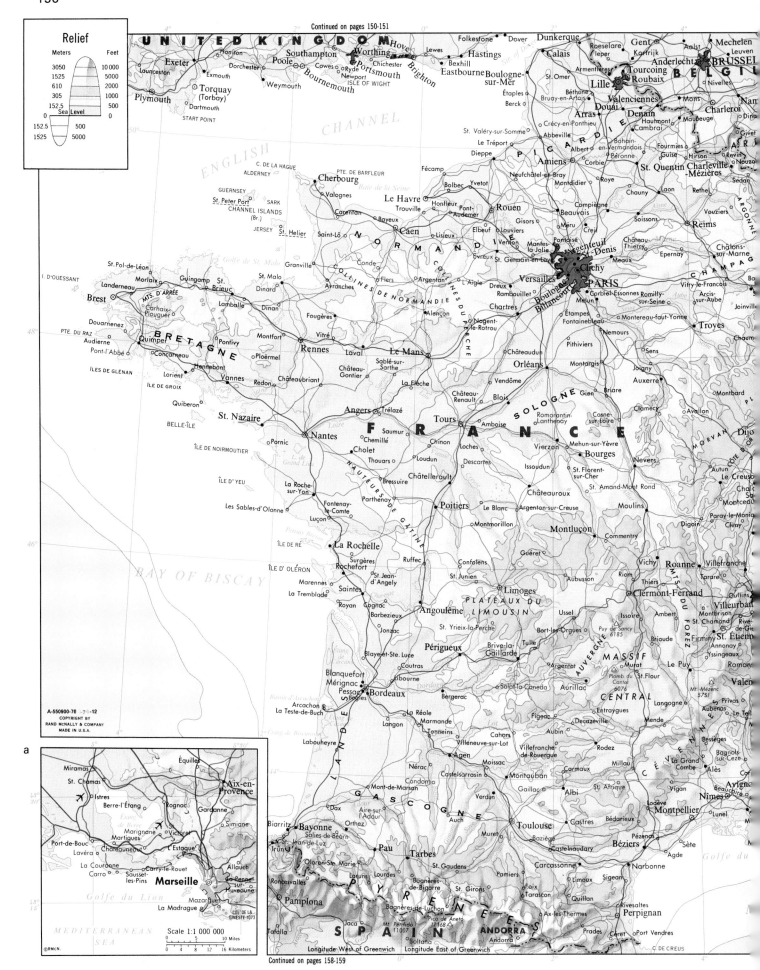

156

Relief

Meters	Feet
3050	10 000
1525	5000
610	2000
305	1000
152.5	500
0 Sea Level	0
152.5	500
1525	5000

Continued on pages 150-151

UNITED KINGDOM

Exeter · Honiton · Southampton · Worthing · Hove · Lewes · Folkestone · Dover · Dunkerque · Roeselare · Gent · Aalst · Mechelen
Launceston · Dorchester · Poole · Cowes · Portsmouth · Chichester · Brighton · Hastings · Eastbourne · Calais · Ieper · Kortrijk · Anderlecht · BRUSSEL · BELGIЇ
Plymouth · Torquay (Torbay) · Weymouth · Bournemouth · Newport · ISLE OF WIGHT · Boulogne-sur-Mer · St. Omer · Armentieres · Tourcoing · Roubaix · Nivelles · Nam
Dartmouth · Exmouth · Ryde · Étaples · Bruay-en-Artois · Lille · Valenciennes · Mons · Charleroi · Dina
START POINT · Berck · Béthune · Douai · Denain · Hautmont · Maubeuge · Givet
Arras · Cambrai · AR

CHANNEL

St. Valéry-sur-Somme · Crécy-en-Ponthieu · PICARDIE · Bohain-en-Vermandois · Fourmies · Revin · Nouzo
C. DE LA HAGUE · Le Tréport · Abbeville · Albert · Péronne · Guise · Hirson · Sedan
ALDERNEY · PTE. DE BARFLEUR · Dieppe · Corbie · Amiens · St. Quentin · Charleville-Mézières
GUERNSEY · Cherbourg · Fécamp · Neufchâtel-en-Bray · Montdidier · Roye · Chauny · Laon · Rethel · ARGONNE
St. Peter Port · SARK · Valognes · Baie de la Seine · Bolbec · Yvetot · Beauvais · Méru · Soissons · Vouziers
CHANNEL ISLANDS (Br.) · Carentan · Le Havre · Honfleur · Pont-Audemer · Rouen · Gisors · Creil · Reims · Châlons-sur-Marne
JERSEY · St. Helier · Bayeux · Trouville · Elbeuf · Louviers · Compiègne · Épernay · CHAMPAG
Saint-Lô · Caen · Lisieux · Vernon · Pontoise · Argenteuil · St-Denis · Château-Thierry · Aube
NORMANDIE · Conde · Flers · Argentan · Évreux · St. Germain-en-Laye · Clichy · Meaux · Vitry-le-François · Ba
Granville · Avranches · L'Aigle · Dreux · Versailles · PARIS · Corbeil-Essonnes · Romilly-sur-Seine · Arcis-sur-Aube · Joinville
COLLINES DE NORMANDIE · Rambouillet · Boulogne-Billancourt · Melun · Étampes · Montereau-faut-Yonne · Troyes
St. Pol-de-Léon · Landerneau · Guingamp · St. Brieuc · St. Malo · Dinard · Fougères · Chartres · Nogent-le-Rotrou · Fontainebleau · Nemours · Chaum
I. D'OUESSANT · Morlaix · MTS. D'ARRÉE · Dinan · Lamballe · Vitré · Alençon · Pithiviers · Sens · Joigny
Brest · Carhaix-Plouguer · Laval · Le Mans · Châteaudun · Montargis · Auxerre · Montbard
Douarnenez · BRETAGNE · Rennes · Sablé-sur-Sarthe · Vendôme · Orléans · Clamecy · Avallon · MORVAN · Dijo
PTE. DU RAZ · Quimper · Pontivy · Montfort · Château-Gontier · La Flèche · Blois · SOLOGNE · Gien · Briare · CÔTE D'OR
Audierne · Ploërmel · Château-Renault · Amboise · Romorantin-Lanthenay · Cosne-sur-Loire · Autun · Le Creuso
Pont-l'Abbé · Concarneau · Redon · Angers · Trélazé · Tours · Vierzon · Nevers · Chal Sa · Montceau
ÎLES DE GLÉNAN · Hennebont · Vannes · Châteaubriant · FRANCE · Saumur · Chinon · Loches · Bourges · Digoin · Paray-le-Monia · Cluny
Lorient · ÎLE DE GROIX · Nantes · Cholet · Chemillé · St. Florent-sur-Cher · Moulins
Quiberon · St. Nazaire · Pornic · Thouars · Loudun · Descartes · St. Amand-Mont Rond
BELLE-ÎLE · ÎLE DE NOIRMOUTIER · La Roche-sur-Yon · HAUTEURS DE GÂTINE · Bressuire · Châtellerault · Châteauroux · Argenton-sur-Creuse
Golfe de St. Malo · Parthenay · Poitiers · Le Blanc · Montluçon · Commentry
ÎLE D'YEU · Fontenay-le-Comte · Montmorillon
Luçon · Niort · Guéret · Vichy · Roanne · Villefranche
ÎLE DE RÉ · La Rochelle · Surgères · Ruffec · Confolens · Aubusson · Riom · Thiers · Tarare
BAY OF BISCAY · ÎLE D'OLÉRON · Rochefort · St. Jean-d'Angély · St. Junien · Limoges · Ussel · Clermont-Ferrand · Villeurban
Marennes · Saintes · PLATEAUX DU · Issoire · Puy de Sancy 6185 · Ambert · Montbrison · St. Chamond · Rive-de-Gie · St. Étien
La Tremblade · Royan · Cognac · Angoulême · LIMOUSIN · Bort-les-Orgues · Brioude · Firminy · St. Étien · Annonay
Barbezieux · St. Yrieix-la-Perche · AUVERGNE · Le Puy · Yssingeaux
Jonzac · Périgueux · Brive-la-Gaillarde · Tulle · Argentat · Plomb du Cantal 6076 · St. Flour · Romans · Valen
Blaye-et-Ste. Luce · Coutras · MASSIF · Murat · Aurillac · Mt. Mézenc 5751 · Privas
Blanquefort · Libourne · Salat-la-Caneda · Langogne · Aubenas · Le Tell
Mérignac · Pessac · Bordeaux · Bergerac · CENTRAL · Entraygues · Mende
Arcachon · Bègles · Figeac · Decazeville · Aubin · CÉVENNES · Bessèges · Bagnols-sur-Cèze
La Teste-de-Buch · La Réole · Marmande · Cahors · Rodez · Millau · La Grand Combe · Alès
Langon · Tonneins · Villefranche-de-Rouergue · Avign
Labouheyre · Villeneuve-sur-Lot · Moissac · Carmaux · St. Afrique · Vigan · Lodève · Nîmes
Agen · Montauban · Gaillac · Albi · Beaucaire
Nérac · LANDES · Castelsarrasin · Condom · Gaillac · Lunel · Montpellier
Mont-de-Marsan · Verdun · Gascogne · Toulouse · Castres · Bédarieux · Pézenas · Béziers · Sète
Dax · Aire-sur-l'Adour · Auch · Bazeige · Castelnaudary · Agde · Golfe du
Biarritz · Bayonne · Salies-de-Béarn · Orthez · Muret · Baziège · Carcassonne · Narbonne
St. Jean-de-Luz · Pau · Tarbes · St. Gaudens · Pamiers · Limoux · Sigean · Rivesaltes
Irún · Oloron-Ste. Marie · Lourdes · Bagnères-de-Bigorre · St. Girons · Foix · Quillan · Perpignan
Roncesvalles · Laruns · St. Gaudens · Bagnères-de-Luchon · Tarascon · Ax-les-Thermes · Prades · Port Vendres
Pamplona · Jaca · Mt. Perdido 11007 · PYRÉNÉES · Pico de Aneto 11168 · ANDORRA · Céret · C. DE CREUS
SPAIN · Boltaña · Andorra
Tafalla

a — Marseille inset

Miramas · Équiller · Aix-en-Provence · St. Chamas · Istres · Rognac · Gardanne · Simiane · Berre-l'Étang · Étang de Berre · Marignane · St. Victoret · Port-de-Bouc · Martigues · L'Estaque · Allauch · Lavéra · Châteauneuf · Penne-sur-Huveaune · La Couronne · Carry-le-Rouet · Sausset-les-Pins · Carro · Marseille · Mazargue · La Madrague

MEDITERRANEAN SEA · Golfe du Lion · COL DE LA GINESTE 1073

Scale 1:1 000 000
0 · 5 · 10 Miles
0 · 4 · 8 · 12 · 16 Kilometers

©RMCN

Continued on pages 158-159

Longitude West of Greenwich · Longitude East of Greenwich

Scale 1:4 000 000; one inch to 64 miles. Conic Projec
Elevations and depressions are given in feet

b

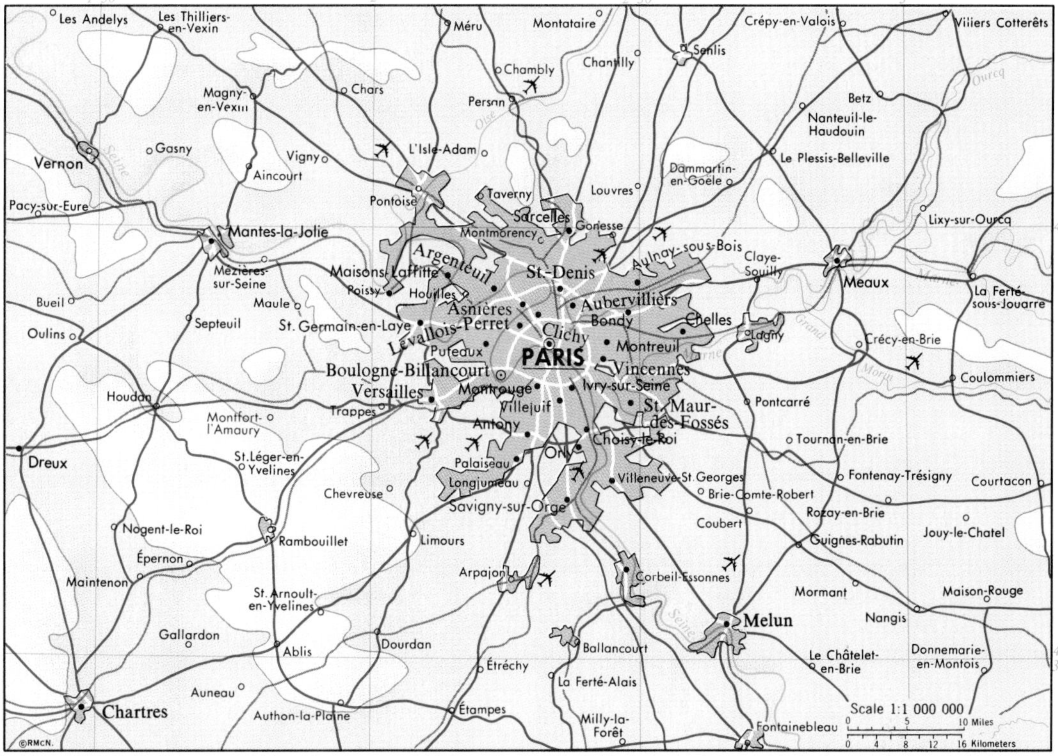

c

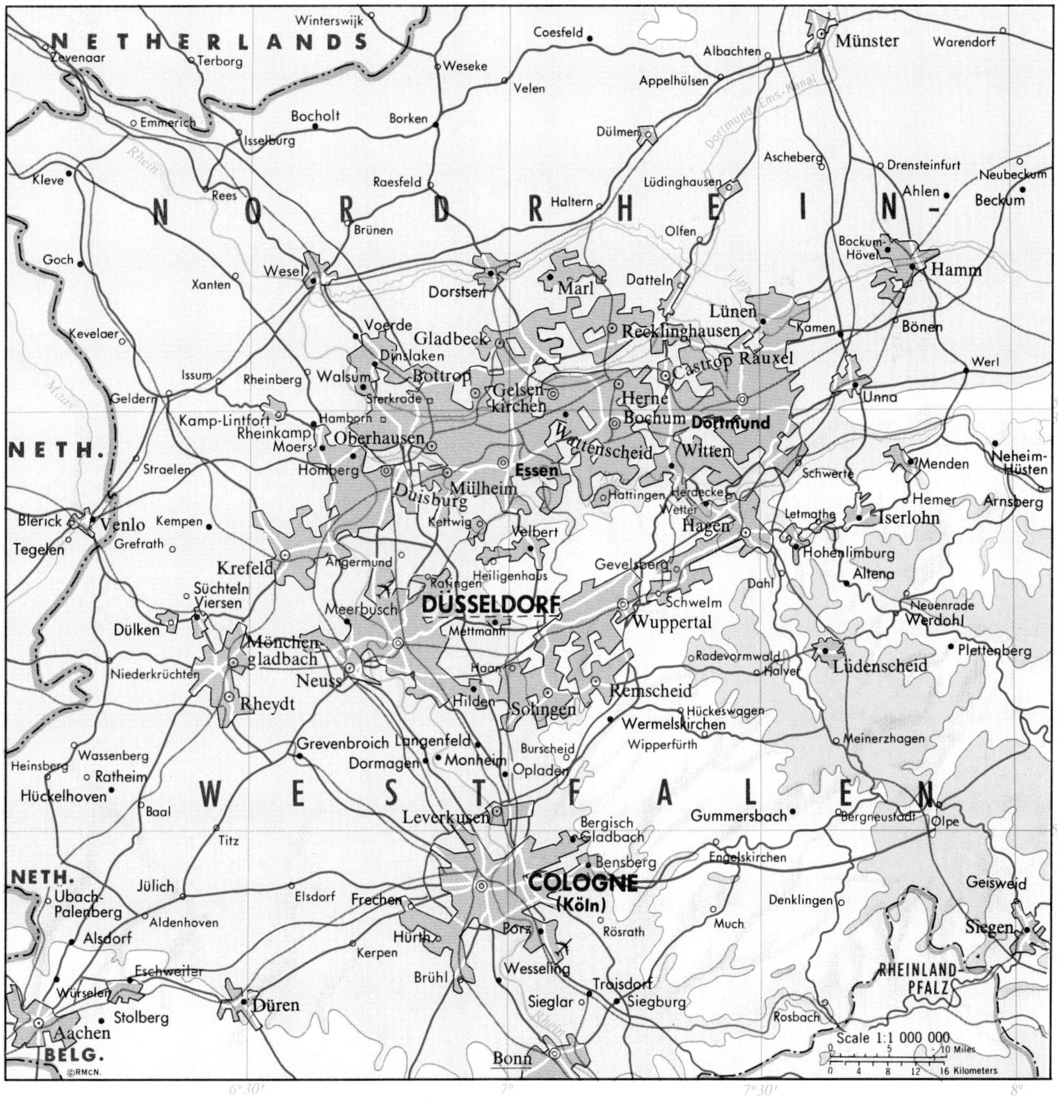

Scale 1:1 000 000

0   4   8   12   16 Kilometers

0   10 Miles

For larger scale coverage of Dusseldorf and Paris see pages 236 and 237.

20   30   40   50   60   70   80   90   100   110   120 Miles

0   40   60   80   100   120   140   160   180   200 Kilometers

Left map (Rhine / Alps region):

COLOGNE (Köln), Siegen, Düren, Siegburg, Aachen, Bonn, Neuwied, Wetzlar, WESTERWALD, RHEINLAND, Koblenz, Andernach, Cochem, EIFEL, PFALZ, FRANKFURT AM MAIN, Wiesbaden, Mainz, Bad Ems, Limburg an der Lahn, Wittlich, Bingen, Bad Kreuznach, Worms, Trier, HUNSRÜCK, Luxembourg, LUX, Esch-sur-Alzette, Thionville, Merzig, SAARLAND, MANNHEIM, Ludwigshafen, Speyer, Kaiserslautern, Neunkirchen, Saarbrücken, Zweibrücken, Landau, Forbach, Metz, Sarreguemines, Wissembourg, Karlsruhe, Rastatt, Pont-à-Mousson, Sarrebourg, Saverne, Haguenau, Baden-Baden, Nancy, Lunéville, Bischeim, Schiltigheim, Strasbourg, Dombasle-sur-Meurthe, Baccarat, Erstein, Offenburg, Charmes, St-Dié, Sélestat, Épinal, Thaon-les-Vosges, Ste-Marie-aux-Mines, Remiremont, Colmar, Guebwiller, Freiburg, Thann, Luxeuil-les-Bains, Mulhouse, Lörrach, Vesoul, Belfort, Beaucourt, Montbéliard, Porrentruy, Olten, Aarau, Basel, Besançon, Solothurn, Biel, Langenthal, Luzern, Salins-les-Bains, Neuchâtel, Burgdorf, Pontarlier, Bern, Yverdon, Moudon, Thun, SWITZERLAND, Lausanne, BERNER ALPEN, Jungfrau 13 642, Geneva, Vevey, Brig, SIMPLON PASS, Thonon-les-Bains, Sion, ALPES PENNINES, Matterhorn 14 692, Monte Rosa 15 203, Genève, Annemasse, Martigny, Chamonix, Mont-Blanc 15 771, Annecy, Mt. Blanc, Aosta, Gran Paradiso 13 323, Ivrea, Albertville, Aix-les-Bains, Villard-Bonnot, Chivasso, Grenoble, Moûtiers, La Mure, Briançon, TURIN (Torino), ALPES, Mt. Viso 12 602, Saluzzo, Gap, Embrun, COTTIENNES, Cuneo, Bra, Mt. Pelat 10 010, MARITIME ALPS, Digne, Breil-sur-Roya, San Remo, Draguignan, Grasse, Menton, Cagnes, Nice, MONACO, en-Provence, Cannes, Antibes, Fréjus, Marseille, Aubagne, Hyères, St. Tropez, Toulon, ILES D'HYÈRES, MEDITERRANEAN SEA

Upper right map (Paris region):

Les Andelys, Les Thilliers-en-Vexin, Méru, Montataire, Crépy-en-Valois, Viliers Cotterêts, Magny-en-Vexin, Chars, Chambly, Chantilly, Senlis, Betz, Ourcq, Vernon, Gasny, Vigny, Aincourt, L'Isle-Adam, Persan, Nanteuil-le-Haudouin, Le Plessis-Belleville, Pacy-sur-Eure, Pontoise, Taverny, Louvres, Dammartin-en-Goele, Lixy-sur-Ourcq, Seine, Mantes-la-Jolie, Montmorency, Sarcelles, Goriesse, Mézières-sur-Seine, Argenteuil, Aulnay-sous-Bois, Claye-Souilly, Meaux, La Ferté-sous-Jouarre, Maisons-Laffitte, Poissy, St-Denis, Aubervilliers, Maule, Asnières, Bondy, Chelles, Lagny, Grand, Septeuil, St. Germain-en-Laye, Levallois-Perret, Clichy, Montreuil, Houilles, Bueil, Oulins, Houdan, PARIS, Vincennes, Crécy-en-Brie, Coulommiers, Boulogne-Billancourt, Montrouge, Ivry-sur-Seine, Pontcarré, Versailles, Trappes, Antony, ORLY, St-Maur-des-Fossés, Tournan-en-Brie, Montfort-l'Amaury, Villejuif, Choisy-le-Roi, Dreux, St. Léger-en-Yvelines, Palaiseau, Longjumeau, Villeneuve St Georges, Brie-Comte-Robert, Fontenay-Trésigny, Courtacon, Chevreuse, Savigny-sur-Orge, Rozay-en-Brie, Jouy-le-Chatel, Nogent-le-Roi, Rambouillet, Limours, Coubert, Guignes-Rabutin, Épernon, Arpajon, Corbeil-Essonnes, Mormant, Maison-Rouge, Maintenon, St. Arnoult-en-Yvelines, Ballancourt, Nangis, Donnemarie-en-Montois, Gallardon, Dourdan, Melun, Le Châtelet-en-Brie, Ablis, Étréchy, Auneau, Authon-la-Plaine, Étampes, Milly-la-Forêt, La Ferté-Alais, Chartres, Fontainebleau, Seine

Lower right map (Ruhr region):

Winterswijk, Coesfeld, Albachten, Münster, Warendorf, NETHERLANDS, Zevenaar, Terborg, Weseke, Velen, Appelhülsen, Emmerich, Isselburg, Bocholt, Borken, Dülmen, Ascheberg, Drensteinfurt, Neubeckum, Kleve, Rees, Raesfeld, Lüdinghausen, Ahlen, Beckum, Goch, Brünen, Haltern, Olfen, Bockum-Hövel, Hamm, NORDRHEIN, Wesel, Xanten, Dorstsen, Datteln, Lünen, Bönen, Werl, Kevelaer, Voerde, Marl, Recklinghausen, Kamen, NETH., Gelderen, Issum, Dinslaken, Gladbeck, Castrop-Rauxel, Unna, Rheinberg, Walsum, Bottrop, Gelsenkirchen, Herne, Bochum, Dortmund, Witten, Kamp-Lintfort, Sterkrade, Hamborn, Oberhausen, Wattenscheid, Straelen, Moers, Homberg, Essen, Mülheim, Schwerte, Menden, Neheim-Hüsten, Blerick, Venlo, Kempen, Duisburg, Kettwig, Hattingen, Herdecke, Wetter, Hagen, Letmathe, Hemer, Arnsberg, NETH., Tegelen, Grefrath, Angermund, Heiligenhaus, Velbert, Gevelsberg, Hohenlimburg, Altena, Krefeld, Ratingen, Schwelm, Dahl, Neuenrade, Werdohl, Süchteln, Viersen, DÜSSELDORF, Remscheid, Dülken, Meerbusch, Mettmann, Haan, Solingen, Wuppertal, Lüdenscheid, Mönchengladbach, Neuss, Hilden, Radevormwald, Halver, Plettenberg, Niederkrüchten, Remscheid, Wermelskirchen, Hückeswagen, Meinerzhagen, Rheydt, Grevenbroich, Langenfeld, Burscheid, Wipperfürth, Heinsberg, Wassenberg, Dormagen, Monheim, Opladen, Engelskirchen, Hückelhoven, Ratheim, WESTFALEN, Leverkusen, Bergisch Gladbach, Gummersbach, Bergneustadt, Olpe, Baal, Titz, Bensberg, NETH., Ubach-Palenberg, Jülich, Elsdorf, Frechen, COLOGNE (Köln), Much, Denklingen, Geisweid, Alsdorf, Aldenhoven, Kerpen, Porz, Rösrath, Siegen, Würselen, Hürth, Wesseling, Troisdorf, RHEINLAND-PFALZ, Eschweiler, Brühl, Siegburg, Aachen, Stolberg, Düren, Sieglar, Rosbach, BELG., Bonn, Rhein, Maas

A-552900-76 -6 -11

Scale 1:4 000 000, one inch to 64 miles. Conic Projection
Elevations and depressions are given in feet

Longitude West of Greenwich

Relief

Meters		Feet
3050		10000
1525		5000
610		2000
305		1000
152.5		500
0	Sea Level	0
152.5		500
1525		5000
3050		10000

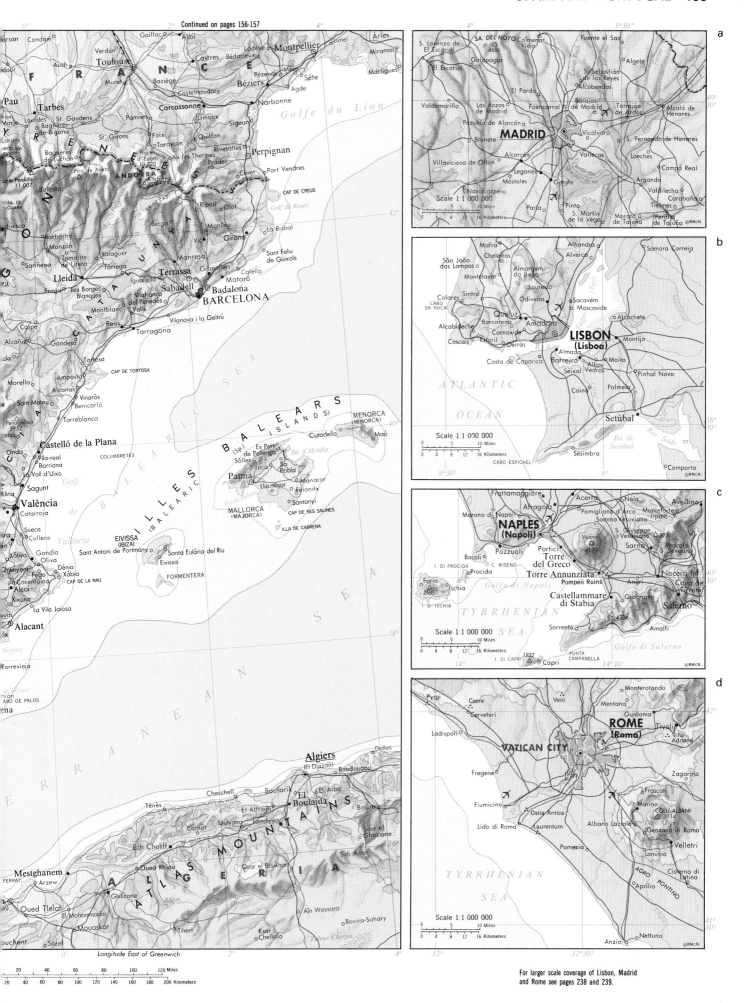

For larger scale coverage of Lisbon, Madrid and Rome see pages 238 and 239.

Relief

Feet	Meters
5000	1525
2000	610
1000	305
500	152.5
Sea Level	0
500	152.5

Continued on pages 152-153

Cities and Towns

| 0 to 50,000 | ○ | 500,000 to 1,000,000 | ◎ |
| 50,000 to 500,000 | ⊙ | 1,000,000 and over | |

Scale 1:4 000 000; one inch to 64 miles. Conic Proj
Elevations and depressions are given in feet

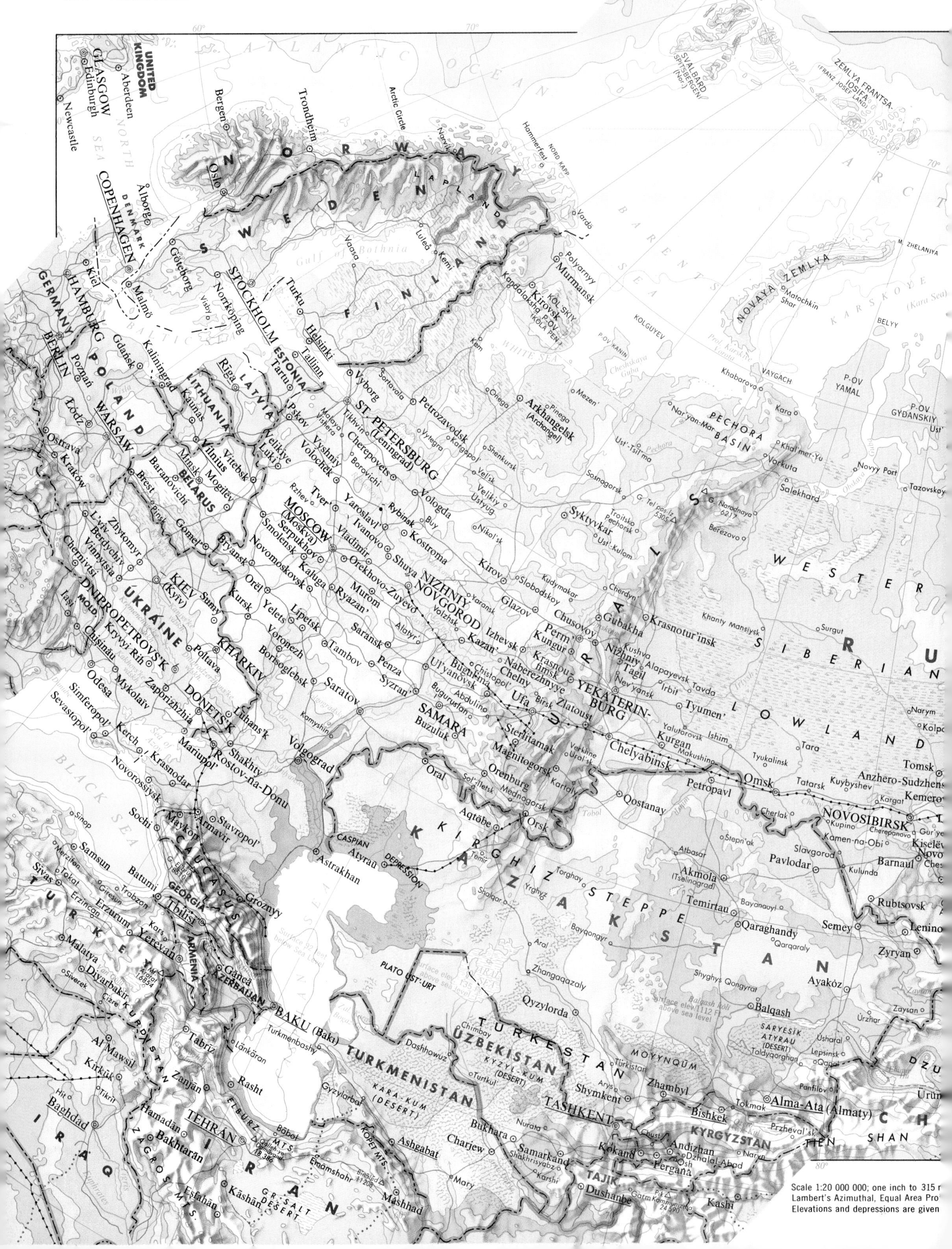

ATLANTIC OCEAN

UNITED KINGDOM
GLASGOW
Aberdeen
Edinburgh
Newcastle

NORTH SEA

NORWAY
SWEDEN
Bergen
Oslo
Trondheim
Göteborg

DENMARK
COPENHAGEN
Ålborg
Kiel
Malmö

GERMANY
HAMBURG
BERLIN
Poznań
Gdańsk

POLAND
WARSAW
Łódź
Kraków
Ostrava

BALTIC SEA
Kaliningrad
Visby
Norrköping

STOCKHOLM
Turku
Helsinki
Tallinn

FINLAND
Vaasa
Gulf of Bothnia
Luleå
Kemi

Lapland

Narvik
Hammerfest
NORD KAPP
Vardø
Kirkenes
Polyarnyy
Murmansk
KOL'SKIY POLUOSTROV
(KOLA PEN.)

BARENTS SEA

SVALBARD
(SPITSBERGEN) (Nor.)
SHTSENBERG
ZEMLYA FRANTSA IOSIFA
(FRANZ JOSEF LAND)

M. ZHELANIYA
NOVAYA ZEMLYA
Matochkin Shar
KARSKOYE (Kara Sea)
BELYY

ARCTIC

ESTONIA
Tartu
LATVIA
Riga
LITHUANIA
Vilnius
Kaunas

BELARUS
Minsk
Mogilev

ST. PETERSBURG
(Leningrad)
Vyborg
Pskov
Novgorod

WHITE SEA
Arkhangelsk
(Archangel)
Onega
Mezen'

PECHORA BASIN
Nar'yan-Mar
Vorkuta
Salekhard

P-OV YAMAL
P-OV GYDANSKIY

Novyy Port
Tazovskoy

Petrozavodsk

MOSCOW
(Moskva)
Tver'
Yaroslavl'
Vladimir
Ivanovo
Kostroma
Rybinsk
Vologda

NIZHNIY NOVGOROD
Kazan'
Kirov
Syktyvkar

WESTERN SIBERIAN LOWLAND
Khanty Mansiysk
Surgut
Narym

Smolensk
Kaluga
Ryazan'
Tula
Orël
Kursk
Lipetsk
Voronezh
Tambov
Penza
Saransk

UKRAINE
KIEV (Kyiv)
KHARKIV
Poltava
DNIPROPETROVS'K
Kryvyi Rih
Zaporizhzhia
DONETS'K
Luhans'k

MOLDOVA
Chişinău
Odesa
Mykolaiv

BLACK SEA
Simferopol'
Sevastopol'
Kerch
Novorossiysk
Sochi

SAMARA
Ul'yanovsk
Saratov
Volgograd
Orenburg
Ufa
Sterlitamak
Magnitogorsk

YEKATERIN-BURG
Nizhniy Tagil
Perm'
Chelyabinsk
Kurgan
Tyumen'
Omsk
NOVOSIBIRSK
Tomsk
Barnaul
Rubtsovsk

CASPIAN DEPRESSION
Astrakhan
Atyraü

CAUCASUS
Maykop
Grozny
Stavropol'
Rostov-na-Donu

GEORGIA
Tbilisi
ARMENIA
Yerevan
AZERBAIJAN
BAKU (Baki)

TURKEY
Erzurum
Kars

KAZAKSTAN
KIRGHIZ STEPPE
Aqtöbe
Orsk
Qostanay
Petropavl
Akmola (Tselinograd)
Qaraghandy
Temirtau
Semey

Aral
Shalqar

PLATO UST'-URT

TURKMENISTAN
KARA-KUM (DESERT)
Ashgabat
Turkmenbashy
Mary

UZBEKISTAN
TASHKENT
Bukhara
Samarkand
KYZYL-KUM (DESERT)
Qyzylorda
Shymkent
Zhambyl

TURKESTAN
SARYESIK ATYRAÜ (DESERT)

KYRGYZSTAN
Bishkek
ALMA-ATA (Almaty)
TIEN SHAN

TAJIKISTAN
Dushanbe

IRAN
TEHRAN
ELBURZ MTS.
Mashhad

IRAQ
Baghdad

Balqash Köli
Balqash
Zaysan

Scale 1:20 000 000; one inch to 315 miles
Lambert's Azimuthal, Equal Area Projection
Elevations and depressions are given

Relief

Meters		Feet
3050		10 000
1525		5000
610		2000
305		1000
152.5		500
0	Sea Level	0
152.5		500
1525		5000 Below
3050		10 000 Sea Level

ARCTIC OCEAN

SEVERNAYA ZEMLYA
(NORTHERN LAND)

P-OV
GORY

TAYMYR
BYRRANGA

M. CHELYUSKIN

Nordvik

BOL'SHOY
BEGICHEV

Ust'-Olenek

LAPTEV SEA

Khatangskiy
Zaliv

Khatanga

Tiksi

KOTEL'NYY

NOVOSIBIRSKIYE O-VA
(NEW SIBERIAN ISLANDS)

DE LONGA

NOVAYA SIBIR'
FADDEYA

MALYY LYAKHOVSKIYE
LYAKHOVSKIYE

M. SVYATOY
NOS

M. BUOR-
KHAYA

EAST SIBERIAN SEA

M. SHELAGSKIY

VRANGELYA
(WRANGEL I.)

M. OMEDVEZHY

AYON

Ambarchik

CHUKOTSKIY

CHUKOTSKOYE NAGORYE

Arctic Circle

P.OV

M. SHMIDTA

Uelen

M. DEZHNEVA

Anadyr

Markovo

Berezhino

KORYAKSKIY KHREBET

M. OLYUTORSKIY

Slautnoye

GORY
PUTORANA

ril'sk

Baykit

Nizhnaya Tunguska

S   I   A

Tura

artsevo

G. Polkan
3543

yysk

Krasnoyarsk

Kansk

Tayshet

Bratsk

Balakhta

Nizhneudinsk

Tulun

Minusinsk

abakan

KHREBET

Munku
Sardyk
11457

Cheremkhovo

Angarsk

Kyren

Piramida
10801

AYAN

TANNU-OLA

Kyzyl

Ur Nuur

HAMS

Tsast Bogd
13419

Khatanga

Balun

Lena

Zhigansk

Olenek

Suntar

Vilyuy

Vilyuysk

Muknuya

Peleduy

Vitim

Bodaybo

PATOM
PLATEAU

Golets
Purpula
5577

Golets
Skalistyy
9186

Kirensk

Ilimsk

Nizhne-Angarsk

Zhigalova

Barguzin

Bratskoye
Vodhr.

Kachuga

Kutulik

Irkutsk

Ulan-Ude

Gorodok

Petrovsk-Zabaykal'skiy

Kyakhta

Selenge

BAYKAL'SKIY KHREBET

Ozero
Baykal (Baikal)
Surface elev 1535 ft
below sea level

YABLONOVYY KHREBET

VERKHOYANSKIY KHREBET

Verkhoyansk

Abyy

Kazachye

Yana

Zashiversk

Zyryanka

KHREBET

Gora Chen
10771

CHERSKOGO

Oymyakon

KHREBET GYDAN (KOLYMSKIY)

Kolyma

Yomsk

Seymchan

Grishiga

Penzhino

Korkovo

M. TAYGONOS

M. ALEVINA

Magadan

Okhotsk

SEA

OF

OKHOTSK

M. YELIZAVETY

Okha

KAMCHATKA

Klyuchevskaya
(Vol.)
15584

Verkhne-Kamchatsk

Petropavlovsk-
Kamchatsky

Ust'-Bol'sheretsk

M. LOPATKA

Aldan

Aldanskoye

Ust'-Maya

Amga

Neit kon

Yakutsk

Olekminsk

Tommot

STANOVOY KHREBET

Tyndinskiy

Yuktali

Skovorodino

Zeya

DZHUGDZHUR KHREBET

Ayan

Chumikan

Udskaya Guba

SHANTAR

Nikolayevsk-na-Amure

KHREBET

BUREINSKIY

Komsomol'sk-
na-Amure

Soyetskaya
Gavan

M. TERPENIYA

SAKHALIN

Aleksandrovsk

Poronaysk

Uglegorsk

Yuzhno-Sakhalinsk

Kholmsk

Korsakov

Tatar Strait

P-OV
KARAGIN

NERCHINSKIY KHREBET

Chita

Nerchinsk

Nerchinskiy
Zavod

Sretensk

Tyrma

Ust'-Tyrma

Belogorsk

Bureya

Svobodnyy

Blagoveshchensk

Birobidzhan

Khabarovsk

Spassk-
Dal'niy

Ussuriysk

Artem

Partizansk

Nakhodka

Vladivostok

SIKHOTE ALIN'

KHREBET

Wakkanai

Soya Kaikyo

HOKKAIDO

Otaru

Sapporo

Asashi

Tsugaru Kaikyo

HONSHU

Aginskoye

Aksha

Borzya

Onon

Kerulen

Ondörhaan

Ulan Bator
(Ulaanbaatar)

MONGOLIA

Sayr Usa

GOBI OR SHAMO
(DESERT)

Hami

Uliastay

HANGAYN NURUU

HANGAY

KHANGAI

Hovd

Har Us Nuur

A

Borzya

Wenquan

Tao'an

Jarud Qi

Nenjiang

Goukou

Qiqihar

Hailun

Suihua

Fuyu

Bali

LESSER KHINGAN
RANGE

HARBIN

Mudanjiang

Jilin

Hunchun

Najin

Chongjin

SEA OF JAPAN

GREATER KHINGAN
RANGE

CHANGCHUN

Shuangliao

Dunhua

NORTH
KOREA

P'yongyang

SOUTH
KOREA

SEOUL

Kaesong

Andong

Taegu

PUSAN

Chifeng

C   H   I   N   A

Weichang

Chengde

Shenyang

Fushun

MANCHURIA

Zhangjiakou

Fengzhen

BEIJING

TIANJIN

Baoding

Lushun

Dalian

Bo Hai

SHANDONG
BANDAO

Korea Bay

YELLOW SEA

JAPAN

Tottori

Matsue

Kanazawa

KYOTO

KOBE

OSAKA

Okayama

Hiroshima

Kochi

Longitude East of Greenwich

| 100 | 200 | 300 | 400 | 500 | 600 Miles |

| 200 | 400 | 600 | 800 | 1000 Kilometers |

Cities and Towns

| 0 to 50,000 | ○ | 500,000 to 1,000,000 |
| 50,000 to 500,000 | ⊙ | 1,000,000 and over |

Relief

Feet	Meters
10000	3050
5000	1525
2000	610
1000	305
500	152.5
Sea Level	0
Below Sea Level	
500	152.5
5000	1525
10000	3050

ARCTIC OCEAN

KARA SEA

BARENTS SEA

Obskaya Guba

NENETS

WESTERN SIBERIAN LOWLAND

YAMAL

KHREBET PAY-KHOY

NOVAYA ZEMLYA

PECHORA BASIN

MALOZEMEL'SKAYA TUNDRA

KOLGUYEV

P-OV KANIN

M. KANIN NOS

MORZHOVETS

Arctic Circle

URAL

U R A L

R U S S I A

YEKATERINBURG

BASHKORTOSTAN

Ufa

Chelyabinsk

Magnitogorsk

Nizhniy Tagil

Krasnotur'insk

Perm'

UDMURTIA

Izhevsk

TATARSTAN

Kazan'

Naberezhnyye Chelny

Syktyvkar

Kirov

MARI EL

Yoshkar-Ola

Cheboksary

CHUVASHIA

NIZHNIY NOVGOROD

Dzerzhinsk

Arkhangelsk (Archangel)

Vologda

Kostroma

Yaroslavl'

Ivanovo

Rybinsk

Cherepovets

Murom

Kovrov

Vladimir

Ryazan'

MOSCOW (Moskva)

Podol'sk

Serpukhov

Kaluga

Tver'

Tula

ST. PETERSBURG (Sankt-Peterburg) (Leningrad)

Kronshtadt

Pushkin

Vyborg

Novgorod

Pskov

Velikiye Luki

Rzhev

Smolensk

Vitebsk

Polotsk

KARELIA

Petrozavodsk

Medvezhegorsk

Belomorsk

Kem'

LAPLAND

Murmansk

Monchegorsk

Kandalaksha

Kirovsk

KOLSKIY P-OV (KOLA PEN.)

SOLOVETSKIYE OSTROVA

Onega

Kargopol'

P-OV ONEZHSKIY

NORWAY

NORD KAPP

MAGERØYA

Hammerfest

Kirkenes

Vardø

Vadsø

SWEDEN

Kiruna

Gällivare

Luleå

Piteå

Skellefteå

Umeå

FINLAND

Oulu

Rovaniemi

Kemi

Kajaani

Kuopio

Joensuu

Jyväskylä

Tampere

Turku

Helsinki

Kotka

Lahti

Pori

Vaasa

ESTONIA

Tallinn

Tartu

Pärnu

Narva

HIIUMAA (DAGO)

SAAREMAA (EZEL)

LATVIA

Riga

Daugavpils

Liepāja

Ventspils

LITHUANIA

Vilnius

Kaunas

Klaipėda

Šiauliai

Panevėžys

BALTIC SEA

GULF OF FINLAND

GULF OF BOTHNIA

| Miles | 0 | 50 | 100 | 150 | 200 | 250 | 300 |

| Kilometers | 0 | 100 | 200 | 300 | 400 | 500 |

Continued on pages 146-147

Scale 1:10 000 000; one inch to 160 miles. Conic Projection
Elevations and depressions are given in feet.

Continued on pages 148-149

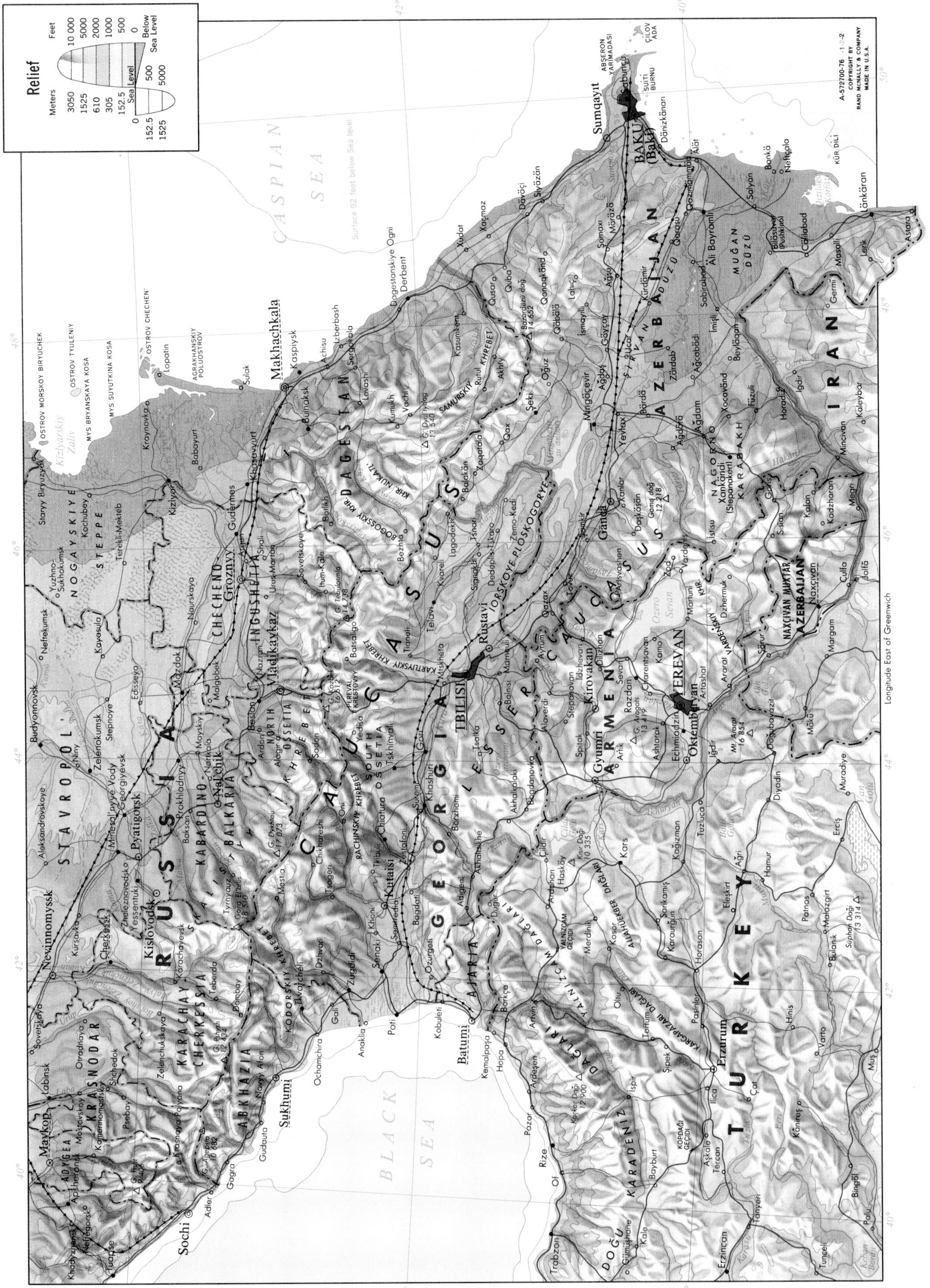

Relief

Feet	Meters
10 000	3050
5000	1525
2000	610
1000	305
500	152.5
0 Sea Level	Sea Level
Below Sea Level	0
500	152.5
5000	1525

A-572700-76 -1-2
COPYRIGHT BY
RAND McNALLY & COMPANY
MADE IN U.S.A.

CASPIAN SEA

BLACK SEA

R U S S I A
STAVROPOL'
KRASNODAR
ADYGEA
KARACHAY-CHERKESSIA
KABARDINO-BALKARIA
NORTH OSSETIA
SOUTH OSSETIA
CHECHENO-INGUSHETIA
DAGESTAN
ABKHAZIA
ADJARA

GEORGIA
ARMENIA
AZERBAIJAN
NAXÇIVAN MUXTAR AZERBAIJAN
NAGORNO-KARABAKH

TURKEY
IRAN

C A U C A S U S
LESSER CAUCASUS

Makhachkala
Groznyy
Vladikavkaz
Sochi
Sukhumi
Batumi
Poti
Kutaisi
TBILISI
Rustavi
YEREVAN
Gyumri
Kirovakan
BAKU (Bakı)
Sumqayıt
Gändä

Mt. Ararat 16 854

Scale 1:4 000 000; one inch to 64 miles. Conic Projection
Elevations and depressions are given in feet

Longitude East of Greenwich

0 10 20 30 40 50 60 70 80 90 100 110 120 Miles
0 20 40 60 80 100 120 140 160 180 200 Kilometers

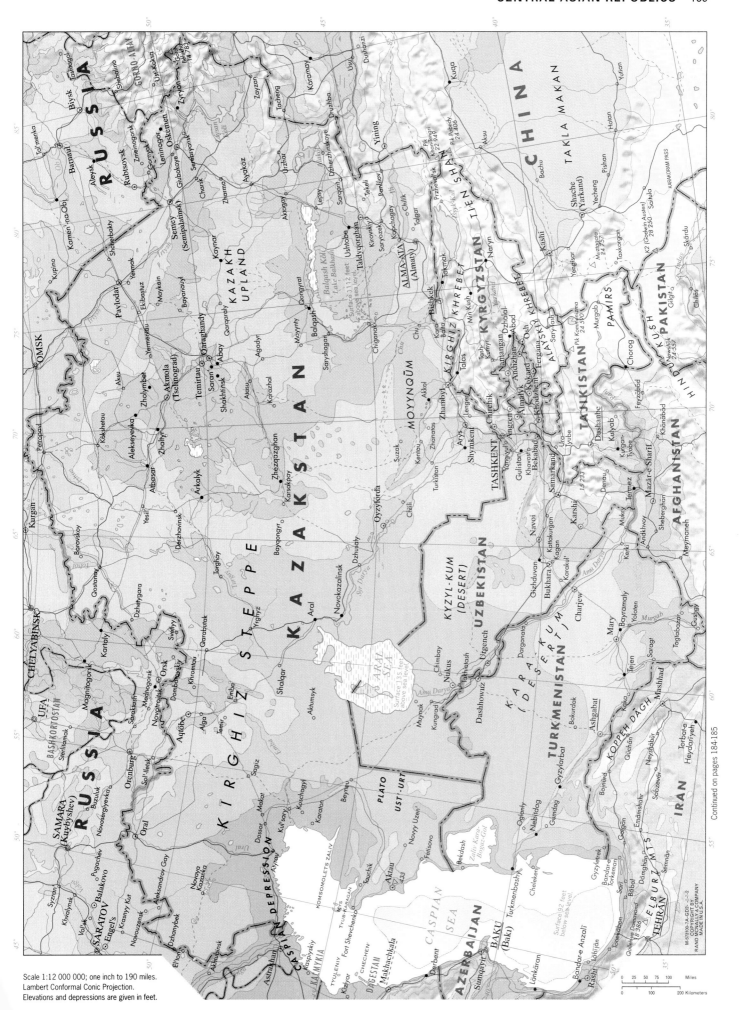

Scale 1:12 000 000; one inch to 190 miles.
Lambert Conformal Conic Projection.
Elevations and depressions are given in feet.

Continued on pages 184-185

RUSSIA

CHINA

TAKLA MAKAN

KAZAKHSTAN

KAZAKH UPLAND

KIRGHIZ STEPPE

KYRGYZSTAN

TIEN SHAN

KIRGHIZ KHREBET

ALAYSKY KHREBET

TAJIKISTAN

PAMIRS

HINDU KUSH

PAKISTAN

AFGHANISTAN

KOPPEH DAGH

IRAN

ELBURZ MTS

TURKMENISTAN

KARA-KUM (DESERT)

UZBEKISTAN

KYZYL-KUM (DESERT)

PLATO UST'-URT

MOYYNQŪM

ARAL SEA

CASPIAN DEPRESSION

CASPIAN SEA

AZERBAIJAN

TASHKENT

ALMA-ATA (Almaty)

OMSK

CHELYABINSK

UFA

SAMARA Kuybyshev

SARATOV

BASHKORTOSTAN

GORNO-ALTAY

KARAKORAM PASS

0 25 50 100 Miles

0 100 200 Kilometers

Bering Strait
180°
175°

SEVERNAYA ZEMLYA
(NORTHERN LAND)
MALYY TAIMYR
M. CHELYUSKIN

VRANGELYA
WRANGELI O. (WRANGEL ISLANDS)
M. SHELAGSKIY
CHUKOTSKIY P-OV
ANADYRSKIY ZALIV

NOVOSIBIRSKIYE O-VA
(NEW SIBERIAN ISLANDS)
FADDEYA
NOVAYA SIBIR

DE LONGA

EAST SIBERIAN SEA

CHUKOTSKOYE NAGORYE

Anadyr

KORYAKSKIY KHREBET

BEL'KOVSKIY
KOTEL'NYY
MALYY LYAKHOVSKIY
LYAKHOVSKIYE
STOLBOVOY

M. SVYATOY NOS

Ambarchik
Nizhne-Kolymsk
Arctic Circle
Sredne-Kolymsk
Zashiversk

AVON
Chumikan Guba
MEDVEZHI

Markovo
Penzhino
Tilichiki

M. OLYUTORSKIY
KABAGIN

RRANGA
YMYR

LAPTEV SEA

Nordvik
Ust'-Olenёk

BOL'SHOY BEGICHEV

G. Sellya Khskata
M. BUOR-KHAYA
Guba Buor-Khaya

Tiksi
Bulun
Kazach'ye

Alazeya
Zyryanka
Kolyma

Gizhiga
Ust' Penzhino

ZALIV SHELEKHOVA

Palana

POLUOSTROV

KAMCHATKA

Ust'-Kamchatsk
Klyuchevskoy
Vol. △ 15 584
Verkhne-Kamchatsk

nga
Olenёk

KHREBET KULAR

Zhigansk

VERKHOYANSKIY

T
U
N
D
R
A

Verkhoyansk

Abyy

KHREBET CHERSKOGO

Gora Chen 10 171

Oymyakon

KHREBET GYDAN (KOLYMSKIY)

Magadan
Yamsk
M. ALEVINA

Petropavlovsk-Kamchatskiy

S I
S A
K H A

Olenёk

Malkha

Vilyuysk

YAKUTSK
(YAKUTIA)
Yakutsk

Aldanskaya

Okhotsk

SEA OF OKHOTSK

M. YELIZAVETY

Okha

SAKHALIN
(Russia)

Tyung
Suntar

Amga
Ust'-Maya

DZHUGDZHUR KHREBET

Ayan

SHANTAR
Udskaya G.

Aleksandrovsk

Mukhtuya
Olёkminsk

Kirensk

Peleduy Vitim
PATOM 5377
G. Golets Purpula
PLATEAU
Bodaybo

A L D A N
P L A T E A U

Tommot
Aldan

Golets Skolistyy 9186

STANOVOY KHREBET

Nel'kan

Chumikan

UDA

Nikolayevsk-na-Amure

TATAR STRAIT

Poronaysk
M. TERPENIYA

Uglegorsk

Dolinsk
Yuzhno-Sakhalinsk

Kholmsk
Korsakov

KURIL ISLANDS
(Russia)

ITURUP

BURYATIA

Nizhne-Angarsk

Barguzin

Baykal
(Lake Baikal)
Surface elev.
above Sea Level

Ulan-Ude

Petrovsk-Zabaykal'skiy

YABLONOVYY KHREBET

Tyndinskiy

Zeya
Zeya

Skovorodino
Beketova

Svobodnyy
Belogorsk

KHREBET BUREINSKIY

Komsomol'sk-na-Amure

Sovetskaya Gavan'

Khabarovsk

SIKHOTE ALIN

HOKKAIDŌ

JAPAN

Chita
Sretensk
Nerchinsk
Nerchinskiy Zavod
Baley

NERCHINSKIY KHREBET

Ust'-Tyrma
Bureya
Raychikhinsk

Zavitinsk

Birobidzhan

KHREBET

Dalnerechensk

SEA OF JAPAN

Aginskoye

Aksha Borzya

GREATER KHINGAN RANGE

NEI MONGGOL

Blagoveshchensk
Aihun

LESSER KHINGAN RANGE

C H I N A

Spassk-Dal'niy
Arsen'yevo
Ussuriysk
Art'ёm

Nakhodka

Manzhouli
Hailar

Qiqihar

Longzhen
Goukou

HEILUNGKIANG

Yilan

Hulan
HARBIN

Shuangcheng
Suifenhe

Vladivostok

I A

Choybalsan

Ulan Bator
Ulaanbaatar
Ondorhaan

Continued on pages 188-189

100   200   300   400   500 Miles
200   400   600   800 Kilometers

A-579300-76 -10-II-19
COPYRIGHT BY
RAND McNALLY & COMPANY
MADE IN U.S.A.

Relief		
Meters		Feet
3050		10 000
1525		5000
610		2000
305		1000
152.5		500
Sea Level		0
152.5		500
1525		5000
3050		10 000

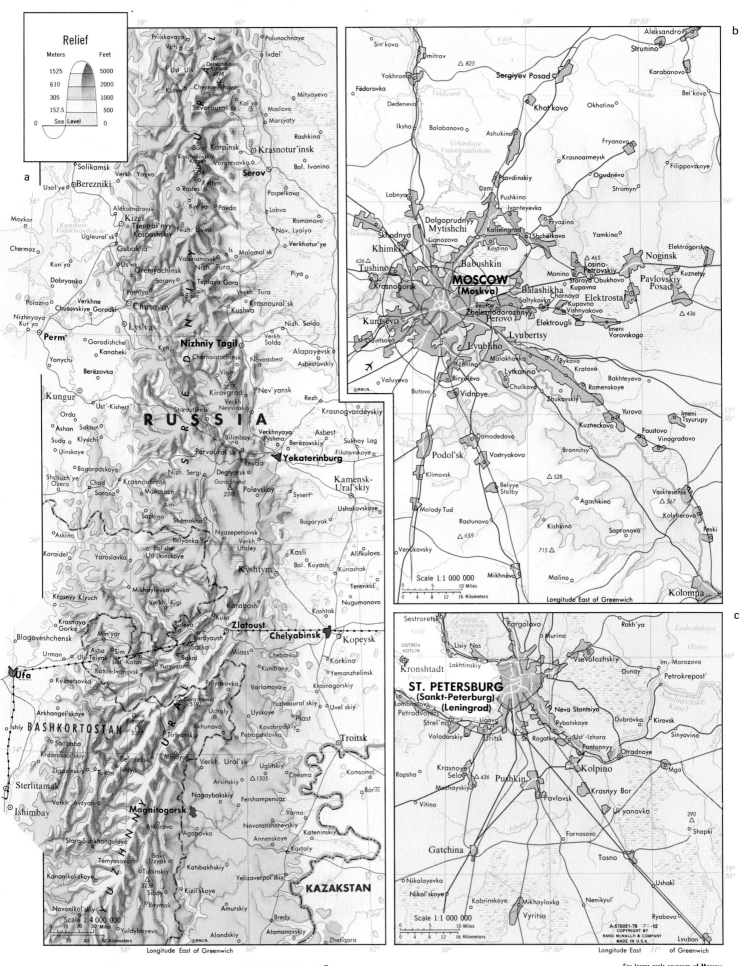

Relief

Meters	Feet
1525	5000
610	2000
305	1000
152.5	500
0 Sea Level	0

a

b

c

Scale 1:1 000 000

0   10 Miles

0 4 8 12 16 Kilometers

Longitude East of Greenwich

Scale 1:1 000 000

0   10 Miles

0 4 8 12 16 Kilometers

Longitude East of Greenwich

Scale 1:4 000 000

0 10 20 30 Miles

0 20 40 60 Kilometers

Longitude East of Greenwich

Cities and Towns

0 to 50,000   ○
50,000 to 500,000   ⊙
500,000 to 1,000,000   ◎
1,000,000 and over

For larger scale coverage of Moscow and St. Petersburg see page 239.

A-570051-76   -12
COPYRIGHT BY
RAND McNALLY & COMPANY
MADE IN U.S.A.

R U S S I A

BASHKORTOSTAN

KAZAKSTAN

Perm'
Berezniki
Solikamsk
Usol'ye
Kizel
Serov
Krasnotur'insk
Severoural'sk
Nizhniy Tagil
Chusovoy
Lys'va
Kungur
Yekaterinburg
Pervoural'sk
Revda
Kamensk-Ural'skiy
Zlatoust
Chelyabinsk
Kopeysk
Miass
Troitsk
Ufa
Magnitogorsk
Sterlitamak
Ishimbay

MOSCOW (Moskva)
Khimki
Tushino
Krasnogorsk
Kuntsevo
Balashikha
Lyubertsy
Podol'sk
Kolomna
Noginsk
Elektrostal'
Sergiyev Posad

ST. PETERSBURG (Sankt-Peterburg) (Leningrad)
Kronshtadt
Pushkin
Kolpino
Gatchina
Tosno

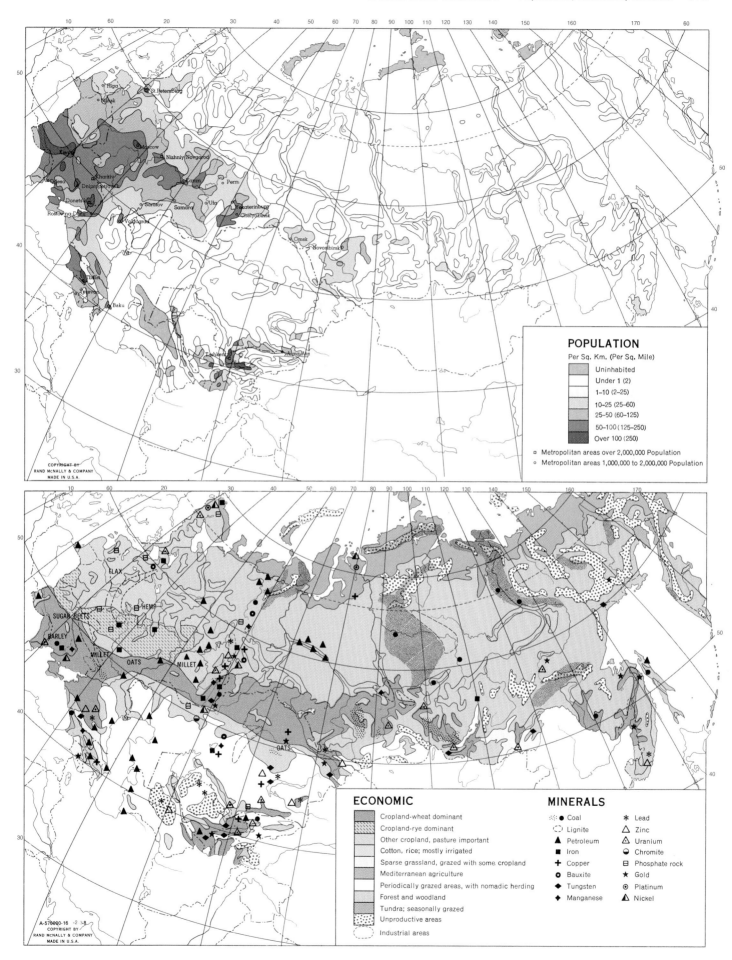

POPULATION

Per Sq. Km. (Per Sq. Mile)

Uninhabited
Under 1 (2)
1–10 (2–25)
10–25 (25–60)
25–50 (60–125)
50–100 (125–250)
Over 100 (250)

▫ Metropolitan areas over 2,000,000 Population
◦ Metropolitan areas 1,000,000 to 2,000,000 Population

ECONOMIC

Cropland-wheat dominant
Cropland-rye dominant
Other cropland, pasture important
Cotton, rice; mostly irrigated
Sparse grassland, grazed with some cropland
Mediterranean agriculture
Periodically grazed areas, with nomadic herding
Forest and woodland
Tundra; seasonally grazed
Unproductive areas

Industrial areas

MINERALS

● Coal
◌ Lignite
▲ Petroleum
■ Iron
✚ Copper
◉ Bauxite
◆ Tungsten
◆ Manganese

✳ Lead
△ Zinc
△ Uranium
⬯ Chromite
⊟ Phosphate rock
★ Gold
⊙ Platinum
▲ Nickel

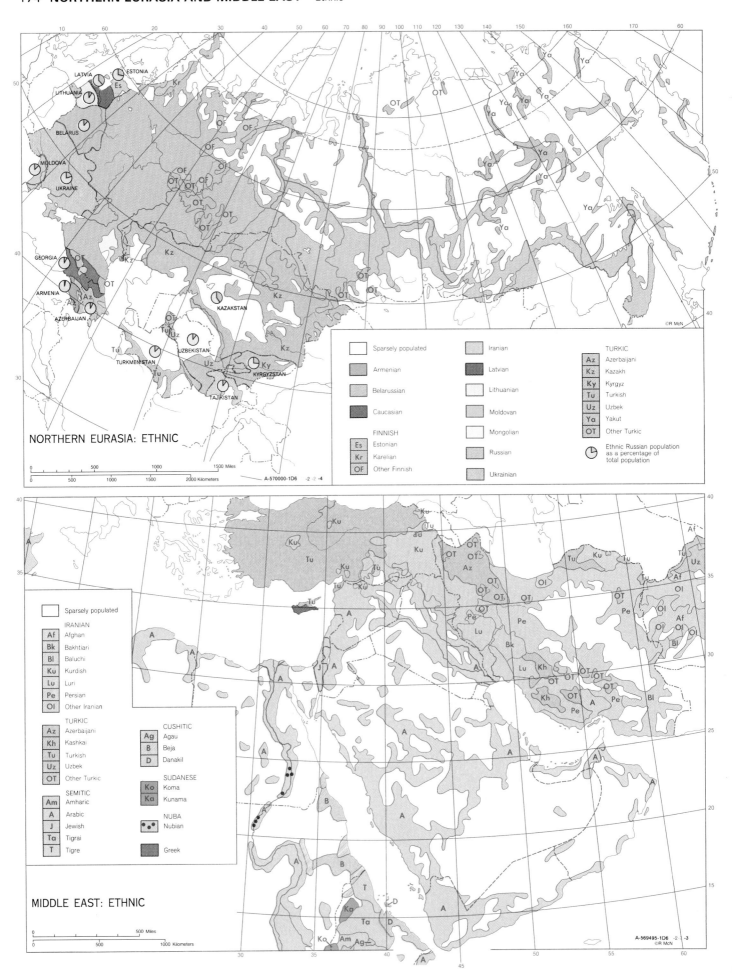

NORTHERN EURASIA: ETHNIC

Sparsely populated	Iranian	**TURKIC**
Armenian	Latvian	Az Azerbaijani
Belarussian	Lithuanian	Kz Kazakh
Caucasian	Moldovan	Ky Kyrgyz
FINNISH	Mongolian	Tu Turkish
Es Estonian	Russian	Uz Uzbek
Kr Karelian	Ukrainian	Ya Yakut
OF Other Finnish		OT Other Turkic

Ethnic Russian population as a percentage of total population

NORTHERN EURASIA: ETHNIC

500 Miles 1000 1500 Miles
0 500 1000 1500 2000 Kilometers

A-570000-1D6 -2 -2 -4

MIDDLE EAST: ETHNIC

	Sparsely populated
	IRANIAN
Af	Afghan
Bk	Bakhtiari
Bl	Baluchi
Ku	Kurdish
Lu	Luri
Pe	Persian
Ol	Other Iranian
	TURKIC
Az	Azerbaijani
Kh	Kashkai
Tu	Turkish
Uz	Uzbek
OT	Other Turkic
	SEMITIC
Am	Amharic
A	Arabic
J	Jewish
Ta	Tigrai
T	Tigre

	CUSHITIC
Ag	Agau
B	Beja
D	Danakil
	SUDANESE
Ko	Koma
Ka	Kunama
	NUBA
•:•	Nubian
	Greek

MIDDLE EAST: ETHNIC

500 Miles
0 500 1000 Kilometers

A-569495-1D6 -2 -2 -3
©R McN

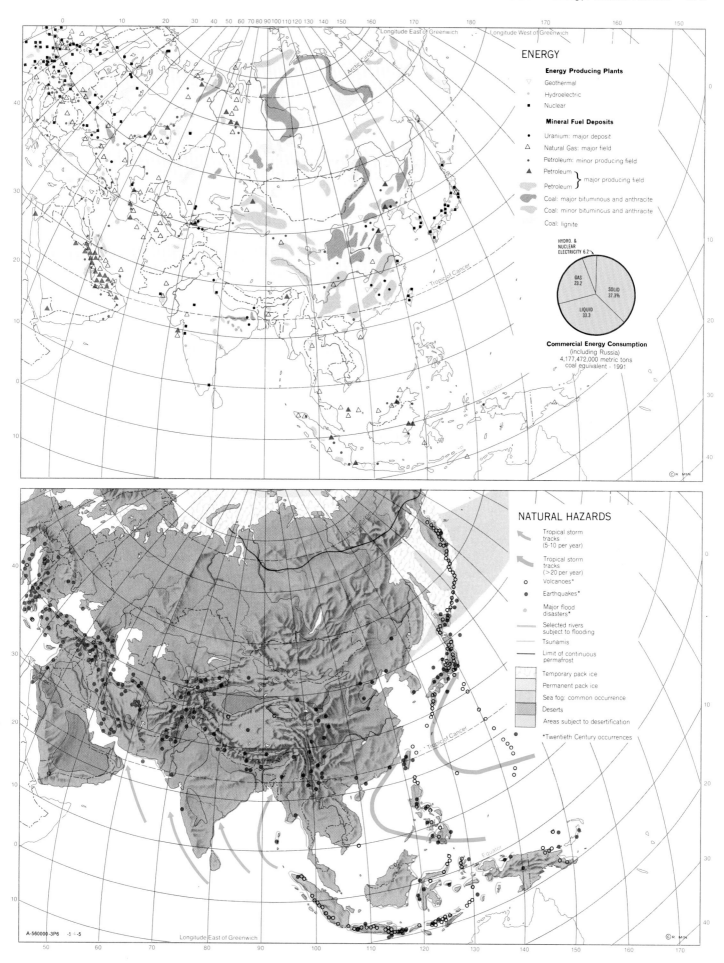

ENERGY

Energy Producing Plants

▽ Geothermal

· Hydroelectric

■ Nuclear

Mineral Fuel Deposits

· Uranium: major deposit

△ Natural Gas: major field

· Petroleum: minor producing field

▲ Petroleum

Petroleum } major producing field

Coal: major bituminous and anthracite

Coal: minor bituminous and anthracite

Coal: lignite

HYDRO. &
NUCLEAR
ELECTRICITY 6.2

GAS
23.2

SOLID
37.3%

LIQUID
33.3

Commercial Energy Consumption
(including Russia)
4,177,472,000 metric tons
coal equivalent - 1991

NATURAL HAZARDS

Tropical storm
tracks
(5-10 per year)

Tropical storm
tracks
(>20 per year)

○ Volcanoes*

● Earthquakes*

● Major flood
disasters*

Selected rivers
subject to flooding

Tsunamis

Limit of continuous
permafrost

Temporary pack ice

Permanent pack ice

Sea fog: common occurrence

Deserts

Areas subject to desertification

*Twentieth Century occurrences

A-560000-3P6 -5-4--5

Longitude East of Greenwich

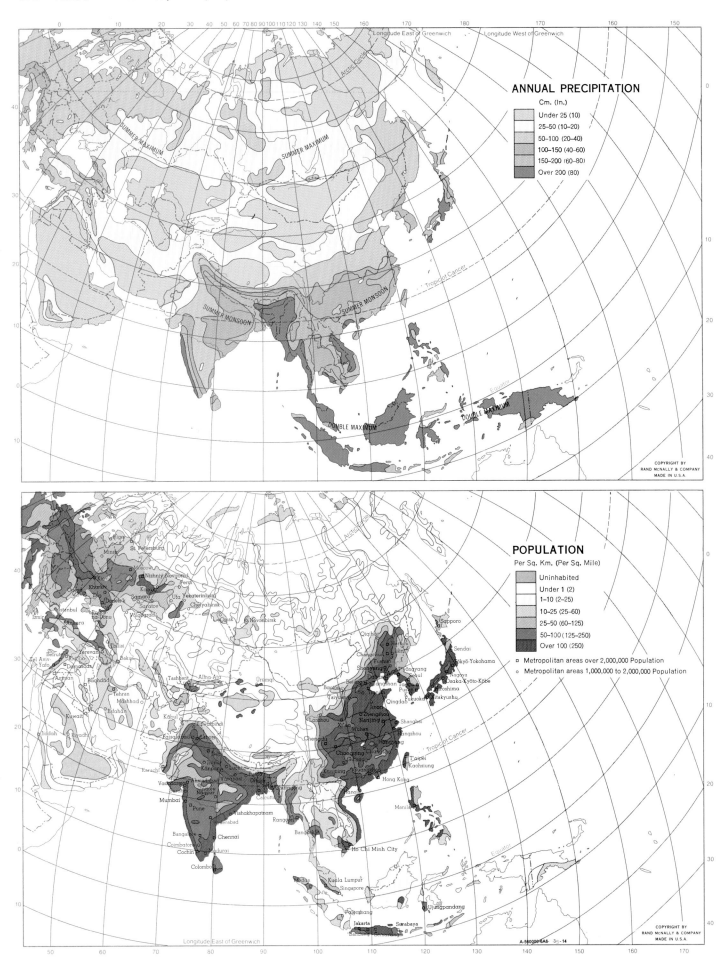

ANNUAL PRECIPITATION
Cm. (In.)
Under 25 (10)
25–50 (10–20)
50–100 (20–40)
100–150 (40–60)
150–200 (60–80)
Over 200 (80)

COPYRIGHT BY
RAND McNALLY & COMPANY
MADE IN U.S.A.

POPULATION
Per Sq. Km. (Per Sq. Mile)
Uninhabited
Under 1 (2)
1–10 (2–25)
10–25 (25–60)
25–50 (60–125)
50–100 (125–250)
Over 100 (250)
□ Metropolitan areas over 2,000,000 Population
○ Metropolitan areas 1,000,000 to 2,000,000 Population

COPYRIGHT BY
RAND McNALLY & COMPANY
MADE IN U.S.A.

A-560000-5A6 3g-14

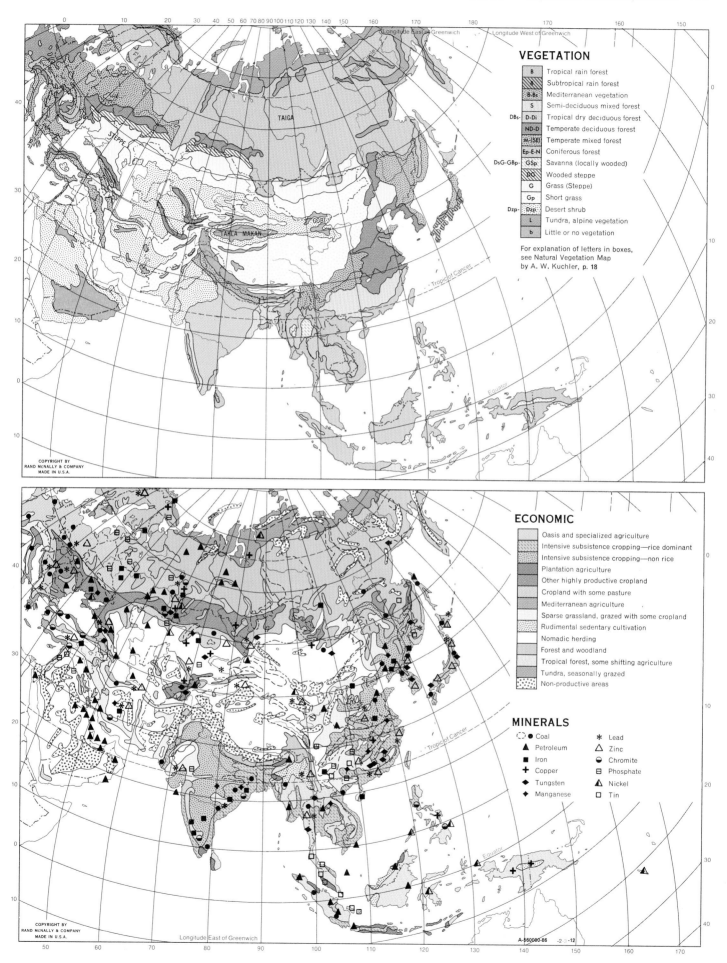

VEGETATION

B	Tropical rain forest
B	Subtropical rain forest
B-Bs	Mediterranean vegetation
S	Semi-deciduous mixed forest
DBs- D-Di	Tropical dry deciduous forest
ND-D	Temperate deciduous forest
M-(SE)	Temperate mixed forest
Ep-E-N	Coniferous forest
DsG-GBp- GSp	Savanna (locally wooded)
DG	Wooded steppe
G	Grass (Steppe)
Gp	Short grass
Dzp- Dzp	Desert shrub
L	Tundra, alpine vegetation
b	Little or no vegetation

For explanation of letters in boxes,
see Natural Vegetation Map
by A. W. Kuchler, p. 18

ECONOMIC

- Oasis and specialized agriculture
- Intensive subsistence cropping—rice dominant
- Intensive subsistence cropping—non rice
- Plantation agriculture
- Other highly productive cropland
- Cropland with some pasture
- Mediterranean agriculture
- Sparse grassland, grazed with some cropland
- Rudimental sedentary cultivation
- Nomadic herding
- Forest and woodland
- Tropical forest, some shifting agriculture
- Tundra, seasonally grazed
- Non-productive areas

MINERALS

⊂⊃ ●	Coal	✳	Lead
▲	Petroleum	△	Zinc
■	Iron	◖	Chromite
✚	Copper	⊟	Phosphate
◆	Tungsten	▲	Nickel
◆	Manganese	□	Tin

TAIGA
STEPPE
GOBI
TAKLA MAKAN

COPYRIGHT BY
RAND McNALLY & COMPANY
MADE IN U.S.A.

COPYRIGHT BY
RAND McNALLY & COMPANY
MADE IN U.S.A.

Longitude East of Greenwich

Longitude West of Greenwich

A-560000-86   -2 3 -12

Urban
Cropland
Cropland & Woodland
Cropland & Grazing Land
Grassland, Grazing Land
Forest, Woodland
Swamp, Marshland
Tundra
Shrub, Sparse Grass, Wasteland
Barren Land
Oasis

Scale 1:36,000,000; one inch to 570 miles. Lambert Azimuthal Equal-Area Projection

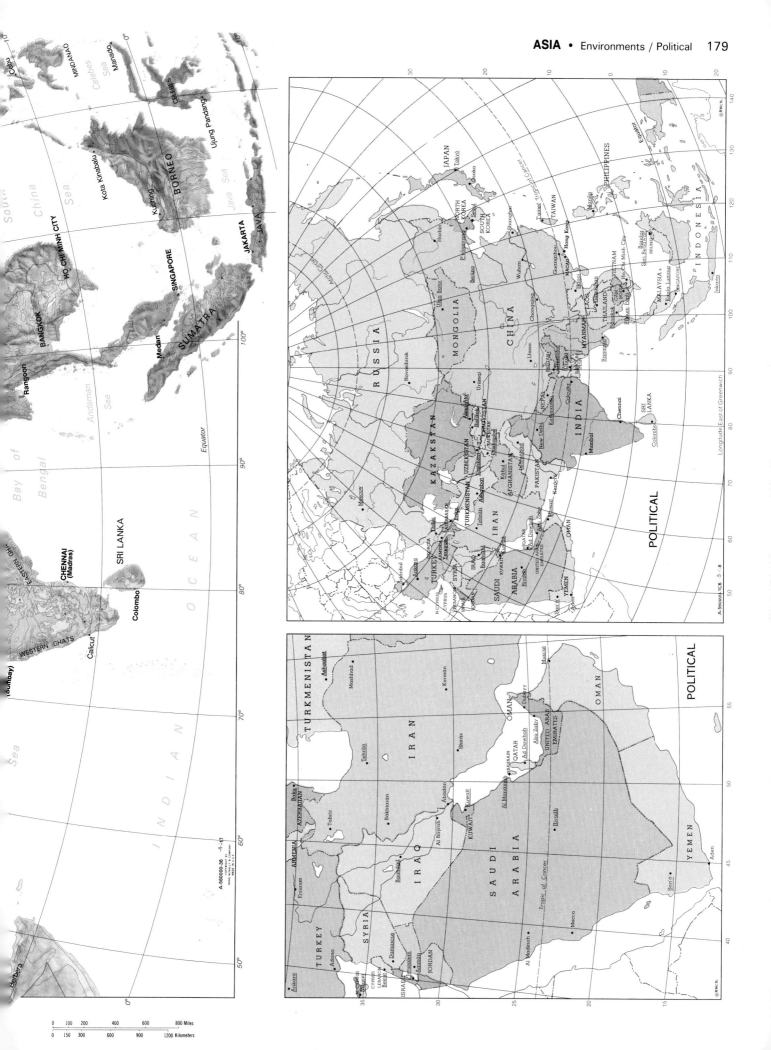

POLITICAL

POLITICAL

Continued on page 209

Relief

Meters   Feet
3050   10 000
1525   5000
610   2000
305   1000
0   Sea Level   0
152.5   Below
              Sea Level
1525   5000
3050   10 000
6100   20 000

A-519695-76   19 7 -40
COPYRIGHT BY
RAND M¢NALLY & COMPANY
MADE IN U.S.A.

Scale 1:40 000 000; one inch to 630 miles. Lambert's Azimuthal, Equal Area Project
Elevations and depressions are given in feet

Longitude East of Greenwich

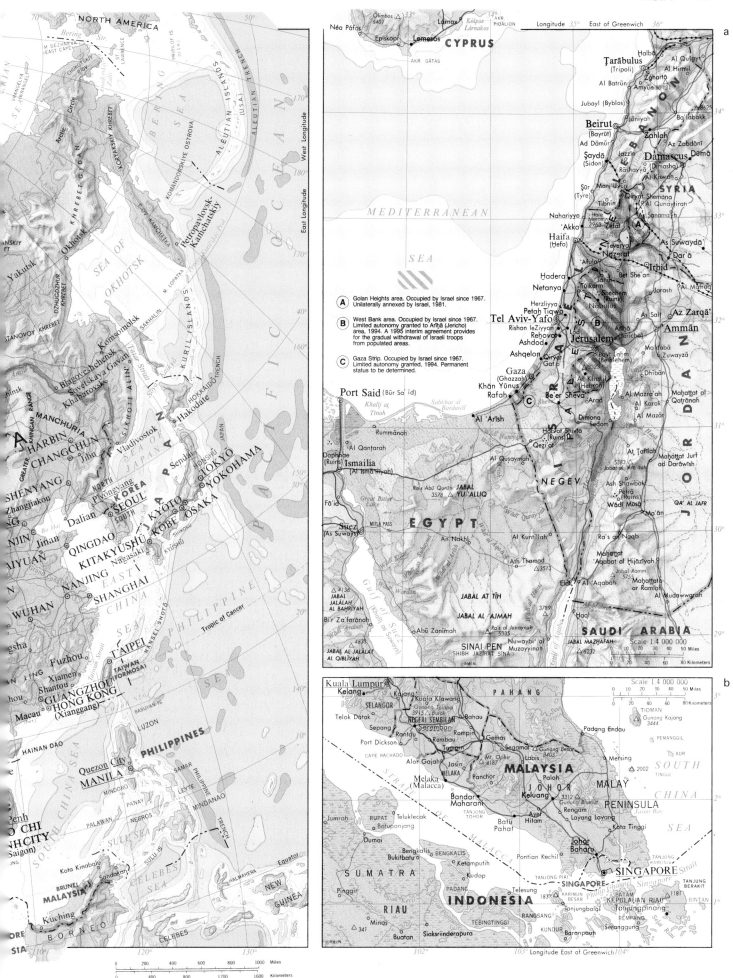

Longitude 35° East of Greenwich 36°

a

CYPRUS
Néa Páfos
Epískopi
Lemesos
Ólimbos △33°
(640)
Lárnax
Kólpos
Lárnakos
AKR.
PIDÁLION
AKR. GÁTAS

Halba
Ṭarābulus
(Tripoli)
Al Qusayr
Al Ḥirmil
Al Batrūn
Zgharta
Amyūn
Jubayl (Byblos)
Pūniyah
Ba'labakk
Beirut
(Bayrūt)
Zaḥlah
Ad Dāmūr
Az Zabdānī
Ṣaydā
(Sidon)
Jazzin
Rāshayyā
Damascus
(Dimashq)
Dūmā
Ṣūr
(Tyre)
Marj 'Uyūn
Al Kiswah
Qiryat Shemona
SYRIA
Tibnin
Al Qunayţirah
An Sanamayn
Nahariyya
Hare
Meron
3963
Zefat
'Akko
Ţeverya
As Suwaydā
Haifa
(Hefa)
Nazerat
Dar'ā
'Afula
Bet She'an
Irbid
Ḥadera
Tulkarm
Janin
Jarash
Al Mafraq
Netanya
Shechem
(Ruins)
As Salt
Herzliyya
Nabulus
Az Zarqā'
Petah Tiqwa
Tel Aviv-Yafo
B
Amman
Rishon leZiyyon
Lod
Ma'daba
Rehovot
Jerusalem
Ashdod
Qiryat
Gat
Bayt Laḥm
(Betlehem)
Zuwayzā
Ashqelon
Al Khalil
(Hebron)
Dhibān
Gaza
(Ghozzah)
Be'er Sheva
Al Mazra'ah
Maḥaṭṭat al
Qaṭrānah
Khān Yūnus
Sedom
'Arad
Al Karak
Rafah
C
Dimona
Al Mazār

MEDITERRANEAN
SEA

(A) Golan Heights area. Occupied by Israel since 1967.
Unilaterally annexed by Israel, 1981.

(B) West Bank area. Occupied by Israel since 1967.
Limited autonomy granted to Arīḥā (Jericho)
area, 1994. A 1995 interim agreement provides
for the gradual withdrawal of Israeli troops
from populated areas.

(C) Gaza Strip. Occupied by Israel since 1967.
Limited autonomy granted, 1994. Permanent
status to be determined.

Port Said (Būr Sa'īd)
Khalīj aṭ
Ṭīnah
Sabkhat al
Bardawīl
Al 'Arīsh
Rummānah
Al Qantarah
Daphnae
(Ruins)
Ismailia
(Al Ismā'īlīyah)
Al Qusaymah
Fā'id
Rais Abū Qurūn JABAL
3578 △ YU 'ALLIQ
Qezi'ot
Ḥorvot Shivta
At Ṭafīlah
Mahaṭṭat Jurf
ad Darāwīsh
Suez
(As Suways)
MITLA PASS
An Nakhl
Ash Shawbak
Petrā
(Ruins)
Wādī Mūsā
Ma'ān
QA' AL JAFR
NEGEV
Al Kuntillah
Ra's an Naqb
Ath Thamad
△3513
Jabal Ramm
575△
Mahaṭṭat
'Aqabat al Ḥijāzīyah
△4136
JABAL
JALĀLAH
AL BAHRĪYAH
JABAL AL AJMAH
3789
Eilat
Al 'Aqabah
Maḥaṭṭat
ar Ramlah
Al Mudawwarah
Bi'r Za'farānah
JORDAN
Abū Zanīmah
JABAL AT TĪH
Ra's al Junaynah
5335
Ḥaql
SAUDI ARABIA
△4835
JABAL AL JALĀLAT
AL QIBLĪYAH
Nuwaybi' al
Muzayyinah
JABAL MAZḤAFAH
△6232
Scale 1:4 000 000
0 10 20 30 40 50 Miles
0 20 40 60 80 Kilometers
SINAI PEN
(SHIBH JAZĪRAT SĪNĀ')
EGYPT

b

Kuala Lumpur
Kelang
Kajang
Kuala Klawang
PAHANG
Scale 1:4 000 000
0 10 20 30 40 50 Miles
0 20 40 60 80 Kilometers
TIOMAN
3°
SELANGOR
Gunong Telapa
3915 △ Burok
Bahau
Gunong Kajang
3444
Telok Datok
NEGERI SEMBILAN
Rantau
Rompin
Padang Endau
Sepang
Seremban
Gemas
PEMANGGIL
Port Dickson
Rembau
Segamat
Gunong Besar
3403
Mersing
CAPE RACHADO
Tampin
AUR
Alor Gajah
Jasin
Mt. Ophir
△4187
Labis
△2002
SOUTH
TINGGI
Melaka
(Malacca)
MELAKA
Panchor
MALAYSIA
MALAY
Bandar
Maharani
JOHOR
Kluang
3312
CHINA
2°
Gunong Blumut
RUPAT
Teluklecak
Batu
Pahat
Ayer
Hitam
Rengam
PENINSULA
Jason Bay
Jumrah
Batupanjang
Layang Layang
Kota Tinggi
SEA
Dumai
Bengkalis
BENGKALIS
Pontian Kechil
Johor
Baharu
TANJONG
TEMINAH
Pinggir
Bukitbatu
Ketamputih
SINGAPORE
TANJONG
SUMATRA
Kudap
TANJONG PIAI
SINGAPORE
Singapore
Strait
TANJUNG
BERAKIT
RIAU
Telesung
△1837
KARIMUN
BESAR
BATAM
KEPULAUAN RIAU
△1181
BINTAN
INDONESIA
△341
Minas
Buatan
Siaksriinderapura
Selat Kechil
Rangsang
KUNDUR
Tanjungbalai
Tanjungpinang
REMPANG
Baranpauh
Serangung
Longitude East of Greenwich 104°
102°
103°

NORTH AMERICA
Bering
Str.
M. DEZHNEVA
(EAST CAPE)
ST. LAWRENCE I.
PRIBILOF IS
(U.S.A.)
WRANGELL
ALEUTIAN ISLANDS
(USA)
ALEUTIAN TRENCH
Arctic Circle
CHUKOTSKIY
60°
50°
West Longitude
170°
East Longitude
180°
West Longitude
170°
KHREBET GYDAN
KORYAKSKIY KHREBET
KOMANDORSKIYE OSTROVA
160°
40°
Yakutsk
SEA OF
OKHOTSK
M. LOPATKA
Petropavlovsk-
Kamchatskiy
Okhotsk
P-OV KAMCHATKA
Komsomolsk
SAKHALIN
KURIL ISLANDS
STANOVOY KHREBET
150°
30°
Blagoveshchensk
Sovetskaya Gavan
Khabarovsk
Hakodate
HOKKAIDO PEN
DZHUGDZHUR KHREBET
MANCHURIA
SIKHOTE ALIN
Vladivostok
HONSHŪ
Sendai
JAPAN
TOKYO
YOKOHAMA
HARBIN
CHANGCHUN
Jilin
SEA OF JAPAN
20°
SHENYANG
NORTH
KOREA
KYOTO
KOBE OSAKA
Pyongyang
SEOUL
SOUTH
KOREA
SHIKOKU
Zhangjiakou
Dalian
Bo Hai
QINGDAO
KITAKYUSHŪ
Nagasaki
KYŪSHŪ
Jinan
NANJING
SHANGHAI
WUHAN
EAST
CHINA
SEA
Tropic of Cancer
PHILIPPINE
SEA
TAIPEI
TAIWAN
(FORMOSA)
Fuzhou
Xiamen
Shantou
GUANGZHOU
HONG KONG
(Xianggang)
Macau
(Port.)
BABUYAN IS
LUZON
10°
HAINAN DAO
PHILIPPINES
Quezon City
MANILA
MINDORO
SAMAR
PANAY
LEYTE
PHILIPPINE
TRENCH
NEGROS
PALAWAN
MINDANAO
SOUTH CHINA SEA
SULU SEA
SULU IS
CELEBES SEA
HALMAHERA
NEW GUINEA
Kota Kinabalu
Sandakan
BRUNEI
MALAYSIA
Kuching
BORNEO
CELEBES
Equator
0 200 400 600 800 1000 Miles
0 400 800 1200 1600 Kilometers

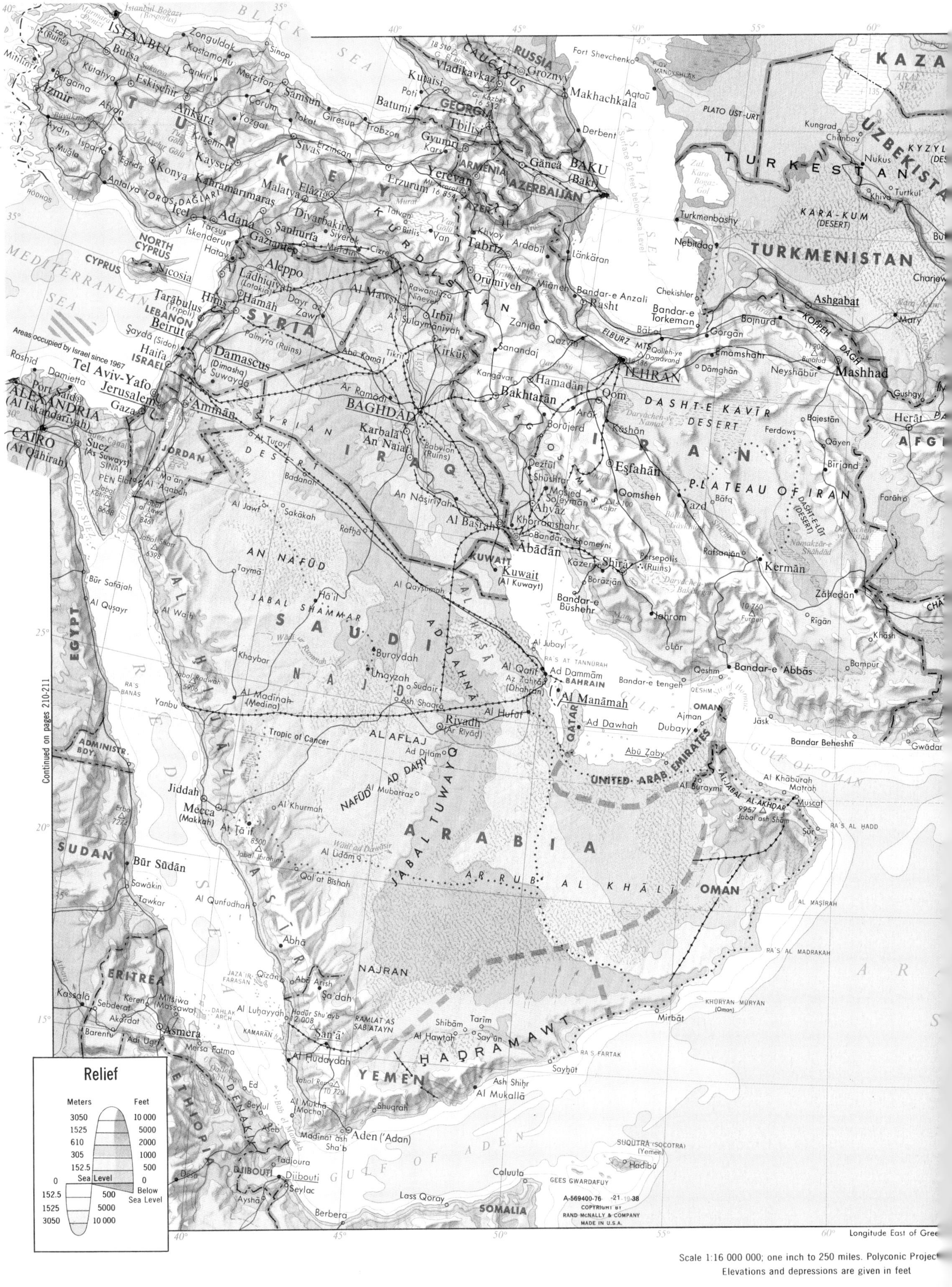

BLACK SEA

RUSSIA

Istanbul Boğazı (Bosporus)
İSTANBUL
Marmara Denizi
Troy (Ruins)
Bursa
İzmir
Bergama
Kütahya
Eskişehir
Afyon
Aydın
Muğla
Isparta
Eğridir
RHODOS
Antalya
İçel
Tarsus
Adana
İskenderun
Hatay
Zonguldak
Kastamonu
Çankırı
Ankara
Merzifon
Samsun
Çorum
Yozgat
Kırşehir
Kayseri
Kahramanmaraş
Gaziantep
Şanlıurfa
Siverek
Diyarbakır
Malatya
Elâzığ
TURKEY
TOROS DAĞLARI
Sinop
Giresun
Trabzon
Erzincan
Sivas
Tokat
Erzurum
Van
Bitlis
Cizre
Talvan
Mardin
CAUCASUS
Kutaisi
Poti
Batumi
GEORGIA
Tbilisi
Gyumri
Kars
ARMENIA
Yerevan
Grozny
Vladikavkaz
Makhachkala
AZERBAIJAN
Gäncä
BAKU (Bakı)
Tabrīz
Khvoy
Orūmiyeh
Ardabīl
Länkäran
Bandar-e Anzali
Rasht
Mīāneh
KURDISTAN
As Sulaymānīyah
Irbīl
Zanjān
Qazvīn
Sanandaj
Hamadān
Bakhtarān
Kangāvar
Qūchān Su
Bandar-e Torkeman
Gorgān
Sārī
Bābol
Dāmghān
Semnān
ELBURZ MTS
TEHRAN
Damāvand
Qom
Arāk
Borūjerd
Kāshān

Fort Shevchenko
KAZA
Aqtaū
PLATO ÜST-URT
Kungrad
Chimbay
Nukus
KYZYL
UZBEKISTA
Turtkul
Khiva
TURKESTAN
KARA-KUM (DESERT)
Nebitdag
Chekishler
Turkmenbashy
Bojnūrd
TURKMENISTAN
KOPPEH DAGH
Ashgabat
Neyshābūr
Mashhad
Gushgy
AFG
Herāt
Qāyen
Birjand
DASHT-E LŪT (DESERT)
Bāfq
Yazd
Kermān
Zāhedān
Khāsh
Bampūr
Gwādar

MEDITERRANEAN SEA
NORTH CYPRUS
CYPRUS
Nicosia
Trābulus (Tripoli)
LEBANON
Beirut
Ladhiqiyah (Latakia)
Aleppo
Hims
Hamāh
SYRIA
Palmyra (Ruins)
Dayr az Zawr
Al Mawşil
Nīneveh
Kirkūk
Tikrīt
Ar Ramādī
BAGHDAD
Karbalā
An Najaf
Babylon (Ruins)
IRAQ
An Nāşirīyah
Al Başrah
Dezfūl
Shūshtar
Masjed Soleymān
Ahvāz
Khorramshahr
Ābādān
Bandar-e Khomeyni
IRAN
Esfahān
Qomsheh
Shīrāz
Kāzerūn
Persepolis (Ruins)
Rafsanjān
Borāzjān
Būshehr
Jahrom
Lār
PLATEAU OF IRAN
Ferdows
Sīrjān
Bandar-e Abbās
Qeshm
QESHM
Bandar-e Lengeh
Jāsk
OMAN

ISRAEL
Tel Aviv-Yafo
Haifa
Sayda (Sidon)
Damascus (Dimashq)
As Suwaydā
Jerusalem
Gaza
Rashīd
Damietta
Port Said
ALEXANDRIA (Al Iskandarīyah)
Suez (As Suways)
CAIRO (Al Qāhirah)
JORDAN
Ammān
Al Turayf
SYRIAN DESERT
EGYPT
SINAI PEN
Al Aqabah
Ma'ān
Jabal Kātrīnah
Būr Safājah
Al Quşayr
RAS BANAS

Al Jawf
Sakākah
Badanah
Rafhā
An Nafūd
Taymā
Ha'il
JABAL SHAMMAR
Al Qayşūmah
KUWAIT (Al Kuwayt)
Al Jubayl
Al Qatīf
Az Zahrān (Dhahran)
Ad Dammām
BAHRAIN
Al Manāmah
RA'S AT TANNŪRAH
Khaybar
Al Madīnah (Medina)
Buraydah
Unayzah
Sudayr
Ash Shaqra
Al Hufūf
QATAR
Ad Dawhah
Abū Zaby
AL HASA
AD DAHNĀ

SAUDI
NAJD
Yanbu
Al Madīnah
Jiddah
Mecca (Makkah)
At Tā'if
Jabal Ibrāhīm
Al Khurmah
Wādī ad Dawāsir
Al Lidām
NAFŪD
AD DAHY
Mubarraz
Ad Dilam
Riyadh (Ar Riyāḍ)
AL AFLAJ
Al Hufūf
Qal'at Bishah
JABAL TUWAYQ
ARABIA
AR RUB' AL KHĀLĪ
OMAN
UNITED ARAB EMIRATES
Ajman
Dubayy
Abū Zaby
Al Buraymī
Al Khābūrah
Matrah
AL JABAL AL AKHDAR
Jabal ash Shām
Muscat
Sūr
RA'S AL HADD
GULF OF OMAN
Bandar Beheshtī

SUDAN
Būr Sūdān
Sawākin
Tawkar
ERITREA
Kassalā
Keren
Mitsiwa
Massawa
DAHLAK ARCH
Sebderat
Akordat
Barentu
Adi Ugri
Asmera
Mersa Fatma
Qīzān
FARASAN
Jāzā IR
Abū Arīsh
Sa'dah
Al Luhayyah
YEMEN
Hajjah
KAMARAN
San'ā
Al Hudaydah
Al Mukhā (Mocha)
Shuqrah
NAJRAN
RAMLAT AS SAB'ATAYN
Shibām
Tarīm
Say'ūn
Al Hawtah
HADRAMAWT
Mirbāt
KHŪRYĀN-MURYĀN (Oman)
Ash Shihr
Al Mukallā
Sayhūt
RA'S FARTAK
RA'S AL MADRAKAH

ETHIOPIA
Ed
Beylul
Madīnat ash Sha'b
Aden ('Adan)
Tadjoura
DJIBOUTI
Seylac
Aysha
Berbera
SOMALIA
Lass Qoray
Caluula
GEES GWARDAFUY
SUQUTRA (SOCOTRA) (Yemen)
Hadibū
GULF OF ADEN

Areas occupied by Israel since 1967

Continued on pages 210-211

ADMINISTR. BDY

Tropic of Cancer

Relief

Meters		Feet
3050		10 000
1525		5000
610		2000
305		1000
152.5		500
0	Sea Level	0
152.5		500 Below
1525		5000 Sea Level
3050		10 000

Longitude East of Gree

Scale 1:16 000 000; one inch to 250 miles. Polyconic Project
Elevations and depressions are given in feet

on pages 170-171

MOYYNQŪM

ylorda

Türkistan
Zhambyl
Shymkent
Arys
Bishkek
QYRGYZ ZHOT
KYRGYZSTAN
SHKENT
Namangan Dzhalal-
Abad
Kokand
Andizhan
Osh
Khudzhand
Fergana
Dzhizak

TAJIKISTAN
Garm
24 590
Pik
Kommunizma
PAMIRS
Dushanbe
Kurgan-Tyube
Khorog
Murgab
Feyzābād
Mazār-e Sharif

HINDU
KUSH
K-YA
KARAKORAM
RANGE

Kābul
Peshāwar
Ghaznī

Chitral
Gilgit
KARAKORAM PASS
K2
(Godwin Austen)
△ 28 250

JAMMU AND KASHMIR
Islāmābād
Srīnagar
Rāwalpindi
Jammu

Jhelum
Siālkot
Gujrānwāla
Amritsar
LAHORE
Jullundur
Ludhiāna
Simla
Gar
Fīrozpur
Chandīgarh
PUNJAB
Patiāla
Dehra Dūn
Ambāla
Saharānpur
Almora
Meerut
Morādābād
Rampur
Bareilly

a

Jalālābad
MORGA RA.
14 930
KHYBER
PASS

AFGHANISTAN
PAKISTAN

Chārsadda
Peshāwar

Scale 1:4 000 000
0 10 20 30 40 Miles
0 20 40 60 Kilometers
© RMCN

b

Scale 1:40 000 000

AFGHANISTAN

PAKISTAN

JAMMU
AND
KASHMIR

HIMACHAL
PRADESH

PUNJAB

HARYANA

UTTAR
PRADESH

RĀJASTHĀN

GUJARAT

MADHYA PRADESH

MAHĀRĀSHTRA

KARNĀTAKA

KERALA

TAMIL NĀDU

SRI LANKA
(CEYLON)

INDIA • POLITICAL

CHINA
XIZANG
(TIBET)

NEPAL

SIKKIM

BHUTAN

ARUNACHAL PRADESH

ASSAM

NĀGALAND

MEGHĀLAYA

MIZORAM

MYANMAR

THAILAND

LAOS

BANGLADESH

WEST
BENGAL

BIHĀR

ORISSA

ANDHRA
PRADESH

Tropic of Cancer

ARABIAN
SEA

BAY
OF
BENGAL

1 - TRIPURA
2 - MANIPUR
3 - LAKSHADWEEP
4 - DELHI
5 - DĀDRA AND NAGAR
    HAVELI
6 - PONDICHERRY
7 - GOA, DAMĀN, AND DIU

Continued on pages 188-189

XIZANG
(TIBET)

GANGDISÊ SHAN

Lhasa

DIPHU
PASS

Mt. Everest
Dhaulāgiri
Kanchenjunga
Gyangzê
Punakha
Thimphu
Kathmandu
Lalitpur
Gangtok
Dārjeeling
Cooch Behār
Gauhāti
Shillong (KHASI HILLS)
Silchar
Imphāl
Kohima
Moggung
Myitkyina
Bhamo

NEPAL

BHUTAN

SIKKIM

ASSAM

NĀGALAND

MEGHĀLAYA

MANIPUR

DELHI
New Delhi
UTTAR
Alīgarh
Mathura
Āgra
Farrukhābād
Bharatpur
Etāwah
Lucknow
Faizābād
Gorakhpur
Darbhanga
Rangpur
Mymensingh
Sirājganj
Tropic of Cancer

Bīkāner
HARYANA

GREAT INDIAN DESERT

RĀJASTHĀN

Jaipur
Ajmer
Jodhpur
Tonk
Kota
Sheopur
Shivpuri
Jhālāwar

Gwalior
Jhānsi
Bānda
PRADESH
KĀNPUR
Allāhābād
Vārānasi
(Benares)
Mirzāpur
Sasarām
Rewa
Murwāra

Patna
Monghyr
Bhāgalpur
Gayā
Giridih
Asānsol
Berhampore
Rājshāhi
BIHĀR
Ranchi
Jamshedpur

DHAKA
Comilla
Noākhāli
BANGLADESH
Burdwān
Bhātpāra
Howrah
CALCUTTA
Khulna
Chittagong

WEST BENGAL
Kharagpur
Balāsore
Cuttack
Bhubaneswar
Puri
Berhampur

MIZORAM
Mt. Victoria
10 018
Shwebo
Monywa
Mandalay
Mogok

MYANMAR
(BURMA)

Myingyan
PEGU YOMA
Magwe
Yenangyaung
Pyinmana

Hyderābād
Abu Road
Pālanpur
Udaipur
KĀTHIĀWĀR

Bhuj
Māndvi
GUJARAT
Rājkot
Jāmnagar
Porbandar
Verāval
Junāgadh
Diu
Daman

AHMADĀBĀD
Ujjain
Bhopāl
Indore
VINDHYA RA.
Baroda
Burhānpur
Bilāspur
MADHYA PRADESH
Sāgar
Jabalpur
Raurkela
Raigarh
Sambalpur
Jājpur

Bhavnagar
Surat
Dhule
Akola
Amrāvati
Wardha
Nāgpur
Raipur
Chandrapur

Gulf of Cambay
Nāsik
Ahmadnagar
Aurangābād

DECCAN

MUMBAI
(Bombay)
MAHĀRĀSHTRA
Pune
HYDERĀBĀD
Nizāmābād
Warangal
Vizianagaram
Vishākhapatnam

Sholāpur
Sāngli
Gulbarga
Rāichūr
Vijayawāda
Elūru
Machilīpatnam
Guntūr
Yanam
Kākināda
Rajahmundry
HYDERĀBĀD

Kolhāpur
Belgaum
Hubli
Bellary
Kurnool
Cuddapah
Nellore

Panaji
(Panjim)
KARNĀTAKA
Mangalore
Mysore
BANGALORE
Vellore
Kolār
CHENNAI (Madras)
Kānchipuram
Pondicherry
Cuddalore
Salem
Kumbakonam
Nāgappattinam
Calicut
Mahé
LAKSHADWEEP
(LACCADIVE IS.
India)
Coimbatore
Tiruchchirāppalli
Thanjāvūr
Madurai
TAMIL NĀDU

ARAVALLI RANGE

GANGES

BAY OF BENGAL

BRAHMAPUTRA

GHĀTS

WESTERN GHĀTS

EASTERN GHĀTS

CORROMANDEL COAST

INDIA

Rangoon
(Yangon)
Pathein
Henzada
Sandoway
Sittwe
Kyaukpyu
Paletwa

PAGODA PT.

ARAKAN YOMA

Area occupied by Pakistan
and claimed by India.

Area claimed and occupied by India;
status disputed by Pakistan.

Area occupied by China
and claimed by India.

Area occupied by India
and claimed by China.

50 100   200   300   400   500 Miles
100   200   400   600   800 Kilometers

c

Tiruchchirāppalli
Thanjāvūr
Nāgappattinam
Ernākulam
TAMIL NĀDU
KERALA
Madurai
Jaffna
Alleppey
Tuticorin
Tirunelveli
Quilon
Trivandrum
CAPE COMORIN
Mannar
Trincomalee
Anurādhapura
Puttalam
Kandy
SRI LANKA
(CEYLON)
Colombo
Galle
Matara
DONDRA HEAD

INDIAN
OCEAN

Same scale as main map

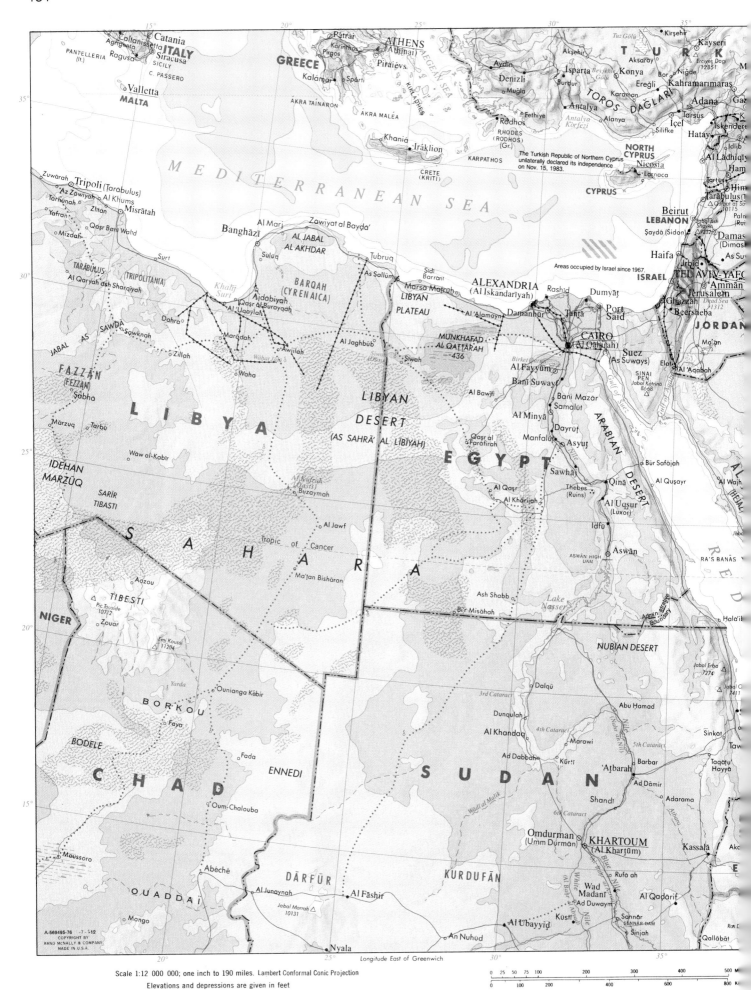

Scale 1:12 000 000; one inch to 190 miles. Lambert Conformal Conic Projection

Elevations and depressions are given in feet

Longitude East of Greenwich

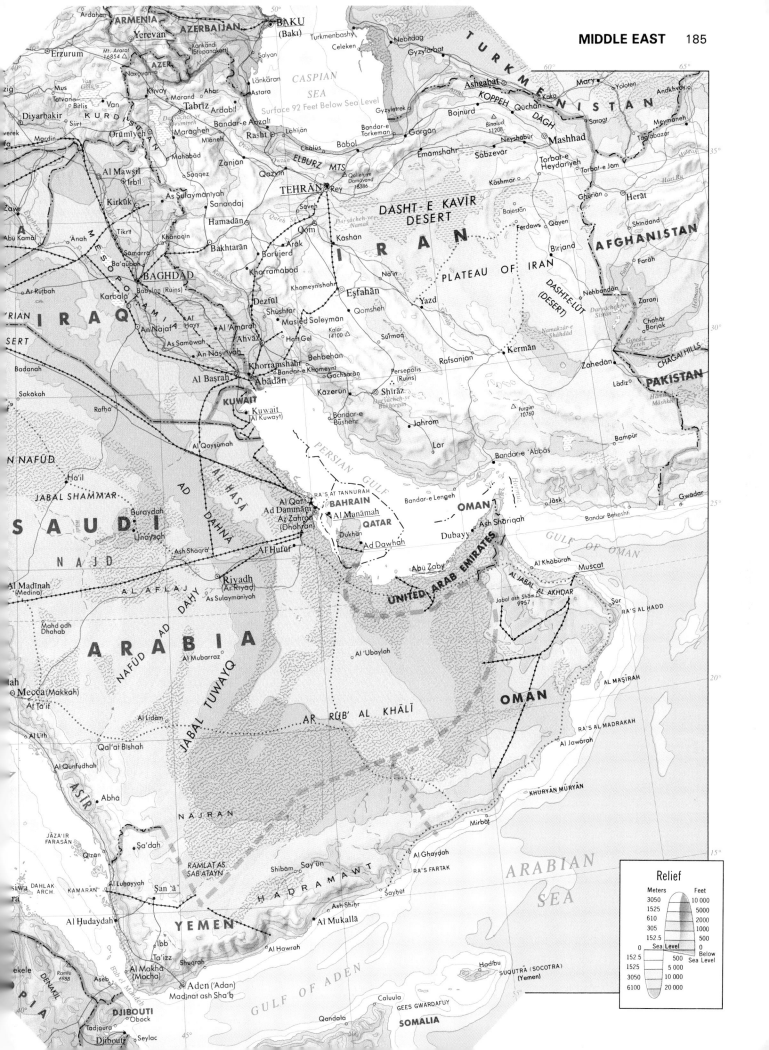

a

CALCUTTA

Scale 1:1 000 000

Relief

Meters	Feet
3050	10 000
1525	5000
610	2000
305	1000
152.5	500
0	Sea Level
152.5	500
1525	5000
3050	10 000

Scale 1:10 000 000; one inch to 160 miles. Lambert Conformal Conic Projecti
Elevations and depressions are given in feet

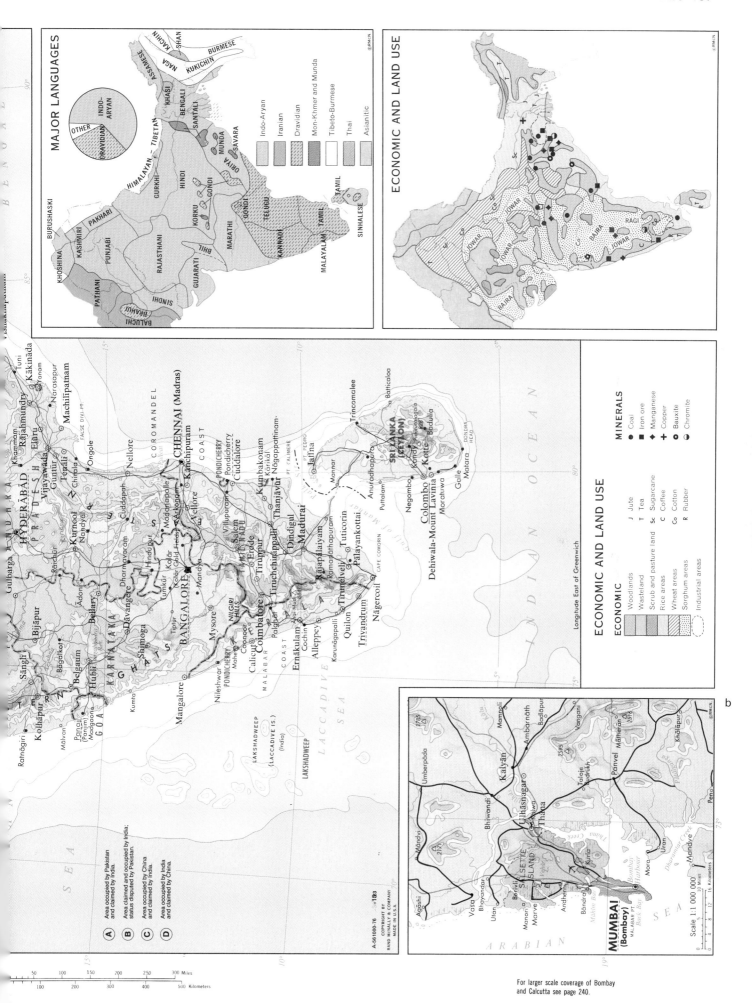

MAJOR LANGUAGES

Indo-Aryan
Iranian
Dravidian
Mon-Khmer and Munda
Tibeto-Burmese
Thai
Asianitic

ECONOMIC AND LAND USE

ECONOMIC

Woodlands
Wasteland
Scrub and pasture land
Rice areas
Wheat areas
Sorghum areas
Industrial areas

J Jute
T Tea
Sc Sugarcane
C Coffee
Co Cotton
R Rubber

MINERALS

● Coal
■ Iron ore
♦ Manganese
✚ Copper
○ Bauxite
◐ Chromite

Longitude East of Greenwich

(A) Area occupied by Pakistan and claimed by India.
(B) Area claimed and occupied by India; status disputed by Pakistan.
(C) Area occupied by China and claimed by India.
(D) Area occupied by India and claimed by China.

A-561000-76
COPYRIGHT BY
RAND McNALLY & COMPANY
MADE IN U.S.A.

MUMBAI (Bombay)

Scale 1:1 000 000

For larger scale coverage of Bombay and Calcutta see page 240.

b

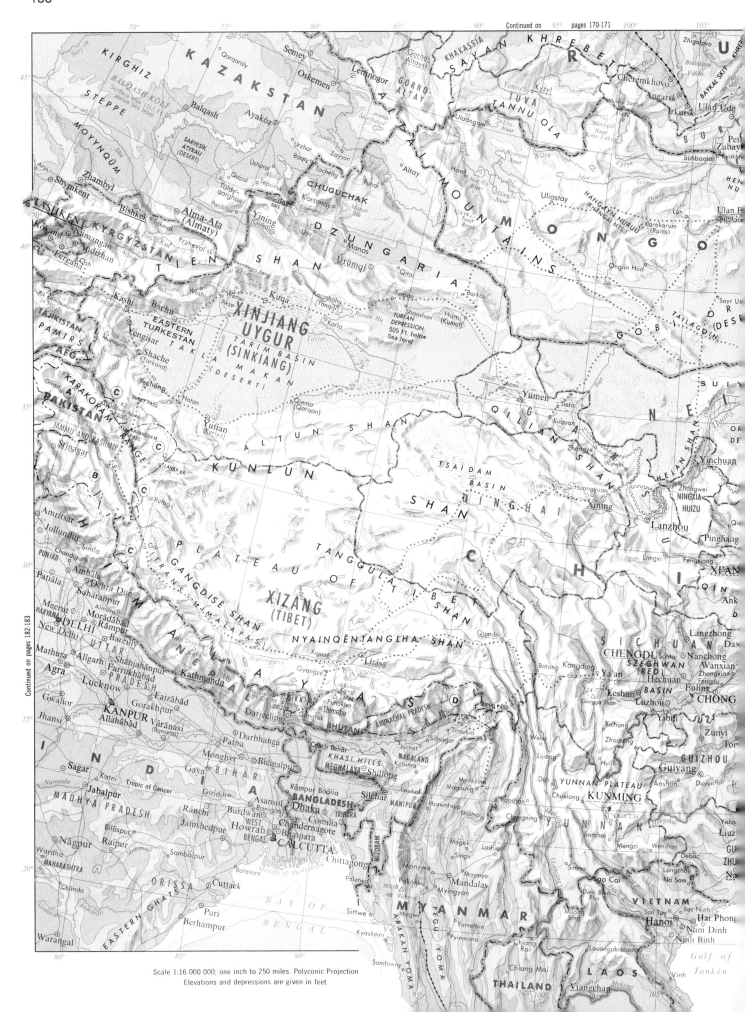

Continued on pages 170-171

Continued on pages 182-183

Scale 1:16 000 000; one inch to 250 miles. Polyconic Projection
Elevations and depressions are given in feet

Chinese Provinces,
Autonomous Regions (AR)
and Municipalities (M)

Conventional Form – Pinyin Form

Conventional	Pinyin
Anhwei	Anhui
Chekiang	Zhejiang
Fukien	Fujian
Heilungkiang	Heilongjiang
Honan	Henan
Hopeh	Hebei
Hunan	Hunan
Hupeh	Hubei
Inner Mongolia (AR)	Nei Monggol
Kansu	Gansu
Kiangsi	Jiangxi
Kiangsu	Jiangsu
Kirin	Jilin
Kwangsi (AR)	Guangxi Zhuangzu
Kwangtung	Guangdong
Kweichow	Guizhou
Liaoning	Liaoning
Ningsia Hui (AR)	Ningxia Huizu
Peking (M)	Beijing
Shanghai (M)	Shanghai
Shansi	Shanxi
Shantung	Shandong
Shensi	Shaanxi
Sinkiang (AR)	Xinjiang Uygur
Szechwan	Sichuan
Tibet (AR)	Xizang
Tientsin (M)	Tianjin
Tsinghai	Qinghai
Yunnan	Yunnan

(A) Area occupied by Pakistan and claimed by India.

(B) Area claimed and occupied by India; status disputed by Pakistan.

(C) Area occupied by China and claimed by India.

(D) Area occupied by India and claimed by China.

Relief

Meters	Feet
3050	10 000
1525	5000
610	2000
305	1000
152.5	500
0 Sea Level	Below Sea Level
152.5	500
1525	5000
3050	10 000
6100	20 000

Habomai, Shikotan, Kunashiri, and Etorofu, occupied since 1945, are claimed by Japan pending a final peace treaty.

A-569700-76 -16-11-28
COPYRIGHT BY
RAND McNALLY & COMPANY
MADE IN U.S.A.

Continued on pages 196-197

Longitude East of Greenwich

| 0 | 50 | 100 | 200 | 300 | 400 | 500 Miles |
| 0 | 100 | 200 | 400 | 600 | 800 Kilometers |

Cities and Towns

| 0 to 50,000 | ○ | 500,000 to 1,000,000 | ◎ |
| 50,000 to 500,000 | ⊙ | 1,000,000 and over | |

Relief

Meters	Feet
1525	5000
610	2000
305	1000
152.5	500
Sea Level	0
0	0

Scale 1:4 000 000 one inch to 64 miles. Conic Projection
Elevations and depressions are given in feet

0 10 20 30 40 Miles
0 10 20 30 40 50 60 Kilometers

A-560796-76 -6-9
COPYRIGHT BY
RAND MCNALLY & COMPANY
MADE IN U.S.A.

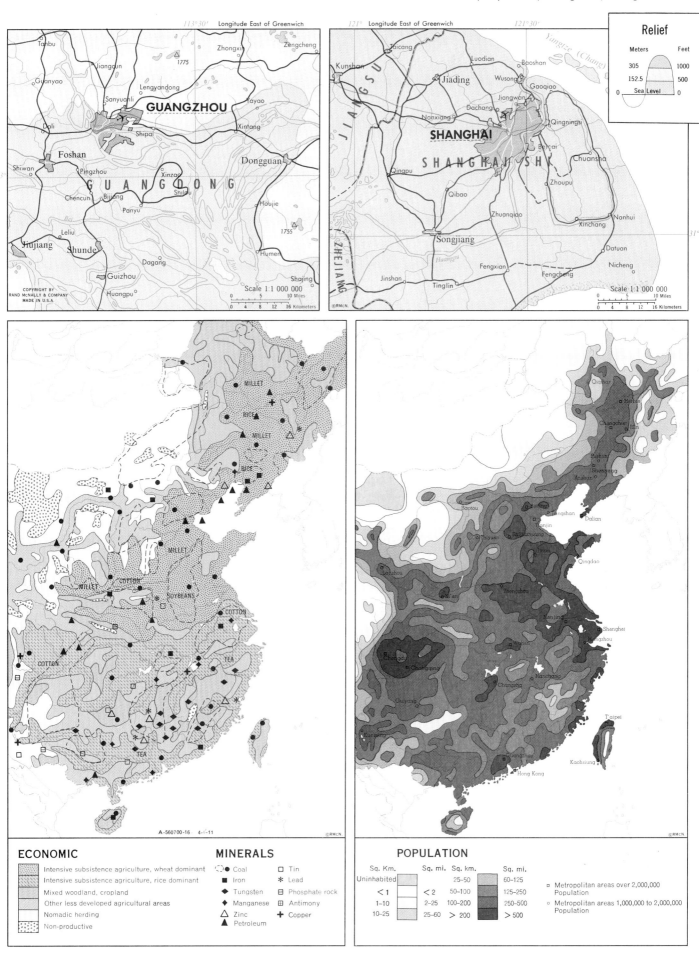

Relief

Meters		Feet
305		1000
152.5		500
0	Sea Level	0

GUANGZHOU map

Tanbu · Zhongxin · Zengcheng · Jianggun · Lengyandong · Guanyao · Sanyuanli · **GUANGZHOU** · Yayao · Xintang · Shipai · Dali · Foshan · Dongguan · Shiwan · Pingzhou · Xinzao · Houjie · Chencun · Bijiang · Shilou · Leliu · Humen · Hujiang · Shunde · Dagang · Guizhou · Shajing · Huangpu

Panyu · GUANGDONG · 1775 · 1755

Scale 1:1 000 000

COPYRIGHT BY
RAND McNALLY & COMPANY
MADE IN U.S.A.

113°30′ Longitude East of Greenwich
23°

SHANGHAI map

Taicang · Kunshan · Luodian · Baoshan · Wusong · Jiading · Gaoqiao · Nanxiang · Dachang · Jiangwan · Qingningsi · Qingpu · Beicai · Chuansha · Qibao · **SHANGHAI** · SHANGHAI SHI · Zhoupu · Zhuanqiao · Songjiang · Nanhui · Xinchang · Jinshan · Fengxian · Datuan · Tinglin · Fengcheng · Nicheng · Huangpu · Yangize (Chang) · JIANGSU · ZHEJIANG

Scale 1:1 000 000

121° Longitude East of Greenwich 121°30′
31°

ECONOMIC

Intensive subsistence agriculture, wheat dominant	
Intensive subsistence agriculture, rice dominant	
Mixed woodland, cropland	
Other less developed agricultural areas	
Nomadic herding	
Non-productive	

MINERALS

● Coal	□ Tin		
■ Iron	✳ Lead		
◆ Tungsten	⊟ Phosphate rock		
◆ Manganese	⊞ Antimony		
△ Zinc	✛ Copper		
▲ Petroleum			

POPULATION

Sq. Km.	Sq. mi.	Sq. km.	Sq. mi.
Uninhabited		25–50	60–125
<1	< 2	50–100	125–250
1–10	2–25	100–200	250–500
10–25	25–60	> 200	> 500

□ Metropolitan areas over 2,000,000 Population
○ Metropolitan areas 1,000,000 to 2,000,000 Population

A-560700-16   4-⸏-11

For larger scale coverage of Shanghai see page 241.

192

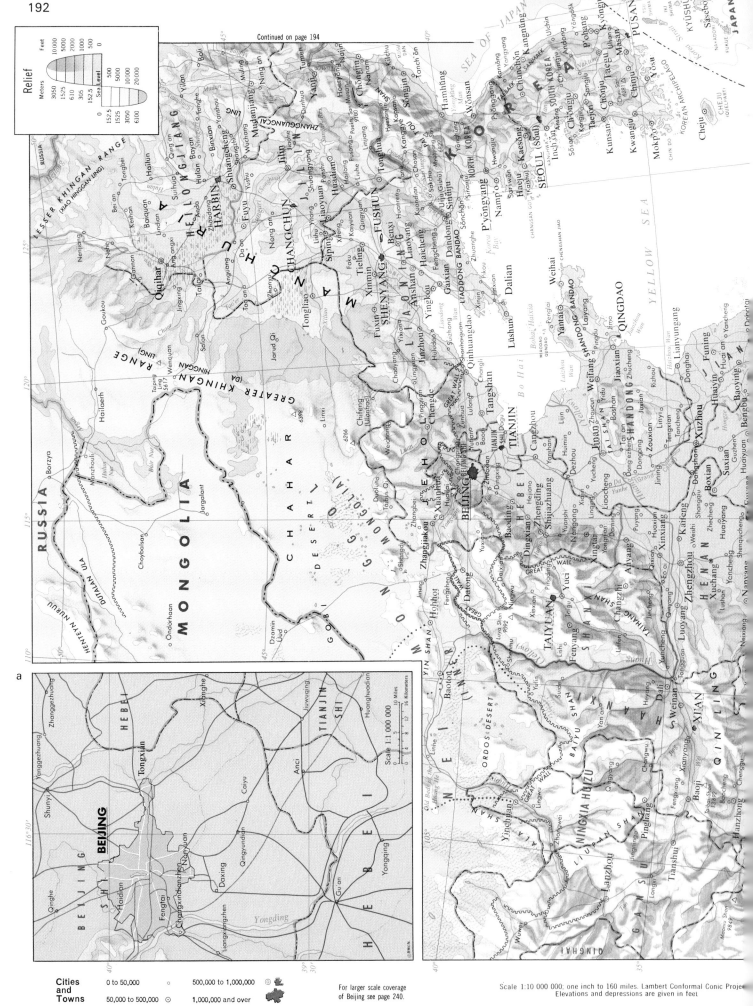

Continued on page 194

Relief

Feet	Meters
10000	3050
5000	1525
2000	610
1000	305
500	152.5
0 Sea level	0
500	152.5
5000	1525
10000	3050
20000	6100

SEA OF JAPAN

JAPAN

RUSSIA

LESSER KHINGAN RANGE (XIAO HINGGAN LING)

HEILONGJIANG

HARBIN

CHANGCHUN

JILIN

MONGOLIA

GREATER KHINGAN RANGE (DA HINGGAN LING)

CHAHAR

GOBI DESERT

DZUNGAN

SHENYANG

LIAONING

FUSHUN

KOREA

NORTH KOREA

P'yŏngyang

SOUTH KOREA

SEOUL (Soul)

YELLOW SEA

Korean Archipelago

CHEJU (QUELPART)

Cheju

Qiqihar

Hailaerh

Borzya

Manzhouli

Choybalsan

Ōndörhaan

LIAODONG BANDAO

Dalian

Lüshun

Bohai Haixia

Bo Hai

QINGDAO

SHANDONG BANDAO

Weihai

Yantai

SHANDONG

Qinhuangdao

Chengde

Tangshan

TIANJIN

BEIJING SHI

BEIJING

JEHOL

HEBEI

Baoding

Shijiazhuang

TAIYUAN

SHANXI

TAIHANG SHAN

Datong

Zhengzhou

HENAN

Kaifeng

Xuzhou

Lianyungang

JIANGSU

Luoyang

XIAN

QIN LING

SHAANXI

NEI MONGGOL (INNER MONGOLIA)

ORDOS DESERT

YIN SHAN

Baotou

GREAT WALL

Yinchuan

NINGXIA HUIZU

LIUPAN SHAN

Lanzhou

GANSU

QINGHAI

Xining

BAIYU SHAN

a

	BEIJING inset	

HEBEI

TIANJIN SHI

BEIJING SHI

BEIJING

Tongxian

Shunyi

Qinghe

Haidian

Fengtai

Changxindianzhen

Daxing

Nanyuan

Yongding

Gu an

Yongqing

Scale 1:1 000 000

0 2 4 6 8 10 Miles

0 4 8 12 16 Kilometers

©RMCN

Cities and Towns

0 to 50,000 ○
50,000 to 500,000 ⊙
500,000 to 1,000,000 ◎
1,000,000 and over

For larger scale coverage of Beijing see page 240.

Scale 1:10 000 000; one inch to 160 miles. Lambert Conformal Conic Projection
Elevations and depressions are given in feet

EAST CHINA SEA

SOUTH CHINA SEA

PHILIPPINE SEA

JAPAN

NANSEI-SHOTO (RYUKYU) ISLANDS

SAKISHIMA-GUNTO

IRIOMOTE-JIMA

Tropic of Cancer

TAIWAN (FORMOSA)

T'AIPEI
Chilung (Kirin)
Ilan
Suao
Hualien
Hsinchu
Miaoli
T'aichung
Changhua
Chiai
Taitung
Tainan
Pingtung
Kaohsiung
Hengchun

PESCADORES

PRATAS ISLAND
(Claimed by China and Taiwan)

PARACEL ISLANDS
(Claimed by China, Taiwan and Vietnam)

BATAN ISLANDS
Batan
Babuyan Channel
BABUYAN ISLANDS
Claveria
Aparri
Luzon Strait
Balintang Channel
Bashi Channel

LUZON

PHILIPPINES

MANILA
Quezon City
Subic
Manila Bay

CATANDUANES

SHANGHAI

ZHEJIANG
Hangzhou
Shaoxing
Ningbo
Ninghai
Linhai
Wenzhou
Lishui
Quxian
Jinhua

FUJIAN
Fuzhou
Quanzhou
Xiamen
Zhangzhou
Putian
Nanping
Yong'an
Dehua
Shantou
Chaozhou

JIANGXI
Nanchang
Qingjiang
Ji'an
Ganzhou
Pingxiang

HUBEI
WUHAN
Wuchang
Hankou
Hanyang
Yichang

HUNAN
Changsha
Xiangtan
Hengyang
Shaoyang
Lingling
Changde

GUIZHOU
Guiyang
Zunyi
Anshun

GUANGDONG
GUANGZHOU (Xiangang)
HONG KONG (Xianggang)
SHENZHEN
Macau (Port.)
Shantou
Huizhou
Foshan
Zhanjiang
Maoming

GUANGXI ZHUANGZU
Nanning
Liuzhou
Guilin
Wuzhou
Beihai

HAINAN
HAINAN DAO
Haikou
Wenchang
LEIZHOU BANDAO

YUNNAN
KUNMING

SZECHWAN (RED) BASIN
Leshan
Wanxian

CHONGQING
Luzhou
Neijiang

VIETNAM
Hanoi
Hai Phong
Vinh
Da Nang (Tourane)
Hue
Qui Nhon

LAOS

CAMBODIA

THAILAND

ANNAMITIC CORDILLERA

Gulf of Tonkin

Longitude East of Greenwich

A-560793-76-10-520
COPYRIGHT BY
RAND McNALLY & COMPANY
MADE IN U.S.A.

0 50 100 150 200 250 300 Miles
0 100 200 300 400 500 Kilometers

Continued on pages 192-193

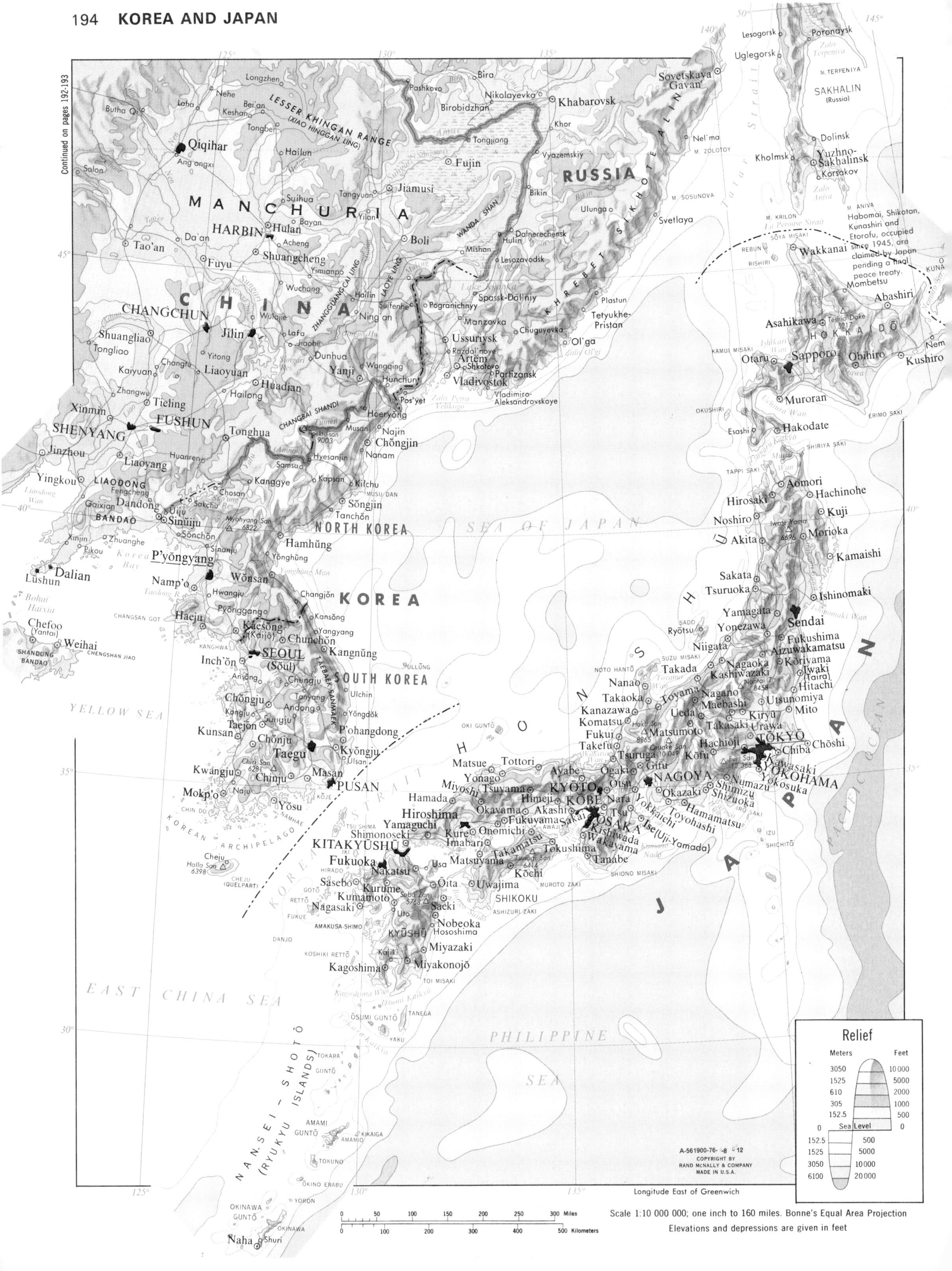

MANCHURIA

CHINA

RUSSIA

Qiqihar
Butha Nehe Longzhen Pashkovo Bira Nikolayevka Khabarovsk Sovetskaya Gavan'
Laha Keshan Bei an LESSER KHINGAN RANGE (XIAO HINGGAN LING) Khor
Tongbei Hailun Birobidzhan Tongjiang SAKHALIN (Russia)
Salon Ang'angxi Suihua Bayan Tangyuan Jiamusi Fujin Vyazemskiy M. TERPENIYA Lesogorsk Poronaysk
HARBIN Hulan Yilan Bikin Zaliv Terpeniya
Tao'an Acheng Wuchang Boli Mishan Lesozavodsk Uglegorsk
Fuyu Shuangcheng Yimianpo Hulin Dalnerechensk Svetlaya Dolinsk
Yitong Huadian Suifenhe Pogranichnyy Spassk-Dal'niy Yuzhno-Sakhalinsk
CHANGCHUN Jilin Lafa Jiaohe Ning'an Plastun Korsakov Kholmsk
Shuangliao Changtu Dunhua Wangqing Manzovka Tetyukhe-Pristan M. ANIVA
Tongliao Liaoyuan Hailong Yanji Hunchun Chuguyevka Habomai, Shikotan, Kunashiri and
Kaiyuan Zhangwu Tonghua Pos'yet Ussuriysk Razdol'noye M. KRILON RUSSIRI Etorofu, occupied
Xinmin Tieling FUSHUN Musan Shkotovo Artëm La Perouse Strait SOYA MISAKI Wakkanai since 1945, are
SHENYANG Huanren Hyesanjin Najin Vladivostok Partizansk REBUN claimed by Japan
Jinzhou Liaoyang CHANGBAI SHANDI Kilchu Chŏngjin Vladimiro- KAMUI MISAKI Asahikawa pending a final
Yingkou LIAODONG Chosan Samsu Nanam Aleksandrovskoye OKUSHIRI Otaru Sapporo HOKKAIDO peace treaty.
Dandong Kanggye Kapsan Tanchŏn OSHIRO Muroran Obihiro Mombetsu
Gaixian BANDAO Sinŭiju Sŏngjin Esashi Kushiro Abashiri
Xinjin Zhuanghe Sinanju Hamhŭng Hakodate KUNA
Pikou Ŭiju Sŏnchŏn Myohyang-san 6822 NORTH KOREA SEA OF JAPAN Aomori
Dalian Sakchu P'yŏngyang Yŏnghŭng Hirosaki Hachinohe
Lüshun Namp'o Wŏnsan KOREA Noshiro Kuji
Bohai Haixia Hwangju Changjin Sakata Akita Morioka
Chefoo (Yantai) Haeju Pyŏnggang Kansŏng Tsuruoka Yamagata Kamaishi
Weihai Kaesŏng (Kaijō) Yangyang Niigata SADO Yonezawa Sendai Ishinomaki
CHANGSAN GOT Inch'ŏn SEOUL (Sŏul) Chunchŏn Kangnŭng Ryotsu Aizuwakamatsu Fukushima
SHANDONG BANDAO Ansŏng SOUTH KOREA Ullŭng Nagaoka Kōriyama
Chŏngju Chungju Yŏngdŏk Nanao Takada Kashiwazaki Iwaki (Taira)
Kongju Tanyang Andong Takaoka Toyama Nagano Maebashi Hitachi
Taejŏn Chŏnju Kyŏngju P'ohangdong Komatsu Matsumoto Ueda Utsunomiya Mito
Kunsan Kŭmje Taegu Fukui Kanazawa Takasaki Urawa Kiryū
Kwangju Chinju Masan Takefu Tsuruga Kōfu TOKYO Chiba Chōshi
Mokp'o Naju PUSAN Matsue Tottori Ayabe Ōgaki Gifu Hachioji Kawasaki Yokohama
Chin Do Yŏsu KYOTO Ōtsu NAGOYA Numazu Yokosuka
Cheju Halla San 6398 Yonago Tsuyama KŌBE Nara OSAKA Okazaki Shizuoka
CHEJU (QUELPART) Miyoshi Himeji Akashi Sakai Ise (Uji-Yamada)
KOREA STRAIT Hamada Okayama Fukuyama Kishiwada Wakayama Yokkaichi Toyohashi Hamamatsu
Hiroshima Onomichi Tokushima Tanabe
Yamaguchi Kure Takamatsu SHIKOKU
Shimonoseki Imabari Matsuyama Kōchi
KITAKYŪSHŪ Usa Ōita MUROTO ZAKI
Fukuoka Nakatsu Uwajima SHIONO MISAKI
Sasebo Kurume Saeki ASHIZURI ZAKI
Kumamoto Nagasaki Nobeoka Hososhima
KYŪSHŪ Miyazaki
Kagoshima Miyakonojō
EAST CHINA SEA

YELLOW SEA

PHILIPPINE SEA

JAPAN

NANSEI SHOTŌ (RYUKYU ISLANDS)
ŌSUMI GUNTŌ TANEGA YAKU
TOKARA GUNTŌ
AMAMI GUNTŌ KIKAIGA AMAMI
OKINAWA GUNTŌ OKINAWA NAHA Shuri
OKINO ERABU YORON

A-561900-76-8 12
COPYRIGHT BY
RAND McNALLY & COMPANY
MADE IN U.S.A.

Longitude East of Greenwich

Scale 1:10 000 000; one inch to 160 miles. Bonne's Equal Area Projection
Elevations and depressions are given in feet

Relief		
Meters		Feet
3050		10 000
1525		5000
610		2000
305		1000
152.5		500
0	Sea Level	0
152.5		500
1525		5000
3050		10 000
6100		20 000

0 50 100 150 200 250 300 Miles
0 100 200 300 400 500 Kilometers

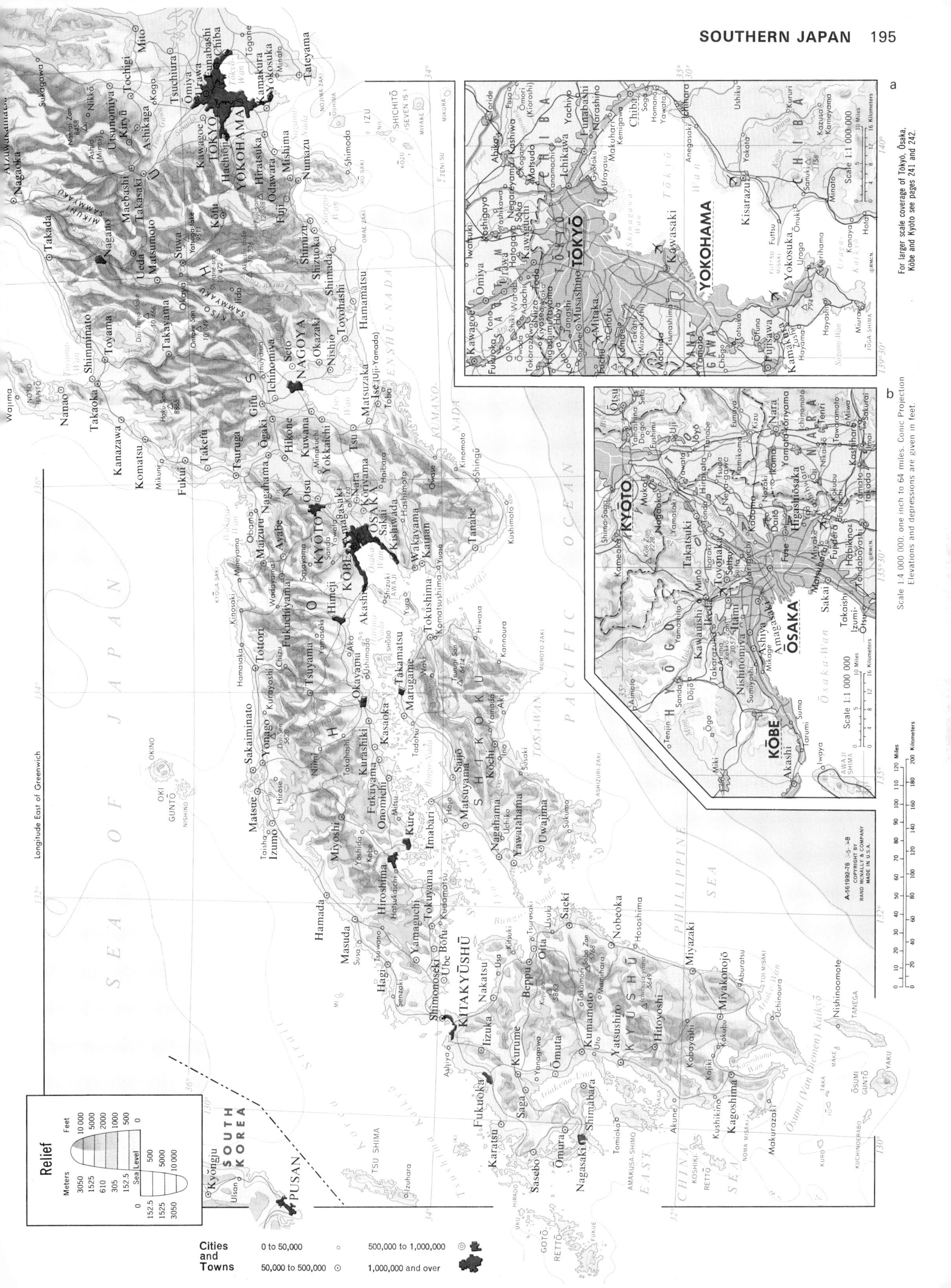

a

For larger scale coverage of Tōkyō, Ōsaka,
Kōbe and Kyōto see pages 241 and 242.

b

Scale 1:4 000 000, one inch to 64 miles. Conic Projection
Elevations and depressions are given in feet.

Scale 1:1 000 000

Relief

Meters	Feet
3050	10 000
1525	5000
610	2000
305	1000
152.5	500
0	Sea Level 0
152.5	500
1525	5000
3050	10 000

Cities and Towns

| 0 to 50,000 | 500,000 to 1,000,000 |
| 50,000 to 500,000 | 1,000,000 and over |

A-561992-76 -5- +8
COPYRIGHT BY
RAND McNALLY & COMPANY
MADE IN U.S.A.

SEA OF JAPAN

PACIFIC OCEAN

PHILIPPINE SEA

EAST CHINA SEA

SOUTH KOREA

TOKYO
YOKOHAMA
NAGOYA
KYOTO
OSAKA
KOBE
KITAKYŪSHŪ

HONSHŪ
SHIKOKU
KYŪSHŪ

Longitude East of Greenwich

196

Relief

Meters | Feet
3050 | 10 000
1525 | 5000
610 | 2000
305 | 1000
152.5 | 500
Sea Level

152.5 | 500
1525 | 5000
3050 | 10 000
6100 | 20 000

A-569800-76 -10-11-30
COPYRIGHT BY
RAND McNALLY & COMPANY
MADE IN U.S.A.

Scale 1:16 000 000; one inch to 250 miles. Polyconic Project
Elevations and depressions are given in feet

Continued on pages 188-189

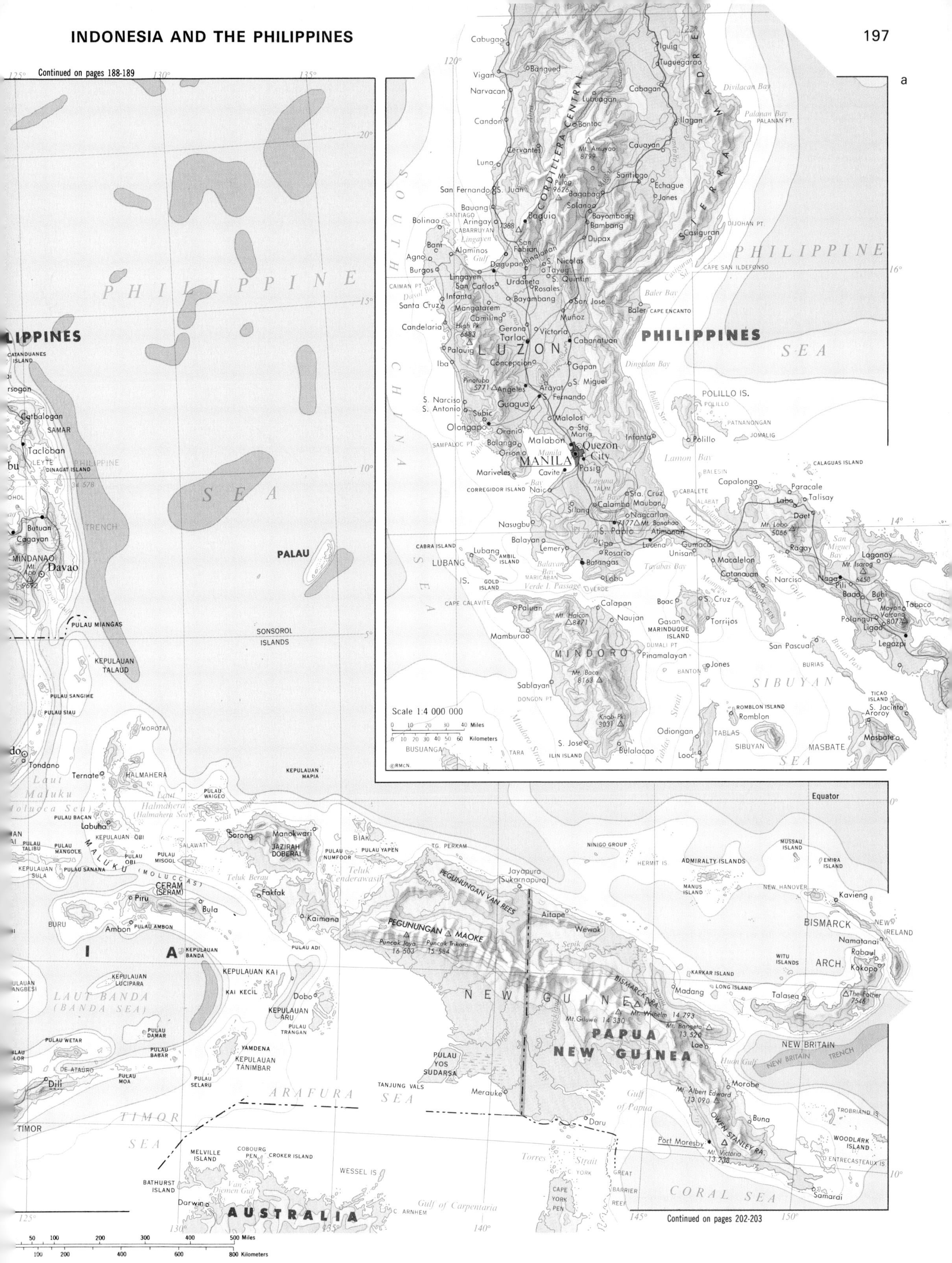

PHILIPPINE

PHILIPPINE SEA

SOUTH CHINA SEA

LUZON

PHILIPPINES

CORDILLERA CENTRAL

SIERRA MADRE

Cabugao
Banguod
Vigan
Narvacan
Candon
Cervantes
Luna
San Fernando · S. Juan
Bauang
Bolinao
Aringay
Alaminos
Agno
Burgos
Lingayen
Santa Cruz
Infanta
Mangatarem
Candelaria
Iba
Palauig
Concepcion
S. Narciso
S. Antonio
Subic
Olongapo
Orani
Orion
Balanga
Mariveles
Corregidor Island

Iguig
Tuguegarao
Bangued
Lubuagan
Bontoc
Cabagan
Ilagan
Palanan Bay
PALANAN PT.
Divilacan Bay
Cauayan
Echague
Santiago
Janes
Bayombong
Bambang
Dupax
Casiguran
DIJOHAN PT.
CAPE SAN ILDEFONSO

Mt. Amuyao 8799
Mt. Pulog 9626
Baguio
Bagabag
Solano
San Nicolas
S. Tayug
S. Quintin
Muñoz
San Jose
Baler Bay
Baler · CAPE ENCANTO

Gerona
Tarlac
Victoria
Cabanatuan
Gapan
S. Miguel
Dingalan Bay
High Pk. 6683
Camiling
Pinatubo 5771
Angeles
Arayat
S. Fernando
Guagua
Sta. Maria
Malolos
Polillo
POLILLO IS.
POLILLO
Patnanongan
JOMALIG

Malabon
MANILA
Quezon City
Pasig
Cavite
Naic
Manila Bay
Laguna TALIM
Sta. Cruz
Mauban
Infanta
Lamon Bay
BALESIN
CALAGUAS ISLAND
Capalonga
Paracale
Talisay
Labo
Daet
CABALETE
ALABAT

Nasugbu
Silang
Calamba
Nagcarlan
Mt. Banahao 7177
Atimonan
S. Pablo
Mt. Labo 5066
S. Narciso
Naga
Mt. Isarog 6450
Pili
Baad
Bula
Ragay
San Miguel Bay
Lagonoy Bay

Cabra Island
Lubang
AMBIL ISLAND
GOLD ISLAND
Batangas
Rosario
Lipa
Balayan
Lemery
Balayan Bay
MARICABAN
Verde I. Passage
VERDE
CAPE CALAVITE
Paluan
Mamburao
MINDORO
Sablayan
Mt. Baco 8163
DONGON PT.
S. Jose
BUSUANGA
TARA

Loba
Lucena
Unisan
Gumaca
Macalelon
Catanauan
S. Narciso
Mt. Halcon 8471
Calapan
Naujan
Gasan
Boac
Torrijos
MARINDUQUE ISLAND
DUMALI PT.
Pinamalayan
Jones
Mamburao
ILIN ISLAND
Mindoro Strait

Tarabas Bay
Pagbilao
S. Cruz PEN.
BONDOC PEN.
San Pascual
Jones
BANTON
SIBUYAN
ROMBLON ISLAND
Romblon
Odiongan
TABLAS
Looc
SIBUYAN SEA
TICAO ISLAND
S. Jacinto
Aroroy
Masbate
MASBATE

BURIAS
Burias Pass
Polangui
Ligao
Moynra Volcano 8077
Tabaco
Legazpi

LIPPINES

PHILIPPINE SEA

CATANDUANES ISLAND
rsogon

Catbalogan
SAMAR
Tacloban
bu
LEYTE
DINAGAT ISLAND
OHOL
Butuan
Cagayan
MINDANAO
Mt. Apo 9692
Davao
PHILIPPINE TRENCH
PULAU MIANGAS
KEPULAUAN TALAUD
PULAU SANGIHE
PULAU SIAU

PALAU

SONSOROL ISLANDS

Scale 1:4 000 000

0   10   20   30   40 Miles
0 10 20 30 40 50 60 Kilometers
©RMCN

Tondano
Ternate
HALMAHERA
MOROTAI
KEPULAUAN MAPIA
Laut Maluku
(Moluca Sea)
PULAU BACAN
Labuha
PULAU TALIBU
PULAU MANGOLE
KEPULAUAN OBI
KEPULAUAN SULA
PULAU SANANA
MALUKU (MOLUCCAS)
BURU
Piru
CERAM (SERAM)
Bula
Ambon
PULAU AMBON
Fakfak
KEPULAUAN BANDA
KEPULAUAN LUCIPARA
LAUT BANDA (BANDA SEA)
PULAU DAMAR
KAI KECIL
Dobo
KEPULAUAN KAI
KEPULAUAN ARU
PULAU TRANGAN
YAMDENA
KEPULAUAN TANIMBAR
PULAU SELARU

PULAU WAIGEO
PULAU WEIGO
Sorong
Manokwari
JAZIRAH DOBERAI
BIAK
PULAU NUMFOOR
PULAU YAPEN
SALAWATI
PULAU MISOOL
Teluk Berau
Teluk Cenderawasih
Kaimana
PULAU ADI

PEGUNUNGAN VAN REES
Jayapura (Sukarnapura)
TG. PERKAM
NINIGO GROUP
HERMIT IS
ADMIRALTY ISLANDS
MUSSAU ISLAND
EMIRA ISLAND
MANUS ISLAND
NEW HANOVER
Kavieng
BISMARCK ARCH.
Namatanai
Rabaul
Kokopo
NEW IRELAND

PEGUNUNGAN MAOKE
Puncak Jaya 16 503
Puncak Trikora 15 584
Aitape
Wewak
Sepik
NEW GUINEA
Madang
KARKAR ISLAND
LONG ISLAND
WITU ISLANDS
Talasea
The Father 7546
NEW BRITAIN

Equator

I   A
PULAU YOS SUDARSA
Mt. Giluwe 14 330
Mt. Wilhelm 14 793
Mt. Bangeta 13 520
PAPUA NEW GUINEA
Lae
Huon Gulf
Morobe
NEW BRITAIN TRENCH
TROBRIAND IS.
WOODLARK ISLAND

Merauke
Daru
Mt. Albert Edward 13 090
Buna
D'ENTRECASTEAUX IS.
TANJUNG VALS
ARAFURA SEA
Gulf of Papua
OWEN STANLEY RA.
Port Moresby
Mt. Victoria 13 238
Samarai
CORAL SEA

DE-ATAURO
PULAU WETAR
PULAU LOR
PULAU MOA
PULAU BABAR
Dili
TIMOR
TIMOR SEA

MELVILLE ISLAND
COBOURG PEN.
CROKER ISLAND
BATHURST ISLAND
Van Diemen Gulf
Darwin
WESSEL IS
Gulf of Carpentaria
CAPE ARNHEM
CAPE YORK PEN.
Torres Strait
GREAT BARRIER REEF
AUSTRALIA

Continued on pages 202-203

50 100   200   300   400   500 Miles
100   200   400   600   800 Kilometers

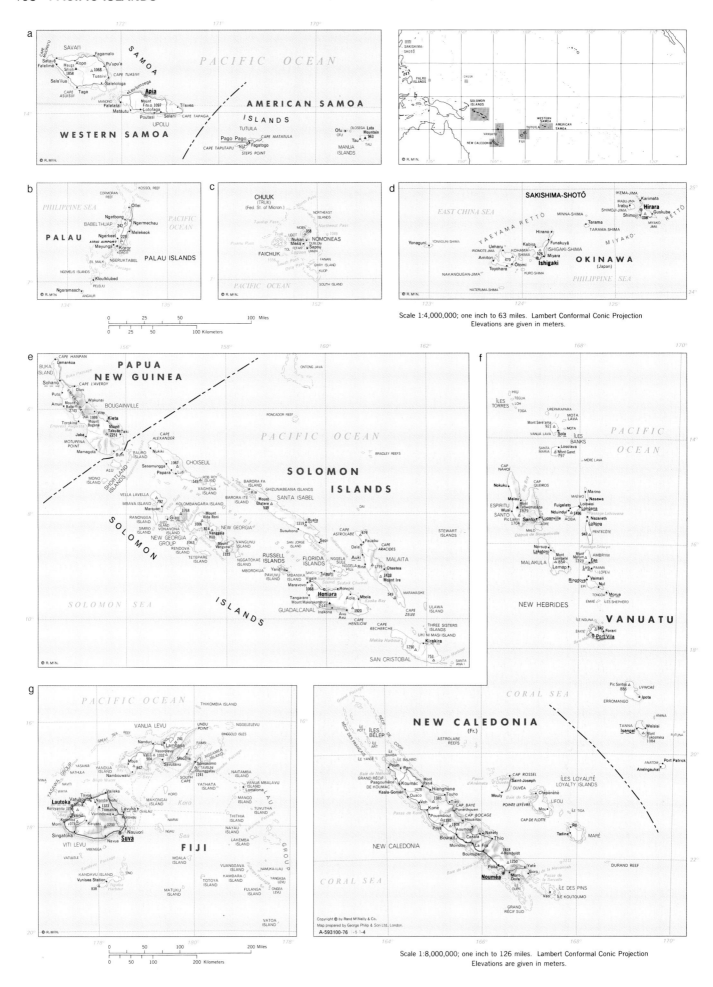

Scale 1:4,000,000; one inch to 63 miles. Lambert Conformal Conic Projection
Elevations are given in meters.

Scale 1:8,000,000; one inch to 126 miles. Lambert Conformal Conic Projection
Elevations are given in meters.

Copyright © by Rand M9Nally & Co.
Map prepared by George Philip & Son Ltd, London.
A-593100-76 -1-I-4

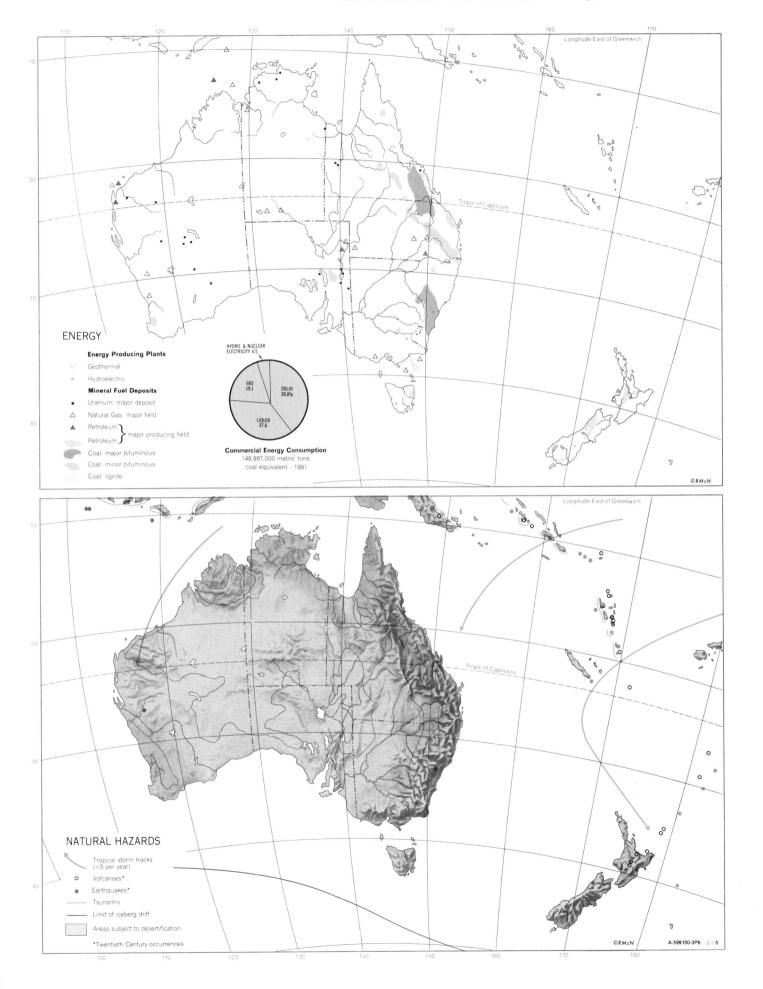

ENERGY

Energy Producing Plants

▽ Geothermal

• Hydroelectric

Mineral Fuel Deposits

• Uranium: major deposit

△ Natural Gas: major field

▲ Petroleum }
Petroleum } major producing field

Coal: major bituminous

Coal: minor bituminous

Coal: lignite

HYDRO. & NUCLEAR
ELECTRICITY 4.5

GAS
19.1

SOLID
38.8%

LIQUID
37.6

Commercial Energy Consumption
148,997,000 metric tons
coal equivalent · 1991

©RMcN

NATURAL HAZARDS

⤻ Tropical storm tracks
(<5 per year)

○ Volcanoes*

• Earthquakes*

Tsunamis

Limit of iceberg drift

Areas subject to desertification

*Twentieth Century occurrences

©RMcN   A-599100-3P6 5-3 5

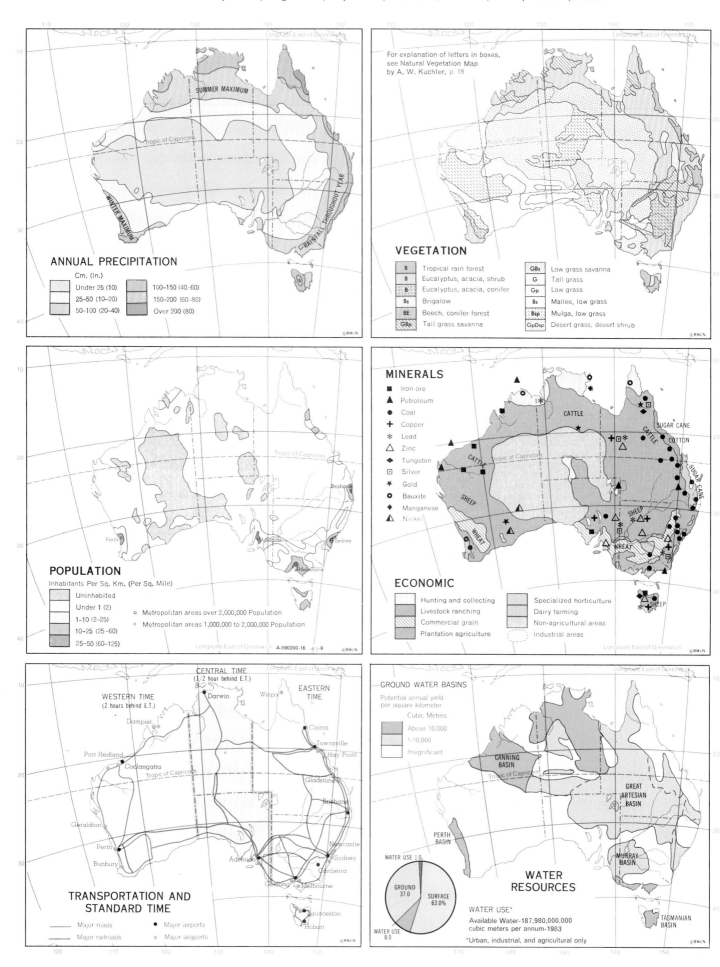

ANNUAL PRECIPITATION

Cm. (In.)

Under 25 (10)	100–150 (40–60)
25–50 (10–20)	150–200 (60–80)
50–100 (20–40)	Over 200 (80)

SUMMER MAXIMUM

WINTER MAXIMUM

RAINFALL THROUGHOUT YEAR

Tropic of Capricorn

VEGETATION

For explanation of letters in boxes, see Natural Vegetation Map by A. W. Kuchler, p. 18

B	Tropical rain forest	GBs	Low grass savanna
B	Eucalyptus, acacia, shrub	G	Tall grass
B	Eucalyptus, acacia, conifer	Gp	Low grass
Bs	Brigalow	Bs	Mallee, low grass
BE	Beech, conifer forest	Bsp	Mulga, low grass
GBp	Tall grass savanna	GpDsp	Desert grass, desert shrub

POPULATION

Inhabitants Per Sq. Km. (Per Sq. Mile)

	Uninhabited
	Under 1 (2)
	1–10 (2–25)
	10–25 (25–60)
	25–50 (60–125)

□ Metropolitan areas over 2,000,000 Population

○ Metropolitan areas 1,000,000 to 2,000,000 Population

A-590200-16   -4-5-9

Perth   Adelaide   Sydney   Melbourne   Brisbane

MINERALS

■	Iron ore
▲	Petroleum
●	Coal
+	Copper
✱	Lead
△	Zinc
◆	Tungsten
⊡	Silver
✶	Gold
⊙	Bauxite
◆	Manganese
◮	Nickel

CATTLE   SUGAR CANE   COTTON   SHEEP   WHEAT

ECONOMIC

	Hunting and collecting		Specialized horticulture
	Livestock ranching		Dairy farming
	Commercial grain		Non-agricultural areas
	Plantation agriculture		Industrial areas

TRANSPORTATION AND STANDARD TIME

WESTERN TIME (2 hours behind E.T.)
CENTRAL TIME (1/2 hour behind E.T.)
EASTERN TIME

Darwin   Weipa   Cairns   Townsville   Hay Point   Gladstone   Brisbane   Newcastle   Sydney   Canberra   Melbourne   Geelong   Adelaide   Coolangatta   Port Hedland   Dampier   Geraldton   Perth   Bunbury   Launceston   Hobart

——	Major roads	●	Major airports
——	Major railroads	○	Major seaports

GROUND WATER BASINS

Potential annual yield per square kilometer

Cubic Meters

	Above 10,000
	1–10,000
	Insignificant

CANNING BASIN   GREAT ARTESIAN BASIN   PERTH BASIN   MURRAY BASIN   TASMANIAN BASIN

WATER RESOURCES

WATER USE 1.0
GROUND 37.0   SURFACE 63.0%
WATER USE 8.0

WATER USE*

Available Water–187,980,000,000 cubic meters per annum-1983

*Urban, industrial, and agricultural only

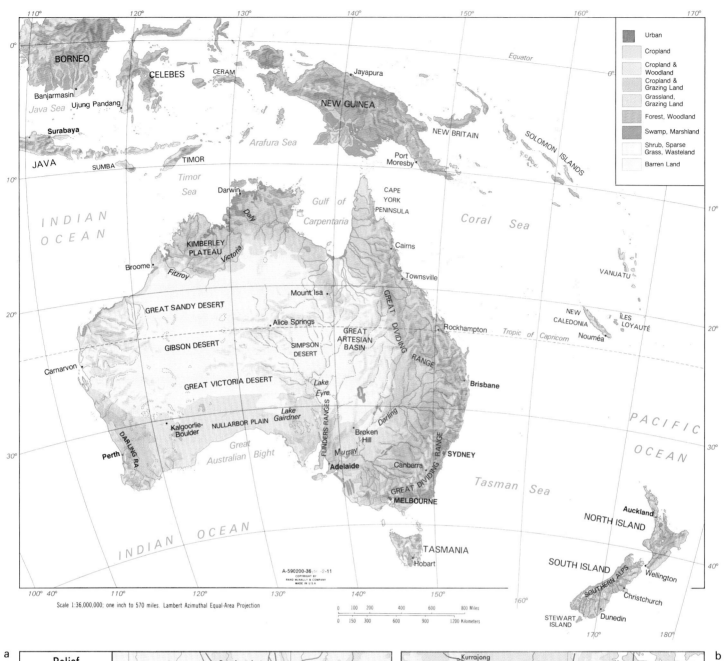

Urban
Cropland
Cropland & Woodland
Cropland & Grazing Land
Grassland, Grazing Land
Forest, Woodland
Swamp, Marshland
Shrub, Sparse Grass, Wasteland
Barren Land

BORNEO
CELEBES
CERAM
Jayapura
Banjarmasin
Ujung Pandang
Java Sea
Surabaya
JAVA
SUMBA
TIMOR
Timor Sea
Arafura Sea
NEW GUINEA
NEW BRITAIN
Port Moresby
SOLOMON ISLANDS
Equator

INDIAN OCEAN
Darwin
Daly
KIMBERLEY PLATEAU
Victoria
Broome
Fitzroy
GREAT SANDY DESERT
Mount Isa
Alice Springs
GIBSON DESERT
SIMPSON DESERT
GREAT ARTESIAN BASIN
Carnarvon
GREAT VICTORIA DESERT
Lake Eyre
Lake Gairdner
Kalgoorlie-Boulder
NULLARBOR PLAIN
FLINDERS RANGES
Broken Hill
Murray
Darling
Great Australian Bight
DARLING RA.
Perth
Adelaide
Canberra
SYDNEY
GREAT DIVIDING RANGE
MELBOURNE
Gulf of Carpentaria
CAPE YORK PENINSULA
Cairns
Townsville
Coral Sea
Rockhampton
Tropic of Capricorn
Brisbane
PACIFIC OCEAN
VANUATU
NEW CALEDONIA
Nouméa
ÎLES LOYAUTÉ
Tasman Sea
INDIAN OCEAN
TASMANIA
Hobart
Auckland
NORTH ISLAND
SOUTH ISLAND
SOUTHERN ALPS
Wellington
Christchurch
STEWART ISLAND
Dunedin

A-590200-36 · ·2-11
COPYRIGHT BY
RAND McNALLY & COMPANY
MADE IN U.S.A.

Scale 1:36,000,000; one inch to 570 miles. Lambert Azimuthal Equal-Area Projection

0 100 200 400 600 800 Miles
0 150 300 600 900 1200 Kilometers

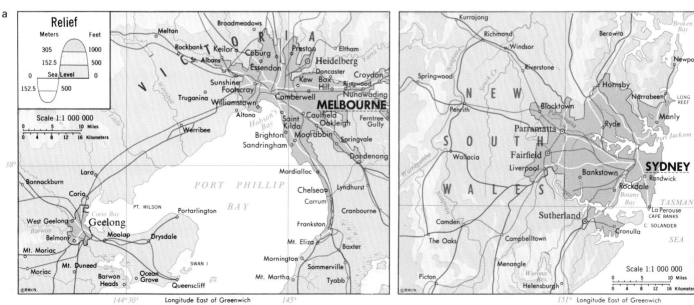

a

Relief

Meters		Feet
305		1000
152.5		500
0	Sea Level	0
152.5		500

Scale 1:1 000 000
0   5   10 Miles
0 4 8 12 16 Kilometers

VICTORIA
Melton
Broadmeadows
Rockbank
Keilor
Coburg
Preston
Eltham
St. Albans
Essendon
Heidelberg
Doncaster
Croydon
Sunshine
Kew
Box Hill
Ringwood
Nunawading
Truganina
Footscray
Camberwell
MELBOURNE
Williamstown
Altona
Caulfield
Oakleigh
Ferntree Gully
Werribee
Saint Kilda
Moorabbin
Springvale
Brighton
Sandringham
Hobson's Bay
Mordialloc
Dandenong
Lara
Bannockburn
PORT PHILLIP BAY
Chelsea
Lyndhurst
Corio
Carrum
Cranbourne
PT. WILSON
Portarlington
Corio Bay
Geelong
West Geelong
Belmont
Moolap
Drysdale
Frankston
Mt. Eliza
Baxter
Barwon
Mt. Moriac
Mt. Duneed
SWAN I.
Mornington
Sommerville
Moriac
Barwon Heads
Ocean Grove
Queenscliff
Mt. Martha
Tyabb
©RMcN.
Little
Werribee
Yarra

144°30'   Longitude East of Greenwich   145°

b

Kurrajong
Richmond
Windsor
Berowra
Broken Bay
Springwood
Riverstone
Newport
NEW
Windsor
Nepean
Hornsby
Narrabeen
LONG REEF
Penrith
South Cr.
Blacktown
SOUTH
Parramatta
Ryde
Manly
Wallacia
Parramatta
Port Jackson
Fairfield
WALES
Liverpool
Bankstown
SYDNEY
Camden
Rockdale
Randwick
Warragamba
Nepean
Botany Bay
Sutherland
TASMAN
The Oaks
La Perouse
CAPE BANKS
Campbelltown
Cronulla
C. SOLANDER
Menangle
SEA
Picton
Georges
Woronora Res.
Helensburgh
©RMcN.
Warragamba

Scale 1:1 000 000
0   5   10 Miles
0 4 8 12 16 Kilometers

151°   Longitude East of Greenwich

For larger scale coverage of Melbourne and Sydney see page 243.

202

Continued on pages 196-197

INDONESIA

Pasuruan
J A V A △ 10 932
G. Mahameru △ 2225
G. Raung
Singaraja
BALI
G. Rinjani
LOMBOK
Sumbawa-Besar
SUMBAWA
Raboo
FLORES
Waingapu
SAVU
SEA
SAWU
ROTI
TIMOR
Kupang
ALOR
LOMBLEN PANTAR
Dili
SELARU
TANJUNG VALS

S U N D A

S U N D A   I S L A N D S

SUMBA

SUNDA TRENCH

TIMOR SEA

A R A F U R A   S E A

C. VAN DIEMEN
CROKER
COBURG PEN.
BATHURST
MELVILLE
Van Diemen Gulf
Clarence Str.
Darwin
Anson Bay
WESSEL IS.
CAPE ARNHEM
Blue Mud Bay
GROOTE EYLANDT
Limmen Bight

CAPE LONDONDERRY
Joseph Bonaparte Gulf
Wyndham
Mt. Hann 2800
KING LEOPOLD RANGES
Pine Creek
Katherine
ARNHEM LAND
Victoria River Downs
Daly Waters
Newcastle Waters
Birdum
Borroloola
SIR EDWARD PELLEW GROUP
GULF
CARPENT
WEL

BUCCANEER ARCH.
CAPE LEVEQUE
DAMPIER LAND
Broome
Derby
GEIKIE RANGE
Fitzroy Crossing
Halls Creek
Roebuck Bay
LaGrange
Tanami
NORTHERN
Alexandria
Burketow

EIGHTY MILE BEACH
LARREY POINT
RIPON
Port Hedland
DAMPIER ARCH.
MONTE BELLO IS.
BARROW
Roebourne
Marble Bar
Nullagine
GREAT SANDY DESERT
TERRITORY
Tennant Creek
Camoowe
Mount
Do

NORTH WEST CAPE
Onslow
Millstream
HAMERSLEY RANGE
Mt. Bruce 4052
Jiggalong
Mt. Ziel 4955
MACDONNELL RANGES
Barrow Creek
Arltunga
Alice Springs
JAMES RANGE
SIMPSON
Q

POINT CLOATES
Tropic of Capricorn
CAPE FARQUHAR
Carnarvon
Peak Hill
GIBSON DESERT
Ayers Rock 2844
Charlotte Waters
DESERT
Birdsvil

BERNIER
DORRE
DIRK HARTOG
STEEP POINT
Meekatharra
Nannine
Wiluna
MUSGRAVE RANGES
Mt. Woodroffe 4724
EVERARD RANGES
The Alberg
Oodnadatta

Cue
Sandstone
Mount Magnet
Laverton
W E S T E R N
Ajana
Northampton
HOUTMAN ROCKS
Geraldton
Dongara
Mingenew
GREAT VICTORIA DESERT
SOUTH AUSTRALI
STUART RANGE
William Creek
Marree
Farin

Menzies
A U S T R A L I A
Oldea Station
Pimba
Woomera

Pithara
Miling
Moora
Lake Brown
Coolgardie
Kalgoorlie-Boulder
Rawlinna
Hughes
NULLARBOR PLAIN
Penong
Ceduna
POINT FOWLER
Whyalla
Port Pirie
FLINDERS RANGE
FL
Part A

DARLING RANGE
Southern Cross
SWANLAND
Norseman
Dundas
Eucla
Eyre
Whyalla
EYRE PENINSULA
Gla
Wollara
Port

Perth
Fremantle
Northam
York
Narrogin
Collie
Salmon Gums
GREAT AUSTRALIAN BIGHT
Port Lincoln
Moonta
Port

CAPE NATURALISTE
Bunbury
Busselton
Katanning
Ravensthorpe
Hopetoun
Esperance
ARCHIPELAGO OF THE RECHERCHE
KANGAROO

CAPE LEEUWIN
Nornalup
Albany
King George Sd.
K
CAPE

PT. D'ENTRECASTEAUX
WEST CAPE HOWE

I N D I A N   O C E A N

I N D I A N

O C E A N

Relief

Meters	Feet
3050	10 000
1525	5000
610	2000
305	1000
152.5	500
0	0
Sea Level	Sea Level
152.5	500
1525	5000
3050	10 000
6100	20 000
	Below Sea Level

A-590200-76 -5 -15

Longitude 115° East of Greenwich

Scale 1:16 000 000; one inch to 250 miles. Lambert's Azimuthal, Equal Area Proj
Elevations and depressions are given in feet

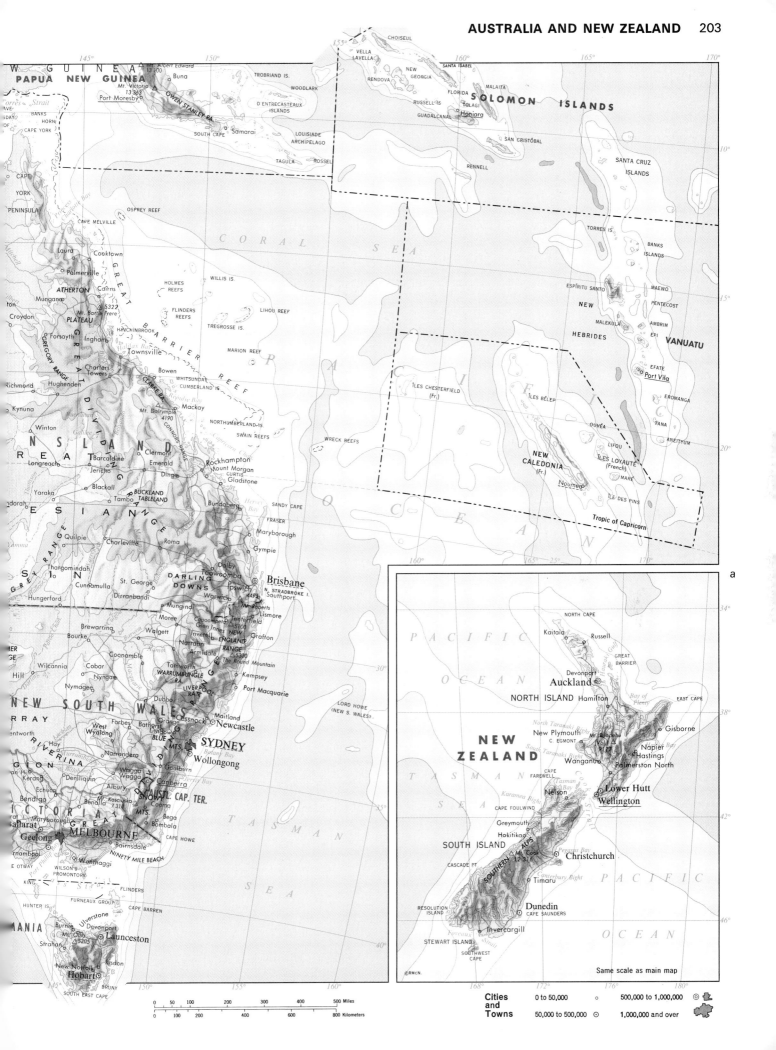

NEW GUINEA
PAPUA NEW GUINEA
Mt. Albert Edward 13100
Buna
Mt. Victoria 13363
Port Moresby
OWEN STANLEY RA.
TROBRIAND IS.
WOODLARK
D ENTRECASTEAUX ISLANDS
SOUTH CAPE
Samarai
LOUISIADE ARCHIPELAGO
TAGULA
ROSSEL

CHOISEUL
VELLA LAVELLA
RENDOVA
NEW GEORGIA
SANTA ISABEL
FLORIDA
RUSSELL IS
TOLAGI
SOLOMON ISLANDS
GUADALCANAL
Honiara
SAN CRISTÓBAL
RENNELL
SANTA CRUZ ISLANDS

Torres Strait
BANKS
THURSDAY I.
HORN I.
CAPE YORK

CAPE YORK PENINSULA

CORAL SEA

OSPREY REEF

CAPE MELVILLE

Laura
Cooktown
Palmerville
ATHERTON
Mungana
Cairns
PLATEAU
Mt. Bartle Frere 5322
HOLMES REEFS
WILLIS IS.
FLINDERS REEFS
TREGROSSE IS.

TORRES IS
BANKS ISLANDS
ESPÍRITU SANTO
MAEWO
NEW
HEBRIDES
PENTECOST
MALEKULA
AMBRIM
EPI
VANUATU
EFATE
Port Vila
EROMANGA

Croydon
Forsayth
Ingham
HINCHINBROOK I.
Halifax Bay
Townsville
Charters Towers
BARRIER REEF
MARION REEF

Richmond
Hughenden
Bowen
CLARKE RA.
Repulse Bay
WHITSUNDAY
CUMBERLAND IS.
Mackay
NORTHUMBERLAND IS.
SWAIN REEFS
ÎLES CHESTERFIELD (Fr.)
ÎLES BÉLEP
OUVÉA
LIFOU
TANA
ANEITYUM

Kynuna
Winton
Mt. Dalrymple 4190
CONNORS RANGE
WRECK REEFS
NEW CALEDONIA (Fr.)
Nouméa
ÎLES LOYAUTÉ (French)
MARÉ
ÎLE DES PINS

QUEENSLAND
GREAT DIVIDING RANGE
Barcaldine
Clermont
Emerald
Dingo
Rockhampton
Mount Morgan
CURTIS
Gladstone

Longreach
Jericho
Blackall
BUCKLAND TABLELAND
Tambo
Bundaberg
SANDY CAPE
FRASER

Yaraka
GREAT RANGE
Quilpie
Charleville
Roma
Maryborough
HERVEY BAY

Thargomindah
DARLING DOWNS
Dalby
Toowoomba
Ipswich
Gympie
Tropic of Capricorn

Hungerford
Cunnamulla
St. George
Dirranbandi
Warwick
BRISBANE
N. STRADBROKE I.
Southport
Mt. Roberts 4495
Lismore

Mungindi
Moree
Capoompeta
Glen Innes 5100
Tenterfield
Inverell
NEW ENGLAND RANGE
Grafton
LORD HOWE (NEW S. WALES)

Brewarrina
Walgett
Narrabri
Armidale
The Round Mountain 5330
Tamworth
Kempsey

Bourke
Coonamble
WARRUMBUNGLE RA.
LIVERPOOL RA.
Port Macquarie

Cobar
Nyngan
NEW SOUTH WALES
Dubbo
Orange
Forbes
Bathurst
Lithgow
BLUE MTS.
Maitland
Cessnock
Newcastle

Wilcannia
Nymagee
Narromine
LIVERPOOL RA.
SYDNEY
Botany Bay
Wollongong

Broken Hill
Cobar
Hay
West Wyalong
Narrandera
Goulburn
Canberra
AUSTL. CAP. TER.

MURRAY
RIVERINA
Wentworth
Kerang
Deniliquin
Wagga Wagga
Albury
Cooma
Bega
Bombala
CAPE HOWE

Echuca
Bendigo
Benalla
Mt. Kosciusko 7316
SNOWY MTS.
Bairnsdale

VICTORIA
Ballarat
Maryborough
GREAT RANGE
Geelong
MELBOURNE
NINETY MILE BEACH

Warrnambool
Wonthaggi
Port Phillip Bay
WILSON'S PROMONTORY
CAPE OTWAY
KING I.
BASS STRAIT
FLINDERS
FURNEAUX GROUP
CAPE BARREN
HUNTER IS.
TASMAN SEA

TASMANIA
Burnie
Ulverstone
Devonport
Launceston
Strahan
Mt. Ossa 5305
New Norfolk
Risdon
HOBART
BRUNY
SOUTH EAST CAPE

a

NEW ZEALAND

PACIFIC OCEAN
NORTH CAPE
Kaitaia
Russell
GREAT BARRIER
Devonport
Auckland
NORTH ISLAND
Hamilton
Bay of Plenty
EAST CAPE
Gisborne
New Plymouth
C. Egmont
Mt. Ruapehu
Napier
Hastings
Wanganui
Palmerston North
CAPE FAREWELL
Nelson
Lower Hutt
Wellington
TASMAN SEA
CAPE FOULWIND
Greymouth
Hokitika
SOUTH ISLAND
SOUTHERN ALPS
Mt. Cook 12316
Christchurch
Pegasus Bay
Timaru
Canterbury Bight
RESOLUTION ISLAND
CASCADE PT
Dunedin
CAPE SAUNDERS
Invercargill
STEWART ISLAND
SOUTHWEST CAPE
PACIFIC OCEAN
Same scale as main map

0 50 100 200 300 400 500 Miles
0 100 200 400 600 800 Kilometers

Cities and Towns
0 to 50,000 ○
50,000 to 500,000 ⊙
500,000 to 1,000,000
1,000,000 and over

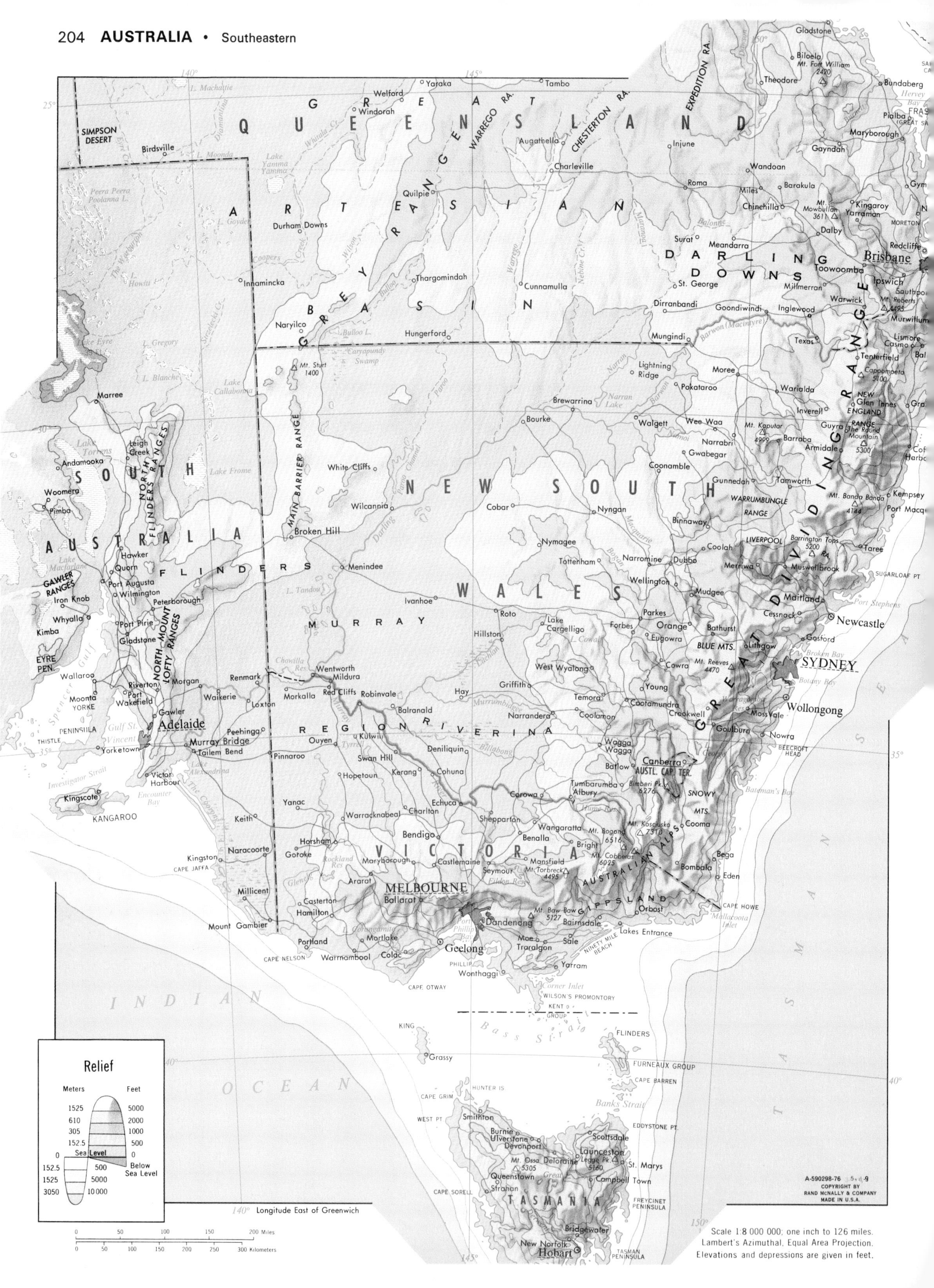

QUEENSLAND

SIMPSON DESERT

GREAT DIVIDING RANGE

WARREGO RA.

GREGORY RANGE

CHESTERTON RA.

EXPEDITION RA.

Yaraka
Welford
Tambo
Windorah
Augathella
Charleville
Injune
Wandoan
Gayndah
Maryborough
Pialba (GREAT IS.)
FRAS
Bundaberg
Hervey Bay
Gym
Gladstone
Biloela
Mt. Fort William 2420
Theodore
Redcliffe
Gympie
MORETON
Kingaroy
Yarraman
Mt. Mowbullan 3611
Dalby
Toowoomba
Ipswich
Brisbane
Southport
Mt. Roberts 4495
Murwillum
Warwick
Millmerran
Surat
Meandarra
Roma
Miles
Barakula
Chinchilla
St. George
Dirranbandi
Goondiwindi
Inglewood
Texas
Lismore
Casino
Bal
Mungindi
Barwon (Macintyre)
Tenterfield
Cappombera 5100
Durham Downs
Thargomindah
Cunnamulla
Innamincka
Naryilco
Hungerford
Carsapundy Swamp
Mt. Sturt 1400
Lightning Ridge
Moree
Pokataroo
Wialda
Glen Innes
NEW
Guyra
The Round Mountain 5300
ENGLAND RANGE
Cof Harbe
Gra

Marree
Birdsville
L. Machattie
L. Moonda
Lake Yamma Yamma
Cooper Creek
Diamantina
Wilson R.
Goyder
Bullo L.
Bulloo
Brewarrina
Narran Lake
Bourke
Walgett
Wee Waa
Narrabri
Mt. Kaputar 4959
Barraba
Gwabegar
Coonamble
Gunnedah
Tamworth
Armidale
Kempsey
Port Macq.

SOUTH AUSTRALIA

NORTH FLINDERS RANGES

FLINDERS RANGES

GAWLER RANGES

EYRE PEN.

Peera Peera Poolanna L.
The Wathwill
L. Howitt
Lake Eyre
Lake Gregory
L. Blanche
Lake Callabonna
Leigh Creek
Andamooka
Woomera
Pimba
Hawker
Quorn
Iron Knob
Whyalla
Kimba
Port Augusta
Wilmington
Peterborough
White Cliffs
Wilcannia
MAIN BARRIER RANGE
Broken Hill
FLINDERS
Menindee
L. Tandou
Ivanhoe
Cobar
Nymagee
Tottenham
Narromine
Dubbo
Wellington
Mudgee
Merriwa
Muswellbrook
Maitland
Cessnock
Newcastle
Port Stephens
BEECROFT HEAD
WARRUMBUNGLE RANGE
Binnaway
Coolah
LIVERPOOL RANGE
Barrington Tops 5200
Taree
SUGARLOAF PT.
Mt. Banda Banda 4144

NEW SOUTH WALES

MURRAY

Lake Torrens
Lake Frome
L. Macfarlane
Wallaroo
Moonta
Port Pirie
Gladstone
Riverton
Morgan
Waikerie
Loxton
Renmark
Wentworth
Mildura
Morkalla
Red Cliffs
Robinvale
Balranald
Hay
Hillston
West Wyalong
L. Cowal
L. Cargelligo
Forbes
Orange
Bathurst
BLUE MTS.
Mt. Reeves 4470
Lithgow
Broken Bay
SYDNEY
Botany Bay
Wollongong
Parkes
Young
Cootamundra
Crookwell
Goulburn
Moss Vale
Nowra
Temora
Narrandera
Coolamon
Wagga Wagga
Batlow
Canberra
AUSTL. CAP. TER.
Bombala
Eden
CAPE HOWE
Mallacoota Inlet
Bateman's Bay

REGION RIVERINA

Chowilla Res.
Waikerie
YORKE PENINSULA
Port Wakefield
Gawler
Adelaide
Murray Bridge
Tailem Bend
Pinnaroo
Peebinga
Ouyen
Kulwin
L. Tyrrell
Swan Hill
Kerang
Hopetoun
Deniliquin
Cohuna
Echuca
Corowa
Albury
Tumbarumba
Bimberi Pk. 6276
SNOWY MTS.
Mt. Kosciusko 7316
Cooma
Bombala
Bega
AUSTRALIAN ALPS
GIPPSLAND

Lake Alexandrina
Lake Albert
Peninsula
Victor Harbour
Encounter Bay
Kingscote
KANGAROO
Gulf St. Vincent
Spencer Gulf
Yorketown
THISTLE
Investigator Strait
Kingston
CAPE JAFFA
Naracoorte
Keith
Yanac
Warracknabeal
Charlton
Shepparton
Wangaratta
Benalla
Bright
Mt. Bogong 6516
Mt. Cobberas 6025
Mt. Hotham
Omeo
Orbost
Bairnsdale
Mt. Baw Baw 5127
Moe
Sale
Lakes Entrance
NINETY MILE BEACH

VICTORIA

Millicent
Mount Gambier
Casterton
Hamilton
Portland
CAPE NELSON
Warrnambool
Colac
Mortlake
Goroke
Horsham
Rocklands Res.
Ararat
Maryborough
Castlemaine
Bendigo
Seymour
Mansfield
Mt. Torbreck 4495
Eildon Res.
Ballarat
MELBOURNE
Dandenong
Geelong
PHILLIP I.
Wonthaggi
CAPE OTWAY
Port Phillip Bay
Corner Inlet
WILSON'S PROMONTORY
Yarram
Traralgon
Glenelg R.

INDIAN OCEAN

KING
Grassy
WEST PT.
CAPE GRIM
Smithton
Burnie
Ulverstone
Devonport
Mt. Ossa 5305
Deloraine
Queenstown
Strahan
CAPE SORELL
Bass Strait
FLINDERS
FURNEAUX GROUP
CAPE BARREN
Banks Strait
EDDYSTONE PT.
Scottsdale
Launceston
Legge Pk. 5160
St. Marys
Campbell Town
FREYCINET PENINSULA
Bridgewater
New Norfolk
Hobart
TASMAN PENINSULA

TASMANIA

GREAT

HUNTER IS.
CAPE BARREN

KENT GROUP

TASMAN SEA

25°
140°
145°
150°
30°
35°
40°
135°

Relief

Meters	Feet
1525	5000
610	2000
305	1000
152.5	500
0 Sea Level	0 Sea Level
152.5	500
1525	5000
3050	10 000

Below Sea Level

140° Longitude East of Greenwich

0   50   100   200 Miles
0   50 100 150 200 250 300 Kilometers

Scale 1:8 000 000; one inch to 126 miles.
Lambert's Azimuthal, Equal Area Projection.
Elevations and depressions are given in feet.

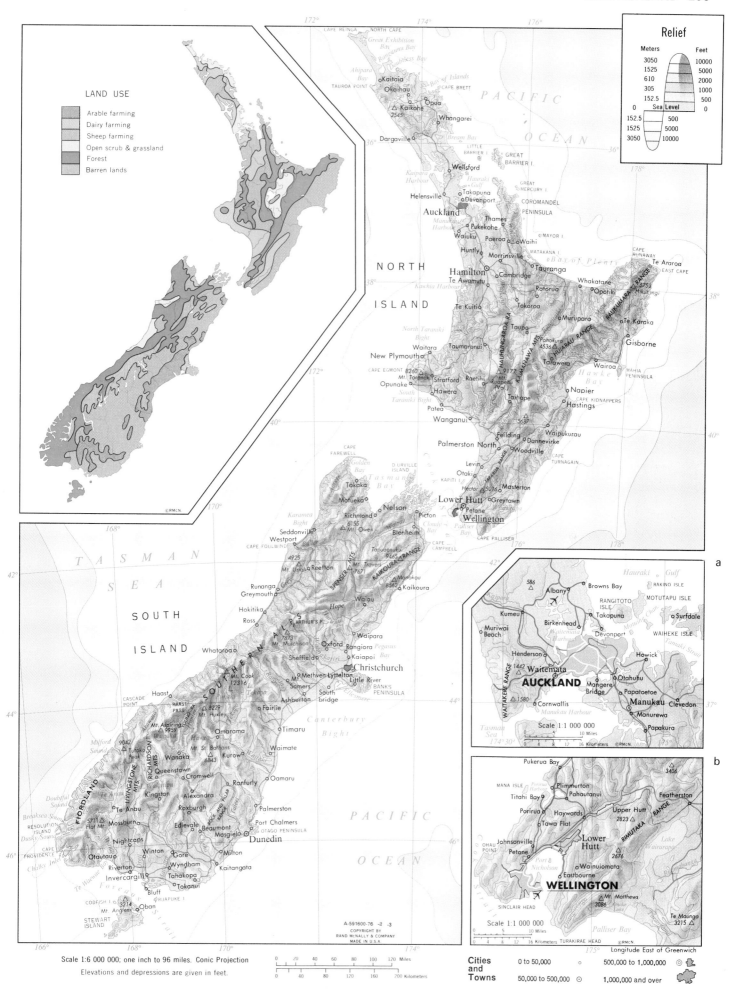

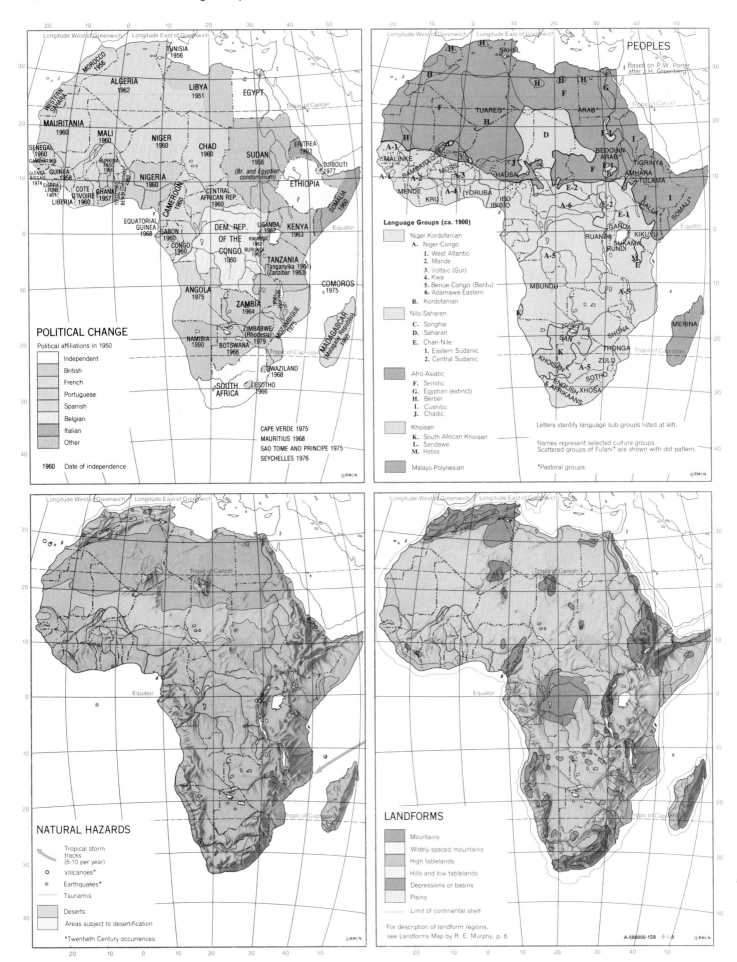

POLITICAL CHANGE

Political affiliations in 1950

- Independent
- British
- French
- Portuguese
- Spanish
- Belgian
- Italian
- Other

1960 Date of independence

CAPE VERDE 1975
MAURITIUS 1968
SAO TOME AND PRINCIPE 1975
SEYCHELLES 1976

TUNISIA 1956
MOROCCO 1956
ALGERIA 1962
LIBYA 1951
EGYPT
WESTERN SAHARA
MAURITANIA 1960
MALI 1960
NIGER 1960
CHAD 1960
SUDAN 1956 (Br. and Egyptian condominium)
ERITREA 1993
DJIBOUTI 1977
SENEGAL 1960
GAMBIA 1965
GUINEA-BISSAU 1974
GUINEA 1958
SIERRA LEONE 1961
LIBERIA 1960
BURKINA FASO 1960
COTE D'IVOIRE 1960
GHANA 1957
TOGO 1960
BENIN (Dahomey) 1960
NIGERIA 1960
CAMEROON 1960
CENTRAL AFRICAN REP. 1960
ETHIOPIA
SOMALIA 1960
EQUATORIAL GUINEA 1968
GABON 1960
CONGO 1960
DEM. REP. OF THE CONGO 1960
UGANDA 1962
RWANDA 1962
BURUNDI 1962
KENYA 1963
TANZANIA (Tanganyika 1961) (Zanzibar 1963)
COMOROS 1975
ANGOLA 1975
ZAMBIA 1964
MOZAMBIQUE 1975
MADAGASCAR (Malagasy Republic) 1960
NAMIBIA 1990
ZIMBABWE (Rhodesia) 1979
BOTSWANA 1966
SWAZILAND 1968
SOUTH AFRICA
LESOTHO 1966

PEOPLES

Based on P.W. Porter after J.H. Greenberg

Language Groups (ca. 1900)

Niger-Kordofanian
  A. Niger-Congo
    1. West Atlantic
    2. Mande
    3. Voltaic (Gur)
    4. Kwa
    5. Benue-Congo (Bantu)
    6. Adamawa-Eastern
  B. Kordofanian

Nilo-Saharan
  C. Songhai
  D. Saharan
  E. Chari-Nile
    1. Eastern Sudanic
    2. Central Sudanic

Afro-Asiatic
  F. Semitic
  G. Egyptian (extinct)
  H. Berber
  I. Cushitic
  J. Chadic

Khoisan
  K. South African Khoisan
  L. Sandawe
  M. Hatsa

Malayo-Polynesian

Letters identify language sub-groups listed at left.

Names represent selected culture groups.
Scattered groups of Fulani* are shown with dot pattern.

*Pastoral groups

SAHEL
TUAREG*
ARAB
BEDOUIN ARAB
TIGRINYA
AMHARA
TULAMA
GALLA
SOMALI
MALINKE
BAMBARA
MOSSI
HAUSA
MENDE
KRU
YORUBA
IBO
IBIBIO
RUANDA
RUNDI
GANDA
SUKAMA
KIKUYU
MBUNDU
SAN
SHONA
THONGA
ZULU
KHOISAN
SOTHO
XHOSA
ENGLISH & AFRIKAANS
MERINA

NATURAL HAZARDS

→ Tropical storm tracks (5-10 per year)
○ Volcanoes*
● Earthquakes*
~ Tsunamis

Deserts
Areas subject to desertification

*Twentieth Century occurrences

LANDFORMS

- Mountains
- Widely spaced mountains
- High tablelands
- Hills and low tablelands
- Depressions or basins
- Plains
--- Limit of continental shelf

For description of landform regions, see Landforms Map by R. E. Murphy, p. 6

A-580000-1S6 -3-2-5

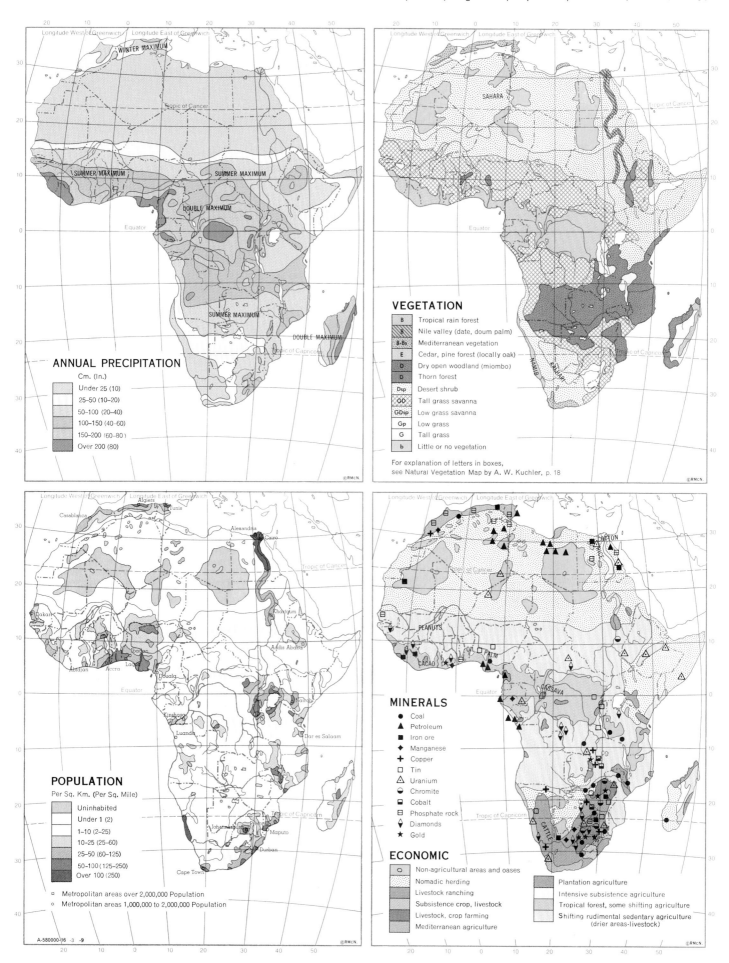

ANNUAL PRECIPITATION

Cm. (In.)

- Under 25 (10)
- 25–50 (10–20)
- 50–100 (20–40)
- 100–150 (40–60)
- 150–200 (60–80)
- Over 200 (80)

VEGETATION

B	Tropical rain forest
B	Nile valley (date, doum palm)
B-B₂	Mediterranean vegetation
E	Cedar, pine forest (locally oak)
D	Dry open woodland (miombo)
D	Thorn forest
Dsp	Desert shrub
GD	Tall grass savanna
GDsp	Low grass savanna
Gp	Low grass
G	Tall grass
b	Little or no vegetation

For explanation of letters in boxes,
see Natural Vegetation Map by A. W. Kuchler, p. 18

POPULATION

Per Sq. Km. (Per Sq. Mile)

- Uninhabited
- Under 1 (2)
- 1–10 (2–25)
- 10–25 (25–60)
- 25–50 (60–125)
- 50–100 (125–250)
- Over 100 (250)

□ Metropolitan areas over 2,000,000 Population
○ Metropolitan areas 1,000,000 to 2,000,000 Population

MINERALS

- ● Coal
- ▲ Petroleum
- ■ Iron ore
- ◆ Manganese
- ✚ Copper
- □ Tin
- △ Uranium
- ◓ Chromite
- ▣ Cobalt
- ⊟ Phosphate rock
- ◈ Diamonds
- ★ Gold

ECONOMIC

- Non-agricultural areas and oases
- Nomadic herding
- Livestock ranching
- Subsistence crop, livestock
- Livestock, crop farming
- Mediterranean agriculture
- Plantation agriculture
- Intensive subsistence agriculture
- Tropical forest, some shifting agriculture
- Shifting rudimental sedentary agriculture (drier areas-livestock)

A-580000-16 -3 -9

20° 10° 0° 10° 20° 30° 40° 50°

MADRID
CORSICA
ROME
SARDINIA
ATLANTIC
SICILY
Athens
İSTANBUL
BAKU
OCEAN
Algiers
MALTA
CRETE
CYPRUS
TEHRAN
Casablanca
Tunis
Medit
Beirut
Baghdad
Tigris
ATLAS MOUNTAINS
Tripoli
ranean
SYRIAN
Euphrates
Banghāzī
Alexandria
DESERT
AN NAFŪD
CANARY ISLANDS
GRAND ERG OCCIDENTAL
CAIRO
ARABIAN DESERT
Nile
Riyadh
El Aaíun
GRAND ERG ORIENTAL
LIBYAN DESERT
Lake Nasser
Red Sea
Mecca
Tropic of Cancer
AHAGGAR
NUBIAN DESERT
Tamenghest
S A H A R A
Nile
ADRAR DES IFÔGHAS
TIBESTI
Khartoum
Asmera
Tombouctou
ENNEDI
White Nile
DANAKIL
Aden
Dakar
S U D A N
Al-Fāshir
Addis Ababa
Berbera
Gulf of Aden
Bamako
Niger
Lake Chad
Kano
N'Djamena
Blue Nile
Freetown
Niger
Mountain Nile
Lake Volta
Yaoundé
Bangui
Uele
Lagos
Ubangi
Congo
Mogadishu
Abidjan
Gulf of Guinea
Kisangani
Equator
Lake Victoria
Nairobi
Congo
Kasai
INDIAN
Kinshasa
Lake Tanganyika
OCEAN
Luanda
Dar es Salaam
ATLANTIC OCEAN
Lubumbashi
Lake Nyasa
COMORO ISLANDS
Zambezi
Lusaka
Blantyre
Moçambique
Harare
MADAGASCAR
Antananariv
Windhoek
KALAHARI DESERT
Limpopo
Tropic of Capricorn
NAMIB DESERT
Johannesburg
Orange
Orange
Durban
INDIAN OCEAN
Cape Town

Legend:
- Urban
- Cropland
- Cropland & Woodland
- Cropland & Grazing Land
- Grassland, Grazing Land
- Forest, Woodland
- Swamp, Marshland
- Shrub, Sparse Grass, Wasteland
- Barren Land
- • Oasis

A-580000-36   -23-11
COPYRIGHT BY
RAND MCNALLY & COMPANY
MADE IN U.S.A.

Scale 1:36,000,000; one inch to 570 miles. Lambert Azimuthal Equal-Area Projection

0 100 200 400 600 800 Miles
0 150 300 600 900 1200 Kilometers

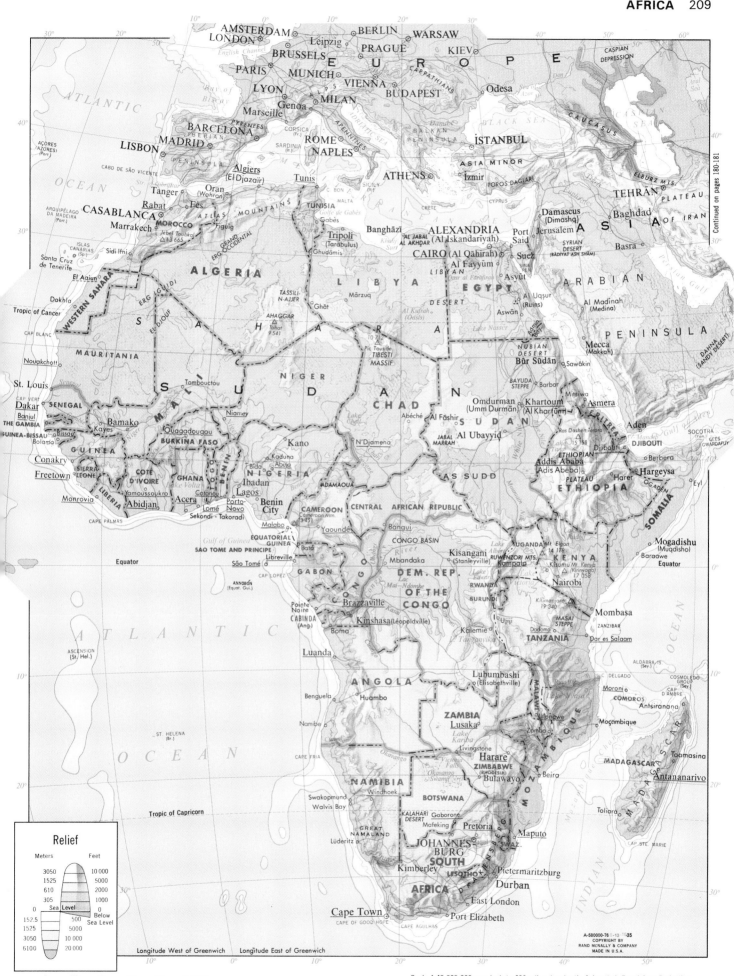

Continued on pages 180-181

Relief

Meters		Feet
3050		10 000
1525		5000
610		2000
305		1000
0	Sea Level	0
152.5		500	Below
1525		5000	Sea Level
3050		10 000
6100		20 000

Longitude West of Greenwich   Longitude East of Greenwich

0   200   400   600   800   1000 Miles
0   400   800   1200   1600 Kilometers

Scale 1:40 000 000; one inch to 630 miles. Lambert's Azimuthal, Equal Area Projection

Elevations and depressions are given in feet.

A-580000-76 9-13-76 35
COPYRIGHT BY
RAND MCNALLY & COMPANY
MADE IN U.S.A.

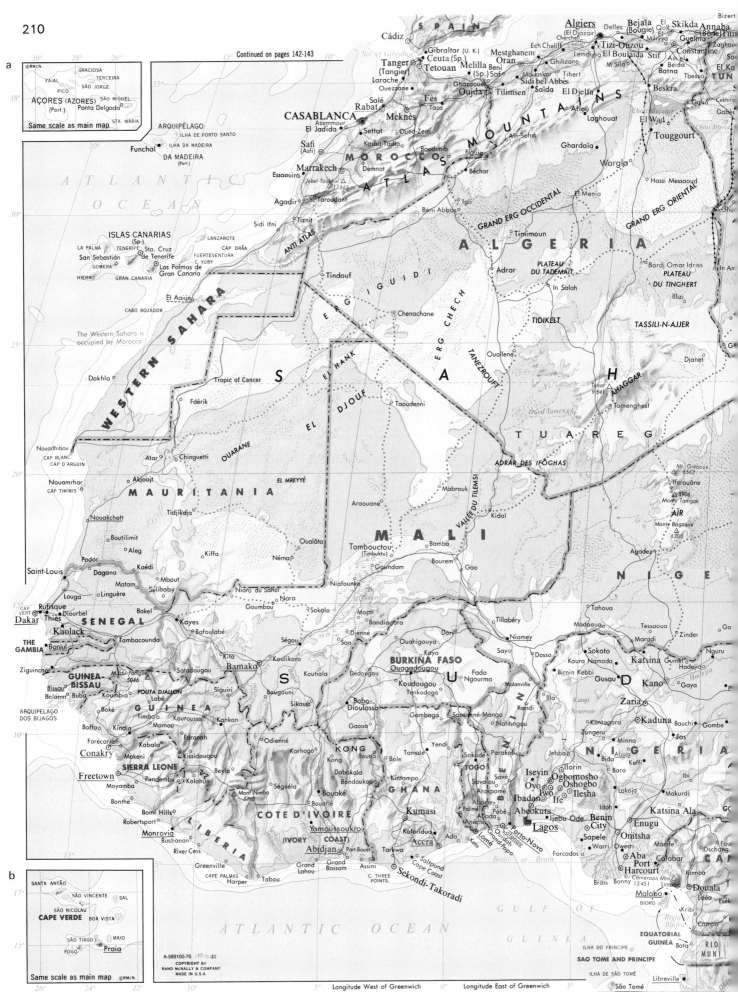

210

210

210

a

AÇORES (AZORES)
(Port.)
GRACIOSA
FAIAL
PICO
SÃO JORGE
TERCEIRA
SÃO MIGUEL
Ponta Delgada
STA. MARIA

Same scale as main map

Continued on pages 142-143

SPAIN
Cádiz
Gibraltar (U.K.)
Str. of Gibraltar
Ceuta (Sp.)
Tanger
(Tangier)
Tetouan
Melilla
(Sp.)
Beni
Larache
Ouezzane
Ghazaouet
Sidi bel Abbes
Oran
Mestghanem
Cherchel
Deltes
Algiers
(El Djazair)
Bejaïa
(Bougie)
Qoll
El
Mihyya
Skikda
Tizi-Ouzou
Stif
El Boulaida
Annaba
Bône Tun
Guelma
Constantine
Beida
Ain-el
Batna
Tbessa
El Ka
TUN

CASABLANCA
Rabat
Salé
Meknès
Fès
Taza
Oujda
Tilimsen
Saïda
El Djelfa
Laghouat
Aflou
Beskra
El Wad
Touggourt

El Jadida
Settat
Kasba-Tadla
Oued-Zem
Boudenib
Aïn-Sefra
Ghardaïa
Wargla
Hassi Messaoud
Figuig
Béchar
Safi
(Asfi)
Marrakech
Essaouira
Demnat
Azemmour
Agadir
Taroudant
Jebel Toubkal
13665
ATLAS MOUNTAINS
MOROCCO
Béni Abbas
Igli
GRAND ERG OCCIDENTAL
Timimoun
Adrar
PLATEAU
DU TADEMAÏT
In Salah
GRAND ERG ORIENTAL
El Menia
Hassi Messaoud
Bordj Omar Idriss
An
PLATEAU
DU TINGHERT
Ghu

Sidi Ifni
Tiznit
ANTI ATLAS
ALGERIA
Tindouf
ERG IGUIDI
Chenachane
ERG CHECH
TIDIKELT
Illizi
TASSILI-N-AJJER

ISLAS CANARIAS
(Sp.)
LANZAROTE
LA PALMA
TENERIFE
Sta. Cruz
de Tenerife
CAP DRÂA
C. YUBY
FUERTEVENTURA
San Sebastián
GOMERA
HIERRO
GRAN CANARIA
Las Palmas de
Gran Canaria
El Aaiún
CABO BOJADOR
The Western Sahara is
occupied by Morocco
WESTERN SAHARA
Tropic of Cancer
Dakhla
Fdérik
SAHARA
EL HANK
EL DJOUF
Taoudenni
Ouallene
TANEZROUFT
AHAGGAR
Tahat
9541
Tamenghest
Djanet
Mt Gréboun
4562
TUAREG

Nouadhibou
CAP BLANC
CAP D'ARGUIN
Atar
Chinguetti
OUARANE
EL MREYYÉ
ADRAR DES IFÔGHAS
Iferouâne
5906
Monts Tamgak
AÏR
Nouamrhar
CAP TIMIRIS
Akjoujt
MAURITANIA
Mabrouk
VALLÉE DU TILEMSI
Monts Bogzane
6300
Nouakchott
Tidjikdja
Araouane
Kidal
Agadez
Boutilimit
Aleg
Kiffa
Néma
Oualâta
Tombouctou
(Timbuktu)
Bamba
MALI
Bourem
Gao
NIGE

Saint-Louis
Podor
Dagana
Kaédi
Mbout
Selibaby
Goundam
Niafounke
Tahoua
Tessaoua
Zinder
Nguru
Louga
Matam
Linguère
Nioro du Sahel
Nara
Goumbou
Sokolo
Mopti
Bandiagara
Dori
Tillabéry
Niamey
Madaoua
Maradi
Katsina
Gumel
Hadejia
Hadeïa
CAP
VERT
Rufisque
Thies
Diourbel
SENEGAL
Bakel
Kayes
Bafoulabé
Ségou
San
Djenné
Ouahigouya
Say
Dosso
Sokoto
Kaura Namoda
Gusau
Kano
Gaya
Dakar
Kaolack
Tambacounda
Kita
Koulikoro
Koutiala
Dédougou
BURKINA FASO
Ouagadougou
Fada
Ngourma
Malanville
Birnin Kebbi
Zaria
THE
GAMBIA
Banjul
M. du Tamgué
5046
Satadougou
Bamako
Bougouni
Sikasso
Bobo-
Dioulasso
Koudougou
Tenkodogo
Gambaga
Sansanné-Mango
Kandi
Illo
Kontagora
Zungeru
Kaduna
Ziguinchor
GUINEA-
BISSAU
Bissau
Bolama
Buba
FOUTA DJALLON
Labé
Siguiri
Kankan
Odienné
Gaoua
Natitingou
Yendi
Minna
Jos
Gombe
Bauchi
ARQUIPÉLAGO
DOS BIJAGÓS
Boké
GUINEA
Timbo
Kouroussa
KONG
Kong
Korhogo
Bouna
Bole
Tamale
Sokodé
Parakou
Jebba
NIGERIA
Abuja
Keffi
Ibi
Boffa
Kindia
Mamou
Faranah
Beyla
Dabakala
Bondoukou
Kintampo
Savalou
Savé
Ilorin
Oyo
Bida
Baro
Lokoja
Makurdi
Forécariah
Kabala
Kissidougou
GHANA
Bouaké
Séguéla
TOGO
Iseyin
Ogbomosho
Oshogbo
Ilesha
Ibadan
Ife
Benin
City
Idah
Conakry
SIERRA LEONE
Mokeni
Pandembu
Kolahun
Mont Nimba
5760
Bouaflé
Kumasi
Koforidua
Abomey
Palimé
Abeokuta
Ijebu-Ode
Enugu
Onitsha
Mamfe
Freetown
Moyamba
Bonthe
Bomi Hills
Robertsport
LIBERIA
COTE D'IVOIRE
(IVORY COAST)
Yamoussoukro
Abidjan
Port-Bouet
Tarkwa
Accra
Ada
Keta
Lomé
Aného
Grand-Popo
Porto-Novo
Lagos
Sapele
Warri
Sapele
Aba
Port
Harcourt
Calabar
Kumba
Dschang
Monrovia
Buchanan
River Cess
Greenville
Harper
CAPE PALMAS
Tabou
Grand
Lahou
Grand
Bassam
Assini
C. THREE
POINTS
Sekondi-Takoradi
Cape Coast
Saltpond
Bight of Benin
Forcados
Brass
Bonny
Cameroon Mtn.
13451
Limbe
Malabo
BIOKO
Kribi
Edea
CAMEROON

ATLANTIC OCEAN
GULF OF GUINEA
EQUATORIAL
GUINEA
SÃO TOMÉ AND PRINCIPE
ILHA DO PRÍNCIPE
ILHA DE SÃO TOMÉ
São Tomé
Libreville
RIO
MUNI
Campo

b

SANTA ANTÃO
SÃO VICENTE
SAL
SÃO NICOLAU
BOA VISTA
CAPE VERDE
MAIO
SÃO TIAGO
FOGO
Praia

Same scale as main map

A-589100-76 17-18-35
COPYRIGHT BY
RAND McNALLY & COMPANY
MADE IN U.S.A.

Longitude West of Greenwich
Longitude East of Greenwich

Scale 1:16 000 000; one inch to 250 miles. Sinusoidal Projec
Elevations and depressions are given in feet

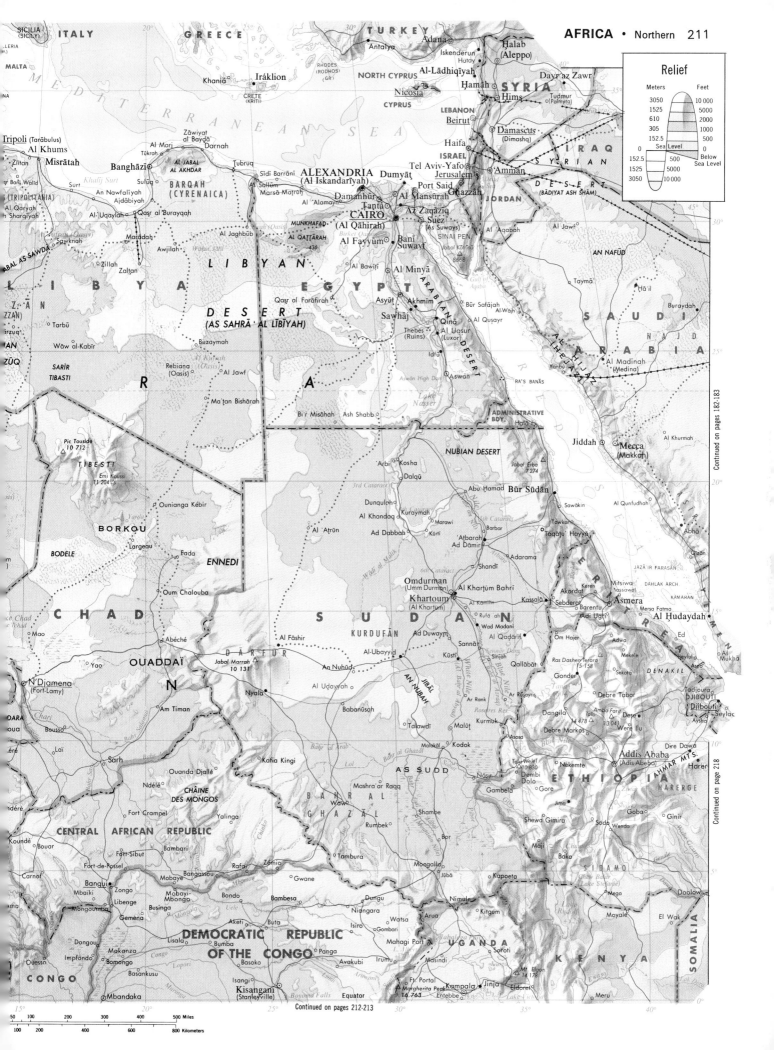

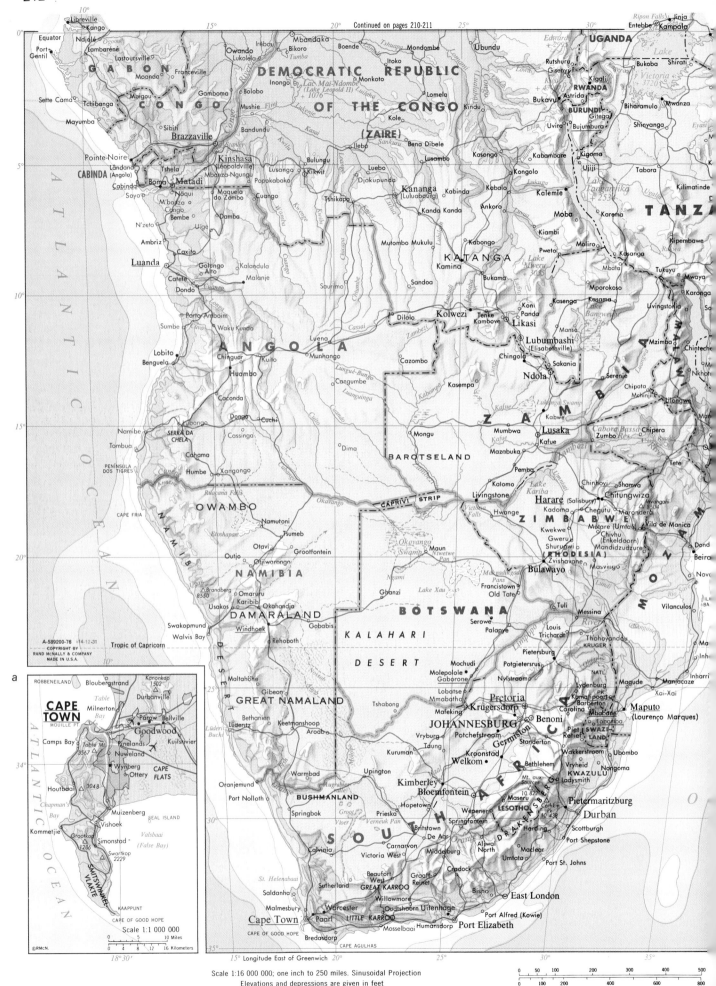

Continued on pages 210-211

Scale 1:16 000 000; one inch to 250 miles. Sinusoidal Projection
Elevations and depressions are given in feet

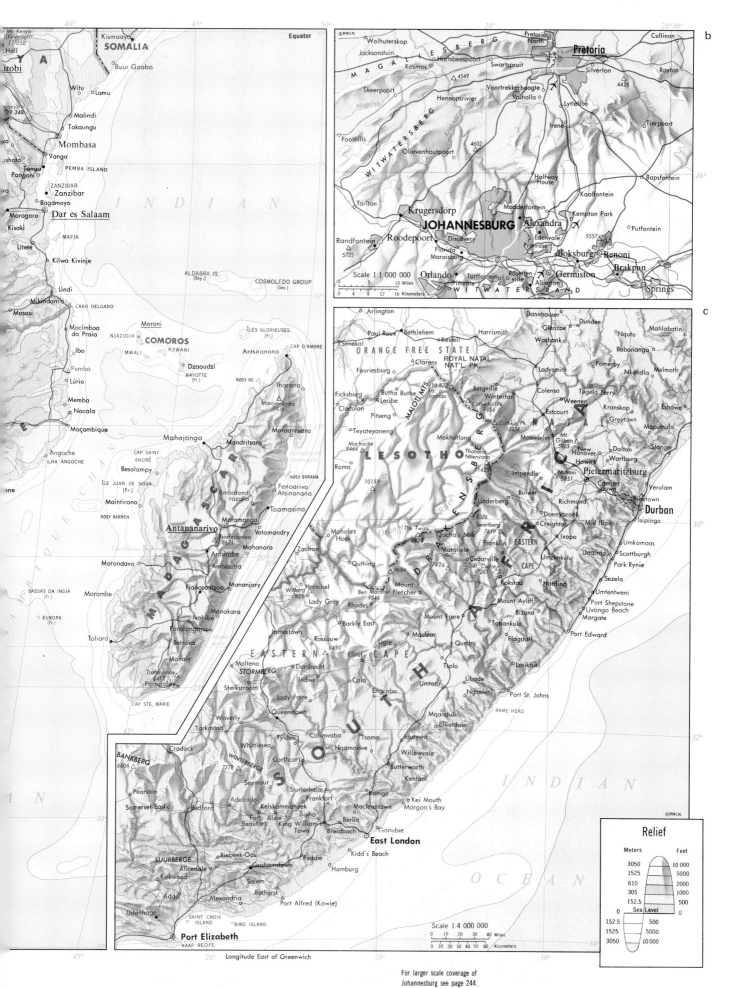

For larger scale coverage of
Johannesburg see page 244.

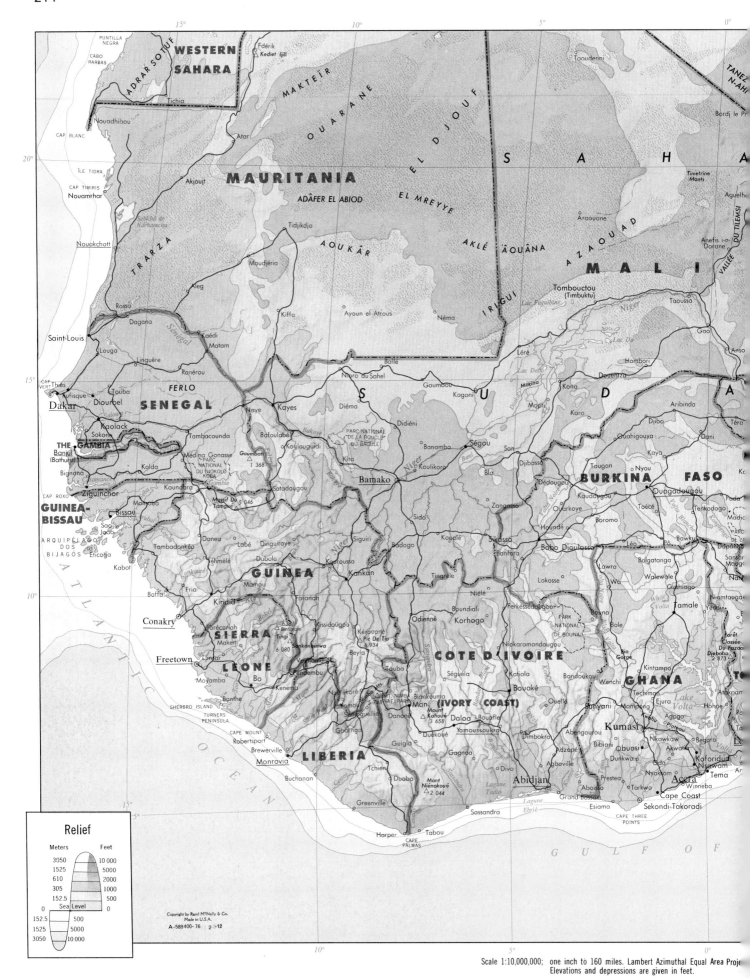

Relief

Meters	Feet
3050	10 000
1525	5000
610	2000
305	1000
152.5	500
0	Sea Level	0
152.5	500
1525	5000
3050	10 000

Copyright by Rand McNally & Co.
Made in U.S.A.
A-589400-76 2 -12

Scale 1:10,000,000; one inch to 160 miles. Lambert Azimuthal Equal Area Proje
Elevations and depressions are given in feet.

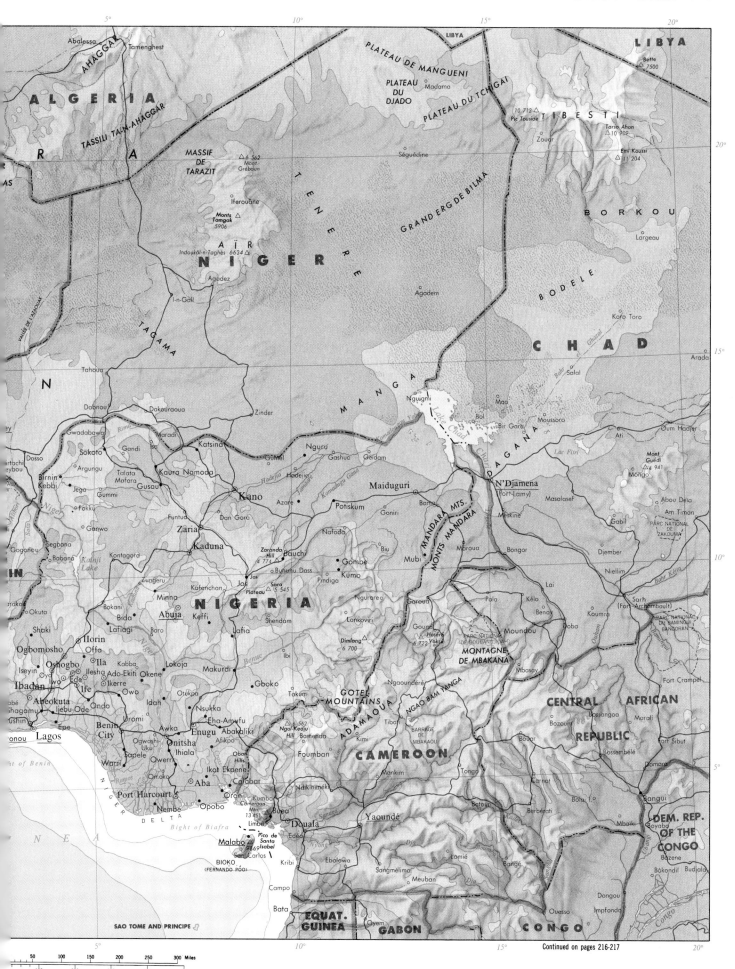

Continued on pages 216-217

Continued on pages 214-215

10°   15°

NIGERIA
Opobo
Bight of Biafra
Douala
Cameroon Mtn. 13,451
Buea
Edéa
Yaoundé
Doumé
Batouri
Berberati
Bolai
Bangui
Boali
Fort de Possel
CENTRAL   AFRICAN   REPUBLIC
Kongbo
Bangassou
Rafai
Git

Malabo
San Carlos
BIOKO
(FERNANDO PÓO)
Kribi
Campo
CAMEROON
Sangmelima
Ebolowa
Lomié
Yokadouma
Bangé
Mbaiki
Boyabe
Mbongoumba
Mongoumba
Gemena
Businga
Bodalang
Yandongi
Aketi
Buta

EQUATORIAL
GUINEA
Bata
Oyem
Meuban
Souanké
Ouesso
Moloundou
Dongou
Impfondo
Bomongo
ILE SUMBA
Budala
Lisala
Bumba
Ibembo
Basoko
Benga

PRÍNCIPE
SAO TOME AND
PRINCIPE
CABO SAN JUAN
ISLA DE CORISCO
Acalayong
MONTS
DE CRISTAL
Makokou
Mekambo
Djokoumatombi
Loka
Mange
Lifanga
Simba
Kisanga
(Stanleyville)

São Tomé
SÃO TOMÉ
Libreville
Kango
Booue
Lebango
Likouala
CONGO
Owando
Mbandaka
(Coquilhatville)
Bikoro
Boende
Lokofa
Bokungu
Ekoli
Litok

0°
GABON
Bifoum
François
de Boundji
DEMOCRATIC
REP. OF
THE CONGO
(ZAIRE)
Yayama

Port-Gentil
CAP LOPEZ
Lambaréné
3360
Koula-Moutou
Franceville
Gamboma
Kiri
Monkoto
Lokolama
Ekanga
Ka

Omboué
Mouila
Mbinda
Lac
Tumba
Inongo
Lac
Mai-Ndombe

Petit Loango
Djambala
Fimi
Makaw
Dekese
Esambo

Tchibanga
Mossendio
Kindanba
Bandundu
Lukenie
Lebo (Port-Francqui)
Domionga

Mayumba
Sibiti
Madingou
Brazzaville
Masi-Manimba
Kwilu
Lusambo

Madingo
Loubomo
Kinshasa
(Léopoldville)
Kikwit
Djokupunda
Demba
Mbuji-M
(Bakwan

Pointe-Noire
Chutes de Livingstone
Livingstone Falls
Kasangulu
Kilembe
Bulunga
Kananga
(Luluabourg)
Kanda-Kanda

CABINDA
(Ang.)
Cabinda
Tshela
Mbanza-Ngungu
Popokabaka
Kitenda
Kahemba
Tshikapa
Chitato

PONTA DO PADRÃO
Boma
Matadi
Noqui
Kimvula
Kwango
Kibenga
Chiluango
Napanga
Ka

Soyo
M'banza Congo
Quimbele
Marimba
Quimbonga
Sambungo

SERRA DO
CONGO
Damba
Quela
Cuilo
Saurimo
Chiumbe
KATANGA
Kangowa

N'zeto
Mabala
Uige
Malanje
Malonga
Na

Ambriz
Caxito
Kalandula
Cambundi-
Catembo
Cacólo
Luau
Lucano

Luanda
Catete
N'dalando
Dondo
Cuango
Mussende
Saútan
Coemba
Luena
Parque Nacional
da Cameia
Calunda

PONTA DAS PALMEIRINHAS
Cuanza
Cacuso

CABO DAS TRÊS PONTAS
Porto Amboim
Sumbe
Gabela
Waku Kundo
Calucinga
Wama
Cuvo
Curunga

Covelo
Lobito
SERRA
CAMBONDA
Serra do Môco
8596
ANGOLA
Huambo
(Nova Lisboa)
Kuito
Coemba
Cangamba
KASHIJI
PLAIN
Chitokoloki

Benguela
Catumbela
Chitembo
Chá Pungana
Mussuma
LIUWA
PLAIN

CABO DE SANTA MARTA
SERRA DA NEVE
SERRE DO CHILENGUE
Caconda
Caluquembe
Caconda
Cacula
Menongue
Cassinga
Lunga
Ninda
Mongu

Bentiaba
Namibe
Lubango
PARQUE
NACIONAL DO
BIKUAR
Folgares
Caiundo
Mavinga
BAROTSE
PLAIN
Nangweshi

PONTA ALBINA
Tômbua
Chiange
Cahama
Oncocua
Cuamato
Catula
Cuito
SILOANA
PLAINS

PONTA DA MARCA
Baía dos Tigres
PARQUE
NACIONAL
DO IONA
Ruacana
Falls
Ruacana
Melunga
Cuangar
Luiana

Foz do Cunene
Cunene
NAMIBIA
Sambusu
Shakawe
Chobe Na
BOTS.
Kasin

CAPRIVI STRIP

Relief

Meters	Feet
3050	10 000
1525	5000
610	2000
305	1000
152.5	500
0	Sea Level 0
152.5	500
1525	5000
3050	10 000

Scale 1:10,000,000; one inch to 160 miles. Lambert Azimuthal Equal Area Projection
Elevations and depressions are given in feet.

10°   15°   20°

SUDAN

ETHIOPIA

Maridi
Yambio
Bagbele
Gobur
Juba
Kapoeta
Keyala
Didinga Hills
Imjero
Lake Stefanie

Bwendi
Niangara
Watsa
Aba
Nimule
Padibe
Langia Mountains
Kinyeti 10,456
Muruasigar △ 7,050
Lokitaung
LOTIKIPI PLAIN
Lokichar
Kaabong
CHALBI DESERT
Moyale
Danisa Hills
Baidoa

Isiro (Paulis)
Mungbere
Nduye
Bunia
Arua
Gulu
Lira
Moroto
Matano 10,118
Lodwar
Marsabit
Wajir
SOMALIA
Baardheere

Panga
Wamba
Mambasa
Butsha
Fort Portal
UGANDA
Nabiswera
Soroti
Mbale
Mount Elgon 14,178
CHERANGANY HILLS
Kitale
Maralal
NDOTO MOUNTAINS
Mado Gashi
BUN PLAINS
Baraawe

Avakubi
datole
Margherita Peak 16,763
MONTS BLEUS
Kabaleka Falls
Mubende
Jinja
Mumias
Kisumu
Eldoret
Thomson's Falls
Nanyuki
Mt Kenya (Kirinyaga) 17,058
Nyeri
Embu
Laisamis
KENYA
Kaninga
Bura
Garissa
Alanga Arba
Solola
Jamaame

Balobe
NATIONAL PARK ALBERT
Kampala
Masaka
Entebbe
Lake George
Mbarara
Kericho
MAU ESCARPMENT
Nakuru
Thika
Machakos
Mwingi
Kolbio
Kismaayo

Rutshuru
Volcan Karisimbi 14,787
Kabale
Ruhengeri
Gisenyi
Kigali
RWANDA
Bukavu
Bukoba
Victoria
BUMBIRE ISLAND
UKEREWE ISLAND
RUBONDO ISLAND
Musoma
Ushashi
Loliondo
Subugo △ 8,668
Magadi
Makindu
YATTA PLATEAU
Makinda
TSAVO NATIONAL PARK
Garsen
Kiunga
LAMU ISLAND
Formosa Bay

Kalima
Kamituga
Mwenga
Butare
Nyanza
Biharamulo
Nyakanazi
Geita
Mwanza
SERENGETI NATIONAL PARK
SERENGETI PLAIN
Loolmalassin 11,969
Longido
Mount Meru 14,978
Kilimanjaro 19,340
Moshi
Kilifi
Malindi

Kampene
BURUNDI
Bujumbura
Shinyanga
Salawe
Nzega
Eyasi
Arusha
Kisiwani
Shimoni
USAMBARA MTS.
Mombasa
Mackinnon Road
PEMBA ISLAND
Chake Chake

Lusangi
Kongolo
Kibondo
Kigoma
Uvinza
Tabora
Igalula
Hanang 11,215
Bereku
MASAI STEPPE
INGURU MOUNTAINS
Mziha
Mvomero
Tanga
ZANZIBAR
Pemba

Kabalo
Nyunzu
Kalemie (Albertville)
Kahia
Karema
MAHALI MTS.
Mpanda
Kituna
Ngoywa
Itigi
Dodoma
Mpwapwa
Kimamba
Bagamoyo
ZANZIBAR
Morogoro
INDIAN OCEAN

Kabila
Ankoro
Kiambi
Lusaka
MLALA HILLS
Mbogo
RUAHA NATIONAL PARK
Mikumi
Kibiti
Dar es Salaam

Manono
Kamudilo
Komeshia
Kasenga
Dubie
Kipili
Sumbawanga
Lake Rukwa
Kipembewe
Iringa
Mahenge
Ngarimbi
Kwangwazi
MAFIA ISLAND
Kilindoni

MONTS MULUMBE
Kialwe
MONTS MITUMBA
MONTS MALIMBA
Moliro
Kasanga
Mbala
USANGU FLATS
Chunya
Mbeya
Sao Hill
Mahenge
Somanga
Kilwa Kisiwani

NATIONAL UPEMBA
Likasi (Jadotville)
Kasama
KIPENGERE RANGE
Njombe
Litoo
Lindi

Lubumbashi (Elisabethville)
Mporokoso
Luwingu
MUCHINGA MOUNTAINS
Chinsali
NYIKA PLATEAU
Livingstonia
Songea
Tunduru
Masasi
Newala
Mtwara
Mikindani
Quionga
CABO DELGADO
COMOROS

Kipushi
Chililabombwe (Bancroft)
Mufulira
Mansa
Lake Bangweulu
Mpika
Mzuzu
Mbamba Bay
Mocimboa da Praia
NJAZIDJA
Moroni
Karthala 7,746
NZWANI

Chingola
Kitwe
Sakania
Kabunda
Chitambo
Mzimba
Côbuè
Ibo
Pemba
MWALI

Luanshya
Ndola
Kapushia
Chamama
Lichinga
Marrupa
Montepuez
Mucata

ZAMBIA
Mkushi
Chipata
Katete
MALAWI
Salima
Mandimba
Maúa
MOZAMBIQUE
Nampuecha

Kabwe (Broken Hill)
Mchinji
Lilongwe
Mkataka
Monkey Bay
Cuamba
Malema
Ribauè
Nacala

Lukanga Swamp
Kapiri Mposhi
Rutunsa
Furancungo
Cásula
Mpimb
Zomba
SERRA NAMÚLI △ 7,936
Nampula
Moçambique

Mumbwa
Lusaka
Chilanga
Mazabuka
Zumbo
Fingoe
Tete
Blantyre
Vila Caldas Xavier
Alto Molócuè
Errego
Nametil
Mogincual

Kafue Flats
Ibwe Munyama
Kariba
Cabora Bassa Res.
Changara
Chemba
MLANJE MTS. Sapitwa 9,843
Macuba
Moma
ANTÓNIO ENES
ILHA ANGOCHE

Sikalongo
Chinhoyi
Kidonan
Bindura
Mtoko
Nsanje
Mucubela
Pebane

Falls
ZIMBABWE
Chegutu
Kadoma
Marondera
Harare (Salisbury)
Chitungwiza
(RHODESIA)

UNVUKWE RANGE
MAVURADONA MTS.
Tendazi △ 4,702

Copyright by Rand McNally & Co.
Made in U.S.A.
A-589500-76 -3|-14

0 50 100 150 200 250 300 Miles
0 100 200 300 400 500 Kilometers

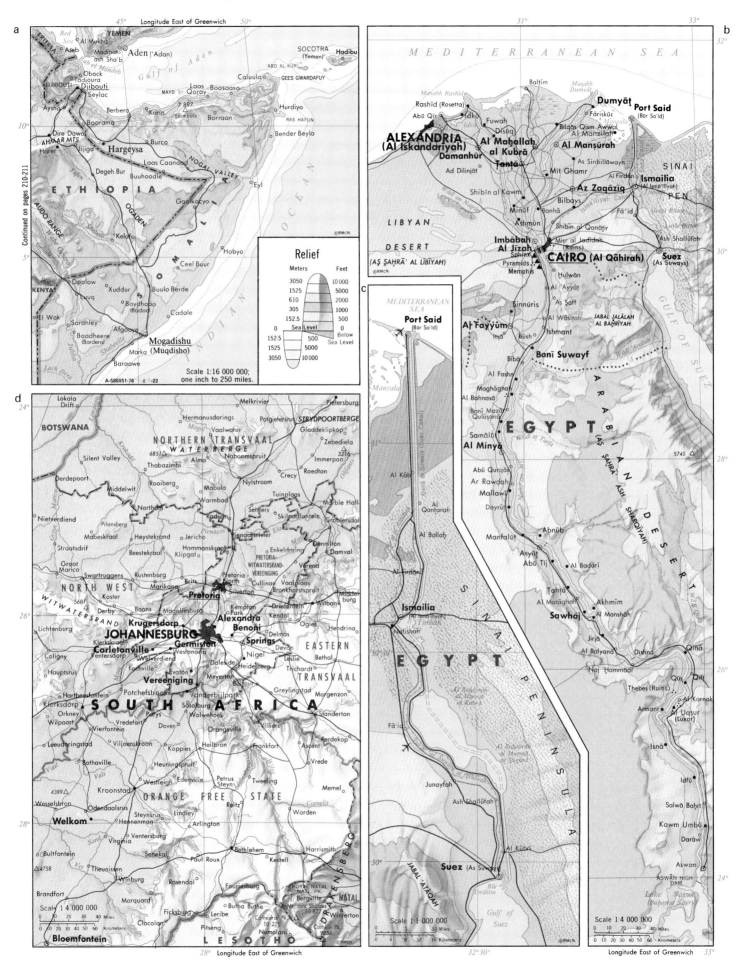

a

Longitude East of Greenwich

Red Sea · YEMEN · Al Mukha · Madīnat ash Sha'b · Aden ('Adan)

ERITREA

DJIBOUTI · Obock · Tadjoura · Djibouti · Seylac · Berbera · Karin · Borraan

Aysha · Boorama

AHMAR MTS. · Dire Dawa · Jijiga · Hargeysa · Harer · Degeh Bur · Laas Caanood · Buuhoodle

ETHIOPIA

OGADEN · NOGAL VALLEY · S O M A L I A

Doolow · Gaalkacyo

KENYA · Xuddur · Luuq · Kelafo · Hobyo

El Wak · Baydhabo (Baidoa) · Cadale

Saraaley · Afgooye · Buulo Berde

Baadheere (Bardera) · Marka (Merca) · Baraawe

Mogadishu (Muqdisho)

INDIAN OCEAN

SOCOTRA (Yemen) · Hadibu · ABD AL-KURI · GEES GWARDAFUY · Caluula · Boosaaso · Hurdiyo · RAS HAFUN · Bender Beyla · Eyl

Relief

Meters	Feet
3050	10 000
1525	5000
610	2000
305	1000
152.5	500
0 Sea Level	0
152.5	500
1525	5000
3050	10 000

Scale 1:16 000 000;
one inch to 250 miles.

A-580051-76

b

M E D I T E R R A N E A N   S E A

Baltīm · Dumyāt · Port Said (Būr Sa'īd)

Rashīd (Rosetta) · Abū Qīr · Idkū · Fuwah

ALEXANDRIA (Al Iskandarīyah) · Damanhūr · Disūq

Al Mahallah al Kubrā · **Tantā** · As Sinbillāwayn · Ismailia (Al Ismā'īlīyah)

Al Mansūrah · Mīt Ghamr · Al Firdān

Ad Dilinjāt · Shibīn al Kawm · Bilbays · Fā'id

SINAI PEN.

LIBYAN · Minūf · Banhā · Shibīn al Qanātir

Az Zaqāzīq

DESERT (AS SAHRĀ' AL LĪBĪYAH) · Imbābah · Al Jīzah · Misr al Jadīdah (Ruins) · Ash Shallūfah

Pyramids · Sphinx · **CAIRO (Al Qāhirah)** · **Suez (As Suways)**

Memphis · Hulwān · Al 'Ayyāt · As Saff

Birkat Qārūn · Sinnūris · Al Wāsitah · JABAL JALĀLAH AL BAHRĪYAH

Al Fayyūm · Itsā · Ishmant · Būsh

Bibā · **Banī Suwayf** · GULF OF SUEZ

Al Fashn

Maghāghah · Al Bahnasā · A R A B I A N

Banī Mazār · Qulūsnā

Samālūt · **Al Minyā** · E G Y P T

Abū Qurqās · (AS SAHRĀ' ASH SHARQĪYAH)

Ar Rawdah · Mallawī · Dayrūt

Abnūb · DESERT

Manfalūt · Asyūt · Abū Tīj · Al Badārī

Tahtā · Al Marāghah · Akhmīm

Sawhāj · Al Manshāh

Jirjā · Al Balyanā · Dishnā

Naj' Hammādī · Qinā

Thebes (Ruins) · Qūs · Qift

Armant · Al Karnak · Al Uqsur (Luxor)

Isnā · Idfū · Salwā Bahrī · Kawm Umbū · Darāw · Aswān

ASWĀN HIGH DAM · Lake Nasser (Buhayrat Nāsir)

c

MEDITERRANEAN SEA

Port Said (Būr Sa'īd)

Manzala · Qanāt as Suways (Suez Canal)

Al Kāb · Al Qantarah · Al Ballah · Al Firdān

Ismailia (Al Ismā'īlīyah) · Nafishah

S I N A I   P E N I N S U L A

E G Y P T · Fā'id

JABAL 'ATAQAH · Junayfah · Ash Shallūfah

Suez (As Suways) · Al Kūbrī

Būr Ibrāhīm · Gulf of Suez

Scale 1:1 000 000

d

Lokala Drift · Melkrivier · Pietersburg

BOTSWANA · Hermanusdorings · Potgietersrus · **STRYDPOORTBERGE** · Gladdeklipkop

NORTHERN TRANSVAAL · **WATERBERGE** · Naboomspruit · Zebediela · Immerpan

Silent Valley · Thabazimbi · Alma · Crecy · Roedtan

Derdepoort · Rooiberg · Mabula · Nylstroom · Marble Hall

Middelwit · Northam · Warmbad · Tuinplaas · Groblersdal

Nietverdiend · Pilansberg · Radium · Settlers · Skilpadfontein

Mabeskraal · Heystekrand · Jericho · Klipgat · Enkeldoring · Dennilton · Verena · Damval

NORTH WEST · Beestekraal · Hammanskraal · PRETORIA-WITWATERSRAND-VEREENIGING

Groot Marico · Swartruggens · Rustenburg · Marikana · Brits · Pretoria North · Cullinan · Vaalplaas · Bronkhorstspruit · Witbank · Middelburg

Lichtenburg · Derby · Boons · Magaliesburg · **Pretoria** · Silverton · Ogies · Hendrina

Coligny · Koster · Kempton Park · Driefontein · Kendal

Krugersdorp · **Alexandra** · **Benoni** · EASTERN

Hauptsrus · Ventersdorp · **JOHANNESBURG** · **Germiston** · **Springs** · Nigel · Devon · Bethal · Trichardt · TRANSVAAL

Carletonville · Westonaria · Evaton · Daleside · Heidelberg · Morgenzon

Hartbeesfontein · Fochville · Meyerton · Balfour · Greylingstad

Vereeniging · Vanderbijlpark · Standerton

Klerksdorp · Orkney · Potchefstroom · Sasolburg · Wolwehoek · Perdekop

Wilport · Vredefort · Dover · Villiers · Ascent

S O U T H   A F R I C A · Parys · Orangeville · Vrede · Memel

Leeudoringstad · Vierfontein · Viljoenskroon · Koppies · Frankfort

Bothaville · Edenville · Tweeling · Warden

Westleigh · Heilbron

O R A N G E   F R E E   S T A T E · Reitz · Harrismith

Wesselsbron · Kroonstad · Petrus Steyn · Lindley · Arlington

Welkom · Odendaalsrus · Steynsrus · Winburg

Bultfontein · Virginia · Ventersburg · Bethlehem · ROYAL NATAL NATL. PK. · Bergville · Winterton

Hennenman · Senekal · Paul Roux · Fouriesburg · Butha Buthe · Leribe

Brandfort · Theunissen · Rosendal · Ficksburg · Clocolan · NATAL · Numolani · Pitseng

Marquard · **LESOTHO** · Clocolan

Bloemfontein

Scale 1:4 000 000

Longitude East of Greenwich

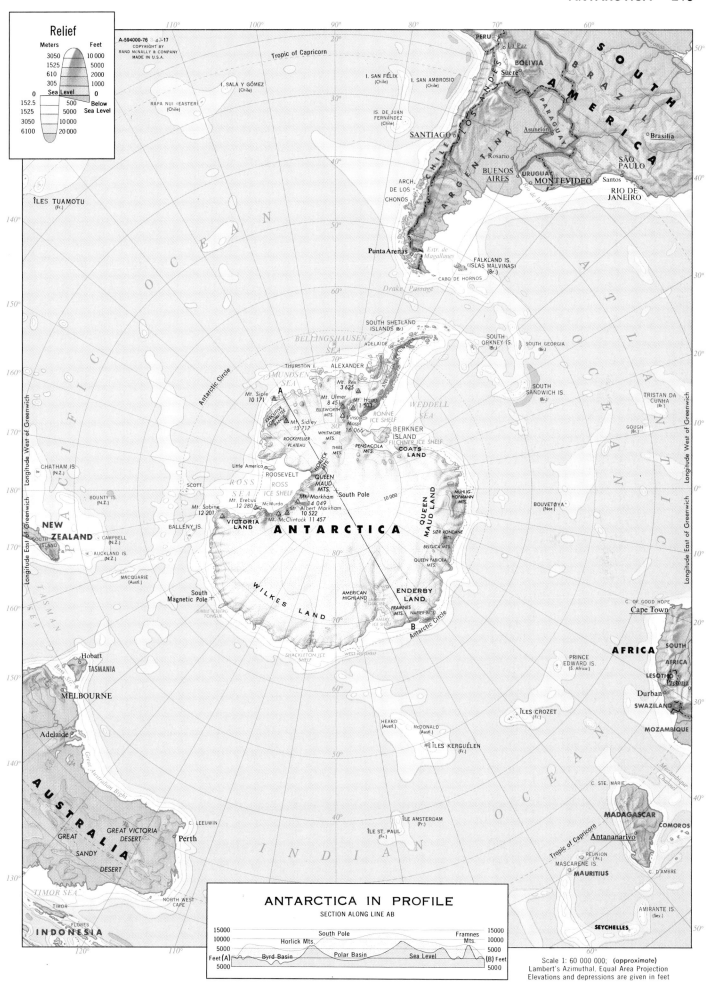

Relief

Meters		Feet
3050		10 000
1525		5000
610		2000
305		1000
0	Sea Level	0
	Below	
152.5	500	Sea Level
1525	5000	
3050	10 000	
6100	20 000	

A-594000-76 3 4-17
COPYRIGHT BY
RAND M<Nally & COMPANY
MADE IN U.S.A.

Tropic of Capricorn

SOUTH AMERICA

PERU
La Paz
BOLIVIA
Sucre
BRAZIL

Santiago
Rosario
BUENOS AIRES
URUGUAY
MONTEVIDEO
RIO DE JANEIRO
SÃO PAULO
Brasilia
Santos
Asunción
PARAGUAY

I. SALA Y GÓMEZ (Chile)
I. SAN FÉLIX (Chile)
I. SAN AMBROSIO (Chile)
IS. DE JUAN FERNÁNDEZ (Chile)

RAPA NUI (EASTER) (Chile)

ÎLES TUAMOTU (Fr.)

ARCH. DE LOS CHONOS

Punta Arenas
Estr. de Magallanes
CABO DE HORNOS
Drake Passage

FALKLAND IS. (ISLAS MALVINAS) (Br.)

SOUTH SHETLAND ISLANDS (Br.)
Adelaide
SOUTH ORKNEY IS. (Br.)
SOUTH GEORGIA (Br.)

SOUTH SANDWICH IS. (Br.)

TRISTAN DA CUNHA (Br.)
GOUGH (Br.)

BELLINGSHAUSEN SEA
Thurston I.
Alexander I.
Mt. Rex 3 625
AMUNDSEN SEA

Mt. Siple 10 171
EXECUTIVE COMMITTEE RANGE
Mt. Ulmer 8 451
Mt. Hagg 1 503
ELLSWORTH MTS.
Vinson Massif 16 066
RONNE ICE SHELF
WEDDELL SEA
BERKNER ISLAND
FILCHNER ICE SHELF

Mt. Sidley 13 717
ROCKEFELLER PLATEAU
WHITMORE MTS.
THIEL MTS.
PENSACOLA MTS.
COATS LAND

Little America
ROOSEVELT I.
ROSS ICE SHELF
HORLICK MTS.
QUEEN MAUD MTS.
South Pole
10 000

SCOTT

BOUNTY IS. (N.Z.)
CHATHAM IS. (N.Z.)

MÜHLIG-HOFMANN MTS.
BOUVETØYA (Nor.)
QUEEN MAUD LAND
SØR RONDANE MTS.
BELGICA MTS.

Mt. Sabine 12 201
Mt. Erebus 12 280
McMurdo
Mt. Markham 14 049
Mt. Albert Markham 10 522
Mt. McClintock 11 457
VICTORIA LAND
ANTARCTICA

NEW ZEALAND
CAMPBELL (N.Z.)
AUCKLAND IS. (N.Z.)

QUEEN FABIOLA MTS.

South Magnetic Pole
WILKES LAND
AMERICAN HIGHLAND
LAMBERT GLACIER
ENDERBY LAND
FRAMNES MTS.
NAPIER MTS.
Antarctic Circle

C. OF GOOD HOPE
Cape Town
AFRICA
SOUTH AFRICA
LESOTHO
Pretoria
Durban
SWAZILAND
MOZAMBIQUE

MACQUARIE (Austl.)
DIBBLE ICEBERG TONGUE
AMERY ICE SHELF
WEST ICE SHELF
SHACKLETON ICE SHELF

PRINCE EDWARD IS. (S. Africa)
ÎLES CROZET (Fr.)

Hobart
TASMANIA
MELBOURNE
Adelaide

HEARD (Austl.)
McDONALD (Austl.)
ÎLES KERGUÉLEN (Fr.)

C. STE. MARIE
MADAGASCAR
COMOROS
Antananarivo
RÉUNION (Fr.)
MASCARENE IS.
MAURITIUS
C. D'AMBRE

AUSTRALIA
GREAT VICTORIA DESERT
GREAT SANDY DESERT
Perth
C. LEEUWIN
NORTH WEST CAPE
Great Australian Bight

ÎLE AMSTERDAM (Fr.)
ÎLE ST. PAUL (Fr.)
Tropic of Capricorn

INDONESIA
TIMOR SEA
TIMOR
FLORES

AMIRANTE IS. (Sey.)
SEYCHELLES

PACIFIC OCEAN
ATLANTIC OCEAN
INDIAN OCEAN

ANTARCTICA IN PROFILE
SECTION ALONG LINE AB

South Pole
Horlick Mts.
Framnes Mts.
Byrd Basin
Polar Basin
Sea Level
Feet (A)
(B) Feet
15000 10000 5000 5000

Scale 1: 60 000 000; (approximate)
Lambert's Azimuthal, Equal Area Projection
Elevations and depressions are given in feet

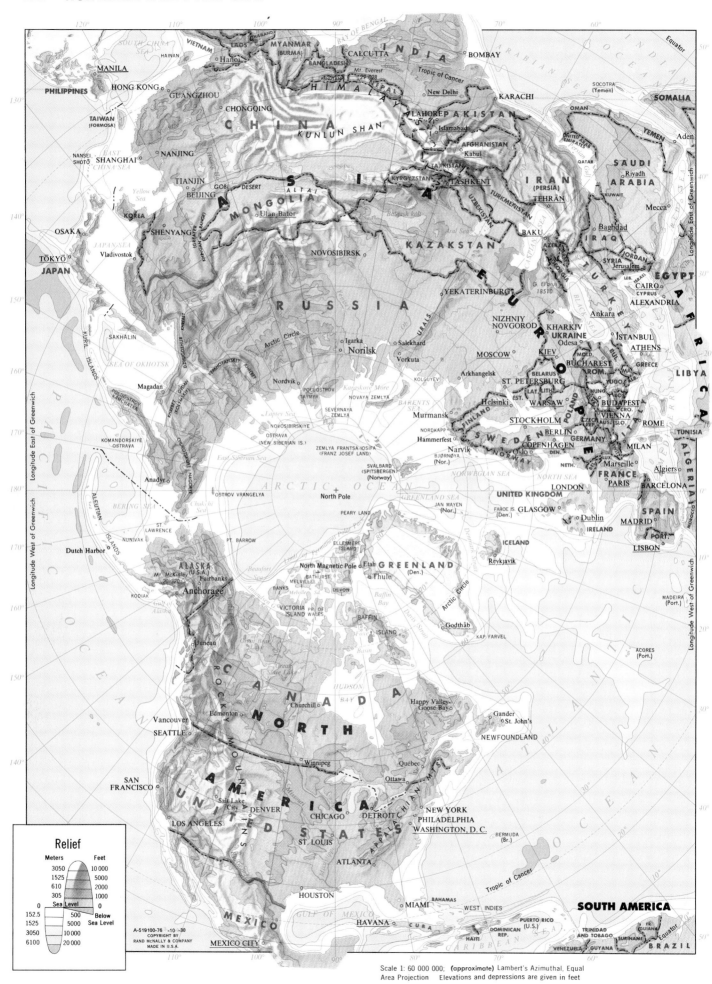

Relief

Meters	Feet
3050	10 000
1525	5000
610	2000
305	1000
0 Sea Level	0
152.5	500 Below
1525	5000 Sea Level
3050	10 000
6100	20 000

A-519100-76 -10 -30
COPYRIGHT BY
RAND McNALLY & COMPANY
MADE IN U.S.A.

Scale 1: 60 000 000; (approximate) Lambert's Azimuthal, Equal
Area Projection   Elevations and depressions are given in feet

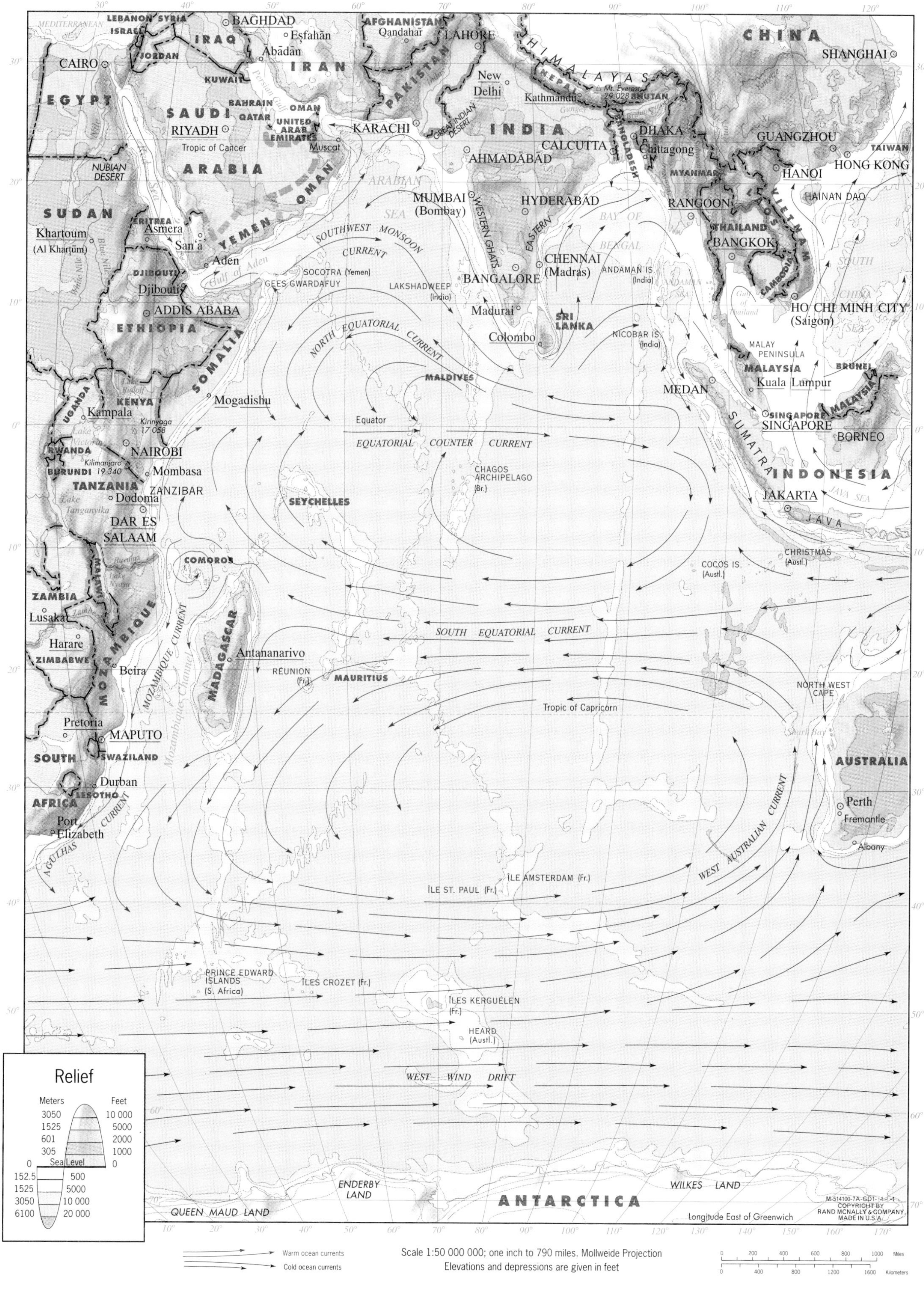

MEDITERRANEAN
LEBANON SYRIA
ISRAEL
JORDAN
IRAQ
BAGHDAD
Esfahān
Abādān
IRAN
Qandahār
AFGHANISTAN
LAHORE
HIMALAYAS
Mt. Everest
29 028
CHINA
SHANGHAI
CAIRO
EGYPT
KUWAIT
BAHRAIN
QATAR
OMAN
UNITED
ARAB
EMIRATES
SAUDI
RIYADH
ARABIA
Tropic of Cancer
Muscat
KARACHI
PAKISTAN
New
Delhi
Kathmandu
NEPAL
BHUTAN
Ganges
INDIA
GUANGZHOU
TAIWAN
HANOI
HONG KONG
NUBIAN
DESERT
AHMADĀBĀD
CALCUTTA
Chittagong
DHAKA
BANGLADESH
SUDAN
Khartoum
(Al Kharţūm)
ERITREA
Asmera
San'a
YEMEN
OMAN
ARABIAN
SEA
MUMBAI
(Bombay)
WESTERN GHATS
HYDERĀBĀD
EASTERN GHATS
RANGOON
MYANMAR
HAINAN DAO
Blue Nile
DJIBOUTI
Djibouti
Aden
Gulf of Aden
SOCOTRA (Yemen)
GEES GWARDAFUY
SOUTHWEST MONSOON
CURRENT
LAKSHADWEEP
(India)
BANGALORE
CHENNAI
(Madras)
ANDAMAN IS.
(India)
THAILAND
BANGKOK
VIETNAM
SOUTH
CAMBODIA
CHINA
ADDIS ABABA
ETHIOPIA
Madurai
Colombo
SRI
LANKA
NICOBAR IS.
(India)
HO CHI MINH CITY
(Saigon)
SEA
Gulf
of
Thailand
MALAY
PENINSULA
MALAYSIA
BRUNEI
NORTH EQUATORIAL CURRENT
SOMALIA
Mogadishu
UGANDA
KENYA
Kampala
Kirinyaga
17 058
Lake
Victoria
Equator
EQUATORIAL COUNTER CURRENT
MALDIVES
CHAGOS
ARCHIPELAGO
(Br.)
MEDAN
SUMATRA
Kuala Lumpur
SINGAPORE
SINGAPORE
BORNEO
INDONESIA
RWANDA
BURUNDI
NAIROBI
Kilimanjaro
19 340
Mombasa
TANZANIA
Dodoma
ZANZIBAR
SEYCHELLES
JAKARTA
JAVA
JAVA SEA
DAR ES
SALAAM
Lake
Tanganyika
Lake
Nyasa
MALAWI
COMOROS
COCOS IS.
(Austl.)
CHRISTMAS
(Austl.)
ZAMBIA
Lusaka
MOZAMBIQUE CURRENT
MADAGASCAR
SOUTH EQUATORIAL CURRENT
Harare
ZIMBABWE
Beira
Antananarivo
RÉUNION
(Fr.)
MAURITIUS
NORTH WEST
CAPE
Tropic of Capricorn
Shark Bay
Pretoria
MAPUTO
SWAZILAND
Mozambique Channel
AUSTRALIA
SOUTH
AFRICA
LESOTHO
Durban
Port
Elizabeth
AGULHAS CURRENT
Perth
Fremantle
Albany
WEST AUSTRALIAN CURRENT
ÎLE AMSTERDAM (Fr.)
ÎLE ST. PAUL (Fr.)
PRINCE EDWARD
ISLANDS
(S. Africa)
ÎLES CROZET (Fr.)
ÎLES KERGUÉLEN
(Fr.)
HEARD
(Austl.)
WEST WIND DRIFT
ENDERBY
LAND
WILKES LAND
QUEEN MAUD LAND
ANTARCTICA
Longitude East of Greenwich

M-514100-7A-GD1-4-4-1
COPYRIGHT BY
RAND MCNALLY & COMPANY
MADE IN U.S.A.

Relief

Meters	Feet
3050	10 000
1525	5000
601	2000
305	1000
0	Sea Level 0
152.5	500
1525	5000
3050	10 000
6100	20 000

→ Warm ocean currents
→ Cold ocean currents

Scale 1:50 000 000; one inch to 790 miles. Mollweide Projection
Elevations and depressions are given in feet

| 0 | 200 | 400 | 600 | 800 | 1000 Miles |
| 0 | 400 | 800 | 1200 | 1600 Kilometers |

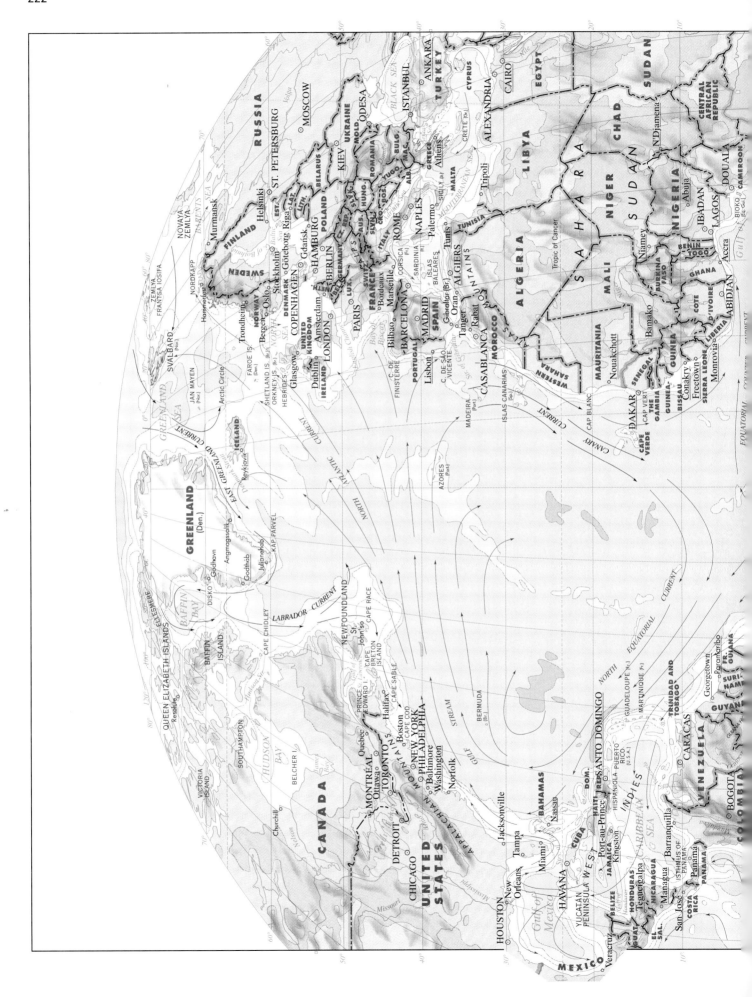

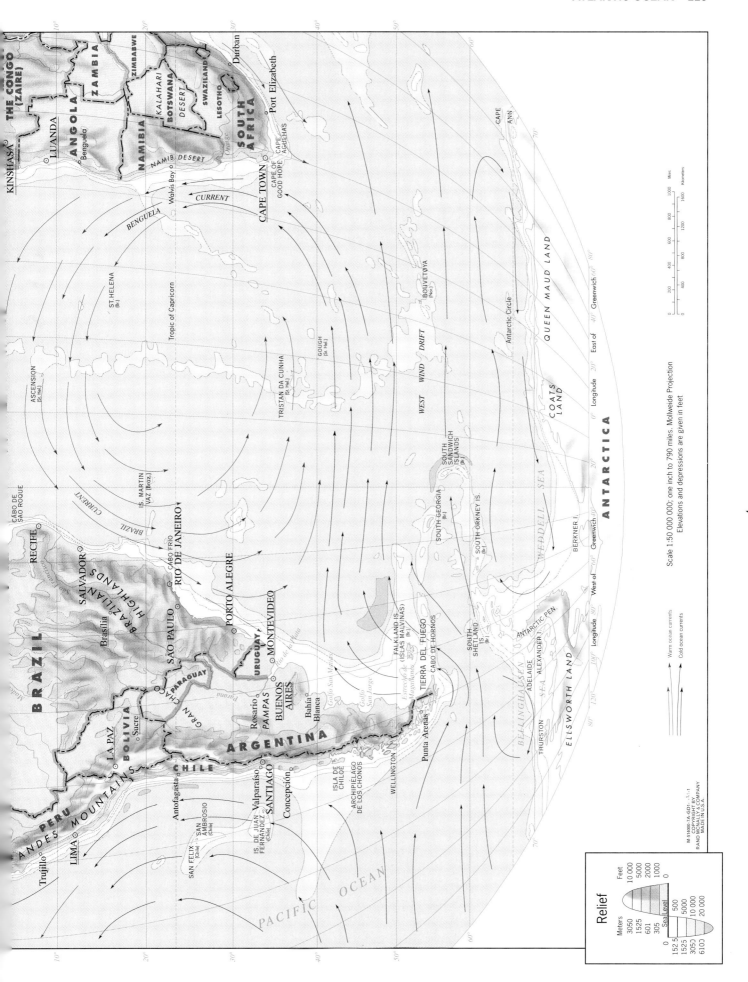

THE CONGO (ZAIRE)
KINSHASA
ANGOLA
LUANDA
Benguela
ZAMBIA
ZIMBABWE
NAMIBIA
KALAHARI DESERT
BOTSWANA
SWAZILAND
LESOTHO
SOUTH AFRICA
Durban
Port Elizabeth
CAPE TOWN
CAPE OF GOOD HOPE
CAPE AGULHAS
NAMIB DESERT
Walvis Bay
CURRENT
BENGUELA
ST HELENA (Br.)
Tropic of Capricorn
ASCENSION (St. Hel.)
CABO DE SAO ROQUE
RECIFE
SALVADOR
BRAZILIAN HIGHLANDS
Brasília
SÃO PAULO
BRAZIL
PERU
Trujillo
LIMA
ANDES MOUNTAINS
CHILE
Antofagasta
SAN FELIX (Chile)
SAN AMBROSIO (Chile)
IS. DE JUAN FERNÁNDEZ (Chile)
Valparaíso
SANTIAGO
Concepción
BOLIVIA
LA PAZ
Sucre
PARAGUAY
GRAN CHACO
Rosario
PAMPAS
BUENOS AIRES
URUGUAY
MONTEVIDEO
Bahía Blanca
Río de la Plata
Paraná
ARGENTINA
IS. MARTIN VAZ (Braz.)
TRISTAN DA CUNHA (St. Hel.)
GOUGH (St. Hel.)
CABO FRIO
RIO DE JANEIRO
PORTO ALEGRE
BRAZIL CURRENT
ISLA DE CHILOÉ
ARCHIPIÉLAGO DE LOS CHONOS
WELLINGTON
Golfo San Matías
Golfo San Jorge
Estrecho de Magallanes
TIERRA DEL FUEGO
CABO DE HORNOS
Punta Arenas
FALKLAND IS. (ISLAS MALVINAS) (Br.)
SOUTH GEORGIA (Br.)
SOUTH ORKNEY IS. (Br.)
SOUTH SANDWICH ISLANDS (Br.)
BOUVETØYA (Nor.)
SOUTH SHETLAND IS.
ANTARCTIC PEN.
ALEXANDER I.
ADELAIDE
THURSTON
BELLINGSHAUSEN SEA
ELLSWORTH LAND
BERKNER I.
COATS LAND
WEDDELL SEA
QUEEN MAUD LAND
ANTARCTICA
Antarctic Circle
WEST WIND DRIFT
CAPE ANN
East of Greenwich
Longitude
West of Greenwich
PACIFIC OCEAN

Scale 1:50 000 000; one inch to 790 miles. Mollweide Projection
Elevations and depressions are given in feet

Warm ocean currents
Cold ocean currents

Miles
Kilometers
0   200   400   600   800   1000
0   400   800   1200   1600

M-514000-7A1GD1-..-1..-1
COPYRIGHT BY
RAND McNALLY & COMPANY
MADE IN U.S.A.

Relief
Meters   Feet
3050   10 000
1525   5000
601   2000
305   1000
0   Sea Level
             Sea Level
152.5   500
1525   5000
3053   10 000
6103   20 000

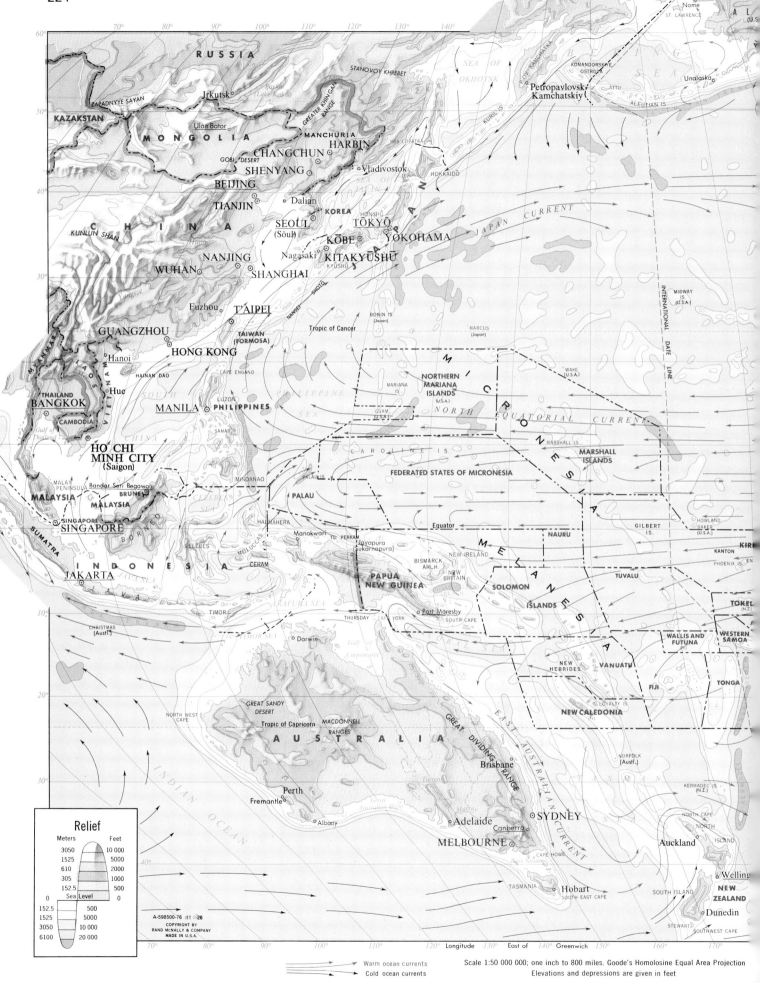

RUSSIA
STANOVOY KHREBET
SEA OF OKHOTSK
KAZAKSTAN
Irkutsk
ZAPADNYYE SAYAN
Baykal (Lake Baykal)
MONGOLIA
Ulan Bator
GREATER KHINGAN RANGE
MANCHURIA
HARBIN
CHANGCHUN
GOBI DESERT
SHENYANG
Vladivostok
BEIJING
HOKKAIDŌ
TIANJIN
Dalian
KOREA
CHINA
KUNLUN SHAN
SEOUL (Sŏul)
TŌKYŌ
HONSHŪ
KŌBE
YOKOHAMA
Nagasaki
KITAKYŪSHŪ
NANJING
SHANGHAI
KYŪSHŪ
WUHAN
Fuzhou
T'AIPEI
Tropic of Cancer
GUANGZHOU
TAIWAN (FORMOSA)
HONG KONG
Hanoi
CAPE ENGANO
Hue
HAINAN DAO
THAILAND
BANGKOK
MANILA
PHILIPPINES
CAMBODIA
SAMAR
HO CHI MINH CITY (Saigon)
MINDANAO
MALAY PENINSULA
Bandar Seri Begawan
BRUNEI
MALAYSIA
PALAU
SINGAPORE
SUMATRA
INDONESIA
JAKARTA
HALMAHERA
Manokwari
CELEBES
MOLUCCAS
CERAM
PETROPAVLOVSK-KAMCHATSKIY
NORTHERN MARIANA ISLANDS (U.S.A.)
GUAM (U.S.A.)
MARIANA IS.
CAROLINE IS.
FEDERATED STATES OF MICRONESIA
MICRONESIA
MARSHALL ISLANDS
Equator
NAURU
MELANESIA
PAPUA NEW GUINEA
Jayapura (Sukarnapura)
BISMARCK ARCH.
NEW IRELAND
NEW BRITAIN
SOLOMON ISLANDS
TUVALU
Port Moresby
THURSDAY
CAPE YORK
Darwin
GREAT SANDY DESERT
Tropic of Capricorn
MACDONNELL RANGES
AUSTRALIA
GREAT DIVIDING RANGE
Brisbane
Perth
Fremantle
Adelaide
Canberra
SYDNEY
MELBOURNE
TASMANIA
Hobart
NEW ZEALAND
Dunedin
Auckland
Wellington

Relief
Meters   Feet
3050   10 000
1525   5 000
610   2 000
305   1 000
152.5   500
0   Sea Level   0
152.5   500
1525   5 000
3050   10 000
6100   20 000

A-598500-76 11 6-26
COPYRIGHT BY
RAND MCNALLY & COMPANY
MADE IN U.S.A.

Warm ocean currents
Cold ocean currents
Scale 1:50 000 000; one inch to 800 miles. Goode's Homolosine Equal Area Projection
Elevations and depressions are given in feet
Longitude   East of   Greenwich

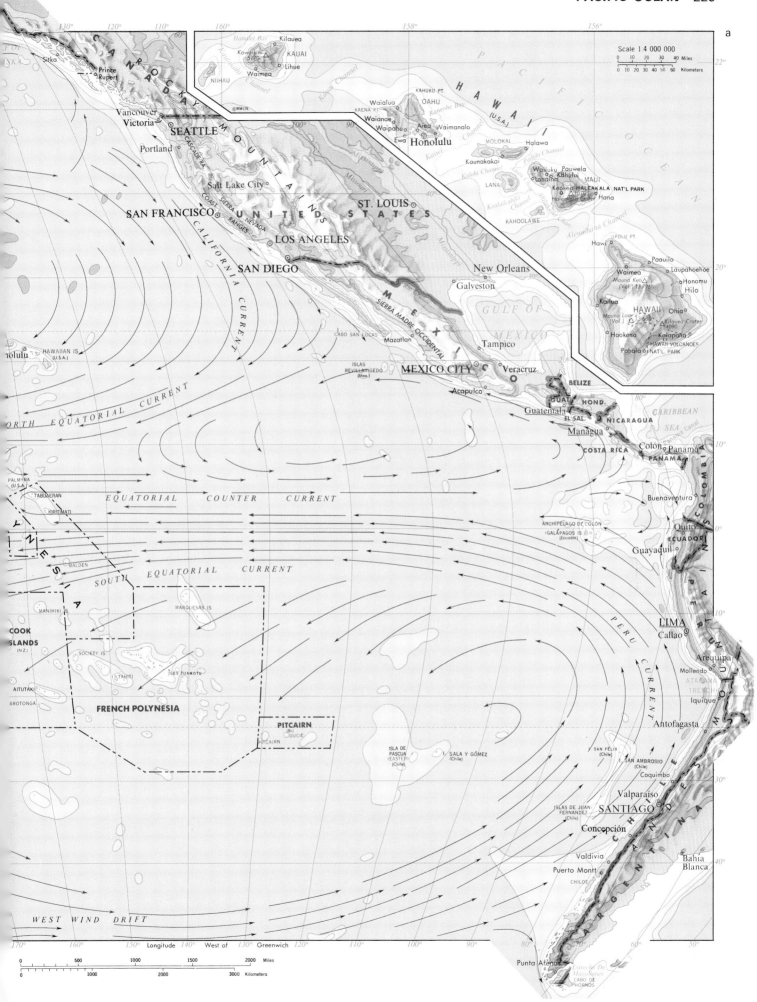

a

Scale 1:4 000 000

0   10   20   30   40 Miles

0 10 20 30 40 50 60 Kilometers

PRINCE RUPERT · Sitka

CANADA · ROCKY · MOUNTAINS

KAUAI · Kilauea · Kawaikini 5170 · Hanalei Bay · Waimea · Lihue · NIIHAU · Kauai Channel

Vancouver · Victoria

SEATTLE

Portland · CASCADE RA.

OAHU · KAHUKU PT. · Waialua · Waianae · Waipahu · Ewa · Honolulu · Area · Waimanalo · Kaneohe Bay

MOLOKAI · Halawa · Kaunakakai · Kaluu Channel · Pailolo Channel

Salt Lake City · SIERRA NEVADA

SAN FRANCISCO · COAST RANGES

UNITED STATES

WAILUKU · Pauwela · Kahului · Lahaina · Keokea · HALEAKALA NAT'L PARK · Hana · Haleakala Crater · MAUI · LANAI · Kealaikahiki Channel · KAHOOLAWE · Alenuihaha Channel

LOS ANGELES

CALIFORNIA CURRENT

SAN DIEGO

ST. LOUIS

HAWI · UPOLU PT. · Paauilo · Waimea · Mauna Kea 13,796 · Laupahoehoe · Honomu · Hilo · Kailua · HAWAII · Ohia · Mauna Loa 13,680 · Kilauea Crater 4090 · Hookena · Kalapana · Pahala · HAWAII VOLCANOES NAT'L PARK

CABO SAN LUCAS · Mazatlan

New Orleans · Galveston

GULF OF MEXICO

SIERRA MADRE OCCIDENTAL

M E X I C O

Tampico

ISLAS REVILLAGIGEDO (Mex.)

MEXICO CITY · Veracruz

Acapulco

BELIZE

GUAT. · HOND. · Guatemala · EL SAL. · NICARAGUA · Managua · CARIBBEAN SEA · COSTA RICA · Colón · Panama · PANAMA · Panama Canal

olulu · HAWAIIAN IS. (U.S.A.)

ORTH EQUATORIAL CURRENT

NORTH EQUATORIAL CURRENT

PALMYRA (U.S.A.) · TABUAERAN · KIRITIMATI

Buenaventura

ARCHIPIÉLAGO DE COLÓN (GALÁPAGOS IS.) (Ecuador)

COLOMBIA · Quito · ECUADOR · Guayaquil

POLYNESIA

EQUATORIAL COUNTER CURRENT

MALDEN

SOUTH EQUATORIAL CURRENT

MANIHIKI · MARQUESAS IS.

COOK ISLANDS (N.Z.)

SOCIETY IS. · TAHITI · ÎLES TUAMOTU

AITUTAKI · AROTONGA

FRENCH POLYNESIA

PITCAIRN (Br.) · DUCIE · PITCAIRN

ISLA DE PASCUA (EASTER) (Chile) · I. SALA Y GÓMEZ (Chile)

LIMA · Callao · PERU CURRENT

Arequipa · Mollendo · ATACAMA TRENCH · Iquique

Antofagasta

SAN FÉLIX (Chile) · I. SAN AMBROSIO (Chile) · Coquimbo

Valparaíso · ISLAS DE JUAN FERNÁNDEZ (Chile) · SANTIAGO · ARGENTINA · CHILE · ANDES

Concepción

Valdivia · Puerto Montt · CHILOE

Bahía Blanca

WEST WIND DRIFT

0   500   1000   1500   2000 Miles

0   1000   2000   3000 Kilometers

170° · 160° · 150° Longitude · 140° West of · 130° Greenwich · 120° · 110° · 100° · 90° · 80° · 70° · 60° · 50°

Punta Arenas · Estrecho De Magallanes · CABO DE HORNOS

MAJOR CITIES MAPS

This section consists of 62 maps of the world's most populous metropolitan areas. In order to make comparison easier, all the metropolitan areas are shown at the same scale, 1:300,000.

Detailed urban maps are an important reference requirement for a world atlas. The names of many large settlements, towns, suburbs, and neighborhoods can be located on these large-scale maps. From a thematic standpoint the maps show generalized land-use patterns. Included were the total urban extent, major industrial areas, parks, public land, wooded areas, airports, shopping centers, streets, and railroads. A special effort was made to portray the various metropolitan areas in a manner as standard and comparable as possible. (For the symbols used, see the legend below.)

Notable differences occur in the forms of cities. In most of North America these forms were conditioned by a rectangular pattern of streets; land-use zones (residential, commercial, industrial) are well defined. The basic structure of most European cities is noticeably different and more complex; street patterns are irregular and zones are less well defined. In Asia, Africa, and South America the form tends to be even more irregular and complex. Widespread dispersion of craft and trade activities has lessened zonation, there may be cities with no identifiable city centers, and sometimes there may be dual centers (old and modern). Higher population densities result in more limited, compact urban places in these areas of the world.

Inhabited Localities

The symbol represents the number of inhabitants within the locality

- · 0—10,000
- ○ 10,000—25,000
- ◉ 25,000—100,000
- ▣ 100,000—250,000
- ▦ 250,000—1,000,000
- ■ >1,000,000

The size of type indicates the relative economic and political importance of the locality

Écommoy	St.-Denis
Trouville	
Lisieux	PARIS

Hollywood   Section of a City,
Westminster   Neighborhood
Northland ■
Center   Major Shopping Center

Urban Area (area of continuous industrial, commercial, and residential development)

Major Industrial Area

Wooded Area

Political Boundaries

International (First-order political unit)

Demarcated, Undemarcated, and Administrative

Demarcation Line

Internal

State, Province, etc.
(Second-order political unit)

County, Oblast, etc.
(Third-order political unit)

Okrug, Kreis, etc.
(Fourth-order political unit)

City or Municipality
(may appear in combination with another boundary symbol)

Capitals of Political Units

BUDAPEST   Independent Nation

Recife   State, Province, etc.

White Plains   County, Oblast, etc.

Iserlohn   Okrug, Kreis, etc.

Transportation

Road

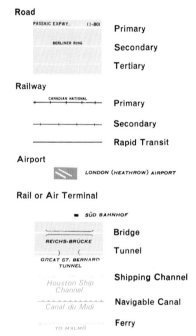

PASSAIC EXPWY.   (I-80)   Primary

BERLINER RING   Secondary

Tertiary

Railway

CANADIAN NATIONAL   Primary

Secondary

Rapid Transit

Airport

LONDON (HEATHROW) AIRPORT

Rail or Air Terminal

■ SÜD BAHNHOF

REICHS-BRÜCKE   Bridge

GREAT ST. BERNARD TUNNEL   Tunnel

Houston Ship Channel   Shipping Channel

Canal du Midi   Navigable Canal

TO MALMÖ   Ferry

Hydrographic Features

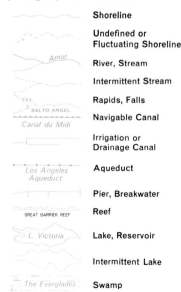

Shoreline

Undefined or Fluctuating Shoreline

Amur   River, Stream

Intermittent Stream

SALTO ÁNGEL   Rapids, Falls

Canal du Midi   Navigable Canal

Irrigation or Drainage Canal

Los Angeles Aqueduct   Aqueduct

Pier, Breakwater

GREAT BARRIER REEF   Reef

L. Victoria   Lake, Reservoir

Intermittent Lake

The Everglades   Swamp

Miscellaneous Cultural Features

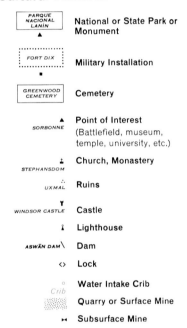

PARQUE NACIONAL LANIN
▲   National or State Park or Monument

FORT DIX
■   Military Installation

GREENWOOD CEMETERY   Cemetery

▲
SORBONNE   Point of Interest (Battlefield, museum, temple, university, etc.)

⚲
STEPHANSDOM   Church, Monastery

⛫
UXMAL   Ruins

Υ
WINDSOR CASTLE   Castle

⚑   Lighthouse

ASWĀN DAM \   Dam

<>   Lock

○
Crib   Water Intake Crib

⠿   Quarry or Surface Mine

⋈   Subsurface Mine

Topographic Features

Mt. Kenya 5199 △   Elevation Above Sea Level

Elevations are given in meters

✶   Rock

A N D E S Mountain Range, Plateau,
KUNLUNSHANMAI   Valley, etc.

BAFFIN ISLAND   Island

POLUOSTROV KAMČATKA   Peninsula, Cape, Point, etc.
CABO DE HORNOS

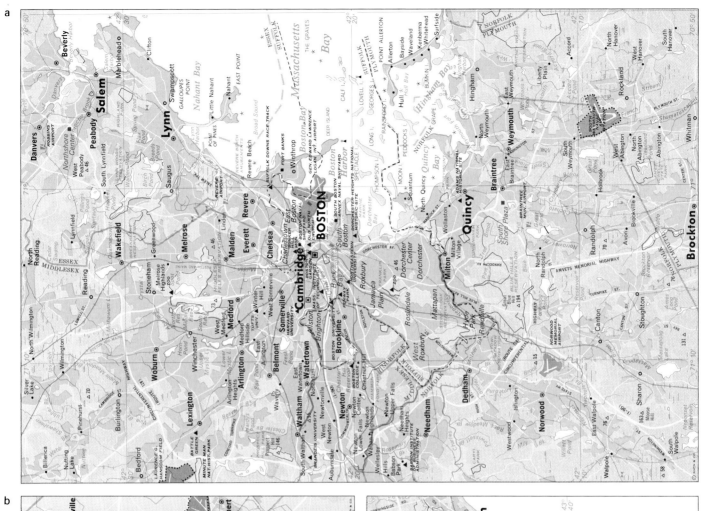

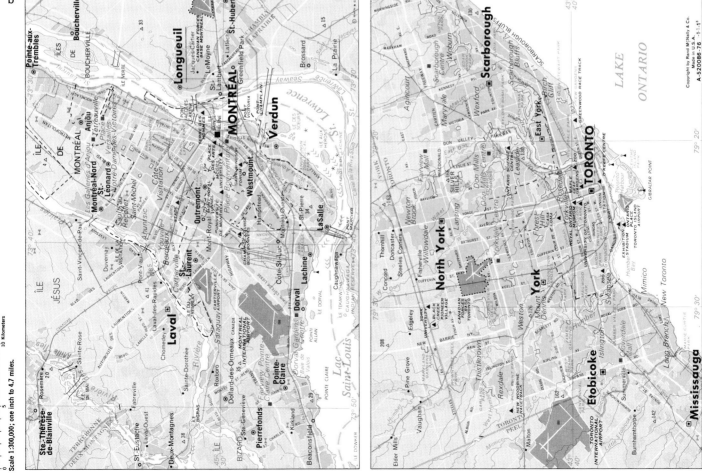

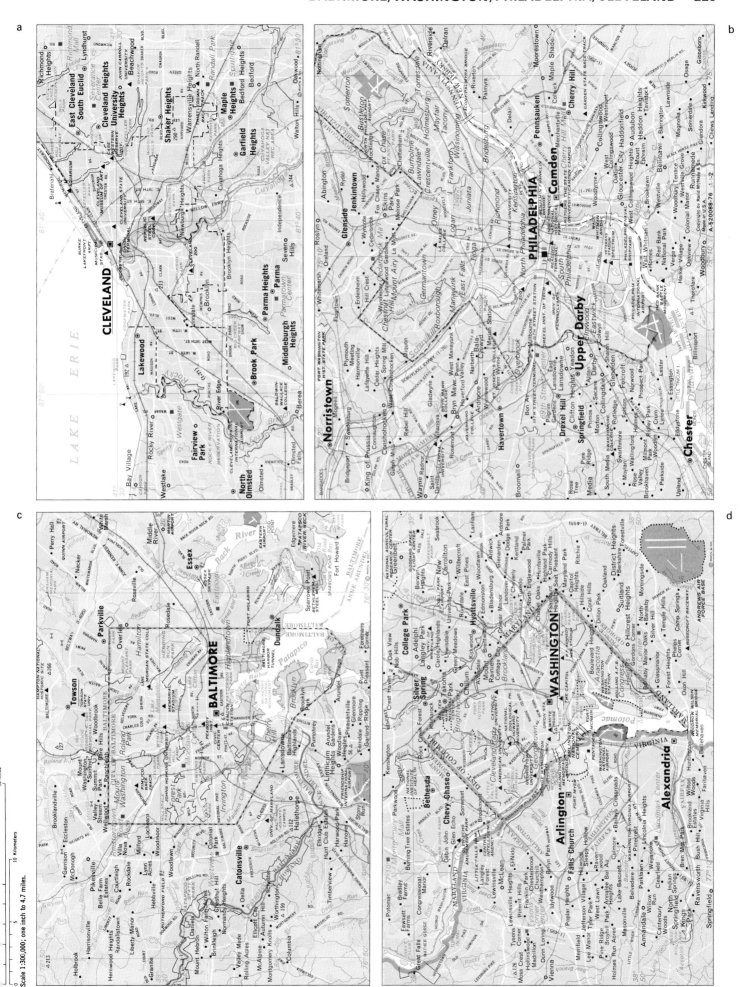

a

b

c

d

Scale 1:300,000; one inch to 4.7 miles.

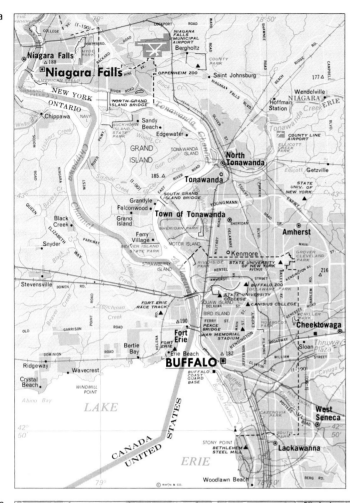

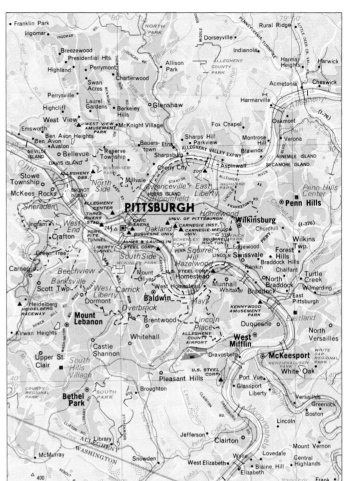

a

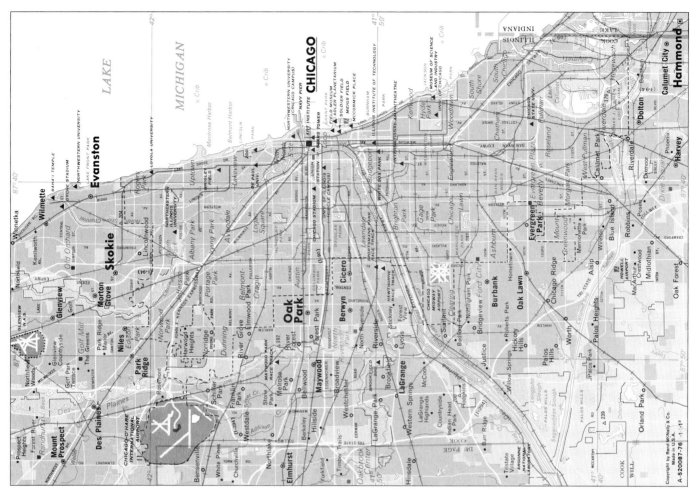

b

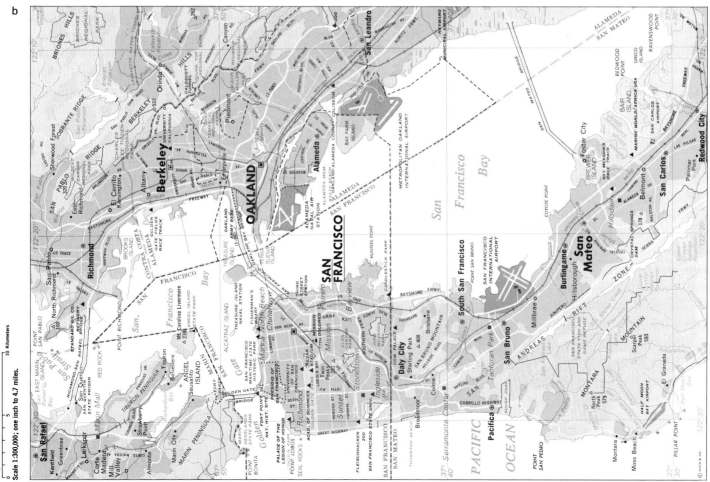

Scale 1:300,000; one inch to 4.7 miles.

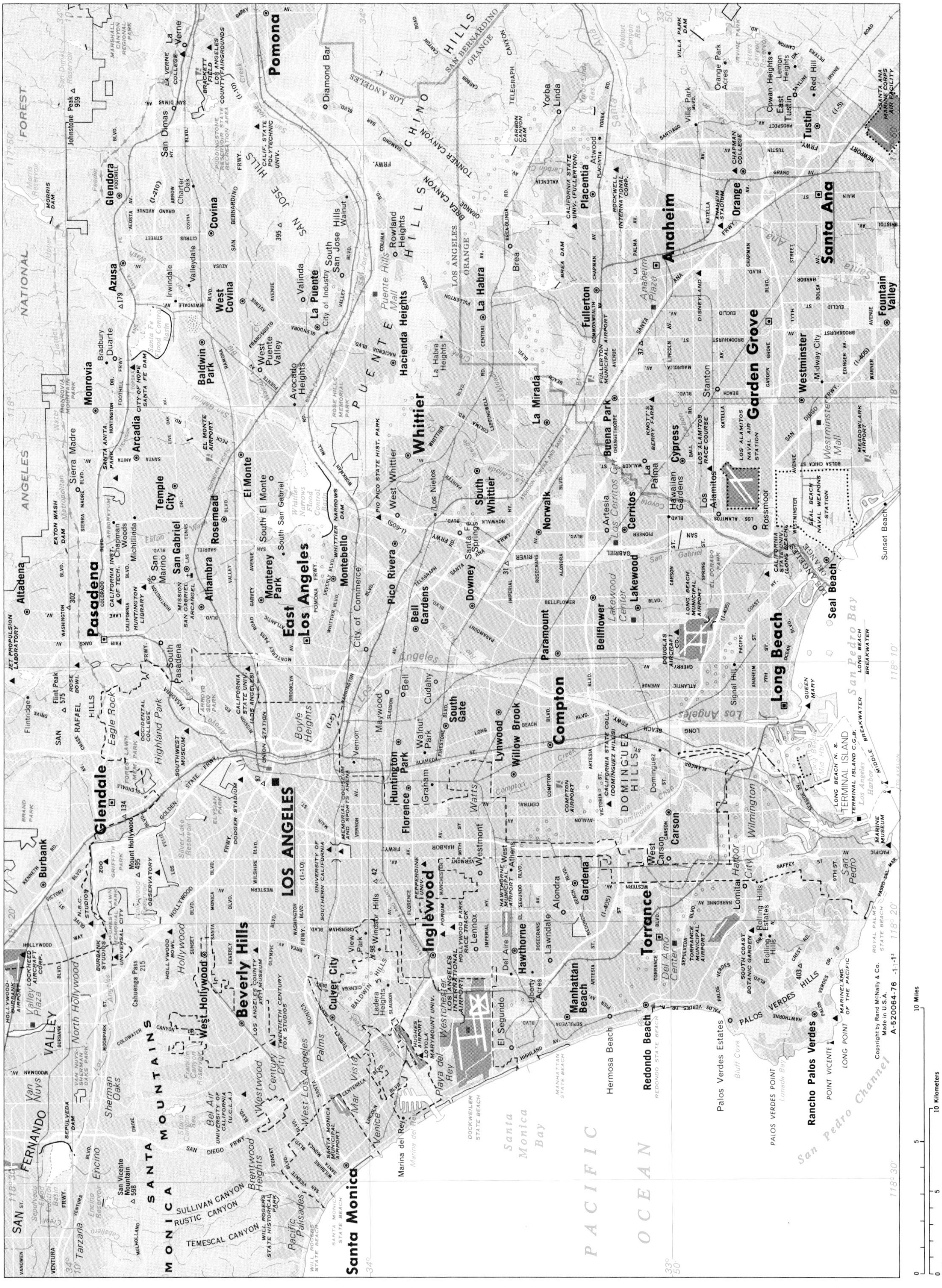

SANTA MONICA MOUNTAINS

SAN FERNANDO VALLEY

LOS ANGELES

Pomona
La Verne
Glendora
Azusa
Covina
West Covina
Baldwin Park
Monrovia
Arcadia
Pasadena
Altadena
Glendale
Burbank
Hollywood
Beverly Hills
West Hollywood
Culver City
Santa Monica
Inglewood
Hawthorne
Manhattan Beach
Redondo Beach
Torrance
Rancho Palos Verdes
Palos Verdes Estates
Gardena
Compton
Carson
Long Beach
Seal Beach
Garden Grove
Westminster
Fountain Valley
Santa Ana
Tustin
Orange
Anaheim
Fullerton
Placentia
Brea
La Habra
La Mirada
Whittier
Norwalk
Cerritos
Cypress
Buena Park
Lakewood
Bellflower
Paramount
Downey
Pico Rivera
Montebello
East Los Angeles
Monterey Park
Alhambra
San Gabriel
Rosemead
Temple City
El Monte
Hacienda Heights
La Puente
Rowland Heights

PACIFIC OCEAN

Santa Monica Bay

San Pedro Bay

San Pedro Channel

ANGELES NATIONAL FOREST

PUENTE HILLS

SAN JOSE HILLS

CHINO HILLS

DOMINGUEZ HILLS

Copyright by Rand McNally & Co.
Made in U.S.A.
A-520064-76

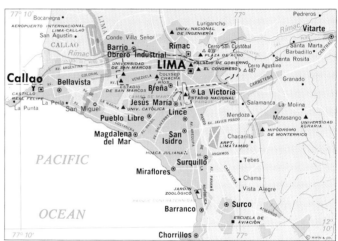

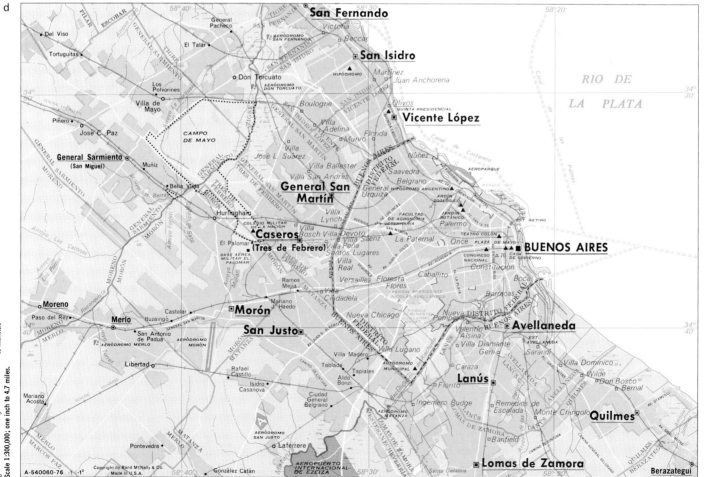

A-540060-76 1 1³

a
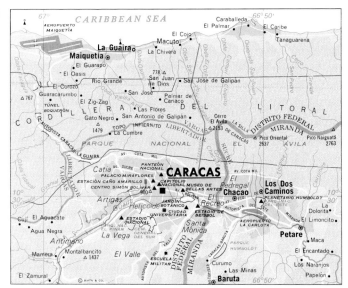

b

c
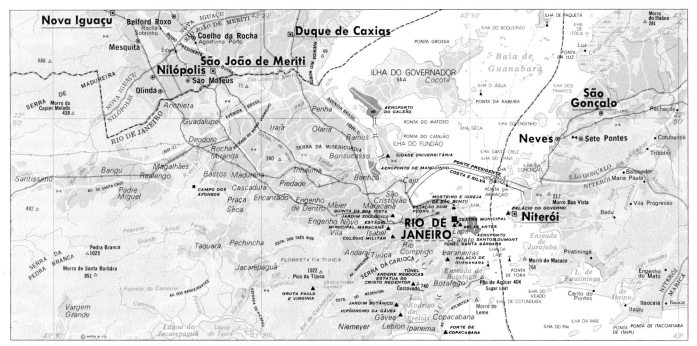

d
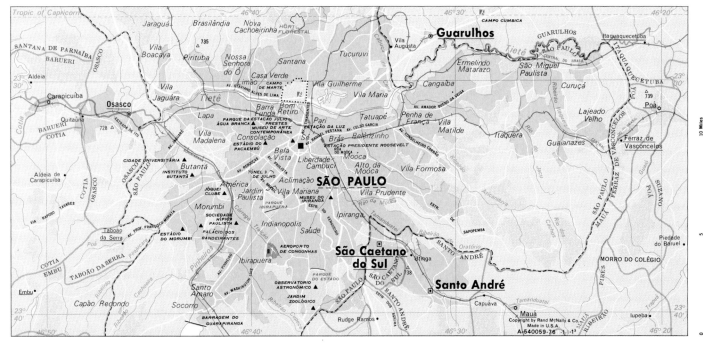

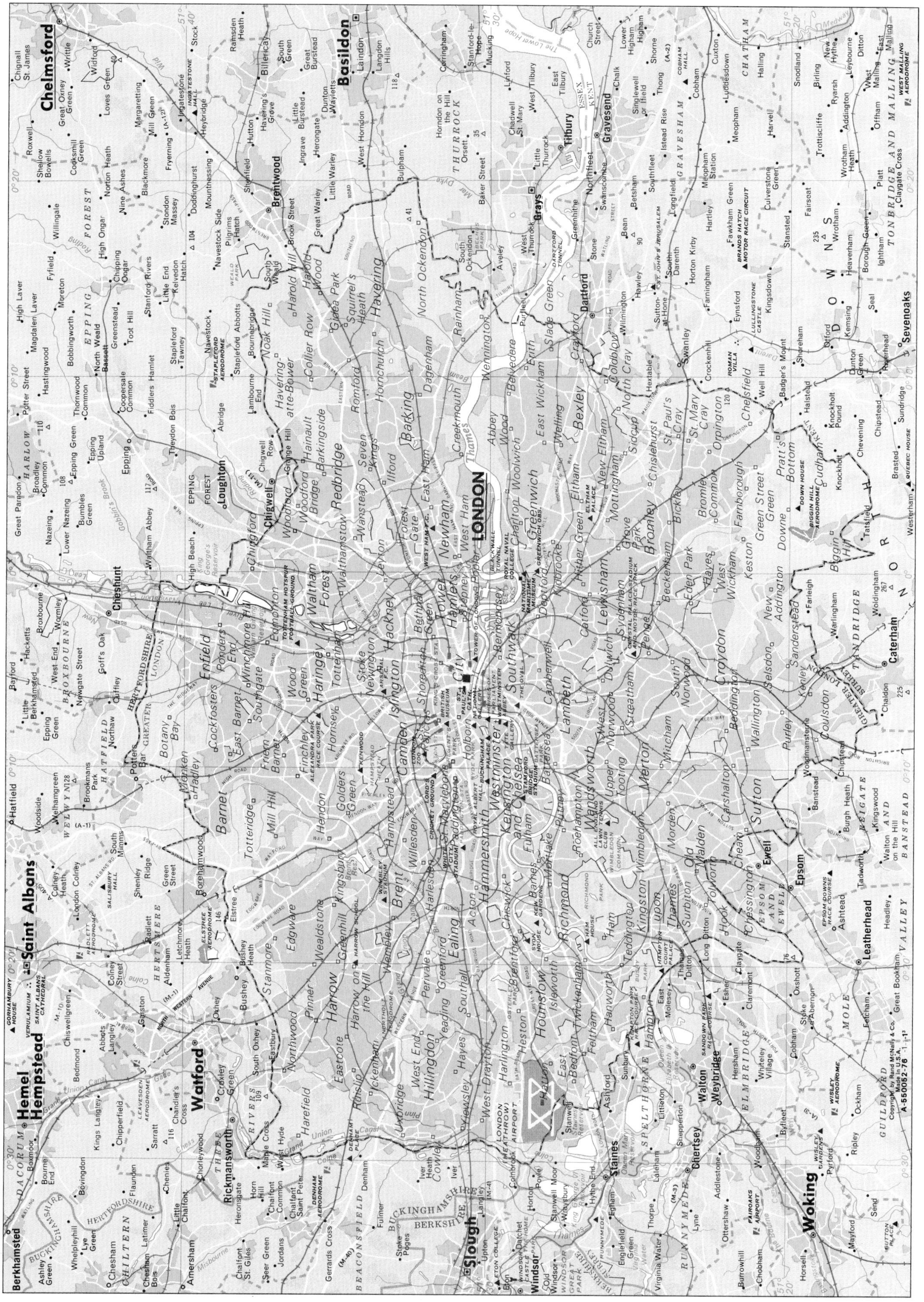

Chelmsford

Basildon

Brentwood

Gravesend

Tilbury

Grays

Dartford

Sevenoaks

LONDON

Loughton

Chigwell

Cheshunt

Saint Albans

Hemel Hempstead

Berkhamsted

Watford

Rickmansworth

Slough

Windsor

Staines

Chertsey

Woking

Weybridge

Walton

Leatherhead

Epsom

Ewell

Scale 1:300,000; one inch to 4.7 miles.

0 ... 5 ... 10 Kilometers

© Copyright by Rand M⁰Nally & Co.
Made in U.S.A.
A-550062-76

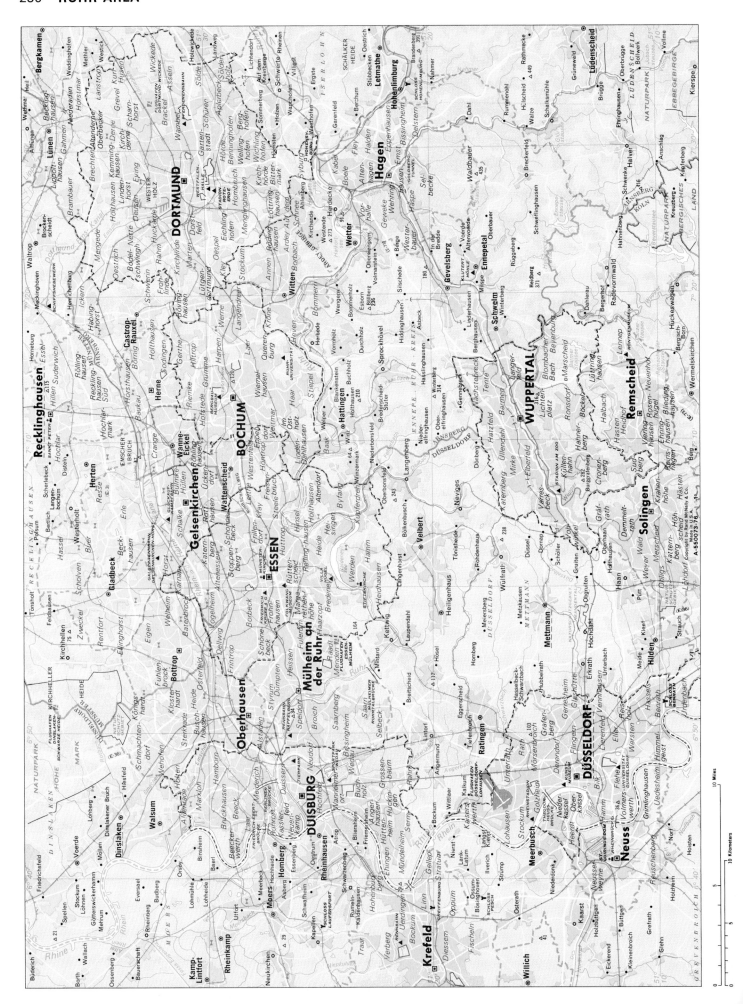

a

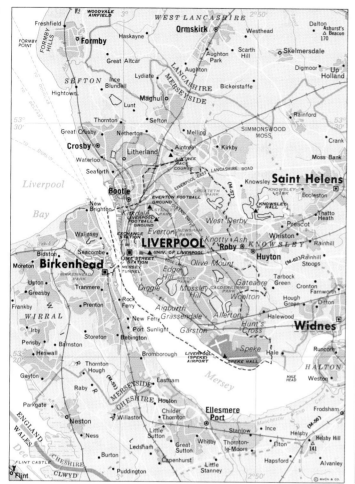

b

c

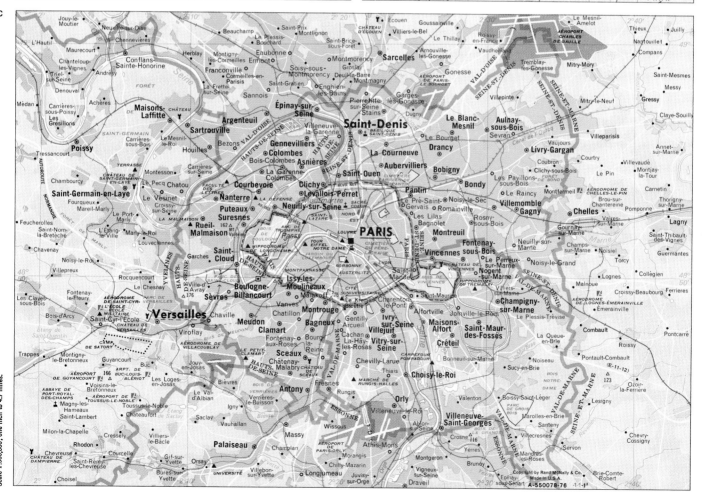

Scale 1:300,000; one inch to 4.7 miles.

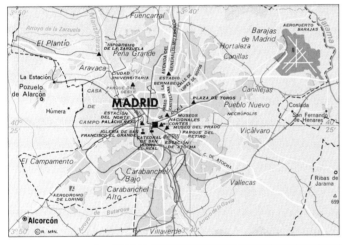

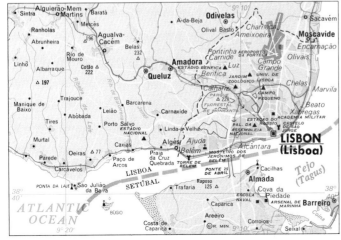

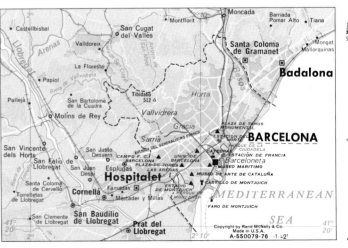

a
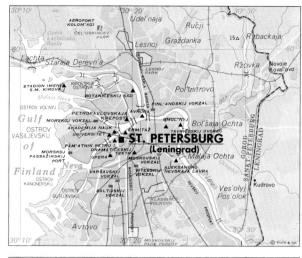

St. Petersburg (Leningrad)

b
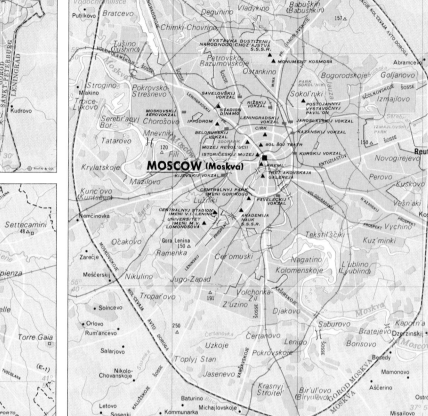

Moscow (Moskva)

c

Rome (Roma)

d
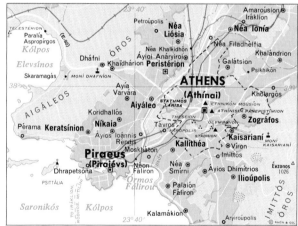

Athens (Athínai)

e

Vienna (Wien)

f

İstanbul

Scale 1:300,000; one inch to 4.7 miles.
Copyright by Rand McNally & Co.
Made in U.S.A.
A-550080-76

g
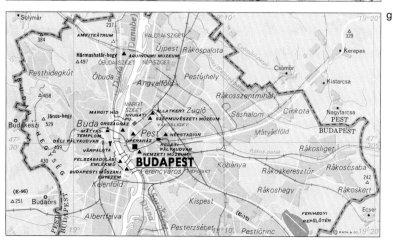

Budapest

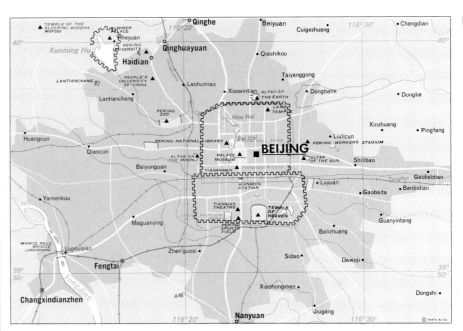

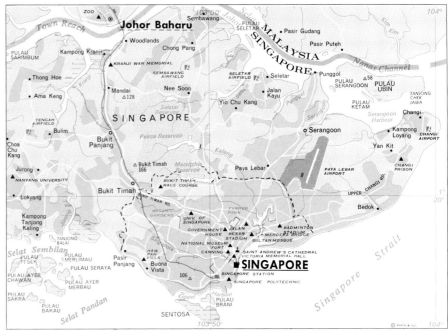

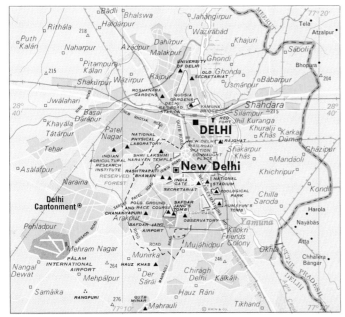

a
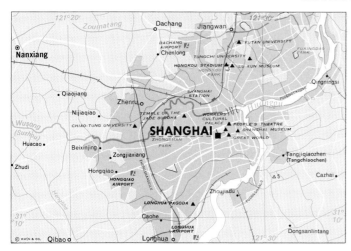

b
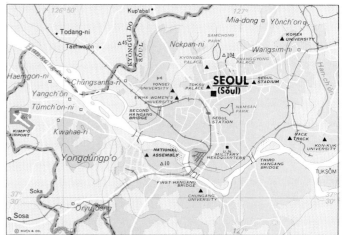

c
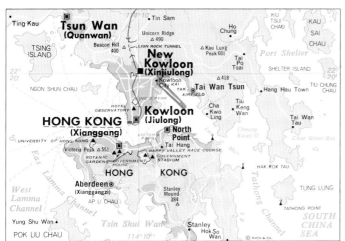

d
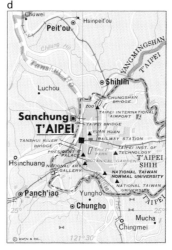

e

f
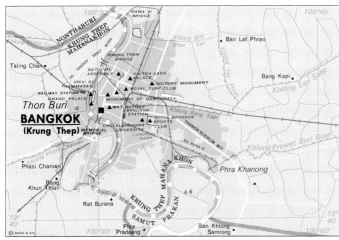

g
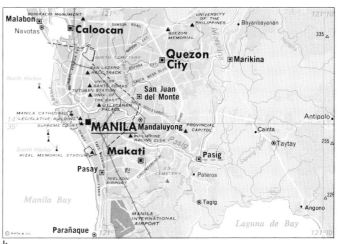

h
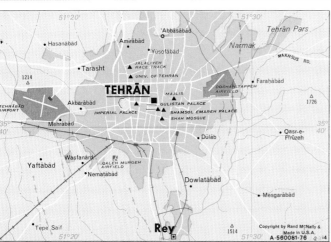

k

m

a

b

a

b

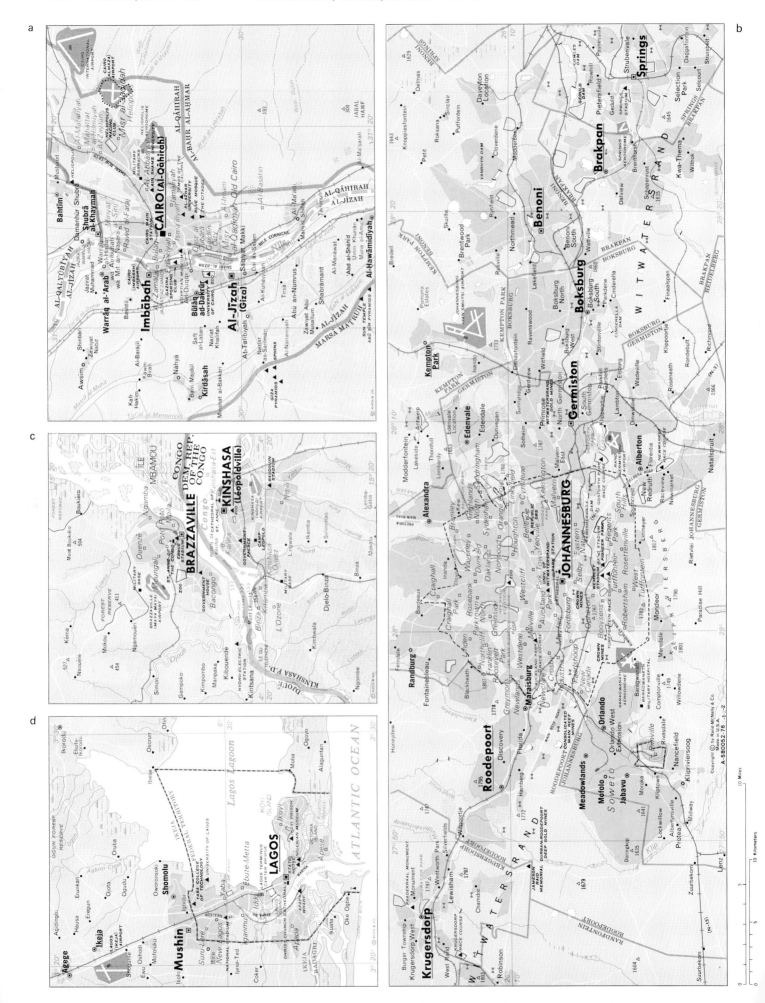

WORLD POLITICAL INFORMATION TABLE

This table gives the area, population, population density, political status, capital, and predominant languages for every country in the world. The political units listed are categorized by political status in the form of government column of the table, as follows: A—independent countries; B—internally independent political entities which are under the protection of another country in matters of defense and foreign affairs; C—colonies and other dependent political units; and D—the major administrative subdivisions of Australia, Canada, China, the United

Kingdom, and the United States. For comparison, the table also includes the continents and the world. A key to abbreviations of country names appears on page 253. All footnotes to this table appear on page 249.

The populations are estimates for January 1, 1997, made by Rand McNally on the basis of official data, United Nations estimates, and other available information. Area figures include inland water.

REGION OR POLITICAL DIVISION	Area Sq. Mi.	Est. Pop. 1/1/97	Pop. Per. Sq. Mi.	Form of Government and Ruling Power		Capital	Predominant Languages
Afars and Issas see Djibouti							
† Afghanistan	251,826	23,230,000	92	Transitional	A	Kābul	Dari, Pashto, Uzbek, Turkmen
Africa	11,700,000	740,600,000	63				
Alabama	52,423	4,297,000	82	State (U.S.)	D	Montgomery	English
Alaska	656,424	614,000	0.9	State (U.S.)	D	Juneau	English, indigenous
† Albania	11,100	3,269,000	295	Republic	A	Tiranë	Albanian, Greek
Alberta	255,287	2,724,000	11	Province (Canada)	D	Edmonton	English
† Algeria	919,595	29,505,000	32	Republic	A	Algiers (El Djazaïr)	Arabic, Berber dialects, French
American Samoa	77	61,000	792	Unincorporated territory (U.S.)	C	Pago Pago	Samoan, English
† Andorra	175	74,000	423	Parliamentary co-principality (Spanish and French protection)	B	Andorra	Catalan, Spanish (Castilian), French
† Angola	481,354	10,475,000	22	Republic	A	Luanda	Portuguese, indigenous
Anguilla	35	11,000	314	Dependent territory (U.K. protection)	B	The Valley	English
Anhui	53,668	60,560,000	1,128	Province (China)	D	Hefei	Chinese (Mandarin)
Antarctica	5,400,000	(¹)					
† Antigua and Barbuda	171	66,000	386	Parliamentary state	A	St. John's	English, local dialects
† Argentina	1,073,519	34,845,000	32	Republic	A	Buenos Aires and Viedma (⁴)	Spanish, English, Italian, German, French
Arizona	114,006	4,305,000	38	State (U.S.)	D	Phoenix	English
Arkansas	53,182	2,509,000	47	State (U.S.)	D	Little Rock	English
† Armenia	11,506	3,464,000	301	Republic	A	Yerevan	Armenian, Russian
Aruba	75	68,000	907	Self-governing territory (Netherlands protection)	B	Oranjestad	Dutch, Papiamento, English, Spanish
Ascension	34	1,100	32	Dependency (St. Helena)	C	Georgetown	English
Asia	17,300,000	3,549,400,000	205				
† Australia	2,966,155	18,350,000	6.2	Federal parliamentary state	A	Canberra	English, indigenous
Australian Capital Territory	927	312,000	337	Territory (Australia)	D	Canberra	English
† Austria	32,377	8,039,000	248	Federal republic	A	Vienna (Wien)	German
† Azerbaijan	33,436	7,708,000	231	Republic	A	Baku (Bakı)	Azeri, Russian, Armenian
† Bahamas	5,382	260,000	48	Parliamentary state	A	Nassau	English, Creole
† Bahrain	267	607,000	2,273	Monarchy	A	Al Manāmah (Manama)	Arabic, English, Farsi, Urdu
† Bangladesh	55,598	124,170,000	2,233	Republic	A	Dhaka (Dacca)	Bangla, English
† Barbados	166	258,000	1,554	Parliamentary state	A	Bridgetown	English
Beijing (Peking)	6,487	11,430,000	1,762	Autonomous city (China)	D	Beijing (Peking)	Chinese (Mandarin)
† Belarus	80,155	10,425,000	130	Republic	A	Minsk	Belarussian, Russian
Belau see Palau							
† Belgium	11,783	10,190,000	865	Constitutional monarchy	A	Brussels (Bruxelles)	Dutch (Flemish), French, German
† Belize	8,867	225,000	25	Parliamentary state	A	Belmopan	English, Spanish, Mayan, Garifuna
† Benin	43,475	5,807,000	134	Republic	A	Porto-Novo and Cotonou	French, Fon, Yoruba, indigenous
Bermuda	21	62,000	2,952	Dependent territory (U.K.)	C	Hamilton	English
† Bhutan	17,954	1,843,000	103	Monarchy (Indian protection)	B	Thimphu	Dzongkha, Tibetan and Nepalese dialects
† Bolivia	424,165	7,619,000	18	Republic	A	La Paz and Sucre	Aymara, Quechua, Spanish
† Bosnia and Herzegovina	19,741	2,595,000	131	Republic	A	Sarajevo	Serbo-Croatian
† Botswana	224,711	1,491,000	6.6	Republic	A	Gaborone	English, Tswana
† Brazil	3,300,171	163,640,000	50	Federal republic	A	Brasília	Portuguese, Spanish, English, French
British Columbia	365,948	3,476,000	9.5	Province (Canada)	D	Victoria	English
British Indian Ocean Territory	23	(¹)		Dependent territory (U.K.)	C		English
British Virgin Islands	59	14,000	237	Dependent territory (U.K.)	C	Road Town	English
† Brunei	2,226	296,000	133	Monarchy	A	Bandar Seri Begawan	Malay, English, Chinese
† Bulgaria	42,855	8,628,000	201	Republic	A	Sofia (Sofiya)	Bulgarian, Turkish
† Burkina Faso	105,869	10,765,000	102	Republic	A	Ouagadougou	French, indigenous
Burma see Myanmar							
† Burundi	10,745	5,953,000	554	Republic	A	Bujumbura	French, Kirundi, Swahili
California	163,707	32,575,000	199	State (U.S.)	D	Sacramento	English
† Cambodia	69,898	11,015,000	158	Constitutional monarchy	A	Phnum Pénh (Phnom Penh)	Khmer, French
† Cameroon	183,568	14,470,000	79	Republic	A	Yaoundé	English, French, indigenous
† Canada	3,849,674	28,975,000	7.5	Federal parliamentary state	A	Ottawa	English, French
† Cape Verde	1,557	456,000	293	Republic	A	Praia	Portuguese, Crioulo
Cayman Islands	100	35,000	350	Dependent territory (U.K.)	C	George Town	English
† Central African Republic	240,535	3,305,000	14	Republic	A	Bangui	French, Sango, Arabic, indigenous
Ceylon see Sri Lanka							
† Chad	495,755	6,628,000	13	Republic	A	N'Djamena	Arabic, French, indigenous
Channel Islands	75	151,000	2,013	Two crown dependencies (U.K. protection)			English, French
† Chile	292,135	14,420,000	49	Republic	A	Santiago	Spanish
† China (excl. Taiwan)	3,690,045	1,222,310,000	331	Socialist republic	A	Beijing (Peking)	Chinese dialects
Christmas Island	52	3,000	58	External territory (Australia)	C	The Settlement	English, Chinese, Malay
Cocos (Keeling) Islands	5.4	600	111	Territory (Australia)	C	West Island	English, Cocos-Malay, Malay
† Colombia	440,831	37,145,000	84	Republic	A	Bogotá	Spanish
Colorado	104,100	3,817,000	37	State (U.S.)	D	Denver	English
† Comoros (excl. Mayotte)	863	688,000	797	Federal Islamic republic	A	Moroni	Arabic, French, Comoran
† Congo	132,047	2,556,000	19	Republic	A	Brazzaville	French, Lingala, Kikongo, indigenous
† Congo, Democratic Republic of the	905,446	47,010,000	52	Military	A	Kinshasa	French, Kikongo, Lingala, Swahili, Tshiluba, Kingwana
Connecticut	5,544	3,309,000	597	State (U.S.)	D	Hartford	English
Cook Islands	91	20,000	220	Self-governing territory (New Zealand protection)	B	Avarua	English, Maori
† Costa Rica	19,730	3,501,000	177	Republic	A	San José	Spanish
† Cote d'Ivoire	124,518	15,015,000	121	Republic	A	Abidjan and Yamoussoukro (⁴)	French, Dioula and other indigenous
† Croatia	21,829	4,543,000	208	Republic	A	Zagreb	Serbo-Croatian

REGION OR POLITICAL DIVISION	Area Sq. Mi.	Est. Pop. 1/1/97	Pop. Per. Sq. Mi.	Form of Government and Ruling Power	Capital	Predominant Languages
† Cuba	42,804	10,985,000	257	Socialist republic . . . . A	Havana (La Habana)	Spanish
† Cyprus	2,276	633,000	278	Republic . . . . A	Nicosia (Levkosía)	Greek, English
Cyprus, North (2)	1,295	183,000	141	Republic . . . . A	Nicosia (Lefkoşa)	Turkish
† Czech Republic	30,450	10,320,000	339	Republic . . . . A	Prague (Praha)	Czech, Slovak
Delaware	2,489	721,000	290	State (U.S.) . . . . D	Dover	English
† Denmark	16,639	5,261,000	316	Constitutional monarchy . . . . A	Copenhagen (København)	Danish
District of Columbia	68	555,000	8,162	Federal district (U.S.) . . . . D	Washington	English
† Djibouti	8,958	431,000	48	Republic . . . . A	Djibouti	French, Arabic, Somali, Afar
† Dominica	305	71,000	233	Republic . . . . A	Roseau	English, French
† Dominican Republic	18,704	8,162,000	436	Republic . . . . A	Santo Domingo	Spanish
† Ecuador	105,037	11,535,000	110	Republic . . . . A	Quito	Spanish, Quechua, indigenous
† Egypt	386,662	64,150,000	166	Republic . . . . A	Cairo (Al Qāhirah)	Arabic
Ellice Islands see Tuvalu	. . . . .	. . . . .	. . .		. . . .	
† El Salvador	8,124	5,881,000	724	Republic . . . . A	San Salvador	Spanish, Nahua
England	50,352	48,830,000	970	Administrative division (U.K.) . . . . D	London	English
† Equatorial Guinea	10,831	437,000	40	Republic . . . . A	Malabo	Spanish, indigenous, English
† Eritrea	36,170	4,082,000	113	Republic . . . . A	Asmera	Tigre, Kunama, Cushitic dialects, Nora Bana, Arabic
† Estonia	17,413	1,450,000	83	Republic . . . . A	Tallinn	Estonian, Latvian, Lithuanian, Russian
† Ethiopia	446,953	57,970,000	130	Republic . . . . A	Addis Ababa	Amharic, Tigrinya, Orominga, Guaraginga, Somali, Arabic
Europe	3,800,000	711,200,000	187			
Falkland Islands (3)	4,700	2,200	0.5	Dependent territory (U.K.) C	Stanley	English
Faroe Islands	540	44,000	81	Self-governing territory (Danish protection) B	Tórshavn	Danish, Faroese
Fiji	7,056	788,000	112	Republic . . . . A	Suva	English, Fijian, Hindustani
† Finland	130,559	5,110,000	39	Republic . . . . A	Helsinki (Helsingfors)	Finnish, Swedish, Lapp, Russian
Florida	65,758	14,445,000	220	State (U.S.) . . . . D	Tallahassee	English
† France (excl. Overseas Departments)	211,208	58,160,000	275	Republic . . . . A	Paris	French
French Guiana	32,253	154,000	4.8	Overseas department (France) C	Cayenne	French
French Polynesia	1,359	227,000	167	Overseas territory (France) C	Papeete	French, Tahitian
Fujian	46,332	32,345,000	698	Province (China) . . . . D	Fuzhou	Chinese dialects
† Gabon	103,347	1,349,000	13	Republic . . . . A	Libreville	French, Fang, indigenous
† Gambia, The	4,127	1,178,000	285	Provisional military government . . . . A	Banjul	English, Malinke, Wolof, Fula, indigenous
Gansu	173,746	24,080,000	139	Province (China) . . . . D	Lanzhou	Chinese (Mandarin), Mongolian, Tibetan dialects
Gaza Strip	139	956,000	6,878	Israeli occupied territory with limited self-government	. . . .	Arabic
† Georgia	59,441	7,319,000	123	State (U.S.) . . . . D	Atlanta	English
† Georgia	26,911	5,189,000	193	Republic . . . . A	Tbilisi	Georgian, Russian, Armenian, Azeri
† Germany	137,822	83,870,000	609	Federal republic . . . . A	Berlin and Bonn	German
† Ghana	92,098	17,895,000	194	Republic . . . . A	Accra	English, Akan and other indigenous
Gibraltar	2.3	29,000	12,609	Dependent territory (U.K.) C	Gibraltar	English, Spanish, Italian, Portuguese, Russian
Gilbert Islands see Kiribati	. . . . .	. . . . .	. . .		. . . .	
Golan Heights	454	31,000	68	Occupied by Israel	. . . .	Arabic, Hebrew
Great Britain see United Kingdom	. .					
† Greece	50,949	10,560,000	207	Republic . . . . A	Athens (Athínai)	Greek, English, French
Greenland	840,004	58,000	0.1	Self-governing territory (Danish protection) B	Godthåb (Nuuk)	Danish, Greenlandic, Inuit dialects
† Grenada	133	95,000	714	Parliamentary state . . . . A	St. George's	English, French
Guadeloupe (incl. Dependencies)	657	410,000	624	Overseas department (France) C	Basse-Terre	French, Creole
Guam	209	159,000	761	Unincorporated territory (U.S.) C	Agana	English, Chamorro, Japanese
Guangdong	68,726	67,740,000	986	Province (China) . . . . D	Guangzhou (Canton)	Chinese dialects, Miao-Yao
Guangxi Zhuangzu	91,236	45,480,000	498	Autonomous region (China) . . . . D	Nanning	Chinese dialects, Thai, Miao-Yao
† Guatemala	42,042	11,425,000	272	Republic . . . . A	Guatemala	Spanish, Amerindian
Guernsey (incl. Dependencies)	30	63,000	2,100	Crown dependency (U.K. protection) . . . . B	St. Peter Port	English, French
† Guinea	94,926	7,523,000	79	Republic . . . . A	Conakry	French, indigenous
† Guinea-Bissau	13,948	1,111,000	80	Republic . . . . A	Bissau	Portuguese, Crioulo, indigenous
Guizhou	65,637	35,025,000	534	Province (China) . . . . D	Guiyang	Chinese (Mandarin), Thai, Miao-Yao
† Guyana	83,000	708,000	8.5	Republic . . . . A	Georgetown	English, indigenous
Hainan	13,127	7,175,000	547	Province (China) . . . . D	Haikou	Chinese, Min, Tai
† Haiti	10,714	6,793,000	634	Republic . . . . A	Port-au-Prince	Creole, French
Hawaii	10,932	1,201,000	110	State (U.S.) . . . . D	Honolulu	English, Hawaiian, Japanese
Hebei	73,359	64,940,000	885	Province (China) . . . . D	Shijiazhuang	Chinese (Mandarin)
Heilongjiang	181,082	37,335,000	206	Province (China) . . . . D	Harbin	Chinese dialects, Mongolian, Tungus
Henan	64,479	91,810,000	1,424	Province (China) . . . . D	Zhengzhou	Chinese (Mandarin)
Holland see Netherlands	. . . . .	. . . . .	. . .		. . . .	
† Honduras	43,277	5,678,000	131	Republic . . . . A	Tegucigalpa	Spanish, indigenous
Hong Kong	414	6,250,000	15,097	Special Administrative Region (China) . . . . D	Hong Kong (Xianggang)	Chinese (Cantonese), English, Putonghua
Hubei	72,356	58,010,000	802	Province (China) . . . . D	Wuhan	Chinese dialects
Hunan	81,081	64,690,000	798	Province (China) . . . . D	Changsha	Chinese dialects, Miao-Yao
† Hungary	35,919	9,963,000	277	Republic . . . . A	Budapest	Hungarian
† Iceland	39,769	271,000	6.8	Republic . . . . A	Reykjavík	Icelandic
Idaho	83,574	1,174,000	14	State (U.S.) . . . . D	Boise	English
Illinois	57,918	11,945,000	206	State (U.S.) . . . . D	Springfield	English
† India (incl. part of Jammu and Kashmir)	1,237,062	961,690,000	777	Federal republic . . . . A	New Delhi	English, Hindi, Telugu, Bengali, indigenous
Indiana	36,420	5,872,000	161	State (U.S.) . . . . D	Indianapolis	English
† Indonesia	752,410	208,060,000	277	Republic . . . . A	Jakarta	Bahasa Indonesia (Malay), English, Dutch, indigenous
Iowa	56,276	2,856,000	51	State (U.S.) . . . . D	Des Moines	English
† Iran	630,578	66,820,000	106	Islamic republic . . . . A	Tehrān	Farsi, Turkish dialects, Kurdish
† Iraq	169,235	21,810,000	129	Republic . . . . A	Baghdād	Arabic, Kurdish, Assyrian, Armenian
† Ireland	27,137	3,576,000	132	Republic . . . . A	Dublin (Baile Átha Cliath)	English, Irish Gaelic
Isle of Man	221	73,000	330	Crown dependency (U.K. protection) . . . . B	Douglas	English, Manx Gaelic
† Israel (excl. Occupied Areas)	8,019	5,575,000	695	Republic . . . . A	Jerusalem (Yerushalayim)	Hebrew, Arabic
† Italy	116,336	57,520,000	494	Republic . . . . A	Rome (Roma)	Italian, German, French, Slovene
Ivory Coast see Cote d'Ivoire	. . . . .	. . . . .	. . .		. . . .	
† Jamaica	4,244	2,605,000	614	Parliamentary state . . . . A	Kingston	English, Creole
† Japan	145,850	125,580,000	861	Constitutional monarchy . . . . A	Tōkyō	Japanese
Jersey	45	88,000	1,956	Crown dependency (U.K. protection) . . . . B	St. Helier	English, French
Jiangsu	39,614	71,500,000	1,805	Province (China) . . . . D	Nanjing (Nanking)	Chinese dialects
Jiangxi	64,325	40,740,000	633	Province (China) . . . . D	Nanchang	Chinese dialects
Jilin	72,201	26,265,000	364	Province (China) . . . . D	Changchun	Chinese (Mandarin), Mongolian, Korean
† Jordan	35,135	5,658,000	161	Constitutional monarchy . . . . A	'Ammān	Arabic
Kansas	82,282	2,600,000	32	State (U.S.) . . . . D	Topeka	English
† Kazakstan	1,049,156	16,900,000	16	Republic . . . . A	Alma-Ata (Almaty) and Akmola (4)	Kazakh, Russian

REGION OR POLITICAL DIVISION	Area Sq. Mi.	Est. Pop. 1/1/97	Pop. Per. Sq. Mi.	Form of Government and Ruling Power	Capital	Predominant Languages
Kentucky	40,411	3,897,000	96	State (U.S.) ....D	Frankfort	English
† Kenya	224,961	28,460,000	127	Republic.............................A	Nairobi	English, Swahili, indigenous
Kiribati	313	82,000	262	Republic.............................A	Bairiki	English, Gilbertese
† Korea, North	46,540	24,550,000	528	Socialist republic...................A	Pyŏngyang	Korean
† Korea, South	38,230	45,710,000	1,196	Republic.............................A	Seoul (Sŏul)	Korean
† Kuwait	6,880	2,018,000	293	Constitutional monarchy ....A	Kuwait	Arabic, English
† Kyrgyzstan	76,641	4,512,000	59	Republic.............................A	Bishkek	Kirghiz, Russian
† Laos	91,429	5,046,000	55	Socialist republic...................A	Viangchan (Vientiane)	Lao, French, English
† Latvia	24,595	2,452,000	100	Republic.............................A	Rīga	Lettish, Lithuanian, Russian, other
† Lebanon	4,015	3,818,000	951	Republic.............................A	Beirut (Bayrūt)	Arabic, French, Armenian, English
† Lesotho	11,720	1,989,000	170	Constitutional monarchy under military rule A	Maseru	English, Sesotho, Zulu, Xhosa
Liaoning	56,255	41,470,000	737	Province (China).....................D	Shenyang	Chinese (Mandarin), Mongolian
† Liberia	38,250	2,074,000	54	Republic.............................A	Monrovia	English, indigenous
† Libya	679,362	5,543,000	8.2	Socialist republic...................A	Tripoli (Ṭarābulus)	Arabic
† Liechtenstein	62	31,000	500	Constitutional monarchy ....A	Vaduz	German
† Lithuania	25,212	3,639,000	144	Republic.............................A	Vilnius	Lithuanian, Polish, Russian
Louisiana	51,843	4,377,000	84	State (U.S.) ....D	Baton Rouge	English
† Luxembourg	998	419,000	420	Constitutional monarchy ....A	Luxembourg	French, Luxembourgish, German
Macau	6.6	426,000	64,545	Chinese territory under Portuguese administration C	Macau	Portuguese, Chinese (Cantonese)
† Macedonia	9,928	2,178,000	219	Republic.............................A	Skopje	Macedonian, Albanian
† Madagascar	226,658	15,390,000	68	Republic.............................A	Antananarivo	Malagasy, French
Maine	35,387	1,254,000	35	State (U.S.) ....D	Augusta	English
† Malawi	45,747	9,462,000	207	Republic.............................A	Lilongwe	Chichewa, English
† Malaysia	127,320	20,770,000	163	Federal constitutional monarchy ....A	Kuala Lumpur	Malay, Chinese dialects, English, Tamil
† Maldives	115	268,000	2,330	Republic.............................A	Male	Divehi
† Mali	482,077	9,798,000	20	Republic.............................A	Bamako	French, Bambara, indigenous
† Malta	122	378,000	3,098	Republic.............................A	Valletta	English, Maltese
Manitoba	250,947	1,159,000	4.6	Province (Canada) ....D	Winnipeg	English
† Marshall Islands	70	59,000	843	Republic (U.S. protection) ....A	Majuro (island)	English, indigenous, Japanese
Martinique	436	401,000	920	Overseas department (France) C	Fort-de-France	French, Creole
Maryland	12,407	5,124,000	413	State (U.S.) ....D	Annapolis	English
Massachusetts	10,555	6,138,000	582	State (U.S.) ....D	Boston	English
† Mauritania	397,956	2,373,000	6.0	Republic.............................A	Nouakchott	Arabic, Pular, Soninke, Wolof
† Mauritius (incl. Dependencies)	788	1,146,000	1,454	Republic.............................A	Port Louis	English, Creole, Bhojpuri, French, Hindi, Tamil, others
Mayotte (5)	144	103,000	715	Territorial collectivity (France) C	Dzaoudzi and Mamoudzou (4)	French, Swahili (Mahorian)
† Mexico	759,534	96,630,000	127	Federal republic ....A	Mexico City (Ciudad de México)	Spanish, indigenous
Michigan	96,810	9,651,000	100	State (U.S.) ....D	Lansing	English
† Micronesia, Federated States of	271	108,000	399	Republic (U.S. protection) ....A	Kolonia and Paliker (4)	English, indigenous
Midway Islands	2.0	20	10	Unincorporated territory (U.S.) C	....	English
Minnesota	86,943	4,671,000	54	State (U.S.) ....D	St. Paul	English
Mississippi	48,434	2,722,000	56	State (U.S.) ....D	Jackson	English
Missouri	69,709	5,388,000	77	State (U.S.) ....D	Jefferson City	English
† Moldova	13,012	4,486,000	345	Republic.............................A	Chişinău (Kishinev)	Romanian (Moldovan), Russian
† Monaco	0.7	32,000	45,714	Constitutional monarchy ....A	Monaco	French, English, Italian, Monegasque
† Mongolia	604,829	2,519,000	4.2	Republic.............................A	Ulan Bator (Ulaanbaatar)	Khalkha Mongol, Turkish dialects, Russian, Chinese
Montana	147,046	881,000	6.0	State (U.S.) ....D	Helena	English
Montserrat	39	13,000	333	Dependent territory (U.K.) C	Plymouth	English
† Morocco (excl. Western Sahara)	172,414	27,955,000	162	Constitutional monarchy ....A	Rabat	Arabic, Berber dialects, French
† Mozambique	308,642	18,270,000	59	Republic.............................A	Maputo	Portuguese, indigenous
† Myanmar (Burma)	261,228	46,400,000	178	Provisional military government ....A	Rangoon (Yangon)	Burmese, indigenous
† Namibia	317,818	1,608,000	5.1	Republic.............................A	Windhoek	English, Afrikaans, German, indigenous
Nauru	8.1	10,000	1,235	Republic.............................A	Yaren District	Nauruan, English
Nebraska	77,358	1,655,000	21	State (U.S.) ....D	Lincoln	English
Nei Monggol (Inner Mongolia)	456,759	22,860,000	50	Autonomous region (China)...........D	Hohhot	Mongolian
† Nepal	56,827	22,720,000	400	Constitutional monarchy ....A	Kathmandu	Nepali, Maithali, Bhojpuri, other indigenous
† Netherlands	16,164	15,615,000	966	Constitutional monarchy ....A	Amsterdam and The Hague ('s-Gravenhage)	Dutch
Netherlands Antilles	309	210,000	680	Self-governing territory (Netherlands protection) ....B	Willemstad	Dutch, Papiamento, English
Nevada	110,567	1,628,000	15	State (U.S.) ....D	Carson City	English
New Brunswick	28,355	782,000	28	Province (Canada) ....D	Fredericton	English, French
New Caledonia	7,172	190,000	26	Overseas territory (France) C	Nouméa	French, indigenous
Newfoundland	156,649	608,000	3.9	Province (Canada) ....D	St. John's	English
New Hampshire	9,351	1,174,000	126	State (U.S.) ....D	Concord	English
New Hebrides see Vanuatu	....	....	....	....	....	....
New Jersey	8,722	8,007,000	918	State (U.S.) ....D	Trenton	English
New Mexico	121,598	1,708,000	14	State (U.S.) ....D	Santa Fe	English, Spanish
New South Wales	309,500	6,216,000	20	State (Australia) ....D	Sydney	English
New York	54,475	18,280,000	336	State (U.S.) ....D	Albany	English
† New Zealand	104,454	3,603,000	34	Parliamentary state ....A	Wellington	English, Maori
† Nicaragua	50,054	4,328,000	86	Republic.............................A	Managua	Spanish, English, indigenous
† Niger	489,191	9,250,000	19	Provisional military government ....A	Niamey	French, Hausa, Djerma, indigenous
† Nigeria	356,669	105,470,000	296	Provisional military government ....A	Lagos and Abuja	English, Hausa, Fulani, Yoruba, Ibo, indigenous
Ningxia Huizu	25,637	5,107,000	199	Autonomous region (China)...........D	Yinchuan	Chinese (Mandarin)
Niue	100	2,300	23	Self-governing territory (New Zealand protection) ....B	Alofi	English, indigenous
Norfolk Island	14	3,000	214	External territory (Australia) C	Kingston	English, Norfolk
North America	9,500,000	462,100,000	49	....	....	....
North Carolina	53,821	7,313,000	136	State (U.S.) ....D	Raleigh	English
North Dakota	70,704	641,000	9.1	State (U.S.) ....D	Bismarck	English
Northern Ireland	5,461	1,640,000	300	Administrative division (U.K.) ....D	Belfast	English
Northern Mariana Islands	184	53,000	288	Commonwealth (U.S. protection) ....B	Saipan (island)	English, Chamorro, Carolinian
Northern Territory	519,771	184,000	0.4	Territory (Australia) ....D	Darwin	English, indigenous
Northwest Territories	1,322,910	58,000	.04	Territory (Canada) ....D	Yellowknife	English, indigenous
† Norway (incl. Svalbard and Jan Mayen)	149,405	4,397,000	29	Constitutional monarchy ....A	Oslo	Norwegian, Lapp, Finnish
Nova Scotia	21,425	956,000	45	Province (Canada) ....D	Halifax	English
Oceania (incl. Australia)	3,300,000	29,100,000	8.8	....	....	....
Ohio	44,828	11,260,000	251	State (U.S.) ....D	Columbus	English
Oklahoma	69,903	3,309,000	47	State (U.S.) ....D	Oklahoma City	English
† Oman	82,030	2,278,000	28	Monarchy ....A	Muscat	Arabic, English, Baluchi, Urdu, Indian dialects
Ontario	412,581	10,665,000	26	Province (Canada) ....D	Toronto	English

REGION OR POLITICAL DIVISION	Area Sq. Mi.	Est. Pop. 1/1/97	Pop. Per. Sq. Mi.	Form of Government and Ruling Power	Capital	Predominant Languages
Oregon	98,386	3,203,000	33	State (U.S.) .....D	Salem	English
† Pakistan (incl. part of Jammu and Kashmir)	339,732	130,700,000	385	Federal Islamic republic .....A	Islāmābād	English, Urdu, Punjabi, Sindhi, Pashto
† Palau (Belau)	196	17,000	87	Republic .....A	Koror and Melekeok (4)	Angaur, English, Japanese, Palauan, Sonsorolese, Tobi
† Panama	29,157	2,679,000	92	Republic .....A	Panamá	Spanish, English
† Papua New Guinea	178,704	4,443,000	25	Parliamentary state .....A	Port Moresby	English, Motu, Pidgin, indigenous
† Paraguay	157,048	5,023,000	32	Republic .....A	Asunción	Spanish, Guarani
Pennsylvania	46,058	12,275,000	267	State (U.S.) .....D	Harrisburg	English
† Peru	496,225	23,565,000	47	Republic .....A	Lima	Quechua, Spanish, Aymara
† Philippines	115,831	75,300,000	650	Republic .....A	Manila	English, Pilipino, Tagalog
Pitcairn (incl. Dependencies)	19	100	5.3	Dependent territory (U.K.) C	Adamstown	English, Tahitian
† Poland	121,196	38,915,000	321	Republic .....A	Warsaw (Warszawa)	Polish
† Portugal	35,516	10,800,000	304	Republic .....A	Lisbon (Lisboa)	Portuguese
Prince Edward Island	2,185	145,000	66	Province (Canada) .....D	Charlottetown	English
Puerto Rico	3,515	3,523,000	1,002	Commonwealth (U.S. protection) .....B	San Juan	Spanish, English
† Qatar	4,412	555,000	126	Monarchy .....A	Doha	Arabic, English
Qinghai	277,994	4,743,000	17	Province (China) .....D	Xining	Tibetan dialects, Mongolian, Turkish dialects, Chinese (Mandarin)
Quebec	594,860	7,330,000	12	Province (Canada) .....D	Québec	French, English
Queensland	666,876	3,335,000	5.0	State (Australia) .....D	Brisbane	English
Reunion	967	686,000	709	Overseas department (France) C	Saint-Denis	French, Creole
Rhode Island	1,545	987,000	639	State (U.S.) .....D	Providence	English
Rhodesia see Zimbabwe						
† Romania	91,699	22,260,000	243	Republic .....A	Bucharest (Bucureşti)	Romanian, Hungarian, German
† Russia	6,592,849	150,500,000	23	Federal republic .....A	Moscow (Moskva)	Russian, Tatar, Ukrainian
† Rwanda	10,169	9,504,000	935	Republic .....A	Kigali	French, Kinyarwanda, Kiswahili
St. Helena (incl. Dependencies)	121	7,000	58	Dependent territory (U.K.) C	Jamestown	English
† St. Kitts and Nevis	104	43,000	413	Parliamentary state .....A	Basseterre	English
† St. Lucia	238	148,000	622	Parliamentary state .....A	Castries	English, French
St. Pierre and Miquelon	93	7,000	75	Territorial collectivity (France) C	Saint-Pierre	French
† St. Vincent and the Grenadines	150	112,000	747	Parliamentary state .....A	Kingstown	English, French
† San Marino	24	25,000	1,042	Republic .....A	San Marino	Italian
† Sao Tome and Principe	372	132,000	355	Republic .....A	São Tomé	Portuguese, Fang
Saskatchewan	251,866	1,043,000	4.1	Province (Canada) .....D	Regina	English
† Saudi Arabia	830,000	18,835,000	23	Monarchy .....A	Riyadh (Ar Riyāḍ)	Arabic
Scotland	30,421	5,152,000	169	Administrative division (U.K.) .....D	Edinburgh	English, Scots Gaelic
† Senegal	75,951	9,111,000	120	Republic .....A	Dakar	French, Wolof, Fulani, Serer, indigenous
† Seychelles	175	78,000	446	Republic .....A	Victoria	English, French, Creole
Shaanxi	79,151	35,385,000	447	Province (China) .....D	Xi'an (Sian)	Chinese (Mandarin)
Shandong	59,074	88,650,000	1,501	Province (China) .....D	Jinan	Chinese (Mandarin)
Shanghai	2,394	13,865,000	5,792	Autonomous city (China) .....D	Shanghai	Chinese (Wu)
Shanxi	60,232	30,890,000	513	Province (China) .....D	Taiyuan	Chinese (Mandarin)
Sichuan	220,078	113,950,000	518	Province (China) .....D	Chengdu	Chinese (Mandarin), Tibetan dialects, Miao-Yao
† Sierra Leone	27,925	4,884,000	175	Provisional military government .....A	Freetown	English, Krio, Mende, Temne, indigenous
† Singapore	246	3,428,000	13,935	Republic .....A	Singapore	Chinese (Mandarin), English, Malay, Tamil
† Slovakia	18,933	5,385,000	284	Republic .....A	Bratislava	Slovak, Hungarian
† Slovenia	7,820	1,947,000	249	Republic .....A	Ljubljana	Slovenian, Serbo-Croatian
† Solomon Islands	10,954	420,000	38	Parliamentary state .....A	Honiara	English, indigenous
† Somalia	246,201	9,880,000	40	None .....A	Mogadishu (Muqdisho)	Arabic, Somali, English, Italian
† South Africa	471,010	42,120,000	89	Republic .....A	Pretoria, Cape Town, and Bloemfontein	Afrikaans, English, Sotho, Tswana, Zulu, others
South America	6,900,000	324,600,000	47			
South Australia	379,925	1,505,000	4.0	State (Australia) .....D	Adelaide	English
South Carolina	32,007	3,710,000	116	State (U.S.) .....D	Columbia	English
South Dakota	77,121	747,000	9.7	State (U.S.) .....D	Pierre	English
South Georgia (incl. Dependencies)	1,450	(1)	.....	Dependent territory (U.K.) C		English
South West Africa see Namibia						
† Spain	194,885	39,220,000	201	Constitutional monarchy .....A	Madrid	Spanish (Castilian), Catalan, Galician, Basque
Spanish North Africa (6)	12	146,000	12,167	Five possessions (Spain) C		Spanish, Arabic, Berber dialects
Spanish Sahara see Western Sahara						
† Sri Lanka	24,962	18,645,000	747	Socialist republic .....A	Colombo and Sri Jayawardenapura	English, Sinhala, Tamil
† Sudan	967,500	29,135,000	30	Provisional military government .....A	Khartoum (Al Kharṭūm)	Arabic, Nubian and other indigenous, English
† Suriname	63,251	439,000	6.9	Republic .....A	Paramaribo	Dutch, Sranan Tongo, English, Hindustani, Javanese
† Swaziland	6,704	1,015,000	151	Monarchy .....A	Mbabane and Lobamba	English, siSwati
† Sweden	173,732	8,928,000	51	Constitutional monarchy .....A	Stockholm	Swedish, Lapp, Finnish
Switzerland	15,943	7,185,000	451	Federal republic .....A	Bern (Berne)	German, French, Italian, Romansch
† Syria	71,498	15,875,000	222	Socialist republic .....A	Damascus (Dimashq)	Arabic, Kurdish, Armenian, Aramaic, Circassian
Taiwan	13,900	21,550,000	1,550	Republic .....A	T'aipei	Chinese (Mandarin), Taiwanese (Min), Hakka
† Tajikistan	55,251	5,957,000	108	Republic .....A	Dushanbe	Tajik, Uzbek, Russian
† Tanzania	364,900	29,320,000	80	Republic .....A	Dar es Salaam and Dodoma	English, Swahili, indigenous
Tasmania	26,178	477,000	18	State (Australia) .....D	Hobart	English
Tennessee	42,146	5,336,000	127	State (U.S.) .....D	Nashville	English
Texas	268,601	19,065,000	71	State (U.S.) .....D	Austin	English, Spanish
† Thailand	198,115	59,150,000	299	Constitutional monarchy .....A	Bangkok (Krung Thep)	Thai, indigenous
Tianjin (Tientsin)	4,363	9,485,000	2,174	Autonomous city (China) .....D	Tianjin (Tientsin)	Chinese (Mandarin)
† Togo	21,925	4,653,000	212	Provisional military government .....A	Lomé	French, Ewe, Mina, Kabye, Dagomba
Tokelau	4.6	1,400	304	Island territory (New Zealand) C		English, Tokelauan
Tonga	288	106,000	368	Constitutional monarchy .....A	Nuku'alofa	Tongan, English
† Trinidad and Tobago	1,980	1,273,000	643	Republic .....A	Port of Spain	English, Hindi, French, Spanish
Tristan da Cunha	40	300	7.5	Dependency (St. Helena) C	Edinburgh	English
† Tunisia	63,170	9,101,000	144	Republic .....A	Tunis	Arabic, French
† Turkey	300,948	63,050,000	210	Republic .....A	Ankara	Turkish, Kurdish, Arabic
† Turkmenistan	188,456	4,186,000	22	Republic .....A	Ashgabat	Turkmen, Russian, Uzbek
Turks and Caicos Islands	193	14,000	73	Dependent territory (U.K.) C	Grand Turk	English
Tuvalu	10	10,000	1,000	Parliamentary state .....A	Funafuti	Tuvaluan, English
† Uganda	93,104	20,485,000	220	Republic .....A	Kampala	English, Luganda, Swahili, indigenous
† Ukraine	233,090	50,760,000	218	Republic .....A	Kiev (Kyyiv)	Ukrainian, Russian, Romanian, Polish
† United Arab Emirates	32,278	3,124,000	97	Federation of monarchs .....A	Abū Ẓaby (Abu Dhabi)	Arabic, Farsi, English, Hindi, Urdu

REGION OR POLITICAL DIVISION	Area Sq. Mi.	Est. Pop. 1/1/97	Pop. Per. Sq. Mi.	Form of Government and Ruling Power	Capital	Predominant Languages
† United Kingdom	94,249	58,550,000	621	Parliamentary monarchy	A London	English, Welsh, Scots Gaelic
† United States	3,787,425	266,890,000	70	Federal republic	A Washington, D.C.	English, Spanish
Upper Volta see Burkina Faso	. . . .	. . . .	. . . .			
† Uruguay	68,500	3,252,000	47	Republic	A Montevideo	Spanish
Utah	84,904	2,002,000	24	State (U.S.)	D Salt Lake City	English
† Uzbekistan	172,742	23,630,000	137	Republic	A Tashkent	Uzbek, Russian
† Vanuatu	4,707	178,000	38	Republic	A Port-Vila	Bislama, English, French
Vatican City	0.2	1,000	5,000	Monarchical-sacerdotal state	A Vatican City	Italian, Latin, other
† Venezuela	352,145	22,180,000	63	Federal republic	A Caracas	Spanish, Amerindian
Vermont	9,615	587,000	61	State (U.S.)	D Montpelier	English
Victoria	87,877	4,564,000	52	State (Australia)	D Melbourne	English
† Vietnam	127,428	74,570,000	585	Socialist republic	A Hanoi	Vietnamese, French, Chinese, English, Khmer, indigenous
Virginia	42,769	6,697,000	157	State (U.S.)	D Richmond	English
Virgin Islands (U.S.)	133	97,000	729	Unincorporated territory (U.S.)	C Charlotte Amalie	English, Spanish, Creole
Wake Island	3.0	7	2.3	Unincorporated territory (U.S.)	C	English
Wales	8,015	2,928,000	365	Administrative division (U.K.)	D Cardiff	English, Welsh Gaelic
Wallis and Futuna	98	15,000	153	Overseas territory (France)	C Mata-Utu	French, Wallisian
Washington	71,303	5,585,000	78	State (U.S.)	D Olympia	English
West Bank (incl. Jericho and East Jerusalem)	2,263	1,466,000	648	Israeli occupied territory with limited self-government	. . . .	Arabic, Hebrew
Western Australia	975,101	1,757,000	1.8	State (Australia)	D Perth	English
Western Sahara	102,703	226,000	2.2	Occupied by Morocco	C	Arabic
† Western Samoa	1,093	217,000	199	Constitutional monarchy	A Apia	English, Samoan
West Virginia	24,231	1,842,000	76	State (U.S.)	D Charleston	English
Wisconsin	65,503	5,178,000	79	State (U.S.)	D Madison	English
Wyoming	97,818	480,000	4.9	State (U.S.)	D Cheyenne	English
Xinjiang Uygur (Sinkiang)	617,764	16,415,000	27	Autonomous region (China)	D Ürümqi	Turkish dialects, Mongolian, Tungus, English
Xizang (Tibet)	471,045	2,432,000	5.2	Autonomous region (China)	D Lhasa	Tibetan dialects
† Yemen	203,850	15,275,000	75	Republic	A Şan'ā'	Arabic
† Yugoslavia	39,449	10,635,000	270	Republic	A Belgrade (Beograd)	Serbo-Croatian, Albanian
Yukon Territory	186,661	29,000	0.2	Territory (Canada)	D Whitehorse	English, Inuktitut, indigenous
Yunnan	152,124	39,885,000	262	Province (China)	D Kunming	Chinese (Mandarin), Tibetan dialects, Khmer, Miao-Yao
† Zambia	290,586	9,260,000	32	Republic	A Lusaka	English, Tonga, Lozi, other indigenous
Zhejiang	39,305	43,780,000	1,114	Province (China)	D Hangzhou	Chinese dialects
† Zimbabwe	150,873	11,695,000	78	Republic	A Harare (Salisbury)	English, Shona, Sindebele
WORLD	57,900,000	5,817,000,000	100	. . . .	. . . .	. . . .

† Member of the United Nations (1997).
. . . None, or not applicable.
(1) No permanent population.
(2) North Cyprus unilaterally declared its independence from Cyprus in 1983.
(3) Claimed by Argentina.
(4) Future capital.
(5) Claimed by Comoros.
(6) Comprises Ceuta, Melilla, and several small islands.

WORLD COMPARISONS

General Information

Equatorial diameter of the earth, 7,926.38 miles.
Polar diameter of the earth, 7,899.80 miles.
Mean diameter of the earth, 7,917.52 miles.
Equatorial circumference of the earth, 24,901.46 miles.
Polar circumference of the earth, 24,855.34 miles.
Mean distance from the earth to the sun, 93,020,000 miles.
Mean distance from the earth to the moon, 238,857 miles.
Total area of the earth, 197,000,000 square miles.

Highest elevation on the earth's surface, Mt. Everest, Asia, 29,028 feet.
Lowest elevation on the earth's land surface, shores of the Dead Sea, Asia, 1,312 feet below sea level.
Greatest known depth of the ocean, southwest of Guam, Pacific Ocean, 35,810 feet.
Total land area of the earth (incl. inland water and Antarctica), 57,900,000 square miles.

Area of Africa, 11,700,000 square miles.
Area of Antarctica, 5,400,000 square miles.
Area of Asia, 17,300,000 square miles.
Area of Europe, 3,800,000 square miles.
Area of North America, 9,500,000 square miles.
Area of Oceania (incl. Australia) 3,300,000 square miles.
Area of South America, 6,900,000 square miles.
Population of the earth (est. 1/1/97), 5,817,000,000.

Principal Islands and Their Areas

ISLAND	Area (Sq. Mi.)
Baffin I., Canada	195,928
Banks I., Canada	27,038
Borneo (Kalimantan), Asia	287,300
Bougainville, Papua New Guinea	3,600
Cape Breton I., Canada	3,981
Celebes (Sulawesi), Indonesia	73,057
Ceram (Seram), Indonesia	7,191
Corsica, France	3,367
Crete, Greece	3,190
Cuba, N. America	42,804
Cyprus, Asia	3,572
Devon I., Canada	21,331
Ellesmere I., Canada	75,767
Flores, Indonesia	5,502
Great Britain, U.K.	88,816
Greenland, N. America	840,004
Guadalcanal, Solomon Is.	2,060
Hainan Dao, China	13,200
Hawaii, U.S.	4,021
Hispaniola, N. America	29,300
Hokkaidō, Japan	32,245
Honshū, Japan	89,176
Iceland, Europe	39,769
Ireland, Europe	32,600
Jamaica, N. America	4,244
Java (Jawa), Indonesia	51,038
Kodiak I., U.S.	3,670
Kyūshū, Japan	17,129
Leyte, Philippines	2,785
Long Island, U.S.	1,401
Luzon, Philippines	40,420
Madagascar, Africa	226,658
Melville I., Canada	16,274
Mindanao, Philippines	36,537
Mindoro, Philippines	3,759
Negros, Philippines	4,907
New Britain, Papua New Guinea	14,093
New Caledonia, Oceania	6,467
Newfoundland, Canada	42,031
New Guinea, Asia-Oceania	309,000
New Ireland, Papua New Guinea	3,500
North East Land, Norway	6,350
North I., New Zealand	44,702
Novaya Zemlya, Russia	31,892
Palawan, Philippines	4,550
Panay, Philippines	4,446
Prince of Wales I., Canada	12,872
Puerto Rico, N. America	3,500
Sakhalin, Russia	29,498
Samar, Philippines	5,100
Sardinia, Italy	9,301
Shikoku, Japan	7,258
Sicily, Italy	9,927
Somerset I., Canada	9,570
Southampton I., Canada	15,913
South I., New Zealand	58,384
Spitsbergen, Norway	15,260
Sri Lanka, Asia	24,962
Sumatra (Sumatera), Indonesia	182,860
Taiwan, Asia	13,900
Tasmania, Australia	26,200
Tierra del Fuego, S. America	18,600
Timor, Indonesia	5,743
Vancouver I., Canada	12,079
Victoria I., Canada	83,897
Vrangelya (Wrangel), Russia	2,819

Principal Lakes, Oceans, Seas, and Their Areas

LAKE Country	Area (Sq. Mi.)
Arabian Sea	1,492,000
Aral Sea, Kazakstan-Uzbekistan	14,900
Arctic Ocean	5,400,000
Athabasca, L., Canada	3,064
Atlantic Ocean	31,800,000
Balqash kölī, (L. Balkhash) Kazakstan	7,066
Baltic Sea, Europe	163,000
Baykal, Ozero, (L. Baikal) Russia	12,162
Bering Sea, Asia-N.A.	876,000
Black Sea, Europe-Asia	178,000
Caribbean Sea, N.A.-S.A.	1,063,000
Caspian Sea, Asia-Europe	143,244
Chad, L., Cameroon-Chad-Nigeria	6,300
Erie, L., Canada-U.S.	9,910
Eyre, L., Australia	3,700
Gairdner, L., Australia	1,660
Great Bear Lake, Canada	12,096
Great Salt Lake, U.S.	1,680
Great Slave Lake, Canada	11,030
Hudson Bay, Canada	475,000
Huron, L., Canada-U.S.	23,000
Indian Ocean	28,900,000
Japan, Sea of, Asia	389,000
Koko Nor, (Qinghai Hu) China	1,770
Ladozhskoye Ozero, (L. Ladoga) Russia	6,834
Manitoba, L., Canada	1,785
Mediterranean Sea, Europe-Africa-Asia	967,000
Mexico, Gulf of, N. America	596,000
Michigan, L., U.S.	22,300
Nicaragua, Lago de, Nicaragua	3,150
North Sea, Europe	222,000
Nyasa, L., Malawi-Mozambique-Tanzania	11,150
Onezhskoye Ozero, (L. Onega) Russia	3,753
Ontario, L., Canada-U.S.	7,540
Pacific Ocean	63,800,000
Red Sea, Africa-Asia	169,000
Rudolf, L., Ethiopia-Kenya	2,473
Superior, L., Canada-U.S.	31,700
Tanganyika. L., Africa	12,350
Titicaca, Lago, Bolivia-Peru	3,200
Torrens, L., Australia	2,280
Vänern, (L.) Sweden	2,156
Van Gölü, (L.) Turkey	1,434
Victoria, L., Kenya-Tanzania-Uganda	26,820
Winnipeg, L., Canada	9,41
Winnipegosis, L., Canada	2,075
Yellow Sea, China-Korea	480,00

Principal Mountains and Their Heights

MOUNTAIN Country	Elev. (Ft.)
Aconcagua, Cerro, Argentina	22,831
Annapurna, Nepal	26,504
Api, Nepal	23,399
Apo, Philippines	9,692
Ararat, Mt., Turkey	16,854
Ayers Rock, Australia	2,844
Barú, Volcán, Panama	11,491
Bangueta, Mt., Papua New Guinea	13,520
Belukha, Gora, Kazakstan-Russia	14,783
Bia, Phu, Laos	9,249
Blanc, Mont, (Monte Bianco) France-Italy	15,771
Blanca Pk., Colorado, U.S.	14,345
Bolívar, Venezuela	16,427
Bonete, Cerro, Argentina	22,546
Borah Pk., Idaho, U.S.	12,662
Boundary Pk., Nevada, U.S.	13,140
Cameroon Mtn., Cameroon	13,451
Carrauntoohil, Ireland	3,406
Chaltel, Cerro, (Monte Fitzroy) Argentina-Chile	10,958
Chimborazo, Ecuador	20,702
Chirripó, Cerro, Costa Rica	12,530
Colima, Nevado de, Mexico	13,911
Cook, Mt., New Zealand	12,316
Cotopaxi, Ecuador	19,347
Cristóbal Colón, Pico, Colombia	19,029
Damāvand, Qolleh-ye, Iran	18,386
Dhawalāgiri, Nepal	26,810
Duarte, Pico, Dominican Rep.	10,417
Dufourspitze, (Monte Rosa) Italy-Switzerland	15,203
Elbert, Mt., Colorado, U.S.	14,433
El'brus, Gora, Russia	18,510
Elgon, Mt., Kenya-Uganda	14,178
Erciyeş Daği, Turkey	12,848
Etna, Mt., Italy	10,902
Everest, Mt., China-Nepal	29,028
Fairweather, Mt., Alaska-Canada	15,300
Foraker, Mt., Alaska, U.S.	17,400
Fuji-san, Japan	12,388
Fūlādī, Kūh-e, Afghanistan	16,872
Galdhøpiggen, Norway	8,100
Gannett Pk., Wyoming, U.S.	13,785
Gasherbrum, China-Pakistan	26,470
Gerlachovský štít, Slovakia	8,710
Giluwe, Mt., Papua New Guinea	14,331
Gongga Shan, China	24,790
Grand Teton Mtn., Wyoming, U.S.	13,770
Grossglockner, Austria	12,461
Hadūr Shu'ayb, Yemen	12,336
Haleakala Crater, Hawaii, U.S.	10,023
Hekla, Iceland	4,892
Hood, Mt., Oregon, U.S.	11,239
Hsinkao Shan, Taiwan	13,113
Huascarán, Nevado, Peru	22,205
Huila, Nevado de, Colombia	18,865
Hvannadalshnúkur, Iceland	6,952
Illampu, Nevado, Bolivia	21,066
Illimani, Nevado, Bolivia	20,741
Iztaccíhuatl, Mexico	17,930
Jaya, Puncak, Indonesia	16,503
Jungfrau, Switzerland	13,642
K2, (Godwin Austen) China-Pakistan	28,250
Kāmet, China-India	25,447
Kānchenjunga, India- Nepal	28,208
Kātrīnā, Jabal, Egypt	8,668
Kebnekaise, Sweden	6,962
Kenya, Mt., (Kirinyaga) Kenya	17,058
Kerinci, Gunung, Indonesia	12,467
Kilimanjaro, Tanzania	19,340
Kinabalu, Gunong, Malaysia	13,455
Klyuchevskaya, Russia	15,584
Kommunizma, Pik, Tajikistan	24,590
Kosciusko, Mt., Australia	7,310
Koussi, Emi, Chad	11,204
Kula Kangri, Bhutan	24,784
La Selle, Massif de, Haiti	8,793
Lassen Pk., California, U.S.	10,457
Llullaillaco, Volcán, Argentina-Chile	22,110
Logan, Mt., Canada	19,551
Longs Pk., Colorado, U.S.	14,255
Makālu, China-Nepal	27,825
Margherita Peak, Congo, D.R.C.-Uganda	16,763
Markham, Mt., Antarctica	14,049
Maromokotro, Madagascar	9,436
Massive, Mt., Colorado, U.S.	14,421
Matterhorn, Italy-Switzerland	14,692
Mauna Kea, Hawaii, U.S.	13,796
Mauna Loa, Hawaii, U.S.	13,679
Mayon Volcano, Philippines	7,943
McKinley, Mt., Alaska, U.S.	20,320
Meron, Hare, Israel	3,693
Meru, Mt., Tanzania	14,978
Misti, Volcán, Peru	19,101
Mitchell, Mt., North Carolina, U.S.	6,684
Môco, Serra do, Angola	8,596
Moldoveanu, Romania	8,343
Mulhacén, Spain (continental)	11,424
Musala, Bulgaria	9,596
Muztag, China	25,338
Muztagata, China	24,757
Namjagbarwa Feng, China	25,446
Nanda Devi, India	25,645
Nānga Parbat, Pakistan	26,650
Narodnaya, Gora, Russia	6,217
Nevis, Ben, United Kingdom	4,406
Ojos del Salado, Nevado, Argentina-Chile	22,615
Ólimbos, Cyprus	6,401
Ólimbos, Greece	9,570
Olympus, Mt., Washington, U.S.	7,965
Orizaba, Pico de, Mexico	18,406
Paektu San, North Korea-China	9,003
Paricutín, Mexico	9,186
Parnassós, Greece	8,061
Pelée, Montagne, Martinique	4,800
Pidurutalagala, Sri Lanka	8,281
Pikes Pk., Colorado, U.S.	14,110
Pobedy, pik, China-Kyrgyzstan	24,406
Popocatépetl, Volcán, Mexico	17,930
Pulog, Mt., Philippines	9,606
Rainier, Mt., Washington, U.S.	14,410
Ramm, Jabal, Jordan	5,755
Ras Dashen Terara, Ethiopia	15,158
Rinjani, Gunung, Indonesia	12,224
Robson, Mt., Canada	12,972
Roraima, Mt., Brazil-Guyana-Venezuela	9,452
Ruapehu, Mt., New Zealand	9,177
St. Elias, Mt., Alaska, U.S.-Canada	18,008
Sajama, Nevado, Bolivia	21,39
Semeru, Gunung, Indonesia	12,06
Shām, Jabal ash, Oman	9,95
Shasta, Mt., California, U.S.	14,16
Snowdon, Wales, U.K.	3,56
Tahat, Algeria	9,54
Tajumulco (Vol.), Guatemala	13,84
Taranaki, Mt., New Zealand	8,26
Tirich Mīr, Pakistan	25,23
Tomanivi (Victoria), (Victoria) Fiji	4,34
Toubkal, Jebel, Morocco	13,66
Triglav, Slovenia	9,39
Trikora, Puncak, Indonesia	15,58
Tupungato, Cerro, Argentina-Chile	21,55
Turquino, Pico, Cuba	6,47
Uncompahgre Pk., Colorado, U.S.	14,30
Vesuvio, (Vesuvius) Italy	4,19
Victoria, Mt., Papua New Guinea	13,23
Vinson Massif, Antarctica	16,06
Waddington, Mt., Canada	13,16
Washington, Mt., New Hampshire, U.S.	6,28
Whitney, Mt., California, U.S.	14,49
Wilhelm, Mt., Papua New Guinea	14,79
Wrangell, Mt., Alaska, U.S.	14,16
Xixabangma Feng (Gosainthan), (Gosainthan) China	26,28
Zugspitze, Austria-Germany	9,72

Principal Rivers and Their Lengths

RIVER Continent	Length (Mi.)
Albany, N. America	610
Aldan, Asia	1,412
Amazonas-Ucayali, S. America	4,000
Amu Darya, Asia	1,578
Amur, Asia	2,744
Amur-Argun, Asia	2,761
Araguaia, S. America	1,400
Arkansas, N. America	1,459
Athabasca, N. America	765
Brahmaputra, Asia	1,770
Branco, S. America	580
Brazos, N. America	870
Canadian, N. America	906
Churchill, N. America	1,000
Colorado, N. America (U.S.-Mexico)	1,450
Columbia, N. America	1,243
Congo, (Zaïre) Africa	2,880
Cumberland, N. America	720
Danube, Europe	1,776
Darling, Australia	864
Dnepr, (Dnieper) Europe	1,367
Dniester, Europe	840
Don, Europe	1,162
Elbe, Europe	724
Euphrates, Asia	1,510
Fraser, N. America	851
Ganges, Asia	1,560
Gila, N. America	630
Godāvari, Asia	930
Green, N. America	730
Huang, (Yellow) Asia	3,395
Indus, Asia	1,800
Irrawaddy, Asia	1,300
Juruá, S. America	1,250
Kama, Europe	1,122
Kasai, Africa	1,338
Kolyma, Asia	1,323
Lena, Asia	2,734
Limpopo, Africa	1,100
Loire, Europe	634
Mackenzie, N. America	2,635
Madeira, S. America	2,013
Magdalena, S. America	950
Marañón, S. America	1,000
Mekong, Asia	2,600
Meuse, Europe	590
Mississippi, N. America	2,348
Mississippi-Missouri, N. America	3,740
Missouri, N. America	2,315
Murray, Australia	1,566
Negro, S. America	1,300
Neman, Europe	582
Niger, Africa	2,600
Nile, Africa	4,145
North Platte, N. America	618
Ob'-Irtysh, Asia	3,362
Oder, Europe	567
Ohio, N. America	981
Oka, Europe	900
Orange, Africa	1,398
Orinoco, S. America	1,600
Ottawa, N. America	790
Paraguay, S. America	1,610
Paraná, S. America	2,800
Parnaíba, S. America	850
Peace, N. America	1,195
Pechora, Europe	1,124
Pecos, N. America	735
Pilcomayo, S. America	1,550
Plata-Paraná, S. America	3,030
Purús, S. America	1,860
Red, N. America	1,270
Rhine, Europe	820
Rhône, Europe	505
Rio Grande, N. America	1,885
Roosevelt, S. America	950
St. Lawrence, N. America	800
Salado, S. America	900
Salween, (Nu) Asia	1,750
São Francisco, S. America	1,988
Saskatchewan-Bow, N. America	1,205
Sava, Europe	584
Snake, N. America	1,038
Sungari, (Songhua) Asia	1,140
Syr Darya, Asia	1,370
Tagus, Europe	625
Tarim, Asia	1,328
Tennessee, N. America	65
Tigris, Asia	1,18
Tisa, Europe	60
Tobol, Asia	98
Tocantins, S. America	1,64
Ucayali, S. America	1,22
Ural, Asia	1,50
Uruguay, S. America	1,02
Verkhnyaya Tunguska, (Angara) Asia	1,10
Vilyuy, Asia	1,64
Volga, Europe	2,19
White, N. America (Ark.-Mo.)	72
Wisła (Vistula), Europe	65
Xiang, Asia	93
Xingu, S. America	1,2
Yangtze, (Chang) Asia	3,9
Yellowstone, N. America	67
Yenisey, Asia	2,54
Yukon, N. America	1,97
Zambezi, Africa	1,7

PRINCIPAL CITIES OF THE WORLD

Abidjan, Cote d'Ivoire	1,929,079
Accra, Ghana (1,390,000)	949,113
Addis Ababa, Ethiopia (1,990,000)	1,912,500
Adelaide, Australia (1,023,597)	14,843
Ahmadābād, India (3,312,216)	2,876,710
Aleppo (Halab), Syria (1,335,000)	1,261,000
Alexandria (Al Iskandarīyah), Egypt (3,350,000)	2,926,859
Algiers (El Djazaïr), Algeria (2,547,983)	1,507,241
Alma-Ata (Almaty), Kazakstan (1,190,000)	1,156,200
'Ammān, Jordan (1,625,000)	936,300
Amsterdam, Netherlands (1,875,000)	713,407
Ankara (Angora), Turkey (2,650,000)	2,559,471
Antananarivo, Madagascar	1,250,000
Antwerp (Antwerpen), Belgium (1,100,000)	479,748
Asmera, Eritrea	358,100
Asunción, Paraguay (700,000)	502,426
Athens (Athínai), Greece (3,096,775)	748,110
Atlanta, Georgia, U.S. (2,833,511)	394,017
Auckland, New Zealand (855,571)	315,668
Baghdād, Iraq	3,841,268
Baku (Bakı), Azerbaijan (2,020,000)	1,080,500
Baltimore, Maryland, U.S. (2,382,172)	736,014
Bamako, Mali	658,275
Bandung, Indonesia (2,220,000)	2,058,122
Bangalore, India (4,130,288)	2,660,088
Bangkok (Krung Thep), Thailand (7,060,000)	5,620,591
Barcelona, Spain (4,040,000)	1,714,355
Beijing (Peking), China (7,320,000)	6,710,000
Beirut, Lebanon (1,675,000)	509,000
Belém, Brazil (1,355,000)	765,476
Belfast, N. Ireland, U.K. (685,000)	295,100
Belgrade (Beograd), Yugoslavia (1,554,826)	1,136,786
Belo Horizonte, Brazil (3,340,000)	1,529,566
Berlin, Germany (4,150,000)	3,433,695
Birmingham, England, U.K. (2,675,000)	1,013,995
Bishkek, Kyrgyzstan	631,300
Bogotá, Colombia (4,260,000)	3,982,941
Bonn, Germany (575,000)	292,234
Boston, Massachusetts, U.S. (4,171,643)	574,283
Brasília, Brazil	1,513,470
Bratislava, Slovakia	441,453
Brazzaville, Congo	693,712
Bremen, Germany (790,000)	551,219
Brisbane, Australia (1,334,017)	751,115
Brussels (Bruxelles), Belgium (2,385,000)	136,920
Bucharest (București), Romania (2,300,000)	2,064,474
Budapest, Hungary (2,515,000)	2,016,774
Buenos Aires, Argentina (11,000,000)	2,960,976
Cairo (Al Qāhirah), Egypt (9,300,000)	6,068,695
Calcutta, India (11,021,918)	4,399,819
Cali, Colombia (1,400,000)	1,350,565
Canberra, Australia (303,846)	276,162
Cape Town, South Africa (1,900,000)	854,616
Caracas, Venezuela (4,000,000)	1,822,465
Casablanca, Morocco (2,475,000)	2,139,204
Changchun, China (2,000,000†)	1,822,000
Chelyabinsk, Russia (1,325,000)	1,148,300
Chengdu, China (2,960,000†)	1,884,000
Chennai (Madras), India (5,421,985)	3,841,396
Chicago, Illinois, U.S. (8,065,633)	2,783,726
Chişinău (Kishinev), Moldova	676,700
Chittagong, Bangladesh (2,342,662)	1,566,070
Chongqing (Chungking), China (2,890,000†)	2,502,000
Cincinnati, Ohio, U.S. (1,744,124)	364,040
Cleveland, Ohio, U.S. (2,759,823)	505,616
Cologne (Köln), Germany (1,810,000)	953,551
Colombo, Sri Lanka (2,050,000)	612,000
Columbus, Ohio, U.S. (1,377,419)	632,910
Conakry, Guinea	800,000
Copenhagen (København), Denmark (1,670,000)	464,566
Cordoba, Argentina (1,260,000)	1,148,305
Curitiba, Brazil (1,815,000)	841,882
Dakar, Senegal	1,490,450
Dalian (Lüda), China	2,280,000
Dallas, Texas, U.S. (3,885,415)	1,006,877
Damascus (Dimashq), Syria (2,000,000)	1,326,000
Dar es Salaam, Tanzania	1,096,000
Delhi, India (8,419,084)	7,206,704
Denver, Colorado, U.S. (1,848,319)	467,610
Detroit, Michigan, U.S. (4,665,236)	1,027,974
Dhaka (Dacca), Bangladesh (6,537,308)	3,637,892
Dnipropetrovs'k, Ukraine (1,600,000)	1,189,300
Donets'k, Ukraine (2,125,000)	1,121,300
Dresden, Germany (870,000)	490,571
Dublin (Baile Átha Cliath), Ireland (1,140,000)	502,749
Durban, South Africa (1,740,000)	715,669
Düsseldorf, Germany (1,225,000)	575,794
Edinburgh, Scotland, U.K. (630,000)	434,520
Essen, Germany (5,050,000)	626,973
Faisalabad, Pakistan	1,104,209
Florence (Firenze), Italy (640,000)	402,316
Fortaleza, Brazil (2,040,000)	743,335
Frankfurt am Main, Germany (1,935,000)	644,865
Fukuoka, Japan (1,750,000)	1,237,067
Gdańsk (Danzig), Poland (909,000)	465,100
Geneva (Génève), Switzerland (470,000)	171,042
Genoa (Genova), Italy (805,000)	675,639
Glasgow, Scotland, U.K. (1,800,000)	689,210
Goiânia, Brazil (1,130,000)	912,136
Guadalajara, Mexico (2,430,000)	1,650,042
Guangzhou (Canton), China (3,420,000†)	3,100,000
Guatemala, Guatemala (1,400,000)	1,057,210
Guayaquil, Ecuador	1,508,444
Hamburg, Germany (2,385,000)	1,652,363
Hannover, Germany (1,000,000)	513,010
Hanoi, Vietnam (1,275,000)	905,939
Harare, Zimbabwe (890,000)	681,000
Harbin, China	2,710,000
Havana (La Habana), Cuba (2,210,000)	2,119,059
Helsinki, Finland (1,040,000)	497,542
Hiroshima, Japan (1,575,000)	1,085,705
Ho Chi Minh City (Saigon), Vietnam (3,300,000)	2,796,229
Hong Kong, Hong Kong (4,770,000)	1,250,993
Honolulu, Hawaii, U.S. (836,231)	365,272
Houston, Texas, U.S. (3,711,043)	1,630,553
Hyderābād, India (4,344,437)	3,058,093
Ibadan, Nigeria	1,144,000
Indianapolis, Indiana, U.S. (1,249,822)	731,327
İstanbul, Turkey (7,550,000)	6,620,241
İzmir, Turkey (1,900,000)	1,757,414
Jakarta, Indonesia (10,200,000)	8,227,746
Jerusalem, Israel (560,000)	524,500
Jiddah, Saudi Arabia	1,300,000
Jinan, China (2,140,000†)	1,546,000
Johannesburg, South Africa (4,000,000)	712,507
Kābul, Afghanistan	1,424,400
Kampala, Uganda	773,463
Kānpur, India (2,029,889)	1,874,409
Kansas City, Missouri, U.S. (1,566,280)	435,146
Kaohsiung, Taiwan (1,900,000)	1,401,239
Karāchi, Pakistan (5,300,000)	4,901,627
Katowice, Poland (2,778,000)	366,800
Kazan', Russia (1,165,000)	1,107,300
Kharkiv, Ukraine (2,050,000)	1,622,800
Khartoum (Al Kharṭūm), Sudan (1,450,000)	473,597
Kiev (Kyïv), Ukraine (3,250,000)	2,635,000
Kingston, Jamaica (820,000)	661,600
Kinshasa, Congo, Democratic Republic of the	3,000,000
Kitakyūshū, Japan (1,525,000)	1,026,455
Kōbe, Japan (*Ōsaka)	1,477,410
Kuala Lumpur, Malaysia (1,475,000)	919,610
Kunming, China (1,550,000†)	1,310,000
Kuwait (Al Kuwayt), Kuwait (1,375,000)	44,335
Kyōto, Japan (*Ōsaka)	1,461,103
Lagos, Nigeria (3,800,000)	1,213,000
Lahore, Pakistan (3,025,000)	2,707,215
La Paz, Bolivia	1,125,600
Leeds, England, U.K. (1,540,000)	445,242
Liège, Belgium (750,000)	200,891
Lille, France (1,050,000)	172,142
Lima, Peru (4,608,010)	371,122
Lisbon (Lisboa), Portugal (2,250,000)	807,167
Liverpool, England, U.K. (1,525,000)	538,809
London, England, U.K. (11,100,000)	6,574,009
Los Angeles, California, U.S. (14,531,529)	3,485,398
Luanda, Angola	1,459,900
Lucknow, India (1,669,204)	1,619,115
Lusaka, Zambia	982,362
Lyon, France (1,335,000)	415,487
Madrid, Spain (4,650,000)	3,102,846
Managua, Nicaragua	682,000
Manaus, Brazil	1,005,634
Manchester, England, U.K. (2,775,000)	437,612
Manila, Philippines (9,650,000)	1,598,918
Mannheim, Germany (1,525,000)	310,411
Maputo, Mozambique	1,069,727
Maracaibo, Venezuela	1,249,670
Marseille, France (1,225,000)	800,550
Mashhad, Iran	1,463,508
Mecca (Makkah), Saudi Arabia	550,000
Medan, Indonesia	1,730,052
Medellín, Colombia (2,095,000)	1,468,089
Melbourne, Australia (3,022,439)	60,475
Memphis, Tennessee, U.S. (981,747)	610,337
Mexico City, Mexico (14,100,000)	8,235,744
Miami, Florida, U.S. (3,192,582)	358,548
Milan (Milano), Italy (3,750,000)	1,371,008
Milwaukee, Wisconsin, U.S. (1,607,183)	628,088
Minneapolis, Minnesota, U.S. (2,464,124)	368,383
Minsk, Belarus (1,694,000)	1,633,600
Mogadishu, Somalia	600,000
Monterrey, Mexico (2,015,000)	1,068,996
Montevideo, Uruguay (1,550,000)	1,251,647
Montréal, Canada (3,127,242)	1,017,666
Moscow (Moskva), Russia (13,150,000)	8,801,500
Mumbai (Bombay), India (12,596,243)	9,925,891
Munich (München), Germany (1,900,000)	1,229,026
Nagoya, Japan (4,800,000)	2,154,793
Nāgpur, India (1,664,006)	1,624,752
Nairobi, Kenya	1,505,000
Nanjing, China	2,390,000
Naples (Napoli), Italy (2,875,000)	1,204,601
Nashville, Tennessee, U.S. (985,026)	487,969
New Delhi, India (*Delhi)	301,297
New Kowloon, Hong Kong (*Hong Kong)	1,526,910
New Orleans, Louisiana, U.S. (1,238,816)	496,938
New York, New York, U.S. (18,087,251)	7,322,564
Nizhniy Novgorod, Russia (2,025,000)	1,445,000
Novosibirsk, Russia (1,600,000)	1,446,300
Nürnberg, Germany (1,065,000)	493,692
Odesa, Ukraine (1,185,000)	1,100,700
Oklahoma City, Oklahoma, U.S. (958,839)	444,719
Omsk, Russia (1,190,000)	1,166,800
Ōsaka, Japan (16,900,000)	2,623,801
Oslo, Norway (720,000)	452,415
Ottawa, Canada (920,857)	313,987
Panamá, Panama (770,000)	411,549
Paris, France (10,275,000)	2,152,423
Perm', Russia (1,180,000)	1,110,400
Perth, Australia (1,143,249)	80,517
Philadelphia, Pennsylvania, U.S. (5,899,345)	1,585,577
Phnum Pénh (Phnom Penh), Cambodia	620,000
Phoenix, Arizona, U.S. (2,122,101)	983,403
Pittsburgh, Pennsylvania, U.S. (2,242,798)	369,879
Port-au-Prince, Haiti (880,000)	797,000
Portland, Oregon, U.S. (1,477,895)	437,319
Porto Alegre, Brazil (2,850,000)	1,247,352
Prague (Praha), Czech Republic (1,328,000)	1,212,010
Pretoria, South Africa (1,100,000)	525,583
Providence, Rhode Island, U.S. (1,141,510)	160,728
Puebla, Mexico (1,200,000)	1,007,170
Pune, India (2,493,987)	1,566,651
Pusan, South Korea (3,800,000)	3,797,566
P'yŏngyang, North Korea	2,355,000
Qingdao, China	1,300,000
Québec, Canada (645,550)	167,517
Quezon City, Philippines (*Manila)	1,666,766
Quito, Ecuador (1,300,000)	1,100,847
Rabat, Morocco (980,000)	518,616
Rangoon (Yangon), Myanmar (2,800,000)	2,705,039
Recife, Brazil (2,880,000)	1,296,995
Rīga, Latvia (1,005,000)	910,200
Rio de Janerio, Brazil (11,050,000)	5,473,909
Riyadh, Saudi Arabia	1,250,000
Rome (Roma), Italy (3,175,000)	2,693,383
Rosario, Argentina (1,190,000)	894,645
Rostov-na-Donu, Russia (1,165,000)	1,027,600
Rotterdam, Netherlands (1,120,000)	589,707
St. Louis, Missouri, U.S. (2,444,099)	396,685
St. Petersburg (Leningrad), Russia (5,525,000)	4,466,800
Salt Lake City, Utah, U.S. (1,072,227)	159,936
Salvador, Brazil (2,340,000)	2,070,296
Samara, Russia (1,505,000)	1,257,300
San Antonio, Texas, U.S. (1,302,099)	935,933
San Diego, California, U.S. (2,949,000)	1,110,549
San Francisco, California, U.S. (6,253,311)	723,959
San José, Costa Rica (1,355,000)	278,600
San Juan, Puerto Rico (1,877,000)	426,832
San Salvador, El Salvador (920,000)	462,652
Santiago, Chile (4,100,000)	232,667
Santo Domingo, Dominican Rep.	2,411,900
Santos, Brazil (1,165,000)	415,554
São Paulo, Brazil (16,925,000)	9,393,753
Sapporo, Japan (1,900,000)	1,671,742
Sarajevo, Bosnia and Herzegovina (479,688†)	341,200
Saratov, Russia (1,155,000)	911,100
Seattle, Washington, U.S. (2,559,164)	516,259
Seoul (Sŏul), South Korea (15,850,000)	10,627,790
Shanghai, China (9,300,000)	7,220,000
Shenyang (Mukden), China (4,370,000†)	3,910,000
Singapore, Singapore (3,025,000)	2,690,100
Skopje, Macedonia (547,214†)	444,900
Sofia (Sofiya), Bulgaria (1,205,000)	1,136,875
Stockholm, Sweden (1,491,726)	674,452
Stuttgart, Germany (2,005,000)	579,988
Surabaya, Indonesia	2,473,272
Sydney, Australia (3,538,749)	13,501
Taegu, South Korea	2,228,834
T'aipei, Taiwan (6,200,000)	2,706,453
Taiyuan, China (1,980,000†)	1,700,000
Tampa, Florida, U.S. (2,067,959)	280,015
Tashkent, Uzbekistan (2,325,000)	2,113,300
Tbilisi, Georgia (1,460,000)	1,279,000
Tegucigalpa, Honduras	576,661
Tehrān, Iran (7,500,000)	6,042,584
Tel Aviv-Yafo, Israel (1,735,000)	339,400
The Hague ('s-Gravenhage), Netherlands (773,000)	445,287
Tianjin (Tientsin), China (5,540,000†)	4,950,000
Tiranë, Albania	238,100
Tōkyō, Japan (30,300,000)	8,163,573
Toronto, Canada (3,893,046)	635,395
Tripoli (Tarābulus), Libya	591,062
Tunis, Tunisia (1,225,000)	596,654
Turin (Torino), Italy (1,550,000)	961,916
Ufa, Russia (1,118,000)	1,097,000
Ulan Bator, Mongolia	548,400
València, Spain (1,270,000)	743,933
Vancouver, Canada (1,602,502)	471,844
Venice (Venezia), Italy (420,000)	85,100
Vienna (Wien), Austria (1,900,000)	1,539,848
Vilnius, Lithuania	596,900
Vladivostok, Russia	648,000
Volgograd (Stalingrad), Russia (1,360,000)	1,007,300
Warsaw (Warszawa), Poland (2,323,000)	1,655,700
Washington, D.C., U.S. (3,923,574)	606,900
Wellington, New Zealand (375,000)	150,301
Winnipeg, Canada (652,354)	616,790
Wuhan, China	3,570,000
Xi'an, China (2,580,000†)	2,210,000
Yekaterinburg, Russia (1,620,000)	1,375,400
Yerevan, Armenia (1,315,000)	1,199,000
Yokohama, Japan (*Tōkyō)	3,220,331
Zagreb, Croatia	697,925
Zurich, Switzerland (870,000)	365,043

Metropolitan area populations are shown in parentheses.
*City is located within the metropolitan area of another city; for example, Kyōto, Japan is located in the Ōsaka metropolitan area.
†Population of entire municipality or district, including rural area.

GLOSSARY OF FOREIGN GEOGRAPHICAL TERMS

Annam ... Annamese
Arab ... Arabic
Bantu ... Bantu
Bur ... Burmese
Camb ... Cambodian
Celt ... Celtic
Chn ... Chinese
Czech ... Czech
Dan ... Danish
Du ... Dutch
Fin ... Finnish
Fr ... French
Ger ... German
Gr ... Greek
Hung ... Hungarian
Ice ... Icelandic
India ... India
Indian ... American Indian
Indon ... Indonesian
It ... Italian
Jap ... Japanese
Kor ... Korean
Mal ... Malayan
Mong ... Mongolian
Nor ... Norwegian
Per ... Persian
Pol ... Polish
Port ... Portuguese
Rom ... Romanian
Rus ... Russian
Siam ... Siamese
So. Slav ... Southern Slavonic
Sp ... Spanish
Swe ... Swedish
Tib ... Tibetan
Tur ... Turkish
Yugo ... Yugoslav

å, Nor., Swe ... brook, river
aa, Dan., Nor ... brook
aas, Dan., Nor ... ridge
āb, Per ... water, river
abad, India, Per ... town, city
ada, Tur ... island
adrar, Berber ... mountain
air, Indon ... stream
akrotírion, Gr ... cape
älf, Swe ... river
alp, Ger ... mountain
altipiano, It ... plateau
alto, Sp ... height
archipel, Fr ... archipelago
archipiélago, Sp ... archipelago
arquipélago, Port ... archipelago
arroyo, Sp ... brook, stream
ås, Nor., Swe ... ridge
austral, Sp ... southern
baai, Du ... bay
bab, Arab ... gate, port
bach, Ger ... brook, stream
backe, Swe ... hill
bad, Ger ... bath, spa
bahía, Sp ... bay, gulf
bahr, Arab ... river, sea, lake
baia, It ... bay, gulf
baía, Port ... bay
baie, Fr ... bay, gulf
bajo, Sp ... depression
bak, Indon ... stream
bakke, Dan., Nor ... hill
balkan, Tur ... mountain range
bana, Jap ... point, cape
banco, Sp ... bank
bandar, Mal., Per. ... town, port, harbor
bang, Siam ... village
bassin, Fr ... basin
batang, Indon., Mal ... river
ben, Celt ... mountain, summit
bender, Arab ... harbor, port
bereg, Rus ... coast, shore
berg, Du., Ger., Nor., Swe. ... mountain, hill
bir, Arab ... well
birkat, Arab ... lake, pond, pool
bit, Arab ... house
bjaerg, Dan., Nor ... mountain
bocche, It ... mouth
boğazı, Tur ... strait
bois, Fr ... forest, wood
boloto, Rus ... marsh
bolsón, Sp. ... flat-floored desert valley
boreal, Sp ... northern
borg, Dan., Nor., Swe ... castle, town
borgo, It ... town, suburb
bosch, Du ... forest, wood
bouche, Fr ... river mouth
bourg, Fr ... town, borough
bro, Dan., Nor., Swe ... bridge
brücke, Ger ... bridge
bucht, Ger ... bay, bight
bugt, Dan., Nor., Swe ... bay, gulf
bulu, Indon ... mountain
burg, Du., Ger ... castle, town
buri, Siam ... town
burun, burnu, Tur ... cape
by, Dan., Nor., Swe ... village
caatinga, Port. (Brazil) ... open brushland
cabezo, Sp ... summit
cabo, Port., Sp ... cape
campo, It., Port., Sp ... plain, field
campos, Port. (Brazil) ... plains
cañón, Sp ... canyon
cap, Fr ... cape
capo, It ... cape
casa, It., Port., Sp ... house
castello, It., Port ... castle, fort
castillo, Sp ... castle
càte, Fr ... hill
çay, Tur ... stream, river
cayo, Sp ... rock, shoal, islet
cerro, Sp ... mountain, hill
champ, Fr ... field
chang, Chn ... village, middle
château, Fr ... castle
chen, Chn ... market town
chiang, Chn ... river
chott, Arab ... salt lake
chou, Chn. ... capital of district; island
chu, Tib ... water, stream
cidade, Port ... town, city
cima, Sp ... summit, peak
città, It ... town, city
ciudad, Sp ... town, city
cochilha, Port ... ridge
col, Fr ... pass
colina, Sp ... hill
cordillera, Sp ... mountain chain
costa, It., Port., Sp ... coast
côte, Fr ... coast
cuchilla, Sp ... mountain ridge
dağ, Tur ... mountain(s)
dake, Jap ... peak, summit
dal, Dan., Du., Nor., Swe ... valley
dan, Kor ... point, cape
danau, Indon ... lake
dar, Arab ... house, abode, country
darya, Per ... river, sea
dasht, Per ... plain, desert
deniz, Tur ... sea
désert, Fr ... desert
deserto, It ... desert
desierto, Sp ... desert
détroit, Fr ... strait
dijk, Du ... dam, dike
djebel, Arab ... mountain
do, Kor ... island
dorf, Ger ... village
dorp, Du ... village
duin, Du ... dune
dzong, Tib. ... fort, administrative capital
eau, Fr ... water
ecuador, Sp ... equator
eiland, Du ... island
elv, Dan., Nor ... river, stream
embalse, Sp ... reservoir
erg, Arab ... dune, sandy desert
est, Fr., It ... east
estado, Sp ... state
este, Port., Sp ... east
estrecho, Sp ... strait
étang, Fr ... pond, lake
état, Fr ... state
eyjar, Ice ... islands
feld, Ger ... field, plain
festung, Ger ... fortress
fiume, It ... river
fjäll, Swe ... mountain
fjärd, Swe ... bay, inlet
fjeld, Nor ... mountain, hill
fjord, Dan., Nor ... fiord, inlet
fjördur, Ice ... fiord, inlet
fleuve, Fr ... river
flod, Dan., Swe ... river
flói, Ice ... bay, marshland
fluss, Ger ... river
foce, It ... river mouth
fontein, Du ... a spring
forêt, Fr ... forest
fors, Swe ... waterfall
forst, Ger ... forest
fos, Dan., Nor ... waterfall
fu, Chn ... town, residence
fuente, Sp ... spring, fountain
fuerte, Sp ... fort
furt, Ger ... ford
gang, Kor ... stream, river
gangri, Tib ... mountain
gat, Dan., Nor ... channel
gàve, Fr ... stream
gawa, Jap ... river
gebergte, Du ... mountain range
gebiet, Ger ... district, territory
gebirge, Ger ... mountains
ghat, India ... pass, mountain range
gobi, Mong ... desert
gol, Mong ... river
göl, gölü, Tur ... lake
golf, Du., Ger ... gulf, bay
golfe, Fr ... gulf, bay
golfo, It., Port., Sp ... gulf, bay
gomba, gompa, Tib ... monastery
gora, Rus., So. Slav ... mountain
góra, Pol ... mountain
gorod, Rus ... town
grad, Rus., So. Slav ... town
guba, Rus ... bay, gulf
gundung, Indon ... mountain
guntō, Jap ... archipelago
gunung, Mal ... mountain
haf, Swe ... sea, ocean
hafen, Ger ... port, harbor
haff, Ger ... gulf, inland sea
hai, Chn ... sea, lake
hama, Jap ... beach, shore
hamada, Arab ... rocky plateau
hamn, Swe ... harbor
hāmūn, Per ... swampy lake, plain
hantō, Jap ... peninsula
hassi, Arab ... well, spring
haus, Ger ... house
haut, Fr ... summit, top
hav, Dan., Nor ... sea, ocean
havn, Dan., Nor ... harbor, port
havre, Fr ... harbor, port
háza, Hung ... house, dwelling of
heim, Ger ... hamlet, home
hem, Swe ... hamlet, home
higashi, Jap ... east
hisar, Tur ... fortress
hissar, Arab ... fort
ho, Chn ... river
hoek, Du ... cape
hof, Ger ... court, farmhouse
höfn, Ice ... harbor
hoku, Jap ... north
holm, Dan., Nor., Swe ... island
hora, Czech ... mountain
horn, Ger ... peak
hoved, Dan., Nor ... cape
hsien, Chn ... district, district capital
hu, Chn ... lake
hügel, Ger ... hill
huk, Dan., Swe ... point
hus, Dan., Nor., Swe ... house
île, Fr ... island
ilha, Port ... island
indsö, Dan., Nor ... lake
insel, Ger ... island
insjö, Swe ... lake
irmak, irmagi, Tur ... river
isla, Sp ... island
isola, It ... island
istmo, It., Sp ... isthmus
järvi, jaur, Fin ... lake
jebel, Arab ... mountain
jima, Jap ... island
jökel, Nor ... glacier
joki, Fin ... river
jökull, Ice ... glacier
kaap, Du ... cape
kai, Jap ... bay, gulf, sea
kaikyō, Jap ... channel, strait
kalat, Per ... castle, fortress
kale, Tur ... fort
kali, Mal ... creek, river
kand, Per ... village
kang, Chn ... mountain ridge; village
kap, Dan., Ger ... cape
kapp, Nor., Swe ... cape
kasr, Arab ... fort, castle
kawa, Jap ... river
kefr, Arab ... village
kei, Jap ... creek, river
ken, Jap ... prefecture
khor, Arab ... bay, inlet
khrebet, Rus ... mountain range
kiang, Chn ... large river
king, Chn ... capital city, town
kita, Jap ... north
ko, Jap ... lake
köbstad, Dan ... market-town
kol, Mong ... lake
kólpos, Gr ... gulf
kong, Chn ... river
kopf, Ger ... head, summit, peak
köpstad, Swe ... market-town
körfezi, Tur ... gulf
kosa, Rus ... spit
kou, Chn ... river mouth
köy, Tur ... village
kraal, Du. (Africa) ... native village
ksar, Arab ... fortified village
kuala, Mal ... bay, river mouth
kuh, Per ... mountain
kum, Tur ... sand
kuppe, Ger ... summit
küste, Ger ... coast
kyo, Jap ... town, capital
la, Tib ... mountain pass
labuan, Mal ... anchorage, port
lac, Fr ... lake
lago, It., Port., Sp ... lake
lagoa, Port ... lake, marsh
laguna, It., Port., Sp ... lagoon, lake
lahti, Fin ... bay, gulf
län, Swe ... county
landsby, Dan., Nor ... village
liehtao, Chn ... archipelago
liman, Tur ... bay, port
ling, Chn ... pass, ridge, mountain
llanos, Sp ... plains
loch, Celt. (Scotland) ... lake, bay
loma, Sp ... long, low hill
lough, Celt. (Ireland) ... lake, bay
machi, Jap ... town
man, Kor ... bay
mar, Port., Sp ... sea
mare, It., Rom ... sea
marisma, Sp ... marsh, swamp
mark, Ger ... boundary, limit
massif, Fr ... block of mountains
mato, Port ... forest, thicket
me, Siam ... river
meer, Du., Ger ... lake, sea
mer, Fr ... sea
mesa, Sp ... flat-topped mountain
meseta, Sp ... plateau
mina, Port., Sp ... mine
minami, Jap ... south
minato, Jap ... harbor, haven
misaki, Jap ... cape, headland
mont, Fr ... mount, mountain
montagna, It ... mountain
montagne, Fr ... mountain
montaña, Sp ... mountain
monte, It., Port., Sp. ... mount, mountain
more, Rus., So. Slav ... sea
morro, Port., Sp ... hill, bluff
mühle, Ger ... mill
mund, Ger ... mouth, opening
mündung, Ger ... river mouth
mura, Jap ... township
myit, Bur ... river
mys, Rus ... cape
nada, Jap ... sea
nadi, India ... river, creek
naes, Dan., Nor ... cape
nafud, Arab ... desert of sand dunes
nagar, India ... town, city
nahr, Arab ... river
nam, Siam ... river, water
nan, Chn., Jap ... south
näs, Nor., Swe ... cape
nez, Fr ... point, cape
nishi, nisi, Jap ... west
njarga, Fin ... peninsula
nong, Siam ... marsh
noord, Du ... north
nor, Mong ... lake
nord, Dan., Fr., Ger., It., Nor., Swe ... north
norte, Port., Sp ... north
nos, Rus ... cape
nyasa, Bantu ... lake
ö, Dan., Nor., Swe ... island
occidental, Sp ... western
ocna, Rom ... salt mine
odde, Dan., Nor ... point, cape
oeste, Port., Sp ... west
oka, Jap ... hill
oost, Du ... east
oriental, Sp ... eastern
óros, Gr ... mountain
ost, Ger., Swe ... east
öster, Dan., Nor., Swe ... eastern
ostrov, Rus ... island
oued, Arab ... river, stream
ouest, Fr ... west
ozero, Rus ... lake
pää, Fin ... mountain
padang, Mal ... plain, field
pampas, Sp. (Argentina) ... grassy plains
pará, Indian (Brazil) ... river
pas, Fr ... channel, passage
paso, Sp ... mountain pass, passage
passo, It., Port. ... mountain pass, passage, strait
patam, India ... city, town
pei, Chn ... north
pélagos, Gr ... open sea
pegunungan, Indon ... mountains
peña, Sp ... rock
peresheyek, Rus ... isthmus
pertuis, Fr ... strait
peski, Rus ... desert
pic, Fr ... mountain peak
pico, Port., Sp ... mountain peak
piedra, Sp ... stone, rock
ping, Chn ... plain, flat
planalto, Port ... plateau
planina, Yugo ... mountains
playa, Sp ... shore, beach
pnom, Camb ... mountain
pointe, Fr ... point
polder, Du., Ger ... reclaimed marsh
polje, So. Slav ... plain, field
poluostrov, Rus ... peninsula
pont, Fr ... bridge
ponta, Port ... point, headland
ponte, It., Port ... bridge
pore, India ... city, town
porthmós, Gr ... strait
porto, It., Port ... port, harbor
potamós, Gr ... river
p'ov, Rus ... peninsula
prado, Sp ... field, meadow
presqu'île, Fr ... peninsula
proliv, Rus ... strait
pu, Chn ... commercial village
pueblo, Sp ... town, village
puerto, Sp ... port, harbor
pulau, Indon ... island
punkt, Ger ... point
punt, Du ... point
punta, It., Sp ... point
pur, India ... city, town
puy, Fr ... peak
qal'a, qal'at, Arab ... fort, village
qasr, Arab ... fort, castle
rann, India ... wasteland
ra's, Arab ... cape, head
reka, Rus., So. Slav ... river
represa, Port ... reservoir
rettō, Jap ... island chain
ría, Sp ... estuary
ribeira, Port ... stream
ribeirão, Port ... river
rio, It., Port ... stream, river
río, Sp ... river
rivière, Fr ... river
roca, Sp ... rock
rt, Yugo ... cape
rūd, Per ... river
saari, Fin ... island
sable, Fr ... sand
sahara, Arab ... desert, plain
saki, Jap ... cape
sal, Sp ... salt
salar, Sp ... salt flat, salt lake
salto, Sp ... waterfall
san, Jap., Kor ... mountain, hill
sat, satul, Rom ... village
schloss, Ger ... castle
sebkha, Arab ... salt marsh
see, Ger ... lake, sea
şehir, Tur ... town, city
selat, Indon ... stream
selvas, Port. (Brazil) ... tropical rain forests
seno, Sp ... bay
serra, Port ... mountain chain
serranía, Sp ... mountain ridge
seto, Jap ... strait
severnaya, Rus ... northern
shahr, Per ... town, city
shan, Chn ... mountain, hill, island
shatt, Arab ... river
shi, Jap ... city
shima, Jap ... island
shōtō, Jap ... archipelago
si, Chn ... west, western
sierra, Sp ... mountain range
sjö, Nor., Swe ... lake, sea
sö, Dan., Nor ... lake, sea
söder, södra, Swe ... south
song, Annam ... river
sopka, Rus ... peak, volcano
source, Fr ... a spring
spitze, Ger ... summit, point
staat, Ger ... state
stad, Dan., Du., Nor., Swe. ... city, town
stadt, Ger ... city, town
stato, It ... state
step', Rus ... treeless plain, steppe
straat, Du ... strait
strand, Dan., Du., Ger., Nor., Swe ... shore, beach
stretto, It ... strait
strom, Ger ... river, stream
ström, Dan., Nor., Swe. ... stream, river
stroom, Du ... stream, river
su, suyu, Tur ... water, river
sud, Fr., Sp ... south
süd, Ger ... south
suidō, Jap ... channel
sul, Port ... south
sund, Dan., Nor., Swe ... sound
sungai, sungei, Indon., Mal ... river
sur, Sp ... south
syd, Dan., Nor., Swe ... south
tafelland, Ger ... plateau
take, Jap ... peak, summit
tal, Ger ... valley
tanjung, tanjong, Mal ... cape
tao, Chn ... island
târg, târgul, Rom ... market, town
tell, Arab ... hill
teluk, Indon ... bay, gulf
terra, It ... land
terre, Fr ... earth, land
thal, Ger ... valley
tierra, Sp ... earth, land
tō, Jap ... east; island
tonle, Camb ... river, lake
top, Du ... peak
torp, Swe ... hamlet, cottage
tsangpo, Tib ... river
tsi, Chn ... village, borough
tso, Tib ... lake
tsu, Jap ... harbor, port
tundra, Rus ... treeless arctic plains
tung, Chn ... east
tuz, Tur ... salt
udde, Swe ... cape
ufer, Ger ... shore, riverbank
ujung, Indon ... point, cape
umi, Jap ... sea, gulf
ura, Jap ... bay, coast, creek
ust'ye, Rus ... river mouth
valle, It., Port., Sp ... valley
vallée, Fr ... valley
valli, It ... lake
vár, Hung ... fortress
város, Hung ... town
varoš, So. Slav ... town
veld, Du ... open plain, field
verkh, Rus ... top, summit
ves, Czech ... village
vest, Dan., Nor., Swe ... west
vik, Swe ... cove, bay
vila, Port ... town
villa, Sp ... town
villar, Sp ... village, hamlet
ville, Fr ... town, city
vostok, Rus ... east
wad, wādī, Arab. ... intermittent stream
wald, Ger ... forest, woodland
wan, Chn., Jap ... bay, gulf
weiler, Ger ... hamlet, village
westersch, Du ... western
wüste, Ger ... desert
yama, Jap ... mountain
yarimada, Tur ... peninsula
yug, Rus ... south
zaki, Jap ... cape
zaliv, Rus ... bay, gulf
zapad, Rus ... west
zee, Du ... sea
zemlya, Rus ... land
zuid, Du ... south

Ab.	Alberta, Can.	Guy.	Guyana
Afg.	Afghanistan		
Afg.	Afghanistan	Hi., U.S.	Hawaii, U.S.
Afr.	Africa	hist.	Historic Site, Ruins
Ak., U.S.	Alaska, U.S.	hist. reg.	Historic Region
Al., U.S.	Alabama, U.S.	Hond.	Honduras
Alb.	Albania	Hung.	Hungary
Alg.	Algeria		
Am. Sam.	American Samoa	i.	Island
And.	Andorra	Ia., U.S.	Iowa, U.S.
Ang.	Angola	ice	Ice Feature, Glacier
Ant.	Antarctica	Ice.	Iceland
Antig.	Antigua and Barbuda	Id., U.S.	Idaho, U.S.
aq.	Aqueduct	Il., U.S.	Illinois, U.S.
Ar., U.S.	Arkansas, U.S.	In., U.S.	Indiana, U.S.
Arg.	Argentina	Indon.	Indonesia
Arm.	Armenia	I. of Man	Isle of Man
arpt.	Airport	I.R.	Indian Reservation
Aus.	Austria	Ire.	Ireland
Austl.	Australia	is.	Islands
Az., U.S.	Arizona, U.S.	Isr.	Israel
Azer.	Azerbaijan	Isr. Occ.	Israeli Occupied Areas
		isth.	Isthmus
b.	Bay, Gulf, Inlet, Lagoon		
Bah.	Bahamas	Jam.	Jamaica
Bahr.	Bahrain	Jord.	Jordan
Barb.	Barbados		
B.A.T.	British Antarctic Territory	Kaz.	Kazakstan
B.C., Can.	British Columbia, Can.	Kir.	Kiribati
Bdi.	Burundi	Ks., U.S.	Kansas, U.S.
Bel.	Belgium	Kuw.	Kuwait
Bela.	Belarus	Ky., U.S.	Kentucky, U.S.
Ber.	Bermuda	Kyrg.	Kyrgyzstan
Bhu.	Bhutan		
bk.	Undersea Bank	l.	Lake, Pond
bldg.	Building	La., U.S.	Louisiana, U.S.
Bngl.	Bangladesh	Lat.	Latvia
Bol.	Bolivia	Leb.	Lebanon
Bos.	Bosnia and Hercegovina	Leso.	Lesotho
Bots.	Botswana	Lib.	Liberia
Braz.	Brazil	Liech.	Liechtenstein
Bru.	Brunei	Lith.	Lithuania
Br. Vir. Is.	British Virgin Islands	Lux.	Luxembourg
bt.	Bight		
Bul.	Bulgaria	Ma., U.S.	Massachusetts, U.S.
Burkina	Burkina Faso	Mac.	Macedonia
		Madag.	Madagascar
c.	Cape, Point	Malay.	Malaysia
Ca., U.S.	California, U.S.	Mald.	Maldives
Cam.	Cameroon	Marsh. Is.	Marshall Islands
Camb.	Cambodia	Mart.	Martinique
can.	Canal	Maur.	Mauritania
Can.	Canada	May.	Mayotte
Cay. Is.	Cayman Islands	Mb., Can.	Manitoba, Canada
Cen. Afr. Rep.	Central African Republic	Md., U.S.	Maryland, U.S.
C. Iv.	Cote d'Ivoire	Me., U.S.	Maine, U.S.
clf.	Cliff, Escarpment	Mex.	Mexico
co.	County, Parish	Mi., U.S.	Michigan, U.S.
Co., U.S.	Colorado, U.S.	Micron.	Micronesia, Federated States of
Col.	Colombia	Mn., U.S.	Minnesota, U.S.
Com.	Comoros	Mo., U.S.	Missouri, U.S.
cont.	Continent	Mol.	Moldova
Cook Is.	Cook Islands	Mong.	Mongolia
C.R.	Costa Rica	Monts.	Montserrat
Cro.	Croatia	Mor.	Morocco
cst.	Coast, Beach	Moz.	Mozambique
Ct., U.S.	Connecticut, U.S.	Ms., U.S.	Mississippi, U.S.
C.V.	Cape Verde	Mt., U.S.	Montana, U.S.
Cyp.	Cyprus	mth.	River Mouth or Channel
Czech Rep.	Czech Republic	mtn.	Mountain
		mts.	Mountains
d.	Delta	Mwi.	Malawi
D.C., U.S.	District of Columbia, U.S.		
De., U.S.	Delaware, U.S.	N.A.	North America
Den.	Denmark	N.B., Can.	New Brunswick, Can.
dep.	Dependency, Colony	N.C., U.S.	North Carolina, U.S.
depr.	Depression	N. Cal.	New Caledonia
dept.	Department, District	N. Cyp.	North Cyprus
des.	Desert	N.D., U.S.	North Dakota, U.S.
Dji.	Djibouti	Ne., U.S.	Nebraska, U.S.
Dom.	Dominica	neigh.	Neighborhood
Dom. Rep.	Dominican Republic	Neth.	Netherlands
D.R.C.	Democratic Republic of the Congo	Nf., Can.	Newfoundland, Can.
		Neth. Ant.	Netherlands Antilles
Ec.	Ecuador	N.H., U.S.	New Hampshire, U.S.
educ.	Educational Facility	Nic.	Nicaragua
El Sal.	El Salvador	Nig.	Nigeria
Eng., U.K.	England, U.K.	N. Ire., U.K.	Northern Ireland, U.K.
Eq. Gui.	Equatorial Guinea	N.J., U.S.	New Jersey, U.S.
Erit.	Eritrea	N. Kor.	North Korea
Est.	Estonia	N.M., U.S.	New Mexico, U.S.
est.	Estuary	N. Mar. Is.	Northern Mariana Islands
Eth.	Ethiopia	Nmb.	Namibia
Eur.	Europe	Nor.	Norway
		N.S., Can.	Nova Scotia, Can.
Falk. Is.	Falkland Islands	N.T., Can.	Northwest Territories, Can.
Faer. Is.	Faroe Islands	Nv., U.S.	Nevada, U.S.
Fin.	Finland	N.Y., U.S.	New York, U.S.
fj.	Fjord	N.Z.	New Zealand
Fl., U.S.	Florida, U.S.		
for.	Forest, Moor	o.	Ocean
Fr.	France	Oc.	Oceania
Fr. Gu.	French Guiana	Oh., U.S.	Ohio, U.S.
Fr. Poly.	French Polynesia	Ok., U.S.	Oklahoma, U.S.
		On., Can.	Ontario, Can.
Ga., U.S.	Georgia, U.S.	Or., U.S.	Oregon, U.S.
Gam.	The Gambia		
Geor.	Georgia	p.	Pass
Ger.	Germany	Pa., U.S.	Pennsylvania, U.S.
Gre.	Greece	Pak.	Pakistan
Gren.	Grenada	Pan.	Panama
Grnld.	Greenland	Pap. N. Gui.	Papua New Guinea
Guad.	Guadeloupe	Para.	Paraguay
Guat.	Guatemala	P.E., Can.	Prince Edward Island, Can.
Gui.	Guinea		
Gui.-B.	Guinea-Bissau		

pen.	Peninsula
Phil.	Philippines
Pit.	Pitcairn
pl.	Plain, Flat
plat.	Plateau, Highland
Pol.	Poland
Port.	Portugal
P.R.	Puerto Rico
prov.	Province, Region
pt. of i.	Point of Interest
Qc., Can.	Quebec, Can.
r.	River, Creek
Reu.	Reunion
rec.	Recreational Site, Park
reg.	Physical Region
rel.	Religious Institution
res.	Reservoir
rf.	Reef, Shoal
R.I., U.S.	Rhode Island, U.S.
Rom.	Romania
Rw.	Rwanda
S.A.	South America
S. Afr.	South Africa
Sau. Ar.	Saudi Arabia
S.C., U.S.	South Carolina, U.S.
sci.	Scientific Station
Scot., U.K.	Scotland, U.K.
S.D., U.S.	South Dakota, U.S.
Sen.	Senegal
sea feat.	Undersea Feature
Sey.	Seychelles
S. Ga.	South Georgia
Sing.	Singapore
Sk., Can.	Saskatchewan, Can.
S. Kor.	South Korea
S.L.	Sierra Leone
Slvk.	Slovakia
Slvn.	Slovenia
S. Mar.	San Marino
Sol. Is.	Solomon Islands
Som.	Somalia
Sp. N. Afr.	Spanish North Africa
Sri L.	Sri Lanka
St. Hel.	St. Helena
St. K./N.	St. Kitts and Nevis
St. Luc.	St. Lucia
St. P./M.	St. Pierre and Miquelon
strt.	Strait, Channel, Sound
S. Tom./P.	Sao Tome and Principe
St. Vin.	St. Vincent and the Grenadines
Sur.	Suriname
Sval.	Svalbard
sw.	Swamp, Marsh
Swaz.	Swaziland
Swe.	Sweden
Switz.	Switzerland
Tai.	Taiwan
Taj.	Tajikistan
Tan.	Tanzania
T./C. Is.	Turks and Caicos Islands
ter.	Territory
Thai.	Thailand
Tn., U.S.	Tennessee, U.S.
trans.	Transportation Facility
Trin.	Trinidad and Tobago
Tun.	Tunisia
Tur.	Turkey
Turk.	Turkmenistan
Tx., U.S.	Texas, U.S.
U.A.E.	United Arab Emirates
Ug.	Uganda
U.K.	United Kingdom
Ukr.	Ukraine
Ur.	Uruguay
U.S.	United States
Ut., U.S.	Utah, U.S.
Uzb.	Uzbekistan
Va., U.S.	Virginia, U.S.
val.	Valley, Watercourse
Vat.	Vatican City
Ven.	Venezuela
Viet.	Vietnam
V.I.U.S.	Virgin Islands (U.S.)
vol.	Volcano
Vt., U.S.	Vermont, U.S.
Wa., U.S.	Washington, U.S.
W. Bank	West Bank
Wi., U.S.	Wisconsin, U.S.
W. Sah.	Western Sahara
W. Sam.	Western Samoa
wtfl.	Waterfall
W.V., U.S.	West Virginia, U.S.
Wy., U.S.	Wyoming, U.S.
Yk. Can.	Yukon Territory, Can.
Yugo.	Yugoslavia
Zam.	Zambia
Zimb.	Zimbabwe
Zam.	Zambia

Key to the Sound Values of Letters and Symbols Used in the Index to Indicate Pronunciation

ă-ăt; băttle
ȧ-finȧl; ȧppeal
ā-rāte; elāte
å-senåte; inanimåte
ä-ärm; cälm
a-ȧsk; bȧth
a̍-sofa̍; ma̍rine (short neutral or indeterminate sound)
â-fâre; prepâre
ch-choose; church
dh-as th in other; either
ē-bē; ēve
ė-ėvent; crėate
ĕ-bĕt; ĕnd
ē̆-recĕnt (short neutral or indeterminate sound)
ẽ-cratẽr; cindẽr
g-gŏ; gāme
gh-guttural g
ĭ-bĭt; wĭll
ĭ-(short neutral or indeterminate sound)
ī-rīde; bīte
κ-guttural k as ch in German ich
ng-sing
ŋ-baŋk; liŋger
N-indicates nasalized
ŏ-nŏd; ŏdd
ŏ-cŏmmit; cŏnnect
ō-ōld; bōld
ô-ôbey; hôtel
ô-ôrder; nôrth
oi-boil
ōō-fōōd; rōōt
o̍-as oo in foot; wood
ou-out; thou
s-soft; so; sane
sh-dish; finish
th-thin; thick
ū-pūre; cūre
ū-ūnite; ūsūrp
û-ûrn; fûr
ŭ-stŭd; ŭp
ū̆-circŭs; sŭbmit
ü-as in French tu
zh-as z in azure
'-indeterminate vowel sound

In many cases the spelling of foreign geographic names does not even remotely indicate the pronunciation to an American, i.e., Słupsk in Poland is pronounced swŏpsk; Jujuy in Argentina is pronounced hōōhwē'; La Spezia in Italy is lä-spē'zyä.

This condition is hardly surprising, however, when we consider that in our own language Worcester, Massachusetts, is pronounced wŏs'tēr; Sioux City, Iowa, sōō si'tĭ; Schuylkill Haven, Pennsylvania, skōōl'kĭl hā-vĕn; Poughkeepsie, New York, pŏ-kĭp'sĕ.

The indication of pronunciation of geographic names presents several peculiar problems:

1. Many foreign tongues use sounds that are not present in the English language and which an American cannot normally articulate. Thus, though the nearest English equivalent sound has been indicated, only approximate results are possible.

2. There are several dialects in each foreign tongue which cause variation in the local pronunciation of names. This also occurs in identical names in the various divisions of a great language group, as the Slavic or the Latin.

3. Within the United States there are marked differences in pronunciation, not only of local geographic names, but also of common words, indicating that the sound and tone values for letters as well as the placing of the emphasis vary considerably from one part of the country to another.

4. A number of different letters and diacritical combinations could be used to indicate essentially the same or approximate pronunciations.

Some variation in pronunciation other than that indicated in this index may be encountered, but such a difference does not necessarily indicate that either is in error, and in many cases it is a matter of individual choice as to which is preferred. In fact, an exact indication of pronunciation of many foreign names using English letters and diacritical marks is extremely difficult and sometimes impossible.

PRONOUNCING INDEX

This universal index includes in a single alphabetical list approximately 34,000 names of features that appear on the reference maps. Each name is followed by a page reference and geographical coordinates.

Abbreviation and Capitalization Abbreviations of names on the maps have been standardized as much as possible. Names that are abbreviated on the maps are generally spelled out in full in the index. Periods are used after all abbreviations regardless of local practice. The abbreviation "St." is used only for "Saint". "Sankt" and other forms of this term are spelled out.

Most initial letters of names are capitalized, except for a few Dutch names, such as "'s-Gravenhage". Capitalization of noninitial words in a name generally follows local practice.

Alphabetization Names are alphabetized in the order of the letters of the English alphabet. Spanish *ll* and *ch,* for example, are not treated as distinct letters. Furthermore, diacritical marks are disregarded in alphabetization — German or Scandinavian *ä* or *ö* are treated as *a* or *o*.

The names of physical features may appear inverted, since they are always alphabetized under the proper, not the generic, part of the name, thus: "Gibraltar, Strait of". Otherwise every entry, whether consisting of one word or more, is alphabetized as a single continuous entity. "Lakeland," for example, appears after "La Crosse" and before "La Salle." Names beginning with articles (Le Havre, Den Helder, Al Manāmah, Ad Dawhah) are not inverted.

In the case of identical names, towns are listed first, then political divisions, then physical features.

Generic Terms Except for cities, the names of all features are followed by terms that represent broad classes of features, for example, Mississippi, r. or Alabama, state. A list of all abbreviations used in the index is on page 253.

Country names and names of features that extend beyond the boundaries of one country are followed by the name of the continent in which each is located. Country designations follow the names of all other places in the index. The locations of places in the United States and the United Kingdom are further defined by abbreviations that indicate the state or political division in which each is located.

Pronunciations Pronunciations are included for most names listed. An explanation of the pronunciation system used appears on page 253.

Page References and Geographical Coordinates The geographical coordinates and page references are found in the last columns of each entry.

If a page contains several maps or insets, a lowercase letter identifies the specific map or inset.

Latitude and longitude coordinates for point features, such as cities and mountain peaks, indicate the locations of the symbols. For extensive areal features, such as countries or mountain ranges, or linear features, such as canals and rivers, locations are given for the position of the type as it appears on the map.

A

PLACE (Pronunciation)	PAGE	LAT.	LONG.
Aachen, Ger. (ä′kĕn)	147	50°46′N	6°07′E
Aalen, Ger. (ä′lĕn)	154	48°49′N	10°08′E
Aalsmeer, Neth.	145a	52°16′N	4°44′E
Aalst, Bel.	151	50°58′N	4°00′E
Aarau, Switz. (ärou)	147	47°22′N	8°03′E
Aarschot, Bel.	145a	50°59′N	4°51′E
Aba, D.R.C.	217	3°52′N	30°14′E
Aba, Nig.	210	5°06′N	7°21′E
Ābādān, Iran (ä-bŭ-dän′)	182	30°15′N	48°30′E
Abaetetuba, Braz. (ä′båĕ-tĕ-tōō′bå)	131	1°44′S	48°45′W
Abajo Peak, mtn., Ut., U.S. (ä-bå′hŏ)	109	37°51′N	109°28′W
Abakaliki, Nig.	215	6°21′N	8°06′E
Abakan, Russia (ŭ-bȧ-kän′)	165	53°43′N	91°28′E
Abakan, r., Russia (u-bȧ-kän′)	170	53°00′N	91°06′E
Abancay, Peru (ä-bän-kä′ė)	130	13°44′S	72°46′W
Abashiri, Japan (ä-bä-shē′rė)	194	44°00′N	144°13′E
Abasolo, Mex. (ä-bä-sō′lå)	112	27°13′N	101°25′W
Abasolo, Mex. (ä-bä-sō′lå)	118	24°05′N	98°24′W
Abaya, Lake, l., Eth. (ȧ-bä′yȧ)	211	6°24′N	38°22′E
'Abbāsābād, Iran	241h	35°44′N	51°25′E
ʻAbbāsah, Turʻat al, can., Egypt	218c	30°45′N	32°15′E
Abbeville, Fr. (ȧb-vēl′)	147	50°08′N	1°49′E
Abbeville, Al., U.S. (ăb′ė-vĭl)	114	31°35′N	85°15′W
Abbeville, Ga., U.S. (ăb′ė-vĭl)	114	31°53′N	83°23′W
Abbeville, La., U.S.	113	29°59′N	92°07′W
Abbeville, S.C., U.S.	115	34°09′N	82°25′W
Abbey Wood, neigh., Eng., U.K.	235	51°29′N	0°08′E
Abbiategrasso, Italy (äb-byä′tå-gräs′sō)	160	45°23′N	8°52′E
Abbots Bromley, Eng., U.K. (ăb′ŭts brŭm′lė)	144a	52°49′N	1°52′W
Abbotsford, Can. (ăb′ŭts-fẽrd)	106d	49°03′N	122°17′W
Abbots Langley, Eng., U.K.	235	51°43′N	0°25′W
ʻAbd al Kūrī, i., Yemen (ăbd-ĕl-kōō′rė)	218a	12°12′N	51°00′E
'Abd al-Shāhīd, Egypt	244a	29°55′N	31°13′E
Abdulino, Russia (äb-dȯ-lē′nō)	166	53°42′N	53°40′E
Abengourou, C. Iv.	214	6°44′N	3°29′W
Abeokuta, Nig. (ä-bå-ȯ-kōō′tä)	210	7°10′N	3°26′E
Abercorn *see* Mbala, Zam.	212	8°50′S	31°22′E
Aberdare, Wales, U.K. (ăb-ẽr-dâr′)	150	51°45′N	3°35′W
Aberdeen, Scot., U.K. (ăb-ẽr-dēn′)	142	57°10′N	2°05′W
Aberdeen, Ms., U.S. (ăb-ẽr-dēn′)	114	33°49′N	88°33′W
Aberdeen, S.D., U.S. (ăb-ẽr-dēn′)	96	45°28′N	98°29′W
Aberdeen, Wa., U.S. (ăb-ẽr-dēn′)	96	47°00′N	123°48′W
Aberford, Eng., U.K. (ăb′ēr-fẽrd)	144a	53°49′N	1°21′W
Abergavenny, Wales, U.K. (ăb′ẽr-gȧ-vĕn′ĭ)	150	51°45′N	3°05′W
Abert, Lake, l., Or., U.S. (ā′bẽrt)	104	42°39′N	120°24′W
Aberystwyth, Wales, U.K. (ă-bẽr-ĭst′wĭth)	150	52°25′N	4°04′W
Abidjan, C. Iv. (ä-bėd-zhäɴ′)	210	5°19′N	4°02′W
Abiko, Japan (ä-bē-kō)	195a	35°53′N	140°01′E
Abilene, Ks., U.S. (ăb′ĭ-lēn)	111	38°54′N	97°12′W
Abilene, Tx., U.S.	96	32°25′N	99°45′W
Abingdon, Eng., U.K.	144b	51°38′N	1°17′W
Abingdon, Il., U.S. (ăb′ĭng-dŭn)	103	40°48′N	90°21′W
Abingdon, Va., U.S.	115	36°42′N	81°57′W
Abington, Ma., U.S. (ăb′ĭng-tŭn)	93a	42°07′N	70°57′W
Abington, Pa., U.S.	229b	40°07′N	75°08′W
Abiquiu Reservoir, res., N.M., U.S.	109	36°26′N	106°42′W
Abitibi, l., Can. (ăb-ĭ-tĭb′ĭ)	85	48°27′N	80°20′W
Abitibi, r., Can.	85	49°30′N	81°10′W
Abkhazia, , Geor.	167	43°10′N	40°45′E
Ablis, Fr. (ȧ-blē′)	157b	48°31′N	1°50′E
Ablon-sur-Seine, Fr.	237c	48°43′N	2°25′E
Abnūb, Egypt (ȧb-nōōb′)	218b	27°18′N	31°11′E
Åbo *see* Turku, Fin.	142	60°28′N	22°12′E
Abóbada, Port.	238d	38°43′N	9°20′W
Abohar, India	186	30°12′N	74°13′E
Aboisso, C. Iv.	214	5°28′N	3°12′W
Abomey, Benin (ȧb-ȯ-mā′)	210	7°11′N	1°59′E
Abony, Hung. (ŏ′bå-ny′)	155	47°12′N	20°00′E
Abou Deïa, Chad	215	11°27′N	19°17′E
Abra, r., Phil. (ä′brä)	197a	17°16′N	120°38′E
Abraão, Braz. (äbrå-ouɴ′)	129a	23°10′S	44°10′W
Abraham's Bay, b., Bah.	123	22°20′N	73°50′W
Abram, Eng., U.K. (ā′brăm)	144a	53°31′N	2°36′W
Abramcevo, Russia	239b	55°50′N	37°50′E
Abrantes, Port. (ȧ-brän′tĕs)	158	39°28′N	8°13′W
Abridge, Eng., U.K.	235	51°39′N	0°07′E
Abrolhos, Arquipélago dos, is., Braz.	131	17°58′S	38°40′W
Abruka, i., Est. (ȧ-brōō′kȧ)	153	58°09′N	22°30′E
Abrunheira, Port.	238d	38°46′N	9°21′W
Abruzzi e Molise, hist. reg., Italy	160	42°10′N	13°55′E
Absaroka Range, mts., U.S. (ȧb-să-rō-kă)	96	44°50′N	109°47′W
Abşeron Yarımadası, pen., Azer.	167	40°20′N	50°30′E
Abū an-Numrus, Egypt	244a	29°57′N	31°12′E
Abū Arīsh, Sau. Ar. (ä-bōō ȧ-rēsh′)	182	16°48′N	43°00′E
Abu Dhabi *see* Abū Ẓaby, U.A.E.	182	24°15′N	54°28′E
Abu Ḥamad, Sudan (ä′bōō hä′-mĕd)	211	19°37′N	33°21′E
Abuja, Nig.	210	9°12′N	7°11′E
Abū Kamāl, Syria	182	34°45′N	40°46′E
Abunã, r., S.A. (ȧ-bōō-nä′)	130	10°25′S	67°00′W
Abū Qīr, Egypt (ä′bōō kēr′)	218b	31°18′N	30°06′E
Abū Qurūn, Ra's, mtn., Egypt	181a	30°22′N	33°32′E
Aburatsu, Japan (ä′bȯ-rät′sōō)	195	31°33′N	131°20′E
Abu Road, India (ȧ′bōō)	183	24°38′N	72°45′E
Abū Şīr Pyramids, hist., Egypt	244a	29°54′N	31°12′E
Abū Tīj, Egypt	218b	27°03′N	31°19′E
Abū Ẓaby, U.A.E.	182	24°15′N	54°28′E
Abū Zanīmah, Egypt	181a	29°03′N	33°08′E
Abyy, Russia	165	68°24′N	134°00′E
Acacias, Col. (ȧ-kȧ′sēäs)	130a	3°59′N	73°44′W
Acadia National Park, rec., Me., U.S. (ă-kā′dĭ-ȧ)	97	44°19′N	68°01′W
Acajutla, El Sal. (ä-kä-hōōt′lä)	120	13°37′N	89°50′W
Acala, Mex. (ä-kä′lä)	119	16°38′N	92°49′W
Acalayong, Eq. Gui.	216	1°05′N	9°40′E
Acámbaro, Mex. (ä-käm′bä-rō)	118	20°03′N	100°42′W
Acancéh, Mex. (ä-kän-sĕ′)	120a	20°50′N	89°27′W
Acapetlahuaya, Mex. (ä-kä-pĕt′lä-hwä′yä)	118	18°24′N	100°04′W
Acaponeta, Mex. (ä-kä-pȯ-nā′tă)	118	22°31′N	105°25′W
Acaponeta, r., Mex. (ä-kä-pȯ-nā′tă)	118	22°47′N	105°23′W
Acapulco, Mex. (ä-kä-pōōl′kō)	116	16°49′N	99°57′W
Acaraí Mountains, mts., S.A.	131	1°30′N	57°40′W
Acarigua, Ven. (äkä-rē′gwä)	130	9°29′N	69°11′W
Acatlán de Osorio, Mex. (ä-kät-län′dā ȯ-sō′rē-ō)	118	18°11′N	98°04′W
Acatzingo de Hidalgo, Mex.	119	18°58′N	97°47′W
Acayucan, Mex. (ä-kä-yōō′kän)	119	17°56′N	94°55′W
Accord, Ma., U.S.	227a	42°10′N	70°53′W
Accoville, W.V., U.S. (äk′kȯ-vĭl)	98	37°45′N	81°50′W
Accra, Ghana (ă′krȧ)	210	5°33′N	0°13′W
Accrington, Eng., U.K. (ăk′rĭng-tŭn)	144a	53°45′N	2°22′W
Acerra, Italy (ä-chĕ′r-rä)	159c	40°42′N	14°22′E
Achacachi, Bol. (ä-chä-kä′chė)	130	16°11′S	68°32′W
Achill Island, i., Ire. (ă-chĭl′)	146	53°55′N	10°05′W
Achinsk, Russia (ȧ-chėnsk′)	170	56°13′N	90°32′E
Acireale, Italy (ä-chė-rā-ä′lā)	160	37°37′N	15°12′E
Acklins, i., Bah. (ăk′lĭns)	117	22°30′N	73°55′W
Acklins, The Bight of, bt., Bah. (ăk′lĭns)	123	22°35′N	74°20′W
Acolman, Mex. (ä-kôl-mȧ′n)	119a	19°38′N	98°56′W
Acoma Indian Reservation, I.R., N.M., U.S.	109	34°52′N	107°40′W
Aconcagua, prov., Chile (ä-kȯn-kä′gwä)	129b	32°20′S	71°00′W
Aconcagua, r., Chile (ä-kȯn-kä′gwä)	129b	32°43′S	70°53′W
Aconcagua, Cerro, mtn., Arg. (ä-kȯn-kä′gwä)	132	32°38′S	70°00′W
Açores (Azores), is., Port.	209	37°44′N	29°25′W
A Coruña, Spain	142	43°20′N	8°20′W
Acoyapa, Nic. (ä-kȯ-yä′pä)	120	11°54′N	85°11′W
Acqui, Italy (äk′kwē)	160	44°41′N	8°22′W
Acre, state, Braz. (ä′krā)	130	8°40′S	70°45′W
Acre, r., S.A.	130	10°33′S	68°34′W
Acton, Can. (ăk′tŭn)	83d	43°38′N	80°02′W
Acton, Al., U.S. (ăk′tŭn)	100h	33°21′N	86°49′W
Acton, Ma., U.S. (ăk′tŭn)	93a	42°29′N	71°26′W
Acton, neigh., Eng., U.K. (ăk′tŭn)	235	51°30′N	0°16′W
Actopan, Mex. (äk-tȯ-pän′)	118	20°16′N	98°57′W
Actópan, r., Mex. (äk-tŏ′pän)	119	19°25′N	96°31′W
Acuitzio del Canje, Mex. (ä-kwēt′zė-ō dĕl kän′hå)	118	19°28′N	101°21′W
Acul, Baie de l', b., Haiti (ä-kōōl′)	123	19°55′N	72°20′W
Ada, Mn., U.S. (ā′dŭ)	102	47°17′N	96°32′W
Ada, Oh., U.S. (ā′dŭ)	98	40°45′N	83°45′W
Ada, Ok., U.S. (ā′dŭ)	111	34°45′N	96°43′W
Ada, Yugo. (ä′dä)	161	45°48′N	20°06′
Adachi, Japan	195a	35°50′N	39°36′
Adachi, neigh., Japan	242a	35°45′N	139°48′
Adak, Ak., U.S. (ă-dăk′)	95a	56°50′N	176°48′
Adak, i., Ak., U.S. (ă-dăk′)	95a	51°40′N	176°28′
Adak Strait, strt., Ak., U.S. (ă-dăk′)	95a	51°42′N	177°16′
Adamaoua, mts., Afr.	210	6°30′N	11°50′
Adams, Ma., U.S. (ăd′ămz)	99	42°35′N	73°10′
Adams, Wi., U.S. (ăd′ămz)	103	43°55′N	89°48′

ăt; finăl; rāte; senåte; ärm; ȧsk; sofȧ; fâre; ch-choose; dh-as th in other; bē; ėvent; bĕt; recĕnt; cratẽr; g-gō; gh-guttural g; bĭt; ĭ-short neutral; rīde; ᴋ-guttural k as ch in German ich;

PLACE (Pronunciation)	PAGE	LAT.	LONG.
Adams, r., Can. (ăd'ămz)	87	51°30'N	119°20'W
Adams, Mount, mtn., Wa., U.S. (ăd'ămz)	96	46°15'N	121°19'W
Adamsville, Al., U.S. (ăd'ămz-vĭl)	100h	33°36'N	86°57'W
Adana, Tur. (ä'dä-nä)	182	37°05'N	35°20'E
Adapazari, Tur. (ä-dä-pä-zä'rė)	149	40°45'N	30°20'E
Adarama, Sudan (ä-dä-rä'mä)	211	17°11'N	34°56'E
Adda, r., Italy (äd'dä)	160	45°43'N	9°31'E
Ad Dabbah, Sudan	211	18°04'N	30°58'E
Ad Dahnā, des., Sau. Ar.	182	26°05'N	47°15'E
Ad-Dāmir, Sudan (ad-dä'mĕr)	211	17°38'N	33°57'E
Ad Dammām, Sau. Ar.	182	26°27'N	49°59'E
Ad Dāmūr, Leb.	181a	33°44'N	35°27'E
Ad Dawhah, Qatar	182	25°02'N	51°28'E
Ad Dilam, Sau. Ar.	182	23°47'N	47°03'E
Ad Dilinjāt, Egypt	218b	30°48'N	30°32'E
Addington, Eng., U.K.	235	51°18'N	0°23'E
Addis Ababa, Eth.	211	9°00'N	38°44'E
Addison, Tx., U.S. (ă'dĭ-sŭn)	107c	32°58'N	96°50'W
Addlestone, Eng., U.K.	235	51°22'N	0°30'W
Addo, S. Afr. (ădō)	213c	33°33'S	25°43'E
Ad Duwaym, Sudan (ad-dò-ām')	211	13°56'N	32°22'E
Addyston, Oh., U.S. (ăd'ė-stŭn)	101f	39°09'N	84°42'W
Adel, Ga., U.S. (ā-dĕl')	114	31°08'N	83°55'W
Adelaide, Austl. (ăd'ė-lād)	202	34°46'S	139°08'E
Adelaide, S. Afr. (ăd-ĕl'ăd)	213c	32°41'S	26°07'E
Adelaide Island, i., Ant. (ăd'ė-lād)	219	67°15'S	68°40'W
Adelphi, Md., U.S.	229d	39°00'N	76°58'W
Aden (ʿAdan), Yemen (ä'dĕn)	182	12°48'N	45°00'E
Aden, Gulf of, b.	182	11°45'N	45°45'E
Aderklaa, Aus.	239e	48°17'N	16°32'E
Adi, Pulau, i., Indon. (ä'dė)	197	4°25'S	133°52'E
Adige, r., Italy (ä'dė-jā)	148	46°38'N	10°43'E
Adigrat, Eth.	185	14°17'N	39°28'E
Adilābād, India (ŭ-dĭl-ä-bäd')	186	19°47'N	78°30'E
Adirondack Mountains, mts., N.Y., U.S. (ăd-ĭ-rŏn'dăk)	97	43°45'N	74°40'W
Adis Abeba *see* Addis Ababa, Eth.	211	9°00'N	38°44'E
Adi Ugri, Erit. (ä-dė ōō'grė)	211	14°54'N	38°52'E
Adjud, Rom. (äd'zhōd)	155	46°05'N	27°12'E
Adkins, Tx., U.S.	107d	29°22'N	98°18'W
Adlershof, neigh., Ger.	238a	52°26'N	13°33'E
Admiralty, i., Ak., U.S. (ăd'mĭrăl-tė)	95	57°50'N	133°50'W
Admiralty Inlet, Wa., U.S. (ăd'mĭrăl-tė)	106a	48°10'N	122°45'W
Admiralty Island National Monument, rec., Ak., U.S. (ăd'mĭrăl-tė)	95	57°50'N	137°30'W
Admiralty Islands, is., Pap. N. Gui. (ăd'mĭrăl-tė)	197	1°40'S	146°45'E
Ado-Ekiti, Nig.	215	7°38'N	5°12'E
Adolph, Mn., U.S. (ā'dolf)	107h	46°47'N	92°17'W
Ādoni, India	187	15°42'N	77°18'E
Adour, r., Fr. (ä-dōōr')	147	43°43'N	0°38'W
Adra, Spain (ä'drä)	158	36°45'N	3°02'W
Adrano, Italy (ä-drä'nō)	160	37°42'N	14°52'E
Adrar, Alg.	210	27°53'N	0°15'W
Adria, Italy (ä'drė-ä)	160	45°03'N	12°01'E
Adrian, Mi., U.S. (ā'drĭ-ăn)	98	41°55'N	84°00'W
Adrian, Mn., U.S. (ā'drĭ-ăn)	102	43°39'N	95°56'W
Adrianople *see* Edirne, Tur.	142	41°41'N	26°35'E
Adriatic Sea, sea, Eur.	142	43°30'N	14°27'E
Adwa, Eth.	211	14°02'N	38°58'E
Adwick-le-Street, Eng., U.K. (ăd'wĭk-lė-strēt')	144a	53°35'N	1°11'W
Adycha, r., Russia (ä'dĭ-chå)	171	66°11'N	136°45'E
Adygea, state, Russia	166	45°00'N	40°00'E
Adz'va, r., Russia (ädz'vå)	166	67°00'N	59°20'E
Aegean Sea, sea (ė-jē'ăn)	142	39°04'N	24°56'E
A Estrada, Spain	158	42°42'N	8°29'W
Affton, Mo., U.S.	107e	38°33'N	90°20'W
Afghanistan, nation, Asia (ăf-găn-ĭ-stăn')	182	33°00'N	63°00'E
Afgooye, Som. (äf-gō'ĭ)	218a	2°08'N	45°08'E
Afikpo, Nig.	215	5°53'N	7°56'E
Aflou, Alg. (ä-flōō')	210	33°59'N	2°04'E
Afognak, i., Ak., U.S. (ä-fŏg-nák')	95	58°28'N	151°35'W
A Fonsagrada, Spain	158	43°08'N	7°07'W
Afonso Claudio, Braz. (äl-fōn'sō-klou'dėō)	129a	20°05'S	41°05'W
Afragola, Italy (ä-frá'gō-lä)	159c	40°40'N	14°19'E
Africa, cont.	209	10°00'N	22°00'E
Afton, Mn., U.S. (ăf'tŭn)	107g	44°54'N	92°47'W
Afton, Ok., U.S. (ăf'tŭn)	111	36°42'N	94°56'W
Afton, Wy., U.S. (ăf'tŭn)	105	42°42'N	110°52'W
ʿAfula, Isr. (ä-fōō'lå)	181a	32°36'N	35°17'E
Afyon, Tur. (ä-fė-ōn)	182	38°45'N	30°20'E
Agadem, Niger (ä'gá-dĕm)	211	16°50'N	13°17'E
Agadez, Niger (ä'gȧ-dĕs)	210	16°58'N	7°59'E
Agadir, Mor. (ä-gȧ-dēr)	210	30°30'N	9°37'W
Agalta, Cordillera de, mts., Hond. (kôr-dēl-yĕ'rä-dĕ-ä-gä'l-tä)	120	15°15'N	85°42'W
Agapovka, Russia (ä-gä-pôv'kä)	172a	53°18'N	59°10'E
Agartala, India	186	23°53'N	91°22'E
Agāshi, India	187b	19°28'N	72°46'E
Agashkino, Russia (á-gäsh'kĭ-nô)	172b	55°18'N	38°13'E
Agattu, i., Ak., U.S. (ä'gä-tōō)	95a	52°14'N	173°40'E
Agboville, C. Iv.	214	5°56'N	4°13'W
Ağdam, Azer. (äg'dăm)	167	40°00'N	47°00'E
Agde, Fr. (ägd)	156	43°19'N	3°30'E
Agege, Nig.	244d	6°37'N	3°20'E
Agen, Fr. (ȧ-zhăN')	147	44°13'N	0°31'E
Agincourt, neigh., Can.	227c	43°48'N	79°17'W
Aginskoye, Russia (ä-hĭn'skô-yĕ)	165	51°15'N	113°15'E
Agno, Phil. (äg'nō)	197a	16°07'N	119°49'E
Agno, r., Phil.	197a	15°42'N	120°28'E
Agnone, Italy (än-yō'nä)	160	41°49'N	14°23'E
Agogo, Ghana	214	6°47'N	1°04'W
Agostinho Pôrto, Braz.	234c	22°47'S	43°23'W
Agra, India (ä'grä)	183	27°18'N	78°00'E
Ağri, Tur.	167	39°50'N	43°10'E
Agri, r., Italy (ä'grē)	160	40°15'N	16°21'E
Agrícola Oriental, Mex.	233a	19°24'N	99°05'W
Agrínion, Grc. (á-grē'nyōn)	149	38°38'N	21°06'E
Agua, vol., Guat. (ä'gwä)	120	14°28'N	90°43'W
Agua Blanca, Río, r., Mex. (rė'ō-ä-gwä-blä'n-kä)	118	21°46'N	102°54'W
Agua Brava, Laguna de, l., Mex.	118	22°04'N	105°40'W
Agua Caliente Indian Reservation, I.R., Ca., U.S. (ä'gwä kal-yĕn'tä)	108	33°50'N	116°24'W
Aguada, Cuba (ä-gwä'dȧ)	122	22°25'N	80°50'W
Aguada, l., Mex. (ä-gwä'dȧ)	120a	18°46'N	89°40'W
Aguadas, Col. (ä-gwä'dȧs)	130	5°37'N	75°27'W
Aguadilla, P.R. (ä-gwä-dēl'yä)	117b	18°27'N	67°10'W
Aguadulce, Pan. (ä-gwä-dōōl'sä)	121	8°15'N	80°33'W
Agua Escondida, Meseta de, plat., Mex.	119	16°54'N	91°35'W
Agua Fria, r., Az., U.S. (ä'gwä frė-ä)	109	33°43'N	112°22'W
Aguai, Braz. (ägwä-ē')	129a	22°04'S	46°57'W
Agualeguas, Mex. (ä-gwä-lā'gwäs)	112	26°19'N	99°33'W
Agualva-Cacém, Port.	238d	38°46'N	9°18'W
Aguán, r., Hond. (ä-gwä'n)	120	15°22'N	87°00'W
Aguanaval, r., Mex. (ä-guä-nä-väl')	112	25°12'N	103°28'W
Aguanus, r., Can. (ä-gwä'nŭs)	93	50°45'N	62°03'W
Aguascalientes, Mex. (ä'gwäs-käl-yĕn'tās)	116	21°52'N	102°17'W
Aguascalientes, state, Mex. (ä'gwäs-käl-yĕn'tās)	118	22°00'N	102°18'W
Águeda, Port. (ä-gwā'dȧ)	158	40°36'N	8°26'W
Agueda, r., Eur. (ä-gĕ-dä)	158	40°50'N	6°44'W
Aguelhok, Mali	214	19°28'N	0°52'E
Aguilar, Spain	158	37°32'N	4°39'W
Aguilar, Co., U.S. (ä-gė-lär')	110	37°24'N	104°38'W
Aguilas, Spain (ä-gė-läs)	148	37°26'N	1°35'W
Aguililla, Mex. (ä-gė-lēl-yä)	118	18°44'N	102°44'W
Aguilillla, r., Mex. (ä-gė-lēl-yä)	118	18°30'N	102°48'W
Aguja, Punta, c., Peru (pŭn'tȧ ä-gōō'hä)	130	6°00'S	81°15'W
Agulhas, Cape, c., S. Afr. (ä-gōōl'yäs)	212	34°47'S	20°00'E
Agusan, r., Phil. (ä-gōō'sän)	197	8°12'N	126°07'E
Ahaggar, mts., Alg. (á-há-gär')	210	23°14'N	6°00'E
Ahar, Iran	185	38°28'N	47°04'E
Ahlen, Ger. (ä'lĕn)	154	51°45'N	7°52'E
Ahlenberg, Ger.	236	51°25'N	7°28'E
Ahmadābād, India (ŭ-mĕd-ä-bäd')	183	23°04'N	72°38'E
Ahmadnagar, India (ä'mûd-nû-gûr)	183	19°09'N	74°45'E
Ahmar Mountains, mts., Eth.	211	9°22'N	42°00'E
Ahoskie, N.C., U.S. (ä-hŏs'kė)	115	36°15'N	77°00'W
Ahrensburg, Ger. (ä'rĕns-bòrg)	145c	53°40'N	10°14'E
Ahrensfelde, Ger.	238a	52°35'N	13°35'E
Ahrweiler, Ger. (är'vī-lĕr)	154	50°34'N	7°05'E
Ähtärinjärvi, l., Fin.	153	62°46'N	24°25'E
Ahuacatlán, Mex. (ä-wä-kät-län')	118	21°05'N	104°28'W
Ahuachapán, El Sal. (ä-wä-chä-pän')	120	13°57'N	89°53'W
Ahualulco, Mex. (ä-wä-lōōl'kō)	118	20°43'N	103°57'W
Ahuatempan, Mex. (ä-wä-tĕm-pän)	118	18°11'N	98°02'W
Ahuntsic, neigh., Can.	227b	45°33'N	73°39'W
Åhus, Swe. (ô'hòs)	152	55°56'N	14°19'E
Ahvāz, Iran	182	31°15'N	48°54'E
Ahvenanmaa (Åland), is., Fin. (ä'vĕ-nán-mô) (ô'länd)	146	60°36'N	19°55'E
Aiea, Hi., U.S.	94a	21°18'N	157°52'W
Aigburth, neigh., Eng., U.K.	237a	53°22'N	2°55'W
Aiken, S.C., U.S. (ā'kĕn)	115	33°32'N	81°43'W
Aimorès, Serra dos, mts., Braz. (sĕ'r-rä-dôs-ī-mō-rē's)	131	17°40'S	42°38'W
Aimoto, Japan (ī-mô-tō)	195b	34°59'N	135°09'E
Aincourt, Fr. (âN-kōō'r)	157b	49°04'N	1°47'E
Aïn el Beïda, Alg.	210	35°57'N	7°25'E
Ainsworth, Eng., U.K.	237b	53°35'N	2°22'W
Ainsworth, Ne., U.S. (ānz'wûrth)	102	42°32'N	99°51'W
Aïn Témouchent, Alg. (ä'ēntĕ-mōō-shaN')	148	35°20'N	1°23'W
Aintree, Eng., U.K.	237a	53°29'N	2°56'W
Aïn Wessara, Alg. (ĕn ōō-sä-rá)	159	35°25'N	2°50'E
Aipe, Col. (ī'pĕ)	130a	3°13'N	75°15'W
Aïr, mts., Niger	210	18°00'N	8°30'E
Aire, r., Eng., U.K.	144a	53°42'N	1°00'W
Aire-sur-l'Adour, Fr. (âr)	156	43°42'N	0°17'W
Airhitam, Selat, strt., Indon.	181b	0°58'N	102°38'E
Airport West, Austl.	243b	37°44'S	144°53'E
Ai Shan, mts., China (äī'shän)	190	37°27'N	120°35'E
Aisne, r., Fr. (ĕn)	147	49°28'N	3°32'E
Aitape, Pap. N. Gui. (ä-ė-tä'pá)	197	3°00'S	142°10'E
Aitkin, Mn., U.S. (āt'kĭn)	103	46°32'N	93°43'W
Aitolikón, Grc. (ā-tō'lĭ-kôn)	161	38°27'N	21°21'E
Aitos, Bul. (ä-ē'tōs)	161	42°42'N	27°17'E
Aitutaki, i., Cook Is. (ī-tōō-tä'kė)	225	19°00'S	162°00'W
Aiud, Rom. (ä'ė-òd)	149	46°19'N	23°40'E
Aiuruoca, Braz. (äē'ōō-rōōō'-kà)	129a	21°57'S	44°36'W
Aiuruoca, r., Braz.	129a	22°11'S	44°35'W
Aix-en-Provence, Fr. (ĕks-prô-văNs)	147	43°32'N	5°27'E
Aix-les-Bains, Fr. (ĕks'-lā-băN')	157	45°42'N	5°56'E
Aiyáleo, Grc.	239d	37°59'N	23°41'E
Aíyina, Grc.	161	37°43'N	23°35'E
Aíyina, i., Grc.	161	37°43'N	23°35'E
Aíyion, Grc.	161	38°13'N	22°04'E
Aizpute, Lat. (ä'ēz-pōō-tĕ)	153	56°44'N	21°37'E
Aizuwakamatsu, Japan	194	37°27'N	139°51'E
Ajaccio, Fr. (ä-yät'chō)	142	41°55'N	8°42'E
Ajalpan, Mex. (ä-häl'pän)	119	18°21'N	97°14'W
Ajana, Austl. (ăj-ăn'ĕr)	202	28°00'S	114°45'E
Ajaria, state, Geor.	168	41°40'N	42°00'E
Ajdābiyah, Libya	211	30°56'N	20°16'E
Ajjer, Tassili-n-, plat., Alg.	210	25°40'N	6°57'E
Ajmah, Jabal al, mts., Egypt	181a	29°12'N	34°03'E
Ajman, U.A.E.	185	25°15'N	54°30'E
Ajmer, India (ŭj-mēr')	183	26°26'N	74°42'E
Ajo, Az., U.S. (ä'hō)	109	32°20'N	112°55'W
Ajuchitlán del Progreso, Mex. (ä-hōō-chet-län)	118	18°11'N	100°32'W
Ajuda, neigh., Port.	238d	38°43'N	9°12'W
Ajusco, Mex. (ä-hōō's-kō)	119a	19°13'N	99°12'W
Ajusco, Cerro, mtn., Mex. (sĕ'r-rô-ä-hōō's-kō)	119a	19°12'N	99°16'W
Akaishi-dake, mtn., Japan (ä-kī-shē dä'kä)	195	35°30'N	138°00'E
Akashi, Japan (ä'kä-shē)	194	34°38'N	134°59'E
Akbarābād, Iran	241h	35°41'N	51°21'E
Aketi, D.R.C. (ä-kå-tē)	211	2°44'N	23°46'E
Akhaltsikhe, Geor. (äkå'l-tsĭ-kĕ)	167	41°40'N	42°50'E
Akhdar, Al Jabal al, mts., Libya	211	32°00'N	22°00'E
Akhḑar, Al Jabal al, mts., Oman	182	23°30'N	56°43'W
Akhelóös, r., Grc. (ä-hĕ'lō-ōs)	161	38°45'N	21°26'E
Akhisar, Tur. (äk-hĭs-sär')	149	38°58'N	27°58'E
Akhtarskaya, Bukhta, b., Russia (bōōk'tä äk-tär'skȧ-yȧ)	163	45°53'N	38°22'E
Akhtopol, Bul. (äk'tō-pōl)	161	42°08'N	27°54'E
Akhunovo, Russia (ä-kû'nô-vô)	172a	54°13'N	59°36'E
Aki, Japan (ä'kė)	195	33°31'N	133°51'E
Akiak, Ak., U.S. (äk'yák)	95	61°00'N	161°02'W
Akimiski, i., Can. (ä-kĭ-mĭ'skĭ)	85	52°54'N	80°22'W
Akishima, Japan	242a	35°41'N	139°22'E
Akita, Japan (ä'kė-tä)	189	39°40'N	140°12'E
Akjoujt, Maur.	210	19°45'N	14°23'W
ʿAkko, Isr.	181a	32°56'N	35°05'E
Aklavik, Can. (äk'lä-vĭk)	84	68°28'N	135°26'W
'Aklé'Âouâna, dunes, Afr.	214	18°07'N	6°00'W
Akmola (Tselinograd), Kaz.	169	51°10'N	71°43'E
Ako, Japan (ä'kō)	195	34°44'N	134°22'E
Akola, India (á-kō'lä)	183	20°47'N	77°00'E
Akordat, Erit.	211	15°34'N	37°54'E
Akpatok, i., Can. (äk'pá-tŏk)	85	60°30'N	67°10'W
Akranes, Ice.	146	64°18'N	21°40'W
Akron, Co., U.S. (äk'rŭn)	110	40°09'N	103°14'W
Akron, Oh., U.S. (äk'rŭn)	97	41°05'N	81°30'W
Akropolis, pt. of i., Grc.	239d	37°58'N	23°43'E
Aksaray, Tur. (äk-sá-rī')	149	38°30'N	34°05'E
Akşehır, Tur. (äk'shå-hĕr)	149	38°20'N	31°20'E
Akşehır Gölü, l., Tur. (äk'shå-hĕr)	182	38°40'N	31°30'E
Aksha, Russia (äk'shå)	165	50°28'N	113°00'E
Aksu, China (ä-kŭ-sōō)	188	41°29'N	80°15'E
Akune, Japan (ä'kò-nä)	195	32°03'N	130°16'E
Akureyri, Ice. (ä-kò-rå'rė)	146	65°39'N	18°01'W
Akutan, i., Ak., U.S. (ä-kōō-tän')	95a	53°58'N	169°54'W
Akwatia, Ghana	214	6°04'N	0°49'W
Alabama, state, U.S. (ăl-ȧ-băm'ȧ)	97	32°50'N	87°30'W
Alabama, r., Al., U.S. (ăl-ȧ-băm'ȧ)	97	31°20'N	87°39'W
Alabat, i., Phil. (ä-lä-bät')	197a	14°14'N	122°05'E
Alacam, Tur. (ä-lä-chäm')	167	41°30'N	35°40'E
Alacant, Spain	148	38°20'N	0°30'W
Alacranes, Cuba (ä-lä-krä'nås)	122	22°45'N	81°35'W
Al Aflaj, des., Sau. Ar.	182	24°00'N	44°47'E
Alagôas, state, Braz. (ä-lä-gō'äzh)	131	9°50'S	36°33'W
Alagoinhas, Braz. (ä-lä-gō-ēn'yäzh)	131	12°13'S	38°12'W
Alagón, Spain (ä-lä-gōn')	158	41°46'N	1°07'W
Alagón, r., Spain (ä-lä-gōn')	158	39°53'N	6°42'W
Alaguntan, Nig.	244d	6°26'N	3°30'E
Alahuatán, r., Mex. (ä-lä-wä-tä'n)	118	18°30'N	100°00'W
Alajuela, C.R. (ä-lä-hwā'lä)	121	10°01'N	84°14'W
Alajuela, Lago, l., Pan. (ä-lä-hwā'lä)	116a	9°15'N	79°34'W
Alaköl, l., Kaz.	169	45°45'N	81°13'E
Alalakeiki Channel, strt., Hi., U.S. (ä-lä-lä-kā'kė)	94a	20°40'N	156°30'W
Al ʿAlamayn, Egypt	211	30°53'N	28°52'E
Al ʿAmārah, Iraq	185	31°50'N	47°09'E
Alameda, Ca., U.S. (ăl-ȧ-mä'dȧ)	96	37°46'N	122°15'W
Alameda, r., Ca., U.S. (ăl-ȧ-mä'dȧ)	106b	37°36'N	122°02'W
Alaminos, Phil. (ä-lä-mē'nôs)	197a	16°09'N	119°58'E
Al ʿAmirīyah, Egypt	149	31°01'N	29°52'E
Alamo, Mex. (ä'lä-mô)	119	20°55'N	97°41'W
Alamo, Ca., U.S. (ă'lȧ-mō)	106b	37°51'N	122°02'W
Alamo, Nv., U.S. (ă'lȧ-mō)	108	37°22'N	115°10'W
Alamo, r., Mex. (ä'lȧ-mō)	112	26°33'N	99°35'W
Alamogordo, N.M., U.S. (ăl-ȧ-mō-gôr'dō)	109	32°55'N	106°00'W
Alamo Heights, Tx., U.S. (ă'lȧ-mō)	107d	29°28'N	98°27'W
Alamo Indian Reservation, I.R., N.M., U.S.	109	34°30'N	107°30'W
Alamo Peak, mtn., N.M., U.S. (ă'lȧ-mō pēk)	112	32°50'N	105°55'W
Alamosa, Co., U.S. (ăl-ȧ-mō'sȧ)	109	37°25'N	105°50'W
Åland *see* Ahvenanmaa, is., Fin.	146	60°36'N	19°55'E
Alandskiy, Russia (ä-länt'skĭ)	172a	52°14'N	59°48'E
Alanga Arba, Kenya	217	0°07'N	40°25'E
Alanya, Tur.	149	36°40'N	32°10'E
Alaotra, l., Madag. (ä-lä-ō'trȧ)	213	17°15'S	48°17'E
Alapayevsk, Russia (ä-lä-pä'yĕfsk)	164	57°50'N	61°35'E
Al ʿAqabah, Jord.	182	29°32'N	35°00'E
Alaquines, Mex. (ä-lä-kē'nås)	118	22°07'N	99°35'W
Al ʿArīsh, Egypt (ä-rēsh')	181a	31°08'N	33°48'E
Alaska, state, U.S. (ȧ-lăs'kȧ)	94a	64°00'N	150°00'W
Alaska, Gulf of, b., Ak., U.S. (ȧ-lăs'kȧ)	95	57°42'N	147°40'W
Alaska Highway, trans., Ak., U.S. (ȧ-lăs'kȧ)	95	63°00'N	142°00'W
Alaska Peninsula, pen., Ak., U.S. (ȧ-lăs'kȧ)	95	55°50'N	162°10'W
Alaska Range, mts., Ak., U.S. (ȧ-lăs'kȧ)	95	62°00'N	152°18'W
Al ʿAtrūn, Sudan	211	18°13'N	26°44'E
Alatyr', Russia (ä'lä-tür)	164	54°55'N	46°30'E
Alazani, r., Asia	168	41°05'N	46°40'E
Alba, Italy (äl'bä)	160	44°41'N	8°02'E
Albacete, Spain (äl-bä-thā'tä)	148	39°00'N	1°49'W
Albachten, Ger. (äl-bä'κ-tĕn)	157c	51°55'N	7°31'E
Alba de Tormes, Spain (äl-bä dā tôr'mās)	158	40°48'N	5°28'W
Alba Iulia, Rom. (äl-bä yōō'lyȧ)	149	46°05'N	23°32'E
Albani, Colli, hills, Italy	159d	41°46'N	12°45'E
Albania, nation, Eur. (ăl-bā'nĭ-ȧ)	142	41°45'N	20°00'E
Albano, Lago, l., Italy (lä'-gō äl-bä'nō)	159d	41°45'N	12°44'E
Albano Laziale, Italy (äl-bä'nō lät-zē-ä'lä)	160	41°44'N	12°43'E
Albany, Austl. (ôl'bȧ-nĭ)	202	35°00'S	118°00'E
Albany, Ca., U.S. (ôl'bȧ-nĭ)	106b	37°54'N	122°18'W
Albany, Ga., U.S. (ôl'bȧ-nĭ)	97	31°35'N	84°10'W

256 Albany – Almería

PLACE (Pronunciation)	PAGE	LAT.	LONG.
Albany, Mo., U.S. (ôl′bȧ-nĭ)	111	40°14′N	94°18′W
Albany, N.Y., U.S. (ôl′bȧ-nĭ)	97	42°40′N	73°50′W
Albany, Or., U.S. (ôl′bȧ-nĭ)	96	44°38′N	123°06′W
Albany, r., Can. (ôl′bȧ-nĭ)	85	51°45′N	83°30′W
Albany Park, neigh., Il., U.S. (ôl′bȧ-nĭ)	231a	41°58′N	87°43′W
Al-Barājīl, Egypt	244a	30°04′N	31°09′E
Al Başrah, Iraq	182	30°35′N	47°59′E
Al Batrūn, Leb. (äl-bä-tro͞on′)	181a	34°16′N	35°39′E
Albemarle, N.C., U.S. (ăl′bė-märl)	115	35°24′N	80°36′W
Albemarle Sound, strt., N.C., U.S. (ăl′bė-märl)	97	36°00′N	76°17′W
Albenga, Italy (äl-bĕŋ′gä)	160	44°04′N	8°13′E
Alberche, r., Spain (äl-bĕr′chå)	158	40°08′N	4°19′W
Alberga, The, r., Austl. (ăl-bŭr′gȧ)	202	27°15′S	135°00′E
Albergaria-a-Velha, Port.	158	40°47′N	8°31′W
Alberhill, Ca., U.S. (ăl′bẽr-hĭl)	107a	33°43′N	117°23′W
Albert, Fr. (ȧl-bâr′)	156	50°00′N	2°49′E
Albert, l., Afr. (ăl′bẽrt) (ȧl-bâr′)	211	1°50′N	30°40′E
Albert, Parc National, rec., D.R.C.	217	0°05′N	29°30′E
Alberta, prov., Can. (ăl-bûr′tȧ)	84	54°33′N	117°10′W
Alberta, Mount, mtn., Can. (ăl-bûr′tȧ)	87	52°18′N	117°28′W
Albert Edward, Mount, mtn., Pap. N. Gui. (ăl′bẽrt ĕd′wẽrd)	197	8°25′S	147°25′E
Albertfalva, neigh., Hung.	239g	47°27′N	19°02′E
Alberti, Arg. (ȧl-bĕ′r-tē)	129c	35°01′S	60°16′W
Albert Kanaal, can., Bel.	145a	51°07′N	5°07′E
Albert Lea, Mn., U.S. (ăl′bẽrt lē′)	103	43°38′N	93°24′W
Albert Nile, r., Ug.	217	3°25′N	31°35′E
Alberton, Can. (ăl′bẽr-tŭn)	92	46°49′N	64°04′W
Alberton, S. Afr.	213b	26°16′S	28°08′E
Albertson, N.Y., U.S.	228	40°46′N	73°39′W
Albertville *see* Kalemie, D.R.C.	212	5°56′S	29°12′E
Albertville, Fr. (ȧl-bêr-vēl′)	157	45°42′N	6°25′E
Albertville, Al., U.S. (ăl′bẽrt-vĭl)	114	34°15′N	86°10′W
Albi, Fr. (äl-bē′)	147	43°54′N	2°07′E
Albia, Ia., U.S. (ăl-bĭ-ȧ)	103	41°01′N	92°44′W
Albina, Sur. (äl-bē′nä)	131	5°30′N	54°33′W
Albina, Ponta, c., Ang.	216	15°51′S	11°44′E
Albino, Point, c., Can. (äl-bē′nō)	101c	42°50′N	79°05′W
Albion, Austl. (ăl′bĭ-ŭn)	243b	37°47′S	144°49′E
Albion, Mi., U.S. (ăl′bĭ-ŭn)	98	42°15′N	84°50′W
Albion, Ne., U.S. (ăl′bĭ-ŭn)	102	41°42′N	98°00′W
Albion, N.Y., U.S. (ăl′bĭ-ŭn)	99	43°15′N	78°10′W
Alboran, Isla del, i., Spain (ė′s-lä-dĕl-äl-bō-rä′n)	142	35°58′N	3°02′W
Ålborg, Den. (ôl′bŏr)	142	57°02′N	9°55′E
Albuquerque, N.M., U.S. (ăl-bů-kûr′kė)	96	35°05′N	106°40′W
Albuquerque, Cayos de, is., Col.	121	12°12′N	81°24′W
Alburquerque, Spain (äl-bo͞or-kĕr′kā)	158	39°13′N	6°58′W
Albury, Austl. (ôl′bẽr-ė)	203	36°00′S	147°00′E
Alcabideche, Port. (äl-kȧ-bē-dā′chå)	159b	38°43′N	9°24′W
Alcácer do Sal, Port. (ăb′ĭ-lēn)	158	38°24′N	8°33′W
Alcalá de Henares, Spain (äl-kä-lä′ dā ā-na′rās)	159a	40°29′N	3°22′W
Alcalá la Real, Spain (äl-kä-lä′lä rā-äl′)	158	37°27′N	3°57′W
Alcamo, Italy (äl′kȧ-mō)	160	37°58′N	13°03′E
Alcanadre, r., Spain (äl-kä-nä′drå)	159	41°41′N	0°18′W
Alcanar, Spain (äl-kä-när′)	159	40°35′N	0°27′E
Alcañiz, Spain (äl-kän-yēth′)	148	41°03′N	0°08′W
Alcântara, Braz. (äl-kän′tȧ-rȧ)	131	2°17′S	44°29′W
Alcântara, neigh., Port. (äl-kän′tȧ-ra)	238d	38°42′N	9°10′W
Alcaraz, Spain (äl-kä-räth′)	158	38°39′N	2°28′W
Alcaudete, Spain (ăb′ĭng-dŭn)	158	37°38′N	4°05′W
Alcázar de San Juan, Spain (äl-kä′thär dā sän hwän′)	148	39°22′N	3°12′W
Alcira, Spain (ä-thē′rä)	159	39°09′N	0°26′W
Alcoa, Tn., U.S. (ăl-kō′ȧ)	114	35°45′N	84°00′W
Alcobendas, Spain (äl-kō-bĕn′dȧs)	159a	40°32′N	3°39′W
Alcochete, Port. (äl-kō-chā′ta)	159b	38°45′N	8°58′W
Alcoi, Spain	148	38°42′N	0°30′W
Alcorcón, Spain	159a	40°22′N	3°50′W
Alcorta, Arg. (ȧl-kôr′tä)	129c	33°32′S	61°08′W
Alcova Reservoir, res., Wy., U.S. (ăl-kō′vȧ)	105	42°31′N	106°33′W
Alcove, Can. (ăl-kōv′)	83c	45°41′N	75°55′W
Alcúdia, Badia d', b., Spain	159	39°48′N	3°20′E
Aldabra Islands, is., Sey. (äl-dä′brä)	213	9°16′S	46°17′E
Aldama, Mex. (äl-dä′mä)	112	28°50′N	105°54′W
Aldama, Mex. (äl-dä′mä)	118	22°54′N	98°04′W
Aldan, Russia	165	58°46′N	125°19′E
Aldan, r., Russia	165	63°00′N	134°00′E
Aldan Plateau, plat., Russia	171	57°42′N	130°28′E
Aldanskaya, Russia	165	61°52′N	135°29′E
Aldeia, Braz.	234d	23°30′S	46°51′E
Aldenham, Eng., U.K.	235	51°40′N	0°21′W
Aldenhoven, Ger. (ȧl′dĕn-hō′vĕn)	157c	50°54′N	6°18′E
Aldenrade, neigh., Ger.	236	51°31′N	6°44′E
Aldergrove, Can. (ôl′dẽr-grōv)	106d	49°03′N	122°28′W
Alderney, i., Guernsey (ôl′dẽr-nĭ)	156	49°43′N	2°11′W
Aldershot, Eng., U.K. (ôl′dẽr-shŏt)	150	51°14′N	0°46′W
Alderson, W.V., U.S. (ôl-dẽr-sŭn)	98	37°40′N	80°40′W
Alderwood Manor, Wa., U.S. (ôl′dẽr-wo͝od män′ŏr)	106a	47°49′N	122°18′W
Aldridge-Brownhills, Eng., U.K.	144a	52°38′N	1°55′W
Aledo, Il., U.S. (ȧ-le′dō)	111	41°12′N	90°47′W
Aleg, Maur.	210	17°03′N	13°55′W
Alegre, Braz. (ȧlĕ′grĕ)	129a	20°41′S	41°32′W
Alegre, r., Braz. (ȧlĕ′grĕ)	132b	22°22′S	43°34′W
Alegrete, Braz. (ä-lå-grā′tā)	132	29°46′S	55°44′W
Aleksandrov, Russia (ä-lyĕk-sän′ drôf)	166	56°24′N	38°45′E
Aleksandrovsk, Russia (ä-lyĕk-sän′drôfsk)	165	51°02′N	142°21′E
Aleksandrovsk, Russia (ä-lyĕk-sän′drôfsk)	172a	59°11′N	57°36′E
Aleksandrów Kujawski, Pol. (ä-lĕk-säh′dro͞ov ko͞o-yav′skē)	155	52°54′N	18°45′E
Alekseyevka, Russia (ä-lyĕk-sā-yĕf′kȧ)	163	50°39′N	38°40′E
Aleksin, Russia (ăb′ĭng-tŭn)	162	54°31′N	37°07′E
Aleksinac, Yugo. (ȧ-lyĕk-sē-nȧk′)	161	43°33′N	21°42′E
Alemán, Presa, res., Mex. (prā′sä-lĕ-mȧ′n)	119	18°20′N	96°35′W
Alem Paraíba, Braz. (ä-lĕ′m-pȧ-räē′bȧ)	129a	21°54′S	42°40′W
Alençon, Fr. (ȧ-läɴ-sôɴ′)	147	48°26′N	0°08′E
Alenquer, Braz. (ä-lĕŋ-kĕr′)	131	1°58′S	54°44′W
Alenquer, Port. (ä-lĕŋ-kĕr′)	158	39°04′N	9°01′W
Alentejo, hist. reg., Port. (ä-lĕŋ-tā′zhȯ)	158	38°05′N	7°45′W
Alenuihaha Channel, strt., Hi., U.S. (ä′lå-no͞o-ė-hä′hä)	94a	20°20′N	156°05′W
Aleppo, Syria (ȧ-lĕp-ō)	182	36°10′N	37°18′E
Alès, Fr. (ä-lĕs′)	147	44°07′N	4°06′E
Alessandria, Italy (ä-lĕs-sän′drė-ä)	148	44°53′N	8°35′E
Ålesund, Nor. (ô′lĕ-sȯn′)	152	62°28′N	6°14′E
Aleutian Islands, is., Ak., U.S. (ȧ-lu′shăn)	94b	52°40′N	177°30′W
Aleutian Trench, deep	95a	50°40′N	177°10′E
Alevina, Mys, c., Russia	165	58°49′N	151°44′E
Alexander Archipelago, is., Ak., U.S. (ăl-ĕg-zăn′dẽr)	95	57°05′N	138°10′W
Alexander City, Al., U.S.	114	32°55′N	85°55′W
Alexander Indian Reserve, I.R., Can.	83g	53°47′N	114°00′W
Alexander Island, i., Ant.	219	71°00′S	71°00′W
Alexandra, S. Afr. (ȧl-ex-än′drȧ)	218d	26°07′S	28°07′E
Alexandria, Austl. (ăl-ĕg-zăn′drĭ-ȧ)	202	19°00′S	136°56′E
Alexandria, Can. (ăl-ĕg-zăn′drĭ-ȧ)	91	45°50′N	74°35′W
Alexandria, Egypt (ăl-ĕg-zăn′drĭ-ȧ)	211	31°12′N	29°58′E
Alexandria, Rom. (ăl-ĕg-zăn′drĭ-ȧ)	161	43°55′N	25°21′E
Alexandria, S. Afr. (ăl-ĕx-än-drĭ-ă)	213c	33°40′S	26°26′E
Alexandria, In., U.S. (ăl-ĕg-zăn′drĭ-ȧ)	98	40°20′N	85°20′W
Alexandria, La., U.S. (ăl-ĕg-zăn′drĭ-ȧ)	97	31°18′N	92°28′W
Alexandria, Mn., U.S. (ăl-ĕg-zăn′drĭ-ȧ)	102	45°53′N	95°23′W
Alexandria, S.D., U.S. (ăl-ĕg-zăn′drĭ-ȧ)	102	43°39′N	97°45′W
Alexandria, Va., U.S. (ăl-ĕg-zăn′drĭ-ȧ)	97	38°50′N	77°05′W
Alexandria Bay, N.Y., U.S. (ăl-ĕg-zăn′drĭ-ȧ)	99	44°20′N	75°55′W
Alexandroúpolis, Grc. (ăb-ĭ-tĭb′ĭ)	149	40°41′N	25°51′E
Alfaro, Spain (äl-färō)	158	42°08′N	1°43′W
Al-Fāshir, Sudan (äl-fä′shēr)	211	13°38′N	25°21′E
Al Fashn, Egypt	218b	28°47′N	30°53′E
Al Fayyūm, Egypt	211	29°14′N	30°48′E
Alfenas, Braz. (äl-fĕ′nȧs)	129a	21°26′S	45°55′W
Alfiós, r., Grc.	161	37°33′N	21°50′E
Al Firdān, Egypt (äl-fer-dän′)	218b	30°43′N	32°20′E
Alfortville, Fr.	237c	48°49′N	2°25′E
Alfred, Can. (ăl′frĕd)	83c	45°34′N	74°52′W
Alfreton, Eng., U.K. (ăl′fẽr-tŭn)	144a	53°06′N	1°23′W
Algarve, hist. reg., Port. (äl-gär′vĕ)	158	37°15′N	8°12′W
Algeciras, Spain (äl-hā-thē′räs)	158	36°08′N	5°25′W
Algeria, nation, Afr. (ăl-gē′rĭ-ȧ)	210	28°45′N	1°00′E
Algés, Port.	238d	38°42′N	9°13′W
Algete, Spain (äl-hā′tā)	159a	40°36′N	3°30′W
Al Ghayḑah, Yemen	185	16°12′N	52°15′E
Alghero, Italy (äl-gâ′rō)	148	40°32′N	8°22′E
Algiers, Alg. (ăl-jērs)	210	36°51′N	2°56′E
Algoa, Tx., U.S. (ăl-gō′ȧ)	113a	29°24′N	95°11′W
Algoma, Wa., U.S.	106a	47°17′N	122°15′W
Algoma, Wi., U.S.	103	44°38′N	87°29′W
Algona, Ia., U.S.	103	43°04′N	94°11′W
Algonac, Mi., U.S. (ăl′gȯ-năk)	98	42°35′N	82°30′W
Algonquin, Il., U.S. (ăl-gŏŋ′kwĭn)	101a	42°10′N	88°17′W
Algonquin Provincial Park, rec., Can.	97	45°50′N	78°20′W
Alhama de Granada, Spain (äl-hä′mä-dĕ-grä-nä′dä)	158	37°00′N	3°59′W
Alhama de Murcia, Spain	158	37°50′N	1°24′W
Alhambra, Ca., U.S. (ăl-hăm′brȧ)	107a	34°05′N	118°08′W
Al Ḩammān, Egypt	149	30°46′N	29°42′E
Alhandra, Port. (äl-yän′drȧ)	159b	38°55′N	9°01′W
Alhaurín, Spain (ä-lou-rēn′)	158	36°40′N	4°40′W
Al Ḩawāmidīyah, Egypt	244a	29°54′N	31°15′E
Al Ḩawrah, Yemen	185	13°49′N	47°37′E
Al Ḩawţah, Yemen	182	15°58′N	48°26′E
Al Ḩayy, Iraq	185	32°10′N	46°03′E
Al Ḩijāz, reg., Sau. Ar.	182	23°45′N	39°08′E
Al Hirmil, Leb.	181a	34°23′N	36°22′E
Alhos Vedros, Port. (äl′yōs′vā′drōs)	159b	38°39′N	9°02′W
Alhucemas, Baie d', b., Afr.	158	35°18′N	3°50′W
Al Ḩudaydah, Yemen	182	14°43′N	43°03′E
Al Hufūf, Sau. Ar.	182	25°15′N	49°43′E
Al Ḩulwān, Egypt (äl-hĕl′wän)	218b	29°51′N	31°20′E
Aliákmon, r., Grc. (ȧl-ė-ȧk′mōn)	149	40°26′N	22°17′E
Äli Bayramlı, Azer.	168	39°56′N	48°56′E
Alibori, r., Benin	215	11°40′N	2°55′E
Alice, S. Afr. (ăl-ĭs)	213c	32°47′S	26°51′E
Alice, Tx., U.S. (ăl′ĭs)	112	27°45′N	98°04′W
Alice, Punta, c., Italy (ä-lē′chĕ)	161	39°23′N	17°10′E
Alice Arm, Can.	86	55°29′N	129°29′W
Alicedale, S. Afr. (ăl′ĭs-dāl)	213c	33°18′S	26°04′E
Alice Springs, Austl. (ăl′ĭs)	202	23°38′S	133°56′E
Alicudi, i., Italy (ä-lē-ko͞o′dē)	160	38°34′N	14°21′E
Alifkulovo, Russia (ä-lĭf-kû′lô-vô)	172a	55°57′N	62°06′E
Alīgarh, India (ä-lė-gŭr′)	183	27°58′N	78°08′E
Al-Imām, neigh., Egypt	244a	30°01′N	31°15′E
Alingsås, Swe. (ȧ′lĭŋ-sȯs)	152	57°57′N	12°30′E
Alipore, neigh., India	240a	22°31′N	88°18′E
Aliquippa, Pa., U.S. (ăl-ĭ-kwĭp′ȧ)	101e	40°37′N	80°15′W
Al Iskandarīyah *see* Alexandria, Egypt	218b	31°12′N	29°58′E
Aliwal North, S. Afr. (ä-lė-wäl′)	212	31°09′S	28°26′E
Al Jafr, Qa'al, pl., Jord.	181a	30°15′N	36°24′E
Al Jaghbūb, Libya	211	29°46′N	24°32′E
Al Jawārah, Oman	185	18°55′N	57°17′E
Al Jawf, Libya	211	24°14′N	23°15′E
Al Jawf, Sau. Ar.	182	29°45′N	39°30′E
Aljezur, Port. (äl-zhā-zo͞or′)	158	37°18′N	8°52′W
Al Jīzah, Egypt	218b	30°01′N	31°12′E
Al Jubayl, Sau. Ar.	182	27°01′N	49°40′E
Al Jufrah, oasis, Libya	211	29°30′N	15°16′E
Al Junaynah, Sudan	184	13°27′N	22°27′E
Aljustrel, Port. (äl-zho͞o-strĕl′)	158	37°44′N	8°23′W
Al Kāb, Egypt	218c	30°56′N	32°19′E
Al Kāmilīn, Sudan (käm-lēn′)	211	15°09′N	33°06′E
Al Karak, Jord. (kĕ-räk′)	181a	31°11′N	35°42′E
Al Karnak, Egypt (kär′nak)	218b	25°42′N	32°43′E
Al Khābūrah, Oman	182	23°45′N	57°30′E
Al Khalīl, W. Bank	181a	31°31′N	35°07′E
Al Khandaq, Sudan (kän-däk′)	211	18°38′N	30°29′E
Al Khārijah, Egypt	184	25°26′N	30°33′E
Al Khums, Libya	211	32°35′N	14°10′E
Al Khurmah, Sau. Ar.	182	21°37′N	41°44′E
Al Kiswah, Syria	181a	33°31′N	36°13′E
Alkmaar, Neth. (älk-mär′)	151	52°39′N	4°42′E
Al Kufrah, oasis, Libya	211	24°45′N	22°45′E
Al-Kunayyisah, Egypt	244a	29°59′N	31°11′E
Al Kuntillah, Egypt	181a	29°59′N	34°42′E
Al Kuwayt, Kuw. (äl-ko͞o-wit)	182	29°04′N	47°59′E
Al Lādhiqīyah, Syria	182	35°32′N	35°51′E
Allagash, r., Me., U.S. (ăl′ȧ-găsh)	92	46°50′N	69°24′W
Allāhābād, India (ŭl-ŭ-hä-bäd′)	183	25°32′N	81°53′E
All American Canal, can., Ca., U.S. (âl ȧ-mĕr′ĭ-kăn)	108	32°43′N	115°12′W
Alland, Aus.	145e	48°04′N	16°05′E
Allariz, Spain (äl-yä-rēth′)	148	42°10′N	7°48′W
Allatoona Lake, res., Ga., U.S. (ăl′ȧ-to͞on′ȧ)	114	34°05′N	84°57′W
Allauch, Fr. (ä-lĕ′ȯ)	156a	43°21′N	5°30′E
Allaykha, Russia (ä-lī′ĸȧ)	165	70°32′N	148°53′E
Allegan, Mi., U.S. (ăl′ė-găn)	98	42°30′N	85°55′W
Allegany Indian Reservation, I.R., N.Y., U.S. (ăl-ė-gā′nĭ)	99	42°05′N	78°55′W
Allegheny, r., Pa., U.S. (ăl-ė-gā′nĭ)	99	41°10′N	79°20′W
Allegheny Front, mtn., U.S. (ăl-ė-gā′nĭ)	98	38°12′N	80°03′W
Allegheny Mountains, mts., U.S. (ăl-ė-gā′nĭ)	97	37°35′N	81°55′W
Allegheny Plateau, plat., U.S. (ăl-ė-gā′nĭ)	98	39°00′N	81°15′W
Allegheny Reservoir, res., U.S. (ăl-ė-gā′nĭ)	99	41°50′N	78°55′W
Allen, Ok., U.S. (ăl′ĕn)	111	34°51′N	96°26′W
Allen, Lough, l., Ire. (lŏk ăl′ĕn)	150	54°07′N	8°09′W
Allendale, N.J., U.S. (ăl′ĕn-dāl)	100a	41°02′N	74°08′W
Allendale, S.C., U.S. (ăl′ĕn-dāl)	115	33°00′N	81°19′W
Allende, Mex.	112	28°20′N	100°50′W
Allende, Mex. (äl-yĕn′då)	119	18°23′N	92°49′W
Allen Park, Mi., U.S.	230c	42°15′N	83°13′W
Allentown, Pa., U.S. (ălėn-toun)	97	40°35′N	75°30′W
Alleppey, India (ȧ-lĕp′ē)	183b	9°33′N	76°22′E
Aller, r., Ger. (äl′ẽr)	154	52°43′N	9°50′E
Allerton, Ma., U.S.	227a	42°18′N	70°53′W
Allerton, neigh., Eng., U.K.	237a	53°22′N	2°53′W
Alliance, Ne., U.S. (ȧ-lī′ăns)	96	42°06′N	102°53′W
Alliance, Oh., U.S. (ȧ-lī′ăns)	98	40°55′N	81°10′W
Al Lidām, Sau. Ar.	182	20°45′N	44°12′E
Allier, r., Fr. (ȧ-lyā′)	156	46°43′N	3°03′E
Alligator Point, c., La., U.S. (al′ĭ-gā-tẽr)	100d	30°57′N	89°41′W
Allinge, Den. (äl′ĭŋ-ĕ)	152	55°16′N	14°48′E
Allison Park, Pa., U.S.	230b	40°34′N	79°57′W
Al Līth, Sau. Ar.	185	20°09′N	40°16′E
All Pines, Belize (ôl pĭnz)	120a	16°55′N	88°15′W
Allston, neigh., Ma., U.S.	227a	42°22′N	71°08′W
Al Luḩayyah, Yemen	182	15°58′N	42°48′E
Alluvial City, La., U.S.	100d	29°51′N	89°42′W
Allyn, Wa., U.S. (ăl′ĭn)	106a	47°23′N	122°51′W
Alma, Can.	85	48°29′N	71°42′W
Alma, Can. (ăl′mȧ)	92	45°36′N	64°59′W
Alma, S. Afr.	218d	24°30′S	28°05′E
Alma, Ga., U.S.	115	31°33′N	82°31′W
Alma, Mi., U.S.	98	43°25′N	84°40′W
Alma, Ne., U.S.	110	40°08′N	99°21′W
Alma, Wi., U.S.	103	44°21′N	91°57′W
Alma-Ata (Almaty), Kaz.	169	43°19′N	77°08′E
Al Mabrak, val., Sau. Ar.	181a	29°16′N	35°12′E
Almada, Port. (äl-mä′dä)	159b	38°40′N	9°09′W
Almadén, Spain (ȧl-mȧ-dhān)	158	38°47′N	4°50′W
Al Madīnah, Sau. Ar.	182	24°26′N	39°42′E
Al Mafraq, Jord.	181a	32°21′N	36°13′E
Almagre, Laguna, l., Mex. (lä-gȯ′nä-ȧl-mä′grĕ)	119	23°48′N	97°45′W
Almagro, Spain (äl-mä′grō)	158	38°52′N	3°41′W
Al Maḩallah al Kubrā, Egypt	218b	30°58′N	31°10′E
Al Manāmah, Bahr.	182	26°01′N	50°33′E
Al-Manāwāt, Egypt	244a	29°55′N	31°14′E
Almanor, Lake, l., Ca., U.S. (ăl-măn′ôr)	108	40°11′N	121°20′W
Almansa, Spain (äl-män′sä)	158	38°52′N	1°09′W
Al Manshāh, Egypt	218b	26°31′N	31°46′E
Almansor, r., Port. (äl-män-sȯr)	158	38°41′N	8°27′W
Al Manşūrah, Egypt	211	31°02′N	31°25′E
Al Manzilah, Egypt (män′za-la)	218b	31°09′N	32°05′E
Almanzora, r., Spain (äl-män-thō′rä)	158	37°20′N	2°25′W
Al Marāghah, Egypt	218b	26°41′N	31°35′E
Almargem do Bispo, Port. (äl-mär-zhĕɴ)	159b	38°51′N	9°16′W
Al-Marj, Libya	211	32°44′N	21°08′E
Al Maşīrah, i., Oman	182	20°43′N	58°58′E
Al Mawşil, Iraq	182	36°00′N	42°53′E
Almazán, Spain (äl-mä-thän′)	158	41°30′N	2°33′W
Al Mazār, Jord.	181a	31°04′N	35°41′E
Al Mazra'ah, Jord.	181a	31°17′N	35°33′E
Almeirim, Port. (äl-māĭ-rēɴ′)	158	39°13′N	8°31′W
Almelo, Neth. (äl′mẽ-lō)	151	52°20′N	6°42′E
Almendra, Embalse de, res., Spain	158	41°15′N	6°10′W
Almendralejo, Spain (äl-män-drä-lā′hō)	158	38°43′N	6°24′W
Almería, Spain (äl-mā-rē′ä)	142	36°52′N	2°28′W
Almería, Golfo de, b., Spain (gȯl-fô-dĕ-äl-māĭ-reɴ′)	158	36°45′N	2°26′W

ăt; finăl; rāte; senåte; ärm; ȧsk; sofȧ; fâre; ch-choose; dh-as th in other; bē; ėvent; bĕt; recĕnt; cratẽr; g-gō; gh-guttural g; bĭt; ĭ-short neutral; rīde; ĸ-guttural k as ch in German ich;

PRONOUNCING INDEX

Älmhult–Andria 257

PLACE (Pronunciation)	PAGE	LAT.	LONG.
Älmhult, Swe. (ălm'hōōlt)	152	56°35'N	14°08'E
Almina, Punta, c., Mor. (äl-mē'nä)	158	35°58'N	5°17'W
Al Minyā, Egypt	211	28°06'N	30°45'E
Almirante, Pan. (äl-mē-rän'tä)	121	9°18'N	82°24'W
Almirante, Bahía de, b., Pan.	121	9°22'N	82°07'W
Almirós, Grc.	161	39°13'N	22°47'E
Almodóvar del Campo, Spain (äl-mō-dhō'vär)	158	38°43'N	4°10'W
Almoloya, Mex. (äl-mō-lō'yä)	118	19°32'N	99°44'W
Almoloya, Mex. (äl-mō-lō'yä)	119a	19°11'N	99°28'W
Almonte, Can. (ăl-mŏn'tė)	91	45°15'N	76°15'W
Almonte, Spain (äl-mōn'tā)	158	37°16'N	6°32'W
Almonte, r., Spain (äl-mōn'tā)	158	39°35'N	5°50'W
Almora, India	183	29°20'N	79°40'E
Al Mubarraz, Sau. Ar.	182	22°31'N	46°27'E
Al Mudawwarah, Jord.	181a	29°20'N	36°01'E
Al Mukhā (Mocha), Yemen	182	13°11'N	43°20'E
Almuñécar, Spain (äl-mōōn-yā'kär)	158	36°44'N	3°43'W
Alnön, i., Swe.	152	62°20'N	17°39'E
Aloha, Or., U.S. (ä'lō-hā)	106c	45°29'N	122°52'W
Alondra, Ca., U.S.	232	33°54'N	118°19'W
Alor, Pulau, i., Indon. (ä'lôr)	197	8°07'S	125°00'E
Álora, Spain (ä'lō-rä)	158	36°49'N	4°42'W
Alor Gajah, Malay.	181b	2°23'N	102°13'E
Alor Setar, Malay. (ä'lor stär)	196	6°10'N	100°16'E
Alouette, r., Can. (ä-lōō-ĕt')	106d	49°16'N	122°32'W
Alpena, Mi., U.S. (ăl-pē'nȧ)	97	45°05'N	83°30'W
Alpes Cotiennes, mts., Eur.	157	44°46'N	7°02'E
Alphen, Neth.	145a	52°07'N	4°38'E
Alpiarça, Port. (äl-pyär'sȧ)	158	39°38'N	8°37'W
Alpine, N.J., U.S. (ăl'pīn)	228	40°56'N	73°56'W
Alpine, Tx., U.S. (ăl'pīn)	112	30°21'N	103°41'W
Alps, mts., Eur. (ălps)	142	46°18'N	8°42'E
Alpujarra, Col. (àl-pōō-ĸa'rä)	130a	3°23'N	74°56'W
Al Qaḑārif, Sudan	211	14°03'N	35°11'E
Al Qāhirah see Cairo, Egypt	211	30°00'N	31°17'E
Al Qanṭarah, Egypt	218c	30°51'N	32°20'E
Al Qaryah Ash Sharqīyah, Libya	211	30°36'N	13°13'E
Al Qaṣr, Egypt	184	25°42'N	28°53'E
Al Qaṭīf, Sau. Ar.	182	26°30'N	50°00'E
Al Qayṣūmah, Sau. Ar.	182	28°15'N	46°20'E
Al Qunaytirah, Syria	181a	33°09'N	35°49'E
Al Qunfudhah, Sau. Ar.	182	19°08'N	41°05'E
Al Quṣaymah, Egypt	181a	30°40'N	34°23'E
Al Quṣayr, Egypt	211	26°14'N	34°11'E
Al Qusayr, Syria	181a	34°32'N	36°33'E
Als, i., Den. (äls)	152	55°06'N	9°40'E
Alsace, hist. reg., Fr. (ăl-sȧ's)	157	48°25'N	7°24'E
Alsip, Il., U.S.	231a	41°40'N	87°44'W
Altadena, Ca., U.S. (ăl-tă-dē'nȧ)	107a	34°12'N	118°08'W
Alta Gracia, Arg. (äl'tä grä'sė-ä)	132	31°41'S	64°19'W
Altagracia, Ven.	130	10°42'N	71°34'W
Altagracia de Orituco, Ven.	131b	9°53'N	66°22'W
Altai Mountains, mts., Asia (äl'tī')	188	49°11'N	87°15'E
Alta Loma, Ca., U.S. (ăl'tă lō'mȧ)	107a	34°07'N	117°35'W
Alta Loma, Tx., U.S. (ăl'tȧ lō-mȧ)	113a	29°22'N	95°05'W
Altamaha, r., Ga., U.S. (ôl-tȧ-mȧ-hô')	115	31°50'N	82°00'W
Altamira, Braz. (äl-tä-mē'rä)	131	3°13'S	52°14'W
Altamira, Mex.	119	22°25'N	97°55'W
Altamirano, Arg. (äl-tä-mė-rä'nō)	132	35°26'S	58°12'W
Altamura, Italy (äl-tä-mōō'rä)	149	40°40'N	16°35'E
Altar of Heaven, pt. of i., China	240b	39°53'N	116°25'E
Altar of the Earth, rel., China	240b	39°57'N	116°24'E
Altar of the Sun, rel., China	240b	39°54'N	116°27'E
Altavista, Va., U.S. (ăl-tä-vĭs'tȧ)	115	37°08'N	79°14'W
Altay, China (äl-tä)	188	47°52'N	86°50'E
Altenburg, Ger. (äl-tĕn-bōōrgh)	154	50°59'N	12°27'E
Altenderne Oberbecker, neigh., Ger.	236	51°35'N	7°33'E
Altenessen, neigh., Ger.	236	51°29'N	7°00'E
Altenhagen, neigh., Ger.	236	51°22'N	7°28'E
Altenmarkt an der Triesting, Aus.	145e	48°02'N	16°00'E
Altenvoerde, Ger.	236	51°18'N	7°22'E
Alter do Chão, Port. (äl-tĕr'dŏ shäɴ'ōɴ)	158	39°13'N	7°38'W
Altiplano, pl., Bol. (äl-tē-plá'nō)	130	18°38'S	68°20'W
Altlandsberg, Ger. (ält länts'bĕrgh)	145b	52°34'N	13°44'E
Altlünen, Ger.	236	51°38'N	7°31'E
Altmannsdorf, neigh., Aus.	239e	48°10'N	16°20'E
Alto, La., U.S. (ăl'tō)	113	32°21'N	91°52'W
Alto da Moóca, neigh., Braz.	234d	23°34'S	46°35'W
Alto Marañón, Río, r., Peru (rē'ō-ȧl'tō-mä-rän-yō'n)	130	8°18'S	77°13'W
Altomünster, Ger. (äl'tō-mün'stĕr)	145d	48°24'N	11°16'E
Alton, Can. (ôl'tŭn)	83d	43°52'N	80°05'W
Alton, Il., U.S. (ôl'tŭn)	97	38°53'N	90°11'W
Altona, Austl.	201a	37°52'S	144°50'E
Altona, Can.	89	49°06'N	97°33'W
Altona, Ger. (äl'tō-nȧ)	145c	53°33'N	9°54'E
Altona North, Austl.	243b	37°50'S	144°51'E
Altoona, Al., U.S. (ăl-tōō'nȧ)	114	34°01'N	86°15'W
Altoona, Pa., U.S. (ăl-tōō'nȧ)	97	40°25'N	78°25'W
Altoona, Wa., U.S. (ăl-tōō'nȧ)	106c	46°16'N	123°39'W
Alto Rio Doce, Braz. (äl'tō-rē'ō-dō'sĕ)	129a	21°02'S	43°23'W
Alto Songo, Cuba (äl-fō-sôŋ'gō)	123	20°10'N	75°45'W
Altotonga, Mex. (ȧl-tō-tôŋ'gä)	119	19°44'N	97°13'W
Alto Velo, i., Dom. Rep. (äl-tō-vĕ'lō)	123	17°30'N	71°35'W
Altrincham, Eng., U.K. (ôl'trĭng-ăm)	144a	53°18'N	2°21'W
Altruppin, Ger. (ält rōō'ppēn)	145b	52°56'N	12°50'E
Altun Shan, mts., China (äl-tōn shän)	188	36°58'N	85°09'E
Alturas, Ca., U.S. (ăl-tōō'rȧs)	104	41°29'N	120°33'W
Altus, Ok., U.S. (ăl'tŭs)	110	34°38'N	99°20'W
Al 'Ubaylah, Sau. Ar.	185	21°59'N	50°57'E
Al-Uḑayyah, Sudan	211	12°06'N	28°16'E
Alūksne, Lat. (ä'lōks-nĕ)	166	57°24'N	27°04'E
Alumette Island, i., Can. (ȧ-lü-mĕt')	91	45°50'N	77°00'W
Alum Rock, Ca., U.S.	106b	37°23'N	121°50'W
Al 'Uqaylah, Libya	211	30°15'N	19°07'E
Al Uqṣur, Egypt	211	25°38'N	32°59'E
Alushta, Ukr. (ä'lshŏ-tȧ)	163	44°39'N	34°23'E
Alva, Ok., U.S. (ăl'vȧ)	110	36°46'N	98°41'W
Alvanley, Eng., U.K.	237a	53°16'N	2°45'W
Alvarado, Mex. (äl-vä-rä'dhō)	119	18°48'N	95°45'W

PLACE (Pronunciation)	PAGE	LAT.	LONG.
Alvarado, Luguna de, l., Mex. (lä-gò'nä-dē-äl-vä-rá'dô)	119	18°44'N	95°45'W
Älvdalen, Swe. (ĕlv'dä-lĕn)	152	61°14'N	14°04'E
Alverca, Port. (al-vĕr'kȧ)	159b	38°53'N	9°02'W
Alvesta, Swe. (äl-vĕs'tä)	152	56°55'N	14°29'E
Alvin, Tx., U.S. (ăl'vĭn)	113a	29°25'N	95°14'W
Alvinópolis, Braz. (äl-vēnō'pō-lės)	129a	20°07'S	43°03'W
Alviso, Ca., U.S. (ăl-vī'sō)	106b	37°26'N	121°59'W
Al Wajh, Sau. Ar.	182	26°15'N	36°32'E
Alwar, India (ŭl'wŭr)	183	27°39'N	76°39'E
Al Wāsiṭah, Egypt	218b	29°21'N	31°15'E
Alytus, Lith. (ä'lė-tós)	153	54°25'N	24°05'E
Alzira, rel., China	240b	39°55'N	116°20'E
Amacuzac, r., Mex. (ä-mä-kōō-zȧk)	118	18°00'N	99°03'W
Amadeus, l., Austl. (ăm-ȧ-dē'ŭs)	202	24°30'S	131°25'E
Amadjuak, l., Can. (ä-mädj'wăk)	85	64°50'N	69°20'W
Amadora, Port.	159b	38°45'N	9°14'W
Amagasaki, Japan (ä'mä-gä-sä'kė)	195	34°43'N	135°25'E
Ama Keng, Sing.	240c	1°24'N	103°42'E
Amakusa-Shimo, i., Japan (ämä-kōō'sä shē-mō)	194	32°24'N	129°35'E
Åmål, Swe. (ô'môl)	152	59°05'N	12°40'E
Amalfi, Col. (ä'mȧ'l-fē)	130a	6°55'N	75°04'W
Amalfi, Italy (ä-mä'l-fē)	159c	40°23'N	14°36'E
Amaliás, Grc. (ȧ-mäl'yȧs)	161	37°48'N	21°23'E
Amalner, India	186	21°07'N	75°06'E
Amambai, Serra de, mts., S.A.	131	20°06'S	57°08'W
Amami, i., Japan	189	28°10'N	129°55'E
Amapala, Hond. (ä-mä-pä'lä)	120	13°16'N	87°39'W
Amarante, Braz. (ä-mä-rän'tä)	131	6°17'S	42°43'W
Amargosa, r., Ca., U.S. (ȧ'mär-gō'sȧ)	108	35°55'N	116°45'W
Amarillo, Tx., U.S. (ăm-ȧ-rĭl'ō)	96	35°14'N	101°49'W
Amaro, Mount, mtn., Italy (ä-mä'rō)	148	42°07'N	14°07'E
Amaroúsion, Grc.	239d	38°03'N	23°49'E
Amasya, Tur. (ä-mä'sė-ȧ)	149	40°40'N	35°50'E
Amatenango, Mex. (ä-mä-tä-naŋ'gō)	119	16°30'N	92°29'W
Amatignak, i., Ak., U.S. (ä-mȧ'tė-näk)	95a	51°12'N	178°30'W
Amatique, Bahía de, b., N.A. (bä-ē'ä-dē-ä-mä-tē'kä)	120	15°58'N	88°50'W
Amatitlán, Guat. (ä-mä-tė-tlän')	120	14°27'N	90°39'W
Amatlán de Cañas, Mex. (ä-mät-län'dā kän-yäs)	118	20°50'N	104°22'W
Amazonas, state, Braz. (ä-mä-thō'näs)	130	4°15'S	64°30'W
Amazonas, Rio (Amazon), r., S.A. (rē'ō-ä-mä-thō'näs)	131	2°03'S	53°18'W
Ambāla, India (ŭm-bä'lŭ)	183	30°31'N	76°48'E
Ambalema, Col. (äm-bä-lā'mä)	130	4°47'N	74°45'W
Ambarchik, Russia (ŭm-bär'chĭk)	165	69°39'N	162°18'E
Ambarnāth, India	187b	19°12'N	73°10'E
Ambato, Ec. (äm-bä'tō)	130	1°15'S	78°30'W
Ambatondrazaka, Madag.	213	17°58'S	48°43'E
Amberg, Ger. (äm'bĕrgh)	154	49°26'N	11°51'E
Ambergris Cay, i., Belize (ăm'bēr-grēs kāz)	120a	18°04'N	87°43'W
Ambergris Cays, is., T./C. Is.	123	21°20'N	71°40'W
Ambérieu-en-Bugey, Fr. (äɴ-bā-rē-u')	157	45°57'N	5°21'E
Ambert, Fr. (äɴ-bĕr')	156	45°32'N	3°41'E
Ambil Island, i., Phil. (äm'bēl)	197a	13°51'N	120°25'E
Ambler, Pa., U.S. (ăm'blēr)	100f	40°09'N	75°13'W
Amboise, Fr. (äɴ-bwăz')	156	47°25'N	0°56'E
Ambon, Indon.	197	3°45'S	128°17'E
Ambon, Pulau, i., Indon.	197	4°50'S	128°45'E
Ambositra, Madag. (äɴ-bō-sē'trä)	213	20°31'S	47°28'E
Amboy, Il., U.S. (ăm'boi)	98	41°41'N	89°15'W
Amboy, Wa., U.S. (ăm'boi)	106c	45°55'N	122°27'W
Ambre, Cap d', c., Madag.	213	12°06'S	49°15'E
Ambridge, Pa., U.S. (ăm'brĭdj)	101e	40°36'N	80°13'W
Ambrim, i., Vanuatu	203	16°25'S	168°15'E
Ambriz, Ang.	212	7°50'S	13°06'E
Amchitka, i., Ak., U.S. (ăm-chĭt'kȧ)	95a	51°25'N	178°10'E
Amchitka Passage, strt., Ak., U.S. (ăm-chĭt'kȧ)	95a	51°30'N	179°36'W
Amealco, Mex. (ä-mā-äl'kō)	118	20°12'N	100°08'W
Ameca, Mex. (ä-mĕ'kä)	118	20°34'N	104°02'W
Amecameca, Mex. (ä-mȧ-kä-mä'kä)	118	19°06'N	98°46'W
Ameide, Neth.	145a	51°57'N	4°57'E
Ameixoera, neigh., Port.	238d	38°47'N	9°10'W
Ameland, i., Neth.	151	53°29'N	5°54'E
Amelia, Oh., U.S. (ȧ-mēl'yȧ)	101f	39°01'N	84°12'W
American, South Fork, r., Ca., U.S. (ȧ-mĕr'ĭ-kăn)	108	38°43'N	120°45'W
Americana, Braz. (ä-mĕ-rė-kȧ'nȧ)	129a	22°46'S	47°19'W
American Falls, Id., U.S. (ȧ-mĕr'ĭ-kăn-fôls')	105	42°45'N	112°53'W
American Falls Reservoir, res., Id., U.S. (ȧ-mĕr'ĭ-kăn-fôls')	96	42°56'N	113°18'W
American Fork, Ut., U.S.	109	40°20'N	111°50'W
American Highland, plat., Ant.	219	72°00'S	79°00'E
American Samoa, dep., Oc.	2	14°20'S	170°00'W
Americus, Ga., U.S. (ȧ-mĕr'ĭ-kŭs)	97	32°04'N	84°15'W
Amersfoort, Neth. (ä'mĕrz-fōrt)	145a	52°08'N	5°23'E
Amersham, Eng., U.K.	235	51°40'N	0°38'W
Amery, Can. (ā'mēr-ė)	85	56°34'N	94°03'W
Amery, Wi., U.S.	103	45°19'N	92°24'W
Ames, Ia., U.S. (āmz)	103	42°00'N	93°36'W
Amesbury, Ma., U.S. (āmz'bĕr-ė)	93a	42°51'N	70°56'W
Amfissa, Grc. (ȧm-fĭ'sȧ)	161	38°32'N	22°26'E
Amga, Russia (ŭm-gä')	165	61°08'N	132°09'E
Amga, r., Russia	171	61°41'N	133°11'E
Amgun', r., Russia	171	52°30'N	138°00'E
Amherst, Can. (ăm'hērst)	85	45°49'N	64°14'W
Amherst, N.Y., U.S.	230a	42°58'N	78°48'W
Amherst, Oh., U.S.	101d	41°24'N	82°13'W
Amherst, i., Can. (ăm'hērst)	91	44°08'N	76°45'W
Amiens, Fr. (ä-myăɴ')	147	49°54'N	2°18'E
Amirante Islands, is., Sey.	5	6°02'S	52°30'E
Amisk Lake, l., Can.	89	54°35'N	102°13'W
Amistad Reservoir, res., N.A.	112	29°20'N	101°00'W
Amite, La., U.S. (ȧ-mēt')	113	30°43'N	90°32'W
Amite, r., La., U.S.	113	30°45'N	90°48'W
Amity, Pa., U.S. (ăm'ĭ-tĭ)	101e	40°02'N	80°11'W

PLACE (Pronunciation)	PAGE	LAT.	LONG.
Amityville, N.Y., U.S. (ăm'ĭ-tĭ-vĭl)	100a	40°41'N	73°24'W
Amlia, i., Ak., U.S. (ȧ'mlėä)	95a	52°00'N	173°28'W
'Ammān, Jord. (ăm'mȧn)	182	31°57'N	35°57'E
Ammersee, l., Ger. (äm'mĕr)	145d	48°00'N	11°08'E
Amnicon, r., Wi., U.S. (ăm'nė-kŏn)	107h	46°35'N	91°56'W
Amorgós, i., Grc. (ä-môr'gōs)	149	36°47'N	25°47'E
Amory, Ms., U.S. (āmō-rē)	114	33°58'N	88°27'W
Amos, Can. (ā'mŭs)	85	48°31'N	78°04'W
Amoy see Xiamen, China	189	24°30'N	118°10'E
Amparo, Braz. (äm-pá'-rô)	129a	22°43'S	46°44'W
Amper, r., Ger. (äm'pĕr)	145d	48°18'N	11°32'E
Amposta, Spain (äm-pōs'tä)	159	40°42'N	0°34'E
Amqui, Can.	92	48°28'N	67°28'W
Amrāvati, India	183	20°58'N	77°47'E
Amritsar, India (ŭm-rĭt'sŭr)	183	31°43'N	74°52'E
Amstelveen, Neth.	145a	52°18'N	4°51'E
Amsterdam, Neth. (äm-stĕr-däm')	142	52°21'N	4°52'E
Amsterdam, N.Y., U.S. (ăm'stĕr-dăm)	99	42°55'N	74°10'W
Amsterdam, Île, i., Afr.	219	37°52'S	77°32'E
Amstetten, Aus. (äm'stĕt-ĕn)	154	48°09'N	14°53'E
Am Timan, Chad (äm'tė-män')	211	11°18'N	20°30'E
Amu Darya, r., Asia (ä-mò-dä'rēä)	164	38°30'N	64°00'E
Amukta Passage, strt., Ak., U.S. (ä-mōōk'tá)	95a	52°30'N	172°00'W
Amundsen Gulf, b., Can. (ä'mŭn-sĕn-gŭlf')	84	70°17'N	123°28'W
Amundsen Sea, sea, Ant. (ä'mŭn-sĕn-sē')	219	72°00'S	110°00'W
Amungen, l., Swe.	152	61°07'N	16°00'E
Amur, r., Asia	165	49°00'N	136°00'E
Amurskiy, Russia (ä-mûr'skĭ)	172a	52°35'N	59°36'E
Amurskiy, Zaliv, b., Russia (zä'lĭf ä-mòr'skĭ)	194	43°20'N	131°40'E
Amusgos, Mex.	118	16°39'N	98°09'W
Amuyao, Mount, mtn., Phil. (ä-mōō-yä'ō)	197a	17°04'N	121°09'E
Amvrakikos Kólpos, b., Grc.	161	39°00'N	21°00'E
Amyun, Leb.	181a	34°18'N	35°48'E
Anabar, r., Russia (ăn-ȧ-bär')	171	71°15'N	113°00'E
Anaco, Ven. (ä-nä'kô)	131b	9°29'N	64°27'W
Anaconda, Mt., U.S. (ăn-ȧ-kŏn'dȧ)	96	46°07'N	112°55'W
Anacortes, Wa., U.S. (ăn-ȧ-kôr'tĕz)	106a	48°30'N	122°37'W
Anacostia, neigh., D.C., U.S.	229d	38°52'N	76°59'W
Anadarko, Ok., U.S. (ăn-ȧ-där'kō)	110	35°05'N	98°14'W
Anadyr', Russia (ŭ-nȧ-dĭr')	165	64°47'N	177°01'E
Anadyr, r., Russia	171	65°30'N	172°45'E
Anadyrskiy Zaliv, b., Russia	164	64°10'N	178°00'W
'Ānah, Iraq	185	34°28'N	41°56'E
Anaheim, Ca., U.S. (ăn'ȧ-hīm)	107a	33°50'N	117°55'W
Anahuac, Tx., U.S. (ä-nä'wäk)	113a	29°46'N	94°41'W
Ānai Mudi, mtn., India	187	10°10'N	77°00'E
Anama Bay, Can.	89	51°56'N	98°05'W
Ana María, Cayos, is., Cuba	122	21°25'N	78°50'W
Anambas, Kepulauan, is., Indon. (ä-näm-bäs)	196	2°41'N	106°38'E
Anamosa, Ia., U.S. (ăn-ȧ-mō'sȧ)	103	42°06'N	91°18'W
Anan'iv, Ukr.	167	47°43'N	29°59'E
Anapa, Russia (ȧ-nä'pä)	167	44°54'N	37°19'E
Anápolis, Braz. (ä-ná'pō-lės)	131	16°17'S	48°47'W
Añatuya, Arg. (ȧ-nyä-tōō'yȧ)	132	28°22'S	62°45'W
Anchieta, Braz. (ȧn-chyĕ'tä)	132b	22°49'S	43°24'W
Ancholme, r., Eng., U.K. (ăn'chŭm)	144a	53°28'N	0°27'W
Anchorage, Ak., U.S. (ăŋ'kēr-åj)	94a	61°12'N	149°48'W
Anchorage, Ky., U.S.	101h	38°16'N	85°32'W
Anci, China (än-tsŭ)	190	39°31'N	116°41'E
Ancienne-Lorette, Can. (äɴ-syĕn' lō-rĕt')	83b	46°48'N	71°21'W
Ancon, Pan. (ăŋ-kōn')	116a	8°55'N	79°32'W
Ancona, Italy (äŋ-kō'nä)	142	43°37'N	13°32'E
Ancud, Chile (äŋ-kōōdh')	132	41°52'S	73°45'W
Ancud, Golfo de, b., Chile (gôl-fô-dē-äŋ-kōōdh')	132	41°15'S	73°00'W
Anda, China	192	46°20'N	125°20'E
Åndalsnes, Nor.	152	62°33'N	7°46'E
Andalucia, hist. reg., Spain (än-dä-lōō-sē'ä)	158	37°35'N	5°40'W
Andalusia, Al., U.S. (ăn-dȧ-lōō'zhĭȧ)	114	31°19'N	86°19'W
Andaman Islands, is., India (ăn-dȧ-măn')	196	11°38'N	92°17'E
Andaman Sea, sea, Asia	196	12°44'N	95°45'E
Andarax, r., Spain	158	37°00'N	2°40'W
Anderlecht, Bel. (än'dĕr-lĕkt)	145a	50°49'N	4°16'E
Andernach, Ger. (än'dĕr-näk)	154	50°25'N	7°23'E
Anderson, Arg. (á'n-dĕr-sōn)	129c	35°15'S	60°15'W
Anderson, Ca., U.S. (ăn'dĕr-sŭn)	104	40°28'N	122°19'W
Anderson, In., U.S. (ăn'dĕr-sŭn)	98	40°05'N	85°50'W
Anderson, S.C., U.S. (ăn'dĕr-sŭn)	97	34°30'N	82°40'W
Anderson, r., Can. (ăn'dĕr-sŭn)	84	68°32'N	125°12'W
Andes Mountains, mts., S.A. (ăn'dēz) (än'dās)	128	13°00'S	75°00'W
Andheri, neigh., India	187b	19°08'N	72°50'E
Andhra Pradesh, state, India	183	16°00'N	79°00'E
Andikíthira, i., Grc.	149	35°50'N	23°20'E
Andizhan, Uzb. (än-dė-zhän')	169	40°45'N	72°22'E
Andong, S. Kor. (än'dŭng')	189	36°31'N	128°42'E
Andongwei, China (än-dôŋ-wā)	190	35°08'N	119°19'E
Andorra, And. (än-dôr'rä)	159	42°38'N	1°30'E
Andorra, nation, Eur. (än-dôr'rä)	142	42°30'N	2°00'E
Andover, Ma., U.S. (ăn'dō-vēr)	93a	42°39'N	71°08'W
Andover, N.J., U.S. (ăn'dō-vēr)	100a	40°59'N	74°45'W
Andøya, i., Nor. (änd-ûē)	146	69°12'N	14°58'E
Andreanof Islands, is., Ak., U.S. (än-drá-ä'nôf-ĭ'ăndz)	94b	51°10'N	177°00'W
Andrelândia, Braz. (än-drĕ-lá'n-dyȧ)	129a	21°45'S	44°18'W
Andrésy, Fr.	237c	48°59'N	2°04'E
Andrew Johnson National Historic Site, rec., Tn., U.S. (ăn'drōō jŏn'sŭn)	115	36°15'N	82°55'W
Andrews, N.C., U.S. (ăn'drōōz)	114	35°12'N	83°48'W
Andrews, S.C., U.S. (ăn'drōōz)	115	33°25'N	79°32'W
Andrews Air Force Base, pt. of i., Md., U.S.	229d	38°48'N	76°52'W
Andria, Italy (än'drė-ä)	149	41°17'N	15°55'E

PLACE (Pronunciation)	PAGE	LAT.	LONG.
Andros, Grc. (än'dhrôs)	161	37°50'N	24°54'E
Ándros, i., Grc. (än'drŏs)	149	37°59'N	24°55'E
Androscoggin, r., Me., U.S. (ăn-drŭs-kŏg'ĭn)	92	44°25'N	70°45'W
Andros Island, i., Bah. (ăn'drŏs)	117	24°30'N	78°00'W
Anefis i-n-Darane, Mali	214	18°03'N	0°36'E
Anegasaki, Japan (ä'nå-gä-sä'kē)	195a	35°29'N	140°02'E
Aneityum, i., Vanuatu (ä-nå-ē'tē-ŭm)	203	20°15'S	169°49'E
Aneta, N.D., U.S. (ă-nē'tȧ)	102	47°41'N	97°57'W
Aneto, Pico de, mtn., Spain (pē'kō-dĕ-ä-nĕ'tô)	142	42°35'N	0°38'E
Angamacutiro, Mex. (än'gä-mä-kōō-tē'rô)	118	20°08'N	101°44'W
Angangueo, Mex. (än-gäŋ'gwå-ō)	118	19°36'N	100°18'W
Ang'angxi, China (äŋ-äŋ-shyē)	189	47°05'N	123°58'E
Angarsk, Russia	165	52°48'N	104°15'E
Ånge, Swe. (ông'ă)	152	62°31'N	15°39'E
Angel, Salto, wtfl., Ven. (säl'tō-ä'n-hĕl)	130	5°44'N	62°27'W
Ángel de la Guarda, i., Mex. (ä'n-hĕl-dĕ-lä-gwä'r-dä)	116	29°30'N	113°00'W
Angeles, Phil. (än'hå-läs)	197a	15°09'N	120°35'E
Ängelholm, Swe. (ĕng'ĕl-hôlm)	152	56°14'N	12°50'E
Angelina, r., Tx., U.S. (ăn-jē lē'nȧ)	113	31°30'N	94°53'W
Angels Camp, Ca., U.S. (ān'jĕls kămp')	108	38°03'N	120°33'W
Angerhausen, neigh., Ger.	236	51°23'N	6°44'E
Ångermanälven, r., Swe.	146	64°10'N	17°30'E
Angermund, Ger. (än'ngĕr-münd)	157c	51°20'N	6°47'E
Angermünde, Ger. (äng'ĕr-mûn-dĕ)	154	53°02'N	14°00'E
Angers, Can. (äɴ-zhā')	83c	45°31'N	75°29'W
Angers, Fr.	156	47°29'N	0°36'W
Angkor, hist., Camb. (äng'kôr)	196	13°52'N	103°50'E
Anglesey, i., Wales, U.K. (ăŋ'g'l-sē)	150	53°35'N	4°28'W
Angleton, Tx., U.S. (aŋ'g'l-tŭn)	113a	29°10'N	95°25'W
Angmagssalik, Grnld. (äŋ-må'så-lĭk)	82	65°40'N	37°40'W
Angoche, Ilha, i., Moz. (ē'lä-än-gō'chå)	213	16°20'S	40°00'E
Angol, Chile (aŋ-gōl')	132	37°47'S	72°43'W
Angola, In., U.S. (ăŋ-gō'lȧ)	98	41°35'N	85°00'W
Angola, nation, Afr. (ăŋ-gō'lȧ)	212	14°15'S	16°00'E
Angono, Phil.	241g	14°31'N	121°08'E
Angora *see* Ankara, Tur.	182	39°55'N	32°50'E
Angoulême, Fr. (äŋ'gōō-lâm')	156	45°40'N	0°09'E
Angra dos Reis, Braz. (aŋ'grä dŏs rā'ēs)	129a	23°01'S	44°17'W
Angri, Italy (ä'n-grē)	159c	40°30'N	14°35'E
Anguang, China (än-gůäŋ)	192	45°28'N	123°42'E
Anguilla, dep., N.A.	117	18°15'N	62°54'W
Anguilla Cays, is., Bah. (ăŋ-gwĭl'ȧ)	122	23°30'N	79°35'W
Anguille, Cape, c., Can. (kăp'-äŋ-gē'yē)	93	47°55'N	59°25'W
Anguo, China (än-gwô)	190	38°27'N	115°19'E
Angyalföld, neigh., Hung.	239g	47°33'N	19°05'E
Anholt, i., Den. (än'hôlt)	152	56°43'N	11°34'E
Anhui, prov., China (än-hwā)	189	31°30'N	117°15'E
Aniak, Ak., U.S. (ä-nyä'k)	95	61°32'N	159°35'W
Aniakchak National Monument, rec., Ak., U.S.	95	56°50'N	157°50'W
Anik, neigh., India	240e	19°02'N	72°53'E
Animas, r., Co., U.S. (ä'nē-mås)	109	37°03'N	107°50'W
Anina, Rom. (ä-nē'nä)	161	45°03'N	21°50'E
Anita, Pa., U.S. (ȧ-nē'ȧ)	99	41°05'N	79°00'W
Aniva, Mys, c., Russia (mĭs ȧ-nē'vȧ)	194	46°08'N	143°13'E
Aniva, Zaliv, b., Russia (zä'lĭf ȧ-nē'vȧ)	194	46°30'N	143°00'E
Anjou, Can.	83a	45°37'N	73°33'W
Ankang, China (än-käŋ)	188	32°38'N	109°10'E
Ankara, Tur. (än'kȧ-rȧ)	182	39°55'N	32°50'E
Anklam, Ger. (än'kläm)	154	53°52'N	13°43'E
Ankoro, D.R.C. (äŋ-kō'rō)	212	6°45'S	26°57'E
Anloga, Ghana	214	5°47'N	0°50'E
Anlong, China (än-loŋ)	193	25°01'N	105°32'E
Anlu, China (än'lōō')	193	31°18'N	113°40'E
Ann, Cape, c., Ma., U.S. (kăp'ăn')	99	42°40'N	70°40'W
Anna, Russia (än'ä)	163	51°31'N	40°27'E
Anna, Il., U.S. (ăn'ȧ)	111	37°28'N	89°15'W
Annaba, Alg.	210	36°57'N	7°39'E
Annaberg-Bucholz, Ger. (än'ä-bĕrgh)	154	50°35'N	13°02'E
An Nafūd, des., Sau. Ar.	182	28°30'N	40°30'E
An Najaf, Iraq (än nä-jäf')	182	32°00'N	44°25'E
An Nakhl, Egypt	181a	29°55'N	33°45'E
Annamese Cordillera, mts., Asia	196	17°34'N	105°38'E
Annandale, Va., U.S.	229d	38°50'N	77°12'W
Annapolis, Md., U.S. (ă-năp'ō-lĭs)	97	39°00'N	76°25'W
Annapolis Royal, Can.	92	44°45'N	65°31'W
Ann Arbor, Mi., U.S. (ăn är'bēr)	97	42°15'N	83°45'W
An-Narrānīyah, Egypt	244a	29°58'N	31°10'E
An Nāṣirīyah, Iraq	182	31°08'N	46°15'E
An Nawfalīyah, Libya	211	30°57'N	17°38'E
Annecy, Fr. (ȧn sē')	157	45°54'N	6°07'E
Annemasse, Fr. (än'mäs')	157	46°09'N	6°13'E
Annen, neigh., Ger.	236	51°27'N	7°22'E
Annenskoye, Kaz. (ä-nĕn'skô-yĕ)	169	53°09'N	60°25'E
Annet-sur-Marne, Fr.	237c	48°56'N	2°43'E
Annette Island, i., Ak., U.S.	86	55°13'N	131°30'W
An Nhon, Viet	196	13°55'N	109°00'E
Annieopsquotch Mountains, mts., Can.	93	48°37'N	57°17'W
Anniston, Al., U.S. (ăn'ĭs-tŭn)	97	33°39'N	85°47'W
Annobón, i., Eq. Gui.	209	2°00'S	3°30'E
Annonay, Fr. (ȧn'ŏ-nĕ)	156	45°16'N	4°36'E
Annotto Bay, Jam. (än-nō'tō)	122	18°15'N	76°45'W
An Nuhūd, Sudan	211	12°39'N	28°18'E
Anoka, Mn., U.S. (ȧ-nō'kȧ)	107g	45°12'N	93°24'W
Anori, Col. (ä-nō'rē)	130a	7°01'N	75°09'W
Áno Viánnos, Grc.	160a	35°02'N	25°26'E
Anpu, China (än-pōō)	188	21°28'N	110°00'E
Anqiu, China (än-chyō)	190	36°26'N	119°12'E
Ansbach, Ger. (äns'bäk)	154	49°18'N	10°35'E
Anschlag, Ger.	236	51°10'N	7°29'E
Anse à Veau, Haiti (äɴs' ä-vō')	123	18°30'N	73°25'W
Anse d'Hainault, Haiti (äɴs'dĕnō)	123	18°30'N	74°25'W
Anserma, Col. (ȧ'n-sĕ'r-mȧ)	130a	5°13'N	75°47'W
Ansermanuevo, Col. (ȧ'n-sĕ'r-mȧ-nwĕ'vō)	130a	4°47'N	75°59'W
Anshan, China	192	41°00'N	123°00'E
Anshun, China (än-shōōn')	188	26°12'N	105°50'E
Anson, Tx., U.S. (ăn'sŭn)	112	32°45'N	99°52'W
Anson Bay, b., Austl.	202	13°10'S	130°00'E
Ansŏng, S. Kor. (än'sŭng')	194	37°00'N	127°12'E
Ansongo, Mali	214	15°40'N	0°30'E
Ansonia, Ct., U.S. (ăn-sōnĭ-ȧ)	99	41°20'N	73°05'W
Antalya, Tur. (än-tä'lē-ä) (ä-dä'lē-ä)	149	37°00'N	30°50'E
Antalya Körfezi, b., Tur.	149	36°40'N	31°20'E
Antananarivo, Madag.	213	18°51'S	47°40'E
Antarctica, cont.	219	80°15'S	127°00'E
Antarctic Peninsula, pen., Ant.	219	70°00'S	65°00'W
Antelope Creek, r., Wy., U.S. (ăn'tē-lōp)	105	43°29'N	105°42'W
Antequera, Spain (än-tē-kĕ'rä)	148	37°01'N	4°34'W
Anthony, Ks., U.S. (ăn'thō-nē)	110	37°08'N	98°01'W
Anthony Peak, mtn., Ca., U.S.	108	39°51'N	122°58'W
Anti Atlas, mts., Mor.	210	28°45'N	9°30'W
Antibes, Fr. (äɴ-tēb')	157	43°36'N	7°12'E
Anticosti, Île d', i., Can. (ăn-tĭ-kŏs'tē)	85	49°30'N	62°00'W
Antigo, Wi., U.S. (ăn'tĭ-gō)	103	45°09'N	89°11'W
Antigonish, Can. (ăn-tĭ-gō-nēsh')	93	45°35'N	61°55'W
Antigua, Guat. (än-tē'gwä)	116	14°32'N	90°43'W
Antigua, r., Mex.	119	19°16'N	96°36'W
Antigua and Barbuda, nation, N.A.	117	17°15'N	61°15'W
Antigua Veracruz, Mex. (än-tē'gwä vä-rä-krōōz')	119	19°18'N	96°17'W
Antilla, Cuba (än-tē'lyä)	123	20°50'N	75°50'W
Antímano, neigh., Ven.	234a	10°28'N	66°59'W
Antioch, Ca., U.S. (ăn'tĭ-ŏk)	106b	38°00'N	121°48'W
Antioch, Il., U.S.	101a	42°29'N	88°06'W
Antioch, Ne., U.S.	102	42°05'N	102°36'W
Antioquia, Col. (än-tē-ō'kēä)	130	6°34'N	75°49'W
Antioquia, dept., Col.	130a	6°48'N	75°42'W
Antlers, Ok., U.S. (ănt'lērz)	111	34°14'N	95°38'W
Antofagasta, Chile (än-tō-fä-gäs'tä)	132	23°32'S	70°21'W
Antofalla, Salar de, pl., Arg. (så-lär'de än-tō-fä'lä)	132	26°00'S	67°52'W
Antón, Pan. (än-tōn')	117	8°24'N	80°15'W
Antongila, Helodrano, b., Madag.	213	16°15'S	50°15'E
Antônio Carlos, Braz. (än-tō'nēō-kà'r-lôs)	129a	21°19'S	43°45'W
António Enes, Moz. (än-to'nyō ĕn'ēs)	213	16°14'S	39°58'E
Antonito, Co., U.S. (ăn-tō-nē'tō)	110	37°04'N	106°01'W
Antonopole, Lat. (än'tō-nō-pō lyĕ)	153	56°19'N	27°11'E
Antony, Fr.	157b	48°45'N	2°18'E
Antsirabe, Madag. (änt-sē-rä'bā)	213	19°49'S	47°16'E
Antsiranana, Madag.	213	12°18'S	49°16'E
Antsla, Est. (änt'slȧ)	153	57°49'N	26°29'E
Antuco, vol., S.A. (än-tōō'kō)	132	37°30'S	72°30'W
Antwerp, Bel.	142	51°13'N	4°24'E
Antwerp, S. Afr.	244b	26°06'S	28°10'E
Antwerpen *see* Antwerp, Bel.	142	51°13'N	4°24'E
Anūpgarh, India (ŭ-nŏp'gŭr)	186	29°22'N	73°20'E
Anuradhapura, Sri L. (ŭ-nōō'rä-dŭ-pōō'rŭ)	183b	8°24'N	80°25'E
Anxi, China (än-shyē)	188	40°36'N	95°49'E
Anyang, China (än'yäng)	189	36°05'N	114°22'E
Anykščiai, Lith. (anīksh-chä'ē)	153	55°34'N	25°04'E
Anzhero-Sudzhensk, Russia (än'zhâ-rō-sōōd'zhĕnsk)	164	56°08'N	86°08'E
Anzio, Italy (änt'zē-ō)	160	41°28'N	12°39'E
Anzoátegui, dept., Ven. (än-zôä'tē-gē)	131b	9°38'N	64°45'W
Aoba, i., Vanuatu	198f	15°25'S	167°50'E
Aomori, Japan (äô-mō'rē)	189	40°45'N	140°52'E
Aosta, Italy (ä-ôs'tä)	160	45°45'N	7°20'E
Aouk, Bahr, r., Afr. (ä-ōk')	211	9°30'N	20°45'E
Aoukâr, reg., Maur.	214	18°00'N	9°40'W
Apalachicola, Fl., U.S. (ăp-ȧ-lăch-ĭ-kō'lȧ)	114	29°43'N	84°59'W
Apan, Mex. (ä-pä'n)	118	19°43'N	98°27'W
Apango, Mex. (ä-päŋ'gō)	118	17°41'N	99°22'W
Apaporis, r., S.A. (ä-pä-pô'rĭs)	130	0°48'N	72°32'W
Aparri, Phil. (ä-pär'rē)	196	18°15'N	121°40'E
Apasco, Mex. (ä-pä's-kō)	118	20°33'N	100°43'W
Apatin, Yugo. (ŏ'pŏ-tĭn)	161	45°40'N	19°00'E
Apatzingán de la Constitución, Mex.	118	19°07'N	102°21'W
Apeldoorn, Neth. (ä'pĕl-dōōrn)	147	52°14'N	5°55'E
Apennines *see* Appennino, mts., Italy	142	43°48'N	11°06'E
Apese, neigh., Nig.	244d	6°25'N	3°25'E
Apía, Col. (ȧ-pē'ȧ)	130a	5°07'N	75°58'W
Apia, W. Sam.	198a	13°50'S	171°44'W
Apipilulco, Mex. (ä-pĭ-pĭ-lōōl'kō)	118	18°09'N	99°40'W
Apishapa, r., Co., U.S. (ăp-ĭ-shä'pȧ)	110	37°40'N	104°08'W
Apizaco, Mex. (ä-pē-zä'kō)	118	19°18'N	98°11'W
Aplerbeck, neigh., Ger.	236	51°29'N	7°33'E
Apo, Mount, mtn., Phil. (ä'pō)	197	6°56'N	125°05'E
Apopka, Fl., U.S. (ä-pŏp'kȧ)	115a	28°37'N	81°30'W
Apopka, Lake, l., Fl., U.S.	115a	28°38'N	81°50'W
Apoquindo, Chile	234b	33°24'S	70°32'W
Apostle Islands, is., Wi., U.S. (ă-pŏs''l)	103	47°05'N	90°55'W
Appalachia, Va., U.S. (ăpȧ-lăch'ĭ-ȧ)	115	36°54'N	82°49'W
Appalachian Mountains, mts., N.A. (ăp-ȧ-lăch'ĭ-ȧn)	97	37°20'N	82°00'W
Appalachicola, r., Fl., U.S. (ăpȧ-lăch'ĭ-cōlä)	97	30°11'N	85°00'W
Äppelbo, Swe. (ĕp-ĕl-bōō)	152	60°30'N	14°02'E
Appelhülsen, Ger. (ä'pĕl-hül'sĕn)	157c	51°55'N	7°26'E
Appennino, mts., Italy (äp-pĕn-nē'nô)	142	43°48'N	11°06'E
Appleton, Mn., U.S. (ăp''l-tŭn)	102	45°10'N	96°01'W
Appleton, Wi., U.S.	97	44°14'N	88°27'W
Appleton City, Mo., U.S.	111	38°10'N	94°02'W
Appomattox, r., Va., U.S. (ăp-ô-măt'ŭks)	115	37°22'N	78°09'W
Aprilia, Italy (ȧ-prē'lyȧ)	160	41°36'N	12°40'E
Apsheronsk, Russia	168	44°28'N	39°44'E
Apt, Fr. (äpt)	157	43°54'N	5°19'E
Apure, r., Ven. (ä-pōō'rä)	130	8°08'N	68°46'W
Apurimac, r., Peru (ä-pōō-rē-mäk')	130	11°39'S	73°48'W
Aqaba, Gulf of, b. (ä'kȧ-bȧ)	182	28°30'N	34°40'E
Aqabah, Wādī al, r., Egypt	181a	29°48'N	34°05'E
Aqtaū, Kaz.	169	43°35'N	51°05'E
Aqtöbe, Kaz.	169	50°20'N	57°00'E
Aquasco, Md., U.S. (ȧ'gwȧ'scō)	100e	38°35'N	76°44'W
Aquidauana, Braz. (ä-kē-däwä'nä)	131	20°24'S	55°46'W
Aquin, Haiti (ä-kăn')	123	18°20'N	73°25'W
Ara, r., Japan (ä-rä)	195a	35°40'N	139°52'E
Arab, Bahr al, r., Sudan	211	9°46'N	26°52'E
'Arabah, Wādī, val., Egypt	218b	29°02'N	32°10'E
Arabats'ka Strilka (Tongue of Arabat), spit, Ukr.	163	45°50'N	35°05'E
Arabi, La., U.S.	100d	29°58'N	90°01'W
Arabian Desert, des., Egypt (ȧ-rā'bĭ-ăn)	211	27°06'N	32°49'E
Arabian Sea, sea (ȧ-rā'bĭ-ăn)	180	16°00'N	65°15'E
Aracaju, Braz. (ä-rä'kä-zhōō')	131	11°00'S	37°01'W
Aracati, Braz. (ä-rä'kä-tē')	131	4°31'S	37°41'W
Araçatuba, Braz. (ä-rä-sȧ-tōō'bä)	131	21°14'S	50°19'W
Aracena, Spain	158	37°53'N	6°34'W
Aracruz, Braz. (ä-rä-krōō's)	131	19°58'S	40°11'W
'Arad, Isr.	181a	31°20'N	35°15'E
Arad, Rom. (ŏ'rŏd)	149	46°10'N	21°18'E
Arafura Sea, sea (ä-rä-fōō'rä)	197	8°40'S	130°00'E
Aragats, Gora, mtn., Arm.	168	40°32'N	44°14'E
Aragon, hist. reg., Spain (ä-rä-gōn')	159	40°55'N	0°45'W
Aragón, r., Spain	158	42°35'N	1°10'W
Aragua, dept., Ven. (ä-rä'gwä)	131b	10°00'N	67°05'W
Aragua de Barcelona, Ven.	130	9°29'N	64°48'W
Araguaia, r., Braz. (ä-rä-gwä'yä)	131	8°37'S	49°43'W
Araguari, Braz. (ä-rä-gwä'rē)	131	18°43'S	48°03'W
Araguatins, Braz. (ä-rä-gwä-tēns)	131	5°41'S	48°04'W
Aragüita, Ven. (ärä-gwē'tä)	131b	10°13'N	66°28'W
Araj, oasis, Egypt (ä-räj')	149	29°05'N	26°51'E
Arāk, Iran	182	34°08'N	49°57'E
Arakan Yoma, mts., Myanmar (ŭ-rŭ-kŭn'yō'mȧ)	183	19°51'N	94°13'E
Arakawa, neigh., Japan	242a	35°47'N	139°44'E
Arakhthos, r., Grc. (är'äĸ-thôs)	161	39°10'N	21°05'E
Arakpur, neigh., India	240d	28°35'N	77°10'E
Aral, Kaz.	169	46°47'N	62°00'E
Aral Sea, sea, Asia	164	45°17'N	60°02'E
Aralsor, l., Kaz. (ä-räl'sôr')	170	49°00'N	48°20'E
Aramberri, Mex. (ä-räm-bĕr-rē')	118	24°05'N	99°47'W
Arana, Sierra, mts., Spain	158	37°17'N	3°28'W
Aranda de Duero, Spain (ä-rän'dä dā dwā'rō)	158	41°43'N	3°45'W
Arandas, Mex. (ä-rän'däs)	118	20°43'N	102°18'W
Aran Island, i., Ire. (ăr'ăn)	150	54°58'N	8°33'W
Aran Islands, is., Ire.	146	53°04'N	9°59'W
Aranjuez, Spain (ä-rän-hwāth')	148	40°02'N	3°24'W
Aransas Pass, Tx., U.S. (ȧ-răn'sȧs pȧs)	113	27°55'N	97°09'W
Araouane, Mali	210	18°54'N	3°33'W
Arapkir, Tur. (ä-räp-kēr')	149	39°00'N	38°10'E
Araraquara, Braz. (ä-rä-rä-kwä'rä)	131	21°47'S	48°08'W
Araras, Braz. (ä-rä'räs)	129a	22°21'S	47°22'W
Araras, Serra das, mts., Braz. (sĕ'r-rä-däs-ä-rä'räs)	131	18°03'S	53°23'W
Araras, Serra das, mts., Braz. (sĕ'r-rä-däs-ä-rä'räs)	132	23°30'S	53°00'W
Araras, Serra das, mts., Braz.	132b	22°24'S	43°15'W
Ararat, Austl. (ăr'ărăt)	203	37°17'S	142°56'E
Ararat, Mount, mtn., Tur.	182	39°50'N	44°20'E
Arari, l., Braz. (ä-rà'rē)	131	0°30'S	48°50'W
Araripe, Chapada do, hills, Braz. (shä-pä'dä-dô-ä-rä-rē'pĕ)	131	5°55'S	40°42'W
Araruama, Braz. (ä-rä-rōō-ä'mä)	129a	22°53'S	42°19'W
Araruama, Lagoa de, l., Braz.	129a	23°00'S	42°15'W
Aras, r., Asia (ä-räs)	182	39°15'N	47°10'E
Aratuípe, Braz. (ä-rä-tōō-ē'pĕ)	131	13°12'S	38°58'W
Arauca, Col. (ä-rou'kä)	130	6°56'N	70°45'W
Arauca, r., S.A.	130	7°13'N	68°43'W
Aravaca, neigh., Spain	238b	40°28'N	3°46'W
Aravalli Range, mts., India (ä-rä'vŭ-lē)	183	24°15'N	72°40'E
Araya, Punta de, c., Ven. (pŭn'tȧ-dĕ-ä-rä'yȧ)	131b	10°40'N	64°15'W
Arayat, Phil. (ä-rä'yät)	197a	15°10'N	120°44'E
'Arbi, Sudan	211	20°36'N	29°57'E
Arboga, Swe. (är-bō'gä)	152	59°26'N	15°50'E
Arborea, Italy (är-bō-rĕ'ä)	160	39°50'N	8°36'E
Arbroath, Scot., U.K. (är-brōth')	150	56°36'N	2°25'W
Arcachon, Fr. (är-kä-shôɴ')	147	44°39'N	1°12'W
Arcachon, Bassin d', Fr. (bä-sĕn' där-kä-shôn')	156	44°42'N	1°50'W
Arcadia, Ca., U.S. (är-kā'dĭ-ȧ)	107a	34°08'N	118°02'W
Arcadia, Fl., U.S.	115a	27°12'N	81°51'W
Arcadia, La., U.S.	113	32°33'N	92°56'W
Arcadia, Wi., U.S.	103	44°15'N	91°30'W
Arcata, Ca., U.S. (är-kȧ'tȧ)	104	40°54'N	124°05'W
Arc de Triomphe, pt. of i., Fr.	237c	48°53'N	2°17'E
Arc Dome Mountain, mtn., Nv., U.S. (ärk dōm)	108	38°51'N	117°21'W
Arcelia, Mex. (är-sā'lē-ä)	118	18°19'N	100°14'W
Archbald, Pa., U.S. (ärch'bôld)	99	41°30'N	75°35'W
Arches National Park, Ut., U.S. (är'ches)	109	38°45'N	109°35'W
Archidona, Ec. (är-chē-do'nä)	130	1°01'S	77°49'W
Archidona, Spain (är-chē-dô'nä)	158	37°08'N	4°24'W
Arcis-sur-Aube, Fr. (är-sēs'sür-ōb')	156	48°31'N	4°04'E
Arco, Id., U.S. (är'kō)	105	43°39'N	113°15'W
Arcola, Tx., U.S.	113a	29°30'N	95°28'W
Arcola, Va., U.S. (ăr'cōlă)	100e	38°57'N	77°32'W
Arcos de la Frontera, Spain (är'kōs-dĕ-lä-frôn-tĕ'rä)	158	36°44'N	5°48'W
Arctic Ocean, o.	220	85°00'N	170°00'E
Arcueil, Fr. (ärk'tĭk)	237c	48°48'N	2°20'E
Arda, r., Bul. (är'dä)	161	41°36'N	25°18'E
Ardabīl, Iran	182	38°15'N	48°00'E
Ardahan, Tur. (är-dȧ-hän')	167	41°10'N	42°40'E
Ardatov, Russia (är-dȧ-tôf')	166	54°58'N	46°10'E

PRONOUNCING INDEX

Ardennes-Atascosa 259

PLACE (Pronunciation)	PAGE	LAT.	LONG.
Ardennes, mts., Eur. (àr-dĕn')	147	50°01'N	5°12'E
Ardey, neigh., Ger.	236	51°26'N	7°23'E
Ardila, r., Eur. (är-dē'là)	158	38°10'N	7°15'W
Ardmore, Md., U.S.	229d	38°56'N	76°52'W
Ardmore, Ok., U.S. (ärd'mōr)	96	34°10'N	97°08'W
Ardmore, Pa., U.S.	100f	40°01'N	75°18'W
Ardrossan, Can. (är-dros'ăn)	83g	53°33'N	113°08'W
Ardsley, Eng., U.K. (ärdz'lē)	144a	53°43'N	1°33'W
Are, Swe.	146	63°12'N	13°12'E
Arecibo, P.R. (ä-rå-sē'bō)	117b	18°28'N	66°45'W
Areeiro, Port.	238d	38°39'N	9°12'W
Areia Branca, Braz. (ä-rē'yä-brå'n-kă)	131	4°58'S	37°02'W
Arena, Point, c., Ca., U.S. (ä-rā'nȧ)	108	38°57'N	123°40'W
Arenas, Punta, c., Ven. (pòn'tä-rē'näs)	131b	10°57'N	64°24'W
Arenas de San Pedro, Spain	158	40°12'N	5°04'W
Arendal, Nor. (ä'rĕn-däl)	152	58°29'N	8°44'E
Arendonk, Bel.	145a	51°19'N	5°07'E
Arequipa, Peru (ä-rå-kē'pä)	130	16°27'S	71°30'W
Arezzo, Italy (ä-rĕt'sō)	148	43°28'N	11°54'E
Arga, r., Spain (är'gä)	158	42°35'N	1°55'W
Arganda, Spain (är-gän'dä)	159a	40°18'N	3°27'W
Argazi, l., Russia (är'gä-zĭ)	172a	55°24'N	60°37'E
Argazi, r., Russia	172a	55°33'N	57°30'E
Argentan, Fr. (àr-zhäN-täN')	156	48°45'N	0°01'W
Argentat, Fr. (àr-zhäN-tä')	156	45°07'N	1°57'E
Argenteuil, Fr. (är-zhäN-tû'y')	156	48°56'N	2°15'E
Argentina, nation, S.A. (är-jĕn-tē'nȧ)	132	35°30'S	67°00'W
Argentino, l., Arg. (är-kĕn-tē'nō)	132	50°15'S	72°45'W
Argenton-sur-Creuse, Fr. (är-zhäN'tôN-sür-krôs)	156	46°34'N	1°28'E
Argolikos Kólpos, b., Grc.	161	37°20'N	23°00'E
Argonne, mts., Fr. (ä'r-gôn)	157	49°21'N	5°54'E
Argos, Grc. (är'gŏs)	161	37°38'N	22°45'E
Argostólion, Grc. (är-gŏs-tŏ'lē-ŏn)	161	38°10'N	20°30'E
Arguello, Point, c., Ca., U.S. (är-gwāl'yō)	108	34°35'N	120°40'W
Arguin, Cap d', c., Maur.	210	20°28'N	17°46'W
Argun', r., Asia (år-gōōn')	165	50°00'N	119°00'E
Argungu, Nig.	215	12°45'N	4°31'E
Argyle, Can. (är'gīl)	83f	50°11'N	97°27'W
Argyle, Mn., U.S.	102	48°21'N	96°48'W
Århus, Den. (ôr'hōōs)	146	56°09'N	10°10'E
Ariakeno-Umi, b., Japan (ä-rē'ä-kä-nō ōō'nē)	195	33°03'N	130°18'E
Ariake-Wan, b., Japan (ä'rē-ä'kä wän)	195	31°19'N	131°15'E
Ariano, Italy (ä-rē-ä'nō)	160	41°09'N	15°11'E
Ariari, r., Col. (ä-ryà'rē)	130a	3°34'N	73°42'W
Aribinda, Burkina	214	14°14'N	0°52'W
Arica, Chile (ä-rē'kä)	130	18°34'S	70°14'W
Arichat, Can. (ä-rĭ-shät')	93	45°31'N	61°01'W
Ariège, r., Fr. (å-rê-ĕzh')	156	43°26'N	1°29'E
Ariel, Wa., U.S. (ā'rĭ-ĕl)	106c	45°57'N	122°34'W
Arieș, r., Rom.	155	46°25'N	23°15'E
Ariguanabo, Lago de, l., Cuba (lä'gô-dĕ-ä-rē-gwä-nä'bô)	123a	22°52'N	82°33'W
Arikaree, r., Co., U.S. (ă-rĭ-kȧ-rē')	110	39°51'N	102°18'W
Arima, Japan (ä'rē-mä')	195b	34°48'N	135°16'E
Aringay, Phil. (ä-rĭŋ-gä'ê)	197a	16°25'N	120°20'E
Arino, neigh., Japan	242b	34°50'N	135°14'E
Arinos, r., Braz. (ä-rē'nôzsh)	131	12°09'S	56°49'W
Aripuanã, r., Braz. (ä-rê-pwän'yȧ)	131	7°06'S	60°29'W
'Arīsh, Wādī al, r., Egypt (å-rēsh')	181a	30°36'N	34°07'E
Aristazabal Island, i., Can.	86	52°30'N	129°20'W
Arizona, state, U.S. (ăr-ĭ-zō'nȧ)	96	34°00'N	113°00'W
Arjona, Spain (är-hō'nä)	158	37°58'N	4°03'W
Arka, r., Russia	171	60°45'N	142°30'E
Arkabutla Lake, res., Ms., U.S. (är-kȧ-bŭt'lȧ)	114	34°48'N	90°00'W
Arkadelphia, Ar., U.S. (är-kȧ-dĕl'fĭ-ȧ)	111	34°06'N	93°05'W
Arkansas, state, U.S. (är'kăn-sô) (är-kăn'sȧs)	97	34°50'N	93°40'W
Arkansas, r., U.S.	96	37°30'N	97°00'W
Arkansas City, Ks., U.S.	111	37°04'N	97°02'W
Arkhangelsk (Archangel), Russia (år-kän'gĕlsk)	164	64°30'N	40°25'E
Arkhangel'skiy, Kaz. (är-kän-gĕl'skĭ)	169	52°52'N	61°53'E
Arkhangel'skoye, Russia (är-kän-gĕl'skô-yĕ)	172a	54°25'N	56°48'E
Arklow, Ire. (ärk'lō)	150	52°47'N	6°10'W
Arkonam, India (är-kō-näm')	187	13°05'N	79°43'E
Arlanza, r., Spain (är-län-thä')	158	42°08'N	3°45'W
Arlanzón, r., Spain (är-län-thōn')	158	42°12'N	3°58'W
Arlberg Tunnel, trans., Aus. (ärl'bĕrgh)	154	47°05'N	10°15'E
Arles, Fr. (ärl)	156	43°42'N	4°38'E
Arlington, S. Afr.	218d	28°02'S	27°52'E
Arlington, Ga., U.S. (är'lĭng-tun')	114	31°25'N	84°42'W
Arlington, Ma., U.S.	93a	42°26'N	71°13'W
Arlington, S.D., U.S. (är'lĕng-tŭn)	102	44°23'N	97°09'W
Arlington, Tx., U.S. (är'lĭng-tŭn)	107c	32°44'N	97°07'W
Arlington, Vt., U.S.	99	43°05'N	73°05'W
Arlington, Va., U.S.	100e	38°55'N	77°10'W
Arlington, Wa., U.S.	106a	48°11'N	122°08'W
Arlington Heights, Il., U.S. (är'lĕng-tŭn-hī'ts)	101a	42°05'N	87°59'W
Arlington National Cemetery, pt. of i., Va., U.S.	229d	38°53'N	77°04'W
Arltunga, Austl. (ärl-tòŋ'gȧ)	202	23°19'S	134°45'E
Arma, Ks., U.S. (är'mȧ)	111	37°34'N	94°43'W
Armagh, Can. (är-mä') (är-mäk')	83b	46°45'N	70°36'W
Armagh, N. Ire., U.K.	146	54°21'N	6°25'W
Armant, Egypt (är-mänt')	218b	25°37'N	32°32'E
Armaro, Col. (är-mà'rō)	130a	4°58'N	74°54'W
Armavir, Russia (är-mȧ-vĭr')	164	45°00'N	41°00'E
Armenia, Col. (är-mē'nēȧ)	130	4°33'N	75°40'W
Armenia, El Sal. (är-mā'nē-ä)	120	13°44'N	89°31'W
Armenia, nation, Asia	164	41°00'N	44°39'E
Armentières, Fr. (år-mäN-tyâr')	156	50°43'N	2°53'E
Armeria, Río de, r., Mex. (rē'ō-dĕ-är-mȧ-rē'ä)	118	19°36'N	104°10'W
Armherstburg, Can. (ärm'hĕrst-bōōrgh)	90	42°06'N	83°06'W
Armians'k, Ukr.	163	46°06'N	33°42'E
Armidale, Austl. (är'mĭ-dāl)	203	30°27'S	151°50'E
Armour, S.D., U.S. (är'mẽr)	102	43°18'N	98°21'W
Armstrong Station, Can. (ärm'strŏng)	85	50°21'N	89°00'W
Arnedo, Spain (är-nā'dō)	158	42°12'N	2°03'W
Arnhem, Neth. (ärn'hĕm)	147	51°58'N	5°56'E
Arnhem, Cape, c., Austl.	202	12°15'S	137°00'E
Arnhem Land, reg., Austl. (ärn'hĕm-lănd)	202	13°15'S	133°00'E
Arno, r., Italy (ä'r-nô)	148	43°30'N	11°00'E
Arnold, Eng., U.K. (är'nŭld)	144a	53°00'N	1°08'W
Arnold, Mn., U.S. (år'nŭld)	107h	46°53'N	92°06'W
Arnold, Pa., U.S.	101e	40°35'N	79°45'W
Arnprior, Can. (ärn-prī'ẽr)	91	45°25'N	76°20'W
Arnsberg, Ger. (ärns'bĕrgh)	157c	51°25'N	8°02'E
Arnstadt, Ger. (ärn'shtät)	154	50°51'N	10°57'E
Aroab, Nmb. (är'ō-áb)	212	25°40'S	19°45'E
Aroostook, r., Me., U.S. (å-rōs'tòk)	92	46°44'N	68°15'W
Aroroy, Phil. (ä-rô-rō'ê)	197a	12°30'N	123°24'E
Arpajon, Fr. (är-pä-jô'n)	157b	48°35'N	2°15'E
Arpoador, Ponta do, c., Braz. (pô'n-tä-dō-är'pōä-dō'r)	132b	22°59'S	43°11'W
Arraiolos, Port. (är-rī-ō'lōzh)	158	38°47'N	7°59'W
Arran, Island of, Scot., U.K. (ă'răn)	150	55°25'N	5°25'W
Ar Rank, Sudan	211	11°45'N	32°53'E
Arras, Fr. (å-räs')	147	50°21'N	2°40'E
Ar Rawḍah, Egypt	218b	27°47'N	30°52'E
Arrecifes, Arg. (är-rå-sē'fās)	129c	34°03'S	60°05'W
Arrecifes, r., Arg.	129c	34°07'S	59°50'W
Arrée, Monts d', mts., Fr. (är-rā')	156	48°27'N	4°00'W
Arriaga, Mex. (är-rēä'gä)	119	16°15'N	93°54'W
Arrone, r., Italy	159d	41°57'N	12°17'E
Arrow Creek, r., Mt., U.S. (ăr'ō)	105	47°29'N	109°53'W
Arrowhead, Lake, l., Ca., U.S. (lăk ăr'ōhĕd)	107a	34°17'N	117°13'W
Arrowrock Reservoir, res., Id., U.S. (ăr'ō-rŏk)	104	43°40'N	115°30'W
Arroya Arena, Cuba (är-rô'yä-rĕ'nä)	123a	23°01'N	82°30'W
Arroyo de la Luz, Spain (är-rō'yō-dĕ-lä-lōō'z)	158	39°39'N	6°46'W
Arroyo Seco, Mex. (är-rō'yō sä'kō)	118	21°31'N	99°44'W
Ar Rub' al Khālī, des., Asia	182	20°00'N	51°00'E
Ar Ruṭbah, Iraq	185	33°02'N	40°17'E
Arsen'yev, Russia	165	44°13'N	133°32'E
Arsinskiy, Russia (är-sĭn'skĭ)	172a	53°46'N	59°54'E
Árta, Grc. (är'tä)	149	39°08'N	21°02'E
Artarmon, Austl.	243a	33°49'S	151°11'E
Arteaga, Mex. (är-tä-ä'gä)	112	25°28'N	100°50'W
Artëm, Russia (ár-tyôm')	165	43°28'N	132°29'E
Artemisa, Cuba (är-tå-mē'sä)	122	22°50'N	82°45'W
Artemivs'k, Ukr.	167	48°37'N	38°00'E
Arteria, Ca., U.S.	232	33°52'N	118°05'W
Artesia, N.M., U.S. (är-tē'sĭ-ȧ)	110	32°44'N	104°23'W
Arthabaska, Can.	91	46°03'N	71°54'W
Arthur's Town, Bah.	123	24°40'N	75°40'W
Arti, Russia (är'tĭ)	172a	56°20'N	58°38'E
Artibonite, r., N.A. (är-tē-bō-nē'tä)	123	19°00'N	72°25'W
Artigas, neigh., Ven.	234a	10°30'N	66°56'W
Aru, Kepulauan, is., Indon.	197	6°20'S	133°00'E
Arua, Ug. (ä'rōō-ä)	211	3°01'N	30°55'E
Aruba, i., Aruba (ä-rōō'bå)	117	12°29'N	70°00'W
Arunachal Pradesh, state, India	183	27°35'N	92°56'E
Arundel Gardens, Md., U.S.	229c	39°13'N	76°37'W
Arundel Village, Md., U.S.	229c	39°13'N	76°36'W
Arusha, Tan. (å-rōō'shä)	212	3°22'S	36°41'E
Arvida, Can.	85	48°26'N	71°11'W
Arvika, Swe. (är-vē'kå)	152	59°41'N	12°35'E
Arzamas, Russia (är-zä-mäs')	166	55°20'N	43°52'E
Arziw, Alg.	148	35°50'N	0°20'W
Arzúa, Spain	158	42°54'N	8°19'W
Aš, Czech Rep. (äsh')	154	50°12'N	12°13'E
Asahi-Gawa, r., Japan (ä-sä'hê-gä'wä)	195	35°01'N	133°40'E
Asahikawa, Japan	189	43°50'N	142°09'E
Asaka, Japan (ä-sä'kä)	195a	35°47'N	139°36'E
Asālafpur, neigh., India	240d	28°38'N	77°05'E
Asansol, India	183	23°45'N	86°58'E
Asbest, Russia (äs-bĕst')	166	57°02'N	61°28'E
Asbestos, Can. (äs-bĕs'tōs)	91	45°49'N	71°52'W
Asbestovskiy, Russia	172a	57°46'N	61°23'E
Asbury Park, N.J., U.S. (ăz'bĕr-ĭ)	100a	40°13'N	74°01'W
Ascención, Bahía de la, b., Mex.	120a	19°39'N	87°30'W
Ascensión, Mex. (äs-sĕn-sė-ōn')	118	24°21'N	99°54'W
Ascension, i., St. Hel. (ȧ-sĕn'shŭn)	209	8°00'S	13°00'W
Ascent, S. Afr. (äs-ĕnt')	218d	27°14'S	29°06'E
Aschaffenburg, Ger. (ä-shäf'ĕn-bòrgh)	154	49°58'N	9°12'E
Ascheberg, Ger. (ä'shĕ-bĕrg)	157c	51°47'N	7°38'E
Aschersleben, Ger. (äsh'ĕrs-lā-bĕn)	154	51°46'N	11°28'E
Ascoli Piceno, Italy (äs'kô-lēpē-chā'nō)	160	42°50'N	13°55'E
Aseb, Erit.	211	12°52'N	43°39'E
Asenovgrad, Bul.	161	42°00'N	24°49'E
Aseri, Est. (ä'sĕ-rĭ)	153	59°26'N	26°58'E
Asha, Russia (ä'shä)	172a	55°01'N	57°17'E
Ashabula, l., N.D., U.S. (äsh'ȧ-bū-lä)	102	47°07'N	97°51'W
Ashan, Russia (ä'shän)	172a	57°08'N	56°25'E
Ashbourne, Eng., U.K. (äsh'bŭrn)	144a	53°01'N	1°44'W
Ashburn, Ga., U.S. (äsh'bŭrn)	114	31°42'N	83°42'W
Ashburn, Va., U.S.	100e	39°02'N	77°30'W
Ashburton, r., Austl. (äsh'bûr-tŭn)	202	22°30'S	115°30'E
Ashby-de-la-Zouch, Eng., U.K. (äsh'bĭ-dē-lȧ zōōsh')	144a	52°44'N	1°23'W
Ashdod, Isr.	181a	31°46'N	34°39'E
Ashdown, Ar., U.S. (äsh'doun)	111	33°41'N	94°07'W
Asheboro, N.C., U.S. (äsh'bŭr-ô)	115	35°41'N	79°50'W
Asherton, Tx., U.S. (äsh'ẽr-tŭn)	112	28°26'N	99°45'W
Asheville, N.C., U.S. (äsh'vĭl)	97	35°35'N	82°35'W
Ashfield, Austl.	243a	33°53'S	151°08'E
Ashford, Eng., U.K.	235	51°26'N	0°27'W
Ash Fork, Az., U.S.	109	35°13'N	112°29'W
Ashgabat, Turk.	169	37°57'N	58°23'E
Ashikaga, Japan (ä'shė-kä'gȧ)	195	36°22'N	139°26'E
Ashiya, Japan (ä'shė-yä')	195	33°54'N	130°40'E
Ashiya, Japan	195b	34°44'N	135°18'E
Ashizuri-Zaki, c., Japan (ä-shē-zò-rē zä-kē)	194	32°43'N	133°04'E
Ashland, Al., U.S. (äsh'lȧnd)	114	33°15'N	85°50'W
Ashland, Ks., U.S.	110	37°11'N	99°46'W
Ashland, Ky., U.S.	98	38°25'N	82°40'W
Ashland, Me., U.S.	92	46°37'N	68°26'W
Ashland, Ma., U.S.	93a	42°16'N	71°28'W
Ashland, Ne., U.S.	102	41°02'N	96°23'W
Ashland, Oh., U.S.	98	40°50'N	82°15'W
Ashland, Or., U.S.	104	42°12'N	122°42'W
Ashland, Pa., U.S.	99	40°45'N	76°20'W
Ashland, Wi., U.S.	97	46°34'N	90°55'W
Ashley, N.D., U.S. (äsh'lē)	102	46°03'N	99°23'W
Ashley, Pa., U.S.	99	41°15'N	75°55'W
Ashley Green, Eng., U.K.	235	51°44'N	0°35'W
Ashmūn, Egypt (äsh-mōōn')	218b	30°19'N	30°57'E
Ashqelon, Isr. (äsh'kĕ-lōn)	181a	31°40'N	34°36'E
Ash Shabb, Egypt (shĕb)	211	22°34'N	29°52'E
Ash Shallūfah, Egypt (shäl'lò-fȧ)	218b	30°09'N	32°33'E
Ash Shaqrā', Sau. Ar.	182	25°10'N	45°08'E
Ash Shāriqah, U.A.E.	185	25°22'N	55°23'E
Ash Shawbak, Jord.	181a	30°31'N	35°35'E
Ash Shiḥr, Yemen	182	14°45'N	49°32'E
Ashtabula, Oh., U.S. (äsh-tȧ-bū'lȧ)	97	41°55'N	80°50'W
Ashtead, Eng., U.K.	235	51°19'N	0°18'W
Ashton, Id., U.S. (äsh'tŭn)	105	44°04'N	111°28'W
Ashton-in-Makerfield, Eng., U.K. (äsh'tŭn-ĭn-māk'ẽr-fēld)	144a	53°29'N	2°39'W
Ashton-under-Lyne, Eng., U.K. (äsh'tŭn-ŭn-dẽr-līn')	144a	53°29'N	2°04'W
Ashuanipi, l., Can. (äsh-wȧ-nĭp'ĭ)	85	52°40'N	67°42'W
Ashukino, Russia (å-shōō'kinô)	172b	56°10'N	37°57'E
Asia, cont.	180	50°00'N	100°00'E
Asia Minor, reg., Tur. (ä'zhȧ)	143	38°18'N	31°18'E
Asientos, Mex. (ä-sė-ĕn'tōs)	118	22°13'N	102°05'W
Asilah, Mor.	158	35°30'N	6°05'W
Asinara, i., Italy	160	41°02'N	8°22'E
Asinara, Golfo dell', b., Italy (gôl'fô-dĕl-ä-sē-nä'rä)	160	40°58'N	8°28'E
Asīr, reg., Sau. Ar. (ä-sēr')	182	19°30'N	42°00'E
Askarovo, Russia (äs-kä-rô'vô)	172a	53°21'N	58°32'E
Askersund, Swe. (äs'kẽr-sònd)	152	58°43'N	14°53'E
Askino, Russia (äs'kĭ-nô)	172a	56°06'N	56°29'E
Asmara *see* Asmera, Erit.	210	15°17'N	38°56'E
Asmera, Erit. (äs-mä'rä)	211	15°17'N	38°56'E
Asnieres, Fr. (ä-nyâr')	157b	48°55'N	2°18'E
Asosa, Eth.	211	10°13'N	34°28'E
Asotin, Wa., U.S. (ȧ-sō'tĭn)	104	46°19'N	117°01'W
Aspen, Co., U.S. (äs'pĕn)	109	39°15'N	106°55'W
Asperen, Neth.	145a	51°52'N	5°07'E
Aspern, neigh., Aus.	239e	48°13'N	16°29'E
Aspinwall, Pa., U.S.	230b	40°30'N	79°55'W
Aspy Bay, b., Can. (äs'pė)	93	46°55'N	60°25'W
Aș Ṣaff, Egypt	218b	29°33'N	31°23'E
As Sallūm, Egypt	211	31°35'N	25°05'E
As Salt, Jord.	181a	32°02'N	35°44'E
Assam, state, India (äs-săm')	183	26°00'N	91°00'E
As Samāwah, Iraq	185	31°18'N	45°17'E
Asseln, neigh., Ger.	236	51°32'N	7°35'E
Assens, Den. (äs'sĕns)	152	55°16'N	9°54'E
As Sinbillāwayn, Egypt	218b	30°53'N	31°37'E
Assini, C. Iv. (å-sė-nē')	210	4°52'N	3°16'W
Assiniboia, Can.	84	49°38'N	105°59'W
Assiniboine, r., Can. (ă-sĭn'ĭ-boin)	89	50°03'N	97°57'W
Assiniboine, Mount, mtn., Can.	87	50°52'N	115°39'W
Assis, Braz. (ä-sė's)	131	22°39'S	50°21'W
Assisi, Italy	148	43°04'N	12°37'E
As-Sudd, reg., Sudan	211	8°45'N	30°45'E
As Sulaymānīyah, Iraq	182	35°47'N	45°23'E
As Sulaymānīyah, Sau. Ar.	185	24°09'N	46°19'E
As Suwaydā', Syria	182	32°41'N	36°41'E
Astakós, Grc. (äs'tä-kôs)	161	38°42'N	21°00'E
Astara, Azer.	167	38°30'N	48°50'E
Asti, Italy (äs'tė)	148	44°54'N	8°12'E
Astipálaia, i., Grc.	149	36°31'N	26°19'E
Astley Bridge, Eng., U.K.	237b	53°36'N	2°26'W
Astorga, Spain (äs-tôr'gä)	158	42°28'N	6°03'W
Astoria, Or., U.S. (äs-tō'rĭ-ȧ)	96	46°11'N	123°51'W
Astoria, neigh., N.Y., U.S.	228	40°46'N	73°55'W
Astrakhan', Russia (äs-trȧ-kän')	164	46°15'N	48°00'E
Astrida, Rw. (äs-trē'dȧ)	212	2°37'S	29°48'E
Asturias, hist. reg., Spain (äs-tōō'ryäs)	158	43°21'N	6°00'W
Asunción *see* Nochistlán, Mex.	118	21°23'N	102°52'W
Asunción *see* Ixtaltepec, Mex.	119	16°33'N	95°04'W
Asunción, Para. (ä-sōōn-syōn')	132	25°25'S	57°30'W
Asunción Mita, Guat. (ä-sōōn-syō'n-mē'tä)	120	14°19'N	89°43'W
Aswān, Egypt (ä-swän')	211	24°05'N	32°57'E
Aswān High Dam, dam, Egypt	211	23°58'N	32°53'E
Atacama, Desierto de, des., Chile (dĕ-syĕ'r-tô-dĕ-ä-tä-kå'mä)	128	23°50'S	69°00'W
Atacama, Puna de, plat., Bol. (pōō'nä-dĕ-ä-tä-kȧ'mä)	130	21°35'S	66°58'W
Atacama, Puna de, reg., Chile (pōō'nä-dĕ-ätä-kȧ'mä)	132	23°15'S	68°45'W
Atacama, Salar de, l., Chile (sȧ-lȧr'dĕ-ätä-kȧ'mä)	132	23°38'S	68°15'W
Atacama Trench, deep	128	25°00'S	71°30'W
Ataco, Col. (ä-tà'kō)	130a	3°36'N	75°22'W
Atacora, Chaîne de l', mts., Benin	214	10°15'N	1°15'E
Atā 'itah, Jabal al, mtn., Jord.	181a	30°48'N	35°19'E
Atamanovskiy, Russia (ä-tä-mä'nôv-skĭ)	172a	52°15'N	60°47'E
'Atāqah, Jabal, mts., Egypt	218c	29°59'N	32°20'E
Atar, Maur. (ä-tär')	210	20°45'N	13°16'W
Atascadero, Ca., U.S. (ăt-äs-kȧ-dâ'rō)	108	35°29'N	120°40'W
Atascosa, r., Tx., U.S. (ăt-äs-kō'sȧ)	112	28°50'N	98°17'W

ng-sing; ŋ-baŋk; N-nasalized n; nŏd; cŏmmit; ōld; ōbey; ôrder; oi-boil; fōōd; ò-as oo in foot; ou-out; s-soft; sh-dish; th-thin; pūre; ûnite; ûrn; stŭd; circŭs; ü-as in French tu; '-indeterminate vowel.

260 Atauro-Bacarra

PLACE (Pronunciation)	PAGE	LAT.	LONG.
Atauro, Ilha de, i., Indon. (dĕ-ä-tä'ōō-rō)	197	8°20'S	126°15'E
Atbara, r., Afr.	211	17°14'N	34°27'E
'Atbarah, Sudan (ät'bȧ-rä)	211	17°45'N	33°15'E
Atbasar, Kaz. (ät'bä-sär')	169	51°42'N	68°28'E
Atchafalaya, r., La., U.S.	113	30°53'N	91°51'W
Atchafalaya Bay, b., La., U.S. (ăch-ȧ-fȧ-lī'ȧ)	113	29°25'N	91°30'W
Atchison, Ks., U.S. (ăch'ĭ-sŭn)	97	39°33'N	95°08'W
Atco, N.J., U.S. (ăt'kō)	100f	39°46'N	74°53'W
Atempan, Mex. (ä-tĕm-pä'n)	119	19°49'N	97°25'W
Atenguillo, r., Mex. (ä-tĕn-gĕ'l-yō)	118	20°18'N	104°35'W
Athabasca, Can. (ăth-ȧ-băs'kȧ)	84	54°43'N	113°17'W
Athabasca, l., Can.	84	59°04'N	109°10'W
Athabasca, r., Can.	84	57°30'N	112°00'W
Athens (Athínai), Grc.	161	38°00'N	23°38'E
Athens, Al., U.S. (ăth'ĕnz)	114	34°47'N	86°58'W
Athens, Ga., U.S.	97	33°55'N	83°24'W
Athens, Oh., U.S.	98	39°20'N	82°10'W
Athens, Pa., U.S.	99	42°00'N	76°30'W
Athens, Tn., U.S.	114	35°26'N	84°36'W
Athens, Tx., U.S.	113	32°13'N	95°51'W
Atherstone, Eng., U.K. (ăth'ẽr-stŭn)	144a	52°34'N	1°33'W
Atherton, Eng., U.K. (ăth'ẽr-tŭn)	144a	53°32'N	2°29'W
Atherton Plateau, plat., Austl. (ădh-ẽr-tŏn)	203	17°00'S	144°30'E
Athi, r., Kenya (ä'tē)	213	2°43'S	38°30'E
Athínai see Athens, Grc.	142	38°00'N	23°38'E
Athis-Mons, Fr.	237c	48°43'N	2°24'E
Athlone, Ire. (ăth-lōn')	146	53°24'N	7°30'W
Athos, mtn., Grc. (ăth'ŏs)	161	40°10'N	24°15'E
Ath Thamad, Egypt	181a	29°41'N	34°17'E
Athy, Ire. (ȧ-thī)	150	52°59'N	7°08'W
Ati, Chad	215	13°13'N	18°20'E
Atibaia, Braz. (ä-tē-bȧ'yȧ)	129a	23°08'S	46°32'W
Atikonak, l., Can.	85	52°34'N	63°49'W
Atimonan, Phil. (ä-tē-mō'nän)	197a	13°59'N	121°56'E
Atiquizaya, El Sal. (ä'tē-kē-zä'yä)	120	14°00'N	89°42'W
Atitlan, vol., Guat. (ä-tē-tlän')	120	14°35'N	91°11'W
Atitlan, Lago, l., Guat. (ä-tē-tlän')	120	14°38'N	91°23'W
Atizapán, Mex. (ä'tē-zà-pän')	119a	19°33'N	99°16'W
Atka, Ak., U.S. (ăt'kȧ)	95a	52°18'N	174°18'W
Atka, i., Ak., U.S.	94b	51°58'N	174°30'W
Atkarsk, Russia (åt-kärsk')	167	51°50'N	45°00'E
Atkinson, Ne., U.S. (ăt'kĭn-sŭn)	102	42°32'N	98°58'W
Atlanta, Ga., U.S. (ăt-lăn'tȧ)	97	33°45'N	84°23'W
Atlanta, Tx., U.S.	111	33°09'N	94°09'W
Atlantic, Ia., U.S. (ăt-lăn'tĭk)	103	41°23'N	94°58'W
Atlantic, N.C., U.S.	115	34°54'N	76°20'W
Atlantic Beach, N.Y., U.S.	228	40°35'N	73°44'W
Atlantic City, N.J., U.S.	97	39°20'N	74°30'W
Atlantic Highlands, N.J., U.S.	100a	40°25'N	74°04'W
Atlantic Ocean, o.	4	5°00'S	25°00'W
Atlas Mountains, mts., Afr. (ăt'lăs)	210	31°22'N	4°57'W
Atliaca, Mex. (ät-lē-ä'kä)	118	17°38'N	99°24'W
Atlin, l., Can. (ăt'lĭn)	84	59°34'N	133°20'W
Atlixco, Mex. (ät-lēz'kō)	118	18°52'N	98°27'W
Atmore, Al., U.S. (ăt'mōr)	114	31°01'N	87°31'W
Atoka, Ok., U.S. (ȧ-tō'kȧ)	111	34°23'N	96°07'W
Atoka Reservoir, res., Ok., U.S.	111	34°30'N	96°05'W
Atotonilco el Alto, Mex.	118	20°35'N	102°32'W
Atotonilco el Grande, Mex.	118	20°17'N	98°41'W
Atoui, r., Afr. (ȧ-tōō-ē')	210	21°00'N	15°32'W
Atoyac, Mex. (ä-tō-yäk')	118	20°01'N	103°28'W
Atoyac, r., Mex.	118	18°35'N	98°16'W
Atoyac, r., Mex.	119	16°27'N	97°28'W
Atoyac de Alvarez, Mex. (ä-tō-yäk'dä äl'vä-räz)	118	17°13'N	100°29'W
Atoyatempan, Mex. (ä-tō'yȧ-tĕm-pän')	119	18°47'N	97°54'W
Atrak, r., Asia	182	37°45'N	56°30'E
Ätran, r., Swe.	152	57°02'N	12°43'E
Atrato, Río, r., Col. (rĕ'ō-ä-trä'tō)	130	7°15'N	77°18'W
Atsugi, Japan	242a	35°27'N	139°22'E
Atta, India	240d	28°34'N	77°20'E
Aṭ Ṭafīlah, Jord. (tä-fē'la)	181a	30°50'N	35°36'E
Aṭ Ṭā'if, Sau. Ar.	182	21°03'N	41°00'E
Aṭ-Ṭalibīyah, Egypt	244a	30°00'N	31°11'E
Attalla, Al., U.S. (ȧ-tăl'yȧ)	114	34°01'N	86°05'W
Attawapiskat, r., Can. (ăt'ȧ-wȧ-pĭs'kăt)	85	52°31'N	86°22'W
Attersee, l., Aus.	154	47°57'N	13°25'E
Attica, N.Y., U.S. (ăt'ĭ-kȧ)	99	42°55'N	78°15'W
Attleboro, Ma., U.S. (ăt''l-bŭr-ō)	100b	41°56'N	71°15'W
Attow, Ben, mtn., Scot., U.K. (bĕn ăt'tō)	150	57°15'N	5°25'W
Attoyac Bay, Tx., U.S. (ă-toi'yăk)	113	31°45'N	94°23'W
Attu, i., Ak., U.S. (ăt-tōō')	94b	53°08'N	173°18'E
Aṭ Ṭūr, Egypt	149	28°09'N	33°47'E
Aṭ Ṭurayf, Sau. Ar.	182	31°32'N	38°30'E
Åtvidaberg, Swe. (ôt-vē'dȧ-bĕrgh)	152	58°12'N	15°55'E
Atwood, Ks., U.S. (ăt'wŏŏd)	110	39°48'N	101°06'W
Atyraū, Kaz.	169	47°10'N	51°50'E
Atzalpur, India	240d	28°43'N	77°21'E
Atzcapotzalco, Mex. (ät'zkä-pō-tzäl'kō)	118	19°29'N	99°11'W
Atzgersdorf, Aus.	145e	48°10'N	16°17'E
Auau Channel, strt., Hi., U.S. (ä'ō-ä'ō)	94a	20°55'N	156°50'W
Aubagne, Fr. (ō-bän'y')	157	43°18'N	5°34'E
Aube, r., Fr. (ōb)	156	48°42'N	3°49'E
Aubenas, Fr. (ōb-nä')	156	44°37'N	4°22'E
Aubervilliers, Fr. (ō-bĕr-vē-yā')	157b	48°54'N	2°23'E
Aubin, Fr. (ō-băN')	156	44°29'N	2°12'E
Aubrey, Can. (ô-brē')	83a	45°08'N	73°47'W
Auburn, Austl.	243a	33°51'S	151°02'E
Auburn, Al., U.S. (ô'bŭrn)	114	32°35'N	85°26'W
Auburn, Ca., U.S.	108	38°52'N	121°05'W
Auburn, Il., U.S.	111	39°36'N	89°46'W
Auburn, In., U.S.	98	41°20'N	85°05'W
Auburn, Me., U.S.	97	44°04'N	70°24'W
Auburn, Ma., U.S.	93a	42°11'N	71°51'W
Auburn, Ne., U.S.	111	40°23'N	95°50'W
Auburn, N.Y., U.S.	99	42°55'N	76°35'W
Auburn, Wa., U.S.	106a	47°18'N	122°14'W
Auburndale, Ma., U.S.	227a	42°21'N	71°22'W
Auburn Heights, Mi., U.S.	101b	42°37'N	83°13'W
Aubusson, Fr. (ō-bü-sôN')	156	45°57'N	2°10'E
Auch, Fr. (ōsh)	147	43°38'N	0°35'E
Aucilla, r., Fl., U.S. (ô-sĭl'ȧ)	114	30°15'N	83°55'W
Auckland, N.Z. (ôk'lănd)	203a	36°53'S	174°45'E
Auckland Islands, is., N.Z.	3	50°30'S	166°30'E
Auckland Park, neigh., S. Afr.	244b	26°11'S	28°00'E
Aude, r., Fr. (ōd)	156	42°55'N	2°08'E
Audenshaw, Eng., U.K.	237b	53°28'N	2°08'W
Audierne, Fr. (ō-dyĕrn')	156	48°02'N	4°31'W
Audincourt, Fr. (ō-dăN-kōōr')	157	47°30'N	6°49'E
Audley, Eng., U.K. (ôd'lĭ)	144a	53°03'N	2°18'W
Audo Range, mts., Eth.	218a	6°58'N	41°18'E
Audubon, Ia., U.S. (ô'dŏŏ-bŏn)	103	41°43'N	94°57'W
Audubon, N.J., U.S.	100f	39°54'N	75°04'W
Aue, Ger. (ou'ĕ)	154	50°35'N	12°44'E
Auf dem Schnee, neigh., Ger.	236	51°26'N	7°25'E
Augathella, Austl. (ôr'gȧ'thĕ-lȧ)	204	25°49'S	146°40'E
Aughton, Eng., U.K.	237a	53°32'N	2°56'W
Augrabiesvalle, wtfl., S. Afr.	212	28°30'S	20°00'E
Augsburg, Ger. (ouks'bŏŏrgh)	147	48°23'N	10°55'E
Augusta, Ar., U.S. (ô-gŭs'tȧ)	111	35°16'N	91°21'W
Augusta, Ga., U.S.	97	33°26'N	82°00'W
Augusta, Ks., U.S.	111	37°41'N	96°58'W
Augusta, Ky., U.S.	98	38°45'N	84°00'W
Augusta, Me., U.S.	97	44°19'N	69°42'W
Augusta, N.J., U.S.	100a	41°07'N	74°44'W
Augusta, Wi., U.S.	103	44°40'N	91°09'W
Augustow, Pol. (ou-gōōs'tōf)	155	53°52'N	23°00'E
Auki, Sol. Is.	198e	8°46'S	160°42'E
Aulnay-sous-Bois, Fr. (ō-nĕ'sōō-bwä')	157b	48°56'N	2°30'E
Aulne, r., Fr. (ōn)	156	48°08'N	3°53'W
Auneau, Fr. (ō-nō')	157b	48°28'N	1°45'E
Auob, r., Afr. (ä'wŏb)	212	25°00'S	19°00'E
Aur, i., Malay.	181b	2°27'N	104°51'E
Aura, Fin.	153	60°38'N	22°32'E
Aurangābād, India (ou-rŭŋ-gä-bäd')	183	19°56'N	75°19'E
Aurdal, Nor. (äŭr-däl)	152	60°54'N	9°24'E
Aurès, Massif de l', mts., Alg.	148	35°16'N	5°53'E
Aurillac, Fr. (ō-rē-yȧk')	147	44°57'N	2°27'E
Aurora, Can.	91	43°59'N	79°25'W
Aurora, Co., U.S.	110	39°44'N	104°50'W
Aurora, Il., U.S. (ô-rō'rȧ)	97	41°45'N	88°18'W
Aurora, In., U.S.	101f	39°04'N	84°55'W
Aurora, Mn., U.S.	103	47°31'N	92°17'W
Aurora, Mo., U.S.	111	36°58'N	93°42'W
Aurora, Ne., U.S.	110	40°54'N	98°01'W
Aursunden, l., Nor. (äûr-sûndĕn)	152	62°42'N	11°10'E
Au Sable, r., Mi., U.S. (ô-sā'b'l)	98	44°40'N	84°25'W
Ausable, r., N.Y., U.S.	99	44°25'N	73°50'W
Austerlitz, trans., Fr.	237c	48°50'N	2°22'E
Austin, Mn., U.S. (ôs'tĭn)	103	43°40'N	92°58'W
Austin, Nv., U.S.	108	39°30'N	117°05'W
Austin, Tx., U.S.	96	30°15'N	97°42'W
Austin, neigh., Il., U.S.	231a	41°54'N	87°45'W
Austin, l., Austl.	202	27°45'S	117°30'E
Austin Bayou, Tx., U.S. (ôs'tĭn bī-ōō')	113a	29°17'N	95°21'W
Austral, Austl.	243a	33°56'S	150°48'E
Australia, nation, Oc.	202	25°00'S	135°00'E
Australian Alps, mts., Austl.	204	37°10'S	147°55'E
Australian Capital Territory, , Austl. (ôs-trā'lĭ-ăn)	203	35°30'S	148°40'E
Austria, nation, Eur. (ôs'trĭ-ȧ)	142	47°15'N	11°53'E
Authon-la-Plaine, Fr. (ō-tôN-lä-plĕ'n)	157b	48°27'N	1°58'E
Autlán, Mex. (ä-ōōt-län')	116	19°47'N	104°24'W
Autun, Fr. (ō-tŭN')	156	46°58'N	4°14'E
Auvergne, mts., Fr. (ō-vĕrn'y')	156	45°12'N	2°31'E
Auxerre, Fr. (ō-sâr')	147	47°48'N	3°32'E
Ava, Mo., U.S. (ā'vȧ)	111	36°56'N	92°40'W
Avakubi, D.R.C. (ä-vȧ-kōō'bē)	211	1°20'N	27°34'E
Avallon, Fr. (ȧ-vȧ-lôN')	156	47°30'N	3°58'E
Avalon, Ca., U.S.	108	33°21'N	118°22'W
Avalon, Pa., U.S. (ăv'ȧ-lŏn)	101e	40°31'N	80°05'W
Aveiro, Port. (ä-vā'rō)	148	40°38'N	8°38'W
Avelar, Braz. (ä'vē-lä'r)	132b	22°20'S	43°25'W
Aveley, Eng., U.K.	235	51°30'N	0°16'E
Avellaneda, Arg. (ä-vĕl-yä-nä'dhä)	132	34°40'S	58°23'W
Avellino, Italy (ä-vĕl-lē'nō)	160	40°40'N	14°46'E
Avenel, N.J., U.S.	228	40°35'N	74°17'W
Averøya, i., Nor. (ävĕr-ûē)	152	63°40'N	7°16'E
Aversa, Italy (ä-vĕr'sä)	160	40°58'N	14°13'E
Avery, Tx., U.S. (ā'vĕr-ĭ)	111	33°34'N	94°46'W
Avesta, Swe. (ä-vĕs'tä)	152	60°16'N	16°09'E
Aveyron, r., Fr. (ȧ-vā-rôN)	156	44°07'N	1°45'E
Avezzano, Italy (ä-vât-sä'nō)	160	42°03'N	13°27'E
Avigliano, Italy (ä-vēl-yä'nō)	160	40°45'N	15°44'E
Avignon, Fr. (ȧ-vē-nyôN')	147	43°55'N	4°50'E
Ávila, Spain (ä-vē-lä)	158	40°39'N	4°42'W
Avilés, Spain (ä-vē-lās')	148	43°33'N	5°55'W
Aviño, Spain	158	43°36'N	8°05'W
Avoca, Ia., U.S. (ȧ-vō'kȧ)	111	41°29'N	95°16'W
Avocado Heights, Ca., U.S.	232	34°03'N	118°00'W
Avon, Ct., U.S. (ā'vŏn)	99	41°40'N	72°50'W
Avon, Ma., U.S. (ā'vŏn)	93a	42°08'N	71°03'W
Avon, Oh., U.S.	101d	41°27'N	82°02'W
Avon, r., Eng., U.K. (ā'vŭn)	150	52°05'N	1°55'W
Avondale, Ga., U.S.	100c	33°47'N	84°16'W
Avondale Heights, Austl.	243b	37°46'S	144°51'E
Avon Lake, Oh., U.S.	101d	41°31'N	82°01'W
Avonmore, Can. (ă'vōN-mōr)	83c	45°11'N	74°58'W
Avon Park, Fl., U.S. (ā'vŏn pärk')	115a	27°35'N	81°29'W
Avranches, Fr. (ȧ-vräNsh')	156	48°43'N	1°34'W
Awaji-Shima, i., Japan	194	34°32'N	135°02'E
Awe, Loch, l., Scot., U.K. (lŏK ôr)	150	56°22'N	5°04'W
Awjilah, Libya	211	29°07'N	21°21'E
Awsīm, Egypt	244a	30°07'N	31°08'E
Ax-les-Thermes, Fr. (äks'lä tĕrm')	156	42°43'N	1°50'E
Axochiapan, Mex. (äks-ō-chyä'pän)	118	18°29'N	98°49'W
Ay, r., Russia	166	55°55'N	57°55'E
Ayabe, Japan (ä'yä-bē)	194	35°16'N	135°17'E
Ayachi, Arin', mtn., Mor.	148	32°29'N	4°57'W
Ayacucho, Arg. (ä-yä-kōō'chō)	132	37°05'S	58°30'W
Ayacucho, Peru	130	13°12'S	74°03'W
Ayaköz, Kaz.	169	48°00'N	80°12'E
Ayamonte, Spain (ä-yä-mô'n-tē)	148	37°14'N	7°28'W
Ayan, Russia (ȧ-yän')	165	56°26'N	138°18'E
Ayase, Japan	242a	35°26'N	139°26'E
Ayata, Bol. (ä-yä'tä)	130	15°17'S	68°43'W
Ayaviri, Peru (ä-yä-vē'rē)	130	14°46'S	70°38'W
Aydar, r., Eur. (ī-där')	163	49°15'N	38°48'E
Ayden, N.C., U.S. (ā'dĕn)	115	35°27'N	77°25'W
Aydın, Tur. (āīy-dĕn)	182	37°40'N	27°40'E
Ayer, Ma., U.S. (âr)	93a	42°33'N	71°36'W
Ayer Hitam, Malay.	181b	1°55'N	103°11'E
Ayers Rock, mtn., Austl.	202	25°23'S	131°05'E
Ayiassos, Grc.	161	39°06'N	26°25'E
Ayía Varvára, Grc.	239d	37°59'N	23°39'E
Áyion Óros (Mount Athos), hist. reg., Grc.	161	40°20'N	24°15'E
Áyios Evstrátios, i., Grc.	149	39°30'N	24°58'E
Ayíou Orous, Kólpos, b., Grc.	161	40°15'N	24°00'E
Aylesbury, Eng., U.K. (ālz'bẽr-ĭ)	150	51°47'N	0°49'W
Aylmer, l., Can. (āl'mẽr)	84	64°27'N	108°22'W
Aylmer, Mount, mtn., Can.	87	51°19'N	115°26'W
Aylmer East, Can. (āl'mẽr)	91	45°24'N	75°50'W
Ayo el Chico, Mex. (ä'yō el chē'kō)	118	20°31'N	102°21'W
Ayon, i., Russia (ī-ôn')	165	69°50'N	168°40'E
Ayorou, Niger	214	14°44'N	0°55'E
Ayotla, Mex. (ä-yōt'lä)	119a	19°18'N	98°55'W
Ayoun el Atrous, Maur.	214	16°40'N	9°37'W
Ayr, Scot., U.K. (âr)	150	55°27'N	4°40'W
Aysha, Eth.	211	10°48'N	42°32'E
Ayutla, Guat. (ȧ-yōōt'lä)	120	14°44'N	92°11'W
Ayutla, Mex.	118	16°50'N	99°16'W
Ayutla, Mex.	118	20°09'N	104°20'W
Ayvalik, Tur. (āīy-wä-lĭk)	149	39°19'N	26°40'E
Azādpur, neigh., India	240d	28°43'N	77°11'E
Azaouad, reg., Mali	214	18°00'N	3°20'W
Azaouak, Vallée de l', val., Afr.	215	15°50'N	3°10'E
Azare, Nig.	215	11°40'N	10°11'E
Azemmour, Mor. (ȧ-zē-mōōr')	210	33°20'N	8°21'W
Azerbaijan, nation, Asia	164	40°30'N	47°30'E
Azle, Tx., U.S. (ăz'lē)	107c	35°54'N	97°33'W
Azogues, Ec. (ä-sō'gās)	130	2°47'S	78°45'W
Azores see Açores, is., Port.	209	37°44'N	29°25'W
Azov, Russia (ȧ-zôf') (ä-zôf)	167	47°07'N	39°19'E
Azov, Sea of, sea, Eur.	164	46°00'N	36°20'E
Aztec, N.M., U.S. (ăz'tĕk)	109	36°40'N	108°00'W
Aztec Ruins National Monument, rec., N.M., U.S.	109	36°50'N	108°00'W
Azua, Dom. Rep. (ä'swä)	123	18°30'N	70°45'W
Azuaga, Spain (ä-thwä'gä)	158	38°15'N	5°42'W
Azucar, Presa de, res., Mex.	112	26°06'N	98°44'W
Azuero, Península de, pen., Pan.	117	7°30'N	80°34'W
Azufre, Cerro (Copiapó), mtn., Chile	132	27°10'S	69°00'W
Azul, Arg. (ä-sōōl')	132	36°46'S	59°51'W
Azul, Cordillera, mts., Peru	130	7°15'S	75°30'W
Azul, Sierra, mts., Mex.	118	23°20'N	98°28'W
Azusa, Ca., U.S. (ȧ-zōō'sȧ)	107a	34°08'N	117°55'W
Az Zahrān (Dhahran), Sau. Ar.	182	26°13'N	50°00'E
Az-Zamālik, neigh., Egypt	244a	30°04'N	31°13'E
Az Zaqāzīq, Egypt	211	30°36'N	31°36'E
Az Zarqā', Jord.	181a	32°03'N	36°07'E
Az Zāwiyah, Libya	210	32°28'N	11°55'E

B

PLACE (Pronunciation)	PAGE	LAT.	LONG.
Baadheere (Bardera), Som.	218a	2°13'N	42°24'E
Baak, Ger.	236	51°25'N	7°10'E
Baal, Ger. (bäl)	157c	51°02'N	6°17'E
Baao, Phil. (bä'ō)	197a	13°27'N	123°22'E
Baarle-Hertog, Bel.	145a	51°26'N	4°57'E
Baarn, Neth.	145a	52°12'N	5°18'E
Babaeski, Tur. (bä'bä-ĕs'kĭ)	161	41°25'N	27°05'E
Babahoyo, Ec. (bä-bä-ō'yō)	130	1°56'S	79°24'W
Babana, Nig.	215	10°36'N	3°50'E
Babanango, S. Afr.	213c	28°24'S	31°11'E
Babanūsah, Sudan	211	11°30'N	27°55'E
Babar, Pulau, i., Indon. (bä'bȧr)	197	7°50'S	129°15'E
Bābarpur, neigh., India	240d	28°41'N	77°17'E
Bab-el-Mandeb see Mandeb, Bab-el-, strt.	182	13°17'N	42°49'E
Babelsberg, neigh., Ger.	238a	52°24'N	13°05'E
Babelthuap, i., Palau	198b	7°30'N	134°36'E
Babia, Arroyo de la, r., Mex.	112	28°26'N	101°50'W
Babine, r., Can.	86	55°10'N	127°00'W
Babine Lake, l., Can. (băb'ēn)	84	54°45'N	126°00'W
Bābol, Iran	182	36°30'N	52°48'E
Babson Park, Ma., U.S.	227a	42°18'N	71°23'W
Babushkin, Russia	162	55°52'N	37°42'E
Babushkin, Russia (bä'bŏŏsh-kĭn)	170	51°47'N	106°08'W
Babuyan Islands, is., Phil. (bä-bōō-yän')	196	19°30'N	122°38'E
Babyak, Bul. (bäb'zhȧk)	161	41°59'N	23°42'E
Babylon, N.Y., U.S. (băb'ĭ-lŏn)	100a	40°42'N	73°19'W
Babylon, hist., Iraq	182	32°15'N	45°23'E
Bacalar, Laguna de, l., Mex. (lä-gōō-nä-dĕ-bä-kä-lär')	120a	18°50'N	88°31'W
Bacan, Pulau, i., Indon.	197	0°30'S	127°00'E
Bacarra, Phil. (bä-kär'rä)	193	18°22'N	120°40'E

ăt; finȧl; rāte; senâte; ärm; åsk; sofȧ; fâre; ch-choose; dh-as th in other; bē; ēvent; bĕt; recĕnt; cratẽr; g-gō; gh-guttural g; bĭt; ĭ-short neutral; rīde; K-guttural k as ch in German ich;

PRONOUNCING INDEX

Bacău–Bangong Co 261

PLACE (Pronunciation)	PAGE	LAT.	LONG.
Bacău, Rom.	149	46°34′N	27°00′E
Baccarat, Fr. (bȧ-kȧ-rȧ′)	157	48°29′N	6°42′E
Bacchus, Ut., U.S. (băk′ŭs)	107b	40°40′N	112°06′W
Bachajón, Mex. (bä-chä-hōn′)	119	17°08′N	92°18′W
Bachu, China (bä-chōō)	188	39°50′N	78°23′E
Back, r., Can.	84	65°30′N	104°15′W
Bačka Palanka, Yugo. (bäch′kä pälän-kä)	161	45°14′N	19°24′E
Bačka Topola, Yugo. (bäch′kä tô′pō-lä′)	161	45°48′N	19°38′E
Back Bay, India (băk)	187b	18°55′N	72°45′E
Back Bay, neigh., Ma., U.S.	227a	42°21′N	71°05′W
Backstairs Passage, strt., Austl. (băk-stârs′)	202	35°50′S	138°15′E
Bac Lieu, Viet	196	9°45′N	105°50′E
Bac Ninh, Viet (bäk′nēn″)	193	21°10′N	106°02′E
Baco, Mount, mtn., Phil. (bä′kō)	197a	12°50′N	121°11′E
Bacoli, Italy (bä-kō-lē′)	159c	40°33′N	14°05′E
Bacolod, Phil. (bä-kō′lōd)	197	10°42′N	123°03′E
Bacongo, neigh., Congo	244c	4°18′S	15°16′E
Bácsalmás, Hung. (bäch′ôl-mäs)	155	46°07′N	19°18′E
Bacup, Eng., U.K. (băk′ŭp)	144a	53°42′N	2°12′W
Bad, r., S.D., U.S. (băd)	102	44°04′N	100°58′W
Badajoz, Spain (bȧ-dhä-hōth′)	148	38°52′N	6°56′W
Badalona, Spain (bä-dhä-lō′nä)	159	41°27′N	2°15′E
Badanah, Sau. Ar.	182	30°49′N	40°45′E
Bad Axe, Mi., U.S. (băd′ ăks)	98	43°50′N	82°55′W
Bad Bramstedt, Ger. (bät bräm′shtĕt)	145c	53°55′N	9°53′E
Baden, Aus. (bä′dĕn)	154	48°00′N	16°14′E
Baden, Switz.	154	47°28′N	8°17′E
Baden-Baden, Ger. (bä′dĕn-bä′dĕn)	147	48°46′N	8°11′E
Baden-Württemberg, hist. reg., Ger. (bä′dĕn vür′tĕm-bĕrgh)	154	48°38′N	9°00′E
Bad Freienwalde, Ger. (bät frī′ĕn-väl′dĕ)	154	52°47′N	14°00′E
Badger's Mount, Eng., U.K.	235	51°20′N	0°09′E
Bad Hersfeld, Ger. (bät hĕrsh′fĕlt)	154	50°53′N	9°43′E
Badīn, Pak.	186	24°47′N	69°51′E
Bad Ischl, Aus. (bät ĭsh″l)	154	47°46′N	13°37′E
Bad Kissingen, Ger. (bät kĭs′ĭng-ĕn)	154	50°12′N	10°05′E
Bad Kreuznach, Ger. (bät kroits′näk)	154	49°52′N	7°53′E
Badlands, reg., N.D., U.S. (băd′ lănds)	102	46°43′N	103°22′W
Badlands, reg., S.D., U.S.	102	43°43′N	102°36′W
Badlands National Park, S.D., U.S.	102	43°56′N	102°37′W
Badlāpur, India	187b	19°12′N	73°12′E
Bādli, India	240d	28°45′N	77°09′E
Badogo, Mali	214	11°02′N	8°13′W
Bad Oldesloe, Ger. (bät ôl′dĕs-lōē)	154	53°48′N	10°21′E
Bad Reichenhall, Ger. (bät rī′kĕn-häl)	154	47°43′N	12°53′E
Bad River Indian Reservation, I.R., Wi., U.S. (băd)	103	46°41′N	90°36′W
Bad Segeberg, Ger. (bät sĕ′gĕ-bōōrgh)	145c	53°56′N	10°18′E
Bad Tölz, Ger. (bät tûltz)	154	47°46′N	11°35′E
Badulla, Sri L.	187	6°55′N	81°07′E
Bad Vöslau, Aus.	145e	47°58′N	16°13′E
Badwater Creek, r., Wy., U.S. (băd′wô-tẽr)	105	43°13′N	107°55′W
Baena, Spain (bä-ā′nä)	148	37°38′N	4°20′W
Baependi, Braz. (bä-ā-pĕn′dĭ)	129a	21°57′S	44°51′W
Baerl, Ger.	236	51°29′N	6°41′E
Baffin Bay, b., N.A. (băf′ĭn)	82	72°00′N	65°00′W
Baffin Bay, b., Tx., U.S.	113	27°11′N	97°35′W
Baffin Island, i., Can.	82	67°20′N	71°00′W
Bāfq, Iran (bäfk)	182	31°48′N	55°23′E
Bafra, Tur. (bäf′rä)	149	41°30′N	35°50′E
Bagabag, Phil. (bä-gä-bäg′)	197a	16°38′N	121°16′E
Bāgalkot, India	187	16°14′N	75°40′E
Bagamoyo, Tan. (bä-gä-mō′yō)	213	6°26′S	38°54′E
Bagaryak, Russia (bȧ-gär-yȧk′)	172a	56°13′N	61°32′E
Bagbele, D.R.C.	217	4°21′N	29°17′E
Bagdad see Baghdād, Iraq	182	33°14′N	44°22′E
Baghdād, Iraq (bȧgh-dȧd′) (băg′dăd)	182	33°14′N	44°22′E
Bagheria, Italy (bä-gå-rē′ä)	160	38°03′N	13°32′E
Bagley, Mn., U.S. (băg′lē)	102	47°31′N	95°24′W
Bagnara, Italy (bän-yä′rä)	160	38°17′N	15°52′E
Bagnell Dam, Mo., U.S. (băg′nĕl)	111	38°13′N	92°40′W
Bagnères-de-Luchon, Fr. (bän-yâr′ dē-lu chôN′)	156	42°46′N	0°36′E
Bagneux, Fr.	237c	48°48′N	2°18′E
Bagnolet, Fr.	237c	48°52′N	2°25′E
Bagnols-sur-Ceze, Fr. (bä-nyôl′)	156	44°09′N	4°37′E
Bago, Myanmar	196	17°17′N	96°29′E
Bagoé, r., Mali (bȧ-gō′å)	210	12°22′N	6°34′W
Baguio, Phil. (bä-gē-ō′)	196	16°24′N	120°36′E
Bagzane, Monts, mtn., Niger	210	18°40′N	8°40′E
Bahamas, nation, N.A. (bȧ-hā′mȧs)	117	26°15′N	76°00′W
Bahau, Malay.	181b	2°48′N	102°25′E
Bahāwalpur, Pak. (bŭ-hä′wŭl-pōōr)	183	29°29′N	71°41′E
Bahia, state, Braz.	131	11°05′S	43°00′W
Bahía, Islas de la, i., Hond. (ē′s-läs-dē-lä-bä-ē′ä)	116	16°15′N	86°30′W
Bahía Blanca, Arg. (bä-ē′ä blän′kä)	132	38°45′S	62°07′W
Bahía de Caráquez, Ec. (bä-e′ä dä kä-rä′kĕz)	130	0°45′S	80°29′W
Bahía Negra, Para. (bä-ē′ä nā′grä)	131	20°11′S	58°05′W
Bahi Swamp, sw., Tan.	217	6°05′S	35°10′E
Bahoruco, Sierra de, mts., Dom. Rep. (sē-ĕ′r-rä-dĕ-bä-ō-rōō′kō)	123	18°10′N	71°25′W
Bahrain, nation, Asia (bä-rān′)	182	26°15′N	51°17′E
Bahr al Ghazāl, hist. reg., Sudan (bär ĕl ghä-zäl′)	211	7°56′N	27°15′E
Bahrīyah, oasis, Egypt (bȧ-hȧ-rē′yä)	149	28°34′N	29°01′E
Bahtīm, Egypt	244a	30°08′N	31°17′E
Baía dos Tigres, Ang.	216	16°36′S	11°43′E
Baia Mare, Rom. (bä′yä mä′rä)	149	47°40′N	23°35′E
Baidyabāti, India	186a	22°47′N	88°21′E
Baie-Comeau, Can.	92	49°13′N	68°10′W
Baie de Wasai, Mi., U.S. (bä dē wä-sä′ē)	107k	46°27′N	84°15′W
Baie-Saint Paul, Can. (bā′sănt-pôl′)	85	47°27′N	70°30′W
Baigou, China (bī-gō)	190	39°08′N	116°02′E
Baihe, China (bī-hŭ)	192	32°30′N	110°15′E
Bai Hu, l., China (bī-hōō)	190	31°22′N	117°38′E
Baiju, China (bī-jyōō)	190	33°04′N	120°17′E
Baikal, Lake see Baykal, Lake, l., Russia	165	53°00′N	109°28′E
Bailén, Spain (bä-ē-lān′)	158	38°05′N	3°48′W
Băileşti, Rom. (bă-ĭ-lĕsh′tē)	161	44°01′N	23°21′E
Baileys Crossroads, Va., U.S.	229d	38°51′N	77°08′W
Bainbridge, Ga., U.S. (bān′brĭj)	114	30°52′N	84°35′W
Bainbridge Island, i., Wa., U.S.	106a	47°39′N	122°32′W
Bainchipota, India	240a	22°52′N	88°16′E
Baipu, China (bī-pōō)	190	32°15′N	120°47′E
Baiquan, China (bī-chyuäŋ)	192	47°22′N	126°00′E
Baird, Tx., U.S. (bârd)	112	32°22′N	99°28′W
Bairdford, Pa., U.S. (bârd′fōrd)	101e	40°37′N	79°53′W
Baird Mountains, mts., Ak., U.S.	95	67°35′N	160°10′W
Bairnsdale, Austl. (bârnz′dāl)	203	37°50′S	147°39′E
Baïse, r., Fr. (bä-ēz′)	156	43°52′N	0°23′E
Baiyang Dian, l., China (bī-yäŋ-dĭĕn)	190	39°00′N	115°45′E
Baiyunguan, China	240b	39°54′N	116°19′E
Baiyu Shan, mts., China (bī-yōō shän)	192	37°02′N	108°30′E
Baja, Hung. (bŏ′yŏ)	155	46°11′N	18°55′E
Baja California, state, Mex. (bä-hä)	116	30°15′N	117°25′W
Baja California, pen., Mex.	82	28°00′N	113°30′E
Baja California Sur, state, Mex.	116	26°00′N	113°30′W
Bajo, Canal, can., Spain	159a	40°36′N	3°41′W
Bakal, Russia (bä′kȧl)	172a	54°57′N	58°50′E
Baker, Mt., U.S. (bā′kẽr)	105	46°21′N	104°12′W
Baker, Or., U.S.	96	44°46′N	117°52′W
Baker, i., Oc.	2	1°00′N	176°00′W
Baker, l., Can.	84	63°51′N	96°10′W
Baker, Mount, mtn., Wa., U.S.	96	48°46′N	121°52′W
Baker Creek, r., Il., U.S.	101a	41°13′N	87°47′W
Bakersfield, Ca., U.S. (bā′kẽrz-fēld)	96	35°23′N	119°00′W
Bakerstown, Pa., U.S. (bā′kerz-toun)	101e	40°39′N	79°56′W
Baker Street, Eng., U.K.	235	51°30′N	0°21′E
Bakewell, Eng., U.K. (bāk′wĕl)	144a	53°12′N	1°40′W
Bakhchysarai, Ukr.	163	44°46′N	33°54′E
Bakhmach, Ukr. (bȧk-mäch′)	163	51°09′N	32°47′E
Bakhtarān, Iran	182	34°01′N	47°00′E
Bakhtegan, Daryācheh-ye, l., Iran	182	29°29′N	54°31′E
Bakhteyevo, Russia	172b	55°35′N	38°32′E
Bakırköy, neigh., Tur.	239f	40°59′N	28°52′E
Bako, Eth. (bä′kō)	211	5°47′N	36°39′E
Bakony, mts., Hung. (bȧ-kôn′y′)	155	46°57′N	17°30′E
Bakoye, r., Afr. (bȧ-kô′ē)	210	12°47′N	9°35′W
Bakr Uzyak, Russia (bȧkr ōō′z′yȧk)	172a	52°59′N	58°43′E
Baku (Bakı), Azer. (bȧ-kōō′)	164	40°28′N	49°45′E
Bakwanga see Mbuji-Mayi, D.R.C.	216	6°09′S	23°28′E
Balabac Island, i., Phil. (bä′lä-bäk)	196	8°00′N	116°28′E
Balabac Strait, strt., Asia	196	7°23′N	116°30′E
Ba'labakk, Leb.	181a	34°00′N	36°13′E
Balabanovo, Russia (bȧ-lȧ-bä′nô-vô)	172b	56°10′N	37°44′E
Bala-Cynwyd, Pa., U.S.	229b	40°00′N	75°14′W
Balagansk, Russia (bä-lä-gänsk′)	170	53°58′N	103°09′E
Balaguer, Spain (bä-lä-gĕr′)	159	41°48′N	0°50′E
Balakhta, Russia (bȧ′lȧk-tȧ′)	165	55°22′N	91°43′E
Balakliia, Ukr.	163	49°28′N	36°51′E
Balakovo, Russia (bȧ′lȧ-kô′vô)	167	52°00′N	47°40′E
Balancán, Mex. (bä-läŋ-kän′)	119	17°47′N	91°32′W
Balanga, Phil. (bä-läŋ′gä)	197a	14°41′N	120°31′E
Ba Lang An, Mui, c., Viet	193	15°18′N	109°10′E
Balashikha, Russia (bȧ-lä′shĭ-kȧ)	172b	55°48′N	37°58′E
Balashov, Russia (bȧ′lȧ-shôf)	167	51°30′N	43°00′E
Balasore, India (bä-lȧ-sōr′)	183	21°38′N	86°59′E
Balassagyarmat, Hung. (bô′lôsh-shô-dyôr′môt)	155	48°04′N	19°19′E
Balaton Lake, l., Hung. (bô′lô-tôn)	149	46°47′N	17°55′E
Balayan, Phil. (bä-lä-yän′)	197a	13°56′N	120°44′E
Balayan Bay, b., Phil.	197a	13°46′N	120°46′E
Balboa Heights, Pan. (bäl-bô′ä)	121	8°59′N	79°33′W
Balboa Mountain, mtn., Pan.	116a	9°05′N	79°44′W
Balcarce, Arg. (bäl-kär′sā)	132	37°49′S	58°17′W
Balchik, Bul.	161	43°24′N	28°13′E
Bald Eagle, Mn., U.S. (bôld ē′g′l)	107g	45°06′N	93°01′W
Bald Eagle Lake, l., Mn., U.S.	107g	45°08′N	93°03′W
Baldock Lake, l., Can.	89	56°33′N	97°57′W
Baldwin, N.Y., U.S.	228	40°39′N	73°37′W
Baldwin, Pa., U.S.	230b	40°23′N	79°58′W
Baldwin Park, Ca., U.S. (bôld′wĭn)	107a	34°05′N	117°58′W
Baldwinsville, N.Y., U.S. (bôld′wĭns-vĭl)	99	43°10′N	76°20′W
Baldy Mountain, mtn., Can.	89	51°28′N	100°44′W
Baldy Peak, mtn., Az., U.S. (bôl′dē)	96	33°55′N	109°35′W
Baldy Peak, mtn., Tx., U.S. (bôl′dē pēk)	112	30°38′N	104°11′W
Balearic Islands see Balears, Illes, is., Spain	142	39°25′N	1°28′E
Balearic Sea, sea, Spain (băl-ē-ăr′ĭk)	159	39°40′N	1°05′E
Balears, Illes, is., Spain	142	39°25′N	1°28′E
Baleine, Grande Rivière de la, r., Can.	85	55°00′N	75°30′W
Baler, Phil. (bä-lar′)	197a	15°46′N	121°33′E
Baler Bay, b., Phil.	197a	15°51′N	121°40′E
Balesin, i., Phil.	197a	14°28′N	122°10′E
Baley, Russia (bȧl-yā′)	171	51°29′N	116°12′E
Balfate, Hond. (bäl-fä′tē)	120	15°48′N	86°24′W
Balfour, S. Afr. (băl′fŏr)	218d	26°41′S	28°37′E
Balgowlah, Austl.	243a	33°48′S	151°16′E
Bali, i., Indon. (bä′lē)	196	8°00′S	115°22′E
Bālihāti, India	240a	22°44′N	88°19′E
Balıkeşir, Tur. (balĭk′ĭysĭr)	167	39°40′N	27°50′E
Balikpapan, Indon. (bä′lēk-pä′pän)	196	1°13′S	116°52′E
Balintang Channel, strt., Phil. (bä-lĭn-täng′)	196	19°50′N	121°08′E
Balizhuang, China	240b	39°52′N	116°28′E
Balkan Mountains see Stara Planina, mts., Bul.	142	42°50′N	24°45′E
Balkh, Afg. (bälk)	183	36°48′N	66°50′E
Ballabhpur, India	240a	22°44′N	88°21′E
Ballancourt, Fr. (bä-äN-kòr′)	157b	48°31′N	2°23′E
Ballarat, Austl. (băl′ȧ-răt)	203	37°37′S	144°00′E
Ballard, l., Austl. (băl′ȧrd)	202	29°15′S	120°45′E
Ballater, Scot., U.K. (băl′ȧ-tẽr)	150	57°05′N	3°06′W
Ballenato, Punta, c., Cuba	233b	23°06′N	82°30′W
Balleny Islands, is., Ant. (băl′ĕ nē)	219	67°00′S	164°00′E
Ballina, Austl. (băl-ĭ-nä′)	204	28°50′S	153°35′E
Ballina, Ire.	150	54°06′N	9°05′W
Ballinasloe, Ire. (băl′ĭ-nȧ-slō′)	150	53°20′N	8°09′W
Ballinger, Tx., U.S. (băl′ĭn-jẽr)	112	31°45′N	99°58′W
Ballston Spa, N.Y., U.S. (bôls′tŭn spä′)	99	43°05′N	73°50′W
Ballygunge, neigh., India	240a	22°31′N	88°21′E
Balmain, Austl.	243a	33°51′S	151°11′E
Balmazújváros, Hung. (bŏl′mŏz-ōō′y′vä′rōsh)	155	47°35′N	21°23′E
Balobe, D.R.C.	217	0°05′N	28°00′E
Balonne, r., Austl. (băl-ōn′)	203	27°00′S	149°10′E
Bālotra, India	186	25°56′N	72°12′E
Balqash, Kaz.	169	46°58′N	75°00′E
Balqash kōlī, l., Kaz.	169	45°58′N	72°15′E
Balranald, Austl. (băl′-rȧn-ăld)	204	34°42′S	143°30′E
Balsam, l., Can. (bôl′sȧm)	91	44°30′N	78°50′W
Balsas, Braz. (bäl′säs)	131	7°09′S	46°04′W
Balsas, r., Mex.	116	18°00′N	101°00′W
Balta, Ukr. (bäl′tä)	167	47°57′N	29°38′E
Bălţi, Mol.	167	47°47′N	27°57′E
Baltic Sea, sea, Eur. (bôl′tĭk)	142	55°20′N	16°50′E
Baltīm, Egypt (bȧl-tēm′)	218b	31°33′N	31°04′E
Baltimore, Md., U.S. (bôl′tĭ-môr)	97	39°20′N	76°38′W
Baltiysk, Russia (bäl-tēysk′)	153	54°40′N	19°55′E
Baluarte, Río del, Mex. (rē′ō-dĕl-bä-lōō′r-tĕ)	118	23°09′N	105°42′W
Baluchistān, hist. reg., Asia (bȧ-lò-chĭ-stän′)	183	27°30′N	65°30′E
Balwyn, Austl.	243b	37°49′S	145°05′E
Balzac, Can. (bôl′zăk)	83e	51°10′N	114°01′W
Bama, Nig.	215	11°30′N	13°41′E
Bamako, Mali (bä-mȧ-kō′)	210	12°39′N	8°00′W
Bambang, Phil. (bäm-bäng′)	197a	16°24′N	121°08′E
Bambari, Cen. Afr. Rep. (bäm-bȧ-rē)	211	5°44′N	20°40′E
Bamberg, Ger. (bäm′bĕrgh)	147	49°53′N	10°52′E
Bamberg, S.C., U.S. (băm′bûrg)	115	33°17′N	81°04′W
Bamenda, Cam.	215	5°56′N	10°10′E
Bamingui, r., Cen. Afr. Rep.	215	7°35′N	19°45′E
Bampton, Eng., U.K. (băm′tŭn)	144b	51°42′N	1°33′W
Bampūr, Iran (bŭm-pōōr′)	182	27°15′N	60°22′E
Bam Yanga, Ngao, mts., Cam.	215	8°20′N	14°40′E
Banahao, Mount, mtn., Phil. (bä-nä-hä′ō)	197a	14°04′N	121°45′E
Banalia, D.R.C.	217	1°33′N	25°20′E
Banamba, Mali	214	13°33′N	7°27′W
Bananal, Braz. (bä-nä-näl′)	129a	22°42′S	44°17′W
Bananal, Ilha do, i., Braz. (ē′lä-dô-bä-nä-näl′)	131	12°09′S	50°27′W
Banās, r., India (băn-äs′)	183	25°20′N	75°20′E
Banās, Ra's, c., Egypt	211	23°48′N	36°39′E
Banat, reg., Rom. (bä-nät′)	161	45°35′N	21°05′E
Banbidian, China	240b	39°54′N	116°32′E
Bancroft, Can. (băn′krŏft)	85	45°05′N	77°55′W
Bancroft see Chililabombwe, Zam.	217	12°18′S	27°43′E
Bānda, India (bän′dä)	183	25°36′N	80°21′E
Banda, Kepulauan, is., Indon.	197	4°40′S	129°56′E
Banda, Laut (Banda Sea), sea, Indon.	197	6°05′S	127°28′E
Banda Aceh, Indon.	196	5°10′N	95°10′E
Banda Banda, Mount, mtn., Austl. (băn′dȧ băn′dȧ)	204	31°09′S	152°15′E
Bandama Blanc, r., C. Iv. (bän-dä′mä)	214	6°15′N	5°00′W
Bandar Beheshtī, Iran	182	25°18′N	60°45′E
Bandar-e 'Abbās, Iran (bän-där′ ȧb-bäs′)	182	27°04′N	56°22′E
Bandar-e Būshehr, Iran	182	28°48′N	50°53′E
Bandar-e Lengeh, Iran	182	26°44′N	54°47′E
Bandar-e Torkeman, Iran	182	37°05′N	54°08′E
Bandar Maharani, Malay. (bän-där′ mä-hä-rä′nē)	181b	2°02′N	102°34′E
Bandar Seri Begawan, Bru.	196	5°00′N	114°59′E
Bande, Spain	158	42°02′N	7°58′W
Bandeira, Pico da, mtn., Braz. (pē′kō dä bän dā′rä)	131	20°27′S	41°47′W
Bāndel, India	240a	22°56′N	88°22′E
Bandelier National Monument, rec., N.M., U.S. (băn-dĕ-lēr′)	109	35°50′N	106°45′W
Banderas, Bahía de, b., Mex. (bä-ē′ä dē bän-dĕ′räs)	118	20°38′N	105°35′W
Bandirma, Tur. (bän-dĭr′mȧ)	149	40°25′N	27°50′E
Bandon, Or., U.S. (băn′dŭn)	104	43°06′N	124°25′W
Bāndra, India	187b	19°04′N	72°49′E
Bandundu, D.R.C.	212	3°18′S	17°20′E
Bandung, Indon.	196	7°00′S	107°22′E
Banes, Cuba (bä′näs)	123	21°00′N	75°45′W
Banff, Can. (bănf)	84	51°10′N	115°34′W
Banff, Scot., U.K.	150	57°39′N	2°37′W
Banff National Park, rec., Can.	84	51°38′N	116°22′W
Bánfield, Arg. (bä′n-fyĕ′ld)	132a	34°44′S	58°24′W
Banfora, Burkina	214	10°38′N	4°46′W
Bangalore, India (băŋ′gȧ′lôr)	183	13°03′N	77°39′E
Bangassou, Cen. Afr. Rep. (bäN-gȧ-sōō′)	211	4°47′N	22°49′E
Bangeta, Mount, mtn., Pap. N. Gui.	197	6°20′S	147°00′E
Banggai, Kepulauan, is., Indon. (bäng-gī′)	197	1°05′S	123°45′E
Banggi, Pulau, i., Malay.	196	7°12′N	117°10′E
Banghāzī, Libya	211	32°07′N	20°04′E
Bangka, i., Indon. (bäŋ′kȧ)	196	2°24′S	106°55′E
Bangkalan, Indon. (bäng-kä-län′)	196	6°07′S	112°50′E
Bang Khun Thian, Thai.	241f	13°42′N	100°28′E
Bangkok, Thai.	196	13°50′N	100°29′E
Bangladesh, nation, Asia	183	24°15′N	90°00′E
Bangong Co, l., Asia (bäŋ-gôŋ tswo)	186	33°40′N	79°30′E

262 Bangor–Bauta

PLACE (Pronunciation)	PAGE	LAT.	LONG.
Bangor, Wales, U.K. (băŋ'ŏr)	150	53°13'N	4°05'W
Bangor, Me., U.S. (băn'gẽr)	97	44°47'N	68°47'W
Bangor, Mi., U.S.	98	42°20'N	86°05'W
Bangor, Pa., U.S.	99	40°55'N	75°10'W
Bangs, Mount, mtn., Az., U.S. (băngs)	109	36°45'N	113°50'W
Bangu, neigh., Braz.	234c	22°52'S	43°27'W
Bangued, Phil. (bän-gād')	197a	17°36'N	120°38'E
Bangui, Cen. Afr. Rep. (bäN-gē')	211	4°22'N	18°35'E
Bangweulu, Lake, l., Zam. (băng-wė-o͞o'lo͞o)	212	10°55'S	30°10'E
Bangweulu Swamp, sw., Zam.	217	11°25'S	30°10'E
Bani, Dom. Rep. (bä'-nė)	123	18°15'N	70°25'W
Bani, Phil. (bä'nē)	197a	16°11'N	119°51'E
Bani, r., Mali	210	13°00'N	5°30'W
Bánica, Dom. Rep. (bä'-nē-kä)	123	19°00'N	71°35'W
Banī Majdūl, Egypt	244a	30°02'N	31°07'E
Banī Mazār, Egypt	184	28°29'N	30°48'E
Banister, r., Va., U.S. (băn'ĭs-tẽr)	115	36°45'N	79°17'W
Banī Suwayf, Egypt	211	29°05'N	31°06'E
Banja Luka, Bos. (bän-yä-lo͞o'kȧ)	149	44°45'N	17°11'E
Banjarmasin, Indon. (bän-jẽr-mä'sĕn)	196	3°18'S	114°32'E
Banjin, China (bän-jyĭn)	190	32°23'N	120°14'E
Banjul, Gam.	210	13°28'N	16°39'W
Bankberg, mts., S. Afr. (băŋk'bûrg)	213c	32°18'S	25°15'E
Banks, Or., U.S. (bănks)	106c	45°37'N	123°07'W
Banks, i., Austl.	203	10°10'S	143°08'E
Banks, Cape, c., Austl.	201b	34°01'S	151°17'E
Banks Island, i., Can.	82	73°00'N	123°00'W
Banks Island, i., Can.	86	53°25'N	130°10'W
Banks Islands, is., Vanuatu	203	13°38'S	168°23'E
Banksmeadow, Austl.	243a	33°58'S	151°13'E
Banks Peninsula, pen., N.Z.	205	43°45'S	172°20'E
Banks Strait, strt., Austl.	204	40°45'S	148°00'E
Bankstown, Austl.	201b	33°55'S	151°02'E
Ban Lat Phrao, Thai.	241f	13°47'N	100°36'E
Bann, r., N. Ire., U.K. (băn)	150	54°50'N	6°29'W
Banning, Ca., U.S. (băn'ĭng)	107a	33°56'N	116°53'W
Bannockburn, Austl.	201a	38°03'S	144°11'E
Bannu, Pak.	186	33°03'N	70°39'E
Baños, Ec. (bä'-nyỏs)	130	1°30'S	78°22'W
Banská Bystrica, Slvk. (bän'skä bė'strė-tzä)	147	48°46'N	19°10'E
Bansko, Bul. (bän'skō)	161	41°51'N	23°33'E
Banstala, India	240a	22°32'N	88°25'E
Banstead, Eng., U.K. (băn'stĕd)	144b	51°18'N	0°09'W
Banton, i., Phil. (bän-tōn')	197a	12°54'N	121°55'E
Bantry, Ire. (băn'trĭ)	150	51°39'N	9°30'W
Bantry Bay, b., Ire.	150	51°25'N	10°09'W
Banyak, Kepulauan, is., Indon.	196	2°08'N	97°15'E
Banyuwangi, Indon. (bän-jỏ-wäŋ'gė)	196	8°15'S	114°15'E
Baocheng, China (bou-chŭŋ)	192	33°15'N	106°58'E
Baodi, China (bou-dē)	192	39°44'N	117°19'E
Baoding, China (bou-dĭŋ)	189	38°52'N	115°31'E
Baoji, China (bou-jyē)	192	34°10'N	106°58'E
Baoshan, China (bou-shän)	188	25°14'N	99°03'E
Baoshan, China	190	31°25'N	121°29'E
Baotou, China (bou-tō)	189	40°28'N	110°10'E
Baoying, China (bou-yĭŋ)	192	33°14'N	119°20'E
Bapsfontein, S. Afr. (băps-fŏn-tān')	213b	26°01'S	28°26'E
Ba 'qūbah, Iraq	185	33°45'N	44°38'E
Ba-queo, Viet	241j	10°48'N	106°38'E
Baqueroncito, Col. (bä-kē-rŏ'n-sē-tỏ)	130a	3°18'N	74°40'W
Bara, India	240a	22°46'N	88°17'E
Baraawe, Som.	218a	1°20'N	44°00'E
Barabinsk, Russia (bȧ'rȧ-bĭnsk)	170	55°18'N	78°00'E
Baraboo, Wi., U.S. (bâr'ȧ-bo͞o)	103	43°29'N	89°44'W
Baracoa, Cuba (bä-rä-kō'ä)	123	20°20'N	74°25'W
Baracoa, Cuba	123a	23°03'N	82°34'W
Baradères, Baie des, b., Haiti (bä-rä-dâr')	123	18°35'N	73°35'W
Baradero, Arg. (bä-rä-dĕ'ỏ)	129c	33°50'S	59°30'W
Baragwanath, S. Afr.	244b	26°16'S	27°59'E
Barahona, Dom. Rep. (bä-rä-ỏ'nä)	123	18°15'N	71°10'W
Barajas de Madrid, Spain (bä-rȧ'häs dā mä-drēdh')	159a	40°28'N	3°35'W
Baranagar, India	186	22°38'N	88°25'E
Baranco, Belize (bä-räŋ'kō)	120	16°01'N	88°55'W
Baranof, i., Ak., U.S. (bä-rä'nỏf)	95	56°48'N	136°08'W
Baranovichi, Bela. (bä'rä-nỏ-vē'chė)	164	53°08'N	25°59'E
Baranpauh, Indon.	181b	0°40'N	103°28'E
Barão de Melgaço, Braz. (bä-rouN-dĕ-mĕl-gä'sỏ)	131	16°12'S	55°48'W
Bārāsat, India	186a	22°42'N	88°29'E
Bārasat, India	240a	22°51'N	88°22'E
Barataria Bay, b., La., U.S.	113	29°13'N	89°50'W
Baraya, Col. (bä-rȧ'yä)	130a	3°10'N	75°04'W
Barbacena, Braz. (bär-bä-sā'nȧ)	131	21°15'S	43°46'W
Barbacoas, Col. (bär-bä-kō'äs)	130	1°39'N	78°12'W
Barbacoas, Ven. (bä-rä-kô'ås)	131b	9°30'N	66°58'W
Barbados, nation, N.A. (bär-bā'dōz)	117	13°30'N	59°00'W
Barbar, Sudan	211	18°11'N	34°00'E
Barbastro, Spain (bär-bäs'trō)	159	42°05'N	0°05'E
Barbeau, Mi., U.S. (bär-bō')	107k	46°17'N	84°16'W
Barberton, S. Afr.	212	25°48'S	31°04'E
Barberton, Oh., U.S. (bär'bẽr-tŭn)	101d	41°01'N	81°37'W
Barbezieux, Fr. (bärb'zyû')	156	45°30'N	0°11'W
Barbosa, Col. (bär-bỏ'-sȧ)	130a	6°26'N	75°19'W
Barboursville, W.V., U.S. (bär'bẽrs-vĭl)	98	38°20'N	82°20'W
Barbourville, Ky., U.S.	114	36°52'N	83°58'W
Barbuda, i., Antig. (bär-bo͞o'dȧ)	117	17°45'N	61°15'W
Barcaldine, Austl. (bär'kôl-dīn)	203	23°33'S	145°17'E
Barcarrota, Spain (bär-kär-rō'tä)	158	38°31'N	6°50'W
Barcellona, Italy (bä-chĕl-lō'nä)	160	38°07'N	15°15'E
Barcelona, Spain (bär-thå-lō'nä)	142	41°25'N	2°08'E
Barcelona, Ven. (bär-så-lō'nä)	130	10°09'N	64°41'W
Barcelos, Braz. (bär-sĕ'lỏs)	130	1°04'S	63°00'W
Barcelos, Port. (bär-thå'lōs)	158	41°34'N	8°39'W
Barcroft, Lake, res., Va., U.S.	229d	38°51'N	77°09'W
Bardawīl, Sabkhat al, b., Egypt	181a	31°20'N	33°24'E
Bardejov, Czech Rep. (bär'dyĕ-yôf)	155	49°18'N	21°18'E
Bardsey Island, i., Wales, U.K. (bärd'sė)	150	52°45'N	4°50'W
Bardstown, Ky., U.S. (bärds'toun)	98	37°50'N	85°30'W
Bardwell, Ky., U.S. (bärd'wĕl)	114	36°51'N	88°57'W
Bare Hills, Md., U.S.	229c	39°23'N	76°40'W
Bareilly, India	183	28°21'N	79°25'E
Barents Sea, sea, Eur. (bä'rĕnts)	164	72°14'N	37°28'E
Barentu, Erit. (bä-rĕn'to͞o)	211	15°06'N	37°39'E
Barfleur, Pointe de, c., Fr. (bȧr-flûr')	156	49°43'N	1°17'W
Barguzin, Russia (bär'go͞o-zĭn)	165	53°44'N	109°28'E
Bar Harbor, Me., U.S. (bär här'bẽr)	92	44°22'N	68°13'W
Bari, Italy (bä'rē)	142	41°08'N	16°53'E
Barinas, Ven. (bä-rē'näs)	130	8°36'N	70°14'W
Baring, Cape, c., Can. (bâr'ĭng)	84	70°07'N	119°48'W
Barisan, Pegunungan, mts., Indon. (bä-rė-sän')	196	2°38'S	101°45'E
Bariti Bil, l., India	240a	22°48'N	88°26'E
Barito, r., Indon. (bä-rē'tō)	196	2°10'S	114°38'E
Barka, r., Afr.	211	16°44'N	37°34'E
Barking, neigh., Eng., U.K.	235	51°33'N	0°06'E
Barkingside, neigh., Eng., U.K.	235	51°36'N	0°05'E
Barkley Sound, strt., Can.	86	48°53'N	125°20'W
Barkly East, S. Afr. (bärk'lē ēst)	213c	30°58'S	27°37'E
Barkly Tableland, plat., Austl. (bär'klė)	202	18°15'S	137°05'E
Barkol, China (bär-kůl)	188	43°43'N	92°50'E
Bârlad, Rom.	149	46°15'N	27°43'E
Bar-le-Duc, Fr. (bär-lē-dük')	157	48°47'N	5°05'E
Barlee, l., Austl. (bär-lē')	202	29°45'S	119°00'E
Barletta, Italy (bär-lĕt'tä)	149	41°19'N	16°20'E
Barmen, neigh., Ger.	236	51°17'N	7°13'E
Barmstedt, Ger. (bärm'shtĕt)	145c	53°47'N	9°46'E
Barnaul, Russia (bär-nä-ŏŏl')	164	53°18'N	83°23'E
Barnes, neigh., Eng., U.K.	235	51°28'N	0°15'W
Barnesboro, Pa., U.S. (bärnz'bẽr-ỏ)	99	40°45'N	78°50'W
Barnesville, Ga., U.S. (bärnz'vĭl)	114	33°03'N	84°10'W
Barnesville, Mn., U.S.	102	46°38'N	96°25'W
Barnesville, Oh., U.S.	98	39°55'N	81°10'W
Barnet, Vt., U.S. (bär'nĕt)	99	44°20'N	72°00'W
Barnetby le Wold, Eng., U.K. (bär'nĕt-bī)	144a	53°34'N	0°26'W
Barnett Harbor, b., Bah.	122	25°40'N	79°20'W
Barnsdall, Ok., U.S. (bärnz'dôl)	111	36°38'N	96°14'W
Barnsley, Eng., U.K. (bärnz'lĭ)	144a	53°33'N	1°29'W
Barnstaple, Eng., U.K. (bärn'stā-p'l)	150	51°06'N	4°05'W
Barnston, Eng., U.K.	237a	53°21'N	3°05'W
Barnum Island, N.Y., U.S.	228	40°36'N	73°39'W
Barnwell, S.C., U.S. (bärn'wĕl)	115	33°14'N	81°23'W
Baro, Nig. (bä'rỏ)	210	8°37'N	6°25'E
Baroda, India (bär-rō'dä)	183	22°21'N	73°12'E
Barotse Plain, pl., Zam.	216	15°50'S	22°55'E
Barqah (Cyrenaica), hist. reg., Libya	211	31°09'N	21°45'E
Barquisimeto, Ven. (bär-kē-sė-mä'tō)	130	10°04'N	69°16'W
Barra, Braz. (bär'rä)	131	11°04'S	43°11'W
Barraba, Austl.	204	30°22'S	150°36'E
Barracas, neigh., Arg.	233d	34°38'S	58°22'W
Barrackpore, India	186a	22°46'N	88°21'E
Barra do Corda, Braz. (bär'rä dỏ cōr-dä)	131	5°33'S	45°13'W
Barra Funda, neigh., Braz.	234d	23°31'S	46°39'W
Barra Mansa, Braz. (bär'rä män'sä)	129a	22°35'S	44°09'W
Barrancabermeja, Col. (bär-räŋ'kä-bēr-mā'hä)	130	7°06'N	73°49'W
Barrancas, Chile	234b	33°27'S	70°46'W
Barranco, Peru	233c	12°09'S	77°02'W
Barranquilla, Col. (bär-rän-kēl'yä)	130	10°57'N	75°00'W
Barras, Braz. (bȧ'r-räs)	131	4°13'S	42°14'W
Barre, Vt., U.S. (băr'ė)	99	44°15'N	72°30'W
Barreiras, Braz. (bär-rā'räs)	131	12°13'S	44°59'W
Barreiro, Port. (bär-rĕ'ė-rỏ)	148	38°39'N	9°05'W
Barren, r., Ky., U.S.	114	37°00'N	86°20'W
Barren, Cape, c., Austl. (băr'ĕn)	203	40°20'S	149°00'E
Barren, Nosy, is., Madag.	213	18°18'S	43°57'E
Barren River Lake, res., Ky., U.S.	114	36°45'N	86°02'W
Barretos, Braz. (bär-rā'tōs)	131	20°40'S	48°36'W
Barrhead, Can. (băr'ĭd)	84	54°08'N	114°24'W
Barriada Pomar Alto, Spain	238e	41°29'N	2°14'E
Barrie, Can. (băr'ĭ)	85	44°25'N	79°45'W
Barrington, Can. (bă-rĕng-tŏn)	83a	45°07'N	73°35'W
Barrington, Il., U.S.	101a	42°09'N	88°08'W
Barrington, N.J., U.S.	229b	39°52'N	75°04'W
Barrington, R.I., U.S.	100b	41°44'N	71°16'W
Barrington Tops, mtn., Austl.	204	32°00'S	151°25'E
Barrio Obrero Industrial, prov., Peru	233c	12°04'S	77°04'W
Bar River, Can. (bär)	107k	46°27'N	84°02'W
Barron, Wi., U.S. (băr'ŭn)	103	45°24'N	91°51'W
Barrow, Ak., U.S. (băr'ō)	94a	71°20'N	156°00'W
Barrow, i., Austl.	202	20°50'S	115°00'E
Barrow, r., Ire. (bå-rå)	150	52°35'N	7°05'W
Barrow, Point, c., Ak., U.S.	95	71°20'N	156°00'W
Barrow Creek, Austl.	202	21°23'S	133°55'E
Barrow-in-Furness, Eng., U.K.	146	54°10'N	3°15'W
Barstow, Ca., U.S. (bär'stō)	108	34°53'N	117°03'W
Barstow, Md., U.S.	100e	38°32'N	76°37'W
Barth, Ger. (bärt)	154	54°20'N	12°43'E
Bartholomew Bayou, r., U.S. (bär-thŏl'ỏ-mū bī-o͞o')	111	33°53'N	91°45'W
Barthurst, Can. (bär-thŭrst')	85	47°38'N	65°40'W
Bartica, Guy. (bär'tĭ-kȧ)	131	6°23'N	58°32'W
Bartin, Tur. (bär'tĭn)	149	41°35'N	32°12'E
Bartle Frere, Mount, mtn., Austl. (bärt''l frēr')	203	17°30'S	145°46'E
Bartlesville, Ok., U.S. (bär'tlz-vĭl)	111	36°44'N	95°58'W
Bartlett, Il., U.S. (bärt'lĕt)	101a	41°59'N	88°11'W
Bartlett, Tx., U.S.	113	30°48'N	97°25'W
Barton, Vt., U.S. (bär'tŭn)	99	44°45'N	72°05'W
Barton-upon-Humber, Eng., U.K. (bär'tŭn-ŭp'ŏn-hŭm'bẽr)	144a	53°41'N	0°26'W
Bartoszyce, Pol. (bär-tỏ-shĭ'tsȧ)	155	54°15'N	20°50'E
Bartow, Fl., U.S. (bär'tō)	115a	27°51'N	81°50'W
Baruta, Ven.	234a	10°26'N	66°53'W
Barvinkove, Ukr.	163	48°55'N	36°59'E
Barwon, r., Austl. (bär'wŭn)	203	30°00'S	147°30'E
Barwon Heads, Austl.	201a	38°17'S	144°29'E
Barycz, r., Pol. (bä'rĭch)	154	51°30'N	16°38'E
Basai Dārāpur, neigh., India	240d	28°40'N	77°08'E
Basankusu, D.R.C. (bä-sän-ko͞o'so͞o)	211	1°14'N	19°45'E
Basbeck, Ger. (bäs'bĕk)	145c	53°40'N	9°11'E
Basdahl, Ger. (bäs'däl)	145c	53°27'N	9°00'E
Basehor, Ks., U.S. (bās'hôr)	107f	39°08'N	94°55'W
Basel, Switz. (bä'z'l)	147	47°32'N	7°35'E
Bashee, r., S. Afr. (bȧ-shē')	213c	31°47'S	28°25'E
Bashi Channel, strt., Asia (băsh'ė)	189	21°20'N	120°22'E
Bashkortostan, state, Russia	166	54°12'N	57°15'E
Bashtanka, Ukr. (bȧsh-tän'kȧ)	163	47°32'N	32°31'E
Bashtīl, Egypt	244a	30°05'N	31°11'E
Basilan Island, i., Phil.	196	6°37'N	122°07'E
Basildon, Eng., U.K.	151	51°35'N	0°25'E
Basilicata, hist. reg., Italy (bä-zē-lė-kä'tä)	160	40°30'N	15°55'E
Basin, Wy., U.S. (bā'sĭn)	105	44°22'N	108°02'W
Basingstoke, Eng., U.K. (bă'zĭng-stōk)	144b	51°14'N	1°06'W
Baška, Cro. (bäsh'ka)	160	44°58'N	14°44'E
Baskale, Tur. (bȧsh-kä'lĕ)	167	38°10'N	44°00'E
Baskatong, Réservoir, res., Can.	91	46°50'N	75°50'W
Baskunchak, l., Russia	167	48°20'N	46°40'E
Basoko, D.R.C. (bȧ-sō'kō)	211	0°52'N	23°50'E
Basque Provinces, hist. reg., Spain	158	43°00'N	2°46'W
Basra *see* Al Başrah, Iraq	182	30°35'N	47°59'E
Bassano, Can. (băs-sän'ō)	84	50°47'N	112°28'W
Bassano del Grappa, Italy	160	45°46'N	11°44'E
Bassari, Togo	214	9°15'N	0°47'E
Bassas da India, i., Reu. (bäs'säs dä ēn'dė-ȧ)	213	21°23'S	39°42'E
Basse Terre, Guad. (bäs' târ')	117	16°00'N	61°43'W
Basseterre, St. K./N.	121b	17°20'N	62°42'W
Basse Terre, i., Guad.	121b	16°10'N	62°14'W
Bassett, Va., U.S. (băs'sĕt)	115	36°45'N	81°58'W
Bass Hill, Austl.	243a	33°54'S	151°00'E
Bass Islands, is., Oh., U.S. (băs)	98	41°40'N	82°50'W
Bass Strait, strt., Austl.	203	39°40'S	145°40'E
Basswood, l., N.A. (băs'wỏd)	103	48°10'N	91°36'W
Båstad, Swe. (bỏ'stät)	152	56°26'N	12°46'E
Bastia, Fr. (bäs'tē-ä)	147	42°43'N	9°27'E
Bastogne, Bel. (bäs-tôn'y')	151	50°02'N	5°45'E
Bastrop, La., U.S. (băs'trŭp)	113	32°47'N	91°55'W
Bastrop, Tx., U.S.	113	30°08'N	97°18'W
Bastrop Bayou, Tx., U.S.	113a	29°07'N	95°22'W
Bāsudebpur, India	240a	22°49'N	88°25'E
Bata, Eq. Gui. (bä'tä)	210	1°51'N	9°45'E
Batabano, Golfo de, b., Cuba (gỏl-fō-dē-bä-tä-bä'nō)	122	22°10'N	83°05'W
Batāla, India	186	31°54'N	75°18'E
Bataly, Kaz. (bȧ-tä'lĭ)	169	52°51'N	62°03'E
Batam, i., Indon. (bä-täm')	181b	1°03'N	104°00'E
Batang, China (bä-täŋ)	188	30°08'N	99°00'E
Batangas, Phil. (bä-tän'gäs)	196	13°45'N	121°04'E
Batan Islands, is., Phil. (bä-tän')	196	20°58'N	122°20'E
Bátaszék, Hung. (bä'tȧ-sāk)	155	46°07'N	18°40'E
Batavia, Il., U.S. (bȧ-tā'vĭ-ȧ)	101a	41°51'N	88°18'W
Batavia, N.Y., U.S.	99	43°00'N	78°15'W
Batavia, Oh., U.S.	101f	39°05'N	84°10'W
Bataysk, Russia (bȧ-tīsk')	167	47°08'N	39°44'E
Bătdâmbâng, Camb. (bȧt-tȧm-bäng')	196	13°14'N	103°15'E
Batenbrock, neigh., Ger.	236	51°31'N	6°57'E
Batesburg, S.C., U.S. (bāts'bûrg)	115	33°53'N	81°34'W
Batesville, Ar., U.S. (bāts'vĭl)	111	35°46'N	91°39'W
Batesville, In., U.S.	98	39°15'N	85°15'W
Batesville, Ms., U.S.	114	34°17'N	89°55'W
Batetska, Russia (bȧ-tĕ'tskȧ)	162	58°36'N	30°21'E
Bath, Can. (bȧth)	92	46°31'N	67°36'W
Bath, Eng., U.K.	147	51°24'N	2°20'W
Bath, Me., U.S.	92	43°54'N	69°50'W
Bath, N.Y., U.S.	99	42°25'N	77°20'W
Bath, Oh., U.S.	101d	41°11'N	81°38'W
Bathsheba, Barb.	121b	13°13'N	60°30'W
Bathurst, Austl. (băth'ŭrst)	203	33°28'S	149°30'E
Bathurst *see* Banjul, Gam.	210	13°28'N	16°39'W
Bathurst, S. Afr. (băt-hûrst)	213c	33°26'S	26°53'E
Bathurst, i., Austl.	202	11°19'S	130°13'E
Bathurst, Cape, c., Can. (băth'-ûrst)	84	70°33'N	127°55'W
Bathurst Inlet, b., Can.	84	68°10'N	108°00'W
Batia, Benin	214	10°54'N	1°29'E
Batley, Eng., U.K. (băt'lĭ)	144a	53°43'N	1°37'W
Batna, Alg. (bät'nä)	210	35°41'N	6°12'E
Baton Rouge, La., U.S. (băt'ŭn ro͞ozh')	97	30°28'N	91°10'W
Battersea, neigh., Eng., U.K.	235	51°28'N	0°10'W
Batticaloa, Sri L.	187	7°40'N	81°10'E
Battle, r., Can.	88	52°20'N	111°59'W
Battle Creek, Mi., U.S. (băt''l krēk')	97	42°20'N	85°15'W
Battle Ground, Wa., U.S. (băt''l ground)	106c	45°47'N	122°32'W
Battle Harbour, Can. (băt''l här'bẽr)	85	52°17'N	55°33'W
Battle Mountain, Nv., U.S.	104	40°40'N	116°56'W
Battonya, Hung. (bät-tỏ'nyä)	155	46°17'N	21°00'E
Batu, Kepulauan, is., Indon. (bä'to͞o)	196	0°10'S	98°00'E
Batumi, Geor. (bŭ-to͞o'mē)	164	41°40'N	41°30'E
Batu Pahat, Malay.	196	1°51'N	102°56'E
Batupanjang, Indon.	181b	1°42'N	101°35'E
Bauang, Phil. (bä'wäng)	197a	16°31'N	120°19'E
Bauchi, Nig. (bȧ-o͞o'chė)	210	10°19'N	9°50'E
Bauerschaft, Ger.	236	51°34'N	6°33'E
Bauerstown, Pa., U.S.	230b	40°30'N	79°59'W
Baukau, neigh., Ger.	236	51°33'N	7°12'E
Bauld, Cape, c., Can.	85a	51°38'N	55°25'W
Baulkham Hills, Austl.	243a	33°46'S	151°00'E
Baumschulenweg, neigh., Ger.	238a	52°28'N	13°29'E
Bāuria, India	186a	22°29'N	88°08'E
Bauru, Braz. (bou-ro͞o')	131	22°21'S	48°57'W
Bauska, Lat. (bou'skȧ)	153	56°24'N	24°12'E
Bauta, Cuba (bȧ'o͞o-tä)	123a	22°59'N	82°33'W

ăt; finȧl; rāte; senāte; ärm; åsk; sofȧ; fâre; ch-choose; dh-as th in other; bē; ėvent; bĕt; recĕnt; cratẽr; g-gō; gh-guttural g; bĭt; ĭ-short neutral; rīde; κ-guttural k as ch in German ich;

PRONOUNCING INDEX Bautzen - Belmont 263

PLACE (Pronunciation)	PAGE	LAT.	LONG.
Bautzen, Ger. (bout'sĕn)	147	51°11'N	14°27'E
Bavaria see Bayern, state, Ger.	154	49°00'N	11°16'E
Baw Baw, Mount, mtn., Austl.	204	37°50'S	146°17'E
Bawean, Pulau, i., Indon. (bȧ'vē-än)	196	5°50'S	112°40'E
Bawtry, Eng., U.K. (bôtrĭ)	144a	53°26'N	1°01'W
Baxley, Ga., U.S. (băks'lĭ)	115	31°47'N	82°22'W
Baxter, Austl.	201a	38°12'S	145°10'E
Baxter Springs, Ks., U.S. (băks'tẽr sprĭngs')	111	37°01'N	94°44'W
Bay, Laguna de, l., Phil. (lä-gōō'nä dȧ bä'ē)	197a	14°24'N	121°13'E
Bayaguana, Dom. Rep. (bä-yä-gwä'nä)	123	18°45'N	69°40'W
Bay al Kabīr, Wadi, val., Libya	148	29°52'N	14°28'E
Bayambang, Phil. (bä-yäm-bäng')	197a	15°50'N	120°26'E
Bayamo, Cuba (bä-yä'mō)	122	20°25'N	76°35'W
Bayamón, P.R.	117b	18°27'N	66°13'W
Bayan, China (bä-yän)	192	46°00'N	127°20'E
Bayanauyl, Kaz.	169	50°43'N	75°37'E
Bayard, Ne., U.S. (bā'ẽrd)	102	41°45'N	103°20'W
Bayard, N.M., U.S.	109	32°45'N	108°07'W
Bayard, W.V., U.S.	99	39°15'N	79°20'W
Bayburt, Tur. (bä'ĭ-bŏort)	167	40°15'N	40°10'E
Bay City, Mi., U.S. (bā)	97	43°35'N	83°55'W
Bay City, Tx., U.S.	113	28°59'N	95°58'W
Baydaratskaya Guba, b., Russia	166	69°20'N	66°10'E
Bay de Verde, Can.	93	48°05'N	52°54'W
Baydhabo (Baidoa), Som.	218a	3°19'N	44°20'E
Baydrag, r., Mong.	188	46°09'N	98°52'E
Bayern (Bavaria), hist. reg., Ger. (bī'ẽrn) (bȧ-vâ-rĭ-ȧ)	154	49°00'N	11°16'E
Bayeux, Fr. (bȧ-yû')	147	49°19'N	0°41'W
Bayfield, Wi., U.S. (bā'fēld)	103	46°48'N	90°51'W
Bayford, Eng., U.K.	235	51°46'N	0°06'W
Baykal, Ozero (Lake Baikal), l., Russia	165	53°00'N	109°28'E
Baykal'skiy Khrebet, mts., Russia	165	53°30'N	107°30'E
Baykit, Russia (bī-kĕt')	165	61°43'N	96°39'E
Baymak, Russia (bày'mäk)	172a	52°35'N	58°21'E
Bay Mills, Mi., U.S. (bā mĭlls)	107k	46°27'N	84°36'W
Bay Mills Indian Reservation, I.R., Mi., U.S.	103	46°19'N	85°03'W
Bay Minette, Al., U.S. (bā'mĭn-ĕt')	114	30°52'N	87°44'W
Bayombong, Phil. (bä-yôm-bŏng')	197a	16°28'N	121°09'E
Bayonne, Fr. (bȧ-yŏn')	142	43°28'N	1°30'W
Bayonne, N.J., U.S. (bā-yōn')	100a	40°40'N	74°07'W
Bayou Bodcau Reservoir, res., La., U.S. (bī'yōō bŏd'kō)	97	32°49'N	93°22'W
Bay Park, N.Y., U.S.	228	40°38'N	73°40'W
Bayport, Mn., U.S. (bā'pōrt)	107g	45°02'N	92°46'W
Bayqongyr, Kaz.	169	47°46'N	66°11'E
Bayramiç, Tur.	161	39°48'N	26°35'E
Bayreuth, Ger. (bī-roit')	154	49°56'N	11°35'E
Bay Ridge, neigh., N.Y., U.S.	228	40°37'N	74°02'W
Bay Roberts, Can. (bā rŏb'ẽrts)	93	47°36'N	53°16'W
Bays, Lake of, l., Can. (bās)	91	45°15'N	79°00'W
Bay Saint Louis, Ms., U.S. (bā' sânt lōō'ĭs)	114	30°19'N	89°20'W
Bay Shore, N.Y., U.S. (bā' shôr)	100a	40°44'N	73°15'W
Bayside, Ma., U.S.	227a	42°18'N	70°53'W
Bayside, neigh., N.Y., U.S.	228	40°46'N	73°46'W
Bayswater, Austl.	243b	37°51'S	145°16'E
Bayswater North, Austl.	243b	37°49'S	145°17'E
Bayt Lahm, W. Bank (bĕth'lē-hĕm)	181a	31°42'N	35°13'E
Baytown, Tx., U.S. (bā'town)	113a	29°44'N	95°01'W
Bayview, Al., U.S. (bā'vū)	100h	33°34'N	86°59'W
Bayview, Wa., U.S.	106a	48°29'N	122°28'W
Bayview, neigh., Ca., U.S.	231b	37°44'N	122°23'W
Bay Village, Oh., U.S. (bā)	101d	41°29'N	81°56'W
Bayville, N.Y., U.S.	228	40°54'N	73°33'W
Baza, Spain (bä'thä)	148	37°29'N	2°46'W
Baza, Sierra de, mts., Spain	158	37°19'N	2°48'W
Bazar-Dyuzi, mtn., Azer. (bä'zär-dyōōz'ē)	167	41°20'N	47°40'E
Bazaruto, Ilha do, i., Moz. (bȧ-zȧ-rō'tō)	212	21°42'S	36°10'E
Bazièrge, Fr.	156	43°25'N	1°41'E
Be, Nosy, i., Madag.	213	13°14'S	47°28'E
Beach, N.D., U.S. (bēch)	102	46°55'N	104°00'W
Beachwood, Oh., U.S.	229a	41°29'N	81°30'W
Beachy Head, c., Eng., U.K. (bēchē hĕd)	151	50°40'N	0°25'E
Beacon, N.Y., U.S. (bē'kŭn)	99	41°30'N	73°55'W
Beacon Hill, Austl.	243a	33°45'S	151°15'E
Beacon Hill, hill, China	241c	22°21'N	114°09'E
Beaconsfield, Can. (bē'kŭnz-fēld)	83a	45°26'N	73°51'W
Beals Creek, r., Tx., U.S. (bēls)	112	32°10'N	101°14'W
Bean, Eng., U.K.	235	51°25'N	0°17'E
Bear, r., U.S.	105	42°17'N	111°42'W
Bear, r., Ut., U.S.	107b	41°28'N	112°10'W
Bear Brook, r., Can.	83c	45°24'N	75°15'W
Bear Creek, Mt., U.S. (bâr krēk)	105	45°11'N	109°07'W
Bear Creek, r., Al., U.S. (bâr)	114	34°27'N	88°00'W
Bear Creek, r., Tx., U.S.	107c	32°56'N	97°09'W
Beardstown, Il., U.S. (bẽrds'toun)	111	40°01'N	90°26'W
Bearfort Mountain, mtn., N.J., U.S. (bē'fōrt)	100a	41°08'N	74°23'W
Bearhead Mountain, mtn., Wa., U.S. (bâr'hĕd)	106a	47°01'N	121°49'W
Bear Lake, l., Can.	89	55°08'N	96°00'W
Bear Lake, l., Id., U.S.	105	41°56'N	111°10'W
Bear River Range, mts., U.S.	105	41°50'N	111°30'W
Beas de Segura, Spain (bā'äs dā sā-gōō'rä)	158	38°16'N	2°53'W
Beata, i., Dom. Rep. (bĕ-ä'tä)	123	17°40'N	71°40'W
Beata, Cabo, c., Dom. Rep. (kȧ'bō-bĕ-ä'tä)	123	17°40'N	71°20'W
Beato, neigh., Port.	238d	38°44'N	9°06'W
Beatrice, Ne., U.S. (bē'ȧ-trĭs)	96	40°16'N	96°45'W
Beatty, Nv., U.S. (bĕt'ē)	108	36°58'N	116°48'W
Beattyville, Ky., U.S. (bĕt'ē-vĭl)	98	37°35'N	83°40'W
Beaucaire, Fr. (bō-kâr')	156	43°49'N	4°37'E
Beaucourt, Fr. (bō-kōōr')	157	47°30'N	6°54'E
Beaufort, N.C., U.S. (bō'frt)	115	34°43'N	76°40'W
Beaufort, S.C., U.S.	115	32°25'N	80°40'W
Beaufort Sea, sea, N.A.	95	70°30'N	138°40'W
Beaufort West, S. Afr.	212	32°20'S	22°45'E
Beauharnois, Can. (bō-är-nwä')	91	45°23'N	73°52'W
Beaumont, Can.	83b	46°50'N	71°01'W
Beaumont, Can.	83g	53°22'N	113°18'W
Beaumont, Ca., U.S. (bō'mŏnt)	107a	33°57'N	116°57'W
Beaumont, Tx., U.S.	97	30°05'N	94°06'W
Beaune, Fr. (bōn)	156	47°02'N	4°49'E
Beauport, Can. (bō-pōr')	83b	46°52'N	71°11'W
Beauséjour, Can.	84	50°04'N	96°33'W
Beauvais, Fr. (bō-vĕ')	156	49°25'N	2°05'E
Beaver, Ok., U.S. (bē'vẽr)	110	36°46'N	100°31'W
Beaver, Pa., U.S.	101e	40°42'N	80°18'W
Beaver, Ut., U.S.	109	38°15'N	112°40'W
Beaver, i., Mi., U.S.	98	45°40'N	85°30'W
Beaver, r., Can.	84	54°20'N	111°10'W
Beaver City, Ne., U.S.	110	40°08'N	99°52'W
Beaver Creek, r., Co., U.S.	110	39°42'N	103°37'W
Beaver Creek, r., Ks., U.S.	110	39°44'N	101°05'W
Beaver Creek, r., Mt., U.S.	102	46°45'N	104°18'W
Beaver Creek, r., Wy., U.S.	102	43°46'N	104°25'W
Beaver Dam, Wi., U.S.	103	43°29'N	88°50'W
Beaverhead, r., Mt., U.S.	105	45°25'N	112°35'W
Beaverhead Mountains, mts., Mt., U.S. (bē'vẽr-hĕd)	105	44°33'N	112°59'W
Beaver Indian Reservation, I.R., Mi., U.S.	98	45°40'N	85°30'W
Beaverton, Or., U.S. (bē'vẽr-tŭn)	106c	45°29'N	122°49'W
Bebek, neigh., Tur.	239f	41°04'N	29°02'E
Bebington, Eng., U.K. (bē'bĭng-tŭn)	144a	53°20'N	2°59'W
Beccar, neigh., Arg.	233d	34°28'S	58°31'W
Bečej, Yugo. (bĕ'chā)	161	45°36'N	20°03'E
Béchar, Alg.	210	31°39'N	2°14'W
Becharof, l., Ak., U.S. (bĕk-ȧ-rôf)	95	57°58'N	156°58'W
Becher Bay, b., Can. (bēch'ẽr)	106a	48°18'N	123°37'W
Beckenham, neigh., Eng., U.K.	235	51°24'N	0°02'W
Beckley, W.V., U.S. (bĕk'lĭ)	98	37°40'N	81°15'W
Bédarieux, Fr. (bā-dȧ-ryû')	156	43°36'N	3°11'E
Beddington, neigh., Eng., U.K.	235	51°22'N	0°08'W
Beddington Creek, r., Can. (bĕd'ĕng tŭn)	83e	51°14'N	114°13'W
Bedford, Can. (bĕd'fẽrd)	91	45°10'N	73°00'W
Bedford, S. Afr.	213c	32°43'S	26°19'E
Bedford, Eng., U.K.	147	52°10'N	0°25'W
Bedford, In., U.S.	98	38°50'N	86°30'W
Bedford, Ia., U.S.	103	40°40'N	94°41'W
Bedford, Ma., U.S.	93a	42°30'N	71°17'W
Bedford, N.Y., U.S.	100a	41°12'N	73°38'W
Bedford, Oh., U.S.	101d	41°23'N	81°32'W
Bedford, Pa., U.S.	99	40°05'N	78°20'W
Bedford, Va., U.S.	115	37°19'N	79°27'W
Bedford Heights, Oh., U.S.	229a	41°22'N	81°30'W
Bedford Hills, N.Y., U.S.	100a	41°14'N	73°41'W
Bedford Park, Il., U.S.	231a	41°46'N	87°49'W
Bedford Park, neigh., N.Y., U.S.	228	40°52'N	73°53'W
Bedford-Stuyvesant, neigh., N.Y., U.S.	228	40°41'N	73°55'W
Bedmond, Eng., U.K.	235	51°43'N	0°25'W
Bedok, Sing.	240c	1°19'N	103°57'E
Beebe, Ar., U.S. (bē'bē)	111	35°04'N	91°54'W
Beecher, Il., U.S. (bē'chŭr)	101a	41°20'N	87°38'W
Beechey Head, c., Can. (bē'chĭ hĕd)	106a	48°19'N	123°40'W
Beech Grove, In., U.S. (bēch grōv)	101g	39°43'N	86°05'W
Beechview, neigh., Pa., U.S.	230b	40°25'N	80°02'W
Beeck, neigh., Ger.	236	51°29'N	6°44'E
Beeckerwerth, neigh., Ger.	236	51°29'N	6°41'E
Beecroft Head, c., Austl. (bē'krûft)	204	35°03'S	151°15'E
Beelitz, Ger. (bē'lētz)	145b	52°14'N	12°59'E
Be'er Sheva', Isr. (bẽr-shē'bȧ)	181a	31°15'N	34°48'E
Be'er Sheva', r., Isr.	181a	31°23'N	34°30'E
Beestekraal, S. Afr.	218d	25°22'S	27°34'E
Beeston, Eng., U.K. (bēs't'n)	144a	52°55'N	1°11'W
Beetz, r., Ger. (bětz)	145b	52°28'N	12°37'E
Beeville, Tx., U.S. (bē'vĭl)	113	28°24'N	97°44'W
Bega, Austl. (bā'gȧ)	203	36°50'S	149°49'E
Beggs, Ok., U.S. (bĕgz)	111	35°46'N	96°06'W
Bègles, Fr. (bĕ'gl')	156	44°47'N	0°34'W
Begoro, Ghana	214	6°23'N	0°23'W
Behala, India	186a	22°31'N	88°19'E
Behbehān, Iran	185	30°35'N	50°14'E
Behm Canal, can., Ak., U.S.	86	55°41'N	131°35'W
Bei, r., China (bā)	191a	22°54'N	113°08'E
Bei'an, China (bā-än)	192	48°05'N	126°26'E
Beicai, China (bā-tsī)	191b	31°12'N	121°33'E
Beifei, r., China (bā-fā)	190	33°14'N	117°03'E
Beihai, China (bā-hī)	188	21°30'N	109°10'E
Beihuangcheng Dao, i., China (bā-hůäŋ-chŭŋ dou)	190	38°23'N	120°55'E
Beijing, China	189	39°55'N	116°23'E
Beijing Shi, China (bā-jyĭŋ shr)	192	40°07'N	116°00'E
Beira, Moz. (bā'rȧ)	212	19°45'N	34°58'E
Beira, hist. reg., Port. (bĕ'y-rä)	158	40°38'N	8°00'W
Beirut, Leb. (bā-rōōt')	182	33°53'N	35°30'E
Beiyuan, China	240b	40°01'N	116°24'E
Beja, Port. (bä'zhä)	148	38°03'N	7°53'W
Béja, Tun.	148	36°52'N	9°20'E
Bejaïa (Bougie), Alg.	210	36°46'N	5°00'E
Bejar, Spain	158	40°25'N	5°43'W
Bejestān, Iran	182	34°30'N	58°22'E
Bejucal, Cuba (bā-hōō-käl')	122	22°56'N	82°23'W
Bejuco, Pan. (bĕ-kōō'kō)	121	8°37'N	79°54'W
Békés, Hung. (bā'kāsh)	155	46°45'N	21°08'E
Békéscsaba, Hung. (bā'kāsh-chô'bô)	149	46°39'N	21°06'E
Beketova, Russia (bĕkĕ-to'vȧ)	171	53°23'N	125°21'E
Bela Crkva, Yugo. (bĕ'lä tsĕrk'vä)	161	44°53'N	21°25'E
Bel Air, Va., U.S.	229d	38°52'N	77°10'W
Bel Air, neigh., Ca., U.S.	232	34°05'N	118°27'W
Belalcázar, Spain (bāl-ȧ-kä'thär)	158	38°35'N	5°12'W
Belarus, nation, Eur.	164	53°30'N	25°33'E
Belas, Port.	238d	38°47'N	9°16'W
Belau see Palau, dep., Oc.	2	7°15'N	134°30'W
Bela Vista, neigh., Braz.	234d	23°33'S	46°38'W
Bela Vista de Goiás, Braz.	131	16°57'S	48°47'W
Belawan, Indon. (bå-lä'wån)	196	3°43'N	98°43'E
Belaya, r., Russia (byĕ'lĭ-yȧ)	167	52°30'N	56°15'E
Belcher Islands, is., Can. (bĕl'chẽr)	85	56°20'N	80°40'W
Belding, Mi., U.S. (bĕl'dĭng)	98	43°05'N	85°25'W
Belebey, Russia (byĕ'lĕ-bā'ĭ)	166	54°00'N	54°10'E
Belém, Braz. (bå-lĕɴ')	131	1°18'S	48°27'W
Belém, neigh., Port.	238d	38°42'N	9°12'W
Belén, Para. (bā-lān')	132	23°30'S	57°09'W
Belen, N.M., U.S. (bĕ-lån')	109	34°40'N	106°45'W
Belènzinho, neigh., Braz.	234d	23°32'S	46°35'W
Bélep, Îles, is., N. Cal.	203	19°30'S	164°00'E
Belëv, Russia (byĕl'yĕf)	166	53°49'N	36°06'E
Belfair, Wa., U.S. (bĕl'far)	106a	47°27'N	122°50'W
Belfast, N. Ire., U.K.	142	54°36'N	5°45'W
Belfast, Me., U.S. (bĕl'fåst)	92	44°25'N	69°01'W
Belfast, Lough, b., N. Ire., U.K. (lŏk bĕl'fåst)	150	54°45'N	6°00'W
Belford Roxo, Braz.	132b	22°46'S	43°24'W
Belfort, Fr. (bā-fôr')	147	47°40'N	7°50'E
Belgaum, India	183	15°57'N	74°32'E
Belgium, nation, Eur. (bĕl'jĭ-ŭm)	142	51°00'N	2°52'E
Belgorod, Russia (byĕl'gŭ-rŭt)	167	50°36'N	36°32'E
Belgorod, prov., Russia	163	50°40'N	36°42'E
Belgrade (Beograd), Yugo.	142	44°48'N	20°32'E
Belgrano, neigh., Arg.	233d	34°34'S	58°28'W
Belgrave, Austl.	243b	37°55'S	145°21'E
Belhaven, N.C., U.S. (bĕl'hā-vĕn)	115	35°33'N	76°37'W
Belington, W.V., U.S. (bĕl'ĭng-tŭn)	99	39°00'N	79°55'W
Belitung, i., Indon.	196	3°30'S	107°30'E
Belize, nation, N.A.	116	17°00'N	88°40'W
Belize, r., Belize	120a	17°16'N	88°56'W
Belize City, Belize (bĕ-lēz')	116	17°31'N	88°10'W
Bel'kovo, Russia (byĕl'kô-vô)	172b	56°15'N	38°49'E
Bel'kovskiy, i., Russia (byĕl-kôf'skĭ)	171	75°45'N	137°00'E
Bell, Ca., U.S.	232	33°58'N	118°11'W
Bell, i., Can. (bĕl)	93	50°45'N	55°35'W
Bell, r., Can.	91	49°25'N	77°15'W
Bella Bella, Can.	86	52°10'N	128°07'W
Bella Coola, Can.	86	52°22'N	126°46'W
Bellaire, Oh., U.S. (bĕl-âr')	98	40°00'N	80°45'W
Bellaire, Tx., U.S.	113a	29°43'N	95°28'W
Bellary, India (bĕl-lä'rė)	183	15°15'N	76°56'E
Bella Union, Ur. (bĕ'l-yȧ-ōō-nyō'n)	132	30°18'S	57°26'W
Bella Vista, Arg.	132	28°35'S	58°53'W
Bella Vista, Arg. (bä'lyȧ vēs'tȧ)	132	27°07'S	65°14'W
Bella Vista, Arg.	132a	34°35'S	58°41'W
Bellavista, Chile	234b	33°31'S	70°37'W
Bella Vista, Para.	131	22°16'S	56°14'W
Bellavista, Peru	233c	12°04'S	77°08'W
Belle-Anse, Haiti	123	18°15'N	72°00'W
Belle Bay, b., Can. (bĕl)	93	47°35'N	55°15'W
Belle Chasse, La., U.S. (bĕl shäs')	100d	29°52'N	90°00'W
Belle Farm Estates, Md., U.S.	229c	39°23'N	76°45'W
Bellefontaine, Oh., U.S. (bĕl-fŏn'tån)	98	40°25'N	83°50'W
Bellefontaine Neighbors, Mo., U.S.	107e	38°46'N	90°13'W
Belle Fourche, S.D., U.S. (bĕl' fōōrsh')	102	44°28'N	103°50'W
Belle Fourche, r., Wy., U.S.	102	44°29'N	104°40'W
Belle Fourche Reservoir, res., S.D., U.S.	102	44°51'N	103°44'W
Bellegarde, Fr. (bĕl-gärd')	157	46°06'N	5°50'E
Belle Glade, Fl., U.S. (bĕl glād)	115a	26°39'N	80°37'W
Bellehaven, Va., U.S.	229d	38°47'N	77°04'W
Belle-Île, i., Fr. (bĕlēl')	147	47°15'N	3°30'W
Belle Isle, Strait of, strt., Can.	85	51°35'N	56°30'W
Belle Mead, N.J., U.S. (bĕl mēd)	100a	40°28'N	74°40'W
Belleoram, Can.	93	47°31'N	55°25'W
Belle Plaine, Ia., U.S. (bĕl plān')	103	41°52'N	92°19'W
Bellerose, N.Y., U.S.	228	40°44'N	73°43'W
Belle Vernon, Pa., U.S. (bĕl vŭr'nŭn)	101e	40°08'N	79°52'W
Belleville, Can. (bĕl'vĭl)	91	44°15'N	77°25'W
Belleville, Il., U.S.	107e	38°31'N	89°59'W
Belleville, Ks., U.S.	111	39°49'N	97°37'W
Belleville, Mi., U.S.	101b	42°12'N	83°29'W
Belleville, N.J., U.S.	100a	40°47'N	74°09'W
Bellevue, Ia., U.S. (bĕl'vū)	103	42°14'N	90°26'W
Bellevue, Ky., U.S.	101f	39°06'N	84°29'W
Bellevue, Mi., U.S.	98	42°30'N	85°00'W
Bellevue, Oh., U.S.	98	41°15'N	82°45'W
Bellevue, Pa., U.S.	101e	40°30'N	80°04'W
Bellevue, Wa., U.S.	106a	47°37'N	122°12'W
Belley, Fr. (bĕ-lē')	157	45°46'N	5°41'E
Bellflower, Ca., U.S. (bĕl-flou'ẽr)	107a	33°53'N	118°08'W
Bell Gardens, Ca., U.S.	107a	33°59'N	118°11'W
Bellingham, Ma., U.S. (bĕl'ĭng-hăm)	93a	42°05'N	71°28'W
Bellingham, Wa., U.S.	96	48°46'N	122°29'W
Bellingham Bay, b., Wa., U.S.	106d	48°44'N	122°34'W
Bellingshausen Sea, sea, Ant. (bĕl'ĭngz houz'n)	219	72°00'S	80°30'W
Bellinzona, Switz. (bĕl-ĭn-tsō'nä)	154	46°10'N	9°09'E
Bellmawr, N.J., U.S.	229b	39°51'N	75°06'W
Bellmore, N.Y., U.S. (bĕl-mōr)	100a	40°40'N	73°31'W
Bello, Col. (bĕ'l-yō)	130	6°20'N	75°33'W
Bello, Cuba	233b	23°07'N	82°24'W
Bellow Falls, Vt., U.S. (bĕl'ōz fôls)	99	43°10'N	72°30'W
Bellpat, Pak.	186	29°08'N	68°00'E
Bell Peninsula, pen., Can.	85	63°50'N	81°16'W
Bells Corners, Can.	83c	45°20'N	75°49'W
Bells Mountain, mtn., Wa., U.S. (bĕls)	106c	45°50'N	122°21'W
Belluno, Italy (bĕl-lōō'nō)	160	46°08'N	12°14'E
Bell Ville, Arg. (bĕl vĕl')	132	32°33'S	62°36'W
Bellville, S. Afr.	212a	33°54'S	18°38'E
Bellville, Tx., U.S. (bĕl'vĭl)	113	29°57'N	96°15'W
Bellwood, Il., U.S.	231a	41°53'N	87°52'W
Bélmez, Spain (bĕl'mĕth)	158	38°17'N	5°17'W
Belmond, Ia., U.S. (bĕl'mŏnd)	103	42°49'N	93°37'W
Belmont, Ca., U.S.	106b	37°34'N	122°18'W
Belmont, Ma., U.S.	227a	42°24'N	71°10'W

ng-sing; ŋ-baŋk; ɴ-nasalized n; nŏd; cŏmmit; ōld; ôbey; ôrder; oi-boil; fōōd; ŏŏ-as oo in foot; ou-out; s-soft; sh-dish; th-thin; pūre; ůnite; ûrn; stŭd; circŭs; ü-as in French tu; '-indeterminate vowel.

PLACE (Pronunciation)	PAGE	LAT.	LONG.
Belmonte, Braz. (bĕl-mōn'tȧ)	131	15°58'S	38°47'W
Belmopan, Belize	116	17°15'N	88°47'W
Belmore, Austl.	243a	33°55'S	151°05'E
Belogorsk, Russia	165	51°09'N	128°32'E
Belo Horizonte, Braz. (bĕ'lôre-sô'n-tĕ)	131	19°54'S	43°56'W
Beloit, Ks., U.S. (bė-loit')	110	39°26'N	98°06'W
Beloit, Wi., U.S.	97	42°31'N	89°04'W
Belomorsk, Russia (byĕl-ô-môrsk')	166	64°30'N	34°42'E
Beloretsk, Russia (byĕ'lō-rĕtsk)	166	53°58'N	58°25'E
Belosarayskaya, Kosa, c., Ukr.	163	46°43'N	37°18'E
Belot, Cuba	233b	23°08'N	82°19'W
Belovo, Russia (byĕ'lŭ-vû)	170	54°25'N	86°18'E
Beloye, l., Russia	166	60°10'N	38°05'E
Belozersk, Russia (byĕ-lŭ-zyôrsk')	166	60°00'N	38°00'E
Belper, Eng., U.K. (bĕl'pĕr)	144a	53°01'N	1°28'W
Belt, Mt., U.S. (bĕlt)	105	47°11'N	110°58'W
Belt Creek, r., Mt., U.S.	105	47°19'N	110°58'W
Belton, Tx., U.S. (bĕl'tŭn)	113	31°04'N	97°27'W
Belton Lake, l., Tx., U.S.	113	31°15'N	97°35'W
Beltsville, Md., U.S. (belts-vĭl)	100e	39°03'N	76°56'W
Belukha, Gora, mtn., Asia	164	49°47'N	86°23'E
Belvedere, Ca., U.S.	231b	37°52'N	122°28'W
Belvedere, Va., U.S.	229d	38°50'N	77°10'W
Belvedere, neigh., Eng., U.K.	235	51°29'N	0°09'E
Belvedere, pt. of i., Aus.	239e	48°11'N	16°23'E
Belvidere, Il., U.S. (bĕl-vē-dēr')	103	42°14'N	88°52'W
Belvidere, N.J., U.S.	99	40°50'N	75°05'W
Belyando, r., Austl. (bĕl-yăn'dō)	203	22°09'S	146°48'E
Belyanka, Russia (byĕl'yȧn-kȧ)	172a	56°04'N	59°16'E
Belynichi, Bela. (byĕl-ĭ-nĭ'chĭ)	162	54°02'N	29°42'E
Belyy, Russia (byĕ'lē)	166	55°52'N	32°58'E
Belyy, i., Russia	164	73°19'N	72°00'E
Belyye Stolby, Russia (byĕ'lĭ-ye stôl'bĭ)	172b	55°20'N	37°52'E
Belzig, Ger. (bĕl'tsēg)	145b	52°08'N	12°35'E
Belzoni, Ms., U.S. (bĕl-zō'nė)	114	33°09'N	90°30'W
Bembe, Ang. (bĕɴ'bĕ)	212	7°00'S	14°20'E
Bembézar, r., Spain (bĕm-bā-thär')	158	38°00'N	5°18'W
Bemidji, Mn., U.S. (bė-mĭj'ĭ)	103	47°28'N	94°54'W
Bena Dibele, D.R.C. (bĕn'ȧ dē-bĕ'lē)	212	4°00'S	22°49'E
Benalla, Austl. (bĕn-ăl'ȧ)	203	36°30'S	146°00'E
Benares *see* Vārānasi, India	183	25°25'N	83°00'E
Benavente, Spain (bā-nä-vĕn'tä)	148	42°01'N	5°43'W
Ben Avon, Pa., U.S.	230b	40°31'N	80°05'W
Benbrook, Tx., U.S. (bĕn'brŏŏk)	107c	32°41'N	97°27'W
Benbrook Reservoir, res., Tx., U.S.	107c	32°35'N	97°30'W
Bend, Or., U.S. (bĕnd)	96	44°04'N	121°17'W
Bendeleben, Mount, mtn., Ak., U.S. (bĕn-dĕl-bĕn)	95	65°18'N	163°45'W
Bender Beyla, Som.	218a	9°40'N	50°45'E
Bendigo, Austl. (bĕn'dĭ-gō)	203	36°39'S	144°20'E
Benedict, Md., U.S. (bĕnĕ'dĭct)	100e	38°31'N	76°41'W
Benešov, Czech Rep. (bĕn'ĕ-shôf)	154	49°48'N	14°40'E
Benevento, Italy (bā-nā-vĕn'tō)	148	41°08'N	14°46'E
Benfica, neigh., Braz.	234c	22°53'S	43°15'W
Benfica, neigh., Port.	238d	38°45'N	9°12'W
Bengal, Bay of, b., Asia (bĕn-gôl')	180	17°30'N	87°00'E
Bengamisa, D.R.C.	217	0°57'N	25°10'E
Bengbu, China (bŭŋ-bōō)	189	32°52'N	117°22'E
Benghazi *see* Banghāzī, Libya	210	32°07'N	20°04'E
Bengkalis, Indon. (bĕng-kä'lĭs)	196	1°29'N	102°06'E
Bengkulu, Indon.	196	3°46'S	102°18'E
Benguela, Ang. (bĕn-gĕl'ȧ)	212	12°35'S	13°25'E
Beni, r., Bol. (bā'nē)	130	13°41'S	67°30'W
Béni-Abbas, Alg. (bā'nē ä-bĕs')	210	30°11'N	2°13'W
Benicia, Ca., U.S. (bė-nĭsh'ĭ-ȧ)	106b	38°03'N	122°09'W
Benin, nation, Afr.	210	8°00'N	2°00'E
Benin, r., Nig. (bĕn-ēn')	215	5°55'N	5°15'E
Benin, Bight of, bt., Afr.	210	5°30'N	3°00'E
Benin City, Nig.	210	6°19'N	5°41'E
Beni Saf, Alg. (bā'nē säf')	210	35°23'N	1°20'W
Benito, r., Eq. Gui.	216	1°35'N	10°45'E
Benkelman, Ne., U.S. (bĕn-kĕl-mȧn)	110	40°05'N	101°35'W
Benkovac, Cro. (bĕn'kō-vȧts)	160	44°02'N	15°41'E
Bennettsville, S.C., U.S. (bĕn'ĕts vĭl)	115	34°35'N	79°41'W
Bennettswood, Austl.	243b	37°51'S	145°07'E
Benninghofen, neigh., Ger.	236	51°29'N	7°31'E
Bennington, Vt., U.S. (bĕn'ĭng-tŭn)	99	42°55'N	73°15'W
Benns Church, Va., U.S. (bĕnz' chûrch')	100g	36°47'N	76°35'W
Benoni, S. Afr. (bĕ-nō'nĭ)	212	26°11'S	28°19'E
Benoni South, S. Afr.	244b	26°13'S	28°18'E
Benoy, Chad	215	8°59'N	16°19'E
Benque Viejo, Belize (bĕn-kĕ bĭĕ'hō)	120a	17°07'N	89°07'W
Benrath, neigh., Ger.	236	51°10'N	6°52'E
Bensberg, Ger.	157c	50°58'N	7°09'E
Bensenville, Il., U.S. (bĕn'sĕn-vĭl)	101a	41°57'N	87°56'W
Bensheim, Ger. (bĕns-hīm)	154	49°42'N	8°38'E
Benson, Az., U.S. (bĕn-sŭn)	109	32°00'N	110°20'W
Benson, Mn., U.S.	102	45°18'N	95°36'W
Bentiaba, Ang.	216	14°15'S	12°21'E
Bentleigh, Austl.	243b	37°55'S	145°02'E
Bentleyville, Pa., U.S. (bent'lē vĭl)	101e	40°07'N	80°01'W
Benton, Can.	92	45°59'N	67°36'W
Benton, Ar., U.S. (bĕn'tŭn)	111	34°34'N	92°34'W
Benton, Ca., U.S.	108	37°44'N	118°22'W
Benton, Il., U.S.	98	38°00'N	88°55'W
Benton Harbor, Mi., U.S. (bĕn'tŭn här'bĕr)	98	42°05'N	86°30'W
Bentonville, Ar., U.S. (bĕn'tŭn-vĭl)	111	36°22'N	94°11'W
Benue, r., Afr. (bā'nōō-ā)	210	8°00'N	8°00'E
Benut, r., Malay.	181b	1°43'N	103°20'E
Benwood, W.V., U.S. (bĕn-wŏŏd)	98	39°55'N	80°45'W
Benxi, China (bŭn-shyē)	192	41°25'N	123°50'E
Beograd *see* Belgrade, Yugo.	142	44°48'N	20°32'E
Beppu, Japan (bĕ'pōō)	195	33°16'N	131°30'E
Bequia Island, i., St. Vin. (bĕk-ē'ä)	121b	13°00'N	61°08'W
Berakit, Tanjung, c., Indon.	181b	1°16'N	104°44'E
Berat, Alb. (bĕ-rät')	161	40°43'N	19°59'E
Berau, Teluk, b., Indon.	197	2°22'S	131°40'E
Berazategui, Arg. (bĕ-rä-zä'tĕ-gē)	132a	34°46'S	58°14'W
Berbera, Som. (bûr'bûr-ȧ)	218a	10°25'N	45°05'E
Berbérati, Cen. Afr. Rep.	215	4°16'N	15°47'E
Berchum, Ger.	236	51°23'N	7°32'E
Berck, Fr. (bĕrk)	156	50°26'N	1°36'E
Berdians'k, Ukr.	167	46°45'N	36°47'E
Berdians'ka kosa, c., Ukr.	163	46°38'N	36°42'E
Berdyaush, Russia (bĕr'dyȧûsh)	172a	55°10'N	59°12'E
Berdychiv, Ukr.	164	49°53'N	28°32'E
Berea, Ky., U.S. (bė-rē'ȧ)	114	37°30'N	84°19'W
Berea, Oh., U.S.	101d	41°22'N	81°51'W
Berehove, Ukr.	155	48°13'N	22°40'E
Bereku, Tan.	217	4°27'S	35°44'E
Berens, r., Can. (bĕr'ĕnz)	89	52°15'N	96°30'W
Berens Island, i., Can.	89	52°18'N	97°40'W
Berens River, Can.	84	52°22'N	97°02'W
Beresford, S.D., U.S. (bĕr'ĕs-fērd)	102	43°05'N	96°46'W
Berettyóújfalu, Hung. (bĕ'rĕt-tyō-ōō'y'fō-lōō)	155	47°14'N	21°33'E
Berëza, Bela. (bĕ-rā'zȧ)	155	52°29'N	24°59'E
Berezhany, Ukr. (bĕr-yĕ'zhȧ-nė)	155	49°25'N	24°58'E
Berezina, r., Bela. (bĕr-yĕ'zē-nȧ)	162	53°20'N	29°05'E
Berezino, Bela. (bĕr-yä'zē-nō)	162	53°51'N	28°54'E
Berezivka, Ukr.	163	47°12'N	30°56'E
Berezna, Ukr. (bĕr-yôz'nȧ)	163	51°32'N	31°47'E
Bereznehuvate, Ukr.	163	47°19'N	32°58'E
Berezniki, Russia (bĕr-yôz'nyē-kė)	166	59°25'N	56°46'E
Berëzovka, Russia	172a	57°35'N	57°19'E
Berëzovo, Russia (bĭr-yô'zē-vû)	164	64°10'N	65°10'E
Berëzovskiy, Russia (bĕr-yô'zôf-skĭ)	172a	56°54'N	60°47'E
Berga, Spain (bĕr'gä)	159	42°05'N	1°52'E
Bergama, Tur. (bĕr'gä-mä)	182	39°08'N	27°09'E
Bergamo, Italy (bĕr'gä-mō)	148	45°43'N	9°41'E
Bergantin, Ven. (bĕr-gän-tē'n)	131b	10°04'N	64°23'W
Bergara, Spain	158	43°08'N	2°23'W
Bergedorf, Ger. (bĕr'gĕ-dôrf)	145c	53°29'N	10°12'E
Bergen, Ger. (bĕr'gĕn)	154	54°26'N	13°26'E
Bergen, Nor.	142	60°24'N	5°20'E
Bergenfield, N.J., U.S.	100a	40°55'N	73°59'W
Bergen op Zoom, Neth.	151	51°29'N	4°16'E
Bergerac, Fr. (bĕr-zhĕ-räk')	147	44°49'N	0°28'E
Bergfelde, Ger.	238a	52°40'N	13°19'E
Berghausen, Ger.	236	51°18'N	7°17'E
Bergholtz, N.Y., U.S.	230a	43°06'N	78°53'W
Bergisch-Born, Ger.	236	51°09'N	7°15'E
Bergisch Gladbach, Ger. (bĕrg'ĭsh-glät'bäk)	157c	50°59'N	7°08'E
Bergkamen, Ger.	236	51°38'N	7°38'E
Berglern, Ger. (bĕrgh'lĕrn)	145d	48°24'N	11°55'E
Bergneustadt, Ger.	157c	51°01'N	7°39'E
Bergville, S. Afr. (bĕrg'vĭl)	213c	28°46'S	29°22'E
Berhampur, India	183	19°19'N	84°48'E
Bering Sea, sea (bē'rĭng)	224	58°00'N	175°00'W
Bering Strait, strt.	94a	64°50'N	169°50'W
Berja, Spain (bĕr'hä)	158	36°50'N	2°56'W
Berkeley, Ca., U.S. (bûrk'lĭ)	96	37°52'N	122°17'W
Berkeley, Il., U.S.	231a	41°53'N	87°55'W
Berkeley, Mo., U.S.	107e	38°45'N	90°20'W
Berkeley Hills, Pa., U.S.	230b	40°32'N	80°00'W
Berkeley Springs, W.V., U.S. (bûrk'lĭ springz)	99	39°40'N	78°10'W
Berkhamsted, Eng., U.K. (bĕrk'hăm'stĕd)	144b	51°44'N	0°34'W
Berkley, Mi., U.S. (bûrk'lĭ)	101b	42°30'N	83°10'W
Berkovitsa, Bul. (bĕ-kō'vē-tsȧ)	161	43°14'N	23°08'E
Berkshire, co., Eng., U.K.	144b	51°23'N	1°07'W
Berland, r., Can.	87	54°00'N	117°10'W
Berlenga, is., Port. (bĕr-lĕn'gȧzh)	158	39°25'N	9°33'W
Berlin, Ger. (bĕr-lēn')	142	52°31'N	13°28'E
Berlin, S. Afr. (bĕr-lĭn)	213c	32°53'S	27°36'E
Berlin, N.H., U.S. (bûr-lĭn)	99	44°25'N	71°10'W
Berlin, N.J., U.S.	100f	39°47'N	74°56'W
Berlin, Wi., U.S. (bûr-lĭn')	103	43°58'N	88°58'W
Berlin-Tempelhof, Zentral Flughafen, arpt., Ger.	238a	52°29'N	13°25'E
Bermejo, r., S.A. (bĕr-mā'hō)	132	25°05'S	61°00'W
Bermeo, Spain (bĕr-mā'yō)	158	43°23'N	2°43'W
Bermuda, dep., N.A.	117	32°20'N	65°45'W
Bern, Switz. (bĕrn)	142	46°55'N	7°25'E
Bernal, Arg. (bĕr-näl')	132a	34°43'S	58°17'W
Bernalillo, N.M., U.S. (bĕr-nä-lē'yō)	109	35°20'N	106°30'W
Bernard, l., Can. (bĕr-närd')	99	45°45'N	79°25'W
Bernardsville, N.J., U.S. (bûr nârds'vĭl)	100a	40°43'N	74°34'W
Bernau, Ger. (bĕr'nou)	154	52°40'N	13°35'E
Bernburg, Ger. (bĕrn'bŏŏrgh)	154	51°48'N	11°43'E
Berndorf, Aus. (bĕrn'dôrf)	154	47°57'N	16°05'E
Berne, In., U.S. (bûrn)	98	40°40'N	84°55'W
Berner Alpen, mts., Switz.	154	46°29'N	7°30'E
Bernier, i., Austl. (bĕr-nēr')	202	24°58'S	113°15'E
Bernina, Pizzo, mtn., Eur.	154	46°23'N	9°58'E
Bero, r., Ang.	216	15°10'S	12°20'E
Beroun, Czech Rep. (bā'rōn)	154	49°57'N	14°03'E
Berounka, r., Czech Rep. (bĕ-rōn'kȧ)	154	49°53'N	13°40'E
Berowra, Austl.	201b	33°36'S	151°10'E
Berre, Étang de, l., Fr. (ā-tôɴ' dĕ bâr')	156a	43°27'N	5°07'E
Berre-l'Étang, Fr. (bâr'lā-tôɴ')	156a	43°28'N	5°11'E
Berriozabal, Mex. (bā'rēō-zä-bäl')	119	16°47'N	93°16'W
Berriyyane, Alg.	148	32°50'N	3°49'E
Berry Creek, r., Can.	88	51°15'N	111°40'W
Berryessa, r., Ca., U.S. (bĕ'rĭ ĕs'ȧ)	108	38°35'N	122°33'W
Berry Islands, is., Bah.	122	25°40'N	77°50'W
Berryville, Ar., U.S. (bĕr'ē-vĭl)	111	36°21'N	93°34'W
Bershad', Ukr. (byĕr'shät)	163	48°22'N	29°31'E
Berthier, Can.	83b	46°56'N	70°44'W
Bertlich, Ger.	236	51°37'N	7°04'E
Bertrand, r., Wa., U.S. (bûr'trȧnd)	106d	48°58'N	122°31'W
Berwick, Pa., U.S. (bûr'wĭk)	99	41°05'N	76°10'W
Berwick-upon-Tweed, Eng., U.K. (bûr'ĭk)	146	55°45'N	2°01'W
Berwyn, Il., U.S. (bûr'wĭn)	101a	41°49'N	87°47'W
Berwyn Heights, Md., U.S.	229d	38°59'N	76°54'W
Beryslav, Ukr.	163	46°49'N	33°24'E
Besalampy, Madag. (bĕz-ȧ-lȧm-pē')	213	16°48'S	44°40'E
Besançon, Fr. (bĕ-säɴ-sôɴ)	147	47°14'N	6°02'E
Besar, Gunong, mtn., Malay.	181b	2°31'N	103°09'E
Besed', r., Eur. (byĕ'syĕt)	162	52°58'N	31°36'E
Besedy, Russia	239b	55°37'N	37°47'E
Beshenkovichi, Bela. (byĕ'shĕn-kōvē'chĭ)	162	55°04'N	29°29'E
Beskid Mountains, mts., Eur.	155	49°23'N	19°00'E
Beskra, Alg.	210	34°52'N	5°39'E
Beskudnikovo, neigh., Russia	239b	55°52'N	37°34'E
Beslan, Russia	168	43°12'N	44°33'E
Besós, r., Spain	238e	41°25'N	2°12'E
Bessarabia, hist. reg., Mol.	163	47°00'N	28°30'E
Bességes, Fr. (bĕ-sĕzh')	156	44°20'N	4°07'E
Bessemer, Al., U.S. (bĕs'ē-mĕr)	100h	33°24'N	86°58'W
Bessemer, Mi., U.S.	103	46°29'N	90°04'W
Bessemer City, N.C., U.S.	115	35°16'N	81°17'W
Bestensee, Ger. (bĕs'tĕn-zā)	145b	52°15'N	13°39'E
Betanzos, Spain (bĕ-tän'thōs)	158	43°18'N	8°14'W
Betatakin Ruin, Az., U.S. (bĕt-ȧ-tăk'ĭn)	109	36°40'N	110°29'W
Bethal, S. Afr. (bĕth'ăl)	218d	26°27'S	29°28'E
Bethalto, Il., U.S. (bȧ-thăl'tō)	107e	38°54'N	90°03'W
Bethanien, Nmb.	212	26°20'S	16°10'E
Bethany, Mo., U.S.	111	40°15'N	94°04'W
Bethel, Ak., U.S. (bĕth'ĕl)	94a	60°50'N	161°50'W
Bethel, Ct., U.S.	100a	41°22'N	73°24'W
Bethel, Vt., U.S.	99	43°50'N	72°40'W
Bethel Park, Pa., U.S.	101e	40°19'N	80°02'W
Bethesda, Md., U.S. (bĕ-thĕs'dȧ)	100e	39°00'N	77°10'W
Bethlehem, S. Afr.	212	28°14'S	28°18'E
Bethlehem, Pa., U.S. (bĕth'lē-hĕm)	99	40°40'N	75°25'W
Bethlehem *see* Bayt Lahm, W. Bank	181a	31°42'N	35°13'E
Bethnal Green, neigh., Eng., U.K.	235	51°32'N	0°03'W
Bethpage, N.Y., U.S.	228	40°45'N	73°29'W
Béthune, Fr. (bā-tün')	156	50°32'N	2°37'E
Betroka, Madag. (bĕ-trōk'ȧ)	213	23°13'S	46°17'E
Betsham, Eng., U.K.	235	51°25'N	0°19'E
Bet She'an, Isr.	181a	32°30'N	35°30'E
Betsiamites, Can.	85	48°57'N	68°36'W
Betsiamites, r., Can.	92	49°11'N	69°20'W
Betsiboka, r., Madag. (bĕt-sĭ-bō'kȧ)	213	16°47'S	46°45'E
Bettles Field, Ak., U.S. (bĕt'tŭls)	95	66°58'N	151°48'W
Betwa, r., India (bĕt'wȧ)	183	25°00'N	78°00'E
Betz, Fr. (bĕ)	157b	49°09'N	2°58'E
Beveren, Bel.	145a	51°13'N	4°14'E
B. Everett Jordan Lake, res., N.C., U.S.	115	35°45'N	79°00'W
Beverly, Ma., U.S.	93a	42°34'N	70°53'W
Beverly, N.J., U.S.	100f	40°03'N	74°56'W
Beverly Hills, Austl.	243a	33°57'S	151°05'E
Beverly Hills, Ca., U.S.	107a	34°05'N	118°24'W
Beverly Hills, Mi., U.S.	230c	42°32'N	83°15'W
Bevier, Mo., U.S. (bė-vēr')	111	39°44'N	92°36'W
Bewdley, Eng., U.K. (būd'lĭ)	144a	52°22'N	2°19'W
Bexhill, Eng., U.K. (bĕks'hĭl)	151	50°49'N	0°25'E
Bexley, Austl.	243a	33°57'S	151°08'E
Bexley, Eng., U.K. (bĕks'ly)	144b	51°26'N	0°09'E
Beyenburg, neigh., Ger.	236	51°15'N	7°18'E
Beyla, Gui. (bā'lȧ)	210	8°41'N	8°37'W
Beylerbeyi, neigh., Tur.	239f	41°03'N	29°03'E
Beylul, Erit.	211	13°15'N	42°21'E
Beyoğlu, neigh., Tur.	239f	41°02'N	28°59'E
Beypazari, Tur. (bā-pȧ-zä'rĭ)	149	40°10'N	31°40'E
Beyşehir, Tur.	167	38°00'N	31°45'E
Beysugskiy, Liman, b., Russia (lĭ-măn' bĕy-sōōg'skĭ)	163	46°07'N	38°35'E
Bezhetsk, Russia (byĕ-zhĕtsk')	166	57°46'N	36°40'E
Bezhitsa, Russia (byĕ-zhĭ'tsȧ)	166	53°19'N	34°18'E
Béziers, Fr. (bā-zyā')	147	43°21'N	3°12'E
Bezons, Fr.	237c	48°56'N	2°13'E
Bhadreswar, India	186a	22°49'N	88°22'E
Bhāgalpur, India (bä'gŭl-pòr)	183	25°15'N	86°59'E
Bhalswa, neigh., India	240d	28°44'N	77°10'E
Bhamo, Myanmar (bŭ-mō')	183	24°00'N	96°15'E
Bhāngar, India	186a	22°30'N	88°36'E
Bharatpur, India (bĕrt'pòr)	183	27°21'N	77°33'E
Bhatinda, India (bŭ-tĭn-dȧ)	183	30°19'N	74°56'E
Bhātpāra, India	183	22°52'N	88°24'E
Bhaunagar, India (bäv-nŭg'ŭr)	183	21°45'N	72°58'E
Bhayandar, India	187b	19°20'N	72°50'E
Bhilai, India	186	21°14'N	81°23'E
Bhīma, r., India (bē'mȧ)	183	18°00'N	74°45'E
Bhiwandi, India	187b	19°18'N	73°03'E
Bhiwāni, India	186	28°53'N	76°08'E
Bhopāl, India (bō-päl)	183	23°20'N	77°25'E
Bhopura, India	240d	28°42'N	77°20'E
Bhubaneswar, India (bō-bŏ-nāsh'vûr)	183	20°21'N	85°53'E
Bhuj, India (bōōj)	183	23°22'N	69°39'E
Bhutan, nation, Asia (bōō-tän')	183	27°15'N	90°30'E
Biafra, Bight of, bt., Afr.	210	4°05'N	7°10'E
Biak, i., Indon. (bē'äk)	197	1°00'S	136°00'E
Biała Podlaska, Pol. (byä'wä pōd-läs'kä)	155	52°01'N	23°08'E
Białograd, Pol.	154	54°00'N	16°01'E
Bialystok, Pol. (byä-wĭs'tōk)	142	53°08'N	23°12'E
Biankouma, C. Iv.	214	7°44'N	7°37'W
Biarritz, Fr. (byä-rēts')	147	43°27'N	1°39'W
Bibb City, Ga., U.S. (bĭb' sĭ'tė)	114	32°31'N	84°56'W
Biberach, Ger. (bē'bĕräk)	154	48°06'N	9°49'E
Bibiani, Ghana	214	6°28'N	2°20'W
Bic, Can. (bĭk)	92	48°22'N	68°42'W
Bickerstaffe, Eng., U.K.	237a	53°32'N	2°50'W
Bickley, neigh., Eng., U.K.	235	51°24'N	0°03'E
Bicknell, In., U.S. (bĭk'nĕl)	98	38°45'N	87°20'W
Bicske, Hung. (bĭsh'kĕ)	155	47°29'N	18°38'E
Bida, Nig. (bē'dä)	210	9°05'N	6°01'E
Biddeford, Me., U.S. (bĭd'ē-fērd)	92	43°29'N	70°29'W
Biddulph, Eng., U.K. (bĭd'ŭlf)	144a	53°07'N	2°10'W
Bidston, Eng., U.K.	237a	53°24'N	3°05'W
Biebrza, r., Pol. (byĕb'zhȧ)	155	53°18'N	22°25'E

ăt; finăl; rāte; senāte; ärm; åsk; sofȧ; fâre; ch-choose; dh-as th in other; bē; ėvent; bĕt; recĕnt; cratēr; g-gō; gh-guttural g; bĭt; ĭ-short neutral; rīde; ᴋ-guttural k as ch in German ich;

PLACE (Pronunciation)	PAGE	LAT.	LONG.
Biel, Switz. (bēl)	154	47°09′N	7°12′E
Bielefeld, Ger. (bē′lē-fĕlt)	147	52°01′N	8°35′E
Biella, Italy (byĕl′lä)	160	45°34′N	8°05′E
Bielsk Podlaski, Pol. (byĕlsk pŭd-lä′skĭ)	147	52°47′N	23°14′E
Bien Hoa, Viet	196	10°59′N	106°49′E
Bienville, Lac, l., Can.	85	55°32′N	72°45′W
Biesenthal, Ger. (bē′sĕn-täl)	145b	52°46′N	13°38′E
Bièvres, Fr.	237c	48°45′N	2°13′E
Biferno, r., Italy (bē-fĕr′nō)	160	41°49′N	14°46′E
Bifoum, Gabon	216	0°22′S	10°23′E
Biga, Tur. (bē′ghà)	161	40°13′N	27°14′E
Big Bay de Noc, Mi., U.S. (bĭg bā dē nok′)	103	45°48′N	86°41′W
Big Bayou, Ar., U.S. (bĭg′bī′yōō)	111	33°04′N	91°28′W
Big Bear City, Ca., U.S. (bĭg bâr)	107a	34°16′N	116°51′W
Big Belt Mountains, mts., Mt., U.S. (bĭg bĕlt)	96	46°53′N	111°43′W
Big Bend Dam, S.D., U.S. (bĭg bĕnd)	102	44°11′N	99°33′W
Big Bend National Park, rec., Tx., U.S.	96	29°15′N	103°15′W
Big Black, r., Ms., U.S. (bĭg blăk)	114	32°05′N	90°49′W
Big Blue, r., Ne., U.S. (bĭg blōō)	111	40°53′N	97°00′W
Big Canyon, Tx., U.S. (bĭg kăn′yŭn)	112	30°27′N	102°19′W
Big Creek, r., Oh., U.S.	229a	41°27′N	81°41′W
Big Cypress Indian Reservation, I.R., Fl., U.S.	115a	26°19′N	81°11′W
Big Cypress Swamp, sw., Fl., U.S. (bĭg sī′prĕs)	115a	26°02′N	81°20′W
Big Delta, Ak., U.S. (bĭg dĕl′tȧ)	95	64°08′N	145°48′W
Big Fork, r., Mn., U.S. (bĭg fôrk)	103	48°08′N	93°47′W
Biggar, Can.	84	52°04′N	108°00′W
Biggin Hill, neigh., Eng., U.K.	235	51°18′N	0°04′E
Big Hole, r., Mt., U.S. (bĭg hōl)	105	45°53′N	113°15′W
Big Hole National Battlefield, Mt., U.S. (bĭg hōl băt′′l-fēld)	105	45°44′N	113°35′W
Bighorn, r., U.S.	96	45°30′N	108°00′W
Bighorn Lake, res., Mt., U.S.	105	45°00′N	108°10′W
Bighorn Mountains, mts., U.S. (bĭg hôrn)	96	44°47′N	107°40′W
Big Island, i., Can.	89	49°10′N	94°40′W
Big Lake, Wa., U.S. (bĭg lāk)	106a	48°24′N	122°14′W
Big Lake, l., Can.	83g	53°35′N	113°47′W
Big Lake, l., Wa., U.S.	106a	48°24′N	122°14′W
Big Lost, r., Id., U.S. (lôst)	105	43°56′N	113°38′W
Big Mossy Point, c., Can.	89	53°45′N	97°50′W
Big Muddy, r., Il., U.S.	98	37°50′N	89°00′W
Big Muddy Creek, r., Mt., U.S. (bĭg mŭd′ĭ)	105	48°53′N	105°02′W
Bignona, Sen.	214	12°49′N	16°14′W
Big Porcupine Creek, r., Mt., U.S. (pôr′kû-pīn)	105	46°38′N	107°04′W
Big Quill Lake, l., Can.	84	51°55′N	104°22′W
Big Rapids, Mi., U.S. (bĭg răp′ĭdz)	98	43°40′N	85°30′W
Big River, Can.	84	53°50′N	107°01′W
Big Sandy, r., Az., U.S. (bĭg sănd′ē)	109	34°59′N	113°36′W
Big Sandy, r., Ky., U.S.	98	38°15′N	82°35′W
Big Sandy, r., Wy., U.S.	105	42°08′N	109°35′W
Big Sandy Creek, r., Co., U.S.	110	39°08′N	103°36′W
Big Sandy Creek, r., Mt., U.S.	105	48°20′N	110°08′W
Bigsby Island, i., Can.	89	49°04′N	94°35′W
Big Sioux, r., U.S. (bĭg sōō)	102	44°34′N	97°00′W
Big Spring, Tx., U.S. (bĭg sprĭng)	112	32°15′N	101°28′W
Big Stone, l., Mn., U.S. (bĭg stōn)	102	45°29′N	96°40′W
Big Stone Gap, Va., U.S.	115	36°50′N	82°50′W
Big Sunflower, r., Ms., U.S. (sŭn-flou′ẽr)	114	32°57′N	90°40′W
Big Timber, Mt., U.S. (bĭg′tĭm-bẽr)	105	45°50′N	109°57′W
Big Wood, r., Id., U.S. (bĭg wo͝od)	105	43°02′N	114°30′W
Bihār, state, India (bē-här′)	186	23°48′N	84°57′E
Biharamulo, Tan. (bē-hä-rä-mōō′lō)	212	2°38′S	31°20′E
Bihorului, Munţii, mts., Rom.	155	46°37′N	22°37′E
Bijagós, Arquipélago dos, is., Gui.-B.	210	11°20′N	17°10′W
Bījāpur, India	187	16°53′N	75°42′E
Bijeljina, Bos.	161	44°44′N	19°15′E
Bijelo Polje, Yugo. (bē′yĕ-lō pô′lyĕ)	161	43°02′N	19°48′E
Bijiang, China (bē-jyän)	191a	22°57′N	113°15′E
Bijie, China (bē-jyĕ)	193	27°20′N	105°18′E
Bijou Creek, r., Co., U.S. (bē′zhōō)	110	39°41′N	104°13′W
Bīkaner, India (bĭ-kă′nûr)	183	28°07′N	73°19′E
Bikin, Russia (bē-kēn′)	194	46°41′N	134°29′E
Bikin, r., Russia	194	46°37′N	135°55′E
Bikoro, D.R.C. (bē-kō′rō)	212	0°45′S	18°07′E
Bikuar, Parque Nacional do, rec., Ang.	216	15°07′S	14°40′E
Bilāspur, India (bē-läs′pōōr)	183	22°08′N	82°12′E
Bila Tserkva, Ukr.	167	49°48′N	30°09′E
Bilauktaung, mts., Asia	196	14°40′N	98°50′E
Bilbao, Spain (bĭl-bä′ō)	142	43°12′N	2°48′W
Bilbays, Egypt	218b	30°26′N	31°37′E
Bileća, Bos. (bē′lĕ-chä)	161	42°52′N	18°26′E
Bilecik, Tur. (bē-lĕd-zhĕk′)	149	40°10′N	29°58′E
Bilé Karpaty, mts., Eur.	155	48°53′N	17°35′E
Biłgoraj, Pol. (bēw-gō′rī)	155	50°31′N	22°43′E
Bilhorod-Dnistrovs′kyi, Ukr.	167	46°09′N	30°19′E
Bilimbay, Russia (bē′lĭm-bȧy)	172a	56°59′N	59°53′E
Billabong, r., Austl. (bĭl′ă-bŏng)	203	35°15′S	145°20′E
Billerica, Ma., U.S. (bĭl′rĭk-ȧ)	93a	42°33′N	71°16′W
Billericay, Eng., U.K.	144b	51°38′N	0°25′E
Billings, Mt., U.S. (bĭl′ĭngz)	96	45°47′N	108°29′W
Billingsport, N.J., U.S.	229b	39°51′N	75°14′W
Bill Williams, r., Az., U.S. (bĭl-wĭl′yumz)	109	34°10′N	113°50′W
Bilma, Niger (bēl′mä)	211	18°41′N	13°20′E
Bilopillia, Ukr.	167	51°10′N	34°19′E
Bilovods′k, Ukr.	163	49°12′N	39°36′E
Biloxi, Ms., U.S. (bĭ-lŏk′sĭ)	97	30°24′N	88°50′W
Bilqās Qism Awwal, Egypt	218b	31°14′N	31°25′E
Bimberi Peak, mtn., Austl. (bĭm′bĕrĭ)	204	35°45′S	148°50′E
Binalonan, Phil. (bē-nä-lō′nän)	197a	16°03′N	120°35′E
Bingen, Ger. (bĭn′gĕn)	154	49°57′N	7°54′E
Bingham, Eng., U.K. (bĭng′ăm)	144a	52°57′N	0°57′W
Bingham, Me., U.S.	92	45°03′N	69°51′W
Bingham Canyon, Ut., U.S.	107b	40°33′N	112°09′W
Bingham Farms, Mi., U.S.	230c	42°32′N	83°16′W
Binghamton, N.Y., U.S. (bĭng′ăm-tŭn)	97	42°05′N	75°55′W
Bingo-Nada, b., Japan (bĭn′gō nä-dä)	195	34°06′N	133°14′E
Binjai, Indon.	196	3°59′N	108°00′E
Binnaway, Austl. (bĭn′ă-wä)	204	31°42′S	149°22′E
Binsheim, Ger.	236	51°31′N	6°42′E
Bintan, i., Indon. (bĭn′tän)	181b	1°09′N	104°43′E
Bintimani, mtn., S.L.	214	9°13′N	11°07′W
Bintulu, Malay. (bēn′tōō-lōō)	196	3°07′N	113°06′E
Binxian, China (bĭn-shyän)	190	37°27′N	117°58′E
Binxian, China	192	45°40′N	127°20′E
Bio Gorge, val., Ghana	214	8°30′N	2°05′W
Bioko (Fernando Póo), i., Eq. Gui.	210	3°35′N	7°45′E
Bira, Russia (bē′rȧ)	194	49°00′N	133°18′E
Bira, r., Russia	194	48°55′N	132°25′E
Birātnagar, Nepal (bĭ-rät′nŭ-gŭr)	186	26°35′N	87°18′E
Birbka, Ukr.	155	49°36′N	24°18′E
Birch, Eng., U.K.	237b	53°34′N	2°13′W
Birch Bay, Wa., U.S. (bûrch)	106d	48°55′N	122°45′W
Birch Bay, b., Wa., U.S.	106d	48°55′N	122°52′W
Birch Island, i., Can.	89	52°25′N	99°55′W
Birch Mountains, mts., Can.	84	57°36′N	113°10′W
Birch Point, c., Wa., U.S.	106d	48°57′N	122°50′W
Bird Island, i., S. Afr. (bĕrd)	213c	33°51′S	26°21′E
Bird Rock, i., Bah. (bûrd)	123	22°50′N	74°20′W
Birds Hill, Can. (bûrds)	83f	49°58′N	97°00′W
Birdsville, Austl. (bûrdz′vĭl)	202	25°50′S	139°31′E
Birdum, Austl. (bûrd′ŭm)	202	15°45′S	133°25′E
Birecik, Tur. (bē-rĕd-zhĕk′)	149	37°10′N	37°50′E
Bir Gara, Chad	215	13°11′N	15°58′E
Bīrjand, Iran (bēr′jänd)	182	33°07′N	59°16′E
Birkenfeld, Or., U.S.	106c	45°59′N	123°20′W
Birkenhead, Eng., U.K. (bûr′kĕn-hĕd)	150	53°23′N	3°02′W
Birkenwerder, Ger. (bēr′kĕn-vĕr-dĕr)	145b	52°41′N	13°22′E
Birkholz, Ger.	238a	52°38′N	13°34′E
Birling, Eng., U.K.	235	51°19′N	0°25′E
Birmingham, Eng., U.K.	142	52°29′N	1°53′W
Birmingham, Al., U.S. (bûr′mĭng-hăm)	97	33°31′N	86°49′W
Birmingham, Mi., U.S.	101b	42°32′N	83°13′W
Birmingham, Mo., U.S.	107f	39°10′N	94°22′W
Birmingham Canal, can., Eng., U.K.	144a	53°07′N	2°40′W
Bi′r Misāhah, Egypt	211	22°16′N	28°04′E
Birnin Kebbi, Nig.	210	12°32′N	4°12′E
Birobidzhan, Russia (bē′rō-bē-jän′)	165	48°42′N	133°28′E
Birsk, Russia (bĭrsk)	164	55°25′N	55°30′E
Birstall, Eng., U.K. (bûr′stôl)	144a	53°44′N	1°39′W
Biryulëvo, Russia (bēr-yōōl′yô-vô)	172b	55°35′N	37°39′E
Biryusa, r., Russia (bēr-yōō′sä)	170	56°43′N	97°30′E
Bi′r Za′farānah, Egypt	181a	29°07′N	32°38′E
Biržai, Lith. (bēr-zhä′ē)	153	56°11′N	24°45′E
Bisbee, Az., U.S. (bĭz′bē)	96	31°30′N	109°55′W
Biscay, Bay of, b., Eur. (bĭs′kā′)	142	45°19′N	3°51′W
Biscayne Bay, b., Fl., U.S. (bĭs-kān′)	115a	25°22′N	80°15′W
Bischeim, Fr. (bĭsh′hīm)	157	48°40′N	7°48′E
Biscotasi Lake, l., Can.	90	47°20′N	81°55′W
Biser, Russia (bē′sẽr)	172a	58°24′N	58°54′E
Biševo, is., Yugo. (bē′shĕ-vō)	160	42°58′N	15°50′E
Bishkek, Kyrg.	169	42°49′N	74°42′E
Bisho, S. Afr.	212	32°50′S	27°20′E
Bishop, Ca., U.S. (bĭsh′ŭp)	108	37°22′N	118°25′W
Bishop, Tx., U.S.	113	27°35′N	97°46′W
Bishop′s Castle, Eng., U.K. (bĭsh′ŏps käs′l)	144a	52°29′N	2°57′W
Bishopville, S.C., U.S. (bĭsh′ŭp-vĭl)	115	34°11′N	80°13′W
Bismarck, N.D., U.S. (bĭz′märk)	96	46°48′N	100°46′W
Bismarck Archipelago, is., Pap. N. Gui.	197	3°15′S	150°45′E
Bismarck Range, mts., Pap. N. Gui.	197	5°15′S	144°15′E
Bissau, Gui.-B. (bē-sa′ōō)	214	11°51′N	15°35′W
Bissett, Can.	89	51°01′N	95°45′W
Bissingheim, neigh., Ger.	236	51°24′N	6°49′E
Bistineau, l., La., U.S. (bĭs-tĭ-nō′)	113	32°19′N	93°45′W
Bistrita, Rom. (bĭs-trĭt-sȧ)	149	47°09′N	24°29′E
Bistrita, r., Rom.	155	47°08′N	25°47′E
Bitlis, Tur. (bĭt-lēs′)	182	38°30′N	42°00′E
Bitola, Mac. (bē′tô-lä) (mō′nä-stēr)	160	41°02′N	21°22′E
Bitonto, Italy (bē-tôn′tō)	160	41°08′N	16°42′E
Bitter Creek, r., Wy., U.S. (bĭt′ẽr)	105	41°36′N	108°29′W
Bitterfeld, Ger. (bĭt′ẽr-fĕlt)	154	51°39′N	12°19′E
Bittermark, neigh., Ger.	236	51°27′N	7°28′E
Bitterroot, r., Mt., U.S.	105	46°28′N	114°10′W
Bitterroot Range, mts., U.S. (bĭt′ẽr-ōōt)	96	47°15′N	115°13′W
Bityug, r., Russia (bĭt′yōōg)	163	51°23′N	40°33′E
Biu, Nig.	215	10°35′N	12°13′E
Biwabik, Mn., U.S. (bē-wä′bĭk)	103	47°32′N	92°24′W
Biwa-ko, l., Japan (bē-wä′kō)	195	35°03′N	135°51′E
Biya, r., Russia (bĭ′yȧ)	170	52°22′N	87°28′E
Biysk, Russia (bēsk)	164	52°32′N	85°28′E
Bizana, S. Afr. (bĭz-änä)	213c	30°51′S	29°54′E
Bizerte, Tun. (bē-zĕrt′)	210	37°23′N	9°52′E
Bjelovar, Cro. (byĕ-lō′vär)	160	45°54′N	16°53′E
Bjørnafjorden, fj., Nor.	152	60°11′N	5°26′E
Bla, Mali	214	12°57′N	5°46′W
Black, l., Mi., U.S. (blăk)	98	45°25′N	84°15′W
Black, l., N.Y., U.S.	99	44°30′N	75°35′W
Black, r., Asia	196	21°00′N	103°30′E
Black, r., Can.	90	49°20′N	81°15′W
Black, r., U.S.	111	35°47′N	91°22′W
Black, r., Az., U.S.	109	33°35′N	109°35′W
Black, r., N.Y., U.S.	99	43°45′N	75°20′W
Black, r., S.C., U.S.	115	33°55′N	80°10′W
Black, r., Wi., U.S.	103	44°07′N	90°56′W
Blackall, Austl. (blăk′ŭl)	203	24°23′S	145°37′E
Black Bay, b., Can. (blăk)	90	48°36′N	88°32′W
Blackburn, Austl.	243b	37°49′S	145°09′E
Blackburn, Eng., U.K. (blăk′bûrn)	150	53°45′N	2°28′W
Blackburn Mount, mtn., Ak., U.S.	95	61°50′N	143°12′W
Black Butte Lake, res., Ca., U.S.	108	39°45′N	122°20′W
Black Creek Pioneer Village, bldg., Can.	227c	43°47′N	79°32′W
Black Diamond, Wa., U.S. (dī′mŭnd)	106a	47°19′N	122°00′W
Black Down Hills, hills, Eng., U.K. (blăk′doun)	150	50°58′N	3°19′W
Blackduck, Mn., U.S. (blăk′dŭk)	103	47°41′N	94°33′W
Blackfeet Indian Reservation, I.R., Mt., U.S.	105	48°40′N	113°00′W
Blackfoot, Id., U.S. (blăk′fo͝ot)	105	43°11′N	112°23′W
Blackfoot, r., Mt., U.S.	105	46°53′N	113°33′W
Blackfoot Indian Reservation, I.R., Mt., U.S.	105	48°49′N	112°53′W
Blackfoot Indian Reserve, I.R., Can.	87	50°45′N	113°00′W
Blackfoot Reservoir, res., Id., U.S.	105	42°53′N	111°23′W
Black Forest *see* Schwarzwald, for., Ger.	154	47°54′N	7°57′E
Black Hills, mts., U.S.	96	44°08′N	103°47′W
Black Island, i., Can.	89	51°10′N	96°30′W
Black Lake, Can.	91	46°02′N	71°24′W
Blackley, neigh., Eng., U.K.	237b	53°31′N	2°13′W
Black Mesa, Az., U.S. (blăk mā′sȧ)	109	36°33′N	110°40′W
Blackmore, Eng., U.K.	235	51°41′N	0°19′E
Blackmud Creek, r., Can. (blăk′mŭd)	83g	53°28′N	113°34′W
Blackpool, Eng., U.K. (blăk′pōōl)	150	53°49′N	3°02′W
Black Range, mts., N.M., U.S.	96	33°15′N	107°55′W
Black River, Jam. (blăk′)	122	18°00′N	77°50′W
Black River Falls, Wi., U.S.	103	44°18′N	90°51′W
Black Rock, Austl.	243b	37°59′S	145°01′E
Black Rock Desert, des., Nv., U.S. (rŏk)	104	40°55′N	119°00′W
Blacksburg, S.C., U.S. (blăks′bûrg)	115	35°09′N	81°30′W
Black Sea, sea	143	43°01′N	32°16′E
Blackshear, Ga., U.S. (blăk′shĭr)	115	31°20′N	82°15′W
Black Springs, Austl.	243b	37°46′S	145°19′E
Blackstone, Va., U.S. (blăk′stōn)	115	37°04′N	78°00′W
Black Sturgeon, r., Can. (stûr′jŭn)	90	49°12′N	88°41′W
Blacktown, Austl. (blăk′toun)	201b	33°47′S	150°55′E
Blackville, Can. (blăk′vĭl)	92	46°44′N	65°50′W
Blackville, S.C., U.S.	115	33°21′N	81°19′W
Black Volta (Volta Noire), r., Afr.	210	11°30′N	4°00′W
Black Warrior, r., Al., U.S. (blăk wŏr′ĭ-ẽr)	114	32°37′N	87°42′W
Blackwater, r., Ire. (blăk-wô′tẽr)	150	52°05′N	9°02′W
Blackwater, r., Mo., U.S.	111	38°53′N	93°22′W
Blackwater, r., Va., U.S.	115	37°07′N	77°10′W
Blackwell, Ok., U.S. (blăk′wĕl)	111	36°47′N	97°19′W
Bladel, Neth.	145a	51°22′N	5°15′E
Bladensburg, Md., U.S.	229d	38°56′N	76°55′W
Blagodarnoye, Russia (blä′gô-där-nō′yĕ)	167	45°00′N	43°30′E
Blagoevgrad, Bul.	161	42°01′N	23°06′E
Blagoveshchensk, Russia (blä′gŏ-vyĕsh′chĕnsk)	165	50°16′N	127°47′E
Blagoveshchensk, Russia	172a	55°03′N	56°00′E
Blaine, Mn., U.S. (blān)	107g	45°11′N	93°14′W
Blaine, Wa., U.S.	106d	48°59′N	122°49′W
Blaine, W.V., U.S.	99	39°25′N	79°10′W
Blaine Hill, Pa., U.S.	230b	40°16′N	79°53′W
Blair, Ne., U.S. (blâr)	102	41°33′N	96°09′W
Blairmore, Can.	87	49°38′N	114°25′W
Blairsville, Pa., U.S. (blârs′vĭl)	99	40°30′N	79°40′W
Blake, i., Wa., U.S. (blāk)	106a	47°37′N	122°28′W
Blakehurst, Austl.	243a	33°59′S	151°07′E
Blakely, Ga., U.S. (blāk′lē)	114	31°22′N	84°55′W
Blanc, Cap, c., Afr.	210	20°39′N	18°08′W
Blanc, Mont, mtn., Eur. (môɴ bläɴ)	142	45°50′N	6°53′E
Blanca, Bahía, b., Arg. (bä-ē′ä-blàn′kä)	132	39°30′S	61°00′W
Blanca Peak, mtn., Co., U.S. (blăŋ′kȧ)	96	37°36′N	105°22′W
Blanche, r., Can.	83c	45°34′N	75°38′W
Blanche, Lake, l., Austl. (blănch)	204	29°20′S	139°12′E
Blanchester, Oh., U.S. (blăn′chĕs-tẽr)	101f	39°18′N	83°58′W
Blanco, r., Mex.	118	24°05′N	99°21′W
Blanco, r., Mex.	119	18°42′N	96°03′W
Blanco, Cabo, c., Arg. (blăŋ′kō)	132	47°08′S	65°47′W
Blanco, Cabo, c., C.R. (kà′bō-blăŋ′kō)	120	9°29′N	85°15′W
Blanco, Cape, c., Or., U.S. (blăn′kō)	104	42°53′N	124°38′W
Blancos, Cayo, i., Cuba (kä′yō-blăŋ′kōs)	122	23°15′N	80°55′W
Blanding, Ut., U.S.	109	37°40′N	109°31′W
Blankenburg, neigh., Ger.	238a	52°35′N	13°28′E
Blankenfelde, Ger. (blän′kĕn-fĕl-dĕ)	145b	52°20′N	13°24′E
Blankenfelde, neigh., Ger.	238a	52°37′N	13°23′E
Blankenstein, Ger.	236	51°24′N	7°14′E
Blanquefort, Fr.	156	44°53′N	0°38′W
Blanquilla, Arrecife, i., Mex. (är-rĕ-sē′fē-blän-kē′l-yä)	119	21°32′N	97°14′W
Blantyre, Mwi. (blăn-tīyr)	212	15°47′S	35°00′E
Blasdell, N.Y., U.S. (bläz′dĕl)	101c	42°48′N	78°51′W
Blato, Cro. (blä′tō)	160	42°55′N	16°47′E
Blawnox, Pa., U.S.	230b	40°29′N	79°52′W
Blaye-et-Sainte Luce, Fr. (blā′ĕ-sănt-lüs′)	156	45°08′N	0°40′W
Blażowa, Pol. (bwä-zhō′vȧ)	155	49°51′N	22°05′E
Bleus, Monts, mts., D.R.C.	217	1°10′N	30°10′E
Bliersheim, Ger.	236	51°23′N	6°43′E
Blind River, Can. (blīnd)	85	46°10′N	83°09′W
Blissfield, Mi., U.S. (blĭs-fēld)	98	41°50′N	83°50′W
Blithe, r., Eng., U.K. (blĭth)	144a	52°22′N	1°49′W
Blitta, Togo	214	8°19′N	0°59′E
Block, i., R.I., U.S. (blŏk)	99	41°05′N	71°35′W
Bloedel, Can.	86	50°07′N	125°23′W
Bloemfontein, S. Afr. (blōōm′fŏn-tān)	212	29°09′S	26°16′E
Blois, Fr. (blwä)	147	47°36′N	1°21′E
Blombacher Bach, neigh., Ger.	236	51°15′N	7°14′E
Blood Indian Reserve, I.R., Can.	87	49°30′N	113°10′W
Bloomer, Wi., U.S. (blōōm′ẽr)	103	45°07′N	91°30′W
Bloomfield, In., U.S. (blōōm′fēld)	98	39°00′N	86°55′W
Bloomfield, Ia., U.S.	103	40°44′N	92°21′W

ng-sing; ŋ-baŋk; ɴ-nasalized n; nŏd; cŏmmit; ōld; ôbey; ôrder; oi-boil; fōōd; o͝o-as oo in foot; ou-out; s-soft; sh-dish; th-thin; pūre; ûnite; ûrn; stŭd; circŭs; ü-as in French tu; ′-indeterminate vowel.

266 Bloomfield-Borovsk

PLACE (Pronunciation)	PAGE	LAT.	LONG.
Bloomfield, Mo., U.S.	111	36°54′N	89°55′W
Bloomfield, Ne., U.S.	102	42°36′N	97°40′W
Bloomfield, N.J., U.S.	100a	40°48′N	74°12′W
Bloomfield Hills, Mi., U.S.	101b	42°35′N	83°15′W
Bloomfield Village, Mi., U.S.	230c	42°33′N	83°15′W
Blooming Prairie, Mn., U.S. (blo͞om′ĭng prâ′rĭ)	103	43°52′N	93°04′W
Bloomington, Ca., U.S. (blo͞om′ĭng-tŭn)	107a	34°04′N	117°24′W
Bloomington, Il., U.S.	97	40°30′N	89°00′W
Bloomington, In., U.S.	98	39°10′N	86°35′W
Bloomington, Mn., U.S.	107g	44°50′N	93°18′W
Bloomsburg, Pa., U.S. (blo͞omz′bûrg)	99	41°00′N	76°25′W
Blossburg, Al., U.S. (blŏs′bûrg)	100h	33°38′N	86°57′W
Blossburg, Pa., U.S.	99	41°45′N	77°00′W
Bloubergstrand, S. Afr.	212a	33°48′S	18°28′E
Blountstown, Fl., U.S. (blŭnts′tun)	114	30°24′N	85°02′W
Bludenz, Aus. (blo͞o-dĕnts′)	154	47°09′N	9°50′E
Blue Ash, Oh., U.S. (blo͞o ăsh)	101f	39°14′N	84°23′W
Blue Earth, Mn., U.S. (blo͞o ûrth)	103	43°38′N	94°05′W
Blue Earth, r., Mn., U.S.	103	43°55′N	94°16′W
Bluefield, W.V., U.S. (blo͞o′fēld)	115	37°15′N	81°11′W
Bluefields, Nic. (blo͞o′fēldz)	117	12°03′N	83°45′W
Blue Island, Il., U.S.	101a	41°39′N	87°41′W
Blue Mesa Reservoir, res., Co., U.S.	109	38°25′N	107°00′W
Blue Mosque, rel., Egypt	244a	30°02′N	31°15′E
Blue Mountain, mtn., Can.	93	50°28′N	57°11′W
Blue Mountains, mts., Austl.	203	33°35′S	149°00′E
Blue Mountains, mts., Jam.	122	18°05′N	76°35′W
Blue Mountains, mts., U.S.	96	45°15′N	118°50′W
Blue Mud Bay, b., Austl. (bo͞o mŭd)	202	13°20′S	136°45′E
Blue Nile, r., Afr.	211	12°30′N	34°00′E
Blue Rapids, Ks., U.S. (blo͞o răp′ĭdz)	111	39°40′N	96°41′W
Blue Ridge, mtn., U.S. (blo͞o rĭj)	97	35°30′N	82°50′W
Blue River, Can.	84	52°05′N	119°17′W
Blue River, r., Mo., U.S.	107f	38°55′N	94°33′W
Bluff, Ut., U.S.	109	37°18′N	109°34′W
Bluff Park, Al., U.S.	100h	33°24′N	86°52′W
Bluffton, In., U.S. (blŭf-tŭn)	98	40°40′N	85°15′W
Bluffton, Oh., U.S.	98	40°50′N	83°55′W
Blumenau, Braz. (blo͞o′mĕn-ou)	132	26°53′S	48°58′W
Blumut, Gunong, mtn., Malay.	181b	2°03′N	103°34′E
Blyth, Eng., U.K. (blīth)	150	55°03′N	1°34′W
Blythe, Ca., U.S.	109	33°37′N	114°37′W
Blytheville, Ar., U.S. (blīth′vĭl)	111	35°55′N	89°51′W
Bo, S.L.	214	7°56′N	11°21′W
Boac, Phil.	197a	13°26′N	121°50′E
Boaco, Nic. (bȯ-ä′kō)	120	12°24′N	85°41′W
Bo'ai, China (bwo-ī)	192	35°10′N	113°08′E
Boa Vista, i., C.V. (bō-ä-vēsh′tà)	210b	16°01′N	23°52′W
Boa Vista do Rio Branco, Braz.	131	2°46′N	60°45′W
Bobbingworth, Eng., U.K.	235	51°44′N	0°13′E
Bobigny, Fr.	237c	48°54′N	2°27′E
Bobo Dioulasso, Burkina (bō′bō-dyo͞o-läs-sō′)	210	11°12′N	4°18′W
Bobr, Bela. (bō′b′r)	162	54°19′N	29°11′E
Bóbr, r., Pol. (bŭ′br)	154	51°44′N	15°13′E
Bobrov, Russia (bŭb-rôf′)	167	51°07′N	40°01′E
Bobrovyts'a, Ukr.	163	50°43′N	31°27′E
Bobruysk, Bela. (bŏ-bro͞o′ĭsk)	166	53°07′N	29°13′E
Bobrynets', Ukr.	163	48°04′N	32°10′E
Boca, neigh., Arg.	233d	34°38′S	58°21′W
Boca del Pozo, Ven. (bô-kä-dĕl-pŏ′zō)	131b	11°00′N	64°21′W
Boca de Uchire, Ven. (bô-kä-dĕ-o͞o-chē′rĕ)	131b	10°09′N	65°27′W
Bocaina, Serra da, mtn., Braz. (sĕ′r-rä-dá-bô-kä′ē-nä)	129a	22°47′S	44°39′W
Bocanegra, Peru	233c	12°01′S	77°07′W
Bocas, Mex. (bō′käs)	118	22°29′N	101°03′W
Bocas del Toro, Pan. (bō′käs dĕl tō′rō)	121	9°24′N	82°15′W
Bochnia, Pol. (bōκ′nyä)	155	49°58′N	20°28′E
Bocholt, Ger. (bō′κōlt)	157c	51°50′N	6°37′E
Bochum, Ger.	154	51°29′N	7°13′E
Böckel, neigh., Ger.	236	51°13′N	7°12′E
Bockum, Ger.	236	51°20′N	6°44′E
Bockum, neigh., Ger.	236	51°21′N	6°38′E
Bockum-Hövel, Ger. (bō′kōm-hû′fĕl)	157c	51°41′N	7°45′E
Bodalang, D.R.C.	216	3°14′N	22°14′E
Bodaybo, Russia (bō-dī′bō)	165	57°12′N	114°46′E
Bodele, depr., Chad (bō-dā-lā′)	211	16°45′N	17°05′E
Bodelschwingh, neigh., Ger.	236	51°33′N	7°22′E
Boden, Swe.	146	65°51′N	21°29′E
Bodensee, l., Eur. (bō′dĕn zā)	142	47°48′N	9°22′E
Bodmin, Eng., U.K. (bŏd′mĭn)	150	50°29′N	4°45′W
Bodmin Moor, Eng., U.K. (bŏd′mĭn mŏr)	150	50°36′N	4°43′W
Bodrum, Tur.	167	37°10′N	27°07′E
Boende, D.R.C. (bô-ĕn′dà)	212	0°13′S	20°52′E
Boerne, Tx., U.S. (bō′ĕrn)	112	29°49′N	98°44′W
Boesmans, r., S. Afr.	213c	33°29′S	26°09′E
Boeuf, r., U.S. (bĕf)	113	32°23′N	91°57′W
Boffa, Gui. (bôf′ä)	210	10°10′N	14°02′W
Bōfu, Japan (bō′fo͞o)	195	34°03′N	131°35′E
Bogalusa, La., U.S. (bō-gá-lo͞o′sà)	113	30°48′N	89°52′W
Bogan, r., Austl. (bō′gĕn)	204	32°10′S	147°40′E
Bogense, Den. (bō′gĕn-sĕ)	152	55°34′N	10°09′E
Boggy Peak, mtn., Antig. (bŏg′ĭ-pēk)	121b	17°03′N	61°50′W
Bogong, Mount, mtn., Austl.	204	36°50′S	147°15′E
Bogor, Indon.	196	6°45′S	106°45′E
Bogoroditsk, Russia (bŏ-gŏ′rô-dĭtsk)	162	53°48′N	38°06′E
Bogorodsk, Russia	166	56°02′N	43°40′E
Bogorodskoje, neigh., Russia	239b	55°49′N	37°44′E
Bogorodskoye, Russia (bô-gô-rôd′skô-yĕ)	172a	56°43′N	56°53′E
Bogotá see Santa Fe de Bogotá, Col.	130	4°36′N	74°05′W
Bogota, N.J., U.S.	228	40°53′N	74°02′W
Bogotol, Russia (bŏ′gō-tŏl)	165	56°15′N	89°45′E
Boguchar, Russia (bŏ′go͞o-chär)	167	49°40′N	41°00′E
Bogue Chitto, Ms., U.S. (nôr′fēld)	114	31°26′N	90°25′W
Boguete, Pan. (bō-gĕ′tē)	121	8°54′N	82°29′W
Bo Hai, b., China	189	38°30′N	120°00′E
Bohai Haixia, strt., China (bwo-hī hī-shyä)	192	38°05′N	121°40′E
Bohain-en-Vermandois, Fr. (bô-ăN-ŏN-vâr-mäN-dwä′)	156	49°58′N	3°22′E
Bohemia see Čechy, hist. reg., Czech Rep.	154	49°51′N	13°55′E
Bohemian Forest, mts., Eur. (bō-hē′mĭ-ăn)	142	49°35′N	12°27′E
Böhnsdorf, neigh., Ger.	238a	52°24′N	13°33′E
Bohodukhiv, Ukr.	167	50°10′N	35°31′E
Bohol, i., Phil. (bō-hôl′)	197	9°28′N	124°35′E
Bohom, Mex. (bō-ô′m)	119	16°47′N	92°42′W
Bohuslav, Ukr.	163	49°34′N	30°51′W
Boiestown, Can. (boiz′toun)	92	46°27′N	66°25′W
Bois Blanc, i., Mi., U.S. (boi′ blăŋk)	98	45°45′N	84°30′W
Boischâtel, Can. (bwä-shä-tĕl′)	83b	46°54′N	71°08′W
Bois-Colombes, Fr.	237c	48°55′N	2°16′E
Bois-des-Filion, Can. (bo͞o-ä′dĕ-fē-yŏN′)	83a	45°40′N	73°46′W
Boise, Id., U.S. (boi′zē)	96	43°38′N	116°12′W
Boise, r., Id., U.S.	104	43°43′N	116°30′W
Boise City, Ok., U.S.	110	36°42′N	102°30′W
Boissevain, Can. (bois′vān)	84	49°14′N	100°03′W
Boissy-Saint-Léger, Fr.	237c	48°45′N	2°31′E
Bojador, Cabo, c., W. Sah.	210	26°21′N	16°08′W
Bojnūrd, Iran	182	37°29′N	57°13′E
Bokani, Nig.	215	9°26′N	5°13′E
Boknafjorden, fj., Nor.	146	59°12′N	5°37′E
Boksburg, S. Afr. (bŏks′bûrgh)	213b	26°13′N	28°15′E
Boksburg North, S. Afr.	244b	26°12′S	28°15′E
Boksburg South, S. Afr.	244b	26°14′S	28°15′E
Boksburg West, S. Afr.	244b	26°13′S	28°14′E
Bokungu, D.R.C.	216	0°41′S	22°19′E
Bol, Chad	215	13°28′N	14°43′E
Bolai I, Cen. Afr. Rep.	215	4°20′N	17°21′E
Bolama, Gui.-B. (bō-lä′mä)	210	11°34′S	15°41′W
Bolan, mtn., Pak. (bō-län′)	186	30°13′N	67°09′E
Bolaños, Mex. (bō-län′yōs)	118	21°40′N	103°48′W
Bolaños, r., Mex.	118	21°26′N	103°54′W
Bolan Pass, p., Pak.	183	29°50′N	67°10′E
Bolbec, Fr. (bôl-bĕk′)	156	49°37′N	0°26′E
Bole, Ghana (bō′lå)	210	9°02′N	2°29′W
Bolesławiec, Pol. (bō-lĕ-slä′vyĕts)	154	51°15′N	15°35′E
Bolgatanga, Ghana	214	10°46′N	0°52′W
Bolhrad, Ukr.	167	45°41′N	28°38′E
Boli, China (bwo-lē)	189	45°40′N	130°38′E
Bolinao, Phil. (bō-lē-nä′ō)	197a	16°24′N	119°53′E
Bolívar, Arg. (bō-lē′vär)	132	36°15′S	61°05′W
Bolívar, Col.	130	1°46′N	76°58′W
Bolivar, Mo., U.S. (bŏl′ĭ-vàr)	111	37°37′N	93°22′W
Bolivar, Tn., U.S.	114	35°14′N	88°56′W
Bolívar, Pico, mtn., Ven.	130	8°44′N	70°54′W
Bolivar Peninsula, pen., Tx., U.S. (bŏl′ĭ-vàr)	113a	29°25′N	94°40′W
Bolivia, nation, S.A. (bō-lĭv′ĭ-à)	130	17°00′S	64°00′W
Bölkenbusch, Ger.	236	51°21′N	7°06′E
Bolkhov, Russia (bŏl-κôf′)	166	53°27′N	35°59′E
Bollate, Italy	238c	45°33′N	9°07′E
Bollensdorf, Ger.	238a	52°31′N	13°43′E
Bollin, r., Eng., U.K. (bŏl′ĭn)	144a	53°18′N	2°11′W
Bollington, Eng., U.K. (bôl′ĭng-tŭn)	144a	53°18′N	2°06′W
Bollington, Eng., U.K.	237b	53°22′N	2°25′W
Bollnäs, Swe. (bôl′nĕs)	152	61°22′N	16°20′E
Bollwerk, Ger.	236	51°10′N	7°35′E
Bolmen, l., Swe. (bôl′mĕn)	152	56°58′N	13°25′E
Bolobo, D.R.C. (bō′lō-bō)	212	2°14′S	16°18′E
Bologna, Italy (bō-lōn′yä)	142	44°30′N	11°18′E
Bologoye, Russia (bŏ-lŏ-gô′yĕ)	166	57°52′N	34°02′E
Bolonchenticul, Mex. (bō-lôn-chĕn-tē-ko͞o′l)	120a	20°03′N	89°47′W
Bolondrón, Cuba (bō-lôn-drōn′)	122	22°45′N	81°25′W
Bol'šaja Ochta, neigh., Russia	239a	59°57′N	30°25′E
Bolseno, Lago di, l., Italy (lä′gō-dē-bôl-sā′nō)	160	42°35′N	11°40′E
Bol'shaya Anyuy, r., Russia	171	67°58′N	161°15′E
Bol'shaya Chuya, r., Russia	171	58°15′N	111°40′E
Bol'shaya Kinel', r., Russia	166	53°20′N	52°40′E
Bol'she Ust'ikinskoye, Russia (bôl′she ōs-tyĭ-kĕn′skô-yĕ)	172a	55°58′N	58°18′E
Bol'shoy Begichëv, i., Russia	165	74°30′N	114°40′E
Bol'shoye Ivonino, Russia (ĭ-vô′nĭ-nō)	172a	59°41′N	61°12′E
Bol'shoy Kuyash, Russia (bôl-shôy ko͞o′yash)	172a	55°52′N	61°07′E
Bol'šoj Teatr, bldg., Russia	239b	55°46′N	37°37′E
Bolsover, Eng., U.K. (bōl′zō-vĕr)	144a	53°14′N	1°17′W
Boltaña, Spain (bôl-tä′nä)	159	42°28′N	0°03′E
Bolton, Can. (bōl′tŭn)	83d	43°53′N	79°44′W
Bolton, Eng., U.K.	150	53°35′N	2°26′W
Bolton-upon-Dearne, Eng., U.K. (bōl′tŭn-ŭp′ŏn-dûrn)	144a	53°31′N	1°19′W
Bolu, Tur. (bō′lò)	149	40°45′N	31°45′E
Bolva, r., Russia (bôl′vä)	162	53°30′N	34°30′E
Bolvadin, Tur. (bôl-vä-dēn′)	149	38°50′N	30°50′E
Bolzano, Italy (bōl-tsä′nō)	148	46°31′N	11°22′E
Boma, D.R.C. (bō′mä)	212	5°51′S	13°03′E
Bombala, Austl. (bŭm-bä′lă)	203	36°55′S	149°07′E
Bombay see Mumbai, India	183	18°58′N	72°50′E
Bombay Harbour, b., India	187b	18°55′N	72°52′E
Bomi Hills, Lib.	210	7°00′N	11°00′W
Bom Jardim, Braz. (bôn zhär-dēN′)	129a	22°10′S	42°25′W
Bom Jesus do Itabapoana, Braz.	129a	21°08′S	41°51′W
Bømlo, i., Nor. (bûmlō)	152	59°47′N	4°57′E
Bommerholz, Ger.	236	51°23′N	7°18′E
Bommern, neigh., Ger.	236	51°25′N	7°20′E
Bomongo, D.R.C.	211	1°22′N	18°21′E
Bom Retiro, neigh., Braz.	234d	23°32′S	46°38′W
Bom Sucesso, Braz. (bôn-so͞o-sĕ′sō)	129a	21°02′S	44°44′W
Bomu see Mbomou, r., Afr.	211	4°50′N	24°00′E
Bon, Cap, c., Tun. (bôN)	148	37°04′N	11°13′E
Bon Air, Pa., U.S.	229b	39°58′N	75°19′W
Bonaire, i., Neth. Ant. (bō-nâr′)	130	12°10′N	68°15′W
Bonavista, Can. (bŏ-nà-vĭs′tà)	85a	48°39′N	53°07′W
Bonavista Bay, b., Can.	85a	48°45′N	53°20′W
Bond, Co., U.S. (bŏnd)	110	39°53′N	106°40′W
Bondi, Austl.	243a	33°53′S	151°17′E
Bondo, D.R.C. (bôn′dō)	170	3°49′N	23°40′E
Bondoc Peninsula, pen., Phil. (bôn-dŏk′)	197a	13°24′N	122°30′E
Bondoukou, C. Iv. (bŏn-do͞o′ko͞o)	210	8°02′N	2°48′W
Bonds Cay, i., Bah. (bŏnds kē)	122	25°30′N	77°45′W
Bondy, Fr.	157b	48°54′N	2°28′E
Bône see Annaba, Alg.	210	36°57′N	7°39′E
Bone, Teluk, b., Indon.	196	4°09′S	121°00′E
Bonete, Cerro, mtn., Arg. (bô′nĕtĕh çĕrrô)	132	27°50′S	68°35′W
Bonfim, Braz. (bôN-fē′N)	129a	20°20′S	44°15′W
Bongor, Chad	215	10°17′N	15°22′E
Bonham, Tx., U.S. (bŏn′ăm)	111	33°35′N	96°09′W
Bonhomme, Pic, mtn., Haiti	123	19°10′N	72°20′W
Bonifacio, Fr. (bō-nē-fä′chō)	160	41°23′N	9°10′E
Bonifacio, Strait of, strt., Eur.	148	41°14′N	9°02′E
Bonifay, Fl., U.S. (bŏn-ĭ-fā′)	114	30°46′N	85°40′W
Bonin Islands, is., Japan (bō′nĭn)	225	26°30′N	141°00′E
Bonn, Ger. (bŏn)	142	50°44′N	7°06′E
Bonne Bay, b., Can. (bŏn)	93	49°33′N	57°55′W
Bonners Ferry, Id., U.S. (bonērz fĕr′ĭ)	104	48°41′N	116°19′W
Bonner Springs, Ks., U.S. (bŏn′ēr sprĭngz)	107f	39°04′N	94°52′W
Bonne Terre, Mo., U.S. (bŏn târ′)	111	37°55′N	90°32′W
Bonnet Peak, mtn., Can. (bŏn′ĭt)	87	51°26′N	115°53′W
Bonneuil-sur-Marne, Fr.	237c	48°46′N	2°29′E
Bonneville Dam, dam, U.S. (bŏn′ē-vĭl)	104	45°37′N	121°57′W
Bonny, Nig. (bŏn′ē)	210	4°29′N	7°13′E
Bonny Lake, Wa., U.S. (bŏn′ē lăk)	106a	47°11′N	122°11′W
Bonnyrigg, Austl.	243a	33°54′S	150°54′E
Bonnyville, Can. (bŏnē-vĭl)	87	54°16′N	110°44′W
Bonorva, Italy (bō-nôr′vä)	160	40°26′N	8°46′E
Bonsúcesso, neigh., Braz.	234c	22°52′S	43°15′W
Bonthain, Indon. (bŏn-tīn′)	196	5°30′S	119°52′E
Bonthe, S.L.	210	7°32′N	12°30′W
Bontoc, Phil. (bŏn-tŏk′)	197a	17°10′N	121°01′E
Booby Rocks, is., Bah. (bo͞o′bĭ rŏks)	122	23°55′N	77°00′W
Booker T. Washington National Monument, rec., Va., U.S. (bo͝ok′ēr tē wŏsh′ĭng-tŭn)	115	37°07′N	79°45′W
Boom, Bel.	145a	51°05′N	4°22′E
Boone, Ia., U.S. (bo͞on)	103	42°04′N	93°51′W
Booneville, Ar., U.S. (bo͞on′vĭl)	111	35°09′N	93°54′W
Booneville, Ky., U.S.	98	37°25′N	83°40′W
Booneville, Ms., U.S.	114	34°37′N	88°35′W
Boons, S. Afr.	218d	25°59′S	27°15′E
Boonton, N.J., U.S. (bo͞on′tŭn)	100a	40°54′N	74°24′W
Boonville, In., U.S.	98	38°00′N	87°15′W
Boonville, Mo., U.S.	111	38°57′N	92°44′W
Boorama, Som.	218a	10°05′N	43°08′E
Boosaaso, Som.	218a	11°19′N	49°10′E
Boothbay Harbor, Me., U.S. (bo͞oth′bā här′bēr)	92	43°51′N	69°39′W
Boothia, Gulf of, b., Can. (bo͞o′thĭ-à)	85	69°04′N	86°04′W
Boothia Peninsula, pen., Can.	82	73°30′N	95°00′W
Boothstown, Eng., U.K.	237b	53°30′N	2°25′W
Bootle, Eng., U.K. (bo͞ot′l)	144a	53°29′N	3°02′W
Booysens, neigh., S. Afr.	244b	26°14′S	28°01′E
Bor, Sudan (bôr)	211	6°13′N	31°35′E
Bor, Tur. (bōr)	167	37°50′N	34°40′E
Boraha, Nosy, i., Madag.	213	16°58′S	50°15′E
Borah Peak, mtn., Id., U.S. (bō′rä)	105	44°12′N	113°47′W
Borås, Swe. (bō′rōs)	146	57°43′N	12°55′E
Borāzjān, Iran (bō-räz-jän′)	182	29°13′N	51°13′E
Borba, Braz. (bôr′bä)	131	4°23′S	59°31′W
Borbeck, neigh., Ger.	236	51°29′N	6°57′E
Borborema, Planalto da, plat., Braz. (plä-näl′tō-dä-bôr-bō-rĕ′mä)	131	7°35′S	36°40′W
Bordeaux, Fr. (bôr-dō′)	142	44°50′N	0°37′W
Bordeaux, S. Afr.	244b	26°06′S	28°01′E
Bordentown, N.J., U.S. (bôr′dĕn-toun)	99	40°05′N	74°40′W
Bordj-bou-Arréridj, Alg. (bŏrj-bo͞o-á-rā-rēj′)	148	36°03′N	4°48′E
Bordj Omar Idriss, Alg.	210	28°06′N	6°34′E
Borehamwood, Eng., U.K.	235	51°40′N	0°16′W
Borgarnes, Ice.	146	64°31′N	21°40′W
Borger, Tx., U.S. (bôr′gēr)	110	35°40′N	101°23′W
Borgholm, Swe. (bôrg-hŏlm′)	152	56°52′N	16°40′E
Borgne, l., La., U.S. (bôrn′y′)	113	30°03′N	89°36′W
Borgomanero, Italy (bôr′gō-mä-nā′rō)	160	45°40′N	8°28′E
Borgo Val di Taro, Italy (bô′r-zhō-väl-dē-tá′rō)	160	44°29′N	9°44′E
Borili, Kaz.	169	53°36′N	61°55′E
Boring, Or., U.S. (bōring)	106c	45°26′N	122°22′W
Borisoglebsk, Russia (bŏ-rē sŏ-glyĕpsk′)	164	51°20′N	42°00′E
Borisov, Bela. (bŏ-rē′sôf)	166	54°16′N	28°33′E
Borisovka, Russia (bŏ-rē-sôf′kà)	167	50°38′N	36°00′E
Borivli, India	187b	19°15′N	72°48′E
Borja, Spain (bôr′hä)	158	41°50′N	1°33′W
Borken, Ger. (bōr′kĕn)	157c	51°50′N	6°51′E
Borkou, reg., Chad (bôr-ko͞o′)	211	18°11′N	18°28′E
Borkum, i., Ger. (bōr′ko͞om)	154	53°31′N	6°50′E
Borlänge, Swe. (bôr-lĕŋ′gĕ)	152	60°30′N	15°24′E
Borle, neigh., India	240e	19°02′N	72°55′E
Borneo, i., Asia	196	0°25′N	112°39′E
Bornholm, i., Den. (bôrn-hôlm)	142	55°16′N	15°15′E
Bornim, neigh., Ger.	238a	52°26′N	13°00′E
Bornstedt, neigh., Ger.	238a	52°25′N	13°02′E
Boromlia, Ukr.	163	50°36′N	34°58′E
Boromo, Burkina	214	11°45′N	2°56′W
Borough Green, Eng., U.K.	235	51°17′N	0°19′E
Borough Park, neigh., N.Y., U.S.	228	40°38′N	74°00′W
Borovan, Bul. (bŏ-rō-vän′)	161	43°24′N	23°47′E
Borovichi, Russia (bŏ-rô-vē′chē)	164	58°22′N	33°56′E
Borovsk, Russia (bô′rŏvsk)	162	55°13′N	36°26′E

ăt; finăl; rāte; senâte; ärm; åsk; sofá; fâre; ch-choose; dh-as th in other; bē; ėvent; bĕt; recĕnt; cratēr; g-gō; gh-guttural g; bĭt; ĭ-short neutral; rīde; κ-guttural k as ch in German ich;

PRONOUNCING INDEX Borraan–Bridgeport 267

PLACE (Pronunciation)	PAGE	LAT.	LONG.
Borraan, Som.	218a	10°38′N	48°30′E
Borracha, Isla la, i., Ven. (ē′s-lä-lä-bôr-rä′chä)	131b	10°18′N	64°44′W
Borriana, Spain	148	39°53′N	0°05′W
Borroloola, Austl. (bŏr-rō-lōō′lȧ)	202	16°15′S	136°19′E
Borshchiv, Ukr.	155	48°47′N	26°04′E
Borth, Ger.	236	51°36′N	6°33′E
Bort-les-Orgues, Fr. (bôr-lā-zôrg)	156	45°26′N	2°26′E
Borūjerd, Iran	182	33°45′N	48°53′E
Boryslav, Ukr.	155	49°17′N	23°24′E
Boryspil′, Ukr.	163	50°17′N	30°54′E
Borzna, Ukr. (bôrz′nȧ)	167	51°15′N	32°26′E
Borzya, Russia (bôrz′yȧ)	165	50°37′N	116°53′E
Bosa, Italy (bō′sä)	160	40°18′N	8°34′E
Bosanska Dubica, Bos. (bō′sän-skä dōō′bĭt-sä)	160	45°10′N	16°49′E
Bosanska Gradiška, Bos. (bō′sän-skä grä-dĭsh′kä)	161	45°08′N	17°15′E
Bosanski Novi, Bos. (bō′s sän-skĭ nō′vē)	160	45°00′N	16°22′E
Bosanski Petrovac, Bos. (bō′sän-skĭ pĕt′rō-väts)	160	44°33′N	16°23′E
Bosanski Šamac, Bos. (bō′sän-skĭ shä′mȧts)	161	45°03′N	18°30′E
Boscobel, Wi., U.S. (bŏs′kȯ-bĕl)	103	43°08′N	90°44′W
Bose, China (bwo-sŭ)	193	24°00′N	106°38′E
Boshan, China (bwo-shan)	189	36°32′N	117°51′E
Boskol′, Kaz. (bȧs-kôl′)	169	53°45′N	61°17′E
Boskoop, Neth.	145a	52°04′N	4°39′E
Boskovice, Czech Rep. (bŏs′kō-vē-tsĕ)	154	49°26′N	16°37′E
Bosna, r., Yugo.	161	44°19′N	17°54′E
Bosnia and Herzegovina, nation, Eur.	161	44°15′N	17°30′E
Bosobolo, D.R.C.	216	4°11′N	19°54′E
Bosporus see İstanbul Boğazi, strt., Tur.	182	41°10′N	29°10′E
Bossangoa, Cen. Afr. Rep.	215	6°29′N	17°27′E
Bossier City, La., U.S. (bŏsh′ēr)	113	32°31′N	93°42′W
Bossley Park, Austl.	243a	33°52′S	150°54′E
Bostanci, neigh., Tur.	239f	40°57′N	29°05′E
Bosten Hu, l., China (bwo-stŭn hōō)	188	42°06′N	88°01′E
Boston, Ga., U.S. (bôs′tŭn)	114	30°47′N	83°47′W
Boston, Ma., U.S.	97	42°15′N	71°07′W
Boston, Pa., U.S.	230b	40°18′N	79°49′W
Boston Bay, b., Ma., U.S.	227a	42°22′N	70°54′W
Boston Garden, pt. of i., Ma., U.S.	227a	42°22′N	71°04′W
Boston Harbor, b., Ma., U.S.	227a	42°20′N	70°58′W
Boston Heights, Oh., U.S.	101d	41°15′N	81°30′W
Boston Mountains, mts., Ar., U.S.	97	35°46′N	93°32′W
Botafogo, neigh., Braz.	234c	22°57′S	43°11′W
Botafogo, Enseada de, b., Braz.	234c	22°57′S	43°10′W
Botany, Austl.	243a	33°57′S	151°12′E
Botany Bay, neigh., Eng., U.K.	235	51°41′N	0°07′W
Botany Bay, b., Austl. (bŏt′ȧ-nĭ)	203	33°58′S	151°11′E
Botevgrad, Bul.	161	42°54′N	23°41′E
Bothaville, S. Afr. (bō′tä-vĭl)	218d	27°24′S	26°38′E
Bothell, Wa., U.S. (bŏth′ĕl)	106a	47°46′N	122°12′W
Bothnia, Gulf of, b., Eur. (bŏth′nĭ-ȧ)	142	63°40′N	21°30′E
Botoşani, Rom. (bō-tō-shän′ĭ)	155	47°46′N	26°40′E
Botswana, nation, Afr. (bŏtswănä)	212	22°10′S	23°13′E
Bottineau, N.D., U.S. (bŏt-ĭ-nō′)	102	48°48′N	100°28′W
Bottrop, Ger. (bŏt′trŏp)	154	51°31′N	6°56′E
Botwood, Can. (bŏt′wo͝od)	85a	49°08′N	55°21′W
Bötzow, Ger.	238a	52°39′N	13°08′E
Bouafle, C. Iv. (bo͝o-ȧ-flā′)	210	6°59′N	5°45′W
Bouar, Cen. Afr. Rep. (bōō-är)	211	5°57′N	15°36′E
Bou Areg, Sebkha, Mor.	158	35°09′N	3°02′W
Boubandjidah, Parc National de, rec., Cam.	215	8°20′N	14°40′E
Boucherville, Can. (bōō-shä-vĕl′)	83a	45°37′N	73°27′W
Boucherville, Îles de, is., Can.	227b	45°37′N	73°28′W
Boudenib, Mor. (bōō-dĕ-nĕb′)	210	32°14′N	3°04′W
Boudette, Mn., U.S. (bōō-dĕt)	103	48°42′N	94°34′W
Boudouaou, Alg.	159	36°44′N	3°25′E
Boufarik, Alg. (bōō-fȧ-rēk′)	159	36°35′N	2°55′E
Bougainville, i., Pap. N. Gui.	198e	6°00′S	155°00′E
Bougainville Trench, deep (bōō-găN-vēl′)	225	7°00′S	152°00′E
Bougie see Bejaïa, Alg.	210	36°46′N	5°00′E
Bougouni, Mali (bōō-gōō-nē′)	210	11°27′N	7°30′W
Bouïra, Alg. (boo-ē′rȧ)	148	36°25′N	3°55′E
Bouïra-Sahary, Alg. (bwē-rȧ sȧ′ä-rē)	159	35°16′N	3°23′E
Bouka, r., Gui.	214	11°05′N	10°40′W
Boukiéro, Congo	244c	4°12′S	15°18′E
Boulder, Co., U.S.	96	40°02′N	105°19′W
Boulder, r., Mt., U.S.	105	46°10′N	112°07′W
Boulder City, Nv., U.S.	96	35°57′N	114°50′W
Boulder Peak, mtn., Id., U.S.	105	43°53′N	114°33′W
Boulogne, neigh., Arg.	233d	34°31′S	58°34′W
Boulogne-Billancourt, Fr. (bōō-lôn′y′-bē-yäN-kōōr′)	156	48°50′N	2°14′E
Boulogne-sur-Mer, Fr. (bōō-lôn′y-sür-mâr′)	147	50°44′N	1°37′E
Boumba, r., Cam.	215	3°20′N	14°40′E
Bouna, C. Iv. (bōō-nä′)	210	9°16′N	3°00′W
Bouna, Parc National de, rec., C. Iv.	214	9°20′N	3°35′W
Boundary Bay, b., N.A. (boun′dȧ-rĭ)	106d	49°03′N	122°59′W
Boundary Peak, mtn., Nv., U.S.	108	37°52′N	118°20′W
Bound Brook, N.J., U.S. (bound bro͝ok)	100a	40°34′N	74°32′W
Bountiful, Ut., U.S. (boun′tĭ-fo͝ol)	107b	40°55′N	111°53′W
Bountiful Peak, mtn., Ut., U.S. (boun′tĭ-fo͝ol)	107b	40°58′N	111°49′W
Bounty Islands, is., N.Z.	5	47°42′S	179°05′E
Bourail, N. Cal.	198f	21°34′S	165°30′E
Bourem, Mali (bōō-rĕm′)	210	16°43′N	0°15′W
Bourg-en-Bresse, Fr. (bōōr-gĕN-brĕs′)	147	46°12′N	5°13′E
Bourges, Fr. (bōōrzh)	147	47°06′N	2°22′E
Bourget, Can. (bōōr-zhĕ′)	83c	45°26′N	75°09′W
Bourg-la-Reine, Fr.	237c	48°47′N	2°19′E
Bourgoin, Fr. (bōōr-gwăN′)	157	45°46′N	5°17′E
Bourke, Austl. (bŭrk)	203	30°10′S	146°00′E
Bourne, Eng., U.K. (bōrn)	144a	52°46′N	0°22′W
Bournebridge, Eng., U.K.	235	51°38′N	0°11′E
Bourne End, Eng., U.K.	235	51°45′N	0°32′W
Bournemouth, Eng., U.K. (bôrn′mŭth)	150	50°44′N	1°55′W
Bou Saâda, Alg. (bōō-sä′dä)	148	35°13′N	4°17′E
Bousso, Chad (bōō-sô′)	211	10°33′N	16°45′E
Boutilimit, Maur.	210	17°30′N	14°54′W
Bouvetøya, i., Ant.	3	55°00′S	3°00′E
Bövinghausen, neigh., Ger.	236	51°31′N	7°19′E
Bow, r., Can. (bō)	84	50°35′N	112°15′W
Bowbells, N.D., U.S. (bō′bĕls)	102	48°50′N	102°16′W
Bowdle, S.D., U.S. (bōd′′l)	102	45°28′N	99°42′W
Bowdon, Eng., U.K.	237b	53°23′N	2°22′W
Bowen, Austl. (bō′ĕn)	203	20°02′S	148°14′E
Bowie, Md., U.S. (bōō′ĭ) (bō′ē)	100e	38°59′N	76°47′W
Bowie, Tx., U.S.	111	33°34′N	97°50′W
Bowling Green, Ky., U.S. (bōlĭng grēn)	97	37°00′N	86°26′W
Bowling Green, Mo., U.S.	111	39°19′N	91°09′W
Bowling Green, Oh., U.S.	98	41°25′N	83°40′W
Bowman, N.D., U.S. (bō′măn)	102	46°11′N	103°23′W
Bowron, r., Can. (bō′rŭn)	87	53°20′N	121°10′W
Boxelder Creek, r., Mt., U.S. (bŏks′ĕl-dēr)	102	45°35′N	104°28′W
Box Elder Creek, r., Mt., U.S.	105	47°17′N	108°37′W
Box Hill, Austl.	201a	37°49′S	145°08′E
Boxian, China (bwo shyĕn)	192	33°52′N	115°47′E
Boxing, China (bwo-shyĭŋ)	190	37°09′N	118°08′E
Boxmoor, Eng., U.K.	235	51°45′N	0°29′W
Boxtel, Neth.	145a	51°40′N	5°21′E
Boyabo, D.R.C.	216	3°43′N	18°46′E
Boyacıköy, neigh., Tur.	239f	41°06′N	29°02′E
Boyang, China (bwo-yäŋ)	193	29°00′N	116°42′E
Boyer, r., Can. (boi′ēr)	83b	46°45′N	70°56′W
Boyer, r., Ia., U.S.	102	41°45′N	95°36′W
Boyle, Ire. (boil)	150	53°59′N	8°15′W
Boyne, r., Ire. (boin)	150	53°40′N	6°40′W
Boyne City, Mi., U.S.	98	45°15′N	85°05′W
Boyoma Falls, wtfl., D.R.C.	211	0°30′N	25°12′E
Boysen Reservoir, res., Wy., U.S.	105	43°19′N	108°11′W
Bozcaada, Tur. (bōz-cä′dä)	161	39°50′N	26°05′E
Bozca Ada, i., Tur.	161	39°50′N	26°00′E
Bozeman, Mt., U.S. (bōz′măn)	96	45°41′N	111°00′W
Bozene, D.R.C.	216	2°56′N	19°12′E
Bozhen, China (bwo-jŭn)	190	38°05′N	116°35′E
Bozoum, Cen. Afr. Rep.	215	6°19′N	16°23′E
Bra, Italy (brä)	160	44°41′N	7°52′E
Bracciano, Lago di, l., Italy (lä′gō-dē-brä-chä′nō)	160	42°05′N	12°00′E
Bracebridge, Can. (brās′brĭj)	91	45°05′N	79°20′W
Braceville, Il., U.S. (brās′vĭl)	101a	41°13′N	88°16′W
Bräcke, Swe. (brĕk′kĕ)	146	62°44′N	15°28′E
Brackenridge, Pa., U.S. (brăk′ĕn-rĭj)	101e	40°37′N	79°44′W
Brackettville, Tx., U.S. (brăk′ĕt-vĭl)	112	29°19′N	100°24′W
Braço Maior, mth., Braz.	131	11°00′S	51°00′W
Braço Menor, mth., Braz. (brä′zō-mē-nō′r)	131	11°38′S	50°00′W
Bradano, r., Italy (brä-dä′nō)	160	40°43′N	16°22′E
Braddock, Pa., U.S. (brăd′ŭk)	101e	40°24′N	79°52′W
Braddock Hills, Pa., U.S.	230b	40°25′N	79°51′W
Bradenburger Tor, pt. of i., Ger.	238a	52°31′N	13°23′E
Bradenton, Fl., U.S. (brā′dĕn-tŭn)	115a	27°28′N	82°35′W
Bradfield, Eng., U.K. (brăd′fēld)	144b	51°25′N	1°08′W
Bradford, Eng., U.K. (brăd′fērd)	146	53°47′N	1°44′W
Bradford, Oh., U.S.	98	40°10′N	84°30′W
Bradford, Pa., U.S.	99	42°00′N	78°40′W
Bradley, Il., U.S. (brăd′lĭ)	101a	41°09′N	87°52′W
Bradner, Can. (brăd′nēr)	106d	49°05′N	122°26′W
Bradshaw, Eng., U.K.	237b	53°36′N	2°24′W
Brady, Tx., U.S. (brā′dĭ)	112	31°09′N	99°21′W
Braga, Port. (brä′gä)	148	41°20′N	8°25′W
Bragado, Arg. (brä-gä′dō)	132	35°07′S	60°28′W
Bragança, Braz. (brä-gän′sä)	131	1°02′S	46°50′W
Bragança, Port.	158	41°48′N	6°46′W
Bragança Paulista, Braz. (brä-gän′sä-pä′ōō-lē′s-tȧ)	132	22°58′S	46°31′W
Bragg Creek, Can. (brăg)	83e	50°57′N	114°35′W
Brahmaputra, r., Asia (brä′mȧ-pōō′trȧ)	183	26°45′N	92°45′E
Brāhui, mts., Pak.	183	28°32′N	66°15′E
Braidwood, Il., U.S. (brād′wo͝od)	101a	41°16′N	88°13′W
Brăila, Rom. (brē′ēlȧ)	142	45°15′N	27°58′E
Brainerd, Mn., U.S. (brān′ērd)	103	46°20′N	94°09′W
Braintree, Ma., U.S. (brān′trē)	93a	42°14′N	71°00′W
Braithwaite, La., U.S. (brīth′wīt)	100d	29°52′N	89°57′W
Brakpan, S. Afr. (brăk′păn)	213b	26°15′S	28°22′E
Bralorne, Can. (brā′lôrn)	87	50°47′N	122°49′W
Bramalea, Can.	83d	43°48′N	79°41′W
Bramhall, Eng., U.K.	237b	53°22′N	2°10′W
Brampton, Can. (brămp′tŭn)	91	43°41′N	79°46′W
Branca, Pedra, mtn., Braz. (pĕ′drä-brä′N-kä)	132b	22°55′S	43°28′W
Branchville, N.J., U.S. (brȧnch′vĭl)	100a	41°09′N	74°44′W
Branchville, S.C., U.S.	115	33°17′N	80°48′W
Branco, r., Braz. (bräŋ′kō)	131	2°21′N	60°38′W
Brandberg, mtn., Nmb.	212	21°15′S	14°15′E
Brandenburg, Ger. (brän′dĕn-bo͝orgh)	147	52°25′N	12°33′E
Brandenburg, hist. reg., Ger.	154	52°12′N	13°31′E
Brandfort, S. Afr. (brăn′d-fôrt)	218d	28°42′S	26°29′E
Brandon, Can. (brăn′dŭn)	84	49°50′N	99°57′W
Brandon, Vt., U.S.	99	43°45′N	73°05′W
Brandon Mountain, mtn., Ire. (brăn-dŏn)	150	52°15′N	10°12′W
Brandywine, Md., U.S. (brăndĭ′wīn)	100e	38°42′N	76°51′W
Branford, Ct., U.S. (brăn′fērd)	99	41°15′N	72°50′W
Braniewo, Pol. (brä-nyĕ′vō)	155	54°23′N	19°50′E
Brańsk, Pol. (brän′ sk)	155	52°44′N	22°51′E
Branson, Mo., U.S.	111	36°39′N	93°13′W
Brantford, Can. (brănt′fērd)	91	43°09′N	80°17′W
Bras d'Or Lake, l., Can. (brä-dôr′)	93	45°52′N	60°50′W
Brasília, Braz. (brä-sē′lvä)	131	15°49′S	47°39′W
Brasília Legal, Braz.	131	3°45′S	55°46′W
Brasópolis, Braz. (brä-sō′pō-lēs)	129a	22°30′S	45°36′W
Braşov, Rom.	149	45°39′N	25°35′E
Brass, Nig. (brăs)	210	4°28′N	6°28′E
Brasschaat, Bel. (bräs′ĸät)	145a	51°19′N	4°30′E
Bratcevo, neigh., Russia	239b	55°51′N	37°24′E
Bratenahl, Oh., U.S. (brä′tĕn-ôl)	101d	41°34′N	81°36′W
Bratislava, Slvk. (brä′tĭs-lä-vä)	142	48°09′N	17°07′E
Bratsk, Russia (brätsk)	165	56°10′N	102°04′E
Bratskoye Vodokhranilishche, res., Russia	165	56°10′N	102°05′E
Bratslav, Ukr. (brät′slȧf)	163	48°48′N	28°59′E
Brattleboro, Vt., U.S. (brăt′′l-bŭr-ō)	99	42°50′N	72°35′W
Braunau, Aus. (brou′nou)	154	48°15′N	13°05′E
Braunschweig, Ger. (broun′shvīgh)	147	52°16′N	10°32′E
Bråviken, r., Swe.	152	58°40′N	16°40′E
Brawley, Ca., U.S. (brô′lĭ)	96	32°59′N	115°32′W
Bray, Ire. (brā)	150	53°10′N	6°05′W
Braybrook, Austl.	243b	37°47′S	144°51′E
Braymer, Mo., U.S. (brā′mēr)	111	39°34′N	93°47′W
Brays Bay, Tx., U.S. (brās′bī′yōō)	113a	29°41′N	95°33′W
Brazeau, r., Can.	87	52°55′N	116°10′W
Brazeau, Mount, mtn., Can. (brä-zō′)	87	52°33′N	117°21′W
Brazil, In., U.S. (brȧ-zĭl′)	98	39°30′N	87°00′W
Brazil, nation, S.A.	131	9°00′S	53°00′W
Brazilian Highlands, mts., Braz. (brȧ zĭl yȧn hī-lăndz)	128	14°00′S	48°00′W
Brazos, r., Tx., U.S. (brä′zōs)	96	33°10′N	98°50′W
Brazos, Clear Fork, r., Tx., U.S.	112	32°56′N	99°14′W
Brazos, Double Mountain Fork, r., Tx., U.S.	110	33°23′N	101°21′W
Brazos, Salt Fork, r., Tx., U.S. (sôlt fôrk)	110	33°20′N	101°57′W
Brazzaville, Congo (brȧ-zȧ-vĕl′)	212	4°16′S	15°17′E
Brčko, Bos. (bērch′kô)	161	44°54′N	18°46′E
Brda, r., Pol. (bēr-dä)	155	53°18′N	17°55′E
Brea, Ca., U.S. (brē′ȧ)	107a	33°55′N	117°54′W
Breakeyville, Can.	83b	46°40′N	71°13′W
Brechten, neigh., Ger.	236	51°35′N	7°28′E
Breckenridge, Mn., U.S. (brĕk′ĕn-rĭj)	102	46°17′N	96°35′W
Breckenridge, Tx., U.S.	112	32°46′N	98°53′W
Breckerfeld, Ger.	236	51°16′N	7°28′E
Brecksville, Oh., U.S. (brĕks′vĭl)	101d	41°19′N	81°38′W
Břeclav, Czech Rep. (brzhĕl′láf)	154	48°46′N	16°54′E
Breda, Neth. (brā-dä′)	151	51°35′N	4°47′E
Bredasdorp, S. Afr. (brä′das-dôrp)	212	34°15′S	20°00′E
Bredbury, Eng., U.K.	237b	53°25′N	2°06′W
Bredell, S. Afr.	244b	26°05′S	28°17′E
Bredeney, neigh., Ger.	236	51°24′N	6°59′E
Bredenscheid-Stüter, Ger.	236	51°22′N	7°11′E
Bredy, Russia (brĕ′dĭ)	172a	52°25′N	60°23′E
Breezewood, Pa., U.S.	230b	40°34′N	80°03′W
Bregenz, Aus. (brā′gĕnts)	154	47°30′N	9°46′E
Bregovo, Bul. (brĕ′gô-vô)	161	44°07′N	22°45′E
Breidafjördur, b., Ice.	146	65°15′N	22°50′W
Breidbach, S. Afr. (brēd′băk)	213c	32°54′S	27°26′E
Breil-sur-Roya, Fr. (brĕ′y′)	157	43°57′N	7°36′E
Breitscheid, Ger.	236	51°22′N	6°52′E
Brejo, Braz. (brȧ′zhō)	131	3°33′S	42°46′W
Bremangerlandet, i., Nor.	152	61°51′N	4°25′E
Bremen, Ger. (brā-mĕn)	142	53°05′N	8°50′E
Bremen, In., U.S. (brē′mĕn)	98	41°25′N	86°05′W
Bremerhaven, Ger. (brām-ēr-hä′fĕn)	146	53°33′N	8°38′E
Bremerton, Wa., U.S. (brĕm′ēr-tŭn)	104	47°34′N	122°38′W
Bremervörde, Ger. (brĕ′mĕr-fûr-dĕ)	145c	53°29′N	9°09′E
Bremner, Can. (brĕm′nēr)	83g	53°34′N	113°14′W
Bremond, Tx., U.S. (brĕm′ŭnd)	113	31°11′N	96°40′W
Breña, Peru	233c	12°04′S	77°04′W
Brenham, Tx., U.S. (brĕn′ăm)	113	30°10′N	96°24′W
Bren Mar Park, Md., U.S.	229d	38°48′N	77°09′W
Brenner Pass, p., Eur. (brĕn′ēr)	147	47°00′N	11°30′E
Brentford, neigh., Eng., U.K.	235	51°29′N	0°18′W
Brenthurst, S. Afr.	244b	26°16′S	28°23′E
Brentwood, Eng., U.K. (brĕnt′wo͝od)	151	51°37′N	0°18′E
Brentwood, Md., U.S.	99	39°00′N	76°55′W
Brentwood, Mo., U.S.	107e	38°37′N	90°21′W
Brentwood, Pa., U.S.	101e	40°22′N	79°59′W
Brentwood Heights, neigh., Ca., U.S.	232	34°04′N	118°30′W
Brentwood Park, S. Afr.	244b	26°08′S	28°18′E
Brescia, Italy (brā′shä)	148	45°33′N	10°15′E
Bressanone, Italy (brĕs-sä-nō′nä)	160	46°42′N	11°40′E
Bresso, Italy	238c	45°32′N	9°11′E
Bressuire, Fr. (grĕ-swēr′)	156	46°49′N	0°14′W
Brest, Bela.	164	52°06′N	23°43′E
Brest, Fr. (brĕst)	142	48°24′N	4°30′W
Brest, prov., Bela.	162	52°30′N	26°50′E
Bretagne, hist. reg., Fr. (brĕ-täN′yĕ)	156	48°00′N	3°00′W
Breton, Pertuis, strt., Fr. (pâr-twē′brĕ-tôN′)	156	46°18′N	1°43′W
Breton Sound, strt., La., U.S. (brĕt′ŭn)	114	29°38′N	89°15′W
Breukelen, Neth.	145a	52°09′N	5°00′E
Brevard, N.C., U.S. (brē-värd′)	115	35°14′N	82°45′W
Breves, Braz. (brā′vĕzh)	131	1°32′S	50°13′W
Brevik, Nor. (brĕ′vĕk)	152	59°04′N	9°39′E
Brewarrina, Austl. (brōō-ēr-rē′nȧ)	203	29°54′S	146°50′E
Brewer, Me., U.S. (brōō′ēr)	92	44°46′N	68°46′W
Brewerville, Lib.	214	6°26′N	10°47′W
Brewster, N.Y., U.S. (brōō′stēr)	100a	41°23′N	73°38′W
Brewster, Cerro, mtn., Pan. (sĕ′r-rō-brōō′stēr)	121	9°19′N	79°15′W
Brewton, Al., U.S. (brōō′tŭn)	114	31°06′N	87°04′W
Brežice, Slvn. (brĕ′zhē-tsĕ)	160	45°55′N	15°37′E
Breznik, Bul. (brĕs′nĕk)	161	42°44′N	22°55′E
Briancon, Fr. (brē-äN-sôN′)	157	44°54′N	6°39′E
Briare, Fr. (brē-är′)	156	47°40′N	2°46′E
Bridal Veil, Or., U.S. (brīd′ȧl vāl)	106c	45°33′N	122°10′W
Bridge Point, c., Bah. (brĭj)	122	25°35′N	76°40′W
Bridgeport, Al., U.S. (brĭj′pôrt)	114	34°55′N	85°42′W
Bridgeport, Ct., U.S.	97	41°12′N	73°12′W
Bridgeport, Il., U.S.	98	38°40′N	87°45′W
Bridgeport, Ne., U.S.	102	41°40′N	103°06′W

268 Bridgeport - Bulalacao

PLACE (Pronunciation)	PAGE	LAT.	LONG.
Bridgeport, Oh., U.S.	98	40°00'N	80°45'W
Bridgeport, Pa., U.S.	100f	40°06'N	75°21'W
Bridgeport, Tx., U.S.	111	33°13'N	97°46'W
Bridgeport, neigh., Il., U.S.	231a	41°51'N	87°39'W
Bridgeton, Al., U.S. (brĭj'tŭn)	100h	33°27'N	86°39'W
Bridgeton, Mo., U.S.	107e	38°45'N	90°23'W
Bridgeton, N.J., U.S.	99	39°30'N	75°15'W
Bridgetown, Barb. (brĭj' toun)	117	13°08'N	59°37'W
Bridgetown, Can.	92	44°51'N	65°18'W
Bridgeview, Il., U.S.	231a	41°45'N	87°48'W
Bridgeville, Pa., U.S. (brĭj'vĭl)	101e	40°22'N	80°07'W
Bridgewater, Austl. (brĭj'wô-tẽr)	204	42°50'S	147°28'E
Bridgewater, Can.	85	44°23'N	64°31'W
Bridgnorth, Eng., U.K. (brĭj'nôrth)	144a	52°32'N	2°25'W
Bridgton, Me., U.S. (brĭj'tŭn)	92	44°04'N	70°45'W
Bridlington, Eng., U.K. (brĭd'lĭng-tŭn)	150	54°06'N	0°10'W
Brie-Comte-Robert, Fr. (brē-kônt-ĕ-rō-bâr')	157b	48°42'N	2°37'E
Brielle, Neth.	145a	51°54'N	4°08'E
Brierfield, Eng., U.K. (brī'ẽr fēld)	144a	53°49'N	2°14'W
Brierfield, Al., U.S. (brī'ẽr-fēld)	114	33°01'N	86°55'W
Brier Island, i., Can. (brī'ẽr)	92	44°16'N	66°24'W
Brieselang, Ger. (brē'zĕ-läng)	145b	52°36'N	12°59'E
Briey, Fr. (brē-ĕ')	157	49°15'N	5°57'E
Brig, Switz. (brēg)	147	46°17'N	7°59'E
Brigg, Eng., U.K. (brĭg)	144a	53°33'N	0°29'W
Brigham City, Ut., U.S. (brĭg'ăm)	107b	41°31'N	112°01'W
Brighouse, Eng., U.K. (brĭg'hous)	144a	53°42'N	1°47'W
Bright, Austl. (brīt)	204	36°43'S	147°00'E
Bright, In., U.S. (brīt)	101f	39°13'N	84°51'W
Brightlingsea, Eng., U.K. (brī't-lĭng-sē)	144b	51°50'N	1°00'E
Brightmoor, neigh., Mi., U.S.	230c	42°24'N	83°14'W
Brighton, Austl.	201a	37°55'S	145°00'E
Brighton, Eng., U.K.	147	50°47'N	0°07'W
Brighton, Al., U.S. (brīt'ŭn)	100h	33°27'N	86°56'W
Brighton, Co., U.S.	110	39°58'N	104°49'W
Brighton, Il., U.S.	107e	39°03'N	90°08'W
Brighton, Ia., U.S.	103	41°11'N	91°47'W
Brighton, neigh., Ma., U.S.	227a	42°21'N	71°08'W
Brighton Indian Reservation, I.R., Fl., U.S.	115a	27°05'N	81°25'W
Brighton Le-Sands, Austl.	243a	33°58'S	151°09'E
Brightwood, neigh., D.C., U.S.	229d	38°58'N	77°02'W
Brigittenau, neigh., Aus.	239e	48°14'N	16°22'E
Brihuega, Spain (brê-wā'gä)	158	40°32'N	2°52'W
Brilyn Park, Va., U.S.	229d	38°54'N	77°10'W
Brimley, Mi., U.S. (brĭm'lē)	107k	46°24'N	84°34'W
Brindisi, Italy (brēn'dē-zē)	142	40°38'N	17°57'E
Brinje, Cro. (brēn'yĕ)	160	45°00'N	15°08'E
Brinkleigh, Md., U.S.	229c	39°18'N	76°50'W
Brinkley, Ar., U.S. (brĭŋk'lĭ)	111	34°52'N	91°12'W
Brinnon, Wa., U.S. (brĭn'ŭn)	106a	47°41'N	122°54'W
Brion, i., Can. (brē-ôn')	93	47°47'N	61°29'W
Brioude, Fr. (brē-ōōd')	156	45°18'N	3°22'E
Brisbane, Austl. (brĭz'bān)	204	27°30'S	153°10'E
Brisbane, Ca., U.S.	231b	37°41'N	122°24'W
Bristol, Eng., U.K.	147	51°29'N	2°39'W
Bristol, Ct., U.S. (brĭs'tŭl)	99	41°40'N	72°55'W
Bristol, Pa., U.S.	100f	40°06'N	74°51'W
Bristol, R.I., U.S.	100b	41°41'N	71°14'W
Bristol, Tn., U.S.	97	36°35'N	82°10'W
Bristol, Vt., U.S.	99	44°10'N	73°00'W
Bristol, Va., U.S.	97	36°36'N	82°00'W
Bristol, Wi., U.S.	101a	42°32'N	88°04'W
Bristol Bay, b., Ak., U.S.	95	58°05'N	158°54'W
Bristol Channel, strt., Eng., U.K.	147	51°20'N	3°47'W
Bristow, Ok., U.S. (brĭs'tō)	111	35°50'N	96°25'W
British Columbia, prov., Can. (brĭt'ĭsh kŏl'ŭm-bĭ-ȧ)	84	56°00'N	124°53'W
British Indian Ocean Territory, dep., Afr.	2	7°00'S	72°00'E
British Isles, is., Eur.	142	54°00'N	4°00'W
Brits, S. Afr.	218d	25°39'S	27°47'E
Britstown, S. Afr. (brĭts'toun)	212	30°30'S	23°40'E
Britt, Ia., U.S. (brĭt)	103	43°05'N	93°47'W
Brittany see Bretagne, hist. reg., Fr.	156	48°00'N	3°00'W
Britton, S.D., U.S. (brĭt'ŭn)	102	45°47'N	97°44'W
Brive-la-Gaillarde, Fr. (brēv-lä-gī-yärd'ĕ)	147	45°10'N	1°31'E
Briviesca, Spain (brê-vyās'kȧ)	158	42°34'N	3°21'W
Brno, Czech Rep. (b'r'nô)	142	49°18'N	16°37'E
Broa, Ensenada de la, b., Cuba	122	22°30'N	82°00'W
Broach, India	186	21°47'N	72°58'E
Broad, r., Ga., U.S. (brôd)	114	34°15'N	83°14'W
Broad, r., N.C., U.S.	115	35°38'N	82°40'W
Broadheath, Eng., U.K.	237b	53°24'N	2°21'W
Broadley Common, Eng., U.K.	235	51°45'N	0°04'E
Broadmeadows, Austl. (brôd'mĕd-ōz)	201a	37°40'S	144°53'E
Broadmoor, Ca., U.S.	231b	37°41'N	122°29'W
Broadview Heights, Oh., U.S. (brôd'vū)	101d	41°18'N	81°41'W
Brockenscheidt, Ger.	236	51°38'N	7°25'E
Brockport, N.Y., U.S. (brŏk'pōrt)	99	43°15'N	77°55'W
Brockton, Ma., U.S. (brŏk'tŭn)	93a	42°04'N	71°01'W
Brockville, Can. (brŏk'vĭl)	85	44°35'N	75°40'W
Brockway, Mt., U.S. (brŏk'wā)	105	47°24'N	105°41'W
Brodnica, Pol. (brôd'nĭt-sȧ)	155	53°16'N	19°26'E
Brody, Ukr. (brô'dĭ)	167	50°05'N	25°10'E
Broich, neigh., Ger.	236	51°25'N	6°51'E
Broken Arrow, Ok., U.S. (brō'kĕn ăr'ō)	111	36°03'N	95°48'W
Broken Bay, b., Austl.	204	33°34'S	151°20'E
Broken Bow, Ne., U.S. (brō'kĕn bō)	102	41°24'N	99°37'W
Broken Bow, Ok., U.S.	111	34°02'N	94°43'W
Broken Hill, Austl. (brōk'ĕn)	203	31°55'S	141°35'E
Broken Hill see Kabwe, Zam.	212	14°27'S	28°27'E
Bromall, Pa., U.S.	229b	39°59'N	75°22'W
Bromborough, Eng., U.K.	237a	53°19'N	2°59'W
Bromley, Eng., U.K. (brŭm'lĭ)	144b	51°23'N	0°01'E
Bromley Common, neigh., Eng., U.K.	235	51°22'N	0°03'E
Bromptonville, Can. (brŭmp'tŭn-vĭl)	91	45°30'N	72°00'W
Brønderslev, Den. (brûn'dẽr-slĕv)	152	57°15'N	9°56'E
Bronkhorstspruit, S. Afr.	218d	25°50'S	28°48'E
Bronnitsy, Russia (brô-nyĭ'tsĭ)	162	55°26'N	38°16'E
Bronson, Mi., U.S. (brŏn'sŭn)	98	41°55'N	85°15'W
Bronte Creek, r., Can.	83d	43°25'N	79°53'W
Bronx, neigh., N.Y., U.S.	228	40°49'N	73°56'W
Bronxville, N.Y., U.S.	228	40°56'N	73°50'W
Brood, r., S.C., U.S. (brōōd)	115	34°46'N	81°25'W
Brookfield, Il., U.S. (brŏŏk'fēld)	101a	41°49'N	87°51'W
Brookfield, Mo., U.S.	111	39°45'N	93°04'W
Brookhaven, Ga., U.S. (brŏŏk'hāv'n)	100c	33°52'N	84°21'W
Brookhaven, Ms., U.S.	114	31°35'N	90°26'W
Brookhaven, Pa., U.S.	229b	39°52'N	75°23'W
Brookings, Or., U.S. (brŏŏk'ĭngs)	104	42°04'N	124°16'W
Brookings, S.D., U.S.	102	44°18'N	96°47'W
Brookland, neigh., D.C., U.S.	229d	38°56'N	76°59'W
Brooklandville, Md., U.S.	229c	39°26'N	76°41'W
Brooklawn, N.J., U.S.	229b	39°53'N	75°08'W
Brookline, Ma., U.S. (brŏŏk'lĭn)	93a	42°20'N	71°08'W
Brookline, N.H., U.S.	93a	42°44'N	71°37'W
Brooklyn, Oh., U.S. (brŏŏk'lĭn)	101d	41°26'N	81°44'W
Brooklyn, neigh., Md., U.S.	229c	39°14'N	76°36'W
Brooklyn Center, Mn., U.S.	107g	45°05'N	93°21'W
Brooklyn Heights, Oh., U.S.	229a	41°24'N	81°40'W
Brooklyn Park, Md., U.S.	229c	39°14'N	76°36'W
Brookmans Park, Eng., U.K.	235	51°43'N	0°12'W
Brookmont, Md., U.S.	229d	38°57'N	77°07'W
Brook Park, Oh., U.S. (brŏŏk)	101d	41°24'N	81°50'W
Brooks, Can.	87	50°35'N	111°53'W
Brooks Range, mts., Ak., U.S. (brŏŏks)	94a	68°20'N	159°00'W
Brook Street, Eng., U.K.	235	51°37'N	0°17'E
Brooksville, Fl., U.S. (brŏŏks'vĭl)	115a	28°32'N	82°28'W
Brookvale, Austl.	243a	33°46'S	151°17'E
Brookville, In., U.S. (brŏŏk'vĭl)	98	39°20'N	85°00'W
Brookville, Ma., U.S.	227a	42°08'N	71°01'W
Brookville, N.Y., U.S.	228	40°49'N	73°35'W
Brookville, Pa., U.S.	99	41°10'N	79°00'W
Brookwood, Al., U.S. (brŏŏk'wŏŏd)	114	33°15'N	87°17'W
Broome, Austl. (brōōm)	202	18°00'S	122°15'E
Brossard, Can.	83a	45°26'N	73°28'W
Brothers, is., Bah. (brŭd'hẽrs)	122	26°05'N	79°00'W
Broughton, Pa., U.S.	230b	40°21'N	79°59'W
Broumov, Czech Rep. (brōō'môf)	154	50°33'N	15°55'E
Brou-sur-Chantereine, Fr.	237c	48°53'N	2°38'E
Brown Bank, bk.	123	21°30'N	74°35'W
Brownfield, Tx., U.S. (broun'fēld)	110	33°11'N	102°16'W
Browning, Mt., U.S. (broun'ĭng)	105	48°37'N	113°05'W
Brownsboro, Ky., U.S. (brounz'bŏ-rô)	101h	38°22'N	85°30'W
Brownsburg, Can. (brouns'bûrg)	83a	45°40'N	74°24'W
Brownsburg, In., U.S.	101g	39°51'N	86°23'W
Brownsmead, Or., U.S. (brounz'-mēd)	106c	46°13'N	123°33'W
Brownstown, In., U.S. (brounz'toun)	98	38°50'N	86°00'W
Brownsville, Pa., U.S. (brounz'vĭl)	101e	40°01'N	79°53'W
Brownsville, Tn., U.S.	114	35°35'N	89°15'W
Brownsville, Tx., U.S.	96	25°55'N	97°30'W
Brownville Junction, Me., U.S. (broun'vĭl)	92	45°20'N	69°04'W
Brownwood, Tx., U.S. (broun'wŏŏd)	96	31°44'N	98°58'W
Brownwood, l., Tx., U.S.	112	31°55'N	99°15'W
Broxbourne, Eng., U.K.	235	51°45'N	0°01'W
Brozas, Spain (brō'thäs)	158	39°37'N	6°44'W
Bruce, Mount, mtn., Austl. (brōōs)	202	22°35'S	118°15'E
Bruce Peninsula, pen., Can.	90	44°50'N	81°20'W
Bruceton, Tn., U.S. (brōōs'tŭn)	114	36°02'N	88°14'W
Bruchmühle, Ger.	238a	52°33'N	13°47'E
Bruchsal, Ger. (brŏŏk'zäl)	154	49°08'N	8°34'E
Bruck, Aus.	154	48°01'N	16°47'E
Bruck, Aus. (brŏŏk)	154	47°25'N	15°14'E
Brück, Ger. (brük)	145b	52°12'N	12°45'E
Bruckhausen, neigh., Ger.	236	51°29'N	6°44'E
Bruderheim, Can. (brōō'dẽr-hīm)	83g	53°47'N	112°56'W
Brugge, Bel.	147	51°13'N	3°05'E
Brügge, Ger.	236	51°13'N	7°34'E
Brugherio, Italy	238c	45°33'N	9°18'E
Brühl, Ger. (brül)	157c	50°49'N	6°54'E
Bruneau, r., Id., U.S. (brōō-nō')	104	42°47'N	115°43'W
Brunei, nation, Asia (brŏŏ-nī')	196	4°52'N	113°38'E
Brünen, Ger. (brü'nĕn)	157c	51°43'N	6°41'E
Brunete, Spain (brōō-nā'tā)	159a	40°24'N	4°00'W
Brunette, i., Can. (brŏŏ-nĕt')	93	47°16'N	55°54'W
Brunn am Gebirge, Aus. (brōōn'äm gĕ-bĭr'gĕ)	145e	48°07'N	16°18'E
Brunoy, Fr.	237c	48°42'N	2°30'E
Brunsbüttel, Ger. (brŏŏns'büt-tĕl)	145c	53°58'N	9°10'E
Brunswick, Austl.	243b	37°46'S	144°58'E
Brunswick, Ga., U.S. (brŭnz'wĭk)	97	31°08'N	81°30'W
Brunswick, Me., U.S.	92	43°54'N	69°57'W
Brunswick, Md., U.S.	99	39°20'N	77°35'W
Brunswick, Mo., U.S.	111	39°25'N	93°07'W
Brunswick, Oh., U.S.	101d	41°14'N	81°50'W
Brunswick, Peninsula de, pen., Chile	132	53°25'S	71°15'W
Bruny, i., Austl. (brōō'nē)	203	43°30'S	147°50'E
Brush, Co., U.S. (brŭsh)	110	40°14'N	103°40'W
Brusque, Braz. (brōō's-kōōĕ)	132	27°15'S	48°45'W
Brussels, Bel.	142	50°51'N	4°21'E
Brussels, Il., U.S. (brŭs'ĕls)	107e	38°57'N	90°36'W
Bruxelles see Brussels, Bel.	142	50°51'N	4°21'E
Bryan, Oh., U.S. (brī'ăn)	98	41°25'N	84°30'W
Bryan, Tx., U.S.	113	30°40'N	96°22'W
Bryansk, Russia	164	53°15'N	34°22'E
Bryansk, prov., Russia	162	52°43'N	32°25'E
Bryant, S.D., U.S. (brī'ănt)	102	44°35'N	97°29'W
Bryant, Wa., U.S.	106a	48°14'N	122°10'W
Bryce Canyon National Park, rec., Ut., U.S. (brīs)	96	37°35'N	112°15'W
Bryn Mawr, Pa., U.S. (brĭn mår')	100f	40°02'N	75°20'W
Bryson City, N.C., U.S. (brīs'ŭn)	114	35°25'N	83°25'W
Bryukhovetskaya, Russia (b'ryŭk'ô-vyĕt-skä'yä)	163	45°56'N	38°58'E
Buala, Sol. Is.	198e	8°08'S	159°35'E
Buatan, Indon.	181b	0°45'N	101°49'E
Buba, Gui.-B. (bōō'bȧ)	210	11°39'N	14°58'W
Buc, Fr.	237c	48°46'N	2°08'E
Bucaramanga, Col. (bōō-kä'rä-mäŋ'gä)	130	7°12'N	73°14'W
Buccaneer Archipelago, is., Austl. (bŭk-ȧ-nēr')	202	16°05'S	122°00'E
Buch, neigh., Ger.	238a	52°38'N	13°30'E
Buchach, Ukr. (bŏŏ'chȧch)	155	49°04'N	25°25'E
Buchanan, Lib. (bů-kăn'ăn)	210	5°57'N	10°02'W
Buchanan, Mi., U.S.	98	41°50'N	86°25'W
Buchanan, l., Austl. (bû-kân'nŏn)	203	21°40'S	145°00'E
Buchanan, l., Tx., U.S. (bû-kăn'ăn)	112	30°55'N	98°40'W
Buchans, Can.	93	48°49'N	56°52'W
Bucharest, Rom.	142	44°23'N	26°10'E
Buchholz, Ger. (bōōk'hôltz)	145c	53°19'N	9°53'E
Buchholz, Ger.	238a	52°35'N	13°47'E
Buchholz, neigh., Ger.	236	51°23'N	6°46'E
Buchholz, neigh., Ger.	238a	52°36'N	13°26'E
Buck Creek, r., In., U.S. (bŭk)	101g	39°43'N	85°58'W
Buckhannon, W.V., U.S. (bŭk-hăn'ŭn)	98	39°00'N	80°10'W
Buckhaven, Scot., U.K. (bŭk-hā'v'n)	150	56°10'N	3°10'W
Buckhorn Island State Park, pt. of i., N.Y., U.S.	230a	43°03'N	78°59'W
Buckie, Scot., U.K. (bŭk'ĭ)	150	57°40'N	2°50'W
Buckingham, Can. (bŭk'ĭng-ăm)	83c	45°35'N	75°25'W
Buckingham, can., India (bŭk'ĭng-ăm)	187	15°18'N	79°50'E
Buckingham Palace, pt. of i., Eng., U.K.	235	51°30'N	0°08'W
Buckinghamshire, co., Eng., U.K.	144b	51°45'N	0°48'W
Buckland, Can. (bŭk'lănd)	83b	46°37'N	70°33'W
Buckland Tableland, reg., Austl.	203	24°31'S	148°00'E
Buckley, Wa., U.S. (buk'lē)	106a	47°10'N	122°02'W
Buckow, neigh., Ger.	238a	52°25'N	13°26'E
Bucksport, Me., U.S. (bŭks'pôrt)	92	44°35'N	68°47'W
Buctouche, Can. (bük-tōōsh')	92	46°28'N	64°43'W
Bucun, China (bōō-tsŏn)	190	36°38'N	117°26'E
București see Bucharest, Rom.	142	44°23'N	26°10'E
Bucyrus, Oh., U.S. (bû-sī'rŭs)	98	40°50'N	82°55'W
Buda, neigh., Hung.	239g	47°30'N	19°02'E
Budakeszi, Hung.	239g	47°31'N	18°56'E
Budaörs, Hung.	239g	47°27'N	18°58'E
Budapest, Hung. (bōō'dá-pĕsht')	142	47°30'N	19°05'E
Budberg, Ger.	236	51°32'N	6°38'E
Büderich, Ger.	236	51°37'N	6°34'E
Budge Budge, India	186a	22°28'N	88°08'E
Budjala, D.R.C.	216	2°39'N	19°42'E
Budyonnovsk, Russia	168	44°46'N	44°09'E
Buea, Cam.	215	4°09'N	9°14'E
Buechel, Ky., U.S. (bĕ-chûl')	101h	38°12'N	85°38'W
Bueil, Fr. (bwā')	157b	48°55'N	1°27'E
Buena Park, Ca., U.S. (bwā'nȧ pärk)	107a	33°52'N	118°00'W
Buenaventura, Col. (bwä'nä-vĕn-tōō'rȧ)	130	3°46'N	77°09'W
Buenaventura, Cuba	123a	22°53'N	82°22'W
Buenaventura, Bahía de, b., Col.	130	3°45'N	79°23'W
Buena Vista, Co., U.S. (bū'nȧ vĭs'tȧ)	110	38°51'N	106°07'W
Buena Vista, Ga., U.S.	114	32°15'N	84°30'W
Buena Vista, Va., U.S.	99	37°45'N	79°20'W
Buena Vista, Bahía, b., Cuba (bä-ē'ä-bwĕ-nä-vē's-tä)	122	22°30'N	79°10'W
Buena Vista Lake Bed, l., Ca., U.S. (bū'nȧ vĭs'tȧ)	108	35°14'N	119°17'W
Buendia, Embalse de, res., Spain	158	40°30'N	2°45'W
Buenos Aires, Arg. (bwā'nōs ī'rās)	132	34°20'S	58°30'W
Buenos Aires, Col.	130a	3°01'N	76°34'W
Buenos Aires, C.R.	121	9°10'N	83°21'W
Buenos Aires, prov., Arg.	132	36°15'S	61°45'W
Buenos Aires, l., S.A.	132	46°30'S	72°15'W
Buer, neigh., Ger.	236	51°36'N	7°03'E
Buffalo, Mn., U.S. (buf'ȧ lō)	103	45°10'N	93°50'W
Buffalo, N.Y., U.S.	97	42°54'N	78°51'W
Buffalo, Tx., U.S.	113	31°28'N	96°04'W
Buffalo, Wy., U.S.	105	44°19'N	106°42'W
Buffalo, r., S. Afr.	213c	28°35'S	30°27'E
Buffalo, r., Ar., U.S.	111	35°56'N	92°58'W
Buffalo, r., Tn., U.S.	114	35°24'N	87°10'W
Buffalo Bayou, Tx., U.S.	113a	29°46'N	95°32'W
Buffalo Creek, r., Mn., U.S.	103	44°46'N	94°28'W
Buffalo Harbor, b., N.Y., U.S.	230a	42°51'N	78°52'W
Buffalo Head Hills, hills, Can.	84	57°16'N	116°18'W
Buford, Can. (bū'fûrd)	83g	53°15'N	113°55'W
Buford, Ga., U.S. (bū'fẽrd)	114	34°05'N	84°00'W
Bug (Zakhidnyy Buh), r., Eur.	155	52°29'N	21°20'E
Buga, Col. (bōō'gä)	130	3°54'N	76°17'W
Buggenhout, Bel.	145a	51°01'N	4°10'E
Buglandsfjorden, l., Nor.	152	58°53'N	7°55'E
Bugojno, Bos. (bŏŏ-gō ĭ nô)	161	44°03'N	17°28'E
Bugul'ma, Russia (bŏŏ-gōl'mȧ)	164	54°40'N	52°40'E
Buguruslan, Russia (bŏŏ-gŏŏ-rŏŏs-lȧn')	164	53°30'N	52°32'E
Buhi, Phil. (bōō'ē)	197a	13°26'N	123°31'E
Buhl, Id., U.S. (būl)	105	42°36'N	114°45'W
Buhl, Mn., U.S.	103	47°28'N	92°49'W
Buin, Chile (bŏŏ-ēn')	129b	33°44'S	70°44'W
Buinaksk, Russia (bŏŏ'ē-näksk)	167	42°40'N	47°20'E
Buir Nur, l., Asia (bōō-ēr nōōr)	189	47°50'N	117°00'E
Bujalance, Spain (bōō-hä-län'thā)	158	37°54'N	4°22'W
Bujumbura, Bdi.	217	3°23'S	29°22'E
Buka Island, i., Pap. N. Gui.	198e	5°15'S	154°35'E
Bukama, D.R.C. (bōō-kä'mä)	212	9°08'S	26°00'E
Bukavu, D.R.C.	212	2°30'S	28°52'E
Bukhara, Uzb. (bŏŏ-kä'rä)	169	39°31'N	64°22'E
Bukitbatu, Indon.	181b	1°25'N	101°58'E
Bukit Panjang, Sing.	240c	1°23'N	103°46'E
Bukit Timah, Sing.	240c	1°20'N	103°47'E
Bukittinggi, Indon.	196	0°25'S	100°28'E
Bukoba, Tan.	212	1°20'S	31°49'E
Bukovina, hist. reg., Eur. (bŏŏ-kō'vĭ-nȧ)	155	48°06'N	25°20'E
Bula, Indon. (bōō'lä)	197	3°00'S	130°30'E
Bulalacao, Phil. (bōō-lȧ-lȧ'kä-ō)	197a	12°30'N	121°20'E

ăt; fĭnȧl; rāte; senȧte; ärm; ȧsk; sofȧ; fâre; ch-choose; dh-as th in other; bē; ēvent; bĕt; recĕnt; cratẽr; g-gō; gh-guttural g; bĭt; ĭ-short neutral; rīde; ĸ-guttural k as ch in German ich;

PRONOUNCING INDEX Bulawayo-Cahuacán 269

PLACE (Pronunciation)	PAGE	LAT.	LONG.
Bulawayo, Zimb. (bo͞o-lȧ-wä'yō)	212	20°12'S	28°43'E
Buldir, i., Ak., U.S. (bŭl dĭr)	95a	52°22'N	175°50'E
Bulgaria, nation, Eur. (bo̤l-gā'rĭ-ȧ)	142	42°12'N	24°13'E
Bulim, Sing.	240c	1°23'N	103°43'E
Bulkley Ranges, mts., Can. (bŭlk'lē)	86	54°30'N	127°30'W
Bullaque, r., Spain (bo̤-lä'kå)	158	39°15'N	4°13'W
Bullas, Spain (bo͞ol'yäs)	158	38°07'N	1°48'W
Bullfrog Creek, r., Ut., U.S. (bŭl'dŏg')	109	37°45'N	110°55'W
Bull Harbour, Can. (hăr'bẽr)	86	50°45'N	127°55'W
Bull Head, mtn., Jam.	122	18°10'N	77°15'W
Bull Run, r., Or., U.S. (bo̤l)	106c	45°26'N	122°11'W
Bull Run Reservoir, res., Or., U.S.	106c	45°29'N	122°11'W
Bull Shoals Reservoir, res., U.S. (bo̤l shōlz)	97	36°35'N	92°57'W
Bulmke-Hüllen, neigh., Ger.	236	51°31'N	7°06'E
Bulpham, Eng., U.K. (bo͞ol'făn)	144b	51°33'N	0°21'E
Bultfontein, S. Afr. (bo̤lt'fŏn-tān')	218d	28°18'S	26°10'E
Bulun, Russia (bo͞o-lo̤n')	165	70°48'N	127°27'E
Bulungu, D.R.C. (bo͞o-lo̤ŋ'go͞o)	216	6°04'S	21°54'E
Bulwer, S. Afr. (bo̤l-wẽr)	213c	29°49'S	29°48'E
Bumba, D.R.C. (bo̤m'bȧ)	211	2°11'N	22°28'E
Bumbire Island, i., Tan.	217	1°40'S	32°05'E
Bumbles Green, Eng., U.K.	235	51°44'N	0°02'E
Buna, Pap. N. Gui. (bo͞o'nȧ)	197	8°58'S	148°38'E
Bunbury, Austl. (bŭn'bŭrĭ)	202	33°25'S	115°45'E
Bundaberg, Austl. (bŭn'dȧ-bûrg)	203	24°45'S	152°18'E
Bundoora, Austl. (Chan.)	243b	37°42'S	145°04'E
Bunguran Utara, Kepulauan, is., Indon.	196	3°22'N	108°00'E
Bunia, D.R.C.	217	1°34'N	30°15'E
Bunker Hill, Il., U.S. (bŭnk'ẽr hĭl)	107e	39°03'N	89°57'W
Bunker Hill Monument, pt. of i., Ma., U.S.	227a	42°22'N	71°04'W
Bunkie, La., U.S. (bŭŋ'kĭ)	113	30°55'N	92°10'W
Bun Plains, pl., Kenya	217	0°55'N	40°35'E
Bununu Dass, Nig.	215	10°00'N	9°31'E
Buona Vista, Sing.	240c	1°16'N	103°47'E
Buor-Khaya, Guba, b., Russia	171	71°45'N	131°00'E
Buor Khaya, Mys, c., Russia	165	71°47'N	133°22'E
Bura, Kenya	217	1°06'S	39°57'E
Buraydah, Sau. Ar.	182	26°23'N	44°14'E
Burbank, Ca., U.S. (bûr'bănk)	107a	34°11'N	118°19'W
Burco, Som.	218a	9°20'N	45°45'E
Burdekin, r., Austl. (bûr'dē-kĭn)	203	19°22'S	145°07'E
Burdur, Tur. (bo͞or-do̤r')	149	37°50'N	30°15'E
Burdwān, India (bo̤d-wän')	183	23°29'N	87°53'E
Bureinskiy, Khrebet, mts., Russia	165	51°15'N	133°30'E
Bures-sur-Yvette, Fr.	237c	48°42'N	2°10'E
Bureya, Russia (bo̤rā'ȧ)	165	49°55'N	130°00'E
Bureya, r., Russia (bo̤-rā'yä)	171	51°00'N	131°15'E
Burford, Eng., U.K. (bûr-fẽrd)	144b	51°46'N	1°38'W
Burg, Ger.	236	51°08'N	7°09'E
Burgas, Bul. (bo̤r-gäs')	149	42°29'N	27°30'E
Burgas, Gulf of, b., Bul.	149	42°30'N	27°40'E
Burgaw, N.C., U.S. (bûr'gô)	115	34°31'N	77°56'W
Burgdorf, Switz. (bo̤rg'dôrf)	154	47°04'N	7°37'E
Burgenland, prov., Aus.	145e	47°58'N	16°57'E
Burgeo, Can.	93	47°36'N	57°34'W
Burger Township, S. Afr.	244b	26°05'S	27°46'E
Burgess, Va., U.S.	99	37°53'N	76°21'W
Burgh Heath, Eng., U.K.	235	51°18'N	0°13'W
Burgo de Osma, Spain	158	41°35'N	3°02'W
Burgos, Mex. (bo̤r'gōs)	112	24°57'N	98°47'W
Burgos, Phil.	197a	16°03'N	119°52'E
Burgos, Spain (bo͞o'r-gôs)	148	42°20'N	3°44'W
Burgsvik, Swe. (bo̤rgs'vĭk)	152	57°04'N	18°18'E
Burhānpur, India (bo̤r'hän-po͞or)	183	21°26'N	76°08'E
Burholme, neigh., Pa., U.S.	229b	40°03'N	75°05'W
Burias Island, i., Phil. (bo͞o'rē-äs)	197a	12°56'N	122°56'E
Burias Pass, strt., Phil. (bo͞o'rē-äs)	197a	13°04'N	123°11'E
Burica, Punta, c., N.A. (po͞o'n-tä-bo͞o'rē-kä)	121	8°02'N	83°12'W
Burien, Wa., U.S. (bū'rĭ-ĕn)	106a	47°28'N	122°20'W
Burin, Can. (bûr'ĭn)	85a	47°02'N	55°10'W
Burin Peninsula, pen., Can.	93	47°00'N	55°40'W
Burkburnett, Tx., U.S. (bûrk-bûr'nĕt)	110	34°04'N	98°35'W
Burke, Vt., U.S. (bûrk)	99	44°40'N	72°00'W
Burke Channel, strt., Can.	86	52°07'N	127°38'W
Burketown, Austl. (bûrk'toun)	202	17°50'S	139°30'E
Burkina Faso, nation, Afr.	210	13°00'N	2°00'W
Burley, Id., U.S. (bûr'lĭ)	105	42°31'N	113°48'W
Burley, Wa., U.S.	106a	47°25'N	122°38'W
Burlingame, Ca., U.S. (bûr'lĭn-gām)	106b	37°35'N	122°22'W
Burlingame, Ks., U.S.	111	38°45'N	95°49'W
Burlington, Can. (bûr'lĭng-tŭn)	91	43°19'N	79°48'W
Burlington, Co., U.S.	110	39°17'N	102°26'W
Burlington, Ia., U.S.	97	40°48'N	91°05'W
Burlington, Ks., U.S.	111	38°10'N	95°46'W
Burlington, Ky., U.S.	101f	39°01'N	84°44'W
Burlington, Ma., U.S.	93a	42°31'N	71°13'W
Burlington, N.J., U.S.	100f	40°04'N	74°52'W
Burlington, N.C., U.S.	115	36°05'N	79°26'W
Burlington, Vt., U.S.	97	44°30'N	73°15'W
Burlington, Wa., U.S.	106a	48°28'N	122°20'W
Burlington, Wi., U.S.	101a	42°41'N	88°16'W
Burma *see* Myanmar, nation, Asia	180	21°00'N	95°15'E
Burnaby, Can.	84	49°14'N	122°58'W
Burnage, Eng., U.K.	237b	53°26'N	2°12'W
Burnet, Tx., U.S. (bûrn'ĕt)	112	30°46'N	98°14'W
Burnham, Il., U.S.	231a	41°39'N	87°34'W
Burnham on Crouch, Eng., U.K. (bûrn'ăm-ŏn-krouch)	144b	51°38'N	0°48'E
Burnhamthorpe, Can.	227c	43°37'N	79°36'W
Burnie, Austl. (bûr'nē)	203	41°15'S	146°05'E
Burning Tree Estates, Md., U.S.	229d	39°01'N	77°12'W
Burnley, Eng., U.K. (bûrn'lē)	150	53°47'N	2°19'W
Burns, Or., U.S. (bûrnz)	104	43°35'N	119°05'W
Burnside, Ky., U.S. (bûrn'sīd)	114	36°57'N	84°33'W
Burns Lake, Can. (bûrnz lăk)	84	54°14'N	125°46'W
Burnsville, Can. (bûrnz'vĭl)	92	47°44'N	65°07'W
Burnt, r., Or., U.S. (bûrnt)	104	44°26'N	117°53'W
Burntwood, r., Can.	89	55°53'N	97°30'W
Burrard Inlet, b., Can. (bûr'ȧrd)	106d	49°19'N	123°15'W
Burr Gaabo, Som.	213	1°14'N	51°47'E
Burro, Serranías del, mts., Mex. (sĕr-rä-nē'äs dĕl bo͞o'r-rô)	112	29°39'N	102°07'W
Burrowhill, Eng., U.K.	235	51°21'N	0°36'W
Burr Ridge, Il., U.S.	231a	41°46'N	87°55'W
Bursa, Tur. (bo͞or'sȧ)	182	40°10'N	28°10'E
Būr Safājah, Egypt	211	26°57'N	33°56'E
Burscheid, Ger. (bo͞or'shīd)	157c	51°05'N	7°07'E
Būr Sūdān, Sudan (so͞o-dån')	211	19°30'N	37°10'E
Burt, N.Y., U.S. (bŭrt)	101c	43°19'N	78°45'W
Burt, l., Mi., U.S. (bŭrt)	98	45°25'N	84°45'W
Burton, Eng., U.K.	237a	53°16'N	3°01'W
Burton, Wa., U.S. (bûr'tŭn)	106a	47°24'N	122°28'W
Burton, Lake, res., Ga., U.S.	114	34°46'N	83°40'W
Burtonsville, Md., U.S. (bûrtŏns-vil)	100e	39°07'N	76°57'W
Burton-upon-Trent, Eng., U.K. (bûr'tŭn-ŭp'-ŏn-trĕnt)	150	52°48'N	1°37'W
Buru, i., Indon.	197	3°30'S	126°30'E
Burullus, l., Egypt	218b	31°20'N	30°58'E
Burundi, nation, Afr.	212	3°00'S	29°30'E
Burwell, Ne., U.S. (bûr'wĕl)	102	41°46'N	99°08'W
Burwood, Austl.	243b	37°51'S	145°06'E
Bury, Eng., U.K. (bĕr'ĭ)	144a	53°36'N	2°17'W
Buryatia, , Russia	171	55°15'N	112°00'E
Bury Saint Edmunds, Eng., U.K. (bĕr'ĭ-sānt ĕd'mŭndz)	151	52°14'N	0°44'E
Burzaco, Arg. (bo͞or-zä'kō)	132a	34°50'S	58°23'W
Busanga Swamp, sw., Zam.	217	14°10'S	25°50'E
Busby, Austl.	243a	33°54'S	150°53'E
Buschhausen, neigh., Ger.	236	51°30'N	6°51'E
Būsh, Egypt (bo͞osh)	218b	29°13'N	31°08'E
Bushey, Eng., U.K.	235	51°39'N	0°22'W
Bushey Heath, Eng., U.K.	235	51°38'N	0°20'W
Bush Hill, Va., U.S.	229d	38°48'N	77°07'W
Bushmanland, hist. reg., S. Afr. (bo̤sh-măn lănd)	212	29°15'S	18°45'E
Bushnell, Il., U.S. (bo̤sh'nĕl)	111	40°33'N	90°28'W
Bushwick, neigh., N.Y., U.S.	228	40°42'N	73°55'W
Businga, D.R.C. (bo̤-sĭŋ'gȧ)	211	3°20'N	20°53'E
Busira, r., D.R.C.	216	0°05'S	19°20'E
Bus'k, Ukr.	155	49°58'N	24°39'E
Busselton, Austl. (bûs'l-tŭn)	202	33°40'S	115°30'E
Bussum, Neth.	145a	52°16'N	5°10'E
Bustamante, Mex. (bo͞os-tä-män'tå)	112	26°34'N	100°30'W
Bustleton, neigh., Pa., U.S.	229b	40°05'N	75°02'W
Busto Arsizio, Italy (bo͞os'tō är-sēd'zē-ō)	160	45°47'N	8°51'E
Busuanga, i., Phil. (bo͞o-swäŋ'gä)	197a	12°20'N	119°43'E
Buta, D.R.C. (bo͞o'tȧ)	211	2°48'N	24°44'E
Butha Buthe, Leso. (bo͞o-thȧ-bo͞o'thȧ)	213c	28°49'S	28°16'E
Butler, Al., U.S. (bŭt'lẽr)	114	32°05'N	88°10'W
Butler, In., U.S.	98	41°25'N	84°50'W
Butler, Md., U.S.	100e	39°32'N	76°46'W
Butler, N.J., U.S.	100a	41°00'N	74°20'W
Butler, Pa., U.S.	99	40°50'N	79°55'W
Butovo, Russia (bo̤-tô'vô)	172b	55°33'N	37°36'E
Butsha, D.R.C.	217	0°57'N	29°13'E
Buttahatchee, r., Al., U.S. (bŭt-ȧ-hăch'ē)	114	34°02'N	88°05'W
Butte, Mt., U.S. (būt)	96	46°00'N	112°31'W
Butterworth, S. Afr. (bŭ tẽr'wûrth)	213c	32°20'S	28°09'E
Büttgen, Ger.	236	51°12'N	6°36'E
Butt of Lewis, c., Scot., U.K. (bŭt ŏv lū'ĭs)	150	58°34'N	6°15'W
Butuan, Phil. (bo͞o-to͞o'än)	197	8°40'N	125°33'E
Buturlinovka, Russia (bo͞o-to͞o'lē-nôf'kȧ)	167	50°47'N	40°35'E
Buuhoodle, Som.	218a	8°15'N	46°20'E
Buulo Berde, Som.	218a	3°53'N	45°30'E
Buxtehude, Ger.	145c	53°29'N	9°42'E
Buxton, Eng., U.K. (bŭks't'n)	144a	53°15'N	1°55'W
Buxton, Or., U.S.	106c	45°41'N	123°11'W
Buy, Russia (bwē)	164	58°30'N	41°48'E
Büyükmenderes, r., Tur.	182	37°50'N	28°20'E
Buzău, Rom. (bo͞o-zĕ'o̤)	161	45°09'N	26°51'E
Buzău, r., Rom.	163	45°17'N	27°22'E
Buzaymah, Libya	211	25°14'N	22°13'E
Buzi, China (bo͞o-dz)	190	33°48'N	118°13'E
Buzuluk, Russia (bo̤-zo̤-lo̤k')	164	52°50'N	52°10'E
Bwendi, D.R.C.	217	4°01'N	26°41'E
Byala, Bul.	161	43°26'N	25°44'E
Byala Slatina, Bul. (byä'la slä'tēnä)	161	43°26'N	23°56'E
Byblos *see* Jubayl, Leb.	181a	34°07'N	35°38'E
Byculla, neigh., India	240e	18°58'N	72°49'E
Bydgoszcz, Pol. (bĭd'gôshch)	146	53°07'N	18°00'E
Byelorussia *see* Belarus, nation, Eur.	164	53°30'N	25°33'E
Byesville, Oh., U.S. (bīz-vĭl)	98	39°55'N	81°35'W
Byfang, neigh., Ger.	236	51°24'N	7°06'E
Byfleet, Eng., U.K.	235	51°20'N	0°29'W
Bygdin, l., Nor. (bügh-dĕn')	152	61°24'N	8°31'E
Byglandsfjord, Nor. (bügh'länds-fyôr)	152	58°40'N	7°49'E
Bykhovo, Bela.	162	53°32'N	30°15'E
Bykovo, Russia (bĭ-kô'vô)	172b	55°38'N	38°05'E
Byrranga, Gory, mts., Russia	170	74°15'N	94°28'E
Bytantay, r., Russia (byän'täy)	171	68°15'N	132°15'E
Bytom, Pol. (bĭ'tŭm)	147	50°21'N	18°55'E
Bytosh', Russia (bĭ-tôsh')	162	53°48'N	34°06'E
Bytow, Pol. (bĭ'tŭf)	155	54°10'N	17°30'E

C

PLACE (Pronunciation)	PAGE	LAT.	LONG.
Cabagan, Phil. (kä-bä-gän')	197a	17°27'N	121°50'E
Cabalete, i., Phil. (kä-bä-lā'tå)	197a	14°19'N	122°00'E
Caballito, neigh., Arg.	233d	34°37'S	58°27'W
Caballones, Canal de, strt., Cuba (kä-näl-dĕ-kä-bäl-yô'nĕs)	122	20°45'N	79°20'W
Caballo Reservoir, res., N.M., U.S. (kä-bä-lyō')	109	33°00'N	107°20'W
Cabanatuan, Phil. (kä-bä-nä-twän')	197a	15°30'N	120°56'E
Cabano, Can. (kä-bä-nō')	92	47°41'N	68°54'W
Cabarruyan, i., Phil. (kä-bä-ro͞o'yän)	197a	16°21'N	120°10'E
Cabedelo, Braz. (kä-bē-dā'lo̤)	131	6°58'S	34°49'W
Cabeza, Arrecife, i., Mex.	119	19°07'N	95°52'W
Cabeza del Buey, Spain (kȧ-bā'thä dĕl bwā')	158	38°43'N	5°18'W
Cabimas, Ven. (kä-bē'mäs)	130	10°21'N	71°27'W
Cabinda, Ang.	212	5°33'S	12°12'E
Cabinda, hist. reg., Ang. (kä-bĭn'dȧ)	212	5°10'S	10°00'E
Cabinet Mountains, mts., Mt., U.S. (kăb'ĭ-nĕt)	104	48°13'N	115°52'W
Cabin John, Md., U.S.	229d	38°58'N	77°09'W
Cabo Frio, Braz. (kä'bō-frē'ō)	129a	22°53'S	42°02'W
Cabo Frio, Ilha do, Braz. (ē'lä-dō-kä'bō frē'ō)	129a	23°01'S	42°00'W
Cabo Gracias a Dios, Hond. (kä'bō-grä-syäs-ä-dyô's)	121	15°00'N	83°13'W
Cabonga, Réservoir, res., Can.	91	47°25'N	76°35'W
Cabora Bassa Reservoir, res., Moz.	212	15°45'S	32°00'E
Cabot Head, c., Can. (kăb'ŭt)	90	45°15'N	81°20'W
Cabot Strait, strt., Can. (kăb'ŭt)	85a	47°35'N	60°00'W
Cabra, Spain (käb'rä)	158	37°28'N	4°29'W
Cabra, i., Phil.	197a	13°55'N	119°55'E
Cabramatta, Austl.	243a	33°54'S	150°56'E
Cabrera, Illa de, i., Spain	159	39°08'N	2°57'E
Cabrera, Sierra de la, mts., Spain	158	42°15'N	6°45'W
Cabriel, r., Spain (kä-brē-ĕl')	158	39°25'N	1°20'W
Cabrillo National Monument, rec., Ca., U.S. (kä-brēl'yō)	108a	32°41'N	117°03'W
Cabuçu, r., Braz. (kä-bo͞o'-so͞o)	132b	22°57'S	43°36'W
Cabugao, Phil. (kä-bo͞o'gä-ō)	197a	17°48'N	120°28'E
Čačak, Yugo. (chä'chåk)	161	43°51'N	20°22'E
Caçapava, Braz. (kä'sä-pá'vä)	129a	23°05'S	45°52'W
Cáceres, Braz. (kà'sē-rĕs)	131	16°11'S	57°32'W
Cáceres, Spain (kà'thå-räs)	148	39°28'N	6°20'W
Cachan, Fr.	237c	48°48'N	2°20'E
Cachapoal, r., Chile (kä-chä-pô-ä'l)	129b	34°23'S	70°19'W
Cache, r., Ar., U.S. (kåsh)	111	35°24'N	91°12'W
Cache Creek, Can.	87	50°48'N	121°19'W
Cache Creek, r., Ca., U.S. (kăsh)	108	38°53'N	122°24'W
Cache la Poudre, r., Co., U.S. (kåsh lȧ po͞od'r')	110	40°43'N	105°39'W
Cachi, Nevados de, mtn., Arg. (nĕ-vá'dôs-dĕ-kå'chē)	132	25°05'S	66°40'W
Cachinal, Chile (kä-chē-näl')	132	24°57'S	69°33'W
Cachoeira, Braz. (kä-shō-ā'rä)	131	12°32'S	38°47'W
Cachoeira do Sul, Braz. (kä-shō-ā'rä-dō-so͞o'l)	132	30°02'S	52°49'W
Cachoeiras de Macacu, Braz. (kä-shō-ā'räs-dĕ-mä-kà'ko͞o)	129a	22°28'S	42°39'W
Cachoeiro de Itapemirim, Braz.	131	20°51'S	41°06'W
Cacilhas, Port.	238d	38°41'N	9°09'W
Cacólo, Ang.	216	10°07'S	19°17'E
Caconda, Ang. (kä-kōn'dä)	212	13°43'S	15°06'E
Cacouna, Can.	92	47°54'N	69°31'W
Cacula, Ang.	216	14°29'S	14°10'E
Cadale, Som.	218a	2°45'N	46°15'E
Caddo, l., La., U.S. (kăd'ō)	113	32°37'N	94°15'W
Cadereyta, Mex. (kä-dä-rā'tä)	118	20°42'N	99°47'W
Cadereyta Jimenez, Mex. (kä-dä-rā'tä hē-mā'nāz)	112	25°36'N	99°59'W
Cadi, Sierra de, mts., Spain (sē-ĕ'r-rä-dĕ-kä'dē)	159	42°17'N	1°34'E
Cadillac, Mi., U.S. (kăd'ĭ-lăk)	98	44°15'N	85°25'W
Cadishead, Eng., U.K.	237b	53°25'N	2°26'W
Cádiz, Spain (kà'dēz)	142	36°34'N	6°20'W
Cadiz, Ca., U.S. (kā'dĭz)	108	34°33'N	115°30'W
Cadiz, Oh., U.S.	98	40°15'N	81°00'W
Cádiz, Golfo de, b., Spain (gôl-fô-dĕ-kä'dēz)	148	36°50'N	7°00'W
Caen, Fr. (käN)	147	49°13'N	0°22'W
Caernarfon, Wales, U.K.	146	53°08'N	4°17'W
Caernarfon Bay, b., Wales, U.K.	150	53°09'N	4°56'W
Cagayan, Phil. (kä-gä-yän')	197	8°13'N	124°30'E
Cagayan, r., Phil.	196	16°45'N	121°55'E
Cagayan Islands, is., Phil.	196	9°40'N	120°30'E
Cagayan Sulu, i., Phil. (kä-gä-yän so͞o'lo͞o)	196	7°00'N	118°30'E
Cagli, Italy (käl'yē)	160	43°35'N	12°40'E
Cagliari, Italy (käl'yä-rē)	142	39°16'N	9°08'E
Cagliari, Golfo di, b., Italy (gôl-fô-dē-käl'yä-rē)	148	39°08'N	9°12'E
Cagnes, Fr. (kän'y')	157	43°40'N	7°14'E
Caguas, Ven. (kä'gwä)	131b	10°12'N	67°27'W
Caguas, P.R. (kä'gwäs)	117b	18°12'N	66°01'W
Cahaba, r., Al., U.S. (kȧ hä-bä)	114	32°50'N	87°15'W
Cahama, Ang. (kä-ä'mä)	212	16°17'S	14°19'E
Cahokia, Il., U.S. (kȧ-hō'kĭ-ȧ)	107e	38°34'N	90°11'W
Cahora-Bassa, wtfl., Moz.	217	15°40'S	32°50'E
Cahors, Fr. (kä-ôr')	147	44°27'N	1°27'E
Cahuacán, Mex. (kä-wä-kä'n)	119a	19°38'N	99°25'W

ng-sing; ŋ-baŋk; N-nasalized n; nŏd; cŏmmit; ōld; ōbey; ôrder; oi-boil; fo͞od; o̤-as oo in foot; ou-out; s-soft; sh-dish; th-thin; pūre; ůnite; ûrn; stŭd; circŭs; ü-as in French tu; '-indeterminate vowel.

270 Cahuita–Canterbury

PLACE (Pronunciation)	PAGE	LAT.	LONG.
Cahuita, Punta, c., C.R. (po͞o′n-tä-kä-wē′tȧ)	121	9°47′N	82°41′W
Cahul, Mol.	163	45°49′N	28°17′E
Caibarién, Cuba (kī-bä-rė-ĕn′)	122	22°35′N	79°30′W
Caicedonia, Col. (kī-sĕ-dȯ-nėä)	130a	4°21′N	75°48′W
Caicos Bank, bk. (kī′kōs)	123	21°35′N	72°00′W
Caicos Islands, is., T./C. Is.	117	21°45′N	71°50′W
Caicos Passage, strt., N.A.	123	21°55′N	72°45′W
Caillou Bay, b., La., U.S. (kȧ-yo͞o′)	113	29°07′N	91°00′W
Caimanera, Cuba (kī-mä-nā′rä)	123	20°00′N	75°10′W
Caiman Point, c., Phil. (kī′mȧn)	197a	15°56′N	119°33′E
Caimito, r., Pan. (kä-ē-mē′tô)	116a	8°50′N	79°45′W
Caimito del Guayabal, Cuba (kä-ē-mė′tō-dĕl-gwä-yä-bä′l)	123a	22°57′N	82°36′W
Cairns, Austl. (kârnz)	203	17°02′S	145°49′E
Cairo, C.R. (kī′rȯ)	121	10°06′N	83°47′W
Cairo, Egypt	211	30°00′N	31°17′E
Cairo, Ga., U.S. (kā′rō)	114	30°48′N	84°12′W
Cairo, Il., U.S.	97	36°59′N	89°11′W
Caistor, Eng., U.K. (kâs′tẽr)	144a	53°30′N	0°20′W
Caiundo, Ang.	216	15°46′S	17°28′E
Caiyu, China (tsī-yo͞o)	190	39°39′N	116°36′E
Cajamarca, Col. (kä-κä-mȧ′r-kä)	130a	4°25′N	75°25′W
Çajamarca, Peru (kä-hä-mär′kä)	130	7°16′S	78°30′W
Čajniče, Bos. (chī′nĭ-chĕ)	161	43°32′N	19°04′E
Cajon, Ca., U.S. (kȧ-hōn′)	107a	34°18′N	117°28′W
Çajuru, Braz. (kȧ-zho͞o′ro͞o)	129a	21°17′S	47°17′W
Čakovec, Cro. (chȧ′kō-vĕts)	160	46°23′N	16°27′E
Cala, S. Afr. (cä-lȧ)	213c	31°33′S	27°41′E
Calabar, Nig. (kăl-ȧ-bär′)	210	4°57′N	8°19′E
Calabazar, Cuba (kä-lä-bä-zä′r)	123a	23°02′N	82°25′W
Calabozo, Ven. (kä-lä-bō′zō)	130	8°48′N	67°27′W
Calabria, hist. reg., Italy (kä-lä′brė-ä)	160	39°26′N	16°23′E
Calafat, Rom. (kȧ-lȧ-fȧt′)	161	43°59′N	22°56′E
Calaguas Islands, is., Phil. (kä-läg′wäs)	197a	14°30′N	123°06′E
Calahoo, Can. (kă-lȧ-ho͞o′)	83g	53°42′N	113°58′W
Calahorra, Spain (kä-lä-ôr′rä)	148	42°18′N	1°58′W
Calais, Fr. (kȧ-lĕ′)	142	50°56′N	1°51′E
Calais, Me., U.S.	97	45°11′N	67°15′W
Calama, Chile (kä-lä′mä)	132	22°17′S	68°58′W
Calamar, Col. (kä-lä-mär′)	130	10°24′N	75°00′W
Calamar, Col.	130	1°55′N	72°33′W
Calamba, Phil. (kä-läm′bä)	197a	14°12′N	121°10′E
Calamian Group, is., Phil. (kä-lä-myän′)	196	12°14′N	118°38′E
Calañas, Spain (kä-län′yäs)	158	37°41′N	6°52′W
Calanda, Spain	159	40°53′N	0°20′W
Calapan, Phil. (kä-lä-pän′)	197a	13°25′N	121°11′E
Călăraşi, Rom. (kŭ-lŭ-rȧsh′ĭ)	149	44°09′N	27°20′E
Calatayud, Spain (kä-lä-tä-yo͞odh′)	148	41°23′N	1°37′W
Calauag Bay, b., Phil.	197a	14°07′N	122°10′E
Calaveras Reservoir, res., Ca., U.S. (kăl-ȧ-vẽr′ăs)	106b	37°29′N	121°47′W
Calavite, Cape, c., Phil. (kä-lä-vē′tā)	197a	13°29′N	120°00′E
Calcasieu, r., La., U.S. (kăl′kȧ-shū)	113	30°22′N	93°08′W
Calcasieu Lake, l., La., U.S.	113	29°58′N	93°08′W
Calcutta, India (kăl-kŭt′ȧ)	183	22°32′N	88°22′E
Caldas, Col. (kȧ′l-dȧs)	130a	6°06′N	75°38′W
Caldas, dept., Col.	130a	5°20′N	75°38′W
Caldas da Rainha, Port. (käl′däs dä rīn′yă)	158	39°25′N	9°08′W
Calder, r., Eng., U.K. (kôl′dẽr)	144a	53°39′N	1°30′W
Caldera, Chile (käl-dā′rä)	132	27°02′S	70°53′W
Calder Canal, can., Eng., U.K.	144a	53°48′N	2°25′W
Caldwell, Id., U.S. (kôld′wĕl)	104	43°40′N	116°43′W
Caldwell, Ks., U.S.	111	37°04′N	97°36′W
Caldwell, N.J., U.S.	228	40°51′N	74°17′W
Caldwell, Oh., U.S.	98	39°40′N	81°30′W
Caldwell, Tx., U.S.	113	30°30′N	96°40′W
Caledon, Can. (kăl′ē-dŏn)	83d	43°52′N	79°59′W
Caledonia, Mn., U.S. (kăl-ē-dō′nĭ-ȧ)	103	43°38′N	91°31′W
Calella, Spain (kä-lĕl′yä)	159	41°37′N	2°39′E
Calera Victor Rosales, Mex. (kä-lā′rä-vē′k-tôr-rô-sȧ′l . . . . . ĕs)	118	22°57′N	102°42′W
Calexico, Ca., U.S. (kȧ-lĕk′sĭ-kō)	96	32°41′N	115°30′W
Calgary, Can. (kăl′gȧ-rĭ)	84	51°03′N	114°05′W
Calhariz, neigh., Port.	238d	38°44′N	9°12′W
Calhoun, Ga., U.S. (kăl-ho͞on′)	114	34°30′N	84°56′W
Cali, Col. (kä′lē)	130	3°26′N	76°30′W
Calicut, India (kăl′ĭ-kŭt)	183	11°19′N	75°49′E
Caliente, Nv., U.S. (käl-yĕn′tā)	109	37°38′N	114°30′W
California, Mo., U.S. (kăl-ĭ-fôr′nĭ-ȧ)	111	38°38′N	92°38′W
California, Pa., U.S.	101e	40°03′N	79°53′W
California, state, U.S.	96	38°10′N	121°20′W
California, Golfo de, b., Mex. (gôl-fô-dĕ-kä-lė-fôr-nyä)	116	30°30′N	113°45′W
California Aqueduct, aq., Ca., U.S.	108	37°10′N	121°10′W
California-Los Angeles, University of (U.C.L.A.), educ., Ca., U.S.	232	34°04′N	118°26′W
Călimani, Munţii, mts., Rom.	155	47°05′N	24°47′E
Calimere, Point, c., India	187	10°20′N	80°20′E
Calimesa, Ca., U.S. (kă-lĭ-mā′sȧ)	107a	34°00′N	117°04′W
Calipatria, Ca., U.S. (kăl-ĭ-pȧt′rĭ-ȧ)	108	33°03′N	115°30′W
Calkini, Mex. (käl-kė-nē′)	119	20°21′N	90°06′W
Callabonna, Lake, l., Austl. (călă′bŏnȧ)	204	29°35′S	140°28′E
Callao, Peru (käl-yä′ō)	130	12°02′S	77°07′W
Calling, l., Can. (kôl′ĭng)	87	55°15′N	113°12′W
Calmar, Can. (kăl′mär)	83g	53°16′N	113°49′W
Calmar, Ia., U.S.	103	43°12′N	91°54′W
Caloocan, Phil.	241g	14°39′N	120°59′E
Caloosahatchee, r., Fl., U.S. (kȧ-loo-sȧ-hăch′ė)	115a	26°45′N	81°41′W
Calotmul, Mex. (kä-lôt-mo͞ol)	120a	20°58′N	88°11′W
Calpulalpan, Mex. (käl-po͞o-läl′pän)	118	19°35′N	98°33′W
Caltagirone, Italy (käl-tä-jē-rō′nȧ)	148	37°14′N	14°32′E
Caltanissetta, Italy (käl-tä-nė-sĕt′tä)	148	37°30′N	14°02′E
Caluango, Ang.	216	8°21′S	19°40′E
Calucinga, Ang.	216	11°18′S	16°12′E
Calumet, Mi., U.S. (kă-lū-mĕt′)	103	47°15′N	88°29′W
Calumet, Lake, l., Il., U.S.	101a	41°43′N	87°36′W
Calumet City, Il., U.S.	101a	41°37′N	87°33′W
Calumet Park, Il., U.S.	231a	41°44′N	87°33′W
Calumet Sag Channel, can., Il., U.S.	231a	41°42′N	87°57′W
Calunda, Ang.	216	12°06′S	23°23′E
Caluquembe, Ang.	216	13°47′S	14°44′E
Caluula, Som.	218a	11°53′N	50°40′E
Calvert, Tx., U.S. (kăl′vẽrt)	113	30°59′N	96°41′W
Calvert Island, i., Can.	84	51°35′N	128°00′W
Calvi, Fr. (käl′vē)	160	42°33′N	8°35′E
Calvillo, Mex. (käl-vēl′yō)	119	21°51′N	102°44′E
Calvinia, S. Afr. (kăl-vĭn′ĭ-ȧ)	212	31°20′S	19°50′E
Cam, r., Eng., U.K. (kăm)	151	52°15′N	0°05′E
Camagüey, Cuba (kä-mä-gwā′)	117	21°25′N	78°00′W
Camagüey, prov., Cuba	122	21°30′N	78°10′W
Camajuani, Cuba (kä-mä-hwä′nė)	122	22°25′N	79°50′W
Camano, Wa., U.S. (kä-mä′no)	106a	48°10′N	122°32′W
Camano Island, i., Wa., U.S.	106a	48°11′N	122°29′W
Camargo, Mex. (kä-mär gō)	112	26°19′N	98°49′W
Camarón, Cabo, c., Hond. (kȧ′bô-kä-mä-rōn′)	120	16°06′N	85°05′W
Camas, Wa., U.S. (kăm′ȧs)	106c	45°36′N	122°24′W
Camas Creek, r., Id., U.S.	105	44°10′N	112°09′W
Camatagua, Ven. (kä-mä-tȧ′gwä)	131b	9°49′N	66°55′W
Ca Mau, Mui, c., Viet	196	8°36′N	104°43′E
Cambay, India (kăm-bā′)	186	22°22′N	72°39′E
Camberwell, Austl.	243b	37°50′S	145°04′E
Cambodia, nation, Asia	196	12°15′N	104°00′E
Cambonda, Serra, mts., Ang.	216	12°10′S	14°15′E
Camborne, Eng., U.K. (kăm′bôrn)	150	50°15′N	5°28′W
Cambrai, Fr. (käɴ-brĕ′)	147	50°10′N	3°15′E
Cambrian Mountains, mts., Wales, U.K. (kăm′brĭ-ăn)	150	52°05′N	4°05′W
Cambridge, Can.	91	43°22′N	80°19′W
Cambridge, Eng., U.K. (kām′brĭj)	147	52°12′N	0°11′E
Cambridge, Md., U.S.	99	38°35′N	76°10′W
Cambridge, Ma., U.S.	93a	42°23′N	71°07′W
Cambridge, Mn., U.S.	103	45°35′N	93°14′W
Cambridge, Ne., U.S.	110	40°17′N	100°10′W
Cambridge, Oh., U.S.	98	40°00′N	81°35′W
Cambridge Bay, Can.	84	69°15′N	105°00′W
Cambridge City, In., U.S.	98	39°45′N	85°15′W
Cambridgeshire, co., Eng., U.K.	144a	52°26′N	0°19′W
Cambuci, Braz. (käm-bo͞o′sē)	129a	21°35′S	41°54′W
Cambuci, neigh., Braz.	234d	23°34′S	46°37′W
Cambundi-Catembo, Ang.	216	10°09′S	17°31′E
Camby, In., U.S. (kăm′bē)	101g	39°40′N	86°19′W
Camden, Austl.	201b	34°03′S	150°42′E
Camden, Al., U.S. (kăm′dĕn)	114	31°58′N	87°15′W
Camden, Ar., U.S.	111	33°36′N	92°49′W
Camden, Me., U.S.	92	44°11′N	69°05′W
Camden, N.J., U.S.	97	39°56′N	75°06′W
Camden, S.C., U.S.	115	34°14′N	80°37′W
Camden, neigh., Eng., U.K.	235	51°33′N	0°10′W
Cameia, Parque Nacional da, rec., Ang.	216	11°40′S	21°20′E
Camenca, Mol.	163	48°02′N	28°43′E
Cameron, Mo., U.S. (kăm′ẽr-ŭn)	111	39°44′N	94°14′W
Cameron, Tx., U.S.	113	30°52′N	96°57′W
Cameron, W.V., U.S.	98	39°40′N	80°35′W
Cameron Hills, hills, Can.	84	60°13′N	120°20′W
Cameroon, nation, Afr.	210	5°48′N	11°00′E
Cameroon Mountain, mtn., Cam.	210	4°12′N	9°11′E
Camiling, Phil. (kä-mė-lĭng′)	197a	15°42′N	120°24′E
Camilla, Ga., U.S. (kȧ-mĭl′ȧ)	114	31°13′N	84°12′W
Caminha, Port. (kä-mĭn′yȧ)	158	41°52′N	8°44′W
Camoçim, Braz. (kä-mô-sēɴ′)	131	2°56′S	40°55′W
Camooweal, Austl.	202	20°00′S	138°13′E
Campana, Arg. (käm-pä′nä)	129c	34°10′S	58°58′W
Campana, i., Chile (käm-pän′yä)	132	48°20′S	75°15′W
Campanario, Spain (kä-pä-nä′rė-ō)	158	38°51′N	5°36′W
Campanella, Punta, c., Italy (pô′n-tä-käm-pä-nĕ′lä)	159c	40°20′N	14°21′E
Campanha, Braz. (käm-pän-yäɴ′)	129a	21°51′S	45°24′W
Campania, hist. reg., Italy (käm-pän′yä)	160	41°00′N	14°40′E
Campbell, Ca., U.S. (kăm′bĕl)	106b	37°17′N	121°57′W
Campbell, Mo., U.S.	111	36°29′N	90°04′W
Campbell, is., N.Z.	3	52°30′S	169°00′E
Campbellfield, Austl.	243b	37°41′S	144°57′E
Campbellpore, Pak.	186	33°49′N	72°24′E
Campbell River, Can.	84	50°01′N	125°15′W
Campbellsville, Ky., U.S. (kăm′bĕlz-vĭl)	114	37°19′N	85°20′W
Campbellton, Can. (kăm′bĕl-tŭn)	85	48°00′N	66°40′W
Campbelltown, Austl. (kăm′bĕl-toun)	201b	34°04′S	150°49′E
Campbelltown, Scot., U.K. (kăm′b′l-toun)	150	55°25′N	5°50′W
Camp Dennison, Oh., U.S. (dĕ′nĭ-sŏn)	101f	39°12′N	84°17′W
Campeche, Mex. (käm-pā′chȧ)	116	19°51′N	90°32′W
Campeche, state, Mex.	116	18°55′N	90°20′W
Campeche, Bahía de, b., Mex. (bä-ē′ä-dĕ-käm-pā′chā)	116	19°30′N	93°40′W
Campechuela, Cuba (käm-pȧ-chwā′lä)	122	20°15′N	77°15′W
Camperdown, S. Afr. (kăm′pẽr-doun)	213c	29°44′S	30°33′E
Câmpina, Rom.	161	45°08′N	25°47′E
Campina Grande, Braz. (käm-pē′nä grän′dĕ)	131	7°15′S	35°49′W
Campinas, Braz. (käm-pē′näzh)	131	22°53′S	47°03′W
Camp Indian Reservation, I.R., Ca., U.S. (kămp)	108	32°39′N	116°26′W
Campo, Cam. (käm′pō)	210	2°22′N	9°49′E
Campoalegre, Col. (kä′m-pȯ-ȧlĕ′grĕ)	130	2°34′N	75°20′W
Campobasso, Italy (käm′pȯ-bäs′sō)	160	41°35′N	14°39′E
Campo Belo, Braz.	129a	20°52′S	45°15′W
Campo de Criptana, Spain (käm′pō dā krėp-tä′nä)	158	39°24′N	3°09′W
Campo Florido, Cuba (kä′m-pō flȯ-rė′dō)	123a	23°07′N	82°07′W
Campo Grande, Braz. (käm-pȯ grän′dĕ)	131	20°28′S	54°32′W
Campo Grande, Braz.	132b	22°54′S	43°33′W
Campo Grande, neigh., Port.	238d	38°45′N	9°09′W
Campo Maior, Braz. (käm-pȯ mä-yôr′)	131	4°48′S	42°12′W
Campo Maior, Port.	158	39°03′N	7°06′W
Campo Real, Spain (käm′pȯ rȧ-äl′)	159a	40°21′N	3°23′W
Campos, Braz. (kä′m-pȯs)	131	21°46′S	41°19′W
Campos do Jordão, Braz. (kä′m-pȯs-dȯ-zhôr-dou′ɴ)	129a	22°45′S	45°35′W
Campos Gerais, Braz. (kä′m-pȯs-zhĕ-rȧės)	129a	21°17′S	45°43′W
Camps Bay, S. Afr. (kămps)	212a	33°57′S	18°22′E
Campsie, Austl.	243a	33°55′S	151°06′E
Camp Springs, Md., U.S. (cămp sprĭngz)	100e	38°48′N	76°55′W
Câmpulung, Rom.	149	45°15′N	25°03′E
Câmpulung Moldovenesc, Rom.	155	47°31′N	25°36′E
Camp Wood, Tx., U.S. (kămp wȯd)	112	29°39′N	100°02′W
Camrose, Can. (kăm-rōz)	84	53°01′N	112°50′W
Camu, r., Dom. Rep. (kä′mo͞o)	123	19°05′N	70°15′W
Canada, nation, N.A. (kăn′ȧ-dȧ)	84	50°00′N	100°00′W
Canada Bay, b., Can.	93	50°43′N	56°10′W
Cañada de Gómez, Arg. (kä-nyä′dä-dĕ-gô′mĕz)	132	32°49′S	61°24′W
Canadian, Tx., U.S. (kȧ-nā′dĭ-ăn)	110	35°54′N	100°24′W
Canadian, r., U.S.	96	35°30′N	102°30′W
Canajoharie, N.Y., U.S. (kăn-ȧ-jȯ-hăr′ė)	99	42°55′N	74°35′W
Çanakkale, Tur. (chä-näk-kä′lĕ)	149	40°10′N	26°26′E
Çanakkale Boğazi (Dardanelles), strt., Tur.	149	40°05′N	25°50′E
Canandaigua, N.Y., U.S. (kăn-ăn-dā′gwȧ)	99	42°55′N	77°20′W
Canandaigua, l., N.Y., U.S.	99	42°45′N	77°20′W
Cananea, Mex. (kä-nä-nĕ′ä)	116	31°00′N	110°20′W
Canarias, Islas (Canary Is.), is., Spain (ė′s-läs-kä-nä′ryäs)	209	29°15′N	16°30′W
Canarreos, Archipiélago de los, is., Cuba	122	21°35′N	82°20′W
Canarsie, neigh., N.Y., U.S.	228	40°38′N	73°53′W
Canary Islands *see* Canarias, Islas, is., Spain	209	29°15′N	16°30′W
Cañas, C.R. (kä′-nyäs)	120	10°26′N	85°06′W
Cañas, r., C.R.	120	10°20′N	85°21′W
Cañasgordas, Col. (kä′nyäs-gȯ′r-däs)	130a	6°44′N	76°01′W
Canastota, N.Y., U.S. (kăn-ȧs-tō′tȧ)	99	43°05′N	75°45′W
Canastra, Serra de, mts., Braz. (sĕ′r-rä-dĕ-kä-nä′s-trä)	131	19°53′S	46°57′W
Canatlán, Mex. (kä-nät-län′)	112	24°30′N	104°45′W
Canaveral, Cape, c., Fl., U.S.	97	28°30′N	80°23′W
Canavieiras, Braz. (kä-nȧ-vē-ā′räs)	131	15°40′S	38°49′W
Canberra, Austl. (kăn′bĕr-ȧ)	203	35°21′S	149°10′E
Canby, Mn., U.S. (kăn′bĭ)	102	44°43′N	96°15′W
Canchyuaya, Cerros de, mts., Peru (sĕ′r-rȯs-dĕ-kän-cho͞o-ȧ′īä)	130	7°30′S	74°30′W
Cancuc, Mex. (kän-ko͞ok)	119	16°58′N	92°17′W
Cancún, Mex.	120a	21°25′N	86°50′W
Candelaria, Cuba (kän-dĕ-lä′ryä)	122	22°45′N	82°55′W
Candelaria, Phil. (kän-dȧ-lä′rė-ä)	197a	15°39′N	119°55′E
Candelaria, r., Mex. (kän-dĕ-lä-ryä)	119	18°25′N	91°21′W
Candeleda, Spain (kän-dhȧ-lā′dhä)	158	40°09′N	5°18′W
Candia *see* Iráklion, Grc.	142	35°20′N	25°10′E
Candle, Ak., U.S. (kăn′d′l)	95	65°00′N	162°04′W
Cando, N.D., U.S. (kăn′dō)	102	48°27′N	99°13′W
Candon, Phil. (kän-dōn′)	197a	17°13′N	120°26′E
Canelones, Ur. (kä-nĕ-lô-nĕs)	129c	34°32′S	56°19′W
Canelones, dept., Ur.	129c	34°34′S	56°15′W
Cañete, Peru (kän-yā′tȧ)	130	13°06′S	76°17′W
Caney, Cuba (kä-nā′) (kā′nĭ)	123	20°05′N	75°45′W
Caney, Ks., U.S. (kā′nĭ)	111	37°00′N	95°57′W
Caney Fork, r., Tn., U.S.	114	36°10′N	85°50′W
Cangamba, Ang.	212	13°40′S	19°54′E
Cangas, Spain (kän′gäs)	158	42°15′N	8°43′W
Cangas de Narcea, Spain (kä′n-gäs-dĕ-när-sĕ-ä)	158	43°08′N	6°36′W
Cangzhou, China (tsäŋ-jō)	192	38°21′N	116°53′E
Caniapiscau, l., Can.	85	54°10′N	71°13′E
Caniapiscau, r., Can.	85	57°00′N	68°45′W
Canicatti, Italy (kä-nė-kät′tē)	160	37°18′N	13°58′E
Canillas, neigh., Spain	238b	40°28′N	3°38′W
Canillejas, neigh., Spain	238b	40°27′N	3°37′W
Cañitas, Mex. (kän-yē′täs)	118	23°38′N	102°44′W
Cannell, Can.	83g	53°35′N	113°38′W
Cannelton, In., U.S. (kăn′ĕl-tŭn)	98	37°55′N	86°45′W
Cannes, Fr. (kȧn)	147	43°34′N	7°05′E
Canning, Can. (kăn′ĭng)	92	45°09′N	64°25′W
Cannock, Eng., U.K. (kăn′ŭk)	144a	52°41′N	2°02′W
Cannock Chase, reg., Eng., U.K. (kăn′ŭk chās)	144a	52°43′N	1°54′W
Cannon, r., Mn., U.S. (kăn′ŭn)	103	44°18′N	93°24′W
Cannonball, r., N.D., U.S. (kăn′ŭn-bäl)	102	46°17′N	101°35′W
Caño, Isla de, i., C.R. (ė′s-lä-dĕ-kä′nō)	121	8°38′N	84°00′W
Canoga Park, Ca., U.S. (kä-nō′gȧ)	107a	34°07′N	118°36′W
Canoncito Indian Reservation, I.R., N.M., U.S.	109	35°00′N	107°05′W
Canon City, Co., U.S. (kăn′yŭn)	110	38°27′N	105°16′W
Canonsburg, Pa., U.S. (kăn′ŭnz-bûrg)	101e	40°16′N	80°11′W
Canoochee, r., Ga., U.S. (kȧ-no͞o′chē)	115	32°25′N	82°11′W
Canora, Can. (kȧ-nōrȧ)	84	51°37′N	102°26′W
Canosa, Italy (kä-nō′sä)	160	41°14′N	16°03′E
Canouan, i., St. Vin.	121b	12°44′N	61°10′W
Cansahcab, Mex.	120a	21°11′N	89°05′W
Canso, Can. (kăn′sō)	93	45°20′N	61°00′W
Canso, Cape, c., Can.	93	45°21′N	60°46′W
Canso, Strait of, strt., Can.	93	45°37′N	61°25′W
Cantabrica, Cordillera, mts., Spain	142	43°05′N	6°05′W
Cantagalo, Braz. (kän-tä-gȧ′lo)	129a	21°59′S	42°22′W
Cantanhede, Port. (kän-täɴ-yā′dȧ)	158	40°22′N	8°35′W
Canterbury, Austl.	243a	33°55′S	151°07′E

ăt; finăl; rāte; senȧte; ärm; ȧsk; sofȧ; fâre; ch-choose; dh-as th in other; bē; ėvent; bĕt; recĕnt; cratẽr; g-gō; gh-guttural g; bĭt; ĭ-short neutral; rīde; ᴋ-guttural k as ch in German ich;

PRONOUNCING INDEX Canterbury-Casselman 271

PLACE (Pronunciation)	PAGE	LAT.	LONG.
Canterbury, Austl.	243b	37°49′S	145°05′E
Canterbury, Eng., U.K. (kăn′tẽr-bẽr-ė)	151	51°17′N	1°06′E
Canterbury Bight, bt., N.Z.	203a	44°15′S	172°08′E
Canterbury Woods, Va., U.S.	229d	38°49′N	77°15′W
Cantiles, Cayo, i., Cuba (ky-ō-kän-tē′lås)	122	21°40′N	82°00′W
Canto do Pontes, Braz.	234c	22°58′S	43°04′W
Canton see Guangzhou, China	189	23°07′N	113°15′E
Canton, Ga., U.S.	114	34°13′N	84°29′W
Canton, Il., U.S.	111	40°34′N	90°02′W
Canton, Ma., U.S.	93a	42°09′N	71°09′W
Canton, Ms., U.S.	114	32°36′N	90°01′W
Canton, Mo., U.S.	111	40°08′N	91°33′W
Canton, N.C., U.S.	115	35°32′N	82°50′W
Canton, Oh., U.S.	97	40°50′N	81°25′W
Canton, Pa., U.S.	99	41°50′N	76°45′W
Canton, S.D., U.S.	102	43°17′N	96°37′W
Cantu, Italy (kän-tōō′)	160	45°43′N	9°09′E
Cañuelas, Arg. (kä-nyòē′-läs)	129c	35°03′S	58°45′W
Canyon, Ca., U.S.	231b	37°49′N	122°09′W
Canyon, Tx., U.S. (kăn′yŭn)	110	34°59′N	101°57′W
Canyon, r., Wa., U.S.	106a	48°09′N	121°48′W
Canyon De Chelly National Monument, rec., Az., U.S.	109	36°14′N	110°00′W
Canyon Ferry Lake, res., Mt., U.S.	105	46°33′N	111°37′W
Canyonlands National Park, Ut., U.S.	109	38°10′N	110°00′W
Caoxian, China (tsou shyĕn)	190	34°48′N	115°33′E
Capalonga, Phil. (kä-pä-lôŋ′gä)	197a	14°20′N	122°30′E
Capannori, Italy (kä-pän′nō-rē)	160	43°50′N	10°30′E
Capão Redondo, neigh., Braz.	234d	23°40′S	46°46′W
Caparica, Port.	238d	38°40′N	9°12′W
Capaya, r., Ven. (kä-pä-ĭä)	131b	10°28′N	66°15′W
Cap-Chat, Can. (kȧp-shȧ′)	85	48°02′N	65°20′W
Cap-de-la-Madeleine, Can. (kȧp dē lȧ mȧ-d′lĕn′)	91	46°23′N	72°30′W
Cape Breton, i., Can. (kāp brĕt′ŭn)	93	45°48′N	59°50′W
Cape Breton Highlands National Park, Can.	85	46°45′N	60°45′W
Cape Charles, Va., U.S. (kāp chärlz)	115	37°13′N	76°02′W
Cape Coast, Ghana	210	5°05′N	1°15′W
Cape Fear, r., N.C., U.S. (kāp fēr)	97	35°00′N	79°00′W
Cape Flats, pl., S. Afr. (kāp flăts)	212a	34°01′S	18°37′E
Cape Girardeau, Mo., U.S. (jē-rär-dō′)	97	37°17′N	89°32′W
Cape Krusenstern National Monument, rec., Ak., U.S.	95	67°30′N	163°40′W
Cape May, N.J., U.S. (kāp mā)	99	38°55′N	74°50′W
Cape May Court House, N.J., U.S.	99	39°05′N	75°00′W
Capenhurst, Eng., U.K.	237a	53°15′N	2°57′W
Cape Romanzof, Ak., U.S. (rō′ män zôf)	95	61°50′N	165°45′W
Capesterre, Guad.	121b	16°02′N	61°37′W
Cape Tormentine, Can.	92	46°08′N	63°47′W
Cape Town, S. Afr. (kāp toun)	212	33°48′S	18°28′E
Cape Verde, nation, Afr.	210b	15°48′N	26°02′W
Cape York Peninsula, pen., Austl. (kāp yôrk)	203	12°30′S	142°35′E
Cap-Haïtien, Haiti (kȧp ȧ-ē-syăn′)	117	19°45′N	72°15′W
Capilla de Señor, Arg. (kä-pēl′yä dā sān-yôr′)	129c	34°18′S	59°07′W
Capitachouane, r., Can.	91	47°50′N	76°45′W
Capitol Heights, Md., U.S.	229d	38°53′N	76°55′W
Capitol Reef National Park, Ut., U.S. (kăp′ĭ-tŏl)	109	38°15′N	111°10′W
Capitol View, Md., U.S.	229d	39°01′N	77°04′W
Capivari, Braz. (kä-pē-vá′rė)	129a	22°59′S	47°29′W
Capivari, r., Braz.	132b	22°39′S	43°19′W
Capoompeta, mtn., Austl. (kȧ-po͞om-pē′tȧ)	203	29°15′S	152°12′E
Capraia, i., Italy (kä-prä′yä)	148	43°02′N	9°51′E
Caprara Point, c., Italy (kä-prä′rä)	160	41°08′N	8°20′E
Capreol, Can.	91	46°43′N	80°56′W
Caprera, i., Italy (kä-prâ′rä)	160	41°12′N	9°28′E
Capri, Italy	159c	40°18′N	14°16′E
Capri, Isola di, i., Italy (ē′-sō-lä-dē-kä′prē)	159c	40°19′N	14°10′E
Capricorn Channel, strt., Austl. (kăp′rĭ-kôrn)	203	22°27′S	151°24′E
Caprivi Strip, hist. reg., Nmb.	212	18°00′S	22°00′E
Cap-Rouge, Can. (kȧp ro͞ozh′)	83b	46°45′N	71°21′W
Cap-Saint Ignace, Can. (kĭp sāɴ-tē-nyȧs′)	83b	47°02′N	70°27′W
Captain Cook Bridge, pt. of i., Austl.	243a	34°00′S	151°08′E
Capua, Italy (kä′pwä)	148	41°07′N	14°14′E
Capuáva, Braz.	234d	23°39′S	46°29′W
Capulhuac, Mex. (kä-pōl-hwäk′)	118	19°33′N	99°43′W
Capulin Mountain National Monument, rec., N.M., U.S. (kȧ-pū′lĭn)	110	36°15′N	103°58′W
Capultitlán, Mex. (kä-pōō′l-tē-tlä′n)	119a	19°15′N	99°40′W
Caputh, Ger.	238a	52°21′N	13°00′E
Caquetá (Japurá), r., S.A.	130	0°20′S	73°00′W
Caraballeda, Ven.	234a	10°37′N	66°50′W
Carabaña, Spain (kä-rä-bän′yä)	159a	40°16′N	3°15′W
Carabanchel Alto, neigh., Spain	238b	40°22′N	3°45′W
Carabanchel Bajo, neigh., Spain	238b	40°23′N	3°47′W
Carabelle, Fl., U.S. (kăr′á-bĕl)	114	29°50′N	84°40′W
Carabobo, dept., Ven. (kä-rä-bô′-bô)	131b	10°07′N	68°06′W
Caracal, Rom. (kȧ-rȧ-kȧl′)	161	44°06′N	24°22′E
Caracas, Ven. (kä-rä′käs)	130	10°30′N	66°58′W
Carácuaro de Morelos, Mex. (kä-rä′kwä-rō-dĕ-mô-rĕ-lôs)	118	18°44′N	101°04′W
Caraguatatuba, Braz. (kä-rä-gwä-tá-to͞o′bä)	129a	23°37′S	45°26′W
Carajás, Serra dos, mts., Braz. (sĕ′r-rä-dôs-kä-rä-zhá′s)	131	5°58′S	51°45′W
Caramanta, Cerro, mtn., Col. (sĕ′r-rô-kä-rä-má′n-tä)	130a	5°29′N	76°01′W
Carangola, Braz. (kä-rän′gŏ′lä)	129a	20°46′S	42°02′W
Carapicuíba, Braz.	234d	23°31′S	46°50′W
Caraquet, Can. (kä-rȧ-kĕt′)	85	47°48′N	64°57′W
Carata, Laguna, l., Nic. (lä-gŏ′nä-kä-rä′tä)	121	13°59′N	83°41′W
Caratasca, Laguna, l., Hond. (lä-gŏ′nä-kä-rä-täs′kä)	121	15°20′N	83°45′W
Caravaca, Spain (kä-rä-vä′kä)	158	38°05′N	1°51′W
Caravelas, Braz. (kȧ-rä-vĕl′äzh)	131	17°46′S	39°06′W
Carayaca, Ven. (kȧ-rä-ĭȧ′kä)	131b	10°32′N	67°07′W
Carȧzinho, Braz. (kä-rȧ′zē-nyō)	132	28°22′S	52°33′W
Carballiño, Spain	148	42°26′N	8°04′W
Carballo, Spain (kär-bäl′yō)	158	43°13′N	8°40′W
Carbet, Pitons du, mtn., Mart.	121b	14°40′N	61°05′W
Carbon, r., Wa., U.S. (kär′bŏn)	106a	47°06′N	122°08′W
Carbonado, Wa., U.S. (kȧr-bō-nā′dō)	106a	47°05′N	122°03′W
Carbonara, Cape, c., Italy (kär-bō-nä′rä)	148	39°08′N	9°33′E
Carbondale, Can. (kär′bŏn-dāl)	83g	53°45′N	113°32′W
Carbondale, Il., U.S.	98	37°42′N	89°12′W
Carbondale, Pa., U.S.	99	41°35′N	75°30′W
Carbonear, Can. (kär-bō-nēr′)	93	47°45′N	53°14′W
Carbon Hill, Al., U.S. (kär′bŏn hĭl)	114	33°53′N	87°34′W
Carcaixent, Spain	159	39°09′N	0°29′W
Carcans, Étang de, l., Fr. (ā-taɴ-dĕ-kär-käɴ)	156	45°12′N	1°00′W
Carcassonne, Fr. (kȧr-kȧ-sŏn′)	147	43°12′N	2°23′E
Carcross, Can. (kär′krôs)	84	60°18′N	134°54′W
Cárdenas, Cuba (kär′dȧ-näs)	117	23°00′N	81°10′W
Cárdenas, Mex.	118	22°01′N	99°38′W
Cárdenas, Mex. (kär-dĕ-näs)	119	17°59′N	93°23′W
Cárdenas, Bahía de, b., Cuba (bä-ē′ä-dĕ-kär′dȧ-näs)	122	23°10′N	81°10′W
Cardiff, Can. (kär′dĭf)	83g	53°46′N	113°36′W
Cardiff, Wales, U.K.	147	51°30′N	3°18′W
Cardigan, Wales, U.K. (kär′dĭ-găn)	147	52°05′N	4°40′W
Cardigan Bay, b., Wales, U.K.	147	52°35′N	4°40′W
Cardston, Can. (kärds′tŭn)	84	49°12′N	113°18′W
Carei, Rom. (kä-rē′)	155	47°42′N	22°28′E
Carentan, Fr. (kä-rôɴ-täɴ′)	156	49°19′N	1°14′W
Carey, Oh., U.S. (kā′rė)	98	40°55′N	83°25′W
Carey, l., Austl. (kâr′ė)	202	29°20′S	123°35′E
Carhaix-Plouguer, Fr. (kär-ĕ′)	156	48°17′N	3°37′W
Caribbean Sea, sea (kăr-ĭ-bē′ăn)	117	14°30′N	75°30′W
Caribe, Arroyo, r., Mex. (är-ro′i-kä-rē′bĕ)	119	18°18′N	90°38′W
Cariboo Mountains, mts., Can. (kă′rĭ-bo͞o)	84	53°00′N	121°00′W
Caribou, Me., U.S.	92	46°51′N	68°01′W
Caribou, i., Can.	90	47°22′N	85°42′W
Caribou Lake, l., Mn., U.S.	107h	46°54′N	92°16′W
Caribou Mountains, mts., Can.	84	59°20′N	115°30′W
Caringbah, Austl.	243a	34°03′S	151°08′E
Carinhanha, Braz. (kä-rĭ-nyän′yä)	131	14°14′S	43°44′W
Carini, Italy (kä-rē′nē)	160	38°09′N	13°10′E
Carinthia see Kärnten, prov., Aus.	154	46°55′N	13°42′E
Carleton Place, Can. (kärl′tŭn)	91	45°15′N	76°10′W
Carletonville, S. Afr.	218d	26°20′S	27°23′E
Carlingford, Austl.	243a	33°47′S	151°03′E
Carlinville, Il., U.S. (kär′lĭn-vĭl)	111	39°16′N	89°52′W
Carlisle, Eng., U.K. (kär-līl′)	142	54°54′N	3°03′W
Carlisle, Ky., U.S.	98	38°20′N	84°00′W
Carlisle, Pa., U.S.	99	40°10′N	77°15′W
Carloforte, Italy (kär′lō-fôr-tȧ)	160	39°11′N	8°28′E
Carlos Casares, Arg. (kär-lôs-kä-sä′rĕs)	132	35°38′S	61°17′W
Carlow, Ire. (kär′lō)	150	52°50′N	7°00′W
Carlsbad, N.M., U.S. (kärlz′băd)	112	32°24′N	104°12′W
Carlsbad Caverns National Park, rec., N.M., U.S.	112	32°08′N	104°30′W
Carlstadt, N.J., U.S.	228	40°50′N	74°06′W
Carlton, Eng., U.K. (kärl′tŭn)	144a	52°58′N	1°05′W
Carlton, Mn., U.S.	107h	46°40′N	92°26′W
Carlton Center, Mi., U.S. (kärl′tŭn sĕn′tẽr)	98	42°45′N	85°20′W
Carlyle, Il., U.S. (kärlīl′)	111	38°37′N	89°23′W
Carmagnolo, Italy (kär-mä-nyô′lä)	160	44°52′N	7°48′E
Carman, Can. (kär′mȧn)	84	49°32′N	98°00′W
Carmarthen, Wales, U.K. (kär-mär′thĕn)	150	51°50′N	4°20′W
Carmaux, Fr. (kȧr-mō′)	156	44°05′N	2°09′E
Carmel, N.Y., U.S. (kär′mĕl)	100a	41°25′N	73°42′W
Carmelo, Ur. (kär-mĕ′lo)	129c	33°59′S	58°15′W
Carmen, Isla del, i., Mex. (ē′s-lä-dĕl-kä′r-mĕn)	116	18°43′N	91°40′W
Carmen, Laguna del, l., Mex. (lä-gŏ′nä-dĕl-kä′r-mĕn)	119	18°15′N	93°26′W
Carmen de Areco, Arg. (kär′mĕn′ dā ä-rā′kō)	129c	34°21′S	59°50′W
Carmen de Patagones, Arg. (kȧ′r-mĕn-dĕ-pä-tä-gô′nĕs)	132	41°00′S	63°00′W
Carmi, Il., U.S. (kär′mī)	98	38°05′N	88°10′W
Carmo, Braz. (kȧ′r-mô)	129a	21°57′S	42°45′W
Carmo do Rio Clara, Braz. (kȧ′r-mô-dô-rē′ō-klä′rä)	129a	20°57′S	46°04′W
Carmona, Spain	158	37°28′N	5°38′W
Carnarvon, Austl. (kär-när′vŭn)	202	24°45′S	113°45′E
Carnarvon, S. Afr.	212	31°00′S	22°15′E
Carnation, Wa., U.S. (kär-nā′shŭn)	106a	47°39′N	121°55′W
Carnaxide, Port. (kär-nä-shē′dĕ)	159b	38°44′N	9°15′W
Carndonagh, Ire. (kärn-dō-nä′)	150	55°15′N	7°15′W
Carnegie, Ok., U.S. (kär-nĕg′ĭ)	110	35°06′N	98°38′W
Carnegie, Pa., U.S.	101e	40°24′N	80°06′W
Carnegie Institute, pt. of i., Pa., U.S.	230b	40°27′N	79°57′W
Carnetin, Fr.	237c	48°54′N	2°42′E
Carneys Point, N.J., U.S. (kär′nēs)	99	39°45′N	75°25′W
Carnic Alps, mts., Eur.	147	46°43′N	12°38′E
Carnide, neigh., Port.	238d	38°46′N	9°11′W
Carnot, Alg. (kär nō′)	159	36°15′N	1°40′E
Carnot, Cen. Afr. Rep.	211	5°00′N	15°52′E
Carnsore Point, c., Ire. (kärn′sôr)	150	52°10′N	6°16′W
Caro, Mi., U.S. (kâ′rō)	98	43°30′N	83°25′W
Carolina, Braz. (kä-rō-lē′nä)	131	7°26′S	47°16′W
Carolina, S. Afr. (kăr-ō-lī′nȧ)	212	26°07′S	30°09′E
Carolina, l., Mex. (kä-rō-lē′nä)	120a	18°41′N	89°40′W
Caroline Islands, is., Oc.	5	8°00′N	140°00′E
Caroni, r., Ven. (kä-rō′nē)	130	5°49′N	62°57′W
Carora, Ven. (kä-rō′rä)	130	10°09′N	70°12′W
Carpathians, mts., Eur. (kär-pā′thĭ-ăn)	142	49°23′N	20°14′E
Carpaţii Meridionali (Transylvanian Alps), mts., Rom.	142	45°30′N	23°30′E
Carpentaria, Gulf of, b., Austl. (kär-pĕn-târ′ĭȧ)	202	14°45′S	138°50′E
Carpentras, Fr. (kär-päɴ-träs′)	157	44°04′N	5°01′E
Carpi, Italy	160	44°48′N	10°54′E
Carrara, Italy (kä-rä′rä)	148	44°05′N	10°05′E
Carrauntoohil, Ire. (kă-rȧn-to͞o′ĭl)	150	52°01′N	9°48′W
Carretas, Punta, c., Peru (po͞o′n-tä-kär-rē′tĕ′rás)	130	14°15′S	76°25′W
Carriacou, i., Gren.	121b	12°28′N	61°20′W
Carrick-on-Sur, Ire. (kăr′-ĭk)	150	52°20′N	7°35′W
Carrier, Can. (kăr′ĭ-ẽr)	83b	46°43′N	71°05′W
Carriere, Ms., U.S. (kȧ-rēr′)	114	30°37′N	89°37′W
Carrières-sous-Bois, Fr.	237c	48°57′N	2°07′E
Carrières-sous-Poissy, Fr.	237c	48°57′N	2°03′E
Carrières-sur-Seine, Fr.	237c	48°55′N	2°11′E
Carriers Mills, Il., U.S. (kăr′ĭ-ẽrs)	98	37°40′N	88°40′W
Carrington, Eng., U.K.	237b	53°26′N	2°24′W
Carrington, N.D., U.S. (kăr′ĭng-tŭn)	102	47°26′N	99°06′W
Carr Inlet, Wa., U.S. (kär ĭn′lĕt)	106a	47°20′N	122°42′W
Carrion Crow Harbor, b., Bah. (kăr′ĭŭn krō)	122	26°35′N	77°55′W
Carrión de los Condes, Spain (kär-rē-ōn′ dā lōs kōn′dås)	158	42°20′N	4°35′W
Carrizo Creek, r., N.M., U.S. (kär-rē′zō)	110	36°22′N	103°39′W
Carrizo Springs, Tx., U.S.	112	28°32′N	99°51′W
Carrizozo, N.M., U.S. (kär-rē-zō′zō)	109	33°40′N	105°55′W
Carroll, Ia., U.S. (kăr′ŭl)	103	42°03′N	94°51′W
Carrollton, Ga., U.S. (kăr-ŭl-tŭn)	114	33°35′N	85°05′W
Carrollton, Il., U.S.	111	39°18′N	90°22′W
Carrollton, Ky., U.S.	98	38°45′N	85°15′W
Carrollton, Mi., U.S.	98	43°30′N	83°55′W
Carrollton, Mo., U.S.	111	39°21′N	93°29′W
Carrollton, Oh., U.S.	98	40°35′N	81°10′W
Carrollton, Tx., U.S.	107c	32°58′N	96°53′W
Carrols, Wa., U.S. (kăr′ŭlz)	106c	46°05′N	122°51′W
Carrot, r., Can.	88	53°12′N	103°50′W
Carry-le-Rouet, Fr. (kä-rē′lĕ-rō-ā′)	156a	43°20′N	5°10′E
Carsamba, Tur. (chär-shäm′bä)	149	41°05′N	36°40′E
Carshalton, neigh., Eng., U.K.	235	51°22′N	0°10′W
Carson, Ca., U.S.	232	33°50′N	118°16′W
Carson, r., Nv., U.S. (kär′sŭn)	108	39°15′N	119°25′W
Carson City, Nv., U.S.	96	39°10′N	119°45′W
Carsondale, Md., U.S.	229d	38°57′N	76°50′W
Carson Sink, Nv., U.S.	108	39°51′N	118°25′W
Cartagena, Col. (kär-tä-hā′nä)	130	10°30′N	75°40′W
Cartagena, Spain (kär-tä-ĸĕ′nä)	142	37°46′N	1°00′W
Cartago, Col. (kär-tä′gō)	130a	4°44′N	75°54′W
Cartago, C.R.	117	9°52′N	83°56′W
Cartaxo, Port. (kär-tä′shō)	158	39°10′N	8°48′W
Carteret, N.J., U.S. (kär′tē-ret)	100a	40°35′N	74°13′W
Cartersville, Ga., U.S. (kär′tẽrs-vĭl)	114	34°09′N	84°47′W
Carthage, Tun.	210	37°04′N	10°18′E
Carthage, Il., U.S. (kär′thȧj)	111	40°27′N	91°09′W
Carthage, Mo., U.S.	111	37°10′N	94°18′W
Carthage, N.Y., U.S.	99	44°00′N	75°45′W
Carthage, N.C., U.S.	115	35°22′N	79°25′W
Carthage, Tx., U.S.	113	32°09′N	94°20′W
Carthcart, S. Afr. (cärth-că′t)	213c	32°18′S	27°11′E
Cartwright, Can. (kärt′rīt)	85	53°36′N	57°00′W
Caruaru, Braz. (kä-rō-á-ro͞o′)	131	8°19′S	35°52′W
Carúpano, Ven. (kä-ro͞o′pä-nō)	130	10°45′N	63°21′W
Caruthersville, Mo., U.S. (kȧ-rŭdh′ẽrz-vĭl)	111	36°09′N	89°41′W
Carver, Or., U.S. (kärv′ẽr)	106c	45°24′N	122°30′W
Carvoeiro, Cabo, c., Port. (kȧ′bō-kär-vō-ĕ′y-rō)	158	39°22′N	9°24′W
Cary, Il., U.S. (kă′rė)	101a	42°13′N	88°14′W
Casablanca, Chile (kä-sä-blăŋ′kä)	129b	33°19′S	71°24′W
Casablanca, Mor.	210	33°32′N	7°41′W
Casa Branca, Braz. (kȧ′sä-brȧ′ɴ-kä)	129a	21°47′S	47°04′W
Casa Grande, Az., U.S. (kä′sä grän′dā)	109	32°50′N	111°45′W
Casa Grande National Monument, rec., Az., U.S.	109	33°00′N	111°33′W
Casale Monferrato, Italy (kä-sä′lā)	160	45°08′N	8°26′E
Casalmaggiore, Italy (kä-säl-mäd-jō′rä)	160	45°00′N	10°24′E
Casa Loma, pt. of i., Can.	227c	43°41′N	79°25′W
Casamance, r., Sen. (kä-sä-mäɴs′)	210	12°30′N	15°00′W
Cascade Mountains, mts., N.A.	87	49°10′N	121°00′W
Cascade Point, c., N.Z. (kăs-kād′)	203a	43°59′S	168°23′E
Cascade Range, mts., N.A.	96	42°50′N	122°20′W
Cascade Tunnel, trans., Wa., U.S.	104	47°41′N	120°53′W
Cascais, Port. (käs-kȧ-ēzh)	158	38°42′N	9°25′W
Case Inlet, Wa., U.S. (kās)	106a	47°22′N	122°47′W
Caseros, Arg. (kä-sā′rōs)	132a	34°35′S	58°34′W
Caserta, Italy (kä-zĕr′tä)	160	41°04′N	14°21′E
Casey, Il., U.S. (kā′sĭ)	98	39°20′N	88°00′W
Cashmere, Wa., U.S. (kăsh′mĭr)	104	47°30′N	120°28′W
Casiguran, Phil. (käs-sē-go͞o′rän)	197a	16°15′N	122°10′E
Casiguran Sound, strt., Phil.	197a	16°02′N	121°51′E
Casilda, Arg. (kä-sē′l-dä)	132	33°02′S	61°11′W
Casilda, Cuba	122	21°50′N	80°00′W
Casimiro de Abreu, Braz. (kȧ′sē-mē′ro-dĕ-ȧ-brĕ′o͞o)	129a	22°30′S	42°11′W
Casino, Austl. (kȧ-sē′nō)	204	28°35′S	153°10′E
Casiquiare, r., Ven. (kä-sē-kyä′rä)	130	2°11′N	66°15′W
Caspe, Spain (käs′pā)	159	41°18′N	0°02′W
Casper, Wy., U.S. (kăs′pẽr)	96	42°51′N	106°18′W
Caspian Depression, depr. (kăs′pĭ-ăn)	164	47°40′N	52°35′E
Caspian Sea, sea	164	40°00′N	52°00′E
Cass, W.V., U.S. (kăs)	99	38°25′N	79°55′W
Cass, l., Mn., U.S.	103	47°23′N	94°28′W
Cassai (Kasai), r., Afr. (kä-sä′ē)	212	11°30′S	21°00′E
Cass City, Mi., U.S. (kăs)	98	43°35′N	83°10′W
Casselman, Can. (kăs′'l-măn)	83c	45°18′N	75°05′W

272 Casselton-Chaldon

PLACE (Pronunciation)	PAGE	LAT.	LONG.
Casselton, N.D., U.S. (kăs''l-tŭn)	102	46°53'N	97°14'W
Cássia, Braz. (ká'syä)	129a	20°36'S	46°53'W
Cassin, Tx., U.S. (kăs'ĭn)	107d	29°16'N	98°29'W
Cassinga, Ang.	212	15°05'S	16°15'E
Cassino, Italy (käs-sē'nō)	148	41°30'N	13°50'E
Cass Lake, Mn., U.S. (kăs)	103	47°23'N	94°37'W
Cassopolis, Mi., U.S. (kăs-ŏ'pô-lĭs)	98	41°55'N	86°00'W
Cassville, Mo., U.S. (kăs'vĭl)	111	36°41'N	93°52'W
Castanheira de Pêra, Port. (käs-tän-yä'rä-dē-pē'rä)	158	40°00'N	8°07'W
Castellammare di Stabia, Italy	159c	40°26'N	14°29'E
Castellbisbal, Spain	238e	41°29'N	1°59'E
Castelli, Arg. (kás-tě'zhē)	129c	36°07'S	57°48'W
Castelló de la Plana, Spain	148	39°59'N	0°05'W
Castelnaudary, Fr. (käs'tĕl-nō-dá-rē')	156	43°20'N	1°57'E
Castelo, Braz. (käs-tĕ'lô)	129a	20°37'S	41°13'W
Castelo Branco, Port. (käs-tä'lò brän'kò)	148	39°48'N	7°37'W
Castelo de Vide, Port. (käs-tä'lò dĭ vē'dĭ)	158	39°25'N	7°25'W
Castelsarrasin, Fr. (kás'tĕl-sá-rá-zăɴ')	156	44°03'N	1°05'E
Castelvetrano, Italy (käs'tĕl-vē-trä'nō)	160	37°43'N	12°50'E
Castilla, Peru (kás-tē'l-yä)	130	5°18'S	80°40'W
Castilla La Nueva, hist. reg., Spain (käs-tē'lyä lä nwä'vä)	158	39°15'N	3°55'W
Castilla La Vieja, hist. reg., Spain (käs-tēl'yä lä vyā'hä)	158	40°48'N	4°24'W
Castillo de San Marcos National Monument, rec., Fl., U.S. (käs-tē'lyā de-sän mär-kōs)	115	29°55'N	81°25'W
Castle, i., Bah. (kás''l)	123	22°05'N	74°20'W
Castlebar, Ire. (kás''l-bär)	150	53°55'N	9°15'W
Castlecrag, Austl.	243a	33°48'S	151°13'E
Castle Dale, Ut., U.S. (kás'l dāl)	109	39°15'N	111°00'W
Castle Donington, Eng., U.K. (dŏn'ĭng-tŭn)	144a	52°50'N	1°21'W
Castleford, Eng., U.K. (kás'l-fērd)	144a	53°43'N	1°21'W
Castlegar, Can. (kás''l-gär)	87	49°19'N	117°40'W
Castle Hill, Austl.	243a	33°44'S	151°00'E
Castlemaine, Austl. (kás''l-mān)	204	37°05'S	144°10'E
Castle Peak, mtn., Co., U.S.	109	39°00'N	106°50'W
Castle Rock, Wa., U.S. (kás''l-rŏk)	104	46°17'N	122°53'W
Castle Rock Flowage, res., Wi., U.S.	103	44°03'N	89°48'W
Castle Shannon, Pa., U.S. (shăn'ŭn)	101e	40°22'N	80°02'W
Castleton, Eng., U.K.	237b	53°35'N	2°11'W
Castleton, In., U.S. (kás''l-tŏn)	101g	39°54'N	86°03'W
Castor, r., Can. (kás'tôr)	83c	45°16'N	75°14'W
Castor, r., Mo., U.S.	111	36°59'N	89°53'W
Castres, Fr. (kás'tr')	156	43°36'N	2°13'E
Castries, St. Luc. (kás-trē')	121b	14°01'N	61°00'W
Castro, Braz. (käs'trô)	131	24°56'S	50°00'W
Castro, Chile (käs'trō)	132	42°27'S	73°48'W
Castro Daire, Port. (käs'trò dīr'ĭ)	158	40°56'N	7°57'W
Castro del Río, Spain (käs-trô-dĕl rē'ō)	158	37°42'N	4°28'W
Castrop Rauxel, Ger. (käs'trōp rou'ksĕl)	157c	51°33'N	7°19'E
Castro-Urdiales, Spain	148	43°23'N	3°11'W
Castro Valley, Ca., U.S.	106b	37°42'N	122°05'W
Castro Verde, Port. (käs-trō vĕr'dĕ)	158	37°43'N	8°05'W
Castrovillari, Italy (kás'trō-vēl-lyä'rē)	160	39°48'N	16°11'E
Castuera, Spain (käs-tò-ā'rä)	158	38°43'N	5°33'W
Casula, Moz.	217	15°25'S	33°40'E
Cat, i., Bah.	123	24°30'N	75°30'W
Catacamas, Hond. (kä-tä-ká'mäs)	120	14°52'N	85°55'W
Cataguases, Braz. (kä-tä-gwá'sĕs)	129a	21°23'S	42°42'W
Catahoula, l., La., U.S. (kăt-á-hò'lá)	113	31°35'N	92°20'W
Catalão, Braz. (kä-tä-louɴ')	131	18°09'S	47°42'W
Catalina, i., Dom. Rep. (kä-tä-lē'nä)	123	18°20'N	69°00'W
Cataluña, Museo de Arte de, bldg., Spain	238e	41°23'N	2°09'E
Catalunya, hist. reg., Spain	159	41°23'N	0°50'E
Catamarca, Arg. (kä-tä-mä'r-kä)	132	28°29'S	65°45'W
Catamarca, prov., Arg. (kä-tä-mär'kä)	132	27°15'S	67°15'W
Catanauan, Phil. (kä-tä-nä'wän)	197a	13°36'N	122°20'E
Catanduanes Island, i., Phil. (kä-tän-dwä'nĕs)	197	13°55'N	125°00'E
Catanduva, Braz. (kä-tán-dōō'vä)	131	21°12'S	48°47'W
Catania, Italy (kä-tä'nyä)	142	37°30'N	15°09'E
Catania, Golfo di, b., Italy (gôl-fô-dē-kä-tä'nyä)	160	37°24'N	15°28'E
Catanzaro, Italy (kä-tän-dzä'rō)	149	38°53'N	16°34'E
Catarroja, Spain (kä-tär-rō'hä)	159	39°24'N	0°25'W
Catawba, r., N.C., U.S. (kă-tô'bá)	115	35°25'N	80°55'W
Catbalogan, Phil. (kät-bä-lō'gän)	197	11°45'N	124°52'E
Catemaco, Mex. (kä-tä-mä'kō)	119	18°26'N	95°06'W
Catemaco, Lago, l., Mex. (lä'gô-kä-tä-mä'kō)	119	18°23'N	95°04'W
Caterham, Eng., U.K. (kā'tēr-ŭm)	144b	51°16'N	0°04'W
Catete, Ang. (kä-tě'tě)	212	9°06'S	13°43'E
Catete, neigh., Braz.	234c	22°55'S	43°10'W
Catford, neigh., Eng., U.K.	235	51°27'N	0°01'W
Cathedral Mountain, mtn., Tx., U.S. (ká-thē'drăl)	112	30°09'N	103°46'W
Cathedral Peak, mtn., Afr. (kă-thē'drăl)	213c	28°53'S	29°04'E
Catherine, Lake, l., Ar., U.S. (kă-thēr-ĭn)	111	34°26'N	92°47'W
Cathkin Peak, mtn., Afr. (kăth'kĭn)	212	29°08'S	29°22'E
Cathlamet, Wa., U.S. (kăth-lăm'ĕt)	106c	46°12'N	123°22'W
Catia, neigh., Ven.	234a	10°31'N	66°57'W
Catlettsburg, Ky., U.S. (kăt'lĕts-bûrg)	98	38°20'N	82°35'W
Catoche, Cabo, c., Mex. (kä-tô'chĕ)	116	21°30'N	87°15'W
Catonsville, Md., U.S. (kā'tŭnz-vĭl)	100e	39°16'N	76°45'W
Catorce, Mex. (kä-tôr'sá)	118	23°41'N	100°51'W
Catskill, N.Y., U.S. (kăts'kĭl)	99	42°15'N	73°50'W
Catskill Mountains, mts., N.Y., U.S.	97	42°20'N	74°35'W
Cattaraugus Indian Reservation, I.R., N.Y., U.S. (kăt'tá-rá-gŭs)	99	42°30'N	79°05'W
Catu, Braz. (ká-tōō)	131	12°26'S	38°12'W
Catuala, Ang.	216	16°29'S	19°03'E
Catumbela, r., Ang. (kă'tŏm-bĕl'á)	216	12°40'S	14°10'E
Cauayan, Phil. (kou-ä'yän)	197a	16°56'N	121°46'E
Cauca, r., Col. (kou'kä)	130	7°30'N	75°26'W
Caucagua, Ven. (käò-ká'gwä)	131b	10°17'N	66°22'W
Caucasus, mts.	164	43°20'N	42°00'E
Cauchon Lake, l., Can. (kô-shŏn')	89	55°25'N	96°30'W
Caughnawaga, Can.	83a	45°24'N	73°41'W
Caulfield, Austl.	201a	37°53'S	145°03'E
Caulonia, Italy (kou-lō'nyä)	160	38°24'N	16°22'E
Cauquenes, Chile (kou-kā'năs)	132	35°54'S	72°14'W
Caura, r., Ven. (kou'rä)	130	6°48'N	64°40'W
Causapscal, Can.	92	48°22'N	67°14'W
Caution, Cape, c., Can. (kô'shŭn)	86	51°10'N	127°47'W
Cauto, r., Cuba (kou'tō)	122	20°33'N	76°20'W
Cauvery, r., India	183	12°00'N	77°00'E
Cava, Braz. (ká'vä)	132b	22°41'S	43°26'W
Cava de' Tirreni, Italy (kä'vä-dĕ-tēr-rĕ'nē)	159c	40°27'N	14°43'E
Cávado, r., Port. (kä-vä'dō)	158	41°43'N	8°08'W
Cavalcante, Braz. (kä-väl-kän'tā)	131	13°45'S	47°33'W
Cavalier, N.D., U.S. (kăv-á-lēr')	102	48°45'N	97°39'W
Cavally, r., Afr.	214	4°40'N	7°30'W
Cavan, Ire. (kăv'ăn)	150	54°01'N	7°00'W
Cavarzere, Italy (kä-vär'dzā-rā)	160	45°08'N	12°06'E
Cavendish, Vt., U.S. (kăv'ĕn-dĭsh)	99	43°25'N	72°35'W
Caviana, Ilha, i., Braz. (kä-vyä'nä)	131	0°45'N	49°33'W
Cavite, Phil. (kä-vē'tä)	197a	14°30'N	120°54'E
Caxambu, Braz. (kä-shá'm-bōō)	131	22°00'S	44°45'W
Caxias, Braz. (kä'shē-äzh)	131	4°48'S	43°16'W
Caxias, Port.	238d	38°42'N	9°16'W
Caxias do Sul, Braz. (kä'shē-äzh-dò-sōō'l)	132	29°13'S	51°03'W
Caxito, Ang. (kä-shē'tò)	212	8°33'S	13°36'E
Cayambe, Ec. (ká-īá'm-bĕ)	130	0°03'N	79°09'W
Cayenne, Fr. Gu. (kā-ĕn')	131	4°56'N	52°18'W
Cayetano Rubio, Mex. (kä-yĕ-tá-nō-rōō'byô)	118	20°37'N	100°21'W
Cayey, P.R.	117b	18°05'N	66°12'W
Cayman Brac, i., Cay. Is. (kī-män' brák)	122	19°45'N	79°50'W
Cayman Islands, dep., N.A.	122	19°30'N	80°30'W
Cay Sal Bank, bk. (kē-săl)	122	23°55'N	80°20'W
Cayuga, l., N.Y., U.S. (kā-yōō'gá)	99	42°35'N	76°35'W
Cazalla de la Sierra, Spain	158	37°55'N	5°48'W
Cazaux, Étang de, l., Fr. (ā-tăn' dĕ kä-zō')	156	44°32'N	0°59'W
Cazenovia, N.Y., U.S. (kăz-ē-nō'vĭ-á)	99	42°55'N	75°50'W
Cazenovia Creek, r., N.Y., U.S.	101c	42°49'N	78°45'W
Čazma, Cro. (chäz'mä)	160	45°44'N	16°39'E
Cazombo, Ang. (kä-zô'm-bō)	212	11°54'S	22°52'E
Cazones, r., Mex. (kä-zô'nĕs)	119	20°37'N	97°28'W
Cazones, Ensenada de, b., Cuba (ĕn-sĕ-nä-dä-dĕ-kä-zō'nás)	122	22°05'N	81°30'W
Cazones, Golfo de, b., Cuba (gôl-fô-dĕ-kä-zō'nás)	122	21°55'N	81°15'W
Cazorla, Spain (kä-thôr'lá)	158	37°55'N	2°58'W
Cea, r., Spain (thā'ä)	158	42°18'N	5°10'W
Ceará-Mirim, Braz. (sā-ä-rä'mē-rē'ɴ)	131	6°00'S	35°13'W
Cebaco, Isla, i., Pan. (ē's-lä-sä-bä'kō)	121	7°27'N	81°08'W
Cebolla Creek, r., Co., U.S. (sē-bōl'yä)	109	38°15'N	107°10'W
Cebreros, Spain (sē-brĕ'rôs)	158	40°28'N	4°28'W
Cebu, Phil. (sā-bōō')	197	10°22'N	123°49'E
Cecchignola, neigh., Italy	239c	41°49'N	12°29'E
Čechy (Bohemia), hist. reg., Czech Rep.	154	49°51'N	13°55'E
Cecil, Pa., U.S. (sē'sĭl)	101e	40°20'N	80°10'W
Cecil Park, Austl.	243a	33°52'S	150°51'E
Cedar, r., Ia., U.S.	103	42°23'N	92°07'W
Cedar, r., Wa., U.S.	106c	45°56'N	122°32'W
Cedar, West Fork, r., Ia., U.S.	103	42°49'N	93°10'W
Cedar Bayou, Tx., U.S.	113a	29°54'N	94°58'W
Cedar Breaks National Monument, rec., Ut., U.S.	109	37°35'N	112°55'W
Cedarbrook, Pa., U.S.	229b	40°05'N	75°10'W
Cedarburg, Wi., U.S. (sē'dēr bûrg)	103	43°23'N	88°00'W
Cedar City, Ut., U.S.	109	37°40'N	113°10'W
Cedar Creek, r., N.D., U.S.	102	46°05'N	102°10'W
Cedar Falls, Ia., U.S.	103	42°31'N	92°29'W
Cedar Grove, N.J., U.S.	228	40°51'N	74°14'W
Cedar Heights, Pa., U.S.	229b	40°05'N	75°17'W
Cedarhurst, N.Y., U.S.	228	40°38'N	73°44'W
Cedar Keys, Fl., U.S.	114	29°06'N	83°03'W
Cedar Lake, In., U.S.	101a	41°22'N	87°27'W
Cedar Lake, l., In., U.S.	101a	41°23'N	87°25'W
Cedar Lake, res., Can.	84	53°10'N	100°00'W
Cedar Rapids, Ia., U.S.	97	42°00'N	91°43'W
Cedar Springs, Mi., U.S.	98	43°15'N	85°40'W
Cedartown, Ga., U.S. (sē'dēr-toun)	114	34°00'N	85°15'W
Cedarville, S. Afr. (cĕdăr'vĭl)	213c	30°23'S	29°04'E
Cedral, Mex. (sā-dräl')	118	23°47'N	100°42'W
Cedros, Hond. (sā'drōs)	120	14°36'N	87°07'W
Cedros, i., Mex.	116	28°10'N	115°10'W
Ceduna, Austl. (sē-dò'nă)	202	32°15'S	133°55'E
Ceel Buur, Som.	218a	4°35'N	46°40'E
Cega, r., Spain (thā'gä)	158	41°25'N	4°27'W
Cegléd, Hung. (tsā'glād)	155	47°10'N	19°49'E
Ceglie, Italy (chĕ'lyĕ)	161	40°39'N	17°32'E
Cehegín, Spain (thā-á-hēn')	158	38°05'N	1°48'W
Ceiba del Agua, Cuba (sā'bä-dĕl-á'gwä)	123a	22°53'N	82°38'W
Cekhira, Tun.	210	34°17'N	10°00'E
Celaya, Mex. (sā-lä'yä)	116	20°33'N	100°49'W
Celebes (Sulawesi), i., Indon.	196	2°15'S	120°30'E
Celebes Sea, sea, Asia	196	3°45'N	121°52'E
Celestún, Mex. (sĕ-lĕs-tōō'n)	120a	20°57'N	90°18'W
Celina, Oh., U.S. (sĕlĭ'na)	98	40°30'N	84°35'W
Celje, Slvn. (tsĕl'yĕ)	160	46°13'N	15°17'E
Celle, Ger. (tsĕl'ĕ)	147	52°37'N	10°05'E
Cement, Ok., U.S. (sē-mĕnt')	110	34°56'N	98°07'W
Cenderawasih, Teluk, b., Indon.	197	2°20'S	135°30'E
Ceniza, Pico, mtn., Ven. (pē'kô-sē-nē'zä)	131b	10°24'N	67°26'W
Center, Tx., U.S. (sĕn'tēr)	113	31°50'N	94°10'W
Center Hill Lake, res., Tn., U.S. (sĕn'tēr-hĭl)	114	36°02'N	86°00'W
Center Line, Mi., U.S. (sĕn'tēr līn)	101b	42°29'N	83°01'W
Centerville, Ia., U.S. (sĕn'tēr-vĭl)	103	40°44'N	92°48'W
Centerville, Mn., U.S.	107g	45°10'N	93°03'W
Centerville, Pa., U.S.	101e	40°02'N	79°58'W
Centerville, S.D., U.S.	102	43°07'N	96°56'W
Centerville, Ut., U.S.	107b	40°55'N	111°53'W
Centocelle, neigh., Italy	239c	41°53'N	12°34'E
Central, Cordillera, mts., Bol. (kôr-dĕl-yĕ'rä-sĕn-trá'l)	130	19°18'S	65°29'W
Central, Cordillera, mts., Col.	130a	3°58'N	75°55'W
Central, Cordillera, mts., Dom. Rep.	123	19°05'N	71°30'W
Central, Cordillera, mts., Phil. (kôr-dĕl-yĕ'rä-sĕn'träl)	197a	17°05'N	120°55'E
Central African Republic, nation, Afr.	211	7°50'N	21°00'E
Central America, reg., N.A. (á-mĕr'ĭ-ká)	116	10°45'N	87°15'W
Central City, Ky., U.S. (sĕn'trăl)	114	37°15'N	87°09'W
Central City, Ne., U.S. (sĕn'trál sĭ'tĭ)	102	41°07'N	98°00'W
Central Falls, R.I., U.S. (sĕn'trăl fôlz)	100b	41°54'N	71°23'W
Central Highlands, Pa., U.S.	230b	40°16'N	79°50'W
Centralia, Il., U.S. (sĕn-trā'lĭ-á)	98	38°35'N	89°05'W
Centralia, Mo., U.S.	111	39°11'N	92°07'W
Centralia, Wa., U.S.	104	46°42'N	122°58'W
Central Intelligence Agency, pt. of i., Va., U.S.	229d	38°57'N	77°09'W
Central Park, pt. of i., N.Y., U.S.	228	40°47'N	73°58'W
Central Plateau, plat., Russia	166	55°00'N	33°30'E
Central Valley, N.Y., U.S.	100a	41°19'N	74°07'W
Centre Island, N.Y., U.S.	228	40°54'N	73°32'W
Centreville, Il., U.S. (sĕn'tēr-vĭl)	107e	38°33'N	90°06'W
Centreville, Md., U.S.	99	39°05'N	76°05'W
Centro Simón Bolívar, pt. of i., Ven.	234a	10°30'N	66°55'W
Century, Fl., U.S. (sĕn'tū-rĭ)	114	30°57'N	87°15'W
Century City, neigh., Ca., U.S.	232	34°03'N	118°26'W
Ceram (Seram), i., Indon.	197	2°45'S	129°30'E
Céret, Fr.	156	42°29'N	2°47'E
Cerignola, Italy (chā-rē-nyō'lä)	160	41°16'N	15°55'E
Cerknica, Slvn. (tsĕr'knē-tsá)	160	45°48'N	14°21'E
Cern'achovsk, Russia (chĕr-nyä'κôfsk)	166	54°38'N	21°49'E
Čer'omuski, neigh., Russia	239b	55°41'N	37°35'E
Cerralvo, Mex. (sĕr-räl'vō)	112	26°05'N	99°37'W
Cerralvo, i., Mex.	116	24°00'N	109°59'W
Cerrito, Col. (sĕr-rē'-tô)	130a	3°41'N	76°17'W
Cerritos, Mex. (sĕr-rē'tôs)	118	22°26'N	100°16'W
Cerro de Pasco, Peru (sĕr'rō dā päs'kō)	130	10°45'S	76°14'W
Cerro Gordo, Arroyo de, r., Mex. (är-rō-yō-dĕ-sĕ'r-rō-gôr-dō)	112	26°12'N	104°06'W
Čertanovo, neigh., Russia	239b	55°38'N	37°37'E
Certegui, Col. (sĕr-tĕ'gē)	130a	5°21'N	76°35'W
Cervantes, Phil. (sĕr-vän'tās)	197a	16°59'N	120°42'E
Cervera del Río Alhama, Spain	158	42°02'N	1°55'W
Cerveteri, Italy (chĕr-vĕ'tĕ-rē)	159d	42°00'N	12°06'E
Cesano Boscone, Italy	238c	45°27'N	9°06'E
Cesena, Italy (chĕ'sĕ-nä)	160	44°08'N	12°16'E
Cēsis, Lat. (sä'sĭs)	153	57°19'N	25°17'E
Česká Lípa, Czech Rep. (chĕs'kä lē'pa)	154	50°41'N	14°31'E
České Budějovice, Czech Rep. (chĕs'kā bōō'dyĕ-yô-vĕt-sĕ)	147	49°00'N	14°30'E
Českomoravská Vysočina, hills, Czech Rep.	154	49°21'N	15°40'E
Český Těšín, Czech Rep.	155	49°43'N	18°22'E
Çeşme, Tur. (chĕsh'mĕ)	161	38°20'N	26°20'E
Cessnock, Austl.	203	32°58'S	151°15'E
Cestos, r., Lib.	214	5°40'N	9°25'W
Cetinje, Yugo. (tsĕt'ĭn-yĕ)	142	42°23'N	18°55'E
Ceuta, Sp. N. Afr. (thā-ōō'tä)	210	36°04'N	5°36'W
Cévennes, reg., Fr. (sā-vĕn')	147	44°20'N	3°48'E
Ceylon see Sri Lanka, nation, Asia	183b	8°45'N	82°30'E
Chabot, Lake, l., Ca., U.S. (sha'bŏt)	106b	37°44'N	122°06'W
Chacabuco, Arg. (chä-kä-bōō'kō)	129c	34°37'S	60°27'W
Chacaltianguis, Mex. (chä-käl-tē-äŋ'gwĕs)	119	18°18'N	95°50'W
Chacao, Ven.	234a	10°30'N	66°51'W
Chachapoyas, Peru (chä-chä-poi'yäs)	130	6°16'S	77°48'W
Chaco, prov., Arg. (chä'kō)	132	26°00'S	60°45'W
Chaco Culture National Historic Park, rec., N.M., U.S. (chä'kô)	109	36°05'N	108°00'W
Chad, Russia (chäd)	172a	56°33'N	57°11'E
Chad, nation, Afr.	211	17°48'N	19°00'E
Chad, Lake, l., Afr.	211	13°55'N	13°40'E
Chadbourn, N.C., U.S. (chăd'bŭrn)	115	34°19'N	78°55'W
Chadderton, Eng., U.K.	237b	53°33'N	2°08'W
Chadron, Ne., U.S. (chăd'rŭn)	96	42°50'N	103°10'W
Chadstone, Austl.	243b	37°53'S	145°05'E
Chadwell Saint Mary, Eng., U.K.	235	51°29'N	0°22'E
Chafarinas, Islas, is., Sp. N. Afr.	158	35°08'N	2°20'W
Chaffee, Mo., U.S. (chăf'ē)	111	37°10'N	89°39'W
Chāgal Hills, hills, Afg.	182	29°15'N	63°28'E
Chagodoshcha, r., Russia (chä-gō-dôsh-chä)	162	59°08'N	35°13'E
Chagres, r., Pan. (chä'grĕs)	121	9°18'N	79°22'W
Chagrin, r., Oh., U.S. (shá'grĭn)	101d	41°34'N	81°24'W
Chagrin Falls, Oh., U.S. (shá'grĭn fôls)	101d	41°26'N	81°23'W
Chahar, hist. reg., China (chä-här)	189	44°25'N	115°00'E
Chahār Borjak, Afg.	185	30°17'N	62°03'E
Chakdaha, India	240a	22°28'N	88°20'E
Chake Chake, Tan.	217	5°15'S	39°46'E
Chalatenango, El Sal. (chäl-ä-tĕ-näŋ'gō)	120	14°04'N	88°54'W
Chalbi Desert, des., Kenya	217	3°40'N	36°50'E
Chalcatongo, Mex. (chäl-kä-tôŋ'gō)	119	17°04'N	97°41'W
Chalchihuites, Mex. (chäl-chē-wē'tás)	118	23°28'N	103°57'W
Chalchuapa, El Sal. (chäl-chwä'pä)	120	14°01'N	89°39'W
Chalco, Mex. (chäl-kō)	119a	19°15'N	98°54'W
Chaldon, Eng., U.K.	235	51°17'N	0°07'W

PRONOUNCING INDEX

Chaleur Bay–Cheremkhovo 273

PLACE (Pronunciation)	PAGE	LAT.	LONG.
Chaleur Bay, b., Can. (shȧ-lûr′)	85	47°58′N	65°33′W
Chalfant, Pa., U.S.	230b	40°25′N	79°52′W
Chalfont Common, Eng., U.K.	235	51°38′N	0°33′W
Chalfont Saint Giles, Eng., U.K.	235	51°38′N	0°34′W
Chalfont Saint Peter, Eng., U.K.	235	51°37′N	0°33′W
Chalgrove, Eng., U.K. (chăl′grȯv)	144b	51°38′N	1°05′W
Chaling, China (chä′lĭng)	193	27°00′N	113°31′E
Chalk, Eng., U.K.	235	51°26′N	0°25′E
Chalmette, La., U.S. (shăl-mĕt′)	100d	29°57′N	89°57′W
Châlons-sur-Marne, Fr. (shȧ-lôɴ′sür-märn)	147	48°57′N	4°23′E
Chalon-sur-Saône, Fr.	147	46°47′N	4°54′E
Chaltel, Cerro (Monte Fitzroy), mtn., S.A. (sĕ′r-rȯ-chäl′tĕl)	132	48°10′S	73°18′W
Chālūs, Iran	185	36°38′N	51°26′E
Chama, Rio, r., N.M., U.S. (chä′mä)	109	36°19′N	106°31′W
Chama, Sierra de, mts., Guat. (sē-ĕ′r-rä-dĕ-chä-mä)	120	15°48′N	90°20′W
Chamama, Mwi.	217	12°55′S	33°43′E
Chaman, Pak. (chŭm-än′)	183	30°58′N	66°21′E
Chambal, r., India (chŭm-bäl′)	183	24°30′N	75°30′E
Chamberlain, S.D., U.S. (chām′bẽr-lĭn)	102	43°48′N	99°21′W
Chamberlain, l., Me., U.S.	92	46°15′N	69°10′W
Chambersburg, Pa., U.S. (chām′bẽrz-bûrg)	99	40°00′N	77°40′W
Chambéry, Fr. (shäm-bā-rē′)	147	45°35′N	5°54′E
Chambeshi, r., Zam.	217	10°35′S	31°20′E
Chamblee, Ga., U.S. (chăm-blē′)	100c	33°55′N	84°18′W
Chambly, Can. (shäɴ-blē′)	83a	45°27′N	73°17′W
Chambly, Fr.	157b	49°11′N	2°14′E
Chambord, Can.	85	48°22′N	72°01′W
Chambourcy, Fr.	237c	48°54′N	2°03′E
Chame, Punta, c., Pan. (pȯ′n-tä-chä′mȧ)	121	8°41′N	79°27′W
Chamelecón, r., Hond. (chä-mĕ-lĕ-kô′n)	120	15°09′N	88°42′W
Chamo, l., Eth.	211	5°58′N	37°00′E
Chamonix-Mont-Blanc, Fr. (shȧ-mȯ-nē′)	157	45°55′N	6°50′E
Champagne, reg., Fr. (shäm-pän′yē)	156	48°53′N	4°48′E
Champaign, Il., U.S. (shăm-pān′)	97	40°10′N	88°15′W
Champdāni, India	186a	22°48′N	88°21′E
Champerico, Guat. (chăm-pȧ-rē′kō)	120	14°18′N	91°55′W
Champigny-sur-Marne, Fr.	237c	48°49′N	2°31′E
Champion, Mi., U.S. (chăm′pĭ-ŭn)	103	46°30′N	87°59′W
Champlain, Lake, l., N.A. (shăm-plān′)	97	44°45′N	73°20′W
Champlan, Fr.	237c	48°43′N	2°16′E
Champlitte-et-le-Prálot, Fr. (shäɴ-plēt′)	157	47°38′N	5°28′E
Champotón, Mex. (chäm-pō-tōn′)	119	19°21′N	90°43′W
Champotón, r., Mex.	119	19°19′N	90°15′W
Champs-sur-Marne, Fr.	237c	48°51′N	2°36′E
Chāmrāil, India	240a	22°38′N	88°18′E
Chañaral, Chile (chän-yä-räl′)	132	26°20′S	70°46′W
Chances Peak, vol., Monts.	121b	16°43′N	62°10′W
Chandannagar, India	240a	22°51′N	88°21′E
Chandeleur Islands, is., La., U.S. (shăn-dĕ-lo͞or′)	114	29°53′N	88°35′W
Chandeleur Sound, strt., La., U.S.	114	29°47′N	89°08′W
Chandīgarh, India	183	30°51′N	77°13′E
Chandler, Can. (chăn′dlẽr)	85	48°21′N	64°41′W
Chandler, Ok., U.S.	111	35°42′N	96°52′W
Chandler's Cross, Eng., U.K.	235	51°40′N	0°27′W
Chandrapur, India	183	19°58′N	79°21′E
Chang *see* Yangtze, r., China	189	30°30′N	117°25′E
Changane, r., Moz.	212	22°42′S	32°46′E
Changara, Moz.	217	16°54′S	33°14′E
Changchun, China (chäŋ-chȯn)	189	43°55′N	125°25′E
Changdang Hu, l., China (chäŋ-däŋ ho͞o)	190	31°37′N	119°29′E
Changde, China (chäŋ-dŭ)	189	29°00′N	111°38′E
Changdian, China	240b	40°01′N	116°32′E
Changhua, Tai. (chäng′hwä′)	193	24°02′N	120°32′E
Changi, Sing.	240c	1°23′N	103°59′E
Changjŏn, N. Kor. (chäng′jŭn′)	194	38°40′N	128°05′E
Changli, China (chäŋ-lē)	192	39°46′N	119°10′E
Changning, China (chäŋ-nĭŋ)	188	24°34′N	99°49′E
Changping, China (chäŋ-pĭŋ)	192	40°12′N	116°10′E
Changqing, China (chäŋ-chyĭŋ)	190	36°33′N	116°42′E
Changsan Got, c., N. Kor.	194	38°06′N	124°50′E
Changsha, China (chäŋ-shä)	189	28°20′N	113°00′E
Changshan Qundao, is., China (chäŋ-shän chyȯn-dou)	190	39°08′N	122°26′E
Changshu, China (chäŋ-sho͞o)	190	31°40′N	120°45′E
Changting, China	193	25°50′N	116°18′E
Changwu, China (chäng′wo͞o′)	192	35°12′N	107°45′E
Changxindianzhen, China (chäŋ-shyĭn-dĭĕn-jŭn)	192a	39°49′N	116°12′E
Changxing Dao, i., China (chäŋ-shyĭŋ dou)	190	39°38′N	121°10′E
Changyi, China (chäŋ-yē)	190	36°51′N	119°23′E
Changyuan, China (chyäŋ-yuän)	190	35°10′N	114°41′E
Changzhi, China (chäŋ-jr)	192	35°58′N	112°58′E
Changzhou, China (chäŋ-jō)	189	31°47′N	119°56′E
Changzhuyuan, China (chäŋ-jo͞o-yuän)	190	31°33′N	115°17′E
Chanhassen, Mn., U.S. (shān′hăs-sĕn)	107g	44°52′N	93°32′W
Chanh-hung, Viet	241j	10°43′N	106°41′E
Channel Islands, is., Eur. (chăn′ĕl)	142	49°15′N	3°30′W
Channel Islands, is., Ca., U.S.	108	33°30′N	119°15′W
Channel-Port-aux-Basques, Can.	85	47°35′N	59°11′W
Channelview, Tx., U.S. (chănĕlvū)	113a	29°46′N	95°07′W
Chantada, Spain (chän-tä′dä)	158	42°38′N	7°36′W
Chanteloup-les-Vignes, Fr.	237c	48°59′N	2°02′E
Chanthaburi, Thai.	196	12°37′N	102°04′E
Chantilly, Fr. (shäɴ-tē-yē′)	157b	49°12′N	2°30′E
Chantilly, Va., U.S. (shăn′tĭlē)	100e	38°53′N	77°26′W
Chantrey Inlet, b., Can. (chăn-trē)	84	67°49′N	95°00′W
Chanute, Ks., U.S. (shȧ-no͞ot′)	97	37°41′N	95°27′W
Chany, l., Russia (chä′nē)	164	54°15′N	77°31′E
Chao'an, China (chou-än)	189	23°48′N	116°35′E
Chao Hu, l., China	193	31°45′N	116°59′E
Chao Phraya, r., Thai.	196	16°13′N	99°33′E
Chaor, r., China (chou-r)	192	47°20′N	121°40′E
Chaoshui, China (chou-shwā)	190	37°43′N	120°56′E
Chaoxian, China (chou shyĕn)	190	31°37′N	117°50′E
Chaoyang, China	189	41°32′N	120°20′E
Chaoyang, China (chou-yäŋ)	193	23°18′N	116°32′E
Chapada, Serra da, mts., Braz. (sĕ′r-rä-dä-shä-pä′dä)	131	14°57′S	54°34′W
Chapadão, Serra do, mtn., Braz. (sĕ′r-rä-dȯ-shä-pȧ-dou′ɴ)	129a	20°31′S	46°20′W
Chapala, Mex. (chä-pä′lä)	118	20°18′N	103°10′W
Chapala, Lago de, l., Mex. (lä′gô-dĕ-chä-pä′lä)	116	20°14′N	103°02′W
Chapalagana, r., Mex. (chä-pä-lä-gȧ′nä)	118	22°11′N	104°09′W
Chaparral, Col. (chä-pär-rȧ′l)	130	3°44′N	75°28′W
Chapayevsk, Russia (châ-pī′ĕfsk)	166	53°00′N	49°30′E
Chapel Hill, N.C., U.S. (chăp′′l hĭl)	115	35°55′N	79°05′W
Chapel Oaks, Md., U.S.	229d	38°54′N	76°55′W
Chapeltown, Eng., U.K.	237b	53°38′N	2°24′W
Chaplain, l., Wa., U.S. (chăp′lĭn)	106a	47°58′N	121°50′W
Chapleau, Can. (chăp-lō′)	85	47°43′N	83°28′W
Chapman, Mount, mtn., Can. (chăp′mȧn)	87	51°50′N	118°20′W
Chapman's Bay, b., S. Afr. (chăp′mȧns bă)	212a	34°06′S	18°17′E
Chapman Woods, Ca., U.S.	232	34°08′N	118°05′W
Chappell, Ne., U.S. (chă-pĕl′)	102	41°06′N	102°29′W
Chapultenango, Mex. (chä-pȯl-tē-näŋ′gō)	119	17°19′N	93°08′W
Chapultepec, Castillo de, hist., Mex.	233a	19°25′N	99°11′W
Chá Pungana, Ang.	216	13°44′S	18°39′E
Charcas, Mex. (chär′käs)	118	23°09′N	101°09′W
Charco de Azul, Bahía, b., Pan.	121	8°14′N	82°45′W
Charente, r., Fr. (shȧ-räɴt′)	156	45°48′N	0°28′W
Charenton-le-Pont, Fr.	237c	48°49′N	2°25′E
Chari, r., Afr. (shä-rē′)	215	12°45′N	14°55′E
Charing, Eng., U.K. (chă′rĭng)	144b	51°13′N	0°49′E
Chariton, Ia., U.S. (châr′ĭ-tŭn)	103	41°02′N	93°16′W
Chariton, r., Mo., U.S.	111	40°24′N	92°38′W
Charjew, Turk.	169	38°52′N	63°37′E
Charlemagne, Can. (shärl-mäny′)	83a	45°43′N	73°29′W
Charleroi, Bel. (shȧr-lē-rwä′)	147	50°25′N	4°35′E
Charleroi, Pa., U.S. (shär′lē-roi)	101e	40°08′N	79°54′W
Charles, Cape, c., Va., U.S. (chärlz)	99	37°05′N	75°48′W
Charlesbourg, Can. (shȧrl-bo͞or′)	83b	46°51′N	71°16′W
Charles City, Ia., U.S. (chärlz)	103	43°03′N	92°40′W
Charles de Gaulle, Aéroport, arpt., Fr.	237c	49°00′N	2°34′E
Charleston, Il., U.S. (chärlz′tŭn)	98	39°30′N	88°10′W
Charleston, Ms., U.S.	114	34°00′N	90°02′W
Charleston, Mo., U.S.	111	36°53′N	89°20′W
Charleston, S.C., U.S.	97	32°47′N	79°56′W
Charleston, W.V., U.S.	97	38°20′N	81°35′W
Charlestown, St. K./N.	121b	17°10′N	62°32′W
Charlestown, In., U.S. (chärlz′toun)	101h	38°46′N	85°39′W
Charleville, Austl. (chär′lē-vĭl)	203	26°16′S	146°28′E
Charleville Mézières, Fr. (shärl-vēl′)	156	49°48′N	4°41′E
Charlevoix, Mi., U.S. (shär′lē-voi)	98	45°20′N	85°15′W
Charlevoix, Lake, l., Mi., U.S.	103	45°17′N	85°43′W
Charlotte, Mi., U.S. (shär′lŏt)	98	42°35′N	84°50′W
Charlotte, N.C., U.S.	97	35°15′N	80°50′W
Charlotte Amalie, V.I.U.S. (shär-lŏt′ĕ ä-mä′lĭ-ȧ)	117	18°21′N	64°54′W
Charlotte Harbor, b., Fl., U.S.	115a	26°49′N	82°00′W
Charlotte Lake, l., Can.	86	52°07′N	125°30′W
Charlottenberg, Swe. (shär-lŭt′ĕn-bĕrg)	152	59°53′N	12°17′E
Charlottenburg, neigh., Ger.	238a	52°31′N	13°16′E
Charlottenburg, Schloss, hist., Ger.	238a	52°31′N	13°14′E
Charlottesville, Va., U.S. (shär′lŏtz-vĭl)	97	38°00′N	78°25′W
Charlottetown, Can. (shär′lŏt-toun)	85	46°14′N	63°08′W
Charlotte Waters, Austl. (shär′lŏt)	202	26°00′S	134°50′E
Charlton, neigh., Eng., U.K.	235	51°29′N	0°02′E
Charmes, Fr. (shärm)	157	48°23′N	6°19′E
Charneca, neigh., Port.	238d	38°47′N	9°08′W
Charnwood Forest, for., Eng., U.K. (chärn′wȯd)	144a	52°42′N	1°15′W
Charny, Can. (shär-nē′)	83b	46°43′N	71°16′W
Chars, Fr. (shär)	157b	49°09′N	1°57′E
Chārsadda, Pak. (chŭr-sä′dä)	183a	34°17′N	71°43′E
Charters Towers, Austl. (chär′tẽrz)	203	20°03′S	146°20′E
Charterwood, Pa., U.S.	230b	40°33′N	80°00′W
Chartres, Fr. (shärt′r′)	147	48°26′N	1°29′E
Chascomús, Arg. (chäs-kō-mo͞os′)	132	35°32′S	58°01′W
Chase City, Va., U.S. (chās)	115	36°45′N	78°27′W
Chashniki, Bela. (chäsh′nyē-kē)	162	54°51′N	29°08′E
Chaska, Mn., U.S. (chăs′kȧ)	107g	44°48′N	93°36′W
Châteaudun, Fr. (shä-tō-dȧɴ′)	156	48°04′N	1°23′E
Châteaufort, Fr.	237c	48°44′N	2°06′E
Château-Gontier, Fr. (chȧ-tō′gôɴ′tyā′)	156	47°48′N	0°43′W
Châteauguay, Can. (chȧ-tō-gā)	83a	45°22′N	73°45′W
Châteauguay, r., N.A.	83a	45°13′N	73°51′W
Châteauneaut, Fr.	156a	43°23′N	5°11′E
Château-Renault, Fr. (shȧ-tō-rē-nō′)	156	47°36′N	0°57′E
Château-Richer, Can. (shȧ-tō′rē-shā′)	83b	47°00′N	71°01′W
Châteauroux, Fr. (shȧ-tō-ro͞o′)	147	46°47′N	1°39′E
Château-Thierry, Fr. (shȧ-tō′ty-ĕr-rē′)	156	49°03′N	3°22′E
Châtellerault, Fr. (shä-tĕl-rō′)	147	46°48′N	0°31′E
Châtenay-Malabry, Fr.	237c	48°46′N	2°17′E
Chatfield, Mn., U.S. (chăt′fēld)	103	43°50′N	92°10′W
Chatham, Can. (chăt′ȧm)	85	42°25′N	82°10′W
Chatham, Can.	85	47°02′N	65°28′W
Chatham, Eng., U.K. (chăt′ŭm)	151	51°23′N	0°32′E
Chatham, N.J., U.S. (chăt′ȧm)	100a	40°44′N	74°23′W
Chatham, Oh., U.S.	101d	41°06′N	82°01′W
Chatham Islands, is., N.Z.	2	44°00′S	178°00′W
Chatham Sound, strt., Can.	86	54°32′N	130°35′W
Chatham Strait, strt., Ak., U.S.	95	57°00′N	134°40′W
Châtillon, Fr.	237c	48°48′N	2°17′E
Chatou, Fr.	237c	48°54′N	2°09′E
Chatpur, neigh., India	240a	22°36′N	88°23′E
Chatswood, Austl.	243a	33°48′S	151°12′E
Chatsworth, Ca., U.S. (chătz′wûrth)	107a	34°16′N	118°36′W
Chatsworth Reservoir, res., Ca., U.S.	107a	34°15′N	118°41′W
Chattahoochee, Fl., U.S. (chăt-tȧ-ho͞o′ cheē)	114	30°42′N	84°47′W
Chattahoochee, r., U.S.	97	32°00′N	85°10′W
Chattanooga, Tn., U.S. (chăt-ȧ-no͞o′gȧ)	97	35°01′N	85°15′W
Chattooga, r., Ga., U.S. (chȧ-to͞o′gȧ)	114	34°47′N	83°13′W
Chaudière, r., Can. (shō-dyĕr′)	91	46°26′N	71°10′W
Chaumont, Fr. (shō-môɴ′)	147	48°08′N	5°07′E
Chaunskaya Guba, b., Russia	171	69°15′N	170°00′E
Chauny, Fr. (shō-nē′)	156	49°40′N	3°09′E
Chau-phu, Viet	196	10°49′N	104°57′E
Chausy, Bela. (chou′sĭ)	162	53°57′N	30°58′E
Chautauqua, l., N.Y., U.S. (shȧ-tô′kwȧ)	99	42°10′N	79°25′W
Chavaniga, Russia	166	66°02′N	37°50′E
Chavenay, Fr.	237c	48°51′N	1°59′E
Chaves, Port. (chä′vĕzh)	158	41°44′N	7°30′W
Chaville, Fr.	237c	48°48′N	2°10′E
Chavinda, Mex. (chä-vē′n-dä)	118	20°01′N	102°27′W
Chazumba, Mex. (chä-zȯm′bä)	119	18°11′N	97°41′W
Cheadle, Eng., U.K. (chē′d′l)	144a	52°59′N	1°59′W
Cheadle Hulme, Eng., U.K.	237b	53°22′N	2°12′W
Cheam, neigh., Eng., U.K.	235	51°21′N	0°13′W
Cheat, W.V., U.S. (chēt)	99	39°35′N	79°40′W
Cheb, Czech Rep. (ĸĕb)	154	50°05′N	12°23′E
Chebarkul', Russia (chĕ-bȧr-kûl′)	172a	54°59′N	60°22′E
Cheboksary, Russia (chyĕ-bôk-sä′rē)	166	56°00′N	47°20′E
Cheboygan, Mi., U.S. (shē-boi′găn)	98	45°40′N	84°30′W
Chech, Erg, des., Alg.	210	24°45′N	2°07′W
Chechen', i., Russia (chyĕch′ĕn)	167	44°00′N	48°10′E
Checheno-Ingushetia, state, Russia	168	43°15′N	45°40′E
Checotah, Ok., U.S. (chē-kō′tȧ)	111	35°27′N	95°32′W
Chedabucto Bay, b., Can. (chĕd-ȧ-bŭk-tō)	93	45°23′N	61°10′W
Cheduba Island, i., Myanmar	196	18°45′N	93°01′E
Cheecham Hills, hills, Can. (chēē′hăm)	88	56°20′N	111°10′W
Cheektowaga, N.Y., U.S. (chēk-tŏ-wä′gȧ)	101c	42°54′N	78°46′W
Cheetham Hill, neigh., Eng., U.K.	237b	53°31′N	2°15′W
Chefoo *see* Yantai, China	189	37°32′N	121°22′E
Chegutu, Zimb.	212	18°18′S	30°10′E
Chehalis, Wa., U.S. (chē-hā′lĭs)	104	46°39′N	122°58′W
Chehalis, r., Wa., U.S.	104	46°47′N	123°17′W
Cheju, S. Kor. (chĕ′jo͞o′)	194	33°29′N	126°40′E
Cheju (Quelpart), i., S. Kor.	194	33°20′N	126°25′E
Chekalin, Russia (chĕ-kä′lĭn)	162	54°05′N	36°13′E
Chela, Serra da, mts., Ang. (sĕr′rȧ dā shā′lȧ)	212	15°30′S	13°30′E
Chelan, Wa., U.S. (chē-lăn′)	104	47°51′N	119°59′W
Chelan, Lake, l., Wa., U.S.	104	48°09′N	120°20′W
Chelas, neigh., Port.	238d	38°45′N	9°07′W
Cheleiros, Port. (shĕ-la′rōzh)	159b	38°54′N	9°19′W
Chéliff, r., Alg. (shā-lēf)	210	36°00′N	2°00′E
Chelles, Fr.	157b	48°53′N	2°36′E
Chełm, Pol. (ĸĕlm)	147	51°08′N	23°30′E
Chełmno, Pol. (ĸĕlm′nō)	155	53°20′N	18°25′E
Chelmsford, Can.	90	46°35′N	81°12′W
Chelmsford, Eng., U.K. (chĕlm′s-fẽrd)	151	51°44′N	0°28′E
Chelmsford, Ma., U.S.	93a	42°36′N	71°21′W
Chelsea, Austl.	201a	38°05′S	145°08′E
Chelsea, Can.	83c	45°30′N	75°46′W
Chelsea, Al., U.S. (chĕl′sē)	100h	33°20′N	86°38′W
Chelsea, Ma., U.S.	93a	42°23′N	71°02′W
Chelsea, Mi., U.S.	98	42°20′N	84°00′W
Chelsea, Ok., U.S.	111	36°32′N	95°23′W
Cheltenham, Eng., U.K. (chĕlt′nŭm)	150	51°57′N	2°06′W
Cheltenham, Md., U.S. (chĕltĕn-hăm)	100e	38°45′N	76°50′W
Chelyabinsk, Russia (chĕl-yä-bēnsk′)	164	55°10′N	61°25′E
Chelyuskin, Mys, c., Russia (chĕl-yȯs′-kĭn)	165	77°45′N	104°45′E
Chemba, Moz.	217	17°08′S	34°52′E
Chembūr, neigh., India	240e	19°04′N	72°54′E
Chemnitz, Ger.	147	50°48′N	12°53′E
Chemung, r., N.Y., U.S. (shē-mŭng)	99	42°20′N	77°25′W
Chën, Gora, mtn., Russia	165	65°13′N	142°12′E
Chenāb, r., Asia (chē-näb)	183	30°30′N	71°30′E
Chenachane, Alg. (shĕ-nȧ-shän′)	210	26°14′N	4°14′W
Chencun, China (chŭn-tsȯn)	191a	22°58′N	113°14′E
Cheney, Wa., U.S. (chē′nȧ)	104	47°29′N	117°34′W
Chengde, China (chŭŋ-dŭ)	189	40°50′N	117°50′E
Chengdong Hu, l., China (chŭŋ-dȯŋ ho͞o)	190	32°22′N	116°32′E
Chengdu, China (chŭŋ-do͞o)	188	30°30′N	104°10′E
Chenggu, China (chŭŋ-go͞o)	192	33°05′N	107°25′E
Chenghai, China (chŭŋ-hī)	193	23°22′N	116°40′E
Chengshan Jiao, c., China (jyou chŭŋ-shän)	192	37°28′N	122°40′E
Chengxi Hu, l., China (chŭŋ-shyē ho͞o)	190	32°31′N	116°04′E
Chenies, Eng., U.K.	235	51°41′N	0°32′W
Chennai, India	183	13°08′N	80°15′E
Chennevières, Fr.	237c	49°00′N	2°07′E
Chenxian, China (chŭn-shyĕn)	193	25°40′N	113°00′E
Chepén, Peru (chĕ-pĕ′n)	130	7°17′S	79°24′W
Chepo, Pan. (chā′pō)	121	9°12′N	79°06′W
Chepo, r., Pan.	121	9°10′N	78°36′W
Cher, r., Fr. (shâr)	147	47°14′N	1°34′E
Cherán, Mex. (chā-rän′)	118	19°41′N	101°54′W
Cherangany Hills, hills, Kenya	217	1°25′N	35°20′E
Cheraw, S.C., U.S. (chē′rô)	115	34°40′N	79°52′W
Cherbourg, Fr. (shär-bȯr′)	142	49°39′N	1°43′W
Cherdyn', Russia (chĕr-dyēn′)	164	60°25′N	56°32′E
Cheremkhovo, Russia (chĕr′yĕm-kô-vō)	165	52°58′N	103°18′E

ŋ-sing; ŋ-baŋk; ɴ-nasalized n; nŏd; cŏmmit; ōld; ȯbey; ôrder; oi-boil; fo͞od; ȯ-as oo in foot; ou-out; s-soft; sh-dish; th-thin; pūre; ůnite; ûrn; stŭd; circŭs; ü-as in French tu; ′-indeterminate vowel.

274 Cherëmukhovo-Chong Pang

PLACE (Pronunciation)	PAGE	LAT.	LONG.
Cherëmukhovo, Russia (chĕr-yĕ-mû-kô-vô)	172a	60°20'N	60°00'E
Cherepanovo, Russia (chĕr'yĕ pä-nô'vō)	164	54°13'N	83°22'E
Cherepovets, Russia (chĕr-yĕ-pô'vyĕtz)	164	59°08'N	37°59'E
Chereya, Bela. (chĕr-ā'yä)	162	54°38'N	29°16'E
Chergui, i., Tun.	148	34°50'N	11°40'E
Chergui, Chott ech, l., Alg. (chĕr gē)	148	34°12'N	0°10'W
Cherikov, Bela. (chĕ'rē-kôf)	162	53°34'N	31°22'E
Cherkasy, Ukr.	163	49°26'N	32°03'E
Cherkasy, prov., Ukr.	163	48°58'N	30°55'E
Cherkessk, Russia	168	44°14'N	42°04'E
Cherlak, Russia (chĭr-läk')	164	54°04'N	74°28'E
Chermoz, Russia (chĕr-môz')	166	58°47'N	56°08'E
Chern', Russia (chĕrn)	162	53°28'N	36°49'E
Chërnaya Kalitva, r., Russia (chôr'ná yá ká-lēt'vá)	163	50°15'N	39°16'E
Chernihiv, Ukr.	167	51°23'N	31°15'E
Chernihiv, prov., Ukr.	163	51°28'N	31°18'E
Chernihivka, Ukr.	163	47°08'N	36°20'E
Chernivtsi, Ukr.	164	48°18'N	25°56'E
Chernobyl' see Chornobai, Ukr.	162	51°17'N	30°14'E
Chernogorsk, Russia (chĕr-nŏ-gôrsk')	170	54°01'N	91°07'E
Chernoistochinsk, Russia (chĕr-nôy-stô'chĭnsk)	172a	57°44'N	59°55'E
Chernyanka, Russia (chĕrn-yäŋ'kä)	163	50°56'N	37°48'E
Cherokee, Ia., U.S. (chĕr-ō-kē')	102	42°43'N	95°33'W
Cherokee, Ks., U.S.	111	37°21'N	94°50'W
Cherokee, Ok., U.S.	110	36°44'N	98°22'W
Cherokee Lake, res., Tn., U.S.	114	36°22'N	83°22'W
Cherokees, Lake of the, res., Ok., U.S. (chĕr-ō-kēz')	97	36°32'N	95°14'W
Cherokee Sound, Bah.	122	26°15'N	76°55'W
Cherry City, Pa., U.S.	230b	40°29'N	79°58'W
Cherryfield, Me., U.S. (chĕr'ĭ-fēld)	92	44°37'N	67°56'W
Cherry Grove, Or., U.S.	106c	45°27'N	123°15'W
Cherry Hill, N.J., U.S.	229b	39°55'N	75°01'W
Cherry Hill, neigh., Md., U.S.	229c	39°15'N	76°38'W
Cherryvale, Ks., U.S.	111	37°16'N	95°33'W
Cherryville, N.C., U.S. (chĕr'ĭ-vĭl)	115	35°32'N	81°22'W
Cherskogo, Khrebet, mts., Russia	165	67°15'N	140°00'E
Chertsey, Eng., U.K.	144b	51°24'N	0°30'W
Cherven', Bela. (chĕr'vyĕn)	162	53°43'N	28°26'E
Chervonoye, l., Bela. (chĕr-vô'nô-yĕ)	162	52°24'N	28°12'E
Chesaning, Mi., U.S. (chĕs'á-nĭng)	98	43°10'N	84°10'W
Chesapeake, Va., U.S. (chĕs'á-pēk)	100g	36°48'N	76°16'W
Chesapeake Bay, b., U.S.	97	38°20'N	76°15'W
Chesapeake Beach, Md., U.S.	100e	38°42'N	76°33'W
Chesham, Eng., U.K. (chĕsh'ŭm)	144b	51°41'N	0°37'W
Chesham Bois, Eng., U.K.	235	51°41'N	0°37'W
Cheshire, Mi., U.S. (chĕsh'ĭr)	98	42°25'N	86°00'W
Cheshire, co., Eng., U.K.	144a	53°16'N	2°30'W
Chëshskaya Guba, b., Russia	164	67°25'N	46°00'E
Cheshunt, Eng., U.K.	144b	51°43'N	0°02'W
Chesma, Russia (chĕs'má)	172a	53°50'N	60°42'E
Chesnokovka, Russia (chĕs-nŏ-kôf'ká)	164	53°28'N	83°41'E
Chessington, neigh., Eng., U.K.	235	51°21'N	0°18'W
Chester, Eng., U.K. (chĕs'tĕr)	150	53°12'N	2°53'W
Chester, Il., U.S.	111	37°54'N	89°48'W
Chester, Pa., U.S.	100f	39°51'N	75°22'W
Chester, S.C., U.S.	115	34°42'N	81°11'W
Chester, Va., U.S.	115	37°20'N	77°24'W
Chester, W.V., U.S.	98	40°35'N	80°30'W
Chesterbrook, Va., U.S.	229d	38°55'N	77°09'W
Chesterfield, Eng., U.K. (chĕs'tĕr-fēld)	150	53°14'N	1°26'W
Chesterfield, Îles, is., N. Cal.	203	19°38'S	160°08'E
Chesterfield Inlet, Can.	85	63°19'N	91°11'W
Chesterfield Inlet, b., Can.	85	63°59'N	92°09'W
Chestermere Lake, l., Can. (chĕs'tē-mēr)	83e	51°03'N	113°45'W
Chesterton, In., U.S. (chĕs'tĕr-tŭn)	98	41°35'N	87°05'W
Chestertown, Md., U.S. (chĕs'tĕr-toun)	99	39°15'N	76°05'W
Chestnut Hill, Md., U.S.	229c	39°17'N	76°47'W
Chestnut Hill, Ma., U.S.	227a	42°20'N	71°10'W
Chesuncook, l., Me., U.S. (chĕs'ŭn-kŏŏk)	92	46°03'N	69°40'W
Cheswick, Pa., U.S.	230b	40°32'N	79°47'W
Chetek, Wi., U.S. (chĕ'tĕk)	103	45°18'N	91°41'W
Chetumal, Bahía de, b., N.A. (bä-ē-ä dĕ chĕt-ōō-mäl')	116	18°07'N	88°05'W
Chevelon Creek, r., Az., U.S. (shĕv'á-lŏn)	109	34°35'N	111°00'W
Chevening, Eng., U.K.	235	51°18'N	0°08'E
Cheverly, Md., U.S.	229d	38°55'N	76°55'W
Chevilly-Larue, Fr.	237c	48°46'N	2°21'E
Cheviot, Oh., U.S. (shĕv'ĭ-ŭt)	101f	39°10'N	84°37'W
Chevreuse, Fr. (shĕ-vrûz')	157b	48°42'N	2°02'E
Chevy Chase, Md., U.S. (shĕvĭ chās)	100e	38°58'N	77°06'W
Chevy Chase View, Md., U.S.	229d	39°01'N	77°05'W
Chew Bahir, Afr. (stĕf-a-nē)	211	4°46'N	37°31'E
Chewelah, Wa., U.S. (chē-wē'lä)	104	48°17'N	117°42'W
Cheyenne, Wy., U.S. (shī-ĕn')	96	41°10'N	104°49'W
Cheyenne, r., U.S.	96	44°20'N	102°15'W
Cheyenne River Indian Reservation, I.R., S.D., U.S.	102	45°07'N	100°46'W
Cheyenne Wells, Co., U.S.	110	38°46'N	102°21'W
Chhalera Bāngar, India	240d	28°33'N	77°20'E
Chhinămor, India	240a	22°48'N	88°18'E
Chhindwāra, India	186	22°08'N	78°57'E
Chiai, Tai. (chī'ī')	193	23°28'N	120°28'E
Chiange, Ang.	216	15°45'S	13°48'E
Chiang Mai, Thai.	196	18°38'N	98°44'E
Chiang Rai, Thai.	196	19°53'N	99°48'E
Chiapa, Río de, r., Mex.	120	16°00'N	92°20'W
Chiapa de Corzo, Mex. (chē-ä'pä dā kôr'zō)	119	16°44'N	93°01'W
Chiapas, state, Mex. (chē-ä'päs)	116	17°10'N	93°00'W
Chiapas, Cordilla de, mts., Mex. (kôr-dēl-yĕ'rä-dĕ-chyä'räs)	119	15°55'N	93°15'W
Chiari, Italy (kyä'rē)	160	45°31'N	9°57'E
Chiasso, Switz.	154	45°50'N	8°57'E
Chiatura, Geor.	168	42°17'N	43°17'E
Chiautla, Mex. (chyä-ōōt'lä)	118	18°16'N	98°37'W
Chiavari, Italy (kyä-vä'rē)	160	44°18'N	9°21'E
Chiba, Japan (chē'bä)	189	35°37'N	140°08'E
Chiba, dept., Japan	195a	35°47'N	140°02'E
Chibougamau, Can. (chē-bōō'gä-mou)	85	49°57'N	74°23'W
Chibougamau, l., Can.	91	49°53'N	74°21'W
Chicago, Il., U.S. (shĭ-kô-gō) (chĭ-kä'gō)	97	41°49'N	87°37'W
Chicago, North Branch, r., Il., U.S.	231a	41°53'N	87°38'W
Chicago Heights, Il., U.S.	101a	41°30'N	87°38'W
Chicago Lawn, neigh., Il., U.S.	231a	41°47'N	87°41'W
Chicago-O'Hare International Airport, arpt., Il., U.S.	231a	41°59'N	87°54'W
Chicago Ridge, Il., U.S.	231a	41°42'N	87°47'W
Chicago Sanitary and Ship Canal, can., Il., U.S.	231a	41°42'N	87°58'W
Chicapa, r., Afr. (chē-kä'pä)	212	7°45'S	20°25'E
Chicbul, Mex. (chēk-bōō'l)	119	18°45'N	90°56'W
Chic-Chocs, Monts, mts., Can.	85	48°38'N	66°37'W
Chichagof, i., Ak., U.S. (chē-chä'gôf)	95	57°50'N	137°00'W
Chichancanab, Lago de, l., Mex. (lä'gô-dĕ-chē-chän-kä-nä'b)	120a	19°50'N	88°28'W
Chichén Itzá, hist., Mex.	120a	20°40'N	88°35'W
Chichester, Eng., U.K. (chĭch'ĕs-tĕr)	150	50°50'N	0°55'W
Chichimilá, Mex. (chē-chē-mē'lä)	120a	20°36'N	88°14'W
Chichiriviche, Ven. (chē-chē-rē-vē-chĕ)	131b	10°56'N	68°17'W
Chickamauga, Ga., U.S. (chĭk-á-mô'gá)	114	34°50'N	85°15'W
Chickamauga Lake, res., Tn., U.S.	114	35°18'N	85°22'W
Chickasawhay, r., Ms., U.S. (chĭk-á-sô'wā)	114	31°45'N	88°45'W
Chickasha, Ok., U.S. (chĭk'á-shā)	96	35°04'N	97°56'W
Chiclana de la Frontera, Spain (chē-klä'nä)	158	36°25'N	6°09'W
Chiclayo, Peru (chē-klä'yō)	130	6°46'S	79°50'W
Chico, Ca., U.S. (chē'kō)	108	39°43'N	121°51'W
Chico, Wa., U.S.	106a	47°37'N	122°43'W
Chico, r., Arg.	132	44°30'S	66°00'W
Chico, r., Arg.	132	49°15'S	69°30'W
Chico, r., Phil.	197a	17°33'N	121°24'E
Chicoloapan, Mex. (chē-kō-lwä'pän)	119a	19°24'N	98°54'W
Chiconautla, Mex.	119a	19°39'N	99°01'W
Chicontepec, Mex. (chē-kōn'tē-pĕk')	118	20°58'N	98°08'W
Chicopee, Ma., U.S. (chĭk'ō-pē)	99	42°10'N	72°35'W
Chicoutimi, Can. (shē-kōō'tē-mē')	85	48°26'N	71°04'W
Chicxulub, Mex. (chēk-sōō-lōō'b)	120a	21°10'N	89°30'W
Chiefland, Fl., U.S. (chēf'lánd)	115	29°30'N	82°50'W
Chiemsee, l., Ger. (κēm zā)	154	47°58'N	12°20'E
Chieri, Italy (kyâ'rē)	160	45°03'N	7°48'E
Chieti, Italy (kyĕ'tē)	148	42°22'N	14°22'E
Chifeng, China (chr-fŭŋ)	189	42°18'N	118°52'E
Chignall Saint James, Eng., U.K.	235	51°46'N	0°25'E
Chignanuapan, Mex. (chē'g-nä-nwä-pá'n)	118	19°49'N	98°02'W
Chignecto Bay, b., Can. (shĭg-nĕk'tō)	92	45°33'N	64°50'W
Chignik, Ak., U.S. (chĭg'nĭk)	95	56°14'N	158°12'W
Chignik Bay, b., Ak., U.S.	95	56°18'N	157°22'W
Chigu Co, l., China (chr-gōō tswo)	186	28°55'N	91°47'E
Chigwell, Eng., U.K.	144b	51°38'N	0°05'E
Chigwell Row, Eng., U.K.	235	51°37'N	0°07'E
Chihe, China (chr-hŭ)	190	32°32'N	117°57'E
Chihuahua, Mex. (chē-wä'wä)	116	28°37'N	106°06'W
Chihuahua, state, Mex.	116	29°00'N	107°30'W
Chikishlyar, Turk. (chē-kēsh-lyär')	170	37°40'N	53°50'E
Chilanga, Zam.	217	15°34'S	28°17'E
Chilapa, Mex. (chē-lä'pä)	118	17°34'N	99°14'W
Chilchota, Mex. (chēl-chō'tä)	118	19°40'N	102°04'W
Chilcotin, r., Can. (chĭl-kō'tĭn)	86	52°20'N	124°15'W
Childer Thornton, Eng., U.K.	237a	53°17'N	2°57'W
Childress, Tx., U.S. (chīld'rĕs)	110	34°26'N	100°11'W
Chile, nation, S.A. (chē'lā)	132	35°00'S	72°00'W
Chilecito, Arg. (chē-lā-sē'tō)	132	29°06'S	67°25'W
Chilengue, Serra do, mts., Ang.	216	13°20'S	15°00'E
Chilibre, Pan. (chē-lē'brĕ)	116a	9°09'N	79°37'W
Chililabombwe, Zam.	217	12°18'S	27°43'E
Chilka, l., India	186	19°26'N	85°42'E
Chilko, r., Can. (chĭl'kō)	86	51°53'N	123°53'W
Chilko Lake, l., Can.	86	51°20'N	124°05'W
Chillán, Chile (chēl-yän')	132	36°44'S	72°06'W
Chillicothe, Il., U.S. (chĭl-ĭ-kŏth'ē)	98	41°55'N	89°30'W
Chillicothe, Mo., U.S.	111	39°46'N	93°32'W
Chillicothe, Oh., U.S.	98	39°20'N	83°00'W
Chilliwack, Can. (chĭl'ĭ-wăk)	84	49°10'N	121°57'W
Chillum, Md., U.S.	229d	38°58'N	76°59'W
Chilly-Mazarin, Fr.	237c	48°42'N	2°19'E
Chiloé, Isla de, i., Chile	132	42°30'S	73°55'W
Chilpancingo de los Bravo, Mex.	116	17°32'N	99°30'W
Chilton, Wi., U.S. (chĭl'tŭn)	103	44°00'N	88°12'W
Chilung, Tai. (chĭ'lung)	189	25°02'N	121°48'E
Chilwa, Lake, l., Afr.	212	15°12'S	36°30'E
Chimacum, Wa., U.S. (chĭm'ä-kŭm)	106a	48°01'N	122°47'W
Chimalpa, Mex. (chē-mäl'pä)	119a	19°26'N	99°22'W
Chimaltenango, Guat. (chē-mäl-tā-näŋ'gō)	120	14°39'N	90°48'W
Chimaltitan, Mex. (chēmäl-tē-tän')	118	21°36'N	103°50'W
Chimbay, Uzb. (chĭm-bī')	169	43°00'N	59°44'E
Chimborazo, mtn., Ec. (chēm-bō-rä'zō)	130	1°35'S	78°45'W
Chimbote, Peru (chēm-bō'tā)	130	9°02'S	78°33'W
Chimki-Chovrino, neigh., Russia	239b	55°51'N	37°30'E
China, Mex. (chē'nä)	112	25°43'N	99°13'W
China, nation, Asia (chī'ná)	188	36°45'N	93°00'E
Chinameca, El Sal. (Chē-nä-mä'kä)	120	13°31'N	88°18'W
Chinandega, Nic. (chē-nän-dä'gä)	120	12°38'N	87°08'W
Chinati Peak, mtn., Tx., U.S. (chĭ-nä'tē)	112	29°56'N	104°29'W
Chinatown, neigh., Ca., U.S.	231b	37°48'N	122°26'W
Chincha Alta, Peru (chĭn'chä äl'tä)	130	13°24'S	76°04'W
Chinchas, Islas, is., Peru (ē's-läs-chē'n-chäs)	130	11°27'S	79°05'W
Chinchilla, Austl. (chĭn-chĭl'á)	204	26°44'S	150°36'E
Chinchorro, Banco, bk., Mex. (bä'n-kô-chēn-chô'r-rō)	120a	18°43'N	87°25'W
Chincilla de Monte Aragon, Spain	158	38°54'N	1°43'W
Chinde, Moz. (shēn'dĕ)	212	17°39'S	36°34'E
Chin Do, i., S. Kor.	194	34°30'N	125°43'E
Chindwin, r., Myanmar (chĭn-dwĭn)	183	23°30'N	94°34'E
Chingford, neigh., Eng., U.K.	235	51°38'N	0°01'E
Chingmei, Tai.	241d	24°59'N	121°32'E
Chingola, Zam. (chĭng-gōlä)	212	12°32'S	27°52'E
Chinguar, Ang. (chĭng-gär)	212	12°35'S	16°15'E
Chinguetti, Maur. (chēŋ-gĕt'ē)	210	20°34'N	12°34'W
Chinhoyi, Zimb.	212	17°22'S	30°12'E
Chinju, S. Kor. (chĭn'jōō)	194	35°13'N	128°10'E
Chinko, r., Cen. Afr. Rep. (shĭn'kō)	211	6°37'N	24°31'E
Chinmen see Quemoy, Tai.	193	24°30'N	118°20'E
Chino, Ca., U.S. (chē'nō)	107a	34°01'N	117°42'W
Chinon, Fr. (shē-nôɴ')	156	47°09'N	0°13'E
Chinook, Mt., U.S. (shĭn-ŏŏk')	105	48°35'N	109°15'W
Chinsali, Zam.	217	10°34'S	32°03'E
Chinteche, Mwi. (chĭn-tĕ'chĕ)	212	11°48'S	34°14'E
Chioggia, Italy (kyôd'jä)	160	45°12'N	12°17'E
Chipata, Zam.	212	13°39'S	32°40'E
Chipera, Moz. (zhē-pĕ'rä)	212	15°16'S	32°30'E
Chipley, Fl., U.S. (chĭp'lĭ)	114	30°45'N	85°33'W
Chipman, Can. (chĭp'mán)	92	46°11'N	65°53'W
Chipola, r., Fl., U.S. (chĭ-pō'lá)	114	30°40'N	85°14'W
Chippawa, Can. (chĭp'ē-wä)	101c	43°03'N	79°03'W
Chipperfield, Eng., U.K.	235	51°42'N	0°29'W
Chippewa, r., Mn., U.S. (chĭp'ē-wä)	102	45°07'N	95°41'W
Chippewa, r., Wi., U.S.	103	45°07'N	91°19'W
Chippewa Falls, Wi., U.S.	103	44°55'N	91°26'W
Chippewa Lake, Oh., U.S.	101d	41°04'N	81°54'W
Chipping Ongar, Eng., U.K.	235	51°43'N	0°15'E
Chipstead, Eng., U.K.	235	51°17'N	0°09'E
Chipstead, Eng., U.K.	235	51°18'N	0°10'W
Chiputneticook Lakes, l., N.A. (chĭ-pōt-nĕt'ĭ-kŏŏk)	92	45°47'N	67°45'W
Chiquimula, Guat. (chē-kē-mōō'lä)	120	14°47'N	89°31'W
Chiquimulilla, Guat. (chē-kē-mōō-lē'l-yä)	120	14°08'N	90°23'W
Chiquinquira, Col. (chē-kēŋ'kē-rä')	130	5°33'N	73°49'W
Chirāgh Delhi, neigh., India	240d	28°32'N	77°14'E
Chirala, India	187	15°52'N	80°22'E
Chirchik, Uzb. (chĭr-chēk')	169	41°28'N	69°18'E
Chire (Shire), r., Afr.	217	17°15'S	35°25'E
Chiricahua National Monument, rec., Az., U.S. (chĭ-rä-cä'hwä)	109	32°02'N	109°18'W
Chirikof, i., Ak., U.S. (chĭ'rĭ-kôf)	95	55°50'N	155°35'W
Chiriquí, Punta, c., Pan. (pŏ'n-tä-chē-rē-kē')	121	9°13'N	81°39'W
Chiriquí Grande, Pan. (chē-rē-kē' grän'dā)	121	8°57'N	82°08'W
Chiri San, mtn., S. Kor. (chĭ'rĭ-sän')	194	35°20'N	127°39'E
Chiromo, Mwi.	212	16°34'S	35°13'E
Chirpan, Bul.	149	42°12'N	25°19'E
Chirripó, Río, r., C.R.	121	9°50'N	83°20'W
Chisasibi, Can.	85	53°40'N	78°58'W
Chisholm, Mn., U.S. (chĭz'ŭm)	103	47°28'N	92°53'W
Chişinău, Mol.	164	47°02'N	28°52'E
Chislehurst, neigh., Eng., U.K.	235	51°25'N	0°04'E
Chistopol', Russia (chĭs-tô'pôl-y')	164	55°21'N	50°37'E
Chiswellgreen, Eng., U.K.	235	51°44'N	0°22'W
Chiswick, neigh., Eng., U.K.	235	51°29'N	0°16'W
Chita, Russia (chē-tá')	165	52°09'N	113°39'E
Chitambo, Zam.	217	12°55'S	30°39'E
Chitato, Ang.	216	7°20'S	20°47'E
Chitembo, Ang.	216	13°34'S	16°40'E
Chitina, Ak., U.S. (chĭ-tē'ná)	95	61°28'N	144°35'W
Chitokoloki, Zam.	216	13°50'S	23°13'E
Chitorgarh, India	186	24°59'N	74°42'E
Chitrāl, Pak. (chē-träl')	183	35°58'N	71°48'E
Chittagong, Bngl. (chĭt-á-gông')	183	22°26'N	90°51'E
Chitungwiza, Zimb.	212	17°51'S	31°05'E
Chiumbe, r., Afr. (chē-ŏm'bā)	212	9°45'S	21°00'E
Chivasso, Italy (kē-väs'sō)	160	45°13'N	7°52'E
Chivhu, Zimb.	212	18°59'S	30°58'E
Chivilcoy, Arg. (chē-vēl-koi')	132	34°51'S	60°03'W
Chixoy, r., Guat. (chē-κoi')	120	15°40'N	90°35'W
Chizu, Japan (chē-zōō')	195	35°16'N	134°15'E
Chloride, Az., U.S. (klō'rīd)	109	35°25'N	114°15'W
Chmielnik, Pol. (κmyĕl'nēk)	155	50°36'N	20°46'E
Choa Chu Kang, Sing.	240c	1°22'N	103°41'E
Choapa, r., Chile (chō-á'pä)	129b	31°56'S	70°48'W
Chobham, Eng., U.K.	235	51°21'N	0°36'W
Choctawhatchee, r., Fl., U.S.	114	30°37'N	85°56'W
Choctawhatchee Bay, b., Fl., U.S. (chôk-tô-hăch'ē)	114	30°15'N	86°32'W
Chodziez, Pol. (κōj'yĕsh)	154	52°59'N	16°55'E
Choele Choel, Arg. (chō-ĕ'lĕ-chōĕ'l)	132	39°14'S	65°46'W
Chōfu, Japan (chō'fōō')	195a	35°39'N	139°33'E
Chōgo, Japan (chō-gō)	195a	35°25'N	139°28'E
Choisel, Fr.	237c	48°41'N	2°01'E
Choiseul, i., Sol. Is. (shwä-zûl')	203	7°30'S	157°30'E
Choisy-le-Roi, Fr.	157b	48°46'N	2°25'E
Chojnice, Pol. (kōĭ-nē-tsĕ)	155	53°41'N	17°34'E
Cholet, Fr. (shō-lĕ')	147	47°06'N	0°54'W
Cho-lon, neigh., Viet	241j	10°46'N	106°40'E
Cholula, Mex. (chō-lōō'lä)	118	19°04'N	98°19'W
Choluteca, Hond. (chō-lōō-tā'kä)	120	13°18'N	87°12'W
Choluteco, r., Hond.	120	13°34'N	86°59'W
Cho-moi, Viet	241j	10°51'N	106°38'E
Chomutov, Czech Rep. (kō'mō-tôf)	154	50°27'N	13°23'E
Chona, r., Russia (chō'nä)	171	60°45'N	109°15'E
Chone, Ec. (chō'nĕ)	130	0°48'S	80°06'W
Chŏngjin, N. Kor. (chŭng-jĭn')	189	41°48'N	129°46'E
Chŏngju, S. Kor. (chŭng-jōō')	194	36°35'N	127°30'E
Chongming Dao, i., China (chōŋ-mĭŋ dou)	193	31°40'N	122°30'E
Chong Pang, Sing.	240c	1°26'N	103°50'E

ăt; finăl; rāte; senāte; ärm; ásk; sofá; fâre; ch-choose; dh-as th in other; bē; ēvent; bĕt; recĕnt; cratẽr; g-gō; gh-guttural g; bĭt; ĭ-short neutral; rīde; κ-guttural k as ch in German ich;

PRONOUNCING INDEX Chongqing-Clocolan 275

PLACE (Pronunciation)	PAGE	LAT.	LONG.
Chongqing, China (chôŋ-chyĭŋ)	188	29°38′N	107°30′E
Chŏnju, S. Kor. (chŭn-jōō′)	194	35°48′N	127°08′E
Chonos, Archipiélago de los, is., Chile	132	44°35′N	76°15′W
Chorley, Eng., U.K. (chôr′lĭ)	144a	53°40′N	2°38′W
Chorleywood, Eng., U.K.	235	51°39′N	0°31′W
Chorlton-cum-Hardy, Eng., U.K.	237b	53°27′N	2°17′W
Chornaya, neigh., Russia	172b	55°45′N	38°04′E
Chornobai, Ukr.	163	51°17′N	30°14′E
Chornobay, Ukr. (chĕr-nō-bī′)	163	49°41′N	32°24′E
Chornomors'ke, Ukr.	167	45°29′N	32°43′E
Chorošovo, neigh., Russia	239b	55°47′N	37°28′E
Chorrera de Managua, Cuba	233b	23°02′N	82°19′E
Chorrillos, Peru (chôr-rē′l-yōs)	130	12°17′S	76°55′W
Chortkiv, Ukr.	155	49°01′N	25°48′E
Chosan, N. Kor. (chō-sän′)	194	40°44′N	125°48′E
Chosen, Fl., U.S. (chō′z′n)	115a	26°41′N	80°41′W
Chōshi, Japan (chō′shē)	194	35°40′N	140°55′E
Choszczno, Pol. (chôsh′chnô)	154	53°10′N	15°25′E
Chota Nagpur, plat., India	186	23°40′N	82°50′E
Choteau, Mt., U.S. (shō′tō)	105	47°51′N	112°10′W
Chowan, r., N.C., U.S. (chô-wän′)	115	36°13′N	76°46′W
Chowilla Reservoir, res., Austl.	204	34°05′S	141°20′E
Chown, Mount, mtn., Can. (choun)	87	53°24′N	119°22′W
Choybalsan, Mong.	189	47°50′N	114°15′E
Christchurch, N.Z. (krīst′chûrch)	203a	43°30′S	172°38′E
Christian, i., Can. (krĭs′chăn)	91	44°50′N	80°00′W
Christiansburg, Va., U.S. (krĭs′chănz-bûrg)	115	37°08′N	80°25′W
Christiansted, V.I.U.S.	117b	17°45′N	64°44′W
Christmas Island, dep., Oc.	196	10°35′S	105°40′E
Christopher, Il., U.S. (krĭs′tô-fẽr)	111	37°58′N	89°04′W
Chrudim, Czech Rep. (krōō′dyĕm)	154	49°57′N	15°46′E
Chrzanów, Pol. (kzhä′nôf)	155	50°08′N	19°24′E
Chuansha, China (chůän-shä)	191b	31°12′N	121°41′E
Chubut, prov., Arg. (chò-bōōt′)	132	44°00′S	69°15′W
Chubut, r., Arg. (chò-bōōt′)	132	43°05′S	69°00′W
Chuckatuck, Va., U.S. (chŭck å-tŭck)	100g	36°51′N	76°35′W
Chucunaque, r., Pan. (chōō-kōō-nä′kå)	121	8°36′N	77°48′W
Chudovo, Russia (chò′dô-vô)	162	59°03′N	31°56′E
Chudskoye Ozero, l., Eur. (chòt′skô-yĕ)	166	58°43′N	26°45′E
Chuguchak, hist. reg., China (chōō′gōō-chäk′)	188	46°09′N	83°58′E
Chuguyevka, Russia (chò-gōō′yĕf-kå)	194	43°58′N	133°49′E
Chugwater Creek, r., Wy., U.S. (chŭg′wô-tẽr)	102	41°43′N	104°54′W
Chuhuïv, Ukr.	167	49°52′N	36°40′E
Chukot National Okrug, , Russia	171	68°15′N	170°00′E
Chukotskiy Poluostrov, pen., Russia	164	66°12′N	175°00′W
Chukotskoye Nagor'ye, mts., Russia	165	66°00′N	166°00′E
Chula Vista, Ca., U.S. (chōō′lå vĭs′tå)	108a	32°38′N	117°05′W
Chulkovo, Russia (chōōl-kô vô)	172b	55°33′N	38°04′E
Chulucanas, Peru	130	5°13′S	80°13′W
Chulum, r., Russia	170	57°52′N	84°45′E
Chumikan, Russia (chōō-mē-kän′)	165	54°47′N	135°09′E
Chun'an, China (chòn-än)	193	29°38′N	119°00′E
Chunchŏn, S. Kor. (chòn-chŭn′)	194	37°51′N	127°46′E
Chungju, S. Kor. (chŭng′jōō′)	194	37°00′N	128°19′E
Chungking *see* Chongqing, China	188	29°38′N	107°30′E
Chŭngsanha-ri, neigh., S. Kor.	241b	37°35′N	126°54′E
Chunya, Tan.	217	8°32′S	33°25′E
Chunya, r., Russia (chòn′yä′)	170	61°45′N	101°28′E
Chuquicamata, Chile (chōō-kē-kä-mä′tä)	132	22°08′S	68°57′W
Chur, Switz. (kōōr)	147	46°51′N	9°32′E
Churchill, Can. (chûrch′ĭl)	85	58°50′N	94°10′W
Churchill, Pa., U.S.	230b	40°27′N	79°51′W
Churchill, Va., U.S.	229d	38°54′N	77°10′W
Churchill, r., Can.	84	58°00′N	95°00′W
Churchill, Cape, c., Can.	85	59°07′N	93°50′W
Churchill Falls, wtfl., Can.	85	53°35′N	64°27′W
Churchill Lake, l., Can.	88	56°12′N	108°40′W
Churchill Peak, mtn., Can.	84	58°10′N	125°14′W
Church Street, Eng., U.K.	235	51°26′N	0°28′E
Church Stretton, Eng., U.K. (chûrch strĕt′ŭn)	144a	52°32′N	2°49′W
Churchton, Md., U.S.	100e	38°49′N	76°33′W
Churu, India	186	28°22′N	75°00′E
Churumuco, Mex. (chōō-rōō-mōō′kō)	118	18°39′N	101°40′W
Chuska Mountains, mts., Az., U.S. (chŭs-kȧ)	109	36°21′N	109°11′W
Chusovaya, r., Russia (chōō-sô-vä′yå)	166	58°08′N	58°35′E
Chusovoy, Russia (chōō-sô-vôy′)	164	58°18′N	57°50′E
Chust, Uzb. (chōōst)	169	41°05′N	71°28′E
Chuvashia, state, Russia	166	55°45′N	46°00′E
Chuviscar, r., Mex. (chōō-vēs-kär′)	112	28°34′N	105°36′W
Chuwang, China (chōō-wäŋ)	190	36°08′N	114°53′E
Chuxian, China (chōō shyĕn)	192	32°19′N	118°19′E
Chuxiong, China (chōō-shyôŋ)	188	25°19′N	101°34′E
Chyhyryn, Ukr.	163	49°02′N	32°39′E
Cicero, Il., U.S. (sĭs′ẽr-ō)	101a	41°50′N	87°46′W
Cide, Tur. (jē′dĕ)	149	41°50′N	33°00′E
Ciechanów, Pol. (tsyĕ-kä′nôf)	155	52°52′N	20°39′E
Ciego de Avila, Cuba (syā′gō dā ä′vē-lä)	117	21°50′N	78°45′W
Ciego de Avila, prov., Cuba	122	22°00′N	78°40′W
Ciempozuelos, Spain (thyĕm-pô-thwā′lōs)	158	40°09′N	3°36′W
Ciénaga, Col. (syā′nä-gä)	130	11°01′N	74°15′W
Cienfuegos, Cuba (syĕn-fwā′gōs)	117	22°10′N	80°30′W
Cienfuegos, prov., Cuba	122	22°15′N	80°40′W
Cienfuegos, Bahía, b., Cuba (bä-ē′ä-syĕn-fwā′gōs)	122	22°00′N	80°35′W
Ciervo, Isla de la, i., Nic. (ē′s-lä-dĕ-lä-syĕ′r-vô)	121	11°56′N	83°20′W
Cieszyn, Pol. (tsyĕ′shĕn)	155	49°47′N	18°45′E
Cieza, Spain (thyā′thä)	158	38°13′N	1°25′W
Cigüela, r., Spain	158	39°53′N	2°54′W
Cihuatlán, Mex. (sē-wä-tlä′n)	118	19°13′N	104°36′W

PLACE (Pronunciation)	PAGE	LAT.	LONG.
Cihuatlán, r., Mex.	118	19°11′N	104°30′W
Cijara, Embalse de, res., Spain	158	39°25′N	5°00′W
Cilician Gates, p., Tur.	167	37°30′N	35°30′E
Cimarron, r., U.S. (sĭm-ȧ-rōn′)	96	36°26′N	98°27′W
Cimarron, r., Co., U.S.	110	37°13′N	102°30′W
Cinca, r., Spain (thēŋ′kä)	159	42°09′N	0°08′E
Cincinnati, Oh., U.S. (sĭn-sĭ-nát′ĭ)	97	39°08′N	84°30′W
Cinco Balas, Cayos, is., Cuba (kä′yōs-thēŋ′kō bä′läs)	122	21°05′N	79°25′W
Cinderella, S. Afr.	244b	26°15′S	28°16′E
Cinisello Balsamo, Italy	238c	45°33′N	9°13′E
Cinkota, neigh., Hung.	239g	47°31′N	19°14′E
Cintalapa, Mex. (sēn-tä-lä′pä)	119	16°41′N	93°44′W
Cinto, Monte, mtn., Fr. (chēn′tō)	147	42°24′N	8°54′E
Circle, Ak., U.S. (sûr′k′l)	94a	65°49′N	144°22′W
Circleville, Oh., U.S. (sûr′k′lvĭl)	98	39°35′N	83°00′W
Cirebon, Indon.	196	6°50′S	108°33′E
Ciri Grande, r., Pan. (sē′rē-grá′n′dĕ)	116a	8°55′N	80°04′W
Cisco, Tx., U.S. (sĭs′kō)	112	32°23′N	98°57′W
Cisliano, Italy	238c	45°27′N	8°59′E
Cisneros, Col. (sēs-nĕ′rôs)	130a	6°33′N	75°05′W
Cisterna di Latina, Italy (chēs-tĕ′r-nä-dē-lä-tē′nä)	159d	41°36′N	12°53′E
Cistierna, Spain (thês-tyĕr′nä)	158	42°48′N	5°08′W
Citronelle, Al., U.S. (cĭt-rō′nĕl)	114	31°05′N	88°15′W
Cittadella, Italy (chēt-tä-dĕl′lä)	160	45°39′N	11°51′E
Città di Castello, Italy (chēt-tä′dē käs-tĕl′lō)	160	43°27′N	12°17′E
City College of New York, pt. of i., N.Y., U.S.	228	40°49′N	73°57′W
City Island, neigh., N.Y., U.S.	228	40°51′N	73°47′W
City of Baltimore, Md., U.S.	229d	39°18′N	76°37′W
City of Commerce, Ca., U.S.	232	33°59′N	118°08′W
City of Industry, Ca., U.S.	232	34°01′N	117°57′W
City of London, neigh., Eng., U.K.	235	51°31′N	0°05′W
City of Westminster, neigh., Eng., U.K.	235	51°30′N	0°09′W
Ciudad Altamirano, Mex. (syōō-dä′d-äl-tä-mē-rä′nô)	118	18°24′N	100°38′W
Ciudad Bolívar, Ven. (syōō-dhädh′ bô-lē′vär)	130	8°07′N	63°41′W
Ciudad Camargo, Mex.	116	27°42′N	105°10′W
Ciudad Chetumal, Mex.	116	18°30′N	88°17′W
Ciudad Darío, Nic. (syōō-dhädh′dä′rē-ō)	120	12°44′N	86°08′W
Ciudad de la Habana, prov., Cuba	122	23°20′N	82°10′W
Ciudad del Carmen, Mex. (syōō-dä′d-dĕl-kå′r-mĕn)	116	18°39′N	91°49′W
Ciudad del Maíz, Mex. (syōō-dhädh′del mä-ēz′)	118	22°24′N	99°37′W
Ciudad Deportive, rec., Mex.	233a	19°24′N	99°06′W
Ciudad Fernández, Mex. (syōō-dhädh′fĕr-nän′dĕz)	118	21°56′N	100°03′W
Ciudad García, Mex. (syōō-dhädh′gär-sē′ä)	116	22°39′N	103°02′W
Ciudad General Belgrano, Arg.	233d	34°44′S	58°32′W
Ciudad Guayana, Ven.	130	8°30′N	62°45′W
Ciudad Guzmán, Mex. (syōō-dhädh′gòz-män)	116	19°40′N	103°29′W
Ciudad Hidalgo, Mex. (syōō-dä′d-ē-dä′l-gô)	118	19°41′N	100°35′W
Ciudad Juárez, Mex. (syōō-dhädh hwä′rāz)	116	31°44′N	106°28′W
Ciudad Madero, Mex. (syōō-dä′d-mä-dĕ′rô)	119	22°16′N	97°52′W
Ciudad Mante, Mex. (syōō-dä′d-mán′tē)	116	22°34′N	98°58′W
Ciudad Manuel Doblado, Mex. (syōō-dä′d-män-wäl′dō-blä′dō)	118	20°43′N	101°57′W
Ciudad Obregón, Mex. (syōō-dhädh-ô-brē-gô′n)	116	27°40′N	109°58′W
Ciudad Real, Spain (thyōō-dhädh′rā-äl′)	158	38°59′N	3°55′W
Ciudad Rodrigo, Spain (thyōō-dhädh′rô-drē′gō)	148	40°38′N	6°34′W
Ciudad Serdán, Mex. (syōō-dä′d-sĕr-dá′n)	119	18°58′N	97°26′W
Ciudad Universitaria, educ., Spain	238b	40°27′N	3°44′W
Ciudad Victoria, Mex. (syōō-dhädh′vēk-tō′rē-ä)	116	23°43′N	99°09′W
Ciutadella, Spain	159	40°00′N	3°52′E
Civitavecchia, Italy (chē′vē-tä-vĕk′kyä)	160	42°06′N	11°49′E
Cixian, China (tsē shyĕn)	190	36°22′N	114°23′E
Clackamas, Or., U.S. (klăc-kȧ′măs)	106c	45°25′N	122°34′W
Claire, l., Can. (klâr)	84	58°33′N	113°16′W
Clair Engle Lake, l., Ca., U.S.	104	40°51′N	122°41′W
Clairton, Pa., U.S. (klârtŭn)	101e	40°17′N	79°53′W
Clamart, Fr.	237c	48°48′N	2°16′E
Clanton, Al., U.S. (klăn′tŭn)	114	32°50′N	86°38′W
Clare, Mi., U.S. (klâr)	98	43°50′N	84°45′W
Clare Island, i., Ire.	150	53°46′N	10°00′W
Claremont, Eng., U.K.	235	51°21′N	0°22′W
Claremont, Ca., U.S. (klâr′mŏnt)	107a	34°06′N	117°43′W
Claremont, N.H., U.S. (klâr′mŏnt)	99	43°20′N	72°20′W
Claremont, W.V., U.S.	98	37°55′N	81°00′W
Claremore, Ok., U.S. (klâr′mōr)	111	36°16′N	95°37′W
Claremorris, Ire. (klâr-mŏr′ĭs)	150	53°46′N	9°05′W
Clarence Strait, strt., Austl. (klăr′ĕns)	202	12°15′S	130°05′E
Clarence Strait, strt., Ak., U.S.	86	55°25′N	132°00′W
Clarence Town, Bah.	123	23°05′N	75°00′W
Clarendon, Ar., U.S. (klâr′ĕn-dŭn)	111	34°42′N	91°17′W
Clarendon, Tx., U.S.	110	34°55′N	100°52′W
Clarens, S. Afr. (clâ-rēns)	213c	28°34′S	28°26′E
Claresholm, Can. (klâr′ĕs-hōlm)	84	50°02′N	113°35′W
Clarinda, Ia., U.S. (klȧ-rĭn′dȧ)	102	40°42′N	95°00′W
Clarines, Ven. (klä-rē′nĕs)	131b	9°57′N	65°10′W
Clarion, Ia., U.S. (klăr′ĭ-ŭn)	103	42°43′N	93°45′W
Clarion, Pa., U.S.	99	41°10′N	79°25′W
Clark, N.J., U.S.	228	40°38′N	74°19′W
Clark, S.D., U.S. (klärk)	102	44°52′N	97°45′W
Clark, Point, c., Can.	90	44°05′N	81°50′W

PLACE (Pronunciation)	PAGE	LAT.	LONG.
Clarkdale, Az., U.S. (klärk-dāl)	109	34°45′N	112°05′W
Clarke City, Can.	85	50°12′N	66°38′W
Clarke Range, mts., Austl.	203	20°30′S	148°00′E
Clark Fork, r., Mt., U.S.	104	47°50′N	115°35′W
Clarksburg, W.V., U.S. (klärkz′bûrg)	97	39°15′N	80°20′W
Clarksdale, Ms., U.S. (klärks-dāl)	114	34°10′N	90°31′W
Clark's Harbour, Can. (klärks)	92	43°26′N	65°38′W
Clarks Hill Lake, res., U.S. (klärk-hĭl)	97	33°50′N	82°35′W
Clarkston, Ga., U.S. (klärks′tŭn)	100c	33°49′N	84°15′W
Clarkston, Wa., U.S.	104	46°24′N	117°01′W
Clarksville, Ar., U.S. (klärks-vĭl)	111	35°28′N	93°26′W
Clarksville, Tn., U.S.	114	36°30′N	87°23′W
Clarksville, Tx., U.S.	111	33°37′N	95°02′W
Clatskanie, Or., U.S.	106c	46°04′N	123°11′W
Clatskanie, r., Or., U.S. (klăt-skă′nē)	106c	46°06′N	123°11′W
Clatsop Spit, Or., U.S. (klăt-sŏp)	106c	46°13′N	124°04′W
Cláudio, Braz. (klou′-dēō)	129a	20°26′S	44°44′W
Claveria, Phil. (klä-vå-rē′ä)	193	18°38′N	121°08′E
Clawson, Mi., U.S. (klô′s′n)	101b	42°32′N	83°09′W
Claxton, Ga., U.S. (klăks′tŭn)	115	32°07′N	81°54′W
Clay, Ky., U.S. (klā)	114	37°28′N	87°50′W
Clay Center, Ks., U.S. (klā sĕn′tẽr)	111	39°23′N	97°08′W
Clay City, Ky., U.S. (klā sĭ′tĭ)	98	37°50′N	83°55′W
Claycomo, Mo., U.S. (kla-kō′mo)	107f	39°12′N	94°30′W
Clay Cross, Eng., U.K. (klā krōs)	144a	53°10′N	1°25′W
Claye-Souilly, Fr. (klĕ-sōō-yĕ′)	157b	48°56′N	2°43′E
Claygate, Eng., U.K.	235	51°22′N	0°20′W
Claygate Cross, Eng., U.K.	235	51°16′N	0°19′E
Claymont, De., U.S. (klā-mŏnt)	100f	39°48′N	75°28′W
Clayton, Eng., U.K.	144a	53°47′N	1°49′W
Clayton, Al., U.S. (klā′tŭn)	114	31°52′N	85°25′W
Clayton, Ca., U.S.	106b	37°56′N	121°56′W
Clayton, Mo., U.S.	107e	38°39′N	90°20′W
Clayton, N.M., U.S.	110	36°26′N	103°12′W
Clayton, N.C., U.S.	115	35°40′N	78°27′W
Clear, l., Ca., U.S.	108	39°05′N	122°50′W
Clear Boggy Creek, r., Ok., U.S. (klēr bŏg′ĭ krēk)	111	34°21′N	96°22′W
Clear Creek, r., Az., U.S.	109	34°40′N	111°05′W
Clear Creek, r., Tx., U.S.	113a	29°34′N	95°13′W
Clear Creek, r., Wy., U.S.	105	44°35′N	106°20′W
Clearfield, Pa., U.S. (klēr-fēld)	99	41°00′N	78°25′W
Clearfield, Ut., U.S.	107b	41°07′N	112°01′W
Clear Hills, Can.	84	57°11′N	119°20′W
Clearing, neigh., Il., U.S.	231a	41°47′N	87°47′W
Clear Lake, Ia., U.S.	103	43°09′N	93°23′W
Clear Lake, Wa., U.S.	106a	48°27′N	122°14′W
Clear Lake Reservoir, res., Ca., U.S.	104	41°53′N	121°00′W
Clearwater, Fl., U.S. (klēr-wô′tẽr)	115a	27°43′N	82°45′W
Clearwater, r., Can.	87	52°00′N	114°50′W
Clearwater, r., Can.	87	52°00′N	120°10′W
Clearwater, r., Can.	88	56°10′N	110°40′W
Clearwater, r., Id., U.S.	104	46°27′N	116°33′W
Clearwater, Middle Fork, r., Id., U.S.	104	46°10′N	115°48′W
Clearwater, North Fork, r., Id., U.S.	104	46°34′N	116°08′W
Clearwater, South Fork, r., Id., U.S.	104	45°46′N	115°53′W
Clearwater Mountains, mts., Id., U.S.	104	45°56′N	115°15′W
Cleburne, Tx., U.S. (klē′bŭrn)	96	32°21′N	97°23′W
Cle Elum, Wa., U.S. (klē ĕl′ŭm)	104	47°12′N	120°55′W
Clementon, N.J., U.S. (klē′mĕn-tŭn)	100f	39°49′N	75°00′W
Cleobury Mortimer, Eng., U.K. (klēō-bĕr′ĭ môr′tĭ-mẽr)	144a	52°22′N	2°29′W
Clermont, Austl. (klẽr′mŏnt)	203	23°02′S	147°46′E
Clermont, Can.	91	47°45′N	70°20′W
Clermont-Ferrand, Fr. (klĕr-môɴ′fĕr-răɴ′)	142	45°47′N	3°03′E
Cleveland, Ms., U.S. (klēv′lănd)	114	33°45′N	90°42′W
Cleveland, Oh., U.S.	97	41°30′N	81°42′W
Cleveland, Ok., U.S.	111	36°18′N	96°28′W
Cleveland, Tn., U.S.	114	35°09′N	84°52′W
Cleveland, Tx., U.S.	113	30°18′N	95°05′W
Cleveland Heights, Oh., U.S.	101d	41°30′N	81°35′W
Cleveland Museum of Art, pt. of i., Oh., U.S.	229a	41°31′N	81°37′W
Cleveland Park, neigh., D.C., U.S.	229d	38°56′N	77°04′W
Cleveland Peninsula, pen., Ak., U.S.	86	55°45′N	132°00′W
Cleves, Oh., U.S. (klē′vĕs)	101f	39°10′N	84°45′W
Clew Bay, b., Ire. (klōō)	150	53°47′N	9°45′W
Clewiston, Fl., U.S. (klē′wĭs-tŭn)	115a	26°44′N	80°55′W
Clichy, Fr. (klē-shē)	156	48°54′N	2°18′E
Clichy-sous-Bois, Fr.	237c	48°55′N	2°33′E
Clifden, Ire. (klĭf′dĕn)	150	53°31′N	10°04′W
Cliffside Park, N.J., U.S.	228	40°49′N	73°59′W
Clifton, Az., U.S. (klĭf′tŭn)	109	33°05′N	109°20′W
Clifton, Ma., U.S.	227a	42°29′N	70°53′W
Clifton, N.J., U.S.	100a	40°52′N	74°09′W
Clifton, S.C., U.S.	115	35°00′N	81°47′W
Clifton, Tx., U.S.	113	31°45′N	97°31′W
Clifton Forge, Va., U.S.	99	37°50′N	79°50′W
Clifton Heights, Pa., U.S.	229b	39°56′N	75°18′W
Clinch, r., Tn., U.S. (klĭnch)	114	36°30′N	83°19′W
Clingmans Dome, mtn., U.S. (klĭng′măns dōm)	114	35°37′N	83°26′W
Clinton, Can. (klĭn-′tŭn)	84	51°05′N	121°35′W
Clinton, Il., U.S.	98	40°10′N	88°55′W
Clinton, In., U.S.	98	39°40′N	87°25′W
Clinton, Ia., U.S.	103	41°50′N	90°13′W
Clinton, Ky., U.S.	114	36°39′N	88°56′W
Clinton, Md., U.S.	100e	38°46′N	76°54′W
Clinton, Ma., U.S.	93a	42°25′N	71°41′W
Clinton, Mo., U.S.	111	38°23′N	93°46′W
Clinton, N.C., U.S.	115	34°58′N	78°20′W
Clinton, Ok., U.S.	110	35°31′N	98°56′W
Clinton, S.C., U.S.	115	34°27′N	81°53′W
Clinton, Tn., U.S.	114	36°05′N	84°08′W
Clinton, Wa., U.S.	106a	47°59′N	122°22′W
Clinton, r., Mi., U.S.	101b	42°36′N	83°00′W
Clinton-Colden, l., Can.	84	63°58′N	106°34′W
Clintonville, Wi., U.S. (klĭn′tŭn-vĭl)	103	44°37′N	88°46′W
Clio, Mi., U.S. (klē′ō)	98	43°10′N	83°45′W
Cloates, Point, c., Austl. (klōts)	202	22°47′S	113°45′E
Clocolan, S. Afr.	218d	28°56′S	27°35′E

PLACE (Pronunciation)	PAGE	LAT.	LONG.
Clonakilty Bay, b., Ire. (klŏn-ȧ-kĭl'tē)	150	51°30'N	8°50'W
Cloncurry, Austl. (klŏn-kŭr'ē)	202	20°58'S	140°42'E
Clonmel, Ire. (klŏn-mĕl)	150	52°21'N	7°45'W
Clontarf, Austl.	243a	33°48'S	151°16'E
Cloquet, Mn., U.S. (klô-kā')	107h	46°42'N	92°28'W
Closter, N.J., U.S. (klōs'tẽr)	100a	40°58'N	73°57'W
Cloud Peak, mtn., Wy., U.S. (kloud)	96	44°23'N	107°11'W
Clover, S.C., U.S. (klō'vẽr)	115	35°08'N	81°08'W
Clover Bar, Can. (klō'vẽr bär)	83g	53°34'N	113°20'W
Cloverdale, Can.	106d	49°06'N	122°44'W
Cloverdale, Ca., U.S. (klō'vẽr-dāl)	108	38°47'N	123°03'W
Cloverdene, S. Afr.	244b	26°09'S	28°22'E
Cloverport, Ky., U.S. (klō'vẽr pōrt)	98	37°50'N	86°35'W
Clovis, N.M., U.S. (klō'vĭs)	96	34°24'N	103°11'W
Cluj-Napoca, Rom.	142	46°46'N	23°34'E
Clun, r., Eng., U.K. (klŭn)	144a	52°25'N	2°56'W
Cluny, Fr. (klü-nē')	156	46°27'N	4°40'E
Clutha, r., N.Z. (kloo'thȧ)	203a	45°52'S	169°30'E
Clwyd, co., Wales, U.K.	144a	53°01'N	2°59'W
Clyde, Ks., U.S.	111	39°34'N	97°23'W
Clyde, Oh., U.S.	98	41°15'N	83°00'W
Clyde, r., Scot., U.K.	150	55°35'N	3°50'W
Clyde, Firth of, b., Scot., U.K. (fûrth ŏv klīd)	150	55°28'N	5°01'W
Côa, r., Port. (kô'ä)	158	40°28'N	6°55'W
Coacalco, Mex. (kō-ä-käl'kō)	119a	19°37'N	99°06'W
Coachella, Canal, can., Ca., U.S. (kō'chĕl-lȧ)	108	33°15'N	115°25'W
Coahuayana, Río de, r., Mex. (rē'ō-dĕ-kô-ä-wä-yä'nä)	118	19°00'N	103°33'W
Coahuayutla, Mex. (kō'ä-wī-yoot'lä)	118	18°19'N	101°44'W
Coahuila, state, Mex. (kō-ä-wē'lȧ)	116	27°30'N	103°00'W
Coal City, Il., U.S. (kōl sĭ'tĭ)	101a	41°17'N	88°17'W
Coalcomán, Río de, r., Mex. (rē'ō-dĕ-kō-äl-kō-män')	118	18°45'N	103°15'W
Coalcomán, Sierra de, mts., Mex.	118	18°30'N	102°45'W
Coalcomán de Matamoros, Mex.	118	18°46'N	103°10'W
Coaldale, Can. (kōl'dāl)	87	49°43'N	112°37'W
Coalgate, Ok., U.S. (kōl'gāt)	111	34°44'N	96°13'W
Coal Grove, Oh., U.S. (kōl grōv)	98	38°20'N	82°40'W
Coal Hill Park, rec., China	240b	39°56'N	116°23'E
Coalinga, Ca., U.S. (kō-ȧ-lĭŋ'gȧ)	108	36°09'N	120°23'W
Coalville, Eng., U.K. (kōl'vĭl)	144a	52°43'N	1°21'W
Coamo, P.R. (kō-ä'mō)	117b	18°05'N	66°21'W
Coari, Braz. (kō-är'ē)	130	4°06'S	63°10'W
Coast Mountains, mts., N.A. (kōst)	84	54°10'N	128°00'W
Coast Ranges, mts., U.S.	96	41°28'N	123°30'W
Coatepec, Mex. (kō-ä-tā-pĕk)	118	19°23'N	98°44'W
Coatepec, Mex.	119	19°26'N	96°56'W
Coatepec, Mex.	119a	19°08'N	99°25'W
Coatepeque, El Sal.	120	13°56'N	89°30'W
Coatepeque, Guat. (kō-ä-tå-pā'kå)	120	14°40'N	91°52'W
Coatesville, Pa., U.S. (kōts'vĭl)	99	40°00'N	75°50'W
Coatetelco, Mex. (kō-ä-tå-tĕl'kō)	118	18°43'N	99°17'W
Coaticook, Can. (kō'tĭ-kŏŏk)	91	45°10'N	71°55'W
Coatlinchán, Mex. (kô-ä-tlē'n-chä'n)	119a	19°26'N	98°52'W
Coats, i., Can. (kōts)	85	62°23'N	82°11'W
Coats Land, reg., Ant.	219	74°00'S	30°00'W
Coatzacoalcos, Mex.	116	18°09'N	94°26'W
Coatzacoalcos, r., Mex.	119	17°40'N	94°41'W
Coba, hist., Mex. (kô'bä)	120a	20°23'N	87°23'W
Cobalt, Can. (kō'bôlt)	85	47°21'N	79°40'W
Cobán, Guat. (kō-bän')	116	15°28'N	90°19'W
Cobar, Austl.	203	31°28'S	145°50'E
Cobberas, Mount, mtn., Austl. (cŏ-bẽr-ăs)	204	36°45'S	148°15'E
Cobequid Mountains, mts., Can.	92	45°35'N	64°10'W
Cobh, Ire. (kôv)	142	51°52'N	8°09'W
Cobham, Eng., U.K.	235	51°23'N	0°24'E
Cobija, Bol. (kō-bē'hä)	130	11°12'S	68°49'W
Cobourg, Can. (kō'bŏŏrgh)	85	43°55'N	78°05'W
Cobre, r., Jam. (kō'brā)	122	18°05'N	77°00'W
Coburg, Austl.	201a	37°45'S	144°58'E
Coburg, Ger. (kō'bŏŏrg)	154	50°16'N	10°57'E
Cocentaina, Spain (kō-thån-tä-ē'nȧ)	159	38°44'N	0°27'W
Cochabamba, Bol.	130	17°24'S	66°09'W
Cochin, India (kō-chĭn')	187	9°58'N	76°19'E
Cochinos, Bahía, b., Cuba (bä-ē'ä-kô-chē'nōs)	122	22°05'N	81°10'W
Cochinos Banks, bk.	122	22°20'N	76°15'W
Cochiti Indian Reservation, I.R., N.M., U.S.	109	35°37'N	106°20'W
Cochran, Ga., U.S. (kŏk'răn)	114	32°23'N	83°23'W
Cochrane, Can.	83e	51°11'N	114°28'W
Cochrane, Can. (kŏk'răn)	85	49°01'N	81°06'W
Cockburn, i., Can. (kŏk-bûrn)	90	45°55'N	83°25'W
Cockeysville, Md., U.S. (kŏk'ĭz-vĭl)	100e	39°30'N	76°40'W
Cockfosters, neigh., Eng., U.K.	235	51°39'N	0°09'W
Cockrell Hill, Tx., U.S. (kŏk'rĕl)	107c	32°44'N	96°53'W
Coco, r., N.A.	117	14°55'N	83°45'W
Coco, Cayo, i., Cuba (kä'-yō-kô'kô)	122	22°30'S	78°30'W
Coco, Isla del, i., C.R. (ē's-lä-dĕl-kô-kô)	116	5°33'N	87°02'W
Cocoa, Fl., U.S. (kō'kō)	115a	28°21'N	80°44'W
Cocoa Beach, Fl., U.S.	115a	28°20'N	80°35'W
Cocoli, Pan. (kŏ-kô'lē)	116a	8°58'N	79°36'W
Coconino, Plateau, plat., Az., U.S. (kō kō nē'nō)	109	35°45'N	112°28'W
Cocos (Keeling) Islands, is., Oc. (kō'kōs) (kē'lĭng)	3	11°50'S	90°50'E
Coco Solito, Pan. (kô-kô-sŏ-lē'tō)	116a	9°21'N	79°53'W
Cocotá, neigh., Braz.	234c	22°49'S	43°11'W
Cocula, Mex. (kō-kōō'lä)	118	20°23'N	103°47'W
Cocula, r., Mex.	118	18°17'N	99°45'W
Cod, Cape, pen., Ma., U.S.	97	41°42'N	70°15'W
Codajás, Braz. (kō-dä-häzh')	130	3°44'S	62°09'W
Codera, Cabo, c., Ven. (kȧ'bō-kō-dĕ'rä)	131b	10°35'N	66°06'W
Codogno, Italy (kô-dō'nyō)	160	45°08'N	9°43'E
Codrington, Antig. (kŏd'rĭng-tŭn)	121b	17°39'N	61°49'W
Cody, Wy., U.S. (kō'dĭ)	105	44°31'N	109°02'W
Coelho da Rocha, Braz.	132b	22°47'S	43°23'W

PLACE (Pronunciation)	PAGE	LAT.	LONG.
Coemba, Ang.	216	12°08'S	18°05'E
Coesfeld, Ger. (kûs'fĕld)	157c	51°56'N	7°10'E
Coeur d'Alene, Id., U.S. (kûr dȧ-lān')	96	47°43'N	116°35'W
Coeur d'Alene, r., Id., U.S.	104	47°26'N	116°35'W
Coeur d'Alene Indian Reservation, I.R., Id., U.S.	104	47°18'N	116°45'W
Coeur d'Alene Lake, l., Id., U.S.	104	47°32'N	116°39'W
Coffeyville, Ks., U.S. (kŏf'ĭ-vĭl)	97	37°01'N	95°38'W
Coff's Harbour, Austl.	204	30°20'S	153°10'E
Cofimvaba, S. Afr. (căfĭm'vä-bȧ)	213c	32°01'S	27°37'E
Coghinas, r., Italy (kō'gē-nås)	160	40°31'N	9°00'E
Cognac, Fr. (kōn-yak')	147	45°41'N	0°22'W
Cohasset, Ma., U.S. (kô-hăs'ĕt)	93a	42°14'N	70°48'W
Cohoes, N.Y., U.S. (kô-hōz')	99	42°50'N	73°40'W
Coig, r., Arg. (kô'ĕk)	132	51°15'N	71°00'W
Coimbatore, India (kô-ēm-bȧ-tôr')	183	11°03'N	76°56'E
Coimbra, Port. (kô-ēm'brä)	142	40°14'N	8°23'W
Coín, Spain (kô-ēn')	158	36°40'N	4°45'W
Coina, Port. (kô-ē'nȧ)	159b	38°35'N	9°03'W
Coina, r., Port. (kô'y-nä)	159b	38°35'N	9°02'W
Coipasa, Salar de, pl., Bol. (sä-lä'r-dĕ-koi-pä'-sä)	130	19°12'S	69°13'W
Coixtlahuaca, Mex. (kō-ēks'tlä-wä'kä)	119	17°42'N	97°17'W
Cojedes, dept., Ven. (kô-kĕ'dĕs)	131b	9°50'N	68°21'W
Cojimar, Cuba (kō-hē-mär')	123a	23°10'N	82°19'W
Cojutepeque, El Sal. (kô-hô-tĕ-pā'kå)	120	13°45'N	88°50'W
Cokato, Mn., U.S. (kô-kā'tō)	103	45°03'N	94°11'W
Cokeburg, Pa., U.S. (kōk bŭgh)	101e	40°06'N	80°03'W
Coker, Nig.	244d	6°29'N	3°20'E
Colāba, neigh., India	240e	18°54'N	72°48'E
Colac, Austl. (kŏ'lăc)	204	38°25'S	143°40'E
Colares, Port. (kô-lä'rĕs)	159b	38°47'N	9°27'W
Colatina, Braz. (kô-lä-tē'nä)	131	19°33'S	40°42'W
Colby, Ks., U.S. (kōl'bĭ)	110	39°23'N	101°04'W
Colchagua, prov., Chile (kōl-chá'gwä)	129b	34°42'S	71°24'W
Colchester, Eng., U.K. (kōl'chĕs-tẽr)	151	51°52'N	0°50'E
Coldblow, neigh., Eng., U.K.	235	51°26'N	0°10'E
Cold Lake, l., Can. (kōld)	88	54°33'N	110°05'W
Coldwater, Ks., U.S. (kōld'wô-tẽr)	110	37°14'N	99°21'W
Coldwater, Mi., U.S.	98	41°55'N	85°00'W
Coldwater, r., Ms., U.S.	114	34°25'N	90°12'W
Coldwater Creek, r., Tx., U.S.	110	36°10'N	101°45'W
Coleman, Tx., U.S. (kōl'mȧn)	112	31°50'N	99°25'W
Colenso, S. Afr. (kŏ-lĕnz'ô)	213c	28°48'S	29°49'E
Coleraine, N. Ire., U.K.	150	55°08'N	6°40'W
Coleraine, Mn., U.S. (kōl-rān')	103	47°16'N	93°29'W
Coleshill, Eng., U.K. (kōlz'hĭl)	144a	52°30'N	1°42'W
Colfax, Ia., U.S. (kōl'făks)	103	41°40'N	93°13'W
Colfax, La., U.S.	113	31°31'N	92°42'W
Colfax, Wa., U.S.	104	46°53'N	117°21'W
Colhué Huapi, l., Arg. (kôl-wä'ŏä'pē)	132	45°30'S	68°45'W
Coligny, S. Afr.	218d	26°20'S	26°18'E
Colima, Mex. (kōlē'mä)	116	19°13'N	103°45'W
Colima, state, Mex.	118	19°10'N	104°00'W
Colima, Nevado de, mtn., Mex. (nĕ-vä'dô-dĕ-kô-lē'mä)	116	19°30'N	103°38'W
Coll, i., Scot., U.K. (kŏl)	150	56°42'N	6°23'W
College, Ak., U.S.	95	64°43'N	147°50'W
College Park, Ga., U.S. (kŏl'ĕj)	100c	33°39'N	84°27'W
College Park, Md., U.S.	100e	38°59'N	76°58'W
College Point, neigh., N.Y., U.S.	228	40°47'N	73°51'W
Collegeville, Pa., U.S. (kŏl'ĕj-vĭl)	100f	40°11'N	75°27'W
Collie, Austl. (kŏl'ē)	202	33°20'S	116°20'E
Collier Bay, b., Austl. (kŏl-yẽr)	202	15°30'S	123°30'E
Collier Row, neigh., Eng., U.K.	235	51°36'N	0°10'E
Collingdale, Pa., U.S.	229b	39°55'N	75°17'W
Collingswood, N.J., U.S. (kŏl'ĭngz-wŏŏd)	100f	39°54'N	75°04'W
Collingwood, Austl.	243b	37°48'S	145°00'E
Collingwood, Can.	91	44°30'N	80°20'W
Collins, Ms., U.S. (kŏl'ĭns)	114	31°40'N	89°34'W
Collinsville, Il., U.S. (kŏl'ĭnz-vĭl)	107e	38°41'N	89°59'W
Collinsville, Ok., U.S.	111	36°21'N	95°50'W
Colmar, Fr. (kôl'mär)	147	48°03'N	7°25'E
Colmenar de Oreja, Spain (kôl-mā-när'dāōrā'hä)	158	40°06'N	3°25'W
Colmenar Viejo, Spain (kôl-mā-när'vyā'hō)	158	40°40'N	3°46'W
Colnbrook, Eng., U.K.	235	51°29'N	0°31'W
Colney Heath, Eng., U.K.	235	51°44'N	0°15'W
Colney Street, Eng., U.K.	235	51°42'N	0°20'W
Cologne, Ger.	142	50°56'N	6°57'E
Cologno Monzese, Italy	238c	45°32'N	9°17'E
Colombes, Fr.	237c	48°55'N	2°15'E
Colombia, Col. (kô-lôm'bē-ä)	130a	3°23'N	74°48'W
Colombia, nation, S.A.	130	3°30'N	72°30'W
Colombo, Sri L. (kô-lôm'bō)	183b	6°58'N	79°52'W
Colón, Arg. (kō-lōn')	129c	33°55'S	61°08'W
Colón, Cuba (kô-lô'n)	122	22°45'N	80°55'W
Colón, Mex. (kō-lōn')	118	20°46'N	100°02'W
Colón, Pan. (kô-lô'n)	117	9°22'N	79°54'W
Colón, Archipiélago de, is., Ec.	130	0°10'S	87°45'W
Colón, Montañas de, mts., Hond. (môn-tä'n-yäs-dĕ-kŏ-lô'n)	121	14°58'N	84°39'W
Colonail Park, Md., U.S.	229c	39°19'N	76°45'W
Colonia, N.J., U.S.	228	40°35'N	74°18'W
Colonia, Ur. (kō-lō'nē-ä)	132	34°27'S	57°50'W
Colonia, dept., Ur.	129c	34°08'S	57°50'W
Colonial Manor, N.J., U.S.	229b	39°51'N	75°09'W
Colonia Suiza, Ur. (kô-lô'nēä-sōē'zä)	129c	34°17'S	57°15'W
Colonna, Capo, c., Italy	161	39°02'N	17°15'E
Colonsay, i., Scot., U.K. (kŏl-ŏn-sā')	151	56°08'N	6°08'E
Coloradas, Lomas, Arg. (lô'mäs-kō-lō-rä'däs)	132	43°30'S	68°00'W
Colorado, state, U.S.	96	39°30'N	106°55'W
Colorado, r., N.A.	96	36°00'N	113°30'W
Colorado, r., Tx., U.S.	96	30°08'N	97°33'W
Colorado, Río, r., Arg.	132	38°30'S	66°00'W
Colorado City, Tx., U.S. (kŏl-ô-rä'dō sĭ'tĭ)	112	32°24'N	100°50'W
Colorado National Monument, rec., Co., U.S.	109	39°00'N	108°40'W

PLACE (Pronunciation)	PAGE	LAT.	LONG.
Colorado Plateau, plat., U.S.	96	36°20'N	109°25'W
Colorado River Aqueduct, aq., Ca., U.S.	108	33°38'N	115°43'W
Colorado River Indian Reservation, I.R., Az., U.S.	109	34°03'N	114°02'W
Colorados, Archipiélago de los, is., Cuba	122	22°25'N	84°25'W
Colorado Springs, Co., U.S. (kŏl-ô-rä'dō)	96	38°49'N	104°48'W
Colosseo, hist., Italy	239c	41°54'N	12°29'E
Colotepec, r., Mex. (kô-lô'tē-pĕk)	119	15°56'N	96°57'W
Colotlán, Mex. (kô-lô-tlän')	118	22°06'N	103°14'W
Colotlán, r., Mex.	118	22°09'N	103°17'W
Colquechaca, Bol. (kôl-kā-chä'kä)	130	18°47'S	66°02'W
Colstrip, Mt., U.S. (kōl'strip)	105	45°54'N	106°38'W
Colton, Ca., U.S. (kōl'tŭn)	107a	34°04'N	117°20'W
Columbia, Il., U.S. (kô-lŭm'bĭ-ȧ)	107e	38°26'N	90°12'W
Columbia, Ky., U.S.	114	37°06'N	85°15'W
Columbia, Md., U.S.	100e	39°15'N	76°51'W
Columbia, Ms., U.S.	114	31°15'N	89°49'W
Columbia, Mo., U.S.	97	38°55'N	92°19'W
Columbia, Pa., U.S.	99	40°00'N	76°25'W
Columbia, S.C., U.S.	97	34°00'N	81°00'W
Columbia, Tn., U.S.	114	35°36'N	87°02'W
Columbia, r., N.A.	84	46°00'N	120°00'W
Columbia, Mount, mtn., Can.	87	52°09'N	117°25'W
Columbia City, In., U.S.	98	41°10'N	85°30'W
Columbia City, Or., U.S.	106c	45°53'N	112°49'W
Columbia Heights, Mn., U.S.	107g	45°03'N	93°15'W
Columbia Icefield, ice., Can.	87	52°08'N	117°26'W
Columbia Mountains, mts., N.A.	87	51°30'N	118°30'W
Columbiana, Al., U.S. (kô-ŭm-bĭ-ă'nȧ)	114	33°10'N	86°35'W
Columbia University, pt. of i., N.Y., U.S.	228	40°48'N	73°58'W
Columbretes, is., Spain (kō-lōōm-brē'tĕs)	159	39°54'N	0°54'E
Columbus, Ga., U.S. (kô-lŭm'bŭs)	97	32°29'N	84°56'W
Columbus, In., U.S.	98	39°15'N	85°55'W
Columbus, Ks., U.S.	111	37°10'N	94°50'W
Columbus, Ms., U.S.	114	33°30'N	88°25'W
Columbus, Mt., U.S.	105	45°39'N	109°15'W
Columbus, Ne., U.S.	102	41°25'N	97°25'W
Columbus, N.M., U.S.	109	31°50'N	107°40'W
Columbus, Oh., U.S.	97	40°00'N	83°00'W
Columbus, Tx., U.S.	113	29°44'N	96°34'W
Columbus, Wi., U.S.	103	43°20'N	89°01'W
Columbus Bank, bk. (kô-lŭm'bŭs)	123	22°05'N	75°30'W
Columbus Grove, Oh., U.S.	98	40°55'N	84°05'W
Columbus Point, c., Bah.	123	24°10'N	75°15'W
Colusa, Ca., U.S. (kô-lū'sȧ)	108	39°12'N	122°01'W
Colville, Wa., U.S. (kŏl'vĭl)	104	48°33'N	117°53'W
Colville, r., Ak., U.S.	95	69°00'N	156°25'W
Colville Indian Reservation, I.R., Wa., U.S.	104	48°15'N	119°00'W
Colville R, Wa., U.S.	104	48°25'N	117°58'W
Colvos Passage, strt., Wa., U.S. (kōl'vōs)	106a	47°24'N	122°32'W
Colwood, Can. (kŏl'wŏŏd)	106a	48°26'N	123°30'W
Colwyn, Pa., U.S.	229b	39°55'N	75°15'W
Comacchio, Italy (kô-mäk'kyō)	160	44°42'N	12°12'E
Comala, Mex. (kō-mä-lä')	118	19°22'N	103°47'W
Comalapa, Guat. (kō-mä-lä'-pä)	120	14°43'N	90°56'W
Comalcalco, Mex. (kō-mäl-käl'kō)	119	18°16'N	93°13'W
Comanche, Ok., U.S. (kō-măn'chē)	111	34°20'N	97°58'W
Comanche, Tx., U.S.	112	31°54'N	98°37'W
Comanche Creek, r., Tx., U.S.	112	31°02'N	102°47'W
Comayagua, Hond. (kō-mä-yä'gwä)	116	14°24'N	87°36'W
Combahee, r., S.C., U.S. (kŏm-bȧ-hē')	115	32°42'N	80°40'W
Comer, Ga., U.S. (kŭm'ẽr)	114	34°02'N	83°07'W
Comete, Cape, c., T./C. Is. (kô-mā'tå)	123	21°45'N	71°25'W
Comilla, Bngl. (kô-mĭl'ä)	183	23°33'N	91°17'E
Comino, Cape, c., Italy (kô-mē'nō)	160	40°30'N	9°48'E
Comitán, Mex. (kô-mē-tän')	116	16°16'N	92°09'W
Commencement Bay, b., Wa., U.S. (kŏ-mĕns'mĕnt bā)	106a	47°17'N	122°21'W
Commentry, Fr. (kô-mäɴ-trē')	156	46°16'N	2°44'E
Commerce, Ga., U.S. (kŏm'ẽrs)	114	34°10'N	83°27'W
Commerce, Ok., U.S.	111	36°57'N	94°54'W
Commerce, Tx., U.S.	111	33°15'N	95°52'W
Como, Austl.	243a	34°00'S	151°04'E
Como, Italy (kō'mō)	148	45°48'N	9°03'E
Como, Lago di, l., Italy (lä'gō-dē-kō'mō)	148	46°00'N	9°30'E
Comodoro Rivadavia, Arg.	132	45°47'S	67°31'W
Como-Est, Can.	83a	45°27'N	74°08'W
Comonfort, Mex. (kô-mōn-fô'rt)	118	20°43'N	100°47'W
Comorin, Cape, c., India (kŏ'mô-rĭn)	183b	8°05'N	78°05'E
Comoros, nation, Afr.	213	12°30'S	42°45'E
Comox, Can. (kō'mŏks)	86	49°40'N	124°55'W
Companario, Cerro, mtn., S.A. (sĕ'r-rô-kôm-pä-nä'ryô)	129b	35°54'S	70°23'W
Compans, Fr.	237c	49°00'N	2°40'E
Compiègne, Fr. (kôɴ-pyĕn'y')	147	49°25'N	2°49'E
Comporta, Port. (kôm-pôr'tȧ)	159b	38°24'N	8°48'W
Compostela, Mex. (kōm-pô-stā'lä)	118	21°14'N	104°54'W
Compton, Ca., U.S. (kŏmpt'tŭn)	107a	33°54'N	118°14'W
Comrat, Mol. (kôm-rät')	167	46°17'N	28°38'E
Conakry, Gui. (kô-nȧ-krē')	210	9°31'N	13°43'W
Conanicut, i., R.I., U.S. (kŏn'ȧ-nĭ-kŭt)	100b	41°34'N	71°20'W
Conasauga, r., Ga., U.S. (kô-nȧ)	114	34°40'N	84°51'W
Concarneau, Fr. (kôɴ-kär-nō')	156	47°54'N	3°52'W
Concepción, Bol. (kôn-sĕp'syōn')	131	15°47'S	61°08'W
Concepción, Chile	132	36°51'S	72°59'W
Concepción, Pan.	121	8°31'N	82°38'W
Concepción, Para.	132	23°29'S	57°18'W
Concepcion, Phil.	197a	15°19'N	120°40'E
Concepción, vol., Nic.	120	11°36'N	85°43'W
Concepción, r., Mex.	116	30°25'N	112°20'W

ăt; finăl; rāte; senāte; ärm; åsk; sofȧ; fâre; ch-choose; dh-as th in other; bē; ēvent; bĕt; recĕnt; cratẽr; g-gō; gh-guttural g; bĭt; ĭ-short neutral; rīde; ᴋ-guttural k as ch in German ich;

PRONOUNCING INDEX

Concepción del Mar–Coubert 277

PLACE (Pronunciation)	PAGE	LAT.	LONG.
Concepción del Mar, Guat. (kôn-sĕp-syōn'dĕl mär')	120	14°07'N	91°23'W
Concepción del Oro, Mex. (kôn-sĕp-syōn' dĕl ō'rō)	116	24°39'N	101°24'W
Concepción del Uruguay, Arg. (kôn-sĕp-syō'n-dĕl-ōō-rōō-gwī')	132	32°31'S	58°10'W
Conception, i., Bah.	123	23°50'N	75°05'W
Conception, Point, c., Ca., U.S.	96	34°27'N	120°28'W
Conception Bay, b., Can. (kŏn-sĕp'shŭn)	93	47°50'N	52°50'W
Conchalí, Chile	234b	33°24'S	70°39'W
Concho, r., Tx., U.S. (kŏn'chō)	112	31°34'N	100°00'W
Conchos, r., Mex. (kōn'chōs)	112	25°03'N	99°00'W
Conchos, r., Mex.	116	29°30'N	105°00'W
Concord, Austl.	243a	33°52'S	151°06'E
Concord, Can.	227c	43°48'N	79°29'W
Concord, Ca., U.S. (kŏŋ'kŏrd)	106b	37°58'N	122°02'W
Concord, Ma., U.S.	93a	42°28'N	71°21'W
Concord, N.H., U.S.	97	43°10'N	71°30'W
Concord, N.C., U.S.	115	35°23'N	80°11'W
Concordia, Arg. (kŏn-kôr'dĭ-à)	132	31°18'S	57°59'W
Concordia, Col.	130a	6°04'N	75°54'W
Concordia, Mex. (kôn-kô'r-dyä)	118	23°17'N	106°06'W
Concordia, Ks., U.S.	111	39°32'N	97°39'W
Concord West, Austl.	243a	33°51'S	151°05'E
Concrete, Wa., U.S. (kŏn-'krēt)	104	48°33'N	121°44'W
Conde, Fr.	156	48°50'N	0°36'W
Conde, S.D., U.S. (kŏn-dē')	102	45°10'N	98°06'W
Condega, Nic. (kŏn-dĕ'gä)	120	13°20'N	86°27'W
Condeúba, Braz. (kōn-dā-ōō'bä)	131	14°47'S	41°44'W
Condom, Fr.	156	43°58'N	0°22'E
Condon, Or., U.S. (kŏn'dŭn)	104	45°14'N	120°10'W
Conecun, r., Al., U.S. (kô-nē'kū)	114	31°05'N	86°52'W
Conegliano, Italy (kō-nâl-yä'nō)	160	45°59'N	12°17'E
Conejos, r., Co., U.S. (kô-nā'hōs)	109	37°07'N	106°19'W
Conemaugh, Pa., U.S. (kŏn'ē-mô)	99	40°25'N	78°50'W
Coney Island, neigh., N.Y., U.S.	228	40°34'N	74°00'W
Coney Island, i., N.Y., U.S. (kō'nĭ)	100a	40°34'N	73°27'W
Conflans-Sainte-Honorine, Fr.	237c	48°59'N	2°06'E
Confolens, Fr. (kôN-fä-läN')	156	46°01'N	0°41'E
Congaree, r., S.C., U.S. (kŏŋ-gá-rē')	115	33°53'N	80°55'W
Conghua, China (tsōŋ-hwä)	193	23°30'N	113°40'E
Congleton, Eng., U.K. (kŏŋ'g'l-tŭn)	144a	53°10'N	2°13'W
Congo, nation, Afr. (kŏn'gō)	212	3°00'S	13°48'E
Congo (Zaire), r., Afr. (kŏn'gō)	209	2°00'S	17°00'E
Congo, Serra do, mts., Ang.	216	6°25'S	13°30'E
Congo, The see Zaire, nation, Afr.	212	1°00'S	22°15'E
Congo Basin, basin, D.R.C.	209	2°47'N	20°58'E
Congress Heights, neigh., D.C., U.S.	229d	38°51'N	77°00'W
Conisbrough, Eng., U.K. (kŏn'ĭs-bŭr-ō)	144a	53°29'N	1°13'W
Coniston, Can.	91	46°29'N	80°51'W
Conklin, Can. (kŏŋk'lĭn)	87	55°38'N	111°05'W
Conley, Ga., U.S. (kŏn'lĭ)	100c	33°38'N	84°19'W
Conn, Lough, l., Ire. (lŏk kŏn)	150	53°56'N	9°25'W
Connacht, hist. reg., Ire. (cŏn'ât)	150	53°50'N	8°45'W
Connaughton, Pa., U.S.	229b	40°05'N	75°19'W
Conneaut, Oh., U.S. (kŏn-ē-ôt')	98	41°55'N	80°35'W
Connecticut, state, U.S. (kŏ-nĕt'ĭ-kŭt)	97	41°40'N	73°10'W
Connecticut, r., U.S.	97	43°55'N	72°15'W
Connellsville, Pa., U.S. (kŏn'nĕlz-vĭl)	99	40°00'N	79°40'W
Connemara, mts., Ire. (kŏn-nê-má'rá)	150	53°30'N	9°54'W
Connersville, In., U.S. (kŏn'ĕrz-vĭl)	98	39°35'N	85°10'W
Connors Range, mts., Austl. (kŏn'nŏrs)	203	22°15'S	149°00'E
Conrad, Mt., U.S. (kŏn'răd)	105	48°11'N	111°56'W
Conrich, Can. (kŏn'rĭch)	83e	51°06'N	113°51'W
Conroe, Tx., U.S. (kŏn'rō)	113	30°18'N	95°23'W
Conselheiro Lafaiete, Braz.	131	20°40'S	43°46'W
Conshohocken, Pa., U.S. (kŏn-shō-hŏk'ĕn)	100f	40°04'N	75°18'W
Consolação, neigh., Braz.	234d	23°33'S	46°39'W
Consolación del Sur, Cuba (kōn-sō-lä-syōn')	122	22°30'N	83°55'W
Consolidated Main Reef Mines, quarry, S. Afr.	244b	26°11'S	27°56'E
Con Son, is., Viet	196	8°30'N	106°28'E
Constance, Mount, mtn., Wa., U.S. (kŏn'stăns)	106a	47°46'N	123°08'W
Constanţa, Rom. (kōn-stán'tsá)	142	44°12'N	28°36'E
Constantina, Spain (kŏn-stän-tē'nä)	158	37°52'N	5°39'W
Constantine, Alg. (kôN-stäN'tēn')	210	36°28'N	6°38'E
Constantine, Mi., U.S. (kŏn'stăn-tēn)	98	41°50'N	85°40'W
Constitución, Chile (kōn'stĭ-tōō-syōn')	132	35°24'S	72°25'W
Constitución, neigh., Arg.	233d	34°37'S	58°23'W
Constitution, Ga., U.S. (kŏn-stĭ-tū'shŭn)	100c	33°41'N	84°20'W
Contagem, Braz. (kōn-tá'zhĕm)	129a	19°54'S	44°05'W
Contepec, Mex. (kōn-tĕ-pĕk')	118	20°04'N	100°07'W
Contreras, Mex. (kôn-trĕ'räs)	119a	19°18'N	99°14'W
Contwoyto, l., Can.	84	65°42'N	110°50'W
Converse, Tx., U.S. (kŏn'vĕrs)	107d	29°31'N	98°17'W
Conway, Ar., U.S. (kŏn'wā)	111	35°06'N	92°27'W
Conway, N.H., U.S.	99	44°00'N	71°10'W
Conway, S.C., U.S.	115	33°49'N	79°01'W
Conway, Wa., U.S.	106a	48°20'N	122°20'W
Conyers, Ga., U.S. (kŏn'yŏrz)	114	33°41'N	84°01'W
Cooch Behār, India (kōoch bē-hār')	183	26°25'N	89°34'E
Coogee, Austl.	243a	33°55'S	151°16'E
Cook, Cape, c., Can. (kŏŏk)	86	50°08'N	127°55'W
Cook, Mount, mtn., N.Z.	203a	43°27'S	170°13'E
Cook, Point, c., Austl.	243b	37°55'S	144°48'E
Cookeville, Tn., U.S. (kŏŏk'vĭl)	114	36°07'N	85°30'W
Cooking Lake, Can. (kōōk'ĭng)	83g	53°25'N	113°08'W
Cooking Lake, l., Can.	83g	53°25'N	113°02'W
Cook Inlet, b., Ak., U.S.	95	60°50'N	151°38'W
Cook Islands, dep., Oc.	2	20°00'S	158°00'W
Cooksmill Green, Eng., U.K.	235	51°44'N	0°22'E
Cook Strait, strt., N.Z.	203a	40°37'S	174°15'E
Cooktown, Austl. (kŏŏk'toun)	203	15°40'S	145°20'E
Cooleemee, N.C., U.S. (kōō-lē'mē)	115	35°50'N	80°32'W

PLACE (Pronunciation)	PAGE	LAT.	LONG.
Coolgardie, Austl. (kōōl-gär'dē)	202	31°00'S	121°25'E
Cooma, Austl. (kōō'mȧ)	203	36°22'S	149°10'E
Coonamble, Austl. (kōō-năm'b'l)	203	31°00'S	148°30'E
Coonoor, India	187	10°22'N	76°15'E
Coon Rapids, Mn., U.S. (kōn)	107g	45°09'N	93°17'W
Cooper, Tx., U.S. (kōōp'ēr)	111	33°23'N	95°40'W
Cooper Center, Ak., U.S.	95	61°54'N	15°30'W
Coopersale Common, Eng., U.K.	235	51°42'N	0°08'E
Coopers Creek, r., Austl. (kōō'pērz)	203	27°32'N	141°19'E
Cooperstown, N.Y., U.S. (kōōp'ērs-toun)	99	42°45'N	74°55'W
Cooperstown, N.D., U.S.	102	47°26'N	98°07'W
Coosa, Al., U.S. (kōō'sȧ)	114	32°43'N	86°25'W
Coosa, r., U.S.	97	34°00'N	86°00'W
Coosawattee, r., Ga., U.S.	114	34°37'N	84°45'W
Coos Bay, Or., U.S. (kōōs)	104	43°21'N	124°12'W
Coos Bay, b., Or., U.S.	104	43°19'N	124°40'W
Cootamundra, Austl. (kŏŏtă-mŭnd'ră)	204	34°25'S	148°00'E
Copacabana, Braz. (kō'pä-kȧ-bä'nä)	132b	22°57'S	43°11'W
Copalita, r., Mex. (kō-pä-lē'tä)	119	15°55'N	96°06'W
Copán, hist., Hond. (kō-pän')	120	14°50'N	89°10'W
Copano Bay, b., Tx., U.S. (kō-pän'ō)	113	28°08'N	97°25'W
Copenhagen (København), Den.	142	55°43'N	12°27'E
Copiapó, Chile (kō-pyä-pō')	132	27°16'S	70°28'W
Copley, Oh., U.S. (kŏp'lē)	101d	41°06'N	81°38'W
Copparo, Italy (kŏp-pä'rō)	160	44°53'N	11°50'E
Coppell, Tx., U.S. (kŏp'pĕl)	107c	32°57'N	97°00'W
Copper, r., Ak., U.S. (kŏp'ēr)	95	62°38'N	145°00'W
Copper Cliff, Can.	90	46°28'N	81°04'W
Copper Harbor, Mi., U.S.	103	47°27'N	87°53'W
Copperhill, Tn., U.S. (kŏp'ēr hĭl)	114	35°00'N	84°22'W
Coppermine, Can. (kŏp'ēr-mīn)	84	67°46'N	115°19'W
Coppermine, r., Can.	84	66°48'N	114°59'W
Copper Mountain, mtn., Ak., U.S.	86	55°14'N	132°36'W
Copperton, Ut., U.S. (kŏp'ēr-tŭn)	107b	40°34'N	112°06'W
Coquilee, Or., U.S. (kō-kēl')	104	43°11'N	124°11'W
Coquilhatville see Mbandaka, D.R.C.	212	0°04'N	18°16'E
Coquimbo, Chile (kō-kēm'bō)	132	29°58'S	71°31'W
Coquimbo, prov., Chile	129b	31°50'S	71°05'W
Coquitlam Lake, l., Can. (kō-kwĭt-lȧm)	106d	49°23'N	122°44'W
Corabia, Rom. (kō-rā'bĭ-ȧ)	149	43°45'N	24°29'E
Coracora, Peru (kō'rä-kō'rä)	130	15°12'S	73°42'W
Coral Gables, Fl., U.S.	115a	25°43'N	80°14'W
Coral Rapids, Can. (kŏr'ăl)	85	50°18'N	81°49'W
Coral Sea, sea, Oc. (kŏr'ăl)	203	13°30'S	150°00'E
Coralville Reservoir, res., Ia., U.S.	103	41°45'N	91°50'W
Corangamite, Lake, l., Austl. (cŏr-ăŋg'á-mĭt)	204	38°05'S	142°55'E
Coraopolis, Pa., U.S. (kō-rä-ŏp'ō-lĭs)	101e	40°30'N	80°09'W
Corato, Italy (kō'rä-tō)	160	41°08'N	16°28'E
Corbeil-Essonnes, Fr. (kôr-bâ'yĕ-sŏn')	156	48°31'N	2°29'E
Corbett, Or., U.S. (kôr'bĕt)	106c	45°31'N	122°17'W
Corbie, Fr. (kôr-bē')	156	49°55'N	2°27'E
Corbin, Ky., U.S. (kôr'bĭn)	114	36°55'N	84°06'W
Corby, Eng., U.K. (kôr'bĭ)	144a	52°29'N	0°38'W
Corcovado, mtn., Braz. (kôr-kō-vä'dō)	132b	22°57'S	43°13'W
Corcovado, Golfo, b., Chile (kôr-kō-vä'dhō)	132	43°40'S	75°00'W
Cordeiro, Braz. (kôr-dā'rō)	129a	22°03'S	42°22'W
Cordele, Ga., U.S. (kôr-dēl')	114	31°55'N	83°50'W
Cordell, Ok., U.S. (kôr-dĕl')	110	35°19'N	98°58'W
Córdoba, Arg. (kôr'dō-vä)	132	30°20'S	64°03'W
Córdoba, Mex. (kô'r-dō-bä)	116	18°53'N	96°54'W
Córdoba, Spain (kô'r-dō-bä)	158	37°55'N	4°45'W
Córdoba, prov., Arg. (kôr'dō-vä)	132	32°00'S	64°00'W
Córdoba, Sierra de, mts., Arg.	132	31°15'S	64°30'W
Cordova, Al., U.S. (kôr'dō-ȧ)	114	33°45'N	86°22'W
Cordova, Ak., U.S. (kôr'dō-vä)	94a	60°34'N	145°38'W
Cordova Bay, b., Ak., U.S.	86	54°55'N	132°35'W
Corfu see Kérkira, i., Grc.	142	39°33'N	19°36'E
Corigliano, Italy (kō-rē-lyä'nō)	160	39°35'N	16°30'E
Corinth see Kórinthos, Grc.	142	37°56'N	22°54'E
Corinth, Ms., U.S. (kŏr'ĭnth)	114	34°55'N	88°30'W
Corinto, Braz. (kō-rē'n-tō)	131	18°20'S	44°16'W
Corinto, Col.	130a	3°09'N	76°12'W
Corinto, Nic. (kōr-ĭn'to)	120	12°30'N	87°12'W
Corio, Austl.	201a	38°05'S	144°22'E
Corio Bay, b., Austl.	201a	38°07'S	144°25'E
Corisco, Isla de, i., Eq. Gui.	216	0°50'N	8°40'E
Cork, Ire. (kôrk)	142	51°54'N	8°25'W
Cork Harbour, b., Ire.	150	51°44'N	8°15'W
Corleone, Italy (kôr-lå-ō'nā)	160	37°48'N	13°18'E
Cormano, Italy	238c	45°33'N	9°10'E
Cormeilles-en-Parisis, Fr.	237c	48°59'N	2°12'E
Cormorant Lake, l., Can.	89	54°13'N	100°47'W
Cornelia, Ga., U.S. (kôr-nē'lyȧ)	114	34°31'N	83°30'W
Cornelis, r., S. Afr. (kôr-nē'lĭs)	218d	27°48'S	29°15'E
Cornell, Ca., U.S. (kôr-nĕl')	107a	34°06'N	118°46'W
Cornell, Wi., U.S.	103	45°10'N	91°10'W
Cornellà, Spain	238e	41°21'N	2°05'E
Corner Brook, Can. (kôr'nēr)	85	48°57'N	57°57'W
Corner Inlet, b., Austl.	204	38°55'S	146°45'E
Corning, Ar., U.S. (kôr'nĭng)	111	36°26'N	90°35'W
Corning, Ia., U.S.	103	40°58'N	94°40'W
Corning, N.Y., U.S.	99	42°10'N	77°05'W
Corno, Monte, mtn., Italy (kôr'nō)	148	42°28'N	13°37'E
Cornwall, Bah.	122	25°55'N	77°15'W
Cornwall, Can. (kôrn'wôl)	91	45°05'N	74°35'W
Coro, Ven. (kō'rō)	130	11°22'N	69°43'W
Corocoro, Bol. (kō-rō-kō'rō)	130	17°15'S	68°21'W
Coromandel Coast, cst., India (kŏr-ō-man'dĕl)	183	13°30'N	80°30'E
Coromandel Peninsula, pen., N.Z.	205	36°50'S	176°00'E
Corona, Al., U.S. (kō-rō'nȧ)	114	33°42'N	87°28'W
Corona, Ca., U.S.	107a	33°52'N	117°34'W
Coronada, Bahía de, b., C.R. (bä-ē'ä-dē-kō-rō-nä'dō)	121	8°47'N	84°04'W
Corona del Mar, Ca., U.S. (kō-rō'nȧ dĕl mär)	107a	33°36'N	117°53'W
Coronado, Ca., U.S. (kŏr-ō-nä'dō)	108a	32°42'N	117°12'W

PLACE (Pronunciation)	PAGE	LAT.	LONG.
Coronation Gulf, b., Can. (kŏr-ō-nā'shŭn)	84	68°07'N	112°50'W
Coronel, Chile (kō-rō-nĕl')	132	37°00'S	73°10'W
Coronel Brandsen, Arg. (kŏ-rō-nĕl-brá'nd-sĕn)	129c	35°09'S	58°15'W
Coronel Dorrego, Arg. (kŏ-rō-nĕl-dŏr-rĕ'gō)	132	38°43'S	61°16'W
Coronel Oviedo, Para. (kō-rō-nĕl-ō-vē'dō)	132	25°28'S	56°22'W
Coronel Pringles, Arg. (kŏ-rō-nĕl-prēn'glĕs)	132	37°54'S	61°22'W
Coronel Suárez, Arg. (kŏ-rō-nĕl-swä'rās)	132	37°27'S	61°49'W
Corowa, Austl. (cŏr-ôwă)	204	36°02'S	146°23'E
Corozal, Belize (cŏr-ŏth-äl')	120a	18°25'N	88°23'W
Corpus Christi, Tx., U.S. (kôr'pŭs krĭstē)	96	27°48'N	97°24'W
Corpus Christi Bay, b., Tx., U.S.	113	27°47'N	97°14'W
Corpus Christi Lake, l., Tx., U.S.	112	28°08'N	98°20'W
Corral, Chile (kō-räl')	132	39°57'S	73°15'W
Corral de Almaguer, Spain (kō-räl'dā äl-mä-gâr')	158	39°45'N	3°10'W
Corralillo, Cuba (kō-rä-lē-yō)	122	23°00'N	80°40'W
Corregidor Island, i., Phil. (kō-rā-hē-dōr')	197a	14°21'N	120°25'E
Correntina, Braz. (kō-rĕn-tē-nȧ)	131	13°18'S	44°33'W
Corrib, Lough, l., Ire. (lŏk kŏr'ĭb)	150	53°25'N	9°19'W
Corrientes, Arg. (kō-ryĕn'tās)	132	27°25'S	58°39'W
Corrientes, prov., Arg.	132	28°45'S	58°00'W
Corrientes, Cabo, c., Col. (kà'bō-kō-ryĕn'tās)	130	5°34'N	77°35'W
Corrientes, Cabo, c., Cuba (kà'bō-kôr-rē-ĕn'tĕs)	122	21°50'N	84°25'W
Corrientes, Cabo, c., Mex.	116	20°25'N	105°41'W
Corringham, Eng., U.K.	235	51°31'N	0°28'E
Corroios, Port.	238d	38°38'N	9°09'W
Corry, Pa., U.S. (kŏr'ĭ)	99	41°55'N	79°40'W
Corse, Cap, c., Fr. (kôrs)	147	42°59'N	9°19'E
Corsica, i., Fr. (kôr'sĭ-kȧ)	142	42°10'N	8°55'E
Corsicana, Tx., U.S. (kôr-sĭ-kăn'ȧ)	96	32°06'N	96°28'W
Corsico, Italy	238c	45°26'N	9°07'E
Cortazar, Mex. (kôr-tä-zär)	118	20°30'N	100°57'W
Corte, Fr. (kôr'tå)	160	42°18'N	9°10'E
Cortegana, Spain (kôr-tå-gä'nä)	158	37°54'N	6°48'W
Corte Madera, Ca., U.S.	231b	37°55'N	122°31'W
Cortes, bldg., Spain	238b	40°25'N	3°41'W
Cortés, Ensendada de, b., Cuba (ĕn-sĕ-nä-dä-dē-kôr-tās')	122	22°05'N	83°45'W
Cortez, Co., U.S.	109	37°21'N	108°35'W
Cortland, N.Y., U.S. (kôrt'lănd)	99	42°35'N	76°10'W
Cortona, Italy (kôr-tō'nä)	160	43°16'N	12°00'E
Corubal, r., Gui.-B.	214	11°43'N	14°40'W
Coruche, Port. (kō-rōō'she)	158	38°58'N	8°34'W
Çoruh, r., Asia (chō-rōōk')	167	40°30'N	41°10'E
Çorum, Tur. (chō-rōōm')	182	40°34'N	34°45'E
Corunna, Mi., U.S. (kō-rŭn'ȧ)	98	43°00'N	84°05'W
Coruripe, Braz. (kō-rō-rē'pĭ)	131	10°09'S	36°13'W
Corvallis, Or., U.S. (kōr-văl'ĭs)	96	44°34'N	123°17'W
Corve, r., Eng., U.K. (kôr'vē)	144a	52°28'N	2°43'W
Corviale, neigh., Italy	239c	41°52'N	12°25'E
Corydon, In., U.S. (kŏr'ĭ-dŭn)	98	38°10'N	86°05'W
Corydon, Ia., U.S.	103	40°45'N	93°20'W
Corydon, Ky., U.S.	98	37°45'N	87°40'W
Cosamaloápan, Mex. (kō-sä-mä-lwä'pän)	119	18°21'N	95°48'W
Coscomatepec, Mex. (kôs'kōmä-tē-pĕk')	119	19°04'N	97°03'W
Cosenza, Italy (kō-zĕnt'sä)	149	39°18'N	16°15'E
Cosfanero, Canal de, strt., Arg.	233d	34°34'S	58°22'W
Coshocton, Oh., U.S. (kō-shŏk'tŭn)	98	40°15'N	81°55'W
Cosigüina, vol., Nic.	120	12°59'N	87°35'W
Cosmoledo Group, is., Sey. (kŏs-mō-lā'dō)	213	9°42'S	47°45'E
Cosmopolis, Wa., U.S. (kŏz-mŏp'ō-lĭs)	104	46°58'N	123°47'W
Cosne-sur-Loire, Fr. (kōn-sür-lwär')	156	47°25'N	2°57'E
Cosoleacaque, Mex. (kō sō lä-ä-kä'kĕ)	119	18°01'N	94°38'W
Costa de Caparica, Port.	159b	38°40'N	9°12'W
Costa Mesa, Ca., U.S. (kŏs'tȧ mā'sȧ)	107a	33°39'N	118°54'W
Costa Rica, nation, N.A. (kŏs'tȧ rē'kȧ)	117	10°30'N	84°30'W
Cosumnes, r., Ca., U.S. (kŏ-sŭm'nĕz)	108	38°21'N	121°17'W
Cotabambas, Peru (kō-tä-bam'bäs)	130	13°49'S	72°17'W
Cotabato, Phil. (kō-tä-bä'tō)	197	7°06'N	124°13'E
Cotaxtla, Mex. (kō-täs'tlä)	119	18°49'N	96°22'W
Cotaxtla, r., Mex.	119	18°54'N	96°21'W
Coteau-du-Lac, Can. (cō-tō'dü-läk)	83a	45°17'N	74°11'W
Coteau-Landing, Can.	83a	45°15'N	74°13'W
Coteaux, Haiti	123	18°15'N	74°05'W
Cote d'Ivoire (Ivory Coast), nation, Afr.	210	7°43'N	6°30'W
Côte d'Or, reg., Fr.	156	47°02'N	4°35'E
Côte-Saint-Luc, Can.	227b	45°28'N	73°40'W
Côte Visitation, neigh., Can.	227b	45°33'N	73°36'W
Cotija de la Paz, Mex. (kō-tē'-ĸä-dĕ-lä-pá'z)	118	19°46'N	102°43'W
Cotonou, Benin (kō-tō-nōō')	210	6°21'N	2°26'E
Cotopaxi, mtn., Ec. (kō-tō-păk'sē)	130	0°40'S	78°26'W
Cotorro, Cuba (kō-tôr-rō)	123a	23°03'N	82°17'W
Cotswold Hills, hills, Eng., U.K. (kŭtz'wōld)	150	51°35'N	2°16'W
Cottage City, Md., U.S.	229d	38°56'N	76°57'W
Cottage Grove, Mn., U.S. (kŏt'āj grōv)	107g	44°50'N	92°52'W
Cottage Grove, Or., U.S.	104	43°48'N	123°04'W
Cottbus, Ger. (kōtt'bōōs)	147	51°47'N	14°20'E
Cottonwood, r., Mn., U.S. (kŏt'ŭn-wŏŏd)	102	44°25'N	95°35'W
Cotulla, Tx., U.S. (kō-tŭl'lȧ)	112	28°26'N	99°14'W
Coubert, Fr. (kōō-bâr')	157b	48°40'N	2°43'E

ŋ-sing; ŋ-baŋk; N-nasalized n; nŏd; cŏmmit; ōld; ôbey; ôrder; oi-boil; fōōd; ŏŏ-as oo in foot; ou-out; s-soft; sh-dish; th-thin; pūre; ûnite; ûrn; stŭd; circŭs; ü-as in French tu; '-indeterminate vowel.

278 Coudersport-Cumaná

PLACE (Pronunciation)	PAGE	LAT.	LONG.
Coudersport, Pa., U.S. (kou'dẽrz-port)	99	41°45'N	78°00'W
Coudres, Île aux, i., Can.	92	47°17'N	70°12'W
Coulommiers, Fr. (ko͞o-lô-myā')	157b	48°49'N	3°05'E
Coulsdon, neigh., Eng., U.K.	235	51°19'N	0°08'W
Coulto, Serra do, mts., Braz. (sĕ'r-rä-dô-kô-ó'tô)	132b	22°33'S	43°27'W
Council Bluffs, Ia., U.S. (koun'sĭl blŭf)	97	41°16'N	95°53'W
Council Grove, Ks., U.S. (koun'sĭl grōv)	111	38°39'N	96°30'W
Coupeville, Wa., U.S. (ko͞op'vĭl)	106a	48°13'N	122°41'W
Courantyne, r., S.A. (kôr'ăntīn)	131	4°28'N	57°42'W
Courbevoie, Fr.	237c	48°54'N	2°15'E
Courcelle, Fr.	237c	48°42'N	2°06'E
Courtenay, Can. (co͞ort-nā')	84	49°41'N	125°00'W
Courtleigh, Md., U.S.	229c	39°22'N	76°46'W
Courtry, Fr.	237c	48°55'N	2°36'E
Coushatta, La., U.S. (kou-shăt'ȧ)	113	32°02'N	93°21'W
Coutras, Fr. (ko͞o-trá')	156	45°02'N	0°07'W
Cova da Piedade, Port.	238d	38°40'N	9°10'W
Covelo, Ang.	216	12°06'S	13°55'E
Cove Neck, N.Y., U.S.	228	40°53'N	73°31'W
Coventry, Eng., U.K. (kŭv'ĕn-trĭ)	150	52°25'N	1°29'W
Covina, Ca., U.S. (kô-vē'nȧ)	107a	34°06'N	117°54'W
Covington, Ga., U.S. (kŭv'ĭng-tŭn)	114	33°36'N	83°50'W
Covington, In., U.S.	98	40°10'N	87°15'W
Covington, Ky., U.S.	97	39°05'N	84°31'W
Covington, La., U.S.	113	30°30'N	90°06'W
Covington, Oh., U.S.	98	40°10'N	84°20'W
Covington, Ok., U.S.	111	36°18'N	97°32'W
Covington, Tn., U.S.	114	35°33'N	89°40'W
Covington, Va., U.S.	98	37°50'N	80°00'W
Cowal, Lake, l., Austl. (kou'ăl)	204	33°30'S	147°10'E
Cowan, l., Austl. (kou'ăn)	202	32°00'S	122°30'E
Cowan Heights, Ca., U.S.	232	33°47'N	117°47'W
Cowansville, Can.	91	45°13'N	72°47'W
Cow Creek, r., Or., U.S. (kou)	104	42°45'N	123°35'W
Cowes, Eng., U.K. (kouz)	150	50°43'N	1°25'W
Cowichan Lake, l., Can.	86	48°54'N	124°20'W
Cowley, neigh., Eng., U.K.	235	51°32'N	0°29'W
Cowlitz, r., Wa., U.S. (kou'lĭts)	104	46°30'N	122°45'W
Cowra, Austl. (kou'rȧ)	204	33°50'S	148°33'E
Coxim, Braz. (kō-shēɴ')	131	18°32'S	54°43'W
Coxquihui, Mex. (kōz-kē-wē')	119	20°10'N	97°34'W
Cox's Bāzār, Bngl.	186	21°32'N	92°00'E
Coyaima, Col. (kō-yäē'mä)	130a	3°48'N	75°11'W
Coyame, Mex. (kō-yä'mā)	112	29°26'N	105°05'W
Coyanosa Draw, Tx., U.S. (kŏ yȧ-nō'sä)	112	30°55'N	103°07'W
Coyoacán, Mex. (kô-yô-á-kän')	118	19°21'N	99°10'W
Coyote, r., Ca., U.S. (kī'ōt)	106b	37°37'N	121°57'W
Coyuca de Benítez, Mex. (kō-yo͞o'kä dā bā-nē'tāz)	118	17°04'N	100°06'W
Coyuca de Catalán, Mex. (kō-yo͞o'kä dā kä-tä-län')	118	18°19'N	100°41'W
Coyutla, Mex. (kō-yo͞o'tlä)	119	20°13'N	97°40'W
Cozad, Ne., U.S. (kō'zăd)	110	40°53'N	99°59'W
Cozaddale, Oh., U.S. (kō-zăd-dāl)	101f	39°16'N	84°09'W
Cozoyoapan, Mex. (kô-zō-yô-ä-pá'n)	118	16°45'N	98°17'W
Cozumel, Mex. (kŏ-zo͞o-mĕ'l)	120a	20°31'N	86°55'W
Cozumel, Isla de, i., Mex. (ē's-lä-dĕ-kŏ-zo͞o-mĕ'l)	116	20°26'N	87°10'W
Crab Creek, r., Wa., U.S.	104	47°21'N	119°09'W
Crab Creek, r., Wa., U.S. (krăb)	104	46°47'N	119°43'W
Cradock, S. Afr. (kră'dŭk)	212	32°12'S	25°38'E
Crafton, Pa., U.S. (krăf'tŭn)	101e	40°26'N	80°04'W
Craig, Co., U.S. (krāg)	105	40°32'N	107°31'W
Craighall Park, neigh., S. Afr.	244b	26°08'S	28°01'E
Craiova, Rom. (krá-yō'vá)	149	44°18'N	23°50'E
Cranberry, l., N.Y., U.S. (krăn'bĕr-ĭ)	99	44°10'N	74°50'W
Cranbourne, Austl.	201a	38°07'S	145°16'E
Cranbrook, Can. (krăn'bro͝ok)	84	49°31'N	115°46'W
Cranbury, N.J., U.S. (krăn'bē-rĭ)	100a	40°19'N	74°31'W
Crandon, Wi., U.S. (krăn'dŭn)	103	45°35'N	88°55'W
Crane Prairie Reservoir, res., Or., U.S.	104	43°50'N	121°55'W
Cranford, N.J., U.S.	228	40°39'N	74°19'W
Crank, Eng., U.K.	237a	53°29'N	2°45'W
Cranston, R.I., U.S. (krăns'tŭn)	100b	41°46'N	71°25'W
Crater Lake, l., Or., U.S. (krā'tẽr)	104	43°00'N	122°08'W
Crater Lake National Park, rec., Or., U.S.	104	42°58'N	122°40'W
Craters of the Moon National Monument, rec., Id., U.S. (krā'tẽr)	105	43°28'N	113°15'W
Crateús, Braz. (krä-tā-o͞ozh')	131	5°09'S	40°35'W
Crato, Braz. (krä'tō)	131	7°19'S	39°13'W
Crawford, Ne., U.S. (krô'fẽrd)	102	42°41'N	103°25'W
Crawford, Wa., U.S.	106c	45°49'N	122°24'W
Crawfordsville, In., U.S. (krô'fẽrdz-vĭl)	98	40°00'N	86°55'W
Crazy Mountains, mts., Mt., U.S. (krā'zĭ)	105	46°11'N	110°25'W
Crazy Woman Creek, r., Wy., U.S.	105	44°08'N	106°40'W
Crecy, S. Afr. (krĕ-sē)	218d	24°38'S	28°52'E
Crécy-en-Brie, Fr. (krā-sē'-ĕɴ-brē')	157b	48°52'N	2°55'E
Crécy-en-Ponthieu, Fr.	156	50°13'N	1°48'E
Credit, r., Can.	83d	43°41'N	79°55'W
Cree, l., Can. (krē)	84	57°35'N	107°52'W
Creekmouth, neigh., Eng., U.K.	235	51°31'N	0°06'E
Creighton, S. Afr. (cre-tŏn)	213c	30°02'S	29°52'E
Creighton, Ne., U.S. (krā'tŭn)	102	42°27'N	97°54'W
Creil, Fr. (krĕ'y')	156	49°18'N	2°28'E
Crema, Italy (krā'mä)	160	45°21'N	9°53'E
Cremona, Italy (krā-mō'nä)	148	45°09'N	10°02'E
Crépy-en-Valois, Fr. (krā-pē'ĕɴ-vä-lwä')	157b	49°14'N	2°53'E
Cres, Cro. (tsrĕs)	160	44°58'N	14°21'E
Cres, i., Yugo.	160	44°50'N	14°31'E
Crescent Beach, Can.	106d	49°03'N	122°58'W
Crescent City, Ca., U.S. (krĕs'ĕnt)	104	41°46'N	124°13'W
Crescent City, Fl., U.S.	115	29°26'N	81°35'W
Crescent Lake, l., Fl., U.S. (krĕs'ĕnt)	115	29°33'N	81°30'W
Crescent Lake, l., Or., U.S.	104	43°25'N	121°58'W
Crescentville, neigh., Pa., U.S.	229b	40°02'N	75°05'W
Cresco, Ia., U.S. (krĕs'kō)	103	43°23'N	92°07'W
Cresskill, N.J., U.S.	228	40°57'N	73°57'W
Crested Butte, Co., U.S. (krĕst'ĕd būt)	109	38°50'N	107°00'W
Crest Haven, Md., U.S.	229d	39°02'N	76°59'W
Crestline, Ca., U.S. (krĕst-līn)	107a	34°15'N	117°17'W
Crestline, Oh., U.S.	98	40°50'N	82°40'W
Crestmore, Ca., U.S. (krĕst'môr)	107a	34°02'N	117°23'W
Creston, Can. (krĕs'tŭn)	84	49°06'N	116°31'W
Creston, Ia., U.S.	103	41°04'N	94°22'W
Creston, Oh., U.S.	101d	40°59'N	81°54'W
Crestview, Fl., U.S. (krĕst'vū)	114	30°44'N	86°35'W
Crestwood, Il., U.S.	231a	41°39'N	87°44'W
Crestwood, Ky., U.S. (krĕst'wo͝od)	101h	38°20'N	85°28'W
Crestwood, Mo., U.S.	107e	38°33'N	90°23'W
Crete, Il., U.S. (krēt)	101a	41°26'N	87°38'W
Crete, Ne., U.S.	111	40°38'N	96°56'W
Crete, i., Grc.	142	35°15'N	24°30'E
Créteil, Fr.	237c	48°48'N	2°28'E
Creus, Cap de, c., Spain	159	42°16'N	3°18'E
Creuse, r., Fr. (krûz)	156	46°51'N	0°49'E
Creve Coeur, Mo., U.S. (krēv kor)	107e	38°40'N	90°27'W
Crevillent, Spain	159	38°12'N	0°48'W
Crewe, Eng., U.K. (kro͞o)	150	53°06'N	2°27'W
Crewe, Va., U.S.	115	37°09'N	78°08'W
Crimean Peninsula see Kryms'kyi Pivostriv, pen., Ukr.	167	45°18'N	33°30'E
Crimmitschau, Ger. (krĭm'ĭt-shou)	154	50°49'N	12°22'E
Cripple Creek, Co., U.S. (krĭp''l)	110	38°44'N	105°12'W
Crisfield, Md., U.S. (krĭs-fēld)	99	38°00'N	75°50'W
Cristal, Monts de, mts., Gabon	216	0°50'N	10°30'E
Cristina, Braz. (krēs-tē'-nä)	129a	22°13'S	45°15'W
Cristóbal Colón, Pico, mtn., Col. (pē'kô-krēs-tô'bäl-kō-lôn')	130	11°00'N	74°00'W
Cristo Redentor, Estatua do, hist., Braz.	234c	22°57'S	43°13'W
Crișul Alb, r., Rom. (krē'sho͞ol älb)	155	46°20'N	22°15'E
Crna, r., Yugo. (ts'r'ná)	161	41°03'N	21°46'E
Crna Gora (Montenegro), hist. reg., Yugo.	161	42°55'N	18°52'E
Črnomelj, Slvn. (ch'r'nō-māl')	160	45°35'N	15°11'E
Croatia, nation, Eur.	160	45°24'N	15°18'E
Crockenhill, Eng., U.K.	235	51°23'N	0°10'E
Crockett, Ca., U.S. (krŏk'ĕt)	106b	38°03'N	122°14'W
Crockett, Tx., U.S.	113	31°19'N	95°28'W
Crofton, Md., U.S.	100e	39°01'N	76°43'W
Crofton, Ne., U.S.	102	42°44'N	97°32'W
Croissy-Beaubourg, Fr.	237c	48°50'N	2°40'E
Croissy-sur-Seine, Fr.	237c	48°53'N	2°09'E
Croix, Lac la, l., N.A. (läk lä kro͞o-ä')	103	48°19'N	91°53'W
Croker, i., Austl. (krō'kȧ)	202	10°45'S	132°25'E
Cromer, Austl.	243a	33°44'S	151°17'E
Cronenberg, neigh., Ger.	236	51°12'N	7°08'E
Cronton, Eng., U.K.	237a	53°23'N	2°46'W
Cronulla, Austl. (krō-nŭl'ȧ)	201b	34°03'S	151°09'E
Crooked, i., Bah.	123	22°45'N	74°10'W
Crooked, l., Can.	93	48°25'N	56°05'W
Crooked, r., Can.	87	54°30'N	122°55'W
Crooked, r., Or., U.S.	104	44°07'N	120°30'W
Crooked Creek, r., Il., U.S. (kro͝ok'ĕd)	111	40°21'N	90°49'W
Crooked Island Passage, strt., Bah.	123	22°40'N	74°50'W
Crookston, Mn., U.S. (kro͝oks'tŭn)	102	47°44'N	96°35'W
Crooksville, Oh., U.S. (kro͝oks'vĭl)	98	39°45'N	82°05'W
Crosby, Eng., U.K.	144a	53°30'N	3°02'W
Crosby, Mn., U.S. (krôz'bĭ)	103	46°29'N	93°58'W
Crosby, N.D., U.S.	102	48°55'N	103°18'W
Crosby, Tx., U.S.	113a	29°55'N	95°04'W
Crosby, neigh., S. Afr.	244b	26°12'S	27°59'E
Crosne, Fr.	237c	48°43'N	2°28'E
Cross, l., La., U.S.	113	32°33'N	93°58'W
Cross, r., Nig.	215	5°35'N	8°05'E
Cross City, Fl., U.S.	114	29°55'N	83°25'W
Crossett, Ar., U.S. (krôs'ĕt)	111	33°08'N	92°00'W
Cross Lake, l., Can.	84	54°45'N	97°30'W
Cross River Reservoir, res., N.Y., U.S. (krôs)	100a	41°14'N	73°34'W
Cross Sound, strt., Ak., U.S. (krŏs)	95	58°12'N	137°20'W
Crosswell, Mi., U.S. (krŏz'wĕl)	98	43°15'N	82°35'W
Crotch, l., Can.	91	44°55'N	76°55'W
Crotone, Italy (krō-tô'nĕ)	161	39°05'N	17°08'E
Croton Falls Reservoir, res., N.Y., U.S. (krōtŭn)	100a	41°22'N	73°44'W
Croton-on-Hudson, N.Y., U.S. (krō'tŭn-ŏn hŭd'sŭn)	100a	41°12'N	73°53'W
Crouse Run, r., Pa., U.S.	230b	40°35'N	79°58'W
Crow, l., Can.	103	49°13'N	93°29'W
Crow Agency, Mt., U.S.	105	45°36'N	107°27'W
Crow Creek, r., Co., U.S.	110	41°08'N	104°25'W
Crow Creek Indian Reservation, I.R., S.D., U.S.	102	44°17'N	99°17'W
Crow Indian Reservation, I.R., Mt., U.S. (krō)	105	45°26'N	108°12'W
Crowle, Eng., U.K. (kroul)	144a	53°36'N	0°49'W
Crowley, La., U.S. (krou'lē)	113	30°13'N	92°22'W
Crown Mountain, mtn., Can. (kroun)	106d	49°24'N	123°05'W
Crown Mountain, mtn., V.I.U.S.	117c	18°22'N	64°58'W
Crown Point, In., U.S. (kroun point')	101a	41°25'N	87°22'W
Crown Point, N.Y., U.S.	99	44°00'N	73°25'W
Crows Nest, Austl.	243a	33°50'S	151°12'E
Crowsnest Pass, p., Can.	87	49°39'N	114°45'W
Crow Wing, r., Mn., U.S. (krō)	103	44°50'N	94°01'W
Crow Wing, r., Mn., U.S.	103	46°42'N	94°48'W
Crow Wing, North Fork, r., Mn., U.S.	103	45°16'N	94°28'W
Crow Wing, South Fork, r., Mn., U.S.	103	44°59'N	94°42'W
Croxley Green, Eng., U.K.	235	51°39'N	0°27'W
Croydon, Austl.	201a	37°48'S	145°17'E
Croydon, Austl. (kroi'dŭn)	203	18°15'S	142°15'E
Croydon, Eng., U.K.	147	51°22'N	0°06'W
Croydon, Pa., U.S.	100f	40°05'N	74°55'W
Crozet, Îles, is., Afr. (krō-zĕ')	3	46°20'S	51°30'E
Cruces, Cuba (kro͞o'sās)	122	22°20'N	80°20'W
Cruces, Arroyo de, r., Mex. (är-rō'yô-dĕ-kro͞o'sĕs)	112	26°17'N	104°32'W
Cruillas, Mex. (kro͞o-ēl'yäs)	112	24°45'N	98°31'W
Crum Lynne, Pa., U.S.	229b	39°52'N	75°20'W
Cruz, Cabo, c., Cuba (ká'-bô-kro͞oz)	117	19°50'N	77°45'W
Cruz, Cayo, i., Cuba (kä'yō-kro͞oz)	122	22°15'N	77°50'W
Cruz Alta, Braz. (kro͞oz äl'tä)	132	28°41'S	54°02'W
Cruz del Eje, Arg. (kro͞o's-dĕl-ĕ-kĕ)	132	30°46'S	64°45'W
Cruzeiro, Braz. (kro͞o-zā'rô)	129a	22°36'S	44°57'W
Cruzeiro do Sul, Braz. (kro͞o-zā'rô dô so͞ol)	130	7°34'S	72°40'W
Crysler, Can.	83c	45°13'N	75°09'W
Crystal Beach, Can.	230a	42°52'N	79°04'W
Crystal City, Tx., U.S. (krĭs'tăl sĭ'tĭ)	112	28°40'N	99°50'W
Crystal Falls, Mi., U.S. (krĭs'tăl fôls)	103	46°06'N	88°21'W
Crystal Lake, Il., U.S. (krĭs'tăl lăk)	101a	42°15'N	88°18'W
Crystal Springs, Ms., U.S. (krĭs'tăl sprĭngz)	114	31°58'N	90°20'W
Crystal Springs, oasis, Ca., U.S.	106b	37°31'N	122°26'W
Csömör, Hung.	239g	47°33'N	19°14'E
Csongrád, Hung. (chôn'gräd)	155	46°42'N	20°09'E
Csorna, Hung. (chôr'nä)	155	47°39'N	17°11'E
Cúa, Ven. (ko͞o'ä)	131b	10°10'N	66°54'W
Cuajimalpa, Mex. (kwä-hē-mäl'pä)	119a	19°21'N	99°18'W
Cuale, Sierra del, mts., Mex. (sē-ĕ'r-rä-dĕl-kwá'lĕ)	118	20°20'N	104°58'W
Cuamato, Ang. (kwä-mä'tō)	216	17°05'S	15°09'E
Cuamba, Moz.	217	14°49'S	36°33'E
Cuando, Ang. (kwän'dō)	216	16°32'S	22°07'E
Cuando, r., Afr.	212	14°30'S	20°00'E
Cuangar, Ang.	216	17°36'S	18°39'E
Cuango, r., Afr.	212	9°00'S	18°00'E
Cuanza, r., Ang. (kwän'zä)	212	9°45'S	15°00'E
Cuarto, r., Arg.	132	33°00'S	63°25'W
Cuatro Caminos, Cuba (kwä'trô-kä-mē'nōs)	123a	23°01'N	82°13'W
Cuatro Ciénegas, Mex. (kwä'trō syā'nā-gās)	112	26°59'N	102°03'W
Cuauhtemoc, Mex. (kwä-o͞o-tē-mŏk')	119	15°43'N	91°57'W
Cuautepec, Mex. (kwä-o͞o-tē-pĕk)	118	16°41'N	99°04'W
Cuautepec, Mex.	118	20°01'N	98°19'W
Cuautepec el Alto, Mex.	233a	19°34'N	99°08'W
Cuautitlán, Mex. (kwä-o͞o-tēt-län')	119a	19°40'N	99°12'W
Cuautla, Mex. (kwä-o͞o'tlä)	118	18°47'N	98°57'W
Cuba, Port. (ko͞o'bȧ)	158	38°10'N	7°55'W
Cuba, nation, N.A. (kū'bȧ)	117	22°00'N	79°00'W
Cubagua, Isla, i., Ven. (ē's-lä-ko͞o-bä'gwä)	131b	10°48'N	64°10'W
Cubango (Okavango), r., Afr. (ko͞o-bäŋ'gō)	212	17°10'S	18°20'E
Cub Hills, hills, Can. (kŭb)	88	54°20'N	104°30'W
Cucamonga, Ca., U.S. (ko͞o-kȧ-mōŋ'gȧ)	107a	34°05'N	117°35'W
Cuchi, Ang.	212	14°40'S	16°50'E
Cuchillo Parado, Mex. (ko͞o-chē'lyō pä-rä'dō)	112	29°26'N	104°52'W
Cuchumatanes, Sierra de los, mts., Guat.	120	15°35'N	91°10'W
Cúcuta, Col. (ko͞o'ko͞o-tä)	130	7°56'N	72°30'W
Cudahy, Wi., U.S. (kŭd'ȧ-hĭ)	101a	42°57'N	87°52'W
Cuddalore, India (kŭd ȧ-lōr')	183	11°49'N	79°46'E
Cuddapah, India (kŭd'ȧ-pä)	183	14°31'N	78°52'E
Cudham, neigh., Eng., U.K.	235	51°19'N	0°05'E
Cue, Austl. (kū)	202	27°30'S	118°10'E
Cuéllar, Spain (kwā'lyär')	158	41°24'N	4°15'W
Cuenca, Ec. (kwĕn'kä)	130	2°52'S	78°54'W
Cuenca, Spain	148	40°05'N	2°07'W
Cuenca, Sierra de, mts., Spain (sē-ĕ'r-rä-dĕ-kwĕ'n-kä)	158	40°02'N	1°50'W
Cuencame, Mex. (kwĕn-kä-mä')	112	24°52'N	103°42'W
Cuerámaro, Mex. (kwā-rä'mä-rō)	118	20°39'N	101°44'W
Cuernavaca, Mex. (kwĕr-nä-vä'kä)	116	18°55'N	99°15'W
Cuero, Tx., U.S. (kwā'rō)	113	29°05'N	97°16'W
Cuetzalá del Progreso, Mex. (kwĕt-zä-lä dĕl prō-grā'sō)	118	18°07'N	99°51'W
Cuetzalan del Progreso, Mex.	119	20°02'N	97°33'W
Cuevas del Almanzora, Spain (kwĕ'väs-dĕl-äl-män-zō-rä)	148	37°19'N	1°54'W
Cuffley, Eng., U.K.	235	51°42'N	0°07'W
Cuglieri, Italy (ko͞o-lyā'rĕ)	160	40°11'N	8°37'E
Cuicatlán, Mex. (kwē-kä-tlän')	119	17°46'N	96°57'W
Cuigezhuang, China	240b	40°01'N	116°28'E
Cuilapa, Guat. (kô-ē-lä'pä)	120	14°16'N	90°20'W
Cuilo (Kwilu), r., Afr.	216	9°15'S	19°30'E
Cuito, r., Ang. (ko͞o-ē'tō)	212	14°45'S	19°00'E
Cuitzeo, Mex. (kwēt'zā-ō)	118	19°57'N	101°11'W
Cuitzeo, Laguna de, l., Mex. (lä-ò'nä-dĕ-kwēt'zā-ō)	118	19°58'N	101°05'W
Cul de Sac, pl., Haiti (ko͞ol-dĕ-sä'k)	123	18°35'N	72°05'W
Culebra, i., P.R. (ko͞o-lā'brä)	117b	18°19'N	65°32'W
Culebra, Sierra de la, mts., Spain (sē-ĕ'r-rä-dĕ-lä-ko͞o-lĕ-brä)	158	41°52'N	6°21'W
Culemborg, Neth.	145a	51°57'N	5°14'E
Culfa, Azer.	168	38°58'N	45°38'E
Culgoa, r., Austl. (kŭl-gō'ȧ)	203	29°21'S	147°00'E
Culiacán, Mex. (ko͞o-lyä-kä'n)	116	24°45'N	107°30'W
Culion, Phil. (ko͞o-lē-ōn')	196	11°43'N	119°58'E
Cúllar de Baza, Spain (ko͞o'l-yär-dĕ-bä'zä)	158	37°36'N	2°35'W
Cullera, Spain (ko͞o-lyā'rä)	148	39°12'N	0°15'W
Cullinan, S. Afr. (kŏ'lĭ-nän)	218d	25°41'S	28°32'E
Cullman, Al., U.S. (kŭl'măn)	114	34°10'N	86°50'W
Culmore, Va., U.S.	229d	38°51'N	77°08'W
Culpeper, Va., U.S. (kŭl'pĕp-ẽr)	99	38°30'N	77°55'W
Culross, Can. (kŭl'rôs)	83f	49°43'N	97°54'W
Culver, In., U.S. (kŭl'vẽr)	98	41°15'N	86°25'W
Culver City, Ca., U.S.	107a	34°00'N	118°23'W
Culverstone Green, Eng., U.K.	235	51°20'N	0°21'E
Cumaná, Ven.	130	10°28'N	64°10'W

ăt; finăl; rāte; senāte; ärm; åsk; sofȧ; fâre; ch-choose; dh-as th in other; bē; ėvent; bĕt; recĕnt; cratẽr; g-gō; gh-guttural g; bĭt; ĭ-short neutral; rīde; ĸ-guttural k as ch in German ich;

PRONOUNCING INDEX

Cumberland-Dawley 279

PLACE (Pronunciation)	PAGE	LAT.	LONG.
Cumberland, Can. (kŭm′bẽr-lănd)	83c	45°31′N	75°25′W
Cumberland, Md., U.S.	97	39°40′N	78°40′W
Cumberland, Wa., U.S.	106a	47°17′N	121°55′W
Cumberland, Wi., U.S.	103	45°31′N	92°01′W
Cumberland, r., U.S.	114	36°45′N	85°33′W
Cumberland, Lake, res., Ky., U.S.	97	36°55′N	85°20′W
Cumberland Islands, is., Austl.	203	20°20′S	149°46′E
Cumberland Peninsula, pen., Can.	85	65°59′N	64°05′W
Cumberland Plateau, plat., U.S.	114	35°25′N	85°30′W
Cumberland Sound, strt., Can.	85	65°27′N	65°44′W
Cundinamarca, dept., Col. (kōōn-dē-nä-mä′r-kȧ)	130a	4°57′N	74°27′W
Cunduacán, Mex. (kōn-dōō-ȧ-kän′)	119	18°04′N	93°23′W
Cunene (Kunene), r., Afr.	212	17°05′S	12°35′E
Cuneo, Italy (kōō′nā-ō)	160	44°24′N	7°31′E
Cunha, Braz. (kōō′nyȧ)	129a	23°05′S	44°56′W
Cunnamulla, Austl. (kŭn-ȧ-mŭl-ȧ)	203	28°00′S	145°55′E
Cupula, Pico, mtn., Mex. (pē′kō-kōō′pōō-lä)	116	24°45′N	111°10′W
Cuquío, Mex. (kōō-kē′ō)	118	20°55′N	103°03′W
Curaçao, i., Neth. Ant. (kōō-rä-sä′ō)	130	12°12′N	68°58′W
Curacautín, Chile (kä-rä-käōō-tē′n)	132	38°25′S	71°53′W
Curaumilla, Punta, c., Chile (kōō-rou-mē′lyä)	129b	33°05′S	71°44′W
Curepto, Chile (kōō-rĕp-tō)	129b	35°06′S	72°02′W
Curitiba, Braz. (kōō-rē-tē′bȧ)	131	25°20′S	49°15′W
Curly Cut Cays, is., Bah.	122	23°40′N	77°40′W
Currais Novos, Braz. (kōōr-rä′ēs nō-vōs)	131	6°02′S	36°39′W
Curran, Can. (kü-räN′)	83c	45°30′N	74°59′W
Current, i., Bah. (kŭ-rĕnt)	122	25°20′N	76°50′W
Current, r., Mo., U.S. (kûr′ĕnt)	111	37°18′N	91°21′W
Currie, Mount, mtn., S. Afr. (kŭ-rē)	213c	30°28′S	29°23′E
Currituck Sound, strt., N.C., U.S. (kûr′ĭ-tŭk)	115	36°27′N	75°42′W
Curtis, Ne., U.S. (kûr′tĭs)	110	40°36′N	100°29′W
Curtis, i., Austl.	203	23°38′S	151°43′E
Curtis B, Md., U.S.	229c	39°13′N	76°35′W
Curtisville, Pa., U.S. (kûr′tĭs-vĭl)	101e	40°38′N	79°50′W
Ćurug, Yugo. (chōō′rŏg)	161	45°27′N	20°03′E
Curunga, Ang.	216	12°51′S	21°12′E
Curupira, Serra, mts., S.A. (sĕr′rȧ kōō-rōō-pē′rȧ)	130	1°00′N	65°30′W
Cururupu, Braz. (kōō-rō-rō-pōō′)	131	1°40′S	44°56′W
Curvelo, Braz. (kōr-vĕl′ō)	131	18°47′S	44°14′W
Cusano Milanino, Italy	238c	45°33′N	9°11′E
Cusco, Peru	130	13°36′S	71°52′W
Cushing, Ok., U.S. (kŏsh′ĭng)	111	35°58′N	96°46′W
Custer, S.D., U.S. (kŭs′tẽr)	102	43°46′N	103°36′W
Custer, Wa., U.S.	106d	48°55′N	122°39′W
Custer Battlefield National Monument, rec., Mt., U.S. (kŭs′tẽr băt″l-fēld)	105	45°44′N	107°15′W
Cut Bank, Mt., U.S. (kŭt bănk)	105	48°38′N	112°19′W
Cuthbert, Ga., U.S. (kŭth′bẽrt)	114	31°47′N	84°48′W
Cuttack, India (kŭ-tăk′)	183	20°38′N	85°53′E
Cutzamala, r., Mex. (kōō-tzä-mä-lä′)	118	18°57′N	100°41′W
Cutzamalá de Pinzón, Mex. (kōō-tzä-mä-lä′dĕ-pēn-zō′n)	118	18°28′N	100°36′W
Cuvo, r., Ang. (kōō′vō)	212	11°00′S	14°30′E
Cuxhaven, Ger. (kŏŏks′hä-fĕn)	146	53°51′N	8°43′E
Cuxton, Eng., U.K.	235	51°22′N	0°27′E
Cuyahoga, r., Oh., U.S. (kī-ȧ-hō′gȧ)	101d	41°22′N	81°38′W
Cuyahoga Falls, Oh., U.S.	101d	41°08′N	81°29′W
Cuyahoga Heights, Oh., U.S.	229a	41°26′N	81°39′W
Cuyapaire Indian Reservation, I.R., Ca., U.S. (kū-yȧ-pâr)	108	32°46′N	116°20′W
Cuyo Islands, is., Phil. (kōō′yō)	196	10°54′N	120°08′E
Cuyotenango, Guat. (kōō-yō-tĕ-năŋ′gō)	120	14°30′N	91°35′W
Cuyuni, r., S.A. (kōō-yōō′nē)	131	6°40′N	60°44′W
Cuyutlán, Mex. (kōō-yōō-tlän′)	118	18°54′N	104°04′W
Cyclades see Kikládhes, is., Grc.	142	37°30′N	24°45′E
Cynthiana, Ky., U.S. (sĭn-thĭ-ăn′ȧ)	98	38°20′N	84°20′W
Cypress, Ca., U.S. (sī′prĕs)	107a	33°50′N	118°03′W
Cypress Hills, hills, Can.	88	49°40′N	110°20′W
Cypress Lake, l., Can.	88	49°28′N	109°43′W
Cyprus, nation, Asia (sī′prŭs)	182	35°00′N	31°00′E
Cyprus, North, nation, Asia	182	35°15′N	33°40′E
Cyrenaica see Barqah, hist. reg., Libya	211	31°09′N	21°45′E
Cyrildene, neigh., S. Afr.	244b	26°11′S	28°06′E
Czech Republic, nation, Eur.	142	50°00′N	15°00′E
Czersk, Pol. (chĕrsk)	155	53°47′N	17°58′E
Częstochowa, Pol. (chăN-stō kô′vȧ)	147	50°49′N	19°10′E

D

PLACE (Pronunciation)	PAGE	LAT.	LONG.
Da'an, China (dä-än)	192	45°25′N	124°22′E
Dabakala, C. Iv. (dä-bä-kä′lä)	210	8°16′N	4°36′W
Daba Shan, mts., China (dä-bä shän)	188	32°25′N	108°20′E
Dabeiba, Col. (dȧ-bā′bä)	130a	7°01′N	76°16′W
Dabie Shan, mts., China (dä-bĭē shän)	189	31°40′N	114°50′E
Dabnou, Niger	215	14°09′N	5°22′E
Dabob Bay, b., Wa., U.S. (dā′bŏb)	106a	47°50′N	122°50′W
Dabola, Gui.	214	10°45′N	11°07′W
Dąbrowa Białostocka, Pol.	155	53°37′N	23°18′E
Dacca see Dhaka, Bngl.	182	23°45′N	90°29′E
Dachang, China (dä-chäŋ)	191b	31°18′N	121°25′E
Dachangshan Dao, i., China (dä-chäŋ-shän dou)	190	39°21′N	122°31′E
Dachau, Ger. (dä′kou)	154	48°16′N	11°26′E
Dacotah, Can. (dȧ-kō′tȧ)	83f	49°52′N	97°38′W
Dadar, neigh., India	240e	19°01′N	72°50′E
Dade City, Fl., U.S. (dād)	115a	28°22′N	82°09′W
Dadeville, Al., U.S. (dăd′vĭl)	114	32°48′N	85°44′W
Dādra & Nagar Haveli, India	183	20°00′N	73°00′E
Dadu, r., China (dä-dōō)	193	29°20′N	103°03′E
Daet, mtn., Phil. (dä′ăt)	197a	14°07′N	122°59′E
Dafoe, r., Can.	89	55°50′N	95°50′W
Dafter, Mi., U.S. (dăf′tẽr)	107k	46°21′N	84°26′W
Dagana, Sen. (dä-gä′nä)	210	16°31′N	15°30′W
Dagana, reg., Chad	215	12°20′N	15°15′E
Dagang, China (dä-gäŋ)	191a	22°48′N	113°24′E
Dagda, Lat. (dȧg′dȧ)	153	56°04′N	27°30′E
Dagenham, Eng., U.K. (dăg′ĕn-ăm)	144b	51°32′N	0°09′E
Dagestan, state, Russia (dä-gĕs-tän′)	167	43°40′N	46°10′E
Daggafontein, S. Afr.	244b	26°18′S	28°28′E
Daggett, Ca., U.S. (dăg′ĕt)	108	34°50′N	116°52′W
Dagu, China (dä-gōō)	192	39°00′N	117°42′E
Dagu, r., China	190	36°29′N	120°06′W
Dagupan, Phil. (dä-gōō′pän)	197a	16°02′N	120°20′E
Daheishan Dao, i., China (dä-hā-shän dou)	190	37°57′N	120°37′E
Dahīrpur, neigh., India	240d	28°43′N	77°12′E
Dahl, Ger. (däl)	157c	51°18′N	7°33′E
Dahlak Archipelago, is., Erit.	211	15°45′N	40°30′E
Dahlem, neigh., Ger.	238a	52°28′N	13°17′E
Dahlerau, Ger.	236	51°13′N	7°19′E
Dahlwitz, Ger.	238a	52°30′N	13°38′E
Dahomey see Benin, nation, Afr.	210	8°00′N	2°00′E
Dahra, Libya	184	29°34′N	17°50′E
Daibu, China (dī-bōō)	190	31°22′N	119°29′E
Daigo, Japan (dī-gō)	195b	34°57′N	135°49′E
Daimiel Manzanares, Spain (dī-myĕl′män-zä-nä′rĕs)	158	39°05′N	3°36′W
Dairen see Dalian, China	188	38°54′N	121°35′E
Dairy, r., Or., U.S. (dâr′ĭ)	106c	45°33′N	123°04′W
Dai-Sen, mtn., Japan (dī′sĕn′)	195	35°22′N	133°35′E
Dai-Tenjo-dake, mtn., Japan (dī-tĕn′jō dä-kȧ)	195	36°21′N	137°38′E
Daiyun Shan, mtn., China (dī-yōn shän)	193	25°40′N	118°08′E
Dajabón, Dom. Rep. (dä-κä-bô′n)	123	19°35′N	71°40′W
Dajarra, Austl. (dȧ-jăr′ȧ)	202	21°45′S	139°30′E
Dakar, Sen. (dȧ-kär′)	210	14°40′N	17°26′W
Dakhla, W. Sah.	210	23°45′N	16°04′W
Dakouraoua, Niger	215	13°58′N	6°15′E
Dakovica, Yugo.	161	42°33′N	20°28′E
Dalälven, r., Swe.	142	60°26′N	15°50′E
Dalby, Austl. (dôl′bē)	203	27°10′S	151°15′E
Dalcour, La., U.S. (dăl-kour)	100d	29°49′N	89°59′W
Dale, Nor. (dä′lĕ)	152	60°35′N	5°55′E
Dale Hollow Lake, res., Tn., U.S. (dăl hŏl′ō)	97	36°33′N	85°03′W
Dalemead, Can. (dä′lē-mēd)	83e	50°53′N	113°38′W
Dalen, Nor. (dä′lĕn)	152	59°28′N	8°01′E
Daleside, S. Afr. (dāl′sīd)	218d	26°30′S	28°03′E
Dalesville, Can. (dālz′vĭl)	83a	45°42′N	74°23′W
Daley Waters, Austl. (dā lē)	202	16°15′N	133°30′E
Dalhart, Tx., U.S. (dăl härt)	110	36°04′N	102°32′W
Dalhousie, Can. (dăl-hōō′zē)	92	48°04′N	66°23′W
Dali, China	188	26°00′N	100°08′E
Dali, China	188	35°00′N	109°38′E
Dali, China (dä-lē)	191a	23°07′N	113°06′E
Dalian, China (lü-dä)	189	38°54′N	121°35′E
Dalian Wan, b., China (dä-lĭĕn wän)	190	38°55′N	121°50′E
Dalías, Spain (dä-lē′ás)	158	36°49′N	2°50′W
Dall, i., Ak., U.S. (dăl)	95	54°50′N	133°10′W
Dallas, Or., U.S. (dăl′lás)	104	44°55′N	123°20′W
Dallas, S.D., U.S.	102	43°13′N	99°34′W
Dallas, Tx., U.S.	96	32°45′N	96°48′W
Dalles Dam, Or., U.S.	104	45°36′N	121°08′W
Dallgow, Ger.	238a	52°32′N	13°05′E
Dall Island, i., Ak., U.S.	86	54°50′N	132°55′W
Dalmacija, hist. reg., Yugo. (däl-mä′tsē-yä)	160	43°25′N	16°37′E
Dalnerechensk, Russia	165	46°07′N	133°21′E
Daloa, C. Iv.	214	6°53′N	6°27′W
Dalroy, Can. (dăl′roi)	83e	51°07′N	113°39′W
Dalrymple, Mount, mtn., Austl. (dăl′rĭm-p′l)	203	21°14′S	148°46′E
Dalton, S. Afr. (dôl′tŏn)	213c	29°21′S	30°41′E
Dalton, Eng., U.K.	237a	53°34′N	2°46′W
Dalton, Ga., U.S. (dôl′tŭn)	114	34°46′N	84°58′W
Daly, r., Austl. (dā′lĭ)	202	14°15′S	131°15′E
Daly City, Ca., U.S. (dā′lē)	106b	37°42′N	122°27′W
Damān, India	183	20°32′N	72°53′E
Damanhūr, Egypt (dä-män-hōōr′)	211	30°59′N	30°31′E
Damar, Pulau, i., Indon.	197	7°15′S	129°15′E
Damara, Cen. Afr. Rep.	215	4°58′N	18°42′E
Damaraland, hist. reg., Nmb. (dă′nȧ-rȧ-lănd)	212	22°15′S	16°15′E
Damas Cays, is., Bah. (dä′mäs)	122	23°50′N	79°50′W
Damascus, Syria	182	33°30′N	36°18′E
Damāvand, Qolleh-ye, mtn., Iran	182	36°05′N	52°05′E
Damba, Ang. (däm′bä)	212	6°41′S	15°08′E
Dâmbovița, r., Rom.	161	44°43′N	25°41′E
Dame Marie, Cap, c., Haiti (dām mȧrē′)	123	18°35′N	74°50′W
Dāmghān, Iran (dăm-gän′)	182	35°50′N	54°15′E
Daming, China (dä-mĭŋ)	192	36°15′N	115°09′E
Dammartin-en-Goële, Fr. (däN-mär-tăN-äN-gō-ĕl′)	157b	49°03′N	2°40′E
Dampier, Selat, strt., Indon. (dăm′pēr)	197	0°40′S	131°15′E
Dampier Archipelago, is., Austl.	202	20°15′S	116°25′E
Dampier Land, reg., Austl.	202	17°30′S	122°25′E
Dan, r., N.C., U.S. (dăn)	115	36°26′N	79°40′W
Dana, Mount, mtn., Ca., U.S.	108	37°54′N	119°13′W
Da Nang, Viet	196	16°08′N	108°22′E
Danbury, Eng., U.K.	144b	51°42′N	0°34′E
Danbury, Ct., U.S. (dăn′bẽr-ĭ)	100a	41°23′N	73°27′W
Danbury, Tx., U.S.	113a	29°14′N	95°22′W
Dandenong, Austl. (dăn′dē-nông)	204	37°59′S	145°13′E
Dandong, China (dän-dôŋ)	189	40°10′N	124°30′E
Dane, r., Eng., U.K. (dān)	144a	53°11′N	2°14′W
Danea, Gui.	214	11°27′N	13°12′W
Danforth, Me., U.S.	92	45°38′N	67°53′W
Dan Gora, Nig.	215	11°30′N	8°09′E
Dangtu, China (däŋ-tōō)	193	31°35′N	118°28′E
Dani, Burkina	210	13°43′N	0°10′W
Dania, Fl., U.S. (dā′nĭ-ȧ)	115a	26°01′N	80°10′W
Daniels, Md., U.S.	229c	39°26′N	77°03′W
Danilov, Russia (dä′nē-lôf)	166	58°12′N	40°08′E
Danissa Hills, hills, Kenya	217	3°20′N	40°55′E
Dänizkänarı, Azer.	168	40°13′N	49°33′E
Dankov, Russia (däŋ′kôf)	166	53°17′N	39°09′E
Dannemora, N.Y., U.S. (dăn-ē-mō′rȧ)	99	44°45′N	73°45′W
Dannhauser, S. Afr. (dän′hou-zẽr)	213c	28°07′S	30°04′E
Dansville, N.Y., U.S. (dănz′vĭl)	99	42°30′N	77°40′W
Danube, r., Eur.	142	43°00′N	24°00′E
Danube, Mouths of the, mth., Rom. (dăn′ūb)	163	45°13′N	29°37′E
Danvers, Ma., U.S. (dăn′vẽrz)	93a	42°34′N	70°57′W
Danville, Ca., U.S. (dăn′vĭl)	106b	37°49′N	122°00′W
Danville, Il., U.S.	98	40°10′N	87°35′W
Danville, In., U.S.	98	39°45′N	86°30′W
Danville, Ky., U.S.	98	37°35′N	84°50′W
Danville, Pa., U.S.	99	41°00′N	76°35′W
Danville, Va., U.S.	97	36°35′N	79°24′W
Danxian, China (dän shyĕn)	193	19°30′N	109°38′E
Danyang, China (dän-yäŋ)	190	32°01′N	119°32′E
Danzig see Gdańsk, Pol.	142	54°20′N	18°40′E
Danzig, Gulf of, b., Eur. (dän′tsĭk)	146	54°41′N	19°01′E
Daoxian, China (dou shyĕn)	193	25°35′N	111°27′E
Dapango, Togo	214	10°52′N	0°12′E
Daphnae, hist., Egypt	181a	30°43′N	32°12′E
Daqin Dao, i., China (dä-chyĭn dou)	190	38°18′N	120°50′E
Darabani, Rom. (dă-rä-băn′ĭ)	155	48°13′N	26°38′E
Daraj, Libya	210	30°12′N	10°14′E
Dār as-Salām, Egypt	244a	29°59′N	31°13′E
Darāw, Egypt (dȧ-rä′ōō)	218b	24°24′N	32°56′E
Darbhanga, India (dŭr-bŭŋ′gä)	183	26°03′N	85°09′E
Darby, Pa., U.S. (där′bĭ)	100f	39°55′N	75°16′W
Darby, i., Bah.	122	23°50′N	76°20′W
Dardanelles see Çanakkale Boğazi, strt., Tur.	149	40°05′N	25°50′E
Dar es Salaam, Tan. (där ĕs sȧ-läm′)	213	6°48′S	39°17′E
Dārfūr, hist. reg., Sudan (där-fōōr′)	211	13°21′N	23°46′E
Dargai, Pak. (dŭr-gä′ē)	186	34°35′N	72°00′E
Darien, Col. (dä-rĭ-ĕn′)	130a	3°56′N	76°30′W
Darien, Ct., U.S. (dâ-rē-ĕn′)	100a	41°04′N	73°28′W
Darién, Cordillera de, mts., Nic.	120	13°00′N	85°42′W
Darien, Serranía del, mts.	121	8°13′N	77°28′W
Darjeeling, India (dŭr-jē′lĭng)	183	27°05′N	88°16′E
Darling, r., Austl.	203	31°50′S	143°20′E
Darling Downs, reg., Austl.	203	27°22′S	150°00′E
Darling Range, mts., Austl.	202	30°30′S	115°45′E
Darlington, Eng., U.K. (där′lĭng-tŭn)	150	54°32′N	1°35′W
Darlington, S.C., U.S.	115	34°15′N	79°52′W
Darlington, Wi., U.S.	103	42°41′N	90°06′W
Darłowo, Pol. (där-lô′vō)	154	54°26′N	16°23′E
Darmstadt, Ger. (därm′shtät)	147	49°53′N	8°40′E
Darnah, Libya	211	32°44′N	22°41′E
Darnley Bay, b., Ak., U.S. (därn′lē)	95	70°00′N	124°00′W
Daroca, Spain (dä-rō-kä)	158	41°08′N	1°24′W
Dartford, Eng., U.K.	144b	51°27′N	0°14′E
Dartmoor, for., Eng., U.K. (därt′mōōr)	150	50°35′N	4°05′W
Dartmouth, Can. (därt′mŭth)	85	44°40′N	63°34′W
Dartmouth, Eng., U.K.	150	50°33′N	3°28′W
Daru, Pap. N. Gui. (dä′rōō)	197	9°04′S	143°21′E
Daruvar, Cro. (där′rōō-vär)	161	45°37′N	17°16′E
Darwen, Eng., U.K. (där′wĕn)	144a	53°42′N	2°28′W
Darwin, Austl. (där′wĭn)	202	12°25′S	131°00′E
Darwin, Cordillera, mts., Chile (kôr-dēl-yĕ′rä-där′wĕn)	132	54°40′S	69°30′W
Dashhowuz, Turk.	169	41°50′N	59°45′E
Dash Point, Wa., U.S. (dăsh)	106a	47°19′N	122°25′W
Dasht, r., Pak. (dŭsht)	182	25°30′N	62°30′E
Dasol Bay, b., Phil. (dä-sōl′)	197a	15°53′N	119°40′E
Datchet, Eng., U.K.	235	51°29′N	0°34′W
Datian Ding, mtn., China (dä-tĭĕn dĭŋ)	193	22°25′N	111°20′E
Datong, China (dä-tôŋ)	192	40°00′N	113°30′E
Dattapukur, India	186a	22°45′N	88°32′E
Datteln, Ger. (dät′tĕln)	157c	51°39′N	7°20′E
Datu, Tandjung, c., Asia	196	2°08′N	110°15′E
Datuan, China (dä-tůän)	191b	30°57′N	121°43′E
Daugava (Zapadnaya Dvina), r., Eur.	153	56°40′N	24°40′E
Daugavpils, Lat. (dä′ŏ-gäv-pēls)	166	55°52′N	26°32′E
Dauphin, Can. (dô′fĭn)	84	51°09′N	100°00′W
Dauphin Lake, l., Can.	89	51°17′N	99°48′W
Dāvangere, India	187	14°30′N	75°55′E
Davao, Phil. (dä′vä-ō)	197	7°05′N	125°30′E
Davao Gulf, b., Phil.	197	6°30′N	125°45′E
Davenport, Ia., U.S. (dăv′ĕn-pōrt)	97	41°34′N	90°38′W
Davenport, Wa., U.S.	104	47°39′N	118°07′W
Daveyton Location, S. Afr.	244b	26°09′S	28°25′E
David, Pan. (dȧ-vēdh′)	117	8°27′N	82°27′W
David City, Ne., U.S. (dā′vĭd)	102	41°15′N	97°10′W
David-Gorodok, Bela. (dȧ-vēt′ gō-rō′dôk)	167	52°02′N	27°14′E
Davis, Ok., U.S. (dā′vĭs)	111	34°34′N	97°08′W
Davis, W.V., U.S.	99	39°15′N	79°25′W
Davis Lake, l., Or., U.S.	104	43°38′N	121°43′W
Davis Mountains, mts., Tx., U.S.	112	30°45′N	104°17′W
Davis Strait, strt., N.A.	82	66°00′N	60°00′W
Davlekanovo, Russia	166	54°15′N	55°05′E
Davos, Switz. (dä′vōs)	154	46°47′N	9°50′E
Davyhulme, Eng., U.K.	237b	53°27′N	2°22′W
Dawa, r., Afr.	211	4°30′N	40°30′E
Dawāsir, Wādī ad, val., Sau. Ar.	182	20°48′N	44°07′E
Dawei, Myanmar	196	14°04′N	98°19′E
Dawen, r., China (dä-wŭn)	190	35°58′N	116°53′E
Dawley, Eng., U.K. (dô′lĭ)	144a	52°38′N	2°28′W

ng-sing; ŋ-baŋk; N-nasalized n; nŏd; cŏmmit; ōld; ôbey; ôrder; oi-boil; fōōd; ŏ-as oo in foot; ou-out; s-soft; sh-dish; th-thin; pūre; ůnite; ûrn; stŭd; circŭs; ü-as in French tu; ′-indeterminate vowel.

280 Dawna Range-Diana Bank

PLACE (Pronunciation)	PAGE	LAT.	LONG.
Dawna Range, mts., Myanmar (dô'nà)	196	17°02'N	98°01'E
Dawson, Can. (dô'sŭn)	84	64°04'N	139°22'W
Dawson, Ga., U.S.	114	31°45'N	84°29'W
Dawson, Mn., U.S.	102	44°54'N	96°03'W
Dawson, r., Austl.	203	24°20'S	149°45'E
Dawson Bay, b., Can.	89	52°55'N	100°50'W
Dawson Creek, Can.	84	55°46'N	120°14'W
Dawson Range, mts., Can.	95	62°15'N	138°10'W
Dawson Springs, Ky., U.S.	114	37°10'N	87°40'W
Dawu, China (dä-wōō)	190	31°33'N	114°07'E
Dawuji, China	240b	39°51'N	116°30'E
Dax, Fr. (dåks)	147	43°42'N	1°06'W
Daxian, China (dä-shyĕn)	188	31°12'N	107°30'E
Daxing, China (dä-shyĭŋ)	192a	39°44'N	116°19'E
Dayiqiao, China (dä-yē-chyou)	190	31°43'N	120°40'E
Dayr az Zawr, Syria (dā-ēz-zôr')	182	35°15'N	40°01'E
Dayton, Ky., U.S. (dā'tŭn)	101f	39°07'N	84°28'W
Dayton, N.M., U.S.	110	32°44'N	104°23'W
Dayton, Oh., U.S.	97	39°54'N	84°15'W
Dayton, Tn., U.S.	114	35°30'N	85°00'W
Dayton, Tx., U.S.	113	30°03'N	94°53'W
Dayton, Wa., U.S.	104	46°18'N	117°59'W
Daytona Beach, Fl., U.S. (dā-tō'nȧ)	97	29°11'N	81°02'W
Dayu, China (dä-yōō)	193	25°20'N	114°20'E
Da Yunhe (Grand Canal), can., China (dä yōn-hŭ)	189	35°00'N	117°00'E
Dayville, Ct., U.S. (dā'vĭl)	99	41°50'N	71°55'W
De Aar, S. Afr. (dē-är')	212	30°45'S	24°05'E
Dead, l., Mn., U.S. (dĕd)	102	46°28'N	96°00'W
Dead Sea, l., Asia	182	31°30'N	35°30'E
Deadwood, S.D., U.S. (dĕd'wo͝od)	96	44°23'N	103°43'W
Deal Island, Md., U.S. (dēl-ī'lănd)	99	38°10'N	75°55'W
Dean, r., Can. (dēn)	86	52°45'N	125°30'W
Dean Channel, strt., Can.	86	52°33'N	127°13'W
Deán Funes, Arg. (dĕ-å'n-fo͞o-nĕs)	132	30°26'S	64°12'W
Dean Row, Eng., U.K.	237b	53°20'N	2°11'W
Dearborn, Mi., U.S. (dēr'bŭrn)	101b	42°18'N	83°15'W
Dearborn Heights, Mi., U.S.	230c	42°19'N	83°14'W
Dearg, Ben, mtn., Scot., U.K. (bĕn dŭrg)	150	57°48'N	4°59'W
Dease Strait, strt., Can. (dēz)	84	68°50'N	108°20'W
Death Valley, Ca., U.S.	108	36°18'N	116°26'W
Death Valley, val., Ca., U.S.	96	36°30'N	117°00'W
Death Valley National Monument, rec., Ca., U.S.	108	36°34'N	117°00'W
Debal'tseve, Ukr.	163	48°23'N	38°29'E
Debao, China (dŭ-bou)	188	23°18'N	106°40'E
Debar, Mac. (dĕ'bär) (då'brä)	161	41°31'N	20°32'E
Dęblin, Pol. (dăɴ'blĭn)	155	51°34'N	21°49'E
Dębno, Pol. (dĕb-nô')	154	52°47'N	13°43'E
Debo, Lac, l., Mali	214	15°15'N	4°40'W
Debrecen, Hung. (dĕ'brĕ-tsĕn)	142	47°32'N	21°40'E
Debre Markos, Eth.	211	10°15'N	37°45'E
Debre Tabor, Eth.	211	11°57'N	38°09'E
Decatur, Al., U.S. (dē-kā'tŭr)	114	34°35'N	87°00'W
Decatur, Ga., U.S.	100c	33°47'N	84°18'W
Decatur, Il., U.S.	97	39°50'N	88°59'W
Decatur, In., U.S.	98	40°50'N	84°55'W
Decatur, Mi., U.S.	98	42°10'N	86°00'W
Decatur, Tx., U.S.	111	33°14'N	97°33'W
Decazeville, Fr. (dē-käz'vēl')	147	44°33'N	2°16'E
Deccan, plat., India (dĕk'ăn)	183	19°05'N	76°40'E
Deception Lake, l., Can.	88	56°33'N	104°15'W
Deception Pass, p., Wa., U.S. (dē-sĕp'shŭn)	106a	48°24'N	122°44'W
Děčín, Czech Rep. (dyĕ'chēn)	154	50°47'N	14°14'E
Decorah, Ia., U.S. (dē-kō'rȧ)	103	43°18'N	91°48'W
Dedenevo, Russia (dyĕ-dyĕ'nyĕ-vô)	172b	56°14'N	37°31'E
Dedham, Ma., U.S. (dĕd'ăm)	93a	42°15'N	71°11'W
Dedo do Deus, mtn., Braz. (dĕ-dô-dô-dĕ'o͞os)	132b	22°30'S	43°02'W
Dédougou, Burkina (dā-dō-go͞o')	210	12°38'N	3°28'W
Dee, r., U.K.	144a	53°15'N	3°05'E
Dee, r., Scot., U.K.	150	57°05'N	2°25'W
Deep, r., N.C., U.S. (dēp)	115	35°36'N	79°32'W
Deep Fork, r., Ok., U.S.	111	35°35'N	96°42'W
Deep River, Can.	91	46°06'N	77°20'W
Deepwater, Mo., U.S. (dep-wô-tēr)	111	38°15'N	93°46'W
Deer, i., Me., U.S.	92	44°07'N	68°38'W
Deerfield, Il., U.S. (dēr'fēld)	101a	42°10'N	87°51'W
Deer Island, Or., U.S.	106c	45°56'N	122°51'W
Deer Lake, Can.	85a	49°10'N	57°25'W
Deer Lake, l., Can.	89	52°40'N	94°30'W
Deer Lodge, Mt., U.S. (dēr lŏj)	105	46°23'N	112°42'W
Deer Park, Oh., U.S.	101f	39°12'N	84°24'W
Deer Park, Wa., U.S.	104	47°58'N	117°28'W
Deer River, Mn., U.S.	103	47°20'N	93°49'W
Dee Why, Austl.	243a	33°45'S	151°17'E
Dee Why Head, c., Austl.	243a	33°46'S	151°19'E
Dee Why Lagoon, b., Austl.	243a	33°45'S	151°18'E
Defiance, Oh., U.S. (dē-fī'ăns)	98	41°15'N	84°20'W
DeFuniak Springs, Fl., U.S. (dē fū'nĭ-ăk)	114	30°42'N	86°06'W
Deganga, India	186a	22°41'N	88°41'E
Degeh Bur, Eth.	218a	8°10'N	43°25'E
Deggendorf, Ger. (dĕ'ghĕn-dôrf)	154	48°50'N	12°59'E
Degollado, Mex. (dä-gō-lyä'dō)	118	20°27'N	102°11'W
DeGrey, r., Austl. (dē grā')	202	20°20'S	119°25'E
Degtyarsk, Russia (dĕg-ty'arsk)	172a	56°42'N	60°05'E
Dehiwala-Mount Lavinia, Sri L.	187	6°47'N	79°55'E
Dehra Dūn, India (dā'rŭ)	183	30°09'N	78°07'E
Dehua, China (dŭ-hwä)	193	25°30'N	118°15'E
Dej, Rom. (dāzh)	149	47°09'N	23°53'E
De Kalb, Il., U.S. (dē kălb')	98	41°54'N	88°46'W
Dekese, D.R.C.	216	3°27'S	21°24'E
Delacour, Can. (dĕ-lä-ko͞or')	83e	51°09'N	113°45'W
Delagua, Co., U.S. (dĕl-ä'gwä)	110	37°19'N	104°42'W
Delair, N.J., U.S.	229b	39°59'N	75°03'W
De Land, Fl., U.S. (dē lănd')	115	29°00'N	81°19'W
Delano, Ca., U.S. (dĕl'ȧ-nō)	108	35°47'N	119°15'W
Delano Peak, mtn., Ut., U.S.	96	38°25'N	112°25'W

PLACE (Pronunciation)	PAGE	LAT.	LONG.
Delavan, Wi., U.S. (dĕl'ȧ-văn)	103	42°39'N	88°38'W
Delaware, Oh., U.S. (dĕl'ȧ-wâr)	98	40°15'N	83°05'W
Delaware, state, U.S.	97	38°40'N	75°30'W
Delaware, r., U.S.	99	41°50'N	75°20'W
Delaware, r., Ks., U.S.	111	39°45'N	95°47'W
Delaware Bay, b., U.S.	97	39°05'N	75°10'W
Delaware Reservoir, res., Oh., U.S.	99	40°30'N	83°05'E
Delémont, Switz. (dē-lā-môɴ')	154	47°21'N	7°18'E
De Leon, Tx., U.S. (dē lē-ŏn')	112	32°06'N	98°33'W
Delft, Neth. (dĕlft)	151	52°01'N	4°20'E
Delfzijl, Neth.	151	53°20'N	6°50'E
Delgada, Punta, c., Arg. (po͞o'n-tä-dĕl-gä'dä)	132	43°46'S	63°46'W
Delgado, Cabo, c., Moz. (kå'bō-dĕl-gä'dō)	213	10°40'S	40°35'E
Delhi, India	183	28°54'N	77°13'E
Delhi, Il., U.S. (dĕl'hī)	107e	39°03'N	90°16'W
Delhi, La., U.S.	113	32°26'N	91°29'W
Delhi, state, India	183	28°30'N	76°50'E
Delhi Cantonment, India	240d	28°36'N	77°08'E
Delitzsch, Ger. (dā'lĭch)	154	51°32'N	12°18'E
Dellansjöarna, l., Swe.	152	61°57'N	16°25'E
Delles, Alg. (dĕ'lĕs')	210	36°59'N	3°40'E
Dell Rapids, S.D., U.S. (dĕl)	102	43°50'N	96°43'W
Dellwig, neigh., Ger.	236	51°29'N	6°56'E
Dellwood, Mn., U.S. (dĕl'wo͝od)	107g	45°05'N	92°58'W
Del Mar, Ca., U.S. (dĕl mär')	108a	32°57'N	117°16'W
Delmas, S. Afr. (dĕl'mȧs)	218d	26°08'S	28°43'E
Delmenhorst, Ger. (dĕl'mĕn-hôrst)	154	53°03'N	8°38'E
Del Norte, Co., U.S. (dĕl nôrt')	109	37°40'N	106°25'W
De-Longa, i., Russia	165	76°21'N	148°56'E
De Long Mountains, mts., Ak., U.S. (dē'lŏng)	95	68°38'N	162°30'W
Deloraine, Austl. (dĕ-lŭ-rān)	204	41°30'S	146°40'E
Delphi, In., U.S. (dĕl'fī)	98	40°35'N	86°40'W
Delphos, Oh., U.S. (dĕl'fŏs)	98	40°50'N	84°20'W
Delran, N.J., U.S.	229b	40°02'N	74°58'W
Delray Beach, Fl., U.S. (dĕl-rā')	115a	26°27'N	80°05'W
Del Rio, Tx., U.S. (dĕl rē'ō)	96	29°21'N	100°52'W
Delson, Can. (dĕl'sŭn)	83a	45°24'N	73°32'W
Delta, Co., U.S.	109	38°45'N	108°05'W
Delta, Ut., U.S.	109	39°20'N	112°35'W
Delta Beach, Can.	83f	50°10'N	98°20'W
Delvine, Alb. (dĕl'vē-nä)	161	39°58'N	20°10'E
Del Viso, Arg.	233d	34°26'S	58°46'W
Dëma, r., Russia (dyĕm'ä)	166	53°40'N	54°30'E
Demarest, N.J., U.S.	228	40°57'N	73°58'W
Demba, D.R.C.	216	5°30'S	22°16'E
Dembi Dolo, Eth.	211	8°46'N	34°46'E
Demidov, Russia (dzyĕ'mē-dô'f)	162	55°16'N	31°32'E
Deming, N.M., U.S. (dĕm'ĭng)	96	32°15'N	107°45'W
Demmeltrath, neigh., Ger.	236	51°11'N	7°03'E
Demmin, Ger. (dĕm'mēn)	154	53°54'N	13°04'E
Demnat, Mor. (dĕm-nät)	210	31°58'N	7°03'W
Demopolis, Al., U.S. (dē-mŏp'ô-lĭs)	114	32°30'N	87°50'W
Demotte, In., U.S. (dē'mŏt)	101a	41°12'N	87°13'W
Dempo, Gunung, mtn., Indon. (dĕm'pō)	196	4°04'S	103°11'E
Dem'yanka, r., Russia (dyĕm-yän'kä)	170	59°07'N	72°58'E
Demyansk, Russia (dyĕm-yänsk')	162	57°39'N	32°26'E
Denain, Fr. (dē-năɴ')	156	50°23'N	3°21'E
Denakil Plain, pl., Eth.	211	12°45'N	41°01'E
Denali National Park, rec., Ak., U.S.	94a	63°48'N	153°02'W
Denbigh, Wales, U.K. (dĕn'bĭ)	150	53°15'N	3°25'W
Dendermonde, Bel.	145a	51°02'N	4°04'E
Dendron, Va., U.S. (dĕn'drŭn)	115	37°02'N	76°53'W
Denenchōfu, neigh., Japan	242a	35°35'N	139°41'E
Denezhkin Kamen, Gora, mtn., Russia (dzyĕ-ŋĕ'zhkĭn kămĭēŋ)	172a	60°26'N	59°35'E
Denham, Mount, mtn., Jam.	117	18°20'N	77°30'W
Den Helder, Neth. (dĕn hĕl'dĕr)	151	52°55'N	5°45'E
Dénia, Spain	159	38°48'N	0°06'E
Deniliquin, Austl. (dĕ-nĭl'ĭ-kwĭn)	203	35°20'S	144°52'E
Denison, Ia., U.S. (dĕn'ĭ-sŭn)	102	42°01'N	95°22'W
Denison, Tx., U.S.	96	33°45'N	97°02'W
Denisovka, Kaz. (dĕ-nē'sof-kȧ)	169	52°26'N	61°45'E
Denizli, Tur. (dĕn-ĭz-lē')	149	37°40'N	29°10'E
Denklingen, Ger. (dĕn'klĕn-gĕn)	157c	50°54'N	7°40'E
Denmark, S.C., U.S. (dĕn'märk)	115	33°18'N	81°09'W
Denmark, nation, Eur.	142	56°14'N	8°30'E
Denmark Strait, strt., Eur.	82	66°30'N	27°00'W
Dennilton, S. Afr. (dĕn-ĭl-tŭn)	218d	25°18'S	29°13'E
Dennison, Oh., U.S. (dĕn'ĭ-sŭn)	98	40°25'N	81°20'W
Denpasar, Indon.	196	8°35'S	115°10'E
Denshaw, Eng., U.K.	237b	53°35'N	2°02'W
Denton, Eng., U.K. (dĕn'tŭn)	144a	53°27'N	2°07'W
Denton, Md., U.S.	99	38°55'N	75°50'W
Denton, Tx., U.S.	111	33°12'N	97°06'W
D'Entrecasteaux, Point, c., Austl. (dăɴ-tr'kȧs-tō')	202	34°50'S	114°45'E
D'Entrecasteaux Islands, is., Pap. N. Gui. (dăɴ-tr'-lȧs-tō')	197	9°45'S	152°00'E
Denver, Co., U.S. (dĕn'vēr)	96	39°44'N	104°59'W
Deoli, India	186	25°52'N	75°23'E
De Pere, Wi., U.S. (dē pēr')	103	44°25'N	88°04'W
Depew, N.Y., U.S. (dē-pū')	101c	42°55'N	78°43'W
Deping, China (dŭ-pĭŋ)	190	37°28'N	116°57'E
Deptford, neigh., Eng., U.K.	235	51°28'N	0°02'W
Depue, Il., U.S. (dē pū)	98	41°15'N	89°55'W
De Queen, Ar., U.S. (dē kwēn')	111	34°02'N	94°21'W
De Quincy, La., U.S. (dē kwĭn'sĭ)	113	30°27'N	93°27'W
Dera, Lach, r., Afr. (läk dā'rä)	218a	0°45'N	41°26'E
Dera, Lak, r., Afr.	211	0°45'N	41°30'E
Dera Ghāzi Khān, Pak. (dā'rŭ gä-zē' ĸan')	183	30°09'N	70°39'E
Dera Ismāīl Khān, Pak. (dā'rŭ ĭs-mä-ēl' ĸän')	186	31°55'N	70°51'E
Derbent, Russia (dĕr-bĕnt')	167	42°00'N	48°10'E
Derby, Austl. (där'bē) (dûr'bē)	202	17°20'S	123°40'E
Derby, S. Afr. (där'bĭ)	218d	25°55'S	27°02'E
Derby, Eng., U.K. (där'bē)	147	52°55'N	1°29'W
Derby, Ct., U.S. (dûr'bē)	99	41°20'N	73°05'W

PLACE (Pronunciation)	PAGE	LAT.	LONG.
Derbyshire, co., Eng., U.K.	144a	53°11'N	1°30'W
Derdepoort, S. Afr.	218d	24°39'S	26°21'E
Derendorf, neigh., Ger.	236	51°15'N	6°48'E
Derg, Lough, l., Ire. (lŏk dĕrg)	150	53°00'N	8°09'W
De Ridder, La., U.S. (dē rĭd'ēr)	113	30°50'N	93°18'W
Dermott, Ar., U.S. (dûr'mŏt)	111	33°32'N	91°24'W
Derne, neigh., Ger.	236	51°34'N	7°31'E
Derry, N.H., U.S. (dâr'ĭ)	93a	42°53'N	71°22'W
Derventa, Bos. (dĕr'ven-tȧ)	161	44°58'N	17°58'E
Derwent, r., Austl. (dĕr'wĕnt)	204	42°21'S	146°30'E
Derwent, r., Eng., U.K.	144a	52°54'N	1°24'W
Desagüe, Gran Canal del, can., Mex.	233a	19°29'N	99°05'W
Des Arc, Ar., U.S. (dāz ärk')	111	34°59'N	91°31'W
Descalvado, Braz. (dĕs-käl-vȧ-dô)	129a	21°55'S	47°37'W
Descartes, Fr.	156	46°58'N	0°42'E
Deschambault Lake, l., Can.	88	54°40'N	103°35'W
Deschênes, Can.	83c	45°23'N	75°47'W
Deschenes, Lake, l., Can.	83c	45°25'N	75°53'W
Deschutes, r., Or., U.S. (dā-sho͞ot')	104	44°25'N	121°21'W
Desdemona, Tx., U.S. (dĕz-dē-mō'nȧ)	112	32°16'N	98°33'W
Dese, Eth.	211	11°00'N	39°51'E
Deseado, Río, r., Arg. (rē-ō-dā-sā-ä'dhō)	132	46°50'S	67°45'W
Desirade Island, i., Guad. (dā-zē-räs')	121b	16°21'N	60°51'W
De Smet, S.D., U.S. (dē smĕt')	102	44°23'N	97°33'W
Des Moines, Ia., U.S. (dē moin')	97	41°35'N	93°37'W
Des Moines, N.M., U.S.	110	36°42'N	103°48'W
Des Moines, Wa., U.S.	106a	46°24'N	122°20'W
Des Moines, r., U.S.	97	42°30'N	94°20'W
Desna, r., Eur. (dyĕs-nȧ')	167	51°55'N	31°45'E
Desolación, i., Chile (dĕ-sô-lä-syô'n)	132	53°05'S	74°00'W
De Soto, Mo., U.S. (dē sō'tō)	111	38°07'N	90°32'W
Des Peres, Mo., U.S. (dĕs pĕr'ĕs)	107e	38°36'N	90°26'W
Des Plaines, Il., U.S. (dĕs plānz')	101a	42°02'N	87°54'W
Des Plaines, r., U.S.	101a	41°39'N	87°56'W
Dessau, Ger. (dĕsou)	147	51°50'N	12°15'E
Detmold, Ger. (dĕt'mōld)	154	51°57'N	8°55'E
Detroit, Mi., U.S. (dē-troit')	97	42°22'N	83°10'W
Detroit, Tx., U.S.	111	33°41'N	95°16'W
Detroit, r., Mi., U.S.	230c	42°06'N	83°08'W
Detroit Lake, res., Or., U.S.	104	44°42'N	122°10'W
Detroit Lakes, Mn., U.S. (dē-troit'lākz)	102	46°48'N	95°51'W
Detroit Metropolitan-Wayne County Airport, arpt., Mi., U.S.	230c	42°13'N	83°22'W
Detva, Slvk. (dyĕt'vȧ)	155	48°32'N	19°21'E
Deuil-la-Barre, Fr.	237c	48°59'N	2°20'E
Deurne, Bel.	145a	51°13'N	4°27'E
Deusen, neigh., Ger.	236	51°33'N	7°26'E
Deutsch Wagram, Aus.	145e	48°19'N	16°34'E
Deux-Montagnes, Can.	83a	45°33'N	73°53'W
Deux Montagnes, Lac des, l., Can.	83a	45°28'N	74°00'W
Deva, Rom. (dā'vä)	149	45°52'N	22°52'E
Dévaványa, Hung. (dā'vô-vän-yô)	155	47°01'N	20°58'E
Develi, Tur. (dĕ'vȧ-lē)	167	38°20'N	35°10'E
Deventer, Neth. (dĕv'ĕn-tēr)	151	52°14'N	6°07'E
Devils, r., Tx., U.S.	112	29°55'N	101°10'W
Devils Island see Diable, Île du, i., Fr. Gu.	131	5°15'N	52°40'W
Devils Lake, N.D., U.S.	96	48°10'N	98°55'W
Devils Lake, l., N.D., U.S. (dĕv''lz)	102	47°57'N	99°04'W
Devils Lake Indian Reservation, I.R., N.D., U.S.	102	48°08'N	99°40'W
Devils Postpile National Monument, rec., Ca., U.S.	108	37°42'N	119°12'W
Devils Tower National Monument, rec., Wy., U.S.	105	44°38'N	105°07'W
Devoll, r., Alb.	161	40°55'N	20°10'E
Devon, Can.	83g	53°23'N	113°43'W
Devon, S. Afr. (dĕv'ŭn)	218d	26°23'S	28°47'E
Devonport, Austl. (dĕv'ŭn-pôrt)	203	41°20'S	146°30'E
Devonport, N.Z.	203a	36°50'S	174°45'E
Devore, Ca., U.S. (dē-vôr')	107a	34°13'N	117°24'W
Dewatto, Wa., U.S. (dē-wät'ō)	106a	47°27'N	123°04'W
Dewey, Ok., U.S. (dū'ĭ)	111	36°48'N	95°55'W
De Witt, Ar., U.S. (dē wĭt')	111	34°17'N	91°22'W
De Witt, Ia., U.S.	103	41°46'N	90°34'W
Dewsbury, Eng., U.K. (dūz'bēr-ĭ)	144a	53°42'N	1°39'W
Dexter, Me., U.S. (dĕks'tēr)	92	45°01'N	69°19'W
Dexter, Mo., U.S.	111	36°46'N	89°56'W
Dezfūl, Iran	182	32°14'N	48°37'E
Dezhnëva, Mys, c., Russia (dyĕzh'nyĭf)	180	68°00'N	172°00'W
Dezhou, China (dŭ-jō)	192	37°28'N	116°17'E
Dháfni, Grc.	239d	38°01'N	23°39'E
Dhahran see Aẓ Ẓahrān, Sau. Ar.	182	26°13'N	50°00'E
Dhaka, Bngl. (dă'kä) (dăk'ȧ)	183	23°45'N	90°29'E
Dharamtar Creek, r., India	187b	18°49'N	72°54'E
Dharmavaram, India	187	14°32'N	77°43'E
Dhawalāgiri, mtn., Nepal	183	28°42'N	83°31'E
Dhenoúsa, i., Grc.	161	37°09'N	25°53'E
Dhībān, Jord.	181a	31°30'N	35°46'E
Dhidhimótikhon, Grc.	161	41°20'N	26°27'E
Dhodhekánisos (Dodecanese), is., Grc.	161	38°00'N	26°10'E
Dhule, India	183	20°58'N	74°43'E
Día, i., Grc. (dē'ä)	160a	35°27'N	25°17'E
Diable, Île du, i., Fr. Gu.	131	5°15'N	52°40'W
Diablo, Mount, mtn., Ca., U.S. (dyä'blō)	106b	37°52'N	121°55'W
Diablo Heights, Pan. (dyȧ'blō)	116a	8°58'N	79°34'W
Diablo Range, mts., Ca., U.S.	106b	37°47'N	121°50'W
Diablotins, Morne, mtn., Dom.	121b	15°31'N	61°24'W
Diaca, Moz.	217	11°30'S	39°59'E
Diaka, r., Mali	215	14°40'N	5°00'E
Diamantina, Braz.	131	18°14'S	43°32'W
Diamantina, r., Austl. (dī'man-tē'nȧ)	202	25°38'S	139°53'E
Diamantino, Braz. (dē-ȧ-män-tē'no)	131	14°22'S	56°23'W
Diamond Creek, Austl.	243b	37°41'S	145°09'E
Diamond Peak, mtn., Or., U.S.	104	43°32'N	122°08'W
Diana Bank, bk. (dī'ăn'ȧ)	123	22°30'N	74°45'W

ăt; finȧl; rāte; senåte; ärm; åsk; sofȧ; fâre; ch-choose; dh-as th in other; bē; ēvent; bĕt; recĕnt; cratēr; g-gō; gh-guttural g; bĭt; ĭ-short neutral; rīde; ĸ-guttural k as ch in German ich;

PRONOUNCING INDEX

Dianbai–Douentza 281

PLACE (Pronunciation)	PAGE	LAT.	LONG.
Dianbai, China (dĭĕn-bī)	193	21°30′N	111°20′E
Dian Chi, l., China (dĭĕn chē)	188	24°58′N	103°18′E
Diancun, China	240b	39°55′N	116°14′E
Dickinson, N.D., U.S. (dĭk′ĭn-sŭn)	96	46°52′N	102°49′W
Dickinson, Tx., U.S. (dĭk′ĭn-sŭn)	113a	29°28′N	95°02′W
Dickinson Bayou, Tx., U.S.	113a	29°26′N	95°08′W
Dickson, Tn., U.S. (dĭk′sŭn)	114	36°03′N	87°24′W
Dickson City, Pa., U.S.	99	41°25′N	75°40′W
Didcot, Eng., U.K. (dĭd′cŏt)	144b	51°35′N	1°15′W
Didiéni, Mali	214	13°53′N	8°06′W
Didsbury, neigh., Eng., U.K.	237b	53°25′N	2°14′W
Die, Fr. (dē)	157	44°45′N	5°22′E
Diefenbaker, res., Can.	84	51°20′N	108°10′W
Diego de Ocampo, Pico, mtn., Dom. Rep. (pē′-kô-dyĕ′gô-dĕ-ô-kä′m-pô)	123	19°40′N	70°45′W
Diego Ramirez, Islas, is., Chile (dē ā′gō rä-mē′räz)	132	56°15′S	70°15′W
Diéma, Mali	214	14°32′N	9°12′W
Dien Bien Phu, Viet	188	21°38′N	102°49′E
Diepensee, Ger.	238a	52°22′N	13°31′E
Dieppe, Can. (dē-ĕp′)	92	46°06′N	64°45′W
Dieppe, Fr.	147	49°54′N	1°05′E
Dierks, Ar., U.S. (dērks)	111	34°06′N	94°02′W
Diessem, neigh., Ger.	236	51°20′N	6°35′E
Diessen, Ger. (dēs′sĕn)	145d	47°57′N	11°06′E
Diest, Bel.	145a	50°59′N	5°05′E
Digby, Can. (dĭg′bĭ)	85	44°37′N	65°46′W
Dighton, Ma., U.S. (dī-tŭn)	100b	41°49′N	71°05′W
Digmoor, Eng., U.K.	237a	53°32′N	2°45′W
Digne, Fr. (dēn′y′)	157	44°07′N	6°16′E
Digoin, Fr. (dē-gwăN′)	156	46°28′N	4°06′E
Digra, India	240a	22°50′N	88°20′E
Digul, r., Indon.	197	7°00′S	140°27′E
Dijohan Point, c., Phil. (dē-kō-än)	197a	16°24′N	122°25′E
Dijon, Fr. (dē-zhôN′)	142	47°21′N	5°02′E
Dikson, Russia (dĭk′sŏn)	164	73°30′N	80°35′E
Dikwa, Nig. (dē′kwà)	211	12°06′N	13°53′E
Dili, Indon. (dĭl′ê)	197	8°35′S	125°35′E
Di Linosa Island, i., Italy (dē-lê-nô′sä)	148	36°01′N	12°43′E
Dilizhan, Arm.	167	40°45′N	45°00′E
Dillingham, Ak., U.S. (dĭl′ĭng-hăm)	94a	59°10′N	158°38′W
Dillon, Mt., U.S. (dĭl′ŭn)	105	45°12′N	112°40′W
Dillon, S.C., U.S.	115	34°24′N	79°28′W
Dillon Park, Md., U.S.	229d	38°52′N	76°56′W
Dillon Reservoir, res., Oh., U.S.	98	40°05′N	82°05′W
Dilolo, D.R.C. (dē-lō′lō)	212	10°19′S	22°23′E
Dimashq see Damascus, Syria	182	33°31′N	36°18′E
Dimbokro, C. Iv.	214	6°39′N	4°42′W
Dimitrovo see Pernik, Bul.	149	42°36′N	23°04′E
Dimlang, mtn., Nig.	215	8°24′N	11°47′E
Dimona, Isr.	181a	31°03′N	35°01′E
Dinagat Island, i., Phil.	197	10°15′N	126°15′E
Dinājpur, Bngl.	186	25°38′N	87°39′E
Dinan, Fr. (dē-näN′)	156	48°27′N	2°03′W
Dinant, Bel. (dē-näN′)	151	50°17′N	4°50′E
Dinara, mts., Yugo. (dē′nä-rä)	149	43°50′N	16°15′E
Dinard, Fr.	156	48°38′N	2°04′W
Dindigul, India	187	10°25′N	78°03′E
Dingalan Bay, b., Phil. (dĭŋ-gä′län)	197a	15°19′N	121°33′E
Dingle, Ire. (dĭng′′l)	150	52°10′N	10°13′W
Dingle, neigh., Eng., U.K.	237a	53°23′N	2°57′W
Dingle Bay, b., Ire.	147	52°02′N	10°15′W
Dingo, Austl. (dĭŋ′gō)	203	23°45′S	149°26′E
Dinguiraye, Gui.	214	11°18′N	10°43′W
Dingwall, Scot., U.K. (dĭng′wôl)	150	57°37′N	4°23′W
Dingxian, China (dĭŋ shyĕn)	192	38°30′N	115°00′E
Dingxing, China (dĭŋ-shyĭŋ)	192	39°18′N	115°50′E
Dingyuan, China (dĭŋ-yüän)	190	32°32′N	117°40′E
Dingzi Wan, b., China	190	36°33′N	121°06′E
Dinosaur National Monument, rec., Co., U.S. (dī′nō-sôr)	105	40°45′N	109°17′W
Dinslaken, Ger. (dēns′lä-kĕn)	157c	51°33′N	6°44′E
Dinslakener Bruch, Ger.	236	51°35′N	6°43′E
Dinteloord, Neth.	145a	51°38′N	4°21′E
Dinuba, Ca., U.S. (dĭ-nū′bà)	108	36°33′N	119°29′W
Dinwiddie, S. Afr.	244b	26°16′S	28°10′E
Dios, Cayo de, i., Cuba (kä′yō-dĕ-dē-ōs′)	122	22°05′N	83°05′W
Diourbel, Sen. (dê-ōōr-bĕl′)	210	14°40′N	16°15′W
Diphu Pass, p., Asia (dĭ-pōō)	188	28°15′N	96°45′E
Diquis, r., C.R. (dê-kēs′)	121	8°59′N	83°24′W
Dire Dawa, Eth.	211	9°40′N	41°47′E
Diriamba, Nic. (dēr-yäm′bä)	120	11°52′N	86°15′W
Dirk Hartog, i., Austl.	202	26°25′S	113°15′E
Dirksland, Neth.	145a	51°45′N	4°04′E
Dirranbandi, Austl. (dĭ-rà-băn′dê)	203	28°24′S	148°29′E
Dirty Devil, r., Ut., U.S. (dûr′tĭ dĕv′′l)	109	38°20′N	110°30′W
Disappointment, l., Austl.	202	23°20′S	123°00′E
Disappointment, Cape, c., Wa., U.S. (dĭs′ă-point′ment)	106c	46°16′N	124°11′W
Discovery, S. Afr. (dĭs-kŭv′ẽr-ĭ)	213b	26°10′S	27°53′E
Discovery, is., Can. (dĭs-kŭv′ẽr-ê)	106a	48°25′N	123°13′W
Disko, i., Grnld. (dĭs′kō)	82	70°00′N	54°00′W
Disna, Bela. (dēs′nà)	166	55°34′N	28°15′E
Disneyland, pt. of i., Ca., U.S.	232	33°48′N	117°55′W
Dispur, India	186	26°00′N	91°50′E
Disraëli, Can. (dĭs-rā′lĭ)	91	45°53′N	71°23′W
Distein, Ger.	236	51°36′N	7°09′E
District Heights, Md., U.S.	229d	38°51′N	76°53′W
District of Columbia, state, U.S.	97	38°50′N	77°00′W
Distrito Federal, dept., Braz. (dēs-trē′tô-fĕ-dĕ-rä′l)	131	15°49′S	47°39′W
Distrito Federal, dept., Mex.	118	19°14′N	99°08′W
Disūq, Egypt (dē-sōōk′)	218b	31°07′N	30°41′E
Ditton, Eng., U.K.	235	51°18′N	0°27′E
Diu, India (dē′ōō)	183	20°48′N	70°58′E
Divilacan Bay, b., Phil. (dê-vê-lä′kän)	197a	17°26′N	122°25′E
Divinópolis, Braz. (dē-vē-nô′pō-lês)	131	20°10′S	44°53′W
Divo, C. Iv.	214	5°50′N	5°22′W
Dixon, Il., U.S. (dĭks′ŭn)	103	41°50′N	89°30′W
Dixon Entrance, strt., N.A.	84	54°25′N	132°00′W
Diyarbakir, Tur. (dê-yär-bĕk′ĭr)	182	38°00′N	40°10′E
Dja, r., Afr.	211	2°30′N	14°00′E
Djakovo, neigh., Russia	239b	55°39′N	37°40′E
Djambala, Congo	216	2°33′S	14°45′E
Djanet, Alg.	210	24°29′N	9°26′E
Djebobo, mtn., Ghana	214	8°20′N	0°37′E
Djedi, Oued, r., Alg.	148	34°18′N	4°39′E
Djelo-Binza, D.R.C.	244c	4°23′S	15°16′E
Djember, Chad	215	10°25′N	17°50′E
Djerba, Île de, i., Tun.	148	33°53′N	11°26′E
Djerid, Chott, l., Tun. (jĕr′ĭd)	210	33°15′N	8°29′E
Djibasso, Burkina	214	13°07′N	4°10′W
Djibo, Burkina	214	14°06′N	1°38′W
Djibouti, Dji. (jē-bōō-tē′)	218a	11°34′N	43°00′E
Djibouti, nation, Afr.	218a	11°35′N	48°08′E
Djokoumatombi, Congo	216	0°47′N	15°22′E
Djokupunda, D.R.C.	212	5°27′S	20°58′E
Djoua, r., Afr.	216	1°25′N	13°40′E
Djursholm, Swe. (djōōrs′hōlm)	152	59°26′N	18°01′E
Dmitriyev-L′govskiy, Russia (d′mē′trĭ-yĕf l′gôf′skĭ)	162	52°07′N	35°05′E
Dmitrov, Russia (d′mē′trôf)	162	56°21′N	37°32′E
Dmitrovsk, Russia (d′mē′trôfsk)	162	52°30′N	35°10′E
Dmytrivka, Ukr.	163	47°57′N	38°56′E
Dnepropetrovsk see Dnipropetrovs′k, Ukr.	164	48°15′N	34°08′E
Dnieper (Dnipro), r., Eur.	167	46°45′N	33°40′E
Dniester, r., Eur.	167	48°21′N	28°10′E
Dniprodzerzhyns′k, Ukr.	167	48°32′N	34°38′E
Dniprodzerzhyns′ke vodoskhovyshche, res., Ukr.	164	49°00′N	34°10′E
Dnipropetrovs′k, Ukr.	164	48°15′N	34°08′E
Dnipropetrovs′k, prov., Ukr.	163	48°15′N	34°10′E
Dniprovs′kyi lyman, b., Ukr.	163	46°33′N	31°45′E
Dnistrovs′kyi lyman, l., Ukr.	163	46°13′N	29°50′E
Dno, Russia (d′nô′)	162	57°49′N	29°59′E
Do, Lac, l., Mali	214	15°50′N	2°20′W
Doba, Chad	215	8°39′N	16°51′E
Dobbs Ferry, N.Y., U.S. (dŏbz′fĕ′rė)	100a	41°01′N	73°53′W
Dobbyn, Austl. (dôb′ĭn)	202	19°45′S	140°02′E
Dobele, Lat. (dŏ′bĕ-lĕ)	153	56°37′N	23°18′E
Doberai, Jazirah, pen., Indon.	197	1°25′S	133°15′E
Döbling, neigh., Aus.	239e	48°15′N	16°22′E
Dobo, Indon.	197	6°00′S	134°18′E
Doboj, Bos. (dō′boi)	161	44°42′N	18°04′E
Dobrich, Bul.	149	43°33′N	27°52′E
Dobryanka, Russia (dôb-ryän′kà)	172a	58°27′N	56°26′E
Dobšina, Slvk. (dôp′shê-nä)	155	48°48′N	20°25′E
Doce, r., Braz. (dō′sā)	131	19°01′S	42°14′W
Doce, Canal Numero, can., Arg.	129c	36°47′S	59°00′W
Doce Leguas, Cayos de las, is., Cuba	122	20°55′N	79°05′W
Doctor Arroyo, Mex. (dŏk-tōr′ är-rō′yō)	118	23°41′N	100°10′W
Doddinghurst, Eng., U.K.	235	51°40′N	0°18′E
Doddington, Eng., U.K. (dŏd′dĭng-tŏn)	144b	51°17′N	0°47′E
Dodecanese see Dhodhekánisos, is., Grc.	161	38°00′N	26°10′E
Dodge City, Ks., U.S. (dŏj)	96	37°44′N	100°01′W
Dodgeville, Wi., U.S. (dŏj′vĭl)	103	42°58′N	90°07′W
Dodoma, Tan. (dō′dō-mà)	212	6°11′S	35°45′E
Dog, l., Can. (dŏg)	90	48°42′N	89°24′W
Dogger Bank, bk. (dŏg′gẽr)	151	55°07′N	2°25′E
Dogubayazit, Tur.	167	39°35′N	44°00′E
Doha see Ad Dawhah, Qatar	182	25°02′N	51°28′E
Dohad, India	186	22°52′N	74°18′E
Doiran, l., Grc.	161	41°10′N	23°00′E
Dokshitsy, Bela. (dôk-shētsē)	162	54°53′N	27°49′E
Dolbeau, Can.	85	48°52′N	72°16′W
Dole, Fr. (dōl)	147	47°07′N	5°28′E
Dolgaya, Kosa, c., Russia (kô′sà dôl-gä′yä)	163	46°42′N	37°42′E
Dolgeville, N.Y., U.S.	99	43°10′N	74°45′W
Dolgiy, i., Russia	166	69°20′N	59°20′E
Dolgoprudnyy, Russia	172b	55°57′N	37°33′E
Dolinsk, Russia (då-lēnsk′)	171	47°29′N	142°31′E
Dollard-des-Ormeaux, Can.	227b	45°29′N	73°49′W
Dollar Harbor, b., Bah.	122	25°30′N	79°15′W
Dolomite, Al., U.S. (dŏl′ô-mīt)	100h	33°28′N	86°57′W
Dolomiti, mts., Italy	160	46°16′N	11°43′E
Dolores, Arg. (dô-lō′rĕs)	132	36°20′S	57°42′W
Dolores, Col.	130a	3°33′N	74°54′W
Dolores, Tx., U.S. (dô-lō′rĕs)	112	27°42′N	99°47′W
Dolores, Ur.	129c	33°32′S	58°15′W
Dolores, r., Co., U.S.	109	38°35′N	108°50′W
Dolores Hidalgo, Mex. (dô-lô′rĕs-ê-däl′gō)	118	21°09′N	100°56′W
Dolphin and Union Strait, strt., Can. (dŏl′fĭn ūn′yŭn)	84	69°22′N	117°10′W
Dolton, Il., U.S.	231a	41°39′N	87°37′W
Dolyna, Ukr.	155	48°57′N	24°01′E
Domažlice, Czech Rep. (dō′mäzh-lê-tsĕ)	154	49°27′N	12°55′E
Dombasle-sur-Meurthe, Fr. (dôN-bäl′)	157	48°38′N	6°18′E
Dombóvár, Hung. (dŏm′bō-vär)	155	46°22′N	18°08′E
Domeyko, Cordillera, mts., Chile (kôr-dēl-yĕ′rä-dô-mä′kō)	130	20°50′S	69°02′W
Dominguez, Ca., U.S.	232	33°50′N	118°31′W
Dominica, nation, N.A. (dŏ-mĭ-nē′kà)	117	15°30′N	60°45′W
Dominica Channel, strt., N.A.	121b	15°00′N	61°30′W
Dominican Republic, nation, N.A. (dô-mĭn′ĭ-kăn)	117	19°00′N	70°45′W
Dominion, Can. (dô-mĭn′yŭn)	93	46°13′N	60°01′W
Domiongo, D.R.C.	216	4°37′S	21°15′E
Domitilla, Catacombe di, pt. of i., Italy	239c	41°52′N	12°31′E
Domodedovo, Russia (dô-mô-dyĕ′do-vô)	172b	55°27′N	37°45′E
Dom Silvério, Braz. (doN-sĕl-vĕ′ryō)	129a	20°09′S	42°57′W
Don, r., Can.	227c	43°39′N	79°21′W
Don, r., Russia	164	49°50′N	41°30′E
Don, r., Eng., U.K.	144a	53°39′N	0°58′W
Don, r., Scot., U.K.	150	57°19′N	2°39′W
Donaldson, Mi., U.S. (dŏn′ăl-sŭn)	107k	46°19′N	84°22′W
Donaldsonville, La., U.S. (dŏn′ăld-sŭn-vĭl)	113	30°05′N	90°58′W
Donalsonville, Ga., U.S.	114	31°02′N	84°50′W
Donaufeld, neigh., Italy	239e	48°15′N	16°25′E
Donaustadt, neigh., Aus.	239e	48°13′N	16°30′E
Donauturm, pt. of i., Aus.	239e	48°14′N	16°25′E
Donawitz, Aus. (dō′ná-vĭts)	154	47°23′N	15°05′E
Don Benito, Spain (dōn′bå-nē′tō)	158	38°55′N	5°52′W
Dönberg, Ger.	236	51°18′N	7°10′E
Don Bosco, neigh., Arg.	233d	34°42′S	58°19′W
Doncaster, Austl. (doŋ′kăs-tẽr)	201a	37°47′S	145°08′E
Doncaster, Can.	227c	43°48′N	79°25′W
Doncaster, Eng., U.K. (doŋ′kăs-tẽr)	150	53°32′N	1°07′W
Doncaster East, Austl.	243b	37°47′S	145°10′E
Dondo, Ang. (dōn′dō)	212	9°38′S	14°25′E
Dondo, Moz.	212	19°33′S	34°47′E
Dondra Head, c., Sri L.	183b	5°52′N	80°52′E
Donegal, Ire. (dŏn-ê-gôl′)	150	54°44′N	8°05′W
Donegal Bay, Ire. (dŏn-ê-gôl′)	146	54°35′N	8°36′W
Donets Coal Basin, reg., Ukr. (dô-nyĕts′)	163	48°15′N	38°50′E
Donets′k, Ukr.	164	48°00′N	37°35′E
Donets′k, prov., Ukr.	163	47°55′N	37°40′E
Dong, r., China (dôŋ)	189	24°13′N	115°08′E
Dongara, Austl. (dôn-gä′rȧ)	202	29°15′S	115°00′E
Dongba, China (dôŋ-bä)	190	31°40′N	119°02′E
Dongba, China	240b	39°58′N	116°32′E
Dongbahe, China	240b	39°58′N	116°27′E
Dong′e, China (dôŋ-ü)	190	36°21′N	116°14′E
Dong′ezhen, China	192	36°11′N	116°16′E
Dongfang, China (dôŋ-fäŋ)	193	19°08′N	108°42′E
Donggala, Indon. (dôŋ-gä′lä)	196	0°45′S	119°32′E
Dongguan, China (dôŋ-gůän)	191a	23°03′N	113°46′E
Dongguang, China (dôŋ-gůäŋ)	190	37°54′N	116°33′E
Donghai, China (dôŋ-hī)	192	34°35′N	119°05′E
Dong Hoi, Viet (dông-hô-ĕ′)	196	17°25′N	106°42′E
Dongila, Eth.	211	11°17′N	37°00′E
Dongming, China (dôŋ-mĭŋ)	190	35°16′N	115°06′E
Dongo, Ang. (dôŋ′gō)	212	14°45′S	15°30′E
Dongon Point, c., Phil. (dŏng-ôn′)	197a	12°43′N	120°35′E
Dongou, Congo (dôŋ-gōō′)	211	2°02′N	18°04′E
Dongping, China (dôŋ-pĭŋ)	192	35°50′N	116°24′E
Dongping Hu, l., China (dôŋ-pĭŋ hōō)	190	36°06′N	116°24′E
Dongshan, China (doŋ-shän)	190	31°05′N	120°24′E
Dongshi, China	240b	39°49′N	116°34′E
Dongtai, China	190	32°51′N	120°20′E
Dongting Hu, l., China (dôŋ-tĭŋ hōō)	189	29°10′N	112°30′E
Dongxiang, China (dôŋ-shyän)	193	28°18′N	116°38′E
Doniphan, Mo., U.S. (dŏn′ĭ-făn)	111	36°37′N	90°50′W
Donji Vakuf, Bos. (dōn′yĭ väk′ōf)	161	44°08′N	17°25′E
Don Martin, Presa de, res., Mex. (prĕ′sä-dĕ-dôn-mär-tē′n)	112	27°35′N	100°38′W
Donnacona, Can.	91	46°40′N	71°46′W
Donnemarie-en-Montois, Fr. (dôn-mä-rē′ĕN-môN-twä′)	157b	48°29′N	3°09′E
Donner und Blitzen, r., Or., U.S. (dŏn′ẽr ŏont′blĭ′tsĕn)	104	42°45′N	118°57′W
Donnybrook, S. Afr. (dŏ-nĭ-brŏŏk)	213c	29°56′S	29°54′E
Donora, Pa., U.S. (dŏ-nō′rä)	101e	40°10′N	79°51′W
Don Torcuato, Arg.	233d	34°29′S	58°37′W
Doolow, Som.	218a	4°10′N	42°05′E
Doonerak, Mount, mtn., Ak., U.S. (dōō′nē-răk)	95	68°00′N	150°34′W
Doorn, Neth.	145a	52°02′N	5°21′E
Door Peninsula, pen., Wi., U.S. (dōr)	103	44°40′N	87°36′W
Dora Baltea, r., Italy (dō′rä bäl′tä-ä)	160	45°40′N	7°34′E
Doraville, Ga., U.S. (dō′rà-vĭl)	100c	33°54′N	84°17′W
Dorchester, Eng., U.K. (dôr′chĕs-tẽr)	150	50°45′N	2°34′W
Dorchester Heights National Historic Site, hist., Ma., U.S.	227a	42°20′N	71°03′W
Dordogne, r., Fr. (dôr-dôn′yĕ)	142	44°53′N	0°16′E
Dordrecht, Neth. (dôr′drĕĸt)	151	51°48′N	4°39′E
Dordrecht, S. Afr. (dôr′drĕĸt)	213c	31°24′S	27°06′E
Doré Lake, l., Can.	88	54°31′N	107°06′W
Dorgali, Italy (dôr′gä-lē)	160	40°18′N	9°37′E
Dörgön Nuur, l., Mong.	188	47°47′N	94°01′E
Dorion-Vaudreuil, Can. (dôr-yō)	83a	45°23′N	74°01′W
Dorking, Eng., U.K. (dôr′kĭng)	144b	51°12′N	0°20′W
Dormont, Pa., U.S. (dôr′mŏnt)	101e	40°24′N	80°02′W
Dornap, Ger.	236	51°15′N	7°04′E
Dornbirn, Aus. (dŏrn′bêrn)	154	47°24′N	9°45′E
Dornoch, Scot., U.K. (dôr′nŏĸ)	146	57°55′N	4°01′W
Dornoch Firth, b., Scot., U.K. (dôr′nŏĸ fûrth)	150	57°55′N	3°55′W
Dorogobuzh, Russia (dôrôgô′-bōō′zh)	162	54°57′N	33°18′E
Dorohoi, Rom. (dō-rô-hoi′)	155	47°57′N	26°28′E
Dorre Island, i., Austl. (dôr)	202	25°19′S	113°10′E
Dorseyville, Pa., U.S.	230b	40°35′N	79°53′W
Dorstfeld, neigh., Ger.	236	51°31′N	7°25′E
Dorstsen, Ger.	157c	51°40′N	6°58′E
Dortmund, Ger. (dôrt′mŏŏnt)	147	51°31′N	7°28′E
Dortmund-Ems-Kanal, can., Ger. (dôrt′mōōnd-ĕms′kä-näl′)	157c	51°50′N	7°25′E
Dörtyol, Tur. (dûrt′yōl)	149	36°50′N	36°20′E
Dorval, Can. (dôr-vál′)	83a	45°26′N	73°44′W
Dos Bahías, Cabo, c., Arg. (kä′bô-dôs-bä-ē′äs)	132	44°55′S	65°35′W
Dos Caminos, Ven. (dôs-kä-mē′nôs)	131b	9°38′N	67°17′W
Dosewallips, r., Wa., U.S. (dō′sê-wäl′lĭps)	106a	47°45′N	123°04′W
Dos Hermanas, Spain (dōsĕr-mä′näs)	158	37°17′N	5°56′W
Dosso, Niger (dôs-ō′)	210	13°03′N	3°12′E
Dothan, Al., U.S. (dō′thăn)	97	31°13′N	85°23′W
Douai, Fr. (dōō-ā′)	147	50°23′N	3°04′E
Douala, Cam. (dōō-ä′lä)	210	4°03′N	9°42′E
Douarnenez, Fr. (dōō-är nē-nĕs′)	156	48°06′N	4°18′W
Double Bayou, Tx., U.S. (dŭb′′l bī′yōō)	113a	29°40′N	94°38′W
Doubs, r., Eur.	157	46°15′N	5°50′E
Douentza, Mali	214	15°00′N	2°57′W

282 Douglas–East

PLACE (Pronunciation)	PAGE	LAT.	LONG.
Douglas, I. of Man (dŭg'lăs)	150	54°10'N	4°24'W
Douglas, Ak., U.S. (dŭg'lăs)	95	58°18'N	134°35'W
Douglas, Az., U.S.	96	31°20'N	109°30'W
Douglas, Ga., U.S.	115	31°30'N	82°53'W
Douglas, Wy., U.S. (dŭg'lăs)	105	42°45'N	105°21'W
Douglas, r., Eng., U.K. (dŭg'lăs)	144a	53°38'N	2°48'W
Douglas Channel, strt., Can.	86	53°30'N	129°12'W
Douglas Lake, res., Tn., U.S. (dŭg'lăs)	114	36°00'N	83°35'W
Douglas Lake Indian Reserve, I.R., Can.	87	50°10'N	120°49'W
Douglasville, Ga., U.S. (dŭg'lăs-vĭl)	114	33°45'N	84°47'W
Dourada, Serra, mts., Braz. (sĕ'r-rä-dôōō-rà'dä)	131	15°11'S	49°57'W
Dourdan, Fr. (dōōr-däN')	157b	48°32'N	2°01'E
Douro, r., Port. (dô'ō-rŏ)	158	41°03'N	8°12'W
Dove, r., Eng., U.K. (dŭv)	144a	52°53'N	1°47'W
Dover, S. Afr.	218d	27°05'S	27°44'E
Dover, Eng., U.K.	142	51°08'N	1°19'E
Dover, De., U.S. (dō vẽr)	97	39°10'N	75°30'W
Dover, N.H., U.S.	99	43°15'N	71°00'W
Dover, N.J., U.S.	100a	40°53'N	74°33'W
Dover, Oh., U.S.	98	40°35'N	81°30'W
Dover, Strait of, strt., Eur.	142	50°50'N	1°15'W
Dover-Foxcroft, Me., U.S. (dō'vẽr fŏks'krôft)	92	45°10'N	69°15'W
Dover Heights, Austl.	243a	33°53'S	151°17'E
Doveton, Austl.	243b	38°00'S	145°14'E
Dovre Fjell, mts., Nor. (dŏv'rĕ fyĕl')	142	62°03'N	8°36'E
Dow, Il., U.S. (dou)	107e	39°01'N	90°20'W
Dowagiac, Mi., U.S. (dô-wô'jăk)	98	42°00'N	86°05'W
Dowlatābād, Iran	241h	35°37'N	51°27'E
Downers Grove, Il., U.S. (dou'nẽrz grōv)	101a	41°48'N	88°00'W
Downey, Ca., U.S. (dou'nĭ)	107a	33°56'N	118°08'W
Downieville, Ca., U.S. (dou'nĭ-nĭl)	108	39°35'N	120°48'W
Downs, Ks., U.S. (dounz)	110	39°29'N	98°32'W
Doylestown, Oh., U.S. (doilz'toun)	101d	40°58'N	81°43'W
Drâa, Cap, c., Mor. (drà)	210	28°39'N	12°15'W
Drâa, Oued, r., Afr.	210	28°00'N	9°31'W
Drabiv, Ukr.	163	49°57'N	32°14'E
Drac, r., Fr. (dräk)	157	44°50'N	5°47'E
Dracut, Ma., U.S. (drā'kŭt)	93a	42°40'N	71°19'W
Draganovo, Bul. (drä-gä-nō'vô)	161	43°13'N	25°45'E
Drăgăşani, Rom. (drä-gà-shän'ĭ)	161	44°39'N	24°18'E
Draguignan, Fr. (drä-gēn-yäN')	157	43°35'N	6°28'E
Drakensberg, mts., Afr. (drä'kĕnz-bĕrgh)	212	29°15'S	29°07'E
Drake Passage, strt. (drāk păs'ĭj)	128	57°00'S	65°00'W
Dráma, Grc. (drä'mä)	149	41°09'N	24°10'E
Drammen, Nor. (dräm'ĕn)	146	59°45'N	10°15'E
Drancy, Fr.	237c	48°56'N	2°27'E
Drau (Drava), r., Eur. (drou)	154	46°44'N	13°45'E
Drava, r., Eur. (drä'vä)	142	45°45'N	17°30'E
Draveil, Fr.	237c	48°41'N	2°25'E
Dravograd, Slvn. (drä'vô-gräd')	160	46°37'N	15°01'E
Dravosburg, Pa., U.S.	230b	40°21'N	79°51'W
Drawsko Pomorskie, Pol. (dräv'skō pō-mōr'skyĕ)	154	53°31'N	15°50'E
Drayton Harbor, b., Wa., U.S. (drā'tŭn)	106d	48°58'N	122°40'W
Drayton Plains, Mi., U.S.	101b	42°41'N	83°23'W
Drayton Valley, Can.	87	53°13'N	114°59'W
Drensteinfurt, Ger. (drĕn'shtīn-fōōrt)	157c	51°47'N	7°44'E
Dresden, Ger. (drās'dĕn)	142	51°05'N	13°45'E
Dreux, Fr. (drû)	156	48°44'N	1°24'E
Drewitz, neigh., Ger.	238a	52°22'N	13°08'E
Drexel Hill, Pa., U.S.	229b	39°57'N	75°19'W
Driefontein, S. Afr.	218d	25°53'S	29°10'E
Drin, r., Alb. (drēn)	161	42°13'N	20°13'E
Drina, r., Yugo. (drē'nä)	149	44°09'N	19°30'E
Drinit, Pellg i, b., Alb.	161	41°42'N	19°17'E
Dr. Ir. W. J. van Blommestein Meer, res., Sur.	131	4°45'N	55°05'W
Drissa, Bela. (drĭs'sä)	162	55°48'N	27°59'E
Drissa, r., Eur.	162	55°44'N	28°58'E
Driver, Va., U.S.	100g	36°50'N	76°30'W
Dröbak, Nor. (drû'bäk)	152	59°40'N	10°35'E
Drobeta-Turnu Severin, Rom. (sĕ-vĕ-rēn')	149	43°54'N	24°49'E
Drogheda, Ire. (drŏ'hē-dȧ)	146	53°43'N	6°15'W
Drogichin, Bela. (drō-gē'chĭn)	155	52°10'N	25°11'E
Drohobych, Ukr.	155	49°21'N	23°31'E
Drôme, r., Fr. (drōm)	156	44°42'N	4°53'E
Dronfield, Eng., U.K. (drŏn'fēld)	144a	53°18'N	1°28'W
Droylsden, Eng., U.K.	237b	53°29'N	2°10'W
Drumheller, Can. (drŭm-hĕl-ẽr)	84	51°28'N	112°42'W
Drummond, i., Mi., U.S. (drŭm'ŭnd)	98	46°00'N	83°50'W
Drummondville, Can. (drŭm'ŭnd-vĭl)	85	45°53'N	72°33'W
Drummoyne, Austl.	243a	33°51'S	151°09'E
Drumright, Ok., U.S. (drŭm'rīt)	111	35°59'N	96°37'W
Drunen, Neth.	145a	51°41'N	5°10'E
Drut', r., Bela. (drōōt)	162	53°40'N	29°45'E
Druya, Bela. (drò'yà)	162	55°45'N	27°26'E
Družba, Russia	239b	55°53'N	37°45'E
Drwęca, r., Pol. (d'r-vän'tsà)	155	53°06'N	19°13'E
Dryden, Can. (drī-dĕn)	85	49°47'N	92°50'W
Drysdale, Austl.	201a	38°11'S	144°34'E
Dry Tortugas, is., Fl., U.S. (tôr-tōō'gäz)	115a	24°37'N	82°45'W
Dschang, Cam. (dshäng)	210	5°34'N	10°09'E
Duabo, Lib.	214	5°40'N	8°05'W
Duagh, Can.	83g	53°43'N	113°24'W
Duarte, Ca., U.S.	232	34°08'N	117°58'W
Duarte, Pico, mtn., Dom. Rep. (dŭĭ'ärtĕh pēcô)	117	19°00'N	71°00'W
Duas Barras, Braz. (dōō'äs-bá'r-räs)	129a	22°03'S	42°30'W
Dubai see Dubayy, U.A.E.	182	25°18'N	55°26'E
Dubăsari, Mol.	163	47°16'N	29°11'E
Dubawnt, l., Can. (dōō-bônt')	84	63°27'N	103°30'W
Dubawnt, r., Can.	84	61°30'N	103°49'W
Dubayy, U.A.E.	182	25°18'N	55°26'E

PLACE (Pronunciation)	PAGE	LAT.	LONG.
Dubbo, Austl. (dŭb'ō)	203	32°20'S	148°42'E
Dubie, D.R.C.	217	8°33'S	28°32'E
Dublin, Ire.	142	53°20'N	6°15'W
Dublin, Ca., U.S. (dŭb'lĭn)	106b	37°42'N	121°56'W
Dublin, Ga., U.S.	115	32°33'N	82°55'W
Dublin, Tx., U.S.	112	32°05'N	98°20'W
Dubno, Ukr. (dōō'b-nô)	155	50°24'N	25°44'E
Du Bois, Pa., U.S. (dò-bois')	99	41°10'N	78°45'W
Dubovka, Russia (dò-bôf'kà)	167	49°00'N	44°50'E
Dubrovka, Russia (dōō-brôf'kà)	172c	59°51'N	30°56'E
Dubrovnik, Cro. (dò'brôv-nĕk) (rä-gōō'sä)	142	42°40'N	18°10'E
Dubrovno, Bela. (dōō-brôf'nö)	162	54°39'N	30°54'E
Dubuque, Ia., U.S. (dò-būk')	97	42°30'N	90°43'W
Duchesne, Ut., U.S. (dò-shān')	109	40°12'N	110°23'W
Duchesne, r., Ut., U.S.	109	40°20'N	110°50'W
Duchess, Austl. (dŭch'ĕs)	202	21°30'S	139°55'E
Ducie Island, i., Pit. (dū-sē')	2	25°30'S	126°20'W
Duck, r., Tn., U.S.	114	35°55'N	87°40'W
Duckabush, r., Wa., U.S. (dŭk'ȧ-bòsh)	106a	47°41'N	123°09'W
Duck Lake, Can.	88	52°47'N	106°13'W
Duck Mountain, mtn., Can.	89	51°35'N	101°00'W
Ducktown, Tn., U.S. (dŭk'toun)	114	35°03'N	84°20'W
Duck Valley Indian Reservation, I.R., Id., U.S.	104	42°02'N	115°49'W
Duckwater Peak, mtn., Nv., U.S. (dŭk-wô-tẽr)	108	39°00'N	115°31'W
Duda, r., Col. (dōō'dä)	130a	3°25'N	74°23'W
Dudinka, Russia (dōō-dĭn'kà)	164	69°15'N	85°42'E
Dudley, Eng., U.K. (dŭd'lĭ)	147	52°28'N	2°07'E
Duero, r., Eur.	142	41°30'N	4°30'W
Dufourspitze, mtn., Eur.	154	45°55'N	7°52'E
Dugger, In., U.S. (dŭg'ẽr)	98	39°00'N	87°10'W
Dugi Otok, i., Yugo. (dōō'gē o'tòk)	160	44°03'N	14°40'E
Dugny, Fr.	237c	48°57'N	2°25'E
Duisburg, Ger. (dōō'ĭs-bòrgh)	147	51°26'N	6°46'E
Duissern, neigh., Ger.	236	51°26'N	6°47'E
Dukhān, Qatar	185	25°25'N	50°48'E
Dukhovshchina, Russia (dōō-kôfsh-'chēnà)	162	55°13'N	32°26'E
Dukinfield, Eng., U.K. (dŭk'ĭn-fēld)	144a	53°28'N	2°05'W
Dukla Pass, p., Eur. (dòk'lä)	147	49°25'N	21°44'E
Dulce, Golfo, b., C.R. (gōl'fō dōōl'sä)	117	8°25'N	83°13'W
Dülken, Ger. (dül'kĕn)	157c	51°15'N	6°21'E
Dülmen, Ger. (dül'mĕn)	157c	51°50'N	7°17'E
Duluth, Mn., U.S. (dò-lōōth')	97	46°50'N	92°07'W
Dulwich, neigh., Eng., U.K.	235	51°26'N	0°05'W
Dumai, Indon.	181b	1°39'N	101°30'E
Dumali Point, c., Phil. (dōō-mä'lē)	197a	13°07'N	121°42'E
Dumas, Tx., U.S.	110	35°52'N	101°58'W
Dumbarton, Scot., U.K. (dŭm'bär-tŭn)	150	56°00'N	4°35'W
Dum-Dum, India	186a	22°37'N	88°25'E
Dumfries, Scot., U.K. (dŭm-frēs')	150	55°05'N	3°40'W
Dumjor, India	186a	22°37'N	88°14'E
Dumont, N.J., U.S. (dōō'mŏnt)	100a	40°56'N	74°00'W
Dümpten, neigh., Ger.	236	51°27'N	6°54'E
Dumyāt, Egypt	211	31°22'N	31°50'E
Dunaföldvár, Hung. (dò'nô-fûld'vär)	155	46°48'N	18°55'E
Dunaïvtsi, Ukr.	163	48°52'N	26°51'E
Dunajec, r., Pol. (dò-nä'yĕts)	155	49°52'N	20°53'E
Dunaújváros, Hung.	155	46°57'N	18°55'E
Dunay, Russia (dōō'nī)	172c	59°59'N	30°57'E
Dunbar, W.V., U.S.	98	38°20'N	81°45'W
Duncan, Can. (dŭŋ'kăn)	84	48°47'N	123°42'W
Duncan, Ok., U.S.	111	34°29'N	97°56'W
Duncan, r., Can.	87	50°30'N	116°45'W
Duncan Dam, dam, Can.	87	50°15'N	116°55'W
Duncan Lake, l., Can.	87	50°20'N	117°00'W
Duncansby Head, c., Scot., U.K. (dŭn'kănz-bĭ)	150	58°40'N	3°01'W
Duncanville, Tx., U.S. (dŭn'kăn-vĭl)	107c	32°39'N	96°55'W
Dundalk, Ire. (dŭn'kôk)	146	54°00'N	6°18'W
Dundalk, Md., U.S.	100e	39°16'N	76°31'W
Dundalk Bay, b., Ire. (dŭn'dôk)	150	53°55'N	6°15'W
Dundas, Austl.	243a	33°48'S	151°02'E
Dundas, Can. (dŭn-dăs')	91	43°16'N	79°58'W
Dundas, l., Austl. (dŭn-dȧs)	202	32°15'S	122°00'E
Dundas Island, i., Can.	86	54°33'N	130°55'W
Dundas Strait, strt., Austl.	202	10°35'S	131°15'E
Dundedin, Fl., U.S. (dŭn-ē'dĭn)	115a	28°00'N	82°43'W
Dundee, S. Afr.	213c	28°14'S	30°16'E
Dundee, Scot., U.K.	142	56°30'N	2°55'W
Dundee, Il., U.S. (dŭn-dē)	101a	42°06'N	88°17'W
Dundrum Bay, b., N. Ire., U.K. (dŭn-drŭm')	150	54°13'N	5°47'W
Dunedin, N.Z.	203a	45°48'S	170°32'E
Dunellen, N.J., U.S. (dŭn-ĕl'l'n)	100a	40°36'N	74°28'W
Dunfermline, Scot., U.K. (dŭn-fẽrm'lĭn)	150	56°05'N	3°30'W
Dungarvan, Ire. (dŭn-gàr'vȧn)	150	52°06'N	7°50'W
Dungeness, Wa., U.S. (dŭnj-nĕs')	106a	48°09'N	123°07'W
Dungeness, r., Wa., U.S.	106a	48°03'N	123°10'W
Dungeness Spit, Wa., U.S.	106a	48°11'N	123°03'W
Dunham Town, Eng., U.K.	237b	53°23'N	2°24'W
Dunheved, Austl.	243a	33°45'S	150°47'E
Dunhua, China (dòn-hwä)	189	43°18'N	128°10'E
Dunkerque, Fr. (dŭn-kĕrk')	147	51°02'N	2°37'E
Dunkirk, In., U.S. (dŭn'kûrk)	98	40°20'N	85°25'W
Dunkwa, Ghana	214	5°22'N	1°12'W
Dun Laoghaire, Ire. (dŭn-lâ'rĕ)	146	53°16'N	6°09'W
Dunlap, Ia., U.S. (dŭn'lăp)	102	41°53'N	95°33'W
Dunlap, Tn., U.S.	114	35°23'N	85°23'W
Dunmore, Pa., U.S. (dŭn'mōr)	99	41°25'N	75°30'W
Dunn, N.C., U.S. (dŭn)	115	35°18'N	78°37'W
Dunnellon, Fl., U.S. (dŭn-ĕl'ŏn)	115	29°02'N	82°28'W
Dunn Loring, Va., U.S.	229d	38°53'N	77°14'W
Dunnville, Can. (dŭn'vĭl)	91	42°55'N	79°40'W
Dunqulah, Sudan	211	19°21'N	30°19'E
Dunsmuir, Ca., U.S. (dŭnz'mūr)	104	41°08'N	122°17'W
Dunton Green, Eng., U.K.	235	51°18'N	0°11'E

PLACE (Pronunciation)	PAGE	LAT.	LONG.
Dunton Wayletts, Eng., U.K.	235	51°35'N	0°24'E
Dunvegan, S. Afr.	244b	26°09'S	28°09'E
Dunwoody, Ga., U.S. (dŭn-wòd'ĭ)	100c	33°57'N	84°20'W
Duolun, China (dwô-lōōn)	189	42°12'N	116°15'E
Duomo, rel., Italy	238c	45°27'N	9°11'E
Du Page, r., Il., U.S. (dōō pàj)	101a	41°41'N	88°11'W
Du Page, East Branch, r., Il., U.S.	101a	41°42'N	88°09'W
Du Page, West Branch, r., Il., U.S.	101a	41°42'N	88°09'W
Dupax, Phil. (dōō'päks)	197a	16°16'N	121°06'E
Dupo, Il., U.S. (dū'pō)	107e	38°31'N	90°12'W
Duque de Caxias, Braz. (dōō'kĕ-dĕ-kà'shyàs)	129a	22°46'S	43°18'W
Duquesne, Pa., U.S. (dò-kān')	101e	40°22'N	79°51'W
Du Quoin, Il., U.S. (dò-kwoin')	111	38°01'N	89°14'W
Durance, r., Fr. (dü-räNs')	147	43°46'N	5°52'E
Durand, Mi., U.S. (dů-rănd')	98	42°50'N	84°00'W
Durand, Wi., U.S.	103	44°37'N	91°58'W
Durango, Mex. (dōō-rä'n-gô)	116	24°02'N	104°42'W
Durango, Co., U.S. (dò-räŋ'gō)	109	37°15'N	107°55'W
Durango, state, Mex.	116	25°00'N	106°00'W
Durant, Ms., U.S. (dů-rănt')	114	33°05'N	89°50'W
Durant, Ok., U.S.	111	33°59'N	96°23'W
Duratón, r., Spain (dōō-rä-tōn')	158	41°30'N	3°55'W
Durazno, Ur. (dōō-räz'nō)	132	33°21'S	56°31'W
Durazno, dept., Ur.	129c	33°00'S	56°35'W
Durban, S. Afr. (dûr'băn)	212	29°48'S	31°00'E
Durbanville, S. Afr. (dûr-bàn'vĭl)	212a	33°50'S	18°39'E
Durbe, Lat. (dōōr'bĕ)	153	56°36'N	21°24'E
Durchholz, Ger.	236	51°23'N	7°17'E
Đurđevac, Cro.	149	46°03'N	17°03'E
Düren, Ger. (dü'rĕn)	157c	50°48'N	6°30'E
Durham, Eng., U.K. (dûr'ăm)	150	54°47'N	1°46'W
Durham, N.C., U.S.	97	36°00'N	78°55'W
Durham Downs, Austl.	204	27°30'S	141°55'E
Durrës, Alb. (dòr'ĕs)	142	41°19'N	19°27'E
Duryea, Pa., U.S. (dōōr-yā')	99	41°20'N	75°50'W
Dushan, China	190	31°38'N	116°16'E
Dushan, China (dōō-shän)	193	25°50'N	107°42'E
Dushanbe, Taj.	169	38°30'N	68°45'E
Düssel, Ger.	236	51°16'N	7°03'E
Düsseldorf, Ger. (düs'ĕl-dôrf)	147	51°14'N	6°47'E
Dussen, Neth.	145a	51°43'N	4°58'E
Dutalan Ula, mts., Mong.	192	49°25'N	112°40'E
Dutch Harbor, Ak., U.S. (dŭch här'bẽr)	94a	53°58'N	166°30'W
Duvall, Wa., U.S. (dōō'vâl)	106a	47°44'N	121°59'W
Duwamish, r., Wa., U.S. (dōō-wăm'ĭsh)	106a	47°24'N	122°18'W
Duyun, China (dōō-yòn)	188	26°18'N	107°40'E
Dvinskaya Guba, b., Russia	166	65°10'N	38°40'E
Dwārka, India	186	22°18'N	68°59'E
Dwight, Il., U.S. (dwĭt)	98	41°00'N	88°20'W
Dworshak Res, Id., U.S.	104	46°45'N	115°50'W
Dyat'kovo, Russia (dyät'kō-vō)	162	53°36'N	34°19'E
Dyer, In., U.S. (dī'ẽr)	101a	41°30'N	87°31'W
Dyersburg, Tn., U.S. (dī'ẽrz-bûrg)	114	36°02'N	89°23'W
Dyersville, Ia., U.S. (dī'ẽrz-vĭl)	103	42°28'N	91°09'W
Dyes Inlet, Wa., U.S. (dīz)	106a	47°37'N	122°45'W
Dykhtau, Gora, mtn., Russia	168	43°03'N	43°08'E
Dyment, Can. (dī'mĕnt)	89	49°37'N	92°19'W
Dzamïn Üüd, Mong.	189	44°38'N	111°32'E
Dzaoudzi, May. (dzou'dzĭ)	213	12°44'S	45°15'E
Dzavhan, r., Mong.	188	48°19'N	94°08'E
Dzerzhinsk, Bela.	162	53°41'N	27°14'E
Dzerzhinsk, Russia	166	56°20'N	43°50'E
Dzerzhyns'k, Ukr.	163	48°26'N	37°50'E
Dzeržinskij, Russia	239b	55°38'N	37°50'E
Dzhalal-Abad, Kyrg. (jȧ-läl'ȧ-bät')	169	40°56'N	73°00'E
Dzhankoi, Ukr.	167	45°43'N	34°22'E
Dzhizak, Uzb. (dzhĕ'zäk)	169	40°13'N	67°58'E
Dzhugdzhur Khrebet, mts., Russia (jòg-jōōr')	165	56°15'N	137°00'E
Działoszyce, Pol. (jyä-wō-shē'tsĕ)	155	50°21'N	20°22'E
Dzibalchen, Mex. (zē-bäl-chĕ'n)	120a	19°25'N	89°39'W
Dzidzantún, Mex. (zēd-zän-tōō'n)	120a	21°18'N	89°00'W
Dzierżoniów, Pol. (dzyĕr-zhôn'yŭf)	154	50°44'N	16°38'E
Dzilam González, Mex. (zē-lä'm-gôn-zä'lĕz)	120a	21°21'N	88°53'W
Dzitás, Mex. (zē-tá's)	120a	20°47'N	88°32'W
Dzungaria, reg., China (dzòŋ-gä'rĭ-ȧ)	188	44°39'N	86°13'E
Dzungarian Gate, p., Asia	188	45°00'N	88°00'E

E

PLACE (Pronunciation)	PAGE	LAT.	LONG.
Eagle, W.V., U.S.	98	38°10'N	81°20'W
Eagle, r., Co., U.S.	109	39°32'N	106°28'W
Eaglecliff, Wa., U.S. (ē'gl-klĭf)	106c	46°10'N	123°13'W
Eagle Creek, r., In., U.S.	101g	39°54'N	86°17'W
Eagle Grove, Ia., U.S.	103	42°39'N	93°55'W
Eagle Lake, Me., U.S.	92	47°03'N	68°38'W
Eagle Lake, Tx., U.S.	113	29°37'N	96°20'W
Eagle Lake, l., Ca., U.S.	104	40°45'N	120°52'W
Eagle Mountain, Ca., U.S.	108	33°49'N	115°27'W
Eagle Mountain L, Tx., U.S.	107c	32°56'N	97°27'W
Eagle Pass, Tx., U.S.	96	28°49'N	100°30'W
Eagle Pk, Ca., U.S.	104	41°18'N	120°11'W
Eagle Rock, neigh., Ca., U.S.	232	34°09'N	118°12'W
Ealing, Eng., U.K. (ē'lĭng)	144b	51°29'N	0°19'W
Earle, Ar., U.S. (ûrl)	111	35°14'N	90°28'W
Earlington, Ky., U.S. (ûr'lĭng-tŭn)	114	37°15'N	87°31'W
Easley, S.C., U.S. (ēz'lĭ)	115	34°48'N	82°37'W
East, r., N.Y., U.S.	228	40°48'N	73°48'W
East, Mount, mtn., Pan.	116a	9°09'N	79°46'W

PRONOUNCING INDEX

East Alton–Elephanta Island (Ghārāpuri) 283

PLACE (Pronunciation)	PAGE	LAT.	LONG.
East Alton, Il., U.S. (ôl'tŭn)	107e	38°53'N	90°08'W
East Angus, Can. (ăŋ'gŭs)	91	45°35'N	71°40'W
East Arlington, Ma., U.S.	227a	42°25'N	71°08'W
East Aurora, N.Y., U.S. (ô-rō'rȧ)	101c	42°46'N	78°38'W
East Barnet, neigh., Eng., U.K.	235	51°38'N	0°09'W
East Bay, b., Tx., U.S.	113a	29°30'N	94°41'W
East Bedfont, neigh., Eng., U.K.	235	51°27'N	0°26'W
East Bernstadt, Ky., U.S. (bûrn'stát)	114	37°09'N	84°08'W
Eastbourne, Eng., U.K. (ēst'bôrn)	151	50°48'N	0°16'E
East Braintree, Ma., U.S.	227a	42°13'N	70°58'W
East Burwood, Austl.	243b	37°51'S	145°09'E
Eastbury, Eng., U.K.	235	51°37'N	0°25'W
East Caicos, i., T./C. Is. (kī'kōs)	123	21°40'N	71°35'W
East Cape, c., N.Z.	203a	37°37'S	178°33'E
East Cape see Dezhnëva, Mys, c., Russia	180	68°00'N	172°00'W
East Carondelet, Il., U.S. (kȧ-rŏn'dĕ-lĕt)	107e	38°33'N	90°14'W
East Cherokee Indian Reservation, I.R., N.C., U.S.	114	35°33'N	83°12'W
Eastchester, N.Y., U.S.	228	40°57'N	73°49'W
East Chicago, In., U.S. (shĭ-kô'gō)	101a	41°39'N	87°29'W
East China Sea, sea, Asia	189	30°28'N	125°52'E
East Cleveland, Oh., U.S. (klēv'lănd)	101d	41°33'N	81°35'W
Eastcote, neigh., Eng., U.K.	235	51°35'N	0°24'W
East Cote Blanche Bay, b., La., U.S. (kōt blänsh')	113	29°30'N	92°07'W
East Des Moines, r., Ia., U.S. (dē moin')	103	42°57'N	94°17'W
East Detroit, Mi., U.S. (dē-troit')	101b	42°28'N	82°57'W
Easter Island see Pascua, Isla de, i., Chile	225	26°50'S	109°00'W
Eastern Ghāts, mts., India	183	13°50'N	78°45'E
Eastern Native, neigh., S. Afr.	244b	26°13'S	28°05'E
Eastern Turkestan, hist. reg., China (tōr-kĕ-stän')(tûr-kĕ-stăn')	188	39°40'N	78°20'E
East Falls, neigh., Pa., U.S.	229b	40°01'N	75°11'W
East Grand Forks, Mn., U.S. (grănd fôrks)	102	47°56'N	97°02'W
East Greenwich, R.I., U.S. (grĭn'ĭj)	100b	41°40'N	71°27'W
Eastham, Eng., U.K.	237a	53°19'N	2°58'W
East Ham, neigh., Eng., U.K.	235	51°32'N	0°03'E
Easthampton, Ma., U.S. (ēst-hămp'tŭn)	99	42°15'N	72°45'W
East Hartford, Ct., U.S. (härt'fērd)	99	41°45'N	72°35'W
East Helena, Mt., U.S. (hĕ-hē'nȧ)	105	46°31'N	111°50'W
East Hills, Austl.	243a	33°58'S	150°59'E
East Hills, N.Y., U.S.	228	40°47'N	73°38'W
East Ilsley, Eng., U.K. (ĭl'slē)	144b	51°30'N	1°18'W
East Jordan, Mi., U.S. (jôr'dăn)	98	45°05'N	85°05'W
East Kansas City, Mo., U.S. (kăn'zȧs)	107f	39°09'N	94°30'W
East Lamma Channel, strt., H.K.	241c	22°15'N	114°07'E
Eastland, Tx., U.S. (ēst'lănd)	112	32°24'N	98°47'W
East Lansdowne, Pa., U.S.	229b	39°56'N	75°16'W
East Lansing, Mi., U.S. (lăn'sĭng)	98	42°45'N	84°30'W
Eastlawn, Mi., U.S.	101b	42°15'N	83°35'W
East Leavenworth, Mo., U.S. (lĕv'ĕn-wûrth)	107f	39°18'N	94°50'W
East Liberty, neigh., Pa., U.S.	230b	40°27'N	79°55'W
East Lindfield, Austl.	243a	33°46'S	151°11'E
East Liverpool, Oh., U.S. (lĭv'ēr-pōōl)	98	40°40'N	80°35'W
East London, S. Afr. (lŭn'dŭn)	212	33°02'S	27°54'E
East Los Angeles, Ca., U.S. (lōs ăŋ'hȧ-lās)	107a	34°01'N	118°09'W
Eastmain, r., Can. (ēst'măn)	85	52°12'N	73°19'W
East Malling, Eng., U.K.	235	51°17'N	0°26'E
Eastman, Ga., U.S. (ēst'măn)	114	32°10'N	83°11'W
East Meadow, N.Y., U.S.	228	40°43'N	73°34'W
East Millstone, N.J., U.S. (mĭl'stōn)	100a	40°30'N	74°35'W
East Molesey, Eng., U.K.	235	51°24'N	0°21'W
East Moline, Il., U.S. (mō-lēn')	103	41°31'N	90°28'W
East Newark, N.J., U.S.	228	40°45'N	74°10'W
East New York, neigh., N.Y., U.S.	228	40°40'N	73°53'W
East Nishnabotna, r., Ia., U.S. (nĭsh-nȧ-bŏt'nȧ)	102	40°53'N	95°23'W
East Norwich, N.Y., U.S.	228	40°50'N	73°32'W
Easton, Md., U.S. (ēs'tŭn)	99	38°45'N	76°05'W
Easton, Pa., U.S.	99	40°45'N	75°15'W
Easton L, Ct., U.S.	100a	41°18'N	73°17'W
East Orange, N.J., U.S. (ŏr'ĕnj)	100a	40°46'N	74°12'W
East Pakistan see Bangladesh, nation, Asia	183	24°15'N	90°00'E
East Palo Alto, Ca., U.S.	106b	37°27'N	122°07'W
East Peoria, Il., U.S. (pē-ō'rĭ-ȧ)	98	40°40'N	89°30'W
East Pittsburgh, Pa., U.S. (pĭts'bûrg)	101e	40°24'N	79°50'W
East Point, Ga., U.S.	100c	33°41'N	84°27'W
Eastport, Me., U.S. (ēst'pōrt)	92	44°53'N	67°01'W
East Providence, R.I., U.S. (prŏv'ĭ-dĕns)	100b	41°49'N	71°22'W
East Retford, Eng., U.K. (rĕt'fērd)	144a	53°19'N	0°56'W
East Richmond, Ca., U.S.	231b	37°57'N	122°19'W
East Rochester, N.Y., U.S. (rŏch'ĕs-tēr)	99	43°10'N	77°30'W
East Rockaway, N.Y., U.S.	228	40°39'N	73°40'W
East Saint Louis, Il., U.S.	97	38°38'N	90°10'W
East Siberian Sea, sea, Russia (sī-bĭr'y'n)	165	73°00'N	153°28'E
Eastsound, Wa., U.S. (ēst-sound)	106d	48°42'N	122°42'W
East Stroudsburg, Pa., U.S. (stroudz'bûrg)	99	41°00'N	75°10'W
East Syracuse, N.Y., U.S. (sĭr'ȧ-kūs)	99	43°05'N	76°00'W
East Tavaputs Plateau, plat., Ut., U.S. (tă-vă'-pŭts)	109	39°25'N	109°45'W
East Tawas, Mi., U.S. (tô'wȧs)	98	44°15'N	83°30'W
East Tilbury, Eng., U.K.	235	51°28'N	0°26'E
East Tustin, Ca., U.S.	232	33°46'N	117°49'W
East Walker, r., U.S. (wôk'ēr)	108	38°36'N	119°02'W
East Walpole, Ma., U.S.	227a	42°10'N	71°13'W
East Watertown, Ma., U.S.	227a	42°22'N	71°10'W
East Weymouth, Ma., U.S.	227a	42°13'N	70°55'W
Eastwick, neigh., Pa., U.S.	229b	39°55'N	75°14'W

PLACE (Pronunciation)	PAGE	LAT.	LONG.
East Wickham, neigh., Eng., U.K.	235	51°28'N	0°07'E
Eastwood, Austl.	243a	33°48'S	151°05'E
East York, Can.	83d	43°41'S	79°20'W
Eaton, Co., U.S. (ē'tŭn)	110	40°31'N	104°42'W
Eaton, Oh., U.S.	98	39°45'N	84°40'W
Eaton Estates, Oh., U.S.	101d	41°19'N	82°01'W
Eaton Rapids, Mi., U.S. (răp'ĭdz)	98	42°30'N	84°40'W
Eatonton, Ga., U.S. (ē'tŭn-tŭn)	114	33°20'N	83°24'W
Eatontown, N.J., U.S. (ē'tŭn-toun)	100a	40°18'N	74°04'W
Eaubonne, Fr.	237c	49°00'N	2°17'E
Eau Claire, Wi., U.S. (ō klâr')	97	44°47'N	91°32'W
Ebeltoft, Den. (ĕ'bĕl-tŭft)	152	56°11'N	10°39'E
Ebensburg, Pa., U.S.	99	40°29'N	78°44'W
Ebersberg, Ger. (ĕ'bĕrs-bĕrgh)	145d	48°05'N	11°58'E
Ebina, Japan	242a	35°26'N	139°25'E
Ebingen, Ger. (ā'bĭng-ĕn)	154	48°13'N	9°04'E
Eboli, Italy (ĕb'ō-lē)	160	40°38'N	15°04'E
Ebolowa, Cam.	210	2°54'N	11°09'E
Ebreichsdorf, Aus.	145e	47°58'N	16°24'E
Ebrié, Lagune, b., C. Iv.	214	5°20'N	4°50'W
Ebro, r., Spain (ā'brō)	142	42°00'N	2°00'W
Ebute-Ikorodu, Nig.	244d	6°37'N	3°30'E
Eccles, Eng., U.K. (ĕk''lz)	144a	53°29'N	2°20'W
Eccles, W.V., U.S.	98	37°45'N	81°10'W
Eccleshall, Eng., U.K.	144a	52°51'N	2°15'W
Eccleston, Eng., U.K.	237a	53°27'N	2°47'W
Eccleston, Md., U.S.	229c	39°24'N	76°44'W
Eceabat, Tur.	161	40°10'N	26°21'E
Echague, Phil. (ā-chä'gwä)	197a	16°43'N	121°40'E
Echandi, Cerro, mtn., N.A. (sĕ'r-rô-ĕ-chä'nd)	121	9°05'N	82°51'W
Ech Cheliff, Alg.	210	36°14'N	1°32'E
Echimamish, r., Can.	89	54°15'N	97°30'W
Echmiadzin, Arm.	168	40°10'N	44°18'E
Echo Bay, Can. (ĕk'ō)	107k	46°29'N	84°04'W
Echoing, r., Can. (ĕk'ō-ĭng)	89	55°15'N	91°30'W
Echternach, Lux. (ĕk'tēr-näk)	157	49°48'N	6°25'E
Echuca, Austl. (ē-chò'kȧ)	203	36°10'S	144°47'E
Écija, Spain (ā'thē-hä)	148	37°20'N	5°07'W
Eckernförde, Ger.	154	54°27'N	9°51'E
Eclipse, Va., U.S. (ē-klĭps')	100g	36°55'N	76°29'W
Ecorse, Mi., U.S. (ē-kôrs')	101b	42°15'N	83°09'W
Ecuador, nation, S.A. (ĕk'wȧ-dôr)	130	0°00'N	78°30'W
Ed, Erit.	211	13°57'N	41°37'E
Eda, neigh., Japan	242a	35°34'N	139°34'E
Eddyville, Ky., U.S. (ĕd'ĭ-vĭl)	114	37°03'N	88°03'W
Ede, Nig.	215	7°44'N	4°27'E
Edéa, Cam. (ĕ-dā'ä)	210	3°48'N	10°08'E
Éden, Braz.	234c	22°48'S	43°24'W
Eden, Tx., U.S.	112	31°13'N	99°51'W
Eden, Ut., U.S.	107b	41°18'N	111°49'W
Eden, r., Eng., U.K. (ē'dĕn)	150	54°40'N	2°35'W
Edenbridge, Eng., U.K. (ē'dĕn-brĭj)	144b	51°11'N	0°05'E
Edendale, S. Afr.	244b	26°09'S	28°09'E
Edenham, Eng., U.K. (ē'd'n-ăm)	144a	52°46'N	0°25'W
Eden Prairie, Mn., U.S. (prâr'ĭ)	107g	44°51'N	93°29'W
Edenton, N.C., U.S. (ē'dĕn-tŭn)	115	36°02'N	76°37'W
Edenton, Oh., U.S.	101f	39°14'N	84°02'W
Edenvale, S. Afr. (ĕd'ĕn-väl)	213b	26°09'S	28°10'E
Edenvale Location, S. Afr.	244b	26°08'S	28°11'E
Edenville, S. Afr. (ĕ'd'n-vĭl)	218d	27°33'S	27°42'E
Eder, r., Ger. (ā'dēr)	154	51°05'N	8°52'E
Edgefield, S.C., U.S. (ĕj'fēld)	115	33°52'N	81°55'W
Edge Hill, neigh., Eng., U.K.	237a	53°24'N	2°57'W
Edgeley, N.D., U.S. (ĕj'lĭ)	102	46°24'N	98°43'W
Edgemere, Md., U.S.	229c	39°14'N	76°27'W
Edgemont, S.D., U.S. (ĕj'mŏnt)	102	43°19'N	103°50'W
Edgerton, Wi., U.S. (ĕj'ēr-tŭn)	103	42°49'N	89°06'W
Edgewater, Al., U.S. (ĕj-wô-tēr)	100h	33°31'N	86°52'W
Edgewater, Md., U.S.	100e	38°58'N	76°35'W
Edgewater, N.J., U.S.	228	40°50'N	73°58'W
Edgewood, Can. (ĕj'wŏd)	87	49°47'N	118°08'W
Edgware, neigh., Eng., U.K.	235	51°37'N	0°17'W
Edgwater, N.Y., U.S.	230a	43°03'N	78°55'W
Edgworth, Eng., U.K.	237b	53°39'N	2°24'W
Édhessa, Grc.	149	40°48'N	22°04'E
Edina, Mn., U.S. (ē-dī'nȧ)	107g	44°55'N	93°20'W
Edina, Mo., U.S.	111	40°10'N	92°11'W
Edinburg, In., U.S. (ĕd''n-bûrg)	98	39°20'N	85°55'W
Edinburg, Tx., U.S.	112	26°18'N	98°08'W
Edinburgh, Scot., U.K. (ĕd''n-bŭr-ō)	142	55°57'N	3°10'W
Edirne, Tur.	161	41°41'N	26°35'E
Edison Park, neigh., Il., U.S.	231a	42°01'N	87°49'W
Edisto, r., S.C., U.S. (ĕd'ĭs-tō)	115	33°10'N	80°50'W
Edisto, North Fork, r., S.C., U.S.	115	33°42'N	81°24'W
Edisto, South Fork, r., S.C., U.S.	115	33°43'N	81°35'W
Edisto Island, S.C., U.S.	115	32°32'N	80°20'W
Edmond, Ok., U.S. (ĕd'mŭnd)	111	35°39'N	97°29'W
Edmonds, Wa., U.S. (ĕd'mŭndz)	106a	47°49'N	122°23'W
Edmonston, Md., U.S.	229d	38°57'N	76°56'W
Edmonton, Can.	84	53°33'N	113°28'W
Edmonton, neigh., Eng., U.K.	235	51°37'N	0°04'W
Edmundston, Can. (ĕd'mŭn-stŭn)	85	47°22'N	68°20'W
Edna, Tx., U.S. (ĕd'nȧ)	113	28°59'N	96°39'W
Edo, r., Japan	242a	35°41'N	139°53'E
Edogawa, neigh., Japan	242a	35°42'N	139°52'E
Edremit, Tur. (ĕd-rĕ-mēt')	149	39°35'N	27°00'E
Edremit Körfezi, b., Tur.	161	39°28'N	26°35'E
Edson, Can. (ĕd'sŭn)	84	53°35'N	116°26'W
Edward, i., Can. (ĕd'wērd)	90	48°21'N	88°29'W
Edward, l., Afr.	212	0°25'S	29°40'E
Edwardsville, Il., U.S. (ĕd'wērdz-vĭl)	107e	38°49'N	89°58'W
Edwardsville, In., U.S.	101h	38°17'N	85°53'W
Edwardsville, Ks., U.S.	107f	39°04'N	94°49'W
Eel, r., Ca., U.S. (ēl)	104	40°39'N	124°15'W
Eel, r., In., U.S.	98	40°50'N	85°55'W
Efate, i., Vanuatu (ā-fä'tä)	203	18°02'S	168°29'E
Effigy Mounds National Monument, rec., Ia., U.S. (ĕf'ĭ-jŭ mounds)	103	43°04'N	91°15'W
Effingham, Il., U.S. (ĕf'ĭng-hăm)	98	39°05'N	88°30'W
Ega, r., Spain (ā'gä)	158	42°40'N	2°20'W
Egadi, Isole, is., Italy (ĕ'sō-lĕ-ĕ'gä-dē)	148	38°01'N	12°00'E

PLACE (Pronunciation)	PAGE	LAT.	LONG.
Egegik, Ak., U.S. (ĕg'ĕ-jĭt)	95	58°10'N	157°22'W
Eger, Hung. (ĕ gĕr)	155	47°53'N	20°24'E
Egersund, Nor. (ĕ'ghĕr-sòn')	146	58°29'N	6°01'E
Egg Harbor, N.J., U.S. (ĕg här'bēr)	99	39°30'N	74°35'W
Egham, Eng., U.K. (ĕg'ŭm)	144b	51°24'N	0°33'W
Egiyn, r., Mong.	188	49°41'N	100°40'E
Egmont, Cape, c., N.Z. (ĕg'mŏnt)	203a	39°18'S	173°49'E
Egota, neigh., Japan	242a	35°43'N	139°40'E
Egypt, nation, Afr. (ē'jĭpt)	211	26°58'N	27°01'E
Eha-Amufu, Nig.	215	6°40'N	7°46'E
Ehingen, neigh., Ger.	236	51°22'N	6°42'E
Ehringhausen, Ger.	236	51°11'N	7°33'E
Ehringhausen, neigh., Ger.	236	51°09'N	7°11'E
Eibar, Spain (ā'ē-bär)	158	43°12'N	2°20'W
Eiche, Ger.	238a	52°34'N	13°36'E
Eichlinghofen, neigh., Ger.	236	51°29'N	7°24'E
Eichstätt, Ger. (īk'shtät)	154	48°54'N	11°14'E
Eichwalde, Ger. (īĸ'väl-dĕ)	145b	52°22'N	13°37'E
Eickerend, Ger.	236	51°13'N	6°34'E
Eidfjord, Nor. (ĕĭd'fyôr)	152	60°28'N	7°04'E
Eidsvoll, Nor. (īdhs'vôl)	146	60°19'N	11°15'E
Eifel, mts., Ger. (ī'fĕl)	154	50°08'N	6°30'E
Eiffel, Tour, pt. of i., Fr.	237c	48°51'N	2°18'E
Eigen, neigh., Ger.	236	51°33'N	6°57'E
Eighty Mile Beach, cst., Austl.	202	19°00'S	121°00'E
Eilenburg, Ger. (ī'lĕn-bòrgh)	154	51°27'N	12°38'E
Einbeck, Ger. (īn'bĕk)	154	51°49'N	9°52'E
Eindhoven, Neth. (īnd'hō-vĕn)	151	51°29'N	5°20'E
Eisenach, Ger. (ī'zĕn-äĸ)	147	50°58'N	10°18'E
Eisenhüttenstadt, Ger.	154	52°08'N	14°40'E
Eivissa, Spain	159	38°55'N	1°24'E
Eivissa, i., Spain	142	38°55'N	1°24'E
Ejea de los Caballeros, Spain	158	42°07'N	1°05'W
Ejura, Ghana	214	7°23'N	1°22'W
Ejutla de Crespo, Mex. (ā-hōt'lä dā krās'pō)	119	16°34'N	96°44'W
Ekanga, D.R.C.	216	2°23'S	23°14'E
Ekenäs, Fin. (ĕ'kĕ-nâs)	153	59°59'N	23°25'E
Ekeren, Bel.	145a	51°17'N	4°27'E
Ekoli, D.R.C.	216	0°23'S	24°16'E
Eksāra, India	240a	22°38'N	88°17'E
El Aaiún, W. Sah.	210	26°45'N	13°15'W
El Affroun, Alg. (ĕl áf-froun')	159	36°28'N	2°38'E
El Aguacate, Ven.	234a	10°28'N	66°59'W
Elands, r., S. Afr. (ēlănds)	213c	31°48'S	26°09'E
Elands, r., S. Afr.	218d	25°11'S	28°52'E
Elandsfontein, S. Afr.	244b	26°10'S	28°12'E
El Arahal, Spain (ĕl ä-rä-äl')	158	37°17'N	5°32'W
El Arba, Alg.	159	36°35'N	3°10'E
Elat, Isr.	182	29°34'N	34°57'E
Elâziğ, Tur. (ĕl-ä'zēz)	182	38°40'N	39°00'E
Elba, Al., U.S. (ĕl'bȧ)	114	31°25'N	86°01'W
Elba, Isola d', i., Italy (ē-sō lä-d-ĕl'bȧ)	148	42°42'N	10°25'E
El Banco, Col. (ĕl băn'cō)	130	8°58'N	74°01'W
Elbansan, Alb. (ĕl-bä-săn')	149	41°08'N	20°05'E
Elbe (Labe), r., Eur. (ĕl'bĕ)(lä'bĕ)	142	52°30'N	11°30'E
Elberfeld, neigh., Ger.	236	51°16'N	7°08'E
Elbert, Mount, mtn., Co., U.S. (ĕl'bērt)	96	39°05'N	106°25'W
Elberton, Ga., U.S. (ĕl'bēr-tŭn)	115	34°05'N	82°53'W
Elbeuf, Fr. (ĕl-bûf')	147	49°16'N	0°59'E
El Beyadh, Alg.	148	33°42'N	1°06'E
Elbistan, Tur. (ĕl-bē-stän')	149	38°20'N	37°10'E
Elblag, Pol. (ĕl'blăng)	146	54°11'N	19°25'E
El Bonillo, Spain (ĕl bō-nēl'yō)	158	38°56'N	2°31'W
El Boulaïda, Alg.	210	36°33'N	2°45'E
Elbow, r., Can. (ĕl'bō)	83e	51°03'N	114°24'W
Elbow Cay, i., Bah.	122	26°25'N	76°55'W
Elbow Lake, Mn., U.S.	102	46°00'N	95°59'W
El'brus, Gora, mtn., Russia (ĕl'brōs')	164	43°20'N	42°25'E
Elbrus, Mount see El'brus, Gora, mtn., Russia	164	43°20'N	42°25'E
Elburz Mountains, mts., Iran (ĕl'bòrz')	182	36°30'N	51°00'E
El Cajon, Col. (ĕl-kä-kō'n)	130a	4°50'N	76°35'W
El Cajon, Ca., U.S.	108a	32°48'N	116°58'W
El Calvario, neigh., Cuba	233b	23°05'N	82°20'W
El Cambur, Ven. (käm-bōōr')	131b	10°24'N	68°06'W
El Campamento, neigh., Spain	238b	40°24'N	3°46'W
El Campo, Tx., U.S. (kăm'pō)	113	29°13'N	96°17'W
El Caribe, Ven.	234a	10°37'N	66°49'W
El Carmen, Chile (ká'r-mĕn)	129b	34°14'S	71°23'W
El Carmen, Col. (ká'r-mĕn)	130	9°54'N	75°12'W
El Casco, Ca., U.S. (kăs'kō)	107a	33°59'N	117°08'W
El Centro, Ca., U.S. (sĕn'trō)	108	32°47'N	115°33'W
El Cerrito, Ca., U.S. (sĕr-rē'tō)	106b	37°55'N	122°19'W
El Cojo, Ven.	234a	10°37'N	66°53'W
El Corozo, Ven.	234a	10°35'N	66°58'W
El Cotorro, Cuba	233b	23°03'N	82°16'W
El Cuyo, Mex.	120a	21°30'N	87°42'W
Elda, Spain (ĕl'dä)	159	38°28'N	0°44'W
Elder Mills, Can.	227c	43°49'N	79°38'W
El Djelfa, Alg.	210	34°40'N	3°17'E
El Djouf, des., Afr. (ĕl djōōf)	210	21°45'N	7°05'W
Eldon, Ia., U.S. (ĕl-dŭn)	103	40°55'N	92°15'W
Eldon, Mo., U.S.	111	38°21'N	92°36'W
Eldora, Ia., U.S. (ĕl-dō'rȧ)	103	42°21'N	93°08'W
El Dorado, Ar., U.S. (ĕl dō-rä'dō)	97	33°13'N	92°39'W
Eldorado, Il., U.S.	98	37°50'N	88°30'W
El Dorado, Ks., U.S.	111	37°49'N	96°51'W
Eldorado Springs, Mo., U.S. (sprĭngz)	111	37°51'N	94°02'W
Eldoret, Kenya (ĕl-dō-rĕt')	217	0°31'N	35°17'E
El Ebano, Mex. (ā-bä'nō)	118	22°13'N	98°26'W
Electra, Tx., U.S. (ē-lĕk'trȧ)	110	34°02'N	98°54'W
Electric Peak, mtn., Mt., U.S. (ē-lĕk'trĭk)	105	45°03'N	110°52'W
Elektrogorsk, Russia (ĕl-yĕk'trô-gôrsk)	172b	55°53'N	38°48'E
Elektrostal', Russia (ĕl-yĕk'trō-stál)	172b	55°47'N	38°27'E
Elektrougli, Russia	172b	55°43'N	38°13'E
El Encantado, Ven.	234a	10°27'N	66°47'W
Elephanta Island (Ghārāpuri), i., India	240e	18°57'N	72°55'E

284 Elephant Butte Reservoir–Erie

PLACE (Pronunciation)	PAGE	LAT.	LONG.
Elephant Butte Reservoir, res., N.M., U.S. (ĕl′ē-fănt būt)	96	33°25′N	107°10′W
El Escorial, Spain (ĕl-ĕs-kō-ryä′l)	159a	40°38′N	4°08′W
El Espino, Nic. (ĕl-ĕs-pē′nō)	120	13°26′N	86°48′W
Eleuthera, i., Bah. (ē-lū′thẽr-ȧ)	117	25°05′N	76°10′W
Eleuthera Point, c., Bah.	122	24°35′N	76°05′W
Eleven Point, r., Mo., U.S. (ē-lĕv′ĕn)	111	36°53′N	91°39′W
Elgin, Scot., U.K.	150	57°40′N	3°30′W
Elgin, Il., U.S. (ĕl′jĭn)	101a	42°03′N	88°16′W
Elgin, Ne., U.S.	102	41°58′N	98°04′W
Elgin, Or., U.S.	104	45°34′N	117°58′W
Elgin, Tx., U.S.	113	30°21′N	97°22′W
Elgin, Wa., U.S.	106a	47°23′N	122°42′W
Elgon, Mount, mtn., Afr. (ĕl′gŏn)	211	1°00′N	34°25′E
El Granada, Ca., U.S.	231b	37°30′N	122°28′W
El Grara, Alg.	148	32°50′N	4°26′E
El Grullo, Mex. (grōō′l-yō)	118	19°46′N	104°10′W
El Guapo, Ven. (gwá′pō)	131b	10°07′N	66°00′W
El Guarapo, Ven.	234a	10°36′N	66°58′W
El Hank, reg., Afr.	210	23°44′N	6°45′W
El Hatillo, Ven. (ä-tē′l-yō)	131b	10°08′N	65°13′W
Elie, Can. (ē′lē)	83f	49°55′N	97°45′W
Elila, r., D.R.C. (ē-lē′lȧ)	212	3°30′S	28°00′E
Elisa, i., Wa., U.S. (ē-lī′sȧ)	106d	48°43′N	122°37′W
Élisabethville see Lubumbashi, D.R.C.	212	11°40′S	27°28′E
Elisenvaara, Russia (ā-lē′sĕn-vä′rȧ)	153	61°25′N	29°46′E
Elizabeth, La., U.S. (ē-lĭz′ȧ-bĕth)	113	30°50′N	92°47′W
Elizabeth, N.J., U.S.	100a	40°40′N	74°13′W
Elizabeth, Pa., U.S.	101e	40°16′N	79°53′W
Elizabeth City, N.C., U.S.	115	36°15′N	76°15′W
Elizabethton, Tn., U.S. (ē-lĭz-ȧ-bĕth′tŭn)	115	36°19′N	82°12′W
Elizabethtown, Ky., U.S. (ē-lĭz′ȧ-bĕth-toun)	98	37°40′N	85°55′W
El Jadida, Mor.	210	33°14′N	8°34′W
Elk, Pol.	146	53°53′N	22°23′E
Elk, r., Can.	87	50°00′N	115°00′W
Elk, r., Tn., U.S.	114	35°05′N	86°36′W
Elk, r., W.V., U.S.	98	38°30′N	81°05′W
El Kairouan, Tun. (kĕr-ō-än)	210	35°46′N	10°04′E
Elk City, Ok., U.S. (ĕlk)	110	35°23′N	99°23′W
El Kef, Tun. (xĕf′)	148	36°14′N	8°42′E
Elkhart, In., U.S. (ĕlk′härt)	98	41°40′N	86°00′W
Elkhart, Ks., U.S.	110	37°00′N	101°54′W
Elkhart, Tx., U.S.	113	31°38′N	95°35′W
Elkhorn, Wi., U.S. (ĕlk′hôrn)	103	42°39′N	88°32′W
Elkhorn, r., Ne., U.S.	102	42°06′N	97°46′W
Elkin, N.C., U.S. (ĕl′kĭn)	115	36°15′N	80°50′W
Elkins Park, Pa., U.S.	229b	40°05′N	75°08′W
Elk Island, i., Can.	89	50°45′N	96°32′W
Elk Island National Park, rec., Can. (ĕlk ī′lănd)	84	53°37′N	112°45′W
Elko, Nv., U.S. (ĕl′kō)	96	40°51′N	115°46′W
Elk Point, S.D., U.S.	102	42°41′N	96°41′W
Elk Rapids, Mi., U.S. (răp′ĭdz)	98	44°55′N	85°25′W
Elkridge, Md., U.S.	229c	39°13′N	76°42′W
Elk River, Id., U.S. (rĭv′ẽr)	104	46°47′N	116°11′W
Elk River, Mn., U.S.	103	45°17′N	93°33′W
Elkton, Ky., U.S. (ĕlk′tŭn)	114	36°47′N	87°08′W
Elkton, Md., U.S.	99	39°35′N	75°50′W
Elkton, S.D., U.S.	102	44°15′N	96°28′W
Elland, Eng., U.K. (el′ănd)	144a	53°41′N	1°50′W
Ellen, Mount, mtn., Ut., U.S. (ĕl′ĕn)	109	38°05′N	110°50′W
Ellendale, N.D., U.S. (ĕl′ĕn-dāl)	102	46°01′N	98°33′W
Ellensburg, Wa., U.S. (ĕl′ĕnz-bûrg)	104	47°00′N	120°31′W
Ellenville, N.Y., U.S. (ĕl′ĕn-vĭl)	99	41°40′N	74°25′W
Ellerslie, Can. (ĕl′ẽrz-lē)	83g	53°25′N	113°30′W
Ellesmere, Eng., U.K. (ĕlz′mẽr)	144a	52°55′N	2°54′W
Ellesmere Island, i., Can.	82	81°00′N	80°00′W
Ellesmere Park, Eng., U.K.	237b	53°29′N	2°20′W
Ellesmere Port, Eng., U.K.	144a	53°17′N	2°54′W
Ellice Islands see Tuvalu, nation, Oc.	3	5°20′S	174°00′E
Ellicott City, is., Md., U.S. (ĕl′ĭ-kŏt sĭ′tē)	100e	39°16′N	76°48′W
Ellicott Creek, r., N.Y., U.S.	101c	43°00′N	78°46′W
El Limoncito, Ven.	234a	10°29′N	66°47′W
Ellinghorst, neigh., Ger.	236	51°34′N	6°57′E
Elliot, S. Afr.	213c	31°19′S	27°52′E
Elliot, Wa., U.S. (ĕl′ĭ-ŭt)	106a	47°28′N	122°08′W
Elliotdale, S. Afr. (ĕl-ĭ-ŏt′dăl)	213c	31°58′S	28°42′E
Elliot Lake, Can.	90	46°23′N	82°39′W
Ellis, Ks., U.S. (ĕl′ĭs)	110	38°56′N	99°34′W
Ellisville, Ms., U.S. (ĕl′ĭs-vĭl)	114	31°37′N	89°10′W
Ellisville, Mo., U.S.	107e	38°35′N	90°35′W
Ellsworth, Ks., U.S. (ĕlz′wûrth)	110	38°43′N	98°14′W
Ellsworth, Me., U.S.	92	44°33′N	68°26′W
Ellsworth Mountains, mts., Ant.	219	77°00′S	90°00′W
Ellwangen, Ger. (ĕl′väŋ-gĕn)	154	48°47′N	10°08′E
Elm, Ger. (ĕlm)	145c	53°31′N	9°13′E
Elm, r., S.D., U.S.	102	45°47′N	98°28′W
Elm, r., W.V., U.S.	98	38°30′N	81°05′W
Elma, Wa., U.S. (ĕl′mȧ)	104	47°02′N	123°20′W
El Mahdia, Tun. (mä-dēȧ)(mä′dē-ȧ)	148	35°30′N	11°09′E
Elmendorf, Tx., U.S. (ĕl′mĕn-dôrf)	107d	29°16′N	98°20′W
El Menia, Alg.	210	30°39′N	2°52′E
Elm Fork, Tx., U.S. (ĕlm fôrk)	107c	32°55′N	96°56′W
Elmhurst, Il., U.S. (ĕlm′hûrst)	101a	41°54′N	87°56′W
Elmhurst, neigh., N.Y., U.S.	228	40°44′N	73°53′W
El Miliyya, Alg. (mē′ä)	210	36°30′N	6°16′E
Elmira, N.Y., U.S. (ĕl-mī′rȧ)	99	42°05′N	76°50′W
Elmira Heights, N.Y., U.S.	99	42°10′N	76°50′W
El Modena, Ca., U.S. (mō-dē′nō)	107a	33°47′N	117°48′W
El Mohammadia, Alg.	159	35°35′N	0°05′E
El Molinito, Mex.	233a	19°27′N	99°15′W
Elmont, N.Y., U.S.	228	40°42′N	73°42′W
El Monte, Ca., U.S. (mŏn′tȧ)	107a	34°04′N	118°02′W
El Morro National Monument, rec., N.M., U.S.	109	35°05′N	108°20′W
Elmshorn, Ger. (ĕlms′hôrn)	154	53°45′N	9°39′E
Elmwood, neigh., Pa., U.S.	229b	39°56′N	75°14′W
Elmwood Park, Il., U.S.	231a	41°55′N	87°49′W

PLACE (Pronunciation)	PAGE	LAT.	LONG.
Elmwood Place, Oh., U.S. (ĕlm′wŏod plās)	101f	39°11′N	84°30′W
Elokomin, r., Wa., U.S. (ē-lō′kō-mĭn)	106c	46°16′N	123°16′W
El Oro, Mex. (ô-rō)	118	19°49′N	100°04′W
El Palmar, Ven.	234a	10°38′N	66°52′W
El Pao, Ven. (ĕl pá′ō)	130	8°08′N	62°37′W
El Paraíso, Hond. (pä-rä-ē′sō)	120	13°55′N	86°35′W
El Pardo, Spain (pä′r-dō)	159a	40°31′N	3°47′W
El Paso, Tx., U.S. (pas′ō)	96	31°47′N	106°27′W
El Pedregal, neigh., Ven.	234a	10°30′N	66°51′W
El Pilar, Ven. (pē-lä′r)	131b	9°56′N	64°48′W
El Plantío, neigh., Spain	238b	40°28′N	3°49′W
El Porvenir, Pan. (pōr-vä-nēr′)	121	9°34′N	78°55′W
El Puerto de Santa María, Spain	158	36°36′N	6°18′W
El Qala, Alg.	148	36°52′N	8°23′E
El Qoll, Alg.	210	37°02′N	6°29′E
El Real, Pan. (rā-äl)	121	8°07′N	77°43′W
El Recreo, neigh., Ven.	234a	10°30′N	66°53′W
El Reloj, Mex.	233a	19°18′N	99°08′W
El Reno, Ok., U.S. (rē′nō)	111	35°31′N	97°57′W
El Rincón de la Florida, Chile	234b	33°33′S	70°34′W
Elroy, Wi., U.S. (ĕl′roi)	103	43°44′N	90°17′W
Elsa, Can.	95	63°55′N	135°25′W
Elsah, Il., U.S. (ĕl′zȧ)	107e	38°57′N	90°22′W
El Salto, Mex. (säl′tō)	118	23°48′N	105°22′W
El Salvador, nation, N.A.	116	14°00′N	89°30′W
El Sauce, Nic. (ĕl-sá′ō-sē)	120	13°00′N	86°40′W
Elsberry, Mo., U.S. (ĕlz′bĕr-ĭ)	111	39°09′N	90°44′W
Elsburg, S. Afr.	244b	26°15′S	28°12′E
Elsdorf, Ger. (ĕls′dōrf)	157c	50°56′N	6°35′E
El Segundo, Ca., U.S. (sĕgŭn′dō)	107a	33°55′N	118°24′W
Elsinore, Ca., U.S. (ĕl′sĭ-nôr)	107a	33°40′N	117°19′W
Elsinore Lake, l., Ca., U.S.	107a	33°38′N	117°21′W
Elstorf, Ger. (ĕls′tōrf)	145c	53°25′N	9°48′E
Elstree, Eng., U.K.	235	51°39′N	0°16′W
Eltham, Austl. (ĕl′thăm)	201a	37°43′S	145°08′E
Eltham, neigh., Eng., U.K.	235	51°27′N	0°04′E
El Tigre, Ven. (tē′grĕ)	130	8°49′N	64°15′W
Elton, Eng., U.K.	237a	53°16′N	2°49′W
El′ton, l., Russia	167	49°10′N	47°00′E
El Toreo, pt. of i., Mex.	233a	19°27′N	99°13′W
El Toro, Ca., U.S. (tō′rō)	107a	33°37′N	117°42′W
El Triunfo, El Sal.	120	13°17′N	88°32′W
El Triunfo, Hond. (ĕl-trē-ōō′n-fō)	120	13°06′N	87°00′W
Elūru, India	183	16°44′N	80°09′E
El Vado Res, N.M., U.S.	109	36°37′N	106°30′W
El Valle, neigh., Ven.	234a	10°27′N	66°55′W
Elvas, Port. (ĕl′väzh)	148	38°53′N	7°11′W
Elverum, Nor. (ĕl′vĕ-rŏŏm)	152	60°53′N	11°33′E
El Viejo, Nic. (ĕl-vyĕ′κō)	120	12°10′N	87°10′W
El Viejo, vol., Nic.	120	12°44′N	87°03′W
Elvins, Mo., U.S. (ĕl′vĭnz)	111	37°49′N	90°31′W
El Wad, Alg.	210	33°23′N	6°49′E
El Wak, Kenya (wäk′)	211	3°00′N	41°00′E
Elwell, Lake, res., Mt., U.S.	105	48°22′N	111°17′W
Elwood, Il., U.S. (ĕ′wŏod)	101a	41°24′N	88°07′W
Elwood, In., U.S.	98	40°15′N	85°50′W
Elx, Spain	159	38°15′N	0°42′W
Ely, Eng., U.K. (ē′lĭ)	151	52°25′N	0°17′E
Ely, Mn., U.S.	103	47°54′N	91°53′W
Ely, Nv., U.S.	96	39°16′N	114°53′W
Elyria, Oh., U.S. (ē-lĭr′ĭ-ȧ)	101d	41°22′N	82°07′W
El Zamural, Ven.	234a	10°27′N	67°00′W
El Zig-Zag, Ven.	234a	10°33′N	66°58′W
Ema, r., Est. (å′mȧ)	153	58°25′N	27°00′E
Emāmshahr, Iran	182	36°25′N	55°01′E
Emån, r., Swe.	152	57°15′N	15°46′E
Embarrass, r., Il., U.S. (ĕm-băr′ăs)	98	39°15′N	88°05′W
Embrun, Can. (ĕm′brŭn)	83c	45°16′N	75°17′W
Embrun, Fr. (äɴ-brûɴ′)	157	44°35′N	6°32′E
Embu, Braz.	234d	23°39′S	46°51′W
Embu, Kenya	217	0°32′S	37°27′E
Emden, Ger. (ĕm′dĕn)	154	53°21′N	7°15′E
Émerainville, Fr.	237c	48°49′N	2°37′E
Emerson, Can. (ĕm′ẽr-sŭn)	84	49°00′N	97°12′W
Emerson, N.J., U.S.	228	40°58′N	74°02′W
Emeryville, Ca., U.S. (ĕm′ẽr-ĭ-vĭl)	106b	37°50′N	122°17′W
Emi Koussi, mtn., Chad (ā′mē kōō-sē′)	211	19°50′N	18°30′E
Emiliano Zapata, Mex. (ĕ-mē-lyá′nō-zä-pá′tá)	119	17°45′N	91°46′W
Emilia-Romagna, hist. reg., Italy (ĕ-mēl′yä rō-má′n-yä)	160	44°35′N	10°48′E
Eminence, Ky., U.S. (ĕm′ĭ-nĕns)	98	38°25′N	85°15′W
Emira Island, i., Pap. N. Gui. (ā-mē-rä′)	197	1°40′S	150°28′E
Emmen, Neth. (ĕm′ĕn)	151	52°48′N	6°55′E
Emmerich, Ger. (ĕm′ẽr-ĭk)	157c	51°51′N	6°16′E
Emmetsburg, Ia., U.S. (ĕm′ĕts-bûrg)	103	43°07′N	94°41′W
Emmett, Id., U.S. (ĕm′ĕt)	104	43°53′N	116°30′W
Emmons, Mount, mtn., Ut., U.S. (ĕm′ŭnz)	96	40°43′N	110°20′W
Emory Peak, mtn., Tx., U.S. (ĕ′mō-rē pēk)	112	29°13′N	103°20′W
Empoli, Italy (ām′pō-lē)	160	43°43′N	10°55′E
Emporia, Ks., U.S. (ĕm-pō′rĭ-ȧ)	96	38°24′N	96°11′W
Emporia, Va., U.S.	115	37°40′N	77°34′W
Emporium, Pa., U.S. (ĕm-pō′rĭ-ŭm)	99	41°30′N	78°15′W
Empty Quarter see Ar Rub′al Khālī, des., Asia	182	20°00′N	51°00′E
Ems, r., Ger. (ĕms)	154	52°52′N	7°16′E
Emst, neigh., Ger.	236	51°21′N	7°30′E
Ems-Weser Kanal, can., Ger.	154	52°23′N	8°11′E
Emsworth, Pa., U.S.	230b	40°30′N	80°04′W
Enånger, Swe. (ĕn-ôŋ′gẽr)	152	61°36′N	16°55′E
Encantada, Cerro de la, mtn., Mex. (sĕ′r-rō-dĕ-lä-ĕn-kän-tä′dä)	116	31°58′N	115°15′W
Encanto, Cape, c., Phil. (ĕn-kän′tō)	197a	15°44′N	121°46′E
Encarnação, neigh., Port.	238d	38°47′N	9°06′W
Encarnación, Para. (ĕn-kär-nä-syōn′)	132	27°26′S	55°52′W
Encarnación de Díaz, Mex. (ĕn-kär-nä-syōn dá dē′áz)	118	21°34′N	102°15′W

PLACE (Pronunciation)	PAGE	LAT.	LONG.
Encinal, Tx., U.S. (ĕn′sĭ-nôl)	112	28°02′N	99°22′W
Encino, neigh., Ca., U.S.	232	34°09′N	118°30′W
Encontrados, Ven. (ĕn-kōn-trä′dōs)	130	9°01′N	72°10′W
Encounter Bay, b., Austl. (ĕn-koun′tẽr)	202	35°50′S	138°45′E
Endako, r., Can.	86	54°05′N	125°30′W
Endau, r., Malay.	181b	2°29′N	103°40′E
Enderbury, i., Kir. (ĕn′dẽr-bûrĭ)	224	2°00′S	171°00′W
Enderby Land, reg., Ant. (ĕn′dẽr bĭĭ)	219	72°00′S	52°00′E
Enderlin, N.D., U.S. (ĕn′dẽr-lĭn)	102	46°38′N	97°37′W
Endicott, N.Y., U.S. (ĕn′dĭ-kŏt)	99	42°05′N	76°00′W
Endicott Mountains, mts., Ak., U.S.	95	67°30′N	153°45′W
Enez, Tur.	161	40°42′N	26°05′E
Enfer, Pointe d′, c., Mart.	121b	14°21′N	60°48′W
Enfield, Austl.	243a	33°53′S	151°06′E
Enfield, Eng., U.K.	144b	51°38′N	0°06′W
Enfield, Ct., U.S. (ĕn′fēld)	99	41°55′N	72°35′W
Enfield, N.C., U.S.	115	36°10′N	77°41′W
Engaño, Cabo, c., Dom. Rep. (kä′-bô- ĕn-gä-nō)	117	18°40′N	68°30′W
Engcobo, S. Afr. (ĕng-cô-bô)	213c	31°41′S	27°59′E
Engel's, Russia (ĕn′gĕls)	167	51°20′N	45°40′E
Engelskirchen, Ger. (ĕn′gĕls-kĕr′κĕn)	157c	50°59′N	7°25′E
Engenho de Dentro, neigh., Braz.	234c	22°54′S	43°18′W
Engenho do Mato, Braz.	234c	22°57′S	43°01′W
Engenho Nofrvo, neigh., Braz.	234c	22°55′S	43°17′W
Enggano, Pulau, i., Indon. (ĕng-gä′nō)	196	5°22′S	102°18′E
Enghien-les-Bains, Fr.	237c	48°58′N	2°19′E
England, Ar., U.S. (ĭŋ′glănd)	111	34°33′N	91°58′W
England, , U.K. (ĭŋ′glănd)	142	51°35′N	1°40′W
Englefield Green, Eng., U.K.	235	51°26′N	0°35′W
Englewood, Co., U.S. (ĕn′g′l-wŏod)	110	39°39′N	105°00′W
Englewood, N.J., U.S.	100a	40°54′N	73°59′W
Englewood, neigh., Il., U.S.	231a	41°47′N	87°39′W
Englewood Cliffs, N.J., U.S.	228	40°53′N	73°57′W
English, In., U.S. (ĭn′glĭsh)	98	38°15′N	86°25′W
English, r., Can.	85	50°31′N	94°12′W
English Channel, strt., Eur.	142	49°45′N	3°06′W
Énguera, Spain (ān′gārä)	159	38°58′N	0°42′W
Enid, Ok., U.S. (ē′nĭd)	96	36°25′N	97°52′W
Enid Lake, res., Ms., U.S.	114	34°13′N	89°47′W
Enkeldoring, S. Afr. (ĕŋ′k′l-dôr-ĭng)	218d	25°24′S	28°43′E
Enköping, Swe. (ĕn′kû-pĭng)	152	59°39′N	17°05′E
Ennedi, mts., Chad (ĕn-nĕd′ē)	211	16°45′N	22°45′E
Ennepetal, Ger.	236	51°18′N	7°22′E
Ennis, Ire. (ĕn′ĭs)	150	52°54′N	9°05′W
Ennis, Tx., U.S.	113	32°20′N	96°38′W
Enniscorthy, Ire. (ĕn-ĭs-kôr′thĭ)	150	52°33′N	6°27′W
Enniskillen, N. Ire., U.K. (ĕn-ĭs-kĭl′ĕn)	150	54°20′N	7°25′W
Ennis Lake, res., Mt., U.S.	105	45°15′N	111°30′W
Enns, r., Aus. (ĕns)	147	47°37′N	14°35′E
Enoree, S.C., U.S. (ē-nō′rē)	115	34°43′N	81°58′W
Enoree, r., S.C., U.S.	115	34°35′N	81°55′W
Enriquillo, Dom. Rep. (ĕn-rē-kē′l-yō)	123	17°55′N	71°15′W
Enriquillo, Lago, l., Dom. Rep. (lä′gô-ĕn-rē-kē′l-yō)	123	18°35′N	71°35′W
Enschede, Neth. (ĕns′κä-dĕ)	147	52°10′N	6°50′E
Enseñada, Arg.	129c	34°50′S	57°55′W
Ensenada, Mex. (ĕn-sĕ-nä′dä)	116	32°00′N	116°30′W
Enshi, China (ŭn-shr)	188	30°18′N	109°25′E
Enshū-Nada, b., Japan (ĕn′shōō nä-dä)	195	34°25′N	137°14′E
Entebbe, Ug.	211	0°04′N	32°28′E
Enterprise, Al., U.S. (ĕn′tẽr-prīz)	114	31°20′N	85°50′W
Enterprise, Or., U.S.	104	45°25′N	117°16′W
Entiat, L, Wa., U.S.	104	45°43′N	120°11′W
Entraygues, Fr. (ĕɴ-trĕg′)	156	44°39′N	2°33′E
Entre Rios, prov., Arg.	132	31°30′S	59°00′W
Enugu, Nig. (ĕ-nōō′gōō)	210	6°27′N	7°27′E
Enumclaw, Wa., U.S. (ĕn′ŭm-klô)	106a	47°12′N	121°59′W
Envigado, Col. (ĕn-vē-gá′dō)	130a	6°10′N	75°34′W
Eolie, Isole, is., Italy (ĕ′sō-lĕ-ĕ-ô′lyĕ)	148	38°43′N	14°43′E
Epe, Nig.	215	6°37′N	3°59′E
Epernay, Fr. (ā-pĕr-nĕ′)	147	49°02′N	3°54′E
Epernon, Fr. (ā-pĕr-nôɴ′)	157b	48°36′N	1°41′E
Ephraim, Ut., U.S. (ē′frā-ĭm)	109	39°20′N	111°40′W
Ephrata, Wa., U.S. (ĕfrā′tȧ)	104	47°18′N	119°35′W
Epi, Vanuatu (ā′pē)	203	16°59′S	168°29′E
Epila, Spain (ā′pē-lä)	158	41°38′N	1°15′W
Épinal, Fr. (ā-pē-nàl′)	147	48°11′N	6°27′E
Épinay-sous-Sénart, Fr.	237c	48°42′N	2°31′E
Épinay-sur-Seine, Fr.	237c	48°57′N	2°19′E
Episkopi, Cyp.	181a	34°38′N	32°55′E
Eppendorf, neigh., Ger.	236	51°27′N	7°11′E
Eppenhausen, neigh., Ger.	236	51°21′N	7°31′E
Epping, Austl.	243a	33°46′S	151°05′E
Epping, Eng., U.K. (ĕp′ĭng)	144b	51°41′N	0°06′E
Epping Green, Eng., U.K.	235	51°44′N	0°05′E
Epping Upland, Eng., U.K.	235	51°43′N	0°06′E
Epsom, Eng., U.K.	144b	51°20′N	0°16′W
Epupa Falls, wtfl., Afr.	216	17°00′S	13°05′E
Epworth, Eng., U.K. (ĕp′wûrth)	144a	53°31′N	0°50′W
Equatorial Guinea, nation, Afr.	210	2°00′N	7°15′E
Equilles, Fr.	156a	43°34′N	5°21′E
Eramosa, r., Can. (ĕr-ȧ-mō′sȧ)	83d	43°39′N	80°08′W
Erba, Jabal, mtn., Sudan (ĕr-bȧ)	211	20°53′N	36°45′E
Erciyeş Daği, mtn., Tur.	149	38°30′N	35°36′E
Erding, Ger. (ĕr′dĕng)	145d	48°19′N	11°54′E
Erechim, Braz. (ĕ-rĕ-shē′ɴ)	132	27°43′S	52°11′W
Ereğli, Tur. (ĕ-rā′ĭ-le)	149	37°40′N	34°00′E
Ereğli, Tur.	149	41°15′N	31°25′E
Erenköy, neigh., Tur.	239f	40°58′N	29°04′E
Erfurt, Ger. (ĕr′fōrt)	147	50°59′N	11°04′E
Ergene, r., Tur. (ĕr′gĕ-nĕ)	161	41°17′N	26°50′E
Erges, r., Eur. (ĕr′-zhĕs)	158	39°45′N	7°01′W
Ergli, Lat.	153	56°54′N	25°38′E
Ergste, Ger.	236	51°25′N	7°34′E
Eria, r., Spain (ā-rē′ä)	158	42°10′N	6°08′W
Erick, Ok., U.S. (âr′ĭk)	110	35°14′N	99°51′W
Erie, Ks., U.S. (ē′rĭ)	111	37°35′N	95°17′W
Erie, Pa., U.S.	97	42°05′N	80°05′W
Erie, Lake, l., N.A.	97	42°15′N	81°25′W

ăt; finăl; rāte; senāte; ärm; ȧsk; sofȧ; fâre; ch-choose; dh-as th in other; bē; ēvent; bĕt; recĕnt; cratẽr; g-gō; gh-guttural g; bĭt; ĭ-short neutral; rīde; κ-guttural k as ch in German ich;

PRONOUNCING INDEX

Erimo Saki–Falmouth 285

PLACE (Pronunciation)	PAGE	LAT.	LONG.
Erimo Saki, c., Japan (ā′rē-mō sä-kē)	189	41°53′N	143°20′E
Erin, Can. (ĕ′rĭn)	83d	43°46′N	80°04′W
Erith, neigh., Eng., U.K.	235	51°29′N	0°10′E
Eritrea, nation, Afr. (ā-rẻ-trā′ȧ)	211	16°15′N	38°30′E
Erkrath, Ger.	236	51°13′N	6°55′E
Erlangen, Ger. (ĕr′läng-ĕn)	154	49°36′N	11°03′E
Erlanger, Ky., U.S. (ẽr′lăng-ẽr)	101f	39°01′N	84°36′W
Erle, neigh., Ger.	236	51°33′N	7°05′E
Ermont, Fr.	237c	48°59′N	2°16′E
Ermoúpolis, Grc.	161	37°30′N	24°56′E
Ernākulam, India	183	9°58′N	76°23′E
Erne, Lower Lough, l., N. Ire., U.K.	150	54°30′N	7°40′W
Erne, Upper Lough, l., N. Ire., U.K. (lŏk ûrn)	150	54°20′N	7°24′W
Erode, India	187	11°20′N	77°45′E
Eromanga, i., Vanuatu	203	18°58′S	169°18′E
Eros, La., U.S. (ē′rōs)	113	32°23′N	92°22′W
Errego, Moz.	217	16°02′S	37°14′E
Errigal, mtn., Ire. (ĕr-ĭ-gôl′)	150	55°02′N	8°07′W
Errol Heights, Or., U.S.	106c	45°29′N	122°38′W
Erskine Park, Austl.	243a	33°49′S	150°47′E
Erstein, Fr. (ĕr′shtīn)	157	48°27′N	7°40′E
Erwin, N.C., U.S. (ûr′wĭn)	115	35°16′N	78°40′W
Erwin, Tn., U.S.	115	36°07′N	82°25′W
Erzgebirge, mts., Eur. (ĕrts′gĕ-bē′gĕ)	142	50°29′N	12°40′E
Erzincan, Tur. (ĕr-zĭn-jän′)	182	39°50′N	39°30′E
Erzurum, Tur. (ĕrz′ro͞om′)	182	39°55′N	41°10′E
Esambo, D.R.C.	216	3°40′S	23°24′E
Esashi, Japan (ĕs′ä-shẻ)	189	41°50′N	140°10′E
Esbjerg, Den. (ĕs′byĕrgh)	146	55°29′N	8°25′E
Esborn, Ger.	236	51°23′N	7°20′E
Escalante, Ut., U.S. (ĕs-kȧ-lăn′tē)	109	37°50′N	111°40′W
Escalante, r., Ut., U.S.	109	37°40′N	111°20′W
Escalón, Mex.	112	26°45′N	104°20′W
Escambia, r., Fl., U.S. (ĕs-kăm′bĭ-ȧ)	114	30°38′N	87°20′W
Escanaba, Mi., U.S. (ĕs-kȧ-nô′bȧ)	97	45°44′N	87°05′W
Escanaba, r., Mi., U.S.	103	46°10′N	87°22′W
Escarpada Point, Phil.	196	18°40′N	122°45′E
Esch-sur-Alzette, Lux.	157	49°32′N	6°21′E
Eschwege, Ger. (ĕsh′vā-gẽ)	154	51°11′N	10°02′E
Eschweiler, Ger. (ĕsh′vī-lẽr)	157c	50°49′N	6°15′E
Escondido, Ca., U.S. (ĕs-kŏn-dē′dō)	108	33°07′N	117°00′W
Escondido, r., Nic.	121	12°04′N	84°09′W
Escondido, Río, r., Mex. (rẻ′ō-ĕs-kōn-dẻ′dô)	112	28°30′N	100°45′W
Escuadrón 201, Mex.	233a	19°22′N	99°06′W
Escudo de Veraguas, i., Pan. (ĕs-ko͞o′dä dā vä-rä′gwäs)	121	9°07′N	81°25′W
Escuinapa, Mex. (ĕs-kwē-nä′pä)	116	22°49′N	105°44′W
Escuintla, Guat. (ĕs-kwēn′tlä)	120	14°16′N	90°47′W
Ese, Cayos de, i., Col.	121	12°24′N	81°07′W
Eşfahān, Iran	182	32°38′N	51°30′E
Esgueva, r., Spain (ĕs-gĕ′vä)	158	41°48′N	4°10′W
Esher, Eng., U.K.	144b	51°23′N	0°22′W
Eshowe, S. Afr. (ĕsh′ỏ-wẻ)	213c	28°54′S	31°28′E
Esiama, Ghana	214	4°56′N	2°21′W
Eskdale, W.V., U.S. (ĕsk′dāl)	98	38°05′N	81°25′W
Eskifjördur, Ice. (ĕs′kẻ-fyŭr′do͞or)	142	65°04′N	14°01′W
Eskilstuna, Swe. (å′shẻl-stü-na)	146	59°23′N	16°28′E
Eskimo Lakes, l., Can. (es′kĭ-mō)	84	69°40′N	130°10′W
Eskişehir, Tur. (ĕs-kẻ-shĕ′h′r)	182	39°40′N	30°20′E
Esko, Mn., U.S. (ĕs′kỏ)	107h	46°27′N	92°22′W
Esla, r., Spain (ĕs-lä)	158	41°50′N	5°48′W
Eslöv, Swe. (ĕs′lûv)	152	55°50′N	13°17′E
Esmeraldas, Ec. (ĕs-må-räl′däs)	130	0°58′N	79°45′W
Espanola, Can. (ĕs-pȧ-nō′lȧ)	85	46°11′N	81°59′W
Esparta, C.R. (ĕs-pär′tä)	121	9°59′N	84°40′W
Esperance, Austl. (ĕs′pẻ-răns)	202	33°45′S	122°07′E
Esperanza, Cuba (ĕs-pĕ-rä′n-zä)	122	22°30′N	80°10′W
Espichel, Cabo, c., Port. (kȧ′bō-ĕs-pē-shĕl′)	158	38°25′N	9°13′W
Espinal, Col. (ĕs-pẻ-näl′)	130	4°10′N	74°53′W
Espinhaço, Serra do, mts., Braz. (sĕ′r-rä-dỏ-ĕs-pẻ-nȧ-sỏ)	131	16°00′S	44°00′W
Espinillo, Punta, c., Ur. (po͞o′n-tä-ĕs-pẻ-nē′l-yỏ)	129c	34°49′S	56°27′W
Espírito Santo, Braz. (ĕs-pẻ′rē-tỏ-sȧn′tỏ)	131	20°27′S	40°18′W
Espírito Santo, state, Braz.	131	19°57′S	40°58′W
Espiritu Santo, i., Vanuatu (ĕs-pē′rẻ-to͞o sän′tō)	203	15°45′S	166°50′E
Espíritu Santo, Bahía del, b., Mex.	120a	19°25′N	87°28′W
Espita, Mex. (ĕs-pē′tä)	120a	20°57′N	88°22′W
Esplugas, Spain	238e	41°23′N	2°06′E
Espoo, Fin.	153	60°13′N	24°41′E
Es Port de Pollença, Spain	159	39°50′N	3°00′E
Esposende, Port. (ĕs-pō-zĕn′dā)	158	41°33′N	8°45′W
Esquel, Arg. (ĕs-kĕ′l)	132	42°47′S	71°22′W
Esquimalt, Can. (ĕs-kwī′mŏlt)	86	48°26′N	123°24′W
Essaouira, Mor.	210	31°34′N	9°44′W
Essel, neigh., Ger.	236	51°37′N	7°15′E
Essen, Bel.	145a	51°28′N	4°27′E
Essen, Ger. (ĕs′sĕn)	142	51°26′N	6°59′E
Essenberg, Ger.	236	51°26′N	6°42′E
Essendon, Austl.	201a	37°46′S	144°55′E
Essequibo, r., Guy. (ĕs-ā-kē′bō)	131	4°26′N	58°17′W
Essex, Il., U.S.	101a	41°11′N	88°11′W
Essex, Md., U.S.	100e	39°19′N	76°29′W
Essex, Ma., U.S.	93a	42°38′N	70°47′W
Essex, Vt., U.S.	99	44°30′N	73°05′W
Essex Fells, N.J., U.S. (ĕs′ĕks fĕlz)	100a	40°50′N	74°16′W
Essexville, Mi., U.S. (ĕs′ĕks-vĭl)	98	43°35′N	83°50′W
Essington, Pa., U.S.	229b	39°52′N	75°18′W
Essling, neigh., Aus.	239e	48°13′N	16°32′E
Esslingen, Ger. (ĕs′slēn-gĕn)	154	48°45′N	9°19′E
Estacado, Llano, pl., U.S. (yȧ-nō ĕs-tȧcȧ-dō′)	96	33°50′N	103°20′W
Estância, Braz. (ĕs-tän′sĭ-ä)	131	11°17′S	37°18′W
Estarreja, Port. (ĕ-tär-rā′zhä)	158	40°44′N	8°39′W
Estats, Pique d′, mtn., Eur.	159	42°43′N	1°30′E
Estcourt, S. Afr. (ĕst-coort)	213c	29°04′S	29°53′E
Este, Italy (ĕs′tā)	160	45°13′N	11°40′E
Estella, Spain (ĕs-tāl′yä)	158	42°40′N	2°01′W
Estepa, Spain (ĕs-tā′pä)	158	37°18′N	4°54′W
Estepona, Spain (ĕs-tå-pō′nä)	158	36°26′N	5°08′W
Esterhazy, Can. (ĕs′tẽr-hā-zē)	89	50°40′N	102°08′W
Estero Bay, b., Ca., U.S. (ĕs-tā′rōs)	108	35°22′N	121°04′W
Estevan, Can. (ĕ-stē′văn)	84	49°07′N	103°05′W
Estevan Group, is., Can.	86	53°05′N	129°40′W
Estherville, Ia., U.S. (ĕs′tẽr-vĭl)	103	43°24′N	94°49′W
Estill, S.C., U.S. (ĕs′tĭl)	115	32°46′N	81°15′W
Eston, Can.	88	51°10′N	108°45′W
Estonia, nation, Eur.	164	59°10′N	25°00′E
Estoril, Port. (ĕs-tô-rēl′)	159b	38°45′N	9°24′W
Estrêla, mtn., Port. (mäl-you′ɴ-dä-ĕs-trĕ′lä)	158	40°20′N	7°38′W
Estrêla, r., Braz. (ĕs-trĕ′lȧ)	132b	22°39′S	43°16′W
Estrêla, Serra da, mts., Port. (sĕr′rȧ dä ĕs-trā′lȧ)	158	40°25′N	7°45′W
Estrella, Cerro de la, mtn., Mex.	233a	19°21′N	99°05′W
Estremadura, hist. reg., Port. (ĕs-trā-mä-do͞o′rȧ)	158	39°00′N	8°36′W
Estremoz, Port. (ĕs-trā-mōzh′)	158	38°50′N	7°35′W
Estrondo, Serra do, mts., Braz. (sĕr′-rȧ dỏ ĕs-trỏn′-dỏ)	131	9°52′S	48°56′W
Esumba, Île, i., D.R.C.	216	2°00′N	21°12′E
Esztergom, Hung. (ĕs′tẽr-gōm)	155	47°46′N	18°45′E
Etah, Grnld. (ē′tă)	82	78°20′N	72°42′W
Étampes, Fr. (ā-tänp′)	156	48°26′N	2°09′E
Étaples, Fr. (ā-täp′l′)	156	50°32′N	1°38′E
Etchemin, r., Can. (ĕch′ĕ-mĭn)	83b	46°39′N	71°03′W
Ethiopa, nation, Afr. (ẻ-thẻ-ō′pẻ-ȧ)	211	7°53′N	37°55′E
Eticoga, Gui.-B.	214	11°09′N	16°08′W
Etiwanda, Ca., U.S. (ĕ-tĭ-wän′dȧ)	107a	34°07′N	117°31′W
Etna, Pa., U.S. (ĕt′nȧ)	101e	40°30′N	79°55′W
Etna, Mount, vol., Italy	142	37°48′N	15°00′E
Etobicoke, Can.	91	43°39′N	79°34′W
Etobicoke Creek, r., Can.	83d	43°44′N	79°48′W
Etolin Strait, strt., Ak., U.S. (ĕt ō lĭn)	95	60°35′S	165°40′W
Eton, Eng., U.K.	235	51°31′N	0°37′W
Eton College, educ., Eng., U.K.	235	51°30′N	0°36′W
Etoshapan, pl., Nmb. (ẻtō′shä)	212	19°07′S	15°30′E
Etowah, Tn., U.S. (ĕt′ỏ-wä)	114	35°18′N	84°31′W
Etowah, r., Ga., U.S.	114	34°23′N	84°19′W
Étréchy, Fr. (ā-trā-shē′)	157b	48°29′N	2°12′E
Etten-Leur, Neth.	145a	51°34′N	4°38′E
Etterbeek, Bel. (ĕt′ẽr-bāk)	145a	50°51′N	4°24′E
Etzatlán, Mex. (ĕt-zä-tlän′)	118	20°44′N	104°04′W
Eucla, Austl. (ū′klȧ)	202	31°45′S	128°50′E
Euclid, Oh., U.S. (ū′klĭd)	101d	41°34′N	81°32′W
Eudora, Ar., U.S. (u-dō′rȧ)	111	33°07′N	91°16′W
Eufaula, Al., U.S. (ů-fô′lȧ)	114	31°53′N	85°09′W
Eufaula, Ok., U.S.	111	35°16′N	95°35′W
Eufaula Reservoir, res., Ok., U.S.	111	35°00′N	94°45′W
Eugene, Or., U.S. (ů-jēn′)	96	44°02′N	123°06′W
Euless, Tx., U.S. (ū′lĕs)	107c	32°50′N	97°05′W
Eunice, La., U.S. (ū′nĭs)	113	30°30′N	92°25′W
Eupen, Bel. (oi′pĕn)	151	50°39′N	6°05′E
Euphrates, r., Asia (ů-frā′tēz)	182	36°00′N	40°00′E
Eure, r., Fr. (ûr)	156	49°03′N	1°22′E
Eureka, Ca., U.S. (û-rē′kȧ)	96	40°45′N	124°10′W
Eureka, Ks., U.S.	111	37°48′N	96°17′W
Eureka, Mt., U.S.	104	48°53′N	115°07′W
Eureka, Nv., U.S.	108	39°33′N	115°58′W
Eureka, S.D., U.S.	102	45°46′N	99°38′W
Eureka, Ut., U.S.	109	39°55′N	112°10′W
Eureka Springs, Ar., U.S.	111	36°24′N	93°43′W
Europe, cont. (ū′rŭp)	142	50°00′N	15°00′E
Eustis, Fl., U.S. (ūs′tĭs)	115	28°50′N	81°41′W
Eutaw, Al., U.S. (ū-tȧ)	114	32°48′N	87°50′W
Eutsuk Lake, l., Can. (o͞ot′sŭk)	86	53°20′N	126°44′W
Evanston, Il., U.S. (ĕv′ăn-stŭn)	97	42°03′N	87°41′W
Evanston, Wy., U.S.	105	41°17′N	111°02′W
Evansville, In., U.S. (ĕv′ănz-vĭl)	97	38°00′N	87°30′W
Evansville, Wi., U.S.	103	42°46′N	89°19′W
Evart, Mi., U.S. (ĕv′ẽrt)	98	43°55′N	85°10′W
Evaton, S. Afr. (ĕv′ȧ-tŏn)	218d	26°32′S	27°53′E
Eveleth, Mn., U.S. (ĕv′ẻ-lĕth)	103	47°27′N	92°35′W
Everard, l., Austl. (ĕv′ẽr-ȧrd)	202	31°20′S	134°10′E
Everard Ranges, mts., Austl.	202	27°15′S	132°00′E
Everest, Mount, mtn., Asia (ĕv′ẽr-ĕst)	183	28°00′N	86°57′E
Everett, Ma., U.S. (ĕv′ēr-ĕt)	93a	42°24′N	71°03′W
Everett, Wa., U.S. (ĕv′ẽr-ĕt)	96	47°59′N	122°11′W
Everett Mountains, mts., Can.	85	62°34′N	68°00′W
Everglades, The, sw., Fl., U.S.	115a	25°35′N	80°55′W
Everglades City, Fl., U.S. (ĕv′ẽr-glādz)	115a	25°50′N	81°25′W
Everglades National Park, rec., Fl., U.S.	97	25°39′N	80°57′W
Evergreen, Al., U.S. (ĕv′ẽr-grēn)	114	31°25′N	87°56′W
Evergreen Park, Il., U.S.	101a	41°44′N	87°42′W
Everman, Tx., U.S. (ĕv′ẽr-măn)	107c	32°38′N	97°17′W
Everson, Wa., U.S. (ĕv′ẽr-sŭn)	106d	48°55′N	122°21′W
Everton, neigh., Eng., U.K.	237a	53°25′N	2°58′W
Eving, neigh., Ger.	236	51°33′N	7°29′E
Évora, Port. (ĕv′ỏ-rä)	148	38°35′N	7°54′W
Évreux, Fr. (ā-vrû′)	147	49°02′N	1°11′E
Evrótas, r., Grc. (ĕv-rō′täs)	161	37°15′N	22°17′E
Évvoia, i., Grc.	149	38°38′N	23°45′E
Ewa Beach, Hi., U.S. (ē′wä)	94a	21°17′N	158°03′E
Ewaso Ng′iro, r., Kenya	211	0°59′N	37°47′E
Ewell, Eng., U.K.	235	51°21′N	0°15′W
Ewu, Nig.	244d	6°33′N	3°19′E
Excelsior, Mn., U.S. (ĕk-sel′sĭ-ŏr)	107g	44°54′N	93°35′W
Excelsior Springs, Mo., U.S.	111	39°20′N	94°13′W
Exe, r., Eng., U.K. (ĕks)	150	50°57′N	3°37′W
Exeter, Eng., U.K.	147	50°45′N	3°33′W
Exeter, Ca., U.S. (ĕk′sẻ-tẽr)	108	36°18′N	119°09′W
Exeter, N.H., U.S.	99	43°00′N	71°00′W
Exmoor, for., Eng., U.K. (ĕks′mȯr)	150	51°10′N	3°55′W
Exmouth, Eng., U.K. (ĕks′mŭth)	150	50°40′N	3°20′W
Exmouth Gulf, b., Austl.	202	21°45′S	114°30′E
Exploits, r., Can. (ĕks-ploits′)	93	48°50′N	56°15′W
Extórrax, r., Mex. (ĕx-tó′rȧx)	118	21°04′N	99°39′W
Extrema, Braz. (ĕsh-trĕ′mä)	129a	22°52′S	46°19′W
Extremadura, hist. reg., Spain (ĕks-trā-mä-doo′rä)	158	38°43′N	6°30′W
Exuma Sound, strt., Bah. (ĕk-so͞o′mä)	122	24°20′N	76°20′W
Eyasi, Lake, l., Tan. (å-yä′sẻ)	212	3°25′S	34°55′E
Eyjafjördur, b., Ice.	146	66°21′N	18°20′W
Eyl, Som.	218a	7°53′N	49°45′E
Eynsford, Eng., U.K.	235	51°22′N	0°13′E
Eyrarbakki, Ice.	146	63°51′N	20°52′W
Eyre, Austl. (âr)	202	32°15′S	126°20′E
Eyre, l., Austl.	202	28°43′S	137°50′E
Eyre Peninsula, pen., Austl.	202	33°30′S	136°00′E
Eyüp, neigh., Tur.	239f	41°03′N	28°55′E
Ezbekīyah, neigh., Egypt	244a	30°03′N	31°15′E
Ezeiza, Arg. (ĕ-zā′zä)	132a	34°52′S	58°31′W
Ezine, Tur. (å′zĭ-nå)	161	39°47′N	26°18′E

F

PLACE (Pronunciation)	PAGE	LAT.	LONG.
Fabens, Tx., U.S. (fā′bĕnz)	112	31°30′N	106°07′W
Fåborg, Den. (fô′bỏrg)	152	55°06′N	10°19′E
Fabreville, neigh., Can.	227b	45°34′N	73°50′W
Fabriano, Italy (fä-brē-ä′nỏ)	160	43°20′N	12°55′E
Fada, Chad (fä′dä)	211	17°06′N	21°18′E
Fada Ngourma, Burkina (fä′dä′′n go͞or′mä)	210	12°04′N	0°21′E
Faddeya, i., Russia (fȧd-yā′)	165	76°12′N	145°00′E
Faenza, Italy (fä-ĕnd′zä)	160	44°16′N	11°53′E
Fafe, Port. (fä′fā)	158	41°30′N	8°10′W
Fafen, r., Eth.	218a	8°15′N	42°40′E
Făgăras, Rom. (fȧ-gä′räsh)	161	45°50′N	24°55′E
Fagerness, Nor. (fä′ghẽr-nĕs)	146	61°00′N	9°10′E
Fagnano, l., S.A. (fäk-nä′nỏ)	132	54°35′S	68°20′W
Faguibine, Lac, l., Mali	214	16°50′N	4°20′W
Fahrland, Ger.	238a	52°28′N	13°01′E
Faial, i., Port. (fä-yä′l)	210a	38°40′N	29°19′W
Fā′id, Egypt (fä-yēd′)	218c	30°19′N	32°18′E
Failsworth, Eng., U.K.	237b	53°31′N	2°09′W
Fairbanks, Ak., U.S. (fâr′bănks)	94a	64°50′N	147°48′W
Fairbury, Il., U.S. (fâr′bĕr-ĭ)	98	40°45′N	88°25′W
Fairbury, Ne., U.S.	111	40°09′N	97°11′W
Fairchild Creek, r., Can. (fâr′chīld)	83d	43°18′N	80°10′W
Fairfax, Mn., U.S. (fâr′făks)	103	44°29′N	94°44′W
Fairfax, S.C., U.S.	115	32°29′N	81°13′W
Fairfax, Va., U.S.	100e	38°51′N	77°20′W
Fairfield, Austl.	201b	33°52′S	150°57′E
Fairfield, Al., U.S. (fâr′fēld)	100h	33°30′N	86°50′W
Fairfield, Ct., U.S.	100a	41°08′N	73°22′W
Fairfield, Il., U.S.	98	38°25′N	88°20′W
Fairfield, Ia., U.S.	103	41°00′N	91°59′W
Fairfield, Me., U.S.	92	44°35′N	69°38′W
Fairfield, N.J., U.S.	228	40°53′N	74°17′W
Fairhaven, Md., U.S.	229d	38°47′N	77°05′W
Fairhaven, Ma., U.S. (fâr-hā′vĕn)	99	41°35′N	70°55′W
Fair Haven, Vt., U.S.	99	43°35′N	73°15′W
Fair Island, i., Scot., U.K. (fâr)	150a	59°34′N	1°41′W
Fair Lawn, N.J., U.S.	228	40°56′N	74°07′W
Fairlee, Md., U.S.	229d	38°52′N	77°16′W
Fairmont, Mn., U.S. (fâr′mŏnt)	103	43°39′N	94°26′W
Fairmont, W.V., U.S.	98	39°30′N	80°10′W
Fairmont City, Il., U.S.	107e	38°39′N	90°05′W
Fairmount, In., U.S.	98	40°25′N	85°45′W
Fairmount, Ks., U.S.	107f	39°12′N	95°55′W
Fairmount Heights, Md., U.S.	229d	38°54′N	76°55′W
Fair Oaks, Ga., U.S. (fâr ōks)	100c	33°56′N	84°33′W
Fairport, N.Y., U.S. (fâr′pōrt)	99	43°05′N	77°30′W
Fairport Harbor, Oh., U.S.	98	41°45′N	81°15′W
Fairseat, Eng., U.K.	235	51°20′N	0°20′E
Fairview, N.J., U.S.	228	40°49′N	74°00′W
Fairview, Ok., U.S. (fâr′vū)	110	36°16′N	98°28′W
Fairview, Or., U.S.	106c	45°32′N	112°26′W
Fairview, Ut., U.S.	109	39°35′N	111°30′W
Fairview Park, Oh., U.S.	101d	41°27′N	81°52′W
Fairweather, Mount, mtn., N.A. (fâr-wĕdh′ẽr)	95	59°12′N	137°22′W
Faisalabad, Pak.	183	31°29′N	73°06′E
Faith, S.D., U.S. (fāth)	102	45°02′N	120°02′W
Faizābād, India	183	26°50′N	82°17′E
Fajardo, P.R.	117b	18°20′N	65°40′W
Fakfak, Indon.	197	2°56′S	132°25′E
Faku, China (fä-ko͞o)	192	42°28′N	123°20′E
Falcón, dept., Ven. (fäl-kô′n)	131b	11°00′N	68°28′W
Falconer, N.Y., U.S. (fô′k′n-ẽr)	99	42°10′N	79°10′W
Falcon Heights, Mn., U.S. (fô′k′n)	107g	44°59′N	93°10′W
Falcon Reservoir, res., N.A. (fôk′n)	112	26°47′N	99°03′W
Făleşti, Mol.	163	47°33′N	27°46′E
Falfurrias, Tx., U.S. (făl′fo͞o-rē′ȧs)	112	27°15′N	98°08′W
Falher, Can. (făl′ẽr)	87	55°44′N	117°12′W
Falkenberg, Swe. (fäl′kĕn-bĕrgh)	152	56°54′N	12°25′E
Falkensee, Ger. (fäl′kĕn-zā)	145b	52°34′N	13°05′E
Falkenthal, Ger. (fäl′kĕn-täl)	145b	52°54′N	13°18′E
Falkirk, Scot., U.K. (fôl′kûrk)	150	55°59′N	3°55′W
Falkland Islands, dep., S.A. (fôk′lănd)	132	50°45′S	61°00′W
Falköping, Swe. (fäl′chûp-ĭng)	152	58°09′N	13°30′E
Fall City, Wa., U.S.	106a	47°34′N	121°53′W
Fall Creek, r., In., U.S. (fôl)	101g	39°52′N	86°04′W
Fallon, Nv., U.S. (făl′ŭn)	108	39°30′N	118°48′W
Fall River, Ma., U.S.	97	41°42′N	71°07′W
Falls Church, Va., U.S. (fălz chûrch)	100e	38°53′N	77°10′W
Falls City, Ne., U.S.	111	40°04′N	95°37′W
Fallston, Md., U.S. (făls′ton)	100e	39°32′N	76°26′W
Falmouth, Jam.	122	18°30′N	77°40′W

286 Falmouth–Floriano

PLACE (Pronunciation)	PAGE	LAT.	LONG.
Falmouth, Eng., U.K. (făl'mŭth)	150	50°08'N	5°04'W
Falmouth, Ky., U.S.	98	38°40'N	84°20'W
False Divi Point, c., India	187	15°45'N	80°50'E
Falster, i., Den. (fäls'tĕr)	152	54°48'N	11°58'E
Fălticeni, Rom. (fŭl-tē-chān'y')	155	47°27'N	26°17'E
Falun, Swe. (fä-lo͞on')	146	60°38'N	15°35'E
Famadas, Spain	238e	41°21'N	2°05'E
Famagusta, N. Cyp. (fä-mä-go͞os'tä)	149	35°08'N	33°59'E
Famatina, Sierra de, mts., Arg.	132	29°00'S	67°50'W
Fangxian, China (fäŋ-shyĕn)	192	32°05'N	110°45'E
Fanning, i., Can.	83f	49°45'N	97°46'W
Fano, Italy (fä'nō)	160	43°49'N	13°01'E
Fanø, i., Den. (fän'û)	152	55°24'N	8°10'E
Fan Si Pan, mtn., Viet	193	22°25'N	103°50'E
Farafangana, Madag. (fä-rä-fäŋ-gä'nä)	213	23°18'S	47°59'E
Farāh, Afg. (fä-rä')	182	32°15'N	62°13'E
Farallón, Punta, c., Mex. (pŏ'n-tä-fä-rä-lōn)	118	19°21'N	105°03'W
Faranah, Gui. (fä-rä'nä)	210	10°02'N	10°44'W
Farasān, Jaza'ir, is., Sau. Ar.	182	16°45'N	41°08'E
Faregh, Wadi al, r., Libya (wădē ĕl fä-rĕg')	149	30°10'N	19°34'E
Farewell, Cape, c., N.Z. (făr-wĕl')	203a	40°37'S	172°40'E
Fargo, N.D., U.S. (fär'gō)	96	46°53'N	96°48'W
Far Hills, N.J., U.S. (fär hĭlz)	100a	40°41'N	74°38'W
Faribault, Mn., U.S. (fâ'rĭ-bō)	103	44°19'N	93°16'W
Farilhões, is., Port. (fä-rē-lyôɴzh')	158	39°28'N	9°32'W
Faringdon, Eng., U.K. (fă'rĭng-dŏn)	144b	51°38'N	1°35'W
Fāriskūr, Egypt (fä-rēs-ko͞or')	218b	31°19'N	31°46'E
Farit, Amba, mtn., Eth.	211	10°51'N	37°52'E
Farley, Mo., U.S. (fär'lē)	107f	39°16'N	94°49'W
Farmers Branch, Tx., U.S.	107c	32°56'N	96°53'W
Farmersburg, In., U.S. (fär'mẽrz-bûrg)	98	39°15'N	87°25'W
Farmersville, Tx., U.S. (fär'mẽrz-vĭl)	111	33°11'N	96°22'W
Farmingdale, N.J., U.S. (färm'ĕng-dāl)	100a	40°11'N	74°10'W
Farmingdale, N.Y., U.S.	100a	40°44'N	73°26'W
Farmingham, Ma., U.S. (färm-ĭng-hăm)	93a	42°17'N	71°25'W
Farmington, Il., U.S. (färm-ĭng-tŭn)	111	40°42'N	90°01'W
Farmington, Me., U.S.	92	44°40'N	70°10'W
Farmington, Mi., U.S.	101b	42°28'N	83°23'W
Farmington, Mo., U.S.	111	37°46'N	90°26'W
Farmington, N.M., U.S.	109	36°40'N	108°10'W
Farmington, Ut., U.S.	107b	40°59'N	111°53'W
Farmington Hills, Mi., U.S.	230c	42°28'N	83°23'W
Farmville, N.C., U.S. (färm-vĭl)	115	35°35'N	77°35'W
Farmville, Va., U.S.	115	37°15'N	78°23'W
Farnborough, Eng., U.K. (färn'bŭr-ô)	144b	51°15'N	0°45'W
Farnborough, neigh., Eng., U.K.	235	51°21'N	0°04'E
Farne Islands, is., Eng., U.K. (färn)	150	55°40'N	1°32'W
Farnham, Can. (fär'năm)	99	45°15'N	72°55'W
Farningham, Eng., U.K. (fär'nĭng-ŭm)	144b	51°22'N	0°14'E
Farnworth, Eng., U.K. (färn'wŭrth)	144a	53°34'N	2°24'W
Faro, Braz. (fä'rò)	131	2°05'S	56°32'W
Faro, Port.	148	37°01'N	7°57'W
Farodofay, Madag.	213	24°59'S	46°58'E
Faroe Islands, is., Eur.	142	62°00'N	5°45'W
Fårön, i., Swe.	153	57°57'N	19°10'E
Farquhar, Cape, c., Austl. (fär'kwȧr)	202	23°50'S	112°55'E
Farrell, Pa., U.S. (făr'ĕl)	98	41°10'N	80°30'W
Far Rockaway, neigh., N.Y., U.S.	228	40°36'N	73°45'W
Farrukhābād, India (fŭ-rŏk-hä-băd')	183	27°29'N	79°35'E
Fársala, Grc.	161	39°18'N	22°25'E
Farsund, Nor. (fär'sŏn)	152	58°05'N	6°47'E
Fartak, Ra's, c., Yemen	182	15°43'N	52°17'E
Fartura, Serra da, mts., Braz. (sĕ'r-rä-dá-făr-to͞o'rä)	132	26°40'S	53°15'W
Farvel, Kap, c., Grnld.	82	60°00'N	44°00'W
Farwell, Tx., U.S. (fär'wĕl)	110	34°24'N	103°03'W
Fasano, Italy (fä-zä'nō)	161	40°50'N	17°22'E
Fastiv, Ukr.	163	50°04'N	29°57'E
Fatëzh, Russia	162	52°06'N	35°51'E
Fatima, Port.	159	39°36'N	9°36'E
Fatsa, Tur. (fät'sä)	149	40°50'N	37°30'E
Faucilles, Monts, mts., Fr. (môɴ fō-sēl')	157	48°07'N	6°13'E
Fauske, Nor.	146	67°15'N	15°24'E
Faust, Can. (foust)	87	55°19'N	115°38'W
Faustovo, Russia	172b	55°27'N	38°29'E
Faversham, Eng., U.K. (fă'vẽr-sh'm)	144b	51°19'N	0°54'E
Favoriten, neigh., Aus.	239e	48°11'N	16°23'E
Fawkham Green, Eng., U.K.	235	51°22'N	0°17'E
Fawkner, Austl.	243b	37°43'S	144°58'E
Fawsett Farms, Md., U.S.	229d	38°59'N	77°14'W
Faxaflói, b., Ice.	146	64°33'N	22°40'W
Fayette, Al., U.S. (fā-yĕt')	114	33°40'N	87°54'W
Fayette, Ia., U.S.	103	42°49'N	91°49'W
Fayette, Ms., U.S.	114	31°43'N	91°00'W
Fayette, Mo., U.S.	111	39°09'N	92°41'W
Fayetteville, Ar., U.S. (fā-yĕt'vĭl)	111	36°03'N	94°08'W
Fayetteville, N.C., U.S.	115	35°02'N	78°54'W
Fayetteville, Tn., U.S.	114	35°10'N	86°33'W
Fazao, Forêt Classée du, for., Togo	214	8°50'N	0°40'E
Fazilka, India	186	30°30'N	74°02'E
Fazzān (Fezzan), hist. reg., Libya	211	26°45'N	13°01'E
Fdérik, Maur.	210	22°45'N	12°38'W
Fear, Cape, c., N.C., U.S. (fēr)	115	33°52'N	77°48'W
Feather, r., Ca., U.S. (fĕth'ẽr)	108	38°56'N	121°41'W
Feather, Middle Fork of, r., Ca., U.S.	108	39°49'N	121°10'W
Feather, North Fork of, r., Ca., U.S.	108	40°00'N	121°20'W
Featherstone, Eng., U.K. (fĕdh'ẽr stŭn)	144a	53°39'N	1°21'W
Fécamp, Fr. (fā-käN')	147	49°45'N	0°20'E
Federal, Distrito, dept., Ven. (dēs-trē'tô-fĕ-dĕ-rä'l)	131b	10°34'N	66°55'W
Federal Way, Wa., U.S.	106a	47°20'N	122°20'W
Fëdorovka, Russia (fyô'dō-rôf-kȧ)	172b	56°15'N	37°14'E
Fehmarn, i., Ger. (fā'märn)	154	54°28'N	11°15'E
Fehrbellin, Ger. (fĕr'bĕl-lēn)	145b	52°49'N	12°46'E
Feia, Logoa, l., Braz. (lō-gôä-fĕ'yä)	129a	21°54'S	41°15'W
Feicheng, China (fā-chŭŋ)	190	36°18'N	116°45'E
Feidong, China (fā-dôŋ)	190	31°53'N	117°28'E
Feira de Santana, Braz. (fĕ'ê-rä dä sänt-än'ä)	131	12°16'S	38°46'W
Feixian, China (fā-shyĕn)	190	35°17'N	117°59'E
Felanitx, Spain (fā-lä-nēch')	148	39°29'N	3°09'E
Feldkirch, Aus. (fĕlt'kĭrk)	154	47°15'N	9°36'E
Feldkirchen, Ger. (fĕld'kēr-kĕn)	145d	48°09'N	11°44'E
Felipe Carrillo Puerto, Mex.	120a	19°36'N	88°04'W
Feltre, Italy (fĕl'trā)	160	46°02'N	11°56'E
Femunden, l., Nor.	146	62°17'N	11°40'E
Fengcheng, China	191b	30°55'N	121°38'E
Fengcheng, China (fŭŋ-chŭŋ)	192	40°28'N	124°03'E
Fengdu, China (fŭŋ-do͞o)	188	29°58'N	107°50'E
Fengjie, China (fŭŋ-jyĕ)	188	31°02'N	109°30'E
Fengming Dao, i., China (fŭŋ-mĭŋ dou)	190	39°19'N	121°15'E
Fengrun, China (fŭŋ-rŏn)	190	39°51'N	118°06'E
Fengtai, China (fŭŋ-tī)	192a	39°51'N	116°19'E
Fengxian, China	190	34°41'N	116°36'E
Fengxian, China (fŭŋ-shyĕn)	191b	30°55'N	121°26'E
Fengxiang, China (fŭŋ-shyäŋ)	188	34°25'N	107°20'E
Fengyang, China (fûng'yäng')	192	32°55'N	117°32'E
Fengzhen, China (fŭŋ-jŭn)	189	40°28'N	113°20'E
Fennimore Pass, strt., Ak., U.S. (fĕn-ĭ-mōr)	95a	51°40'N	175°38'W
Fenoarivo Atsinanana, Madag.	213	17°30'S	49°31'E
Fenton, Mi., U.S. (fĕn-tŭn)	98	42°50'N	83°40'W
Fenton, Mo., U.S.	107e	38°31'N	90°27'W
Fenyang, China	189	37°20'N	111°48'E
Feodosiia, Ukr.	167	45°02'N	35°21'E
Ferbitz, Ger.	238a	52°30'N	13°01'E
Ferdows, Iran	182	34°00'N	58°13'E
Ferencváros, neigh., Hung.	239g	47°28'N	19°06'E
Ferentino, Italy (fā-rĕn-tē'nō)	160	41°42'N	13°18'E
Fergana, Uzb.	169	40°23'N	71°46'E
Fergus Falls, Mn., U.S. (fûr'gŭs)	96	46°17'N	96°03'W
Ferguson, Mo., U.S. (fûr-gŭ-sŭn)	107e	38°45'N	90°18'W
Ferkéssédougou, C. Iv.	214	9°36'N	5°12'W
Fermo, Italy (fĕr'mō)	160	43°10'N	13°43'E
Fermoselle, Spain (fĕr-mō-säl'yâ)	158	41°20'N	6°23'W
Fermoy, Ire. (fûr-moi')	150	52°05'N	8°06'W
Fernandina Beach, Fl., U.S. (fûr-năn-dē'nȧ)	115	30°38'N	81°29'W
Fernando de Noronha, , Braz.	131	3°51'S	32°25'W
Fernando Póo see Bioko, i., Eq. Gui.	210	3°35'N	7°45'E
Fernán-Núñez, Spain (fĕr-nän'no͞on'yâth)	158	37°42'N	4°43'W
Fernão Veloso, Baia de, b., Moz.	217	14°20'S	40°55'E
Ferndale, Ca., U.S. (fûrn'dāl)	104	40°34'N	124°18'W
Ferndale, Md., U.S.	229c	39°11'N	76°38'W
Ferndale, Mi., U.S.	101b	42°27'N	83°08'W
Ferndale, Wa., U.S.	106d	48°51'N	122°36'W
Fernie, Can. (fûr'nĭ)	84	49°30'N	115°03'W
Fern Prairie, Wa., U.S. (fûrn prâr'ĭ)	106c	45°38'N	122°25'W
Ferny Creek, Austl.	243b	37°53'S	145°21'E
Ferrara, Italy (fĕr-rä'rä)	148	44°50'N	11°37'E
Ferrat, Cap, c., Alg. (kăp fĕr-rät)	159	35°49'N	0°29'W
Ferraz de Vasconcelos, Braz.	234d	23°32'S	46°22'W
Ferreira do Alentejo, Port.	158	38°03'N	8°06'W
Ferreira do Zezere, Port. (fĕr-rĕ'ê-rä dò zâ-zä'rĕ)	158	39°49'N	8°17'W
Ferrelview, Mo., U.S. (fĕr'rĕl-vū)	107f	39°18'N	94°40'W
Ferreñafe, Peru (fĕr-rĕn-yá'fĕ)	130	6°38'S	79°48'W
Ferriday, La., U.S. (fĕr'ĭ-dā)	113	31°38'N	91°33'W
Ferrieres, Fr.	237c	48°49'N	2°42'E
Ferrol, Spain	142	43°30'N	8°12'W
Ferry Village, N.Y., U.S.	230a	43°58'N	78°57'W
Fershampenuaz, Russia (fĕr-shàm'pĕn-wäz)	172a	53°32'N	59°50'E
Fertile, Mn., U.S. (fur'tĭl)	102	47°33'N	96°18'W
Fès, Mor. (fĕs)	210	34°08'N	5°00'W
Fessenden, N.D., U.S. (fĕs'ĕn-dĕn)	102	47°39'N	99°40'W
Festus, Mo., U.S. (fĕst'ŭs)	111	38°12'N	90°22'W
Fetcham, Eng., U.K.	235	51°17'N	0°22'W
Fethiye, Tur. (fĕt-hē'yĕ)	149	36°40'N	29°05'E
Feuilles, Rivière aux, r., Can.	85	58°30'N	70°50'W
Ffestiniog, Wales, U.K.	150	52°59'N	3°58'W
Fianarantsoa, Madag. (fyȧ-nä'rȧn-tsō'ȧ)	213	21°21'S	47°15'E
Fichtenau, Ger.	238a	52°27'N	13°42'E
Ficksburg, S. Afr. (fĭks'bûrg)	218d	28°53'S	27°53'E
Fidalgo Island, i., Wa., U.S. (fĭ-dăl'gō)	106a	48°28'N	122°39'W
Fiddlers Hamlet, Eng., U.K.	235	51°41'N	0°08'E
Fieldbrook, Ca., U.S. (fēld'brŏk)	104	40°59'N	124°02'W
Fier, Alb. (fyĕr)	161	40°43'N	19°34'E
Fife Ness, c., Scot., U.K. (fīf'nes')	150	56°15'N	2°19'W
Fifth Cataract, wtfl., Sudan	211	18°27'N	33°38'E
Figeac, Fr. (fē-zhȧk')	156	44°37'N	2°02'E
Figeholm, Swe. (fē-ghĕ-hōlm)	152	57°24'N	16°33'E
Figueira da Foz, Port. (fē-gwĕy-rä-dȧ-fô'z)	158	40°10'N	8°50'W
Figuig, Mor.	210	32°20'N	1°30'W
Fiji, nation, Oc. (fē'jē)	3	18°40'S	175°00'E
Filadelfia, C.R. (fĭl-ȧ-dĕl'fĭ-ȧ)	120	10°26'N	85°37'W
Filatovskoye, Russia (fĭ-lä'tōf-skô-yĕ)	172a	56°49'N	62°20'E
Filchner Ice Shelf, ice., Ant. (fĭlk'nẽr)	219	80°00'S	35°00'W
Fili, neigh., Russia	239b	55°45'N	37°31'E
Filicudi, i., Italy (fē'le-ko͞o'dē)	160	38°34'N	14°39'E
Filippovskoye, Russia (fĭ-lĭ-pôf'skô-yĕ)	172b	56°06'N	38°38'E
Filipstad, Swe. (fĭl'ĭps-städh)	152	59°44'N	14°09'E
Fillmore, Ut., U.S. (fĭl'môr)	109	39°00'N	112°20'W
Filsa, Nor.	152	60°35'N	12°03'E
Fimi, r., D.R.C.	212	2°43'S	17°50'E
Finaalspan, S. Afr.	244b	26°17'S	28°15'E
Finch, Can. (fĭnch)	83c	45°09'N	75°06'W
Finchley, neigh., Eng., U.K.	235	51°36'N	0°10'W
Findlay, Oh., U.S. (fĭnd'lȧ)	98	41°05'N	83°40'W
Fingoe, Moz.	217	15°12'S	31°50'E
Finke, r., Austl. (fĭŋ'kē)	202	25°25'S	134°30'E
Finkenkrug, Ger.	238a	52°34'N	13°03'E
Finland, nation, Eur. (fĭn'lȧnd)	142	62°45'N	26°13'E
Finland, Gulf of, b., Eur. (fĭn'lȧnd)	142	59°35'N	23°35'E
Finlandia, Col. (fēn-lä'n-dēä)	130a	4°38'N	75°39'W
Finlay, r., Can. (fĭn'lā)	84	57°45'N	125°30'W
Finow, Ger. (fē'nōv)	145b	52°50'N	13°44'E
Finowfurt, Ger. (fē'nō-fo͞ort)	145b	52°50'N	13°41'E
Fircrest, Wa., U.S. (fûr'krĕst)	106a	47°14'N	122°31'W
Firenze see Florence, Italy	142	43°47'N	11°15'E
Firenzuola, Italy (fē-rĕnt-swô'lä)	160	44°08'N	11°21'E
Firgrove, Eng., U.K.	237b	53°37'N	2°08'W
Firozpur, India	183	30°58'N	74°39'E
Fischa, r., Aus.	145e	48°04'N	16°33'E
Fischamend Markt, Aus.	145e	48°07'N	16°37'E
Fischeln, neigh., Ger.	236	51°18'N	6°35'E
Fish, r., Nmb. (fĭsh)	212	28°00'S	17°30'E
Fish Cay, i., Bah.	123	22°30'N	74°20'W
Fish Creek, r., Can. (fĭsh)	83e	50°52'N	114°21'W
Fisher, La., U.S. (fĭsh'ẽr)	113	31°28'N	93°30'W
Fisher Bay, b., Can.	89	51°30'N	97°16'W
Fisher Channel, strt., Can.	86	52°10'N	127°42'W
Fisherman's Wharf, pt. of i., Ca., U.S.	231b	37°48'N	122°25'W
Fisher Strait, strt., Can.	85	62°43'N	84°28'W
Fisherville, Can.	227c	43°47'N	79°28'W
Fishpool, Eng., U.K.	237b	53°35'N	2°17'W
Fisterra, Cabo de, c., Spain	142	42°52'N	9°48'W
Fitchburg, Ma., U.S. (fĭch'bûrg)	99	42°35'N	71°48'W
Fitri, Lac, l., Chad	215	12°50'N	17°28'E
Fitzgerald, Ga., U.S. (fĭts-jĕr'ăld)	114	31°42'N	83°17'W
Fitz Hugh Sound, strt., Can. (fĭts hū)	86	51°40'N	127°57'W
Fitzroy, Austl.	243b	37°48'S	144°59'E
Fitzroy, r., Austl. (fĭts-roi')	202	18°00'S	124°05'E
Fitzroy, r., Austl.	203	23°45'S	150°02'E
Fitzroy, Monte (Cerro Chaltel), mtn., S.A.	132	48°10'S	73°18'W
Fitzroy Crossing, Austl.	202	18°08'S	126°00'E
Fitzwilliam, i., Can. (fĭts-wĭl'yŭm)	90	45°30'N	81°45'W
Fiume see Rijeka, Cro.	148	45°22'N	14°24'E
Fiumicino, Italy (fyo͞o-mē-chē'nô)	159d	41°47'N	12°19'E
Five Dock, Austl.	243a	33°52'S	151°08'E
Fjällbacka, Swe. (fyĕl'băk-ȧ)	152	58°37'N	11°17'E
Flagstaff, S. Afr. (flăg'stăf)	213c	31°06'S	29°31'E
Flagstaff, Az., U.S. (flăg-stȧf)	96	35°15'N	111°40'W
Flagstaff, l., Me., U.S. (flăg-stȧf)	99	45°05'N	70°30'W
Flåm, Nor. (flôm)	152	60°50'N	7°00'E
Flambeau, r., Wi., U.S. (flăm-bō')	103	45°32'N	91°05'W
Flaming Gorge Reservoir, res., U.S.	96	41°13'N	109°30'W
Flamingo, Fl., U.S. (flȧ-mĭŋ'gȯ)	115	25°10'N	80°55'W
Flamingo Cay, i., Bah. (flȧ-mĭŋ'gȯ)	123	22°50'N	75°50'W
Flamingo Point, c., V.I.U.S.	117c	18°19'N	65°00'W
Flanders, hist. reg., Fr. (flăn'dẽrz)	151	50°53'N	2°29'E
Flandreau, S.D., U.S. (flăn'drō)	102	44°02'N	96°35'W
Flatbush, neigh., N.Y., U.S.	228	40°39'N	73°56'W
Flathead, r., N.A.	87	49°30'N	114°30'W
Flathead, Middle Fork, r., Mt., U.S.	105	48°30'N	113°47'W
Flathead, North Fork, r., N.A.	105	48°45'N	114°20'W
Flathead, South Fork, r., Mt., U.S.	105	48°05'N	113°45'W
Flathead Indian Reservation, I.R., Mt., U.S.	105	47°30'N	114°25'W
Flathead Lake, l., Mt., U.S. (flăt'hĕd)	96	47°57'N	114°20'W
Flatow, Ger.	145b	52°44'N	12°58'E
Flat Rock, Mi., U.S. (flăt rŏk)	101b	42°06'N	83°17'W
Flattery, Cape, c., Wa., U.S. (flăt'ẽr-ĭ)	104	48°22'N	124°45'W
Flatwillow Creek, r., Mt., U.S. (flat wĭl'ô)	105	46°45'N	108°47'W
Flaunden, Eng., U.K.	235	51°42'N	0°32'W
Flehe, neigh., Ger.	236	51°12'N	6°47'E
Flekkefjord, Nor. (flăk'kĕ-fyôr)	152	58°19'N	6°38'E
Flemingsburg, Ky., U.S. (flĕm'ĭngz-bûrg)	98	38°25'N	83°45'W
Flensburg, Ger. (flĕns'bōrgh)	146	54°48'N	9°27'E
Flers, Fr. (flĕr)	147	48°43'N	0°37'W
Fletcher, N.C., U.S.	115	35°26'N	82°30'W
Fley, neigh., Ger.	236	51°23'N	7°30'E
Flinders, i., Austl.	203	39°35'S	148°10'E
Flinders, r., Austl.	203	18°48'S	141°07'E
Flinders, reg., Austl. (flĭn'dẽrz)	202	32°15'S	138°45'E
Flinders Reefs, rf., Austl.	203	17°30'S	149°02'E
Flin Flon, Can. (flĭn flŏn)	84	54°46'N	101°53'W
Flingern, neigh., Ger.	236	51°14'N	6°49'E
Flint, Wales, U.K.	144a	53°15'N	3°07'W
Flint, Mi., U.S.	97	43°00'N	83°45'W
Flint, r., Ga., U.S. (flĭnt)	97	31°25'N	84°15'W
Flora, Il., U.S. (flō'rȧ)	98	38°40'N	88°25'W
Flora, In., U.S.	98	40°25'N	86°30'W
Florala, Al., U.S. (flŏr-ăl'ȧ)	114	31°01'N	86°19'W
Floral Park, N.Y., U.S. (flôr'ăl pärk)	100a	40°42'N	73°42'W
Florence, Italy	142	43°47'N	11°15'E
Florence, Al., U.S. (flŏr'ĕns)	97	34°46'N	87°40'W
Florence, Az., U.S.	109	33°00'N	111°25'W
Florence, Ca., U.S.	232	33°58'N	118°15'W
Florence, Co., U.S.	110	38°23'N	105°08'W
Florence, Ks., U.S.	111	38°14'N	96°56'W
Florence, S.C., U.S.	115	34°10'N	79°45'W
Florence, Wa., U.S.	106a	48°13'N	122°21'W
Florencia, Col. (flō-rĕn'sē-ȧ)	130	1°31'N	75°13'W
Florencio Sánchez, Ur. (flō-rĕn-sēō-sȧ'n-chĕz)	129c	33°52'S	57°24'W
Florencio Varela, Arg. (flō-rĕn'sē-o vä-rā'lä)	132a	34°50'S	58°16'W
Florentia, S. Afr.	244b	26°16'S	28°08'E
Flores, Braz. (flō'rĕzh)	131	7°57'S	37°48'W
Flores, Guat.	120a	16°53'N	89°54'W
Flores, dept., Ur.	129c	33°33'S	57°00'W
Flores, neigh., Arg.	233d	34°38'S	58°28'W
Flores, i., Indon.	196	8°14'S	121°08'E
Flores, r., Arg.	129c	36°13'S	60°28'W
Flores, Laut (Flores Sea), sea, Indon.	196	7°09'S	120°30'E
Floresta, neigh., Arg.	233d	34°38'S	58°29'W
Floresville, Tx., U.S. (flō'rĕs-vĭl)	112	29°10'N	98°08'W
Floriano, Braz. (flō-rä-ä'nō)	131	6°17'S	42°58'W

ăt; finȧl; rāte; senȧte; ärm; ȧsk; sofȧ; fâre; ch-choose; dh-as th in other; bē; ēvent; bĕt; recĕnt; cratẽr; g-gō; gh-guttural g; bĭt; ĭ-short neutral; rīde; ᴋ-guttural k as ch in German ich;

PRONOUNCING INDEX
Florianópolis–Frankford 287

PLACE (Pronunciation)	PAGE	LAT.	LONG.
Florianópolis, Braz. (flō-rē-ä-nō'pō-lês)	132	27°30'S	48°30'W
Florida, Col. (flō-rē'dä)	130a	3°20'N	76°12'W
Florida, Cuba	122	22°10'N	79°50'W
Florida, S. Afr.	213b	26°11'S	27°56'E
Florida, N.Y., U.S. (flŏr'ĭ-dȧ)	100a	41°20'N	74°21'W
Florida, Ur. (flō-rē-dhä)	132	34°06'S	56°14'W
Florida, dept., Ur. (flō-rē'dhä)	129c	33°48'S	56°15'W
Florida, state, U.S. (flŏr'ĭ-dȧ)	97	30°30'N	84°40'W
Florida, i., Sol. Is.	203	8°56'S	159°45'E
Florida, Straits of, strt., N.A.	117	24°10'N	81°00'W
Florida Bay, b., Fl., U.S. (flŏr'ĭ-dȧ)	115a	24°55'N	80°55'W
Florida Keys, is., Fl., U.S.	97	24°33'N	81°20'W
Florida Mountains, mts., N.M., U.S.	109	32°10'N	107°35'W
Florido, Río, r., Mex. (flō-rē'dō)	112	27°21'N	104°48'W
Floridsdorf, Aus. (flō'rĭds-dôrf)	145e	48°16'N	16°25'E
Florina, Grc. (flō-rē'nä)	149	40°48'N	21°24'E
Florissant, Mo., U.S. (flŏr'ĭ-sănt)	107e	38°47'N	90°20'W
Flotantes, Jardines, rec., Mex.	233a	19°16'N	99°06'W
Flourtown, Pa., U.S.	229b	40°07'N	75°13'W
Flower Hill, N.Y., U.S.	228	40°49'N	73°41'W
Floyd, r., Ia., U.S. (floid)	102	42°38'N	96°15'W
Floydada, Tx., U.S. (floi-dā'dȧ)	110	33°59'N	101°19'W
Floyds Fork, r., Ky., U.S. (floi-dz)	101h	38°08'N	85°30'W
Flumendosa, r., Italy	160	39°45'N	9°18'E
Flushing, Mi., U.S. (flûsh'ĭng)	98	43°05'N	83°50'W
Flushing, neigh., N.Y., U.S.	228	40°45'N	73°49'W
Fly, r. (flī)	197	8°00'S	141°45'E
Foča, Bos. (fō'chä)	161	43°29'N	18°48'E
Fochville, S. Afr. (fŏk'vĭl)	218d	26°29'S	27°29'E
Focşani, Rom. (fōk-shä'nē)	155	45°41'N	27°17'E
Fogang, China (fwo-gäŋ)	193	23°50'N	113°35'E
Foggia, Italy (fōd'jä)	149	41°30'N	15°34'E
Fogo, Can. (fō'gō)	93	49°43'N	54°17'W
Fogo, i., Can.	91	49°40'N	54°13'W
Fogo, i., C.V.	210b	14°46'N	24°51'W
Fohnsdorf, Aus. (fōns'dôrf)	154	47°13'N	14°40'E
Föhr, i., Ger. (fûr)	154	54°47'N	8°30'E
Foix, Fr. (fwä)	156	42°58'N	1°34'E
Fokku, Nig.	215	11°40'N	4°31'E
Folcroft, Pa., U.S.	229b	39°54'N	75°17'W
Folgares, Ang.	216	14°54'S	15°08'E
Foligno, Italy (fō-lēn'yō)	160	42°58'N	12°41'E
Folkeston, Eng., U.K.	151	51°05'N	1°18'E
Folkingham, Eng., U.K. (fō'kĭng-ăm)	144a	52°53'N	0°24'W
Folkston, Ga., U.S.	115	30°50'N	82°01'W
Folsom, Ca., U.S.	108	38°40'N	121°10'W
Folsom, N.M., U.S. (fōl'sŭm)	110	36°47'N	103°56'W
Folsom, Pa., U.S.	229b	39°54'N	75°19'W
Fomento, Cuba (fō-mĕ'n-tō)	122	21°35'N	78°20'W
Fómeque, Col. (fō'mĕ-kĕ)	130a	4°29'N	73°52'W
Fonda, Ia., U.S. (fōn'dȧ)	103	42°33'N	94°51'W
Fond du Lac, Wi., U.S. (fŏn dū lăk')	97	43°47'N	88°29'W
Fond du Lac Indian Reservation, I.R., Mn., U.S.	103	46°44'N	93°04'W
Fondi, Italy (fōn'dē)	160	41°23'N	13°25'E
Fonseca, Golfo de, b., N.A. (gôl-fō-dĕ-fōn-sā'kä)	116	13°09'N	87°55'W
Fontainebleau, Fr. (fōn-tĕn-blō')	147	48°24'N	2°42'E
Fontainebleau, S. Afr.	244b	26°07'S	27°59'E
Fontana, Ca., U.S. (fŏn-tă'nȧ)	107a	34°06'N	117°27'W
Fonte Boa, Braz. (fōn'tȧ bō'ă)	130	2°32'S	66°05'W
Fontenay-aux-Roses, Fr.	237c	48°47'N	2°17'E
Fontenay-le-Comte, Fr. (fônt-nĕ'lē-kônt')	156	46°28'N	0°53'W
Fontenay-le-Fleury, Fr.	237c	48°49'N	2°03'E
Fontenay-sous-Bois, Fr.	237c	48°51'N	2°29'E
Fontenay-Trésigny, Fr. (fôn-te-nā' tra-sēn-yē')	157b	48°43'N	2°53'E
Fontenelle Reservoir, res., Wy., U.S.	105	42°05'N	110°05'W
Fontera, Punta, c., Mex. (pōō'n-tä-fôn-tĕ'rä)	119	18°36'N	92°43'W
Fontibón, Col. (fōn-tē-bôn')	130a	4°42'N	74°09'W
Fontur, c., Ice.	142	66°21'N	14°02'W
Foothills, S. Afr. (fōt-hĭls)	213b	25°55'S	27°36'E
Footscray, Austl.	201a	37°48'S	144°54'E
Fora, Ponta de, c., Braz.	234c	22°57'S	43°07'W
Foraker, Mount, mtn., Ak., U.S. (fôr'ȧ-kĕr)	95	62°40'N	152°40'W
Forbach, Fr. (fôr'bäk)	157	49°12'N	6°54'E
Forbes, Austl. (fôrbz)	203	33°24'S	148°05'E
Forbes, Mount, mtn., Can.	87	51°52'N	116°56'W
Forbidden City, bldg., China	240b	39°55'N	116°23'E
Forchheim, Ger. (fôrk'hīm)	154	49°43'N	11°05'E
Fordham University, pt. of i., N.Y., U.S.	228	40°51'N	73°53'W
Fords, N.J., U.S.	228	40°32'N	74°19'W
Fordsburg, neigh., S. Afr.	244b	26°13'S	28°02'E
Fordyce, Ar., U.S. (fôr'dīs)	111	33°48'N	92°24'W
Forécariah, Gui. (fōr-kȧ-rē'ä')	210	9°26'N	13°06'W
Forel, Mont, mtn., Grnld.	82	65°50'N	37°41'W
Forest, Ms., U.S. (fŏr'ĕst)	114	32°22'N	89°29'W
Forest, r., N.D., U.S.	102	48°08'N	97°45'W
Forest City, Ia., U.S.	103	43°14'N	93°40'W
Forest City, N.C., U.S.	115	35°20'N	81°52'W
Forest City, Pa., U.S.	99	41°35'N	75°30'W
Forest Gate, neigh., Eng., U.K.	235	51°33'N	0°02'E
Forest Grove, Or., U.S. (grōv)	106c	45°31'N	123°07'W
Forest Heights, Md., U.S.	229d	38°49'N	77°00'W
Forest Hill, Austl.	243b	37°50'S	145°11'E
Forest Hill, Md., U.S.	100e	39°35'N	76°26'W
Forest Hill, Tx., U.S.	107c	32°40'N	97°16'W
Forest Hill, neigh., Can.	227c	43°42'N	79°24'W
Forest Hills, Pa., U.S.	230b	40°26'N	79°52'W
Forest Hills, neigh., N.Y., U.S.	228	40°42'N	73°51'W
Forest Park, Il., U.S.	231a	41°53'N	87°50'W
Forest Park, neigh., Md., U.S.	229c	39°19'N	76°41'W
Forestville, Austl.	243a	33°46'S	151°13'E
Forestville, Can. (fŏr'ĕst-vĭl)	92	48°45'N	69°06'W
Forestville, Md., U.S.	100e	38°51'N	76°55'W
Forez, Monts du, mts., Fr. (môn dü fō-rā')	156	44°55'N	3°43'E

PLACE (Pronunciation)	PAGE	LAT.	LONG.
Forfar, Scot., U.K. (fôr'fȧr)	150	57°10'N	2°55'W
Forillon, Parc National, rec., Can.	92	48°50'N	64°05'W
Forio, mtn., Italy (fô'ryō)	159c	40°29'N	13°55'E
Forked Creek, r., Il., U.S. (fôrk'd)	101a	41°16'N	88°01'W
Forked Deer, r., Tn., U.S.	114	35°53'N	89°29'W
Forli, Italy (fôr-lē')	148	44°13'N	12°03'E
Formby, Eng., U.K. (fôrm'bē)	144a	53°34'N	3°04'W
Formby Point, c., Eng., U.K.	144a	53°33'N	3°06'W
Formentera, Isla de, i., Spain (ĕ's-lä-dĕ-fôr-mĕn-tā'rä)	148	38°43'N	1°25'E
Formiga, Braz. (fôr-mē'gȧ)	131	20°27'S	45°25'W
Formigas Bank, bk. (fôr-mē'gäs)	123	18°30'N	75°40'W
Formosa, Arg. (fōr-mō'sä)	132	27°25'S	58°12'W
Formosa, Braz.	131	15°32'S	47°10'W
Formosa, prov., Arg.	132	24°30'S	60°45'W
Formosa, Serra, mts., Braz. (sĕ'r-rä)	131	12°59'S	55°11'W
Formosa Bay, b., Kenya	217	2°45'S	40°30'E
Formosa Strait *see* Taiwan Strait, strt., Asia	189	24°30'N	120°00'E
Fornosovo, Russia (fôr-nô'sō vō)	172c	59°35'N	30°34'E
Forrest City, Ar., U.S. (for'ĕst sĭ'tĭ)	111	35°00'N	90°46'W
Forsayth, Austl. (fôr-sīth')	203	18°33'S	143°42'E
Forshaga, Swe. (fôrs'hä'gä)	152	59°34'N	13°25'E
Forst, Ger. (fôrst)	147	51°45'N	14°38'E
Forsyth, Ga., U.S. (fôr-sīth')	114	33°02'N	83°56'W
Forsyth, Mt., U.S.	105	46°15'N	106°41'W
Fort, neigh., India	240e	18°56'N	72°50'E
Fort Albany, Can. (fôrt ôl'bȧ nĭ)	85	52°20'N	81°30'W
Fort Alexander Indian Reserve, I.R., Can.	89	50°27'N	96°15'W
Fortaleza, Braz. (fôr'tä-lā'zȧ) (sä-ä-rä')	131	3°35'S	38°31'W
Fort Atkinson, Wi., U.S. (ăt'kĭn-sŭn)	103	42°55'N	88°46'W
Fort Beaufort, S. Afr. (bō'fôrt)	213c	32°47'S	26°39'E
Fort Belknap Indian Reservation, I.R., Mt., U.S.	105	48°16'N	108°38'W
Fort Bellefontaine, Mo., U.S. (bĕl-fōn-tān')	107f	38°50'N	90°15'W
Fort Benton, Mt., U.S. (bĕn'tŭn)	105	47°51'N	110°40'W
Fort Berthold Indian Reservation, I.R., N.D., U.S. (bĕrth'ôld)	102	47°47'N	103°28'W
Fort Bragg, Ca., U.S.	108	39°26'N	123°48'W
Fort Branch, In., U.S. (brănch)	98	38°15'N	87°35'W
Fort Chipewyan, Can.	84	58°46'N	111°15'W
Fort Cobb Reservoir, res., Ok., U.S.	110	35°12'N	98°28'W
Fort Collins, Co., U.S. (kŏl'ĭns)	96	40°36'N	105°04'W
Fort Crampel, Cen. Afr. Rep. (kràm-pĕl')	211	6°59'N	19°11'E
Fort-de-France, Mart. (dĕ fräns)	117	14°37'N	61°06'W
Fort Deposit, Al., U.S. (dē-pŏz'ĭt)	114	31°58'N	86°35'W
Fort-de-Possel, Cen. Afr. Rep. (dĕ pō-sĕl')	211	5°03'N	19°11'E
Fort Dodge, Ia., U.S. (dŏj)	97	42°31'N	94°10'W
Fort Edward, N.Y., U.S. (wĕrd)	99	43°15'N	73°30'W
Fort Erie, Can. (ē'rĭ)	101c	42°55'N	78°56'W
Fortescue, r., Austl. (fôr'tĕs-kū)	202	21°25'S	116°50'E
Fort Fairfield, Me., U.S. (fâr'fēld)	92	46°46'N	67°53'W
Fort Fitzgerald, Can. (fĭts-jĕr'ăld)	84	59°48'N	111°50'W
Fort Frances, Can. (frăn'sĕs)	85	48°36'N	93°24'W
Fort Frederica National Monument, rec., Ga., U.S. (frĕd'ĕ-rĭ-kȧ)	114	31°13'N	85°25'W
Fort Gaines, Ga., U.S. (gānz)	114	31°35'N	85°03'W
Fort Gibson, Ok., U.S. (gĭb'sŭn)	111	35°50'N	95°13'W
Fort Good Hope, Can. (gŏŏd hōp)	84	66°19'N	128°52'W
Forth, Firth of, b., Scot., U.K. (fûrth ŏv fôrth)	142	56°04'N	3°03'W
Fort Hall, Kenya (hôl)	213	0°47'S	37°13'E
Fort Hall Indian Reservation, I.R., Id., U.S.	105	43°02'N	112°21'W
Fort Howard, Md., U.S.	229c	39°12'N	76°27'W
Fort Huachuca, Az., U.S. (wä-chōō'kä)	109	31°30'N	110°25'W
Fortier, Can. (fôr'tyā')	83f	49°56'N	97°55'W
Fort Jefferson National Monument, rec., Fl., U.S. (jĕf'ĕr-sŭn)	115a	24°42'N	83°02'W
Fort Kent, Me., U.S. (kĕnt)	92	47°14'N	68°37'W
Fort Langley, Can. (lăng'lĭ)	106d	49°10'N	122°35'W
Fort Lauderdale, Fl., U.S. (lô'dĕr-dāl)	115a	26°07'N	80°09'W
Fort Lee, N.J., U.S.	100a	40°50'N	73°58'W
Fort Liard, Can.	84	60°16'N	123°34'W
Fort Loudoun Lake, res., Tn., U.S. (fôrt lou'dĕn)	114	35°52'N	84°10'W
Fort Lupton, Co., U.S. (lŭp'tŭn)	110	40°04'N	104°54'W
Fort Macleod, Can. (mȧ-kloud')	84	49°43'N	113°25'W
Fort Madison, Ia., U.S. (măd'ĭ-sŭn)	103	40°40'N	91°17'W
Fort Matanzas, Fl., U.S. (mä-tän'zäs)	115	29°39'N	81°17'W
Fort McDermitt Indian Reservation, I.R., Or., U.S. (mȧk dĕr'mĭt)	104	42°04'N	118°07'W
Fort McHenry National Monument, pt. of i., Md., U.S.	229c	39°16'N	76°35'W
Fort McMurray, Can. (mȧk-mŭr'ĭ)	84	56°44'N	111°23'W
Fort McPherson, Can. (mȧk-fŭr's'n)	84	67°37'N	134°59'W
Fort Meade, Fl., U.S. (mēd)	115a	27°45'N	81°48'W
Fort Mill, S.C., U.S. (mĭl)	115	35°03'N	80°57'W
Fort Mojave Indian Reservation, I.R., Ca., U.S. (mō-hä'vâ)	108	34°59'N	115°02'W
Fort Morgan, Co., U.S. (môr'gȧn)	110	40°14'N	103°49'W
Fort Myers, Fl., U.S. (mī'ĕrz)	115a	26°36'N	81°45'W
Fort Nelson, Can. (nĕl'sŭn)	84	58°57'N	122°30'W
Fort Nelson, r., Can. (nĕl'sŭn)	84	58°44'N	122°20'W
Fort Payne, Al., U.S. (pān)	114	34°26'N	85°41'W
Fort Peck, Mt., U.S. (pĕk)	105	47°58'N	106°30'W
Fort Peck Indian Reservation, I.R., Mt., U.S.	102	48°22'N	105°40'W
Fort Peck Lake, res., Mt., U.S.	96	47°52'N	106°59'W
Fort Pierce, Fl., U.S. (pērs)	115a	27°25'N	80°20'W
Fort Portal, Ug. (pôr'tàl)	211	0°40'N	30°16'E
Fort Providence, Can. (prŏv'ĭ-dĕns)	84	61°27'N	117°59'W
Fort Pulaski National Monument, rec., Ga., U.S. (pu-läs'kĭ)	115	31°59'N	80°56'W
Fort Qu'Appelle, Can.	88	50°46'N	103°55'W
Fort Randall Dam, dam, S.D., U.S.	102	42°48'N	98°35'W

PLACE (Pronunciation)	PAGE	LAT.	LONG.
Fort Resolution, Can. (rĕz'ō-lū'shŭn)	84	61°08'N	113°42'W
Fort Riley, Ks., U.S. (rī'lĭ)	111	39°05'N	96°46'W
Fort Saint James, Can. (fôrt sānt jāmz)	84	54°26'N	124°15'W
Fort Saint John, Can. (sānt jŏn)	84	56°15'N	120°51'W
Fort Sandeman, Pak. (săn'da-măn)	183	31°28'N	69°29'E
Fort Saskatchewan, Can. (săs-kăt'chōō-ån)	83g	53°43'N	113°13'W
Fort Scott, Ks., U.S. (skŏt)	97	37°50'N	94°43'W
Fort Severn, Can. (sĕv'ĕrn)	85	55°58'N	87°50'W
Fort Shevchenko, Kaz. (shĕv-chĕn'kō)	170	44°30'N	50°18'E
Fort Sibut, Cen. Afr. Rep. (fôr sē-bü')	211	5°44'N	19°05'E
Fort Sill, Ok., U.S. (fôrt sĭl)	110	34°41'N	98°25'W
Fort Simpson, Can. (sĭmp'sŭn)	84	61°52'N	121°48'W
Fort Smith, Can.	84	60°09'N	112°08'W
Fort Smith, Ar., U.S. (smĭth)	97	35°23'N	94°24'W
Fort Stockton, Tx., U.S. (stŏk'tŭn)	112	30°54'N	102°51'W
Fort Sumner, N.M., U.S. (sŭm'nĕr)	110	34°30'N	104°17'W
Fort Sumter National Monument, rec., S.C., U.S. (sŭm'tĕr)	115	32°43'N	79°54'W
Fort Thomas, Ky., U.S. (tŏm'ăs)	101f	39°05'N	84°27'W
Fortuna, Ca., U.S. (fŏr-tū'nȧ)	104	40°36'N	124°10'W
Fortune, Can. (fôr'tŭn)	93	47°04'N	55°51'W
Fortune, i., Bah.	123	22°35'N	74°20'W
Fortune Bay, b., Can.	85a	47°25'N	55°25'W
Fort Union National Monument, rec., N.M., U.S. (ūn'yŭn)	110	35°51'N	104°57'W
Fort Valley, Ga., U.S. (văl'ĭ)	114	32°33'N	83°53'W
Fort Vermilion, Can. (vĕr-mĭl'yŭn)	84	58°23'N	115°50'W
Fort Victoria *see* Masvingo, Zimb.	212	20°07'S	30°47'E
Fort Wayne, In., U.S. (wān)	97	41°00'N	85°10'W
Fort Wayne Military Museum, pt. of i., Mi., U.S.	230c	42°18'N	83°06'W
Fort William, Scot., U.K. (wĭl'yŭm)	150	56°50'N	3°00'W
Fort William, hist., India	240a	22°33'N	88°20'E
Fort William, Mount, mtn., Austl. (wĭ'ĭ-ăm)	204	24°45'S	151°15'E
Fort Worth, Tx., U.S. (wûrth)	96	32°45'N	97°20'W
Fort Yukon, Ak., U.S. (yōō'kŏn)	94a	66°30'N	145°00'W
Fort Yuma Indian Reservation, I.R., Ca., U.S. (yōō'mä)	109	32°54'N	114°47'W
Foshan, China	189	23°02'N	113°07'E
Fossano, Italy (fôs-sä'nō)	160	44°34'N	7°42'E
Fossil Creek, r., Tx., U.S. (fŏs-ĭl)	107c	32°53'N	97°19'W
Fossombrone, Italy (fōs-sôm-brō'nā)	160	43°41'N	12°48'E
Foss Res, Ok., U.S.	110	35°38'N	99°11'W
Fosston, Mn., U.S. (fôs'tŭn)	102	47°34'N	95°44'W
Fosterburg, Il., U.S. (fŏs'tĕr-bûrg)	107e	38°58'N	90°04'W
Foster City, Ca., U.S.	231b	37°34'N	122°16'W
Fostoria, Oh., U.S. (fŏs-tō'rĭ-ȧ)	98	41°10'N	83°20'W
Fougéres, Fr. (fōō-zhâr')	147	48°23'N	1°14'W
Foula, i., Scot., U.K. (fou'lȧ)	150a	60°08'N	2°04'W
Foulwind, Cape, c., N.Z. (foul'wĭnd)	203a	41°45'S	171°00'E
Foumban, Cam. (fōōm-bän')	210	5°43'N	10°55'E
Fountain Creek, r., Co., U.S. (foun'tĭn)	110	38°36'N	104°37'W
Fountain Valley, Ca., U.S.	107a	33°42'N	117°57'W
Fourche la Fave, r., Ar., U.S. (fōōrsh lä fāv')	111	34°46'N	93°45'W
Fouriesburg, S. Afr. (fō'rēz-bûrg)	218d	28°38'S	28°13'E
Fourmies, Fr. (fōōr-mē')	156	50°01'N	4°01'E
Four Mountains, Islands of the, is., Ak., U.S.	95a	52°58'N	170°40'W
Fourqueux, Fr.	237c	48°53'N	2°04'E
Fourth Cataract, wtfl., Sudan	211	18°52'N	32°07'E
Fouta Djallon, mts., Gui. (fōō'tä jä-lôn)	210	11°37'N	12°29'W
Foveaux Strait, strt., N.Z. (fō-vō')	203a	46°30'S	167°43'E
Fowler, Co., U.S. (foul'ĕr)	110	38°04'N	104°02'W
Fowler, In., U.S.	98	40°35'N	87°20'W
Fowler, Point, c., Austl.	202	32°05'S	132°30'E
Fowlerton, Tx., U.S. (foul'ĕr-tŭn)	112	28°26'N	98°48'W
Fox, i., Wa., U.S. (fŏks)	106a	47°15'N	122°08'W
Fox, r., Il., U.S.	103	41°35'N	88°43'W
Fox, r., Wi., U.S.	103	44°18'N	88°23'W
Foxboro, Ma., U.S. (fŏks'bŭrō)	93a	42°04'N	71°15'W
Fox Chapel, Pa., U.S.	230b	40°30'N	79°55'W
Foxe Basin, b., Can. (fŏks)	85	67°35'N	79°21'W
Foxe Channel, strt., Can.	85	64°30'N	79°23'W
Foxe Peninsula, pen., Can.	85	64°57'N	77°26'W
Fox Islands, is., Ak., U.S. (fŏks)	95a	53°04'N	167°30'W
Fox Lake, Il., U.S. (lāk)	101a	42°24'N	88°11'W
Fox Lake, l., Il., U.S.	101a	42°24'N	88°07'W
Fox Point, Wi., U.S.	101a	43°10'N	87°54'W
Fox Valley, Austl.	243a	33°45'S	151°06'E
Foyle, Lough, b., Eur. (lŏk foil')	150	55°07'N	7°08'W
Foz do Cunene, Ang.	216	17°16'S	11°50'E
Fraga, Spain (frä'gä)	159	41°31'N	0°20'E
Fragoso, Cayo, i., Cuba (kä'yō-frä-gō'sō)	122	22°45'N	79°30'W
Framnes Mountains, mts., Ant.	219	67°50'S	62°35'E
Franca, Braz. (frä'n-kä)	131	20°28'S	47°20'W
Francavilla, Italy (fräŋ-kä-vēl'lä)	161	40°32'N	17°37'E
France, nation, Eur. (fräns)	142	46°39'N	0°47'E
Frances, l., Can. (frăn'sĭs)	84	61°27'N	128°28'W
Frances, Cabo, c., Cuba (kä'bō-frän-sĕ's)	122	21°55'N	84°05'W
Frances, Punta, c., Cuba (pōō'n-tä-frän-sĕ's)	122	21°45'N	83°10'W
Francés Viejo, Cabo, c., Dom. Rep. (kä'bō-frän'sås vyā'hō)	123	19°40'N	69°35'W
Franceville, Gabon (fräns-vēl')	212	1°38'S	13°35'E
Francis Case, Lake, res., S.D., U.S. (frăn'sĭs)	96	43°15'N	99°00'W
Francisco Sales, Braz. (frän-sē's-kō-sà'lĕs)	129a	21°42'S	44°26'W
Francistown, Bots. (frăn'sis-toun)	212	21°17'S	27°28'E
Franconville, Fr.	237c	48°59'N	2°14'E
Frank, Pa., U.S.	230b	40°16'N	79°48'W
Frankby, Eng., U.K.	237a	53°22'N	3°08'W
Frankford, neigh., Pa., U.S.	229b	40°01'N	75°05'W

PLACE (Pronunciation)	PAGE	LAT.	LONG.
Frankfort, S. Afr. (frănk'fŏrt)	213c	32°43'S	27°28'E
Frankfort, S. Afr.	218d	27°17'S	28°30'E
Frankfort, Il., U.S. (frăŋk'fŭrt)	101a	41°30'N	87°51'W
Frankfort, In., U.S.	98	40°15'N	86°30'W
Frankfort, Ks., U.S.	111	39°42'N	96°27'W
Frankfort, Ky., U.S.	97	38°10'N	84°55'W
Frankfort, Mi., U.S.	98	44°40'N	86°15'W
Frankfort, N.Y., U.S.	99	43°05'N	75°05'W
Frankfurt am Main, Ger.	142	50°07'N	8°40'E
Frankfurt an der Oder, Ger.	147	52°20'N	14°31'E
Franklin, S. Afr.	213c	30°19'S	29°28'E
Franklin, In., U.S. (frănk'lĭn)	98	39°25'N	86°00'W
Franklin, Ky., U.S.	114	36°42'N	86°34'W
Franklin, La., U.S.	113	29°47'N	91°31'W
Franklin, Ma., U.S.	93a	42°05'N	71°24'W
Franklin, Mi., U.S.	230c	42°31'N	83°18'W
Franklin, Ne., U.S.	110	40°06'N	99°01'W
Franklin, N.H., U.S.	99	43°25'N	71°40'W
Franklin, N.J., U.S.	100a	41°08'N	74°35'W
Franklin, Oh., U.S.	98	39°30'N	84°20'W
Franklin, Pa., U.S.	99	41°25'N	79°50'W
Franklin, Tn., U.S.	114	35°54'N	86°54'W
Franklin, Va., U.S.	115	36°41'N	76°57'W
Franklin, l., Nv., U.S.	108	40°23'N	115°10'W
Franklin D. Roosevelt Lake, res., Wa., U.S.	104	48°12'N	118°43'W
Franklin Mountains, mts., Can.	84	65°36'N	125°55'W
Franklin Park, Il., U.S.	101a	41°56'N	87°53'W
Franklin Park, Pa., U.S.	230b	40°35'N	80°06'W
Franklin Park, Va., U.S.	229d	38°55'N	77°09'W
Franklin Roosevelt Park, neigh., S. Afr.	244b	26°09'S	27°59'E
Franklin Square, N.Y., U.S.	100a	40°43'N	73°40'W
Franklinton, La., U.S. (frăŋk'lĭn-tŭn)	113	30°49'N	90°09'W
Frankston, Austl.	201a	38°09'S	145°08'E
Franksville, Wi., U.S. (frănkz'vĭl)	101a	42°46'N	87°55'W
Fransta, Swe.	152	62°30'N	16°04'E
Franz Josef Land see Zemlya Frantsa-Iosifa, is., Russia	164	81°32'N	40°00'E
Frascati, Italy (fräs-kä'tē)	160	41°49'N	12°45'E
Fraser, Mi., U.S. (frā'zēr)	101b	42°32'N	82°57'W
Fraser, i., Austl.	203	25°12'S	153°00'E
Fraser, r., Can.	84	51°30'N	122°00'W
Fraserburgh, Scot., U.K. (frā'zēr-bûrg)	150	57°40'N	2°01'W
Fraser Plateau, plat., Can.	87	51°30'N	122°00'W
Frattamaggiore, Italy (frät-tä-mäg-zhyô'rē)	159c	40°41'N	14°16'E
Fray Bentos, Ur. (frī bĕn'tōs)	132	33°10'S	58°19'W
Frazee, Mn., U.S. (frā-zē')	102	46°42'N	95°43'W
Fraziers Hog Cay, i., Bah.	122	25°25'N	77°55'W
Frechen, Ger. (frĕ'κĕn)	157c	50°54'N	6°49'E
Fredericia, Den. (frĕdh-ĕ-rē'tsē-ȧ)	152	55°35'N	9°45'E
Frederick, Md., U.S. (frĕd'ēr-ĭk)	97	39°25'N	77°25'W
Frederick, Ok., U.S.	110	34°23'N	99°01'W
Frederick House, r., Can.	90	49°05'N	81°20'W
Fredericksburg, Tx., U.S. (frĕd'ēr-ĭkz-bûrg)	112	30°16'N	98°52'W
Fredericksburg, Va., U.S.	99	38°20'N	77°30'W
Fredericktown, Mo., U.S. (frĕd'ēr-ĭk-toun)	111	37°32'N	90°16'W
Fredericton, Can. (frĕd'-ēr-ĭk-tŭn)	85	45°48'N	66°39'W
Frederikshavn, Den. (frĕdh'ĕ-rĕks-houn)	146	57°27'N	10°31'E
Frederikssund, Den. (frĕdh'ĕ-rĕks-sōn)	152	55°51'N	12°04'E
Fredersdorf bei Berlin, Ger.	238a	52°31'N	13°44'E
Fredonia, Col. (frĕ-dō'nyȧ)	130a	5°55'N	75°40'W
Fredonia, Ks., U.S. (frē-dō'nĭ-ȧ)	111	36°31'N	95°50'W
Fredonia, N.Y., U.S.	99	42°25'N	79°20'W
Fredrikstad, Nor. (frĕdh'rĕks-städ)	146	59°14'N	10°58'E
Freeburg, Il., U.S. (frē'bûrg)	107e	38°26'N	89°59'W
Freehold, N.J., U.S. (frē'hōld)	100a	40°15'N	74°16'W
Freeland, Pa., U.S. (frē'lănd)	99	41°00'N	75°50'W
Freeland, Wa., U.S.	106a	48°01'N	122°32'W
Freels, Cape, c., Can. (frēlz)	93	46°37'N	53°45'W
Freelton, Can. (frēl'tŭn)	83d	43°24'N	80°02'W
Freeport, Bah.	122	26°30'N	78°45'W
Freeport, Il., U.S. (frē'pōrt)	97	42°19'N	89°30'W
Freeport, N.Y., U.S.	100a	40°39'N	73°35'W
Freeport, Tx., U.S.	113	28°56'N	95°21'W
Freetown, S.L. (frē'toun)	210	8°30'N	13°15'W
Fregenal de la Sierra, Spain (frā-hȧ-näl' dā lä syĕr'rä)	158	38°09'N	6°40'W
Fregene, Italy (frĕ-zhĕ'-nĕ)	159d	41°52'N	12°12'E
Freiberg, Ger. (frī'bĕrgh)	147	50°54'N	13°18'E
Freiburg, Ger.	147	48°00'N	7°50'E
Freienried, Ger. (frī'ĕn-rēd)	145d	48°20'N	11°08'E
Freirina, Chile (frā-ĭ-rē'nä)	132	28°35'S	71°26'W
Freisenbruch, neigh., Ger.	236	51°27'N	7°06'E
Freising, Ger. (frī'zĭng)	154	48°25'N	11°45'E
Fréjus, Fr. (frā-zhüs')	157	43°28'N	6°46'E
Fremantle, Austl. (frē'măn-t'l)	202	32°03'S	116°05'E
Fremont, Ca., U.S. (frē-mŏnt')	106b	37°33'N	122°00'W
Fremont, Mi., U.S.	98	43°25'N	85°55'W
Fremont, Ne., U.S.	102	41°26'N	96°30'W
Fremont, Oh., U.S.	98	41°20'N	83°05'W
Fremont, r., Ut., U.S.	109	38°20'N	111°30'W
Fremont Peak, mtn., Wy., U.S.	105	43°05'N	109°35'W
French Broad, r., Tn., U.S. (frĕnch brôd)	114	35°59'N	83°01'W
French Frigate Shoals, Hi., U.S.	94b	23°30'N	167°10'W
French Guiana, dep., S.A. (gē-ä'nä)	131	4°20'N	53°00'W
French Lick, In., U.S. (frĕnch lĭk)	98	38°35'N	86°35'W
Frenchman, r., N.A.	88	49°25'N	108°30'W
Frenchman Creek, r., Mt., U.S. (frĕnch-măn)	105	48°51'N	107°20'W
Frenchman Creek, r., Ne., U.S.	110	40°24'N	101°50'W
Frenchman Flat, Nv., U.S.	108	36°55'N	116°11'W
French Polynesia, dep., Oc.	2	15°00'S	140°00'W
French River, Mn., U.S.	107h	46°54'N	91°54'W
French's Forest, Austl.	243a	33°45'S	151°14'E

PLACE (Pronunciation)	PAGE	LAT.	LONG.
Freshfield, Eng., U.K.	237a	53°34'N	3°04'W
Freshfield, Mount, mtn., Can. (frĕsh'fēld)	87	51°44'N	116°57'W
Fresh Meadows, neigh., N.Y., U.S.	228	40°44'N	73°48'W
Fresnes, Fr.	237c	48°45'N	2°19'E
Fresnillo, Mex. (frås-nēl'yō)	116	23°10'N	102°52'W
Fresno, Col. (frĕs'nō)	130a	5°10'N	75°01'W
Fresno, Ca., U.S.	96	36°44'N	119°46'W
Fresno, r., Ca., U.S. (frĕz'nō)	108	37°00'N	120°24'W
Fresno Slough, Ca., U.S.	108	36°39'N	120°12'W
Freudenstadt, Ger. (froi'den-shtät)	154	48°28'N	8°26'E
Freycinet Peninsula, pen., Austl. (frā-sē-nĕ')	204	42°13'S	148°56'E
Fria, Gui.	214	10°05'N	13°32'W
Fria, r., Az., U.S. (frē-ä)	109	34°03'N	112°12'W
Fria, Cape, c., Nmb. (frĭȧ)	212	18°15'S	12°10'E
Friant-Kern Canal, can., Ca., U.S. (kûrn)	108	36°57'N	119°37'W
Frias, Arg. (frē-äs)	132	28°43'S	65°03'W
Fribourg, Switz. (frē-bōōr')	147	46°48'N	7°07'E
Fridley, Mn., U.S. (frĭd'lĭ)	107g	45°05'N	93°16'W
Friedberg, Ger. (frēd'bĕrgh)	145d	48°22'N	11°00'E
Friedenau, neigh., Ger.	238a	52°28'N	13°20'E
Friedland, Ger. (frēt'länt)	154	53°39'N	13°34'E
Friedrichsfeld, Ger.	236	51°38'N	6°39'E
Friedrichsfelde, neigh., Ger.	238a	52°31'N	13°31'E
Friedrichshafen, Ger. (frē-drĕks-häf'ĕn)	154	47°39'N	9°28'E
Friedrichshagen, neigh., Ger.	238a	52°27'N	13°38'E
Friedrichshain, neigh., Ger.	238a	52°31'N	13°27'E
Friemersheim, Ger.	236	51°23'N	6°42'E
Friend, Ne., U.S. (frĕnd)	111	40°40'N	97°16'W
Friends Colony, neigh., India	240d	28°34'N	77°16'E
Friendship International Airport, arpt., Md., U.S.	229c	39°11'N	76°40'W
Friendswood, Tx., U.S. (frĕnds'wŏd)	113a	29°31'N	95°11'W
Friern Barnet, neigh., Eng., U.K.	235	51°37'N	0°10'W
Fries, Va., U.S. (frēz)	115	36°42'N	80°59'W
Friesack, Ger. (frē'säk)	145b	52°44'N	12°35'E
Frillendorf, neigh., Ger.	236	51°28'N	7°05'E
Frio, Cabo, c., Braz. (kä'bō-frē'ō)	131	22°58'S	42°08'W
Frio R, Tx., U.S.	112	29°00'N	99°15'W
Frisian Islands, is., Neth. (frē'zhăn)	146	53°30'N	5°20'E
Friuli-Venezia Giulia, hist. reg., Italy	160	46°20'N	13°20'E
Frobisher Bay, b., Can.	85	62°49'N	66°41'W
Frobisher Lake, l., Can. (frŏb'ĭsh'ēr)	84	56°25'N	108°20'W
Frodsham, Eng., U.K. (frŏdz'ăm)	144a	53°18'N	2°48'W
Frohavet, b., Nor.	146	63°49'N	9°12'E
Frohnau, neigh., Ger.	238a	52°38'N	13°18'E
Frohnhausen, neigh., Ger.	236	51°27'N	6°58'E
Frome, Lake, l., Austl. (frōōm)	202	30°40'S	140°13'E
Frontenac, Ks., U.S. (frŏn'tē-năk)	111	37°27'N	94°41'W
Frontera, Mex. (frŏn-tā'rä)	119	18°34'N	92°38'W
Front Range, mts., Co., U.S. (frŭnt)	110	40°59'N	105°29'W
Front Royal, Va., U.S. (frŭnt)	99	38°55'N	78°10'W
Frosinone, Italy (frō-zē-nō'nā)	160	41°38'N	13°22'E
Frostburg, Md., U.S. (frôst'bûrg)	99	39°40'N	78°55'W
Fruita, Co., U.S. (frōōt-ȧ)	109	39°10'N	108°45'W
Frunze see Bishkek, Kyrg.	169	42°49'N	74°42'E
Fryanovo, Russia (f'ryä'nô-vô)	172b	56°08'N	38°28'E
Fryazino, Russia (f'ryä'zĭ-nô)	172b	55°58'N	38°05'E
Frydlant, Czech Rep. (frēd'länt)	154	50°56'N	15°05'E
Fryerning, Eng., U.K.	235	51°41'N	0°22'E
Fucheng, China (fōō-chŭŋ)	190	37°53'N	116°08'E
Fuchu, Japan (fōō'chōō)	195a	35°41'N	139°29'E
Fuchun, r., China (fōō-chōn)	193	29°50'N	120°00'E
Fuego, vol., Guat. (fwā'gō)	120	14°29'N	90°52'W
Fuencarral, Spain (fuān-kär-räl')	159a	40°29'N	3°42'W
Fuensalida, Spain (fwān-sä-lē'dä)	158	40°04'N	4°15'W
Fuente, Mex. (fwĕ'n-tĕ')	112	28°39'N	100°34'W
Fuente de Cantos, Spain (fwĕn'tå dā kän'tōs)	158	38°15'N	6°18'W
Fuente el Saz, Spain (fwĕn'tå ĕl säth')	159a	40°39'N	3°30'W
Fuenteobejuna, Spain	158	38°15'N	5°30'W
Fuentesaúco, Spain (fwĕn-tå-sä-ōō'kō)	158	41°18'N	5°25'W
Fuerte, Río del, r., Mex. (rē'ō-dĕl-fōō-ĕ'r-tĕ)	116	26°15'N	108°50'W
Fuerte Olimpo, Para. (fwĕr'tå ō-lēm-pō)	132	21°10'S	57°49'W
Fuerteventura Island, i., Spain (fwĕr'tå-vĕn-tōō'rä)	210	28°24'N	13°21'W
Fuhai, China	188	47°01'N	87°07'E
Fuhlenbrock, neigh., Ger.	236	51°32'N	6°54'E
Fuji, Japan (jōō'jē)	195	35°11'N	138°44'E
Fuji, r., Japan	195	35°20'N	138°23'E
Fujian, prov., China (fōō-jyĕn)	189	25°40'N	117°30'E
Fujidera, Japan	195b	34°34'N	135°37'E
Fujiidera, Japan	242b	34°34'N	135°36'E
Fujin, China (fōō-jyĭn)	189	47°13'N	132°11'E
Fuji San, mtn., Japan (fōō'jē sän)	189	35°23'N	138°44'E
Fujisawa, Japan (fōō'jē-sä'wä)	195a	35°20'N	139°29'E
Fujiyama see Fuji San, mtn., Japan	189	35°23'N	138°44'E
Fukagawa, neigh., Japan	242a	35°40'N	139°48'E
Fukiai, neigh., Japan	242b	34°42'N	135°12'E
Fukuchiyama, Japan (fōō'kō-chē-yä'ma)	195	35°18'N	135°07'E
Fukue, i., Japan (fō-kōō'ā)	194	32°40'N	129°02'E
Fukui, Japan (fōō'kōō-ē)	189	36°05'N	136°14'E
Fukuoka, Japan (fōō'kō-ō'kȧ)	189	33°35'N	130°23'E
Fukuoka, Japan	195a	35°52'N	139°31'E
Fukushima, Japan (fōō'kō-shē'mȧ)	194	37°45'N	140°29'E
Fukushima, neigh., Japan	242b	34°42'N	135°29'E
Fukuyama, Japan (fōō'kō-yä'mȧ)	194	34°31'N	133°21'E
Fulda, Ger.	147	50°33'N	9°41'E
Fulda, r., Ger. (fōl'dä)	154	51°05'N	9°40'E
Fulerum, neigh., Ger.	236	51°26'N	6°57'E
Fuling, China (fōō-lĭŋ)	188	29°40'N	107°30'E
Fullerton, Ca., U.S. (fōl'ēr-tŭn)	107a	33°53'N	117°56'W
Fullerton, La., U.S.	113	31°00'N	93°00'W
Fullerton, Ne., U.S.	102	41°21'N	97°59'W

PLACE (Pronunciation)	PAGE	LAT.	LONG.
Fulmer, Eng., U.K.	235	51°33'N	0°34'W
Fulton, Ky., U.S. (fŭl'tŭn)	114	36°30'N	88°53'W
Fulton, Mo., U.S.	111	38°51'N	91°56'W
Fulton, N.Y., U.S.	99	43°20'N	76°25'W
Fultondale, Al., U.S. (fŭl'tŭn-dāl)	100h	33°37'N	86°48'W
Funabashi, Japan (fōō'nȧ-bä'shē)	195	35°43'N	139°59'E
Funasaka, Japan	242b	34°49'N	135°17'E
Funaya, Japan (fōō-nä'yä)	195b	34°45'N	135°52'E
Funchal, Port. (fŏn-shäl')	210	32°41'N	16°15'W
Fundación, Col. (fōōn-dä-syō'n)	130	10°43'N	74°13'W
Fundão, Port. (fŏn-douɴ')	158	40°08'N	7°32'W
Fundão, Ilha do, i., Braz.	234c	22°51'S	43°14'W
Funde, India	240e	18°54'N	72°58'E
Fundy, Bay of, b., Can. (fŭn'dĭ)	85	45°00'N	66°00'W
Fundy National Park, rec., Can.	85	45°38'N	65°00'W
Funing, China	190	39°55'N	119°16'E
Funing, China (fōō-nĭŋ)	192	33°55'N	119°54'E
Funing Wan, b., China	193	26°48'N	120°35'E
Funtua, Nig.	215	11°31'N	7°17'E
Furancungo, Moz.	217	14°55'S	33°35'E
Furbero, Mex. (fōōr-bĕ'rô)	119	20°21'N	97°32'W
Furgun, mtn., Iran	182	28°47'N	57°00'E
Furmanov, Russia (fûr-mä'nôf)	166	57°14'N	41°11'E
Furnas, Reprêsa de, res., Braz.	131	21°00'S	46°00'W
Furneaux Group, is., Austl. (fûr'nō)	203	40°15'S	146°27'E
Fürstenfeld, Aus. (für'stĕn-fĕlt)	154	47°02'N	16°03'E
Fürstenfeldbruck, Ger. (fur'stĕn-fĕld'brōōk)	145d	48°11'N	11°16'E
Fürstenwalde, Ger. (für'stĕn-väl-dĕ)	154	52°21'N	14°04'E
Fürth, Ger. (fürt)	147	49°28'N	11°03'E
Furuichi, Japan (fōō'rō-ĕ'chē)	195b	34°33'N	135°37'E
Fusa, Japan (fōō'sä)	195a	35°52'N	140°08'E
Fuse, Japan	195b	34°40'N	135°33'E
Fushimi, Japan (fōō'shē-mē)	195b	34°57'N	135°47'E
Fushun, China (fōō'shōōn')	189	41°50'N	124°00'E
Fusong, China (fōō-sôŋ)	192	42°12'N	127°12'E
Futatsubashi, Japan	242a	35°29'N	139°30'E
Futtsu, Japan (fōō'tsōō')	195a	35°19'N	139°49'E
Futtsu Misaki, c., Japan (fōōt'tsōō' mē-sä'kē)	195a	35°19'N	139°46'E
Fuwah, Egypt (fōō'wȧ)	218b	31°13'N	30°35'E
Fuxian, China (fōō shyĕn)	190	39°36'N	121°59'E
Fuxin, China (fōō-shyĭn)	192	42°05'N	121°40'E
Fuyang, China (fōō-yäŋ)	189	32°53'N	115°48'E
Fuyang, China	193	30°10'N	119°58'E
Fuyang, r., China (fōō-yäŋ)	190	36°59'N	114°48'E
Fuyu, China (fōō-yōō)	189	45°20'N	125°00'E
Fuzhou, China (fōō-jō)	189	26°02'N	119°18'E
Fuzhou, r., China	190	39°38'N	121°43'E
Fuzhoucheng, China (fōō-jō-chŭŋ)	190	39°46'N	121°44'E
Fyfield, Eng., U.K.	235	51°45'N	0°16'E
Fyn, i., Den. (fü''n)	152	55°24'N	10°33'E
Fyne, Loch, l., Scot., U.K. (fīn)	150	56°14'N	5°10'W
Fyresvatn, l., Nor.	152	59°04'N	7°55'E

G

PLACE (Pronunciation)	PAGE	LAT.	LONG.
Gaalkacyo, Som.	218a	7°00'N	47°30'E
Gabela, Ang.	216	10°48'S	14°20'E
Gabès, Tun. (gä'bĕs)	210	33°51'N	10°04'E
Gabès, Golfe de, b., Tun.	210	32°22'N	10°59'E
Gabil, Chad	215	11°09'N	18°12'E
Gąbin, Pol. (gôɴ'bēn)	155	52°23'N	19°47'E
Gabon, nation, Afr. (gȧ-bôɴ')	212	0°30'S	10°45'E
Gaborone, Bots.	212	24°28'S	25°59'E
Gabriel, r., Tx., U.S. (gā'brĭ-ĕl)	113	30°38'N	97°15'W
Gabrovo, Bul. (gäb'rô-vō)	161	42°52'N	25°19'E
Gachsārān, Iran	185	30°12'N	50°47'E
Gacko, Bos. (gäts'kô)	161	43°10'N	18°34'E
Gadsden, Al., U.S. (gădz'dĕn)	97	34°00'N	86°00'W
Găeşti, Rom. (gä-yĕsh'tē)	161	44°43'N	25°21'E
Gaeta, Italy (gä-ā'tä)	160	41°18'N	13°34'E
Gaffney, S.C., U.S. (găf'nĭ)	115	35°04'N	81°47'W
Gafsa, Tun. (găf'sä)	210	34°16'N	8°37'E
Gagarin, Russia	162	55°32'N	34°58'E
Gagnoa, C. Iv.	214	6°08'N	5°56'W
Gagny, Fr.	237c	48°53'N	2°32'E
Gagra, Geor.	168	43°20'N	40°15'E
Gahmen, neigh., Ger.	236	51°36'N	7°32'E
Gaillac-sur-Tarn, Fr. (gȧ-yăk'sür-tärn')	156	43°54'N	1°52'E
Gaillard Cut, reg., Pan. (gä-ēl-yä'rd)	116a	9°03'N	79°42'W
Gainesville, Fl., U.S. (gānz'vĭl)	97	29°40'N	82°20'W
Gainesville, Ga., U.S.	114	34°16'N	83°48'W
Gainesville, Tx., U.S.	111	33°38'N	97°08'W
Gainsborough, Eng., U.K. (gānz'bŭr-ô)	144a	53°23'N	0°46'W
Gairdner, Lake, l., Austl. (gârd'nēr)	202	32°20'S	136°30'E
Gaithersburg, Md., U.S. (gā'thērs'bûrg)	100e	39°08'N	77°13'W
Gaixian, China (gī-shyĕn)	192	40°25'N	122°20'E
Galana, r., Kenya	217	3°00'S	39°30'E
Galapagar, Spain (gä-lä-pä-gär')	159a	40°36'N	4°00'W
Galapagos Islands see Colón, Archipiélago de, is., Ec.	130	0°10'S	87°45'W
Galaria, r., Italy	159d	41°58'N	12°21'E
Galashiels, Scot., U.K. (găl-ȧ-shēlz)	150	55°40'N	2°57'W
Galata, neigh., Tur.	239f	41°01'N	28°58'E
Galați, Rom.	142	45°25'N	28°05'E
Galatina, Italy (gä-lä-tē'nä)	161	40°10'N	18°12'E
Galátsion, Grc.	239d	38°01'N	23°45'E
Galaxídhion, Grc.	161	38°26'N	22°22'E
Galdhøpiggen, mtn., Nor.	152	61°37'N	8°17'E
Galeana, Mex. (gä-lā-ā'nä)	112	24°50'N	100°04'W

PLACE (Pronunciation)	PAGE	LAT.	LONG.
Galena, Il., U.S. (gȧ-lē'nȧ)	103	42°26'N	90°27'W
Galena, In., U.S.	101h	38°21'N	85°55'W
Galena Peak, mtn., Tx., U.S.	113a	29°44'N	95°14'W
Galera, Cerro, mtn., Pan. (sĕ'r-rô-gä-lĕ'rä)	116a	8°55'N	79°38'W
Galeras, vol., Col. (gä-lĕ'räs)	130	0°57'N	77°27'W
Gales, r., Or., U.S. (gālz)	106c	45°33'N	123°11'W
Galesburg, Il., U.S. (gālz'bûrg)	97	40°56'N	90°21'W
Galesville, Wi., U.S. (gālz'vĭl)	103	44°04'N	91°22'W
Galeton, Pa., U.S. (gā'l'tŭn)	99	41°45'N	77°40'W
Galich, Russia (gȧl'ĭch)	166	58°20'N	42°38'E
Galicia, hist. reg., Pol. (gȧ-lĭsh'ĭ-ȧ)	155	49°48'N	21°05'E
Galicia, hist. reg., Spain (gä-lē'thyä)	158	43°35'N	8°03'W
Galilee, l., Austl. (găl'ĭ-lē)	203	22°23'S	145°09'E
Galilee, Sea of, l., Isr.	181a	32°53'N	35°45'E
Galina Point, c., Jam. (gä-lē'nä)	122	18°25'N	76°50'W
Galion, Oh., U.S. (găl'ĭ-ŭn)	98	40°45'N	82°50'W
Galisteo, N.M., U.S. (gä-lĭs-tā'ō)	110	35°20'N	106°00'W
Gallarate, Italy (gäl-lä-rä'tä)	160	45°37'N	8°48'E
Gallardon, Fr. (gä-lär-dôɴ')	157b	48°31'N	1°40'E
Gallatin, Mo., U.S. (găl'ȧ-tĭn)	111	39°55'N	93°58'W
Gallatin, Tn., U.S.	114	36°23'N	86°28'W
Gallatin, r., Mt., U.S.	105	45°12'N	111°10'W
Galle, Sri L. (gäl)	183b	6°13'N	80°10'E
Gállego, r., Spain (gäl-yā'gō)	159	42°27'N	0°37'W
Gallinas, Punta de, c., Col. (gä-lyē'näs)	130	12°10'N	72°10'W
Gallipoli, Italy (gäl-lē'pô-lē)	161	40°03'N	17°58'E
Gallipoli see Gelibolu, Tur.	149	40°25'N	26°40'E
Gallipoli Peninsula, pen., Tur.	161	40°23'N	25°10'E
Gallipolis, Oh., U.S. (găl-ĭ-pō-lēs)	98	38°50'N	82°10'W
Gällivare, Swe. (yĕl-ĭ-vär'ĕ)	146	68°06'N	20°29'E
Gallo, r., Spain (gäl'yō)	158	40°43'N	1°42'W
Gallup, N.M., U.S. (găl'ŭp)	96	35°30'N	108°45'W
Galty Mountains, mts., Ire.	150	52°19'N	8°20'W
Galva, Il., U.S. (găl'vȧ)	111	41°11'N	90°02'W
Galveston, Tx., U.S. (găl'vĕs-tŭn)	97	29°18'N	94°48'W
Galveston Bay, b., Tx., U.S.	97	29°39'N	94°45'W
Galveston I, Tx., U.S.	113a	29°12'N	94°53'W
Galvin, Austl.	243b	37°51'S	144°49'E
Galway, Ire.	142	53°16'N	9°05'W
Galway Bay, b., Ire. (gôl'wā)	150	53°10'N	9°47'W
Gamba, China (gäm-bä)	186	28°23'N	89°42'E
Gambaga, Ghana (gäm-bä'gä)	210	10°32'N	0°26'W
Gambela, Eth. (găm-bā'lȧ)	211	8°15'N	34°33'E
Gambia (Gambie), r., Afr.	214	13°20'N	15°55'W
Gambia, The, nation, Afr.	210	13°38'N	19°38'W
Gambie, r., Afr.	210	12°30'N	13°00'W
Gamboma, Congo (gäm-bō'mä)	212	1°53'S	15°51'E
Gamleby, Swe. (gäm'lĕ-bü)	152	57°54'N	16°20'E
Gan, r., China (gän)	193	26°50'N	115°00'E
Gäncä, Azer.	166	40°40'N	46°22'E
Gandak, r., India	186	26°37'N	84°22'E
Gander, Can. (găn'dĕr)	85	48°57'N	54°34'W
Gander, r., Can.	93	49°10'N	54°35'W
Gander Lake, l., Can.	93	48°55'N	55°40'W
Gandhinagar, India	186	23°30'N	72°47'E
Gandi, Nig.	215	12°55'N	5°49'E
Gandía, Spain (gän-dē'ä)	159	38°56'N	0°10'W
Gangdisê Shan (Trans Himalayas), mts., China	188	30°25'N	83°43'E
Ganges, r., Asia (găn'jēz)	183	24°00'N	89°30'E
Ganges, Mouths of the, mth., Asia (găn'jēz)	183	21°18'N	88°40'E
Gangi, Italy (gän'jē)	160	37°48'N	14°15'E
Gangtok, India	183	27°15'N	88°30'E
Gannan, China (gän-nän)	192	47°50'N	123°30'E
Gannett Peak, mtn., Wy., U.S. (găn'ĕt)	96	43°10'N	109°38'W
Gano, Oh., U.S. (g'nō)	101f	39°18'N	84°24'W
Gänserndorf, Aus.	145e	48°21'N	16°43'E
Gansu, prov., China (gän-sōō)	188	38°50'N	101°10'E
Ganwo, Nig.	215	11°13'N	4°42'E
Ganyu, China (gän-yōō)	190	34°52'N	119°07'E
Ganzhou, China (gän-jō)	189	25°50'N	114°30'E
Gao, Mali (gä'ō)	210	16°16'N	0°03'W
Gao'an, China (gou-än)	193	28°30'N	115°02'E
Gaobaita, China	240b	39°53'N	116°30'E
Gaobeidian, China	240b	39°54'N	116°33'E
Gaomi, China (gou-mē)	190	36°23'N	119°46'E
Gaoqiao, China (gou-chyou)	191b	31°21'N	121°35'E
Gaoshun, China (gou-shòn)	190	31°22'N	118°50'E
Gaotang, China (gou-täŋ)	190	36°52'N	116°12'E
Gaoyao, China (gou-you)	193	23°08'N	112°25'E
Gaoyi, China (gou-yē)	190	37°37'N	114°39'E
Gaoyou, China (gou-yō)	192	32°46'N	119°26'E
Gaoyou Hu, l., China (kä'ō-yōō'hōō)	189	32°42'N	118°40'E
Gap, Fr. (gȧp)	147	44°34'N	6°08'E
Gapan, Phil. (gä-pän)	197a	15°18'N	120°56'E
Gar, China	188	31°11'N	80°35'E
Garanhuns, Braz. (gä-rän-yòɴsh')	131	8°49'S	36°28'W
Garbagnate Milanese, Italy	238c	45°35'N	9°05'E
Garbatella, neigh., Italy	239c	41°52'N	12°29'E
Garber, Ok., U.S. (gȧr'bĕr)	111	36°28'N	97°35'W
Garches, Fr.	237c	48°51'N	2°11'E
Garching, Ger. (gär'ĸēng)	145d	48°15'N	11°39'E
Garcia, Mex. (gär-sē'ä)	112	25°50'N	100°37'W
García de la Cadena, Mex.	118	21°14'N	103°26'W
Garda, Lago di, l., Italy (lä-gō-dē-gär'dä)	148	45°43'N	10°26'E
Gardanne, Fr. (gȧr-dȧn')	156a	43°28'N	5°29'E
Gardelegen, Ger. (gär-dē-lā'ghĕn)	154	52°32'N	11°22'E
Garden, i., Mi., U.S. (gär'd'n)	98	45°50'N	85°50'W
Gardena, Ca., U.S. (gär-dē'nȧ)	107a	33°53'N	118°19'W
Garden City, Ks., U.S.	110	37°58'N	100°52'W
Garden City, Mi., U.S.	101b	42°20'N	83°21'W
Garden City, N.Y., U.S.	228	40°43'N	73°37'W
Garden City Park, N.Y., U.S.	228	40°44'N	73°40'W
Garden Grove, Ca., U.S. (gär'd'n grōv)	107a	33°47'N	117°56'W
Garden Reach, India	186a	22°33'N	88°17'E
Garden River, Can.	107k	46°33'N	84°10'W
Gardēz, Afg.	186	33°43'N	69°09'E
Gardiner, Me., U.S. (gärd'nĕr)	92	44°12'N	69°46'W
Gardiner, Mt., U.S.	105	45°03'N	110°43'W
Gardiner, Wa., U.S.	106a	48°03'N	122°55'W
Gardiner Dam, dam, Can.	88	51°17'N	106°51'W
Gardner, Ma., U.S.	99	42°35'N	72°00'W
Gardner Canal, strt., Can.	86	53°28'N	128°15'W
Gardner Pinnacles, Hi., U.S.	94b	25°10'N	167°00'W
Gareloi, i., Ak., U.S. (gär-lōō-ä')	95a	51°40'N	178°48'W
Garenfeld, Ger.	236	51°24'N	7°31'E
Garfield, N.J., U.S. (gär'fēld)	100a	40°53'N	74°06'W
Garfield, Ut., U.S.	107b	40°45'N	112°10'W
Garfield Heights, Oh., U.S.	101d	41°25'N	81°36'W
Gargaliánoi, Grc. (gȧr-gä-lyä'nē)	161	37°07'N	21°50'E
Garges-lès-Gonesse, Fr.	237c	48°58'N	2°25'E
Gargždai, Lith. (gärgzh'dī)	153	55°43'N	20°09'E
Garibaldi, Mount, mtn., Can. (gâr-ĭ-băl'dē)	86	49°51'N	123°01'W
Garin, Arg. (gä-rē'n)	132a	34°25'S	58°44'W
Garissa, Kenya	217	0°28'S	39°38'E
Garland, Md., U.S.	229c	39°11'N	76°39'W
Garland, Tx., U.S. (gär'lănd)	107c	32°55'N	96°39'W
Garland, Ut., U.S.	105	41°45'N	112°10'W
Garm, Taj.	169	39°12'N	70°28'E
Garmisch-Partenkirchen, Ger. (gär'mēsh pär'tĕn-kĕr'ĸĕn)	154	47°38'N	11°10'E
Garnett, Ks., U.S. (gär'nĕt)	111	38°16'N	95°15'W
Garonne, r., Fr. (gȧ-rôn)	142	44°00'N	1°00'E
Garoua, Cam. (gär'wä)	211	9°18'N	13°24'E
Garrett, In., U.S. (găr'ĕt)	98	41°20'N	85°10'W
Garrison, Md., U.S.	229c	39°24'N	76°45'W
Garrison, N.Y., U.S. (găr'ĭ-sŭn)	100a	41°23'N	73°57'W
Garrison, N.D., U.S.	102	47°38'N	101°24'W
Garrovillas, Spain (gä-rô-vēl'yäs)	158	39°42'N	6°30'W
Garry, l., Can. (găr'ĭ)	84	66°16'N	99°23'W
Garsen, Kenya	217	2°16'S	40°07'E
Garson, Can.	91	46°34'N	80°52'W
Garstedt, Ger. (gär'shtĕt)	145c	53°40'N	9°58'E
Garston, Eng., U.K.	235	51°41'N	0°23'W
Garston, neigh., Eng., U.K.	237a	53°21'N	2°53'W
Gartenstadt, neigh., Ger.	236	51°30'N	7°26'E
Garulia, India	186a	22°48'N	88°23'E
Garwolin, Pol. (gär-vō'lēn)	155	51°54'N	21°40'E
Garwood, N.J., U.S.	228	40°39'N	74°19'W
Gary, In., U.S. (gā'rĭ)	97	41°35'N	87°21'W
Gary, W.V., U.S. (fĭl'bĕrt)	115	37°21'N	81°33'W
Garzón, Col. (gär-thōn')	130	2°13'N	75°44'W
Gasan, Phil. (gä-sän')	197a	13°19'N	121°52'E
Gasan-Kuli, Turk.	170	37°25'N	53°55'E
Gas City, In., U.S. (găs)	98	40°30'N	85°40'W
Gascogne, reg., Fr. (gäs-kôn'yĕ)	156	43°45'N	1°49'W
Gasconade, r., Mo., U.S. (găs-kô-nād')	111	37°46'N	92°15'W
Gascoyne, r., Austl. (găs-koin')	202	25°15'S	117°00'E
Gashland, Mo., U.S. (găsh'-lănd)	107f	39°15'N	94°35'W
Gashua, Nig.	215	12°54'N	11°00'E
Gasny, Fr. (gäs-nē')	157b	49°05'N	1°36'E
Gaspé, Can.	85	48°50'N	64°29'W
Gaspé, Péninsule de, pen., Can.	85	48°30'N	65°00'W
Gasper Hernández, Dom. Rep. (gäs-pär' ĕr-nän'dāth)	123	19°40'N	70°15'W
Gassaway, W.V., U.S. (găs'ȧ-wā)	98	38°40'N	80°45'W
Gaston, Or., U.S. (găs'tŭn)	106c	45°26'N	123°08'W
Gastonia, N.C., U.S. (găs-tō'nĭ-ȧ)	115	35°15'N	81°14'W
Gastre, Arg. (gäs-trĕ)	132	42°12'S	68°50'W
Gata, Cabo de, c., Spain (kȧ'bô-dĕ-gä'tä)	148	36°42'N	2°00'W
Gata, Sierra de, mts., Spain (syĕr'rȧ dā gä'tä)	148	40°12'N	6°39'W
Gatchina, Russia (gä-chē'nȧ)	166	59°33'N	30°08'E
Gateacre, neigh., Eng., U.K.	237a	53°23'N	2°51'W
Gátes, Akrotírion, c., Cyp.	181a	34°30'N	33°15'E
Gateshead, Eng., U.K. (gāts'hĕd)	150	54°56'N	1°38'W
Gates of the Arctic National Park, rec., Ak., U.S.	95	67°45'N	153°30'W
Gatesville, Tx., U.S. (gāts'vĭl)	113	31°26'N	97°34'W
Gateway of India, hist., India	240e	18°55'N	72°50'E
Gâtine, Hauteurs de, hills, Fr.	156	46°40'N	0°50'W
Gatineau, Can. (gȧ'tē-nō)	83c	45°29'N	75°38'W
Gatineau, r., Can.	91	45°45'N	75°50'W
Gatineau, Parc de la, rec., Can.	91	45°32'N	75°53'W
Gatley, Eng., U.K.	237b	53°23'N	2°14'W
Gato Negro, Ven.	234a	10°33'N	66°57'W
Gattendorf, Aus.	145e	48°01'N	17°00'E
Gatun, Pan. (gä-tōōn')	121	9°16'N	79°25'W
Gatun, r., Pan.	116a	9°21'N	79°40'W
Gatún, Lago, l., Pan.	121	9°13'N	79°24'W
Gatun Locks, trans., Pan.	116a	9°16'N	79°57'W
Gauhāti, India	183	26°09'N	91°51'E
Gauja, r., Lat. (gȧ'ò-yȧ)	153	57°10'N	24°30'E
Gaula, r., Nor.	152	62°55'N	10°45'E
Gāvānpada, India	240e	18°57'N	73°01'E
Gávdhos, i., Grc. (gäv'dôs)	149	34°48'N	24°08'E
Gavins Point Dam, Ne., U.S. (gă'-vĭns)	102	42°47'N	97°47'W
Gāvkhūnī, Bātlāq-e, l., Iran	182	31°40'N	52°48'E
Gävle, Swe. (yĕv'lĕ)	142	60°40'N	17°07'E
Gävlebukten, b., Swe.	152	60°45'N	17°30'E
Gavrilov Posad, Russia (gȧ'vrê-lôf'ka po-sȧt)	162	56°34'N	40°09'E
Gavrilov-Yam, Russia (gȧ'vrê-lôf yäm')	162	57°17'N	39°49'E
Gawler, Austl. (gô'lĕr)	202	34°35'S	138°47'E
Gawler Ranges, mts., Austl.	204	32°35'S	136°30'E
Gaya, India (gŭ'yä)(gī'ȧ)	183	24°53'N	85°00'E
Gaya, Nig. (gä'yä)	210	11°58'N	9°05'E
Gaylord, Mi., U.S. (gā'lôrd)	98	45°00'N	84°35'W
Gayndah, Austl. (gān'däh)	204	25°43'S	151°33'E
Gayton, Eng., U.K.	237a	53°19'N	3°06'W
Gaza, Gaza	182	31°30'N	34°29'E
Gaziantep, Tur. (gä-zē-än'tĕp)	182	37°10'N	37°30'E
Gbarnga, Lib.	214	7°00'N	9°29'W
Gdańsk, Pol. (g'dänsk)	142	54°20'N	18°40'E
Gdov, Russia (g'dôf')	166	58°44'N	27°51'E
Gdynia, Pol. (g'dēn'yȧ)	146	54°29'N	18°30'E
Geary, Ok., U.S. (gē'rĭ)	110	35°36'N	98°19'W
Géba, r., Gui.-B.	214	12°25'N	14°35'W
Gebo, Wy., U.S. (gĕb'ō)	105	43°49'N	108°13'W
Ged, La., U.S. (gĕd)	113	30°07'N	93°36'W
Gediz, r., Tur.	149	38°44'N	28°45'E
Gedney, i., Wa., U.S. (gĕd-nē)	106a	48°01'N	122°18'W
Gedser, Den.	152	54°35'N	12°08'E
Gee Cross, Eng., U.K.	237b	53°26'N	2°04'W
Geel, Bel.	145a	51°09'N	5°01'E
Geelong, Austl. (jē-lông')	203	38°06'S	144°13'E
Gegu, China (gŭ-gōō)	190	39°00'N	117°30'E
Ge Hu, l., China (gŭ hōō)	190	31°37'N	119°57'E
Geidam, Nig.	210	12°57'N	11°57'E
Geikie Range, mts., Austl. (gē'kē)	202	17°35'S	125°32'E
Geislingen, Ger. (gis'lĭng-ĕn)	154	48°37'N	9°52'E
Geist Reservoir, res., In., U.S. (gēst)	101g	39°57'N	85°59'W
Geita, Tan.	217	2°52'S	32°10'E
Gejiu, China (gŭ-jīo)	193	23°32'N	102°50'E
Geldermalsen, Neth.	145a	51°53'N	5°18'E
Geldern, Ger. (gĕl'dĕrn)	157c	51°31'N	6°20'E
Gelibolu, Tur. (gĕl-lē'pô-lē)(gĕ-lĭb'ō-lò)	149	40°25'N	26°40'E
Gellep-Stratum, neigh., Ger.	236	51°20'N	6°41'E
Gellibrand, Point, c., Austl.	243b	37°52'S	144°54'E
Gelsenkirchen, Ger. (gĕl-zĕn-kĭrk-ĕn)	154	51°31'N	7°05'E
Gemas, Malay. (jĕm'ās)	181b	2°35'N	102°37'E
Gemena, D.R.C.	211	3°15'N	19°46'E
Gemlik, Tur. (gĕm'lĭk)	149	40°30'N	29°10'E
Genale (Jubba), r., Afr.	218a	5°15'N	41°00'E
General Alvear, Arg. (gĕ-nĕ-räl'äl-vĕ-ä'r)	129c	36°04'S	60°02'W
General Arenales, Arg. (ä-rē-nä'lĕs)	129c	34°19'S	61°16'W
General Belgrano, Arg. (bĕl-grá'nô)	129c	35°45'S	58°32'W
General Cepeda, Mex. (sĕ-pĕ'dä)	112	25°24'N	101°29'W
General Conesa, Arg. (kô-nĕ'sä)	129c	36°30'S	57°19'W
General Guido, Arg. (gē'dô)	129c	36°41'S	57°48'W
General Lavalle, Arg. (lá-vá'l-yĕ)	129c	36°25'S	56°55'W
General Madariaga, Arg. (män-dä-rēä'gä)	132	36°59'S	57°14'W
General Pacheco, Arg.	233d	34°28'S	58°37'W
General Paz, Arg. (pá'z)	129c	35°30'S	58°20'W
General Pedro Antonio Santos, Mex.	118	21°37'N	98°58'W
General Pico, Arg. (pē'kô)	132	36°46'S	63°44'W
General Roca, Arg. (rô-kä)	132	39°01'S	67°31'W
General San Martín, Arg. (sän-mår-tē'n)	132a	34°35'S	58°32'W
General Sarmiento (San Miguel), Arg.	132a	34°33'S	58°43'W
General Urquiza, neigh., Arg.	233d	34°34'S	58°29'W
General Viamonte, Arg. (vēä'môn-tĕ)	129c	35°01'S	60°59'W
General Zuazua, Mex. (zwä'zwä)	112	25°54'N	100°07'W
Genesee, r., N.Y., U.S. (jĕn-ē-sē')	99	42°25'N	78°10'W
Geneseo, Il., U.S. (jē-nĕsēō)	98	41°28'N	90°11'W
Geneva (Genève), Switz.	142	46°14'N	6°04'E
Geneva, Al., U.S. (jē-nē'vȧ)	114	31°03'N	85°50'W
Geneva, Il., U.S.	101a	41°53'N	88°18'W
Geneva, Ne., U.S.	111	40°32'N	97°37'W
Geneva, N.Y., U.S.	99	42°50'N	77°00'W
Geneva, Oh., U.S.	98	41°45'N	80°55'W
Geneva, Lake, l., Switz.	147	46°28'N	6°30'E
Genève see Geneva, Switz.	142	46°14'N	6°04'E
Genil, r., Spain (hå-nēl')	158	37°15'N	4°05'W
Gennebreck, Ger.	236	51°19'N	7°12'E
Gennevilliers, Fr.	237c	48°56'N	2°18'E
Genoa, Italy	142	44°23'N	9°52'E
Genoa, Ne., U.S. (jen'ō-ȧ)	111	41°26'N	97°43'W
Genoa City, Wi., U.S.	101a	42°31'N	88°19'W
Genova, Golfo di, b., Italy (gòl-fô-dē-jĕn'ō-vä)	142	44°10'N	8°45'E
Genovesa, i., Ec. (ĕ's-lä-gē-nō-vĕ-sä)	130	0°08'N	90°15'W
Gent, Bel.	147	51°05'N	3°40'E
Genthin, Ger. (gĕn-tēn')	154	52°24'N	12°10'E
Gentilly, Fr.	237c	48°49'N	2°21'E
Genzano di Roma, Italy (gzhĕnt-zä'-nô-dē-rô'mä)	159d	41°43'N	12°49'E
Geographe Bay, b., Austl. (jē-ō-grăf')	202	33°00'S	114°00'E
Geographe Channel, strt., Austl. (jēō'grä-fĭk)	202	24°15'S	112°50'E
George, l., N.Y., U.S. (jôrj)	99	43°40'N	73°30'W
George, Lake, l., N.A. (jôrg)	107k	46°26'N	84°09'W
George, Lake, l., Ug.	217	0°02'N	30°25'E
George, Lake, l., Fl., U.S. (jôr-ĭj)	115	29°10'N	81°50'W
George, Lake, l., In., U.S.	101a	41°31'N	87°17'W
Georges, r., Austl.	201b	33°57'S	151°00'E
Georges Hall, Austl.	243a	33°55'S	150°59'E
George Town, Bah.	123	23°30'N	75°50'W
Georgetown, Can. (jôrg-toun)	83d	43°39'N	79°56'W
Georgetown, Can. (jôr-ĭj-toun)	93	46°11'N	62°32'W
George Town, Cay. Is.	122	19°20'N	81°20'W
Georgetown, Guy. (jôrj'toun)	131	7°45'N	58°04'W
George Town, Malay.	196	5°21'N	100°09'E
Georgetown, Ct., U.S.	100a	41°15'N	73°25'W
Georgetown, De., U.S.	99	38°40'N	75°20'W
Georgetown, Il., U.S.	98	40°00'N	87°40'W
Georgetown, Ky., U.S.	98	38°10'N	84°35'W
Georgetown, Md., U.S.	99	39°25'N	75°55'W
Georgetown, Ma., U.S. (jôrg-toun)	93a	42°43'N	71°00'W
Georgetown, S.C., U.S. (jôr-ĭj-toun)	115	33°22'N	79°17'W
Georgetown, Tx., U.S. (jôrg-toun)	113	30°37'N	97°40'W
Georgetown, neigh., D.C., U.S.	229d	38°54'N	77°03'W
Georgetown University, pt. of i., D.C., U.S.	229d	38°54'N	77°04'W
George Washington Birthplace National Monument, rec., Va., U.S. (jôrj wŏsh'ĭng-tŭn)	99	38°10'N	77°00'W
George Washington Carver National Monument, rec., Mo., U.S. (jôrg wăsh-ĭng-tŭn kär'vĕr)	111	36°58'N	94°21'W
George West, Tx., U.S.	112	28°20'N	98°07'W
Georgia, nation, Asia	164	42°17'N	43°00'E

ng-sing; ŋ-baŋk; ɴ-nasalized n; nŏd; cŏmmit; ōld; ôbey; ôrder; oi-boil; fōōd; ò-as oo in foot; ou-out; s-soft; sh-dish; th-thin; pūre; ûnite; ûrn; stŭd; circŭs; ü-as in French tu; '-indeterminate vowel.

290 Georgia–Gooseberry Creek

PLACE (Pronunciation)	PAGE	LAT.	LONG.
Georgia, state, U.S. (jôr′ji-ă)	97	32°40′N	83°50′W
Georgia, Strait of, strt., N.A.	86	49°20′N	124°00′W
Georgiana, Al., U.S. (jôr-jē-ăn′ȧ)	114	31°39′N	86°44′W
Georgian Bay, b., Can.	85	45°15′N	80°50′W
Georgian Bay Islands National Park, rec., Can.	90	45°20′N	81°40′W
Georgina, r., Austl. (jôr-jē′nȧ)	202	22°00′S	138°15′E
Georgiyevsk, Russia (gyôr-gyĕfsk′)	167	44°05′N	43°30′E
Gera, Ger. (gā′rä)	147	50°52′N	12°06′E
Geral, Serra, mts., Braz. (sĕr′rȧ zhȧ-räl′)	132	28°30′S	51°00′W
Geral de Goiás, Serra, mts., Braz. (zhȧ-räl′-dĕ-gô-yá′s)	131	14°22′S	45°40′W
Geraldton, Austl. (jĕr′ăld-tŭn)	202	28°40′S	114°35′E
Geraldton, Can.	85	49°43′N	87°00′W
Gerdview, S. Afr.	244b	26°10′S	28°11′E
Gérgal, Spain (gĕr′gäl)	158	37°08′N	2°29′W
Gering, Ne., U.S. (gē′rĭng)	102	41°49′N	103°41′W
Gerlachovský štít, mtn., Slvk.	155	49°12′N	20°08′E
Gerli, neigh., Arg.	233d	34°41′S	58°23′W
Germantown, Oh., U.S. (jûr′mȧn-toun)	98	39°35′N	84°25′W
Germantown, neigh., Pa., U.S.	229b	40°03′N	75°11′W
Germany, nation, Eur. (jûr′mȧ-nĭ)	142	51°00′N	10°00′E
Germiston, S. Afr. (jûr′mĭs-tŭn)	212	26°19′S	28°11′E
Gerona, Phil. (hā-rō′nä)	197a	15°36′N	120°36′E
Gerrards Cross, Eng., U.K. (jĕrȧrds krŏs)	144b	51°34′N	0°33′W
Gers, r., Fr. (zhĕr)	159	43°25′N	0°30′E
Gersthofen, Ger. (gĕrst-hō′fĕn)	145d	48°26′N	10°54′E
Getafe, Spain (hä-tä′fā)	158	40°19′N	3°44′W
Gettysburg, Pa., U.S. (gĕt′ĭs-bûrg)	99	39°50′N	77°15′W
Gettysburg, S.D., U.S.	102	45°01′N	99°59′W
Getzville, N.Y., U.S.	230a	43°01′N	78°46′W
Gevelsberg, Ger. (gĕ-fĕls′bĕrgh)	157c	51°18′N	7°20′E
Geweke, neigh., Ger.	236	51°22′N	7°25′E
Ghāghra, r., India	183	26°00′N	83°00′E
Ghana, nation, Afr. (gän′ä)	210	8°00′N	2°00′W
Ghanzi, Bots. (gän′zē)	212	21°30′S	22°00′E
Ghārāpuri, India	240e	18°57′N	72°56′E
Ghardaïa, Alg. (gär-dä′ē-ä)	210	32°29′N	3°38′E
Gharo, Pak.	186	24°50′N	68°35′E
Ghāt, Libya	210	24°52′N	10°16′E
Ghātkopar, neigh., India	240e	19°05′N	72°54′E
Ghazāl, Bahr al-, r., Sudan	211	9°30′N	30°00′E
Ghazal, Bahr el, r., Chad (bär ĕl ghä-zäl′)	215	14°30′N	17°00′E
Ghāzipur, neigh., India	240d	28°38′N	77°19′E
Ghazzah see Gaza, Gaza	182	31°30′N	34°29′E
Gheorgheni, Rom.	149	46°48′N	25°30′E
Gherla, Rom. (gĕr′lä)	155	47°01′N	23°55′E
Ghilizane, Alg.	210	35°43′N	0°43′E
Ghonda, neigh., India	240d	28°41′N	77°16′E
Ghondi, neigh., India	240d	28°42′N	77°16′E
Ghost Lake, Can.	83e	51°15′N	114°46′W
Ghudāmis, Libya	210	30°07′N	9°26′E
Ghūrīān, Afg.	185	34°21′N	61°30′E
Ghushuri, India	240a	22°37′N	88°22′E
Gia-dinh, Viet	241j	10°48′N	106°42′E
Giannutri, Isola di, i., Italy (jän-nōō′trē)	160	42°15′N	11°06′E
Gibara, Cuba (hē-bä′rä)	122	21°05′N	76°10′W
Gibbsboro, N.J., U.S.	229b	39°50′N	74°58′W
Gibeon, Nmb. (gĭb′ē-ŭn)	212	25°15′S	17°30′E
Gibraleón, Spain (hē-brä-lā-ōn′)	158	37°24′N	7°00′W
Gibraltar, dep., Eur. (gĭ-bräl-tä′r)	142	36°08′N	5°22′W
Gibraltar, Strait of, strt.	142	35°55′N	5°45′W
Gibraltar Point, c., Can.	227c	43°36′N	79°23′W
Gibson City, Il., U.S. (gĭb′sŭn)	98	40°25′N	88°20′W
Gibson Desert, des., Austl.	202	24°45′S	123°15′E
Gibson Island, Md., U.S.	100e	39°05′N	76°26′W
Gibson Reservoir, res., Ok., U.S.	111	36°07′N	95°08′W
Giddings, Tx., U.S. (gĭd′ĭngz)	113	30°11′N	96°55′W
Gidea Park, neigh., Eng., U.K.	235	51°35′N	0°12′E
Gideon, Mo., U.S. (gĭd′ē-ŭn)	111	36°27′N	89°56′W
Gien, Fr. (zhē-ăN′)	147	47°43′N	2°37′E
Giessen, Ger. (gēs′sĕn)	154	50°35′N	8°40′E
Gif-sur-Yvette, Fr.	237c	48°42′N	2°08′E
Gifu, Japan (gē′fōō)	189	35°25′N	136°45′E
Gig Harbor, Wa., U.S. (gĭg)	106a	47°20′N	122°36′W
Giglio, Isola del, i., Italy (jēl′yō)	160	42°23′N	10°55′E
Gijón, Spain (hē-hōn′)	142	43°33′N	5°37′W
Gila, r., U.S. (hē′lȧ)	96	33°00′N	110°00′W
Gila Bend, Az., U.S.	109	32°59′N	112°41′W
Gila Cliff Dwellings National Monument, rec., N.M., U.S.	109	33°15′N	108°20′W
Gila River Indian Reservation, I.R., Az., U.S.	109	33°11′N	112°38′W
Gilbert, Mn., U.S. (gĭl′bērt)	103	47°27′N	92°29′W
Gilbert, r., Austl. (gĭl-bĕrt)	203	17°15′S	142°09′E
Gilbert, Mount, mtn., Can.	86	50°51′N	124°20′W
Gilbert Islands, is., Kir.	225	0°30′S	174°00′E
Gilboa, Mount, mtn., S. Afr. (gĭl-bōȧ)	213c	29°13′N	30°17′W
Gilford Island, i., Can. (gĭl′fērd)	86	50°45′N	126°25′W
Gilgit, Pak. (gĭl′gĭt)	183	35°58′N	73°48′E
Gil Island, i., Can. (gĭl)	86	53°13′N	129°15′W
Gillen, l., Austl. (jĭl′ĕn)	202	26°15′S	125°15′E
Gillett, Ar., U.S. (jĭ-lĕt′)	111	34°07′N	91°22′W
Gillette, Wy., U.S.	105	44°17′N	105°30′W
Gillingham, Eng., U.K. (gĭl′ĭng ăm)	151	51°23′N	0°33′E
Gilman, Il., U.S. (gĭl′măn)	98	40°45′N	87°55′W
Gilman Hot Springs, Ca., U.S.	107a	33°49′N	116°57′W
Gilmer, Tx., U.S. (gĭl′mẽr)	113	32°43′N	94°57′W
Gilmore, Ga., U.S. (gĭl′môr)	100c	33°51′N	84°29′W
Gilo, r., Eth.	211	7°40′N	34°17′E
Gilroy, Ca., U.S. (gĭl-roi′)	108	37°00′N	121°34′W
Giluwe, Mount, mtn., Pap. N. Gui.	197	6°04′S	144°00′E
Gimli, Can. (gĭm′lē)	89	50°39′N	97°00′W
Gimone, r., Fr. (zhē-mōn′)	156	43°26′N	0°36′E
Ginir, Eth.	211	7°13′N	40°44′E
Ginosa, Italy (jē-nō′zä)	160	40°35′N	16°48′E
Ginza, neigh., Japan	242a	35°40′N	139°47′E
Gioia del Colle, Italy (jô′yä dĕl kôl′lā)	160	40°48′N	16°55′E
Girard, Ks., U.S. (jĭ-rärd′)	111	37°30′N	94°50′W
Girardot, Col. (hē-rär-dōt′)	130	4°19′N	74°47′W
Giresun, Tur. (ghĕr′ĕ-sōn′)	182	40°55′N	38°20′E
Girgaum, neigh., India	240e	18°57′N	72°48′E
Giridih, India (jē-rē-dē)	183	24°12′N	86°18′E
Girona, Spain	148	41°55′N	2°48′E
Gironde, r., Fr. (zhē-rôNd′)	142	45°31′N	1°00′W
Girvan, Scot., U.K. (gûr′văn)	150	55°15′N	5°01′W
Gisborne, N.Z. (gĭz′bŭrn)	203a	38°40′S	178°08′E
Gisenyi, Rw.	212	1°43′S	29°15′E
Gisors, Fr. (zhē-zôr′)	156	49°19′N	1°47′E
Gitambo, D.R.C.	216	4°21′N	24°45′E
Gitega, Bdi.	212	3°39′S	30°05′E
Giurgiu, Rom. (jôr′jô)	161	43°53′N	25°58′E
Givet, Fr. (zhē-vĕ′)	156	50°08′N	4°47′E
Givors, Fr. (zhē-vôr′)	156	45°35′N	4°46′E
Giza see Al Jīzah, Egypt	218b	30°01′N	31°12′E
Gizhiga, Russia (gē′zhi-gȧ)	165	61°59′N	160°46′E
Gizo, Sol. Is.	198e	8°06′S	156°51′E
Gizycko, Pol. (gĭ′zhĭ-ko)	146	54°03′N	21°48′E
Gjirokastër, Alb.	149	40°04′N	20°10′E
Gjøvik, Nor. (gyû′vĕk)	146	60°47′N	10°36′E
Glabeek-Zuurbemde, Bel.	145a	50°52′N	4°59′E
Glace Bay, Can. (glās bā)	93	46°12′N	59°57′W
Glacier Bay National Park, rec., Ak., U.S. (glā′shẽr)	94a	58°40′N	136°50′W
Glacier National Park, rec., Can.	84	51°45′N	117°35′W
Glacier Peak, mtn., Wa., U.S.	104	48°07′N	121°10′W
Glacier Point, c., Can.	106a	48°24′N	123°59′W
Gladbeck, Ger. (gläd′bĕk)	154	51°35′N	6°59′E
Gladdeklipkop, S. Afr.	218d	24°17′S	29°36′E
Gladesville, Austl.	243a	33°50′S	151°08′E
Gladstone, Austl.	202	33°15′S	138°20′E
Gladstone, Austl. (glăd′stōn)	203	23°45′S	152°00′E
Gladstone, Mi., U.S.	103	45°50′N	87°04′W
Gladstone, N.J., U.S.	100a	40°43′N	74°39′W
Gladstone, Or., U.S.	106c	45°23′N	122°36′W
Gladwin, Mi., U.S. (glăd′wĭn)	98	44°00′N	84°25′W
Gladwyne, Pa., U.S.	229b	40°02′N	75°17′W
Glåma, r., Nor.	142	61°30′N	10°30′E
Glarus, Switz. (glä′rōs)	154	47°02′N	9°03′E
Glasgow, Scot., U.K. (glås′gō)	142	55°54′N	4°25′W
Glasgow, Ky., U.S.	114	37°00′N	85°55′W
Glasgow, Mo., U.S.	111	39°14′N	92°48′W
Glasgow, Mt., U.S.	105	48°14′N	106°39′W
Glashütte, neigh., Ger.	236	51°13′N	6°52′E
Glassmanor, Md., U.S.	229d	38°49′N	76°59′W
Glassport, Pa., U.S. (glás′pōrt)	101e	40°19′N	79°53′W
Glauchau, Ger. (glou′κou)	154	50°51′N	12°28′E
Glazov, Russia (glä′zôf)	164	58°05′N	52°52′E
Glehn, Ger.	236	51°10′N	6°35′E
Glen, r., Eng., U.K. (glĕn)	144a	52°44′N	0°18′W
Glénan, Îles de, is., Fr. (ĕl-dĕ-glā-näN′)	156	47°43′N	4°42′W
Glenarden, Md., U.S.	229d	38°56′N	76°52′W
Glen Burnie, Md., U.S. (bûr′nē)	100e	39°10′N	76°38′W
Glen Canyon, val., Ut., U.S.	109	37°10′N	110°50′W
Glen Canyon Dam, dam, Az., U.S. (glĕn kăn′yŭn)	96	36°57′N	111°25′W
Glen Canyon National Recreation Area, rec., U.S.	109	37°00′N	111°20′W
Glen Carbon, Il., U.S. (kär′bōn)	107e	38°45′N	89°59′W
Glencoe, S. Afr. (glĕn-cō)	213c	28°14′S	30°09′E
Glencoe, Il., U.S.	101a	42°08′N	87°45′W
Glencoe, Mn., U.S. (glĕn′kō)	103	44°44′N	94°07′W
Glen Cove, N.Y., U.S. (kōv)	100a	40°51′N	73°38′W
Glendale, Az., U.S. (glĕn′dāl)	109	33°30′N	112°15′W
Glendale, Ca., U.S.	96	34°09′N	118°15′W
Glendale, Oh., U.S.	101f	31°16′N	84°22′W
Glendive, Mt., U.S. (glĕn′dīv)	96	47°08′N	104°41′W
Glendo, Wy., U.S.	105	42°32′N	104°54′W
Glendora, Ca., U.S. (glĕn-dō′rȧ)	107a	34°08′N	117°52′W
Glendora, N.J., U.S.	229b	39°50′N	75°04′W
Glen Echo, Md., U.S.	229d	38°58′N	77°08′W
Glenelg, r., Austl.	204	37°20′S	141°30′E
Glen Ellyn, Il., U.S. (glĕn ĕl′-lĕn)	101a	41°53′N	88°04′W
Glenfield, Austl.	243a	33°58′S	150°54′E
Glen Head, N.Y., U.S.	228	40°50′N	73°37′W
Glenhuntly, Austl.	243b	37°54′S	145°03′E
Glen Innes, Austl. (ĭn′ĕs)	203	29°45′S	152°02′E
Glenmore, Md., U.S.	229c	39°11′N	76°36′W
Glenns Ferry, Id., U.S. (fĕr′ĭ)	104	42°58′N	115°21′W
Glen Olden, Pa., U.S. (ōl′d′n)	100f	39°54′N	75°17′W
Glenomra, La., U.S. (glĕn-mō′rȧ)	113	30°58′N	92°36′W
Glen Ridge, N.J., U.S.	228	40°49′N	74°13′W
Glen Rock, N.J., U.S.	228	40°58′N	74°08′W
Glenrock, Wy., U.S. (glĕn′rŏk)	105	42°50′N	105°53′W
Glenroy, Austl.	243b	37°42′S	144°55′E
Glens Falls, N.Y., U.S. (glĕnz fôlz)	99	43°20′N	73°40′W
Glenshaw, Pa., U.S. (glĕn′shô)	101e	40°33′N	79°57′W
Glenside, Pa., U.S.	229b	40°06′N	75°09′W
Glen Valley, Can.	106d	49°09′N	122°30′W
Glenview, Il., U.S. (glĕn′vū)	101a	42°04′N	87°48′W
Glenville, Ga., U.S. (glĕn′vĭl)	115	31°55′N	81°56′W
Glen Waverley, Austl.	243b	37°53′S	145°10′E
Glenwood, Ia., U.S.	102	41°03′N	95°44′W
Glenwood, Mn., U.S.	102	45°39′N	95°23′W
Glenwood, N.M., U.S.	109	33°19′N	108°52′W
Glenwood Landing, N.Y., U.S.	228	40°50′N	73°39′W
Glenwood Springs, Co., U.S.	109	39°35′N	107°20′W
Glienicke, Ger. (glē′nē-kĕ)	145b	52°38′N	13°19′E
Glinde, Ger. (glēn′dĕ)	145c	53°32′N	10°13′E
Glittertinden, mtn., Nor.	152	61°39′N	8°12′E
Gliwice, Pol. (gwĭ-wĭt′sĕ)	147	50°18′N	18°40′E
Globe, Az., U.S. (glōb)	96	33°20′N	110°50′W
Głogów, Pol. (gwō′gōōv)	147	51°40′N	16°04′E
Glommen, r., Nor. (glôm′ĕn)	152	60°03′N	11°15′E
Glonn, Ger. (glônn)	145d	47°59′N	11°52′E
Glorieuses, Îles, is., Reu.	213	11°28′S	47°50′E
Glossop, Eng., U.K. (glŏs′ŭp)	144a	53°26′N	1°57′W
Gloster, Ms., U.S. (glŏs′tẽr)	114	31°10′N	91°00′W
Gloucester, Eng., U.K. (glŏs′tẽr)	147	51°54′N	2°11′W
Gloucester, Ma., U.S.	93a	42°37′N	70°40′W
Gloucester City, N.J., U.S.	100f	39°53′N	75°08′W
Glouster, Oh., U.S. (glŏs′tẽr)	98	39°35′N	82°05′W
Glover Island, i., Can. (glŭv′ẽr)	93	48°44′N	57°45′W
Gloversville, N.Y., U.S. (glŭv′ẽrz-vĭl)	99	43°05′N	74°20′W
Glovertown, Can. (glŭv′ẽr-toun)	93	48°41′N	54°02′W
Glubokoye, Bela. (glōō-bô-kō′yĕ)	166	55°08′N	27°44′E
Glückstadt, Ger. (glük-shtät)	145c	53°47′N	9°25′E
Glushkovo, Russia (glôsh′kô-vō)	163	51°21′N	34°43′E
Gmünden, Aus. (g′mōn′dĕn)	154	47°57′N	13°47′E
Gniezno, Pol. (g′nyåz′nô)	147	52°32′N	17°34′E
Gnjilane, Yugo. (gnyē′lȧ-nĕ)	161	42°28′N	21°27′E
Goa, , India (gō′ȧ)	183	15°45′N	74°00′E
Goascorán, Hond. (gō-äs′kō-rän′)	120	13°37′N	87°43′W
Goba, Eth. (gō′bä)	211	7°17′N	39°58′E
Gobabis, Nmb. (gō-bä′bĭs)	212	22°25′S	18°50′E
Gobi (Shamo), des., Asia (gō′be)	188	43°29′N	103°15′E
Goble, Or., U.S. (gō′b′l)	106c	46°01′N	122°53′W
Goch, Ger. (gôk)	157c	51°35′N	6°10′E
Godāvari, r., India (gō-dä′vŭ-rē)	183	19°00′N	78°30′E
Goddards Soak, sw., Austl. (gŏd′ȧrdz)	202	31°20′S	123°30′E
Goderich, Can. (gōd′rĭch)	90	43°45′N	81°45′W
Godfrey, Il., U.S. (gŏd′frē)	107e	38°57′N	90°12′W
Godhavn, Grnld. (gōdh′hávn)	82	69°15′N	53°30′W
Gods, r., Can. (gŏdz)	89	55°17′N	93°35′W
Gods Lake, Can.	85	54°40′N	94°09′W
Godthåb, Grnld. (gŏt′hôb)	82	64°10′N	51°32′W
Godwin Austen see K2, mtn., Asia	182	36°06′N	76°38′E
Goéland, Lac au, l., Can.	91	49°47′N	76°41′W
Goffs, Ca., U.S. (gôfs)	108	34°57′N	115°06′W
Goff's Oak, Eng., U.K.	235	51°43′N	0°05′W
Gogebic, l., Mi., U.S. (gō-gē′bĭk)	103	46°24′N	89°25′W
Gogebic Range, mts., Mi., U.S.	103	46°37′N	89°48′W
Göggingen, Ger. (gûg′gĕn-gĕn)	145d	48°21′N	10°53′E
Gogland, i., Russia	153	60°04′N	26°55′E
Gogonou, Benin	215	10°50′N	2°50′E
Gogorrón, Mex. (gō-gô-rōn′)	118	21°51′N	100°54′W
Goiânia, Braz. (gō-yá′nyä)	131	16°41′S	48°57′W
Goiás, Braz. (gō-yá′s)	131	15°57′S	50°10′W
Goiás, state, Braz.	131	16°00′S	48°00′W
Goirle, Neth.	145a	51°31′N	5°06′E
Gökçeada, i., Tur.	161	40°10′N	25°27′E
Göksu, r., Tur. (gûk′sōō′)	167	36°40′N	33°30′E
Gol, Nor. (gûl)	152	60°58′N	8°54′E
Golabāri, India	240a	22°36′N	88°20′E
Golax, Va., U.S. (gō′lăks)	115	36°41′N	80°56′W
Golcar, Eng., U.K. (gōl′kȧr)	144a	53°38′N	1°52′W
Golconda, Il., U.S. (gŏl-kŏn′dȧ)	111	37°21′N	88°32′W
Gołdap, Pol. (gôl′dăp)	155	54°17′N	22°17′E
Golden, Can.	87	51°18′N	116°58′W
Golden, Co., U.S.	110	39°44′N	105°15′W
Goldendale, Wa., U.S. (gōl′dĕn-dāl)	104	45°49′N	120°48′W
Golden Gate, strt., Ca., U.S. (gōl′dĕn gāt)	106b	37°48′N	122°32′W
Golden Hinde, mtn., Can. (hīnd)	86	49°40′N	125°45′W
Golden's Bridge, N.Y., U.S.	100a	41°17′N	73°41′W
Golden Valley, Mn., U.S.	107g	44°58′N	93°23′W
Golders Green, neigh., Eng., U.K.	235	51°35′N	0°12′W
Goldfield, Nv., U.S. (gōld′fēld)	108	37°42′N	117°15′W
Gold Hill, mtn., Pan.	116a	9°03′N	79°08′W
Gold Mountain, mtn., Wa., U.S. (gōld)	106a	47°33′N	122°48′W
Goldsboro, N.C., U.S. (gōldz-bûr′ô)	115	35°23′N	77°59′W
Goldthwaite, Tx., U.S. (gōld′thwāt)	112	31°27′N	98°34′W
Goleniów, Pol. (gô-lĕ-nyŭf′)	154	53°33′N	14°51′E
Golets-Purpula, Gora, mtn., Russia	165	59°08′N	115°22′E
Golf, Il., U.S.	231a	42°03′N	87°48′W
Golfito, C.R. (gōl-fē′tō)	121	8°40′N	83°12′W
Golf Park Terrace, Il., U.S.	231a	42°03′N	87°51′W
Goliad, Tx., U.S. (gō-lĭ-ăd′)	113	28°40′N	97°12′W
Golo, r., Fr.	160	42°28′N	9°18′E
Golo Island, i., Phil. (gō′lō)	197a	13°38′N	120°17′E
Golovchino, Russia (gō-lôf′chē-nō)	163	50°34′N	35°52′E
Golyamo Konare, Bul. (gō′lȧ-mō-kō′nä-rĕ)	161	42°16′N	24°33′E
Golzow, Ger. (gōl′tsōv)	145b	52°17′N	12°36′E
Gombe, Nig.	210	10°19′N	11°02′E
Gomel′, Bela. (go′mĕl′)	164	52°20′N	31°03′E
Gomel′, prov., Bela. (Oblast)	162	52°18′N	29°00′E
Gomera Island, i., Spain (gō-mā′rä)	210	28°00′N	18°01′W
Gomez Farias, Mex. (gō′māz fä-rē′ás)	112	24°59′N	101°02′W
Gómez Palacio, Mex. (pä-lä′syō)	116	25°35′N	103°30′W
Gonaïves, Haiti (gō-nȧ-ēv′)	117	19°25′N	72°45′W
Gonaïves, Golfe des, b., Haiti (gō-nȧ-ēv′)	123	19°20′N	73°20′W
Gonâve, Île de la, i., Haiti (gō-náv′)	117	18°50′N	73°30′W
Gonda, India	186	27°13′N	82°00′E
Gondal, India	186	22°02′N	70°47′E
Gonder, Eth.	211	12°39′N	37°30′E
Gonesse, Fr. (gō-nĕs′)	157b	48°59′N	2°28′E
Gongga Shan, mtn., China (gôŋ-gä shän)	188	29°16′N	101°46′E
Goniri, Nig.	215	11°30′N	12°20′E
Gonō, r., Japan (gō′nō)	195	35°00′N	132°25′E
Gonor, Can. (gō′nôr)	83f	50°04′N	96°57′W
Gonubie, S. Afr. (gŏn′ōō-bē)	213c	32°56′S	28°02′E
Gonzales, Mex. (gôn-zá′lĕs)	118	22°47′N	98°26′W
Gonzales, Tx., U.S. (gŏn-zä′lĕz)	113	29°31′N	97°25′W
González Catán, Arg. (gōn-zá′lĕz-kä-tá′n)	132a	34°47′S	58°39′W
Good Hope, Cape of, c., S. Afr. (kāp ov gŏŏd hōp)	212	34°21′S	18°29′E
Good Hope Mountain, mtn., Can.	86	51°09′N	124°10′W
Gooding, Id., U.S. (gŏŏd′ĭng)	105	42°55′N	114°43′W
Goodland, In., U.S. (gŏŏd′lănd)	98	40°50′N	87°15′W
Goodland, Ks., U.S.	110	39°19′N	101°43′W
Goodwood, S. Afr. (gŏŏd′wŏŏd)	212a	33°54′S	18°33′E
Goole, Eng., U.K. (gōōl)	144a	53°42′N	0°52′W
Goose, r., N.D., U.S.	102	47°40′N	97°41′W
Gooseberry Creek, r., Wy., U.S. (gōōs-bĕr′ĭ)	105	44°04′N	108°35′W

PRONOUNCING INDEX Goose Creek-Great Plains 291

PLACE (Pronunciation)	PAGE	LAT.	LONG.
Goose Creek, r., Id., U.S. (gōōs)	105	42°07′N	113°53′W
Goose Lake, l., Ca., U.S.	104	41°56′N	120°35′W
Gorakhpur, India (gō'rŭk-pōōr)	183	26°45′N	82°39′E
Gorda, Punta, c., Cuba (pōō'n-tä-gôr-dä)	122	22°25′N	82°10′W
Gorda Cay, i., Bah. (gôr'dä)	122	26°05′N	77°30′W
Gordon, Can. (gôr'dŭn)	83f	50°00′N	97°20′W
Gordon, Ne., U.S.	102	42°47′N	102°14′W
Gordons Corner, Md., U.S.	229d	39°50′N	76°57′W
Gore, Eth. (gō'rē)	211	8°12′N	35°34′E
Gore Hill, Austl.	243a	33°49′S	151°11′E
Gorgān, Iran	182	36°44′N	54°30′E
Gorgona, Isola di, Italy (gôr-gō'nä)	148	43°27′N	9°55′E
Gori, Geor. (gō'rē)	167	42°00′N	44°08′E
Gorinchem, Neth. (gō'rĭn-kĕm)	145a	51°50′N	4°59′E
Goring, Eng., U.K. (gôr'ĭng)	144b	51°30′N	1°08′W
Gorizia, Italy (gō-rē'tsē-yä)	160	45°56′N	13°40′E
Gor'kiy see Nizhniy Novgorod, Russia	164	56°15′N	44°05′E
Gor'kovskoye, res., Russia	164	56°38′N	43°40′E
Gorlice, Pol. (gôr-lē'tsĕ)	155	49°38′N	21°11′E
Görlitz, Ger. (gür'lĭts)	147	51°10′N	15°01′E
Gorman, Tx., U.S. (gôr'măn)	112	32°13′N	98°40′W
Gorna Oryakhovitsa, Bul. (gôr'nä-ôr-yĕk'ô-vē-tsä)	161	43°08′N	25°40′E
Gornji Milanovac, Yugo. (gôrn'yē-mē'la-nô-väts)	161	44°02′N	20°29′E
Gorno-Altay, state, Russia	170	51°00′N	86°00′E
Gorno-Altaysk, Russia (gôr'nŭ'ŭl-tĭsk')	164	51°58′N	85°58′E
Gorodishche, Russia (gō-rô'dĭsh-chĕ)	172a	57°57′N	57°03′E
Gorodok, Bela.	162	55°27′N	29°58′E
Gorodok, Russia	165	50°30′N	103°58′E
Gorontalo, Indon. (gō-rōn-tä'lo)	197	0°40′N	123°04′E
Gorton, neigh., Eng., U.K.	237b	53°27′N	2°10′W
Goryn', r., Eur. (gō'rĕn')	155	50°55′N	26°07′E
Gorzów Wielkopolski, Pol. (gō-zhōōv'vyĕl-ko-pōl'skē)	146	53°44′N	15°15′E
Gosely, Eng., U.K.	144a	52°33′N	2°10′W
Gosen, Ger.	238a	52°24′N	13°43′E
Goshen, In., U.S. (gō'shĕn)	98	41°35′N	85°50′W
Goshen, Ky., U.S.	101h	38°24′N	85°34′W
Goshen, N.Y., U.S.	100a	41°24′N	74°19′W
Goshen, Oh., U.S.	101f	39°14′N	84°09′W
Goshute Indian Reservation, I.R., Ut., U.S. (gō-shōōt')	109	39°50′N	114°00′W
Goslar, Ger. (gôs'lär)	154	51°55′N	10°25′E
Gospa, r., Ven. (gôs-pä)	131b	9°43′N	64°23′W
Gostivar, Mac. (gos'tĕ-vär)	161	41°46′N	20°58′E
Gostynin, Pol. (gôs-tē'nĭn)	155	52°24′N	19°30′E
Göta, r., Swe. (gōētä)	152	58°11′N	12°03′E
Göta Kanal, can., Swe. (yû'tȧ)	152	58°35′N	15°24′E
Gotanno, neigh., Japan	242a	35°46′N	139°49′E
Göteborg, Swe. (yû'tĕ-bôrgh)	142	57°39′N	11°56′E
Gotel Mountains, mts., Afr.	215	7°05′N	11°20′E
Gotera, El Sal. (gō-tā'rä)	120	13°41′N	88°06′W
Gotha, Ger. (gō'tȧ)	147	50°47′N	10°43′E
Gothenburg see Göteborg, Swe.	142	57°39′N	11°56′E
Gothenburg, Ne., U.S. (gŏth'ĕn-bûrg)	110	40°57′N	100°08′W
Gotland, i., Swe.	142	57°35′N	17°35′E
Gotska Sandön, i., Swe.	153	58°24′N	19°15′E
Götterswickerhamm, Ger.	236	51°35′N	6°40′E
Göttingen, Ger. (gŭt'ĭng-ĕn)	154	51°32′N	9°57′E
Gouda, Neth. (gou'dä)	145a	52°00′N	4°42′E
Gough, i., St. Hel. (gŏf)	2	40°00′S	10°00′W
Gouin, Réservoir, res., Can.	85	48°15′N	74°15′W
Goukou, China (gō-kō)	189	48°45′N	121°42′E
Goulais, r., Can.	90	46°45′N	84°10′W
Goulburn, Austl. (gōl'bŭrn)	203	34°47′S	149°40′E
Goumbati, mtn., Sen.	214	13°08′N	12°06′W
Goumbou, Mali (gōōm-bōō')	210	14°59′N	7°27′W
Gouna, Cam.	215	8°32′N	13°34′E
Goundam, Mali (gōōn-däN')	210	16°29′N	3°37′W
Gournay-sur-Marne, Fr.	237c	48°52′N	2°34′E
Goussainville, Fr.	237c	49°01′N	2°28′E
Gouverneur, N.Y., U.S. (gŭv-ēr-nōōr')	99	44°20′N	75°25′W
Go-vap, Viet	241j	10°49′N	106°42′E
Govenlock, Can. (gŭvĕn-lŏk)	84	49°15′N	109°48′W
Governador, Ilha do, i., Braz. (gō-vĕr-nä-dō-'r-ē-lä'dō)	132b	22°48′S	43°13′W
Governador Portela, Braz. (pōr-tĕ'lä)	132b	22°28′S	43°30′W
Governador Valadares, Braz. (vä-lä-dä'rĕs)	131	18°47′S	41°45′W
Governor's Harbour, Bah.	122	25°15′N	76°15′W
Gowanda, N.Y., U.S. (gō-wŏn'dȧ)	99	42°30′N	78°55′W
Goya, Arg. (gō'yä)	132	29°06′S	59°12′W
Göyçay, Azer. (gĕ-ôk'chī)	167	40°40′N	47°40′E
Goyt, r., Eng., U.K. (goit)	144a	53°19′N	2°03′W
Graaff-Reinet, S. Afr. (gräf'rī'nĕt)	212	32°10′S	24°40′E
Gračac, Cro. (grä'chäts)	160	44°16′N	15°50′E
Gračanica, Bos.	161	44°42′N	18°18′E
Graceville, Fl., U.S. (grās'vĭl)	114	30°57′N	85°30′W
Graceville, Mn., U.S.	102	45°33′N	96°25′W
Gracias, Hond. (grä'sē-äs)	120	14°35′N	88°37′W
Graciosa Island, i., Port. (grä-syō'sä)	210a	39°07′N	27°30′W
Gradačac, Bos. (gra-dä'chats)	149	44°50′N	18°28′E
Grado, Spain (grä'dō)	158	43°24′N	6°04′W
Gräfelfing, Ger. (grä'fĕl-fēng)	145d	48°07′N	11°27′E
Grafenberg, neigh., Ger.	236	51°14′N	6°50′E
Grafing bei München, Ger. (grä'fēng)	145d	48°03′N	11°58′E
Grafton, Austl. (graf'tŭn)	203	29°38′S	153°05′E
Grafton, Il., U.S.	107e	38°58′N	90°26′W
Grafton, Ma., U.S.	93a	42°13′N	71°41′W
Grafton, N.D., U.S.	102	48°24′N	97°25′W
Grafton, Oh., U.S.	101d	41°16′N	82°04′W
Grafton, W.V., U.S.	98	39°20′N	80°00′W
Gragnano, Italy (grän-yä'nō)	159c	40°27′N	14°32′E
Graham, N.C., U.S. (grā'ăm)	115	36°03′N	79°23′W
Graham, Tx., U.S.	110	33°07′N	98°34′W
Graham, Wa., U.S.	106a	47°03′N	122°18′W
Graham, i., Can.	84	53°50′N	132°40′W
Grahamstown, S. Afr. (grā'ăms'toun)	213c	33°19′S	26°33′E
Grajewo, Pol. (grä-yā'vo)	155	53°38′N	22°28′E
Grama, Serra de, mtn., Braz. (sĕ'r-rä-dĕ-grá'mà)	129a	20°42′S	42°28′W
Gramada, Bul. (grä'mä-dä)	161	43°46′N	22°41′E
Gramatneusiedl, Aus.	145e	48°02′N	16°29′E
Grampian Mountains, mts., Scot., U.K. (grăm'pĭ-ăn)	142	56°30′N	4°55′W
Granada, Nic. (grä-nä'dhä)	116	11°55′N	85°58′W
Granada, Spain (grä-nä'dä)	148	37°13′N	3°37′W
Gran Bajo, reg., Arg. (grán'bä'kŏ)	132	47°35′S	68°45′W
Granbury, Tx., U.S. (grăn'bĕr-ĭ)	113	32°26′N	97°45′W
Granby, Can. (grăn'bĭ)	85	45°30′N	72°40′W
Granby, Mo., U.S.	111	36°54′N	94°15′W
Granby, l., Co., U.S.	110	40°07′N	105°40′W
Gran Canaria Island, i., Spain (grän'kä-nä'rē-ä)	210	27°39′N	15°39′W
Gran Chaco, reg., S.A. (grán'chá'kŏ)	132	25°30′S	62°15′W
Grand, i., Mi., U.S.	103	46°37′N	86°38′W
Grand, l., Can.	92	45°59′N	66°15′W
Grand, l., Me., U.S.	92	45°17′N	67°42′W
Grand, r., Can.	91	43°45′N	80°20′W
Grand, r., Mi., U.S.	98	42°58′N	85°13′W
Grand, r., Mo., U.S.	111	39°50′N	93°52′W
Grand, r., S.D., U.S.	102	45°40′N	101°55′W
Grand, North Fork, r., U.S.	102	45°52′N	102°49′W
Grand, South Fork, r., S.D., U.S.	102	45°38′N	102°56′W
Grand Bahama, i., Bah.	117	26°35′N	78°30′W
Grand Bank, Can. (grănd băngk)	85a	47°06′N	55°47′W
Grand Bassam, C. Iv. (grän bá-säN')	210	5°12′N	3°44′W
Grand Bourg, Guad. (grän bōōr')	121b	15°54′N	61°20′W
Grand Caicos, i., T./C. Is. (grănd kä-ē'kōs)	123	21°45′N	71°50′W
Grand Canal see Da Yunhe, can., China	189	35°00′N	117°00′E
Grand Canal, can., Ire.	150	53°21′N	7°15′W
Grand Canyon, Az., U.S.	109	36°05′N	112°10′W
Grand Canyon, val., Az., U.S.	96	35°50′N	113°16′W
Grand Canyon National Park, rec., Az., U.S.	96	36°15′N	112°20′W
Grand Cayman, i., Cay. Is. (kā'măn)	117	19°15′N	81°15′W
Grand Coulee Dam, dam, Wa., U.S. (kōō'lē)	96	47°58′N	119°28′W
Grande, r., Arg.	129b	35°25′S	70°14′W
Grande, r., Mex.	119	17°37′N	96°41′W
Grande, r., Nic. (grän'dĕ)	121	13°01′N	84°21′W
Grande, r., Ur.	129c	33°19′S	57°15′W
Grande, Arroyo, r., Mex. (är-rō'yō-grä'n-dĕ)	118	23°30′N	98°45′W
Grande, Bahía, b., Arg. (bä-ē'ä-grán'dĕ)	132	50°45′S	68°00′W
Grande, Boca, mth., Ven. (bŏ'kä-grä'n-dĕ)	131	8°46′N	60°17′W
Grande, Cuchilla, mts., Ur. (kōō-chē'l-yä)	132	33°00′S	55°15′W
Grande, Ilha, i., Braz. (grän'dĕ)	129a	23°11′S	44°14′W
Grande, Río, r., Bol.	130	16°49′S	63°19′W
Grande, Rio, r., Braz.	131	19°48′S	49°54′W
Grande, Rio, r., N.A. (grän'dȧ)	96	26°50′N	99°10′W
Grande, Salinas, l., Arg. (sä-lē'näs)	132	29°45′S	65°00′W
Grande, Salto, wtfl., Braz. (säl-tō)	131	16°18′S	39°38′W
Grande Cayemite, Île, i., Haiti	123	18°45′N	73°45′W
Grande de Otoro, r., Hond. (grä'dą dā ô-tō'rō)	120	14°42′N	88°21′W
Grande de Santiago, Río, r., Mex. (rēō-grä'n-dĕ-dĕ-sän-tyá'gô)	116	20°30′N	104°00′W
Grande Pointe, Can. (grănd point')	83f	49°47′N	97°03′W
Grande Prairie, Can. (prâr'ĭ)	84	55°10′N	118°48′W
Grand Erg Occidental, des., Alg.	210	30°00′N	1°00′E
Grand Erg Oriental, des., Alg.	210	30°00′N	7°00′E
Grande Rivière du Nord, Haiti (rē-vyâr' dü nôr')	123	19°35′N	72°10′W
Grande Ronde, r., Or., U.S. (rŏnd')	104	45°32′N	117°52′W
Gran Desierto, des., Mex. (grän-dĕ-syĕ'r-tô)	109	32°14′N	114°28′W
Grande Terre, i., Guad.	121b	16°28′N	61°13′W
Grande Vigie, Pointe de la, c., Guad. (grănd vē-gē')	121b	16°32′N	61°25′W
Grand Falls, Can. (fôlz)	85a	48°56′N	55°40′W
Grandfather Mountain, mtn., N.C., U.S. (grănd-fä-thēr)	115	36°07′N	81°48′W
Grandfield, Ok., U.S. (grănd'fēld)	110	34°13′N	98°39′W
Grand Forks, Can. (fôrks)	84	49°02′N	118°27′W
Grand Forks, N.D., U.S.	96	47°55′N	97°05′W
Grand Haven, Mi., U.S. (hā'v'n)	98	43°05′N	86°15′W
Grand I, N.Y., U.S.	101c	43°03′N	78°58′W
Grand Island, Ne., U.S. (ī'lănd)	96	40°56′N	98°20′W
Grand Island, N.Y., U.S.	230a	42°49′N	78°58′W
Grand Junction, Co., U.S. (jŭngk'shŭn)	96	39°05′N	108°35′W
Grand Lake, l., Can. (lāk)	85a	49°00′N	57°10′W
Grand Lake, l., La., U.S.	113	29°57′N	91°25′W
Grand Lake, l., Mn., U.S.	107h	46°54′N	92°26′W
Grand Ledge, Mi., U.S. (lĕj)	98	42°45′N	84°50′W
Grand Lieu, Lac de, l., Fr. (grăN'-lyû)	156	47°00′N	1°45′W
Grand Manan, i., Can. (mȧ-năn)	92	44°40′N	66°50′W
Grand Mère, Can. (grăn mâr')	85	46°36′N	72°43′W
Grândola, Port. (grăN'dō-lȧ)	158	38°10′N	8°36′W
Grand Portage Indian Reservation, I.R., Mn., U.S. (pōr'tĭj)	103	47°54′N	89°34′W
Grand Portage National Monument, rec., Mi., U.S.	103	47°59′N	89°47′W
Grand Prairie, Tx., U.S. (prĕ'rē)	107c	32°45′N	97°00′W
Grand Rapids, Can.	89	53°08′N	99°20′W
Grand Rapids, Mi., U.S. (răp'ĭdz)	97	43°00′N	85°45′W
Grand Rapids, Mn., U.S.	103	47°16′N	93°33′W
Grand-Riviere, Can.	92	48°26′N	64°30′W
Grand Staircase-Escalante National Monument, rec., Ut., U.S.	108	37°25′N	111°30′E
Grand Teton, mtn., Wy., U.S.	96	43°46′N	110°50′W
Grand Teton National Park, Wy., U.S. (tē'tŏn)	105	43°54′N	110°15′W
Grand Traverse Bay, b., Mi., U.S. (trăv'ērs)	98	45°00′N	85°30′W
Grand Turk, T./C. Is. (tûrk)	123	21°30′N	71°10′W
Grand Turk, i., T./C. Is.	123	21°30′N	71°10′W
Grandview, Mo., U.S. (grănd'vyōō)	107f	38°53′N	94°32′W
Grandyle, N.Y., U.S.	230a	43°00′N	78°57′W
Grange Hill, Eng., U.K.	235	51°37′N	0°05′E
Granger, Wy., U.S. (grān'jēr)	105	41°37′N	109°58′W
Grangeville, Id., U.S. (grānj'vĭl)	104	45°56′N	116°08′W
Granite, Md., U.S.	229c	39°21′N	76°51′W
Granite City, Il., U.S. (grăn'ĭt sĭt'ĭ)	107e	38°42′N	90°09′W
Granite Falls, Mn., U.S. (fôlz)	102	44°46′N	95°34′W
Granite Falls, N.C., U.S.	115	35°49′N	81°25′W
Granite Falls, Wa., U.S.	106a	48°05′N	121°59′W
Granite Lake, l., Can.	93	48°01′N	57°00′W
Granite Peak, mtn., Mt., U.S.	96	45°13′N	109°48′W
Graniteville, S.C., U.S. (grăn'ĭt-vĭl)	115	33°35′N	81°50′W
Granito, Braz. (grä-nē'tō)	131	7°39′S	39°34′W
Granma, prov., Cuba	122	20°10′N	76°50′W
Gränna, Swe. (grĕn'á)	152	58°02′N	14°38′E
Granollers, Spain (grä-nōl-yĕrs')	159	41°36′N	2°19′E
Gran Pajonal, reg., Peru (grä'n-pä-kō-näl')	130	11°14′S	71°45′W
Gran Paradiso, mtn., Italy	160	45°32′N	7°16′E
Gran Piedra, mtn., Cuba (grän-pyĕ'drä)	123	20°00′N	75°40′W
Grantham, Eng., U.K. (grăn'tăm)	150	52°54′N	0°38′W
Grant Park, Il., U.S. (grănt pärk)	101a	41°14′N	87°39′W
Grant Park, pt. of i., Il., U.S.	231a	41°52′N	87°37′W
Grants Pass, Or., U.S. (grȧnts pȧs)	104	42°26′N	123°20′W
Granville, Austl.	243a	33°50′S	151°01′E
Granville, Fr. (grăN-vēl')	147	48°52′N	1°35′W
Granville, N.Y., U.S. (grăn'vĭl)	99	43°25′N	73°15′W
Granville, l., Can.	84	56°18′N	100°30′W
Grão Mogol, Braz. (grouN' mŏ-gôl')	131	16°34′S	42°35′W
Grapevine, Tx., U.S. (grāp'vīn)	107c	32°56′N	97°05′W
Gräso, i., Swe.	152	60°30′N	18°35′E
Grass, r., N.Y., U.S.	99	44°45′N	75°10′W
Grass Cay, i., V.I.U.S.	117c	18°22′N	64°50′W
Grasse, Fr. (gräs)	157	43°39′N	6°57′E
Grassendale, neigh., Eng., U.K.	237a	53°21′N	2°54′W
Grass Mountain, mtn., Wa., U.S. (gràs)	106a	47°13′N	121°48′W
Grates Point, c., Can. (grāts)	93	48°09′N	52°57′W
Gravelbourg, Can. (grăv'ĕl-bôrg)	84	49°53′N	106°34′W
Gravesend, Eng., U.K. (grāvz'ĕnd')	144b	51°26′N	0°22′E
Gravina, Italy (grä-vē'nä)	160	40°48′N	16°27′E
Gravois, Pointe à, c., Haiti (grá-vwä')	123	18°00′N	74°20′W
Gray, Fr. (grå)	157	47°26′N	5°35′E
Grayling, Mi., U.S. (grā'lĭng)	98	44°40′N	84°40′W
Grays, Eng., U.K.	235	51°29′N	0°20′E
Grays Harbor, b., Wa., U.S. (grās)	96	46°55′N	124°23′W
Grayslake, Il., U.S. (grāz'lāk)	101a	42°20′N	88°20′W
Grays Peak, mtn., Co., U.S. (grāz)	110	39°29′N	105°52′W
Grays Thurrock, Eng., U.K. (thŭ'rŏk)	144b	51°28′N	0°19′E
Grayvoron, Russia (grá-ē'vō-rôn)	163	50°28′N	35°41′E
Graz, Aus. (gräts)	142	47°05′N	15°26′E
Greasby, Eng., U.K.	237a	53°23′N	3°07′W
Great Abaco, i., Bah. (ä'bä-kō)	117	26°30′N	77°05′W
Great Altcar, Eng., U.K.	237a	53°33′N	3°01′W
Great Artesian Basin, basin, Austl. (är-tēzh-ăn bā-sĭn)	203	23°16′S	143°37′E
Great Australian Bight, bt., Austl. (ôs-trā'lĭ-ăn bĭt)	202	33°30′S	127°00′E
Great Bahama Bank, bk. (bȧ-hā'mȧ)	122	25°00′N	78°50′W
Great Barrier, i., N.Z. (băr'ĭ-ēr)	203a	36°10′S	175°30′E
Great Barrier Reef, rf., Austl. (bȧ-rĭ-ĕr rēf)	203	16°43′S	146°34′E
Great Basin, basin, U.S. (grāt bā's'n)	96	40°08′N	117°10′W
Great Bear Lake, l., Can. (bâr)	84	66°10′N	119°53′W
Great Bend, Ks., U.S. (bĕnd)	110	38°41′N	98°46′W
Great Bitter Lake, l., Egypt	218b	30°24′N	32°27′E
Great Blasket Island, i., Ire. (blăs'kĕt)	150	52°05′N	10°55′W
Great Bookham, Eng., U.K.	235	51°16′N	0°22′W
Great Burstead, Eng., U.K.	235	51°36′N	0°25′E
Great Corn Island, i., Nic.	121	12°10′N	82°54′W
Great Crosby, Eng., U.K.	237a	53°29′N	3°01′W
Great Dismal Swamp, sw., U.S. (dĭz'mȧl)	115	36°35′N	76°34′W
Great Divide Basin, basin, Wy., U.S. (dĭ-vīd' bā's'n)	105	42°10′N	108°10′W
Great Dividing Range, mts., Austl. (dĭ-vī-dĭng rānj)	203	35°16′S	146°38′E
Great Duck, i., Can. (dŭk)	90	45°40′N	83°22′W
Greater Antilles, is., N.A.	117	20°30′N	79°15′W
Greater Khingan Range, mts., China (dä hĭŋ-gän lĭŋ)	189	46°30′N	120°00′E
Greater Leech Indian Reservation, I.R., Mn., U.S. (grāt'ēr lēch)	103	47°39′N	94°27′W
Greater Manchester, co., Eng., U.K.	144a	53°34′N	2°41′W
Greater Sunda Islands, is., Asia	196	4°00′S	108°00′E
Great Exuma, i., Bah. (ĕk-sōō'mä)	122	23°35′N	76°00′W
Great Falls, Mt., U.S. (fôlz)	96	47°30′N	111°15′W
Great Falls, S.C., U.S.	115	34°32′N	80°53′W
Great Falls, Va., U.S.	229d	39°00′N	77°17′W
Great Guana Cay, i., Bah. (gwä'nä)	122	24°00′N	76°20′W
Great Harbor Cay, i., Bah. (kē)	122	25°45′N	77°50′W
Great Inagua, i., Bah. (ē-nä'gwä)	117	21°00′N	73°15′W
Great Indian Desert, des., Asia	183	27°35′N	71°37′E
Great Isaac, i., Bah. (ī'zȧk)	122	26°05′N	79°05′W
Great Karroo, plat., S. Afr. (grāt kȧ'rōō)	212	32°45′S	22°00′E
Great Kills, neigh., N.Y., U.S.	228	40°33′N	74°10′W
Great Namaland, hist. reg., Nmb.	212	25°45′S	16°15′E
Great Neck, N.Y., U.S. (nĕk)	100a	40°48′N	73°44′W
Great Nicobar Island, i., India (nĭk-ō-bär')	196	7°00′N	94°18′E
Great Oxney Green, Eng., U.K.	235	51°44′N	0°25′E
Great Parndon, Eng., U.K.	235	51°45′N	0°05′E
Great Pedro Bluff, c., Jam.	122	17°50′N	78°05′W
Great Pee Dee, r., S.C., U.S. (pē-dē')	97	34°01′N	79°26′W
Great Plains, pl., N.A. (plāns)	82	45°00′N	104°00′W

ng-sing; ŋ-baŋk; N-nasalized n; nŏd; cŏmmit; ōld; ôbey; ôrder; oi-boil; fōōd; ŏ-as oo in foot; ou-out; s-soft; sh-dish; th-thin; pūre; ůnite; ûrn; stŭd; circŭs; ü-as in French tu; '-indeterminate vowel.

292 Great Ragged–Guara

PLACE (Pronunciation)	PAGE	LAT.	LONG.
Great Ragged, i., Bah.	123	22°10′N	75°45′W
Great Ruaha, r., Tan.	212	7°30′S	37°00′E
Great Salt Lake, l., Ut., U.S. (sôlt lāk)	96	41°19′N	112°48′W
Great Salt Lake Desert, des., Ut., U.S.	96	41°00′N	113°30′W
Great Salt Plains Reservoir, res., Ok., U.S.	110	36°56′N	98°14′W
Great Sand Dunes National Monument, rec., Co., U.S.	110	37°56′N	105°25′W
Great Sand Hills, hills, Can. (sănd)	88	50°35′N	109°05′W
Great Sandy Desert, des., Austl. (săn'dē)	202	21°50′S	123°10′E
Great Sandy Desert, des., Or., U.S. (săn'dĭ)	104	43°43′N	120°44′W
Great Sitkin, i., Ak., U.S. (sĭt-kĭn)	95a	52°18′N	176°22′W
Great Slave Lake, l., Can. (slāv)	84	61°37′N	114°58′W
Great Smoky Mountains National Park, rec., U.S. (smōk-ē)	97	35°43′N	83°20′W
Great Stirrup Cay, i., Bah. (stĭr-ŭp)	122	25°50′N	77°55′W
Great Sutton, Eng., U.K.	237a	53°17′N	2°56′W
Great Victoria Desert, des., Austl. (vĭk-tō'rĭ-ȧ)	202	29°45′S	124°30′E
Great Wall, hist., China	188	38°00′N	109°00′E
Great Waltham, Eng., U.K. (wôl'thŭm)	144b	51°47′N	0°27′E
Great Warley, Eng., U.K.	235	51°35′N	0°17′E
Great Yarmouth, Eng., U.K. (yär-mŭth)	147	52°35′N	1°45′E
Grebbestad, Swe. (grĕb-bĕ-städh)	152	58°42′N	11°15′E
Gréboun, Mont, mtn., Niger	210	20°00′N	8°35′E
Greco, neigh., Italy	238c	45°30′N	9°13′E
Gredos, Sierra de, mts., Spain (syĕr'rä dā grā'dōs)	158	40°13′N	5°30′W
Greece, nation, Eur. (grēs)	142	39°00′N	21°30′E
Greeley, Co., U.S. (grē'lĭ)	96	40°25′N	104°41′W
Green, r., U.S.	96	38°30′N	110°10′W
Green, r., Ky., U.S. (grēn)	114	37°13′N	86°30′W
Green, r., N.D., U.S.	102	47°05′N	103°05′W
Green, r., Ut., U.S.	109	38°30′N	110°05′W
Green, r., Wa., U.S.	106a	47°17′N	121°57′W
Green, r., Wy., U.S.	105	41°08′N	110°27′W
Greenbank, Wa., U.S. (grēn'bănk)	106a	48°06′N	122°35′W
Green Bay, Wi., U.S.	97	44°30′N	88°04′W
Green Bay, b., U.S.	97	44°55′N	87°40′W
Green Bayou, Tx., U.S.	113a	29°53′N	95°13′W
Greenbelt, Md., U.S. (grēn'bĕlt)	100e	38°59′N	76°53′W
Greenbrae, Ca., U.S.	231b	37°57′N	122°31′W
Greencastle, In., U.S. (grēn-kȧs''l)	98	39°40′N	86°50′W
Green Cay, i., Bah.	122	24°05′N	77°10′W
Green Cove Springs, Fl., U.S. (kōv)	115	29°56′N	81°42′W
Greendale, Wi., U.S. (grēn'dāl)	101a	42°56′N	87°59′W
Greenfield, In., U.S. (grēn'fēld)	98	39°45′N	85°40′W
Greenfield, Ia., U.S.	103	41°16′N	94°30′W
Greenfield, Ma., U.S.	99	42°35′N	72°35′W
Greenfield, Mo., U.S.	111	37°23′N	93°48′W
Greenfield, Oh., U.S.	98	39°15′N	83°25′W
Greenfield, Tn., U.S.	114	36°08′N	88°45′W
Greenfield Park, Can.	83a	45°29′N	73°29′W
Greenhills, Oh., U.S. (grēn-hĭls)	101f	39°16′N	84°31′W
Greenhithe, Eng., U.K.	235	51°27′N	0°17′E
Greenland, dep., N.A. (grēn'lănd)	82	74°00′N	40°00′W
Greenland Sea, sea	220	77°00′N	1°00′W
Green Meadows, Md., U.S.	229d	38°58′N	76°57′W
Greenmount, Eng., U.K.	237b	53°37′N	2°20′W
Green Mountain, mtn., Or., U.S.	106c	45°52′N	123°24′W
Green Mountain Reservoir, res., Co., U.S.	109	39°50′N	106°20′W
Green Mountains, mts., N.A.	97	43°10′N	73°05′W
Greenock, Scot., U.K. (grēn'ŭk)	146	55°55′N	4°45′W
Green Peter Lake, res., Or., U.S.	104	44°28′N	122°30′W
Green Pond Mountain, mtn., N.J., U.S. (pŏnd)	100a	41°00′N	74°32′W
Greenport, N.Y., U.S.	99	41°06′N	72°22′W
Green River, Ut., U.S. (grēn rĭv'ēr)	109	39°00′N	110°05′W
Green River, Wy., U.S.	105	41°32′N	109°26′W
Green River Lake, res., Ky., U.S.	114	37°15′N	85°15′W
Greensboro, Al., U.S. (grēnz'bŭro)	114	32°42′N	87°36′W
Greensboro, Ga., U.S. (grēns-bûr'ō)	114	33°34′N	83°11′W
Greensboro, N.C., U.S.	97	36°04′N	79°45′W
Greensborough, Austl.	243b	37°42′S	145°06′E
Greensburg, In., U.S. (grēnz'bûrg)	98	39°20′N	85°30′W
Greensburg, Ks., U.S. (grēns-bûrg)	110	37°36′N	99°17′W
Greensburg, Pa., U.S.	99	40°20′N	79°30′W
Greenside, neigh., S. Afr.	244b	26°09′S	28°01′E
Greenstead, Eng., U.K.	235	51°42′N	0°14′E
Green Street, Eng., U.K.	235	51°40′N	0°16′W
Green Street Green, neigh., Eng., U.K.	235	51°21′N	0°04′E
Greenvale, N.Y., U.S.	228	40°49′N	73°38′W
Greenville, Lib.	210	5°01′N	9°03′W
Greenville, Al., U.S. (grēn'vĭl)	114	31°49′N	86°39′W
Greenville, Il., U.S.	111	38°52′N	89°22′W
Greenville, Ky., U.S.	114	37°11′N	87°11′W
Greenville, Me., U.S.	92	45°26′N	69°35′W
Greenville, Mi., U.S.	98	43°10′N	85°25′W
Greenville, Ms., U.S.	97	33°25′N	91°00′W
Greenville, N.C., U.S.	115	35°35′N	77°22′W
Greenville, Oh., U.S.	98	40°05′N	84°35′W
Greenville, Pa., U.S.	98	41°20′N	80°25′W
Greenville, S.C., U.S.	97	34°50′N	82°25′W
Greenville, Tn., U.S.	115	36°08′N	82°50′W
Greenville, Tx., U.S.	113	33°09′N	96°07′W
Greenwich, Eng., U.K.	144b	51°28′N	0.00
Greenwich, Ct., U.S.	100a	41°01′N	73°37′W
Greenwich Observatory, pt. of i., Eng., U.K.	235	51°28′N	0.00
Greenwich Village, neigh., N.Y., U.S.	228	40°44′N	74°00′W
Greenwood, Ar., U.S. (grēn-wŏd)	111	35°13′N	94°15′W
Greenwood, In., U.S.	101g	39°37′N	86°07′W
Greenwood, Ma., U.S.	227a	42°29′N	71°04′W
Greenwood, Ms., U.S.	114	33°30′N	90°09′W
Greenwood, S.C., U.S.	115	34°10′N	82°10′W
Greenwood, Lake, res., S.C., U.S.	115	34°17′N	81°55′W
Greenwood Lake, l., N.Y., U.S.	100a	41°13′N	74°20′W
Greer, S.C., U.S. (grēr)	115	34°55′N	81°56′W
Grefrath, Ger. (grĕf'rät)	157c	51°20′N	6°21′E
Gregory, S.D., U.S. (grĕg'ō-rĭ)	102	43°12′N	99°27′W
Gregory, Lake, l., Austl. (grĕg'ō-rē)	202	28°47′S	139°15′E
Gregory Range, mts., Austl.	203	19°23′S	143°45′E
Greifenberg, Ger. (grī'fĕn-bĕrgh)	145d	48°04′N	11°06′E
Greiffenburg, hist., Ger.	236	51°20′N	6°38′E
Greifswald, Ger. (grīfs'vält)	154	54°05′N	13°24′E
Greiz, Ger. (grīts)	154	50°39′N	12°14′E
Gremyachinsk, Russia (grâ'myà-chĭnsk)	172a	58°35′N	57°53′E
Grenada, Ms., U.S. (grē-nä'da)	114	33°45′N	89°47′W
Grenada, nation, N.A.	117	12°02′N	61°15′W
Grenada Lake, res., Ms., U.S.	114	33°52′N	89°30′W
Grenadines, The, is., N.A. (grĕn'ȧ-dēnz)	121b	12°37′N	61°35′W
Grenen, c., Den.	146	57°43′N	10°31′E
Grenoble, Fr. (grē-nō'bl')	147	45°14′N	5°45′E
Grenora, N.D., U.S. (grē-nō'rȧ)	102	48°38′N	103°55′W
Grenville, Can. (grĕn'vĭl)	99	45°40′N	74°35′W
Grenville, Gren.	121b	12°07′N	61°38′W
Gresham, Or., U.S. (grĕsh'ăm)	106c	45°30′N	122°25′W
Gretna, La., U.S. (grĕt'nȧ)	100d	29°56′N	90°03′W
Grevel, neigh., Ger.	236	51°34′N	7°33′E
Grevelingen Krammer, r., Neth.	145a	51°42′N	4°03′E
Grevenbroich, Ger. (grĕ'fen-broik)	157c	51°05′N	6°36′E
Grey, r., Can. (grā)	93	47°53′N	57°00′W
Grey, Point, c., Can.	106d	49°22′N	123°16′W
Greybull, Wy., U.S. (grā'bŏŏl)	105	44°28′N	108°05′W
Greybull, r., Wy., U.S.	105	44°13′N	108°43′W
Greylingstad, S. Afr. (grā-lĭng'shtát)	218d	26°40′S	29°13′E
Greymouth, N.Z. (grā'mouth)	203a	42°27′S	171°17′E
Grey Range, mts., Austl.	203	28°40′S	142°05′E
Greystanes, Austl.	243a	33°49′S	150°58′E
Greytown, S. Afr. (grā'toun)	213c	29°07′S	30°38′E
Grey Wolf Peak, mtn., Wa., U.S. (grā wŏlf)	106a	48°53′N	123°12′W
Gridley, Ca., U.S. (grĭd'lĭ)	108	39°22′N	121°43′W
Griffin, Ga., U.S. (grĭf'ĭn)	114	33°15′N	84°16′W
Griffith, Austl. (grĭf-ĭth)	204	34°16′S	146°10′E
Griffith, In., U.S.	101a	41°31′N	87°26′W
Grigoriopol', Mol. (grĭ'gor-i-ō'pŏl)	163	47°09′N	29°18′E
Grijalva, r., Mex. (grē-häl'vä)	119	17°25′N	93°23′W
Grim, Cape, c., Austl. (grĭm)	204	40°43′S	144°30′E
Grimma, Ger. (grĭm'ȧ)	154	51°14′N	12°43′E
Grimsby, Can. (grĭmz'bĭ)	83d	43°11′N	79°33′W
Grimsby, Eng., U.K.	146	53°35′N	0°05′W
Grímsey, i., Ice. (grĭms'ȧ)	146	66°30′N	17°50′W
Grimstad, Nor. (grĭm-städh)	146	58°21′N	8°30′E
Grindstone Island, Can.	93	47°25′N	61°51′W
Grinnel, Ia., U.S. (grĭ-nĕl')	103	41°44′N	92°44′W
Grinzing, neigh., Aus.	239e	48°15′N	16°21′E
Griswold, Ia., U.S. (grĭz'wŭld)	102	41°11′N	95°05′W
Groais Island, i., Can.	93	50°57′N	55°35′W
Grobina, Lat. (grō'bĭnĭa)	153	56°35′N	21°10′E
Groblersdal, S. Afr.	218d	25°11′S	29°25′E
Grodno, Bela. (grŏd'nō)	166	53°40′N	23°49′E
Grodzisk, Pol. (grō'jĕsk)	154	52°14′N	16°22′E
Grodzisk Masowiecki, Pol. (grō'jēsk mä-zō-vyĕts'ke)	155	52°06′N	20°40′E
Groesbeck, Tx., U.S. (grōs'bĕk)	113	31°32′N	96°31′W
Groix, Île de, i., Fr. (ēl dē grwä')	156	47°39′N	3°28′W
Grójec, Pol. (grō'yĕts)	155	51°53′N	20°52′E
Gronau, Ger. (grō'nou)	154	52°12′N	7°05′E
Groningen, Neth. (grō'nĭng-ĕn)	146	53°13′N	6°30′E
Groote Eylandt, i., Austl. (grō'tē ī'länt)	202	13°50′S	137°30′E
Grootfontein, Nmb. (grōt'fōn-tān')	212	19°30′S	18°15′E
Groot-Kei, r., Afr. (kē)	213c	32°17′S	27°30′E
Grootkop, mtn., S. Afr.	212a	34°11′S	18°23′E
Groot Marico, S. Afr.	218d	25°36′S	26°23′E
Groot Marico, r., Afr.	218d	25°13′S	26°20′E
Groot-Vis, r., S. Afr.	213c	33°04′S	26°08′E
Groot Vloer, pl., S. Afr. (grōt' vlôr')	212	30°00′S	21°00′E
Gros-Mécatina, i., Can.	93	50°50′N	58°33′W
Gros Morne, mtn., Can. (grō môrn')	93	49°36′N	57°48′W
Gros Morne National Park, rec., Can.	85a	49°45′N	59°15′W
Gros Pate, mtn., Can.	93	50°16′N	57°25′W
Grossbeeren, Ger.	238a	52°21′N	13°18′E
Grosse Island, i., Mi., U.S. (grōs)	101b	42°08′N	83°09′W
Grosse Isle, Can. (īl')	83f	50°04′N	97°27′W
Grossenbaum, neigh., Ger.	236	51°22′N	6°47′E
Grossenhain, Ger. (grōs'ĕn-hīn)	154	51°17′N	13°33′E
Gross-Enzersdorf, Aus.	145e	48°13′N	16°33′E
Grosse Pointe, Mi., U.S. (point')	101b	42°23′N	82°54′W
Grosse Pointe Farms, Mi., U.S. (färm)	101b	42°25′N	82°53′W
Grosse Pointe Park, Mi., U.S. (pärk)	101b	42°23′N	82°55′W
Grosse Pointe Woods, Mi., U.S.	230c	42°27′N	82°55′W
Grosseto, Italy (grōs-sā'tō)	160	42°46′N	11°09′E
Grossglockner, mtn., Aus.	147	47°06′N	12°45′E
Gross Höbach, Ger. (hû'bäk)	145d	48°21′N	11°36′E
Grossjedlersdorf, neigh., Aus.	239e	48°17′N	16°25′E
Gross Kreutz, Ger. (kroitz)	145b	52°24′N	12°47′E
Gross Schönebeck, Ger. (shō'nē-bĕk)	145b	52°54′N	13°32′E
Gross Ziethen, Ger.	238a	52°24′N	13°27′E
Gros Ventre, r., Wy., U.S. (grōvĕn't'r)	105	43°38′N	110°34′W
Groton, Ct., U.S. (grŏt'ŭn)	99	41°20′N	72°00′W
Groton, Ma., U.S.	93a	42°37′N	71°34′W
Groton, S.D., U.S.	102	45°25′N	98°04′W
Grottaglie, Italy (grôt-täl'yā)	161	40°32′N	17°26′E
Grouard Mission, Can.	84	55°31′N	116°09′W
Groveland, Ma., U.S. (grōv'land)	93a	42°25′N	71°02′W
Groveton, N.H., U.S. (grōv'tŭn)	99	44°35′N	71°30′W
Groveton, Tx., U.S.	113	31°04′N	95°07′W
Groznyy, Russia (grŏz'nĭ)	164	43°20′N	45°40′E
Grudziądz, Pol. (grŏ'jyŏnts)	146	53°30′N	18°48′E
Grues, Île aux, i., Can. (ō grü)	83b	47°05′N	70°32′W
Gruiten, Ger.	236	51°14′N	7°01′E
Grumme, neigh., Ger.	236	51°30′N	7°14′E
Grünau, neigh., Ger.	238a	52°25′N	13°34′E
Grundy Center, Ia., U.S. (grŭn'dĭ sĕn'tēr)	103	42°22′N	92°45′W
Grünewald, Ger.	236	51°13′N	7°37′E
Grunewald, neigh., Ger.	238a	52°30′N	13°17′E
Gruñidora, Mex. (grōō-nyē-dō'rō)	118	24°10′N	101°49′W
Grünwald, Ger. (grōōn'väld)	145d	48°04′N	11°34′E
Gryazi, Russia (gryä'zĭ)	162	52°31′N	39°59′E
Gryazovets, Russia (gryä'zō-vĕts)	166	58°52′N	40°14′E
Gryfice, Pol. (grĭ'fĭ-tsĕ)	154	53°55′N	15°11′E
Gryfino, Pol. (grĭ'fē-nō)	154	53°16′N	14°30′E
Guabito, Pan. (gwä-bē'tō)	121	9°30′N	82°33′W
Guacanayabo, Golfo de, b., Cuba (gôl-fô-dĕ-gwä-kä-nä-yä'bō)	122	20°30′N	77°40′W
Guacara, Ven. (gwä'kä-rä)	131b	10°16′N	67°48′W
Guadalajara, Mex. (gwä-dhä-lä-hä'rä)	116	20°41′N	103°21′W
Guadalajara, Spain (gwä-dä-lä-kä'rä)	148	40°37′N	3°10′W
Guadalcanal, Spain (gwä-dhäl-kä-näl')	158	38°05′N	5°48′W
Guadalcanal, i., Sol. Is.	203	9°48′S	158°43′E
Guadalcázar, Mex. (gwä-dhäl-kä'zär)	118	22°38′N	100°24′W
Guadalete, r., Spain (gwä-dhä-lā'tā)	158	36°53′N	5°38′W
Guadalhorce, r., Spain (gwä-dhäl-ôr'thā)	158	37°05′N	4°50′W
Guadalimar, r., Spain (gwä-dhä-lē-mär')	158	38°29′N	2°53′W
Guadalope, r., Spain (gwä-dä-lō-pē)	159	40°48′N	0°10′W
Guadalquivir, Río, r., Spain (rē'ō-gwä-dhäl-kē-vēr')	142	37°30′N	5°00′W
Guadalupe, Mex.	112	31°23′N	106°06′W
Guadalupe, i., Mex.	116	29°00′N	118°45′W
Guadalupe, r., Tx., U.S. (gwä-dhä-lōō'pä)	112	29°54′N	99°03′W
Guadalupe, Basílica de, rel., Mex.	233a	19°29′N	99°07′W
Guadalupe, Sierra de, mts., Spain (syĕr'rä dā gwä-dhä-lōō'pä)	148	39°30′N	5°25′W
Guadalupe Mountains, mts., N.M., U.S.	112	32°00′N	104°55′W
Guadalupe Peak, mtn., Tx., U.S.	112	31°55′N	104°55′W
Guadarrama, r., Spain (gwä-dhär-rä'mä)	159a	40°34′N	3°58′W
Guadarrama, Sierra de, mts., Spain (gwä-dhär-rä'mä)	142	41°00′N	3°40′W
Guadatentin, r., Spain	158	37°43′N	1°58′W
Guadeloupe, dep., N.A. (gwä-dē-lōōp)	117	16°40′N	61°10′W
Guadeloupe Passage, strt., N.A.	121b	16°26′N	62°00′W
Guadiana, r., Eur. (gwä-dvä'nä)	142	39°00′N	6°00′W
Guadiana, Bahía de, b., Cuba (bä-ē'ä-dē-gwä-dhē-ä'nä)	122	22°10′N	84°35′W
Guadiana Alto, r., Spain (äl'tō)	158	39°02′N	2°52′W
Guadiana Menor, r., Spain (mā'nôr)	158	37°43′N	2°45′W
Guadiaro, r., Spain (gwä-dhē-ä'rō)	158	36°38′N	5°25′W
Guadiela, r., Spain (gwä-dhē-ā'lä)	158	40°27′N	2°05′W
Guadix, Spain (gwä-dēsh')	158	37°18′N	3°09′W
Guaianazes, neigh., Braz.	234d	23°33′S	46°25′W
Guaira, Braz. (gwä-ē-rä)	131	24°03′S	54°02′W
Guaire, r., Ven. (gwī'rĕ)	131b	10°25′N	66°43′W
Guajaba, Cayo, i., Cuba (kä'yō-gwä-hä'bä)	122	21°50′N	77°35′W
Guajará Mirim, Braz. (gwä-zhä-rä'mē-rēɴ')	130	10°58′S	65°12′W
Guajira, Península de, pen., S.A.	130	12°35′N	73°00′W
Gualán, Guat. (gwä-län')	120	15°08′N	89°21′W
Gualeguay, Arg. (gwä-lĕ-gwä'y)	132	33°10′S	59°20′W
Gualeguay, r., Arg.	132	32°49′S	59°05′W
Gualicho, Salina, l., Arg. (sä-lē'nä-gwä-lē'chō)	132	40°20′S	65°15′W
Guam, i., Oc. (gwäm)	3	14°00′N	143°20′E
Guamo, Col. (gwä'mō)	130a	4°02′N	74°58′W
Gu'an, China (gōō-än)	192a	39°25′N	116°18′E
Guan, r., China (gŭän)	190	31°56′N	115°19′E
Guanabacoa, Cuba (gwä-nä-bä-kō'ä)	117	23°08′N	82°19′W
Guanabara, Baía de, b., Braz.	129a	22°44′S	43°09′W
Guanacaste, Cordillera, mts., C.R.	120	10°54′N	85°27′W
Guanacevi, Mex. (gwä-nä-sĕ-vē')	116	25°30′N	105°45′W
Guanahacabibes, Península de, pen., Cuba	122	21°55′N	84°35′W
Guanajay, Cuba (gwä-nä-hī')	122	22°55′N	82°40′W
Guanajuato, Mex. (gwä-nä-hwä'tō)	116	21°01′N	101°16′W
Guanajuato, state, Mex.	116	21°00′N	101°00′W
Guanape, Ven. (gwä-nä'pĕ)	131b	9°55′N	65°32′W
Guanape, r., Ven.	131b	9°52′N	65°20′W
Guanare, Ven. (gwä-nä'rä)	130	8°57′N	69°47′W
Guanduçu, r., Braz. (gwä'n-dōō'sōō)	132b	22°50′S	43°40′W
Guane, Cuba (gwä'nā)	122	22°10′N	84°05′W
Guangchang, China (gŭäŋ-chäŋ)	193	26°50′N	116°18′E
Guangde, China (gŭäŋ-dŭ)	193	30°40′N	119°20′E
Guangdong, prov., China (gŭäŋ-dōŋ)	189	23°45′N	113°15′E
Guanglu Dao, i., China (gŭäŋ-lōō dou)	190	39°13′N	122°21′E
Guangping, China (gŭäŋ-pĭŋ)	190	36°30′N	114°57′E
Guangrao, China (gŭaŋ-rou)	190	37°04′N	118°24′E
Guangshan, China (gŭäŋ-shän)	190	32°02′N	114°53′E
Guangxi Zhuangzu, prov., China (gŭäŋ-shyē)	188	24°00′N	108°30′E
Guangzhou, China	188	23°07′N	113°15′E
Guanhu, China (gŭän-hōō)	190	34°26′N	117°59′E
Guannan, China (gŭän-nän)	190	34°17′N	119°17′E
Guanta, Ven. (gwän'tä)	131b	10°15′N	64°35′W
Guantánamo, Cuba (gwän-tä'nä-mō)	123	20°10′N	75°10′W
Guantánamo, prov., Cuba	123	20°10′N	75°05′W
Guantánamo, Bahía de, b., Cuba	123	19°35′N	75°35′W
Guantao, China (gŭän-tou)	190	36°39′N	115°25′E
Guanxian, China (gŭän-shyĕn)	190	36°30′N	115°28′E
Guanyao, China (gŭän-you)	191a	23°13′N	113°04′E
Guanyintang, China	240b	39°52′N	116°31′E
Guanyun, China (gŭän-yōn)	190	34°28′N	119°16′E
Guapiles, C.R. (gwä-pē-lĕs)	121	10°05′N	83°54′W
Guapimirim, Braz. (gwä-pē-mē-rē'ɴ)	132b	22°31′S	42°59′W
Guaporé, r., S.A. (gwä-pō-rā')	130	12°11′S	63°47′W
Guaqui, Bol. (guä'kē)	130	16°42′S	68°47′W
Guara, Sierra de, mts., Spain (sē-ĕ'r-rä-dĕ-gwä'rä)	159	42°24′N	0°15′W

ăt; finăl; rāte; senāte; ärm; ȧsk; sofȧ; fâre; ch-choose; dh-as th in other; bē; ēvent; bĕt; recĕnt; cratēr; g-gō; gh-guttural g; bĭt; ĭ-short neutral; rīde; ĸ-guttural k as ch in German ich;

PRONOUNCING INDEX Guarabira – Hamilton 293

PLACE (Pronunciation)	PAGE	LAT.	LONG.
Guarabira, Braz. (gwä-rä-bē'rȧ)	131	6°49'S	35°27'W
Guaracarumbo, Ven.	234a	10°34'N	66°59'W
Guaranda, Ec. (gwä-rån'dä)	130	1°39'S	78°57'W
Guarapari, Braz. (gwä-rä-pä'rė)	131	20°34'S	40°31'W
Guarapiranga, Represa do, res., Braz.	129a	23°45'S	46°44'W
Guarapuava, Braz. (gwä-rä-pwä'vȧ)	132	25°29'S	51°26'W
Guarda, Port. (gwär'dä)	158	40°32'N	7°17'W
Guardiato, r., Spain	158	38°10'N	5°05'W
Guarena, Spain (gwä-rā'nyä)	158	38°52'N	6°08'W
Guaribe, r., Ven. (gwä-rė'bĕ)	131b	9°48'N	65°17'W
Guárico, dept., Ven.	131b	9°42'N	67°25'W
Guarulhos, Braz. (gwȧ-rò'l-yôs)	129a	23°28'S	46°30'W
Guarus, Braz. (gwȧ'ro͞os)	129a	21°44'S	41°19'W
Guasca, Col. (gwäs'kä)	130a	4°52'N	73°52'W
Guasipati, Ven. (gwä-sė-pä'tē)	131	7°26'N	61°57'W
Guastalla, Italy (gwäs-täl'lä)	160	44°53'N	10°39'E
Guasti, Ca., U.S. (gwäs'tĭ)	107a	34°04'N	117°35'W
Guatemala, Guat. (guä-tå-mä'lä)	116	14°37'N	90°32'W
Guatemala, nation, N.A.	116	15°45'N	91°45'W
Guatire, Ven. (gwä-tė'rĕ)	131b	10°28'N	66°34'W
Guaviare, r., Col.	130	3°35'N	69°28'W
Guayabal, Cuba (gwä-yä-bä'l)	122	20°40'N	77°40'W
Guayalejo, r., Mex. (gwä-yä-lĕ'hô)	118	23°24'N	99°09'W
Guayama, P.R. (gwä-yä'mä)	117b	18°00'N	66°08'W
Guayamouc, r., Haiti	123	19°05'N	72°00'W
Guayaquil, Ec. (gwī-ä-kēl')	130	2°16'S	79°53'W
Guayaquil, Golfo de, b., Ec. (gôl-fô-dĕ)	130	3°03'S	82°12'W
Guaymas, Mex. (gwȧ'y-mäs)	116	27°49'N	110°58'W
Guayubin, Dom. Rep. (gwȧ-yo͞o-bė'n)	123	19°40'N	71°25'W
Guazacapán, Guat. (gwä-zä-kä-pän')	120	14°04'N	90°26'W
Gubakha, Russia (go͞o-bä'kå)	164	58°53'N	57°35'E
Gubbio, Italy (go͞ob'byô)	160	43°23'N	12°36'E
Guben, Ger.	154	51°57'N	14°43'E
Gucheng, China (go͞o-chŭŋ)	190	39°09'N	115°43'E
Gúdar, Sierra de, mts., Spain	159	40°28'N	0°47'W
Gudena, r., Den.	152	56°20'N	9°47'E
Gudermes, Russia	168	43°20'N	46°08'E
Gudvangen, Nor. (go͞odh'väŋ-gĕn)	152	60°52'N	6°45'E
Guebwiller, Fr. (gĕb-vė-lâr')	157	47°53'N	7°10'E
Guédi, Mont, mtn., Chad	215	12°14'N	18°58'E
Guelma, Alg. (gwĕl'mä)	210	36°32'N	7°17'E
Guelph, Can. (gwĕlf)	91	43°33'N	80°15'W
Güere, r., Ven. (gwĕ'rĕ)	131b	9°39'N	65°00'W
Guéret, Fr. (gā-rĕ')	156	46°09'N	1°52'E
Guermantes, Fr.	237c	48°51'N	2°42'E
Guernsey, dep., Eur.	156	49°28'N	2°35'W
Guernsey, i., Guernsey (gûrn'zĭ)	147	49°27'N	2°36'W
Guerrero, Mex.	112	28°20'N	100°24'W
Guerrero, Mex. (gĕr-rā'rō)	112	26°47'N	99°20'W
Guerrero, state, Mex.	116	17°45'N	100°15'W
Gueydan, La., U.S. (gā'dăn)	113	30°01'N	92°31'W
Guia de Pacobaíba, Braz. (gwė'ä-dĕ-pä'kō-bī'bä)	132b	22°42'S	43°10'W
Guiana Highlands, mts., S.A.	128	3°20'N	60°00'W
Guichi, China (gwā-chr)	193	30°35'N	117°28'E
Guichicovi, Mex. (gwē-chė-kō'vė)	119	16°58'N	95°10'W
Guidonia, Italy (gwē-dō'nyȧ)	160	42°00'N	12°45'E
Guiglo, C. Iv.	214	6°33'N	7°29'W
Guignes-Rabutin, Fr. (gēɴ'yĕ)	157b	48°38'N	2°48'E
Güigüe, Ven. (gwė'gwĕ)	131b	10°05'N	67°48'W
Guija, Lago, l., N.A. (gē'hä)	120	14°16'N	89°21'W
Guildford, Austl.	243a	33°51'S	150°59'E
Guildford, Eng., U.K. (gĭl'fērd)	150	51°13'N	0°34'W
Guilford, In., U.S. (gĭl'fērd)	101f	39°10'N	84°55'W
Guilin, China (gwā-lĭn)	189	25°18'N	110°22'E
Guimarães, Port. (gē-mä-răɴsh')	158	41°27'N	8°22'W
Guinea, nation, Afr. (gĭn'ė)	210	10°48'N	12°28'W
Guinea, Gulf of, b., Afr.	210	2°00'N	1°00'E
Guinea-Bissau, nation, Afr. (gĭn'ė)	210	12°00'N	20°00'W
Guingamp, Fr. (găɴ-gäɴ')	156	48°35'N	3°10'W
Guir, r., Mor.	148	31°55'N	2°48'W
Güira de Melena, Cuba (gwē'rä dā må-lā'nä)	122	22°45'N	82°30'W
Güiria, Ven. (gwė-rē'ä)	130	10°43'N	62°16'W
Guise, Fr. (guēz)	156	49°54'N	3°37'E
Guisisil, vol., Nic. (gė-sė-sēl')	120	12°40'N	86°11'W
Guiyang, China (gwā-yäŋ)	188	26°45'N	107°00'E
Guizhou, China (gwā-jō)	191a	22°46'N	113°15'E
Guizhou, prov., China	188	27°00'N	106°10'E
Gujānwāla, Pak. (gòj-rän'va-lȧ)	183	32°08'N	74°14'E
Gujarat, India	183	22°54'N	72°00'E
Gulbarga, India (gòl-bûr'gȧ)	183	17°25'N	76°52'E
Gulbene, Lat. (gòl-bă'nĕ)	153	57°09'N	26°49'E
Gulfport, Ms., U.S. (gŭlf'pōrt)	114	30°24'N	89°05'W
Gulja *see* Yining, China	188	43°58'N	80°40'E
Gull Lake, Can.	88	50°10'N	108°25'W
Gull Lake, l., Can.	87	52°35'N	114°00'W
Gulph Mills, Pa., U.S.	229b	40°04'N	75°21'W
Gulu, Ug.	217	2°47'N	32°18'E
Gumaca, Phil. (go͞o-mä-kä')	197a	13°55'N	122°06'E
Gumbeyka, r., Russia (gòm-bĕy'kȧ)	172a	53°20'N	59°42'E
Gumel, Nig.	210	12°39'N	9°22'E
Gummersbach, Ger. (gòm'ĕrs-bäk)	154	51°02'N	7°34'E
Gummi, Nig.	215	12°09'N	5°09'E
Gumpoldskirchen, Aus.	145e	48°04'N	16°15'E
Guna, India	186	24°44'N	77°17'E
Gunisao, r., Can. (gŭn-*i*-sā'ō)	89	53°40'N	97°35'W
Gunisao Lake, l., Can.	89	53°35'N	96°10'W
Gunnedah, Austl. (gŭ'nē-dä)	204	31°00'S	150°10'E
Gunnison, Co., U.S. (gŭn'ĭ-sŭn)	109	38°33'N	106°56'W
Gunnison, Ut., U.S.	109	39°10'N	111°50'W
Gunnison, r., Co., U.S.	109	38°45'N	108°20'W
Guntersville, Al., U.S. (gŭn'tērz-vĭl)	114	34°20'N	86°19'W
Guntersville Lake, res., Al., U.S.	114	34°30'N	86°20'W
Guntramsdorf, Aus.	145e	48°04'N	16°19'E
Guntūr, India (gòn'to͞or)	183	16°22'N	80°29'E
Guoyang, China (gwô-yäŋ)	190	33°32'N	116°10'E
Gurdon, Ar., U.S. (gûr'dŭn)	111	33°56'N	93°10'W
Gurgueia, r., Braz.	131	8°12'S	43°49'W
Guri, Embalse, res., Ven.	130	7°30'N	63°00'W
Gurnee, Il., U.S. (gûr'nē)	101a	42°22'N	87°55'W
Gurskøy, i., Nor. (go͞orskûė)	152	62°18'N	5°20'E
Gurupi, Serra do, mts., Braz. (sĕ'r-rä-dô-go͞o-ro͞o-pē')	131	5°32'S	47°02'W
Guru Sikhar, mtn., India	186	29°42'N	72°50'E
Gur'yevsk, Russia (go͞or-yĭfsk')	164	54°17'N	85°56'E
Gusau, Nig. (go͞o-zä'o͞o)	210	12°12'N	6°40'E
Gusev, Russia (go͞o'sĕf)	153	54°35'N	22°15'E
Gushi, China (go͞o-shr)	190	32°11'N	115°39'E
Gushiago, Ghana	214	9°55'N	0°12'W
Gusinje, Yugo. (go͞o-sēn'yĕ)	161	42°34'N	19°54'E
Gus'-Khrustal'nyy, Russia (go͞os-ĸro͞o-stäl'ny')	166	55°39'N	40°41'E
Gustavo A. Madero, Mex. (go͞os-tä'vô-å-mä-dĕ'rô)	118	19°29'N	99°07'W
Güstrow, Ger. (güs'trō)	154	53°48'N	12°12'E
Gütersloh, Ger. (gü'tērs-lo)	154	51°54'N	8°22'E
Guthrie, Ok., U.S. (gŭth'rĭ)	111	35°52'N	97°26'W
Guthrie Center, Ia., U.S.	103	41°41'N	94°33'W
Gutiérrez Zamora, Mex. (go͞o-tĭ-âr'rāz zä-mō'rä)	119	20°27'N	97°17'W
Guttenberg, Ia., U.S. (gŭt'ĕn-bûrg)	103	42°48'N	91°09'W
Guttenberg, N.J., U.S.	228	40°48'N	74°01'W
Guyana, nation, S.A. (gŭy'ănă)	131	7°45'N	59°00'W
Guyancourt, Fr.	237c	48°46'N	2°04'E
Guyang, China (go͞o-yäŋ)	190	34°56'N	114°57'E
Guye, China (go͞o-yŭ)	190	39°46'N	118°23'E
Guymon, Ok., U.S. (gī'mŏn)	110	36°41'N	101°29'W
Guysborough, Can. (gīz'bŭr-ô)	93	45°23'N	61°30'W
Guzhen, China (go͞o-jŭn)	192	33°20'N	117°18'E
Gvardeysk, Russia (gvȧr-dĕysk')	153	54°39'N	21°11'E
Gwadabawa, Nig.	215	13°20'N	5°15'E
Gwādar, Pak. (gwä'dŭr)	182	25°15'N	62°29'E
Gwalior, India	183	26°13'N	78°10'E
Gwane, D.R.C. (gwän)	211	4°43'N	25°50'E
Gwardafuy, Gees, c., Som.	218a	11°55'N	51°30'E
Gwda, r., Pol.	154	53°27'N	16°52'E
Gwembe, Zam.	217	16°30'S	27°35'E
Gweru, Zimb.	212	19°15'S	29°48'E
Gwinn, Mi., U.S. (gwĭn)	103	46°15'N	87°30'W
Gyandzha, Azer.	164	40°40'N	46°20'E
Gyaring Co, l., China	186	30°37'N	88°33'E
Gydan, Khrebet (Kolymskiy), mts., Russia	165	61°45'N	155°00'E
Gydanskiy Poluostrov, pen., Russia	164	70°42'N	76°03'E
Gympie, Austl. (gĭm'pė)	203	26°20'S	152°50'E
Gyöngyös, Hung. (dyûn'dvûsh)	149	47°47'N	19°55'E
Györ, Hung. (dyûr)	149	47°40'N	17°37'E
Gyōtoku, Japan (gyō'tô-ko͞o')	195a	35°42'N	139°56'E
Gypsumville, Can. (jĭp'sŭm'vĭl)	84	51°45'N	98°35'W
Gyula, Hung. (dyò'lä)	155	46°38'N	21°18'E
Gyumri, Arm.	167	40°40'N	43°50'E
Gyzylarbat, Turk.	169	38°55'N	56°33'E

H

PLACE (Pronunciation)	PAGE	LAT.	LONG.
Haan, Ger. (hän)	157c	51°12'N	7°00'E
Haapamäki, Fin. (häp'ä-mĕ-kē)	153	62°16'N	24°20'E
Haapsalu, Est. (häp'sä-lò)	153	58°56'N	23°33'E
Haar, Ger. (här)	145d	48°06'N	11°44'E
Haar, neigh., Ger.	236	51°26'N	7°13'E
Ha'Arava (Wādī al Jayb), val., Asia	181a	30°33'N	35°10'E
Haarlem, Neth. (här'lĕm)	151	52°22'N	4°37'E
Habana, prov., Cuba (hä-vä'nä)	122	22°45'N	82°25'W
Haberfield, Austl.	243a	33°53'S	151°08'E
Hābra, India	186a	22°49'N	88°38'E
Hachinohe, Japan (hä'chē-nō'hå)	194	40°29'N	141°40'E
Hachiōji, Japan (hä'chė-ō'jė)	194	35°39'N	139°18'E
Hacienda Heights, Ca., U.S.	232	33°58'N	117°58'W
Hackensack, N.J., U.S. (hăk'ĕn-săk)	100a	40°54'N	74°03'W
Hacketts, Eng., U.K.	235	51°45'N	0°05'W
Hackney, neigh., Eng., U.K.	235	51°33'N	0°03'W
Ḥadd, Ra's al, c., Oman	182	22°29'N	59°46'E
H̉addonfield, N.J., U.S. (hăd'ŭn-fēld)	100f	39°53'N	75°02'W
Haddon Heights, N.J., U.S. (hăd'ŭn hīts)	100f	39°53'N	75°03'W
Hadejia, Nig. (hä-dā'jä)	210	12°30'N	9°59'E
Hadejia, r., Nig.	210	12°15'N	10°00'E
H̱adera, Isr. (ĸå-dĕ'rå)	181a	32°26'N	34°55'E
Hadersdorf, neigh., Aus.	239e	48°13'N	16°14'E
Haderslev, Den. (hä'dhĕrs-lĕv)	152	55°17'N	9°28'E
Hadfield, Austl.	243b	37°42'S	144°56'E
Hadiach, Ukr.	167	50°22'N	33°59'E
Ḥadīdū, Yemen	182	12°40'N	53°50'E
H̉adlock, Wa., U.S. (hăd'lŏk)	106a	48°02'N	122°46'W
Ḥaḍramawt, reg., Yemen	182	15°22'N	48°40'E
H̉adūr Shu'ayb, mtn., Yemen	182	15°45'N	43°45'E
Haeju, N. Kor. (hä'ĕ-jŭ)	194	38°03'N	125°42'E
Hafnarfjördur, Ice.	146	64°02'N	21°32'W
Haft Gel, Iran	185	31°27'N	49°27'E
Hafun, Ras, c., Som. (hä-fo͞on')	218a	10°15'N	51°35'E
Hageland, Mt., U.S. (hăge'lând)	105	48°53'N	108°43'W
Hagen, Ger. (hä'gĕn)	154	51°21'N	7°29'E
Hagerstown, In., U.S. (hā'gērz-toun)	98	39°55'N	85°10'W
Hagerstown, Md., U.S.	97	39°40'N	77°45'W
Hagi, Japan (hä'gĭ)	195	34°25'N	131°25'E
Hague, Cap de la, c., Fr. (dē lȧ ȧg')	156	49°44'N	1°55'W
Haguenau, Fr. (ȧg'nō')	157	48°47'N	7°48'E
Hahnenberg, Ger.	236	51°12'N	7°24'E
Hai'an, China (hī-än)	190	32°35'N	120°25'E
Haibara, Japan (hä'ė-bä'rä)	195	34°29'N	135°57'E
Haicheng, China (hī-chŭŋ)	192	40°58'N	122°45'E
Haidārpur, neigh., India	240d	28°43'N	77°09'E
Haidian, China (hī-dĭĕn)	190	39°59'N	116°17'E
Haifa, Isr. (hä'ē-fȧ)	182	32°48'N	35°00'E
Haifeng, China (hä'ė-fĕng')	193	23°00'N	115°20'E
Haifuzhen, China (hī-fo͞o-jŭn)	190	31°57'N	121°48'E
Haijima, Japan	242a	35°42'N	139°21'E
Haikou, China (hī-kō)	193	20°00'N	110°20'E
Ḥā'il, Sau. Ar.	182	27°30'N	41°47'E
H̉ailar, China	189	49°10'N	118°40'E
Hailey, Id., U.S. (hā'lĭ)	105	43°31'N	114°19'W
Haileybury, Can.	91	47°27'N	79°38'W
Haileyville, Ok., U.S. (hā'lĭ-vĭl)	111	34°51'N	95°34'W
Hailing Dao, i., China (hī-lĭŋ dou)	193	21°30'N	112°15'E
Hailong, China (hī-loŋ)	192	42°32'N	125°52'E
Hailun, China (hä'ė-lo͞on')	189	47°18'N	126°50'E
Hainan, prov., China	188	19°00'N	109°30'E
Hainan Dao, i., China (hī-nän dou)	189	19°00'N	111°10'E
Hainault, neigh., Eng., U.K.	235	51°36'N	0°06'E
Hainburg, Aus.	154	48°09'N	16°57'E
Haines, Ak., U.S. (hānz)	95	59°10'N	135°38'W
Haines City, Fl., U.S.	115a	28°05'N	81°38'W
Hai Phong, Viet (hī'fông')(hä'ėp-hŏng)	196	20°52'N	106°40'E
Haisyn, Ukr.	167	48°46'N	29°22'E
Haiti, nation, N.A. (hā'tĭ)	117	19°00'N	72°15'W
Haizhou, China	190	34°34'N	119°11'E
Haizhou Wan, b., China	192	34°49'N	120°35'E
Hajduböszormény, Hung. (hôl'dò-bû'sûr-mān')	155	47°41'N	21°30'E
Hajdúhadház, Hung. (hô'ĭ-dò-hôd'häz)	155	47°32'N	21°32'E
Hajdúnánás, Hung. (hô'ĭ-dò-nä'näsh)	155	47°52'N	21°27'E
Hakodate, Japan (hä-kō-dä't å)	189	41°46'N	140°42'E
Haku-San, mtn., Japan (hä'ko͞o-sän')	194	36°11'N	136°45'E
Halā'ib, Egypt (hä-lä'ėb)	211	22°10'N	36°40'E
Halbe, Ger. (häl'bĕ)	145b	52°07'N	13°43'E
Halberstadt, Ger. (häl'bĕr-shtät)	154	51°54'N	11°07'E
Halcon, Mount, mtn., Phil. (häl-kōn')	197a	13°19'N	120°55'E
Halden, Nor. (häl'dĕn)	146	59°10'N	11°21'E
Halden, neigh., Ger.	236	51°23'N	7°31'E
Haldensleben, Ger.	154	52°18'N	11°23'E
Hale, Eng., U.K. (hāl)	144a	53°22'N	2°20'W
Haleakala Crater, Hi., U.S. (hä'lå-ä'kä-lä)	94a	20°44'N	156°15'W
Haleakala National Park, Hi., U.S.	94a	20°46'N	156°00'W
Halebarns, Eng., U.K.	237b	53°22'N	2°19'W
Haledon, N.J., U.S.	228	40°56'N	74°11'W
Hales Corners, Wi., U.S. (hālz kŏr'nērz)	101a	42°56'N	88°03'W
Halesowen, Eng., U.K. (hālz'ô-wĕn)	144a	52°26'N	2°03'W
Halethorpe, Md., U.S. (hāl-thôrp)	100e	39°15'N	76°40'W
Halewood, Eng., U.K.	237a	53°22'N	2°49'W
Haleyville, Al., U.S. (hā'lĭ-vĭl)	114	34°11'N	87°36'W
Half Moon Bay, Ca., U.S. (hăf'mo͞on)	106b	37°28'N	122°26'W
Halfway House, S. Afr. (häf-wā hous)	213b	26°00'S	28°08'E
Halfweg, Neth.	145a	52°23'N	4°45'E
Halifax, Can. (hăl'ĭ-făks)	85	44°39'N	63°36'W
Halifax, Eng., U.K.	150	53°44'N	1°52'W
Halifax Bay, b., Austl. (hăl'ĭ-făx)	203	18°56'S	147°07'E
Halifax Harbour, b., Can.	92	44°35'N	63°31'W
Halkett, Cape, c., Ak., U.S.	95	70°50'N	151°15'W
Hallam, Austl.	243b	38°01'S	145°16'E
Hallam Peak, mtn., Can.	87	52°11'N	118°46'E
Halla San, mtn., S. Kor. (häl'lȧ-sän)	194	33°20'N	126°37'E
Halle, Bel. (häl'lĕ)	145a	50°45'N	4°13'E
Halle, Ger.	147	51°30'N	11°59'E
Hallettsville, Tx., U.S. (hăl'ĕts-vĭl)	113	29°26'N	96°55'W
Hallock, Mn., U.S. (hăl'ŭk)	102	48°46'N	96°57'W
Hall Peninsula, pen., Can. (hôl)	85	63°14'N	65°40'W
Halls Bayou, Tx., U.S.	113a	29°55'N	95°23'W
Hallsberg, Swe. (häls'bĕrgh)	152	59°04'N	15°04'E
Halls Creek, Austl. (hôlz)	202	18°15'S	127°45'E
Halmahera, i., Indon. (häl-mä-hā'rä)	197	0°45'N	128°45'E
Halmahera, Laut, Indon.	197	1°00'S	129°00'E
Halmstad, Swe. (hälm'städ)	146	56°40'N	12°46'E
Halsafjorden, fj., Nor. (häl'sĕ fyôrd)	152	63°03'N	8°23'E
Halstead, Eng., U.K.	235	51°20'N	0°08'E
Halstead, Ks., U.S. (hôl'stĕd)	111	38°02'N	97°36'W
Haltern, Ger. (häl'tĕrn)	157c	51°45'N	7°10'E
Haltom City, Tx., U.S. (hôl'tŏm)	107c	32°48'N	97°13'W
Halver, Ger.	157c	51°11'N	7°30'E
Ham, neigh., Eng., U.K.	235	51°26'N	0°19'W
Hamada, Japan	194	34°53'N	132°05'E
Hamadān, Iran (hŭ-mŭ-dän')	182	34°45'N	48°07'E
Ḥamāh, Syria (hä'mä)	182	35°08'N	36°53'E
H̉amamatsu, Japan (hä'mä-mät'sò)	194	34°41'N	137°43'E
Hamar, Nor. (hä'mär)	146	60°49'N	11°05'E
Hamasaka, Japan (hă'mȧ-sä'kȧ)	195	35°57'N	134°27'E
Hamberg, S. Afr.	244b	26°11'S	27°53'E
Hamborn, Ger. (häm'bōrn)	157c	51°30'N	6°43'E
Hamburg, Ger. (häm'bo͞orgh)	142	53°34'N	10°02'E
Hamburg, S. Afr. (hăm'bürg)	213c	33°18'S	27°28'E
Hamburg, Ar., U.S. (hăm'bûrg)	111	33°15'N	91°49'W
Hamburg, N.J., U.S.	100a	41°09'N	74°35'W
Hamburg, N.Y., U.S.	101c	42°44'N	78°51'W
Hamburg, state, Ger.	145c	53°35'N	10°00'E
Hamden, Ct., U.S. (hăm'dĕn)	99	41°20'N	72°55'W
Hämeenlinna, Fin. (hĕ'mån-lĭn-nȧ)	146	61°00'N	24°29'E
Hameln, Ger. (hä'mĕln)	154	52°06'N	9°23'E
Hamelwörden, Ger. (hä'mĕl-vûr-dĕn)	145c	53°47'N	9°19'E
Hamersley Range, mts., Austl. (hăm'ērz-lė)	202	22°15'S	117°50'E
Hamhŭng, N. Kor. (häm'hòng')	189	39°57'N	127°35'E
Hami, China (hä-mē)	188	42°58'N	93°14'E
Hamilton, Austl. (hăm'ĭl-tŭn)	203	37°50'S	142°10'E
Hamilton, Can.	85	43°15'N	79°52'W
Hamilton, N.Z.	203a	37°45'S	175°28'E
Hamilton, Al., U.S.	114	34°09'N	88°01'W
Hamilton, Ma., U.S.	93a	42°37'N	70°52'W
Hamilton, Mo., U.S.	111	39°43'N	93°59'W
Hamilton, Mt., U.S.	105	46°15'N	114°09'W
Hamilton, Oh., U.S.	97	39°22'N	84°33'W
Hamilton, Tx., U.S.	112	31°42'N	98°07'W

ng-sing; ŋ-baŋk; ɴ-nasalized n; nŏd; cŏmmit; ōld; ôbey; ôrder; oi-boil; fo͞od; ò-as oo in foot; ou-out; s-soft; sh-dish; th-thin; pūre; ůnite; ûrn; stŭd; circŭs; ü-as in French tu; '-indeterminate vowel.

294 Hamilton–Hazard

PLACE (Pronunciation)	PAGE	LAT.	LONG.
Hamilton, Lake, l., Ar., U.S.	111	34°25′N	93°32′W
Hamilton Harbour, b., Can.	83d	43°17′N	79°50′W
Hamilton Inlet, b., Can.	85	54°20′N	56°57′W
Hamina, Fin. (hä′mē-nȧ)	153	60°34′N	27°15′E
Hamlet, N.C., U.S. (hăm′lĕt)	115	35°52′N	79°46′W
Hamlin, Tx., U.S. (hăm′lĭn)	110	32°54′N	100°08′W
Hamm, Ger. (häm)	154	51°40′N	7°48′E
Hamm, neigh., Ger.	236	51°12′N	6°44′E
Hammanskraal, S. Afr. (hä-mȧns-kräl′)	218d	25°24′S	28°17′E
Hamme, Bel.	145a	51°06′N	4°07′E
Hamme-Oste Kanal, can., Ger. (hä′mĕ-ōs′tĕ kä-näl)	145c	53°20′N	8°59′E
Hammerfest, Nor. (hä′mĕr-fĕst)	142	70°38′N	23°59′E
Hammersmith, neigh., Eng., U.K.	235	51°30′N	0°14′W
Hammond, In., U.S. (hăm′ŭnd)	97	41°37′N	87°31′W
Hammond, La., U.S.	113	30°30′N	90°28′W
Hammond, Or., U.S.	106c	46°12′N	123°57′W
Hammondville, Austl.	243a	33°57′S	150°57′E
Hammonton, N.J., U.S. (hăm′ŭn-tŭn)	99	39°40′N	74°45′W
Hampden, Me., U.S. (hăm′dĕn)	92	44°44′N	68°51′W
Hampstead, Md., U.S.	100e	39°36′N	76°54′W
Hampstead, neigh., Eng., U.K.	235	51°33′N	0°11′W
Hampstead Heath, pt. of i., Eng., U.K.	235	51°34′N	0°10′W
Hampstead Norris, Eng., U.K. (hămp-stĕd nŏ′rĭs)	144b	51°27′N	1°14′W
Hampton, Austl.	243b	37°56′S	145°00′E
Hampton, Can. (hămp′tŭn)	92	45°32′N	65°51′W
Hampton, Ia., U.S.	103	42°43′N	93°15′W
Hampton, Va., U.S.	99	37°02′N	76°21′W
Hampton, neigh., Eng., U.K.	235	51°25′N	0°22′W
Hampton National Historic Site, pt. of i., Md., U.S.	229c	39°25′N	76°35′W
Hampton Roads, b., Va., U.S.	100g	36°56′N	76°23′W
Hams Fork, r., Wy., U.S.	105	41°55′N	110°40′W
Hamtramck, Mi., U.S. (hăm-trăm′ĭk)	101b	42°24′N	83°03′W
Han, r., China	189	31°40′N	112°04′E
Han, r., China (hän)	193	25°00′N	116°35′E
Han, r., S. Kor.	194	37°10′N	127°40′E
Hana, Hi., U.S. (hä′nä)	94a	20°43′N	155°59′W
Hanábana, r., Cuba (hä-nä-bä′nä)	122	22°30′N	80°55′W
Hanalei Bay, b., Hi., U.S. (hä-nä-lä′ē)	94a	22°15′N	159°40′W
Hanang, mtn., Tan.	217	4°26′S	35°24′E
Hanau, Ger. (hä′nou)	154	50°08′N	8°56′E
Hancock, Mi., U.S. (hăn′kŏk)	97	47°08′N	88°37′W
Handan, China (hän-dän)	190	36°37′N	114°30′E
Handforth, Eng., U.K.	237b	53°21′N	2°13′W
Haney, Can. (hā-nē)	87	49°13′N	122°36′W
Hanford, Ca., U.S. (hăn′fērd)	108	36°20′N	119°38′W
Hangayn Nuruu, mts., Mong.	188	48°03′N	99°45′E
Hang Hau Town, H.K.	241c	22°19′N	114°16′E
Hango, Fin. (häŋ′gû)	142	59°49′N	22°56′E
Hangzhou, China (häng′chō′)	189	30°17′N	120°12′E
Hangzhou Wan, b., China (häŋ-jō wän)	193	30°20′N	121°25′E
Hankamer, Tx., U.S. (hăn′kȧ-mēr)	113a	29°52′N	94°42′W
Hankinson, N.D., U.S. (häŋ′kĭn-sŭn)	102	46°04′N	96°54′W
Hankou, China (hän-kō)	193	30°42′N	114°22′E
Hann, Mount, mtn., Austl. (hän)	202	16°05′S	126°07′E
Hanna, Can. (hăn′ȧ)	84	51°38′N	111°54′W
Hanna, Wy., U.S.	105	41°51′N	106°34′W
Hannah, N.D., U.S.	102	48°58′N	98°42′W
Hannibal, Mo., U.S. (hăn′ĭ bȧl)	97	39°42′N	91°22′W
Hannover, Ger. (hän-ō′vēr)	142	52°22′N	9°45′E
Hanöbukten, b., Swe.	152	55°54′N	14°55′E
Hanoi, Viet (hä-noi′)	196	21°04′N	105°50′E
Hanover, Can. (hăn′ō-vēr)	90	44°10′N	81°05′W
Hanover, Md., U.S.	229c	39°11′N	76°42′W
Hanover, Ma., U.S.	93a	42°07′N	70°49′W
Hanover, N.H., U.S.	99	43°45′N	72°15′W
Hanover, Pa., U.S.	99	39°50′N	77°00′W
Hanover, i., Chile	132	51°00′S	74°45′W
Hanshan, China (hän′shän′)	190	31°43′N	118°06′E
Hans Lollick, i., V.I.U.S. (häns′lôl′ĭk)	117c	18°24′N	64°55′W
Hanson, Ma., U.S. (hăn′sŭn)	93a	42°04′N	70°53′W
Hansville, Wa., U.S. (hăns′-vĭl)	106a	47°55′N	122°33′W
Hantengri Feng, mtn., Asia (hän-tŭŋ-rē fŭŋ)	188	42°10′N	80°20′E
Hantsport, Can. (hănts′pōrt)	92	45°04′N	64°11′W
Hanworth, neigh., Eng., U.K.	235	51°26′N	0°23′W
Hanyang, China (han′yäng′)	189	30°30′N	114°10′E
Hanzhong, China (hän-jôŋ)	192	33°02′N	107°00′E
Haocheng, China (hou-chŭŋ)	190	33°19′N	117°33′E
Haparanda, Swe. (hä-pa-rän′dä)	146	65°54′N	23°57′E
Hapeville, Ga., U.S. (hăp′vĭl)	100c	33°39′N	84°25′W
Happy Camp, Ca., U.S.	104	41°47′N	123°22′W
Happy Valley-Goose Bay, Can.	85	53°19′N	60°33′W
Hapsford, Eng., U.K.	237a	53°16′N	2°48′W
Ḩaql, Sau. Ar.	181a	29°15′N	34°57′E
Ḩar, Laga, r., Kenya	217	2°15′N	39°30′E
Haramachida, Japan	242a	35°33′N	139°27′E
Harare, Zimb.	212	17°50′S	31°03′E
Harbin, China	189	45°40′N	126°30′E
Harbor Beach, Mi., U.S. (här′bẽr bēch)	98	43°50′N	82°40′W
Harbor City, neigh., Ca., U.S.	232	33°48′N	118°17′W
Harbord, Austl.	243a	33°47′S	151°17′E
Harbor Isle, N.Y., U.S.	228	40°36′N	73°40′W
Harbor Springs, Mi., U.S.	98	45°25′N	85°05′W
Harbour Breton, Can. (brĕt′ŭn) (brĕ-tôn′)	93	47°29′N	55°48′W
Harbour Grace, Can. (grās)	93	47°32′N	53°13′W
Harburg, Ger. (här-bōrgh)	145c	53°28′N	9°58′E
Hardangerfjorden, Nor. (här-däng′ẽr fyôrd)	146	59°58′N	6°30′E
Hardin, Mt., U.S. (här′dĭn)	105	45°44′N	107°36′W
Harding, S. Afr. (här′dĭng)	212	30°34′S	29°54′E
Harding, Lake, res., U.S.	114	32°43′N	85°00′W
Hardwār, India (hŭr′dvär)	183	29°56′N	78°06′E
Hardy, r., Mex. (här′dĭ)	108	32°04′N	115°10′W
Hare Bay, b., Can. (hâr)	93	51°18′N	55°50′W
Harefield, neigh., Eng., U.K.	235	51°36′N	0°29′W
Harer, Eth.	211	9°43′N	42°10′E
Harerge, hist. reg., Eth.	211	8°15′N	41°00′E
Hargeysa, Som. (här-gā′ē-sȧ)	218a	9°20′N	43°57′E
Harghita, Munţii, mts., Rom.	155	46°25′N	25°40′E
Harima-Nada, b., Japan (hä′rē-mä nä-dä)	195	34°34′N	134°37′E
Haringey, neigh., Eng., U.K.	235	51°35′N	0°07′W
Haringvliet, r., Neth.	145a	51°49′N	4°03′E
Hari Rud, r., Asia	182	34°29′N	61°16′E
Harker Village, N.J., U.S.	229b	39°51′N	75°09′W
Harlan, Ia., U.S. (här′lăn)	111	41°40′N	95°10′W
Harlan, Ky., U.S.	114	36°50′N	83°19′W
Harlan County Reservoir, res., Ne., U.S.	110	40°03′N	99°51′W
Harlem, Mt., U.S. (hȧr′lĕm)	105	48°33′N	108°50′W
Harlem, neigh., N.Y., U.S.	228	40°49′N	73°56′W
Harlesden, neigh., Eng., U.K.	235	51°32′N	0°15′W
Harlingen, Neth. (här′lĭng-ĕn)	151	53°10′N	5°24′E
Harlingen, Tx., U.S.	96	26°12′N	97°42′W
Harlington, neigh., Eng., U.K.	235	51°29′N	0°26′W
Harlow, Eng., U.K. (här′lō)	144b	51°46′N	0°08′E
Harlowton, Mt., U.S. (hȧr′lō-tun)	105	46°26′N	109°50′W
Harmar Heights, Pa., U.S.	230b	40°33′N	79°49′W
Harmarville, Pa., U.S.	230b	40°32′N	79°51′W
Harmony, In., U.S. (här′mō-nĭ)	98	39°35′N	87°00′W
Harney Basin, Or., U.S. (här′nĭ)	104	43°26′N	120°19′W
Harney Lake, l., Or., U.S.	104	43°11′N	119°23′W
Harney Peak, mtn., S.D., U.S.	96	43°52′N	103°32′W
Härnosand, Swe. (hĕr-nû-sänd)	146	62°37′N	17°54′E
Haro, Spain (ä′rō)	158	42°35′N	2°49′W
Harola, India	240d	28°36′N	77°19′E
Harold Hill, neigh., Eng., U.K.	235	51°36′N	0°13′E
Harold Wood, neigh., Eng., U.K.	235	51°36′N	0°14′E
Haro Strait, strt., N.A. (hă′rō)	106a	48°27′N	123°11′W
Harpen, neigh., Ger.	236	51°29′N	7°16′E
Harpenden, Eng., U.K. (här′pĕn-d′n)	144b	51°48′N	0°22′W
Harper, Lib.	210	4°25′N	7°43′W
Harper, Ks., U.S. (här′pēr)	110	37°17′N	98°02′W
Harper, Wa., U.S.	106a	47°31′N	122°32′W
Harpers Ferry, W.V., U.S. (här′pērz)	99	39°20′N	77°45′W
Harper Woods, Mi., U.S.	230c	42°24′N	82°55′W
Harpurhey, neigh., Eng., U.K.	237b	53°31′N	2°13′W
Harricana, r., Can.	91	50°10′N	78°50′W
Harriman, Tn., U.S. (hă′ĭ-măn)	114	35°55′N	84°34′W
Harrington, De., U.S. (hăr′ĭng-tŭn)	99	38°55′N	75°35′W
Harris, i., Scot., U.K. (hăr′ĭs)	150	57°55′N	6°40′W
Harris, Lake, l., Fl., U.S.	115a	28°43′N	81°40′W
Harrisburg, Il., U.S. (hăr′ĭs-bûrg)	98	37°45′N	88°35′W
Harrisburg, Pa., U.S.	97	40°15′N	76°50′W
Harrismith, S. Afr. (hă-rĭs′mĭth)	218d	28°17′S	29°08′E
Harrison, Ar., U.S. (hăr′ĭ-sŭn)	111	36°13′N	93°06′W
Harrison, N.J., U.S.	228	40°45′N	74°10′W
Harrison, N.Y., U.S.	228	40°58′N	73°43′W
Harrison, Oh., U.S.	101f	39°16′N	84°45′W
Harrisonburg, Va., U.S. (hăr′ĭ-sŭn-bûrg)	99	38°30′N	78°50′W
Harrison Lake, l., Can.	87	49°31′N	121°59′W
Harrisonville, Md., U.S.	229c	39°23′N	77°50′W
Harrisonville, Mo., U.S. (hăr-ĭ-sŭn-vĭl)	111	38°39′N	94°21′W
Harris Park, Austl.	243a	33°49′S	151°01′E
Harrisville, Ut., U.S. (hăr′ĭs-vĭl)	107b	41°17′N	112°00′W
Harrisville, W.V., U.S.	98	39°10′N	81°05′W
Harrodsburg, Ky., U.S. (hăr′ŭdz-bûrg)	98	37°45′N	84°50′W
Harrods Creek, r., Ky., U.S. (hăr′ŭdz)	101h	38°24′N	35°33′W
Harrow, Eng., U.K. (hăr′ō)	144b	51°34′N	0°21′W
Harrow on the Hill, neigh., Eng., U.K.	235	51°34′N	0°20′W
Harsefeld, Ger. (här′zĕ-fĕld′)	145c	53°27′N	9°30′E
Harstad, Nor. (här′städh)	146	68°49′N	16°10′E
Hart, Mi., U.S. (härt)	98	43°40′N	86°25′W
Hartbeesfontein, S. Afr.	218d	26°46′S	26°25′E
Hartbeespoortdam, res., S. Afr.	213b	25°47′S	27°43′E
Hartford, Al., U.S. (härt′fẽrd)	114	31°05′N	85°42′W
Hartford, Ar., U.S.	111	35°01′N	94°21′W
Hartford, Ct., U.S.	97	41°45′N	72°40′W
Hartford, Il., U.S.	107e	38°50′N	90°06′W
Hartford, Ky., U.S.	114	37°25′N	86°50′W
Hartford, Mi., U.S.	98	42°15′N	86°15′W
Hartford, Wi., U.S.	103	43°19′N	88°25′W
Hartford City, In., U.S.	98	40°35′N	85°25′W
Hartington, Eng., U.K. (härt′ĭng-tŭn)	144a	53°08′N	1°48′W
Hartington, Ne., U.S.	102	42°37′N	97°18′W
Hartland Point, c., Eng., U.K.	150	51°03′N	4°40′W
Hartlepool, Eng., U.K. (här′t′l-pōōl)	146	54°40′N	1°12′W
Hartley, Eng., U.K.	235	51°23′N	0°19′E
Hartley, Ia., U.S. (härt′lĭ)	102	43°12′N	95°29′W
Hartley Bay, Can.	86	53°25′N	129°15′W
Hart Mountain, mtn., Can. (härt)	89	52°25′N	101°30′W
Hartsbeespoort, S. Afr.	213b	25°44′S	27°51′E
Hartselle, Al., U.S. (härt′sĕl)	114	34°24′N	86°55′W
Hartshorne, Ok., U.S. (härts′hôrn)	111	34°49′N	95°34′W
Hartsville, S.C., U.S. (härts′vĭl)	115	34°20′N	80°04′W
Hartwell, Ga., U.S. (härt′wĕl)	115	34°21′N	82°56′W
Hartwell Lake, res., U.S.	97	34°30′N	83°00′W
Hārua, India	186a	22°36′N	88°40′E
Harvard, Il., U.S. (här′vȧrd)	103	42°25′N	88°39′W
Harvard, Ma., U.S.	93a	42°30′N	71°35′W
Harvard, Ne., U.S.	110	40°36′N	98°08′W
Harvard, Mount, mtn., Co., U.S.	109	38°55′N	106°20′W
Harvel, Eng., U.K.	235	51°21′N	0°22′E
Harvey, Can.	92	45°44′N	64°46′W
Harvey, Il., U.S.	101a	41°37′N	87°39′W
Harvey, La., U.S.	100d	29°54′N	90°05′W
Harvey, N.D., U.S.	102	47°46′N	99°55′W
Harwich, Eng., U.K. (här′wĭch)	151	51°53′N	1°13′E
Harwick, Pa., U.S.	230b	40°34′N	79°48′W
Harwood, Eng., U.K.	237b	53°35′N	2°23′W
Harwood, Md., U.S.	229c	38°52′N	76°37′W
Harwood Heights, Il., U.S.	231a	41°59′N	87°48′W
Harwood Park, Md., U.S.	229c	39°12′N	76°44′W
Haryana, state, India	183	29°00′N	75°45′E
Harz Mountains, mts., Ger. (härts)	154	51°42′N	10°50′E
Ḩasanābād, Iran	241h	35°44′N	51°19′E
Hasbrouck Heights, N.J., U.S.	228	40°52′N	74°04′W
Hashimoto, Japan (hä′shē-mō′tō)	195	34°19′N	135°37′E
Haskayne, Eng., U.K.	237a	53°34′N	2°58′W
Haskell, Ok., U.S. (hăs′kĕl)	111	35°49′N	95°41′W
Haskell, Tx., U.S.	110	33°09′N	99°43′W
Hasköy, neigh., Tur.	239f	41°02′N	28°58′E
Haslingden, Eng., U.K. (hăz′lĭng dĕn)	144a	53°43′N	2°19′W
Hasselbeck-Schwarzbach, Ger.	236	51°16′N	6°53′E
Hassels, neigh., Ger.	236	51°10′N	6°53′E
Hassi Messaoud, Alg.	210	31°17′N	6°13′E
Hässleholm, Swe. (hăs′lĕ-hōlm)	152	56°10′N	13°44′E
Hasslinghausen, Ger.	236	51°20′N	7°17′E
Hästen, neigh., Ger.	236	51°09′N	7°06′E
Hasten, neigh., Ger.	236	51°12′N	7°09′E
Hastings, N.Z.	203a	39°33′S	176°53′E
Hastings, Eng., U.K. (hās′tĭngz)	147	50°52′N	0°28′E
Hastings, Mi., U.S.	98	42°40′N	85°20′W
Hastings, Mn., U.S.	107g	44°44′N	92°51′W
Hastings, Ne., U.S.	96	40°34′N	98°42′W
Hastings-on-Hudson, N.Y., U.S. (ŏn-hŭd′sŭn)	100a	40°59′N	75°53′W
Hastingwood, Eng., U.K.	235	51°45′N	0°09′E
Hatay, Tur.	182	36°20′N	36°10′E
Hatchie, r., Tn., U.S. (hăch′ē)	114	35°28′N	89°14′W
Haţeg, Rom. (kät-säg′)	161	45°35′N	22°57′E
Hatfield Broad Oak, Eng., U.K. (hăt-fēld brôd ōk)	144b	51°50′N	0°14′E
Hatogaya, Japan (hä′tō-gä-yä)	195a	35°50′N	139°45′E
Hatsukaichi, Japan (hät′sōō-kȧ′ē-chē)	195	34°22′N	132°19′E
Hatteras, Cape, c., N.C., U.S. (hăt′ẽr-ȧs)	97	35°15′N	75°24′W
Hattiesburg, Ms., U.S. (hăt′ĭz-bûrg)	97	31°20′N	89°18′W
Hattingen, Ger. (hä′tĕn-gĕn)	157c	51°24′N	7°11′E
Hatton, neigh., Eng., U.K.	235	51°28′N	0°25′W
Hattori, Japan	242b	34°46′N	135°27′E
Hatvan, Hung. (hôt′vôn)	155	47°39′N	19°44′E
Hatzfeld, neigh., Ger.	236	51°17′N	7°11′E
Haugesund, Nor. (hou′gĕ-soon′)	146	59°26′N	5°20′E
Haughton Green, Eng., U.K.	237b	53°27′N	2°06′W
Haukivesi, l., Fin. (hou′kē-vĕ′sē)	153	62°02′N	29°02′E
Haultain, r., Can.	88	56°15′N	106°35′W
Hauptsrus, S. Afr.	218d	26°35′S	26°16′E
Hauraki Gulf, b., N.Z. (hä-ōō-rä′kē)	203a	36°30′S	175°00′E
Haut, Isle au, Me., U.S. (hō)	92	44°03′N	68°13′W
Haut Atlas, mts., Mor.	148	32°10′N	5°49′W
Hauterive, Can.	92	49°11′N	68°16′W
Hauula, Hi., U.S.	94a	21°37′N	157°45′W
Hauz Rāni, neigh., India	240d	28°32′N	77°13′E
Havana, Cuba	117	23°08′N	82°23′W
Havana, Il., U.S. (hȧ-vă′nȧ)	111	40°17′N	90°02′W
Havasu, Lake, res., U.S. (hăv′ȧ-sōō)	109	34°26′N	114°09′W
Havel, r., Ger. (hä′fĕl)	154	53°09′N	13°10′E
Havel-Kanal, can., Ger.	145b	52°36′N	13°12′E
Haverford, Pa., U.S.	229b	40°01′N	75°18′W
Haverhill, Ma., U.S. (hā′vẽr-hĭl)	93a	42°46′N	71°05′W
Haverhill, N.H., U.S.	99	44°00′N	72°05′W
Havering, neigh., Eng., U.K.	235	51°34′N	0°14′E
Havering's Grove, Eng., U.K.	235	51°38′N	0°23′E
Haverstraw, N.Y., U.S. (hā′vẽr-strô)	100a	41°11′N	73°58′W
Havertown, Pa., U.S.	229b	39°59′N	75°18′W
Havlíckuv Brod, Czech Rep.	147	49°38′N	15°34′E
Havre, Mt., U.S. (hăv′ẽr)	96	48°34′N	109°42′W
Havre-Boucher, Can. (hăv′rȧ-bōō-shā′)	93	45°42′N	61°30′W
Havre de Grace, Md., U.S. (hăv′ẽr dē gràs′)	99	39°35′N	76°05′W
Havre-Saint Pierre, Can.	92	50°15′N	63°36′W
Haw, r., N.C., U.S. (hô)	115	36°17′N	79°46′W
Hawaii, state, U.S.	96c	20°00′N	157°40′W
Hawaii, i., Hi., U.S. (hä-wī′ē)	96c	19°50′N	157°15′W
Hawaiian Gardens, Ca., U.S.	232	33°50′N	118°04′W
Hawaiian Islands, is., Hi., U.S. (hä-wī′ȧn)	96c	22°00′N	158°00′W
Hawaii Volcanoes National Park, rec., Hi., U.S.	96c	19°30′N	155°25′W
Hawarden, Ia., U.S. (hā′wȧr-dĕn)	102	43°00′N	96°28′W
Ḩawf, Jabal, hills, Egypt	244a	29°55′N	31°21′E
Hawi, Hi., U.S. (hä′wē)	94a	20°16′N	155°48′W
Hawick, Scot., U.K. (hô′ĭk)	150	55°25′N	2°55′W
Hawke Bay, b., N.Z. (hôk)	203a	39°17′S	177°20′E
Hawker, Austl. (hô′kẽr)	204	31°58′S	138°12′E
Hawkesbury, Can. (hôks′bẽr-ĭ)	91	45°35′N	74°35′W
Hawkinsville, Ga., U.S. (hô′kĭnz-vĭl)	114	32°15′N	83°30′W
Hawks Nest Point, c., Bah.	123	24°05′N	75°30′W
Hawley, Eng., U.K.	235	51°25′N	0°14′E
Hawley, Mn., U.S. (hô′lĭ)	102	46°52′N	96°18′W
Haworth, Eng., U.K. (hä′wûrth)	144a	53°50′N	1°57′W
Haworth, N.J., U.S.	228	40°58′N	73°59′W
Hawthorn, Austl.	243b	37°49′S	145°02′E
Hawthorne, Ca., U.S. (hô′thôrn)	107a	33°55′N	118°22′W
Hawthorne, Nv., U.S.	108	38°33′N	118°39′W
Hawthorne, N.J., U.S.	228	40°57′N	74°09′W
Haxtun, Co., U.S. (hăks′tŭn)	110	40°39′N	102°38′W
Hay, r., Austl. (hā)	202	23°00′S	136°45′E
Hay, r., Can.	84	60°21′N	117°14′W
Hayama, Japan (hä-yä′mä)	195a	35°16′N	139°35′E
Hayashi, Japan (hä-yä′shē)	195a	35°13′N	139°38′E
Hayden, Az., U.S. (hā′dĕn)	109	33°00′N	110°50′W
Hayes, neigh., Eng., U.K.	235	51°23′N	0°01′E
Hayes, r., Can.	85	55°25′N	93°55′W
Hayes, Mount, mtn., Ak., U.S. (hāz)	95	63°32′N	146°40′W
Haynesville, La., U.S. (hānz′vĭl)	113	32°55′N	93°08′W
Hayrabolu, Tur.	161	41°14′N	27°05′E
Hay River, Can.	84	60°50′N	115°53′W
Hays, Ks., U.S. (hāz)	110	38°51′N	99°20′W
Haystack Mountain, mtn., Wa., U.S. (hā-stăk′)	106a	48°26′N	122°07′W
Hayward, Ca., U.S. (hā′wẽrd)	106b	37°40′N	122°06′W
Hayward, Wi., U.S.	103	46°01′N	91°31′W
Hazard, Ky., U.S. (hăz′ȧrd)	114	37°13′N	83°10′W

PRONOUNCING INDEX Hazel Grove–Himeji 295

PLACE (Pronunciation)	PAGE	LAT.	LONG.
Hazel Grove, Eng., U.K.	237b	53°23'N	2°08'W
Hazelhurst, Ga., U.S. (hā'z'l-hûrst)	115	31°50'N	82°36'W
Hazelhurst, Ms., U.S.	114	31°52'N	90°23'W
Hazel Park, Mi., U.S.	101b	42°28'N	83°06'W
Hazelton, Can. (hā'z'l-tŭn)	84	55°15'N	127°40'W
Hazelton Mountains, mts., Can.	86	55°00'N	128°00'W
Hazleton, Pa., U.S.	99	41°00'N	76°00'W
Headland, Al., U.S. (hĕd'lănd)	114	31°22'N	85°20'W
Headley, Eng., U.K.	235	51°17'N	0°16'W
Heald Green, Eng., U.K.	237b	53°22'N	2°14'W
Healdsburg, Ca., U.S. (hēldz'bûrg)	108	38°37'N	122°52'W
Healdton, Ok., U.S. (hēld'tŭn)	111	34°13'N	97°28'W
Heanor, Eng., U.K. (hēn'ŏr)	144a	53°01'N	1°22'W
Heard Island, i., Austl. (hûrd)	3	53°10'S	74°35'E
Hearne, Tx., U.S. (hûrn)	113	30°53'N	96°35'W
Hearst, Can. (hûrst)	85	49°36'N	83°40'W
Heart, r., N.D., U.S. (härt)	102	46°46'N	102°34'W
Heart Lake Indian Reserve, I.R., Can.	87	55°02'N	111°30'W
Heart's Content, Can. (härts kŏn'tĕnt)	93	47°52'N	53°22'W
Heathmont, Austl.	243b	37°49'S	145°15'E
Heaton Moor, Eng., U.K.	237b	53°25'N	2°11'W
Heavener, Ok., U.S. (hēv'nēr)	111	34°52'N	94°36'W
Heaverham, Eng., U.K.	235	51°18'N	0°15'E
Heaviley, Eng., U.K.	237b	53°24'N	2°09'W
Hebbronville, Tx., U.S. (hē'brŭn-vĭl)	112	27°18'N	98°40'W
Hebbville, Md., U.S.	229c	39°20'N	77°46'W
Hebei, prov., China (hŭ-bā)	189	39°15'N	115°40'E
Heber City, Ut., U.S. (hē'bēr)	109	40°30'N	111°25'W
Heber Springs, Ar., U.S.	111	35°28'N	91°59'W
Hebgen Lake, res., Mt., U.S. (hĕb'gĕn)	105	44°47'N	111°38'W
Hebrides, is., Scot., U.K.	142	57°00'N	6°30'W
Hebrides, Sea of the, sea, Scot., U.K.	150	57°00'N	7°00'W
Hebron, Can. (hĕb'rŭn)	85	58°11'N	62°56'W
Hebron, In., U.S.	101a	41°19'N	87°13'W
Hebron, Ky., U.S.	101f	39°04'N	84°43'W
Hebron, Ne., U.S.	111	40°11'N	97°36'W
Hebron, N.D., U.S.	102	46°54'N	102°04'W
Hebron *see* Al Khalīl, W. Bank	181a	31°31'N	35°07'E
Heby, Swe. (hĭ'bü)	152	59°56'N	16°48'E
Hecate Strait, strt., Can. (hĕk'ā-tē)	84	53°00'N	131°00'W
Hecelchakán, Mex. (ā-sĕl-chä-kän')	119	20°10'N	90°09'W
Hechi, China (hŭ-chr)	193	24°50'N	108°18'E
Hechuan, China (hŭ-chyuän)	188	30°00'N	106°20'E
Hecla Island, i., Can.	89	51°08'N	96°45'W
Hedemora, Swe. (hĭ-dĕ-mō'rä)	152	60°16'N	15°55'E
Hedon, Eng., U.K. (hĕ-dŭn)	144a	53°44'N	0°12'W
Heemstede, Neth.	145a	52°20'N	4°36'E
Heerdt, neigh., Ger.	236	51°13'N	6°43'E
Heerlen, Neth.	151	50°55'N	5°58'E
Hefei, China (hŭ-fā)	189	31°51'N	117°15'E
Heflin, Al., U.S. (hĕf'lĭn)	114	33°40'N	85°33'W
Heide, Ger. (hī'dĕ)	154	54°13'N	9°06'E
Heide, neigh., Ger.	236	51°31'N	6°52'E
Heidelberg, Austl. (hī'dĕl-bûrg)	201a	37°45'S	145°04'E
Heidelberg, Ger. (hīdĕl-bĕrgh)	147	49°24'N	8°43'E
Heidelberg, S. Afr.	218d	26°32'S	28°22'E
Heidelberg, Pa., U.S.	230b	40°23'N	80°05'W
Heidenheim, Ger. (hī'dĕn-hīm)	154	48°41'N	10°09'E
Heil, Ger.	236	51°38'N	7°35'E
Heilbron, S. Afr. (hĭl'brŏn)	218d	27°17'S	27°58'E
Heilbronn, Ger. (hīl'brōn)	147	49°09'N	9°16'E
Heiligenhaus, Ger. (hī'lē-gĕn-houz)	157c	51°19'N	6°58'E
Heiligensee, neigh., Ger.	238a	52°36'N	13°13'E
Heiligenstadt, Ger. (hī'lē-gĕn-shtät)	154	51°21'N	10°10'E
Heilongjiang, prov., China (hā-lôŋ-jyäŋ)	189	46°36'N	128°07'E
Heinersdorf, Ger.	238a	52°23'N	13°20'E
Heinersdorf, neigh., Ger.	238a	52°34'N	13°27'E
Heinola, Fin. (hå-nō'lå)	153	61°13'N	26°03'E
Heinsberg, Ger. (hīnz'bĕrgh)	157c	51°04'N	6°07'E
Heisingen, neigh., Ger.	236	51°25'N	7°04'E
Heist-op-den-Berg, Bel.	145a	51°05'N	4°14'E
Hejaz *see* Al Ḥijāz, reg., Sau. Ar.	182	23°45'N	39°08'E
Hejian, China (hŭ-jyĕn)	192	38°28'N	116°05'E
Hekla, vol., Ice.	142	63°53'N	19°37'W
Hel, Pol. (hāl)	155	54°37'N	18°53'E
Helagsfjället, mtn., Swe.	146	62°54'N	12°24'E
Helan Shan, mts., China (hŭ-län shän)	188	38°02'N	105°20'E
Helena, Ar., U.S. (hē-lē'nȧ)	97	34°33'N	90°35'W
Helena, Mt., U.S. (hĕ-lē'nȧ)	96	46°35'N	112°01'W
Helensburgh, Austl. (hĕl'ĕnz-bŭr-ō)	201b	34°11'S	150°59'E
Helensburgh, Scot., U.K.	150	56°01'N	4°53'W
Helgoland, i., Ger. (hĕl'gō-länd)	154	54°13'N	7°30'E
Heliopolis, hist., Egypt	244a	30°08'N	31°17'E
Hellier, Ky., U.S. (hĕl'yēr)	115	37°16'N	82°27'W
Hellín, Spain (ĕl-yēn')	148	38°30'N	1°40'W
Hells Canyon, val., U.S.	104	45°20'N	116°45'W
Helmand, r., Afg. (hĕl'mŭnd)	182	31°00'N	63°48'E
Hel'miaziv, Ukr.	163	49°49'N	31°54'E
Helmond, Neth. (hĕl'mōnt) (ĕl'môɴ')	151	51°35'N	5°04'E
Helmstedt, Ger. (hĕlm'shtĕt)	154	52°14'N	11°03'E
Helotes, Tx., U.S. (hē'lōts)	107d	29°35'N	98°41'W
Helper, Ut., U.S. (hĕlp'ēr)	109	39°40'N	110°55'W
Helsby, Eng., U.K.	237a	53°16'N	2°46'W
Helsingborg, Swe. (hĕl'sĭng-bôrgh)	146	56°04'N	12°40'E
Helsingfors *see* Helsinki, Fin.	142	60°10'N	24°53'E
Helsingør, Den. (hĕl-sĭng-ûr')	146	56°03'N	12°33'E
Helsinki, Fin. (hĕl'sĕn-kē) (hĕl'sĭng-fôrs')	142	60°10'N	24°53'E
Hemel Hempstead, Eng., U.K. (hĕm'ĕl hĕmp'stĕd)	144b	51°43'N	0°29'W
Hemer, Ger.	157c	51°22'N	7°46'E
Hemet, Ca., U.S. (hĕm'ĕt)	107a	33°45'N	116°57'W
Hemingford, Ne., U.S. (hĕm'ĭng-fērd)	102	42°21'N	103°30'W
Hemphill, Tx., U.S. (hĕmp'hĭl)	113	31°20'N	93°48'W
Hempstead, N.Y., U.S. (hĕmp'stĕd)	100a	40°42'N	73°37'W
Hempstead, Tx., U.S.	113	30°07'N	96°05'W
Hemse, Swe. (hĕm'sĕ)	152	57°15'N	18°25'E
Hemsön, i., Swe.	152	62°43'N	18°22'E
Henan, prov., China (hŭ-nän)	189	33°58'N	112°33'E
Henares, r., Spain (å-nä'rås)	158	40°50'N	2°55'W
Henderson, Ky., U.S. (hĕn'dĕr-sŭn)	98	37°50'N	87°30'W
Henderson, Nv., U.S.	108	36°09'N	115°04'W
Henderson, N.C., U.S.	115	36°18'N	78°24'W
Henderson, Tn., U.S.	114	35°25'N	88°40'W
Henderson, Tx., U.S.	113	32°09'N	94°48'W
Hendersonville, N.C., U.S. (hĕn'dēr-sŭn-vĭl)	115	35°17'N	82°28'W
Hendersonville, Tn., U.S.	114	36°18'N	86°37'W
Hendon, Eng., U.K. (hĕn'dŭn)	144b	51°34'N	0°13'W
Hendrina, S. Afr. (hĕn-drē'nȧ)	218d	26°10'S	29°44'E
Hengch'un, Tai. (hĕng'chŭn')	193	22°00'N	120°42'E
Hengelo, Neth. (hĕngĕ-lō)	151	52°20'N	6°45'E
Hengshan, China (hĕng'shän')	193	27°20'N	112°40'E
Hengshui, China (hĕng'shōō-ĕ')	190	37°43'N	115°42'E
Hengxian, China (hŭŋ shyĕn)	193	22°40'N	109°20'E
Hengyang, China	189	26°58'N	112°30'E
Heniches'k, Ukr.	167	46°11'N	34°47'E
Henley on Thames, Eng., U.K. (hĕn'lē ŏn tĕmz)	144b	51°31'N	0°54'W
Henlopen, Cape, c., De., U.S. (hĕn-lō'pĕn)	99	38°45'N	75°05'W
Hennebont, Fr. (ĕn-bôɴ')	156	47°47'N	3°16'W
Hennenman, S. Afr.	218d	27°59'S	27°03'E
Hennessey, Ok., U.S. (hĕn'ĕ-sĭ)	111	36°04'N	97°53'W
Hennigsdorf, Ger. (hĕ'nĕngz-dōrf))	145b	52°39'N	13°12'E
Hennops, r., S. Afr. (hĕn'ŏps)	213b	25°51'S	27°57'E
Hennopsrivier, S. Afr.	213b	25°50'S	27°59'E
Henrietta, Ok., U.S. (hĕn-rĭ-ĕt'ȧ)	111	35°25'N	95°58'W
Henrietta, Tx., U.S. (hen-rĭ-ĕ'tȧ)	110	33°47'N	98°11'W
Henrietta Maria, Cape, c., Can. (hĕn-rĭ-ĕt'ȧ)	85	55°10'N	82°20'W
Henry Mountains, mts., Ut., U.S. (hĕn'rĭ)	96	37°55'N	110°45'W
Henrys Fork, r., Id., U.S.	105	43°52'N	111°55'W
Henteyn Nuruu, mtn., Russia	192	49°40'N	111°00'E
Hentiyn Nuruu, mts., Mong.	188	49°25'N	107°51'E
Henzada, Myanmar	183	17°38'N	95°28'E
Heppner, Or., U.S. (hĕp'nēr)	104	45°21'N	119°33'W
Hepu, China (hŭ-pōō)	193	21°28'N	109°10'E
Herāt, Afg. (hĕ-rät')	182	34°28'N	62°13'E
Herbede, Ger.	236	51°25'N	7°16'E
Hercules, Can.	83g	53°27'N	113°20'W
Herdecke, Ger. (hĕr'dĕ-kĕ)	157c	51°24'N	7°26'E
Heredia, C.R. (ā-rā'dhē-ä)	121	10°04'N	84°06'W
Hereford, Eng., U.K. (hĕrĕ'fērd)	150	52°05'N	2°44'W
Hereford, Md., U.S.	100e	39°35'N	76°42'W
Hereford, Tx., U.S. (hĕr'ĕ-fērd)	110	34°47'N	102°25'W
Hereford and Worcester, co., Eng., U.K.	144a	52°24'N	2°15'W
Herencia, Spain (å-rān'thē-ä)	158	39°23'N	3°22'W
Herentals, Bel.	145a	51°10'N	4°51'E
Herford, Ger. (hĕr'fōrt)	154	52°06'N	8°42'E
Herington, Ks., U.S. (hĕr'ĭng-tŭn)	111	38°41'N	96°57'W
Herisau, Switz. (hā'rē-zou)	154	47°23'N	9°18'E
Herk-de-Stad, Bel.	145a	50°56'N	5°13'E
Herkimer, N.Y., U.S. (hûr'kĭ-mēr)	99	43°05'N	75°00'W
Hermannskogel, mtn., Aus.	239e	48°16'N	16°18'E
Hermansville, Mi., U.S. (hûr'mȧns-vĭl)	98	45°40'N	87°35'W
Hermantown, Mn., U.S. (hĕr'mȧn-toun)	107h	46°46'N	92°12'W
Hermanusdorings, S. Afr.	218d	24°08'S	27°46'E
Herminie, Pa., U.S. (hûr-mĭ'nē)	101e	40°16'N	79°45'W
Hermitage Bay, b., Can. (hûr'mĭ-tĕj)	93	47°35'N	56°05'W
Hermit Islands, is., Pap. N. Gui. (hûr'mĭt)	197	1°48'S	144°55'E
Hermosa Beach, Ca., U.S. (hĕr-mō'sȧ)	107a	33°51'N	118°24'W
Hermosillo, Mex. (ĕr-mō-sē'l-yō)	116	29°00'N	110°57'W
Hermsdorf, neigh., Ger.	238a	52°37'N	13°18'E
Hernals, neigh., Aus.	239e	48°13'N	16°20'E
Herndon, Va., U.S. (hĕrn'don)	100e	38°58'N	77°22'W
Herne, Ger. (hĕr'nĕ)	157c	51°32'N	7°13'E
Herning, Den. (hĕr'nĭng)	146	56°08'N	8°55'E
Hernwood Heights, Md., U.S.	229c	39°22'N	77°50'W
Héroes Chapultepec, Mex.	233a	19°28'N	99°04'W
Héroes de Churubusco, Mex.	233a	19°22'N	99°06'W
Heron, l., Mn., U.S. (hĕr'ŭn)	102	43°42'N	95°23'W
Herongate, Eng., U.K.	235	51°36'N	0°21'E
Heron Lake, Mn., U.S.	102	43°48'N	95°20'W
Heronsgate, Eng., U.K.	235	51°38'N	0°31'W
Herrero, Punta, Mex. (pô'n-tä-ĕr-rĕ'rô)	120a	19°18'N	87°24'W
Herrin, Il., U.S. (hĕr'ĭn)	98	37°50'N	89°00'W
Herschel, S. Afr. (hĕr'-shĕl)	213c	30°37'S	27°12'E
Herscher, Il., U.S. (hēr'shēr)	101a	41°03'N	88°06'W
Hersham, Eng., U.K.	235	51°22'N	0°23'W
Herstal, Bel. (hĕr'stäl)	151	50°42'N	5°32'E
Herten, Ger.	236	51°35'N	7°07'E
Hertford, Eng., U.K.	150	51°48'N	0°05'W
Hertford, N.C., U.S. (hûrt'fērd)	115	36°10'N	76°30'W
Hertfordshire, co., Eng., U.K.	144b	51°46'N	0°05'W
Hertzberg, Ger. (hĕrtz'bĕrgh)	145b	52°54'N	12°58'E
Hervás, Spain	158	40°16'N	5°51'W
Herzliyya, Isr.	181a	32°10'N	34°49'E
Hessen, hist. reg., Ger. (hĕs'ĕn)	154	50°42'N	9°00'E
Heswall, Eng., U.K.	237a	53°20'N	3°06'W
Hetch Hetchy Aqueduct, Ca., U.S. (hĕtch hĕt'chĭ ăk'wē-dŭkt)	108	37°27'N	120°54'W
Hettinger, N.D., U.S. (hĕt'ĭn-jēr)	102	45°58'N	102°36'W
Hetzendorf, neigh., Aus.	239e	48°10'N	16°18'E
Heuningspruit, S. Afr.	218d	27°28'S	27°26'E
Heven, neigh., Ger.	236	51°26'N	7°17'E
Hewlett, N.Y., U.S.	228	40°38'N	73°42'W
Hewlett Harbor, N.Y., U.S.	228	40°38'N	73°41'W
Hexian, China	190	31°44'N	118°20'E
Hexian, China (hŭ shyĕn)	193	24°20'N	111°28'E
Hextable, Eng., U.K.	235	51°25'N	0°11'E
Heyang, China (hŭ-yäŋ)	192	35°18'N	110°18'E
Heystekrand, S. Afr.	218d	25°16'S	27°14'E
Heyuan, China (hŭ-yůän)	193	23°48'N	114°45'E
Heywood, Eng., U.K. (hā'wŏod)	144a	53°36'N	2°12'W
Heze, China (hŭ-dzŭ)	190	35°13'N	115°28'E
Hialeah, Fl., U.S. (hī-ȧ-lē'ăh)	115a	25°49'N	80°18'W
Hiawatha, Ks., U.S. (hī-ȧ-wô'thȧ)	111	39°50'N	95°33'W
Hiawatha, Ut., U.S.	109	39°25'N	111°05'W
Hibbing, Mn., U.S. (hĭb'ĭng)	97	47°26'N	92°58'W
Hickman, Ky., U.S. (hĭk'mȧn)	114	34°33'N	89°10'W
Hickory, N.C., U.S. (hĭk'ō-rĭ)	115	35°43'N	81°21'W
Hickory Hills, Il., U.S.	231a	41°43'N	87°49'W
Hicksville, N.Y., U.S.	98	41°15'N	84°45'W
Hicksville, N.Y., U.S. (hĭks'vĭl)	100a	40°47'N	73°25'W
Hico, Tx., U.S. (hī'kō)	112	32°00'N	98°02'W
Hidalgo, Mex.	112	27°49'N	99°53'W
Hidalgo, Mex. (ē-dhäl'gō)	118	24°14'N	99°25'W
Hidalgo, state, Mex.	116	20°45'N	99°30'W
Hidalgo del Parral, Mex. (ē-dä'l-gō-dĕl-pär-rä'l)	116	26°55'N	105°40'W
Hidalgo Yalalag, Mex. (ē-dhäl'gō-yä-lä-läg)	119	17°12'N	96°11'W
Hiddinghausen, Ger.	236	51°22'N	7°17'E
Hierro Island, i., Spain (yĕ'r-rô)	210	27°37'N	18°29'W
Hiesfeld, Ger.	236	51°33'N	6°46'E
Hietzing, neigh., Aus.	239e	48°11'N	16°18'E
Higashi, neigh., Japan	242b	34°41'N	135°31'E
Higashimurayama, Japan	195a	35°46'N	139°28'E
Higashinada, neigh., Japan	242b	34°43'N	135°16'E
Higashinakano, Japan	242a	35°38'N	139°25'E
Higashinari, neigh., Japan	242b	34°40'N	135°33'E
Higashiōizumi, neigh., Japan	242a	35°45'N	139°36'E
Higashiōsaka, Japan	195b	34°40'N	135°44'E
Higashisumiyoshi, neigh., Japan	242b	34°37'N	135°32'E
Higashiyama, neigh., Japan	241e	35°00'N	135°48'E
Higashiyodogawa, neigh., Japan	242b	34°44'N	135°29'E
Higgins, l., Mi., U.S. (hĭg'ĭnz)	98	44°20'N	84°45'W
Higginsville, Mo., U.S. (hĭg'ĭnz-vĭl)	111	39°05'N	93°44'W
High, i., Mi., U.S.	98	45°45'N	85°45'W
Higham, Eng., U.K.	235	51°26'N	0°28'E
High Beach, Eng., U.K.	235	51°39'N	0°02'E
High Bluff, Can.	83f	50°01'N	98°08'W
Highborne Cay, i., Bah. (hībōrn kē)	122	24°45'N	76°50'W
Highcliff, Pa., U.S.	230b	40°32'N	80°03'W
Higher Broughton, neigh., Eng., U.K.	237b	53°30'N	2°15'W
Highgrove, Ca., U.S. (hī'grōv)	107a	34°01'N	117°20'W
High Island, Tx., U.S.	113a	29°34'N	94°24'W
Highland, Ca., U.S. (hī'lănd)	107a	34°08'N	117°13'W
Highland, Il., U.S.	111	38°44'N	89°41'W
Highland, In., U.S.	101a	41°33'N	87°28'W
Highland, Mi., U.S.	101b	42°38'N	83°37'W
Highland, Pa., U.S.	230b	40°33'N	80°04'W
Highland Park, Il., U.S.	101a	42°11'N	87°47'W
Highland Park, Md., U.S.	229d	38°54'N	76°54'W
Highland Park, Mi., U.S.	101b	42°24'N	83°06'W
Highland Park, N.J., U.S.	100a	40°30'N	74°25'W
Highland Park, Tx., U.S.	107c	32°49'N	96°48'W
Highlands, N.J., U.S. (hī-lăndz)	100a	40°24'N	73°59'W
Highlands, Tx., U.S.	113a	29°49'N	95°01'W
High Laver, Eng., U.K.	235	51°45'N	0°13'E
Highmore, S.D., U.S. (hī'mōr)	102	44°30'N	99°26'W
High Ongar, Eng., U.K. (on'gĕr)	144b	51°43'N	0°15'E
High Peak, mtn., Phil.	197a	15°38'N	120°05'E
High Point, N.C., U.S.	115	35°55'N	80°00'W
High Prairie, Can.	84	55°26'N	116°29'W
High Ridge, Mo., U.S.	107e	38°27'N	90°32'W
High River, Can.	84	50°35'N	113°52'W
High Rock Lake, res., N.C., U.S. (hī'-rŏk)	115	35°40'N	80°15'W
High Springs, Fl., U.S.	115	29°48'N	82°38'W
High Tatra Mountains, mts., Eur.	155	49°15'N	19°40'E
Hightown, Eng., U.K.	237a	53°32'N	3°04'W
Hightstown, N.J., U.S. (hīts-toun)	100a	40°16'N	74°32'W
High Wycombe, Eng., U.K. (wĭ-kŭm)	150	51°36'N	0°45'W
Higuero, Punta, c., P.R.	117b	18°21'N	67°11'W
Higuerote, Ven. (ē-gē-rô'tĕ)	131b	10°29'N	66°06'W
Higüey, Dom. Rep. (ē-gwĕ'y)	123	18°40'N	68°45'W
Hiiumaa, i., Est. (hē'ŏm-ô)	166	58°47'N	22°05'E
Hikone, Japan (hē'kō-nĕ)	195	35°15'N	136°15'E
Hildburghausen, Ger. (hĭld'bŏorg hou-zĕn)	154	50°26'N	10°45'E
Hilden, Ger. (hĕl'dĕn)	157c	51°10'N	6°56'E
Hildesheim, Ger. (hĭl'dĕs-hīm)	147	52°08'N	9°56'E
Hillaby, Mount, mtn., Barb. (hĭl'ȧ-bĭ)	121b	13°15'N	59°35'W
Hill City, Ks., U.S. (hĭl)	110	39°22'N	99°54'W
Hill City, Mn., U.S.	103	46°58'N	93°38'W
Hill Crest, Pa., U.S.	229b	40°05'N	75°11'W
Hillcrest Heights, Md., U.S.	229d	38°52'N	76°57'W
Hillegersberg, Neth.	145a	51°57'N	4°29'E
Hillen, neigh., Ger.	236	51°37'N	7°13'E
Hillerød, Den. (hē'lĕ-rûdh)	152	55°56'N	12°17'E
Hillingdon, neigh., Eng., U.K.	235	51°32'N	0°27'W
Hillsboro, Il., U.S. (hĭlz'bŭr-ō)	111	39°09'N	89°28'W
Hillsboro, Ks., U.S.	111	38°22'N	97°11'W
Hillsboro, N.H., U.S.	99	43°05'N	71°55'W
Hillsboro, N.D., U.S.	102	47°23'N	97°05'W
Hillsboro, Oh., U.S.	98	39°10'N	83°40'W
Hillsboro, Or., U.S.	106c	45°31'N	122°59'W
Hillsboro, Tx., U.S.	113	32°01'N	97°06'W
Hillsboro, Wi., U.S.	103	43°39'N	90°20'W
Hillsburgh, Can. (hĭlz'bûrg)	83d	43°48'N	80°09'W
Hills Creek Lake, res., Or., U.S.	104	43°41'N	122°26'W
Hillsdale, Mi., U.S. (hĭls-dāl)	109	41°55'N	84°35'W
Hillside, Md., U.S.	229d	38°52'N	76°55'W
Hillside, neigh., N.Y., U.S.	228	40°42'N	73°47'W
Hillwood, Va., U.S.	229d	38°52'N	77°10'W
Hilo, Hi., U.S. (hē'lō)	96c	19°44'N	155°01'W
Hiltrop, neigh., Ger.	236	51°30'N	7°15'E
Hilvarenbeek, Neth.	145a	51°29'N	5°10'E
Hilversum, Neth. (hĭl'vēr-sŭm)	145a	52°13'N	5°10'E
Himachal Pradesh, India	183	32°00'N	77°30'E
Himalayas, mts., Asia	183	29°30'N	85°02'E
Himeji, Japan (hē'mȧ-jē)	194	34°50'N	134°42'E

ng-sing; ŋ-baŋk; ɴ-nasalized n; nŏd; cŏmmit; ōld; ôbey; ôrder; oi-boil; fōōd; ŏo-as oo in foot; ou-out; s-soft; sh-dish; th-thin; pūre; ůnite; ûrn; stŭd; circŭs; ü-as in French tu; '-indeterminate vowel.

296 Himmelgeist-Howard

PLACE (Pronunciation)	PAGE	LAT.	LONG.
Himmelgeist, neigh., Ger.	236	51°10′N	6°49′E
Himmelpforten, Ger. (hĕ'mĕl-pfōr-tĕn)	145c	53°37′N	9°19′E
Ḩimş, Syria	182	34°44′N	36°43′E
Hinche, Haiti (hĕn'chȧ) (äɴsh)	123	19°10′N	72°05′W
Hinchinbrook, i., Austl. (hĭn-chĭn-bro͝ok)	202	18°23′S	146°57′E
Hinckley, Eng., U.K. (hĭnk'lĭ)	144a	52°32′N	1°21′W
Hindley, Eng., U.K. (hĭnd'lĭ)	144a	53°32′N	2°35′W
Hindu Kush, mts., Asia (hĭn'do͞o ko͞osh')	183	35°15′N	68°44′E
Hindupur, India (hĭn'do͞o-po͞or)	187	13°52′N	77°34′E
Hingham, Ma., U.S. (hĭng'ăm)	93a	42°14′N	70°53′W
Hinkley, Oh., U.S. (hĭnk'-lĭ)	101d	41°14′N	81°45′W
Hino, Japan	242a	35°41′N	139°24′E
Hinojosa del Duque, Spain (ē-nō-kō'sä)	158	38°30′N	5°09′W
Hinsdale, Il., U.S. (hĭnz'dāl)	101a	41°48′N	87°56′W
Hinsel, neigh., Ger.	236	51°26′N	7°05′E
Hinton, Can. (hĭn'tŭn)	87	53°25′N	117°34′W
Hinton, W.V., U.S. (hĭn'tŭn)	98	37°40′N	80°55′W
Hirado, i., Japan (hē'rä-dō)	194	33°19′N	129°18′E
Hirakata, Japan (hē'rä-kä'tä)	195b	34°49′N	135°40′E
Hirara, Japan	198d	24°48′N	125°17′E
Hiratsuka, Japan (hē-rät-so͞o'kȧ)	195	35°20′N	139°19′E
Hirosaki, Japan (hē'rō-sä'kē)	189	40°31′N	140°38′E
Hirose, Japan (hē'rō-sä)	195	35°20′N	133°11′E
Hiroshima, Japan (hē-rō-shē'mȧ)	189	34°22′N	132°25′E
Hirota, Japan	242b	34°45′N	135°21′E
Hirschstetten, neigh., Aus.	239e	48°14′N	16°29′E
Hirson, Fr. (ēr-sôɴ')	156	49°54′N	4°00′E
Hisar, India	186	29°15′N	75°47′E
Hispaniola, i., N.A. (hĭ'spăn-ĭ-ō-lȧ)	117	17°30′N	73°15′W
Hitachi, Japan (hē-tä'chē)	194	36°42′N	140°47′E
Hitchcock, Tx., U.S. (hĭch'kŏk)	113a	29°21′N	95°01′W
Hither Green, neigh., Eng., U.K.	235	51°27′N	0°01′W
Hitoyoshi, Japan (hē'tō-yō'shē)	195	32°13′N	130°45′E
Hitra, i., Nor. (hĭträ)	146	63°34′N	7°37′E
Hittefeld, Ger. (hē'tĕ-fĕld)	145c	53°23′N	9°59′E
Hiwasa, Japan (hē'wȧ-sä)	195	33°44′N	134°31′E
Hiwassee, r., Tn., U.S. (hī-wôs'sē)	114	35°10′N	84°35′W
Hjälmaren, l., Swe.	146	59°07′N	16°05′E
Hjo, Swe. (yō)	152	58°19′N	14°11′E
Hjørring, Den. (jûr'ĭng)	146	57°27′N	9°59′E
Hlobyne, Ukr.	163	49°22′N	33°17′E
Hlohovec, Slvk. (hlō'ho-vĕts)	155	48°24′N	17°49′E
Hlukhiv, Ukr.	167	51°42′N	33°52′E
Hobart, Austl. (hō'bȧrt)	203	43°00′S	147°30′E
Hobart, In., U.S.	101a	41°31′N	87°15′W
Hobart, Ok., U.S.	110	35°02′N	99°06′W
Hobart, Wa., U.S.	106a	47°25′N	121°58′W
Hobbs, N.M., U.S. (hŏbs)	110	32°41′N	103°15′W
Hoboken, Bel. (hō'bō-kĕn)	145a	51°11′N	4°20′E
Hoboken, N.J., U.S.	100a	40°43′N	74°03′W
Hobro, Den. (hō-brō')	152	56°38′N	9°47′E
Hobson, Va., U.S. (hŏb'sŭn)	100g	36°54′N	76°31′W
Hobson's Bay, b., Austl. (hŏb'sŭnz)	201a	37°54′S	144°45′E
Hobyo, Som.	218a	5°24′N	48°28′E
Hochdahl, Ger.	236	51°13′N	6°56′E
Hochheide, Ger.	236	51°27′N	6°41′E
Ho Chi Minh City, Viet	196	10°46′N	106°34′E
Hochlar, neigh., Ger.	236	51°36′N	7°10′E
Höchsten, Ger.	236	51°27′N	7°29′E
Hockinson, Wa., U.S. (hŏk'ĭn-sŭn)	106c	45°44′N	122°29′W
Hoctún, Mex. (ôk-to͞o'n)	120a	20°52′N	89°10′W
Hodgenville, Ky., U.S. (hŏj'ĕn-vĭl)	98	37°35′N	85°45′W
Hodges Hill, mtn., Can. (hŏj'ĕz)	93	49°04′N	55°53′W
Hodgkins, Il., U.S.	231a	41°46′N	87°51′W
Hódmezövásárhely, Hung. (hōd'mĕ-zû-vô'shôr-hĕl-y')	155	46°24′N	20°21′E
Hodna, Chott el, l., Alg.	148	35°20′N	3°27′E
Hodonin, Czech Rep. (hē'dō-nēn)	155	48°50′N	17°06′E
Hoegaarden, Bel.	145a	50°46′N	4°55′E
Hoek van Holland, Neth.	145a	51°59′N	4°05′E
Hoeryŏng, N. Kor. (hwĕr'yŭng)	194	42°28′N	129°39′E
Hof, Ger. (hōf)	154	50°19′N	11°55′E
Hofburg, pt. of i., Aus.	239e	48°12′N	16°22′E
Hofsjökull, ice., Ice. (hôfs'yü'ko͞ol)	146	64°55′N	18°40′W
Hog, i., Mi., U.S.	98	45°50′N	85°20′W
Hogansville, Ga., U.S. (hō'gănz-vĭl)	114	33°10′N	84°54′W
Hogar y Redención, Mex.	233a	19°22′N	99°13′W
Hog Cay, i., Bah.	123	23°35′N	75°30′W
Hogsty Reef, rf., Bah.	123	21°45′N	73°50′W
Hohenbrunn, Ger. (hō'hĕn-bro͞on)	145d	48°03′N	11°42′E
Hohenlimburg, Ger. (hō'hĕn lĕm'bo͞org)	157c	51°20′N	7°35′E
Hohen Neuendorf, Ger. (hō'hĕn noi'ĕn-dōrf)	145b	52°40′N	13°22′E
Hohenschönhausen, neigh., Ger.	238a	52°33′N	13°30′E
Hohensyburg, hist., Ger.	236	51°25′N	7°29′E
Hohe Tauern, mts., Aus. (hō'ĕ tou'ĕrn)	154	47°11′N	12°12′E
Hohhot, China (hŭ-ho͞o-tŭ)	189	41°05′N	111°50′E
Hohoe, Ghana	214	7°09′N	0°28′E
Hohokus, N.J., U.S. (hō-hō-kŭs)	100a	41°01′N	74°08′W
Höhscheid, neigh., Ger.	236	51°09′N	7°04′E
Hoi An, Viet	193	15°48′N	108°30′E
Hoisington, Ks., U.S. (hoi'zĭng-tŭn)	110	38°30′N	98°46′W
Hoisten, Ger.	236	51°08′N	6°42′E
Hojo, Japan (hō'jō)	195	33°58′N	132°50′E
Hokitika, N.Z. (hō-kĭ-tē'kä)	203a	42°43′S	170°59′E
Hokkaidō, i., Japan (hŏk'kī-dō)	194	43°30′N	142°45′E
Holbaek, Den. (hôl'bĕk)	152	55°42′N	11°40′E
Holborn, neigh., Eng., U.K.	235	51°31′N	0°07′W
Holbox, Mex. (ôl-bō'x)	120a	21°33′N	87°19′W
Holbox, Isla, i., Mex. (ē's-lä-ôl-bō'x)	120a	21°40′N	87°21′W
Holbrook, Az., U.S. (hōl'brŏk)	109	34°55′N	110°15′W
Holbrook, Ma., U.S.	93a	42°10′N	71°01′W
Holden, Ma., U.S. (hōl'dĕn)	93a	42°21′N	71°51′W
Holden, Mo., U.S.	111	38°42′N	94°00′W
Holden, W.V., U.S.	98	37°45′N	82°05′W
Holdenville, Ok., U.S. (hōl'dĕn-vĭl)	111	35°05′N	96°25′W
Holdrege, Ne., U.S. (hōl'drĕj)	110	40°25′N	99°28′W
Holguín, Cuba (ôl-gēn')	117	20°55′N	76°15′W
Holguín, prov., Cuba	122	20°40′N	76°15′W
Holidaysburg, Pa., U.S. (hŏl'ĭ-dāz-bûrg)	99	40°30′N	78°30′W
Hollabrunn, Aus.	154	48°33′N	16°04′E
Holland, Mi., U.S. (hŏl'ănd)	98	42°45′N	86°10′W
Hollands Diep, strt., Neth.	145a	51°43′N	4°25′E
Hollenstedt, Ger. (hō'lĕn-shtĕt)	145c	53°22′N	9°43′E
Hollins, Eng., U.K.	237b	53°34′N	2°17′W
Hollis, N.H., U.S. (hŏl'ĭs)	93a	42°30′N	71°29′W
Hollis, Ok., U.S.	110	34°39′N	99°56′W
Hollis, neigh., N.Y., U.S.	228	40°43′N	73°46′W
Hollister, Ca., U.S. (hŏl'ĭs-tẽr)	108	36°50′N	121°25′W
Holliston, Ma., U.S. (hŏl'ĭs-tŭn)	93a	42°12′N	71°25′W
Holly, Mi., U.S. (hŏl'ĭ)	98	42°45′N	83°30′W
Holly, Wa., U.S.	106a	47°34′N	122°58′W
Holly Springs, Ms., U.S. (hŏl'ĭ sprĭngz)	114	34°45′N	89°28′W
Hollywood, Ca., U.S. (hŏl'ē-wo͝od)	107a	34°06′N	118°20′W
Hollywood, Fl., U.S.	115a	26°00′N	80°11′W
Hollywood Bowl, pt. of i., Ca., U.S.	232	34°07′N	118°20′W
Holmes, Pa., U.S.	229b	39°54′N	75°19′W
Holmes Reefs, rf., Austl. (hōmz)	203	16°33′S	148°43′E
Holmes Run Acres, Va., U.S.	229d	38°51′N	77°13′W
Holmestrand, Nor. (hŏl'mĕ-strän)	152	59°29′N	10°17′E
Holmsbu, Nor. (hōlms'bo͞o)	152	59°36′N	10°26′E
Holmsjön, l., Swe.	152	62°23′N	15°43′E
Holroyd, Austl.	243a	33°50′S	150°58′E
Holstebro, Den. (hôl'stĕ-brô)	146	56°22′N	8°39′E
Holston, r., Tn., U.S. (hōl'stŭn)	114	36°02′N	83°42′W
Holt, Eng., U.K. (hōlt)	144a	53°05′N	2°53′W
Holten, neigh., Ger.	236	51°31′N	6°48′E
Holthausen, neigh., Ger.	236	51°34′N	7°26′E
Holton, Ks., U.S. (hōl'tŭn)	111	39°27′N	95°43′W
Holy Cross, Ak., U.S. (hō'lĭ krôs)	95	62°10′N	159°40′W
Holyhead, Wales, U.K. (hŏl'ē-hĕd)	150	53°18′N	4°45′W
Holy Island, i., Eng., U.K.	150	55°43′N	1°48′W
Holy Island, i., Wales, U.K. (hō'lĭ)	150	53°15′N	4°45′W
Holyoke, Co., U.S. (hōl'yōk)	110	40°36′N	102°18′W
Holyoke, Ma., U.S.	99	42°10′N	72°40′W
Holzen, Ger.	236	51°26′N	7°31′E
Holzheim, Ger.	236	51°09′N	6°39′E
Holzwickede, Ger.	236	51°30′N	7°36′E
Homano, Japan (hō-mä'nō)	195a	35°33′N	140°08′E
Homberg, Ger. (hōm'bĕrgh)	157c	51°27′N	6°42′E
Hombori, Mali	214	15°17′N	1°42′W
Home Gardens, Ca., U.S. (hōm gär'd'nz)	107a	33°53′N	117°32′W
Homeland, Ca., U.S. (hōm'lănd)	107a	33°44′N	117°07′W
Homer, Ak., U.S. (hō'mẽr)	95	59°42′N	151°30′W
Homer, La., U.S.	113	32°46′N	93°05′W
Homer Youngs Peak, mtn., Mt., U.S.	105	45°19′N	113°41′W
Homestead, Fl., U.S. (hōm'stĕd)	115a	25°27′N	80°28′W
Homestead, Mi., U.S.	107k	46°20′N	84°07′W
Homestead, Pa., U.S.	101e	40°29′N	79°55′W
Homestead National Monument of America, rec., Ne., U.S.	111	40°16′N	96°51′W
Hometown, Il., U.S.	231a	41°44′N	87°44′W
Homewood, Al., U.S. (hōm'wo͝od)	100h	33°28′N	86°48′W
Homewood, Il., U.S.	101a	41°34′N	87°40′W
Homewood, neigh., Pa., U.S.	230b	40°27′N	79°54′W
Hominy, Ok., U.S. (hŏm'ĭ-nĭ)	111	36°25′N	96°24′W
Homochitto, r., Ms., U.S. (hō-mō-chĭt'ō)	114	31°23′N	91°15′W
Honda, Col. (hōn'dȧ)	130	5°13′N	74°45′W
Honda, Bahía, b., Cuba (bä-ē'ä-ô'n-dä)	122	23°10′N	83°20′W
Hondo, Tx., U.S.	112	29°20′N	99°08′W
Hondo, r., N.M., U.S.	110	33°22′N	105°06′W
Hondo, Río, r., N.A. (hon-dō')	120a	18°16′N	88°32′W
Honduras, nation, N.A. (hŏn-do͞o'rȧs)	116	14°30′N	88°00′W
Honduras, Gulf of, b., N.A.	116	16°30′N	87°30′W
Honea Path, S.C., U.S. (hŭn'ĭ păth)	115	34°25′N	82°16′W
Hønefoss, Nor. (hē'nē-fōs)	146	60°10′N	10°15′E
Honesdale, Pa., U.S. (hōnz'dāl)	99	41°30′N	75°15′W
Honey Grove, Tx., U.S. (hŭn'ĭ grōv)	111	33°35′N	95°54′W
Honey Lake, l., Ca., U.S. (hŭn'ĭ)	108	40°11′N	120°34′W
Honfleur, Can. (ôɴ-flûr')	83b	46°39′N	70°53′W
Honfleur, Fr. (ôɴ-flûr')	156	49°26′N	0°13′E
Hon Gay, Viet	193	20°58′N	107°10′E
Hong Kong (Xianggang), China	189	21°45′N	115°00′E
Hongshui, r., China (hōŋ-shwā)	188	24°30′N	105°00′E
Honguedo, Détroit d', strt., Can.	92	49°08′N	63°45′W
Hongze Hu, l., China	189	33°17′N	118°37′E
Honiara, Sol. Is.	203	9°26′S	159°57′E
Honiton, Eng., U.K. (hŏn'ĭ-tŏn)	150	50°49′N	3°10′W
Honolulu, Hi., U.S. (hŏn-ō-lo͞o'lo͞o)	96c	21°18′N	157°50′W
Honomu, Hi., U.S. (hŏn'ō-mo͞o)	94a	19°50′N	155°04′W
Honshū, i., Japan	189	36°00′N	138°00′E
Höntrop, neigh., Ger.	236	51°27′N	7°08′E
Hood, Mount, mtn., Or., U.S.	96	45°20′N	121°43′W
Hood Canal, b., Wa., U.S. (ho͝od)	106a	47°45′N	122°45′W
Hood River, Or., U.S.	96	45°42′N	121°30′W
Hoodsport, Wa., U.S. (ho͝odz'pōrt)	106a	47°25′N	123°09′W
Hooghly-Chinsura, India	240a	22°54′N	88°24′E
Hoogly, r., India (ho͞og'lĭ)	183	21°35′N	87°50′E
Hoogstraten, Bel.	145a	51°24′N	4°46′E
Hooker, Ok., U.S. (ho͝ok'ẽr)	110	36°49′N	101°13′W
Hool, Mex. (o͞o'l)	120a	19°32′N	90°22′W
Hoonah, Ak., U.S. (ho͞o'nȧ)	95	58°05′N	135°25′W
Hoopa Valley Indian Reservation, I.R., Ca., U.S.	104	41°18′N	123°35′W
Hooper, Ne., U.S. (ho͝op'ẽr)	111	41°37′N	96°31′W
Hooper, Ut., U.S.	107b	41°10′N	112°08′W
Hooper Bay, Ak., U.S.	95	61°32′N	166°02′W
Hoopeston, Il., U.S. (ho͞ops'tŭn)	98	40°35′N	87°40′W
Hoosick Falls, N.Y., U.S. (ho͞o'sĭk)	99	42°55′N	73°15′W
Hooton, Eng., U.K.	237a	53°18′N	2°57′W
Hoover Dam, Nv., U.S. (ho͞o'vẽr)	108	36°00′N	115°06′W
Hoover Dam, dam, U.S.	96	36°00′N	114°27′W
Hopatcong, Lake, l., N.J., U.S. (hō-păt'kong)	100a	40°57′N	74°38′W
Hope, Ak., U.S. (hōp)	95	60°54′N	149°48′W
Hope, Ar., U.S.	111	33°41′N	93°35′W
Hope, N.D., U.S.	102	47°17′N	97°45′W
Hope, Ben, mtn., Scot., U.K. (bĕn hōp)	150	58°25′N	4°25′W
Hopedale, Can. (hōp'dāl)	85	55°26′N	60°11′W
Hopedale, Ma., U.S. (hōp'dāl)	93a	42°08′N	71°33′W
Hopelchén, Mex. (o-pĕl-chĕ'n)	120a	19°47′N	89°51′W
Hopes Advance, Cap, c., Can. (hōps ăd-vans')	85	61°05′N	69°35′W
Hopetoun, Austl. (hōp'toun)	202	33°50′S	120°15′E
Hopetown, S. Afr. (hōp'toun)	212	29°35′S	24°10′E
Hopewell, Va., U.S. (hōp'wĕl)	115	37°14′N	77°15′W
Hopewell Culture National Historical Park, rec., Oh., U.S.	98	39°25′N	83°00′W
Hopi Indian Reservation, I.R., Az., U.S. (hō'pē)	109	36°20′N	110°30′W
Hopkins, Mn., U.S. (hŏp'kĭns)	107g	44°55′N	93°24′W
Hopkinsville, Ky., U.S. (hŏp'kĭns-vĭl)	97	36°50′N	87°28′W
Hopkinton, Ma., U.S. (hŏp'kĭn-tŭn)	93a	42°14′N	71°31′W
Hoppegarten, Ger.	238a	52°31′N	13°40′E
Hoquiam, Wa., U.S. (hō'kwĭ-ăm)	96	47°00′N	123°53′W
Horconcitos, Pan. (ŏr-kôn-sē'-tôs)	121	8°18′N	82°11′W
Hörde, neigh., Ger.	236	51°29′N	7°30′E
Horgen, Switz. (hôr'gĕn)	154	47°16′N	8°35′E
Horicon, Wi., U.S. (hŏr'ĭ-kŏn)	103	43°26′N	88°40′W
Horinouchi, neigh., Japan	242a	35°41′N	139°40′E
Horlivka, Ukr.	167	48°17′N	38°03′E
Hormuz, Strait of, strt., Asia (hôr'mŭz')	182	26°30′N	56°30′E
Horn, i., Austl. (hôrn)	203	10°30′S	143°30′E
Horn, Cape see Hornos, Cabo de, c., Chile	132	56°00′S	67°00′W
Hornavan, l., Swe.	146	65°54′N	16°17′E
Hornchurch, neigh., Eng., U.K.	235	51°34′N	0°12′E
Horndon on the Hill, Eng., U.K.	235	51°31′N	0°25′E
Horneburg, Ger. (hōr'nĕ-bōrgh)	145c	53°30′N	9°35′E
Horneburg, Ger.	236	51°38′N	7°18′E
Hornell, N.Y., U.S. (hôr-nĕl')	99	42°20′N	77°40′W
Horn Hill, Eng., U.K.	235	51°37′N	0°32′W
Hornos, Cabo de, c., Chile	132	56°00′S	67°00′W
Horn Plateau, plat., Can.	84	62°12′N	120°29′W
Hornsby, Austl. (hôrnz'bĭ)	201b	33°43′S	151°06′E
Hornsey, neigh., Eng., U.K.	235	51°35′N	0°07′W
Horodenka, Ukr.	155	48°40′N	25°30′E
Horodnia, Ukr.	163	51°54′N	31°31′E
Horodok, Ukr.	155	49°47′N	23°39′E
Horqueta, Para. (ŏr-kĕ'tä)	132	23°20′S	57°00′W
Horse Creek, r., Co., U.S. (hôrs)	110	38°49′N	103°48′W
Horse Creek, r., Wy., U.S.	102	41°33′N	104°39′W
Horse Islands, is., Can.	93	50°11′N	55°45′W
Horsell, Eng., U.K.	235	51°19′N	0°34′W
Horsens, Den. (hôrs'ĕns)	152	55°50′N	9°49′E
Horseshoe Bay, Can. (hôrs-sho͞o)	106d	49°23′N	123°16′W
Horsforth, Eng., U.K. (hôrs'fŭrth)	144a	53°50′N	1°38′W
Horsham, Austl. (hôr'shăm) (hôrs'ăm)	203	36°42′S	142°17′E
Horsley, Austl.	243a	33°51′S	150°51′E
Horst, Ger. (hôrst)	145c	53°49′N	9°37′E
Horst, neigh., Ger.	236	51°32′N	7°02′E
Horsthausen, neigh., Ger.	236	51°33′N	7°13′E
Horstmar, neigh., Ger.	236	51°36′N	7°33′E
Hortaleza, neigh., Spain	238b	40°28′N	3°39′W
Horten, Nor. (hōr'tĕn)	152	59°26′N	10°27′E
Horton, Ks., U.S. (hôr'tŭn)	111	39°38′N	95°32′W
Horton, r., Ak., U.S. (hôr'tŭn)	95	68°38′N	122°00′W
Horton Kirby, Eng., U.K.	235	51°23′N	0°15′E
Horwich, Eng., U.K. (hŏr'ĭch)	144a	53°36′N	2°33′W
Hösel, Ger.	236	51°19′N	6°54′E
Hososhima, Japan (hō'sō-shē'mä)	194	32°25′N	131°40′E
Hospitalet, Spain	238e	41°22′N	2°08′E
Hoste, i., Chile (ŏs'tä)	132	55°20′S	70°45′W
Hostotipaquillo, Mex. (ôs-tō-tĭ-pä-kēl'yō)	118	21°09′N	104°05′W
Hota, Japan (hō'tä)	195a	35°08′N	139°50′E
Hotan, China (hwō-tän)	188	37°11′N	79°50′E
Hotan, r., China	188	39°09′N	81°08′E
Hoto Mayor, Dom. Rep. (ô-tô-mä-yō'r)	123	18°45′N	69°10′W
Hot Springs, Ak., U.S. (hŏt sprĭngs)	95	65°00′N	150°20′W
Hot Springs, Ar., U.S.	97	34°29′N	93°02′W
Hot Springs, S.D., U.S.	102	43°28′N	103°32′W
Hot Springs, Va., U.S.	99	38°00′N	79°55′W
Hot Springs National Park, rec., Ar., U.S.	97	34°30′N	93°00′W
Hotte, Massif de la, mts., Haiti	123	18°25′N	74°00′W
Hotville, Ca., U.S. (hŏt'vĭl)	108	32°50′N	115°24′W
Houdan, Fr. (o͞o-däɴ')	157b	48°47′N	1°36′E
Hough Green, Eng., U.K.	237a	53°23′N	2°47′W
Houghton, Mi., U.S. (hō'tŭn)	103	47°06′N	88°36′W
Houghton, l., Mi., U.S.	98	44°20′N	84°45′W
Houilles, Fr. (o͞o-yĕs')	157b	48°55′N	2°11′E
Houjie, China (hwō-jyĕ)	191a	22°58′N	113°39′E
Houlton, Me., U.S. (hōl'tŭn)	92	46°07′N	67°50′W
Houma, La., U.S. (ho͞o'mȧ)	113	29°36′N	90°43′W
Hounslow, neigh., Eng., U.K.	235	51°29′N	0°22′W
Housatonic, r., U.S. (ho͞o-sȧ-tŏn'ĭk)	99	41°50′N	73°25′W
House Springs, Mo., U.S. (hous sprĭngs)	107e	38°24′N	90°34′W
Houston, Ms., U.S. (hūs'tŭn)	114	33°53′N	89°00′W
Houston, Tx., U.S.	97	29°46′N	95°21′W
Houston Ship Channel, strt., Tx., U.S.	113a	29°38′N	94°57′W
Houtbaai, S. Afr.	212a	34°03′S	18°22′E
Houtman Rocks, is., Austl. (hout'män)	202	28°15′S	112°45′E
Houzhen, China (hwō-jŭn)	190	36°59′N	118°59′E
Hovd, Mong.	188	48°08′N	91°40′E
Hovd Gol, r., Mong.	188	49°06′N	91°16′E
Hove, Eng., U.K. (hōv)	150	50°50′N	0°09′W
Hövsgöl Nuur, l., Mong.	188	51°11′N	99°11′E
Howard, Ks., U.S. (hou'ȧrd)	111	37°27′N	96°10′W

PLACE (Pronunciation)	PAGE	LAT.	LONG.
Howard, S.D., U.S.	102	44°01'N	97°31'W
Howard Beach, neigh., N.Y., U.S.	228	40°40'N	73°51'W
Howden, Eng., U.K. (hou'dĕn)	144a	53°44'N	0°52'W
Howe, Cape, c., Austl. (hou)	203	37°30'S	150°40'E
Howell, Mi., U.S. (hou'ĕl)	98	42°40'N	84°00'W
Howe Sound, strt., Can.	86	49°22'N	123°18'W
Howick, Can. (hou'ĭk)	83a	45°11'N	73°51'W
Howick, S. Afr.	213c	29°29'S	30°16'E
Howland, i., Oc. (hou'lănd)	2	1°00'N	176°00'W
Howrah, India (hou'rä)	183	22°33'N	88°20'E
Howrah Bridge, trans., India	240a	22°35'N	88°21'E
Howse Peak, mtn., Can.	87	51°30'N	116°40'W
Howson Peak, mtn., Can.	86	54°25'N	127°45'W
Hoxie, Ar., U.S. (kŏh'sĭ)	111	36°03'N	91°00'W
Hoxton Park, Austl.	243a	33°55'S	150°51'E
Hoy, i., Scot., U.K. (hoi)	150a	58°53'N	3°10'W
Hōya, Japan	195a	35°45'N	139°35'E
Hoylake, Eng., U.K. (hoi-lāk')	144a	53°23'N	3°11'W
Hoyo, Sierra del, mts., Spain (sē-ĕ'r-rä-dĕl-ô'yô)	159a	40°39'N	3°56'W
Hradec Králové, Czech Rep.	147	50°12'N	15°50'E
Hradyz'k, Ukr.	163	49°12'N	33°06'E
Hranice, Czech Rep. (hrän'yĕ-tsĕ)	155	49°33'N	17°45'E
Hröby, Swe. (hûr'bü)	152	55°50'N	13°41'E
Hron, r., Slvk.	155	48°22'N	18°42'E
Hrubieszów, Pol. (hrōō-byă'shōōf)	155	50°48'N	23°54'E
Hsawnhsup, Myanmar	188	24°29'N	94°45'E
Hsinchu, Tai. (hsĭn'chōō')	193	24°48'N	121°00'E
Hsinchuang, Tai.	241d	25°02'N	121°26'E
Hsinkao Shan, mtn., Tai.	189	23°38'N	121°05'E
Huadian, China (hwä-dĭĕn)	192	42°38'N	126°45'E
Huai, r., China (hwī)	189	32°07'N	114°38'E
Huai'an, China (hwī-än)	192	33°31'N	119°11'E
Huailai, China	192	40°20'N	115°45'E
Huailin, China (hwī-lĭn)	190	31°27'N	117°36'E
Huainan, China	190	32°38'N	117°02'E
Huaiyang, China (hōōăĭ'yang)	192	33°45'N	114°54'E
Huaiyuan, China (hwī-yůän)	192	32°53'N	117°13'E
Huajicori, Mex. (wä-jē-kō'rē)	118	22°41'N	105°24'W
Huajuapan de León, Mex. (wäj-wä'päm dā lā-ón')	119	17°46'N	97°45'W
Hualapai Indian Reservation, I.R., Az., U.S. (wälåpī)	109	35°41'N	113°38'W
Hualapai Mountains, mts., Az., U.S.	109	34°53'N	113°54'W
Hualien, Tai. (hwä'lyĕn')	193	23°58'N	121°58'E
Huallaga, r., Peru (wäl-yä'gä)	130	8°12'S	76°34'W
Huamachuco, Peru (wä-mä-chōō'kō)	130	7°52'S	78°11'W
Huamantla, Mex. (wä-män'tlà)	119	19°18'N	97°54'W
Huambo, Ang.	212	12°44'S	15°47'E
Huamuxtitlán, Mex. (wä-mōōs-tē-tlän')	118	17°49'N	98°38'W
Huancavelica, Peru (wän'kä-vä-lē'kä)	130	12°47'S	75°02'W
Huancayo, Peru (wän-kä'yō)	130	12°09'S	75°04'W
Huanchaca, Bol. (wän-chä'kä)	130	20°09'S	66°40'W
Huang (Yellow), r., China (hůäŋ)	189	35°06'N	113°39'E
Huang, Old Beds of the, mth., China	188	40°28'N	106°34'E
Huang, Old Course of the, r., China	190	34°28'N	116°59'E
Huangchuan, China (hůäŋ-chůän)	192	32°07'N	115°01'E
Huangcun, China	240b	39°56'N	116°11'E
Huanghua, China (hůäŋ-hwä)	190	38°28'N	117°18'E
Huanghuadian, China (hůäŋ-hwä-dĭĕn)	190	39°22'N	116°53'E
Huangli, China (hōōäɴg'lē)	190	31°39'N	119°42'E
Huangpu, China (hůäŋ-pōō)	191a	22°44'N	113°20'E
Huangpu, r., China	191b	30°56'N	121°16'E
Huangqiao, China (hůän-chyou)	190	32°15'N	120°13'E
Huangxian, China (hůäŋ shyĕn)	190	37°39'N	120°32'E
Huangyuan, China (hůäŋ-yůän)	188	37°00'N	101°01'E
Huanren, China (hůän-rŭn)	192	41°10'N	125°30'E
Huánuco, Peru (wä-nōō'kō)	130	9°50'S	76°17'W
Huánuni, Bol. (wä-nōō'nē)	130	18°11'S	66°43'W
Huaquechula, Mex. (wä-kĕ-chōō'lä)	118	18°44'N	98°37'W
Huaral, Peru (wä-rä'l)	130	11°28'S	77°11'W
Huarás, Peru (óä'rá's)	130	9°32'S	77°29'W
Huascarán, Nevados, mts., Peru (wäs-kä-rän')	130	9°05'S	77°50'W
Huasco, Chile (wäs'kō)	132	28°32'S	71°16'W
Huatla de Jiménez, Mex. (wá'tlä-dĕ-κĕ-mĕ'nĕz)	119	18°08'N	96°49'W
Huatlatlauch, Mex. (wä'tlä-tlä-ōō'ch)	118	18°40'N	98°04'W
Huatusco, Mex. (wä-tōōs'kō)	119	19°09'N	96°57'W
Huauchinango, Mex. (wä-ōō-chē-näŋ'gō)	118	20°09'N	98°03'W
Huaunta, Nic. (wä-ó'n-tä)	121	13°30'N	83°32'W
Huaunta, Laguna, l., Nic. (lä-gò'nä-wä-ó'n-tä)	121	13°35'N	83°46'W
Huautla, Mex. (wä-ōō'tlä)	118	21°04'N	98°13'W
Huaxian, China (hwä shyĕn)	192	35°34'N	114°32'E
Huaynamota, Río de, r., Mex. (rē'ō-dĕ-wäy-nä-mŏ'tä)	118	22°10'N	104°36'W
Huazolotitlán, Mex. (wäzō-lō-tlē-tlän')	119	16°18'N	97°55'W
Hubbard, N.H., U.S. (hŭb'ērd)	93a	42°53'N	71°12'W
Hubbard, Tx., U.S.	113	31°53'N	96°46'W
Hubbard, l., Mi., U.S.	98	44°45'N	83°30'W
Hubbard Creek Reservoir, res., Tx., U.S.	112	32°50'N	98°55'W
Hubbelrath, Ger.	236	51°16'N	6°55'E
Hubei, prov., China (hōō-bā)	189	31°20'N	111°58'E
Hubli, India (hò'blē)	183	15°25'N	75°09'E
Hückeswagen, Ger. (hü'kĕs-vä'gĕn)	157c	51°09'N	7°20'E
Hucknall, Eng., U.K. (hŭk'năl)	144a	53°02'N	1°12'W
Huddersfield, Eng., U.K. (hŭd'ērz-fēld)	150	53°39'N	1°47'W
Hudiksvall, Swe. (hōō'dĭks-väl)	146	61°44'N	17°05'E
Hudson, Can. (hŭd'sŭn)	83a	45°26'N	74°08'W
Hudson, Ma., U.S.	93a	42°24'N	71°34'W
Hudson, Mi., U.S.	98	41°50'N	84°15'W
Hudson, N.Y., U.S.	99	42°15'N	73°45'W
Hudson, Oh., U.S.	101d	41°15'N	81°27'W
Hudson, Wi., U.S.	107g	44°59'N	92°45'W
Hudson, r., U.S.	97	42°30'N	73°55'W
Hudson Bay, Can.	89	52°52'N	102°25'W
Hudson Bay, b., Can.	85	60°15'N	85°30'W
Hudson Falls, N.Y., U.S.	99	43°20'N	73°30'W
Hudson Heights, Can.	83a	45°28'N	74°09'W
Hudson Strait, strt., Can.	85	63°25'N	74°05'W
Hue, Viet (ü-ā')	196	16°28'N	107°42'E
Huebra, r., Spain (wĕ'brä)	158	40°44'N	6°17'W
Huehuetenango, Guat. (wā-wå-tå-näŋ'gō)	120	15°19'N	91°26'W
Huejotzingo, Mex. (wā-hō-tzĭŋ'gō)	118	19°09'N	98°24'W
Huejúcar, Mex. (wā-hōō'kär)	118	22°26'N	103°12'W
Huejuquilla el Alto, Mex. (wā-hōō-kēl'yä ĕl äl'tō)	118	22°42'N	103°54'W
Huejutla, Mex. (wā-hōō'tlä)	118	21°08'N	98°26'W
Huelma, Spain (wĕl'mä)	158	37°39'N	3°36'W
Huelva, Spain (wĕl'vä)	148	37°16'N	6°58'W
Huércal-Overa, Spain (wĕr-käl' ō-vä'rä)	158	37°12'N	1°58'W
Huerfano, r., Co., U.S. (wâr'fá-nō)	110	37°41'N	105°13'W
Huésca, Spain (wĕs-kä)	148	42°07'N	0°25'W
Huéscar, Spain (wās'kär)	158	37°50'N	2°34'W
Huetamo de Núñez, Mex.	118	18°34'N	100°53'W
Huete, Spain (wā'tå)	158	40°09'N	2°42'W
Hueycatenango, Mex. (wĕy-kå-tĕ-nä'n-gô)	118	17°31'N	99°10'W
Hueytlalpan, Mex. (wā'ĭ-tlàl'păn)	119	20°03'N	97°41'W
Hueytown, Al., U.S.	100h	33°28'N	86°59'W
Huffman, Al., U.S. (hŭf'măn)	100h	33°36'N	86°42'W
Hügel, Villa, pt. of i., Ger.	236	51°25'N	7°01'E
Hugh Butler, l., Ne., U.S.	110	40°21'N	100°40'W
Hughenden, Austl. (hū'ĕn-dĕn)	203	20°58'S	144°13'E
Hughes, Austl. (hūz)	202	30°45'S	129°30'E
Hughesville, Md., U.S.	100e	38°32'N	76°48'W
Hugo, Mn., U.S. (hū'gō)	107g	45°10'N	93°00'W
Hugo, Ok., U.S.	111	34°01'N	95°32'W
Hugoton, Ks., U.S. (hū'gō-tŭn)	110	37°10'N	101°28'W
Hugou, China (hōō-gō)	190	33°22'N	117°07'E
Huichapan, Mex. (wē-chä-pän')	118	20°22'N	99°39'W
Huila, dept., Col. (wē'lä)	130a	3°10'N	75°20'W
Huila, Nevado de, mtn., Col. (nĕ-vä-dô-de-wē'lä)	130a	2°59'N	76°01'W
Huilai, China	193	23°02'N	116°18'E
Huili, China	188	26°48'N	102°20'E
Huimanguillo, Mex. (wē-män-gēl'yō)	119	17°50'N	93°16'W
Huimin, China (hōōĭ mĭn)	189	37°29'N	117°32'E
Huipulco, Mex.	233a	19°17'N	99°09'W
Huitzilac, Mex. (òē't-zē-lä'k)	119a	19°01'N	99°16'W
Huitzitzilingo, Mex. (wē-tzē-tzē-lē'n-go)	118	21°11'N	98°42'W
Huitzuco, Mex. (wē-tzōō'kō)	118	18°16'N	99°20'W
Huixquilucan, Mex. (òē'x-kē-lōō-kä'n)	119a	19°21'N	99°22'W
Huiyang, China	193	23°05'N	114°25'E
Hukou, China (hōō-kō)	189	29°58'N	116°20'E
Hulan, China (hōō'län')	189	45°58'N	126°32'E
Hulan, r., China	192	47°20'N	126°30'E
Huliaipole, Ukr.	163	47°39'N	36°12'E
Hulin, China (hōō'lĭn')	194	45°45'N	133°25'E
Hull, Can. (hŭl)	85	45°26'N	75°43'W
Hull, Ma., U.S.	93a	42°18'N	70°54'W
Hull, r., Eng., U.K.	144a	53°47'N	0°20'W
Hülscheid, Ger.	236	51°16'N	7°34'E
Hulst, Neth. (hōlst)	145a	51°17'N	4°01'E
Huludao, China (hōō-lōō-dou)	189	40°40'N	120°55'E
Hulun Nur, l., China (hōō-lòn nòr)	189	48°50'N	116°45'E
Humacao, P.R. (ōō-mä-kä'ō)	117b	18°09'N	65°49'W
Humansdorp, S. Afr. (hōō'mäns-dôrp)	212	33°57'S	24°45'E
Humbe, Ang. (hòm'bâ)	212	16°50'S	14°55'E
Humber, r., Can.	83d	43°53'N	79°40'W
Humber, r., Eng., U.K. (hŭm'bēr)	146	53°30'N	0°30'E
Humbermouth, Can. (hŭm'bēr-mŭth)	93	48°58'N	57°55'W
Humberside, co., Eng., U.K.	144a	53°47'N	0°36'W
Humble, Tx., U.S. (hŭm'b'l)	113	29°58'N	95°15'W
Humboldt, Can. (hŭm'bōlt)	84	52°12'N	105°07'W
Humboldt, Ia., U.S.	103	42°43'N	94°11'W
Humboldt, Ks., U.S.	111	37°48'N	95°26'W
Humboldt, Ne., U.S.	111	40°10'N	95°57'W
Humboldt, r., Nv., U.S.	96	40°30'N	116°50'W
Humboldt, East Fork, r., Nv., U.S.	104	40°59'N	115°21'W
Humboldt, North Fork, r., Nv., U.S.	104	41°25'N	115°45'W
Humboldt, Planetario, bldg., Ven.	234a	10°30'N	66°50'W
Humboldt Bay, b., Ca., U.S.	104	40°48'N	124°25'W
Humboldt Range, mts., Nv., U.S.	108	40°12'N	118°16'W
Humbolt, Tn., U.S.	114	35°47'N	88°55'W
Humbolt Salt Marsh, Nv., U.S.	108	39°49'N	117°41'W
Humboldt Sink, Nv., U.S.	108	39°58'N	118°54'W
Humen, China (hōō-mŭn)	191a	22°49'N	113°39'E
Humphreys Peak, mtn., Az., U.S. (hŭm'frĭs)	96	35°20'N	111°40'W
Humpolec, Czech Rep. (hòm'pô-lĕts)	154	49°33'N	15°21'E
Humuya, r., Hond. (ōō-mōō'yä)	120	14°38'N	87°36'W
Húnaflói, b., Ice. (hōō'nä-flō'ĭ)	146	65°41'N	20°44'W
Hunan, prov., China (hōō'nän')	189	28°08'N	111°25'E
Hunchun, China (hòn-chùn)	189	42°53'N	130°34'E
Hunedoara, Rom. (κōō'nĕd-wä'rå)	161	45°45'N	22°54'E
Hungary, nation, Eur. (hŭŋ'gå-rĭ)	142	46°44'N	17°55'E
Hungerford, Austl. (hŭn'gēr-fērd)	203	28°50'S	144°32'E
Hungry Horse Reservoir, res., Mt., U.S. (hŭŋ'gá-rĭ hôrs)	105	48°11'N	113°30'W
Hunsrück, mts., Ger. (hōōns'rûk)	154	49°43'N	7°12'E
Hunte, r., Ger. (hòn'tĕ)	154	52°45'N	8°26'E
Hunter Islands, is., Austl. (hŭn-tēr)	203	40°33'S	143°36'E
Hunters Hill, Austl.	243a	33°50'S	151°09'E
Huntingburg, In., U.S. (hŭnt'ĭng-bûrg)	98	38°15'N	86°55'W
Huntingdon, Can. (hŭnt'ĭng-dŭn)	91	45°10'N	74°05'W
Huntingdon, Can.	106d	49°00'N	122°16'W
Huntingdon, Tn., U.S.	114	36°00'N	88°23'W
Huntington, In., U.S.	98	40°55'N	85°30'W
Huntington, Pa., U.S.	99	40°30'N	78°00'W
Huntington, Va., U.S.	229d	38°48'N	77°15'W
Huntington, W.V., U.S.	97	38°25'N	82°25'W
Huntington Beach, Ca., U.S.	107a	33°39'N	118°00'W
Huntington Park, Ca., U.S.	107a	33°59'N	118°14'W
Huntington Station, N.Y., U.S.	100a	40°51'N	73°25'W
Huntington Woods, Mi., U.S.	230c	42°29'N	83°10'W
Huntley, Mt., U.S.	105	45°54'N	108°01'W
Hunt's Cross, neigh., Eng., U.K.	237a	53°21'N	2°51'W
Huntsville, Can.	85	45°20'N	79°15'W
Huntsville, Al., U.S. (hŭnts'vĭl)	114	34°44'N	86°36'W
Huntsville, Md., U.S.	229d	38°55'N	76°54'W
Huntsville, Mo., U.S.	111	39°24'N	92°32'W
Huntsville, Tx., U.S.	113	30°44'N	95°34'W
Huntsville, Ut., U.S.	107b	41°16'N	111°46'W
Huolu, China (hòŭ lōō)	190	38°05'N	114°20'E
Huon Gulf, b., Pap. N. Gui.	197	7°15'S	147°45'E
Huoqiu, China (hwô-chyô)	190	32°19'N	116°17'E
Huoshan, China (hwô-shän)	193	31°30'N	116°25'E
Huraydin, Wādī, r., Egypt	181a	30°55'N	34°12'E
Hurd, Cape, c., Can. (hûrd)	90	45°15'N	81°45'W
Hurdiyo, Som.	218a	10°43'N	51°05'E
Hurley, Wi., U.S. (hûr'lĭ)	103	46°26'N	90°11'W
Hurlingham, Arg. (ōō'r-lēn-gäm)	132a	34°36'S	58°38'W
Huron, Oh., U.S. (hū'rŏn)	98	41°20'N	82°35'W
Huron, S.D., U.S.	96	44°22'N	98°15'W
Huron, r., Mi., U.S.	101b	42°12'N	83°26'W
Huron, Lake, l., N.A. (hū'rŏn)	97	45°15'N	82°40'W
Huron Mountains, mts., Mi., U.S. (hū'rŏn)	103	46°47'N	87°52'W
Hurricane, Ak., U.S. (hŭr'ĭ-kān)	95	63°00'N	149°30'W
Hurricane, Ut., U.S.	109	37°10'N	113°20'W
Hurricane Flats, bk. (hŭ-rĭ-kăn flăts)	122	23°35'N	78°30'W
Hurst, Tx., U.S.	107c	32°48'N	97°12'W
Hurstville, Austl.	243a	33°58'S	151°06'E
Húsavik, Ice.	146	66°00'N	17°10'W
Husen, neigh., Ger.	236	51°33'N	7°36'E
Huşi, Rom. (kósh')	163	46°52'N	28°04'E
Huskvarna, Swe. (hòsk-vär'nȧ)	152	57°48'N	14°16'E
Husum, Ger. (hōō'zòm)	154	54°29'N	9°04'E
Hutchins, Tx., U.S. (hŭch'ĭnz)	107c	32°38'N	96°43'W
Hutchinson, Ks., U.S. (hŭch'ĭn-sŭn)	96	38°02'N	97°56'W
Hutchinson, Mn., U.S.	103	44°53'N	94°23'W
Hütteldorf, neigh., Aus.	239e	48°12'N	16°16'E
Hüttenheim, neigh., Ger.	236	51°22'N	6°43'E
Hutton, Eng., U.K.	235	51°38'N	0°22'E
Huttrop, neigh., Ger.	236	51°27'N	7°03'E
Hutuo, r., China	192	38°10'N	114°00'E
Huy, Bel. (ü-ē') (hû'ē)	151	50°33'N	5°14'E
Huyton, Eng., U.K.	237a	53°24'N	2°50'W
Hvannadalshnúkur, mtn., Ice.	146	64°09'N	16°46'W
Hvar, i., Yugo. (κhvär)	160	43°08'N	16°28'E
Hwange, Zimb.	212	18°22'S	26°29'E
Hwangju, N. Kor. (hwäng'jōō')	194	38°39'N	125°49'E
Hyargas Nuur, l., Mong.	188	48°00'N	92°32'E
Hyattsville, Md., U.S. (hī'ăt's-vĭl)	100e	38°57'N	76°58'W
Hyco Lake, res., N.C., U.S. (rōks' bŭr-ō)	115	36°22'N	78°58'W
Hydaburg, Ak., U.S. (hī-dă'bûrg)	95	55°12'N	132°49'W
Hyde, Eng., U.K. (hīd)	144a	53°27'N	2°05'W
Hyde Park, neigh., Il., U.S.	231a	41°48'N	87°36'W
Hyderābād, India (hī-dēr-å-băd')	183	17°29'N	78°28'E
Hyderabad, India	183	18°30'N	76°50'E
Hyderābād, Pak.	183	25°29'N	68°28'E
Hyéres, Fr. (ē-âr')	147	43°09'N	6°08'E
Hyéres, Îles d', is., Fr. (ēl'dyâr')	147	42°57'N	6°17'E
Hyesanjin, N. Kor. (hyĕ'sän-jĭn')	194	41°11'N	128°12'E
Hymera, In., U.S. (hī-mē'rá)	98	39°10'N	87°20'W
Hyndman Peak, mtn., Id., U.S. (hīnd'măn)	96	43°38'N	114°04'W
Hyōgo, dept., Japan (hĭyō'gō)	195b	34°54'N	135°15'E
Hyōgo, neigh., Japan	242b	34°47'N	135°10'E
Hythe End, Eng., U.K.	235	51°27'N	0°32'W

I

PLACE (Pronunciation)	PAGE	LAT.	LONG.
Ia, r., Japan (ĕ'ä)	195b	34°54'N	135°34'E
Iahotyn, Ukr.	163	50°18'N	31°46'E
Ialomiţa, r., Rom.	161	44°37'N	26°42'E
Iaşi, Rom. (yä'shē)	142	47°10'N	27°40'E
Iasinia, Ukr.	155	48°17'N	24°21'E
Iavoriv, Ukr.	155	49°56'N	23°24'E
Iba, Phil. (ē'bä)	197a	15°20'N	119°59'E
Ibadan, Nig. (ē-bä'dän)	210	7°17'N	3°30'E
Ibagué, Col.	130	4°27'N	75°14'W
Ibar, r., Yugo. (ē'bär)	161	43°22'N	20°35'E
Ibaraki, Japan (ē-bä'rä-gē)	195b	34°49'N	135°35'E
Ibarra, Ec. (ē-bär'rä)	130	0°19'N	78°08'W
Ibb, Yemen	185	14°01'N	44°10'E
Iberoamericana, Universidad, educ., Mex.	233a	19°21'N	99°08'W
Iberville, Can. (ē-bår-vēl') (ĭ'bēr-vĭl)	91	45°14'N	73°01'W
Ibese, Nig.	244d	6°33'N	3°29'E
Ibi, Nig. (ē'bē)	210	8°12'N	9°45'E
Ibiapaba, Serra da, mts., Braz. (sĕ'r-rä-dä-ē-byä-pá'bä)	131	3°30'S	40°55'W
Ibirapuera, neigh., Braz.	234d	23°37'S	46°40'W
Ibiza see Eivissa, i., Spain	142	38°55'N	1°24'E
Ibo, Moz. (ē'bō)	213	12°20'S	40°35'E
Ibrāhīm, Būr, b., Egypt	218c	29°57'N	32°33'E
Ibrahim, Jabal, mtn., Sau. Ar.	182	20°31'N	41°17'E
Ibwe Munyama, Zam.	217	16°09'S	28°34'E
Ica, Peru (ē'kä)	130	14°09'S	75°42'W
Içá (Putumayo), r., S.A.	130	3°00'S	69°00'W
Içana, Braz. (ē-sä'nä)	130	0°15'N	67°19'W
Ice Harbor Dam, Wa., U.S.	104	46°15'N	118°54'W
İçel, Tur.	182	37°00'N	34°40'E
Iceland, nation, Eur. (īs'lănd)	142	65°12'N	19°45'W

ng-sing; ŋ-baŋk; ɴ-nasalized n; nŏd; cŏmmit; ōld; ôbey; ôrder; oi-boil; fōōd; ó-as oo in foot; ou-out; s-soft; sh-dish; th-thin; pūre; ůnite; ûrn; stŭd; circŭs; ü-as in French tu; '-indeterminate vowel.

ăt; fīnăl; rāte; senáte; ärm; ásk; sofá; fâre;　ch-choose;　dh-as th in other;　bē; ēvent; bĕt; recĕnt; cratĕr;　g-gō; gh-guttural g;　bĭt; ĭ-short neutral; rīde;　κ-guttural k as ch in German ich;

PLACE (Pronunciation)	PAGE	LAT.	LONG.
Iron Cove, b., Austl.	243a	33°52'S	151°10'E
Irondale, Al., U.S. (ī'ērn-dāl)	100h	33°32'N	86°43'W
Iron Gate, val., Eur.	161	44°43'N	22°32'E
Iron Knob, Austl. (ī-ǎn nŏb)	204	32°47'S	137°10'E
Iron Mountain, Mi., U.S. (ī'ērn)	103	45°49'N	88°04'W
Iron River, Mi., U.S.	103	46°09'N	88°39'W
Ironton, Oh., U.S. (ī'ērn-tŭn)	98	38°30'N	82°45'W
Ironwood, Mi., U.S. (ī'ērn-wo͝od)	103	46°28'N	90°10'W
Iroquois, r., Il., U.S. (ĭr'ô-kwoi)	98	40°55'N	87°20'W
Iroquois Falls, Can.	85	48°41'N	80°39'W
Irō-Saki, c., Japan (ē'rō sä'kē)	194	34°35'N	138°54'E
Irpin, r., Ukr.	163	50°13'N	29°55'E
Irrawaddy, r., Myanmar (ĭr-ȧ-wäd'ē)	183	23°27'N	96°25'E
Irtysh, r., Asia (ĭr-tĭsh')	164	59°00'N	69°00'E
Irumu, D.R.C. (ē-rō'mo͞o)	211	1°30'N	29°52'E
Irun, Spain (ē-ro͞on')	158	43°20'N	1°47'W
Irvine, Scot., U.K.	150	55°39'N	4°40'W
Irvine, Ca., U.S. (ûr'vĭn)	107a	33°40'N	117°45'W
Irvine, Ky., U.S.	98	37°40'N	84°00'W
Irving, Tx., U.S. (ûr'vēng)	107c	32°49'N	96°57'W
Irving Park, neigh., Il., U.S.	231a	41°57'N	87°43'W
Irvington, N.J., U.S. (ûr'vēng-tŭn)	100a	40°43'N	74°15'W
Irvington, neigh., Md., U.S.	229c	39°17'N	76°41'W
Irwin, Pa., U.S. (ûr'wĭn)	101e	40°19'N	79°42'W
Is, Russia (ēs)	172a	58°48'N	59°44'E
Isa, Nig.	215	13°14'N	6°24'E
Isaacs, Mount, mtn., Pan. (ē-sä-ä'ks)	116a	9°22'N	79°31'W
Isabela, i., Ec. (ē-sä-bā'lä)	130	0°47'S	91°35'W
Isabela, Cabo, c., Dom. Rep. (kä'bô-ē-sä-bĕ'lä)	123	20°00'N	71°00'W
Isabella, Cordillera, mts., Nic. (kôr-dēl-yĕ'rä-ē-sä-bēlä)	120	13°20'N	85°37'W
Isabella Indian Reservation, I.R., Mi., U.S. (ĭs-ȧ-bĕl'-lȧ)	98	43°35'N	84°55'W
Isaccea, Rom. (ē-säk'chä)	163	45°16'N	28°26'E
Ísafjördur, Ice. (ēs'ȧ-fy̆r-dôr)	146	66°09'N	22°39'W
Isando, S. Afr.	244b	26°09'S	28°12'E
Isangi, D.R.C. (ē-säŋ'gē)	188	0°46'N	24°15'E
Isar, r., Ger. (ē'zär)	147	48°30'N	12°30'E
Isarco, r., Italy (ē-sär'kō)	160	46°37'N	11°25'E
Isarog, Mount, mtn., Phil. (ē-sä-rô-g)	197a	13°40'N	123°23'E
Ischia, Italy (ēs'kyä)	159c	40°29'N	13°58'E
Ischia, Isola d', i., Italy (dē'sh-kyä)	148	40°26'N	13°55'E
Ise, Japan (ĭs'hē) (ū'gē-yä'mä'dȧ)	194	34°30'N	136°43'E
Iselin, N.J., U.S.	228	40°34'N	74°19'W
Iseo, Lago d', l., Italy (lä-'gō-dē-ē-zĕ'ō)	160	45°50'N	9°55'E
Isére, r., Fr. (ē-zâr')	147	45°15'N	5°15'E
Iserlohn, Ger. (ē'zĕr-lōn)	157c	51°22'N	7°42'E
Isernia, Italy (ē-zĕr'nyä)	160	41°35'N	14°14'E
Ise-Wan, b., Japan (ē'sĕ wän)	194	34°49'N	136°44'E
Iseyin, Nig.	210	7°58'N	3°36'E
Ishigaki, Japan	198d	24°20'N	124°09'E
Ishikari Wan, b., Japan (ē'shē-kä-rē wän)	194	43°30'N	141°05'E
Ishim, Russia (ĭsh-ēm')	164	56°07'N	69°13'E
Ishim, r., Asia	164	53°17'N	67°45'E
Ishimbay, Russia (ē-shēm-bī')	172a	53°28'N	56°02'E
Ishinomaki, Japan (ĭsh-nō-mä'kē)	189	38°22'N	141°22'E
Ishinomaki Wan, b., Japan (ē-shē-nō-mä'kē wän)	194	38°10'N	141°40'E
Ishly, Russia (ĭsh'lĭ)	172a	54°13'N	55°55'E
Ishlya, Russia (ĭsh'lyȧ)	172a	53°54'N	57°48'E
Ishmant, Egypt	218b	29°17'N	31°15'E
Ishpeming, Mi., U.S. (ĭsh'pē-mĭng)	103	46°28'N	87°42'W
Isidro Casanova, Arg.	233d	34°42'S	58°35'W
Isipingo, S. Afr. (ĭs-ĭ-pĭŋg-gō)	213c	29°59'S	30°58'E
Isiro, D.R.C.	211	2°47'N	27°37'E
İskenderun, Tur. (ĭs-kĕn'dĕr-o͞on)	182	36°45'N	36°15'E
İskenderun Körfezi, b., Tur.	149	36°22'N	35°25'E
İskilip, Tur. (ēs'kĭ-lēp')	149	40°40'N	34°30'E
Iskūr, r., Bul. (ĭs'k'r)	161	43°05'N	23°37'E
Isla-Cristina, Spain (ī'lä-krē-stē'nä)	158	37°13'N	7°20'W
Islāmābād, Pak.	183	33°55'N	73°05'E
Isla Mujeres, Mex. (ē's-lä-mo͞o-kĕ'rĕs)	120a	21°25'N	86°53'W
Island Lake, l., Can.	85	53°47'N	94°25'W
Island Park, N.Y., U.S.	228	40°36'N	73°40'W
Islands, Bay of, b., Can. (ī'lǎndz)	93	49°10'N	58°15'W
Islay, i., Scot., U.K. (ī'lā)	146	55°55'N	6°35'W
Isle, r., Fr. (ēl)	156	45°02'N	0°29'E
Isle of Axholme, reg., Eng., U.K. (äks'-hōm)	144a	53°33'N	0°48'W
Isle of Man, dep., Eur. (măn)	150	54°26'N	4°21'W
Isle Royale National Park, rec., Mi., U.S. (īl'roi-ǎl')	97	47°57'N	88°37'W
Isleta, N.M., U.S. (ēs-lā'tȧ) (ī-lē'tȧ)	109	34°55'N	106°45'W
Isleta Indian Reservation, I.R., N.M., U.S.	109	34°55'N	106°45'W
Isleworth, neigh., Eng., U.K.	235	51°28'N	0°20'W
Islington, neigh., Can.	227c	43°39'N	79°32'W
Islington, neigh., Eng., U.K.	235	51°34'N	0°06'W
Ismailia, Egypt (ēs-mä-ēl'ēȧ)	218b	30°35'N	32°17'E
Ismā'īlīyah, neigh., Egypt	244a	30°03'N	31°14'E
Ismā'īlīyah Canal, can., Egypt	218b	30°25'N	31°45'E
Ismaning, Ger. (ēz'mä-nēng)	145d	48°14'N	11°41'E
Isparta, Tur. (ē-spär'tȧ)	182	37°50'N	30°40'E
Israel, nation, Asia	182	32°40'N	34°00'E
Issaquah, Wa., U.S. (ĭz'sä-kwäh)	106a	47°32'N	122°02'W
Isselburg, Ger. (ē'sĕl-bo͞org)	157c	51°50'N	6°28'E
Issoire, Fr. (ē-swȧr')	156	45°32'N	3°13'E
Issoudun, Fr. (ē-so͞o-däN')	156	46°56'N	2°00'E
Issum, Ger. (ē'so͞om)	157c	51°32'N	6°24'E
Issyk-Kul, Ozero, l., Kyrg.	169	42°13'N	76°12'E
Issy-les-Moulineaux, Fr.	237c	48°49'N	2°17'E
Īstādeh-ye Moqor, Āb-e, l., Afg.	186	32°35'N	68°00'E
İstanbul, Tur. (ē-stän-bo͞ol')	182	41°02'N	29°00'E
İstanbul Boğazi (Bosporus), strt., Tur.	182	41°10'N	29°10'E
Istead Rise, Eng., U.K.	235	51°24'N	0°22'E
Istiaía, Grc. (ĭs-tyī'yä)	161	38°58'N	23°11'E
Istmina, Col. (ēst-mē'nä)	130a	5°10'N	76°40'W
Istokpoga, Lake, l., Fl., U.S. (ĭs-tŏk-pō'gȧ)	115a	27°20'N	81°33'W
Istra, pen., Yugo. (ē-strä)	160	45°18'N	13°48'E
Istranca Dağlari, mts., Eur. (ĭ-strän'jȧ)	161	41°50'N	27°25'E
Istres, Fr. (ēs'tr')	156a	43°30'N	5°00'E
Itabaiana, Braz. (ē-tä-bä-yä-nä)	131	10°42'S	37°17'W
Itabapoana, Braz. (ē-tä'-bä-pôä'nä)	129a	21°19'S	40°58'W
Itabapoana, r., Braz.	129a	21°11'S	41°18'W
Itabirito, Braz. (ē-tä-bē-rē'tô)	129a	20°15'S	43°46'W
Itabuna, Braz. (ē-tä-bo͞o'nȧ)	131	14°47'S	39°17'W
Itacoara, Braz. (ē-tä-kô'ä-rä)	129a	21°41'S	42°04'W
Itacoatiara, Braz. (ē-tȧ-kwȧ-tyä'rȧ)	131	3°03'S	58°18'W
Itagüí, Col. (ē-tä'gwē)	130a	6°11'N	75°36'W
Itagui, r., Braz.	132b	22°53'S	43°43'W
Itaipava, Braz. (ē-tī-pȧ'-vä)	132b	22°23'S	43°09'W
Itaipu, Braz. (ē-tī'po͞o)	132b	22°58'S	43°02'W
Itaipu, Ponta de, c., Braz.	234c	22°59'S	43°03'W
Itaituba, Braz. (ē-tä'ī-to͞o'bȧ)	131	4°12'S	56°00'W
Itajaí, Braz. (ē-tä-zhī')	132	26°52'S	48°39'W
Italy, Tx., U.S.	113	32°11'N	96°51'W
Italy, nation, Eur. (ĭt'ȧ-lē)	142	43°58'N	11°14'E
Itambi, Braz. (ē-tä'm-bē)	132b	22°44'S	42°57'W
Itami, Japan (ē'tä'mē')	195b	34°47'N	135°25'E
Itapecerica, Braz. (ē-tä-pē-sē-rē'kȧ)	129a	20°29'S	45°08'W
Itapecuru-Mirim, Braz. (ē-tä-pĕ'ko͞o-ro͞o-mē-rēN')	131	3°17'S	44°15'W
Itaperuna, Braz. (ē-tä'pä-ro͞o'nä)	131	21°12'S	41°53'W
Itapetininga, Braz. (ē-tä-pē-tē-nē'N-gä)	131	23°37'S	48°03'W
Itapira, Braz.	129a	22°27'S	46°47'W
Itapira, Braz. (ē-tȧ-pē'rȧ)	131	20°42'S	51°19'W
Itaquaquecetuba, Braz.	234d	23°29'S	46°21'W
Itarsi, India	186	22°43'N	77°45'E
Itasca, Tx., U.S. (ī-tăs'kȧ)	113	32°09'N	97°08'W
Itasca, l., Mn., U.S.	102	47°13'N	95°14'W
Itatiaia, Pico da, mtn., Braz. (pē'-kô-dȧ-ē-tä-tyȧ'ēä)	131	22°18'S	44°41'W
Itatiba, Braz. (ē-tä-tē'bä)	129a	23°01'S	46°48'W
Itaúna, Braz. (ē-tä-o͞o'nä)	129a	20°05'S	44°35'W
Ithaca, Mi., U.S. (ĭth'ȧ-kȧ)	98	43°20'N	84°35'W
Ithaca, N.Y., U.S.	97	42°25'N	76°30'W
Itháka, i., Grc. (ē'thä-kē)	161	38°27'N	20°48'E
Itigi, Tan.	217	5°42'S	34°29'E
Itimbiri, r., D.R.C.	216	2°40'N	23°30'E
Itire, Nig.	244d	6°31'N	3°21'E
Itoko, D.R.C. (ē-tō'kō)	212	1°13'S	22°07'E
Itu, Braz. (ē-to͞o')	129a	23°16'S	47°16'W
Ituango, Col. (ē-twäŋ'gō)	130	7°07'N	75°44'W
Ituiutaba, Braz. (ē-to͞o-ēo͞o-tä'bä)	131	18°56'S	49°17'W
Itumirim, Braz. (ē-to͞o-mē-rē'N)	129a	21°20'S	44°51'W
Itundujia Santa Cruz, Mex. (ē-to͞on-do͞o-hē'ȧ sä'n-tä kro͞o'z)	119	16°50'N	97°43'W
Iturbide, Mex. (ē'to͞or-bē'dhȧ)	120a	19°38'N	89°31'W
Iturup, i., Russia (ē-to͞o-ro͞op')	171	45°35'N	147°15'E
Ituzaingo, Arg. (ē-to͞o-zä-ē'n-gō)	132a	34°40'S	58°40'W
Itzehoe, Ger. (ē'tzē-hō)	154	53°55'N	9°31'E
Iuka, Ms., U.S. (ī-ū'kȧ)	114	34°47'N	88°10'W
Iúna, Braz. (ē-o͞o'-nä)	129a	20°22'S	41°32'W
Iupeba, Braz.	234d	23°41'S	46°22'W
Ivanhoe, Austl. (ĭv'ăn-hō)	204	32°53'S	144°10'E
Ivanhoe, Austl.	243b	37°46'S	145°03'E
Ivanivka, Ukr.	162	46°43'N	34°33'E
Ivano-Frankivs'k, Ukr.	167	48°53'N	24°46'E
Ivanopil', Ukr.	163	49°51'N	28°11'E
Ivanovo, Russia (ē-vä'nô-vō)	164	57°02'N	41°54'E
Ivanovo, prov., Russia	162	56°55'N	40°30'E
Ivanteyevka, Russia (ē-vän-tyē'yĕf-kȧ)	172b	55°58'N	37°56'E
Ivdel', Russia (ĭv'dyĕl)	172a	60°42'N	60°27'E
Iver, Eng., U.K.	235	51°31'N	0°30'W
Iver Heath, Eng., U.K.	235	51°32'N	0°31'W
Iviza *see* Eivissa, i., Spain	142	38°55'N	1°24'E
Ivohibé, Madag. (ē-vô-hē-bā')	213	22°28'S	46°59'E
Ivory Coast *see* Cote d'Ivoire, nation, Afr.	210	7°43'N	6°30'W
Ivrea, Italy (ē-vrĕ'ä)	148	45°25'N	7°54'E
Ivry-sur-Seine, Fr.	157b	48°49'N	2°23'E
Ivujivik, Can.	85	62°17'N	77°52'W
Iwaki, Japan	194	37°03'N	140°57'E
Iwate Yama, mtn., Japan (ē-wä-tē-yä'mä)	194	39°50'N	140°56'E
Iwatsuki, Japan	195a	35°48'N	139°43'E
Iwaya, Japan (ē'wȧ-yȧ)	195b	34°35'N	135°01'E
Iwo, Nig.	210	7°38'N	4°11'E
Ixcateopán, Mex. (ēs-kä-tä-ō-pän')	118	18°29'N	99°49'W
Ixelles, Bel.	145a	50°49'N	4°23'E
Ixhautlán, Mex. (ēs-wȧt-län')	118	20°41'N	98°01'W
Ixhuatán, Mex. (ēs-hwä-tän')	119	16°19'N	94°30'W
Ixmiquilpan, Mex. (ēs-mē-kēl'pän)	118	20°30'N	99°12'W
Ixopo, S. Afr.	213c	30°10'S	30°04'E
Ixtacalco, Mex. (ēs-tä-käl'kō)	119a	19°23'N	99°07'W
Ixtaltepec, Mex. (ēs-täl-tē-pĕk')	119	16°33'N	95°04'W
Ixtapalapa, Mex. (ēs'tä-pä-lä'pä)	119a	19°21'N	99°06'W
Ixtapaluca, Mex. (ēs'tä-pä-lo͞o'kä)	119a	19°18'N	98°53'W
Ixtepec, Mex. (ēks-tĕ'pĕk)	119	16°37'N	95°09'W
Ixtlahuaca, Mex. (ēs-tlä-wä'kä)	118	19°34'N	99°46'W
Ixtlán de Juárez, Mex. (ēs-tlän' dā hwä'râz)	119	17°20'N	96°29'W
Ixtlán del Río, Mex. (ēs-tlän'dĕl rē'ō)	118	21°05'N	104°22'W
Iya, r., Russia	170	53°45'N	99°30'E
Iyo-Nada, b., Japan (ē'yō nä-dä)	195	33°33'N	132°07'E
Izabal, Guat. (ē'zä-bäl')	120	15°23'N	89°10'W
Izabal, Lago, l., Guat.	120	15°30'N	89°04'W
Izalco, El Sal. (ē-zäl'kō)	120	13°50'N	89°40'W
Izamal, Mex. (ē-zä-mä'l)	120a	20°55'N	89°00'W
Izberbash, Russia	168	42°33'N	47°52'E
Izhevsk, Russia (ē-zhyĕfsk')	164	56°50'N	53°15'E
Izhma, Russia (ĭzh'mȧ)	166	65°00'N	54°05'E
Izhma, r., Russia	166	64°00'N	53°00'E
Izhora, r., Russia (ĕz'hô-rȧ)	172c	59°36'N	30°20'E
Izmaïl, Ukr.	167	45°00'N	28°49'E
İzmir, Tur. (ĭz-mēr')	182	38°25'N	27°05'E
İzmit, Tur. (ĭz-mēt')	149	40°45'N	29°45'E
Iznajar, Embalse de, res., Spain	158	37°15'N	4°30'W
Iztaccíhuatl, mtn., Mex.	118	19°10'N	98°38'W
Izuhara, Japan (ē'zo͞o-hä'rä)	195	34°11'N	129°18'E
Izumi-Ōtsu, Japan (ē'zo͞o-mo͞o ō'tso͞o)	195b	34°30'N	135°24'E
Izumo, Japan (ē'zo͞o-mō)	195	35°22'N	132°45'E
Izu Shichitō, is., Japan	189	34°32'N	139°25'E

J

PLACE (Pronunciation)	PAGE	LAT.	LONG.
Jabal, Bahr al, r., Sudan	211	7°30'N	31°00'E
Jabalpur, India	183	23°18'N	79°59'E
Jabavu, S. Afr.	244b	26°15'S	27°53'E
Jablonec nad Nisou, Czech Rep. (yäb'lô-nyĕts)	154	50°43'N	15°12'E
Jablunkov Pass, p., Eur. (yäb'lôn-kôf)	155	49°31'N	18°35'E
Jaboatão, Braz. (zhä-bô-ȧ-touN)	131	8°14'S	35°08'W
Jaca, Spain (hä'kä)	159	42°35'N	0°30'W
Jacala, Mex. (hä-kȧ'lä)	118	21°01'N	99°11'W
Jacaltenango, Guat. (hä-käl-tē-näŋ'gō)	120	15°39'N	91°41'W
Jacarézinho, Braz. (zhä-kä-rĕ'zē-nyô)	131	23°13'S	49°58'W
Jáchymov, Czech Rep. (yä'chī-môf)	154	50°22'N	12°51'E
Jacinto City, Tx., U.S. (hä-sĕn'tō) (jȧ-sĭn'tō)	113a	29°45'N	95°14'W
Jacksboro, Tx., U.S. (jăks'bŭr-ō)	110	33°13'N	98°11'W
Jackson, Al., U.S. (jăk'sŭn)	114	31°31'N	87°52'W
Jackson, Ca., U.S.	108	38°22'N	120°47'W
Jackson, Ga., U.S.	114	33°19'N	83°55'W
Jackson, Ky., U.S.	114	37°32'N	83°17'W
Jackson, La., U.S.	113	30°50'N	91°13'W
Jackson, Mi., U.S.	97	42°15'N	84°25'W
Jackson, Mn., U.S.	102	43°37'N	95°00'W
Jackson, Ms., U.S.	97	32°17'N	90°10'W
Jackson, Mo., U.S.	111	37°23'N	89°40'W
Jackson, Oh., U.S.	98	39°00'N	82°40'W
Jackson, Tn., U.S.	97	35°37'N	88°49'W
Jackson, Port, b., Austl.	201b	33°50'S	151°18'E
Jackson Heights, neigh., N.Y., U.S.	228	40°45'N	73°53'W
Jackson Lake, l., Wy., U.S.	105	43°57'N	110°28'W
Jacksonville, Al., U.S. (jăk'sŭn-vĭl)	114	33°52'N	85°45'W
Jacksonville, Fl., U.S.	97	30°20'N	81°40'W
Jacksonville, Il., U.S.	97	39°43'N	90°12'W
Jacksonville, Tx., U.S.	113	31°58'N	95°18'W
Jacksonville Beach, Fl., U.S.	115	31°18'N	81°25'W
Jacmel, Haiti (zhȧk-mĕl')	123	18°15'N	72°30'W
Jaco, l., Mex. (hä'kō)	112	27°51'N	103°50'W
Jacobābād, Pak.	186	28°22'N	68°30'E
Jacobina, Braz. (zhä-kô-bē'nȧ)	131	11°13'S	40°30'W
Jacomino, Cuba	233b	23°06'N	82°20'W
Jacques-Cartier, r., Can.	83b	47°04'N	71°28'W
Jacques Cartier, Détroit de, strt., Can.	92	50°07'S	63°58'W
Jacques-Cartier, Mont, mtn., Can.	92	48°59'N	66°00'W
Jacquet River, Can. (zhȧ-kĕ') (jăk'ĕt)	92	47°55'N	66°00'W
Jacutinga, Braz. (zhȧ-ko͞o-tēn'gä)	129a	22°17'S	46°36'W
Jade Buddha, Temple of the (Yufosi), rel., China	241a	31°14'N	121°26'E
Jadebusen, b., Ger.	154	53°28'N	8°17'E
Jadotville *see* Likasi, D.R.C.	212	10°59'S	26°44'E
Jaén, Peru (kä-ĕ'n)	130	5°38'S	78°49'W
Jaen, Spain	148	37°45'N	3°48'W
Jaffa, Cape, c., Austl. (jăf'ȧ)	202	36°58'S	139°29'E
Jaffna, Sri L. (jăf'nȧ)	183b	9°44'N	80°09'E
Jagüey Grande, Cuba (hä'gwā grän'dā)	122	22°35'N	81°05'W
Jahore Strait, strt., Asia	181b	1°22'N	103°37'E
Jahrom, Iran	182	28°30'N	53°28'E
Jaibo, r., Cuba (hä-ē'bō)	123	20°10'N	75°20'W
Jaipur, India	183	27°00'N	75°50'E
Jaisalmer, India	186	27°00'N	70°54'E
Jajce, Bos. (yī'tsĕ)	161	44°20'N	17°19'E
Jajpur, India	183	20°49'N	86°37'E
Jakarta, Indon. (yä-kär'tä)	196	6°17'S	106°45'E
Jakobstad, Fin. (yȧ'kôb-städh)	146	63°33'N	22°31'E
Jalacingo, Mex. (hä-lä-sĭŋ'gō)	119	19°47'N	97°16'W
Jalālābād, Afg. (jŭ-lä-lȧ-bäd)	183a	34°25'N	70°27'E
Jalālah al Baḩrīyah, Jabal, mts., Egypt	218b	29°20'N	32°00'E
Jalapa, Guat. (hä-lä'pȧ)	120	14°38'N	89°58'W
Jalapa de Díaz, Mex.	119	18°06'N	96°33'W
Jalapa del Marqués, Mex. (dĕl mär-kās')	119	16°30'N	95°29'W
Jaleswar, Nepal	186	26°50'N	85°55'E
Jalgaon, India	186	21°08'N	75°33'E
Jalisco, Mex. (hä-lēs'kō)	118	21°27'N	104°54'W
Jalisco, state, Mex.	116	20°07'N	104°45'W
Jalón, r., Spain (hä-lōn')	158	41°22'N	1°46'W
Jalostotitlán, Mex. (hä-lōs-tē-tlȧn')	118	21°09'N	102°30'W
Jalpa, Mex. (häl'pä)	118	21°40'N	103°04'W
Jalpa, Mex. (häl'pā)	118	18°12'N	93°06'W
Jalpan, Mex. (häl'pän)	118	21°13'N	99°31'W
Jaltepec, Mex. (häl-tä-pĕk')	119	17°20'N	95°15'W
Jaltipan, Mex. (häl-tȧ-pän')	119	17°59'N	94°42'W
Jaltocan, Mex. (häl-tō-kän')	118	21°08'N	98°32'W
Jamaare, r., Nig.	215	11°50'N	10°10'E
Jamaica, nation, N.A.	117	17°45'N	78°00'W
Jamaica Bay, b., N.Y., U.S.	228	40°36'N	73°51'W
Jamaica Cay, i., Bah.	123	22°45'N	75°55'W
Jamālīyah, neigh., Egypt	244a	30°03'N	31°16'E
Jamālpur, Bngl.	186	24°56'N	89°58'E
Jamay, Mex. (hä-mī')	118	20°16'N	102°43'W
Jambi, Indon. (mäm'bē)	196	1°45'S	103°28'E

ng-sing; ŋ-baŋk; N-nasalized n; nŏd; cŏmmit; ōld; ôbey; ôrder; oi-boil; fo͞od; o͝o-as oo in foot; ou-out; s-soft; sh-dish; th-thin; pūre; ůnite; ûrn; stŭd; circŭs; ü-as in French tu; '-indeterminate vowel.

300 James-Jos Plateau

PLACE (Pronunciation)	PAGE	LAT.	LONG.
James, r., U.S.	96	46°25'N	98°55'W
James, r., Mo., U.S.	111	36°51'N	93°22'W
James, r., Va., U.S.	97	37°35'N	77°50'W
James, Lake, res., N.C., U.S.	115	36°07'N	81°48'W
James Bay, b., Can. (jāmz)	85	53°53'N	80°40'W
Jamesburg, N.J., U.S. (jāmz'bûrg)	100a	40°21'N	74°26'W
Jameson Raid Memorial, hist., S. Afr.	244b	26°11'S	27°49'E
James Point, c., Bah.	122	25°20'N	76°30'W
James Range, mts., Austl.	202	24°15'S	133°30'E
James Ross, i., Ant.	128	64°20'S	58°20'W
Jamestown, S. Afr.	213c	31°07'S	26°49'E
Jamestown, N.Y., U.S. (jāmz'toun)	97	42°05'N	79°15'W
Jamestown, N.D., U.S.	96	46°54'N	98°42'W
Jamestown, R.I., U.S.	100b	41°30'N	71°21'W
Jamestown Reservoir, res., N.D., U.S.	102	47°16'N	98°40'W
Jamiltepec, Mex. (hä-mēl-tå-pĕk)	119	16°16'N	97°54'W
Jammerbugten, b., Den.	152	57°20'N	9°28'E
Jammu, India	183	32°50'N	74°52'E
Jammu and Kashmīr, hist. reg., Asia (kåsh-mēr')	183	39°10'N	75°05'E
Jāmnagar, India (jäm-nŭ'gŭr)	183	22°33'N	70°03'E
Jamshedpur, India (jäm'shĕd-pōōr)	183	22°52'N	86°11'E
Jándula, r., Spain (hän'dōō-lå)	158	38°28'N	3°52'W
Janesville, Wi., U.S. (jānz'vĭl)	103	42°41'N	89°03'W
Janin, W. Bank	181a	32°27'N	35°19'E
Jan Mayen, i., Nor. (yän mī'ĕn)	146	70°59'N	8°05'W
Jánoshalma, Hung. (yä'nôsh-hôl-mô)	155	46°17'N	19°18'E
Janów Lubelski, Pol. (yä'nōōf lŭ-bĕl'skĭ)	155	50°40'N	22°25'E
Januária, Braz. (zhä-nwä'rē-ä)	131	15°31'S	44°17'W
Japan, nation, Asia (jȧ-păn')	189	36°30'N	133°30'E
Japan, Sea of, sea, Asia (jȧ-păn')	189	40°08'N	132°55'E
Japeri, Braz. (zhå-pĕ'rê)	132b	22°38'S	43°40'W
Japurá (Caquetá), r., S.A.	130	2°00'S	68°00'W
Jarabacoa, Dom. Rep. (ĸä-rä-bä-kō'ä)	123	19°05'N	70°40'W
Jaral del Progreso, Mex. (hä-räl dĕl prō-grā'sō)	118	20°21'N	101°05'W
Jarama, r., Spain (hä-rä'mä)	158	40°33'N	3°30'W
Jarash, Jord.	181a	32°17'N	35°53'E
Jardim Paulista, neigh., Braz.	234d	23°35'S	46°40'W
Jardines, Banco, bk., Cuba (bä'n-kō-här-dē'nås)	122	21°45'N	81°40'W
Jargalant, Mong.	192	46°28'N	115°10'E
Jari, r., Braz. (zhä-rē)	131	0°28'N	53°00'W
Jarocin, Pol. (yä-rō'tsyēn)	155	51°58'N	17°31'E
Jarosław, Pol. (yå-rôs-wäf)	147	50°01'N	22°41'E
Jarud Qi, China (jya-lōō-tŭ shyē)	189	44°35'N	120°40'E
Jasenevo, neigh., Russia	239b	55°36'N	37°33'E
Jasin, Malay.	181b	2°19'N	102°26'E
Jašiūnai, Lith. (dzá-shōō-ná'yē)	153	54°27'N	25°25'E
Jāsk, Iran (jäsk)	182	25°46'N	57°48'E
Jasło, Pol. (yås'wō)	155	49°44'N	21°28'E
Jason Bay, b., Malay.	181b	1°53'N	104°14'E
Jasonville, In., U.S. (jā'sŭn-vĭl)	98	39°10'N	87°15'W
Jasper, Can.	84	52°53'N	118°05'W
Jasper, Al., U.S. (jăs'pẽr)	114	33°50'N	87°17'W
Jasper, Fl., U.S.	115	30°30'N	82°56'W
Jasper, In., U.S.	98	38°20'N	86°55'W
Jasper, Mn., U.S.	102	43°51'N	96°22'W
Jasper, Tx., U.S.	113	30°55'N	93°59'W
Jasper National Park, rec., Can.	84	53°09'N	117°45'W
Jászapáti, Hung. (yäs'ô-pä-tê)	155	47°29'N	20°10'E
Jászberény, Hung.	155	47°30'N	19°56'E
Jatibonico, Cuba (hä-tē-bô-nē'kô)	122	22°00'N	79°15'W
Jauja, Peru (ĸä-ō'ĸ)	130	11°43'S	75°32'W
Jaumave, Mex. (hou-mä'vå)	118	23°23'N	99°24'W
Jaunjelgava, Lat. (youn'yĕl'gá-vá)	166	56°37'N	25°06'E
Java (Jawa), i., Indon.	196	8°35'S	111°11'E
Javari, r., S.A. (ĸá-vä-rē)	130	4°25'S	72°07'W
Java Trench, deep	196	9°45'S	107°30'E
Jawa, Laut (Java Sea), sea, Indon.	196	5°10'S	110°30'E
Jawor, Pol. (yä'vôr)	154	51°04'N	16°12'E
Jaworzno, Pol. (yä-vôzh'nō)	155	50°11'N	19°18'E
Jaya, Puncak, mtn., Indon.	197	4°00'S	137°00'E
Jayapura, Indon.	196	2°30'S	140°45'W
Jayb, Wādī al (Ha'Arava), val., Asia	181a	30°33'N	35°10'E
Jazīrat Muhammad, Egypt	244a	30°07'N	31°12'E
Jazzīn, Leb.	181a	33°34'N	35°37'E
Jeanerette, La., U.S. (jĕn-ẽr-et') (zhän-rĕt')	113	29°54'N	91°41'W
Jebba, Nig. (jĕb'ȧ)	210	9°07'N	4°46'E
Jeddore Lake, l., Can.	93	48°07'N	55°35'W
Jedlesee, neigh., Aus.	239e	48°16'N	16°23'E
Jędrzejów, Pol. (yăɴ-dzhā'yōf)	155	50°38'N	20°18'E
Jefferson, Ga., U.S. (jĕf'ẽr-sŭn)	114	34°05'N	83°35'W
Jefferson, Ia., U.S.	103	42°10'N	94°22'W
Jefferson, La., U.S.	100d	29°57'N	90°04'W
Jefferson, Pa., U.S.	230b	39°56'N	80°04'W
Jefferson, Tx., U.S.	113	32°47'N	94°21'W
Jefferson, Wi., U.S.	103	42°59'N	88°45'W
Jefferson, r., Mt., U.S.	105	45°37'N	112°22'W
Jefferson, Mount, mtn., Or., U.S.	104	44°41'N	121°50'W
Jefferson City, Mo., U.S.	97	38°34'N	92°10'W
Jefferson Park, neigh., Il., U.S.	231a	41°59'N	87°46'W
Jeffersontown, Ky., U.S. (jĕf'ẽr-sŭn-toun)	101h	38°11'N	85°34'W
Jeffersonville, In., U.S. (jĕf'ẽr-sŭn-vĭl)	101h	38°17'N	85°44'W
Jega, Nig.	215	12°15'N	4°23'E
Jehol, hist. reg., China (jĕ-hŏl)	189	42°31'N	118°12'E
Jēkabpils, Lat. (yĕk'ȧb-pĭls)	166	56°29'N	25°50'E
Jelenia Góra, Pol. (yĕ-lĕn'yȧ gō'rȧ)	154	50°53'N	15°43'E
Jelgava, Lat.	153	56°39'N	23°42'E
Jellico, Tn., U.S. (jĕl'ĭ-kō)	114	36°34'N	84°06'W
Jemez Indian Reservation, I.R., N.M., U.S.	109	35°35'N	106°45'W
Jena, Ger. (yā'nä)	147	50°55'N	11°37'E
Jenkins, Ky., U.S. (jĕŋ'kĭnz)	115	37°09'N	82°38'W
Jenkintown, Pa., U.S. (jĕŋ'kĭn-toun)	100f	40°06'N	75°08'W
Jennings, La., U.S. (jĕn'ĭngz)	113	30°14'N	92°40'W
Jennings, Mi., U.S.	98	44°20'N	85°20'W

PLACE (Pronunciation)	PAGE	LAT.	LONG.
Jennings, Mo., U.S.	107e	38°43'N	90°16'W
Jequitinhonha, r., Braz. (zhĕ-kē-tēŋ-ō'n-yä)	131	16°47'S	41°19'W
Jérémie, Haiti (zhā-rå-mē')	123	18°40'N	74°10'W
Jeremoabo, Braz. (zhĕ-rā-mō-á'bō)	131	10°03'S	38°13'W
Jerez, Punta, c., Mex. (pōō'n-tä-ĸĕ-räz')	119	23°04'N	97°44'W
Jerez de la Frontera, Spain	148	36°42'N	6°09'W
Jerez de los Caballeros, Spain	158	38°20'N	6°45'W
Jericho, Austl. (jĕr'ĭ-kō)	203	23°38'S	146°24'E
Jericho, S. Afr. (jĕr-ĭkō)	218d	25°16'N	27°47'E
Jericho, N.Y., U.S.	228	40°48'N	73°32'W
Jericho *see* Arīḩā, W. Bank	181a	31°51'N	35°28'E
Jerome, Az., U.S. (jē-rōm')	96	34°45'N	112°10'W
Jerome, Id., U.S.	105	42°44'N	114°31'W
Jersey, dep., Eur.	156	49°15'N	2°10'W
Jersey, i., Jersey (jûr'zĭ)	147	49°13'N	2°07'W
Jersey City, N.J., U.S.	97	40°43'N	74°05'W
Jersey Shore, Pa., U.S.	99	41°10'N	77°15'W
Jerseyville, Il., U.S. (jẽr'zē-vĭl)	111	39°07'N	90°18'W
Jerusalem, Isr. (jē-rōō'sá-lĕm)	182	31°46'N	35°14'E
Jesup, Ga., U.S. (jĕs'ŭp)	115	31°36'N	81°53'W
Jésus, Île, i., Can.	227b	45°35'N	73°45'W
Jesús Carranza, Mex. (hē-sōō's-kär-rä'n-zä)	119	17°26'N	95°01'W
Jesús del Monte, neigh., Cuba	233b	23°06'N	82°22'W
Jesús María, Peru	233c	12°04'S	77°04'W
Jewel, Or., U.S. (jū'ĕl)	106c	45°56'N	123°30'W
Jewel Cave National Monument, rec., S.D., U.S.	102	43°44'N	103°52'W
Jhālawār, India	183	24°30'N	76°00'E
Jhang Maghiāna, Pak.	186	31°21'N	72°19'E
Jhānsi, India (jän'sē)	183	25°29'N	78°32'E
Jhārsuguda, India	186	22°51'N	84°13'E
Jhelum, Pak.	183	32°59'N	73°43'E
Jhelum, r., Asia (jā'lŭm)	183	31°40'N	71°51'E
Jhenkāri, India	240a	22°46'N	88°18'E
Jhil Kuranga, neigh., India	240d	28°40'N	77°17'E
Jiading, China (jyä-dĭŋ)	190	31°23'N	121°15'E
Jialing, r., China (jyä-lĭŋ)	188	32°30'N	105°30'E
Jiamusi, China	194	46°50'N	130°21'E
Ji'an, China (jyē-än)	189	27°15'N	115°10'E
Ji'an, China	192	41°00'N	126°04'E
Jianchangying, China (jyĕn-chäŋ-yĭŋ)	190	40°09'N	118°47'E
Jiangcun, China (jyän-tsòn)	191a	23°16'N	113°14'E
Jiangling, China (jyäŋ-lĭŋ)	189	30°30'N	112°10'E
Jiangshanzhen, China (jyäŋ-shän-jŭn)	190	36°39'N	120°31'E
Jiangsu, prov., China (jyäŋ-sōō)	189	33°45'N	120°30'E
Jiangwan, China (jyäŋ-wän)	191b	31°18'N	121°29'E
Jiangxi, prov., China (jyäŋ-shyē)	189	28°15'N	116°00'E
Jiangyin, China (jyäŋ-yĭn)	193	31°54'N	120°15'E
Jianli, China (jyĕn-lē)	193	29°50'N	112°52'E
Jianning, China (jyĕn-nĭŋ)	193	26°50'N	116°55'E
Jian'ou, China (jyĕn-ō)	193	27°10'N	118°18'E
Jianshi, China (jyĕn-shr)	193	30°40'N	109°45'E
Jiaohe, China	190	38°03'N	116°18'E
Jiaohe, China (jyou-hŭ)	192	43°40'N	127°20'E
Jiaoxian, China (jyou shyĕn)	189	36°18'N	120°01'E
Jiaozuo, China (jyou-dzwō)	190	35°15'N	113°18'E
Jiashan, China (jyä-shän)	190	32°41'N	118°00'E
Jiaxing, China (jyä-shyĭŋ)	189	30°45'N	120°50'E
Jiayu, China (jyä-yōō)	193	30°00'N	114°00'E
Jiazhou Wan, b., China (jyä-jō wän)	189	36°10'N	119°55'E
Jicarilla Apache Indian Reservation, I.R., N.M., U.S. (ĸē-kȧ-rēl'yȧ)	109	36°45'N	107°00'W
Jicarón, Isla, i., Pan. (ĸē-kä-rōn')	121	7°14'N	81°41'W
Jiddah, Sau. Ar.	182	21°30'N	39°15'E
Jieshou, China	190	33°17'N	115°20'E
Jieyang, China (jyĕ-yäŋ)	189	23°38'N	116°20'E
Jiggalong, Austl. (jĭg'ȧ-lông)	202	23°20'S	120°45'E
Jiguani, Cuba (ĸē-gwä-nē')	122	20°20'N	76°30'W
Jigüey, Bahía, b., Cuba (bä-ē'ä-ĸē'gwā)	122	22°15'N	78°10'W
Jihlava, Czech Rep. (yē'hlá-vá)	147	49°23'N	15°33'E
Jijel, Alg.	147	36°49'N	5°47'E
Jijia, r., Rom.	155	47°35'N	27°02'E
Jijiashi, China (jyē-jyä-shr)	190	32°10'N	120°17'E
Jijiga, Eth.	218a	9°15'N	42°48'E
Jilin, China (jyē-lĭn)	189	43°58'N	126°40'E
Jilin, prov., China	189	44°20'N	124°50'E
Jiloca, r., Spain (ĸē-lō'kä)	158	41°13'N	1°30'W
Jilotepeque, Guat. (ĸē-lô-tĕ-pĕ'kĕ)	120	14°39'N	89°36'W
Jima, Eth.	211	7°41'N	36°52'E
Jimbolia, Rom. (zhĭm-bô'lyä)	161	45°45'N	20°44'E
Jiménez, Mex.	112	27°09'N	104°55'W
Jiménez, Mex.	112	29°03'N	100°42'W
Jiménez, Mex. (ĸē-mā'nåz)	118	24°12'N	98°29'W
Jiménez del Téul, Mex. (tĕ-ōō'l)	118	21°28'N	103°51'W
Jimo, China (jyē-mwo)	192	36°22'N	120°28'E
Jim Thorpe, Pa., U.S. (jĭm' thôrp')	99	40°50'N	75°45'W
Jinan, China (jyē-nän)	189	36°40'N	117°01'E
Jincheng, China (jyĭn-chŭŋ)	192	35°30'N	112°50'E
Jindřichův Hradec, Czech Rep. (yĕn'd'r-zhĭ-kōōf hrä'dĕts)	154	49°09'N	15°02'E
Jing, r., China (jyĭŋ)	192	34°40'N	108°20'E
Jing'anji, China (jyĭŋ-än-jē)	190	34°30'N	116°55'E
Jingdezhen, China (jyĭn-dŭ-jŭn)	193	29°18'N	117°18'E
Jingjiang, China (jyĭŋ-jyäŋ)	190	32°02'N	120°15'E
Jingning, China (jyĭŋ-nĭŋ)	192	35°28'N	105°50'E
Jingpo Hu, l., China (jyĭŋ-pwo hōō)	192	44°10'N	129°00'E
Jingxian, China	190	37°43'N	116°17'E
Jingxian, China (jyĭŋ shyĕn)	193	26°32'N	109°45'E
Jingxing, China (jyĭŋ-shyĭŋ)	192	47°00'N	123°00'E
Jingzhi, China (jyĭŋ-jr)	190	36°19'N	119°23'E
Jinhua, China (jyĭn-hwä)	189	29°10'N	119°42'E
Jining, China (jyē-nĭŋ)	189	35°26'N	116°34'E
Jining, China	192	41°00'N	113°10'E
Jinja, Ug. (jĭn'jä)	211	0°26'N	33°12'E
Jinotega, Nic. (ĸē-nō-tā'gä)	120	13°07'N	86°00'W
Jinotepe, Nic. (ĸē-nō-tā'på)	120	11°52'N	86°12'W
Jinqiao, China (jyĭn-chyou)	190	31°46'N	116°46'E
Jinshan, China (jyĭn-shän)	191b	30°53'N	121°09'E

PLACE (Pronunciation)	PAGE	LAT.	LONG.
Jinta, China (jyĭn-tä)	188	40°11'N	98°45'E
Jintan, China (jyĭn-tän)	190	31°47'N	119°34'E
Jin Xian, China (jyĭn shyĕn)	192	39°04'N	121°40'E
Jinxiang, China (jyĭn-shyäŋ)	190	35°03'N	116°20'E
Jinyun, China (jyĭn-yòn)	193	28°40'N	120°08'E
Jinzhai, China (jyĭn-jī)	190	31°41'N	115°51'E
Jinzhou, China (jyĭn-jō)	189	41°00'N	121°00'E
Jinzhou Wan, b., China (jyĭn-jō wän)	190	39°07'N	121°17'E
Jinzū-Gawa, r., Japan (jēn'zōō gä'wä)	195	36°26'N	137°18'E
Jipijapa, Ec. (ĸē-pē-hä'pä)	130	1°36'S	80°52'W
Jiquilisco, El Sal. (ĸē-kē-lē's-kô)	120	13°18'N	88°32'W
Jiquilpan de Juárez, Mex. (ĸē-kēl'pän dā hwä'räz)	118	20°00'N	102°43'W
Jiquipilco, Mex. (hē-kē-pē'l-kô)	119a	19°32'N	99°37'W
Jitotol, Mex. (ĸē-tô-tōl')	119	17°03'N	92°54'W
Jiu, r., Rom.	161	44°45'N	23°17'E
Jiugang, China	240b	39°49'N	116°27'E
Jiujiang, China	189	29°43'N	116°00'E
Jiujiang, China (jyô-jyän)	191a	22°50'N	113°02'E
Jiuquan, China (jyô-chyän)	188	39°46'N	98°26'E
Jiurongcheng, China (jyô-rôŋ-chŭŋ)	190	37°23'N	122°31'E
Jiushouzhang, China (jyô-shō-jäŋ)	190	35°59'N	115°52'E
Jiuwuqing, China (jyô-wōō-chyĭŋ)	192a	32°31'N	116°51'E
Jiuyongnian, China (jyô-yôŋ-nĭĕn)	190	36°41'N	114°46'E
Jixian, China (jyē shyĕn)	190	35°25'N	114°03'E
Jixian, China	190	37°37'N	115°33'E
Jixian, China	190	40°03'N	117°25'E
Jiyun, r., China (jyē-yōōm)	190	39°35'N	117°34'E
Joachimsthal, Ger.	145b	52°58'N	13°45'E
João Pessoa, Braz.	131	7°09'S	34°45'W
João Ribeiro, Braz. (zhô-uɴ-rē-bā'rō)	129a	20°42'S	44°03'W
Jobabo, r., Cuba (hō-bä'bä)	122	20°50'N	77°15'W
Jock, r., Can. (jŏk)	83c	45°08'N	75°51'W
Jocotepec, Mex. (jô-kō-tå-pĕk')	118	20°17'N	103°26'W
Jodar, Spain (hō'där)	158	37°54'N	3°20'W
Jodhpur, India (hōd'pōōr)	183	26°23'N	73°00'E
Joensuu, Fin. (yō-ĕn'sōō)	153	62°35'N	29°46'E
Joffre, Mount, mtn., Can. (jŏ'f'r)	87	50°32'N	115°13'W
Jõgeva, Est. (yû'gĕ-vá)	153	58°45'N	26°23'E
Joggins, Can. (jŏ'gĭnz)	92	45°42'N	64°27'W
Johannesburg, S. Afr. (yô-hän'ĕs-bòrgh)	212	26°08'S	27°54'E
Johannisthal, neigh., Ger.	238a	52°26'N	13°30'E
John Carroll University, pt. of i., Oh., U.S.	229a	41°29'N	81°32'W
John Day, r., Or., U.S. (jŏn'dā)	104	44°46'N	120°15'W
John Day, Middle Fork, r., Or., U.S.	104	44°53'N	119°04'W
John Day, North Fork, r., Or., U.S.	104	45°03'N	118°50'W
John Day Dam, Or., U.S.	104	45°40'N	120°15'W
John F. Kennedy International Airport, arpt., N.Y., U.S.	228	40°38'N	73°47'W
John H. Kerr Reservoir, res., U.S.	97	36°30'N	78°38'W
John Martin Reservoir, res., Co., U.S. (jŏn mär'tĭn)	110	37°57'N	103°04'W
Johns Hopkins University, pt. of i., Md., U.S.	229c	39°20'N	76°37'W
Johnson, r., Or., U.S. (jŏn'sŭn)	106c	45°27'N	122°20'W
Johnsonburg, Pa., U.S. (jŏn'sŭn-bûrg)	99	41°30'N	78°40'W
Johnson City, Il., U.S. (jŏn'sŭn)	98	37°50'N	88°55'W
Johnson City, N.Y., U.S.	99	42°10'N	76°00'W
Johnson City, Tn., U.S.	97	36°17'N	82°23'W
Johnston, i., Oc. (jŏn'stŭn)	2	17°00'N	168°00'W
Johnstone Strait, strt., Can.	86	50°25'N	126°00'W
Johnston Falls, wtfl., Afr.	217	10°35'S	28°50'E
Johnstown, N.Y., U.S. (jonz'toun)	99	43°00'N	74°20'W
Johnstown, Pa., U.S.	97	40°20'N	78°50'W
Johor, r., Malay. (jŭ-hōr')	181b	1°39'N	103°52'E
Johor Baharu, Malay.	196	1°28'N	103°46'E
Jõhvi, Est. (yû'vĭ)	153	59°21'N	27°21'E
Joigny, Fr. (zhwän-yē')	156	47°58'N	3°26'E
Joinville, Braz. (zhwăɴ-vēl')	132	26°18'S	48°47'W
Joinville, Fr.	157	48°28'N	5°05'E
Joinville, i., Ant.	128	63°00'S	53°30'W
Joinville-le-Pont, Fr.	237c	48°49'N	2°28'E
Jojutla, Mex. (hō-hōō'tlå)	118	18°39'N	99°11'W
Jola, Mex. (ĸō'lä)	118	21°08'N	104°26'W
Joliet, Il., U.S. (jō-lĭ-ĕt')	101a	41°32'N	88°05'W
Joliette, Can. (zhō-lyĕt')	85	46°01'N	73°30'W
Jolo, Phil. (hō-lō)	196	5°59'N	121°05'E
Jolo Island, i., Phil.	196	5°55'N	121°15'E
Jomalig, i., Phil. (hô-mä'lēg)	197a	14°44'N	122°34'E
Jomulco, Mex. (hô-mōōl'kô)	118	21°08'N	104°24'W
Jonacatepec, Mex.	118	18°39'N	98°46'W
Jonava, Lith. (yō-nä'vá)	153	55°05'N	24°15'E
Jones, Phil. (jōnz)	197a	12°56'N	122°05'E
Jones, Phil.	197a	16°35'N	121°39'E
Jonesboro, Ar., U.S. (jōnz'bŭro)	97	35°49'N	90°42'W
Jonesboro, La., U.S.	113	32°14'N	92°43'W
Jonesville, La., U.S. (jōnz'vĭl)	113	31°35'N	91°50'W
Jonesville, Mi., U.S.	98	42°00'N	84°45'W
Jong, r., S.L.	214	8°10'N	12°10'W
Joniškis, Lith. (yô'nĭsh-kĭs)	153	56°14'N	23°36'E
Jönköping, Swe. (yûn'chû-pĭng)	146	57°47'N	14°10'E
Jonquiere, Can. (zhôɴ-kyâr')	85	48°25'N	71°15'W
Jonuta, Mex. (hō-nōō'tä)	119	18°07'N	92°09'W
Jonzac, Fr. (zhôɴ-zák')	156	45°27'N	0°27'W
Joplin, Mo., U.S. (jŏp'lĭn)	97	37°05'N	94°31'W
Jordan, nation, Asia (jôr'dăn)	182	30°15'N	38°00'E
Jordan, r., Asia	181a	32°05'N	35°35'E
Jordan, r., Ut., U.S.	107b	40°42'N	111°56'W
Jorhāt, India (jōr-hät')	183	26°43'N	94°16'E
Jorullo, Volcán de, vol., Mex. (vôl-ká'n-dĕ-hō-rōōl'yō)	118	18°54'N	101°38'W
José C. Paz, Arg.	132a	34°32'S	58°44'W
Joseph Bonaparte Gulf, b., Austl. (jō'sĕf bō'ná-pärt)	202	13°30'S	128°40'E
Josephburg, Can.	83g	53°45'N	113°06'W
Joseph Lake, l., Can. (jō'sĕf lăk)	83g	53°18'N	113°06'W
Joshua Tree National Monument, rec., Ca., U.S. (jō'shŭ-ȧ trē)	108	34°02'N	115°53'W
Jos Plateau, plat., Nig. (jŏs)	215	9°53'N	9°05'E

ăt; finăl; rāte; senāte; ärm; åsk; sofȧ; fâre; ch-choose; dh-as th in other; bē; ēvent; bĕt; recĕnt; cratẽr; g-gō; gh-guttural g; bĭt; ĭ-short neutral; rīde; ĸ-guttural k as ch in German ich;

PRONOUNCING INDEX

Jostedalsbreen – Kanā'is 301

PLACE (Pronunciation)	PAGE	LAT.	LONG.
Jostedalsbreen, ice., Nor. (yôstě-däls-brěěn)	146	61°40'N	6°55'E
Jotunheimen, mts., Nor.	146	61°44'N	8°11'E
Joulter's Cays, is., Bah. (jōl'tẽrz)	122	25°20'N	78°10'W
Jouy-en-Josas, Fr.	237c	48°46'N	2°10'E
Jouy-le-Chatel, Fr. (zhwē-lẽ-shä-tĕl')	157b	48°40'N	3°07'E
Jovellanos, Cuba (hō-vĕl-yä'nōs)	122	22°50'N	81°10'W
J. Percy Priest Lake, res., Tn., U.S.	114	36°00'N	86°45'W
Juan Aldama, Mex. (kòá'n-äl-dá'mä)	118	24°16'N	103°21'W
Juan Anchorena, neigh., Arg.	233d	34°29'S	58°30'W
Juan de Fuca, Strait of, strt., N.A. (hwän' dā fōō'kä)	84	48°25'N	124°37'W
Juan de Nova, Île, i., Reu.	213	17°18'S	43°07'E
Juan Díaz, r., Pan. (kōōá'n-dē'äz)	116a	9°05'N	79°30'W
Juan Fernández, Islas de, is., Chile	128	33°30'S	79°00'W
Juan González Romero, Mex.	233a	19°30'N	99°04'W
Juan L. Lacaze, Ur. (hōōá'n-ĕ'lĕ-lä-kä'zĕ)	129c	34°25'S	57°28'W
Juan Luis, Cayos de, is., Cuba (ka-yōs-dĕ-hwän lōō-ēs')	122	22°15'N	82°00'W
Juárez, Arg. (hōōá'rĕz)	132	37°42'S	59°46'W
Juázeiro, Braz. (zhōōá'zā'rò)	131	9°27'S	40°28'W
Juazeiro do Norte, Braz. (zhōōá'zā'rò-dò-nôr-tĕ)	131	7°16'S	38°57'W
Jubayl, Leb. (jōō-bīl')	181a	34°07'N	35°38'E
Jubba (Genale), r., Afr.	218a	1°30'N	42°25'E
Juby, Cap, c., Mor. (yōō'bē)	210	28°01'N	13°21'W
Júcar, r., Spain (hōō'kär)	148	39°10'N	1°22'W
Júcaro, Cuba (hōō'kà-rò)	122	21°40'N	78°50'W
Juchipila, Mex. (hōō-chē-pē'lä)	118	21°26'N	103°09'W
Juchitán, Mex. (hōō-chē-tän')	116	16°15'N	95°00'W
Juchitlán, Mex. (hōō-chē-tlän)	118	20°05'N	104°07'W
Jucuapa, El Sal. (kōō-kwä'pä)	120	13°30'N	88°24'W
Judenburg, Aus. (jōō'dĕn-bûrg)	154	47°10'N	14°40'E
Judith, r., Mt., U.S. (jōō'dĭth)	105	47°20'N	109°36'W
Jugo-Zapad, neigh., Russia	239b	55°40'N	37°32'E
Juhua Dao, i., China (jyōō-hwä dou)	190	40°30'N	120°47'E
Juigalpa, Nic. (hwē-gäl'pä)	120	12°02'N	85°24'W
Juilly, Fr.	237c	49°01'N	2°42'E
Juiz de Fora, Braz. (zhò-ēzh' dā fō'rä)	131	21°47'S	43°20'W
Jujuy, Arg. (hōō-hwē')	132	24°14'S	65°15'W
Jujuy, prov., Arg. (hōō-hwē')	132	23°00'S	65°45'W
Jukskei, r., S. Afr.	213b	25°58'S	27°58'E
Julesburg, Co., U.S. (jōōlz'bûrg)	110	40°59'N	102°16'W
Juliaca, Peru (hōō-lē-ä'kä)	130	15°26'S	70°12'W
Julian Alps, mts., Yugo.	148	46°05'N	14°05'E
Julianehåb, Grnld.	82	60°07'N	46°20'W
Jülich, Ger. (yü'lĕk)	157c	50°55'N	6°22'E
Jullundur, India	183	31°29'N	75°39'E
Julpaiguri, India	186	26°35'N	88°48'E
Jumento Cays, is., Bah. (hōō-mĕn'tō)	123	23°05'N	75°40'W
Jumilla, Spain (hōō-mēl'yä)	158	38°28'N	1°20'W
Jump, r., Wi., U.S. (jŭmp)	103	45°18'N	90°53'W
Jumpingpound Creek, r., Can. (jŭmp-ĭng-pound)	83e	51°01'N	114°34'W
Jumrah, Indon.	181b	1°48'N	101°04'E
Junagādh, India (jò-nä'gŭd)	183	21°33'N	70°25'E
Junayfah, Egypt	218c	30°11'N	32°26'E
Junaynah, Ra's al, mtn., Egypt	181a	29°02'N	33°58'E
Junction, Tx., U.S. (jŭŋk'shŭn)	112	30°29'N	99°48'W
Junction City, Ks., U.S.	111	39°01'N	96°49'W
Jundiaí, Braz.	131	23°11'S	46°52'W
Juneau, Ak., U.S. (jōō'nō)	94a	58°25'N	134°30'W
Jungfrau, mtn., Switz. (yòng'frou)	154	46°30'N	7°59'E
Juniata, neigh., Pa., U.S.	229b	40°01'N	75°07'W
Junín, Arg. (hōō-nē'n)	132	34°35'S	60°56'W
Junín, Col.	130a	4°47'N	73°39'W
Juniyah, Leb. (jōō-nē'ĕ)	181a	33°59'N	35°38'E
Jupiter, r., Can.	92	49°40'N	63°20'W
Jupiter, Mount, mtn., Wa., U.S.	106a	47°42'N	123°04'W
Jur, r., Sudan (jòr)	211	6°38'N	27°52'E
Jura, mts., Eur. (zhü-rà')	147	46°55'N	6°49'E
Jura, i., Scot., U.K. (jōō'rà)	150	56°09'N	6°45'W
Jura, Sound of, strt., Scot., U.K. (jōō'rȧ)	150	55°45'N	5°55'W
Jurbarkas, Lith. (yōōr-bär'käs)	153	55°06'N	22°50'E
Jūrmala, Lat.	153	56°57'N	23°37'E
Jurong, China (jyōō-roŋ)	190	31°58'N	119°12'E
Jurong, Sing.	240c	1°21'N	103°42'E
Juruá, r., S.A.	130	5°30'S	67°30'W
Juruena, r., Braz. (zhōō-rōōĕ'nä)	131	12°22'S	58°34'W
Justice, Il., U.S.	231a	41°45'N	87°50'W
Jutiapa, Guat. (hōō-tē-ä'pä)	120	14°16'N	89°55'W
Juticalpa, Hond. (hōō-tē-käl'pä)	116	14°35'N	86°17'W
Jutland *see* Jylland, reg., Den.	146	56°04'N	9°00'E
Juventino Rosas, Mex.	118	20°38'N	101°02'W
Juventud, Isla de la, i., Cuba	117	21°40'N	82°45'W
Juvisy-sur-Orge, Fr.	237c	48°41'N	2°23'E
Juxian, China (jyōō shyĕn)	192	35°35'N	118°50'E
Juxtlahuaca, Mex. (hōōs-tlä-hwä'kä)	118	17°20'N	98°02'W
Juye, China (jyōō-yü)	190	35°25'N	116°05'E
Južna Morava, r., Yugo. (ŭ'zhnä mô'rä-vä)	161	42°30'N	22°00'E
Jwālahari, neigh., India	240d	28°40'N	77°06'E
Jylland, reg., Den.	146	56°04'N	9°00'E

K

PLACE (Pronunciation)	PAGE	LAT.	LONG.
K2, mtn., Asia	183	36°06'N	76°38'E
Kaabong, Ug.	217	3°31'N	34°08'E
Kaalfontein, S. Afr. (kärl-fōn-tān)	213b	26°02'S	28°16'E
Kaappunt, c., S. Afr.	212a	34°21'S	18°30'E
Kaarst, Ger.	236	51°14'N	6°37'E
Kabaena, Pulau, i., Indon. (kä-bȧ-ā'nȧ)	196	5°35'S	121°07'E
Kabala, S.L. (kȧ-bà'lȧ)	210	9°43'N	11°39'W
Kabale, Ug.	217	1°15'S	29°59'E
Kabalega Falls, wtfl., Ug.	211	2°15'N	31°41'E
Kabalo, D.R.C. (kä-bä'lō)	212	6°03'S	26°55'E
Kabambare, D.R.C. (kä-bäm-bä'rȧ)	212	4°47'S	27°45'E
Kabardino-Balkaria, state, Russia	166	43°30'N	43°30'E
Kabba, Nig.	215	7°50'N	6°03'E
Kabe, Japan (kä'bā)	195	34°32'N	132°30'E
Kabel, neigh., Ger.	236	51°24'N	7°29'E
Kabinakagami, r., Can.	90	49°00'N	84°15'W
Kabinda, D.R.C. (kä-bēɴ'dä)	212	6°08'S	24°29'E
Kabompo, r., Zam. (kȧ-bôm'pō)	212	14°00'S	23°40'E
Kabongo, D.R.C. (kȧ-bông'ō)	212	7°58'S	25°10'E
Kabot, Gui.	214	10°48'N	14°57'W
Kaboudia, Ra's, c., Tun.	148	35°17'N	11°28'E
Kābul, Afg. (kä'bòl)	183	34°39'N	69°14'E
Kabul, r., Asia (kä'bòl)	183	34°44'N	69°43'E
Kabunda, D.R.C.	217	12°25'S	29°22'E
Kabwe, Zam.	212	14°27'S	28°27'E
Kachuga, Russia (kȧ-chōō-gȧ)	165	54°09'N	105°43'E
Kadei, r., Afr.	215	4°00'N	15°10'E
Kadıköy, neigh., Tur.	239f	40°59'N	29°01'E
Kadnikov, Russia (käd'nē-kôf)	166	59°30'N	40°10'E
Kadoma, Japan	195b	34°43'N	135°36'E
Kadoma, Zimb.	212	18°21'S	29°55'E
Kaduna, Nig. (kä-dōō'nä)	210	10°33'N	7°27'E
Kaduna, r., Nig.	215	9°30'N	6°00'E
Kaédi, Maur. (kä-ā-dē')	210	16°09'N	13°30'W
Kaena Point, c., Hi., U.S. (kä'ā-nä)	96d	21°33'N	158°19'W
Kaesŏng, N. Kor. (kä'ĕ-sŭng) (kĭ'jō)	189	38°00'N	126°35'E
Kafanchan, Nig.	215	9°36'N	8°17'E
Kafia Kingi, Sudan (kä'fē-ȧ kĭŋ'gē)	211	9°17'N	24°28'E
Kafue, Zam. (kä'fōō)	212	15°45'S	28°17'E
Kafue, r., Zam.	212	15°45'S	26°30'E
Kafue Flats, sw., Zam.	217	16°15'S	26°30'E
Kafue National Park, rec., Zam.	217	15°00'S	25°35'E
Kafwira, D.R.C.	217	12°10'S	27°33'E
Kagal'nik, r., Russia (kä-gäl''nēk)	163	46°58'N	39°25'E
Kagera, r., Afr. (kä-gā'rȧ)	212	1°10'S	31°10'E
Kagoshima, Japan (kä'gō-shē'mȧ)	189	31°35'N	130°31'E
Kagoshima-Wan, b., Japan (kä'gō-shē'mä wän)	194	31°24'N	130°39'E
Kagran, neigh., Aus.	239e	48°15'N	16°27'E
Kahayan, r., Indon.	196	1°45'S	113°40'E
Kahemba, D.R.C.	216	7°17'S	19°00'E
Kahia, D.R.C.	217	6°21'S	28°24'E
Kahoka, Mo., U.S. (kȧ-hō'kȧ)	111	40°26'N	91°42'W
Kahoolawe, Hi., U.S. (kä-hōō-lä'wē)	94a	20°28'N	156°48'W
Kahramarımaraş, Tur.	182	37°40'N	36°50'W
Kahshahpiwi, r., Can.	103	48°24'N	90°56'W
Kahuku Point, c., Hi., U.S. (kä-hōō'kōō)	96d	21°50'N	157°50'W
Kahului, Hi., U.S.	96c	20°53'N	156°28'W
Kai, Kepulauan, is., Indon.	197	5°35'S	132°45'E
Kaiang, Malay.	181b	3°00'N	101°47'E
Kaiashk, r., Can.	90	49°40'N	89°30'W
Kaibab Indian Reservation, I.R., Az., U.S. (kä'ē-bȧb)	109	36°55'N	112°45'W
Kaibab Plat, Az., U.S.	109	36°30'N	112°10'W
Kaidori, Japan	242a	35°37'N	139°27'E
Kaidu, r., China (kī-dōō)	188	42°35'N	84°04'E
Kaieteur Fall, wtfl., Guy. (kī-ĕ-tōōr')	131	4°48'N	59°24'W
Kaifeng, China (kī-fŭŋ)	189	34°48'N	114°22'E
Kai Kecil, i., Indon.	197	5°45'S	132°40'E
Kailua, Hi., U.S. (kä'ē-lōō'ä)	96c	21°18'N	157°43'W
Kailua Kona, Hi., U.S.	94a	19°49'N	155°59'W
Kaimana, Indon.	197	3°32'S	133°47'E
Kaimanawa Mountains, mts., N.Z.	205	39°10'S	176°00'E
Kainan, Japan (kä'ē-nän')	195	34°09'N	135°14'E
Kainji Lake, res., Nig.	210	10°25'N	4°50'E
Kaisermühlen, neigh., Aus.	239e	48°14'N	16°26'E
Kaiserslautern, Ger. (kī-zẽrs-lou'tẽrn)	147	49°26'N	7°46'E
Kaiserwerth, neigh., Ger.	236	51°18'N	6°44'E
Kaitaia, N.Z. (kä-ē-tä'ē-ȧ)	203a	35°30'S	173°28'E
Kaiwi Channel, strt., Hi., U.S. (käē-wē)	96c	21°10'N	157°38'W
Kaiyuan, China	192	42°30'N	124°00'E
Kaiyuan, China (kū-yuän)	193	23°42'N	103°20'E
Kaiyuh Mountains, mts., Ak., U.S. (kī-yōō')	95	64°25'N	157°38'W
Kajaani, Fin. (kä'yȧ-nē)	146	64°15'N	27°16'E
Kajang, Gunong, mtn., Malay.	181b	2°47'N	104°05'E
Kajiki, Japan (kä'jē-kē)	194	31°44'N	130°41'E
Kakhovka, Ukr. (kä-κôf'kȧ)	163	46°46'N	33°32'E
Kakhovskoye, res., Ukr. (kä-κôf'skô-yĕ)	164	47°21'N	33°33'E
Kākināda, India	183	16°58'N	82°18'E
Kaktovik, Ak., U.S. (käk-tō'vĭk)	95	70°08'N	143°51'W
Kakwa, r., Can. (käk'wȧ)	87	54°00'N	118°55'W
Kalach, Russia (kȧ-lȧch')	167	50°15'N	40°55'E
Kaladan, r., Asia	188	21°07'N	93°04'E
Ka Lae, c., Hi., U.S.	94a	18°55'N	155°41'W
Kalahari Desert, des., Afr. (kä-lä-hä'rē)	212	23°00'S	22°03'E
Kalama, Wa., U.S. (kȧ-lăm'ȧ)	106c	46°01'N	122°50'W
Kalama, r., Wa., U.S.	106c	46°03'N	122°47'W
Kalámai, Grc. (kä-lä-mī')	142	37°04'N	22°08'E
Kalamákion, Grc.	239d	37°55'N	23°43'E
Kalamazoo, Mi., U.S. (kăl-ȧ-mȧ-zōō')	97	42°20'N	85°40'W
Kalamazoo, r., Mi., U.S.	98	42°35'N	86°00'W
Kalanchak, Ukr. (kä-län-chäk')	163	46°17'N	33°14'E
Kalandula, Ang. (dōō'kȧ dȧ brä-gäɴ'sä)	212	9°06'S	15°57'E
Kalaotoa, Pulau, i., Indon.	196	7°22'S	122°30'E
Kalapana, Hi., U.S. (kä-lä-pá'nä)	94a	19°25'N	155°00'W
Kalar, mtn., Iran	182	31°43'N	51°41'E
Kalāt, Pak. (kŭ-lät')	183	29°05'N	66°36'E
Kalemie, D.R.C.	212	5°56'S	29°12'E
Kalgan *see* Zhangjiakou, China	189	40°45'N	114°58'E
Kalgoorlie-Boulder, Austl. (kăl-gōōr'lē)	202	30°45'S	121°35'E
Kaliakra, Nos, c., Bul.	149	43°25'N	28°42'E
Kalima, D.R.C.	217	2°34'S	26°37'E
Kalina, neigh., D.R.C.	244c	4°18'S	15°16'E
Kaliningrad, Russia	164	54°42'N	20°32'E
Kaliningrad, Russia (kä-lē-nēn'grät)	172b	55°55'N	37°49'E
Kalinkovichi, Bela. (kä-lēn-ko-vē'chē)	162	52°07'N	29°19'E
Kalispel Indian Reservation, I.R., Wa., U.S. (kăl-ĭ-spĕl')	104	48°25'N	117°30'W
Kalispell, Mt., U.S. (kăl'ĭ-spĕl)	96	48°12'N	114°18'W
Kalisz, Pol. (kä'lēsh)	147	51°45'N	18°05'E
Kaliua, Tan.	217	5°04'S	31°48'E
Kalixälven, r., Swe.	146	67°12'N	22°00'E
Kālkāji, neigh., India	240d	28°33'N	77°16'E
Kalksburg, neigh., Aus.	239e	48°08'N	16°15'E
Kalkum, Ger.	236	51°18'N	6°46'E
Kallithéa, Grc.	239d	37°57'N	23°42'E
Kalmar, Swe. (käl'mär)	146	56°40'N	16°19'E
Kalmarsund, strt., Swe. (käl'mär)	152	56°30'N	16°17'E
Kal'mius, r., Ukr. (käl'myōōs)	163	47°15'N	37°38'E
Kalmykia, state, Russia	167	46°56'N	46°00'E
Kalocsa, Hung. (kä'lō-chä)	155	46°32'N	19°00'E
Kalohi Channel, strt., Hi., U.S. (kä-lō'hĭ)	94a	20°55'N	157°15'W
Kaloko, D.R.C.	217	6°47'S	25°48'E
Kalomo, Zam. (kä-lō'mō)	212	17°02'S	26°30'E
Kalsubai Mount, mtn., India	186	19°43'N	73°47'E
Kaltenkirchen, Ger. (käl'tĕn-kēr-κĕn)	145c	53°50'N	9°57'E
Kālu, r., India	187b	19°18'N	73°14'E
Kaluga, Russia (kȧ-lò'gä)	164	54°29'N	36°12'E
Kaluga, prov., Russia	162	54°10'N	35°00'E
Kalundborg, Den. (kȧ-lòn''bôr')	152	55°42'N	11°07'E
Kalush, Ukr. (kä'lòsh)	155	49°02'N	24°24'E
Kalvarija, Lith. (käl-vä-rē'yȧ)	153	54°24'N	23°17'E
Kalwa, India	187b	19°12'N	72°59'E
Kal'ya, Russia (käl'yȧ)	172a	60°17'N	59°58'E
Kalyān, India	186	19°16'N	73°07'E
Kalyazin, Russia (käl-yȧ'zĭn)	162	57°13'N	37°55'E
Kama, r., Russia (kä'mä)	164	56°10'N	53°50'E
Kamaishi, Japan (kä'mä-ē'shē)	194	39°16'N	142°03'E
Kamakura, Japan (kä'mä-kōō'rä)	195	35°19'N	139°33'E
Kamarān, i., Yemen	182	15°19'N	41°47'E
Kāmārhāti, India	186a	22°41'N	88°23'E
Kamata, neigh., Japan	242a	35°33'N	139°43'E
Kambove, D.R.C. (käm-bō'vĕ)	212	10°58'S	26°43'E
Kamchatka, r., Russia	171	54°15'N	158°38'E
Kamchatka, Poluostrov, pen., Russia	171	55°19'N	157°45'E
Kāmdebpur, India	240a	22°54'N	88°20'E
Kameari, neigh., Japan	242a	35°46'N	139°51'E
Kameido, neigh., Japan	242a	35°42'N	139°50'E
Kamen, Ger. (kä'mĕn)	157c	51°35'N	7°40'E
Kamenjak, Rt, c., Cro. (kä'mĕ-nyäk)	160	44°45'N	13°57'E
Kamen'-na-Obi, Russia (kä-mĭny'nŭ ô'bē)	164	53°43'N	81°28'E
Kamensk-Shakhtinskiy, Russia (kä'mĕnsk shäk'tĭn-skĭ)	163	48°17'N	40°16'E
Kamensk-Ural'skiy, Russia (kä'mĕnsk ōō-räl'skĭ)	166	56°27'N	61°55'E
Kamenz, Ger. (kä'mĕnts)	154	51°16'N	14°05'E
Kameoka, Japan (kä'mā-ōkä)	195b	35°01'N	135°35'E
Kāmet, mtn., Asia	186	30°50'N	79°42'E
Kamiakatsuka, neigh., Japan	242a	35°46'N	139°39'E
Kamianets'-Podil's'kyi, Ukr.	167	48°41'N	26°34'E
Kamianka-Buz'ka, Ukr.	155	50°06'N	24°20'E
Kamiasao, Japan	242a	35°35'N	139°30'E
Kamień Pomorski, Pol.	154	53°57'N	14°48'E
Kamiishihara, Japan	242a	35°39'N	139°32'E
Kamikitazawa, neigh., Japan	242a	35°40'N	139°38'E
Kamikoma, Japan (kä'mē-kō'mä)	195b	34°45'N	135°50'E
Kamina, D.R.C.	212	8°44'S	25°00'E
Kaministikwia, r., Can. (kȧ-mĭ-nĭ-stĭk'wĭ-ȧ)	103	48°40'N	89°41'W
Kamioyamada, Japan	242a	35°35'N	139°24'E
Kamitsuruma, Japan	242a	35°31'N	139°25'E
Kamituga, D.R.C.	217	3°04'S	28°11'E
Kamloops, Can. (kăm'lōōps)	84	50°40'N	120°20'W
Kamoshida, neigh., Japan	242a	35°34'N	139°30'E
Kamp, r., Aus. (kämp)	154	48°30'N	15°45'E
Kampala, Ug. (käm-pä'lä)	211	0°19'N	32°25'E
Kampar, r., Indon. (käm'pär)	196	0°30'N	101°30'E
Kampene, D.R.C.	217	3°36'S	26°40'E
Kampenhout, Bel.	145a	50°56'N	4°33'E
Kamp-Lintfort, Ger. (kämp-lĕnt'fōrt)	157c	51°30'N	6°34'E
Kampong Kranji, Sing.	240c	1°26'N	103°46'E
Kampong Loyang, Sing.	240c	1°22'N	103°58'E
Kâmpóng Saôm, Camb.	196	10°40'N	103°50'E
Kampong Tanjong Keling, Sing.	240c	1°18'N	103°42'E
Kâmpóng Thum, Camb. (kŏm'pŏng-tŏm)	196	12°41'N	104°29'E
Kâmpôt, Camb. (käm'pŏt)	196	10°41'N	104°07'E
Kampuchea *see* Cambodia, nation, Asia	196	12°15'N	104°00'E
Kamsack, Can. (kăm'săk)	84	51°34'N	101°54'W
Kamskoye, res., Russia	164	59°08'N	56°30'E
Kamudilo, D.R.C.	217	7°42'S	27°18'E
Kamuela, Hi., U.S.	94a	20°01'N	155°40'W
Kamui Misaki, c., Japan	194	43°25'N	139°35'E
Kámuk, Cerro, mtn., C.R. (sĕ'r-rô-kä-mōō'k)	121	9°18'N	83°02'W
Kamyshevatskaya, Russia	163	46°24'N	37°58'E
Kamyshin, Russia (kä-mwēsh'ĭn)	164	50°08'N	45°20'E
Kamyshlov, Russia (kä-mēsh'lôf)	164	56°50'N	62°32'E
Kan, r., Russia (kän)	170	56°30'N	94°17'E
Kanab, Ut., U.S. (kăn'ăb)	109	37°00'N	112°30'W
Kanabeki, Russia (kȧ-nä'byĕ-kĭ)	172a	57°48'N	57°16'E
Kanab Plateau, plat., Az., U.S.	109	36°31'N	112°55'W
Kanaga, i., Ak., U.S. (kă-nä'gä)	95a	52°02'N	177°38'W
Kanagawa, dept., Japan (kä'nä-gä'wä)	195a	35°29'N	139°32'E
Kanai, Japan	242a	35°35'N	139°28'E
Kanā'is, Ra's al, c., Egypt	149	31°14'N	28°08'E

302 Kanamachi–Keluang

PLACE (Pronunciation)	PAGE	LAT.	LONG.
Kanamachi, Japan (kä-nä-mä′chē)	195a	35°46′N	139°52′E
Kanamori, Japan	242a	35°32′N	139°28′E
Kananga, D.R.C.	212	6°14′S	22°17′E
Kananikol′skoye, Russia	172a	52°48′N	57°29′E
Kanasín, Mex. (kä-nä-sē′n)	120a	20°54′N	89°31′W
Kanatak, Ak., U.S. (kă-nă′tŏk)	95	57°35′N	155°48′W
Kanawha, r., W.V., U.S. (kȧ-nô′wȧ)	97	37°55′N	81°50′W
Kanaya, Japan (kä-nä′yä)	195a	35°10′N	139°49′E
Kanazawa, Japan (kä′nȧ-zä′wȧ)	189	36°34′N	136°38′E
Kānchenjunga, mtn., Asia (kĭn-chĭn-jŏn′gȧ)	183	27°30′N	88°18′E
Kānchipuram, India	183	12°55′N	79°43′E
Kanda Kanda, D.R.C. (kän′dȧ kän′dȧ)	212	6°56′S	23°36′E
Kandalaksha, Russia (kȧn-dȧ-lȧk′shȧ)	164	67°10′N	33°05′E
Kandalakshskiy Zaliv, b., Russia	166	66°20′N	35°00′E
Kandava, Lat. (kän′dȧ-vȧ)	153	57°03′N	22°45′E
Kandi, Benin (kän-dē′)	210	11°08′N	2°56′E
Kandiāro, Pak.	186	27°09′N	68°12′E
Kandla, India (kŭnd′lŭ)	186	23°00′N	70°20′E
Kandy, Sri L. (kän′dē)	183b	7°18′N	80°42′E
Kane, Pa., U.S. (kān)	99	41°40′N	78°50′W
Kaneohe, Hi., U.S. (kä-nā-ō′hā)	94a	21°25′N	157°47′W
Kaneohe Bay, b., Hi., U.S.	96d	21°32′N	157°40′W
Kanevskaya, Russia (kä-nyĕf′skȧ)	163	46°07′N	38°58′E
Kangaroo, i., Austl. (kăŋ-gȧ-rōō′)	202	36°05′S	137°05′E
Kangaroo Ground, Austl.	243b	37°41′S	145°13′E
Kangāvar, Iran (kŭŋ′gä-vär)	182	34°37′N	46°45′E
Kangean, Kepulauan, is., Indon. (käŋ′gē-än)	196	6°50′S	116°22′E
Kanggye, N. Kor. (käng′gyĕ)	189	40°55′N	126°40′E
Kanghwa, i., S. Kor. (käng′hwä)	194	37°38′N	126°00′E
Kangnŭng, S. Kor. (käng′nŏ ng)	194	37°42′N	128°50′E
Kango, Gabon (kän-gō)	212	0°09′N	10°08′E
Kangowa, D.R.C.	216	9°55′S	22°48′E
Kanin, Poluostrov, pen., Russia	164	68°00′N	45°00′E
Kaningo, Kenya	217	0°49′S	38°32′E
Kanin Nos, Mys, c., Russia	166	68°40′N	44°00′E
Kaniv, Ukr.	163	49°46′N	31°27′E
Kanivs′ke vodoskhovyshche, res., Ukr.	164	50°10′N	30°40′E
Kanjiža, Yugo. (kä′nyē-zhä)	161	46°05′N	20°02′E
Kankakee, Il., U.S. (kăŋ-kȧ-kē′)	98	41°07′N	87°53′W
Kankakee, r., Il., U.S.	98	41°15′N	88°15′W
Kankan, Gui. (kän-kän) (kän-kän′)	210	10°23′N	9°18′W
Kannapolis, N.C., U.S. (kăn-ăp′ō-lĭs)	115	35°30′N	80°38′W
Kannoura, Japan (kä′nō-ōō′rä)	195	33°34′N	134°18′E
Kano, Nig. (kä′nō)	210	12°00′N	8°30′E
Kanonkop, mtn., S. Afr.	212a	33°49′S	18°37′E
Kanopolis Reservoir, res., Ks., U.S. (kăn-ŏp′ō-lĭs)	110	38°44′N	98°01′W
Kānpur, India (kän′pûr)	186	26°30′N	80°10′E
Kansas, state, U.S. (kăn′zȧs)	96	38°30′N	99°40′W
Kansas, r., Ks., U.S.	111	39°08′N	95°52′W
Kansas City, Ks., U.S.	97	39°06′N	94°39′W
Kansas City, Mo., U.S.	97	39°05′N	94°35′W
Kansk, Russia	165	56°14′N	95°43′E
Kansŏng, S. Kor.	194	38°09′N	128°29′E
Kantang, Thai. (kän′täng′)	196	7°26′N	99°28′E
Kantchari, Burkina	214	12°29′N	1°31′E
Kanton, i., Kir.	224	3°50′S	174°00′W
Kantunilkín, Mex. (kän-tōō-nēl-kē′n)	120a	21°07′N	87°30′W
Kanzaki, r., Japan	242b	34°42′N	135°25′E
Kanzhakovskiy Kamen, Gora, mtn., Russia (kȧn-zhä′kôvs-kēē kämĭen)	172a	59°38′N	59°12′E
Kaohsiung, Tai. (kä-ō-syŏng′)	189	22°35′N	120°25′E
Kaolack, Sen.	210	14°09′N	16°04′W
Kaouar, oasis, Niger	211	19°16′N	13°09′E
Kapaa, Hi., U.S.	94a	22°06′N	159°20′W
Kapanga, D.R.C.	216	8°21′S	22°35′E
Kapellen, Ger.	236	51°25′N	6°35′E
Kapfenberg, Aus. (käp′fĕn-bĕrgh)	154	47°27′N	15°16′E
Kapiri Mposhi, Zam.	217	13°58′S	28°41′E
Kapoeta, Sudan	211	4°45′N	33°35′E
Kaposvár, Hung. (kô′pôsh-vär)	155	46°21′N	17°45′E
Kapotn′a, neigh., Russia	239b	55°38′N	37°48′E
Kapsan, N. Kor. (käp′sän′)	194	40°59′N	128°22′E
Kapuskasing, Can.	85	49°28′N	82°22′W
Kapuskasing, r., Can.	90	48°55′N	82°55′W
Kapustin Yar, Russia (kä′pŏs-tēn yär′)	167	48°30′N	45°40′E
Kaputar, Mount, mtn., Austl. (kă-pû-tăr)	204	30°11′S	150°11′E
Kapuvár, Hung. (kô′pōō-vär)	155	47°35′N	17°02′E
Kara, Russia (kärȧ)	164	68°42′N	65°30′E
Kara, r., Russia	166	68°30′N	65°20′E
Karabalā′, Iraq (kŭr′bȧ-lä)	182	32°31′N	43°58′E
Karabanovo, Russia (kä′rȧ-bȧ-nō-vō)	162	56°19′N	38°43′E
Karabash, Russia (kô-rȧ-bäsh′)	172a	55°27′N	60°14′E
Kara-Bogaz-Gol, Zaliv, b., Turk. (kȧ-rä′ bŭ-gäs′)	169	41°30′N	53°40′E
Karachay-Cherkessia, state, Russia	168	44°00′N	42°00′E
Karachev, Russia (kȧ-rȧ-chôf′)	166	53°08′N	34°54′E
Karāchi, Pak.	183	24°59′N	68°56′E
Karaidel′, Russia (kä′rī-dĕl)	172a	55°52′N	56°54′E
Kara-Khobda, r., Kaz. (kä-rȧ kôb′dȧ)	170	50°40′N	55°00′E
Karakoram Pass, p., Asia	183	35°35′N	77°45′E
Karakoram Range, mts., India (kä′rä kō′rŏm)	183	35°24′N	76°38′E
Karakorum, hist., Mong.	188	47°25′N	102°22′E
Kara-Kum, des., Turk.	169	40°00′N	57°00′E
Kara Kum Canal, can., Turk.	169	37°35′N	61°50′E
Karaman, Tur. (kä-rä-män′)	149	37°10′N	33°00′E
Karamay, China (kär-äm-ā)	188	45°37′N	84°53′E
Karamea Bight, bt., N.Z. (kȧ-rȧ-mē′ȧ bĭt)	203a	41°20′S	171°30′E
Kara Sea see Karskoye More, sea, Russia	164	74°00′N	68°00′E
Karashahr (Yanqui), China (kä-rä-shä-är) (yän-chyē)	188	42°14′N	86°28′E
Karatsu, Japan (kä′rȧ-tsōō)	195	33°28′N	129°59′E
Karaul, Russia (kä-rä-ōl′)	170	70°13′N	83°46′E

PLACE (Pronunciation)	PAGE	LAT.	LONG.
Karave, India	240e	19°01′N	73°01′E
Karawanken, mts., Eur.	154	46°32′N	14°07′E
Karcag, Hung. (kär′tsäg)	155	47°18′N	20°58′E
Kardhítsa, Grc.	161	39°23′N	21°57′E
Kärdla, Est. (kĕrd′lȧ)	153	58°59′N	22°44′E
Karelia, state, Russia	170	62°30′N	32°35′E
Karema, Tan.	212	6°49′S	30°26′E
Kargat, Russia (kär-gät′)	164	55°17′N	80°07′E
Karghalik see Yecheng, China	188	37°54′N	77°25′E
Kargopol′, Russia (kär-gō-pōl″)	164	61°30′N	38°50′E
Kariba, Lake, res., Afr.	212	17°15′S	27°55′E
Karibib, Nmb. (kȧr′ȧ-bĭb)	212	21°55′S	15°50′E
Kārikāl, India (kä-rē-käl′)	187	10°58′N	79°49′E
Karimata, Kepulauan, is., Indon. (kä-rē-mä′tȧ)	196	1°08′S	108°10′E
Karimata, Selat, strt., Indon.	196	1°00′S	107°10′E
Karimun Besar, i., Indon.	181b	1°10′N	103°28′E
Karimunjawa, Kepulauan, is., Indon. (kä′rē-mōōn-yä′vä)	196	5°36′S	110°15′E
Karin, Som. (kȧr′ĭn)	218a	10°43′N	45°50′E
Karkar Dūmān, neigh., India	240d	28°39′N	77°18′E
Karkar Island, i., Pap. N. Gui. (kär′kär)	197	4°50′S	146°45′E
Karkheh, r., Iran	182	32°45′N	47°50′E
Karkinits′ka zatoka, b., Ukr.	163	45°50′N	32°45′E
Karlivka, Ukr.	163	49°26′N	35°08′E
Karlobag, Cro. (kär-lō-bäg′)	160	44°30′N	15°03′E
Karlovac, Cro. (kär′lō-väts)	149	45°29′N	15°16′E
Karlovo, Bul. (kär′lō-vō)	161	42°39′N	24°48′E
Karlovy Vary, Czech Rep. (kär′lō-vē vä′rē)	147	50°13′N	12°53′E
Karlshamn, Swe. (kärls′häm)	152	56°11′N	14°50′E
Karlskrona, Swe. (kärls′krō-nä)	146	56°10′N	15°33′E
Karlsruhe, Ger. (kärls′rōō-ē)	147	49°00′N	8°23′E
Karlstad, Swe. (kärl′städ)	142	59°25′N	13°28′E
Karluk, Ak., U.S. (kär′lŭk)	95	57°30′N	154°22′W
Karmøy, i., Nor. (kärm-ûe)	152	59°14′N	5°00′E
Karnataka, state, India	183	14°55′N	75°00′E
Karnobat, Bul. (kär-nô′bät)	161	42°39′N	26°59′E
Kärnten (Carinthia), prov., Aus. (kĕrn′tĕn)	154	46°55′N	13°42′E
Karolinenhof, neigh., Ger.	238a	52°23′N	13°38′E
Karonga, Mwi. (kȧ-rōŋ′gȧ)	212	9°52′S	33°57′E
Kárpathos, i., Grc.	149	35°34′N	27°26′E
Karpinsk, Russia (kär′pĭnsk)	172a	59°46′N	60°00′E
Kars, Tur. (kärs)	182	40°35′N	43°00′E
Kārsava, Lat. (kär′sä-vä)	153	56°46′N	27°39′E
Karshi, Uzb. (kär′shē)	169	38°30′N	66°08′E
Karskiye Vorota, Proliv, strt., Russia	164	70°30′N	58°07′E
Karskoye More (Kara Sea), sea, Russia	164	74°00′N	68°00′E
Kartaly, Russia (kȧr′tȧ lē)	164	53°05′N	60°40′E
Karunagapalli, India	187	9°09′N	76°34′E
Karvina, Czech Rep.	155	49°50′N	18°30′E
Kasaan, Ak., U.S.	87	55°32′N	132°24′E
Kasai, neigh., Japan	242a	35°39′N	139°53′E
Kasai (Cassai), r., Afr.	212	3°45′S	19°10′E
Kasama, Zam. (kȧ-sä′mȧ)	212	10°13′S	31°12′E
Kasanga, Tan. (kȧ-säŋ′gȧ)	212	8°28′S	31°09′E
Kasaoka, Japan (kä′sȧ-ō′kȧ)	195	34°33′N	133°29′E
Kasba-Tadla, Mor. (käs′bȧ-täd′lȧ)	210	32°37′N	5°57′W
Kasempa, Zam. (kȧ-sĕm′pȧ)	212	13°27′S	25°50′E
Kasenga, D.R.C. (kȧ-seŋ′gȧ)	212	10°22′S	28°38′E
Kasese, D.R.C.	217	1°38′S	27°07′E
Kasese, Ug.	217	0°10′N	30°05′E
Kāshān, Iran (kä-shän′)	182	33°52′N	51°15′E
Kashgar see Kashi, China	188	39°29′N	76°00′E
Kashi (Kashgar), China (kä-shr) (käsh-gär)	188	39°29′N	76°00′E
Kashihara, Japan (kä′shē-hä′rä)	195b	34°31′N	135°48′E
Kashiji Plain, pl., Zam.	216	13°25′S	22°30′E
Kashin, Russia (kä-shēn′)	162	57°20′N	37°38′E
Kashira, Russia (kä-shē′rȧ)	162	54°49′N	38°11′E
Kashiwa, Japan (kä′shē-wä)	195a	35°51′N	139°58′E
Kashiwara, Japan	195b	34°35′N	135°38′E
Kashiwazaki, Japan (kä′shē-wä-zä′kē)	194	37°06′N	138°17′E
Kāshmar, Iran	185	35°12′N	58°27′E
Kashmir see Jammu and Kashmir, hist. reg., Asia	183	39°10′N	75°05′E
Kashmor, Pak.	186	28°33′N	69°34′E
Kashtak, Russia (käsh′tăk)	172a	55°18′N	61°25′E
Kasimov, Russia (kȧ-sē′môf)	166	54°56′N	41°23′E
Kaskanak, Ak., U.S. (kăs-kă′năk)	95	60°00′N	158°00′W
Kaskaskia, r., Il., U.S. (kăs-kăs′kĭ-ȧ)	98	39°10′N	88°50′W
Kaskattama, r., Can. (kăs-kȧ-tä′mȧ)	89	56°28′N	90°55′W
Kaskö (Kaskinen), Fin. (kȧs′kû) (käs′kē-nĕn)	153	62°24′N	21°18′E
Kasli, Russia (käs′lĭ)	166	55°53′N	60°46′E
Kasongo, D.R.C. (kä-sôŋ′gō)	212	4°31′S	26°42′E
Kásos, i., Grc.	149	35°20′N	26°55′E
Kaspiysk, Russia	168	42°52′N	47°38′E
Kassándras, Kólpos, b., Grc.	161	40°10′N	23°35′E
Kassel, Ger. (käs′ĕl)	147	51°19′N	9°30′E
Kasslerfeld, neigh., Ger.	236	51°26′N	6°45′E
Kasson, Mn., U.S. (kăs′ŭn)	103	44°01′N	92°45′W
Kastamonu, Tur. (kä-stȧ-mō′nōō)	182	41°20′N	33°50′E
Kastoría, Grc. (kȧs-tō′rĭ-ȧ)	149	40°28′N	21°17′E
Kasūr, Pak.	186	31°10′N	74°29′E
Kataba, Zam.	217	16°05′S	25°10′E
Katahdin, Mount, mtn., Me., U.S. (kȧ-tä′dĭn)	92	45°56′N	68°57′W
Katanga, hist. reg., D.R.C. (kȧ-täŋ′gȧ)	212	8°30′S	25°00′E
Katanning, Austl. (kȧ-tăn′ĭng)	202	33°45′S	117°45′E
Katano, Japan	242b	34°48′N	135°42′E
Katav-Ivanovsk, Russia (kä′tȧf ĭ-vä′nôfsk)	172a	54°46′N	58°13′E
Katayama, neigh., Japan	242a	35°46′N	139°34′E
Kateninskiy, Russia (kȧtyĕ′nĭs-kĭ)	172a	53°12′N	61°05′E
Kateríni, Grc.	161	40°18′N	22°36′E
Katernberg, neigh., Ger.	236	51°29′N	7°04′E
Katete, Zam.	217	14°05′S	32°07′E
Katherine, Austl. (kăth′ēr-ĭn)	202	14°15′S	132°20′E

PLACE (Pronunciation)	PAGE	LAT.	LONG.
Kāthiāwār, pen., India (kä′tyȧ-wär′)	183	22°10′N	70°20′E
Kathmandu, Nepal (kăt-măn-dōō′)	183	27°49′N	85°21′E
Kathryn, Can. (kăth′rĭn)	83e	51°13′N	113°42′W
Kathryn, Ca., U.S.	107a	33°42′N	117°45′W
Katihār, India	186	25°39′N	87°39′E
Katiola, C. Iv.	214	8°08′N	5°06′W
Katmai National Park, rec., Ak., U.S. (kăt′mī)	94a	58°38′N	155°00′W
Katompi, D.R.C.	217	6°11′S	26°20′E
Katopa, D.R.C.	217	2°45′S	25°06′E
Katowice, Pol.	142	50°15′N	19°00′E
Katrineholm, Swe. (kȧ-trē′nĕ-hōlm)	152	59°01′N	16°10′E
Katsbakhskiy, Russia (kȧts-băk′skĭ)	172a	52°57′N	59°37′E
Katsina, Nig. (kăt′sē-nȧ)	210	13°00′N	7°32′E
Katsina Ala, Nig.	210	7°10′N	9°17′E
Katsura, r., Japan (kä′tsŏ-rä)	195b	34°55′N	135°43′E
Katsushika, neigh., Japan	242a	35°43′N	139°51′E
Katta-Kurgan, Uzb. (kȧ-tȧ-kŏr-gän′)	169	39°45′N	66°42′E
Kattegat, strt., Eur. (kăt′ĕ-gät)	142	56°57′N	11°25′E
Katternberg, neigh., Ger.	236	51°09′N	7°02′E
Katumba, D.R.C.	217	7°45′S	25°18′E
Katun′, r., Russia (kȧ-tōn′)	170	51°30′N	86°18′E
Katwijk aan Zee, Neth.	145a	52°12′N	4°23′E
Kauai, i., Hi., U.S.	96c	22°09′N	159°15′W
Kauai Channel, strt., Hi., U.S. (kä-ōō-ä′ē)	96c	21°35′N	158°52′W
Kaufbeuren, Ger. (kouf′boi-rĕn)	154	47°52′N	10°38′E
Kaufman, Tx., U.S. (kôf′măn)	113	32°36′N	96°18′W
Kaukauna, Wi., U.S. (kô-kô′nȧ)	103	44°17′N	88°15′W
Kaulakahi Channel, strt., Hi., U.S. (kä′ōō-lȧ-kä′hē)	94a	22°00′N	159°55′W
Kaulsdorf-Süd, neigh., Ger.	238a	52°29′N	13°34′E
Kaunakakai, Hi., U.S. (kä′ōō-nȧ-kä′kī)	94a	21°06′N	156°59′W
Kaunas, Lith. (kou′nȧs) (kôv′nō)	164	54°42′N	23°54′E
Kaura Namoda, Nig.	210	12°35′N	6°35′E
Kavála, Grc. (kä-vä′lä)	149	40°55′N	24°24′E
Kavieng, Pap. N. Gui. (kä-vē-ĕng′)	197	2°44′S	151°02′E
Kavīr, Dasht-e, des., Iran (dŭsht-ē-ka-vēr′)	182	34°41′N	53°30′E
Kawagoe, Japan (kä-wä-gō′ā)	195	35°55′N	139°29′E
Kawaguchi, Japan (kä-wä-gōō-chē)	195a	35°48′N	139°44′E
Kawaikini, mtn., Hi., U.S. (kä-wä′ē-kĭ-nĭ)	94a	22°05′N	159°33′W
Kawanishi, Japan (kä-wä′nē-shē)	195b	34°49′N	135°26′E
Kawasaki, Japan (kä-wä-sä′kē)	194	35°32′N	139°43′E
Kawashima, neigh., Japan	242a	35°28′N	139°35′E
Kaxgar, r., China	188	39°30′N	75°00′E
Kaya, Burkina (kä′yä)	210	13°05′N	1°05′W
Kayan, r., Indon.	196	1°45′N	115°38′E
Kaycee, Wy., U.S. (kā-sē′)	105	43°43′N	106°38′W
Kayes, Mali (kāz)	210	14°27′N	11°26′W
Kayseri, Tur. (kī′sĕ-rē)	182	38°45′N	35°20′E
Kazach′ye, Russia	165	70°46′N	135°47′E
Kazakstan, nation, Asia	164	48°45′N	59°00′E
Kazan′, Russia (kȧ-zän′)	164	55°50′N	49°18′E
Kazanka, Ukr. (kȧ-zän′kȧ)	163	47°49′N	32°50′E
Kazanlŭk, Bul. (kä′zȧn-lĕk)	161	42°47′N	25°23′E
Kazbek, Gora, mtn. (kȧz-bĕk′)	167	42°42′N	44°31′E
Kāzerūn, Iran	182	29°37′N	51°44′E
Kazincbarcika, Hung. (kô′zĭnts-bôr-tsĭ-ko)	155	48°15′N	20°39′E
Kazungula, Zam.	217	17°45′S	25°20′E
Kazusa Kameyama, Japan (kä-zōō-sä kä-mȧ′yä-mä)	195a	35°14′N	140°06′E
Kazym, r., Russia (kä-zēm′)	170	63°30′N	67°41′E
Kéa, i., Grc.	161	37°36′N	24°13′E
Kealaikahiki Channel, strt., Hi., U.S. (kā-ä′lä-ē-kä-hē′kē)	94a	20°38′N	157°00′W
Keansburg, N.J., U.S. (kēnz′bûrg)	100a	40°26′N	74°08′W
Kearney, Ne., U.S. (kär′nĭ)	102	40°42′N	99°05′W
Kearny, N.J., U.S.	100a	40°46′N	74°09′W
Kearsley, Eng., U.K.	237b	53°32′N	2°23′W
Keasey, Or., U.S. (kēz′ĭ)	106c	45°51′N	123°20′W
Kebayoran, neigh., Indon.	241i	6°14′S	106°46′E
Kebnekaise, mtn., Swe. (kĕp′nĕ-kȧ-ĕs′ĕ)	142	67°53′N	18°10′E
Kecskemét, Hung. (kĕch′kĕ-māt)	149	46°52′N	19°42′E
Kedah, hist. reg., Malay. (kä′dä)	196	6°00′N	100°31′E
Kėdainiai, Lith. (kē-dī′nĭ-ī)	153	55°16′N	23°58′E
Kedgwick, Can. (kĕdj′wĭk)	92	47°39′N	67°21′W
Keenbrook, Ca., U.S. (kēn′brŏŏk)	107a	34°16′N	117°29′W
Keene, N.H., U.S. (kēn)	99	42°55′N	72°15′W
Keetmanshoop, Nmb. (kāt′mȧns-hōp)	212	26°30′S	18°05′E
Keet Seel Ruin, Az., U.S. (kēt sēl)	109	36°46′N	110°32′W
Keewatin, Mn., U.S. (kē-wä′tĭn)	103	47°24′N	93°03′W
Kefallinía, i., Grc.	149	38°08′N	20°58′E
Keffi, Nig. (kĕf′ē)	210	8°51′N	7°52′E
Ke Ga, Mui, c., Viet	196	12°58′N	109°50′E
Kei, r., Afr. (kā)	213c	32°57′S	26°50′E
Keila, Est. (kā′lȧ)	153	59°19′N	24°25′E
Keilor, Austl.	201a	37°43′S	144°50′E
Kei Mouth, S. Afr.	213c	32°40′S	28°23′E
Keiskammahoek, S. Afr. (kās′kämä-hōōk′)	213c	32°42′S	27°11′E
Kéita, Bahr, r., Chad	215	9°30′N	19°17′E
Keitele, l., Fin. (kā′tĕ-lĕ)	153	62°50′N	25°40′E
Kekaha, Hi., U.S.	94a	21°57′N	159°42′W
Kelafo, Eth.	218a	5°40′N	44°00′E
Kelang, Malay.	196	3°20′N	101°27′E
Kelang, r., Malay.	181b	3°00′N	101°40′E
Kelenföld, neigh., Hung.	239g	47°28′N	19°03′E
Kelkit, r., Tur.	149	40°38′N	37°03′E
Keller, Tx., U.S. (kĕl′ēr)	107c	32°56′N	97°15′W
Kellinghusen, Ger. (kĕ′lĕng-hōō-zĕn)	145c	53°57′N	9°43′E
Kellogg, Id., U.S. (kĕl′ŏg)	104	47°32′N	116°07′W
Kellyville, Austl.	243a	33°43′S	150°57′E
Kelme′, Lith. (kĕl-mȧ)	153	55°36′N	22°53′E
Kélo, Chad	215	9°19′N	15°48′E
Kelowna, Can.	84	49°53′N	119°29′W
Kelsey Bay, Can. (kĕl′sē)	86	50°24′N	125°57′W
Kelso, Wa., U.S.	106c	46°09′N	122°54′W
Keluang, Malay.	181b	2°01′N	103°19′E

ăt; finăl; rāte; senāte; ärm; ȧsk; sofȧ; fâre; ch-choose; dh-as th in other; bē; ēvent; bĕt; recĕnt; cratẽr; g-gō; gh-guttural g; bĭt; ĭ-short neutral; rīde; ĸ-guttural k as ch in German ich;

PRONOUNCING INDEX

Kelvedon Hatch-King's Lynn 303

PLACE (Pronunciation)	PAGE	LAT.	LONG.
Kelvedon Hatch, Eng., U.K.	235	51°40'N	0°16'E
Kem', Russia (kĕm)	164	65°00'N	34°48'E
Kemah, Tx., U.S. (kē'mȧ)	113a	29°32'N	95°01'W
Kemerovo, Russia	164	55°31'N	86°05'E
Kemi, Fin. (kā'mē)	146	65°48'N	24°38'E
Kemi, r., Fin.	146	67°02'N	27°50'E
Kemigawa, Japan (kĕ'mē-gä'wä)	195a	35°38'N	140°07'E
Kemijarvi, Fin. (kĕ'mē-yĕr-vē)	146	66°48'N	27°21'E
Kemi-joki, I., Fin.	146	66°37'N	28°13'E
Kemmerer, Wy., U.S. (kĕm'ẽr-ẽr)	105	41°48'N	110°36'W
Kemp, I., Tx., U.S. (kĕmp)	110	33°55'N	99°22'W
Kempen, Ger. (kĕm'pĕn)	157c	51°22'N	6°25'E
Kempsey, Austl. (kĕmp'sē)	203	30°59'S	152°50'E
Kempt, I., Can. (kĕmpt)	91	47°28'N	74°00'W
Kempten, Ger. (kĕmp'tĕn)	147	47°44'N	10°17'E
Kempton Park, S. Afr. (kĕmp'tŏn pärk)	218d	26°07'S	28°29'E
Kemsing, Eng., U.K.	235	51°18'N	0°14'E
Ken, r., India	186	25°00'N	79°55'E
Kenai, Ak., U.S. (kĕ-nī')	95	60°38'N	151°18'W
Kenai Fjords National Park, rec., Ak., U.S.	95	59°45'N	150°00'W
Kenai Mountains, mts., Ak., U.S.	95	60°00'N	150°00'W
Kenai Pen, Ak., U.S.	95	64°40'N	150°18'W
Kenberma, Ma., U.S.	227a	42°17'N	70°52'W
Kendal, S. Afr.	218d	26°03'S	28°58'E
Kendal, Eng., U.K. (kĕn'dăl)	150	54°20'N	1°48'W
Kendallville, In., U.S. (kĕn'dăl-vĭl)	98	41°25'N	85°20'W
Kenedy, Tx., U.S. (kĕn'ĕ-dĭ)	113	28°49'N	97°50'W
Kenema, S.L.	214	7°52'N	11°12'W
Kenilworth, Il., U.S.	231a	42°05'N	87°43'W
Kenilworth, N.J., U.S.	228	40°41'N	74°18'W
Kenitra, Mor. (kĕ-nē'trȧ)	148	34°21'N	6°34'W
Kenley, neigh., Eng., U.K.	235	51°19'N	0°06'W
Kenmare, N.D., U.S. (kĕn-mâr')	102	48°41'N	102°05'W
Kenmore, N.Y., U.S. (kĕn'mōr)	101c	42°58'N	78°53'W
Kennebec, r., Me., U.S. (kĕn-ē-bĕk')	92	44°23'N	69°48'W
Kennebunk, Me., U.S. (kĕn-ē-buŋk')	92	43°24'N	70°33'W
Kennedale, Tx., U.S. (kĕn'-ē-dāl)	107c	32°38'N	97°13'W
Kennedy, Cape see Canaveral, Cape, c., Fl., U.S.	97	28°30'N	80°23'W
Kennedy, Mount, mtn., Can.	95	60°25'N	138°50'W
Kenner, La., U.S. (kĕn'ẽr)	113	29°58'N	90°15'W
Kennett, Mo., U.S. (kĕn'ĕt)	111	36°14'N	90°01'W
Kennewick, Wa., U.S. (kĕn'ē-wĭk)	104	46°12'N	119°06'W
Kenney Dam, dam, Can.	86	53°37'N	124°58'W
Kennydale, Wa., U.S. (kĕn-nē'dāl)	106a	47°31'N	122°12'W
Kénogami, Can. (kĕn-ŏ'gä-mē)	85	48°26'N	71°14'W
Kenogamissi Lake, I., Can.	90	48°15'N	81°31'W
Keno Hill, Can.	95	63°58'N	135°18'W
Kenora, Can. (kē-nō'rȧ)	85	49°47'N	94°29'W
Kenosha, Wi., U.S. (kē-nō'shȧ)	97	42°34'N	87°50'W
Kenova, W.V., U.S. (kē-nō'vȧ)	98	38°20'N	82°35'W
Kensico Reservoir, res., N.Y., U.S. (kĕn'sĭ-kō)	100a	41°08'N	73°45'W
Kensington, Austl.	243a	33°55'S	151°14'E
Kensington, Ca., U.S.	231b	37°54'N	122°16'W
Kensington, Md., U.S.	229d	39°02'N	77°03'W
Kensington, neigh., S. Afr.	244b	26°12'S	28°06'E
Kensington, neigh., N.Y., U.S.	228	40°39'N	73°58'W
Kensington, neigh., Pa., U.S.	229b	39°58'N	75°08'W
Kensington and Chelsea, neigh., Eng., U.K.	235	51°29'N	0°11'W
Kent, Oh., U.S. (kĕnt)	98	41°05'N	81°20'W
Kent, Wa., U.S.	106a	47°23'N	122°14'W
Kentani, S. Afr. (kĕnt-änĭ')	213c	32°31'S	28°19'E
Kentland, In., U.S. (kĕnt'lănd)	98	40°50'N	87°25'W
Kentland, Md., U.S.	229d	38°55'N	76°53'W
Kenton, Oh., U.S. (kĕn'tŭn)	98	40°40'N	83°35'W
Kent Peninsula, pen., Can.	84	68°28'N	108°10'W
Kentucky, state, U.S. (kĕn-tŭk'ĭ)	97	37°30'N	87°35'W
Kentucky, res., U.S.	97	36°20'N	88°50'W
Kentucky, r., Ky., U.S.	97	38°15'N	85°01'W
Kentwood, La., U.S. (kĕnt'wŏŏd)	113	30°56'N	90°31'W
Kenya, nation, Afr. (kĕn'yȧ)	212	1°00'N	36°53'E
Kenya, Mount (Kirinyaga), mtn., Kenya	213	0°10'S	37°20'E
Kenyon, Mn., U.S. (kĕn'yŭn)	103	44°15'N	92°58'W
Keokuk, Ia., U.S. (kē'ō-kŭk)	97	40°24'N	91°34'W
Keoma, Can. (kē-ō'mȧ)	83e	51°13'N	113°39'W
Keon Park, Austl.	243b	37°42'S	145°01'E
Kepenkeck Lake, I., Can.	93	48°13'N	54°45'W
Kępno, Pol. (kaŋ'pnō)	155	51°17'N	17°59'E
Kerala, state, India	183	16°38'N	76°00'E
Kerang, Austl. (kē-răng')	203	35°32'S	143°58'E
Keratsínion, Grc.	239d	37°58'N	23°37'E
Kerch, Ukr.	164	45°20'N	36°26'E
Kerchenskiy Proliv, strt., Eur. (kĕr-chĕn'skĭ prō'lĭf)	163	45°08'N	36°35'E
Kerempe Burun, c., Tur.	149	42°00'N	33°20'E
Keren, Erit.	211	15°46'N	38°28'E
Kerguélen, Îles, is., Afr. (kĕr'gā-lĕn)	3	49°50'S	69°30'E
Kericho, Kenya	217	0°22'S	35°17'E
Kerinci, Gunung, mtn., Indon.	196	1°45'S	101°18'E
Keriya see Yutian, China	188	36°55'N	81°39'E
Keriya, r., China (kē'rē-yä)	188	37°13'N	81°59'E
Kerkebet, Erit.	184	16°18'N	37°24'E
Kerkenna, Îles, i., Tun. (kĕr'kĕn-nä)	210	34°49'N	11°37'E
Kerki, Turk. (kĕr'kē)	170	37°52'N	65°15'E
Kérkira, Grc.	149	39°36'N	19°56'E
Kérkira, i., Grc.	142	39°33'N	19°36'E
Kermadec Islands, is., N.Z. (kẽr-măd'ĕk)	3	30°30'S	177°00'E
Kermān, Iran (kĕr-män')	182	30°23'N	57°08'E
Kermānshāh see Bakhtarān, Iran	182	34°01'N	47°00'E
Kern, r., Ca., U.S.	108	35°31'N	118°37'W
Kern, South Fork, r., Ca., U.S.	108	35°40'N	118°15'W
Kerpen, Ger. (kĕr'pĕn)	157c	50°52'N	6°42'E
Kerrobert, Can.	88	51°53'N	109°13'W
Kerrville, Tx., U.S. (kûr'vĭl)	112	30°02'N	99°07'W
Kerulen, r., Asia (kĕr'o͞o-lĕn)	189	47°52'N	113°22'E
Kesagami Lake, I., Can.	91	50°23'N	80°15'W

PLACE (Pronunciation)	PAGE	LAT.	LONG.
Keşan, Tur. (kĕ'shȧn)	161	40°50'N	26°37'E
Keshan, China (kŭ-shän)	189	48°00'N	126°30'E
Kesour, Monts des, mts., Alg.	148	32°51'N	0°30'W
Kestell, S. Afr. (kĕs'tĕl)	218d	28°19'N	28°43'E
Keszthely, Hung. (kĕst'hĕl-lĭ)	155	46°46'N	17°12'E
Ket', r., Russia (kyĕt)	170	58°30'N	84°15'E
Keta, Ghana	210	6°00'N	1°00'E
Ketamputih, Indon.	181b	1°25'N	102°19'E
Ketapang, Indon. (kĕ-tȧ-päng')	196	2°00'S	109°57'E
Ketchikan, Ak., U.S. (kĕch-ĭ-kăn')	94a	55°21'N	131°35'W
Kętrzyn, Pol. (kaŋ't'r-zĭn)	155	54°04'N	21°24'E
Kettering, Eng., U.K. (kĕt'ẽr-ĭng)	144a	52°23'N	0°43'W
Kettering, Oh., U.S.	98	39°40'N	84°15'W
Kettle, r., Can.	87	49°40'N	119°00'W
Kettle, r., Mn., U.S. (kĕt''l)	103	46°20'N	92°57'W
Kettwig, Ger. (kĕt'vĕg)	157c	51°22'N	6°56'E
Kęty, Pol. (kaŋ tĭ)	155	49°54'N	19°16'E
Ketzin, Ger. (kĕ'tzēn)	145b	52°29'N	12°51'E
Keuka, I., N.Y., U.S. (kē-ū'kȧ)	99	42°30'N	77°10'W
Kevelaer, Ger. (kĕ'fĕ-lăr)	157c	51°35'N	6°15'E
Kew, Austl.	201a	37°49'S	145°02'E
Kew, S. Afr.	244b	26°08'S	28°06'E
Kewanee, Il., U.S. (kē-wä'nē)	103	41°15'N	89°55'W
Kewaunee, Wi., U.S. (kē-wô'nē)	103	44°27'N	87°33'W
Keweenaw Bay, b., Mi., U.S. (kē'wē-nô)	103	46°59'N	88°15'W
Keweenaw Peninsula, pen., Mi., U.S.	103	47°28'N	88°12'W
Kew Gardens, pt. of i., Eng., U.K.	235	51°28'N	0°18'W
Keya Paha, r., S.D., U.S. (kē-yȧ pä'hä)	102	43°11'N	100°10'W
Key Largo, i., Fl., U.S.	115a	25°11'N	80°15'W
Keyport, N.J., U.S. (kē'pōrt)	100a	40°26'N	74°12'W
Keyport, Wa., U.S.	106a	47°42'N	122°38'W
Keyser, W.V., U.S. (kī'sẽr)	99	39°25'N	79°00'W
Key West, Fl., U.S. (kē wĕst')	97	24°31'N	81°47'W
Kežmarok, Slvk. (kĕzh'mȧ-rŏk)	155	49°10'N	20°27'E
Khabarovo, Russia (kŭ-bȧr-ôvŏ)	164	69°31'N	60°41'E
Khabarovsk, Russia (kä-bä'rôfsk)	165	48°35'N	135°12'E
Khaïdhárion, Grc.	239d	38°01'N	23°39'E
Khajuri, neigh., India	240d	28°43'N	77°16'E
Khakassia, state, Russia	170	52°32'N	89°33'E
Khalándrion, Grc.	239d	38°01'N	23°48'E
Khālāpur, India	187b	18°48'N	73°17'E
Khalkidhiki, pen., Grc.	161	40°30'N	23°18'E
Khalkís, Grc. (ĸăl'kĭs)	149	38°28'N	23°38'E
Khal'mer-Yu, Russia (kŭl-myĕr'-yo͞o')	164	67°52'N	64°25'E
Khalturin, Russia (ĸäl'to͞o-rĕn)	166	58°28'N	49°00'E
Khambhāt, Gulf of, b., India	183	21°20'N	72°27'E
Khammam, India	187	17°09'N	80°13'E
Khānābād, Afg.	186	36°43'N	69°11'E
Khānaqīn, Iraq	185	34°21'N	45°22'E
Khandwa, India	186	21°53'N	76°22'E
Khaníon, Kólpos, b., Grc.	160a	35°35'N	23°55'E
Khanka, I., Asia (ĸän'kȧ)	165	45°09'N	133°28'E
Khānpur, Pak.	186	28°42'N	70°42'E
Khanty-Mansiysk, Russia (ĸŭn-te'mŭn-sēsk')	164	61°02'N	69°01'E
Khān Yūnus, Gaza	181a	31°21'N	34°19'E
Kharagpur, India (kŭ-rŭg'pŏŏr)	183	22°26'N	87°21'E
Khardah, India	240a	22°44'N	88°22'E
Kharkiv, Ukr.	164	50°00'N	36°10'E
Kharkiv, prov., Ukr.	163	49°33'N	35°55'E
Kharkov see Kharkiv, Ukr.	164	50°00'N	36°10'E
Kharlovka, Russia	166	68°47'N	37°20'E
Kharmanli, Bul. (ĸȧr-män'lē)	161	41°54'N	25°55'E
Khartoum, Sudan	211	15°34'N	32°36'E
Khasavyurt, Russia	168	43°15'N	46°37'E
Khāsh, Iran	182	28°08'N	61°08'E
Khāsh, r., Afg.	182	32°30'N	64°27'E
Khasi Hills, hills, India	183	25°38'N	91°55'E
Khaskovo, Bul. (ĸȧs'kō-vō)	149	41°56'N	25°32'E
Khatanga, Russia (kȧ-tän'gȧ)	165	71°48'N	101°47'E
Khatangskiy Zaliv, b., Russia (kȧ-täŋ'g-skē)	165	73°45'N	108°30'E
Khayāla, neigh., India	240d	28°40'N	77°06'E
Khaybār, Sau. Ar.	182	25°45'N	39°28'E
Kherson, Ukr. (kĕr-sôn')	167	46°38'N	32°34'E
Kherson, prov., Ukr.	163	46°32'N	32°55'E
Khichripur, neigh., India	240d	28°37'N	77°19'E
Khiitola, Russia (khē'tō-lȧ)	153	61°14'N	29°40'E
Khimki, Russia (ĸēm'kĭ)	172b	55°54'N	37°27'E
Khíos, Grc. (kē'ŏs)	149	38°23'N	26°09'E
Khíos, i., Grc.	149	38°20'N	25°45'E
Khmel'nyts'kyi, Ukr.	167	49°29'N	26°54'E
Khmel'nyts'kyi, prov., Ukr.	163	49°27'N	26°30'E
Khmil'nyk, Ukr.	163	49°34'N	27°58'E
Kholargós, Grc.	239d	38°00'N	23°48'E
Kholm, Russia (ĸôlm)	162	57°09'N	31°07'E
Kholmsk, Russia (kŭlmsk)	165	47°09'N	142°33'E
Khomeynīshahr, Iran	185	32°41'N	51°31'E
Khon Kaen, Thai.	196	16°37'N	102°41'E
Khopër, r., Russia (kô'pẽr)	167	52°00'N	43°00'E
Khor, Russia (kôr')	194	47°50'N	134°52'E
Khor, r., Russia	194	47°23'N	135°20'E
Khóra Sfakíon, Grc.	160a	35°12'N	24°10'E
Khorel, India	240a	22°42'N	88°19'E
Khorog, Taj.	169	37°30'N	71°36'E
Khorol, Ukr. (ĸō'rôl)	163	49°48'N	33°17'E
Khorol, r., Ukr.	163	49°50'N	33°21'E
Khorramābād, Iran	185	33°30'N	48°20'E
Khorramshahr, Iran (kō-ram'shär)	182	30°36'N	48°15'E
Khot'kovo, Russia	172b	56°15'N	38°00'E
Khotyn, Ukr.	167	48°29'N	26°32'E
Khoyniki, Bela.	163	51°54'N	30°00'E
Khudzhand, Taj.	169	40°17'N	69°37'E
Khulna, Bngl.	183	22°50'N	89°38'E
Khūryān Mūryān, is., Oman	182	17°27'N	56°02'E
Khust, Ukr. (kŏŏst)	155	48°10'N	23°18'E
Khvalynsk, Russia (ĸvȧ-lĭnsk')	167	52°30'N	48°00'E
Khvoy, Iran	182	38°32'N	45°01'E
Khyber Pass, p., Asia (kī'bẽr)	183	34°28'N	71°18'E
Kialwe, D.R.C.	217	9°22'S	27°08'E

PLACE (Pronunciation)	PAGE	LAT.	LONG.
Kiambi, D.R.C. (kyăm'bē)	212	7°20'S	28°01'E
Kiamichi, r., Ok., U.S. (kyȧ-mē'chē)	111	34°31'N	95°34'W
Kianta, I., Fin. (kyȧn'tȧ)	166	65°00'N	28°15'E
Kibenga, D.R.C.	216	7°55'S	17°35'E
Kibiti, Tan.	217	7°44'S	38°57'E
Kibombo, D.R.C.	217	3°54'S	25°55'E
Kibondo, Tan.	217	3°35'S	30°42'E
Kičevo, Mac. (kē'chĕ-vŏ)	161	41°30'N	20°59'E
Kichijōji, Japan	242a	35°42'N	139°35'E
Kickapoo, r., Wi., U.S. (kĭk'ȧ-po͞o)	103	43°20'N	90°55'W
Kicking Horse Pass, p., Can.	87	51°25'N	116°10'W
Kidal, Mali (kē-dȧl')	210	18°33'N	1°00'E
Kidderminster, Eng., U.K. (kĭd'ẽr-mĭn-stẽr)	144a	52°23'N	2°14'W
Kidderpore, neigh., India	240a	22°31'N	88°19'E
Kidd's Beach, S. Afr. (kĭdz)	213c	33°09'S	27°43'E
Kidsgrove, Eng., U.K. (kĭdz'grōv)	144a	53°05'N	2°15'W
Kiel, Ger. (kēl)	142	54°19'N	10°08'E
Kiel, Wi., U.S.	103	43°52'N	88°04'W
Kiel Bay, b., Ger.	154	54°33'N	10°19'E
Kiel Canal see Nord-Ostsee Kanal, can., Ger.	154	54°03'N	9°23'E
Kielce, Pol. (kyĕl'tsĕ)	155	50°50'N	20°41'E
Kieldrecht, Bel. (kēl'drĕĸt)	145a	51°17'N	4°09'E
Kierspe, Ger.	236	51°08'N	7°35'E
Kiev (Kyïv), Ukr.	164	50°27'N	30°30'E
Kiffa, Maur. (kēf'ȧ)	210	16°37'N	11°24'W
Kigali, Rw. (kē-gä'lē)	212	1°59'S	30°05'E
Kigoma, Tan. (kē-gō'mä)	212	4°57'S	29°38'E
Kii-Suido, strt., Japan (kē so͞o-ē'dō)	194	33°53'N	134°55'E
Kikaiga, i., Japan	194	28°25'N	130°10'E
Kikinda, Yugo. (kē'kēn-dä)	161	45°49'N	20°30'E
Kikládhes, is., Grc.	142	37°30'N	24°45'E
Kikwit, D.R.C. (kē'kwēt)	212	5°02'S	18°49'E
Kil, Swe. (kēl)	152	59°30'N	13°15'E
Kilauea, Hi., U.S. (kē-lä-o͞o-ā'ä)	94a	22°12'N	159°25'W
Kilauea Crater, Hi., U.S.	94a	19°28'N	155°18'W
Kilbuck Mountains, mts., Ak., U.S. (kĭl-bŭk)	95	60°05'N	160°00'W
Kilchu, N. Kor. (kĭl'chŏ)	194	40°59'N	129°23'E
Kildare, Ire. (kĭl-dâr')	150	53°09'N	7°05'W
Kilembe, D.R.C.	216	5°42'S	19°55'E
Kilgore, Tx., U.S.	113	32°23'N	94°53'W
Kilia, Ukr.	163	45°28'N	29°17'E
Kilifi, Kenya	217	3°38'S	39°51'E
Kilimanjaro, mtn., Tan. (kyl-ē-män-jä'rō)	213	3°09'S	37°19'E
Kilimatinde, Tan. (kĭl-ē-mä-tĭn'dȧ)	212	5°48'S	34°58'E
Kilindoni, Tan.	217	7°55'S	39°39'E
Kilingi-Nõmme, Est. (kē'lĭn-gē-nôm'mē)	153	58°08'N	25°03'E
Kilis, Tur. (kē'lĕs)	149	36°50'N	37°20'E
Kilkenny, Ire. (kĭl-kĕn-ĭ)	147	52°40'N	7°30'W
Kilkís, Grc. (kĭl'kĭs)	161	40°59'N	22°51'E
Killala, Ire. (kĭ-lă'lȧ)	150	54°11'N	9°10'W
Killara, Austl.	243a	33°46'S	151°09'E
Killarney, Ire.	150	52°03'N	9°05'W
Killarney Heights, Austl.	243a	33°46'S	151°13'E
Killdeer, N.D., U.S. (kĭl'dēr)	102	47°22'N	102°45'W
Killiniq Island, i., Can.	85	60°32'N	63°56'W
Kilmarnock, Scot., U.K. (kĭl-mär'nŭk)	150	55°38'N	4°25'W
Kilrush, Ire. (kĭl'rŭsh)	150	52°40'N	9°16'W
Kilwa Kisiwani, Tan.	217	8°58'S	39°30'E
Kilwa Kivinje, Tan.	213	8°43'S	39°18'E
Kim, r., Cam.	215	5°40'N	11°17'E
Kimamba, Tan.	217	6°47'S	37°08'E
Kimba, Austl. (kĭm'bȧ)	204	33°08'S	136°25'E
Kimball, Ne., U.S. (kĭm-băl)	102	41°14'N	103°41'W
Kimball, S.D., U.S.	102	43°44'N	98°58'W
Kimberley, Can. (kĭm'bẽr-lĭ)	84	49°41'N	115°59'W
Kimberley, S. Afr.	212	28°40'S	24°50'E
Kimi, Cam.	215	6°05'N	11°30'E
Kími, Grc.	161	38°38'N	24°05'E
Kímolos, i., Grc. (kē'mō-lōs)	161	36°52'N	24°20'E
Kimry, Russia (kĭm'rē)	166	56°53'N	37°24'E
Kimvula, D.R.C.	216	5°44'S	15°58'E
Kinabalu, Gunong, mtn., Malay.	196	5°45'N	115°26'E
Kincardine, Can. (kĭn-kär'dĭn)	85	44°10'N	81°15'W
Kinda, D.R.C.	217	9°18'S	25°04'E
Kindanba, Congo	216	3°44'S	14°31'E
Kinder, La., U.S. (kĭn'dẽr)	113	30°30'N	92°50'W
Kindersley, Can. (kĭn'dẽrz-lē)	84	51°27'N	109°10'W
Kindia, Gui. (kĭn'dē-ȧ)	210	10°04'N	12°51'W
Kindu, D.R.C.	212	2°57'S	25°56'E
Kinel'-Cherkassy, Russia	166	53°32'N	51°32'E
Kineshma, Russia (kē-nĕsh'mȧ)	166	57°27'N	41°02'E
King, i., Austl. (kĭng)	203	39°35'S	143°40'E
Kingaroy, Austl. (kĭŋ'gȧ-roi)	204	26°37'S	151°50'E
King City, Can.	83d	43°56'N	79°32'W
King City, Ca., U.S. (kĭng sĭ'tĭ)	108	36°12'N	121°08'W
Kingcome Inlet, b., Can. (kĭng'kŭm)	86	50°50'N	126°10'W
Kingfisher, Ok., U.S. (kĭng'fĭsh-ẽr)	111	35°51'N	97°55'W
King George Sound, strt., Austl. (jôrj)	202	35°17'S	118°30'E
King George's Reservoir, res., Eng., U.K.	235	51°39'N	0°01'W
Kingisepp, Russia (kĭŋ-gē-sep')	166	59°22'N	28°38'E
King Leopold Ranges, mts., Austl. (lē'ō-pōld)	202	16°25'S	125°00'E
Kingman, Az., U.S. (kĭng'măn)	109	35°10'N	114°05'W
Kingman, Ks., U.S. (kĭng'măn)	110	37°38'N	98°07'W
King of Prussia, Pa., U.S.	229b	40°05'N	75°23'W
Kings, r., Ca., U.S.	108	36°28'N	119°43'W
Kingsbury, neigh., Eng., U.K.	235	51°35'N	0°17'W
Kings Canyon National Park, rec., Ca., U.S. (kăn'yŭn)	96	36°52'N	118°53'W
Kingsclere, Eng., U.K. (kĭngs-clēr)	144b	51°18'N	1°15'W
Kingscote, Austl. (kĭngz'kŭt)	204	35°45'S	137°32'E
Kingsdown, Eng., U.K.	235	51°21'N	0°17'E
Kingsford, Austl.	243a	33°56'S	151°14'E
Kingsgrove, Austl.	243a	33°57'S	151°06'E
Kings Langley, Eng., U.K.	235	51°43'N	0°28'W
King's Lynn, Eng., U.K. (kĭngz lĭn')	151	52°45'N	0°20'E

PLACE (Pronunciation)	PAGE	LAT.	LONG.
Kings Mountain, N.C., U.S.	115	35°13′N	81°30′W
Kings Norton, Eng., U.K. (nôr′tŭn)	144a	52°25′N	1°54′W
King Sound, strt., Austl.	202	16°50′S	123°35′E
Kings Park, N.Y., U.S. (kĭngz pärk)	100a	40°53′N	73°16′W
Kings Park, Va., U.S.	229d	38°48′N	77°15′W
Kings Peak, mtn., Ut., U.S.	96	40°46′N	110°20′W
Kings Point, N.Y., U.S.	228	40°49′N	73°45′W
Kingsport, Tn., U.S. (kĭngz′pōrt)	115	36°33′N	82°36′W
Kingston, Austl. (kĭngz′tŭn)	202	37°52′S	139°52′E
Kingston, Can.	85	44°15′N	76°30′W
Kingston, Jam.	117	18°00′N	76°45′W
Kingston, N.Y., U.S.	97	42°00′N	74°00′W
Kingston, Pa., U.S.	99	41°15′N	75°50′W
Kingston, Wa., U.S.	106a	47°04′N	122°29′W
Kingston upon Hull, Eng., U.K.	142	53°45′N	0°25′W
Kingston upon Thames, neigh., Eng., U.K.	235	51°25′N	0°19′W
Kingstown, St. Vin. (kĭngz′toun)	117	13°10′N	61°14′W
Kingstree, S.C., U.S. (kĭngz′trē)	115	33°30′N	79°50′W
Kingsville, Tx., U.S. (kĭngz′vĭl)	113	27°32′N	97°52′W
King William Island, i., Can. (kĭng wĭl′yăm)	84	69°25′N	97°00′W
King William's Town, S. Afr. (kĭng-wĭl′-yŭmz-toun)	213c	32°53′S	27°24′E
Kinira, r., S. Afr.	213c	30°37′S	28°52′E
Kinloch, Mo., U.S. (kĭn-lŏk)	107e	38°44′N	90°19′W
Kinnaird, Can. (kĭn-ärd′)	87	49°17′N	117°39′W
Kinnairds Head, c., Scot., U.K. (kĭn-ârds′hĕd)	146	57°42′N	3°55′W
Kinomoto, Japan (kē′nō-mōtō)	195	33°53′N	136°07′E
Kinosaki, Japan (kē′nō-sä′kē)	195	35°38′N	134°47′E
Kinshasa, D.R.C.	212	4°18′S	15°18′E
Kinshasa-Est, neigh., D.R.C.	244c	4°18′S	15°18′E
Kinshasa-Ouest, neigh., D.R.C.	244c	4°20′S	15°15′E
Kinsley, Ks., U.S. (kĭnz′lĭ)	110	37°55′N	99°24′W
Kinston, N.C., U.S. (kĭnz′tŭn)	115	35°15′N	77°35′W
Kintamo, Rapides de, wtfl., Afr.	244c	4°19′S	15°15′E
Kintampo, Ghana (kēn-täm′pō)	210	8°03′N	1°43′W
Kintsana, Congo	244c	4°19′S	15°10′E
Kintyre, pen., Scot., U.K.	150	55°50′N	5°40′W
Kiowa, Ks., U.S. (kī′ô-wȧ)	110	37°01′N	98°30′W
Kiowa, Ok., U.S.	111	34°42′N	95°53′W
Kiparissía, Grc.	149	37°17′N	21°43′E
Kiparissiakós Kólpos, b., Grc.	161	37°28′N	21°15′E
Kipawa, Lac, l., Can.	91	46°55′N	79°00′W
Kipembawe, Tan. (kē-pĕm-bä′wȧ)	212	7°39′S	33°24′E
Kipengere Range, mts., Tan.	217	9°10′S	34°00′E
Kipili, Tan.	217	7°26′S	30°36′E
Kipushi, D.R.C.	217	11°46′S	27°14′E
Kirakira, Sol. Is.	198e	10°27′S	161°55′E
Kirby, Tx., U.S. (kûr′bĭ)	107d	29°29′N	98°23′W
Kirbyville, Tx., U.S. (kûr′bĭ-vĭl)	113	30°39′N	93°54′W
Kirchderne, neigh., Ger.	236	51°33′N	7°30′E
Kirchende, Ger.	236	51°25′N	7°26′E
Kirchhellen, Ger.	236	51°36′N	6°55′E
Kirchheller Heide, for., Ger.	236	51°36′N	6°53′E
Kirchhörde, neigh., Ger.	236	51°27′N	7°27′E
Kirchlinde, neigh., Ger.	236	51°32′N	7°22′E
Kirdāsah, Egypt	244a	30°02′N	31°07′E
Kirenga, r., Russia (kē-rĕŋ′gȧ)	171	56°30′N	108°18′E
Kirensk, Russia (kē-rĕnsk′)	165	57°47′N	108°22′E
Kirghiz Steppe, plat., Kyrg.	169	49°28′N	57°07′E
Kirgizskiy Khrebet, mts., Asia	183	37°58′N	72°23′E
Kiri, D.R.C.	216	1°27′S	19°00′E
Kiribati, nation, Oc.	3	1°30′S	173°00′E
Kirin see Chilung, Tai.	189	25°02′N	121°48′E
Kiritimati, i., Kir.	2	2°20′N	157°40′W
Kirkby, Eng., U.K.	144a	53°29′N	2°54′W
Kirkby-in-Ashfield, Eng., U.K. (kûrk′bē-ĭn-ăsh′fēld)	144a	53°06′N	1°16′W
Kirkcaldy, Scot., U.K. (kēr-kô′dĭ)	150	56°06′N	3°15′W
Kirkdale, neigh., Eng., U.K.	237a	53°26′N	2°59′W
Kirkenes, Nor.	146	69°40′N	30°03′E
Kirkham, Eng., U.K. (kûrk′ăm)	144a	53°47′N	2°53′W
Kirkland, Can.	227b	45°27′N	73°52′W
Kirkland, Wa., U.S. (kûrk′lănd)	106a	47°41′N	122°12′W
Kirklareli, Tur. (kērk′lár-ĕ′lē)	149	41°44′N	27°15′E
Kirksville, Mo., U.S. (kûrks′vĭl)	97	40°12′N	92°35′W
Kirkūk, Iraq (kĭr-ko͝ok′)	182	35°28′N	44°22′E
Kirkwall, Scot., U.K. (kûrk′wôl)	146	58°58′N	2°59′W
Kirkwood, S. Afr.	213c	33°26′S	25°24′E
Kirkwood, Md., U.S.	229d	38°57′N	76°58′W
Kirkwood, Mo., U.S. (kûrk′wo͝od)	107e	38°35′N	90°24′W
Kirn, Ger. (kērn)	154	49°47′N	7°23′E
Kirov, Russia	162	54°04′N	34°19′E
Kirov, Russia	164	58°35′N	49°35′E
Kirovakan, Arm.	168	40°48′N	44°30′E
Kirovgrad, Russia (kē′rŭ-vŭ-grad)	172a	57°26′N	60°03′E
Kirovohrad, Ukr.	167	48°33′N	32°17′E
Kirovohrad, prov., Ukr.	163	48°23′N	31°10′E
Kirovsk, Russia	164	67°40′N	33°58′E
Kirovsk, Russia (kē-rôfsk′)	172c	59°52′N	30°59′E
Kirsanov, Russia (kēr-sȧ′nôf)	167	52°40′N	42°40′E
Kirşehir, Tur. (kēr-shĕ′hēr)	182	39°10′N	34°00′E
Kirtachi Seybou, Niger	215	12°48′N	2°29′E
Kīrthar Range, mts., Pak. (kĭr-tŭr)	183	27°00′N	67°10′E
Kirton, Eng., U.K. (kûr′tŭn)	144a	53°29′N	0°35′W
Kiruna, Swe. (kē-ro͞o′nä)	146	67°49′N	20°08′E
Kirundu, D.R.C.	217	0°44′S	25°32′E
Kirwan Heights, Pa., U.S.	230b	40°22′N	80°06′W
Kirwin Reservoir, res., Ks., U.S. (kûr′wĭn)	110	39°34′N	99°04′W
Kiryū, Japan	194	36°24′N	139°20′E
Kirzhach, Russia (kēr-zhák′)	162	56°08′N	38°53′E
Kisaki, Tan. (kē-sä′kē)	213	7°37′S	37°43′E
Kisangani, D.R.C.	211	0°30′N	25°12′E
Kisarazu, Japan (kē′sȧ-rȧ′zo͞o)	195a	35°23′N	139°55′E
Kiselëvsk, Russia (kē-sĭ-lyôfsk′)	164	54°00′N	86°39′E
Kishiwada, Japan (kē′shē-wä′dä)	194	34°25′N	135°18′E
Kishkino, Russia (kēsh′kĭ-nô)	172b	55°15′N	38°04′E
Kisiwani, Tan.	217	4°08′S	37°57′E
Kiska, i., Ak., U.S. (kĭs′kä)	94b	52°08′N	177°10′E
Kiskatinaw, r., Can.	87	55°10′N	120°20′W
Kiskittogisu Lake, l., Can.	89	54°05′N	99°00′W
Kiskitto Lake, l., Can. (kĭs-kĭ′tō)	89	54°16′N	98°34′W
Kiskunfélegyháza, Hung. (kĭsh′kon-fā′lĕd-y′hä′zô)	155	46°42′N	19°52′E
Kiskunhalas, Hung. (kĭsh′kon-hô′lôsh)	155	46°24′N	19°26′E
Kiskunmajsa, Hung. (kĭsh′kon-mī′shô)	155	46°29′N	19°42′E
Kislovodsk, Russia	168	43°55′N	42°44′E
Kismaayo, Som.	213	0°18′S	42°30′E
Kiso, Japan	242a	35°34′N	139°26′E
Kiso-Gawa, r., Japan (kē′sō-gä′wä)	195	35°29′N	137°12′E
Kiso-Sammyaku, mts., Japan (kē′sō säm′myȧ-ko͞o)	195	35°47′N	137°39′E
Kissamos, Grc.	160a	35°13′N	23°35′E
Kissidougou, Gui. (kē′sē-do͞o′go͞o)	210	9°11′N	10°06′W
Kissimmee, Fl., U.S. (kĭ-sĭm′ē)	115a	28°17′N	81°25′W
Kissimmee, r., Fl., U.S.	115a	27°45′N	81°07′W
Kissimmee, Lake, l., Fl., U.S.	115a	27°58′N	81°17′W
Kistarcsa, Hung.	239g	47°33′N	19°16′E
Kisujszallás, Hung.	155	47°12′N	20°47′E
Kisumu, Kenya (kē′so͞o-mo͞o)	212	0°06′S	34°45′E
Kita, Mali (kē′tȧ)	210	13°03′N	9°29′W
Kita, neigh., Japan	242a	35°45′N	139°44′E
Kitakami Gawa, r., Japan	194	39°20′N	141°10′E
Kitakyūshū, Japan	189	33°53′N	130°50′E
Kitale, Kenya	217	1°01′N	35°00′E
Kitamachi, neigh., Japan	242a	35°46′N	139°39′E
Kitamba, neigh., D.R.C.	244c	4°19′S	15°14′E
Kitatawara, Japan	242b	34°44′N	135°42′E
Kit Carson, Co., U.S.	110	38°46′N	102°48′W
Kitchener, Can. (kĭch′ĕ-nēr)	85	43°25′N	80°35′W
Kitenda, D.R.C.	216	6°53′S	17°21′E
Kitgum, Ug. (kĭt′go͝om)	211	3°29′N	33°04′E
Kithira, i., Grc.	149	36°15′N	22°56′E
Kíthnos, i., Grc.	161	37°24′N	24°10′E
Kitimat, Can. (kĭ′tĭ-măt)	84	54°03′N	128°33′W
Kitimat, r., Can.	86	53°50′N	129°00′W
Kitimat Ranges, mts., Can.	86	53°30′N	128°50′W
Kitlope, r., Can. (kĭt′lōp)	86	53°00′N	128°00′W
Kitsuki, Japan (kēt′sō-kē)	195	33°24′N	131°35′E
Kittanning, Pa., U.S. (kĭ-tăn′ĭng)	99	40°50′N	79°30′W
Kittatinny Mountains, mts., N.J., U.S. (kĭ-tȧ-tĭ′nē)	100a	41°16′N	74°44′W
Kittery, Me., U.S. (kĭt′ēr-ĭ)	92	43°07′N	70°45′W
Kittsee, Aus.	145e	48°05′N	17°05′E
Kitty Hawk, N.C., U.S. (kĭt′tē hôk)	115	36°04′N	75°42′W
Kitunda, Tan.	217	6°48′S	33°13′E
Kitwe, Zam.	217	12°49′S	28°13′E
Kitzingen, Ger. (kĭt′zĭng-ĕn)	154	49°44′N	10°08′E
Kiunga, Kenya	217	1°45′S	41°29′E
Kivu, Lac, l., Afr.	212	1°45′S	28°55′E
Kiyose, Japan	195a	35°47′N	139°32′E
Kizel, Russia (kē′zĕl)	166	59°05′N	57°42′E
Kızıl, r., Tur.	182	40°00′N	34°00′E
Kizil′skoye, Russia (kĭz′ĭl-skô-yĕ)	172a	52°43′N	58°53′E
Kizlyar, Russia (kĭz-lyär′)	167	44°00′N	46°50′E
Kizlyarskiy Zaliv, b., Russia	168	44°33′N	46°55′E
Kizu, Japan (kē′zo͞o)	195	34°43′N	135°49′E
Kizuki, Japan	242a	35°34′N	139°40′E
Kizuri, Japan	242b	34°39′N	135°34′E
Klaas Smits, r., S. Afr.	213c	31°45′S	26°33′E
Klaaswaal, Neth.	145a	51°46′N	4°25′E
Kladno, Czech Rep. (kläd′nō)	154	50°10′N	14°05′E
Klagenfurt, Aus. (klä′gĕn-fo͝ort)	147	46°38′N	14°19′E
Klaipėda, Lith. (klī′pȧ-dȧ)	166	55°43′N	21°10′E
Klamath, r., U.S.	104	41°40′N	123°25′W
Klamath Falls, Or., U.S.	96	42°13′N	121°49′W
Klamath Mountains, mts., Ca., U.S.	104	42°00′N	123°25′W
Klarälven, r., Swe.	146	60°40′N	13°00′E
Klaskanine, r., Or., U.S. (klăs′kȧ-nīn)	106c	46°02′N	123°43′W
Klatovy, Czech Rep. (klä′tô-vē)	147	49°23′N	13°18′E
Klawock, Ak., U.S. (klă′wăk)	95	55°32′N	133°10′W
Kleef, Ger.	236	51°11′N	6°56′E
Kleinebroich, Ger.	236	51°12′N	6°35′E
Kleinmachnow, Ger. (klīn-mäĸ′nō)	145b	52°22′N	13°12′E
Klein Ziethen, Ger.	238a	52°23′N	13°27′E
Klerksdorp, S. Afr. (klĕrks′dôrp)	218d	26°52′S	26°40′E
Klerksraal, S. Afr. (klĕrks′kräl)	218d	26°15′N	27°10′E
Kletnya, Russia (klyĕt′nyȧ)	162	53°19′N	33°14′E
Kletsk, Bela. (klĕtsk)	162	53°04′N	26°43′E
Kleve, Ger. (klĕ′fĕ)	154	51°47′N	6°09′E
Kley, neigh., Ger.	236	51°30′N	7°22′E
Klickitat, r., Wa., U.S.	104	46°01′N	121°07′W
Klimovichi, Bela. (klē-mô-vē′chē)	162	53°37′N	31°21′E
Klimovsk, Russia (klĭ′môfsk)	172b	55°21′N	37°32′E
Klin, Russia (klēn)	162	56°18′N	36°43′E
Klintehamn, Swe. (klēn′tē-häm)	152	57°24′N	18°14′E
Klintsy, Russia (klĭn′tsĭ)	167	52°46′N	32°14′E
Klip, r., S. Afr. (klĭp)	218d	27°18′N	29°25′E
Klipgat, S. Afr.	218d	25°26′S	27°57′E
Klippan, Swe. (klyp′pȧn)	152	56°08′N	13°09′E
Klippoortje, S. Afr.	244b	26°17′S	28°14′E
Kliptown, S. Afr.	244b	26°17′S	27°53′E
Kłodzko, Pol. (klôd′skô)	154	50°26′N	16°38′E
Klondike Region, hist. reg., N.A. (klŏn′dīk)	84	64°12′N	142°38′W
Klosterfelde, Ger. (klōs′tēr-fĕl-dĕ)	145b	52°47′N	13°29′E
Klosterneuburg, Aus. (klōs-tēr-noi′bo͝orgh)	145e	48°19′N	16°20′E
Kluane, l., Can.	84	61°15′N	138°40′W
Kluane National Park, rec., Can.	84	60°25′N	137°53′W
Kluczbork, Pol. (klo͞och′bōrk)	155	50°59′N	18°15′E
Klyaz′ma, r., Russia (klyäz′mȧ)	162	55°49′N	39°19′E
Klyuchevskaya, vol., Russia (klyo͞o-chĕfskä′yä)	165	56°13′N	160°00′E
Klyuchi, Russia (klyo͞o′chĭ)	172a	57°03′N	57°20′E
Knezha, Bul. (knyä′zhȧ)	149	43°27′N	24°03′E
Knife, r., N.D., U.S. (nīf)	102	47°06′N	102°33′W
Knight Inlet, b., Can. (nīt)	86	50°41′N	125°40′W
Knightstown, In., U.S. (nīts′toun)	98	39°45′N	85°30′W
Knin, Cro. (knēn)	160	44°02′N	16°14′E
Knittelfeld, Aus.	147	47°13′N	14°50′E
Knob Peak, mtn., Phil. (nŏb)	197a	12°30′N	121°20′E
Knockholt, Eng., U.K.	235	51°18′N	0°06′E
Knockholt Pound, Eng., U.K.	235	51°19′N	0°08′E
Knoppiesfontein, S. Afr.	244b	26°05′S	28°25′E
Knottingley, Eng., U.K. (nŏt′ĭng-lĭ)	144a	53°42′N	1°14′W
Knott's Berry Farm, pt. of i., Ca., U.S.	232	33°50′N	118°00′W
Knotty Ash, neigh., Eng., U.K.	237a	53°25′N	2°54′W
Knowsley, Eng., U.K.	237a	53°27′N	2°51′W
Knox, Austl.	243b	37°53′S	145°18′E
Knox, In., U.S. (nŏks)	98	41°15′N	86°40′W
Knox, Cape, c., Can.	86	54°12′N	133°20′W
Knoxville, Ia., U.S. (nŏks′vĭl)	103	41°19′N	93°05′W
Knoxville, Tn., U.S.	97	35°58′N	83°55′W
Knutsford, Eng., U.K. (nŭts′fērd)	144a	53°18′N	2°22′W
Knyszyn, Pol. (knĭ′shĭn)	155	53°16′N	22°59′E
Kobayashi, Japan (kō′bȧ-yä′shē)	195	31°58′N	130°59′E
Kōbe, Japan (kō′bĕ)	189	34°30′N	135°10′E
Kobeliaky, Ukr.	167	49°11′N	34°12′E
København see Copenhagen, Den.	142	55°43′N	12°27′E
Koblenz, Ger. (kō′blĕntz)	147	50°18′N	7°36′E
Kobozha, r., Russia (kô-bō′zhȧ)	162	58°55′N	35°18′E
Kobrin, Bela. (kō′brēn′)	167	52°13′N	24°23′E
Kobrinskoye, Russia (kô-brĭn′skô-yĕ)	172c	59°25′N	30°07′E
Kobuk, r., Ak., U.S. (kō′bŭk)	95	66°58′N	158°48′W
Kobuk Valley National Park, rec., Ak., U.S.	95	67°20′N	159°00′W
Kobuleti, Geor. (kô-bô-lyä′tē)	167	41°50′N	41°40′E
Kočani, Mac. (kô′chä-nĕ)	161	41°54′N	22°25′E
Kočevje, Slvn. (kô′chäv-ye)	160	45°38′N	14°51′E
Kocher, r., Ger. (kôĸ′ēr)	154	49°00′N	9°52′E
Kōchi, Japan (kō′chē)	189	33°35′N	133°32′E
Kodaira, Japan	195a	35°43′N	139°29′E
Kodiak, Ak., U.S. (kō′dyăk)	94a	57°50′N	152°30′W
Kodiak Island, i., Ak., U.S.	95	57°24′N	153°32′W
Kodok, Sudan (ko′dŏk)	211	9°57′N	32°08′E
Koforidua, Ghana (kō fō-rĭ-do͞o′ȧ)	210	6°03′N	0°17′W
Kōfu, Japan (kō′fo͞o′)	194	35°41′N	138°34′E
Koga, Japan (kō′gȧ)	195	36°13′N	139°40′E
Kogan, r., Gui.	214	11°30′N	14°05′W
Kogane, Japan (kō′gä-nȧ)	195a	35°50′N	139°56′E
Koganei, Japan (kō′gä-nā)	195a	35°42′N	139°31′E
Kogarah, Austl.	243a	33°58′S	151°08′E
Køge, Den. (kû′gĕ)	152	55°27′N	12°09′E
Køge Bugt, b., Den.	152	55°30′N	12°25′E
Kogoni, Mali	214	14°44′N	6°02′W
Kohīma, India (kô-ē′mȧ)	183	25°45′N	94°41′E
Kohyl′nyk, r., Eur.	163	46°08′N	29°10′E
Koito, r., Japan (kô′ē-tō)	195a	35°19′N	139°58′E
Kŏje, i., S. Kor. (kû′jĕ)	194	34°53′N	129°00′E
Kokand, Uzb. (kô-känt′)	169	40°27′N	71°07′E
Kokemäenjoki, r., Fin.	153	61°23′N	22°03′E
Kokhma, Russia (kôĸ′mȧ)	162	56°57′N	41°08′E
Kokkola, Fin. (kô′kô-lȧ)	146	63°47′N	22°58′E
Kokomo, In., U.S. (kō′kô-mō)	98	40°30′N	86°20′W
Koko Nor (Qinghai Hu), l., China (kō′kô nor) (chyĭŋ-hī ho͞o)	188	37°26′N	98°30′E
Kokopo, Pap. N. Gui. (kô-kō′pō)	197	4°25′S	152°27′E
Kökshetau, Kaz.	169	53°15′N	69°13′E
Koksoak, r., Can. (kôk′sô-ăk)	85	57°42′N	69°50′W
Kokstad, S. Afr. (kôk′shtät)	213c	30°33′S	29°27′E
Kokubu, Japan (kō′ko͞o-bo͞o)	195	31°42′N	130°46′E
Kokubunji, Japan	242a	35°42′N	139°29′E
Kokuou, Japan (kō′ko͞o-ō′o͞o)	195b	34°34′N	135°39′E
Kola Peninsula see Kol′skiy Poluostrov, pen., Russia	164	67°15′N	37°40′E
Kolār (Kolār Gold Fields), India (kôl-är′)	183	13°39′N	78°33′E
Kolárvo, Slvk. (kôl-árōvō)	155	47°54′N	17°59′E
Kolbio, Kenya	217	1°10′S	41°15′E
Kol′chugino, Russia (kôl-chô′gē-nô)	162	56°19′N	39°29′E
Kolda, Sen.	214	12°53′N	14°57′W
Kolding, Den. (kŭl′dĭng)	152	55°29′N	9°24′E
Kole, D.R.C. (kō′lȧ)	212	3°19′S	22°46′E
Kolguyev, i., Russia (kôl-gô′yĕf)	164	69°00′N	49°00′E
Kolhāpur, India	187	16°48′N	74°15′E
Kolín, Czech Rep. (kō′lēn)	154	50°01′N	15°11′E
Kolkasrags, c., Lat. (kôl-käs′rágz)	153	57°46′N	22°39′E
Köln see Cologne, Ger.	157c	50°56′N	6°57′E
Kolno, Pol. (kôw′nō)	155	53°23′N	21°56′E
Koło, Pol. (kô′wō)	155	52°11′N	18°37′E
Kołobrzeg, Pol. (kô-lôb′zhĕk)	146	54°10′N	15°35′E
Kolomenskoje, neigh., Russia	239b	55°40′N	37°41′E
Kolomna, Russia (kál-ôm′nȧ)	166	55°06′N	38°47′E
Kolomyia, Ukr.	155	48°32′N	25°04′E
Kolonie Stolp, Ger.	238a	52°28′N	13°46′E
Kolp′, r., Russia (kôlp)	162	59°18′N	35°32′E
Kolpashevo, Russia (kŭl pȧ shô′vȧ)	164	58°16′N	82°43′E
Kolpino, Russia (kôl′pē-nô)	166	59°45′N	30°37′E
Kolpny, Russia (kôlp′nyē)	162	52°14′N	36°54′E
Kol′skiy Poluostrov, pen., Russia	164	67°15′N	37°40′E
Kolva, r., Russia	166	61°00′N	57°00′E
Kolwezi, D.R.C. (kôl-wĕ′zē)	212	10°43′S	25°28′E
Kolyberovo, Russia (kô-lĭ-byâ′rô-vô)	172b	55°16′N	38°45′E
Kolyma, r., Russia	165	66°30′N	151°45′E
Kolymskiy Mountains see Gydan, Khrebet, mts., Russia	165	61°45′N	155°00′E
Kom, r., Afr.	216	2°15′N	12°05′E
Komadugu Gana, r., Nig.	215	12°15′N	11°10′E
Komae, Japan	195a	35°37′N	139°35′E
Komagome, neigh., Japan	242a	35°44′N	139°45′E
Komandorskiye Ostrova, is., Russia	181	55°40′N	167°13′E
Komárno, Slvk. (kô′mär-nô)	155	47°46′N	18°08′E
Komarno, Ukr.	155	49°38′N	23°42′E
Komárom, Hung. (kô′mä-rôm)	155	47°45′N	18°06′E
Komatipoort, S. Afr. (kō-mä′tē-pōrt)	212	25°21′S	32°00′E
Komatsu, Japan (kō-mät′so͞o)	194	36°23′N	136°26′E
Komatsushima, Japan (kō-mät′so͞o-shē′mä)	195	34°04′N	134°32′E
Komeshia, D.R.C.	217	8°01′S	27°07′E

ăt; finăl; rāte; senāte; ärm; ȧsk; sofȧ; fâre; ch-choose; dh-as th in other; bē; ėvent; bĕt; recĕnt; cratēr; g-gō; gh-guttural g; bĭt; ĭ-short neutral; rīde; ĸ-guttural k as ch in German ich;

PLACE (Pronunciation)	PAGE	LAT.	LONG.
Komga, S. Afr. (kōm'gȧ)	213c	32°36'S	27°54'E
Komi, state, Russia (kô'mê)	170	63°00'N	55°00'E
Kommetjie, S. Afr.	212a	34°09'S	18°19'E
Kommunizma, Pik, mtn., Taj.	169	38°57'N	72°01'E
Komoé, r., C. Iv.	214	5°40'N	3°40'W
Komsomol, Kaz.	169	53°45'N	62°04'E
Komsomol'sk-na-Amure, Russia	165	50°46'N	137°14'E
Kona, Mali	214	14°57'N	3°53'W
Konda, r., Russia (kôn'dȧ)	166	60°50'N	64°00'E
Kondas, r., Russia (kôn'dȧs)	172a	59°30'N	56°28'E
Kondli, neigh., India	240d	28°37'N	77°19'E
Kondoa, Tan. (kôn-dō'ȧ)	212	4°52'S	36°00'E
Kondolole, D.R.C.	217	1°20'N	25°58'E
Koné, N. Cal.	198f	21°04'S	164°52'E
Kong, C. Iv. (kông)	210	9°05'N	4°41'W
Kongbo, Cen. Afr. Rep.	216	4°44'N	21°23'E
Kongolo, D.R.C. (kôŋ'gō'lō)	212	5°23'S	27°00'E
Kongsberg, Nor. (kŭngs'bĕrg)	152	59°40'N	9°36'E
Kongsvinger, Nor. (kŭngs'vĭŋ-gĕr)	152	60°12'N	12°00'E
Koni, D.R.C. (kō'nē)	212	10°32'S	27°27'E
Königsberg see Kaliningrad, Russia	164	54°42'N	20°32'E
Königsbrunn, Ger. (kû'nēgs-brōōn)	145d	48°16'N	10°53'E
Königshardt, neigh., Ger.	236	51°33'N	6°51'E
Königs Wusterhausen, Ger. (kû'nēgs vōōs'tĕr-hou-zĕn)	145b	52°18'N	13°38'E
Konin, Pol. (kô'nyĕn)	147	52°11'N	18°17'E
Kónitsa, Grc. (kô'nyē'tsȧ)	161	40°03'N	20°46'E
Konjic, Bos. (kôn'yēts)	161	43°38'N	17°59'E
Konju, S. Kor.	194	36°21'N	127°05'E
Konnagar, India	186a	22°41'N	88°22'E
Konohana, neigh., Japan	242b	34°41'N	135°26'E
Konoike, Japan	242b	34°42'N	135°37'E
Konotop, Ukr. (kô-nô-tôp')	167	51°13'N	33°14'E
Konpienga, r., Burkina	214	11°15'N	0°35'E
Konqi, r., China (kôn-chyē)	188	41°09'N	87°46'E
Końskie, Pol. (koin''skyĕ)	155	51°12'N	20°26'E
Konstanz, Ger. (kôn'shtänts)	154	47°39'N	9°10'E
Kontagora, Nig. (kōn-tá-gō'rä)	210	10°24'N	5°28'E
Konya, Tur. (kōn'yȧ)	182	36°55'N	32°25'E
Koocanusa, Lake, res., N.A.	104	49°00'N	115°10'W
Kootenay (Kootenai), r., N.A.	87	49°45'N	117°05'W
Kootenay Lake, l., Can.	87	49°35'N	116°50'W
Kootenay National Park, Can. (kōō'tē-nā)	84	51°06'N	117°02'W
Kooyong, Austl.	243b	37°50'S	145°02'E
Kōō-zan, mtn., Japan (kōō'zän)	195b	34°53'N	135°32'E
Kopervik, Nor. (kô'pĕr-vêk)	152	59°18'N	5°20'E
Kopeysk, Russia (kô-päsk')	170	55°07'N	61°37'E
Köping, Swe. (chû'pĭng)	152	59°32'N	15°58'E
Kopparberg, Swe. (kŏp'pár-bĕrgh)	152	59°53'N	15°00'E
Koppeh Dāgh, mts., Asia	182	37°28'N	58°29'E
Koppies, S. Afr.	218d	27°15'S	27°35'E
Koprivnica, Cro. (kô'prēv-nē'tsȧ)	160	46°10'N	16°48'E
Kopychyntsi, Ukr.	155	49°06'N	25°55'E
Korčula, i., Yugo. (kôr'chōō-lȧ)	161	42°50'N	17°05'E
Korea, North, nation, Asia	189	40°00'N	127°00'E
Korea, South, nation, Asia	189	36°30'N	128°00'E
Korea Bay, b., Asia	192	39°18'N	123°50'E
Korean Archipelago, is., S. Kor.	189	34°05'N	125°35'E
Korea Strait, strt., Asia	189	33°30'N	128°30'E
Korets', Ukr.	155	50°35'N	27°13'E
Korhogo, C. Iv. (kôr-hō'gō)	210	9°27'N	5°38'W
Kōri, Japan	242b	34°47'N	135°39'E
Koridhallós, Grc.	239d	37°59'N	23°39'E
Korinthiakós Kólpos, b., Grc.	149	38°15'N	22°33'E
Kórinthos, Grc. (kô-rēn'thôs) (kŏr'ĭnth)	142	37°56'N	22°54'E
Koriukivka, Ukr.	163	51°44'N	32°24'E
Kōriyama, Japan (kō'rē-yä'mä)	194	37°18'N	140°25'E
Korkino, Russia (kôr'kē-nŭ)	172a	54°53'N	61°25'E
Korla, China (kōr-lä)	188	41°37'N	86°03'E
Körmend, Hung. (kûr'mĕnt)	154	47°02'N	16°36'E
Kornat, i., Yugo. (kôr-nät')	160	43°46'N	15°10'E
Korneuburg, Aus. (kôr'noi-bôrgh)	145e	48°22'N	16°21'E
Koro, Mali	214	14°04'N	3°05'W
Korocha, Russia (kô-rō'chȧ)	163	50°50'N	37°13'E
Korop, Ukr. (kō'rôp)	163	51°33'N	32°54'E
Koro Sea, sea, Fiji	198g	18°00'S	179°50'E
Korosten', Ukr. (kô'rôs-tĕn)	167	50°51'N	28°39'E
Korostyshiv, Ukr.	163	50°19'N	29°05'E
Koro Toro, Chad	215	16°05'N	18°30'E
Korotoyak, Russia (kô'rô-tô-yȧk')	163	51°00'N	39°06'E
Korsakov, Russia (kôr'sȧ-kôf')	165	46°42'N	143°16'E
Korsnäs, Fin. (kôrs'nĕs)	153	62°51'N	21°17'E
Korsør, Den. (kôrs'ûr')	152	55°19'N	11°08'E
Kortrijk, Bel.	151	50°49'N	3°10'E
Koryakskiy Khrebet, mts., Russia	165	62°00'N	168°45'E
Kosa Byriuchyi ostriv, i., Ukr.	163	46°07'N	35°12'E
Kościan, Pol. (kŭsh'tsyän)	154	52°05'N	16°38'E
Kościerzyna, Pol. (kŭsh-tsyĕ-zhē'nȧ)	155	54°08'N	17°59'E
Kosciusko, Ms., U.S. (kŏs-ĭ-ŭs'kō)	114	33°04'N	89°35'W
Kosciusko, Mount, mtn., Austl.	203	36°26'S	148°20'E
Kosha, Sudan	211	20°49'N	30°27'E
Koshigaya, Japan (kō'shē-gä'yä)	195a	35°53'N	139°48'E
Koshim, r., Kaz.	170	50°30'N	50°40'E
Kosi, r., India (kō'sē)	186	26°00'N	86°20'E
Košice, Slvk. (kō'shē-tsĕ')	147	48°43'N	21°17'E
Kosino, Russia	239b	55°43'N	37°52'E
Kosmos, S. Afr. (kŏz'mŏs)	213b	25°45'S	27°51'E
Kosmosa, Monument, hist., Russia	239b	55°49'N	37°38'E
Kosobrodskiy, Russia (kä-sô'brôd-skĭ)	172a	54°14'N	60°53'E
Kosovo, hist. reg., Yugo.	161	42°35'N	21°00'E
Kosovska Mitrovica, Yugo. (kô'sôv-skä' mē'trô-vē-tsä')	161	42°51'N	20°50'E
Kostajnica, Cro. (kôs'tä-ē-nē'tsȧ)	160	45°14'N	16°32'E
Koster, S. Afr.	218d	25°52'S	26°52'E
Kostiantynivka, Ukr.	163	48°33'N	37°42'E
Kostino, Russia (kôs'tĭ-nô)	172b	55°54'N	37°51'E
Kostroma, Russia (kôs-trô-mȧ')	164	57°46'N	40°55'E
Kostroma, prov., Russia	162	57°50'N	41°10'E
Kostrzyn, Pol. (kôst'chĕn)	147	52°35'N	14°38'E
Kos'va, r., Russia (kôs'vȧ)	172a	58°44'N	57°08'E
Koszalin, Pol. (kô-shä'lĭn)	146	54°12'N	16°10'E
Kőszeg, Hung. (kû'sĕg)	154	47°21'N	16°32'E
Kota, India	183	25°17'N	75°49'E
Kota Baharu, Malay. (kō'tä bä'rōō)	196	6°15'N	102°23'E
Kotabaru, Indon.	196	3°22'S	116°15'E
Kota Kinabalu, Malay.	196	5°55'N	116°05'E
Kota Tinggi, Malay.	181b	1°43'N	103°54'E
Kotel, Bul. (kō-tĕl')	161	42°54'N	26°28'E
Kotel'nich, Russia (kô-tyĕl'nĕch)	166	58°15'N	48°20'E
Kotel'nyy, i., Russia (kô-tyĕl'nē)	165	74°51'N	134°09'E
Kotka, Fin. (kŏt'kȧ)	146	60°28'N	26°56'E
Kotlas, Russia (kôt'lȧs)	166	61°10'N	46°50'E
Kotlin, Ostrov, i., Russia (ôs-trôf' kôt'lĭn)	172c	60°02'N	29°49'E
Kōtō, neigh., Japan	242a	35°41'N	139°48'E
Kotor, Yugo.	161	42°25'N	18°46'E
Kotorosl', r., Russia (kô-tô'rôsl)	162	57°18'N	39°08'E
Kotovs'k, Ukr.	163	47°49'N	29°31'E
Kotte, Sri L.	187	6°50'N	80°05'E
Kotto, r., Cen. Afr. Rep.	211	5°17'N	22°04'E
Kotuy, r., Russia (kô-tōō')	170	71°00'N	103°15'E
Kotzebue, Ak., U.S. (kŏt'sĕ-bōō)	94a	66°48'N	162°42'W
Kotzebue Sound, strt., Ak., U.S.	95	67°00'N	164°28'W
Kouchibouguac National Park, rec., Can.	92	46°53'N	65°35'W
Koudougou, Burkina (kōō-dōō'gōō)	210	12°15'N	2°22'W
Kouilou, r., Congo	212	4°30'S	12°00'E
Koula-Moutou, Gabon	216	1°08'S	12°29'E
Koulikoro, Mali (kōō-lē-kō'rō)	210	12°53'N	7°33'W
Koulouguidi, Mali	215	13°27'N	17°33'E
Koumac, N. Cal.	198f	20°33'S	164°17'E
Koumra, Chad	215	8°55'N	17°33'E
Koundara, Gui.	214	12°29'N	13°18'W
Kouroussa, Gui. (kōō-rōō'sä)	210	10°39'N	9°53'W
Koutiala, Mali (kōō-tē-ä'lä)	210	12°29'N	5°29'W
Kouvola, Fin. (kō'ô-vô-lä)	153	60°51'N	26°40'E
Kouzhen, China (kō-jŭn)	190	36°19'N	117°37'E
Kovda, l., Russia (kôv'dȧ)	166	66°45'N	32°00'E
Kovel', Ukr. (kō'vĕl)	167	51°13'N	24°45'E
Kovno see Kaunas, Lith.	164	54°42'N	23°54'E
Kovrov, Russia (kôv-rôf')	166	56°23'N	41°21'E
Kowloon (Jiulong), H.K.	242c	22°18'N	114°10'E
Koyuk, Ak., U.S. (kô-yōōk')	95	65°00'N	161°18'W
Koyukuk, r., Ak., U.S. (kô-yōō'kŏk)	95	66°25'N	153°50'W
Kozáni, Grc.	149	40°16'N	21°51'E
Kozelets', Ukr. (kôzĕ-lyĕts)	163	50°53'N	31°07'E
Kozel'sk, Russia (kô-zĕlsk')	162	54°01'N	35°49'E
Koziatyn, Ukr.	167	49°43'N	28°50'E
Kozienice, Pol. (kō-zyĕ-nē'tsĕ)	155	51°34'N	21°35'E
Koźle, Pol. (kôzh'lĕ)	155	50°19'N	18°10'E
Kozloduy, Bul. (kŭz'lô-dwĕ)	161	43°45'N	23°42'E
Kōzu, i., Japan (kō'zōō)	195	34°16'N	139°03'E
Kra, Isthmus of, isth., Asia	196	9°30'S	99°45'E
Kraai, r., S. Afr. (krä'ē)	213c	30°50'S	27°03'E
Krabbendijke, Neth.	145a	51°26'N	4°05'E
Krâchéh, Camb.	196	12°28'N	106°06'E
Kragujevac, Yugo. (krä'gōō'yĕ-vȧts)	149	44°01'N	20°55'E
Krahenhöhe, neigh., Ger.	236	51°10'N	7°06'E
Kraków, Pol. (krä'kôf)	142	50°05'N	20°00'E
Kraljevo, Yugo. (kräl'ye-vô)	149	43°39'N	20°48'E
Kramators'k, Ukr.	163	48°43'N	37°32'E
Kramfors, Swe. (kräm'fôrs)	152	62°54'N	17°49'E
Krampnitz, Ger.	238a	52°28'N	13°04'E
Kranj, Slvn. (krän')	148	46°16'N	14°23'E
Kranskop, S. Afr. (kränz'kŏp)	213c	28°57'S	30°54'E
Krāslava, Lat. (kräs'lä-vä)	153	55°53'N	27°12'E
Kraslice, Czech Rep. (kräs'lē-tsĕ)	154	50°19'N	12°30'E
Krasnaya Gorka, Russia	172a	55°12'N	56°40'E
Krasnaya Sloboda, Russia	167	48°25'N	44°35'E
Kraśnik, Pol. (kräsh'nĭk)	155	50°53'N	22°15'E
Krasnoarmeysk, Russia (kräs'nô-är-maśk')	172b	56°06'N	38°09'E
Krasnoarmiis'k, Ukr.	163	48°19'N	37°04'E
Krasnodar, Russia (kräs'nô-dár)	164	45°03'N	38°55'E
Krasnodarskiy, prov., Russia (krȧs-nô-där'skĭ ôb'lást)	163	45°25'N	38°10'E
Krasnogorsk, Russia	172b	55°49'N	37°20'E
Krasnogorskiy, Russia (kräs-nô-gôr'skĭ)	172a	54°36'N	61°15'E
Krasnogvardeyskiy, Russia (krȧ'sno-gvär-dzyĕ ĕs-kēē)	172a	57°17'N	62°05'E
Krasnohrad, Ukr.	163	49°23'N	35°26'E
Krasnokamsk, Russia (kräs-nô-kämsk')	166	58°00'N	55°45'E
Krasnokuts'k, Ukr.	163	50°03'N	35°05'E
Krasnoslobodsk, Russia (kräs-nô-slôbôtsk')	166	54°20'N	43°50'E
Krasnotur'insk, Russia (krŭs-nŭ-tōō-rensk')	164	59°47'N	60°15'E
Krasnoufimsk, Russia (krŭs-nŭ-ōō-fēmsk')	164	56°38'N	57°46'E
Krasnoural'sk, Russia (kräs'nô-ōō-rälsk')	166	58°21'N	60°05'E
Krasnousol'skiy, Russia (kräs-nô-ô-sôl'skĭ)	172a	53°54'N	56°27'E
Krasnovishersk, Russia (kräs-nô-vêshersk')	166	60°22'N	57°20'E
Krasnoyarsk, Russia (kräs-nô-yársk')	165	56°13'N	93°12'E
Krasnoye Selo, Russia (kräs'nŭ-yŭ sâ'lō)	172c	59°44'N	30°06'E
Krasnyj Stroitel', neigh., Russia	239b	55°35'N	37°37'E
Krasny Kholm, Russia (kräs'nē kôlm)	162	58°03'N	37°11'E
Krasnystaw, Pol. (kräs-nē-stáf')	155	50°59'N	23°11'E
Krasnyy Bor, Russia (kräs'nē bôr)	172c	59°41'N	30°40'E
Krasnyy Klyuch, Russia (kräs'nē'klyûch')	172a	55°24'N	56°43'E
Krasnyy Kut, Russia (krȧs-nē kōōt')	167	50°50'N	47°00'E
Kratovo, Mac. (krä'tô-vô)	161	42°04'N	22°12'E
Kratovo, Russia (krä'tô-vô)	172b	55°35'N	38°10'E
Kray, neigh., Ger.	236	51°28'N	7°05'E
Krefeld, Ger. (krā'fĕlt)	157c	51°20'N	6°34'E
Kremenchuk, Ukr.	167	49°04'N	33°26'E
Kremenchuts'ke vodoskhovyshche, res., Ukr.	167	49°20'N	32°45'E
Kremenets', Ukr.	155	50°06'N	25°43'E
Kreml', bldg., Russia	239b	55°45'N	37°37'E
Kremmen, Ger. (krĕ'mĕn)	145b	52°45'N	13°02'E
Krempe, Ger. (krĕm'pē)	145c	53°50'N	9°29'E
Krems, Aus. (krĕms)	154	48°25'N	15°36'E
Krestovyy, Pereval, p., Geor.	168	42°32'N	44°28'E
Kresttsy, Russia (krȧst'sė)	162	58°16'N	32°25'E
Kretinga, Lith. (krĕ-tĭŋ'gȧ)	153	55°55'N	21°17'E
Kreuzberg, Ger.	236	51°09'N	7°27'E
Kreuzberg, neigh., Ger.	238a	52°30'N	13°23'E
Kribi, Cam. (krē'bē)	210	2°57'N	9°55'E
Krichëv, Bela. (krē'chôf)	162	53°44'N	31°39'E
Krilon, Mys, c., Russia (mĭs krĭl'ôn)	194	45°58'N	142°00'E
Krimpen aan de IJssel, Neth.	145a	51°55'N	4°34'E
Krishna, r., India	183	16°00'N	79°00'E
Krishnanagar, India	186	23°29'N	88°33'E
Krishnapur, India	240a	22°36'N	88°26'E
Kristiansand, Nor. (krĭs-tyȧn-sän'')	142	58°09'N	7°59'E
Kristianstad, Swe. (krĭs-tyȧn-städ')	146	56°02'N	14°09'E
Kristiansund, Nor. (krĭs-tyȧn-sôn'')	146	63°07'N	7°49'E
Kristinehamn, Swe. (krēs-tē'nĕ-häm')	146	59°20'N	14°05'E
Kristinestad, Fin. (krĭs-tē'nĕ-städh)	153	62°16'N	21°28'E
Kriva-Palanka, Mac. (krē-vȧ-pȧ-läŋ'kȧ)	161	42°12'N	22°21'E
Križevci, Cro. (krē'zhĕv-tsĭ)	160	46°02'N	16°30'E
Krk, i., Yugo. (k'rk)	160	45°06'N	14°33'E
Krnov, Czech Rep. (k'r'nôf)	155	50°05'N	17°41'E
Krokodil, r., S. Afr. (krŏ'kō-dĭ)	218d	24°25'S	27°08'E
Krolevets', Ukr.	167	51°33'N	33°21'E
Kromy, Russia (krô'mē)	162	52°44'N	35°41'E
Kronshtadt, Russia (krōn'shtät)	166	59°59'N	29°47'E
Kroonstad, S. Afr. (krōn'shtät)	212	27°40'S	27°15'E
Kropotkin, Russia (krȧ-pôt'kĭn)	167	45°25'N	40°30'E
Krosno, Pol. (krôs'nô)	155	49°41'N	21°46'E
Krotoszyn, Pol. (krō-tō'shĭn)	155	51°41'N	17°25'E
Krško, Slvn. (k'rsh'kô)	160	45°58'N	15°30'E
Kruger National Park, rec., S. Afr. (krōō'gĕr) (krü'gĕr)	212	23°22'S	30°18'E
Krugersdorp, S. Afr. (krōō'gĕrz-dôrp)	212	26°06'S	27°46'E
Krugersdorp West, S. Afr.	244b	26°06'S	27°45'E
Krummensee, Ger.	238a	52°36'N	13°42'E
Krung Thep see Bangkok, Thai.	196	13°50'N	100°29'E
Kruševac, Yugo. (krŏ'shĕ-vȧts)	161	43°34'N	21°21'E
Kruševo, Mac.	161	41°20'N	21°15'E
Krylatskoje, neigh., Russia	239b	55°45'N	37°26'E
Krylbo, Swe. (krül'bô)	152	60°07'N	16°14'E
Krym, Respublika, prov., Ukr.	163	45°08'N	34°05'E
Krymskaya, Russia (krĭm'skȧ-yȧ)	163	44°58'N	38°01'E
Kryms'kyi Pivostriv (Crimean Peninsula), pen., Ukr.	167	45°18'N	33°30'E
Krynki, Pol. (krĭn'kė)	155	53°15'N	23°47'E
Kryve Ozero, Ukr.	163	47°57'N	30°21'E
Kryvyi Rih, Ukr.	164	47°54'N	33°22'E
Ksar Chellala, Alg.	159	35°12'N	2°20'E
Ksar-el-Kebir, Mor.	148	35°01'N	5°48'W
Ksar-es-Souk, Mor.	148	31°58'N	4°25'W
Kuai, r., China (kōō-ī)	190	33°30'N	116°56'E
Kuala Klawang, Malay.	181b	2°57'N	102°04'E
Kuala Lumpur, Malay. (kwä'lä lōm-pōōr')	196	3°08'N	101°42'E
Kuandian, China (kûän-dĭĕn)	192	40°40'N	124°50'E
Kuban, r., Russia	167	45°20'N	40°05'E
Kubenskoye, l., Russia	166	59°40'N	39°40'E
Kuching, Malay. (kōō'chĭng)	196	1°30'N	110°26'E
Kuchinoerabo, i., Japan (kōō'chē nō ĕr'ȧ-bō)	195	30°31'N	129°53'E
Kudamatsu, Japan (kōō'dȧ-mä'tsōō)	195	34°00'N	131°51'E
Kudap, Indon.	181b	1°14'N	102°30'E
Kudat, Malay. (kōō-dät')	196	6°56'N	116°48'E
Kudbrooke, neigh., Eng., U.K.	235	51°28'N	0°03'E
Kudirkos Naumietis, Lith. (kōōdĭr-kôs nå'ô-mĕ'tĭs)	153	54°51'N	23°00'E
Kudymkar, Russia (kōō-dĭm-kär')	164	58°43'N	54°52'E
Kufstein, Aus. (kōōf'shtĭn)	154	47°34'N	12°11'E
Kuhstedt, Ger. (kōō'shtĕ)	145c	53°23'N	8°58'E
Kuibyshev see Kuybyshev, Russia	164	53°10'N	50°05'E
Kuilsrivier, S. Afr.	212a	33°56'S	18°41'E
Kuito, Ang.	212	12°22'S	16°56'E
Kuji, Japan	189	40°11'N	141°46'E
Kujū-san, mtn., Japan (kōō'jô-sän')	195	33°07'N	131°14'E
Kukës, Alb. (kōō'kĕs)	161	42°03'N	20°25'E
Kula, Bul. (kōō'lȧ)	161	43°52'N	23°13'E
Kula, Tur.	149	38°32'N	28°30'E
Kula Kangri, mtn., Bhu.	183	33°11'N	90°36'E
Kular, Khrebet, mts., Russia (kō-lär')	171	69°00'N	131°45'E
Kuldīga, Lat. (kŏl'dē-gȧ)	153	56°59'N	21°59'E
Kulebaki, Russia (kōō-lĕ-bäk'ĭ)	166	55°22'N	42°30'E
Küllenhahn, neigh., Ger.	236	51°14'N	7°08'E
Kulmbach, Ger. (klōlm'bäĸ)	154	50°07'N	11°28'E
Kulunda, Russia (kô-lôn'dȧ)	164	52°38'N	79°00'E
Kulundinskoye, l., Russia	170	52°45'N	77°18'E
Kum, r., S. Kor. (kôm)	194	36°50'N	127°30'E
Kuma, r., Russia (kōō'mä)	167	44°50'N	45°10'E
Kumamoto, Japan (kōō'mä-mō'tô)	189	32°49'N	130°40'E
Kumano-Nada, b., Japan (kōō-mä'nō nä-dä)	195	34°03'N	136°36'E
Kumanovo, Mac. (kô-mä'nô-vô)	161	42°10'N	21°41'E
Kumasi, Ghana (kōō-mä'sē)	210	6°41'N	1°35'W
Kumba, Cam. (kôm'bȧ)	210	4°38'N	9°25'E
Kumbakonam, India (kôm'bŭ-kō'nŭm)	183	10°59'N	79°25'E
Kumkale, Tur.	161	39°59'N	26°10'E
Kumo, Nig.	215	10°03'N	11°13'E
Kumta, India	187	14°19'N	75°28'E
Kumul see Hami, China	188	42°58'N	93°14'E
Kunashak, Russia (kû-nä'shák)	172a	55°43'N	61°35'E
Kunashir (Kunashiri), i., Russia (kōō-nŭ-shēr')	189	44°00'N	145°45'E
Kunda, Est.	153	59°30'N	26°28'E

306 Kundravy–Laje

PLACE (Pronunciation)	PAGE	LAT.	LONG.
Kundravy, Russia (ko͞on′drȧ-vĭ)	172a	54°50′N	60°14′E
Kundur, i., Indon.	181b	0°49′N	103°20′E
Kunene (Cunene), r., Afr.	212	17°05′S	12°35′E
Kungälv, Swe. (kŭng′ĕlf)	152	57°53′N	12°01′E
Kungsbacka, Swe. (kŭngs′bä-kȧ)	152	57°31′N	12°04′E
Kungur, Russia (kȯn-go͞or′)	164	57°27′N	56°53′E
Kunitachi, Japan	242a	35°41′N	139°26′E
Kunlun Shan, mts., China (ko͞on-lo͞on shän)	188	35°26′N	83°09′E
Kunming, China (ko͞on-mĭŋ)	188	25°10′N	102°50′E
Kunsan, S. Kor. (kȯn′sän′)	189	35°54′N	126°46′E
Kunshan, China (ko͞onshän)	191b	31°23′N	120°57′E
Kuntsëvo, Russia (kȯn-tsyô′vȯ)	162	55°43′N	37°27′E
Kun'ya, Russia	172a	58°42′N	56°47′E
Kun'ya, r., Russia (kȯn′yȧ)	162	56°45′N	30°53′E
Kuopio, Fin. (kȯ-ô′pė-ŏ)	146	62°48′N	28°30′E
Kupa, r., Yugo.	160	45°32′N	14°50′E
Kupang, Indon.	197	10°14′S	123°37′E
Kupavna, Russia	172b	55°49′N	38°11′E
Kupferdreh, neigh., Ger.	236	51°23′N	7°05′E
Kupians'k, Ukr.	167	49°44′N	37°38′E
Kupino, Russia (ko͞o-pĭ′nȯ)	164	54°00′N	77°47′E
Kupiškis, Lith. (kȯ-pĭsh′kĭs)	153	55°50′N	24°55′E
Kuqa, China (ko͞o-chyä)	188	41°34′N	82°44′E
Kür, r., Asia	167	41°10′N	45°40′E
Kurashiki, Japan (ko͞o′rä-shē′kė)	195	34°37′N	133°44′E
Kuraymah, Sudan	211	18°34′N	31°49′E
Kurayoshi, Japan (ko͞o′rȧ-yō′shė)	195	35°25′N	133°49′E
Kurdistan, hist. reg., Asia (kûrd′ĭ-stăn)	182	37°40′N	43°30′E
Kurdufān, hist. reg., Sudan (kôr-dȯ-făn′)	211	14°08′N	28°39′E
Kŭrdzhali, Bul.	161	41°39′N	25°21′E
Kure, Japan (ko͞o′rĕ)	189	34°17′N	132°35′E
Kuressaare, Est. (kȯ′rĕ-sä′rĕ)	153	58°15′N	22°26′E
Kurgan, Russia (kȯr-găn′)	164	55°28′N	65°14′E
Kurgan-Tyube, Taj. (kȯr-gän′ tyȯ′bĕ)	169	38°00′N	68°49′E
Kurihama, Japan (ko͞o-rē-hä′mä)	195a	35°14′N	139°42′E
Kuril Islands, is., Russia (ko͞o′rĭl)	171	46°20′N	149°30′E
Ku-ring-gai, Austl.	243a	33°45′S	151°08′E
Kurisches Haff, b., Eur.	153	55°10′N	21°08′E
Kurl, neigh., Ger.	236	51°35′N	7°35′E
Kurla, neigh., India	187b	19°03′N	72°53′E
Kurmuk, Sudan (kȯr′mo͞ok)	211	10°40′N	34°13′E
Kurnell, Austl.	243a	34°01′S	151°13′E
Kurnool, India (kȯr-no͞ol′)	183	16°00′N	78°04′E
Kurrajong, Austl.	201b	33°33′S	150°40′E
Kuršenai, Lith. (kȯr′shå-nī)	153	56°01′N	22°56′E
Kursk, Russia (kȯrsk)	164	51°44′N	36°08′E
Kuršumlija, Yugo. (kȯr′shȯm′lĭ-yȧ)	161	43°08′N	21°18′E
Kuruçeşme, neigh., Tur.	239f	41°03′N	29°02′E
Kuruman, S. Afr. (ko͞o-ro͞o-män′)	212	27°25′S	23°30′E
Kurume, Japan (ko͞o′rȯ-mĕ)	189	33°10′N	130°30′E
Kurume, Japan	242a	35°45′N	139°32′E
Kururi, Japan (ko͞o′rȯ-rė)	195a	35°17′N	140°05′E
Kusa, Russia (ko͞o′sȧ)	172a	55°19′N	59°27′E
Kushchëvskaya, Russia	163	46°34′N	39°40′E
Kushikino, Japan (ko͞o′shĭ-kē′nō)	195	31°44′N	130°19′E
Kushimoto, Japan (ko͞o′shĭ-mō′tō)	195	33°29′N	135°47′E
Kushiro, Japan (ko͞o′shē-rō)	189	43°00′N	144°22′E
Kushva, Russia (ko͞osh′vȧ)	164	58°18′N	59°51′E
Kuskokwim, r., Ak., U.S.	95	61°32′N	160°36′W
Kuskokwim Bay, b., Ak., U.S. (kŭs′kȯ-kwĭm)	95	59°25′N	163°14′W
Kuskokwim Mountains, mts., Ak., U.S.	95	62°08′N	158°00′W
Kuskovak, Ak., U.S. (kŭs-kō′văk)	95	60°10′N	162°50′W
Kuskovo, neigh., Russia	239b	55°44′N	37°49′E
Kütahya, Tur. (kû-tä′hyȧ)	182	39°20′N	29°50′E
Kutaisi, Geor. (ko͞o-tŭ-ē′sē)	167	42°15′N	42°40′E
Kutch, Gulf of, b., India	183	22°45′N	68°33′E
Kutch, Rann of, sw., Asia	183	23°59′N	69°13′E
Kutenholz, Ger. (ko͞o′tĕn-hōlts)	145c	53°29′N	9°20′E
Kutim, Russia (ko͞o′tĭm)	172a	60°22′N	58°51′E
Kutina, Cro. (ko͞o′tė-nȧ)	160	45°29′N	16°48′E
Kutno, Pol. (kȯt′nô)	147	52°14′N	19°22′E
Kutno, l., Russia	166	65°15′N	31°30′E
Kutulik, Russia (kȯ to͞o′lyĭk)	165	53°12′N	102°51′E
Kuujjuaq, Can.	85	58°06′N	68°25′W
Kuusamo, Fin. (ko͞o′sȧ-mȯ)	146	65°59′N	29°10′E
Kuvshinovo, Russia (kȯv-shē′nô-vȯ)	162	57°01′N	34°09′E
Kuwait *see* Al Kuwait, Kuw.	182	29°04′N	47°59′E
Kuwait, nation, Asia	182	29°00′N	48°45′E
Kuwana, Japan (ko͞o′wȧ-nȧ)	195	35°02′N	136°40′E
Kuybyshev *see* Samara, Russia	166	53°10′N	50°05′E
Kuybyshevskoye, res., Russia	164	53°40′N	49°00′E
Kuz'minki, neigh., Russia	239b	55°42′N	37°48′E
Kuzneckovo, Russia	172b	55°29′N	38°22′E
Kuznetsk, Russia (ko͞oz-nyĕtsk′)	166	53°00′N	46°30′E
Kuznetsk Basin, basin, Russia	164	56°30′N	86°15′E
Kuznetsovka, Russia (kȯz-nyĕt′sôf-kȧ)	172a	54°41′N	56°40′E
Kuznetsovo, Russia (kȯz-nyĕt-sô′vȯ)	162	56°39′N	36°55′E
Kuznetsy, Russia	172b	55°50′N	38°39′E
Kvarner Zaliv, b., Yugo. (kvär′nĕr)	160	44°41′N	14°05′E
Kvichak, Ak., U.S. (vĭc′-hăk)	95	59°00′N	156°48′W
Kwa, r., D.R.C.	216	3°00′S	16°45′E
Kwahu Plateau, plat., Ghana	214	7°00′N	1°35′W
Kwando (Cuando), r., Afr.	216	16°50′S	22°40′E
Kwangju, S. Kor.	194	35°09′N	126°54′E
Kwango (Cuango), r., Afr. (kwäng′ō′)	216	6°35′S	16°50′E
Kwangwazi, Tan.	217	7°47′S	38°15′E
Kwa-Thema, S. Afr.	244b	26°18′S	28°23′E
Kwekwe, Zimb.	212	18°49′S	29°45′E
Kwenge, r., Afr. (kwĕŋ′gĕ)	212	6°45′S	18°23′E
Kwilu, r., Afr. (kwē′lo͞o)	212	4°00′S	18°00′E
Kyakhta, Russia (kyäκ′ta)	165	51°00′N	107°30′E
Kyaukpyu, Myanmar (chouk′pyoo′)	183	19°19′N	93°33′E
Kybartai, Lith. (kē′bär-tī′)	153	54°40′N	22°46′E
Kyïv *see* Kiev, Ukr.	164	50°27′N	30°30′E
Kyïvs'ke vodoskhovyshche, res., Ukr.	164	51°00′N	30°20′E
Kyn, Russia (kĭn′)	172a	57°52′N	58°42′E
Kynuna, Austl. (kī-no͞o′nȧ)	203	21°30′S	142°12′E
Kyoga, Lake, l., Ug.	211	1°30′N	32°45′E
Kyōga-Saki, c., Japan (kyō′gä sa′kė)	195	35°46′N	135°14′E
Kyŏngju, S. Kor. (kyŭng′yo͞o)	189	35°48′N	129°12′E
Kyōto, Japan (kyō′tō′)	189	35°00′N	135°46′E
Kyōto, dept., Japan	195b	34°56′N	135°42′E
Kyren, Russia (kĭ-rĕn′)	165	51°46′N	102°13′E
Kyrgyzstan, nation, Asia	164	41°45′N	74°38′E
Kyrönjoki, r., Fin.	153	63°03′N	22°20′E
Kyrya, Russia (kēr′yȧ)	172a	59°18′N	59°03′E
Kyshtym, Russia (kĭsh-tĭm′)	166	55°42′N	60°34′E
Kytlym, Russia (kĭt′lĭm)	172a	59°30′N	59°15′E
Kyūhōji, neigh., Japan	242b	34°38′N	135°35′E
Kyūshū, i., Japan	189	33°00′N	131°00′E
Kyustendil, Bul. (kyȯs-tĕn-dĭl′)	149	42°16′N	22°39′E
Kyyiv, prov., Ukr.	163	50°05′N	30°40′E
Kyzyl, Russia (kĭ zĭl)	165	51°37′N	93°38′E
Kyzyl-Kum, des., Asia	164	42°47′N	64°45′E

L

PLACE (Pronunciation)	PAGE	LAT.	LONG.
Laa, Aus.	154	48°42′N	16°23′E
Laab im Walde, Aus.	239e	48°09′N	16°11′E
La Almunia de Doña Godina, Spain	158	41°29′N	1°22′W
Laas Caanood, Som.	218a	8°24′N	47°20′E
La Asunción, Ven. (lä ä-so͞on-syōn′)	130	11°02′N	63°57′W
La Baie, Can.	91	48°21′N	70°53′W
La Banda, Arg. (lä bän′dä)	132	27°48′S	64°12′W
La Bandera, Chile	234b	33°34′S	70°39′W
La Barca, Mex. (lä bär′kȧ)	118	20°17′N	102°33′W
Laberge, Lake, l., Can. (lȧ-bĕrzh′)	84	61°08′N	136°42′W
Laberinto de las Doce Leguas, is., Cuba	122	20°40′N	78°35′W
Labinsk, Russia	167	44°30′N	40°40′E
Labis, Malay. (läb′ĭs)	181b	2°23′N	103°01′E
La Bisbal, Spain (lä bēs-bäl′)	159	41°55′N	3°00′E
Labo, Phil. (lä′bȯ)	197a	14°11′N	122°49′E
Labo, Mount, mtn., Phil.	197a	14°00′N	122°47′E
Labouheyre, Fr. (lȧ-bo͞o-âr′)	156	44°14′N	0°58′W
Laboulaye, Arg. (lä-bô′o͞o-lä-yĕ)	132	34°01′S	63°10′W
Labrador, reg., Can. (lăb′rȧ-dôr)	85	53°05′N	63°30′W
Labrador Sea, sea, Can.	93	50°38′N	55°00′W
Lábrea, Braz. (lä-brā′ä)	130	7°28′S	64°39′W
Labuan, Pulau, i., Malay. (lä-bȯ-än′)	196	5°28′N	115°11′E
Labuha, Indon.	197	0°43′S	127°35′E
L'Acadie, Can. (lȧ-kȧ-dē′)	83a	45°18′N	73°22′W
L'Acadie, r., Can.	83a	45°24′N	73°21′W
La Calera, Chile (lä-kä-lĕ-rä)	129b	32°47′S	71°11′W
La Calera, Col.	130a	4°43′N	73°58′W
Lac Allard, Can.	92	50°38′N	63°28′W
La Canada, Ca., U.S. (lä kän-yä′dä)	107a	34°13′N	118°12′W
La Candelaria, Mex.	233a	19°20′N	99°09′W
Lacantum, r., Mex. (lä-kän-to͞o′m)	119	16°13′N	90°52′W
La Carolina, Spain (lä kä-rȯ-lē′nä)	158	38°16′N	3°48′W
La Catedral, Cerro, mtn., Mex. (sĕ′r-rȯ-lä-kä-tĕ-drȧ′l)	119a	19°32′N	99°31′W
Lac-Beauport, Can. (läk-bō-pōr′)	83b	46°58′N	71°17′W
Laccadive Islands *see* Lakshadweep, is., India	183	11°00′N	73°02′E
Laccadive Sea, sea, Asia	187	9°10′N	75°17′E
Lac Court Oreille Indian Reservation, I.R., Wi., U.S.	103	46°04′N	91°18′W
Lac du Flambeau Indian Reservation, I.R., Wi., U.S.	103	46°12′N	89°50′W
La Ceiba, Hond. (lȧ sēbä)	116	15°45′N	86°52′W
La Ceja, Col. (lä-sĕ-κä)	130a	6°02′N	75°25′W
Lac-Frontière, Can.	85	46°42′N	70°00′W
Lacha, l., Russia (lȧ′chä)	166	61°15′N	39°05′E
La Chaux de Fonds, Switz. (lȧ shō dẽ-fôɴ′)	154	47°07′N	6°47′E
L'Achigan, r., Can. (lä-shē-gäɴ)	83a	45°49′N	73°48′W
Lachine, Can. (lȧ-shēn′)	83a	45°26′N	73°40′W
Lachlan, r., Austl. (läk′lăn)	203	34°00′S	145°00′E
La Chorrera, Pan. (lȧchȯr-rā′rä)	121	8°54′N	79°47′W
Lachta, neigh., Russia	239a	60°00′N	30°10′E
Lachute, Can. (lȧ-sho͞ot′)	91	45°39′N	74°20′W
La Ciotat, Fr. (lȧ syȯ-tȧ′)	157	43°13′N	5°35′E
La Cisterna, Chile	234b	33°33′S	70°41′W
Lackawanna, N.Y., U.S. (lak-ȧ-wŏn′á)	101c	42°49′N	78°50′W
Lac La Biche, Can.	84	54°46′N	112°58′W
Lacombe, Can.	84	52°28′N	113°44′W
Laconia, N.H., U.S. (lȧ-kō′nĭ-ȧ)	99	43°30′N	71°30′W
La Conner, Wa., U.S. (lȧ kŏn′ẽr)	106a	48°23′N	122°30′W
La Courneuve, Fr.	237c	48°56′N	2°23′E
Lacreek, l., S.D., U.S. (lå′krēk)	102	43°04′N	101°46′W
La Cresenta, Ca., U.S. (lȧ krĕs′ĕnt-å)	107a	34°14′N	118°13′W
La Cross, Ks., U.S. (lȧ-krôs′)	110	38°30′N	99°20′W
La Crosse, Wi., U.S.	97	43°48′N	91°14′W
La Cruz, Col. (lȧ kro͞oz′)	130	1°37′N	77°00′W
La Cruz, C.R. (lä-kro͞o′z)	120	11°05′N	85°37′W
Lacs, Riviere des, r., N.D., U.S. (rẽ-vyĕr′ de läk)	102	48°30′N	101°45′W
La Cuesta, C.R. (lä-kwĕ′s-tä)	121	8°32′N	82°51′W
La Cygne, Ks., U.S. (lȧ-sēn′y') (lȧ-sēn′)	111	38°20′N	94°45′W
Ladd, Il., U.S. (lăd)	98	41°25′N	89°25′W
Ladíspoli, Italy (lä-dė′s-pô-lē)	159d	41°57′N	12°05′E
Lādīz, Iran	185	28°56′N	61°19′E
Ladner, Can. (lăd′nẽr)	86	49°05′N	123°05′W
Lādnun, India (läd′nȯn)	186	27°45′N	74°20′E
Ladoga, Lake *see* Ladozhskoye Ozero, l., Russia	164	60°59′N	31°30′E
La Dolorita, Ven.	234a	10°29′N	66°47′W
La Dorado, Col. (lä dȯ-rä′dȧ)	130	5°28′N	74°42′W
Ladozhskoye Ozero, Russia (lȧ-dôsh′skô-yē ô′zĕ-rô)	164	60°59′N	31°30′E
La Durantaye, Can. (lä dü-räɴ-tā′)	83b	46°51′N	70°51′W
Lady Frere, S. Afr. (lā-dē frâ′r')	213c	31°48′S	27°16′E
Lady Grey, S. Afr.	213c	30°44′S	27°17′E
Ladysmith, Can. (lā′dĭ-smĭth)	86	48°58′N	123°49′W
Ladysmith, S. Afr.	212	28°38′S	29°48′E
Ladysmith, Wi., U.S.	103	45°27′N	91°07′W
Lae, Pap. N. Gui. (lä′å)	197	6°15′S	146°57′E
Laerdalsøyri, Nor.	152	61°08′N	7°26′E
La Esperanza, Hond. (lä ĕs-på-rän′zä)	120	14°20′N	88°21′W
Lafayette, Al., U.S.	114	32°52′N	85°25′W
Lafayette, Ca., U.S.	106b	37°53′N	122°07′W
Lafayette, Ga., U.S. (lă-fā-yĕt′)	114	34°41′N	85°19′W
Lafayette, In., U.S.	97	40°25′N	86°55′W
Lafayette, La., U.S.	97	30°15′N	92°02′W
La Fayette, R.I., U.S.	100b	41°34′N	71°29′W
Lafayette Hill, Pa., U.S.	229b	40°05′N	75°15′W
Laferrere, Arg.	233d	34°45′S	58°35′W
La Ferté-Alais, Fr. (lä-fĕr-tā′ä-lā′)	157b	48°29′N	2°19′E
La Ferté-sous-Jouarre, Fr. (lȧ fĕr-tā′so͞o-zho͞o-är′)	157b	48°56′N	3°07′E
Lafia, Nig.	215	8°30′N	8°30′E
Lafiagi, Nig.	215	8°52′N	5°25′E
Laflèche, Can.	227b	45°30′N	73°28′W
La Flèche, Fr. (lȧ flāsh′)	156	47°43′N	0°03′W
La Floresta, Spain	238e	41°27′N	2°04′E
La Florida, Chile	234b	33°32′S	70°33′W
La Follete, Tn., U.S. (lä-fŏl′ĕt)	114	36°23′N	84°07′W
Lafourche, Bayou, r., La., U.S. (bă-yo͞o′lȧ-fo͞orsh′)	113	29°25′N	90°15′W
La Frette-sur-Seine, Fr.	237c	48°58′N	2°11′E
La Gaiba, Braz. (lä-gī′bä)	131	17°54′S	57°32′W
La Galite, i., Tun. (gä-lēt)	148	37°36′N	8°03′E
Lågan, r., Nor. (lô′ghĕn)	142	61°00′N	10°00′E
Lagan, r., Swe.	152	56°34′N	13°25′E
Lagan, r., N. Ire., U.K. (lā′găn)	150	54°30′N	6°00′W
La Garenne-Colombes, Fr.	237c	48°55′N	2°15′E
Lagarto, r., Pan. (lä-gä′r-tô)	116a	9°08′N	80°05′W
Lagartos, l., Mex. (lä-gä′r-tôs)	120a	21°32′N	88°15′W
Laghouat, Alg. (lä-gwät′)	210	33°45′N	2°49′E
Lagny, Fr. (län-yē′)	157b	48°53′N	2°41′E
Lagoa da Prata, Braz. (lȧ-gô′ä-dȧ-prä′tȧ)	129a	20°04′S	45°33′W
Lagoa Dourada, Braz. (lȧ-gô′ä-dȯ-rä′dä)	129a	20°55′S	44°03′W
Lagogne, Fr. (laɴ-gōn′y')	156	44°43′N	3°50′E
Lagonay, Phil.	197a	13°44′N	123°31′E
Lagos, Nig. (lä′gōs)	210	6°27′N	3°24′E
Lagos, Port. (lä′gȯzh)	158	37°08′N	8°43′W
Lagos de Moreno, Mex. (lä′gōs dā mȯ-rā′nō)	116	21°21′N	101°55′W
La Grand' Combe, Fr. (lȧ gräɴ kaɴb′)	156	44°12′N	4°03′E
La Grande, Or., U.S. (lȧ grănd′)	96	45°20′N	118°06′W
La Grande, r., Can.	85	53°55′N	77°30′W
La Grange, Austl. (lä grānj)	202	18°40′S	122°00′E
La Grange, Ga., U.S. (lȧ-grānj′)	97	33°01′N	85°00′W
La Grange, Il., U.S.	101a	41°49′N	87°53′W
Lagrange, In., U.S.	98	41°40′N	85°25′W
La Grange, Ky., U.S.	98	38°20′N	85°25′W
La Grange, Mo., U.S.	111	40°04′N	91°30′W
Lagrange, Oh., U.S.	101d	41°14′N	82°07′W
Lagrange, Tx., U.S.	113	29°55′N	96°50′W
La Grange Highlands, Il., U.S.	231a	41°48′N	87°53′W
La Grange Park, Il., U.S.	231a	41°50′N	87°52′W
La Granja, Chile	234b	33°32′S	70°39′W
La Grita, Ven. (lä grē′tȧ)	130	8°02′N	71°59′W
La Guaira, Ven. (lä gwä′ė-rä)	130	10°36′N	66°54′W
La Guardia, Spain (lä gwär′dė-ȧ)	158	41°55′N	8°48′W
La Guardia Airport, arpt., N.Y., U.S.	228	40°46′N	73°53′W
Laguna, Braz. (lä-go͞o′nä)	132	28°19′S	48°42′W
Laguna, Cayos, is., Cuba (kä′yōs-lä-gȯ′nă)	122	22°15′N	82°45′W
Laguna Indian Reservation, I.R., N.M., U.S.	109	35°00′N	107°30′W
Lagunillas, Bol. (lä-go͞o-nēl′yäs)	130	19°42′S	63°38′W
Lagunillas, Mex. (lä-go͞o-nė′l-yäs)	118	21°34′N	99°41′W
La Habana *see* Havana, Cuba	117	23°08′N	82°23′W
La Habra, Ca., U.S. (lȧ hȧb′rȧ)	107a	34°56′N	117°57′W
La Habra Heights, Ca., U.S.	232	33°57′N	117°57′W
Lahaina, Hi., U.S. (lä-hä′ē-nä)	94a	20°52′N	156°39′W
La Häy-les-Roses, Fr.	237c	48°47′N	2°21′E
Lāhījān, Iran	185	37°12′N	50°01′E
Laholm, Swe. (lä′hȯlm)	152	56°30′N	13°00′E
La Honda, Ca., U.S. (lā hôn′dă)	106b	37°20′N	122°16′W
Lahore, Pak. (lä-hōr′)	183	32°00′N	74°18′E
Lahr, Ger. (lär)	154	48°19′N	7°52′E
Lahti, Fin. (lä′tė)	146	60°59′N	27°39′E
Lai, Chad	211	9°29′N	16°18′E
Lai'an, China (lī-än)	190	32°27′N	118°25′E
Laibin, China (lī-bĭn)	193	23°42′N	109°20′E
L'Aigle, Fr. (lĕ′gl')	156	48°45′N	0°37′E
Lainate, Italy	238c	45°34′N	9°02′E
Lainz, neigh., Aus.	239e	48°11′N	16°17′E
Laisamis, Kenya	217	1°36′N	37°48′E
Laiyang, China (läī′yäɴg)	192	36°59′N	120°42′E
Laizhou Wan, b., China (lī-jō wän)	189	37°22′N	119°19′E
Laja, Río de la, r., Mex. (rė′ō-dĕ-lä-lȧ′κä)	118	21°17′N	100°57′W
Lajas, Cuba (lä′häs)	122	22°25′N	80°20′W
Laje, Ponta da, c., Port.	238d	38°40′N	9°19′W

ăt; finăl; rāte; senåte; ärm; åsk; sofȧ; fâre; ch-choose; dh-as th in other; bē; ėvent; bĕt; recĕnt; cratẽr; g-gō; gh-guttural g; bĭt; ĭ-short neutral; rīde; κ-guttural k as ch in German ich;

PRONOUNCING INDEX

Lajeado – Las Juntas 307

PLACE (Pronunciation)	PAGE	LAT.	LONG.
Lajeado, Braz. (lä-zhĕä'dô)	132	29°24'S	51°46'W
Lajeado Velho, neigh., Braz.	234d	23°32'S	46°23'W
Lajes, Braz. (lä'zhĕs)	132	27°47'S	50°17'W
Lajinha, Braz. (lä-zhē'nyä)	129a	20°08'S	41°36'W
La Jolla, Ca., U.S. (lá hoi'yá)	108a	32°51'N	117°16'W
La Jolla Indian Reservation, I.R., Ca., U.S.	108	33°19'N	116°21'W
La Junta, Co., U.S. (lá hōōn'tá)	110	37°59'N	103°35'W
Lake Arrowhead, Ca., U.S.	232	33°52'N	118°05'W
Lake Arthur, La., U.S. (är'thŭr)	113	30°06'N	92°40'W
Lake Barcroft, Va., U.S.	229d	38°51'N	77°09'W
Lake Barkley, res., U.S.	114	36°45'N	88°00'W
Lake Benton, Mn., U.S. (bĕn'tŭn)	102	44°15'N	96°17'W
Lake Bluff, Il., U.S. (blŭf)	101a	42°17'N	87°50'W
Lake Brown, Austl. (broun)	202	31°03'S	118°30'E
Lake Charles, La., U.S. (chärlz')	97	30°15'N	93°14'W
Lake City, Fl., U.S.	115	30°09'N	82°40'W
Lake City, Ia., U.S.	103	42°14'N	94°43'W
Lake City, Mn., U.S.	103	44°28'N	92°19'W
Lake City, S.C., U.S.	115	33°57'N	79°45'W
Lake Clark National Park, rec., Ak., U.S.	95	60°30'N	153°15'W
Lake Cowichan, Can. (kou'ĭ-chăn)	86	48°50'N	124°03'W
Lake Crystal, Mn., U.S. (krĭs'tăl)	103	44°05'N	94°12'W
Lake District, reg., Eng., U.K. (lāk)	150	54°25'N	3°20'W
Lake Elmo, Mn., U.S. (ĕlmō)	107g	45°00'N	92°53'W
Lake Forest, Il., U.S. (fŏr'ĕst)	101a	42°16'N	87°50'W
Lake Fork, r., Ut., U.S.	109	40°30'N	110°25'W
Lake Geneva, Wi., U.S. (jĕ-nē'vá)	103	42°36'N	88°28'W
Lake Harbour, Can. (här'bĕr)	85	62°43'N	69°40'W
Lake Havasu City, Az., U.S.	109	34°27'N	114°22'W
Lake June, Tx., U.S. (jōōn)	107c	32°43'N	96°45'W
Lakeland, Fl., U.S. (lāk'lănd)	97	28°02'N	81°58'W
Lakeland, Ga., U.S.	114	31°02'N	83°02'W
Lakeland, Mn., U.S.	107g	44°57'N	92°47'W
Lake Linden, Mi., U.S. (lĭn'dĕn)	103	47°11'N	88°26'W
Lake Louise, Can. (lōō-ēz')	87	51°26'N	116°11'W
Lakemba, Austl.	243a	33°55'S	151°05'E
Lake Mead National Recreation Area, rec., U.S.	109	36°00'N	114°30'W
Lake Mills, Ia., U.S. (mĭlz')	103	43°25'N	93°32'W
Lakemore, Oh., U.S. (lāk-mōr)	101d	41°01'N	81°24'W
Lake Odessa, Mi., U.S.	98	42°50'N	85°15'W
Lake Oswego, Or., U.S. (ŏs-wē'go)	106c	45°25'N	122°40'W
Lake Placid, N.Y., U.S.	99	44°17'N	73°59'W
Lake Point, Ut., U.S.	107b	40°41'N	112°16'W
Lakeport, Ca., U.S. (lāk'pōrt)	108	39°03'N	122°54'W
Lake Preston, S.D., U.S. (prĕs'tŭn)	102	44°21'N	97°23'W
Lake Providence, La., U.S. (prŏv'ĭ-dĕns)	113	32°48'N	91°12'W
Lake Red Rock, res., Ia., U.S.	103	41°30'N	93°15'W
Lake Sharpe, res., S.D., U.S.	102	44°30'N	100°00'W
Lakeside, S. Afr.	244b	26°06'S	28°09'E
Lakeside, Ca., U.S. (lāk'sīd)	108a	32°52'N	116°55'W
Lake Station, In., U.S.	101a	41°34'N	87°15'W
Lake Stevens, Wa., U.S.	106a	48°01'N	122°04'W
Lake Success, N.Y., U.S. (sŭk-sĕs')	100a	40°46'N	73°43'W
Lakeview, Or., U.S.	104	42°11'N	120°21'W
Lakeview, neigh., Il., U.S.	231a	41°57'N	87°39'W
Lake Village, Ar., U.S.	111	33°20'N	91°17'W
Lake Wales, Fl., U.S. (wālz')	115a	27°54'N	81°35'W
Lakewood, Ca., U.S. (lāk'wŏŏd)	107a	33°50'N	118°09'W
Lakewood, Co., U.S.	110	39°44'N	105°06'W
Lakewood, Oh., U.S.	97	41°29'N	81°48'W
Lakewood, Pa., U.S.	99	40°05'N	74°10'W
Lakewood, Wa., U.S.	106a	48°09'N	122°13'W
Lakewood Center, Wa., U.S.	106a	47°10'N	122°31'W
Lake Worth, Fl., U.S. (wûrth')	115a	26°37'N	80°04'W
Lake Worth Village, Tx., U.S.	107c	32°49'N	97°26'W
Lake Zurich, Il., U.S. (tsü'rĭk)	101a	42°11'N	88°05'W
Lakhdenpokh'ya, Russia (l'äk-dĭe'npoκyȧ)	153	61°33'N	30°10'E
Lakhtinskiy, Russia (lák-tĭn'skĭ)	172c	59°59'N	30°10'E
Lakota, N.D., U.S. (lá-kō'tá)	102	48°04'N	98°21'W
Lakshadweep, state, India	183	10°10'N	72°50'E
Lakshadweep, is., India	183	11°00'N	73°02'E
Laleham, Eng., U.K.	235	51°25'N	0°30'W
La Libertad, El Sal.	120	13°29'N	89°20'W
La Libertad, Guat. (lä lē-bĕr-tädh')	120	15°31'N	91°44'W
La Libertad, Guat.	120a	16°46'N	90°12'W
La Ligua, Chile (lä lē'gwä)	129b	32°21'S	71°13'W
Lalín, Spain (lä-lē'n)	158	42°40'N	8°05'W
La Línea, Spain (lä lē'nȧ-ä)	148	36°11'N	5°22'W
La Lisa, Cuba	233b	23°04'N	82°26'W
Lalitpur, Nepal	183	27°23'N	85°24'E
La Louviere, Bel. (lá lōō-vyâr')	151	50°30'N	4°10'E
La Luz, Mex. (lä lōōz')	118	21°04'N	101°19'W
Lama-Kara, Togo	214	9°33'N	1°12'E
La Malbaie, Can. (lá mäl-bā')	85	47°39'N	70°10'W
La Mancha, reg., Spain (lä män'chä)	158	38°55'N	4°20'W
Lamar, Co., U.S. (lá-mär')	110	38°04'N	102°44'W
Lamar, Mo., U.S.	111	37°28'N	94°15'W
La Marmora, Punta, mtn., Italy (lä-mä'r-mô-rä)	148	40°00'N	9°28'E
La Marque, Tx., U.S. (lá-märk)	113a	29°23'N	94°58'W
Lamas, Peru (lä'mȧs)	130	6°24'S	76°41'W
Lamballe, Fr. (läN-bäl')	156	48°29'N	2°36'W
Lambari, Braz. (läm-bá'rē)	129a	21°58'S	45°22'W
Lambasa, Fiji	198g	16°26'S	179°24'E
Lambayeque, Peru (läm-bä-yā'kå)	130	6°41'S	79°58'W
Lambert, Ms., U.S. (lăm'bẽrt)	114	34°10'N	90°16'W
Lambertville, N.J., U.S. (lăm'bẽrt-vĭl)	99	40°20'N	75°00'W
Lambeth, neigh., Eng., U.K.	235	51°28'N	0°07'W
Lambourne End, Eng., U.K.	235	51°38'N	0°08'E
Lambrate, neigh., Italy	238c	45°29'N	9°15'E
Lambro, r., Italy	238c	45°26'N	9°16'E
Lambton, S. Afr.	244b	26°15'S	28°10'E
Lame Deer, Mt., U.S. (lām dēr')	105	45°36'N	106°40'W
Lamego, Port. (lä-mā'gō)	158	41°07'N	7°47'W
La Mesa, Col.	130a	4°38'N	74°27'W
La Mesa, Ca., U.S. (lä mā'sä)	108a	32°46'N	117°01'W
Lamesa, Tx., U.S.	110	32°44'N	101°54'W
Lamía, Grc. (lá-mē'á)	149	38°54'N	22°25'E
La Mirada, Ca., U.S.	232	33°54'N	118°01'W
Lamon Bay, b., Phil. (lä-mōn')	196	14°35'N	121°52'E
La Mora, Chile (lä-mō'rä)	129b	32°28'S	70°56'W
La Mott, Pa., U.S.	229b	40°04'N	75°08'W
La Moure, N.D., U.S. (lá mōōr')	102	46°23'N	98°17'W
Lampa, r., Chile (lá'm-pä)	129b	33°15'S	70°55'W
Lampasas, Tx., U.S. (lăm-păs'ás)	112	31°06'N	98°10'W
Lampasas, r., Tx., U.S.	112	31°18'N	98°08'W
Lampazos, Mex. (läm-pä'zōs)	116	27°03'N	100°30'W
Lampedusa, i., Italy (läm-pȧ-dōō'sä)	148	35°29'N	12°58'E
Lamstedt, Ger. (läm'shtĕt)	145c	53°38'N	9°06'E
Lamu, Kenya (lä'mōō)	213	2°16'S	40°54'E
Lamu Island, i., Kenya	217	2°25'S	40°50'E
La Mure, Fr. (lá mür')	157	44°55'N	5°50'E
Lan', r., Bela. (lán')	162	52°38'N	27°05'E
Lanai, i., Hi., U.S. (lä-nä'ē)	96c	20°48'N	157°06'W
Lanai City, Hi., U.S.	94a	20°50'N	156°56'W
Lanak La, p., China	188	34°40'N	79°50'E
Lanark, Scot., U.K. (lăn'árk)	150	55°40'N	3°50'W
Lancashire, co., Eng., U.K. (lăŋ'kă-shĭr)	144a	53°49'N	2°42'W
Lancaster, Eng., U.K.	146	54°04'N	2°55'W
Lancaster, Ky., U.S.	98	37°35'N	84°30'W
Lancaster, Ma., U.S.	93a	42°28'N	71°40'W
Lancaster, N.H., U.S.	99	44°25'N	71°30'W
Lancaster, N.Y., U.S.	101c	42°54'N	78°42'W
Lancaster, Oh., U.S.	98	39°40'N	82°35'W
Lancaster, Pa., U.S.	97	40°05'N	76°20'W
Lancaster, Tx., U.S.	107c	32°36'N	96°45'W
Lancaster, Wi., U.S.	103	42°51'N	90°44'W
Lândana, Ang. (län-dä'nä)	212	5°15'S	12°07'E
Landau, Ger. (län'dou)	154	49°13'N	8°07'E
Lander, Wy., U.S. (lăn'dẽr)	105	42°49'N	108°24'W
Landerneau, Fr. (läN-dĕr-nō')	156	48°28'N	4°14'W
Landes, reg., Fr. (länd)	156	44°22'N	0°52'W
Landover, Md., U.S.	229d	38°56'N	76°54'W
Landsberg, Ger. (länds'bōōrgh)	154	48°03'N	10°53'E
Lands End, c., Eng., U.K.	142	50°03'N	5°45'W
Landshut, Ger. (länts'hōōt)	147	48°32'N	12°09'E
Landskrona, Swe. (lȧns-krō'nȧ)	152	55°51'N	12°47'E
Lane Cove, Austl.	243a	33°49'S	151°10'E
Lanett, Al., U.S. (lȧ-nĕt')	114	32°52'N	85°13'W
Langadhás, Grc.	161	40°44'N	23°10'E
Langat, r., Malay.	181b	2°46'N	101°33'E
Langdon, Can. (lăng'dŭn)	83e	50°58'N	113°40'W
Langdon, Mn., U.S.	107g	44°49'N	92°56'W
Langdon Hills, Eng., U.K.	235	51°34'N	0°25'E
L'Ange-Gardien, Can. (länzh gȧr-dyăN')	83b	46°55'N	71°06'W
Langeland, i., Den.	152	54°52'N	10°46'E
Langenberg, Ger.	236	51°21'N	7°09'E
Langenbochum, Ger.	236	51°37'N	7°07'E
Langendreer, neigh., Ger.	236	51°28'N	7°19'E
Langenhorst, Ger.	236	51°22'N	7°02'E
Langenzersdorf, Aus.	145e	48°30'N	16°22'E
Langesund, Nor. (läng'ĕ-sōn')	152	58°59'N	9°38'E
Langfjorden, fj., Nor.	152	62°40'N	7°45'E
Langhorne, Pa., U.S. (lăng'hôrn)	100f	40°10'N	74°55'W
Langhorne Acres, Md., U.S.	229d	38°51'N	77°16'W
Langia Mountains, mts., Ug.	217	3°35'N	33°35'E
Langjökull, ice., Ice. (läng-yû'kōōl)	146	64°40'N	20°31'W
Langla Co, l., China (läŋ-lä tswo)	186	30°42'N	80°40'E
Langley, Can. (lăng'lĭ)	87	49°06'N	122°39'W
Langley, Md., U.S.	229d	38°57'N	77°10'W
Langley, S.C., U.S.	115	33°32'N	81°52'W
Langley, Wa., U.S.	106a	48°02'N	122°25'W
Langley Indian Reserve, I.R., Can.	106d	49°12'N	122°31'W
Langley Park, Md., U.S.	229d	38°59'N	76°59'W
Langnau, Switz. (läng'nou)	154	46°56'N	7°46'E
Langon, Fr. (läN-gôN')	156	44°34'N	0°16'W
Langres, Fr. (läN'gr')	157	47°53'N	5°20'E
Langres, Plateau de, plat., Fr. (plä-tō'dĕ-läN'grĕ)	156	47°39'N	5°00'E
Langsa, Indon. (läng'sȧ)	196	4°33'N	97°52'E
Lang Son, Viet (läng'sŏn')	196	21°52'N	106°42'E
Langst-Kierst, Ger.	236	51°18'N	6°43'E
L'Anguille, r., Ar., U.S. (läN-gē'y')	111	35°23'N	90°52'W
Langxi, China (läŋ-shyē)	190	31°10'N	119°09'E
Langzhong, China (läŋ-jȯŋ)	188	31°40'N	106°05'E
Lanham, Md., U.S. (lăn'ăm)	100e	38°58'N	76°54'W
Lanigan, Can. (lăn'ĭ-găn)	84	51°52'N	105°02'W
Länkäran, Azer. (lĕn-kô-rän')	164	38°52'N	48°58'E
Lank-Latum, Ger.	236	51°18'N	6°41'E
Lankoviri, Nig.	215	9°00'N	11°25'E
Lankwitz, neigh., Ger.	238a	52°26'N	13°21'E
Lansdale, Pa., U.S. (lănz'dāl)	99	40°20'N	75°15'W
Lansdowne, Austl.	243a	33°54'S	150°59'E
Lansdowne, Md., U.S.	229c	39°15'N	76°40'W
Lansdowne, Pa., U.S.	100f	39°57'N	75°17'W
L'Anse, Mi., U.S. (làns)	103	46°43'N	88°28'W
L'Anse and Vieux Desert Indian Reservation, I.R., Mi., U.S.	103	46°41'N	88°12'W
Lansford, Pa., U.S. (lănz'fẽrd)	99	40°50'N	75°50'W
Lansing, Il., U.S.	101a	41°34'N	87°33'W
Lansing, Ia., U.S.	103	43°22'N	91°16'W
Lansing, Ks., U.S.	107f	39°15'N	94°53'W
Lansing, Mi., U.S.	97	42°45'N	84°35'W
Lansing, neigh., Can.	227c	43°45'N	79°25'W
Lantianchang, China	240b	39°58'N	116°17'E
Lanús, Arg. (lä-nōōs')	132a	34°42'S	58°24'W
Lanusei, Italy (lä-nōō-sĕ'y)	160	39°51'N	9°34'E
Lanúvio, Italy (lä-nōō'vyô)	159d	41°41'N	12°42'E
Lanzarote Island, i., Spain (län-zá-rō'tä)	210	29°04'N	13°03'W
Lanzhou, China (län-jō)	188	35°55'N	103°55'E
Laoag, Phil. (lä-wäg')	196	18°13'N	120°38'E
Laohumiao, China	240b	39°58'N	116°20'E
Laon, Fr. (läN)	156	49°36'N	3°35'E
La Oroya, Peru (lä-ô-rō'yă)	130	11°30'S	76°00'W
Laos, nation, Asia (lä-ōs) (lá-ōs')	196	20°15'N	102°00'E
Laoshan Wan, b., China (lou-shän wän)	190	36°21'N	120°48'E
Lapa, neigh., Braz.	234c	22°55'S	43°11'W
La Palma, Pan. (lä-päl'mä)	121	8°25'N	78°07'W
La Palma, Spain	158	37°24'N	6°36'W
La Palma Island, i., Spain	210	28°42'N	19°03'W
La Pampa, prov., Arg.	132	37°25'S	67°00'W
Lapa Rio Negro, Braz. (lä-pä-rē'ō-nĕ'grô)	132	26°12'S	49°56'W
La Paternal, neigh., Arg.	233d	34°36'S	58°28'W
La Paz, Arg. (lä päz')	132	30°48'S	59°47'W
La Paz, Bol.	130	16°31'S	68°03'W
La Paz, Hond.	120	14°15'N	87°40'W
La Paz, Mex.	116	24°00'N	110°15'W
La Paz, Mex. (lä-pá'z)	118	23°39'N	100°44'W
Lapeer, Mi., U.S. (lá-pēr')	98	43°05'N	83°15'W
La-Penne-sur-Huveaune, Fr. (la-pĕn'sür-ü-vōn')	156a	43°18'N	5°33'E
La Perouse, Austl.	201b	33°59'S	151°14'E
La Piedad Cabadas, Mex. (lä pyä-dhädh' kä-bä'dhäs)	118	20°20'N	102°04'W
Lapland, hist. reg., Eur. (lăp'lănd)	142	68°20'N	22°00'E
La Plata, Arg. (lä plä'tä)	132	34°54'S	57°57'W
La Plata, Mo., U.S. (lá plā'tá)	111	40°03'N	92°28'W
La Plata Peak, mtn., Co., U.S.	109	39°00'N	106°25'W
La Playa, Cuba	233b	23°06'N	82°27'W
La Pocatière, Can. (lá pô-kà-tyȧr')	91	47°24'N	70°01'W
La Poile Bay, b., Can. (lá pwäl')	93	47°38'N	58°20'W
La Porte, In., U.S. (lá pōrt')	98	41°35'N	86°45'W
Laporte, Oh., U.S.	101d	41°19'N	82°05'W
La Porte, Tx., U.S.	113a	29°40'N	95°01'W
La Porte City, Ia., U.S.	103	42°20'N	92°10'W
Lappeenranta, Fin. (lä'pĕn-rän'tä)	153	61°04'N	28°08'E
La Prairie, Can. (lá-prâ-rē')	83a	45°24'N	73°30'W
Lâpseki, Tur. (läp'sȧ-kē)	161	40°20'N	26°41'E
Laptev Sea, sea, Russia (läp'tyĭf)	165	75°39'N	120°00'E
La Puebla de Montalbán, Spain	158	39°54'N	4°21'W
La Puente, Ca., U.S. (pwĕn'tē)	107a	34°01'N	117°57'W
La Punta, Peru	233c	12°05'S	77°10'W
Lapuşul, r., Rom. (lä'pōō-shōōl)	155	47°29'N	23°46'E
La Queue-en-Brie, Fr.	237c	48°47'N	2°35'E
La Quiaca, Arg. (lä kē-ä'kä)	132	22°15'S	65°44'W
L'Aquila, Italy (lá'kē-lä)	148	42°22'N	13°24'E
Lār, Iran (lär)	182	27°31'N	54°12'E
Lara, Austl.	201a	38°02'S	144°24'E
Larache, Mor. (lä-räsh')	210	35°15'N	6°09'W
Laramie, Wy., U.S. (lăr'á-mĭ)	96	41°20'N	105°40'W
Laramie, r., Co., U.S.	110	40°56'N	105°55'W
Laranjeiras, neigh., Braz.	234c	22°56'S	43°11'W
Larchmont, N.Y., U.S. (lärch'mŏnt)	100a	40°56'N	73°46'W
Larch Mountain, mtn., Or., U.S. (lärch)	106c	45°32'N	122°06'W
Laredo, Spain (lá-rā'dhō)	158	43°24'N	3°24'W
Laredo, Tx., U.S.	96	27°31'N	99°29'W
La Reina, Chile	234b	33°27'S	70°33'W
La Réole, Fr. (lá rȧ-ōl')	156	44°37'N	0°03'W
Largeau, Chad (lär-zhō')	211	17°55'N	19°07'E
Largo, Cayo, Cuba (kä'yō-lär'gō)	122	21°40'N	81°30'W
Larimore, N.D., U.S. (lăr'ĭ-môr)	102	47°53'N	97°38'W
Larino, Italy (lä-rē'nô)	160	41°48'N	14°54'E
La Rioja, Arg. (lä rē-ōhä)	132	29°18'S	67°42'W
La Rioja, prov., Arg. (lä-rē-ô'kä)	132	28°45'S	68°00'W
Lárisa, Grc. (lä'rē-sá)	149	39°38'N	22°25'E
Lārkāna, Pak.	186	27°40'N	68°12'E
Larkspur, Ca., U.S.	231b	37°56'N	122°32'W
Larnaca, Cyp.	149	34°55'N	33°37'E
Lárnakos, Kólpos, b., Cyp.	181a	36°50'N	33°45'E
Larned, Ks., U.S. (lär'nĕd)	110	38°09'N	99°07'W
La Robla, Spain (lä rōb'lä)	158	42°48'N	5°36'W
La Rochelle, Fr. (lá rô-shĕl')	142	46°10'N	1°09'W
La Roche-sur-Yon, Fr. (lá rôsh'sûr-yôN')	147	46°39'N	1°27'W
La Roda, Spain (lä rō'dä)	158	39°13'N	2°08'W
La Romona, Dom. Rep. (lä-rä-mō'nä)	123	18°25'N	69°00'W
Larrey Point, c., Austl. (lăr'ē)	202	19°15'S	118°15'E
Laruns, Fr. (lá-räNs')	156	42°58'N	0°28'W
Larvik, Nor. (lär'vēk)	146	59°06'N	10°03'E
La Sabana, Ven. (lä-sä-bá'nä)	131b	10°38'N	66°24'W
La Sabina, Cuba (lä-sä-bē'nä)	123a	22°51'N	82°05'W
La Sagra, mtn., Spain (lä sä'grä)	148	37°56'N	2°35'W
La Sal, Ut., U.S. (lá sál')	109	38°10'N	109°20'W
La Salle, Can.	83a	45°26'N	73°39'W
La Salle, Can.	83f	49°41'N	97°16'W
La Salle, Can. (lá säl')	101b	42°14'N	83°06'W
La Salle, Il., U.S.	98	41°20'N	89°05'W
Las Animas, Co., U.S. (lás ă'nĭ-más)	110	38°03'N	103°16'W
La Sarre, Can.	85	48°43'N	79°12'W
Lascahobas, Haiti (läs-kä-ō'bȧs)	123	19°00'N	71°55'W
Las Cruces, Mex. (läs-krōō'sĕs)	119	16°37'N	93°54'W
Las Cruces, N.M., U.S.	96	32°20'N	106°50'W
La Selle, Massif de, mtn., Haiti (lá'sĕl')	123	18°25'N	72°05'W
La Serena, Chile (lä-sĕ-rĕ'nä)	132	29°55'S	71°24'W
La Seyne, Fr. (lä-sån')	147	43°07'N	5°52'E
Las Flores, Arg. (läs flō'rĕs)	132	36°01'S	59°07'W
Las Flores, Ven.	234a	10°34'N	66°56'W
Lashio, Myanmar (lăsh'ē-ō)	188	22°58'N	98°03'E
Las Juntas, C.R. (läs-κōō'n-täs)	120	10°15'N	85°00'W

308 Las Maismas – Le Pré-Saint-Gervais

PLACE (Pronunciation)	PAGE	LAT.	LONG.
Las Maismas, sw., Spain (läs-mī′s-mäs)	158	37°05′N	6°25′W
Las Minas, Ven.	234a	10°27′N	66°52′W
La Solana, Spain (lä-sȯ-lä-nä)	158	38°56′N	3°13′W
Las Palmas, Pan.	121	8°08′N	81°30′W
Las Palmas de Gran Canaria, Spain (läs päl′mäs)	210	28°07′N	15°28′W
La Spezia, Italy (lä-spĕ′zyä)	142	44°07′N	9°48′E
Las Piedras, Ur. (läs-pyĕ′dräs)	129c	34°42′S	56°08′W
Las Pilas, vol., Nic. (läs-pē′läs)	120	12°32′N	86°43′W
Las Rejas, Chile	234b	33°28′S	70°44′W
Las Rosas, Mex. (läs rō thäs)	119	16°24′N	92°23′W
Las Rozas de Madrid, Spain (läs rō′thas dā mä-dhrēd′)	159a	40°29′N	3°53′W
Lassee, Aus.	145e	48°14′N	16°50′E
Lassen Peak, mtn., Ca., U.S. (lăs′ĕn)	96	40°30′N	121°32′W
Lassen Volcanic National Park, rec., Ca., U.S.	96	40°43′N	121°35′W
L'Assomption, Can. (lȧs-sôm-syôɴ)	83a	45°50′N	73°25′W
Lass Qoray, Som.	218a	11°13′N	48°19′E
Las Tablas, Pan. (läs tä′bläs)	121	7°48′N	80°16′W
Last Mountain, l., Can. (lȧst moun′tĭn)	84	51°05′N	105°10′W
Lastoursville, Gabon (lȧs-to͞or-vēl′)	212	1°00′S	12°49′E
Las Tres Vírgenes, Volcán, vol., Mex. (vē′r-hĕ-nĕs)	116	26°00′N	111°45′W
Las Tunas, prov., Cuba	122	21°05′N	77°00′W
Las Vacas, Mex. (läs-vȧ′käs)	119	16°24′N	95°48′W
Las Vegas, Chile (läs-vĕ′gäs)	129b	32°50′S	70°59′W
Las Vegas, Nv., U.S. (läs vā′gäs)	96	36°12′N	115°10′W
Las Vegas, N.M., U.S.	96	35°36′N	105°13′W
Las Vegas, Ven. (läs-vĕ′gäs)	131b	10°26′N	64°08′W
Las Vigas, Mex.	119	19°38′N	97°03′W
Las Vizcachas, Meseta de, plat., Arg.	132	49°35′S	71°00′W
Latacunga, Ec. (lä-tä-ko͝oŋ′gä)	130	1°02′S	78°33′W
Latakia *see* Al Lādhiqīyah, Syria	182	35°32′N	35°51′E
La Teste-de-Buch, Fr. (lä-tĕst-dĕ-büsh)	156	44°38′N	1°11′W
Lathrop, Mo., U.S. (lā′thrŭp)	111	39°32′N	94°21′W
Latimer, Eng., U.K.	235	51°41′N	0°33′W
La Tortuga, Isla, i., Ven. (ē′s-lä-lä-tôr-to͞o′gä)	130	10°55′N	65°18′W
Latorytsia, r., Eur.	155	48°27′N	22°30′E
Latourell, Or., U.S. (lȧ-tou′rĕl)	106c	45°32′N	122°13′W
La Tremblade, Fr. (lä-trĕɴ-bläd′)	156	45°45′N	1°12′W
Latrobe, Pa., U.S. (lȧ-trōb′)	99	40°25′N	79°15′W
Lattingtown, N.Y., U.S.	228	40°54′N	73°36′W
La Tuque, Can. (lȧ′tük′)	85	47°27′N	72°49′W
Lātūr, India (lä-to͞or′)	186	18°20′N	76°35′E
Latvia, nation, Eur.	164	57°28′N	24°29′E
Lau Group, is., Fiji	198g	18°20′S	178°30′W
Launceston, Austl. (lôn′sĕs-tŭn)	203	41°35′S	147°22′E
Launceston, Eng., U.K. (lôrn′stŏn)	150	50°38′N	4°26′W
La Unión, Chile (lä-o͞o-nyô′n)	132	40°15′S	73°04′W
La Unión, El Sal.	120	13°18′N	87°51′W
La Unión, Mex. (lä o͞on-nyōn′)	118	17°59′N	101°48′W
La Unión, Spain	148	37°38′N	0°50′W
Laupendahl, Ger.	236	51°21′N	6°56′E
Laura, Austl. (lôrȧ)	203	15°40′S	144°45′E
Laurel, De., U.S. (lô′rĕl)	99	38°30′N	75°40′W
Laurel, Md., U.S.	100e	39°06′N	76°51′W
Laurel, Ms., U.S.	97	31°42′N	89°07′W
Laurel, Mt., U.S.	105	45°41′N	108°45′W
Laurel, Wa., U.S.	106d	48°52′N	122°29′W
Laurel Gardens, Pa., U.S.	230b	40°31′N	80°01′W
Laurel Hollow, N.Y., U.S.	228	40°52′N	73°28′W
Laurelwood, Or., U.S. (lô′rĕl-wo͝od)	106c	45°25′N	123°05′W
Laurens, S.C., U.S. (lô′rĕnz)	115	34°29′N	82°03′W
Laurentian Highlands, hills, Can. (lô′rĕn-tĭ-ȧn)	82	49°00′N	74°50′W
Laurentides, Can. (lô′rĕn-tīdz)	83a	45°51′N	73°46′W
Lauria, Italy (lou′rē-ä)	149	40°03′N	15°02′E
Laurinburg, N.C., U.S. (lô′rĭn-bûrg)	115	34°45′N	79°27′W
Laurium, Mi., U.S. (lô′rĭ-ŭm)	103	47°13′N	88°28′W
Lausanne, Switz. (lō-zȧn′)	142	46°32′N	6°35′E
Laut, Pulau, i., Indon.	196	3°39′S	116°07′E
Lautaro, Chile (lou-tä′rō)	132	38°40′S	72°24′W
Laut Kecil, Kepulauan, is., Indon.	196	4°44′S	115°43′E
Lautoka, Fiji	198g	17°37′S	177°27′E
Lauzon, Can. (lō-zōɴ′)	83b	46°50′N	71°10′W
Lava Beds National Monument, rec., Ca., U.S. (lä′vȧ bĕds)	104	41°38′N	121°44′W
Lavaca, r., Tx., U.S. (lȧ-vák′ȧ)	113	29°05′N	96°50′W
Lava Hot Springs, Id., U.S.	105	42°37′N	111°58′W
Laval, Can.	85	45°31′N	73°44′W
Laval, Fr. (lä-väl′)	147	48°05′N	0°47′W
Laval-des-Rapides, neigh., Can.	227b	45°33′N	73°42′W
Laval-Ouest, neigh., Can.	227b	45°33′N	73°52′W
La Vecilla de Curueño, Spain	158	42°53′N	5°18′W
La Vega, Dom. Rep. (lä-vĕ′gä)	123	19°15′N	70°35′W
La Vega, neigh., Ven.	234a	10°28′N	66°57′W
Lavello, Italy (lä-vĕl′lō)	160	41°05′N	15°50′E
La Verne, Ca., U.S. (lȧ vûrn′)	107a	34°06′N	117°46′W
Laverton, Austl. (lā′vẽr-tŭn)	202	28°45′S	122°30′E
La Victoria, Peru	233c	12°04′S	77°02′W
La Victoria, Ven. (lä vēk-tō′rē-ä)	130	10°14′N	67°20′W
La Vila Joiosa, Spain	159	38°30′N	0°14′W
Lavonia, Ga., U.S. (lȧ-vō′nĭ-ȧ)	114	34°26′N	83°05′W
Lavon Reservoir, res., Tx., U.S.	113	33°06′N	96°20′W
Lavras, Braz. (lä′vräzh)	129a	21°15′S	44°59′W
Lávrion, Grc. (läv′rĭ-ŏn)	161	37°44′N	24°05′E
Lavry, Russia (lou′rȧ)	162	57°35′N	27°28′E
Lawndale, Ca., U.S. (lôn′dāl)	107a	33°54′N	118°22′W
Lawndale, neigh., Il., U.S.	231a	41°51′N	87°43′W
Lawndale, neigh., Pa., U.S.	229b	40°03′N	75°05′W
Lawnside, N.J., U.S.	229b	39°52′N	75°03′W
Lawra, Ghana	214	10°39′N	2°52′W
Lawrence, In., U.S. (lô′rĕns)	101g	39°59′N	86°01′W
Lawrence, Ks., U.S.	97	38°57′N	95°13′W
Lawrence, Ma., U.S.	93a	42°42′N	71°09′W
Lawrence, Pa., U.S.	101e	40°18′N	80°07′W
Lawrenceburg, In., U.S. (lô′rĕns-bûrg)	101f	39°06′N	84°47′W
Lawrenceburg, Ky., U.S.	98	38°00′N	85°00′W
Lawrenceburg, Tn., U.S.	114	35°13′N	87°20′W
Lawrenceville, Ga., U.S. (lô-rĕns-vĭl)	114	33°56′N	83°57′W
Lawrenceville, Il., U.S.	98	38°45′N	87°45′W
Lawrenceville, N.J., U.S.	100a	40°17′N	74°44′W
Lawrenceville, Va., U.S.	115	36°43′N	77°52′W
Lawrenceville, neigh., Pa., U.S.	230b	40°28′N	79°57′W
Lawsonia, Md., U.S. (lô-sō′nĭ-ȧ)	99	38°00′N	75°50′W
Lawton, Ok., U.S. (lô′tŭn)	96	34°36′N	98°25′W
Lawz, Jabal al, mtn., Sau. Ar.	182	28°46′N	35°37′E
Layang Layang, Malay. (lä-yäng′ lä-yäng′)	181b	1°49′N	103°28′E
Laysan, i., Hi., U.S.	94b	26°00′N	171°00′W
Layton, Ut., U.S. (lā′tŭn)	107b	41°04′N	111°58′W
Lazdijai, Lith. (läzh′dē-yī′)	153	54°12′N	23°35′E
Lazio (Latium), hist. reg., Italy	160	42°05′N	12°25′E
Lead, S.D., U.S. (lēd)	96	44°22′N	103°47′W
Leader, Can.	88	50°55′N	109°32′W
Leadville, Co., U.S. (lĕd′vĭl)	110	39°14′N	106°18′W
Leaf, r., Ms., U.S. (lēf)	114	31°43′N	89°20′W
League City, Tx., U.S. (lēg)	113a	29°31′N	95°05′W
Leamington, Can. (lĕm′ĭng-tŭn)	90	42°05′N	82°35′W
Leamington, Eng., U.K. (lĕ′mĭng-tŭn)	150	52°17′N	1°25′W
Leatherhead, Eng., U.K. (lĕdh′ẽr-hĕd′)	144b	51°17′N	0°20′W
Leavenworth, Ks., U.S. (lĕv′ĕn-wûrth)	97	39°19′N	94°54′W
Leavenworth, Wa., U.S.	104	47°35′N	120°39′W
Leawood, Ks., U.S. (lē′wo͝od)	107f	38°58′N	94°37′W
Łeba, Pol. (lā′bä)	155	54°45′N	17°34′E
Lebam, r., Malay.	181b	1°35′N	104°09′E
Lebango, Congo	216	0°22′N	14°49′E
Lebanon, Il., U.S. (lĕb′ȧ-nŭn)	107e	38°36′N	89°49′W
Lebanon, In., U.S.	98	40°00′N	86°30′W
Lebanon, Ky., U.S.	114	37°32′N	85°15′W
Lebanon, Mo., U.S.	111	37°40′N	92°43′W
Lebanon, N.H., U.S.	99	43°40′N	72°15′W
Lebanon, Oh., U.S.	98	39°25′N	84°10′W
Lebanon, Or., U.S.	104	44°31′N	122°53′W
Lebanon, Pa., U.S.	99	40°20′N	76°20′W
Lebanon, Tn., U.S.	114	36°10′N	86°16′W
Lebanon, nation, Asia	182	34°00′N	34°00′E
Lebedyan', Russia (lyĕ′bĕ-dyän′)	166	53°03′N	39°08′E
Lebedyn, Ukr.	167	50°34′N	34°27′E
Le Blanc, Fr. (lĕ-bläɴ′)	156	46°38′N	0°59′E
Le Blanc-Mesnil, Fr.	237c	48°56′N	2°28′E
Leblon, neigh., Braz.	234c	22°59′S	43°13′W
Le Borgne, Haiti (lẽ bōrn′y')	123	19°50′N	72°30′W
Lębork, Pol. (lăɴ-bo͝ork′)	155	54°33′N	17°46′E
Le Bourget, Fr.	237c	48°56′N	2°26′E
Lebrija, Spain (lå-brē′hä)	158	36°55′N	6°06′W
Lecce, Italy (lĕt′chā)	149	40°22′N	18°11′E
Lecco, Italy (lĕk′kō)	160	45°52′N	9°28′E
Lech, r., Ger. (lĕk)	154	47°41′N	10°52′E
Le Châtelet-en-Brie, Fr. (lĕ-shä-tĕ-lā′ĕɴ-brē′)	157b	48°29′N	2°50′E
Leche, Laguna de, l., Cuba (lä-go͝o′nä-dĕ-lĕ′chĕ)	122	22°10′N	78°30′W
Leche, Laguna de la, l., Mex.	112	27°16′N	102°45′W
Lecompte, La., U.S.	113	31°06′N	92°25′W
Le Creusot, Fr. (lĕkrû-zō)	147	46°48′N	4°23′E
Ledesma, Spain (lå-dĕs′mä)	158	41°05′N	5°59′W
Ledsham, Eng., U.K.	237a	53°16′N	2°58′W
Leduc, Can. (lĕ-do͞ok′)	87	53°16′N	113°33′W
Leech, l., Mn., U.S. (lēch)	103	47°06′N	94°16′W
Leeds, Eng., U.K.	142	53°48′N	1°33′W
Leeds, Al., U.S. (lēdz)	100h	33°33′N	86°33′W
Leeds, N.D., U.S.	102	48°18′N	99°24′W
Leeds and Liverpool Canal, can., Eng., U.K. (lĭv′ẽr-po͞ol)	144a	53°36′N	2°38′W
Leegebruch, Ger. (lĕh′gĕn-bro͞oĸ)	145b	52°43′N	13°12′E
Leek, Eng., U.K. (lēk)	144a	53°06′N	2°01′W
Lee Manor, Va., U.S.	229d	38°52′N	77°15′W
Leer, Ger. (lār)	154	53°14′N	7°27′E
Lees, Eng., U.K.	237b	53°32′N	2°04′W
Leesburg, Fl., U.S. (lēz′bûrg)	115	28°49′N	81°53′W
Leesburg, Va., U.S.	99	39°10′N	77°30′W
Lees Summit, Mo., U.S.	107f	38°55′N	94°23′W
Lee Stocking, i., Bah.	122	23°45′N	76°05′W
Leesville, La., U.S. (lēz′vĭl)	113	31°09′N	93°17′W
Leetonia, Oh., U.S. (lė-tō′nĭ-ȧ)	98	40°50′N	80°45′W
Leeuwarden, Neth. (lā′wär-dĕn)	147	52°12′N	5°50′E
Leeuwin, Cape, c., Austl. (lo͞o′wĭn)	202	34°15′S	114°30′E
Leeward Islands, is., N.A. (lē′wẽrd)	113	17°00′N	62°15′W
Le François, Mart.	121b	14°37′N	60°55′W
Lefroy, l., Austl. (lē-froi′)	202	31°30′S	122°00′E
Leganés, Spain (lå-gä′nås)	159a	40°20′N	3°46′W
Legazpi, Phil. (lå-gäs′pė)	197	13°09′N	123°44′E
Legge Peak, mtn., Austl. (lĕg)	204	41°33′S	148°10′E
Leggett, Ca., U.S.	108	39°51′N	123°42′W
Leghorn *see* Livorno, Italy	142	43°32′N	11°18′E
Legnano, Italy (lå-nyä′nō)	160	45°35′N	8°53′E
Legnica, Pol. (lĕk-nĭt′sȧ)	147	51°13′N	16°10′E
Leh, India (lā)	186	34°10′N	77°40′E
Le Havre, Fr. (lẽ ȧv′r′)	142	49°31′N	0°07′E
Lehi, Ut., U.S. (lē′hī)	109	40°25′N	111°55′W
Lehman Caves National Monument, rec., Nv., U.S. (lē′măn)	109	38°54′N	114°08′W
Lehnin, Ger. (lĕh′nēn)	145b	52°19′N	12°45′E
Leião, Port.	238d	38°44′N	9°18′W
Leicester, Eng., U.K. (lĕs′tẽr)	142	52°37′N	1°08′W
Leicestershire, co., Eng., U.K.	144a	52°40′N	1°12′W
Leichhardt, Austl.	243a	33°53′S	151°09′E
Leichhardt, r., Austl. (līk′härt)	202	18°30′S	139°45′E
Leiden, Neth. (lī′dĕn)	151	52°09′N	4°29′E
Leigh Creek, Austl. (lē krēk)	204	30°33′S	138°30′E
Leikanger, Nor. (lī′käŋ′gẽr)	152	61°11′N	6°51′E
Leimuiden, Neth.	145a	52°13′N	4°40′E
Leine, r., Ger. (lī′nĕ)	154	51°58′N	9°56′E
Leinster, hist. reg., Ire. (lĕn-stẽr)	150	52°45′N	7°19′W
Leipsic, Oh., U.S. (līp′sĭk)	98	41°05′N	84°00′W
Leipzig, Ger. (līp′tsĭk)	142	51°20′N	12°24′E
Leiria, Port. (lā-rē′ä)	158	39°45′N	8°50′W
Leitchfield, Ky., U.S. (lēch′fēld)	114	37°28′N	86°20′W
Leitha, r., Aus.	145e	48°04′N	16°57′E
Leithe, neigh., Ger.	236	51°29′N	7°06′E
Leitrim, Can.	83c	45°20′N	75°36′W
Leizhou Bandao, pen., China (lā-jō bän-dou)	188	20°42′N	109°10′E
Le Kremlin-Bicêtre, Fr.	237c	48°49′N	2°21′E
Leksand, Swe. (lĕk′sänd)	152	60°45′N	14°56′E
Leland, Wa., U.S. (lē′lănd)	106a	47°54′N	122°53′W
Leliu, China (lŭ-lĭō)	191a	22°52′N	113°09′E
Le Locle, Switz. (lẽ lō′kl′)	154	47°03′N	6°43′E
Le Maire, Estrecho de, strt., Arg. (ĕs-trĕ′chō-dĕ-lĕ-mī′rĕ)	132	55°15′S	65°30′W
Le Mans, Fr. (lẽ mäɴ′)	147	48°01′N	0°12′E
Le Marin, Mart.	121b	14°28′N	60°55′W
Le Mars, Ia., U.S. (lė märz′)	102	42°46′N	96°09′W
Lemay, Mo., U.S.	107e	38°32′N	90°17′W
Lemdiyya, Alg.	210	36°18′N	2°40′E
Leme, Morro do, mtn., Braz.	234c	22°58′S	43°10′W
Lemery, Phil. (lā-mā-rē′)	197a	13°51′S	120°55′E
Le Mesnil-Amelot, Fr.	237c	49°01′N	2°36′E
Le Mesnil-le-Roi, Fr.	237c	48°56′N	2°08′E
Lemhi, r., Id., U.S.	105	44°40′N	113°27′W
Lemhi Range, mts., Id., U.S. (lĕm′hī)	105	44°35′N	113°33′W
Lemmon, S.D., U.S. (lĕm′ŭn)	102	45°55′N	102°10′W
Le Môle, Haiti (lẽ mōl′)	123	19°50′N	73°20′W
Lemon Grove, Ca., U.S. (lĕm′ŭn-grōv)	108a	32°44′N	117°02′W
Lemon Heights, Ca., U.S.	232	33°46′N	117°48′W
Le Moule, Guad. (lẽ mo͞ol′)	121b	16°19′N	61°22′W
LeMoyne, Can.	227b	45°31′N	73°29′W
Lempa, r., N.A. (lĕm′pä)	120	13°20′N	88°46′W
Lemvig, Den. (lĕm′vēgh)	152	56°33′N	8°16′E
Lena, r., Russia	165	68°00′N	123°00′E
Lençóes Paulista, Braz. (lĕɴ-sôɴs′ pou-lēs′tȧ)	132	22°30′S	48°45′W
Lençóis, Braz. (lĕn-sóis)	131	12°38′S	41°28′W
Lenexa, Ks., U.S. (lē′nĕx-ă)	107f	38°58′N	99°44′W
Lengyandong, China (lŭŋ-yän-dōŋ)	191a	23°12′N	113°21′E
Lenik, r., Malay.	181b	1°59′N	102°51′E
Lenina, Gora, hill, Russia	239b	55°42′N	37°31′E
Leningrad *see* Saint Petersburg, Russia	164	59°57′N	30°20′E
Leningrad, prov., Russia	162	59°15′N	30°30′E
Leningradskaya, Russia (lyĕ-nĭn-gräd′skȧ-yȧ)	163	46°19′N	39°23′E
Lenino, Russia (lyĕ′nĭ-nô)	172b	55°37′N	37°41′E
Leninogor, Kaz.	169	50°29′N	83°25′E
Leninsk, Russia (lyĕ-nēnsk′)	167	48°40′N	45°10′E
Leninsk-Kuznetski, Russia (lyĕ-nēnsk′ko͞oz-nyĕt′skĭ)	164	54°28′N	86°48′E
Lennox, Ca., U.S.	232	33°56′N	118°21′W
Lennox, S.D., U.S. (lĕn′ŭks)	102	43°22′N	96°53′W
Lenoir, N.C., U.S. (lė-nōr′)	115	35°54′N	81°35′W
Lenoir City, Tn., U.S.	114	35°47′N	84°16′W
Lenox, Ia., U.S.	103	40°51′N	94°29′W
Lenz, S. Afr.	244b	26°19′S	27°49′E
Léo, Burkina	214	11°06′N	2°06′W
Leoben, Aus. (lå-ō′bĕn)	154	47°22′N	15°09′E
Léogane, Haiti (lā-ō-gan′)	123	18°30′N	72°35′W
Leola, S.D., U.S. (lė-ō′lȧ)	102	45°43′N	99°55′W
Leominster, Ma., U.S. (lĕm′ĭn-stẽr)	99	42°32′N	71°45′W
León, Mex. (lå-ōn′)	116	21°08′N	101°41′W
León, Nic. (lĕ-ô′n)	116	12°28′N	86°53′W
León, Spain (lĕ-ô′n)	148	42°38′N	5°33′W
Leon, Ia., U.S. (lē′ŏn)	103	40°43′N	93°44′W
León, hist. reg., Spain	158	41°18′N	5°50′W
Leon, r., Tx., U.S. (lē′ōn)	112	31°54′N	98°20′W
Leonforte, Italy (lā-ōn-fōr′tā)	160	37°40′N	14°27′E
Leonia, N.J., U.S.	228	40°52′N	73°59′W
Léopold, Mont, D.R.C.	244c	4°19′S	15°15′E
Leopoldau, neigh., Aus.	239e	48°16′N	16°27′E
Leopold II, Lac *see* Mai-Ndombe, Lac, l., D.R.C.	212	2°16′S	19°00′E
Leopoldina, Braz. (lā-ō-pōl-dē′nä)	129a	21°32′S	42°38′W
Leopoldsburg, Bel.	145a	51°07′N	5°18′E
Leopoldsdorf im Marchfelde, Aus. (lā′ō-pōlts-dōrf′)	145e	48°14′N	16°42′E
Leopoldstadt, neigh., Aus.	239e	48°13′N	16°23′E
Léopoldville *see* Kinshasa, D.R.C.	212	4°18′S	15°18′E
Leova, Mol.	163	46°30′N	28°16′E
Lepe, Spain (lā′pā)	158	37°15′N	7°12′W
Le Pecq, Fr.	237c	48°54′N	2°07′E
Lepel', Bela. (lyĕ-pĕl′)	162	54°52′N	28°41′E
Le Perreux-sur-Marne, Fr.	237c	48°51′N	2°30′E
Leping, China (lŭ-pĭŋ)	193	29°02′N	117°12′E
L'Épiphanie, Can. (lā-pė-fä-nē′)	83a	45°51′N	73°29′W
Le Plessis-Belleville, Fr. (lĕ-plĕ-sē′bĕl-vēl′)	157b	49°05′N	2°46′E
Le Plessis-Bouchard, Fr.	237c	49°00′N	2°14′E
Le Plessis-Trévise, Fr.	237c	48°49′N	2°34′E
Le Port-Marly, Fr.	237c	48°53′N	2°06′E
Lepreau, Can. (lė-prō′)	92	45°10′N	66°28′W
Le Pré-Saint-Gervais, Fr.	237c	48°53′N	2°25′E

ăt; finăl; rāte; senåte; ärm; åsk; sofȧ; fâre; ch-choose; dh-as th in other; bē; ėvent; bĕt; recĕnt; cratẽr; g-gō; gh-guttural g; bĭt; ĭ-short neutral; rīde; ĸ-guttural k as ch in German ich;

PRONOUNCING INDEX Lepsinsk – Lindian 309

PLACE (Pronunciation)	PAGE	LAT.	LONG.
Lepsinsk, Kaz.	169	45°32'N	80°47'E
Le Puy, Fr. (lē pwē')	147	45°02'N	3°54'E
Le Raincy, Fr.	237c	48°54'N	2°31'E
Lercara Friddi, Italy (lĕr-kä'rä)	160	37°47'N	13°36'E
Lerdo, Mex. (lĕr'dō)	116	25°31'N	103°30'W
Leribe, Leso.	213c	28°53'S	28°02'E
Lerma, Mex. (lĕr'mä)	119	19°49'N	90°34'W
Lerma, Mex.	119a	19°17'N	99°30'W
Lerma, Spain (lĕ'r-mä)	158	42°03'N	3°45'W
Lerma, r., Mex.	118	20°14'N	101°50'W
Le Roy, N.Y., U.S. (lē roi')	99	43°00'N	78°00'W
Lerwick, Scot., U.K. (lĕr'ĭk) (lûr'wĭk)	142	60°08'N	1°27'W
Léry, Can. (lā-rī')	83a	45°21'N	73°49'W
Lery, Lake, l., La., U.S. (lĕ'rē)	100d	29°48'N	89°45'W
Les Andelys, Fr. (lā-zäN-dē-lē')	157b	49°15'N	1°25'E
Les Borges Blanques, Spain	159	41°29'N	0°53'E
Lesbos see Lésvos, i., Grc.	142	39°15'N	25°40'E
Les Cayes, Haiti	123	18°15'N	73°45'W
Les Cèdres, Can. (lā-sĕdr'')	83a	45°18'N	74°03'W
Les Clayes-sous-Bois, Fr.	237c	48°49'N	1°59'E
Les Grésillons, Fr.	237c	48°56'N	2°01'E
Lesh, Alb. (lĕshē) (ä-lă'sē-ō)	161	41°47'N	19°40'E
Leshan, China (lŭ-shän)	188	29°40'N	103°40'E
Lésigny, Fr.	237c	48°45'N	2°37'E
Lésina, Lago di, l., Italy (lä'gō dē lā'zē-nä)	160	41°48'N	15°12'E
Leskovac, Yugo. (lĕs'kō-váts)	149	43°00'N	21°58'E
Leslie, S. Afr.	218d	26°23'S	28°57'E
Leslie, Ar., U.S. (lĕz'lĭ)	111	35°49'N	92°32'W
Les Lilas, Fr.	237c	48°53'N	2°25'E
Les Loges-en-Josas, Fr.	237c	48°46'N	2°09'E
Lesnoj, neigh., Russia	239a	60°00'N	30°20'E
Lesnoy, Russia (lĕs'noi)	166	66°45'N	34°45'E
Lesogorsk, Russia (lyĕs'ō-gôrsk)	194	49°28'N	141°59'E
Lesotho, nation, Afr. (lĕsō'thō)	212	29°45'S	28°07'E
Lesozavodsk, Russia (lyĕ-sô-zá-vôdsk')	194	45°21'N	133°19'E
Les Pavillons-sous-Bois, Fr.	237c	48°55'N	2°30'E
Les Sables-d'Olonne, Fr. (lā sá'bl'dō-lŭn')	147	46°30'N	1°47'W
Les Saintes Islands, is., Guad. (lā-sănt')	121b	15°50'N	61°40'W
Lesser Antilles, is.	117	12°15'N	65°00'W
Lesser Caucasus, mts., Asia	168	41°00'N	44°35'E
Lesser Khingan Range, mts., China	189	49°50'N	129°26'E
Lesser Slave, r., Can.	87	55°15'N	114°30'W
Lesser Slave Lake, l., Can. (lĕs'ĕr slāv)	84	55°25'N	115°30'W
Lesser Sunda Islands, is., Indon.	196	9°00'S	120°00'E
L'Estaque, Fr. (lĕs-täl)	156a	43°22'N	5°20'E
Lester, Pa., U.S.	229b	39°52'N	75°17'W
Les Thilliers-en-Vexin, Fr. (lā-tē-yā'ĕN-vĕ-sán')	157b	49°19'N	1°36'E
Le Sueur, Mn., U.S. (lē sōōr')	103	44°27'N	93°53'W
Lésvos, i., Grc.	142	39°15'N	25°40'E
Leszno, Pol. (lĕsh'nō)	147	51°51'N	16°35'E
L'Étang-la-Ville, Fr.	237c	48°52'N	2°05'E
Letchmore Heath, Eng., U.K.	235	51°40'N	0°20'W
Le Teil, Fr. (lē tā'y')	156	44°34'N	4°39'E
Lethbridge, Austl.	243a	33°44'S	150°48'E
Lethbridge, Can. (lĕth'brĭj)	84	49°42'N	112°50'W
Le Thillay, Fr.	237c	49°00'N	2°28'E
Leticia, Col. (lē-tē'syá)	130	4°04'S	69°57'W
Leting, China (lŭ-tĭŋ)	190	39°26'N	118°53'E
Le Tréport, Fr. (lē-trā'pôr')	156	50°03'N	1°21'E
Letychiv, Ukr.	163	49°22'N	27°29'E
Leuven, Bel.	151	50°53'N	4°42'E
Levack, Can.	90	46°38'N	81°23'W
Levádhia, Grc.	161	38°25'N	22°51'E
Le Val-d'Albian, Fr.	237c	48°45'N	2°11'E
Levallois-Perret, Fr. (lē-vál-wä'pĕ-rĕ')	157b	48°53'N	2°17'E
Levanger, Nor. (lĕ-väng'ĕr)	146	63°42'N	11°01'E
Levanna, mtn., Eur. (lå-vä'nä)	160	45°25'N	7°14'E
Levenshulme, neigh., Eng., U.K.	237b	53°27'N	2°10'W
Leveque, Cape, c., Austl. (lē-vĕk')	202	16°26'S	123°08'E
Leverkusen, Ger. (lĕ'fĕr-kōō-zĕn)	157c	51°01'N	6°59'E
Le Vésinet, Fr.	237c	48°54'N	2°08'E
Levice, Slvk. (lā'vĕt-sĕ)	155	48°13'N	18°37'E
Levico, Italy (lā'vē-kō)	160	46°02'N	11°20'E
Le Vigan, Fr. (lē vē-gäN')	156	43°59'N	3°36'E
Lévis, Can. (lā-vē') (lĕ'vĭs)	85	46°49'N	71°11'W
Levittown, N.Y., U.S.	228	40°41'N	73°31'W
Levittown, Pa., U.S. (lĕ'vĭt-toun)	100f	40°08'N	74°50'W
Levkás, Grc. (lyĕfkäs')	161	38°49'N	20°43'E
Levkás, i., Grc.	149	38°42'N	20°22'E
Levoča, Slvk. (lā'vō-chá)	155	49°03'N	20°38'E
Levuka, Fiji	198g	17°41'S	178°50'E
Lewes, Eng., U.K.	151	50°51'N	0°01'E
Lewes, De., U.S. (lōō'ĭs)	99	38°45'N	75°10'W
Lewinsville, Va., U.S.	229d	38°54'N	77°12'W
Lewinsville Heights, Va., U.S.	229d	38°53'N	77°12'W
Lewis, r., Wa., U.S.	104	46°05'N	122°09'W
Lewis, East Fork, r., Wa., U.S.	106c	45°52'N	122°40'W
Lewis, Island of, i., Scot., U.K. (lōō'ĭs)	150	58°05'N	6°07'W
Lewisburg, Tn., U.S. (lū'ĭs-bûrg)	114	35°27'N	86°47'W
Lewisburg, W.V., U.S.	98	37°50'N	80°20'W
Lewisdale, Md., U.S.	229d	38°58'N	76°58'W
Lewisham, S. Afr.	244b	26°07'S	27°49'E
Lewisham, neigh., Eng., U.K.	235	51°27'N	0°01'E
Lewis Hills, hills, Can.	93	48°48'N	58°30'W
Lewisporte, Can. (lū'ĭs-pōrt)	93	49°15'N	55°04'W
Lewis Range, mts., Mt., U.S. (lū'ĭs)	105	48°15'N	113°20'W
Lewis Smith Lake, res., Al., U.S.	114	34°05'N	87°07'W
Lewiston, Id., U.S. (lū'ĭs-tŭn)	96	46°24'N	116°59'W
Lewiston, Me., U.S.	97	44°05'N	70°14'W
Lewiston, N.Y., U.S.	101c	43°11'N	79°02'W
Lewiston, Ut., U.S.	105	41°58'N	111°51'W
Lewistown, Il., U.S. (lū'ĭs-toun)	111	40°23'N	90°06'W
Lewistown, Mt., U.S.	96	47°05'N	109°25'W
Lewistown, Pa., U.S.	99	40°35'N	77°30'W
Lexington, Ky., U.S. (lĕk'sĭng-tŭn)	97	38°05'N	84°30'W
Lexington, Ma., U.S.	93a	42°27'N	71°14'W
Lexington, Ms., U.S.	114	33°08'N	90°02'W
Lexington, Mo., U.S.	111	39°11'N	93°52'W
Lexington, Ne., U.S.	110	40°46'N	99°44'W
Lexington, N.C., U.S.	115	35°47'N	80°15'W
Lexington, Tn., U.S.	114	35°37'N	88°24'W
Lexington, Va., U.S.	99	37°45'N	79°20'W
Leybourne, Eng., U.K.	235	51°18'N	0°25'E
Leyte, i., Phil. (lā'tā)	197	10°35'N	125°35'E
Leżajsk, Pol. (lĕ'zhä-ĭsk)	155	50°14'N	22°25'E
Lezha, r., Russia (lĕ-zhä')	162	58°59'N	40°27'E
L'gov, Russia (lgôf)	163	51°42'N	35°15'E
Lhasa, China (läs'ä)	188	29°41'N	91°12'E
L'Hautil, Fr.	237c	49°00'N	2°01'E
Liangxiangzhen, China (lĭäŋ-shyäŋ-jŭn)	192a	39°43'N	116°08'E
Lianjiang, China (lĭĕn-jyäŋ)	193	21°38'N	110°15'E
Lianozovo, Russia (lĭ-a-nô'zô-vô)	172b	55°54'N	37°36'E
Lianshui, China (lĭĕn-shwā)	190	33°46'N	119°15'E
Lianyungang, China (lĭĕn-yòn-gäŋ)	189	34°35'N	119°09'E
Liao, r., China	189	43°37'N	120°05'E
Liao, r., China	192	41°40'N	122°40'E
Liaocheng, China (lĭou-chŭŋ)	192	36°27'N	115°56'E
Liaodong Bandao, pen., China (lĭou-dôŋ bän-dou)	189	39°45'N	122°22'E
Liaodong Wan, b., China (lĭou-dôŋ wäŋ)	192	40°25'N	121°15'E
Liaoning, prov., China	189	41°31'N	122°11'E
Liaoyang, China (lyä'ō-yäng')	189	41°18'N	123°10'E
Liaoyuan, China (lĭou-yůän)	192	43°00'N	124°59'E
Liard, r., Can. (lē-är')	84	59°43'N	126°42'W
Libano, Col. (lē'bá-nō)	130a	4°55'N	75°05'W
Libby, Mt., U.S. (lĭb'ē)	104	48°27'N	115°35'W
Libenge, D.R.C. (lē-bĕŋ'gä)	211	3°39'N	18°40'E
Liberal, Ks., U.S. (lĭb'ĕr-ăl)	110	37°01'N	100°56'W
Liberdade, neigh., Braz.	234d	23°35'S	46°37'W
Liberec, Czech Rep. (lē'bĕr-ĕts)	147	50°45'N	15°06'E
Liberia, C.R.	120	10°38'N	85°28'W
Liberia, nation, Afr. (lī-bē'rĭ-á)	210	6°30'N	9°55'W
Libertad, Arg.	132a	34°42'S	58°42'W
Libertad de Orituco, Ven. (lē-bĕr-tä'd-dĕ-ō-rē-tōō'kō)	131b	9°32'N	66°24'W
Liberty, In., U.S. (lĭb'ĕr-tĭ)	98	39°35'N	84°55'W
Liberty, Mo., U.S.	107f	39°15'N	94°25'W
Liberty, Pa., U.S.	230b	40°20'N	79°51'W
Liberty, S.C., U.S.	115	34°47'N	82°41'W
Liberty, Tx., U.S.	113	30°03'N	94°46'W
Liberty, Ut., U.S.	107b	41°20'N	111°52'W
Liberty Bay, b., Wa., U.S.	106a	47°43'N	122°41'W
Liberty Lake, l., Md., U.S.	100e	39°25'N	76°56'W
Liberty Manor, Md., U.S.	229c	39°21'N	76°47'W
Libertyville, Il., U.S. (lĭb'ĕr-tĭ-vĭl)	101a	42°17'N	87°57'W
Libode, S. Afr. (lĭ-bō'dĕ)	213c	31°33'S	29°03'E
Libón, r., N.A.	123	19°30'N	71°45'W
Libourne, Fr. (lē-bōōrn')	147	44°55'N	0°12'W
Library, Pa., U.S.	230b	40°18'N	80°02'W
Libres, Mex. (lē'bräs)	119	19°26'N	97°41'W
Libreville, Gabon (lē-br'vēl')	212	0°23'N	9°27'E
Liburn, Ga., U.S. (lĭb'ûrn)	100c	33°53'N	84°09'W
Libya, nation, Afr. (lĭb'ē-ä)	211	27°38'N	15°00'E
Libyan Desert, des., Afr. (lĭb'ē-ăn)	211	28°23'N	23°34'E
Libyan Plateau, plat., Afr.	184	30°58'N	26°20'E
Licancábur, Cerro, mtn., S.A. (sĕ'r-rô-lē-kän-ká'bōōr)	132	22°45'S	67°45'W
Licanten, Chile (lē-kän-tē'n)	129b	34°58'S	72°00'W
Lichfield, Eng., U.K. (lĭch'fēld)	144a	52°41'N	1°49'W
Lichinga, Moz.	217	13°18'S	35°14'E
Lichtenberg, neigh., Ger.	238a	52°31'N	13°29'E
Lichtenburg, S. Afr. (lĭk'tĕn-bĕrgh)	218d	26°09'S	26°10'E
Lichtendorf, Ger.	236	51°28'N	7°37'E
Lichtenplatz, neigh., Ger.	236	51°15'N	7°12'E
Lichtenrade, neigh., Ger.	238a	52°23'N	13°25'E
Lichterfelde, neigh., Ger.	238a	52°26'N	13°19'E
Lick Creek, r., In., U.S. (lĭk)	101g	39°43'N	86°06'W
Licking, r., Ky., U.S. (lĭk'ĭng)	98	38°30'N	84°10'W
Lida, Bela. (lē'dá)	155	53°53'N	25°19'E
Lidcombe, Austl.	243a	33°52'S	151°03'E
Lidgerwood, N.D., U.S. (lĭj'ĕr-wood)	102	46°04'N	97°10'W
Lidköping, Swe. (lēt'chû-pĭng)	152	58°31'N	13°06'E
Lido Beach, N.Y., U.S.	228	40°35'N	73°38'W
Lido di Roma, Italy (lē'dō-dē-rō'mä)	159d	41°19'N	12°17'E
Lidzbark, Pol. (lĭts'bärk)	155	54°07'N	20°36'E
Liebenbergsvlei, r., S. Afr.	218d	27°35'S	28°25'E
Liebenwalde, Ger. (lē'bĕn-väl-dĕ)	145b	52°52'N	13°24'E
Liechtenstein, nation, Eur. (lĕk'tĕn-shtīn)	147	47°10'N	10°00'E
Liège, Bel.	147	50°38'N	5°34'E
Lienz, Aus. (lē-ĕnts')	154	46°49'N	12°45'E
Liepāja, Lat. (le'pä-yä')	166	56°31'N	20°59'E
Lier, Bel.	145a	51°08'N	4°34'E
Lierenfeld, neigh., Ger.	236	51°13'N	6°51'E
Liesing, Aus. (lē'sĭng)	145e	48°09'N	16°17'E
Liestal, Switz. (lēs'täl)	154	47°28'N	7°44'E
Lifanga, D.R.C.	216	0°19'N	21°57'E
Lifou, i., N. Cal.	203	21°15'S	167°32'E
Ligao, Phil. (lē-gä'ō)	197a	13°14'N	123°33'E
Lightning Ridge, Austl.	204	29°23'S	147°50'E
Ligonha, r., Moz. (lē-gō'nyá)	213	16°14'S	39°00'E
Ligonier, In., U.S. (lĭg-ō-nēr)	98	41°30'N	85°35'W
Ligovo, Russia (lē'gô-vô)	172c	59°51'N	30°13'E
Liguria, hist. reg., Italy (lē-gōō-rē-ä)	160	44°24'N	8°27'E
Ligurian Sea, sea, Eur. (lĭ-gū'rĭ-ăn)	148	43°42'N	8°32'E
Lihou Reef, rf., Austl. (lē-hōō')	203	17°23'S	152°43'E
Lihuang, China (lē'hōōăng)	190	31°32'N	115°46'E
Lihue, Hi., U.S. (lē-hōō'ā)	96c	21°59'N	159°23'W
Lihula, Est. (lē'hò-lå)	153	58°41'N	23°50'E
Liji, China (lē-jyē)	190	33°47'N	117°47'E
Lijiang, China (lē-jyäŋ)	188	27°00'N	100°08'E
Lijin, China (lē-jyĭn)	192	37°30'N	118°15'E
Likasi, D.R.C.	212	10°59'S	26°44'E
Likhoslavl', Russia (lyē-kôsläv''l)	162	57°07'N	35°27'E
Likouala, r., Congo	216	0°10'S	16°30'E
Lille, Fr. (lēl)	142	50°38'N	3°01'E
Lille Baelt, strt., Den.	152	55°09'N	9°53'E
Lillehammer, Nor. (lēl'ĕ-häm'mĕr)	146	61°07'N	10°25'E
Lillesand, Nor. (lēl'ĕ-sän')	152	58°16'N	8°19'E
Lilleström, Nor. (lēl'ĕ-strûm)	152	59°56'N	11°04'E
Lilliwaup, Wa., U.S. (lĭl'ĭ-wŏp)	106a	47°28'N	123°07'W
Lillooet, Can. (lĭ'lōō-ĕt)	84	50°30'N	121°55'W
Lillooet, r., Can.	87	49°50'N	122°10'W
Lilongwe, Mwi. (lē-lō-än)	212	13°59'S	33°44'E
Liluāh, India	240a	22°37'N	88°20'E
Lilydale, Austl.	243b	37°45'S	145°21'E
Lilyfield, Austl.	243a	33°52'S	151°10'E
Lima, Peru (lē'mä)	130	12°06'S	76°55'W
Lima, Swe.	152	60°54'N	13°24'E
Lima, Oh., U.S. (lī'má)	97	40°40'N	84°05'W
Lima, r., Eur.	158	41°45'N	8°22'W
Lima Duarte, Braz. (dwä'r-tĕ)	129a	21°52'S	43°47'W
Limão, neigh., Braz.	234d	23°30'S	46°40'W
Lima Reservoir, res., Mt., U.S.	105	44°45'N	112°15'W
Limassol, Cyp.	149	34°39'N	33°02'E
Limay, r., Arg. (lē-mä'ē)	132	39°50'S	69°15'W
Limbazi, Lat. (lēm'bä-zĭ)	153	57°32'N	24°44'E
Limbdi, India	186	22°37'N	71°52'E
Limbe, Cam.	210	4°01'N	9°12'E
Limburg an der Lahn, Ger. (lem-bòrg')	154	50°22'N	8°03'E
Limefield, Eng., U.K.	237b	53°37'N	2°18'W
Limeira, Braz. (lē-mā'rä)	129a	22°34'S	47°24'W
Limerick, Ire. (lĭm'nák)	147	52°39'N	8°35'W
Limestone Bay, b., Can. (lĭm'stōn)	89	53°50'N	98°50'W
Limfjorden, Den.	146	56°55'N	8°56'E
Limmen Bight, bt., Austl. (lĭm'ĕn)	202	14°45'S	136°00'E
Limni, Grc. (lēm'nē)	161	38°47'N	23°22'E
Limnos, i., Grc.	149	39°58'N	24°48'E
Limoges, Can. (lē-môzh')	83c	45°20'N	75°15'W
Limoges, Fr.	147	45°50'N	1°15'E
Limón, C.R. (lē-mōn')	117	10°01'N	83°02'W
Limón, Hond. (lē-mô'n)	120	15°53'N	85°34'W
Limon, Co., U.S. (lī'mŏn)	110	39°15'N	103°41'W
Limon, r., Dom. Rep.	123	18°20'N	71°40'W
Limón, Bahía, b., Pan.	116a	9°21'N	79°58'W
Limours, Fr. (lē-mōōr')	157b	48°39'N	2°05'E
Limousin, Plateaux du, plat., Fr. (plä-tō' dü lē-mōō-zäN')	156	45°44'N	1°09'E
Limoux, Fr. (lē-mōō')	156	43°03'N	2°14'E
Limpopo, r., Afr. (lĭm-pō'pō)	212	23°15'S	27°46'E
Linares, Chile (lē-nä'räs)	132	35°51'S	71°35'W
Linares, Mex.	116	24°53'N	99°34'W
Linares, Spain (lē-nä'rĕs)	148	38°07'N	3°38'W
Linares, prov., Chile	129b	35°53'S	71°30'W
Linaro, Cape, c., Italy (lē-nä'rä)	160	42°02'N	11°53'E
Lince, Peru	233c	12°05'S	77°03'W
Linchuan, China (lĭn-chůän)	189	27°58'N	116°18'E
Lincoln, Arg. (lĭŋ'kŭn)	132	34°51'S	61°29'W
Lincoln, Can.	83d	43°10'N	79°29'W
Lincoln, Eng., U.K.	146	53°14'N	0°33'W
Lincoln, Ca., U.S.	108	38°51'N	121°19'W
Lincoln, Il., U.S.	111	40°09'N	89°21'W
Lincoln, Ks., U.S.	110	39°02'N	98°08'W
Lincoln, Me., U.S.	92	45°23'N	68°31'W
Lincoln, Ma., U.S.	93a	42°25'N	71°19'W
Lincoln, Ne., U.S.	96	40°49'N	96°43'W
Lincoln, Pa., U.S.	230b	40°18'N	79°51'W
Lincoln, Mount, mtn., Co., U.S.	110	39°20'N	106°19'W
Lincoln Center, pt. of i., N.Y., U.S.	228	40°46'N	73°59'W
Lincoln Heath, reg., Eng., U.K.	144a	53°23'N	0°39'W
Lincolnia Heights, Va., U.S.	229d	38°50'N	77°09'W
Lincoln Park, Mi., U.S.	101b	42°14'N	83°11'W
Lincoln Park, N.J., U.S.	100a	40°56'N	74°18'W
Lincoln Park, pt. of i., Il., U.S.	231a	41°56'N	87°38'W
Lincoln Place, neigh., Pa., U.S.	230b	40°22'N	79°55'W
Lincolnshire, co., Eng., U.K.	144a	53°12'N	0°29'W
Lincolnshire Wolds, Eng., U.K. (woldz')	150	53°25'N	0°23'W
Lincolnton, N.C., U.S. (lĭŋ'kŭn-tŭn)	115	35°27'N	81°15'W
Lincolnwood, Il., U.S.	231a	42°00'N	87°46'W
Linda-a-Velha, Port.	238d	38°43'N	9°14'W
Lindale, Ga., U.S. (lĭn'dāl)	114	34°10'N	85°10'W
Lindau, Ger. (lĭn'dou)	154	47°33'N	9°40'E
Linden, Al., U.S. (lĭn'dĕn)	114	32°16'N	87°47'W
Linden, Ma., U.S.	227a	42°26'N	71°02'W
Linden, Mo., U.S.	107f	39°13'N	94°35'W
Linden, N.J., U.S.	100a	40°39'N	74°14'W
Linden, neigh., S. Afr.	244b	26°08'S	28°00'E
Lindenberg, Ger.	238a	52°36'N	13°31'E
Linden-Dahlhausen, neigh., Ger.	236	51°26'N	7°09'E
Lindenhorst, neigh., Ger.	236	51°33'N	7°27'E
Lindenhurst, N.Y., U.S. (lĭn'dĕn-hûrst)	100a	40°41'N	73°23'W
Lindenwold, N.J., U.S. (lĭn'dĕn-wōld)	100f	39°50'N	75°00'W
Linderhausen, Ger.	236	51°18'N	7°17'E
Lindesberg, Swe. (lĭn'dĕs-bĕrgh)	152	59°37'N	15°14'E
Lindesnes, c., Nor. (lĭn'ĕs-nĕs)	142	58°00'N	7°05'E
Lindfield, Austl.	243a	33°47'S	151°10'E
Lindi, Tan. (lĭn'dē)	213	10°00'S	39°43'E
Lindi, r., D.R.C.	211	1°00'N	27°13'E
Lindian, China (lĭn-dĭĕn)	192	47°08'N	124°59'E

310 Lindley–Lokoja

PLACE (Pronunciation)	PAGE	LAT.	LONG.
Lindley, S. Afr. (lĭnd'lė)	218d	27°52'S	27°55'E
Lindow, Ger. (lēn'dōv)	145b	52°58'N	12°59'E
Lindsay, Can. (lĭn'zė)	91	44°20'N	78°45'W
Lindsay, Ok., U.S.	111	34°50'N	97°38'W
Lindsborg, Ks., U.S. (lĭnz'bôrg)	111	38°34'N	97°42'W
Lineville, Al., U.S. (lĭn'vĭl)	114	33°18'N	85°45'W
Linfen, China	189	36°00'N	111°38'E
Linga, Kepulauan, is., Indon.	196	0°35'S	105°05'E
Lingao, China (lĭn-gou)	193	19°58'N	109°40'E
Lingayen, Phil. (lĭŋ'gä-yän')	196	16°01'N	120°13'E
Lingayen Gulf, b., Phil.	197a	16°18'N	120°11'E
Lingdianzhen, China	190	31°52'N	121°28'E
Lingen, Ger. (lĭŋ'gĕn)	154	52°32'N	7°20'E
Lingling, China (lĭŋ-lĭŋ)	193	26°10'N	111°40'E
Lingshou, China (lĭŋ-shō)	190	38°21'N	114°41'E
Linguère, Sen. (lĭŋ-gĕr')	210	15°24'N	15°07'W
Lingwu, China	192	38°05'N	106°18'E
Lingyuan, China (lĭŋ-yůän)	192	41°12'N	119°20'E
Linhai, China	193	28°52'N	121°08'E
Linhe, China (lĭn-hŭ)	192	40°49'N	107°45'E
Linhuaiguan, China (lĭn-hwī-gůän)	190	32°55'N	117°38'E
Linhuanji, China	190	33°42'N	116°33'E
Linjiang, China (lĭn-jyäŋ)	192	41°45'N	127°00'E
Linköping, Swe. (lĭn'chû-pĭng)	146	58°25'N	15°35'E
Linksfield, neigh., S. Afr.	244b	26°10'S	28°06'E
Linmeyer, S. Afr.	244b	26°16'S	28°04'E
Linn, neigh., Ger.	236	51°20'N	6°38'E
Linnhe, Loch, b., Scot., U.K. (lĭn'ė)	150	56°35'N	4°30'W
Linqing, China (lĭn-chyĭŋ)	189	36°49'N	115°42'E
Linqu, China (lĭn-chyōō)	190	36°31'N	118°33'E
Lins, Braz. (lė'ns)	131	21°42'S	49°41'W
Linthicum Heights, Md., U.S. (lĭn'thĭ-kŭm)	100e	39°12'N	76°39'W
Linton, In., U.S. (lĭn'tŭn)	98	39°05'N	87°15'W
Linton, N.D., U.S.	102	46°16'N	100°15'W
Lintorf, Ger.	236	51°20'N	6°49'E
Linwu, China (lĭn'wōō')	193	25°20'N	112°30'E
Linxi, China (lĭn-shyē)	192	43°30'N	118°02'E
Linyi, China (lĭn-yē)	189	35°04'N	118°21'E
Linying, China (lĭn'yĭng')	190	33°48'N	113°56'E
Linz, Aus. (lĭnts)	147	48°18'N	14°18'E
Linzhang, China (lĭn-jäŋ)	190	36°19'N	114°40'E
Lion, Golfe du, b., Fin.	142	43°00'N	4°00'E
Lipa, Phil. (lė-pä')	196	13°55'N	121°10'E
Lipari, Italy (lē'pä-rė)	160	38°29'N	15°00'E
Lipari, i., Italy	160	38°32'N	15°04'E
Lipetsk, Russia (lyē'pĕtsk)	164	52°26'N	39°34'E
Lipetsk, prov., Russia	162	52°18'N	38°30'E
Liping, China (lē-pĭŋ)	188	26°18'N	109°00'E
Lipno, Pol. (lēp'nō)	155	52°50'N	19°12'E
Lippe, r., Ger. (lĭp'ĕ)	157b	51°36'N	6°45'E
Lippolthausen, neigh., Ger.	236	51°37'N	7°29'E
Lippstadt, Ger. (lĭp'shtät)	154	51°39'N	8°20'E
Lipscomb, Al., U.S. (lĭp'skŭm)	100h	33°26'N	86°56'W
Lipu, China (lē-pōō)	193	24°38'N	110°35'E
Lira, Ug.	217	2°15'N	32°54'E
Liri, r., Italy (lē'rē)	160	41°49'N	13°30'E
Lisala, D.R.C. (lė-sä'lä)	211	2°09'N	21°31'E
Lisboa see Lisbon, Port.	142	38°42'N	9°05'W
Lisbon (Lisboa), Port.	142	38°42'N	9°05'W
Lisbon, N.D., U.S.	102	46°21'N	97°43'W
Lisbon, Oh., U.S.	98	40°45'N	80°50'W
Lisbon Falls, Me., U.S.	92	43°59'N	70°03'W
Lisburn, N. Ire., U.K. (lĭs'bŭrn)	150	54°35'N	6°05'W
Lisburne, Cape, c., Ak., U.S.	94a	68°20'N	165°40'W
Lishi, China (lē-shr)	192	37°32'N	111°12'E
Lishu, China	192	43°12'N	124°18'E
Lishui, China	189	28°28'N	120°00'E
Lishui, China (lĭ'shwĭ')	190	31°41'N	119°01'E
Lisianski Island, i., Hi., U.S.	94b	25°30'N	174°00'W
Lisieux, Fr. (lē-zyû')	156	49°10'N	0°13'E
Lisiy Nos, Russia (lĭ'sĭy-nôs)	172c	60°01'N	30°00'E
Liski, Russia (lyēs'kė)	163	50°56'N	39°28'E
Lisle, Il., U.S. (līl)	101a	41°48'N	88°04'W
L'Isle-Adam, Fr. (lēl-ädäN')	157b	49°05'N	2°13'E
Lismore, Austl. (lĭz'môr)	203	28°48'S	153°18'E
Litani, r., Leb.	181a	33°28'N	35°42'E
Litchfield, Il., U.S. (lĭch'fēld)	111	39°10'N	89°38'W
Litchfield, Mn., U.S.	103	45°08'N	94°34'W
Litchfield, Oh., U.S.	101d	41°10'N	82°01'W
Litherland, Eng., U.K.	237a	53°28'N	2°59'W
Lithgow, Austl. (lĭth'gō)	203	33°23'S	149°31'E
Lithinon, Akra, c., Grc.	160a	34°59'N	24°35'E
Lithonia, Ga., U.S. (lĭ-thō'nĭ-ȧ)	100c	33°43'N	84°07'W
Lithuania, nation, Eur. (lĭth-ů-ā'nĭ-ȧ)	164	55°42'N	23°30'E
Litókhoron, Grc. (lē'tô-ĸô'rôn)	161	40°05'N	22°29'E
Litoko, D.R.C.	216	1°13'S	24°47'E
Litoměřice, Czech Rep. (lē'tô-myĕr'zhĭ-tsĕ)	154	50°33'N	14°10'E
Litomyšl, Czech Rep. (lē'tô-mēsh'l)	154	49°52'N	16°14'E
Litoo, Tan.	217	9°45'S	38°24'E
Little, r., Austl.	201a	37°54'S	144°27'E
Little, r., Tn., U.S.	114	36°28'N	89°39'W
Little, r., Tx., U.S.	113	30°48'N	96°50'W
Little Abaco, i., Bah. (ä'bä-kō)	122	26°55'N	77°45'W
Little Abitibi, r., Can.	90	50°15'N	81°30'W
Little America, sci., Ant.	219	78°30'S	161°30'W
Little Andaman, i., India (ăn-dȧ-măn')	196	10°39'N	93°08'E
Little Bahama Bank, bk. (bȧ-hā'mȧ)	122	26°55'N	78°40'W
Little Belt Mountains, mts., Mt., U.S. (bĕlt)	96	47°00'N	110°50'W
Little Berkhamsted, Eng., U.K.	235	51°45'N	0°08'W
Little Bighorn, r., Mt., U.S. (bĭg-hôrn)	105	45°08'N	107°30'W
Little Bitter Lake, l., Egypt	218b	30°10'N	32°36'E
Little Bitterroot, r., Mt., U.S. (bĭt'ẽr-ōōt)	105	47°45'N	114°45'W
Little Blue, r., Ia., U.S. (blōō)	107f	38°52'N	94°25'W
Little Blue, r., Ne., U.S.	110	40°15'N	98°01'W
Littleborough, Eng., U.K. (lĭt''l-bŭr-ô)	144a	53°39'N	2°06'W
Little Burstead, Eng., U.K.	235	51°36'N	0°24'E
Little Calumet, r., Il., U.S. (kăl-ů-mĕt')	101a	41°38'N	87°38'W
Little Cayman, i., Cay. Is. (kā'mȧn)	122	19°40'N	80°05'W
Little Chalfont, Eng., U.K.	235	51°40'N	0°34'W
Little Colorado, r., Az., U.S. (kŏl-ô-rä'dō)	96	36°05'N	111°35'W
Little Compton, R.I., U.S. (kŏmp'tŏn)	100b	41°31'N	71°07'W
Little Corn Island, i., Nic.	121	12°19'N	82°50'W
Little End, Eng., U.K.	235	51°41'N	0°14'E
Little Exuma, i., Bah. (ĕk-sōō'mä)	123	23°25'N	75°40'W
Little Falls, Mn., U.S. (fôlz)	103	45°58'N	94°23'W
Little Falls, N.J., U.S.	228	40°53'N	74°14'W
Little Falls, N.Y., U.S.	99	43°05'N	74°55'W
Little Ferry, N.J., U.S.	228	40°51'N	74°03'W
Littlefield, Tx., U.S. (lĭt''l-fēld)	110	33°55'N	102°17'W
Little Fork, r., Mn., U.S. (fôrk)	103	48°24'N	93°30'W
Little Goose Dam, dam, Wa., U.S.	104	46°35'N	118°02'W
Little Hans Lollick, i., V.I.U.S. (häns lôl'lĭk)	117c	18°25'N	64°54'W
Little Hulton, Eng., U.K.	237b	53°32'N	2°25'W
Little Humboldt, r., Nv., U.S. (hŭm'bōlt)	104	41°10'N	117°40'W
Little Inagua, i., Bah. (ė-nä'gwä)	123	21°30'N	73°00'W
Little Isaac, i., Bah. (ī'zȧk)	122	25°55'N	79°00'W
Little Kanawha, r., W.V., U.S. (kȧ-nô'wȧ)	98	39°05'N	81°30'W
Little Karroo, plat., S. Afr. (kä-rōō)	212	33°50'S	21°02'E
Little Lever, Eng., U.K.	237b	53°34'N	2°22'W
Little Mecatina, r., Can. (mĕ cȧ tĭ nȧ)	85	52°40'N	62°21'W
Little Miami, r., Oh., U.S. (mī-ăm'ĭ)	101f	39°19'N	84°15'W
Little Minch, strt., Scot., U.K.	150	57°35'N	6°45'W
Little Missouri, r., U.S.	96	46°00'N	104°00'W
Little Missouri, r., Ar., U.S. (mĭ-sōō'rĭ)	111	34°15'N	93°54'W
Little Nahant, Ma., U.S.	227a	42°25'N	70°56'W
Little Neck, neigh., N.Y., U.S.	228	40°46'N	73°44'W
Little Pee Dee, r., S.C., U.S. (pē-dē')	115	34°35'N	79°21'W
Little Powder, r., Wy., U.S. (pou'dẽr)	105	44°51'N	105°20'W
Little Red, r., Ar., U.S. (rĕd)	111	35°25'N	91°55'W
Little Red, r., Ok., U.S.	111	33°53'N	94°38'W
Little Rock, Ar., U.S. (rôk)	97	34°42'N	92°16'W
Little Sachigo Lake, l., Can. (să'chĭ-gō)	89	54°09'N	92°11'W
Little Salt Lake, l., Ut., U.S.	109	37°55'N	112°53'W
Little San Salvador, i., Bah. (săn săl'vȧ-dôr)	123	24°35'N	75°55'W
Little Satilla, r., Ga., U.S. (sȧ-tĭl'ȧ)	115	31°43'N	82°47'W
Little Sioux, r., Ia., U.S. (sōō)	102	42°22'N	95°47'W
Little Smoky, r., Can. (smōk'ĭ)	87	55°10'N	116°55'W
Little Snake, r., Co., U.S. (snāk)	105	40°40'N	108°21'W
Little Stanney, Eng., U.K.	237a	53°15'N	2°53'W
Little Sutton, Eng., U.K.	237a	53°17'N	2°57'W
Little Tallapoosa, r., Al., U.S. (tăl-ȧ-pōō'sä)	114	32°25'N	85°28'W
Little Tennessee, r., Tn., U.S. (tĕn-ĕ-sē')	114	35°36'N	84°05'W
Little Thurrock, Eng., U.K.	235	51°28'N	0°21'E
Littleton, Eng., U.K.	235	51°24'N	0°28'W
Littleton, Co., U.S. (lĭt''l-tŭn)	110	39°34'N	105°01'W
Littleton, Ma., U.S.	93a	42°32'N	71°29'W
Littleton, N.H., U.S.	99	44°15'N	71°45'W
Little Wabash, r., Il., U.S. (wô'băsh)	98	38°50'N	88°30'W
Little Warley, Eng., U.K.	235	51°35'N	0°19'E
Little Wood, r., Id., U.S. (wŏod)	105	43°00'N	114°08'W
Lityn, Ukr.	163	49°16'N	28°11'E
Liubar, Ukr.	163	49°56'N	27°44'E
Liuhe, China	192	42°10'N	125°38'E
Liuli, Tan.	217	11°05'S	34°38'E
Liulicun, China	240b	39°56'N	116°28'E
Liupan Shan, mts., China	192	36°20'N	105°30'E
Liuwa Plain, pl., Zam.	216	14°30'S	22°40'E
Liuyang, China (lyōō'yäng')	193	28°10'N	113°35'E
Liuyuan, China (liô-yůän)	190	36°09'N	114°37'E
Liuzhou, China (liô-jō)	188	24°25'N	109°30'E
Līvāni, Lat. (lē'vá-nė)	153	56°24'N	26°12'E
Lively, Can.	90	46°26'N	81°09'W
Livengood, Ak., U.S. (lĭv'ĕn-gŏd)	95	65°30'N	148°35'W
Live Oak, Fl., U.S. (lĭv'ōk)	114	30°15'N	83°00'W
Livermore, Ca., U.S. (lĭv'ẽr-mōr)	106b	37°41'N	121°46'W
Livermore, Ky., U.S.	98	37°30'N	87°05'W
Liverpool, Austl. (lĭv'ẽr-pōōl)	201b	33°55'S	150°56'E
Liverpool, Can.	85	44°02'N	64°41'W
Liverpool, Eng., U.K.	142	53°25'N	2°52'W
Liverpool, Tx., U.S.	113a	29°18'N	95°17'W
Liverpool Bay, b., Can.	95	69°45'N	130°00'W
Liverpool Range, mts., Austl.	203	31°47'S	151°00'E
Livindo, r., Afr.	211	1°09'N	13°30'E
Livingston, Guat.	120	15°50'N	88°45'W
Livingston, Al., U.S. (lĭv'ĭng-stŭn)	114	32°35'N	88°09'W
Livingston, Il., U.S.	107e	38°58'N	89°51'W
Livingston, Mt., U.S.	96	45°40'N	110°35'W
Livingston, N.J., U.S.	100a	40°47'N	74°20'W
Livingston, Tn., U.S.	114	36°23'N	85°20'W
Livingstone, Zam. (lĭv-ĭng-stôn)	212	17°50'S	25°53'E
Livingstone, Chutes de, wtfl., Afr.	216	4°50'S	14°30'E
Livingstonia, Mwi. (lĭv-ĭng-stō'nĭ-ȧ)	212	10°36'S	34°07'E
Livno, Bos. (lēv'nō)	149	43°50'N	17°03'E
Livny, Russia (lĕv'nė)	167	52°28'N	37°36'E
Livonia, Mi., U.S. (lĭ-vō-nĭ-ȧ)	101b	42°25'N	83°23'W
Livorno, Italy (lė-vôr'nō) (lĕg'hôrn)	142	43°32'N	11°18'E
Livramento, Braz. (lē-vrá-mĕ'n-tô)	132	30°46'S	55°21'W
Livry-Gargan, Fr.	237c	48°56'N	2°33'E
Lixian, China	190	38°30'N	115°38'E
Lixian, China (lē shyĕn)	193	29°42'N	111°40'E
Liyang, China (lē'yäng')	193	31°30'N	119°29'E
Lizard Point, c., Eng., U.K. (lĭz'ȧrd)	147	49°55'N	5°09'W
Lizy-sur-Ourcq, Fr. (lēk-sē'sür-ōōrk')	157b	49°01'N	3°02'E
Ljubljana, Slvn. (lyōō'blyȧ'na)	142	46°04'N	14°29'E
Ljubuški, Bos. (lyōō'bŏsh-kė)	161	43°11'N	17°29'E
Ljungan, r., Swe.	152	62°50'N	13°45'E
Ljungby, Swe. (lyŏng'bü)	152	56°49'N	13°56'E
Ljusdal, Swe. (lyōōs'däl)	152	61°50'N	16°11'E
Ljusnan, r., Swe.	146	61°55'N	15°33'E
Llandudno, Wales, U.K. (lăn-düd'nō)	150	53°20'N	3°46'W
Llanelli, Wales, U.K. (lȧ-nĕl'ĭ)	147	51°44'N	4°09'W
Llanes, Spain (lyä'nȧs)	148	43°25'N	4°41'W
Llano, Tx., U.S. (lă'nō) (lyä'nō)	112	30°45'N	98°41'W
Llano, r., Tx., U.S.	112	30°38'N	99°04'W
Llanos, reg., S.A. (lyȧ'nōs)	130	4°00'N	71°15'W
Lleida, Spain	148	41°38'N	0°37'E
Llera, Mex. (lyā'rä)	118	23°16'N	99°03'W
Llerena, Spain (lyā-rā'nä)	158	38°14'N	6°02'W
Lliria, Spain	159	39°35'N	0°34'W
Llobregat, r., Spain (lyô-brē-gät')	159	41°55'N	1°55'E
Lloyd Lake, l., Can. (loid)	83e	50°52'N	114°13'W
Lloydminster, Can.	84	53°17'N	110°00'W
Llucena, Spain	159	40°08'N	0°18'W
Llucmajor, Spain	159	39°28'N	2°53'E
Llullaillaco, Volcán, vol., S.A. (lyōō-lyī-lyä'kō)	132	24°50'S	68°30'W
Loange, r., Afr. (lô-äŋ'gä)	212	5°00'S	20°15'E
Lo Aranguiz, Chile	234b	33°23'S	70°40'W
Lobamba, Swaz.	212	26°27'S	31°12'E
Lobatse, Bots. (lō-bä'tsē)	212	25°13'S	25°35'E
Lobau, reg., Aus.	239e	48°10'N	16°32'E
Lobería, Arg. (lô-bĕ'rē'ä)	132	38°13'S	58°48'W
Lobito, Ang. (lô-bē'tō)	212	12°30'S	13°34'E
Lobnya, Russia (lôb'nyȧ)	172b	56°01'N	37°29'E
Lobo, Phil.	197a	13°39'N	121°14'E
Lobos, Arg. (lō'bôs)	129c	35°10'S	59°08'W
Lobos, Cayo, i., Bah. (lō'bôs)	122	22°25'N	77°40'W
Lobos, Isla de, i., Mex. (ė's-lä-dĕ-lō'bōs)	119	21°24'N	97°11'W
Lobos de Tierra, i., Peru (lō'bō-dĕ-tyĕ'r-rä)	130	6°29'S	80°55'W
Lobva, Russia (lôb'vȧ)	172a	59°12'N	60°28'E
Lobva, r., Russia	172a	59°14'N	60°17'E
Locarno, Switz. (lô-kär'nō)	154	46°10'N	8°43'E
Lochearn, Md., U.S.	229c	39°21'N	76°43'W
Loches, Fr. (lôsh)	156	47°08'N	0°56'E
Loch Raven Reservoir, res., Md., U.S.	100e	39°28'N	76°38'W
Lockeport, Can.	92	43°42'N	65°07'W
Lockhart, S.C., U.S. (lŏk'hȧrt)	115	34°47'N	81°30'W
Lockhart, Tx., U.S.	113	29°54'N	97°40'W
Lock Haven, Pa., U.S. (lŏk'hā-vĕn)	99	41°05'N	77°30'W
Lockland, Oh., U.S. (lŏk'lănd)	101f	39°14'N	84°27'W
Lockport, Il., U.S.	101a	41°35'N	88°04'W
Lockport, N.Y., U.S.	99	43°11'N	78°43'W
Lockwillow, S. Afr.	244b	26°17'S	27°50'E
Loc Ninh, Viet (lōk'nĭng')	196	12°00'N	106°30'E
Locust Grove, N.Y., U.S.	228	40°48'N	73°30'W
Locust Valley, N.Y., U.S.	228	40°53'N	73°36'W
Lod, Isr. (lôd)	181a	31°57'N	34°55'E
Lodève, Fr. (lô-dĕv')	156	43°43'N	3°18'E
Lodeynoye Pole, Russia (lô-dĕy-nô'yĕ)	166	60°43'N	33°24'E
Lodge Creek, r., N.A. (lŏj)	105	49°20'N	110°20'W
Lodge Creek, r., Mt., U.S.	105	48°51'N	109°30'W
Lodgepole Creek, r., Wy., U.S. (lŏj'pōl)	102	41°22'N	104°48'W
Lodhran, Pak.	186	29°40'N	71°39'E
Lodi, Italy (lô'dė)	160	45°18'N	9°30'E
Lodi, Ca., U.S. (lō'dī)	108	38°07'N	121°17'W
Lodi, N.J., U.S.	228	40°53'N	74°05'W
Lodi, Oh., U.S. (lō'dī)	101d	41°02'N	82°01'W
Lodosa, Spain (lô-dô'sä)	158	42°27'N	2°04'W
Lodwar, Kenya	217	3°07'N	35°36'E
Łódź, Pol.	142	51°46'N	19°30'E
Loeches, Spain (lô-āch'ĕs)	159a	40°22'N	3°25'W
Loffa, r., Afr.	214	7°10'N	10°35'W
Lofoten, is., Nor. (lô'fô-tĕn)	142	68°26'N	13°42'E
Logan, Oh., U.S. (lō'gȧn)	98	39°35'N	82°25'W
Logan, Ut., U.S.	96	41°46'N	111°51'W
Logan, W.V., U.S.	98	37°50'N	82°00'W
Logan, Mount, mtn., Can.	84	60°54'N	140°33'W
Logansport, In., U.S. (lō'gănz-pōrt)	97	40°45'N	86°25'W
Logan Square, neigh., Il., U.S.	231a	41°56'N	87°42'W
Lognes, Fr.	237c	48°50'N	2°38'E
Logone, r., Afr. (lō-gō'nä) (lô-gôn')	211	10°20'N	15°30'E
Logroño, Spain (lô-grō'nyō)	148	42°28'N	2°25'W
Logrosán, Spain (lô-grô-sän')	158	39°22'N	5°29'W
Løgstør, Den. (lügh-stûr')	152	56°56'N	9°15'E
Lohausen, neigh., Ger.	236	51°16'N	6°44'E
Lohberg, Ger.	236	51°35'N	6°46'E
Lo Hermida, Chile	234b	33°29'S	70°33'W
Lohheide, Ger.	236	51°30'N	6°40'E
Löhme, Ger.	238a	52°37'N	13°40'E
Lohmühle, Ger.	236	51°31'N	6°40'E
Löhnen, Ger.	236	51°36'N	6°39'E
Loir, r., Fr. (lwår)	156	47°40'N	0°07'E
Loire, r., Fr.	142	47°30'N	2°00'E
Loja, Ec. (lô'hä)	130	3°49'S	79°13'W
Loja, Spain (lô'-kä)	158	37°10'N	4°11'W
Loka, D.R.C.	216	0°20'N	17°57'E
Lokala Drift, Bots. (lô'kä-lȧ drĭft)	218d	24°00'S	26°38'E
Lokandu, D.R.C.	217	2°31'S	25°47'E
Lokhvytsia, Ukr.	167	50°21'N	33°16'E
Lokichar, Kenya	217	2°23'N	35°39'E
Lokitaung, Kenya	217	4°16'N	35°45'E
Lokofa-Bokolongo, D.R.C.	216	0°12'N	19°22'E
Lokoja, Nig. (lô-kō'yä)	210	7°47'N	6°45'E

ăt; fĭnȧl; rāte; senāte; ärm; åsk; sofȧ; fâre; ch-choose; dh-as th in other; bē; ėvent; bĕt; recĕnt; cratẽr; g-gō; gh-guttural g; bĭt; ĭ-short neutral; rīde; ĸ-guttural k as ch in German ich;

PRONOUNCING INDEX

Lokolama–Ludlow 311

PLACE (Pronunciation)	PAGE	LAT.	LONG.
Lokolama, D.R.C.	216	2°34′S	19°53′E
Lokosso, Burkina	214	10°19′N	3°40′W
Lol, r., Sudan (lŏl)	211	9°06′N	28°09′E
Loliondo, Tan.	217	2°03′S	35°37′E
Lolland, i., Den. (lôl′än′)	152	54°41′N	11°00′E
Lolo, Mt., U.S.	105	46°45′N	114°05′W
Lom, Bul. (lôm)	149	43°48′N	23°15′E
Loma Linda, Ca., U.S. (lō′mȧ lĭn′dȧ)	107a	34°04′N	117°16′W
Lomami, r., D.R.C.	212	0°50′S	24°40′E
Lomas Chapultepec, neigh., Mex.	233a	19°26′N	99°13′W
Lomas de Zamora, Arg. (lō′mäs dā zä-mō′rä)	129c	34°46′S	58°24′W
Lombard, Il., U.S. (lŏm-bärd)	101a	41°53′N	88°01′W
Lombardia, hist. reg., Italy (lôm-bär-dē′ä)	160	45°20′N	9°30′E
Lombardy, S. Afr.	244b	26°07′S	28°08′E
Lomblen, Pulau, i., Indon. (lŏm-blĕn′)	197	8°08′S	123°45′E
Lombok, i., Indon. (lŏm-bŏk′)	196	9°15′S	116°15′E
Lomé, Togo	210	6°08′N	1°13′E
Lomela, D.R.C. (lô-mā′lȧ)	212	2°19′S	23°33′E
Lomela, r., D.R.C.	212	0°35′S	21°20′E
Lometa, Tx., U.S. (lô-mē′tȧ)	112	31°10′N	98°25′W
Lomié, Cam. (lô-mē-ā′)	215	3°10′N	13°37′E
Lomita, Ca., U.S. (lō-mē′tȧ)	107a	33°48′N	118°20′W
Lommel, Bel.	145a	51°14′N	5°21′E
Lommond, Loch, l., Scot., U.K. (lôk lŏ′mŭnd)	150	56°15′N	4°40′W
Lomonosov, Russia (lô-mô′nô-sof)	172c	59°54′N	29°47′E
Lompoc, Ca., U.S. (lŏm-pŏk′)	108	34°39′N	120°30′W
Łomża, Pol. (lôm′zhȧ)	155	53°11′N	22°04′E
Lonaconing, Md., U.S. (lō-nă-kō′nĭng)	99	39°35′N	78°55′W
London, Can. (lŭn′dŭn)	85	43°00′N	81°20′W
London, Eng., U.K.	142	51°30′N	0°07′W
London, Ky., U.S.	114	37°07′N	84°06′W
London, Oh., U.S.	98	39°50′N	83°30′W
London (Heathrow) Airport, arpt., Eng., U.K.	235	51°27′N	0°28′W
London Colney, Eng., U.K.	235	51°43′N	0°18′W
Londonderry, Can. (lŭn′dŭn-dĕr-ĭ)	92	45°29′N	63°36′W
Londonderry, N. Ire., U.K.	146	55°00′N	7°19′W
Londonderry, Cape, c., Austl.	202	13°30′S	127°00′E
London Zoo, pt. of i., Eng., U.K.	235	51°32′N	0°09′W
Londrina, Braz. (lôn-drē′nä)	131	21°53′S	51°17′W
Lonely, i., Can. (lōn′lĭ)	85	45°35′N	81°30′W
Lone Pine, Ca., U.S.	108	36°36′N	118°03′W
Lone Star, Nic.	121	13°58′N	84°25′W
Long, i., Bah.	117	23°25′N	75°10′W
Long, i., Can.	92	44°21′S	66°25′W
Long, l., N.D., U.S.	102	46°47′N	100°14′W
Long, l., Wa., U.S.	106a	47°29′N	122°36′W
Longa, r., Ang. (lôŋ′gȧ)	212	10°20′S	15°15′E
Long Bay, b., S.C., U.S.	115	33°30′N	78°54′W
Long Beach, Ca., U.S. (lông bēch)	96	33°46′N	118°12′W
Long Beach, N.Y., U.S.	100a	40°35′N	73°38′W
Long Branch, N.J., U.S. (lông brȧnch)	100a	40°18′N	73°59′W
Long Ditton, Eng., U.K.	235	51°23′N	0°20′W
Longdon, N.D., U.S. (lông′-dŭn)	102	48°45′N	98°23′W
Long Eaton, Eng., U.K. (ē′tŭn)	144a	52°54′N	1°16′W
Longfield, Eng., U.K.	235	51°24′N	0°18′E
Longford, Ire. (lông′fērd)	150	53°43′N	7°40′W
Longgu, China (lôŋ-gōō)	190	34°52′N	116°48′E
Longhorn, Tx., U.S. (lông-hôrn)	107d	29°33′N	98°23′W
Longhua, China	241a	31°09′N	121°26′E
Longido, Tan.	217	2°44′S	36°41′E
Long Island, i., Pap. N. Gui.	197	5°10′S	147°30′E
Long Island, i., Ak., U.S.	86	54°54′N	132°45′W
Long Island, i., N.Y., U.S. (lông)	97	40°50′N	72°50′W
Long Island City, neigh., N.Y., U.S.	228	40°45′N	73°56′W
Long Island Sound, strt., U.S. (lông ī′lănd)	97	41°05′N	72°45′W
Longjumeau, Fr. (lôN-zhü-mō′)	157b	48°42′N	2°17′E
Longkou, China (lôŋ-kō)	190	37°39′N	120°21′E
Longlac, Can. (lông′lȧk)	85	49°41′N	86°28′W
Longlake, S.D., U.S. (lông-lāk)	102	45°52′N	99°06′W
Long Lake, l., Can.	90	49°10′N	86°45′W
Longmont, Co., U.S. (lông′mŏnt)	110	40°11′N	105°07′W
Longnor, Eng., U.K. (lông′nôr)	144a	53°11′N	1°52′W
Long Pine, Ne., U.S. (lông pīn)	102	42°31′N	99°42′W
Long Point, Austl.	243a	34°01′S	150°54′E
Long Point, c., Can.	89	53°02′N	98°40′W
Long Point, c., Can.	91	42°35′N	80°05′W
Long Point, c., Can.	93	48°48′N	58°46′W
Long Point Bay, b., Can.	91	42°40′N	80°10′W
Long Range Mountains, mts., Can.	85a	48°00′N	58°30′W
Longreach, Austl. (lông′rēch)	203	23°32′S	144°17′E
Long Reach, r., Can.	92	45°26′N	66°05′W
Long Reef, c., Austl.	201b	33°45′S	151°22′E
Longridge, Eng., U.K. (lông′rĭj)	144a	53°51′N	2°37′W
Longs Peak, mtn., Co., U.S. (lôngz)	96	40°17′N	105°37′W
Longtansi, China (lôŋ-tä-sz)	190	32°12′N	115°53′E
Longton, Eng., U.K. (lông′tŭn)	144a	52°59′N	2°08′W
Longueuil, Can. (lôN-gû′y′)	91	45°32′N	73°30′W
Longueville, Austl.	243a	33°50′S	151°10′E
Longview, Tx., U.S.	113	32°29′N	94°44′W
Longview, Wa., U.S. (lông-vū)	104	46°06′N	123°02′W
Longville, La., U.S. (lông′vĭl)	113	30°36′N	93°14′W
Longwy, Fr. (lôN-wē′)	157	49°32′N	6°14′E
Longxi, China (lôŋ-shyē)	188	35°00′N	104°40′E
Long Xuyen, Viet (loung′ sōō′yĕn)	196	10°31′N	105°28′E
Longzhou, China (lôŋ-jō)	188	22°20′N	107°02′E
Lonoke, Ar., U.S. (lō′nōk)	111	34°48′N	91°52′W
Lons-le-Saunier, Fr. (lôN-lē-sō-nyā′)	157	46°40′N	5°33′E
Lontue, r., Chile (lōn-tòĕ′)	129b	35°20′S	70°45′W
Looc, Phil. (lō-ōk′)	197a	12°16′N	121°59′E
Loogootee, In., U.S.	98	38°40′N	86°55′W
Lookout, Cape, c., N.C., U.S. (lòk′out)	115	34°34′N	76°38′W
Lookout Point Lake, res., Or., U.S.	104	43°51′N	122°38′W
Loolmalasin, mtn., Tan.	217	3°03′S	35°46′E
Looma, Can. (ō′mă)	83g	53°22′N	113°15′W
Loop, neigh., Il., U.S.	231a	41°53′N	87°38′W
Loop Head, c., Ire. (lōōp)	150	52°32′N	9°59′W
Loosahatchie, r., Tn., U.S. (lōz-ȧ-hă′chē)	114	35°20′N	89°45′W
Loosdrechtsche Plassen, l., Neth.	145a	52°11′N	5°09′E
Lopatka, Mys, c., Russia (lō-păt′kȧ)	181	51°00′N	156°52′E
Lopez, Cap, c., Gabon	216	0°37′N	8°43′E
Lopez Bay, b., Phil. (lō′pāz)	197a	14°04′N	122°00′E
Lopez I, Wa., U.S.	106a	48°25′N	122°53′W
Lopori, r., D.R.C. (lō-pō′rē)	211	1°35′N	20°43′E
Lo Prado Arriba, Chile	234b	33°26′S	70°45′W
Lora, Spain (lō′rä)	158	37°40′N	5°31′W
Lorain, Oh., U.S. (lō-rān′)	101d	41°28′N	82°10′W
Loralai, Pak. (lō-rŭ-lī′)	183	30°31′N	68°35′E
Lorca, Spain (lôr′kä)	148	37°39′N	1°40′W
Lord Howe, i., Austl. (lôrd hou)	202	31°44′S	157°56′W
Lordsburg, N.M., U.S. (lôrdz′bûrg)	109	32°20′N	108°45′W
Lorena, Braz. (lō-rā′nȧ)	129a	22°45′S	45°07′W
Loreto, Braz. (lō-rā′tō)	131	7°09′S	45°10′W
Loretteville, Can. (lō-rĕt-vēl′)	83b	46°51′N	71°21′W
Lorica, Col. (lō-rē′kä)	130	9°14′N	75°54′W
Lorient, Fr. (lō-rē′äN′)	147	47°45′N	3°22′W
Lorn, Firth of, b., Scot., U.K. (fûrth ŏv lôrn′)	150	56°10′N	6°09′W
Lörrach, Ger. (lûr′äĸ)	154	47°36′N	7°38′E
Lorraine, hist. reg., Fr.	157	49°00′N	6°00′E
Los Alamitos, Ca., U.S. (lōs ăl-ȧ-mē′tōs)	107a	33°48′N	118°04′W
Los Alamos, N.M., U.S. (ăl-ȧ-mōs′)	109	35°53′N	106°20′W
Los Altos, Ca., U.S. (ăl-tôs′)	106b	37°23′N	122°06′W
Los Andes, Chile (ȧn′dĕs)	129b	32°44′S	70°36′W
Los Angeles, Chile (äŋ′hȧ-lās)	132	37°27′S	72°15′W
Los Angeles, Ca., U.S.	108	34°03′N	118°14′W
Los Angeles, r., Ca., U.S.	107a	33°50′N	118°13′W
Los Angeles Aqueduct, Ca., U.S.	108	35°12′N	118°02′W
Los Angeles International Airport, arpt., Ca., U.S.	232	33°56′N	118°24′W
Los Bronces, Chile (lōs brō′n-sĕs)	129b	33°09′S	70°18′W
Loscha, r., Id., U.S. (lŏs′chă)	104	46°20′N	115°11′W
Los Cuatro Álamos, Chile	234b	33°32′S	70°44′W
Los Dos Caminos, Ven.	234a	10°31′N	66°50′W
Los Estados, Isla de, i., Arg. (ē′s-lä dĕ lōs ĕs-dōs)	132	54°45′S	64°25′W
Los Gatos, Ca., U.S. (gă′tōs)	108	37°13′N	121°59′W
Los Herreras, Mex. (ĕr-rā-räs)	112	25°55′N	99°23′W
Los Ilanos, Dom. Rep. (lōs ē-lä′nōs)	123	18°35′N	69°30′W
Los Indios, Cayos de, is., Cuba (kä′vōs dĕ lōs ē′n-dvō′s)	122	21°50′N	83°10′W
Lošinj, i., Yugo.	160	44°35′N	14°34′E
Losino Petrovskiy, Russia	172b	55°52′N	38°12′E
Los Nietos, Ca., U.S. (nyā′tōs)	107a	33°57′N	118°05′W
Los Palacios, Cuba	122	22°35′N	83°15′W
Los Pinos, r., Co., U.S. (pē′nōs)	109	36°58′N	107°35′W
Los Reyes, Mex.	116	19°35′N	102°29′W
Los Reyes, Mex.	119a	19°21′N	98°58′W
Los Santos, Pan. (săn′tōs)	121	7°57′N	80°24′W
Los Santos de Maimona, Spain (săn′tōs)	158	38°38′N	6°30′W
Lost, r., Or., U.S.	104	42°07′N	121°30′W
Los Teques, Ven. (tĕ′kĕs)	130	10°22′N	67°04′W
Lost River Range, mts., Id., U.S. (rĭ′vĕr)	105	44°23′N	113°48′W
Los Vilos, Chile (vē′lōs)	132	31°56′S	71°29′W
Lot, r., Fr. (lôt)	147	44°30′N	1°30′E
Lota, Chile (lō′tä)	132	37°11′S	73°14′W
Lothian, Md., U.S. (lōth′ĭăn)	100e	38°50′N	76°38′W
Lotikipi Plain, pl., Afr.	217	4°25′N	34°55′E
Lötschberg Tunnel, trans., Switz.	154	46°26′N	7°54′E
Louangphrabang, Laos (lōō-ang′prä-bäng′)	196	19°47′N	102°15′E
Loudon, Tn., U.S. (lou′dŭn)	114	35°43′N	84°20′W
Loudonville, Oh., U.S. (lou′dŭn-vĭl)	98	40°40′N	82°15′W
Loudun, Fr.	156	47°03′N	0.00
Loughborough, Eng., U.K. (lŭf′bŭr-ō)	144a	52°46′N	1°12′W
Loughton, Eng., U.K.	235	51°39′N	0°03′E
Louisa, Ky., U.S. (lōō′ēz-ȧ)	98	38°05′N	82°40′W
Louisade Archipelago, is., Pap. N. Gui.	203	10°44′S	153°58′E
Louisburg, N.C., U.S. (lōō′ĭs-bûrg)	115	36°05′N	79°19′W
Louisburg, Can. (lōō′ĭs-bourg)	93	45°55′N	59°58′W
Louiseville, Can.	91	46°17′N	72°58′W
Louisiana, Mo., U.S. (lōō-ē-zē-ăn′ȧ)	111	39°24′N	91°03′W
Louisiana, state, U.S.	97	30°50′N	92°50′W
Louis Trichardt, S. Afr. (lōō′ĭs trĭchȧrt)	212	22°52′S	29°53′E
Louisville, Co., U.S. (lōō′ĭs-vĭl) (lōō′ē-vĭl)	110	39°58′N	105°08′W
Louisville, Ga., U.S.	115	33°00′N	82°25′W
Louisville, Ky., U.S.	97	38°15′N	85°45′W
Louisville, Ms., U.S.	114	33°07′N	89°02′W
Louis XIV, Pointe, c., Can.	85	54°35′N	79°51′W
Louny, Czech Rep. (lō′nē)	154	50°20′N	13°47′E
Loup, r., Ne., U.S. (lōōp)	102	41°17′N	97°58′W
Loup City, Ne., U.S.	102	41°15′N	98°59′W
Lourdes, Fr. (lōōrd)	147	43°06′N	0°03′W
Lourenço Marques see Maputo, Moz.	212	26°50′S	32°30′E
Loures, Port. (lō′rĕzh)	159b	38°49′N	9°10′W
Lousa, Port. (lō′zȧ)	158	40°05′N	8°12′W
Louth, Eng., U.K. (louth)	150	53°27′N	0°02′W
Louvain see Leuven, Bel.	151	50°53′N	4°42′E
Louveciennes, Fr.	237c	48°52′N	2°07′E
Louviers, Fr. (lōō-vyā′)	156	49°13′N	1°11′E
Louvre, bldg., Fr.	237c	48°52′N	2°20′E
Lovech, Bul. (lō′vĕts)	161	43°10′N	24°40′E
Lovedale, Pa., U.S.	230b	40°17′N	79°52′W
Loveland, Co., U.S. (lŭv′lănd)	110	40°24′N	105°04′W
Loveland, Oh., U.S.	101f	39°16′N	84°15′W
Lovell, Wy., U.S. (lŭv′ĕl)	105	44°50′N	108°23′W
Lovelock, Nv., U.S. (lŭv′lŏk)	108	40°10′N	118°37′W
Loves Green, Eng., U.K.	235	51°43′N	0°24′E
Lovick, Al., U.S. (lŭ′vĭk)	100h	33°34′N	86°38′W
Loviisa, Fin. (lô′vē-sȧ)	153	60°28′N	26°10′E
Low, Cape, c., Can. (lō)	85	62°58′N	86°50′W
Lowa, r., D.R.C. (lō′wȧ)	212	1°30′S	27°18′E
Lowell, In., U.S.	101a	41°17′N	87°26′W
Lowell, Ma., U.S.	97	42°38′N	71°18′W
Lowell, Mi., U.S.	98	42°55′N	85°20′W
Löwenberg, Ger. (lû′vĕn-bĕrgh)	145b	52°53′N	13°09′E
Lower Broughton, neigh., Eng., U.K.	237b	53°29′N	2°15′W
Lower Brule Indian Reservation, I.R., S.D., U.S. (brü′lā)	102	44°15′N	100°21′W
Lower California see Baja CAlifornia, pen., Mex.	82	28°00′N	113°30′W
Lower Granite Dam, dam, Wa., U.S.	104	46°40′N	117°26′W
Lower Higham, Eng., U.K.	235	51°26′N	0°28′E
Lower Hutt, N.Z. (hŭt)	203a	41°10′S	174°55′E
Lower Klamath Lake, l., Ca., U.S. (klăm′ăth)	104	41°55′N	121°50′W
Lower Lake, l., Ca., U.S.	104	41°21′N	119°53′W
Lower Marlboro, Md., U.S. (lō′ēr mărl′bōrō)	100e	38°40′N	76°42′W
Lower Monumental Dam, dam, Wa., U.S.	104	46°34′N	118°32′W
Lower Nazeing, Eng., U.K.	235	51°44′N	0°01′E
Lower New York Bay, b., N.Y., U.S.	228	40°33′N	74°02′W
Lower Otay Lake, res., Ca., U.S. (ō′tā)	108a	32°37′N	116°46′W
Lower Place, Eng., U.K.	237b	53°36′N	2°09′W
Lower Red Lake, l., Mn., U.S.	103	47°58′N	94°31′W
Lower Saxony see Niedersachsen, hist. reg., Ger.	154	52°52′N	8°27′E
Lowestoft, Eng., U.K. (lō′stŏf)	151	52°31′N	1°45′E
Łowicz, Pol. (lô′vĭch)	155	52°06′N	19°57′E
Lowville, N.Y., U.S. (lou′vĭl)	99	43°45′N	75°30′W
Loxicha, Mex.	119	16°03′N	96°46′W
Loxton, Austl. (lôks′tŭn)	204	34°25′S	140°38′E
Loyauté, Îles, is., N. Cal.	203	21°00′S	167°00′E
Loznica, Yugo. (lōz′nē-tsȧ)	149	44°31′N	19°16′E
Lozova, Ukr.	167	48°53′N	36°23′E
Luama, r., D.R.C. (lōō′ä-mȧ)	212	4°17′S	27°45′E
Lu'an, China (lōō-ăn)	193	31°45′N	116°29′E
Luan, r., China	189	41°25′N	117°15′E
Luanda, Ang. (lōō-än′dä)	212	8°48′S	13°14′E
Luanguinga, r., Afr. (lōō-ä-gĭŋ′gȧ)	212	14°00′S	20°45′E
Luanshya, Zam.	217	13°08′S	28°24′E
Luanxian, China (luän shyĕn)	190	39°47′N	118°40′E
Luao, Ang.	216	10°42′S	22°12′E
Luarca, Spain (lwä′kä)	148	43°33′N	6°30′W
Lubaczów, Pol. (lōō-bä′chóf)	155	50°08′N	23°10′E
Lubán, Pol. (lōō′bän′)	154	51°08′N	15°17′E
Lubānas Ezers, l., Lat. (lōō-bä′nȧs ā′zĕrs)	153	56°48′N	26°30′E
Lubang, Phil. (lōō-bäng′)	197a	13°49′N	120°07′E
Lubang Islands, is., Phil.	196	13°47′N	119°56′E
Lubango, Ang.	212	14°55′S	13°30′E
Lubartów, Pol. (lōō-bär′tóf)	155	51°27′N	22°37′E
Lubawa, Pol. (lōō-bä′vä)	155	53°31′N	19°47′E
Lübben, Ger. (lüb′ĕn)	154	51°56′N	13°53′E
Lubbock, Tx., U.S.	97	33°35′N	101°50′E
Lubec, Me., U.S. (lū′bĕk)	92	44°49′N	67°01′W
Lübeck, Ger. (lü′bĕk)	142	53°53′N	10°42′E
Lübecker Bucht, b., Ger. (lü′bĕ-kĕr bōōĸt)	146	54°10′N	11°20′E
Lubilash, r., D.R.C. (lōō-bē-lȧsh′)	212	7°35′S	23°55′E
Lubin, Pol. (lyò′bĭn)	154	51°24′N	16°14′E
Lublin, Pol. (lyòb′lēn′)	142	51°14′N	22°33′E
Lubny, Ukr. (lòb′nē)	167	50°01′N	33°02′E
Lubuagan, Phil. (lō-bwä-gä′n)	197a	17°24′N	121°11′E
Lubudi, D.R.C.	217	9°57′S	25°58′E
Lubudi, r., D.R.C. (lō-bò′dē)	212	10°00′S	24°30′E
Lubumbashi, D.R.C.	212	11°40′S	27°28′E
Lucano, Ang.	216	11°16′S	21°38′E
Lucca, Italy (lōōk′kä)	148	43°51′N	10°29′E
Lucea, Jam.	122	18°25′N	78°10′W
Luce Bay, b., Scot., U.K. (lūs)	150	54°45′N	4°45′W
Lucena, Phil. (lōō-sä′nä)	197a	13°55′N	121°36′E
Lucena, Spain (lōō-thā′nä)	148	37°25′N	4°28′W
Lučenec, Slvk. (lōō′châ-nyĕts)	147	48°19′N	19°41′E
Lucera, Italy (lōō-châ′rä)	160	41°31′N	15°22′E
Luchi, China	193	28°18′N	110°10′E
Luchou, Tai.	241d	25°05′N	121°28′E
Lucin, Ut., U.S. (lù-sēn′)	105	41°23′N	113°59′W
Lucipara, Kepulauan, is., Indon.	197	5°45′S	128°15′E
Luckenwalde, Ger.	154	52°05′N	13°10′E
Lucknow, India (lŭk′nou)	183	26°54′N	80°58′E
Lucky Peak Lake, res., Id., U.S.	104	43°33′N	116°00′W
Luçon, Fr. (lü-sôN′)	156	46°27′N	1°12′W
Lucrecia, Cabo, c., Cuba	123	21°05′N	75°30′W
Luda Kamchiya, r., Bul.	161	42°46′N	27°13′E
Luddesdown, Eng., U.K.	235	51°22′N	0°24′E
Lüdenscheid, Ger. (lü′dĕn-shīt)	157c	51°13′N	7°38′E
Lüderitz, Nmb. (lü′dēr-ĭts) (lü′dĕ-rĭts)	212	26°35′S	15°15′E
Lüderitz Bucht, b., Nmb.	212	26°35′S	14°30′E
Ludhiāna, India	183	31°00′N	75°52′E
Lüdinghausen, Ger.	157c	51°46′N	7°27′E
Ludington, Mi., U.S. (lŭd′ĭng-tŭn)	98	44°00′N	86°25′W
Ludlow, Eng., U.K. (lŭd′lō)	144a	52°22′N	2°43′W
Ludlow, Ky., U.S.	101f	39°05′N	84°33′W

312 Ludvika–Maeno

PLACE (Pronunciation)	PAGE	LAT.	LONG.
Ludvika, Swe. (loodh-vē'kȧ)	152	60°10'N	15°09'E
Ludwigsburg, Ger.	154	48°53'N	9°14'E
Ludwigsfelde, Ger.	145b	52°18'N	13°16'E
Ludwigshafen, Ger.	154	49°29'N	8°26'E
Ludwigslust, Ger.	154	53°18'N	11°31'E
Ludza, Lat. (lo͞od'zȧ)	153	56°33'N	27°45'E
Luebo, D.R.C. (lo͞o-ā'bō)	212	5°15'S	21°22'E
Luena, Ang.	212	11°45'S	19°55'E
Luena, D.R.C.	217	9°27'S	25°47'E
Lufira, r., D.R.C. (lo͞o-fē'rȧ)	212	9°32'S	27°15'E
Lufkin, Tx., U.S. (lŭf'kĭn)	113	31°21'N	94°43'W
Luga, Russia (lo͞o'gȧ)	166	58°43'N	29°52'E
Luga, r., Russia	162	59°00'N	29°25'E
Lugano, Switz. (lo͞o-gä'nō)	154	46°01'N	8°52'E
Lugarno, Austl.	243a	33°59'S	151°03'E
Lugenda, r., Moz.	213	12°05'S	38°15'E
Lugo, Italy (lo͞o'gô)	160	44°28'N	11°57'E
Lugo, Spain (lo͞o'gō)	148	43°01'N	7°32'W
Lugoj, Rom.	149	45°51'N	21°56'E
Lugouqiao, China	240b	39°51'N	116°13'E
Luhans'k, Ukr.	164	48°34'N	39°18'E
Luhans'k, prov., Ukr.	163	49°30'N	38°35'E
Luhe, China (lo͞o-hŭ)	190	32°22'N	118°50'E
Luiana, Ang.	216	17°23'S	23°03'E
Luilaka, r., D.R.C. (lo͞o-ē-lä'kȧ)	212	2°18'S	21°15'E
Luis Moya, Mex. (lo͞oē's-mô-yä)	118	22°26'N	102°14'W
Luján, Arg. (lo͞o'hän')	129c	34°36'S	59°07'W
Luján, r., Arg.	129c	34°33'S	58°59'W
Lujia, China (lo͞o-jyä)	190	31°17'N	120°54'W
Lukanga Swamp, sw., Zam. (lo͞o-käŋ'gȧ)	212	14°30'S	27°25'E
Lukenie, r., D.R.C. (lo͞o-kā'nyȧ)	212	3°10'S	19°05'E
Lukolela, D.R.C.	212	1°03'S	17°01'E
Lukovit, Bul. (lo͞o'kō-vēt')	161	43°13'N	24°07'E
Łuków, Pol. (wō'kōf)	155	51°57'N	22°25'E
Lukuga, r., D.R.C. (lo͞o-ko͞o'gȧ)	212	5°50'S	27°35'E
Lüleburgaz, Tur. (lü'lĕ-bŏr-gäs')	161	41°25'N	27°23'E
Luling, Tx., U.S. (lū'lĭng)	113	29°41'N	97°38'W
Lulong, China (lo͞o-lôŋ)	189	39°54'N	118°53'E
Lulonga, r., D.R.C.	216	1°00'N	18°37'E
Luluabourg *see* Kananga, D.R.C.	212	6°14'S	22°17'E
Lulu Island, i., Can.	106d	49°09'N	123°05'W
Lulu Island, i., Ak., U.S.	84	55°28'N	133°30'W
Lumajangdong Co, l., China	186	34°00'N	81°47'E
Lumber, r., N.C., U.S. (lŭm'bẽr)	115	34°45'N	79°10'W
Lumberton, Ms., U.S. (lŭm'bẽr-tŭn)	114	31°00'N	89°25'W
Lumberton, N.C., U.S.	115	34°47'N	79°00'W
Luminárias, Braz. (lo͞o-mē-ná'ryäs)	129a	21°32'S	44°53'W
Lummi, i., Wa., U.S.	106d	48°42'N	122°43'W
Lummi Bay, b., Wa., U.S. (lŭm'ĭ)	106d	48°47'N	122°44'W
Lummi Island, Wa., U.S.	106d	48°44'N	122°42'W
Lumwana, Zam.	217	11°50'S	25°10'E
Lün, Mong.	188	47°58'N	104°52'E
Luna, Phil. (lo͞o'nȧ)	197a	16°51'N	120°22'E
Lund, Swe. (lŭnd)	146	55°42'N	13°10'E
Lundy, i., Eng., U.K. (lŭn'dē)dep)	150	51°12'N	4°50'W
Lüneburg, Ger. (lü'nĕ-bŏrgh)	154	53°16'N	10°25'E
Lunel, Fr. (lü-nĕl')	156	43°41'N	4°07'E
Lünen, Ger. (lü'nĕn)	157c	51°36'N	7°30'E
Lunenburg, Can. (lo͞o'nĕn-bûrg)	85	44°23'N	64°19'W
Lunenburg, Ma., U.S.	93a	42°36'N	71°44'W
Lunéville, Fr. (lü-nȧ-vel')	157	48°37'N	6°29'E
Lunga, Ang.	216	14°42'S	18°32'E
Lungué-Bungo, r., Afr.	212	13°00'S	20°30'E
Lunsar, S.L.	214	8°41'N	12°32'W
Lunt, Eng., U.K.	237a	53°31'N	2°59'W
Luodian, China (lwô-dĭĕn)	190	31°25'N	121°20'E
Luoding, China (lwô-dĭŋ)	193	23°42'N	111°35'E
Luohe, China (lwô-hŭ)	190	33°35'N	114°02'E
Luoyang, China (lwô-yäŋ)	189	34°45'N	112°32'E
Luozhen, China (lwô-jŭn)	190	37°45'N	118°29'E
Luque, Para. (loo'kā)	132	25°18'S	57°17'W
Luray, Va., U.S. (lū-rā')	99	38°40'N	78°25'W
Lurgan, N. Ire., U.K. (lûr'găn)	146	54°27'N	6°28'W
Lurigancho, Peru	233c	12°02'S	77°01'W
Lúrio, Moz. (lo͞o'rê-ŏ)	213	13°17'S	40°29'E
Lúrio, Moz.	213	14°00'S	38°45'E
Lurnea, Austl.	243a	33°56'S	150°54'E
Lusaka, D.R.C.	217	7°10'S	29°27'E
Lusaka, Zam. (lō-sä'kȧ)	212	15°25'S	28°17'E
Lusambo, D.R.C. (lo͞o-säm'bō)	212	4°58'S	23°27'E
Lusanga, D.R.C.	212	5°13'S	18°43'E
Lusangi, D.R.C.	217	4°37'S	27°08'E
Lushan, China	192	33°45'N	113°00'E
Lushiko, r., Afr.	216	6°35'S	19°45'E
Lushoto, Tan. (lo͞o-shō'tō)	213	4°47'S	38°17'E
Lüshun, China (lü-shŭn)	189	38°49'N	121°15'E
Lusikisiki, S. Afr. (lo͞o-sē-kē-sē'kē)	213c	31°22'S	29°37'E
Lusk, Wy., U.S. (lŭsk)	102	42°46'N	104°27'W
Lūt, Dasht-e, des., Iran (dăsht-ē-lo͞ot)	182	31°47'N	58°38'E
Lutcher, La., U.S. (lŭch'ẽr)	113	30°03'N	90°43'W
Lütgendortmund, neigh., Ger.	236	51°30'N	7°21'E
Luton, Eng., U.K. (lū'tŭn)	150	51°55'N	0°28'W
Luts'k, Ukr.	167	50°45'N	25°20'E
Lüttringhausen, neigh., Ger.	236	51°13'N	7°14'E
Luuq, Som.	218a	3°38'N	42°35'E
Luverne, Al., U.S. (lū-vûn')	114	31°42'N	86°15'W
Luverne, Mn., U.S.	102	43°40'N	96°13'W
Luwingu, Zam.	217	10°15'S	29°55'E
Luxapallila Creek, r., U.S. (lŭk-sȧ-pôl'ĭ-lȧ)	114	33°36'N	88°08'W
Luxembourg, Lux.	142	49°38'N	6°30'E
Luxembourg, nation, Eur.	142	49°30'N	6°22'E
Luxeuil-les-Baines, Fr.	157	47°49'N	6°19'E
Luxomni, Ga., U.S. (lŭx'ŏm-nī)	100c	33°54'N	84°07'W
Luxor *see* Al Uqṣur, Egypt	211	25°38'N	32°59'E
Lu Xun Museum, bldg., China	241a	31°16'N	121°28'E
Luya Shan, mtn., China	192	38°50'N	111°40'E
Luyi, China (lo͞o-yē)	190	33°52'N	115°32'E
Luyuan, China	240b	39°54'N	116°27'E
Luz, Braz.	234c	22°48'S	43°05'W
Luz, neigh., Port.	238d	38°46'N	9°10'W
Luzern, Switz. (lō-tsĕrn)	147	47°03'N	8°18'E
Luzhou, China (lo͞o-jō)	188	28°58'N	105°25'E
Luziânia, Braz. (lo͞o-zyá'nēä)	131	16°17'S	47°44'W
Lužniki, neigh., Russia	239b	55°43'N	37°33'E
Luzon, i., Phil. (lo͞o-zŏn')	196	17°10'N	119°45'E
Luzon Strait, strt., Asia	193	20°40'N	121°00'E
L'viv, Ukr.	164	49°50'N	24°00'E
Lyalta, Can.	83e	51°07'N	113°36'W
Lyalya, r., Russia (lyá'lyȧ)	172a	58°58'N	60°17'E
Lyaskovets, Bul.	161	43°07'N	25°41'E
Lydenburg, S. Afr. (lī'dĕn-bûrg)	212	25°06'S	30°21'E
Lydiate, Eng., U.K.	237a	53°32'N	2°57'W
Lye Green, Eng., U.K.	235	51°43'N	0°35'W
Lyell, Mount, mtn., Ca., U.S. (lī'ĕl)	108	37°44'N	119°22'W
Lykens, Pa., U.S. (lī'kĕnz)	99	40°35'N	76°45'W
Lykhivka, Ukr.	163	48°52'N	33°57'E
Lyna, r., Eur. (lĭn'á)	155	53°56'N	20°30'E
Lynbrook, N.Y., U.S.	228	40°39'N	73°41'W
Lynch, Ky., U.S. (lĭnch)	115	36°56'N	82°55'W
Lynchburg, Va., U.S. (lĭnch'bûrg)	97	37°23'N	79°08'W
Lynch Cove, Wa., U.S. (lĭnch)	106a	47°26'N	122°54'W
Lynden, Can. (lĭn'dĕn)	83d	43°14'N	80°08'W
Lynden, Wa., U.S.	106d	48°56'N	122°27'W
Lyndhurst, Austl.	201a	38°03'S	145°14'E
Lyndhurst, N.J., U.S.	228	40°49'N	74°07'W
Lyndhurst, Oh., U.S.	229a	41°31'N	81°30'W
Lyndon, Ky., U.S. (lĭn'dŭn)	101h	38°15'N	85°36'W
Lyndonville, Vt., U.S. (lĭn'dŭn-vĭl)	99	44°35'N	72°00'W
Lyne, Eng., U.K.	235	51°23'N	0°33'W
Lynn, Ma., U.S. (lĭn)	97	42°28'N	70°57'W
Lynnewood Gardens, Pa., U.S.	229b	40°04'N	75°09'W
Lynnfield, Ma., U.S.	227a	42°32'N	71°03'W
Lynn Lake, Can. (lăk)	84	56°51'N	101°05'W
Lynwood, Ca., U.S. (lĭn'wŏd)	107a	33°56'N	118°13'W
Lyon, Fr. (lē-ôɴ')	142	45°44'N	4°52'E
Lyons, Ga., U.S. (lī'ŭnz)	115	32°08'N	82°19'W
Lyons, Il., U.S.	231a	41°49'N	87°50'W
Lyons, Ks., U.S.	110	38°20'N	98°11'W
Lyons, Ne., U.S.	102	41°57'N	96°28'W
Lyons, N.J., U.S.	100a	40°41'N	74°33'W
Lyons, N.Y., U.S.	99	43°05'N	77°00'W
Lyptsi, Ukr.	163	50°11'N	36°25'E
Lysefjorden, fj., Nor.	152	58°59'N	6°35'E
Lysekil, Swe. (lü'sĕ-kēl)	152	58°17'N	11°22'E
Lysterfield, Austl.	243b	37°56'S	145°18'E
Lys'va, Russia (lĭs'vȧ)	166	58°07'N	57°47'E
Lytham, Eng., U.K. (lĭth'ăm)	144a	53°44'N	2°58'W
Lytkarino, Russia	172b	55°35'N	37°55'E
Lyttelton, S. Afr. (lĭt'l'ton)	213b	25°51'S	28°13'E
Lyuban', Russia (lyo͞o'bȧn)	162	59°21'N	31°15'E
Lyubertsy, Russia (lyo͞o'bĕr-tsē)	162	55°40'N	37°55'E
Lyubim, Russia (lyo͞o-bēm')	162	58°24'N	40°39'E
Lyublino, Russia (lyo͞ob'lĭ-nō)	172b	55°41'N	37°45'E
Lyudinovo, Russia (lū-dē'novō)	162	53°52'N	34°28'E

M

PLACE (Pronunciation)	PAGE	LAT.	LONG.
Ma'ān, Jord. (mä-än')	182	30°12'N	35°45'E
Maartensdijk, Neth.	145a	52°09'N	5°10'E
Maas (Meuse), r., Eur.	151	51°50'N	5°40'E
Maastricht, Neth. (mäs'trĭkt)	151	50°51'N	5°35'E
Mabaia, Ang.	216	7°13'S	14°03'E
Mabana, Wa., U.S. (mä-bä-nä)	106a	48°06'N	122°25'W
Mabank, Tx., U.S. (mā'bănk)	113	32°21'N	96°05'W
Mabeskraal, S. Afr.	218d	25°12'S	26°47'E
Mableton, Ga., U.S. (mā'b'l-tŭn)	100c	33°49'N	84°34'W
Mabrouk, Mali	210	19°27'N	1°16'W
Mabula, S. Afr. (mä'bo͞o-la)	218d	24°49'S	27°59'E
Macalelon, Phil. (mä-kä-lā-lōn')	197a	13°46'N	122°09'E
Macau, Braz. (mä-kà'ō)	131	5°12'S	36°34'W
Macau, dep., Asia	189	22°00'N	113°00'E
Macaya, Pico de, mtn., Haiti	123	18°25'N	74°00'W
Macclesfield, Eng., U.K. (măk''lz-fēld)	144a	53°15'N	2°07'W
Macclesfield Canal, can., Eng., U.K. (măk''lz-fēld)	144a	53°14'N	2°07'W
Macdona, Tx., U.S. (măk-dō'nȧ)	107d	29°20'N	98°42'W
Macdonald, l., Austl. (măk-dŏn'ăld)	202	23°40'S	127°40'E
Macdonnell Ranges, mts., Austl. (măk-dŏn'ĕl)	202	23°40'S	131°30'E
MacDowell Lake, l., Can. (măk-dou ĕl)	89	52°15'N	92°45'W
Macdui, Ben, mtn., Scot., U.K. (bĕn măk-do͞o'ê)	146	57°06'N	3°45'W
Macedonia, Oh., U.S. (măs-ê-dō'nĭ-ȧ)	101d	41°19'N	81°30'E
Macedonia, hist. reg., Eur. (măs-ê-dō'nĭ-ȧ)	149	41°05'N	22°15'E
Macedonia, nation, Eur.	161	41°50'N	22°00'E
Maceió, Braz.	131	9°40'S	35°43'W
Macerata, Italy (mä-chä-rä'tä)	160	43°18'N	13°28'E
Macfarlane, Lake, l., Austl. (măc'fär-lăn)	204	32°10'S	137°00'E
Machache, mtn., Leso.	213c	29°22'S	27°53'E
Machado, Braz. (mä-shá-dô)	129a	21°42'S	45°55'W
Machakos, Kenya	217	1°31'S	37°16'E
Machala, Ec. (mä-chá'lä)	130	3°18'S	78°54'W
Machens, Mo., U.S. (măk'ĕns)	107e	38°54'N	90°20'W
Machias, Me., U.S. (mȧ-chī'ăs)	92	44°22'N	67°29'W
Machida, Japan (mä-chē'dä)	195a	35°32'N	139°28'E
Machilīpatnam, India	183	16°22'N	81°10'E
Machu Picchu, Peru (mä'chō-pē'k-chō)	130	13°07'S	72°34'W
Măcin, Rom. (mȧ-chēn')	163	45°15'N	28°09'E
Macina, reg., Mali	214	14°50'N	4°40'W
Mackay, Austl. (mă-kī')	203	21°15'S	149°08'E
Mackay, Id., U.S. (măk-kā')	105	43°55'N	113°38'W
Mackay, l., Austl. (mă-kī')	202	22°30'S	127°45'E
MacKay, l., Can. (măk-kā')	84	64°10'N	112°35'W
Mackenzie, r., Can.	84	63°38'N	124°23'W
Mackenzie Bay, b., Can.	95	69°20'N	137°10'W
Mackenzie Mountains, mts., Can. (mȧ-kĕn'zĭ)	84	63°41'N	129°27'W
Mackinaw, r., Il., U.S.	98	40°35'N	89°25'W
Mackinaw City, Mi., U.S. (măk'ĭ-nô)	98	45°45'N	84°45'W
Mackinnon Road, Kenya	217	3°44'S	39°03'E
Macleantown, S. Afr. (măk-lăn'toun)	213c	32°48'S	27°48'E
Maclear, S. Afr. (mȧ-klẽr')	212	31°06'S	28°23'E
Macleod, Austl.	243b	37°43'S	145°04'E
Macomb, Il., U.S. (mȧ-ko͞om')	111	40°27'N	90°40'W
Mâcon, Fr. (mä-kôɴ)	147	46°19'N	4°51'E
Macon, Ga., U.S. (mā'kŏn)	97	32°49'N	83°39'W
Macon, Ms., U.S.	114	32°07'N	88°31'W
Macon, Mo., U.S.	111	39°42'N	92°29'W
Macquarie, r., Austl.	203	31°43'S	148°04'E
Macquarie Fields, Austl.	243a	33°59'S	150°53'E
Macquarie Islands, is., Austl. (mȧ-kwŏr'ê)	3	54°36'S	158°45'E
Macquarie University, educ., Austl.	243a	33°46'S	151°06'E
Macritchie Reservoir, res., Sing.	240c	1°21'N	103°50'E
Macuelizo, Hond. (mä-kwĕ-lē'zō)	120	15°22'N	88°32'W
Macuto, Ven.	234a	10°37'N	66°53'W
Mad, r., Ca., U.S. (măd)	104	40°38'N	123°37'W
Madagascar, nation, Afr. (măd-ȧ-găs'kȧr)	213	18°05'S	43°12'E
Madame, i., Can. (mȧ-dȧm')	93	45°33'N	61°02'W
Madanapalle, India	187	13°06'N	78°09'E
Madang, Pap. N. Gui. (mä-däng')	197	5°15'S	145°45'E
Madaoua, Niger (mȧ-dou'ȧ)	210	14°04'N	6°03'E
Madawaska, r., Can. (măd-ȧ-wôs'kȧ)	91	45°20'N	77°25'W
Madeira, r., S.A.	130	6°48'S	62°43'W
Madeira, Arquipélago da, is., Port.	209	33°26'N	16°44'W
Madeira, Ilha da, i., Port. (mä-dā'rä)	210	32°41'N	16°15'W
Madelia, Mn., U.S. (mȧ-dē'lĭ-ȧ)	103	44°03'N	94°23'W
Madeline, i., Wi., U.S. (măd'ĕ-lĭn)	103	46°47'N	91°30'W
Madera, Ca., U.S. (mȧ-dā'rȧ)	108	36°57'N	120°04'W
Madera, vol., Nic.	120	11°27'N	85°30'W
Madgaon, India	187	15°09'N	73°58'E
Madhya Pradesh, state, India (mŭd'vŭ prŭ-dāsh')	183	22°04'N	77°48'E
Madill, Ok., U.S. (mȧ-dĭl')	111	34°04'N	96°45'W
Madīnat ash Sha'b, Yemen	182	12°45'N	44°00'E
Madingo, Congo	216	4°07'S	11°22'E
Madingou, Congo	216	4°09'S	13°34'E
Madison, Fl., U.S. (măd'ĭ-sŭn)	114	30°28'N	83°25'W
Madison, Ga., U.S.	114	33°34'N	83°29'W
Madison, Il., U.S.	107e	38°40'N	90°09'W
Madison, In., U.S.	98	38°45'N	85°25'W
Madison, Ks., U.S.	111	38°08'N	96°07'W
Madison, Me., U.S.	92	44°47'N	69°52'W
Madison, Mn., U.S.	102	44°59'N	96°13'W
Madison, Ne., U.S.	102	41°49'N	97°27'W
Madison, N.J., U.S.	100a	40°46'N	74°25'W
Madison, N.C., U.S.	115	36°22'N	79°59'W
Madison, S.D., U.S.	102	44°01'N	97°08'W
Madison, Wi., U.S.	97	43°05'N	89°23'W
Madison Heights, Mi., U.S.	230c	42°30'N	83°06'W
Madison Res, Mt., U.S.	105	45°25'N	111°28'W
Madisonville, Ky., U.S. (măd'ĭ-sŭn-vĭl)	98	37°20'N	87°30'W
Madisonville, La., U.S.	113	30°22'N	90°10'W
Madisonville, Tx., U.S.	113	30°57'N	95°55'W
Madjori, Burkina	214	11°26'N	1°15'E
Mado Gashi, Kenya	217	0°44'N	39°10'E
Madona, Lat. (mȧ'dō'nȧ)	153	56°50'N	26°14'E
Madrakah, Ra's al, c., Oman	182	18°53'N	57°48'E
Madras *see* Chennai, India	183	13°08'N	80°15'E
Madre, Laguna, l., Mex. (lä-go͞o'nä mä'drå)	113	25°08'N	97°41'W
Madre, Sierra, mts., N.A. (sē-ĕ'r-rä-mä'drĕ)	119	15°55'N	92°40'W
Madre, Sierra, mts., Phil.	197a	16°40'N	122°10'E
Madre de Dios, Archipiélago, is., Chile (mä'drå dā dē-ōs')	132	50°40'S	76°30'W
Madre de Dios, Río, r., S.A. (rê'ō-mä'drå dā dē-ōs)	130	12°07'S	68°02'W
Madre del Sur, Sierra, mts., Mex. (sē-ĕ'r-rä-mä'drå dĕlso͞or')	116	17°35'N	100°35'W
Madre Occidental, Sierra, mts., Mex.	116	29°30'N	107°30'W
Madre Oriental, Sierra, mts., Mex.	116	25°30'N	100°45'W
Madrid, Spain (mä-drē'd)	142	40°26'N	3°42'W
Madrid, Ia., U.S. (măd'rĭd)	103	41°51'N	93°48'W
Madridejos, Spain (mä-dhrē-dhä'hōs)	158	39°29'N	3°32'W
Madrillon, Va., U.S.	229d	38°55'N	77°14'W
Madura, i., Indon. (mȧ-do͞o'rä)	196	6°45'S	113°30'E
Madurai, India (mä-do͞o'rä)	183	9°57'N	78°04'E
Madureira, neigh., Braz.	234c	22°53'S	43°21'W
Madureira, Serra do, mtn., Braz. (sĕ'r-rä-dô-mä-do͞o-rä'rȧ)	132b	22°49'S	43°30'W
Maebashi, Japan (mä-ĕ-bä'shē)	189	36°26'N	139°04'E
Maeno, neigh., Japan	242a	35°46'N	139°42'E

PRONOUNCING INDEX Maestra–Mandve 313

PLACE (Pronunciation)	PAGE	LAT.	LONG.
Maestra, Sierra, mts., Cuba (sē-ĕ′r-rä-mä-ās′trä)	117	20°05′N	77°05′W
Maewo, i., Vanuatu	203	15°17′S	168°16′E
Mafeking, S. Afr. (măf′ĕ′kĭng)	212	25°46′S	24°45′E
Mafra, Braz. (mä′frä)	132	26°21′N	49°59′W
Mafra, Port. (mäf′rȧ)	159b	38°56′N	9°20′W
Magadan, Russia (má-gá-dän′)	165	59°39′N	150°43′E
Magadan Oblast, Russia	171	65°00′N	160°00′E
Magadi, Kenya	217	1°54′S	36°17′E
Magalhães Bastos, neigh., Braz.	234c	22°53′S	43°23′W
Magalies, r., S. Afr. (mä-gä′lyĕs)	213b	25°51′S	27°42′E
Magaliesberg, mts., S. Afr.	213b	25°45′S	27°43′E
Magaliesburg, S. Afr.	218d	26°01′S	27°32′E
Magallanes, Estrecho de, strt., S.A.	132	52°30′S	68°45′W
Magat, r., Phil. (mä-gät′)	197a	16°45′N	121°16′E
Magdalena, Arg. (mäg-dä-lā′nä)	129c	35°05′S	57°32′W
Magdalena, Bol.	130	13°17′S	63°57′W
Magdalena, Mex.	96	30°34′N	110°50′W
Magdalena, N.M., U.S.	109	34°10′N	107°45′W
Magdalena, i., Chile	132	44°45′S	73°15′W
Magdalena, Bahía, b., Mex. (bä-ē′ä-mäg-dä-lā′nä)	116	24°30′N	114°00′W
Magdalena, Río, r., Col.	130	7°45′N	74°04′W
Magdalena del Mar, Peru	233c	12°06′S	77°05′W
Magdalen Laver, Eng., U.K.	235	51°45′N	0°11′E
Magdeburg, Ger. (mäg′dĕ-bòrgh)	142	52°07′N	11°39′E
Magellan, Strait of see Magallanes, Estrecho de, strt., S.A.	132	52°30′S	68°45′W
Magenta, Italy (mȧ-jĕn′tȧ)	160	45°26′N	8°53′E
Magerøya, i., Nor.	146	71°10′N	24°11′E
Maggiore, Lago, l., Italy	148	46°03′N	8°25′E
Maghāghah, Egypt	218b	28°38′N	30°50′W
Maghniyya, Alg.	148	34°52′N	1°40′W
Maghull, Eng., U.K.	237a	53°32′N	2°57′W
Maginu, Japan	242a	35°35′N	139°36′E
Magiscatzin, Mex. (mä-kēs-kät-zēn′)	118	22°48′N	98°42′W
Maglaj, Bos. (má′glä-ē)	161	44°34′N	18°12′E
Magliana, neigh., Italy	239c	41°50′N	12°25′E
Maglie, Italy (mäl′yā)	161	40°06′N	18°20′E
Magna, Ut., U.S. (măg′ná)	107b	40°43′N	112°06′W
Magnitogorsk, Russia (mág-nyĕ′tô-gôrsk)	164	53°26′N	59°05′E
Magnolia, Ar., U.S. (măg-nō′lĭ-ȧ)	111	33°16′N	93°13′W
Magnolia, Ms., U.S.	114	31°08′N	90°27′W
Magnolia, N.J., U.S.	229b	39°51′N	75°02′W
Magny-en-Vexin, Fr. (mä-nyē′ĕN-vĕ-săN′)	157b	49°09′N	1°45′E
Magny-les-Hameaux, Fr.	237c	48°44′N	2°04′E
Magog, Can. (mȧ-gŏg′)	91	45°15′N	72°10′W
Magome, neigh., Japan	242a	35°35′N	139°43′E
Magpie, r., Can.	90	48°13′N	84°50′W
Magpie, r., Can.	92	50°40′N	64°30′W
Magpie, Lac, l., Can.	92	50°55′N	64°39′W
Magrath, Can.	84	49°25′N	112°52′W
Maguanying, China	240b	39°52′N	116°17′E
Magude, Moz. (mä-gōō′dä)	212	24°58′S	32°39′E
Magwe, Myanmar (mŭg-wā′)	183	20°19′N	94°57′E
Mahābād, Iran	185	36°55′N	45°50′E
Mahahi Port, D.R.C. (mä-hä′gē)	211	2°14′N	31°12′E
Mahajanga, Madag.	213	15°12′S	46°26′E
Mahakam, r., Indon.	196	0°30′S	116°15′E
Mahali Mountains, mts., Tan.	217	6°20′S	30°00′E
Mahaly, Madag. (má-hál-ē′)	213	24°09′S	46°20′E
Mahanoro, Madag. (má-há-nō′rō)	213	19°57′S	48°47′E
Mahanoy City, Pa., U.S. (mä-hȧ-noi′)	99	40°50′N	76°10′W
Maḥaṭṭat al-Ḥilmīyah, neigh., Egypt	244a	30°07′N	31°19′E
Maḥaṭṭat al Qaṭrānah, Jord.	181a	31°15′N	36°04′E
Maḥaṭṭat ʻAqabat al Ḥijāzīyah, Jord.	181a	29°45′N	35°55′E
Maḥaṭṭat ar Ramlah, Jord.	181a	29°31′N	35°57′E
Maḥaṭṭat Jurf ad Darāwīsh, Jord.	181a	30°41′N	35°51′E
Mahd adh-Dhahab, Sau. Ar.	185	23°30′N	40°52′E
Mahe, India (mä-ā′)	183	11°42′N	75°39′E
Mahenge, Tan. (mä-hĕŋ′gȧ)	212	7°38′S	36°16′E
Mahi, r., India	186	23°16′N	73°20′E
Māhīm, neigh., India	240e	19°03′N	72°49′E
Māhīm Bay, b., India	187b	19°03′N	72°45′E
Mahlabatini, S. Afr. (mä′lá-bá-tē′nē)	213c	28°15′S	31°29′E
Mahlow, Ger. (mä′lōv)	145b	52°23′N	13°24′E
Mahlsdorf, neigh., Ger.	238a	52°31′N	13°37′E
Mahlsdorf-Süd, neigh., Ger.	238a	52°29′N	13°36′E
Mahnomen, Mn., U.S. (mô-nō′mĕn)	102	47°18′N	95°58′W
Mahone Bay, Can. (mȧ-hōn′)	92	44°27′N	64°23′W
Mahone Bay, b., Can.	92	44°30′N	64°15′W
Mahopac, Lake, l., N.Y., U.S. (mä-hō′păk)	100a	41°24′N	73°45′W
Mahrauli, neigh., India	240d	28°31′N	77°11′E
Māhul, neigh., India	240e	19°01′N	72°53′E
Mahwah, N.J., U.S. (mȧ-wă′)	100a	41°05′N	74°09′W
Maidenhead, Eng., U.K. (mād′ĕn-hĕd)	144b	51°30′N	0°44′W
Maidstone, Austl.	243b	37°47′S	144°52′E
Maidstone, Eng., U.K.	151	51°17′N	0°32′E
Maiduguri, Nig. (mä′ē-dá-gōō′rē)	211	11°51′N	13°10′E
Maigualida, Sierra, mts., Ven. (sē-ĕ′r-rä-mī-gwä′lē-dē)	130	6°30′N	65°50′W
Maijdi, Bngl.	186	22°59′N	91°08′E
Maikop see Maykop, Russia	164	44°35′N	40°07′E
Main, r., Ger. (mīn)	154	49°49′N	9°20′E
Main Barrier Range, mts., Austl. (băr″ĭ-ĕr)	203	31°25′S	141°40′E
Mai-Ndombe, Lac, l., D.R.C.	212	2°16′S	19°00′E
Maine, state, U.S. (mān)	97	45°25′N	69°50′W
Mainland, i., Scot., U.K. (măn-lănd)	146	60°19′N	2°40′W
Maintenon, Fr. (măN-tĕ-nôN′)	157b	48°35′N	1°35′E
Maintirano, Madag. (mä′ēn-tē-rä′nō)	213	18°05′S	44°08′E
Mainz, Ger. (mīnts)	142	49°59′N	8°16′E
Maio, i., C.V. (mä′yo)	210b	15°15′N	22°50′W
Maipo, S.A.	132	34°08′S	69°51′W
Maipo, r., Chile (mī′pô)	129b	33°45′S	71°08′W
Maiquetía, Ven. (mī-kĕ-tē′ä)	130	10°37′N	66°56′W
Maison-Rouge, Fr. (mā-zôN-rōōzh′)	157b	48°34′N	3°09′E
Maisons-Alfort, Fr.	237c	48°48′N	2°26′E
Maisons-Laffitte, Fr.	157b	48°57′N	2°09′E
Maitani, Japan	242b	34°49′N	135°22′E
Maitland, Austl. (măt′lănd)	203	32°45′S	151°40′E
Maizuru, Japan (mä-ĭ′zōō-rōō)	195	35°26′N	135°15′E
Majene, Indon.	196	3°34′S	119°00′E
Maji, Eth.	211	6°14′N	35°34′E
Majorca see Mallorca, i., Spain	142	39°18′N	2°22′E
Makah Indian Reservation, I.R., Wa., U.S.	104	48°17′N	124°52′W
Makala, D.R.C.	244c	4°25′S	15°15′E
Makanya, Tan. (mä-kän′yä)	213	4°15′S	37°49′E
Makanza, D.R.C.	211	1°42′N	19°08′E
Makarakomburu, Mount, mtn., Sol. Is.	198e	9°43′S	160°02′E
Makarska, Cro. (má′kär-ská)	161	43°17′N	17°05′E
Makar'yev, Russia	166	57°50′N	43°48′E
Makasar see Ujung Pandang, Indon.	196	5°08′S	119°28′E
Makasar, Selat (Makassar Strait), strt., Indon.	196	2°00′S	118°07′E
Makati, Phil.	241g	14°34′N	121°01′E
Makaw, D.R.C.	216	3°29′S	18°19′E
Make, i., Japan (mä′kȧ)	195	30°43′N	130°49′E
Makeni, S.L.	210	8°53′N	12°03′W
Makgadikgadi Pans, pl., Bots.	212	20°38′S	21°31′E
Makhachkala, Russia (mäk′äch-kä′lä)	167	43°00′N	47°40′E
Makhaleng, r., Leso.	213c	29°53′S	27°33′E
Makiïvka, Ukr.	167	48°03′N	38°00′E
Makindu, Kenya	217	2°17′S	37°49′E
M'akino, Russia	239b	55°48′N	37°22′E
Makkah see Mecca, Sau. Ar.	182	21°27′N	39°45′E
Makkovik, Can.	85	55°01′N	59°10′W
Makokou, Gabon (mȧ-kȯ-kōō′)	210	0°34′N	12°52′E
Maków Mazowiecki, Pol. (mä′kōov mä-zō-vyĕts′kē)	155	52°51′N	21°07′E
Makuhari, Japan (mä-kōō-hä′rē)	195a	35°39′N	140°04′E
Makurazaki, Japan (mä′kò-rä-zä′kē)	195	31°16′N	130°18′E
Makurdi, Nig.	210	7°45′N	8°32′E
Makushin, Ak., U.S. (mȧ-kò′shĭn)	95	53°57′N	166°28′W
Makushino, Russia (mȧ-kò-shēn′ô)	164	55°03′N	67°43′E
Mala, Punta, c., Pan. (pò′n-tä-mä′lä)	121	7°32′N	79°44′W
Malabar Coast, cst., India (măl′á-bär)	187	11°19′N	75°33′E
Malabar Point, c., India	187b	18°57′N	72°47′E
Malabo, Eq. Gui.	210	3°45′N	8°47′E
Malabon, Phil.	197a	14°39′N	120°57′E
Malacca, Strait of, strt., Asia (mȧ-lăk′ȧ)	196	4°15′N	99°44′E
Malad City, Id., U.S. (mȧ-lăd′)	105	42°11′N	112°15′W
Málaga, Col. (má′lä-gä)	130	6°41′N	72°46′W
Málaga, Spain	142	36°45′N	4°25′W
Malagón, Spain (mä-lä-gōn′)	158	39°12′N	3°52′W
Malaita, i., Sol. Is. (mȧ-lä′ē-tȧ)	203	8°38′S	161°15′E
Malakāl, Sudan (mȧ-lȧ-käl′)	211	9°46′N	31°54′E
Malakhovka, Russia (mȧ-lăk′ôf-kȧ)	172b	55°38′N	38°01′E
Malakoff, Fr.	237c	48°49′N	2°19′E
Malakpur, neigh., India	240d	28°42′N	77°12′E
Malang, Indon.	196	8°06′S	112°50′E
Malanje, Ang. (mä-läŋ-gȧ)	212	9°32′S	16°20′E
Malanville, Benin	210	12°04′N	3°09′E
Mälaren, l., Swe.	146	59°38′N	16°55′E
Malartic, Can.	85	48°07′N	78°11′W
Malatya, Tur. (mȧ-lä′tyȧ)	182	38°30′N	38°15′E
Malawi, nation, Afr.	212	11°15′S	33°45′E
Malawi, Lake see Nyasa, Lake, l., Afr.	212	10°45′S	34°30′E
Malaya Vishera, Russia (vē-shā′rä)	164	58°51′N	32°13′E
Malay Peninsula, pen., Asia (mȧ-lā′) (mā′lā)	196	6°00′N	101°00′E
Malaysia, nation, Asia (mȧ-lā′zhȧ)	196	4°10′N	101°22′E
Malbon, Austl. (măl′bŭn)	202	21°15′S	140°30′E
Malbork, Pol. (mäl′bòrk)	146	54°02′N	19°04′E
Malcabran, r., Port. (mäl-kä-brän′)	159b	38°47′N	8°46′W
Malden, Ma., U.S. (môl′dĕn)	93a	42°26′N	71°04′W
Malden, Mo., U.S.	111	36°32′N	89°56′W
Malden, i., Kir.	2	4°20′S	154°30′W
Maldives, nation, Asia	180	4°30′N	71°30′E
Maldon, Eng., U.K. (môrl′dŏn)	144b	51°44′N	0°39′E
Maldonado, Ur. (mäl-dŏ-nä′dô)	132	34°54′S	54°57′W
Maldonado, Punta, c., Mex. (pōō′n-tä)	118	16°18′N	98°34′W
Maléa, Ákra, c., Grc.	149	36°31′N	23°13′E
Mālegaon, India	186	20°35′N	74°30′E
Malé Karpaty, mts., Slvk.	155	48°31′N	17°15′E
Malekula, i., Vanuatu (mä-lā-kōō′lä)	203	16°44′S	167°45′E
Malema, Moz.	217	14°57′S	37°20′E
Malheur, r., Or., U.S. (mȧ-lōōr′)	104	43°45′N	117°41′W
Malheur Lake, l., Or., U.S. (mȧ-lōōr′)	104	43°16′N	118°37′W
Mali, nation, Afr.	210	15°45′N	0°15′W
Malibu, Ca., U.S. (mă′lĭ-bōō)	107a	34°03′N	118°38′W
Malik, Wādī al, r., Sudan	211	16°48′N	29°30′E
Malimba, Monts, mts., D.R.C.	217	7°45′S	29°15′E
Malinalco, Mex. (mä-lē-näl′kō)	118	18°54′N	99°31′W
Malinaltepec, Mex. (mä-lē-näl-tȧ-pĕk′)	118	17°01′N	98°41′W
Malindi, Kenya (mä-lēn′dē)	213	3°14′S	40°04′E
Malin Head, c., Ire.	146	55°23′N	7°24′W
Malino, Russia (mä′lĭ-nô)	172b	55°07′N	38°12′E
Malkara, Tur. (mäl′kȧ-rȧ)	161	40°51′N	26°52′E
Malko Tŭrnovo, Bul. (mäl′kō-t′r′nô-vȧ)	161	41°59′N	27°28′E
Mallaig, Scot., U.K.	150	56°59′N	5°55′W
Mallet Creek, Oh., U.S. (măl′ĕt)	101d	41°10′N	81°55′W
Mallorca, i., Spain	142	39°30′N	3°00′E
Mallorquinas, Spain	238e	41°28′N	2°16′E
Mallow, Ire. (măl′ō)	150	52°07′N	9°04′W
Malmédy, Bel. (mȧl-mā-dē′)	151	50°25′N	6°01′E
Malmesbury, S. Afr. (mämz′bĕr-ĭ)	212	33°30′S	18°35′E
Malmköping, Swe. (mälm′chû′pĭng)	152	59°09′N	16°39′E
Malmö, Swe.	142	55°36′N	13°00′E
Malmyzh, Russia (mȧl-mĕzh′)	165	49°58′N	137°07′E
Malmyzh, Russia	166	56°30′N	50°48′E
Malnoue, Fr.	237c	48°50′N	2°36′E
Maloarkhangelsk, Russia (mä′lô-ȧr-κäŋ′gĕlsk)	162	52°26′N	36°29′E
Malolos, Phil. (mä-lô′lôs)	197a	14°51′N	120°49′E
Malomal'sk, Russia (mȧ-lô-mälsk″)	172a	58°47′N	59°55′E
Malone, N.Y., U.S. (mȧ-lōn′)	99	44°50′N	74°20′W
Malonga, D.R.C.	216	10°24′S	23°10′E
Maloti Mountains, mts., Leso.	213c	29°00′S	28°29′E
Maloyaroslavets, Russia (mä′lô-yä-rô-slä-vyĕts)	162	55°01′N	36°25′E
Malozemel'skaya Tundra, reg., Russia	166	67°30′N	50°00′E
Malpas, Eng., U.K. (măl′pȧz)	144a	53°01′N	2°46′W
Malpelo, Isla de, i., Col. (mäl-pā′lō)	130	3°55′N	81°30′W
Malpeque Bay, b., Can. (môl-pĕk′)	92	46°30′N	63°47′W
Malta, Mt., U.S. (môl′tȧ)	105	48°20′N	107°50′W
Malta, nation, Eur.	142	35°52′N	13°30′E
Maltahöhe, Nmb. (mäl′tä-hō′ĕ)	212	24°45′S	16°45′E
Maltrata, Mex. (mäl-trä′tä)	119	18°48′N	97°16′W
Maluku (Moluccas), is., Indon.	197	2°22′S	128°25′E
Maluku, Laut (Molucca Sea), sea, Indon.	197	0°15′N	125°41′E
Malūṭ, Sudan	211	10°30′N	32°17′E
Mālvan, India	187	16°08′N	73°32′E
Malvern, Austl.	243b	37°52′S	145°02′E
Malvern, Ar., U.S. (măl′vĕrn)	111	34°21′N	92°47′W
Malvern, neigh., S. Afr.	244b	26°12′S	28°06′E
Malverne, N.Y., U.S.	228	40°40′N	73°40′W
Malvern East, S. Afr.	244b	26°12′S	28°08′E
Malyn, Ukr.	163	50°44′N	29°15′E
Malynivka, Ukr.	163	49°50′N	36°43′E
Malyy Anyuy, r., Russia	171	67°52′N	164°30′E
Malyy Tamir, i., Russia	171	78°10′N	107°30′E
Mamantel, Mex. (mä-mȧn-tĕl′)	119	18°36′N	91°06′W
Mamaroneck, N.Y., U.S. (măm′ȧ-rō-nĕk)	100a	40°57′N	73°44′W
Mambasa, D.R.C.	217	1°21′N	29°03′E
Mamburao, Phil. (mäm-bōō′rä-ō)	197a	13°14′N	120°35′E
Mamera, Ven.	234a	10°27′N	66°59′W
Mamfe, Cam. (mäm′fĕ)	210	5°46′N	9°17′E
Mamihara, Japan (mä′mē-hä-rä)	195	32°41′N	131°12′E
Mammoth Cave, Ky., U.S. (măm′ŏth)	114	37°10′N	86°04′W
Mammoth Cave National Park, rec., Ky., U.S.	97	37°20′N	86°21′W
Mammoth Hot Springs, Wy., U.S. (măm′ŭth hôt sprĭngz)	105	44°55′N	110°50′W
Mamnoli, India	187b	19°17′N	73°15′E
Mamoré, r., S.A.	130	13°00′S	65°20′W
Mamou, Gui.	210	10°26′N	12°07′W
Mampong, Ghana	214	7°04′N	1°24′W
Mamry, Jezioro, l., Pol. (mäm′rĭ)	155	54°10′N	21°28′E
Man, C. Iv.	214	7°24′N	7°33′W
Manacor, Spain (mä-nä-kôr′)	159	39°35′N	3°15′E
Manado, Indon.	197	1°29′N	124°50′E
Managua, Cuba (mä-nä′gwä)	123a	22°58′N	82°17′W
Managua, Nic.	116	12°10′N	86°16′W
Managua, Lago de, l., Nic. (lá′gô-dĕ)	120	12°28′N	86°10′W
Manakara, Madag. (mä-nä-kä′rŭ)	213	22°17′S	48°06′E
Manama see Al Manāmah, Bahr.	182	26°01′N	50°33′E
Mananara, r., Madag. (mä-nä-nä′rŭ)	213	23°15′S	48°15′E
Mananjary, Madag. (mä-nän-zhä′rē)	213	20°16′S	48°13′E
Manas, China	188	44°30′N	86°00′E
Manassas, Va., U.S. (mȧ-năs′ȧs)	99	38°45′N	77°30′W
Manaus, Braz. (mä-nä′ōōzh)	131	3°01′S	60°00′W
Manayunk, neigh., Pa., U.S.	229b	40°01′N	75°13′W
Mancelona, Mi., U.S. (măn-sē-lō′nȧ)	98	44°50′N	85°05′W
Mancha Real, Spain (män′chä rā-äl′)	158	37°48′N	3°37′W
Manchazh, Russia (män′chȧsh)	172a	56°30′N	58°10′E
Manchester, Eng., U.K.	142	53°28′N	2°14′W
Manchester, Ct., U.S. (măn′chĕs-tĕr)	99	41°45′N	72°30′W
Manchester, Ga., U.S.	114	32°50′N	84°37′W
Manchester, Ia., U.S.	103	42°30′N	91°30′W
Manchester, Ma., U.S.	93a	42°35′N	70°47′W
Manchester, Mo., U.S.	107e	38°36′N	90°31′W
Manchester, N.H., U.S.	97	43°00′N	71°30′W
Manchester, Oh., U.S.	98	38°40′N	83°35′W
Manchester Docks, pt. of i., Eng., U.K.	237b	53°28′N	2°17′W
Manchester Ship Canal, Eng., U.K.	144a	53°20′N	2°40′W
Manchuria, hist. reg., China (măn-chōō′rē-ȧ)	189	48°00′N	124°58′E
Mandal, Nor. (män′däl)	152	58°03′N	7°28′E
Mandalay, Myanmar (măn′dȧ-lā)	183	22°00′N	96°08′E
Mandalselva, r., Nor.	152	58°25′N	7°30′E
Mandaluyong, Phil.	241g	14°35′N	121°02′E
Mandan, N.D., U.S. (măn′dăn)	96	46°49′N	100°54′W
Mandāoli, neigh., India	240d	28°38′N	77°18′E
Mandara Mountains, mts., Afr. (män-dä′rä)	211	10°15′N	13°23′E
Mandau Siak, r., Indon.	181b	1°03′N	101°25′E
Mandeb, Bab-el-, strt. (băb′ĕl măn-dĕb′)	182	13°17′N	42°49′E
Mandimba, Moz.	217	14°21′S	35°39′E
Mandinga, Pan. (män-dĭŋ′gä)	121	9°32′N	79°04′W
Mandla, India	186	22°43′N	80°23′E
Mándra, Grc. (män′drä)	161	38°06′N	23°32′E
Mandres-les-Roses, Fr.	237c	48°42′N	2°33′E
Mandritsara, Madag. (mȧn-drĕt-sä′rȧ)	213	15°49′S	48°47′E
Manduria, Italy (män-dōō′rē-ä)	161	40°23′N	17°41′E
Mandve, India	187b	18°47′N	72°52′E

314 Māndvi–Market Deeping

PLACE (Pronunciation)	PAGE	LAT.	LONG.
Māndvi, India (mŭnd'vē)	183	22°54'N	69°23'E
Māndvi, India (mŭnd'vē)	187b	19°29'N	72°53'E
Mandvi, neigh., India	240e	18°57'N	72°50'E
Mandya, India	187	12°40'N	77°00'E
Manfredonia, Italy (män-frå-dô'nyä)	160	41°39'N	15°55'E
Manfredónia, Golfo di, b., Italy (gôl-fô-dē)	160	41°34'N	16°05'E
Mangabeiras, Chapada das, pl., Braz.	131	8°05'S	47°32'W
Mangalore, India (mŭŋ-gŭ-lōr')	183	12°53'N	74°52'E
Manganji, Japan	242a	35°40'N	139°26'E
Mangaratiba, Braz. (män-gä-rä-tē'bȧ)	129a	22°56'S	44°03'W
Mangatarem, Phil. (män'gȧ-tä'rĕm)	197a	15°48'N	120°18'E
Mange, D.R.C.	216	0°54'N	20°30'E
Mangkalihat, Tanjung, c., Indon.	196	1°25'N	119°55'E
Mangles, Islas de, Cuba (ē's-läs-dĕ-mäŋ'gläs) (măŋ'g'lz)	122	22°05'N	82°50'W
Mangoche, Mwi.	212	14°16'S	35°14'E
Mangoky, r., Madag. (män-gō'kē)	213	22°02'S	44°11'E
Mangole, Pulau, i., Indon.	197	1°35'S	126°22'E
Mangualde, Port. (män-gwäl'dĕ)	158	40°38'N	7°44'W
Mangueira, Lagoa da, l., Braz.	132	33°15'S	52°45'W
Mangum, Ok., U.S. (măŋ'gŭm)	110	34°52'N	99°31'W
Mangzhangdian, China (mäŋ-jäŋ-dĭĕn)	190	32°07'N	114°44'E
Manhasset, N.Y., U.S.	228	40°48'N	73°42'W
Manhattan, Il., U.S.	101a	41°25'N	87°29'W
Manhattan, Ks., U.S. (măn-hăt'ăn)	96	39°11'N	96°34'W
Manhattan Beach, Ca., U.S.	107a	33°53'N	118°24'W
Manhuaçu, Braz. (män-ŏŏä'sōō)	129a	20°17'S	42°01'W
Manhumirim, Braz. (män-ōō-mê-rē'N)	129a	22°30'S	41°57'W
Manicouagane, r., Can.	85	50°00'N	68°35'W
Manicouagane, Lac, res., Can.	85	51°30'N	68°19'W
Manicuare, Ven. (mä-nē-kwä'rĕ)	131b	10°35'N	64°10'W
Manihiki Islands, is., Cook Is. (mä'nē-hē'kê)	225	9°40'S	158°00'W
Manila, Phil.	196	14°37'N	121°00'E
Manila Bay, b., Phil. (mȧ-nĭl'ȧ)	197a	14°38'N	120°46'E
Manique de Baixo, Port.	238d	38°44'N	9°22'W
Manisa, Tur. (mä'nê-sȧ)	149	38°40'N	27°30'E
Manistee, Mi., U.S. (măn-ĭs-tē')	98	44°15'N	86°20'W
Manistee, r., Mi., U.S.	98	44°25'N	85°45'W
Manistique, Mi., U.S. (măn-ĭs-tēk')	103	45°58'N	86°16'W
Manistique, l., Mi., U.S.	103	46°14'N	85°30'W
Manistique, r., Mi., U.S.	103	46°05'N	86°09'W
Manitoba, prov., Can. (măn-ĭ-tō'bȧ)	84	55°12'N	97°29'W
Manitoba, Lake, l., Can.	84	51°00'N	98°45'W
Manito Lake, l., Can. (măn'ĭ-tō)	88	52°45'N	109°45'W
Manitou, i., Mi., U.S. (măn'ĭ-tōō)	103	47°21'N	87°33'W
Manitou, l., Can.	103	49°21'N	93°01'W
Manitou Islands, is., Mi., U.S.	98	45°05'N	86°00'W
Manitoulin Island, i., Can. (măn-ĭ-tōō'lĭn)	85	45°45'N	81°30'W
Manitou Springs, Co., U.S.	110	38°51'N	104°58'W
Manitowoc, Wi., U.S. (măn-ĭ-tô-wŏk')	103	44°05'N	87°42'W
Manitqueira, Serra da, mts., Braz.	129a	22°40'S	45°12'W
Maniwaki, Can.	91	46°23'N	76°00'W
Manizales, Col. (mä-nê-zä'lås)	130	5°05'N	75°31'W
Manjacaze, Moz. (man'yä-kä'zĕ)	212	24°37'S	33°49'E
Mankato, Ks., U.S. (măn-kā'tō)	110	39°45'N	98°12'W
Mankato, Mn., U.S.	97	44°10'N	93°59'W
Mankim, Cam.	215	5°01'N	12°00'E
Manlléu, Spain (män-lyā'ōō)	159	42°00'N	2°16'E
Manly, Austl.	243a	33°48'S	151°17'E
Mannar, Sri L. (mȧ-när')	183b	9°48'N	80°03'E
Mannar, Gulf of, b., Asia	183	8°47'N	78°33'E
Mannheim, Ger. (män'hīm)	147	49°30'N	8°31'E
Manning, Ia., U.S. (măn'ĭng)	102	41°53'N	95°04'W
Manning, S.C., U.S.	115	33°41'N	80°12'W
Mannington, W.V., U.S. (măn'ĭng-tŭn)	98	39°30'N	80°55'W
Mannswörth, neigh., Aus.	239e	48°09'N	16°31'E
Mano, r., Afr.	214	7°00'N	11°25'W
Man of War Bay, b., Bah.	123	21°05'N	74°05'W
Man of War Channel, strt., Bah.	122	22°45'N	76°10'W
Manokwari, Indon. (mȧ-nŏk-wä'rê)	197	0°56'S	134°10'E
Manono, D.R.C.	217	7°18'S	27°25'E
Manor, Can. (măn'ẽr)	89	49°36'N	102°05'W
Manor, Wa., U.S.	106c	45°45'N	122°36'W
Manorhaven, N.Y., U.S.	228	40°50'N	73°42'W
Manori, neigh., India	187b	19°13'N	72°43'E
Manosque, Fr. (mȧ-nôsk')	157	43°51'N	5°48'E
Manotick, Can.	83c	45°13'N	75°41'W
Manouane, r., Can.	91	50°15'N	70°30'W
Manouane, Lac, l., Can. (mä-nōō'ån)	92	50°36'N	70°50'W
Manresa, Spain (män-rā'sä)	148	41°44'N	1°52'E
Mansa, Zam.	212	11°12'S	28°53'E
Mansel, i., Can. (măn'sĕl)	85	61°56'N	81°10'W
Manseriche, Pongo de, reg., Peru (pŏ'n-gô-dĕ-män-sĕ-rē'chĕ)	130	4°15'S	77°45'W
Mansfield, Eng., U.K. (mănz'fēld)	144a	53°08'N	1°12'W
Mansfield, La., U.S.	113	32°02'N	93°43'W
Mansfield, Oh., U.S.	98	40°45'N	82°30'W
Mansfield, Wa., U.S.	104	47°48'N	119°39'W
Mansfield, Mount, mtn., Vt., U.S.	99	44°30'N	72°45'W
Mansfield Woodhouse, Eng., U.K. (wŏd-hous)	144a	53°08'N	1°12'W
Manta, Ec. (män'tä)	130	1°03'S	80°16'W
Manteno, Il., U.S. (măn-tē-nō)	101a	41°15'N	87°50'W
Manteo, N.C., U.S.	115	35°55'N	75°40'W
Mantes-la-Jolie, Fr. (mänt-ĕ-lä-zhō-lē')	156	48°59'N	1°42'E
Manti, Ut., U.S. (măn'tī)	109	39°15'N	11°40'W
Mantilla, neigh., Cuba	233b	23°04'N	82°20'W
Mantova, Italy (män'tô-vä) (măn'tŭ-ȧ)	148	45°09'N	10°47'E
Mantua, Cuba (män-tōō'ä)	122	22°20'N	84°15'W

PLACE (Pronunciation)	PAGE	LAT.	LONG.
Mantua see Mantova, Italy	148	45°09'N	10°47'E
Mantua, Md., U.S.	229d	38°51'N	77°15'W
Mantua, Ut., U.S. (măn'tŭ-ȧ)	107b	41°30'N	111°57'W
Manua Islands, is., Am. Sam.	198a	14°13'S	169°35'W
Manui, Pulau, i., Indon. (mä-nōō'ē)	197	3°35'S	123°38'E
Manus Island, i., Pap. N. Gui. (mä'nōōs)	197	2°22'S	146°22'E
Manvel, Tx., U.S. (măn'vel)	113a	29°28'N	95°22'W
Manville, N.J., U.S. (măn'vĭl)	100a	40°33'N	74°36'W
Manville, R.I., U.S.	100b	41°57'N	71°27'W
Manyal Shīhah, Egypt	244a	29°57'N	31°14'E
Manzala Lake, l., Egypt	218b	31°14'N	32°04'E
Manzanares, Col. (män-sä-nä'rĕs)	130a	5°15'N	75°09'W
Manzanares, r., Spain (mänz-nä'rĕs)	159a	40°36'N	3°48'W
Manzanares, Canal del, Spain (kä-nä'l-dĕl-män-thä-nä'rĕs)	159a	40°20'N	3°38'W
Manzanillo, Cuba (män'zä-nēl'yō)	117	20°20'N	77°05'W
Manzanillo, Mex.	116	19°02'N	104°21'W
Manzanillo, Bahía de, b., Mex. (bä-ē'ä-dĕ-män-zä-nē'l-yō)	118	19°00'N	104°38'W
Manzanillo, Bahía de, b., N.A.	123	19°55'N	71°50'W
Manzanillo, Punta, c., Pan.	121	9°40'N	79°33'W
Manzhouli, China (män-jō-lē)	189	49°25'N	117°15'E
Manzovka, Russia (mȧn-zhô'f-kȧ)	194	44°16'N	132°13'E
Mao, Chad (mä'ō)	211	14°07'N	15°19'E
Mao, Dom. Rep.	123	19°35'N	71°10'W
Maó, Spain	148	39°52'N	4°15'E
Maoke, Pegunungan, mts., Indon.	197	4°00'S	138°00'E
Maoming, China	189	21°55'N	110°40'E
Maoniu Shan, mtn., China (mou-nĭō shän)	192	32°45'N	104°09'E
Mapastepec, Mex. (ma-päs-tå-pĕk')	119	15°24'N	92°52'W
Mapia, Kepulauan, i., Indon.	197	0°57'N	134°22'E
Mapimí, Mex. (mä-pê-mē')	112	25°50'N	103°50'W
Mapimí, Bolsón de, des., Mex. (bôl-sŏ'n-dĕ-mä-pē'mē)	112	27°27'N	103°20'W
Maple Creek, Can. (mā'p'l) (crēk)	84	49°55'N	109°27'W
Maple Cross, Eng., U.K.	235	51°37'N	0°30'W
Maple Grove, Can. (grōv)	83a	45°19'N	73°51'W
Maple Heights, Oh., U.S.	101d	41°25'N	81°34'W
Maple Leaf Gardens, rec., Can.	227c	43°40'N	79°23'W
Maple Shade, N.J., U.S. (shād)	100f	39°57'N	75°01'W
Maple Valley, Wa., U.S. (văl'ê)	106a	47°24'N	122°02'W
Maplewood, Mn., U.S. (wŏd)	107g	45°00'N	93°03'W
Maplewood, Mo., U.S.	107e	38°37'N	90°20'W
Maplewood, N.J., U.S.	228	40°44'N	74°17'W
Mapocho, r., Chile	234b	33°25'S	70°47'W
Mapumulo, S. Afr. (mä-pä-mōō'lō)	213c	29°12'S	31°05'E
Maputo, Moz.	212	26°50'S	32°30'E
Maquela do Zombo, Ang. (mȧ-kā'lȧ dô zŏm'bô)	212	6°08'S	15°15'E
Maquoketa, Ia., U.S. (mȧ-kō-kê-tȧ)	103	42°04'N	90°42'W
Maquoketa, r., Ia., U.S.	103	42°08'N	90°40'W
Mar, Serra do, mts., Braz. (sĕr'rȧ dô mär')	132	26°30'S	49°15'W
Maracaibo, Ven. (mä-rä-kī'bō)	130	10°38'N	71°45'W
Maracaibo, Lago de, l., Ven. (lä'gô-dĕ-mä-rä-kī'bō)	130	9°55'N	72°13'W
Maracay, Ven. (mä-rä-käy')	130	10°15'N	67°35'W
Marādah, Libya	211	29°10'N	19°07'E
Maradi, Niger (mȧ-rȧ-dē')	210	13°29'N	7°06'E
Marāgheh, Iran	185	37°20'N	46°10'E
Maraisburg, S. Afr.	213b	26°12'S	27°57'E
Marais des Cygnes, r., Ks., U.S.	111	38°30'N	95°30'W
Marajó, Ilha de, i., Braz.	131	1°00'S	49°30'W
Maralal, Kenya	217	1°06'N	36°42'E
Marali, Cen. Afr. Rep.	215	6°01'N	18°24'E
Marand, Iran	185	38°26'N	45°46'E
Maranguape, Braz. (mä-räŋ-gwä'pĕ)	131	3°48'S	38°38'W
Maranhão, state, Braz. (mä-rän-youN)	131	5°15'S	45°52'W
Maranoa, r., Austl. (mä-rä-nō'ä)	203	27°01'S	148°03'E
Marano di Napoli, Italy (mä-rä'nô-dē-nä'pô-lē)	159c	40°39'N	14°12'E
Marañón, Río, r., Peru (rē'ō-mä-rä-nyŏn')	130	4°26'S	75°08'W
Maraoli, neigh., India	240e	19°03'N	72°54'E
Marapanim, Braz. (mä-rä-pä-nē'N)	131	0°45'S	47°42'W
Marathon, Can.	85	48°50'N	86°10'W
Marathon, Fl., U.S. (măr'ȧ-thŏn)	115a	24°41'N	81°06'W
Marathon, Oh., U.S.	101f	39°09'N	83°59'W
Maravatío, Mex. (mä-rȧ-vä'tē-ō)	118	19°54'N	100°25'W
Marawi, Sudan	211	18°07'N	31°57'E
Marayong, Austl.	243a	33°45'S	150°54'E
Marble Bar, Austl. (märb''l bär)	202	21°15'S	119°15'E
Marble Canal, can., Az., U.S. (mär'b'l)	109	36°21'N	111°48'W
Marblehead, Ma., U.S. (mär'b'l-hĕd)	93a	42°30'N	70°51'W
Marburg an der Lahn, Ger.	154	50°49'N	8°46'E
Marca, Ponta da, c., Ang.	216	16°31'S	11°42'E
Marcala, Hond. (mär-kä-lä)	120	14°08'N	88°01'W
Marceline, Mo., U.S. (mär-sê-lēn')	111	39°42'N	92°56'W
Marche, hist. reg., Italy (mär'kā)	160	43°35'N	12°33'E
Marchegg, Aus.	145e	48°18'N	16°55'E
Marchena, Spain (mär-chā'nä)	148	37°20'N	5°25'W
Marchena, i., Ec. (ē's-lä-mär-chĕ'nä)	130	0°29'N	90°31'W
Marchfeld, reg., Aus.	145e	48°14'N	16°37'E
Mar Chiquita, Laguna, l., Arg. (lä-gōō'nä-mär-chê-kē'tä)	129c	34°25'S	61°10'W
Marco Polo Bridge, trans., China	240b	39°52'N	116°12'E
Marcos Paz, Arg. (mär-kōs' päz)	129c	34°49'S	58°51'W
Marcus, i., Japan (mär'kŭs)	225	24°00'N	155°00'E
Marcus Hook, Pa., U.S. (mär'kŭs hŏk)	100f	39°49'N	75°25'W
Marcy, Mount, mtn., N.Y., U.S. (mär'sê)	99	44°10'N	73°55'W

PLACE (Pronunciation)	PAGE	LAT.	LONG.
Mar de Espanha, Braz. (mär-dĕ-ĕs-pä'nyȧ)	129a	21°53'S	43°00'W
Mar del Plata, Arg. (mär dĕl- plä'ta)	132	37°59'S	57°35'W
Mardin, Tur. (mär-dēn')	182	37°25'N	40°40'E
Maré, i., N. Cal. (mȧ-rā')	203	21°53'S	168°30'E
Maree, Loch, b., Scot., U.K. (mȧ-rē')	150	57°40'N	5°44'W
Mareil-Marly, Fr.	237c	48°53'N	2°05'E
Marengo, Ia., U.S. (mȧ-rĕŋ'gō)	103	41°47'N	92°04'W
Marennes, Fr. (mȧ-rĕn')	156	45°49'N	1°08'W
Marfa, Tx., U.S. (mär'fȧ)	112	30°19'N	104°01'W
Margarethenhöhe, neigh., Ger.	236	51°26'N	6°58'E
Margaretting, Eng., U.K.	235	51°41'N	0°25'E
Margarita, Pan. (mär-gōō-rē'tä)	116a	9°20'N	79°55'W
Margarita, Isla de, i., Ven. (mä-gȧ-rē'tȧ)	130	11°00'N	64°15'W
Margate, S. Afr. (mä-gāt')	213c	30°52'S	30°21'E
Margate, Eng., U.K. (mär'gāt)	151	51°21'N	1°17'E
Margherita Peak, mtn., Afr.	211	0°22'N	29°51'E
Marguerite, r., Can.	92	50°39'N	66°42'W
Marhanets', Ukr.	163	47°41'N	34°33'E
Maria, Can. (mȧ-rē'ȧ)	92	48°10'N	66°04'W
Mariager, Den. (mä-rê-ägh'ẽr)	152	56°38'N	10°00'E
Mariana, Braz. (mä-ryȧ'nä)	129a	20°23'S	43°24'W
Mariana Islands, is., Oc.	5	16°00'N	145°30'E
Marianao, Cuba (mä-rê-ä-nä'ō)	117	23°05'N	82°26'W
Mariana Trench, deep	225	12°00'N	144°00'E
Marianna, Ar., U.S. (mä-rĭ-ăn'ȧ)	111	34°45'N	90°45'W
Marianna, Fl., U.S.	114	30°46'N	85°14'W
Marianna, Pa., U.S.	101e	40°01'N	80°05'W
Mariano Acosta, Arg. (mä-rêä'nô-ȧ-kôs'tä)	132a	34°28'S	58°48'W
Mariano J. Haedo, Arg.	233d	34°39'S	58°36'W
Mariánské Lázně, Czech Rep. (mär'yȧn-skĕ'läz'nyĕ)	154	49°58'N	12°42'E
Maria Paula, Braz.	234c	22°54'S	43°02'W
Marias, r., Mt., U.S. (mȧ-rī'ȧz)	105	48°15'N	110°50'W
Marias, Islas, is., Mex. (mä-rē'äs)	116	21°30'N	106°40'W
Mariato, Punta, c., Pan.	121	7°17'N	81°09'W
Maribo, Den. (mä'rê-bô)	152	54°46'N	11°29'E
Maribor, Slvn. (mä're-bôr)	142	46°33'N	15°37'E
Maribyrnong, Austl.	243b	37°46'S	144°54'E
Maricaban, i., Phil. (mä-rê-kä-bän')	197a	13°40'N	120°44'E
Mariefred, Swe. (mä-rē'ĕ-frĭd)	152	59°17'N	17°09'E
Marie Galante, i., Guad. (mȧ-rē' gȧ-länt')	121b	15°58'N	61°05'W
Mariehamn, Fin. (mȧ-rē'ĕ-häm''n)	153	60°07'N	19°57'E
Mari El, state, Russia	166	56°30'N	48°00'E
Mariendorf, neigh., Ger.	238a	52°26'N	13°23'E
Marienfelde, neigh., Ger.	238a	52°25'N	13°22'E
Mariestad, Swe. (mä-rē'ĕ-städ')	152	58°43'N	13°45'E
Marietta, Ga., U.S. (mā-rĭ-ĕt'ȧ)	100c	33°57'N	84°33'W
Marietta, Oh., U.S.	98	39°25'N	81°30'W
Marietta, Ok., U.S.	111	33°53'N	97°07'W
Marietta, Wa., U.S.	106d	48°48'N	122°35'W
Mariinsk, Russia (mȧ-rē'ĭnsk)	170	56°15'N	87°28'E
Marijampole, Lith. (mä-rê-yäm-pô'lĕ)	153	54°33'N	23°26'E
Marikana, S. Afr. (mä'-rĭ-kä-nȧ)	218d	25°40'S	27°28'E
Marikina, Phil.	241g	14°37'N	121°06'E
Marília, Braz. (mä-rē'lyȧ)	131	22°02'S	49°48'W
Marimba, Ang.	216	8°28'S	17°08'E
Marín, Spain	158	42°24'N	8°40'W
Marina del Rey, Ca., U.S.	232	33°59'N	118°28'W
Marina del Rey, b., Ca., U.S.	232	33°58'N	118°27'W
Marin City, Ca., U.S.	231b	37°52'N	122°21'W
Marinduque Island, i., Phil. (mä-rên-dōō'kä)	197a	13°14'N	121°45'E
Marine, Il., U.S. (mȧ-rēn')	107e	38°48'N	89°47'W
Marine City, Mi., U.S.	98	42°45'N	82°30'W
Marine Lake, l., Mn., U.S.	107g	45°13'N	92°55'W
Marineland of the Pacific, pt. of i., Ca., U.S.	232	33°44'N	118°24'W
Marine on Saint Croix, Mn., U.S.	107g	45°11'N	92°47'W
Marinette, Wi., U.S. (mär-ĭ-nĕt')	97	45°04'N	87°40'W
Maringa, r., D.R.C. (mä-riŋ'gä)	211	0°30'N	21°00'E
Marinha Grande, Port. (mä-rēn'yȧ grän'dĕ)	158	39°49'N	8°53'W
Marion, Al., U.S. (măr'ĭ-ŭn)	114	32°36'N	87°19'W
Marion, Il., U.S.	98	37°40'N	88°55'W
Marion, In., U.S.	97	40°35'N	85°45'W
Marion, Ia., U.S.	103	42°01'N	91°39'W
Marion, Ks., U.S.	111	38°21'N	97°02'W
Marion, Ky., U.S.	114	37°19'N	88°05'W
Marion, N.C., U.S.	115	35°40'N	82°00'W
Marion, N.D., U.S.	102	46°37'N	98°20'W
Marion, Oh., U.S.	98	40°35'N	83°10'W
Marion, S.C., U.S.	115	34°08'N	79°23'W
Marion, Va., U.S.	115	36°48'N	81°33'W
Marion, Lake, res., S.C., U.S.	115	33°25'N	80°35'W
Marion Reef, rf., Austl.	203	18°57'S	151°31'E
Mariposa, Chile (mä-rê-pô'sä)	129b	35°33'S	71°21'W
Mariposa Creek, r., Ca., U.S.	108	37°14'N	120°30'W
Mariquita, Col. (mä-rē-kē'tä)	130a	5°13'N	74°52'W
Mariscal Estigarribia, Para.	132	22°03'S	60°28'W
Marisco, Ponta do, c., Braz. (pô'n-tä-dô-mä-rē's-kō)	132b	23°01'S	43°17'W
Maritime Alps, mts., Eur. (mă'rĭ-tīm ălps)	147	44°20'N	7°02'E
Mariupol', Ukr.	164	47°07'N	37°32'E
Mariveles, Phil.	197a	14°27'N	120°29'E
Marj Uyan, Leb.	181a	33°21'N	35°36'E
Marka, Som.	218a	1°45'N	44°47'E
Markaryd, Swe. (mär'kä-rüd)	152	56°30'N	13°34'E
Marked Tree, Ar., U.S. (märkt trē)	111	35°31'N	90°26'W
Marken, i., Neth.	145a	52°26'N	5°08'E
Market Bosworth, Eng., U.K. (bŏz'wûrth)	144a	52°37'N	1°23'W
Market Deeping, Eng., U.K. (dēp'ĭng)	144a	52°40'N	0°19'W

ăt; finăl; rāte; senåte; ärm; åsk; sofȧ; fâre; ch-choose; dh-as th in other; bē; ėvent; bĕt; recĕnt; cratẽr; g-gō; gh-guttural g; bĭt; ĭ-short neutral; rīde; K-guttural k as ch in German ich;

PRONOUNCING INDEX

Market Drayton-Mayran 315

PLACE (Pronunciation)	PAGE	LAT.	LONG.
Market Drayton, Eng., U.K. (drā'tŭn)	144a	52°54'N	2°29'W
Market Harborough, Eng., U.K. (här'bŭr-ō)	144a	52°28'N	0°55'W
Market Rasen, Eng., U.K. (rā'zĕn)	144a	53°23'N	0°21'W
Markham, Can. (märk'ăm)	91	43°53'N	79°15'W
Markham, Mount, mtn., Ant.	219	82°59'S	159°30'E
Markivka, Ukr.	163	49°32'N	39°34'E
Markovo, Russia (mär'kô-vô)	165	64°46'N	170°48'E
Markrāna, India	186	27°08'N	74°43'E
Marks, Russia	167	51°42'N	46°46'E
Marksville, La., U.S. (märks'vĭl)	113	31°09'N	92°05'W
Markt Indersdorf, Ger. (märkt ēn'dĕrs-dōrf)	145d	48°22'N	11°23'E
Marktredwitz, Ger. (märk-rĕd'vĕts)	154	50°02'N	12°05'E
Markt Schwaben, Ger. (märkt shvä'bĕn)	145d	48°12'N	11°52'E
Marl, Ger. (märl)	157c	51°40'N	7°05'E
Marlboro, N.J., U.S.	100a	40°18'N	74°15'W
Marlborough, Ma., U.S.	93a	42°21'N	71°33'W
Marlette, Mi., U.S. (mär-lĕt')	98	43°25'N	83°05'W
Marlin, Tx., U.S. (mär'lĭn)	113	31°18'N	96°52'W
Marlinton, W.V., U.S. (mär'lĭn-tŭn)	98	38°15'N	80°10'W
Marlow, Eng., U.K. (mär'lō)	144b	51°33'N	0°46'W
Marlow, Ok., U.S.	111	34°38'N	97°56'W
Marls, The, b., Bah. (märls)	122	26°30'N	77°15'W
Marly-le-Roi, Fr.	237c	48°52'N	2°05'E
Marmande, Fr. (mȧr-mäNd')	156	44°30'N	0°10'E
Marmara Denizi, sea, Tur.	182	40°40'N	28°00'E
Marmarth, N.D., U.S. (mär'mȧrth)	102	46°19'N	103°57'W
Mar Muerto, l., Mex. (mär-mōĕ'r-tô)	119	16°13'N	94°22'W
Marne, Ger. (mär'nĕ)	145c	53°57'N	9°01'E
Marne, r., Fr. (märn)	147	49°00'N	4°30'E
Maroa, Ven. (mä-rō'ä)	130	2°43'N	67°37'W
Maroantsetra, Madag. (mȧ-rō-äŋ-tsā'trȧ)	213	15°18'S	49°48'E
Maro Jarapeto, mtn., Col. (mä-rô-hä-rä-pĕ'tô)	130a	6°29'N	76°39'W
Marolles-en-Brie, Fr.	237c	48°44'N	2°33'E
Maromokotro, mtn., Madag.	213	14°00'S	49°11'E
Marondera, Zimb.	212	18°10'S	31°36'E
Maroni, r., S.A. (mä-rō'nē)	131	3°02'N	53°54'W
Maro Reef, rf., Hi., U.S.	94b	25°15'N	170°00'W
Maroua, Cam. (mär'wä)	211	10°36'N	14°20'E
Maroubra, Austl.	243a	33°57'S	151°16'E
Marple, Eng., U.K. (mär'p'l)	144a	53°24'N	2°04'W
Marquard, S. Afr.	218d	28°41'S	27°26'E
Marquesas Islands, is., Fr. Poly. (mär-kĕ'säs)	2	8°50'S	141°00'W
Marquesas Keys, is., Fl., U.S. (mär-kē'zȧs)	115a	24°37'N	82°15'W
Marquês de Valença, Braz. (mär-kĕ's-dĕ-vä-lĕ'n-sȧ)	129a	22°16'S	43°42'W
Marquette, Can. (mȧr-kĕt')	83f	50°04'N	97°43'W
Marquette, Mi., U.S.	97	46°32'N	87°25'W
Marquez, Tx., U.S. (mär-kāz')	113	31°14'N	96°15'W
Marra, Jabal, mtn., Sudan (jĕb'ĕl mär'ä)	211	13°00'N	23°47'E
Marrakech, Mor. (mȧr-rä'kĕsh)	210	31°38'N	8°00'W
Marree, Austl. (mär'rē)	202	29°38'S	137°55'E
Marrero, La., U.S.	100d	29°55'N	90°06'W
Marrickville, Austl.	243a	33°55'S	151°09'E
Marrupa, Moz.	217	13°08'S	37°30'E
Mars, Pa., U.S. (märz)	101e	40°42'N	80°01'W
Marsabit, Kenya	217	2°20'N	37°59'E
Marsala, Italy (mär-sä'lä)	148	37°48'N	12°28'E
Marscheid, neigh., Ger.	236	51°14'N	7°14'E
Marsden, Eng., U.K. (märz'dĕn)	144a	53°36'N	1°55'W
Marseille, Fr. (mȧr-sâ'y')	142	43°18'N	5°25'E
Marseilles, Il., U.S. (mär-sĕlz')	98	41°20'N	88°40'W
Marsfield, Austl.	243a	33°47'S	151°07'E
Marshall, Il., U.S. (mär'shăl)	98	39°20'N	87°40'W
Marshall, Mi., U.S.	98	42°20'N	84°55'W
Marshall, Mn., U.S.	102	44°28'N	95°49'W
Marshall, Mo., U.S.	111	39°07'N	93°12'W
Marshall, Tx., U.S.	97	32°33'N	94°22'W
Marshall Islands, nation, Oc.	3	10°00'N	165°00'E
Marshalltown, Ia., U.S. (mär'shăl-toun)	103	42°02'N	92°55'W
Marshallville, Ga., U.S. (mär'shăl-vĭl)	114	32°29'N	83°55'W
Marshfield, Ma., U.S. (märsh'fēld)	93a	42°06'N	70°43'W
Marshfield, Mo., U.S.	111	37°20'N	92°53'W
Marshfield, Wi., U.S.	103	44°40'N	90°10'W
Marsh Harbour, Bah.	122	26°30'N	77°00'W
Mars Hill, In., U.S. (märz'hĭl')	101g	39°43'N	86°15'W
Mars Hill, Me., U.S.	92	46°34'N	67°54'W
Marstrand, Swe. (mär'stränd)	152	57°54'N	11°33'E
Marsyaty, Russia (märs'yȧ-tĭ)	172a	60°03'N	60°28'E
Mart, Tx., U.S. (märt)	113	31°32'N	96°49'W
Martaban, Gulf of, b., Myanmar (mär-tŭ-bän')	196	16°34'N	96°58'E
Martapura, Indon.	196	3°19'S	114°45'E
Marten, neigh., Ger.	236	51°31'N	7°23'E
Martha's Vineyard, i., Ma., U.S. (mär'thȧz vĭn'yȧrd)	99	41°25'N	70°35'W
Martigny, Switz. (mȧr-tē-nyē')	154	46°06'N	7°00'E
Martigues, Fr.	157	43°24'N	5°05'E
Martin, Tn., U.S. (mär'tĭn)	114	36°20'N	88°45'W
Martina Franca, Italy (mär-tē'nä fräŋ'kä)	161	40°43'N	17°21'E
Martinez, Ca., U.S. (mär-tē'nĕz)	106b	38°01'N	122°08'W
Martinez, Tx., U.S.	107d	29°25'N	98°20'W
Martínez, neigh., Arg.	233d	34°29'S	58°30'W
Martinique, dep., N.A. (mȧr-tē-nēk')	117	14°50'N	60°40'W
Martin Lake, res., Al., U.S.	114	32°40'N	86°05'W
Martin Point, c., Ak., U.S.	95	70°10'N	142°00'W
Martinsburg, W.V., U.S. (mär'tĭnz-bûrg)	99	39°30'N	78°00'W
Martins Ferry, Oh., U.S. (mär'tĭnz)	98	40°05'N	80°45'W
Martinsville, In., U.S. (mär'tĭnz-vĭl)	98	39°25'N	86°25'W
Martinsville, Va., U.S.	115	36°40'N	79°53'W
Martos, Spain (mär'tōs)	158	37°43'N	3°58'W
Martre, Lac la, l., Can. (läk la märtr)	84	63°24'N	119°58'W
Marugame, Japan (mä'ro͞o-gä'mä)	195	34°19'N	133°48'E
Marungu, mts., D.R.C.	217	7°50'S	29°50'E
Marve, neigh., India	187b	19°12'N	72°43'E
Marwitz, Ger.	238a	52°41'N	13°09'E
Mary, Turk. (mä'rē)	169	37°45'N	61°47'E
Mar'yanskaya, Russia (mȧr-yän'skȧ-yȧ)	163	45°04'N	38°39'E
Maryborough, Austl. (mâ'rĭ-bŭr-ô)	203	25°35'S	152°40'E
Maryborough, Austl.	203	37°00'S	143°50'E
Maryland, state, U.S. (mĕr'ĭ-lănd)	97	39°10'N	76°25'W
Maryland Park, Md., U.S.	229d	38°53'N	76°54'W
Marys, r., Nv., U.S. (mā'rĭz)	104	41°25'N	115°10'W
Marystown, Can. (mâr'ĭz-toun)	93	47°11'N	55°10'W
Marysville, Can.	92	45°59'N	66°35'W
Marysville, Ca., U.S.	108	39°09'N	121°37'W
Marysville, Oh., U.S.	98	40°15'N	83°25'W
Marysville, Wa., U.S.	106a	48°03'N	122°11'W
Maryville, Il., U.S. (mā'rĭ-vĭl)	107e	38°44'N	89°57'W
Maryville, Mo., U.S.	111	40°21'N	94°51'W
Maryville, Tn., U.S.	114	35°44'N	83°59'W
Marzahn, neigh., Ger.	238a	52°33'N	13°33'E
Mārzuq, Libya	211	26°00'N	14°09'E
Marzūq, Idehan, des., Libya	210	24°30'N	13°00'E
Masai Steppe, plat., Tan.	217	4°30'S	36°40'E
Masaka, Ug.	217	0°20'S	31°44'E
Masalasef, Chad	215	11°43'N	17°08'E
Masalembo-Besar, i., Indon.	196	5°40'S	114°28'E
Masan, S. Kor. (mä-sän')	189	35°10'N	128°31'E
Masangwe, Tan.	217	5°28'S	30°05'E
Masasi, Tan. (mä-sä'sē)	213	10°43'S	38°48'E
Masatepe, Nic. (mä-sä-tĕ'pĕ)	120	11°57'N	86°10'W
Masaya, Nic. (mä-sä'yä)	120	11°58'N	86°05'W
Masbate, Phil. (mäs-bä'tä)	197a	12°21'N	123°38'E
Masbate, i., Phil.	197	12°19'N	123°03'E
Mascarene Islands, is., Afr.	5	20°20'S	56°40'E
Mascot, Austl.	243a	33°56'S	151°12'E
Mascot, Tn., U.S. (măs'kŏt)	114	36°04'N	83°45'W
Mascota, Mex. (mäs-kō'tä)	118	20°33'N	104°45'W
Mascota, r., Mex.	118	20°33'N	104°52'W
Mascouche, Can. (mȧs-ko͞osh')	83a	45°45'N	73°36'W
Mascouche, r., Can.	83a	45°44'N	73°45'W
Mascoutah, Il., U.S. (măs-kū'tä)	107e	38°29'N	89°48'W
Maseru, Leso. (măz'ēr-o͞o)	212	29°09'S	27°11'E
Mashhad, Iran	182	36°17'N	59°30'E
Māshkel, Hāmūn-i-, l., Asia (hä-mo͞on'ē māsh-kĕl')	182	28°28'N	64°13'E
Mashra'ar Raqq, Sudan	211	8°28'N	29°15'E
Masi-Manimba, D.R.C.	216	4°46'S	17°55'E
Masindi, Ug. (mä-sēn'dē)	211	1°44'N	31°43'E
Masjed Soleymān, Iran	182	31°45'N	49°17'E
Mask, Lough, b., Ire. (lŏk măsk)	150	53°35'N	9°23'W
Maslovo, Russia (mäs'lô-vô)	172a	60°08'N	60°28'E
Mason, Mi., U.S. (mā'sŭn)	98	42°35'N	84°25'W
Mason, Oh., U.S.	101f	39°22'N	84°18'W
Mason, Tx., U.S.	112	30°46'N	99°14'W
Mason City, Ia., U.S.	97	43°08'N	93°14'W
Masonville, Va., U.S.	229d	38°51'N	77°12'W
Maspeth, neigh., N.Y., U.S.	228	40°43'N	73°55'W
Massa, Italy (mäs'sä)	160	44°02'N	10°08'E
Massachusetts, state, U.S. (măs-ȧ-cho͞o'sĕts)	97	42°20'N	72°30'W
Massachusetts Bay, b., Ma., U.S.	92	42°26'N	70°20'W
Massafra, Italy (mäs-sä'frä)	161	40°35'N	17°05'E
Massa Marittima, Italy	160	43°03'N	10°55'E
Massapequa, N.Y., U.S.	100a	40°41'N	73°28'W
Massaua *see* Mitsiwa, Erit.	211	15°40'N	39°19'E
Massena, N.Y., U.S. (mă-sē'nȧ)	99	44°55'N	74°55'W
Masset, Can. (măs'ĕt)	84	54°02'N	132°09'W
Masset Inlet, b., Can.	87	53°42'N	132°20'E
Massif Central, Fr. (mȧ-sēf' säN-trȧl')	142	45°12'N	3°02'E
Massillon, Oh., U.S. (măs'ĭ-lŏn)	98	40°50'N	81°35'W
Massinga, Moz. (mä-sĭn'gä)	212	23°18'S	35°18'E
Massive, Mount, mtn., Co., U.S. (măs'ĭv)	96	39°05'N	106°30'W
Masson, Can. (mäs-sŭn)	83c	45°33'N	75°25'W
Massy, Fr.	237c	48°44'N	2°17'E
Masuda, Japan (mä-so͞o'dȧ)	195	34°42'N	131°53'E
Masuria, reg., Pol.	155	53°40'N	21°10'E
Masvingo, Zimb.	212	20°07'S	30°47'E
Matadi, D.R.C. (mȧ-tä'dē)	212	5°49'S	13°27'E
Matagalpa, Nic. (mä-tä-gäl'pä)	116	12°52'N	85°57'W
Matagami, l., Can. (mȧ-tä-gȧ'mē)	85	50°10'N	78°28'W
Matagorda Bay, b., Tx., U.S. (măt-ȧ-gôr'dȧ)	113	28°32'N	96°13'W
Matagorda Island, i., Tx., U.S.	113	28°13'N	96°27'W
Matam, Sen. (mä-tăm')	210	15°40'N	13°15'W
Matamoros, Mex. (mä-tä-mō'rôs)	112	25°32'N	103°13'W
Matamoros, Mex.	116	25°52'N	97°30'W
Matane, Can. (mȧ-tȧn')	85	48°51'N	67°32'W
Matanzas, Cuba (mä-tän'zäs)	117	23°05'N	81°35'W
Matanzas, prov., Cuba	122	22°45'N	81°20'W
Matanzas, Bahía, b., Cuba (bä-ē'ä)	122	23°10'N	81°30'W
Matapalo, Cabo, c., C.R. (kȧ'bô-mä-tä-pä'lō)	121	8°22'N	83°25'W
Matapédia, Can. (mă-tȧ-pā'dē-ȧ)	92	47°58'N	66°56'W
Matapédia, l., Can.	92	48°33'N	67°32'W
Matapédia, r., Can.	92	48°10'N	67°10'W
Mataquito, r., Chile (mä-tä-kē'tô)	129b	35°08'S	71°35'W
Matara, Sri L. (mä-tä'rä)	183b	5°59'N	80°35'E
Mataram, Indon.	196	8°45'S	116°15'E
Matatiele, S. Afr. (mä-tä-tyā'lā)	213c	30°21'S	28°49'E
Matawan, N.J., U.S.	100a	40°24'N	74°13'W
Matehuala, Mex. (mä-tȧ-wä'lä)	116	23°38'N	100°39'W
Matera, Italy (mä-tâ'rä)	160	40°42'N	16°37'E
Mateur, Tun. (mȧ-tûr')	148	37°09'N	9°43'E
Māthěrān, India	187b	18°58'N	73°16'E
Matheson, Can.	91	48°35'N	80°33'W
Mathews, Lake, l., Ca., U.S. (măth ūz)	107a	33°50'N	117°24'W
Mathura, India (mu-to͝o'rŭ)	183	27°39'N	77°39'E
Matias Barbosa, Braz. (mä-tē'äs-bär-bô-sä)	129a	21°53'S	43°19'W
Matillas, Laguna, l., Mex. (lä-gō'nä-mä-tē'l-yäs)	119	18°02'N	92°36'W
Matina, C.R. (mä-tē'nä)	121	10°06'N	83°20'W
Matiši, Lat. (mä'tē-sē)	153	57°43'N	25°09'E
Matlalcueyetl, Cerro, mtn., Mex. (sĕ'r-rä-mä-tläl-kwĕ'yĕtl)	118	19°13'N	98°02'W
Matlock, Eng., U.K. (măt'lŏk)	144a	53°08'N	1°33'W
Matochkin Shar, Russia (mä'tŏch-kĭn)	164	73°57'N	56°16'E
Mato Grosso, Braz. (măt'ō grōs'ō)	131	15°04'S	59°58'W
Mato Grosso, state, Braz.	131	14°38'S	55°36'W
Mato Grosso, Chapada de, hills, Braz. (shä-pä'dä-dĕ)	131	13°39'S	55°42'W
Mato Grosso do Sul, state, Braz.	131	20°00'S	56°00'W
Matosinhos, Port.	158	41°10'N	8°48'W
Maṭraḥ, Oman (mȧ-trä')	182	23°36'N	58°27'E
Matsubara, Japan	195b	34°34'N	135°34'E
Matsudo, Japan (mät'sō-dō)	195a	35°48'N	139°55'E
Matsue, Japan (mät'sō-ĕ)	189	35°29'N	133°04'E
Matsumoto, Japan (mät'sō-mō'tō)	194	36°15'N	137°59'E
Matsuyama, Japan (mät'sō-yä'mä)	189	33°48'N	132°45'E
Matsuzaka, Japan (mät'sō-zä'kä)	195	34°35'N	136°34'E
Mattamuskeet, Lake, l., N.C., U.S. (măt-tȧ-mŭs'kēt)	115	35°34'N	76°03'W
Mattaponi, r., Va., U.S. (măt'ȧ-ponī')	99	37°45'N	77°00'W
Mattawa, Can. (măt'ȧ-wȧ)	85	46°15'N	78°49'W
Matterhorn, mtn., Eur. (măt'ĕr-hôrn)	154	45°57'N	7°36'E
Matteson, Il., U.S. (măt'ē-sŭn)	101a	41°30'N	87°42'W
Matthew Town, Bah. (măth'ū toun)	123	21°00'N	73°40'W
Mattoon, Il., U.S. (mă-to͞on')	97	39°30'N	88°20'W
Maturín, Ven. (mä-to͞o-rēn')	130	9°48'N	63°16'W
Mátyásföld, neigh., Hung.	239g	47°31'N	19°13'E
Mátyas-Templom, rel., Hung.	239g	47°30'N	19°02'E
Maúa, Moz.	217	13°51'S	37°10'E
Mauban, Phil. (mä'o͞o-bän')	197a	14°11'N	121°44'E
Maubeuge, Fr. (mō-bûzh')	156	50°18'N	3°57'E
Maud, Oh., U.S. (môd)	101f	39°21'N	84°23'W
Mauer, Aus. (mou'ĕr)	145e	48°09'N	16°16'E
Maués, Braz. (mȧ-wĕ's)	131	3°34'S	57°30'W
Mau Escarpment, cliff, Kenya	217	0°45'S	35°50'E
Maui, i., Hi., U.S. (mä'o͞o-ē)	96c	20°52'N	156°02'W
Maule, r., Chile (mà'ō-lĕ)	129b	35°45'S	70°50'W
Maumee, Oh., U.S. (mô-mē')	98	41°30'N	83°40'W
Maumee, r., In., U.S.	98	41°10'N	84°50'W
Maumee Bay, b., Oh., U.S.	98	41°50'N	83°20'W
Maun, Bots. (mä-ōn')	212	19°52'S	23°40'E
Mauna Kea, mtn., Hi., U.S. (mä'ō-nä-kā'ä)	96c	19°52'N	155°30'W
Mauna Loa, mtn., Hi., U.S. (mä'ō-nä-lō'ä)	96c	19°28'N	155°38'W
Maurecourt, Fr.	237c	49°00'N	2°04'E
Maurepas Lake, l., La., U.S. (mō-rē-pä')	113	30°18'N	90°40'W
Mauricie, Parc National de la, rec., Can.	91	46°46'N	73°00'W
Mauritania, nation, Afr. (mô-rē-tā'nĭ-ȧ)	210	19°38'N	13°30'W
Mauritius, nation, Afr. (mô-rĭsh'ĭ-ŭs)	3	20°18'S	57°36'E
Maury, Wa., U.S. (mô'rĭ)	106a	47°22'N	122°23'W
Mauston, Wi., U.S. (môs'tŭn)	103	43°46'N	90°05'W
Maverick, r., Az., U.S. (mă-vûr'ĭk)	109	33°40'N	109°30'W
Mavinga, Ang.	216	15°50'S	20°21'E
Mawlamyine, Myanmar	196	16°30'N	97°39'E
Maxville, Can. (măks'vĭl)	83c	45°17'N	74°52'W
Maxville, Mo., U.S.	107e	38°26'N	90°24'W
Maya, r., Russia (mä'yä)	171	58°00'N	135°45'E
Mayaguana, i., Bah.	123	22°25'N	73°00'W
Mayaguana Passage, strt., Bah.	123	22°20'N	73°25'W
Mayagüez, P.R. (mä-yä-gwāz')	117	18°12'N	67°10'W
Mayari, r., Cuba	123	20°25'N	75°35'W
Mayas, Montañas, mts., N.A. (mōntăn'äs mä'äs)	120a	16°43'N	89°00'W
Mayd, i., Som.	218a	11°24'N	46°38'E
Mayen, Ger. (mī'ĕn)	154	50°19'N	7°14'E
Mayenne, r., Fr. (mȧ-yĕn)	156	48°14'N	0°45'W
Mayfair, neigh., S. Afr.	244b	26°12'S	28°01'E
Mayfair, neigh., Pa., U.S.	229b	40°02'N	75°03'W
Mayfield, Ky., U.S. (mā'fēld)	114	36°44'N	88°19'W
Mayfield Creek, r., Ky., U.S.	114	36°54'N	88°47'W
Mayfield Heights, Oh., U.S.	101d	41°31'N	81°26'W
Mayfield Lake, res., Wa., U.S.	104	46°31'N	122°34'W
Maykop, Russia	164	44°35'N	40°07'E
Maykor, Russia (mī-kôr')	172a	59°01'N	55°52'E
Maymyo, Myanmar (mī'myō)	188	22°14'N	96°32'E
Maynard, Ma., U.S. (mā'nȧrd)	93a	42°25'N	71°27'W
Mayne, Can. (mān)	106d	48°51'N	123°18'W
Mayne, i., Can.	106d	48°52'N	123°14'W
Mayo, Can. (mä-yō')	84	63°40'N	135°51'W
Mayo, Fl., U.S.	114	30°02'N	83°08'W
Mayo, Md., U.S.	100e	38°54'N	76°31'W
Mayodan, N.C., U.S. (mā-yō'dăn)	115	36°25'N	79°59'W
Mayon Volcano, vol., Phil. (mä-yōn')	197a	13°21'N	123°43'E
Mayotte, dep., Afr. (mȧ-yôt')	213	13°07'S	45°32'E
May Pen, Jam.	122	18°00'N	77°25'W
Mayraira Point, c., Phil.	193	18°40'N	120°45'E
Mayran, Laguna de, l., Mex. (lä-ō'nä-dĕ-mī-rän')	116	25°40'N	102°35'W

PRONOUNCING INDEX Meppel–Millersburg 317

PLACE (Pronunciation)	PAGE	LAT.	LONG.
Meppel, Neth. (mĕp'ĕl)	151	52°41'N	6°08'E
Meppen, Ger. (mĕp'ĕn)	154	52°40'N	7°18'E
Merabéllou, Kólpos, b., Grc.	160a	35°16'N	25°55'E
Meramec, r., Mo., U.S. (mĕr'ȧ-mĕk)	111	38°06'N	91°06'W
Merano, Italy (mā-rä'nō)	148	46°39'N	11°10'E
Merasheen, i., Can. (mē'rȧ-shēn)	93	47°30'N	54°15'W
Merauke, Indon. (mā-rou'kā)	197	8°32'S	140°17'E
Meraux, La., U.S. (mē-ro')	100d	29°56'N	89°56'W
Mercader y Millás, Spain	238e	41°21'N	2°05'E
Mercato San Severino, Italy	159c	40°34'N	14°38'E
Merced, Ca., U.S. (mĕr-sĕd')	108	37°17'N	120°30'W
Merced, r., Ca., U.S.	108	37°25'N	120°31'W
Mercedario, Cerro, mtn., Arg. (mĕr-så-dhä'rē-ō)	132	31°58'S	70°07'W
Mercedes, Arg.	129c	34°41'S	59°26'W
Mercedes, Arg. (mĕr-sā'dhās)	132	29°04'S	58°01'W
Mercedes, Tx., U.S.	113	26°09'N	97°55'W
Mercedes, Ur.	132	33°17'S	58°04'W
Mercedita, Chile (mĕr-sĕ-dē'tä)	129b	33°51'S	71°10'W
Mercer Island, Wa., U.S. (mûr'sẽr)	106a	47°35'N	122°15'W
Mercês, Braz. (mĕ-sĕ's)	129a	21°13'S	43°20'W
Mercês, Port.	238d	38°47'N	9°19'W
Merchtem, Bel.	145a	50°57'N	4°13'E
Mercier, Can.	83a	45°19'N	73°45'W
Mercy, Cape, c., Can.	85	64°48'N	63°22'W
Merdeka Palace, bldg., Indon.	241i	6°10'S	106°49'E
Mere, Eng., U.K.	237b	53°20'N	2°25'W
Meredale, S. Afr.	244b	26°17'S	27°59'E
Meredith, N.H., U.S. (mĕr'ē-dĭth)	99	43°35'N	71°35'W
Merefa, Ukr. (må-rĕf'ȧ)	163	49°49'N	36°04'E
Merendón, Serranía de, mts., Hond.	120	15°01'N	89°05'W
Mereworth, Eng., U.K. (mĕ-rĕ wûrth)	144b	51°15'N	0°23'E
Mergui, Myanmar (mĕr-gē')	196	12°29'N	98°39'E
Mergui Archipelago, is., Myanmar	196	12°04'N	97°02'E
Meric (Maritsa), r., Eur.	153	40°43'N	26°19'E
Mérida, Mex.	116	20°58'N	89°37'W
Mérida, Ven.	130	8°30'N	71°15'W
Mérida, Cordillera de, mts., Ven. (mĕ'rē-dhä)	130	8°30'N	70°45'W
Meriden, Ct., U.S. (mĕr'ĭ-dĕn)	99	41°30'N	72°50'W
Meridian, Ms., U.S. (mē-rĭd-ĭ-ăn)	97	32°21'N	88°41'W
Meridian, Tx., U.S.	113	31°56'N	97°37'W
Mérignac, Fr.	156	44°50'N	0°40'W
Merikarvia, Fin. (mä'rē-kår'vē-å)	153	61°51'N	21°30'E
Mering, Ger. (mĕ'rēng)	145d	48°16'N	11°00'E
Merion Station, Pa., U.S.	229b	40°00'N	75°15'W
Merkel, Tx., U.S. (mûr'kĕl)	112	32°26'N	100°02'W
Merkinė, Lith.	153	54°10'N	24°10'E
Merksem, Bel.	145a	51°15'N	4°27'E
Merkys, r., Lith. (măr'kĭs)	155	54°23'N	25°00'E
Merlo, Arg. (mĕr-lō)	132a	34°40'S	58°44'W
Merlynston, Austl.	243b	37°43'S	144°58'E
Meron, Hare, mtn., Isr.	181a	32°58'N	35°25'E
Merriam, Ks., U.S. (mĕr-rĭ-yăm)	107f	39°01'N	94°42'W
Merriam, Mn., U.S.	107g	44°44'N	93°36'W
Merrick, N.Y., U.S. (mĕr'ĭk)	100a	40°40'N	73°33'W
Merri Creek, r., Austl.	243b	37°48'S	144°59'E
Merrifield, Va., U.S. (mĕr'ĭ-fēld)	100e	38°50'N	77°12'W
Merrill, Wi., U.S. (mĕr'ĭl)	103	45°11'N	89°42'W
Merrimac, Ma., U.S. (mĕr'ĭ-măk)	93a	45°20'N	71°00'W
Merrimack, N.H., U.S.	93a	42°51'N	71°25'W
Merrimack, r., Ma., U.S. (mĕr'ĭ-măk)	99	43°10'N	71°30'W
Merrionette Park, Il., U.S.	231a	41°41'N	87°42'W
Merritt, Can. (mĕr'ĭt)	84	50°07'N	120°47'W
Merrylands, Austl.	243a	33°50'S	150°59'E
Merryville, La., U.S. (mĕr'ĭ-vĭl)	113	30°46'N	93°34'W
Mersa Fatma, Erit.	211	14°54'N	40°14'E
Merscheid, neigh., Ger.	236	51°10'N	7°01'E
Merseburg, Ger. (mĕr'zĕ-bŏŏrgh)	154	51°21'N	11°59'E
Mersey, r., Eng., U.K. (mûr'zē)	144a	53°20'N	2°55'W
Merseyside, co., Eng., U.K.	144a	53°29'N	2°59'W
Mersing, Malay.	181b	2°25'N	103°51'E
Merta Road, India (mâr'tŭ rōd)	186	26°50'N	73°54'E
Merthyr Tydfil, Wales, U.K. (mûr'thẽr tĭd'vĭl)	150	51°46'N	3°30'W
Mértola Almodóvar, Port. (mĕr-tô-lȧ-äl-mô-dô'vär)	158	37°39'N	8°04'W
Merton, neigh., Eng., U.K.	235	51°25'N	0°12'W
Méru, Fr. (mā-rü')	156	49°14'N	2°08'E
Meru, Kenya (mā'rōō)	211	0°01'N	37°45'E
Meru, Mount, mtn., Tan.	217	3°15'S	36°43'E
Merume Mountains, mts., Guy. (mĕr-ü'mĕ)	131	5°45'N	60°15'W
Merwede Kanaal, can., Neth.	145a	52°15'N	5°01'E
Merwin, l., Wa., U.S. (mĕr'wĭn)	106c	45°58'N	122°27'W
Merzifon, Tur. (mĕr'ze-fōn)	182	40°50'N	35°30'E
Mesa, Az., U.S. (mā'sȧ)	109	33°25'N	111°50'W
Mesabi Range, mts., Mn., U.S. (mā-sŏb'bē)	103	47°17'N	93°04'W
Mesagne, Italy (mā-sän'yå)	161	40°34'N	17°51'E
Mesa Verde National Park, rec., Co., U.S. (vĕr'dē)	96	37°22'N	108°27'W
Mescalero Apache Indian Reservation, I.R., N.M., U.S. (mĕs-kä-lā'rō)	109	33°10'N	105°45'W
Meščerskij, Russia	239b	55°40'N	37°25'E
Meshchovsk, Russia (myĕsh'chĕfsk)	162	54°17'N	35°19'E
Mesilla, N.M., U.S. (må-sē'yä)	109	32°15'N	106°45'W
Meskine, Chad	215	11°25'N	15°21'E
Mesolóngion, Grc. (mĕ-sô-lôŋ'gē-ôn)	161	38°23'N	21°28'E
Mesopotamia, hist. reg., Asia	185	34°00'N	44°00'E
Mesquita, Braz.	132b	22°48'S	43°26'W
Messina, Italy (mĕ-sē'nȧ)	142	38°11'N	15°34'E
Messina, S. Afr.	212	22°17'S	30°13'E
Messina, Stretto di, strt., Italy (strĕ't-tô dē)	149	38°10'N	15°34'E
Messíni, Grc.	161	37°05'N	22°00'E
Messy, Fr.	237c	48°58'N	2°42'E

PLACE (Pronunciation)	PAGE	LAT.	LONG.
Mestaganem, Alg.	210	36°04'N	0°11'E
Mestre, Italy (mĕs'trā)	160	45°29'N	12°15'E
Meta, dept., Col. (mĕ'tä)	130a	3°28'N	74°07'W
Meta, r., S.A.	130	4°33'N	72°09'W
Métabetchouane, r., Can. (mĕ-tȧ-bĕt-chōō-än')	91	47°45'N	72°00'W
Metairie, La., U.S.	113	30°00'N	90°11'W
Metán, Arg. (mĕ-tȧ'n)	132	25°32'S	64°51'W
Metangula, Moz.	212	12°42'S	34°48'E
Metapán, El Sal. (må-täpän')	120	14°21'N	89°26'W
Metcalfe, Can. (mĕt-käf)	83c	45°14'N	75°27'W
Metchosin, Can.	106a	48°22'N	123°33'W
Metepec, Mex. (må-tĕ-pĕk')	118	18°56'N	98°31'W
Metepec, Mex.	118	19°15'N	99°36'W
Methow, r., Wa., U.S. (mĕt'hou) (mĕt hou')	104	48°26'N	120°15'W
Methuen, Ma., U.S. (mē-thū'ĕn)	93a	42°44'N	71°11'W
Metković, Cro. (mĕt'kō-vĭch)	161	43°02'N	17°40'E
Metlakatla, Ak., U.S. (mĕt-lȧ-kăt'lȧ)	95	55°08'N	131°35'W
Metropolis, Il., U.S. (mē-trŏp'ō-lĭs)	111	37°09'N	88°46'W
Metropolitan Museum of Art, pt. of i., N.Y., U.S.	228	40°47'N	73°58'W
Metter, Ga., U.S. (mĕt'ẽr)	115	32°21'N	82°05'W
Mettmann, Ger. (mĕt'män)	157c	51°15'N	6°58'E
Metuchen, N.J., U.S. (mē-tŭ'chĕn)	100a	40°32'N	74°21'W
Metz, Fr. (mĕtz)	147	49°08'N	6°10'E
Metztitlán, Mex. (mĕtz-tĕt-län)	118	20°36'N	98°45'W
Meuban, Cam.	215	2°27'N	12°41'E
Meudon, Fr.	237c	48°48'N	2°14'E
Meuse (Maas), r., Eur. (mûz) (müz)	151	50°32'N	5°22'E
Mexborough, Eng., U.K. (mĕks'bŭr-ō)	144a	53°30'N	1°17'W
Mexia, Tx., U.S. (må-hē'ä)	113	31°32'N	96°29'W
Mexian, China	189	24°20'N	116°10'E
Mexicalcingo, Mex. (mĕ-kē-käl-sēn'go)	119a	19°13'N	99°34'W
Mexicali, Mex. (mäk-sē-kä'lē)	116	32°28'N	115°29'W
Mexicana, Altiplanicie, plat., Mex.	118	22°38'N	102°33'W
Mexican Hat, Ut., U.S. (mĕk'sĭ-kăn hăt)	109	37°10'N	109°55'W
Mexico, Me., U.S. (mĕk'sĭ-kō)	92	44°34'N	70°33'W
Mexico, Mo., U.S.	111	39°09'N	91°51'W
Mexico, nation, N.A.	116	23°45'N	104°00'W
Mexico, Gulf of, b., N.A.	116	25°15'N	93°45'W
Mexico City, Mex. (mĕk'sĭ-kō)	116	19°28'N	99°09'W
Mexticacán, Mex. (mĕs'tē-kä-kän')	118	21°12'N	102°43'W
Meyers Chuck, Ak., U.S.	86	55°44'N	132°15'W
Meyersdale, Pa., U.S. (mī'ẽrz-dāl)	99	39°55'N	79°00'W
Meyerton, S. Afr. (mī'ẽr-tŭn)	218d	26°35'S	28°01'E
Meymaneh, Afg.	182	35°53'N	64°38'E
Mezen', Russia	164	65°50'N	44°05'E
Mezen', r., Russia	166	65°20'N	44°45'E
Mézenc, Mont, mtn., Fr. (mŏn-mā-zĕn')	156	44°55'N	4°12'E
Mezha, r., Eur. (myâ'zhȧ)	162	55°53'N	31°44'E
Mézieres-sur-Seine, Fr. (mā-zyâr'sür-sån')	157b	48°58'N	1°49'E
Mezőkövesd, Hung. (mĕ'zû-kû'vĕsht)	155	47°49'N	20°36'E
Mezőtur, Hung. (mĕ'zû-tōōr)	155	47°00'N	20°36'E
Mezquital, Mex. (måz-kē-täl')	118	23°30'N	104°20'W
Mezquitic, Mex. (måz-kē-tēk')	118	22°25'N	103°43'W
Mezquitic, r., Mex.	118	22°25'N	103°45'W
Mfangano Island, i., Kenya	217	0°28'S	33°35'E
Mga, Russia (m'gȧ)	172c	59°45'N	31°04'E
Mglin, Russia (m'glĕn')	162	53°03'N	32°52'W
Mia, Oued, r., Alg.	148	29°26'N	3°15'E
Miacatlán, Mex. (mē'ä-kä-tlän')	118	18°42'N	99°17'W
Mia-dong, neigh., S. Kor.	241b	37°37'N	127°01'E
Miahuatlán, Mex. (mē'ä-wä-tlän')	119	16°20'N	96°38'W
Miajadas, Spain (mē-ä-hä'däs)	158	39°10'N	5°53'W
Miami, Az., U.S.	96	33°20'N	110°55'W
Miami, Fl., U.S.	97	25°45'N	80°11'W
Miami, Ok., U.S.	111	36°51'N	94°51'W
Miami, Tx., U.S.	110	35°41'N	100°39'W
Miami Beach, Fl., U.S.	115a	25°47'N	80°07'W
Miamisburg, Oh., U.S. (mī-ăm'ĭz-bûrg)	98	39°40'N	84°20'W
Miamitown, Oh., U.S. (mī-ăm'ĭ-toun)	101f	39°13'N	84°43'W
Mīāneh, Iran	182	37°15'N	47°13'E
Miangas, Pulau, i., Indon.	197	5°30'N	127°00'E
Miaoli, Tai. (mē-ou'lĭ)	193	24°30'N	120°48'E
Miaozhen, China (mĭou-jŭn)	190	31°44'N	121°28'E
Miass, Russia (mī-äs')	170	54°59'N	60°06'E
Miastko, Pol. (myäst'kō)	154	54°01'N	17°00'E
Miccosukee Indian Reservation, I.R., Fl., U.S.	115a	26°10'N	80°50'W
Michajlovskoje, Russia	239b	55°35'N	37°35'E
Michalovce, Slvk. (mē'kä-lôf'tsĕ)	155	48°44'N	21°56'E
Michel Peak, mtn., Can.	86	53°35'N	126°25'W
Michelson, Mount, mtn., Ak., U.S. (mĭch'ĕl-sŭn)	95	69°11'N	144°12'W
Michendorf, Ger. (mē'kĕn-dōrf)	145b	52°19'N	13°02'E
Miches, Dom. Rep. (mē'chĕs)	123	19°00'N	69°05'W
Michigan, state, U.S. (mĭsh-'ĭ-găn)	97	45°55'N	87°00'W
Michigan, Lake, l., U.S.	97	43°20'N	87°10'W
Michigan City, In., U.S.	98	41°40'N	86°55'W
Michillinda, Ca., U.S.	232	34°07'N	118°05'W
Michipicoten, r., Can.	103	47°56'N	84°42'W
Michipicoten Harbour, Can.	103	47°58'N	84°58'W
Michurinsk, Russia (mĭ-chōō-rĭnsk')	167	52°53'N	40°32'E
Mico, Punta, c., Nic. (pōō'n-tä-mē'kô)	121	11°38'N	83°24'W
Micronesia, is., Oc.	224	11°00'N	159°00'E
Micronesia, Federated States Of, nation, Oc.	3	5°00'N	152°00'E
Midas, Nv., U.S. (mī'dȧs)	104	41°15'N	116°50'W
Middelfart, Den. (mēd'"l-färt)	152	55°30'N	9°45'E
Middle, r., Can.	86	55°00'N	125°50'W

PLACE (Pronunciation)	PAGE	LAT.	LONG.
Middle Andaman, i., India (ăn-dȧ-măn')	196	12°44'N	93°21'E
Middle Bayou, Tx., U.S.	113a	29°38'N	95°06'W
Middleburg, S. Afr. (mĭd'ĕl-bûrg)	212	31°30'S	25°00'E
Middleburg, S. Afr.	218d	25°47'S	29°30'E
Middleburg Heights, Oh., U.S.	229a	41°22'N	81°48'W
Middlebury, Vt., U.S. (mĭd''l-bĕr-ĭ)	99	44°00'N	73°10'W
Middle Concho, Tx., U.S. (kōn'chō)	112	31°21'N	100°50'W
Middle River, Md., U.S.	100e	39°20'N	76°27'W
Middlesboro, Ky., U.S. (mĭd''lz-bŭr-ō)	114	36°36'N	83°42'W
Middlesbrough, Eng., U.K. (mĭd''lz-brŭ)	146	54°35'N	1°18'W
Middlesex, N.J., U.S. (mĭd''l-sĕks)	100a	40°34'N	74°30'W
Middleton, Can. (mĭd''l-tŭn)	92	44°57'N	65°04'W
Middleton, Eng., U.K.	144a	53°34'N	2°12'W
Middletown, Ct., U.S.	99	41°35'N	72°40'W
Middletown, De., U.S.	99	39°30'N	75°40'W
Middletown, Ma., U.S.	93a	42°35'N	71°01'W
Middletown, N.Y., U.S.	99	41°26'N	74°25'W
Middletown, Oh., U.S.	98	39°30'N	84°25'W
Middlewich, Eng., U.K. (mĭd''l-wĭch)	144a	53°11'N	2°27'W
Middlewit, S. Afr. (mĭd'l'wĭt)	218d	24°50'S	27°00'E
Midfield, Al., U.S.	100h	33°28'N	86°54'W
Midi, Canal du, Fr. (kä-näl-dü-mē-dē')	147	43°22'N	1°35'E
Mid Illovo, S. Afr. (mĭd ĭl'ō-vō)	213c	29°59'S	30°32'E
Midland, Can. (mĭd'lănd)	85	44°45'N	79°50'W
Midland, Mi., U.S.	98	43°40'N	84°20'W
Midland, Tx., U.S.	112	32°05'N	102°05'W
Midland Beach, neigh., N.Y., U.S.	228	40°34'N	74°05'W
Midlothian, Il., U.S.	231a	41°38'N	87°42'W
Midvale, Ut., U.S. (mĭd'vāl)	107b	40°37'N	111°54'W
Midway, S. Afr.	244b	26°18'S	27°51'E
Midway, Al., U.S. (mĭd'wā)	114	32°03'N	85°30'W
Midway City, Ca., U.S.	232	33°45'N	118°00'W
Midway Islands, is., Oc.	2	28°00'N	179°00'W
Midwest, Wy., U.S. (mĭd-wĕst')	105	43°25'N	106°15'W
Midye, Tur. (mēd'yĕ)	167	41°35'N	28°10'E
Międzyrzecz, Pol. (myăn-dzû'zhĕch)	154	52°26'N	15°35'E
Mielec, Pol. (myĕ'lĕts)	155	50°17'N	21°27'E
Mier, Mex. (myâr)	112	26°26'N	99°08'W
Mieres, Spain (myā'rās)	158	43°14'N	5°45'W
Mier y Noriega, Mex. (myâr'ē nō-rē-ā'gä)	118	23°28'N	100°08'W
Miguel Auza, Mex.	118	24°17'N	103°27'W
Miguel Pereira, Braz.	132b	22°27'S	43°28'W
Mijares, r., Spain	159	39°55'N	0°01'W
Mikage, Japan (mē'kȧ-gȧ)	195b	34°42'N	135°15'E
Mikawa-Wan, b., Japan (mē'kä-wä wän)	195	34°43'N	137°09'E
Mikhaylov, Russia (mē-κäy'lôf)	166	54°14'N	39°03'E
Mikhaylovka, Russia	167	50°05'N	43°10'E
Mikhaylovka, Russia	172a	55°35'N	57°57'E
Mikhaylovka, Russia	172c	59°20'N	30°21'E
Mikhnëvo, Russia (mĭk-nyô'vô)	172b	55°08'N	37°57'E
Miki, Japan (mē'kē)	195b	34°47'N	134°59'E
Mikindani, Tan. (mē-kēn-dä'nē)	213	10°17'S	40°07'E
Mikkeli, Fin. (mĕk'ĕ-lĭ)	146	61°42'N	27°14'E
Míkonos, i., Grc.	161	37°26'N	25°30'E
Mikulov, Czech Rep. (mĭ'kōō-lôf)	154	48°47'N	16°39'E
Mikumi, Tan.	217	7°24'S	36°59'E
Mikuni, Japan (mē'kōō-nē)	195	36°09'N	136°14'E
Mikuni-Sammyaku, mts., Japan (säm'myä-kōō)	195	36°51'N	138°38'E
Mikura, i., Japan (mē'kōō-rȧ)	195	33°53'N	139°26'E
Milaca, Milaca, Mn., U.S. (mē-lăk'ȧ)	103	45°45'N	93°41'W
Milan (Milano), Italy (mē-lä'nō)	160	45°29'N	9°12'E
Milan, Mi., U.S. (mī'lăn)	98	42°05'N	83°40'W
Milan, Mo., U.S.	111	40°13'N	93°07'W
Milan, Tn., U.S.	114	35°54'N	88°47'W
Milâs, Tur. (mē'lăs)	149	37°10'N	27°25'E
Milazzo, Italy	160	38°13'N	15°17'E
Milbank, S.D., U.S. (mĭl'băŋk)	102	45°13'N	96°38'W
Mildura, Austl. (mĭl-dū'rȧ)	203	34°10'S	142°18'E
Miles City, Mt., U.S. (mīlz)	96	46°24'N	105°50'W
Milford, Ct., U.S. (mĭl'fẽrd)	99	41°15'N	73°05'W
Milford, De., U.S.	99	38°55'N	75°25'W
Milford, Md., U.S.	229c	39°21'N	76°44'W
Milford, Ma., U.S.	93a	42°09'N	71°31'W
Milford, Mi., U.S.	101b	42°35'N	83°36'W
Milford, N.H., U.S.	99	42°50'N	71°40'W
Milford, Oh., U.S.	101f	39°11'N	84°18'W
Milford, Ut., U.S.	109	38°20'N	113°05'W
Milford Sound, strt., N.Z.	205	44°35'S	167°47'E
Miling, Austl. (mĭl'"ng)	202	30°30'S	116°25'E
Milipitas, Ca., U.S. (mĭl-ĭ-pĭ'tăs)	106b	37°26'N	121°54'W
Milk, r., N.A.	96	48°30'N	107°00'W
Millau, Fr. (mē-yō')	147	44°06'N	3°04'E
Millbourne, Pa., U.S.	229b	39°58'N	75°15'W
Millbrae, Ca., U.S. (mĭl'brā)	106b	37°36'N	122°23'W
Millburn, N.J., U.S.	228	40°44'N	74°20'W
Millbury, Ma., U.S. (mĭl'bĕr-ĭ)	93a	42°12'N	71°46'W
Mill Creek, r., Can. (mĭl)	83g	53°28'N	113°25'W
Mill Creek, r., Ca., U.S.	108	40°07'N	121°55'W
Milledgeville, Ga., U.S. (mĭl'ĕj-vĭl)	114	33°05'N	83°15'W
Mille Îles, Rivière des, r., Can. (rê-vyâr' dā mēl'ĭl')	83a	45°41'N	73°40'W
Mille Lac Indian Reservation, I.R., Mn., U.S. (mĭl lăk')	103	46°14'N	94°13'W
Mille Lacs, l., Mn., U.S.	103	46°25'N	93°22'W
Mille Lacs, Lac des, l., Can. (läk dē mēl läks)	90	48°52'N	90°53'W
Millen, Ga., U.S. (mĭl'ĕn)	115	32°47'N	81°55'W
Miller, S.D., U.S. (mĭl'ẽr)	102	44°31'N	99°00'W
Millerovo, Russia (mĭl'ĕ-rô-vô)	167	48°58'N	40°27'E
Millersburg, Ky., U.S. (mĭl'ẽrz-bûrg)	98	38°15'N	84°10'W
Millersburg, Oh., U.S.	98	40°35'N	81°55'W
Millersburg, Pa., U.S.	99	40°35'N	76°55'W

PLACE (Pronunciation)	PAGE	LAT.	LONG.
Millerton, Can. (mĭl'ẽr-tŭn)	92	46°56'N	65°40'W
Millertown, Can. (mĭl'ẽr-toun)	93	48°49'N	56°32'W
Mill Green, Eng., U.K.	235	51°41'N	0°22'E
Mill Hill, neigh., Eng., U.K.	235	51°37'N	0°13'W
Millicent, Austl. (mĭl-ĭ-sĕnt)	204	37°30'S	140°20'E
Millinocket, Me., U.S. (mĭl-ĭ-nŏk'ĕt)	92	45°40'N	68°44'W
Millis, Ma., U.S. (mĭl-ĭs)	93a	42°10'N	71°22'W
Mill Neck, N.Y., U.S.	228	40°52'N	73°34'W
Millstadt, Il., U.S. (mĭl'stăt)	107e	38°27'N	90°06'W
Millstone, r., N.J., U.S. (mĭl'stōn)	100a	40°27'N	74°38'W
Millstream, Austl. (mĭl'strēm)	202	21°45'S	117°10'E
Milltown, Can. (mĭl'toun)	92	45°13'N	67°19'W
Millvale, Pa., U.S.	230b	40°29'N	79°58'W
Mill Valley, Ca., U.S. (mĭl)	106b	37°54'N	122°32'W
Millwood Reservoir, res., Ar., U.S.	111	33°00'N	94°00'W
Milly-la-Forêt, Fr. (mē-yē'-la-fô-rĕ')	157b	48°24'N	2°28'E
Milmont Park, Pa., U.S.	229b	39°53'N	75°20'W
Milnerton, S. Afr. (mĭl'nẽr-tŭn)	212a	33°52'S	18°30'E
Milnor, N.D., U.S. (mĭl'nẽr)	102	46°17'N	97°29'W
Milnrow, Eng., U.K.	237b	53°37'N	2°06'W
Milo, Me., U.S.	92	44°16'N	69°01'W
Milon-la-Chapelle, Fr.	237c	48°44'N	2°03'E
Milos, i., Grc. (mē'lŏs)	149	36°45'N	24°35'E
Milpa Alta, Mex. (mē'l-pä-ä'l-tä)	119a	19°11'N	99°01'W
Milspe, Ger.	236	51°18'N	7°21'E
Milton, Can.	83d	43°31'N	79°53'W
Milton, Fl., U.S. (mĭl'tŭn)	114	30°37'N	87°02'W
Milton, Pa., U.S.	99	41°00'N	76°50'W
Milton, Ut., U.S.	107b	41°04'N	111°44'W
Milton, Wa., U.S.	106a	47°15'N	122°20'W
Milton, Wi., U.S.	103	42°45'N	89°00'W
Milton-Freewater, Or., U.S.	104	45°57'N	118°25'W
Milvale, Pa., U.S. (mĭl'văl)	101e	40°29'N	79°58'W
Milville, N.J., U.S. (mĭl'vĭl)	99	39°25'N	75°00'W
Milwaukee, Wi., U.S.	97	43°03'N	87°55'W
Milwaukee, r., Wi., U.S.	101a	43°10'N	87°56'W
Milwaukie, Or., U.S. (mĭl-wô'kē)	104	45°27'N	122°38'W
Mimiapan, Mex. (mē-myä-pån')	119a	19°26'N	99°28'W
Mimoso do Sul, Braz. (mē-mô'sō-dô-sōō'l)	129a	21°03'S	41°21'W
Min, r., China (mĕn)	189	26°03'N	118°30'E
Min, r., China	193	29°30'N	104°00'E
Mina, r., Alg. (mē'nȧ)	159	35°24'N	0°51'E
Minago, r., Can. (mĭ-nä'gō)	89	54°25'N	98°45'W
Minakuchi, Japan (mē'nȧ-kōō'chē)	195	34°59'N	136°06'E
Minami, neigh., Japan	241e	34°58'N	135°45'E
Minamisenju, neigh., Japan	242a	35°44'N	139°48'E
Minas, Cuba (mē'näs)	122	21°30'N	77°35'W
Minas, Indon.	181b	0°52'N	101°29'E
Minas, Ur. (mē'näs)	132	34°18'S	55°12'W
Minas, Sierra de las, mts., Guat. (syĕr'rȧ dā läs mē'näs)	120	15°08'N	90°25'W
Minas Basin, b., Can. (mī'nȧs)	92	45°20'N	64°00'W
Minas Channel, strt., Can.	92	45°15'N	64°45'W
Minas de Oro, Hond. (mē'näs-dĕ-dĕ-ō-rô)	120	14°52'N	87°19'W
Minas de Riotinto, Spain (mē'näs dā rē-ō-tēn'tō)	158	37°43'N	6°35'W
Minas Novas, Braz. (mē'näzh nō'väzh)	131	17°20'S	42°19'W
Minatare, l., Ne., U.S. (mĭn'ȧ-târ)	102	41°56'N	103°07'W
Minatitlán, Mex. (mē-nä-tē-tlän')	116	17°59'N	94°33'W
Minatitlán, Mex.	118	19°21'N	104°02'W
Minato, Japan (mē'nȧ-tō)	195	35°13'N	139°52'E
Minato, neigh., Japan	242a	35°39'N	139°45'E
Minato, neigh., Japan	242b	34°39'N	135°26'E
Minch, The, strt., Scot., U.K.	142	58°04'N	6°04'W
Mindanao, i., Phil.	197	8°00'N	125°00'E
Mindanao Sea, sea, Phil.	197	8°55'N	124°00'E
Minden, Ger. (mĭn'dĕn)	154	52°17'N	8°58'E
Minden, La., U.S.	113	32°36'N	93°19'W
Minden, Ne., U.S.	110	40°30'N	98°54'W
Mindoro, i., Phil.	196	12°50'N	121°05'E
Mindoro Strait, strt., Phil.	197a	12°28'N	120°33'E
Mindyak, Russia (mēn'dyák)	172a	54°01'N	58°48'E
Mineola, N.Y., U.S. (mĭn-ē-ō'lȧ)	100a	40°43'N	73°38'W
Mineola, Tx., U.S.	113	32°39'N	95°31'W
Mineral del Chico, Mex. (mē-nȧ-räl'dĕl chē'kō)	118	20°13'N	98°46'W
Mineral del Monte, Mex. (mē-nȧ-räl dĕl mōn'tȧ)	118	20°18'N	98°39'W
Mineral'nyye Vody, Russia	167	44°10'N	43°15'E
Mineral Point, Wi., U.S. (mĭn'ẽr-ăl)	103	42°50'N	90°10'W
Mineral Wells, Tx., U.S. (mĭn'ẽr-ăl wĕlz)	112	32°48'N	98°06'W
Minerva, Oh., U.S. (mĭ-nur'vȧ)	98	40°45'N	81°10'W
Minervino, Italy (mē-nĕr-vē'nō)	160	41°07'N	16°05'E
Mineyama, Japan (mē-nĕ-yä'mä)	195	35°38'N	135°05'E
Mingäçevir, Azer.	168	40°45'N	47°03'E
Mingäçevir su anbarı, res., Azer.	168	40°50'N	46°50'E
Mingan, Can.	85	50°18'N	64°02'W
Mingenew, Austl. (mĭn'gĕ-nū)	202	29°15'S	115°45'E
Mingo Junction, Oh., U.S. (mĭŋ'gō)	98	40°15'N	80°40'W
Minho, hist. reg., Port. (mēn yō)	158	41°32'N	8°13'W
Minho (Miño), r., Eur. (mē'n-yō)	158	41°28'N	9°05'W
Ministik Lake, l., Can. (mĭ-nĭs'tĭk)	83g	53°23'N	113°05'W
Minna, Nig. (mĭn'ȧ)	210	9°37'N	6°33'E
Minneapolis, Ks., U.S. (mĭn-ē-ăp'ō-lĭs)	111	39°07'N	97°41'W
Minneapolis, Mn., U.S.	97	44°58'N	93°15'W
Minnedosa, Can. (mĭn-ē-dō'sȧ)	84	50°14'N	99°51'W
Minneota, Mn., U.S. (mĭn-ē-ō'tȧ)	102	44°34'N	95°59'W
Minnesota, state, U.S. (mĭn-ē-sō'tȧ)	97	46°10'N	90°20'W
Minnesota, r., Mn., U.S.	97	44°30'N	95°00'W
Minnetonka, l., Mn., U.S. (mĭn-ē-tôŋ'kȧ)	103	44°52'N	93°34'W
Minnitaki Lake, l., Can. (mĭ-nĭ-tä'kē)	89	49°58'N	92°00'W
Mino, r., Japan	195b	34°56'N	135°06'E
Minonk, Il., U.S. (mī'nŏnk)	98	40°55'N	89°00'W
Minooka, Il., U.S. (mĭ-nōō'kȧ)	101a	41°27'N	88°15'W
Minot, N.D., U.S.	96	48°13'N	101°17'W
Minsk, Bela. (mēnsk)	164	53°54'N	27°35'E
Minsk, prov., Bela.	162	53°50'N	27°43'E
Mińsk Mazowiecki, Pol. (mēn'sk mä-zō-vyĕt'skĭ)	155	52°10'N	21°35'E
Minsterley, Eng., U.K. (mĭnstẽr-lē)	144a	52°38'N	2°55'W
Mintard, Ger.	236	51°22'N	6°54'E
Minto, Austl.	243a	34°01'S	150°51'E
Minto, Can.	92	46°05'N	66°05'W
Minto, l., Can.	85	57°18'N	75°50'W
Minturno, Italy (mēn-tōōr'nō)	160	41°17'N	13°44'E
Minūf, Egypt (mē-nōōf')	218b	30°26'N	30°55'E
Minusinsk, Russia (mē-nò-sēnsk')	165	53°47'N	91°45'E
Min'yar, Russia	172a	55°06'N	57°33'E
Miquelon Lake, l., Can. (mĭ'kĕ-lôn)	83g	53°16'N	112°55'W
Miquihuana, Mex. (mē-kē-wä'nä)	118	23°36'N	99°45'W
Miquon, Pa., U.S.	229b	40°04'N	75°16'W
Mir, Bela. (mēr)	155	53°27'N	26°25'E
Miracema, Braz. (mē-rä-sĕ'mä)	129a	21°24'S	42°10'W
Miracema do Norte, Braz.	131	9°34'S	48°24'W
Mirador, Braz. (mē-rȧ-dōr')	131	6°19'S	44°12'W
Miraflores, Col. (mē-rä-flō'räs)	130	5°10'N	73°13'W
Miraflores, Peru	130	16°19'S	71°20'W
Miraflores, Peru	233c	12°08'S	77°03'W
Miraflores Locks, trans., Pan.	116a	9°00'N	79°35'W
Miragoâne, Haiti (mē-rȧ-gwän')	123	18°25'N	73°05'W
Mira Loma, Ca., U.S. (mĭ'rȧ lō'mȧ)	107a	34°01'N	117°32'W
Miramar, Ca., U.S. (mĭr'ȧ-mär)	108a	32°53'N	117°08'W
Miramar, neigh., Cuba	233b	23°07'N	82°25'W
Miramas, Fr.	156	43°35'N	5°00'E
Miramichi Bay, b., Can. (mĭr'ȧ-mē'shē)	92	47°08'N	65°08'W
Miranda, Austl.	243a	34°02'S	151°06'E
Miranda, Col. (mē-rä'n-dä)	130a	3°14'N	76°11'W
Miranda, Ca., U.S.	108	40°14'N	123°49'W
Miranda, Ven.	131b	10°09'N	68°24'W
Miranda, dept., Ven.	131b	10°17'N	66°41'W
Miranda de Ebro, Spain (mē-rá'n-dä-dĕ-ĕ'brō)	158	42°42'N	2°59'W
Miranda do Douro, Port. (mē-rän'dä dò-dwĕ'rō)	158	41°30'N	6°17'W
Mirandela, Port. (mē-rän-dä'lȧ)	158	41°28'N	7°10'W
Mirando City, Tx., U.S. (mĭr-ån'dō)	112	27°25'N	99°03'W
Mira Por Vos Islets, is., Bah. (mē'rä pôr vōs)	123	22°05'N	74°30'W
Mira Por Vos Pass, strt., Bah.	123	22°10'N	74°35'W
Mirbāţ, Oman	182	16°58'N	54°42'E
Mirebalais, Haiti (mēr-bȧ-lĕ')	123	18°50'N	72°05'W
Mirecourt, Fr. (mēr-kōōr')	157	48°20'N	6°08'E
Mirfield, Eng., U.K. (mûr'fēld)	144a	53°41'N	1°42'W
Miri, Malay. (mē'rē)	196	4°13'N	113°56'E
Mirim, Lagoa, l., S.A. (mē-rēɴ')	132	33°00'S	53°15'W
Mírina, Grc.	161	39°52'N	25°01'E
Miropol'ye, Ukr. (mē-rō-pôl'yĕ)	163	51°02'N	35°13'E
Mīrpur Khās, Pak. (mēr'pōōr ĸäs)	186	25°36'N	69°10'E
Mirzāpur, India (mēr'zä-pōōr)	183	25°12'N	82°38'E
Mirzāpur, India	240a	22°50'N	88°24'E
Misailovo, Russia	239b	55°34'N	37°49'E
Misantla, Mex. (mē-sän'tlä)	119	19°55'N	96°49'W
Miscou, i., Can. (mĭs'kō)	92	47°58'N	64°35'W
Miscou Point, c., Can.	92	48°04'N	64°32'W
Miseno, Cape, c., Italy (mē-zĕ'nō)	159c	40°33'N	14°12'E
Misery, Mount, mtn., St. K./N. (mĭz'rē-ĭ)	121b	17°28'N	62°47'W
Mishan, China (mĭ'shäɴ)	194	45°32'N	132°19'E
Mishawaka, In., U.S. (mĭsh-ȧ-wôk'ȧ)	98	41°45'N	86°15'W
Mishina, Japan (mē'shē-mä)	195	35°09'N	138°56'E
Misiones, prov., Arg. (mē-syō'näs)	132	27°00'S	54°30'W
Miskito, Cayos, is., Nic.	121	14°34'N	82°30'W
Miskolc, Hung. (mĭsh'kōlts)	142	48°07'N	20°50'E
Misool, Pulau, i., Indon. (mē-sōl')	197	2°00'S	130°05'E
Misquah Hills, Mn., U.S. (mĭs-kwä' hĭlz)	103	47°50'N	90°30'W
Mişr al Jadīdah, Egypt	218b	30°06'N	31°35'E
Mişr al-Qadīmah (Old Cairo), neigh., Egypt	244a	30°00'N	31°14'E
Misrātah, Libya	211	32°23'N	14°58'E
Missinaibi, r., Can. (mĭs'ĭn-ä'ē-bē)	85	50°27'N	83°01'W
Missinaibi Lake, l., Can.	90	48°23'N	83°40'W
Mission, Ks., U.S. (mĭsh'ŭn)	107f	39°02'N	94°39'W
Mission, Tx., U.S.	112	26°14'N	98°19'W
Mission City, Can. (sĭ'tĭ)	87	49°08'N	112°18'W
Missisagi, r., Can.	90	46°35'N	83°30'W
Mississauga, Can.	91	43°34'N	79°37'W
Mississippi, state, U.S. (mĭs-ĭ-sĭp'ē)	97	32°30'N	89°45'W
Mississippi, l., Can.	91	45°05'N	76°15'W
Mississippi, r., U.S.	97	32°00'N	91°30'W
Mississippi Sound, strt., Ms., U.S.	114	34°16'N	89°10'W
Missoula, Mt., U.S. (mĭ-zōō'lȧ)	96	46°55'N	114°00'W
Missouri, state, U.S. (mĭ-sōō'rē)	97	38°00'N	93°40'W
Missouri, r., U.S.	96	40°40'N	96°00'W
Missouri City, Tx., U.S.	113a	29°37'N	95°32'W
Missouri Coteau, hills, U.S.	96	47°30'N	101°00'W
Missouri Valley, Ia., U.S.	102	41°35'N	95°53'W
Mist, Or., U.S. (mĭst)	106c	46°00'N	123°15'W
Mistassini, Can. (mĭs-tȧ-sĭ'nē)	91	48°56'N	71°55'W
Mistassini, l., Can. (mĭs-tȧ-sĭ'nē)	85	50°48'N	73°30'W
Mistelbach, Aus. (mĭs'tĕl-bäk)	154	48°34'N	16°33'E
Misteriosa, Lago, l., Mex. (mēs-tē-ryō'sä)	120a	18°05'N	90°15'W
Misti, Volcán, vol., Peru	130	16°04'S	71°20'W
Mistretta, Italy (mē-strĕt'tä)	160	37°54'N	14°22'E
Misty Fjords National Monument, rec., Ak., U.S.	95	51°00'N	131°00'W
Mita, Punta de, c., Mex. (pōō'n-tä-dĕ-mē'tä)	118	20°44'N	105°34'W
Mitaka, Japan (mē'tä-kä)	195a	35°42'N	139°34'E
Mitcham, Austl.	243b	37°49'S	145°12'E
Mitcham, neigh., Eng., U.K.	235	51°24'N	0°10'W
Mitchell, Il., U.S. (mĭch'ĕl)	107e	38°46'N	90°05'W
Mitchell, In., U.S.	98	38°45'N	86°25'W
Mitchell, Ne., U.S.	102	41°56'N	103°49'W
Mitchell, S.D., U.S.	96	43°42'N	98°01'W
Mitchell, Mount, mtn., N.C., U.S.	97	35°47'N	82°15'W
Mīt Ghamr, Egypt	218b	30°43'N	31°20'E
Mitilíni, Grc.	149	39°09'N	26°35'E
Mitla Pass, p., Egypt	181a	30°03'N	32°40'E
Mito, Japan (mē'tō)	194	36°20'N	140°23'E
Mitry-Mory, Fr.	237c	48°59'N	2°37'E
Mitsiwa, Erit.	211	15°40'N	39°19'E
Mitsu, Japan (mēt'sò)	195	34°21'N	132°49'E
Mitte, neigh., Ger.	238a	52°31'N	13°24'E
Mittelland Kanal, can., Ger. (mĭt'ĕl-lănd)	154	52°18'N	10°42'E
Mittenwalde, Ger. (mē'tĕn-väl-dĕ)	145b	52°16'N	13°33'E
Mittweida, Ger. (mĭt-vī'dä)	154	50°59'N	12°58'E
Mitumba, Monts, mts., D.R.C.	217	10°50'S	27°00'E
Mityayevo, Russia (mĭt-yä'yĕ-vô)	172a	60°17'N	61°02'E
Miura, Japan	195a	35°08'N	139°37'E
Miwa, Japan (mē'wä)	195b	34°32'N	135°51'E
Mixcoac, neigh., Mex.	233a	19°23'N	99°12'W
Mixico, Guat. (mēs'kò)	120	14°37'N	90°37'W
Mixquiahuala, Mex. (mēs-kē-wä'lä)	118	20°12'N	99°13'W
Mixteco, r., Mex. (mēs-tā'kō)	118	17°45'N	98°10'W
Miyake, Japan (mē'yä-kå)	195b	34°35'N	135°34'E
Miyake, i., Japan (mē'yä-kå)	195	34°06'N	139°21'E
Miyakojima, neigh., Japan	242b	34°43'N	135°33'E
Miyakonojō, Japan	194	31°44'N	131°04'E
Miyazaki, Japan (mē'yä-zä'kē)	194	31°55'N	131°27'E
Miyoshi, Japan (mē-yō'shē')	194	34°48'N	132°49'E
Mizdah, Libya (mēz'dä)	184	31°29'N	13°09'E
Mizil, Rom. (mē'zēl)	161	45°01'N	26°30'E
Mizonuma, Japan	242a	35°48'N	139°36'E
Mizoram, state, India	183	23°25'N	92°45'E
Mizue, neigh., Japan	242a	35°41'N	139°54'E
Mizuho, Japan	242a	35°46'N	139°21'E
Mjölby, Swe. (myûl'bü)	152	58°20'N	15°09'E
Mjörn, l., Swe.	152	57°55'N	12°22'E
Mjösa, l., Nor. (myûsä)	146	60°41'N	11°25'E
Mkalama, Tan.	212	4°07'S	34°38'E
Mkushi, Zam.	217	13°40'S	29°20'E
Mkwaja, Tan.	217	5°47'S	38°51'E
Mladá Boleslav, Czech Rep. (mlä'dä bô'lĕ-slàf)	154	50°26'N	14°52'E
Mlala Hills, hills, Tan.	217	6°47'S	31°45'E
Mlanje Mountains, mts., Mwi.	217	15°55'S	35°30'E
Mława, Pol. (mwä'vȧ)	146	53°07'N	20°25'E
Mmabatho, S. Afr.	212	25°42'S	25°43'E
Mnevniki, neigh., Russia	239b	55°45'N	37°28'E
Moa, r., Afr.	214	7°40'N	11°15'W
Moa, Pulau, i., Indon.	197	8°30'S	128°30'E
Moab, Ut., U.S. (mō'ăb)	109	38°35'N	109°35'W
Moanda, Gabon	212	1°37'S	13°09'E
Moar Lake, l., Can. (môr)	89	52°00'N	95°09'W
Moba, D.R.C.	212	7°12'S	29°39'E
Moba, Nig.	244d	6°27'N	3°28'E
Mobaye, Cen. Afr. Rep. (mô-bä'y')	211	4°19'N	21°11'E
Mobayi-Mbongo, D.R.C.	211	4°14'N	21°11'E
Moberly, Mo., U.S. (mō'bẽr-lĭ)	97	39°24'N	92°25'W
Mobile, Al., U.S. (mō-bēl')	97	30°42'N	88°03'W
Mobile, r., Al., U.S.	114	31°15'N	88°00'W
Mobile Bay, b., Al., U.S.	97	30°26'N	87°56'W
Mobridge, S.D., U.S. (mō'brĭj)	102	45°32'N	100°26'W
Moca, Dom. Rep. (mô'kä)	123	19°25'N	70°35'W
Moçambique, Moz. (mō-säɴ-bē'kĕ)	217	15°03'S	40°42'E
Moçâmedes, Ang. (mô-zȧ-mĕ-dĕs)	212	15°10'S	12°09'E
Moçâmedes, hist. reg., Ang.	212	16°00'S	12°15'E
Mochitlán, Mex. (mō-chē-tlän')	118	17°10'N	99°19'W
Mochudi, Bots. (mō-chōō'dē)	212	24°13'S	26°07'E
Mocímboa da Praia, Moz. (mô-sē'ēm-bô-ȧ prä'ēȧ)	213	11°20'S	40°21'E
Moclips, Wa., U.S.	104	47°14'N	124°13'W
Môco, Serra do, mtn., Ang.	216	12°25'S	15°10'E
Mococa, Braz. (mô-kô'kȧ)	129a	21°29'S	46°58'W
Moctezuma, Mex. (mòk'tȧ-zōō'mä)	118	22°44'N	101°06'W
Mocuba, Moz.	217	16°50'S	36°59'E
Modderbee, S. Afr.	244b	26°10'S	28°24'E
Modderfontein, S. Afr.	213b	26°06'S	28°10'E
Modena, Italy (mô'dĕ-nä)	148	44°38'N	10°54'E
Modesto, Ca., U.S. (mò-dĕs'tō)	108	37°39'N	121°00'W
Modjeska, Ca., U.S.	232	33°43'N	117°37'W
Mödling, Aus. (mûd'lĭng)	145e	48°06'N	16°17'E
Moelv, Nor.	152	60°55'N	10°40'E
Moengo, Sur.	131	5°43'N	54°19'W
Moenkopi, Az., U.S.	109	36°07'N	111°13'W
Moers, Ger. (mûrs)	157c	51°27'N	6°38'E
Moffat Tunnel, trans., Co., U.S. (môf'ăt)	110	39°52'N	106°20'W
Mofolo, S. Afr.	244b	26°14'S	27°53'E
Mogadishu (Muqdisho), Som.	218a	2°08'N	45°22'E
Mogadore, Oh., U.S. (mŏg-ȧ-dōr')	101d	41°04'N	81°23'E
Mogaung, Myanmar (mō-gä'òng)	183	25°30'N	96°52'E
Mogi das Cruzes, Braz. (mô-gē-däs-krōō'sĕs)	131	23°33'S	46°10'W
Mogi-Guaçu, r., Braz. (mô-gē-gwä'sōō)	129a	22°06'S	47°12'W
Mogilëv, Bela. (mō-gē-lyôf')	164	53°53'N	30°22'E
Mogilëv, prov., Bela. (mô-gê-lyôf')	162	53°28'N	30°15'E
Mogilno, Pol. (mô-gēl'nō)	154	52°38'N	17°58'W
Mogi-Mirim, Braz. (mô-gē-mē-rē'ɴ)	129a	22°26'S	46°57'W
Mogok, Myanmar (mō-gōk')	183	23°14'N	96°38'E

ăt; finăl; rāte; senâte; ärm; åsk; sofȧ; fâre; ch-choose; dh-as th in other; bē; ēvent; bĕt; recĕnt; cratẽr; g-gō; gh-guttural g; bĭt; ĭ-short neutral; rīde; ĸ-guttural k as ch in German ich;

PRONOUNCING INDEX Mogol – Moonachie 319

PLACE (Pronunciation)	PAGE	LAT.	LONG.
Mogol, r., S. Afr. (mô-gŏl)	218d	24°12′S	27°55′E
Mogollon Plateau, plat., Az., U.S.	96	34°15′N	110°45′W
Mogollon Rim, cliff, Az., U.S. (mō-gô-yōn′)	109	34°26′N	111°17′W
Moguer, Spain (mô-gĕr′)	158	37°15′N	6°50′W
Mohács, Hung. (mō′häch)	155	45°59′N	18°38′E
Mohale's Hoek, Leso.	213c	30°09′S	27°28′E
Mohall, N.D., U.S. (mō′hôl)	102	48°46′N	101°29′W
Mohave, l., Nv., U.S. (mô-hä′vä)	109	35°23′N	114°40′W
Mohe, China (mwo-hŭ)	189	53°33′N	122°30′E
Mohenjo-Dero, hist., Pak.	183	27°20′N	68°10′E
Mohili, neigh., India	240e	19°06′N	72°53′E
Mohyliv-Podil's'kyi, Ukr.	167	48°27′N	27°51′E
Mõisaküla, Est. (mẽẽ′sȧ-kü′lä)	153	58°07′N	25°12′E
Moissac, Fr. (mwä-sȧk′)	156	44°07′N	1°05′E
Moita, Port. (mô-ē′tȧ)	159b	38°39′N	9°00′W
Mojave, Ca., U.S.	108	35°06′N	118°09′W
Mojave, r., Ca., U.S. (mô-hä′vä)	108	34°46′N	117°24′W
Mojave Desert, Ca., U.S.	108	35°05′N	117°30′W
Mojave Desert, des., Ca., U.S.	96	35°00′N	117°00′W
Mokhotlong, Leso.	213c	29°18′S	29°06′E
Mokp'o, S. Kor. (môk′pō′)	189	34°50′N	126°30′E
Mol, Bel.	145a	51°21′N	5°09′E
Moldavia, hist. reg., Rom.	155	47°20′N	27°12′E
Moldavia see Moldova, nation, Eur.	164	48°00′N	28°00′E
Molde, Nor. (môl′dĕ)	146	62°44′N	7°15′E
Moldova, nation, Eur.	164	48°00′N	28°00′E
Moldova, r., Rom.	155	47°17′N	26°27′E
Moldoveanu, Vârful, mtn., Rom.	161	45°33′N	24°38′E
Molepolole, Bots. (mō-lå-pô-lō′lå)	212	24°15′S	25°33′W
Molfetta, Italy (môl-fĕt′tä)	149	41°11′N	16°38′E
Molina, Chile (mō-lē′nä)	129b	35°07′S	71°17′W
Molina de Aragón, Spain (mô-lē′nä dĕ ä-rä-gôn)	158	40°40′N	1°54′W
Molina de Segura, Spain (mô-lē′nä dĕ sē-gōō′rä)	158	38°03′N	1°07′W
Moline, Il., U.S. (mō-lēn′)	111	41°31′N	90°34′W
Molino de Rosas, Mex.	233a	19°22′N	99°13′W
Molíns de Rey, Spain	238e	41°25′N	2°01′E
Moliro, D.R.C.	212	8°13′S	30°34′E
Moliterno, Italy (mōl-ē-tĕr′nō)	160	40°13′N	15°54′W
Möllen, Ger.	236	51°35′N	6°42′E
Mollendo, Peru (mō-lyĕn′dō)	130	17°02′S	71°59′W
Moller, Port, Ak., U.S. (pōrt mōl′ẽr)	95	56°18′N	161°30′W
Mölndal, Swe. (mûln′däl)	152	57°39′N	12°01′E
Molochna, r., Ukr.	163	47°05′N	35°22′E
Molochnyĭ lyman, l., Ukr.	163	46°35′N	35°32′E
Molodechno, Bela. (mô-lô-dĕch′nô)	166	54°18′N	26°57′E
Molody Tud, Russia (mō-lō-dô′ĕ tōō′d)	172b	55°17′N	37°31′E
Molokai, i., Hi., U.S. (mō-lô kä′ē)	96c	21°15′N	157°05′E
Molokcha, r., Russia (mô′lôk-chä)	172b	56°15′N	38°29′E
Molopo, r., Afr. (mō-lō-pō)	212	27°45′S	20°45′E
Molson Lake, l., Can. (mōl′sŭn)	89	54°12′N	96°45′W
Molteno, S. Afr. (môl-tä′nô)	213c	31°24′S	26°23′E
Moluccas see Maluku, is., Indon.	197	2°22′S	128°25′E
Moma, Moz.	217	16°44′S	39°14′E
Mombasa, Kenya (mōm-bä′sä)	213	4°03′S	39°40′E
Mombetsu, Japan (mōm′bĕt-sōō′)	194	44°21′N	142°48′E
Momence, Il., U.S. (mô-mĕns′)	101a	41°09′N	87°40′W
Momostenango, Guat. (mô-môs-tā-näŋ′gô)	120	15°02′N	91°25′W
Momotombo, Nic.	120	12°25′N	86°43′W
Mompog Pass, strt., Phil. (mōm-pŏg′)	197a	13°35′N	122°09′E
Mompos, Col. (mōm-pōs′)	130	9°05′N	74°30′W
Momtblanc, Spain	159	41°20′N	1°08′E
Møn, i., Den. (mûn)	152	54°54′N	12°30′E
Monaca, Pa., U.S. (mŏ-nȧ′kō)	101e	40°41′N	80°17′W
Monaco, nation, Eur. (mŏn′ȧ-kō)	142	43°43′N	7°47′E
Monaghan, Ire. (mŏ′ȧ-gän)	150	54°16′N	7°20′W
Mona Passage, strt., N.A. (mō′nä)	117	18°00′N	68°10′W
Monarch Mountain, mtn., Can. (mŏn′ẽrk)	86	51°41′N	125°53′W
Monashee Mountains, mts., Can. (mŏ-nă′shē)	87	50°30′N	118°30′W
Monastir see Bitola, Mac.	160	41°02′N	21°22′E
Monastir, Tun. (mŏn-ȧs-tēr′)	148	35°49′N	10°56′E
Monastyrshchina, Russia (mô-nȧs-tērsh′chĭ-nȧ)	162	54°19′N	31°49′E
Monastyryshche, Ukr.	163	48°57′N	29°53′E
Moncada, Spain	238e	41°29′N	2°11′E
Monção, Braz. (mon-souɴ′)	131	3°39′S	45°23′W
Moncayo, mtn., Spain (môn-kä′yō)	158	41°44′N	1°48′W
Monchegorsk, Russia (mōn′chĕ-gôrsk)	166	69°00′N	33°35′E
Mönchengladbach, Ger. (mûn′kĕn gläd′bäk)	154	51°12′N	6°28′E
Moncique, Serra de, mts., Port. (sĕr′rä dä môn-chē′kĕ)	158	37°22′N	8°37′W
Monclova, Mex. (môn-klō′vä)	116	26°53′N	101°25′W
Moncton, Can. (mŭŋk′tŭn)	85	46°06′N	64°47′W
Mondêgo, r., Port. (môn-dĕ′gō)	158	40°10′N	8°36′W
Mondego, Cabo, c., Port. (kä′bō môn-dā′gô)	158	40°12′N	8°55′W
Mondeor, S. Afr.	244b	26°17′S	28°00′E
Mondombe, D.R.C. (môn-dôm′bȧ)	212	0°45′S	23°06′E
Mondoñedo, Spain (môn-dô-nyā′dō)	158	43°35′N	7°18′W
Mondovi, Wi., U.S. (mŏn-dō′vĭ)	103	44°35′N	91°42′W
Monee, Il., U.S. (mŏ-nĭ)	101a	41°25′N	87°45′W
Monessen, Pa., U.S. (mŏ-nĕs′sĕn)	101e	40°09′N	79°53′W
Monett, Mo., U.S. (mŏ-nĕt′)	111	36°55′N	93°55′W
Monfalcone, Italy	160	45°49′N	13°30′E
Monforte de Lemos, Spain (môn-fôr′tä dĕ lĕ′môs)	158	42°30′N	7°30′W
Mongala, r., D.R.C. (mŏŋ-gäl′ȧ)	211	3°20′N	21°30′E
Mongalla, Sudan	211	5°11′N	31°46′E
Mongat, Spain	238e	41°28′N	2°17′E
Monghyr, India (mŏn-gēr′)	183	25°23′N	86°34′E
Mongo, r., Afr.	214	9°50′N	11°50′W
Mongolia, nation, Asia (mŏŋ-gō′lĭ-ȧ)	188	46°00′N	100°00′E
Mongos, Chaîne des, mts., Cen. Afr. Rep.	211	8°04′N	21°59′E
Mongoumba, Cen. Afr. Rep. (mŏŋ-gōōm′bȧ)	211	3°38′N	18°36′E
Mongu, Zam. (mŏŋ-gōō′)	212	15°15′S	23°09′E
Monken Hadley, neigh., Eng., U.K.	235	51°40′N	0°11′W
Monkey Bay, Mwi.	217	14°05′S	34°55′E
Monkey River, Belize (mŭŋ′kĭ)	120a	16°22′N	88°33′W
Monkland, Can. (mŭngk-lănd)	83c	45°12′N	74°52′W
Monkoto, D.R.C. (môn-kō′tô)	212	1°38′S	20°39′E
Monmouth, Il., U.S. (mŏn′mŭth)(mŏn′mouth)	111	40°54′N	90°38′W
Monmouth Junction, N.J., U.S. (mŏn′mouth jŭngk′shŭn)	100a	40°23′N	74°33′W
Monmouth Mountain, mtn., Can. (mŏn′mŭth)	86	51°00′N	123°47′W
Mono, r., Afr.	214	7°20′N	1°25′E
Mono Lake, l., Ca., U.S. (mō′nō)	108	38°04′N	119°00′W
Monon, In., U.S. (mō′nŏn)	98	40°55′N	86°55′W
Monongah, W.V., U.S. (mô-nŏŋ′gȧ)	98	39°25′N	80°10′W
Monongahela, Pa., U.S. (mô-nŏn-gȧ-hē′lȧ)	101a	40°11′N	79°55′W
Monongahela, r., W.V., U.S.	98	39°30′N	80°10′W
Monopoli, Italy (mô-nô′pô-lê)	161	40°55′N	17°17′E
Monóvar, Spain (mô-nō′vär)	159	38°26′N	0°50′W
Monreale, Italy (mōn-rå-ä′lå)	160	38°04′N	13°15′E
Monroe, Ga., U.S. (mŭn-rō′)	114	33°47′N	83°43′W
Monroe, La., U.S.	97	32°30′N	92°06′W
Monroe, Mi., U.S.	98	41°55′N	83°25′W
Monroe, N.Y., U.S.	100a	41°19′N	74°11′W
Monroe, N.C., U.S.	115	34°58′N	80°34′W
Monroe, Ut., U.S.	109	38°35′N	112°10′W
Monroe, Wa., U.S.	106a	47°52′N	121°58′W
Monroe, Wi., U.S.	103	42°35′N	89°40′W
Monroe, Lake, l., Fl., U.S.	115	28°50′N	81°15′W
Monroe City, Mo., U.S.	111	39°38′N	91°41′W
Monroeville, Al., U.S. (mŭn-rō′vĭl)	114	31°33′N	87°19′W
Monrovia, Lib.	210	6°18′N	10°47′W
Monrovia, Ca., U.S. (mŏn-rō′vĭ-ȧ)	107a	34°09′N	118°00′W
Mons, Bel. (môɴ′)	147	50°29′N	3°55′E
Monson, Me., U.S. (mŏn′sŭn)	92	45°17′N	69°28′W
Mönsterås, Swe. (mŭn′stĕr-ôs)	152	57°04′N	16°24′E
Montagne Tremblant Provincial Park, rec., Can.	97	46°30′N	75°51′W
Montague, Can. (mŏn′tȧ-gū)	93	46°10′N	62°39′W
Montague, Mi., U.S.	98	43°30′N	86°25′W
Montague, i., Ak., U.S.	95	60°10′N	147°00′W
Montalbán, Ven. (mōnt-äl-bän)	131b	10°14′N	68°19′W
Montalbancito, Ven.	234a	10°28′N	66°59′W
Montalegre, Port. (mōn-tä-lā′grĕ)	158	41°49′N	7°48′W
Montana, state, U.S. (mŏn-tăn′ȧ)	96	47°10′N	111°50′W
Montánchez, Spain (môn-tän′chāth)	158	39°18′N	6°09′W
Montara, Ca., U.S.	231b	37°33′N	122°31′W
Montargis, Fr. (môɴ-tȧr-zhē′)	147	47°59′N	2°42′E
Montataire, Fr. (môɴ-tȧ-tȧr)	157b	49°15′N	2°26′E
Montauban, Fr. (môn-tô-bäɴ′)	147	44°01′N	1°22′E
Montauk, N.Y., U.S.	99	41°03′N	71°57′W
Montauk Point, c., N.Y., U.S. (mŏn-tôk′)	99	41°05′N	71°55′W
Montbard, Fr. (môɴ-bȧr′)	156	47°40′N	4°19′E
Montbéliard, Fr. (môɴ-bā-lyȧr′)	157	47°32′N	6°45′E
Mont Belvieu, Tx., U.S. (mŏnt bĕl′vū)	113a	29°51′N	94°53′W
Montbrison, Fr. (môɴ-brē-zoɴ′)	156	45°38′N	4°06′E
Montceau, Fr. (môɴ-sō′)	156	46°39′N	4°22′E
Montclair, Ca., U.S.	232	34°06′N	117°41′W
Montclair, N.J., U.S. (mŏnt-klâr′)	100a	40°49′N	74°13′W
Mont-de-Marsan, Fr. (môɴ-dē-mȧr-säɴ′)	147	43°54′N	0°32′W
Montdidier, Fr. (môɴ-dē-dyā′)	156	49°42′N	2°33′E
Monte, Arg. (mŏ′n-tĕ)	129c	35°25′S	58°49′W
Monteagudo, Bol. (mōn′tå-ä-gōō′dhō)	130	19°49′S	63°48′W
Montebello, Can.	83c	45°40′N	74°56′W
Montebello, Ca., U.S. (mŏn-tē-bĕl′ō)	107a	34°01′N	118°06′W
Monte Bello Islands, is., Austl.	202	20°30′S	114°10′E
Monte Caseros, Arg. (mŏ′n-tĕ-kä-sĕ′rôs)	132	30°16′S	57°39′W
Monte Chingolo, neigh., Arg.	233d	34°45′S	58°20′W
Montecillos, Cordillera de, mts., Hond.	120	14°19′N	87°52′W
Monte Cristi, Dom. Rep. (mŏ′n-tĕ-krē′s-tē)	123	19°50′N	71°40′W
Montecristo, Isola di, i., Italy (mōn′tå-krēs′tō)	160	42°20′N	10°19′E
Monte Escobedo, Mex. (mōn′tå ĕs-kô-bā′dhō)	118	22°18′N	103°34′W
Monteforte Irpino, Italy (mōn-tĕ-fô′r-tĕ ē′r-pē′nō)	159c	40°39′N	14°42′E
Montefrío, Spain (mōn-tå-frē′ō)	158	37°20′N	4°02′W
Montego Bay, Jam. (mŏn-tē′gō)	117	18°30′N	77°55′W
Montelavar, Port. (mōn-tĕ-lȧ-vär′)	159b	38°51′N	9°20′W
Montélimar, Fr. (môɴ-tā-lē-mär′)	147	44°33′N	4°47′E
Montellano, Spain (mōn-tå-lyä′nō)	158	37°00′N	5°34′W
Montello, Wi., U.S. (mŏn-tĕl′ō)	103	43°47′N	89°20′W
Montemorelos, Mex. (mōn′tå-mō-rā′lōs)	116	25°14′N	99°50′W
Montemor-o-Novo, Port. (mōɴ-tĕ-môr′ō-nô′vō)	158	38°39′N	8°11′W
Montenegro see Crna Gora, state, Yugo.	161	42°55′N	18°52′E
Montenegro, reg., Moz.	217	13°07′S	39°00′E
Montepulciano, Italy (mōn′tå-pōōl-chä′nō)	160	43°05′N	11°48′E
Montereau-faut-Yonne, Fr. (môɴ-t′rō′fō-yôn′)	156	48°24′N	2°57′E
Monterey, Ca., U.S. (mŏn-tĕ-rā′)	96	36°36′N	121°53′W
Monterey, Tn., U.S.	114	36°06′N	85°15′W
Monterey Bay, b., Ca., U.S.	96	36°48′N	122°01′W
Monterey Park, Ca., U.S.	107a	34°04′N	118°08′W
Montería, Col. (mōn-tā-rā′ä)	130	8°47′N	75°57′W
Monteros, Arg. (mōn-tĕ′rôs)	132	27°14′S	65°29′W
Monterotondo, Italy (môn-tĕ-rô-tô′n-dō)	159d	42°03′N	12°39′E
Monterrey, Mex. (mōn-tĕr-rā′)	116	25°43′N	100°19′W
Montesano, Wa., U.S. (mŏn-tē-sä′nō)	104	46°59′N	123°35′W
Monte Sant'Angelo, Italy (mô′n-tĕ sän ä′n-gzhĕ-lô)	149	41°43′N	15°59′E
Montes Claros, Braz. (môn-tĕs-klä′rôs)	131	16°44′S	43°41′W
Montespaccato, neigh., Italy	239c	41°54′N	12°23′E
Montevallo, Al., U.S. (mŏn-tē-văl′ō)	114	33°05′N	86°49′W
Montevarchi, Italy (mōn-tå-vär′kē)	160	43°30′N	11°45′E
Monteverde Nuovo, neigh., Italy	239c	41°51′N	12°27′E
Montevideo, Mn., U.S. (mŏn′tå-vē-dhā′ō)	102	44°56′N	95°42′W
Montevideo, Ur. (mōn′tå-vē-dhā′ō)	132	34°50′S	56°10′W
Monte Vista, Co., U.S. (mŏn′tē vĭs′tȧ)	109	37°35′N	106°10′W
Montezuma, Ga., U.S. (mŏn-tē-zōō′mȧ)	114	32°17′N	84°00′W
Montezuma Castle National Monument, rec., Az., U.S.	109	34°38′N	111°50′W
Montfermeil, Fr.	237c	48°54′N	2°34′E
Montflorit, Spain	238e	41°29′N	2°08′E
Montfoort, Neth.	145a	52°02′N	4°56′E
Montfor-l'Amaury, Fr. (môɴ-fôr′lä-mō-rē′)	157b	48°47′N	1°49′E
Montfort, Fr. (môn-fôr)	156	48°09′N	1°58′W
Montgeron, Fr.	237c	48°42′N	2°27′E
Montgomery, Al., U.S. (mŏnt-gŭm′ẽr-ĭ)	97	32°23′N	86°17′W
Montgomery, W.V., U.S.	98	38°10′N	81°25′W
Montgomery City, Mo., U.S.	111	38°58′N	91°29′W
Montgomery Knolls, Md., U.S.	229c	39°14′N	76°48′W
Monticello, Ar., U.S. (mŏn-tĭ-sĕl′ō)	111	33°38′N	91°47′W
Monticello, Fl., U.S.	114	30°32′N	83°53′W
Monticello, Ga., U.S.	114	33°00′N	83°11′W
Monticello, Il., U.S.	98	40°05′N	88°35′W
Monticello, In., U.S.	98	40°40′N	86°50′W
Monticello, Ia., U.S.	103	42°14′N	91°13′W
Monticello, Ky., U.S.	114	36°47′N	84°50′W
Monticello, Me., U.S.	92	46°19′N	67°53′W
Monticello, Mn., U.S.	103	45°18′N	93°48′W
Monticello, N.Y., U.S.	99	41°35′N	74°40′W
Monticello, Ut., U.S.	109	37°55′N	109°25′W
Montigny-le-Bretonneux, Fr.	237c	48°46′N	2°02′E
Montigny-lés-Cormeilles, Fr.	237c	48°59′N	2°12′E
Montijo, Port. (môn-tē′zhō)	159b	38°42′N	8°58′W
Montijo, Spain (môn-tē′hō)	158	38°55′N	6°35′W
Montijo, Bahía, b., Pan. (bä-ē′ä môn-tē′hō)	117	7°36′N	81°11′W
Mont-Joli, Can. (môɴ zhô-lē′)	85	48°35′N	68°11′W
Montjuich, Castillo de, hist., Spain	238e	41°22′N	2°10′E
Montluçon, Fr. (môɴ-lü-sôɴ′)	147	46°20′N	2°35′E
Montmagny, Can. (môɴ-män-yē′)	91	46°59′N	70°33′W
Montmagny, Fr.	237c	48°58′N	2°21′E
Montmartre, neigh., Fr.	237c	48°53′N	2°21′E
Montmorency, Austl.	243b	37°43′S	145°07′E
Montmorency, Fr. (môɴ′mô-räɴ-sē′)	157b	48°59′N	2°19′E
Montmorency, r., Can. (mŏnt-mô-rĕn′sĭ)	83b	47°03′N	71°10′W
Montmorillon, Fr. (môɴ′mô-rē-yôɴ′)	156	46°26′N	0°50′E
Montone, r., Italy (môn-tô′nĕ)	160	44°03′N	11°45′E
Montoro, Spain (môn-tō′rō)	158	38°01′N	4°22′W
Montpelier, Id., U.S.	105	42°19′N	111°19′W
Montpelier, In., U.S. (mŏnt-pēl′yẽr)	98	40°35′N	85°20′W
Montpelier, Oh., U.S.	98	41°35′N	84°35′W
Montpelier, Vt., U.S.	97	44°20′N	72°35′W
Montpellier, Fr. (môɴ-pĕ-lyā′)	147	43°38′N	3°53′E
Montréal, Can. (mŏn-trē-ôl′)	85	45°30′N	73°35′W
Montreal, r., Can.	90	47°15′N	84°20′W
Montreal, r., Can.	91	47°50′N	80°30′W
Montreal Lake, l., Can.	88	54°20′N	105°40′W
Montréal-Nord, Can.	83a	45°36′N	73°38′W
Montréal-Ouest, Can.	227b	45°27′N	73°39′W
Montreuil, Fr.	157b	48°52′N	2°27′E
Montreux, Switz. (môn-trû′)	154	46°26′N	6°52′E
Montrose, Austl.	243b	37°49′S	145°21′E
Montrose, Scot., U.K.	150	56°45′N	2°25′W
Montrose, Ca., U.S. (mŏnt-rōz)	107a	34°13′N	118°13′W
Montrose, Co., U.S. (mŏn-trōz′)	109	38°30′N	107°55′W
Montrose, Oh., U.S.	101d	41°08′N	81°38′W
Montrose, Pa., U.S. (mŏnt-rōz′)	99	41°50′N	75°50′W
Montrose Hill, Pa., U.S.	230b	40°30′N	79°51′W
Montrouge, Fr.	157b	48°49′N	2°19′E
Mont-Royal, Can.	83a	47°31′N	73°39′W
Monts, Pointe des, c., Can. (pwăɴt′ dā môɴ′)	92	49°19′N	67°22′W
Mont Saint Martin, Fr. (môɴ sâɴ mär-tăɴ′)	157	49°34′N	6°13′E
Montserrat, dep., N.A. (mŏnt-sĕ-răt′)	117	16°48′N	63°15′W
Montvale, N.J., U.S. (mŏnt-văl′)	100a	41°02′N	74°01′W
Monywa, Myanmar (mōn′yōō-wȧ)	183	22°02′N	95°16′E
Monza, Italy (mōn′tsä)	160	45°34′N	9°17′E
Monzón, Spain (mōn-thōn′)	159	41°54′N	0°09′E
Moóca, neigh., Braz.	234d	23°33′S	46°35′W
Moody, Tx., U.S. (mōō′dĭ)	113	31°18′N	97°20′W
Mooi, r., S. Afr.	213c	29°00′S	30°15′E
Mooi, r., S. Afr. (mōō′ĭ)	218d	26°34′S	27°03′E
Mooirivier, S. Afr.	213c	29°14′S	29°59′E
Moolap, Austl.	201a	38°11′S	144°26′E
Moonachie, N.J., U.S.	228	40°50′N	74°03′W

ng-sing; ŋ-baŋk; ɴ-nasalized n; nŏd; cŏmmit; ōld; ôbey; ôrder; oi-boil; fōōd; ŏ-as oo in foot; ou-out; s-soft; sh-dish; th-thin; pūre; ůnite; ûrn; stŭd; circŭs; ü-as in French tu; ′-indeterminate vowel.

320 Moonta–Moyynqūm

PLACE (Pronunciation)	PAGE	LAT.	LONG.
Moonta, Austl. (mo͞on'tȧ)	202	34°05'S	137°42'E
Moora, Austl. (mo͝or'ȧ)	202	30°35'S	116°12'E
Moorabbin, Austl.	201a	37°56'S	145°02'E
Moore, l., Austl. (mōr)	202	29°50'S	118°12'E
Moorebank, Austl.	243a	33°56'S	150°56'E
Moorenweis, Ger. (mō'rĕn-vīz)	145d	48°10'N	11°05'E
Moore Reservoir, res., Vt., U.S.	99	44°20'N	72°10'W
Moorestown, N.J., U.S. (morz'toun)	100f	39°58'N	74°56'W
Mooresville, In., U.S. (mōrz'vĭl)	101g	39°37'N	86°22'W
Mooresville, N.C., U.S.	115	35°34'N	80°48'W
Moorhead, Mn., U.S. (mōr'hĕd)	102	46°52'N	96°44'W
Moorhead, Ms., U.S.	114	33°25'N	90°30'W
Mooroolbark, Austl.	243b	37°47'S	145°19'E
Moorside, Eng., U.K.	237b	53°34'N	2°04'W
Moose, r., Can.	85	51°01'N	80°42'W
Moose Creek, Can.	83c	45°16'N	74°58'W
Moosehead, Me., U.S. (mo͞os'hĕd)	92	45°37'N	69°15'W
Moose Island, i., Can.	89	51°50'N	97°09'W
Moose Jaw, Can. (mo͞os jô)	84	50°23'N	105°32'W
Moose Jaw, r., Can.	88	50°34'N	105°17'W
Moose Lake, Can.	89	53°40'N	100°28'W
Moose Mountain, mtn., Can.	89	49°45'N	102°37'W
Moose Mountain Creek, r., Can.	89	49°12'N	102°10'W
Moosilauke, mtn., N.H., U.S. (mo͞o-sĭ-lô'kē)	99	44°00'N	71°50'W
Moosinning, Ger. (mō'zē-nēng)	145d	48°17'N	11°51'E
Moosomin, Can. (mo͞o'sô-mĭn)	89	50°07'N	101°40'W
Moosonee, Can. (mo͞o'sô-nė)	85	51°20'N	80°44'W
Mopti, Mali (mŏp'tė)	210	14°30'N	4°12'W
Moquegua, Peru (mô-kā'gwä)	130	17°15'S	70°54'W
Mór, Hung. (mōr)	155	47°25'N	18°14'E
Mora, India	187b	18°54'N	72°56'E
Mora, Spain (mô-rä)	158	39°42'N	3°45'W
Mora, Swe. (mō'rä)	152	61°00'N	14°29'E
Mora, Mn., U.S. (mō'rȧ)	103	45°52'N	93°18'W
Mora, N.M., U.S.	110	35°58'N	105°17'W
Morādābād, India (mô-rä-dä-bäd')	183	28°57'N	78°48'E
Morales, Guat. (mô-rä'lĕs)	120	15°29'N	88°46'W
Moramanga, Madag. (mō-rä-mäŋ'gä)	213	18°48'S	48°09'E
Morangis, Fr.	237c	48°42'N	2°20'E
Morant Point, c., Jam. (mô-ränt')	122	17°55'N	76°10'W
Morata de Tajuña, Spain (mô-rä'tä dā tä-ho͞o'nyä)	159a	40°14'N	3°27'W
Moratuwa, Sri L.	187	6°35'N	79°59'E
Morava (Moravia), hist. reg., Czech Rep.	154	49°21'N	16°57'E
Morava, r., Eur.	147	49°00'N	17°30'E
Moravia *see* Morava, hist. reg., Czech Rep.	154	49°21'N	16°57'E
Morawhanna, Guy. (mō-rȧ-hwä'nȧ)	131	8°12'N	59°33'W
Moray Firth, b., Scot., U.K. (mŭr'ā)	142	57°41'N	3°55'W
Mörbylånga, Swe. (mûr'bü-lôŋ'gȧ)	152	56°32'N	16°23'E
Morden, Can. (môr'dĕn)	84	49°11'N	98°05'W
Mordialloc, Austl. (môr-dĭ-äl'ŏk)	201a	38°00'S	145°05'E
Mordvinia, state, Russia	166	54°18'N	43°50'E
More, Ben, mtn., Scot., U.K. (bĕn môr)	150	58°09'N	5°01'W
Moreau, r., S.D., U.S. (mô-rō')	102	45°13'N	102°22'W
Moree, Austl. (mō'rē)	203	29°20'S	149°50'E
Morehead, Ky., U.S.	98	38°10'N	83°25'W
Morehead City, N.C., U.S. (mōr'hĕd)	115	34°43'N	76°43'W
Morehouse, Mo., U.S. (mōr'hous)	111	36°49'N	89°41'W
Morelia, Mex. (mô-rā'lyä)	116	19°43'N	101°12'W
Morella, Spain (mô-räl'yä)	159	40°38'N	0°07'W
Morelos, Mex.	112	28°24'N	100°51'W
Morelos, Mex. (mô-rā'lōs)	118	22°46'N	102°36'W
Morelos, Mex.	119a	19°41'N	99°29'W
Morelos, neigh., Mex.	233a	19°27'N	99°07'W
Morelos, r., Mex.	112	25°27'N	99°35'W
Morena, Sierra, mtn., Ca., U.S. (syĕr'rä mô-rā'nä)	106b	37°24'N	122°19'W
Morena, Sierra, mts., Spain (syĕr'rä mô-rā'nä)	142	38°15'N	5°45'W
Morenci, Az., U.S. (mô-rĕn'sĭ)	109	33°05'N	109°25'W
Morenci, Mi., U.S.	98	41°50'N	84°50'W
Moreno, Arg. (mô-rĕ'nō)	132a	34°39'S	58°47'W
Moreno, Ca., U.S.	107a	33°55'N	117°09'W
Mores, i., Bah. (mōrz)	122	26°20'N	77°35'W
Moresby, i., Can. (mōrz'bĭ)	106d	48°43'N	123°15'W
Moresby Island, i., Can.	84	52°50'N	131°55'W
Moreton, Eng., U.K.	237a	53°24'N	3°07'W
Moreton, i., Austl. (môr'tŭn)	204	26°53'S	152°42'E
Moreton Bay, b., Austl. (môr'tŭn)	204	27°12'S	153°10'E
Morewood, Can. (mōr'wo͝od)	83c	45°11'N	75°17'W
Morgan, Mt., U.S. (môr'găn)	105	48°55'N	107°56'W
Morgan, Ut., U.S.	105	41°04'N	111°42'W
Morgan City, La., U.S.	113	29°41'N	91°11'W
Morganfield, Ky., U.S. (môr'găn-fēld)	98	37°40'N	87°55'W
Morgan's Bay, S. Afr.	213c	32°42'S	28°19'E
Morganton, N.C., U.S. (môr'găn-tŭn)	115	35°44'N	81°42'W
Morgantown, W.V., U.S. (môr'găn-toun)	99	39°40'N	79°55'W
Morga Range, mts., Afg.	183a	34°02'N	70°38'E
Morgenzon, S. Afr. (môr'gănt-sŏn)	218d	26°44'S	29°39'E
Moriac, Austl.	201a	38°15'S	144°20'E
Morice Lake, l., Can.	86	54°00'N	127°37'W
Moriguchi, Japan (mō'rē-go͞o'chė)	195b	34°44'N	135°34'E
Morinville, Can. (mō'rĭn-vĭl)	83g	53°48'N	113°39'W
Morioka, Japan (mō'rē-ō'kȧ)	189	39°40'N	141°21'E
Morivione, neigh., Italy	238c	45°26'N	9°12'E
Morkoka, r., Russia (mōr-kô'kȧ)	171	65°35'N	111°00'E
Morlaix, Fr. (mŏr-lĕ')	147	48°36'N	3°48'W
Morley, Can. (mŏr'lė)	83e	51°10'N	114°51'W
Morley Green, Eng., U.K.	237b	53°20'N	2°16'W
Mormant, Fr.	157b	48°35'N	2°54'E
Morne Gimie, St. Luc. (mōrn' zhė-mē')	121b	13°53'N	61°03'W
Morningside, Md., U.S.	229d	38°50'N	76°53'W
Mornington, Austl.	201a	38°13'S	145°02'E
Morobe, Pap. N. Gui.	197	8°03'S	147°45'E
Morocco, nation, Afr. (mô-rŏk'ō)	210	32°00'N	7°00'W
Morogoro, Tan. (mō-rō-gō'rō)	213	6°49'S	37°40'E
Moroleón, Mex. (mô-rō-lā-ōn')	118	20°07'N	101°15'W
Morombe, Madag. (mo͞o-ro͞om'bā)	213	21°39'S	43°34'E
Morón, Arg. (mo-rŏ'n)	129c	34°39'S	58°37'W
Morón, Cuba (mô-rōn')	122	22°05'N	78°35'W
Morón, Ven. (mô-rŏ'n)	131b	10°29'N	68°11'W
Morondava, Madag. (mō-rōn-dȧ'vȧ)	213	20°17'S	44°18'E
Morón de la Frontera, Spain (mô-rōn'dā läf rōn-tā'rä)	158	37°08'N	5°20'W
Morongo Indian Reservation, I.R., Ca., U.S. (mō-rôŋ'gō)	108	33°54'N	116°47'W
Moroni, Com.	213	11°41'S	43°16'E
Moroni, Ut., U.S. (mô-rō'nĭ)	109	39°30'N	111°40'W
Morotai, i., Indon. (mō-rô-tä'ė)	197	2°12'N	128°30'E
Moroto, Ug.	217	2°32'N	34°39'E
Morozovsk, Russia	167	48°20'N	41°50'E
Morrill, Ne., U.S. (mŏr'ĭl)	102	41°59'N	103°54'W
Morrilton, Ar., U.S. (mŏr'ĭl-tŭn)	111	35°09'N	92°42'W
Morrinhos, Braz. (mô-rēn'yōzh)	131	17°45'S	48°56'W
Morris, Can. (mŏr'ĭs)	84	49°21'N	97°22'W
Morris, Il., U.S.	98	41°20'N	88°25'W
Morris, Mn., U.S.	102	45°35'N	95°53'W
Morris, r., Can.	89	49°30'N	97°30'W
Morrison, Il., U.S. (mŏr'ĭ-sŭn)	103	41°48'N	89°58'W
Morris Reservoir, res., Ca., U.S.	107a	34°11'N	117°49'W
Morristown, N.J., U.S. (mŏr'rĭs-toun)	100a	40°48'N	74°29'W
Morristown, Tn., U.S.	114	36°10'N	83°18'W
Morrisville, Pa., U.S. (mŏr'ĭs-vĭl)	100f	40°12'N	74°46'W
Morro, Castillo del, hist., Cuba	233b	23°09'N	82°21'W
Morro do Chapéu, Braz. (môr-ŏ dô-shä-pĕ'o͞o)	131	11°34'S	41°03'W
Morrow, Oh., U.S. (mŏr'ō)	101f	39°21'N	84°07'W
Mors, i., Den.	152	56°46'N	8°38'E
Mörsenbroich, neigh., Ger.	236	51°15'N	6°48'E
Morshansk, Russia (môr-shánsk')	166	53°25'N	41°35'E
Mortara, Italy (môr-tä'rä)	160	45°13'N	8°47'E
Morteros, Arg. (môr-tĕ'tôs)	132	30°47'S	62°00'W
Mortes, Rio das, r., Braz. (rēō-däs-mô'r-tĕs)	129a	21°04'S	44°29'W
Mortlake, Austl.	243a	33°51'S	151°07'E
Mortlake, neigh., Eng., U.K.	235	51°28'N	0°16'W
Morton, Pa., U.S.	229b	39°55'N	75°20'W
Morton Grove, Il., U.S.	231a	42°02'N	87°47'W
Morton Indian Reservation, I.R., Mn., U.S. (mŏr'tŭn)	103	44°35'N	94°48'W
Mortsel, Bel. (môr-sĕl')	145a	51°10'N	4°28'E
Morvan, mts., Fr. (mōr-väɴ')	156	47°11'N	4°10'E
Morzhovets, i., Russia (môr'zhô-vyĕts')	166	66°40'N	42°30'E
Mosal'sk, Russia (mō-zálsk')	162	54°27'N	34°57'E
Moscavide, Port.	159b	38°47'N	9°06'W
Moscow (Moskva), Russia	164	55°45'N	37°37'E
Moscow, Id., U.S. (mŏs'kō)	96	46°44'N	116°57'W
Mosel (Moselle), r., Eur. (mō'sĕl) (mô-zĕl)	154	49°49'N	7°00'E
Moses, r., S. Afr.	218d	25°17'S	29°04'E
Moses Lake, Wa., U.S.	104	47°08'N	119°15'W
Moses Lake, l., Wa., U.S. (mō'zĕz)	104	47°09'N	119°30'W
Moshchnyy, is., Russia (môsh'chnĭ)	153	59°56'N	28°07'E
Moshi, Tan. (mō'shė)	213	3°21'S	37°20'E
Mosjøen, Nor.	146	65°50'N	13°10'E
Moskháton, Grc.	239d	37°57'N	23°41'E
Moskva *see* Moscow, Russia	164	55°45'N	37°37'E
Moskva, prov., Russia	162	55°38'N	36°48'E
Moskva, r., Russia	166	55°30'N	37°05'E
Mosman, Austl.	243a	33°49'S	151°14'E
Mosonmagyaróvár, Hung.	155	47°51'N	17°16'E
Mosquitos, Costa de, cst., Nic. (kôs-tä-dĕ-mōs-kē'tōs)	121	12°05'N	83°49'W
Mosquitos, Gulfo de los, b., Pan. (go͞o'l-fô-dĕ-lôs-mōs-kē'tōs)	117	9°17'N	80°59'W
Moss, Nor. (môs)	146	59°29'N	10°39'E
Moss Bank, Eng., U.K.	237a	53°29'N	2°44'W
Moss Beach, Ca., U.S. (môs bēch)	106b	37°32'N	122°31'W
Moss Crest, mtn., Va., U.S.	229d	38°55'N	77°15'W
Mosselbaai, S. Afr. (mô'sŭl bā)	212	34°06'S	22°23'E
Mossendjo, Congo	216	2°57'S	12°44'E
Mossley, Eng., U.K. (môs'lĭ)	144a	53°31'N	2°02'W
Mossley Hill, neigh., Eng., U.K.	237a	53°23'N	2°55'W
Moss Point, Ms., U.S. (môs)	114	30°25'N	88°32'W
Most, Czech Rep. (môst)	154	50°32'N	13°37'E
Mostar, Bos. (môs'tär)	149	43°20'N	17°51'E
Móstoles, Spain (môs-tō'läs)	159a	40°19'N	3°52'W
Mostoos Hills, hills, Can. (mŏs'to͞os)	88	54°50'N	108°45'W
Mosvatnet, l., Nor.	152	59°55'N	7°50'E
Motagua, r., N.A. (mô-tä'gwä)	120	15°29'N	88°39'W
Motala, Swe. (mô-tô'lä)	152	58°34'N	15°00'E
Motherwell, Scot., U.K. (mŭdh'ĕr-wĕl)	146	55°45'N	4°05'W
Motril, Spain (mô-trēl')	148	36°44'N	3°32'W
Mottingham, neigh., Eng., U.K.	235	51°26'N	0°03'E
Motul, Mex. (mō-to͞o'l)	120a	21°07'N	89°14'W
Mouaskar, Alg.	210	35°25'N	0°08'E
Mouchoir Bank, bk. (mo͞o-shwär')	123	21°35'N	70°40'W
Mouchoir Passage, strt., T./C. Is.	123	21°05'N	71°05'W
Moudjéria, Maur.	214	17°53'N	12°20'W
Mouila, Gabon	216	1°52'S	11°01'E
Mouille Point, c., S. Afr.	212a	33°54'S	18°19'E
Moulins, Fr. (mo͞o-läɴ')	147	46°34'N	3°19'E
Moulouya, Oued, r., Mor. (mo͞o-lo͞o'yȧ)	210	34°00'N	4°00'W
Moultrie, Ga., U.S. (mōl'trĭ)	114	31°10'N	83°48'W
Moultrie, Lake, l., S.C., U.S.	115	33°12'N	80°00'W
Mound City, Il., U.S.	111	37°06'N	89°13'W
Mound City, Mo., U.S.	111	40°08'N	95°13'W
Moundou, Chad	215	8°34'N	16°05'E
Moundsville, W.V., U.S. (moundz'vĭl)	98	39°50'N	80°50'W
Mount, Cape, c., Lib.	214	6°47'N	11°20'W
Mountain Brook, Al., U.S. (moun'tĭn bro͝ok)	100h	33°30'N	86°45'W
Mountain Creek Lake, l., Tx., U.S.	107c	32°43'N	97°03'W
Mountain Grove, Mo., U.S. (grōv)	111	37°07'N	92°16'W
Mountain Home, Id., U.S. (hōm)	104	43°08'N	115°43'W
Mountain Park, Can. (pärk)	84	52°55'N	117°14'W
Mountain View, Ca., U.S. (moun'tĭn vū)	106b	37°25'N	122°07'W
Mountain View, Mo., U.S.	111	36°59'N	91°46'W
Mount Airy, N.C., U.S. (âr'ĭ)	115	36°28'N	80°37'W
Mount Ayliff, S. Afr. (ā'lĭf)	213c	30°48'S	29°24'E
Mount Ayr, Ia., U.S. (âr)	103	40°43'N	94°06'W
Mount Baldy, Ca., U.S.	232	34°14'N	117°40'W
Mount Carmel, Il., U.S. (kär'mĕl)	98	38°25'N	87°45'W
Mount Carmel, Pa., U.S.	99	40°50'N	76°25'W
Mount Carooll, Il., U.S.	103	42°05'N	89°55'W
Mount Clemens, Mi., U.S. (klĕm'ĕnz)	101b	42°36'N	82°52'W
Mount Dennis, neigh., Can.	227c	43°42'N	79°30'W
Mount Desert, i., Me., U.S. (dė-zûrt')	92	44°15'N	68°08'W
Mount Dora, Fl., U.S. (dō'rȧ)	115a	28°45'N	81°38'W
Mount Druitt, Austl.	243a	33°46'S	150°49'E
Mount Duneed, Austl.	201a	38°15'S	144°20'E
Mount Eliza, Austl.	201a	38°11'S	145°05'E
Mount Ephraim, N.J., U.S.	229b	39°53'N	75°06'W
Mount Fletcher, S. Afr. (flĕ'chĕr)	213c	30°42'S	28°32'E
Mount Forest, Can. (fŏr'ĕst)	91	44°00'N	80°45'W
Mount Frere, S. Afr. (frâr')	213c	30°54'S	29°02'E
Mount Gambier, Austl. (găm'bēr)	202	37°30'S	140°53'E
Mount Gilead, Oh., U.S. (gĭl'ėăd)	98	40°30'N	82°50'W
Mount Greenwood, neigh., Il., U.S.	231a	41°42'N	87°43'W
Mount Healthy, Oh., U.S. (hĕlth'ė)	101f	39°14'N	84°32'W
Mount Hebron, Md., U.S.	229c	39°18'N	76°50'W
Mount Holly, N.J., U.S. (hŏl'ĭ)	100f	39°59'N	74°47'W
Mount Hope, Can.	83d	43°09'N	79°55'W
Mount Hope, N.J., U.S. (hōp)	100a	40°55'N	74°32'W
Mount Hope, W.V., U.S.	98	37°55'N	81°10'W
Mount Isa, Austl. (ī'zȧ)	202	21°00'S	139°45'E
Mount Kisco, N.Y., U.S. (kĭs'ko)	100a	41°12'N	73°44'W
Mountlake Terrace, Wa., U.S. (mount lāk tĕr'ĭs)	106a	47°48'N	122°19'W
Mount Lebanon, Pa., U.S. (lĕb'ȧ-nŭn)	101e	40°22'N	80°03'W
Mount Magnet, Austl. (măg-nĕt)	202	28°00'S	118°00'E
Mount Martha, Austl.	201a	38°17'S	145°01'E
Mount Morgan, Austl. (môr-găn)	203	23°42'S	150°45'E
Mount Moriac, Austl.	201a	38°13'S	144°12'E
Mount Morris, Mi., U.S. (mŏr'ĭs)	98	43°10'N	83°45'W
Mount Morris, N.Y., U.S.	99	42°45'N	77°50'W
Mountnessing, Eng., U.K.	235	51°39'N	0°21'E
Mount Nimba National Park, rec., C. Iv.	214	7°35'N	8°10'W
Mount Olive, N.C., U.S. (ŏl'ĭv)	115	35°11'N	78°05'W
Mount Oliver, Pa., U.S.	230b	40°28'N	79°59'W
Mount Peale, Ut., U.S.	109	38°26'N	109°16'W
Mount Pleasant, Ia., U.S. (plĕz'ănt)	103	40°59'N	91°34'W
Mount Pleasant, Mi., U.S.	98	43°35'N	84°45'W
Mount Pleasant, S.C., U.S.	115	32°46'N	79°51'W
Mount Pleasant, Tn., U.S.	114	35°31'N	87°12'W
Mount Pleasant, Tx., U.S.	113	33°10'N	94°56'W
Mount Pleasant, Ut., U.S.	109	39°35'N	111°20'W
Mount Pritchard, Austl.	243a	33°54'S	150°54'E
Mount Prospect, Il., U.S. (prŏs'pĕkt)	101a	42°03'N	87°56'W
Mount Rainier, Md., U.S.	229d	38°56'N	76°58'W
Mount Rainier National Park, rec., Wa., U.S. (rȧ-nēr')	96	46°47'N	121°17'W
Mount Revelstoke National Park, Can. (rĕv'ĕl-stōk)	84	51°22'N	120°15'W
Mount Savage, Md., U.S. (săv'āj)	99	39°45'N	78°55'W
Mount Shasta, Ca., U.S. (shăs'tȧ)	104	41°18'N	122°17'W
Mount Sterling, Il., U.S. (stûr'lĭng)	111	39°59'N	90°44'W
Mount Sterling, Ky., U.S.	98	38°05'N	84°00'W
Mount Stewart, Can. (stū'ărt)	93	46°22'N	62°52'W
Mount Union, Pa., U.S. (ūn'yŭn)	99	40°25'N	77°50'W
Mount Vernon, Il., U.S. (vûr'nŭn)	98	38°20'N	88°50'W
Mount Vernon, In., U.S.	98	37°55'N	87°50'W
Mount Vernon, Mo., U.S.	111	37°09'N	93°48'W
Mount Vernon, N.Y., U.S.	100a	40°55'N	73°51'W
Mount Vernon, Oh., U.S.	98	40°25'N	82°30'W
Mount Vernon, Pa., U.S.	230b	40°17'N	79°48'W
Mount Vernon, Va., U.S.	100e	38°43'N	77°06'W
Mount Vernon, Wa., U.S.	104	48°25'N	122°20'W
Mount Washington, neigh., Md., U.S.	229c	39°22'N	76°40'W
Mount Washington Summit, Md., U.S.	229c	39°23'N	76°40'W
Mount Waverley, Austl.	243b	37°53'S	145°08'E
Moura, Braz. (mō'rȧ)	131	1°33'S	61°38'W
Moura, Port.	158	38°08'N	7°28'W
Mourne Mountains, mts., N. Ire., U.K. (môrn)	150	54°10'N	6°09'W
Moussoro, Chad	215	13°39'N	16°29'E
Moûtiers, Fr. (mo͞o-tyâr')	157	45°31'N	6°34'E
Mowbullan, Mount, mtn., Austl.	204	26°50'S	151°34'E
Moyahua, Mex. (mô-yä'wä)	118	21°16'N	103°10'W
Moyale, Kenya (mô-yä'lä)	211	3°28'N	39°04'E
Moyamba, S.L. (mô-yäm'bä)	210	8°10'N	12°26'W
Moyen Atlas, mts., Mor.	148	32°49'N	5°28'W
Moyeuvre-Grande, Fr.	157	49°15'N	6°26'E
Moyie, r., Id., U.S. (moi'yė)	104	38°50'N	116°10'W
Moylan, Pa., U.S.	229b	39°54'N	75°23'W
Moyobamba, Peru (mō-yō-bäm'bä)	130	6°12'S	76°56'W
Moyuta, Guat. (mô-ē-o͞o'tä)	120	14°01'N	90°05'W
Moyyero, r., Russia	170	67°15'N	104°10'E
Moyynqūm, des., Kaz.	169	44°30'N	70°00'E

ăt; fināl; rāte; senâte; ärm; ȧsk; sofȧ; fâre; ch-choose; dh-as th in other; bē; ėvent; bĕt; recĕnt; cratĕr; g-gō; gh-guttural g; bĭt; ĭ-short neutral; rīde; ĸ-guttural k as ch in German ich;

PRONOUNCING INDEX Mozambique-Nagatino 321

PLACE (Pronunciation)	PAGE	LAT.	LONG.
Mozambique, nation, Afr. (mō-zăm-bēk′)	212	20°15′S	33°53′E
Mozambique Channel, strt., Afr. (mō-zăm-bek′)	213	24°00′S	38°00′E
Mozdok, Russia (mōz-dôk′)	167	43°45′N	44°35′E
Mozhaysk, Russia (mō-zhäysk′)	162	55°31′N	36°02′E
Mozhayskiy, Russia (mō-zhá′y′skĭ)	172c	59°42′N	30°08′E
Mozyr′, Bela. (mō-zür′)	167	52°03′N	29°14′E
Mpanda, Tan.	217	6°22′S	31°02′E
Mpika, Zam.	217	11°54′S	31°26′E
Mpimbe, Mwi.	217	15°18′S	35°04′E
Mporokoso, Zam. ('m-pō-rō-kō′sō)	212	9°23′S	30°05′E
Mpwapwa, Tan. ('m-pwä′pwä)	212	6°21′S	36°29′E
Mqanduli, S. Afr. ('m-kän′dōō-lē)	213c	31°50′S	28°42′E
Mrągowo, Pol. (mrän′gô-vô)	155	53°52′N	21°18′E
M'Sila, Alg. (m′sē′lȧ)	210	35°47′N	4°34′E
Msta, r., Russia (m′stá′)	166	58°30′N	33°00′E
Mstislavl′, Bela. (m′stē-slävl′)	162	54°01′N	31°42′E
Mtakataka, Mwi.	217	14°12′S	34°32′E
Mtamvuna, r., Afr.	213c	30°43′S	29°53′E
Mtata, r., S. Afr.	213c	31°48′S	29°03′E
Mtsensk, Russia (m′tsĕnsk)	166	53°17′N	36°33′E
Mtwara, Tan.	217	10°16′S	40°11′E
Muar, r., Malay.	181b	2°18′N	102°43′E
Mubende, Ug.	217	0°35′N	31°23′E
Mubi, Nig.	215	10°18′N	13°20′E
Mucacata, Moz.	217	13°20′S	39°59′E
Much, Ger. (mōōĸ)	157c	50°54′N	7°24′E
Muchinga Mountains, mts., Zam.	217	12°40′S	30°50′E
Much Wenlock, Eng., U.K. (mŭch wĕn′lŏk)	144a	52°35′N	2°33′W
Muckalee Creek, r., Ga., U.S. (mŭk′ă lē)	114	31°55′N	84°10′W
Mucking, Eng., U.K.	235	51°30′N	0°26′E
Muckleshoot Indian Reservation, I.R., Wa., U.S. (mŭck″l-shōōt)	106a	47°21′N	122°04′W
Mucubela, Moz.	217	16°55′S	37°52′E
Mud, l., Mi., U.S. (mŭd)	103	46°12′N	84°32′W
Mudan, r., China (mōō-dän)	192	45°30′N	129°40′E
Mudanjiang, China (mōō-dän-jyäŋ)	192	44°28′N	129°38′E
Muddy, r., Nv., U.S. (mŭd′ĭ)	109	36°56′N	114°42′W
Muddy Boggy Creek, r., Ok., U.S. (mud′ĭ bôg′ĭ)	111	34°42′N	96°11′W
Muddy Creek, r., Ut., U.S. (mŭd′ĭ)	109	38°45′N	111°10′W
Mudgee, Austl. (mŭ-jē)	204	32°47′S	149°10′E
Mudjatik, r., Can.	88	56°23′N	107°40′W
Mufulira, Zam.	217	12°33′S	28°14′E
Muğla, Tur. (mōōg′lä)	182	37°10′N	28°20′E
Mühileiten, Aus.	239e	48°10′N	16°34′E
Mühldorf, Ger. (mül-dôrf)	154	48°15′N	12°33′E
Mühlenbeck, Ger.	238a	52°40′N	13°22′E
Mühlhausen, Ger. (mül′hou-zĕn)	154	51°13′N	10°25′E
Muhu, i., Est. (mōō′hōō)	153	58°41′N	22°55′E
Muir Woods National Monument, rec., Ca., U.S. (mūr)	108	37°54′N	123°22′W
Muizenberg, S. Afr. (mwĭz-ĕn-bûrg′)	212a	34°07′S	18°28′E
Mujāhidpur, neigh., India	240d	28°34′N	77°13′E
Mukacheve, Ukr.	155	48°25′N	22°43′E
Mukden see Shenyang, China	188	41°45′N	123°22′E
Mukhtuya, Russia (mōk-tōō′yȧ)	165	61°00′N	113°00′E
Mukilteo, Wa., U.S. (mū-kĭl-tā′ō)	106a	47°57′N	122°18′W
Muko, Japan (mōō′kō)	195b	34°57′N	135°43′E
Muko, r., Japan (mōō′kō)	195b	34°52′N	135°17′E
Mukutawa, r., Can.	89	53°10′N	97°28′W
Mukwonago, Wi., U.S. (mū-kwō-nȧ′gō)	101a	42°52′N	88°19′W
Mula, Spain (mōō′lä)	158	38°05′N	1°12′W
Mula, Al., U.S. (mŭl′gȧ)	100h	33°33′N	86°59′W
Mulde, r., Ger. (mōōl′dĕ)	154	50°30′N	12°30′E
Muleros, Mex. (mōō-lā′rōs)	118	23°44′N	104°00′W
Muleshoe, Tx., U.S.	110	34°13′N	102°43′W
Mulgrave, Can. (mŭl′grāv)	93	45°37′N	61°23′W
Mulhacén, mtn., Spain	148	37°04′N	3°18′W
Mülheim, Ger. (mül′hīm)	157c	51°25′N	6°53′E
Mulhouse, Fr. (mü-lōōz′)	147	47°46′N	7°20′E
Muling, China (mōō-lĭŋ)	192	44°32′N	130°18′E
Muling, r., China	192	44°40′N	130°30′E
Mull, Island of, i., Scot., U.K. (mŭl)	150	56°40′N	6°19′W
Mullan, Id., U.S. (mŭl′ăn)	104	47°26′N	115°50′W
Müller, Pegunungan, mts., Indon. (mül′ĕr)	196	0°22′N	113°05′E
Mullingar, Ire. (mŭl-ĭn-gär)	150	53°31′N	7°26′W
Mullins, S.C., U.S. (mŭl′ĭnz)	115	34°11′N	79°13′W
Mullins River, Belize	120a	17°08′N	88°18′W
Multān, Pak. (mōō-tän′)	183	30°17′N	71°13′E
Multnomah Channel, strt., Or., U.S. (mŭl nō mȧ)	106c	45°41′N	122°53′W
Mulumbe, Monts, mts., D.R.C.	217	8°47′S	27°20′E
Mulvane, Ks., U.S. (mŭl-vān′)	111	37°30′N	97°13′W
Mumbai, India	183	18°58′N	72°50′E
Mumbwa, Zam. (mōm′bwä)	212	14°59′S	27°04′E
Mumias, Kenya	217	0°20′N	34°29′E
Muna, Mex. (mōō′nȧ)	120a	20°28′N	89°42′W
Münchehofe, Ger.	238a	52°30′N	13°40′E
München see Munich, Ger.	142	48°08′N	11°35′E
Muncie, In., U.S. (mŭn′sĭ)	97	40°10′N	85°30′W
Mundelein, Il., U.S. (mŭn-dē-līn′)	101a	42°16′N	88°00′W
Mündelheim, neigh., Ger.	236	51°21′N	6°41′E
Mundonueva, Pico de, mtn., Col. (pē′kō-dĕ-mōō′n-dō-nwĕ′vä)	130a	4°18′N	74°12′W
Muneco, Cerro, mtn., Mex. (sĕ′r-rō-mōō-nĕ′kō)	119a	19°13′N	99°20′W
Mungana, Austl. (mŭn-găn′ȧ)	203	17°15′S	144°18′E
Mungbere, D.R.C.	217	2°38′N	28°30′E
Munger, Mn., U.S. (mŭn′gĕr)	107h	46°48′N	92°20′W
Mungindi, Austl. (mŭn-gĭn′dē)	203	29°00′S	148°45′E
Munhall, Pa., U.S. (mŭn′hôl)	101e	40°24′N	79°53′W
Munhango, Ang. (mōn-häŋ′gȧ)	212	12°15′S	18°55′E
Munich, Ger.	142	48°08′N	11°35′E
Munirka, neigh., India	240d	28°34′N	77°10′E
Munising, Mi., U.S. (mū′nĭ-sĭng)	103	46°24′N	86°41′W
Muniz Freire, Braz.	129a	20°29′S	41°25′W
Munku Sardyk, mtn., Asia (mōn′kō sär-dĭk′)	165	51°45′N	100°30′E
Muñoz, Phil. (mōō-nyōth′)	197a	15°44′N	120°53′E
Munro, neigh., Arg.	233d	34°32′S	58°31′W
Münster, Ger. (mün′stĕr)	147	51°57′N	7°38′E
Munster, In., U.S. (mŭn′stĕr)	101a	41°34′N	87°31′W
Munster, hist. reg., Ire. (mŭn-stĕr)	150	52°30′N	9°24′W
Muntok, Indon. (mōn-tŏk′)	196	2°05′S	105°11′E
Muong Sing, Laos (mōō′ông-sĭng′)	196	21°06′N	101°17′E
Muping, China (mōō-pĭŋ)	190	37°23′N	121°36′E
Muqui, Braz. (mōō-kōē)	129a	20°56′S	41°20′W
Mur, r., Eur. (mōōr)	147	47°00′N	15°00′E
Muradiye, Tur. (mōō-rä′dē-yĕ)	167	39°00′N	43°40′E
Murat, Fr. (mü-rä′)	156	45°05′N	2°56′E
Murat, r., Tur. (mōō-rät′)	182	39°00′N	42°00′E
Murayama, Japan	242a	35°45′N	139°23′E
Murchison, r., Austl. (mûr′chĭ-sŭn)	202	26°45′S	116°15′E
Murcia, Spain (mōōr′thyä)	142	38°00′N	1°10′W
Murcia, hist. reg., Spain	158	38°35′N	1°51′W
Murdo, S.D., U.S. (mûr′dō)	102	43°53′N	100°42′W
Mureș, r., Rom. (mōō′rĕsh)	149	46°02′N	21°50′E
Muret, Fr. (mü-rĕ′)	156	43°28′N	1°17′E
Murfreesboro, Tn., U.S. (mûr′frēz-bŭr-ō)	114	35°50′N	86°19′W
Murgab, Taj.	169	38°10′N	73°59′E
Murgab, r., Asia (mōōr-gäb′)	182	37°07′N	62°32′E
Muriaé, r., Braz.	129a	21°20′S	41°40′W
Murino, Russia (mōō′rĭ-nō)	172c	60°03′N	30°28′E
Müritz, l., Ger. (mür′its)	154	53°20′N	12°33′E
Murmansk, Russia (mōōr-mänsk′)	164	69°00′N	33°20′E
Murom, Russia (mōō′rôm)	164	55°30′N	42°00′W
Muroran, Japan (mōō′rō-rän)	189	42°21′N	141°05′E
Muros, Spain (mōō′rōs)	158	42°48′N	9°00′W
Muroto-Zaki, c., Japan (mōō′rō-tō zä′kē)	194	33°14′N	134°12′E
Murphy, Mo., U.S. (mŭr′fĭ)	107e	38°29′N	90°29′W
Murphy, N.C., U.S.	114	35°05′N	84°00′W
Murphysboro, Il., U.S. (mŭr′fĭz-bŭr-ō)	111	37°46′N	89°21′W
Murray, Ky., U.S. (mŭr′ĭ)	114	36°39′N	88°17′W
Murray, Ut., U.S.	107b	40°40′N	111°53′W
Murray, r., Austl.	202	34°20′S	140°00′E
Murray, r., Can.	87	55°00′N	121°00′W
Murray, Lake, res., S.C., U.S. (mŭr′ĭ)	115	34°07′N	81°18′W
Murray Bridge, Austl.	202	35°10′S	139°35′E
Murray Harbour, Can.	93	46°00′N	62°31′W
Murray Region, reg., Austl. (mŭ′rē)	203	33°20′S	142°30′E
Murrumbidgee, r., Austl. (mŭr-ŭm-bĭd′jē)	203	34°30′S	145°20′E
Murrupula, Moz.	217	15°27′S	38°47′E
Murshidābād, India (mōr′shē-dä-bäd′)	186	24°08′N	88°11′E
Murska Sobota, Slvn. (mōōr′skä sô′bô-tä)	160	46°40′N	16°14′E
Murtal, Port.	238d	38°42′N	9°22′W
Muruasigar, mtn., Kenya	217	3°08′N	35°02′E
Murwāra, India	183	23°54′N	80°23′E
Murwillumbah, Austl. (mŭr-wĭl′lŭm-bŭ)	204	28°15′S	153°30′E
Mürz, r., Aus. (mürts)	154	47°30′N	15°21′E
Mürzzuschlag, Aus. (mürts′tsōō-shlägh)	154	47°37′N	15°41′E
Mus, Tur. (mōōsh)	167	38°55′N	41°30′E
Musala, mtn., Bul.	161	42°05′N	23°24′E
Musan, N. Kor. (mō′sän)	189	41°11′N	129°10′E
Musashino, Japan (mōō-sä′shē-nō)	195a	35°43′N	139°35′E
Muscat, Oman (mŭs-kăt′)	182	23°23′N	58°30′E
Muscat and Oman see Oman, nation, Asia	182	20°00′N	57°45′E
Muscatine, Ia., U.S. (mŭs-kȧ-tēn)	103	41°26′N	91°00′W
Muscle Shoals, Al., U.S. (mŭs″l shōlz)	114	34°44′N	87°38′W
Musgrave Ranges, mts., Austl. (mŭs′grāv)	202	26°15′S	131°15′E
Mushie, D.R.C. (mŭsh′ē)	212	3°04′S	16°50′E
Mushin, Nig.	215	6°32′N	3°22′E
Musi, r., Indon. (mōō′sē)	196	2°40′S	103°42′E
Musinga, Alto, mtn., Col. (ä′l-tō-mōō-sē′n-gä)	130a	6°40′N	76°13′W
Muskego Lake, l., Wi., U.S. (mŭs-kē′gō)	101a	42°53′N	88°10′W
Muskegon, Mi., U.S. (mŭs-kē′gŭn)	97	43°15′N	86°20′W
Muskegon, r., Mi., U.S.	98	43°20′N	85°55′W
Muskegon Heights, Mi., U.S.	98	43°10′N	86°20′W
Muskingum, r., Oh., U.S. (mŭs-kĭŋ′gŭm)	98	39°45′N	81°55′W
Muskogee, Ok., U.S. (mŭs-kō′gē)	97	35°44′N	95°21′W
Muskoka, l., Can. (mŭs-kō′kȧ)	91	45°00′N	79°30′W
Musoma, Tan.	217	1°30′S	33°48′E
Mussau Island, i., Pap. N. Gui. (mōō-sä′ōō)	197	1°30′S	149°32′E
Musselshell, r., Mt., U.S. (mŭs″l-shĕl)	105	46°25′N	108°20′W
Mussende, Ang.	216	10°32′S	16°05′E
Mussuma, Ang.	216	14°14′S	21°59′E
Mustafakemalpaşa, Tur.	149	40°05′N	28°30′E
Mustang Bayou, Tx., U.S.	113a	29°22′N	95°12′W
Mustang Creek, r., Tx., U.S. (mŭs′tăng)	110	36°22′N	102°46′W
Mustang Island, i., Tx., U.S.	113	27°43′N	97°00′W
Mustique, i., St. Vin. (müs-tēk′)	121b	12°53′N	61°03′W
Musturud, Egypt	244a	30°08′N	31°17′E
Mustvee, Est. (mōōst′vĕ-ĕ)	153	58°50′N	26°54′E
Musu Dan, c., N. Kor. (mō′sō dän)	189	40°51′N	130°00′E
Muswellbrook, Austl. (mŭs′wŭnl-brōk)	204	32°15′S	150°50′E
Mutare, Zimb.	212	18°49′S	32°39′E
Mutombo Mukulu, D.R.C. (mōō-tôm′bō mōō-kōō′lōō)	212	8°12′S	23°56′E
Mutsu Wan, b., Japan (mōōt′sōō wän)	194	41°20′N	140°55′E
Mutton Bay, Can. (mŭt″n)	93	50°48′N	59°02′W
Mutum, Braz. (mōō-tōō′m)	129a	19°48′S	41°24′W
Muzaffargarh, Pak.	186	30°09′N	71°15′E
Muzaffarpur, India	186	26°13′N	85°20′E
Muzon, Cape, c., Ak., U.S.	86	54°41′N	132°44′W
Muzquiz, Mex. (mōōz′kēz)	112	27°53′N	101°31′W
Muztagata, mtn., China	188	38°20′N	75°28′E
Mvomero, Tan.	217	6°20′S	37°25′E
Mvoti, r., S. Afr.	213c	29°18′S	30°52′E
Mwali, i., Com.	213	12°15′S	43°45′E
Mwanza, Tan. (mwän′zä)	212	2°31′S	32°54′E
Mwaya, Tan. (mwä′yä)	212	9°19′S	33°51′E
Mwenga, D.R.C.	217	3°02′S	28°26′E
Mweru, l., Afr.	212	8°50′S	28°50′E
Mwingi, Kenya	217	0°56′S	38°04′E
Myanmar (Burma), nation, Asia	180	21°00′N	95°15′E
Myingyan, Myanmar (myĭng-yŭn′)	183	21°37′N	95°26′E
Myitkyina, Myanmar (myĭ′chē-nȧ)	183	25°33′N	97°25′E
Myjava, Slvk. (mûē′yȧ-vä)	155	48°45′N	17°33′E
Mykhailivka, Ukr.	163	47°16′N	35°12′E
Mykolaïv, Ukr.	164	46°58′N	32°02′E
Mykolaïv, prov., Ukr.	163	47°27′N	31°25′E
Mymensingh, Bngl.	183	24°48′N	90°28′E
Mynämäki, Fin.	153	60°41′N	21°58′E
Myohyang San, mtn., N. Kor. (myō′hyang)	194	40°00′N	126°12′E
Mýrdalsjökull, ice., Ice. (mür′däls-yû′kôl)	146	63°34′N	18°04′W
Myrhorod, Ukr.	167	49°56′N	33°36′E
Myrtle Beach, S.C., U.S. (mûr′t′l)	115	33°42′N	78°53′W
Myrtle Point, Or., U.S.	104	43°04′N	124°08′W
Mysen, Nor.	152	59°32′N	11°16′E
Myshikino, Russia (mēsh′kē-nō)	162	57°48′N	38°21′E
Mysore, India (mī-sōr′)	183	12°31′N	76°42′E
Mysovka, Russia (mē′ sôf-kȧ)	153	55°11′N	21°17′E
Mystic, Ia., U.S. (mĭs′tĭk)	103	40°47′N	92°54′W
Mytishchi, Russia (mē-tēsh′chi)	172b	55°55′N	37°46′E
Mziha, Tan.	217	5°54′S	37°47′E
Mzimba, Mwi. ('m-zĭm′bä)	212	11°52′S	33°34′E
Mzimkulu, r., Afr.	213c	30°12′S	29°57′E
Mzimvubu, r., S. Afr.	213c	31°22′S	29°20′E
Mzuzu, Mwi.	217	11°30′S	34°10′E

N

PLACE (Pronunciation)	PAGE	LAT.	LONG.
Naab, r., Ger. (näp)	154	49°38′N	12°15′E
Naaldwijk, Neth.	145a	52°00′N	4°11′E
Naalehu, Hi., U.S.	94a	19°00′N	155°35′W
Naantali, Fin. (nän′tȧ-lē)	153	60°29′N	22°03′E
Nabberu, l., Austl. (năb′ēr-ōō)	202	26°05′S	120°35′E
Naberezhnyye Chelny, Russia	164	55°42′N	52°19′E
Nabeul, Tun. (nä-bûl′)	210	36°34′N	10°45′E
Nabiswera, Ug.	217	1°28′N	32°16′E
Naboomspruit, S. Afr.	218d	24°32′S	28°43′E
Nābulus, W. Bank	181a	32°13′N	35°16′E
Nacala, Moz. (nă-kȧ′lȧ)	213	14°34′S	40°41′E
Nacaome, Hond. (nä-kä-ō′mȧ)	120	13°32′N	87°28′W
Na Cham, Viet (nä chäm′)	193	22°02′N	106°30′E
Naches, r., Wa., U.S. (năch′ĕz)	104	46°51′N	121°03′W
Náchod, Czech Rep. (näk′ôt)	154	50°25′N	16°08′E
Nächstebreck, neigh., Ger.	236	51°18′N	7°14′E
Nacimiento, Lake, res., Ca., U.S. (nȧ-sĭ-myĕn′tō)	108	35°50′N	121°00′W
Nacogdoches, Tx., U.S. (năk′ō-dō′chĕz)	113	31°36′N	94°40′W
Nadadores, Mex. (nä-dä-dō′rās)	112	27°04′N	101°36′W
Nadiād, India	186	22°45′N	72°51′E
Nadir, V.I.U.S.	117c	18°19′N	64°53′W
Nădlac, Rom.	161	46°09′N	20°52′E
Nadvirna, Ukr.	155	48°37′N	24°35′E
Nadym, r., Russia (nȧ′dĭm)	170	64°30′N	72°48′E
Naestved, Den. (nĕst′vĭdh)	146	55°14′N	11°46′E
Nafada, Nig.	215	11°08′N	11°20′E
Nafishah, Egypt	218c	30°34′N	32°15′E
Nafūd ad Dahy, des., Sau. Ar.	182	22°15′N	44°15′E
Nag, Co, l., China	186	31°38′N	91°18′E
Naga, Phil. (nä′gä)	197	13°37′N	123°12′E
Naga, i., Japan	195	32°09′N	130°16′E
Nagahama, Japan (nä′gä-hä′mä)	195	33°32′N	132°29′E
Nagahama, Japan	195	35°23′N	136°16′E
Nagaland, India	183	25°47′N	94°15′E
Nagano, Japan (nä′gä-nō)	189	36°42′N	138°12′E
Nagao, Japan	242b	34°50′N	135°43′E
Nagaoka, Japan (nä′gȧ-ō′kȧ)	189	37°22′N	138°49′E
Nagaoka, Japan	195b	34°54′N	135°42′E
Nagappattinam, India	183	10°48′N	79°51′E
Nagarote, Nic. (nä-gä-rō′tē)	120	12°17′N	86°35′W
Nagasaki, Japan (nä′gȧ-sä′kē)	189	32°48′N	129°53′E
Nagata, neigh., Japan	242b	34°40′N	135°09′E
Nagatino, neigh., Russia	239b	55°41′N	37°41′E

ng-sing; ŋ-baŋk; ɴ-nasalized n; nŏd; cŏmmit; ōld; ôbey; ôrder; oi-boil; fōōd; ȯ-as oo in foot; ou-out; s-soft; sh-dish; th-thin; pūre; ûnite; ûrn; stŭd; circŭs; ü-as in French tu; ′-indeterminate vowel.

PLACE (Pronunciation)	PAGE	LAT.	LONG.
Nagatsuta, neigh., Japan	242a	35°32′N	139°30′E
Nāgaur, India	186	27°19′N	73°41′E
Nagaybakskiy, Russia (nȧ-gȧy-bäk′skĭ)	172a	53°33′N	59°33′E
Nagcarlan, Phil. (näg-kär-län′)	197a	14°07′N	121°24′E
Nāgercoil, India	187	8°15′N	77°29′E
Nagorno Karabakh, hist. reg., Azer. (nu-gôr′nŭ-kŭ-rŭ-bäk′)	167	40°10′N	46°50′E
Nagoya, Japan	189	35°09′N	136°53′E
Nāgpur, India (näg′po͞or)	183	21°12′N	79°09′E
Nagua, Dom. Rep. (nȧ′gwä)	123	19°20′N	69°40′W
Nagykanizsa, Hung. (nôd′y’kô′nė-shô)	149	46°27′N	17°00′E
Nagykōrōs, Hung. (nôd′y’kŭ-rŭsh)	155	47°02′N	19°46′E
Nagytarcsa, Hung.	239g	47°32′N	19°17′E
Naha, Japan (nä′hä)	189	26°02′N	127°43′E
Nahanni National Park, rec., Can.	84	62°10′N	125°15′W
Nahant, Ma., U.S. (nȧ-hănt)	93a	42°26′N	70°55′W
Nahant Bay, b., Ma., U.S.	227a	42°27′N	70°55′W
Nahariyya, Isr.	181a	33°01′N	35°06′E
Nahaut, Ma., U.S.	227a	42°25′N	70°55′W
Nahmer, Ger.	236	51°20′N	7°35′E
Nahuel Huapi, l., Arg. (nä′wl wä′pė)	132	41°00′S	71°30′W
Nahuizalco, El Sal. (nä-wė-zäl′kō)	120	13°50′N	89°43′W
Naic, Phil. (nä-ēk)	197a	14°20′N	120°46′E
Naica, Mex. (nä-ē′kä)	112	27°53′N	105°30′W
Naiguata, Pico, mtn., Ven. (pē′kȯ)	131b	10°32′N	66°44′W
Naihāti, India	240a	22°54′N	88°25′E
Nain, Can. (nīn)	85	56°29′N	61°52′W
Nā′īn, Iran	185	32°52′N	53°05′E
Nairn, Scot., U.K. (nârn)	150	57°35′N	3°54′W
Nairobi, Kenya (nī-rō′bė)	212	1°17′S	36°49′E
Naivasha, Kenya (nī-vä′shȧ)	212	0°47′S	36°29′E
Najd, hist. reg., Sau. Ar.	182	25°18′N	42°38′E
Najin, N. Kor. (nä′jĭn)	189	42°04′N	130°35′E
Najran, des., Sau. Ar. (nŭj-rän′)	182	17°29′N	45°30′E
Naju, S. Kor. (nä′jo͞o′)	194	35°02′N	126°42′E
Najusa, r., Cuba (nä-ho͞o′sä)	122	20°55′N	77°55′W
Naka, r., Japan	242a	35°39′N	139°51′E
Nakajima, Japan	242a	35°26′N	139°56′E
Nakanobu, neigh., Japan	242a	35°36′N	139°43′E
Nakatsu, Japan (nä′käts-o͞o)	194	33°34′N	131°10′E
Nakhodka, Russia (nŭ-κôt′kŭ)	165	43°03′N	133°08′E
Nakhon Ratchasima, Thai.	196	14°56′N	102°14′E
Nakhon Sawan, Thai.	196	15°42′N	100°06′E
Nakhon Si Thammarat, Thai.	196	8°27′N	99°58′E
Nakło nad Notecia, Pol.	155	53°10′N	17°35′E
Nakskov, Den. (näk′skou)	146	54°51′N	11°06′E
Naktong, r., S. Kor. (näk′tŭng)	194	36°10′N	128°30′E
Nal′chik, Russia (nȧl-chēk′)	167	43°30′N	43°35′E
Nalón, r., Spain (nä-lōn′)	158	43°15′N	5°38′W
Nālūt, Libya (nä-lo͞ot′)	210	31°51′N	10°49′E
Namak, Daryacheh-ye, l., Iran	182	34°58′N	51°33′E
Namakan, l., Mn., U.S. (nă′mȧ-kȧn)	103	48°20′N	92°43′W
Namamugi, neigh., Japan	242a	35°29′N	139°41′E
Namangan, Uzb. (nȧ-mȧn-gän′)	169	41°08′N	71°59′E
Namao, Can.	83g	53°43′N	113°30′W
Namatanai, Pap. N. Gui. (nä′mä-tȧ-nä′ė)	197	3°43′S	152°26′E
Nambour, Austl. (năm′bȯr)	204	26°48′S	153°00′E
Nam Co, l., China (näm tswo)	188	30°30′N	91°10′E
Nam Dinh, Viet (näm dēnκ′)	196	20°30′N	106°10′E
Nametil, Moz.	217	15°43′S	39°21′E
Namhae, i., S. Kor. (näm′hī′)	194	34°23′N	128°05′E
Namib Desert, des., Nmb. (nä-mēb′)	212	18°45′S	12°45′E
Namibia, nation, Afr.	212	19°30′S	16°13′E
Namoi, r., Austl. (nămȯi)	203	30°10′S	148°43′E
Namous, Oued en, r., Alg. (nȧ-mo͞os′)	148	31°48′N	0°19′W
Nampa, Id., U.S. (năm′pȧ)	96	43°35′N	116°35′W
Namp′o, N. Kor.	189	38°47′N	125°28′E
Nampuecha, Moz.	217	13°59′S	40°18′E
Nampula, Moz.	217	15°07′S	39°15′E
Namsos, Nor. (näm′sȯs)	146	64°28′N	11°14′E
Namu, Can.	86	51°53′N	127°50′W
Namuli, Serra, mts., Moz.	217	15°05′S	37°05′E
Namur, Bel. (nȧ-mür′)	147	50°29′N	4°55′E
Namutoni, Nmb. (nȧ-mo͞o-tō′nė)	212	18°45′S	17°00′E
Nan, r., Thai.	196	18°11′N	100°29′E
Nanacamilpa, Mex. (nä-nä-kä-mė′l-pä)	119a	19°30′N	98°33′W
Nanaimo, Can. (nȧ-nī′mō)	84	49°10′N	123°56′W
Nanam, N. Kor. (nä′nän′)	194	41°38′N	129°37′E
Nanao, Japan (nä′nä-ō)	194	37°03′N	136°59′E
Nan′ao Dao, i., China (nän-ou dou)	193	23°30′N	117°30′E
Nancefield, S. Afr.	244b	26°17′S	27°53′E
Nanchang, China (nän′chäng′)	189	28°38′N	115°48′E
Nanchangshan Dao, i., China (nän-chäŋ-shän dou)	190	37°56′N	120°42′E
Nancheng, China (nän-chäŋ)	189	26°50′N	116°40′E
Nanchong, China (nän-chȯŋ)	188	30°45′N	106°05′E
Nancy, Fr. (näɴ-sē′)	147	48°42′N	6°11′E
Nancy Creek, r., Ga., U.S. (năn′cē)	100c	33°51′N	84°25′W
Nanda Devi, mtn., India (nän′dä dā′vē)	183	30°30′N	80°25′E
Nānded, India	186	19°13′N	77°21′E
Nandurbār, India	186	21°29′N	74°13′E
Nandyāl, India	187	15°54′N	78°09′E
Nanga Parbat, mtn., Pak.	186	35°20′N	74°35′E
Nangi, India	186a	22°30′N	88°14′E
Nangis, Fr. (näɴ-zhē′)	157b	48°33′N	3°01′E
Nangong, China (nän-gȯŋ)	192	37°22′N	115°22′E
Nangweshi, Zam.	216	16°26′S	23°17′E
Nanhuangcheng Dao, i., China (nän-hůäŋ-chŭŋ dou)	190	38°22′N	120°54′E
Nanhui, China	190	31°03′N	121°45′E
Naniwa, neigh., Japan	242b	34°39′N	135°30′E
Nanjing, China (nän-jyĭŋ)	189	32°04′N	118°46′E

PLACE (Pronunciation)	PAGE	LAT.	LONG.
Nanjuma, r., China (nän-jyo͞o-mä)	190	39°37′N	115°45′E
Nanking *see* Nanjing, China	188	32°04′N	118°46′E
Nanle, China (nän-lŭ)	190	36°03′N	115°13′E
Nan Ling, mts., China	189	25°15′N	111°40′E
Nanliu, r., China (nän-lĭȯ)	193	22°00′N	109°18′E
Nannine, Austl. (nă-nēn′)	202	25°50′S	118°30′E
Nanning, China (nän′nĭng′)	188	22°56′N	108°10′E
Nānole, neigh., India	240e	19°01′N	72°55′E
Nanpan, r., China (nän-pän)	193	24°50′N	105°30′E
Nanping, China (nän-pĭŋ)	189	26°40′N	118°05′E
Nansei-shotō, is., Japan	189	27°30′N	127°00′E
Nansemond, Va., U.S. (năn′sė-mŭnd)	100g	36°46′N	76°32′W
Nantai Zan, mtn., Japan (nän-täė zän)	194	36°47′N	139°28′E
Nanterre, Fr.	237c	48°53′N	2°12′E
Nantes, Fr. (näɴt′)	142	47°13′N	1°37′W
Nanteuil-le-Haudouin, Fr. (näɴ-tû-lĕ-ō-dwȧɴ′)	157b	49°08′N	2°49′E
Nanticoke, Pa., U.S. (năn′tī-kōk)	99	41°10′N	76°00′W
Nantong, China (nän-tȯŋ)	190	32°02′N	120°51′E
Nantong, China	190	32°08′N	121°06′E
Nantouillet, Fr.	237c	49°00′N	2°42′E
Nantucket, i., Ma., U.S. (năn-tŭk′ĕt)	97	41°15′N	70°05′W
Nantwich, Eng., U.K. (nănt′wĭch)	144a	53°04′N	2°31′W
Nanxiang, China (nän-shyäŋ)	190	31°17′N	121°17′E
Nanxiong, China (nän-shȯŋ)	193	25°10′N	114°20′E
Nanyang, China	189	33°00′N	112°42′E
Nanyang Hu, l., China (nän-yäŋ ho͞o)	190	35°14′N	116°24′E
Nanyuan, China (nän-yůän)	192a	39°48′N	116°24′E
Naoābād, India	240a	22°28′N	88°27′E
Naolinco, Mex. (nä-o-lēŋ′kō)	119	19°39′N	96°50′W
Naopukuria, India	240a	22°55′N	88°16′E
Náousa, Grc. (nä′o͞o-sȧ)	161	40°38′N	22°05′E
Naozhou Dao, i., China (nou-jō dou)	193	20°58′N	110°58′E
Napa, Ca., U.S. (năp′ȧ)	96	38°20′N	122°17′W
Napanee, Can. (năp′ȧ-nē)	91	44°15′N	77°00′W
Naperville, Il., U.S. (nā′pẽr-vĭl)	101a	41°46′N	88°09′W
Napier, N.Z. (nā′pĭ-ẽr)	203a	39°30′S	177°00′E
Napierville, Can. (nā′pī-ẽ-vĭl)	83a	45°11′N	73°24′W
Naples (Napoli), Italy	142	40°37′N	14°12′E
Naples, Fl., U.S. (nă′p’lz)	115a	26°07′N	81°46′W
Napo, r., S.A. (nä′pō)	130	1°49′S	74°20′W
Napoleon, Oh., U.S. (nȧ-pō′lē-ŭn)	98	41°20′N	84°10′W
Napoleonville, La., U.S. (nȧ-pō′lė-ŭn-vĭl)	113	29°56′N	91°03′W
Napoli *see* Naples, Italy	142	40°37′N	14°12′E
Napoli, Golfo di, b., Italy	148	40°29′N	14°08′E
Nappanee, In., U.S. (năp′ȧ-nē)	98	41°30′N	86°00′W
Nara, Japan (nä′rä)	189	34°41′N	135°50′E
Nara, Mali	210	15°09′N	7°27′W
Nara, dept., Japan	195b	34°36′N	135°49′E
Nara, r., Russia	162	55°05′N	37°16′E
Naracoorte, Austl. (nȧ-rȧ-ko͞on′tė)	202	36°50′S	140°50′E
Narashino, Japan	195a	35°41′N	140°01′E
Naraspur, India	187	16°32′N	81°43′E
Nārāyanpāra, India	240a	22°54′N	88°19′E
Narbėrth, Pa., U.S. (när′bûrth)	100f	40°01′N	75°17′W
Narbonne, Fr. (nȧr-bȯn′)	147	43°12′N	3°00′E
Nare, Col. (nä′rĕ)	130a	6°12′N	74°37′W
Narew, r., Pol. (när′ĕf)	155	52°43′N	21°19′E
Narmada, r., India	183	22°30′N	75°30′E
Naroch′, l., Bela. (nä′rôch)	162	54°51′N	27°00′E
Narodnaya, Gora, mtn., Russia (nȧ-rôd′nȧ-yȧ)	164	65°10′N	60°10′E
Naro-Fominsk, Russia (nä′rȯ-mēnsk′)	166	55°23′N	36°43′E
Narrabeen, Austl. (năr-ȧ-bĭn)	201b	33°44′S	151°18′E
Narragansett, R.I., U.S. (năr-ă-găn′sĕt)	100b	41°26′N	71°27′W
Narragansett Bay, b., R.I., U.S.	99	41°20′N	71°15′W
Narrandera, Austl. (nȧ-rȧn-dē′rȧ)	203	34°40′S	146°40′E
Narraweena, Austl.	243a	33°45′S	151°16′E
Narre Warren North, Austl.	243b	37°59′S	145°19′E
Narrogin, Austl. (năr′ȯ-gĭn)	202	33°00′S	117°15′E
Naruo, Japan	242b	34°43′N	135°23′E
Narva, Est. (nȧr′vȧ)	166	59°24′N	28°12′E
Narvacan, Phil. (när-vä-kän′)	197a	17°27′N	120°29′E
Narva Jõesuu, Est. (nȧr′vȧ ȯ-ô-ă′so͞o-ȯ)	153	59°26′N	28°02′E
Narvik, Nor. (när′vėk)	142	68°21′N	17°18′E
Narvskiy Zaliv, b., Eur. (nȧr′vskĭ zä′lĭf)	153	59°35′N	27°25′E
Narvskoye, res., Eur.	153	59°18′N	28°14′E
Nar′yan-Mar, Russia (när′yȧn mär′)	164	67°42′N	53°30′E
Naryilco, Austl. (năr-ĭl′kȯ)	204	28°40′S	141°50′E
Narym, Russia (nä-rēm′)	164	58°47′N	82°05′E
Naryn, r., Asia (nŭ-rĭn′)	170	41°20′N	76°00′E
Naseby, Eng., U.K. (nāz′bĭ)	144a	52°23′N	0°59′W
Nashua, Mo., U.S. (năsh′ŭ-ȧ)	107f	39°18′N	94°34′W
Nashua, N.H., U.S.	97	42°47′N	71°23′W
Nashville, Ar., U.S. (năsh′vĭl)	111	33°56′N	93°50′W
Nashville, Ga., U.S.	114	31°12′N	83°15′W
Nashville, Il., U.S.	111	38°21′N	89°42′W
Nashville, Mi., U.S.	98	42°35′N	85°50′W
Nashville, Tn., U.S.	97	36°10′N	86°48′W
Nashwauk, Mn., U.S. (năsh′wôk)	103	47°21′N	93°12′W
Näsi, l., Fin.	146	61°42′N	24°05′E
Našice, Cro. (nä′shė-tsĕ)	149	45°29′N	18°06′E
Nasielsk, Pol. (nä′syĕlsk)	155	52°35′N	20°50′E
Nāsik, India (nä′sĭk)	183	20°02′N	73°49′E
Nāşir, Sudan (nä-zēr′)	211	8°30′N	33°06′E
Nasirabād, India	186	26°13′N	74°48′E
Naskaupi, r., Can. (näs′kô-pĭ)	85	53°59′N	61°10′W
Nasondoye, D.R.C.	217	10°22′S	25°06′E
Nass, r., Can. (năs)	86	55°00′N	129°30′W
Nassau, Bah. (năs′ô)	117	25°05′N	77°20′W
Nassenheide, Ger. (nä′sĕn-hī-dĕ)	145b	52°49′N	13°13′E
Nasser, Lake, res., Egypt	211	23°50′N	32°50′E

PLACE (Pronunciation)	PAGE	LAT.	LONG.
Nasugbu, Phil. (nȧ-sȯg-bo͞o′)	197a	14°05′N	120°37′E
Nasworthy Lake, l., Tx., U.S. (năz′wûr-thė)	112	31°17′N	100°30′W
Natagaima, Col. (nä-tä-gī′mä)	130a	3°38′N	75°07′W
Nātāgarh, India	240a	22°42′N	88°25′E
Natal, Braz. (nä-täl′)	131	6°00′S	35°13′W
Natalspruit, S. Afr.	244b	26°19′S	28°09′E
Natashquan, Can. (nä-tăsh′kwän)	85	50°11′N	61°49′W
Natashquan, r., Can.	93	50°35′N	61°35′W
Natchez, Ms., U.S. (năch′ĕz)	97	31°35′N	91°20′W
Natchitoches, La., U.S. (năk′ĭ-tŏsh)(nȧch-ĭ-tōsh′)	113	31°46′N	93°06′W
Natick, Ma., U.S. (nā′tĭk)	93a	42°17′N	71°21′W
National Bison Range, I.R., Mt., U.S. (năsh′ŭn-ăl bī′s’n)	105	47°18′N	113°58′W
National City, Ca., U.S.	108a	32°38′N	117°01′W
National Park, Pa., U.S.	229b	39°51′N	75°12′W
Natitingou, Benin	210	10°19′N	1°22′E
Natividade, Braz. (nä-tė-vė-dä′dĕ)	131	11°43′S	47°34′W
Natron, Lake, l., Tan. (nā′trŏn)	212	2°17′S	36°10′E
Natrona Heights, Pa., U.S. (nā′trŏ nā)	101e	40°38′N	79°43′W
Naţrūn, Wādī an, val., Egypt	218b	30°33′N	30°12′E
Natuna Besar, i., Indon.	196	4°00′N	106°50′E
Natural Bridges National Monument, rec., Ut., U.S. (năt′ů-răl brĭj′ĕs)	109	37°20′N	110°20′W
Naturaliste, Cape, c., Austl. (năt-ů-rȧ-lĭst′)	202	33°30′S	115°10′E
Nau, Cap de la, c., Spain	142	38°43′N	0°14′E
Naucalpan de Juárez, Mex.	119a	19°28′N	99°14′W
Nauchampatepetl, mtn., Mex. (näo͞o-chäm-pä-tĕ′pĕtl)	119	19°32′N	97°09′W
Nauen, Ger. (nou′ĕn)	145b	52°36′N	12°53′E
Naugatuck, Ct., U.S. (nô′gȧ-tŭk)	99	41°25′N	73°05′W
Naujan, Phil. (nä-ȯ-hän′)	197a	13°19′N	121°17′E
Naumburg, Ger. (noum′bȯrgh)	154	51°10′N	11°50′E
Naupada, neigh., India	240e	19°04′N	72°50′E
Nauru, nation, Oc.	3	0°30′S	167°00′E
Nautla, Mex. (nä-o͞ot′lä)	116	20°14′N	96°44′W
Nava, Mex. (nä′vä)	112	28°25′N	100°44′W
Nava del Rey, Spain (nä-vä dĕl rā′ė)	158	41°22′N	5°04′W
Navahermosa, Spain (nä-vä-ĕr-mō′sä)	158	39°39′N	4°28′W
Navajas, Cuba (nä-vä-häs′)	122	22°40′N	81°20′W
Navajo Hopi Joint Use Area, I.R., Az., U.S.	109	36°15′N	110°30′W
Navajo Indian Reservation, I.R., U.S. (năv′ȧ-hō)	109	36°31′N	109°24′W
Navajo National Monument, rec., Az., U.S.	109	36°43′N	110°39′W
Navajo Reservoir, res., N.M., U.S.	109	36°57′N	107°26′W
Navalcarnero, Spain (nä-väl′kär-nā′rō)	159a	40°17′N	4°05′W
Navalmoral de la Mata, Spain	158	39°53′N	5°32′W
Navan, Can. (nă′vȧn)	83c	45°25′N	75°26′W
Navarino, i., Chile (nȧ-vä-rė′nȯ)	132	55°30′S	68°15′W
Navarra, hist. reg., Spain (nä-vär′rä)	158	42°40′N	1°35′W
Navarro, Arg. (nä-vȧ′r-rō)	129c	35°00′S	59°16′W
Navasota, Tx., U.S. (năv-aȧ-sō′tȧ)	113	30°24′N	96°05′W
Navasota, r., Tx., U.S.	113	31°03′N	96°11′W
Navassa, i., N.A. (nȧ-vȧs′ȧ)	123	18°25′N	75°15′W
Navestock, Eng., U.K.	235	51°39′N	0°13′E
Navestock Side, Eng., U.K.	235	51°39′N	0°16′E
Navia, r., Spain (nä-vē′ä)	158	43°10′N	6°45′W
Navidad, Chile (nä-vė-dä′d)	129b	33°57′S	71°51′W
Navidad Bank, bk. (nä-vė-dädh′)	123	20°05′N	69°00′W
Navidade do Carangola, Braz. (nȧ-vē-dä′dȯ-kȧ-rän-gô′la)	129a	21°04′S	41°58′W
Navojoa, Mex. (nä-vȯ-kô′ä)	116	27°00′N	109°40′W
Navotas, Phil.	241g	14°40′N	120°57′E
Nàvplion, Grc.	161	37°33′N	22°46′E
Nawābshāh, Pak. (nȧ-wäb′shä)	186	26°20′N	68°30′E
Naxçıvan, Azer.	167	39°10′N	45°30′E
Naxçıvan Muxtar, state, Azer.	168	39°20′N	45°30′E
Náxos, i., Grc. (nȧk′sȯs)	149	37°15′N	25°20′E
Nayābās, India	240d	28°35′N	77°19′E
Nayarit, state, Mex. (nä-yä-rēt′)	116	22°00′N	105°15′W
Nayarit, Sierra de, mts., Mex. (sē-ĕ′r-rä-dĕ)	118	23°20′N	105°07′W
Naye, Sen.	214	14°25′N	12°12′W
Naylor, Md., U.S. (nā′lŏr)	100e	38°43′N	76°46′W
Nazaré da Mata, Braz. (dä-mä-tä)	131	7°46′S	35°13′W
Nazas, Mex. (nä′zäs)	112	25°14′N	104°08′W
Nazas, r., Mex.	116	25°30′N	104°40′W
Nazerat, Isr.	181a	32°43′N	35°19′E
Nazilli, Tur. (nȧ-zĭ-lē′)	167	37°40′N	28°10′E
Naziya, r., Russia (nȧ-zē′yȧ)	172c	59°48′N	31°18′E
Nazko, r., Can.	86	52°35′N	123°10′W
Nazlat as-Sammān, Egypt	244a	29°59′N	31°08′E
Nazlat Khalīfah, Egypt	244a	30°01′N	31°10′E
N′dalatando, Ang.	216	9°18′S	14°54′E
Ndali, Benin	215	9°51′N	2°43′E
Ndikiniméki, Cam.	215	4°46′N	10°50′E
N′Djamena, Chad	211	12°07′N	15°03′E
Ndjili, neigh., D.R.C.	244c	4°21′S	15°19′E
Ndola, Zam. (n’dō′lä)	212	12°58′S	28°38′E
Ndoto Mountains, mts., Kenya	217	1°55′N	37°05′E
Ndrhamcha, Sebkha de, l., Maur.	214	18°50′N	15°15′W
Nduye, D.R.C.	217	1°50′N	29°01′E
Neagh, Lough, l., N. Ire., U.K. (lŏk nā)	146	54°40′N	6°47′W
Néa Ionía, Grc.	239d	38°02′N	23°45′E
Néa Liósia, Grc.	239d	38°02′N	23°42′E
Néa Páfos, Cyp.	181a	34°46′N	32°27′E
Neapean, r., Austl.	201b	33°40′S	150°39′E
Neápolis, Grc.	160a	35°17′N	25°37′E
Neápolis, Grc. (nȧ-ŏp′ ȯ-lĭs)	161	36°35′N	23°08′E
Near Islands, is., Ak., U.S. (nēr)	95a	52°20′N	172°40′E

PRONOUNCING INDEX Near North Side–New Mills 323

PLACE (Pronunciation)	PAGE	LAT.	LONG.
Near North Side, neigh., Il., U.S.	231a	41°54'N	87°38'W
Néa Smírni, Grc.	239d	37°57'N	23°43'E
Neath, Wales, U.K. (nēth)	150	51°41'N	3°50'W
Nebine Creek, r., Austl. (nĕ-bēne')	204	27°50'S	147°00'E
Nebitdag, Turk.	170	39°30'N	54°20'E
Nebraska, state, U.S. (nē-brăs'kȧ)	96	41°45'N	101°30'W
Nebraska City, Ne., U.S.	111	40°40'N	95°50'W
Nechako, r., Can.	86	53°45'N	124°55'W
Nechako Plateau, plat., Can. (nĭ-chă'kō)	86	54°00'N	124°30'W
Nechako Range, mts., Can.	86	53°20'N	124°30'W
Nechako Reservoir, res., Can.	86	53°25'N	125°10'W
Neches, r., Tx., U.S. (nĕch'ĕz)	113	31°03'N	94°40'W
Neckar, r., Ger. (nĕk'är)	154	49°16'N	9°06'E
Necker Island, i., Hi., U.S.	94b	24°00'N	164°00'W
Necochea, Arg. (nā-kô-chā'ä)	132	38°30'S	58°45'W
Nedlitz, neigh., Ger.	238a	52°26'N	13°03'E
Nedryhailiv, Ukr.	163	50°49'N	33°52'E
Needham, Ma., U.S. (nēd'ăm)	93a	42°17'N	71°14'W
Needham Heights, Ma., U.S.	227a	41°28'N	71°14'W
Needles, Ca., U.S. (nē'd'lz)	109	34°51'N	114°39'W
Neenah, Wi., U.S. (nē'nȧ)	103	44°10'N	88°30'W
Neepawa, Can.	84	50°13'N	99°29'W
Nee Reservoir, res., Co., U.S. (nee)	110	38°26'N	102°56'W
Nee Soon, Sing.	240c	1°24'N	103°49'E
Negareyama, Japan (nā'gā-rå-yä'mä)	195a	35°52'N	139°54'E
Negaunee, Mi., U.S. (nē-gô'nē)	103	46°30'N	87°37'W
Negeri Sembilan, state, Malay. (nā'grē-sĕm-bē-län')	181b	2°46'N	101°54'E
Negev, des., Isr. (nĕ'gĕv)	181a	30°34'N	34°43'E
Negombo, Sri L.	187	7°39'N	79°49'E
Negotin, Yugo. (nĕ'gô-tēn)	161	44°13'N	22°33'E
Negro, r., Arg.	132	39°50'S	65°00'W
Negro, r., N.A.	120	13°01'N	87°10'W
Negro, r., S.A.	129c	33°17'S	58°18'W
Negro, Cerro, mtn., Pan. (sĕ'-rrô-nā'grō)	121	8°44'N	80°37'W
Negro, Rio, r., S.A. (rē'ō nā'grō)	130	0°18'S	63°21'W
Negros, i., Phil. (nā'grōs)	196	9°50'N	121°45'E
Nehalem, r., Or., U.S. (nē-hăl'ĕm)	104	45°52'N	123°37'W
Nehaus an der Oste, Ger. (noi'houz)(ōz'tē)	145c	53°48'N	9°02'E
Nehbandān, Iran	185	31°32'N	60°02'E
Nehe, China (nŭ-hŭ)	192	48°23'N	124°58'E
Neheim-Hüsten, Ger. (nĕ'hīm)	157c	51°28'N	7°58'E
Neiba, Dom. Rep. (nå-ē'bä)	123	18°30'N	71°20'W
Neiba, Bahía de, b., Dom. Rep.	123	18°10'N	71°00'W
Neiba, Sierra de, mts., Dom. Rep. (sē-ĕr'rä-dĕ)	123	18°40'N	71°40'W
Neihart, Mt., U.S. (nī'hårt)	105	46°54'N	110°39'W
Neijiang, China (nā-jyäŋ)	193	29°38'N	105°01'E
Neillsville, Wi., U.S. (nēlz'vĭl)	103	44°35'N	90°37'W
Neiqiu, China (nā-chyō)	190	37°17'N	114°32'E
Neira, Col. (nā'rä)	130a	5°10'N	75°32'W
Neisse, r., Eur. (nēs)	154	51°30'N	15°00'E
Neiva, Col. (nå-ē'vä)(nā'vä)	130	2°55'N	75°16'W
Neixiang, China (nā-shyäŋ)	192	33°00'N	111°38'E
Nekemte, Eth.	211	9°09'N	36°29'E
Nekoosa, Wi., U.S. (nē-ko͞o'sȧ)	103	44°19'N	89°54'W
Neligh, Ne., U.S. (nē'-lē)	102	42°06'N	98°02'W
Nel'kan, Russia (nĕl-kän')	165	57°45'N	136°36'E
Nellore, India (nĕl-lōr')	183	14°28'N	79°59'E
Nel'ma, Russia (nĕl-mä')	194	47°34'N	139°05'E
Nelson, Can. (nĕl'sŭn)	84	49°29'N	117°17'W
Nelson, N.Z.	203a	41°15'S	173°22'E
Nelson, Eng., U.K.	144a	53°50'N	2°13'W
Nelson, i., Ak., U.S.	95	60°38'N	164°42'W
Nelson, r., Can.	89	56°50'N	93°40'W
Nelson, Cape, c., Austl.	204	38°29'S	141°20'E
Nelsonville, Oh., U.S. (nĕl'sŭn-vĭl)	98	39°30'N	82°15'W
Néma, Maur. (nā'mä)	210	16°37'N	7°15'W
Nemadji, r., Wi., U.S. (nĕ-măd'jē)	107h	46°33'N	92°16'W
Neman, Russia (nyĕ'-mȧn)	153	55°02'N	22°01'E
Neman, r., Eur.	166	53°28'N	24°45'E
Nematābād, Iran	241h	35°38'N	51°21'E
Nembe, Nig.	215	4°35'N	6°26'E
Nemčinovka, Russia	239b	55°43'N	37°23'E
Nemeiben Lake, l., Can. (nĕ-mē'bȧn)	88	55°20'N	105°20'W
Nemours, Fr.	156	48°16'N	2°41'E
Nemuro, Japan (nā'mō-rō)	189	43°13'N	145°10'E
Nemuro Strait, strt., Asia	194	43°07'N	145°10'E
Nemyriv, Ukr.	163	48°56'N	28°51'E
Nen, r., China (nŭn)	189	47°07'N	123°28'E
Nen, r., Eng., U.K. (nĕn)	144a	52°32'N	0°19'W
Nenagh, Ire. (nē'nȧ)	150	52°50'N	8°05'W
Nenana, Ak., U.S. (nå-nä'nȧ)	95	64°28'N	149°18'W
Nenikyul', Russia (nĕ-nyĕ'kyûl)	172c	59°26'N	30°40'E
Nenjiang, China (nŭn-jyäŋ)	189	49°02'N	125°15'E
Neodesha, Ks., U.S. (nē-ô-dĕ-shô')	111	37°24'N	95°41'W
Neosho, Mo., U.S.	111	36°51'N	94°22'W
Neosho, r., Ks., U.S. (nē-ō'shō)	111	38°07'N	95°40'W
Nepal, nation, Asia (nĕ-pôl')	183	28°45'N	83°00'E
Nephi, Ut., U.S. (nē'fī)	109	39°40'N	111°50'W
Nepomuceno, Braz. (nĕ-pô-mo͞o-sĕ'no)	129a	21°15'S	45°13'W
Nera, r., Italy (nā'rä)	160	42°45'N	12°54'E
Nérac, Fr. (nā-råk')	156	44°08'N	0°19'E
Nerchinsk, Russia (nyĕr' chĕnsk)	165	51°47'N	116°17'E
Nerchinskiy Khrebet, mts., Russia	165	50°30'N	118°30'E
Nerchinskiy Zavod, Russia (nyĕr'chĕn-skĭzá-vôt')	165	51°35'N	119°46'E
Nerekhta, Russia (nyĕ-rĕk'tá)	162	57°29'N	40°34'E
Neretva, r., Yugo. (nĕ'rĕt-vá)	161	43°08'N	17°50'E
Nerja, Spain (nĕr'hä)	158	36°45'N	3°53'W
Nerl', r., Russia (nyĕrl)	162	56°59'N	37°57'E
Nerskaya, r., Russia (nyĕr'ská-yȧ)	172b	55°31'N	38°46'E
Nerussa, r., Russia (nyå-ro͞o'sȧ)	162	52°24'N	34°20'E
Ness, Eng., U.K.	237a	53°17'N	3°03'W
Ness, Loch, l., Scot., U.K. (lŏĸ nĕs)	150	57°23'N	4°20'W
Ness City, Ks., U.S. (nĕs)	110	38°27'N	99°55'W
Nesterov, Russia (nyĕs-tă'rôf)	153	54°39'N	22°38'E
Neston, Eng., U.K.	237a	53°18'N	3°04'W
Néstos (Mesta), r., Eur. (nās'tōs)	161	41°25'N	24°12'E
Nesvizh, Bela. (nyĕs'vēsh)	162	53°13'N	26°44'E
Netanya, Isr.	181a	32°19'N	34°52'E
Netcong, N.J., U.S. (nĕt'cŏnj)	100a	40°54'N	74°42'W
Netherlands, nation, Eur. (nĕdh'ĕr-lăndz)	142	53°01'N	3°57'E
Netherlands Guiana see Suriname, nation, S.A.	131	4°00'N	56°00'W
Netherton, Eng., U.K.	237a	53°30'N	2°58'W
Nette, neigh., Ger.	236	51°33'N	7°25'E
Nettilling, l., Can.	85	66°30'N	70°40'W
Nett Lake Indian Reservation, I.R., Mn., U.S. (nĕt lāk)	103	48°23'N	93°19'W
Nettuno, Italy (nĕt-to͞o'nô)	159d	41°28'N	12°40'E
Neubeckum, Ger. (noi'bĕ-ko͞om)	157c	51°48'N	8°01'E
Neubrandenburg, Ger. (noi-brän'dĕn-bôrgh)	154	53°33'N	13°16'E
Neuburg, Ger. (noi'bôrgh)	154	48°43'N	11°12'E
Neuchâtel, Switz. (nû-shá-tĕl')	147	47°00'N	6°52'E
Neuchâtel, Lac de, l., Switz.	154	46°48'N	6°53'E
Neudorf, neigh., Ger.	236	51°25'N	6°47'E
Neuenhagen, Ger. (noi'ĕn-hä-gĕn)	145b	52°31'N	13°41'E
Neuenhof, neigh., Ger.	236	51°10'N	7°13'E
Neuenkamp, neigh., Ger.	236	51°26'N	6°44'E
Neuenrade, Ger. (noi'ĕn-rä-dĕ)	157c	51°17'N	7°47'E
Neu-Erlaa, neigh., Aus.	239e	48°08'N	16°19'E
Neu Fahrland, Ger.	238a	52°26'N	13°03'E
Neufchâtel-en-Bray, Fr. (nû-shä-tĕl'ĕɴ-brā')	156	49°43'N	1°25'E
Neuilly-sur-Marne, Fr.	237c	48°51'N	2°32'E
Neuilly-sur-Seine, Fr.	237c	48°53'N	2°16'E
Neukirchen, Ger.	236	51°27'N	6°33'E
Neulengbach, Aus.	145e	48°13'N	15°55'E
Neumarkt, Ger. (noi'märkt)	154	49°17'N	11°30'E
Neumünster, Ger. (noi'münstĕr)	146	54°04'N	10°00'E
Neunkirchen, Aus. (noin'kĭrĸ-ĕn)	154	47°43'N	16°05'E
Neuquén, Arg. (nĕ-ō-kān')	132	38°52'S	68°12'W
Neuquén, prov., Arg.	132	39°40'S	70°45'W
Neuquén, r., Arg.	132	38°45'S	69°00'W
Neuruppin, Ger. (noi'ro͞o-pēn)	154	52°55'N	12°48'E
Neuse, r., N.C., U.S. (nūz)	115	36°12'N	78°50'W
Neusiedler See, l., Eur. (noi-zēd'lĕr)	154	47°54'N	16°31'E
Neuss, Ger. (nois)	157c	51°12'N	6°41'E
Neusserweyhe, neigh., Ger.	236	51°13'N	6°39'E
Neustadt, Ger. (noi'shtät)	154	49°21'N	8°08'E
Neustadt bei Coburg, Ger. (bī kō'bo͞orgh)	154	50°20'N	11°09'E
Neustadt in Holstein, Ger.	154	54°06'N	10°50'E
Neustift am Walde, neigh., Aus.	239e	48°15'N	16°18'E
Neustrelitz, Ger. (noi-strā'lĭts)	154	53°21'N	13°05'E
Neutral Hills, hills, Can. (nū'trăl)	88	52°10'N	110°50'W
Neu Ulm, Ger. (noi ō lm')	154	48°23'N	10°01'E
Neuva Pompeya, neigh., Arg.	233d	34°39'S	58°25'W
Neuville, Can. (nū'vĭl)	83b	46°39'N	71°35'W
Neuville-sur-Oise, Fr.	237c	49°01'N	2°04'E
Neuwaldegg, neigh., Aus.	239e	48°14'N	16°17'E
Neuwied, Ger. (noi'vēdt)	154	50°26'N	7°28'E
Neva, r., Russia (nyĕ-vä')	162	59°49'N	30°54'E
Nevada, Ia., U.S. (nē-vä'dȧ)	103	42°01'N	93°27'W
Nevada, Mo., U.S.	111	37°49'N	94°21'W
Nevada, state, U.S. (nē vá'dá)	96	39°30'N	117°00'W
Nevada, Sierra, mts., Spain (syĕr'rä nā-vä'dhä)	142	37°01'N	3°28'W
Nevada, Sierra, mts., U.S. (sē-ĕ'r-rä nē-vä'dá)	96	39°20'N	120°05'W
Nevado, Cerro el, mtn., Col. (sĕ'r-rô-ĕl-nē-vä'dô)	130a	4°02'N	74°08'W
Neva Stantsiya, Russia (nyĕ-vä' stän'tsĭ-yȧ)	172c	59°53'N	30°30'E
Neve, Serra da, mts., Ang.	216	13°40'S	13°20'E
Nevel', Russia (nyĕ'vĕl)	166	56°03'N	29°57'E
Neveri, r., Ven. (nĕ-vĕ-rē)	131b	10°13'N	64°18'W
Nevers, Fr. (nĕ-vår')	147	46°59'N	3°10'E
Neves, Braz.	132b	22°51'S	43°06'W
Nevesinje, Bos. (nĕ-vĕ'sēn-yĕ)	161	43°15'N	18°08'E
Neviges, Ger.	236	51°19'N	7°05'E
Neville Island, i., Pa., U.S.	230b	40°31'N	80°08'W
Nevinnomyssk, Russia	168	44°38'N	41°56'E
Nevis, i., St. K./N. (nē'vĭs)	117	17°05'N	62°38'W
Nevis, Ben, mtn., Scot., U.K. (bĕn)	146	56°47'N	5°00'W
Nevis Peak, mtn., St. K./N.	121b	17°11'N	62°33'W
Nevşehir, Tur. (nĕv-shĕ'hĕr)	149	38°40'N	34°35'E
Nev'yansk, Russia (nĕv-yänsk')	164	57°29'N	60°14'E
New, r., Va., U.S. (nū)	115	37°20'N	80°35'W
Newabāgam, India	240a	22°48'N	88°24'E
New Addington, neigh., Eng., U.K.	235	51°21'N	0°01'W
Newala, Tan.	217	10°56'S	39°18'E
New Albany, In., U.S. (nū ôl'bȧ-nĭ)	101h	38°17'N	85°49'W
New Albany, Ms., U.S.	115	34°28'N	89°00'W
New Amsterdam, Guy. (ăm'stĕr-dăm)	131	6°14'N	57°30'W
Newark, Eng., U.K. (nū'ĕrk)	144a	53°04'N	0°49'W
Newark, Ca., U.S. (nū'ĕrk)	106b	37°32'N	122°02'W
Newark, De., U.S. (no͞o'ärk)	99	39°40'N	75°45'W
Newark, N.J., U.S. (no͞o'ûrk)	97	40°44'N	74°10'W
Newark, N.Y., U.S. (nū'ĕrk)	99	43°05'N	77°10'W
Newark, Oh., U.S.	98	40°05'N	82°25'W
Newaygo, Mi., U.S. (nū'wā-go)	98	43°25'N	85°50'W
New Bedford, Ma., U.S. (bĕd'fĕrd)	97	41°35'N	70°55'W
Newberg, Or., U.S. (nū'bûrg)	98	45°17'N	122°58'W
New Bern, N.C., U.S. (bûrn)	97	35°05'N	77°05'W
Newbern, Tn., U.S.	114	36°05'N	89°12'W
Newberry, Mi., U.S. (nū'bĕr-ĭ)	103	46°22'N	85°31'W
Newberry, S.C., U.S.	115	34°15'N	81°40'W
New Boston, Mi., U.S. (bôs'tŭn)	101b	42°10'N	83°24'W
New Boston, Oh., U.S.	98	38°45'N	82°55'W
New Braunfels, Tx., U.S. (nū broun'fĕls)	112	29°43'N	98°07'W
New Brighton, Eng., U.K.	237a	53°26'N	3°03'W
New Brighton, Mn., U.S. (brī'tŭn)	107g	45°04'N	93°12'W
New Brighton, Pa., U.S.	101e	40°34'N	80°18'W
New Brighton, neigh., N.Y., U.S.	228	40°38'N	74°06'W
New Britain, Ct., U.S. (brĭt''n)	99	41°40'N	72°45'W
New Britain, i., Pap. N. Gui.	197	6°45'S	149°38'E
New Brunswick, N.J., U.S. (brŭnz'wĭk)	100a	40°29'N	74°27'W
New Brunswick, prov., Can.	85	47°14'N	66°30'W
Newburg, In., U.S.	98	38°00'N	87°25'W
Newburg, Mo., U.S.	111	37°54'N	91°53'W
Newburgh, N.Y., U.S.	99	41°30'N	74°00'W
Newburgh Heights, Oh., U.S.	101d	41°27'N	81°40'W
Newbury, Eng., U.K. (nū'bĕr-ĭ)	150	51°24'N	1°26'W
Newbury, Ma., U.S.	93a	42°48'N	70°52'W
Newburyport, Ma., U.S. (nū'bĕr-ĭ-pōrt)	93a	42°48'N	70°53'W
New Caledonia, dep., Oc.	203	21°28'S	164°40'E
New Canaan, Ct., U.S. (kā-nȧn)	100a	41°06'N	73°30'W
New Carlisle, Can. (kär-līl')	85	48°01'N	65°20'W
New Carrollton, Md., U.S.	229d	35°58'N	76°53'W
Newcastle, Austl. (nū-kås''l)	204	33°00'S	151°55'E
Newcastle, Can.	85	47°00'N	65°34'W
New Castle, De., U.S.	99	39°40'N	75°35'W
New Castle, In., U.S.	98	39°55'N	85°25'W
New Castle, Oh., U.S.	98	40°20'N	82°10'W
New Castle, Pa., U.S.	98	41°00'N	80°25'W
Newcastle, Tx., U.S.	110	33°13'N	98°44'W
Newcastle, Wy., U.S.	102	43°51'N	104°11'W
Newcastle under Lyme, Eng., U.K. (nū-kås''l) (nŭ-kås''l)	144a	53°01'N	2°14'W
Newcastle upon Tyne, Eng., U.K.	142	55°00'N	1°45'W
Newcastle Waters, Austl. (wô'tĕrz)	202	17°10'S	133°25'E
Newclare, neigh., S. Afr.	244b	26°11'S	27°58'E
Newcomerstown, Oh., U.S. (nū'kŭm-ĕrz-toun)	98	40°15'N	81°40'W
New Croton Reservoir, res., N.Y., U.S. (krŏ'tôn)	100a	41°15'N	73°47'W
New Delhi, India (dĕl'hī)	183	28°43'N	77°18'E
Newell, S.D., U.S. (nū'ĕl)	102	44°43'N	103°26'W
New Eltham, neigh., Eng., U.K.	235	51°26'N	0°04'E
New England Range, mts., Austl. (nŭ ĭŋ'glȧnd)	203	29°32'S	152°30'E
Newenham, Cape, c., Ak., U.S. (nū-ĕn-hăm)	95	58°40'N	162°32'W
Newfane, N.Y., U.S. (nū-fān)	101c	43°17'N	78°44'W
New Ferry, Eng., U.K.	237a	53°22'N	2°59'W
Newfoundland, prov., Can.	85a	48°15'N	56°53'W
Newgate, Can. (nů'gāt)	87	49°01'N	115°10'W
Newgate Street, Eng., U.K.	235	51°44'N	0°07'W
New Georgia, i., Sol. Is. (jôr'jĭ-ȧ)	203	8°08'S	158°00'E
New Georgia Group, is., Sol. Is.	198e	8°30'S	157°20'E
New Georgia Sound, strt., Sol. Is.	198e	8°00'S	158°10'E
New Glasgow, Can. (glås'gō)	85	45°35'N	62°36'W
New Guinea, i. (gĭne)	197	5°45'S	140°00'E
Newhalem, Wa., U.S. (nū hā'lŭm)	104	48°44'N	121°11'W
Newham, neigh., Eng., U.K.	235	51°32'N	0°03'E
New Hampshire, state, U.S. (hămp'shĭr)	97	43°55'N	71°40'W
New Hampton, Ia., U.S. (hămp'tŭn)	103	43°03'N	92°20'W
New Hanover, S. Afr. (hăn'ôvĕr)	213c	29°23'S	30°32'E
New Hanover, i., Pap. N. Gui.	197	2°37'S	150°15'E
New Harmony, In., U.S. (nū hār'mô-nĭ)	98	38°10'N	87°55'W
New Haven, Ct., U.S. (hā'vĕn)	97	41°20'N	72°55'W
New Haven, In., U.S. (nū hāv''n)	98	41°05'N	85°00'W
New Hebrides, is., Vanuatu	203	16°00'S	167°00'E
New Hey, Eng., U.K.	237b	53°36'N	2°06'W
New Holland, Eng., U.K. (hŏl'ănd)	144a	53°42'N	0°21'W
New Holland, N.C., U.S.	115	35°27'N	76°14'W
New Hope Mountain, mtn., Al., U.S. (hōp)	100h	33°23'N	86°45'W
New Hudson, Mi., U.S. (hŭd'sŭn)	101b	42°30'N	83°36'W
New Hyde Park, N.Y., U.S.	228	40°44'N	73°41'W
New Hythe, Eng., U.K.	235	51°19'N	0°27'E
New Iberia, La., U.S. (ī-bē'rĭ-ȧ)	113	30°00'N	91°50'W
Newington, Can. (nū'ĕng-tŏn)	83c	45°07'N	75°00'W
New Ireland, i., Pap. N. Gui. (ĭr'lănd)	197	3°15'S	152°30'E
New Jersey, state, U.S. (jûr'zĭ)	97	40°30'N	74°50'W
New Kensington, Pa., U.S. (kĕn'zĭng-tŭn)	101e	40°34'N	79°35'W
Newkirk, Ok., U.S. (nū'kûrk)	111	36°52'N	97°03'W
New Kowloon (Xinjiulong), H.K.	241c	22°20'N	114°10'E
New Lagos, neigh., Nig.	244d	6°30'N	3°22'E
New Lenox, Il., U.S. (lĕn'ŭk)	101a	41°31'N	87°58'W
New Lexington, Oh., U.S. (lĕk'sĭng-tŭn)	98	39°40'N	82°10'W
New Lisbon, Wi., U.S. (lĭz'bŭn)	103	43°52'N	90°11'W
New Liskeard, Can.	91	47°30'N	79°40'W
New London, Ct., U.S. (lŭn'dŭn)	99	41°20'N	72°05'W
New London, Wi., U.S.	103	44°24'N	88°45'W
New Madrid, Mo., U.S. (măd'rĭd)	111	36°34'N	89°31'W
Newman's Grove, Ne., U.S. (nū'măn grōv)	102	41°46'N	97°44'W
Newmarket, Can. (nū'mär-kĕt)	91	44°00'N	79°30'W
Newmarket, S. Afr.	244b	26°17'S	28°08'E
New Martinsville, W.V., U.S. (mär'tĭnz-vĭl)	98	39°35'N	80°50'W
New Meadows, Id., U.S.	104	44°58'N	116°20'W
New Mexico, state, U.S. (mĕk'sĭ-kō)	96	34°30'N	107°10'W
New Milford, N.J., U.S.	228	40°56'N	74°01'W
New Mills, Eng., U.K. (mĭlz)	144a	53°22'N	2°00'W

ng-sing; ŋ-baŋk; ɴ-nasalized n; nŏd; cŏmmit; ōld; ōbey; ôrder; oi-boil; fo͞od; ŏ-as oo in foot; ou-out; s-soft; sh-dish; th-thin; pūre; ůnite; ûrn; stŭd; circŭs; ü-as in French tu; '-indeterminate vowel.

324 New Munster–Noma Misaki

PLACE (Pronunciation)	PAGE	LAT.	LONG.
New Munster, Wi., U.S. (mŭn′stẽr)	101a	42°35′N	88°13′W
Newnan, Ga., U.S. (nū′năn)	114	33°22′N	84°47′W
New Norfolk, Austl. (nôr′fŏk)	203	42°50′S	147°17′E
New Orleans, La., U.S. (ôr′lê-ănz)	97	30°00′N	90°05′W
New Philadelphia, Oh., U.S. (fĭl-á-dĕl′fĭ-á)	98	40°30′N	81°30′W
New Plymouth, N.Z. (plĭm′ŭth)	203a	39°04′S	174°13′E
Newport, Austl.	201b	33°39′S	151°19′E
Newport, Austl.	243b	37°51′S	144°53′E
Newport, Eng., U.K.	144a	52°46′N	2°22′W
Newport, Eng., U.K. (nū-pôrt)	150	50°41′N	1°25′W
Newport, Wales, U.K.	147	51°36′N	3°05′W
Newport, Ar., U.S. (nū′pōrt)	111	35°35′N	91°16′W
Newport, Ky., U.S.	97	39°05′N	84°30′W
Newport, Me., U.S.	92	44°49′N	69°20′W
Newport, Mn., U.S.	107g	44°52′N	92°59′W
Newport, N.H., U.S.	99	43°20′N	72°10′W
Newport, Or., U.S.	104	44°39′N	124°02′W
Newport, R.I., U.S.	99	41°29′N	71°16′W
Newport, Tn., U.S.	114	35°55′N	83°12′W
Newport, Vt., U.S.	99	44°55′N	72°15′W
Newport, Wa., U.S.	104	48°12′N	117°01′W
Newport Beach, Ca., U.S. (bēch)	107a	33°36′N	117°55′W
Newport News, Va., U.S.	97	36°59′N	76°24′W
New Prague, Mn., U.S. (nū prāg)	103	44°33′N	93°35′W
New Providence, i., Bah. (prŏv′ĭ-dĕns)	122	25°00′N	77°25′W
New Redruth, S. Afr.	244b	26°16′S	28°07′E
New Richmond, Oh., U.S. (rĭch′mŭnd)	98	38°55′N	84°15′W
New Richmond, Wi., U.S.	103	45°07′N	92°34′W
New Roads, La., U.S. (rōds)	113	30°42′N	91°26′W
New Rochelle, N.Y., U.S. (rū-shĕl′)	100a	40°55′N	73°47′W
New Rockford, N.D., U.S. (rŏk′fērd)	102	47°40′N	99°08′W
New Ross, Ire. (rôs)	150	52°25′N	6°55′W
New Sarepta, Can.	83g	53°17′N	113°09′W
New Siberian Islands *see* Novosibirskiye Ostrova, is., Russia	165	74°00′N	140°30′E
New Smyrna Beach, Fl., U.S. (smûr′nȧ)	115	29°00′N	80°57′W
New South Wales, state, Austl. (wālz)	203	32°45′S	146°14′E
Newton, Can. (nū′tŭn)	83f	49°56′N	98°04′W
Newton, Eng., U.K.	144a	53°27′N	2°37′W
Newton, Il., U.S.	98	39°00′N	88°10′W
Newton, Ia., U.S.	103	41°42′N	93°04′W
Newton, Ks., U.S.	111	38°03′N	97°22′W
Newton, Ma., U.S.	93a	42°21′N	71°13′W
Newton, Ms., U.S.	114	32°18′N	89°10′W
Newton, N.J., U.S.	100a	41°03′N	74°45′W
Newton, N.C., U.S.	115	35°40′N	81°19′W
Newton, Tx., U.S.	113	30°47′N	93°45′W
Newton Brook, neigh., Can.	227c	43°48′N	79°24′W
Newton Highlands, Ma., U.S.	227a	41°19′N	71°13′W
Newton Lower Falls, Ma., U.S.	227a	42°19′N	71°23′W
Newtonsville, Oh., U.S. (nū′tŭnz-vĭl)	101f	39°11′N	84°04′W
Newton Upper Falls, Ma., U.S.	227a	42°19′N	71°13′W
Newtonville, Ma., U.S.	227a	42°21′N	71°13′W
Newtown, N.D., U.S. (nū′toun)	102	47°57′N	102°25′W
Newtown, Oh., U.S.	101f	39°08′N	84°22′W
Newtown, Pa., U.S.	100f	40°13′N	74°56′W
Newtown, neigh., Austl.	243a	33°54′S	151°11′E
Newtownards, N. Ire., U.K. (nu-t′n-ardz′)	150	54°35′N	5°39′W
New Ulm, Mn., U.S. (ŭlm)	103	44°18′N	94°27′W
New Utrecht, neigh., N.Y., U.S.	228	40°36′N	73°59′W
New Waterford, Can. (wô′tẽr-fẽrd)	85	46°15′N	60°05′W
New Westminster, Can. (wĕst′mĭn-stẽr)	87	49°12′N	122°55′W
New York, N.Y., U.S. (yôrk)	97	40°40′N	73°58′W
New York, state, U.S.	97	42°45′N	78°05′W
New Zealand, nation, Oc. (zē′lănd)	203a	42°00′S	175°00′E
Nexapa, r., Mex. (nĕks-ä′pä)	118	18°32′N	98°29′W
Neya-gawa, Japan (nā′yä gä′wä)	195b	34°47′N	135°38′E
Neyshābūr, Iran	182	36°06′N	58°45′E
Neyva, r., Russia (nĕy′vȧ)	172a	57°39′N	60°37′E
Nezahualcóyotl, Mex.	119a	19°27′N	99°03′W
Nez Perce, Id., U.S. (nĕz′ pûrs′)	104	46°16′N	116°15′W
Nez Perce Indian Reservation, I.R., Id., U.S.	104	46°20′N	116°30′W
Ngami, l., Bots. (n′gä′mē)	212	20°56′S	22°31′E
Ngamouéri, Congo	244c	4°14′S	15°14′E
Ngangerabeli Plain, pl., Kenya	217	1°20′S	40°10′E
Ngangla Ringco, l., China (ŋäŋ-lä rĭŋ-tswo)	186	31°42′N	82°53′E
Ngarimbi, Tan.	217	8°28′S	38°36′E
Ngoko, r., Afr.	216	1°55′N	15°53′E
Ngol-Kedju Hill, mtn., Cam.	215	6°20′N	9°45′E
Ngombe, D.R.C.	244c	4°24′S	15°11′E
Ngong, Kenya ('n-gông)	212	1°27′S	36°39′E
Ngounié, r., Gabon	216	1°15′S	10°43′E
Ngoywa, Tan.	217	5°56′S	32°48′E
Ngqeleni, S. Afr. ('ng-kĕ-lā′nē)	213c	31°41′S	29°04′E
Nguigmi, Niger ('n-gĕg′mē)	211	14°15′N	13°07′E
Ngurore, Nig.	215	9°18′N	12°14′E
Nguru, Nig. ('n-gōō′rōō)	210	12°53′N	10°26′E
Nguru Mountains, mts., Tan.	217	6°10′S	37°35′E
Nha Trang, Viet (nyä-träng′)	196	12°08′N	108°56′E
Niafounke, Mali	210	16°03′N	4°17′W
Niagara, Wi., U.S. (nī-ăg′ȧ-rȧ)	103	45°45′N	88°05′W
Niagara, r., N.A.	101c	43°12′N	79°03′W
Niagara Falls, Can.	101c	43°05′N	79°05′W
Niagara Falls, N.Y., U.S.	97	43°06′N	79°02′W
Niagara-on-the-Lake, Can.	83d	43°16′N	79°05′W
Niakaramandougou, C. Iv.	214	8°40′N	5°17′W
Niamey, Niger (nē-ä-mā′)	210	13°31′N	2°07′E
Niamtougou, Togo	214	9°46′N	1°06′E
Niangara, D.R.C. (nē-äŋ-gá′rá)	211	3°42′N	27°52′E
Niangua, r., Mo., U.S. (nī-ăŋ′gwȧ)	111	37°30′N	93°05′W
Nias, Pulau, i., Indon. (nē′ās′)	196	0°58′N	97°43′E
Nibe, Den. (nē′bĕ)	152	56°57′N	9°36′E
Nicaragua, nation, N.A. (nĭk-á-rä′gwȧ)	116	12°45′N	86°15′W
Nicaragua, Lago de, l., Nic. (lä′gô dĕ)	116	11°45′N	85°28′W
Nicastro, Italy (nē-käs′trō)	149	38°39′N	16°15′E
Nicchehabin, Punta, c., Mex. (pōō′n-tä-nĕk-chĕ-ä-bē′n)	120a	19°50′N	87°20′W
Nice, Fr. (nēs)	142	43°42′N	7°21′E
Nicheng, China (nē-chŭŋ)	191b	30°54′N	121°48′E
Nichicun, l., Can. (nĭch′ĭ-kŭn)	85	53°07′N	72°10′W
Nicholas Channel, strt., N.A. (nĭk′ô-lȧs)	122	23°30′N	80°20′W
Nicholasville, Ky., U.S. (nĭk′ô-lȧs-vĭl)	98	37°55′N	84°35′W
Nicobar Islands, is., India (nĭk-ô-bär′)	196	8°28′N	94°04′E
Nicolai Mountain, mtn., Or., U.S. (nē-cō lī′)	106c	46°05′N	123°27′W
Nicolás Romero, Mex. (nē-kō-lá′s rô-mĕ′rô)	119a	19°38′N	99°20′W
Nicolet, Lake, l., Mi., U.S. (nĭ′kō-lĕt)	107k	46°22′N	84°14′W
Nicolls Town, Bah.	122	25°10′N	78°00′W
Nicols, Mn., U.S. (nĭk′ĕls)	107g	44°50′N	93°12′W
Nicomeki, r., Can.	106d	49°04′N	122°47′W
Nicosia, Cyp. (nē-kô-sē′á)	182	35°10′N	33°22′E
Nicoya, C.R. (nē-kō′yä)	120	10°08′N	85°27′W
Nicoya, Golfo de, b., C.R. (gôl-fô-dĕ)	120	10°03′N	85°04′W
Nicoya, Península de, pen., C.R.	120	10°05′N	86°00′W
Nidzica, Pol. (nē-jĕt′sȧ)	155	53°21′N	20°30′E
Niederaden, neigh., Ger.	236	51°36′N	7°34′E
Niederbonsfeld, Ger.	236	51°23′N	7°08′E
Niederdonk, Ger.	236	51°14′N	6°41′E
Niedereifringhausen, Ger.	236	51°21′N	7°10′E
Niedere Tauern, mts., Aus.	154	47°15′N	13°41′E
Niederkrüchten, Ger. (nē′dĕr-krük-tĕn)	157c	51°12′N	6°14′E
Nieder-Neuendorf, Ger.	238a	52°37′N	13°12′E
Niederösterreich, prov., Aus.	145e	48°24′N	16°20′E
Niedersachsen (Lower Saxony), hist. reg., Ger. (nē′dĕr-zäκ-sĕn)	154	52°52′N	8°27′E
Niederschöneweide, neigh., Ger.	238a	52°27′N	13°31′E
Niederschönhausen, neigh., Ger.	238a	52°35′N	13°23′E
Niellim, Chad	215	9°42′N	17°49′E
Niemeyer, neigh., Braz.	234c	23°00′S	43°15′W
Nienburg, Ger. (nē′ĕn-bōrgh)	154	52°40′N	9°15′E
Nierst, Ger.	236	51°19′N	6°43′E
Nietverdiend, S. Afr.	218d	25°02′S	26°10′E
Nieuw Nickerie, Sur. (nē-nē′kĕ-rē′)	131	5°51′N	57°00′W
Nieves, Mex. (nyā′vȧs)	118	24°00′N	102°57′W
Niğde, Tur. (nĭg′dĕ)	149	37°55′N	34°40′E
Nigel, S. Afr. (nī′jĕl)	218d	26°26′S	28°27′E
Niger, nation, Afr. (nī′jẽr)	210	18°02′N	8°30′E
Niger, r., Afr.	210	8°00′N	6°00′E
Niger Delta, d., Nig.	215	4°45′N	5°20′E
Nigeria, nation, Afr. (nī-jē′rĭ-á)	210	8°57′N	6°30′E
Nihoa, i., Hi., U.S.	94b	23°15′N	161°30′W
Nihonbashi, neigh., Japan	242a	35°41′N	139°47′E
Nii, i., Japan (nē)	195	34°26′N	139°23′E
Niigata, Japan (nē′ē-gä′tȧ)	189	37°47′N	139°04′E
Niihau, i., Hi., U.S. (nē′ē-ha′ōō)	96c	21°50′N	160°05′W
Niimi, Japan (nē′mē)	195	34°59′N	133°28′E
Niiza, Japan	195a	35°48′N	139°34′E
Nijmegen, Neth. (nī′mā-gĕn)	151	51°50′N	5°52′E
Nikaia, Grc.	239d	37°58′N	23°39′E
Nikitinka, Russia (nē-kĭ′tĭn-kȧ)	162	55°33′N	33°19′E
Nikolayevka, Russia (nē-kô-lä′yĕf-ká)	172c	59°29′N	29°48′E
Nikolayevka, Russia	194	48°37′N	134°09′E
Nikolayevskiy, Russia	167	50°00′N	45°30′E
Nikolayevsk-na-Amure, Russia	165	53°18′N	140°49′E
Nikolo-Chovanskoje, Russia	239b	55°36′N	37°27′E
Nikol′sk, Russia (nē-kôlsk′)	164	59°30′N	45°40′E
Nikol′skoye, Russia (nē-kôl′skô-yĕ)	172c	59°27′N	30°00′E
Nikopol, Bul. (nē′kô-pôl′)	149	43°41′N	24°52′E
Nikopol′, Ukr.	167	47°36′N	34°24′E
Nilahue, r., Chile (nē-lá′wĕ)	129b	34°36′S	71°50′W
Nile, r., Afr. (nīl)	211	27°30′N	31°00′E
Niles, Il., U.S.	231a	42°01′N	87°49′W
Niles, Mi., U.S. (nīlz)	98	41°50′N	86°15′W
Niles, Oh., U.S.	98	41°15′N	80°45′W
Nileshwar, India	187	12°08′N	74°14′E
Nilgani, India	240a	22°46′N	88°26′E
Nilgiri Hills, hills, India	187	12°05′N	76°22′E
Nilópolis, Braz. (nē-lô′pō-lēs)	129a	22°48′S	43°25′W
Nīmach, India	186	24°32′N	74°51′E
Nimba, Mont, mtn., Afr. (nĭm′bȧ)	210	7°40′N	8°33′W
Nimba Mountains, mts., Afr.	214	7°30′N	8°35′W
Nîmes, Fr. (nēm)	142	43°49′N	4°22′E
Nimrod Reservoir, res., Ar., U.S. (nĭm′rŏd)	111	34°58′N	93°46′W
Nimule, Sudan (nē-mōō′lā)	211	3°38′N	32°12′E
Ninda, Ang.	216	14°47′S	21°24′E
Nine Ashes, Eng., U.K.	235	51°42′N	0°18′E
Nine Mile Creek, r., Ut., U.S. (mīn′īmôd′)	109	39°50′N	110°30′W
Ninety Mile Beach, cst., Austl.	203	38°20′S	147°30′E
Nineveh, Iraq (nĭn′ē-vȧ)	182	36°30′N	43°10′E
Ning′an, China (nĭŋ-än)	189	44°20′N	129°20′E
Ningbo, China (nĭŋ-bwo)	189	29°56′N	121°30′E
Ningde, China (nĭŋ-dŭ)	189	26°38′N	119°33′E
Ninghai, China (nĭng′hī′)	193	29°20′N	121°20′E
Ninghe, China (nĭŋ-hŭ)	190	39°20′N	117°50′E
Ningjin, China (nĭŋ-jyĭn)	190	37°39′N	116°47′E
Ningjin, China	190	37°37′N	114°55′E
Ningming, China	193	22°22′N	107°06′E
Ningwu, China (nĭng′wōō′)	189	39°00′N	112°12′E
Ningxia Huizu, prov., China (nĭŋ-shyä)	188	37°10′N	106°00′E
Ningyang, China (nĭng′yäng′)	190	35°46′N	116°48′E
Ninh Binh, Viet (nĕn bĕnk′)	196	20°22′N	106°00′E
Ninigo Group, is., Pap. N. Gui.	197	1°15′S	143°30′E
Ninnescah, r., Ks., U.S. (nĭn′ĕs-kä)	110	37°37′N	98°31′W
Nioaque, Braz. (nēô-á′-kĕ)	131	21°14′S	55°41′W
Niobrara, r., U.S. (nī-ô-brâr′ȧ)	96	42°46′N	98°46′W
Niokolo Koba, Parc National du, rec., Sen.	214	13°05′N	13°00′W
Nioro du Sahel, Mali (nē-ō′rō)	210	15°15′N	9°35′W
Nipawin, Can.	84	53°22′N	104°00′W
Nipe, Bahía de, b., Cuba (bä-ē′ä-dĕ-nē′pā)	123	20°50′N	75°30′W
Nipe, Sierra de, mts., Cuba (sē-ĕ′r-rá-dĕ)	123	20°20′N	75°50′W
Nipigon, Can. (nĭp′ĭ-gŏn)	85	48°58′N	88°17′W
Nipigon, l., Can.	85	49°37′N	89°55′W
Nipigon Bay, b., Can.	90	48°56′N	88°00′W
Nipisiguit, r., Can. (nĭ-pĭ′sĭ-kwĭt)	92	47°26′N	66°15′W
Nipissing, l., Can. (nĭp′ĭ-sĭng)	85	45°59′N	80°19′W
Niquero, Cuba (nē-kā′rō)	122	20°00′N	77°35′W
Nirmali, India	186	26°30′N	86°43′E
Niš, Yugo.	142	43°19′N	21°54′E
Nisa, Port. (nē′sȧ)	158	39°32′N	7°41′W
Nišava, r., Eur. (nē′shȧ-vȧ)	161	43°17′N	22°17′E
Nishi, Japan	242b	34°41′N	135°30′E
Nishinari, neigh., Japan	242b	34°38′N	135°28′E
Nishino, i., Japan (nēsh′ē-nō)	195	36°06′N	132°49′E
Nishinomiya, Japan (nēsh′ē-nô-mē′yȧ)	195b	34°44′N	135°21′E
Nishio, Japan (nēsh′ē-ô)	195	34°50′N	137°01′E
Nishiyodogawa, neigh., Japan	242b	34°42′N	135°27′E
Niska Lake, l., Can. (nĭs′kȧ)	88	55°35′N	108°38′W
Nisko, Pol. (nēs′kô)	155	50°30′N	22°07′E
Nisku, Can. (nĭs-kū′)	83g	53°21′N	113°33′W
Nisqually, r., Wa., U.S. (nĭs-kwôl′ĭ)	104	46°51′N	122°33′W
Nissan, r., Swe.	152	57°06′N	13°22′E
Nisser, l., Nor. (nĭs′ĕr)	152	59°14′N	8°35′E
Nissum Fjord, fj., Den.	152	56°24′N	7°35′E
Niterói, Braz. (nē-tĕ-rô′ĭ)	131	22°53′S	43°07′W
Nith, r., Scot., U.K. (nĭth)	150	55°13′N	3°55′W
Nitra, Slvk. (nē′trȧ)	155	48°18′N	18°04′E
Nitra, r., Slvk.	155	48°13′N	18°14′E
Nitro, W.V., U.S. (nī′trō)	98	38°25′N	81°50′W
Niue, dep., Oc. (nĭ′ô)	225	19°50′S	167°00′W
Nivelles, Bel. (nē-vĕl′)	151	50°33′N	4°17′E
Nixon, Tx., U.S. (nĭk′sŭn)	113	29°16′N	97°48′W
Nizāmābād, India	183	18°48′N	78°07′E
Nizhne-Angarsk, Russia (nyĕzh′nyĭ-ŭngärsk′)	165	55°49′N	108°46′E
Nizhne-Chirskaya, Russia	167	48°20′N	42°50′E
Nizhne-Kolymsk, Russia (kô-lēmsk′)	165	68°32′N	160°56′E
Nizhneudinsk, Russia (nĕzh′nyĭ-ōōdēnsk′)	165	54°58′N	99°15′E
Nizhniye Sergi, Russia (nyĕzh′ nyĕ sĕr′gĕ)	166	56°41′N	59°19′E
Nizhniy Novgorod (Gor′kiy), Russia	164	56°15′N	44°05′E
Nizhniy Tagil, Russia (tŭgēl′)	164	57°54′N	59°59′E
Nizhnyaya Kur′ya, Russia (nyĕ′zhnyȧ-yȧ koōr′yȧ)	172a	58°01′N	56°00′E
Nizhnyaya Salda, Russia (nyĕ′zhnya′ya säl′da′)	172a	58°05′N	60°43′E
Nizhnyaya Taymyra, r., Russia	170	72°30′N	95°18′E
Nizhnyaya Tunguska, r., Russia	165	64°13′N	91°30′E
Nizhnyaya Tura, Russia (tōō′rȧ)	172a	58°38′N	59°50′E
Nizhnyaya Us′va, Russia (ōo′vȧ)	172a	59°05′N	58°53′E
Nizhyn, Ukr.	167	51°03′N	31°52′E
Nízke Tatry, mts., Slvk.	155	48°57′N	19°18′E
Njazidja, i., Com.	213	11°44′S	42°38′E
Njombe, Tan.	217	9°20′S	34°46′E
Njurunda, Swe. (nyōō-rŏn′dȧ)	152	62°15′N	17°24′E
Nkala Mission, Zam.	217	15°55′S	26°00′E
Nkandla, S. Afr. ('n-känd′lȧ)	213c	28°40′S	31°06′E
Nkawkaw, Ghana	214	6°33′N	0°47′W
Nkhota, Mwi. (kō-tȧ kō-tȧ)	212	12°52′S	34°16′E
Noākhāli, Bngl.	183	22°52′N	91°08′E
Noatak, Ak., U.S. (nô-ä′tȧk)	95	67°22′N	163°28′W
Noatak, r., Ak., U.S.	95	67°58′N	162°15′W
Nobeoka, Japan (nō-bȧ-ō′kȧ)	194	32°36′N	131°41′E
Noblesville, In., U.S. (nō′bl′z-vĭl)	98	40°00′N	86°00′W
Nobleton, Can. (nō′bl′tŭn)	83d	43°54′N	79°39′W
Noborito, Japan	242a	35°37′N	139°34′E
Nocera Inferiore, Italy (ēn-fĕ-ryô′rĕ)	159c	40°30′N	14°38′E
Nochistlán, Mex. (nô-chēs-tlän′)	118	21°23′N	102°52′W
Nochixtlón, Mex. (ä-sôn-syôn′)	119	17°28′N	97°12′W
Nogales, Mex.	116	31°15′N	111°00′W
Nogales, Mex. (nō-gä′lĕs)	119	18°49′N	97°09′W
Nogales, Az., U.S. (nô-gä′lĕs)	96	31°20′N	110°55′W
Nogal Valley, val., Som. (nō′gäl)	218a	8°30′N	47°50′E
Nogent-le-Roi, Fr. (nŏ-zhŏN-lĕ-rwä′)	157b	48°39′N	1°32′E
Nogent-le-Rotrou, Fr. (rō-trōō′)	156	48°22′N	0°47′E
Nogent-sur-Marne, Fr.	237c	48°50′N	2°29′E
Noginsk, Russia (nô-gēnsk′)	166	55°52′N	38°28′E
Noguera Pallaresa, r., Spain	159	42°18′N	1°03′E
Noia, Spain	158	42°46′N	8°50′W
Noirmoutier, Île de, i., Fr. (nwȧr-mōō-tyā′)	147	47°03′N	3°08′W
Noisy-le-Grand, Fr.	237c	48°51′N	2°33′E
Noisy-le-Roi, Fr.	237c	48°51′N	2°04′E
Noisy-le-Sec, Fr.	237c	48°53′N	2°28′E
Nojima-Zaki, c., Japan (nō′jē-mä zä-kē)	195	34°54′N	139°48′E
Nokomis, Il., U.S. (nô-kō′mĭs)	98	39°15′N	89°10′W
Nola, Italy (nô′lä)	160	40°41′N	14°32′E
Nolinsk, Russia (nô-lēnsk′)	166	57°32′N	49°50′E
Noma Misaki, c., Japan (nō′mä mē′sä-kē)	195	31°25′N	130°09′E

ăt; finăl; rāte; senāte; ärm; ȧsk; sofȧ; fâre; ch-choose; dh-as th in other; bē; ēvent; bĕt; recĕnt; cratẽr; g-gō; gh-guttural g; bĭt; ĭ-short neutral; rīde; κ-guttural k as ch in German ich;

PRONOUNCING INDEX Nombre de Dios–Norwood 325

PLACE (Pronunciation)	PAGE	LAT.	LONG.
Nombre de Dios, Mex. (nôm-brĕ-dĕ-dyō's)	118	23°50'N	104°14'W
Nombre de Dios, Pan. (nô'm-brĕ)	121	9°34'N	79°28'W
Nome, Ak., U.S. (nōm)	94a	64°30'N	165°20'W
Nonacho, l., Can.	84	61°48'N	111°20'W
Nonantum, Ma., U.S.	227a	42°20'N	71°12'W
Nong'an, China (nôŋ-än)	192	44°25'N	125°10'E
Nongoma, S. Afr. (nŏn-gō'mȧ)	212	27°48'S	31°45'E
Nooksack, Wa., U.S. (nòk'săk)	106d	48°55'N	122°19'W
Nooksack, r., Wa., U.S.	106d	48°54'N	122°31'W
Noordwijk aan Zee, Neth.	145a	52°14'N	4°25'E
Noordzee Kanaal, can., Neth.	145a	52°27'N	4°42'E
Nootka, i., Can. (nōōt'kȧ)	84	49°32'N	126°42'W
Nootka Sound, strt., Can.	86	49°33'N	126°38'W
Nóqui, Ang. (nô-kē')	212	5°51'S	13°25'E
Nor, r., China (nou')	194	46°55'N	132°45'E
Nora, Swe.	152	59°32'N	14°56'E
Nora, In., U.S. (nō'rä)	101g	39°54'N	86°08'W
Noranda, Can.	91	48°15'N	79°01'W
Norbeck, Md., U.S. (nōr'bĕk)	100e	39°06'N	77°05'W
Norborne, Mo., U.S. (nôr'bôrn)	111	39°17'N	93°39'W
Norco, Ca., U.S. (nôr'kō)	107a	33°57'N	117°33'W
Norcross, Ga., U.S. (nôr'krôs)	100c	33°56'N	84°13'W
Nord, Riviere du, Can. (rēv-yĕr' dü nōr)	83a	45°45'N	74°02'W
Nordegg, Can. (nûr'dĕg)	87	52°28'N	116°04'W
Norden, Ger. (nôr'dĕn)	154	53°35'N	7°14'E
Norden, Eng., U.K.	237b	53°38'N	2°13'W
Norderney, i., Ger. (nōr'dĕr-nĕy)	154	53°45'N	6°58'E
Nordfjord, fj., Nor. (nô'fyôr)	152	61°50'N	5°35'E
Nordhausen, Ger. (nôrt'hau-zĕn)	147	51°30'N	10°48'E
Nordhorn, Ger. (nôrt'hôrn)	154	52°26'N	7°05'E
Nordland, Wa., U.S. (nôrd'lȧnd)	106a	48°03'N	122°41'W
Nördlingen, Ger. (nûrt'lĭng-ĕn)	154	48°51'N	10°30'E
Nord-Ostsee Kanal (Kiel Canal), can., Ger. (nōrd-ōzt-zā) (kēl)	154	54°03'N	9°23'E
Nordrhein-Westfalen (North Rhine-Westphalia), hist. reg., Ger. (nōrd'hīn-vĕst-fä-lĕn)	154	50°50'N	6°53'E
Nordvik, Russia (nôrd'vēk)	165	73°57'N	111°15'E
Nore, r., Ire. (nōr)	150	52°34'N	7°15'W
Norf, Ger.	236	51°09'N	6°43'E
Norfolk, Ma., U.S. (nôr'fŏk)	93a	42°07'N	71°19'W
Norfolk, Ne., U.S.	96	42°10'N	97°25'W
Norfolk, Va., U.S.	97	36°55'N	76°15'W
Norfolk, i., Oc.	225	27°10'S	166°50'E
Norfork, Lake, l., Ar., U.S.	111	36°25'N	92°09'W
Noril'sk, Russia (nô rēlsk')	164	69°00'N	87°11'E
Normal, Il., U.S. (nôr'măl)	98	40°35'N	89°00'W
Norman, r., Austl.	203	18°27'S	141°29'E
Norman, Lake, res., N.C., U.S.	97	35°30'N	80°53'W
Normandie, hist. reg., Fr. (nōr-män-dē')	156	49°02'N	0°17'E
Normandie, Collines de, hills, Fr. (kō-lēn'dĕ-nōr-män-dē')	156	48°46'N	0°50'W
Normandy *see* Normandie, hist. reg., Fr.	156	49°02'N	0°17'E
Normandy Heights, Md., U.S.	229c	39°17'N	76°48'W
Normanhurst, Austl.	243a	33°43'S	151°06'E
Normanton, Austl. (nôr'mȧn-tŭn)	203	17°45'S	141°10'E
Normanton, Eng., U.K.	144a	53°40'N	1°21'W
Norman Wells, Can.	84	65°26'N	127°00'W
Nornalup, Austl. (nôr-năl'ŭp)	202	35°00'S	117°00'E
Nørresundby, Den. (nû-rĕ-sòn'bü)	152	57°04'N	9°55'E
Norridge, Il., U.S.	231a	41°57'N	87°49'W
Norris, Tn., U.S. (nŏr'ĭs)	114	36°09'N	84°05'W
Norris Lake, res., Tn., U.S.	97	36°17'N	84°10'W
Norristown, Pa., U.S. (nŏr'ĭs-town)	100f	40°07'N	75°21'W
Norrköping, Swe. (nôr'chûp'ĭng)	142	58°37'N	16°10'E
Norrtälje, Swe. (nôr-tĕl'yĕ)	146	59°47'N	18°39'E
Norseman, Austl. (nôrs'măn)	202	32°15'S	122°00'E
Norte, Punta, c., Arg. (pōō'n-tä-nōr'tĕ)	129c	36°17'S	56°46'W
Norte, Serra do, mts., Braz. (sĕ'r-rä-dô-nôr'te)	131	12°04'S	59°08'W
North, Cape, c., Can.	93	47°02'N	60°25'W
North Abington, Ma., U.S.	227a	42°08'N	70°57'W
North Adams, Ma., U.S. (ăd'ămz)	99	42°40'N	73°05'W
Northam, Austl. (nôr-dhăm)	202	31°50'S	116°45'E
Northam, S. Afr. (nôr'thăm)	218d	24°52'S	27°16'E
North America, cont.	82	45°00'N	100°00'W
North American Basin, deep (ȧ-mĕr'ĭ-kȧn)	4	23°45'N	62°45'W
Northampton, Austl. (nôr-thămp'tŭn)	202	28°22'S	114°45'E
Northampton, Eng., U.K. (nôrth-ămp'tŭn)	147	52°14'N	0°56'W
Northampton, Ma., U.S.	99	42°20'N	72°45'W
Northampton, Pa., U.S.	99	40°45'N	75°30'W
Northamptonshire, co., Eng., U.K.	144a	52°25'N	0°47'W
North Andaman Island, i., India (ăn-dȧ-măn')	196	13°15'N	93°30'E
North Andover, Ma., U.S. (ăn'dô-vĕr)	93a	42°42'N	71°07'W
North Arlington, N.J., U.S.	228	40°47'N	74°08'W
North Arm, mth., Can. (ärm)	106d	49°13'N	123°01'W
North Atlanta, Ga., U.S. (ăt-lăn'tȧ)	100c	33°52'N	84°20'W
North Attleboro, Ma., U.S. (ăt''l-bŭr-ō)	100b	41°59'N	71°18'W
North Auburn, Austl.	243a	33°50'S	151°02'E
North Baltimore, Oh., U.S. (bôl'tĭ-môr)	98	41°10'N	83°40'W
North Balwyn, Austl.	243b	37°48'S	145°05'E
North Barnaby, Md., U.S.	229d	38°49'N	76°57'W
North Barrackpore, India	240a	22°46'N	88°22'E
North Basque, Tx., U.S. (băsk)	112	31°56'N	98°01'W
North Battleford, Can. (băt''l-fērd)	84	52°47'N	108°17'W
North Bay, Can.	85	46°13'N	79°26'W
North Beach, neigh., Ca., U.S.	231b	37°48'N	122°25'W
North Bellmore, N.Y., U.S.	228	40°41'N	73°32'W
North Bend, Or., U.S. (bĕnd)	104	43°23'N	124°13'W
North Bergen, N.J., U.S.	228	40°48'N	74°01'W
North Berwick, Me., U.S. (bûr'wĭk)	92	43°18'N	70°46'W
North Bight, bt., Bah. (bīt)	122	24°30'N	77°40'W
North Bimini, i., Bah. (bĭ'mĭ-nē)	122	25°45'N	79°20'W
North Borneo *see* Sabah, hist. reg., Malay.	196	5°10'N	116°25'E
Northborough, Ma., U.S.	93a	42°19'N	71°39'W
North Box Hill, Austl.	243b	37°48'S	145°07'E
North Braddock, Pa., U.S.	230b	40°24'N	79°52'W
Northbridge, Austl.	243a	33°49'S	151°13'E
Northbridge, Ma., U.S. (nôrth'brĭj)	93a	42°09'N	71°39'W
North Caicos, i., T./C. Is. (kī'kōs)	123	21°55'N	72°00'W
North Caldwell, N.J., U.S.	228	40°52'N	74°16'W
North Cape, c., N.Z.	203a	34°31'S	173°02'E
North Carolina, state, U.S. (kăr-ô-lī'nȧ)	97	35°40'N	81°30'W
North Cascades National Park, rec., Wa., U.S.	87	48°50'N	120°50'W
North Cat Cay, i., Bah.	122	25°35'N	79°20'W
North Channel, strt., Can.	90	46°10'N	83°20'W
North Channel, strt., U.K.	142	55°15'N	7°56'W
North Charleston, S.C., U.S. (chärlz'tŭn)	115	32°49'N	79°57'W
North Chicago, Il., U.S. (shĭ-kô'gō)	101a	42°19'N	87°51'W
Northcliff, neigh., S. Afr.	244b	26°09'S	27°58'E
North College Hill, Oh., U.S. (kŏl'ĕj hĭl)	101f	39°13'N	84°33'W
North Concho, Tx., U.S. (kŏn'chō)	112	31°40'N	100°48'W
North Cooking Lake, Can. (kòk'ĭng lăk)	83g	53°28'N	112°57'W
Northcote, Austl.	243b	37°46'S	145°00'E
North Cyprus, nation, Asia	182	35°15'N	33°40'E
North Dakota, state, U.S. (dȧ-kō'tȧ)	96	47°20'N	101°55'W
North Downs, Eng., U.K. (dounz)	150	51°11'N	0°01'W
North Dum-Dum, India	186a	22°38'N	88°23'E
Northeast Cape, c., Ak., U.S. (nôrth-ēst)	95	63°15'N	169°04'W
Northeast Point, c., Bah.	123	21°25'N	73°00'W
Northeast Point, c., Bah.	123	22°45'N	73°50'W
Northeast Providence Channel, strt., Bah. (prŏv'ĭ-dĕns)	122	25°45'N	77°00'W
Northeim, Ger. (nôrt'hīm)	154	51°42'N	9°59'E
North Elbow Cays, is., Bah.	122	23°55'N	80°30'W
North Englewood, Md., U.S.	229d	38°55'N	76°55'W
Northern Cheyenne Indian Reservation, I.R., Mt., U.S.	105	45°32'N	106°43'W
Northern Dvina *see* Severnaya Dvina, r., Russia	164	63°00'N	42°40'E
Northern Ireland, , U.K. (ĭr'lănd)	142	54°48'N	7°00'W
Northern Land *see* Severnaya Zemlya, is., Russia	165	79°33'N	101°15'E
Northern Mariana Islands, dep., Oc. (mä-rē-ä'nȧ)	3	17°20'N	145°00'E
Northern Territory, , Austl.	202	18°15'S	133°00'E
Northern Yukon National Park, rec., Can.	95	69°00'N	140°00'W
North Essendon, Austl.	243b	37°45'S	144°54'E
Northfield, Il., U.S.	231a	42°06'N	87°46'W
Northfield, Mn., U.S. (nôrth'fēld)	103	44°28'N	93°11'W
North Fitzroy, Austl.	243b	37°47'S	144°59'E
Northfleet, Eng., U.K.	235	51°27'N	0°21'E
North Flinders Ranges, mts., Austl. (flĭn'dērz)	204	31°55'S	138°45'E
North Foreland, Eng., U.K. (nôrth-fōr'lȧnd)	151	51°20'N	1°30'E
North Franklin Mountain, mtn., Tx., U.S. (frăŋ'klĭn)	112	31°55'N	106°30'W
North Frisian Islands, is., Eur.	146	55°16'N	8°15'E
North Gamboa, Pan. (gäm-bô'ä)	121	9°07'N	79°40'W
North Germiston, S. Afr.	244b	26°14'S	28°09'E
North Gower, Can. (gŏw'ēr)	83c	45°08'N	75°43'W
North Haledon, N.J., U.S.	228	40°58'N	74°11'W
North Hanover, Ma., U.S.	227a	42°09'N	70°52'W
North Hills, N.Y., U.S.	228	40°47'N	73°41'W
North Hollywood, Ca., U.S. (hŏl'ē-wòd)	107a	34°10'N	118°23'W
North Island, i., N.Z.	203a	37°20'S	173°30'E
North Island, i., Ca., U.S.	108a	32°39'N	117°14'W
North Judson, In., U.S. (jŭd'sŭn)	98	41°15'N	86°50'W
North Kansas City, Mo., U.S. (kăn'zȧs)	107f	39°08'N	94°34'W
North Kingstown, R.I., U.S.	100b	41°34'N	71°26'W
Northlake, Il., U.S.	231a	41°55'N	87°54'W
North Little Rock, Ar., U.S. (lĭt''l rŏk)	111	34°46'N	92°13'W
North Loup, r., Ne., U.S. (lōōp)	102	42°05'N	100°10'W
North Magnetic Pole, pt. of i.	220	77°19'N	101°49'W
North Manchester, In., U.S. (măn'chĕs-tēr)	98	41°00'N	85°45'W
North Manly, Austl.	243a	33°46'S	151°16'E
Northmead, Austl.	243a	33°47'S	151°00'E
Northmead, S. Afr.	244b	26°10'S	28°20'E
North Merrick, N.Y., U.S.	228	40°41'N	73°34'W
Northmoor, Mo., U.S. (nôth'mōōr)	107f	39°10'N	94°37'W
North Moose Lake, l., Can.	89	54°09'N	100°20'W
North Mount Lofty Ranges, mts., Austl.	204	33°50'S	138°30'E
North Ockendon, neigh., Eng., U.K.	235	51°32'N	0°18'E
North Ogden, Ut., U.S. (ŏg'dĕn)	107b	41°18'N	111°58'W
North Ogden Peak, mtn., Ut., U.S.	107b	41°23'N	111°59'W
North Olmsted, Oh., U.S. (ōlm-stĕd)	101d	41°25'N	81°55'W
North Ossetia, state, Russia	166	43°00'N	44°15'E
North Parramatta, Austl.	243a	33°48'S	151°00'E
North Pease, r., Tx., U.S. (pēz)	110	34°19'N	100°58'W
North Pender, i., Can. (pĕn'dēr)	106d	48°48'N	123°16'W
North Philadelphia, neigh., Pa., U.S.	229b	39°58'N	75°09'W
North Plains, Or., U.S. (plānz)	106c	45°36'N	123°00'W
North Platte, Ne., U.S. (plăt)	96	41°08'N	100°45'W
North Platte, r., U.S.	96	41°20'N	102°40'W
North Point, H.K.	241c	22°17'N	114°12'E
North Point, c., Barb.	121b	13°22'N	59°36'W
North Point, c., Mi., U.S.	98	45°00'N	83°20'W
North Pole, pt. of i.	220	90°00'N	0.00
Northport, Al., U.S. (nôrth'pōrt)	114	33°12'N	87°35'W
Northport, N.Y., U.S.	100a	40°53'N	73°20'W
Northport, Wa., U.S.	104	48°53'N	117°47'W
North Quincy, Ma., U.S.	227a	42°17'N	71°01'W
North Randolph, Ma., U.S.	227a	42°12'N	71°04'W
North Reading, Ma., U.S. (rĕd'ĭng)	93a	42°34'N	71°04'W
North Richland Hills, Tx., U.S.	107c	32°50'N	97°13'W
North Richmond, Ca., U.S.	231b	37°57'N	122°22'W
Northridge, Ca., U.S. (nôrth'ridj)	107a	34°14'N	118°32'W
North Ridgeville, Oh., U.S. (rĭj-vĭl)	101d	41°23'N	82°01'W
North Riverside, Il., U.S.	231a	41°51'N	87°49'W
North Ronaldsay, i., Scot., U.K.	150a	59°21'N	2°23'W
North Royalton, Oh., U.S. (roi'ăl-tŭn)	101d	41°19'N	81°44'W
North Ryde, Austl.	243a	33°48'S	151°07'E
North Saint Paul, Mn., U.S. (sånt pôl')	103	45°01'N	92°59'W
North Santiam, r., Or., U.S. (săn'tyăm)	104	44°42'N	122°50'W
North Saskatchewan, r., Can. (săn-kăch'ē-wän)	84	54°00'N	111°30'W
North Sea, Eur.	142	56°09'N	3°16'E
North Side, neigh., Pa., U.S.	230b	40°28'N	80°01'W
North Skunk, r., Ia., U.S. (skŭnk)	103	41°39'N	92°46'W
North Springfield, Va., U.S.	229d	38°48'N	77°13'W
North Stradbroke Island, i., Austl. (străd'brōk)	203	27°45'S	154°18'E
North Sydney, Austl.	243a	33°50'S	151°13'E
North Sydney, Can. (sĭd'nē)	93	46°13'N	60°15'W
North Taranaki Bight, N.Z. (tȧ-rȧ-nä'kĭ bīt)	203a	38°40'S	174°00'E
North Tarrytown, N.Y., U.S. (tăr'ĭ-toun)	100a	41°05'N	73°52'W
North Thompson, r., Can.	87	50°50'N	120°10'W
North Tonawanda, N.Y., U.S. (tŏn-ȧ-wŏn'dȧ)	101c	43°02'N	78°53'W
North Truchas Peaks, mtn., N.M., U.S. (trōō'chäs)	96	35°58'N	105°40'W
North Twillingate, i., Can. (twĭl'ĭn-gāt)	92	35°58'N	105°37'W
North Uist, i., Scot., U.K. (ū'ĭst)	150	57°37'N	7°22'W
Northumberland, N.H., U.S.	99	44°30'N	71°30'W
Northumberland Islands, is., Austl.	203	21°42'S	151°30'E
Northumberland Strait, strt., Can. (nôr thŭm'bēr-lȧnd)	92	46°25'N	64°20'W
North Umpqua, r., Or., U.S. (ŭmp'kwȧ)	104	43°20'N	122°50'W
North Valley Stream, N.Y., U.S.	228	40°41'N	73°41'W
North Vancouver, Can. (văn-kōō'vēr)	84	49°19'N	123°04'W
North Vernon, In., U.S. (vûr'nŭn)	98	39°05'N	85°45'W
North Versailles, Pa., U.S.	230b	40°22'N	79°48'W
Northville, Mi., U.S. (nôrth-vĭl)	101b	42°26'N	83°28'W
North Wales, Pa., U.S. (wālz)	100f	40°12'N	75°16'W
North Weald Bassett, Eng., U.K.	235	51°43'N	0°10'E
North West Cape, c., Austl. (nôrth'wĕst)	202	21°50'S	112°25'E
Northwest Cape Fear, r., N.C., U.S. (căp fēr)	115	34°34'N	79°46'W
Northwestern University, pt. of i., Il., U.S.	231a	42°04'N	87°40'W
North West Gander, r., Can. (găn'dēr)	93	48°40'N	55°15'W
Northwest Harbor, b., Md., U.S.	229c	39°16'N	76°35'W
Northwest Providence Channel, strt., Bah. (prŏv'ĭ-dĕns)	122	26°15'N	78°45'W
Northwest Territories, , Can. (tĕr'ĭ-tō'rĭs)	84	64°42'N	119°09'W
North Weymouth, Ma., U.S.	227a	42°15'N	70°57'W
Northwich, Eng., U.K. (nôrth'wĭch)	144a	53°15'N	2°31'W
North Wilkesboro, N.C., U.S. (wĭlks'bûrō)	115	36°08'N	81°10'W
North Wilmington, Ma., U.S.	227a	42°34'N	71°10'W
Northwood, Ia., U.S. (nôrth'wòd)	103	43°26'N	93°13'W
Northwood, N.D., U.S.	102	47°44'N	97°36'W
Northwood, neigh., Eng., U.K.	235	51°37'N	0°25'W
North Yamhill, r., Or., U.S. (yăm' hĭl)	106c	45°22'N	123°21'W
North York, Can.	91	43°47'N	79°25'W
North York Moors, for., Eng., U.K. (yôrk mōrz')	150	54°20'N	0°40'W
North Yorkshire, co., Eng., U.K.	144a	53°50'N	1°10'W
Norton, Ks., U.S. (nôr'tŭn)	110	39°40'N	99°54'W
Norton, Ma., U.S.	100b	41°58'N	71°08'W
Norton, Va., U.S.	115	36°54'N	82°36'W
Norton Bay, b., Ak., U.S.	95	64°22'N	162°18'W
Norton Heath, Eng., U.K.	235	51°43'N	0°19'E
Norton Reservoir, res., Ma., U.S.	100b	42°01'N	71°07'W
Norton Sound, strt., Ak., U.S.	95	63°48'N	164°50'W
Norval, Can. (nôr'vål)	83d	43°39'N	79°52'W
Norwalk, Ca., U.S. (nôr'wôk)	107a	33°54'N	118°05'W
Norwalk, Ct., U.S.	100a	41°06'N	73°25'W
Norwalk, Oh., U.S.	98	41°15'N	82°35'W
Norway, Me., U.S.	92	44°11'N	70°35'W
Norway, Mi., U.S.	103	45°47'N	87°55'W
Norway, nation, Eur. (nôr'wā)	142	63°48'N	11°17'E
Norway House, Can.	84	53°59'N	97°50'W
Norwegian Sea, sea, Eur. (nôr-wē'jăn)	146	66°54'N	1°43'E
Norwell, Ma., U.S. (nôr'wĕl)	93a	42°10'N	70°47'W
Norwich, Eng., U.K.	147	52°40'N	1°15'E
Norwich, Ct., U.S. (nôr'wĭch)	99	41°20'N	72°00'W
Norwich, N.Y., U.S.	99	42°35'N	75°30'W
Norwood, Ma., U.S. (nôr'wōōd)	93a	42°11'N	71°13'W

326 Norwood-Obion

PLACE (Pronunciation)	PAGE	LAT.	LONG.
Norwood, N.C., U.S.	115	35°15′N	80°08′W
Norwood, Oh., U.S.	101f	39°10′N	84°27′W
Norwood, Pa., U.S.	229b	39°53′N	75°18′W
Norwood Park, neigh., Il., U.S.	231a	41°59′N	87°48′W
Nose, neigh., Japan	242b	34°49′N	135°09′E
Nose Creek, r., Can. (nōz)	83e	51°09′N	114°02′W
Noshiro, Japan (nō′shė-rȯ)	194	40°09′N	140°02′E
Nosivka, Ukr. (nô′sôf-kȧ)	163	50°54′N	31°35′E
Nossob, r., Afr. (nȯ′sŏb)	212	24°15′S	19°10′E
Noteć, r., Pol. (nȯ′tĕcn)	154	52°50′N	16°19′E
Notodden, Nor. (nōt′ôd′n)	152	59°35′N	9°15′E
Notre-Dame, rel., Fr.	237c	48°51′N	2°21′E
Notre Dame, Monts, mts., Can.	92	46°35′N	70°35′W
Notre Dame Bay, b., Can. (nō′t'r dȧm′)	85a	49°45′N	55°15′W
Notre-Dame-des-Victoires, neigh., Can.	227b	45°35′N	73°34′W
Notre-Dame-du-Lac, Can.	92	47°37′N	68°51′W
Nottawasaga Bay, b., Can. (nŏt′ȧ-wȧ-sā′gȧ)	91	44°45′N	80°35′W
Nottaway, r., Can. (nôt′ȧ-wā)	85	50°58′N	78°02′W
Nottingham, Eng., U.K. (nŏt′ĭng-ăm)	147	52°58′N	1°09′W
Nottingham, Pa., U.S.	229b	40°07′N	74°58′W
Nottingham Island, i., Can.	85	62°58′N	78°53′W
Nottingham Park, Il., U.S.	231a	41°46′N	87°48′W
Nottinghamshire, co., Eng., U.K.	144a	53°03′N	1°05′W
Notting Hill, Austl.	243b	37°54′S	145°08′E
Nottoway, r., Va., U.S. (nôt′ȧ-wā)	115	36°53′N	77°47′W
Notukeu Creek, r., Can.	88	49°55′N	106°30′W
Nouadhibou, Maur.	210	21°02′N	17°09′W
Nouakchott, Maur.	210	18°06′N	15°57′W
Nouamrhar, Maur.	210	19°22′N	16°31′W
Nouméa, N. Cal. (no͞o-mā′ä)	203	22°16′S	166°27′E
Nouvelle, Can. (no͞o-vĕl′)	92	48°09′N	66°22′W
Nouvelle-France, Cap de, c., Can.	85	62°03′N	74°00′W
Nouzonville, Fr. (no͞o-zôɴ-vēl′)	156	49°51′N	4°43′E
Nova Cachoeirinha, neigh., Braz.	234d	23°28′S	46°40′W
Nova Cruz, Braz. (nō′vȧ-kro͞o′z)	131	6°22′S	35°20′W
Nova Friburgo, Braz. (frė-bo͞or′gȯ)	131	22°18′S	42°31′W
Nova Iguaçu, Braz. (nō′vä-ē-gwä-so͞o′)	131	22°45′S	43°27′W
Nova Lima, Braz. (lē′mä)	129a	19°59′S	43°51′W
Nova Lisboa *see* Huambo, Ang.	212	12°44′S	15°47′E
Nova Mambone, Moz. (nō′vȧ-mȧm-bŏ′nĕ)	212	21°04′S	35°13′E
Nova Odesa, Ukr.	163	47°18′N	31°48′E
Nova Praha, Ukr.	163	48°34′N	32°54′E
Novara, Italy (nȯ-vä′rä)	148	45°24′N	8°38′E
Nova Resende, Braz.	129a	21°12′S	46°25′W
Nova Scotia, prov., Can. (skō′shȧ)	85	44°28′N	65°00′W
Novate Milanese, Italy	238c	45°32′N	9°08′E
Nova Vodolaha, Ukr.	163	49°43′N	35°51′E
Novaya Ladoga, Russia (nô′vȧ-ya lȧ-dô-gȧ)	153	60°06′N	32°16′E
Novaya Lyalya, Russia (lyȧ′lyȧ)	172a	59°03′N	60°36′E
Novaya Sibir, i., Russia (sė-bēr′)	165	75°00′N	149°00′E
Novaya Zemlya, i., Russia (zĕm-lyȧ′)	164	72°00′N	54°46′E
Nova Zagora, Bul. (zä′gȯ-rȧ)	161	42°30′N	26°01′E
Novelda, Spain (nō-vĕl′dȧ)	159	38°22′N	0°46′W
Nové Mesto nad Váhom, Slvk. (nȯ′vĕ myĕs′tō)	155	48°44′N	17°47′E
Nové Zámky, Slvk. (zȧm′kė)	147	47°58′N	18°10′E
Novgorod, Russia (nôv′gȯ-rŏt)	166	58°32′N	31°16′E
Novgorod, prov., Russia	162	58°27′N	31°55′E
Novhorod-Sivers'kyi, Ukr.	167	52°01′N	33°14′E
Novi, Mi., U.S. (nō′vĭ)	101b	42°29′N	83°28′W
Novigrad, Cro. (nō′vĭ grȧd)	160	44°09′N	15°34′E
Novi Ligure, Italy (nô′vė)	160	44°43′N	8°48′E
Novinger, Mo., U.S. (nŏv′ĭn-jẽr)	111	40°14′N	92°43′W
Novi Pazar, Bul. (pä-zär′)	161	43°22′N	27°26′E
Novi Pazar, Yugo. (pȧ-zär′)	149	43°08′N	20°30′E
Novi Sad, Yugo. (säd′)	142	45°15′N	19°53′E
Novoaidar, Ukr.	163	48°57′N	39°01′E
Novoarchangel'skoje, Russia	239b	55°55′N	37°33′E
Novoasbest, Russia (nô-vȯ-äs-bĕst′)	172a	57°43′N	60°14′E
Novocherkassk, Russia (nô′vȯ-chĕr-kȧsk′)	167	47°25′N	40°04′E
Novochovrino, neigh., Russia	239b	55°52′N	37°30′E
Novogirejevo, neigh., Russia	239b	55°45′N	37°49′E
Novokuznetsk, Russia (nō′vȯ-kȯ′z-nyĕ′tsk) (stȧ′lênsk)	164	53°43′N	86°59′E
Novo-Ladozhskiy Kanal, can., Russia (nȯ-vȯ-lä′dȯzh-skĭ kȧ-näl′)	153	59°54′N	31°19′E
Novo Mesto, Slvn. (nôvȯ mās′tȯ)	160	45°48′N	15°13′E
Novomoskovsk, Russia (nô′vȯ-mȯs-kôfsk′)	164	54°06′N	38°08′E
Novomoskovs'k, Ukr.	167	48°37′N	35°12′E
Novomyrhorod, Ukr.	163	48°46′N	31°44′E
Novonikol'skiy, Russia (nô′vȯ-nyĭ-kôl′skĭ)	172a	52°28′N	57°12′E
Novorossiysk, Russia (nô′vȯ-rô-sēsk′)	164	44°43′N	37°48′E
Novorzhev, Russia (nô′vȯ-rzhêv′)	162	57°01′N	29°17′E
Novo-Selo, Bul. (nô′vȯ-sĕ′lȯ)	161	44°09′N	22°46′E
Novosibirsk, Russia (nô′vȯ-sė-bērsk′)	164	55°09′N	82°58′E
Novosibirskiye Ostrova (New Siberian Islands), is., Russia	165	74°00′N	140°30′E
Novosil', Russia (nô′vȯ-sĭl)	162	52°58′N	37°03′E
Novosokol'niki, Russia (nô′vȯ-sȯ-kôl′nė-kė)	162	56°18′N	30°07′E
Novotatishchevskiy, Russia (nô′vȯ-tȧ-tyĭsh′chĕv-skĭ)	172a	53°22′N	60°24′E
Novoukraïnka, Ukr.	167	48°18′N	31°33′E
Novouzensk, Russia (nô-vȯ-ȯ-zĕnsk′)	167	50°40′N	48°08′E
Novozybkov, Russia (nô′vȯ-zėp′kôf)	167	52°31′N	31°54′E
Novyi Buh, Ukr.	163	47°43′N	32°33′E
Nový Jičín, Czech Rep. (nȯ′vē yė′chėn)	155	49°36′N	18°02′E
Novyy Oskol, Russia (ȯs-kôl′)	163	50°46′N	37°53′E
Novyy Port, Russia (nô′vē)	164	67°19′N	72°28′E
Nowa Sól, Pol. (nô′vȧ sŭl′)	154	51°49′N	15°41′E
Nowata, Ok., U.S. (nȯ-wä′tȧ)	111	36°42′N	95°38′W
Nowood Creek, r., Wy., U.S.	105	44°02′N	107°37′W
Nowra, Austl. (nou′rȧ)	204	34°55′S	150°45′E
Nowy Dwór Mazowiecki, Pol. (nō′vĭ dvo͞or mä-zo-vyĕts′ke)	155	52°26′N	20°46′E
Nowy Sącz, Pol. (nȯ′vė sôɴch′)	155	49°36′N	20°42′E
Nowy Targ, Pol. (tärk′)	155	49°29′N	20°02′E
Noxon Reservoir, res., Mt., U.S.	104	47°50′N	115°40′W
Noxubee, r., Ms., U.S. (nŏks′ů-bē)	114	33°20′N	88°55′W
Noyes Island, i., Ak., U.S. (noiz)	86	55°30′N	133°40′W
Nozaki, Japan (nō′zä-kė)	195b	34°43′N	135°39′E
Nozuta, Japan	242a	35°35′N	139°27′E
Nqamakwe, S. Afr. ('n-gä-mä′ᴋwȧ)	213c	32°13′S	27°57′E
Nqutu, S. Afr. ('n-ko͞o′to͞o)	213c	28°17′S	30°41′E
Nsawam, Ghana	214	5°50′N	0°20′W
Ntshoni, mtn., S. Afr.	213c	29°34′S	30°03′E
Ntwetwe Pan, pl., Bots.	212	20°00′S	24°18′E
Nubah, Jibāl an, mts., Sudan	211	12°22′N	30°39′E
Nubian Desert, des., Sudan (no͞o′bĭ-ăn)	211	21°13′N	33°09′E
Nudo Coropuna, mtn., Peru (no͞o′dô kō-rō-po͞o′nä)	130	15°53′S	72°04′W
Nudo de Pasco, mtn., Peru (dĕ pȧs′kô)	130	10°34′S	76°12′W
Nueces, r., Tx., U.S. (nů-ā′sȧs)	96	28°20′N	98°08′W
Nueltin, l., Can. (nwĕl′tin)	84	60°14′N	101°00′W
Nueva Armenia, Hond. (nwā′vä är-mā′nė-ȧ)	120	15°47′N	86°32′W
Nueva Atzacoalco, Mex.	233a	19°29′N	99°05′W
Nueva Chicago, neigh., Arg.	233d	34°40′S	58°30′W
Nueva Coronela, Cuba	233b	23°04′N	82°28′W
Nueva Esparta, dept., Ven. (nwĕ′vä ĕs-pä′r-tä)	131b	10°50′N	64°35′W
Nueva Gerona, Cuba (ᴋĕ-rȯ′nä)	122	21°55′N	82°45′W
Nueva Palmira, Ur. (päl-mē′rä)	129c	33°53′S	58°23′W
Nueva Rosita, Mex. (nȯĕ′vä rô-sė′tä)	96	27°55′N	101°10′W
Nueva San Salvador, El Sal.	120	13°41′N	89°16′W
Nueve, Canal Numero, can., Arg.	129c	36°22′S	58°19′W
Nueve de Julio, Arg. (nwā′vȧ dā ho͞o′lyȯ)	132	35°26′S	60°51′W
Nuevitas, Cuba (nwā-vē′täs)	117	21°35′N	77°15′W
Nuevitas, Bahía de, b., Cuba (bä-ē′ä dĕ nwā-vē′täs)	122	21°30′N	77°05′W
Nuevo, Ca., U.S. (nwā′vō)	107a	33°48′N	117°09′W
Nuevo Laredo, Mex. (lä-rā′dhō)	116	27°29′N	99°30′W
Nuevo Leon, state, Mex. (lȧ-ōn′)	116	26°00′N	100°00′W
Nuevo San Juan, Pan. (nwĕ′vȯ sän ᴋo͞o-ä′n)	116a	9°14′N	79°43′W
Nugumanovo, Russia (nû-gû-mä′nô-vô)	172a	55°28′N	61°50′E
Nulato, Ak., U.S. (no͞o-lä′tō)	95	64°40′N	158°18′W
Nullagine, Austl. (nŭ-lă′jēn)	202	22°00′S	120°07′E
Nullarbor Plain, pl., Austl. (nŭ-lär′bȯr)	202	31°45′S	126°30′E
Numabin Bay, b., Can. (no͞o-mä′bĭn)	88	56°30′N	103°08′W
Numansdorp, Neth.	145a	51°43′N	4°25′E
Numazu, Japan (no͞o′mä-zo͞o)	194	35°06′N	138°55′E
Numfoor, Pulau, i., Indon.	197	1°20′S	134°48′E
Nun, r., Nig.	215	5°05′N	6°10′E
Nunawading, Austl.	201a	37°49′S	145°10′E
Nuneaton, Eng., U.K. (nūn′ē-tŭn)	150	52°31′N	1°28′W
Nunivak, i., Ak., U.S. (no͞o′nĭ-văk)	94a	60°25′N	167°42′W
Ñuñoa, Chile	234b	33°28′S	70°36′W
Nunyama, Russia (nûn-yä′mȧ)	95	65°49′N	170°32′W
Nuoro, Italy (nwô′rō)	160	40°29′N	9°20′E
Nūra, r., Kaz.	169	49°48′N	73°54′E
Nurata, Uzb. (no͞or′ät′ȧ)	169	40°33′N	65°28′E
Nuremberg *see* Nürnberg, Ger.	142	49°28′N	11°07′E
Nürnberg, Ger. (nürn′bĕrgh)	142	49°28′N	11°07′E
Nurse Cay, i., Bah.	123	22°30′N	75°50′W
Nusabyin, Tur. (no͞o′sī-bėn)	167	37°05′N	41°10′E
Nushagak, r., Ak., U.S. (nū-shă-găk′)	95	59°28′N	157°40′W
Nushan Hu, l., China	190	32°50′N	117°59′E
Nushki, Pak. (nŭsh′kė)	183	29°30′N	66°02′E
Nussdorf, neigh., Aus.	239e	48°15′N	16°22′E
Nuthe, r., Ger. (no͞o′tė)	145b	52°15′N	13°11′E
Nutley, N.J., U.S. (nŭt′lė)	100a	40°49′N	74°09′W
Nutter Fort, W.V., U.S. (nŭt′ẽr fôrt)	98	39°15′N	80°15′W
Nutwood, Il., U.S. (nŭt′wȯd)	107e	39°05′N	90°34′W
Nuwaybi 'al Muzayyinah, Egypt	181a	28°59′N	34°40′E
Nuweland, S. Afr.	212a	33°58′S	18°28′E
Nyack, N.Y., U.S. (nī′ăk)	100a	41°05′N	73°55′W
Nyainqêntanglha Shan, mts., China (nyä-ĭn-chyŭn-täŋ-lä shän)	188	29°55′N	88°08′E
Nyakanazi, Tan.	217	3°00′S	31°15′E
Nyala, Sudan	211	12°00′N	24°52′E
Nyanga, r., Gabon	216	2°45′S	10°30′E
Nyanza, Rw.	217	2°21′S	29°45′E
Nyasa, Lake, l., Afr. (nyä′sä)	212	10°45′S	34°30′E
Nyazepetrovsk, Russia (nyä′zĕ-pĕ-trôvsk′)	172a	56°04′N	59°38′E
Nyborg, Den. (nü′bôr″)	152	55°20′N	10°45′E
Nybro, Swe. (nü′brȯ)	152	56°44′N	15°56′E
Nyeri, Kenya	217	0°25′S	36°57′E
Nyika Plateau, plat., Mwi.	217	10°30′S	35°50′E
Nyíregyháza, Hung. (nyē′rĕd-y'hä′zä)	149	47°58′N	21°45′E
Nykøbing, Den. (nü′kû-bĭng)	146	56°46′N	8°47′E
Nykøbing, Den.	152	54°45′N	11°54′E
Nykøbing Sjaelland, Den.	152	55°55′N	11°37′E
Nyköping, Swe. (nü′chû-pĭng)	146	58°46′N	16°58′E
Nylstroom, S. Afr. (nĭl′strōm)	212	24°42′S	28°25′E
Nymagee, Austl. (nī-mȧ-gē′)	203	32°17′S	146°18′E
Nymburk, Czech Rep. (nėm′bȯrk)	147	50°12′N	15°03′E
Nynäshamn, Swe. (nü-nĕs-hȧm'n)	152	58°53′N	17°55′E
Nyngan, Austl. (nĭŋ′găn)	203	31°31′S	147°25′E
Nyong, r., Cam. (nyông)	210	4°00′N	12°00′E
Nyou, Burkina	214	12°46′N	1°56′W
Nýřany, Czech Rep. (nėr-zhä′nė)	154	49°43′N	13°13′E
Nysa, Pol. (nē′sȧ)	155	50°29′N	17°20′E
Nytva, Russia	166	58°00′N	55°10′E
Nyungwe, Mwi.	217	10°16′S	34°07′E
Nyunzu, D.R.C.	217	5°57′S	28°01′E
Nyuya, r., Russia (nyo͞o′yȧ)	171	60°30′N	111°45′E
Nyzhni Sirohozy, Ukr.	163	46°51′N	34°25′E
Nzega, Tan.	217	4°13′S	33°11′E
N'zeto, Ang.	212	7°14′S	12°52′E
Nzi, r., C. Iv.	214	7°00′N	4°27′W
Nzwani, i., Com. (äɴ-zhwäɴ)	213	12°14′S	44°47′E

O

PLACE (Pronunciation)	PAGE	LAT.	LONG.
Oahe, Lake, res., U.S.	96	45°20′N	100°00′W
Oahu, i., Hi., U.S. (ō-ä′ho͞o) (ō-ā′hü)	96c	21°38′N	157°48′W
Oak Bay, Can.	86	48°27′N	123°18′W
Oak Bluff, Can. (ōk blŭf)	83f	49°47′N	97°21′W
Oak Creek, Co., U.S. (ōk krēk′)	105	40°20′N	106°50′W
Oakdale, Ca., U.S. (ōk′dāl)	108	37°45′N	120°52′W
Oakdale, Ky., U.S.	98	38°15′N	85°50′W
Oakdale, La., U.S.	113	30°49′N	92°40′W
Oakdale, Pa., U.S.	101e	40°24′N	80°11′W
Oakengates, Eng., U.K. (ōk′ĕn-gāts)	144a	52°41′N	2°27′W
Oakes, N.D., U.S. (ōks)	102	46°10′N	98°50′W
Oakfield, Me., U.S. (ōk′fēld)	92	46°08′N	68°10′W
Oakford, Pa., U.S. (ōk′fŏrd)	100f	40°08′N	74°58′W
Oak Forest, Il., U.S.	231a	41°36′N	87°45′W
Oak Grove, Or., U.S. (grōv)	106c	45°25′N	122°38′W
Oakham, Eng., U.K. (ōk′ăm)	144a	52°40′N	0°38′W
Oak Harbor, Oh., U.S. (ōk′här′bẽr)	98	41°30′N	83°05′W
Oak Harbor, Wa., U.S.	106a	48°18′N	122°39′W
Oakland, Ca., U.S. (ōk′lănd)	96	37°48′N	122°16′W
Oakland, Md., U.S.	229d	38°52′N	76°55′W
Oakland, Ne., U.S.	102	41°50′N	96°28′W
Oakland, neigh., Pa., U.S.	230b	40°26′N	79°58′W
Oakland City, In., U.S.	98	38°20′N	87°20′W
Oakland Gardens, neigh., N.Y., U.S.	228	40°45′N	73°45′W
Oak Lawn, Il., U.S.	101a	41°43′N	87°45′W
Oakleigh, Austl. (ōk′lȧ)	201a	37°54′S	145°05′E
Oakleigh South, Austl.	243b	37°56′S	145°05′E
Oakley, Id., U.S. (ōk′lĭ)	104	42°15′N	135°53′W
Oakley, Ks., U.S.	110	39°08′N	100°49′W
Oakman, Al., U.S. (ōk′măn)	114	33°42′N	87°20′W
Oakmont, Pa., U.S. (ōk′mōnt)	101e	40°31′N	79°50′W
Oak Mountain, mtn., Al., U.S.	100h	33°22′N	86°42′W
Oak Park, Il., U.S. (pärk)	101a	41°53′N	87°48′W
Oak Park, Mi., U.S.	230c	42°28′N	83°11′W
Oak Point, Wa., U.S.	106c	46°11′N	123°11′W
Oak Ridge, Tn., U.S. (rĭj)	114	36°01′N	84°15′W
Oak View, Md., U.S.	229d	39°01′N	76°59′W
Oakview, N.J., U.S.	229b	39°51′N	75°09′W
Oakville, Can.	83f	49°56′N	97°58′W
Oakville, Can. (ōk′vĭl)	91	43°27′N	79°40′W
Oakville, Mo., U.S.	107e	38°27′N	90°18′W
Oakville Creek, r., Can.	83d	43°34′N	79°54′W
Oakwood, Oh., U.S.	229a	41°06′N	84°23′W
Oakwood, Tx., U.S. (ōk′wȯd)	113	31°36′N	95°48′W
Oatley, Austl.	243a	33°59′S	151°05′E
Oatman, Az., U.S. (ōt′măn)	109	34°00′N	114°25′W
Oaxaca, Mex.	116	17°03′N	96°42′W
Oaxaca, state, Mex. (wä-hä′kä)	116	16°45′N	97°00′W
Oaxaca, Sierra de, mts., Mex. (sē-ĕ′r-rä dĕ)	119	16°15′N	97°25′W
Ob', r., Russia	164	62°15′N	67°00′E
Oba, Can. (ō′bȧ)	85	48°58′N	84°09′W
Obama, Japan (ō′bȧ-mä)	195	35°29′N	135°44′E
Oban, Scot., U.K. (ō′băn)	150	56°25′N	5°35′W
Oban Hills, hills, Nig.	215	5°35′N	8°30′E
O'Bannon, Ky., U.S. (ō-băn′nŏn)	101h	38°17′N	85°30′W
O Barco de Valdeorras, Spain	158	42°26′N	6°58′W
Obatogamau, l., Can. (ō-bȧ-tō′găm-ô)	91	49°38′N	74°10′W
Oberbauer, Ger.	236	51°17′N	7°26′E
Oberbonsfeld, Ger.	236	51°22′N	7°08′E
Oberelfringhausen, Ger.	236	51°20′N	7°11′E
Oberhaan, Ger.	236	51°13′N	7°02′E
Oberhausen, Ger. (ō′bĕr-hou′zĕn)	157c	51°27′N	6°51′E
Oberkassel, neigh., Ger.	236	51°14′N	6°46′E
Ober-kirchbach, Aus.	239e	48°17′N	16°12′E
Oberlaa, neigh., Aus.	239e	48°08′N	16°24′E
Oberlin, Ks., U.S. (o′bẽr-lĭn)	110	39°49′N	100°30′W
Oberlin, Oh., U.S.	98	41°15′N	82°15′W
Oberösterreich, prov., Aus.	154	48°05′N	13°15′E
Oberroth, Ger. (ō′bĕr-rōt)	145d	48°19′N	11°20′E
Ober Sankt Veit, neigh., Aus.	239e	48°11′N	16°16′E
Oberschöneweide, neigh., Ger.	238a	52°28′N	13°31′E
Oberwengern, Ger.	236	51°23′N	7°22′E
Obgruiten, Ger.	236	51°13′N	7°01′E
Obi, Kepulauan, is., Indon. (ō′bė)	197	1°25′S	128°15′E
Obi, Pulau, i., Indon.	197	1°30′S	127°45′E
Óbidos, Braz. (ō′bė-dȯzh)	131	1°57′S	55°32′W
Obihiro, Japan (ō′bē-hē′rō)	194	42°55′N	142°50′E
Obion, r., Tn., U.S.	114	36°10′N	89°25′W
Obion, North Fork, r., Tn., U.S. (ȯ-bī′ŏn)	114	35°49′N	89°06′W

PLACE (Pronunciation)	PAGE	LAT.	LONG.
Obitsu, r., Japan (ō'bět'sōō)	195a	35°19'N	140°03'E
Obock, Dji. (ō-bŏk')	218a	11°55'N	43°15'E
Obol', r., Bela. (ō-bŏl')	162	55°24'N	29°24'E
Oboyan', Russia (ô-bô-yän')	167	51°14'N	36°16'E
Obskaya Guba, b., Russia	164	67°13'N	73°45'E
Obu, neigh., Japan	242b	34°44'N	135°09'E
Obuasi, Ghana	214	6°14'N	1°39'W
Óbuda, neigh., Hung.	239g	47°33'N	19°02'E
Obukhiv, Ukr.	163	50°07'N	30°36'E
Obukhovo, Russia	172b	55°50'N	38°17'E
Obytichna kosa, spit, Ukr.	163	46°32'N	36°07'E
Očakovo, neigh., Russia	239b	55°41'N	37°27'E
Ocala, Fl., U.S. (ô-kä'là)	115	29°11'N	82°09'W
Ocampo, Mex. (ô-käm'pō)	118	22°49'N	99°23'W
Ocaña, Col. (ô-kän'yä)	130	8°15'N	73°37'W
Ocaña, Spain (ô-kä'n-yä)	158	39°58'N	3°31'W
Occidental, Cordillera, mts., Col.	130a	5°05'N	76°04'W
Occidental, Cordillera, mts., Peru	130	10°12'S	76°58'W
Ocean Beach, Ca., U.S. (ō'shăn bēch)	108a	32°44'N	117°14'W
Ocean Bight, bt., Bah.	123	21°15'N	73°15'W
Ocean City, Md., U.S.	99	38°20'N	75°10'W
Ocean City, N.J., U.S.	99	39°15'N	74°35'W
Ocean Falls, Can. (Fôls)	84	52°21'N	127°40'W
Ocean Grove, Austl.	201a	38°16'S	144°32'E
Ocean Grove, N.J., U.S. (grōv)	99	40°10'N	74°00'W
Oceanside, Ca., U.S. (ō'shăn-sīd)	108	33°11'N	117°22'W
Oceanside, N.Y., U.S.	100a	40°38'N	73°39'W
Ocean Springs, Ms., U.S. (sprĭngs)	114	30°25'N	88°49'W
Ochakiv, Ukr.	163	46°38'N	31°33'E
Ochamchira, Geor.	168	42°44'N	41°28'E
Ochiai, neigh., Japan	242a	35°43'N	139°42'E
Ochlockonee, r., Fl., U.S. (ŏk-lô-kō'nē)	114	30°10'N	84°38'W
Ocilla, Ga., U.S. (ô-sĭl'à)	114	31°36'N	83°15'W
Ockelbo, Swe. (ôk'ĕl-bô)	152	60°54'N	16°35'E
Ockham, Eng., U.K.	235	51°18'N	0°27'W
Ocklawaha, Lake, res., Fl., U.S.	115	29°30'N	81°50'W
Ocmulgee, r., Ga., U.S.	114	32°25'N	83°30'W
Ocmulgee National Monument, rec., Ga., U.S. (ôk-mŭl'gē)	114	32°45'N	83°28'W
Ocoa, Bahía de, b., Dom. Rep.	123	18°20'N	70°40'W
Ococingo, Mex. (ô-kô-sē'n-gô)	119	17°03'N	92°18'W
Ocom, Lago, l., Mex. (ô-kŏ'm)	120a	19°26'N	88°18'W
Oconee, r., Ga., U.S. (ô-kō'nē)	97	32°45'N	83°00'W
Oconee, Lake, res., Ga., U.S.	114	33°30'N	83°15'W
Oconomowoc, Wi., U.S. (ô-kŏn'ô-mô-wŏk')	103	43°06'N	88°24'W
Oconto, Wi., U.S. (ô-kŏn'tō)	103	44°54'N	87°55'W
Oconto, r., Wi., U.S.	103	45°08'N	88°24'W
Oconto Falls, Wi., U.S.	103	44°53'N	88°11'W
Ocós, Guat. (ô-kōs')	120	14°31'N	92°12'W
Ocotal, Nic. (ô-kô-täl')	120	13°36'N	86°31'W
Ocotepeque, Hond. (ô-kō-tâ-pā'kâ)	120	14°25'N	89°13'W
Ocotlán, Mex. (ô-kô-tlän')	118	20°19'N	102°44'W
Ocotlán de Morelos, Mex. (dā mô-rā'lōs)	119	16°46'N	96°41'W
Ocozocoautla, Mex. (ô-kō'zô-kwä-ōō'tlä)	119	16°44'N	93°22'W
Ocumare del Tuy, Ven. (ō-kōō-mä'ra del twē')	130	10°07'N	66°47'W
Oda, Ghana	214	5°55'N	0°59'W
Odawara, Japan (ō'dà-wä'rä)	195	35°15'N	139°10'E
Odda, Nor. (ôdh-à)	152	60°04'N	6°30'E
Odebolt, Ia., U.S. (ō'dė-bōlt)	102	42°20'N	95°14'W
Odemira, Port. (ō-dà-mē'rà)	158	37°35'N	8°40'W
Ödemiş, Tur. (û'dě-mēsh)	149	38°12'N	28°00'E
Odendaalsrus, S. Afr. (ō'dĕn-däls-rûs')	218d	27°52'S	26°41'E
Odense, Den. (ō'dhĕn-sĕ)	146	55°24'N	10°20'E
Odenton, Md., U.S. (ō'dĕn-tŭn)	100e	39°05'N	76°43'W
Odenwald, for., Ger. (ō'dĕn-väld)	154	49°39'N	8°55'E
Oder, r., Eur. (ō'dēr)	142	52°40'N	14°19'E
Oderhaff, l., Eur.	154	53°47'N	14°02'E
Odesa, Ukr.	164	46°28'N	30°44'E
Odessa, Tx., U.S. (ô-dĕs'à)	112	31°52'N	102°21'W
Odessa, Wa., U.S.	104	47°20'N	118°42'W
Odessa, prov., Ukr.	163	46°05'N	29°48'E
Odiel, r., Spain (ō-dė-ĕl')	158	37°47'N	6°42'W
Odiham, Eng., U.K. (ŏd'ē-ăm)	144b	51°14'N	0°56'W
Odintsovo, Russia (ô-dēn'tsô-vô)	172b	55°40'N	37°16'E
Odiongan, Phil. (ō-dė-ôŋ'gän)	197a	12°24'N	121°59'E
Odivelas, Port. (ō-dė-vā'lyäs)	159b	38°47'N	9°11'W
Odobeşti, Rom. (ō-dô-bĕsh't')	155	45°46'N	27°08'E
O'Donnell, Tx., U.S. (ō-dŏn'ĕl)	110	32°59'N	101°51'W
Odorhei, Rom. (ō-dôr-hā')	155	46°18'N	25°17'E
Odra see Oder, r., Eur. (ô'drà)	142	52°40'N	14°19'E
Oeiras, Braz. (wà-ė-räzh')	131	7°05'S	42°01'W
Oeirás, Port. (ô-ē'y-rá's)	159b	38°42'N	9°18'W
Oella, Md., U.S.	229c	39°16'N	76°47'W
Oelwein, Ia., U.S. (ōl'wīn)	103	42°40'N	91°56'W
Oespel, neigh., Ger.	236	51°30'N	7°23'E
Oestrich, Ger.	236	51°22'N	7°38'E
Oestrich, neigh., Ger.	236	51°34'N	7°22'E
Oestrum, Ger.	236	51°25'N	6°40'E
O'Fallon, Il., U.S. (ō-făl'ŭn)	107e	38°36'N	89°55'W
O'Fallon Creek, r., Mt., U.S.	105	46°25'N	104°47'W
Ofanto, r., Italy (ō-făn'tō)	160	41°08'N	15°33'E
Offa, Nig.	215	8°09'N	4°44'E
Offenbach, Ger. (ôf'ĕn-bäk)	154	50°06'N	8°50'E
Offenburg, Ger. (ôf'ĕn-bòrgh)	154	48°28'N	7°57'E
Ofin, Nig.	244d	6°33'N	3°30'E
Ofomori, neigh., Japan	242a	35°34'N	139°44'E
Ofuna, Japan (ō'fōō-nä)	195a	35°21'N	139°32'E
Ogaden Plateau, plat., Eth.	218a	6°45'N	44°53'E
Ogaki, Japan	194	35°21'N	136°36'E
Ogallala, Ne., U.S. (ō-gä-lä'lä)	102	41°08'N	101°44'W

PLACE (Pronunciation)	PAGE	LAT.	LONG.
Ogawa, Japan	242a	35°44'N	139°28'E
Ogbomosho, Nig. (ŏg-bô-mō'shō)	210	8°08'N	4°15'E
Ogden, Ia., U.S. (ŏg'dĕn)	103	42°10'N	94°20'W
Ogden, Ut., U.S.	96	41°14'N	111°58'W
Ogden, r., Ut., U.S.	107b	41°16'N	111°54'W
Ogden Peak, mtn., Ut., U.S.	107b	41°11'N	111°51'W
Ogdensburg, N.J., U.S. (ŏg'dĕnz-bûrg)	100a	41°05'N	74°36'W
Ogdensburg, N.Y., U.S.	97	44°40'N	75°30'W
Ogeechee, r., Ga., U.S. (ô-gē'chė)	115	32°35'N	81°50'W
Ogies, S. Afr.	218d	26°03'S	29°04'E
Ogilvie Mountains, mts., Can. (ō'g'l-vĭ)	84	64°45'N	138°10'W
Oglesby, Il., U.S. (ō'g'lz-bĭ)	98	41°20'N	89°00'W
Oglio, r., Italy (ôl'yō)	160	45°15'N	10°19'E
Ōgo, Japan (ō'gô)	195b	34°49'N	135°06'E
Ogou, r., Togo	214	8°05'N	1°30'E
Ogoyo, Nig.	244d	6°26'N	3°29'E
Ogudnëvo, Russia (ŏg-ód-nyô'vô)	172b	56°04'N	38°17'E
Ogudu, Nig.	244d	6°34'N	3°24'E
Ogulin, Cro. (ō-gōō-lēn')	160	45°17'N	15°11'E
Ogwashi-Uku, Nig.	215	6°10'N	6°31'E
O'Higgins, prov., Chile (ô-kė'gēns)	129b	34°17'S	70°52'W
Ohio, state, U.S. (ô'hī'ō)	97	40°30'N	83°15'W
Ohio, r., U.S.	97	37°25'N	88°05'W
Ohoopee, r., Ga., U.S. (ô-hōō'pe-mc)	115	32°32'N	82°38'W
Ohře, r., Eur. (ôr'zhě)	154	50°08'N	12°45'E
Ohrid, Mac. (ō'krēd)	161	41°08'N	20°46'E
Ohrid, Lake, l., Eur.	161	40°58'N	20°35'E
Ōi, Japan (oi')	195a	35°51'N	139°31'E
Oi-Gawa, r., Japan (ō'ē-gä'wà)	195	35°09'N	138°05'E
Oil City, Pa., U.S. (oil sĭ'tĭ)	99	41°25'N	79°40'W
Oirschot, Neth.	145a	51°30'N	5°20'E
Oise, r., Fr. (wäz)	147	49°30'N	2°56'E
Oisterwijk, Neth.	145a	51°34'N	5°13'E
Oita, Japan (ō'ē-tä)	194	33°14'N	131°38'E
Oji, Japan (ō'jė)	195b	34°36'N	135°43'E
Ojinaga, Mex. (ō-kē-nä'gä)	116	29°34'N	104°26'W
Ojitlán, Mex. (ōkė-tlän') (sän-lōō'käs)	119	18°04'N	96°23'W
Ojo Caliente, Mex. (ōkō käl-yĕn'tâ)	118	21°50'N	100°43'W
Ojocaliente, Mex. (ô-kō-kä-lyĕ'n-tĕ)	118	22°39'N	102°15'W
Ojo del Toro, Pico, mtn., Cuba (pē'kô-ô-kō-dĕl-tô'rô)	122	19°55'N	77°25'W
Oka, Can. (ō-kä)	83a	45°28'N	74°05'W
Oka, r., Russia (ô-kà')	166	55°10'N	42°10'E
Oka, r., Russia (ô-kä')	167	52°10'N	35°20'E
Oka, r., Russia (ō-kä')	170	53°28'N	101°09'E
Okahandja, Nmb.	212	21°50'S	16°45'E
Okanagan (Okanogan), r., N.A. (ō'kà-näg'ăn)	87	49°06'N	119°43'W
Okanagan Lake, l., Can.	84	50°00'N	119°28'W
Okano, r., Gabon (ō'kä'nō)	210	0°15'N	11°08'E
Okanogan, Wa., U.S.	104	48°20'N	119°34'W
Okanogan, r., Wa., U.S.	104	48°36'N	119°33'W
Okatibbee, r., Ms., U.S. (ō'kä-tĭb'ē)	114	32°37'N	88°54'W
Okatoma Creek, r., Ms., U.S. (ô-kà-tō'mă)	114	31°43'N	89°34'W
Okavango (Cubango), r., Afr.	212	18°00'S	20°00'E
Okavango Swamp, sw., Bots.	212	19°30'S	23°02'E
Okaya, Japan (ō'kà-yà)	195	36°04'N	138°01'E
Okayama, Japan (ō'kà-yä'mà)	189	34°39'N	133°54'E
Okazaki, Japan (ō'kà-zä'kė)	194	34°58'N	137°09'E
Okeechobee, Fl., U.S. (ō-kė-chō'bē)	115	27°15'N	80°50'W
Okeechobee, Lake, l., Fl., U.S.	97	27°00'N	80°49'W
O'Keefe Centre, bldg., Can.	227c	43°37'N	79°22'W
Okeene, Ok., U.S. (ô-kēn')	110	36°06'N	98°19'W
Okefenokee Swamp, sw., U.S. (ō'kē-fē-nō'kē)	115	30°54'N	82°20'W
Okemah, Ok., U.S. (ô-kē'mä)	111	35°26'N	96°18'W
Okene, Nig.	215	7°33'N	6°15'E
Oke Ogbe, Nig.	244d	6°24'N	3°23'E
Okha, Russia (ŭ-ĸä')	165	53°44'N	143°12'E
Okhotino, Russia (ô-kô'tĭ-nô)	172b	56°14'N	38°24'E
Okhotsk, Russia (ô-kôtsk')	165	59°28'N	143°32'E
Okhotsk, Sea of, sea, Asia (ô-kôtsk')	165	56°45'N	146°00'E
Okhtyrka, Ukr.	167	50°18'N	34°53'E
Okinawa, i., Japan	189	26°30'N	128°00'E
Okino, i., Japan (ō'kē-nô)	195	36°22'N	133°27'E
Ōkino Erabu, i., Japan (ō-kē'nô-â-rä'bōō)	194	27°18'N	129°00'E
Oklahoma, state, U.S. (ô-klá-hō'mà)	96	36°00'N	98°20'W
Oklahoma City, Ok., U.S.	96	35°27'N	97°32'W
Oklawaha, r., Fl., U.S. (ŏk-lȧ-wô'hô)	115	29°13'N	82°00'W
Okmulgee, Ok., U.S. (ôk-mŭl'gē)	111	35°37'N	95°58'W
Okolona, Ky., U.S. (ō-kô-lō'nȧ)	101h	38°08'N	85°41'W
Okolona, Ms., U.S.	114	33°59'N	88°43'W
Oktemberyan, Arm.	168	40°09'N	44°02'E
Okushiri, i., Japan (ō'koo-shē'rē)	194	42°12'N	139°30'E
Okuta, Nig.	215	9°14'N	3°15'E
Olalla, Wa., U.S. (ō-lä'lä)	106a	47°26'N	122°33'W
Olanchito, Hond. (ō'län-chē'tô)	120	15°28'N	86°35'W
Öland, i., Swe. (û-länd')	142	57°03'N	17°15'E
Olathe, Ks., U.S. (ô-lā'thė)	107f	38°53'N	94°49'W
Olavarría, Arg. (ō-lä-vär-rē'ä)	132	36°49'N	60°15'W
Oława, Pol. (ô-lä'và)	155	50°57'N	17°18'E
Olazoago, Arg. (ō-läz-kôä'gô)	129c	35°14'S	60°37'W
Olbia, Italy (ô'l-byä)	160	40°55'N	9°28'E
Olching, Ger. (ōl'kĕng)	145d	48°13'N	11°21'E
Old Bahama Channel, strt., N.A. (bȧ-hā'mȧ)	122	22°45'N	78°30'W
Old Bight, Bah.	123	24°15'N	75°20'W
Old Bridge, N.J., U.S. (brĭj)	100a	40°24'N	74°22'W
Old Brookville, N.Y., U.S.	228	40°49'N	73°36'W
Old Crow, Can. (crō)	84	67°51'N	139°58'W
Oldenburg, Ger. (ôl'dĕn-bòrgh)	146	53°09'N	8°13'E
Old Forge, Pa., U.S. (fôrj)	99	41°20'N	75°50'W
Oldham, Eng., U.K. (ōld'ăm)	150	53°32'N	2°07'W

PLACE (Pronunciation)	PAGE	LAT.	LONG.
Oldham Pond, l., Ma., U.S.	227a	42°03'N	70°51'W
Old Harbor, Ak., U.S. (här'bēr)	95	57°18'N	153°20'W
Old Head of Kinsale, c., Ire. (ōld hĕd ŏv kĭn-sāl)	150	51°35'N	8°35'W
Old Malden, neigh., Eng., U.K.	235	51°23'N	0°15'W
Old North Church, pt. of i., Ma., U.S.	227a	42°22'N	71°03'W
Old R, Tx., U.S.	113a	29°54'N	94°52'W
Olds, Can. (ōldz)	84	51°47'N	114°06'W
Old Tate, Bots.	212	21°18'S	27°43'E
Old Town, Me., U.S. (toun)	92	44°55'N	68°42'W
Old Westbury, N.Y., U.S.	228	40°47'N	73°37'W
Old Windsor, Eng., U.K.	235	51°28'N	0°35'W
Old Wives Lake, l., Can. (wīvz)	88	50°05'N	106°00'W
Olean, N.Y., U.S. (ō-lė-ăn')	97	42°05'N	78°25'W
Olecko, Pol. (ô-lĕt'skô)	155	54°02'N	22°29'E
Olekma, r., Russia (ô-lyĕk-má')	171	55°41'N	120°33'E
Olëkminsk, Russia (ô-lyĕk-mênsk')	165	60°39'N	120°40'E
Oleksandriia, Ukr.	162	48°40'N	33°07'E
Olenëk, r., Russia (ô-lyĕ-nyôk')	165	68°00'N	113°00'E
Oléron Île, d', i., Fr. (ēl' dō lā-rôɴ')	147	45°52'N	1°58'W
Oleśnica, Pol. (ô-lĕsh-nĭ'tsà)	147	51°13'N	17°24'E
Olfen, Ger. (ōl'fĕn)	157c	51°43'N	7°22'E
Ol'ga, Russia (ôl'gà)	165	43°48'N	135°44'E
Ol'gi, Zaliv, b., Russia (zä'lĭf ôl'gĭ)	194	43°43'N	135°25'E
Olhão, Port. (ôl-youɴ')	148	37°02'N	7°54'W
Ol'hopil', Ukr.	163	48°11'N	29°28'E
Olievenhoutpoort, S. Afr.	213b	25°58'S	27°55'E
Ólimbos, Grc.	149	40°03'N	22°22'E
Ólimbos, mtn., Cyp.	181a	34°56'N	32°52'E
Olinda, Austl.	243b	37°51'S	145°22'E
Olinda, Braz. (ô-lē'n-dä)	131	8°00'S	34°58'W
Olinda, Braz.	132b	22°49'S	43°25'W
Oliva, Spain (ô-lē'vä)	159	38°54'N	0°07'W
Oliva de la Frontera, Spain (ô-lē'vä dā)	158	38°33'N	6°55'W
Olivais, neigh., Port.	238d	34°46'N	9°06'W
Olive Hill, Ky., U.S. (ŏl'ĭv)	98	38°15'N	83°10'W
Oliveira, Braz. (ô-lē-vā'rä)	129a	20°42'S	44°49'W
Olive Mount, neigh., Eng., U.K.	237a	53°24'N	2°55'W
Olivenza, Spain (ō-lē-vĕn'thä)	158	38°42'N	7°06'W
Oliver, Can.	83g	53°38'N	113°21'W
Oliver, Can. (ŏ'lĭ-vẽr)	84	49°11'N	119°33'W
Oliver, Wi., U.S. (ŏ'lĭvẽr)	107h	46°39'N	92°12'W
Oliver Lake, l., Can.	83g	53°19'N	113°00'W
Olivia, Mn., U.S. (ō-lĭv'ē-ȧ)	102	44°46'N	95°00'W
Olivos, Arg. (ōlē'vōs)	132a	34°30'S	58°29'W
Ollagüe, Chile (ō-lyä'gâ)	130	21°17'S	68°17'W
Ollerton, Eng., U.K. (ôl'ẽr-tŭn)	144a	53°12'N	1°02'W
Olmos Park, Tx., U.S. (ōl'mŭs pärk')	107d	29°27'N	98°32'W
Olmsted, Oh., U.S.	229a	41°24'N	81°44'W
Olmsted Falls, Oh., U.S.	229a	41°22'N	81°55'W
Olney, Il., U.S. (ŏl'nĭ)	98	38°45'N	88°05'W
Olney, Or., U.S. (ŏl'nē)	106c	46°06'N	123°45'W
Olney, Tx., U.S.	110	33°24'N	98°43'W
Olney, neigh., Pa., U.S.	229b	40°02'N	75°08'W
Olomane, r., Can. (ō'lô mà'nĕ)	93	51°05'N	60°50'W
Olomouc, Czech Rep. (ô'lô-mōts)	147	49°37'N	17°15'E
Olonets, Russia (ô-lô'nĕts)	153	60°58'N	32°54'E
Olongapo, Phil.	196	14°49'S	120°17'E
Oloron, Gave d', r., Fr. (gäv-dō-lō-rôɴ')	156	43°21'N	0°44'W
Oloron-Sainte Marie, Fr. (ō-lō-rôɴt'săɴt mà-rē')	156	43°11'N	1°37'W
Olot, Spain (ô-lōt')	148	42°09'N	2°30'E
Olpe, Ger. (ōl'pĕ)	157c	51°02'N	7°51'E
Olsnitz, Ger. (ōlz'nētz)	154	50°25'N	12°11'E
Olsztyn, Pol. (ōl'shtĕn)	146	53°47'N	20°28'E
Olt, r., Rom.	149	44°09'N	24°40'E
Olten, Switz. (ōl'tĕn)	154	47°20'N	7°53'E
Oltenița, Rom. (ôl-tā'nĭ-tsà)	161	44°05'N	26°39'E
Olvera, Spain (ôl-vĕ'rä)	158	36°55'N	5°16'W
Olympia, Wa., U.S. (ô-lĭm'pĭ-à)	96	47°02'N	122°52'W
Olympic Mountains, mts., Wa., U.S.	104	47°54'N	123°58'W
Olympic National Park, rec., Wa., U.S. (ô-lĭm'pĭk)	96	47°54'N	123°00'W
Olympieion, pt. of i., Grc.	239d	37°58'N	23°44'E
Olympus, Mount, mtn., Wa., U.S. (ô-lĭm'pŭs)	104	47°43'N	123°30'W
Olyphant, Pa., U.S. (ŏl'ĭ-fănt)	99	41°30'N	75°40'W
Olyutorskiy, Mys, c., Russia (ŭl-yōō'tôr-skė)	165	59°49'N	167°16'E
Omae-Zaki, c., Japan (ō'mä-å zä'kė)	195	34°37'N	138°15'E
Omagh, N. Ire., U.K. (ō'mä)	150	54°35'N	7°25'W
Omaha, Ne., U.S. (ō'mà-hä)	97	41°18'N	95°57'W
Omaha Indian Reservation, I.R., Ne., U.S.	102	42°09'N	96°08'W
Oman, nation, Asia	182	20°00'N	57°45'E
Oman, Gulf of, b., Asia	182	24°24'N	58°58'E
Omaruru, Nmb. (ō-mä-rōō'rōō)	212	21°25'S	16°50'E
Ombrone, r., Italy (ôm-brō'nā)	160	42°48'N	11°18'E
Omdurman, Sudan	211	15°45'N	32°30'E
Omealca, Mex. (ōmā-äl'kō)	119	18°44'N	96°45'W
Ometepec, Mex. (ô-mā-tà-pĕk')	118	16°41'N	98°27'W
Om Hajer, Eth.	211	14°06'N	36°46'E
Omineca, r., Can. (ō-mĭ-nĕk'ȧ)	86	55°50'N	125°45'W
Omineca Mountains, mts., Can.	86	56°00'N	125°00'W
Ōmiya, Japan (ō'mē-yà)	195	35°54'S	139°38'E
Omo, r., Eth. (ō'mō)	211	5°54'N	36°09'E
Omoa, Hond. (ô-mō'rä)	120	15°43'N	88°03'W
Omoko, Nig.	215	5°20'N	6°39'E
Omolon, r., Russia (ō'mô-lôn)	171	67°43'N	159°15'E
Omori, Japan (ō'mō-rē)	195a	35°50'N	140°09'E
Ometepe, Isla de, i., Nic. (ē's-lä-dĕ-ō-mō-tā'pà)	120	11°32'N	85°30'W
Omro, Wi., U.S. (ŏm'rō)	103	44°01'N	89°46'W
Omsk, Russia (ômsk)	164	55°12'N	73°19'E
Ōmura, Japan (ō'mōō-rà)	195	32°56'N	129°57'E

ng-sing; ŋ-baŋk; ɴ-nasalized n; nŏd; cŏmmit; ōld; ôbey; ôrder; oi-boil; fōōd; ŏo-as oo in foot; ou-out; s-soft; sh-dish; th-thin; pūre; ůnite; ûrn; stŭd; circŭs; ü-as in French tu; '-indeterminate vowel.

328 Ōmuta-Oświęcim

PLACE (Pronunciation)	PAGE	LAT.	LONG.
Ōmuta, Japan (ō-mò-tá)	195	33°02'N	130°28'E
Omutninsk, Russia (ŏ'mōō-tnēnsk)	166	58°38'N	52°10'E
Onawa, Ia., U.S. (ŏn-à-wà)	102	42°02'N	96°05'W
Onaway, Mi., U.S.	98	45°25'N	84°10'W
Once, neigh., Arg.	233d	34°36'S	58°24'W
Oncócua, Ang.	216	16°34'S	13°28'E
Onda, Spain (ōn'dä)	159	39°58'N	0°13'W
Ondava, r., Slvk. (ōn'dá-vá)	155	48°51'N	21°40'E
Ondo, Nig.	215	7°04'N	4°47'E
Öndörhaan, Mong.	189	47°20'N	110°40'E
Onega, Russia (ô-nyě'gá)	164	63°50'N	38°08'E
Onega, r., Russia	166	63°20'N	39°20'E
Onega, Lake *see* Onezhskoye Ozero, l., Russia	166	62°02'N	34°35'E
Oneida, N.Y., U.S. (ô-nī'dà)	99	43°05'N	75°40'W
Oneida, l., N.Y., U.S.	99	43°10'N	76°00'W
O'Neill, Ne., U.S. (ō-nēl')	102	42°28'N	98°38'W
Oneonta, N.Y., U.S. (ō-nē-ŏn'tà)	99	42°25'N	75°05'W
Onezhskaja Guba, b., Russia	166	64°30'N	36°00'E
Onezhskiy, Poluostrov, pen., Russia	166	64°30'N	37°40'E
Onezhskoye Ozero, Russia (ô-năsh'skô-yě ô'zě-rō)	166	62°02'N	34°35'E
Ongiin Hiid, Mong.	188	46°00'N	102°46'E
Ongole, India	187	15°36'N	80°03'E
Onilahy, r., Madag.	213	23°41'S	45°00'E
Onitsha, Nig. (ô-nĭt'shá)	210	6°09'N	6°47'W
Onomichi, Japan (ō'nô-mē'chê)	194	34°27'N	133°12'E
Onon, r., Asia (ô'nôn)	165	49°00'N	112°00'E
Onoto, Ven. (ō-nŏ'tō)	131b	9°38'N	65°03'W
Onslow, Austl. (ŏnz'lō)	202	21°53'S	115°00'E
Onslow B, N.C., U.S. (ônz'lō)	115	34°22'N	77°35'W
Ontake San, mtn., Japan (ôn'tä-kä sän)	194	35°55'N	137°29'E
Ontario, Ca., U.S. (ŏn-tā'rĭ-ō)	107a	34°04'N	117°39'E
Ontario, Or., U.S.	104	44°02'N	116°57'W
Ontario, prov., Can.	85	50°47'N	88°50'W
Ontario, Lake, l., N.A.	97	43°35'N	79°05'W
Ontario Science Centre, bldg., Can.	227c	43°43'N	79°21'W
Ontinyent, Spain	159	38°48'N	0°35'W
Ontonagon, Mi., U.S. (ŏn-tô-năg'ŏn)	103	46°50'N	89°20'W
Ōnuki, Japan (ō'nōō-kê)	195a	35°17'N	139°51'E
Oodnadatta, Austl. (ōōd'nâ-dá'tá)	202	27°38'S	135°40'E
Ooldea Station, Austl. (ōōl-dā'ä)	202	30°35'S	132°08'E
Oologah Reservoir, res., Ok., U.S.	97	36°43'N	95°32'W
Ooltgensplaat, Neth.	145a	51°41'N	4°19'E
Oostanaula, r., Ga., U.S. (ōō-stá-nô'lá)	114	34°25'N	85°10'W
Oostende, Bel. (ōst-ĕn'dē)	147	51°14'N	2°55'E
Oosterhout, Neth.	145a	51°38'N	4°52'E
Ooster Schelde, r., Neth.	145a	51°40'N	3°40'E
Ootsa Lake, l., Can.	86	53°49'N	126°18'W
Opalaca, Sierra de, mts., Hond. (sē-sě'r-rä-dě-ô-pä-lä'kä)	120	14°30'N	88°29'W
Opasquia, Can. (ō-păs'kwê-à)	89	53°16'N	93°53'W
Opatów, Pol. (ō-pä'tôf)	155	50°47'N	21°25'E
Opava, Czech Rep. (ō'pä-vä)	155	49°56'N	17°52'E
Opelika, Al., U.S. (ŏp-ê-lī'kà)	114	32°39'N	85°23'W
Opelousas, La., U.S. (ŏp-ē-lōō'sås)	113	30°33'N	92°04'W
Opeongo, l., Can. (ŏp-ê-ôŋ'gō)	91	45°40'N	78°20'W
Opheim, Mt., U.S. (ô-fīm')	105	48°51'N	106°19'W
Ophir, Ak., U.S. (ō'fēr)	95	63°10'N	156°28'W
Ophir, Mount, mtn., Malay.	181b	2°22'N	102°37'E
Ophirton, neigh., S. Afr.	244b	26°14'S	28°01'E
Opico, El Sal. (ô-pē'kō)	120	13°50'N	89°23'W
Opinaca, r., Can. (ŏp-ĭ-nä'kå)	85	52°28'N	77°40'W
Opishnia, Ukr.	163	49°57'N	34°34'E
Opladen, Ger. (ōp'lä-děn)	157c	51°04'N	7°00'E
Opobo, Nig.	215	4°34'N	7°27'E
Opochka, Russia (ô-pôch'kå)	166	56°43'N	28°39'E
Opoczno, Pol. (ô-pôch'nō)	155	51°22'N	20°18'E
Opole, Pol. (ô-pôl'å)	147	50°42'N	17°55'E
Opole Lubelskie, Pol. (ô-pō'lä lōō-běl'skyě)	155	51°09'N	21°58'E
Opp, Al., U.S. (ŏp)	114	31°18'N	86°15'W
Oppdal, Nor. (ôp'däl)	152	62°37'N	9°41'E
Opportunity, Wa., U.S. (ŏp-ŏr tū'nĭ tĭ)	104	47°37'N	117°20'W
Oppum, neigh., Ger.	236	51°19'N	6°37'E
Oquirrh Mountains, mts., Ut., U.S. (ō'kwēr)	107b	40°38'N	112°11'W
Oradea, Rom. (ô-räd'yä)	142	47°02'N	21°55'E
Oradell, N.J., U.S.	228	40°57'N	74°02'W
Oral, Kaz.	169	51°14'N	51°22'E
Oran, Alg. (ō-rän)(ō-rän')	210	35°46'N	0°45'W
Orán, Arg. (ō-rá'n)	132	23°13'S	64°17'W
Oran, Mo., U.S. (ôr'àn)	111	37°05'N	89°39'W
Oran, Sebkha d', l., Alg.	159	35°28'N	0°28'W
Orange, Austl. (ŏr'ěnj)	203	33°15'S	149°08'E
Orange, Fr. (ô-ranzh')	147	44°08'N	4°48'E
Orange, Ca., U.S.	107a	33°48'N	117°51'W
Orange, Ct., U.S.	99	41°15'N	73°00'W
Orange, N.J., U.S.	100a	40°46'N	74°14'W
Orange, Tx., U.S.	111	30°07'N	93°44'W
Orange, r., Afr.	212	29°15'S	17°30'E
Orange, Cabo, c., Braz. (kä-bô-rá'n-zhě)	131	4°25'N	51°30'W
Orangeburg, S.C., U.S. (ŏr'ěnj-bûrg)	115	33°30'N	80°50'W
Orange Cay, i., Bah. (ŏr-ěnj kē)	122	24°55'N	79°05'W
Orange City, Ia., U.S.	102	43°01'N	96°06'W
Orange Grove, neigh., S. Afr.	244b	26°10'S	28°05'E
Orange Lake, l., Fl., U.S.	115	29°30'N	82°12'W
Orangeville, Can. (ŏr'ěnj-vĭl)	91	43°55'N	80°06'W
Orangeville, S. Afr.	218d	27°05'S	28°13'E
Orange Walk, Belize (wôl''k)	120a	18°09'N	88°32'W
Orani, Phil. (ō-rä'nê)	197a	14°47'N	120°32'E
Oranienburg, Ger. (ō-rä'nê-ěn-bòrgh)	154	52°45'N	13°14'E
Oranjemund, Nmb.	212	28°33'S	16°20'E
Orăştie, Rom. (ô-rûsh'tyå)	161	45°50'N	23°14'E
Orbetello, Italy (ôr-bå-těl'lō)	160	42°27'N	11°15'E
Orbigo, r., Spain (ôr-bē'gō)	158	42°30'N	5°55'W
Orbost, Austl. (ôr'bŭst)	204	37°43'S	148°20'E
Orcas, i., Wa., U.S. (ôr'kås)	106d	48°43'N	122°52'W
Orchard Farm, Mo., U.S. (ôr'chērd färm)	107e	38°53'N	90°27'W
Orchard Park, N.Y., U.S.	101c	42°46'N	78°46'W
Orchards, Wa., U.S. (ôr'chēdz)	106c	45°40'N	122°33'W
Orchila, Isla, i., Ven.	130	11°47'N	66°34'W
Ord, Ne., U.S. (ôrd)	102	41°35'N	98°57'W
Ord, r., Austl.	202	17°30'S	128°40'E
Ord, Mount, mtn., Az., U.S.	109	33°55'N	109°40'W
Orda, Russia (ôr'dá)	172a	57°10'N	57°12'E
Ordes, Spain	158	43°00'N	8°24'W
Ordos Desert, des., China	188	39°12'N	108°10'E
Ordu, Tur. (ôr'dò)	149	41°00'N	37°50'E
Ordway, Co., U.S. (ôrd'wā)	110	38°11'N	103°46'W
Örebro, Swe. (û'rē-brō)	146	59°16'N	15°11'E
Oredezh, r., Russia (ō'rě-dězh)	172c	59°23'N	30°21'E
Oregon, Il., U.S.	103	42°01'N	89°21'W
Oregon, state, U.S.	96	43°40'N	121°50'W
Oregon Caves National Monument, rec., Or., U.S. (cāvz)	104	42°05'N	123°13'W
Oregon City, Or., U.S.	106c	45°21'N	122°36'W
Öregrund, Swe. (û-rě-grònd)	152	60°20'N	18°26'E
Orekhovo, Bul.	161	43°43'N	23°59'E
Orekhovo-Zuyevo, Russia (ôr-yě'kô-vô zò'yě-vô)	164	55°46'N	39°00'E
Orël, Russia (ôr-yôl')	164	52°59'N	36°05'E
Orël, prov., Russia	162	52°35'N	36°08'E
Oreland, Pa., U.S.	229b	40°07'N	75°11'W
Orem, Ut., U.S. (ō'rěm)	109	40°15'N	111°50'W
Ore Mountains *see* Erzgebirge, mts., Eur.	142	50°29'N	12°40'E
Orenburg, Russia (ô'rěn-bōōrg)	164	51°50'N	55°05'E
Øresund, strt., Eur.	152	55°50'N	12°40'E
Órganos, Sierra de los, mts., Cuba (sē-ě'r-rá-dě-lôs-ŏ'r-gä-nôs)	122	22°20'N	84°10'W
Organ Pipe Cactus National Monument, rec., Az., U.S. (ôr'găn pīp kăk'tŭs)	109	32°14'N	113°05'W
Orgãos, Serra das, mtn., Braz. (sě'r-rä-däs-ôr-gouɴ's)	129a	22°30'S	43°01'W
Orhei, Mol.	167	47°27'N	28°49'E
Orhon, r., Mong.	188	48°33'N	103°07'E
Oriental, Cordillera, mts., Col. (kôr-dēl-yě'rä)	130a	3°30'N	74°27'W
Oriental, Cordillera, mts., Dom. Rep. (kôr-dēl-yě'rä-ô-ryě'n-täl)	123	18°55'N	69°40'W
Oriental, Cordillera, mts., S.A. (kôr-dēl-yě'rä ō-rê-ěn-täl')	130	14°00'S	68°33'W
Orikhiv, Ukr.	163	47°34'N	35°51'E
Oril', r., Ukr.	163	49°08'N	34°55'E
Orillia, Can. (ô-rĭl'ĭ-à)	85	44°35'N	79°25'W
Orin, Wy., U.S.	105	42°40'N	105°10'W
Orinda, Ca., U.S.	106b	37°53'N	122°11'W
Orinoco, Río, r., Ven. (rē'ō-ō-rĭ-nō'kō)	130	8°32'N	63°13'W
Oriola, Spain	159	38°04'N	0°55'W
Orion, Phil. (ō-rê-ōn')	197a	14°37'N	120°34'E
Orissa, state, India (ŏ-rĭs'á)	183	25°09'N	83°50'E
Oristano, Italy (ô-rês-tä'nō)	148	39°53'N	8°38'E
Oristano, Golfo di, b., Italy (gôl-fô-dē-ô-rês-tä'nō)	160	39°53'N	8°12'E
Orituco, r., Ven. (ô-rē-tōō'kō)	131b	9°37'N	66°25'W
Oriuco, r., Ven. (ô-rēōō'kō)	131b	9°36'N	66°25'W
Orivesi, l., Fin.	153	62°15'N	29°55'E
Orizaba, Mex. (ô-rê-zä'bä)	117	18°52'N	97°05'W
Orizaba, Pico de, vol., Mex.	116	19°04'N	97°14'W
Orkanger, Nor.	152	63°19'N	9°54'W
Orkla, r., Nor. (ôr'klå)	152	62°55'N	9°50'E
Orkney, S. Afr. (ôrk'nĭ)	218d	26°58'S	26°39'E
Orkney Islands, is., Scot., U.K.	142	59°01'N	2°08'W
Orlando, S. Afr. (ôr-län-dò)	213b	26°15'S	27°56'E
Orlando, Fl., U.S. (ôr-lăn'dō)	97	28°32'N	81°22'W
Orlando West Extension, S. Afr.	244b	26°15'S	27°54'E
Orland Park, Il., U.S. (ôr-lăn')	101a	41°38'N	87°52'W
Orleans, Can. (ôr-lå-äɴ')	83c	45°28'N	75°31'W
Orléans, Fr. (ôr-lā-äɴ')	142	47°55'N	1°56'E
Orleans, In., U.S. (ôr-lênz')	98	38°40'N	86°25'W
Orléans, Île d', i., Can.	91	46°56'N	70°57'W
Orly, Fr.	157b	48°45'N	2°24'E
Ormond, Austl.	243b	37°54'S	145°03'E
Ormond Beach, Fl., U.S. (ôr'mŏnd)	115	29°15'N	81°05'W
Ormskirk, Eng., U.K. (ôrms'kěrk)	144a	53°34'N	2°53'W
Ormstown, Can. (ôrms'toun)	83a	45°07'N	74°00'W
Orneta, Pol. (ôr-nyě'tä)	155	54°07'N	20°10'E
Örnsköldsvik, Swe. (ûrn'skôlts-vēk)	146	63°10'N	18°32'E
Oro, Río del, r., Mex.	109	26°04'N	105°40'W
Oro, Río del, r., Mex. (rē'ō děl ō'rō)	118	18°04'N	100°59'W
Orobie, Alpi, mts., Italy (äl'pē-ô-rŏ'byě)	160	46°05'N	9°47'E
Oron, Nig.	215	4°48'N	8°14'E
Orosei, Golfo di, b., Italy (gôl-fô-dē-ô-rô-sā'ē)	160	40°12'N	9°45'E
Orosháza, Hung. (ô-rôsh-hä'sô)	155	46°33'N	20°31'E
Orosi, vol., C.R. (ō-rō'sē)	120	11°00'N	85°30'W
Oroville, Ca., U.S. (ŏr'ō-vĭl)	108	39°29'N	121°34'W
Oroville, Wa., U.S.	104	48°55'N	119°25'W
Oroville, Lake, res., Ca., U.S.	108	39°32'N	121°25'W
Orpington, neigh., Eng., U.K.	235	51°23'N	0°06'E
Orreagal, Spain	158	43°00'N	1°17'W
Orrville, Oh., U.S. (ôr'vĭl)	98	40°45'N	81°50'W
Orsa, Swe. (ōr'sä)	152	61°08'N	14°35'E
Orsay, Fr.	237c	48°42'N	2°11'E
Orsett, Eng., U.K.	235	51°31'N	0°22'E
Orsha, Bela. (ôr'shá)	166	54°29'N	30°28'E
Orsk, Russia (ôrsk)	164	51°15'N	58°50'E
Orşova, Rom. (ôr'shô-vä)	161	44°43'N	22°26'E
Orsoy, Ger.	236	51°31'N	6°41'E
Ortega, Col. (ôr-tě'gä)	130a	3°56'N	75°12'W
Ortegal, Cabo, c., Spain (kå'bô-ôr-tå-gäl')	148	43°46'N	8°15'W
Orth, Aus.	145e	48°09'N	16°42'E
Orthez, Fr. (ôr-těz')	157	43°29'N	0°43'W
Ortigueira, Spain (ôr-tê-gā'ê-rä)	148	43°40'N	7°50'W
Orting, Wa., U.S. (ôrt'ĭng)	106a	47°06'N	122°12'W
Ortona, Italy (ôr-tō'nä)	160	42°22'N	14°22'E
Ortonville, Mn., U.S. (ôr-tŭn-vĭl)	102	45°18'N	96°26'W
Oruba, Nig.	244d	6°35'N	3°25'E
Orūmīyeh, Iran	182	37°30'N	45°15'E
Orūmīyeh, Daryacheh-ye, l., Iran	182	38°01'N	45°17'E
Oruro, Bol. (ō-rōō'rō)	130	17°57'S	66°59'W
Orvieto, Italy (ôr-vyå'tō)	160	42°43'N	12°08'E
Oryu-dong, neigh., S. Kor.	241b	37°29'N	126°51'E
Osa, Russia (ô'sá)	166	57°18'N	55°25'E
Osa, Península de, pen., C.R. (ō'sä)	121	8°30'N	83°25'W
Osage, Ia., U.S. (ō'sāj)	103	43°16'N	92°49'W
Osage, N.J., U.S.	229b	39°51'N	75°01'W
Osage, r., Mo., U.S.	111	38°10'N	93°12'W
Osage City, Ks., U.S. (ō'sāj sĭ'tĭ)	111	38°28'N	95°53'W
Ōsaka, Japan (ō'sä-kä)	189	34°40'N	135°27'E
Ōsaka, dept., Japan	195b	34°45'N	135°36'E
Osaka Castle, hist., Japan	242b	34°41'N	135°32'E
Ōsaka-Wan, b., Japan (wän)	194	34°34'N	135°16'E
Osakis, Mn., U.S. (ô-sā'kĭs)	102	45°51'N	95°09'W
Osakis, l., Mn., U.S.	103	45°55'N	94°55'W
Osasco, Braz.	234d	23°32'S	46°46'W
Osawatomie, Ks., U.S. (ŏs-à-wăt'ō-mê)	111	38°29'N	94°57'W
Osborne, Ks., U.S. (ŏz'bŭrn)	110	39°25'N	98°42'W
Osceola, Ar., U.S. (ŏs-ê-ō'lá)	111	35°42'N	89°58'W
Osceola, Ia., U.S.	103	41°04'N	93°45'W
Osceola, Mo., U.S.	111	38°02'N	93°41'W
Osceola, Ne., U.S.	102	41°11'N	97°34'W
Oscoda, Mi., U.S. (ŏs-kō'dà)	98	44°25'N	83°20'W
Osëtr, r., Russia (ô'sět'r)	162	54°27'N	38°15'E
Osgood, In., U.S. (ŏz'gòd)	98	39°10'N	85°20'W
Osgoode, Can.	83c	45°09'N	75°37'W
Osh, Kyrg. (ôsh)	169	40°33'N	72°48'E
Oshawa, Can. (ŏsh'à-wà)	85	43°50'N	78°50'W
Ōshima, i., Japan (ō'shē'mä)	195	34°47'N	139°35'E
Oshkosh, Ne., U.S. (ŏsh'kŏsh)	102	41°24'N	102°22'W
Oshkosh, Wi., U.S.	97	44°01'N	88°35'W
Oshmyany, Bela. (ôsh-myä'nĭ)	153	54°27'N	25°55'E
Oshodi, Nig.	244d	6°34'N	3°21'E
Oshogbo, Nig.	210	7°47'N	4°34'E
Osijek, Cro. (ôs'ĭ-yěk)	149	45°33'N	18°48'E
Osinniki, Russia (ŭ-sě'nyĭ-kē)	170	53°37'N	87°21'E
Oskaloosa, Ia., U.S. (ŏs-kà-lōō'sà)	103	41°16'N	92°40'W
Oskarshamm, Swe. (ôs'kärs-häm'n)	152	57°16'N	16°24'E
Oskarström, Swe. (ôs'kärs-strûm)	152	56°48'N	12°55'E
Oskemen, Kaz.	169	49°58'N	82°38'E
Oskil, r., Eur.	167	51°00'N	37°41'E
Oslo, Nor. (ŏs'lō)	142	59°56'N	10°41'E
Oslofjorden, fj., Nor.	152	59°03'N	10°35'E
Osmaniye, Tur.	149	37°10'N	36°30'E
Osnabrück, Ger. (ôs-nä-brük')	154	52°16'N	8°05'E
Osorno, Chile (ô-sō'r-nō)	132	40°42'S	73°13'W
Osorun, Nig.	244d	6°33'N	3°29'E
Osøyra, Nor.	152	60°24'N	5°22'E
Osprey Reef, rf., Austl. (ŏs'prå)	203	14°00'S	146°45'E
Ossa, Mount, mtn., Austl. (ŏsà)	203	41°45'S	146°05'E
Ossenberg, Ger.	236	51°34'N	6°35'E
Osseo, Mn., U.S. (ŏs'sě-ō)	107g	45°07'N	93°24'W
Ossining, N.Y., U.S. (ŏs'ĭ-nĭng)	100a	41°09'N	73°51'W
Ossipee, N.H., U.S. (ŏs'ĭ-pê)	92	43°42'N	71°08'W
Ossjøen, l., Nor. (ôs-syûěn)	152	61°20'N	12°00'E
Ossum-Bösinghoven, Ger.	236	51°18'N	6°39'E
Ostankino, neigh., Russia	239b	55°49'N	37°37'E
Ostashkov, Russia (ôs-tăsh'kôf)	166	57°07'N	33°04'E
Oster, Ukr. (ōs'těr)	163	50°55'N	30°52'E
Osterdalälven, r., Swe.	146	61°40'N	13°00'E
Osterfeld, neigh., Ger.	236	51°30'N	6°53'E
Osterfjord, fj., Nor. (ûs'těr fyôr')	152	60°40'N	5°25'E
Östersund, Swe. (ûs'těr-sōōnd)	146	63°09'N	14°49'E
Östhammar, Swe. (ûst'häm'är)	152	60°16'N	18°21'E
Ostrava, Czech Rep.	142	49°51'N	18°18'E
Ostróda, Pol. (ôs'tròt-à)	155	53°41'N	19°58'E
Ostrogozhsk, Russia (ôs-tr-gôzhk')	167	50°53'N	39°03'E
Ostroh, Ukr.	167	50°21'N	26°40'E
Ostrołęka, Pol. (ôs-trô-woɴ'kå)	155	53°04'N	21°35'E
Ostrov, Russia (ôs-trôf')	166	57°21'N	28°22'E
Ostrov, Russia	239b	55°35'N	37°51'E
Ostrowiec Świętokrzyski, Pol. (ôs-trō'vyěts shvyěn-tō-kzhĭ'ske)	147	50°55'N	21°24'E
Ostrów Lubelski, Pol. (ôs'trôf lōō'běl-skĭ)	155	51°32'N	22°49'E
Ostrów Mazowiecka, Pol. (mä-zô-vyět'skä)	147	52°47'N	21°54'E
Ostrów Wielkopolski, Pol. (ôs'trōōf vyěl-kô-pōl'skē)	147	51°38'N	17°49'E
Ostrzeszów, Pol. (ôs-tzhä'shôf)	155	51°26'N	17°56'E
Ostuni, Italy (ôs-tōō'nē)	161	40°44'N	17°35'E
Osum, r., Alb. (ō'sòm)	161	40°37'N	20°00'E
Osuna, Spain (ô-sōō'nä)	158	37°18'N	5°05'W
Osveya, Bela. (ôs'vě-yá)	162	56°00'N	28°08'E
Oswaldtwistle, Eng., U.K. (ŏz-wàld-twĭs''l)	144a	53°44'N	2°23'W
Oswegatchie, r., N.Y., U.S. (ŏs-wê-găch'ĭ)	99	44°15'N	75°20'W
Oswego, Ks., U.S. (ŏs-wē'gō)	111	37°10'N	95°08'W
Oswego, N.Y., U.S.	97	43°25'N	76°30'W
Oświęcim, Pol. (ôsh-vyăɴ'tsyĭm)	155	50°02'N	19°17'E

PRONOUNCING INDEX Otaru–Palmeirinhas 329

PLACE (Pronunciation)	PAGE	LAT.	LONG.
Otaru, Japan (ō'tȧ-rò)	189	43°07'N	141°00'E
Otavalo, Ec. (ōtä-vä'lō)	130	0°14'N	78°16'W
Otavi, Nmb. (ô-tä'vė)	212	19°35'S	17°20'E
Otay, Ca., U.S. (ō'tā)	108a	32°36'N	117°04'W
Otepää, Est.	153	58°03'N	26°30'E
Otford, Eng., U.K.	235	51°19'N	0°12'E
Óthris, Óros, mtn., Grc.	161	39°00'N	22°15'E
Oti, r., Afr.	214	9°00'N	0°10'E
Otish, Monts, mts., Can. (ô-tĭsh')	85	52°15'N	70°20'W
Otjiwarongo, Nmb. (ŏt-jė-wȧ-rôn'gō)	212	20°20'S	16°25'E
Otočac, Cro. (ō'tō-chȧts)	160	44°53'N	15°15'E
Otra, r., Nor.	152	59°13'N	7°20'E
Otra, r., Russia (ôt'rȧ)	172b	55°22'N	38°20'E
Otradnoye, Russia (ô-trȧ'd-nô-yĕ)	172c	59°46'N	30°50'E
Otranto, Italy (ô'trän-tô) (ô-trän'tō)	161	40°07'N	18°30'E
Otranto, Strait of, strt., Eur.	142	40°30'N	18°45'E
Otsego, Mi., U.S. (ŏt-sē'gō)	98	42°25'N	85°45'W
Otsu, Japan (ō'tsò)	194	35°00'N	135°54'E
Otta, I., Nor. (ôt'tȧ)	152	61°53'N	8°40'E
Ottakring, neigh., Aus.	239e	48°12'N	16°19'E
Ottavia, neigh., Italy	239c	41°58'N	12°24'E
Ottawa, Can. (ŏt'ȧ-wȧ)	85	45°25'N	75°43'W
Ottawa, Il., U.S.	98	41°20'N	88°50'W
Ottawa, Ks., U.S.	111	38°37'N	95°16'W
Ottawa, Oh., U.S.	98	41°00'N	84°00'W
Ottawa, r., Can.	85	46°05'N	77°20'W
Otter Creek, r., Ut., U.S. (ŏt'ẽr)	109	38°20'N	111°55'W
Otter Creek, r., Vt., U.S.	99	44°05'N	73°15'W
Otter Point, c., Can.	106a	48°21'N	123°50'W
Ottershaw, Eng., U.K.	235	51°22'N	0°32'W
Otter Tail, I., Mn., U.S.	102	46°21'N	95°52'W
Otterville, Il., U.S. (ŏt'ẽr-vĭl)	107e	39°03'N	90°24'W
Ottery, S. Afr. (ŏt'ẽr-ĭ)	212a	34°02'S	18°31'E
Ottumwa, Ia., U.S. (ô-tŭm'wȧ)	97	41°00'N	92°26'W
Otukpa, Nig.	215	7°09'N	7°41'E
Otumba, Mex. (ô-tūm'bä)	118	19°41'N	98°46'W
Otway, Cape, c., Austl. (ŏt'wā)	203	38°55'S	153°40'E
Otway, Seno, b., Chile (sĕ'nō-ô't-wä'y)	132	53°00'S	73°00'W
Otwock, Pol. (ôt'vôtsk)	155	52°05'N	21°18'E
Ouachita, r., U.S.	97	33°25'N	92°30'W
Ouachita Mountains, mts., U.S. (wŏsh'ĭ-tô)	97	34°29'N	95°01'W
Ouagadougou, Burkina (wä'gȧ-do͞o'go͞o)	210	12°22'N	1°31'W
Ouahigouya, Burkina (wä-ė-go͞o'yä)	210	13°35'N	2°25'W
Oualâta, Maur. (wä-lä'tä)	210	17°11'N	6°50'W
Ouallene, Alg. (wäl-lân')	210	24°43'N	1°15'E
Ouanaminthe, Haiti	123	19°35'N	71°45'W
Ouarane, reg., Maur.	210	20°44'N	10°27'W
Ouarkoye, Burkina	214	12°05'N	3°40'W
Ouassel, r., Alg.	159	35°30'N	1°55'E
Oubangui (Ubangi), r., Afr. (o͞o-bäŋ'gė)	216	4°30'N	20°35'E
Oude Rijn, r., Neth.	145a	52°09'N	4°33'E
Oudewater, Neth.	145a	52°01'N	4°52'E
Oud-Gastel, Neth.	145a	51°35'N	4°27'E
Oudtshoorn, S. Afr. (outs'hōrn)	212	33°33'S	23°36'E
Oued Rhiou, Alg.	159	35°55'N	0°57'E
Oued Tlelat, Alg.	159	35°33'N	0°28'W
Oued-Zem, Mor. (wĕd-zĕm')	210	33°05'N	5°49'W
Ouessant, Island d', i., Fr. (ĕl-dwĕ-säN')	147	48°28'N	5°00'W
Ouesso, Congo	211	1°37'N	16°04'E
Ouest, Point, c., Haiti	123	19°00'N	73°25'W
Ouezzane, Mor. (wĕ-zan')	210	34°48'N	5°40'W
Ouham, r., Afr.	215	8°30'N	17°50'E
Ouidah, Benin (wē-dä')	210	6°25'N	2°05'E
Oujda, Mor.	210	34°41'N	1°45'W
Oulins, Fr. (o͞o-lăN')	157b	48°52'N	1°27'E
Oullins, Fr. (o͞o-lăN')	156	45°44'N	4°46'E
Oulu, Fin. (ō'lò)	142	64°58'N	25°43'E
Oulujärvi, I., Fin.	146	64°20'N	25°48'E
Oum Chalouba, Chad (o͞om shä-lo͞o'bä)	211	15°48'N	20°30'E
Oum Hadjer, Chad	215	13°18'N	19°41'E
Ounas, r., Fin. (ō'nȧs)	146	67°46'N	24°40'E
Oundle, Eng., U.K. (ôn'd'l)	144a	52°28'N	0°28'W
Ounianga Kébir, Chad (o͞o-nė-äŋ'gȧ kē-bēr')	211	19°04'N	20°22'E
Ouray, Co., U.S. (o͞o-rā')	110	38°00'N	107°40'W
Ourense, Spain	158	42°20'N	7°52'W
Ourinhos, Braz. (ôò-rē'nyôs)	131	23°04'S	49°45'W
Ourique, Port. (ō-rē'kĕ)	158	37°39'N	8°10'W
Ouro Fino, Braz. (ōŭ-rô-fē'nō)	129a	22°18'S	46°21'W
Ouro Prêto, Braz. (ō'rò prä'tò)	132	20°24'S	43°30'W
Outardes, Rivière aux, r., Can.	85	50°53'N	68°50'W
Outer, i., Wi., U.S. (out'ẽr)	103	47°03'N	90°20'W
Outer Brass, i., V.I.U.S. (bräs)	117c	18°24'N	64°58'W
Outer Hebrides, is., Scot., U.K.	150	57°20'N	7°50'W
Outjo, Nmb. (ōt'yō)	212	20°05'S	17°10'E
Outlook, Can.	88	51°31'N	107°05'W
Outremont, Can. (o͞o-trē-môN')	83a	45°31'N	73°36'W
Ouvéa, i., N. Cal.	203	20°43'S	166°48'E
Ouyen, Austl. (o͞o-ĕn)	204	35°05'S	142°10'E
Ovalle, Chile (ō-väl'yā)	132	30°43'S	71°16'W
Ovando, Bahía de, b., Cuba (bä-ē'ä-dĕ-ô-vä'n-dō)	123	20°10'N	74°05'W
Ovar, Port. (ō-vär')	158	40°52'N	8°38'W
Overbrook, neigh., Pa., U.S.	229b	39°58'N	75°16'W
Overbrook, neigh., Pa., U.S.	230b	40°24'N	79°59'W
Overijse, Bel.	145a	50°46'N	4°32'E
Overland, Mo., U.S. (ō-vẽr-lănd)	107e	38°42'N	90°22'W
Overland Park, Ks., U.S.	107f	38°59'N	94°40'W
Overlea, Md., U.S. (ō'vẽr-lā)(ō'vẽr-lē)	100e	39°21'N	76°31'W
Övertornea, Swe.	146	66°19'N	23°31'E
Ovidiopol', Ukr.	163	46°15'N	30°28'E
Oviedo, Dom. Rep. (ô-vyĕ'dō)	123	17°50'N	71°25'W
Oviedo, Spain (ō-vė-ā'dhō)	142	43°22'N	5°50'W
Ovruch, Ukr.	163	51°19'N	28°51'E
Owada, Japan (ō'wä-dȧ)	195a	35°49'N	139°33'E
Owambo, hist. reg., Nmb.	212	18°10'S	15°00'E
Owando, Congo	212	0°29'S	15°55'E
Owasco, I., N.Y., U.S. (ō-wăsk'kō)	99	42°50'N	76°30'W
Owase, Japan (ō'wä-shė)	195	34°03'N	136°12'E
Owego, N.Y., U.S. (ō-wē'gō)	99	42°05'N	76°15'W
Owen, Wi., U.S. (ō'ĕn)	103	44°56'N	90°35'W
Owensboro, Ky., U.S. (ō'ĕnz-bŭr-ô)	97	37°45'N	87°05'W
Owens Lake, I., Ca., U.S.	108	37°13'N	118°20'W
Owen Sound, Can. (ō'ĕn)	85	44°30'N	80°55'W
Owen Stanley Range, mts., Pap. N. Gui. (stăn'lė)	197	9°00'S	147°30'E
Owensville, In., U.S. (ō'ĕnz-vĭl)	98	38°15'N	87°40'W
Owensville, Mo., U.S.	111	38°20'N	91°29'W
Owensville, Oh., U.S.	101f	39°08'N	84°07'W
Owenton, Ky., U.S. (ō'ĕn-tŭn)	98	38°35'N	84°55'W
Owerri, Nig. (ô-wĕr'ė)	210	5°26'N	7°04'E
Owings Mill, Md., U.S. (ōwĭngz mĭl)	100e	39°25'N	76°50'W
Owl Creek, r., Wy., U.S. (oul)	105	43°45'N	108°46'W
Owo, Nig.	215	7°15'N	5°37'E
Oworonsoki, Nig.	244d	6°33'N	3°24'E
Owosso, Mi., U.S. (ô-wŏs'ō)	98	43°00'N	84°15'W
Owyhee, r., U.S.	96	43°04'N	117°45'W
Owyhee, Lake, res., Or., U.S.	96	43°27'N	117°30'W
Owyhee, South Fork, r., Id., U.S.	104	42°07'N	116°43'W
Owyhee Mountains, mts., Id., U.S. (ô-wī'hė)	96	43°15'N	116°48'W
Oxbow, Can.	89	49°12'N	102°11'W
Oxchuc, Mex. (ôs-cho͞ok')	119	16°47'N	92°24'W
Oxford, Can. (ŏks'fẽrd)	92	45°44'N	63°52'W
Oxford, Eng., U.K.	147	51°43'N	1°16'W
Oxford, Al., U.S. (ŏks'fẽrd)	115	33°38'N	80°46'W
Oxford, Ma., U.S.	93a	42°07'N	71°52'W
Oxford, Mi., U.S.	98	42°50'N	83°15'W
Oxford, Ms., U.S.	114	34°22'N	89°30'W
Oxford, N.C., U.S.	115	36°17'N	78°35'W
Oxford, Oh., U.S.	98	39°30'N	84°45'W
Oxford Falls, Austl.	243a	33°44'S	151°15'E
Oxford Lake, I., Can.	89	54°51'N	95°37'W
Oxfordshire, co., Eng., U.K.	144b	51°36'N	1°30'W
Oxkutzcab, Mex. (ôx-ko͞o'tz-käb)	120a	20°18'N	89°22'W
Oxmoor, Al., U.S. (ŏks'mòr)	100h	33°25'N	86°52'W
Oxnard, Ca., U.S. (ŏks'närd)	108	34°08'N	119°12'W
Oxon Hill, Md., U.S. (ōks'ōn hĭl)	100e	38°48'N	77°00'W
Oxshott, Eng., U.K.	235	51°20'N	0°21'W
Oyama, Japan	242a	35°36'N	139°22'E
Oyapock, r., S.A. (ō-yȧ-pŏk')	131	2°45'N	52°15'W
Oyem, Gabon	210	1°37'N	11°35'E
Øyeren, I., Nor. (ûĭĕrĕn)	152	59°50'N	11°25'E
Oymyakon, Russia (oi-myŭ-kôn')	165	63°14'N	142°58'E
Oyo, Nig. (ō'yō)	210	7°51'N	3°56'E
Oyodo, neigh., Japan	242b	34°43'N	135°30'E
Oyonnax, Fr. (ô-yô-nȧks')	157	46°16'N	5°40'E
Oyster Bay, N.Y., U.S.	100a	40°52'N	73°32'W
Oyster Bay Cove, N.Y., U.S.	228	40°52'N	73°31'W
Oyster Bayou, Tx., U.S.	113a	29°41'N	94°33'W
Oyster Creek, r., Tx., U.S. (ois'tẽr)	113a	29°13'N	95°29'W
Oyyl, r., Kaz.	170	49°30'N	55°10'E
Ozama, r., Dom. Rep. (ô-zä'mä)	123	18°45'N	69°55'W
Ozamiz, Phil. (ô-zä'mēz)	197	8°06'N	123°43'E
Ozark, Al., U.S. (ō'zärk)	114	31°28'N	85°28'W
Ozark, Ar., U.S.	111	35°29'N	93°49'W
Ozark Plateau, plat., U.S.	97	36°37'N	93°56'W
Ozarks, Lake of the, I., Mo., U.S. (ō'zärksz)	97	38°06'N	93°26'W
Ozëry, Russia (ô-zyô'rė)	162	54°53'N	38°31'E
Ozieri, Italy	148	40°38'N	8°53'E
Ozoir-la-Ferrière, Fr.	237c	48°46'N	2°40'E
Ozone Park, neigh., N.Y., U.S.	228	40°40'N	73°51'W
Ozorków, Pol. (ô-zôr'kôf)	155	51°58'N	19°20'E
Ozuluama, Mex.	119	21°34'N	97°52'W
Ozumba, Mex.	119a	19°02'N	98°48'W
Ozurgeti, Geor.	168	41°56'N	42°00'E

P

PLACE (Pronunciation)	PAGE	LAT.	LONG.
Paarl, S. Afr. (pärl)	212	33°45'S	18°55'E
Paarlshoop, neigh., S. Afr.	244b	26°13'S	27°59'E
Paauilo, Hi., U.S. (pä-ä-o͞o'ė-lō)	94a	20°03'N	155°25'W
Pabianice, Pol. (pä-byȧ-nē'tsĕ)	155	51°40'N	19°29'E
Pacaás Novos, Massiço de, mts., Braz.	130	11°03'S	64°02'W
Pacaraima, Serra, mts., S.A. (sĕr'rȧ pä-kä-rä-ē'mȧ)	130	3°45'N	62°30'W
Pacasmayo, Peru (pä-käs-mä'yō)	130	7°24'S	79°30'W
Pachuca, Mex. (pä-cho͞o'kä)	116	20°07'N	98°43'W
Pacific, Wa., U.S. (pȧ-sĭf'ĭk)	106a	47°16'N	122°15'W
Pacifica, Ca., U.S. (pȧ-sĭf'ĭ-kä)	106b	37°38'N	122°29'W
Pacific Beach, Ca., U.S.	108a	32°47'N	117°22'W
Pacific Grove, Ca., U.S.	108	36°37'N	121°54'W
Pacific Islands, Trust Territory of the *see* Palau, nation, Oc.	3	7°15'N	134°30'E
Pacific Ocean, o.	2	0.00	170°00'W
Pacific Palisades, neigh., Ca., U.S.	232	34°03'N	118°32'W
Pacific Ranges, mts., Can.	86	51°00'N	125°30'W
Pacific Rim National Park, rec., Can.	86	49°00'N	126°00'W
Paço de Arcos, Port.	238d	38°42'N	9°17'W
Pacolet, r., S.C., U.S. (pā'cō-lĕt)	115	34°55'N	81°49'W
Pacy-sur-Eure, Fr. (pä-sē-sür-ûr')	157b	49°01'N	1°24'E
Padang, Indon. (pä-däng')	196	1°01'S	100°28'E
Padang, i., Indon.	181b	1°12'N	102°21'E
Padang Endau, Malay.	181b	2°39'N	103°38'E
Paddington, neigh., Eng., U.K.	235	51°31'N	0°10'W
Paden City, W.V., U.S. (pā'dĕn)	98	39°30'N	80°55'W
Paderborn, Ger. (pä-dĕr-bòrn')	154	51°43'N	8°46'E
Paderno Dugnano, Italy	238c	45°34'N	9°10'E
Padibe, Ug.	217	3°28'N	32°50'E
Padiham, Eng., U.K. (păd'ĭ-hăm)	144a	53°48'N	2°19'W
Padilla, Mex. (pä-dēl'yä)	118	24°00'N	98°45'W
Padilla Bay, b., Wa., U.S. (pä-dĭl'lȧ)	106a	48°31'N	122°34'W
Padova, Italy (pä'dô-vä)(păd'û-ȧ)	148	45°24'N	11°53'E
Padre Island, i., Tx., U.S. (pä'drā)	113	27°09'N	97°15'W
Padre Miguel, neigh., Braz.	234c	22°53'S	43°26'W
Padua *see* Padova, Italy	148	45°24'N	11°53'E
Paducah, Ky., U.S.	97	37°05'N	88°36'W
Paducah, Tx., U.S.	110	34°01'N	100°18'W
Paektu-san, mtn., Asia (pâk'to͞o-sän')	194	42°00'N	128°03'E
Pag, i., Yugo. (päg)	160	44°30'N	14°48'E
Pagai Selatan, Pulau, i., Indon.	196	2°48'S	100°22'E
Pagai Utara, Pulau, i., Indon.	196	2°45'S	100°02'E
Pagasitikós Kólpos, b., Grc.	161	39°15'N	23°00'E
Page, Az., U.S.	109	36°57'N	111°27'W
Pago Pago, Am. Sam.	198a	14°16'S	170°42'W
Pagosa Springs, Co., U.S. (pȧ-gō'sȧ)	110	37°15'N	107°05'W
Pagote, India	240e	18°54'N	72°59'E
Pahala, Hi., U.S. (pä-hä'lä)	94a	19°11'N	155°28'W
Pahang, state, Malay.	181b	3°02'N	102°57'E
Pahang, r., Malay.	196	3°39'N	102°41'E
Pahokee, Fl., U.S. (pȧ-hō'kē)	115a	26°45'N	80°40'W
Paide, Est. (pī'dĕ)	153	58°54'N	25°30'E
Päijänne, I., Fin. (pĕ'ĕ-yĕn-nĕ)	146	61°38'N	25°05'E
Pailolo Channel, strt., Hi., U.S. (pä-ė-lō'lō)	94a	21°05'N	156°41'W
Paine, Chile (pī'nĕ)	129b	33°49'S	70°44'W
Painesville, Oh., U.S. (pānz'vĭl)	98	41°40'N	81°15'W
Painted Desert, des., Az., U.S. (pānt'ĕd)	110	36°15'N	111°35'W
Painted Rock Reservoir, res., Az., U.S.	109	33°00'N	113°05'W
Paintsville, Ky., U.S. (pānts'vĭl)	98	37°50'N	82°50'W
Paisley, Austl.	243b	37°51'S	144°51'E
Paisley, Scot., U.K. (pāz'lĭ)	146	55°50'N	4°30'W
Paita, Peru (pä-ē'tä)	130	5°11'S	81°12'W
Pai T'ou Shan, mts., N. Kor.	189	40°30'N	127°20'E
Paiute Indian Reservation, I.R., Ut., U.S.	109	38°17'N	113°50'W
Pajápan, Mex. (pä-hä'pän)	119	18°16'N	94°41'W
Pakanbaru, Indon.	196	0°43'N	101°15'E
Pakhra, r., Russia (päk'rȧ)	172b	55°29'N	37°51'E
Pakistan, nation, Asia	183	28°00'N	67°30'E
Pakokku, Myanmar (pȧ-kŏk'kò)	188	21°29'N	95°00'E
Paks, Hung. (pôksh)	155	46°38'N	18°53'E
Pala, Chad	215	9°22'N	14°54'E
Palacios, Tx., U.S. (pä-lä'syōs)	113	28°42'N	96°12'W
Palagruža, Otoci, is., Cro.	160	42°20'N	16°23'E
Palaión Fáliron, Grc.	239d	37°55'N	23°41'E
Palaiseau, Fr. (pȧ-lĕ-zō')	157b	48°44'N	2°16'E
Palana, Russia	165	59°07'N	159°58'E
Palanan Bay, b., Phil. (pä-lä'nän)	197a	17°14'N	122°35'E
Palanan Point, c., Phil.	197a	17°12'N	122°40'E
Pālanpur, India (pä'lŭn-po͞or)	183	24°08'N	73°29'E
Palapye, Bots. (pȧ-läp'yĕ)	212	22°34'S	27°28'E
Palatine, Il., U.S. (păl'ȧ-tīn)	101a	42°07'N	88°03'W
Palatka, Fl., U.S. (pȧ-lăt'kȧ)	115	29°39'N	81°40'W
Palau (Belau), nation, Oc. (pä-lä'ò)	3	7°15'N	134°30'E
Palauig, Phil. (pä-lou'ĕg)	197a	15°27'N	119°54'E
Palawan, i., Phil. (pä-lä'wȧn)	196	9°50'N	117°38'E
Pālayankottai, India	187	8°50'N	77°50'E
Paldiski, Est. (päl'dĭ-skĭ)	153	59°22'N	24°04'E
Palembang, Indon. (pä-lĕm-bäng')	196	2°57'S	104°40'E
Palencia, Guat. (pä-lĕn'sė-ȧ)	120	14°40'N	90°22'W
Palencia, Spain (pä-lĕ'n-syä)	148	42°02'N	4°32'W
Palenque, Mex. (pä-lĕŋ'kȧ)	119	17°34'N	91°58'W
Palenque, Punta, c., Dom. Rep. (po͞o'n-tä)	123	18°10'N	70°10'W
Palermo, Col. (pä-lĕr'mô)	130a	2°53'N	75°26'W
Palermo, Italy	142	38°08'N	13°24'E
Palermo, neigh., Arg.	233d	34°35'S	58°25'W
Palestine, Tx., U.S.	97	31°46'N	95°38'W
Palestine, hist. reg., Asia (păl'ĕs-tīn)	181a	31°33'N	35°00'E
Paletwa, Myanmar (pŭ-lĕt'wä)	183	21°19'N	92°52'E
Palghāt, India	187	10°49'N	76°40'E
Pāli, India	186	25°53'N	73°18'E
Palín, Guat. (pä-lēn')	120	14°42'N	90°42'W
Palisades Park, N.J., U.S.	228	40°51'N	74°00'W
Palizada, Mex. (pä-lė-zä'dä)	119	18°17'N	92°04'W
Palk Strait, strt., Asia (pôk)	183	10°00'N	79°23'E
Palma, Braz. (päl'mä)	129a	21°23'S	42°18'W
Palma, Spain	142	39°35'N	2°38'E
Palma, Bahía de, b., Spain	159	39°24'N	2°37'E
Palma del Río, Spain	158	37°43'N	5°19'W
Palmar de Cariaco, Ven.	234a	10°34'N	66°55'W
Palmares, Braz. (päl-mȧ'rĕs)	131	8°46'S	35°28'W
Palmas, Braz.	131	10°08'S	48°18'W
Palmas, Braz. (päl'mäs)	132	26°20'S	51°56'W
Palmas, Cape, c., Lib.	210	4°22'N	7°44'W
Palma Soriano, Cuba (sô-rē-ä'nō)	122	20°15'N	76°00'W
Palm Beach, Fl., U.S. (päm bēch')	115a	26°43'N	80°03'W
Palmeira dos Índios, Braz. (pä-mā'rä-dôs-ē'n-dyôs)	131	9°26'S	36°33'W
Palmeirinhas, Ponta das, c., Ang.	216	9°05'S	13°00'E

ng-sing; ŋ-baŋk; N-nasalized n; nŏd; cŏmmit; ōld; ôbey; ôrder; oi-boil; fo͞od; ò-as oo in foot; ou-out; s-soft; sh-dish; th-thin; pūre; ûnite; ûrn; stŭd; circŭs; ü-as in French tu; '-indeterminate vowel.

330 Palmela-Passau

PLACE (Pronunciation)	PAGE	LAT.	LONG.
Palmela, Port. (päl-mā′lä)	158	38°34′N	8°54′W
Palmer, Ak., U.S. (päm′ẽr)	95	61°38′N	149°15′W
Palmer, Wa., U.S.	106a	47°19′N	121°53′W
Palmer Park, Md., U.S.	229d	38°55′N	76°52′W
Palmerston North, N.Z. (päm′ẽr-stŭn)	203a	40°20′S	175°35′E
Palmerville, Austl. (päm′ẽr-vĭl)	203	16°08′S	144°15′E
Palmetto, Fl., U.S. (pȧl-mĕt′ō)	115a	27°32′N	82°34′W
Palmetto Point, c., Bah.	123	21°15′N	73°25′W
Palmi, Italy (päl′mē)	160	38°21′N	15°54′E
Palmira, Col. (päl-mē′rä)	130	3°33′N	76°17′W
Palmira, Cuba	122	22°15′N	80°25′W
Palmyra, Mo., U.S. (päl-mī′rȧ)	111	39°45′N	91°32′W
Palmyra, N.J., U.S.	100f	40°01′N	75°00′W
Palmyra, i., Oc.	2	6°00′N	162°20′W
Palmyra, hist., Syria	182	34°25′N	38°28′E
Palmyras Point, c., India	186	20°42′N	87°45′E
Palo Alto, Ca., U.S. (pä′lō äl′tō)	106b	37°27′N	122°09′W
Paloduro Creek, r., Tx., U.S. (pă-lō-dōō′rō)	110	36°16′N	101°12′W
Paloh, Malay.	181b	2°11′N	103°12′E
Paloma, l., Mex. (pä-lō′mä)	112	26°53′N	104°02′W
Palomar Park, Ca., U.S.	231b	37°29′N	122°16′W
Palomo, Cerro el, mtn., Chile (sĕ′r-rō-ĕl-pä-lô′mô)	129b	34°36′S	70°20′W
Palos, Cabo de, c., Spain (kä′bô-dĕ-pä′lôs)	148	39°38′N	0°43′W
Palos Heights, Il., U.S.	231a	41°40′N	87°48′W
Palos Hills, Il., U.S.	231a	41°41′N	87°49′W
Palos Park, Il., U.S.	231a	41°40′N	87°50′W
Palos Verdes Estates, Ca., U.S. (pă′lŭs vûr′dĭs)	107a	33°48′N	118°24′W
Palouse, Wa., U.S. (pȧ-lōōz′)	104	46°54′N	117°04′W
Palouse, r., Wa., U.S.	104	47°02′N	117°35′W
Palu, Tur. (pä-loo′)	167	38°55′N	40°10′E
Paluan, Phil. (pä-lōō′än)	197a	13°25′N	120°29′E
Pamiers, Fr. (pȧ-myā′)	147	43°07′N	1°34′E
Pamirs, mts., Asia	183	38°14′N	72°27′E
Pamlico, r., N.C., U.S. (păm′lĭ-kō)	115	35°25′N	76°59′W
Pamlico Sound, strt., N.C., U.S.	97	35°10′N	76°10′W
Pampa, Tx., U.S. (păm′pȧ)	96	35°32′N	100°56′W
Pampa de Castillo, pl., Arg. (pä′m-pä-dĕ-käs-tē′l-yō)	132	45°30′S	67°30′W
Pampana, r., S.L.	214	8°35′N	11°55′W
Pampanga, r., Phil. (päm-päŋ′gä)	197a	15°20′N	120°48′E
Pampas, reg., Arg. (päm′päs)	132	37°00′S	64°30′W
Pampilhosa do Botão, Port. (päm-pē-lyō′sȧ-dô-bō-touɴ)	158	40°21′N	8°32′W
Pamplona, Col. (päm-plō′nä)	130	7°19′N	72°41′W
Pamplona, Spain (päm-plō′nä)	148	42°49′N	1°39′W
Pamunkey, r., Va., U.S. (pȧ-mŭŋ′kĭ)	99	37°40′N	77°20′W
Pana, Il., U.S. (pā′nȧ)	98	39°25′N	89°05′W
Panagyurishte, Bul. (pȧ-nȧ-gyōō′rēsh-tĕ)	161	42°30′N	24°11′E
Panaji (Panjim), India	183	15°33′N	73°52′E
Panamá, Pan.	117	8°58′N	79°32′W
Panama, nation, N.A.	117	9°00′N	80°00′W
Panamá, Istmo de, isth., Pan.	117	9°00′N	80°00′W
Panama Canal, can., Pan.	116a	9°20′N	79°55′W
Panama City, Fl., U.S. (păn-ȧ mä′ sĭ′tĭ)	114	30°08′N	85°39′W
Panamint Range, mts., Ca., U.S. (păn-ȧ-mĭnt′)	108	36°40′N	117°30′W
Panarea, i., Italy (pä-nä′rĕ-ä)	160	38°37′N	15°05′E
Panaro, r., Italy (pä-nä′rô)	160	44°47′N	11°06′E
Panay, i., Phil. (pä-nī′)	196	11°15′N	121°38′E
Pančevo, Yugo. (pȧn′chĕ-vô)	149	44°52′N	20°42′E
Pānchghara, India	240a	22°44′N	88°16′E
Panch′iao, Tai.	241d	25°01′N	121°27′E
Panchor, Malay.	181b	2°11′N	102°43′E
Pānchur, India	186a	22°31′N	88°17′E
Panda, D.R.C. (pän′dä′)	212	10°59′S	27°24′E
Pan de Guajaibon, mtn., Cuba (pän dā gwä-jȧ-bōn′)	122	22°50′N	83°20′W
Panevėžys, Lith. (pä′nyĕ-vāzh′ēs)	166	55°44′N	24°21′E
Panfilov, Kaz. (pŭn-fē′lôf)	169	44°12′N	79°58′E
Panga, D.R.C. (päŋ′gä)	211	1°51′N	26°25′E
Pangani, Tan. (pän-gä′nē)	213	5°28′S	38°58′E
Pangani, r., Tan.	217	4°40′S	37°45′E
Pangkalpinang, Indon. (päng-käl′pē-näng′)	196	2°11′S	106°04′E
Pangnirtung, Can.	85	66°08′N	65°26′W
Panguitch, Ut., U.S. (păn′gwĭch)	109	37°50′N	112°30′W
Panié, Mont, mtn., N. Cal.	198f	20°36′S	164°46′E
Pānihāti, India	186a	22°42′N	88°23′E
Panimávida, Chile (pä-nē-mà′vē-dä)	129b	35°44′S	71°26′W
Panje, India	240e	18°54′N	72°57′E
Pankow, neigh., Ger.	238a	52°34′N	13°24′E
Panshi, China (pän-shē)	192	42°50′N	126°48′E
Pantar, Pulau, i., Indon. (pän′tär)	197	8°40′S	123°45′E
Pantelleria, i., Italy (pän-tĕl-lȧ-rē′ä)	148	36°43′N	11°59′E
Pantepec, Mex. (pän-tȧ-pĕk′)	119	17°11′N	93°04′W
Pantheon, hist., Italy	239c	41°55′N	12°29′E
Pantin, Fr.	237c	48°54′N	2°24′E
Pantitlán, Mex.	233a	19°25′N	99°05′W
Panuco, Mex. (pä′nōō-kô)	118	22°04′N	98°11′W
Pánuco, Mex. (pä′nōō-kô)	118	23°25′N	105°55′W
Panuco, r., Mex.	116	21°59′N	98°20′W
Pánuco de Coronado, Mex. (pä′nōō-kô dā kō-rô-nä′dhō)	112	24°33′N	104°20′W
Panvel, India	187b	18°59′N	73°06′E
Panyu, China (pä-yōō)	191a	22°56′N	113°22′E
Panzós, Guat. (pä-zós′)	120	15°26′N	89°40′W
Pao, r., Ven. (pà′ō)	131b	9°52′N	67°57′W
Paola, Ks., U.S. (pȧ-ō′lȧ)	111	38°34′N	94°51′W
Paoli, In., U.S. (pȧ-ō′lĭ)	98	38°35′N	86°30′W
Paoli, Pa., U.S.	100f	40°03′N	75°29′W
Paonia, Co., U.S. (pā-ō′nyȧ)	109	38°50′N	107°40′W
Pápa, Hung. (pä′pô)	149	47°18′N	17°27′E
Papagayo, r., Mex. (pä-pä-gä′yō)	118	16°52′N	99°41′W
Papagayo, Golfo del, b., C.R. (gôl-fô-dĕl-pä-pä-gä′yō)	120	10°44′N	85°56′W
Papagayo, Laguna, l., Mex. (lä-ò-nä)	118	16°44′N	99°44′W
Papago Indian Reservation, I.R., Az., U.S. (pä′pä′gō)	109	32°33′N	112°12′W
Papantla de Olarte, Mex. (pä-pän′tlä dā-ô-lä′r-tĕ)	116	20°30′N	97°15′W
Papatoapan, r., Mex. (pä-pä-tô-ä-pà′n)	119	18°00′N	96°22′W
Papelón, Ven.	234a	10°27′N	66°47′W
Papenburg, Ger. (päp′ĕn-bòrgh)	154	53°05′N	7°23′E
Papinas, Arg. (pä-pē′näs)	129c	35°30′S	57°19′W
Papineauville, Can. (pä-pē-nō′vĕl)	83c	45°38′N	75°01′W
Papua, Gulf of, b., Pap. N. Gui. (păp-ōō-ȧ)	197	8°20′S	144°45′E
Papua New Guinea, nation, Oc. (păp-ōō-ȧ)(gĭne)	197	7°00′S	142°15′E
Papudo, Chile (pä-pōō′dô)	129b	32°30′S	71°25′W
Paquequer Pequeno, Braz. (pä-kĕ-kĕ′r-pĕ-kĕ′nô)	132b	22°19′S	43°02′W
Para, r., Russia	162	53°45′N	40°58′E
Paracale, Phil. (pä-rä-kä′lȧ)	197a	14°17′N	122°47′E
Paracambi, Braz.	132b	22°36′S	43°43′W
Paracatu, Braz. (pä-rä-kä-tōō′)	131	17°17′S	46°43′W
Paracel Islands, is., Asia	196	16°40′N	113°00′E
Paraćin, Yugo. (pá′rä-chĕn)	149	43°51′N	21°26′E
Para de Minas, Braz. (pä-rä-dĕ-mē′näs)	131	19°52′S	44°37′W
Paradise, i., Bah.	122	25°05′N	77°20′W
Paradise Valley, Nv., U.S. (păr′ȧ-dīs)	104	41°28′N	117°32′W
Parados, Cerro de los, mtn., Col. (sĕ′r-rô-dĕ-lôs-pä-rä′dōs)	130a	5°44′N	75°13′W
Paragould, Ar., U.S. (păr′ȧ-gōōld)	111	36°03′N	90°29′W
Paraguaçu, r., Braz. (pä-rä-gwä-zōō′)	131	12°25′S	39°46′W
Paraguay, nation, S.A. (păr′ȧ-gwā)	132	24°00′S	57°00′W
Paraguay, Río, r., S.A. (rē′ō-pä-rä-gwä′y)	132	21°12′S	57°31′W
Paraíba, state, Braz. (pä-rä-ē′bä)	131	7°11′S	37°05′W
Paraíba, r., Braz.	129a	23°02′S	45°43′W
Paraíba do Sul, Braz. (dô-sōō′l)	129a	22°10′S	43°18′W
Paraibuna, Braz. (pä-räē-bōō′nä)	129a	23°23′S	45°38′W
Paraíso, C.R.	121	9°50′N	83°53′W
Paraíso, Mex.	119	18°24′N	93°11′W
Paraiso, Pan. (pä-rä-ē′sō)	116a	9°02′N	79°38′W
Paraisópolis, Braz. (pä-räē-sô′pō-lēs)	129a	22°35′S	45°45′W
Paraitinga, r., Braz. (pä-rä-ē-tē′n-gä)	129a	23°15′S	45°24′W
Parakou, Benin (pȧ-rȧ-kōō′)	210	9°21′N	2°37′E
Paramaribo, Sur. (pȧ-rȧ-mä′rē-bō)	131	5°50′N	55°15′W
Paramatta, Austl. (păr-ȧ-măt′ȧ)	201b	33°49′S	150°59′E
Paramillo, mtn., Col. (pä-rä-mē′l-yō)	130a	7°06′N	75°55′W
Paramount, Ca., U.S.	232	33°53′N	118°09′W
Paramus, N.J., U.S.	100a	40°56′N	74°04′W
Paran, r., Asia	181a	30°05′N	34°50′E
Paraná, Arg.	132	31°44′S	60°32′W
Paraná, Río, r., S.A.	132	24°00′S	54°00′W
Paranaíba, Braz. (pä-rä-nȧ-ē′bȧ)	131	19°43′S	51°13′W
Paranaíba, r., Braz.	131	18°58′S	50°44′W
Paraná Ibicuy, r., Arg.	129c	33°27′S	59°26′W
Paranam, Sur.	131	5°39′N	55°13′W
Paranápanema, r., Braz. (pä-rä′nä′pä-nĕ-mä)	131	22°28′S	52°15′W
Parañaque, Phil.	241g	14°30′N	120°59′E
Paraopeba, r., Braz. (pä-rä-o-pĕ′dä)	129a	20°09′S	44°14′W
Parapara, Ven. (pä-rä-pä-rä)	131b	9°44′N	67°17′W
Parati, Braz. (pä-rätē)	129a	23°14′S	44°43′W
Paray-le-Monial, Fr. (pȧ-rĕ′lē-mô-nyäl′)	156	46°27′N	4°14′E
Pārbati, r., India	186	24°50′N	76°44′E
Parchim, Ger. (par′kĭm)	154	53°25′N	11°52′E
Parczew, Pol. (pär′chĕf)	155	51°38′N	22°53′E
Pardo, r., Braz.	129a	21°32′S	46°40′W
Pardo, r., Braz. (pär′dō)	131	15°25′S	39°40′W
Pardubice, Czech Rep. (pär′dò-bĭt-sĕ)	154	50°02′N	15°47′E
Parecis, Serra dos, mts., Braz. (sĕr′rȧ dōs pä-rā-sēzh′)	131	13°45′S	59°28′W
Paredes de Nava, Spain (pä-rā′dås dä nä′vä)	158	42°10′N	4°41′W
Paredón, Mex.	112	25°56′N	100°58′W
Parent, Can.	85	47°59′N	74°30′W
Parent, Lac, l., Can.	91	48°40′N	77°00′W
Parepare, Indon.	196	4°01′S	119°38′E
Pargolovo, Russia (pár-gô′lô vô)	172c	60°04′N	30°18′E
Pari, neigh., Braz.	234d	23°32′S	46°37′W
Paria, r., Az., U.S.	109	37°07′N	111°51′W
Paria, Golfo de, b. (gôl-fô-dĕ-br-pä-rē-ä)	130	10°33′N	62°14′W
Paricutín, Volcán, vol., Mex.	118	19°27′N	102°14′W
Parida, Río de la, r., Mex. (rē′ō-dĕ-lä-pä-rē′dä)	112	26°23′N	104°40′W
Parima, Serra, mts., S.A. (sĕr′rȧ pä-rē′mȧ)	130	3°45′N	64°00′W
Pariñas, Punta, c., Peru (pōō′n-tä-pä-rē′n-yäs)	130	4°30′S	81°23′W
Parintins, Braz. (pä-rĭn-tĭɴzh′)	131	2°34′S	56°30′W
Paris, Can.	91	43°15′N	80°23′W
Paris, Fr. (pȧ-rē′)	142	48°51′N	2°20′E
Paris, Ar., U.S. (păr′ĭs)	111	35°17′N	93°43′W
Paris, Il., U.S.	98	39°35′N	87°40′W
Paris, Ky., U.S.	98	38°15′N	84°15′W
Paris, Mo., U.S.	111	39°27′N	91°59′W
Paris, Tn., U.S.	114	36°16′N	88°20′W
Paris, Tx., U.S.	97	33°39′N	95°33′W
Paris-le-Bourget, Aéroport de, arpt., Fr.	237c	48°57′N	2°25′E
Paris-Orly, Aéroport de, arpt., Fr.	237c	48°45′N	2°25′E
Parita, Golfo de, b., Pan. (gôl-fô-dĕ-pä-rē′tä)	121	8°06′N	80°10′W
Park City, Ut., U.S.	105	40°39′N	111°33′W
Parkdene, S. Afr.	244b	26°14′S	28°16′E
Parker, S.D., U.S. (pär′kẽr)	102	43°24′N	97°10′W
Parker Dam, dam, U.S.	96	34°20′N	114°00′W
Parkersburg, W.V., U.S. (pär′kẽrz-bûrg)	97	39°15′N	81°35′W
Parkes, Austl. (pärks)	204	33°10′S	148°10′E
Park Falls, Wi., U.S. (pärk)	103	45°55′N	90°29′W
Park Forest, Il., U.S.	101a	41°29′N	87°41′W
Parkgate, Eng., U.K.	237a	53°18′N	3°05′W
Parkhill Gardens, S. Afr.	244b	26°14′S	28°11′E
Parkland, Wa., U.S. (pärk′lănd)	106a	47°09′N	122°26′W
Parklawn, Va., U.S.	229d	38°50′N	77°09′W
Parklea, Austl.	243a	33°44′S	150°57′E
Park Orchards, Austl.	243b	37°46′S	145°13′E
Park Range, mts., Co., U.S.	105	40°54′N	106°40′W
Park Rapids, Mn., U.S.	102	46°53′N	95°05′W
Park Ridge, Il., U.S.	101a	42°00′N	87°50′W
Park Ridge Manor, Il., U.S.	231a	42°02′N	87°50′W
Park River, N.D., U.S.	102	48°22′N	97°43′W
Parkrose, Or., U.S. (pärk′rōz)	106c	45°33′N	122°33′W
Park Rynie, S. Afr.	213c	30°22′S	30°43′E
Parkston, S.D., U.S. (pärks′tŭn)	102	43°22′N	97°59′W
Park Town, neigh., S. Afr.	244b	26°11′S	28°03′E
Parktown North, neigh., S. Afr.	244b	26°09′S	28°02′E
Parkview, Pa., U.S.	230b	40°30′N	79°56′W
Parkville, Md., U.S.	100e	39°22′N	76°32′W
Parkville, Mo., U.S.	107f	39°12′N	94°41′W
Parkwood, Md., U.S.	229d	39°01′N	77°05′W
Parla, Spain (pär′lä)	159a	40°14′N	3°46′W
Parliament, Houses of, pt. of i., Eng., U.K.	235	51°30′N	0°07′W
Parma, Italy (pär′mä)	148	44°48′N	10°20′E
Parma, Oh., U.S.	101d	41°23′N	81°44′W
Parma Heights, Oh., U.S.	101d	41°23′N	81°36′W
Parnaíba, Braz. (pär-nä-ē′bä)	131	3°00′S	41°42′W
Parnaíba, r., Braz.	131	3°57′S	42°30′W
Parnassós, mtn., Grc.	161	38°36′N	22°35′E
Parndorf, Aus.	145e	48°00′N	16°52′E
Pärnu, Est. (pĕr′nōō)	166	58°24′N	24°29′E
Pärnu, r., Est.	153	58°40′N	25°05′E
Pärnu Laht, b., Est. (läkt)	153	58°15′N	24°17′E
Paro, Bhu. (pä′rô)	186	27°30′N	89°30′E
Paroo, r., Austl. (pä′rōō)	203	30°00′S	144°00′E
Paropamisus, mts., Afg.	182	34°45′N	63°58′E
Páros, Grc. (pä′rôs) (pā′rŏs)	161	37°05′N	25°14′E
Páros, i., Grc.	149	37°11′N	25°00′E
Parow, S. Afr. (pă′rò)	212a	33°54′S	18°36′E
Parowan, Ut., U.S. (păr′ô-wăn)	109	37°50′N	112°50′W
Parral, Chile (pär-rä′l)	132	36°07′S	71°47′W
Parral, r., Mex.	112	27°25′N	105°08′W
Parramatta, r., Austl. (păr-ȧ-măt′ȧ)	201b	33°42′S	150°58′E
Parras, Mex. (pär-räs′)	112	25°28′N	102°08′W
Parrita, C.R. (pär-rē′tä)	121	9°32′N	84°17′W
Parrsboro, Can. (pärz′bŭr-ô)	92	45°24′N	64°20′W
Parry, i., Can. (păr′ĭ)	91	45°15′N	80°00′W
Parry, Mount, mtn., Can.	86	52°53′N	128°45′W
Parry Islands, is., Can.	82	75°30′N	110°00′W
Parry Sound, Can.	85	45°20′N	80°00′W
Parsnip, r., Can. (pärs′nĭp)	87	54°45′N	122°20′W
Parsons, Ks., U.S. (pär′s′nz)	97	37°20′N	95°16′W
Parsons, W.V., U.S.	99	39°05′N	79°40′W
Parthenay, Fr. (pȧr-t′nĕ′)	156	46°39′N	0°16′W
Partington, Eng., U.K.	237b	53°25′N	2°26′W
Partinico, Italy (pär-tē′nē-kô)	160	38°02′N	13°11′E
Partizansk, Russia	165	43°15′N	133°19′E
Parys, S. Afr. (pȧ-rīs′)	218d	26°53′S	27°28′E
Pasadena, Ca., U.S. (păs-ȧ-dē′nȧ)	96	34°09′N	118°09′W
Pasadena, Md., U.S.	100e	39°06′N	76°35′W
Pasadena, Tx., U.S.	113a	29°43′N	95°13′W
Pasay, Phil.	241g	14°33′N	121°00′E
Pascagoula, Ms., U.S. (păs-kȧ-gōō′lȧ)	114	30°22′N	88°33′W
Pascagoula, r., Ms., U.S.	114	30°52′N	88°48′W
Paşcani, Rom. (päsh-kän′)	155	47°46′N	26°42′E
Pasco, Wa., U.S. (păs′kō)	104	46°13′N	119°04′W
Pascoe Vale, Austl.	243b	37°44′S	144°56′E
Pascua, Isla de (Easter Island), i., Chile	225	26°50′S	109°00′W
Pasewalk, Ger. (pä′zĕ-välk)	154	53°31′N	14°01′E
Pashiya, Russia (pä′shĭ-yȧ)	172a	58°27′N	58°17′E
Pashkovo, Russia (pásh-kô′vô)	194	48°52′N	131°09′E
Pashkovskaya, Russia (pȧsh-kôf′skȧ-yȧ)	163	45°00′N	39°04′E
Pasig, Phil.	197a	14°34′N	121°05′E
Pasion, Río de la, r., Guat. (rē′ō-dĕ-lä-pä-syōn′)	120a	16°31′N	90°11′W
Pasir Gudang, Malay.	240c	1°27′N	103°53′E
Pasir Panjang, Sing.	240c	1°17′N	103°47′E
Pasir Puteh, Malay.	240c	1°26′N	103°56′E
Paso de los Libres, Arg. (pä-sô-dĕ-lôs-lē′brĕs)	132	29°33′S	57°05′W
Paso de los Toros, Ur. (tō′rôs)	129c	32°43′S	56°33′W
Paso del Rey, Arg.	233d	34°39′S	58°45′W
Paso Robles, Ca., U.S. (pă′sō rō′blĕs)	108	35°38′N	120°44′W
Pasquia Hills, hills, Can. (păs′kwē-ȧ)	89	53°13′N	102°37′W
Passaic, N.J., U.S. (pă-sā′ĭk)	100a	40°52′N	74°08′W
Passaic, r., N.J., U.S.	100a	40°42′N	74°26′W
Passamaquoddy Bay, b., N.A. (păs′ȧ-mȧ-kwŏd′ĭ)	92	45°06′N	66°59′W
Passa Tempo, Braz. (pä′s-sä-tĕ′m-pô)	129a	20°40′S	44°29′W
Passau, Ger. (päs′ou)	147	48°34′N	13°27′E

ăt; finăl; rāte; senāte; ärm; ȧsk; sofȧ; fâre; ch-choose; dh-as th in other; bē; ēvent; bĕt; recĕnt; cratẽr; g-gō; gh-guttural g; bĭt; ĭ-short neutral; rīde; ĸ-guttural k as ch in German ich;

PLACE (Pronunciation)	PAGE	LAT.	LONG.
Pass Christian, Ms., U.S. (pȧs krĭs'tyĕn)	114	30°20'N	89°15'W
Passero, Cape, c., Italy (päs-sĕ'rō)	142	36°34'N	15°13'E
Passo Fundo, Braz. (pä'sŏ fōn'dŏ)	132	28°16'S	52°13'W
Passos, Braz. (pä's-sōs)	131	20°45'S	46°37'W
Pastaza, r., S.A. (päs-tä'zä)	130	3°05'S	76°18'W
Pasto, Col. (päs'tō)	130	1°15'N	77°19'W
Pastora, Mex. (päs-tō-rä)	118	22°08'N	100°04'W
Pasuruan, Indon.	196	7°45'S	112°50'E
Pasvalys, Lith. (päs-vä-lēs')	153	56°04'N	24°23'E
Patagonia, reg., Arg. (păt-ȧ-gō'nĭ-ȧ)	132	46°45'S	69°30'W
Pātālganga, r., India	187b	18°52'N	73°08'E
Patapsco, r., Md., U.S. (pȧ-tăps'kō)	100e	39°12'N	76°30'W
Pateros, Lake, res., Wa., U.S.	104	48°05'N	119°45'W
Paterson, N.J., U.S. (păt'ēr-sŭn)	100a	40°55'N	74°10'W
Pathein, Myanmar	183	16°46'N	94°47'E
Pathfinder Reservoir, res., Wy., U.S. (păth'fīn-dēr)	105	42°22'N	107°10'W
Patiāla, India (pŭt-ē-ä'lŭ)	183	30°25'N	76°28'E
Pati do Alferes, Braz. (pä-tē-dō-äl-fĕ'rĕs)	132b	22°25'S	43°25'W
Patna, India (pŭt'nŭ)	183	25°33'N	85°18'E
Patnanongan, i., Phil. (pät-nä-nōŋ'gän)	197a	14°50'N	122°25'E
Patoka, r., In., U.S. (pȧ-tō'kȧ)	98	38°25'N	87°25'W
Patom Plateau, plat., Russia	165	59°30'N	115°00'E
Patos, Braz. (pä'tōzh)	131	7°03'S	37°14'W
Patos, Wa., U.S. (pä'tōs)	106d	48°47'N	122°57'W
Patos, Lagoa dos, l., Braz. (lä'gō-ȧ dozh pä'tōzh)	132	31°15'S	51°30'W
Patos de Minas, Braz. (dĕ-mē'năzh)	131	18°39'S	46°31'W
Pátrai, Grc. (pä-trī') (pä-träs')	149	38°15'N	21°48'E
Patraïkós Kólpos, b., Grc.	161	38°16'N	21°19'E
Patras see Pátrai, Grc.	149	38°15'N	21°48'E
Patrocínio, Braz. (pä-trō-sē'nē-ō)	131	18°48'S	46°47'W
Pattani, Thai. (pät'ȧ-nē)	196	6°56'N	101°13'E
Patten, Me., U.S. (păt''n)	92	45°59'N	68°27'W
Patterson, La., U.S. (păt'ēr-sŭn)	113	29°41'N	91°20'W
Patterson, i., Can.	90	48°38'N	87°14'W
Patton, Pa., U.S.	99	40°40'N	78°45'W
Patuca, r., Hond.	121	15°22'N	84°31'W
Patuca, Punta, c., Hond. (po͞o'n-tä-pä-to͞o'kä)	121	15°55'N	84°05'W
Patuxent, r., Md., U.S. (pȧ-tŭk'sĕnt)	99	39°10'N	77°10'W
Pátzcuaro, Mex. (päts'kwä-rō)	118	19°30'N	101°36'W
Pátzcuaro, Lago de, l., Mex. (lä'gô-dĕ)	118	19°36'N	101°38'W
Patzicia, Guat. (pät-zē'syä)	120	14°36'N	90°57'W
Patzún, Guat. (pät-zo͞on')	120	14°40'N	91°00'W
Pau, Fr. (pō)	147	43°18'N	0°23'W
Pau, Gave de, r., Fr. (gäv-dĕ)	156	43°33'N	0°51'W
Paulding, Oh., U.S. (pôl'dĭng)	98	41°05'N	84°35'W
Paulinenaue, Ger. (pou'lē-nĕ-nou-ĕ)	145b	52°40'N	12°43'E
Paulistano, Braz. (pá'ō-lēs-tá-nä)	131	8°13'S	41°06'W
Paulo Afonso, Salto, wtfl., Braz. (säl-tō-pou'lō äf-fōɴ'sō)	131	9°33'S	38°32'W
Paul Roux, S. Afr. (pôrl ro͞o)	218d	28°18'S	27°57'E
Paulsboro, N.J., U.S. (pôlz'bē-rō)	100f	39°50'N	75°16'W
Pauls Valley, Ok., U.S. (pôlz văl'ē)	111	34°43'N	97°13'W
Pavarandocito, Col. (pä-vä-rän-dō-sē'tō)	130a	7°18'N	76°32'W
Pavda, Russia (päv'da)	172a	59°16'N	59°32'E
Pavia, Italy (pä-vē'ä)	148	45°12'N	9°11'E
Pavlodar, Kaz. (pȧv-lō-dȧr')	169	52°17'N	77°23'E
Pavlof Bay, b., Ak., U.S. (păv-lŏf)	95	55°20'N	161°20'W
Pavlohrad, Ukr.	167	48°32'N	35°52'E
Pavlovsk, Russia (pȧv-lôfsk')	163	50°28'N	40°05'E
Pavlovsk, Russia	172c	59°41'N	30°27'E
Pavlovskiy Posad, Russia (pȧv-lôf'skĭ pô-sȧt')	166	55°47'N	38°39'E
Pavuna, Braz. (pä-vo͞o'nȧ)	132b	22°48'S	43°21'W
Päwesin, Ger. (pă'vĕ-zēn)	145b	52°31'N	12°44'E
Pawhuska, Ok., U.S. (pô-hŭs'kȧ)	111	36°41'N	96°20'W
Pawnee, Ok., U.S. (pô-nē')	111	36°20'N	96°47'W
Pawnee, r., Ks., U.S.	110	38°18'N	99°42'W
Pawnee City, Ne., U.S.	111	40°08'N	96°09'W
Paw Paw, Mi., U.S. (pô'pô)	98	42°15'N	85°55'W
Paw Paw, r., Mi., U.S.	103	42°14'N	86°21'W
Pawtucket, R.I., U.S. (pô-tŭk'ĕt)	99	41°53'N	71°23'W
Paxoi, i., Grc.	161	39°14'N	20°15'E
Paxton, Il., U.S. (păks'tŭn)	98	40°35'N	88°00'W
Paya Lebar, Sing.	240c	1°22'N	103°53'E
Payette, Id., U.S. (pȧ-ĕt')	104	44°05'N	116°55'W
Payette, r., Id., U.S.	104	43°57'N	116°26'W
Payette, North Fork, r., Id., U.S.	104	44°10'N	116°10'W
Payette, South Fork, r., Id., U.S.	104	44°07'N	115°43'W
Pay-Khoy, Khrebet, mts., Russia	166	68°08'N	63°04'E
Payne, l., Can. (pān)	85	59°22'N	73°16'W
Paynesville, S. Afr.	244b	26°14'S	28°28'E
Paynesville, Mn., U.S. (pānz'vĭl)	103	45°23'N	94°43'W
Paysandú, Ur. (pī-sän-do͞o')	132	32°16'S	57°55'W
Payson, Ut., U.S. (pā's'n)	109	40°05'N	111°45'W
Pazardzhik, Bul. (pä-zȧr-dzhek')	149	42°10'N	24°22'E
Pazin, Cro. (pä'zēn)	160	45°14'N	13°57'E
Peabody, Ks., U.S. (pē'bŏd-ĭ)	111	38°09'N	97°09'W
Peabody, Ma., U.S.	93a	42°32'N	70°56'W
Peabody Institute, pt. of i., Md., U.S.	229c	39°18'N	76°37'W
Peace, r., Can.	84	57°30'N	117°30'W
Peace Creek, r., Fl., U.S. (pēs)	115a	27°16'N	81°53'W
Peace Dale, R.I., U.S. (dāl)	100b	41°27'N	71°30'W
Peace River, Can. (rĭv'ēr)	84	56°14'N	117°17'W
Peacock Hills, hills, Can. (pē-kŏk' hĭlz)	84	66°08'N	109°55'W
Peak Hill, Austl.	202	25°38'S	118°50'E
Peakhurst, Austl.	243a	33°58'S	151°04'E
Pearl, r., U.S. (pûrl)	97	30°30'N	89°45'W
Pearland, Tx., U.S. (pûrl'ănd)	113a	29°34'N	95°17'W
Pearl Harbor, Hi., U.S.	94a	21°20'N	157°53'W
Pearl Harbor, b., Hi., U.S.	96d	21°22'N	157°58'W
Pearsall, Tx., U.S. (pēr'sôl)	112	28°53'N	99°06'W
Pearse Island, i., Can. (pērs)	86	54°51'N	130°21'W
Pearston, S. Afr. (pē'ērstŏn)	213c	32°36'S	25°09'E
Peary Land, reg., Grnld. (pēr'ĭ)	220	82°00'N	40°00'W
Pease, r., Tx., U.S. (pēz)	110	34°07'N	99°53'W
Peason, La., U.S. (pēz''n)	113	31°25'N	93°19'W
Pebane, Moz. (pĕ-bá'nē)	213	17°10'S	38°08'E
Pecan Bay, Tx., U.S. (pē-kăn')	112	32°04'N	99°15'W
Peçanha, Braz. (pā-kän'yȧ)	131	18°37'S	42°26'W
Pecatonica, r., Il., U.S. (pĕk-ȧ-tŏn-ĭ-kȧ)	103	42°21'N	89°28'W
Pechenga, Russia (pyĕ'chĕŋ-gȧ)	166	69°30'N	31°10'E
Pechincha, neigh., Braz.	234c	22°56'S	43°21'W
Pechora, r., Russia	164	66°00'N	54°00'E
Pechora Basin, Russia (pyĕ-chô'rá)	164	67°55'N	58°37'E
Pechori, Russia (pĕt'sē-rē)	162	57°48'N	27°33'E
Pecos, N.M., U.S. (pā'kōs)	109	35°29'N	105°41'W
Pecos, Tx., U.S.	112	31°26'N	103°30'W
Pecos, r., U.S.	96	31°10'N	103°10'W
Pécs, Hung. (pāch)	149	46°04'N	18°15'E
Peddie, S. Afr.	213c	33°13'S	27°09'E
Pedley, Ca., U.S. (pĕd'lē)	107a	33°59'N	117°29'W
Pedra Azul, Braz. (pā'drä-zo͞o'l)	131	16°03'S	41°13'W
Pedreiras, Braz. (pĕ-drā'räs)	131	4°30'S	44°31'W
Pedro, Point, c., Sri L. (pē'drō)	187	9°50'N	80°14'E
Pedro Antonio Santos, Mex.	120a	18°55'N	88°13'W
Pedro Betancourt, Cuba (bā-täŋ-kōrt')	122	22°40'N	81°15'W
Pedro de Valdivia, Chile (pĕ'drō-dĕ-väl-dē'vē-ä)	132	22°32'S	69°55'W
Pedro do Rio, Braz. (dō-rē'ō)	132b	22°20'S	43°09'W
Pedro II, Braz. (pā'drō sá-gōn'dō)	131	4°20'S	41°27'W
Pedro Juan Caballero, Para. (hòá'n-kä-bäl-yĕ'rō)	132	22°40'S	55°42'W
Pedro Miguel, Pan. (mē-gāl')	116a	9°01'N	79°36'W
Pedro Miguel Locks, trans., Pan. (mē-gāl')	116a	9°01'N	79°36'W
Peebinga, Austl. (pē-bĭng'ȧ)	202	34°43'S	140°55'E
Peebles, Scot., U.K. (pē'b'lz)	150	55°40'N	3°15'W
Peekskill, N.Y., U.S. (pēks'kĭl)	100a	41°17'N	73°55'W
Pegasus Bay, b., N.Z. (pĕg'ȧ-sŭs)	203a	43°18'S	173°25'E
Pegnitz, r., Ger. (pĕgh-nēts)	154	49°38'N	11°40'E
Pego, Spain (pā'gō)	159	38°50'N	0°09'W
Peguis Indian Reserve, I.R., Can.	89	51°20'N	97°35'W
Pegu Yoma, mts., Myanmar (pĕ-go͞o'yō'mä)	183	19°16'N	95°59'E
Pehčevo, Mac. (pĕk'chĕ-vō)	161	41°42'N	22°57'E
Pehladpur, neigh., India	240d	28°35'N	77°06'E
Peigan Indian Reserve, I.R., Can.	87	49°35'N	113°40'W
Peipus, Lake see Chudskoye Ozero, l., Eur.	166	58°43'N	26°45'E
Peit'ou, Tai.	241d	25°08'N	121°29'E
Pekin, Il., U.S. (pē'kĭn)	98	40°35'N	89°30'W
Peking see Beijing, China	189	39°55'N	116°23'E
Pelagie, Isole, is., Italy	148	35°46'N	12°32'E
Pélagos, i., Grc.	161	39°17'N	24°05'E
Pelahatchie, Ms., U.S. (pĕl-ȧ-hăch'ē)	114	32°17'N	89°48'W
Pelat, Mont, mtn., Fr. (pē-lá')	147	44°16'N	6°43'E
Peleduy, Russia (pyĕl-yĭ-do͞o'ē)	165	59°50'N	112°47'E
Pelée, Mont, mtn., Mart. (pē-lā')	121b	14°49'N	61°10'W
Pelee, Point, c., Can.	90	41°55'N	82°30'W
Pelee Island, i., Can. (pē'lē)	90	41°45'N	82°30'W
Pelequén, Chile (pĕ-lĕ-kĕ'n)	129b	34°26'S	71°52'W
Pelham, Ga., U.S. (pĕl'hăm)	114	31°07'N	84°10'W
Pelham, N.H., U.S.	93a	42°43'N	71°22'W
Pelham, N.Y., U.S.	228	40°55'N	73°49'W
Pelham Manor, N.Y., U.S.	228	40°54'N	73°48'W
Pelican, l., Mn., U.S.	103	46°36'N	94°00'W
Pelican Bay, b., Can.	89	52°45'N	100°20'W
Pelican Harbor, b., Bah. (pĕl'ĭ-kăn)	122	26°20'N	76°45'W
Pelican Rapids, Mn., U.S. (pĕl'ĭ-kăn)	102	46°34'N	96°05'W
Pella, Ia., U.S. (pĕl'ȧ)	103	41°25'N	92°50'W
Pellworm, i., Ger. (pĕl'vôrm)	154	54°33'N	8°25'E
Pelly, l., Can.	84	66°08'N	102°57'W
Pelly, r., Can.	84	62°20'N	133°00'W
Pelly Bay, b., Can. (pĕl'ĭ)	85	68°57'N	91°05'W
Pelly Crossing, Can.	95	62°50'N	136°50'W
Pelly Mountains, mts., Can.	84	61°50'N	133°05'W
Peloncillo Mountains, mts., Az., U.S. (pĕl-ōn-sĭl'lō)	109	32°40'N	109°20'W
Peloponnisos, pen., Grc.	161	37°28'N	22°14'E
Pelotas, Braz. (pā-lō'tăzh)	132	31°45'S	52°18'W
Pelton, Can. (pĕl'tŭn)	101b	42°15'N	82°57'W
Pelym, r., Russia	166	60°20'N	63°05'E
Pelzer, S.C., U.S. (pĕl'zēr)	115	34°38'N	82°30'W
Pemanggil, i., Malay.	181b	2°37'N	104°41'E
Pematangsiantar, Indon.	196	2°58'N	99°03'E
Pemba, Moz. (pĕm'bá)	213	12°58'S	40°30'E
Pemba, Zam.	212	15°29'S	27°22'E
Pemba Channel, strt., Afr.	217	5°10'S	39°30'E
Pemba Island, i., Tan.	217	5°20'S	39°57'E
Pembina, N.D., U.S. (pĕm'bĭ-ná)	102	48°58'N	97°15'W
Pembina, r., Can.	87	53°05'N	114°30'W
Pembina, r., N.A.	89	49°08'N	98°20'W
Pembroke, Can. (pĕm' brōk)	85	45°50'N	77°00'W
Pembroke, Wales, U.K.	150	51°40'N	5°00'W
Pembroke, Ma., U.S. (pĕm'brōk)	93a	42°05'N	70°49'W
Pen, India	187b	18°44'N	73°06'E
Penafiel, Port. (pā-ná-fyĕl')	158	41°12'N	8°19'W
Peñafiel, Spain (pā-nyá-fyĕl')	158	41°38'N	4°08'W
Peña Grande, neigh., Spain	238b	40°23'N	3°44'W
Peñalara, mtn., Spain (pā-nyä-lä'rä)	148	40°52'N	3°57'W
Pena Nevada, Cerro, Mex.	118	23°47'N	99°52'W
Peñaranda de Bracamonte, Spain	158	40°54'N	5°11'W
Peñarroya-Pueblonuevo, Spain (pĕn-yär-rō'yä-pwĕ'blō-nwĕ'vō)	158	38°18'N	5°18'W
Peñas, Cabo de, c., Spain (ká'bō-dĕ-pā'nyäs)	158	43°42'N	6°12'W
Penas, Golfo de, b., Chile (gôl-fô-dĕ-pĕ'n-äs)	132	47°15'S	77°30'W
Penasco, r., Tx., U.S. (pā-nás'kō)	112	32°50'N	104°45'W
Pendembu, S.L. (pĕn-dĕm'bo͞o)	210	8°06'N	10°42'W
Pender, Ne., U.S. (pĕn'dēr)	102	42°08'N	96°43'W
Penderisco, r., Col. (pĕn-dĕ-rē's-kō)	130a	6°30'N	76°21'W
Pendjari, Parc National de la, rec., Benin	214	11°25'N	1°30'E
Pendlebury, Eng., U.K.	237b	53°31'N	2°20'W
Pendleton, Or., U.S. (pĕn'd'l-tŭn)	96	45°41'N	118°47'W
Pend Oreille, r., Wa., U.S.	104	48°44'N	117°20'W
Pend Oreille, Lake, l., Id., U.S. (pŏn-dō-rā') (pĕn-dō-rĕl')	96	48°09'N	116°38'W
Penedo, Braz. (pā-nā'dō)	131	10°17'S	36°28'W
Penetanguishene, Can. (pĕn'ē-tăŋ-gĭ-shēn')	91	44°45'N	79°55'W
Pengcheng, China (pŭŋ-chŭŋ)	190	36°24'N	114°11'E
Penglai, China (pŭŋ-lī)	192	37°49'N	120°45'E
Penha, neigh., Braz.	234c	22°49'S	43°17'W
Penha de França, neigh., Braz.	234d	23°32'S	46°32'W
Peniche, Port. (pĕ-nē'chä)	158	39°22'N	9°24'W
Peninsula, Oh., U.S. (pĕn-ĭn'sū-lȧ)	101d	41°14'N	81°32'W
Penistone, Eng., U.K. (pĕn'ĭ-stŭn)	144a	53°31'N	1°38'W
Penjamillo, Mex. (pĕn-hä-mēl'yō)	118	20°06'N	101°56'W
Pénjamo, Mex. (pān'hä-mō)	118	20°27'N	101°43'W
Penk, r., Eng., U.K. (pĕnk)	144a	52°41'N	2°10'W
Penkridge, Eng., U.K. (pĕnk'rĭj)	144a	52°43'N	2°07'W
Pennant Hills, Austl.	243a	33°44'S	151°04'E
Penne, Italy (pĕn'nā)	160	42°28'N	13°57'E
Penner, r., India (pĕn'ēr)	183	14°43'N	79°09'E
Penn Hills, Pa., U.S.	230b	40°28'N	79°53'W
Pennines, hills, Eng., U.K. (pĕn-īn')	150	54°30'N	2°10'W
Pennines, Alpes, mts., Eur.	154	46°02'N	7°07'E
Pennsauken, N.J., U.S.	229b	39°58'N	75°04'W
Pennsboro, W.V., U.S. (pĕnz'bŭr-ō)	98	39°10'N	81°00'W
Penns Grove, N.J., U.S. (pĕnz grōv)	100f	39°44'N	75°28'W
Pennsylvania, state, U.S. (pĕn-sĭl-vā'nĭ-ȧ)	97	41°00'N	78°10'W
Penn Valley, Pa., U.S.	229b	40°01'N	75°16'W
Penn Wynne, Pa., U.S.	229b	39°59'N	75°16'W
Penn Yan, N.Y., U.S. (pĕn yăn')	99	42°40'N	77°00'W
Pennycutaway, r., Can.	89	56°10'N	93°25'W
Peno, l., Russia (pā'nō)	162	56°55'N	32°28'E
Penobscot, r., Me., U.S.	97	45°00'N	68°36'W
Penobscot Bay, b., Me., U.S. (pē-nŏb'skŏt)	92	44°20'N	69°00'W
Penong, Austl. (pē-nông')	202	32°00'S	133°00'E
Penrith, Austl.	201b	33°45'S	150°42'E
Pensacola, Fl., U.S. (pĕn-sȧ-kō'lȧ)	97	30°25'N	87°13'W
Pensacola Dam, Ok., U.S.	111	36°27'N	95°02'W
Pensby, Eng., U.K.	237a	53°21'N	3°06'W
Pensilvania, Col. (pĕn-sēl-vá'nyä)	130a	5°31'N	75°05'W
Pentagon, pt. of i., Va., U.S.	229d	38°52'N	77°03'W
Pentecost, i., Vanuatu (pĕn'tē-kōst)	203	16°05'S	168°28'E
Penticton, Can.	84	49°30'N	119°35'W
Pentland Firth, strt., Scot., U.K. (pĕnt'lănd)	150	58°44'N	3°25'W
Penza, Russia (pĕn'zȧ)	164	53°10'N	45°00'E
Penzance, Eng., U.K. (pĕn-zăns')	150	50°07'N	5°40'W
Penzberg, Ger. (pĕnts'bĕrgh)	154	47°43'N	11°21'E
Penzhina, r., Russia (pyĭn-zē-nŭ)	171	62°15'N	166°30'E
Penzhino, Russia	165	63°42'N	168°00'E
Penzhinskaya Guba, b., Russia	171	60°30'N	161°30'E
Penzing, neigh., Aus.	239e	48°12'N	16°18'E
Peoria, Il., U.S. (pē-ō'rĭ-ȧ)	97	40°45'N	89°35'W
Peotillos, Mex. (pā-ō-tel'yōs)	118	22°30'N	100°39'W
Peotone, Il., U.S. (pē'ō-tōn)	101a	41°20'N	87°47'W
Pepacton Reservoir, res., N.Y., U.S. (pĕp-ác'tŭn)	99	42°05'N	74°40'W
Pepe, Cabo, c., Cuba (kä'bō-pĕ'pĕ)	122	21°30'N	83°10'W
Pepperell, Ma., U.S. (pĕp'ēr-ĕl)	93a	42°40'N	71°36'W
Peqin, Alb. (pĕ-kēn')	161	41°03'N	19°48'E
Pequannock, N.J., U.S.	228	40°57'N	74°18'W
Perales, r., Spain (pā-rä'lās)	159a	40°24'N	4°07'W
Perales de Tajuña, Spain (dā tä-ho͞o'nyä)	159a	40°14'N	3°22'W
Perche, Collines du, hills, Fr.	156	48°25'N	0°40'E
Perchtoldsdorf, Aus. (pĕrk'tōlts-dôrf)	145e	48°07'N	16°17'E
Perdekop, S. Afr.	218d	27°11'S	29°38'E
Perdido, r., Al., U.S. (pĕr-dī'dō)	114	30°45'N	87°38'W
Perdido, Monte, mtn., Spain (pĕr-dē'dō)	159	42°40'N	0.00
Perdões, Braz. (pĕr-dô'ĕs)	129a	21°05'S	45°05'W
Pereiaslav-Khmel'nyts'kyi, Ukr.	167	50°05'N	31°25'E
Pereira, Col. (pā-rā'rä)	130	4°49'N	75°42'W
Pere Marquette, Mi., U.S.	98	43°55'N	86°10'W
Pereshchepyne, Ukr.	163	49°02'N	35°19'E
Pereslavl'-Zalesskiy, Russia (pȧ-rȧ-slăv''l zȧ-lyĕs'kĭ)	166	56°43'N	38°52'E
Pergamino, Arg. (pĕr-gä-mē'nō)	132	33°53'S	60°36'W
Perham, Mn., U.S. (pĕr'hăm)	102	46°37'N	95°35'W
Peribonca, r., Can. (pĕr-ĭ-bŏŋ'kȧ)	85	50°30'N	71°00'W
Périgueux, Fr. (pā-rē-gû')	147	45°12'N	0°43'E
Perija, Sierra de, mts., Col. (sē-ĕ'r-rä-dĕ-pĕ-rē'kä)	130	9°25'N	73°30'W
Peristérion, Grc.	239d	38°01'N	23°42'E
Perivale, neigh., Eng., U.K.	235	51°32'N	0°19'W
Perkam, Tanjung, c., Indon.	197	1°20'S	138°45'E
Perkins, Can. (pĕr'kĕns)	83c	45°37'N	75°37'W
Perlas, Archipiélago de las, is., Pan.	121	8°29'N	79°15'W
Perlas, Laguna las, l., Nic. (lä-gŏ'nä-dĕ-läs)	121	12°34'N	83°19'W
Perleberg, Ger. (pĕr'lē-bĕrg)	154	53°06'N	11°51'E

PLACE (Pronunciation)	PAGE	LAT.	LONG.
Perm', Russia (pěrm)	164	58°00'N	56°15'E
Pernambuco see Recife, Braz.	131	8°09'S	34°59'W
Pernambuco, state, Braz. (pěr-näm-bōō'kō)	131	8°08'S	38°54'W
Pernik, Bul. (pěr-nêk')	149	42°36'N	23°04'E
Péronne, Fr. (pā-rôn')	156	49°57'N	2°49'E
Perote, Mex. (pě-rô'tě)	119	19°33'N	97°13'W
Perovo, Russia (pâ'rô-vô)	172b	55°43'N	37°47'E
Perpignan, Fr. (pěr-pē-nyäɴ')	147	42°42'N	2°48'E
Perris, Ca., U.S. (pěr'ĭs)	107a	33°46'N	117°14'W
Perros, Bahía, b., Cuba (bä-ē'ä-pā'rōs)	122	22°25'N	78°35'W
Perrot, Île, i., Can.	83a	45°23'N	73°57'W
Perry, Fl., U.S. (pěr'ĭ)	114	30°06'N	83°35'W
Perry, Ga., U.S.	114	32°27'N	83°44'W
Perry, Ia., U.S.	103	41°49'N	94°40'W
Perry, N.Y., U.S.	99	42°45'N	78°00'W
Perry, Ok., U.S.	111	36°17'N	97°18'W
Perry, Ut., U.S.	107b	41°27'N	112°02'W
Perry Hall, Md., U.S.	100e	39°24'N	76°29'W
Perrymont, Pa., U.S.	230b	40°33'N	80°02'W
Perryopolis, Pa., U.S. (pě-rê-ŏ'pô-lĭs)	101e	40°05'N	79°45'W
Perrysburg, Oh., U.S. (pěr ĭz-bûrg)	98	41°35'N	83°35'W
Perryton, Tx., U.S. (pěr'ĭ-tŭn)	110	36°23'N	100°48'W
Perryville, Ak., U.S. (pěr-ĭ-vĭl)	95	55°58'N	159°28'W
Perryville, Mo., U.S.	111	37°41'N	89°52'W
Persan, Fr. (pěr-säɴ')	157b	49°09'N	2°15'E
Persepolis, hist., Iran (pěr-sěpō-lĭs)	182	30°15'N	53°08'E
Persian Gulf, b., Asia (pûr'zhăn)	182	27°38'N	50°30'E
Perth, Austl. (pûrth)	202	31°50'S	116°10'E
Perth, Can.	91	44°40'N	76°15'W
Perth, Scot., U.K.	146	56°24'N	3°25'W
Perth Amboy, N.J., U.S. (ăm'boi)	100a	40°31'N	74°16'W
Pertuis, Fr. (pěr-tüē')	157	43°43'N	5°29'E
Peru, Il., U.S. (pē-rōō')	98	41°20'N	89°10'W
Peru, In., U.S.	98	40°45'N	86°00'W
Peru, nation, S.A.	130	10°00'S	75°00'W
Perugia, Italy (pā-rōō'jä)	148	43°08'N	12°24'E
Peruque, Mo., U.S. (pě rō'kě)	107e	38°52'N	90°36'W
Pervomais'k, Ukr.	167	48°04'N	30°52'E
Pervoural'sk, Russia (pěr-vô-ô-rálsk')	172a	56°54'N	59°58'E
Perwenitz, Ger.	238a	52°40'N	13°01'E
Pesaro, Italy (pā'zä-rō)	148	43°54'N	12°55'E
Pescado, r., Ven. (pěs-kä'dō)	131b	9°33'N	65°32'W
Pescara, Italy (pās-kä'rä)	160	42°26'N	14°15'E
Pescara, r., Italy	160	42°18'N	13°22'E
Peschanyy mŭis, c., Kaz.	170	43°10'N	51°20'E
Pescia, Italy (pā'shä)	160	43°53'N	11°42'E
Peshāwar, Pak. (pě-shä'wŭr)	183	34°01'N	71°34'E
Peshtera, Bul.	161	42°03'N	24°19'E
Peshtigo, Wi., U.S. (pěsh'tê-gō)	103	45°03'N	87°46'W
Peshtigo, r., Wi., U.S.	103	45°15'N	88°14'W
Peski, Russia (pyâs'kĭ)	172b	55°13'N	38°48'E
Pêso da Régua, Port. (pā-sò-dä-rā'gwä)	158	41°09'N	7°47'W
Pespire, Hond. (pās-pē'rā)	120	13°35'N	87°20'W
Pesqueria, r., Mex. (pās-kā-rē'ā)	112	25°55'N	100°25'W
Pessac, Fr.	156	44°48'N	0°38'W
Pesterzsébet, neigh., Hung.	239g	47°26'N	19°07'E
Pestlorinc, neigh., Hung.	239g	47°26'N	19°12'E
Pestújhely, neigh., Hung.	239g	47°32'N	19°07'E
Petacalco, Bahía de, b., Mex. (bä-ē'ä-dě-pě-tä-käl'kō)	118	17°55'N	102°00'W
Petah Tiqwa, Isr.	181a	32°05'N	34°53'E
Petaluma, Ca., U.S. (pét-ȧ-lò'mȧ)	108	38°15'N	122°38'W
Petare, Ven. (pě-tä'rě)	131b	10°28'N	66°48'W
Petatlán, Mex. (pā-tä-tlän')	118	17°31'N	101°17'W
Petawawa, Can.	91	45°54'N	77°17'W
Petén, Laguna de, l., Guat. (lä-gò'nä-dě-pā-tān')	120a	17°05'N	89°54'W
Petenwell Reservoir, res., Wi., U.S.	103	44°10'N	89°55'W
Peterborough, Austl.	202	32°53'S	138°58'E
Peterborough, Can. (pē'tēr-bŭr-ô)	85	44°20'N	78°20'W
Peterborough, Eng., U.K.	150	52°35'N	0°14'W
Peterhead, Scot., U.K. (pē-tēr-hěd')	150	57°36'N	3°47'W
Peter Pond Lake, l., Can. (pŏnd)	84	55°55'N	108°44'W
Petersburg, Ak., U.S. (pē'tērz-bûrg)	95	56°52'N	133°10'W
Petersburg, Il., U.S.	111	40°01'N	89°51'W
Petersburg, In., U.S.	98	38°30'N	87°15'W
Petersburg, Ky., U.S.	101f	39°04'N	84°52'W
Petersburg, Va., U.S.	97	37°12'N	77°30'W
Peters Creek, r., Pa., U.S.	230b	40°18'N	79°52'W
Petershagen, Ger. (pě'tērs-hä-gěn)	145b	52°32'N	13°46'E
Petersham, Austl.	243a	33°54'S	151°09'E
Petershausen, Ger. (pě'těrs-hou-zěn)	145d	48°25'N	11°29'E
Pétionville, Haiti	123	18°30'N	72°20'W
Petit, S. Afr.	244b	26°06'S	28°22'E
Petitcodiac, Can. (pē-tē-kō-dyȧk')	92	45°56'N	65°10'W
Petite Terre, i., Guad. (pē-tēt'târ')	121b	16°12'N	61°00'W
Petit Goâve, Haiti (pē-tē' gō-áv')	123	18°25'N	72°50'W
Petit Jean Creek, r., Ar., U.S. (pē-tē'zhäɴ')	111	35°05'N	93°55'W
Petit Loango, Gabon	216	2°16'S	9°35'E
Petlalcingo, Mex. (pě-tläl-sēŋ'gō)	119	18°05'N	97°53'W
Peto, Mex. (pě'tô)	120a	20°07'N	88°49'W
Petorca, Chile (pā-tōr'kȧ)	129b	32°14'S	70°55'W
Petoskey, Mi., U.S. (pē-tŏs-kĭ)	98	45°25'N	84°55'W
Petra, hist., Jord.	181a	30°21'N	35°25'E
Petra Velikogo, Zaliv, b., Russia	194	42°40'N	131°50'E
Petre, Point, c., Can.	91	43°50'N	77°00'W
Petrich, Bul. (pā'trĭch)	149	41°24'N	23°13'E
Petrified Forest National Park, rec., Az., U.S. (pět'rĭ-fīd fôr'ěst)	109	34°58'N	109°35'W
Petrikov, Bela. (pyě'trê-kô-v)	162	52°09'N	28°30'E
Petrinja, Cro. (pā'trēn-yȧ)	160	45°25'N	16°17'E
Petrodvorets, Russia (pyě-trô-dvô-ryěts')	172c	59°53'N	29°55'E
Petrokrepost', Russia (pyě'trô-krě-pôst)	166	59°56'N	31°03'E
Petrolia, Can. (pē-trō'lĭ-ȧ)	90	42°50'N	82°10'W
Petrolina, Braz. (pě-trō-lē'nȧ)	131	9°18'S	40°28'W
Petronell, Aus.	145e	48°07'N	16°52'E
Petropavl, Kaz.	169	54°44'N	69°07'E
Petropavlivka, Ukr.	163	48°24'N	36°23'E
Petropavlovka, Russia	172a	54°10'N	59°50'E
Petropavlovsk-Kamchatskiy, Russia (käm-chät'skĭ)	165	53°13'N	158°56'E
Petrópolis, Braz. (på-trò-pò-lēzh')	131	22°31'S	43°10'W
Petroşani, Rom.	161	45°24'N	23°24'E
Petrovsk, Russia (pyě-trôfsk')	167	52°20'N	45°15'E
Petrovskaya, Russia (pyě-trôf'ská-yȧ)	163	45°25'N	37°50'E
Petrovsko-Razumovskoje, neigh., Russia	239b	55°50'N	37°34'E
Petrovskoye, Russia	167	45°20'N	43°00'E
Petrovsk-Zabaykal'skiy, Russia (pyě-trôfskzä-bī-käl'skĭ)	165	51°13'N	109°08'E
Petrozavodsk, Russia (pyä'trô-zȧ-vôtsk')	164	61°46'N	34°25'E
Petrus Steyn, S. Afr.	218d	27°40'S	28°09'E
Petrykivka, Ukr.	163	48°43'N	34°29'E
Pewaukee, Wi., U.S. (pĭ-wô'kē)	101a	43°05'N	88°15'W
Pewaukee Lake, l., Wi., U.S.	101a	43°03'N	88°18'W
Pewee Valley, Ky., U.S. (pe wē)	101h	38°19'N	85°29'W
Peza, r., Russia (pyâ'zȧ)	166	65°35'N	46°50'E
Pézenas, Fr. (pā-zē-nä')	156	43°26'N	3°24'E
Pforzheim, Ger. (pfōrts'hīm)	147	48°52'N	8°43'E
Phalodi, India	186	27°13'N	72°22'E
Phan Thiet, Viet (p'hän')	196	11°30'N	108°43'E
Phelps Corner, Md., U.S.	229d	38°48'N	76°58'W
Phelps Lake, l., N.C., U.S.	115	35°46'N	76°27'W
Phenix City, Al., U.S. (fē'nĭks)	114	32°29'N	85°00'W
Philadelphia, Ms., U.S. (fĭl-ȧ-děl'phĭ-ȧ)	114	32°45'N	89°07'W
Philadelphia, Pa., U.S.	97	40°00'N	75°13'W
Philip, S.D., U.S. (fĭl'ĭp)	102	44°03'N	101°35'W
Philippeville see Skikda, Alg.	210	36°58'N	6°51'E
Philippines, nation, Asia (fĭl'ĭ-pēnz)	197	14°25'N	125°00'E
Philippine Sea, sea (fĭl'ĭ-pēn)	225	16°00'N	133°00'E
Philippine Trench, deep	197	10°30'N	127°15'E
Philipsburg, Pa., U.S. (fĭl'lĭps-bērg)	99	40°55'N	78°10'W
Philipsburg, Wy., U.S.	105	46°19'N	113°19'W
Phillip, i., Austl. (fĭl'ĭp)	204	38°32'S	145°10'E
Phillip Channel, strt., Indon.	181b	1°04'N	103°40'E
Phillipi, W.V., U.S. (fĭ-lĭp'ĭ)	98	39°10'N	80°00'W
Phillips, Wi., U.S. (fĭl'ĭps)	103	45°41'N	90°24'W
Phillipsburg, Ks., U.S. (fĭl'lĭps-bērg)	110	39°44'N	99°19'W
Phillipsburg, N.J., U.S.	99	40°45'N	75°10'W
Phinga, India	240a	22°41'N	88°25'E
Phitsanulok, Thai.	196	16°51'N	100°15'E
Phnom Penh see Phnum Pénh, Camb.	196	11°39'N	104°53'E
Phnum Pénh, Camb. (nŏm'pěn')	196	11°39'N	104°53'E
Phoenix, Az., U.S. (fē'nĭks)	96	33°30'N	112°00'W
Phoenix, Md., U.S.	100e	39°31'N	76°40'W
Phoenix Islands, is., Kir.	2	4°00'S	174°00'W
Phoenixville, Pa., U.S. (fē'nĭks-vĭl)	100f	40°08'N	75°31'W
Phou Bia, mtn., Laos	196	19°36'N	103°00'E
Phra Nakhon Si Ayutthaya, Thai.	196	14°16'N	100°37'E
Phuket, Thai.	196	7°57'N	98°19'E
Phu Quoc, Dao, i., Viet	196	10°13'N	104°00'E
Phu-tho-hoa, Viet	241j	10°46'N	106°39'E
Pi, r., China (bē)	190	32°06'N	116°31'E
Piacenza, Italy (pyä-chěnt'sä)	148	45°02'N	9°42'E
Pianosa, i., Italy (pyä-nō'sä)	160	42°13'N	15°45'E
Piave, r., Italy (pyä'vā)	160	45°45'N	12°15'E
Piazza Armerina, Italy (pyät'sä är-må-rē'nä)	160	37°23'N	14°26'E
Pibor, r., Sudan (pē'bôr)	211	7°21'N	32°54'E
Pic, r., Can. (pěk)	90	48°48'N	86°28'W
Picara Point, c., V.I.U.S. (pē-kä'rä)	117c	18°23'N	64°57'W
Picayune, Ms., U.S. (pĭk'á yōōn)	114	30°32'N	89°41'W
Picher, Ok., U.S. (pĭch'ēr)	111	36°58'N	94°49'W
Pichilemu, Chile (pē-chē-lě'mōō)	129b	34°22'S	72°01'W
Pichucalco, Mex. (pē-chōō-käl'kō)	119	17°34'N	93°06'W
Pickerel, l., Can. (pĭk'ēr-ěl)	90	48°35'N	91°10'W
Pickwick Lake, res., U.S. (pĭk'wĭck)	114	35°04'N	88°05'W
Pico, Ca., U.S. (pē'kō)	107a	34°01'N	118°05'W
Pico Island, i., Port. (pē'kō)	210a	38°16'N	28°49'W
Pico Rivera, Ca., U.S.	107a	34°01'N	118°05'W
Picos, Braz. (pē'kōzh)	131	7°13'S	41°23'W
Picton, Austl. (pĭk'tŭn)	201b	34°11'S	150°37'E
Picton, Can.	91	44°00'N	77°15'W
Pictou, Can. (pĭk-tōō')	93	45°41'N	62°43'W
Pidálion, Akrotírion, c., Cyp.	181a	34°50'N	34°05'E
Pidurutalagala, mtn., Sri L. (pē'dò-rò-tä'lȧ-gä'lȧ)	183	7°00'N	80°46'E
Pidvolochys'k, Ukr.	163	49°32'N	26°16'E
Pie, i., Can. (pī)	90	48°10'N	89°07'W
Piedade, Braz. (pyä-dä'dě)	129a	23°42'S	47°25'W
Piedade do Baruel, Braz.	234d	23°37'S	46°18'W
Piedmont, Al., U.S. (pēd'mŏnt)	114	33°54'N	85°36'W
Piedmont, Ca., U.S.	106b	37°50'N	122°14'W
Piedmont, Mo., U.S.	111	37°09'N	90°42'W
Piedmont, S.C., U.S.	115	34°40'N	82°27'W
Piedmont, W.V., U.S.	99	39°30'N	79°05'W
Piedrabuena, Spain (pyä-drä-bwä'nä)	158	39°01'N	4°10'W
Piedras, Punta, c., Arg. (pōō'n-tä-pyě'dräs)	129c	35°25'S	57°10'W
Piedras Negras, Mex. (pyä'dräs nā'gräs)	116	28°41'N	100°33'W
Pieksämäki, Fin. (pyěk'sě-mě-kě)	153	62°18'N	27°14'E
Piemonte, hist. reg., Italy (pyě-mô'n-tě)	160	44°30'N	7°42'E
Pienaars, r., S. Afr.	218d	25°13'S	28°05'E
Pienaarsrivier, S. Afr.	218d	25°12'S	28°18'E
Pierce, Ne., U.S. (pērs)	102	42°11'N	97°33'W
Pierce, W.V., U.S.	99	39°15'N	79°30'W
Piermont, N.Y., U.S. (pēr'mŏnt)	100a	41°03'N	73°55'W
Pierre, S.D., U.S. (pēr)	96	44°22'N	100°20'W
Pierrefitte-sur-Seine, Fr.	237c	48°58'N	2°22'E
Pierrefonds, Can.	83a	45°29'N	73°52'W
Piešt'any, Slvk.	155	48°36'N	17°48'E
Pietermaritzburg, S. Afr. (pē-tēr-mȧ-rĭts-bûrg)	212	29°36'S	30°23'E
Pietersburg, S. Afr. (pē'tērz-bûrg)	212	23°56'S	29°30'E
Pietersfield, S. Afr.	244b	26°14'S	28°26'E
Piet Retief, S. Afr. (pēt rē-tēf')	212	27°00'S	30°58'E
Pietrosu, Vârful, mtn., Rom.	155	47°35'N	24°49'E
Pieve di Cadore, Italy (pyā'vā dē kä-dō'rā)	148	46°26'N	12°22'E
Pigeon, r., N.A. (pĭj'ŭn)	103	48°05'N	90°13'W
Pigeon Lake, Can.	83f	49°57'N	97°36'W
Pigeon Lake, l., Can.	87	53°00'N	114°00'W
Piggott, Ar., U.S. (pĭg-ŭt)	111	36°22'N	90°10'W
Pijijiapan, Mex. (pēkē-kē-ä'pän)	119	15°40'N	93°12'W
Pijnacker, Neth.	145a	52°01'N	4°25'E
Pikes Peak, mtn., Co., U.S. (pīks)	96	38°49'N	105°03'W
Pikesville, Md., U.S.	229c	39°23'N	76°44'W
Pikeville, Ky., U.S. (pīk'vĭl)	98	37°28'N	82°31'W
Pikou, China (pē-kō)	192	39°25'N	122°19'E
Pikwitonei, Can. (pĭk'wĭ-tōn)	89	55°35'N	97°09'W
Piła, Pol. (pē'lä)	154	53°09'N	16°44'E
Pilansberg, mtn., S. Afr. (pĕ'ăns'bûrg)	218d	25°08'S	26°55'E
Pilar, Arg. (pē'lär)	129c	34°27'S	58°55'W
Pilar, Para.	132	27°00'S	58°15'W
Pilar de Goiás, Braz. (dě-gô'yá's)	131	14°47'S	49°33'W
Pilchuck, r., Wa., U.S.	106a	48°03'N	121°58'W
Pilchuck Creek, r., Wa., U.S. (pĭl'chŭck)	106a	48°19'N	122°11'W
Pilchuck Mountain, mtn., Wa., U.S.	106a	48°03'N	121°48'W
Pilcomayo, r., S.A. (pēl-cō-mī'ō)	132	24°45'S	59°15'W
Pilgrim Gardens, N.J., U.S.	229b	39°57'N	75°19'W
Pilgrims Hatch, Eng., U.K.	235	51°38'N	0°17'E
Pili, Phil. (pē'lē)	197a	13°34'N	123°17'E
Pilica, r., Pol. (pē-lēt'sä)	155	51°00'N	19°48'E
Pillar Point, c., Wa., U.S. (pĭl'ȧr)	106a	48°14'N	124°06'W
Pillar Rocks, Wa., U.S.	106c	46°16'N	123°35'W
Pilón, r., Mex. (pē-lōn')	118	24°13'N	99°03'W
Pilot Point, Tx., U.S. (pī'lŭt)	111	33°24'N	97°00'W
Pilsen see Plzeň, Czech Rep.	142	49°46'N	13°25'E
Piltene, Lat. (pĭl'tě-ně)	153	57°17'N	21°40'E
Pimal, Cerra, mtn., Mex. (sě'r-rä-pē-mäl')	118	22°58'N	104°19'W
Pimba, Austl. (pĭm'bá)	202	31°15'S	137°50'E
Pimville, neigh., S. Afr. (pĭm'vĭl)	213b	26°17'S	27°54'E
Pinacate, Cerro, mtn., Mex. (sě'r-rô-pē-nä-kä'tě)	116	31°45'N	113°30'W
Pinamalayan, Phil. (pē-nä-mä-lä'yän)	197a	13°04'N	121°31'E
Pinang see George Town, Malay.	196	5°21'N	100°09'E
Pinarbaşi, Tur. (pē'när-bä'shĭ)	149	38°50'N	36°10'E
Pinar del Río, Cuba (pē-när' děl rē'ō)	117	22°25'N	83°35'W
Pinar del Río, prov., Cuba	122	22°45'N	83°25'W
Pinatubo, mtn., Phil. (pē-nä-tōō'bō)	197a	15°09'N	120°19'E
Pincher Creek, Can. (pĭn'chěr krēk)	87	49°29'N	113°57'W
Pinckneyville, Il., U.S. (pĭnk'nĭ-vĭl)	111	38°06'N	89°22'W
Pińczów, Pol. (pēn''chŏf)	155	50°32'N	20°33'E
Pindamonhangaba, Braz. (pē'n-dä-mōnyä'n-gä-bä)	129a	22°56'S	45°26'W
Pinder Point, c., Bah.	122	26°35'N	78°35'W
Píndhos Oros, mts., Grc.	142	39°48'N	21°19'E
Pindiga, Nig.	215	9°59'N	10°54'E
Pine, r., Can. (pīn)	87	55°30'N	122°20'W
Pine, r., Wi., U.S.	103	45°50'N	88°37'W
Pine Bluff, Ar., U.S. (pīn blŭf)	97	34°13'N	92°01'W
Pine Brook, N.J., U.S.	228	40°52'N	74°20'W
Pine City, Mn., U.S. (pīn)	103	45°50'N	93°01'W
Pine Creek, Austl.	202	13°45'S	132°00'E
Pine Creek, r., Nv., U.S.	108	40°15'N	116°17'W
Pinecrest, Va., U.S.	229d	38°50'N	77°09'W
Pine Falls, Can.	89	50°35'N	96°15'W
Pine Flat Lake, res., Ca., U.S.	108	36°52'N	119°18'W
Pine Forest Range, mts., Nv., U.S.	104	41°35'N	118°45'W
Pinega, Russia (pě-nyě'gȧ)	164	64°40'N	43°30'E
Pinega, r., Russia	166	64°10'N	42°30'E
Pine Grove, Can.	227c	43°48'N	79°35'W
Pine Hill, N.J., U.S. (pīn hĭl)	100f	39°47'N	74°59'W
Pinehurst, Ma., U.S.	227a	42°32'N	71°14'W
Pine Island Sound, strt., Fl., U.S.	115a	26°32'N	82°30'W
Pine Lake Estates, Ga., U.S. (lāk ěs-tāts')	100c	33°47'N	84°13'W
Pinelands, S. Afr. (pīn'lănds)	212a	33°57'S	18°30'E
Pine Lawn, Mo., U.S. (lôn)	107e	38°42'N	90°17'W
Pine Pass, p., Can.	87	55°22'N	122°40'W
Pine Ridge, Va., U.S.	229d	38°52'N	77°14'W
Pinerolo, Italy (pē-nå-rō'lō)	160	44°47'N	7°18'E
Pines, Lake o' the, Tx., U.S.	113	32°50'N	94°40'W
Pinetown, S. Afr. (pīn'toun)	213c	29°47'S	30°52'E
Pine View Reservoir, res., Ut., U.S. (vū)	107b	41°17'N	111°54'W
Pineville, Ky., U.S. (pīn'vĭl)	114	36°48'N	83°43'W
Pineville, La., U.S.	113	31°20'N	92°25'W
Ping, r., Thai.	196	17°54'N	98°29'E
Pingding, China (pĭŋ-dĭŋ)	192	37°50'N	113°30'E
Pingdu, China (pĭŋ-dōō)	192	36°46'N	119°57'E
Pingfang, China	240b	39°56'N	116°33'E
Pinggir, Indon.	181b	1°05'N	101°12'E
Pinghe, China (pĭŋ-hŭ)	193	24°30'N	117°02'E
Pingle, China (pĭŋ-lŭ)	193	24°30'N	110°22'E
Pingliang, China (pĭng'lyäng')	188	35°12'N	106°50'E
Pingquan, China (pĭŋ-chyůän)	192	40°58'N	118°40'E

ăt; finăl; rāte; senâte; ärm; åsk; sofȧ; fâre; ch-choose; dh-as th in other; bē; ėvent; bět; recěnt; cratēr; g-gō; gh-guttural g; bĭt; ĭ-short neutral; rīde; ᴋ-guttural k as ch in German ich;

PRONOUNCING INDEX
Pingtan–Pont-Audemer 333

PLACE (Pronunciation)	PAGE	LAT.	LONG.
Pingtan, China (pĭŋ-tän)	193	25°30'N	119°45'E
Pingtan Dao, i., China (pĭŋ-tän dou)	193	25°40'N	119°45'E
P'ingtung, Tai.	193	22°40'N	120°35'E
Pingwu, China (pĭŋ-wo͞o)	192	32°20'N	104°40'E
Pingxiang, China (pĭŋ-shyäŋ)	193	27°40'N	113°50'E
Pingyi, China (pĭŋ-yē)	190	35°30'N	117°38'E
Pingyuan, China (pĭŋ-yủän)	190	37°11'N	116°26'E
Pingzhou, China (pĭŋ-jō)	191a	23°01'N	113°11'E
Pinhal, Braz. (pē-nyä'l)	129a	22°11'S	46°43'W
Pinhal Novo, Port. (nô vô)	159b	38°38'N	8°54'W
Pinheiros, r., Braz.	234d	23°38'S	46°43'W
Pinhel, Port. (pēn-yĕl')	158	40°45'N	7°03'W
Pini, Pulau, i., Indon.	196	0°07'S	98°38'E
Piniós, r., Grc.	161	39°30'N	21°40'E
Pinnacles National Monument, rec., Ca., U.S. (pĭn'ȧ-k'lz)	108	36°30'N	121°00'W
Pinneberg, Ger. (pĭn'ĕ-bĕrg)	145c	53°40'N	9°48'E
Pinner, neigh., Eng., U.K.	235	51°36'N	0°23'W
Pinole, Ca., U.S. (pĭ-nō'lē)	106b	38°01'N	122°17'W
Pinos-Puente, Spain (pwān'tå)	158	37°15'N	3°43'W
Pinotepa Nacional, Mex. (pē-nō-tā'pä nä-syô-näl')	118	16°21'N	98°04'W
Pins, Île des, i., N. Cal.	203	22°44'S	167°44'E
Pinsk, Bela. (pēn'sk)	164	52°07'N	26°05'E
Pinta, i., Ec.	130	0°41'N	90°47'W
Pintendre, Can. (pĕɴ-tändr')	83b	46°45'N	71°07'W
Pinto, Spain (pēn'tō)	159a	40°14'N	3°42'W
Pinto Butte, Can. (pĭn'tō)	88	49°22'N	107°25'W
Pioche, Nv., U.S. (pī-ō'chē)	109	37°56'N	114°28'W
Piombino, Italy (pyôm-bē'nō)	148	42°56'N	10°33'E
Pioneer Mountains, mts., Mt., U.S. (pī'ô-nēr')	105	45°23'N	112°51'W
Piotrków Trybunalski, Pol. (pyōtr'ko͝ov trĭ-bo͞o-nal'skē)	147	51°23'N	19°44'E
Piper, Al., U.S. (pī'pēr)	114	33°04'N	87°00'W
Piper, Ks., U.S.	107f	39°09'N	94°51'W
Pipéri, i., Grc. (pē'per-ē)	161	39°19'N	24°20'E
Pipe Spring National Monument, rec., Az., U.S. (pīp sprĭng)	109	36°50'N	112°45'W
Pipestone, Mn., U.S. (pīp'stōn)	102	44°00'N	96°19'W
Pipestone National Monument, rec., Mn., U.S.	102	44°03'N	96°24'W
Pipmuacan, Réservoir, res., Can. (pĭp-mä-kän')	91	49°45'N	70°00'W
Piqua, Oh., U.S. (pĭk'wȧ)	98	40°10'N	84°15'W
Piracaia, Braz. (pē-rä-kä'yä)	129a	23°04'S	46°20'W
Piracicaba, Braz. (pē-rä-sē-kä'bä)	131	22°43'S	47°39'W
Piraíba, r., Braz. (pä-rä-ē'bä)	129a	21°38'S	41°29'W
Piraiévs, Grc.	149	37°57'N	23°38'E
Piramida, mtn., Russia	165	54°00'N	96°00'E
Pirámide de Cuicuilco, hist., Mex.	233a	19°18'N	99°11'W
Piran, Slvn. (pē-rä'n)	160	45°31'N	13°34'E
Piranga, Braz. (pē-rä'n-gä)	129a	20°41'S	43°17'W
Pirapetinga, Braz. (pē-rä-pĕ-tē'n-gä)	129a	21°40'S	42°20'W
Pirapora, Braz. (pē-rä-pō'rȧ)	131	17°39'S	44°54'W
Pirassununga, Braz. (pē-rä-so͞o-no͞o'n-gä)	129a	22°00'S	47°24'W
Pirenópolis, Braz. (pē-rĕ-nô'pō-lēs)	131	15°56'S	48°49'W
Pírgos, Grc.	149	37°51'N	21°28'E
Piritu, Laguna de, l., Ven. (lä-gô'nä-dĕ-pē-rē'to͞o)	131b	10°00'N	64°57'W
Pirmasens, Ger. (pĭr-mä-zĕns')	154	49°12'N	7°34'E
Pirna, Ger. (pĭr'nä)	154	50°57'N	13°56'E
Pirot, Yugo. (pē'rōt)	149	43°09'N	22°35'E
Pirtleville, Az., U.S. (pûr't'l-vĭl)	109	31°25'N	109°35'W
Piru, Indon. (pē-ro͞o')	197	3°15'S	128°25'E
Pisa, Italy (pē'sä)	148	43°52'N	10°24'E
Pisagua, Chile (pē-sä'gwä)	130	19°43'S	70°12'W
Piscataway, Md., U.S. (pĭs-kă-tă-wā)	100e	38°42'N	76°59'W
Piscataway, N.J., U.S.	100a	40°35'N	74°27'W
Pisco, Peru (pēs'kō)	130	13°43'S	76°07'W
Pisco, Bahía de, b., Peru	130	13°43'S	77°48'W
Piseco, l., N.Y., U.S. (pĭ-sā'kô)	99	43°25'N	74°35'W
Pisek, Czech Rep. (pē'sĕk)	147	49°18'N	14°08'E
Pisticci, Italy (pēs-tē'chē)	160	40°24'N	16°34'E
Pistoia, Italy (pēs-tô'yä)	148	43°57'N	11°54'E
Pisuerga, r., Spain (pē-swĕr'gä)	158	41°48'N	4°28'W
Pit, r., Ca., U.S. (pĭt)	104	40°58'N	121°42'W
Pitalito, Col. (pē-tä-lē'tō)	130	1°45'N	75°09'W
Pitampura Kālan, neigh., India	240d	28°42'N	77°08'E
Pitcairn, Pa., U.S. (pĭt'kârn)	101e	40°29'N	79°47'W
Pitcairn, dep., Oc.	2	25°04'S	130°05'W
Piteälven, r., Swe.	146	66°08'N	18°51'E
Pitești, Rom. (pē-tĕsht'')	161	44°51'N	24°51'E
Pithara, Austl. (pĭt'ără)	202	30°27'S	116°45'E
Pithiviers, Fr. (pē-tē-vyā')	156	48°12'N	2°14'E
Pitman, N.J., U.S. (pĭt'mȧn)	100f	39°44'N	75°08'W
Pitseng, Leso.	213c	29°03'S	28°13'E
Pitt, r., Can.	106d	49°19'N	122°39'W
Pitt Island, i., Can.	86	53°35'N	129°45'W
Pittsburg, Ca., U.S. (pĭts'bûrg)	106b	38°01'N	121°52'W
Pittsburg, Ks., U.S.	97	37°25'N	94°43'W
Pittsburg, Tx., U.S.	111	32°00'N	94°57'W
Pittsburgh, Pa., U.S.	97	40°26'N	80°01'W
Pittsfield, Il., U.S. (pĭts'fēld)	111	39°37'N	90°47'W
Pittsfield, Me., U.S.	92	44°45'N	69°44'W
Pittsfield, Ma., U.S.	99	42°25'N	73°15'W
Pittston, Pa., U.S. (pĭts'tŭn)	99	41°20'N	75°50'W
Piũi, Braz. (pē-o͞o'ē)	129a	20°27'S	45°57'W
Piura, Peru (pē-o͞o'rä)	130	5°13'S	80°46'W
Pivdennyi Buh, r., Ukr.	167	48°12'N	30°13'E
Piya, Russia (pē'yȧ)	172a	58°34'N	61°12'E
Placentia, Can.	93	47°15'N	53°58'W
Placentia, Ca., U.S. (plă-sĕn'shĭ-ȧ)	107a	33°52'N	117°50'W
Placentia Bay, b., Can.	85a	47°14'N	54°30'W
Placerville, Ca., U.S. (plăs'ēr-vĭl)	108	38°43'N	120°47'W
Placetas, Cuba (plä-thā'täs)	122	22°10'N	79°40'W
Placid, l., N.Y., U.S. (plăs'ĭd)	99	44°20'N	74°00'W
Plain City, Ut., U.S. (plān)	107b	41°18'N	112°06'W
Plainfield, Il., U.S. (plān'fēld)	101a	41°37'N	88°12'W
Plainfield, In., U.S.	101g	39°42'N	86°23'W
Plainfield, N.J., U.S.	100a	40°38'N	74°25'W
Plainview, Ar., U.S. (plān'vū)	111	34°59'N	93°15'W
Plainview, Mn., U.S.	103	44°09'N	93°12'W
Plainview, Ne., U.S.	102	42°20'N	97°47'W
Plainview, Tx., U.S.	110	34°11'N	101°42'W
Plainwell, Mi., U.S. (plan'wĕl)	98	42°25'N	85°40'W
Plaisance, Can. (plĕ-zäɴs')	83c	45°37'N	75°07'W
Plana or Flat Cays, is., Bah. (plä'nä)	123	22°35'N	73°35'W
Plandome Manor, N.Y., U.S.	228	40°49'N	73°42'W
Planegg, Ger. (plä'nĕg)	145d	48°06'N	11°27'E
Plano, Tx., U.S. (plā'nō)	111	33°01'N	96°42'W
Plantagenet, Can. (plăɴ-täzh-nē')	83c	45°33'N	75°00'W
Plant City, Fl., U.S. (plȧnt sĭ'tĭ)	115a	28°00'N	82°07'W
Plaquemine, La., U.S. (pläk'mēn')	113	30°17'N	91°14'W
Plasencia, Spain (plä-sĕn'thē-ä)	158	40°02'N	6°07'W
Plast, Russia (plást)	166	54°22'N	60°48'E
Plaster Rock, Can. (plȧs'tēr rŏk)	92	46°54'N	67°24'W
Plastun, Russia (plȧs-to͞on')	194	44°41'N	136°08'E
Plata, Río de la, est., S.A. (dälä plä'tä)	132	34°35'S	58°15'W
Platani, r., Italy (plä-tä'nē)	160	37°26'N	13°28'E
Plateforme, Pointe, c., Haiti	123	19°35'N	73°50'W
Platinum, Ak., U.S. (plăt'ĭ-nŭm)	95	59°00'N	161°27'W
Plato, Col. (plä'tō)	130	9°49'N	74°48'W
Platón Sánchez, Mex. (plä-tōn' sän'chĕz)	118	21°14'N	98°20'W
Platt, Eng., U.K.	235	51°17'N	0°20'E
Platte, S.D., U.S. (plăt)	102	43°22'N	98°51'W
Platte, r., Mo., U.S.	111	40°09'N	94°40'W
Platte, r., Ne., U.S.	96	40°50'N	100°40'W
Platteville, Wi., U.S. (plăt'vĭl)	103	42°44'N	90°31'W
Plattsburg, Mo., U.S. (plăts'bûrg)	111	39°33'N	94°26'W
Plattsburg, N.Y., U.S.	99	44°40'N	73°30'W
Plattsmouth, Ne., U.S. (plăts'mŭth)	102	41°00'N	95°53'W
Plauen, Ger. (plou'ĕn)	147	50°30'N	12°08'E
Playa de Guanabo, Cuba (plä-yä-dĕ-gwä-nä'bō)	123a	23°10'N	82°07'W
Playa del Rey, neigh., Ca., U.S.	232	33°58'N	118°26'W
Playa de Santa Fé, Cuba	123a	23°05'N	82°31'W
Playas Lake, l., N.M., U.S. (plä'yȧs)	109	31°50'N	108°30'W
Playa Vicente, Mex. (vē-sĕn'tå)	119	17°49'N	95°49'W
Playa Vicente, r., Mex.	119	17°36'N	96°13'W
Playgreen Lake, l., Can. (plā'grēn)	89	54°00'N	98°10'W
Plaza de Toros Monumental, rec., Spain	238e	41°24'N	2°11'E
Pleasant, l., N.Y., U.S. (plĕz'ănt)	99	43°25'N	74°25'W
Pleasant Grove, Al., U.S.	100h	33°29'N	86°57'W
Pleasant Hill, Ca., U.S.	106b	37°57'N	122°04'W
Pleasant Hill, Mo., U.S.	111	38°46'N	94°18'W
Pleasant Hills, Pa., U.S.	230b	40°20'N	79°58'W
Pleasanton, Ca., U.S. (plĕz'ăn-tŭn)	106b	37°40'N	121°53'W
Pleasanton, Ks., U.S.	111	38°10'N	94°41'W
Pleasanton, Tx., U.S.	112	28°58'N	98°30'W
Pleasant Plain, Oh., U.S. (plĕz'ănt)	101f	39°17'N	84°06'W
Pleasant Ridge, Mi., U.S.	101b	42°28'N	83°09'W
Pleasant View, Ut., U.S. (plĕz'ănt vū)	107b	41°20'N	112°02'W
Pleasantville, Md., U.S.	229c	39°11'N	76°38'W
Pleasantville, N.Y., U.S. (plĕz'ănt-vĭl)	100a	41°08'N	73°47'W
Pleasure Ridge Park, Ky., U.S. (plĕzh'ĕr rĭj)	101h	38°09'N	85°49'W
Plenty, Bay of, b., N.Z. (plĕn'tē)	203a	37°30'S	177°10'E
Plentywood, Mt., U.S. (plĕn'tē-wŏŏd)	105	48°47'N	104°38'W
Ples, Russia (plyĕs)	162	57°26'N	41°29'E
Pleshcheyevo, l., Russia (plĕsh-chā'yĕ-vô)	162	56°50'N	38°22'E
Plessisville, Can. (plĕ-sē'vēl')	91	46°12'N	71°47'W
Pleszew, Pol. (plĕ'zhĕf)	155	51°54'N	17°48'E
Plettenberg, Ger. (plĕ'tĕn-bĕrgh)	157c	51°13'N	7°53'E
Pleven, Bul. (plĕ'vĕn)	149	43°24'N	24°26'E
Pljevlja, Yugo. (plēv'lyä)	149	43°20'N	19°21'E
Płock, Pol. (pwôtsk)	147	52°32'N	19°44'E
Ploërmel, Fr. (plô-ĕr-mĕl')	156	47°56'N	2°25'W
Ploiești, Rom. (plô-yĕsht'')	142	44°56'N	26°01'E
Plomárion, Grc. (plô-mä'rĭ-ŏn)	161	38°51'N	26°24'E
Plomb du Cantal, mtn., Fr. (plôɴ'dükän-täl')	147	45°30'N	2°49'E
Plonge, Lac la, l., Can. (plōɴzh)	88	55°08'N	107°25'W
Plovdiv, Bul. (plôv'dĭf) (fĭl-ĭp-ŏp'ō-lĭs)	142	42°09'N	24°43'E
Pluma Hidalgo, Mex. (plo͞o'mä ē-däl'gō)	119	15°54'N	96°23'W
Plumpton, Austl.	243a	33°45'S	150°50'E
Plunge, Lith. (plo̤n'gā)	153	55°56'N	21°45'E
Plymouth, Monts.	121b	16°43'N	62°12'W
Plymouth, Eng., U.K. (plĭm'ŭth)	147	50°25'N	4°14'W
Plymouth, In., U.S.	98	41°20'N	86°20'W
Plymouth, Ma., U.S.	99	42°00'N	70°45'W
Plymouth, Mi., U.S.	101b	42°23'N	83°27'W
Plymouth, N.H., U.S.	99	43°50'N	71°40'W
Plymouth, N.C., U.S.	115	35°50'N	76°44'W
Plymouth, Pa., U.S.	99	41°15'N	75°55'W
Plymouth, Wi., U.S.	103	43°45'N	87°59'W
Plyussa, r., Russia (plyo͞o'sȧ)	162	58°33'N	28°30'E
Plzeň, Czech Rep.	142	49°45'N	13°23'E
Po, r., Italy	142	45°10'N	11°00'E
Pocahontas, Ar., U.S. (pō-kȧ-hŏn'tȧs)	111	36°15'N	91°01'W
Pocahontas, Ia., U.S.	103	42°43'N	94°41'W
Pocatello, Id., U.S. (pō-kȧ-tĕl'ō)	96	42°54'N	112°30'W
Pochëp, Russia (pô-chĕp')	167	52°56'N	33°27'E
Pochinok, Russia (pô-chē'nôk)	162	54°14'N	32°27'E
Pochinski, Russia	166	54°40'N	44°50'E
Pochotitán, Mex. (pô-chô-tē-tá'n)	118	21°37'N	104°33'W
Pochutla, Mex.	119	15°46'N	96°28'W
Pocomoke City, Md., U.S. (pō-kō-mōk')	99	38°05'N	75°35'W
Pocono Mountains, mts., Pa., U.S. (pō-cō'nō)	99	41°10'N	75°30'W
Poços de Caldas, Braz. (pō-sôs-dĕ-käl'dás)	131	21°48'S	46°34'W
Poder, Sen. (pô-dôr')	210	16°35'N	15°04'W
Podgorica, Yugo.	161	42°25'N	19°15'E
Podkamennaya Tunguska, r., Russia	165	61°43'N	93°45'E
Podol'sk, Russia (pô-dôl''sk)	166	55°26'N	37°33'E
Poggibonsi, Italy (pôd-jē-bôn'sē)	160	43°27'N	11°12'E
Pogodino, Bela. (pô-gô'dē-nô)	166	54°17'N	31°00'E
P'ohangdong, S. Kor.	194	35°57'N	129°23'E
Point Cook, Austl.	243b	37°56'S	144°45'E
Pointe-à-Pitre, Guad. (pwăɴt' ȧ pē-tr')	117	16°15'N	61°32'W
Pointe-aux-Trembles, Can. (po͞o-ăɴt' ō-träɴbl)	83a	45°39'N	73°30'W
Pointe Claire, Can. (po͞o-ăɴt' klĕr)	83a	45°27'N	73°48'W
Pointe-des-Cascades, Can. (kȧs-kȧdz')	83a	45°19'N	73°58'W
Pointe Fortune, Can. (fôr'tūn)	83a	45°34'N	74°23'W
Pointe-Gatineau, Can. (po͞o-ăɴt'gä-tē-nō')	83c	45°28'N	75°42'W
Pointe Noire, Congo	212	4°48'S	11°51'E
Point Hope, Ak., U.S. (hōp)	95	68°18'N	166°38'W
Point Pleasant, Md., U.S.	229c	39°11'N	76°35'W
Point Pleasant, W.V., U.S. (plĕz'ănt)	98	38°50'N	82°10'W
Point Roberts, Wa., U.S. (rŏb'ērts)	106d	48°59'N	123°04'W
Poissy, Fr. (pwȧ-sē')	157b	48°55'N	2°02'E
Poitiers, Fr. (pwȧ-tyā')	147	46°35'N	0°18'E
Pokaran, India (pō'kŭr-ŭn)	186	27°00'N	72°05'E
Pokrov, Russia (pô-krôf)	162	55°56'N	39°09'E
Pokrovsko-Strešnevo, neigh., Russia	239b	55°49'N	37°29'E
Pokrovskoye, Russia (pô-krôf'skô-yĕ)	163	47°27'N	38°54'E
Pola, r., Russia (pō'lä)	162	57°44'N	31°53'E
Pola de Laviana, Spain (dĕ-lä-vyä'nä)	158	43°15'N	5°29'W
Pola de Siero, Spain	158	43°24'N	5°39'W
Poland, nation, Eur. (pō'lănd)	142	52°37'N	17°01'E
Polangui, Phil. (pô-läŋ'gē)	197a	13°18'N	123°29'E
Polazna, Russia (pô'láz-ná)	172a	58°18'N	56°25'E
Polessk, Russia (pô'lĕsk)	153	54°50'N	21°14'E
Poles'ye (Pripyat Marshes), sw., Eur.	167	52°10'N	27°30'E
Polevskoy, Russia (pô-lē'vs-kô'ē)	172a	56°28'N	60°14'E
Polgár, Hung. (pôl'gär)	155	47°54'N	21°10'E
Policastro, Golfo di, b., Italy	160	40°00'N	13°23'E
Poligny, Fr. (pō-lē-nyē')	157	46°48'N	5°42'E
Polikhnitos, Grc.	161	39°05'N	26°11'E
Polillo, Phil. (pô-lēl'yō)	197a	14°42'N	121°56'W
Polillo Islands, is., Phil.	183	15°05'N	122°15'E
Polillo Strait, strt., Phil.	197a	15°02'N	121°40'E
Polist', r., Russia (pô'lĭst)	162	57°42'N	31°02'E
Polistena, Italy (pō-lēs-tā'nä)	160	38°25'N	16°05'E
Poliyiros, Grc.	161	40°23'N	23°27'E
Polkan, Gora, mtn., Russia	165	60°18'N	92°08'E
Polochic, r., Guat. (pō-lô-chēk')	120	15°19'N	89°45'W
Polonne, Ukr.	163	50°07'N	27°31'E
Polotsk, Bela. (pô'lôtsk)	166	55°30'N	28°48'E
Polpaico, Chile (pôl-pá'y-kô)	129b	33°10'S	70°53'W
Polson, Mt., U.S. (pōl'sŭn)	105	47°40'N	114°10'W
Polsum, Ger.	236	51°37'N	7°03'E
Poltava, Ukr. (pŏl-tä'vä)	164	49°35'N	34°33'E
Poltava, prov., Ukr.	163	49°53'N	32°58'E
Põltsamaa, Est. (pôlt'sȧ-mä)	153	58°39'N	26°00'E
Polunochnoye, Russia (pô-lo͞o-nô'ch-nô'yĕ)	172a	60°52'N	60°27'E
Poluy, r., Russia (pôl'wē)	170	65°45'N	68°15'E
Polyakovka, Russia (pŭl-yä'kôv-kȧ)	172a	54°38'N	59°42'E
Polyarnyy, Russia (pŭl-yär'nē)	164	69°10'N	33°30'E
Polynesia, is., Oc.	224	4°00'S	156°00'W
Pomba, r., Braz. (pô'm-bȧ)	129a	21°28'S	42°28'W
Pomerania, hist. reg., Pol. (pŏm-ē-rā'nĭ-ȧ)	154	53°50'N	15°20'E
Pomeroy, S. Afr. (pŏm'ēr-roi)	213c	28°36'S	30°26'E
Pomeroy, Wa., U.S. (pŏm'ēr-oi)	104	46°28'N	117°35'W
Pomezia, Italy (pô-mĕ't-zyä)	159d	41°41'N	12°31'E
Pomigliano d'Arco, Italy (pô-mē-lyȧ'nô-d-ä'r-kô)	159c	40°39'N	14°23'E
Pomme de Terre, Mn., U.S. (pôm dē tĕr')	102	45°22'N	95°52'W
Pomona, Ca., U.S. (pō-mō'nȧ)	96	34°04'N	117°45'W
Pomona Estates, S. Afr.	244b	26°06'S	28°15'E
Pomorie, Bul.	149	42°24'N	27°41'E
Pompano Beach, Fl., U.S. (pŏm'pȧ-nō)	115a	26°12'N	80°07'W
Pompeii Ruins, hist., Italy	159c	40°31'N	14°29'E
Pomponne, Fr.	237c	48°53'N	2°41'E
Pompton Lakes, N.J., U.S. (pŏmp'tŏn)	100a	41°01'N	74°16'W
Pompton Plains, N.J., U.S.	228	40°58'N	74°18'W
Pomuch, Mex. (pô-mo͞o'ch)	120a	20°12'N	90°10'W
Ponca, Ne., U.S. (pŏn'kȧ)	102	42°34'N	96°43'W
Ponca City, Ok., U.S.	111	36°42'N	97°07'W
Ponce, P.R. (pōn'sä)	117	18°01'N	66°43'W
Ponders End, neigh., Eng., U.K.	235	51°39'N	0°03'W
Pondicherry, India	183	11°58'N	79°48'E
Pondicherry, state, India	183	11°50'N	74°50'E
Ponferrada, Spain (pôn-fĕr-rä'dhä)	148	42°33'N	6°38'W
Ponoka, Can. (pŏ-nō'kȧ)	84	52°42'N	113°35'W
Ponoy, Russia	166	66°58'N	41°00'E
Ponoy, r., Russia	166	67°00'N	39°00'E
Ponta Delgada, Port. (pôn'tȧ dĕl-gä'dȧ)	210a	37°40'N	25°45'W
Ponta Grossa, Braz. (grō'sȧ)	131	25°09'S	50°05'W
Pont-à-Mousson, Fr. (pôɴ'tȧ-mo͞o-sôɴ')	157	48°55'N	6°02'E
Pontarlier, Fr. (pôɴ'tár-lyā')	157	46°53'N	6°22'E
Pont-Audemer, Fr. (pôɴ'tōd'mâr')	156	49°23'N	0°28'E

ng-sing; ŋ-baŋk; ɴ-nasalized n; nŏd; cŏmmit; ōld; ôbey; ôrder; oi-boil; fo͞od; o̤-as oo in foot; ou-out; s-soft; sh-dish; th-thin; pūre; ủnite; ûrn; stŭd; circŭs; ü-as in French tu; '-indeterminate vowel.

PLACE (Pronunciation)	PAGE	LAT.	LONG.
Pontault-Combault, Fr.	237c	48°47′N	2°36′E
Pontchartrain Lake, l., La., U.S. (pôn-shár-trăn′)	113	30°10′N	90°10′W
Ponteareas, Spain	158	42°09′N	8°23′W
Pontedera, Italy (pōn-tå-dā′rä)	160	43°37′N	10°37′E
Ponte de Sor, Port.	158	39°14′N	8°03′W
Pontefract, Eng., U.K. (pŏn′tė-frăkt)	144a	53°41′N	1°18′W
Ponte Nova, Braz. (pô′n-tĕ-nô′và)	131	20°26′S	42°52′W
Pontevedra, Arg.	233d	34°46′S	58°43′W
Pontevedra, Spain (pōn-tĕ-vĕ-drä)	148	42°28′N	8°38′W
Ponthierville *see* Ubundi, D.R.C.	212	0°21′S	25°29′E
Pontiac, Il., U.S. (pŏn′tĭ-ăk)	98	40°55′N	88°35′W
Pontiac, Mi., U.S.	97	42°37′N	83°17′W
Pontianak, Indon. (pōn-tė-ä′nåk)	196	0°04′S	109°20′E
Pontian Kechil, Malay.	181b	1°29′N	103°24′E
Pontic Mountains, mts., Tur.	167	41°20′N	34°30′E
Pontinha, neigh., Port.	238d	38°46′N	9°11′W
Pontivy, Fr. (pôɴ-tē-vē′)	156	48°05′N	2°57′W
Pontoise, Fr. (pôɴ-twàz′)	156	49°03′N	2°05′E
Pontonnyy, Russia (pôn′tôn-nyĭ)	172c	59°47′N	30°39′E
Pontotoc, Ms., U.S. (pŏn-tô-tŏk′)	114	34°11′N	88°59′W
Pontremoli, Italy (pōn-trĕm′ô-lē)	160	44°21′N	9°50′E
Ponziane, Isole, i., Italy (ē′sō-lĕ)	148	40°55′N	12°58′E
Poole, Eng., U.K. (po͞ol)	150	50°43′N	2°00′W
Poolesville, Md., U.S. (poolĕs-vĭl)	100e	39°08′N	77°26′W
Pooley Island, i., Can. (po͞o′lė)	86	52°44′N	128°16′W
Poopó, Lago de, l., Bol.	130	18°45′S	67°07′W
Popayán, Col. (pō-pä-yän′)	130	2°21′N	76°43′W
Poplar, Mt., U.S. (pŏp′lẽr)	105	48°08′N	105°10′W
Poplar, neigh., Eng., U.K.	235	51°31′N	0°01′W
Poplar, r., Mt., U.S.	105	48°34′N	105°20′W
Poplar, West Fork, r., Mt., U.S.	105	48°59′N	106°06′W
Poplar Bluff, Mo., U.S. (blŭf)	111	36°43′N	90°22′W
Poplar Heights, Va., U.S.	229d	38°53′N	77°12′W
Poplar Plains, Ky., U.S. (plāns)	98	38°20′N	83°40′W
Poplar Point, Can.	83f	50°04′N	97°57′W
Poplarville, Ms., U.S. (pŏp′lẽr-vĭl)	114	30°50′N	89°33′W
Popocatépetl Volcán, Mex. (pô-pô-kä-tā′pĕ′t′l)	116	19°01′N	98°38′W
Popokabaka, D.R.C. (pō′pô-kà-bä′kà)	212	5°42′S	16°35′E
Popovo, Bul. (pô′pô-vō)	161	43°23′N	26°17′E
Porbandar, India (pōr-bŭn′dŭr)	183	21°44′N	69°40′E
Porce, r., Col. (pôr-sĕ)	130a	7°11′N	74°55′W
Porcher Island, i., Can. (pôr′kẽr)	86	53°57′N	130°30′W
Porcuna, Spain (pôr-ko͞o′nä)	158	37°54′N	4°10′W
Porcupine, r., N.A.	95	67°38′N	140°07′W
Porcupine Creek, r., Mt., U.S.	105	48°27′N	106°24′W
Porcupine Hills, hills, Can.	89	52°30′N	101°45′W
Pordenone, Italy (pōr-då-nō′nå)	160	45°58′N	12°38′E
Pori, Fin. (pô′rē)	146	61°29′N	21°45′E
Poriúncula, Braz.	129a	20°58′S	42°02′W
Porkhov, Russia (pôr′κôf)	166	57°46′N	29°33′E
Porlamar, Ven. (pōr-lä-mär′)	130	11°00′N	63°55′W
Pornic, Fr. (pôr-nēk′)	156	47°08′N	2°07′W
Poronaysk, Russia (pô′rô-nīsk)	165	49°21′N	143°23′E
Porrentruy, Switz. (pô-räɴ-trüē′)	154	47°25′N	7°02′E
Porsgrunn, Nor. (pôrs′grôn′)	152	59°09′N	9°36′E
Portachuelo, Bol. (pôrt-ä-chwā′lō)	130	17°20′S	63°12′W
Portage, Pa., U.S. (pôr′tåj)	99	40°25′N	78°35′W
Portage, Wi., U.S.	103	43°33′N	89°29′W
Portage Des Sioux, Mo., U.S. (dē so͞o)	107e	38°56′N	90°21′W
Portage la Prairie, Can. (lä-prā′rĭ)	84	49°57′N	98°25′W
Port Alberni, Can. (pōr äl-bĕr-nē′)	84	49°14′N	124°48′W
Portalegre, Port. (pôr-tä-lā′grĕ)	148	39°18′N	7°26′W
Portales, N.M., U.S. (pôr-tä′lĕs)	110	34°10′N	103°11′W
Port Alfred, S. Afr.	212	33°36′S	26°55′E
Port Alice, Can. (ăl′ĭs)	84	50°23′N	127°27′W
Port Allegany, Pa., U.S. (ăl-ė-gā′nĭ)	99	41°50′N	78°10′W
Port Angeles, Wa., U.S. (ăn′jė-lĕs)	96	48°07′N	123°26′W
Port Antonio, Jam.	117	18°10′N	76°25′W
Portarlington, Austl.	201a	38°07′S	144°39′E
Port Arthur, Tx., U.S.	97	29°52′N	93°59′W
Port Augusta, Austl. (ô-gŭs′tă)	204	32°28′S	137°50′E
Port au Port Bay, b., Can. (pôr′tō pōr′)	93	48°41′N	58°45′W
Port-au-Prince, Haiti (präɴs′)	117	18°35′N	72°20′W
Port Austin, Mi., U.S. (ôs′tĭn)	98	44°00′N	83°00′W
Port Blair, India (blâr)	196	12°07′N	92°45′E
Port Bolivar, Tx., U.S. (bŏl′ĭ-vàr)	113a	29°22′N	94°46′W
Port Borden, Can. (bôr′dĕn)	92	46°15′N	63°42′W
Port-Bouët, C. Iv.	210	5°24′N	3°56′W
Port-Cartier, Can.	92	50°01′N	66°53′W
Port Chester, N.Y., U.S. (chĕs′tẽr)	100a	40°59′N	73°40′W
Port Chicago, Ca., U.S. (shĭ-kô′gō)	106b	38°03′N	122°01′W
Port Clinton, Oh., U.S. (klĭn′tŭn)	98	41°30′N	83°00′W
Port Colborne, Can.	91	42°53′N	79°13′W
Port Coquitlam, Can. (kô-kwĭt′lăm)	87	49°16′N	122°46′W
Port Credit, Can. (krĕd′ĭt)	83d	43°33′N	79°35′W
Port-de-Bouc, Fr. (pôr-dē-bo͝ok′)	156a	43°24′N	5°00′E
Port de Paix, Haiti (pĕ)	123	19°55′N	72°50′W
Port Dickson, Malay. (dĭk′sŭn)	181b	2°33′N	101°49′E
Port Discovery, b., Wa., U.S. (dĭs-kŭv′ẽr-ĭ)	106a	48°05′N	122°55′W
Port Edward, S. Afr. (ĕd′wẽrd)	213c	31°04′S	30°14′E
Port Elgin, Can. (ĕl′jĭn)	92	46°03′N	64°05′W
Port Elizabeth, S. Afr. (ė-lĭz′ȧ-bĕth)	212	33°57′S	25°37′E
Porterdale, Ga., U.S. (pōr′tẽr-dāl)	114	33°34′N	83°53′W
Porterville, Ca., U.S. (pōr′tẽr-vĭl)	108	36°03′N	119°05′W
Port Francqui *see* Ilebo, D.R.C.	212	4°19′S	20°35′E
Port Gamble, Wa., U.S. (găm′bŭl)	106a	47°52′N	122°36′W
Port Gamble Indian Reservation, I.R., Wa., U.S.	106a	47°54′N	122°33′W
Port-Gentil, Gabon (zhäɴ-tē′)	212	0°43′S	8°47′E
Port Gibson, Ms., U.S.	114	31°56′N	90°57′W
Port Harcourt, Nig. (här′kŭrt)	210	4°43′N	7°05′E
Port Hardy, Can. (här′dĭ)	86	50°43′N	127°29′W
Port Hawkesbury, Can.	93	45°37′N	61°21′W
Port Hedland, Austl. (hĕd′lănd)	202	20°30′S	118°30′E
Porthill, Id., U.S.	104	49°00′N	116°30′W
Port Hood, Can. (ho͝od)	93	46°01′N	61°32′W
Port Hope, Can. (hōp)	91	43°55′N	78°10′W
Port Huron, Mi., U.S. (hū′rŏn)	97	43°00′N	82°30′W
Portici, Italy (pôr′tė-chė)	159c	40°34′N	14°20′E
Portillo, Chile (pôr-tē′l-yô)	129b	32°51′S	70°09′W
Portimão, Port. (pôr-tē-moùɴ)	158	37°09′N	8°34′W
Port Jervis, N.Y., U.S. (jûr′vĭs)	100a	41°22′N	74°41′W
Portland, Austl. (pōrt′lănd)	203	38°20′S	142°40′E
Portland, In., U.S.	98	40°25′N	85°00′W
Portland, Me., U.S.	97	43°40′N	70°16′W
Portland, Mi., U.S.	98	42°50′N	85°00′W
Portland, Or., U.S.	96	45°31′N	122°41′W
Portland, Tx., U.S.	113	27°53′N	97°20′W
Portland Bight, bt., Jam.	122	17°45′N	77°05′W
Portland Canal, can., Ak., U.S.	86	55°10′N	130°08′W
Portland Inlet, b., Can.	86	54°50′N	130°15′W
Portland Point, c., Jam.	122	17°40′N	77°20′W
Port Lavaca, Tx., U.S. (lȧ-vä′kȧ)	113	28°36′N	96°38′W
Port Lincoln, Austl. (lĭŋ-kŭn)	202	34°39′S	135°50′E
Port Ludlow, Wa., U.S. (lŭd′lō)	106a	47°26′N	122°41′W
Port Macquarie, Austl. (mȧ-kwŏ′rĭ)	203	31°25′S	152°45′E
Port Madison Indian Reservation, I.R., Wa., U.S. (măd′ĭ-sŭn)	106a	47°46′N	122°38′W
Port Maria, Jam. (mȧ-rī′ȧ)	122	18°20′N	76°55′W
Port Melbourne, Austl.	243b	37°51′S	144°56′E
Port Moody, Can. (mo͞od′ĭ)	87	49°17′N	122°51′W
Port Moresby, Pap. N. Gui. (mōrz′bė)	197	9°34′S	147°20′E
Port Neches, Tx., U.S. (nĕch′ĕz)	113	29°59′N	93°57′W
Port Nelson, Can. (nĕl′sŭn)	89	57°03′N	92°36′W
Portneuf-Sur-Mer, Can. (pôr-nûf′sür mĕr)	92	48°36′N	69°06′W
Port Nolloth, S. Afr. (nŏl′ŏth)	212	29°10′S	17°00′E
Porto (Oporto), Port. (pōr′tò)	142	41°10′N	8°38′W
Porto Acre, Braz. (ä′krĕ)	130	9°38′S	67°34′W
Porto Alegre, Braz. (ä-lā′grĕ)	132	29°58′S	51°11′W
Porto Amboim, Ang.	212	11°01′S	13°45′E
Portobelo, Pan. (pôr′tô-bā′lô)	117	9°32′N	79°40′W
Pôrto de Pedras, Braz. (pä′dräzh)	131	9°09′S	35°20′W
Pôrto Feliz, Braz. (fĕ-lē′s)	129a	23°12′S	47°30′W
Portoferraio, Italy (pōr′tô-fĕr-rä′yō)	160	42°47′N	10°20′E
Port of Spain, Trin. (spān)	131	10°44′N	61°24′W
Portogruaro, Italy (pōr′tô-grô-ä′rō)	160	45°48′N	12°49′E
Portola, Ca., U.S. (pôr′tō-là)	108	39°47′N	120°29′W
Porto Mendes, Braz. (mĕ′n-dĕs)	131	24°41′S	54°13′W
Porto Murtinho, Braz. (mòr-tēn′yô)	131	21°43′S	57°43′W
Porto Nacional, Braz. (nä-syô-näl′)	131	10°43′S	48°14′W
Porto Novo, Benin (pōr′tô-nō′vō)	210	6°29′N	2°37′E
Port Orchard, Wa., U.S. (ôr′chẽrd)	106a	47°32′N	122°38′W
Port Orchard, b., Wa., U.S.	106a	47°40′N	122°39′W
Porto Salvo, Port.	238d	38°43′N	9°18′W
Porto Santo, Ilha de, i., Port. (săɴ′tô)	210	32°41′N	16°15′W
Porto Seguro, Braz. (sā-go͞o′rô)	131	16°26′S	38°59′W
Porto Torres, Italy (tôr′rĕs)	160	40°49′N	8°25′E
Porto-Vecchio, Fr. (vĕk′ė-ô)	160	41°36′N	9°17′E
Porto Velho, Braz. (vāl′yô)	130	8°45′S	63°43′W
Portoviejo, Ec. (pôr-tō-vyā′hō)	130	1°11′S	80°28′W
Port Phillip Bay, b., Austl. (fĭl′ĭp)	203	37°57′S	144°50′E
Port Pirie, Austl. (pĭ′rė)	202	33°10′S	138°00′E
Port Reading, N.J., U.S.	228	40°34′N	74°16′W
Port Royal, b., Jam. (roi′ăl)	122	17°50′N	76°45′W
Port Said, Egypt	218c	31°15′N	32°19′E
Port Saint Johns, S. Afr. (sānt jŏnz)	212	31°37′S	29°32′E
Port Saint Lucie, Fl., U.S.	115a	27°20′N	80°20′W
Port Shepstone, S. Afr. (shĕps′tŭn)	212	30°45′S	30°23′E
Portsmouth, Dom.	121b	15°33′N	61°28′W
Portsmouth, Eng., U.K. (pôrts′mŭth)	142	50°45′N	1°03′W
Portsmouth, N.H., U.S.	97	43°05′N	70°50′W
Portsmouth, Oh., U.S.	97	38°45′N	83°00′W
Portsmouth, Va., U.S.	97	36°50′N	76°19′W
Port Sulphur, La., U.S. (sŭl′fẽr)	114	29°28′N	89°41′W
Port Sunlight, Eng., U.K.	237a	53°21′N	2°59′W
Port Susan, b., Wa., U.S. (sū-zàn′)	106a	48°11′N	122°25′W
Port Townsend, Wa., U.S. (tounz′ĕnd)	106a	48°07′N	122°46′W
Port Townsend, b., Wa., U.S.	106a	48°05′N	122°47′W
Portugal, nation, Eur. (pōr′tu-găl)	142	38°15′N	8°08′W
Portugalete, Spain (pōr-to͞o-gä-lā′tā)	158	43°18′N	3°05′W
Portuguese West Africa *see* Angola, nation, Ang.	212	14°15′S	16°00′E
Port Vendres, Fr.	156	42°32′N	3°07′E
Port Vila, Vanuatu	203	17°44′S	168°19′E
Port Vue, Pa., U.S.	230b	40°20′N	79°52′W
Port Wakefield, Austl. (wāk′fēld)	202	34°12′S	138°10′E
Port Washington, N.Y., U.S. (wŏsh′ĭng-tŭn)	100a	40°49′N	73°42′W
Port Washington, Wi., U.S.	103	43°24′N	87°52′W
Posadas, Arg. (pō-sä′dhäs)	132	27°32′S	55°56′W
Posadas, Spain (pō-sä-däs)	158	37°48′N	5°09′W
Poshekhon′ye Volodarsk, Russia (pô-shyĕ′κôn-yĕ vôl′ô-dàrsk)	162	58°31′N	39°07′E
Poso, Danau, l., Indon. (pō′sō)	196	2°00′S	119°40′E
Pospelokova, Russia (pôs-pyĕl′kô-và)	172a	59°25′N	60°50′E
Possession Sound, strt., Wa., U.S. (pŏ-zĕsh-ŭn)	106a	47°59′N	122°17′W
Possum Kingdom Reservoir, res., Tx., U.S. (pŏs′ŭm kĭng′dŭm)	112	32°58′N	98°12′W
Post, Tx., U.S. (pōst)	110	33°12′N	101°21′W
Postojna, Slvn. (pōs-tôyná)	160	45°45′N	14°13′E
Pos′yet, Russia (pos-yĕt′)	194	42°27′N	130°47′E
Potawatomi Indian Reservation, I.R., Ks., U.S. (pŏt-å-wä′tō mē)	111	39°30′N	96°11′W
Potchefstroom, S. Afr. (pŏch′ĕf-strōm)	212	26°42′S	27°06′E
Poteau, Ok., U.S. (pō-tō′)	111	35°03′N	94°37′W
Poteet, Tx., U.S. (pō-tēt)	112	29°05′N	98°35′W
Potenza, Italy (pô-tĕnt′sä)	149	40°39′N	15°49′E
Potenza, r., Italy	160	43°09′N	13°00′E
Potgietersrus, S. Afr. (pôt-κē′tĕrs-rûs)	212	24°09′S	29°04′E
Potholes Reservoir, res., Wa., U.S.	104	47°00′N	119°20′W
Poti, Geor. (pô′tė)	167	42°10′N	41°40′E
Potiskum, Nig.	210	11°43′N	11°05′E
Potomac, Md., U.S. (pô-tō′măk)	100e	39°01′N	77°13′W
Potomac, r., U.S. (pō-tō′măk)	97	38°15′N	76°55′W
Poto Poto, neigh., Congo	244c	4°15′S	15°18′E
Potosí, Bol.	130	19°35′S	65°45′W
Potosi, Mo., U.S. (pŏ-tō′sĭ)	111	37°56′N	90°46′W
Potosi, r., Mex. (pō-tō-sē′)	112	25°04′N	99°36′W
Potrerillos, Hond. (pō-trā-rēl′yōs)	120	15°13′N	87°58′W
Potsdam, Ger. (pôts′dăm)	147	52°24′N	13°04′E
Potsdam, N.Y., U.S. (pŏts′dăm)	99	44°40′N	75°00′W
Pottenstein, Aus.	145e	47°58′N	16°06′E
Potters Bar, Eng., U.K. (pŏt′ẽz bär)	144b	51°41′N	0°12′W
Potter Street, Eng., U.K.	235	51°46′N	0°08′E
Pottstown, Pa., U.S. (pŏts′toun)	99	40°15′N	75°40′W
Pottsville, Pa., U.S. (pôts′vĭl)	99	40°40′N	76°15′W
Poughkeepsie, N.Y., U.S. (pŏ-kĭp′sė)	97	41°45′N	73°55′W
Poulsbo, Wa., U.S. (pōlz′bò)	106a	47°44′N	122°38′W
Poulton-le-Fylde, Eng., U.K. (pōl′tŭn-lē-fīld′)	144a	53°52′N	2°59′W
Pouso Alegre, Braz. (pō′zò ä-lā′grĕ)	131	22°13′S	45°56′W
Póvoa de Varzim, Port. (pō-vō′ȧ dā vär′zēɴ)	148	41°23′N	8°44′W
Powder, r., U.S. (pou′dẽr)	96	45°18′N	105°37′W
Powder, r., Or., U.S.	104	44°55′N	117°35′W
Powder, South Fork, r., Wy., U.S.	105	43°13′N	106°54′W
Powder River, Wy., U.S.	105	43°06′N	106°55′W
Powell, Wy., U.S. (pou′ĕl)	105	44°44′N	108°44′W
Powell, Lake, res., U.S.	96	37°26′N	110°25′W
Powell Lake, l., Can.	86	50°10′N	124°13′W
Powell Point, c., Bah.	122	24°50′N	76°20′W
Powell Reservoir, res., Ky., U.S.	114	36°30′N	83°35′W
Powell River, Can.	84	49°52′N	124°33′W
Poyang Hu, l., China	189	29°20′N	116°28′E
Poygan, r., Wi., U.S. (poi′gȧn)	103	44°10′N	89°05′W
Poyle, Eng., U.K.	235	51°28′N	0°31′W
Poynton, Eng., U.K.	237b	53°21′N	2°07′W
Požarevac, Yugo. (pô′zhá′rĕ-våts)	161	44°38′N	21°12′E
Poza Rica, Mex. (pô-zô-rē′kä)	119	20°32′N	97°25′W
Poznań, Pol.	142	52°25′N	16°55′E
Pozoblanco, Spain (pô-thō-bläŋ′kō)	158	38°23′N	4°50′W
Pozos, Mex. (pŏ′zōs)	118	22°05′N	100°50′W
Pozuelo de Alarcón, Spain (pō-thwā′lō dā ä-lär-kōn′)	159a	40°27′N	3°49′W
Pozzuoli, Italy (pôt-swô′lē)	160	40°34′N	14°08′E
Pra, r., Ghana (prȧ)	214	5°45′N	1°35′W
Pra, r., Russia	162	55°00′N	40°13′E
Prachin Buri, Thai. (prä′chĕn)	196	13°59′N	101°15′E
Pradera, Col. (prä-dĕ′rä)	130a	3°24′N	76°13′W
Prades, Fr. (pråd)	156	42°37′N	2°23′E
Prado, Col. (prä′dô)	130a	3°44′N	74°55′W
Prado, Museo del, bldg., Spain	238b	40°25′N	3°41′W
Prado Churubusco, Mex.	233a	19°21′N	99°07′W
Prado Reservoir, res., Ca., U.S. (prä′dō)	107a	33°45′N	117°40′W
Prados, Braz. (prá′dôs)	129a	21°05′S	44°04′W
Prague, Czech Rep.	154	50°05′N	14°26′E
Praha *see* Prague, Czech Rep.	142	50°05′N	14°26′E
Prahran, Austl.	243b	37°51′S	144°59′E
Praia, C.V. (prä′yȧ)	210b	15°00′N	23°30′W
Praia Funda, Ponta da, c., Braz. (pôn′tä-dȧ-prä′yȧ-fo͞o′n-dä)	132b	23°04′S	43°34′W
Prairie du Chien, Wi., U.S. (prā′rĭ dò shēn′)	103	43°02′N	91°10′W
Prairie Grove, Can. (prā′rĭ grōv)	83f	49°48′N	96°57′W
Prairie Island Indian Reservation, I.R., Mn., U.S.	103	44°42′N	92°32′W
Prairies, Rivière des, r., Can. (rē-vyâr′ dā prå-rē′)	83a	45°40′N	73°34′W
Pratas Island, i., Asia	193	20°40′N	116°30′E
Prat del Llobregat, Spain	238e	41°20′N	2°06′E
Prato, Italy (prä′tō)	160	43°53′N	11°03′E
Pratt, Ks., U.S. (prăt)	110	37°37′N	98°43′W
Pratt's Bottom, neigh., Eng., U.K.	235	51°20′N	0°07′E
Prattville, Al., U.S. (prăt′vĭl)	114	32°28′N	86°27′W
Pravdinsk, Russia	153	54°26′N	21°00′E
Pravdinskiy, Russia (pråv-dĕn′skĭ)	172b	56°03′N	37°52′E
Pravia, Spain (prä′vė-ä)	158	43°30′N	6°08′W
Pregolya, r., Russia (prĕ-gô′lä)	153	54°37′N	20°50′E
Premont, Tx., U.S. (prė-mŏnt′)	112	27°20′N	98°07′W
Prenton, Eng., U.K.	237a	53°22′N	3°03′W
Prenzlau, Ger. (prĕnts′lou)	154	53°19′N	13°52′E
Prenzlauer Berg, neigh., Ger.	238a	52°32′N	13°26′E
Přerov, Czech Rep. (przhě′rôf)	147	49°28′N	17°28′E
Prescot, Eng., U.K. (prĕs′kŭt)	144a	53°25′N	2°48′W
Prescott, Can. (prĕs′kŭt)	99	44°45′N	75°35′W
Prescott, Az., U.S. (prĕs′kŏt)	96	34°30′N	112°30′W
Prescott, Ar., U.S.	111	33°47′N	93°23′W
Prescott, Wi., U.S. (prĕs′kŭt)	107g	44°45′N	92°48′W
Presho, S.D., U.S. (prĕsh′ô)	102	43°56′N	100°04′W
Presidencia Rogue Sáenz Peña, Arg.	132	26°52′S	60°15′W
Presidente Epitácio, Braz. (prā-sė-dĕn′tĕ å-pē-tä′syô)	131	21°56′S	52°01′W
Presidente Roosevelt, Estação, trans., Braz.	234d	23°33′S	46°36′W
Presidio, Tx., U.S. (prĕ-sĭ′dĭ-ô)	112	29°33′N	104°23′W
Presidio, Río del, r., Mex. (rĕ′ō-dĕl-prĕ-sĕ′dyô)	118	23°54′N	105°44′W
Presidio of San Francisco, pt. of i., Ca., U.S.	231b	37°48′N	122°28′W
Prešov, Slvk. (prĕ′shôf)	147	49°00′N	21°18′E
Prespa, Lake, l., Eur. (prĕs′pä)	161	40°49′N	20°50′E

ăt; finăl; rāte; senåte; ärm; åsk; sofȧ; fâre; ch-choose; dh-as th in other; bē; ėvent; bĕt; recĕnt; cratẽr; g-gō; gh-guttural g; bĭt; ĭ-short neutral; rīde; κ-guttural k as ch in German ich;

PRONOUNCING INDEX Prespuntal – Putaendo 335

PLACE (Pronunciation)	PAGE	LAT.	LONG.
Prespuntal, r., Ven.	131b	9°55'N	64°32'W
Presque Isle, Me., U.S. (prěsk'ēl')	92	46°41'N	68°03'W
Pressbaum, Aus.	145e	48°12'N	16°06'E
Prestea, Ghana	214	5°27'N	2°08'W
Preston, Austl.	201a	37°45'S	145°01'E
Preston, Eng., U.K. (prěs'tŭn)	150	53°46'N	2°42'W
Preston, Id., U.S. (pres'tŭn)	105	42°05'N	111°54'W
Preston, Mn., U.S. (prěs'tŭn)	103	43°42'N	92°06'W
Preston, Wa., U.S.	106a	47°31'N	121°56'W
Prestonburg, Ky., U.S. (prěs'tŭn-bûrg)	98	37°35'N	82°50'W
Prestwich, Eng., U.K. (prěst'wĭch)	144a	53°32'N	2°17'W
Pretoria, S. Afr. (prê-tō'rĭ-ȧ)	212	25°43'S	28°16'E
Pretoria North, S. Afr. (prě-tô'rĭ-ȧ no͞ord)	218d	25°41'S	28°11'E
Préveza, Grc. (prě'vȧ-zä)	161	38°58'N	20°44'E
Pribilof Islands, is., Ak., U.S. (prĭ'bĭ-lof)	95	57°00'N	169°20'W
Priboj, Yugo. (prē'boi)	161	43°33'N	19°33'E
Price, Ut., U.S. (prīs)	109	39°35'N	110°50'W
Price, r., Ut., U.S.	109	39°21'N	110°35'W
Prichard, Al., U.S. (prĭt'chârd)	114	30°44'N	88°04'W
Priddis, Can. (prĭd'dĭs)	83e	50°53'N	114°20'W
Priddis Creek, r., Can.	83e	50°56'N	114°32'W
Priego, Spain (prê-ā'gō)	158	37°27'N	4°13'W
Prienai, Lith. (prê-ĕn'ī)	153	54°38'N	23°56'E
Prieska, S. Afr. (prê-ĕs'kȧ)	212	29°40'S	22°50'E
Priest Lake, l., Id., U.S. (prēst)	104	48°30'N	116°43'W
Priest Rapids Dam, Wa., U.S.	104	46°39'N	119°55'W
Priest Rapids Lake, res., Wa., U.S.	104	46°42'N	119°58'W
Priiskovaya, Russia (prĭ-ĕs'kô-vȧ-yȧ)	172a	60°50'N	58°55'E
Prijedor, Bos. (prē'yĕ-dôr)	160	44°58'N	16°43'E
Prijepolje, Yugo. (prē'yĕ-pô'lyĕ)	161	43°22'N	19°41'E
Prilep, Mac. (prē'lĕp)	149	41°20'N	21°35'E
Primorsk, Russia (prē-môrsk')	153	60°24'N	28°35'E
Primorsko-Akhtarskaya, Russia (prē-môr'skô äĸ-tär'skĭ-ê)	167	46°03'N	38°09'E
Primos, Pa., U.S.	229b	39°55'N	75°18'W
Primrose, S. Afr.	213b	26°11'S	28°11'E
Primrose Lake, l., Can.	88	54°55'N	109°45'W
Prince Albert, Can. (prĭns ăl'bērt)	84	53°12'N	105°46'W
Prince Albert National Park, rec., Can.	84	54°10'N	105°25'W
Prince Albert Sound, strt., Can.	84	70°23'N	116°57'W
Prince Charles Island, i., Can. (chärlz)	85	67°41'N	74°10'W
Prince Edward Island, prov., Can.	85	46°45'N	63°10'W
Prince Edward Islands, is., S. Afr.	219	46°36'S	37°57'E
Prince Edward National Park, rec., Can. (ĕd'wērd)	85	46°33'N	63°35'W
Prince Edward Peninsula, pen., Can.	99	44°00'N	77°15'W
Prince Frederick, Md., U.S. (prĭnce frĕdĕrĭk)	100e	38°33'N	76°35'W
Prince George, Can. (jôrj)	84	53°51'N	122°57'W
Prince of Wales, i., Austl.	203	10°47'S	142°15'E
Prince of Wales, i., Ak., U.S.	95	55°47'N	132°50'W
Prince of Wales, Cape, c., Ak., U.S. (wālz)	95	65°48'N	169°08'W
Prince Rupert, Can. (roo'pērt)	84	54°19'N	130°19'W
Princes Risborough, Eng., U.K. (prĭns'ĕz rĭz'brŭ)	144b	51°41'N	0°51'W
Princess Charlotte Bay, b., Austl. (shär'lŏt)	203	13°45'S	144°15'E
Princess Royal Channel, strt., Can. (roi'ăl)	86	53°10'N	128°37'W
Princess Royal Island, i., Can.	86	52°57'N	128°49'W
Princeton, Can. (prĭns'tŭn)	86	49°27'N	120°31'W
Princeton, Il., U.S.	98	41°20'N	89°25'W
Princeton, In., U.S.	98	38°20'N	87°35'W
Princeton, Ky., U.S.	114	37°07'N	87°52'W
Princeton, Mi., U.S.	103	46°16'N	87°33'W
Princeton, Mn., U.S.	103	45°34'N	93°36'W
Princeton, Mo., U.S.	111	40°23'N	93°34'W
Princeton, N.J., U.S.	99	40°21'N	74°40'W
Princeton, W.V., U.S.	115	37°21'N	81°05'W
Princeton, Wi., U.S.	103	43°50'N	89°09'W
Prince William Sound, strt., Ak., U.S. (wĭl'yăm)	95	60°40'N	147°10'W
Príncipe, i., S. Tom./P. (prēn'sē-pě)	210	1°37'N	7°25'E
Principe Channel, strt., Can. (prĭn'sĭ-pē)	86	53°28'N	129°45'W
Prineville, Or., U.S. (prīn'vĭl)	104	44°17'N	120°48'W
Prineville Reservoir, res., Or., U.S.	104	44°07'N	120°45'W
Prinzapolca, Nic. (prēn-zä-pōl'kä)	121	13°18'N	83°35'W
Prinzapolca, r., Nic.	121	13°23'N	84°23'W
Prior Lake, Mn., U.S. (prī'ēr)	107g	44°43'N	93°26'W
Priozërsk, Russia (prĭ-ô'zĕrsk)	153	61°03'N	30°08'E
Pripet, r., Eur.	167	51°50'N	29°45'E
Pripyat Marshes *see* Poles'ye, sw., Eur.	167	52°10'N	27°30'E
Priština, Yugo. (prēsh'tĭ-nä)	149	42°39'N	21°12'E
Pritzwalk, Ger. (prēts'välk)	154	53°09'N	12°12'E
Privas, Fr. (prē-väs')	156	44°44'N	4°37'E
Prizren, Yugo. (prē'zrĕn)	149	42°11'N	20°45'E
Procida, Italy (prô'chê-dä)	159c	40°31'N	14°02'E
Procida, Isola di, i., Italy	159c	40°32'N	13°57'E
Proctor, Mn., U.S. (prŏk'tēr)	107h	46°45'N	92°14'W
Proctor, Vt., U.S.	99	43°40'N	73°00'W
Proebstel, Wa., U.S. (prōb'stĕl)	106c	45°40'N	122°29'W
Proenca-a-Nova, Port. (prô-ān'sȧ-ä-nō'vȧ)	158	39°44'N	7°55'W
Progreso, Hond. (prô-grĕ'sô)	120	15°28'N	87°49'W
Progreso, Mex.	112	27°29'N	101°05'W
Progreso, Mex. (prô-grā'sō)	116	21°14'N	89°39'W
Prokhladnyy, Russia	168	43°46'N	44°00'E
Prokop'yevsk, Russia	170	53°53'N	86°45'E
Prokuplje, Yugo. (prô'kōp'l-yĕ)	161	43°16'N	21°40'E
Prome, Myanmar	196	18°46'N	95°15'E
Pronya, r., Bela. (prô'nyä)	162	54°08'N	30°58'E
Pronya, r., Russia	162	54°08'N	39°30'E
Prospect, Austl.	243a	33°48'S	150°56'E
Prospect, Ky., U.S. (prŏs'pĕkt)	101h	38°21'N	85°36'W
Prospect Heights, Il., U.S.	231a	42°06'N	87°56'W
Prospect Park, N.J., U.S.	228	40°56'N	74°10'W
Prospect Park, Pa., U.S. (prŏs'pĕkt pärk)	100f	39°53'N	75°18'W
Prosser, Wa., U.S. (prŏs'ēr)	104	46°10'N	119°46'W
Prostějov, Czech Rep. (prôs'tyĕ-yôf)	155	49°28'N	17°08'E
Protea, S. Afr.	244b	26°17'S	27°51'E
Protection, i., Wa., U.S. (prô-tĕk'shŭn)	106a	48°07'N	122°56'W
Protoka, r., Russia (prôt'ô-kȧ)	162	55°00'N	36°42'E
Provadiya, Bul. (prō-väd'ê-yȧ)	161	43°13'N	27°28'E
Providence, Ky., U.S. (prŏv'ĭ-dĕns)	98	37°25'N	87°45'W
Providence, R.I., U.S.	97	41°50'N	71°23'W
Providence, Ut., U.S.	105	41°42'N	111°50'W
Providencia, Chile	234b	33°26'S	70°37'W
Providencia, Isla de, i., Col.	121	13°21'N	80°55'W
Providenciales, i., T./C. Is.	123	21°50'N	72°15'W
Provideniya, Russia (prô-vĭ-dă'nĭ-yȧ)	95	64°30'N	172°54'W
Provincetown, Ma., U.S.	99	42°03'N	70°11'W
Provo, Ut., U.S. (prō'vō)	96	40°15'N	111°40'W
Prozor, Bos. (prô'zôr)	161	43°48'N	17°59'E
Prudence Island, i., R.I., U.S. (pro͞o'dĕns)	100b	41°38'N	71°20'W
Prudhoe Bay, b., Ak., U.S.	95	70°40'N	147°25'W
Prudnik, Pol. (prôd'nĭk)	155	50°19'N	17°34'E
Prussia, hist. reg., Eur. (prŭsh'ȧ)	154	50°43'N	8°35'E
Pruszków, Pol. (prósh'kôf)	155	52°09'N	20°50'E
Prut, r., Eur. (pro͞ot)	142	48°05'N	27°07'E
Pryluky, Ukr.	167	50°36'N	32°21'E
Prymors'k, Ukr.	163	46°43'N	36°21'E
Pryor, Ok., U.S. (prī'ēr)	111	36°16'N	95°19'W
Pryvil'ne, Ukr.	163	47°30'N	32°21'E
Przedbórz, Pol.	155	51°05'N	19°53'E
Przemyśl, Pol. (pzhě'mĭsh'l)	142	49°47'N	22°45'E
Przheval'sk, Kyrg. (p'r-zhĭ-välsk')	169	42°29'N	78°24'E
Psel, r., Eur.	167	49°45'N	33°42'E
Psikhikón, Grc.	239d	38°00'N	23°47'E
Pskov, Russia (pskôf)	164	57°48'N	28°19'E
Pskov, prov., Russia	162	57°33'N	29°05'E
Pskovskoye Ozero, l., Eur. (p'skôv'skô'yĕ ôzê-rô)	166	58°05'N	28°15'E
Ptich', r., Bela. (p'têch)	166	53°17'N	28°16'E
Ptuj, Slvn. (pto͞o'ê)	160	46°24'N	15°54'E
Pucheng, China (po͞o-chŭŋ)	190	35°43'N	115°22'E
Pucheng, China (po͞o'chĕng')	193	28°02'N	118°25'E
Puck, Pol. (pŏtsk)	155	54°43'N	18°23'E
Puddington, Eng., U.K.	237a	53°15'N	3°00'W
Pudozh, Russia (po͞o'dôzh)	166	61°50'N	36°50'E
Puebla, Mex. (pwā'blä)	116	19°02'N	98°11'W
Puebla, state, Mex.	119	19°00'N	97°45'W
Puebla de Don Fadrique, Spain	158	37°55'N	2°55'W
Pueblo, Co., U.S. (pwā'blō)	96	38°15'N	104°36'W
Pueblo Libre, Peru	233c	12°05'S	77°05'W
Pueblo Nuevo, Mex. (nwā'vô)	118	23°23'N	105°21'W
Pueblo Nuevo, neigh., Spain	238b	40°26'N	3°39'W
Pueblo Viejo, Mex. (vyā'hô)	119	17°23'N	93°46'W
Puente Alto, Chile (pwĕ'n-tĕ ál'tô)	129b	33°36'S	70°34'W
Puentedeume, Spain (pwĕn-tå-dhå-o͞o'må)	158	43°28'N	8°09'W
Puente-Genil, Spain (pwĕn'tå-hå-nēl')	158	37°25'N	4°18'W
Puerco, Rio, r., N.M., U.S. (pwĕr'kō)	109	35°15'N	107°05'W
Puerto Aisén, Chile (pwĕ'r-tô ä'y-sĕ'n)	132	45°28'S	72°44'W
Puerto Angel, Mex. (pwĕ'r-tô äŋ'hál)	119	15°42'N	96°32'W
Puerto Armuelles, Pan. (pwe'r-tô är-mo͞o-ā'lyās)	121	8°18'N	82°52'W
Puerto Barrios, Guat. (pwĕ'r-tô bär'rê-ôs)	116	15°43'N	88°36'W
Puerto Bermúdez, Peru (pwĕ'r-tō bĕr-mo͞o'dāz)	130	10°17'S	74°57'W
Puerto Berrío, Col. (pwĕ'r-tô bĕr-rē'ō)	130	6°29'N	74°27'W
Puerto Cabello, Ven. (pwĕ'r-tô kä-bĕl'yô)	130	10°28'N	68°01'W
Puerto Cabezas, Nic. (pwĕ'r-tô kä-bā'zäs)	121	14°01'N	83°26'W
Puerto Casado, Para. (pwĕ'r-tô kä-sä'dō)	132	22°16'S	57°57'W
Puerto Castilla, Hond. (pwĕ'r-tô käs-tēl'yō)	120	16°01'N	86°01'W
Puerto Chicama, Peru (pwĕ'r-tō chê-kä'mä)	130	7°46'S	79°18'W
Puerto Colombia, Col. (pwĕr'tô kô-lôm'bê-ä)	130	11°08'N	75°09'W
Puerto Cortés, C.R. (pwĕ'r-tô kôr-tās')	121	9°00'N	83°37'W
Puerto Cortés, Hond. (pwĕ'r-tô kôr-tās')	116	15°48'N	87°57'W
Puerto Cumarebo, Ven. (pwĕ'r-tō ko͞o-mä-rē'bô)	130	11°25'N	69°17'W
Puerto de Luna, N.M., U.S. (pwĕr'tô dȧ lo͞o'nä)	110	34°49'N	104°36'W
Puerto de Nutrias, Ven. (pwĕ'r-tō dĕ no͞o-trê-äs')	130	8°02'N	69°19'W
Puerto Deseado, Arg. (pwĕ'r-tō dā-sā-ä'dhō)	132	47°38'S	66°00'W
Puerto de Somport, p., Eur.	159	42°51'N	0°25'W
Puerto Eten, Peru (pwĕ'r-tō ĕ-tĕ'n)	130	6°59'S	79°51'W
Puerto Jiménez, C.R. (pwĕ'r-tô ĸê-mĕ'nĕz)	121	8°35'N	83°23'W
Puerto La Cruz, Ven. (pwĕ'r-tô lä kro͞o'z)	130	10°14'N	64°38'W
Puertollano, Spain (pwĕ-tôl-yä'nō)	148	38°41'N	4°05'W
Puerto Madryn, Arg. (pwĕ'r-tō mä-drĕn')	132	42°45'S	65°01'W
Puerto Maldonado, Peru (pwĕ'r-tô mäl-dō-nä'dô)	130	12°43'S	69°01'W
Puerto Miniso, Mex. (pwĕ'r-tō mē-nē'sô)	118	16°06'N	98°02'W
Puerto Montt, Chile (pwĕ'r-tō mô'nt)	132	41°29'S	73°00'W
Puerto Natales, Chile (pwĕ'r-tō nä-tá'lĕs)	132	51°48'S	72°01'W
Puerto Niño, Col. (pwĕ'r-tō nē'n-yō)	130a	5°57'N	74°36'W
Puerto Padre, Cuba (pwĕ'r-tō pä'drā)	122	21°10'N	76°40'W
Puerto Peñasco, Mex. (pwĕ'r-tô pĕn-yä's-kô)	116	31°39'N	113°15'W
Puerto Pinasco, Para. (pwĕ'r-tō pē-ná's-kô)	132	22°31'S	57°50'W
Puerto Píritu, Ven. (pwĕ'r-tō pē'rē-to͞o)	131b	10°05'N	65°04'W
Puerto Plata, Dom. Rep. (pwĕ'r-tô plä'tä)	117	19°50'N	70°40'W
Puerto Princesa, Phil. (pwĕr-tô prēn-sā'sä)	196	9°45'N	118°41'E
Puerto Rico, dep., N.A. (pwĕr'tô rē'kō)	117	18°16'N	66°50'W
Puerto Rico Trench, deep	117	19°45'N	66°30'W
Puerto Salgar, Col. (pwĕ'r-tō säl-gär')	130a	5°30'N	74°39'W
Puerto Santa Cruz, Arg. (pwĕ'r-tō sän'tä kro͞oz')	132	50°04'S	68°32'W
Puerto Suárez, Bol. (pwĕ'r-tō swä'râz)	131	18°55'S	57°39'W
Puerto Tejada, Col. (pwĕ'r-tō tĕ-ĸä'dä)	130	3°13'N	76°23'W
Puerto Vallarta, Mex. (pwĕ'r-tō väl-yär'tä)	118	20°36'N	105°13'W
Puerto Varas, Chile (pwĕ'r-tō vä'räs)	132	41°16'S	73°03'W
Puerto Wilches, Col. (pwĕ'r-tô vēl'c-hĕs)	130	7°19'N	73°54'W
Pugachëv, Russia (po͞o'gȧ-chyôf)	167	52°00'N	48°40'E
Puget, Wa., U.S. (pū'jĕt)	106c	46°10'N	123°23'W
Puget Sound, strt., Wa., U.S.	104	47°49'N	122°26'W
Puglia (Apulia), hist. reg., Italy (po͞o'lyä) (ä-po͞o'lyä)	160	41°13'N	16°10'E
Pukaskwa National Park, rec., Can.	85	48°22'N	85°55'W
Pukeashun Mountain, mtn., Can.	87	51°12'N	119°14'W
Pukin, r., Malay.	181b	2°53'N	102°54'E
Pula, Cro. (po͞o'lä)	148	44°52'N	13°55'E
Pulacayo, Bol. (po͞o-lä-kä'yō)	130	20°12'N	66°33'W
Pulaski, Tn., U.S. (pů-lăs'kĭ)	114	35°11'N	87°03'W
Pulaski, Va., U.S.	115	37°00'N	81°45'W
Puławy, Pol. (pó-wä'vê)	155	51°24'N	21°59'E
Pulicat, r., India	187	13°58'N	79°52'E
Pullman, Wa., U.S. (pŏl'măn)	104	46°44'N	117°10'W
Pullman, neigh., Il., U.S.	231a	41°43'N	87°36'W
Pulog, Mount, mtn., Phil. (po͞o'lôg)	197a	16°38'N	120°53'E
Puma Yumco, l., China (po͞o-mä yo͞om-tswo)	186	28°30'N	90°10'E
Pumphrey, Md., U.S.	229c	39°13'N	76°38'W
Pumpkin Creek, r., Mt., U.S. (pŭmp'kĭn)	105	45°47'N	105°35'W
Punakha, Bhu. (po͞o-nŭk'ŭ)	183	27°45'N	89°59'E
Punata, Bol. (po͞o-nä'tä)	130	17°43'S	65°43'W
Punchbowl, Austl.	243a	33°56'S	151°03'E
Pune, India	183	18°38'N	73°53'E
Punggol, Sing.	240c	1°25'N	103°55'E
Punjab, state, India (pŭn'jäb')	183	31°00'N	75°30'E
Puno, Peru (po͞o'nô)	130	15°58'S	70°02'W
Punta Arenas, Chile (po͞o'n-tä-rĕ'näs)	132	53°09'S	70°48'W
Punta Brava, Cuba	233b	23°01'N	82°30'W
Punta de Piedras, Ven. (po͞o'n-tä dĕ pyĕ'dräs)	131b	10°54'N	64°06'W
Punta Gorda, Belize (pón'tä gôr'dä)	120	16°07'N	88°50'W
Punta Gorda, Fl., U.S. (pŭn'tȧ gôr'dȧ)	115a	26°55'N	82°02'W
Punta Gorda, Río, r., Nic. (po͞o'n-tä gô'r-dä)	121	11°34'N	84°13'W
Punta Indio, Canal, strt., Arg. (po͞o'n-tä- ĕ'n-dyô)	129c	34°56'S	57°20'W
Puntarenas, C.R. (pónt-ä-rā'näs)	117	9°59'N	84°49'W
Punto Fijo, Ven. (po͞o'n-tô fē'ĸô)	130	11°48'N	70°14'W
Punxsutawney, Pa., U.S. (pŭnk-sŭ-tô'nê)	99	40°55'N	79°00'W
Puquio, Peru (po͞o'kyô)	130	14°43'S	74°02'W
Pur, r., Russia	170	65°30'N	77°30'E
Purcell, Ok., U.S. (pûr-sĕl')	111	35°01'N	97°22'W
Purcell Mountains, mts., N.A. (pûr-sĕl')	87	50°00'N	116°30'W
Purdy, Wa., U.S. (pûr'dê)	106a	47°23'N	122°37'W
Purépero, Mex. (po͞o-rā'pâ-rō)	118	19°56'N	102°02'W
Purfleet, Eng., U.K.	235	51°29'N	0°15'E
Purgatoire, r., Co., U.S. (pûr-gȧ-twär')	110	37°25'N	103°53'W
Puri, India (pò'rê)	183	19°52'N	85°51'E
Purial, Sierra de, mts., Cuba (sē-ĕ'r-rä-dĕ-po͞o-rê-äl')	123	20°15'N	74°40'W
Purificación, Col. (po͞o-rê-fê-kä-syōn')	130	3°52'N	74°54'W
Purificación, Mex. (po͞o-rē-fê-kä-syô'n)	118	19°44'N	104°38'W
Purificación, r., Mex.	118	19°30'N	104°54'W
Purkersdorf, Aus.	145e	48°13'N	16°11'E
Purley, neigh., Eng., U.K.	235	51°20'N	0°07'W
Puruandiro, Mex. (pó-ro͞o-än'dê-rō)	118	20°04'N	101°33'W
Purús, r., S.A. (po͞o-ro͞o's)	130	6°45'S	64°34'W
Pusan, S. Kor.	189	35°08'N	129°05'E
Pushkin, Russia (pósh'kĭn)	166	59°43'N	30°25'E
Pushkino, Russia (po͞osh'kê-nô)	162	56°01'N	37°51'E
Pustoshka, Russia (pûs-tôsh'kȧ)	162	56°20'N	29°33'E
Pustunich, Mex. (po͞os-to͞o'nêch)	119	19°10'N	90°29'W
Putaendo, Chile (po͞o-tä-ĕn-dô)	129b	32°37'S	70°42'W

ng-sing; ŋ-baŋk; ɴ-nasalized n; nŏd; cŏmmit; ōld; ôbey; ôrder; oi-boil; fo͞od; ó-as oo in foot; ou-out; s-soft; sh-dish; th-thin; pūre; ůnite; ûrn; stŭd; circ*ŭ*s; ü-as in French tu; '-indeterminate vowel.

336 Puteaux–Rainy

PLACE (Pronunciation)	PAGE	LAT.	LONG.
Puteaux, Fr. (pü-tō′)	157b	48°52′N	2°12′E
Putfontein, S. Afr. (pót′fŏn-tān)	213b	26°08′S	28°24′E
Puth Kalān, neigh., India	240d	28°43′N	77°05′E
Putian, China (po͞o-tĭĕn)	193	25°40′N	119°02′E
Putilkovo, Russia	239b	55°52′N	37°23′E
Putla de Guerrero, Mex. (po͞o′tlä-dĕ-gĕr-rĕ′rō)	119	17°03′N	97°55′W
Putnam, Ct., U.S. (pŭt′n*ă*m)	99	41°55′N	71°55′W
Putney, neigh., Eng., U.K.	235	51°28′N	0°13′W
Putorana, Gory, mts., Russia	165	68°45′N	93°15′E
Pütt, Ger.	236	51°11′N	6°59′E
Puttalam, Sri L.	183b	8°02′N	79°44′E
Putumayo, r., S.A. (po-to͞o-mä′yō)	130	1°02′S	73°50′W
Putung, Tanjung, c., Indon.	196	3°35′S	111°50′E
Putyvl′, Ukr.	163	51°21′N	33°52′E
Puulavesi, l., Fin.	153	61°49′N	27°10′E
Puyallup, Wa., U.S. (pū-ăl′ŭp)	106a	47°12′N	122°18′W
Puyang, China (po͞o-yäŋ)	192	35°42′N	114°58′E
Pweto, D.R.C. (pwā′tō)	212	8°29′S	28°58′E
Pyasina, r., Russia (pyä-sē′nȧ)	170	72°45′N	87°37′E
Pyatigorsk, Russia (pyä-tē-gôrsk′)	167	44°00′N	43°00′E
Pyhäjärvi, l., Fin.	153	60°57′N	21°50′E
Pyinmana, Myanmar (pyēn-mä′n*ŭ*)	183	19°47′N	96°15′E
Pymatuning Reservoir, res., Pa., U.S. (pī-mȧ-tŭn′ĭng)	98	41°40′N	80°30′W
Pymble, Austl.	243a	33°45′S	151°09′E
Pyŏnggang, N. Kor. (pyŭng′gäng′)	194	38°21′N	127°18′E
P′yŏngyang, N. Kor.	189	39°03′N	125°48′E
Pyramid, l., Nv., U.S. (pĭ′r*ȧ*-mĭd)	108	40°02′N	119°50′W
Pyramid Lake Indian Reservation, I.R., Nv., U.S.	108	40°17′N	119°52′W
Pyramids, hist., Egypt	218b	29°53′N	31°10′E
Pyrenees, mts., Eur. (pĭr-e-nēz′)	142	43°00′N	0°05′E
Pyrford, Eng., U.K.	235	51°19′N	0°30′W
Pyriatyn, Ukr.	167	50°13′N	32°31′E
Pyrzyce, Pol. (pězhĭ′tsě)	154	53°09′N	14°53′E

Q

PLACE (Pronunciation)	PAGE	LAT.	LONG.
Qal′at Bishah, Sau. Ar.	182	20°01′N	42°30′E
Qamdo, China (chyäm-dwō)	188	31°06′N	96°30′E
Qandahār, Afg.	183	31°43′N	65°58′E
Qandala, Som.	185	11°28′N	49°52′E
Qapal, Kaz.	169	45°13′N	79°08′E
Qaraghandy, Kaz.	169	49°42′N	73°18′E
Qarqan *see* Qiemo, China	188	38°02′N	85°16′E
Qarqan, r., China	188	38°55′N	87°15′E
Qarqaraly, Kaz.	169	49°18′N	75°28′E
Qārūn, Birket, l., Egypt	211	29°34′N	30°34′E
Qaşr al Burayqah, Libya	211	30°25′N	19°20′E
Qasr al-Farāfirah, Egypt	211	27°04′N	28°13′E
Qaşr Banī Walīd, Libya	211	31°45′N	14°04′E
Qasr-e Fīrūzeh, Iran	241h	35°40′N	51°32′E
Qasr el Boukhari, Alg.	148	35°50′N	2°48′E
Qatar, nation, Asia (kä′tȧr)	182	25°00′N	52°45′E
Qaţţārah, Munkhafaḑ al, depr., Egypt	211	30°07′N	27°30′E
Qāyen, Iran	182	33°45′N	59°08′E
Qazvīn, Iran	182	36°10′N	49°59′E
Qeshm, Iran	182	26°51′N	56°10′E
Qeshm, i., Iran	182	26°52′N	56°15′E
Qezel Owzan, r., Iran	182	36°30′N	49°00′E
Qezi′ot, Isr.	181a	30°53′N	34°28′E
Qianwei, China (chyĕn-wā)	190	40°11′N	120°05′E
Qi′anzhen, China (chyē-än-jŭn)	190	32°16′N	120°59′E
Qibao, China (chyē-bou)	191b	31°06′N	121°16′E
Qiblīyah, Jabal al Jalālat al, mts., Egypt	181a	28°49′N	32°21′E
Qieshikou, China	240b	39°59′N	116°24′E
Qijiang, China (chyē-jyäŋ)	193	29°05′N	106°40′E
Qikou, China (chyē-kō)	190	38°37′N	117°33′E
Qilian Shan, mts., China (chyē-lĭĕn shän)	188	38°43′N	98°00′E
Qiliping, China (chyē-lē-pĭŋ)	190	31°28′N	114°41′E
Qindao, China (chyĭn-dou)	189	36°05′N	120°10′E
Qing′an, China (chyĭŋ-än)	192	46°50′N	127°30′E
Qingcheng, China (chyĭŋ-chŭŋ)	190	37°12′N	117°43′E
Qingfeng, China (chyĭŋ-fŭŋ)	190	35°52′N	115°05′E
Qinghai, prov., China (chyĭŋ-hī)	188	36°14′N	95°30′E
Qinghai Hu *see* Koko Nor, l., China	188	37°26′N	98°30′E
Qinghe, China (chyĭŋ-hŭ)	192a	40°08′N	116°16′E
Qinghuayuan, China	240b	40°00′N	116°19′E
Qingjiang, China	190	33°34′N	118°58′E
Qingjiang, China (chyĭŋ-jyäŋ)	193	28°00′N	115°30′E
Qingliu, China (chyĭŋ-lĭō)	193	26°15′N	116°50′E
Qingningsi, China (chyĭŋ-nĭŋ-sz)	191b	31°16′N	121°33′E
Qingping, China (chyĭŋ-pĭŋ)	190	36°46′N	116°03′E
Qingpu, China (chyĭŋ-po͞o)	193	31°08′N	121°06′E
Qingxian, China (chyĭŋ shyĕn)	190	38°37′N	116°48′E
Qingyang, China (chyĭŋ-yäŋ)	188	36°02′N	107°42′E
Qingyuan, China	192	42°05′N	125°00′E
Qingyuan, China (chyĭŋ-yoăn)	193	23°43′N	113°10′E
Qingyun, China (chyĭŋ-yón)	190	37°52′N	117°26′E
Qingyundian, China (chĭŋ-yón-dĭĕn)	192a	39°41′N	116°31′E
Qinhuangdao, China (chyĭn-huaŋ-dou)	189	39°57′N	119°34′E
Qin Ling, mts., China (chyĭn lĭŋ)	188	33°25′N	108°58′E
Qinyang, China (chyĭn-yäŋ)	192	35°00′N	112°55′E
Qinzhou, China (chyĭn-jō)	193	22°00′N	108°35′E
Qionghai, China (chyôŋ-hī)	193	19°10′N	110°28′E
Qiqian, China (chyē-chyĕn)	189	52°23′N	121°04′E
Qiqihar, China	189	47°18′N	124°00′E
Qiryat Gat, Isr.	181a	31°38′N	34°36′E
Qiryat Shemona, Isr.	181a	33°12′N	35°34′E
Qitai, China (chyē-tī)	188	44°07′N	89°04′E
Qiuxian, China (chyô shyĕn)	190	36°43′N	115°13′E
Qixian, China (chyē-shyĕn)	190	34°33′N	114°47′E
Qixian, China	192	35°36′N	114°13′E
Qiyang, China (chyē-yäŋ)	193	26°40′N	112°00′E
Qom, Iran	182	34°28′N	50°53′E
Qostanay, Kaz.	169	53°10′N	63°39′E
Quabbin Reservoir, res., Ma., U.S. (kwā′bĭn)	99	42°20′N	72°10′W
Quachita, Lake, l., Ar., U.S. (kwä shĭ′tô)	111	34°47′N	93°37′W
Quadra Island, i., Can.	86	50°08′N	125°16′W
Quadraro, neigh., Italy	239c	41°51′N	12°33′E
Quakers Hill, Austl.	243a	33°43′S	150°53′E
Quakertown, Pa., U.S. (kwā′kẽr-toun)	99	40°30′N	75°20′W
Quanah, Tx., U.S. (kwä′nȧ)	110	34°19′N	99°43′W
Quang Ngai, Viet (kwäng n′gä′ē)	196	15°05′N	108°58′E
Quang Ngai, mtn., Viet	193	15°10′N	108°20′E
Quanjiao, China (chyuăn-jyou)	190	32°06′N	118°17′E
Quanzhou, China (chyuăn-jō)	189	24°58′N	118°40′E
Quanzhou, China	193	25°58′N	111°02′E
Qu′Appelle, r., Can.	84	50°30′N	104°00′W
Qu′Appelle Dam, dam, Can.	88	51°00′N	106°25′W
Quartu Sant′Elena, Italy (kwär-to͞o′ sänt a′lā-nä)	160	39°16′N	9°12′E
Quartzsite, Az., U.S.	109	33°40′N	114°13′W
Quatsino Sound, strt., Can. (kwŏt-sē′nō)	86	50°25′N	128°10′W
Quba, Azer. (ko͞o′bȧ)	167	41°05′N	48°30′E
Qūchān, Iran	185	37°06′N	58°30′E
Qudi, China	190	37°06′N	117°15′E
Québec, Can. (kwē-bĕk′) (kā-bĕk′)	83b	46°49′N	71°13′W
Quebec, prov., Can.	85	51°07′N	70°25′W
Quedlinburg, Ger. (kvĕd′lĕn-bo͞orgh)	154	51°45′N	11°10′E
Queen Bess, Can.	86	51°16′N	124°34′W
Queen Charlotte Islands, is., Can. (kwēn shär′lŏt)	84	53°30′N	132°25′W
Queen Charlotte Ranges, mts., Can.	86	53°00′N	132°00′W
Queen Charlotte Sound, strt., Can.	86	51°30′N	129°30′W
Queen Charlotte Strait, strt., Can. (strāt)	84	50°40′N	127°25′W
Queen Elizabeth Islands, is., Can. (ē-lĭz′ȧ-bĕth)	82	78°20′N	110°00′W
Queen Maud Gulf, b., Can. (mȯd)	84	68°27′N	102°55′W
Queen Maud Land, reg., Ant.	219	75°00′S	10°00′E
Queen Maud Mountains, mts., Ant.	219	85°00′S	179°00′W
Queens Channel, strt., Austl. (kwēnz)	202	14°25′S	129°10′E
Queenscliff, Austl.	201a	38°16′S	144°39′E
Queensland, state, Austl. (kwēnz′l*ă*nd)	203	22°45′S	141°01′E
Queenstown, Austl. (kwēnz′toun)	204	42°00′S	145°40′E
Queenstown, S. Afr.	213c	31°54′S	26°53′E
Queimados, Braz. (kā-mȧ′dōs)	132b	22°42′S	43°34′W
Quela, Ang.	216	9°16′S	17°02′E
Quelimane, Moz. (kā-lē-mä′n*ĕ*)	213	17°48′S	37°05′E
Queluz, Port.	159b	38°45′N	9°15′W
Quemado de Güines, Cuba (kā-mä′dhä-dē-gwē′nĕs)	122	22°45′N	80°20′W
Quemoy, Tai.	193	24°30′N	118°20′E
Quemoy, i., Tai.	193	24°27′N	118°23′E
Quepos, C.R. (kā′pōs)	121	9°26′N	84°10′W
Quepos, Punta, c., C.R. (po͞o′n-tä)	121	9°23′N	84°20′W
Querenburg, neigh., Ger.	236	51°27′N	7°16′E
Querétaro, Mex. (kå-rā′tä-rō)	116	20°37′N	100°25′W
Querétaro, state, Mex.	118	21°00′N	100°00′W
Quesada, Spain (kå-sä′dhä)	158	37°51′N	3°04′W
Quesnel, Can. (kā-nĕl′)	84	52°59′N	122°30′W
Quesnel, r., Can.	87	52°15′N	122°00′W
Quesnel Lake, l., Can.	84	52°32′N	121°05′W
Quetame, Col. (kĕ-tä′mĕ)	130a	4°20′N	73°50′W
Quetta, Pak. (kwĕt′ä)	183	30°19′N	67°01′E
Quezaltenango, Guat. (kå-zäl′tå-näŋ′gō)	116	14°50′N	91°30′W
Quezaltepeque, El Sal. (kĕ-zäl′tĕ′pĕ-kĕ)	120	13°50′N	89°17′W
Quezaltepeque, Guat. (kå-zäl′tå-pā′kå)	120	14°39′N	89°26′W
Quezon City, Phil. (kā-zōn)	196	14°40′N	121°02′E
Qufu, China (chyo͞o-fo͞o)	190	35°37′N	116°54′E
Quibdo, Col. (kēb′dō)	130	5°42′N	76°41′W
Quiberon, Fr. (kē-bē-rôɴ′)	156	47°29′N	3°08′W
Quiçama, Parque Nacional de, rec., Ang.	216	10°00′S	13°25′E
Quicksborn, Ger. (kvēks′bōrn)	145c	53°44′N	9°54′E
Quilcene, Wa., U.S. (kwĭl-sēn′)	106a	47°50′N	122°53′W
Quilimari, Chile (kē-lē-mä′rē)	129b	32°06′S	71°28′W
Quillan, Fr. (kē-yäɴ′)	156	42°53′N	2°13′E
Quillota, Chile (kēl-yō′tä)	132	32°52′S	71°14′W
Quilmes, Arg. (kēl′mās)	129c	34°43′S	58°16′W
Quilon, India (kwē-lōn′)	183b	8°58′N	76°16′E
Quilpie, Austl. (kwĭl′pē)	203	26°34′S	149°20′E
Quimbaya, Col. (kēm-bä′yä)	130a	4°38′N	75°46′W
Quimbele, Ang.	216	6°28′S	16°13′E
Quimbonge, Ang.	216	8°36′S	18°30′E
Quimper, Fr. (kăɴ-pĕr′)	147	47°59′N	4°04′W
Quinalt, r., Wa., U.S.	104	47°23′N	124°10′W
Quinault Indian Reservation, I.R., Wa., U.S.	104	47°27′N	124°34′W
Quincy, Fl., U.S. (kwĭn′sē)	114	30°35′N	84°35′W
Quincy, Il., U.S.	97	39°55′N	91°23′W
Quincy, Ma., U.S.	93a	42°15′N	71°00′W
Quincy, Mi., U.S.	98	42°00′N	84°50′W
Quincy, Or., U.S.	106c	46°08′N	123°10′W
Quincy Bay, b., Ma., U.S.	227a	42°17′N	70°58′W
Qui Nhon, Viet (kwĭnyôn)	196	13°51′N	109°03′E
Quinn, r., Nv., U.S. (kwĭn)	104	41°42′N	117°45′W
Quintanar de la Orden, Spain (kēn-tä-när′)	158	39°36′N	3°02′W
Quintana Roo, state, Mex. (rô′ô)	116	19°30′N	88°30′W
Quinta Normal, Chile	234b	33°27′S	70°42′W
Quintero, Chile (kēn-tĕ′rô)	129b	32°48′S	71°30′W
Quinto Romano, neigh., Italy	238c	45°29′N	9°05′E
Quionga, Moz.	217	10°37′S	40°30′E
Quiroga, Mex. (kē-rō′gä)	118	19°39′N	101°30′W
Quiroga, Spain (kē-rō′gä)	158	42°28′N	7°18′W
Quitauna, Braz.	234d	23°31′S	46°47′W
Quitman, Ga., U.S. (kwĭt′m*ă*n)	114	30°46′N	83°35′W
Quitman, Ms., U.S.	114	33°02′N	88°43′W
Quito, Ec. (kē′tō)	130	0°17′S	78°32′W
Qumbu, S. Afr. (kȯm′bo͞o)	213c	31°10′S	28°48′E
Quorn, Austl. (kwôrn)	204	32°20′S	138°00′E
Qurayyah, Wādī, r., Egypt	181a	30°08′N	34°27′E
Qūsmūryn Köli, l., Kaz.	169	52°30′N	64°15′E
Qutang, China (chyo͞o-täŋ)	190	32°33′N	120°07′E
Quthing, Leso.	213c	30°35′S	27°42′E
Quxian, China (chyo͞o-shyĕn)	189	28°58′N	118°58′E
Quxian, China	193	30°40′N	106°48′E
Quzhou, China (chyoō-jō)	190	36°47′N	114°58′E
Qyzylorda, Kaz.	169	44°58′N	65°45′E

R

PLACE (Pronunciation)	PAGE	LAT.	LONG.
Raab (Raba), r., Eur. (räp)	154	46°55′N	15°55′E
Raadt, neigh., Ger.	236	51°24′N	6°56′E
Raahe, Fin. (rä′ĕ)	146	64°39′N	24°22′E
Raasdorf, Aus.	239e	48°15′N	16°34′E
Rab, i., Yugo. (räb)	160	44°45′N	14°40′E
Raba, Indon.	196	8°32′S	118°49′E
Raba (Raab), r., Eur.	155	47°28′N	17°12′E
Rabat, Mor. (rȧ-bät′)	210	33°59′N	6°47′W
Rabaul, Pap. N. Gui. (rä′boul)	197	4°15′S	152°19′E
Rābigh, Sau. Ar.	185	22°48′N	39°01′E
Raby, Eng., U.K.	237a	53°19′N	3°02′W
Raccoon, r., Ia., U.S. (ră-ko͞on′)	103	42°07′N	94°45′W
Raccoon Cay, i., Bah.	123	22°25′N	75°50′W
Race, Cape, c., Can. (rās)	93	46°40′N	53°10′W
Raceview, S. Afr.	244b	26°17′S	28°08′E
Rachado, Cape, c., Malay.	181b	2°26′N	101°29′E
Racibórz, Pol. (rä-chē′bo͞ozh)	155	50°06′N	18°14′E
Racine, Wi., U.S. (r*ȧ*-sēn′)	97	42°43′N	87°49′W
Raco, Mi., U.S. (r*ȧ* cō)	107k	46°22′N	84°43′W
Rădăuţi, Rom.	149	47°53′N	25°55′E
Radcliffe, Eng., U.K. (răd′klĭf)	144a	53°34′N	2°20′W
Radevormwald, Ger. (rä′dĕ-fōrm-väld)	157c	51°12′N	7°22′E
Radford, Va., U.S. (răd′fẽrd)	115	37°06′N	81°33′W
Rādhanpur, India	186	23°57′N	71°38′E
Radium, S. Afr. (rā′dĭ-*ŭ*m)	218d	25°06′S	28°18′E
Radlett, Eng., U.K.	235	51°42′N	0°20′W
Radnor, Pa., U.S.	229b	40°02′N	75°21′W
Radom, Pol. (rä′dôm)	147	51°24′N	21°11′E
Radomir, Bul. (rä′dô-mêr)	161	42°33′N	22°58′E
Radomsko, Pol. (rä-dôm′skô)	147	51°04′N	19°27′E
Radomyshl, Ukr. (rä-dô-mēsh″l)	167	50°30′N	29°13′E
Radul′, Ukr. (rä′do͞ol)	163	51°52′N	30°46′E
Radviliškis, Lith. (räd′vē-lēsh′kēs)	153	55°49′N	23°31′E
Radwah, Jabal, mtn., Sau. Ar.	182	24°44′N	38°14′E
Radzyń Podlaski, Pol. (räd′zēn-y′ pŭd-lä′skĭ)	155	51°49′N	22°40′E
Raeford, N.C., U.S. (rā′fẽrd)	115	34°57′N	79°15′W
Raesfeld, Ger. (r*ăz*′fĕld)	157c	51°46′N	6°50′E
Raeside, l., Austl. (rā′sīd)	202	29°20′S	122°30′E
Rae Strait, strt., Can. (rā)	84	68°40′N	95°03′W
Rafaela, Arg. (rä-fä-ā′lä)	132	31°15′S	61°21′W
Rafael Castillo, Arg.	233d	34°42′S	58°37′W
Rafah, Pak. (rä′fä)	181a	31°14′N	34°12′E
Rafsanjān, Iran	182	30°45′N	56°30′E
Raft, r., Id., U.S. (răft)	105	42°20′N	113°17′W
Ragay, Phil. (rä-gī′)	197a	13°49′N	122°45′E
Ragay Gulf, b., Phil.	197a	13°44′N	122°38′E
Ragunda, Swe. (rä-gón′dä)	152	63°07′N	16°24′E
Ragusa, Italy (rä-go͞o′sä)	148	36°58′N	14°41′E
Rahm, neigh., Ger.	236	51°21′N	6°47′E
Rahnsdorf, neigh., Ger.	238a	52°26′N	13°42′E
Rahway, N.J., U.S. (rô′wā)	100a	40°37′N	74°16′W
Rāichūr, India (rä′ē-cho͞or′)	183	16°23′N	77°18′E
Raigarh, India (rī′gŭr)	183	21°57′N	83°32′E
Rainbow Bridge National Monument, rec., Ut., U.S. (rān′bō)	109	37°05′N	111°00′W
Rainbow City, Pan.	116a	9°20′N	79°53′W
Rainford, Eng., U.K.	237a	53°30′N	2°48′W
Rainhill, Eng., U.K.	237a	53°26′N	2°46′W
Rainhill Stoops, Eng., U.K.	237a	53°24′N	2°45′W
Rainier, Or., U.S.	106c	46°05′N	122°56′W
Rainier, Mount, mtn., Wa., U.S. (rā-nēr′)	96	46°52′N	121°46′W
Rainy, r., N.A.	97	48°50′N	94°41′W

PRONOUNCING INDEX

Rainy Lake–Remiremont 337

PLACE (Pronunciation)	PAGE	LAT.	LONG.
Rainy Lake, l., N.A. (rān'ē)	85	48°43'N	94°29'W
Rainy River, Can.	85	48°43'N	94°29'W
Raipur, India (rä'jŭ-bōō-rē')	186	21°25'N	81°37'E
Raisin, r., Mi., U.S. (rā'zĭn)	98	42°00'N	83°35'W
Raitan, N.J., U.S. (rā-tăn)	100a	40°34'N	74°40'W
Rājahmundry, India (räj-ŭ-mŭn'drē)	183	17°03'N	81°51'E
Rajang, r., Malay.	196	2°10'N	113°30'E
Rājapālaiyam, India	187	9°30'N	77°33'E
Rājasthān, state, India (rä'jŭs-tän)	183	26°00'N	72°00'E
Rājkot, India (räj'kōt)	183	22°20'N	70°48'E
Rājpur, India	186a	22°24'N	88°25'E
Rājpur, neigh., India	240d	28°41'N	77°12'E
Rājshāhi, Bngl.	183	24°26'S	88°39'E
Rakhiv, Ukr.	155	48°02'N	24°13'E
Rakh'oya, Russia (räk'yȧ)	172c	60°06'N	30°50'E
Rakitnoye, Russia (rȧ-kēt'nô-yĕ)	167	50°51'N	35°53'E
Rákoscsaba, neigh., Hung.	239g	47°29'N	19°17'E
Rákoshegy, neigh., Hung.	239g	47°28'N	19°14'E
Rákoskeresztúr, neigh., Hung.	239g	47°29'N	19°15'E
Rákosliget, neigh., Hung.	239g	47°30'N	19°16'E
Rákospalota, neigh., Hung.	239g	47°34'N	19°08'E
Rákosszentmihály, neigh., Hung.	239g	47°32'N	19°11'E
Rakovník, Czech Rep.	154	50°07'N	13°45'E
Rakvere, Est. (rȧk'vĕ-rĕ)	166	59°22'N	26°14'E
Raleigh, N.C., U.S.	97	35°45'N	78°39'W
Ram, r., Can.	87	52°10'N	115°05'W
Rama, Nic. (rä'mä)	121	12°11'N	84°14'W
Ramallo, Arg. (rä-mä'l-yô)	129c	33°28'S	60°02'W
Ramanāthapuram, India	187	9°13'N	78°52'E
Rambouillet, Fr. (rän-bōō-yĕ')	156	48°39'N	1°49'E
Rame Head, c., S. Afr.	213c	31°48'S	29°22'E
Ramenka, neigh., Russia	239b	55°41'N	37°30'E
Ramenskoye, Russia (rá'mĕn-skô-yĕ)	162	55°34'N	38°15'E
Ramlat as Sab'atayn, reg., Asia	182	16°08'N	45°15'E
Ramm, Jabal, mtn., Jord.	181a	29°37'N	35°32'E
Râmnicu Sărat, Rom.	149	45°24'N	27°06'E
Râmnicu Vâlcea, Rom.	161	45°07'N	24°22'E
Ramos, Mex. (rä'mōs)	118	22°46'N	101°52'W
Ramos, r., Nig.	215	5°10'N	5°40'E
Ramos Arizpe, Mex. (ä-rēz'pȧ)	112	25°33'N	100°57'W
Rampart, Ak., U.S. (răm'pärt)	95	65°28'N	150°18'W
Rampo Mountains, mts., N.J., U.S. (răm'pō)	100a	41°06'N	72°12'W
Rāmpur, India (räm'pōōr)	183	28°53'N	79°03'E
Ramree Island, i., Myanmar (răm'rē')	196	19°01'N	93°23'E
Ramsayville, Can. (răm'zē vĭl)	83c	45°23'N	75°34'W
Ramsbottom, Eng., U.K. (rămz'bŏt-ŭm)	144a	53°39'N	2°20'W
Ramsden Heath, Eng., U.K.	235	51°38'N	0°28'E
Ramsey, I. of Man (răm'zē)	150	54°20'N	4°25'W
Ramsey, N.J., U.S.	100a	41°03'N	74°09'W
Ramsey Lake, l., Can.	90	47°15'N	82°16'W
Ramsgate, Austl.	243a	33°59'S	151°08'E
Ramsgate, Eng., U.K. (rămz''gāt)	151	51°19'N	1°20'E
Ramu, r., Pap. N. Gui. (rä'mōō)	197	5°35'S	145°16'E
Rancagua, Chile (rän-kä'gwä)	132	34°10'S	70°43'W
Rance, r., Fr. (räns)	156	48°17'N	2°30'W
Rānchī, India	183	23°21'N	85°20'E
Ranchleigh, Md., U.S.	229c	39°22'N	76°40'W
Rancho Boyeros, Cuba (rä'n-chô-bô-yĕ'rôs)	123a	23°00'N	82°23'W
Rancho Palos Verdes, Ca., U.S.	232	33°45'N	118°24'W
Randallstown, Md., U.S. (răn'dălz-toun)	100e	39°22'N	76°48'W
Randburg, S. Afr.	244b	26°06'S	27°59'E
Randers, Den. (rän'ĕrs)	146	56°28'N	10°03'E
Randfontein, S. Afr. (rănt'fŏn-tān)	213b	26°10'S	27°42'E
Randleman, N.C., U.S. (răn'd'l-măn)	115	35°49'N	79°50'W
Randolph, Ma., U.S. (răn'dôlf)	93a	42°10'N	71°03'W
Randolph, Ne., U.S.	102	42°22'N	97°22'W
Randolph, Vt., U.S.	99	43°55'N	72°40'W
Random Island, i., Can. (răn'dŭm)	93	48°12'N	53°25'W
Randsfjorden, Nor.	152	60°35'N	10°10'E
Randwick, Austl.	201b	33°55'S	151°15'E
Ranérou, Sen.	214	15°18'N	13°58'W
Rangeley, Me., U.S. (rānj'lē)	92	44°56'N	70°38'W
Rangeley, l., Me., U.S.	92	45°00'N	70°25'W
Ranger, Tx., U.S. (rān'jēr)	96	32°26'N	98°41'W
Rangia, India	186	26°32'N	91°39'E
Rangoon (Yangon), Myanmar (răŋ-gōōn')	183	16°46'N	96°09'E
Rangpur, Bngl. (rŭng'pōōr)	183	25°48'N	89°19'E
Rangsang, i., Indon. (räng'säng')	181b	0°53'N	103°05'E
Rangsdorf, Ger. (rängs'dōrf)	145b	52°17'N	13°25'E
Ranholas, Port.	238d	38°47'N	9°22'W
Rānīganj, India (rä-nē-gŭnj')	186	23°40'N	87°08'E
Rankin, Pa., U.S.	230b	40°25'N	79°53'W
Rankin Inlet, b., Can. (răŋ'kĕn)	85	62°45'N	94°27'W
Ranova, r., Russia (rä'nô-vȧ)	162	53°55'N	40°03'E
Rantau, Malay.	181b	2°35'N	101°58'E
Rantekombola, Bulu, mtn., Indon.	196	3°22'S	119°50'E
Rantoul, Il., U.S. (răn-tōōl')	98	40°25'N	88°05'W
Raoyang, China (rou-yäŋ)	190	38°16'N	115°45'E
Rapallo, Italy (rä-päl'lō)	160	44°21'N	9°14'E
Rapel, r., Chile (rä-pål')	129b	34°05'S	71°30'W
Rapid, r., Mn., U.S. (răp'ĭd)	103	48°21'N	94°50'W
Rapid City, S.D., U.S.	96	44°06'N	103°14'W
Rapla, Est. (räp'lȧ)	153	59°02'N	24°46'E
Rappahannock, r., Va., U.S. (răp'ȧ-hăn'ŭk)	99	38°20'N	75°25'W
Raquette, l., N.Y., U.S. (răk'ĕt)	99	43°50'N	74°35'W
Raritan, r., N.J., U.S. (răr'ĭ-tăn)	100a	40°32'N	74°27'W
Rarotonga, Cook Is. (rä'rô-tŏŋ'gȧ)	2	20°40'S	163°00'W
Ra's an Naqb, Jord.	181a	30°00'N	35°29'E
Raşcov, Mol.	163	47°55'N	28°51'E
Ras Dashen Terara, mtn., Eth. (räs dä-shän')	211	12°49'N	38°14'E
Raseiniai, Lith. (rä-syā'nyī)	153	55°23'N	23°04'E
Rashayya, Leb.	181a	33°30'N	35°50'E
Rashīd, Egypt (rȧ-shēd') (rō-zĕt'ȧ)	184	31°22'N	30°25'E
Rashīd, Masabb, mth., Egypt	218b	31°30'N	29°58'E
Rashkina, Russia (rásh'kĭ-nȧ)	172a	59°57'N	61°30'E
Rasht, Iran	182	37°13'N	49°45'E
Raška, Yugo. (räsh'kȧ)	161	43°16'N	20°40'E
Rasskazovo, Russia (räs-kä'sô-vô)	167	52°40'N	41°40'E
Rastatt, Ger. (rä-shtät)	154	48°51'N	8°12'E
Rastes, Russia (rás'tĕs)	172a	59°24'N	58°49'E
Rastunovo, Russia (rás-tōō'nô-vô)	172b	55°15'N	37°50'E
Ratangarh, India (rŭ-tŭn'gŭr)	186	28°10'N	74°30'E
Ratcliff, Tx., U.S. (răt'klĭf)	113	31°22'N	95°09'W
Rath, neigh., Ger.	236	51°17'N	6°49'E
Rathenow, Ger. (rä'tĕ-nō)	154	52°36'N	12°20'E
Rathlin Island, i., N. Ire., U.K. (răth-lĭn)	150	55°18'N	6°13'W
Rathmecke, Ger.	236	51°15'N	7°38'E
Ratingen, Ger. (rä'tēn-gĕn)	157c	51°18'N	6°51'E
Rat Islands, is., Ak., U.S. (răt)	95a	51°35'N	176°48'E
Ratlām, India	186	23°19'N	75°05'E
Ratnāgiri, India	187	17°04'N	73°24'E
Raton, N.M., U.S. (rȧ-tōn')	96	36°52'N	104°26'W
Rattlesnake Creek, r., Or., U.S. (răt''l snāk)	104	42°38'N	117°39'W
Rättvik, Swe. (rĕt'vĕk)	152	60°54'N	15°07'E
Rauch, Arg. (rá'ōōch)	132	36°47'S	59°05'W
Raufoss, Nor. (rou'fôs)	152	60°44'N	10°30'E
Raúl Soares, Braz. (rä-ōō'l-sôá'rĕs)	129a	20°05'S	42°28'W
Rauma, Fin. (rä'ô-mȧ)	146	61°07'N	21°31'E
Rauna, Lat. (rȧŭ'nȧ)	153	57°21'N	25°31'E
Raurkela, India	183	22°15'N	84°53'E
Rautalampi, Fin. (rä'ōō-tē-läm'pô)	153	62°39'N	26°25'E
Rava-Rus'ka, Ukr.	155	50°14'N	23°40'E
Ravenna, Italy (rä-vĕn'nä)	148	44°27'N	12°13'E
Ravenna, Ne., U.S. (rȧ-vĕn'ȧ)	102	41°20'N	98°50'W
Ravenna, Oh., U.S.	98	41°10'N	81°20'W
Ravensburg, Ger. (rä'vĕns-bōōrgh)	154	47°48'N	9°35'E
Ravensdale, Wa., U.S. (rā'vĕnz-dāl)	106a	47°22'N	121°58'W
Ravensthorpe, Austl. (rā'vĕns-thôrp)	202	33°30'S	120°20'E
Ravenswood, S. Afr.	244b	26°11'S	28°15'E
Ravenswood, W.V., U.S. (rā'vĕnz-wŏŏd)	98	38°55'N	81°50'W
Ravensworth, Va., U.S.	229d	38°48'N	77°13'W
Ravenwood, Va., U.S.	229d	38°52'N	77°09'W
Rāwalpindi, Pak. (rä-wŭl-pēn'dē)	183	33°40'N	73°10'E
Rawa Mazowiecka, Pol.	155	51°46'N	20°17'E
Rawāndūz, Iraq	182	36°37'N	44°30'E
Rawicz, Pol. (rä'vēch)	154	51°36'N	16°51'E
Rawlina, Austl. (rôr-lĕn ȧ)	202	31°13'S	125°45'E
Rawlins, Wy., U.S. (rô'lĭnz)	96	41°46'N	107°15'W
Rawson, Arg.	129c	34°36'S	60°03'W
Rawson, Arg. (rô'sŭn)	132	43°16'S	65°09'W
Rawtenstall, Eng., U.K. (rô'tĕn-stôl)	144a	53°42'N	2°17'W
Ray, Cape, c., Can. (rā)	85a	47°40'N	59°18'W
Raya, Bukit, mtn., Indon.	196	0°45'S	112°11'E
Raychikinsk, Russia (rī'chĭ-kēnsk)	171	49°52'N	129°17'E
Rayleigh, Eng., U.K. (rā'lē)	144b	51°35'N	0°36'E
Raymond, Can. (rā'mŭnd)	87	49°27'N	112°39'W
Raymond, Wa., U.S.	104	46°41'N	123°42'W
Raymondville, Tx., U.S. (rā'mŭnd-vĭl)	111	26°30'N	97°46'W
Ray Mountains, mts., Ak., U.S.	95a	65°40'N	151°45'W
Rayne, La., U.S. (rān)	113	30°12'N	92°15'W
Rayón, Mex. (rä-yōn')	118	21°49'N	99°39'W
Rayton, S. Afr. (rā'tŭn)	213b	25°45'S	28°33'E
Raytown, Mo., U.S. (rā'toun)	107f	39°01'N	94°48'W
Rayville, La., U.S. (rā-vĭl)	113	32°28'N	91°46'W
Raz, Pointe du, c., Fr. (pwänt dü rä)	147	48°02'N	4°43'W
Razdan, Arm.	168	40°30'N	44°46'E
Razdol'noye, Russia (räz-dôl'nô-yĕ)	194	43°38'N	131°58'E
Razgrad, Bul.	149	43°32'N	26°32'E
Razlog, Bul. (räz'lôk)	161	41°54'N	23°32'E
Razorback Mountain, mtn., Can. (rā'zēr-băk)	86	51°35'N	124°42'W
Rea, r., Eng., U.K. (rē)	144a	52°25'N	2°31'W
Reaburn, Can. (rā'bûrn)	83f	50°06'N	97°53'W
Reading, Eng., U.K. (rĕd'ĭng)	147	51°25'N	0°58'W
Reading, Ma., U.S.	93a	42°32'N	71°07'W
Reading, Mi., U.S.	98	41°45'N	84°45'W
Reading, Oh., U.S.	101f	39°14'N	84°26'W
Reading, Pa., U.S.	97	40°20'N	75°55'W
Readville, neigh., Ma., U.S.	227a	42°14'N	71°08'W
Realengo, Braz. (rē-ä-län-gô)	129a	23°50'S	43°25'W
Real Felipe, Castillo, hist., Peru	233c	12°04'S	77°09'W
Rebel Hill, Pa., U.S.	229b	40°04'N	75°20'W
Rebiana, Libya	211	24°10'N	22°03'E
Rebun, i., Japan (rē'bōōn)	194	45°25'N	140°54'E
Recanati, Italy (rā-kä-nä'tē)	160	43°25'N	13°35'E
Recherche, Archipelago of the, is., Austl. (rē-shârsh')	202	34°17'S	122°30'E
Rechitsa, Bela. (ryĕ'chĕt-sȧ)	167	52°22'N	30°24'E
Recife, Braz. (rå-sē'fē)	131	8°09'S	34°59'W
Recife, Kapp, c., S. Afr. (rå-sē'fē)	213c	34°03'S	25°43'E
Recklinghausen, Ger. (rĕk'lĭng-hou-zĕn)	157c	51°36'N	7°13'E
Recklinghausen Süd, neigh., Ger.	236	51°34'N	7°13'E
Reconquista, Arg. (rā-kôn-kēs'tä)	132	29°01'S	59°41'W
Reconquista, r., Arg.	233d	34°39'S	58°45'W
Rector, Ar., U.S. (rĕk'tēr)	111	36°16'N	90°21'W
Red, r., Asia	196	21°00'N	103°00'E
Red, r., N.A. (rĕd)	96	48°00'N	97°00'W
Red, r., U.S.	97	31°40'N	92°55'W
Red, r., Tn., U.S.	114	36°35'N	86°55'W
Red, North Fork, r., U.S.	110	35°20'N	100°08'W
Red, Prairie Dog Town Fork, r., U.S. (prā'rĭ)	110	34°54'N	101°31'W
Red, Salt Fork, r., U.S.	110	35°04'N	100°31'W
Redan, Ga., U.S. (rē-dăn') (rĕd'ăn)	100c	33°44'N	84°09'W
Red Bank, N.J., U.S. (băngk)	100a	40°21'N	74°06'W
Red Bank National Park, N.J., U.S.	229b	39°52'N	75°10'W
Red Bluff Reservoir, res., Tx., U.S.	112	32°03'N	103°52'W
Redbridge, neigh., Eng., U.K.	235	51°34'N	0°05'E
Redby, Mn., Mn., U.S. (rĕd'bē)	103	47°52'N	94°55'W
Red Cedar, r., Wi., U.S. (sē'dēr)	103	45°03'N	91°48'W
Redcliff, Can. (rĕd'clĭf)	84	50°05'N	110°47'W
Redcliffe, Austl. (rĕd'clĭf)	204	27°20'S	153°12'E
Red Cliff Indian Reservation, I.R., Wi., U.S.	103	46°48'N	91°22'W
Red Cloud, Ne., U.S. (kloud)	110	40°06'N	98°32'W
Red Deer, Can. (dēr)	84	52°16'N	113°48'W
Red Deer, r., Can.	84	51°00'N	111°00'W
Red Deer, r., Can.	89	52°55'N	102°10'W
Red Deer Lake, l., Can.	89	52°58'N	101°28'W
Reddick, Il., U.S. (rĕd'dĭk)	101a	41°06'N	88°16'W
Redding, Ca., U.S. (rĕd'ĭng)	104	40°36'N	122°25'W
Reddish, Eng., U.K.	237b	53°26'N	2°09'W
Redenção da Serra, Braz. (rĕ-dĕn-soun-dä-sĕ'r-rä)	129a	23°17'S	45°31'W
Redfield, S.D., U.S. (rĕd'fēld)	102	44°53'N	98°30'W
Red Fish Bar, Tx., U.S.	113a	29°29'N	94°53'W
Redford, neigh., Mi., U.S.	230c	42°25'N	83°16'W
Redford Township, Mi., U.S.	230c	42°25'N	83°16'W
Red Hill, Ca., U.S.	232	33°45'N	117°48'W
Red Indian Lake, l., Can. (ĭn'dĭ-ăn)	85a	48°40'N	56°50'W
Red Lake, Can. (lāk)	85	51°02'N	93°49'W
Red Lake, r., Mn., U.S.	102	48°02'N	96°04'W
Red Lake Falls, Mn., U.S. (lăk fôls)	102	47°52'N	96°17'W
Red Lake Indian Reservation, I.R., Mn., U.S.	102	48°09'N	95°55'W
Redlands, Ca., U.S. (rĕd'lăndz)	107a	34°04'N	117°11'W
Red Lion, Pa., U.S. (lī'ŭn)	99	39°55'N	76°30'W
Red Lodge, Mt., U.S.	105	45°13'N	107°16'W
Redmond, Wa., U.S. (rĕd'mŭnd)	106a	47°40'N	122°07'W
Rednitz, r., Ger. (rĕd'nētz)	154	49°10'N	11°00'E
Red Oak, Ia., U.S. (ōk)	102	41°00'N	95°12'W
Redon, Fr. (rē-dôn')	156	47°42'N	2°03'W
Redonda, Isla, i., Braz. (ē's-lä-rĕ-dô'n-dä)	132b	23°05'S	43°11'W
Redonda Island, i., Antig. (rĕ-dŏn'dȧ)	121b	16°55'N	62°28'W
Redondela, Spain (rā-dhōn-dā'lä)	158	42°16'N	8°34'W
Redondo, Port. (rā-dôn'dō)	158	38°40'N	7°32'W
Redondo, Wa., U.S. (rē-dŏn'dō)	106a	47°21'N	122°19'W
Redondo Beach, Ca., U.S.	107a	33°50'N	118°23'W
Red Pass, Can. (pȧs)	87	52°59'N	118°59'W
Red Rock, r., Mt., U.S.	105	44°54'N	112°44'W
Red Sea, sea	182	23°15'N	37°00'E
Redstone, Can. (rĕd'stōn)	86	52°08'N	123°42'W
Red Sucker Lake, l., Can. (sŭk'ēr)	89	54°09'N	93°40'W
Redwater, r., Mt., U.S.	105	47°37'N	105°25'W
Red Willow Creek, r., Ne., U.S.	110	40°34'N	100°48'W
Red Wing, Mn., U.S.	103	44°34'N	92°35'W
Redwood City, Ca., U.S. (rĕd' wŏŏd)	106b	37°29'N	122°13'W
Redwood Falls, Mn., U.S.	102	44°32'N	95°06'W
Redwood Valley, Ca., U.S.	108	39°15'N	123°12'W
Ree, Lough, l., Ire. (lŏk'rē')	146	53°30'N	7°45'W
Reed City, Mi., U.S. (rēd)	98	43°50'N	85°35'W
Reed Lake, l., Can.	89	54°37'N	100°30'W
Reedley, Ca., U.S. (rēd'lē)	108	36°37'N	119°27'W
Reedsburg, Wi., U.S. (rēdz'bûrg)	103	43°32'N	90°01'W
Reedsport, Or., U.S. (rēdz'pôrt)	104	43°42'N	124°08'W
Reelfoot Lake, res., Tn., U.S. (rēl'fŏŏt)	114	36°18'N	89°20'W
Rees, Ger. (rĕz)	157c	51°46'N	6°25'E
Reeves, Mount, mtn., Austl. (rēv's)	204	33°50'S	149°56'E
Reform, Al., U.S. (rē-fôrm')	114	33°23'N	88°00'W
Refugio, Tx., U.S. (rå-fōō'hyō) (rē-fū'jō)	113	28°18'N	97°15'W
Rega, r., Pol. (rĕ-gä)	154	53°48'N	15°30'E
Regen, r., Ger. (rā'ghĕn)	154	49°09'N	12°21'E
Regensburg, Ger. (rā'ghĕns-bŏrgh)	147	49°02'N	12°06'E
Regents Park, Austl.	243a	33°53'S	151°02'E
Regent's Park, pt. of i., Eng., U.K.	235	51°32'N	0°09'W
Reggio, La., U.S. (rĕg'jĭ-ō)	100d	29°50'N	89°46'W
Reggio di Calabria, Italy (rĕ'jô dē kä-lä'brē-ä)	149	38°07'N	15°42'E
Reggio nell' Emilia, Italy	148	44°43'N	10°34'E
Reghin, Rom. (rå-gēn')	155	46°47'N	24°44'E
Regina, Can. (rē-jī'nȧ)	88	50°25'N	104°39'W
Regla, Cuba (răg'lä)	122	23°08'N	82°20'W
Regnitz, r., Ger. (rĕg'nētz)	154	49°50'N	10°55'E
Rego Park, neigh., N.Y., U.S.	228	40°44'N	73°52'W
Reguengos de Monsaraz, Port.	158	38°26'N	7°30'W
Rehoboth, Nmb.	212	23°10'S	17°15'E
Reḥovot, Isr.	181a	31°53'N	34°49'E
Reichenbach, Ger. (rī'kĕn-bäk)	154	50°36'N	12°18'E
Reidsville, N.C., U.S. (rēdz'vĭl)	115	36°20'N	79°37'W
Reigate, Eng., U.K. (rī'gāt)	150	51°12'N	0°12'W
Reims, Fr. (răns)	142	49°16'N	4°00'E
Reina Adelaida, Archipiélago, is., Chile	132	52°00'S	74°15'W
Reinbeck, Ia., U.S. (rīn'bĕk)	103	42°22'N	92°34'W
Reindeer, l., Can. (rān'dēr)	84	57°36'N	101°23'W
Reindeer, r., Can.	88	55°45'N	103°30'W
Reindeer Island, i., Can.	89	52°25'N	98°00'W
Reinosa, Spain (rå-ē-nō'sä)	158	43°01'N	4°08'W
Reisholz, neigh., Ger.	236	51°11'N	6°52'E
Reistertown, Md., U.S. (rēs'tēr-toun)	100e	39°28'N	76°50'W
Reitz, S. Afr.	218d	27°48'S	28°25'E
Rema, Jabal, mtn., Yemen	182	14°13'N	44°38'E
Rembau, Malay.	181b	2°36'N	102°06'E
Remedios, Col. (rĕ-mĕ'dyôs)	130a	7°03'N	74°42'W
Remedios, Cuba (rā-mā'dhē-ōs)	122	22°30'N	79°35'W
Remedios, Pan. (rĕ-mĕ'dyôs)	121	8°14'N	81°46'W
Remedios de Escalada, neigh., Arg.	233d	34°43'S	58°23'W
Remiremont, Fr. (rē-mēr-môn')	157	48°01'N	6°35'E

ng-sing; ŋ-baŋk; n-nasalized n; nŏd; cŏmmit; ōld; ôbey; ôrder; oi-boil; fōōd; ŏŏ-as oo in foot; ou-out; s-soft; sh-dish; th-thin; pūre; ūnite; ûrn; stŭd; circŭs; ü-as in French tu; '-indeterminate vowel.

PLACE (Pronunciation)	PAGE	LAT.	LONG.
Rempang, i., Indon.	181b	0°51'N	104°04'E
Remscheid, Ger. (rĕm'shīt)	157c	51°10'N	7°11'E
Rena, Nor.	152	61°08'N	11°17'E
Renca, Chile	234b	33°24'S	70°44'W
Renca, Cerro, mtn., Chile	234b	33°23'S	70°43'W
Rendova, i., Sol. Is. (rĕn'dô-vȧ)	203	8°38'S	156°26'E
Rendsburg, Ger. (rĕnts'bòrgh)	154	54°19'N	9°39'E
Renfrew, Can. (rĕn'frōō)	85	45°30'N	76°30'W
Rengam, Malay. (rĕn'gäm')	181b	1°53'N	103°24'E
Rengo, Chile (rĕn'gō)	129b	34°22'S	70°50'W
Reni, Ukr. (ran')	163	45°26'N	28°18'E
Renmark, Austl. (rĕn'märk)	202	34°10'S	140°50'E
Rennel, i., Sol. Is. (rĕn-nĕl')	203	11°50'S	160°38'E
Rennes, Fr. (rĕn)	142	48°07'N	1°02'W
Reno, Nv., U.S. (rē'nō)	96	39°32'N	119°49'W
Reno, r., Italy (rā'nô)	160	44°10'N	10°55'E
Renovo, Pa., U.S. (rē-nō'vō)	99	41°20'N	77°50'W
Renqiu, China (rŭn-chyô)	190	38°44'N	116°05'E
Rensselaer, In., U.S. (rĕn'sē-lâr)	98	41°00'N	87°10'W
Rensselaer, N.Y., U.S. (rĕn'sē-lâr)	99	42°40'N	73°45'W
Rentchler, Il., U.S. (rĕnt'chlẽr)	107e	38°30'N	89°52'W
Renton, Wa., U.S. (rĕn'tŭn)	106a	47°29'N	122°13'W
Repentigny, Can.	83a	45°47'N	73°26'W
Republic, Al., U.S. (rē-pŭb'lĭk)	100h	33°37'N	86°54'W
Republic, Wa., U.S.	104	48°38'N	118°44'W
Republican, r., U.S.	96	40°15'N	100°00'W
Republican, South Fork, r., Co., U.S. (rē-pŭb'lĭ-kăn)	110	39°35'N	102°28'W
Repulse Bay, b., Austl. (rē-pŭls')	203	20°56'S	149°22'E
Requena, Spain (rå-kā'nä)	148	39°29'N	1°03'W
Reseda, neigh., Ca., U.S.	232	34°12'N	118°31'W
Resende, Braz. (rĕ-sĕ'n-dĕ)	129a	22°30'S	44°26'W
Resende Costa, Braz. (kôs-tä)	129a	20°55'S	44°12'W
Reservoir, Austl.	243b	37°43'S	145°00'E
Reshetylivka, Ukr.	163	49°34'N	34°04'E
Resistencia, Arg. (rā-sēs-tĕn'syä)	132	27°24'S	58°54'W
Reşiţa, Rom. (rå'shē-tȧ)	161	45°18'N	21°56'E
Resolute, Can. (rĕz-ō-lūt')	82	74°41'N	95°00'W
Resolution, i., Can. (rĕz-ō-lū'shŭn)	85	61°30'N	63°58'W
Resolution Island, i., N.Z. (rĕz-ŏl-ûshûn)	203a	45°43'S	166°20'E
Resse, neigh., Ger.	236	51°34'N	7°07'E
Restigouche, r., Can.	92	47°35'N	67°35'W
Restrepo, Col. (rĕs-trĕ'pô)	130a	3°49'N	76°31'W
Restrepo, Col.	130a	4°16'N	73°32'W
Retalhuleu, Guat. (rā-tāl-ōō-lān')	120	14°31'N	91°41'W
Rethel, Fr. (r-tl')	156	49°34'N	4°20'E
Réthimnon, Grc.	160a	35°21'N	24°30'E
Retie, Bel.	145a	51°16'N	5°08'E
Retiro, Parque del, rec., Spain	238b	40°25'N	3°41'W
Retsil, Wa., U.S. (rĕt'sĭl)	106a	47°33'N	122°37'W
Reunion, dep., Afr. (rā-ü-nyôn')	3	21°06'S	55°36'E
Reus, Spain (rā'ōōs)	148	41°08'N	1°05'E
Reutlingen, Ger. (roit'lĭng-ĕn)	154	48°29'N	9°14'E
Reutov, Russia (rĕ-ōō'ôf)	172b	55°45'N	37°52'E
Revda, Russia (ryâv'dá)	172a	56°48'N	59°57'E
Revelstoke, Can. (rĕv'ĕl-stōk)	84	51°00'N	118°12'W
Reventazón, Río, r., C.R. (rå-vĕn-tä-zōn')	121	10°10'N	83°30'W
Revere, Ma., U.S. (rē-vēr')	93a	42°24'N	71°01'W
Revesby, Austl.	243a	33°57'S	151°01'E
Revillagigedo, Islas, is., Mex. (ĕ's-läs-rē-vēl-yä-hĕ'gĕ-dô)	116	18°45'N	111°00'W
Revillagigedo Chan, Ak., U.S. (rē-vĭl'ȧ-gĭ-gē'dō)	86	55°10'N	131°13'W
Revillagigedo Island, i., Ak., U.S.	86	55°35'N	131°23'W
Revin, Fr. (rē-văɴ)	156	49°56'N	4°34'E
Rewa, India (rā'wä)	183	24°41'N	81°11'E
Rewāri, India	186	28°19'N	76°39'E
Rexburg, Id., U.S. (rĕks'bûrg)	105	43°50'N	111°48'W
Rey, Iran	185	35°35'N	51°25'E
Rey, I., Mex. (rā)	112	27°00'N	103°33'W
Rey, Isla del, i., Pan. (ē's-lä-dĕl-rā'ē)	121	8°20'N	78°40'W
Reyes, Bol. (rā'yĕs)	130	14°19'S	67°16'W
Reyes, Point, c., Ca., U.S.	108	38°00'N	123°00'W
Reykjanes, c., Ice. (rā'kyá-nĕs)	142	63°37'N	24°33'W
Reykjavík, Ice. (rā'kyá-vĕk)	142	64°09'N	21°39'W
Reynosa, Mex. (rā-ē-nō'sä)	112	26°05'N	98°21'W
Rēzekne, Lat. (rå'zĕk-nĕ)	166	56°31'N	27°19'E
Rezh, Russia (rĕzh')	172a	57°22'N	61°23'E
Rezina, Mol. (ryĕzh'ĕ-nĭ)	163	47°44'N	28°56'E
Rhaetian Alps, mts., Eur.	154	46°30'N	10°00'E
Rhaetien Alps, mts., Eur.	160	46°22'N	10°33'E
Rheinberg, Ger. (rīn'bĕrgh)	157c	51°33'N	6°37'E
Rheine, Ger. (rī'nĕ)	154	52°16'N	7°26'E
Rheinen, Ger.	236	51°27'N	7°38'E
Rheinhausen, Ger.	236	51°24'N	6°44'E
Rhein-Herne-Kanal, can., Ger.	236	51°27'N	6°47'E
Rheinkamp, Ger.	157c	51°30'N	6°37'E
Rheinland-Pfalz (Rhineland-Palatinate), hist. reg., Ger.	154	50°05'N	6°40'E
Rheydt, Ger. (rĕ'yt)	157c	51°10'N	6°28'E
Rhin, r., Ger. (rēn)	145b	52°52'N	12°49'E
Rhine, r., Eur.	142	50°34'N	7°21'E
Rhinelander, Wi., U.S. (rīn'lăn-dẽr)	103	45°39'N	89°25'W
Rhin Kanal, can., Ger. (rēn kä-näl')	145b	52°47'N	12°40'E
Rhiou, r., Alg.	159	35°45'N	1°18'E
Rho, Italy	238c	45°32'N	9°02'E
Rhode Island, state, U.S. (rōd ī'lănd)	97	41°35'N	71°40'W
Rhode Island, i., R.I., U.S.	100b	41°31'N	71°14'W
Rhodes, Austl.	243a	33°50'S	151°05'E
Rhodes, S. Afr. (rōdz)	213c	30°48'S	27°56'E
Rhodes, Eng., U.K.	237b	53°33'N	2°14'W
Rhodes *see* Ródhos, i., Grc.	142	36°00'N	28°29'E
Rhodesia *see* Zimbabwe, nation, Afr.	212	17°50'S	29°30'E
Rhodon, Fr.	237c	48°43'N	2°04'E
Rhodope Mountains, mts., Eur. (rô'dô-pē)	142	42°00'N	24°08'E
Rhondda, Wales, U.K. (rŏn'dhá)	150	51°40'N	3°40'W
Rhône, r., Fr. (rōn)	142	44°30'N	4°45'E
Rhoon, Neth.	145a	51°52'N	4°24'E
Rhum, i., Scot., U.K. (rŭm)	150	57°00'N	6°20'W
Riachão, Braz. (rē-ä-chouɴ')	131	7°15'S	46°30'W
Rialto, Ca., U.S. (rē-ăl'tō)	107a	34°06'N	117°23'W
Riau, prov., Indon.	181b	0°56'N	101°25'E
Riau, Kepulauan, i., Indon.	196	0°30'N	104°55'E
Riau, Selat, strt., Indon.	181b	0°40'N	104°27'E
Riaza, r., Spain (rē-ä'thä)	158	41°25'N	3°25'W
Ribadavia, Spain (rē-bä-dhä'vē-ä)	158	42°18'N	8°06'W
Ribadeo, Spain (rē-bä-dhā'ō)	158	43°32'N	7°05'W
Ribadesella, Spain (rē'bä-dā-sāl'yä)	158	43°30'N	5°02'W
Ribe, Den. (rē'bĕ)	152	55°20'N	8°45'E
Ribeirão Prêto, Braz. (rē-bā-rouɴ-prē'tô)	131	21°11'S	47°47'W
Ribera, N.M., U.S. (rē-bē'rä)	110	35°23'N	105°27'W
Riberalta, Bol. (rē-bā-räl'tä)	130	11°06'S	66°02'W
Rib Lake, Wi., U.S. (rĭb lāk)	103	45°20'N	90°11'W
Rîbniţa, Mol.	163	47°45'N	29°02'E
Rice, l., Can.	91	44°05'N	78°10'W
Rice Lake, Wi., U.S.	103	45°30'N	91°44'W
Rice Lake, l., Mn., U.S.	107g	45°10'N	93°09'W
Richards Island, i., Can. (rĭch'ẽrds)	95	69°45'N	135°30'W
Richards Landing, Can. (lănd'ĭng)	107k	46°18'N	84°02'W
Richardson, Tx., U.S. (rĭch'ẽrd-sŭn)	107c	32°56'N	96°44'W
Richardson, Wa., U.S.	106a	48°27'N	122°54'W
Richardson Mountains, mts., Can.	84	66°58'N	136°19'W
Richardson Mountains, mts., N.Z.	205	44°50'S	168°30'E
Richardson Park, De., U.S. (pärk)	99	39°45'N	75°35'W
Richelieu, r., Can. (rēsh'lyû')	91	45°05'N	73°25'W
Richfield, Mn., U.S.	107g	44°53'N	93°17'W
Richfield, Oh., U.S.	101d	41°14'N	81°38'W
Richfield, Ut., U.S.	109	38°45'N	112°05'W
Richford, Vt., U.S. (rĭch'fẽrd)	99	45°00'N	72°35'W
Rich Hill, Mo., U.S. (rĭch hĭl)	111	38°05'N	94°21'W
Richibucto, Can. (rĭ-chĭ-bŭk'tō)	85	46°41'N	64°52'W
Richland, Ga., U.S. (rĭch'lănd)	114	32°05'N	84°40'W
Richland, Wa., U.S.	104	46°17'N	119°19'W
Richland Center, Wi., U.S. (sĕn'tẽr)	103	43°20'N	90°25'W
Richmond, Austl.	201b	33°36'S	150°45'E
Richmond, Austl. (rĭch'mŭnd)	203	20°47'S	143°14'E
Richmond, Austl.	243b	37°49'S	145°00'E
Richmond, Can.	83c	45°12'N	75°49'W
Richmond, Can.	91	45°40'N	72°07'W
Richmond, S. Afr.	213c	29°52'S	30°17'E
Richmond, Il., U.S.	101a	42°29'N	88°18'W
Richmond, In., U.S.	98	39°50'N	85°00'W
Richmond, Ky., U.S.	98	37°45'N	84°20'W
Richmond, Mo., U.S.	111	39°16'N	93°58'W
Richmond, Tx., U.S.	113	29°35'N	95°45'W
Richmond, Ut., U.S.	105	41°55'N	111°50'W
Richmond, Va., U.S.	97	37°35'N	77°30'W
Richmond, neigh., Eng., U.K.	235	51°28'N	0°18'W
Richmond, neigh., N.J., U.S.	229b	39°59'N	75°06'W
Richmond Beach, Wa., U.S.	106a	47°47'N	122°23'W
Richmond Heights, Mo., U.S.	107e	38°38'N	90°20'W
Richmond Heights, Oh., U.S.	229a	41°33'N	81°29'W
Richmond Highlands, Wa., U.S.	106a	47°46'N	122°22'W
Richmond Hill, Can. (hĭl)	91	43°53'N	79°26'W
Richmondtown Restoration, pt. of i., N.Y., U.S.	228	40°34'N	74°09'W
Richmond Valley, neigh., N.Y., U.S.	228	40°31'N	74°13'W
Richton, Ms., U.S. (rĭch'tŭn)	114	31°20'N	89°54'W
Richwood, W.V., U.S. (rĭch'wŏod)	98	38°10'N	80°30'W
Ricketts Point, c., Austl.	243b	38°00'S	145°02'E
Rickmansworth, Eng., U.K.	235	51°39'N	0°29'W
Ridderkerk, Neth.	145a	51°52'N	4°35'E
Rideau, r., Can.	83c	45°17'N	75°41'W
Rideau Lake, l., Can. (rē-dō')	91	44°40'N	76°20'W
Ridge, Eng., U.K.	235	51°41'N	0°15'W
Ridgefield, Ct., U.S. (rĭj'fēld)	100a	41°16'N	73°30'W
Ridgefield, N.J., U.S.	228	40°50'N	74°00'W
Ridgefield, Wa., U.S.	106c	45°49'N	122°40'W
Ridgefield Park, N.J., U.S.	228	40°51'N	74°01'W
Ridgeway, Can. (rĭj'wā)	101c	42°53'N	79°02'W
Ridgewood, N.J., U.S. (rĭdj'wŏod)	100a	40°59'N	74°08'W
Ridgewood, neigh., N.Y., U.S.	228	40°42'N	73°53'W
Ridgway, Pa., U.S.	99	41°25'N	78°40'W
Riding Mountain, mtn., Can. (rīd'ĭng)	89	50°37'N	99°37'W
Riding Mountain National Park, rec., Can. (rīd'ĭng)	84	50°59'N	99°19'W
Riding Rocks, is., Bah.	122	25°20'N	79°10'W
Ridley Park, Pa., U.S.	229b	39°53'N	75°19'W
Riebeek-Oos, S. Afr.	213c	33°14'S	26°09'E
Ried, Aus. (rēd)	154	48°13'N	13°30'E
Riemke, neigh., Ger.	236	51°30'N	7°13'E
Riesa, Ger. (rē'zȧ)	154	51°17'N	13°17'E
Rieti, Italy (rē-ā'tē)	148	42°25'N	12°51'E
Rietvlei, S. Afr.	244b	26°18'S	28°03'E
Rievleidam, res., S. Afr.	213b	25°52'S	28°18'E
Riffe Lake, res., Wa., U.S.	104	46°20'N	122°10'W
Rifle, Co., U.S. (rī'f'l)	109	39°35'N	107°50'W
Riga, Lat. (rē'gȧ)	164	56°55'N	24°05'E
Riga, Gulf of, b., Eur.	166	57°56'N	23°05'E
Rīgān, Iran	182	28°45'N	58°55'E
Rigaud, Can. (rē-gō')	83a	45°29'N	74°18'W
Rigby, Id., U.S. (rĭg'bē)	105	43°40'N	111°55'W
Rigeley, W.V., U.S. (rĭj'lē)	99	39°40'N	78°45'W
Rīgestān, des., Afg.	182	30°53'N	64°42'E
Rigolet, Can. (rĭg-ō-lā')	85	54°10'N	58°40'W
Riihimäki, Fin.	153	60°44'N	24°44'E
Rijeka, Cro. (rĭ-yĕ'kä)	148	45°22'N	14°24'E
Rijkevorsel, Bel.	145a	51°21'N	4°46'E
Rijswijk, Neth.	145a	52°03'N	4°19'E
Rika, r., Ukr. (rĕ'kȧ)	155	48°21'N	23°37'E
Rima, r., Nig.	215	13°30'N	5°50'E
Rímac, Peru	233c	12°02'S	77°03'W
Rímac, r., Peru	233c	12°02'S	77°09'W
Rimavska Sobota, Slvk. (rē'máf-ská sô'bô-tá)	155	48°25'N	20°01'E
Rimbo, Swe. (rēm'bô)	152	59°45'N	18°22'E
Rimini, Italy (rē'mē-nē)	148	44°03'N	12°33'E
Rimouski, Can. (rē-mōōs'kē)	85	48°27'N	68°32'W
Rincón de Romos, Mex. (rēn-kōn dā rô-mōs')	118	22°13'N	102°21'W
Ringkøbing, Den. (rĭng'kûb-ĭng)	146	56°06'N	8°14'E
Ringkøbing Fjord, fj., Den.	152	55°55'N	8°04'E
Ringsted, Den. (rĭng'stĕdh)	152	55°27'N	11°49'E
Ringvassøya, i., Nor. (rĭng'väs-ûê)	146	69°58'N	16°43'E
Ringwood, Austl.	201a	37°49'S	145°14'E
Ringwood North, Austl.	243b	37°48'S	145°14'E
Rinjani, Gunung, mtn., Indon.	196	8°39'S	116°22'E
Río Abajo, Pan. (rĕ'ō-ä-bä'κô)	116a	9°01'N	78°30'W
Río Balsas, Mex. (rĕ'ō-bäl-säs)	118	17°59'N	99°45'W
Riobamba, Ec. (rē'ō-bäm-bä)	130	1°45'S	78°37'W
Rio Bonito, Braz. (rē'ō bō-nē'tô)	129a	22°44'S	42°38'W
Rio Branco, Braz. (rē'ō brăŋ'kô)	130	9°57'S	67°50'W
Río Branco, Ur. (rīō brănco)	132	32°33'S	53°29'W
Río Casca, Braz. (rē'ō-kà's-kä)	129a	20°15'S	42°39'W
Río Chico, Ven. (rē'ō chē'kō)	131b	10°20'N	65°58'W
Rio Claro, Braz. (rē'ō klä'rô)	131	22°25'S	47°33'W
Rio Comprido, neigh., Braz.	234c	22°55'S	43°12'W
Río Cuarto, Arg. (rē'ō kwär'tō)	132	33°05'S	64°15'W
Rio das Flores, Braz. (rē'ō-däs-flô-rĕs)	129a	22°10'S	43°35'W
Rio de Janeiro, Braz. (rē'ô dā zhä-nâ'ê-rô)	132b	22°50'S	43°20'W
Rio de Janeiro, state, Braz.	131	22°27'S	42°43'W
Río de Jesús, Pan.	121	7°54'N	80°59'W
Rio de Mouro, Port.	238d	38°46'N	9°20'W
Río Frío, Mex. (rē'ō-frē'ô)	119a	19°21'N	98°40'W
Río Gallegos, Arg. (rē'ō gä-lā'gōs)	132	51°43'S	69°15'W
Río Grande, Braz. (rē'ō grän'dĕ)	132	31°04'S	52°14'W
Río Grande, Mex. (rē'ō grän'dā)	118	23°51'N	102°59'W
Riogrande, Tx., U.S. (rē'ō grán-dā)	112	26°23'N	98°48'W
Río Grande, Ven.	234a	10°35'N	66°57'W
Rio Grande do Norte, state, Braz.	131	5°26'S	37°20'W
Rio Grande do Sul, state, Braz. (rē'ô grän'dĕ-dô-sōō'l)	132	29°00'S	54°00'W
Ríohacha, Col. (rē'ō-ä'chä)	130	11°30'N	72°54'W
Río Hato, Pan. (rē'ō-ä'tô)	121	8°19'N	80°11'W
Riom, Fr. (rē-ôɴ')	156	45°54'N	3°08'E
Rio Muni, hist. reg., Eq. Gui. (rē'ō mōō'nē)	210	1°47'N	8°33'E
Rionegro, Col. (rē'ō-nĕ'grô)	130a	6°09'N	75°22'W
Río Negro, prov., Arg. (rē'ō nā'grō)	132	40°15'S	68°15'W
Río Negro, dept., Ur. (rē'ō-nĕ'grō)	129c	32°48'S	57°45'W
Río Negro, Embalse del, res., Ur.	132	32°45'S	55°50'W
Rionero, Italy (rē-ō-nā'rô)	160	40°55'N	15°42'E
Rioni, r., Geor.	168	42°08'N	41°39'E
Rio Novo, Braz. (rē'ō-nô'vô)	129a	21°30'S	43°08'W
Rio Pardo de Minas, Braz. (rē'ō pär'dō-dĕ-mē'näs)	131	15°43'S	42°24'W
Rio Pombo, Braz. (rē'ō pôm'bä)	129a	21°17'S	43°09'W
Rio Sorocaba, Represa do, res., Braz.	129a	23°37'S	47°19'W
Ríosucio, Col. (rē'ō-sōō'syô)	130a	5°25'N	75°41'W
Río Tercero, Arg. (rē'ō dĕr-sĕ'rô)	132	32°12'S	63°59'W
Rio Verde, Braz. (vĕr'dĕ)	131	17°47'S	50°49'W
Ríoverde, Mex. (rē'ō-vĕr'dā)	116	21°54'N	99°59'W
Ripley, Eng., U.K. (rĭp'lē)	144a	53°03'N	1°24'W
Ripley, Eng., U.K.	235	51°18'N	0°29'W
Ripley, Ms., U.S.	114	34°44'N	88°55'W
Ripley, Tn., U.S.	114	35°44'N	89°34'W
Ripoll, Spain (rē-pōl'')	159	42°10'N	2°10'E
Ripon, Wi., U.S. (rĭp'ŏn)	103	43°49'N	88°50'W
Ripon, i., Austl.	202	20°05'S	118°10'E
Ripon Falls, wtfl., Ug.	212	0°38'N	33°02'E
Risaralda, dept., Col.	130a	5°15'N	76°00'W
Risdon, Austl. (rĭz'dŭn)	203	42°37'S	147°32'E
Rishiri, i., Japan (rē-shē'rē)	194	45°10'N	141°08'E
Rishon le Ziyyon, Isr.	181a	31°57'N	34°48'E
Rishra, India	186a	22°42'N	88°22'E
Rising Sun, In., U.S. (rīz'ĭng sŭn)	98	38°55'N	84°55'W
Risor, Nor. (rēs'ûr)	146	58°44'N	9°10'E
Ritacuva, Alto, mtn., Col. (ä'l-tô-rē-tä-kōō'vä)	130	6°22'N	72°13'W
Ritchie, Va., U.S.	229d	38°52'N	76°52'W
Rithāla, neigh., India	240d	28°43'N	77°06'E
Rittman, Oh., U.S. (rĭt'năn)	101d	40°58'N	81°47'W
Ritzville, Wa., U.S. (rĭts'vĭl)	104	47°08'N	118°23'W
Riva, Dom. Rep. (rē'vä)	123	19°10'N	69°55'W
Riva, Italy (rē'vä)	160	45°54'N	10°49'E
Riva, Md., U.S. (rĭ'vä)	100e	38°57'N	76°36'W
Rivas, Nic. (rē'väs)	120	11°25'N	85°51'W
Rive-de-Gier, Fr. (rēv-dē-zhē-ā')	156	45°32'N	4°37'E
Rivera, Ur. (rē-vā'rä)	132	30°52'S	55°32'W
River Cess, Lib. (rĭv'ẽr sĕs)	210	5°46'N	9°52'W
Riverdale, Il., U.S. (rĭv'ẽr dăl)	101a	41°38'N	87°36'W
Riverdale, Md., U.S.	229d	38°58'N	76°55'W
Riverdale, Ut., U.S.	107b	41°11'N	112°00'W
Riverdale, neigh., N.Y., U.S.	228	40°54'N	73°54'W
River Edge, N.J., U.S.	228	40°56'N	74°02'W
River Falls, Al., U.S.	114	31°20'N	86°25'W
River Falls, Wi., U.S.	103	44°48'N	92°38'W
River Forest, Il., U.S.	231a	41°53'N	87°49'W
River Grove, Il., U.S.	231a	41°56'N	87°50'W
Riverhead, Eng., U.K.	235	51°17'N	0°10'E
Riverhead, N.Y., U.S. (rĭv'ẽr hĕd)	99	40°55'N	72°40'W
Riverina, reg., Austl. (rĭv-ẽr-ē'nä)	203	34°55'S	144°30'E
River Jordan, Can. (jôr'dăn)	106a	48°25'N	124°03'W

PRONOUNCING INDEX

River Oaks-Roses 339

PLACE (Pronunciation)	PAGE	LAT.	LONG.
River Oaks, Tx., U.S. (ōkz)	107c	32°47′N	97°24′W
River Rouge, Mi., U.S. (ro͞ozh)	101b	42°16′N	83°09′W
Rivers, Can.	89	50°01′N	100°15′W
Riverside, Ca., U.S. (rĭv′ẽr-sīd)	96	33°59′N	117°21′W
Riverside, Il., U.S.	231a	41°50′N	87°49′W
Riverside, N.J., U.S.	100f	40°02′N	74°58′W
Rivers Inlet, Can.	86	51°45′N	127°15′W
Riverstone, Austl.	201b	33°41′S	150°52′E
Riverton, Va., U.S.	99	39°00′N	78°15′W
Riverton, Wy., U.S.	105	43°02′N	108°24′W
Rivesaltes, Fr. (rēv′zält′)	156	42°48′N	2°48′E
Riviera Beach, Fl., U.S. (rĭv-ĭ-ĕr′á bēch)	115a	26°46′N	80°04′W
Riviera Beach, Md., U.S.	100e	39°10′N	76°32′W
Rivière-Beaudette, Can.	83a	45°14′N	74°20′W
Rivière-du-Loup, Can. (rē-vyâr′ dü lo͞o′)	85	47°50′N	69°32′W
Rivière Qui Barre, Can. (rēv-yĕr′ kē-băr)	83g	53°47′N	113°51′W
Rivière-Trois-Pistoles, Can. (trwä′pēs-tôl′)	92	48°07′N	69°10′W
Rivne, Ukr.	163	48°11′N	31°46′E
Rivne, Ukr.	167	50°37′N	26°17′E
Rivne, prov., Ukr.	163	50°55′N	27°00′E
Riyadh, Sau. Ar.	182	24°31′N	46°47′E
Rize, Tur. (rē′zĕ)	149	41°00′N	40°30′E
Rizhao, China (rē-jou)	192	35°27′N	119°28′E
Rizzuto, Cape, c., Italy (rēt-so͞o′tō)	161	38°53′N	17°05′E
Rjukan, Nor. (ryo͞o′kän)	146	59°53′N	8°30′E
Roanne, Fr. (rō-än′)	147	46°02′N	4°04′E
Roanoke, Al., U.S. (rō′á-nōk)	114	33°08′N	85°21′W
Roanoke, Va., U.S.	97	37°16′N	79°55′W
Roanoke, r., U.S.	97	36°17′N	77°22′W
Roanoke Rapids, N.C., U.S.	115	36°25′N	77°40′W
Roanoke Rapids Lake, res., N.C., U.S.	115	36°28′N	77°37′W
Roan Plateau, plat., Co., U.S. (rōn)	109	39°25′N	110°00′W
Roatan, Hond. (rō-ä-tän′)	120	16°18′N	86°33′W
Roatán, i., Hond.	120	16°19′N	86°46′W
Robbeneiland, i., S. Afr.	212a	33°48′S	18°22′E
Robbins, Il., U.S. (rŏb′ĭnz)	101a	41°39′N	87°42′W
Robbinsdale, Mn., U.S. (rŏb′ĭnz-dāl)	107g	45°03′N	93°22′W
Robe, Wa., U.S. (rōb)	106a	48°06′N	121°50′W
Roberts, Mount, mtn., Austl. (rŏb′ẽrts)	203	28°05′S	152°30′E
Roberts, Point, c., Wa., U.S. (rŏb′ẽrts)	106d	48°58′N	123°05′W
Robertsham, neigh., S. Afr.	244b	26°15′S	28°00′E
Robertson, Lac, l., Can.	93	51°00′N	59°10′W
Robertsport, Lib. (rŏb′ẽrts-pōrt)	210	6°45′N	11°22′W
Roberval, Can. (rŏb′ẽr-văl) (rô-bĕr-vál′)	85	48°32′N	72°15′W
Robinson, Can.	93	48°16′N	58°50′W
Robinson, S. Afr.	244b	26°09′S	27°43′E
Robinson, Il., U.S. (rŏb′ĭn-sŭn)	98	39°00′N	87°45′W
Robinvale, Austl. (rŏb-ĭn′vāl)	204	34°45′S	142°45′E
Roblin, Can.	89	51°15′N	101°25′W
Robson, Mount, mtn., Can. (rŏb′sŭn)	87	53°07′N	119°09′W
Robstown, Tx., U.S. (rŏbz′toun)	113	27°46′N	97°41′W
Roby, Eng., U.K.	237a	53°25′N	2°51′W
Roca, Cabo da, c., Port. (kå′bō-dä-rô′kä)	158	38°47′N	9°30′W
Rocas, Atol das, atoll, Braz. (ä-tôl-däs-rō′kás)	131	3°50′S	33°46′W
Rocha, Ur. (rō′chás)	132	34°26′S	54°14′W
Rocha Miranda, neigh., Braz.	234c	22°52′S	43°22′W
Rocha Sobrinho, Braz.	234c	22°47′S	43°25′W
Rochdale, Eng., U.K. (rŏch′dāl)	150	53°37′N	2°09′W
Roche à Bateau, Haiti (rôsh á bá-tō′)	123	18°10′N	74°00′W
Rochefort, Fr. (rôsh-fôr′)	147	45°55′N	0°57′W
Rochelle, Il., U.S. (rō-shĕl′)	103	41°53′N	89°06′W
Rochelle Park, N.J., U.S.	228	40°55′N	74°04′W
Rochester, Eng., U.K.	144a	51°24′N	0°30′E
Rochester, In., U.S. (rŏch′ĕs-tẽr)	98	41°05′N	86°20′W
Rochester, Mi., U.S.	101b	42°41′N	83°09′W
Rochester, Mn., U.S.	97	44°01′N	92°30′W
Rochester, N.H., U.S.	99	43°20′N	71°00′W
Rochester, N.Y., U.S.	97	43°15′N	77°35′W
Rochester, Pa., U.S.	101e	40°42′N	80°16′W
Rock, r., U.S.	97	41°40′N	90°00′W
Rock, r., Ia., U.S.	102	43°17′N	96°13′W
Rock, r., Or., U.S.	106c	45°34′N	122°52′W
Rock, r., Or., U.S.	106c	45°52′N	123°14′W
Rockaway, N.J., U.S. (rŏck′á-wā)	100a	40°54′N	74°30′W
Rockaway Park, neigh., N.Y., U.S.	228	40°35′N	73°50′W
Rockaway Point, neigh., N.Y., U.S.	228	40°33′N	73°55′W
Rockbank, Austl.	201a	37°44′S	144°40′E
Rockcliffe Park, Can. (rok′klĭf pärk)	83c	45°27′N	75°40′W
Rock Creek, r., Can. (rŏk)	105	49°01′N	107°00′W
Rock Creek, r., Il., U.S.	101a	41°16′N	87°54′W
Rock Creek, r., Mt., U.S.	105	46°25′N	113°40′W
Rock Creek, r., Or., U.S.	104	45°30′N	120°06′W
Rock Creek, r., Wa., U.S.	104	47°09′N	117°50′W
Rock Creek Park, pt. of i., D.C., U.S.	229d	38°58′N	77°03′W
Rockdale, Austl.	201b	33°57′S	151°08′E
Rockdale, Md., U.S.	100e	39°22′N	76°49′W
Rockdale, Tx., U.S. (rŏk′dāl)	113	30°39′N	97°00′W
Rockefeller Center, pt. of i., N.Y., U.S.	228	40°45′N	74°00′W
Rock Falls, Il., U.S. (rŏk fôlz)	103	41°45′N	89°42′W
Rock Ferry, Eng., U.K.	237a	53°22′N	3°00′W
Rockford, Il., U.S. (rŏk′fẽrd)	97	42°16′N	89°07′W
Rockhampton, Austl. (rŏk-hămp′tŭn)	203	23°26′S	150°29′E
Rock Hill, S.C., U.S. (rŏk′hĭl)	97	34°55′N	81°01′W
Rockingham, N.C., U.S. (rŏk′ĭng-hăm)	115	34°54′N	79°45′W
Rockingham Forest, for., Eng., U.K. (rok′ĭng-hăm)	144a	52°29′N	0°43′W
Rock Island, Il., U.S.	97	41°31′N	90°37′W
Rock Island Dam, Wa., U.S. (ĭ lănd)	104	47°17′N	120°33′W
Rockland, Can. (rŏk′lănd)	83c	45°33′N	75°17′W
Rockland, Me., U.S.	92	44°06′N	69°09′W
Rockland, Ma., U.S.	93a	42°07′N	70°55′W
Rockland Reservoir, res., Austl.	204	36°55′S	142°20′E
Rockledge, Pa., U.S.	229b	40°03′N	75°05′W
Rockmart, Ga., U.S. (rŏk′märt)	114	33°58′N	85°00′W
Rockmont, Wi., U.S. (rŏk′mŏnt)	107h	46°34′N	91°54′W
Rockport, In., U.S. (rŏk′pōrt)	98	38°20′N	87°00′W
Rockport, Ma., U.S.	93a	42°39′N	70°37′W
Rockport, Mo., U.S.	111	40°25′N	95°30′W
Rockport, Tx., U.S.	113	28°03′N	97°03′W
Rock Rapids, Ia., U.S. (răp′ĭdz)	102	43°26′N	96°10′W
Rock Sound, strt., Bah.	122	24°50′N	76°05′W
Rocksprings, Tx., U.S. (rŏk sprĭngs)	112	30°02′N	100°12′W
Rock Springs, Wy., U.S.	96	41°35′N	109°13′W
Rockstone, Guy. (rŏk′stōn)	131	5°55′N	57°27′W
Rock Valley, Ia., U.S. (văl′ĭ)	102	43°13′N	96°17′W
Rockville, In., U.S. (rŏk′vĭl)	98	39°45′N	87°15′W
Rockville, Md., U.S.	100e	39°05′N	77°11′W
Rockville Centre, N.Y., U.S. (sĕn′tẽr)	100a	40°39′N	73°39′W
Rockwall, Tx., U.S. (rŏk′wôl)	111	32°55′N	96°23′W
Rockwell City, Ia., U.S. (rŏk′wĕl)	103	42°22′N	94°37′W
Rockwood, Can. (rŏk-wo͝od)	83d	43°37′N	80°08′W
Rockwood, Me., U.S.	92	45°39′N	69°45′W
Rockwood, Tn., U.S.	114	35°51′N	84°41′W
Rocky, r., Oh., U.S.	229a	41°30′N	81°49′W
Rocky, East Branch, r., Oh., U.S.	101d	41°13′N	81°43′W
Rocky, West Branch, r., Oh., U.S.	101d	41°17′N	81°54′W
Rocky Boys Indian Reservation, I.R., Mt., U.S.	105	48°08′N	109°34′W
Rocky Ford, Co., U.S.	110	38°02′N	103°43′W
Rocky Hill, N.J., U.S. (hĭl)	100a	40°24′N	74°38′W
Rocky Island Lake, l., Can.	90	46°56′N	83°04′W
Rocky Mount, N.C., U.S.	115	35°55′N	77°47′W
Rocky Mountain House, Can.	87	52°22′N	114°55′W
Rocky Mountain National Park, rec., Co., U.S.	96	40°29′N	106°06′W
Rocky Mountains, mts., N.A.	82	50°00′N	114°00′W
Rocky River, Oh., U.S.	101d	41°29′N	81°51′W
Rocquencourt, Fr.	237c	48°50′N	2°07′E
Rodas, Cuba (rō′dhás)	122	22°20′N	80°35′W
Roden, r., Eng., U.K. (rō′dĕn)	144a	52°49′N	2°38′W
Rodeo, Mex. (rō-dā′ō)	112	25°12′N	104°34′W
Rodeo, Ca., U.S. (rō′dêō)	106b	38°02′N	122°16′W
Roderick Island, i., Can. (rŏd′ẽ-rĭk)	86	52°40′N	128°22′W
Rodez, Fr. (rō-dĕz′)	147	44°22′N	2°34′E
Rōdhos, Grc.	149	36°24′N	28°15′E
Ródhos, i., Grc.	142	36°00′N	28°29′E
Rodnei, Munţii, mts., Rom.	155	47°41′N	24°05′E
Rodniki, Russia (rôd′nē-kē)	166	57°08′N	41°48′E
Rodonit, Kep I, c., Alb.	161	41°38′N	19°01′E
Roebling, N.J., U.S. (rōb′lĭng)	100f	40°07′N	74°48′W
Roebourne, Austl. (rō′bŭrn)	202	20°50′S	117°15′E
Roebuck Bay, b., Austl. (rō′bŭck)	202	18°15′S	121°10′E
Roedtan, S. Afr.	218d	24°37′S	29°08′E
Roehampton, neigh., Eng., U.K.	235	51°27′N	0°14′W
Roeselare, Bel.	151	50°55′N	3°05′E
Roesiger, l., Wa., U.S. (rōz′ĭ-gẽr)	106a	47°59′N	121°56′W
Roes Welcome Sound, strt., Can. (rōz)	85	64°10′N	87°23′W
Rogachëv, Bela. (rôg′á-chyôf)	166	53°07′N	30°04′E
Rogans Hill, Austl.	243a	33°44′S	151°01′E
Rogatica, Bos. (rō-gä′tē-tsä)	161	43°46′N	19°00′E
Rogers, Ar., U.S. (rŏj-ẽrz)	111	36°19′N	94°07′W
Rogers City, Mi., U.S.	98	45°30′N	83°50′W
Rogers Park, neigh., Il., U.S.	231a	42°01′N	87°40′W
Rogersville, Tn., U.S.	114	36°21′N	83°00′W
Rognac, Fr. (rōn-yäk′)	156a	43°29′N	5°15′E
Rogoaguado, l., Bol. (rō′gō-ä-gwä-dō)	130	12°42′S	66°46′W
Rogovskaya, Russia (rô-gôf′ská-yá)	163	45°43′N	38°42′E
Rogózno, Pol. (rō′gôzh-nō)	154	52°44′N	16°53′E
Rogue, r., Or., U.S. (rōg)	104	42°32′N	124°13′W
Rohatyn, Ukr.	155	49°22′N	24°37′E
Rohdenhaus, Ger.	236	51°18′N	7°01′E
Röhlinghausen, neigh., Ger.	236	51°31′N	7°08′E
Rohrbeck, Ger.	238a	52°32′N	13°02′E
Roissy, Fr.	237c	48°47′N	2°39′E
Roissy-en-France, Fr.	237c	49°00′N	2°31′E
Rojas, Arg. (rō′häs)	129c	34°11′S	60°42′W
Rojo, Cabo, c., Mex. (rō′hō)	119	21°35′N	97°16′W
Rojo, Cabo, c., P.R. (rō′hō)	117b	17°55′N	67°14′W
Rokel, r., S.L.	214	9°00′N	11°55′W
Rokkō-Zan, mtn., Japan (rôk′kō zän)	195b	34°46′N	135°16′E
Roksana, S. Afr.	244b	26°07′S	28°04′E
Rokycany, Czech Rep. (rô′kĭ′tsá-nĭ)	154	49°44′N	13°37′E
Roldanillo, Col. (rôl-dä-nē′l-yō)	130a	4°24′N	76°09′W
Rolla, Mo., U.S.	111	37°56′N	91°45′W
Rolla, N.D., U.S.	102	48°52′N	99°32′W
Rolleville, Bah.	122	23°40′N	76°00′W
Rolling Acres, Md., U.S.	229c	39°17′N	76°52′W
Röllinghausen, neigh., Ger.	236	51°36′N	7°14′E
Rolling Hills, Ca., U.S.	232	33°46′N	118°21′W
Roma, Austl. (rō′má)	203	26°30′S	148°48′E
Roma *see* Rome, Italy	142	41°52′N	12°37′E
Roma, Leso.	213c	29°28′S	27°43′E
Romaine, r., Can. (rō-mĕn′)	85	51°22′N	63°23′W
Romainville, Fr.	237c	48°53′N	2°26′E
Roman, Rom. (rō′män)	155	46°56′N	26°57′E
Romania, nation, Eur. (rō-mä′nē-á)	142	46°18′N	22°53′E
Romano, Cape, c., Fl., U.S. (rō-mä′nō)	115a	25°48′N	82°00′W
Romano, Cayo, i., Cuba (kä′yō-rô-má′nō)	122	22°15′N	78°00′W
Romanovo, Russia (rô-mä′nô-vô)	172a	59°09′N	61°24′E
Romans, Fr. (rō-mäN′)	156	45°04′N	4°49′E
Romblon, Phil. (rōm-blōn′)	197a	12°34′N	122°16′E
Romblon Island, i., Phil.	197a	12°33′N	122°17′E
Rome (Roma), Italy	142	41°52′N	12°37′E
Rome, Ga., U.S. (rōm)	97	34°14′N	85°10′W
Rome, N.Y., U.S.	99	43°15′N	75°25′W
Romeo, Mi., U.S. (rō′mē-ō)	98	42°50′N	83°00′W
Romford, Eng., U.K. (rŭm′fẽrd)	144b	51°35′N	0°11′E
Romiley, Eng., U.K.	237b	53°25′N	2°05′W
Romilly-sur-Seine, Fr. (rō-mē-yē′sür-săn′)	156	48°32′N	3°41′E
Romita, Mex. (rō-mē′tä)	118	20°53′N	101°32′W
Romny, Ukr. (rôm′nĭ)	167	50°46′N	33°31′E
Rømø, i., Den. (rûm′û)	152	55°08′N	8°17′E
Romoland, Ca., U.S. (rō′mō′lănd)	107a	33°44′N	117°11′W
Romorantin-Lanthenay, Fr. (rō-mō-räN-tăN′)	156	47°24′N	1°46′E
Rompin, Malay.	181b	2°42′N	102°30′E
Rompin, r., Malay.	181b	2°54′N	103°10′E
Romsdalsfjorden, Nor.	152	62°40′N	7°05′W
Romulus, Mi., U.S. (rom′ū lŭs)	101b	42°14′N	83°24′W
Ron, Mui, c., Viet	193	18°05′N	106°45′E
Ronan, Mt., U.S. (rō′năn)	105	47°28′N	114°03′W
Roncador, Serra do, mts., Braz. (sĕr′rá dō rōn-kä-dōr′)	131	12°44′S	52°19′W
Ronceverte, W.V., U.S. (rŏn′sē-vûrt)	98	37°45′N	80°30′W
Ronda, Spain (rōn′dä)	167	36°45′N	5°10′W
Ronda, Sierra de, mts., Spain	158	36°35′N	5°03′W
Rondebult, S. Afr.	244b	26°18′S	28°14′E
Rondônia, , Braz.	130	10°15′S	63°07′W
Ronge, Lac la, l., Can. (rōnzh)	84	55°10′N	105°00′W
Rongjiang, China (rōŋ-jyäŋ)	193	25°52′N	108°45′E
Rongxian, China	193	22°50′N	110°32′E
Rønne, Den. (rûn′ĕ)	146	55°08′N	14°46′E
Ronneby, Swe. (rōn′ĕ-bü)	152	56°13′N	15°17′E
Ronne Ice Shelf, ice., Ant.	219	77°30′S	38°00′W
Ronsdorf, neigh., Ger.	236	51°14′N	7°12′E
Roodepoort, S. Afr. (rō′dĕ-pōrt)	213b	26°10′S	27°52′E
Roodhouse, Il., U.S. (ro͞od′hous)	111	39°29′N	90°21′W
Rooiberg, S. Afr.	218d	24°46′S	27°42′E
Roosendaal, Neth. (rō′zĕn-dāl)	145a	51°32′N	4°27′E
Roosevelt, N.Y., U.S.	228	40°41′N	73°36′W
Roosevelt, Ut., U.S. (rōz″vĕlt)	109	40°20′N	110°00′W
Roosevelt, r., Braz. (rô′sĕ-vĕlt)	131	9°22′S	60°28′W
Roosevelt Island, i., Ant.	219	79°30′S	168°00′W
Root, r., Wi., U.S.	101a	42°49′N	87°54′W
Rooty Hill, Austl.	243a	33°46′S	150°50′E
Roper, r., Austl. (rōp′ẽr)	202	14°50′S	134°00′E
Ropsha, Russia (rôp′shá)	172c	59°44′N	29°53′E
Roque Pérez, Arg. (rô′kĕ-pĕ′rĕz)	129c	35°23′S	59°22′W
Roques, Islas los, is., Ven.	130	12°25′N	67°40′W
Roraima, , Braz. (rō′rīy-mă)	130	2°00′N	62°15′W
Roraima, Mount, mtn., S.A. (rō-rä-ē′mä)	131	5°12′N	60°52′W
Røros, Nor. (rûr′ōs)	146	62°36′N	11°25′E
Ros′, r., Ukr. (rôs)	163	49°40′N	30°22′E
Rosa, Monte, mtn., Italy (mōn′tä rō′zä)	148	45°56′N	7°51′E
Rosales, Mex. (rō-zä′läs)	112	28°15′N	100°43′W
Rosales, Phil. (rō-sä′lēs)	197a	15°54′N	120°38′E
Rosamorada, Mex. (rō′zä-mō-rä′dhä)	118	22°06′N	105°16′W
Rosanna, Austl.	243b	37°45′S	145°04′E
Rosaria, Laguna, l., Mex. (lä-gō′nä-rō-sä′ryä)	119	17°50′N	93°51′W
Rosario, Arg. (rō-zä′rē-ō)	132	32°58′S	60°42′W
Rosario, Braz. (rō-zä′rē-ō)	131	2°49′S	44°15′W
Rosario, Mex.	112	26°31′N	105°40′W
Rosario, Mex.	118	22°58′N	105°54′W
Rosario, Phil.	197a	13°49′N	121°13′W
Rosario, Ur.	129c	34°19′S	57°24′E
Rosario, Cayo, i., Cuba (kä′yō-rō-sä′ryō)	122	21°40′N	81°55′W
Rosário do Sul, Braz. (rō-zä′rē-ō-dō-so͞o′l)	132	30°17′S	54°52′W
Rosário Oeste, Braz. (ō′ĕst′ĕ)	131	14°47′S	56°20′W
Rosario Strait, strt., Wa., U.S.	106a	48°27′N	122°45′W
Rosbach, Ger. (rōz′bäk)	157c	50°47′N	7°38′E
Roscoe, Tx., U.S. (rôs′kō)	112	32°26′N	100°38′W
Roseau, Dom.	121b	15°17′N	61°23′W
Roseau, Mn., U.S. (rō-zō′)	102	48°52′N	95°47′W
Roseau, r., Mn., U.S.	102	48°52′N	96°11′W
Rosebank, neigh., S. Afr.	244b	26°09′S	28°02′E
Roseberg, Or., U.S. (rōz′bûrg)	96	43°13′N	123°30′W
Rosebery, neigh., Austl.	243a	33°55′S	151°12′E
Rosebud, r., Can. (rōz′bŭd)	87	51°20′N	112°20′W
Rosebud Creek, r., Mt., U.S.	105	45°48′N	106°34′W
Rosebud Indian Reservation, I.R., S.D., U.S.	102	43°13′N	100°42′W
Rosedale, Ms., U.S.	114	33°49′N	90°56′W
Rosedale, Wa., U.S.	106a	47°20′N	122°39′W
Rosedale, neigh., Can.	227c	43°41′N	79°22′W
Rosedale, neigh., N.Y., U.S.	228	40°39′N	73°45′W
Roseires Reservoir, res., Sudan	211	11°15′N	34°45′E
Roseland, neigh., Il., U.S.	231a	41°42′N	87°38′W
Roselle, Il., U.S. (rō-zĕl′)	101a	41°59′N	88°05′W
Roselle, N.J., U.S.	228	40°40′N	74°16′W
Rosemead, Ca., U.S.	232	34°04′N	118°03′W
Rosemère, Can. (rōz′mĕr)	83a	45°38′N	73°48′W
Rosemont, Il., U.S.	231a	41°59′N	87°52′W
Rosemont, Pa., U.S.	229b	40°01′N	75°19′W
Rosemount, Mn., U.S. (rōz′mount)	107g	44°44′N	93°08′W
Rosendal, S. Afr. (rō-sĕn′täl)	218d	28°32′S	27°56′E
Roseneath, S. Afr.	244b	26°17′S	28°11′E
Rosenheim, Ger. (rō′zĕn-hīm)	147	47°52′N	12°06′E
Rosenthal, neigh., Ger.	238a	52°36′N	13°23′E
Roses, Golf de, b., Spain	159	42°10′N	3°20′E

340 Rosetown–Saburovo

PLACE (Pronunciation)	PAGE	LAT.	LONG.
Rosetown, Can. (rōz'toun)	84	51°33'N	108°00'W
Rose Tree, Pa., U.S.	229b	39°56'N	75°23'W
Rosetta *see* Rashīd, Egypt	184	31°22'N	30°25'E
Rosettenville, neigh., S. Afr.	213b	26°15'S	28°04'E
Roseville, Austl.	243a	33°47'S	151°11'E
Roseville, Ca., U.S. (rōz'vĭl)	108	38°44'N	121°19'W
Roseville, Mi., U.S.	101b	42°30'N	82°55'W
Roseville, Mn., U.S.	107g	45°01'N	93°10'W
Rosiclare, Il., U.S. (rōz'y-klâr)	98	37°30'N	88°15'W
Rosignol, Guy. (rŏs-ĭg-nél)	131	6°16'N	57°37'W
Roșiori de Vede, Rom. (rô-shôr'ĕ dĕ vĕ-dĕ)	161	44°06'N	25°00'E
Roskilde, Den. (rôs'kĕl-dĕ)	152	55°39'N	12°04'E
Roslavl', Russia (rôs'läv'l)	166	53°56'N	32°52'E
Roslyn, N.Y., U.S.	228	40°48'N	73°39'W
Roslyn, Wa., U.S. (rŏz'lĭn)	104	47°14'N	121°00'W
Roslyn Estates, N.Y., U.S.	228	40°47'N	73°40'W
Roslyn Heights, N.Y., U.S.	228	40°47'N	73°39'W
Rosny-sous-Bois, Fr.	237c	48°53'N	2°29'E
Rösrath, Ger. (rûz'rät)	157c	50°53'N	7°11'E
Ross, Oh., U.S. (rôs)	101f	39°19'N	84°39'W
Rossano, Italy (rô-sä'nō)	149	39°34'N	16°38'E
Rossan Point, c., Ire.	150	54°45'N	8°30'W
Ross Creek, r., Can.	83g	53°40'N	113°08'W
Rosseau, l., Can. (rôs-sō')	91	45°15'N	79°30'W
Rossel, i., Pap. N. Gui. (rô-sĕl')	203	11°31'S	154°00'E
Rosser, Can. (rôs'sẽr)	83f	49°59'N	97°27'W
Ross Ice Shelf, ice., Ant.	219	81°30'S	175°00'W
Rossignol, Lake, l., Can.	92	44°10'N	65°10'W
Ross Island, i., Can.	89	54°14'N	97°45'W
Ross Lake, res., Wa., U.S.	104	48°40'N	121°07'W
Rossland, Can. (rôs'lănd)	84	49°05'N	118°48'W
Rossmore, Austl.	243a	33°57'S	150°46'E
Rossosh', Russia (rôs'sŭsh)	167	50°12'N	39°32'E
Rossouw, S. Afr.	213c	31°12'S	27°18'E
Ross Sea, sea, Ant.	219	76°00'S	178°00'W
Rossvatnet, l., Nor.	146	65°36'N	13°08'E
Rossville, Ga., U.S. (rôs'vĭl)	114	34°57'N	85°22'W
Rossville, Md., U.S.	229c	39°20'N	76°29'W
Rosthern, Can.	88	52°41'N	106°25'W
Rostherne, Eng., U.K.	237b	53°21'N	2°23'W
Rostock, Ger. (rôs'tŭk)	146	54°04'N	12°06'E
Rostov, Russia	166	57°13'N	39°23'E
Rostov, prov., Russia	163	47°38'N	39°15'E
Rostov-na-Donu, Russia (rôstôv-nà-dô-nōō)	164	47°16'N	39°47'E
Roswell, Ga., U.S. (rŏz'wĕl)	114	34°02'N	84°21'W
Roswell, N.M., U.S.	96	33°23'N	104°32'W
Rosyln, Pa., U.S.	229b	40°07'N	75°08'W
Rotan, Tx., U.S. (rô-tăn')	110	32°51'N	100°27'W
Rothenburg, Ger.	154	49°20'N	10°10'E
Rotherham, Eng., U.K. (rŏdh'ẽr-ăm)	144a	53°26'N	1°21'W
Rothesay, Can. (rôth'sâ)	92	45°23'N	66°00'W
Rothesay, Scot., U.K.	150	55°50'N	3°14'W
Rothneusiedl, neigh., Aus.	239e	48°08'N	16°23'E
Rothwell, Eng., U.K.	144a	53°44'N	1°30'W
Roti, Pulau, i., Indon. (rō'tē)	196	10°30'S	122°52'E
Roto, Austl. (rō'tō)	204	33°07'S	145°30'E
Rotorua, N.Z.	205	38°07'S	176°17'E
Rotterdam, Neth. (rôt'ẽr-däm')	142	51°55'N	4°27'E
Rottweil, Ger. (rōt'vīl)	154	48°10'N	8°36'E
Roubaix, Fr. (rōō-bĕ')	156	50°42'N	3°10'E
Rouen, Fr. (rōō-äN')	142	49°25'N	1°05'E
Rouge, r., Can. (rōōzh)	83d	43°53'N	79°21'W
Rouge, r., Can.	91	46°40'N	74°50'W
Rouge, r., Mi., U.S.	101b	42°30'N	83°15'W
Rough River Reservoir, res., Ky., U.S.	98	37°45'N	86°10'W
Round Lake, Il., U.S.	101a	42°21'N	88°05'W
Round Pond, l., Can.	93	48°15'N	55°57'W
Round Rock, Tx., U.S.	113	30°31'N	97°41'W
Round Top, mtn., Or., U.S. (tŏp)	106c	45°41'N	123°22'W
Roundup, Mt., U.S. (round'ŭp)	105	46°25'N	108°35'W
Rousay, i., Scot., U.K. (rōō'zȧ)	150a	59°10'N	3°04'W
Rouyn, Can. (rōōn)	85	48°22'N	79°03'W
Rovaniemi, Fin. (rô'vȧ-nyĕ'mĭ)	146	66°29'N	25°45'E
Rovato, Italy (rô-vä'tō)	160	45°33'N	10°00'E
Roven'ki, Russia	163	49°54'N	38°54'E
Roven'ky, Ukr.	163	48°06'N	39°44'E
Rovereto, Italy (rō-vā-rā'tō)	160	45°53'N	11°05'E
Rovigo, Italy (rô-vē'gô)	160	45°05'N	11°48'E
Rovinj, Cro. (rô'ēn')	160	45°05'N	13°40'E
Rovira, Col. (rô-vē'rä)	130a	4°14'N	75°13'W
Rovuma (Ruvuma), r., Afr.	217	10°50'S	39°50'E
Rowland Heights, Ca., U.S.	232	33°59'N	117°54'W
Rowley, Ma., U.S. (rou'lē)	93a	42°43'N	70°53'W
Rowville, Austl.	243b	37°56'S	145°14'E
Roxana, Il., U.S. (rŏks'ăn-nȧ)	107e	38°51'N	90°05'W
Roxas, Phil. (rô-xäs)	196	11°30'N	122°47'E
Roxboro, Can.	227b	45°31'N	73°48'W
Roxborough, neigh., Pa., U.S.	229b	40°02'N	75°13'W
Roxbury, neigh., N.Y., U.S.	228	40°34'N	73°54'W
Roxo, Cap, c., Sen.	214	12°20'N	16°43'W
Roy, N.M., U.S. (roi)	110	35°54'N	104°09'W
Roy, Ut., U.S.	107b	41°10'N	112°02'W
Royal, i., Bah.	122	25°30'N	76°50'W
Royal Albert Hall, pt. of i., Eng., U.K.	235	51°30'N	0°11'W
Royal Canal, can., Ire. (roi-ăl)	150	53°28'N	6°45'W
Royal Natal National Park, rec., S. Afr.	213c	28°35'S	28°54'E
Royal Naval College, pt. of i., Eng., U.K.	235	51°29'N	0°01'W
Royal Oak, Can. (roi'ăl ōk)	106a	48°30'N	123°24'W
Royal Oak, Mi., U.S.	101b	42°29'N	83°09'W
Royal Oak Township, Mi., U.S.	230c	42°27'N	83°10'W
Royal Ontario Museum, bldg., Can.	227c	43°40'N	79°24'W
Royalton, Mi., U.S. (roi'ăl-tŭn)	98	42°00'N	86°25'W
Royan, Fr. (rwä-yäN')	156	45°40'N	1°02'W
Roye, Fr. (rwä)	156	49°43'N	2°40'E
Royersford, Pa., U.S. (rô' yẽrz-fẽrd)	100f	40°11'N	75°32'W
Royston, Ga., U.S. (roiz'tŭn)	114	34°15'N	83°06'W
Royton, Eng., U.K. (roi'tŭn)	144a	53°34'N	2°07'W
Rozay-en-Brie, Fr. (rô-zā-ĕN-brē')	157b	48°41'N	2°57'E
Rozdil'na, Ukr.	163	46°47'N	30°08'E
Rozelle, Austl.	243a	33°52'S	151°10'E
Rozhaya, r., Russia (rô'zhá-yá)	172b	55°20'N	37°37'E
Rozivka, Ukr.	163	47°14'N	36°35'E
Rožňava, Slvk. (rôzh'nyá-vá)	155	48°39'N	20°32'E
Rtishchevo, Russia ('r-tĭsh'chĕ-vô)	167	52°15'N	43°40'E
Ru, r., China (rōō)	190	33°07'N	114°18'E
Ruacana Falls, wtfl., Afr.	212	17°15'S	14°45'E
Ruaha National Park, rec., Tan.	217	7°15'S	34°50'E
Ruapehu, vol., N.Z. (rò-á-pā'hōō)	203a	39°15'S	175°37'E
Rub' al Khali *see* Ar Rub' al Khālī, des., Asia	182	20°00'N	51°00'E
Rubeho Mountains, mts., Tan.	217	6°45'S	36°15'E
Rubidoux, Ca., U.S.	107a	33°59'N	117°24'W
Rubizhne, Ukr.	163	48°53'N	38°29'E
Rubondo Island, i., Tan.	217	2°10'S	31°55'E
Rubtsovsk, Russia	164	51°31'N	81°17'E
Ruby, Ak., U.S. (rōō'bē)	94a	64°38'N	155°22'W
Ruby, l., Nv., U.S.	108	40°11'N	115°20'W
Ruby, r., Mt., U.S.	105	45°06'N	112°10'W
Ruby Mountains, mts., Nv., U.S.	108	40°11'N	115°36'W
Rüdersdorf, Ger.	238a	52°29'N	13°47'E
Rudge Ramos, Braz.	234d	23°41'S	46°34'W
Rüdinghausen, neigh., Ger.	236	51°27'N	7°25'E
Rudkøbing, Den. (rōōdh'kûb-ĭng)	152	54°56'N	10°44'E
Rüdnitz, Ger. (rüd'nētz)	145b	52°44'N	13°38'E
Rudolf, Lake, l., Afr. (rōō'dŏlf)	211	3°30'N	36°05'E
Rudow, neigh., Ger.	238a	52°25'N	13°30'E
Rueil-Malmaison, Fr.	237c	48°53'N	2°11'E
Rufā'ah, Sudan (rōō-fä'ä)	211	14°52'N	33°30'E
Ruffec, Fr. (rü-fĕk')	156	46°03'N	0°11'E
Rufiji, r., Tan. (rò-fē'jē)	213	8°00'S	38°00'E
Rufisque, Sen. (rü-fēsk')	210	14°43'N	17°17'W
Rufunsa, Zam.	217	15°05'S	29°40'E
Rufus Woods, Wa., U.S.	104	48°02'N	119°33'W
Rugao, China (rōō-gou)	192	32°24'N	120°33'E
Rugby, Eng., U.K. (rŭg'bē)	144a	52°22'N	1°15'W
Rugby, N.D., U.S.	102	48°22'N	100°00'W
Rugeley, Eng., U.K. (rōōj'lē)	144a	52°46'N	1°56'W
Rügen, i., Ger. (rü'ghĕn)	142	54°28'N	13°47'E
Rüggeberg, Ger.	236	51°16'N	7°22'E
Ruhlsdorf, Ger.	238a	52°23'N	13°16'E
Ruhnu-Saar, i., Est. (rōōnò-sá'âr)	153	57°46'N	23°15'E
Ruhr, r., Ger. (ròr)	154	51°18'N	8°17'E
Ruhrort, neigh., Ger.	236	51°26'N	6°45'E
Rui'an, China (rwā-än)	193	27°48'N	120°40'E
Ruislip, neigh., Eng., U.K.	235	51°34'N	0°25'W
Ruiz, Mex. (ròē'z)	118	21°55'N	105°09'W
Ruiz, Nevado del, vol., Col. (nĕ-vá'dô-dĕl-rōōē'z)	130a	4°52'N	75°20'W
Rūjiena, Lat. (rò'yĭ-ă-ná)	153	57°54'N	25°19'E
Ruki, r., D.R.C.	216	0°05'S	18°55'E
Rukwa, Lake, l., Tan. (rōōk-wä')	212	8°00'S	32°25'E
Rum, r., Mn., U.S. (rŭm)	103	45°52'N	93°45'W
Ruma, Yugo. (rōō'má)	161	45°00'N	19°53'E
Rum'ancevo, Russia	239b	55°38'N	37°26'E
Rumbek, Sudan (rŭm'bĕk)	211	6°52'N	29°43'E
Rum Cay, i., Bah.	123	23°40'N	74°50'W
Rumelihisari, neigh., Tur.	239f	41°05'N	29°03'E
Rumford, Me., U.S. (rŭm'fẽrd)	92	44°32'N	70°35'W
Rummah, Wādī ar, val., Sau. Ar.	182	26°17'N	41°45'E
Rummānah, Egypt	181a	31°01'N	32°39'E
Rummelsburg, neigh., Ger.	238a	52°30'N	13°29'E
Rummenohl, Ger.	236	51°17'N	7°32'E
Runan, China (rōō-nän)	192	32°59'N	114°22'E
Runcorn, Eng., U.K. (rŭŋ'kôrn)	144a	53°20'N	2°44'W
Runnemede, N.J., U.S.	229b	39°51'N	75°04'W
Runnymede, pt. of i., Eng., U.K.	235	51°26'N	0°34'W
Ruo, r., China (rwô)	188	41°15'N	100°46'E
Rupat, i., Indon. (rōō'pät)	181b	1°55'N	101°35'E
Rupat, Selat, strt., Indon.	181b	1°55'N	101°17'E
Rupert, Id., U.S. (rōō'pẽrt)	105	42°36'N	113°41'W
Rupert, Rivière de, r., Can.	85	51°35'N	76°30'W
Rural Ridge, Pa., U.S.	230b	40°35'N	79°50'W
Ruse, Bul. (rōō'sĕ) (rò'sĕ)	142	43°50'N	25°59'E
Rushan, China (rōō-shän)	190	36°54'N	121°31'E
Rush City, Mn., U.S.	103	45°40'N	92°59'W
Rusholme, neigh., Eng., U.K.	237b	53°27'N	2°12'W
Rushville, Il., U.S. (rŭsh'vĭl)	111	40°08'N	90°34'W
Rushville, In., U.S.	98	39°35'N	85°30'W
Rushville, Ne., U.S.	102	42°43'N	102°27'W
Rusizi, r., Afr.	217	3°00'S	29°05'E
Rusk, Tx., U.S. (rŭsk)	113	31°49'N	95°09'W
Ruskin, Can. (rŭs'kĭn)	106d	49°10'N	122°25'W
Russ, r., Aus.	145e	48°12'N	16°55'E
Russas, Braz. (rōō's-säs)	131	4°48'S	37°50'W
Russell, Can.	83c	45°15'N	75°22'W
Russell, Can. (rŭs'ĕl)	84	50°47'N	101°15'W
Russell, Ca., U.S.	106b	37°39'N	122°08'W
Russell, Ks., U.S.	110	38°51'N	98°51'W
Russell, Ky., U.S.	98	38°30'N	82°45'W
Russel Lake, l., Can.	89	56°15'N	101°30'W
Russell Gardens, N.Y., U.S.	228	40°47'N	73°43'W
Russell Islands, is., Sol. Is.	203	9°16'S	158°30'E
Russellville, Al., U.S. (rŭs'ĕl-vĭl)	114	34°29'N	87°44'W
Russellville, Ar., U.S.	111	35°16'N	93°08'W
Russellville, Ky., U.S.	114	36°48'N	86°51'W
Russia, nation, Russia	164	61°00'N	60°00'E
Russian, r., Ca., U.S. (rŭsh'ăn)	108	38°59'N	123°10'W
Rustavi, Geor.	168	41°33'N	45°02'E
Rustenburg, S. Afr. (rŭs'tĕn-bûrg)	218d	25°40'S	27°15'E
Ruston, La., U.S. (rŭs'tŭn)	113	32°32'N	92°39'W
Ruston, Wa., U.S.	106a	47°18'N	122°30'W
Rusville, S. Afr.	244b	26°10'S	28°18'E
Rute, Spain (rōō'tä)	158	38°20'N	4°34'W
Ruth, Nv., U.S. (rōōth)	108	39°17'N	115°00'W
Ruthenia, hist. reg., Ukr.	155	48°25'N	23°00'E
Rutherford, N.J., U.S.	228	40°49'N	74°07'W
Rutherfordton, N.C., U.S. (rŭdh'ẽr-fẽrd-tŭn)	115	35°23'N	81°58'W
Rutland, Vt., U.S.	99	43°35'N	72°55'W
Rutledge, Md., U.S. (rût'lĕdj)	100e	39°34'N	76°33'W
Rutledge, Pa., U.S.	229b	39°54'N	75°20'W
Rutog, China	188	33°29'N	79°26'E
Rutshuru, D.R.C. (rōōt-shōō'rōō)	212	1°11'S	29°27'E
Rüttenscheid, neigh., Ger.	236	51°26'N	7°00'E
Ruvo, Italy (rōō'vô)	160	41°07'N	16°32'E
Ruvuma, r., Afr.	212	11°30'S	37°00'E
Ruza, Russia (rōō'zá)	162	55°42'N	36°12'E
Ruzhany, Bela. (rò-zhän'ĭ)	155	52°49'N	24°54'E
Rwanda, nation, Afr.	212	2°10'S	29°37'E
Ryabovo, Russia (ryä'bô-vô)	172c	59°24'N	31°08'E
Ryarsh, Eng., U.K.	235	51°19'N	0°24'E
Ryazan', Russia (ryä-zän'')	164	54°37'N	39°43'E
Ryazan', prov., Russia	162	54°10'N	39°37'E
Ryazhsk, Russia (ryäzh'sk')	166	53°43'N	40°04'E
Rybachiy, Poluostrov, pen., Russia	166	69°50'N	33°20'E
Rybatskoye, Russia	172c	59°50'N	30°31'E
Rybinsk, Russia	164	58°02'N	38°52'E
Rybinskoye, res., Russia	164	58°23'N	38°15'E
Rybnik, Pol. (rĭb'nĕk)	155	50°06'N	18°37'E
Rydal, Pa., U.S.	229b	40°06'N	75°06'W
Rydalmere, Austl.	243a	33°49'S	151°02'E
Ryde, Austl.	243a	33°49'S	151°06'E
Ryde, Eng., U.K. (rīd)	150	50°43'N	1°16'W
Rye, N.Y., U.S. (rī)	100a	40°58'N	73°42'W
Ryl'sk, Russia (rēl''sk)	167	51°33'N	34°42'E
Rynfield, S. Afr.	244b	26°09'S	28°20'E
Ryōtsu, Japan (ryōt'sōō)	194	38°02'N	138°23'E
Rypin, Pol. (rĭ'pĕn)	155	53°04'N	19°25'E
Rysy, mtn., Eur.	155	49°12'N	20°04'E
Ryukyu Islands *see* Nansei-shotō, is., Japan	189	27°30'N	127°00'E
Rzeszów, Pol. (zhá-shóf)	147	50°02'N	22°00'E
Rzhev, Russia ('r-zhĕf)	164	56°16'N	34°17'E
Rzhyshchiv, Ukr.	163	49°58'N	31°05'E

S

PLACE (Pronunciation)	PAGE	LAT.	LONG.
Saale, r., Ger. (sä-lē)	154	51°14'N	11°52'E
Saalfeld, Ger. (säl'fĕlt)	154	50°38'N	11°20'E
Saarbrücken, Ger. (zähr'brü-kĕn)	147	49°15'N	7°01'E
Saaremaa, i., Est.	166	58°25'N	22°30'E
Saarland, state, Ger.	154	49°25'N	6°50'E
Saarn, neigh., Ger.	236	51°24'N	6°53'E
Saarnberg, neigh., Ger.	236	51°25'N	6°53'E
Saavedra, Arg. (sä-ä-vā'drä)	132	37°45'S	62°23'W
Şaba, i., Neth. Ant. (sä'bä)	121b	17°39'N	63°20'W
Šabac, Yugo. (shä'bàts)	149	44°45'N	19°49'E
Sabadell, Spain (sä-bä-dhāl')	148	41°32'N	2°07'E
Sabah, hist. reg., Malay.	196	5°10'N	116°25'E
Sabana, Archipiélago de, is., Cuba	122	23°05'N	80°00'W
Sabana, Río, r., Pan. (sä-bä'nä)	121	8°40'N	78°02'W
Sabana de la Mar, Dom. Rep. (sä-bä'nä dā lä mär')	123	19°05'N	69°30'W
Sabana de Uchire, Ven. (sä-bá'nä dĕ ōō-chē'rĕ)	131b	10°02'N	65°32'W
Sabanagrande, Hond. (sä-bä'nä-grä'n-dĕ)	120	13°47'N	87°16'W
Sabanalarga, Col. (sä-bá'nä-lär'gä)	130	10°38'N	75°02'W
Sabanas Páramo, mtn., Col. (sä-bá'näs pá'rä-mô)	130a	6°28'N	76°08'W
Sabancuy, Mex. (sä-bäŋ-kwē')	119	18°58'N	91°09'W
Sabang, Indon. (sä'bäng)	196	5°52'N	95°26'E
Sabaudia, Italy (sá-bou'dē-ä)	160	41°19'N	13°00'E
Sabetha, Ks., U.S. (sȧ-bĕth'ȧ)	111	39°54'N	95°49'W
Sabi (Rio Save), r., Afr. (sä'bē)	212	20°18'S	32°07'E
Sabile, Lat. (sá'bē-lĕ)	153	57°03'N	22°34'E
Sabinal, Tx., U.S. (sá-bī'năl)	112	29°19'N	99°27'W
Sabinal, Cayo, i., Cuba (kä'yō sä-bē-näl')	122	21°40'N	77°20'W
Sabinas, Mex.	116	28°05'N	101°30'W
Sabinas, r., Mex. (sä-bē'näs)	112	26°37'N	99°52'W
Sabinas, Río, r., Mex. (rē'ō sä-bē'näs)	112	27°25'N	100°33'W
Sabinas Hidalgo, Mex. (ē-däl'gô)	112	26°30'N	100°10'W
Sabine, Tx., U.S. (sá-bēn')	113	29°44'N	93°54'W
Sabine, r., U.S.	97	32°00'N	94°30'W
Sabine, Mount, mtn., Ant.	219	72°05'S	169°10'E
Sabine Lake, l., La., U.S.	113	29°53'N	93°41'W
Sablayan, Phil. (säb-lä-yän')	197a	12°49'N	120°47'E
Sable, Cape, c., Can. (sā'b'l)	85	43°25'N	65°24'W
Sable, Cape, c., Fl., U.S.	97	25°12'N	81°10'W
Sables, Rivière aux, r., Can.	91	49°00'N	70°20'W
Sablé-sur-Sarthe, Fr. (säb-lā-sür-särt')	156	47°50'N	0°17'W
Sablya, Gora, mtn., Russia	166	64°50'N	59°00'E
Sâbor, r., Port. (sä-bōr')	158	41°18'N	6°54'W
Sabunchu, Azer.	168	40°26'N	49°56'E
Saburovo, neigh., Russia	239b	55°38'N	37°42'E

ăt; finăl; rāte; senāte; ärm; àsk; sofȧ; fâre; ch-choose; dh-as th in other; bē; ēvent; bĕt; recĕnt; cratẽr; g-gō; gh-guttural g; bĭt; ĭ-short neutral; rīde; K-guttural k as ch in German ich;

PLACE (Pronunciation)	PAGE	LAT.	LONG.
Sabzevār, Iran	185	36°13′N	57°42′E
Sac, r., Mo., U.S. (sŏk)	111	38°11′N	93°45′W
Sacandaga Reservoir, res., N.Y., U.S.	99	43°10′N	74°15′W
Sacavém, Port. (sä-kä-vĕn′)	159b	38°47′N	9°06′W
Sacavém, r., Port.	159b	38°52′N	9°06′W
Sac City, Ia., U.S. (sŏk)	102	42°25′N	95°00′W
Sachigo Lake, l., Can. (săch′ĭ-gō)	89	53°49′N	92°08′W
Sachsen, hist. reg., Ger. (zäk′sĕn)	154	50°45′N	12°17′E
Sacketts Harbor, N.Y., U.S. (săk′ĕts)	99	43°55′N	76°05′W
Sackville, Can. (săk′vĭl)	92	45°54′N	64°22′W
Saco, Me., U.S. (sô′kō)	92	43°30′N	70°28′W
Saco, r., Braz. (sä′kô)	132b	22°20′S	43°26′W
Saco, r., Me., U.S.	92	43°53′N	70°46′W
Sacramento, Mex.	112	25°45′N	103°22′W
Sacramento, Mex.	112	27°05′N	101°45′W
Sacramento, Ca., U.S. (săk-rá-mĕn′tō)	96	38°35′N	121°30′W
Sacramento, r., Ca., U.S.	108	40°20′N	122°07′W
Sacrow, neigh., Ger.	238a	52°26′N	13°06′E
Sa′dah, Yemen	182	16°50′N	43°45′E
Saddle Brook, N.J., U.S.	228	40°54′N	74°06′W
Saddle Lake Indian Reserve, I.R., Can.	87	54°00′N	111°40′W
Saddle Mountain, mtn., Or., U.S. (săd′′l)	106c	45°58′N	123°40′W
Saddle Rock, N.Y., U.S.	228	40°48′N	73°45′W
Sadiya, India (sŭ-dē′yä)	183	27°53′N	95°35′E
Sado, i., Japan (sä′dō)	189	38°05′N	138°26′E
Sado, r., Port. (sä′dō)	158	38°15′N	8°20′W
Saeby, Den. (sĕ′bü)	152	57°21′N	10°29′E
Saeki, Japan (sä′á-kĕ)	194	32°56′N	131°51′E
Safdar Jang′s Tomb, rel., India	240d	28°36′N	77°13′E
Säffle, Swe.	152	59°10′N	12°55′E
Safford, Az., U.S. (săf′fĕrd)	109	32°50′N	109°45′W
Safi, Mor. (sä′fē)(äs′fē)	210	32°24′N	9°09′W
Saga, Japan (sä′gä)	195	33°15′N	130°18′E
Sagamihara, Japan	242a	35°34′N	139°23′E
Sagami-Nada, b., Japan (sä′gä′mĕ nä-dä)	195	35°06′N	139°24′E
Sagamore Hills, Oh., U.S. (săg′á-môr hĭlz)	101d	41°19′N	81°34′W
Saganaga, l., N.A. (sä-gá-nä′gá)	103	48°13′N	91°17′W
Sāgar, India	183	23°55′N	78°45′E
Saghyz, r., Kaz.	170	48°30′N	56°10′E
Saginaw, Mi., U.S. (săg′ĭ-nô)	97	43°25′N	84°00′W
Saginaw, Mn., U.S.	107h	46°51′N	92°26′W
Saginaw, Tx., U.S.	107c	32°52′N	97°22′W
Saginaw Bay, b., Mi., U.S.	97	43°50′N	83°40′W
Saguache, Co., U.S. (sá-wäch′)	109	38°05′N	106°10′W
Saguache Creek, r., Co., U.S.	98	38°05′N	106°40′W
Sagua de Tánamo, Cuba (sä-gwä dĕ tá′nä-mō)	123	20°40′N	75°15′W
Sagua la Grande, Cuba (sä-gwä lä grä′n-dĕ)	122	22°45′N	80°05′W
Saguaro National Monument, rec., Az., U.S. (säg-wä′rō)	109	32°12′N	110°40′W
Saguenay, r., Can. (säg-ē-nä′)	85	48°20′N	70°15′W
Sagunt, Spain	159	38°58′N	1°29′E
Sagunto, Spain (sä-gòn′tō)	148	39°40′N	0°17′W
Sahara, des., Afr. (sá-hä′rá)	210	23°44′N	1°40′W
Saharan Atlas, mts., Afr.	148	33°31′N	1°02′W
Sahāranpur, India (sŭ-hä′rŭn-pōōr′)	183	29°58′N	77°41′E
Sahara Village, Ut., U.S. (sá-hä′rá)	107b	41°06′N	111°58′W
Sahel see Sudan, reg., Afr.	210	15°00′N	7°00′E
Sāhiwāl, Pak.	186	30°43′N	73°04′E
Sahuayo de Dias, Mex.	118	20°03′N	102°43′W
Saigon see Ho Chi Minh City, Viet.	196	10°46′N	106°34′E
Saijō, Japan (sä′è-jō)	195	33°55′N	133°13′E
Saimaa, l., Fin. (sä′ĭ-mä)	146	61°24′N	28°45′E
Sain Alto, Mex. (sä-ēn′ äl′tō)	118	23°35′N	103°13′W
Saint Adolphe, Can. (sånt a′dôlf)(săn′ tá-dôlf′)	83f	49°40′N	97°07′W
Saint Afrique, Fr. (săn′ tá-frēk′)	156	43°58′N	2°52′E
Saint Albans, Austl. (sånt ôl′bănz)	201a	37°44′S	144°47′E
Saint Albans, Eng., U.K.	150	51°44′N	0°20′W
Saint Albans, Vt., U.S.	99	44°50′N	73°05′W
Saint Albans, W.V., U.S.	98	38°20′N	81°50′W
Saint Albans, neigh., N.Y., U.S.	228	40°42′N	73°46′W
Saint Albans Cathedral, pt. of i., Eng., U.K.	235	51°45′N	0°20′W
Saint Albert, Can. (sånt ăl′bĕrt)	87	53°38′N	113°38′W
Saint Amand-Mont Rond, Fr. (săn′t á-män′ môn-rôn′)	156	46°44′N	2°28′E
Saint André-Est, Can.	83a	45°33′N	74°19′W
Saint Andrews, Can.	85	45°05′N	67°03′W
Saint Andrews, Scot., U.K.	150	56°20′N	2°40′W
Saint Andrew′s Channel, strt., Can.	93	46°06′N	60°28′W
Saint Anicet, Can. (sĕnt ä-nē-sĕ′)	83a	45°07′N	74°23′W
Saint Ann, Mo., U.S.	107e	38°44′N	90°23′W
Sainte Anne, Guad.	121b	16°15′N	61°23′W
Saint Anne, Il., U.S.	101a	41°07′N	87°44′W
Sainte-Anne, r., Can.	83b	47°07′N	70°50′W
Sainte Anne, r., Can. (sånt än′)(sănt än′)	91	46°55′N	71°46′W
Sainte Anne-des-Plaines, Can. (dä plĕn)	83a	45°46′N	73°49′W
Saint Anne of the Congo, rel., Congo	244c	4°16′S	15°17′E
Saint Ann′s Bay, Jam.	122	18°25′N	77°15′W
Saint Anns Bay, b., Can. (ănz)	93	46°20′N	60°30′W
Saint Anselme, Can. (sănt′ tän-sĕlm′)	83b	46°37′N	70°58′W
Saint Anthony, Can. (săn än′thô-nē)	85	51°24′N	55°35′W
Saint Anthony, Id., U.S. (sånt än′thô-nē)	105	43°59′N	111°42′W
Saint Antoine-de-Tilly, Can.	83b	46°40′N	71°31′W
Saint Apollinaire, Can. (săn′ tá-pôl-ė-nâr′)	83b	46°36′N	71°30′W
Saint Arnoult-en-Yvelines, Fr. (săN-tär-nōō′ĕn-nĕv-lēn′)	157b	48°33′N	1°55′E
Saint Augustin-de-Québec, Can. (sĕn tō-güs-tĕn′)	83b	46°45′N	71°27′W
Saint Augustin-Deux-Montagnes, Can.	83a	45°38′N	73°59′W
Saint Augustine, Fl., U.S. (sånt ō′gŭs-tēn)	97	29°53′N	81°21′W
Sainte Barbe, Can. (sånt bärb′)	83a	45°14′N	74°12′W
Saint Barthélemy, i., Guad.	121b	17°55′N	62°32′W
Saint Bees Head, c., Eng., U.K. (sånt bēz′ hĕd)	150	54°30′N	3°40′W
Saint Benoit, Can. (sĕn bĕ-nōō-ä′)	83a	45°34′N	74°05′W
Saint Bernard, La., U.S. (bĕr-närd′)	100d	29°52′N	89°52′W
Saint Bernard, Oh., U.S.	101f	39°10′N	84°30′W
Saint Bride, Mount, mtn., Can. (sånt brīd)	87	51°30′N	115°57′W
Saint Brieuc, Fr. (săn′ brēs′)	147	48°32′N	2°47′W
Saint Bruno, Can. (brü′nō)	83a	45°31′N	73°20′W
Saint Canut, Can. (săn′ ká-nü′)	83a	45°43′N	74°04′W
Saint Casimir, Can. (ká-zĕ-mēr′)	91	46°45′N	72°34′W
Saint Catharines, Can. (kăth′á-rĭnz)	85	43°10′N	79°14′W
Saint Catherine, Mount, mtn., Gren.	121b	12°10′N	61°42′W
Saint Chamas, Fr. (săn-shä-mä′)	156a	43°32′N	5°03′E
Saint Chamond, Fr. (săn′ shá-môn′)	147	45°30′N	4°17′E
Saint Charles, Can. (săn′ shärlz′)	83b	46°47′N	70°57′W
Saint Charles, Il., U.S. (sånt chärlz′)	101a	41°55′N	88°19′W
Saint Charles, Mi., U.S.	98	43°20′N	84°10′W
Saint Charles, Mn., U.S.	103	43°56′N	92°05′W
Saint Charles, Mo., U.S.	107e	38°47′N	90°29′W
Saint Charles, Lac, l., Can.	83b	46°56′N	71°21′W
Saint Christopher-Nevis see Saint Kitts and Nevis, nation, N.A.	116	17°24′N	63°30′W
Saint Clair, Mi., U.S. (sånt klâr′)	98	42°55′N	82°30′W
Saint Clair, l., Can.	97	42°25′N	82°30′W
Saint Clair, r., Can.	98	42°45′N	82°25′W
Saint Clair Shores, Mi., U.S.	101b	42°30′N	82°54′W
Saint Claude, Fr. (săn′ klōd′)	157	46°24′N	5°53′E
Saint Clet, Can. (sånt′ klä′)	83a	45°22′N	74°21′W
Saint-Cloud, Fr.	237c	48°51′N	2°13′E
Saint Cloud, Fl., U.S. (sånt kloud′)	115a	28°13′N	81°17′W
Saint Cloud, Mn., U.S.	97	45°33′N	94°08′W
Saint Constant, Can. (kōn′stănt)	83a	45°23′N	73°34′W
Saint Croix, i., V.I.U.S. (sånt kroi′)	117	17°40′N	64°43′W
Saint Croix, r., N.A. (kroi′)	92	45°28′N	67°32′W
Saint Croix, r., U.S. (sånt kroi′)	97	45°45′N	93°00′W
Saint Croix Indian Reservation, I.R., Wi., U.S.	103	45°40′N	92°21′W
Saint Croix Island, i., S. Afr. (săn krwä)	213c	33°48′S	25°45′E
Saint-Cyr-l'Ecole, Fr.	237c	48°48′N	2°04′E
Saint Damien-de-Buckland, Can. (sånt dä′mĕ-ĕn)	83b	46°37′N	70°39′W
Saint David, Can. (da′vĭd)	83b	46°47′N	71°11′W
Saint Davids, Fr.	229b	40°02′N	75°22′W
Saint David′s Head, c., Wales, U.K.	150	51°54′N	5°25′W
Saint-Denis, Fr. (săn′dĕ-nē′)	147	48°26′N	2°22′E
Saint Dizier, Fr. (dĕ-zyä′)	147	48°49′N	4°55′E
Saint Dominique, Can. (sĕn dō-mē-nēk′)	83a	45°19′N	74°09′W
Sainte-Dorothée, neigh., Can.	227b	45°32′N	73°49′W
Saint Edouard-de-Napierville, Can. (sĕn-tĕ-dōō-är′)	83a	45°14′N	73°31′W
Saint Elias, Mount, mtn., N.A. (sånt ė-lī′ăs)	84	60°25′N	141°00′W
Saint Étienne, Fr.	147	45°26′N	4°22′E
Saint Etienne-de-Lauzon, Can. (săN′ tā-tyĕn′)	83b	46°39′N	71°19′W
Sainte Euphémie, Can. (sĕnt û-fĕ-mē′)	83b	46°47′N	70°27′W
Saint Eustache, Can. (săn′ tû-stäsh′)	83a	45°34′N	73°54′W
Saint Eustache, Can.	83f	46°58′N	97°47′W
Sainte Famille, Can. (săN′t fä-mē′y)	83b	46°58′N	70°58′W
Saint Félicien, Can. (săn fä-lē-syăn′)	85	48°39′N	72°28′W
Sainte Felicite, Can.	92	48°54′N	67°20′W
Saint Féréol, Can. (fa-rä-ôl′)	83b	47°07′N	70°52′W
Saint Florent-sur-Cher, Fr. (săn′ flô-rän′sür-shâr′)	156	46°58′N	2°15′E
Saint Flour, Fr. (săn flōōr′)	156	45°02′N	3°09′E
Sainte Foy, Can. (sånt fwä)	91	46°47′N	71°18′W
Saint Francis, r., Ar., U.S.	111	35°56′N	90°27′W
Saint Francis Lake, l., Can.	91	45°00′N	74°00′W
Saint François, Can. (săn′frän-swä′)	83b	47°01′N	70°49′W
Saint François de Boundji, Congo	216	1°03′S	15°22′E
Saint François Xavier, Can.	83f	49°55′N	97°32′W
Saint Gaudens, Fr. (gō-däns′)	156	43°07′N	0°43′E
Sainte-Geneviève, Can.	227b	45°29′N	73°23′W
Sainte Genevieve, Mo., U.S. (sånt jĕn′ė-vēv)	111	37°58′N	90°02′W
Saint George, Austl. (sånt jôrj′)	203	28°02′S	148°40′E
Saint George, Can. (săn′zhôrzh′)	83d	45°08′N	66°49′W
Saint George, Can. (sånt jôrj′)	85	45°08′N	66°49′W
Saint George, S.C., U.S. (sånt jôrj′)	115	33°11′N	80°35′W
Saint George, Ut., U.S.	109	37°06′N	113°40′W
Saint George, neigh., N.Y., U.S.	228	40°39′N	74°05′W
Saint George, i., Ak., U.S.	95	56°30′N	169°40′W
Saint George, Cape, c., Can.	85a	48°28′N	59°15′W
Saint George, Cape, c., Fl., U.S.	114	29°30′N	85°00′W
Saint George′s, Fr. Gu.	131	3°48′N	51°47′W
Saint George′s, Gren.	121b	12°02′N	61°57′W
Saint George′s Bay, b., Can.	85a	45°49′N	61°45′W
Saint Georges Bay, b., Can.	93	45°49′N	61°45′W
Saint George′s Channel, strt., Eur. (jôr-jĕz)	142	51°45′N	6°30′W
Saint Germain-en-Laye, Fr. (săn′ zhĕr-măn-äN-lā′)	156	48°53′N	2°05′E
Saint Gervais, Can. (zhĕr-vĕ′)	83b	46°43′N	70°53′W
Saint Girons, Fr. (zhē-rôn′)	156	42°58′N	1°08′E
Saint Gotthard Pass, p., Switz.	154	46°33′N	8°34′E
Saint-Gratien, Fr.	237c	48°58′N	2°17′E
Saint Gregory, Mount, mtn., Can. (sånt grĕg′ĕr-ė)	93	49°19′N	58°13′W
Saint Helena, St. Hel.	209	16°01′S	5°16′W
Saint Helenabaai, b., S. Afr.	212	32°25′S	17°15′E
Sainte-Hélène, Île, i., Can.	227b	45°31′N	73°32′W
Saint Helens, Eng., U.K.	144a	53°27′N	2°44′W
Saint Helens, Or., U.S. (hĕl′ĕnz)	106c	45°52′N	122°49′W
Saint Helens, Mount, vol., Wa., U.S.	104	46°13′N	122°10′W
Saint Helier, Jersey (hyĕl′yĕr)	156	49°12′N	2°06′W
Saint Henri, Can. (săn′ hĕn′rė)	83b	46°41′N	71°04′W
Saint Hubert, Can.	83a	45°29′N	73°24′W
Saint Hyacinthe, Can.	85	45°35′N	72°55′W
Saint Ignace, Mi., U.S. (sånt ĭg′nás)	103	45°51′N	84°39′W
Saint Ignace, i., Can. (sånt ĭg′nás)	90	48°47′N	88°14′W
Saint Irenee, Can. (săn′ tĕ-rä-nä′)	91	47°34′N	70°15′W
Saint Isidore-de-Laprairie, Can.	83a	45°18′N	73°41′W
Saint Isidore-de-Prescott, Can. (săn′ ĭz′ĭ-dôr-près-kōt)	83c	45°23′N	74°54′W
Saint Isidore-Dorchester, Can. (dôr-chĕs′tĕr)	83b	46°35′N	71°05′W
Saint Ives, Austl.	243a	33°44′S	151°10′E
Saint Jacob, Il., U.S. (jä-kŏb)	107e	38°43′N	89°46′W
Saint James, Mn., U.S. (sånt jämz′)	103	43°58′N	94°37′W
Saint James, Cape, c., Can.	86	51°58′N	131°00′W
Saint Janvier, Can. (săn′ zhän-vyä′)	83a	45°43′N	73°56′W
Saint Jean, Can.	83b	46°55′N	70°54′W
Saint Jean, Can. (săn′ zhän′)	85	45°20′N	73°15′W
Saint Jean, Lac, l., Can.	85	48°35′N	72°00′W
Saint Jean-Chrysostome, Can. (krī-zōs-tōm′)	83b	46°43′N	71°12′W
Saint Jean-d′Angely, Fr. (dän-zhä-lē′)	156	45°56′N	0°33′W
Saint Jean-de-Luz, Fr. (dĕ lüz′)	156	43°23′N	1°40′W
Saint Jérôme, Can. (sånt jĕ-rōm′)(săn zhä-rōm′)	83a	45°47′N	74°00′W
Saint Joachim-de-Montmorency, Can. (sånt jō′á-kĭm)	83b	47°04′N	70°51′W
Saint John, Can. (sånt jŏn)	85	45°16′N	66°03′W
Saint John, In., U.S.	101a	41°27′N	87°29′W
Saint John, Ks., U.S.	110	37°59′N	98°44′W
Saint John, N.D., U.S.	102	48°57′N	99°42′W
Saint John, i., V.I.U.S.	117b	18°16′N	64°48′W
Saint John, r., N.A.	85	47°00′N	68°00′W
Saint John, Cape, c., Can.	93	50°00′N	55°32′W
Saint Johns, Antig.	121b	17°07′N	61°50′W
Saint John′s, Can. (jŏns)	85a	47°34′N	52°43′W
Saint Johns, Az., U.S. (jŏnz)	109	34°30′N	109°25′W
Saint Johns, Mi., U.S.	98	43°05′N	84°35′W
Saint Johns, r., Fl., U.S.	97	29°54′N	81°32′W
Saint Johnsburg, N.Y., U.S.	230a	43°05′N	78°53′W
Saint Johnsbury, Vt., U.S. (jŏnz′bĕr-ė)	99	44°25′N	72°00′W
Saint John′s University, pt. of i., N.Y., U.S.	228	40°43′N	73°48′W
Saint Joseph, Dom.	121b	15°25′N	61°26′W
Saint Joseph, Mi., U.S.	98	42°05′N	86°30′W
Saint Joseph, Mo., U.S.	97	39°44′N	94°49′W
Saint Joseph, l., Can.	98	46°15′N	83°55′W
Saint Joseph, l., Can. (jō′zhŭf)	85	51°31′N	90°40′W
Saint Joseph, r., Mi., U.S. (sånt jō′sĕf)	98	41°45′N	85°50′W
Saint Joseph Bay, b., Fl., U.S. (jō′zhŭf)	114	29°48′N	85°26′W
Saint Joseph-de-Beauce, Can. (sĕn zhō-zĕf′dĕ bōs)	83b	46°18′N	70°52′W
Saint Joseph-du-Lac, Can. (sĕn zhō-zĕf′ dü läk)	83a	45°32′N	74°00′W
Saint Joseph Island, i., Tx., U.S. (sånt jō-sĕf)	113	27°58′N	96°50′W
Saint Junien, Fr. (săn′zhü-nyän′)	156	45°53′N	0°54′E
Sainte Justine-de-Newton, Can. (sånt jüs-tēn′)	83a	45°22′N	74°22′W
Saint Kilda, Austl.	201a	37°52′S	144°59′E
Saint Kilda, i., Scot., U.K. (kĭl′dá)	150	57°50′N	8°32′W
Saint Kitts, i., St. K./N. (sånt kĭtts)	117	17°24′N	63°30′W
Saint Kitts and Nevis, nation, N.A.	117	17°24′N	63°30′W
Saint Lambert, Can.	99	45°29′N	73°29′W
Saint Lambert-de-Lévis, Can.	83b	46°35′N	71°12′W
Saint Laurent, Fr. Gu.	131	5°27′N	53°56′W
Saint Laurent-d′Orleans, Can.	83f	45°55′N	73°23′W
Saint Lawrence, i., Ak., U.S.	94a	63°10′N	172°12′W
Saint Lawrence, r., N.A.	85	48°24′N	69°30′W
Saint Lawrence, Gulf of, b., Can.	85	48°00′N	62°00′W
Saint Lazare, Can. (săn′lá-zär′)	83b	46°39′N	70°48′W
Saint Lazare-Vaudreuil, Can.	83a	45°24′N	74°08′W
Saint Léger-en-Yvelines, Fr. (săn-lä-zhĕ′ĕn-nĕv-lēn′)	157b	48°43′N	1°45′E
Saint Léonard, Can. (sånt lĕn′ärd)	92	47°10′N	67°56′W
Saint Leonard, Md., U.S.	100e	38°29′N	76°31′W
Saint Lô, Fr.	156	49°07′N	1°04′W
Saint-Louis, Sen.	210	16°02′N	16°30′W
Saint Louis, Mi., U.S. (sånt lōō′ĭs)	98	43°25′N	84°35′W
Saint Louis, Mo., U.S. (sånt lōō′ĭs)(lōō′ė)	97	38°39′N	90°15′W

ng-sing; ŋ-baŋk; N-nasalized n; nŏd; cŏmmit; ōld; ŏbey; ôrder; oi-boil; fōōd; ȯ-as oo in foot; ou-out; s-soft; sh-dish; th-thin; pūre; ūnite; ûrn; stŭd; circŭs; ü-as in French tu; ′-indeterminate vowel.

342 Saint Louis-Samana or Atwood Cay

PLACE (Pronunciation)	PAGE	LAT.	LONG.
Saint Louis, r., Mn., U.S. (sånt lo͞o'ĭs)	103	46°57'N	92°58'W
Saint Louis, Lac, l., Can. (săn' lo͞o-ē')	83a	45°24'N	73°51'W
Saint Louis-de-Gonzague, Can. (săn' lo͞o ē')	83a	45°13'N	74°00'W
Saint Louis Park, Mn., U.S.	107g	44°56'N	93°21'W
Saint Lucia, nation, N.A.	117	13°54'N	60°40'W
Saint Lucia Channel, strt., N.A. (lū'shĭ-ȧ)	121b	14°15'N	61°00'W
Saint Lucie Canal, can., Fl., U.S. (lū'sė)	115a	26°57'N	80°25'W
Saint Magnus Bay, b., Scot., U.K. (măg'nŭs)	150a	60°25'N	2°09'W
Saint Malo, Fr. (săn' må-lō')	147	48°40'N	2°02'W
Saint Malo, Golfe de, b., Fr. (gôlf-dē-săn-mä-lō')	147	48°50'N	2°49'W
Saint Marc, Haiti (săn' mark')	123	19°10'N	72°40'W
Saint-Marc, Canal de, strt., Haiti	123	19°05'N	73°15'W
Saint Marcellin, Fr. (mär-sē-lăn')	157	45°08'N	5°15'E
Saint Margarets, Md., U.S.	100e	39°02'N	76°30'W
Sainte Marie, Cap, c., Madag.	213	25°31'S	45°00'E
Sainte-Marie-aux-Mines, Fr. (săn'tē-mä-rē'ō-mēn')	157	48°14'N	7°08'E
Sainte Marie-Beauce, Can. (sănt'må-rē')	91	46°27'N	71°03'W
Saint Maries, Id., U.S. (sånt mā'rēs)	104	47°18'N	116°34'W
Saint Martin, i., N.A. (mär'tĭn)	121b	18°06'N	62°54'W
Sainte Martine, Can.	83a	45°14'N	73°37'W
Saint Martins, Can. (mär'tĭnz)	92	45°21'N	65°32'W
Saint Martinville, La., U.S. (mär'tĭn-vĭl)	113	30°08'N	91°50'W
Saint Mary, r., Can. (mā'rė)	87	49°25'N	113°00'W
Saint Mary, Cape, c., Gam.	214	13°28'N	16°40'W
Saint Mary Cray, neigh., Eng., U.K.	235	51°23'N	0°07'E
Saint Marylebone, neigh., Eng., U.K.	235	51°31'N	0°10'W
Saint Mary Reservoir, res., Can.	87	49°30'N	113°00'W
Saint Marys, Austl. (mā'rėz)	204	41°40'S	148°10'E
Saint Marys, Austl.	243a	33°47'S	150°47'E
Saint Marys, Can.	90	43°15'N	81°10'W
Saint Marys, Ga., U.S.	115	30°43'N	81°35'W
Saint Mary's, Ks., U.S.	111	39°12'N	96°03'W
Saint Mary's, Oh., U.S.	98	40°30'N	84°25'W
Saint Marys, Pa., U.S.	99	41°25'N	78°30'W
Saint Marys, W.V., U.S.	98	39°20'N	81°15'W
Saint Marys, r., N.A.	107k	46°27'N	84°33'W
Saint Marys, r., U.S.	115	30°37'N	82°05'W
Saint Mary's Bay, b., Can.	92	44°20'N	66°10'W
Saint Mary's Bay, b., Can.	93	46°50'N	53°47'W
Saint Mathew, S.C., U.S. (măth'ū)	115	33°40'N	80°46'W
Saint Matthew, i., Ak., U.S.	95	60°25'N	172°10'W
Saint Matthews, Ky., U.S. (măth'ūz)	101h	38°15'N	85°39'W
Saint Maur-des-Fossés, Fr.	157b	48°48'N	2°29'E
Saint-Maurice, Fr.	237c	48°49'N	2°25'E
Saint Maurice, r., Can. (săn' mō-rēs') (sånt mô'rĭs)	85	47°20'N	72°55'W
Saint-Mesmes, Fr.	237c	48°59'N	2°42'E
Saint Michael, Ak., U.S. (sånt mī'kĕl)	95	63°22'N	162°20'W
Saint Michel, Can. (săn'mė-shĕl')	83b	46°52'N	70°54'W
Saint-Michel, neigh., Can.	227b	45°35'N	73°35'W
Saint Michel, Bras, r., Can.	83b	46°47'N	70°51'W
Saint Michel-de-l'Atalaye, Haiti	123	19°25'N	72°20'W
Saint Michel-de-Napierville, Can.	83a	45°14'N	73°34'W
Saint Mihiel, Fr. (săn' mē-yĕl')	157	48°53'N	5°30'E
Saint Nazaire, Fr. (săn'nå-zâr')	142	47°18'N	2°13'W
Saint Nérée, Can. (nā-rā')	83b	46°43'N	70°43'W
Saint Nicolas, Can. (ne-kô-lä')	83b	46°42'N	71°22'W
Saint Nicolas, Cap, c., Haiti	123	19°45'N	73°35'W
Saint Omer, Fr. (săn'tō-mâr')	156	50°44'N	2°16'E
Saint-Ouen, Fr.	237c	48°54'N	2°20'E
Saint Pancras, neigh., Eng., U.K.	235	51°32'N	0°07'W
Saint Pascal, Can. (sĕn pä-skäl')	92	47°32'N	69°48'W
Saint Paul, Can. (sånt pôl')	84	53°59'N	111°17'W
Saint Paul, Mn., U.S.	97	44°57'N	93°05'W
Saint Paul, Ne., U.S.	102	41°13'N	98°28'W
Saint Paul, i., Can.	93	47°15'N	60°10'W
Saint Paul, i., Ak., U.S.	95	57°10'N	170°20'W
Saint Paul, r., Lib.	214	7°10'N	10°00'W
Saint Paul, Île, i., Afr.	3	38°43'S	77°31'E
Saint Paul Park, Mn., U.S. (pärk)	107g	44°51'N	93°00'W
Saint Pauls, N.C., U.S. (pôls)	115	34°47'N	78°57'W
Saint Paul's Cathedral, pt. of i., Eng., U.K.	235	51°31'N	0°06'W
Saint Paul's Cray, neigh., Eng., U.K.	235	51°24'N	0°07'E
Saint Peter, Mn., U.S. (pē tẽr)	103	44°20'N	93°56'W
Saint Peter Port, Guernsey	156	49°27'N	2°35'W
Saint Petersburg (Sankt-Peterburg) (Leningrad), Russia	164	59°57'N	30°20'E
Saint Petersburg, Fl., U.S. (pē'tẽrz-bûrg)	97	27°47'N	82°38'W
Sainte Pétronille, Can. (sĕnt pět-rō-nēl')	83b	46°51'N	71°08'W
Saint Philémon, Can. (sĕn fēl-mōn')	83b	46°41'N	70°28'W
Saint Philippe-d'Argenteuil, Can. (săn'fē-lēp')	83a	45°38'N	74°25'W
Saint Philippe-de-Lapairie, Can.	83a	45°20'N	73°28'W
Saint-Pierre, Can.	227b	45°27'N	73°39'W
Saint Pierre, Mart. (săn'pyâr')	121b	14°45'N	61°12'W
Saint Pierre, St. P./M.	93	46°47'N	56°11'W
Saint Pierre, i., St. P./M.	93	46°47'N	56°11'W
Saint Pierre, Lac, l., Can.	91	46°07'N	72°45'W
Saint Pierre and Miquelon, dep., N.A.	85a	46°53'N	56°40'W
Saint Pierre-d'Orléans, Can.	83b	46°53'N	71°04'W
Saint Pierre-Montmagny, Can.	83b	46°55'N	70°37'W
Saint Placide, Can. (plās'ĭd)	83a	45°32'N	74°11'W
Saint Pol-de-Léon, Fr. (săn-pô'dē-lā-ôn')	156	48°41'N	4°00'W
Saint-Prix, Fr.	237c	49°01'N	2°16'E
Saint Quentin, Fr. (săn'kän-tăn')	147	49°52'N	3°16'E
Saint Raphaël, Can. (rä-fä-ĕl')	83b	46°48'N	70°46'W
Saint Raymond, Can.	91	46°50'N	71°51'W
Saint Rédempteur, Can. (săn rā-dänp-tûr')	83b	46°42'N	71°18'W
Saint Rémi, Can. (sĕn rē-mē')	83a	45°15'N	73°36'W
Saint-Rémy-lès-Chevreuse, Fr.	237c	48°42'N	2°04'E
Saint Romuald-d'Etchemin, Can. (sĕn rō'mo͞o-äl)	91	46°45'N	71°14'W
Sainte Rose, Guad.	121b	16°19'N	61°45'W
Sainte-Rose, neigh., Can.	227b	45°36'N	73°47'W
Saintes, Fr.	156	45°44'N	0°41'W
Sainte Scholastique, Can. (skô-lås-tēk')	83a	45°39'N	74°05'W
Saint Siméon, Can.	91	47°51'N	69°55'W
Saint Stanislas-de-Kostka, Can.	83a	45°11'N	74°08'W
Saint Stephen, Can. (stē'vĕn)	85	45°12'N	66°17'W
Saint Sulpice, Can.	83a	45°50'N	73°21'W
Saint Thérèse-de-Blainville, Can. (tē-rĕz' dē blĕn-vēl')	91	45°38'N	73°51'W
Saint-Thibault-des-Vignes, Fr.	237c	48°52'N	2°41'E
Saint Thomas, Can. (tŏm'ȧs)	85	42°45'N	81°15'W
Saint Thomas, i., V.I.U.S.	117	18°22'N	64°57'W
Saint Thomas Harbor, b., V.I.U.S. (tŏm'ȧs)	117c	18°19'N	64°56'W
Saint Timothée, Can. (tē-mô-tā')	83a	45°17'N	74°03'W
Saint Tropez, Fr. (trô-pĕ')	157	43°15'N	6°42'E
Saint Valentin, Can. (väl-ĕn-tĭn)	83a	45°07'N	73°19'W
Saint Valéry-sur-Somme, Fr. (vå-lā-rē')	156	50°10'N	1°39'E
Saint Vallier, Can. (väl-yā')	83b	46°54'N	70°49'W
Saint Victor, Can. (vĭk'tẽr)	91	46°09'N	70°56'W
Saint Vincent, Gulf, b., Austl. (vĭn'sĕnt)	204	34°55'S	138°00'E
Saint Vincent and the Grenadines, nation, N.A.	117	13°20'N	60°50'W
Saint-Vincent-de-Paul, neigh., Can.	227b	45°37'N	73°39'W
Saint Vincent Passage, strt., N.A.	121b	13°35'N	61°10'W
Saint Walburg, Can.	84	53°39'N	109°12'W
Saint Yrieix-la-Perche, Fr. (ē-rē-ĕ)	156	45°30'N	1°08'E
Saitama, dept., Japan (sī'tä-mä)	195a	35°52'N	139°40'E
Saitbaba, Russia (så-ĕt'bå-bå)	172a	54°06'N	56°42'E
Sajama, Nevada, mtn., Bol. (nĕ-vå'dä-sä-hä'mä)	130	18°13'S	68°53'W
Sakai, Japan (sä'kä-ė)	194	34°34'N	135°28'E
Sakaiminato, Japan	195	35°33'N	133°15'E
Sakākah, Sau. Ar.	182	29°58'N	40°03'E
Sakakawea, Lake, res., N.D., U.S.	96	47°49'N	101°58'W
Sakania, D.R.C. (så-kä'nĭ-å)	212	12°45'S	28°34'E
Sakarya, r., Tur. (så-kär'yå)	182	40°10'N	31°00'E
Sakata, Japan (sä'kä-tä)	189	38°56'N	139°57'E
Sakchu, N. Kor. (säk'chò)	194	40°29'N	125°09'E
Sakha (Yakutia), state, Russia	171	65°21'N	117°13'E
Sakhalin, i., Russia (så-kå-lēn')	165	52°00'N	143°00'E
Šakiai, Lith. (shä'kĭ-ī)	153	54°59'N	23°05'E
Sakishima-guntō, is., Japan (sä'kė-shē'ma gòn'tō')	189	24°25'N	125°00'E
Sakmara, r., Russia	167	52°00'N	56°10'E
Sakomet, r., R.I., U.S. (sä-kō'mĕt)	100b	41°32'N	71°11'W
Sakurai, Japan	195b	34°31'N	135°51'E
Sakwaso Lake, l., Can. (sȧ-kwȧ'sō)	89	53°01'N	91°55'W
Sal, i., C.V. (säal)	210b	16°45'N	22°39'W
Sal, r., Russia (sål)	167	47°30'N	43°00'E
Sal, Cay, i., Bah. (kē săl)	122	23°45'N	80°25'W
Sala, Swe. (sô'lä)	152	59°56'N	16°34'E
Sala Consilina, Italy (sä'lä kôn-sė-lē'nä)	160	40°24'N	15°38'E
Salada, Laguna, l., Mex. (lä-gò'nä-sä-lä'dä)	108	32°34'N	115°45'W
Saladillo, Arg. (sä-lä-dēl'yō)	132	35°38'S	59°48'W
Salado, Hond. (sä-lä'dhō)	120	15°44'N	87°03'W
Salado, r., Arg.	129c	35°53'S	58°12'W
Salado, r., Arg. (sä-lä'dô)	132	26°05'S	63°35'W
Salado, r., Arg.	132	37°00'S	67°00'W
Salado, r., Mex.	116	28°00'N	102°00'W
Salado, r., Mex. (sä-lä'dô)	119	18°30'N	97°29'W
Salado Creek, r., Tx., U.S.	107d	29°23'N	98°25'W
Salado de los Nadadores, Río, r., Mex. (dĕ-lôs-nä-dä-dô'rĕs)	112	27°26'N	101°35'W
Salal, Chad	215	14°51'N	17°13'E
Salamanca, Chile (sä-lä-mä'n-kä)	129b	31°48'S	70°57'W
Salamanca, Mex.	116	20°36'N	101°10'W
Salamanca, Spain (sä-lä-mä'n-kå)	142	40°54'N	5°42'W
Salamanca, N.Y., U.S. (săl-å-măŋ'kå)	99	42°10'N	78°45'W
Salamat, Bahr, r., Chad (bär sä-lä-mät')	211	10°06'N	19°16'E
Salamina, Col. (sä-lä-mē'-nä)	130a	5°25'N	75°29'W
Salamis, Grc. (săl'å-mĭs)	161	37°58'N	23°30'E
Salat-la-Canada, Fr.	156	44°52'N	1°13'E
Salaverry, Peru (sä-lä-vă'rė)	130	8°16'S	78°54'W
Salawati, i., Indon. (sä-lä-wä'tė)	197	1°07'S	130°52'E
Salawe, Tan.	217	3°19'S	32°52'E
Sala y Gómez, Isla, i., Chile	225	26°50'S	105°50'W
Salcedo, Dom. Rep. (säl-sä'dō)	123	19°25'N	70°30'W
Saldaña, r., Col. (säl-då'n-yä)	130a	3°42'N	75°16'W
Saldanha, S. Afr.	212	32°55'S	18°05'E
Saldus, Lat. (sål'dòs)	153	56°39'N	22°30'E
Sale, Austl. (sāl)	204	38°10'S	147°07'E
Sale, Eng., U.K.	144a	53°24'N	2°20'W
Sale, r., Can. (sål'rē-vyâr')	83f	49°44'N	97°11'W
Salekhard, Russia (sŭ-lyĭ-kärt)	166	66°35'N	66°50'E
Salem, India	183	11°39'N	78°11'E
Salem, S. Afr.	213c	33°29'S	26°30'E
Salem, Il., U.S. (sā'lĕm)	98	38°40'N	89°00'W
Salem, In., U.S.	98	38°35'N	86°00'W
Salem, Ma., U.S.	93a	42°31'N	70°54'W
Salem, Mo., U.S.	111	37°36'N	91°33'W
Salem, N.H., U.S.	93a	42°46'N	71°16'W
Salem, N.J., U.S.	99	39°35'N	75°30'W
Salem, Oh., U.S.	98	40°55'N	80°50'W
Salem, Or., U.S.	96	44°55'N	123°03'W
Salem, S.D., U.S.	102	43°43'N	97°23'W
Salem, Va., U.S.	115	37°16'N	80°05'W
Salem, W.V., U.S.	98	39°15'N	80°35'W
Salemi, Italy (sä-lā'mē)	160	37°49'N	12°48'E
Salerno, Italy (sä-lĕr'nò)	148	40°27'N	14°46'E
Salerno, Golfo di, b., Italy (gôl-fô-dē)	148	40°30'N	14°40'E
Salford, Eng., U.K. (săl'fẽrd)	150	53°26'N	2°19'W
Salgótarján, Hung. (shôl'gō-tôr-yän)	155	48°06'N	19°50'E
Salhyr, r., Ukr.	163	45°25'N	34°22'E
Salida, Co., U.S. (sȧ-lī'dȧ)	110	38°31'N	106°01'W
Salies-de-Béan, Fr.	156	43°27'N	0°58'W
Salima, Mwi.	217	13°47'S	34°26'E
Salina, Ks., U.S. (sȧ-lī'nȧ)	96	38°50'N	97°37'W
Salina, Ut., U.S.	109	39°00'N	111°55'W
Salina, i., Italy (sä-lē'nä)	160	38°35'N	14°48'E
Salina Cruz, Mex. (sä-lē'nä kro͞oz')	116	16°10'N	95°12'W
Salina Point, c., Bah.	123	22°10'N	74°20'W
Salinas, Mex.	116	22°38'N	101°42'W
Salinas, P.R.	117b	17°58'N	66°16'W
Salinas, Ca., U.S. (sȧ-lē'nȧs)	108	36°41'N	121°40'W
Salinas, r., Mex. (sä-lē'näs)	119	16°15'N	90°31'W
Salinas, r., Ca., U.S.	108	36°33'N	121°29'W
Salinas, Bahía de, b., N.A. (bä-ē'ä-dĕ-sȧ-lē'nȧs)	120	11°05'N	85°55'W
Salinas National Monument, rec., N.M., U.S.	109	34°10'N	106°05'W
Salinas Victoria, Mex. (sä-lē'näs vėk-tō'rē-ä)	112	25°59'N	100°19'W
Saline, r., Ar., U.S. (sȧ-lēn')	111	34°06'N	92°30'W
Saline, r., Ks., U.S.	110	39°05'N	99°43'W
Salins-les-Bains, Fr. (så-lăn'-lā-băn')	157	46°55'N	5°54'E
Salisbury, Can.	92	46°03'N	65°05'W
Salisbury, Eng., U.K. (sôlz'bē-rė)	147	50°35'N	1°51'W
Salisbury, Md., U.S.	99	38°20'N	75°40'W
Salisbury, Mo., U.S.	111	39°24'N	92°47'W
Salisbury, N.C., U.S.	115	35°40'N	80°29'W
Salisbury *see* Harare, Zimb.	212	17°50'S	31°03'E
Salisbury Island, i., Can.	85	63°36'N	76°20'W
Salisbury Plain, pl., Eng., U.K.	150	51°15'N	1°52'W
Salkehatchie, r., S.C., U.S. (sô-kė-hăch'ė)	115	33°09'N	81°10'W
Salkhia, India	240a	22°35'N	88°21'E
Sallisaw, Ok., U.S. (săl'ĭ-sô)	111	35°27'N	94°48'W
Salmon, Id., U.S. (săm'ŭn)	105	45°11'N	113°54'W
Salmon, r., Can.	86	54°00'N	123°50'W
Salmon, r., Can.	92	46°19'N	65°36'W
Salmon, r., Id., U.S.	96	45°30'N	115°45'W
Salmon, r., N.Y., U.S.	99	44°35'N	74°15'W
Salmon, r., Wa., U.S.	106c	45°44'N	122°36'W
Salmon Arm, Can.	87	50°42'N	119°16'W
Salmon Falls Creek, r., Id., U.S.	105	42°22'N	114°53'W
Salmon Gums, Austl. (gŭmz)	202	33°00'S	122°00'E
Salmon River Mountains, mts., Id., U.S.	96	44°15'N	115°44'W
Salon-de-Provence, Fr. (så-lôn-dē-prô-văns')	157	43°48'N	5°09'E
Salonika *see* Thessaloníki, Grc.	142	40°38'N	22°59'E
Salonta, Rom. (sä-lôn'tä)	155	46°46'N	21°38'E
Salop, co., Eng., U.K.	144a	52°36'N	2°45'W
Saloum, r., Sen.	214	14°10'N	15°45'W
Salsette Island, i., India	187b	19°12'N	72°52'E
Sal'sk, Russia (sälsk)	167	46°30'N	41°20'E
Salt, r., Az., U.S. (sôlt)	96	33°28'N	111°35'W
Salt, r., Mo., U.S.	111	39°54'N	92°11'W
Salta, Arg. (säl'tä)	132	24°50'S	65°16'W
Salta, prov., Arg.	132	25°15'S	65°00'W
Saltair, Ut., U.S. (sôlt'âr)	107b	40°46'N	112°09'W
Salt Cay, i., T./C. Is.	123	21°20'N	71°15'W
Salt Creek, r., Il., U.S. (sôlt)	101a	42°01'N	88°01'W
Saltillo, Mex. (säl-tēl'yō)	116	25°24'N	100°59'W
Salt Lake City, Ut., U.S. (sôlt lāk sĭ'tĭ)	96	40°45'N	111°52'W
Salto, Arg. (säl'tō)	129c	34°17'S	60°15'W
Salto, Ur.	132	31°18'S	57°45'W
Salto, r., Mex.	118	22°16'N	99°18'W
Salto, Serra do, mtn., Braz. (sĕ'r-rä-dô)	129a	20°26'S	43°28'W
Salto Grande, Braz. (grän'dä)	131	22°57'S	49°58'W
Salton Sea, Ca., U.S. (sôlt'ŭn)	108	33°28'N	115°43'W
Salton Sea, l., Ca., U.S.	96	33°19'N	115°50'W
Saltpond, Ghana	210	5°16'N	1°07'W
Salt River Indian Reservation, I.R., Az., U.S. (sôlt rĭv'ẽr)	109	33°40'N	112°01'W
Saltsjöbaden, Swe. (sält'shû-bäd'ĕn)	152	59°15'N	18°20'E
Saltspring Island, i., Can. (sält'sprĭng)	86	48°47'N	123°30'W
Saltville, Va., U.S. (sôlt'vĭl)	115	36°50'N	81°45'W
Saltykovka, Russia (sål-tē'kôf-kå)	172b	55°45'N	37°56'E
Salud, Mount, mtn., Pan. (sä-lo͞o'th)	116a	9°14'N	79°42'W
Saluda, S.C., U.S. (sȧ-lo͞o'dȧ)	115	34°02'N	81°46'W
Saluda, r., S.C., U.S.	115	34°07'N	81°48'W
Saluzzo, Italy (sä-lo͞ot'sō)	160	44°39'N	7°31'E
Salvador, Braz. (säl-vä-dōr') (bä-ē'å)	131	12°59'S	38°27'W
Salvador Lake, l., La., U.S.	113	29°45'N	90°20'W
Salvador Point, c., Bah.	122	24°30'N	77°45'W
Salvatierra, Mex. (säl-vä-tyĕr'rä)	118	20°13'N	100°52'W
Salween, r., Asia	180	21°00'N	98°00'E
Salyan, Azer.	167	39°40'N	49°10'E
Salzburg, Aus. (sälts'bòrgh)	147	47°48'N	13°04'E
Salzburg, state, Aus.	154	47°30'N	13°18'E
Salzwedel, Ger. (sälts-vä'dĕl)	154	52°51'N	11°10'E
Samāika, neigh., India	240d	28°32'N	77°05'E
Samālūt, Egypt (så-mä-lo͞ot')	184	28°17'N	30°43'E
Samana, Cabo, c., Dom. Rep.	117	19°20'N	69°00'W
Samana or Atwood Cay, i., Bah.	123	23°05'N	73°45'W

ăt; finȧl; rāte; senåte; ärm; åsk; sofȧ; fâre; ch-choose; dh-as th in other; bē; ėvent; bĕt; recĕnt; cratẽr; g-gō; gh-guttural g; bĭt; ĭ-short neutral; rīde; K-guttural k as ch in German ich;

PLACE (Pronunciation)	PAGE	LAT.	LONG.
Samar, i., Phil. (sä'mär)	197	11°30'N	126°07'E
Samara (Kuybyshev), Russia	166	53°10'N	50°05'E
Samara, r., Russia	167	52°50'N	50°35'E
Samara, r., Ukr. (så-mä'rå)	163	48°47'N	35°30'E
Samarai, Pap. N. Gui. (sä-mä-rä'ê)	197	10°45'S	150°49'E
Samarinda, Indon.	196	0°30'S	117°10'E
Samarkand, Uzb. (så-mår-känt')	169	39°42'N	67°00'E
Şamaxı, Azer.	167	40°35'N	48°40'E
Šamba, D.R.C.	217	4°38'S	26°22'E
Sambalpur, India (sŭm'bŭl-pòr)	183	21°30'N	84°05'E
Sāmbhar, r., India	186	27°00'N	74°58'E
Sambir, Ukr.	155	49°31'N	23°12'E
Samborombón, r., Arg.	129c	35°20'S	57°52'W
Samborombón, Bahía, b., Arg. (bä-ē'ä-säm-bô-rôm-bô'n)	129c	35°57'S	57°05'W
Sambre, r., Eur. (säɴ'br')	151	50°20'N	4°15'E
Sambungo, Ang.	216	8°39'S	20°43'E
Sammamish, r., Wa., U.S.	106a	47°43'N	122°08'W
Sammamish, Lake, l., Wa., U.S. (så-măm'ĭsh)	106a	47°35'N	122°02'W
Samoa Islands, is., Oc.	198a	14°00'S	171°00'W
Samokov, Bul. (sä'mô-kôf)	161	42°20'N	23°33'E
Samora Correia, Port. (så-mô'rä-kôr-rē'yä)	159b	38°55'N	8°52'W
Samorovo, Russia (så-må-rô'vô)	170	60°47'N	69°13'E
Sámos, i., Grc. (sä'mŏs)	149	37°53'N	26°35'E
Samothráki, i., Grc.	149	40°23'N	25°10'E
Sampaloc Point, c., Phil. (säm-pä'lôk)	197a	14°43'N	119°56'E
Sam Rayburn Reservoir, res., Tx., U.S.	113	31°10'N	94°15'W
Samson, Al., U.S. (săm'sŭn)	114	31°06'N	86°02'W
Samsu, N. Kor. (säm'so͞o')	194	41°12'N	128°00'E
Samsun, Tur. (såm'so͞on')	182	41°20'N	36°05'E
Samtredia, Geor. (såm'trĕ-dê)	167	42°18'N	42°25'E
Samuel, i., Can. (såm'ū-ĕl)	106d	48°50'N	123°10'W
Samur, r. (sä-mo͞or')	167	41°40'N	47°20'E
San, Mali (sän)	210	13°18'N	4°54'W
San, r., Eur.	147	50°33'N	22°12'E
Şan'ā', Yemen (sän'ä)	182	15°17'N	44°05'E
Sanaga, r., Cam. (sä-nä'gä)	210	4°30'N	12°00'E
San Ambrosio, Isla, i., Chile (ē's-lä-dĕ-sän äm-brō'zê-ō)	128	26°40'S	80°00'W
Sanana, Pulau, i., Indon.	197	2°15'S	126°38'E
Sanandaj, Iran	182	36°44'N	46°43'E
San Andreas, Ca., U.S. (săn ăn'drê-ăs)	108	38°10'N	120°42'W
San Andreas, l., Ca., U.S.	106b	37°36'N	122°26'W
San Andrés, Col. (sän-än-drĕ's)	130a	6°57'N	75°41'W
San Andrés, Mex. (sän än-drās')	119a	19°15'N	99°10'W
San Andrés, i., Col.	121	12°32'N	81°34'W
San Andrés, Laguna de, l., Mex.	119	22°40'N	97°50'W
San Andres Mountains, mts., N.M., U.S. (săn ăn'drê-ăs)	96	33°00'N	106°40'W
San Andrés Tuxtla, Mex. (sän-än-drā's-to͞os'tlä)	116	18°27'N	95°12'W
San Angelo, Tx., U.S. (săn ăn-jĕ-lō)	96	31°28'N	100°22'W
San Antioco, Isola di, i., Italy (ē'sō-lä-dē-sän-än-tyŏ'kô)	160	39°00'N	8°25'E
San Antonio, Chile (sän-án-tō'nyō)	132	33°34'S	71°36'W
San Antonio, Col.	130a	2°57'N	75°06'W
San Antonio, Col.	130a	3°55'N	75°28'W
San Antonio, Phil.	197a	14°57'N	120°05'E
San Antonio, Tx., U.S. (săn ăn-tō'nê-ō)	96	29°25'N	98°30'W
San Antonio, r., Tx., U.S.	113	29°00'N	97°58'W
San Antonio, Cabo, c., Cuba (kå'bô-sän-än-tō'nyô)	117	21°55'N	84°55'W
San Antonio, Lake, res., Ca., U.S.	108	36°00'N	121°13'W
San Antonio Bay, b., Tx., U.S.	113	28°20'N	97°08'W
San Antonio de Areco, Arg. (dā ä-rā'kō)	129c	34°16'S	59°30'W
San Antonio de Galipán, Ven.	234a	10°33'N	66°53'W
San Antonio de las Vegas, Cuba	123a	22°51'N	82°23'W
San Antonio de los Baños, Cuba (dā lōs bän'yōs)	122	22°54'N	82°30'W
San Antonio de los Cobres, Arg. (dā lōs kō'brås)	132	24°15'S	66°29'W
San Antônio de Pádua, Braz. (dĕ-pá'dwä)	129a	21°32'S	42°09'W
San Antonio de Tamanaco, Ven.	131b	9°42'N	66°03'W
San Antonio Heights, Ca., U.S.	232	34°10'N	117°40'W
San Antonio Oeste, Arg. (sän-nä-tō'nyō ô-ĕs'tå)	132	40°49'S	64°56'W
San Antonio Peak, mtn., Ca., U.S. (săn ăn-tō'nĭ-ō)	107a	34°17'N	117°39'W
Sanarate, Guat. (sä-nä-rä'tĕ)	120	14°47'N	90°12'W
San Augustine, Tx., U.S. (săn ô'gŭs-tēn)	113	31°33'N	94°08'W
San Bartolo, Mex.	112	24°43'N	103°12'W
San Bartolo, Mex. (sän bär-tō'lô)	119a	19°36'N	99°43'W
San Bartolomé de la Cuadra, Spain	238e	41°26'N	2°02'E
San Bartolomeo, Italy (bär-tô-lô-mā'ô)	160	41°25'N	15°04'E
San Baudilio de Llobregat, Spain	238e	41°21'N	2°03'E
San Benedetto del Tronto, Italy (bä'nå-dĕt'tô dĕl trōn'tô)	160	42°58'N	13°54'E
San Benito, Tx., U.S. (săn bĕ-nē'tō)	113	26°07'N	97°37'W
San Benito, r., Ca., U.S.	108	36°40'N	121°20'W
San Bernardino, Ca., U.S. (bûr-när-dē'nō)	96	34°07'N	117°19'W
San Bernardino Mountains, mts., Ca., U.S.	108	34°05'N	116°23'W
San Bernardo, Chile (sän bĕr-när'dô)	129b	33°35'S	70°42'W
San Blas, Mex. (sän bläs')	116	21°33'N	105°19'W
San Blas, Cape, c., Fl., U.S.	97	29°38'N	85°38'W
San Blas, Cordillera de, mts., Pan.	121	9°17'N	78°20'W
San Blas, Golfo de, b., Pan.	121	9°33'N	78°42'W
San Blas, Punta, c., Pan.	121	9°35'N	78°55'W
San Bruno, Ca., U.S. (săn brū-nô)	106b	37°38'N	122°25'W
San Buenaventura, Mex. (bwā'nà-vĕn-to͞o'rä)	112	27°07'N	101°30'W
San Carlos, Chile (sän-ká'r-lôs)	132	36°23'S	71°58'W
San Carlos, Col.	130a	6°11'N	74°58'W
San Carlos, Eq. Gui.	216	3°27'N	8°33'E
San Carlos, Mex.	112	24°36'N	98°52'W
San Carlos, Mex. (sän kär'lōs)	119	17°49'N	92°33'W
San Carlos, Nic. (sän-kä'r-lôs)	121	11°08'N	84°48'W
San Carlos, Phil.	197a	15°56'N	120°20'E
San Carlos, Ca., U.S. (săn kär'lōs)	106b	37°30'N	122°15'W
San Carlos, Ven.	130	9°36'N	68°35'W
San Carlos, r., C.R.	121	10°36'N	84°18'W
San Carlos de Bariloche, Arg.	132	41°15'S	71°26'W
San Carlos Indian Reservation, I.R., Az., U.S. (săn kär'lōs)	109	33°27'N	110°15'W
San Carlos Lake, res., Az., U.S.	109	33°05'N	110°29'W
San Casimiro, Ven. (kä-sē-mê'rō)	131b	10°01'N	67°02'W
San Cataldo, Italy (kä-täl'dō)	160	37°30'N	13°59'E
Sánchez, Dom. Rep. (sän'chĕz)	117	19°15'N	69°40'W
Sanchez, Río de los, r., Mex. (rê'ō-dĕ-lōs)	118	20°31'N	102°29'W
Sánchez Román, Mex. (rô-má'n)	118	21°48'N	103°20'W
Sanchung, Tai.	241d	25°04'N	121°29'E
San Clemente, Spain (sän klå-mĕn'tå)	158	39°25'N	2°24'W
San Clemente de Llobregat, Spain	238e	41°20'N	2°00'E
San Clemente Island, i., Ca., U.S.	96	32°54'N	118°29'W
San Cristóbal, Dom. Rep. (krēs-tô'bäl)	123	18°25'N	70°05'W
San Cristóbal, Guat.	120	15°22'N	90°26'W
San Cristóbal, Ven.	130	7°43'N	72°15'W
San Cristobal, i., Sol. Is.	203	10°47'S	162°17'E
San Cristóbal de las Casas, Mex.	116	16°44'N	92°39'W
Sancti Spíritus, Cuba (säŋk'tê spē'rê-to͞os)	117	21°55'N	79°25'W
Sancti Spiritus, prov., Cuba	122	22°05'N	79°20'W
San Cugat del Vallés, Spain	238e	41°28'N	2°05'E
Sancy, Puy de, mtn., Fr. (pwē-dĕ-säɴ-sē')	147	45°30'N	2°53'E
Sand, i., Or., U.S. (sănd)	106c	46°16'N	124°01'W
Sand, i., Wi., U.S.	103	46°03'N	91°09'W
Sand, r., S. Afr.	213c	28°30'S	29°30'E
Sand, r., S. Afr.	218d	28°09'S	26°46'E
Sanda, Japan (sän'dä)	195	34°53'N	135°14'E
Sandakan, Malay. (sån-dä'kån)	196	5°51'N	118°03'E
Sanday, i., Scot., U.K. (sănd'ā)	150a	59°17'N	2°25'W
Sandbach, Eng., U.K. (sănd'băch)	144a	53°08'N	2°22'W
Sandefjord, Nor. (sän'dĕ-fyôr')	152	59°09'N	10°14'E
San de Fuca, Wa., U.S. (de-fo͞o-cä)	106a	48°14'N	122°44'W
Sanders, Az., U.S.	109	35°13'N	109°20'W
Sanderson, Tx., U.S. (săn'dẽr-sŭn)	112	30°09'N	102°24'W
Sanderstead, neigh., Eng., U.K.	235	51°20'N	0°05'W
Sandersville, Ga., U.S. (săn'dẽrz-vĭl)	115	32°57'N	82°50'W
Sandhammaren, c., Swe. (sänt'häm-măr)	146	55°24'N	14°37'E
Sand Hills, reg., Ne., U.S. (sănd)	102	41°57'N	101°29'W
Sand Hook, N.J., U.S. (sănd hòk)	100a	40°29'N	74°05'W
Sandhurst, Eng., U.K. (sănd'hûrst)	144b	51°20'N	0°48'W
Sandia Indian Reservation, I.R., N.M., U.S.	109	35°15'N	106°30'W
San Diego, Ca., U.S. (săn dê-ā'gô)	96	32°43'N	117°10'W
San Diego, Tx., U.S.	110	27°47'N	98°13'W
San Diego, r., Ca., U.S.	108	32°53'N	116°57'W
San Diego de la Unión, Mex. (sän dê-ā-gô dā lä o͞o-nyōn')	118	21°27'N	100°52'W
Sandies Creek, r., Tx., U.S. (sănd'êz)	113	29°13'N	97°34'W
San Dimas, Mex. (dê-mäs')	118	24°08'N	105°57'W
San Dimas, Ca., U.S. (săn dē-más)	107a	34°07'N	117°49'W
Sandnes, Nor. (sänd'nĕs)	152	58°52'N	5°44'E
Sandoa, D.R.C. (sän-dō'ä)	212	9°39'S	23°00'E
Sandomierz, Pol. (sån-dô'myĕzh)	155	50°39'N	21°45'E
San Doná di Piave, Italy (sän dô nà' dê pyä'vĕ)	160	45°38'N	12°34'E
Sandoway, Myanmar (sän-dô-wī')	183	18°24'N	94°28'E
Sandpoint, Id., U.S. (sănd point)	104	48°17'N	116°34'W
Sandringham, Austl. (săn'drĭng-ăm)	201a	37°57'S	145°01'E
Sandringham, neigh., S. Afr.	244b	26°09'S	28°07'E
Sandrio, Italy (sä'n-dryô)	160	46°11'N	9°53'E
Sands Point, N.Y., U.S.	228	40°51'N	73°43'W
Sand Springs, Ok., U.S. (sănd sprĭnz)	111	36°08'N	96°06'W
Sandstone, Austl. (sănd'stōn)	202	28°00'S	119°25'E
Sandstone, Mn., U.S.	103	46°08'N	92°53'W
Sanduo, China (sän-dwô)	190	32°49'N	119°39'E
Sandusky, Al., U.S. (săn-dŭs'kê)	100h	33°32'N	86°50'W
Sandusky, Mi., U.S.	98	43°25'N	82°50'W
Sandusky, Oh., U.S.	97	41°25'N	82°45'W
Sandusky, r., Oh., U.S.	98	41°10'N	83°20'W
Sandwich, Il., U.S. (sănd'wĭch)	98	42°35'N	88°53'W
Sandy, Or., U.S. (sănd'ê)	106c	45°24'N	122°16'W
Sandy, Ut., U.S.	107b	40°36'N	111°53'W
Sandy, r., Or., U.S.	106c	45°28'N	122°17'W
Sandy Cape, c., Austl.	203	24°25'S	153°10'E
Sandy Hook, Ct., U.S. (hòk)	100a	41°25'N	73°17'W
Sandy Lake, l., Can.	83g	53°46'N	113°58'W
Sandy Lake, l., Can.	89	53°00'N	93°07'W
Sandy Lake, l., Can.	93	49°16'N	57°00'W
Sandy Point, Tx., U.S.	113a	29°22'N	95°27'W
Sandy Point, c., Wa., U.S.	106d	48°48'N	122°42'W
Sandy Springs, Ga., U.S. (springz)	100c	33°55'N	84°23'W
San Estanislao, Para. (ĕs-tä-nês-lá'ô)	132	24°38'S	56°20'W
San Esteban, Hond. (ĕs-tĕ'bän)	120	15°13'N	85°53'W
San Fabian, Phil. (fä-byä'n)	197a	16°14'N	120°28'E
San Felipe, Chile (få-lē'på)	132	32°45'S	70°43'W
San Felipe, Mex.	118	22°21'N	105°26'W
San Felipe, Mex. (fĕ-lê'pĕ)	118	21°29'N	101°13'W
San Felipe, Ven. (fĕ-lē'pĕ)	130	10°13'N	68°45'W
San Felipe, Cayos de, is., Cuba (kä'yōs-dĕ-sän-fĕ-lē'pĕ)	122	22°00'N	83°30'W
San Felipe Creek, r., Ca., U.S. (săn fĕ-lēp'å)	108	33°10'N	116°03'W
San Felipe Indian Reservation, I.R., N.M., U.S.	109	35°26'N	106°26'W
San Félix, Isla, i., Chile (ē's-lä-dĕ-sän fā-lēks')	128	26°20'S	80°10'W
San Fernanda, Spain (fĕr-nä'n-dä)	158	36°28'N	6°13'W
San Fernando, Arg. (fĕr-ná'n-dô)	132a	34°26'S	58°34'W
San Fernando, Chile	129b	35°36'S	70°58'W
San Fernando, Mex. (fĕr-nän'dô)	112	24°52'N	98°10'W
San Fernando, Phil. (sän fĕr-nä'n-dô)	196	16°38'N	120°19'E
San Fernando, Ca., U.S. (fĕr-nän'dô)	107a	34°17'N	118°27'W
San Fernando, r., Mex. (sän fĕr-nän'dô)	112	25°07'N	98°25'W
San Fernando de Apure, Ven. (sän-fĕr-nä'n-dō-dĕ-ä-po͞o'rä)	130	7°46'N	67°29'W
San Fernando de Atabapo, Ven. (dĕ-ä-tä-bä'pô)	130	3°58'N	67°41'W
San Fernando de Henares, Spain (dĕ-ā-nä'râs)	159a	40°23'N	3°31'W
Sånfjället, mtn., Swe.	146	62°19'N	13°30'E
Sanford, Can. (săn'fẽrd)	83f	49°41'N	97°27'W
Sanford, Fl., U.S. (săn'fôrd)	97	28°46'N	81°18'W
Sanford, Me., U.S. (săn'fẽrd)	92	43°26'N	70°47'W
Sanford, N.C., U.S.	115	35°26'N	79°10'W
San Francisco, Arg. (săn frăn'sĭs'kô)	132	31°23'S	62°09'W
San Francisco, El Sal.	120	13°48'N	88°11'W
San Francisco, Ca., U.S.	96	37°45'N	122°26'W
San Francisco, r., N.M., U.S.	109	33°35'N	108°55'W
San Francisco Bay, b., Ca., U.S. (săn frăn'sĭs'kô)	108	37°45'N	122°21'W
San Francisco Culhuacán, Mex.	233a	19°20'N	99°06'W
San Francisco del Oro, Mex. (dĕl ō'rō)	116	27°00'N	106°37'W
San Francisco del Rincón, Mex. (dĕl rēn-kōn')	118	21°01'N	101°51'W
San Francisco de Macaira, Ven. (dĕ-mä-kī'rä)	131b	9°58'N	66°17'W
San Francisco de Macoris, Dom. Rep. (dā-mä-kô'rēs)	123	19°20'N	70°15'W
San Francisco de Paula, Cuba (dā pou'lä)	123a	23°04'N	82°18'W
San Francisco el Grande, Iglesia de, rel., Spain	238b	40°25'N	3°43'W
San Gabriel, Ca., U.S. (săn gä-brê-ĕl') (gā'brê-ĕl)	107a	34°06'N	118°06'W
San Gabriel, r., Ca., U.S.	107a	33°47'N	118°06'W
San Gabriel Chilac, Mex. (sän-gä-brē-ĕl-chê-läk')	119	18°19'N	97°22'W
San Gabriel Mts, Ca., U.S.	107a	34°17'N	118°03'W
San Gabriel Reservoir, res., Ca., U.S.	107a	34°14'N	117°48'W
Sangamon, r., Il., U.S. (săn'gá-msion)	111	40°08'N	90°08'W
Sangenjaya, neigh., Japan	242a	35°38'N	139°40'E
Sanger, Ca., U.S. (săng'ẽr)	108	36°42'N	119°33'W
Sangerhausen, Ger. (säng'ẽr-hou-zĕn)	154	51°28'N	11°17'E
Sangha, r., Afr.	211	2°40'N	16°10'E
Sangihe, Pulau, i., Indon.	197	3°30'N	125°30'E
San Gil, Col. (sän-кĕ'l)	130	6°32'N	73°13'W
San Giovanni in Fiore, Italy (sän jô-văn'nê ēn fyô'rå)	160	39°15'N	16°40'E
San Giuseppe Vesuviano, Italy	159c	40°36'N	14°31'E
Sangju, S. Kor. (säng'jo͞o')	194	36°20'N	128°07'E
Sāngli, India	183	16°56'N	74°38'E
Sangmélima, Cam.	215	2°56'N	11°59'E
San Gorgonio Mountain, mtn., Ca., U.S. (săn gôr-gō'nĭ-ō)	107a	34°06'N	116°50'W
Sangre de Cristo Mountains, mts., U.S.	96	37°45'N	105°50'W
San Gregoria, Ca., U.S. (săn grĕ-gôr'ä)	106b	37°20'N	122°23'W
San Gregorio Atlapulco, Mex.	233a	19°15'N	99°03'W
Sangro, r., Italy (säŋ'grô)	160	41°38'N	13°56'E
Sangüesa, Spain (sän-gwĕ'sä)	158	42°36'N	1°15'W
Sanhe, China (sän-hŭ)	190	39°59'N	117°06'E
Sanibel Island, i., Fl., U.S. (săn'ĭ-bĕl)	115a	26°26'N	82°15'W
San Ignacio, Belize	120a	17°11'N	89°04'W
San Ildefonso, Cape, c., Phil. (sän-ēl-dĕ-fôn-sô)	197a	16°03'N	122°10'E
San Ildefonso o la Granja, Spain (ō lä grän'khä)	158	40°54'N	4°02'W
San Isidro, Arg. (ē-sê'drô)	129c	34°28'S	58°31'W
San Isidro, C.R.	121	9°24'N	83°43'W
San Isidro, Peru	233c	12°07'S	77°03'W
San Jacinto, Phil. (sän hä-sēn'tô)	197a	12°33'N	123°43'E
San Jacinto, Ca., U.S. (săn jȧ-sĭn'tô)	107a	33°47'N	116°57'W
San Jacinto, r., Ca., U.S. (săn jȧ-sĭn'tô)	107a	33°44'N	117°14'W
San Jacinto, r., Tx., U.S.	113	30°25'N	95°05'W
San Jacinto, West Fork, r., Tx., U.S.	113	30°35'N	95°37'W
San Javier, Chile (sän-hå-vē'ĕr)	129b	35°35'S	71°43'W
San Jerónimo, Mex.	119a	19°31'N	98°46'W
San Jerónimo de Juárez, Mex. (hå-rō'nê-mô dā hwä'râz)	118	17°08'N	100°30'W
San Jerónimo Lídice, Mex.	233a	19°20'N	99°13'W
San Joaquin, Ven.	131b	10°16'N	67°47'W
San Joaquin, r., Ca., U.S. (săn hwä-kēn')	108	37°10'N	120°51'W
San Joaquin Valley, Ca., U.S.	108	36°45'N	120°30'W
San Jorge, Golfo, b., Arg. (gôl-fô-sän-кô'r-kĕ)	132	46°15'S	66°45'W
San José, C.R. (sän hô-sā')	117	9°57'N	84°05'W
San Jose, Phil.	197a	12°22'N	121°04'E
San Jose, Phil.	197a	15°49'N	120°57'E

ng-sing; ŋ-baŋk; ɴ-nasalized n; nŏd; cŏmmit; ōld; ôbey; ôrder; oi-boil; fo͞od; ò-as oo in foot; ou-out; s-soft; sh-dish; th-thin; pūre; ûnite; ûrn; stŭd; circŭs; ü-as in French tu; '-indeterminate vowel.

344 San Jose-Santa Fe de Bogotá

PLACE (Pronunciation)	PAGE	LAT.	LONG.
San Jose, Ca., U.S. (săn hō-zā')	96	37°20'N	121°54'W
San José, i., Mex. (kō-sĕ')	116	25°00'N	110°35'W
San José, Isla de, i., Pan. (ē's-lä-dĕ-sän hō-sā')	121	8°17'N	79°20'W
San Jose, Rio, r., N.M., U.S. (săn hō-zā')	109	35°15'N	108°10'W
San José de Feliciano, Arg. (dā lä ēs-kē'nä)	132	30°26'S	58°44'W
San José de Galipán, Ven.	234a	10°35'N	66°54'W
San José de Gauribe, Ven. (sän-hô-sĕ'dĕ-gäōō-rĕ'bĕ)	131b	9°51'N	65°49'W
San José de las Lajas, Cuba (sän-κô-sĕ'dĕ-läs-lä'käs)	123a	22°58'N	82°10'W
San José Iturbide, Mex. (ē-tōōr-bē'dĕ)	118	21°00'N	100°24'W
San Juan, Arg. (hwän')	132	31°36'S	68°29'W
San Juan, Col. (hōä'n)	130a	3°23'N	73°48'W
San Juan, Dom. Rep. (sän hwän')	123	18°50'N	71°15'W
San Juan, Phil.	197a	16°41'N	120°20'E
San Juan, P.R. (sän hwän')	117	18°30'N	66°10'W
San Juan, prov., Arg.	132	31°00'S	69°30'W
San Juan, r., Mex. (sän-hōō-än')	119	18°10'N	95°23'W
San Juan, r., N.A.	117	10°58'N	84°18'W
San Juan, r., U.S.	96	36°30'N	109°00'W
San Juan, Cabezas de, c., P.R.	117b	18°29'N	65°30'W
San Juan, Cabo, c., Eq. Gui.	216	1°08'N	9°23'E
San Juan, Pico, mtn., Cuba (pē'kō-sän-kōä'n)	122	21°55'N	80°00'W
San Juan, Río, r., Mex. (rē'ō-sän-hwän)	112	25°35'N	99°15'W
San Juan Bautista, Para. (sän hwän' bou-tēs'tä)	132	26°48'S	57°09'W
San Juan Capistrano, Mex. (sän-hōō-än' kä-pēs-trä'nō)	118	22°41'N	104°07'W
San Juan Creek, r., Ca., U.S. (săn hwän')	108	35°24'N	120°12'W
San Juan de Aragón, Mex.	233a	19°28'N	99°05'W
San Juan de Aragón, Bosque, rec., Mex.	233a	19°28'N	99°04'W
San Juan de Aragón, Zoológico de, rec., Mex.	233a	19°28'N	99°05'W
San Juan de Dios, Ven.	234a	10°35'N	66°57'W
San Juan de Guadalupe, Mex. (sän hwan dā gwä-dhä-lōō'pā)	112	24°37'N	102°43'W
San Juan del Monte, Phil.	241g	14°36'N	121°02'E
San Juan del Norte, Nic.	121	10°55'N	83°44'W
San Juan del Norte, Bahía de, b., Nic.	121	11°12'N	83°40'W
San Juan de los Lagos, Mex. (sän-hōō-än'dā lōs lä'gōs)	118	21°15'N	102°18'W
San Juan de los Lagos, r., Mex. (dā lōs lä'gōs)	118	21°13'N	102°12'W
San Juan de los Morros, Ven. (dĕ-lôs-mô'r-rôs)	131b	9°54'N	67°22'W
San Juan del Río, Mex. (sän hwän del rē'ō)	112	24°47'N	104°29'W
San Juan del Río, Mex.	118	20°21'N	99°59'W
San Juan del Sur, Nic. (dĕl sōōr)	116	11°15'N	85°53'W
San Juan Evangelista, Mex. (sän-hōō-ä'n-å-väŋ-kå-lĕs'ta')	119	17°57'N	95°08'W
San Juan Island, i., Wa., U.S.	106a	48°28'N	123°08'W
San Juan Islands, is., Can. (săn hwän)	86	48°49'N	123°14'W
San Juan Islands, is., Wa., U.S.	172a	48°36'N	122°50'W
San Juan Ixtenco, Mex. (ēx-tĕ'n-kō)	119	19°14'N	97°52'W
San Juan Martínez, Cuba	122	22°15'N	83°50'W
San Juan Mountains, mts., Co., U.S. (san hwän')	96	37°50'N	107°30'W
San Julián, Arg. (sän hōō-lyä'n)	132	49°17'S	68°02'W
San Justo, Arg. (hōōs'tō)	132a	34°40'S	58°33'W
San Justo Desvern, Spain	238e	41°23'N	2°05'E
Sankanbiriwa, mtn., S.L.	214	8°56'N	10°48'W
Sankarani, r., Afr. (sän'kä-rä'nē)	210	11°10'N	8°35'W
Sankt Gallen, Switz.	147	47°25'N	9°22'E
Sankt Moritz, Switz. (sånt mō'rĭts) (zäŋkt mō'rēts)	154	46°31'N	9°50'E
Sankt Pölten, Aus. (zäŋkt-pûl'tĕn)	154	48°12'N	15°38'E
Sankt Veit, Aus. (zäŋκt vĭt')	154	46°46'N	14°20'E
Sankuru, r., D.R.C. (säŋ-kōō'rōō)	212	4°00'S	22°35'E
San Lázaro, Cabo, c., Mex. (sän-lä'zä-rō)	116	24°58'N	113°30'W
San Leandro, Ca., U.S. (săn lē-ăn'drō)	106b	37°43'N	122°10'W
Şanlıurfa, Tur.	182	37°20'N	38°45'E
San Lorenzo, Arg. (sän lō-rĕn'zō)	132	32°46'S	60°44'W
San Lorenzo, Hond. (sän lō-rĕn'zō)	120	13°24'N	87°24'W
San Lorenzo, Ca., U.S. (săn lō-rĕn'zō)	106b	37°41'N	122°08'W
San Lorenzo de El Escorial, Spain	158	40°36'N	4°09'W
San Lorenzo Tezonco, Mex.	233a	19°18'N	99°04'W
Sanlúcar de Barrameda, Spain (sän-lōō'kär)	148	36°46'N	6°21'W
San Lucas, Bol. (lōō'kås)	130	20°12'S	65°06'W
San Lucas, Cabo, c., Mex.	116	22°45'N	109°45'W
San Luis, Arg. (lō-ēs')	132	33°16'S	66°15'W
San Luis, Col. (lôē's)	130a	6°03'N	74°57'W
San Luis, Cuba	123	20°15'N	75°50'W
San Luis, Guat.	120	14°38'N	89°42'W
San Luis, prov., Arg.	132	32°45'S	66°00'W
San Luis, neigh., Cuba	233b	23°05'N	82°20'W
San Luis de la Paz, Mex. (dā lä päz')	118	21°17'N	100°32'W
San Luis del Cordero, Mex. (dĕl kōr-dā'rō)	112	25°25'N	104°20'W
San Luis Obispo, Ca., U.S. (ō-bĭs'pō)	96	35°18'N	120°40'W
San Luis Obispo Bay, b., Ca., U.S.	108	35°07'N	121°05'W
San Luis Potosí, Mex.	116	22°08'N	100°58'W
San Luis Potosí, state, Mex.	116	22°45'N	101°45'W
San Luis Rey, r., Ca., U.S. (rā'ē)	108	33°22'N	117°06'W
San Luis Tlaxialtemalco, Mex.	233a	19°15'N	99°03'W
San Manuel, Az., U.S. (sän măn'ū-ĕl)	109	32°30'N	110°45'W
San Marcial, N.M., U.S. (săn mår-shäl')	109	33°40'N	107°00'W
San Marco, Italy (sän mär'kō)	160	41°53'N	15°50'E
San Marcos, Guat. (mär'kōs)	120	14°57'N	91°49'W
San Marcos, Mex.	118	16°46'N	99°23'W
San Marcos, Tx., U.S. (săn mär'kōs)	113	29°53'N	97°56'W
San Marcos, r., Tx., U.S.	112	30°08'N	98°15'W
San Marcos, Universidad de, educ., Peru	233c	12°03'S	77°05'W
San Marcos de Colón, Hond. (sän-må'r-kōs-dĕ-kō-lô'n)	120	13°17'N	86°50'W
San Maria di Léuca, Cape, c., Italy (dē-lĕ'ōō-kä)	149	39°47'N	18°20'E
San Marino, S. Mar. (sän mä-rē'nō)	160	44°55'N	12°26'E
San Marino, Ca., U.S. (săn mẽr-ē'nō)	107a	34°07'N	118°06'W
San Marino, nation, Eur.	142	43°40'N	13°00'E
San Martín, Col. (sän mär-tē'n)	130a	3°42'N	73°44'W
San Martín, vol., Mex. (mär-tē'n)	119	18°36'N	95°11'W
San Martín, l., S.A.	132	48°15'S	72°30'W
San Martín Chalchicuautla, Mex.	118	21°22'N	98°39'W
San Martin de la Vega, Spain (sän mär ten' dā lä vā'gä)	159a	40°12'N	3°34'W
San Martín Hidalgo, Mex. (sän mär-tē'n-ē-däl'gō)	118	20°27'N	103°55'W
San Mateo, Mex.	119	16°59'N	97°04'W
San Mateo, Ca., U.S. (săn mă-tā'ō)	106b	37°34'N	122°20'W
San Mateo, Ven. (sän mä-tĕ'ō)	131b	9°45'N	64°34'W
San Matías, Golfo, b., Arg. (sän mä-tē'äs)	132	41°30'S	63°45'W
Sanmen Wan, b., China	193	29°00'N	122°15'E
San Miguel, Chile	234b	33°30'S	70°40'W
San Miguel, El Sal. (sän mē-gål')	116	13°28'N	88°11'W
San Miguel, Mex. (sän mē-gål')	119	18°18'N	97°09'W
San Miguel, Pan.	121	8°26'N	78°55'W
San Miguel, Peru	233c	12°06'S	77°06'W
San Miguel, Phil. (sän mē-gĕ'l)	197a	15°09'N	120°56'E
San Miguel, Ven. (sän mē-gĕ'l)	131b	9°56'N	64°58'W
San Miguel, vol., El Sal.	120	13°27'N	88°17'W
San Miguel, i., Ca., U.S.	108	34°03'N	120°23'W
San Miguel, r., Bol. (sän-mē-gĕl')	130	13°34'S	63°58'W
San Miguel, r., N.A. (sän mē-gål')	119	15°27'N	92°00'W
San Miguel, r., Co., U.S. (săn mē-gĕl')	109	38°15'N	108°40'W
San Miguel, Bahía, b., Pan. (bä-ē'ä-sän mē-gål')	121	8°17'N	78°26'W
San Miguel Bay, b., Phil.	197a	13°55'N	123°12'E
San Miguel de Allende, Mex. (dā ä-lyĕn'dā)	118	20°54'N	100°44'W
San Miguel del Padrón, Cuba	233b	23°05'N	82°19'W
San Miguel el Alto, Mex. (ĕl äl'tō)	118	21°03'N	102°26'W
Sannār, Sudan	211	14°25'N	33°30'E
San Narcisco, Phil. (sän när-sē'sō)	197a	15°01'N	120°05'E
San Narcisco, Phil.	197a	13°34'N	122°33'E
San Nicolás, Arg. (sän nē-kō-lä's)	132	33°20'S	60°14'W
San Nicolas, Phil. (nē-kō-läs')	197a	16°05'N	120°45'E
San Nicolas, i., Ca., U.S. (săn nĭ'kō-là)	108	33°14'N	119°10'W
San Nicolás, r., Mex.	118	19°40'N	105°08'W
Sanniquellie, Lib.	214	7°22'N	8°43'W
Sannois, Fr.	237c	48°58'N	2°15'E
Sannūr, Wādī, Egypt	218b	28°48'N	31°12'E
Sanok, Pol. (sä'nŏk)	155	49°31'N	22°13'E
San Pablo, Phil. (sän-pä-blō)	197a	14°05'N	121°20'E
San Pablo, Ca., U.S. (săn păb'lō)	106b	37°58'N	122°21'W
San Pablo, Ven. (sän-på'blô)	131b	9°46'N	65°04'W
San Pablo, r., Pan. (sän päb'lō)	121	8°12'N	81°12'W
San Pablo Bay, b., Ca., U.S. (săn păb'lō)	106b	38°04'N	122°25'W
San Pablo Res, Ca., U.S.	106b	37°55'N	122°12'W
San Pascual, Phil. (päs-kwäl')	197a	13°08'N	122°59'E
San Pedro, Arg.	129c	33°41'S	59°42'W
San Pedro, Arg. (sän pā'drō)	132	24°15'S	64°15'W
San Pedro, Chile (sän pĕ'drō)	129b	33°54'S	71°27'W
San Pedro, El Sal. (sän pā'drō)	120	13°49'N	88°58'W
San Pedro, Mex. (sän pā'drō)	119	18°38'N	92°25'W
San Pedro, Para. (sän-pĕ'drō)	132	24°13'S	57°00'W
San Pedro, Ca., U.S. (săn pē'drō)	107a	33°44'N	118°17'W
San Pedro, r., Cuba (sän-pĕ'drō)	122	21°05'N	78°15'W
San Pedro, r., Mex.	112	27°56'N	105°50'W
San Pedro, r., Mex. (sän pä'drō)	118	22°08'N	104°59'W
San Pedro, r., Az., U.S.	109	32°48'N	110°37'W
San Pedro, Río de, r., Mex.	118	21°51'N	102°24'W
San Pedro, Río de, r., N.A.	119	18°23'N	92°13'W
San Pedro Bay, b., Ca., U.S. (săn pē'drō)	107a	33°42'N	118°12'W
San Pedro de las Colonias, Mex. (dē-läs-kō-lô'nyäs)	112	25°47'N	102°58'W
San Pedro de Macorís, Dom. Rep. (sän-pĕ'drō-dā mä-kō-rēs')	123	18°30'N	69°30'W
San Pedro Lagunillas, Mex. (sän pā'drō lä-gōō-nēl'yäs)	118	21°12'N	104°47'W
San Pedro Sula, Hond. (sän pā'drō sōō'lä)	120	15°29'N	88°01'W
San Pedro Xalostoc, Mex.	233a	19°32'N	99°05'W
San Pedro Zacatenco, Mex.	233a	19°31'N	99°08'W
San Pietro, Isola di, i., Italy (ē'sō-lä-dē-sän pyā'trō)	160	39°09'N	8°15'E
San Pietro in Vaticano, rel., Vat.	239c	41°54'N	12°28'E
San Quentin, Ca., U.S. (săn kwĕn-tĕn')	106b	37°57'N	122°29'W
San Quintin, Phil. (sän kēn-tēn')	197a	15°59'N	120°47'E
San Rafael, Arg. (sän rä-fä-ĕl')	132	34°30'S	68°13'W
San Rafael, Col. (sän-rä-fä-ĕ'l)	130a	6°18'N	75°02'W
San Rafael, Ca., U.S. (săn rå-fĕl)	106b	37°58'N	122°31'W
San Rafael, r., Ut., U.S. (săn rå-fĕl')	109	39°05'N	110°50'W
San Rafael, Cabo, c., Dom. Rep. (kà'bō)	123	19°00'N	68°50'W
San Ramón, C.R.	121	10°07'N	84°30'W
San Ramon, Ca., U.S. (săn rä-mōn')	106b	37°47'N	122°59'W
San Remo, Italy (sän rā'mō)	160	43°48'N	7°46'E
San Roque, Col. (sän-rô'kĕ)	130a	6°29'N	75°00'W
San Roque, Spain	158	36°13'N	5°23'W
San Saba, Tx., U.S. (săn să'bå)	112	31°12'N	98°43'W
San Saba, r., Tx., U.S.	112	30°58'N	99°12'W
San Salvador, El Sal. (sän säl-vä-dōr')	116	13°45'N	89°11'W
San Salvador (Watling), i., Bah. (săn săl'vá-dôr)	123	24°05'N	74°30'W
San Salvador, i., Ec.	130	0°14'S	90°50'W
San Salvador, r., Ur. (sän-säl-vä-dô'r)	129c	33°42'S	58°04'W
Sansanné-Mango, Togo (sän-så-nā' mäŋ'gō)	210	10°21'N	0°28'E
San Sebastián, Spain	142	43°19'N	1°59'W
San Sebastian, Spain (sän så-bås-tyän')	210	28°09'N	17°11'W
San Sebastián, Ven. (sän-sĕ-bäs-tyà'n)	131b	9°58'N	67°11'W
San Sebastiàn de los Reyes, Spain	159a	40°33'N	3°38'W
San Severo, Italy (sän sĕ-vå'rō)	149	41°43'N	15°24'E
Sanshui, China (sän-shwā)	189	23°14'N	112°51'E
San Simon Creek, r., Az., U.S. (sån sī-mōn')	109	32°45'N	109°30'W
San Siro, neigh., Italy	238c	45°29'S	9°07'E
Sanssouci, Schloss, hist., Ger.	238a	52°24'N	13°02'E
Santa Ana, El Sal.	116	14°02'N	89°35'W
Santa Ana, Mex. (sän'tä ä'nä)	118	19°18'N	98°10'W
Santa Ana, Ca., U.S. (săn'tå ăn'å)	96	33°45'N	117°52'W
Santa Ana, r., Ca., U.S.	107a	33°41'N	117°57'W
Santa Ana Mountains, mts., Ca., U.S.	107a	33°44'N	117°36'W
Santa Anna, Tx., U.S.	112	31°44'N	99°18'W
Santa Antão, i., C.V. (sä-tä-ä'n-zhĕ-lō)	210b	17°20'N	26°05'W
Santa Bárbara, Braz. (sän-tä-bà'r-bä-rä)	131	19°57'S	43°25'W
Santa Bárbara, Hond.	120	14°52'N	88°20'W
Santa Barbara, Mex.	112	26°48'N	105°50'W
Santa Barbara, Ca., U.S.	96	34°26'N	119°43'W
Santa Barbara, i., Ca., U.S.	108	33°30'N	118°44'W
Santa Barbara Channel, strt., Ca., U.S.	108	34°15'N	120°00'W
Santa Branca, Braz. (sän-tä-brä'N-kä)	129a	23°25'S	45°52'W
Santa Catalina, i., Ca., U.S.	96	33°29'N	118°37'W
Santa Catalina, Cerro de, mtn., Pan.	121	8°39'N	81°36'W
Santa Catalina, Gulf of, b., Ca., U.S. (săn'tȧ kă-tȧ-lē'nȧ)	108	33°00'N	117°58'W
Santa Catarina, Mex. (săn'tå kä-tä-rē'nä)	112	25°41'N	100°27'W
Santa Catarina, state, Braz. (sän-tä-kä-tä-rē'nå)	132	27°15'S	50°30'W
Santa Catarina, r., Mex.	118	16°31'N	98°39'W
Santa Clara, Cuba (sän't klä'rá)	117	22°25'N	80°00'W
Santa Clara, Mex.	112	24°29'N	103°22'W
Santa Clara, Ca., U.S. (săn'tȧ klârȧ)	104	37°21'N	121°56'W
Santa Clara, Ur.	132	32°46'S	54°51'W
Santa Clara, vol., Nic.	120	12°44'N	87°00'W
Santa Clara, r., Ca., U.S. (săn'tȧ klä'rȧ)	108	34°22'N	118°53'W
Santa Clara, Bahía de, b., Cuba (bä-ē'ä-dĕ-sän-tä-klä-rä)	122	23°05'N	80°50'W
Santa Clara, Sierra, mts., Mex. (sē-ĕ'r-rä-sän'tå klä'rá)	116	27°30'N	113°50'W
Santa Clara Indian Reservation, I.R., N.M., U.S.	109	35°59'N	106°10'W
Santa Coloma de Gramanet, Spain	238e	41°27'N	2°13'E
Santa Cruz, Bol. (săn'tå krōōz')	130	17°45'S	63°03'W
Santa Cruz, Braz. (sän-tä-krōō's)	132	29°43'S	52°15'W
Santa Cruz, Braz.	132b	22°55'S	43°41'W
Santa Cruz, Chile	129b	34°38'S	71°21'W
Santa Cruz, C.R.	120	10°16'N	85°37'W
Santa Cruz, Mex.	112	25°50'N	105°25'W
Santa Cruz, Phil.	197a	13°28'N	122°02'E
Santa Cruz, Phil.	197a	14°17'N	121°25'E
Santa Cruz, Phil.	197a	15°46'N	119°53'E
Santa Cruz, Ca., U.S.	96	36°59'N	122°02'W
Santa Cruz, prov., Arg.	132	48°00'S	70°00'W
Santa Cruz, i., Ec. (sän-tä-krōō'z)	130	0°38'S	90°20'W
Santa Cruz, r., Arg. (săn'tå krōōz')	132	50°05'S	71°00'W
Santa Cruz, r., Az., U.S. (săn'tȧ krōōz')	109	32°30'N	111°30'W
Santa Cruz Barillas, Guat. (sän-tä-krōō'z-bä-rē'l-yäs)	120	15°47'N	91°22'W
Santa Cruz del Sur, Cuba (sän-tä-krōō's-dĕl-sō'r)	122	20°45'N	78°00'W
Santa Cruz de Tenerife, Spain (săn'tä krōōz dā tä-nå-rē'fā)	209	28°07'N	15°27'W
Santa Cruz Islands, is., Sol. Is.	203	10°58'S	166°47'E
Santa Cruz Meyehualco, Mex.	233a	19°20'N	99°03'W
Santa Cruz Mountains, mts., Ca., U.S. (săn'tå krōōz')	106b	37°30'N	122°19'W
Santa Domingo, Cay, i., Bah.	123	21°50'N	75°45'W
Santa Eduviges, Chile	234b	33°33'S	70°39'W
Santa Elena del Gomero, Chile	234b	33°29'S	70°46'W
Santa Fe, Arg. (sän'tä fā')	132	31°33'S	60°45'W
Santa Fé, Cuba (sän-tä-fĕ')	122	21°45'N	82°40'W
Santa Fe, Mex.	233a	19°23'N	99°14'W
Santa Fe, Spain (sän'tä-fā')	158	37°12'N	3°43'W
Santa Fe, N.M., U.S. (săn'tȧ fā')	96	35°40'N	106°00'W
Santa Fe, prov., Arg. (sän'tä fā')	132	32°00'S	61°15'W
Santa Fe de Bogotá, Col.	130	4°36'N	74°05'W

ăt; fĭnăl; rāte; senåte; ärm; åsk; sofȧ; fâre; ch-choose; dh-as th in other; bē; ėvent; bĕt; recĕnt; cratẽr; g-gō; gh-guttural g; bĭt; ĭ-short neutral; rīde; κ-guttural k as ch in German ich;

PLACE (Pronunciation)	PAGE	LAT.	LONG.
Santa Filomena, Braz. (sän-tä-fĕ-lŏ-mĕ'nä)	131	9°09'S	44°45'W
Santa Genoveva, mtn., Mex. (sän-tä-hĕ-nô-vĕ'vä)	116	23°30'N	110°00'W
Santai, China (san-tī)	188	31°02'N	105°02'E
Santa Inés, Ven. (sän'tä ĕ-nĕ's)	131b	9°54'N	64°21'W
Santa Inés, i., Chile (sän'tä ĕ-nās')	132	53°45'S	74°15'W
Santa Isabel, i., Sol. Is.	203	7°57'S	159°28'E
Santa Isabel, Pico de, mtn., Eq. Gui.	215	3°35'N	8°46'E
Santa Lucia, Cuba (sän'tä lōō-sē'ä)	122	21°15'N	77°30'W
Santa Lucia, Ur. (sän-tä-lōō-sē'ä)	132	34°27'S	56°23'W
Santa Lucia, Ven.	131b	10°18'N	66°40'W
Santa Lucia, r., Ur.	129c	34°19'S	56°13'W
Santa Lucia Bay, b., Cuba (sän'tä lōō-sē'ä)	122	22°55'N	84°20'W
Santa Margarita, i., Mex. (sän'tä mär-gá-rē'tä)	116	24°15'N	112°00'W
Santa Maria, Braz. (sän'tä mä-rē'ä)	132	29°40'S	54°00'W
Santa Maria, Italy (sän-tä-mä-rē'ä)	160	41°05'N	14°15'E
Santa Maria, Phil. (sän-tä-mä-rē'ä)	197a	14°48'N	120°57'E
Santa Maria, Ca., U.S. (sän-tä mä-rē'ä)	108	34°57'N	120°28'W
Santa María, vol., Guat.	120	14°45'N	91°33'W
Santa Maria, r., Mex. (sän'tä mä-rē'ä)	118	21°33'N	100°17'W
Santa Maria, Cabo de, c., Port. (kä'bō-dĕ-sän-tä-mä-rē'ä)	158	36°58'N	7°54'W
Santa Maria, Cape, c., Bah.	123	23°45'N	75°00'W
Santa Maria, Cayo, i., Cuba	122	22°40'N	79°00'W
Santa María del Oro, Mex. (sän'tä-mä-rē'ä-dĕl-ô-ró)	118	21°21'N	104°35'W
Santa María de los Angeles, Mex. (dĕ-lôs-ä'n-hĕ-lĕs)	118	22°10'N	103°34'W
Santa María del Río, Mex.	118	21°46'N	100°43'W
Santa María del Rosario, Cuba	233b	23°04'N	82°15'W
Santa María de Ocotán, Mex.	118	22°56'N	104°30'W
Santa Maria Island, i., Port. (sän-tä-mä-rē'ä)	210a	37°09'N	26°02'W
Santa Maria Madalena, Braz.	129a	22°00'S	42°00'W
Santa Marta, Col. (sän'tä mär'tä)	130	11°15'N	74°13'W
Santa Marta, Peru	233c	12°02'S	76°56'W
Santa Marta, Cabo de, c., Ang.	216	13°52'S	12°25'E
Santa Martha Acatitla, Mex.	233a	19°22'N	99°01'W
Santa Monica, Ca., U.S. (sän'tä mŏn'ĭ-ká)	96	34°01'N	118°29'W
Santa Mónica, neigh., Ven.	234a	10°29'N	66°53'W
Santa Monica Bay, b., Ca., U.S.	232	33°54'N	118°25'W
Santa Monica Mountains, mts., Ca., U.S.	107a	34°08'N	118°38'W
Santana, r., Braz.	132b	22°33'S	43°37'W
Santander, Col. (sän-tän'dĕr')	130a	3°00'N	76°25'W
Santander, Spain (sän-tän-dâr')	142	43°27'N	3°50'W
Sant Antoni de Portmany, Spain	159	38°59'N	1°17'E
Santa Paula, Ca., U.S. (sän'tä pô'lá)	108	34°24'N	119°05'W
Santarém, Braz. (sän-tä-rěn')	131	2°28'S	54°37'W
Santarém, Port.	158	39°18'N	8°48'W
Santaren Channel, strt., Bah. (sän-tä-rěn')	122	24°15'N	79°30'W
Santa Rita do Sapucai, Braz. (sä-pô-ká'ē)	129a	22°15'S	45°41'W
Santa Rosa, Arg. (sän-tä-rô-sä)	132	36°45'S	64°10'W
Santa Rosa, Col. (sän-tä-rô-sä)	130a	6°38'N	75°24'W
Santa Rosa, Ec.	130	3°29'S	79°55'W
Santa Rosa, Guat. (sän'tä rō'sá)	120	14°21'N	90°16'W
Santa Rosa, Hond.	120	14°45'N	88°51'W
Santa Rosa, Ca., U.S. (sän'tä rō'zá)	96	38°27'N	122°42'W
Santa Rosa, N.M., U.S. (sän'tä rō'sá)	110	34°55'N	104°41'W
Santa Rosa, Ven. (sän-tä-rô-sä)	131b	9°37'N	64°10'W
Santa Rosa de Cabal, Col. (sän-tä-rô-sä-dĕ-kä-bä'l)	130a	4°53'N	75°38'W
Santa Rosa de Viterbo, Braz. (sän-tä-rô-sä-dĕ-vē-tĕr'-bó)	129a	21°30'S	47°21'W
Santa Rosa Indian Reservation, I.R., Ca., U.S. (sän'tä rō'zá')	108	33°28'N	116°50'W
Santa Rosalía, Mex. (sän'tä rô-zä'lē-ä)	116	27°13'N	112°15'W
Santa Rosa Range, mts., Nv., U.S. (sän'tä rō'zá)	104	41°33'N	117°50'W
Santa Susana, Ca., U.S. (sän'tä sōō-zä'ná)	107a	34°16'N	118°42'W
Santa Teresa, Arg. (sän-tä-tĕ-rĕ'sä)	129c	33°27'S	60°47'W
Santa Teresa, Ven.	131b	10°14'N	66°40'W
Santa Teresa de lo Ovalle, Chile	234b	33°23'S	70°47'W
Santa Úrsula Coapa, Mex.	233a	19°17'N	99°11'W
Santa Uxia, Spain	158	42°34'N	8°55'W
Santa Vitória do Palmar, Braz. (sän-tä-vē-tô'ryä-dô-päl-már)	132	33°30'S	53°16'W
Santa Ynez, r., Ca., U.S. (sän'tä ē-něz')	108	34°40'N	120°20'W
Santa Ysabel Indian Reservation, I.R., Ca., U.S. (sän'tä ĭ-zá-bĕl')	108	33°05'N	116°46'W
Santee, Ca., U.S. (sän tē')	108a	32°50'N	116°58'W
Santee, r., S.C., U.S.	97	33°00'N	79°45'W
Santeny, Fr.	237c	48°43'N	2°34'E
Sant' Eufemia, Golfo di, b., Italy (gôl-fō-dē-sän-tĕ'ô-fĕ'myä)	160	38°53'N	15°53'E
Sant Feliu de Guixols, Spain	159	41°45'N	3°01'E
Santiago, Braz. (sän-tyä'gô)	132	29°05'S	54°46'W
Santiago, Chile (sän-tē-ä'gô)	132	33°26'S	70°40'W
Santiago, Pan.	117	8°07'N	80°58'W
Santiago, Phil. (sän-tyä'gô)	197a	16°42'N	121°33'E
Santiago, prov., Chile (sän-tyä'gô)	129b	33°28'S	70°55'W
Santiago, i., Phil. (sän-tyä'gô)	197a	16°29'N	120°03'E
Santiago de Compostela, Spain	148	42°52'N	8°32'W
Santiago de Cuba, Cuba (sän-tyä'gô-dä kōō'bä)	117	20°00'N	75°50'W
Santiago de Cuba, prov., Cuba	122	20°20'N	76°05'W
Santiago de las Vegas, Cuba (sän-tyä'gô-dĕ-läs-vĕ'gäs)	123a	22°58'N	82°23'W
Santiago del Estero, Arg.	132	27°50'S	64°14'W
Santiago del Estero, prov., Arg. (sän-tē-ä'gô-dĕl ĕs-tä-ró)	132	27°15'S	63°30'W
Santiago de los Cabelleros, Dom. Rep.	117	19°30'N	70°45'W
Santiago Mountains, mts., Tx., U.S. (sän-tē-ä'gô)	96	30°00'N	103°30'W
Santiago Reservoir, res., Ca., U.S.	107a	33°47'N	117°42'W
Santiago Rodriguez, Dom. Rep. (sän-tyä'gô-rô-drē'gĕz)	123	19°30'N	71°25'W
Santiago Tepalcatlalpan, Mex.	233a	19°15'N	99°08'W
Santiago Tuxtla, Mex. (sän-tyä'gô-tōō'x-tlä)	119	18°28'N	95°18'W
Santiaguillo, Laguna de, l., Mex. (lä-oō'nä-dĕ-sän-tĕ-ä-gēl'yó)	112	24°51'N	104°43'W
Santissimo, neigh., Braz.	234c	22°53'S	43°31'W
Santisteban del Puerto, Spain (sän'tĕ stä-bän'dĕl pwĕr'tó)	158	38°15'N	3°12'W
Sant Mateu, Spain	159	40°26'N	0°09'E
Santo Amaro, Braz. (sän'tô ä-mä'ró)	131	12°32'S	38°33'W
Santo Amaro, neigh., Braz.	234d	23°39'S	46°42'W
Santo Amaro de Campos, Braz.	129a	22°01'S	41°05'W
Santo André, Braz.	129a	23°40'S	46°31'W
Santo Angelo, Braz. (sän-tô-á'n-zhĕ-lô)	132	28°16'S	53°59'W
Santo Antônio do Monte, Braz. (sän-tô-än-tô'nyô-dô-môn'tĕ)	129a	20°06'S	45°18'W
Santo Domingo, Cuba (sän'tô-dōmĭn'gó)	122	22°35'N	80°20'W
Santo Domingo, Dom. Rep. (sän'tô dô-mĭn'gó)	117	18°30'N	69°55'W
Santo Domingo, Nic. (sän-tô-dô-mĕ'n-gō)	121	12°15'N	84°56'W
Santo Domingo de la Caizada, Spain (dä lä käl-thä'dä)	158	42°27'N	2°55'W
Santoña, Spain (sän-tô'nyä)	158	43°25'N	3°27'W
Sant' Onofrio, neigh., Italy	239c	41°56'N	12°25'E
Santos, Braz. (sän'tozh)	131	23°58'S	46°20'W
Santos Dumont, Braz. (sän-tôs-dô-mô'nt)	131	21°28'S	43°33'W
Sanuki, Japan (sä'nōō-kē)	195a	35°16'N	139°53'E
San Urbano, Arg. (sän-ôr-bä'nô)	129c	33°39'S	61°28'W
San Valentin, Monte, mtn., Chile (sän-vä-lĕn-tē'n)	132	46°41'S	73°30'W
San Vicente, Arg. (sän-vē-sĕn'tĕ)	129c	35°00'S	58°26'W
San Vicente, Chile	129b	34°25'S	71°06'W
San Vicente, El Sal. (sän ysī-drô)	120	13°41'N	88°43'W
San Vicente de Alcántara, Spain	158	39°24'N	7°08'W
San Vicente dels Horts, Spain	238e	41°24'N	2°01'E
San Vito al Tagliamento, Italy (san vē'tô)	160	45°53'N	12°52'E
San Xavier Indian Reservation, I.R., Az., U.S. (x-ä'vĭēr')	109	32°07'N	111°12'W
San Ysidro, Ca., U.S. (sän ysī-drô)	108a	32°33'N	117°02'W
Sanyuanli, China (sän-yûän-lē)	191a	23°11'N	113°16'E
São Bernardo do Campo, Braz. (soun-bĕr-när'dô-dô-ká'm-pô)	129a	23°44'S	46°33'W
São Borja, Braz. (soun-bôr-zhä)	132	28°44'S	55°59'W
São Caetano do Sul, Braz.	234d	23°37'S	46°34'W
São Carlos, Braz. (soun kär'lôzh)	131	22°02'S	47°54'W
São Cristovão, Braz. (soun-krĕs-tō-voun)	131	11°04'S	37°11'W
São Cristóvão, neigh., Braz.	234c	22°54'S	43°14'W
São Fidélis, Braz. (soun-fĕ-dĕ'lĕs)	129a	21°41'S	41°45'W
São Francisco, Braz. (soun frän-sĕsh'kô)	131	15°59'S	44°42'W
São Francisco, Rio, r., Braz. (rĕ'ô-sän-frän-sĕ's-kô)	131	8°56'S	40°20'W
São Francisco do Sul, Braz. (soun frän-sĕsh-kô-dô-sōō'l)	132	26°15'S	48°42'W
São Gabriel, Braz. (soun'gä-brĕ-ĕl')	132	30°28'S	54°11'W
São Geraldo, Braz. (soun-zhĕ-rä'l-dô)	129a	21°01'S	42°49'W
São Gonçalo, Braz. (soun'gôn-sä'lô)	129a	22°55'S	43°04'W
Sao Hill, Tan.	217	8°20'S	35°12'E
São João, Gui.-B.	214	11°32'N	15°26'W
São João da Barra, Braz. (soun-zhōun-dä-bä'rä)	129a	21°40'S	41°03'W
São João da Boa Vista, Braz. (soun-zhōun-dä-bôä-vē's-tä)	129a	21°58'S	46°45'W
São João del Rei, Braz. (soun zhōun'dĕl-rä)	132	21°08'S	44°14'W
São João de Meriti, Braz. (soun-zhōun-dĕ-mĕ-rē-tĕ)	132b	22°47'S	43°22'W
São João do Araguaia, Braz. (soun zhô-oun'dô-ä-rä-gwä'yä)	131	5°29'S	48°44'W
São João dos Lampas, Port. (soun' zhô-oun' dôzh län-päzh')	159b	38°52'N	9°24'W
São João Nepomuceno, Braz. (soun-zhōun-nĕ-pô-mōō-sĕ-nô)	129a	21°33'S	43°00'W
São Jorge Island, i., Port. (soun zhôr'zhĕ)	210a	38°28'N	27°34'W
São José do Rio Pardo, Braz. (soun zhô-sĕ'dô-rē'ô-pä'r-dô)	129a	21°36'S	46°50'W
São José do Rio Prêto, Braz. (soun zhô-zĕ'dô-rē'ô-prē-tô)	131	20°57'S	49°12'W
São José dos Campos, Braz. (soun zhô-zĕ'dôzh kän pôzh')	129a	23°12'S	45°53'W
São Julião da Barra, Port.	238d	38°40'N	9°21'W
São Leopoldo, Braz. (soun-lĕ-ô-pôl'dô)	132	29°46'S	51°09'W
São Luis, Braz.	131	2°31'S	43°14'W
São Luis do Paraitinga, Braz. (soun-loō'ēs-dô-pä-rä-ē-tē'n-gä)	129a	23°15'S	45°18'W
São Manuel, r., Braz.	131	8°28'S	57°07'E
São Mateus, Braz. (soun mä-tä'ôzh)	131	18°44'S	39°45'W
São Mateus, Braz.	132b	22°49'S	43°23'W
São Miguel Arcanjo, Braz. (soun-mĕ-gĕ'l-är-kän-zhô)	129a	23°54'S	47°59'W
São Miguel Island, i., Port.	210a	37°59'N	26°38'W
Saona, i., Dom. Rep. (sä-ô'nä)	123	18°10'N	68°55'W
Saône, r., Fr. (sōn)	142	47°00'N	5°30'E
São Nicolau, i., C.V. (soun' nĕ-kô-loun')	210b	16°19'N	25°19'W
São Paulo, Braz. (soun' pou'lô)	131	23°34'S	46°38'W
São Paulo, state, Braz. (soun pou'lô)	131	21°45'S	50°47'W
São Paulo de Olivença, Braz. (soun'pou'lôdä ô-lĕ-vĕn'sá)	130	3°32'S	68°46'W
São Pedro, Braz. (soun-pĕ'drô)	129a	22°34'S	47°54'W
São Pedro de Aldeia, Braz. (soun-pĕ'drô-dĕ-äl-dĕ'yä)	129a	22°50'S	42°04'W
São Pedro e São Paulo, Rocedos, rocks, Braz.	128	1°50'N	30°00'W
São Raimundo Nonato, Braz. (soun' rī-mô'n-do nô-nä'tô)	131	9°09'S	42°32'W
São Roque, Braz. (soun' rô'kĕ)	129a	23°32'S	47°08'W
São Roque, Cabo de, c., Braz. (kä'bo-dĕ-soun' rô'kĕ)	131	5°06'S	35°11'W
São Sebastião, Braz. (soun sä-bäs-tĕ-oun')	129a	23°48'S	45°25'W
São Sebastião, Ilha de, i., Braz.	129a	23°52'S	45°22'W
São Sebastião do Paraíso, Braz.	129a	20°54'S	46°33'W
São Simão, Braz. (soun-sē-moun)	129a	21°30'S	47°33'W
São Tiago, i., C.V. (soun tē-ä'gò)	210b	15°09'N	24°45'W
São Tomé, S. Tom./P.	210	0°20'N	6°44'E
Sao Tome and Principe, nation, Afr. (prēn'sĕ-pē)	210	1°00'N	6°00'E
Saoura, Oued, r., Alg.	210	29°39'N	1°42'W
São Vicente, Braz. (soun ve-sĕ'n-tĕ)	131	23°57'S	46°25'W
São Vicente, i., C.V. (soun vĕ-sĕn'tä)	210b	16°51'N	24°35'W
São Vicente, Cabo de, c., Port. (kä'bō-dĕ-sän-vĕ-sĕ'n-tĕ)	142	37°03'N	9°31'W
Sapele, Nig. (sä-pā'lä)	210	5°54'N	5°41'E
Sapitwa, mtn., Mwi.	217	15°58'S	35°38'E
Sa Pobla, Spain	159	39°46'N	3°02'E
Sapozhok, Russia (sä-pô-zhôk')	162	53°58'N	40°44'E
Sapporo, Japan (säp-pô'rô)	189	43°02'N	141°29'E
Sapronovo, Russia (sáp-rô'nô-vô)	172b	55°13'N	38°25'E
Sapucaí, r., Braz. (sä-pōō-kä-ē')	129a	22°20'S	45°53'W
Sapucaia, Braz. (sä-pōō-kä'yä)	129a	22°01'S	42°54'W
Sapucaí Mirim, r., Braz. (sä-pōō-kä-ē'mē-rēn)	129a	21°06'S	47°03'W
Sapulpa, Ok., U.S. (sá-pŭl'pá)	111	36°01'N	96°05'W
Saqqez, Iran	185	36°14'N	46°16'E
Saquarema, Braz. (sä-kwä-rĕ-mä)	129a	22°56'S	42°32'W
Sara, Wa., U.S. (sä'rä)	106c	45°45'N	122°42'W
Sara, Bahr, r., Chad (bär)	211	8°19'N	17°44'E
Sarajevo, Bos. (sä-rä-yĕv'ó) (sä-rä'ya-vô)	142	43°50'N	18°26'E
Sarakhs, Iran	185	36°32'N	61°11'E
Sarana, Russia (sá-rä'ná)	172a	56°31'N	57°44'E
Saranac Lake, N.Y., U.S.	99	44°20'N	74°05'W
Saranac Lake, l., N.Y., U.S. (sär'á-näk)	99	44°15'N	74°20'W
Sarandi, Arg. (sä-rän'dĕ)	132a	34°41'S	58°21'W
Sarandi Grande, Ur. (sä-rän'dĕ-gränd')	129c	33°42'S	56°21'W
Saranley, Som.	218a	2°28'N	42°15'E
Saransk, Russia (sä-ränsk')	164	54°10'N	45°10'E
Sarany, Russia (sä-rä'nī)	172a	58°33'N	58°48'E
Sara Peak, mtn., Nig.	215	9°37'N	9°25'E
Sarapul, Russia (sä-räpôl')	166	56°28'N	53°50'E
Sarasota, Fl., U.S. (sär-á-sōtá)	115a	27°27'N	82°30'W
Saratoga, Tx., U.S. (sär-á-tō'gá)	113	30°17'N	94°31'W
Saratoga, Wa., U.S.	106a	48°04'N	122°29'W
Saratoga Pass, Wa., U.S.	106a	48°09'N	122°33'W
Saratoga Springs, N.Y., U.S. (springz)	99	43°05'N	74°50'W
Saratov, Russia (sá rä'tôf)	164	51°30'N	45°30'E
Saravane, Laos	193	15°48'N	106°40'E
Sarawak, hist. reg., Malay.	196	2°30'N	112°45'E
Sárbogárd, Hung. (shär'bô-gärd)	155	46°53'N	18°38'E
Sarcee Indian Reserve, I.R., Can.	83e	50°58'N	114°23'W
Sarcelles, Fr.	157b	49°00'N	2°23'E
Sardalas, Libya	210	25°59'N	10°33'E
Sardinia, i., Italy (sär-dĭn'ĭá)	142	40°08'N	9°05'E
Sardis, Ms., U.S. (sär'dĭs)	114	34°26'N	89°55'W
Sardis Lake, res., Ms., U.S.	114	34°27'N	89°43'W
Sargent, Ne., U.S. (sär'jĕnt)	102	41°40'N	99°38'W
Sarh, Chad (är-chän-bō')	211	9°09'N	18°23'E
Sarikamis, Tur.	167	40°20'N	42°40'E
Sariñena, Spain (sä-rēn-yĕ'nä)	159	41°46'N	0°11'W
Sark, i., Guernsey (särk)	156	49°28'N	2°22'W
Şarköy, Tur. (shär'kû-ĕ)	161	40°39'N	27°07'E
Sarmiento, Monte, mtn., Chile (mô'n-tĕ-sär-myĕn'tô)	132	54°28'S	70°40'W
Sarnia, Can. (sär'nē-á)	85	43°00'N	82°23'W
Sarno, Italy (sär'nô)	159c	40°35'N	14°38'E
Sarny, Ukr. (sär'nĕ)	167	51°17'N	26°39'E
Saronikós Kólpos, b., Grc.	161	37°53'N	23°30'E
Saros Körfezi, b., Tur. (sä'rôs)	161	40°20'N	26°20'E
Sárospatak, Hung. (shä'rôsh-pô'tôk)	155	48°19'N	21°35'E
Šar Planina, mts., Yugo. (shär plä'nē-ä)	161	42°07'N	21°30'E
Sarpsborg, Nor. (särps'bôrg)	152	59°17'N	11°07'E
Sarratt, Eng., U.K.	235	51°41'N	0°29'W
Sarrebourg, Fr. (sär-bōōr')	151	48°43'N	7°00'E
Sarreguemines, Fr. (sär-gĕ-mēn')	147	49°06'N	7°05'E
Sarria, Spain (sär'rēä)	158	42°54'N	7°37'W
Sarstun, r., N.A. (särs-tōō'n)	115	15°50'N	89°26'W
Sartène, Fr. (sär-tĕn')	160	41°36'N	8°59'E

346 Sarthe-Sekota

PLACE (Pronunciation)	PAGE	LAT.	LONG.
Sarthe, r., Fr. (särt)	147	47°44′N	0°32′W
Sartrouville, Fr.	237c	48°57′N	2°10′E
Şärur, Azer.	168	39°33′N	44°58′E
Sárvár, Hung. (shär′vär)	154	47°14′N	16°55′E
Sarych, Mys, c., Ukr. (mĭs sȧ-rēch′)	167	44°25′N	33°00′E
Sary-Ishikotrau, Peski, des., Kyrg. (sä′rē ē′ shĕk-ō′trou)	169	46°12′N	75°30′E
Sarysu, r., Kaz. (sä′rē-sōō)	169	47°47′N	69°14′E
Sasarām, India (sŭs-ŭ-räm′)	183	25°00′N	84°00′E
Sasayama, Japan (sä′sä-yä′mä)	195	35°05′N	135°14′E
Sasebo, Japan (sä′sȧ-bō)	189	33°12′N	129°43′E
Sashalom, neigh., Hung.	239g	47°31′N	19°11′E
Saskatchewan, prov., Can.	84	54°46′N	107°40′W
Saskatchewan, r., Can. (săs-kăch′ē-wän)	84	53°45′N	103°20′W
Saskatoon, Can. (săs-kȧ-tōōn′)	84	52°07′N	106°38′W
Sasolburg, S. Afr.	218d	26°52′S	27°47′E
Sasovo, Russia (sás′ō-vō)	166	54°20′N	42°00′E
Saspamco, Tx., U.S. (săs-păm′cō)	107d	29°13′N	98°18′W
Sassafras, Austl.	243b	37°52′S	145°21′E
Sassandra, C. Iv.	214	4°58′N	6°05′W
Sassandra, r., C. Iv. (sás-sän′drȧ)	210	5°35′N	6°25′W
Sassari, Italy (säs′sä-rē)	148	40°44′N	8°33′E
Sassnitz, Ger. (säs′nēts)	154	54°31′N	13°37′E
Satadougou, Mali (sä-tȧ-dōō-gōō′)	214	12°21′N	12°07′W
Säter, Swe. (sĕ′tĕr)	152	60°21′N	15°50′E
Sātghara, India	240a	22°44′N	88°21′E
Satilla, r., Ga., U.S. (sȧ-tĭl′ȧ)	115	31°15′N	82°13′W
Satka, Russia (sät′kȧ)	166	55°03′N	59°02′E
Sátoraljaujhely, Hung. (shä′tō-rō-lyō-ōō′yĕl′)	155	48°24′N	21°40′E
Satu Mare, Rom. (sȧ′tōō-mȧ′rĕ)	149	47°50′N	22°53′E
Saturna, Can. (să-tûr′nȧ)	106d	48°48′N	123°12′W
Saturna, i., Can.	106d	48°47′N	123°03′W
Sauda, Nor.	146	59°40′N	6°21′E
Saudárkrókur, Ice.	142	65°41′N	19°38′W
Saudi Arabia, nation, Asia (sȧ-ō′dĭ ȧ-rä′bĭ-ȧ)	182	22°40′N	46°00′E
Sauerlach, Ger. (zou′ĕr-läĸ)	145d	47°58′N	11°39′E
Saugatuck, Mi., U.S. (sô′gȧ-tŭk)	98	42°40′N	86°10′W
Saugeen, r., Can.	90	44°20′N	81°20′W
Saugerties, N.Y., U.S. (sô′gēr-tēz)	99	42°05′N	73°55′W
Saugus, Ma., U.S. (sô′gŭs)	93a	42°28′N	71°01′W
Sauk, r., Mn., U.S. (sôk)	103	45°30′N	94°45′W
Sauk Centre, Mn., U.S.	103	45°43′N	94°58′W
Sauk City, Wi., U.S.	103	43°16′N	89°45′W
Sauk Rapids, Mn., U.S. (răp′ĭd)	103	45°35′N	94°08′W
Sault Sainte Marie, Can.	85	46°31′N	84°20′W
Sault Sainte Marie, Mi., U.S. (sōō sānt mȧ-rē′)	97	46°29′N	84°21′W
Saumatre, Étang, l., Haiti	123	18°40′N	72°10′W
Saunders Lake, l., Can. (sän′dērs)	83g	53°18′N	113°25′W
Saurimo, Ang.	212	9°39′S	20°24′E
Sausalito, Ca., U.S. (sô-sȧ-lē′tō)	106b	37°51′N	122°29′W
Sausset-les-Pins, Fr. (sō-sĕ′lā-păɴ′)	156a	43°20′N	5°08′E
Saútar, Ang.	216	11°06′S	18°27′E
Sauvie Island, i., Or., U.S. (sô′vē)	106c	45°43′N	123°49′W
Sava, r., Yugo. (sä′vä)	142	44°50′N	18°30′E
Savage, Md., U.S. (să′vĕj)	100e	39°07′N	76°49′W
Savage, Mn., U.S.	107g	44°47′N	93°20′W
Savai'i, i., W. Sam.	198a	13°35′S	172°25′W
Savalen, l., Nor.	152	62°19′N	10°15′E
Savalou, Benin	210	7°56′N	1°58′E
Savanna, Il., U.S. (sȧ-văn′ȧ)	103	42°05′N	90°09′W
Savannah, Ga., U.S. (sȧ-văn′ȧ)	97	32°04′N	81°07′W
Savannah, Mo., U.S.	111	39°58′N	94°49′W
Savannah, Tn., U.S.	114	35°13′N	88°14′W
Savannah, r., U.S.	97	33°11′N	81°51′W
Savannakhét, Laos	196	16°33′N	104°45′E
Savanna la Mar, Jam. (sȧ-vän′ȧ lȧ mär′)	122	18°10′N	78°10′W
Save, r., Fr.	156	43°32′N	0°50′E
Save, Rio (Sabi), r., Afr. (rē′ō-sä′vē)	212	21°28′S	34°14′E
Sāveh, Iran	185	35°01′N	50°20′E
Saverne, Fr. (sȧ-vĕrn′)	157	48°40′N	7°22′E
Savigliano, Italy (sä-vēl-yä′nō)	160	44°38′N	7°42′E
Savigny-sur-Orge, Fr.	157b	48°41′N	2°22′E
Savona, Italy (sä-nō′nä)	148	44°19′N	8°28′E
Savonlinna, Fin. (sȧ′vôn-lēn′nȧ)	153	61°53′N	28°49′E
Savran′, Ukr. (säv-rän′)	163	48°07′N	30°09′E
Sawahlunto, Indon.	196	0°37′S	100°50′E
Sawākin, Sudan	211	19°02′N	37°19′E
Sawda, Jabal as, mts., Libya	211	28°14′N	13°46′E
Sawhāj, Egypt	211	26°34′N	31°40′E
Sawknah, Libya	211	29°04′N	15°53′E
Sawu, Laut (Savu Sea), sea, Indon.	196	9°15′S	122°15′E
Sawyer, l., Wa., U.S. (sô′yĕr)	106a	47°20′N	122°02′W
Saxony *see* Sachsen, hist. reg., Ger.	154	50°45′N	12°17′E
Say, Niger (sä′ē)	210	13°09′N	2°16′E
Sayan Khrebet, mts., Russia (sŭ-yän′)	165	51°30′N	90°00′E
Sayḩūt, Yemen	182	15°23′N	51°28′E
Sayre, Ok., U.S. (sā′ēr)	110	35°19′N	99°40′W
Sayre, Pa., U.S.	99	41°55′N	76°30′W
Sayreton, Al., U.S. (sā′ēr-tŭn)	100h	33°34′N	86°51′W
Sayreville, N.J., U.S. (sâr′vĭl)	100a	40°28′N	74°21′W
Sayr Usa, Mong.	188	44°15′N	107°00′E
Sayula, Mex.	118	19°50′N	103°33′W
Sayula, Mex. (sä-yōō′lä)	119	17°51′N	94°56′W
Sayula, Luguna de, l., Mex. (lä-gō′nä-dē)	118	20°00′N	103°33′W
Say'un, Yemen	182	16°00′N	48°59′E
Sayville, N.Y., U.S. (sā′vĭl)	99	40°45′N	73°10′W
Sazanit, i., Alb.	149	40°30′N	19°17′E
Sázava, r., Czech Rep.	154	49°36′N	15°24′E
Sazhino, Russia (sáz-hē′nō)	172a	56°20′N	58°15′E
Scala, Teatro alla, bldg., Italy	238c	45°28′N	9°11′E
Scandinavian Peninsula, pen., Eur.	180	62°00′N	14°00′E
Scanlon, Mn., U.S. (skăn′lôn)	107h	46°27′N	92°26′W
Scappoose, Or., U.S. (skă-pōōs′)	106c	45°46′N	122°53′W
Scappoose, r., Or., U.S.	106c	45°47′N	122°57′W
Scarborough, Can. (skär′bēr-ō)	91	43°45′N	79°12′W
Scarborough, Eng., U.K. (skär′bŭr-ō)	150	54°16′N	0°19′W
Scarsdale, N.Y., U.S. (skärz′dāl)	100a	41°01′N	73°47′W
Scarth Hill, Eng., U.K.	237a	53°33′N	2°52′W
Scatari I, Can. (skăt′ȧ-rē)	93	46°00′N	59°44′W
Sceaux, Fr.	237c	48°47′N	2°17′E
Schaerbeek, Bel. (skär′bāk)	145a	50°50′N	4°23′E
Schaffhausen, Switz. (shäf′hou-zĕn)	147	47°42′N	8°38′E
Schalksmühle, Ger.	236	51°14′N	7°31′E
Schapenrust, S. Afr.	244b	26°16′S	28°22′E
Scharnhorst, neigh., Ger.	236	51°32′N	7°32′E
Schefferville, Can.	85	54°52′N	67°01′W
Scheiblingstein, Aus.	239e	48°16′N	16°13′E
Schelde,, r., Eur.	151	51°04′N	3°55′E
Schenectady, N.Y., U.S. (skē-nĕk′tȧ-dē)	97	42°50′N	73°55′W
Scheveningen, Neth.	145a	52°06′N	4°15′E
Schiedam, Neth.	145a	51°55′N	4°23′E
Schildow, Ger.	238a	52°38′N	13°23′E
Schiller Park, Il., U.S.	231a	41°58′N	87°52′W
Schiltigheim, Fr. (shēl′tegh-hīm)	157	48°48′N	7°47′E
Schio, Italy (skē′ō)	160	45°43′N	11°23′E
Schleswig, Ger. (shlĕs′vēgh)	146	54°32′N	9°32′E
Schleswig-Holstein, hist. reg., Ger. (shlĕs′vēgh-hōl′shtīn)	154	54°40′N	9°10′E
Schmalkalden, Ger. (shmäl′käl-dĕn)	154	50°41′N	10°25′E
Schneider, In., U.S. (schnīd′ēr)	101a	41°12′N	87°26′W
Schofield, Wi., U.S. (skō′fēld)	103	44°52′N	89°37′W
Schöller, Ger.	236	51°14′N	7°01′E
Scholven, neigh., Ger.	236	51°36′N	7°01′E
Schönbrunn, Schloss, pt. of i., Aus.	239e	48°11′N	16°19′E
Schönebeck, Ger. (shû′nē-bergh)	154	52°01′N	11°44′E
Schönebeck, neigh., Ger.	236	51°28′N	6°56′E
Schöneberg, neigh., Ger.	238a	52°29′N	13°21′E
Schönefeld, Ger.	238a	52°23′N	13°30′E
Schöneiche, Ger.	238a	52°28′N	13°41′E
Schönerlinde, Ger.	238a	52°39′N	13°27′E
Schonnebeck, neigh., Ger.	236	51°29′N	7°04′E
Schönow, Ger.	238a	52°40′N	13°32′E
Schönwalde, Ger.	238a	52°37′N	13°07′E
Schoonhoven, Neth.	145a	51°56′N	4°51′E
Schramberg, Ger. (shräm′bĕrgh)	154	48°14′N	8°24′E
Schreiber, Can.	90	48°50′N	87°10′W
Schroon, l., N.Y., U.S. (skrōōn)	99	43°50′N	73°50′W
Schultzendorf, Ger. (shōōl′tzĕn-dōrf)	145b	52°21′N	13°55′E
Schumacher, Can.	90	48°30′N	81°30′W
Schüren, neigh., Ger.	236	51°30′N	7°32′E
Schuyler, Ne., U.S. (slī′ler)	102	41°28′N	97°05′W
Schuylkill, r., Pa., U.S. (skōōl′kĭl)	100f	40°10′N	75°31′W
Schuylkill-Haven, Pa., U.S. (skōōl′kĭl hā-vĕn)	99	40°35′N	76°10′W
Schwabach, Ger. (shvä′bäk)	154	49°19′N	11°02′E
Schwäbische Alb, mts., Ger. (shvă′bē-shĕ älb)	154	48°11′N	9°09′E
Schwäbisch Gmünd, Ger. (shvă′bēsh gmünd)	154	48°47′N	9°49′E
Schwäbisch Hall, Ger. (häl)	154	49°08′N	9°44′E
Schwafheim, Ger.	236	51°25′N	6°39′E
Schwandorf, Ger. (shvän′dôrf)	154	49°19′N	12°08′E
Schwanebeck, Ger.	238a	52°37′N	13°32′E
Schwanenwerder, neigh., Ger.	238a	52°27′N	13°10′E
Schwaner, Pegunungan, mts., Indon. (sĸvän′ĕr)	196	1°05′S	112°30′E
Schwarzenberg, Ger.	236	51°24′N	6°42′E
Schwarzwald, for., Ger. (shvärts′väld)	154	47°54′N	7°57′E
Schwaz, Aus.	154	47°20′N	11°45′E
Schwechat, Aus. (shvĕk′át)	154	48°09′N	16°29′E
Schwedt, Ger. (shvĕt)	154	53°04′N	14°17′E
Schweflinghausen, Ger.	236	51°16′N	7°25′E
Schweinfurt, Ger. (shvīn′fôrt)	154	50°03′N	10°14′E
Schwelm, Ger. (shvĕlm)	157c	51°17′N	7°18′E
Schwenke, Ger.	236	51°11′N	7°26′E
Schwerin, Ger. (shvĕ-rēn′)	154	53°36′N	11°25′E
Schwerin, neigh., Ger.	236	51°33′N	7°20′E
Schweriner See, l., Ger. (shvĕ′rē-nĕr zā)	154	53°40′N	11°06′E
Schwerte, Ger. (shvĕr′tĕ)	157c	51°26′N	7°34′E
Schwielowsee, l., Ger. (shvē′lōv zā)	145b	52°20′N	12°52′E
Schwyz, Switz. (schēts)	154	47°01′N	8°38′E
Sciacca, Italy (shē-äk′kä)	160	37°30′N	13°09′E
Science and Industry, Museum of, pt. of i., Il., U.S.	231a	41°47′N	87°35′W
Scilly, Isles of, is., Eng., U.K. (sĭl′ē)	142	49°56′N	6°50′W
Scioto, r., Oh., U.S. (sī-ō′tō)	97	39°10′N	82°55′W
Scituate, Ma., U.S. (sĭt′ū-āt)	93a	42°12′N	70°45′W
Scobey, Mt., U.S. (skō′bē)	105	48°48′N	105°29′W
Scoggin, Or., U.S. (skŏ′gĭn)	106c	45°28′N	123°14′W
Scoresby, Austl.	243b	37°54′S	145°14′E
Scotch, r., Can. (skŏch)	83c	45°21′N	74°56′W
Scotia, Ca., U.S. (skō′shȧ)	104	40°29′N	124°06′W
Scotland, S.D., U.S.	102	43°08′N	97°43′W
Scotland, , U.K. (skŏt′lȧnd)	142	57°05′N	5°10′W
Scotland Neck, N.C., U.S. (nĕk)	115	36°06′N	77°25′W
Scotstown, Can. (skŏts′toun)	99	45°35′N	71°15′W
Scott, r., Ca., U.S.	104	41°20′N	122°55′W
Scott, Cape, c., Can. (skŏt)	84	50°47′N	128°26′W
Scott, Mount, mtn., Or., U.S.	104	42°55′N	122°00′W
Scott, Mount, mtn., Or., U.S.	106c	45°27′N	122°33′W
Scott Air Force Base, Il., U.S.	107e	38°33′N	89°52′W
Scottburgh, S. Afr. (skŏt′bŭr-ō)	212	30°18′S	30°42′E
Scott City, Ks., U.S.	110	38°28′N	100°54′W
Scottdale, Ga., U.S. (skŏt′dāl)	100c	33°47′N	84°16′W
Scott Islands, is., Ant.	219	67°00′S	178°00′E
Scottsbluff, Ne., U.S. (skŏts′blŭf)	102	41°52′N	103°40′W
Scottsboro, Al., U.S. (skŏts′bŭro)	114	34°40′N	86°03′W
Scottsburg, In., U.S. (skŏts′bûrg)	98	38°40′N	85°50′W
Scottsdale, Austl. (skŏts′dāl)	204	41°12′S	147°37′E
Scottsville, Ky., U.S. (skŏts′vĭl)	114	36°45′N	86°10′W
Scott Township, Pa., U.S.	230b	40°24′N	80°06′W
Scottville, Mi., U.S.	98	44°00′N	86°20′W
Scranton, Pa., U.S. (skrăn′tŭn)	97	41°15′N	75°45′W
Scugog, l., Can. (skū′gôg)	91	44°05′N	78°55′W
Scunthorpe, Eng., U.K. (skŭn′thôrp)	144a	53°36′N	0°38′W
Scutari *see* Shkodër, Alb.	142	42°04′N	19°30′E
Scutari, Lake, l., Eur. (skōō′tä-rē)	149	42°14′N	19°33′E
Seabeck, Wa., U.S. (sē′bĕck)	106a	47°38′N	122°50′W
Sea Bright, N.J., U.S. (sē brīt)	100a	40°22′N	73°58′W
Seabrook, Md., U.S.	229d	38°58′N	76°51′W
Seabrook, Tx., U.S. (sē′brŏk)	113	29°34′N	95°01′W
Sea Cliff, N.Y., U.S.	228	40°51′N	73°38′W
Seacombe, Eng., U.K.	237a	53°25′N	3°01′W
Seaford, De., U.S. (sē′fērd)	99	38°35′N	75°40′W
Seaford, N.Y., U.S.	228	40°40′N	73°30′W
Seaforth, Austl.	243a	33°48′S	151°15′E
Seaforth, Eng., U.K.	237a	53°28′N	3°01′W
Seagraves, Tx., U.S. (sē′grāvs)	110	32°51′N	102°38′W
Sea Islands, is., Ga., U.S. (sē)	115	31°21′N	81°05′W
Seal, Eng., U.K.	235	51°17′N	0°14′E
Seal, r., Can.	84	59°08′N	96°37′W
Seal Beach, Ca., U.S.	107a	33°44′N	118°06′W
Seal Cays, is., Bah.	123	22°40′N	75°55′W
Seal Cays, is., T./C. Is.	123	21°10′N	71°45′W
Seal Island, i., S. Afr. (sēl)	212a	34°07′S	18°36′E
Seal Rocks, Ca., U.S.	231b	37°47′N	122°31′W
Sealy, Tx., U.S. (sē′lē)	113	29°46′N	96°10′W
Searcy, Ar., U.S. (sûr′sē)	111	35°13′N	91°43′W
Searles, l., Ca., U.S. (sûrl′s)	108	35°44′N	117°22′W
Searsport, Me., U.S. (sērz′pōrt)	92	44°28′N	68°55′W
Seaside, Or., U.S. (sē′sīd)	104	45°59′N	123°55′W
Seat Pleasant, Md., U.S.	229d	38°53′N	76°52′W
Seattle, Wa., U.S. (sē-ăt′'l)	96	47°36′N	122°20′W
Sebaco, Nic. (sĕ-bä′kō)	120	12°50′N	86°03′W
Sebago, Me., U.S. (sē-bā′gō)	92	43°52′N	70°20′W
Sebastián Vizcaíno, Bahía, b., Mex.	116	28°45′N	115°15′W
Sebastopol, Ca., U.S. (sē-bás′tō-pōl)	108	38°27′N	122°50′W
Sebderat, Erit.	211	15°30′N	36°45′E
Sebewaing, Mi., U.S. (se′bē-wăng)	98	43°45′N	83°25′W
Sebezh, Russia (syĕ′bĕzh)	162	56°16′N	28°29′E
Sebinkarahisar, Tur.	149	40°15′N	38°10′E
Sebnitz, Ger. (zĕb′nēts)	154	51°01′N	14°16′E
Sebou, Oued, r., Mor.	210	34°23′N	5°18′W
Sebree, Ky., U.S. (sē-brē′)	98	37°35′N	87°30′W
Sebring, Fl., U.S. (sē′brĭng)	115a	27°30′N	81°26′W
Sebring, Oh., U.S.	98	40°55′N	81°05′W
Secane, Pa., U.S.	229b	39°55′N	75°18′W
Secaucus, N.J., U.S.	228	40°47′N	74°04′W
Secchia, r., Italy (sĕ′kyä)	160	44°25′N	10°25′E
Seco, r., Mex. (sĕ′kō)	119	18°11′N	93°18′W
Sedalia, Mo., U.S.	97	38°42′N	93°12′W
Sedan, Fr. (sē-dăɴ)	147	49°49′N	4°55′E
Sedan, Ks., U.S. (sē-dăn′)	111	37°07′N	96°08′W
Sedom, Isr.	181a	31°04′N	35°24′E
Sedro Woolley, Wa., U.S. (sē′drō-wŏŏl′ē)	106a	48°30′N	122°14′W
Šeduva, Lith. (shĕ′dŏ-vȧ)	153	55°46′N	23°45′E
Seeberg, Ger.	238a	52°33′N	13°41′E
Seeburg, Ger.	238a	52°31′N	13°07′E
Seefeld, Ger.	238a	52°37′N	13°40′E
Seer Green, Eng., U.K.	235	51°37′N	0°36′W
Seestall, Ger. (zā′shtäl)	145d	47°58′N	10°52′E
Sefrou, Mor. (sĕ-frōō′)	148	33°49′N	4°46′W
Sefton, Eng., U.K.	237a	53°30′N	2°58′W
Seg, l., Russia (syĕgh)	166	63°20′N	33°30′E
Segamat, Malay. (sā′gȧ-mát)	181b	2°30′N	102°49′E
Segang, China (sŭ-gäŋ)	190	31°59′N	114°13′E
Segbana, Benin	215	10°56′N	3°42′E
Segorbe, Spain (sĕ-gôr-bē)	159	39°50′N	0°30′W
Ségou, Mali (sā-gōō′)	210	13°27′N	6°16′W
Segovia, Col. (sĕ-gō′vēä)	130a	7°08′N	74°42′W
Segovia, Spain (sā-gō′vē-ä)	148	40°58′N	4°05′W
Segre, r., Spain (sā′grä)	159	41°54′N	1°10′E
Seguam, i., Ak., U.S. (sē′gwäm)	95a	52°16′N	172°10′W
Seguam Passage, strt., Ak., U.S.	95a	52°20′N	173°00′W
Séguédine, Niger	215	20°12′N	12°59′E
Séguéla, C. Iv. (sā-gā-lä′)	210	7°57′N	6°40′W
Seguin, Tx., U.S. (sē-gēn′)	113	29°35′N	97°58′W
Segula, i., Ak., U.S. (sē-gū′lá)	95a	52°08′N	178°35′E
Segura, r., Spain	148	38°24′N	2°12′W
Segura, Sierra de, mts., Spain (sē-ĕ′r-rä-dē)	158	38°05′N	2°45′W
Sehwān, Pak.	186	26°33′N	67°51′E
Seibeeshiden, Japan	242a	35°34′N	139°22′E
Seibo, Dom. Rep. (sĕ′y-bō)	123	18°45′N	69°05′W
Seiling, Ok., U.S.	110	36°09′N	98°56′W
Seim, r., Eur.	167	51°23′N	33°22′E
Seinäjoki, Fin. (sâ′ē-nĕ-yō′kē)	153	62°47′N	22°50′E
Seine, r., Can. (sân)	83f	49°48′N	97°03′W
Seine, r., Can. (sân)	90	49°04′N	91°00′W
Seine, r., Fr.	142	48°00′N	4°30′E
Seine, Baie de la, b., Fr. (bī dē lä sån)	156	49°37′N	0°53′W
Seio do Venus, mtn., Braz. (sĕ-yō-dō-vĕ′nōōs)	132b	22°28′S	43°12′W
Seixal, Port. (sâ-ê-shäl′)	159b	38°38′N	9°06′W
Sekenke, Tan.	217	4°16′S	34°10′E
Şeki, Azer.	168	41°12′N	47°12′E
Sekondi-Takoradi, Ghana (sĕ-kôn′dē tä-kō-rä′dē)	210	4°59′N	1°43′W
Sekota, Eth.	211	12°47′N	38°59′E

ăt; finăl; rāte; senāte; ärm; ȧsk; sofȧ; fâre; ch-choose; dh-as th in other; bē; ēvent; bĕt; recĕnt; cratĕr; g-gō; gh-guttural g; bĭt; ĭ-short neutral; rīde; ĸ-guttural k as ch in German ich;

PRONOUNCING INDEX

Selangor–Sheffield Lake 347

PLACE (Pronunciation)	PAGE	LAT.	LONG.
Selangor, state, Malay. (så-län'gōr)	181b	2°53'N	101°29'E
Selanovtsi, Bul. (sál'á-nôv-tsĭ)	161	43°42'N	24°05'E
Selaru, Pulau, i., Indon.	197	8°30'S	130°30'E
Selatan, Tanjung, c., Indon. (så-lä'tän)	196	4°09'S	114°40'E
Selawik, Ak., U.S. (sē-lá-wĭk)	95	66°30'N	160°09'W
Selayar, Pulau, i., Indon.	196	6°15'S	121°15'E
Selbecke, neigh., Ger.	236	51°20'N	7°28'E
Selbusjøen, l., Nor. (sĕl'bōō)	152	63°18'N	11°55'E
Selby, Eng., U.K. (sĕl'bē)	144a	53°47'N	1°03'W
Selby, neigh., S. Afr.	244b	26°13'S	28°02'E
Seldovia, Ak., U.S. (sĕl-dō'vē-ȧ)	95	59°26'N	151°42'W
Selection Park, S. Afr.	244b	26°18'S	28°27'E
Selemdzha, r., Russia (sâ-lĕmt-zhä')	171	52°28'N	131°50'E
Selenga (Selenge), r., Asia (sĕ lĕŋ gä')	165	49°00'N	102°00'E
Selenge, r., Asia	188	49°04'N	102°23'E
Selennyakh, r., Russia (sĕl-yĭn-yäk)	171	67°42'N	141°45'E
Sélestat, Fr. (sẽ-lẽ-stä')	157	48°16'N	7°27'E
Seletar, Sing.	240c	1°25'N	103°53'E
Sélibaby, Maur. (så-lē-bȧ-bē')	210	15°21'N	12°11'W
Seliger, l., Russia (sĕl'lĕ-gĕr)	166	57°14'N	33°18'E
Selizharovo, Russia (sâ'lē-zhä'rô-vô)	162	56°51'N	33°28'E
Selkirk, Can. (sĕl'kûrk)	84	50°09'N	96°52'W
Selkirk Mountains, mts., Can.	84	51°00'N	117°40'W
Selleck, Wa., U.S. (sĕl'ĕck)	106a	47°22'N	121°52'W
Sellersburg, In., U.S. (sĕl'ĕrs-bûrg)	101h	38°25'N	85°45'W
Sellya Khskaya, Guba, b., Russia (sĕl-yäk'skȧ-yȧ)	171	72°30'N	136°00'E
Selma, Al., U.S. (sĕl'mȧ)	97	32°25'N	87°00'W
Selma, Ca., U.S.	108	36°34'N	119°37'W
Selma, N.C., U.S.	115	35°33'N	78°16'W
Selma, Tx., U.S.	107d	29°33'N	98°19'W
Selmer, Tn., U.S.	114	35°11'N	88°36'W
Selsingen, Ger. (zĕl'zĕn-gĕn)	145c	53°22'N	9°13'E
Selway, r., Id., U.S. (sĕl'wȧ)	104	46°07'N	115°12'W
Selwyn, l., Can. (sĕl'wĭn)	84	59°41'N	104°30'W
Seman, r., Alb.	161	40°48'N	19°53'E
Semarang, Indon. (sĕ-mä'räng)	196	7°03'S	110°27'E
Sembawang, Sing.	240c	1°27'N	103°50'E
Semenivka, Ukr.	167	52°10'N	32°34'E
Semeru, Gunung, mtn., Indon.	196	8°06'S	112°55'E
Semey, Kaz.	169	50°28'N	80°29'E
Semiahmoo Indian Reserve, I.R., Can.	106d	49°01'N	122°43'W
Semiahmoo Spit, Wa., U.S. (sĕm'ĭ-á-mōō)	106d	48°59'N	122°52'W
Semichi Islands, is., Ak., U.S. (sē-mē'chī)	95a	52°40'N	174°50'E
Seminoe Reservoir, res., Wy., U.S. (sĕm'ĭ nô)	105	42°08'N	107°10'W
Seminole, Ok., U.S. (sĕm'ĭ-nōl)	111	35°13'N	96°41'W
Seminole, Tx., U.S.	112	32°43'N	102°39'W
Seminole, Lake, res., U.S.	114	30°57'N	84°46'W
Semisopochnoi, i., Ak., U.S. (sē-mē-sȧ-pōsh' noi)	95a	51°45'N	179°25'E
Semliki, r., Afr. (sĕm'lē-kē)	211	0°45'N	29°36'E
Semmering Pass, p., Aus. (sĕm'ĕr-ĭng)	154	47°39'N	15°50'E
Senador Pompeu, Braz. (sĕ-nä-dōr-pôm-pĕ'ō)	131	5°34'S	39°18'W
Senaki, Geor.	168	42°17'N	42°04'E
Senatobia, Ms., U.S. (sĕ-nȧ-tō'bē-ȧ)	114	34°36'N	89°56'W
Send, Eng., U.K.	235	51°17'N	0°31'W
Sendai, Japan (sĕn-dī')	189	38°18'N	141°02'E
Seneca, Ks., U.S. (sĕn'ĕ-kȧ)	111	39°49'N	96°03'W
Seneca, Md., U.S.	100e	39°04'N	77°20'W
Seneca, S.C., U.S.	115	34°40'N	82°58'W
Seneca, l., N.Y., U.S.	99	42°30'N	76°55'W
Seneca Falls, N.Y., U.S.	99	42°55'N	76°55'W
Senegal, nation, Afr. (sĕn-ĕ-gôl')	210	14°53'N	14°58'W
Sénégal, r., Afr.	210	16°00'N	14°00'W
Senekal, S. Afr. (sĕn'ĕ-kȧl)	218d	28°20'S	27°37'E
Senftenberg, Ger. (zĕnf'tĕn-bĕrgh)	154	51°32'N	14°00'E
Sengunyane, r., Leso.	213c	29°35'S	28°08'E
Senhor do Bonfim, Braz. (sĕn-yôr dô bôN-fē'N)	131	10°21'S	40°09'W
Senigallia, Italy (så-nē-gäl'lyä)	160	43°42'N	13°16'E
Senj, Cro. (sĕn')	160	44°58'N	14°55'E
Senja, i., Nor. (sĕnyä)	146	69°28'N	16°10'E
Senlis, Fr. (säN-lĕs')	157b	49°13'N	2°35'E
Sennar Dam, dam, Sudan	211	13°38'N	33°38'E
Senneterre, Can.	85	48°20'N	77°22'W
Senno, Bela. (syĕ'nô)	162	54°48'N	29°43'E
Senriyama, Japan	242b	34°47'N	135°30'E
Sens, Fr. (säNs)	156	48°05'N	3°18'E
Sensuntepeque, El Sal. (sĕn-sōōn-tå-pä'kå)	120	13°53'N	88°34'W
Senta, Yugo. (sĕn'tä)	149	45°54'N	20°05'E
Sentosa, i., Sing.	240c	1°15'N	103°50'E
Senzaki, Japan (sĕn'zä-kē)	195	34°22'N	131°09'E
Seoul (Sŏul), S. Kor.	189	37°35'N	127°03'E
Sepang, Malay.	181b	2°43'N	101°45'E
Sepetiba, Baía de, b., Braz. (bäē'ä dĕ så-pȧ-tē'bȧ)	132b	23°01'S	43°42'W
Sepik, r. (sĕp-ĕk')	197	4°07'S	142°40'E
Septentrional, Cordillera, mts., Dom. Rep.	123	19°50'N	71°15'W
Septeuil, Fr. (sĕ-tû')	157b	48°53'N	1°40'E
Sept-Îles, Can. (sĕ-tēl')	92	50°12'N	66°23'W
Sequatchie, r., Tn., U.S. (sė-kwăch'ė)	114	35°33'N	85°14'W
Sequim, Wa., U.S. (sē'kwĭm)	106a	48°05'N	123°07'W
Sequim Bay, b., Wa., U.S.	106a	48°04'N	122°58'W
Sequoia National Park, rec., Ca., U.S. (sė-kwoi'ȧ)	96	36°34'N	118°37'W
Seraing, Bel. (sẽ-räN')	151	50°38'N	5°28'E
Serāmpore, India	186a	22°44'N	88°21'E
Serang, Indon. (så-räng')	196	6°13'S	106°10'E
Seranggung, Indon.	181b	0°49'N	104°11'E
Serangoon, Sing.	240c	1°22'N	103°54'E
Serangoon Harbour, b., Sing.	240c	1°23'N	103°57'E
Serbia see Srbija, hist. reg., Yugo.	161	44°05'N	20°35'E
Serdobsk, Russia (sĕr-dôpsk')	167	52°30'N	44°20'E
Serebr'anyj Bor, neigh., Russia	239b	55°47'N	37°25'E
Sered', Slvk.	155	48°17'N	17°43'E
Seredyna-Buda, Ukr.	162	52°11'N	34°03'E
Seremban, Malay. (sĕr-ĕm-bän')	181b	2°44'N	101°57'E
Serengeti National Park, rec., Tan.	217	2°20'S	34°50'E
Serengeti Plain, pl., Tan.	217	2°40'S	34°55'E
Serenje, Zam. (sē-rĕn'yė)	212	13°12'S	30°49'E
Seret, r., Ukr. (sĕr'ĕt)	155	49°45'N	25°30'E
Sergeya Kirova, i., Russia (sĕr-gyĕ'yȧ kė'rô-vȧ)	170	77°30'N	86°10'E
Sergipe, state, Braz. (sĕr-zhē'pĕ)	131	10°27'S	37°04'W
Sergiyev Posad, Russia	172b	56°18'N	38°08'E
Sergiyevsk, Russia	166	53°58'N	51°00'E
Sérifos, Grc.	161	37°10'N	24°32'E
Sérifos, i., Grc.	161	37°42'N	24°17'E
Serodino, Arg. (sĕ-rô-dē'nō)	129c	32°36'S	60°56'W
Seropédica, Braz. (sĕ-rô-pĕ'dē-kä)	132b	22°44'S	43°43'W
Serov, Russia (syĕ-rôf')	170	59°36'N	60°30'E
Serowe, Bots. (sĕ-rō'wĕ)	212	22°18'S	26°39'E
Serpa, Port. (sĕr-pä)	158	37°56'N	7°38'W
Serpukhov, Russia (syĕr'pò-kôf)	164	54°53'N	37°27'E
Sérrai, Grc. (sĕr'rĕ) (sĕr'ĕs)	149	41°06'N	23°36'E
Serrinha, Braz. (sĕr-rēn'yȧ)	131	11°43'S	38°49'W
Serta, Port. (sĕr'tȧ)	158	39°48'N	8°01'W
Sertânia, Braz. (sĕr-tȧ'nyä)	131	8°28'S	37°13'W
Sertãozinho, Braz. (sĕr-touN-zē'n-yō)	129a	21°10'S	47°58'W
Serting, r., Malay.	181b	3°01'N	102°32'E
Servon, Fr.	237c	48°43'N	2°35'E
Sese Islands, is., Ug.	217	0°30'S	32°30'E
Sesia, r., Italy (sâz'yä)	160	45°33'N	8°25'E
Sesimbra, Port. (sĕ-sē'm-brä)	159b	38°27'N	9°06'W
Sesmyl, r., S. Afr.	213b	25°51'S	28°06'E
Ses Salines, Cap de, c., Spain	159	39°16'N	3°03'E
Sesto San Giovanni, Italy	238c	45°32'N	9°14'E
Sestri Levante, Italy (sĕs'trē lå-vän'tå)	160	44°15'N	9°24'E
Sestroretsk, Russia (sĕs-trô-rĕtsk)	166	60°06'N	29°58'E
Sestroretskiy Razliv, Ozero, l., Russia	172c	60°05'N	30°07'E
Seta, Japan (sĕ'tä)	195b	34°58'N	135°56'W
Setagaya, neigh., Japan	242a	35°39'N	139°40'E
Séte, Fr. (sĕt)	147	43°24'N	3°42'E
Sete Lagoas, Braz. (sĕ-tĕ lä-gô'äs)	131	19°23'S	43°58'W
Sete Pontes, Braz.	132b	22°51'S	43°05'W
Seto, Japan (sē'tō)	195	35°11'N	137°07'E
Seto-Naikai, sea, Japan (sĕ'tô nī'kī)	195	33°50'N	132°25'E
Seton Hall University, pt. of i., N.Y., U.S.	228	40°45'N	74°15'W
Settat, Mor. (sĕt-ät') (sĕ-tȧ')	210	33°02'N	7°30'W
Sette-Cama, Gabon (sĕ-tĕ-kä-mä')	212	2°29'S	9°40'E
Settecamini, neigh., Italy	239c	41°56'N	12°37'E
Settimo Milanese, Italy	238c	45°29'N	9°03'E
Settlement Point, c., Bah. (sĕt'l-mĕnt)	122	26°40'N	79°00'W
Settlers, S. Afr. (sĕt'lĕrs)	218d	24°57'S	28°33'E
Settsu, Japan	195b	34°46'N	135°33'E
Setúbal, Port. (så-tōō'bäl)	148	30°32'N	8°54'W
Setúbal, Baía de, b., Port.	158	38°27'N	9°08'W
Seul, Lac, l., Can. (läk sûl)	85	50°20'N	92°30'W
Sevan, l., Arm. (syĭ-vän')	167	40°10'N	45°20'E
Sevastopol', Ukr. (syĕ-vás-tô'pôl'')	164	44°34'N	33°34'E
Seven Hills, Austl.	243a	33°46'S	150°57'E
Seven Hills, Oh., U.S.	229a	41°22'N	81°41'W
Seven Kings, neigh., Eng., U.K.	235	51°34'N	0°05'E
Sevenoaks, Eng., U.K. (sĕ-vĕn-ôks')	144b	51°16'N	0°12'E
Severka, r., Russia (sâ'vĕr-kȧ)	172b	55°11'N	38°41'E
Severn, r., Can. (sĕv'ĕrn)	85	55°21'N	88°42'W
Severn, r., U.K.	150	51°50'N	2°25'W
Severna Park, Md., U.S. (sĕv'ĕrn-â)	100e	39°04'N	76°33'W
Severnaya Dvina, r., Russia	164	63°00'N	42°40'E
Severnaya Zemlya (Northern Land), is., Russia (sĕ-vyĭr-nŭ zĭ-m'lyä')	165	79°33'N	101°15'E
Severoural'sk, Russia (sĕ-vyĭ-rŭ-ōō-rälsk')	170	60°08'N	59°53'E
Sevier, r., Ut., U.S.	96	39°25'N	112°20'W
Sevier, East Fork, r., Ut., U.S.	109	37°45'N	112°10'W
Sevier Lake, l., Ut., U.S. (sė-vēr')	109	38°55'N	113°10'W
Sevilla, Col. (sĕ-vē'l-yä)	130a	4°16'N	75°56'W
Sevilla, Spain (sâ-vēl'yä)	142	37°29'N	5°58'W
Seville, Oh., U.S. (sĕ'vĭl)	101d	41°01'N	81°45'W
Sevlievo, Bul. (sĕv'lyĕ-vô)	149	43°02'N	25°05'E
Sevran, Fr.	237c	48°56'N	2°32'E
Sèvres, Fr.	237c	48°49'N	2°12'E
Sevsk, Russia (syĕfsk)	162	52°08'N	34°28'E
Seward, Ak., U.S. (sū'árd)	94a	60°18'N	149°28'W
Seward, Ne., U.S.	111	40°55'N	97°06'W
Seward Peninsula, pen., Ak., U.S.	95	65°40'N	164°00'W
Sewell, Chile (sĕ'ŏ-ĕl)	132	34°01'S	70°18'W
Sewickley, Pa., U.S. (sė-wĭk'lė)	101e	40°33'N	80°11'W
Seybaplaya, Mex. (sā-ė-bä-plä'yä)	119	19°38'N	90°40'W
Seychelles, nation, Afr. (sā-shĕl')	3	5°20'S	55°10'E
Seydisfjördur, Ice. (sä'dēs-fyûr-dòr)	146	65°21'N	14°08'W
Seyhan, r., Tur.	149	37°28'N	35°40'E
Seylac, Som.	218a	11°19'N	43°20'E
Seymour, S. Afr. (sē'môr)	213c	32°33'S	26°48'E
Seymour, In., U.S. (sē'mōr)	98	38°55'N	85°55'W
Seymour, Ia., U.S.	103	40°41'N	93°03'W
Seymour, Tx., U.S.	110	33°35'N	99°16'W
Sezela, S. Afr.	213c	30°33'S	30°37'E
Sezze, Italy (sĕt'så)	160	41°32'N	13°00'E
Sfântu Gheorghe, Rom.	149	45°53'N	25°49'E
Sfax, Tun. (sfäks)	210	34°51'N	10°45'E
's-Gravenhage see The Hague, Neth. ('s krä'vĕn-hä'kĕ) (häg)	142	52°05'N	4°16'E
Sha, r., China (shä)	189	33°33'N	114°30'E
Shaanxi, prov., China (shän-shyĕ)	188	35°30'N	109°10'E
Shabeelle (Shebele), r., Afr.	218a	1°38'N	43°50'E
Shache, China (shä-chū)	188	38°15'N	77°15'E
Shackleton Ice Shelf, ice., Ant. (shăk''l-tŭn)	219	65°00'S	100°00'E
Shades Creek, r., Al., U.S. (shādz)	100h	33°20'N	86°55'W
Shades Mountain, mtn., Al., U.S.	100h	33°22'N	86°51'W
Shagamu, Nig.	215	6°51'N	3°39'E
Shāhdād, Namakzār-e, l., Iran (nŭ-mŭk-zär')	182	31°00'N	58°30'E
Shāhdara, neigh., India	240d	28°40'N	77°18'E
Shāhjahānpur, India (shä-jŭ-hän'pōōr)	183	27°58'N	79°58'E
Shah Mosque, rel., Iran	241h	35°40'N	51°25'E
Shajing, China (shä-jyĭŋ)	191a	22°44'N	113°48'E
Shakarpur Khās, neigh., India	240d	28°38'N	77°17'E
Shaker Heights, Oh., U.S. (shā'kĕr)	101d	41°28'N	81°34'W
Shakhty, Russia (shäK'tė)	164	47°41'N	40°11'E
Shaki, Nig.	215	8°39'N	3°25'E
Shakopee, Mn., U.S. (shăk'ô-pe)	107g	44°48'N	93°31'W
Shakūrpur, neigh., India	240d	28°41'N	77°09'E
Shala Lake, l., Eth. (shä'lȧ)	211	7°34'N	39°00'E
Shalqar, Kaz.	169	47°52'N	59°41'E
Shalqar kölī, l., Kaz.	170	50°30'N	51°30'E
Shām, Jabal ash, mtn., Oman	182	23°01'N	57°45'E
Shambe, Sudan (shäm'bȧ)	211	7°08'N	30°46'E
Shammar, Jabal, mts., Sau. Ar. (jĕb'ĕl shŭm'ár)	182	27°13'N	40°16'E
Shamokin, Pa., U.S. (shȧ-mō'kĭn)	99	40°45'N	76°30'W
Shamrock, Tx., U.S. (shăm'rŏk)	110	35°14'N	100°12'W
Shamva, Zimb. (shäm'vȧ)	212	17°18'S	31°35'E
Shandon, Oh., U.S. (shăn-dŭn)	101f	39°20'N	84°13'W
Shandong, prov., China (shän-dôŋ)	189	36°08'N	117°09'E
Shandong Bandao, pen., China (shän-dôŋ bän-dou)	189	37°00'N	120°10'E
Shangcai, China (shäŋ-tsī)	190	33°16'N	114°16'E
Shangcheng, China (shäŋ-chŭŋ)	190	31°47'N	115°22'E
Shangdu, China (shäŋ-dōō)	192	41°38'N	113°22'E
Shanghai, China (shäng'hī')	189	31°14'N	121°27'E
Shanghai-Shi, prov., China (shäŋ-hī shr)	189	31°30'N	121°45'E
Shanghe, China (shäŋ-hŭ)	190	37°18'N	117°10'E
Shanglin, China (shäŋ-lĭn)	190	38°20'N	116°05'E
Shangqiu, China (shäŋ-chyô)	192	34°24'N	115°39'E
Shangrao, China (shäŋ-rou)	193	28°25'N	117°58'E
Shangzhi, China (shäŋ-jr)	192	45°18'N	127°52'E
Shanhaiguan, China	192	40°01'N	119°45'E
Shannon, Al., U.S. (shăn'ŭn)	100h	33°23'N	86°52'W
Shannon, r., Ire. (shăn'ŏn)	147	52°30'N	10°15'W
Shanshan, China (shän'shän')	188	42°51'N	89°53'E
Shantar, i., Russia (shän'tär)	171	55°13'N	138°42'E
Shantou, China (shän-tō)	189	23°20'N	116°40'E
Shanxi, prov., China (shän-shyĕ)	189	37°30'N	112°00'E
Shan Xian, China (shän shyĕn)	190	34°47'N	116°04'E
Shaobo, China (shou-bwo)	192	32°33'N	119°30'E
Shaobo Hu, l., China (shou-bwo hōō)	190	32°47'N	119°13'E
Shaoguan, China (shou-guän)	189	24°58'N	113°42'E
Shaoxing, China (shou-shyĭŋ)	189	30°00'N	120°40'E
Shaoyang, China	189	27°15'N	111°28'E
Shapki, Russia (shäp'kĭ)	172c	59°36'N	31°11'E
Shark Bay, b., Austl. (shärk)	202	25°30'S	113°00'E
Sharon, Ma., U.S. (shăr'ŏn)	93a	42°07'N	71°11'W
Sharon, Pa., U.S.	98	41°15'N	80°30'W
Sharon Hill, Pa., U.S.	229b	39°55'N	75°16'W
Sharon Springs, Ks., U.S.	110	38°51'N	101°45'W
Sharonville, Oh., U.S. (shăr'ŏn vĭl)	101f	39°16'N	84°24'W
Sharpsburg, Pa., U.S. (shärps'bûrg)	101e	40°30'N	79°54'W
Sharps Hill, Pa., U.S.	230b	40°30'N	79°56'W
Sharr, Jabal, mtn., Sau. Ar.	182	28°00'N	36°07'E
Shashi, China (shä-shē)	189	30°20'N	112°18'E
Shasta, Mount, mtn., Ca., U.S.	96	41°35'N	122°12'W
Shasta Lake, res., Ca., U.S. (shăs'tȧ)	96	40°51'N	122°32'W
Shatsk, Russia (shȧtsk)	166	54°00'N	41°40'E
Shattuck, Ok., U.S. (shăt'ŭk)	110	36°16'N	99°53'W
Shaunavon, Can.	84	49°40'N	108°25'W
Shaw, Eng., U.K.	237b	53°35'N	2°06'W
Shaw, Ms., U.S. (shô)	114	33°36'N	90°44'W
Shawano, Wi., U.S. (shȧ-wô'nô)	103	44°41'N	88°13'W
Shawinigan, Can.	85	46°32'N	72°46'W
Shawnee, Ks., U.S. (shô-nē')	107f	39°01'N	94°43'W
Shawnee, Ok., U.S.	96	35°20'N	96°54'W
Shawneetown, Il., U.S. (shô'nē-toun)	98	37°40'N	88°05'W
Shayang, China	193	31°00'N	112°38'E
Shchara, r., Bela. (sh-chä'rȧ)	155	53°17'N	25°12'E
Shchëlkovo, Russia (shchĕl'kô-vô)	162	55°55'N	38°00'E
Shchigry, Russia (shchē'grė)	163	51°52'N	36°54'E
Shchors, Ukr. (shchôrs)	163	51°38'N	31°58'E
Shchuch'ye Ozero, Russia (shchōōch'yĕ ô'zĕ-rō)	172a	56°31'N	56°35'E
Sheakhala, India	186a	22°47'N	88°10'E
Shebele (Shabeelle), r., Afr. (shā'bȧ-lē)	218a	6°07'N	43°10'E
Sheboygan, Wi., U.S. (shė-boi'gȧn)	97	43°45'N	87°44'W
Sheboygan Falls, Wi., U.S.	103	43°43'N	87°51'W
Shechem, hist., W. Bank	181a	32°15'N	35°22'E
Shedandoah, Pa., U.S.	99	40°50'N	76°15'W
Shediac, Can. (shē'dē-ăk)	92	46°13'N	64°32'W
Shedin Peak, mtn., Can. (shĕd'ĭn)	86	55°55'N	127°32'W
Sheepshead Bay, neigh., N.Y., U.S.	228	40°35'N	73°56'W
Sheerness, Eng., U.K. (shēr'nĕs)	144b	51°26'N	0°46'E
Sheffield, Can.	83d	43°20'N	80°13'W
Sheffield, Eng., U.K.	146	53°23'N	1°28'W
Sheffield, Al., U.S. (shĕf'fēld)	114	35°42'N	87°42'W
Sheffield, Oh., U.S.	101d	41°26'N	82°05'W
Sheffield Lake, Oh., U.S.	101d	41°30'N	82°03'W

ng-sing; ŋ-baŋk; N-nasalized n; nŏd; cŏmmit; ōld; ōbey; ôrder; oi-boil; fōōd; ò-as oo in foot; ou-out; s-soft; sh-dish; th-thin; pūre; ůnite; ûrn; stŭd; circŭs; ü-as in French tu; '-indeterminate vowel.

PLACE (Pronunciation)	PAGE	LAT.	LONG.
Sheksna, r., Russia (shěks'nȧ)	166	59°50'N	38°40'E
Shelagskiy, Mys, c., Russia (shĭ-lăg'skē)	165	70°08'N	170°52'E
Shelbina, Ar., U.S. (shěl-bī'nȧ)	111	39°41'N	92°03'W
Shelburn, In., U.S. (shěl'bŭrn)	98	39°10'N	87°30'W
Shelburne, Can.	85	43°46'N	65°19'W
Shelburne, Can.	91	44°04'N	80°12'W
Shelby, In., U.S. (shěl'bė)	101a	41°12'N	87°21'W
Shelby, Mi., U.S.	98	43°35'N	86°20'W
Shelby, Ms., U.S.	114	33°56'N	90°44'W
Shelby, Mt., U.S.	105	48°35'N	111°55'W
Shelby, N.C., U.S.	115	35°16'N	81°35'W
Shelby, Oh., U.S.	98	40°50'N	82°40'W
Shelbyville, Il., U.S. (shěl'bė-vĭl)	98	39°20'N	88°45'W
Shelbyville, In., U.S.	98	39°30'N	85°45'W
Shelbyville, Ky., U.S.	98	38°10'N	85°15'W
Shelbyville, Tn., U.S.	114	35°30'N	86°28'W
Shelbyville Reservoir, res., Il., U.S.	98	39°30'N	88°45'W
Sheldon, Ia., U.S. (shěl'dŭn)	102	43°10'N	95°50'W
Sheldon, Tx., U.S.	113a	29°52'N	95°07'W
Shelekhova, Zaliv, b., Russia	165	60°00'N	156°00'E
Shelikof Strait, strt., Ak., U.S. (shě'lė-kôf)	95	57°56'N	154°20'W
Shellbrook, Can.	88	53°15'N	106°22'W
Shelley, Id., U.S. (shěl'lė)	105	43°24'N	112°06'W
Shellow Bowells, Eng., U.K.	235	51°45'N	0°20'E
Shellrock, r., Ia., U.S. (shěl'rŏk)	103	43°25'N	93°19'W
Shelon', r., Russia (shȧ'lôn)	162	57°50'N	29°40'E
Shelter, Port, b., H.K.	241c	22°21'N	114°17'E
Shelton, Ct., U.S. (shěl'tŭn)	99	41°15'N	73°05'W
Shelton, Ne., U.S.	110	40°46'N	98°41'W
Shelton, Wa., U.S.	104	47°14'N	123°05'W
Shemakha, Russia (shě-mȧ-kä')	172a	56°16'N	59°19'E
Shenandoah, Ia., U.S. (shěn-ăn-dō'ȧ)	111	40°46'N	95°23'W
Shenandoah, Va., U.S.	99	38°30'N	78°30'W
Shenandoah, r., Va., U.S.	99	38°55'N	78°05'W
Shenandoah National Park, rec., Va., U.S.	97	38°35'N	78°25'W
Shendam, Nig.	215	8°53'N	9°32'E
Shenfield, Eng., U.K.	235	51°38'N	0°19'E
Shengfang, China (shengfäŋ)	190	39°05'N	116°40'E
Shenkursk, Russia (shěn-ko͞orsk')	164	62°10'N	43°08'E
Shenmu, China	192	38°55'N	110°35'E
Shenqiu, China	192	33°11'N	115°06'E
Shenxian, China (shŭn shyän)	190	38°02'N	115°33'E
Shenxian, China (shŭn shyěn)	190	36°14'N	115°38'E
Shenyang, China (shŭn-yäŋ)	189	41°45'N	123°22'E
Shenze, China (shŭn-dzŭ)	190	38°12'N	115°12'E
Shenzhen, China	193	22°32'N	114°08'E
Sheopur, India	183	25°37'N	77°10'E
Shepard, Can. (shě'pȧrd)	83e	50°57'N	113°55'W
Shepetivka, Ukr.	167	50°10'N	27°01'E
Shepparton, Austl. (shěp'ȧr-tŭn)	204	36°15'S	145°25'E
Shepperton, Eng., U.K.	235	51°24'N	0°27'W
Sherborn, Ma., U.S. (shûr'bŭrn)	93a	42°15'N	71°22'W
Sherbrooke, Can.	85	45°24'N	71°54'W
Sherburn, Eng., U.K. (shûr'bŭrn)	144a	53°47'N	1°15'W
Shereshevo, Bela. (shě-rě-shě-vô)	155	52°31'N	24°08'E
Sheridan, Ar., U.S. (shěr'ĭ-dăn)	111	34°19'N	92°21'W
Sheridan, Or., U.S.	104	45°06'N	123°22'W
Sheridan, Wy., U.S.	96	44°48'N	106°56'W
Sherman, Tx., U.S. (shěr'măn)	96	33°39'N	96°37'W
Sherman Oaks, neigh., Ca., U.S.	232	34°09'N	118°26'W
Sherna, r., Russia (shěr'nȧ)	172b	56°08'N	38°45'E
Sherridon, Can.	89	55°10'N	101°10'W
's Hertogenbosch, Neth. (sěr-tō'ghěn-bôs)	151	51°41'N	5°19'E
Sherwood, Or., U.S.	106c	45°21'N	122°50'W
Sherwood Forest, for., Eng., U.K.	144a	53°11'N	1°07'W
Sherwood Park, Can.	87	53°31'N	113°19'W
Shetland Islands, is., Scot., U.K. (shět'lănd)	142	60°35'N	2°10'W
Sheva, India	240e	18°56'N	72°57'E
Shewa Gimira, Eth.	211	7°13'N	35°49'E
Shexian, China (shŭ shyěn)	190	36°34'N	113°42'E
Sheyang, r., China (she-yäŋ)	190	33°42'N	119°40'E
Sheyenne, r., N.D., U.S. (shī-ěn')	102	46°42'N	97°52'W
Shi, r., China (shr)	190	31°58'N	115°50'E
Shi, r., China	190	32°09'N	114°11'E
Shiawassee, r., Mi., U.S. (shī-ȧ-wôs'ē)	98	43°15'N	84°05'W
Shibām, Yemen (shē'bäm)	182	16°02'N	48°40'E
Shibīn al Kawn, Egypt (shė-bēn'ěl kōm')	218b	30°31'N	31°01'E
Shibīn al Qanāṭir, Egypt (kȧ-nä'tēr)	218b	30°18'N	31°21'E
Shibuya, neigh., Japan	242a	35°40'N	139°42'E
Shicun, China (shr-tsòn)	190	33°47'N	117°18'E
Shields, r., Mt., U.S. (shēldz)	105	45°54'N	110°40'W
Shifnal, Eng., U.K. (shĭf'năl)	144a	52°40'N	2°22'W
Shihlin, Tai.	241d	25°05'N	121°31'E
Shijian, China (shr-jyěn)	190	31°27'N	117°51'E
Shijiazhuang, China (shr-jyä-jůäŋ)	189	38°04'N	114°31'E
Shijiu Hu, l., China (shr-jyō ho͞o)	190	31°29'N	119°07'E
Shijōnawate, Japan	242b	34°45'N	135°39'E
Shikārpur, Pak.	183	27°51'N	68°52'E
Shiki, Japan (shė'kė)	195a	35°50'N	139°35'E
Shikoku, i., Japan (shē'kō'ko͞o)	189	33°43'N	133°33'E
Shilibao, China	240b	39°55'N	116°29'E
Shilka, r., Russia (shĭl'kȧ)	171	53°00'N	118°45'E
Shilla, mtn., India	186	32°18'N	78°17'E
Shillong, India (shěl-lông')	183	25°39'N	91°58'E
Shiloh, Il., U.S. (shī'lō)	107e	38°34'N	89°54'W
Shilong, China (shr-lôŋ)	193	23°05'N	113°58'E
Shilou, China	191a	22°58'N	113°29'E
Shimabara, Japan (shē'mä-bä'rä)	195	32°46'N	130°22'E
Shimada, Japan (shē'mä-dä)	195	34°49'N	138°13'E
Shimbiris, mtn., Som.	218a	10°40'N	47°23'E

PLACE (Pronunciation)	PAGE	LAT.	LONG.
Shimizu, Japan (shē'mė-zo͞o)	194	35°00'N	138°29'E
Shimminato, Japan (shěm'mė'nä-tô)	195	36°47'N	137°05'E
Shimoda, Japan (shē'mō-dȧ)	195	34°41'N	138°58'E
Shimoga, India	187	13°59'N	75°38'E
Shimohōya, Japan	242a	35°45'N	139°34'E
Shimoigusa, neigh., Japan	242a	35°43'N	139°37'E
Shimomizo, Japan	242a	35°31'N	139°23'E
Shimoni, Kenya	217	4°39'S	39°23'E
Shimonoseki, Japan	189	33°58'N	130°55'E
Shimo-Saga, Japan (shė'mô sä'gä)	195b	35°01'N	135°41'E
Shimo-shakujii, neigh., Japan	242a	35°45'N	139°37'E
Shimotsuruma, Japan	242a	35°29'N	139°28'E
Shimoyugi, Japan	242a	35°38'N	139°23'E
Shin, Loch, l., Scot., U.K. (lŏĸ shĭn)	150	58°08'N	4°02'W
Shinagawa-Wan, b., Japan (shė'nä-gä'wä wän)	195a	35°37'N	139°49'E
Shinano-Gawa, r., Japan (shė-nä'nō gä'wä)	195	36°43'N	138°22'E
Shīndand, Afg.	185	33°18'N	62°08'E
Shinji, l., Japan (shĭn'jė)	195	35°23'N	133°05'E
Shinjuku, neigh., Japan	242a	35°41'N	139°42'E
Shinkolobwe, D.R.C.	217	11°02'S	26°35'E
Shinyanga, Tan. (shĭn-yäŋ'gä)	212	3°40'S	33°26'E
Shiono Misaki, c., Japan (shė-ô'nō mė'sä-kė)	194	33°20'N	136°10'E
Shipai, China (shr-pī)	191a	23°07'N	113°23'E
Ship Channel Cay, i., Bah. (shĭp chă-něl kē)	122	24°50'N	76°50'W
Shipley, Eng., U.K. (shĭp'lė)	144a	53°50'N	1°47'W
Shippegan, Can. (shĭ'pė-găn)	92	47°45'N	64°42'W
Shippegan Island, i., Can.	92	47°50'N	64°38'W
Shippenburg, Pa., U.S. (shĭp'ěn bûrg)	99	40°00'N	77°30'W
Shipshaw, r., Can. (shĭp'shô)	91	48°50'N	71°03'W
Shiqma, r., Isr.	181a	31°31'N	34°40'E
Shirane-san, mtn., Japan (shē'rä'nȧ-sän')	195	35°44'N	138°14'E
Shirati, Tan. (shė-rä'tē)	212	1°15'S	34°02'E
Shīrāz, Iran (shē-räz')	182	29°32'N	52°27'E
Shire, r., Afr. (shē'rȧ)	212	15°00'S	35°00'E
Shiriya Saki, c., Japan (shė'rä sä'kė)	194	41°25'N	142°10'E
Shirley, Ma., U.S. (shûr'lė)	93a	42°33'N	71°39'W
Shishaldin Volcano, vol., Ak., U.S. (shī-shăl'dĭn)	95a	54°48'N	164°00'W
Shively, Ky., U.S. (shīv'lė)	101h	38°11'N	85°47'W
Shivpuri, India	183	25°31'N	77°46'E
Shivta, Horvot, hist., Isr.	181a	30°54'N	34°36'E
Shivwits Plateau, plat., Az., U.S.	109	36°13'N	113°42'W
Shiwan, China (shr-wän)	191a	23°01'N	113°04'E
Shiwan Dashan, mts., China (shr-wän dä-shän)	193	22°10'N	107°30'E
Shizuki, Japan (shĭ'zo͞o-kė)	195	34°29'N	134°51'E
Shizuoka, Japan (shē'zo͞o'ōkȧ)	194	34°58'N	138°24'E
Shklov, Bela. (shklôf)	162	54°11'N	30°23'E
Shkodër, Alb. (shkô'dûr) (sko͞o'tȧrē)	142	42°04'N	19°30'E
Shkotovo, Russia (shkô'tô-vô)	194	43°15'N	132°21'E
Shoal Creek, r., Il., U.S. (shōl)	111	38°37'N	89°25'W
Shoal Lake, l., Can.	89	49°32'N	95°00'W
Shoals, In., U.S. (shōlz)	98	38°40'N	86°45'W
Shōdai, Japan	242b	34°51'N	135°42'E
Shōdo, i., Japan (shō'dō)	195	34°27'N	134°27'E
Shogunle, Nig.	244d	6°35'N	3°21'E
Sholāpur, India (shō'lä-po͞or)	183	17°42'N	75°51'E
Shomolu, Nig.	244d	6°32'N	3°23'E
Shoreham, Eng., U.K.	235	51°20'N	0°11'E
Shorewood, Wi., U.S. (shōr'wo͝od)	101a	43°05'N	87°54'W
Shoshone, Id., U.S. (shō-shōn'tė)	105	42°56'N	114°24'W
Shoshone, r., Wy., U.S.	105	44°35'N	108°50'W
Shoshone Lake, l., Wy., U.S.	105	44°17'N	110°50'W
Shoshoni, Wy., U.S.	105	43°14'N	108°05'W
Shostka, Ukr. (shôst'kȧ)	163	51°51'N	33°31'E
Shouguang, China (shō-gůäŋ)	190	36°53'N	118°45'E
Shouxian, China (shō shyěn)	190	32°36'N	116°45'E
Shpola, Ukr. (shpô'lȧ)	167	49°01'N	31°36'E
Shreveport, La., U.S. (shrēv'pôrt)	97	32°30'N	93°46'W
Shrewsbury, Eng., U.K. (shro͞oz'bēr-ĭ)	150	52°43'N	2°44'W
Shrewsbury, Ma., U.S.	93a	42°18'N	71°43'W
Shroud Cay, i., Bah.	122	24°20'N	76°40'W
Shuangcheng, China (shůäŋ-chŭŋ)	192	45°18'N	126°18'E
Shuanghe, China (shůäŋ-hŭ)	190	31°33'N	116°48'E
Shuangliao, China	189	43°37'N	123°30'E
Shuangyang, China	192	43°28'N	125°45'E
Shubrā al-Khaymah, Egypt	244a	30°06'N	31°15'E
Shuhedun, China (sho͞o-hŭ-dòn)	190	31°33'N	117°01'E
Shuiye, China (shwā-yŭ)	190	36°08'N	114°07'E
Shule, r., China (sho͞o-lŭ)	188	40°53'N	94°55'E
Shullsburg, Wi., U.S. (shŭlz'bûrg)	103	42°35'N	90°16'W
Shumagin, is., Ak., U.S. (sho͞o'mȧ-gěn)	95	55°22'N	159°20'W
Shumen, Bul.	149	43°15'N	26°54'E
Shunde, China (shòn-dŭ)	191a	22°50'N	113°15'E
Shungnak, Ak., U.S. (shŭng'nȧk)	95	66°55'N	157°20'W
Shunut, Gora, mtn., Russia (gȧ-rä sho͞o'nòt)	172a	56°33'N	59°45'E
Shunyi, China (shòn-yē)	190	40°09'N	116°38'E
Shuqrah, Yemen	182	13°32'N	46°02'E
Shūrāb, r., Iran (sho͞o räb)	182	31°08'N	55°30'E
Shuri, Japan (sho͞o'rė)	194	26°10'N	127°48'E
Shurugwi, Zimb.	212	19°34'S	30°03'E
Shūshtar, Iran (sho͞osh'tŭr)	182	31°50'N	48°46'E
Shuswap Lake, l., Can. (sho͞os'wŏp)	87	50°57'N	119°15'W
Shuya, Russia (sho͞o'yȧ)	164	56°52'N	41°23'E
Shuyang, China (sho͞o yäng)	190	34°09'N	118°47'E
Shweba, Myanmar	183	22°23'N	96°13'E
Shyghys Qongyrat, Kaz.	169	47°25'N	75°10'E
Shymkent, Kaz.	169	42°17'N	69°42'E
Shyroke, Ukr.	163	47°40'N	33°18'E
Siak Kecil, r., Indon.	181b	1°01'N	101°45'E

PLACE (Pronunciation)	PAGE	LAT.	LONG.
Siaksriinderapura, Indon. (sė-äks'rĭ ĕn'drȧ-po͞o'rä)	181b	0°48'N	102°05'E
Siālkot, Pak. (sė-äl'kōt)	183	32°39'N	74°30'E
Siátista, Grc. (syä'tĭs-ta)	161	40°15'N	21°32'E
Siau, Pulau, i., Indon.	197	2°40'N	126°00'E
Šiauliai, Lith. (shė-ou'lė-ī)	166	55°57'N	23°19'E
Sibay, Russia (sē'bȧy)	172a	52°41'N	58°40'E
Šibenik, Cro. (shė-bā'něk)	149	43°44'N	15°55'E
Siberia, reg., Russia	180	57°00'N	97°00'E
Siberut, Pulau, i., Indon. (sē'bȧ-ro͞ot)	196	1°22'S	99°45'E
Sibiti, Congo (sė-bė-tē')	212	3°41'S	13°21'E
Sibiu, Rom. (sė-bĭ-o͞o')	149	45°47'N	24°09'E
Sibley, Ia., U.S. (sĭb'lė)	102	43°24'N	95°33'W
Sibolga, Indon. (sė-bō'gä)	196	1°45'N	98°45'E
Sibpur, India	240a	22°34'N	88°19'E
Sibsāgar, India (sėb-sŭ'gŭr)	183	26°47'N	94°45'E
Sibutu Island, i., Phil.	196	4°40'N	119°30'E
Sibuyan, i., Phil. (sė-bo͞o-yän')	197a	12°19'N	122°25'E
Sibuyan Sea, sea, Phil.	196	12°43'N	122°38'E
Sichuan, prov., China (sz-chůän)	188	31°20'N	103°00'E
Sicily, i., Italy (sĭs'ĭ-lė)	142	37°38'N	13°30'E
Sico, r., Hond. (sė-kô)	120	15°32'N	85°42'W
Sidamo, hist. reg., Eth. (sē-dä'mô)	211	5°08'N	37°45'E
Sidao, China	240b	39°51'N	116°26'E
Sidcup, neigh., Eng., U.K.	235	51°25'N	0°06'E
Siderno Marina, Italy (sė-děr'nô mä-rē'nä)	160	38°18'N	16°19'E
Sídheros, Ákra, c., Grc.	160a	35°19'N	26°20'E
Sidhirókastron, Grc.	161	41°13'N	23°27'E
Sidi Aïssa, Alg.	159	35°53'N	3°44'E
Sidi bel Abbès, Alg. (sē'dė-běl ȧ-běs')	210	35°15'N	0°43'W
Sidi Ifni, Mor. (ĕf'nė)	210	29°22'N	10°15'W
Sidley, Mount, mtn., Ant. (sĭd'lė)	219	77°25'S	129°00'W
Sidney, Can.	86	48°39'N	123°24'W
Sidney, Mt., U.S. (sĭd'nė)	105	47°43'N	104°07'W
Sidney, Ne., U.S.	102	41°10'N	103°00'W
Sidney, Oh., U.S.	98	40°20'N	84°10'W
Sidney Lanier, Lake, res., Ga., U.S. (lăn'yẽr)	97	34°27'N	83°56'W
Sido, Mali	214	11°40'N	7°36'W
Sidon *see* Saydā, Leb.	182	33°34'N	35°23'E
Sidr, Wādī, r., Egypt	181a	29°43'N	32°58'E
Sidra, Gulf of *see* Surt, Khalīj, b., Libya	211	31°30'N	18°28'E
Siedlce, Pol. (syĕd''l-tsě)	155	52°09'N	22°20'E
Siegburg, Ger. (zēg'bo͞orgh)	154	50°48'N	7°13'E
Siegen, Ger. (zē'ghěn)	154	50°52'N	8°01'E
Sieghartskirchen, Aus.	145e	48°16'N	16°00'E
Siemensstadt, neigh., Ger.	238a	52°32'N	13°17'E
Siemiatycze, Pol. (syěm'yä'tė-chě)	155	52°26'N	22°52'E
Siemionówka, Pol. (sěě-mēō'nôf-kä)	155	52°53'N	23°50'E
Siem Reap, Camb. (syěm'rā'äp)	196	13°32'N	103°54'E
Siena, Italy (sė-ěn'ä)	148	43°19'N	11°21'E
Sieradz, Pol. (syě'rädz)	155	51°35'N	18°45'E
Sierpc, Pol. (syěrpts)	155	52°51'N	19°42'E
Sierra Blanca, Tx., U.S. (sė-ě'rȧ blaŋ-kä)	112	31°10'N	105°20'W
Sierra Blanca Peak, mtn., N.M., U.S. (blăn'kȧ)	96	33°25'N	105°50'W
Sierra Leone, nation, Afr. (sė-ěr'rä lȧ-ō'nȧ)	210	8°48'N	12°30'W
Sierra Madre, Ca., U.S. (mă'drē)	107a	34°10'N	118°03'W
Sierra Mojada, Mex. (sė-ě'r-rä-mô-kä'dä)	112	27°22'N	103°42'W
Sífnos, i., Grc.	161	36°58'N	24°30'E
Sigean, Fr. (sē-zhôɴ')	156	43°02'N	2°56'E
Sigeurney, Ia., U.S. (sē-gûr-nĭ)	103	41°16'N	92°10'W
Sighetu Marmaţiei, Rom.	155	47°57'N	23°55'E
Sighişoara, Rom. (sē-gė-shwä'rȧ)	155	46°11'N	24°48'E
Siglufjördur, Ice.	146	66°06'N	18°45'W
Signakhi, Geor.	167	41°45'N	45°50'E
Signal Hill, Ca., U.S. (sĭg'năl hĭl)	107a	33°48'N	118°11'W
Sigsig, Ec. (sėg-sēg')	130	3°04'S	78°44'W
Sigtuna, Swe. (sēgh-to͞o'nȧ)	152	59°40'N	17°39'E
Siguanea, Ensenada de la, b., Cuba	122	21°45'N	83°15'W
Siguatepeque, Hond. (sē-gwȧ'tě-pě-kě)	120	14°33'N	87°51'W
Sigüenza, Spain (sē-gwě'n-zä)	148	41°03'N	2°38'W
Siguiri, Gui. (sė-gė-rē')	210	11°25'N	9°10'W
Sihong, China (sz-hôŋ)	190	33°25'N	118°13'E
Siirt, Tur. (sĭ-ĕrt')	167	38°00'N	42°00'E
Sikalongo, Zam.	217	16°46'S	27°07'E
Sikasso, Mali (sė-käs'sō)	210	11°19'N	5°40'W
Sikeston, Mo., U.S. (sīks'tŭn)	111	36°50'N	89°35'W
Sikhote Alin', Khrebet, mts., Russia (se-ĸô'ta a-lēn')	165	45°00'N	135°45'E
Síkinos, i., Grc. (sĭ'kĭ-nōs)	161	36°45'N	24°55'E
Sikkim, state, India	183	27°42'N	88°25'E
Siklós, Hung. (sĭ'klōsh)	155	45°51'N	18°18'E
Sil, r., Spain (sė'l)	158	42°20'N	7°13'W
Silāmpur, neigh., India	240d	28°40'N	77°16'E
Silang, Phil. (sė-läng')	197a	14°14'N	120°58'E
Silao, Mex. (sė-lä'ō)	118	20°56'N	101°25'W
Silchar, India (sĭl-chär')	183	24°52'N	92°50'E
Silent Valley, S. Afr. (sī'lěnt vă'lė)	218d	24°32'S	26°40'E
Siler City, N.C., U.S. (sī'lẽr)	115	35°45'N	79°29'W
Silesia, hist. reg., Pol. (sĭ-lē'shȧ)	154	50°58'N	16°53'E
Silifke, Tur.	149	36°20'N	34°00'E
Siling Co, l., China	188	32°05'N	89°10'E
Silistra, Bul. (sė-lės'trȧ)	149	44°01'N	27°13'E
Siljan, l., Swe. (sėl'yän)	146	60°48'N	14°28'E
Silkeborg, Den. (sĭl'kě-bôr')	152	56°10'N	9°33'E
Sillery, Can. (sěl'-re')	83b	46°46'N	71°15'W
Siloam Springs, Ar., U.S. (sī-lōm)	111	36°10'N	94°32'W
Siloana Plains, pl., Zam.	216	16°55'S	23°10'E
Silocayoápan, Mex. (sė-lô-kä-yô-ȧ'pän)	118	17°29'N	98°09'W

PRONOUNCING INDEX Silsbee–Snowden 349

PLACE (Pronunciation)	PAGE	LAT.	LONG.
Silsbee, Tx., U.S. (sĭlz′ bē)	113	30°19′N	94°09′W
Şilschede, Ger.	236	51°21′N	7°19′E
Šilutė, Lith.	153	55°21′N	21°29′E
Silva Jardim, Braz. (sē′l-vä-zhär-dēN)	129a	22°40′N	42°24′W
Silvana, Wa., U.S. (sĭ-văn′ ă)	106a	48°12′N	122°16′W
Silvânia, Braz. (sēl-vá′nyä)	131	16°43′S	48°33′W
Silvassa, India	186	20°10′N	73°00′E
Silver, l., Mo., U.S.	111	39°38′N	93°12′W
Silverado, Ca., U.S. (sĭl-vẽr-ä′dō)	107a	33°45′N	117°40′W
Silver Bank, bk.	123	20°40′N	69°40′W
Silver Bank Passage, strt., N.A.	123	20°40′N	70°20′W
Silver Bay, Mn., U.S.	103	47°24′N	91°07′W
Silver City, Pan.	121	9°20′N	79°54′W
Silver City, N.M., U.S. (sĭl′vẽr sĭ′tĭ)	109	32°45′N	108°20′W
Silver Creek, N.Y., U.S. (crēk)	99	42°35′N	79°10′W
Silver Creek, r., Az., U.S.	109	34°30′N	110°05′W
Silver Creek, r., In., U.S.	101h	38°20′N	85°45′W
Silver Creek, Muddy Fork, r., In., U.S.	101h	38°26′N	85°52′W
Silverdale, Wa., U.S. (sĭl′vẽr-dāl)	106a	49°39′N	122°42′W
Silver Hill, Md., U.S.	229d	38°51′N	76°57′W
Silver Lake, Ma., U.S.	227a	42°00′N	70°48′W
Silver Lake, Wi., U.S. (lăk)	101a	42°33′N	88°10′W
Silver Lake, l., Wi., U.S.	101a	42°35′N	88°08′W
Silver Spring, Md., U.S. (sprĭng)	100e	39°00′N	77°00′W
Silver Star Mountain, mtn., Wa., U.S.	106c	45°45′N	122°15′W
Silverthrone Mountain, mtn., Can. (sĭl′vẽr-thrōn)	86	51°31′N	126°06′W
Silverton, S. Afr.	218d	25°45′S	28°13′E
Silverton, Co., U.S. (sĭl′vẽr-tŭn)	109	37°50′N	107°40′W
Silverton, Oh., U.S.	101f	39°12′N	84°24′W
Silverton, Or., U.S.	104	45°02′N	122°46′W
Silves, Port. (sēl′vĕzh)	148	37°15′N	8°24′W
Silvies, r., Or., U.S. (sĭl′vēz)	104	43°44′N	119°15′W
Sim, Russia (sĭm)	172a	55°00′N	57°42′E
Sim, r., Russia	172a	54°50′N	56°50′E
Simao, China (sz-mou)	188	22°56′N	101°07′E
Simard, Lac, l., Can.	91	47°38′N	78°40′W
Simba, D.R.C.	216	0°36′N	22°55′E
Simcoe, Can. (sĭm′kō)	150	42°50′N	80°20′W
Simcoe, l., Can.	85	44°30′N	79°20′W
Simeulue, Pulau, i., Indon.	196	2°27′N	95°30′E
Simferopol′, Ukr.	164	44°58′N	34°04′E
Simi, i., Grc.	149	36°27′N	27°41′E
Similk Beach, Wa., U.S. (sē′mĭlk)	106a	48°27′N	122°35′W
Simla, India (sĭm′là)	183	31°09′N	77°15′E
Simla, neigh., India	240a	22°35′N	88°22′E
Şimleu Silvaniei, Rom.	149	47°14′N	22°46′E
Simms Point, c., Bah.	122	25°00′N	77°40′W
Simojovel, Mex. (sē-mō-hō-vĕl′)	119	17°12′N	92°43′W
Simonésia, Braz. (sē-mō-nĕ′syä)	129a	20°04′S	41°53′W
Simonette, r., Can. (sī-mŏn-ĕt′)	87	54°15′N	118°00′W
Simonstad, S. Afr.	212a	34°11′S	18°25′E
Simood Sound, Can.	86	50°45′N	126°25′W
Simplon Pass, p., Switz. (sĭm′plŏn) (săN-plôN′)	154	46°13′N	7°53′E
Simpson, i., Can.	103	48°43′N	87°44′W
Simpson Desert, des., Austl. (sĭmp-sŭn)	202	24°40′S	136°40′E
Simrishamn, Swe. (sēm′rēs-häm′n)	152	55°35′N	14°19′E
Sims Bayou, Tx., U.S. (sĭmz bī-yōō′)	113a	29°37′N	95°23′W
Simushir, i., Russia (se-mōō′shēr)	189	47°15′N	150°47′E
Sinaia, Rom. (sĭ-nä′yà)	161	45°20′N	25°30′E
Sinai Peninsula, pen., Egypt (sī′nī)	211	29°24′N	33°29′E
Sinaloa, state, Mex. (sē-nä-lō-ä)	116	25°15′N	107°45′W
Sinan, China (sz-nän)	188	27°50′N	108°30′E
Sinanju, N. Kor. (sĭ′năn-jŏ′)	194	39°39′N	125°41′E
Sincelejo, Col. (sēn-sâ-lā′hō)	130	9°12′N	75°30′W
Sinclair Inlet, Wa., U.S. (sĭn-klâr′)	106a	47°31′N	122°41′W
Sinclair Mills, Can.	87	54°02′N	121°41′W
Sindi, Est. (sēn′dē)	153	58°20′N	24°40′E
Sines, Port. (sē′năzh)	158	37°57′N	8°50′W
Singapore, Sing. (sĭn′gá-pōr′)	196	1°18′N	103°52′E
Singapore, nation, Asia	196	1°22′N	103°45′E
Singapore Strait, strt., Asia	181b	1°14′N	104°20′E
Singlewell or Ifield, Eng., U.K.	235	51°25′N	0°23′E
Singu, Myanmar (sĭn′gŭ)	188	22°37′N	96°04′E
Siniye Lipyagi, Russia (sēn′ĭ-ē lēp′yä-gē)	163	51°24′N	38°29′E
Sinj, Cro. (sēn′)	160	43°42′N	16°39′E
Sinjah, Sudan	211	13°09′N	33°52′E
Sinkāt, Sudan	184	18°50′N	36°50′E
Sinkiang see Xinjiang Uygur, , China	188	40°15′N	82°15′E
Sin′kovo, Russia (sĭn-kô′vô)	172b	56°23′N	37°19′E
Sinnamary, Fr. Gu.	131	5°15′N	52°52′W
Sinni, r., Italy (sēn′nē)	160	40°05′N	16°15′E
Sinnūris, Egypt	218b	29°25′N	30°52′E
Sino, Pedra de, mtn., Braz. (pĕ′drä-dō-sē′nō)	132b	22°27′S	43°02′W
Sinop, Tur.	182	42°00′N	35°05′E
Sint Eustatius, i., Neth. Ant.	121b	17°32′N	62°45′W
Sint Niklaas, Bel.	145a	51°10′N	4°07′E
Sinton, Tx., U.S. (sĭn′tŭn)	113	28°03′N	97°30′W
Sintra, Port. (sēn′trá)	158	38°48′N	9°23′W
Sint Truiden, Bel.	145a	50°49′N	5°14′E
Sinŭiju, N. Kor. (sĭ′nŏĭ-jōō)	189	40°04′N	124°33′E
Sinyavino, Russia (sĭn-yä′vĭ-nô)	172c	59°50′N	31°07′E
Sinyaya, r., Eur. (sēn′yá-yá)	162	56°40′N	28°20′E
Sion, Switz. (sē′ôN′)	154	46°15′N	7°17′E
Sioux City, Ia., U.S. (sōō sĭ′tĭ)	96	42°30′N	96°25′W
Sioux Falls, S.D., U.S. (fôlz)	96	43°33′N	96°43′W
Sioux Lookout, Can.	85	50°06′N	91°55′W
Siping, China (sz-pĭŋ)	189	43°05′N	124°24′E
Sipiwesk, Can.	84	55°27′N	97°24′W
Sipsey, r., Al., U.S. (sĭp′sē)	114	33°26′N	87°42′W
Sipura, Pulau, i., Indon.	196	2°15′S	99°33′E
Siqueros, Mex. (sē-kā′rōs)	118	23°19′N	106°14′W
Siquia, Río, r., Nic. (sē-kē′ä)	121	12°23′N	84°36′W
Siracusa, Italy (sē-rä-koo′sä)	149	37°02′N	15°19′E
Sirājganj, Bngl. (sĭ-räj′gŭnj)	183	24°23′N	89°43′E
Sirama, El Sal. (Sē-rä-mä)	120	13°23′N	87°55′W
Sir Douglas, Mount, mtn., Can. (sûr dŭg′lăs)	87	50°44′N	115°20′W
Sir Edward Pellew Group, is., Austl. (pĕl′ū)	202	15°15′S	137°15′E
Siret, Rom.	155	47°58′N	26°01′E
Siret, r., Eur.	149	47°00′N	27°00′E
Sirhān, Wadi, depr., Sau. Ar.	182	31°02′N	37°16′E
Síros, i., Grc.	149	37°23′N	24°55′E
Sirsa, India	186	29°39′N	75°02′E
Sir Sandford, Mount, mtn., Can. (sûr sănd′fẽrd)	87	51°40′N	117°52′W
Sirvintos, Lith. (shēr′vĭn-tôs)	153	55°02′N	24°59′E
Sir Wilfrid Laurier, Mount, mtn., Can. (sûr wĭl′frĭd lôr′yẽr)	87	52°47′N	119°45′W
Sisak, Cro. (sē′sák)	149	45°29′N	16°20′E
Sisal, Mex. (sē-säl′)	116	21°09′N	90°03′W
Sishui, China (sz-shwā)	190	35°40′N	117°17′E
Sisquoc, r., Ca., U.S. (sĭs′kwŏk)	108	34°47′N	120°13′W
Sisseton, S.D., U.S. (sĭs′tŭn)	102	45°39′N	97°04′W
Sistān, Daryacheh-ye, l., Asia	182	31°45′N	61°15′E
Sisteron, Fr. (sēst′rôN′)	157	44°10′N	5°55′E
Sisterville, W.V., U.S. (sĭs′tẽr-vĭl)	98	39°30′N	81°00′W
Sitía, Grc. (sē′tĭ-à)	160a	35°09′N	26°10′E
Sitka, Ak., U.S. (sĭt′kà)	94a	57°08′N	135°18′W
Sittingbourne, Eng., U.K. (sĭt-ĭng-bôrn)	144b	51°20′N	0°44′E
Sittwe, Myanmar	183	20°09′N	92°54′E
Sivas, Tur. (sē′väs)	182	39°50′N	36°50′E
Siverek, Tur. (sē′vĕ-rĕk)	182	37°50′N	39°20′E
Siverskaya, Russia (sē′vẽr-ská-yá)	153	59°17′N	30°03′E
Sivers′kyi Donets′, r., Eur.	163	48°48′N	38°42′E
Sīwah, Egypt	184	29°12′N	25°31′E
Siwah, oasis, Egypt (sē′wä)	211	29°33′N	25°11′E
Sixaola, r., C.R.	121	9°31′N	83°07′W
Sixian, China (sz shyĕn)	190	33°37′N	117°51′E
Sixth Cataract, wtfl., Sudan	211	16°26′N	32°44′E
Siyang, China (sz-yäŋ)	190	33°43′N	118°42′E
Sjaelland, i., Den. (shĕl′lán′)	152	55°34′N	11°35′E
Sjenica, Yugo. (syĕ′nē-tsà)	161	43°15′N	20°02′E
Skadovs′k, Ukr.	163	46°08′N	32°54′E
Skagen, Den. (skä′ghĕn)	152	57°43′N	10°32′E
Skagerrak, strt., Eur. (skä-ghĕ-räk′)	142	57°43′N	8°28′E
Skagit, r., Wa., U.S.	104	48°29′N	121°52′W
Skagit Bay, b., Wa., U.S. (skăg′ĭt)	106a	48°20′N	122°32′W
Skagway, Ak., U.S. (skăg-wā)	94a	59°30′N	135°28′W
Skälderviken, b., Swe.	152	56°20′N	12°25′E
Skalistyy, Golets, mtn., Russia	165	57°28′N	119°48′E
Skalistyy Khrebet, mts., Russia	168	43°15′N	43°00′E
Skamania, Wa., U.S. (skă-mā′nĭ-ă)	106c	45°37′N	112°03′W
Skamokawa, Wa., U.S.	106c	46°16′N	123°27′W
Skanderborg, Den. (skän-ẽr-bôr′)	152	56°04′N	9°55′E
Skaneateles, N.Y., U.S. (skăn-ē-ăt′lĕs)	99	42°55′N	76°25′W
Skaneateles, l., N.Y., U.S.	99	42°50′N	76°20′W
Skänninge, Swe. (shĕn′ĭng-ĕ)	152	58°24′N	15°02′E
Skanör-Falsterbo, Swe. (skän′ûr)	152	55°24′N	12°49′E
Skara, Swe. (skä′rà)	152	58°25′N	13°24′E
Skeena, r., Can. (skē′nà)	84	54°30′N	129°00′W
Skeena Mountains, mts., Can.	86	56°00′N	128°00′W
Skeerpoort, S. Afr.	213b	25°49′S	27°45′E
Skeerpoort, r., S. Afr.	213b	25°58′S	27°41′E
Skeldon, Guy. (skĕl′dŭn)	131	5°49′N	57°15′W
Skellefteå, Swe. (shĕl′ĕf-tĕ-a′)	146	64°47′N	20°48′E
Skellefteälven, r., Swe.	146	65°15′N	19°30′E
Skelmersdale, Eng., U.K.	237a	53°33′N	2°48′W
Skhodnya, Russia (skôd′nyà)	172b	55°57′N	37°21′E
Skhodnya, r., Russia	172b	55°55′N	37°16′E
Skíathos, i., Grc. (skē′á-thôs)	161	39°15′N	23°25′E
Skibbereen, Ire. (skĭb′ẽr-ēn)	150	51°32′N	9°25′W
Skidegate, b., Can. (skĭ′-dē-gāt′)	86	53°15′N	132°00′W
Skidmore, Tx., U.S. (skĭd′mōr)	113	28°16′N	97°40′W
Skien, Nor. (skē′ĕn)	146	59°13′N	9°35′E
Skierniewice, Pol. (skyĕr-nyĕ-vēt′sĕ)	155	51°58′N	20°13′E
Skihist Mountain, mtn., Can.	87	50°11′N	121°54′W
Skikda, Alg.	210	36°58′N	6°51′E
Skilpadfontein, S. Afr.	218d	25°02′S	28°50′E
Skíros, Grc.	161	38°53′N	24°32′E
Skiros, i., Grc.	149	38°50′N	24°43′E
Skive, Den. (skē′vĕ)	152	56°34′N	8°56′E
Skjálfandafljót, r., Ice. (skyäl′fánd-ō)	146	65°24′N	16°40′W
Skjerstad, Nor. (skyĕr-städ)	146	67°12′N	15°37′E
Škofja Loka, Slvn. (shkôf′yá lō′kà)	160	46°10′N	14°20′E
Skokie, Il., U.S. (skō′kē)	101a	42°02′N	87°45′W
Skokomish Indian Reservation, I.R., Wa., U.S. (Skō-kō′mĭsh)	106a	47°22′N	123°07′W
Skole, Ukr. (skô′lĕ)	155	49°03′N	23°32′E
Skópelos, i., Grc. (skô′pá-lôs)	161	39°04′N	23°31′E
Skopin, Russia (skô′pēn)	166	53°49′N	39°35′E
Skopje, Mac. (skôp′yĕ)	160	42°02′N	21°26′E
Skövde, Swe. (shûv′dĕ)	146	58°25′N	13°48′E
Skovorodino, Russia (skô′vô-rô′dĭ-nô)	165	53°53′N	123°56′E
Skowhegan, Me., U.S. (skou-hē′găn)	92	44°45′N	69°27′W
Skradin, Cro. (skrä′dēn)	161	43°49′N	17°58′E
Skreia, Nor. (skrā′à)	152	60°40′N	10°55′E
Skudeneshavn, Nor. (skōō′dĕ-nes-houn′)	152	59°10′N	5°19′E
Skuilte, S. Afr.	244b	26°07′S	28°19′E
Skull Valley Indian Reservation, I.R., Ut., U.S. (skŭl)	109	40°25′N	112°50′W
Skuna, r., Ms., U.S. (skŭ′nà)	114	33°57′N	89°36′W
Skunk, r., Ia., U.S. (skŭnk)	103	41°12′N	92°14′W
Skuodas, Lith. (skwô′dás)	153	56°16′N	21°32′E
Skurup, Swe. (skû′rŏp)	152	55°29′N	13°27′E
Skvyra, Ukr.	167	49°43′N	29°41′E
Skwierzyna, Pol. (skvē-ĕr′zhĭ-ná)	154	52°35′N	15°30′E
Skye, Island of, i., Scot., U.K. (skī)	146	57°25′N	6°17′W
Skykomish, r., Wa., U.S. (skī′kō-mĭsh)	106a	47°50′N	121°55′W
Skyring, Seno de, b., Chile (sĕ′nō-s-krē′ng)	132	52°35′S	72°30′W
Slade Green, neigh., Eng., U.K.	235	51°28′N	0°12′E
Slagese, Den.	152	55°25′N	11°19′E
Slamet, Gunung, mtn., Indon. (slä′mĕt)	196	7°15′S	109°15′E
Slănic, Rom. (slŭ′nĕk)	161	45°13′N	25°56′E
Slater, Mo., U.S. (slāt′ẽr)	111	39°13′N	93°03′W
Slatina, Rom. (slä′tē-nä)	161	44°26′N	24°21′E
Slaton, Tx., U.S. (slā′tŭn)	110	33°26′N	101°38′W
Slattocks, Eng., U.K.	237b	53°35′N	2°10′W
Slave, r., Can. (slāv)	84	59°40′N	111°21′W
Slavgorod, Russia (sláf′gō-rôt)	164	52°58′N	78°43′E
Slavonija, hist. reg., Yugo. (slä-vō′nē-yä)	161	45°29′N	17°31′E
Slavonska Požega, Cro. (slä-vôn′skä pô′zhĕ-gä)	161	45°18′N	17°42′E
Slavonski Brod, Cro. (skä-vôn′skē brôd)	149	45°10′N	18°01′E
Slavuta, Ukr. (slá-vōō′tá)	163	50°18′N	27°01′E
Slavyanskaya, Russia (slâv-yán′ská-yá)	163	45°14′N	38°09′E
Sławno, Pol. (swav′nō)	154	54°21′N	16°38′E
Slayton, Mn., U.S. (slā′tŭn)	102	44°00′N	95°44′W
Sleaford, Eng., U.K. (slē′fẽrd)	144a	53°00′N	0°25′W
Sleepy Eye, Mn., U.S. (slēp′ĭ ī)	103	44°17′N	94°44′W
Sleepy Hollow, Ca., U.S.	232	33°57′N	117°47′W
Slidell, La., U.S. (slī-dĕl′)	113	30°17′N	89°47′W
Sliedrecht, Neth.	145a	51°49′N	4°46′E
Sligo, Ire. (slī′gō)	146	54°17′N	8°19′W
Slite, Swe. (slē′tĕ)	152	57°41′N	18°47′E
Sliven, Bul. (slē′vĕn)	149	42°41′N	26°20′E
Sloan, N.Y., U.S.	230a	42°54′N	78°47′W
Sloatsburg, N.Y., U.S. (slōts′bûrg)	100a	41°09′N	74°11′W
Slobodka, Bela. (slô′bôd-ká)	153	54°34′N	26°12′E
Slonim, Bela. (swō′nēm)	155	53°05′N	25°19′E
Slough, Eng., U.K. (slou)	144b	51°29′N	0°36′W
Slovakia, nation, Eur.	155	48°50′N	20°00′E
Slovenia, nation, Eur.	160	45°58′N	14°43′E
Slovians′k, Ukr.	167	48°52′N	37°34′E
Sluch, r., Ukr.	167	50°56′N	26°48′E
Slunj, Cro. (slōn′)	160	45°08′N	15°46′E
Słupsk, Pol. (swópsk)	146	54°28′N	17°02′E
Slutsk, Bela. (slōtsk)	166	53°02′N	27°34′E
Slyne Head, c., Ire. (slīn)	146	53°25′N	10°05′W
Smackover, Ar., U.S. (smăk′ō-vẽr)	111	33°22′N	92°42′W
Smederevo, Yugo.	161	44°39′N	20°54′E
Smederevska Palanka, Yugo. (smĕ-dĕ-rĕv′skä pä-län′kä)	161	44°21′N	21°00′E
Smedjebacken, Swe. (smĭ′tyĕ-bä-kĕn)	152	60°09′N	15°19′E
Smethport, Pa., U.S. (smĕth′pōrt)	99	41°50′N	78°25′W
Smethwick, Eng., U.K.	150	52°31′N	2°04′W
Smila, Ukr.	167	49°14′N	31°52′E
Smile, Ukr.	163	50°55′N	33°36′E
Smiltene, Lat. (smĕl′tĕ-nĕ)	153	57°26′N	25°57′E
Smith, Can. (smĭth)	84	55°10′N	114°02′W
Smith, i., Wa., U.S.	106a	48°20′N	122°53′W
Smith, r., Mt., U.S.	105	47°00′N	111°20′W
Smith Center, Ks., U.S. (sĕn′tẽr)	110	39°45′N	98°46′W
Smithers, Can. (smĭth′ẽrs)	84	54°47′N	127°10′W
Smithfield, Austl.	243a	33°51′S	150°57′E
Smithfield, N.C., U.S. (smĭth′fēld)	115	35°30′N	78°21′W
Smithfield, Ut., U.S.	105	41°50′N	111°49′W
Smithland, Ky., U.S. (smĭth′lănd)	98	37°10′N	88°25′W
Smith Mountain Lake, res., Va., U.S.	115	37°00′N	79°45′W
Smith Point, Tx., U.S.	113a	29°32′N	94°45′W
Smiths Falls, Can. (smĭths)	85	44°55′N	76°05′W
Smithton, Austl. (smĭth′tŭn)	204	40°55′S	145°12′E
Smithton, Il., U.S.	107e	38°24′N	89°59′W
Smithville, Tx., U.S. (smĭth′vĭl)	113	30°00′N	97°08′W
Smitswinkelvlakte, pl., S. Afr.	212a	34°16′S	18°25′E
Smoke Creek Desert, des., Nv., U.S. (smōk crēk)	108	40°28′N	119°40′W
Smoky, r., Can. (smōk′ĭ)	87	55°30′N	117°30′W
Smoky Hill, r., U.S. (smōk′ĭ hĭl)	96	38°40′N	100°00′W
Smøla, i., Nor. (smûlà)	146	63°16′N	7°40′E
Smolensk, Russia (smô-lyĕnsk′)	164	54°46′N	32°03′E
Smolensk, prov., Russia	162	55°00′N	32°18′E
Smyadovo, Bul.	161	43°04′N	27°00′E
Smyrna see İzmir, Tur.	182	38°25′N	27°05′E
Smyrna, De., U.S. (smûr′nă)	99	39°20′N	75°35′W
Smyrna, Ga., U.S.	100c	33°53′N	84°31′W
Snag, Can. (snăg)	95	62°18′N	140°30′W
Snake, r., U.S.	96	45°30′N	117°00′W
Snake, r., Mn., U.S. (snāk)	103	45°58′N	93°20′W
Snake Range, mts., Nv., U.S.	109	39°20′N	114°15′W
Snake River Plain, pl., Id., U.S.	105	43°08′N	114°46′W
Snap Point, c., Bah.	122	23°45′N	77°30′W
Sneffels, Mount, mtn., Co., U.S. (snĕf′ĕlz)	109	38°00′N	107°50′W
Snelgrove, Can. (snĕl′grōv)	83d	43°44′N	79°50′W
Sniardwy, Jezioro, l., Pol. (snyärt′vĭ)	155	53°46′N	21°59′E
Snodland, Eng., U.K.	235	51°20′N	0°27′E
Snöhetta, mtn., Nor. (snû-hĕttä)	146	62°18′N	9°12′E
Snohomish, Wa., U.S. (snô-hō′mĭsh)	106a	47°55′N	122°05′W
Snohomish, r., Wa., U.S.	106a	47°53′N	122°04′W
Snoqualmie, Wa., U.S. (snō qwăl′mē)	106a	47°32′N	121°50′W
Snoqualmie, r., Wa., U.S.	104	47°32′N	121°53′W
Snov, r., Eur. (snôf)	163	51°38′N	31°38′E
Snowden, Pa., U.S.	230b	40°16′N	79°58′W

350 Snowdon-South Sandwich Trench

PLACE (Pronunciation)	PAGE	LAT.	LONG.
Snowdon, mtn., Wales, U.K.	150	53°05'N	4°04'W
Snow Hill, Md., U.S. (hĭl)	99	38°15'N	75°20'W
Snow Lake, Can.	89	54°50'N	100°10'W
Snowy Mountains, mts., Austl. (snō'ē)	203	36°17'S	148°30'E
Snyder, Ok., U.S. (snī'dẽr)	110	34°40'N	98°57'W
Snyder, Tx., U.S.	112	32°48'N	100°53'W
Soar, r., Eng., U.K. (sōr)	144a	52°44'N	1°09'W
Sobat, r., Sudan (sō'bät)	211	9°04'N	32°02'E
Sobinka, Russia (sô-bĭŋ'kȧ)	162	55°59'N	40°02'E
Sobo Zan, mtn., Japan (sô'bô zän)	194	32°47'N	131°27'E
Sobral, Braz. (sô-brä'l)	131	3°39'S	40°16'W
Sochaczew, Pol. (sô-ĸä'chĕf)	155	52°14'N	20°18'E
Sochi, Russia (sôch'ĭ)	164	43°35'N	39°50'E
Society Islands, is., Fr. Poly. (sô-sī'ĕ-tē)	225	15°00'S	157°30'W
Socoltenango, Mex. (sô-kôl-tĕ-näŋ'gō)	119	16°17'N	92°20'W
Socorro, Braz. (sô-kô'r-rō)	129a	22°35'S	46°32'W
Socorro, Col. (sô-kôr'rō)	130	6°23'N	73°19'W
Socorro, N.M., U.S.	109	34°05'N	106°55'W
Socúellamos, Spain (sô-kōō-āl'yä-môs)	158	39°18'N	2°48'W
Soda, l., Ca., U.S. (sō'dȧ)	108	35°12'N	116°25'W
Soda Peak, mtn., Wa., U.S.	106c	45°53'N	122°04'W
Soda Springs, Id., U.S. (sprĭngz)	105	42°39'N	111°37'W
Söderhamn, Swe. (sû-dĕr-häm''n)	146	61°20'N	17°00'E
Söderköping, Swe.	152	58°30'N	16°14'E
Södertälje, Swe. (sû-dĕr-tĕl'yĕ)	146	59°12'N	17°35'E
Sodingen, neigh., Ger.	236	51°32'N	7°15'E
Sodo, Eth.	211	7°03'N	37°46'E
Sodpur, India	240a	22°42'N	88°23'E
Soest, Ger. (zōst)	154	51°35'N	8°05'E
Soeurs, Île des, i., Can.	227b	45°28'N	73°33'W
Sofia (Sofiya), Bul. (sô'fē-yȧ) (sô'fē-ȧ)	142	42°43'N	23°20'E
Sofiïvka, Ukr.	163	48°03'N	33°53'E
Sofiya see Sofia, Bul.	142	42°43'N	23°20'E
Soga, Japan (sô'gä)	195a	35°35'N	140°08'E
Sogamoso, Col. (sô-gä-mô'sō)	130	5°42'N	72°51'W
Sognafjorden, fj., Nor.	142	61°09'N	5°30'E
Sogozha, r., Russia (sô'gô-zhȧ)	162	58°35'N	39°08'E
Sohano, Pap. N. Gui.	198e	5°27'S	154°40'E
Soissons, Fr. (swä-sôN')	156	49°23'N	3°17'E
Soisy-sous-Montmorency, Fr.	237c	48°59'N	2°18'E
Sōka, Japan (sō'kä)	195a	35°50'N	139°49'E
Sokal', Ukr. (sô'käl')	155	50°28'N	24°20'E
Söke, Tur. (sû'kĕ)	149	37°40'N	27°10'E
Sokólka, Pol. (sô-kōl'kȧ)	155	53°23'N	23°30'E
Sokol'niki, neigh., Russia	239b	55°48'N	37°41'E
Sokolo, Mali (sô-kô-lō')	210	14°51'N	6°09'W
Sokołów Podlaski, Pol. (sô-kô-wôf' pŭd-lä'skĭ)	155	52°24'N	22°15'E
Sokone, Sen.	214	13°53'N	16°22'W
Sokoto, Nig. (sō'kô-tō)	210	13°04'N	5°16'E
Sola de Vega, Mex.	119	16°31'N	96°58'W
Solander, Cape, c., Austl.	201b	34°03'S	151°16'E
Solano, Phil. (sō-lä'nō)	197a	16°31'N	121°11'E
Sölderholz, neigh., Ger.	236	51°29'N	7°35'E
Soledad, Col. (sō-lĕ-dä'd)	130	10°47'N	75°00'W
Soledad Díez Gutiérrez, Mex.	118	22°19'N	100°54'W
Soleduck, r., Wa., U.S. (sōl'dŭk)	104	47°59'N	124°28'W
Solentiname, Islas de, is., Nic. (ē's-läs-dĕ-sô-lĕn-tē-nä'mȧ)	120	11°15'N	85°16'W
Solheim, S. Afr.	244b	26°11'S	28°10'E
Solihull, Eng., U.K. (sō'lĭ-hŭl)	144a	52°25'N	1°46'W
Solikamsk, Russia (sô-lē-kȧmsk')	166	59°38'N	56°48'E
Sol'-Iletsk, Russia	164	51°10'N	55°05'E
Solimões, Rio, r., Braz. (rē'ō-sô-lē-mô'ĕs)	130	2°45'S	67°44'W
Solingen, Ger. (zō'lĭng-ĕn)	154	51°10'N	7°05'E
Sóller, Spain (sō'lyĕr)	159	39°45'N	2°40'E
Solncevo, Russia	239b	55°39'N	37°24'E
Sologne, reg., Fr. (sō-lōn'yĕ)	156	47°36'N	1°53'E
Solola, Guat. (sô-lō'lä)	120	14°45'N	91°12'W
Solomon, r., Ks., U.S.	110	39°24'N	98°19'W
Solomon, North Fork, r., Ks., U.S.	110	39°34'N	99°52'W
Solomon, South Fork, r., Ks., U.S.	110	39°19'N	99°52'W
Solomon Islands, nation, Oc. (sŏl'ō-mŭn)	3	7°00'S	160°00'E
Solon, China (swo-lōōn)	189	46°32'N	121°18'E
Solon, Oh., U.S. (sō'lŭn)	101d	41°23'N	81°26'W
Solothurn, Switz. (zô'lō-thōōrn)	154	47°13'N	7°30'E
Solovetskiye Ostrova, is., Russia	166	65°10'N	35°40'E
Šolta, i., Yugo. (shôl'tä)	160	43°20'N	16°15'E
Soltau, Ger. (sôl'tou)	154	53°00'N	9°50'E
Sol'tsy, Russia (sôl'tsē)	162	58°04'N	30°13'E
Solvay, N.Y., U.S. (sŏl'vā)	99	43°05'N	76°10'W
Sölvesborg, Swe. (sûl'vĕs-bôrg)	152	56°04'N	14°35'E
Sol'vychegodsk, Russia (sôl'vē-chĕ-gôtsk')	166	61°18'N	46°58'E
Solway Firth, b., U.K. (sŏl'wā fûrth')	146	54°42'N	3°55'W
Solwezi, Zam.	217	12°11'S	26°25'E
Somalia, nation, Afr. (sō-ma'lē-ă)	218a	3°28'N	44°47'E
Somanga, Tan.	217	8°24'S	39°17'E
Sombor, Yugo. (sôm'bôr)	149	45°45'N	19°10'E
Sombrerete, Mex. (sōm-brå-rā'tå)	118	23°38'N	103°37'W
Sombrero, Cayo, i., Ven. (kä-yô-sôm-brĕ'rô)	131b	10°52'N	68°12'W
Somerdale, N.J., U.S.	229b	39°51'N	75°01'W
Somerset, Ky., U.S. (sŭm'ẽr-sĕt)	114	37°05'N	84°35'W
Somerset, Md., U.S.	229d	38°58'N	77°05'W
Somerset, Ma., U.S.	100b	41°46'N	71°05'W
Somerset, Pa., U.S.	99	40°00'N	79°05'W
Somerset, Tx., U.S.	107d	29°13'N	98°39'W
Somerset East, S. Afr.	213c	32°44'S	25°36'E
Somersworth, N.H., U.S. (sŭm'ẽrz-wûrth)	92	43°16'N	70°53'W
Somerton, Az., U.S. (sŭm'ẽr-tŭn)	109	32°36'N	114°43'W
Somerton, neigh., Pa., U.S.	229b	40°06'N	75°01'W
Somerville, Ma., U.S. (sŭm'ẽr-vĭl)	93a	42°23'N	71°06'W
Somerville, N.J., U.S.	100a	40°34'N	74°37'W
Somerville, Tn., U.S.	114	35°14'N	89°21'W
Somerville, Tx., U.S.	113	30°21'N	96°31'W
Someș, r., Eur.	155	47°43'N	23°09'E
Somma Vesuviana, Italy (sôm'mä vä-zōō-vē-ä'nä)	159c	40°38'N	14°27'E
Somme, r., Fr. (sŏm)	156	50°02'N	2°04'E
Sommerberg, Ger.	236	51°27'N	7°32'E
Sommerfeld, Ger. (zō'mĕr-fĕld)	145b	52°48'N	13°02'E
Sommerville, Austl.	201a	38°14'S	145°10'E
Somoto, Nic. (sô-mō'tō)	120	13°28'N	86°37'W
Son, r., India (sōn)	183	24°40'N	82°35'E
Sonari, India	240e	18°52'N	72°59'E
Sŏnchŏn, N. Kor. (sŭn'shŭn)	194	39°49'N	124°56'E
Sondags, r., S. Afr.	213c	33°17'S	25°14'E
Sønderborg, Den. (sûn''ẽr-bôrgh)	146	54°55'N	9°47'E
Sondershausen, Ger. (zôn'dẽrz-hou'zĕn)	154	51°17'N	10°45'E
Song Ca, r., Viet	193	19°15'N	105°00'E
Songea, Tan. (sôn-gā'ä)	212	10°41'S	35°39'E
Songjiang, China	189	31°01'N	121°14'E
Sŏngjin, N. Kor. (sŭng'jĭn')	194	40°38'N	129°10'E
Songkhla, Thai. (sông'klä')	196	7°09'N	100°34'E
Songwe, D.R.C.	217	12°25'S	29°40'E
Sonneberg, Ger. (sôn'ĕ-bĕrgh)	154	50°20'N	11°14'E
Sonora, Ca., U.S. (sô-nō'rȧ)	108	37°58'N	120°22'W
Sonora, Tx., U.S.	112	30°33'N	100°38'W
Sonora, state, Mex.	116	29°45'N	111°15'W
Sonora, r., Mex.	116	28°45'N	111°35'W
Sonora Peak, mtn., Ca., U.S.	96	38°22'N	119°39'W
Sonseca, Spain (sôn-sā'kä)	158	39°41'N	3°56'W
Sonsón, Col. (sôn-sôn')	130	5°42'N	75°28'W
Sonsonate, El Sal. (sōn-sô-nä'tå)	120	13°46'N	89°43'W
Sonsorol Islands, is., Palau (sŏn-sô-rōl')	197	5°03'N	132°33'E
Sooke Basin, b., Can. (sŏŏk)	106a	48°21'N	123°47'W
Soo Locks, trans., Mi., U.S. (sōō lŏks)	107a	46°30'N	84°30'W
Sopetrán, Col. (sô-pĕ-trä'n)	130a	6°30'N	75°44'W
Sopot, Pol. (sô'pôt)	155	54°26'N	18°25'E
Sopron, Hung. (shŏp'rŏn)	149	47°41'N	16°36'E
Sora, Italy (sō'rä)	160	41°43'N	13°37'E
Sorbas, Spain (sôr'bäs)	158	37°05'N	2°07'W
Sorbonne, educ., Fr.	237c	48°51'N	2°21'E
Sordo, r., Mex. (sô'r-dō)	119	16°39'N	97°33'W
Sorel, Can. (sô-rĕl')	85	46°01'N	73°07'W
Sorell, Cape, c., Austl.	204	42°10'S	144°50'E
Soresina, Italy (sō-rå-zē'nä)	160	45°17'N	9°51'E
Soria, Spain (sō'rē-ä)	148	41°46'N	2°28'W
Soriano, dept., Ur. (sŏ-rēä'nō)	129c	33°25'S	58°00'W
Soroca, Mol.	167	48°09'N	28°17'E
Sorocaba, Braz. (sô-rô-kä'bȧ)	131	23°29'S	47°27'W
Sorong, Indon. (sō-rông')	197	1°00'S	131°20'E
Sorot', r., Russia (sō-rō'tzh)	162	57°08'N	29°23'E
Soroti, Ug. (sō-rō'tē)	211	1°43'N	33°37'E
Sørøya, i., Nor.	146	70°37'N	20°58'E
Sorraia, r., Port. (sôr-rī'ȧ)	158	38°55'N	8°42'W
Sorrento, Italy (sôr-rĕn'tō)	160	40°23'N	14°23'E
Sorsogon, Phil. (sôr-sôgōn')	197	12°51'N	124°02'E
Sortavala, Russia (sôr'tä-vä-lä)	164	61°43'N	30°40'E
Sosenki, Russia	239b	55°34'N	37°26'E
Sosna, r., Russia (sôs'nȧ)	163	50°33'N	38°15'E
Sosnogorsk, Russia	164	63°13'N	54°09'E
Sosnowiec, Pol. (sôs-nô'vyĕts)	155	50°17'N	19°10'E
Sosnytsia, Ukr.	163	51°30'N	32°29'E
Sosunova, Mys, c., Russia (mĭs sô'sô-nôf'ȧ)	194	46°28'N	138°06'E
Sos'va, r., Russia (sôs'vȧ)	166	63°10'N	63°30'E
Sos'va, r., Russia (sôs'vȧ)	172a	59°55'N	60°40'E
Sota, r., Benin	215	11°10'N	3°20'E
Sota la Marina, Mex. (sô-tä-lä-mä-rē'nä)	118	23°45'N	98°11'W
Soteapan, Mex. (sō-tå-ä'pän)	119	18°14'N	94°51'W
Soto la Marina, Río, r., Mex. (rē'ō-so'tō lä mä-rē'nä)	118	23°55'N	98°30'W
Sotuta, Mex. (sô-tōō'tä)	120a	20°35'N	89°00'W
Soublette, Ven. (sô-ōō-blĕ'tē)	131b	9°55'N	66°06'W
Souflion, Grc.	161	41°12'N	26°17'E
Soufrière, St. Luc. (sōō-frē-âr')	121b	13°50'N	61°03'W
Soufrière, mtn., St. Vin.	121b	13°19'N	61°12'W
Soufrière, vol., Guad. (sōō-frē-ăr')	121b	16°06'N	61°42'W
Sŏul see Seoul, S. Kor.	189	37°35'N	127°03'E
Sounding Creek, r., Can. (soun'dĭng)	88	51°35'N	111°00'W
Souq Ahras, Alg.	147	36°23'N	8°00'E
Sources, Mount aux, mtn., Afr. (môn'tō sôrs')	212	28°47'S	29°04'E
Soure, Port. (sōr-ĕ)	158	40°04'N	8°37'W
Souris, Can.	84	49°38'N	100°15'W
Souris, Can. (sōō'rē')	93	46°20'N	62°17'W
Souris, r., N.A.	84	48°30'N	101°30'W
Sourlake, Tx., U.S. (sour'lăk)	113	30°09'N	94°24'W
Sousse, Tun. (sōōs)	210	36°00'N	10°39'E
South, r., Ga., U.S.	100c	33°40'N	84°15'W
South, r., N.C., U.S.	115	34°49'N	78°33'W
South Africa, nation, Afr.	212	28°00'S	24°50'E
Southall, neigh., Eng., U.K.	235	51°31'N	0°23'W
South Amboy, N.J., U.S. (south'ăm'boi)	100a	40°28'N	74°17'W
South America, cont.	128	15°00'S	60°00'W
Southampton, Eng., U.K. (south-ămp'tŭn)	142	50°54'N	1°30'W
Southampton, N.Y., U.S.	99	40°53'N	72°24'W
Southampton Island, i., Can.	85	64°38'N	84°00'W
South Andaman Island, i., India (ăn-dȧ-măn')	196	11°57'N	93°24'E
South Australia, state, Austl. (ôs-trā'lĭ-ȧ)	202	29°45'S	132°00'E
South Bay, b., Bah.	123	20°55'N	73°35'W
South Bend, In., U.S. (bĕnd)	97	41°40'N	86°20'W
South Bend, Wa., U.S. (bĕnd)	104	46°39'N	123°48'W
South Bight, bt., Bah.	122	24°20'N	77°35'W
South Bimini, i., Bah. (bē'mē-nē)	122	25°40'N	79°20'W
Southborough, Ma., U.S. (south'bŭr-ō)	93a	42°18'N	71°33'W
South Boston, Va., U.S. (bôs'tŭn)	115	36°41'N	78°55'W
South Boston, neigh., Ma., U.S.	227a	42°20'N	71°03'W
Southbridge, Ma., U.S. (south'brĭj)	99	42°05'N	72°00'W
South Brooklyn, neigh., N.Y., U.S.	228	40°41'N	73°59'W
South Caicos, i., T./C. Is. (kī'kōs)	123	21°30'N	71°35'W
South Carolina, state, U.S. (kăr-ô-lī'nȧ)	97	34°15'N	81°10'W
South Cave, Eng., U.K. (cāv)	144a	53°45'N	0°35'W
South Charleston, W.V., U.S.	98	38°20'N	81°40'W
South Chicago, neigh., Il., U.S.	231a	41°44'N	87°33'W
South China Sea, sea, Asia (chī'nȧ)	196	15°23'N	114°12'E
South Creek, r., Austl.	201b	33°43'S	150°50'E
Southcrest, S. Afr.	244b	26°15'S	28°07'E
South Dakota, state, U.S. (dȧ-kō'tȧ)	96	44°20'N	101°55'W
South Darenth, Eng., U.K.	235	51°24'N	0°15'E
South Downs, Eng., U.K. (dounz)	150	50°55'N	1°13'W
South Dum-Dum, India	186a	22°36'N	88°25'E
South East Cape, c., Austl.	203	43°47'S	146°03'E
Southend-on-Sea, Eng., U.K. (south-ĕnd')	151	51°33'N	0°41'E
Southern Alps, mts., N.Z. (sŭ-thûrn ălps)	203a	43°35'S	170°00'E
Southern California, University of, pt. of i., Ca., U.S.	232	34°02'N	118°17'W
Southern Cross, Austl.	202	31°13'S	119°30'E
Southern Indian, l., Can. (sŭth'ẽrn ĭn'dĭ-ăn)	84	56°46'N	98°57'W
Southern Pines, N.C., U.S. (sŭth'ẽrn pīnz)	115	35°10'N	79°23'W
Southern Ute Indian Reservation, I.R., Co., U.S. (ūt)	109	37°05'N	108°23'W
South Euclid, Oh., U.S. (ū'klĭd)	101d	41°30'N	81°34'W
Southfield, Mi., U.S.	230c	42°29'N	83°17'W
Southfleet, Eng., U.K.	235	51°25'N	0°19'E
South Fox, i., Mi., U.S. (fŏks)	98	45°25'N	85°55'W
South Gate, Ca., U.S. (gāt)	107a	33°57'N	118°13'W
Southgate, neigh., Eng., U.K.	235	51°38'N	0°08'W
South Georgia, i., S. Geor. (jôr'jȧ)	128	54°00'S	37°00'W
South Germiston, S. Afr.	244b	26°15'S	28°10'E
South Green, Eng., U.K.	235	51°37'N	0°26'E
South Haven, Mi., U.S. (hāv''n)	98	42°25'N	86°15'W
South Head, c., Austl.	243a	33°50'S	151°17'E
South Hempstead, N.Y., U.S.	228	40°41'N	73°37'W
South Hill, Va., U.S.	115	36°44'N	78°08'W
South Hills, neigh., S. Afr.	244b	26°15'S	28°05'E
South Holston Lake, res., U.S.	115	36°35'N	82°00'W
South Indian Lake, Can.	89	56°50'N	99°00'W
Southington, Ct., U.S. (sŭdh'ĭng-tŭn)	99	41°35'N	72°55'W
South Island, i., N.Z.	203a	42°40'S	169°00'E
South Loup, r., Ne., U.S. (lōōp)	102	41°21'N	100°08'W
South Lynnfield, Ma., U.S.	227a	42°31'N	71°00'W
South Magnetic Pole, pt. of i.	219	65°18'S	139°30'E
South Media, Pa., U.S.	229b	39°54'N	75°23'W
South Melbourne, Austl.	243b	37°50'S	144°57'E
South Merrimack, N.H., U.S. (mĕr'ĭ-măk)	93a	42°47'N	71°36'W
South Milwaukee, Wi., U.S. (mĭl-wô'kē)	101a	42°55'N	87°52'W
South Mimms, Eng., U.K.	235	51°42'N	0°14'W
South Moose Lake, l., Can.	89	53°51'N	100°20'W
South Nation, r., Can.	91	45°00'N	75°25'W
South Negril Point, c., Jam. (nå-grĕl')	122	18°15'N	78°25'W
South Ockendon, Eng., U.K.	235	51°32'N	0°18'E
South Ogden, Ut., U.S. (ŏg'dĕn)	107b	41°12'N	111°58'W
South Orange, N.J., U.S.	228	40°45'N	74°15'W
South Orkney Islands, is., Ant.	128	57°00'S	45°00'W
South Ossetia, hist. reg., Geor.	168	42°20'N	44°00'E
South Oxhey, Eng., U.K.	235	51°38'N	0°23'W
South Paris, Me., U.S. (păr'ĭs)	92	44°13'N	70°32'W
South Park, Ky., U.S. (pärk)	101h	38°06'N	85°43'W
South Pasadena, Ca., U.S. (păs-ȧ-dē'nȧ)	107a	34°06'N	118°08'W
South Pease, r., Tx., U.S. (pēz)	110	33°54'N	100°45'W
South Pender, i., Can. (pĕn'dẽr)	106d	48°45'N	123°09'W
South Philadelphia, neigh., Pa., U.S.	229b	39°56'N	75°10'W
South Pittsburg, Tn., U.S. (pĭs'bûrg)	114	35°00'N	85°42'W
South Platte, r., U.S. (plăt)	96	40°40'N	102°40'W
South Point, c., Barb.	121b	13°00'N	59°43'W
South Point, c., Mi., U.S.	98	44°50'N	83°20'W
South Pole, pt. of i., Ant.	219	90°00'S	0.00
South Porcupine, Can.	90	48°28'N	81°13'W
Southport, Austl. (south'pōrt)	203	27°57'S	153°27'E
Southport, Eng., U.K. (south'pôrt)	150	53°38'N	3°00'W
Southport, In., U.S.	101g	39°40'N	86°07'W
Southport, N.C., U.S.	115	35°55'N	78°02'W
South Portland, Me., U.S. (pōrt-lănd)	92	43°37'N	70°15'W
South Prairie, Wa., U.S. (prâ'rĭ)	106a	47°08'N	122°06'W
South Range, Wi., U.S. (rānj)	107h	46°37'N	91°59'W
South River, N.J., U.S. (rĭv'ẽr)	100a	40°27'N	74°23'W
South Ronaldsay, i., Scot., U.K. (rŏn'ăld-s'ā)	150a	58°48'N	2°55'W
South Saint Paul, Mn., U.S.	107g	44°54'N	93°02'W
South Salt Lake, Ut., U.S. (sôlt lāk)	107b	40°44'N	111°53'W
South Sandwich Islands, is., S. Geor. (sănd'wĭch)	128	58°00'S	27°00'W
South Sandwich Trench, deep	128	55°00'S	27°00'W

ăt; finăl; rāte; senåte; ärm; ȧsk; sofȧ; fâre; ch-choose; dh-as th in other; bē; ėvent; bĕt; recĕnt; cratẽr; g-gō; gh-guttural g; bĭt; ĭ-short neutral; rīde; ĸ-guttural k as ch in German ich;

PRONOUNCING INDEX

South San Francisco-Sterling 351

PLACE (Pronunciation)	PAGE	LAT.	LONG.
South San Francisco, Ca., U.S. (săn frăn-sĭs'kō)	106b	37°39'N	122°24'W
South San Jose Hills, Ca., U.S.	232	34°01'N	117°55'W
South Saskatchewan, r., Can. (sās-kach'ĕ-wän)	84	50°30'N	110°30'W
South Shetland Islands, is., Ant.	128	62°00'S	70°00'W
South Shields, Eng., U.K. (shēldz)	146	55°00'N	1°22'W
South Shore, neigh., Il., U.S.	231a	41°46'N	87°35'W
South Side, neigh., Pa., U.S.	230b	40°26'N	79°58'W
South Sioux City, Ne., U.S. (soo sĭt'ē)	102	42°48'N	96°26'W
South Taranaki Bight, bt., N.Z. (tä-rä-nä'kē)	203a	39°35'S	173°50'E
South Thompson, r., Can. (tŏmp'sŭn)	87	50°41'N	120°21'W
Southton, Tx., U.S. (south'tŭn)	107d	29°18'N	98°26'W
South Uist, i., Scot., U.K. (û'ĭst)	150	57°15'N	7°24'W
South Umpqua, r., Or., U.S. (ŭmp'kwȧ)	104	43°00'N	122°54'W
South Walpole, Ma., U.S.	227a	42°06'N	71°16'W
South Waltham, Ma., U.S.	227a	42°22'N	71°15'W
Southwark, neigh., Eng., U.K.	235	51°30'N	0°06'W
South Weald, Eng., U.K.	235	51°37'N	0°16'E
Southwell, Eng., U.K. (south'wĕl)	144a	53°04'N	0°56'W
South West Africa see Namibia, nation, Afr.	212	19°30'S	16°13'E
South Westbury, N.Y., U.S.	228	40°45'N	73°35'W
Southwest Miramichi, r., Can. (mĭr ȧ-mē'shē)	92	46°35'N	66°17'W
Southwest Point, c., Bah.	122	25°50'N	77°10'W
Southwest Point, c., Bah.	123	23°55'N	74°30'W
South Weymouth, Ma., U.S.	227a	42°10'N	70°57'W
South Whittier, Ca., U.S.	232	33°56'N	118°03'W
South Yorkshire, co., Eng., U.K.	144a	53°29'N	1°35'W
Sovetsk, Russia (sô-vyĕtsk')	166	55°04'N	21°54'E
Sovetskaya Gavan', Russia (sŭ-vyĕt'skĭ-u gä'vŭn')	165	48°59'N	140°14'E
Sow, r., Eng., U.K. (sou)	144a	52°45'N	2°12'W
Soweto, neigh., S. Afr.	244b	26°14'S	27°54'E
Soya Kaikyō, strt., Asia	194	45°45'N	141°38'E
Sōya Misaki, c., Japan (sō'yȧ mē'sä-kē)	194	45°35'N	141°25'E
Soyo, Ang.	212	6°10'S	12°25'E
Sozh, r., Eur. (sôzh)	167	52°50'N	31°00'E
Sozopol, Bul. (sôz'ō-pōl')	161	42°18'N	27°50'E
Spa, Bel. (spä)	151	50°30'N	5°50'E
Spain, nation, Eur. (spān)	142	40°15'N	4°30'W
Spalding, Ne., U.S. (spôl'dĭng)	102	41°43'N	98°23'W
Spanaway, Wa., U.S. (spăn'ȧ-wā)	106a	47°06'N	122°26'W
Spandau, neigh., Ger.	238a	52°32'N	13°12'E
Spangler, Pa., U.S. (spăng'lẽr)	99	40°40'N	78°50'W
Spanish Fork, Ut., U.S. (spăn'ĭsh fôrk)	109	40°10'N	111°40'W
Spanish Town, Jam.	117	18°00'N	76°55'W
Sparks, Nv., U.S. (spärks)	108	39°34'N	119°45'W
Sparrows Point, Md., U.S. (spăr'ōz)	100e	39°13'N	76°29'W
Sparta see Spárti, Grc.	149	37°07'N	22°28'E
Sparta, Ga., U.S. (spär'tȧ)	115	33°16'N	82°59'W
Sparta, Il., U.S.	111	38°07'N	89°42'W
Sparta, Mi., U.S.	98	43°10'N	85°45'W
Sparta, Tn., U.S.	114	35°54'N	85°26'W
Sparta, Wi., U.S.	103	43°56'N	90°50'W
Sparta Mountains, mts., N.J., U.S.	100a	41°00'N	74°38'W
Spartanburg, S.C., U.S. (spär'tăn-bûrg)	97	34°57'N	82°13'W
Spartel, Cap, c., Mor. (spär-tĕl')	158	35°48'N	5°50'W
Spárti, Grc. (Sparta)	149	37°07'N	22°28'E
Spartivento, Cape, c., Italy	142	38°54'N	8°52'E
Spartivento, Cape, c., Italy (spär-tē-vĕn'tô)	160	37°55'N	16°09'E
Spas-Demensk, Russia (spȧs dyĕ-mĕnsk')	162	54°24'N	34°02'E
Spas-Klepiki, Russia (spȧs klĕp'ē-kē)	162	55°09'N	40°11'E
Spassik-Ryazanskiy, Russia (ryä-zän'skĭ)	162	54°24'N	40°21'E
Spassk-Dal'niy, Russia (spŭsk'däl'nyē)	165	44°30'N	133°00'E
Spátha, Ákra, c., Grc.	160a	35°42'N	23°45'E
Spaulding, Al., U.S. (spôl'dĭng)	100h	33°27'N	86°50'W
Spear, Cape, c., Can. (spēr)	93	47°32'N	52°32'W
Spearfish, S.D., U.S. (spēr'fĭsh)	102	44°28'N	103°52'W
Speed, In., U.S. (spēd)	101h	38°25'N	85°45'W
Speedway, In., U.S. (spēd'wā)	101g	39°47'N	86°14'W
Speichersee, l., Ger.	145d	48°12'N	11°47'E
Speke, neigh., Eng., U.K.	237a	53°21'N	2°51'W
Speldorf, neigh., Ger.	236	51°25'N	6°52'E
Spellen, Ger.	236	51°37'N	6°37'E
Spencer, In., U.S. (spĕn'sẽr)	98	39°15'N	86°45'W
Spencer, Ia., U.S.	102	43°09'N	95°08'W
Spencer, N.C., U.S.	115	35°43'N	80°25'W
Spencer, W.V., U.S.	98	38°55'N	81°20'W
Spencer Gulf, b., Austl. (spĕn'sẽr)	202	34°20'S	136°55'E
Sperenberg, Ger. (shpĕ'rĕn-bĕrgh)	145b	52°09'N	13°22'E
Sperkhiós, r., Grc.	161	38°54'N	22°02'E
Spey, l., Scot., U.K. (spā)	150	57°25'N	3°29'W
Speyer, Ger. (shpī'ẽr)	154	49°18'N	8°26'E
Sphinx, hist., Egypt (sfĭnks)	218b	29°57'N	31°08'E
Spijkenisse, Neth.	145a	51°51'N	4°18'E
Spinazzola, Italy (spē-nät'zō-lä)	160	40°58'N	16°05'E
Spirit Lake, Id., U.S. (spĭr'ĭt)	104	47°58'N	116°51'W
Spirit Lake, Ia., U.S. (lāk)	102	43°25'N	95°08'W
Spišská Nová Ves, Slvk. (spēsh'skä nō'vä vĕs)	147	48°56'N	20°35'E
Spitsbergen see Svalbard, dep., Nor.	164	77°00'N	20°00'E
Split, Cro. (splēt)	142	43°30'N	16°28'E
Split Lake, l., Can.	89	56°08'N	96°15'W
Spokane, Wa., U.S. (spōkăn')	96	47°39'N	117°25'W
Spokane, r., Wa., U.S.	104	47°47'N	118°00'W

PLACE (Pronunciation)	PAGE	LAT.	LONG.
Spokane Indian Reservation, I.R., Wa., U.S.	104	47°55'N	118°00'W
Spoleto, Italy (spō-lā'tō)	160	42°44'N	12°44'E
Spoon, r., Il., U.S. (spo͞on)	111	40°36'N	90°22'W
Spooner, Wi., U.S. (spo͞on'ẽr)	103	45°50'N	91°53'W
Sportswood, Austl.	243b	37°50'S	144°53'E
Spotswood, N.J., U.S. (spŏtz'wo͝od)	100a	40°23'N	74°22'W
Sprague, r., Or., U.S. (sprāg)	104	42°30'N	121°42'W
Spratly, i., Asia (sprăt'lē)	196	9°21'N	113°58'E
Spray, N.C., U.S. (sprā)	115	36°30'N	79°44'W
Spree, r., Ger. (shprā)	154	51°53'N	14°08'E
Spremberg, Ger. (shprĕm'bĕrgh)	154	51°35'N	14°23'E
Spring, r., Ar., U.S.	111	36°25'N	91°35'W
Springbok, S. Afr. (sprĭng'bŏk)	212	29°35'S	17°55'E
Spring Creek, r., Nv., U.S. (sprĭng)	108	40°18'N	117°45'W
Spring Creek, r., Tx., U.S.	112	31°08'N	100°50'W
Spring Creek, r., Tx., U.S.	113	30°03'N	95°43'W
Springdale, Can.	93	49°30'N	56°05'W
Springdale, Ar., U.S. (sprĭng'dāl)	111	36°10'N	94°07'W
Springdale, Pa., U.S.	101e	40°33'N	79°46'W
Springer, N.M., U.S. (sprĭng'ẽr)	110	36°21'N	104°37'W
Springerville, Az., U.S.	109	34°08'N	109°17'W
Springfield, Co., U.S. (sprĭng'fēld)	110	37°24'N	102°04'W
Springfield, Il., U.S.	97	39°46'N	89°37'W
Springfield, Ky., U.S.	98	37°35'N	85°10'W
Springfield, Ma., U.S.	97	42°05'N	72°35'W
Springfield, Mn., U.S.	103	44°14'N	94°59'W
Springfield, Mo., U.S.	97	37°13'N	93°17'W
Springfield, Oh., U.S.	97	39°55'N	83°50'W
Springfield, Or., U.S.	104	44°01'N	123°02'W
Springfield, Pa., U.S.	229b	39°55'N	75°24'W
Springfield, Tn., U.S.	114	36°30'N	86°53'W
Springfield, Vt., U.S.	99	43°20'N	72°35'W
Springfield, Va., U.S.	229d	38°45'N	77°13'W
Springfontein, S. Afr. (sprĭng'fŏn-tīn)	212	30°16'S	25°45'E
Springhill, Can. (sprĭng-hĭl')	85	45°39'N	64°03'W
Spring Mill, Pa., U.S.	229b	40°04'N	75°17'W
Spring Mountains, mts., Nv., U.S.	108	36°18'N	115°49'W
Springs, S. Afr. (sprĭngs)	218d	26°16'S	28°27'E
Springstein, Can. (sprĭng'stīn)	83f	49°49'N	97°29'W
Springton Reservoir, res., Pa., U.S. (sprĭng-tŭn)	100f	39°57'N	75°26'W
Springvale, Austl.	201a	37°57'S	145°09'E
Springvale South, Austl.	243b	37°58'S	145°09'E
Spring Valley, Ca., U.S.	108a	32°46'N	117°01'W
Springvalley, Il., U.S. (sprĭng-văl'ĭ)	98	41°20'N	89°15'W
Spring Valley, Mn., U.S.	103	43°41'N	92°26'W
Spring Valley, N.Y., U.S.	100a	41°07'N	74°03'W
Springville, Ut., U.S. (sprĭng-vĭl)	109	40°10'N	111°40'W
Springwood, Austl.	201b	33°42'S	150°34'E
Sprockhövel, Ger.	236	51°22'N	7°15'E
Spruce Grove, Can. (spro͞os grōv)	83g	53°32'N	113°55'W
Spur, Tx., U.S. (spûr)	110	33°29'N	100°51'W
Squam, l., N.H., U.S. (skwôm)	99	43°45'N	71°30'W
Squamish, Can. (skwŏ'mĭsh)	86	49°42'N	123°09'W
Squamish, r., Can.	86	50°10'N	123°30'W
Squillace, Golfo di, b., Italy (go͞o'l-fō-dē skwēl-lä'chā)	160	38°44'N	16°47'E
Squirrel Hill, neigh., Pa., U.S.	230b	40°26'N	79°55'W
Squirrel's Heath, neigh., Eng., U.K.	235	51°35'N	0°13'E
Srbija (Serbia), hist. reg., Yugo. (sr bē-yä) (sĕr'bē-ä)	161	44°05'N	20°35'E
Srbobran, Yugo. (s'r'bô-brän')	161	45°32'N	19°50'E
Sredne-Kolymsk, Russia (s'rĕd'nyĕ kô-lēmsk')	165	67°49'N	154°55'E
Sredne Rogatka, Russia (s'red'ná-ya) (rô gär'tkȧ)	172c	59°49'N	30°20'E
Sredniy Ik, r., Russia (srĕd'nĭ ĭk)	172a	55°46'N	58°50'E
Sredniy Ural, mts., Russia (ö'ràl)	172a	57°47'N	59°00'E
Śrem, Pol. (shrĕm)	155	52°06'N	17°01'E
Sremska Karlovci, Yugo. (srĕm'skē kär'lov-tsē)	161	45°10'N	19°57'E
Sremska Mitrovica, Yugo. (srĕm'skä mē'trô-vē-tsä')	161	44°59'N	19°39'E
Sretensk, Russia (s'rĕ'tĕnsk)	165	52°13'N	117°39'E
Sri Lanka, nation, Asia	183b	8°45'N	82°30'E
Srīnagar, India (srē-nŭg'ŭr)	183	34°11'N	74°49'E
Środa, Pol. (shrō'dȧ)	155	52°14'N	17°17'E
Staaken, neigh., Ger.	238a	52°32'N	13°08'E
Stabroek, Bel.	145a	51°20'N	4°21'E
Stade, Ger. (shtä'dē)	154	53°36'N	9°28'E
Städjan, mtn., Swe. (stĕd'yän)	152	61°53'N	12°50'E
Stadlau, neigh., Aus.	239e	48°14'N	16°28'E
Stafford, Eng., U.K. (stăf'fẽrd)	150	52°48'N	2°06'W
Stafford, Ks., U.S.	110	37°58'N	98°37'W
Staffordshire, co., Eng., U.K.	144a	52°45'N	2°00'W
Stahnsdorf, Ger. (shtäns'dôrf)	145b	52°22'N	13°10'E
Staines, Eng., U.K.	144b	51°26'N	0°13'W
Stains, Fr.	237c	48°57'N	2°23'E
Stakhanov, Ukr.	167	48°34'N	38°37'E
Stalingrad see Volgograd, Russia	164	48°40'N	42°20'E
Stalybridge, Eng., U.K.	144a	53°29'N	2°03'W
Stambaugh, Mi., U.S. (stăm'bô)	103	46°03'N	88°38'W
Stamford, Eng., U.K.	144a	52°39'N	0°28'W
Stamford, Ct., U.S. (stăm'fẽrd)	100a	41°03'N	73°32'W
Stamford, Tx., U.S.	110	32°57'N	99°48'W
Stammersdorf, Aus. (shtäm'ĕrs-dôrf)	145e	48°19'N	16°25'E
Stamps, Ar., U.S. (stămps)	111	33°22'N	93°31'W
Stanberry, Mo., U.S. (stan'bĕr-ē)	111	40°12'N	94°34'W
Standerton, S. Afr. (stăn'dẽr-tŭn)	212	26°57'S	29°17'E
Standing Rock Indian Reservation, I.R., N.D., U.S. (stănd'ĭng rŏk)	102	47°07'N	101°05'W
Standish, Eng., U.K. (stăn'dĭsh)	144a	53°36'N	2°39'W
Stanford, Ky., U.S. (stăn'fẽrd)	114	37°29'N	84°40'W
Stanford le Hope, Eng., U.K.	235	51°31'N	0°26'E
Stanford Rivers, Eng., U.K.	235	51°41'N	0°13'E
Stanger, S. Afr. (stăŋ-ger)	213c	29°22'S	31°18'E

PLACE (Pronunciation)	PAGE	LAT.	LONG.
Staniard Creek, Bah.	122	24°50'N	77°55'W
Stanislaus, r., Ca., U.S. (stăn'ĭs-lô)	108	38°10'N	120°16'W
Stanley, Can. (stăn'lē)	92	46°17'N	66°44'W
Stanley, Falk. Is.	132	51°46'S	57°59'W
Stanley, H.K.	241c	22°13'N	114°12'E
Stanley, N.D., U.S.	102	48°20'N	102°25'W
Stanley, Wi., U.S.	103	44°56'N	90°56'W
Stanley Mound, hill, H.K.	241c	22°14'N	114°12'E
Stanley Pool, l., Afr.	212	4°07'S	15°40'E
Stanley Reservoir, res., India (stăn'lē)	187	12°07'N	77°27'E
Stanleyville see Kisangani, D.R.C.	211	0°30'S	25°12'E
Stanlow, Eng., U.K.	237a	53°17'N	2°52'W
Stanmore, neigh., Eng., U.K.	235	51°37'N	0°19'W
Stann Creek, Belize (stăn krēk)	120a	17°01'N	88°14'W
Stanovoy Khrebet, mts., Russia (stŭn-ȧ-voi')	165	56°12'N	127°12'E
Stansted, Eng., U.K.	235	51°20'N	0°18'E
Stanton, Ca., U.S. (stăn'tŭn)	107a	33°48'N	118°00'W
Stanton, Ne., U.S.	102	41°57'N	97°15'W
Stanton, Tx., U.S.	112	32°08'N	101°46'W
Stanwell, Eng., U.K.	235	51°27'N	0°29'W
Stanwell Moor, Eng., U.K.	235	51°28'N	0°30'W
Stanwood, Wa., U.S. (stăn'wōd)	106a	48°14'N	122°23'W
Stapleford Abbots, Eng., U.K.	235	51°38'N	0°10'E
Stapleford Tawney, Eng., U.K.	235	51°40'N	0°11'E
Staples, Mn., U.S. (stā'p'lz)	103	46°21'N	94°48'W
Stapleton, Al., U.S.	114	30°45'N	87°48'W
Stara Planina, mts., Bul.	142	42°50'N	24°45'E
Staraya Kupavna, Russia (stä'rȧ-yȧ kû-päf'nȧ)	172b	55°48'N	38°10'E
Staraya Russa, Russia (stä'rȧ-yȧ ro͞osȧ)	166	57°58'N	31°21'E
Stara Zagora, Bul. (zä'gô-rȧ)	149	42°26'N	25°37'E
Starbuck, Can. (stär'bŭk)	83f	49°46'N	97°36'W
Stargard Szczeciński, Pol. (shtär'gärt shchĕ-chyn'skē)	146	53°19'N	15°03'E
Staritsa, Russia (stä'rē-tsȧ)	162	56°29'N	34°58'E
Starke, Fl., U.S. (stärk)	115	29°55'N	82°07'W
Starkville, Co., U.S. (stärk'vĭl)	110	37°06'N	104°34'W
Starkville, Ms., U.S.	114	33°27'N	88°47'W
Starnberg, Ger. (shtärn-bĕrgh)	145d	47°59'N	11°20'E
Starnberger See, l., Ger.	154	47°58'N	11°30'E
Starobil's'k, Ukr.	167	49°19'N	38°57'E
Starodub, Russia (stä-rô-dróp')	162	52°25'N	32°49'E
Starogard Gdański, Pol. (stä'rō-grad gdĕn'skē)	146	53°58'N	18°33'E
Starokostiantyniv, Ukr.	167	49°45'N	27°12'E
Staro-Minskaya, Russia (stä'rô mĭn'skȧ-yȧ)	167	46°19'N	38°51'E
Staro-Shcherbinovskaya, Russia	163	46°38'N	38°38'E
Staro-Subkhangulovo, Russia (stäro-so͞ob-kan-go͞o'lôvō)	172a	53°08'N	57°24'E
Staroutkinsk, Russia (stȧ-rô-o͞ot'kĭnsk)	172a	57°14'N	59°21'E
Starovirivka, Ukr.	163	49°31'N	35°48'E
Start Point, c., Eng., U.K. (stärt)	147	50°14'N	3°34'W
Staryi Ostropil', Ukr.	163	49°48'N	27°32'E
Stary Sącz, Pol. (stä-rē sônch')	155	49°32'N	20°36'E
Staryy Oskol, Russia (stä'rē ôs-kôl')	167	51°18'N	37°51'E
Stassfurt, Ger. (shtäs'fo͞ort)	154	51°52'N	11°35'E
Staszów, Pol. (stä'shôf)	155	50°32'N	21°13'E
State College, Pa., U.S. (stāt kŏl'ĕj)	99	40°50'N	77°55'W
State Line, Mn., U.S. (līn)	107h	46°36'N	92°18'W
Staten Island, i., N.Y., U.S. (stăt'ĕn)	100a	40°35'N	74°10'W
Statesboro, Ga., U.S. (stāts'bŭr-ō)	115	32°26'N	81°47'W
Statesville, N.C., U.S. (stās'vĭl)	115	34°45'N	80°54'W
Statue of Liberty National Monument, rec., N.Y., U.S.	228	40°41'N	74°03'W
Staunton, Il., U.S. (stôn'tŭn)	107e	39°01'N	89°47'W
Staunton, Va., U.S.	99	38°10'N	79°05'W
Stavanger, Nor. (stä'văng'ẽr)	142	58°59'N	5°44'E
Stave, r., Can. (stāv)	106d	49°12'N	122°24'W
Staveley, Eng., U.K. (stāv'lē)	144a	53°17'N	1°21'W
Stavenisse, Neth.	145a	51°35'N	3°59'E
Stavropol', Russia	164	45°05'N	41°50'E
Steamboat Springs, Co., U.S. (stēm'bōt')	110	40°30'N	106°48'W
Stebliv, Ukr.	163	49°23'N	31°03'E
Steel, r., Can. (stēl)	90	49°08'N	86°55'W
Steelton, Pa., U.S. (stēl'tŭn)	99	40°15'N	76°45'W
Steenbergen, Neth.	145a	51°35'N	4°18'E
Steens Mountain, mts., Or., U.S. (stēnz)	104	42°15'N	118°52'W
Steep Point, c., Austl. (stēp)	202	26°15'N	112°05'E
Stefanie, Lake see Chew Bahir, l., Afr.	211	4°46'N	37°31'E
Steglitz, neigh., Ger.	238a	52°28'N	13°19'E
Steiermark (Styria), prov., Aus. (shtī'ẽr-märk)	154	47°22'N	14°40'E
Steinbach, Can.	84	49°32'N	96°41'W
Steinkjer, Nor. (stēĭn-kyĕr)	146	64°00'N	11°19'E
Steinstücken, neigh., Ger.	238a	52°23'N	13°08'E
Stella, Wa., U.S. (stĕl'ȧ)	106c	46°11'N	123°12'W
Stellarton, Can. (stĕl'ȧr-tŭn)	85	45°34'N	62°40'W
Stendal, Ger. (shtĕn'däl)	154	52°37'N	11°51'E
Stepanakert see Xankändi, Azer.	166	39°50'N	46°40'E
Stephens, Port, b., Austl. (stē'fĕns)	204	32°43'N	152°55'E
Stephenville, Can. (stē'vĕn-vĭl)	85a	48°33'N	58°35'W
Stepn'ak, Kaz.	169	52°50'N	70°50'E
Stepney, neigh., Eng., U.K.	235	51°31'N	0°02'W
Sterkrade, Ger. (shtĕr'krädĕ)	157c	51°31'N	6°51'E
Sterkstroom, S. Afr.	213c	31°33'S	26°36'E
Sterling, Co., U.S. (stûr'lĭng)	96	40°38'N	103°14'W
Sterling, Il., U.S.	98	41°48'N	89°42'W
Sterling, Ks., U.S.	110	38°11'N	98°11'W
Sterling, Ma., U.S.	93a	42°26'N	71°41'W
Sterling, Tx., U.S.	112	31°53'N	100°58'W

PLACE (Pronunciation)	PAGE	LAT.	LONG.
Sterling Park, Ca., U.S.	231b	37°41'N	122°26'W
Sterlitamak, Russia (styĕr'lĭ-ta-mäk')	164	53°38'N	55°56'E
Šternberk, Czech Rep. (shtĕrn'bĕrk)	155	49°44'N	17°18'E
Stettin *see* Szczecin, Pol.	142	53°25'N	14°35'E
Stettler, Can.	84	52°19'N	112°43'W
Steubenville, Oh., U.S. (stū'bĕn-vĭl)	98	40°20'N	80°40'W
Stevens, l., Wa., U.S. (stē'vĕnz)	106a	47°59'N	122°06'W
Stevens Point, Wi., U.S.	103	44°30'N	89°35'W
Stevensville, Mt., U.S. (stē'vĕnz-vĭl)	105	46°31'N	114°03'E
Stewart, r., Can. (stū'ērt)	84	63°27'N	138°48'W
Stewart Island, i., N.Z.	203a	46°56'S	167°40'E
Stewart Manor, N.Y., U.S.	228	40°43'N	73°41'W
Stewiacke, Can. (stū'wē-ăk)	92	45°08'N	63°21'W
Steynsrus, S. Afr. (stīns'rōōs)	218d	27°58'S	27°33'E
Steyr, Aus. (shtīr)	147	48°03'N	14°24'E
Stickney, Il., U.S.	231a	41°49'N	87°47'W
Stiepel, neigh., Ger.	236	51°25'N	7°15'E
Stif, Alg.	210	36°18'N	5°21'E
Stikine, r., Can. (stĭ-kēn')	84	58°17'N	130°10'W
Stikine Ranges, Can.	84	59°05'N	130°00'W
Stillaguamish, r., Wa., U.S.	106a	48°11'N	122°18'W
Stillaguamish, South Fork, r., Wa., U.S. (stĭl-ȧ-gwä'mĭsh)	106a	48°05'N	121°59'W
Stillwater, Mn., U.S. (stĭl'wô-tēr)	107g	45°04'N	92°48'W
Stillwater, Mt., U.S.	105	45°23'N	109°45'W
Stillwater, Ok., U.S.	111	36°06'N	97°03'W
Stillwater, r., Mt., U.S.	105	48°47'N	114°40'W
Stillwater Range, mts., Nv., U.S.	108	39°43'N	118°11'W
Stintonville, S. Afr.	244b	26°14'S	28°13'E
Štip, Mac. (shtĭp)	161	41°43'N	22°07'E
Stirling, Scot., U.K. (stûr'lĭng)	150	56°05'N	3°59'W
Stittsville, Can. (stĭts'vĭl)	83c	45°15'N	75°54'W
Stizef, Alg. (mĕr-syā' lȧ-kônb)	159	35°18'N	0°11'W
Stjördalshalsen, Nor. (styûr-däls-hälsĕn)	152	63°26'N	11°00'E
Stockbridge Munsee Indian Reservation, I.R., Wi., U.S. (stŏk'brĭdj mŭn-sē)	103	44°49'N	89°00'W
Stockerau, Aus. (shtô'kĕ-rou)	154	48°24'N	16°13'E
Stockholm, Swe. (stŏk'hōlm)	142	59°23'N	18°00'E
Stockholm, Me., U.S. (stŏk'hōlm)	92	47°05'N	68°08'W
Stockport, Eng., U.K. (stŏk'pôrt)	150	53°24'N	2°09'W
Stockton, Eng., U.K.	150	54°35'N	1°25'W
Stockton, Ca., U.S. (stŏk'tŭn)	96	37°56'N	121°16'W
Stockton, Ks., U.S.	110	39°26'N	99°16'W
Stockton, i., Wi., U.S.	103	46°56'N	90°25'W
Stockton Plateau, plat., Tx., U.S.	96	30°34'N	102°35'W
Stockton Reservoir, res., Mo., U.S.	111	37°40'N	93°45'W
Stockum, neigh., Ger.	236	51°28'N	7°22'E
Stöde, Swe. (stû'dĕ)	152	62°26'N	16°35'E
Stoeng Trêng, Camb. (stŏng'trĕng')	196	13°36'N	106°00'E
Stoke d'Abernon, Eng., U.K.	235	51°19'N	0°23'W
Stoke Newington, neigh., Eng., U.K.	235	51°34'N	0°05'W
Stoke-on-Trent, Eng., U.K. (stōk-ŏn-trĕnt)	146	53°01'N	2°12'W
Stoke Poges, Eng., U.K.	235	51°33'N	0°35'W
Stokhid, r., Ukr.	155	51°24'N	25°20'E
Stolac, Bos. (stô'läts)	161	43°03'N	17°59'E
Stolbovoy, is., Russia (stôl-bô-voi')	171	74°05'N	136°00'E
Stolin, Bela. (stô'lēn)	155	51°54'N	26°52'E
Stolpe, Ger.	238a	52°40'N	13°16'E
Stömstad, Swe.	152	58°58'N	11°09'E
Stondon Massey, Eng., U.K.	235	51°41'N	0°18'E
Stone, Eng., U.K.	144a	52°54'N	2°09'W
Stone, Eng., U.K.	235	51°27'N	0°16'E
Stoneham, Can. (stōn'ȧm)	83b	46°59'N	71°22'W
Stoneham, Ma., U.S.	93a	42°30'N	71°05'W
Stonehaven, Scot., U.K. (stōn'hā-v'n)	150	56°57'N	2°09'W
Stone Mountain, Ga., U.S. (stōn)	100c	33°49'N	84°10'W
Stone Park, Il., U.S.	231a	41°45'N	87°53'W
Stonewall, Can. (stōn'wôl)	83f	50°09'N	97°21'W
Stonewall, Ms., U.S.	114	32°08'N	88°44'W
Stoney Creek, Can. (stō'nē)	83d	43°13'N	79°45'W
Stonington, Ct., U.S. (stōn'ĭng-tŭn)	99	41°20'N	71°55'W
Stony Indian Reserve, I.R., Can.	83e	51°10'N	114°45'W
Stony Mountain, Can.	83f	50°05'N	97°13'W
Stony Plain, Can. (stō'nē plān)	83g	53°32'N	114°00'W
Stony Plain Indian Reserve, I.R., Can.	83g	53°29'N	113°48'W
Stony Point, N.Y., U.S.	100a	41°13'N	73°58'W
Stony Run, Md., U.S.	229c	39°11'N	76°42'W
Stora Sotra, i., Nor.	152	60°24'N	4°35'E
Stord, i., Nor. (stōrd)	152	59°54'N	5°15'E
Store Baelt, strt., Den.	152	55°25'N	10°50'E
Storeton, Eng., U.K.	237a	53°21'N	3°03'W
Storfjorden, fj., Nor.	152	62°17'N	6°19'E
Stormberg, mts., S. Afr. (stôrm'bûrg)	213c	31°28'S	26°35'E
Storm Lake, Ia., U.S.	102	42°39'N	95°12'W
Stormy Point, c., V.I.U.S. (stôr'mē)	117c	18°22'N	65°01'W
Stornoway, Scot., U.K. (stôr'nō-wā)	146	58°13'N	6°21'W
Storozhynets', Ukr.	155	48°10'N	25°44'E
Störsjo, Swe. (stôr'shû)	152	62°49'N	13°08'E
Störsjoen, l., Nor. (stôr-syûĕn)	152	61°32'N	11°30'E
Störsjon, l., Swe.	146	63°06'N	14°00'E
Storvik, Swe.	152	60°37'N	16°31'E
Stoughton, Wi., U.S.	103	42°54'N	89°15'W
Stour, r., Eng., U.K. (stour)	151	52°09'N	0°29'E
Stourbridge, Eng., U.K. (stour'brĭj)	144a	52°27'N	2°08'W
Stow, Ma., U.S. (stō)	93a	42°56'N	71°31'W
Stow, Oh., U.S.	101d	41°09'N	81°26'W
Stowe Township, Pa., U.S.	230b	40°29'N	80°04'W
Straatsdrif, S. Afr.	218d	25°19'S	26°22'E
Strabane, N. Ire., U.K. (stră-băn')	150	54°59'N	7°27'W
Straelen, Ger. (shtră'lĕn)	157c	51°26'N	6°16'E
Strahan, Austl. (strā'ăn)	203	42°08'S	145°28'E
Strakonice, Czech Rep. (strä'kô-nyē-tsĕ)	154	49°18'N	13°52'E

PLACE (Pronunciation)	PAGE	LAT.	LONG.
Straldzha, Bul. (sträl'dzhȧ)	161	42°37'N	26°44'E
Stralsund, Ger. (shräl'sŏont)	146	54°18'N	13°04'E
Strangford Lough, l., N. Ire., U.K.	150	54°30'N	5°34'W
Strängnäs, Swe. (strĕng'nĕs)	152	59°23'N	16°59'E
Stranraer, Scot., U.K. (străn-rär')	150	54°55'N	5°05'W
Strasbourg, Fr. (strȧs-bōōr')	142	48°36'N	7°49'E
Stratford, Can. (străt'fērd)	90	43°20'N	81°05'W
Stratford, Ct., U.S.	99	41°10'N	73°05'W
Stratford, Wi., U.S.	103	44°16'N	90°02'W
Stratford-upon-Avon, Eng., U.K.	150	52°13'N	1°41'W
Strathfield, Austl.	243a	33°52'S	151°06'E
Strathmoor, neigh., Mi., U.S.	230c	42°23'N	83°11'W
Straubing, Ger. (strou'bĭng)	154	48°52'N	12°36'E
Strauch, Ger.	236	51°09'N	6°56'E
Strausberg, Ger. (strous'bĕrgh)	154	52°35'N	13°50'E
Strawberry, r., Ut., U.S.	109	40°05'N	110°55'W
Strawberry Point, Ca., U.S.	231b	37°54'N	122°31'W
Strawn, Tx., U.S. (strôn)	112	32°38'N	98°28'W
Streatham, neigh., Eng., U.K.	235	51°26'N	0°08'W
Streator, Il., U.S. (strē'tēr)	98	41°05'N	88°50'W
Streeter, N.D., U.S.	102	46°40'N	99°22'W
Streetsville, Can. (strētz'vĭl)	83d	43°34'N	79°43'W
Strehaia, Rom. (strĕ-кä'yȧ)	161	44°37'N	23°13'E
Strel'na, Russia (strĕl'nȧ)	172c	59°52'N	30°01'E
Stretford, Eng., U.K. (strĕt'fērd)	144a	53°25'N	2°19'W
Strickland, r., Pap. N. Gui. (strĭk'lănd)	197	6°15'S	142°00'E
Strijen, Neth.	145a	51°44'N	4°32'E
Stromboli, Italy (strôm'bô-lē)	149	38°46'N	15°16'E
Stromyn, Russia (strô'mĭn)	172b	56°02'N	38°29'E
Strong, r., Ms., U.S. (strông)	114	32°03'N	89°42'W
Strongsville, Oh., U.S. (strôngz'vĭl)	101d	41°19'N	81°50'W
Stronsay, i., Scot., U.K. (strŏn'sā)	150a	59°09'N	2°35'W
Stroudsburg, Pa., U.S. (stroudz'bûrg)	99	41°00'N	75°15'W
Strubenvale, S. Afr.	244b	26°16'S	28°28'E
Struer, Den.	152	56°29'N	8°34'E
Strugi Krasnyye, Russia (strōō'gĭ krä's-ny'yĕ)	162	58°14'N	29°10'E
Struisbelt, S. Afr.	244b	26°19'S	28°29'E
Struma, r., Eur. (strōō'mȧ)	161	41°55'N	23°05'E
Strumica, Mac. (strōō'mĭ-tsȧ)	161	41°26'N	22°38'E
Strümp, Ger.	236	51°17'N	6°40'E
Strunino, Russia	172b	56°23'N	38°34'E
Struthers, Oh., U.S. (strŭdh'ērz)	98	41°00'N	80°35'W
Struvenhütten, Ger. (shtrōō'vĕn-hü-tĕn)	145c	53°52'N	10°04'E
Strydpoortberge, mts., S. Afr.	218d	24°08'N	29°18'E
Stryi, Ukr.	155	49°16'N	23°51'E
Strzelce Opolskie, Pol. (stzhĕl'tsĕ ō-pōl'skyĕ)	155	50°31'N	18°20'E
Strzelin, Pol. (stzhĕ-lĭn)	155	50°48'N	17°06'E
Strzelno, Pol. (stzhål'nō)	155	52°37'N	18°10'E
Stuart, Fl., U.S. (stū'ērt)	115a	27°10'N	80°14'W
Stuart, Ia., U.S.	103	41°31'N	94°20'W
Stuart, i., Ak., U.S.	95	63°25'N	162°45'W
Stuart, i., Wa., U.S.	106d	48°42'N	123°10'W
Stuart Lake, l., Can.	86	54°32'N	124°35'W
Stuart Range, mts., Austl.	202	29°00'S	134°30'E
Sturgeon, r., Can.	83g	53°41'N	113°46'W
Sturgeon, r., Mi., U.S.	103	46°43'N	88°43'W
Sturgeon Bay, Wi., U.S.	103	44°50'N	87°22'W
Sturgeon Bay, b., Can.	89	52°00'N	98°00'W
Sturgeon Falls, Can.	85	46°19'N	79°49'W
Sturgis, Ky., U.S.	98	37°35'N	88°00'W
Sturgis, Mi., U.S.	98	41°45'N	85°25'W
Sturgis, S.D., U.S.	102	44°25'N	103°31'W
Sturt Creek, r., Austl.	202	19°40'S	127°40'E
Sturtevant, Wi., U.S. (stûr'tĕ-vănt)	101a	42°42'N	87°54'W
Stutterheim, S. Afr. (stûrt'ĕr-hĭm)	213c	32°34'S	27°27'E
Stuttgart, Ger. (shtōōt'gärt)	142	48°48'N	9°15'E
Stuttgart, Ar., U.S. (stŭt'gärt)	111	34°30'N	91°33'W
Styal, Eng., U.K.	237b	53°21'N	2°15'W
Stykkishólmur, Ice.	146	65°00'N	21°48'W
Styr', r., Eur. (stēr)	155	51°44'N	26°07'E
Styria *see* Steiermark, prov., Aus.	154	47°22'N	14°40'E
Styrum, neigh., Ger.	236	51°27'N	6°51'E
Suao, Tai. (sōōou)	193	24°35'N	121°45'E
Subarnarekha, r., India	186	22°38'N	86°26'E
Subata, Lat. (sō'bȧ-tȧ)	153	56°02'N	25°54'E
Subic, Phil. (sōō'bĭk)	197a	14°52'N	120°15'E
Subic Bay, b., Phil.	197a	14°41'N	120°11'E
Subotica, Yugo. (sōō'bô'tē-tsȧ)	142	46°06'N	19°41'E
Subugo, mtn., Kenya	217	1°40'S	35°49'E
Succasunna, N.J., U.S. (sŭk'kȧ-sŭn'nȧ)	100a	40°52'N	74°37'W
Suceava, Rom. (sōō-chȧ-ä'vȧ)	155	47°39'N	26°17'E
Suceava, r., Rom.	155	47°45'N	26°10'E
Sucha, Pol. (sōō'кȧ)	155	49°44'N	19°40'E
Suchiapa, Mex. (sōō-chē-ä'pä)	119	16°38'N	93°08'W
Suchiapa, r., Mex.	119	16°27'N	93°26'W
Suchitoto, El Sal. (sōō-chē-tō'tō)	120	13°58'N	89°03'W
Sucio, r., Col. (sōō'syō)	130a	6°55'N	76°15'W
Suck, r., Ire. (sŭk)	150	53°34'N	8°16'W
Sucre, Bol. (sōō'krā)	130	19°06'S	65°16'W
Sucre, dept., Ven. (sōō'krĕ)	131b	10°18'N	64°12'W
Sucy-en-Brie, Fr.	237c	48°46'N	2°32'E
Sud, Canal du, strt., Haiti	123	18°40'N	73°15'W
Sud, Rivière du, r., Can. (rē-vyâr'dü süd')	83b	46°56'N	70°35'W
Suda, Russia (sō'dȧ)	172a	56°58'N	56°45'E
Suda, r., Russia (sō'dȧ)	162	59°24'N	36°40'E
Sudair, Sau. Ar. (sü-dä'ēr)	182	25°48'N	46°28'E
Sudalsvatnet, l., Nor.	152	59°35'N	6°59'E
Sudan, nation, Afr.	211	14°00'N	28°00'E
Sudan, reg., Afr. (sōō-dän')	210	15°00'N	7°00'E
Sudberg, neigh., Ger.	236	51°11'N	7°08'E
Sudbury, Can. (sŭd'bēr-ē)	85	46°28'N	81°00'W

PLACE (Pronunciation)	PAGE	LAT.	LONG.
Sudbury, Ma., U.S.	93a	42°23'N	71°25'W
Suderwich, neigh., Ger.	236	51°37'N	7°15'E
Sudetes, mts., Eur.	142	50°41'N	15°37'E
Sudogda, Russia (sō'dôk-dȧ)	162	55°57'N	40°29'E
Sudost', r., Eur. (sō-dôst')	162	52°43'N	33°13'E
Sudzha, Russia (sŏd'zhȧ)	163	51°14'N	35°11'E
Sueca, Spain (swā'kä)	159	39°12'N	0°18'W
Suez, Egypt	211	29°58'N	32°34'E
Suez, Gulf of, b., Egypt (sōō-ĕz')	211	29°53'N	32°33'E
Suez Canal, can., Egypt	211	30°53'N	32°21'E
Suffern, N.Y., U.S. (sŭf'fērn)	100a	41°07'N	74°09'W
Suffolk, Va., U.S. (sŭf'ŭk)	100g	36°43'N	76°35'W
Sugandha, India	240a	22°54'N	88°20'E
Sugar City, Co., U.S.	110	38°12'N	103°42'W
Sugar Creek, Mo., U.S.	107f	39°07'N	94°27'W
Sugar Creek, r., Il., U.S. (shŏg'ēr)	111	40°14'N	89°28'W
Sugar Creek, r., In., U.S.	98	39°55'N	87°10'W
Sugar Island, i., Mi., U.S.	107k	46°31'N	84°12'W
Sugarloaf Point, c., Austl. (shŏg'ēr'lōf)	204	32°19'S	153°04'E
Suggi Lake, l., Can.	89	54°22'N	102°47'W
Suginami, neigh., Japan	242a	35°42'N	139°38'E
Sühbaatar, Mong.	188	50°18'N	106°31'E
Suhl, Ger. (zōōl)	154	50°37'N	10°41'E
Suichuan, mtn., China	193	26°25'N	114°10'E
Suide, China (swā-dü)	192	37°32'N	110°12'E
Suifenhe, China (swā-fŭn-hŭ)	189	44°47'N	131°13'E
Suihua, China	189	46°38'N	126°50'E
Suining, China (sōō'ē-nĭng')	190	33°54'N	117°57'E
Suipacha, Arg. (swē-pä'chä)	129c	34°45'S	59°43'W
Suiping, China (swā-pĭŋ)	190	33°09'N	113°58'E
Suir, r., Ire. (sūr)	150	52°20'N	7°32'W
Suisun Bay, b., Ca., U.S. (sōōē-sōōn')	106b	38°07'N	122°02'W
Suita, Japan (sō'ē-tä)	195b	34°45'N	135°32'E
Suitland, Md., U.S. (sōōt'lănd)	100e	38°51'N	76°57'W
Suixian, China (swā shyĕn)	193	31°42'N	113°20'E
Suiyüan, hist. reg., China (swā-yüĕn)	188	41°31'N	107°04'E
Suizhong, China (swā-jôŋ)	192	40°22'N	120°20'E
Sukabumi, Indon.	196	6°52'S	106°56'E
Sukadana, Indon.	196	1°15'S	110°30'E
Sukagawa, Japan (sōō'kä-gä'wä)	195	37°08'N	140°07'E
Sukhinichi, Russia (sōō'кē'nē-chē)	166	54°07'N	35°18'E
Sukhona, r., Russia (sō-кô'nȧ)	166	59°30'N	42°20'E
Sukhoy Log, Russia (sōō'kôy lôg)	172a	56°55'N	62°03'E
Sukhumi, Geor. (sō-kōm')	167	43°00'N	41°00'E
Sukkur, Pak. (sŭk'ŭr)	183	27°49'N	68°50'E
Sukkwan Island, i., Ak., U.S.	86	55°05'N	132°45'W
Suksun, Russia (sōk'sōn)	172a	57°08'N	57°22'E
Sukumo, Japan (sōō'kō-mō)	195	32°58'N	132°45'E
Sukunka, r., Can.	87	55°00'N	121°50'W
Sula, r., Ukr. (sōō-lä')	163	50°36'N	33°13'E
Sula, Kepulauan, is., Indon.	197	2°20'S	125°20'E
Sulaco, r., Hond. (sōō-lä'kō)	120	14°55'N	87°31'W
Sulaimān Range, mts., Pak. (sō-lä-ē-män')	183	29°47'N	69°10'E
Sulak, r., Russia (sōō-läk')	167	43°30'N	47°00'E
Sulfeld, Ger. (zōōl'fĕld)	145c	53°48'N	10°13'E
Sulina, Rom. (sōō-lē'nȧ)	149	45°08'N	29°38'E
Sulitelma, mtn., Eur. (sōō-lē-tyĕl'mȧ)	146	67°03'N	16°35'E
Sullana, Peru (sōō-lyä'nä)	130	4°57'S	80°47'W
Sulligent, Al., U.S. (sŭl'ĭ-jĕnt)	114	33°52'N	88°06'W
Sullivan, Il., U.S. (sŭl'ĭ-văn)	98	41°35'N	88°35'W
Sullivan, In., U.S.	98	39°05'N	87°20'W
Sullivan, Mo., U.S.	111	38°13'N	91°09'W
Sulmona, Italy (sōōl-mō'nä)	160	42°02'N	13°58'E
Sulphur, Ok., U.S. (sŭl'fŭr)	111	34°31'N	96°58'W
Sulphur, r., Tx., U.S.	111	33°26'N	95°06'W
Sulphur Springs, Tx., U.S. (sprĭngz)	111	33°09'N	95°36'W
Sultan, Wa., U.S. (sŭl'tăn)	106a	47°52'N	121°49'W
Sultan, r., Wa., U.S.	106a	47°55'N	121°49'W
Sultepec, Mex. (sōōl-tȧ-pĕk')	118	18°50'N	99°51'W
Sulu Archipelago, is., Phil. (sōō'lōō)	196	5°52'N	122°00'E
Suluntah, Libya	149	32°39'N	21°49'E
Sulūq, Libya	211	31°39'N	20°15'E
Sulu Sea, sea, Asia	196	8°25'N	119°00'E
Suma, Japan (sōō'mä)	195b	34°39'N	135°08'E
Sumas, Wa., U.S. (sū'mȧs)	106d	49°00'N	122°16'W
Sumatera, i., Indon. (sō-mä-trȧ)	196	2°06'N	99°40'E
Sumatra *see* Sumatera, i., Indon.	196	2°06'N	99°40'E
Sumba, i., Indon. (sŭm'bȧ)	196	9°52'S	119°00'E
Sumba, Île, i., D.R.C.	216	1°44'N	19°32'E
Sumbawa, i., Indon. (sōm-bä'wä)	196	9°00'S	118°18'E
Sumbawa-Besar, Indon.	196	8°32'S	117°20'E
Sumbawanga, Tan.	217	7°58'S	31°37'E
Sumbe, Ang.	212	11°13'S	13°50'E
Sümeg, Hung. (shü'mĕg)	155	46°59'N	17°19'E
Sumida, r., Japan (sōō'mē-dä)	195	36°01'N	139°24'E
Sumidouro, Braz. (sōō-mē-dō'rō)	129a	22°04'S	42°41'W
Sumiyoshi, Japan (sōō'mē-yō'shē)	195b	34°43'N	135°16'E
Sumiyoshi, neigh., Japan	242b	34°36'N	135°31'E
Summer Lake, l., Or., U.S. (sŭm'ēr)	104	42°50'N	120°35'W
Summerland, Can. (sŭ'mĕr-lănd)	87	49°39'N	119°40'W
Summerseat, Eng., U.K.	237b	53°38'N	2°19'W
Summerside, Can. (sŭm'ēr-sīd)	85	46°25'N	63°47'W
Summerton, S.C., U.S. (sŭm'ēr-tŭn)	115	33°37'N	80°22'W
Summerville, S.C., U.S. (sŭm'ēr-vĭl)	115	33°00'N	80°10'W
Summit, Il., U.S. (sŭm'mĭt)	101a	41°47'N	87°48'W
Summit, N.J., U.S.	100a	40°43'N	74°21'W
Summit Lake Indian Reservation, I.R., Nv., U.S.	104	41°35'N	119°30'W
Summit Park, Md., U.S.	229c	39°23'N	76°41'W
Summit Peak, mtn., Co., U.S.	109	37°20'N	106°40'W
Sumner, Wa., U.S. (sŭm'nēr)	106a	47°12'N	122°14'W
Šumperk, Czech Rep. (shōm'pĕrk)	155	49°57'N	17°02'E
Sumqayıt, Azer.	168	40°36'N	49°38'E
Sumrall, Ms., U.S. (sŭm'rôl)	114	31°25'N	89°34'W
Sumter, S.C., U.S. (sŭm'tēr)	115	33°55'N	80°21'W
Sumy, Ukr. (sōō'mĭ)	164	50°54'N	34°47'E

ăt; finȧl; rāte; senāte; ärm; ȧsk; sofȧ; fâre; ch-choose; dh-as th in other; bē; ēvent; bĕt; recĕnt; cratẽr; g-gō; gh-guttural g; bĭt; ĭ-short neutral; rīde; к-guttural k as ch in German ich;

PLACE (Pronunciation)	PAGE	LAT.	LONG.
Sumy, prov., Ukr.	163	51°02′N	34°05′E
Sun, r., Mt., U.S. (sŭn)	105	47°34′N	111°53′W
Sunburst, Mt., U.S.	105	48°53′N	111°55′W
Sunbury, Eng., U.K.	235	51°25′N	0°26′W
Sunda, Selat, strt., Indon.	196	5°45′S	106°15′E
Sundance, Wy., U.S. (sŭn′dăns)	105	44°24′N	104°27′W
Sundarbans, sw., Asia (sòn′dẽr-bŭns)	183	21°50′N	89°00′E
Sunday Strait, strt., Austl. (sŭn′dā)	202	15°50′S	122°45′E
Sundbyberg, Swe. (sòn′bü-bĕrgh)	152	59°24′N	17°56′E
Sunderland, Eng., U.K. (sŭn′dẽr-lănd)	146	54°55′N	1°25′W
Sunderland, Md., U.S.	100e	38°41′N	76°36′W
Sundridge, Eng., U.K.	235	51°17′N	0°08′E
Sundsvall, Swe. (sònds′väl)	142	62°24′N	19°19′E
Sungari (Songhua), r., China	189	46°09′N	127°53′E
Sungari Reservoir, res., China	192	42°55′N	127°50′E
Sungurlu, Tur. (sōōn′gòr-lò′)	149	40°08′N	34°20′E
Sun Kosi, r., Nepal	186	27°13′N	85°52′E
Sunland, Ca., U.S. (sŭn-lănd)	107a	34°16′N	118°18′W
Sunne, Swe. (sōōn′ĕ)	152	59°51′N	13°07′E
Sunninghill, Eng., U.K. (sŭnĭng′hĭl)	144b	51°23′N	0°40′W
Sunnymead, Ca., U.S. (sŭn′ĭ-mēd)	107a	33°56′N	117°15′W
Sunnyside, Ut., U.S.	109	39°35′N	110°20′W
Sunnyside, Wa., U.S.	104	46°19′N	120°00′W
Sunnyvale, Ca., U.S. (sŭn-nē-väl)	106b	37°23′N	122°02′W
Sunol, Ca., U.S. (sōō′nŭl)	106b	37°36′N	122°53′W
Sunset, Ut., U.S. (sŭn-sĕt)	107b	41°08′N	112°02′W
Sunset Beach, Ca., U.S.	232	33°43′N	118°04′W
Sunset Crater National Monument, rec., Az., U.S. (krā′tẽr)	109	35°20′N	111°30′W
Sunshine, Austl.	201a	37°47′S	144°50′E
Suntar, Russia (sòn-tär′)	165	62°14′N	117°49′E
Sunyani, Ghana	214	7°20′N	2°20′W
Suoyarvi, Russia (sōō′ò-yĕr′vē)	166	62°12′N	32°29′E
Superior, Az., U.S. (su-pē′rĭ-ẽr)	109	33°15′N	111°10′W
Superior, Ne., U.S.	110	40°04′N	98°05′W
Superior, Wi., U.S.	97	46°44′N	92°06′W
Superior, Wy., U.S.	105	41°45′N	108°57′W
Superior, Laguna, l., Mex. (lä-gōō′nä sōō-pā-rē-ōr′)	119	16°20′N	94°55′W
Superior, Lake, l., N.A.	97	47°38′N	89°20′W
Superior Village, Wi., U.S.	107h	46°38′N	92°07′W
Sup′ung Reservoir, res., Asia (sōō′pōōng)	194	40°35′N	126°00′E
Suqian, China (sōō-chyĕn)	190	33°57′N	118°17′E
Suquamish, Wa., U.S. (sōō-gwä′mĭsh)	106a	47°44′N	122°34′W
Suquṭrā (Socotra), i., Yemen (sò-kō′trà)	182	13°00′N	52°30′E
Ṣūr, Leb. (sōōr) (tīr)	181a	33°16′N	35°13′E
Ṣūr, Oman	182	22°23′N	59°28′E
Sura, neigh., India	240a	22°33′N	88°25′E
Surabaya, Indon.	196	7°23′S	112°45′E
Surakarta, Indon.	196	7°35′S	110°45′E
Šurany, Slvk. (shōō′rà-nû′)	155	48°05′N	18°11′E
Surat, Austl. (sū-rät)	204	27°18′S	149°00′E
Surat, India (sò′rŭt)	183	21°08′N	73°22′E
Surat Thani, Thai.	196	8°59′N	99°14′E
Surazh, Bela.	162	55°24′N	30°46′E
Surazh, Russia (sōō-ràzh′)	162	53°02′N	32°27′E
Surbiton, neigh., Eng., U.K.	235	51°24′N	0°18′W
Surco, Peru	233c	12°09′S	77°01′W
Suresnes, Fr.	237c	48°52′N	2°14′E
Surgères, Fr. (sür-zhâr′)	156	46°06′N	0°51′W
Surgut, Russia (sòr-gòt′)	164	61°18′N	73°38′E
Suriname, nation, S.A. (sōō-rē-näm′)	131	4°00′N	56°00′W
Sūrmaq, Iran	185	31°03′N	52°48′E
Surquillo, Peru	233c	12°07′S	77°02′W
Surt, Libya	211	31°14′N	16°37′E
Surt, Khalīj, b., Libya	211	31°30′N	18°28′E
Suruga-Wan, b., Japan (sōō′rōō-gä wän)	194	34°52′N	138°36′E
Suru-Lere, neigh., Nig.	244d	6°31′N	3°22′E
Susa, Japan	195	34°40′N	131°39′E
Sušak, i., Yugo.	160	42°45′N	16°30′E
Susak, Otok, i., Yugo.	160	44°31′N	14°15′E
Susaki, Japan (sōō′sä-kē)	195	33°23′N	133°16′E
Sušice, Czech Rep.	154	49°14′N	13°31′E
Susitna, Ak., U.S. (sōō-sĭt′nȧ)	95	61°28′N	150°28′W
Susitna, r., Ak., U.S.	95	62°00′N	150°28′W
Susong, China (sōō-sôŋ)	193	30°18′N	116°08′E
Susquehanna, Pa., U.S. (sŭs′kwē-hăn′ȧ)	99	41°55′N	73°55′W
Susquehanna, r., U.S.	99	39°50′N	76°20′W
Sussex, Can. (sŭs′ĕks)	85	45°43′N	65°31′W
Sussex, N.J., U.S.	100a	41°12′N	74°36′W
Sussex, Wi., U.S.	101a	43°08′N	88°12′W
Sutherland, Austl. (sŭdh′ẽr-lănd)	201b	34°02′S	151°04′E
Sutherland, S. Afr. (sŭ′thẽr-lănd)	212	32°25′S	20°40′E
Sutlej, r., Asia (sŭt′lĕj)	183	30°15′N	73°00′E
Sutton, Eng., U.K. (sut′′n)	144b	51°21′N	0°12′W
Sutton, Ma., U.S.	93a	42°09′N	71°46′W
Sutton-at-Hone, Eng., U.K.	235	51°25′N	0°14′E
Sutton Coldfield, Eng., U.K. (kōld′fēld)	144a	52°34′N	1°49′W
Sutton-in-Ashfield, Eng., U.K. (ĭn-ăsh′fēld)	144a	53°07′N	1°15′W
Suurbekom, S. Afr.	244b	26°19′S	27°44′E
Suurberge, mts., S. Afr.	213c	33°15′S	25°32′E
Suva, Fiji	198g	18°08′S	178°25′E
Suwa, Japan (sōō′wä)	195	36°03′N	138°08′E
Suwałki, Pol. (sò-vou′kē)	155	54°05′N	22°58′E
Suwanee Lake, l., Can.	89	56°08′N	100°10′W
Suwannee, r., U.S. (sò-wô′nē)	97	29°42′N	83°00′W
Suways al Ḥulwah, Tur′ at as, can., Egypt	218c	30°15′N	32°20′E
Suxian, China (sōō shyĕn)	192	33°29′N	117°51′E
Suzdal′, Russia (sōōz′dàl)	162	56°26′N	40°29′E
Suzhou, China (sōō-jō)	189	31°19′N	120°37′E
Suzuki-shinden, Japan	242a	35°43′N	139°31′E
Suzu Misaki, c., Japan (sōō′zōō mē′sä-kē)	194	37°30′N	137°35′E
Svalbard (Spitsbergen), dep., Nor. (sväl′bärt) (spĭts′bûr-gĕn)	164	77°00′N	20°00′E
Svaneke, Den. (svä′nĕ-kĕ)	152	55°08′N	15°07′E
Svatove, Ukr.	167	49°23′N	38°10′E
Svedala, Swe. (svĕ′dä-lä)	152	55°29′N	13°11′E
Sveg, Swe.	152	62°03′N	14°22′E
Svelvik, Nor. (svĕl′vĕk)	152	59°37′N	10°18′E
Svenčionys, Lith.	153	55°09′N	26°09′E
Svendborg, Den. (svĕn-bôrgh)	152	55°05′N	10°35′E
Svensen, Or., U.S. (svĕn′sĕn)	106c	46°10′N	123°39′W
Sverdlovsk see Yekaterinburg, Russia	164	56°51′N	60°36′E
Svetlaya, Russia (svyĕt′lá-yà)	194	46°09′N	137°53′E
Svicha, r., Ukr.	155	49°09′N	24°10′E
Svilajnac, Yugo. (svē′lá-ē-náts)	161	44°12′N	21°14′E
Svilengrad, Bul. (svĕl′ĕn-grát)	161	41°44′N	26°11′E
Svir′, r., Russia	166	60°55′N	33°40′E
Svir Kanal, can., Russia (ká-näl′)	153	60°10′N	32°40′E
Svishtov, Bul. (svēsh′tôf)	149	43°36′N	25°21′E
Svisloch′, r., Bela. (svēs′lôκ)	162	53°38′N	28°10′E
Svitavy, Czech Rep.	154	49°46′N	16°28′E
Svobodnyy, Russia (svò-bôd′nĭ)	165	51°28′N	128°28′E
Svolvaer, Nor. (svôl′vĕr)	146	68°15′N	14°29′E
Svyatoy Nos, Mys, c., Russia (svyŭ′toi nôs)	165	72°18′N	139°28′E
Swadlincote, Eng., U.K. (swŏd′lĭn-kôt)	144a	52°46′N	1°33′W
Swain Reefs, rf., Austl. (swān)	203	22°12′S	152°08′E
Swainsboro, Ga., U.S. (swānz′bŭr-ō)	115	32°37′N	82°21′W
Swakopmund, Nmb. (svä′kôp-mònt) (swá′kôp-mònd)	212	22°40′S	14°30′E
Swallowfield, Eng., U.K. (swŏl′ō-fēld)	144b	51°21′N	0°58′W
Swampscott, Ma., U.S. (swômp′skŏt)	93a	42°28′N	70°55′W
Swan, r., Austl.	202	31°30′S	116°30′E
Swan, r., Can.	89	51°58′N	101°45′W
Swan, r., Mt., U.S.	105	47°50′N	113°40′W
Swan Acres, Pa., U.S.	230b	40°33′N	80°02′W
Swan Hill, Austl.	203	35°20′S	143°30′E
Swan Hills, Can. (hĭlz)	84	54°52′N	115°45′W
Swan Island, i., Austl. (swŏn)	201a	38°15′S	144°41′E
Swan Lake, l., Can.	89	52°30′N	100°45′W
Swanland, reg., Austl. (swŏn′lănd)	202	31°45′S	119°15′E
Swanley, Eng., U.K.	235	51°24′N	0°12′E
Swan Range, mts., Mt., U.S.	105	47°50′N	113°40′W
Swan River, Can. (swŏn rĭv′ẽr)	84	52°06′N	101°16′W
Swanscombe, Eng., U.K.	235	51°26′N	0°18′E
Swansea, Wales, U.K.	147	51°37′N	3°59′W
Swansea, Il., U.S. (swŏn′sē)	107e	38°32′N	89°59′W
Swansea, Ma., U.S.	100b	41°45′N	71°09′W
Swansea, neigh., Can.	227c	43°38′N	79°28′W
Swanson Reservoir, res., Ne., U.S. (swŏn′sŭn)	110	40°13′N	101°30′W
Swartberg, mtn., Afr.	213c	30°08′S	29°34′E
Swarthmore, Pa., U.S.	229b	39°54′N	75°21′W
Swartkop, mtn., S. Afr.	212a	34°13′S	18°27′E
Swartruggens, S. Afr.	218d	25°40′S	26°40′E
Swartspruit, S. Afr.	213b	25°44′S	28°01′E
Swatow see Shantou, China	189	23°20′N	116°40′E
Swaziland, nation, Afr. (Swä′zē-lănd)	212	26°45′S	31°30′E
Sweden, nation, Eur. (swē′dĕn)	142	60°10′N	14°10′E
Swedesboro, N.J., U.S. (swēdz′bē-rō)	100f	39°45′N	75°22′W
Sweetwater, Tn., U.S. (swēt′wô-tẽr)	114	35°36′N	84°29′W
Sweetwater, Tx., U.S.	96	32°28′N	100°25′W
Sweetwater, l., N.D., U.S.	102	48°15′N	98°35′W
Sweetwater, r., Wy., U.S.	105	42°19′N	108°35′W
Sweetwater Reservoir, res., Ca., U.S.	108a	32°42′N	116°54′W
Świdnica, Pol. (shvĭd-nē′tsä)	154	50°50′N	16°30′E
Świdwin, Pol. (shvĭd′vĭn)	154	53°46′N	15°48′E
Świebodzice, Pol.	154	50°51′N	16°17′E
Świebodzin, Pol. (shvyĕn-bo′jĕts)	154	52°16′N	15°36′E
Świecie, Pol. (shvyän′tsyĕ)	155	53°23′N	18°26′E
Świętokrzyskie, Góry, mts., Pol. (shvyĕɴ-tō-kzhĭ′skyĕ gōō′rĭ)	155	50°57′N	21°02′E
Swift, r., Eng., U.K.	144a	52°26′N	1°08′W
Swift, r., Me., U.S. (swĭft)	93	44°42′N	70°40′E
Swift Creek Reservoir, res., Wa., U.S.	104	46°03′N	122°10′W
Swift Current, Can. (swĭft kûr′ĕnt)	84	50°17′N	107°50′W
Swindle Island, i., Can.	86	52°32′N	128°35′W
Swindon, Eng., U.K. (swĭn′dŭn)	150	51°35′N	1°55′W
Swinomish Indian Reservation, I.R., Wa., U.S. (swĭ-nō′mĭsh)	106a	48°25′N	122°27′W
Świnoujście, Pol. (shvĭ-nĭ-ō-wēsh′chyĕ)	154	53°56′N	14°14′E
Swinton, Eng., U.K. (swĭn′tŭn)	144a	53°30′N	1°19′W
Swinton, Eng., U.K.	237b	53°31′N	2°20′W
Swissvale, Pa., U.S. (swĭs′văl)	101e	40°25′N	79°53′W
Switzerland, nation, Eur. (swĭt′zẽr-lănd)	142	46°30′N	7°43′E
Syas′, r., Russia (syäs)	162	59°28′N	33°24′E
Sycamore, Il., U.S. (sĭk′ȧ-mōr)	103	42°00′N	88°42′W
Sycan, r., Or., U.S.	104	42°45′N	121°00′W
Sychëvka, Russia (sē-chôf′kȧ)	162	55°52′N	34°18′E
Sydenham, Austl.	243b	37°42′S	144°46′E
Sydenham, neigh., S. Afr.	244b	26°09′S	28°06′E
Sydenham, neigh., Eng., U.K.	235	51°26′N	0°03′W
Sydney, Austl. (sĭd′nē)	203	33°55′S	151°17′E
Sydney, Can.	85	46°09′N	60°11′W
Sydney Mines, Can.	85	46°14′N	60°14′W
Syktyvkar, Russia (sük-tüf′kär)	164	61°35′N	50°40′E
Sylacauga, Al., U.S. (sĭl-ȧ-kô′gȧ)	114	33°10′N	86°15′W
Sylarna, mtn., Eur.	152	63°00′N	12°10′E
Sylt, i., Ger. (sĭlt)	154	54°55′N	8°30′E
Sylvania, Austl.	243a	34°01′S	151°07′E
Sylvania, Ga., U.S. (sĭl-vā′nĭ-à)	115	32°44′N	81°40′W
Sylvania Heights, Austl.	243a	34°02′S	151°06′E
Sylvester, Ga., U.S. (sĭl-vĕs′tẽr)	114	31°32′N	83°50′W
Syndal, Austl.	243b	37°53′S	145°09′E
Synel′nykove, Ukr.	167	48°19′N	35°33′E
Syosset, N.Y., U.S.	228	40°50′N	73°30′W
Syracuse, Ks., U.S. (sĭr′ȧ-kūs)	110	37°59′N	101°44′W
Syracuse, N.Y., U.S.	97	43°05′N	76°10′W
Syracuse, Ut., U.S.	107b	41°06′N	112°04′W
Syr Darya, r., Asia	164	44°15′N	65°45′E
Syria, nation, Asia (sĭr′ĭ-à)	182	35°00′N	37°15′E
Syrian Desert, des., Asia	182	32°00′N	40°00′E
Sysert′, Russia (sĕ′sĕrt)	172a	56°30′N	60°48′E
Sysola, r., Russia	166	60°50′N	50°40′E
Syukunosho, Japan	242b	34°50′N	135°32′E
Syvash, zatoka, b., Ukr.	163	45°55′N	34°42′E
Syzran′, Russia (sĕz-rän′)	164	53°09′N	48°27′E
Szamotuły, Pol. (shá-mō-tōō′wĕ)	154	52°36′N	16°34′E
Szarvas, Hung. (sôr′vôsh)	155	46°51′N	20°36′E
Szczebrzeszyn, Pol. (shchĕ-bzhä′shĕn)	155	50°41′N	22°58′E
Szczecin, Pol. (shchĕ′tsĭn)	142	53°25′N	14°35′E
Szczecinek, Pol. (shchĕ-tsĭ′nĕk)	146	53°41′N	16°42′E
Szczuczyn, Pol. (shchōō′chĕn)	155	53°32′N	22°17′E
Szczytno, Pol. (shchĭt′nô)	155	53°33′N	21°00′E
Szechwan Basin, basin, China	188	30°45′N	104°40′E
Szeged, Hung. (sĕ′gĕd)	142	46°15′N	20°12′E
Székesfehérvár, Hung. (sā′kĕsh-fĕ′hār-vär)	149	47°12′N	18°26′E
Szekszárd, Hung. (sĕk′särd)	149	46°19′N	18°42′E
Szentendre, Hung. (sĕnt′ĕn-drĕ)	155	47°40′N	19°07′E
Szentes, Hung. (sĕn′tĕsh)	155	46°38′N	20°18′E
Szigetvar, Hung. (sĕ′gĕt-vär)	155	46°05′N	17°50′E
Szolnok, Hung.	155	47°11′N	20°12′E
Szombathely, Hung. (sòm′bôt-hĕl′)	149	47°13′N	16°35′E
Szprotawa, Pol. (shprō-tä′vä)	154	51°34′N	15°29′E
Szydłowiec, Pol. (shid-wô′vyets)	155	51°13′N	20°53′E

T

PLACE (Pronunciation)	PAGE	LAT.	LONG.
Taal, l., Phil. (tä-äl′)	197a	13°58′N	121°06′E
Tabaco, Phil. (tä-bä′kō)	197a	13°27′N	123°40′E
Tabankulu, S. Afr. (tä-bän-kōō′la)	213c	30°56′S	29°19′E
Tabasará, Serranía de, mts., Pan.	121	8°29′N	81°22′W
Tabasco, Mex. (tä-bäs′kō)	118	21°47′N	103°04′W
Tabasco, state, Mex.	116	18°10′N	93°00′W
Taber, Can.	84	49°47′N	112°08′W
Tablas, i., Phil. (täb′läs)	197a	12°26′N	122°00′E
Tablas Strait, strt., Phil.	197a	12°17′N	121°41′E
Table Bay, b., S. Afr. (tā′b′l)	212a	33°41′S	18°27′E
Table Mountain, mtn., S. Afr.	212a	33°58′S	18°26′E
Table Rock Lake, Mo., U.S.	111	36°37′N	93°29′W
Tabligbo, Togo	214	6°35′N	1°30′E
Taboão da Serra, Braz.	234d	23°38′S	46°46′W
Taboga, i., Pan. (tä-bō′gä)	116a	8°48′N	79°35′W
Taboguilla, i., Pan. (tä-bō-gē′l-yä)	116a	8°48′N	79°31′W
Tábor, Czech Rep. (tä′bôr)	154	49°25′N	14°40′E
Tabora, Tan. (tä-bō′rä)	212	5°01′S	32°48′E
Tabou, C. Iv. (tá-bōō′)	210	4°25′N	7°21′W
Tabrīz, Iran (tà-brēz′)	182	38°00′N	46°13′E
Tabuaeran, i., Kir.	2	3°52′N	159°20′W
Tabwémasana, Mont, mtn., Vanuatu	198f	15°20′S	166°44′E
Tacámbaro, r., Mex. (tä-käm′bä-rō)	118	18°55′N	101°25′W
Tacámbaro de Codallos, Mex.	118	19°12′N	101°28′W
Tacarigua, Laguna de la, l., Ven.	131b	10°18′N	65°43′W
Tacheng, China (tä-chŭŋ)	188	46°50′N	83°24′E
Tachie, r., Can.	86	54°30′N	125°00′W
Tachikawa, Japan	242a	35°42′N	139°25′E
Tacloban, Phil. (tä-klō′bän)	197	11°06′N	124°58′E
Tacna, Peru (täk′nä)	130	18°34′S	70°16′W
Tacoma, Wa., U.S. (tȧ-kō′mȧ)	96	47°14′N	122°27′W
Taconic Range, mts., N.Y., U.S. (tȧ-kŏn′ĭk)	99	41°55′N	73°40′W
Tacony, neigh., Pa., U.S.	229b	40°02′N	75°03′W
Tacotalpa, Mex. (tä-kō-täl′pä)	119	17°37′N	92°51′W
Tacotalpa, r., Mex.	119	17°24′N	92°38′W
Tacuba, neigh., Mex.	233a	19°28′N	99°12′W
Tacubaya, neigh., Mex.	233a	19°25′N	99°12′W
Tademaït, Plateau du, plat., Alg. (tä-dē-mä′ēt)	210	28°00′N	2°15′E
Tadio, Lagune, b., C. Iv.	214	5°20′N	5°25′W
Tadjoura, Dji. (tåd-zhōō′rá)	218a	11°48′N	42°54′E
Tadley, Eng., U.K. (tăd′lē)	144b	51°19′N	1°08′W
Tadotsu, Japan (tä′dò-tsò)	195	34°14′N	133°43′E
Tadoussac, Can. (tà-dōō-sák′)	91	48°09′N	69°43′W
Tadworth, Eng., U.K.	235	51°17′N	0°14′W
Tadzhikistan see Tajikistan, nation, Asia	164	39°22′N	69°30′E
Taebaek Sanmaek, mts., Asia (tī-bīk′ sän-mīk′)	194	37°20′N	128°50′E
Taedong, r., N. Kor. (tī-dŏng)	194	38°38′N	124°32′E
Taegu, S. Kor. (tī′gōō′)	189	35°49′N	128°41′E
Taejŏn, S. Kor.	194	36°20′N	127°26′E
Tafalla, Spain (tä-fäl′yä)	158	42°30′N	1°42′W
Tafna, r., Alg. (täf′nä)	158	35°28′N	1°00′W
Taft, Ca., U.S. (táft)	108	35°09′N	119°27′W

354 Tagama–Tarkastad

PLACE (Pronunciation)	PAGE	LAT.	LONG.
Tagama, reg., Niger	215	15°50'N	6°30'E
Taganrog, Russia (tá-gán-rôk')	167	47°12'N	38°56'E
Taganrogskiy Zaliv, b., Eur. (tá-gán-rôk'skĭ zä'lĭf)	167	46°55'N	38°17'E
Tagula, i., Pap. N. Gui. (tä'gōō-lá)	203	11°45'S	153°46'E
Tagus (Tajo), r., Eur. (tā'gŭs)	142	39°40'N	5°07'W
Tahan, Gunong, mtn., Malay.	196	4°33'N	101°52'E
Tahat, mtn., Alg. (tä-hät')	210	23°22'N	5°21'E
Tahiti, i., Fr. Poly. (tä-hē'tē) (tä'ē-tē')	2	17°30'S	149°30'W
Tahkuna Nina, c., Est. (táh-kōō'ná nē'ná)	153	59°08'N	22°03'E
Tahlequah, Ok., U.S. (tă-lē-kwä')	111	35°54'N	94°58'W
Tahoe, l., U.S. (tä'hō)	96	39°09'N	120°18'W
Tahoua, Niger (tä'ōō-ä)	210	14°54'N	5°16'E
Tahtsa Lake, l., Can.	86	53°33'N	127°47'W
Tahuya, Wa., U.S. (tȧ-hū-yă')	106a	47°23'N	123°03'W
Tahuya, r., Wa., U.S.	106a	47°28'N	122°55'W
Tai'an, China (tī-än)	192	36°13'N	117°08'E
Taibai Shan, mtn., China (tī-bī shän)	192	33°42'N	107°25'E
Taibus Qi, China (tī-bōō-sz chyē)	192	41°52'N	115°25'E
Taicang, China (tī-tsäŋ)	190	31°26'N	121°06'E
T'aichung, Tai. (tī'chóng)	189	24°10'N	120°42'E
Tai'erzhuang, China (tī-är-jůäŋ)	190	34°34'N	117°44'E
Taigu, China (tī-gōō)	192	37°25'N	112°35'E
Taihang Shan, mts., China (tī-häŋ shän)	192	35°45'N	112°00'E
Taihe, China (tī-hŭ)	190	33°10'N	115°38'E
Tai Hu, l., China (tī hōō)	189	31°13'N	120°00'E
Tailagoin, reg., Mong. (tī'lȧ-gän' kä'rä)	188	43°39'N	105°54'E
Tailai, China (tī-lī)	192	46°20'N	123°10'E
Tailem Bend, Austl. (tā-lĕm)	204	35°15'S	139°30'E
T'ainan, Tai. (tī'nan')	189	23°08'N	120°18'E
Taínaron, Ákra, c., Grc.	142	37°45'N	22°00'E
Taining, China (tī'nĭng')	193	26°58'N	117°15'E
T'aipei, Tai. (tī'pā')	189	25°02'N	121°38'E
Taipei Institute of Technology, educ., Tai.	241d	25°02'N	121°32'E
Taiping, pt. of i., Malay.	196	4°56'N	100°39'E
Taiping Ling, mtn., China	192	47°03'N	120°30'E
Tai Po Tsai, H.K.	241c	22°21'N	114°15'E
Taisha, Japan (tī'shä)	195	35°23'N	132°40'E
Taishan, China (tī-shän)	193	22°15'N	112°50'E
Tai Shan, mts., China (tī shän)	192	36°16'N	117°05'E
Taitao, Península de, pen., Chile	132	46°20'S	77°15'W
Taitō, neigh., Japan	242a	35°43'N	139°47'E
T'aitung, Tai. (tī'tōōng')	193	22°45'N	121°02'E
Taiwan, nation, Asia (tī-wän) (fŏr-mō'sȧ)	189	23°30'N	122°20'E
Taiwan Normal University, educ., Tai.	241d	25°02'N	121°31'E
Taiwan Strait, strt., Asia	189	24°30'N	120°00'E
Tai Wan Tau, H.K.	241c	22°18'N	114°17'E
Tai Wan Tsun, H.K.	241c	22°19'N	114°12'E
Taixian, China (tī shyĕn)	190	32°31'N	119°54'E
Taixing, China (tī-shyĭŋ)	190	32°12'N	119°58'E
Taiyanggong, China	240b	39°58'N	116°25'E
Taiyuan, China (tī-yůän)	189	37°32'N	112°38'E
Taizhou, China (tī-jō)	190	32°23'N	119°41'E
Ta'izz, Yemen	185	13°38'N	44°04'E
Tajano de Morais, Braz. (tē-zhä'nô-dĕ-mô-rä'ēs)	129a	22°05'S	42°04'W
Tajikistan, nation, Asia	164	39°22'N	69°30'E
Tajninka, Russia	239b	55°54'N	37°45'E
Tajumulco, vol., Guat. (tä-hōō-mōōl'kō)	120	15°03'N	91°53'W
Tajuña, r., Spain (tä-ĸōō'n-yä)	158	40°23'N	2°36'W
Tājūrā', Libya	148	32°56'N	13°24'W
Tak, Thai.	196	16°57'N	99°12'E
Taka, i., Japan (tä'kä)	195	30°47'N	130°23'E
Takada, Japan (tä'kȧ-dä)	194	37°08'N	138°30'E
Takahashi, Japan (tä'kä'hä-shĭ)	195	34°47'N	133°35'E
Takaishi, Japan	195b	34°32'N	135°27'E
Takamatsu, Japan (tä'kä'mä-tsōō')	189	34°20'N	134°02'E
Takamori, Japan (tä'kä'mô-rē')	195	32°50'N	131°08'E
Takaoka, Japan (ta'kä'ô-kä')	194	36°45'N	136°59'E
Takapuna, N.Z.	205	36°48'S	174°47'E
Takarazuka, Japan (tä'kä-rä-zōō'kä)	195b	34°48'N	135°22'E
Takasaki, Japan (tä'kät'sōō-kē')	194	36°20'N	139°00'E
Takatsu, Japan (tä-kät'sōō) (mē'zō-nô-kō'chē)	195a	35°36'N	139°37'E
Takatsuki, Japan (tä'kät'sōō-kē')	195b	34°51'N	135°38'E
Takayama, Japan (tä'kä'yä'mä)	195	36°11'N	137°16'E
Takefu, Japan (tä'kĕ-fōō)	194	35°57'N	136°09'E
Takenotsuka, neigh., Japan	242a	35°48'N	139°48'E
Takla Lake, l., Can.	84	55°25'N	125°53'W
Takla Makan, des., China (mä-kȧn')	188	39°22'N	82°34'E
Takoma Park, Md., U.S. (tă'kōmȧ pärk)	100e	38°59'N	77°00'W
Takum, Nig.	215	7°17'N	9°59'E
Tala, Mex. (tä'lä)	118	20°39'N	103°42'W
Talagante, Chile (tä-lä-gá'n-tĕ)	129b	33°39'S	70°54'W
Talamanca, Cordillera de, mts., C.R.	121	9°37'N	83°55'W
Talanga, Hond. (tä-lä'n-gä)	120	14°21'N	87°09'W
Talara, Peru (tä-lä'rä)	130	4°32'S	81°17'W
Talasea, Pap. N. Gui. (tä-lä-sā'ä)	197	5°20'S	150°00'E
Talata Mafara, Nig.	215	12°35'N	6°04'E
Talaud, Kepulauan, is., Indon. (tä-lout')	197	4°17'N	127°30'E
Talavera de la Reina, Spain	148	39°58'N	4°51'W
Talca, Chile (täl'kä)	132	35°25'S	71°39'W
Talca, prov., Chile	129b	35°23'S	71°15'W
Talca, Punta, c., Chile (pōō'n-tä-täl'kä)	129b	33°25'S	71°42'W
Talcahuano, Chile (täl-kä-wä'nō)	132	36°41'S	73°05'W
Taldom, Russia (täl-dôm)	162	56°44'N	37°33'E
Taldyqorghan, Kaz.	169	45°03'N	77°18'E
Talea de Castro, Mex. (tä'lā-ä dā käs'trō)	119	17°22'N	96°14'W
Talibu, Pulau, i., Indon.	197	1°30'S	125°00'E
Talim, i., Phil. (tä-lēm')	197a	14°21'N	121°14'E
Talisay, Phil. (tä-lē'sī)	197a	14°08'N	122°56'E
Talkeetna, Ak., U.S. (tál-kēt'ná)	95	62°18'N	150°02'W
Talladega, Al., U.S. (tăl-á-dē'gȧ)	114	33°25'N	86°06'W
Tallahassee, Fl., U.S. (tăl-ȧ-hăs'ē)	97	30°25'N	84°17'W
Tallahatchie, r., Ms., U.S. (tal-ȧ hăch'ē)	114	34°21'N	90°03'W
Tallapoosa, Ga., U.S. (tăl-ȧ-pōō'sȧ)	114	33°44'N	85°15'W
Tallapoosa, r., Al., U.S.	114	32°22'N	86°08'W
Tallassee, Al., U.S. (tăl'ȧ-sē)	114	32°30'N	85°54'W
Tallinn, Est. (tȧl'lĕn) (rä'väl)	164	59°26'N	24°44'E
Tallmadge, Oh., U.S. (tăl'mĭj)	101d	41°06'N	81°26'W
Tallulah, La., U.S. (tă-lōō'lȧ)	113	32°25'N	91°13'W
Tally Ho, Austl.	243b	37°52'S	145°09'E
Tal'ne, Ukr.	163	48°52'N	30°43'E
Talo, mtn., Eth.	211	10°45'N	37°55'E
Taloje Budrukh, India	187b	19°05'N	73°05'E
Talpa de Allende, Mex. (täl'pä dā äl-yĕn'dā)	118	20°25'N	104°48'W
Talquin, Lake, res., Fl., U.S.	114	30°26'N	84°33'W
Talsi, Lat. (tal'sĭ)	153	57°16'N	22°35'E
Taltal, Chile (täl-täl')	132	25°26'S	70°32'W
Taly, Russia (täl'ĭ)	163	49°51'N	40°07'E
Tama, Ia., U.S. (tā'mä)	103	41°57'N	92°36'W
Tama, r., Japan	195a	35°38'N	139°35'E
Tamagawa, neigh., Japan	242a	35°37'N	139°39'E
Tama-kyūryō, mts., Japan	242a	35°35'N	139°30'E
Tamale, Ghana (tä-mä'lå)	210	9°25'N	0°50'W
Taman', Russia (tá-män')	163	45°13'N	36°46'E
Tamanaco, r., Ven. (tä-mä-nä'kō)	131b	9°32'N	66°00'W
Tamaqua, Pa., U.S. (tȧ-mô'kwă)	99	40°45'N	75°50'W
Tamar, r., Eng., U.K. (tā'mär)	150	50°35'N	4°15'W
Tamarite de Litera, Spain (tä-mä-rē'tā)	159	41°52'N	0°24'E
Tamaulipas, state, Mex. (tä-mä-ōō-lē'päs')	116	23°45'N	98°30'W
Tamazula de Gordiano, Mex.	118	19°44'N	103°09'W
Tamazulapan del Progreso, Mex.	119	17°41'N	97°34'W
Tamazunchale, Mex. (tä-mä-zōn-chä'lå)	118	21°16'N	98°46'W
Tambacounda, Sen. (täm-bä-kōōn'dä)	210	13°47'N	13°40'W
Tambador, Serra do, mts., Braz. (sĕ'r-rä-dô-täm'bä-dōr)	131	10°33'S	41°16'W
Tambelan, Kepulauan, is., Indon. (täm-bȧ-län')	196	0°38'N	107°38'E
Tambo, Austl. (tăm'bō)	203	24°50'S	146°15'E
Tambov, Russia (tám-bôf')	164	52°45'N	41°10'E
Tambov, prov., Russia	162	52°50'N	40°42'E
Tambre, r., Spain (täm'brā)	158	42°59'N	8°33'W
Tambura, Sudan (täm-bōō'rä)	211	5°34'N	27°30'E
Tame, r., Eng., U.K. (tām)	144a	52°41'N	1°42'W
Tâmega, r., Port. (tá-mā'gá)	158	41°30'N	7°45'W
Tamenghest, Alg.	210	22°34'N	5°34'E
Tamenghest, Oued, r., Alg.	210	22°15'N	2°51'E
Tamgak, Monts, mtn., Niger (tam-gäk')	210	18°40'N	8°40'E
Tamgué, Massif du, mtn., Gui.	210	12°15'N	12°35'W
Tamiahua, Mex. (tä-myä-wä)	119	21°17'N	97°26'W
Tamiahua, Laguna, l., Mex. (lä-gō'nä-tä-myä-wä)	119	21°38'N	97°33'W
Tamiami Canal, can., Fl., U.S. (tă-mī-ăm'ĭ)	115a	25°52'N	80°08'W
Tamil Nadu, state, India	183	11°30'N	78°00'E
Tampa, Fl., U.S. (tăm'pȧ)	97	27°57'N	82°25'W
Tampa Bay, b., Fl., U.S.	97	27°35'N	82°38'W
Tampere, Fin. (tȧm'pĕ-rĕ)	146	61°21'N	23°39'E
Tampico, Mex. (täm-pē'kō)	116	22°14'N	97°51'W
Tampico Alto, Mex. (täm-pē'kō äl'tō)	119	22°07'N	97°48'W
Tampin, Malay.	181b	2°28'N	102°15'E
Tam Quan, Viet	193	14°20'N	109°10'E
Tamuín, Mex. (tä-mōō-ē'n)	118	22°04'N	98°47'W
Tamworth, Austl. (tăm'wûrth)	203	31°01'S	151°00'E
Tamworth, Eng., U.K.	144a	52°38'N	1°41'W
Tana, i., Vanuatu	203	19°32'S	169°27'E
Tana, r., Kenya (tä'nä)	213	0°30'S	39°30'E
Tanabe, Japan (tä-nä'bā)	194	33°45'N	135°21'E
Tanabe, Japan	195b	34°49'N	135°46'E
Tanacross, Ak., U.S. (tă'nȧ-crŏs)	95	63°20'N	143°30'W
Tanaga, i., Ak., U.S. (tä-nä'gä)	95a	51°28'N	178°10'W
Tanahbala, Pulau, i., Indon. (tá-nä-bä'lä)	196	0°30'S	98°22'E
Tanahmasa, Pulau, i., Indon. (tá-nä-mä'sä)	196	0°03'S	97°30'E
Tanakpur, India (tăn'ăk-pōr)	186	29°10'N	80°07'E
Tana Lake, l., Eth.	211	12°09'N	36°41'E
Tanami, Austl. (tá-nä'mē)	202	19°45'S	129°50'E
Tanana, Ak., U.S. (tă'ná-nô)	95	65°18'N	152°20'W
Tanana, r., Ak., U.S.	95	64°26'N	148°40'W
Tanaro, r., Italy (tä-nä'rô)	160	44°45'N	8°02'E
Tanashi, Japan	195a	35°44'N	139°34'E
Tan-binh, Viet	241j	10°48'N	106°40'E
Tanbu, China (tän-bōō)	191a	23°20'N	113°06'E
Tancheng, China (tän-chŭŋ)	192	34°37'N	118°22'E
Tanchŏn, N. Kor. (tän'chŭn)	194	40°29'N	128°50'E
Tancítaro, Mex. (tän-sē'tä-rō)	118	19°16'N	102°24'W
Tancítaro, Cerro de, mtn., Mex. (sĕ'r-rô-dĕ)	118	19°24'N	102°19'W
Tancoco, Mex. (tän-kō'kō)	119	21°16'N	97°45'W
Tandil, Arg. (tän-dēl')	132	36°16'S	59°01'W
Tandil, Sierra del, mts., Arg.	132	38°40'S	59°40'W
Tanega, i., Japan (tä'nå-gä')	189	30°36'N	131°11'E
Tanezrouft, reg., Alg. (tä'nĕz-rōft)	210	24°17'N	0°30'W
Tang, r., China (täŋ)	190	33°38'N	117°29'E
Tang, r., China	190	39°13'N	114°45'E
Tanga, Tan. (täŋ'gȧ)	213	5°04'S	39°06'E
Tangancícuaro, Mex. (täŋ-gän-sē'kwa-rô)	118	19°52'N	102°13'W
Tanganyika, Lake, l., Afr.	212	5°15'S	29°40'E
Tanger, Mor. (tăn-jēr')	210	35°52'N	5°55'W
Tangermünde, Ger. (täŋ'ĕr-mün'de)	154	52°33'N	11°58'E
Tanggu, China (täŋ-gōō)	190	39°04'N	117°41'E
Tanggula Shan, mts., China (täŋ-gōō-lä shän)	188	33°15'N	89°07'E
Tanghe, China	192	32°40'N	112°50'E
Tangier *see* Tanger, Mor.	210	35°52'N	5°55'W
Tangipahoa, r., La., U.S. (tăn'jē-pȧ-hō'ȧ)	113	30°48'N	90°28'W
Tangra Yumco, l., China (täŋ-rä yōōm-tswo)	186	30°50'N	85°40'E
T'angshan, China	192	39°38'N	118°11'E
Tangxian, China (täŋ shyĕn)	190	38°49'N	115°00'E
Tangzha, China (täŋ-jä)	190	32°06'N	120°48'E
Tanimbar, Kepulauan, is., Indon.	197	8°00'S	132°00'E
Tanjong Piai, c., Malay.	181b	1°16'N	103°11'E
Tanjong Ramunia, c., Malay.	181b	1°27'N	104°44'E
Tanjungbalai, Indon. (tän'jông-bä'lä)	181b	1°00'N	103°26'E
Tanjungkarang-Telukbetung, Indon.	196	5°16'S	105°06'E
Tanjungpandan, Indon.	196	2°47'S	107°51'E
Tanjungpinang, Indon. (tän'jŏng-pē'näng)	181b	0°55'N	104°29'E
Tanjungpriok, neigh., Indon.	241i	6°06'S	106°53'E
Tannu-Ola, mts., Asia	165	51°00'N	94°00'E
Tannūrah, Ra's at, c., Sau. Ar.	182	26°45'N	49°59'E
Tano, r., Afr.	214	5°40'N	2°30'W
Tan-qui-dong, Viet	241j	10°44'N	106°43'E
Tanquijo, Arrecife, i., Mex. (är-rĕ-sē'fĕ-tän-kē'kô)	119	21°07'N	97°16'W
Tanshui Ho, r., Tai.	241d	25°08'N	121°27'E
Tan Son Nhut Airport, arpt., Viet	241j	10°49'N	106°40'E
Ţanţā, Egypt	211	30°47'N	31°00'E
Tan-thuan-dong, Viet	241j	10°45'N	106°44'E
Tantoyuca, Mex. (tän-tō-yōō'kä)	118	21°22'N	98°13'W
Tanyang, S. Kor.	194	36°53'N	128°20'E
Tanzania, nation, Afr.	212	6°48'S	33°58'E
Tao, r., China (tou)	192	35°30'N	103°40'E
Tao'an, China (tou-än)	189	45°15'N	122°45'E
Tao'er, r., China (tou-är)	189	45°40'N	122°00'E
Taormina, Italy (tä-ôr-mē'nä)	160	37°53'N	15°18'E
Taos, N.M., U.S. (tä'ôs)	109	36°25'N	105°35'W
Taoudenni, Mali (tä'ōō-dē-nē')	210	22°57'N	3°37'W
Taoussa, Mali	214	16°55'N	0°35'W
Taoyuan, China (tou-yůän)	193	29°00'N	111°15'E
Tapa, Est. (tá'pá)	153	59°16'N	25°56'E
Tapachula, Mex.	120	14°55'N	92°20'W
Tapajós, r., Braz. (tä-pä-zhô's)	131	3°27'S	55°33'W
Tapalque, Arg. (tä-päl-kē')	129c	36°22'S	60°05'W
Tapanatepec, Mex. (tä-pä-nä-tē-pĕk)	119	16°22'N	94°19'W
Tāpi, r., India	183	21°00'N	76°30'E
Tapiales, Arg.	233d	34°42'S	58°30'W
Tappi Saki, c., Japan (täp'pē sä'kē)	194	41°05'N	139°40'E
Tapps, l., Wa., U.S. (tăpz)	106a	47°20'N	122°12'W
Taquara, neigh., Braz.	234c	22°55'S	43°21'W
Taquara, Serra de, mts., Braz. (sĕ'r-rä-dĕ-tä-kwä'rä)	131	15°28'S	54°33'W
Taquari, r., Braz. (tä-kwä'rĭ)	131	18°35'S	56°50'W
Tar, r., N.C., U.S. (tär)	115	35°58'N	78°06'W
Tara, Russia (tä'rȧ)	164	56°58'N	74°13'E
Tara, i., Phil. (tä'rä)	197a	12°18'N	120°28'E
Tara, r., Russia (tä'rá)	170	56°32'N	76°13'E
Ţarābulus, Leb. (tȧ-rä'bō-lōōs)	182	34°25'N	35°50'E
Ţarābulus (Tripolitania), hist. reg., Libya	210	31°00'N	12°26'E
Tarakan, Indon.	196	3°17'N	118°04'E
Taranaki, Mount, vol., N.Z.	205	39°18'S	174°04'E
Tarancón, Spain (tä-rän-kōn')	158	40°01'N	3°00'W
Taranto, Italy (tä'rän-tô)	149	40°30'N	17°15'E
Taranto, Golfo di, b., Italy (gôl-fô-dē tä'rän-tô)	142	40°03'N	17°10'E
Tarapoto, Peru (tä-rä-pô'tô)	130	6°29'S	76°26'W
Tarare, Fr. (tȧ-rär')	156	45°55'N	4°23'E
Tarascon, Fr. (tȧ-rás-kôn')	156	42°53'N	1°35'E
Tarascon, Fr. (tä-räs-kôɴ)	156	43°47'N	4°41'E
Tarashcha, Ukr. (tä'räsh-chȧ)	163	49°34'N	30°52'E
Tarasht, Iran	241h	35°42'N	51°21'E
Tarata, Bol. (tä-rä'tä)	130	17°43'S	66°00'W
Taravo, r., Fr.	160	41°54'N	8°58'E
Tarazit, Massif de, mts., Niger	215	20°05'N	7°35'E
Tarazona, Spain (tä-rä-thō'nä)	158	41°54'N	1°45'W
Tarazona de la Mancha, Spain (tä-rä-zō'nä-dĕ-lä-mä'n-chä)	158	39°13'N	1°50'W
Tarbes, Fr. (tärb)	147	43°04'N	0°05'E
Tarbock Green, Eng., U.K.	237a	53°23'N	2°49'W
Tarboro, N.C., U.S. (tär'bŭr-ô)	115	35°53'N	77°34'W
Taredo, neigh., India	240e	19°58'N	72°49'E
Taree, Austl. (tä-rē')	204	31°52'S	152°21'E
Tarentum, Pa., U.S. (tȧ-rĕn'tŭm)	101e	40°36'N	79°44'W
Tarfa, Wādī at, val., Egypt	218b	28°14'N	31°00'E
Târgovişte, Rom.	149	44°54'N	25°29'E
Târgu Jiu, Rom.	149	45°02'N	23°17'E
Târgu Mureş, Rom.	149	46°33'N	24°33'E
Târgu Neamţ, Rom.	155	47°14'N	26°23'E
Târgu Ocna, Rom.	155	46°18'N	26°38'E
Târgu Secuiesc, Rom.	155	46°04'N	26°06'E
Tarhūnah, Libya	184	32°26'N	13°38'E
Tarija, Bol. (tär-rē'hä)	130	21°42'S	64°52'W
Tarīm, Yemen (tä-rĭm')	182	16°13'N	49°08'E
Tarim, r., China (tá-rĭm')	188	40°45'N	85°39'E
Tarim Basin, basin, China (tá-rĭm')	188	39°52'N	82°34'E
Tarka, r., S. Afr. (tä'kȧ)	213c	32°15'S	26°00'E
Tarkastad, S. Afr.	213c	32°01'S	26°18'E

ăt; finăl; rāte; senåte; ärm; åsk; sofȧ; fâre; ch-choose; dh-as th in other; bē; ēvent; bĕt; recĕnt; cratĕr; g-gō; gh-guttural g; bĭt; ĭ-short neutral; rīde; ĸ-guttural k as ch in German ich;

PRONOUNCING INDEX

Tarkhankut–Teslin 355

PLACE (Pronunciation)	PAGE	LAT.	LONG.
Tarkhankut, Mys, c., Ukr. (mĭs tår-ĸän′kòt)	167	45°21′N	32°30′E
Tarkio, Mo., U.S. (tär′kĭ-ō)	111	40°27′N	95°22′W
Tarkwa, Ghana (tärk′wä)	210	5°19′N	1°59′W
Tarlac, Phil. (tär′läk)	196	15°29′N	120°36′E
Tarlton, S. Afr. (tärl′tŭn)	213b	26°05′S	27°38′E
Tarma, Peru (tär′mä)	130	11°26′S	75°40′W
Tarn, r., Fr. (tärn)	147	43°45′N	2°00′E
Târnăveni, Rom.	155	46°19′N	24°18′E
Tarnów, Pol. (tär′nòf)	147	50°02′N	21°00′E
Taro, r., Italy (tä′rō)	160	44°41′N	10°03′E
Taroudant, Mor. (tå-ro͞o-dänt′)	210	30°39′N	8°52′W
Tarpon Springs, Fl., U.S. (tär′pŏn)	115a	28°07′N	82°44′W
Tarporley, Eng., U.K. (tär′pĕr-lė)	144a	53°09′N	2°40′W
Tarpum Bay, b., Bah. (tär′pŭm)	122	25°05′N	76°20′W
Tarquinia, Italy (tär-kwē′nē-ä)	160	42°16′N	11°46′E
Tarragona, Spain (tär-rä-gō′nä)	142	41°05′N	1°15′E
Tarrant, Al., U.S. (tăr′ănt)	100h	33°35′N	86°46′W
Tárrega, Spain (tä rå-gä)	159	41°40′N	1°09′E
Tarrejón de Ardoz, Spain (tär-rĕ-ĸō′n-dĕ-är-dôz)	159a	40°28′N	3°29′W
Tarrytown, N.Y., U.S. (tăr′ĭ-toun)	100a	41°04′N	73°52′W
Tarsus, Tur. (tår′sòs) (tär′sŭs)	182	37°00′N	34°50′E
Tartagal, Arg. (tär-tä-gà′l)	132	23°31′S	63°47′W
Tartu, Est. (tär′to͞o) (dôr′pät)	164	58°23′N	26°44′E
Ţarţūs, Syria	184	34°54′N	35°59′E
Tarumi, Japan (tä′ro͞o-mė)	195b	34°38′N	135°04′E
Tarusa, Russia (tä-ro͞os′á)	162	54°43′N	37°11′E
Tarzana, Ca., U.S. (tär-ză′ă)	107a	34°10′N	118°32′W
Tashkent, Uzb. (tåsh′kĕnt)	169	41°23′N	69°04′E
Tasman Bay, b., N.Z. (tăz′măn)	203a	40°50′S	173°20′E
Tasmania, state, Austl.	203	41°28′S	142°30′E
Tasman Peninsula, pen., Austl.	204	43°00′S	148°30′E
Tasman Sea, sea, Oc.	225	29°30′S	155°00′E
Tasquillo, Mex. (täs-kē′lyō)	118	20°34′N	99°21′W
Tatarsk, Russia (tå-tärsk′)	164	55°13′N	75°58′E
Tatar Strait, strt., Russia	165	51°00′N	141°45′E
Tate Gallery, pt. of i., Eng., U.K.	235	51°29′N	0°08′W
Tater Hill, mtn., Or., U.S. (tāt′ẽr hĭl)	106c	45°47′N	123°02′W
Tateyama, Japan (tä′tė-yä′mä)	195	35°04′N	139°52′E
Tathong Channel, strt., H.K.	241c	22°15′N	114°15′E
Tatlow, Mount, mtn., Can.	86	51°23′N	123°52′W
Tatsfield, Eng., U.K.	235	51°18′N	0°02′E
Tau, Nor.	152	59°05′N	5°59′E
Tauern Tunnel, trans., Aus.	154	47°12′N	13°17′E
Taung, S. Afr. (tä′òng)	212	27°25′S	24°47′E
Taunton, Ma., U.S. (tän′tŭn)	99	41°54′N	71°03′W
Taunton, r., R.I., U.S.	100b	41°50′N	71°02′W
Taupo, Lake, l., N.Z. (tä′o͞o-pō)	203a	38°42′S	175°55′E
Taurage, Lith. (tou′rå-gā)	153	55°15′N	22°18′E
Taurus Mountains *see* Toros Dağlari, mts., Tur.	182	37°00′N	32°40′E
Tauste, Spain (tä-o͞os′tå)	158	41°55′N	1°15′W
Tavda, Russia (táv-dá′)	164	58°00′N	64°44′E
Tavda, r., Russia	170	58°30′N	64°15′E
Taverny, Fr. (tå-vĕr-nē′)	157b	49°02′N	2°13′E
Taviche, Mex. (tä-vē′chĕ)	119	16°43′N	96°35′W
Tavira, Port. (tä-vē′rȧ)	158	37°09′N	7°42′W
Tavistock, N.J., U.S.	229b	39°53′N	75°02′W
Tavşanli, Tur. (táv′shän-lĭ)	167	39°30′N	29°30′E
Tawakoni, l., Tx., U.S.	113	32°51′N	95°59′W
Tawaramoto, Japan (tä′wä-rä-mô-tô)	195b	34°33′N	135°48′E
Tawas City, Mi., U.S.	98	44°15′N	83°30′W
Tawas Point, c., Mi., U.S. (tô′wȧs)	98	44°15′N	83°25′W
Tawitawi Group, is., Phil. (tä′wē-tä′wē)	196	4°52′N	120°35′E
Tawkar, Sudan	211	18°28′N	37°46′E
Taxco de Alarcón, Mex. (täs′kō dĕ ä-lär-kō′n)	118	18°34′N	99°37′W
Tay, r., Scot., U.K.	150	56°35′N	3°37′W
Tay, Loch, l., Scot., U.K.	150	56°25′N	4°07′W
Tayabas Bay, b., Phil. (tä-yä′bäs)	197a	13°44′N	121°40′E
Tayga, Russia (tī′gä)	170	56°12′N	85°47′E
Taygonos, Mys, c., Russia	165	60°37′N	160°17′E
Taylor, Mi., U.S.	230c	42°13′N	83°16′W
Taylor, Tx., U.S.	113	30°35′N	97°25′W
Taylor, Mount, mtn., N.M., U.S.	96	35°20′N	107°40′W
Taylorville, Il., U.S. (tā′lẽr-vĭl)	98	39°30′N	89°20′W
Taymyr, l., Russia (tī-mĭr′)	165	74°13′N	100°45′E
Taymyr, Poluostrov, pen., Russia	165	75°15′N	95°00′E
Táyros, Grc.	239d	37°58′N	23°42′E
Tayshet, Russia (tī-shĕt′)	165	56°09′N	97°49′E
Taytay, Phil.	241g	14°34′N	121°08′E
Tayug, Phil.	197a	16°01′N	120°45′E
Taz, r., Russia (táz)	170	67°15′N	80°45′E
Taza, Mor. (tä′zä)	210	34°08′N	4°00′W
Tazovskoye, Russia	164	66°58′N	78°28′E
Tbessa, Alg.	210	35°27′N	8°13′E
Tbilisi, Geor. (′tbĭl-yē′sē)	167	41°40′N	44°45′E
Tchentlo Lake, l., Can.	86	55°11′N	125°00′W
Tchibanga, Gabon (chė-bäŋ′gä)	212	2°51′S	11°02′E
Tchien, Lib.	214	6°04′N	8°08′W
Tchigai, Plateau du, plat., Afr.	215	21°20′N	14°50′E
Tczew, Pol. (t′chĕf′)	146	54°06′N	18°48′E
Teabo, Mex. (tĕ-ä′bô)	120a	20°25′N	89°14′W
Teague, Tx., U.S.	113	31°39′N	96°16′W
Teaneck, N.J., U.S.	228	40°53′N	74°01′W
Teapa, Mex. (tā-ä′pä)	119	17°35′N	92°56′W
Tebing Tinggi, i., Indon. (teb′ĭng-tĭng′gä)	181b	0°54′N	102°39′E
Tecalitlán, Mex. (tā-kä-lė-tlän′)	118	19°28′N	103°17′W
Techiman, Ghana	214	7°35′N	1°56′W
Tecoanapa, Mex. (tāk-wä-nä-pä′)	118	16°33′N	98°46′W
Tecoh, Mex. (tĕ-kô)	120a	20°46′N	89°27′W
Tecolotlán, Mex. (tā-kô-lô-tlän′)	118	20°13′N	103°57′W
Tecolutla, Mex. (tā-kô-lo͞o′tlä)	119	20°33′N	97°00′W
Tecolutla, r., Mex.	119	20°16′N	97°14′W

PLACE (Pronunciation)	PAGE	LAT.	LONG.
Tecomán, Mex. (tā-kô-män′)	118	18°53′N	103°53′W
Tecómitl, Mex. (tĕ-kô′mētl)	119a	19°13′N	98°59′W
Tecozautla, Mex. (tā′kô-zä-o͞o′tlä)	118	20°33′N	99°38′W
Tecpan de Galeana, Mex. (tĕk-pän′ dā gä-lā-ä′nä)	118	17°13′N	100°41′W
Tecpatán, Mex. (tĕk-pä-tá′n)	119	17°08′N	93°18′W
Tecuala, Mex. (tĕ-kwä-lä)	118	22°24′N	105°29′W
Tecuci, Rom. (ta-kòch′)	149	45°51′N	27°30′E
Tecumseh, Can. (tė-kŭm′sĕ)	101b	42°19′N	82°53′W
Tecumseh, Mi., U.S.	98	42°00′N	84°00′W
Tecumseh, Ne., U.S.	111	40°21′N	96°09′W
Tecumseh, Ok., U.S.	111	35°18′N	96°55′W
Teddington, neigh., Eng., U.K.	235	51°25′N	0°20′W
Tees, r., Eng., U.K. (tēz)	150	54°40′N	2°10′W
Teganuna, l., Japan (tā′gä-no͞o′nä)	195a	35°50′N	140°02′E
Tegel, neigh., Ger.	238a	52°35′N	13°17′E
Tegeler See, l., Ger.	238a	52°35′N	13°15′E
Tegucigalpa, Hond. (tå-go͞o-sė-gäl′pä)	116	14°08′N	87°15′W
Tehachapi Mountains, mts., Ca., U.S. (tė-hă-shă′pĭ)	108	34°50′N	118°55′W
Tehar, neigh., India	240d	28°38′N	77°07′E
Tehrān, Iran (tĕ-hrän′)	182	35°45′N	51°30′E
Tehuacan, Mex. (tā-wä-kän′)	116	18°27′N	97°23′W
Tehuantepec, Mex.	116	16°20′N	95°14′W
Tehuantepec, r., Mex.	119	16°30′N	95°23′W
Tehuantepec, Golfo de, b., Mex. (gôl-fô dĕ)	116	15°45′N	95°00′W
Tehuantepec, Istmo de, isth., Mex. (ē′st-mô dĕ)	119	17°55′N	94°35′W
Tehuehuetla, Arroyo, r., Mex. (tĕ-wĕ-wĕ′tlä ar-rô-yô)	118	17°54′N	100°26′W
Tehuitzingo, Mex. (tā-wē-tzĭŋ′gō)	118	18°21′N	98°16′W
Tejeda, Sierra de, mts., Spain (sē-ĕ′r-rä dĕ tĕ-kĕ′dä)	158	36°55′N	4°00′W
Tejúpan, Mex. (tĕ-ĸo͞o-pä′n) (sän-tyå′gô)	119	17°39′N	97°34′W
Tejúpan, Punta, c., Mex.	118	18°19′N	103°30′W
Tejupilco de Hidalgo, Mex. (tā-ho͞o-pēl′kō dā ė-dhäl′gō)	118	18°52′N	100°07′W
Tekamah, Ne., U.S. (tė-kā′mȧ)	102	41°46′N	96°13′W
Tekax de Alvaro Obregon, Mex.	120a	20°12′N	89°11′W
Tekeze, r., Afr.	211	13°38′N	38°00′E
Tekit, Mex. (tĕ-kē′t)	120a	20°35′N	89°18′W
Tekoa, Wa., U.S. (tė-kō′ȧ)	104	47°15′N	117°03′W
Tekstil′ščiki, neigh., Russia	239b	55°42′N	37°44′E
Tela, Hond. (tā′lä)	116	15°45′N	87°25′W
Tela, India	240d	28°44′N	77°20′E
Tela, Bahía de, b., Hond.	120	15°53′N	87°29′W
Telapa Burok, Gunong, mtn., Malay.	181b	2°51′N	102°04′E
Telavi, Geor.	167	42°00′N	45°20′E
Tel Aviv-Yafo, Isr. (tĕl-ä-vēv′já′fȧ)	182	32°03′N	34°46′E
Telegraph Creek, Can. (tĕl′ė-gráf)	84	57°59′N	131°22′W
Teleneşti, Mol.	163	47°31′N	28°22′E
Telescope Peak, mtn., Ca., U.S. (tĕl′ė skōp)	96	36°12′N	117°05′W
Telesung, Indon.	181b	1°07′N	102°53′E
Telica, vol., Nic. (tå-lē′kä)	120	12°38′N	86°52′W
Tell City, In., U.S. (tĕl)	98	38°00′N	86°45′W
Teller, Ak., U.S. (tĕl′ẽr)	95	65°17′N	166°28′W
Tello, Col. (tĕ′l-yô)	130a	3°05′N	75°08′W
Telluride, Co., U.S. (tĕl′ū-rīd)	109	37°55′N	107°50′W
Telok Datok, Malay.	181b	2°51′N	101°33′E
Teloloapan, Mex. (tā′lô-lô-ä′pän)	118	18°19′N	99°54′W
Tel′pos-Iz, Gora, mtn., Russia (tyĕl′pôs-ēz′)	164	63°50′N	59°20′E
Telšiai, Lith. (tĕl′sha′ė)	153	55°59′N	22°17′E
Teltow, Ger. (tĕl′tō)	145b	52°24′N	13°12′E
Teltower Hochfläche, reg., Ger.	238a	52°22′N	13°20′E
Teluklecak, Indon.	181b	1°53′N	101°45′E
Tema, Ghana	214	5°38′N	0°01′E
Temascalcingo, Mex. (tā′mäs-käl-sĭŋ′gō)	118	19°55′N	100°00′W
Temascaltepec, Mex. (tā′mäs-käl-tå pĕk)	118	19°00′N	100°03′W
Temax, Mex. (tĕ′mäx)	116	21°10′N	88°51′W
Temir, Kaz.	169	49°10′N	57°15′E
Temirtau, Kaz.	169	50°08′N	73°13′E
Témiscouata, l., Can. (tĕ′mĭs-kô-ä′tä)	92	47°40′N	68°50′W
Témiskaming, Can. (tė-mĭs′kȧ-mĭng)	85	46°41′N	79°01′W
Temoaya, Mex. (tĕ-mô-a-um-yä)	119a	19°28′N	99°36′W
Tempe, Az., U.S.	109	33°24′N	111°54′W
Tempelhof, neigh., Ger.	238a	52°28′N	13°23′E
Temperley, Arg. (tĕ′m-pĕr-lā)	132a	34°47′S	58°24′W
Tempio Pausania, Italy (tĕm′pē-ō pou-sä′nē-ä)	160	40°55′N	9°05′E
Temple, Tx., U.S. (tĕm′p′l)	113	31°06′N	97°20′W
Temple City, Ca., U.S.	107a	34°07′N	118°02′W
Temple Hills, Md., U.S.	229d	38°49′N	76°57′W
Temple of Heaven, rel., China	240b	39°53′N	116°25′E
Templestowe, Austl.	243b	37°45′S	145°07′E
Templeton, Can. (tĕm′p′l-tŭn)	83c	45°29′N	75°37′W
Temple University, pt. of i., Pa., U.S.	229b	39°59′N	75°09′W
Templin, Ger. (tĕm-plēn′)	154	53°08′N	13°30′E
Tempoal, r., Mex. (tĕm-pô-ä′l)	118	21°38′N	98°23′W
Temryuk, Russia (tyĕm-ryòk′)	167	45°17′N	37°21′E
Temuco, Chile (tå-mo͞o′kō)	132	38°46′S	72°38′W
Temyasovo, Russia (tĕm-yä′sô-vô)	172a	53°00′N	58°06′E
Tenafly, N.J., U.S.	228	40°56′N	73°58′W
Tenāli, India	187	16°10′N	80°32′E
Tenamaxtlán, Mex. (tā′nä-mäs-tlän′)	118	20°13′N	104°06′W
Tenancingo, Mex. (tå-nän-sēŋ′gō)	118	18°54′N	99°36′W
Tenango, Mex. (tā-näŋ′gō)	119a	19°09′N	98°51′W
Tenasserim, Myanmar (tĕn-ăs′ẽr-ĭm)	196	12°09′N	99°01′E
Tendrivs′ka Kosa, ostriv, i., Ukr.	163	46°12′N	31°17′E
Tenerife Island, i., Spain (tå-nå-rē′fā) (tĕn-ẽr-ĭf′)	210	28°41′N	17°02′W
Tènés, Alg. (tā-nĕs′)	147	36°28′N	1°22′E

PLACE (Pronunciation)	PAGE	LAT.	LONG.
Tengiz kōlī, l., Kaz.	169	50°45′N	68°39′E
Tengxian, China (tŭŋ shyĕn)	192	35°07′N	117°08′E
Tenjin, Japan (tĕn′jĕn)	195b	34°54′N	135°04′E
Tenke, D.R.C. (tĕŋ′kå)	212	11°26′S	26°45′E
Tenkiller Ferry Reservoir, res., Ok., U.S. (tĕn-kĭl′ẽr)	111	35°42′N	94°47′W
Tenkodogo, Burkina (tĕŋ-kô-dō′gô)	210	11°47′N	0°22′W
Tenmile, r., Wa., U.S. (tĕn mīl)	106d	48°52′N	122°32′W
Tennant Creek, Austl. (tĕn′ănt)	202	19°45′S	134°00′E
Tennessee, state, U.S. (tĕn-ĕ-sē′)	97	35°50′N	88°00′W
Tennessee, r., U.S.	97	35°35′N	88°20′W
Tennille, Ga., U.S. (tĕn′ĭl)	114	32°55′N	86°50′W
Tennōji, neigh., Japan	242b	34°39′N	135°31′E
Teno, r., Chile (tĕ′nô)	129b	34°55′S	71°00′W
Tenora, Austl. (tĕn-ôră)	204	34°23′S	147°33′E
Tenosique, Mex. (tā-nô-sē′kå)	119	17°27′N	91°25′W
Tenri, Japan	195b	34°36′N	135°50′E
Tenryū-Gawa, r., Japan (tĕn′ryo͞o′gä′wä)	195	35°16′N	137°54′E
Tensas, r., La., U.S. (tĕn′sô)	113	31°54′N	91°30′W
Tensaw, r., Al., U.S. (tĕn′sô)	114	30°45′N	87°52′W
Tenterfield, Austl. (tĕn′tẽr-fēld)	203	29°00′S	152°06′E
Ten Thousand, Islands, is., Fl., U.S. (tĕn thou′zănd)	115a	25°45′N	81°35′W
Teocaltiche, Mex. (tā′ô-käl-tē′chå)	118	21°27′N	102°38′W
Teocelo, Mex. (tā-ô-sā′lō)	119	19°22′N	96°57′W
Teocuitatlán de Corona, Mex.	118	20°06′N	103°22′W
Teófilo Otoni, Braz. (tē-ô′fē-lō-tô′nė)	131	17°49′S	41°18′W
Teoloyucan, Mex. (tā′ô-lô-yo͞o′kän)	118	19°43′N	99°12′W
Teopisca, Mex. (tā-ô-pēs′kä)	119	16°30′N	92°33′W
Teotihuacán, Mex. (tĕ-ô-tē-wá-kà′n)	119a	19°40′N	98°52′W
Teotitlán del Camino, Mex. (tā-ô-tė-tlän′ dĕl kä-mē′nô)	119	18°07′N	97°04′W
Tepalcatepec, Mex. (tā′päl-kä-tā′pĕk)	118	19°11′N	102°51′W
Tepalcatepec, r., Mex.	118	18°54′N	102°25′W
Tepalcates, Mex.	233a	19°23′N	99°04′W
Tepalcingo, Mex. (tā-päl-sēŋ′gô)	118	18°34′N	98°49′W
Tepatitlán de Morelos, Mex. (tā-pä-tē-tlän′ dā mô-rā′lôs)	116	20°55′N	102°47′W
Tepeaca, Mex. (tā-på-ä′kä)	119	18°57′N	97°54′W
Tepecoacuilco de Trujano, Mex.	118	18°15′N	99°29′W
Tepeji del Río, Mex. (tā-på-ĸe′ dĕl rē′ō)	118	19°55′N	99°22′W
Tepelmeme, Mex. (tā′pĕl-mā′må)	119	17°51′N	97°23′W
Tepepan, Mex.	233a	19°16′N	99°08′W
Tepetlaoxtoc, Mex. (tā′på-tlä′ôs-tōk′)	118	19°34′N	98°49′W
Tepezala, Mex. (tā-på-zä-lä′)	118	22°12′N	102°12′W
Tepic, Mex. (tā-pēk′)	116	21°32′N	104°53′W
Tëplaya Gora, Russia (tyôp′lå-yå gô-rä)	172a	58°32′N	59°08′E
Teplice, Czech Rep.	147	50°39′N	13°50′E
Teposcolula, Mex.	119	17°33′N	97°29′W
Tequendama, Salto de, wtfl., Col. (sä′l-tô dĕ tĕ-kĕn-dä′mä)	130	4°34′N	74°18′W
Tequila, Mex. (tå-kē′lä)	118	20°53′N	103°48′W
Tequisistlán, r., Mex. (tĕ-kē-sės-tlä′n)	119	16°20′N	95°40′W
Tequisquiapan, Mex. (tå-kēs-kė-ä′pän)	118	20°33′N	99°57′W
Ter, r., Spain (tĕr)	159	42°04′N	2°52′E
Téra, Niger	214	14°01′N	0°45′E
Tera, r., Spain (tā′rä)	158	42°05′N	6°24′W
Teramo, Italy (tā′rä-mô)	160	42°40′N	13°41′E
Terborg, Neth. (tĕr-bōrg)	157c	51°55′N	6°23′E
Tercan, Tur. (tĕr′jän)	167	39°40′N	40°12′E
Terceira Island, i., Port. (tĕr-sā′rä)	210a	38°49′N	26°36′W
Terebovlia, Ukr.	155	49°18′N	25°43′E
Terek, r., Russia	167	43°30′N	45°10′E
Terenkul′, Russia (tĕ-rĕn′kòl)	172a	55°38′N	62°18′E
Teresina, Braz. (tĕr-å-sē′nȧ)	131	5°04′S	42°42′W
Teresópolis, Braz. (tĕr-ā-sô′pō-lēzh)	129a	22°25′S	42°59′W
Teriberka, Russia (tyĕr-ê-byôr′kå)	166	69°00′N	35°15′E
Terme, Tur. (tĕr′mĕ)	167	41°05′N	37°00′E
Termez, Uzb. (tyĕr′mĕz)	170	37°19′N	67°20′E
Terminal, Ca., U.S.	232	33°45′N	118°15′W
Termini, Italy (tĕr′mē-nē)	160	37°58′N	13°39′E
Términos, Laguna de, l., Mex. (lä-gô′nä dĕ tĕ′r-mē-nôs)	116	18°37′N	91°32′W
Termoli, Italy (tĕr′mô-lė)	160	42°00′N	15°01′E
Tern, r., Eng., U.K. (tûrn)	144a	52°49′N	2°31′W
Ternate, Indon. (tĕr-nä′tä)	197	0°52′N	127°25′E
Terni, Italy (tĕr′nė)	148	42°38′N	12°41′E
Ternopil′, Ukr.	167	49°32′N	25°36′E
Terpeniya, Mys, c., Russia	165	48°44′N	144°42′E
Terpeniya, Zaliv, b., Russia (zä′lĭf tĕr-pä′nĭ-yå)	194	49°10′N	143°05′E
Terrace, Can. (tĕr′ĭs)	84	54°31′N	128°35′W
Terracina, Italy (tĕr-rä-chē′nä)	148	41°18′N	13°14′E
Terra Nova National Park, rec., Can.	85a	48°37′N	54°15′W
Terrassa, Spain	159	41°34′N	2°01′E
Terrebonne, Can. (tĕr-bŏn′)	99	45°42′N	73°38′W
Terrebonne Bay, b., La., U.S.	113	28°55′N	90°30′W
Terre Haute, In., U.S. (tĕr-ē hōt′)	97	39°25′N	87°25′W
Terrell, Tx., U.S. (tĕr′ĕl)	113	32°44′N	96°15′W
Terrell, Wa., U.S.	106d	48°53′N	122°44′W
Terrell Hills, Tx., U.S. (tĕr′ĕl hĭlz)	107d	29°28′N	98°27′W
Terschelling, i., Neth. (tĕr-sĸĕl′ĭng)	151	53°25′N	5°12′E
Teruel, Spain (tå-ro͞o-ĕl′)	148	40°20′N	1°05′W
Tešanj, Bos. (tĕ′shän′)	161	44°36′N	17°59′E
Teschendorf, Ger. (tĕ′shĕn-dōrf)	145b	52°51′N	13°10′E
Tesecheacan, Mex. (tĕ-sĕ-chĕ-ä-kà′n)	119	18°10′N	95°41′W
Teshekpuk, l., Ak., U.S. (tē-shĕk′pŭk)	95	70°18′N	152°36′W
Teshio Dake, mtn., Japan (tĕsh′ē-ō-dä′kä)	194	44°00′N	142°50′E
Teshio Gawa, r., Japan (tĕsh′ė-ô gä′wä)	194	44°53′N	144°55′E
Tesiyn, r., Asia	188	49°45′N	96°00′E
Teslin, Can. (tĕs-lĭn)	95	60°10′N	132°30′W

356 Teslin–Tires

PLACE (Pronunciation)	PAGE	LAT.	LONG.
Teslin, l., Can.	84	60°12′N	132°08′W
Teslin, r., Can.	84	61°18′N	134°14′W
Tessaoua, Niger (tĕs-sä′ō-ä)	210	13°53′N	7°53′E
Tessenderlo, Bel.	145a	51°04′N	5°08′E
Test, r., Eng., U.K. (tĕst)	150	51°10′N	1°30′W
Testa del Gargano, c., Italy (tās′tä dĕl gär-gä′nō)	160	41°48′N	16°13′E
Tetachuck Lake, l., Can.	86	53°20′N	125°50′W
Tete, Moz. (tā′tĕ)	212	16°13′S	33°35′E
Tête Jaune Cache, Can. (tĕt′zhŏn-kăsh)	87	52°57′N	119°26′W
Teterboro, N.J., U.S.	228	40°52′N	74°03′W
Teteriv, r., Ukr.	167	51°05′N	29°30′E
Teterow, Ger. (tā′tĕ-rō)	154	53°46′N	12°33′E
Teteven, Bul. (tĕt′ĕ-ven′)	161	42°57′N	24°15′E
Teton, r., Mt., U.S. (tē′tŏn)	105	47°54′N	111°37′W
Tétouan, Mor.	210	35°42′N	5°34′W
Tetovo, Mac. (tä′tō-vō)	161	42°01′N	21°00′E
Tetyukhe-Pristan, Russia (tĕt-yōō′kĕ prĭ-stän′)	194	44°21′N	135°44′E
Tetyushi, Russia (tyĕt-yō′shĭ)	166	54°57′N	48°50′E
Teupitz, Ger. (toi′pētz)	145b	42°08′N	13°37′E
Tevere, r., Italy	148	42°30′N	12°14′E
Teverya, Isr.	181a	32°48′N	35°32′E
Tewksbury, Ma., U.S. (tūks′bĕr-ĭ)	93a	42°37′N	71°14′W
Texada Island, i., Can.	86	49°40′N	124°24′W
Texarkana, Ar., U.S. (tĕk-sär-kăn′ā)	97	33°26′N	94°02′W
Texarkana, Tx., U.S.	97	33°26′N	94°04′W
Texas, state, U.S.	96	31°00′N	101°00′W
Texas City, Tx., U.S.	113	29°23′N	94°54′W
Texcaltitlán, Mex. (tās-käl′tē-tlän′)	118	18°54′N	99°51′W
Texcoco, Mex. (tās-kō′kō)	118	19°31′N	98°53′W
Texcoco, Lago de, l., Mex.	119a	19°30′N	99°00′W
Texel, i., Neth. (tĕk′sĕl)	151	53°10′N	4°45′E
Texistepec, Mex. (tĕk-sēs-tā-pĕk′)	119	17°51′N	94°46′W
Texmelucan, Mex.	118	19°17′N	98°26′W
Texoma, Lake, res., U.S. (tĕk′ō-mă)	96	34°03′N	96°28′W
Texontepec, Mex. (tā-zōn-tā-pĕk′)	118	19°52′N	98°48′W
Texontepec de Aldama, Mex. (dā äl-dä′mä)	118	20°19′N	99°19′W
Teyateyaneng, Leso.	213c	29°11′S	27°43′E
Teykovo, Russia (tĕy-kō′vō)	166	56°52′N	40°34′E
Teziutlán, Mex. (tā-zē-ōō-tlän′)	119	19°48′N	97°21′W
Tezpur, India	186	26°42′N	92°52′E
Tha-anne, r., Can.	84	60°50′N	96°56′W
Thabana Ntlenyana, mtn., Leso.	213c	29°28′S	29°17′E
Thabazimbi, S. Afr.	218d	24°36′S	27°22′E
Thailand, nation, Asia	196	16°30′N	101°00′E
Thailand, Gulf of, b., Asia	196	11°37′N	100°46′E
Thākurpukur, India	240a	22°28′N	88°19′E
Thale Luang, l., Thai.	196	7°51′N	99°39′E
Thame, Eng., U.K. (tām)	144b	51°43′N	0°59′W
Thames, r., Can. (tĕmz)	90	42°40′N	81°45′W
Thames, r., Eng., U.K.	142	51°30′N	1°30′W
Thames Ditton, Eng., U.K.	235	51°23′N	0°21′W
Thāmit, Wadi, r., Libya	149	30°39′N	16°23′E
Thāna, India (thä′nŭ)	186	19°13′N	72°58′E
Thāna Creek, r., India	187b	19°03′N	72°58′E
Thanh Hoa, Viet (tän′hō′ä)	196	19°46′N	105°42′E
Thanjāvūr, India	183	10°51′N	79°11′E
Thann, Fr. (tän)	157	47°49′N	7°05′E
Thaon-les-Vosges, Fr. (tä-ŏn-lā-vōzh′)	157	48°16′N	6°24′E
Thargomindah, Austl. (thär′gō-mĭn′dȧ)	203	27°58′S	143°57′E
Thásos, i., Grc. (thă′sōs)	149	40°41′N	24°53′E
Thatch Cay, i., V.I.U.S. (thăch)	117c	18°22′N	64°53′W
Thatto Heath, Eng., U.K.	237a	53°26′N	2°45′W
Thaya, r., Eur. (tä′yȧ)	154	48°48′N	15°40′E
Thayer, Mo., U.S. (thâ′ēr)	111	36°30′N	91°34′W
The Basin, Austl.	243b	37°51′S	145°19′E
Thebes see Thívai, Grc.	149	38°20′N	23°18′E
Thebes, hist., Egypt (thēbz)	211	25°47′N	32°39′E
The Brothers, mtn., Wa., U.S.	106a	47°39′N	123°08′W
The Capital, pt. of i., D.C., U.S.	229d	38°53′N	77°00′W
The Coorong, l., Austl. (kō′rŏng)	204	36°07′S	139°45′E
The Coteau, hills, Can.	88	51°10′N	107°30′W
The Dalles, Or., U.S. (dălz)	96	45°36′N	121°10′W
The Father, mtn., Pap. N. Gui.	197	5°05′S	151°30′E
The Hague ('s-Gravenhage), Neth.	142	52°05′N	4°16′E
The Narrows, strt., N.Y., U.S.	228	40°37′N	74°03′W
The Oaks, Austl.	201b	34°04′S	150°36′E
Theodore, Austl. (thēō′dôr)	204	24°51′S	150°09′E
Theodore Roosevelt Dam, dam, Az., U.S. (thē-ō-dōr rōō-sȧ-vĕlt)	109	33°46′N	111°25′W
Theodore Roosevelt Lake, res., Az., U.S.	109	33°45′N	111°00′W
Theodore Roosevelt National Park, N.D., U.S.	102	47°20′N	103°42′W
Theológos, Grc.	161	40°37′N	24°41′E
The Oval, pt. of i., Eng., U.K.	235	51°29′N	0°07′W
The Pas, Can. (pä)	84	53°50′N	101°15′W
Thermopolis, Wy., U.S. (thēr-mŏp′ō-lĭs)	105	43°38′N	108°11′W
The Round Mountain, mtn., Austl.	204	30°17′S	152°19′E
The Sound, strt., Austl.	243a	33°49′S	151°17′E
Thessalía, hist. reg., Grc.	161	39°50′N	22°09′E
Thessalon, Can.	85	46°11′N	83°37′W
Thessaloníki, Grc. (thĕs-sȧ-lō-nē′kē)	142	40°38′N	22°59′E
Thetford Mines, Can. (thĕt′fērd mīns)	91	46°05′N	71°20′W
The Twins, mtn., Afr. (twĭnz)	213c	30°09′S	28°29′E
Theunissen, S. Afr.	218d	28°25′S	26°44′E
Theydon Bois, Eng., U.K.	235	51°40′N	0°06′E
Thiais, Fr.	237c	48°46′N	2°23′E
Thibaudeau, Can. (tĭ′bō-dō′)	89	57°05′N	94°08′W
Thibodaux, La., U.S. (tē-bō-dō′)	113	29°48′N	90°48′W
Thief, l., Mn., U.S. (thēf)	102	48°32′N	95°46′W
Thief, r., Mn., U.S.	103	48°18′N	96°07′E
Thief River Falls, Mn., U.S. (thēf rĭv′ēr fôlz)	102	48°07′N	96°11′W
Thiers, Fr. (tyâr)	156	45°51′N	3°32′E
Thiès, Sen. (tē-ĕs′)	210	14°48′N	16°56′W
Thika, Kenya	217	1°03′S	37°05′E
Thimphu, Bhu.	183	27°33′N	89°42′E
Thingvallavatn, l., Ice.	146	64°12′N	20°22′W
Thio, N. Cal.	198f	21°37′S	166°14′E
Thionville, Fr. (tyôn-vēl′)	147	49°23′N	6°31′E
Third Cataract, wtfl., Sudan	211	19°53′N	30°11′E
Thisted, Den. (tēs′tĕdh)	152	56°57′N	8°38′E
Thistilfjördur, b., Ice.	146	66°29′N	14°59′W
Thistle, i., Austl. (thĭs″l)	204	34°55′S	136°11′E
Thistletown, neigh., Can.	227c	43°44′N	79°33′W
Thjórsá, r., Ice. (tyûr′sȧ)	146	64°23′N	19°18′W
Thohoyandou, S. Afr.	212	23°00′S	30°29′E
Tholen, Neth.	145a	51°32′N	4°11′E
Thomas, Ok., U.S. (tŏm′ăs)	110	35°44′N	98°43′W
Thomas, W.V., U.S.	99	39°15′N	79°30′W
Thomaston, Ga., U.S. (tŏm′ăs-tŭn)	114	32°51′N	84°17′W
Thomaston, N.Y., U.S.	228	40°47′N	73°43′W
Thomastown, Austl.	243b	37°41′S	145°01′E
Thomasville, Al., U.S. (tŏm′ăs-vĭl)	114	31°55′N	87°43′W
Thomasville, N.C., U.S.	115	35°52′N	80°05′W
Thomlinson, Mount, mtn., Can.	86	55°33′N	127°29′W
Thompson, Can.	84	55°48′N	97°59′W
Thompson, r., Can.	87	50°15′N	121°20′W
Thompson, r., Mo., U.S.	111	40°32′N	93°49′W
Thompson Falls, Mt., U.S.	104	47°35′N	115°20′W
Thomson, r., Austl. (tŏm-sŏn)	203	24°30′S	143°07′E
Thomson's Falls, Kenya	217	0°02′N	36°22′E
Thon Buri, neigh., Thai.	241f	13°43′N	100°29′E
Thong, Eng., U.K.	235	51°24′N	0°24′E
Thong Hoe, Sing.	240c	1°25′N	103°42′E
Thong-tay-hoi, Viet	241j	10°50′N	106°39′E
Thonon-les-Bains, Fr. (tō-nôn′lā-băn′)	157	46°22′N	6°27′E
Thorigny-sur-Marne, Fr.	237c	48°53′N	2°42′E
Thornbury, Austl.	243b	37°45′S	145°00′E
Thorne, Eng., U.K. (thôrn)	144a	53°37′N	0°58′W
Thornhill, S. Afr.	244b	26°07′S	28°09′E
Thornleigh, Austl.	243a	33°44′S	151°05′E
Thornton, Eng., U.K.	237a	53°30′N	3°00′W
Thornton Hough, Eng., U.K.	237a	53°19′N	3°03′W
Thornton-le-Moors, Eng., U.K.	237a	53°16′N	2°50′W
Thorntown, In., U.S. (thôrn′tŭn)	98	40°05′N	86°35′W
Thornwood Common, Eng., U.K.	235	51°43′N	0°08′E
Thorold, Can. (thō′rōld)	91	43°13′N	79°12′W
Thouars, Fr. (tōō-är′)	156	47°00′N	0°17′W
Thousand Islands, is., N.Y., U.S. (thou′zănd)	99	44°15′N	76°10′W
Thrace, hist. reg. (thrās)	161	41°20′N	26°07′E
Thrapston, Eng., U.K. (thrăp′stŭn)	144a	52°23′N	0°32′W
Three Forks, Mt., U.S. (thrē fôrks)	105	45°56′N	111°35′W
Three Oaks, Mi., U.S. (thrē ōks)	98	41°50′N	86°40′W
Three Points, Cape, c., Ghana	210	4°45′N	2°06′W
Three Rivers, Mi., U.S.	98	42°00′N	83°40′W
Thule, Grnld.	82	76°34′N	68°47′W
Thun, Switz. (tōōn)	154	46°46′N	7°34′E
Thunder Bay, Can.	90	48°28′N	89°12′W
Thunder Bay, b., Can. (thŭn′dēr)	90	48°29′N	88°52′W
Thunder Hills, hills, Can.	88	54°30′N	106°00′W
Thunersee, l., Switz.	154	46°40′N	7°30′E
Thurber, Tx., U.S. (thûr′bēr)	112	32°30′N	98°23′W
Thüringen (Thuringia), hist. reg., Ger. (tü′rĭng-ĕn)	154	51°07′N	10°45′E
Thurles, Ire. (thûrlz)	150	52°44′N	7°45′W
Thursday, i., Austl. (thûrz-dā)	203	10°17′S	142°23′E
Thurso, Can. (thŭn′sō)	83c	45°36′N	75°15′W
Thurso, Scot., U.K.	150	58°35′N	3°40′W
Thurston Island, i., Ant. (thûrs′tŭn)	219	71°20′S	98°00′W
Tiachiv, Ukr.	155	48°01′N	23°42′E
Tiananmen, hist., China	240b	39°55′N	116°23′E
Tiandong, China (tĭĕn-dôŋ)	193	23°32′N	107°10′E
Tianjin, China	189	39°08′N	117°14′E
Tianjin Shi, China (tĭĕn-jyĭn shr)	192	39°30′N	117°13′E
Tianmen, China (tĭĕn-mŭn)	193	30°40′N	113°10′E
Tianshui, China (tĭĕn-shwā)	192	34°25′N	105°40′E
Tiasmyn, r., Ukr.	163	49°14′N	32°23′E
Tibagi, Braz. (tē′bä-zhē)	131	24°40′S	50°35′W
Tibasti, Sarir, des., Libya	211	24°00′N	16°30′E
Tibati, Cam.	215	6°27′N	12°38′E
Tiber see Tevere, r., Italy	148	42°30′N	12°14′E
Tibesti, mts., Chad	211	20°40′N	17°48′E
Tibet see Xizang, prov., China (tĭ-bĕt′)	188	32°22′N	83°30′E
Tibnīn, Leb.	181a	33°12′N	35°23′E
Tiburon, Haiti	123	18°35′N	74°25′W
Tiburon, Ca., U.S. (tē-bōō-rōn′)	106b	37°53′N	122°27′W
Tiburon, Ca., U.S.	231b	36°04′N	119°19′W
Tiburón, i., Mex.	116	28°45′N	113°10′W
Tiburón, Cabo, c. (kȧ′bō)	121	8°42′N	77°19′W
Tiburon Island, i., Ca., U.S.	106b	37°52′N	122°26′W
Ticao Island, i., Phil. (tē-kä′ō)	197a	12°40′N	123°30′E
Tickhill, Eng., U.K. (tĭk′ĭl)	144a	53°26′N	1°06′W
Ticonderoga, N.Y., U.S. (tī-kŏn-dēr-ō′gȧ)	99	43°50′N	73°30′W
Ticul, Mex. (tē-kōō′l)	120a	20°22′N	89°32′W
Tidaholm, Swe. (tē′dȧ-hōlm)	152	58°11′N	13°53′E
Tideswell, Eng., U.K. (tīdz′wĕl)	144a	53°17′N	1°47′W
Tidikelt, reg., Alg. (tē-dē-kĕlt′)	210	25°53′N	2°11′E
Tidjikdja, Maur. (tē-jĭk′jä)	210	18°33′N	11°25′W
Tidra, Île, i., Maur.	214	19°50′N	16°45′W
Tiefenbroich, Ger.	236	51°18′N	6°49′E
Tieling, China (tĭĕ-lĭŋ)	189	42°18′N	123°50′E
Tielmes, Spain (tyâl-màs′)	159a	40°15′N	3°20′W
Tienen, Bel.	145a	50°49′N	4°58′E
Tien Shan, mts., Asia	188	42°00′N	78°46′E
Tientsin see Tianjin, China	189	39°08′N	117°14′E
Tiergarten, neigh., Ger.	238a	52°31′N	13°21′E
Tierp, Swe. (tyĕrp)	152	60°21′N	17°28′E
Tierpoort, S. Afr.	213b	25°53′S	28°26′E
Tierra Blanca, Mex. (tyĕ′r-rä-blä′n-kä)	119	18°28′N	96°19′W
Tierra del Fuego, i., S.A. (tyĕr′rä dĕl fwā′gō)	132	53°50′S	68°45′W
Tiétar, r., Spain (tē-ā′tär)	158	39°56′N	5°44′W
Tiffin, Oh., U.S. (tĭf′ĭn)	98	41°10′N	83°15′W
Tifton, Ga., U.S. (tĭf′tŭn)	114	31°25′N	83°34′W
Tigard, Or., U.S. (tī′gärd)	106c	45°25′N	122°46′W
Tighina, Mol.	167	46°49′N	29°29′E
Tignish, Can. (tĭg′nĭsh)	92	46°57′N	64°02′W
Tigoda, r., Russia (tē′gô-dȧ)	172c	59°29′N	31°15′E
Tigre, r., Peru	130	2°20′S	75°41′W
Tigres, Península dos, pen., Ang. (pĕ-nē′ŋ-sōō-lä-dōs-tē′grĕs)	212	16°30′S	11°45′E
Tigris, r., Asia	182	34°45′N	44°10′E
Tīh, Jabal at, mts., Egypt	181a	29°23′N	34°05′E
Tihert, Alg.	210	35°28′N	1°15′E
Tihuatlán, Mex. (tē-wä-tlän′)	119	20°43′N	97°34′W
Tijuana, Mex. (tē-hwä′nä)	116	32°32′N	117°02′W
Tijuca, Pico da, mtn., Braz. (pē′kō-dä-tē-zhōō′kȧ)	132b	22°56′S	43°17′W
Tikal, hist., Guat. (tē-käl′)	120a	17°16′N	89°49′W
Tikhoretsk, Russia (tē-ĸôr-yĕtsk′)	167	45°55′N	40°05′E
Tikhvin, Russia (tēĸ-vēn′)	164	59°36′N	33°38′E
Tikrīt, Iraq	182	34°36′N	43°31′E
Tiksi, Russia (tēk-sē′)	165	71°42′N	128°32′E
Tilburg, Neth. (tĭl′bûrg)	147	51°33′N	5°05′E
Tilbury, Eng., U.K.	144b	51°28′N	0°23′E
Tilemsi, Vallée du, val., Mali	214	17°50′N	0°25′E
Tilichiki, Russia (tyĭ-le-chĭ-kē)	165	60°49′N	166°14′E
Tilimsen, Alg.	210	34°53′N	1°21′W
Tillabéry, Niger (tē-yȧ-bā-rē′)	210	14°14′N	1°30′E
Tillamook, Or., U.S. (tĭl′ȧ-mŏŏk)	104	45°27′N	123°50′W
Tillamook Bay, b., Or., U.S.	104	45°32′N	124°26′W
Tillberga, Swe. (tĕl-bĕr′ghȧ)	152	59°40′N	16°34′E
Tillsonburg, Can. (tĭl′sŭn-bûrg)	91	42°50′N	80°50′W
Tim, Russia (tēm)	163	51°39′N	37°07′E
Timaru, N.Z. (tĭm′ȧ-rōō)	203a	44°26′S	171°17′E
Timashevskaya, Russia (tēmä-shĕfs-kä′yȧ)	167	45°47′N	38°57′E
Timbalier Bay, b., La., U.S. (tĭm′bȧ-lēr)	113	28°55′N	90°14′W
Timber, Or., U.S. (tĭm′bēr)	106c	45°43′N	123°17′W
Timberview, Md., U.S.	229c	39°13′N	76°45′W
Timbo, Gui. (tĭm′bō)	210	10°41′N	11°51′W
Timbuktu see Tombouctou, Mali	210	16°46′N	3°01′W
Times Square, pt. of i., N.Y., U.S.	228	40°45′N	74°00′W
Timétrine Monts, mts., Mali	214	19°50′N	0°30′W
Timimoun, Alg. (tē-mē-mōōn′)	210	29°14′N	0°22′E
Timiris, Cap, c., Maur.	210	19°23′N	16°32′W
Timiş, r., Eur.	161	45°28′N	21°06′E
Timişoara, Rom.	149	45°44′N	21°21′E
Timmins, Can. (tĭm′ĭnz)	85	48°25′N	81°22′W
Timmonsville, S.C., U.S. (tĭm′ŭnz-vĭl)	115	34°09′N	79°55′W
Timok, r., Eur.	161	43°35′N	22°13′E
Timor, i., Indon. (tē-mōr′)	197	10°08′S	125°00′E
Timor Sea, sea	202	12°40′S	125°00′E
Timpanogos Cave National Monument, rec., Ut., U.S. (tĭ-măn′ō-gŏz)	109	40°25′N	111°45′W
Timperley, Eng., U.K.	237b	53°24′N	2°19′W
Timpson, Tx., U.S. (tĭmp′sŭn)	113	31°55′N	94°24′W
Timsāh, l., Egypt (tĭm′sä)	218b	30°34′N	32°22′E
Tina, r., S. Afr. (tē′nȧ)	213c	30°50′S	28°44′E
Tina, Monte, mtn., Dom. Rep. (mô′n-tĕ-tē′nȧ)	123	18°50′N	70°40′W
Tinaguillo, Ven. (tē-nä-gē′l-yō)	131b	9°55′N	68°18′W
Tīnah, Khalīj at, b., Egypt	181a	31°06′N	32°42′E
Tindouf, Alg. (tĕn-dōōf′)	210	27°43′N	7°44′W
Tinggi, i., Malay.	181b	2°16′N	104°16′E
Tinghert, Plateau du, plat., Alg.	210	27°30′N	7°30′E
Tingi Mountains, mts., S.L.	214	9°00′N	10°50′W
Ting Kau, H.K.	241c	22°23′N	114°04′E
Tinglin, China	191b	30°53′N	121°18′E
Tingo María, Peru (tē′ngô-mä-rē′ä)	130	9°15′S	76°04′W
Tingréla, C. Iv.	214	10°29′N	6°24′W
Tingsryd, Swe. (tĭngs′rüd)	152	56°32′N	14°58′E
Tinguindio, Mex.	118	19°38′N	102°02′W
Tinguiririca, r., Chile (tē′n-gē-rē-rē′kä)	129b	34°48′S	70°45′W
Tinley Park, Il., U.S. (tĭn′lē)	101a	41°34′N	87°47′W
Tinnoset, Nor. (tĕn′nōs′sĕt)	152	59°44′N	9°00′E
Tinogasta, Arg. (tē-nō-gäs′tä)	132	28°07′S	67°30′W
Tínos, i., Grc.	149	37°45′N	25°12′E
Tinsukia, India (tin-sōō′kĭ-ȧ)	182	27°18′N	95°29′W
Tintic, Ut., U.S. (tĭn′tĭk)	109	39°55′N	112°15′W
Tio, Pic de, mtn., Gui.	214	8°55′N	8°55′W
Tioga, neigh., Pa., U.S.	229b	40°00′N	75°10′W
Tioman, i., Malay.	181b	2°50′N	104°15′E
Tipitapa, Nic. (tē-pē-tä′pä)	120	12°14′N	86°05′W
Tipitapa, r., Nic.	120	12°13′N	85°57′W
Tippah Creek, r., Ms., U.S. (tĭp′pȧ)	114	34°43′N	88°15′W
Tippecanoe, r., In., U.S. (tĭp-ē-kȧ-nōō′)	98	40°55′N	86°45′W
Tipperary, Ire. (tĭ-pē-râ′rē)	147	52°28′N	8°13′W
Tippo Bay, Ms., U.S. (tĭp′ō bīōō′)	111	33°35′N	90°06′W
Tipton, In., U.S.	98	40°15′N	86°00′W
Tipton, Ia., U.S.	103	41°46′N	91°10′W
Tiranë, Alb. (tē-rä′nä)	142	41°48′N	19°50′E
Tirano, Italy (tē-rä′nō)	160	46°12′N	10°09′E
Tiraspol, Mol.	167	46°52′N	29°38′E
Tire, Tur. (tē′rĕ)	149	38°05′N	27°48′E
Tiree, i., Scot., U.K. (tī-rē′)	146	56°34′N	6°30′W
Tires, Port.	238d	38°43′N	9°21′W

ăt; finăl; rāte; senāte; ärm; ȧsk; sofȧ; fâre; ch-choose; dh-as th in other; bē; ēvent; bĕt; recĕnt; cratēr; g-gō; gh-guttural g; bĭt; ĭ-short neutral; rīde; ĸ-guttural k as ch in German ich;

PRONOUNCING INDEX Tirlyanskiy–Tottington 357

PLACE (Pronunciation)	PAGE	LAT.	LONG.
Tirlyanskiy, Russia (tĭr-lyän'skĭ)	172a	54°13'N	58°37'E
Tírnavos, Grc.	161	39°50'N	22°14'E
Tirol, prov., Aus. (tė-rōl')	154	47°13'N	11°10'E
Tiruchchirāppalli, India (tĭr'ō-chĭ-rä'pȧ-lĭ)	183	10°49'N	78°48'E
Tirunelveli, India	183b	8°53'N	77°43'E
Tiruppur, India	187	11°11'N	77°08'E
Tisdale, Can. (tĭz'dāl)	84	52°51'N	104°04'W
Tista, r., Asia	186	26°00'N	89°30'E
Tisza, r., Eur. (tė'sä)	142	47°30'N	21°00'E
Titāgarh, India	186a	22°44'N	88°23'E
Titicaca, Lago, l., S.A. (lä'gō-tē-tē-kä'kä)	130	16°12'S	70°33'W
Titiribi, Col. (tē-tē-rē-bė')	130a	6°05'N	75°47'W
Tito, Lagh, r., Kenya	217	2°25'N	39°05'E
Titov Veles, Mac. (tė'tôv vĕ'lĕs)	161	41°42'N	21°50'E
Titterstone Clee Hill, hill, Eng., U.K. (klė)	144a	52°24'N	2°37'W
Titule, D.R.C.	217	3°17'N	25°32'E
Titusville, Fl., U.S. (tĭ'tŭs-vĭl)	115a	28°37'N	80°44'W
Titusville, Pa., U.S.	99	40°40'N	79°40'W
Titz, Ger. (tētz)	157c	51°00'N	6°26'E
Tiu Keng Wan, H.K.	241c	22°18'N	114°15'E
Tiverton, R.I., U.S. (tĭv'ẽr-tun)	100b	41°38'N	71°11'W
Tivoli, Italy (tē'vô-lė)	148	41°38'N	12°48'E
Tixkokob, Mex. (tēx-kō-kō'b)	120a	21°01'N	89°23'W
Tixtla de Guerrero, Mex. (tē'x-tlä-dĕ-gĕr-rĕ'rô)	118	17°36'N	99°24'W
Tizapán, Mex.	233a	19°20'N	99°13'W
Tizard Bank and Reef, rf., Asia (tĭz'ȧrd)	196	10°51'N	113°20'E
Tizimín, Mex. (tē-zē-mē'n)	120a	21°08'N	88°10'W
Tizi-Ouzou, Alg. (tē'zė-o͞o-zo͞o')	210	36°44'N	4°04'E
Tiznados, r., Ven. (tėz-nä'dôs)	131b	9°53'N	67°49'W
Tiznit, Mor. (tėz-nēt)	210	29°52'N	9°39'W
Tkvarcheli, Geor.	168	42°15'N	41°41'E
Tlacolula de Matamoros, Mex.	119	16°56'N	96°29'W
Tlacotálpan, Mex. (tlä-kō-täl'pän)	119	18°39'N	95°40'W
Tlacotepec, Mex. (tlä-kô-tā-pĕ'k)	118	17°46'N	99°57'W
Tlacotepec, Mex.	118	19°11'N	99°41'W
Tlacotepec, Mex.	119	18°41'N	97°40'W
Tláhuac, Mex. (tlä-wäk')	119a	19°16'N	99°00'W
Tlajomulco de Zúñiga, Mex. (tlä-hô-mo͞o'l-ko-dĕ-zo͞o'n-yē-gä)	118	20°30'N	103°27'W
Tlalchapa, Mex. (tläl-chä'pä)	118	18°26'N	100°29'W
Tlalixcoyan, Mex. (tlä-lēs'kô-yän')	119	18°53'N	96°04'W
Tlalmanalco, Mex. (tläl-mä-nä'l-kô)	119a	19°12'N	98°48'W
Tlalnepantla, Mex.	119a	19°32'N	99°13'W
Tlalnepantla, Mex. (tläl-nȧ-pȧn'tlä)	119a	18°59'N	99°01'W
Tlalpan, Mex. (tläl-pä'n)	118	19°17'N	99°10'W
Tlalpujahua, Mex. (tläl-po͞o-ĸä'wä)	118	19°50'N	100°10'W
Tlaltenco, Mex.	233a	19°17'N	99°01'W
Tlapa, Mex. (tlä'pä)	118	17°30'N	98°30'W
Tlapacoyan, Mex. (tlä-pä-kô-yä'n)	119	19°57'N	97°11'W
Tlapehuala, Mex. (tlä-pȧ-wä'lä)	118	18°17'N	100°30'W
Tlaquepaque, Mex. (tlä-kĕ-pä'kĕ)	118	20°39'N	103°17'W
Tlatlaya, Mex. (tlä-tlä'yä)	118	18°36'N	100°14'W
Tlaxcala, Mex. (tläs-kä'lä)	116	19°16'N	98°14'W
Tlaxcala, state, Mex.	118	19°30'N	98°15'W
Tlaxco, Mex. (tläs'kō)	118	19°37'N	98°06'W
Tlaxiaco Santa María Asunción, Mex.	118	17°16'N	97°41'W
Tlayacapan, Mex. (tlä-yä-kä-pä'n)	119a	18°57'N	99°00'W
Tlevak Strait, strt., Ak., U.S.	86	53°03'N	132°58'W
Tlumach, Ukr. (t'lû-mäch')	155	48°47'N	25°00'E
Toa, r., Cuba (tō'ä)	123	20°25'N	74°35'W
Toamasina, Madag.	213	18°14'S	49°25'E
Toar, Cuchillas de, mts., Cuba (ko͞o-chė'l-lyäs-dĕ-tô-ä'r)	123	20°20'N	74°50'W
Tobago, i., Trin. (tō-bā'gō)	117	11°15'N	60°30'W
Toba Inlet, b., Can.	86	50°20'N	124°50'W
Tobarra, Spain (tō-bär'rä)	158	38°37'N	1°42'W
Tobol, r., Asia	164	52°00'N	62°00'E
Tobol'sk, Russia (tô-bôlsk')	170	58°09'N	68°28'E
Tocaima, Col. (tô-kä'y-mä)	130a	4°28'N	74°38'W
Tocantinópolis, Braz. (tō-kän-tē-nō'pō-lės)	131	6°27'S	47°18'W
Tocantins, state, Braz.	131	10°00'S	48°00'W
Tocantins, r., Braz. (tō-kän-tēns')	131	3°28'S	49°22'W
Toccoa, Ga., U.S. (tŏk'ō-ȧ)	114	34°35'N	83°20'W
Toccoa, r., Ga., U.S.	114	34°53'N	84°24'W
Tochigi, Japan (tō'chē-gĭ)	195	36°25'N	139°45'E
Tocoa, Hond. (tō-kō'ä)	120	15°37'N	86°01'W
Tocopilla, Chile (tō-kō-pēl'yä)	132	22°03'S	70°08'W
Tocuyo de la Costa, Ven. (tô-ko͞o'yō-dĕ-lä-kôs'tä)	131b	11°03'N	68°24'W
Toda, Japan	195a	35°48'N	139°42'E
Todmorden, Eng., U.K. (tŏd'môr-dĕn)	144a	53°43'N	2°05'W
Tofino, Can. (tō-fē'nō)	86	49°09'N	125°54'W
Töfsingdalens National Park, rec., Swe.	152	62°09'N	13°05'E
Tōgane, Japan (tō'gä-nä)	195	35°29'N	140°16'E
Togian, Kepulauan, is., Indon.	196	0°20'S	122°00'E
Togo, nation, Afr. (tō'gō)	210	8°00'N	0°52'E
Toguzak, r., Russia (tō'gô-zák)	172a	53°40'N	61°42'E
Tohopekaliga, Lake, l., Fl., U.S. (tō'hō-pē'kȧ-lī'gȧ)	115a	28°16'N	81°09'W
Tohor, Tanjong, c., Malay.	181b	1°53'N	102°29'E
Toijala, Fin. (toi'yȧ-lȧ)	153	61°11'N	23°46'E
Toi-Misaki, c., Japan (toi mė'sä-kė)	194	31°20'N	131°20'E
Toiyabe, Nv., U.S. (toi'yă-bē)	108	38°59'N	117°22'W
Tokachi Gawa, r., Japan (tō-kä'chė gä'wä)	194	43°10'N	142°30'E
Tokaj, Hung. (tô'kô-ė)	155	48°06'N	21°24'E
Tokat, Tur. (tō-ĸät')	182	40°20'N	36°30'E
Tokelau, dep., Oc. (tō-kĕ-lä'ō)	2	8°00'S	176°00'W
Tokmak, Kyrg. (tôk'mȧk)	169	42°44'N	75°41'E
Tokmak, Ukr.	163	47°17'N	35°48'E

PLACE (Pronunciation)	PAGE	LAT.	LONG.
Tokorozawa, Japan (tô'kô-rô-zä'wä)	195a	35°47'N	139°29'E
Toksu Palace, bldg., S. Kor.	241b	37°35'N	126°58'E
Tokuno, i., Japan (tô-ko͞o'nō)	189	27°42'N	129°25'E
Tokushima, Japan (tō'kô'shē-mä)	189	34°06'N	134°31'E
Tokuyama, Japan (tō'kô'yä-mä)	195	34°04'N	131°49'E
Tōkyō, Japan	189	35°42'N	139°46'E
Tōkyō-Wan, b., Japan (tō'kyō wän)	195	35°56'N	139°56'E
Tolcayuca, Mex. (tôl-kä-yo͞o'kä)	118	19°55'N	98°54'W
Toledo, Spain (tô-lĕ'dô)	148	39°53'N	4°02'W
Toledo, Ia., U.S. (tō-lē'dō)	103	41°59'N	92°35'W
Toledo, Oh., U.S.	97	41°40'N	83°35'W
Toledo, Or., U.S.	104	44°37'N	123°58'W
Toledo, Montes de, mts., Spain (mô'n-tĕs-dĕ-tô-lĕ'dô)	158	39°33'N	4°40'W
Toledo Bend Reservoir, res., U.S.	97	31°30'N	93°30'W
Toliara, Madag.	213	23°16'S	43°44'E
Tolima, dept., Col. (tô-lē'mä)	130a	4°07'N	75°20'W
Tolima, Nevado del, mtn., Col. (nĕ-vä-dô-dĕl-tô-lē'mä)	130a	4°40'N	75°20'W
Tolimán, Mex. (tô-lė-män')	118	20°54'N	99°54'W
Tollesbury, Eng., U.K. (tōl'z-bĕrĭ)	144b	51°46'N	0°49'E
Tollygunge, neigh., India	240a	22°30'N	88°21'E
Tolmezzo, Italy (tôl-mĕt'zô)	160	46°25'N	13°03'E
Tolmin, Slvn. (tôl'mĕn)	160	46°12'N	13°45'E
Tolna, Hung. (tôl'nô)	155	46°25'N	18°47'E
Tolo, Teluk, b., Indon. (tō'lō)	196	2°00'S	122°06'E
Tolosa, Spain (tô-lō'sä)	148	43°10'N	2°05'W
Tolt, r., Wa., U.S. (tōlt)	106a	47°13'N	121°49'W
Toluca, Mex. (tô-lo͞o'kȧ)	116	19°17'N	99°40'W
Toluca, Il., U.S. (tô-lo͞o'kȧ)	98	41°00'N	89°10'W
Toluca, Nevado de, mtn., Mex. (nĕ-vä-dô-dĕ-tô-lo͞o'kä)	116	19°09'N	99°42'W
Tolworth, neigh., Eng., U.K.	235	51°23'N	0°17'W
Tolyatti, Russia	166	53°30'N	49°10'E
Tom', r., Russia	170	55°33'N	85°00'E
Tomah, Wi., U.S. (tō'mȧ)	103	43°58'N	90°31'W
Tomahawk, Wi., U.S. (tŏm'ȧ-hôk)	103	45°27'N	89°44'W
Tomakivka, Ukr.	163	47°49'N	34°43'E
Tomanivi, mtn., Fiji	198g	17°37'S	178°01'E
Tomar, Port. (tō-mär')	158	39°36'N	8°26'W
Tomashevka, Bela. (tô-mȧ'shĕf-kȧ)	155	51°34'N	23°37'E
Tomaszów Lubelski, Pol. (tô-mä'shôf lo͞o-bĕl'skĭ)	155	50°20'N	23°27'E
Tomaszów Mazowiecki, Pol. (tô-mä'shôf mä-zô'vyĕt-skĭ)	155	51°33'N	20°00'E
Tomatlán, Mex. (tô-mä-tlä'n)	118	19°54'N	105°14'W
Tombadonkéa, Gui.	214	11°00'N	14°23'W
Tombador, Serra do, mts., Braz. (sĕr'rȧ dô tōm-bä-dôr')	131	11°31'S	57°33'W
Tombigbee, r., U.S. (tŏm-bĭg'bė)	97	33°00'N	88°30'W
Tombos, Braz. (tô'm-bōs)	129a	20°53'S	42°00'W
Tombouctou, Mali	210	16°46'N	3°01'W
Tombs of the Caliphs, pt. of i., Egypt	244a	30°03'N	31°17'E
Tombstone, Az., U.S. (to͞om'stōn)	109	31°40'N	110°00'W
Tombua, Ang. (ȧ-lĕ-zhän'drĕ)	212	15°49'S	11°53'E
Tomelilla, Swe. (tô'mĕ-lēl-lä)	152	55°34'N	13°55'E
Tomelloso, Spain (tō-mål-lyō'sō)	158	39°09'N	3°02'W
Tommot, Russia (tŏm-mŏt')	165	59°13'N	126°22'E
Tomsk, Russia (tŏmsk)	164	56°29'N	84°57'E
Tonala, Mex.	118	20°38'N	103°14'W
Tonalá, r., Mex.	119	18°05'N	94°08'W
Tonawanda, N.Y., U.S. (tŏn-ȧ-wŏn'dȧ)	101c	43°01'N	78°53'W
Tonawanda, Town of, N.Y., U.S.	230a	42°59'N	78°52'W
Tonawanda Creek, r., N.Y., U.S.	101c	43°05'N	78°43'W
Tonbridge, Eng., U.K. (tŭn-brij)	144b	51°11'N	0°17'E
Tonda, Japan (tôn'dä)	195b	34°51'N	135°38'E
Tondabayashi, Japan (tôn-dä-bä'yä-shė)	195b	34°29'N	135°36'E
Tondano, Indon. (tôn-dä'nō)	197	1°15'N	124°50'E
Tønder, Den. (tûn'nĕr)	152	54°47'N	8°49'E
Tone-Gawa, r., Japan (tô'nĕ gä'wa)	195	36°12'N	139°19'E
Tonga, nation, Oc. (tŏŋ'gȧ)	224	18°50'S	175°20'W
Tong'an, China (tōŋ-än)	193	24°48'N	118°02'E
Tonga Trench, deep	224	23°00'S	172°30'W
Tongbei, China (tōŋ-bā)	189	48°00'N	126°48'E
Tongguan, China (tōŋ-gūän)	190	34°48'N	110°25'E
Tonghe, China (tōŋ-hŭ)	192	45°58'N	128°40'E
Tonghua, China (tōŋ-hwä)	189	41°43'N	125°50'E
Tongjiang, China (tōŋ-jyäŋ)	189	47°38'N	132°54'E
Tongliao, China (tōŋ-lĭou)	192	43°30'N	122°15'E
Tongo, Cam.	215	5°11'N	14°00'E
Tongoy, Chile (tōn-goi')	132	30°16'S	71°29'W
Tongren, China (tōŋ-rŭn)	188	27°45'N	109°12'E
Tongshan, China (tōŋ-shän)	190	34°27'N	116°27'E
Tongtian, r., China (tōŋ-tĭĕn)	188	33°00'N	97°00'E
Tongue, r., Mt., U.S. (tŭng)	105	45°08'N	106°40'W
Tongxian, China (tōŋ shyĕn)	190	39°55'N	116°40'E
Tonj, r., Sudan (tōnj)	211	6°18'N	28°33'E
Tonk, India (tŏŋk)	183	26°13'N	75°45'E
Tonkawa, Ok., U.S. (tŏŋ kȧ-wô)	111	36°42'N	97°19'W
Tonkin, Gulf of, b., Asia (tôn-kăn')	196	20°30'N	108°10'E
Tonle Sap, l., Camb. (tôn'lä säp')	196	13°03'N	102°49'E
Tonneins, Fr. (tô-näɴ')	156	44°24'N	0°18'E
Tönning, Ger. (tû'nēng)	154	54°20'N	8°55'E
Tonopah, Nv., U.S. (tō-nō-pä')	96	38°04'N	117°15'W
Tönsberg, Nor. (tûns'bĕrgh)	146	59°19'N	10°25'E
Tönsholt, Ger.	236	51°38'N	6°58'E
Tonto, r., Mex. (tôn'tō)	119	18°15'N	96°13'W
Tonto Creek, r., Az., U.S.	109	34°05'N	111°15'W
Tonto National Monument, rec., Az., U.S. (tôn'tô)	109	33°33'N	111°08'W
Tooele, Ut., U.S. (tö-ĕl ė)	107b	40°33'N	112°17'W
Toongabbie, Austl.	243a	33°47'S	150°57'E
Toot Hill, Eng., U.K.	235	51°42'N	0°12'E
Toowoomba, Austl. (tò wo͝om'bȧ)	203	27°32'S	152°10'E

PLACE (Pronunciation)	PAGE	LAT.	LONG.
Topanga, Ca., U.S. (tō'păn-gȧ)	107a	34°05'N	118°36'W
Topeka, Ks., U.S. (tô-pē'kȧ)	97	39°02'N	95°41'W
Topilejo, Mex. (tō-pē-lĕ'hô)	119a	19°12'N	99°09'W
Topkapi, neigh., Tur.	239f	41°02'N	28°54'E
Topkapi Müzesi, bldg., Tur.	239f	41°00'N	28°59'E
T'oplyj Stan, neigh., Russia	239b	55°37'N	37°30'E
Topock, Az., U.S.	109	34°40'N	114°20'W
Top of Hebers, Eng., U.K.	237b	53°34'N	2°12'W
Topol'čany, Slvk. (tô-pôl'chä-nü)	155	48°38'N	18°10'E
Topolobampo, Mex. (tō-pō-lô-bä'm-pô)	116	25°45'N	109°00'W
Topolovgrad, Bul.	161	42°05'N	26°19'E
Toppenish, Wa., U.S. (tôp'ĕn-ĭsh)	104	46°22'N	120°00'W
Toppings, Eng., U.K.	237b	53°37'N	2°25'W
Torbat-e Ḩeydarīyeh, Iran	185	35°16'N	59°13'E
Torbat-e Jām, Iran	185	35°14'N	60°36'E
Torbay, Can. (tôr-bā')	93	47°40'N	52°43'W
Torbay *see* Torquay, Eng., U.K.	150	50°30'N	3°26'W
Torbreck, Mount, mtn., Austl. (tōr-brĕk)	204	37°05'S	146°55'E
Torch, l., Mi., U.S. (tôrch)	98	45°00'N	85°30'W
Torcy, Fr.	237c	48°51'N	2°39'E
Tor di Quinto, neigh., Italy	239c	41°56'N	12°28'E
Töreboda, Swe. (tû'rĕ-bō'dä)	152	58°44'N	14°04'E
Torhout, Bel.	151	51°01'N	3°04'E
Toribío, Col. (tô-rē-bė'ō)	130a	2°58'N	76°14'W
Toride, Japan (tô'rē-dā)	195a	35°54'N	104°04'E
Torino *see* Turin, Italy	142	45°05'N	7°44'E
Tormes, r., Spain (tōr'mās)	158	41°12'N	6°15'W
Torneälven, r., Eur.	142	67°00'N	22°30'E
Torneträsk, l., Swe. (tôr'nĕ trĕsk)	146	68°10'N	20°36'E
Torngat Mountains, mts., Can.	85	59°18'N	64°35'W
Tornio, Fin. (tôr'nĭ-ō)	142	65°55'N	24°09'E
Toro, Lac, l., Can.	91	46°53'N	73°46'W
Toronto, Can. (tô-rŏn'tō)	85	43°40'N	79°23'W
Toronto, Oh., U.S.	98	40°30'N	80°35'W
Toronto, res., Mex.	112	27°35'N	105°37'W
Toropets, Russia (tô'rô-pyĕts)	166	56°31'N	31°37'E
Toros Dağlari, Tur. (tô'rŭs)	182	37°00'N	32°40'E
Torote, r., Spain (tô-rō'tä)	159a	40°36'N	3°24'W
Tor Pignatara, neigh., Italy	239c	41°52'N	12°32'E
Torquay, Eng., U.K. (tôr-kē')	150	50°30'N	3°26'W
Torra, Cerro, mtn., Col. (sĕ'r-rô-tō'r-rä)	130a	4°41'N	76°22'W
Torrance, Ca., U.S. (tŏr'rănc)	107a	33°50'N	118°20'W
Torre Annunziata, Italy (tôr'rä ä-no͞on-tsė-ä'tä)	159c	40°31'N	14°27'E
Torreblanca, Spain	159	40°18'N	0°12'E
Torre del Greco, Italy (tôr'rȧ dĕl grā'kō)	160	40°32'N	14°23'E
Torrejoncillo, Spain (tôr'rā-hōn-thē'lyō)	158	39°54'N	6°26'W
Torrelavega, Spain (tôr-rā'lä-vä'gä)	158	43°22'N	4°02'W
Torrellas de Llobregat, Spain	238e	41°21'N	1°59'E
Torre Maggiore, Italy (tôr'rä mäd-jō'rä)	160	41°41'N	15°18'E
Torrens, Lake, l., Austl. (tŏr-ĕns)	202	30°07'S	137°40'E
Torrent, Spain	159	39°25'N	0°28'W
Torreón, Mex. (tôr-rā-ōn')	116	25°32'N	103°26'W
Torres Islands, is., Vanuatu (tôr'rĕs) (tŏr'ĕz)	203	13°18'N	165°59'E
Torres Martinez Indian Reservation, I.R., Ca., U.S. (tôr'ĕz mär-tē'nĕz)	108	33°33'N	116°21'W
Torres Novas, Port. (tôr'rĕzh nō'väzh)	158	39°28'N	8°37'W
Torres Strait, strt., Austl. (tôr'rĕs)	203	10°30'S	141°30'E
Torres Vedras, Port. (tôr'rĕsh vă'dräzh)	158	39°08'N	9°18'W
Torrevieja, Spain (tôr-rā-vyā'hä)	159	37°58'N	0°40'W
Torrijos, Phil. (tôr-rē'hōs)	197a	13°19'N	122°06'E
Torrington, Ct., U.S. (tŏr'ĭng-tŭn)	99	41°50'N	73°10'W
Torrington, Wy., U.S.	102	42°04'N	104°11'W
Torro, Spain (tô'r-rō)	158	41°27'N	5°23'W
Tor Sapienza, neigh., Italy	239c	41°54'N	12°35'E
Torsby, Swe. (tôrs'bü)	152	60°07'N	12°56'E
Torshälla, Swe. (tôrs'hĕl-ä)	152	59°26'N	16°21'E
Tórshavn, Far. Is. (tôrs-houn')	142	62°00'N	6°55'W
Tortola, i., Br. Vir. Is. (tôr-tō'lä)	117b	18°34'N	64°40'W
Tortona, Italy (tôr-tō'nä)	160	44°52'N	8°52'W
Tortosa, Spain (tôr-tō'sä)	142	40°59'N	0°33'E
Tortosa, Cap de, c., Spain	159	40°42'N	0°55'E
Tortue, Canal de la, strt., Haiti (tôr-tü')	123	20°05'N	73°20'W
Tortue, Île de la, i., Haiti	123	20°10'N	73°00'W
Tortue, Rivière de la, r., Can. (lä tōr-tü')	83a	45°12'N	73°32'W
Tortuguitas, Arg.	233d	34°28'S	58°45'W
Toruń, Pol.	142	53°02'N	18°35'E
Tõrva, Est. (t'r'vȧ)	153	58°02'N	25°56'E
Torzhok, Russia (tôr'zhôk)	166	57°03'N	34°53'E
Toscana, hist. reg., Italy (tôs-kä'nä)	160	43°23'N	11°08'E
Toshima, neigh., Japan	242a	35°44'N	139°43'E
Tosna, r., Russia	172c	59°28'N	30°53'E
Tosno, Russia (tôs'nō)	162	59°32'N	30°52'E
Tostado, Arg. (tôs-tä'dô)	132	29°10'S	61°43'W
Tosya, Tur. (tôz'yȧ)	149	41°00'N	34°00'E
Totana, Spain (tô-tä-nä)	158	37°45'N	1°28'W
Tot'ma, Russia (tôt'mȧ)	166	60°00'N	42°20'E
Totness, Sur.	131	5°51'N	56°17'W
Totonicapán, Guat. (tôtō-nē-kä'pän)	116	14°55'N	91°20'W
Totoras, Arg. (tô-tô'räs)	129c	32°33'S	61°13'W
Totowa, N.J., U.S.	228	40°54'N	74°13'W
Totsuka, Japan (tôt'so͞o-kä)	195a	35°24'N	139°32'E
Tottenham, Eng., U.K. (tŏt'ĕn-ȧm)	144b	51°35'N	0°06'W
Tottenville, neigh., N.Y., U.S.	228	40°31'N	74°15'W
Totteridge, neigh., Eng., U.K.	235	51°38'N	0°12'W
Tottington, Eng., U.K.	237b	53°37'N	2°20'W

358 Tottori–Tulaghi

PLACE (Pronunciation)	PAGE	LAT.	LONG.
Tottori, Japan (tŏt'tô-rē)	189	35°30'N	134°15'E
Touba, C. Iv.	214	8°17'N	7°41'W
Touba, Sen.	214	14°51'N	15°53'W
Toubkal, Jebel, mtn., Mor.	210	31°15'N	7°46'W
Tougan, Burkina	214	13°04'N	3°04'W
Touggourt, Alg. (tŏ-go͞ort') (to͞o-go͞or')	210	33°09'N	6°07'E
Touil, Oued, r., Alg. (to͞o-ēl')	148	34°42'N	2°16'E
Toul, Fr. (to͞ol)	147	48°39'N	5°51'E
Toulon, Fr. (to͞o-lôn')	142	43°09'N	5°54'E
Toulouse, Fr. (to͞o-lo͞oz')	142	43°37'N	1°27'E
Toungoo, Myanmar (tŏ-ŏŋ-go͞o')	196	19°00'N	96°29'E
Tourcoing, Fr. (tŏr-kwăn')	147	50°44'N	3°06'E
Tournan-en-Brie, Fr. (to͞or-nän-ĕn-brē')	157b	48°45'N	2°47'E
Tours, Fr. (to͞or)	142	47°23'N	0°39'E
Touside, Pic, mtn., Chad (to͞o-sē-dā')	211	21°10'N	16°30'E
Toussus-le-Noble, Fr.	237c	48°45'N	2°07'E
Tovdalselva, r., Nor. (tôv-däls-ĕlvå)	152	58°23'N	8°16'E
Towaco, N.J., U.S.	228	40°56'N	74°21'W
Towanda, Pa., U.S. (tô-wän'dȧ)	99	41°45'N	76°30'W
Tower Hamlets, neigh., Eng., U.K.	235	51°32'N	0°03'W
Tower of London, pt. of i., Eng., U.K.	235	51°30'N	0°05'W
Towers of Silence, rel., India	240e	18°58'N	72°48'E
Town Bluff Lake, l., Tx., U.S.	113	30°52'N	94°30'W
Towner, N.D., U.S. (tou'nẽr)	102	48°21'N	100°24'W
Town Reach, strt., Asia	240c	1°28'N	103°44'E
Townsend, Ma., U.S. (toun'zĕnd)	93a	42°41'N	71°42'W
Townsend, Mt., U.S.	105	46°19'N	111°35'W
Townsend, Mount, mtn., Wa., U.S.	106a	47°52'N	123°03'W
Townsville, Austl. (tounz'vĭl)	203	19°18'S	146°50'E
Towson, Md., U.S. (tou'sŭn)	100e	39°24'N	76°36'W
Towuti, Danau, l., Indon. (tô-wo͞o'tē)	196	3°00'S	121°45'E
Toxkan, r., China	188	40°34'N	77°15'E
Toyah, Tx., U.S. (tô'yȧ)	112	31°19'N	103°46'W
Toyama, Japan (tō'yä-mä)	189	36°42'N	137°14'E
Toyama-Wan, b., Japan	195	36°58'N	137°16'E
Toyoda, Japan	242a	35°39'N	139°23'E
Toyohashi, Japan (tō'yō-hä'shē)	194	34°44'N	137°21'E
Toyonaka, Japan (tō'yō-nä'kȧ)	195b	34°47'N	135°28'E
Tozeur, Tun. (tō-zûr')	148	33°59'N	8°11'E
Traar, neigh., Ger.	236	51°23'N	6°36'E
Trabzon, Tur. (tràb'zôn)	182	41°00'N	39°45'E
Tracy, Can.	91	46°00'N	73°13'W
Tracy, Ca., U.S. (trā'sē)	108	37°45'N	121°27'W
Tracy, Mn., U.S.	102	44°13'N	95°37'W
Tracy City, Tn., U.S.	114	35°15'N	85°44'W
Trafalgar, Cabo, c., Spain (kå'bô-trä-fäl-gä'r)	158	36°10'N	6°02'W
Trafaria, Port.	238d	38°40'N	9°14'W
Trafford Park, Eng., U.K.	237b	53°28'N	2°20'W
Trafonomby, mtn., Madag.	213	24°32'S	46°35'E
Trail, Can. (trāl)	84	49°06'N	117°42'W
Traisen, r., Aus.	145e	48°15'N	15°55'E
Traiskirchen, Aus.	145e	48°01'N	16°18'E
Trakai, Lith. (trá-kāy)	153	54°38'N	24°59'E
Trakiszki, Pol. (trá-kē'-sh-kē)	155	54°16'N	23°07'E
Tralee, Ire. (trȧ-lē')	147	52°16'N	9°20'W
Tranås, Swe. (trän'ôs)	152	58°03'N	14°56'E
Trancoso, Port. (träŋ-kō'sŏ)	158	40°46'N	7°23'W
Trangan, Pulau, i., Indon. (träŋ'gän)	197	6°52'S	133°30'E
Trani, Italy (trä'nē)	160	41°15'N	16°25'E
Tranmere, Eng., U.K.	237a	53°23'N	3°01'W
Transylvania, hist. reg., Rom. (trăn-sĭl-vā'nĭ-ȧ)	155	46°30'N	22°35'E
Trapani, Italy	148	38°01'N	12°31'E
Trappes, Fr. (tràp)	157b	48°47'N	2°01'E
Traralgon, Austl. (trä'răl-gŏn)	204	38°15'S	146°33'E
Trarza, reg., Maur.	214	17°35'N	15°15'W
Trasimeno, Lago, l., Italy (lä'gō trä-sē-mā'nō)	160	43°00'N	12°12'E
Trás-os-Montes, hist. reg., Port. (träzh'ōzh mōn'tāzh)	148	41°33'N	7°13'W
Traun, r., Aus. (troun)	154	48°10'N	14°15'E
Traunstein, Ger. (troun'stīn)	154	47°52'N	12°38'E
Traverse, Lake, l., Mn., U.S. (trăv'ẽrs)	102	45°46'N	96°53'W
Traverse City, Mi., U.S.	98	44°45'N	85°40'W
Travnik, Bos. (träv'nēk)	161	44°13'N	17°43'E
Treasure Island, i., Ca., U.S. (trĕzh'ẽr)	106b	37°49'N	122°22'W
Trebbin, Ger. (trĕ'bēn)	145b	52°13'N	13°13'E
Trebinje, Bos. (trå'bēn-yĕ)	161	42°43'N	18°21'E
Trebišov, Slvk. (trĕ'bē-shôf)	155	48°36'N	21°32'E
Tregrosse Islands, is., Austl. (trē-grōs')	203	18°08'S	150°53'E
Treinta y Tres, Ur. (trå-ēn'tä ē träs')	132	33°14'S	54°17'W
Trelew, Arg. (trē'lū)	132	43°15'S	65°25'W
Trelleborg, Swe.	152	55°24'N	13°07'E
Tremblay-lès-Gonnesse, Fr.	237c	48°59'N	2°34'E
Tremiti, Isole, is., Italy (ē'sō-lĕ trä-mē'tē)	160	42°07'N	16°33'E
Tremont, neigh., N.Y., U.S.	228	40°51'N	73°55'W
Trenčín, Czech Rep. (trĕn'chēn)	147	48°52'N	18°02'E
Trenque Lauquén, Arg. (trĕn'kĕ-lá'ō-kĕ'n)	132	35°50'S	62°44'W
Trent, r., Can. (trĕnt)	91	44°15'N	77°55'W
Trent, r., Eng., U.K.	144a	53°25'N	0°45'W
Trent and Mersey Canal, can., Eng., U.K. (trĕnt) (mûr zē)	144a	53°11'N	2°24'W
Trentino-Alto Adige, hist. reg., Italy	160	46°16'N	10°47'E
Trento, Italy (trĕn'tô)	148	46°04'N	11°07'E
Trenton, Can. (trĕn'tŭn)	85	44°05'N	77°35'W
Trenton, Can.	93	45°37'N	62°38'W
Trenton, Mi., U.S.	101b	42°08'N	83°12'W
Trenton, Mo., U.S.	111	40°05'N	93°36'W
Trenton, N.J., U.S.	97	40°13'N	74°46'W
Trenton, Tn., U.S.	114	35°57'N	88°55'W
Trepassey, Can. (trē-păs'ē)	93	46°44'N	53°22'W
Trepassey Bay, b., Can.	93	46°40'N	53°20'W
Treptow, neigh., Ger.	238a	52°29'N	13°29'E
Tres Arroyos, Arg. (trās'är-rō'yōs)	132	38°18'S	60°16'W
Três Corações, Braz. (trĕ's kō-rä-zō'ĕs)	129a	21°41'S	45°14'W
Tres Cumbres, Mex. (trĕ's ko͞o'm-brĕs)	119a	19°03'N	99°14'W
Três Lagoas, Braz. (trĕ's lä-gô'ás)	131	20°48'S	51°42'W
Tres Marias, Reprêsa, res., Braz.	131	18°15'S	45°30'W
Tres Morros, Alto de, mtn., Col. (á'l-tō dĕ trĕ's mô'r-rôs)	130a	7°08'N	76°10'W
Três Pontas, Braz. (trĕ'pô'n-täs)	129a	21°22'S	45°30'W
Três Pontas, Cabo das, c., Ang.	216	10°23'S	13°32'E
Três Rios, Braz. (trĕ's rē'ōs)	129a	22°07'S	43°13'W
Très-Saint Rédempteur, Can. (săn rā-dänp-tûr')	83a	45°26'N	74°23'W
Tressancourt, Fr.	237c	48°55'N	2°00'E
Treuenbrietzen, Ger. (troi'ĕn-brē-tzĕn)	145b	52°06'N	12°52'E
Treviglio, Italy (trā-vē'lyô)	160	45°30'N	9°34'E
Treviso, Italy (trĕ-vē'sō)	148	45°39'N	12°15'E
Trichardt, S. Afr. (trĭ-kärt')	218d	26°32'N	29°16'E
Triel-sur-Seine, Fr.	237c	48°59'N	2°00'E
Trier, Ger.	147	49°45'N	6°38'E
Trieste, Italy (trē-ĕs'tā)	142	45°39'N	13°48'E
Triglav, mtn., Slvn.	160	46°23'N	13°50'E
Trigueros, Spain (trē-gā'rōs)	158	37°23'N	6°50'W
Trikala, Grc.	149	39°33'N	21°49'E
Trikora, Puncak, mtn., Indon.	197	4°15'S	138°45'E
Trim Creek, r., Il., U.S. (trĭm)	101a	41°19'N	87°39'W
Trincomalee, Sri L. (trĭŋ-kô-mȧ-lē')	183b	8°39'N	81°12'E
Tring, Eng., U.K. (trĭng)	144b	51°46'N	0°40'W
Trinidad, Bol. (trē-nē-dhädh')	130	14°48'S	64°43'W
Trinidad, Cuba (trē-nē-dhädh')	117	21°50'N	80°00'W
Trinidad, Co., U.S. (trĭn'ĭdăd)	96	37°11'N	104°31'W
Trinidad, Ur.	132	33°29'S	56°55'W
Trinidad, i., Trin. (trĭn'ĭ-dăd)	131	10°00'N	61°00'W
Trinidad, r., Pan.	116a	8°55'N	80°01'W
Trinidad, Sierra de, mts., Cuba (sē-ĕ'r-rä dĕ trē-nē-dä'd)	122	21°50'N	79°55'W
Trinidad and Tobago, nation, N.A. (trĭn'ĭ-dăd) (tô-bā'gō)	117	11°00'N	61°00'W
Trinitaria, Mex. (trē-nē-tä'ryä)	119	16°09'N	92°04'W
Trinity, Can. (trĭn'ĭ-tē)	93	48°59'N	53°55'W
Trinity, Tx., U.S.	113	30°52'N	95°27'W
Trinity, is., Ak., U.S.	95	56°25'N	153°15'W
Trinity, r., Ca., U.S.	104	40°50'N	123°20'W
Trinity, r., Tx., U.S.	97	30°50'N	95°09'W
Trinity, East Fork, r., Tx., U.S.	111	33°24'N	96°42'W
Trinity, West Fork, r., Tx., U.S.	110	33°22'N	98°26'W
Trinity Bay, b., Can.	85	48°00'N	53°40'W
Trino, Italy (trē'nô)	160	45°11'N	8°16'E
Trion, Ga., U.S. (trī'ŏn)	114	34°32'N	85°18'W
Tripoli (Tarābulus), Libya	211	32°50'N	13°13'E
Tripolis, Grc. (trĭ'pô-lĭs)	149	37°32'N	22°32'E
Tripolitania *see* Tarābulus, hist. reg., Libya	210	31°00'N	12°26'E
Tripura, state, India	183	24°00'N	92°00'E
Tristan da Cunha Islands, is., St. Hel. (três-tän'dä ko͞on'yȧ)	2	35°30'S	12°15'W
Triste, Golfo, b., Ven. (gôl-fô trē's-tĕ)	131b	10°40'N	68°05'W
Triticus Reservoir, res., N.Y., U.S. (trī tĭ-cŭs)	100a	41°20'N	73°36'W
Trivandrum, India (trē-vŭn'drŭm)	183b	8°34'N	76°58'E
Trnava, Slvk. (t'r'nȧ-vȧ)	155	48°22'N	17°34'E
Trobriand Islands, is., Pap. N. Gui. (trō-brē-ănd')	197	8°25'S	151°45'E
Trogir, Cro. (trō'gēr)	160	43°32'N	16°17'E
Troice-Lykovo, neigh., Russia	239b	55°47'N	37°24'E
Trois Fourches, Cap des, c., Mor.	158	35°28'N	2°58'W
Trois-Rivières, Can. (trwä'rē-vyâ')	85	46°21'N	72°35'W
Troitsk, Russia (trô'ĭtsk)	170	54°06'N	61°35'E
Troits'ke, Ukr.	163	47°39'N	30°16'E
Troitsko-Pechorsk, Russia (trô'ĭtsk-ô-pyĕ-chôrsk')	164	62°18'N	56°07'E
Trollhättan, Swe. (trôl'hĕt-ĕn)	146	58°17'N	12°17'E
Trollheimen, mts., Nor. (trôll-hĕĭm)	152	62°48'N	9°05'E
Trombay, neigh., India	240e	19°02'N	72°57'E
Trona, Ca., U.S. (trō'nȧ)	108	35°49'N	117°20'W
Tronador, Cerro, mtn., S.A. (sĕ'r-rô trō-nä'dôr)	132	41°17'S	71°56'W
Troncoso, Mex. (trôn-kô'sŏ)	118	22°43'N	102°22'W
Trondheim, Nor. (trôn'hâm)	142	63°25'N	11°35'E
Tropar'ovo, neigh., Russia	239b	55°39'N	37°29'E
Trosa, Swe. (trô'sä)	152	58°54'N	17°25'E
Trottiscliffe, Eng., U.K.	235	51°19'N	0°21'E
Trout, l., Can.	84	61°10'N	121°30'W
Trout, l., Can.	85	51°16'N	92°46'W
Trout Creek, r., Or., U.S.	104	42°18'N	118°31'W
Troutdale, Or., U.S. (trout'dāl)	106c	45°32'N	122°23'W
Trout Lake, Mi., U.S.	103	46°20'N	85°02'W
Trouville, Fr. (tro͞o-vēl')	156	49°23'N	0°05'E
Troy, Al., U.S. (troi)	114	31°47'N	85°46'W
Troy, Il., U.S.	107e	38°44'N	89°53'W
Troy, Ks., U.S.	111	39°46'N	95°07'W
Troy, Mo., U.S.	110	38°56'N	99°57'W
Troy, Mt., U.S.	104	48°28'N	115°56'W
Troy, N.Y., U.S.	97	42°45'N	73°45'W
Troy, N.C., U.S.	115	35°21'N	79°58'W
Troy, Oh., U.S.	98	40°00'N	84°10'W
Troy, hist., Tur.	182	39°59'N	26°14'E
Troyes, Fr. (trwä)	147	48°18'N	4°03'E
Trstenik, Yugo. (t'r'stĕ-nēk)	149	43°36'N	21°00'E
Trubchëvsk, Russia (trŏp'chĕfsk)	167	52°36'N	33°46'E
Trucial States *see* United Arab Emirates, nation, Asia	182	24°00'N	54°00'E
Truckee, Ca., U.S. (trŭk'ē)	108	39°20'N	120°12'W
Truckee, r., Ca., U.S.	108	39°25'N	120°07'W
Truganina, Austl.	201a	37°49'S	144°44'E
Trujillo, Col. (tro͞o-kē'l-yō)	130a	4°10'N	76°20'W
Trujillo, Peru	130	8°08'S	79°00'W
Trujillo, Spain (tro͞o-kē'l-yô)	148	39°27'N	5°50'W
Trujillo, Ven.	130	9°15'N	70°28'W
Trujillo, r., Mex.	118	23°12'N	103°10'W
Trujin, Lago, l., Dom. Rep. (tro͞o-kĕn')	123	17°45'N	71°25'W
Truk Islands, is., Micron.	198c	7°25'N	151°47'E
Trumann, Ar., U.S. (tro͞o'măn)	111	35°41'N	90°31'W
Trŭn, Bul. (trŭn)	161	42°49'N	22°39'E
Truro, Can. (tro͞o'rō)	85	45°22'N	63°16'W
Truro, Eng., U.K.	150	50°17'N	5°05'W
Trussville, Al., U.S. (trŭs'vĭl)	100h	33°37'N	86°37'W
Truth or Consequences, N.M., U.S. (tro͞oth ŏr kŏn'sē-kwĕn-sĭs)	109	33°10'N	107°20'W
Trutnov, Czech Rep. (trŏt'nôf)	154	50°36'N	15°36'E
Trzcianka, Pol. (tchyän'kȧ)	154	53°02'N	16°27'E
Trzebiatów, Pol. (tchĕ-byä'tŏ-v)	154	54°03'N	15°16'E
Tsaidam Basin, basin, China (tsī-däm)	188	37°19'N	94°08'E
Tsala Apopka Lake, r., Fl., U.S. (tsă'lȧ ă-pŏp'kȧ)	115	28°57'N	82°11'W
Tsast Bogd, mtn., Mong.	188	46°44'N	92°34'E
Tsavo National Park, rec., Kenya	217	2°35'S	38°45'E
Tsawwassen Indian Reserve, I.R., Can.	106d	49°03'N	123°11'W
Tsentral'nyy-Kospashskiy, Russia (tsĕn-träl'nyĭ-kôs-pash'skĭ)	172a	59°03'N	57°48'E
Tshela, D.R.C. (tshā'lȧ)	212	4°59'S	12°56'E
Tshikapa, D.R.C. (tshē-kä'pä)	212	6°25'S	20°48'E
Tshofa, D.R.C.	217	5°14'S	25°15'E
Tshuapa, r., D.R.C.	212	0°30'S	22°00'E
Tsiafajovona, mtn., Madag.	213	19°17'S	47°27'E
Tsing Island, i., H.K.	241c	22°21'N	114°05'E
Tsin Shui Wan, b., H.K.	241c	22°13'N	114°10'E
Tsiribihina, r., Madag. (tsē'rē-bē-hē-nä')	213	19°45'S	43°30'E
Tsitsa, r., S. Afr. (tsē'tsȧ)	213c	31°28'S	28°53'E
Tskhinvali, Geor.	168	42°13'N	43°56'E
Tsolo, S. Afr. (tsō'lō)	213c	31°19'S	28°47'E
Tsomo, S. Afr.	213c	32°03'S	27°49'E
Tsomo, r., S. Afr.	213c	31°53'S	27°48'E
Tsu, Japan (tso͞o)	194	34°42'N	136°31'E
Tsuchiura, Japan (tso͞o'chē-o͞o-rä)	195	36°04'N	140°09'E
Tsuda, Japan (tso͞o'dä)	195b	34°48'N	135°43'E
Tsugaru Kaikyō, strt., Japan	189	41°25'N	140°20'E
Tsukumono, neigh., Japan	242b	34°50'N	135°11'E
Tsumeb, Nmb. (tso͞o'mĕb)	212	19°10'S	17°45'E
Tsunashima, Japan (tso͞o'nä-shē'mä)	195a	35°32'N	139°37'E
Tsuruga, Japan (tso͞o'rō-gä)	194	35°39'N	136°04'E
Tsurugi San, mtn., Japan (tso͞o'rō-gē sän)	194	33°52'N	134°07'E
Tsurumi, r., Japan	242a	35°29'N	139°41'E
Tsuruoka, Japan (tso͞o'rō-ō'kä)	194	38°43'N	139°51'E
Tsurusaki, Japan (tso͞o'rō-sä'kē)	195	33°15'N	131°42'E
Tsu Shima, is., Japan (tso͞o shē'mä)	189	34°28'N	129°30'E
Tsushima Strait, strt., Asia	189	34°00'N	129°00'E
Tsu Wan (Quanwan), H.K.	241c	22°22'N	114°07'E
Tsuwano, Japan (tso͞o'wȧ-nō')	195	34°28'N	131°47'E
Tsuyama, Japan (tso͞o'yä-mä')	194	35°05'N	134°00'E
Tua, r., Port. (to͞o'ä)	158	41°23'N	7°18'W
Tualatin, r., Or., U.S. (to͞o'á-lȧ-tĭn)	106c	45°25'N	122°54'W
Tuamoto, Îles, Fr. Poly. (to͞o-ä-mō'to͞o)	225	19°00'S	141°20'W
Tuapse, Russia (tŏ'áp-sē)	167	44°00'N	39°10'E
Tuareg, hist. reg., Alg.	210	21°26'N	2°51'E
Tubarão, Braz. (to͞o-bä-roun')	132	28°23'N	48°56'W
Tübingen, Ger. (tü'bĭng-ĕn)	154	48°33'N	9°05'E
Tubinskiy, Russia (tû bĭn'skĭ)	172a	52°53'N	58°15'E
Tubruq, Libya	211	32°03'N	24°04'E
Tucacas, Ven. (to͞o-kä'käs)	130	10°48'N	68°20'W
Tuckahoe, N.Y., U.S.	228	40°57'N	73°50'W
Tucker, Ga., U.S. (tŭk'ẽr)	100c	33°51'N	84°13'W
Tucson, Az., U.S. (to͞o-sŏn')	96	32°15'N	111°00'W
Tucumán, Arg. (to͞o-ko͞o-män')	132	26°52'S	65°08'W
Tucumán, prov., Arg.	132	26°30'S	65°30'W
Tucumcari, N.M., U.S. (to͞o'kŭm-kâr-ē)	110	35°11'N	103°43'W
Tucupita, Ven. (to͞o-ko͞o-pē'tä)	130	9°00'N	62°09'W
Tudela, Spain (to͞o-dhā'lä)	148	42°03'N	1°37'W
Tugaloo, r., Ga., U.S. (tŭg'ȧ-lo͞o)	114	34°35'N	83°05'W
Tugela, r., S. Afr. (to͞o-gel'ȧ)	213c	28°50'S	30°52'E
Tugela Ferry, S. Afr.	213c	28°44'S	30°27'E
Tug Fork, r., U.S. (tŭg)	98	37°50'N	82°30'W
Tuguegarao, Phil. (to͞o-gā-gȧ-rä'ō)	196	17°37'N	121°44'E
Tuhai, r., China (to͞o-hī)	190	37°05'N	116°56'E
Tui, Slvn.	158	42°03'N	8°38'W
Tuinplaas, S. Afr.	218d	24°54'S	28°46'E
Tujunga, Ca., U.S. (to͞o-jŭŋ'gȧ)	107a	34°15'N	118°16'W
Tukan, Russia (to͞o'kȧn)	172a	53°52'N	57°25'E
Tukangbesi, Kepulauan, is., Indon.	197	6°00'S	124°15'E
Tūkrah, Libya	211	32°34'N	20°47'E
Tuktoyaktuk, Can.	84	69°32'N	132°37'W
Tuktut Nogait National Park, rec., Can.	84	69°00'N	122°00'W
Tukums, Lat. (to͞o'koms)	166	56°57'N	23°09'E
Tukuyu, Tan. (to͞o-ko͞o'yȧ)	212	9°13'S	33°43'E
Tukwila, Wa., U.S. (tŭk'wĭ-lȧ)	106a	47°28'N	122°16'W
Tula, Mex. (to͞o'lä)	118	20°04'N	99°22'W
Tula, Russia (to͞o'lä)	166	54°12'N	37°37'E
Tula, prov., Russia	162	53°45'N	37°19'E
Tula, r., Mex. (to͞o'lä)	118	20°40'N	99°27'W
Tulagai, i., Sol. Is. (to͞o-lä'gē)	203	9°15'S	160°17'E
Tulaghi, Sol. Is.	198e	9°06'S	160°09'E

ăt; finȧl; rāte; senåte; ärm; ásk; sofȧ; fâre; ch-choose; dh-as th in other; bē; ēvent; bĕt; recĕnt; cratẽr; g-gō; gh-guttural g; bĭt; ĭ-short neutral; rīde; ĸ-guttural k as ch in German ich;

PRONOUNCING INDEX

Tulalip – Ulm 359

PLACE (Pronunciation)	PAGE	LAT.	LONG.
Tulalip, Wa., U.S. (tū-lā'lĭp)	106a	48°04'N	122°18'W
Tulalip Indian Reservation, I.R., Wa., U.S.	106a	48°06'N	122°16'W
Tulancingo, Mex. (tōō-län-sĭŋ'gō)	116	20°04'N	98°24'W
Tulangbawang, r., Indon.	196	4°17'S	105°00'E
Tulare, Ca., U.S. (tōō-lä'rȧ) (tul-âr')	108	36°12'N	119°22'W
Tulare Lake Bed, l., Ca., U.S.	108	35°57'N	120°18'W
Tularosa, N.M., U.S. (tōō-lȧ-rō'zȧ)	109	33°05'N	106°05'W
Tulcán, Ec. (tōōl-kän')	130	0°44'N	77°52'W
Tulcea, Rom. (tōōl'chȧ)	149	45°10'N	28°47'E
Tul'chyn, Ukr.	167	48°42'N	28°53'E
Tulcingo, Mex. (tōōl-sĭŋ'gō)	118	18°03'N	98°27'W
Tule, r., Ca., U.S. (tōōl'lȧ)	108	36°08'N	118°50'W
Tule River Indian Reservation, I.R., Ca., U.S. (tōō'lȧ)	108	36°05'N	118°35'W
Tuli, Zimb. (tōō'lē)	212	20°58'S	29°12'E
Tulia, Tx., U.S. (tōō'lĭ-ȧ)	110	34°32'N	101°46'W
Tulik Volcano, vol., Ak., U.S. (tōō'lĭk)	95a	53°28'N	168°10'W
Tūlkarm, W. Bank (tōōl kärm)	181a	32°19'N	35°02'E
Tullahoma, Tn., U.S. (tŭl-ȧ-hō'mȧ)	114	35°21'N	86°12'W
Tullamarine, Austl.	243b	37°41'S	144°52'E
Tullamore, Ire. (tŭl-ȧ-mōr')	150	53°15'N	7°29'W
Tulle, Fr. (tül)	156	45°15'N	1°45'E
Tulln, Aus. (tōōln)	154	48°21'N	16°04'E
Tullner Feld, reg., Aus.	145e	48°20'N	15°59'E
Tulpetlac, Mex. (tōōl-pȧ-tlȧk')	119a	19°33'N	99°04'W
Tulsa, Ok., U.S. (tŭl'sȧ)	97	36°08'N	95°58'W
Tulum, Mex. (tōō-lōō'm)	120a	20°17'N	87°26'W
Tulun, Russia (tōō-lōōn')	165	54°29'N	100°43'E
Tuma, r., Nic. (tōō'mä)	120	13°07'N	85°32'W
Tumba, Lac, l., D.R.C. (tōōm'bä)	212	0°50'S	17°45'E
Tumbes, Peru (tōō'm-bĕs)	130	3°39'S	80°27'W
Tumbiscatío, Mex. (tōōm-bē-skä-tē'ō)	118	18°32'N	102°23'W
Tumbo, i., Can.	106d	48°49'N	123°04'W
Tumen, China (tōō-mŭn)	192	43°00'N	129°50'E
Tumen, r., Asia	194	42°08'N	128°40'E
Tumeremo, Ven. (tōō-mȧ-rā'mō)	131	7°15'N	61°28'W
Tumkūr, India	187	13°22'N	77°05'E
Tumuacacori National Monument, rec., Az., U.S. (tōō-mä-kä'kȧ-rē)	109	31°36'N	110°20'W
Tumuc-Humac Mountains, mts., S.A. (tōō-mōk'ōō-mäk')	131	2°15'N	54°50'W
Tunas de Zaza, Cuba (tōō'näs dā zä'zä)	122	21°40'N	79°35'W
Tunbridge Wells, Eng., U.K. (tŭn'brĭj welz')	151	51°05'N	0°09'E
Tunduru, Tan.	217	11°07'S	37°21'E
Tungabhadra Reservoir, res., India	187	15°26'N	75°57'E
Tuni, India	187	17°29'N	82°38'E
Tunica, Ms., U.S. (tū'nĭ-kȧ)	114	34°41'N	90°23'W
Tunis, Tun. (tū'nĭs)	210	36°59'N	10°06'E
Tunis, Golfe de, b., Tun.	148	37°06'N	10°43'E
Tunisia, nation, Afr. (tu-nĭzh'ē-ȧ)	210	35°00'N	10°11'E
Tunja, Col. (tōō'n-hä)	130	5°32'N	73°19'W
Tunkhannock, Pa., U.S. (tŭnk-hăn'ŭk)	99	41°35'N	75°55'W
Tunnel, r., Wa., U.S. (tŭn'ĕl)	106a	47°48'N	123°04'W
Tuoji Dao, i., China (twô-jyē dou)	190	38°11'N	120°45'E
Tuolumne, r., Ca., U.S. (twô-lŭm'nē)	108	37°35'N	120°37'W
Tuostakh, r., Russia	171	67°09'N	137°30'E
Tupelo, Ms., U.S. (tū'pĕ-lō)	114	34°14'N	88°43'W
Tupinambaranas, Ilha, i., Braz.	131	3°04'S	58°09'W
Tupiza, Bol. (tōō-pē'zä)	130	21°26'S	65°43'W
Tupper Lake, N.Y., U.S. (tŭp'ēr)	99	44°15'N	74°25'W
Tūpqaraghan tübek, pen., Kaz.	170	44°30'N	50°40'E
Tupungato, Cerro, vol., S.A.	132	33°30'S	69°52'W
Tuquerres, Col. (tōō-kĕ'r-rĕs)	130	1°12'N	77°44'W
Tura, Russia (tŏŏr'ȧ)	165	64°08'N	99°58'E
Turbio, r., Mex. (tōōr-byō)	118	20°28'N	101°40'W
Turbo, Col. (tōōr'bō)	130	8°02'N	76°43'W
Turda, Rom. (tŏŏr'dȧ)	155	46°35'N	23°47'E
Turfan Depression, depr., China	188	42°16'N	90°00'E
Turffontein, neigh., S. Afr.	213b	26°15'S	28°02'E
Tŭrgovishte, Bul.	161	43°14'N	26°36'E
Turgutlu, Tur.	167	38°30'N	27°20'E
Türi, Est. (tü'rĭ)	153	58°49'N	25°29'E
Turia, r., Spain (tōō'ryä)	158	40°12'N	1°18'W
Turicato, Mex. (tōō-rē-kä'tō)	118	19°03'N	101°24'W
Turiguano, i., Cuba (tōō-rē-gwä'nō)	122	22°20'N	78°35'W
Turin, Italy	142	45°05'N	7°44'E
Turiya, r., Ukr.	155	51°18'N	24°55'E
Turka, Ukr. (tŏŏr'kȧ)	155	49°10'N	23°02'E
Turkestan, hist. reg., Asia	164	43°27'N	62°14'E
Turkey, nation, Asia	143	38°45'N	32°00'E
Turkey, r., Ia., U.S. (tûrk'ē)	103	43°20'N	92°16'W
Türkistan, Kaz.	169	44°00'N	68°00'E
Turkmenbashy, Turk.	169	40°00'N	52°50'E
Turkmenistan, nation, Asia	164	40°46'N	56°01'E
Turks, is., T./C. Is. (tûrks)	117	21°40'N	71°45'W
Turks Island Passage, strt., T./C. Is.	123	21°15'N	71°25'W
Turku, Fin. (tòrgokò)	142	60°28'N	22°12'E
Turlock, Ca., U.S. (tûr'lŏk)	108	37°30'N	120°51'W
Turneffe, i., Belize	116	17°25'N	87°43'W
Turner, Ks., U.S. (tûr'nēr)	107f	39°05'N	94°42'W
Turner Sound, strt., Bah.	122	24°20'N	78°05'W
Turners Peninsula, pen., S.L.	214	7°20'N	12°40'W
Turnhout, Bel. (tŭrn-hout')	151	51°19'N	4°58'E
Turnov, Czech Rep. (tŏŏr'nôf)	154	50°36'N	15°12'E
Turnu Măgurele, Rom.	149	43°54'N	24°49'E
Turpan, China (tōō-är-pän)	188	43°06'N	88°41'E
Turquino, Pico, mtn., Cuba (pē'kō dä tōōr-kē'nō)	122	20°00'N	76°50'W
Turramurra, Austl.	243a	33°44'S	151°08'E
Turrialba, C.R. (tōōr-ryä'l-bä)	121	9°54'N	83°41'W
Turtkul', Uzb. (tŏŏrt-kōōl')	169	41°28'N	61°02'E
Turtle, r., Can.	89	49°20'N	92°30'W
Turtle Bay, b., Tx., U.S.	113a	29°48'N	94°38'W

PLACE (Pronunciation)	PAGE	LAT.	LONG.
Turtle Creek, Pa., U.S.	230b	40°25'N	79°49'W
Turtle Creek, r., S.D., U.S.	102	44°40'N	98°53'W
Turtle Mountain Indian Reservation, I.R., N.D., U.S.	102	48°45'N	99°57'W
Turtle Mountains, mts., N.D., U.S.	102	48°57'N	100°11'W
Turukhansk, Russia (tōō-rōō-känsk')	164	66°03'N	88°39'E
Tuscaloosa, Al., U.S. (tŭs-kȧ-lōō'sȧ)	97	33°10'N	87°35'W
Tuscarora, Nv., U.S. (tŭs-kȧ-rō'rȧ)	104	41°18'N	116°15'W
Tuscarora Indian Reservation, I.R., N.Y., U.S.	101c	43°10'N	78°51'W
Tuscola, Il., U.S. (tŭs-kō-lȧ)	98	39°50'N	88°20'W
Tuscumbia, Al., U.S. (tŭs-kŭm'bĭ-ȧ)	114	34°41'N	87°42'W
Tushino, Russia (tōō'shĭ-nô)	172b	55°51'N	37°24'E
Tuskegee, Al., U.S. (tŭs-kē'gē)	114	32°25'N	85°40'W
Tustin, Ca., U.S. (tŭs'tĭn)	107a	33°44'N	117°49'W
Tutayev, Russia (tōō-tȧ-yĕf')	166	57°53'N	39°34'E
Tutbury, Eng., U.K. (tŭt'bēr-ē)	144a	52°52'N	1°51'W
Tuticorin, India (tōō-tē-kō-rĭn')	183b	8°51'N	78°09'E
Tutitlan, Mex. (tōō-tē-tlä'n)	119a	19°38'N	99°10'W
Tutóia, Braz. (tōō-tō'yȧ)	131	2°42'S	42°21'W
Tutrakan, Bul.	149	44°02'N	26°36'E
Tuttle Creek Reservoir, res., Ks., U.S.	111	39°30'N	96°38'W
Tuttlingen, Ger. (tŏŏt'lĭng-ĕn)	154	47°58'N	8°50'E
Tutuila, i., Am. Sam.	198a	14°18'S	170°42'W
Tutwiler, Ms., U.S. (tŭt'wĭ-lēr)	114	34°01'N	90°25'W
Tuva, state, Russia	170	51°15'N	90°45'E
Tuvalu, nation, Oc.	3	5°20'S	174°00'E
Tuwayq, Jabal, mts., Sau. Ar.	182	20°45'N	46°30'E
Tuxedo, Md., U.S.	229d	38°55'N	76°55'W
Tuxedo Park, N.Y., U.S. (tŭk-sē'dō pärk)	100a	41°11'N	74°11'W
Tuxford, Eng., U.K. (tŭks'fērd)	144a	53°14'N	0°54'W
Túxpan, Mex.	116	20°57'N	97°26'W
Tuxpan, Mex. (tōōs'pän)	118	19°34'N	103°22'W
Túxpan, r., Mex. (tōōs'pän)	119	20°55'N	97°52'W
Túxpan, Arrecife, i., Mex. (är-rē-sē'fē-tōō'x-pä'n)	119	21°01'N	97°12'W
Tuxtepec, Mex. (tōōs-tȧ-pĕk')	119	18°06'N	96°09'W
Tuxtla Gutiérrez, Mex. (tōōs'tlä gōō-tyâr'rĕs)	116	16°44'N	93°08'W
Tuy, r., Ven. (tōō'ē)	131b	10°15'N	66°03'W
Tuyra, r., Pan. (tōō-ē'rȧ)	121	7°55'N	77°37'W
Tuz Gölü, l., Tur.	166	38°45'N	33°25'E
Tuzigoot National Monument, rec., Az., U.S.	109	34°40'N	111°52'W
Tuzla, Bos. (tōōz'lȧ)	149	44°33'N	18°46'E
Tvedestrand, Nor. (tvĭ'dhĕ-stränd)	152	58°39'N	8°54'E
Tveitsund, Nor. (tvåt'sŏŏnd)	152	59°03'N	8°29'E
Tver', Russia	164	56°52'N	35°57'E
Tver', prov., Russia	162	56°50'N	33°08'E
Tvertsa, r., Russia (tvĕr'tsȧ)	162	56°58'N	35°22'E
Tweed, r., U.K. (twēd)	150	55°32'N	2°35'W
Tweeling, S. Afr. (twē'lĭng)	218d	27°34'S	28°31'E
Twenty Mile Creek, r., Can. (twĕn'tĭ mīl)	83d	43°09'N	79°49'W
Twickenham, Eng., U.K. (twĭk''n-ăm)	144b	51°26'N	0°20'W
Twillingate, Can. (twĭl'ĭn-gāt)	85a	49°39'N	54°46'W
Twin Bridges, Mt., U.S. (twĭn brĭ-jĕz)	105	45°34'N	112°17'W
Twin Falls, Id., U.S. (fôls)	96	42°33'N	114°29'W
Twinsburg, Oh., U.S. (twĭnz'bûrg)	101d	41°19'N	81°26'W
Twitchell Reservoir, res., Ca., U.S.	108	34°50'N	120°10'W
Two Butte Creek, r., Co., U.S. (tōō būt)	110	37°39'N	102°45'W
Two Harbors, Mn., U.S.	103	47°00'N	91°42'W
Two Prairie Bay, Ar., U.S. (prâ'rĭ bī ōō')	111	34°48'N	92°07'W
Two Rivers, Wi., U.S. (rĭv'ērz)	103	44°09'N	87°36'W
Tyabb, Austl.	201a	38°16'S	145°11'E
Tylden, S. Afr. (tĭl-dĕn)	213c	32°08'S	27°06'E
Tyldesley, Eng., U.K. (tĭldz'lē)	144a	53°32'N	2°28'W
Tyler, Mn., U.S. (tī'lēr)	102	44°18'N	96°08'W
Tyler, Tx., U.S.	97	32°21'N	95°19'W
Tyler Park, Va., U.S.	229d	38°52'N	77°12'W
Tylertown, Ms., U.S. (tī'lēr-toun)	114	31°08'N	90°06'W
Tylihul, r., Ukr.	163	47°25'N	30°27'E
Tyndall, S.D., U.S. (tĭn'dȧl)	102	42°58'N	97°52'W
Tyndinskiy, Russia	165	55°22'N	124°45'E
Tyne, r., Eng., U.K. (tīn)	150	54°59'N	1°56'W
Tynemouth, Eng., U.K. (tīn'mŭth)	146	55°04'N	1°39'W
Tyngsboro, Ma., U.S. (tĭnj-bûr'ō)	93a	42°40'N	71°27'W
Tynset, Nor. (tün'sĕt)	146	62°17'N	10°45'E
Tyre see Şūr, Leb.	181a	33°16'N	35°13'E
Tyrifjorden, l., Nor.	152	60°03'N	10°25'E
Tyrone, Pa., U.S.	99	40°40'N	78°15'W
Tyrrell, Lake, l., Austl. (tĭr'ĕll)	204	35°12'S	143°00'E
Tyrrhenian Sea, sea, Italy (tĭr-rē'nĭ-ȧn)	142	40°10'N	12°15'E
Tysons Corner, Va., U.S.	229d	38°55'N	77°14'W
Tyukalinsk, Russia (tyŏŏ-kȧ-lĭnsk')	164	56°03'N	71°43'E
Tyukyan, r., Russia (tyŏŏk'yȧn)	171	65°42'N	116°09'E
Tyuleniy, i., Russia	167	44°30'N	48°00'E
Tyumen', Russia (tyōō-mĕn')	164	57°02'N	65°28'E

PLACE (Pronunciation)	PAGE	LAT.	LONG.
Tzucacab, Mex. (tzōō-kä-kä'b)	120a	20°06'N	89°03'W

U

PLACE (Pronunciation)	PAGE	LAT.	LONG.
Uaupés, Braz. (wä-ōō'pās)	130	0°02'S	67°03'W
Ubangi, r., Afr. (ōō-bäŋ'gē)	211	3°00'N	18°00'E
Ubatuba, Braz. (ōō-bȧ-tōō'bȧ)	129a	23°25'S	45°06'W
Ubeda, Spain (ōō'bȧ-dä)	158	38°01'N	3°23'W
Uberaba, Braz. (ōō-bȧ-rä'bȧ)	131	19°47'S	47°47'W
Uberlândia, Braz. (ōō-bĕr-lȧ'n-dyä)	131	18°54'S	48°11'W
Ubombo, S. Afr. (ōō-bôm'bō)	212	27°33'S	32°13'E
Ubon Ratchathani, Thai. (ōō'bŭn rä'chätá-nē)	196	15°15'N	104°52'E
Ubort', r., Eur. (ōō-bôrt')	163	51°18'N	27°43'E
Ubrique, Spain (ōō-brē'kā)	158	36°43'N	5°36'W
Ubundu, D.R.C.	212	0°21'S	25°29'E
Ucayali, r., Peru (ōō'kä-yä'lē)	130	8°58'S	74°13'W
Uccle, Bel. (ū'kl')	145a	50°48'N	4°17'E
Uchaly, Russia (û-chä'lĭ)	172a	54°22'N	59°28'E
Uchiko, Japan (ōō'chē-kō)	195	33°30'N	132°39'E
Uchinoura, Japan (ōō'chē-nō-ōō'rȧ)	195	31°16'N	131°03'E
Uchinskoye Vodokhranilishche, res., Russia	172b	56°08'N	37°44'E
Uchiura-Wan, b., Japan (ōō'chē-ōō'rä wän)	194	42°20'N	140°44'E
Uchur, r., Russia (ŏŏ-chŏŏr')	171	57°25'N	130°35'E
Ückendorf, neigh., Ger.	236	51°30'N	7°07'E
Uda, r., Russia (ŏŏ'dȧ)	171	52°28'N	110°51'E
Uda, r., Russia	171	53°54'N	131°29'E
Udai, r., Ukr.	163	50°45'N	32°13'E
Udaipur, India (ŏŏ-dŭ'ē-pōōr)	186	24°41'N	73°41'E
Uddevalla, Swe. (ŏŏd'dĕ-väl-ȧ)	146	58°21'N	11°55'E
Udine, Italy (ōō'dē-nȧ)	148	46°05'N	13°14'E
Udmurtia, state, Russia	166	57°00'N	53°00'E
Udon Thani, Thai.	196	17°31'N	102°51'E
Udskaya Guba, b., Russia	165	55°00'N	136°30'E
Ueckermünde, Ger.	154	53°43'N	14°01'E
Ueda, Japan (wä'dä)	194	36°26'N	138°16'E
Uedesheim, neigh., Ger.	236	51°10'N	6°48'E
Uele, r., D.R.C. (wä'lȧ)	211	3°55'N	23°30'E
Uelzen, Ger. (ült'sĕn)	154	52°58'N	10°34'E
Uerdingen, neigh., Ger.	236	51°21'N	6°39'E
Ufa, Russia (ŏŏ'fȧ)	164	54°45'N	55°57'E
Ufa, r., Russia	166	56°00'N	57°05'E
Ugab, r., Nmb. (ōō'gäb)	212	21°10'S	14°00'E
Ugalla, r., Tan. (ōō-gä'lä)	212	6°15'S	32°30'E
Uganda, nation, Afr. (ōō-gän'dä) (û-găn'dȧ)	211	2°00'N	32°28'E
Ugashik Lake, l., Ak., U.S. (ōō'gȧ-shēk)	95	57°36'N	157°10'W
Ugie, S. Afr. (ŏ'jē)	213c	31°13'S	28°14'E
Uglegorsk, Russia (ōō-glĕ-gôrsk)	165	49°00'N	142°31'E
Ugleural'sk, Russia (ŏŏg-lĕ-ŏŏ-rälsk')	172a	58°58'N	57°35'E
Uglich, Russia (ōōg-lēch')	162	57°33'N	38°19'E
Uglitskiy, Russia (ŏŏg-lĭt'skĭ)	172a	53°50'N	60°18'E
Uglovka, Russia (ōōg-lôf'kȧ)	162	58°14'N	33°24'E
Ugra, r., Russia (ōōg'rȧ)	166	54°43'N	34°20'E
Ugŭrchin, Bul.	161	43°06'N	24°23'E
Uhrichsville, Oh., U.S. (ū'rĭks-vĭl)	98	40°25'N	81°20'W
Uíge, Ang.	212	7°37'S	15°03'E
Uiju, N. Kor. (ŏ'ējōō)	189	40°09'N	124°33'E
Uinkaret Plateau, plat., Az., U.S. (û-ĭn'kâr-ēt)	109	36°43'N	113°15'W
Uinskoye, Russia (ŏ-ĭn'skô-yĕ)	172a	56°53'N	56°25'E
Uinta, r., Ut., U.S. (û-ĭn'tȧ)	109	40°25'N	109°55'W
Uintah and Ouray Indian Reservation, I.R., Ut., U.S.	109	40°20'N	110°20'W
Uinta Mountains, mts., Ut., U.S.	96	40°35'N	111°00'W
Uitenhage, S. Afr.	212	33°46'S	25°26'E
Uithoorn, Neth.	145a	52°13'N	4°49'E
Uji, Japan (ōō'jē)	195b	34°53'N	135°49'E
Ujiji, Tan. (ōō-jē'jē)	212	4°55'S	29°41'E
Ujjain, India (ōō-jŭēn)	183	23°18'N	75°37'E
Ujungpandang, Indon.	196	5°08'S	119°28'E
Ukerewe Island, i., Tan.	217	2°00'S	32°40'E
Ukhta, Russia (ōōk'tȧ)	166	65°22'N	31°30'E
Ukhta, Russia	166	63°08'N	53°42'E
Ukiah, Ca., U.S. (ū-kī'ȧ)	108	39°09'N	123°12'W
Ukita, neigh., Japan	242a	35°40'N	139°52'E
Ukmerge, Lith. (ŏŏk-mĕr-ghå)	166	55°16'N	24°45'E
Ukraine, nation, Eur.	164	49°15'N	30°15'E
Uku, i., Japan (ōōk'ōō)	195	33°18'N	129°02'E
Ulaangom, Mong.	188	50°23'N	92°14'E
Ulan Bator (Ulaanbaatar), Mong.	188	47°56'N	107°00'E
Ulan-Ude, Russia (ōō'län ōō'dȧ)	165	51°59'N	107°41'E
Ulchin, S. Kor. (ōōl'chĕn')	194	36°57'N	129°26'E
Ulcinj, Yugo. (ōōl'tsēn')	149	41°56'N	19°15'E
Ulhās, r., India	187b	19°13'N	73°03'E
Ulhāsnagar, India	186	19°10'N	73°07'E
Uliastay, Mong.	188	47°49'N	97°00'E
Ulindi, r., D.R.C. (ōō-lĭn'dē)	212	1°55'S	26°17'E
Ülkenözen, r.	167	49°50'N	49°35'E
Ulla, Bela. (ŏŏl'ȧ)	162	55°14'N	29°15'E
Ulla, r., Bela.	162	54°58'N	29°03'E
Ulla, r., Spain (ōō'lä)	158	42°45'N	8°33'W
Ullŭng, i., S. Kor. (ōōl'lōng')	194	37°29'N	130°50'E
Ulm, Ger. (ŏŏlm)	147	48°24'N	9°59'E

ng-sing; ŋ-baŋk; ᴋ-nasalized n; nŏd; cŏmmit; ōld; ôbey; ôrder; oi-boil; fōōd; ŏ-as oo in foot; ou-out; s-soft; sh-dish; th-thin; pūre; ůnite; ûrn; stŭd; circŭs; ü-as in French tu; '-indeterminate vowel.

360 Ulmer–Valence

PLACE (Pronunciation)	PAGE	LAT.	LONG.
Ulmer, Mount, mtn., Ant. (ŭl'mûr')	219	77°30'S	86°00'W
Ulricehamn, Swe. (ōōl-rē'sĕ-häm)	152	57°49'N	13°23'E
Ulsan, S. Kor. (ōōl'sän')	194	35°35'N	129°22'E
Ulster, hist. reg., Eur. (ŭl'stẽr)	150	54°41'N	7°10'W
Ulua, r., Hond. (ōō-lōō'ä)	120	15°49'N	87°45'W
Ulubāria, India	186a	22°27'N	88°09'E
Ulukişla, Tur. (ōō-lōō-kēsh'la)	149	36°40'N	34°30'E
Ulunga, Russia (ò-lōōn'gá)	194	46°16'N	136°29'E
Ulungur, r., China (ōō-lōōn-gůr)	188	46°31'N	88°00'E
Ulu-Telyak, Russia (ōō lò'tĕlyák)	172a	54°54'N	57°01'E
Ulverstone, Austl. (ŭl'vẽr-stŭn)	203	41°20'S	146°22'E
Ul'yanovka, Russia	172c	59°38'N	30°47'E
Ul'yanovsk, Russia (ōō-lyä'nôfsk)	164	54°20'N	48°24'E
Ulysses, Ks., U.S. (ū-lĭs'ēz)	110	37°34'N	101°25'W
Umán, Mex. (ōō-män')	120a	20°52'N	89°44'W
Uman', Ukr. (ò-mán')	167	48°44'N	30°13'E
Umatilla Indian Reservation, I.R., Or., U.S. (ū-má-tĭl'á)	104	45°38'N	118°35'W
Umberpāda, India	187b	19°28'N	73°04'E
Umbria, hist. reg., Italy (ŭm'brĭ-ă)	160	42°53'N	12°22'E
Umeälven, r., Swe.	142	64°57'N	18°51'E
Umhlatuzi, r., S. Afr. (òm'hlá-tōō'zĭ)	213c	28°47'S	31°17'E
Umiat, Ak., U.S. (ōō'mĭ-ăt)	94a	69°20'N	152°28'W
Umkomaas, S. Afr. (òm-kō'mäs)	213c	30°12'S	30°48'E
Umnak, i., Ak., U.S. (ōōm'nák)	94b	53°10'N	169°08'W
Umnak Pass, Ak., U.S.	95a	53°10'N	168°04'W
Umniati, r., Zimb.	212	17°08'S	29°11'E
Umpqua, r., Or., U.S. (ŭmp'kwá)	104	43°42'N	123°50'W
Umtata, S. Afr. (òm-tä'tä)	212	31°36'S	28°47'E
Umtentweni, S. Afr.	213c	30°41'S	30°29'E
Umzimkulu, S. Afr. (òm-zēm-kōō'lōō)	213c	30°12'S	29°53'E
Umzinto, S. Afr. (òm-zĭn'tò)	213c	30°19'S	30°41'E
Una, r., Yugo. (ōō'ná)	160	44°38'N	16°10'E
Unalakleet, Ak., U.S. (ū-ná-lák'lēt)	95	63°50'N	160°42'W
Unalaska, Ak., U.S. (ū-ná-lás'ká)	95a	53°30'N	166°20'W
Unare, r., Ven.	131b	9°45'N	65°12'W
Unare, Laguna de, l., Ven. (lä-gò'nä-de-ōō-ná'rĕ)	131b	10°07'N	65°23'W
Unayzah, Sau. Ar.	182	25°50'N	44°02'E
Uncas, Can. (ŭŋ'kăs)	83g	53°30'N	113°02'W
Uncia, Bol. (ōōn'sē-ä)	130	18°28'S	66°32'W
Uncompahgre, r., Co., U.S.	109	38°20'N	107°45'W
Uncompahgre Peak, mtn., Co., U.S. (ŭn-kŭm-pä'grē)	109	38°00'N	107°30'W
Uncompahgre Plateau, plat., Co., U.S.	109	38°40'N	108°40'W
Underberg, S. Afr. (ŭn'dẽr-bûrg)	213c	29°51'S	29°32'E
Unecha, Russia (ò-nĕ'chá)	162	52°51'N	32°44'E
Ungava, Péninsule d', pen., Can.	85	59°55'N	74°00'W
Ungava Bay, b., Can. (ŭŋ-gā'vá)	85	59°46'N	67°18'W
União da Vitória, Braz. (ōō-nē-oun' dä vē-tô'ryä)	132	26°17'S	51°13'W
Unidad Sante Fe, Mex.	233a	19°23'N	99°15'W
Unije, i., Yugo. (ōō'nē-yĕ)	160	44°39'N	14°10'E
Unimak, i., Ak., U.S. (ōō-nē-mák')	95	54°30'N	163°35'W
Unimak Pass, Ak., U.S.	95a	54°22'N	165°22'W
Union, Ms., U.S. (ūn'yŭn)	114	32°35'N	89°07'W
Union, Mo., U.S.	111	38°28'N	90°59'W
Union, N.J., U.S.	228	40°42'N	74°16'W
Union, N.C., U.S.	115	34°42'N	81°40'W
Union, Or., U.S.	104	45°13'N	117°52'W
Union City, Ca., U.S.	106b	37°36'N	122°01'W
Union City, In., U.S.	98	40°10'N	85°00'W
Union City, Mi., U.S.	98	42°00'N	85°10'W
Union City, N.J., U.S.	228	40°46'N	74°02'W
Union City, Pa., U.S.	99	41°50'N	79°50'W
Union City, Tn., U.S.	114	36°25'N	89°04'W
Uniondale, N.Y., U.S.	228	40°43'N	73°36'W
Unión de Reyes, Cuba	122	22°45'N	81°30'W
Unión de San Antonio, Mex.	118	21°07'N	101°56'W
Unión de Tula, Mex.	118	19°57'N	104°14'W
Union Grove, Wi., U.S. (ūn-yŭn grōv)	101a	42°41'N	88°03'W
Unión Hidalgo, Mex. (ē-dä'lgō)	119	16°29'N	94°51'W
Union Point, Ga., U.S.	114	33°37'N	83°08'W
Union Springs, Al., U.S. (sprĭngz)	114	32°08'N	85°43'W
Uniontown, Al., U.S. (ūn'yŭn-toun)	114	32°26'N	87°30'W
Uniontown, Oh., U.S.	101d	40°58'N	81°25'W
Uniontown, Pa., U.S.	99	39°55'N	79°45'W
Unionville, Mo., U.S. (ūn'yŭn-vĭl)	111	40°28'N	92°58'W
Unisan, Phil. (ōō-nē'sän)	197a	13°50'N	121°59'E
United Arab Emirates, nation, Asia	182	24°00'N	54°00'E
United Kingdom, nation, Eur.	142	56°30'N	1°40'W
United Nations Headquarters, pt. of i., N.Y., U.S.	228	40°45'N	73°58'W
United States, nation, N.A.	96	38°00'N	110°00'W
Unity, Can.	88	52°27'N	109°10'W
Universal, In., U.S. (ū-nĭ-vûr'sál)	98	39°35'N	87°30'W
University City, Mo., U.S. (ū'nĭ-vûr'sĭ-tĭ)	107e	38°40'N	90°19'W
University Heights, Oh., U.S.	229a	41°30'N	81°32'W
University Park, Md., U.S.	229d	38°58'N	76°57'W
University Park, Tx., U.S.	107c	32°51'N	96°48'W
Unna, Ger. (ōō'nä)	157c	51°32'N	7°41'E
Uno, Canal Numero, can., Arg.	129c	36°43'S	58°14'W
Unterhaching, Ger. (ōōn'tĕr-hä-kĕng)	145d	48°03'N	11°38'E
Untermauerbach, Aus.	239e	48°14'N	16°12'E
Ünye, Tur. (ün'yĕ)	149	41°00'N	37°10'E
Unzha, r., Russia (òn'zhá)	166	57°45'N	44°10'E
Upa, r., Russia (ò'pá)	162	53°54'N	36°48'E
Upata, Ven. (ōō-pä'tä)	130	7°58'N	62°27'W
Upemba, Parc National de l', rec., D.R.C.	217	9°10'S	26°15'E
Up Holland, Eng., U.K.	237a	53°33'N	2°44'W
Upington, S. Afr. (ŭp'ĭng-tŭn)	212	28°25'S	21°15'E
Upland, Ca., U.S. (ŭp'lănd)	107a	34°06'N	117°38'W
Upland, Pa., U.S.	229b	39°51'N	75°23'W
Upolu, i., W. Sam.	198a	13°55'S	171°45'W
Upolu Point, c., Hi., U.S. (ōō-pô'lōō)	94a	20°15'N	155°48'W
Upper Arrow Lake, l., Can. (ăr'ō)	87	50°30'N	117°55'W
Upper Brookville, N.Y., U.S.	228	40°51'N	73°34'W
Upper Darby, Pa., U.S. (där'bĭ)	100f	39°58'N	75°16'W
Upper des Lacs, l., N.A. (dĕ läk)	102	48°58'N	101°55'W
Upper Ferntree Gully, Austl.	243b	37°54'S	145°19'E
Upper Kapuas Mountains, mts., Asia	196	1°45'N	112°06'E
Upper Klamath Lake, l., Or., U.S.	104	42°23'N	122°55'W
Upper Lake, l., Nv., U.S. (ŭp'ẽr)	104	41°42'N	119°59'W
Upper Marlboro, Md., U.S. (ūpẽr märl'bōrō)	100e	38°49'N	76°46'W
Upper Mill, Wa., U.S. (mĭl)	106a	47°11'N	121°55'W
Upper New York Bay, b., N.Y., U.S.	228	40°41'N	74°03'W
Upper Red Lake, l., Mn., U.S. (rĕd)	103	48°14'N	94°53'W
Upper Saint Clair, Pa., U.S.	230b	40°21'N	80°05'W
Upper Sandusky, Oh., U.S. (săn-dŭs'kē)	98	40°50'N	83°20'W
Upper San Leandro Reservoir, res., Ca., U.S. (ŭp'ẽr săn lē-ăn'drō)	106b	37°47'N	122°04'W
Upper Tooting, neigh., Eng., U.K.	235	51°26'N	0°10'W
Upper Volta *see* Burkina Faso, nation, Afr.	210	13°00'N	2°00'W
Uppingham, Eng., U.K. (ŭp'ĭng-ăm)	144a	52°35'N	0°43'W
Uppsala, Swe. (ōōp'sà-lä)	142	59°53'N	17°39'E
Upton, Eng., U.K.	235	51°30'N	0°35'W
Uptown, Ma., U.S. (ŭp'toun)	93a	42°10'N	71°36'W
Uptown, neigh., Il., U.S.	231a	41°58'N	87°40'W
Upwey, Austl.	243b	37°54'S	145°20'E
Uraga, Japan (ōō'rá-gá')	195a	35°15'N	139°43'E
Ural, r. (ò-räl'') (ū-rôl)	164	48°00'N	51°00'E
Urals, mts., Russia	164	56°28'N	58°13'E
Uran, India (ōō-rän')	187b	18°53'N	72°46'E
Uranium City, Can.	84	59°34'N	108°59'W
Urawa, Japan (ōō'rä-wä')	194	35°52'N	139°39'E
Urayasu, Japan (ōō'rä-yä'sōō)	195a	35°40'N	139°54'W
Urazovo, Russia (ò-rá'zô-vô)	163	50°08'N	38°03'E
Urbana, Il., U.S. (ûr-băn'á)	98	40°10'N	88°15'W
Urbana, Oh., U.S.	98	40°05'N	83°50'W
Urbino, Italy (ōōr-bē'nò)	160	43°43'N	12°37'E
Urda, Kaz. (òr'dá)	170	48°50'N	47°30'E
Urdaneta, Phil. (ōōr-dä-nä'tä)	197a	15°59'N	120°34'E
Urdinarrain, Arg. (ōōr-dē-när-rāē'n)	129c	32°43'S	58°53'W
Uritsk, Russia (ōō'rĭtsk)	172c	59°50'N	30°11'E
Urla, Tur. (òr'là)	161	38°20'N	26°44'E
Urman, Russia (òr'mán)	172a	54°53'N	56°52'E
Urmi, r., Russia (òr'mē)	194	48°50'N	134°00'E
Urmston, Eng., U.K.	237b	53°27'N	2°21'W
Uromi, Nig.	215	6°44'N	6°18'E
Urrao, Col. (ōōr-rá'ō)	130	6°19'N	76°11'W
Urshel'skiy, Russia (ōōr-shĕl'skēē)	162	55°50'N	40°11'E
Ursus, Pol.	155	52°12'N	20°53'E
Urubamba, r., Peru (ōō-rōō-bäm'bä)	130	11°48'S	72°34'W
Uruguaiana, Braz.	132	29°45'S	57°00'W
Uruguay, nation, S.A. (ōō-rōō-gwī') (ū'rōō-gwā)	132	32°45'S	56°00'W
Uruguay, Rio, r., S.A. (rē'ō-ò-rōō-gwī)	132	27°05'S	55°15'W
Ürümqi, China (ū-rům-chyē)	188	43°49'N	87°43'E
Urup, i., Russia (ò'ròp')	189	46°00'N	150°00'E
Uryupinsk, Russia (òr'yò-pēn-sk')	167	50°50'N	42°00'E
Ürzhar, Kaz.	169	47°28'N	82°00'E
Urziceni, Rom. (ò-zē-chĕn'')	161	44°45'N	26°42'E
Usa, Japan	194	33°31'N	131°22'E
Usa, r., Russia (ò'sá)	166	66°00'N	58°20'E
Uşak, Tur. (ōō'shák)	149	38°45'N	29°15'E
Usakos, Nmb. (ōō-sä'kōs)	212	22°00'S	15°40'E
Usambara Mountains, mts., Tan.	217	4°40'S	38°25'E
Usangu Flats, sw., Tan.	217	8°10'S	34°00'E
Ushaki, Russia (ōō'shá-kĭ)	172c	59°28'N	31°00'E
Ushakovskoye, Russia (ò-shá-kôv'skô-yĕ)	172a	56°18'N	62°23'E
Usharal, Kaz.	169	46°14'N	80°58'E
Ushashi, Tan.	217	2°00'S	33°57'E
Ushiku, Japan (ōō'shē-kōō)	195a	35°24'N	140°09'E
Ushimado, Japan (ōō'shē-mä'dō)	195	34°37'N	134°09'E
Ushuaia, Arg. (ōō-shōō-ī'ä)	132	54°46'S	68°24'W
Usman', Russia (ōōs-mán')	167	52°03'N	39°40'E
Usmānpur, neigh., India	240d	28°41'N	77°15'E
Usol'ye, Russia (ò-sô'lyĕ)	172a	59°24'N	56°40'E
Usol'ye-Sibirskoye, Russia (ò-sô'lyĕsĭ' bẽr'skô-yĕ)	170	52°44'N	103°46'E
Uspallata Pass, p., S.A. (ōōs-pä-lyä'tä)	132	32°47'S	70°08'W
Uspanapa, r., Mex. (ōōs-pä-nä'pä)	119	17°43'N	94°14'W
Ussel, Fr. (üs'ĕl)	156	45°33'N	2°17'E
Ussuri, r., Asia (ōō-sōō'rē)	171	47°30'N	134°00'E
Ussuriysk, Russia	165	43°48'N	132°09'E
Ust'-Bol'sheretsk, Russia	165	52°41'N	157°00'E
Ustica, Isola di, i., Italy	160	38°43'N	12°11'E
Ústí nad Labem, Czech Rep.	154	50°40'N	14°02'E
Ust'-Izhora, Russia (òst-ĕz'hô-rá)	172c	59°49'N	30°35'E
Ustka, Pol. (ōōst'ká)	154	54°34'N	16°52'E
Ust'-Kamchatsk, Russia	165	56°13'N	162°18'E
Ust'-Katav, Russia (òst ká'táf)	172a	54°55'N	58°12'E
Ust'-Kishert', Russia (òst kē'shĕrt)	172a	57°21'N	57°13'E
Ust'-Kulom, Russia (kō'lŭm)	164	61°38'N	54°00'E
Ust'-Maya, Russia (má'yă)	165	60°33'N	134°43'E
Ust' Olenëk, Russia	165	72°52'N	120°15'E
Ust-Ordynskiy, Russia (òst-ôr-dyĕnsk'ĭ)	170	52°47'N	104°39'E
Ust' Penzhino, Russia	171	63°00'N	165°10'E
Ust' Port, Russia (òst'pôrt')	164	69°20'N	83°41'E
Ust'-Tsil'ma, Russia (tsĭl'má)	164	65°25'N	52°10'E
Ust'-Tyrma, Russia (tur'má)	165	50°27'N	131°17'E
Ust' Uls, Russia	172a	60°35'N	58°32'E
Ust'-Urt, Plato, plat., Asia	164	44°03'N	54°58'E
Ustynivka, Ukr.	163	47°59'N	32°31'E
Ustyuzhna, Russia (yōōzh'ná)	166	58°49'N	36°19'E
Usu, China (ů-sōō)	188	44°28'N	84°07'E
Usuki, Japan (ōō'sōō-kē')	195	33°06'N	131°47'E
Usulutan, El Sal. (ōō-sōō-lä-tän')	120	13°22'N	88°25'W
Usumacinta, r., N.A. (ōō'sōō-mä-sēn'tō)	119	18°24'N	92°30'W
Us'va, Russia (ōōs'vá)	172a	58°41'N	57°38'E
Utah, state, U.S. (ū'tô)	96	39°25'N	112°40'W
Utah Lake, l., Ut., U.S.	109	40°10'N	111°55'W
Utan, India	187b	19°17'N	72°43'E
Ute Mountain Indian Reservation, I.R., N.M., U.S.	109	36°57'N	108°34'W
Utena, Lith. (ōō'tá-nä)	153	55°32'N	25°40'E
Utete, Tan. (ōō-tā'tá)	213	8°05'S	38°47'E
Utfort, Ger.	236	51°28'N	6°38'E
Utica, In., U.S. (ū'tĭ-kă)	101h	38°20'N	85°39'W
Utica, N.Y., U.S.	97	43°05'N	75°10'W
Utiel, Spain (ōō-tyāl')	158	39°34'N	1°13'W
Utika, Mi., U.S. (ū'tĭ-kă)	101b	42°37'N	83°02'W
Utik Lake, l., Can.	89	55°16'N	96°00'W
Utikuma Lake, l., Can.	87	55°50'N	115°25'W
Utila, i., Hond. (ōō-tē'lä)	120	16°07'N	87°05'W
Utinga, Braz.	234d	23°38'S	46°32'W
Uto, Japan (ōō'tō')	194	32°43'N	130°39'E
Utrecht, Neth. (ū'trĕkt) (ü'trĕkt)	147	52°05'N	5°06'E
Utrera, Spain (ōō-trā'rä)	148	37°12'N	5°48'W
Utsunomiya, Japan (ōōt'sò-nò-mē-yá')	189	36°35'N	139°52'E
Uttaradit, Thai.	196	17°47'N	100°10'E
Uttarpara-Kotrung, India	186a	22°40'N	88°21'E
Uttar Pradesh, state, India (òt-tär-prä-dĕsh)	183	27°00'N	80°00'E
Uttoxeter, Eng., U.K. (ŭt-tôk'sē-tẽr)	144a	52°54'N	1°52'W
Utuado, P.R. (ōō-tōō-ä'dhō)	117b	18°16'N	66°40'W
Uusikaupunki, Fin.	153	60°48'N	21°24'E
Uvalde, Tx., U.S. (ū-văl'dē)	112	29°14'N	99°47'W
Uvel'skiy, Russia (ò-vyĕl'skĭ)	172a	54°27'N	61°22'E
Uvinza, Tan.	217	5°06'S	30°22'E
Uvira, D.R.C. (ōō-vē'rä)	212	3°28'S	29°03'E
Uvod', r., Russia (ò-vôd')	162	56°40'N	41°10'E
Uvongo Beach, S. Afr.	213c	30°49'S	30°23'E
Uvs Nuur, l., Asia	188	50°29'N	93°32'E
Uwajima, Japan (ōō-wä'jē-mä)	194	33°12'N	132°35'E
Uxbridge, Ma., U.S. (ŭks'brĭj)	93a	42°05'N	71°38'W
Uxbridge, neigh., Eng., U.K.	235	51°33'N	0°29'W
Uxmal, hist., Mex. (ōō'x-mä'l)	120a	20°22'N	89°44'W
Uy, r., Russia (ōōy)	172a	54°05'N	62°11'E
Uyama, Japan	242b	34°50'N	135°41'E
Uyskoye, Russia (ûy'skô-yĕ)	172a	54°22'N	60°01'E
Uyuni, Bol. (ōō-yōō'nē)	130	20°28'S	66°45'W
Uyuni, Salar de, pl., Bol. (sä-lär-dĕ)	130	20°58'S	67°09'W
Uzbekistan, nation, Asia	164	42°42'N	60°00'E
Uzh, r., Ukr. (òzh)	163	51°07'N	29°05'E
Uzhhorod, Ukr.	155	48°38'N	22°18'E
Užice, Yugo. (ōō'zhĕ-tsĕ)	161	43°51'N	19°53'E
Uzunköprü, Tur.	161	41°17'N	26°42'E

V

PLACE (Pronunciation)	PAGE	LAT.	LONG.
Vaal, r., S. Afr. (väl)	212	28°15'S	24°30'E
Vaaldam, res., S. Afr.	218d	26°58'S	28°37'E
Vaalplaas, S. Afr.	218d	25°39'S	28°56'E
Vaalwater, S. Afr.	218d	24°17'S	28°08'E
Vaasa, Fin. (vä'sá)	142	63°06'N	21°39'E
Vác, Hung. (väts)	155	47°46'N	19°10'E
Vache, Île à, i., Haiti	123	18°05'N	73°40'W
Vadstena, Swe. (väd'stĭ'ná)	152	58°27'N	14°53'E
Vaduz, Liech. (vä'dòts)	154	47°10'N	9°32'E
Vaga, r., Russia (va'gá)	166	61°55'N	42°30'E
Vah, r., Slvk. (väκ)	147	48°07'N	17°52'E
Vaigai, r., India	187	10°20'N	78°13'E
Vaires-sur-Marne, Fr.	237c	48°52'N	2°39'E
Vakh, r., Russia (vàκ)	170	61°30'N	81°33'E
Valachia, hist. reg., Rom.	161	44°45'N	24°17'E
Valcanuta, neigh., Italy	239c	41°53'N	12°25'E
Valcartier-Village, Can. (väl-kärt-yĕ'vē-läzh')	83b	46°56'N	71°28'W
Valdai Hills, hills, Russia (vál-dī' gô'rĭ)	166	57°50'N	32°35'E
Valday, Russia (vál-dī')	166	57°58'N	33°13'E
Valdecañas, Embalse de, res., Spain	158	39°45'N	5°30'W
Valdemārpils, Lat.	153	57°22'N	22°34'E
Valdemorillo, Spain (väl-dā-mô-rēl'yō)	159a	40°30'N	4°04'W
Valdepeñas, Spain (väl-dā-pān'yäs)	148	38°46'N	3°22'W
Valderaduey, r., Spain (väl-dĕ-rä-dwĕ'y)	158	41°39'N	5°35'W
Valdés, Península, pen., Arg. (vál-dĕ's)	132	42°15'S	63°15'W
Valdez, Ak., U.S. (văl'dēz)	95	61°10'N	146°18'W
Valdilecha, Spain (väl-dē-lā'chä)	159a	40°17'N	3°19'W
Valdivia, Chile (väl-dē'vä)	132	39°47'S	73°13'W
Valdivia, Col. (väl-dē'vēä)	130a	7°10'N	75°26'W
Val-d'Or, Can.	85	48°03'N	77°50'W
Valdosta, Ga., U.S. (văl-dŏs'tă)	97	30°50'N	83°18'W
Vale, Or., U.S. (vāl)	104	43°59'N	117°14'W
Valença, Braz. (vä-lĕn'să)	131	13°43'S	38°58'W
Valença, Port.	158	42°03'N	8°36'W
Valence, Fr. (vä-lĕnns)	147	44°56'N	4°54'E

ăt; finăl; rāte; senāte; ärm; ȧsk; sofȧ; fâre; ch-choose; dh-as th in other; bē; ėvent; bĕt; recĕnt; cratẽr; g-gō; gh-guttural g; bĭt; ĭ-short neutral; rīde; κ-guttural k as ch in German ich;

PRONOUNCING INDEX València - Vero Beach 361

PLACE (Pronunciation)	PAGE	LAT.	LONG.
València, Spain	142	39°26′N	0°23′W
Valencia, Ven. (vä-lĕn′syä)	130	10°11′N	68°00′W
València, hist. reg., Spain	159	39°08′N	0°43′W
València, Golf de, b., Spain	159	39°50′N	0°30′E
Valencia, Lago de, l., Ven.	131b	10°11′N	67°45′W
Valencia de Alcántara, Spain	158	39°34′N	7°13′W
Valenciennes, Fr. (vȧ-läN-syĕn′)	156	50°24′N	3°36′E
Valentín Alsina, neigh., Arg.	233d	34°40′S	58°25′W
Valentine, Ne., U.S. (vȧ läN-tē-nyē′)	96	42°52′N	100°34′W
Valera, Ven. (vä-lĕ′rä)	130	9°12′N	70°45′W
Valerianovsk, Russia (vȧ-lĕ-rĭ-ä′nôvsk)	172a	58°47′N	59°34′E
Valérien, Mont, hill, Fr.	237c	48°53′N	2°13′E
Valga, Est. (väl′gȧ)	166	57°47′N	26°03′E
Valhalla, S. Afr. (vál-hăl-*ȧ*)	213b	25°49′S	28°09′E
Valier, Mt., U.S. (vă-lēr′)	105	48°17′N	112°14′W
Valjevo, Yugo. (väl′yȧ-vȯ)	161	44°17′N	19°57′E
Valky, Ukr.	163	49°49′N	35°40′E
Valladolid, Mex. (väl-yä-dhȯ-lēdh′)	116	20°39′N	88°13′W
Valladolid, Spain (väl-yä-dhȯ-lēdh′)	142	41°41′N	4°41′W
Valldoreix, Spain	238e	41°28′N	2°04′E
Valle, Arroyo del, Ca., U.S. (ä-rō′yō dĕl väl′yȧ)	108	37°36′N	121°43′W
Vallecas, Spain (väl-yä′käs)	159a	40°23′N	3°37′W
Valle de Allende, Mex. (väl′yā dā äl-yĕn′dȧ)	112	26°55′N	105°25′W
Valle de Bravo, Mex. (brä′vȯ)	118	19°12′N	100°07′W
Valle de Guanape, Ven. (vä′l-yĕ-dĕ-gwä-nä′pĕ)	131b	9°54′N	65°41′W
Valle de la Pascua, Ven. (lä-pä′s-kōōä)	130	9°12′N	65°08′W
Valle del Cauca, dept., Col. (vä′l-yĕ del kou′kä)	130a	4°03′N	76°13′W
Valle de Santiago, Mex. (sän-tē-ä′gȯ)	118	20°23′N	101°11′W
Valledupar, Col. (dōō-pär′)	130	10°13′N	73°39′W
Valle Grande, Bol. (grän′dā)	130	18°27′S	64°03′W
Vallejo, Ca., U.S. (vă-yā′hō) (vă-lā′hō)	96	38°06′N	122°15′W
Vallejo, Sierra de, mts., Mex. (sē-ĕ′r-rä-dĕ-väl-yĕ′kȯ)	118	21°00′N	105°10′W
Vallenar, Chile (väl-yȧ-när′)	132	28°39′S	70°52′W
Valles, Mex.	116	21°59′N	99°02′W
Valletta, Malta (väl-lĕt′ä)	148	35°50′N	14°29′E
Valle Vista, Ca., U.S. (väl′yä vĭs′t*ȧ*)	107a	33°45′N	116°53′W
Valley City, N.D., U.S.	96	46°55′N	97°59′W
Valley City, Oh., U.S. (văl′ĭ)	101d	41°14′N	81°56′W
Valleydale, Ca., U.S.	232	34°06′N	117°56′W
Valley Falls, Ks., U.S.	111	39°25′N	95°26′W
Valleyfield, Can. (văl′ē-fēld)	85	45°16′N	74°09′W
Valley Mede, Md., U.S.	229c	39°17′N	76°50′W
Valley Park, Mo., U.S. (văl′ē pärk)	107e	38°33′N	90°30′W
Valley Stream, N.Y., U.S. (văl′ĭ strēm)	100a	40°39′N	73°42′W
Valli di Comácchio, l., Italy (vä′lē-dē-kô-mä′chyȯ)	160	44°38′N	12°15′E
Vallière, Haiti (väl-yâr′)	123	19°30′N	71°55′W
Vallimanca, r., Arg. (väl-yē-mä′n-kä)	129c	36°21′S	60°55′W
Valls, Spain (väls)	148	41°15′N	1°15′E
Valmiera, Lat. (vál′myĕ-rȧ)	166	57°34′N	25°54′E
Valognes, Fr. (vȧ-lôn′y′)	156	49°32′N	1°30′W
Valona see Vlorë, Alb.	149	40°28′N	19°31′E
Valparaíso, Chile (väl′pä-rä-ē′sȯ)	132	33°02′S	71°32′W
Valparaíso, Mex.	118	22°49′N	103°33′W
Valparaiso, In., U.S. (văl-p*ȧ*-rā′zȯ)	98	41°25′N	87°05′W
Valpariso, prov., Chile	129b	32°58′S	71°23′W
Valréas, Fr. (vál-rȧ-ä′)	156	44°25′N	4°56′E
Vals, r., S. Afr.	218d	27°32′S	26°51′E
Vals, Tanjung, c., Indon.	197	8°30′S	137°15′E
Valsbaai, b., S. Afr.	212a	34°14′S	18°35′E
Valuyevo, Russia (vá-lōō′yĕ-vȯ)	172b	55°34′N	37°21′E
Valuyki, Russia (vȧ-lȯ-ē′kē)	167	50°14′N	38°04′E
Valverde del Camino, Spain (väl-vĕr-dĕ-dĕl-kä-mē′nō)	158	37°34′N	6°44′W
Vammala, Fin.	153	61°19′N	22°51′E
Van, Tur. (vȧn)	182	38°04′N	43°10′E
Van Buren, Ar., U.S. (văn bū′rĕn)	111	35°26′N	94°20′W
Van Buren, Me., U.S.	92	47°09′N	67°58′W
Vanceburg, Ky., U.S. (văns′bûrg)	98	38°35′N	83°20′W
Vancouver, Can. (văn-kōō′vĕr)	84	49°16′N	123°06′W
Vancouver, Wa., U.S.	96	45°37′N	122°40′W
Vancouver Island, i., Can.	84	49°50′N	125°05′W
Vancouver Island Ranges, mts., Can.	86	49°25′N	125°25′W
Vandalia, Il., U.S. (văn-dā′lĭ-*ȧ*)	98	39°00′N	89°00′W
Vandalia, Mo., U.S.	111	39°19′N	91°30′W
Vanderbijlpark, S. Afr.	218d	26°43′S	27°50′E
Vanderhoof, Can.	84	54°01′N	124°01′W
Van Diemen, Cape, c., Austl. (văndē′mĕn)	202	11°05′S	130°15′E
Van Diemen Gulf, b., Austl.	202	11°50′S	131°30′E
Vanegas, Mex. (vä-nĕ′gäs)	116	23°54′N	100°54′W
Vänern, l., Swe.	142	58°52′N	13°17′E
Vänersborg, Swe. (vĕ′nĕrs-bôr′)	146	58°24′N	12°15′E
Vanga, Kenya (väŋ′gä)	213	4°38′S	39°10′E
Vangani, India	187b	19°07′N	73°15′E
Van Gölü, l., Tur.	166	38°33′N	42°46′E
Van Horn, Tx., U.S.	112	31°03′N	104°50′W
Vanier, Can.	83c	45°27′N	75°39′W
Vaniköy, neigh., Tur.	239f	41°04′N	29°04′E
Van Lear, Ky., U.S. (văn lēr′)	98	37°45′N	82°50′W
Vannes, Fr. (vȧn)	147	47°42′N	2°46′W
Van Nuys, Ca., U.S. (văn nīz′)	107a	34°11′N	118°27′W
Van Rees, Pegunungan, mts., Indon.	197	2°30′S	138°45′E
Vantaan, r., Fin.	153	60°25′N	24°43′E
Vanua Levu, i., Fiji	198g	16°33′S	179°15′E
Vanuatu, nation, Oc.	203	16°02′S	169°15′E
Vanves, Fr.	237c	48°50′N	2°18′E
Van Wert, Oh., U.S. (văn wûrt′)	98	40°50′N	84°35′W
Vanzago, Italy	238c	45°32′N	9°00′E
Vara, Swe. (vä′rä)	152	58°17′N	12°55′E
Varaklāni, Lat.	153	56°38′N	26°46′E
Varallo, Italy (vä-räl′lô)	160	45°44′N	8°14′E
Vārānasi (Benares), India	183	25°25′N	83°00′E
Varangerfjorden, b., Nor.	143	70°05′N	30°20′E
Varano, Lago di, l., Italy (lä′gō-dē-vä-rä′nȯ)	160	41°52′N	15°55′E
Varaždin, Cro. (vä′räzh′dĕn)	149	46°17′N	16°20′E
Varazze, Italy (vä-rät′sä)	160	44°23′N	8°34′E
Varberg, Swe. (vär′bĕrg)	152	57°06′N	12°16′E
Vardar, r., Yugo. (vär′där)	161	41°40′N	21°50′E
Varėna, Lith. (vä-rā′nȧ)	153	54°16′N	24°35′E
Varennes, Can. (vȧ-rĕn′)	83a	45°41′N	73°27′W
Vareš, Bos. (vä′rĕsh)	161	44°10′N	18°20′E
Varese, Italy (vä-rā′sȧ)	160	45°45′N	8°49′E
Vargem Grande, neigh., Braz.	234c	22°59′S	43°29′W
Varginha, Braz. (vär-zhē′n-yä)	131	21°33′S	45°25′W
Varkaus, Fin. (vär′kous)	153	62°19′N	27°51′E
Varlamovo, Russia (vár-lá′mô-vô)	172a	54°37′N	60°41′E
Varna, Bul. (vär′n*ȧ*)	142	43°14′N	27°58′E
Varna, Russia	172a	53°22′N	60°59′E
Värnamo, Swe. (vĕr′ná-mȯ)	152	57°11′N	13°45′E
Varnsdorf, Czech Rep. (värns′dôrf)	154	50°54′N	14°36′E
Varnville, S.C., U.S. (värn′vĭl)	115	32°49′N	81°05′W
Várpalota, pt. of i., Hung.	239g	47°30′N	19°02′E
Vasa, India	187b	19°20′N	72°47′E
Vascongadas see Basque Provinces, hist. reg., Spain	158	43°00′N	2°46′W
Vashka, r., Russia	166	64°00′N	48°00′E
Vashon, Wa., U.S. (văsh′*ŭ*n)	106a	47°27′N	122°28′W
Vashon Heights, Wa., U.S. (hītz)	106a	47°30′N	122°28′W
Vashon Island, i., Wa., U.S.	106a	47°27′N	122°27′W
Vasiljevskij, Ostrov, i., Russia	239a	59°56′N	30°15′E
Vaslui, Rom. (vȧs-lōō′ē)	155	46°39′N	27°49′E
Vassar, Mi., U.S. (văs′ẽr)	98	43°25′N	83°35′W
Vassouras, Braz. (väs-sō′räzh)	129a	22°25′S	43°40′W
Västerås, Swe. (vĕs′tĕr-ôs)	146	59°39′N	16°30′E
Västerdalälven, r., Swe.	146	61°06′N	13°10′E
Västervik, Swe. (vĕs′tĕr-vēk)	146	57°45′N	16°35′E
Vasto, Italy (väs′tô)	148	42°06′N	12°42′E
Vasyl′kiv, Ukr.	167	50°10′N	30°22′E
Vasyugan, r., Russia (vȧs-yōō-gȧn′)	170	58°52′N	77°30′E
Vatican City, nation, Eur.	160	41°54′N	12°22′E
Vaticano, Cape, c., Italy (vä-tē-kä′nô)	160	38°38′N	15°52′E
Vatnajökull, ice., Ice. (vät′nȧ-yû-kôl)	146	64°34′N	16°41′W
Vatomandry, Madag.	213	18°53′S	48°13′E
Vatra Dornei, Rom. (vät′rȧ dôr′nȧ′)	155	47°22′N	25°20′E
Vättern, l., Swe.	142	58°15′N	14°24′E
Vattholma, Swe.	152	60°01′N	17°40′E
Vaucluse, Austl.	243a	33°51′S	151°17′E
Vaudreuil, Can. (vô-drû′y′)	83a	45°24′N	74°02′W
Vaugh, Wa., U.S. (vôn)	106a	47°21′N	122°47′W
Vaughan, Can.	83d	43°47′N	79°36′W
Vaughn, N.M., U.S.	110	34°37′N	105°13′W
Vauhallan, Fr.	237c	48°44′N	2°12′E
Vaujours, Fr.	237c	48°56′N	2°35′E
Vaupés, r., S.A. (vá′ōō-pē′s)	130	1°18′N	71°14′W
Vaxholm, Swe. (väks′hôlm)	152	59°26′N	18°19′E
Växjo, Swe. (vĕks′shû)	146	56°53′N	14°46′E
Vaygach, i., Russia (vī-gách′)	164	70°00′N	59°00′E
Veadeiros, Chapadas dos, hills, Braz. (shä-pä′däs-dôs-vĕ-á-dá′rōs)	131	14°00′S	47°00′W
Vedea, r., Rom. (vá′dyȧ)	161	44°25′N	24°45′E
Vedia, Arg. (vĕ′dyä)	129c	34°29′S	61°30′W
Veedersburg, In., U.S. (vē′dĕrz-bûrg)	98	40°05′N	87°15′W
Vega, i., Nor.	146	65°38′N	10°51′E
Vega de Alatorre, Mex. (vā′gä dā ä-lä-tōr′rȧ)	119	20°02′N	96°39′W
Vega Real, reg., Dom. Rep. (vĕ′gä-rĕ-ä′l)	123	19°30′N	71°05′W
Vegreville, Can.	84	53°30′N	112°03′W
Vehār Lake, l., India	187b	19°11′N	72°52′E
Veinticinco de Mayo, Arg.	129c	35°26′S	60°09′W
Vejer de la Frontera, Spain	158	36°15′N	5°58′W
Vejle, Den. (vī′l*ĕ*)	146	55°41′N	9°29′E
Velbert, Ger. (fĕl′bĕrt)	157c	51°20′N	7°03′E
Velebit, mts., Yugo. (vā′lĕ-bēt)	149	44°25′N	15°23′E
Velen, Ger. (fĕ′lĕn)	157c	51°54′N	7°00′E
Vélez-Málaga, Spain (vā′lāth-mä′lä-gä)	158	36°48′N	4°05′W
Vélez-Rubio, Spain (rōō′bē-ȯ)	158	37°38′N	2°05′W
Velika Kapela, mts., Yugo. (vĕ′lē-kä kä-pĕ′lä)	149	45°03′N	15°20′E
Velika Morava, r., Yugo. (mô′rä-vä)	149	44°00′N	21°30′E
Velikaya, r., Russia (vȧ-lē′kȧ-yȧ)	162	57°25′N	28°07′E
Velikiye Luki, Russia (vyē-lē′-kyē lōō′ke)	164	56°19′N	30°32′E
Velikiy Ustyug, Russia (vȧ-lē′kĭ ōōs-tyôg′)	164	60°45′N	46°38′E
Veliko Tŭrnovo, Bul.	149	43°06′N	25°38′E
Velikoye, Russia (vȧ-lē′kô-yĕ)	162	57°21′N	39°45′E
Velikoye, l., Russia	162	57°00′N	36°53′E
Veli Lošinj, Cro. (lô′shēn′)	160	44°30′N	14°29′E
Velizh, Russia (vå′lēzh)	166	55°37′N	31°11′E
Vella Lavella, i., Sol. Is.	203	8°00′S	156°42′E
Velletri, Italy (vĕl-lā′trē)	160	41°42′N	12°48′E
Vellore, India (vĕl-lōr′)	183	12°57′N	79°09′E
Vels, Russia (vĕls)	172a	60°35′N	58°47′E
Vel′sk, Russia (vĕlsk)	164	61°00′N	42°18′E
Velten, Ger. (fel′tĕn)	145b	52°41′N	13°11′E
Velya, r., Russia (vĕl′yȧ)	172b	56°23′N	37°54′E
Velyka Lepetykha, Ukr.	163	47°11′N	33°58′E
Velykyi Bychkiv, Ukr.	155	47°59′N	24°01′E
Venadillo, Col. (vĕ-nä-dē′l-yō)	130a	4°43′N	74°55′W
Venado, Mex. (vȧ-mä′dō)	118	22°54′N	101°07′W
Venado Tuerto, Arg. (vĕ-nä′dô-tōōĕ′r-tô)	132	33°28′S	61°47′W
Vendôme, Fr. (väN-dōm′)	156	47°46′N	1°05′E
Veneto, hist. reg., Italy (vĕ-nĕ′tȯ)	160	45°58′N	11°24′E
Venëv, Russia (vĕn-ĕf′)	166	54°19′N	38°14′E
Venezia see Venice, Italy	142	45°25′N	12°18′E
Venezuela, nation, S.A. (vĕn-ē-zwē′l*ȧ*)	130	8°00′N	65°00′W
Venezuela, Golfo de, b., S.A. (gôl-fô-dĕ)	130	11°34′N	71°02′W
Veniaminof, Mount, mtn., Ak., U.S.	95	56°12′N	159°20′W
Venice, Italy	142	45°25′N	12°18′E
Venice, Ca., U.S. (vĕn′ĭs)	107a	33°59′N	118°28′W
Venice, Il., U.S.	107e	38°40′N	90°10′W
Venice, neigh., Ca., U.S.	232	34°00′N	118°29′W
Venice, Gulf of, b., Italy	148	45°23′N	13°00′E
Venlo, Neth.	157c	51°22′N	6°11′E
Vennhausen, neigh., Ger.	236	51°13′N	6°51′E
Venta, r., Eur. (vĕn′tȧ)	153	57°05′N	21°45′E
Ventana, Sierra de la, mts., Arg. (sē-ĕ-rá-dĕ-lä-vĕn-tȧ′nä)	132	38°00′S	63°00′W
Ventersburg, S. Afr. (vĕn-tĕrs′bûrg)	218d	28°06′S	27°10′E
Ventersdorp, S. Afr. (vĕn-tĕrs′dôrp)	218d	26°20′S	26°48′E
Ventimiglia, Italy (vĕn-tē-mēl′yä)	160	43°46′N	7°37′E
Ventnor, N.J., U.S. (vĕnt′nẽr)	99	39°20′N	74°25′W
Ventspils, Lat. (vĕnt′spĕls)	166	57°24′N	21°41′E
Ventuari, r., Ven. (vĕn-tōōá′rē)	130	4°47′N	65°56′W
Ventura, Ca., U.S. (vĕn-tōō′r*ȧ*)	108	34°18′N	119°18′W
Venukovsky, Russia (vĕ-nōō′kôv-skĭ)	172b	55°10′N	37°26′E
Venustiano Carranza, Mex. (vĕ-nōōs-tyä′nō-kär-rä′n-zä)	118	19°44′N	103°48′W
Venustiano Carranza, Mex. (kär-rä′n-zȯ)	119	16°21′N	92°36′W
Vera, Arg. (vĕ-rä)	132	29°22′S	60°09′W
Vera, Spain (vā′rä)	158	37°18′N	1°53′W
Veracruz, Mex.	116	19°13′N	96°07′W
Vera Cruz, state, Mex. (vā-rä-krōōz′)	116	20°30′N	97°15′W
Verāval, India (vĕr′vŭ-väl)	183	20°59′N	70°49′E
Verberg, neigh., Ger.	236	51°22′N	6°36′E
Vercelli, Italy (vĕr-chĕl′lē)	160	45°18′N	8°27′E
Verchères, Can. (vĕr-shâr′)	83a	45°46′N	73°21′W
Verde, i., Phil. (vĕr′dȧ)	197a	13°34′N	121°11′E
Verde, r., Mex.	118	21°48′N	99°50′W
Verde, r., Mex.	118	20°50′N	103°00′W
Verde, r., Mex.	119	16°05′N	97°44′W
Verde, r., Az., U.S. (vûrd)	109	34°04′N	111°40′W
Verde, Cap, c., Bah.	123	22°50′N	75°00′W
Verde, Cay, i., Bah.	123	22°00′N	75°05′W
Verde Island Passage, strt., Phil. (vĕr′dē)	197a	13°36′N	120°39′E
Verdemont, Ca., U.S. (vûr′dē-mŏnt)	107a	34°12′N	117°22′W
Verden, Ger. (fĕr′dĕn)	154	52°55′N	9°15′E
Verdigris, r., Ok., U.S. (vûr′dē-grēs)	111	36°50′N	95°29′W
Verdun, Can. (vĕr′dŭN′)	91	45°27′N	73°34′W
Verdun, Fr. (vâr-dûN′)	147	49°09′N	5°21′E
Verdun, Fr.	157	43°48′N	1°10′E
Vereeniging, S. Afr. (vĕ-rä′nĭ-gĭng)	218d	26°40′S	27°56′E
Verena, S. Afr. (vĕr-ĕn *ȧ*)	218d	25°30′S	29°02′E
Vereya, Russia (vĕ-rá′yȧ)	162	55°21′N	36°08′E
Verga, N.J., U.S.	229b	39°52′N	75°10′W
Verín, Spain (vå-rēn′)	158	41°56′N	7°26′W
Verkhne-Kamchatsk, Russia (vyĕrk′nyĕ kȧm-chatsk′)	165	54°42′N	158°41′E
Verkhne Neyvinskiy, Russia (nā-vĭn′skĭ)	172a	57°17′N	60°10′E
Verkhne Ural′sk, Russia (ö-ralsk′)	164	53°53′N	59°13′E
Verkhniy Avzyan, Russia (vyĕrk′nyē áv-zyȧn′)	172a	53°32′N	57°30′E
Verkhniye Kigi, Russia (vyĕrk′nĭ-yĕ kĭ′gĭ)	172a	55°23′N	58°37′E
Verkhniy Ufaley, Russia (ö-fá′lā)	172a	56°04′N	60°15′E
Verkhnyaya Pyshma, Russia (vyĕrk′nyä-yä pōōsh′má)	172a	56°57′N	60°37′E
Verkhnyaya Salda, Russia (säl′dȧ)	172a	58°03′N	60°33′E
Verkhnyaya Tunguska (Angara), r., Russia (tŏn-gōs′kȧ)	170	58°13′N	97°00′E
Verkhnyaya Tura, Russia (tô′rȧ)	172a	58°22′N	59°51′E
Verkhnyaya Yayva, Russia (yäy′vá)	172a	59°28′N	57°38′E
Verkhotur′ye, Russia (vyĕr-kô-tōōr′yĕ)	172a	58°52′N	60°47′E
Verkhoyansk, Russia (vyĕr-kȯ-yänsk′)	165	67°43′N	133°33′E
Verkhoyanskiy Khrebet, mts., Russia (vyĕr-kȯ-yänskĭ)	165	67°45′N	128°00′E
Vermilion, Can. (vĕr-mĭl′y*ŭ*n)	84	53°22′N	110°51′W
Vermilion, l., Mn., U.S.	103	47°49′N	92°35′W
Vermilion, r., Can.	88	53°30′N	111°00′W
Vermilion, r., Can.	91	47°30′N	73°15′W
Vermilion, r., Il., U.S.	98	41°05′N	89°00′W
Vermilion, r., Mn., U.S.	103	48°09′N	92°31′W
Vermilion Hills, hills, Can.	88	50°43′N	106°50′W
Vermilion Range, mts., Mn., U.S.	103	47°55′N	91°59′W
Vermillion, S.D., U.S.	102	42°46′N	96°56′W
Vermillion, r., S.D., U.S.	102	43°54′N	97°14′W
Vermillion Bay, b., La., U.S.	113	29°47′N	92°00′W
Vermont, Austl.	243b	37°50′S	145°12′E
Vermont, state, U.S. (vĕr-mŏnt′)	97	43°50′N	72°50′W
Vernal, Ut., U.S. (vûr′n*ȧ*l)	105	40°29′N	109°40′W
Verneuk Pan, pl., S. Afr. (vĕr-nŭk′)	212	30°10′S	21°46′E
Vernon, Can.	83c	45°10′N	75°27′W
Vernon, Can. (vĕr-nôN′)	84	50°18′N	119°15′W
Vernon, Ca., U.S. (vûr′n*ŭ*n)	107a	34°01′N	118°12′W
Vernon, In., U.S. (vûr′n*ŭ*n)	98	39°00′N	85°40′W
Vernon, N.J., U.S.	100a	39°00′N	85°40′W
Vernon, Tx., U.S.	110	34°09′N	99°16′W
Vernonia, Or., U.S. (vûr-nō′ny*ȧ*)	106c	45°52′N	123°12′W
Vero Beach, Fl., U.S. (vē′rō)	115a	27°36′N	80°25′W

ng-sing; ŋ-baŋk; N-nasalized n; nŏd; cŏmmit; ōld; ôbey; ôrder; oi-boil; fōōd; ȯ-as oo in foot; ou-out; s-soft; sh-dish; th-thin; pūre; ûnite; ûrn; stŭd; circ*ŭ*s; ü-as in French tu; ′-indeterminate vowel.

362 Véroia-Virac

PLACE (Pronunciation)	PAGE	LAT.	LONG.
Véroia, Grc.	161	40°30′N	22°13′E
Verona, Italy (vā-rō′nä)	148	45°28′N	11°02′E
Verona, N.J., U.S.	228	40°50′N	74°12′W
Verona, Pa., U.S.	230b	40°30′N	79°50′W
Verrières-le-Buisson, Fr.	237c	48°45′N	2°16′E
Versailles, Fr. (vĕr-sī′y′)	147	48°48′N	2°07′E
Versailles, Ky., U.S. (vẽr-sālz′)	98	38°05′N	84°45′W
Versailles, Mo., U.S.	111	38°27′N	92°52′W
Versailles, Pa., U.S.	230b	40°21′N	79°51′W
Versailles, neigh., Arg.	233d	34°38′S	58°31′W
Versailles, Château de, hist., Fr.	237c	48°48′N	2°07′E
Vert, Cap, c., Sen.	210	14°43′N	17°30′W
Verulam, S. Afr. (vĕ-ro͞o-lăm)	213c	29°39′S	31°08′E
Verulamium, pt. of i., Eng., U.K.	235	51°45′N	0°22′W
Verviers, Bel. (vĕr-vyā′)	151	50°35′N	5°57′E
Vesele, Ukr.	163	46°59′N	34°56′E
Vesijärvi, l., Fin.	153	61°09′N	25°10′E
Vešn'aki, neigh., Russia	239b	55°44′N	37°49′E
Vesoul, Fr. (vē-so͞ol′)	157	47°38′N	6°11′E
Vestavia Hills, Al., U.S.	100h	33°26′N	86°46′W
Vesterålen, is., Nor. (vĕs′tĕr ô′lĕn)	146	68°54′N	14°03′E
Vestfjord, fj., Nor.	142	67°33′N	12°59′E
Vestmannaeyjar, Ice. (vĕst′män-ā-ā′yär)	146	63°12′N	20°17′W
Vesuvio, vol., Italy (vĕ-so͞o′vyä)	142	40°35′N	14°26′E
Ves'yegonsk, Russia (vĕ-syĕ-gônsk′)	162	58°42′N	37°09′E
Veszprem, Hung. (vĕs′prām)	155	47°05′N	17°53′E
Vészto, Hung. (vĕs′tû)	155	46°55′N	21°18′E
Vet, r., S. Afr. (vĕt)	218d	28°25′S	26°37′E
Vetka, Bela. (vyĕt′kȧ)	162	52°36′N	31°05′E
Vetlanda, Swe. (vĕt-län′dä)	152	57°26′N	15°05′E
Vetluga, Russia (vyĕt-lo͞o′gȧ)	166	57°50′N	45°42′E
Vetluga, r., Russia	166	56°50′N	45°50′E
Vetovo, Bul. (vā′tô-vô)	161	43°42′N	26°18′E
Vetren, Bul. (vĕt′rĕn′)	161	42°16′N	24°04′E
Vevay, In., U.S. (vē′vā)	98	38°45′N	85°05′W
Veynes, Fr. (vān″)	157	44°31′N	5°47′E
Vézère, r., Fr. (vā-zer′)	156	45°01′N	1°00′E
Viacha, Bol. (vēȧ′chȧ)	130	16°43′S	68°16′W
Viadana, Italy (vē-ä-dä′nä)	160	44°55′N	10°30′E
Vian, Ok., U.S. (vī′ăn)	111	35°30′N	95°00′W
Viana, Braz. (vē-ä′nä)	131	3°09′S	44°44′W
Viana do Alentejo, Port. (vē-ä′nȧ dò ä-lĕn-tā′hò)	158	38°20′N	8°02′W
Viana do Bolo, Spain	158	42°10′N	7°07′W
Viana do Castelo, Port. (dò käs-tā′lò)	148	41°41′N	8°45′W
Viangchan, Laos	196	18°07′N	102°33′E
Viar, r., Spain (vē-ä′rä)	158	38°15′N	6°08′W
Viareggio, Italy (vē-ä-rĕd′jô)	160	43°52′N	10°14′E
Viborg, Den. (vē′bôr)	152	56°27′N	9°22′E
Vibo Valentia, Italy (vē′bô-vä-lĕ′n-tyä)	160	38°47′N	16°06′E
Vic, Spain	159	41°55′N	2°14′E
Vicálvaro, Spain	159a	40°25′N	3°37′W
Vicente López, Arg. (vē-sĕ′n-tĕ-lŏ′pĕz)	132a	34°31′S	58°29′W
Vicenza, Italy (vē-chĕnt′sä)	148	45°33′N	11°33′E
Vichuga, Russia (vē-cho͞o′gȧ)	166	57°13′N	41°58′E
Vichy, Fr. (vē-shē′)	147	46°06′N	3°28′E
Vickersund, Nor.	152	60°00′N	9°59′E
Vicksburg, Mi., U.S. (vĭks′bûrg)	98	42°10′N	85°30′W
Vicksburg, Ms., U.S.	97	32°20′N	90°50′W
Viçosa, Braz. (vē-sô′sä)	129a	20°46′S	42°51′W
Victoria, Arg. (vēk-tô′rēä)	132	32°36′S	60°09′W
Victoria, Can. (vĭk-tō′rĭ-ȧ)	84	48°26′N	123°23′W
Victoria, Chile (vēk-tô-rēä)	132	38°15′S	72°16′W
Victoria, Col. (vēk-tô′rēä)	130a	5°19′N	74°54′W
Victoria, Phil. (vēk-tô-ryä′)	197a	15°34′N	120°41′E
Victoria, Tx., U.S. (vĭk-tō′rĭ-ȧ)	113	28°48′N	97°00′W
Victoria, Va., U.S.	115	36°57′N	78°13′W
Victoria, state, Austl.	203	36°46′S	143°15′E
Victoria, neigh., Arg.	233d	34°28′S	58°31′W
Victoria, l., Afr.	212	0°50′S	32°50′E
Victoria, r., Austl.	202	17°25′S	130°50′E
Victoria, Mount, mtn., Myanmar	183	21°26′N	93°59′E
Victoria, Mount, mtn., Pap. N. Gui.	197	9°35′S	147°45′E
Victoria de las Tunas, Cuba (vēk-tô′rē-ä dā läs to͞o′näs)	122	20°55′N	77°05′W
Victoria Falls, wtfl., Afr.	212	17°55′S	25°51′E
Victoria Island, i., Can.	82	70°13′N	107°45′W
Victoria Island, i., Nig.	244d	6°26′N	3°26′E
Victoria Lake, l., Can.	93	48°20′N	57°40′W
Victoria Land, reg., Ant.	219	75°00′S	160°00′E
Victoria Nile, r., Ug.	217	2°20′N	31°35′E
Victoria Peak, mtn., Belize (vēk-tōrĭ′ȧ)	120a	16°47′N	88°40′W
Victoria Peak, mtn., Can.	86	50°03′N	126°06′W
Victoria Peak, mtn., H.K.	241c	22°17′N	114°08′E
Victoria River Downs, Austl. (vĭc-tôr′ĭȧ)	202	16°30′S	131°10′E
Victoria Station, pt. of i., Eng., U.K.	237b	53°29′N	2°15′W
Victoria Strait, strt., Can. (vĭk-tō′rĭ-ȧ)	84	69°10′N	100°58′W
Victoriaville, Can. (vĭk-tō′rĭ-ȧ-vĭl)	85	46°04′N	71°59′W
Victoria West, S. Afr. (wĕst)	212	31°25′S	23°10′E
Vidalia, Ga., U.S. (vĭ-dā′lĭ-ȧ)	115	32°10′N	82°26′W
Vidalia, La., U.S.	113	31°33′N	91°28′W
Vidin, Bul. (vĭ′dĭn)	149	44°00′N	22°53′E
Vidnoye, Russia	172b	55°33′N	37°41′E
Vidzy, Bela. (vē′dzĭ)	162	55°23′N	26°46′E
Viedma, Arg. (vyād′mä)	132	40°55′S	63°03′W
Viedma, l., Arg.	132	49°40′S	72°35′W
Viejo, r., Nic. (vyā′hō)	120	12°45′N	86°19′W
Vienna (Wien), Aus.	142	48°13′N	16°22′E
Vienna, Ga., U.S. (vē-ĕn′ȧ)	114	32°03′N	83°50′W
Vienna, Il., U.S.	111	37°24′N	88°50′W
Vienna, Va., U.S.	100e	38°54′N	77°16′W
Vienne, Fr. (vyĕn′)	147	45°31′N	4°54′E
Vienne, r., Fr.	156	47°06′N	0°20′E
Vientiane *see* Viangchan, Laos	196	18°07′N	102°33′E
Vieques, P.R. (vyā′kås)	117b	18°09′N	65°27′W
Vieques, i., P.R. (vyā′kås)	117b	18°05′N	65°28′W
Vierfontein, S. Afr. (vēr′fŏn-tān)	218d	27°06′S	26°45′E
Vieringhausen, neigh., Ger.	236	51°11′N	7°10′E
Viersen, Ger. (fēr′zĕn)	157c	51°15′N	6°24′E
Vierwaldstätter See, l., Switz.	154	46°54′N	8°36′E
Vierzon, Fr. (vyâr-zôN′)	147	47°14′N	2°04′E
Viesca, Mex. (vē-ās′kä)	112	25°21′N	102°47′W
Viesca, Laguna de, l., Mex. (lä-ò′nä-dĕ)	112	25°30′N	102°40′W
Vieste, Italy (vyĕs′tå)	160	41°52′N	16°10′E
Vietnam, nation, Asia (vyĕt′näm′)	196	18°00′N	107°00′E
View Park, Ca., U.S.	232	34°00′N	118°21′W
Vigan, Phil. (vēgän)	196	17°36′N	120°22′E
Vigentino, neigh., Italy	238c	45°25′N	9°11′E
Vigevano, Italy (vē-jā-vä′nô)	160	45°18′N	8°52′E
Vigny, Fr. (vēn-y′ē′)	157b	49°05′N	1°54′E
Vigo, Spain (vē′gō)	142	42°18′N	8°42′W
Vihti, Fin. (vĭ′tĭ)	153	60°27′N	24°18′E
Vijayawāda, India	183	16°31′N	80°37′E
Viksøyri, Nor.	152	61°06′N	6°35′E
Vila Augusta, Braz.	234d	23°28′S	46°32′W
Vila Boacaya, neigh., Braz.	234d	23°29′S	46°44′W
Vila Caldas Xavier, Moz.	217	15°59′S	34°12′E
Vila de Manica, Moz. (vē′lä dā mä-nē′kȧ)	212	18°48′S	32°49′E
Vila de Rei, Port. (vē′lȧ dā rā′ĭ)	158	39°42′N	8°03′W
Vila do Conde, Port. (vē′lȧ dò kōn′dĕ)	158	41°21′N	8°44′W
Vilafranca del Penedès, Spain	159	41°20′N	1°40′E
Vilafranca de Xira, Port. (fräŋ′kȧ dā shē′rȧ)	158	38°58′N	8°59′W
Vila Guilherme, neigh., Braz.	234d	23°30′S	46°36′W
Vilaine, r., Fr. (vē-lân′)	156	47°34′N	2°15′W
Vila Isabel, neigh., Braz.	234c	22°55′S	43°15′W
Vila Jaguára, neigh., Braz.	234d	23°31′S	46°45′W
Vilalba, Spain	158	43°18′N	7°43′W
Vila Madalena, neigh., Braz.	234d	23°33′S	46°42′W
Vila Mariana, neigh., Braz.	234d	23°35′S	46°38′W
Vilanculos, Moz. (vē-län-ko͞o′lòs)	212	22°03′S	35°13′E
Vilāni, Lat. (vē′lȧ-nĭ)	153	56°31′N	27°00′E
Vila Nova de Foz Côa, Port. (nō′vȧ dā fôz-kō′ȧ)	158	41°08′N	7°11′W
Vila Nova de Gaia, Port. (vē′lȧ nō′vȧ dā gä′yȧ)	158	41°08′N	8°40′W
Vila Nova de Milfontes, Port. (nō′vȧ dā mēl-fōn′tāzh)	158	37°44′N	8°48′W
Vila Progresso, Braz.	234c	22°55′S	43°03′W
Vila Prudente, neigh., Braz.	234d	23°35′S	46°33′W
Vila Real, Port. (rā-äl′)	148	41°18′N	7°48′W
Vila-real, Spain	159	39°55′N	0°07′W
Vila Real de Santo Antonio, Port.	158	37°14′N	7°25′W
Vila Viçosa, Port. (vē-sō′zȧ)	158	38°47′N	7°24′W
Vileyka, Bela. (vē-lā′ē-kȧ)	162	54°19′N	26°58′E
Vilhelmina, Swe.	146	64°37′N	16°30′E
Viljandi, Est. (vēl′yän-dē)	166	58°24′N	25°34′E
Viljoenskroon, S. Afr.	218d	27°13′S	26°58′E
Vilkaviškis, Lith. (vēl-kȧ-vēsh′kēs)	153	54°40′N	23°08′E
Vil'kitskogo, i., Russia (vyl-kēts-kōgō)	170	73°25′N	76°00′E
Villa Acuña, Mex. (vēl′yä-ko͞o′n-yä)	112	29°20′N	100°56′W
Villa Adelina, neigh., Arg.	233d	34°31′S	58°32′W
Villa Ahumada, Mex. (ä-o͞o-mä′dä)	112	30°43′N	106°30′W
Villa Alta, Mex. (äl′tä)(sän ēl-dä-fōn′sō)	119	17°20′N	96°08′W
Villa Angela, Arg. (vē′l-yä á′n-кĕ-lä)	132	27°31′S	60°42′W
Villa Ballester, Arg. (vē′l-yä-bäl-yĕs-tĕr)	132a	34°33′S	58°33′W
Villa Bella, Bol. (bĕ′l-yä)	130	10°25′S	65°22′W
Villablino, Spain (vēl-yä-blē′nò)	158	42°58′N	6°18′W
Villa Borghese, pt. of i., Italy	239c	41°55′N	12°29′E
Villa Bosch, neigh., Arg.	233d	34°36′S	58°34′W
Villacañas, Spain (vēl-yä-kän′yäs)	158	39°39′N	3°20′W
Villacarrillo, Spain (vēl-yä-kä-rēl′yò)	158	38°09′N	3°07′W
Villach, Aus. (fē′läк)	147	46°38′N	13°50′E
Villacidro, Italy (vē-lä-chē′drò)	160	39°28′N	8°41′E
Villa Ciudadela, neigh., Arg.	233d	34°38′S	58°34′W
Villa Clara, prov., Cuba	122	22°40′N	80°10′W
Villa Constitución, Arg. (kōn-stē-to͞o-syōn′)	129c	33°15′S	60°19′W
Villa Coronado, Mex. (kō-rō-nä′dhō)	112	26°45′N	105°10′W
Villa Cuauhtémoc, Mex. (vēl′yä-ko͞o-äò-tĕ′mòk)	119	22°11′N	97°50′W
Villa de Allende, Mex. (vēl′yä′dā äl-yĕn′dā)	112	25°18′N	100°01′W
Villa de Alvarez, Mex. (vēl′yä-dĕ-ä′l-vä-rĕz)	118	19°17′N	103°44′W
Villa de Cura, Ven. (dĕ-ko͞o′rä)	131b	10°03′N	67°29′W
Villa de Guadalupe, Mex. (dĕ-gwä-dhä-lo͞o′på)	118	23°22′N	100°44′W
Villa de Mayo, Arg.	132a	34°31′S	58°41′W
Villa Devoto, neigh., Arg.	233d	34°36′S	58°31′W
Villa Diamante, neigh., Arg.	233d	34°41′S	58°26′W
Villa Dolores, Arg. (vēl′yä dò-lō′räs)	132	31°50′S	65°05′W
Villa Domínico, neigh., Arg.	233d	34°41′S	58°20′W
Villa Escalante, Mex. (vēl′yä-ĕs-kä-lán′tĕ)	118	19°24′N	101°36′W
Villa Flores, Mex. (vēl′yä-flō′räs)	119	16°13′N	93°17′W
Villafranca, Italy (vēl-lä-fräŋ′kä)	160	45°22′N	10°53′E
Villafranca del Bierzo, Spain	158	42°37′N	6°49′W
Villafranca de los Barros, Spain	158	38°34′N	6°22′W
Villafranche-de-Rouergue, Fr. (dē-ro͞o-ĕrg′)	156	44°21′N	2°02′E
Villa García, Mex. (gär-sē′ä)	118	22°07′N	101°55′W
Villagarcía, Spain	158	42°38′N	8°43′W
Villagrán, Mex.	112	24°28′N	99°30′W
Villa Grove, Il., U.S. (vĭl′ȧ grōv)	98	39°55′N	88°15′W
Villaguay, Arg. (vē′l-yä-gwī)	132	31°47′S	58°53′W
Villa Hayes, Para. (vĕl′yä äyås)(hāz)	132	25°07′S	57°31′W
Villahermosa, Mex. (vēl′yä-ĕr-mō′sä)	116	17°59′N	92°56′W
Villa Hidalgo, Mex. (vēl′yäē-däl′gō)	118	21°39′N	102°41′W
Villa José L. Suárez, neigh., Arg.	233d	34°32′S	58°34′W
Villaldama, Mex. (vēl-yäl-dä′mä)	116	26°30′N	100°26′W
Villa Lopez, Mex. (vēl′yä lō′pĕz)	112	27°00′N	105°02′W
Villalpando, Spain (vēl-yäl-pän′dō)	158	41°54′N	5°24′W
Villa Lugano, neigh., Arg.	233d	34°41′S	58°28′W
Villa Lynch, neigh., Arg.	233d	34°36′S	58°32′W
Villa Madero, Arg.	233d	34°41′S	58°30′W
Villa María, Arg. (vē′l-yä-mä-rē′ä)	132	32°17′S	63°08′W
Villamatín, Spain (vēl-yä-mä-tē′n)	158	36°50′N	5°38′W
Villa Mercedes, Arg. (mĕr-sā′dås)	132	33°38′S	65°16′W
Villa Montes, Bol. (vē′l-yä-mô′n-tĕs)	130	21°13′S	63°26′W
Villa Morelos, Mex. (mô-rĕ′lomcs)	118	20°01′N	101°24′W
Villa Nova, Md., U.S.	229c	39°21′N	76°44′W
Villanova, Pa., U.S.	229b	40°02′N	75°21′W
Villanueva, Col. (vē′l-yä-nòĕ′vä)	130	10°44′N	73°08′W
Villanueva, Hond. (vēl′yä-nwā′vä)	120	15°19′N	88°02′W
Villanueva, Mex. (vēl′yä-nòĕ′vä)	118	22°25′N	102°53′W
Villanueva de Córdoba, Spain (vēl-yä-nwĕ′vä-dä kôr′dò-bä)	158	38°18′N	4°38′W
Villanueva de la Serena, Spain (lä sā-rā′nä)	158	38°59′N	5°56′W
Villa Obregón, Mex. (vē′l-yä-ô-brĕ-gô′n)	119a	19°21′N	99°11′W
Villa Ocampo, Mex. (ô-käm′pō)	112	26°26′N	105°30′W
Villa Pedro Montoya, Mex. (vēl′yä-pĕ′drô-môn-tô′yȧ)	118	21°38′N	99°51′W
Villard-Bonnot, Fr. (vēl-yär′bōn-nō′)	157	45°15′N	5°53′E
Villa Real, neigh., Arg.	233d	34°37′S	58°31′W
Villarrica, Para. (vēl-yä-rē′kä)	132	25°55′S	56°23′W
Villarrobledo, Spain (vēl-yär-rô-blā′dhō)	148	39°15′N	2°37′W
Villa Sáenz Peña, neigh., Arg.	233d	34°36′S	58°31′W
Villa San Andrés, neigh., Arg.	233d	34°33′S	58°32′W
Villa Santos Lugares, neigh., Arg.	233d	34°36′S	58°32′W
Villa Unión, Mex. (vĕl′yä-o͞o-nyōn′)	118	23°10′N	106°14′W
Villaverde, neigh., Spain	238b	40°21′N	3°42′W
Villavicencio, Col. (vē′l-yä-vē-sĕ′n-syō)	130	4°09′N	73°38′W
Villaviciosa de Odón, Spain	159a	40°22′N	3°38′W
Villavieja, Col. (vē′l-yä-vē-ĕ′kȧ)	130a	3°13′N	75°13′W
Villazón, Bol. (vē′l-yä-zô′n)	130	22°02′S	65°42′W
Villecresnes, Fr.	237c	48°43′N	2°32′E
Ville-d'Avray, Fr.	237c	48°50′N	2°11′E
Villefranche, Fr.	147	45°59′N	4°43′E
Villejuif, Fr. (vēl′zhüst′)	157b	48°48′N	2°22′E
Ville-Marie, Can.	85	47°18′N	79°22′W
Villemomble, Fr.	237c	48°53′N	2°31′E
Villena, Spain (vē-lyā′nȧ)	148	38°37′N	0°52′W
Villenbon-sur-Yvette, Fr.	237c	48°42′N	2°15′E
Villeneuve, Can. (vēl′nûv′)	83g	53°40′N	113°49′W
Villeneuve-le-Roi, Fr.	237c	48°44′N	2°25′E
Villeneuve-Saint Georges, Fr. (săN-zhôrzh′)	157b	48°43′N	2°27′E
Villeneuve-sur-Lot, Fr. (sür-lō′)	156	44°25′N	0°41′E
Villeparisis, Fr.	237c	48°56′N	2°37′E
Ville Platte, La., U.S. (vēl plăt′)	113	30°41′N	92°17′W
Villers Cotterêts, Fr. (vē-âr′kô-trĕ′)	157b	49°15′N	3°05′E
Villers-sur-Marne, Fr.	237c	48°50′N	2°33′E
Villerupt, Fr. (vēl′rüp′)	157	49°28′N	6°16′E
Ville-Saint Georges, Can. (vĭl-sĕN-zhôrzh′)	91	46°07′N	70°40′W
Villeta, Col. (vē′l-yĕ′tȧ)	130a	5°02′N	74°29′W
Villeurbanne, Fr. (vēl-ûr-băn′)	147	45°43′N	4°55′E
Villiers, S. Afr. (vĭl′ĭ-ĕrs)	218d	27°03′S	28°38′E
Villiers-le-Bâcle, Fr.	237c	48°44′N	2°08′E
Villiers-le-Bel, Fr.	237c	49°00′N	2°23′E
Villingen-Schwenningen, Ger.	154	48°04′N	8°33′E
Villisca, Ia., U.S. (vĭ′lĭs′kȧ)	103	40°56′N	94°56′W
Villupuram, India	187	11°59′N	79°33′E
Vilnius, Lith. (vĭl′nē-òs)	164	54°40′N	25°26′E
Vilppula, Fin. (vĭl′pŭ-lȧ)	153	62°01′N	24°24′E
Vil'shanka, Ukr.	163	48°14′N	30°52′E
Vil'shany, Ukr.	163	50°02′N	35°54′E
Vilvoorde, Bel.	145a	50°56′N	4°25′E
Vilyuy, r., Russia (vēl′yĭ)	165	63°00′N	121°00′E
Vilyuysk, Russia (vē-lyo͞o′ĭsk′)	165	63°41′N	121°47′E
Vimmerby, Swe. (vĭm′ĕr-bü)	152	57°41′N	15°51′E
Vimperk, Czech Rep. (vĭm-pĕrk′)	154	49°04′N	13°41′E
Viña del Mar, Chile (vē′nyä dĕl mär′)	132	33°00′S	71°33′W
Vinalhaven, Me., U.S. (vī-năl-hā′vĕn)	92	44°03′N	68°49′W
Vinaròs, Spain	159	40°29′N	0°27′E
Vincennes, Fr. (văN-sĕn′)	157b	48°51′N	2°27′E
Vincennes, In., U.S. (vĭn-zĕnz′)	97	38°40′N	87°30′W
Vincennes, Château de, hist., Fr.	237c	48°51′N	2°26′E
Vincent, Al., U.S. (vĭn′sĕnt)	114	33°21′N	86°25′W
Vindelälven, r., Swe.	146	65°02′N	18°30′E
Vindeln, Swe. (vĭn′dĕln)	146	64°10′N	19°52′E
Vindhya Range, mts., India (vĭnd′yä)	183	22°30′N	75°50′E
Vineland, N.J., U.S. (vīn′lănd)	99	39°30′N	75°00′W
Vinh, Viet (vĕn′y′)	196	18°38′N	105°42′E
Vinhais, Port. (vĕn-yä′ēzh)	158	41°51′N	7°00′W
Vinings, Ga., U.S. (vī′nĭngz)	100c	33°52′N	84°28′W
Vinita, Ok., U.S. (vĭ-nē′tȧ)	111	36°38′N	95°09′W
Vinkovci, Cro. (vēn′kôv-tsē)	161	45°17′N	18°47′E
Vinnytsia, Ukr.	164	49°13′N	28°31′E
Vinnytsia, prov., Ukr.	163	48°45′N	28°01′E
Vinogradovo, Russia (vĭ-nô-grä′do-vô)	172b	55°25′N	38°33′E
Vinson Massif, mtn., Ant.	219	77°40′S	87°00′W
Vinton, Ia., U.S. (vĭn′tŭn)	103	42°08′N	92°01′W
Vinton, La., U.S.	113	30°12′N	93°35′W
Violet, La., U.S. (vī′ō-lĕt)	100d	29°54′N	89°54′W
Virac, Phil. (vē-räk′)	193	13°38′N	124°20′E

PRONOUNCING INDEX Virbalis - Walled Lake 363

PLACE (Pronunciation)	PAGE	LAT.	LONG.
Virbalis, Lith. (vėr'bá-lės)	153	54°38'N	22°55'E
Virden, Can. (vûr'dĕn)	84	49°51'N	101°55'W
Virden, Il., U.S.	111	39°28'N	89°46'W
Vírgen del San Cristóbal, rel., Chile	234b	33°26'S	70°39'W
Virgin, r., U.S.	109	36°51'N	113°50'W
Virginia, S. Afr.	218d	28°07'S	26°54'E
Virginia, Mn., U.S. (vĕr-jĭn'yȧ)	97	47°32'N	92°36'W
Virginia, state, U.S.	97	37°00'N	80°45'W
Virginia Beach, Va., U.S.	99	36°50'N	75°58'W
Virginia City, Nv., U.S.	108	39°18'N	119°40'W
Virginia Hills, Va., U.S.	229d	38°47'N	77°06'W
Virginia Water, Eng., U.K.	235	51°24'N	0°34'W
Virgin Islands, is., N.A. (vûr'jĭn)	117	18°15'N	64°00'W
Viroflay, Fr.	237c	48°48'N	2°10'E
Víron, Grc.	239d	37°57'N	23°45'E
Viroqua, Wi., U.S. (vĭ-rō'kwȧ)	103	43°33'N	90°54'W
Virovitica, Cro. (vė-rô-vē'tė-tsȧ)	161	45°50'N	17°24'E
Virpazar, Yugo. (vėr'pä-zär')	161	42°16'N	19°06'E
Virrat, Fin. (vĭr'ät)	153	62°15'N	23°45'E
Virserum, Swe. (vĭr'sĕ-ro͝om)	152	57°22'N	15°35'E
Vis, Cro. (vės)	160	43°03'N	16°11'E
Vis, i., Yugo.	149	43°00'N	16°10'E
Visalia, Ca., U.S. (vĭ-sā'lĭ-ȧ)	108	36°20'N	119°18'W
Visby, Swe. (vĭs'bü)	142	57°39'N	18°19'E
Viscount Melville Sound, strt., Can.	82	74°00'N	110°00'W
Višegrad, Bos. (vē'shĕ-gräd)	161	43°48'N	19°17'E
Vishākhapatnam, India	183	17°48'N	83°21'E
Vishera, r., Russia (vĭ'shĕ-rȧ)	172a	60°40'N	58°46'E
Vishnyakovo, Russia	172b	55°44'N	38°10'E
Vishoek, S. Afr.	212a	34°13'S	18°26'E
Visim, Russia (vē'sĭm)	172a	57°38'N	59°32'E
Viskan, r., Swe.	152	57°20'N	12°25'E
Višķi, Lat. (vēs'kĭ)	153	56°02'N	26°47'E
Visoko, Bos. (vē'sô-kô)	161	43°59'N	18°10'E
Vistula see Wisła, r., Pol.	142	52°30'N	20°00'E
Vitarte, Peru	233c	12°02'S	76°54'W
Vitebsk, Bela. (vē'tyĕpsk)	164	55°12'N	30°16'E
Vitebsk, prov., Bela.	162	55°05'N	29°18'E
Viterbo, Italy (vė-tĕr'bō)	148	42°24'N	12°08'E
Viti Levu, i., Fiji	198g	18°00'S	178°00'E
Vitim, Russia (vē'tėm)	165	59°22'N	112°43'E
Vitim, r., Russia (vē'tėm)	165	54°00'N	115°00'E
Vitino, Russia (vē'tĭ-nô)	172c	59°40'N	29°51'E
Vitória, Braz. (vė-tō'rė-ä)	131	20°09'S	40°17'W
Vitoria, Spain (vē-tô-ryä)	148	42°43'N	2°43'W
Vitória de Conquista, Braz. (vė-tō'rė-ä-dä-kōn-kwē's-tä)	131	14°51'S	40°44'W
Vitry-le-François, Fr. (vė-trē'lĕ-frän-swȧ')	156	48°44'N	4°34'E
Vitry-sur-Seine, Fr.	237c	48°48'N	2°24'E
Vittorio, Italy (vė-tô'rė-ô)	160	45°59'N	12°17'E
Viveiro, Spain	158	43°39'N	7°37'W
Vivian, La., U.S. (vĭv'ĭ-ȧn)	113	32°51'N	93°59'W
Vizianagaram, India	183	18°10'N	83°29'E
Vlaardingen, Neth. (vlär'dĭng-ĕn)	151	51°54'N	4°20'E
Vladikavkaz, Russia	167	43°05'N	44°35'E
Vladimir, Russia (vlá-dyē'mėr)	164	56°08'N	40°24'E
Vladimir, prov., Russia (vlä-dyē'mĕr)	162	56°08'N	39°53'E
Vladimiro-Aleksandrovskoye, Russia	194	42°50'N	133°00'E
Vladivostok, Russia (vlá-dė-vôs-tŏk')	165	43°06'N	131°47'E
Vladykino, neigh., Russia	239b	55°52'N	37°36'E
Vlasenica, Bos. (vlä'sĕ-nēt'sȧ)	161	44°11'N	18°58'E
Vlasotince, Yugo. (vlä'sô-tėn-tsĕ)	161	42°58'N	22°08'E
Vlieland, i., Neth. (vlē'länt)	151	53°19'N	4°55'E
Vlissingen, Neth. (vlĭs'sĭng-ĕn)	151	51°30'N	3°34'E
Vlorë, Alb.	149	40°27'N	19°30'E
Vltava, r., Czech Rep.	154	49°24'N	14°18'E
Vodl, l., Russia (vôd''l)	166	62°20'N	37°20'E
Voerde, Ger.	157c	51°35'N	6°41'E
Vogelheim, neigh., Ger.	236	51°29'N	6°59'E
Voghera, Italy (vô-gā'rä)	160	44°58'N	9°02'E
Vohwinkel, neigh., Ger.	236	51°14'N	7°09'E
Voight, r., Wa., U.S.	106a	47°03'N	122°08'W
Voinjama, Lib.	214	8°25'N	9°45'W
Voiron, Fr. (vwȧ-rôɴ')	157	45°23'N	5°48'E
Voisin, Lac, l., Can. (vwŏ'-zĭn)	88	54°13'N	107°15'W
Volchansk, Ukr. (vôl-chänsk')	167	50°18'N	36°56'E
Volchonka-Zil, neigh., Russia	239b	55°40'N	37°37'E
Volga, r., Russia (vôl'gä)	164	47°30'N	46°20'E
Volga, Mouths of the, mth.	167	46°00'N	49°10'E
Volgograd, Russia (vŏl-gō-grä't)	164	48°40'N	42°20'E
Volgogradskoye, res., Russia (vôl-gô-grad'skô-yĕ)	164	51°10'N	45°10'E
Volkhov, Russia (vôl'kôf)	153	59°54'N	32°21'E
Volkhov, r., Russia	166	58°45'N	31°40'E
Volkovysk, Bela. (vôl-kô-vėsk')	155	53°11'N	24°29'E
Vollme, Ger.	236	51°10'N	7°36'E
Volmarstein, Ger.	236	51°22'N	7°23'E
Volmerswerth, neigh., Ger.	236	51°11'N	6°46'E
Volodarskiy, Russia (vô-lô-där'skĭ)	172c	59°49'N	30°06'E
Volodymyr-Volyns'kyi, Ukr.	155	50°50'N	24°20'E
Vologda, Russia (vô'lôg-dȧ)	164	59°12'N	39°52'E
Vologda, prov., Russia	162	59°00'N	37°26'E
Volokolamsk, Russia (vô-lô-kôlámsk)	162	56°02'N	35°58'E
Volokonovka, Russia (vô-lô-kô'nôf-kȧ)	163	50°28'N	37°52'E
Volozhin, Bela. (vô'lô-shėn)	162	54°04'N	26°38'E
Vol'sk, Russia (vôl'sk)	167	52°02'N	47°23'E
Volta, r., Ghana	214	6°05'N	0°30'E
Volta, Lake, res., Ghana (vôl'tȧ)	210	7°10'N	0°30'W
Volta Blanche (White Volta), r., Afr.	214	11°30'N	0°40'W
Volta Noire see Black Volta, r., Afr.	210	11°30'N	4°00'W
Volta Redonda, Braz. (vōl'tä-rā-dôn'dä)	131	22°32'S	44°05'W
Volterra, Italy (vôl-tĕr'rä)	160	43°22'N	10°51'E
Voltri, Italy (vōl'trē)	160	44°25'N	8°45'E
Volturno, r., Italy (vôl-to͞or'nô)	160	41°12'N	14°20'E
Vólvi, Límni, l., Grc.	161	40°41'N	23°23'E
Volzhskoye, l., Russia (vôl'sh-skô-yĕ)	162	56°43'N	36°18'E
Von Ormy, Tx., U.S. (vōn ôr'mė)	107d	29°18'N	98°36'W
Võõpsu, Est. (vo͞op'sò)	153	58°06'N	27°30'E
Voorburg, Neth.	145a	52°04'N	4°21'E
Voortrekkerhoogte, S. Afr.	213b	25°48'S	28°10'E
Vop', r., Russia (vôp)	162	55°20'N	32°55'E
Vopnafjördur, Ice.	146	65°43'N	14°58'W
Vorarlberg, prov., Aus.	154	47°20'N	9°55'E
Vordingborg, Den. (vôr'dĭng-bôr)	152	55°10'N	11°55'E
Vorhalle, neigh., Ger.	236	51°23'N	7°28'E
Vorías Sporádhes, is., Grc.	161	38°55'N	24°05'E
Vorkuta, Russia (vôr-ko͞o'tȧ)	164	67°28'N	63°40'E
Vormholz, Ger.	236	51°24'N	7°18'E
Vormsi, i., Est. (vôrm'sĭ)	153	59°06'N	23°05'E
Vórois Evvoïkós Kólpos, b., Grc.	161	38°48'N	23°02'E
Vorona, r., Russia (vô-rō'na)	167	51°50'N	42°00'E
Voronezh, Russia (vô-rō'nyĕzh)	164	51°39'N	39°11'E
Voronezh, prov., Russia	163	51°10'N	39°13'E
Voronezh, r., Russia	167	52°17'N	39°32'E
Voronovo, Bela. (vô'rô-nô-vô)	155	54°07'N	25°16'E
Vorontsovka, Russia (vô-rônt'sôv-kȧ)	172a	59°40'N	60°14'E
Voron'ya, r., Russia (vô-rô'nyȧ)	166	68°20'N	35°20'E
Võrts-Järv, l., Est. (vôrts yärv)	153	58°15'N	26°12'E
Võru, Est. (vô'rû)	166	57°50'N	26°58'E
Vorya, r., Russia (vôr'yȧ)	172b	55°55'N	38°15'E
Vosges, mts., Fr. (vōzh)	147	48°09'N	6°57'E
Voskresensk, Russia (vôs-krĕ-sĕnsk')	172b	55°20'N	38°42'E
Voss, Nor. (vôs)	146	60°40'N	6°24'E
Vostryakovo, Russia	172b	55°23'N	37°49'E
Votkinsk, Russia (vôt-kēnsk')	166	57°00'N	54°00'E
Votkinskoye Vodokhranilishche, res., Russia	166	57°30'N	55°00'E
Vouga, r., Port. (vō'gȧ)	158	40°43'N	7°51'W
Vouziers, Fr. (vo͞o-zyā')	156	49°25'N	4°40'E
Voxnan, r., Swe.	152	61°30'N	15°24'E
Voyageurs National Park, Mn., U.S.	103	48°30'N	92°40'W
Vozhe, l., Russia (vôzh'yĕ)	166	60°40'N	39°00'E
Voznesens'k, Ukr.	167	47°34'N	31°22'E
Vradiïvka, Ukr.	163	47°51'N	30°38'E
Vrangelya (Wrangel), i., Russia	164	71°25'N	178°30'W
Vranje, Yugo. (vrän'yĕ)	161	42°33'N	21°55'E
Vratsa, Bul. (vrät'tsȧ)	149	43°12'N	23°31'E
Vrbas, Yugo. (v'r'bäs)	161	45°34'N	19°43'E
Vrbas, r., Yugo.	161	44°25'N	17°17'E
Vrchlabí, Czech Rep. (v'r'chlä-bė)	154	50°32'N	15°51'E
Vrede, S. Afr. (vrĭ'dĕ)(vrēd)	218d	27°25'S	29°11'E
Vredefort, S. Afr. (vrĭ'dĕ-fôrt)(vrĕd'fōrt)	218d	27°00'S	27°21'E
Vreeswijk, Neth.	145a	52°00'N	5°06'E
Vršac, Yugo. (v'r'shäts)	149	45°08'N	21°18'E
Vrutky, Slvk. (vro͞ot'kė)	155	49°09'N	18°55'E
Vryburg, S. Afr. (vrĭ'bûrg)	212	26°55'S	24°45'E
Vryheid, S. Afr. (vrĭ'hīt)	212	27°43'S	30°58'E
Vsetín, Czech Rep. (fsĕt'yēn)	155	49°21'N	18°01'E
Vsevolozhskiy, Russia (vsyĕ'vôlô'zh-skēē)	172c	60°01'N	30°41'E
Vuelta Abajo, reg., Cuba (vwĕl'tä ä-bä'hō)	122	22°20'N	83°45'W
Vught, Neth.	145a	51°38'N	5°18'E
Vukovar, Cro. (vô'kô-vär)	161	45°20'N	19°00'E
Vulcan, Mi., U.S. (vŭl'kăn)	98	45°45'N	87°50'W
Vulcano, i., Italy (vo͞ol-kä'nô)	160	38°23'N	15°00'E
Vûlchedrŭma, Bul.	161	43°43'N	23°29'E
Vyartsilya, Russia (vyär-tsē'lyȧ)	153	62°10'N	30°40'E
Vyatka, r., Russia (vyát'kȧ)	166	59°20'N	51°25'E
Vyazemskiy, Russia (vyá-zĕm'skĭ)	194	47°29'N	134°39'E
Vyaz'ma, Russia (vyáz'mȧ)	166	55°12'N	34°17'E
Vyazniki, Russia (vyáz'nė-kė)	166	56°10'N	42°10'E
Vyborg, Russia (vwē'bôrk)	164	60°43'N	28°46'E
Vychegda, r., Russia (vė'chĕg-dȧ)	166	61°40'N	48°00'E
Vylkove, Ukr.	167	45°24'N	29°36'E
Vym, r., Russia (vwĕm)	166	63°15'N	51°20'E
Vyritsa, Russia (vē'rĭ-tsȧ)	172c	59°24'N	30°20'E
Vyshnevolotskoye, l., Russia (vŭy'sh-ņē'vôlôt's-kô'yĕ)	162	57°30'N	34°27'E
Vyshniy Volochëk, Russia (vėsh'nyĭ vôl-ô-chĕk')	164	57°34'N	34°35'E
Vyškov, Czech Rep. (vėsh'kôf)	154	49°17'N	16°58'E
Vysoké Mýto, Czech Rep. (vû'sô-kā mū'tô)	154	49°58'N	16°07'E
Vysokovsk, Russia (vĭ-sô'kôfsk)	162	56°16'N	36°32'E
Vytegra, Russia (vû'tĕg-rȧ)	164	61°00'N	36°20'E
Vyzhnytsia, Ukr.	155	48°16'N	25°12'E
W			
W, Parcs Nationaux du, rec., Niger	215	12°20'N	2°40'E
Waal, r., Neth. (väl)	151	51°46'N	5°00'E
Waalwijk, Neth.	145a	51°41'N	5°05'E
Wabamun, Grc.	149	39°23'N	22°56'E
Wabamuno, Can. (wŏ'bă-mŭn)	87	53°33'N	114°28'W
Wabasca, Can. (wŏ-bás'kȧ)	87	56°00'N	113°53'W
Wabash, In., U.S. (wô'băsh)	98	40°45'N	85°50'W
Wabash, r., U.S.	97	38°00'N	88°00'W
Wabasha, Mn., U.S. (wä'bȧ-shô)	103	44°24'N	92°04'W
Wabe Gestro, r., Eth.	211	6°25'N	41°21'E
Wabowden, Can. (wä-bō'd'n)	89	54°55'N	98°38'W
Wąbrzeźno, Pol. (vôŋ-bzĕzh'nô)	155	53°17'N	18°59'E
Wabu Hu, l., China (wä-bo͞o ho͞o)	190	32°25'N	116°35'E
W. A. C. Bennett Dam, dam, Can.	87	56°01'N	122°10'W
Waccamaw, r., S.C., U.S. (wăk'ȧ-mô)	115	33°47'N	78°55'W
Waccasassa Bay, b., Fl., U.S. (wă-kȧ-să'sȧ)	114	29°02'N	83°10'W
Wachow, Ger. (vä'kōv)	145b	53°32'N	12°46'E
Waco, Tx., U.S. (wā'kō)	96	31°35'N	97°06'W
Waconda Lake, res., Ks., U.S.	110	39°45'N	98°15'W
Wadayama, Japan (wä'dä'yä-mä)	195	35°19'N	134°49'E
Waddenzee, sea, Neth.	151	53°00'N	4°50'E
Waddington, Mount, mtn., Can. (wŏd'dĭng-tŭn)	84	51°23'N	125°15'W
Wadena, Can.	88	51°57'N	103°50'W
Wadena, Mn., U.S. (wŏ-dē'nȧ)	102	46°26'N	95°09'W
Wadesboro, N.C., U.S. (wādz'bŭr-ô)	115	34°57'N	80°05'W
Wadeville, S. Afr.	244b	26°16'S	28°11'E
Wadley, Ga., U.S. (wŭd'lė)	115	32°54'N	82°25'W
Wad Madani, Sudan (wäd mē-dä'nē)	211	14°27'N	33°31'E
Wadowice, Pol. (vá-dô'vēt-sĕ)	155	49°53'N	19°31'E
Wadsworth, Oh., U.S. (wŏdz'wûrth)	101d	41°01'N	81°44'W
Wager Bay, b., Can. (wā'jēr)	85	65°48'N	88°19'W
Wagga Wagga, Austl. (wôg'ȧ wôg'ȧ)	203	35°10'S	147°30'E
Wagoner, Ok., U.S. (wăg'ŭn-ēr)	111	35°58'N	95°22'W
Wagon Mound, N.M., U.S. (wăg'ŭn mound)	110	35°59'N	104°45'W
Wągrowiec, Pol. (vôŋ-grô'vyĕts)	155	52°47'N	17°14'E
Waha, Libya	184	28°16'N	19°54'E
Wahiawa, Hi., U.S.	96d	21°30'N	158°03'W
Wahoo, Ne., U.S. (wä-ho͞o')	102	41°14'N	96°39'W
Wahpeton, N.D., U.S. (wô'pė-tŭn)	102	46°17'N	96°38'W
Währing, neigh., Aus.	239e	48°14'N	16°21'E
Wahroonga, Austl.	243a	33°43'S	150°07'E
Waialua, Hi., U.S. (wä'ē-ä-lo͞o'ä)	94a	21°33'N	158°08'W
Waianae, Hi., U.S. (wä'ē-á-nä'ā)	94a	21°25'N	158°11'W
Waidhofen, Aus. (vĭd'hôf-ĕn)	154	47°58'N	14°46'E
Waidmannslust, neigh., Ger.	238a	52°36'N	13°20'E
Waigeo, Pulau, i., Indon. (wä-ė-gä'ô)	197	0°07'N	131°00'E
Waikato, r., N.Z. (wä'ė-kä'to)	203a	38°10'S	175°35'E
Waikerie, Austl. (wā'kĕr-ē)	204	34°15'S	140°00'E
Wailuku, Hi., U.S. (wä'ė-lo͞o'ko͞o)	96c	20°55'N	156°30'W
Waimanalo, Hi., U.S. (wä-ė-mä'nä-lo)	94a	21°19'N	157°53'W
Waimea, Hi., U.S. (wä-ė-mä'ä)	94a	21°56'N	159°38'W
Wainganga, r., India (wä-ēn-gŭŋ'gä)	183	20°30'N	80°15'E
Waingapu, Indon.	196	9°32'S	120°00'E
Wainwright, Can.	84	52°49'N	110°52'W
Wainwright, Ak., U.S. (wān-rīt)	95	74°40'N	159°00'W
Waipahu, Hi., U.S. (wä'ė-pä'ho͞o)	96d	21°20'N	158°02'W
Waiska, r., Mi., U.S. (wȧ-ĭz-kȧ)	107k	46°20'N	84°38'W
Waitara, Austl.	243a	33°43'S	150°06'E
Waitsburg, Wa., U.S. (wāts'bûrg)	104	46°17'N	118°08'W
Wajima, Japan (wä'jė-mȧ)	195	37°23'N	136°56'E
Wajir, Kenya	217	1°45'N	40°04'E
Wakami, r., Can.	90	47°43'N	82°22'W
Wakasa-Wan, b., Japan (wä'kä-sä wän)	194	35°43'N	135°39'E
Wakatipu, l., N.Z. (wä-kä-tē'po͞o)	203a	45°04'S	168°30'E
Wakayama, Japan (wä-kä'yä-mä)	189	34°14'N	135°11'E
Wake, i., Oc. (wāk)	3	19°25'N	167°00'E
Wa Keeney, Ks., U.S. (wô-kē'nė)	110	39°01'N	99°53'W
Wakefield, Can. (wāk-fēld)	83c	45°39'N	75°55'W
Wakefield, Eng., U.K.	150	53°41'N	1°25'W
Wakefield, Ma., U.S.	93a	42°31'N	71°05'W
Wakefield, Mi., U.S.	103	46°28'N	89°55'W
Wakefield, Ne., U.S.	102	42°15'N	96°52'W
Wakefield, R.I., U.S.	100b	41°26'N	71°30'W
Wake Forest, N.C., U.S. (wāk fŏr'ĕst)	115	35°58'N	78°31'W
Waki, Japan (wä'kė)	195	34°05'N	134°10'E
Wakkanai, Japan (wä'kä-nä'ė)	189	45°19'N	141°43'E
Wakkerstroom, S. Afr. (vák'ēr-strōm)(wăk'ēr-stro͞om)	212	27°19'S	30°04'E
Wakonassin, r., Can.	90	46°35'N	82°10'W
Waku Kundo, Ang.	212	11°25'S	15°07'E
Wałbrzych, Pol. (väl'bzhûk)	154	50°46'N	16°16'E
Walcott, Lake, res., Id., U.S.	105	42°40'N	113°23'W
Wałcz, Pol. (välch)	154	53°11'N	16°30'E
Waldbauer, neigh., Ger.	236	51°18'N	7°28'E
Waldoboro, Me., U.S. (wôl'dô-bŭr-ô)	92	44°06'N	69°22'W
Waldo Lake, l., Or., U.S. (wôl'dō)	104	43°46'N	122°10'W
Waldorf, Md., U.S. (wăl'dôrf)	100e	38°37'N	76°57'W
Waldron, Mo., U.S.	107f	39°14'N	94°47'W
Waldron, i., Wa., U.S.	106d	48°42'N	123°02'W
Wales, Ak., U.S. (wālz)	95	65°35'N	168°14'W
Wales, , U.K.	142	52°12'N	3°40'W
Walewale, Ghana	214	10°21'N	0°48'W
Walgett, Austl. (wôl'gĕt)	203	30°00'S	148°10'E
Walhalla, S.C., U.S. (wŭl-hăl'ȧ)	114	34°45'N	83°04'W
Walikale, D.R.C.	217	1°25'S	28°03'E
Walkden, Eng., U.K.	144a	53°32'N	2°24'W
Walker, Mn., U.S. (wôk'ēr)	103	47°06'N	94°37'W
Walker, r., Nv., U.S.	108	39°07'N	119°10'W
Walker, Mount, mtn., Wa., U.S.	106a	47°47'N	122°54'W
Walker Lake, l., Can.	89	54°42'N	96°57'W
Walker Lake, l., Nv., U.S.	108	38°46'N	118°30'W
Walker River Indian Reservation, I.R., Nv., U.S.	108	39°06'N	118°20'W
Walkerville, Mt., U.S. (wôk'ēr-vĭl)	105	46°20'N	112°32'W
Wallace, Id., U.S. (wŏl'ås)	104	47°27'N	115°55'W
Wallaceburg, Can.	90	42°39'N	82°25'W
Wallach, Ger.	236	51°35'N	6°34'E
Wallacia, Austl.	201b	33°52'S	150°40'E
Wallaroo, Austl. (wŏl-ȧ-ro͞o)	202	33°52'S	137°45'E
Wallasey, Eng., U.K. (wŏl'ȧ-sė)	144a	53°25'N	3°03'W
Walla Walla, Wa., U.S. (wŏl'ȧ wŏl'ȧ)	96	46°03'N	118°20'W
Walled Lake, Mi., U.S. (wôl'd lăk)	101b	42°32'N	83°29'W

ăt; fīnăl; rāte; senâte; ärm; àsk; sofȧ; fâre;   ch-choose;   dh-as th in other;   bē; ĕvent; bĕt; recĕnt; cratẽr;   g-gō; gh-guttural g;   bĭt; ĭ-short neutral; rīde;   ᴋ-guttural k as ch in German ich;

PRONOUNCING INDEX Weddinghofen-West Yorkshire 365

PLACE (Pronunciation)	PAGE	LAT.	LONG.
Weddinghofen, Ger.	236	51°36'N	7°37'E
Wedel, Ger. (vā'dĕl)	145c	53°35'N	9°42'E
Wedge Mountain, mtn., Can. (wĕj)	87	50°10'N	122°50'W
Wedgeport, Can. (wĕj'pōrt)	92	43°44'N	65°59'W
Wednesfield, Eng., U.K. (wĕd''nz-fēld)	144a	52°36'N	2°04'W
Weed, Ca., U.S. (wēd)	104	41°35'N	122°21'W
Weehawken, N.J., U.S.	228	40°46'N	74°01'W
Weenen, S. Afr. (vā'nĕn)	213c	28°52'S	30°05'E
Weert, Neth.	151	51°16'N	5°39'E
Weesow, Ger.	238a	52°39'N	13°43'E
Weesp, Neth.	145a	52°18'N	5°01'E
Wegendorf, Ger.	238a	52°36'N	13°45'E
Węgorzewo, Pol. (vôn-gô'zhĕ-vô)	155	54°14'N	21°46'E
Węgrow, Pol. (vôn'gróf)	155	52°23'N	22°02'E
Wehofen, neigh., Ger.	236	51°32'N	6°46'E
Wehringhausen, neigh., Ger.	236	51°21'N	7°27'E
Wei, r., China (wā)	188	34°00'N	108°10'E
Wei, r., China (wā)	190	35°47'N	114°27'E
Weichang, China (wā-chäŋ)	189	41°50'N	118°00'E
Weiden, Ger.	154	49°41'N	12°09'E
Weidling, Aus.	239e	48°17'N	16°19'E
Weidlingau, neigh., Aus.	239e	48°13'N	16°13'E
Weidlingbach, Aus.	239e	48°16'N	16°15'E
Weifang, China	189	36°43'N	119°08'E
Weihai, China (wa'hăī')	189	37°30'N	122°05'E
Weilheim, Ger. (vīl'hīm')	154	47°50'N	11°06'E
Weimar, Ger. (vī'mär)	147	50°59'N	11°20'E
Weinan, China	192	34°32'N	109°40'E
Weipa, Austl.	203	12°25'S	141°54'E
Weir, r., Can. (wēr-rĭv-ēr)	89	56°49'N	94°04'W
Weirton, W.V., U.S.	98	40°25'N	80°35'W
Weiser, Id., U.S. (wē'zēr)	104	44°15'N	116°58'W
Weiser, r., Id., U.S.	104	44°26'N	116°40'W
Weishi, China (wā-shr)	192	34°23'N	114°12'E
Weissenburg, Ger.	154	49°04'N	11°20'E
Weissenfels, Ger. (vī'sĕn-fĕlz)	154	51°13'N	11°58'E
Weiss Lake, res., Al., U.S.	114	34°15'N	85°35'W
Weitmar, neigh., Ger.	236	51°27'N	7°12'E
Weixi, China (wā-shyē)	188	27°27'N	99°30'E
Weixian, China (wā shyĕn)	190	36°59'N	115°17'E
Wejherowo, Pol. (vā-hĕ-rô'vô)	155	54°36'N	18°15'E
Welch, W.V., U.S. (wĕlch)	115	37°24'N	81°28'W
Welcome Monument, hist., Indon.	241i	6°11'S	106°49'E
Weldon, N.C., U.S. (wĕl'dŭn)	115	36°24'N	77°36'W
Weldon, r., Mo., U.S.	111	40°22'N	93°39'W
Weleetka, Ok., U.S. (wē-lēt'kȧ)	111	35°19'N	96°08'W
Welford, Austl. (wĕl'fērd)	204	25°08'S	144°43'E
Welhamgreen, Eng., U.K.	235	51°44'N	0°13'W
Welheim, neigh., Ger.	236	51°32'N	6°59'E
Welkom, S. Afr. (wĕl'kŏm)	212	27°57'S	26°45'E
Welland, Can. (wĕl'ănd)	91	42°59'N	79°13'W
Wellesley, Ma., U.S. (wĕlz'lē)	93a	42°18'N	71°17'W
Wellesley Hills, Ma., U.S.	227a	42°19'N	71°17'W
Wellesley Islands, is., Austl.	202	16°15'S	139°25'E
Well Hill, Eng., U.K.	235	51°21'N	0°09'E
Wellinghofen, neigh., Ger.	236	51°28'N	7°29'E
Wellington, Austl. (wĕl'lĭng-tŭn)	204	32°40'S	148°50'E
Wellington, N.Z.	203a	41°15'S	174°45'E
Wellington, Eng., U.K.	144a	52°42'N	2°30'W
Wellington, Ks., U.S.	111	37°16'N	97°24'W
Wellington, Oh., U.S.	98	41°10'N	82°10'W
Wellington, Tx., U.S.	110	34°51'N	100°12'W
Wellington, i., Chile (ŏŏ'lĕng-tŏn)	132	49°30'S	76°30'W
Wells, Can.	84	53°06'N	121°34'W
Wells, Mi., U.S.	98	45°50'N	87°00'W
Wells, Mn., U.S.	103	43°44'N	93°43'W
Wells, Nv., U.S.	104	41°07'N	115°04'W
Wells, l., Austl. (wĕlz)	202	26°35'S	123°40'E
Wellsboro, Pa., U.S. (wĕlz'bŭ-rô)	99	41°45'N	77°15'W
Wellsburg, W.V., U.S. (wĕlz'bûrg)	98	40°10'N	80°40'W
Wells Dam, dam, Wa., U.S.	104	48°00'N	119°39'W
Wellston, Oh., U.S. (wĕlz'tŭn)	98	39°05'N	82°30'W
Wellsville, Mo., U.S. (wĕlz'vĭl)	111	39°04'N	91°33'W
Wellsville, N.Y., U.S.	99	42°10'N	78°00'W
Wellsville, Oh., U.S.	98	40°35'N	80°40'W
Wellsville, Ut., U.S.	105	41°38'N	111°57'W
Welper, Ger.	236	51°25'N	7°12'E
Wels, Aus. (vĕls)	147	48°10'N	14°01'E
Welshpool, Wales, U.K. (wĕlsh'po͞ol)	150	52°44'N	3°10'W
Welverdiend, S. Afr. (vĕl-vēr-dēnd')	218d	26°23'S	27°16'E
Welwyn Garden City, Eng., U.K. (wĕlĭn)	144b	51°46'N	0°17'W
Wem, Eng., U.K. (wĕm)	144a	52°51'N	2°44'W
Wembere, r., Tan.	217	4°35'S	33°55'E
Wembley, neigh., Eng., U.K.	235	51°33'N	0°18'W
Wen, r., China (wŭn)	190	36°24'N	119°00'E
Wenan Wa, sw., China (wĕn'än' wä)	190	38°56'N	116°29'E
Wenatchee, Wa., U.S. (wē-năch'ē)	104	47°24'N	120°18'W
Wenatchee Mountains, mts., Wa., U.S.	104	47°28'N	121°10'W
Wenchang, China (wŭn-chäŋ)	193	19°32'N	110°42'E
Wenchi, Ghana	214	7°42'N	2°07'W
Wendelville, N.Y., U.S.	230a	43°04'N	78°47'W
Wendeng, China (wŭn-dŭŋ)	190	37°14'N	122°03'E
Wendo, Eth.	211	6°37'N	38°29'E
Wendorer, Ut., U.S.	105	40°47'N	114°01'W
Wendover, Can. (wĕn-dōv'ēr)	83c	45°34'N	75°07'W
Wendover, Eng., U.K.	144b	51°44'N	0°45'W
Wengern, Ger.	236	51°24'N	7°21'E
Wenham, Ma., U.S. (wĕn'ăm)	93a	42°36'N	70°53'W
Wennington, neigh., Eng., U.K.	235	51°30'N	0°13'E
Wenquan, China (wŭn-chyůän)	189	47°10'N	120°00'E
Wenshan, China	188	23°20'N	104°15'E
Wenshang, China (wĕn'shäng)	190	35°43'N	116°31'E
Wensu, China (wĕn-sō)	188	41°45'N	80°30'E
Wentworth, Austl. (wĕnt'wûrth)	203	34°03'S	141°53'E
Wentworthville, Austl.	243a	33°49'S	150°58'E
Wenzhou, China (wŭn-jō)	189	28°00'N	120°40'E
Wepener, S. Afr. (wē'pĕn-ēr) (vā'pĕn-ēr)	212	29°43'S	27°04'E
Werden, neigh., Ger.	236	51°23'N	7°00'E
Werder, Ger. (vĕr'dēr)	145b	52°23'N	12°56'E
Were Ilu, Eth.	211	10°39'N	39°21'E
Werl, Ger. (vĕrl)	157c	51°33'N	7°55'E
Wermelskirchen, Ger.	157c	51°08'N	7°13'E
Werne, neigh., Ger.	236	51°29'N	7°18'E
Werneuchen, Ger. (vĕr'hoi-kĕn)	145b	52°38'N	13°44'E
Wernsdorf, Ger.	238a	52°22'N	13°43'E
Werra, r., Ger. (vĕr'ä)	154	51°16'N	9°54'E
Werribee, Austl.	201a	37°54'S	144°40'E
Werribee, r., Austl.	201a	37°40'S	144°37'E
Wersten, neigh., Ger.	236	51°11'N	6°49'E
Wertach, r., Ger. (vĕr'täk)	154	48°12'N	10°40'E
Weseke, Ger. (vĕ'zĕ-kĕ)	157c	51°54'N	6°51'E
Wesel, Ger. (vā'zĕl)	157c	51°39'N	6°37'E
Weser, r., Ger. (vā'zēr)	142	51°00'N	10°30'E
Weslaco, Tx., U.S. (wĕs-lā'kō)	113	26°10'N	97°59'W
Weslemkoon, l., Can.	91	45°02'N	77°25'W
Wesleyville, Can. (wĕs'lē-vĭl)	93	49°09'N	53°34'W
Wessel Islands, is., Austl. (wĕs'ĕl)	202	11°45'S	136°25'E
Wesselsbron, S. Afr. (wĕs'ĕl-brŏn)	218d	27°51'S	26°22'E
Wessington Springs, S.D., U.S. (wĕs'ĭng-tŭn)	102	44°06'N	98°35'W
West, Mount, mtn., Pan.	116a	9°10'N	79°52'W
West Abington, Ma., U.S.	227a	42°08'N	70°59'W
West Allis, Wi., U.S. (wĕst-ăl'ĭs)	101a	43°01'N	88°01'W
West Alton, Mo., U.S. (ôl'tŭn)	107e	38°52'N	90°13'W
West Athens, Ca., U.S.	232	33°55'N	118°18'W
West Bay, b., Fl., U.S.	114	30°20'N	85°45'W
West Bay, b., Tx., U.S.	113a	29°11'N	95°03'W
West Bend, Wi., U.S. (wĕst bĕnd)	103	43°25'N	88°13'W
West Bengal, state, India (bĕn-gôl')	183	23°30'N	87°30'E
West Blocton, Al., U.S. (blŏk'tŭn)	114	33°05'N	87°05'W
Westborough, Ma., U.S. (wĕst'bŭr-ô)	93a	42°17'N	71°37'W
West Boylston, Ma., U.S. (boil'stŭn)	93a	42°22'N	71°46'W
West Branch, Mi., U.S. (wĕst branch)	98	44°15'N	84°10'W
West Bridgford, Eng., U.K. (brĭj'fērd)	144a	52°55'N	1°08'W
West Bromwich, Eng., U.K. (wĕst brŭm'ĭj)	144a	52°32'N	1°59'W
Westbrook, Me., U.S. (wĕst'brŏk)	92	43°41'N	70°23'W
Westbury, N.Y., U.S.	228	40°45'N	73°35'W
Westby, Wi., U.S. (wĕst'bē)	103	43°40'N	90°52'W
West Caicos, i., T./C. Is. (käē'kō) (kī'kōs)	123	21°40'N	72°30'W
West Caldwell, N.J., U.S.	228	40°51'N	74°17'W
West Cape Howe, c., Austl.	202	35°15'S	117°30'E
West Carson, Ca., U.S.	232	33°50'N	118°18'W
Westchester, Il., U.S.	231a	41°51'N	87°53'W
West Chester, Oh., U.S. (chĕs'tēr)	101f	39°20'N	84°24'W
West Chester, Pa., U.S.	100f	39°57'N	75°36'W
Westchester, neigh., Ca., U.S.	232	33°55'N	118°25'W
Westchester, neigh., N.Y., U.S.	228	40°51'N	73°52'W
West Chicago, Il., U.S. (chĭ-kȧ'gō)	101a	41°53'N	88°12'W
West Collingswood, N.J., U.S.	229b	39°54'N	75°06'W
West Columbia, S.C., U.S. (cŏl'ŭm-bē-ȧ)	115	33°58'N	81°05'W
West Columbia, Tx., U.S.	113	29°08'N	95°39'W
West Conshohocken, N.J., U.S.	229b	40°04'N	75°19'W
West Cote Blanche Bay, b., La., U.S.	113	29°30'N	92°17'W
West Covina, Ca., U.S. (wĕst kō-vē'nȧ)	107a	34°04'N	117°55'W
Westdale, Il., U.S.	231a	41°56'N	87°55'W
West Derby, neigh., Eng., U.K.	237a	53°26'N	2°54'W
West Des Moines, Ia., U.S. (dē moin')	103	41°35'N	93°42'W
West Des Moines, r., Ia., U.S.	103	42°52'N	94°32'W
West Drayton, neigh., Eng., U.K.	235	51°30'N	0°29'W
West Elizabeth, Pa., U.S.	230b	40°17'N	79°54'W
West End, Bah.	122	26°40'N	78°55'W
West End, Eng., U.K.	235	51°44'N	0°04'W
West End, neigh., Eng., U.K.	235	51°32'N	0°24'W
West End, neigh., Pa., U.S.	230b	40°27'N	80°02'W
Westende, Ger.	236	51°25'N	7°24'E
Westenfeld, neigh., Ger.	236	51°28'N	7°09'E
Westerbauer, neigh., Ger.	236	51°20'N	7°23'E
Westerham, Eng., U.K. (wĕ'stēr'ŭm)	144b	51°15'N	0°05'E
Westerholt, Ger.	236	51°36'N	7°05'E
Westerhörn, Ger. (vĕs'tĕr-hōrn)	145c	53°52'N	9°41'E
Westerlo, Bel.	145a	51°05'N	4°57'E
Westerly, R.I., U.S. (wĕs'tēr-lē)	99	41°25'N	71°50'W
Western Australia, state, Austl. (ôs-trā'lĭ-ȧ)	202	24°15'S	121°30'E
Western Dvina *see* Zapadnaya Dvina, r., Eur.	153	55°30'N	28°27'E
Western Ghāts, mts., India	183	17°35'N	74°00'E
Western Port, Md., U.S. (wĕs'tērn pōrt)	99	39°30'N	79°00'W
Western Sahara, dep., Afr. (sȧ-hä'rȧ)	210	23°05'N	15°33'W
Western Samoa, nation, Oc.	2	14°30'S	172°00'W
Western Siberian Lowland, depr., Russia	164	63°37'N	72°45'E
Western Springs, Il., U.S.	231a	41°47'N	87°53'W
Westerville, Oh., U.S. (wĕs'tēr-vĭl)	98	40°10'N	83°00'W
Westerwald, for., Ger. (vĕs'tēr-väld)	154	50°35'N	7°45'E
Westfalenhalle, pt. of i., Ger.	236	51°30'N	7°27'E
Westfield, Ma., U.S. (wĕst'fēld)	99	42°05'N	72°45'W
Westfield, N.J., U.S.	100a	40°39'N	74°21'W
Westfield, N.Y., U.S. (wĕst'fēld)	100a	42°20'N	79°40'W
Westford, Ma., U.S. (wĕst'fērd)	93a	42°35'N	71°26'W
West Frankfort, Il., U.S. (frăŋk'fŭrt)	98	37°55'N	88°55'W
West Ham, Eng., U.K.	144b	51°30'N	0°00'W
West Hanover, Ma., U.S.	227a	42°07'N	70°53'W
West Hartford, Ct., U.S. (härt'fērd)	99	41°45'N	72°45'W
Westhead, Eng., U.K.	237a	53°34'N	2°51'W
West Heidelberg, Austl.	243b	37°45'S	145°02'E
West Helena, Ar., U.S. (hĕl'ĕn-ȧ)	111	34°32'N	90°39'W
West Hempstead, N.Y., U.S.	228	40°42'N	73°39'W
Westhofen, Ger.	236	51°25'N	7°31'E
West Hollywood, Ca., U.S.	232	34°05'N	118°24'W
West Homestead, Pa., U.S.	230b	40°24'N	79°55'W
West Horndon, Eng., U.K.	235	51°34'N	0°21'E
West Hoxton, Austl.	243a	33°55'S	150°50'E
West Hyde, Eng., U.K.	235	51°37'N	0°30'W
Westick, Ger.	236	51°35'N	7°38'E
West Indies, is. (ĭn'dēz)	117	19°00'N	78°30'W
West Jordon, Ut., U.S. (jôr'dăn)	107b	40°37'N	111°56'W
West Kirby, Eng., U.K. (kûr'bē)	144a	53°22'N	3°11'W
West Lafayette, In., U.S. (lä-fā-yĕt')	98	40°25'N	86°55'W
Westlake, Oh., U.S.	101d	41°27'N	81°55'W
Westland, Mi., U.S.	230c	42°19'N	83°23'W
West Lawn, Va., U.S.	229d	38°52'N	77°11'W
Westleigh, S. Afr. (wĕst-lē)	218d	27°39'S	27°18'E
West Liberty, Ia., U.S. (wĕst lĭb'ēr-tĭ)	103	41°34'N	91°15'W
West Liberty, neigh., Pa., U.S.	230b	40°24'N	80°01'W
West Linn, Or., U.S. (lĭn)	106c	45°22'N	122°37'W
Westlock, Can. (wĕst'lŏk)	87	54°09'N	113°52'W
West Los Angeles, neigh., Ca., U.S.	232	34°03'N	118°28'W
West Malling, Eng., U.K.	235	51°18'N	0°25'E
West Manayunk, Pa., U.S.	229b	40°01'N	75°14'W
West Memphis, Ar., U.S.	111	35°08'N	90°11'W
West Midlands, co., Eng., U.K.	144a	52°26'N	1°50'W
West Mifflin, Pa., U.S.	230b	40°22'N	79°52'W
Westminster, Ca., U.S. (wĕst'min-stēr)	107a	33°45'N	117°59'W
Westminster, Md., U.S.	99	39°40'N	76°55'W
Westminster, S.C., U.S.	114	34°38'N	83°10'W
Westminster Abbey, pt. of i., Eng., U.K.	235	51°30'N	0°07'W
Westmont, Ca., U.S.	232	33°56'N	118°18'W
Westmount, Can. (wĕst'mount)	83a	45°29'N	73°36'W
West Newbury, Ma., U.S. (nū'bēr-ē)	93a	42°47'N	70°57'W
West Newton, Ma., U.S.	227a	42°21'N	71°14'W
West Newton, Pa., U.S. (nū'tŭn)	101e	40°12'N	79°45'W
West New York, N.J., U.S. (nů yŏrk)	100a	40°47'N	74°01'W
West Nishnabotna, r., Ia., U.S. (nĭsh-nȧ-bŏt'nȧ)	102	40°56'N	95°37'W
West Norwood, neigh., Eng., U.K.	235	51°26'N	0°06'W
Weston, Ma., U.S. (wĕs'tŭn)	93a	42°22'N	71°18'W
Weston, W.V., U.S.	98	39°00'N	80°30'W
Westonaria, S. Afr.	218d	26°19'S	27°38'E
Weston-super-Mare, Eng., U.K. (wĕs'tŭn sū'pēr-mā'rē)	150	51°23'N	3°00'W
West Orange, N.J., U.S. (wĕst ŏr'ĕnj)	100a	40°46'N	74°14'W
West Palm Beach, Fl., U.S. (päm bēch)	97	26°44'N	80°04'W
West Peabody, Ma., U.S.	227a	42°30'N	70°57'W
West Pensacola, Fl., U.S. (pĕn-sȧ-kō'lȧ)	114	30°24'N	87°18'W
West Pittsburg, Ca., U.S. (pĭts'bûrg)	106b	38°02'N	121°56'W
Westplains, Mo., U.S. (wĕst-plānz')	111	36°42'N	91°51'W
West Point, Ga., U.S.	114	32°52'N	85°10'W
West Point, Ms., U.S.	114	33°36'N	88°39'W
Westpoint, Ne., U.S.	102	41°50'N	96°00'W
West Point, N.Y., U.S.	100a	41°23'N	73°58'W
West Point, Ut., U.S.	107b	41°07'N	112°05'W
West Point, Va., U.S.	99	37°25'N	76°50'W
West Point Lake, res., U.S.	114	33°00'N	85°10'W
Westport, Ire.	150	53°44'N	9°36'W
Westport, Ct., U.S. (wĕst'pōrt)	100a	41°07'N	73°22'W
Westport, Or., U.S. (wĕst'pôrt)	106c	46°08'N	123°22'W
West Puente Valley, Ca., U.S.	232	34°04'N	117°59'W
West Pymble, Austl.	243a	33°46'S	151°08'E
Westray, i., Scot., U.K. (wĕs'trā)	150a	59°19'N	3°05'W
West Road, r., Can. (rōd)	86	53°00'N	124°00'W
West Ryde, Austl.	243a	33°48'S	151°05'E
West Saint Paul, Mn., U.S. (sånt pôl')	107g	44°55'N	93°05'W
West Sand Spit, i., T./C. Is.	123	21°25'N	72°10'W
West Seneca, N.Y., U.S.	230a	42°50'N	78°45'W
West Slope, Or., U.S.	106c	45°30'N	122°46'W
West Somerville, Ma., U.S.	227a	42°24'N	71°07'W
West Tavaputs Plateau, plat., Ut., U.S. (wĕst tăv'ȧ-pōts)	109	39°45'N	110°35'W
West Terre Haute, In., U.S. (tĕr-ē hōt')	98	39°30'N	87°30'W
West Thurrock, Eng., U.K.	235	51°29'N	0°16'E
West Tilbury, Eng., U.K.	235	51°29'N	0°24'E
West Turffontein, neigh., S. Afr.	244b	26°16'S	28°02'E
West Union, Ia., U.S. (ūn'yŭn)	103	42°58'N	91°48'W
West University Place, Tx., U.S.	113a	29°43'N	95°26'W
Westview, Oh., U.S. (wĕst'vū)	101d	41°21'N	81°54'W
West View, Pa., U.S.	101e	40°31'N	80°02'W
Westville, Can. (wĕst'vĭl)	93	45°35'N	62°43'W
Westville, Il., U.S.	98	40°00'N	87°40'W
Westville, N.J., U.S.	229b	39°52'N	75°08'W
Westville Grove, N.J., U.S.	229b	39°51'N	75°07'W
West Virginia, state, U.S. (wĕst vēr-jĭn'ĭ-ȧ)	97	39°00'N	80°50'W
West Walker, r., Ca., U.S. (wôk'ēr)	108	38°25'N	119°25'W
West Warwick, R.I., U.S. (wŏr'ĭk)	100b	41°42'N	71°31'W
Westwego, La., U.S. (wĕst-wē'gō)	100d	29°55'N	90°09'W
West Whittier, Ca., U.S.	232	33°59'N	118°04'W
West Wickham, neigh., Eng., U.K.	235	51°22'N	0°01'W
Westwood, Ca., U.S. (wĕst'wŏd)	108	40°18'N	121°00'W
Westwood, Ks., U.S.	107f	39°03'N	94°37'W
Westwood, Ma., U.S.	93a	42°13'N	71°14'W
Westwood, N.J., U.S.	100a	40°59'N	74°02'W
Westwood, neigh., Ca., U.S.	232	34°04'N	118°27'W
West Wyalong, Austl. (wīălông)	203	34°00'S	147°20'E
West Yorkshire, co., Eng., U.K.	144a	53°37'N	1°48'W

ng-sing; ŋ-baŋk; ɴ-nasalized n; nŏd; cŏmmit; ōld; ôbey; ôrder; oi-boil; fo͞od; ŏŏ-as oo in foot; ou-out; s-soft; sh-dish; th-thin; pūre; ůnite; ûrn; stŭd; circŭs; ü-as in French tu; '-indeterminate vowel.

366 Wetar–Wind River Range

PLACE (Pronunciation)	PAGE	LAT.	LONG.
Wetar, Pulau, i., Indon. (wĕt′ȧr)	197	7°34′S	126°00′E
Wetaskiwin, Can. (wĕ-tăs′kė-wŏn)	84	52°58′N	113°22′W
Wetherill Park, Austl.	243a	33°51′S	150°54′E
Wethmar, Ger.	236	51°37′N	7°33′E
Wetmore, Tx., U.S. (wĕt′mōr)	107d	29°34′N	98°25′W
Wetter, Ger.	157c	51°23′N	7°23′E
Wetumpka, Al., U.S. (wė-tŭmp′kȧ)	114	32°33′N	86°12′W
Wetzlar, Ger. (vets′lär)	154	50°35′N	8°30′E
Wewak, Pap. N. Gui. (wȧ-wăk′)	197	3°19′S	143°30′E
Wewoka, Ok., U.S. (wė-wō′kȧ)	111	35°09′N	96°30′W
Wexford, Ire. (wĕks′fẽrd)	147	52°20′N	6°30′W
Weybridge, Eng., U.K. (wā′brĭj)	144b	51°20′N	0°26′W
Weyburn, Can. (wā′bûrn)	84	49°41′N	103°52′W
Weyer, neigh., Ger.	236	51°10′N	7°01′E
Weymouth, Eng., U.K. (wā′mŭth)	150	50°37′N	2°34′W
Weymouth, Ma., U.S.	93a	42°44′N	70°57′W
Weymouth, Oh., U.S.	101d	41°11′N	81°48′W
Whalan, Austl.	243a	33°45′S	150°49′E
Whale Cay, i., Bah.	122	25°20′N	77°45′W
Whale Cay Channels, strt., Bah.	122	26°45′N	77°10′W
Wharton, N.J., U.S. (hwôr′tŭn)	100a	40°54′N	74°35′W
Wharton, Tx., U.S.	113	29°19′N	96°06′W
What Cheer, Ia., U.S. (hwŏt chēr)	103	41°23′N	92°24′W
Whatcom, Lake, l., Wa., U.S. (hwät′kŭm)	106c	48°44′N	123°34′W
Whatshan Lake, l., Can. (wŏt′shăn)	87	50°00′N	118°03′W
Wheatland, Wy., U.S. (hwēt′lănd)	105	42°04′N	104°52′W
Wheatland Reservoir Number 2, res., Wy., U.S.	105	41°52′N	105°36′W
Wheaton, Il., U.S. (hwē′tŭn)	101a	41°52′N	88°06′W
Wheaton, Md., U.S.	100e	39°05′N	77°05′W
Wheaton, Mn., U.S.	102	45°48′N	96°29′W
Wheeler Peak, mtn., Nv., U.S.	96	38°58′N	114°15′W
Wheeler Peak, mtn., N.M., U.S.	110	36°34′N	105°25′W
Wheeling, Il., U.S. (hwēl′ĭng)	101a	42°08′N	87°54′W
Wheeling, W.V., U.S.	98	40°05′N	80°45′W
Wheelwright, Arg. (ȯė′l-rē′gt)	129c	33°46′S	61°14′W
Whelpleyhill, Eng., U.K.	235	51°44′N	0°33′W
Whidbey Island, i., Wa., U.S. (hwĭd′bė)	106a	48°13′N	122°50′W
Whippany, N.J., U.S. (hwĭp′ȧ-nē)	100a	40°49′N	74°25′W
Whiston, Eng., U.K.	237a	53°25′N	2°50′W
Whitaker, Pa., U.S.	230b	40°24′N	79°53′W
Whitby, Can. (hwĭt′bė)	85	43°50′N	79°00′W
Whitby, Eng., U.K.	237a	53°17′N	2°54′W
Whitchurch, Eng., U.K. (hwĭt′chûrch)	144a	52°58′N	2°49′W
White, l., Can.	90	48°47′N	85°50′W
White, l., Can.	91	45°15′N	76°35′W
White, r., Can.	90	48°34′N	85°46′W
White, r., U.S.	97	35°30′N	92°00′W
White, r., U.S.	102	43°41′N	99°48′W
White, r., U.S.	109	40°10′N	108°55′W
White, r., In., U.S.	98	39°15′N	86°45′W
White, r., S.D., U.S.	102	43°13′N	101°04′W
White, r., Tx., U.S.	110	36°25′N	102°20′W
White, r., Vt., U.S.	99	43°45′N	72°35′W
White, r., Wa., U.S.	104	47°07′N	121°48′W
White, East Fork, r., In., U.S.	98	38°45′N	86°20′W
White Bay, b., Can.	85a	50°00′N	56°30′W
White Bear Indian Reserve, I.R., Can.	89	49°50′N	102°15′W
White Bear Lake, l., Mn., U.S.	107g	45°04′N	92°58′W
White Castle, La., U.S.	113	30°10′N	91°09′W
White Center, Wa., U.S.	106a	47°31′N	122°21′W
White Cloud, Mi., U.S.	98	43°35′N	85°45′W
Whitecourt, Can. (wīt′côrt)	84	54°09′N	115°41′W
White Earth, r., N.D., U.S.	102	48°30′N	102°44′W
White Earth Indian Reservation, I.R., Mn., U.S.	102	47°18′N	95°42′W
Whiteface, r., Mn., U.S. (whīt′fās)	103	47°12′N	92°13′W
Whitefield, Eng., U.K.	237b	53°33′N	2°18′W
Whitefield, N.H., U.S. (hwīt′fēld)	99	44°20′N	71°35′W
Whitefish Bay, Wi., U.S.	101a	43°07′N	77°54′W
Whitefish Bay, b., Can.	89	49°26′N	94°14′W
Whitefish Bay, b., N.A.	103	46°36′N	84°50′W
White Hall, Il., U.S.	111	39°26′N	90°23′W
Whitehall, Mi., U.S. (hwīt′hôl)	98	43°20′N	86°20′W
Whitehall, N.Y., U.S.	99	43°30′N	73°25′W
Whitehall, Pa., U.S.	230b	40°22′N	79°59′W
Whitehaven, Eng., U.K. (hwīt′hā-vĕn)	150	54°35′N	3°30′W
Whitehead, Ma., U.S.	227a	42°17′N	70°52′W
Whitehorn, Point, c., Wa., U.S. (hwīt′hôrn)	106d	48°54′N	122°48′W
Whitehorse, Can. (whīt′hôrs)	84	60°39′N	135°01′W
White House, pt. of i., D.C., U.S.	229d	38°54′N	77°02′W
White Lake, l., La., U.S.	113	29°40′N	92°35′W
Whiteley Village, Eng., U.K.	235	51°21′N	0°26′W
Whiteman, Ma., U.S.	227a	42°05′N	70°56′W
Whitemarsh, Pa., U.S.	229b	40°07′N	75°13′W
White Mountain Peak, mtn., Ca., U.S.	108	37°38′N	118°13′W
White Mountains, mts., Me., U.S.	92	44°22′N	71°15′W
White Mountains, mts., N.H., U.S.	99	42°20′N	71°05′W
Whitemouth, l., Can.	89	49°14′N	95°40′W
White Nile (Al Bahr al Abyad), r., Sudan	211	12°30′N	32°30′E
White Oak, Pa., U.S.	230b	40°21′N	79°48′W
White Otter, l., Can.	90	49°15′N	91°48′W
White Pass, p., N.A.	95	59°35′N	135°03′W
White Plains, N.Y., U.S.	100a	41°02′N	73°47′W
White River, Can.	90	48°38′N	85°23′W
White Rock, Can.	87	49°01′N	122°49′W
Whiterock Reservoir, res., Tx., U.S. (hwīt′rŏk)	107c	32°51′N	96°40′W
White Russia, nation, Eur.	164	53°30′N	25°33′E
Whitesail Lake, l., Can. (whīt′sāl)	86	53°30′N	127°00′W
White Sands National Monument, rec., N.M., U.S.	109	32°50′N	106°20′W
White Sea, sea, Russia	164	66°00′N	40°00′E
White Settlement, Tx., U.S.	107c	32°45′N	97°28′W
Whitestone, neigh., N.Y., U.S.	228	40°47′N	73°49′W
White Sulphur Springs, Mt., U.S.	105	46°32′N	110°49′W
White Umfolzi, r., S. Afr. (ŭm-fô-lō′zė)	213c	28°12′S	30°55′E
Whiteville, N.C., U.S. (hwīt′vĭl)	115	34°18′N	78°45′W
White Volta (Volta Blanche), r., Afr.	214	9°40′N	1°10′W
Whitewater, Wi., U.S. (whīt-wŏt′ẽr)	103	42°49′N	88°40′W
Whitewater, l., Can.	89	49°14′N	100°39′W
Whitewater, r., In., U.S.	101f	39°19′N	84°55′W
Whitewater Bay, b., Fl., U.S.	115a	25°16′N	80°21′W
Whitewater Creek, r., Mt., U.S.	105	48°50′N	107°50′W
Whitewell, Tn., U.S. (hwīt′wĕl)	114	35°11′N	85°31′W
Whitewright, Tx., U.S. (hwīt′rīt)	111	33°33′N	96°25′W
Whitham, r., Eng., U.K. (wĭth′ŭm)	144a	53°08′N	0°15′W
Whiting, In., U.S. (hwīt′ĭng)	101a	41°41′N	87°30′W
Whitinsville, Ma., U.S. (hwīt′ĕns-vĭl)	93a	42°06′N	71°40′W
Whitman, Ma., U.S. (hwĭt′măn)	93a	42°05′N	70°57′W
Whitmire, S.C., U.S. (hwĭt′mīr)	115	34°30′N	81°40′W
Whitney, Mount, mtn., Ca., U.S.	96	36°34′N	118°18′W
Whitney Lake, l., Tx., U.S. (hwĭt′nė)	113	32°02′N	97°36′W
Whitstable, Eng., U.K. (wĭt′stȧb′l)	144b	51°22′N	1°03′E
Whitsunday, i., Austl. (hwĭt′s′n-dā)	203	20°16′S	149°00′E
Whittier, Ca., U.S. (hwĭt′ĭ-ẽr)	107a	33°58′N	118°02′W
Whittier South, Ca., U.S.	232	33°57′N	118°01′W
Whittlesea, S. Afr. (wĭt′l′sē)	213c	32°11′S	26°51′E
Whitworth, Eng., U.K. (hwĭt′wŭrth)	144a	53°40′N	2°10′W
Whyalla, Austl. (hwī-ăl′ȧ)	202	33°00′S	137°32′E
Whymper, Mount, mtn., Can. (wĭm′pẽr)	86	48°57′N	124°10′W
Wiarton, Can. (wī′ȧr-tŭn)	85	44°45′N	80°45′W
Wichita, Ks., U.S. (wĭch′i-tô)	96	37°42′N	97°21′W
Wichita, r., Tx., U.S.	110	33°50′N	99°38′W
Wichita Falls, Tx., U.S. (fôls)	96	33°54′N	98°29′W
Wichita Mountains, mts., Ok., U.S.	96	34°48′N	98°43′W
Wichlinghofen, neigh., Ger.	236	51°27′N	7°30′E
Wick, Scot., U.K. (wĭk)	146	58°25′N	3°05′W
Wickatunk, N.J., U.S. (wĭk′ȧ-tŭnk)	100a	40°21′N	74°15′W
Wickede, neigh., Ger.	236	51°32′N	7°37′E
Wickenburg, Az., U.S.	109	33°58′N	112°44′W
Wickiup Reservoir, res., Or., U.S.	104	43°40′N	121°43′W
Wickliffe, Oh., U.S. (wĭk′klĭf)	101d	41°37′N	81°29′W
Wicklow, Ire.	150	52°59′N	6°06′W
Wicklow Mountains, mts., Ire. (wĭk′lō)	150	52°49′N	6°20′W
Wickup Mountain, mtn., Or., U.S. (wĭk′ŭp)	106c	46°06′N	123°35′W
Wiconisco, Pa., U.S. (wĭ-kŏn′ĭs-kō)	99	43°35′N	76°45′W
Widen, W.V., U.S. (wī′dĕn)	98	38°25′N	80°55′W
Widnes, Eng., U.K. (wĭd′nĕs)	144a	53°21′N	2°44′W
Wieliczka, Pol. (vyĕ-lēch′kȧ)	155	49°58′N	20°06′E
Wiemelhausen, neigh., Ger.	236	51°28′N	7°13′E
Wien *see* Vienna, Aus.	142	48°13′N	16°22′E
Wien, prov., Aus.	145e	48°11′N	16°23′E
Wiener Berg, Aus.	239e	48°10′N	16°22′E
Wiener Neustadt, Aus. (vē′nĕr noi′shtät)	147	47°48′N	16°15′E
Wiener Wald, for., Aus.	145e	48°09′N	16°05′E
Wieprz, r., Pol. (vyĕpzh)	155	51°25′N	22°45′E
Wiergate, Tx., U.S. (wēr′gāt)	113	31°00′N	93°42′W
Wiesbaden, Ger. (vēs′bä-dĕn)	147	50°05′N	8°15′E
Wigan, Eng., U.K. (wĭg′ăn)	150	53°33′N	2°37′W
Wiggins, Ms., U.S. (wĭg′ĭnz)	114	30°51′N	89°05′W
Wight, Isle of, i., Eng., U.K. (wīt)	150	50°44′N	1°17′W
Wilber, Ne., U.S. (wĭl′bẽr)	111	40°29′N	96°57′W
Wilburton, Ok., U.S. (wĭl′bẽr-tŭn)	111	34°54′N	95°18′W
Wilcannia, Austl. (wĭl-cān-ĭȧ)	203	31°30′S	143°30′E
Wildau, Ger. (vēl′dou)	145b	52°20′N	13°39′E
Wildberg, Ger. (vēl′bĕrgh)	145b	52°52′N	12°39′E
Wildcat Hill, hill, Can. (wīld′kăt)	89	53°17′N	102°30′W
Wildercroft, Md., U.S.	229d	38°58′N	76°53′W
Wildhay, r., Can. (wīld′hā)	87	53°15′N	117°20′W
Wildomar, Ca., U.S. (wĭl′dȯ-mär)	107a	33°35′N	117°17′W
Wild Rice, r., Mn., U.S.	102	47°10′N	96°40′W
Wild Rice, r., N.D., U.S.	102	46°10′N	97°12′W
Wild Rice Lake, l., Mn., U.S.	107h	46°54′N	92°10′W
Wildspitze, mtn., Aus.	154	46°55′N	10°50′E
Wildwood, N.J., U.S.	99	39°00′N	74°50′W
Wildwood Manor, Md., U.S.	229d	39°01′N	77°07′W
Wiley, Co., U.S. (wī′lė)	110	38°08′N	102°41′W
Wilge, r., S. Afr. (wĭl′jė)	218d	25°38′S	29°09′E
Wilge, r., S. Afr.	218d	27°27′S	28°46′E
Wilhelm, Mount, mtn., Pap. N. Gui.	197	5°58′S	144°58′E
Wilhelmina Gebergte, mts., Sur.	131	4°30′N	57°00′W
Wilhelmina Kanaal, can., Neth.	145a	51°37′N	4°55′E
Wilhelmshaven, Ger. (vėl-hĕlms-hä′fĕn)	146	53°30′N	8°10′E
Wilhelmstadt, neigh., Ger.	238a	52°31′N	13°11′E
Wilkes-Barre, Pa., U.S. (wĭlks′băr-ė)	97	41°15′N	75°50′W
Wilkes Land, reg., Ant.	219	71°00′S	126°00′E
Wilkeson, Wa., U.S. (wĭl-kē′sŭn)	106a	47°06′N	122°03′W
Wilkie, Can. (wĭlk′ē)	84	52°25′N	108°43′W
Wilkinsburg, Pa., U.S. (wĭl′kĭnz-bûrg)	101e	40°26′N	79°53′W
Wilkins Township, Pa., U.S.	230b	40°25′N	79°50′W
Willamette, r., Or., U.S.	96	45°00′N	123°00′W
Willapa Bay, b., Wa., U.S.	104	46°37′N	124°00′W
Willard, Oh., U.S. (wĭl′ȧrd)	98	41°00′N	82°50′W
Willard, Ut., U.S.	107b	41°24′N	112°02′W
Willaston, Eng., U.K.	237a	53°18′N	3°00′W
Willcox, Az., U.S. (wĭl′kŏks)	109	32°15′N	109°50′W
Willcox Playa, l., Az., U.S.	109	32°08′N	109°51′W
Willemstad, Neth. Ant.	130	12°12′N	68°58′W
Willesden, Eng., U.K. (wĭlz′dĕn)	144b	51°31′N	0°17′W
William Bill Dannelly Reservoir, res., Al., U.S.	114	32°10′N	87°15′W
William Creek, Austl. (wĭl′yăm)	202	28°45′S	136°20′E
Williams, Az., U.S. (wĭl′yămz)	109	35°15′N	112°15′W
Williams, i., Bah.	122	24°30′N	78°30′W
Williamsburg, Ky., U.S. (wĭl′yămz-bŭrg)	114	36°42′N	84°09′W
Williamsburg, Oh., U.S.	101f	39°04′N	84°02′W
Williamsburg, Va., U.S.	115	37°15′N	76°41′W
Williamsburg, neigh., N.Y., U.S.	228	40°42′N	73°57′W
Williams Lake, Can.	87	52°08′N	122°09′W
Williamson, W.V., U.S. (wĭl′yăm-sŭn)	98	37°40′N	82°15′W
Williamsport, Md., U.S.	99	39°35′N	77°45′W
Williamsport, Pa., U.S.	99	41°15′N	77°05′W
Williamston, N.C., U.S. (wĭl′yămz-tŭn)	115	35°50′N	77°04′W
Williamston, S.C., U.S.	115	34°36′N	82°30′W
Williamstown, Austl.	201a	37°52′S	144°54′E
Williamstown, W.V., U.S. (wĭl′yămz-toun)	98	39°20′N	81°30′W
Williamsville, N.Y., U.S. (wĭl′yăm-vĭl)	101c	42°58′N	78°46′W
Willich, Ger.	236	51°16′N	6°33′E
Willimantic, Ct., U.S. (wĭl-ĭ-măn′tĭk)	99	41°40′N	72°10′W
Willingale, Eng., U.K.	235	51°44′N	0°19′E
Willis, Tx., U.S. (wĭl′ĭs)	113	30°24′N	95°29′W
Willis Islands, is., Austl.	203	16°15′S	150°30′E
Williston, N.D., U.S. (wĭl′ĭs-tŭn)	96	48°08′N	103°38′W
Williston, Lake, l., Can.	84	55°40′N	123°40′W
Williston Park, N.Y., U.S.	228	40°45′N	73°39′W
Willmar, Mn., U.S. (wĭl′mär)	102	45°07′N	95°05′W
Willmersdorf, Ger.	238a	52°40′N	13°41′E
Willoughby, Austl.	243a	33°48′S	151°12′E
Willoughby, Oh., U.S. (wĭl′ȯ-bė)	101d	41°39′N	81°25′W
Willow, Ak., U.S.	95	61°50′N	150°00′W
Willow Brook, Ca., U.S.	232	33°55′N	118°14′W
Willow Creek, r., Or., U.S.	104	44°21′N	117°34′W
Willow Grove, Pa., U.S.	100f	40°07′N	75°07′W
Willowick, Oh., U.S. (wĭl′ȯ-wĭk)	101d	41°39′N	81°28′W
Willowmore, S. Afr. (wĭl′ȯ-môr)	212	33°15′S	23°37′E
Willow Run, Mi., U.S. (wĭl′ȯ rŭn)	101b	42°16′N	83°34′W
Willow Run, Va., U.S.	229d	38°49′N	77°10′W
Willows, Ca., U.S. (wĭl′ōz)	108	39°32′N	122°11′W
Willow Springs, Il., U.S.	231a	41°44′N	87°52′W
Willow Springs, Mo., U.S. (sprĭngz)	111	36°59′N	91°56′W
Willowvale, S. Afr. (wĭ-lȯ′vāl)	213c	32°17′S	28°32′E
Wills Point, Tx., U.S. (wĭlz point)	113	32°42′N	96°02′W
Wilmer, Tx., U.S. (wĭl′mẽr)	107c	32°35′N	96°40′W
Wilmette, Il., U.S. (wĭl-mĕt′)	101a	42°04′N	87°42′W
Wilmington, Austl.	204	32°39′S	138°07′E
Wilmington, Eng., U.K.	235	51°26′N	0°12′E
Wilmington, Ca., U.S. (wĭl′mĭng-tŭn)	107a	33°46′N	118°16′W
Wilmington, De., U.S.	97	39°45′N	75°33′W
Wilmington, Il., U.S.	101a	41°19′N	88°09′W
Wilmington, Ma., U.S.	93a	42°34′N	71°10′W
Wilmington, N.C., U.S.	97	34°12′N	77°56′W
Wilmington, Oh., U.S.	98	39°20′N	83°50′W
Wilmore, Ky., U.S. (wĭl′mōr)	98	37°50′N	84°35′W
Wilmslow, Eng., U.K. (wĭlmz′lō)	144a	53°19′N	2°14′W
Wilno *see* Vilnius, Lith.	164	54°40′N	25°26′E
Wilpoort, S. Afr.	218d	26°57′S	26°17′E
Wilson, Ar., U.S. (wĭl′sŭn)	111	35°35′N	90°02′W
Wilson, N.C., U.S.	115	35°42′N	77°55′W
Wilson, Ok., U.S.	111	34°09′N	97°27′W
Wilson, r., Al., U.S.	114	34°53′N	87°28′W
Wilson, Mount, mtn., Ca., U.S.	107a	34°15′N	118°06′W
Wilson, Point, c., Austl.	201a	38°05′S	144°31′E
Wilson Lake, res., Al., U.S.	97	34°45′N	87°30′W
Wilson's Promontory, pen., Austl. (wĭl′sŭnz)	203	39°05′S	146°50′E
Wilsonville, Il., U.S. (wĭl′sŭn-vĭl)	107e	39°04′N	89°52′W
Wilstedt, Ger. (vēl′shtĕt)	145c	53°45′N	10°04′E
Wilster, Ger. (vēl′stẽr)	145c	53°55′N	9°23′E
Wilton, Ct., U.S. (wĭl′tŭn)	100a	41°11′N	73°25′W
Wilton, N.D., U.S.	102	47°09′N	100°47′W
Wilton Woods, Va., U.S.	229d	38°47′N	77°06′W
Wiluna, Austl. (wĭ-lōō′nȧ)	202	26°35′S	120°25′E
Wimbledon, neigh., Eng., U.K.	235	51°25′N	0°12′W
Wimbledon Common, pt. of i., Eng., U.K.	235	51°26′N	0°14′W
Winamac, In., U.S. (wĭn′ȧ măk)	98	41°05′N	86°40′W
Winburg, S. Afr. (wĭm-bûrg)	218d	28°31′S	27°02′E
Winchester, Eng., U.K.	150	51°04′N	1°20′W
Winchester, Ca., U.S. (wĭn′chĕs-tẽr)	107a	33°41′N	117°06′W
Winchester, Id., U.S.	104	46°14′N	116°39′W
Winchester, In., U.S.	98	40°10′N	84°50′W
Winchester, Ky., U.S.	98	38°00′N	84°15′W
Winchester, Ma., U.S.	93a	42°28′N	71°09′W
Winchester, N.H., U.S.	99	42°45′N	72°25′W
Winchester, Tn., U.S.	114	35°11′N	86°06′W
Winchester, Va., U.S.	99	39°10′N	78°10′W
Wind, r., Wy., U.S.	105	43°17′N	109°02′W
Windber, Pa., U.S. (wĭnd′bẽr)	99	40°15′N	78°45′W
Wind Cave National Park, rec., S.D., U.S.	102	43°36′N	103°53′W
Winder, Ga., U.S. (wīn′dẽr)	114	33°58′N	83°43′W
Windermere, Eng., U.K. (wĭn′dẽr-mēr)	150	54°25′N	2°59′W
Windham, Ct., U.S. (wĭnd′ăm)	99	41°45′N	72°05′W
Windham, N.H., U.S.	93a	42°49′N	71°21′W
Windhoek, Nmb. (vĭnt′hȯk)	212	22°05′S	17°10′E
Wind Lake, l., Wi., U.S.	101a	42°49′N	88°06′W
Wind Mountain, mtn., N.M., U.S.	112	32°02′N	105°30′W
Windom, Mn., U.S. (wĭn′dŭm)	102	43°50′N	95°04′W
Windora, Austl. (wĭn-dō′rȧ)	203	25°15′S	142°50′E
Wind River Indian Reservation, I.R., Wy., U.S.	105	43°07′N	109°08′W
Wind River Range, mts., Wy., U.S.	96	43°19′N	109°47′W

ăt; finăl; rāte; senåte; ärm; åsk; sofȧ; fâre; ch-choose; dh-as th in other; bē; ėvent; bĕt; recĕnt; cratẽr; g-gō; gh-guttural g; bĭt; ĭ-short neutral; rīde; κ-guttural k as ch in German ich;

PRONOUNCING INDEX

Windsor–Wynnewood 367

PLACE (Pronunciation)	PAGE	LAT.	LONG.
Windsor, Austl. (wĭn′zẽr)	201b	33°37′S	150°49′E
Windsor, Can.	85	42°19′N	83°00′W
Windsor, Can.	85	44°59′N	64°08′W
Windsor, Can.	85a	48°57′N	55°40′W
Windsor, Eng., U.K.	150	51°27′N	0°37′W
Windsor, Co., U.S.	110	40°27′N	104°51′W
Windsor, Mo., U.S.	111	38°32′N	93°31′W
Windsor, N.C., U.S.	115	35°58′N	76°57′W
Windsor, Vt., U.S.	99	43°30′N	72°25′W
Windsor, University of, educ., Can.	230c	42°18′N	83°04′W
Windsor Airport, arpt., Can.	230c	42°17′N	82°58′W
Windsor Castle, hist., Eng., U.K.	235	51°29′N	0°36′W
Windsor Hills, Ca., U.S.	232	33°59′N	118°21′W
Windward Islands, is., N.A. (wĭnd′wẽrd)	117	12°45′N	61°40′W
Windward Passage, strt., N.A.	117	19°30′N	74°20′W
Winefred Lake, l., Can.	88	55°30′N	110°35′W
Winfield, Ks., U.S.	111	37°14′N	97°00′W
Wing Lake Shores, Mi., U.S.	230c	42°33′N	83°17′W
Winifred, Mt., U.S. (wĭn ĭ frĕd)	105	47°35′N	109°20′W
Winisk, r., Can.	85	54°30′N	86°30′W
Wink, Tx., U.S. (wĭŋk)	112	31°48′N	103°06′W
Winkler, Can. (wĭnk′lẽr)	89	49°11′N	97°56′W
Winneba, Ghana (wĭn′ē-bȧ)	214	5°25′N	0°36′W
Winnebago, Mn., U.S. (wĭn′ē-bā′gō)	103	43°45′N	94°08′W
Winnebago, Lake, l., Wi., U.S.	103	44°09′N	88°10′W
Winnebago Indian Reservation, I.R., Ne., U.S.	102	42°15′N	96°06′W
Winnemucca, Nv., U.S. (wĭn-ē-mŭk′ȧ)	96	40°59′N	117°43′W
Winnemucca, l., Nv., U.S.	108	40°06′N	119°07′W
Winner, S.D., U.S. (wĭn′ẽr)	102	43°22′N	99°50′W
Winnetka, Il., U.S. (wĭ-nĕtkȧ)	101a	42°07′N	87°44′W
Winnett, Mt., U.S. (wĭn′ĕt)	105	47°01′N	108°20′W
Winnfield, La., U.S. (wĭn′fēld)	113	31°56′N	92°39′W
Winnibigoshish, l., Mn., U.S. (wĭn′ĭ-bĭ-gō′shĭsh)	103	47°30′N	93°45′W
Winnipeg, Can. (wĭn′ĭ-pĕg)	84	49°53′N	97°09′W
Winnipeg, r., Can.	84	50°30′N	95°00′W
Winnipeg, Lake, l., Can.	84	52°00′N	97°00′W
Winnipegosis, Can. (wĭn′ĭ-pē-gō′sĭs)	84	51°39′N	99°56′W
Winnipegosis, l., Can.	84	52°30′N	100°00′W
Winnipesaukee, l., N.H., U.S. (wĭn′ē-pē-sô′kē)	99	43°40′N	71°20′W
Winnsboro, La., U.S. (wĭnz′bŭr′ō)	113	32°09′N	91°42′W
Winnsboro, S.C., U.S.	115	34°29′N	81°05′W
Winnsboro, Tx., U.S.	111	32°56′N	95°15′W
Winona, Can. (wĭ-nō′nȧ)	83d	43°13′N	79°39′W
Winona, Mn., U.S.	97	44°03′N	91°40′W
Winona, Ms., U.S.	114	33°29′N	89°43′W
Winooski, Vt., U.S. (wĭ-no͞os′kē)	99	44°30′N	73°10′W
Winsen, Ger. (vēn′zĕn)	145c	53°22′N	10°13′E
Winsford, Eng., U.K. (wĭnz′fẽrd)	144a	53°11′N	2°30′W
Winslow, Az., U.S. (wĭnz′lō)	109	35°00′N	110°45′W
Winslow, Wa., U.S.	106a	47°38′N	122°31′W
Winsted, Ct., U.S. (wĭn′stĕd)	99	41°55′N	73°05′W
Winster, Eng., U.K. (wĭn′stẽr)	144a	53°08′N	1°38′W
Winston-Salem, N.C., U.S. (wĭn stŭn-sā′lĕm)	97	36°05′N	80°15′W
Winterberg, Ger.	236	51°17′N	7°18′E
Winterberge, mts., Afr.	213c	32°18′S	26°25′E
Winter Garden, Fl., U.S. (wĭn′tẽr gär′d′n)	115a	28°32′N	81°35′W
Winter Haven, Fl., U.S. (hā′vĕn)	115a	28°01′N	81°38′W
Winter Park, Fl., U.S. (pärk)	115a	28°35′N	81°21′W
Winters, Tx., U.S. (wĭn′tẽrz)	112	31°59′N	99°58′W
Winterset, Ia., U.S. (wĭn′tẽr-sĕt)	103	41°19′N	94°03′W
Winterswijk, Neth.	157c	51°58′N	6°44′E
Winterthur, Switz. (vĭn′tĕr-to͞or)	154	47°30′N	8°32′E
Winterton, S. Afr.	213c	28°51′S	29°33′E
Winthrop, Me., U.S. (wĭn′thrŭp)	92	44°19′N	70°00′W
Winthrop, Ma., U.S.	93a	42°23′N	70°59′W
Winthrop, Mn., U.S.	103	44°31′N	94°20′W
Winton, Austl. (wĭn-tŭn)	203	22°17′S	143°08′E
Winz, Ger.	236	51°23′N	7°09′E
Wipperfürth, Ger. (vē′pĕr-fürt)	157c	51°07′N	7°23′E
Wirksworth, Eng., U.K. (wûrks′wûrth)	144a	53°05′N	1°35′W
Wisconsin, state, U.S. (wĭs-kŏn′sĭn)	97	44°30′N	91°00′W
Wisconsin, r., Wi., U.S.	97	43°14′N	90°34′W
Wisconsin Dells, Wi., U.S.	103	43°38′N	89°46′W
Wisconsin Rapids, Wi., U.S.	103	44°24′N	89°50′W
Wishek, N.D., U.S. (wĭsh′ĕk)	102	46°15′N	99°34′W
Wisła, r., Pol. (vēs′wȧ)	142	52°30′N	20°00′E
Wisłoka, r., Pol. (vēs-wô′kȧ)	155	49°55′N	21°26′E
Wismar, Ger. (vĭs′mär)	146	53°53′N	11°28′E
Wismar, Guy. (wĭs′mȧr)	131	5°58′N	58°15′W
Wisner, Ne., U.S. (wĭz′nẽr)	102	42°00′N	96°55′W
Wissembourg, Fr. (vē-säɴ-bo͞or′)	157	49°03′N	7°58′E
Wissinoming, neigh., Pa., U.S.	229b	40°01′N	75°04′W
Wissous, Fr.	237c	48°44′N	2°20′E
Wister, Lake, l., Ok., U.S. (vĭs′tẽr)	111	35°02′N	94°52′W
Witbank, S. Afr. (wĭt-băŋk)	218d	25°53′S	29°14′E
Witberg, mtn., Afr.	213c	30°32′S	27°18′E
Witfield, S. Afr.	244b	26°11′S	28°12′E
Witham, Eng., U.K. (wĭdh′ăm)	144b	51°48′N	0°37′E
Witham, r., Eng., U.K.	144a	53°11′N	0°20′W
Withamsville, Oh., U.S. (wĭdh′ămz-vĭl)	101f	39°04′N	84°16′W
Withington, neigh., Eng., U.K.	237b	53°26′N	2°14′W
Withlacoochee, r., Fl., U.S. (wĭth-lȧ-ko͞o′chē)	115a	28°58′N	82°30′W
Withlacoochee, r., Ga., U.S.	114	31°15′N	83°30′W
Withrow, Mn., U.S. (wĭdh′rō)	107g	45°08′N	92°54′W
Witney, Eng., U.K. (wĭt′nē)	144b	51°45′N	1°30′W
Witpoortje, S. Afr.	244b	26°08′S	27°50′E
Witt, Il., U.S. (vĭt)	98	39°10′N	89°15′W
Witten, Ger. (vē′tĕn)	157c	51°26′N	7°19′E
Wittenau, neigh., Ger.	238a	52°35′N	13°20′E
Wittenberg, Ger. (vē′tĕn-bĕrgh)	154	51°53′N	12°40′E
Wittenberge, Ger. (vĭt-ĕn-bĕr′gē)	154	52°59′N	11°45′E
Wittlaer, Ger.	236	51°19′N	6°44′E
Wittlich, Ger. (vĭt′lĭk)	154	49°58′N	6°54′E
Witu, Kenya (wē′to͞o)	213	2°18′S	40°28′E
Witu Islands, is., Pap. N. Gui.	197	4°45′S	149°50′E
Witwatersberg, mts., S. Afr. (wĭt-wôr-tẽrz-bûrg)	213b	25°58′S	27°53′E
Witwatersrand, mtn., S. Afr. (wĭt-wôr′tẽrs-rănd)	218d	25°55′S	26°27′E
Witwatersrand, University of, educ., S. Afr.	244b	26°12′S	28°02′E
Witwatersrand Gold Mines, quarry, S. Afr.	244b	26°12′S	28°10′E
Wkra, r., Pol. (f′krȧ)	155	52°40′N	20°35′E
Włocławek, Pol. (vwô-tswä′vĕk)	155	52°38′N	19°08′E
Włodawa, Pol. (vwô-dä′vä)	155	51°33′N	23°33′E
Włoszczowa, Pol. (vwôsh-chô′vä)	155	50°51′N	19°58′E
Woburn, Ma., U.S. (wō′bŭrn) (wŏ′bŭrn)	93a	42°29′N	71°10′W
Woburn, neigh., Can.	227c	43°46′N	79°13′W
Woerden, Neth.	145a	52°05′N	4°52′E
Woking, Eng., U.K.	144b	51°18′N	0°33′W
Wokingham, Eng., U.K. (wō′kĭng-hăm)	144b	51°23′N	0°50′W
Wolcott, Ks., U.S. (wōl′kŏt)	107f	39°12′N	94°47′W
Woldingham, Eng., U.K.	235	51°17′N	0°02′W
Wolf, i., Can. (wo͝olf)	91	44°10′N	76°25′W
Wolf, r., Ms., U.S.	114	30°45′N	89°36′W
Wolf, r., Wi., U.S.	103	45°14′N	88°45′W
Wolfenbüttel, Ger. (vôl′fĕn-büt-ĕl)	154	52°10′N	10°32′E
Wolf Lake, l., Il., U.S.	101a	41°39′N	87°33′W
Wolf Point, Mt., U.S. (wo͝olf point)	105	48°07′N	105°40′W
Wolfratshausen, Ger. (vōlf′räts-hou-zĕn)	145d	47°55′N	11°25′E
Wolfsburg, Ger. (vōlfs′bo͞orgh)	154	52°30′N	10°37′E
Wolfville, Can. (wo͝olf′vĭl)	92	45°05′N	64°22′W
Wolgast, Ger. (vôl′gäst)	154	54°04′N	13°46′E
Wolhuterskop, S. Afr.	213b	25°41′S	27°40′E
Wolkersdorf, Aus.	145e	48°24′N	16°31′E
Wollaston, Ma., U.S.	227a	42°16′N	71°01′W
Wollaston, l., Can. (wo͝ol′ȧs-tŭn)	84	58°15′N	103°20′W
Wollaston Peninsula, pen., Can.	84	70°00′N	115°00′W
Wollongong, Austl. (wo͝ol′ŭn-gŏng)	203	34°26′S	151°05′E
Wołomin, Pol. (vô-wō′mēn)	155	52°19′N	21°17′E
Wolseley, Can.	88	50°25′N	103°15′W
Woltersdorf, Ger. (vōl′tĕs-dōrf)	145b	52°07′N	13°13′E
Woltersdorf, Ger.	238a	52°26′N	13°45′E
Wolverhampton, Eng., U.K. (wo͝ol′vẽr-hămp-tŭn)	147	52°35′N	2°07′W
Wolverine, Mi., U.S.	230c	42°33′N	83°29′W
Wolwehoek, S. Afr.	218d	26°55′S	27°50′E
Wonga Park, Austl.	243b	37°44′S	145°16′E
Wŏnsan, N. Kor. (wŭn′sän′)	189	39°08′N	127°24′E
Wonthaggi, Austl. (wŏnt-hăg′ē)	203	38°45′S	145°42′E
Wood, S.D., U.S. (wo͝od)	102	43°26′N	100°25′W
Woodbine, Ia., U.S. (wo͝od′bīn)	102	41°44′N	95°42′W
Woodbridge, N.J., U.S. (wo͝od′brĭj′)	100a	40°33′N	74°18′W
Woodbrook, Md., U.S.	229c	39°23′N	76°37′W
Wood Buffalo National Park, rec., Can.	84	59°50′N	118°53′W
Woodburn, Il., U.S. (wo͝od′bûrn)	107e	39°03′N	90°01′W
Woodburn, Or., U.S.	104	45°10′N	122°51′W
Woodbury, N.J., U.S. (wo͝od′bĕr-ē)	100f	39°50′N	75°14′W
Woodbury, N.Y., U.S.	228	40°49′N	73°28′W
Woodbury Terrace, N.J., U.S.	229b	39°51′N	75°08′W
Woodcrest, Ca., U.S. (wo͝od′krĕst)	107a	33°53′N	117°18′W
Woodford, Eng., U.K.	237b	53°21′N	2°10′W
Woodford Bridge, neigh., Eng., U.K.	235	51°36′N	0°04′E
Wood Green, neigh., Eng., U.K.	235	51°36′N	0°07′W
Woodhaven, neigh., N.Y., U.S.	228	40°41′N	73°51′W
Woodinville, Wa., U.S. (wo͝od′ĭn-vĭl)	106a	47°46′N	122°09′W
Woodland, Ca., U.S. (wo͝od′lănd)	108	38°41′N	121°47′W
Woodland, Wa., U.S.	106c	45°54′N	122°45′W
Woodland Hills, Ca., U.S.	107a	34°10′N	118°36′W
Woodlands, Sing.	240c	1°27′N	103°46′E
Woodlark Island, i., Pap. N. Gui. (wo͝od′lärk)	197	9°07′S	152°00′E
Woodlawn, Md., U.S.	229c	39°19′N	76°43′W
Woodlawn, Md., U.S.	229d	38°57′N	76°53′W
Woodlawn, neigh., Il., U.S.	231a	41°47′N	87°36′W
Woodlawn Beach, N.Y., U.S. (wo͝od′lôn bēch)	101c	42°48′N	78°51′W
Woodlawn Heights, Md., U.S.	229c	39°11′N	76°39′W
Woodlyn, Pa., U.S.	229b	39°52′N	75°21′W
Woodlynne, N.J., U.S.	229b	39°55′N	75°05′W
Woodmansterne, Eng., U.K.	235	51°19′N	0°10′W
Woodmere, N.Y., U.S.	228	40°38′N	73°43′W
Woodmoor, Md., U.S.	229c	39°20′N	76°44′W
Wood Mountain, mtn., Can.	88	49°14′N	106°20′W
Wood Ridge, N.J., U.S.	228	40°51′N	74°05′W
Wood River, Il., U.S.	107e	38°52′N	90°06′W
Woodroffe, Mount, mtn., Austl. (wo͝od′rŭf)	202	26°05′S	132°00′E
Woodruff, S.C., U.S. (wo͝od′rŭf)	115	34°43′N	82°03′W
Woods, l., Austl. (wo͝odz)	202	18°00′S	133°18′E
Woods, Lake of the, l., N.A.	85	49°25′N	93°25′W
Woodsburgh, N.Y., U.S.	228	40°37′N	73°42′W
Woods Cross, Ut., U.S. (krôs)	107b	40°53′N	111°54′W
Woodsfield, Oh., U.S. (wo͝odz-fēld)	98	39°45′N	81°10′W
Woodside, neigh., N.Y., U.S.	228	40°45′N	73°55′W
Woodson, Or., U.S. (wo͝odsŭn)	106c	46°07′N	123°20′W
Woodstock, Can.	85	46°09′N	67°34′W
Woodstock, Can. (wo͝od′stŏk)	91	43°10′N	80°50′W
Woodstock, Eng., U.K.	144b	51°48′N	1°22′W
Woodstock, Il., U.S.	103	42°20′N	88°29′W
Woodstock, Va., U.S.	99	38°55′N	78°25′W
Woodsville, N.H., U.S. (wo͝odz′vĭl)	99	44°10′N	72°00′W
Woodville, Ms., U.S. (wo͝od′vĭl)	114	31°06′N	91°11′W
Woodville, Tx., U.S.	113	30°48′N	94°25′W
Woodward, Ok., U.S. (wo͝od′wôrd)	110	36°25′N	99°24′W
Woollahra, Austl.	243a	33°53′S	151°15′E
Woolton, neigh., Eng., U.K.	237a	53°23′N	2°52′W
Woolwich, Eng., U.K. (wo͝ol′ĭj)	144b	51°28′N	0°05′E
Woomera, Austl. (wo͞om′ĕrȧ)	202	31°15′S	136°43′E
Woonsocket, R.I., U.S. (wo͞on-sŏk′ĕt)	100b	42°00′N	71°30′W
Woonsocket, S.D., U.S.	102	44°03′N	98°17′W
Wooster, Oh., U.S. (wo͝os′tẽr)	98	40°50′N	81°55′W
Worcester, S. Afr. (wo͞os′tẽr)	212	33°35′S	19°31′E
Worcester, Eng., U.K. (wo͝os′tẽr)	147	52°09′N	2°14′W
Worcester, Ma., U.S. (wo͝os′tẽr)	97	42°16′N	71°49′W
Worden, Il., U.S. (wôr′dĕn)	107e	38°56′N	89°50′W
Workington, Eng., U.K. (wûr′kĭng-tŭn)	150	54°40′N	3°30′W
Worksop, Eng., U.K. (wûrk′sŏp) (wûr′sŭp)	144a	53°18′N	1°07′W
Worland, Wy., U.S. (wûr′lănd)	105	44°02′N	107°56′W
Wormley, Eng., U.K.	235	51°44′N	0°01′W
Worms, Ger. (vōrms)	147	49°37′N	8°22′E
Worona Reservoir, res., Austl.	201b	34°12′S	150°55′E
Woronora, Austl.	243a	34°01′S	151°03′E
Worsley, Eng., U.K.	237b	53°30′N	2°23′W
Worth, Il., U.S. (wûrth)	101a	41°42′N	87°47′W
Wortham, Tx., U.S. (wûr′dhăm)	113	31°46′N	96°22′W
Worthing, Eng., U.K. (wûr′dhĭng)	150	50°48′N	0°29′W
Worthington, In., U.S. (wûr′dhĭng-tŭn)	98	39°05′N	87°00′W
Worthington, Md., U.S.	229c	39°14′N	76°47′W
Worthington, Mn., U.S.	102	43°38′N	95°36′W
Worth Lake, l., Tx., U.S.	107c	32°48′N	97°32′W
Wowoni, Pulau, i., Indon. (wō-wō′nē)	197	4°05′S	123°45′E
Wragby, Eng., U.K. (răg′bē)	144a	53°17′N	0°19′W
Wrangell, Ak., U.S. (răn′gĕl)	94a	56°28′N	132°25′W
Wrangell, Mount, mtn., Ak., U.S.	95	61°58′N	143°50′W
Wrangell Mountains, mts., Ak., U.S.	95	62°28′N	142°40′W
Wrangell-Saint Elias National Park, rec., Ak., U.S.	95	61°00′N	142°00′W
Wrath, Cape, c., Scot., U.K. (răth)	150	58°34′N	5°01′W
Wray, Co., U.S. (rā)	110	40°06′N	102°14′W
Wraysbury, Eng., U.K.	235	51°27′N	0°33′W
Wreak, r., Eng., U.K. (rēk)	144a	52°45′N	0°59′W
Wreck Reefs, rf., Austl. (rĕk)	203	22°00′S	155°52′E
Wrekin, The, mtn., Eng., U.K. (rĕk′ĭn)	144a	52°40′N	2°33′W
Wrens, Ga., U.S. (rĕnz)	115	33°15′N	82°25′W
Wrentham, Ma., U.S.	93a	42°04′N	71°20′W
Wrexham, Wales, U.K. (rĕk′săm)	150	53°03′N	3°00′W
Wrights Corners, N.Y., U.S. (rītz kôr′nẽrz)	101c	43°14′N	78°42′W
Wrightsville, Ga., U.S. (rīts′vĭl)	115	32°44′N	82°44′W
Writtle, Eng., U.K.	235	51°44′N	0°26′E
Wrocław, Pol. (vrôtsläv) (brĕs′lou)	155	51°07′N	17°10′E
Wrotham, Eng., U.K. (ro͞ot′ŭm)	144b	51°18′N	0°19′E
Wrotham Heath, Eng., U.K.	235	51°18′N	0°21′E
Września, Pol. (vzhăsh′nyȧ)	155	52°19′N	17°33′E
Wu, r., China (wo͞o′)	188	27°30′N	107°00′E
Wuchang, China (wo͞o-chäŋ)	189	30°32′N	114°25′E
Wuchang, China	192	44°59′N	127°00′E
Wucheng, China (wo͞o-chŭŋ)	190	37°14′N	116°03′E
Wuhan, China	189	30°30′N	114°15′E
Wuhu, China (wo͞o′ho͞o)	193	31°22′N	118°22′E
Wuji, China (wo͞o-jyĭ)	190	38°12′N	114°57′E
Wujiang, China (wo͞o-jyäŋ)	190	31°10′N	120°38′E
Wuleidao Wan, b., China (wo͞o-lā-dou wän)	190	36°55′N	122°00′E
Wülfrath, Ger.	236	51°17′N	7°02′E
Wulidian, China (wo͞o-lē-dĭĕn)	190	32°09′N	114°17′E
Wünsdorf, Ger. (vüns′dorf)	145b	52°10′N	13°29′E
Wupatki National Monument, rec., Az., U.S.	109	35°35′N	111°45′W
Wuping, China (wo͞o-pĭŋ)	193	25°05′N	116°01′E
Wupper, r., Ger.	236	51°14′N	7°06′E
Wuppertal, Ger. (vo͝op′ẽr-täl)	147	51°16′N	7°14′E
Wuqiao, China (wo͞o-chyou)	190	37°37′N	116°29′E
Würm, r., Ger. (vürm)	145d	48°07′N	11°20′E
Würselen, Ger. (vür′zĕ-lĕn)	157c	50°49′N	6°09′E
Würzburg, Ger. (vürts′bo͝orgh)	147	49°48′N	9°57′E
Wurzen, Ger. (vo͝ort′sĕn)	147	51°22′N	12°45′E
Wushi, China (wo͞o-shr)	188	41°13′N	79°08′E
Wusong, China (wo͞o-sôŋ)	190	31°23′N	121°29′E
Wustermark, Ger. (vo͞os′tĕr-märk)	145b	52°33′N	12°57′E
Wustrau, Ger. (vo͞ost′rou)	145b	52°40′N	12°51′E
Wuustwezel, Bel.	145a	51°23′N	4°36′E
Wuwei, China (wo͞o-wā′)	193	31°19′N	117°53′E
Wuxi, China (wo͞o-shyē)	189	31°36′N	120°17′E
Wuxing, China (wo͞o-shyĭŋ)	189	30°38′N	120°10′E
Wuyi Shan, mts., China (wo͞o-yē shän)	193	26°38′N	116°35′E
Wuyou, China (wo͞o-yō)	190	33°18′N	120°15′E
Wuzhi Shan, mtn., China (wo͞o-jr shän)	193	18°48′N	109°30′E
Wuzhou, China (wo͞o-jō)	189	23°32′N	111°25′E
Wyandotte, Mi., U.S. (wī′ăn-dŏt)	101b	42°12′N	83°10′W
Wye, Eng., U.K. (wī)	144b	51°12′N	0°57′E
Wye, r., Eng., U.K.	144a	53°14′N	1°46′W
Wylie, Lake, res., S.C., U.S.	115	35°02′N	81°21′W
Wymore, Ne., U.S. (wī′mōr)	111	40°09′N	96°41′W
Wynberg, S. Afr. (wĭn′bĕrg)	212a	34°00′S	18°28′E
Wyncote, Pa., U.S.	229b	40°05′N	75°09′W
Wyndham, Austl. (wĭnd′ăm)	202	15°30′S	128°15′E
Wyndmoor, Pa., U.S.	229b	40°05′N	75°12′W
Wynne, Ar., U.S. (wĭn)	111	35°12′N	90°46′W
Wynnewood, Ok., U.S. (wĭn′wo͝od)	111	34°39′N	97°10′W
Wynnewood, Pa., U.S.	229b	40°01′N	75°17′W

ng-sing; ŋ-baŋk; ɴ-nasalized n; nŏd; cŏmmit; ōld; ōbey; ôrder; oi-boil; fo͞od; o͝o-as oo in foot; ou-out; s-soft; sh-dish; th-thin; pūre; ûnite; ûrn; stŭd; circŭs; ü-as in French tu; ′-indeterminate vowel.

368 Wynona–Yeniseysk

PLACE (Pronunciation)	PAGE	LAT.	LONG.
Wynona, Ok., U.S. (wī-nō'nȧ)	111	36°33'N	96°19'W
Wynyard, Can. (wīn'yẽrd)	84	51°47'N	104°10'W
Wyoming, Oh., U.S. (wī-ō'mĭng)	101f	39°14'N	84°28'W
Wyoming, state, U.S.	96	42°50'N	108°30'W
Wyoming Range, mts., Wy., U.S.	96	42°43'N	110°35'W
Wyre Forest, for., Eng., U.K. (wīr)	144a	52°24'N	2°24'W
Wysokie Mazowieckie, Pol. (vē-sô'kyĕ mä-zô-vyĕts'kyĕ)	155	52°55'N	22°42'E
Wyszków, Pol. (vēsh'kôf)	155	52°35'N	21°29'E
Wythenshawe, neigh., Eng., U.K.	237b	53°24'N	2°17'W
Wytheville, Va., U.S. (wĭth'vĭl)	115	36°55'N	81°06'W

X

PLACE (Pronunciation)	PAGE	LAT.	LONG.
Xàbia, Spain	159	38°45'N	0°07'E
Xabregas, neigh., Port.	238d	38°44'N	9°07'W
Xagua, Banco, bk., Cuba (bä'n-kō-sä'gwä)	122	21°35'N	80°50'W
Xai Xai, Moz.	212	25°00'S	33°45'E
Xalapa, Mex.	116	19°32'N	96°53'W
Xangongo, Ang.	212	16°50'S	15°05'E
Xankändi (Stepanakert), Azer. (styĕ'pän-á-kĕrt)	167	39°50'N	46°40'E
Xanten, Ger. (ksän'tĕn)	157c	51°40'N	6°28'E
Xánthi, Grc.	149	41°08'N	24°53'E
Xàtiva, Spain	148	38°58'N	0°31'W
Xau, Lake, l., Bots.	212	21°15'S	24°38'E
Xcalak, Mex. (sä-lä'k)	120a	18°15'N	87°50'W
Xelva, Spain	158	39°43'N	1°00'W
Xenia, Oh., U.S. (zē'nĭ-ȧ)	98	39°40'N	83°55'W
Xi, r., China (shyē)	193	23°15'N	112°10'E
Xiajin, China (shyä-jyĭn)	192	36°58'N	115°59'E
Xiamen, China	189	24°30'N	118°10'E
Xiamen, i., Tai. (shyä-mŭn)	193	24°28'N	118°20'E
Xi'an, China (shyē-än)	188	34°20'N	109°00'E
Xiang, r., China (shyäŋ)	189	27°30'N	112°30'E
Xianghe, China (shyäŋ-hŭ)	190	39°46'N	116°59'E
Xiangtan, China (shyäŋ-tän)	189	27°55'N	112°45'E
Xianyang, China (shyĕn-yäŋ)	192	34°20'N	108°40'E
Xiaoxingkai Hu, l., China (shyou-shyĭŋ-kī hōō)	194	42°25'N	132°45'E
Xiaoxintian, China	240b	39°58'N	116°22'E
Xiapu, China (shyä-pōō)	189	27°00'N	120°00'E
Xiayi, China (shyä-yē)	190	34°15'N	116°07'E
Xicotencatl, Mex. (sē-kō-tĕn-kät''l)	118	23°00'N	98°58'W
Xifeng, China (shyē-fŭŋ)	192	42°40'N	124°40'E
Xiheying, China (shyē-hŭ-yĭŋ)	190	39°58'N	114°50'E
Xiliao, r., China	192	43°23'N	121°40'E
Xilitla, Mex. (sē-lē'tlä)	118	21°24'N	98°59'W
Xinchang, China (shyn-chäŋ)	191b	31°02'N	121°38'E
Xing'an, China (shyĭŋ-än)	193	25°44'N	110°32'E
Xingcheng, China (shyĭŋ-chŭŋ)	190	40°38'N	120°41'E
Xinghua, China (shyĭŋ-hwä)	190	32°58'N	119°48'E
Xingjiawan, China (shyĭŋ-jyä-wän)	190	37°16'N	114°54'E
Xingtai, China (shyĭŋ-tī)	192	37°04'N	114°33'E
Xingu, r., Braz. (zhĕŋ-gō')	131	6°20'S	52°34'W
Xinhai, China (shyĭn-hī)	190	36°59'N	117°33'E
Xinhua, China (shyĭn-hwä)	193	27°45'N	111°20'E
Xinhuai, r., China (shyĭn-hwī)	190	33°48'N	119°39'E
Xinhui, China (shyn-hwā)	193	22°40'N	113°08'E
Xining, China (shyē-nĭŋ)	188	36°52'N	101°36'E
Xinjiang Uygur (Sinkiang), prov., China (shyĭn-jyäŋ)	188	40°15'N	82°15'E
Xinjin, China (shyĭn-jyĭn)	192	39°23'N	121°57'E
Xinmin, China (shyĭn-mĭn)	192	42°00'N	122°42'E
Xintai, China (shyĭn-tī)	190	35°55'N	117°44'E
Xintang, China (shyĭn-täŋ)	191a	23°08'N	113°36'E
Xinxian, China (shyĭn shyĕn)	190	31°47'N	114°50'E
Xinxian, China	192	38°20'N	112°45'E
Xinxiang, China (shyĭn-shyäŋ)	192	35°17'N	113°49'E
Xinyang, China (shyĭn-yäŋ)	189	32°08'N	114°04'E
Xinye, China (shyĭn-yŭ)	192	32°40'N	112°20'E
Xinzao, China (shyĭn-dzou)	191a	23°01'N	113°25'E
Xinzheng, China (shyĭn-jŭŋ)	190	34°24'N	113°43'E
Xinzhuang, China	240b	39°56'N	116°31'E
Xinzo de Limia, Spain	158	42°03'N	7°43'W
Xiongyuecheng, China (shyôŋ-yûĕ-chŭŋ)	190	40°10'N	122°08'E
Xiping, China (shyē-pĭŋ)	190	33°21'N	114°01'E
Xishui, China (shyē-shwā)	193	30°30'N	115°10'E
Xixian, China (shyē shyĕn)	190	32°20'N	114°42'E
Xixona, Spain	159	38°31'N	0°29'W
Xiyang, China (shyē-yäŋ)	190	37°37'N	113°42'E
Xiyou, China (shyē-yō)	190	37°21'N	119°59'E
Xizang (Tibet), prov., China (shyē-dzäŋ)	188	31°15'N	87°30'E
Xizhong Dao, i., China (shyē-jôŋ dou)	190	39°27'N	121°06'E
Xochihuehuetlán, Mex. (sô-chē-wē-wē-tlà'n)	119	17°53'N	98°29'E
Xochimilco, Mex. (sō-chē-mēl'kō)	119a	19°15'N	99°06'W
Xochimilco, Lago de, l., Mex.	233a	19°16'N	99°06'W
Xuancheng, China (shyůän-chŭŋ)	193	30°52'N	118°48'E
Xuanhua, China (shyůän-hwä)	192	40°35'N	115°05'E
Xuanhuadian, China (shyůän-hwä-dĭĕn)	190	31°42'N	114°29'E
Xuchang, China (shyōō-chäŋ)	192	34°02'N	113°49'E
Xudat, Azer.	168	41°38'N	48°42'E
Xuddur, Som.	218a	3°55'N	43°45'E
Xun, r., China (shyòn)	193	23°28'N	110°30'E
Xuzhou, China	189	34°17'N	117°10'E

Y

PLACE (Pronunciation)	PAGE	LAT.	LONG.
Ya'an, China (yä-än)	188	30°00'N	103°20'E
Yablonovyy Khrebet, mts., Russia (yȧ-blô-nô-vē')	165	51°15'N	111°30'E
Yablunivskiyi, Pereval, p., Ukr.	155	48°20'N	24°25'E
Yacheng, China (yä-chŭŋ)	193	18°20'N	109°10'E
Yachiyo, Japan	195a	35°43'N	140°07'E
Yacolt, Wa., U.S. (yă'kōlt)	106c	45°52'N	122°24'W
Yacolt Mountain, mtn., Wa., U.S.	106c	45°52'N	122°27'W
Yacona, r., Ms., U.S. (yá'cō nä)	114	34°13'N	89°30'W
Yacuiba, Bol. (yà-kōō-ē'bà)	130	22°02'S	63°44'W
Yadkin, r., N.C., U.S. (yăd'kĭn)	115	36°12'N	80°40'W
Yafran, Libya	210	31°57'N	12°04'E
Yaguajay, Cuba (yä-guä-hä'ē)	122	22°20'N	79°20'W
Yahagi-Gawa, r., Japan (yä'hä-gē gä'wä)	195	35°16'N	137°22'E
Yaho, Japan	242a	35°41'N	139°27'E
Yahongqiao, China (yä-hôŋ-chyou)	190	39°45'N	117°52'E
Yahualica, Mex. (yä-wä-lē'kä)	118	21°08'N	102°53'W
Yajalón, Mex. (yä-hä-lōn')	119	17°16'N	92°20'W
Yakhroma, Russia (yäl'rô-ma)	172b	56°17'N	37°30'E
Yakhroma, r., Russia	172b	56°15'N	37°38'E
Yakima, Wa., U.S. (yăk'ĭmȧ)	96	46°35'N	120°30'W
Yakima, r., Wa., U.S. (yăk'ĭ-mȧ)	104	46°48'N	120°22'W
Yakima Indian Reservation, I.R., Wa., U.S.	104	46°16'N	121°03'W
Yakō, neigh., Japan	242a	35°32'N	139°41'E
Yakoma, D.R.C.	216	4°05'N	22°27'E
Yaku, i., Japan (yä'kōō)	189	30°15'N	130°41'E
Yakutat, Ak., U.S. (yăk'ô-tát)	95	59°32'N	139°35'W
Yakutsk, Russia (yá-kòtsk')	165	62°13'N	129°49'E
Yale, Mi., U.S.	98	43°05'N	82°45'W
Yale, Ok., U.S.	111	36°07'N	96°42'W
Yale Lake, res., Wa., U.S.	104	46°00'N	122°20'W
Yalinga, Cen. Afr. Rep. (yá-lĭŋ'gá)	211	6°56'N	23°22'E
Yalobusha, r., Ms., U.S. (yá-lô-bòsh'ȧ)	114	33°48'N	90°02'W
Yalong, r., China (yä-lôŋ)	188	32°29'N	98°41'E
Yalta, Ukr. (yäl'tá)	167	44°29'N	34°12'E
Yalu, r., Asia	189	41°20'N	126°35'E
Yalutorovsk, Russia (yä-lōō-tô'rôfsk)	164	56°42'N	66°32'E
Yamada, Japan (yä'mȧ-dȧ)	195	33°37'N	133°39'E
Yamagata, Japan (yä-mȧ'gä-tȧ)	189	38°12'N	140°24'E
Yamaguchi, Japan (yä-mȧ'gōō-chê)	194	34°10'N	131°30'E
Yamaguchi, Japan	242b	34°50'N	135°15'E
Yamal, Poluostrov, pen., Russia (yä-mäl')	164	71°15'N	70°00'E
Yamal Nenets, state, Russia	170	67°00'N	75°00'E
Yamantau, Gora, mtn., Russia (gȧ-rä' yä'man-tàw)	172a	54°16'N	58°08'E
Yamasaki, Japan (yä'mȧ'sä-kê)	195	35°01'N	134°33'E
Yamasaki, Japan	195b	34°53'N	135°41'E
Yamashina, Japan (yä'mä-shê'nä)	195b	34°59'N	135°50'E
Yamashita, Japan (yä'mä-shê'tä)	195b	34°53'N	135°25'E
Yamato, Japan	195a	35°28'N	139°28'E
Yamato, Japan	242a	35°44'N	139°26'E
Yamato, Japan	242a	35°47'N	139°37'E
Yamato, r., Japan	242b	34°36'N	135°26'E
Yamato-Kōriyama, Japan	195b	34°39'N	135°48'E
Yamato-takada, Japan (yä'mä-tô tä'kä-dä)	195b	34°31'N	135°45'E
Yambi, Mesa de, mtn., Col. (mĕ'sä-dĕ-yà'm-bē)	130	1°55'N	71°45'W
Yambol, Bul. (yàm'bòl)	149	42°28'N	26°31'E
Yamdena, i., Indon.	197	7°23'S	130°30'E
Yamenkou, China	240b	39°53'N	116°12'E
Yamethin, Myanmar (yŭ-mē'thĕn)	183	20°14'N	96°27'E
Yamhill, Or., U.S. (yăm'hĭl)	106c	45°20'N	123°11'W
Yamkino, Russia (yäm'kĭ-nô)	172b	55°56'N	38°25'E
Yamma Yamma, Lake, l., Austl. (yăm'ȧ yăm'ȧ)	203	26°15'S	141°30'E
Yamoussoukro, C. Iv.	210	6°49'N	5°17'W
Yamsk, Russia (yämsk)	165	59°41'N	154°09'E
Yamuna, r., India	183	25°30'N	80°30'E
Yamzho Yumco, l., China (yäm-jwo yōōm-tswo)	188	29°11'N	91°26'E
Yana, r., Russia (yä'nȧ)	165	71°00'N	136°00'E
Yanac, Austl. (yăn'ăk)	203	36°10'S	141°30'E
Yanagawa, Japan (yä-nä'gä-wä)	195	33°11'N	130°24'E
Yanam, India (yŭnŭm')	183	16°48'N	82°15'E
Yan'an, China (yän-än)	188	36°46'N	109°15'E
Yanbu', Sau. Ar.	182	23°57'N	38°02'E
Yancheng, China (yän-chŭŋ)	192	33°23'N	120°11'E
Yancheng, China	192	33°38'N	113°59'E
Yandongi, D.R.C.	216	2°51'N	22°16'E
Yangcheng Hu, l., China (yäŋ-chŭŋ hōō)	190	31°30'N	120°31'E
Yangchun, China (yäŋ-chòn)	193	22°08'N	111°48'E
Yang'erzhuang, China (yäŋ-är-jůäŋ)	190	38°18'N	117°31'E
Yanggezhuang, China (yäŋ-gŭ-jůäŋ)	192a	40°10'N	116°48'E
Yanggu, China (yäŋ-gōō)	190	36°06'N	115°46'E
Yanghe, China (yäŋ-hŭ)	190	33°48'N	118°23'E
Yangjiang, China (yäŋ-jyäŋ)	193	21°52'N	111°58'E
Yangjiaogou, China (yäŋ-jyou-gō)	190	37°17'N	118°53'E
Yangon *see* Rangoon, Myanmar	183	16°46'N	96°09'E
Yangquan, China (yäŋ-chyůän)	190	37°52'N	113°36'E
Yangtze (Chang), r., China (yăng'tse) (chäŋ)	189	30°30'N	117°25'E
Yangxin, China (yäŋ-shyĭn)	190	37°39'N	117°34'E
Yangyang, S. Kor. (yäng'yäng')	194	38°02'N	128°38'E
Yangzhou, China (yäŋ-jō)	189	32°24'N	119°24'E
Yanji, China (yän-jyē)	189	42°55'N	129°35'E
Yanjiahe, China (yän-jyä-hŭ)	190	31°55'N	114°47'E
Yanjin, China (yän-jyĭn)	190	35°09'N	114°13'E
Yankton, S.D., U.S. (yănk'tŭn)	96	42°51'N	97°24'W
Yanling, China (yän-lĭŋ)	190	34°07'N	114°12'E
Yanshan, China (yän-shän)	192	38°05'N	117°15'E
Yanshou, China (yän-shō)	192	45°25'N	128°43'E
Yantai, China	189	37°32'N	121°22'E
Yanychi, Russia (yä'nĭ-chĭ)	172a	57°42'N	56°24'E
Yanzhou, China (yäŋ-jō)	189	35°35'N	116°50'E
Yanzhuang, China (yän-jůäŋ)	190	36°08'N	117°47'E
Yao, Chad (yä'ō)	202	13°00'N	17°38'E
Yao, Japan	195b	34°37'N	135°37'E
Yaoundé, Cam.	210	3°52'N	11°31'E
Yap, i., Micron. (yăp)	3	11°00'N	138°00'E
Yapen, Pulau, i., Indon.	197	1°30'S	136°15'E
Yaque del Norte, r., Dom. Rep. (yä'kȧ dĕl nôr'tȧ)	117	19°40'N	71°25'W
Yaque del Sur, r., Dom. Rep. (yä-kĕ-dĕl-sōō'r)	123	18°35'N	71°05'W
Yaqui, r., Mex. (yä'kē)	116	28°15'N	109°40'W
Yaracuy, dept., Ven. (yä-rä-kōō'ē)	131b	10°10'N	68°31'W
Yaraka, Austl. (yȧ-răk'ȧ)	203	24°50'S	144°08'E
Yaransk, Russia (yä-ränsk')	164	57°18'N	48°05'E
Yarda, oasis, Chad (yär'dȧ)	211	18°29'N	19°13'E
Yare, r., Eng., U.K.	151	52°40'N	1°32'E
Yarkand *see* Shache, China (yär'mŭth)	188	38°15'N	77°15'E
Yaroslavka, Russia (yȧ-rô-släv'kȧ)	172a	55°52'N	57°59'E
Yaroslavl', Russia (yȧ-rô-släv''l)	164	57°37'N	39°54'E
Yaroslavl', prov., Russia	162	58°05'N	38°05'E
Yarra, r., Austl.	201a	37°51'S	144°54'E
Yarra Canal, can., Austl.	243b	37°49'S	144°55'E
Yarraville, Austl.	243b	37°49'S	144°53'E
Yarro-to, l., Russia (yá'rô-tô')	166	67°55'N	71°35'E
Yartsevo, Russia	165	60°13'N	89°52'E
Yartsevo, Russia (yär'tsyĕ-vô)	166	55°04'N	32°38'E
Yarumal, Col. (yä-rōō-mäl')	130	6°57'N	75°24'W
Yasawa Group, is., Fiji	198g	17°00'S	177°23'E
Yasel'da, r., Bela. (yä-syŭl'dȧ)	155	52°13'N	25°53'E
Yateras, Cuba (yä-tā'räs)	123	20°00'N	75°00'W
Yates Center, Ks., U.S. (yāts)	111	37°53'N	95°44'W
Yathkyed, l., Can. (yáth-kī-ĕd')	84	62°41'N	98°00'W
Yatsuga-take, mtn., Japan (yät'sōō-gä dä'kä)	195	36°01'N	138°21'W
Yatsushiro, Japan (yät'sōō'shê-rô)	195	32°30'N	130°35'E
Yatta Plateau, plat., Kenya	217	1°55'S	38°10'E
Yautepec, Mex. (yä-ōō-tà-pĕk')	118	18°53'N	99°04'W
Yawata, Japan (yä'wä-tä)	195	34°52'N	135°43'E
Yawatahama, Japan (yä'wä'tä'hä-mä)	195	33°24'N	132°25'E
Yaxian, China (yä shyĕn)	193	18°10'N	109°32'E
Yayama, D.R.C.	216	1°16'S	23°07'E
Yayao, China (yä-you)	191a	23°10'N	113°40'E
Yazd, Iran	182	31°59'N	54°03'E
Yazoo, r., Ms., U.S. (yă'zōō)	97	32°32'N	90°40'W
Yazoo City, Ms., U.S.	114	32°50'N	90°18'W
Ye, Myanmar (yā)	196	15°13'N	97°52'E
Yeading, neigh., Eng., U.K.	235	51°32'N	0°24'W
Yeadon, Pa., U.S. (yē'dŭn)	100f	39°56'N	75°16'W
Yecla, Spain (yā'klä)	158	38°35'N	1°09'W
Yedikule, neigh., Tur.	239f	40°59'N	28°55'E
Yefremov, Russia (yĕ-frä'môf)	162	53°08'N	38°04'E
Yegor'yevsk, Russia (yĕ-gôr'yĕfsk)	166	55°23'N	38°59'E
Yeji, China (yŭ-jyē)	190	31°52'N	115°57'E
Yekaterinburg, Russia	164	56°51'N	60°36'E
Yelabuga, Russia (yĕ-lä'bô-gȧ)	166	55°50'N	52°18'E
Yelan, Russia	167	50°50'N	44°00'E
Yelek, r.	167	51°20'N	53°10'E
Yelets, Russia (yĕ-lyĕts')	164	52°35'N	38°28'E
Yelizavetpol'skiy, Russia (yĕ'lĭ-za-vĕt-pôl-skĭ)	172a	52°51'N	60°38'E
Yelizavety, Mys, c., Russia (yĕ-lyĕ-sȧ-vyĕ'tĭ)	165	54°28'N	142°59'E
Yell, i., Scot., U.K. (yĕl)	150a	60°35'N	1°27'W
Yellow *see* Huang, r., China	189	35°06'N	113°39'E
Yellow, r., Fl., U.S. (yĕl'ō)	114	30°33'N	86°53'W
Yellowhead Pass, p., Can. (yĕl'ô-hĕd)	87	52°52'N	118°35'W
Yellowknife, Can. (yĕl'ô-nīf)	84	62°29'N	114°38'W
Yellow Sea, sea, Asia	189	35°20'N	122°15'E
Yellowstone, r., U.S.	96	46°00'N	108°00'W
Yellowstone, Clarks Fork, r., U.S.	105	44°55'N	109°05'W
Yellowstone Lake, l., Wy., U.S.	96	44°27'N	110°03'W
Yellowstone National Park, rec., U.S. (yĕl'ô-stōn)	96	44°45'N	110°35'W
Yel'nya, Russia (yĕl'nyȧ)	162	54°34'N	33°12'E
Yemanzhelinsk, Russia (yĕ-mán-zhâ'lĭnsk)	172a	54°47'N	61°24'E
Yemen, nation, Asia (yĕm'ĕn)	182	15°00'N	47°00'E
Yemetsk, Russia	166	63°28'N	41°28'E
Yenangyaung, Myanmar (yă'nän-d oung)	183	20°27'N	94°59'E
Yencheng, China	188	37°30'N	79°26'E
Yendi, Ghana (yĕn'dê)	210	9°26'N	0°01'W
Yengisar, China (yŭn-gē-sär)	188	39°01'N	75°29'E
Yenice, r., Tur.	167	41°10'N	33°00'E
Yenikapi, neigh., Tur.	239f	41°00'N	28°57'E
Yenisey, r., Russia (yĕ-nê-sĕ'ê)	164	71°00'N	82°00'E
Yeniseysk, Russia (yĕ-nĭĕsă'ĭsk)	165	58°27'N	90°28'E

ăt; finȧl; rāte; senāte; ärm; ȧsk; sofȧ; fâre; ch-choose; dh-as th in other; bē; ėvent; bĕt; recĕnt; cratẽr; g-gō; gh-guttural g; bĭt; ĭ-short neutral; rīde; ĸ-guttural k as ch in German ich;

PLACE (Pronunciation)	PAGE	LAT.	LONG.
Yeo, I., Austl. (yō)	202	28°15′S	124°00′E
Yerevan, Arm. (yĕ-rĕ-vän′)	167	40°10′N	44°30′E
Yerington, Nv., U.S. (yē′rĭng-t*ŭ*n)	108	38°59′N	119°10′W
Yermak, i., Russia	166	66°45′N	71°30′E
Yeste, Spain (yĕs′tå)	158	38°23′N	2°19′W
Yeu, Île d′, i., Fr. (ēl dyû)	147	46°43′N	2°45′W
Yevlax, Azer.	168	40°36′N	47°09′E
Yexian, China (yŭ-shyĕn)	190	37°09′N	119°57′E
Yeya, r., Russia (yä′yå)	163	46°25′N	39°17′E
Yeysk, Russia (yĕysk)	167	46°41′N	38°13′E
Yi, r., China	190	34°38′N	118°07′E
Yiannitsá, Grc.	161	40°47′N	22°26′E
Yiaros, i., Grc.	161	37°52′N	24°42′E
Yibin, China (yē-bĭn)	188	28°50′N	104°40′E
Yichang, China (yē-chäŋ)	189	30°38′N	111°22′E
Yidu, China (yē-dōō)	192	36°42′N	118°30′E
Yiewsley, neigh., Eng., U.K.	235	51°31′N	0°28′W
Yilan, China (yē-län)	189	46°10′N	129°40′E
Yinchuan, China (yĭn-chůän)	188	38°22′N	106°22′E
Yingkou, China (yĭŋ-kō)	189	40°35′N	122°10′E
Yining, China (yē-nĭŋ)	188	43°58′N	80°40′E
Yin Shan, mts., China (yĭng′shän′)	192	40°50′N	110°30′E
Yio Chu Kang, Sing.	240c	1°23′N	103°51′E
Yishan, China (yē-shän)	188	24°32′N	108°42′E
Yishui, China (yē-shwā)	190	35°49′N	118°40′E
Yíthion, Grc.	161	36°50′N	22°37′E
Yitong, China (yē-tôŋ)	189	43°15′N	125°10′E
Yixian, China (yē shyĕn)	192	41°30′N	121°15′E
Yixing, China	190	31°26′N	119°57′E
Yiyang, China (yē-yäŋ)	193	28°52′N	112°12′E
Yoakum, Tx., U.S. (yō′k*ŭ*m)	113	29°18′N	97°09′W
Yockanookany, r., Ms., U.S. (yŏk′å-nōō-kă-nī)	114	32°47′N	89°38′W
Yodo-Gawa, strt., Japan (yō′dō′gä-wä)	195b	34°46′N	135°35′E
Yog Point, c., Phil. (yōg)	193	14°00′N	124°30′E
Yogyakarta, Indon. (yŏg-yå-kär′tå)	196	7°50′S	110°20′E
Yoho National Park, Can. (yō′hō)	84	51°26′N	116°30′W
Yojoa, Lago de, l., Hond. (lä′gô dĕ yô-hō′ä)	120	14°49′N	87°53′W
Yokkaichi, Japan (yô′kä′ê-chê)	194	34°58′N	136°35′E
Yokohama, Japan (yō′kô-hä′mą)	189	35°37′N	139°40′E
Yokosuka, Japan (yô-kō′sò-kä)	194	35°17′N	139°40′E
Yokota, Japan (yô-kō′tä)	195a	35°23′N	140°02′E
Yola, Nig. (yō′lä)	210	9°13′N	12°27′E
Yolaina, Cordillera de, mts., Nic.	121	11°34′N	84°34′W
Yomou, Gui.	214	7°34′N	9°16′W
Yonago, Japan (yō′nä-gō)	194	35°27′N	133°19′E
Yŏnch′on, neigh., S. Kor.	241b	37°38′N	127°04′E
Yonezawa, Japan (yō′nĕ′zá-wä)	194	37°50′N	140°07′E
Yong′an, China (yôŋ-än)	193	26°00′N	117°22′E
Yongding, r., China (yôŋ-dĭŋ)	192	40°25′N	115°00′E
Yŏngdŏk, S. Kor. (yŭng′dŭk′)	194	36°28′N	129°25′E
Yongdŭngp′o, neigh., S. Kor.	241b	37°32′N	126°54′E
Yŏnghŭng, N. Kor. (yŭng′hông′)	194	39°31′N	127°11′E
Yonghŭng Man, b., N. Kor.	194	39°10′N	128°00′E
Yongnian, China (yôŋ-nĭĕn)	192	36°47′N	114°32′E
Yongqing, China (yôŋ-chyĭŋ)	192a	39°18′N	116°27′E
Yongshun, China (yôŋ-shòn)	188	29°05′N	109°58′E
Yonkers, N.Y., U.S. (yŏŋ′kĕrz)	100a	40°57′N	73°54′W
Yonne, r., Fr. (yòn)	156	48°18′N	3°15′E
Yono, Japan (yō′nō)	195a	35°53′N	139°36′E
Yorba Linda, Ca., U.S. (yôr′bă lĭn′då)	107a	33°55′N	117°51′W
York, Austl.	202	32°00′S	117°00′E
York, Can.	83d	43°41′N	79°29′W
York, Eng., U.K.	146	53°58′N	1°10′W
York, Al., U.S. (yôrk)	114	32°33′N	88°16′W
York, Ne., U.S.	111	40°52′N	97°36′W
York, Pa., U.S.	97	40°00′N	76°40′W
York, S.C., U.S.	115	34°59′N	81°14′W
York, Cape, c., Austl.	203	10°45′S	142°35′E
York, Kap, c., Grnld.	82	75°30′N	73°00′W
Yorke Peninsula, pen., Austl.	204	34°24′S	137°20′E
Yorketown, Austl.	204	35°00′S	137°28′E
York Factory, Can.	89	57°05′N	92°18′W
Yorkfield, Il., U.S.	231a	41°52′N	87°56′W
Yorkshire Wolds, Eng., U.K. (yôrk′shĭr)	150	54°00′N	0°35′W
Yorkton, Can. (yôrk′t*ŭ*n)	84	51°13′N	102°28′W
Yorktown, Tx., U.S. (yôrk′toun)	113	28°57′N	97°30′W
Yorktown, Va., U.S.	115	37°12′N	76°31′W
Yorkville, neigh., Can.	227c	43°40′N	79°24′W
Yoro, Hond. (yō′rò)	120	15°09′N	87°05′W
Yoron, i., Japan	194	26°48′N	128°40′E
Yosemite National Park, rec., Ca., U.S. (yò-sĕm′ĭ-tê)	96	38°03′N	119°36′W
Yoshida, Japan (yō′shê-då)	195	34°39′N	132°41′E
Yoshikawa, Japan (yō-shê′kä′wä′)	195a	35°53′N	139°51′E
Yoshino, r., Japan (yō′shē-nō)	195	34°04′N	133°57′E
Yoshkar-Ola, Russia (yôsh-kär′ô-lä′)	166	56°35′N	48°05′E
Yos Sudarsa, Pulau, i., Indon.	197	7°20′S	138°30′E
Yŏsu, S. Kor. (yŭ′sōō′)	194	34°42′N	127°42′E
You, r., China (yō)	193	23°55′N	106°50′E
Youghal, Ire. (yōō′ôl) (yôl)	151	51°58′N	7°57′E
Youghal Bay, b., Ire.	150	51°52′N	7°46′W
Young, Austl. (yŭng)	204	34°15′S	148°18′E
Young, Ur. (yô-ōō′ng)	129c	32°42′S	57°38′W
Youngs, l., Wa., U.S. (yŭngz)	106a	47°25′N	122°08′W
Youngstown, N.Y., U.S.	101c	43°15′N	79°02′W
Youngstown, Oh., U.S.	98	41°05′N	80°40′W
Yozgat, Tur. (yôz′gád)	182	39°50′N	34°50′E
Ypsilanti, Mi., U.S. (ĭp-sĭ-lăn′tĭ)	101b	42°15′N	83°37′W
Yreka, Ca., U.S. (wī-rē′k*á*)	104	41°43′N	122°36′W
Yrghyz, Kaz.	169	48°30′N	61°17′E
Yrghyz, r., Kaz.	169	49°30′N	60°32′E
Ysleta, Tx., U.S. (ēz-lĕ′tå)	112	31°42′N	106°18′W
Yssingeaux, Fr. (ē-sän-zhō)	156	45°09′N	4°08′E
Ystad, Swe.	146	55°25′N	13°49′E
Yu′alliq, Jabal, mts., Egypt	181a	30°12′N	33°42′E
Yuan, r., China (yůän)	189	28°50′N	110°50′E
Yuan′an, China (yůän-än)	193	31°08′N	111°28′E
Yuan Huan, pt. of i., Tai.	241d	25°03′N	121°31′E
Yuanling, China (yůän-lĭŋ)	193	28°30′N	110°18′E
Yuanshi, China (yůän-shr)	192	37°45′N	114°32′E
Yuasa, Japan	195	34°02′N	135°10′E
Yuba City, Ca., U.S. (yōō′b*á*)	108	39°08′N	121°38′W
Yucaipa, Ca., Ca., U.S. (yū-k*á*-ē′p*á*)	107a	34°02′N	117°02′W
Yucatán, state, Mex. (yōō-kä-tän′)	116	20°45′N	89°00′W
Yucatan Channel, strt., N.A.	116	22°30′N	87°00′W
Yucatan Peninsula, pen., N.A.	120	19°30′N	89°00′W
Yucheng, China (yōō-chŭŋ)	190	34°31′N	115°54′E
Yucheng, China	192	36°55′N	116°39′E
Yuci, China (yōō-tsz)	192	37°32′N	112°40′E
Yudoma, r., Russia (yōō-dô′må)	171	59°13′N	137°00′E
Yueqing, China (yůĕ-chyĭn)	193	28°02′N	120°40′E
Yueyang, China (yůĕ-yäŋ)	189	29°25′N	113°05′E
Yuezhuang, China (yůĕ-jůäŋ)	190	36°13′N	118°17′E
Yug, r., Russia (yòg)	166	59°50′N	45°55′E
Yugoslavia, nation, Eur. (yōō-gô-slä-vĭ-*ă*)	142	44°00′N	21°00′E
Yukhnov, Russia (yòk′nof)	162	54°44′N	35°15′E
Yukon, , Can. (yōō′kŏn)	84	63°16′N	135°30′W
Yukon, r., N.A.	94a	64°00′N	159°30′W
Yukutat Bay, b., Ak., U.S. (yōō-kū tăt′)	95	59°34′N	140°50′W
Yuldybayevo, Russia (yòld′bä′yĕ-vô)	172a	52°20′N	57°52′E
Yulin, China	188	38°18′N	109°45′E
Yulin, China (yōō-lĭn)	193	22°38′N	110°10′E
Yuma, Az., U.S. (yōō′mä)	96	32°40′N	114°40′W
Yuma, Co., U.S.	110	40°08′N	102°50′W
Yuma, r., Dom. Rep.	123	19°05′N	70°05′W
Yumbi, D.R.C.	217	1°14′S	26°14′E
Yumen, China (yōō-mŭn)	188	40°14′N	96°56′E
Yuncheng, China (yòn-chŭŋ)	192	35°00′N	110°40′E
Yungho, Tai.	241d	25°01′N	121°31′E
Yung Shu Wan, H.K.	241c	22°14′N	114°06′E
Yunnan, prov., China (yun′nän′)	188	24°23′N	101°03′E
Yunnan Plat, plat., China (yò-nän)	188	26°03′N	101°26′E
Yunxian, China (yòn shyĕn)	189	32°50′N	110°55′E
Yunxiao, China (yòn-shyou)	193	24°00′N	117°20′E
Yura, Japan (yōō′rä)	195	34°18′N	134°54′E
Yurécuaro, Mex. (yōō-rā′kwä-rò)	118	20°21′N	102°16′W
Yurimaguas, Peru (yōō-rê-mä′gwäs)	130	5°59′S	76°12′W
Yuriria, Mex. (yōō′rê-rē′ä)	118	20°11′N	101°08′W
Yurovo, Russia	172b	55°30′N	38°24′E
Yur′yevets, Russia	166	57°15′N	43°08′E
Yuscarán, Hond. (yōōs-kä-rän′)	120	13°57′N	86°48′W
Yushan, China (yōō-shän)	193	28°42′N	118°20′E
Yushu, China (yōō-shōō)	192	44°58′N	126°32′E
Yutian, China (yōō-tĭĕn) (kŭ-r-yä)	188	36°55′N	81°39′E
Yutian, China (yōō-tĭĕn)	192	39°54′N	117°45′E
Yuty, Para. (yōō-tē′)	132	26°45′S	56°13′W
Yuwangcheng, China (yü′wäng′chĕng)	190	31°32′N	114°26′E
Yuxian, China (yōō shyĕn)	192	39°40′N	114°38′E
Yuzha, Russia (yōō′zhá)	166	56°38′N	42°20′E
Yuzhno-Sakhalinsk, Russia (yōōzh′nô-sä-kä-lĭnsk′)	165	47°11′N	143°04′E
Yuzhnoural′skiy, Russia (yōōzh-nô-ô-rál′skĭ)	172a	54°26′N	61°17′E
Yuzhnyy Ural, mts., Russia (yōō′zhnĭ ò-räl′)	172a	52°51′N	57°48′E
Yverdon, Switz. (ê-vĕr-dôn)	154	46°46′N	6°35′E
Yvetot, Fr. (ēv-tō′)	156	49°39′N	0°45′E

Z

PLACE (Pronunciation)	PAGE	LAT.	LONG.
Za, r., Mor.	148	34°19′N	2°23′W
Zaachila, Mex. (sä-ä-chē′lå)	119	16°56′N	96°45′W
Zaandam, Neth. (zän′dám)	151	52°25′N	4°49′E
Ząbkowice Śląskie, Pol.	154	50°35′N	16°48′E
Zabrze, Pol. (zäb′zhĕ)	147	50°18′N	18°48′E
Zacapa, Guat. (sä-kä′pä)	120	14°56′N	89°30′W
Zacapoaxtla, Mex. (sä-kä-pō-äs′tlä)	119	19°51′N	97°34′W
Zacatecas, Mex. (sä-kä-tā′käs)	116	22°44′N	102°32′W
Zacatecas, state, Mex.	116	24°00′N	102°45′W
Zacatecoluca, El Sal. (sä-kä-tå-kô-lōō′kä)	120	13°31′N	88°50′W
Zacatelco, Mex.	118	19°12′N	98°12′W
Zacatepec, Mex. (sä-kä-tå-pĕk′) (sän-tê-ä′gô)	119	17°10′N	95°53′W
Zacatlán, Mex. (sä-kä-tlän′)	119	19°55′N	97°57′W
Zacoalco de Torres, Mex. (sä-kô-äl′kô dä tōr′rĕs)	118	20°12′N	103°33′W
Zacualpan, Mex. (sä-kô-äl-pän′)	118	18°43′N	99°46′W
Zacualtipan, Mex. (sá-kò-äl-tē-pän′)	118	20°38′N	98°39′W
Zadar, Cro. (zä′där)	142	44°08′N	15°16′E
Zadonsk, Russia (zä-dônsk′)	162	52°22′N	38°55′E
Žagare, Lat. (zhágårĕ)	153	56°21′N	23°14′E
Zagarolo, Italy (tzä-gä-rō′lô)	159d	41°51′N	12°53′E
Zaghouan, Tun. (zá-gwän′)	210	36°30′N	10°04′E
Zagreb, Cro. (zä′grĕb)	142	45°50′N	15°58′E
Zagros Mountains, mts., Iran	182	33°30′N	46°30′E
Zāhedān, Iran (zä′hå-dän)	182	29°37′N	60°31′E
Zahlah, Leb. (zä′lä′)	181a	33°50′N	35°54′E
Zaire, nation, Afr.	212	1°00′S	22°15′E
Zaječar, Yugo. (zä′yĕ-chär′)	161	43°54′N	22°16′E
Zakhidnyi Buh (Bug), r., Eur.	154	52°29′N	21°20′E
Zákinthos, Grc.	161	37°48′N	20°55′E
Zákinthos, i., Grc.	149	37°45′N	20°32′E
Zakopane, Pol. (zá-kô-pä′nĕ)	155	49°18′N	19°57′E
Zakouma, Parc National de, rec., Chad	215	10°50′N	19°20′E
Zalaegerszeg, Hung. (zŏ′lô-ĕ′gĕr-sĕg)	154	46°50′N	16°50′E
Zalău, Rom. (z*á*-lŭ′ò)	155	47°11′N	23°06′E
Zalțan, Libya	211	28°20′N	19°40′E
Zaltbommel, Neth.	145a	51°48′N	5°15′E
Zama, Japan	242a	35°29′N	139°24′E
Zambezi, r., Afr. (zám-bā′zê)	212	16°00′S	29°45′E
Zambia, nation, Afr. (zăm′bê-å)	212	14°23′S	24°15′E
Zamboanga, Phil. (säm-bô-aŋ′gä)	196	6°58′N	122°02′E
Zambrów, Pol. (zäm′bròf)	155	52°29′N	22°17′E
Zamora, Mex. (sä-mō′rä)	116	19°59′N	102°16′W
Zamora, Spain (thä-mō′rä)	148	41°32′N	5°43′W
Zanatepec, Mex.	119	16°30′N	94°22′W
Zandvoort, Neth.	145a	52°22′N	4°30′E
Zanesville, Oh., U.S. (zānz′vĭl)	98	39°55′N	82°00′W
Zangasso, Mali	214	12°09′N	5°37′W
Zanjān, Iran	182	36°26′N	48°24′E
Zanzibar, Tan. (zăn′zĭ-bär)	213	6°10′S	39°11′E
Zanzibar, i., Tan.	213	6°20′S	39°37′E
Zanzibar Channel, strt., Tan.	217	6°05′S	39°00′E
Zaozhuang, China (dzou-jůäŋ)	190	34°51′N	117°34′E
Zapadnaya Dvina, r., Eur. (zä′påd-nå-yå dvē′nà)	153	55°30′N	28°27′E
Zapala, Arg. (zä-pä′lä)	132	38°53′S	70°02′W
Zapata, Tx., U.S. (sä-pä′tä)	112	26°52′N	99°18′W
Zapata, Ciénaga de, sw., Cuba (syĕ′nä-gä-dĕ-zä-pá′tä)	122	22°30′N	81°20′W
Zapata, Península de, pen., Cuba (pĕ-nē′n-sōō-lä-dĕ-zä-pá′tä)	122	22°20′N	81°30′W
Zapatera, Isla, i., Nic. (ê′s-lä-sä-pä-tā′rō)	120	11°45′N	85°45′W
Zapopan, Mex. (sä-pō′pän)	118	20°42′N	103°23′W
Zaporizhzhia, Ukr.	164	47°50′N	35°10′E
Zaporizhzhia, prov., Ukr.	163	47°20′N	35°05′E
Zaporoshskoye, Russia (zá-pô-rôsh-skô-yĕ)	153	60°36′N	30°31′E
Zapotiltic, Mex. (sä-pô-tēl-tēk′)	118	19°37′N	103°25′W
Zapotitlán, Mex. (sä-pô-tê-tlän′)	118	17°13′N	98°58′W
Zapotitlán, Mex.	233a	19°18′N	99°02′W
Zapotitlán, Punta, c., Mex.	119	18°34′N	94°48′W
Zapotlanejo, Mex. (sä-pô-tlä-nā′hô)	118	20°38′N	103°05′W
Zaragoza, Mex. (sä-rä-gō′sä)	118	23°59′N	99°45′W
Zaragoza, Mex.	118	22°02′N	100°45′W
Zaragoza, Spain (thä-rä-gō′thä)	142	41°39′N	0°53′W
Zarand, Munții, mts., Rom.	155	46°07′N	22°21′E
Zaranda Hill, mtn., Nig.	215	10°15′N	9°35′E
Zaranj, Afg.	185	31°06′N	61°53′E
Zarasai, Lith. (zä-rä-sī′)	153	55°45′N	26°18′E
Zárate, Arg. (zä-rä′tä)	132	34°05′S	59°05′W
Zaraysk, Russia (zä-rä′ėsk)	166	54°46′N	38°53′E
Zarečje, Russia	239b	55°41′N	37°23′E
Zaria, Nig. (zä′rē-ä)	210	11°07′N	7°44′E
Zarqā′, r., Jord.	181a	32°13′N	35°43′E
Zarzal, Col. (zär-zà′l)	130a	4°23′N	76°04′W
Zashiversk, Russia (zá′shĭ-vĕrsk′)	165	67°08′N	144°02′E
Zastavna, Ukr. (zàs-täf′nà)	155	48°32′N	25°50′E
Zastron, S. Afr. (zàs′tr*ŭ*n)	213c	30°19′S	27°07′E
Žatec, Czech Rep. (zhä′těts)	154	50°19′N	13°32′E
Zavitinsk, Russia	171	50°12′N	129°44′E
Zawiercie, Pol. (zá-vyĕr′tsyĕ)	155	50°28′N	19°25′E
Zāwiyat al-Baydā′, Libya	211	32°49′N	21°46′E
Zāwiyat Nābit, Egypt	244a	30°07′N	31°09′E
Zāyandeh, r., Iran	182	32°15′N	51°00′E
Zaysan, Kaz. (zī′sán)	169	47°43′N	84°44′E
Zaysan, l., Kaz.	169	48°16′N	84°05′E
Zaza, r., Cuba (zá′zà)	122	21°40′N	79°25′W
Zbarazh, Ukr. (zbä-räzh′)	155	49°39′N	25°48′E
Zbruch, r., Ukr. (zbròch)	155	48°56′N	26°18′E
Zdolbuniv, Ukr.	155	50°31′N	26°17′E
Zduńska Wola, Pol. (zdōōn″skä vō′lä)	155	51°36′N	18°27′E
Zebediela, S. Afr.	218d	24°19′S	29°21′E
Zeeland, Mi., U.S. (zē′l*ă*nd)	98	42°50′N	86°00′W
Zefat, Isr.	181a	32°58′N	35°30′E
Zehdenick, Ger. (tsā′dē-nĕk)	154	52°59′N	13°20′E
Zehlendorf, Ger. (tsā′lĕn-dôrf)	145b	52°47′N	13°23′E
Zehlendorf, neigh., Ger.	238a	52°26′N	13°15′E
Zeist, Neth.	145a	52°05′N	5°14′E
Zelenogorsk, Russia (zĕ-lä′nô-gôrsk)	153	60°13′N	29°39′E
Zella-Mehlis, Ger. (tsâl′å-mā′lês)	154	50°40′N	10°38′E
Zémio, Cen. Afr. Rep. (za-myō′)	211	5°03′N	25°11′E
Zemlya Frantsa-Iosifa (Franz Josef Land), is., Russia	164	81°32′N	40°00′E
Zempoala, Punta, c., Mex. (pōō′n-tä-sĕm-pô-ä′lä)	119	19°30′N	96°18′W
Zempoatlépetl, mtn., Mex. (sĕm-pô-ä-tlā′pĕt′l)	119	17°13′N	95°59′W
Zemun, Yugo. (zĕ′mōōn) (sĕm′lĭn)	149	44°50′N	20°25′E
Zengcheng, China (dzŭŋ-chŭŋ)	191a	23°18′N	113°49′E
Zenica, Bos. (zĕ′nēt-sä)	161	44°10′N	17°54′E
Zeni-Su, is., Japan (zĕ′nē sōō)	195	33°55′N	138°55′E
Žepče, Bos. (zhĕp′chĕ)	163	44°26′N	18°01′E
Zepernick, Ger. (tsĕ′pĕr-nĕk)	145b	52°39′N	13°32′E
Zerbst, Ger. (tsĕrbst)	154	51°58′N	12°03′E
Zerpenschleuse, Ger. (tsĕr′pĕn-shloi-zĕ)	145b	52°51′N	13°30′E
Zeuthen, Ger. (tsoi′tĕn)	145b	52°21′N	13°38′E
Zevenaar, Neth.	157c	51°56′N	6°06′E
Zevenbergen, Neth.	145a	51°38′N	4°36′E

ng-sing; ŋ-baŋk; N-nasalized n; nŏd; c*ŏ*mmit; ōld; ôbey; ôrder; oi-boil; fōōd; ò-as oo in foot; ou-out; s-soft; sh-dish; th-thin; pūre; ůnite; ûrn; stŭd; circ*ŭ*s; ü-as in French tu; ′-indeterminate vowel.

PLACE (Pronunciation)	PAGE	LAT.	LONG.
Zeya, Russia (zā'yà)	165	53°43'N	127°29'E
Zeya, r., Russia	171	52°31'N	128°30'E
Zeytinburnu, neigh., Tur.	239f	40°59'N	28°54'E
Zeytun, Tur. (zā-tōōn')	167	38°00'N	36°40'E
Zezere, r., Port. (zě'zå-rě)	158	39°54'N	8°12'W
Zgierz, Pol. (zgyězh)	155	51°51'N	19°26'E
Zhambyl, Kaz.	169	42°51'N	71°29'E
Zhangaqazaly, Kaz.	169	45°47'N	62°00'E
Zhangbei, China (jän-bā)	189	41°12'N	114°50'E
Zhanggezhuang, China (jän-gǔ-jùän)	190	40°09'N	116°56'E
Zhangguangcai Ling, mts., China (jän-gŭän-tsī lǐŋ)	192	43°50'N	127°55'E
Zhangjiakou, China	189	40°45'N	114°58'E
Zhangqiu, China (jän-chyỏ)	190	36°50'N	117°29'E
Zhangye, China (jän-yu)	188	38°46'N	101°00'E
Zhangzhou, China (jän-jỏ)	189	24°35'N	117°45'E
Zhangzi Dao, i., China (jän-dz dou)	190	39°02'N	122°44'E
Zhanhua, China (jän-hwä)	190	37°42'N	117°49'E
Zhanjiang, China (jän-jyän)	189	21°20'N	110°28'E
Zhanyu, China (jän-yōō)	192	44°30'N	122°30'E
Zhao'an, China (jou-än)	193	23°48'N	117°10'E
Zhaodong, China (jou-dỏŋ)	192	45°58'N	126°00'E
Zhaotong, China (jou-tỏŋ)	188	27°18'N	103°50'E
Zhaoxian, China (jou shyěn)	190	37°46'N	114°48'E
Zhaoyuan, China (jou-yuän)	190	37°22'N	120°23'E
Zhecheng, China (jǔ-chǔŋ)	192	34°05'N	115°19'E
Zhegao, China (jǔ-gou)	190	31°47'N	117°44'E
Zhejiang, prov., China (jǔ-jyäŋ)	189	29°30'N	120°00'E
Zhelaniya, Mys, c., Russia (zhě'lä-nǐ-yá)	164	75°43'N	69°10'E
Zhem, r., Kaz.	170	46°50'N	54°10'E
Zhengding, China (jŭŋ-dǐŋ)	192	38°10'N	114°35'E
Zhen'guosi, China	240b	39°51'N	116°21'E
Zhengyang, China (jŭŋ-yäŋ)	190	32°34'N	114°22'E
Zhengzhou, China (jŭŋ-jỏ)	189	34°46'N	113°42'E
Zhenjiang, China (jŭŋ-jyäŋ)	189	32°13'N	119°24'E
Zhenru, China	241a	31°15'N	121°24'E
Zhenyuan, China (jŭŋ-yuän)	193	27°08'N	108°30'E
Zhetíqara, Kaz.	169	52°12'N	61°18'E
Zhigalovo, Russia (zhě-gä'lỏ-vỏ)	165	54°52'N	105°05'E
Zhigansk, Russia (zhě-gänsk')	165	66°45'N	123°20'E
Zhijiang, China (jr-jyäŋ)	193	27°25'N	109°45'E
Zhizdra, Russia (zhěz'drá)	162	53°47'N	34°41'E
Zhizhitskoye, l., Russia (zhě-zhět'skỏ-yě)	162	56°08'N	31°34'E
Zhmerynka, Ukr.	167	49°02'N	28°09'E
Zhongshan Park, rec., China	241a	31°13'N	121°25'E
Zhongwei, China (jỏŋ-wä)	188	37°32'N	105°10'E
Zhongxian, China (jỏŋ shyěn)	188	30°20'N	108°00'E
Zhongxin, China (jỏŋ-shyǐn)	191a	23°16'N	113°38'E
Zhoucun, China (jỏ-tsōōn)	192	36°49'N	117°52'E
Zhoukouzhen, China (jỏ-kỏ-jǔn)	190	33°39'N	114°40'E
Zhoupu, China (jỏ-pōō)	190	31°07'N	121°33'E
Zhoushan Qundao, is., China (jỏ-shän-chyón-dou)	189	30°00'N	123°00'E
Zhouxian, China (jỏ shyěn)	192	39°30'N	115°59'E
Zhovkva, Ukr.	155	50°03'N	23°58'E
Zhu, r., China (jōō)	191a	22°48'N	113°36'E
Zhuanghe, China (jůäŋ-hǔ)	192	39°40'N	123°00'E
Zhuanqiao, China (jůäŋ-chyou)	191b	31°02'N	121°24'E
Zhucheng, China (jōō-chǔŋ)	192	36°01'N	119°24'E
Zhuji, China (jōō-jyě)	193	29°58'N	120°10'E
Zhujiang Kou, b., Asia (jōō-jyäŋ kỏ)	193	22°00'N	114°00'E
Zhukovskiy, Russia (zhỏ-kôf'skī)	172b	55°33'N	38°09'E
Zhurivka, Ukr.	163	50°31'N	31°43'E
Zhytomyr, Ukr.	164	50°15'N	28°40'E
Zhytomyr, prov., Ukr.	163	50°40'N	28°07'E
Zi, r., China (dzě)	193	26°50'N	111°00'E
Zia Indian Reservation, I.R., N.M., U.S.	109	35°30'N	106°43'W
Zibo, China (dzě-bwo)	190	36°48'N	118°04'E
Ziel, Mount, mtn., Austl. (zěl)	202	23°15'S	132°45'E
Zielona Góra, Pol. (zhyě-lỏ'nä gōō'rä)	154	51°56'N	15°30'E
Zigazinskiy, Russia (zǐ-gazinskěě)	172a	53°50'N	57°18'E
Ziguinchor, Sen.	210	12°35'N	16°16'W
Zile, Tur. (zē-lě')	149	40°20'N	35°50'E
Žilina, Slvk. (zhě'lǐ-nä)	147	49°14'N	18°45'E
Zillah, Libya	211	28°26'N	17°52'E
Zima, Russia (zě'má)	170	53°58'N	102°08'E
Zimapan, Mex. (sē-mä'pän)	118	20°43'N	99°23'W
Zimatlán de Alvarez, Mex.	119	16°52'N	96°47'W
Zimba, Zam.	217	17°19'S	26°13'E
Zimbabwe, nation, Afr. (rỏ-dē'zhǐ-á)	212	17°50'S	29°30'E
Zimnicea, Rom. (zěm-nē'chá)	161	43°39'N	25°22'E
Zin, r., Isr.	181a	30°50'N	35°12'E
Zinacatepec, Mex. (zē-nä-kä-tě'pěk)	119	18°19'N	97°15'W
Zinapécuaro, Mex. (sē-nä-pā'kwá-rỏ)	118	19°50'N	100°49'W
Zinder, Niger (zǐn'děr)	210	13°48'N	8°59'E
Zin'kiv, Ukr.	163	50°13'N	34°23'E
Zion, Il., U.S. (zī'ǔn)	101a	42°27'N	87°50'W
Zion National Park, rec., Ut., U.S.	96	37°20'N	113°00'W
Zionsville, In., U.S. (zīǔnz-vǐl)	101g	39°57'N	86°15'W
Zirandaro, Mex. (sē-rän-dä'rỏ)	118	18°28'N	101°02'W
Zitacuaro, Mex. (sē-tá-kwä'rỏ)	118	19°25'N	100°22'W
Zitlala, Mex. (sē-tlä'lä)	118	17°38'N	99°09'W
Zittau, Ger. (tsē'tou)	154	50°55'N	14°48'E
Ziway, l., Eth.	211	8°08'N	39°11'E
Ziya, r., China (dzē-yä)	190	38°38'N	116°31'E
Zlatograd, Bul.	161	41°24'N	25°05'E
Zlatoust, Russia (zlá-tỏ-ȯst')	164	55°13'N	59°39'E
Zlītan, Libya	211	32°27'N	14°33'E
Złoczew, Pol. (zwỏ'chěf)	155	51°23'N	18°34'E
Zlynka, Russia (zlěn'ká)	162	52°28'N	31°39'E
Znamensk, Russia (znä'měnsk)	153	54°37'N	21°13'E
Znamianka, Ukr.	163	48°43'N	32°35'E
Znojmo, Czech Rep. (znoí'mô)	147	48°52'N	16°03'E
Zoetermeer, Neth.	145a	52°08'N	4°29'E
Zoeterwoude, Neth.	145a	52°08'N	4°29'E
Zográfos, Grc.	239d	37°59'N	23°46'E
Zolochiv, Ukr.	155	49°48'N	24°55'E
Zolotonosha, Ukr. (zỏ'lỏ-tỏ-nỏ'shá)	167	49°41'N	32°03'E
Zolotoy, Mys, c., Russia (mǐs zỏ-lỏ-tôy')	194	47°24'N	139°10'E
Zomba, Mwi. (zŏm'bá)	212	15°23'S	35°18'E
Zongo, D.R.C. (zỏŋ'gỏ)	211	4°19'N	18°36'E
Zonguldak, Tur. (zỏŋ'gŏōl'dák)	182	41°25'N	31°50'E
Zonhoven, Bel.	145a	50°59'N	5°24'E
Zoquitlán, Mex. (sỏ-kēt-län')	119	18°09'N	97°02'W
Zorita, Spain (thỏ-rē'tä)	158	39°18'N	5°41'W
Zossen, Ger. (tsỏ'sěn)	145b	52°13'N	13°27'E
Zouar, Chad	215	20°27'N	16°32'E
Zouxian, China (dzỏ shyěn)	192	35°24'N	116°54'E
Zubtsov, Russia (zỏp-tsôf')	162	56°13'N	34°34'E
Zuera, Spain (thwä'rä)	159	41°40'N	0°48'W
Zugdidi, Geor.	168	42°30'N	41°53'E
Zuger See, l., Switz. (tsōōg)	154	47°10'N	8°40'E
Zugspitze, mtn., Eur.	154	47°25'N	11°00'E
Zuidelijk Flevoland, reg., Neth.	145a	52°22'N	5°20'E
Zújar, r., Spain (zōō'kär)	158	38°55'N	5°05'W
Zújar, Embalse del, res., Spain	158	38°50'N	5°20'W
Zulueta, Cuba (zōō-lỏ-ě'tä)	122	22°20'N	79°35'W
Zumbo, Moz.	212	15°36'S	30°25'E
Zumbro, r., Mn., U.S. (zǔm'brỏ)	103	44°18'N	92°14'W
Zumbrota, Mn., U.S. (zǔm-brỏ'tá)	103	44°16'N	92°39'W
Zumpango, Mex. (sỏm-päŋ-gỏ)	118	19°48'N	99°06'W
Zundert, Neth.	145a	51°28'N	4°39'E
Zungeru, Nig. (zỏŋ-gā'rōō)	210	9°48'N	6°09'E
Zunhua, China (dzỏn-hwä)	192	40°12'N	117°55'E
Zuni, r., Az., U.S.	109	34°40'N	109°30'W
Zuni Indian Reservation, I.R., N.M., U.S. (zōō'nē)	109	35°10'N	108°40'W
Zuni Mountains, mts., N.M., U.S.	109	35°10'N	108°10'W
Zunyi, China	188	27°58'N	106°40'E
Zürich, Switz. (tsü'rǐk)	142	47°22'N	8°32'E
Zürichsee, l., Switz.	154	47°18'N	8°47'E
Zushi, Japan (zōō'shě)	195a	35°17'N	139°35'E
Zuurbekom, S. Afr.	244b	26°19'S	27°49'E
Zuwārah, Libya	210	32°58'N	12°07'E
Zuwayzā, Jord.	181a	31°42'N	35°55'E
Zvenigorod, Russia (zvä-nē'gỏ-rôt)	162	55°46'N	36°54'E
Zvenyhorodka, Ukr.	167	49°07'N	30°59'E
Zvishavane, Zimb.	212	20°15'S	30°28'E
Zvolen, Slvk. (zvỏ'lěn)	155	48°35'N	19°10'E
Zvornik, Bos. (zvôr'něk)	161	44°24'N	19°08'E
Zweckel, neigh., Ger.	236	51°36'N	6°59'E
Zweibrücken, Ger. (tsvī-brük'ěn)	154	49°16'N	7°20'E
Zwickau, Ger. (tsvǐkỏu)	154	50°43'N	12°30'E
Zwolle, Neth. (zvỏl'ě)	147	52°33'N	6°05'E
Żyradów, Pol. (zhě-rär'dỏf)	155	52°04'N	20°28'E
Zyryan, Kaz.	169	49°43'N	84°20'E
Zyryanka, Russia (zě-ryän'ká)	165	65°45'N	151°15'E

SUBJECT INDEX

Listed below are major topics covered by the thematic maps, graphs and/or statistics.
Page citations are for world, continent and country maps and for world tables.

SOURCES

The sources listed below have been consulted during the process of creating and updating the thematic maps and statistics for the 19th edition.

AAMA Motor Vehicle Facts and Figures, American Automobile Manufacturers Association

Agricultural Atlas of the United States, U.S. Dept. of Commerce, Bureau of the Census

Agricultural Statistics, U.S. Dept. of Agriculture

Air Carrier Traffic and Canadian Airports, Statistics Canada, Minister of Industry, Science and Technology

Annual Report series (various titles), U.S. Dept. of the Interior, Bureau of Mines

Anuario Estatistico do Brasil, Fundacao Instituto Brasileiro de Geografia e Estatistica

Atlas of African Agriculture, United Nations, Food and Agriculture Organization

Atlas of Economic Mineral Deposits, Cornell University Press

Atlas of India, TT Maps and Publications\Government of India

Atlas of the Middle East, U.S. Central Intelligence Agency

Canada Year Book, Statistics Canada, Minister of Industry, Science and Technology

Catalog of Significant Earthquakes, National Oceanic and Atmospheric Administration, National Geophysical Data Center

Census of Agriculture, Dept. of Commerce, Bureau of the Census

Census of Population Characteristics: United States, U.S. Dept. of Commerce, Economics and Statistics Administration

China Statistical Yearbook, State Statistical Bureau of the People's Republic of China

City and County Data Book, U.S. Dept of Commerce, Bureau of the Census

Coal Fields of the United States, U.S. Dept. of the Interior, Geological Survey

Coal Production U.S., U.S. Dept. of Energy, Energy Information Administration

Commercial Nuclear Power Plants Around the World, Nuclear News

Commercial Nuclear Power Plants in the United States, Nuclear News

Compendium of Social Statistics and Indicators, United Nations, Department of International Economic and Social Affairs

The Copper Industry of the U.S.S.R., U.S. Dept. of the Interior, Bureau of Mines

Demographic Yearbook, United Nations, Dept. of Economic and Social Development

Earthquakes and Volcanoes, U.S. Dept. of the Interior, U.S. Geological Survey

Eastern Europe Coal Infrastructure, U.S. Central Intelligence Agency

Ecoregions of the Continents, U.S. Dept. of Agriculture, Forest Service

Energy in the Newly Independent States of Eurasia, U.S. Central Intelligence Agency

Energy Map of Central Asia, Petroleum Economist

Energy Map of the World, Petroleum Economist

Energy Statistics Yearbook, United Nations, Dept. of Economic and Social Information and Policy Analysis

FAA Statistical Handbook of Aviation, U.S. Dept. of Transportation, Federal Aviation Administration

FAO Atlas of the Living Resources of the Seas, United Nations, Food and Agriculture Organization

FAO Fertilizer Yearbook, United Nations, Food and Agriculture Organization

FAO Production Yearbook, United Nations, Food and Agriculture Organization

FAO Trade Yearbook, United Nations, Food and Agriculture Organization

FAO Yearbook of Fishery Statistics, United Nations, Food and Agriculture Organization

FAO Yearbook of Forest Products, United Nations, Food and Agriculture Organization

Fiber Organon, Fiber Economics Bureau, Inc.

Geothermal Energy in the Western United States and Hawaii, U.S. Dept. of Energy/Energy Information Administration

Geothermal Resources Council, unpublished data

A Guide to Your National Forests, U.S. Dept. of Agriculture, Forest Service

Handbook of International Economic Statistics, U.S. Central Intelligence Agency

Handbook of International Trade and Development Statistics, United Nations, Conference on Trade and Development

International Data Base, U.S. Bureau of the Census, Center for International Research

International Energy Annual, U.S. Dept. of Energy, Energy Information Administration

International Energy Outlook, Dept. of Energy, Energy Information Administration

International Petroleum Encyclopedia, PennWell Publishing Co.

International Trade Statistics Yearbook, United Nations, Dept. of Economic and Social Development

International Water Power and Dam Construction Yearbook, Reed Business Publishing

Largest U.S. Oil and Gas Fields, U.S. Dept. of Energy, Energy Information Administration

Major Coalfields of the World, International Energy Agency Coal Research

Maritime Transport, Organization for Economic Co-operation and Development

Merchant Fleets of the World, U.S. Dept. of Transportation, Maritime Administration

Mineral Industries of Africa, U.S. Dept. of the Interior, Bureau of Mines

Mineral Industries of Asia and the Pacific, U.S. Dept. of the Interior, Bureau of Mines

Mineral Industries of Europe and Central Eurasia, U.S. Dept. of the Interior, Bureau of Mines

Mineral Industries of Latin America and Canada, U.S. Dept. of the Interior, Bureau of Mines

Mineral Industries of the Middle East, U.S. Dept. of the Interior, Bureau of Mines

Minerals Yearbook, U.S. Dept. of the Interior, Bureau of Mines

Monthly Bulletin of Statistics, United Nations, Dept. of Economic and Social Development

National Atlas - Canada, Dept. of Energy, Mines, and Resources

National Atlas - Chile, Instituto Geografico Militar

National Atlas - China, Cartographic Publishing House

National Atlas - Japan, Geographical Survey Institute

National Atlas - United States, U.S. Dept. of the Interior, Geological Survey

National Atlas - U.S.S.R., Central Administration of Geodesy and Cartography

National Priorities List, U.S. Environmental Protection Agency

Natural Gas Annual, U.S. Dept. of Energy, Energy Information Administration

Non-Ferrous Metal Data, American Bureau of Metal Statistics

Nuclear Power Reactors in the World, International Atomic Energy Agency

Oxford Economic Atlas of the World, Oxford University Press

The People's Republic of China - A New Industrial Power, U.S. Dept. of the Interior, Bureau of Mines

Petroleum Supply Annual, U.S. Dept. of Energy, Energy Information Administration

Population and Dwelling Counts: A National Overview, Minister of Industry, Science and Technology, Statistics Canada

Population and Vital Statistics Reports, United Nations, Dept. for Economic and social Information and Policy Analysis

Post-Soviet Geography, V.H. Winston and Son, Inc.

Primary Aluminum Plants Worldwide, U.S. Dept. of the Interior, Bureau of Mines

Public Land Surveys, U.S. Dept. of the Interior, Geological Survey

Rail in Canada, Statistics Canada, Transportation Section

Rand McNally Road Atlas, Rand McNally

Refugees, United Nations High Commissioner for Refugees

Refugee Survey Quarterly, United Nations, Centre for Documentation on Refugees

The State of the World's Refugees, United Nations High Commissioner for Refugees

The States of the Former Soviet Union: An Updated Overview, U.S. Central Intelligence Agency, Directorate of Intelligence

Statistical Abstract of India, Central Statistical Organisation

Statistical Abstract of the United States, U.S. Dept. of Commerce, Bureau of the Census

Statistical Pocket-Book of Yugoslavia, Federal Statistical Office

Statistical Yearbook, United National Educational, Scientific and Cultural Organization (UNESCO)

Sugar Yearbook, International Sugar Organization

Survey of Energy Resources, World Energy Council

This Dynamic Planet: World Map of Volcanoes, Earthquakes and Plate Tectonics, Smithsonian Institution/U.S. Geological Survey

Tin Ore Resources of Asia and Australia, United Nations, Economic Commission for Asia and the Far East

Uranium Resources, Production and Demand, Organization for Economic Co-operation and Development/International Atomic Energy Agency

U.S.S.R. Energy Atlas, U.S. Central Intelligence Agency

World Atlas of Agriculture, Isituto Geografico De Agostini

World Atlas of Geology and Mineral Deposits, Mining Journal Books, Ltd.

World Coal Resources and Major Trade Routes, Miller Freeman Publications, Inc.

World Development Report, The World Bank

The World Factbook, U.S. Central Intelligence Agency

World Gas Map, Petroleum Economist

World Mineral Statistics, British Geological Survey

World Mining Porphyry Copper, Miller Freeman Publications, Inc.

World Oil, Gulf Publishing Company

World Population Prospects, United Nations, Dept. for Economic and Social Information and Policy Analysis

World Refugee Report, U.S. Dept. of Stats, Bureau for Refugee Programs

World Transport Data, International Road Transport Union

World Urbanization Prospects, United Nations, Dept. of Economic and Social Information and Policy Analysis

Year Book Australia, Australian Bureau of Statistics

Year Book of Labour Statistics, International Labour Organization